Business Law with UCC Applications

Paul A. Sukys
PROFESSOR EMERITUS OF LAW AND APPLIED PHILOSOPHY
NORTH CENTRAL STATE COLLEGE | MANSFIELD, OHIO

15e

BUSINESS LAW WITH UCC APPLICATIONS, FIFTEETH EDITION

Published by McGraw-Hill Education, 2 Penn Plaza, New York, NY 10121. Copyright © 2020 by McGraw-Hill Education. All rights reserved. Printed in the United States of America. Previous editions © 2017, 2013, and 2009. No part of this publication may be reproduced or distributed in any form or by any means, or stored in a database or retrieval system, without the prior written consent of McGraw-Hill Education, including, but not limited to, in any network or other electronic storage or transmission, or broadcast for distance learning.

Some ancillaries, including electronic and print components, may not be available to customers outside the United States.

This book is printed on acid-free paper.

1 2 3 4 5 6 7 8 9 LWI 21 20 19 18

ISBN 978-1-259-99816-4 (bound edition)
MHID 1-259-99816-9 (bound edition)
ISBN 978-1-260-47137-3 (loose-leaf edition)
MHID 1-260-47137-3 (loose-leaf edition)

Executive Portfolio Manager: *Kathleen Klehr*
Product Developers: *Jaroslaw Szymanski / Allie Kukla*
Senior Marketing Manager: *Michelle Williams*
Lead Content Project Manager: *Dana M. Pauley*
Senior Content Project Manager: *Angela Norris*
Senior Buyer: *Susan K. Culbertson*
Design: *Jessica Cuevas*
Lead Content Licensing Specialist: *Carrie Burger*
Cover Image: *©Rawpixel.com/Shutterstock*
Compositor: *Aptara, Inc.*

All credits appearing on page or at the end of the book are considered to be an extension of the copyright page.

Library of Congress Cataloging-in-Publication Data

Name: Brown, Gordon W., 1928- author. | Sukys, Paul, author.
Title: Business law with UCC applications / Paul A. Sukys, Professor of Law
   and Applied Philosophy, North Central State College, Mansfield, Ohio;
   Gordon W. Brown, Professor Emeritus, North Shore Community College,
   Danvers, Massachusetts.
Description: Fifteenth edition. | New York, NY : McGraw-Hill Education, [2020]
Identifiers: LCCN 2018034715 | ISBN 9781259998164 (alk. paper) | ISBN
   1259998169 (alk. paper)
Subjects: LCSH: Commercial law–United States.
Classification: LCC KF889.85 .B76 2020 | DDC 346.7307–dc23 LC record available at https://lccn.loc.gov/2018034715

The Internet addresses listed in the text were accurate at the time of publication. The inclusion of a website does not indicate an endorsement by the authors or McGraw-Hill Education, and McGraw-Hill Education does not guarantee the accuracy of the information presented at these sites.

mheducation.com/highered

This book is dedicated with much love and many thanks to my wife, Susan. As I've learned during our life together—as a team—the possibilities are limitless.

Also to Jennifer, Ashley, and Megan, all three of whom have grown up to be excellent educators in their own right. They have made me very proud.

Finally, to Austin, Marena, Ariya, Veda, and Forest the newest additions to our family, who have reminded me how wonderful it is to feel young again.

Paul Sukys

About the Author

Courtesy Jennifer A. Chiocco

Paul A. Sukys is an attorney and professor emeritus of applied philosophy, humanities, and law at North Central State College in Mansfield, Ohio, where he has taught courses in business law; the legal and ethical aspects of health care; leadership and the humanities; American government; philosophy and science; ethics; science, art, and literature; introduction to the humanities; Eastern philosophy; the philosophy of religion; and Western philosophy. He has also taught at Mount Vernon Nazarene University, Ashland University, and Cuyahoga Community College in Cleveland. He is the sole author of *Lifting the Scientific Veil: Science Appreciation for the Nonscientist* and *Business Law with UCC Applications* and co-author of *Civil Litigation* and *Understanding Business and Personal Law*. He has written numerous articles, including "The *Hobby Lobby* Teachable Moment: Veil Piercing, Corporate Rights, and the Legal Debate," (*Business Education Forum*) and "Robinson's Theological Catch 22 and Emerson's Divine Man: When Good Intentions Go Wrong," (*Community College Humanities Review*). He has also made various presentations at professional conferences, including a session at the National Business Education Association convention in 2018, entitled, "Employment Law in the 21st Century: Can Basic Principles Survive Under Social, Religious, and Political Pressure?" Sukys earned his doctorate in applied philosophy and art history at the Union Institute and University in Cincinnati. He received undergraduate and graduate degrees in English Literature from John Carroll University in Cleveland, where he taught as a graduate associate. He earned his law degree at the Cleveland-Marshall College of Law, the law school of Cleveland State University. Sukys is a member of the Ohio Bar, the National Business Education Association (NBEA), the Community College Humanities Association (CCHA), the Christian Legal Society, the Ohio State Bar Association (OSBA), and the Chautauqua Literary and Scientific Circle (CLSC). Sukys lives in Cleveland.

Preface

Business Law with UCC Applications has reached its fifteenth edition. Over the last four decades, the text has undergone many changes. When it was first printed, photographs were rarely used and sometimes completely forbidden by the editorial staff. Ancillaries were limited to teacher-friendly test banks and transparencies, and the language used, in an attempt to mimic "legalese," was often just a bit too formal. Today, the pages are filled with photographs, charts, diagrams, and features, and multiple digital ancillaries are available to both the instructor and the student. As for the language, it is familiar and informal, while maintaining a practical approach designed to teach students the proper terms in a way that is both instructive and accessible. Through the years, the authors and editors have attempted to build a text that provides students with an overview of procedural and substantive legal principles that will help them navigate the difficult waters of the law as it relates to the issues they can expect to face in their everyday lives. As in previous editions, a great deal of care has been taken to present legal concepts in the most coherent and accessible way and to provide up-to-date coverage of both business and general law topics that are essential to today's students. All of the chapters for this edition have been updated, and we have continued to enhance our coverage of these important topics. Included in these updates are the following new additions to the text.

- Two critically important topics have been added to Chapter 2, the Sources of the Law. The first new feature explains the nature of executive orders, looks at various types of executive orders, and examines several theories of presidential power. The new section also considers the question of whether the president has the constitutional authority to issue such orders in the first place.

- Another new section added to Chapter 2 investigates the charge that the president's authority has been undermined by the Deep State. The new section investigates the nature of the Deep State from historical and contemporary points of views, explores the motives of Deep State agents, and looks at how the president and Congress can counteract the effects of the Deep State.

- Chapter 5 on Criminal Law and Cybercrimes tackles one of the most distressing and complicated issues of our day—guns in schools. The section investigates the dangers of guns in schools and explores the various attempts by both state and federal authorities to enact laws that will protect school children from gun-related violence.

- Chapter 15, Product Liability and Consumer Protection, includes a new section on the Consumer Finance Protection Bureau (CFPB). The CFPB is important because it is responsible for ensuring that financial consumers are knowledgeable enough to make smart decisions regarding things like credit cards, loans from banks, and other areas of the financial world. An in-depth look at the CFPB is warranted because the bureau has been the focus of much controversy over the last few years.

- Chapter 23, Employment Law, features a controversial case that some legal experts predict will rewrite the relationship between employment law and civil rights. The new case, *Kimberly Hively v. Ivy Tech Community College*, hinges on the question of whether sexual orientation qualifies as gender discrimination under the Civil Rights Act of 1964, something the Equal Employment Opportunity Commission has supported for some time but the courts have been reluctant to embrace, at least until now.

- Chapter 33, Science, Technology, and Law in the 21st Century, now includes expanded coverage of legislative and executive efforts to deal with the threat of climate change. New coverage in that chapter includes the California Delta Water Twin Tunnel Project; the Solid Waste Act; the Toxic Substance Abuse Act; the Comprehensive Environmental Response, Compensation, and Liability Act (CERCLA); the Oil Pollution Act; and the Paris Climate Agreement.

More details follow in the "Important Changes in the Fifteenth Edition of *Business Law with UCC Applications*" section.

The popular format of previous editions has been preserved, with learning objectives identified in the margin where that material appears in the text. Each chapter begins with an outline followed by the Opening Case, with numbered questions and Chapter Objectives. An Opening Case is chosen to appear at the start of a chapter because that case illustrates multiple legal points within the chapter. Often, the case will feature a look at both the positive and negative consequences of the court's ruling. This approach is meant to emphasize the fact that cases often have legal and social consequences that stretch beyond the effects on the litigants in that individual case.

In other areas in each chapter, titles have been given to every example. Major headings and chapter summaries continue to be numbered, following the chapter outline. The popular case illustrations, presenting either hypothetical or actual situations based on well-founded court decisions, have been retained and updated. Our Quick Quiz feature appears in each chapter and allows students to test their knowledge of the chapter topics while they actively study the text. A new feature entitled *Business Law with UCC Applications—and Now the Applications* looks at some of the ethical, political, social, and practical applications of the UCC related to the content of those chapters in which the feature is located. For example, the installment in Chapter 7 takes a look at how to solve the conflicts that can arise when the parties to a contract are not sure whether a contract is for the sale of goods or for services rendered.

The popular Classic Cases feature has been continued, giving not only the the instructor, but also the students an opportunity to explore topics related to the content of the chapter in a provocative and stimulating way. Classic cases are chosen to remind learners that, despite the passage of time and changes in social customs, many—perhaps most—legal principles remain stable and predictable. Nor is this meant to downplay the advent of new cases and new principles, many of which appear at key points within the pages of the text.

We also have retained case studies pertaining to each of the nine parts of the book that summarize an actual litigated case, present a lengthy extract from the justice's or the judge's decision, and provide follow-up questions that are pertinent to the cases and are appropriate as a review of the legal concepts involved. Most of these cases are chosen because they stand—or will stand—as landmark decisions that have altered—or will alter—the course of jurisprudence for generations to come. The Activities at the end of each chapter, including Key Terms, Questions for Review and Discussion, and Cases for Analysis, help students self-check their understanding of the terms and concepts presented in the chapter. We also have continued to include the *Question of Ethics* element at various strategic points throughout the text. The U.S. Constitution appears in Appendix A. Included in Appendix B is information about how to access the Uniform Commercial Code. Marginal references within the chapters tie these specific documents to the content. The fifteenth edition of *Business Law* thus offers a comprehensive package of materials to meet both instructors' and students' needs.

Important Changes in the Fifteenth Edition of *Business Law with UCC Applications*

Chapter 1 Ethics and the Law

- A new Opening Case, *Ziglar v. Abbasi*, 582 U.S. —— (2017), which focuses on the conflict between preserving national security and protecting human rights.
- A new look at the ethical decision-making process by explaining the difference between being tolerant and being nonjudgmental. The material focuses on the illogical and self-contradictory nature of nonjudgmentalism.
- A creative look at the threat of failed and unstable states on the international scene with an emphasis on the difference between the duty to protect one's own citizens and the duty to protect the citizens of a nation whose government threatens those citizens, as is the case in the current civil war in Syria.
- A novel example discussing the relationship between promoting human rights and dealing with nation-states that fail to do so yet, on another level, are helping to eliminate an even greater evil.
- A note on the new Responsibility to Protect (R2P) protocol instituted and supported by the United Nations.

Chapter 2 Sources of the Law

- A new Opening Case, *States of New York, et al. v. Trump*, Civil Action No. 17-CV-5228 (2017), which involves 15 states and the District of Columbia that filed a joint lawsuit in the U.S. District Court asking that court to grant an injunction that would stop the enforcement of what they called President Trump's unconstitutional DACA order.
- A new take on the development of the two central theories of legal interpretation, textualism and pragmatism.
- A new major addition that explains the nature of executive orders, looks at the types of executive orders, examines the various theories of presidential power, and explores the current challenges to executive power.
- The introduction of a new feature entitled *Business Law with UCC Applications–and Now the Applications.* The installment in Chapter 2 takes a look at the dangers associated with placing legislative power in the hands of a semi-independent body such as the Uniform Law Commission.
- A new section that examines the nature of the Deep State from historical and contemporary points of views, explores the motives of the Deep State agents, and looks at how to counteract the effects of the Deep State.
- A new section that studies the goals and the operation of the Regulatory Flexibility Act.

Chapter 3 The Judicial Process and Cyber-Procedure

- A new Opening Case, *The European Community (EC) v. RJR Nabisco, Inc. (RJR)*, 579 U.S. —— (2016), in which the European Community (EC), acting for itself and for its members, brought suit in federal court in New York against the American corporation RJR Nabisco under the Racketeer Influenced and Corrupt Organizations (RICO) Act, claiming that RJR had, in furtherance of its illegal scheme, committed numerous acts of money laundering, wire fraud, mail fraud, and violations of the Travel Act. For good measure, the EC added several allegations of wrongdoing under the state laws of New York.

- A discussion about how to determine whether a non-nation-state configuration qualifiers as a "foreign state" and, thus, has the right to bring a lawsuit in U.S. District Courts. These non-nation-state configurations include non-governmental organizations, unified international institutions, and conglomerates.
- A discussion about choosing which law applies in a lawsuit in the context of the new Defend Trade Secrets Act (DTSA).
- An examination of *Bristol-Myers Squibb v. Superior Court of California*, a landmark case that redefines the nature of forum shopping in class action lawsuits.
- A look at the new amendments to the federal rules of civil procedure that are designed to limit the amount of information gathering that is conducted by both sides in a civil case.
- Some new details that explore what happens during an arrest in a criminal case, including a look at the exclusionary rule, the fruit of the poisonous tree rule, the attenuation doctrine, the independent source rule, and the inevitable discovery doctrine.
- The addition of new material on the jury selection process as it occurs in a criminal trial.
- The addition of new material on the consequences of a hung jury and about what happens when the judge declares a mistrial.

Chapter 4 Alternative Dispute Resolution and Cyber-ADR

- A new Opening Case, *Considie v. Brookdale Senior Living, Inc*, 124 F. Supp 3d 83 (2015), which discusses whether arbitration can ever be truly mandatory.
- A look at the Federal Arbitration Act (FAA), which is designed to make sure that properly initiated arbitration agreements are enforced by the courts.

Chapter 5 Criminal Law and Cybercrimes

- A new Opening Case, *United States v. Hearst*, 563 F.2d 1313 (9th Cir. 1978), in which the world-renown defense attorney F. Lee Bailey uses the creative defense of coercive persuasion in an ill-fated attempt to earn a not-guilty verdict for heiress-turned-urban guerilla Patty Hearst.
- An ethics feature that focuses on the infamous "texting suicide case" in which a teenage boy killed himself by carbon monoxide poisoning after being told on his cell phone by his girlfriend to "get back in the car."
- A detailed reexamination of the nature of "recklessness" in the law in the context of the Philadelphia Amtrak Derailment tragedy that killed eight people.
- A consideration of the controversial third requirement that some states have added to the three-step test of corporate criminal liability. The third requirement adds that the directors or officers of a corporation must have authorized, approved, or recklessly tolerated the criminal actions of the employees.
- A reconsideration of corporate criminal liability in the context of the Grenfell Tower fire in London, the worst fire in England for more than 100 years.
- A look at the unintended consequences that can emerge from variations in the law that exist from jurisdiction to jurisdiction, especially at the international level.

- A new examination of several legal theories under which corporations can be held criminally liable for their conduct.
- A new study of the dangers of guns in schools and attempts at both the state and federal level to enact laws that will protect school children from gun-related violence.
- An in-depth look at the global cyber-crime wave in cyber-extortion, using malware, ransomware, and other serious cyber-attack strategies.
- A look at the civil cause of action available under the Computer Fraud and Abuse Act (CFAA).
- An examination of state and federal legislation designed to regulate drone activity.
- A discussion of the Stockholm syndrome and coercive persuasion as defenses to criminal liability.

Chapter 6 Tort Law and Cybertorts

- An introduction to the case of *Jailynn Brown, et al. v. Andre T. Harris Sr., et al*, Appellate Case No. 27069, Trial Court Case No. 2014-CV-5144 (2014) which examines the issue of duty, the nature of negligence, and the viability of the defense of assumption of the risk.
- A new examination of the concept of the temporary public figure (also known as the limited-purpose public figure) as it was involved in a false story about the the University of Virginia printed in *Rolling Stone Magazine*.
- The introduction of the two relatively new intentional torts of civil theft and food disparagement.
- A discussion of the actual malice test in a defamation case as it played out in the story of an anti-violence editorial published in the *The New York Times* that falsely accused Sara Palin's political action committee of inspiring the shooting of Democratic Congresswoman Gabby Giffords in 2011.
- A look at the Federal Employers Liability Act (FELA), which established a negligence standard for railroads that all but eliminates the foreseeability causation doctrine in such cases.
- An examination of the doctrine of *ferae naturae* (wild nature) that helps determine the liability of a property owner when people are injured on the owner's property by wild animals.
- A new discussion of the Federal Torts Claims Act, sovereign immunity, and public duty doctrine.
- A new Case Study for Part I, *Barbara Schneider, Plaintiff-Appellant v. Mark Kumpf, Defendant-Appellee,* Court of Appeals of Ohio Second District, Montgomery County, No. 26855. Decided July 29, 2016, 2016-Ohio-5161.

Chapter 7 The Essentials of Contract Law

- A new Opening Case, *Grondin v. Rossington*, 690 F. Supp. 200, which discusses some of the essential elements of a written contract.
- Another installment of the new feature, *Business Law with UCC Applications–and Now the Applications*, which takes a look at the conflicts that can arise when the parties to a contract are not sure whether a contract is for the sale of goods or for services rendered.

Chapter 8 Offer, Acceptance, and Mutual Assent

- A new Opening Case, *B.J. Kadrmas, Inc. v. Oxbow Energy LLC*, 727 N.W. 2d 279 (2007), which discusses the nature of offer and acceptance.
- Another installment of the new feature, *Business Law with UCC Applications—and Now the Applications,* that focuses on UCC 2-204 (1) and (3), which explain the simple nature of a contract and, in doing so, help establish a sane and stable economy.
- A discussion of a new statute titled The Fair and Accurate Credit Transactions Act (FACT Act). The FACT Act, which is actually an amendment to the Fair Credit Reporting Act (FCRA), is designed to cut down on identity theft related to the use of credit and debit cards.
- The examination of a new type of identify theft called catfishing. Catfishing is not identity theft, *per se*. Instead, catfishing involves the creation of an entirely new online identity, a cyber-ghost, who then snags a gullible, but innocent, victim who becomes involved with the cyber-ghost and is then deliberately conned out of large amounts of money.

Chapter 9 Consideration and Cyber-Payments

- A new Opening Case, *Stein v. Gelfand*, 476 F. Supp. 2d. 427 (2007), which explores what happens when the amount of consideration is not known at the time that a contract is made.
- An introductory discussion about a new form of consideration called bitcoin, which is actually a subset of cryptocurrency.

Chapter 10 Capacity and Legality: The Final Elements

- A new Opening Case, *AK Steel Corp. v. ArcelorMittal USA, L.L.C*, 2016-Ohio-3285 (Court of Appeals, 12th Appellate District of Ohio, Butler County), which looks at the nature of restrictive employment agreements.
- A new, more detailed, more complete discussion of noncompete agreements (also referred to as restrictive employment covenants).

Chapter 11 Written Contracts and Cyber-Commerce

- A new Opening Case, *Charlotte Eastland Mall LLC v. Sole Survivor Inc.*, No. COA03-1422, Court of Appeals of North Carolina (October 19, 2004), which looks at those contracts must be in writing to be enforceable.
- Another installment of the new feature, *Business Law with UCC Applications—and Now the Applications*, which takes a look at the conflicts that can arise when the parties to a contract for specially manufactured goods have not reduced that contract to writing.

Chapter 12 Third Parties, Discharge, and Remedies

- A new Opening Case, *Lake Ridge v. Carney*, 66 Ohio St. 3d 376, No. 2464, which looks at the concept of contract repudiation.

Chapter 13 Sales Contracts: Formation, Title, and Risk of Loss

- A new Opening Case, *ePresence, Inc. v. Evolve Software, Inc.*, 190 F. Supp. 2d 159 U.S. District Court, D. Massachusetts (February 27, 2002), which looks at the differences between service contracts and sale of goods contracts.

- Another installment of the new feature, *Business Law with UCC Applications—and Now the Applications*, which takes a look at the question of when to apply the UCC to a case and when to look to other forms of contract law such as common law, consumer protection law, real property law, employment law, or the United Nations Convention on Contracts for the International Sale of Goods.

Chapter 14 Sales Contracts Rights, Duties, Breach, and Warranties

- A new Opening Case, *Hooten Equipment Company v. Trimat, Inc.*, 4th District No. 03CA16 2004-Ohio-1128), which explores the nature of nonconforming goods.
- Another installment of the new feature, *Business Law with UCC Applications—and Now the Applications*, which takes a look at the standards used to measure when, under the UCC, a buyer's rejection of the goods purchased in a sales contract has been effective.

Chapter 15 Product Liability and Consumer Protection

- A new Opening Case, *Peter Macrie, Sr., Peter Macrie, Jr. and Toni Marie Macrie, Plaintiffs-Appellants v. SDS Biotech Corp., Aka Fermenta Plant Protection, Defendant-Respondent,* 267 N.J. Super. 34, which examines the duty to warn and the concept of risk analysis.
- A new in-depth discussion of the the Consumer Finance Protection Bureau (CFPB, or simply the Bureau) and its troubled history.
- An ethical study that focuses on a new Deep State attack on the authority of the president. This attack challenged the power of the president to appoint a new director for the Consumer Finance Protection Bureau.
- The addition of a section on the Military Lending Act (MLA), a statute enacted to protect members the military, especially those on active duty, as well as their spouses and dependents, from being targeted by certain financial organizations and institutions that use questionable lending strategies to take advantage of military personnel who often find themselves in a vulnerable position because of their highly mobile, somewhat unpredictable lifestyles.
- New Case Study for Part 3, *Norcold, Inc. v. Gateway Supply Company*, 298 N.E. 2d 618, 154 Ohio App. 594 (2003).

Chapter 16 The Nature of Negotiable Instruments

- A new Opening Case, *N. E. Guthrie, Petitioner v. National Homes Corporation* 394 S. W. 2d 494 (1965); *N. E. Guthrie, Appellant v. National Homes Corporation, Appellee,* 387 S. W. 2d 158, which looks at the nature of promissory notes.
- A more in-depth discussion of section UCC 3-106, which explains in detail the characteristics that make an instrument unconditional and, therefore, a negotiable instrument.

Chapter 17 Holders in Due Course, Defenses, and Liabilities

- A new Opening Case, *Williams v. Stansbury,* 649 S.W.2d 293, Supreme Court of Texas (1983); and, in the Texas appellate court, *Williams v. Stansbury* 634 S.W.2d 924, (Tex. App. 1982), which takes a look at the relationship between promissory notes and garnishment orders.

- The addition of new material on consumer credit contracts and the FTC legend.
- Another installment of the new feature, *Business Law with UCC Applications—and Now the Applications*, which examines the question of whether the addition of UCC 1-106 (d) to Article 3 makes obsolete most of the other rules laid down in that article.

Chapter 18 Bank–Depositor Relationships and Cyber-Banking

- A new Opening Case, *Spacemakers of America Inc. v. Suntrust Bank*, No: A04A2080 (Court of Appeals of Georgia), which examines the dangers that result from ignoring the activities of those employees who handle the firm's money.
- A new, more detailed discussion clarifying the changing roles of a bank from creditor to debtor and back again.
- A new, more detailed discussion clarifying the roles of a bank as agent and principal.
- A new section on Project Sheltered Harbor, a national protocol designed to stave off a potentially catastrophic run on the banks of the country, similar to the ones that ushered in the Great Depression of the 20th century.
- New Case Study for Part 4, *Read v. South Carolina National Bank*, 86 S. C. 534, 335 S.E.2d 359, Supreme Court of South Carolina.

Chapter 19 Insurance

- A new Opening Case, *State Farm Fire and Casualty Company v. Ramsey*, 719 F.Supp. 1337 (1989) United States District Court, S.D. Mississippi, E.D., which highlights the need to be able to distinguish between tenants-in-common and tenants by the entirety.
- A new discussion of the four types of co-tenancy: tenancy in common, joint tenancy, community property, and tenancy by the entirety.
- A new discussion of the homestead, a type of ownership unique to American law.
- A new discussion of the homestead exemption.
- A new discussion of the proof of loss form, which is designed to detail the personal property destroyed during an incident that gives rise to an insurance claim.
- A new discussion of renters' insurance, which protects tenants against the damage or loss of personal property, stolen personal property, liability for a visitor's personal injury, and liability for negligent destruction of the rented premises.
- A new discussion on the changes that have been made to the federal Affordable Care Act.
- A new discussion on the nature and the extent of of cyber insurance coverage.

Chapter 20 Mortgages, Land Contracts, and the 21st-Century Financial Crisis

- A new Opening Case that was literally ripped from the morning headlines, found in James Leggate, "Cincinnati Sues Company over 'Predatory' Land Sales Contracts, Blighted Properties," *WCPO Cincinnati* (April 14, 2017), which examines the dangers associated with manipulating land contracts.
- A new section explaining land contracts.
- An addition to the discussion of the 21st-century financial crisis and the backlash against the Dodd-Frank Act.

- A new section that discusses the plan, introduced by the administration and the Senate, to alter the operation of both Fannie Mae and Freddie Mac, in order to minimize the role that the federal government has in overseeing the operation of these two government-sponsored enterprises (GSEs).

Chapter 21 Bankruptcy Law: In Theory, in History, and in Practice

- Updated, in-depth coverage of the current state of bankruptcy law in the United States.
- New coverage of the changes in Chapter 13 Bankruptcy filings as initiated under the authority of the Bankruptcy Abuse Prevention and Consumer Protection Act (BAPCPA).

Chapter 22 Agency Law

- A new Opening Case, *Latty v. St. Joseph's Society*, 17 A.3d 155 (2011), 198 Md. App. 254 (2011), which explores the nature of agency law and the extent of vicarious liability under tort law principles.
- Addition of new material on agency law in the health care setting that includes a look at living wills, durable health care power of attorney, DNR identification, and anatomical gift documents.
- Additional material on agency in the health care setting, including the legal definitions of death, terminal condition, and a permanently unconscious state.

Chapter 23 Employment Law

- A new Opening Case, *Kimberly Hively v. Ivy Tech Community College*, No. 15-1720 (2017), which explores the question of whether sexual orientation qualifies as gender discrimination under the Civil Rights Act of 1964.
- New coverage concerning what questions can and cannot be asked by an employer during a job interview process.
- Coverage concerning new guidelines issued by the Occupational Safety and Health Administration (OSHA) concerning what employers can and cannot do in relation to drug and alcohol testing after workplace injuries.
- New coverage concerning the status of private collective actions filed under the Fair Labor Standards Act.
- New coverage concerning the status of the overtime minimum salary increase proposal made by the administration under the FLSA.
- New coverage concerning the Working Families Flexibility Act of 2017.
- New coverage concerning the Strategic Enforcement Plan of the EEOC. The goal of this initiative is to make certain that the legal system is open and accessible to all.
- New coverage concerning the stated objectives of the new Strategic Enforcement Plan.

Chapter 24 Labor Law

- A new Opening Case, chronicled in "About the IDG," *IDG The Independent Drivers Guild*, https://drivingguild.org/about (2017), which involves a look at the new Uber Drivers' Union, the Independent Drivers Guild (the IDG or the Guild),

- A new "Soon to Be a Classic Case" feature on *Janus v. AFSCME*, in which the governor of Illinois challenged a state statute that gave public unions like the American Federation of State, County, and Municipal Employees (AFSCME) the exclusive authority to represent all state employees, even those who were opposed to the very idea of a union.
- New Case Study for Part 5, *Evans v. Georgia Regional Hospital*, 803 F. 3d 1248, U.S. Court of Appeals, Eleventh Circuit.

Chapter 25 The Business Entity: An Introduction

- A new Opening Case, *Van Hooser, et al. v. Keenoin, et al.*, 271 S.W. 2d 270 (Court of Appeals of Kentucky), which involves a study of the differences between a partnership and a corporation.
- The addition of material on a new corporate structure known as the private, religiously based corporate entity.
- The addition of material on a new breed of business entities known collectively as economic development special-purpose entities (EDSPEs), including such diverse corporate structures as special improvement districts, port authorities, new community authorities, joint economic development districts, municipal utility districts, and community improvement corporations.

Chapter 26 The Corporate Entity

- A new Opening Case, *Messick v. Moring* 514 So. 2d 892 (the Supreme Court of Alabama), which involves a close examination of the corporate law doctrine of piercing the corporate veil.
- New coverage of the "Delaware Factor," which is an attempt to explain why many promoters still flock to Delaware to incorporate, despite the fact that most other states have incorporation statutes that are just as easy, economical, effective, and efficient as Delaware's original ground-breaking statute.

Chapter 27 Managing the Corporate Entity

- A new Opening Case, *Unocal Corporation v. Mesa Petroleum Company*, 493 A. 2d 946, (1985), which involves a close examination of the Business Judgment Rule.
- New coverage that examines the many recent challenges to the Sarbanes-Oxley Act.
- Coverage of a new concept known as American legal imperialism.
- New coverage of the unintended consequences that have emerged in the wake of the passage of the Sarbanes-Oxley Act.
- New coverage that examines the environmental, social, and governance (ESG) movement in support of stakeholder corporate control.
- New coverage of the Wells Fargo compensation recovery case, a case that is the most vivid example of a change in corporate policy motivated by a shareholder proposal that was never voted upon.
- New coverage of the Financial Choice Act of 2017 (FCA), which is an attempt to limit the number of shareholders eligible to submit shareholder proposals.

Chapter 28 Government Regulation of the Corporate Entity

- A new Opening Case, *Asadi v. GE Energy (USA) L.L.C.*, No. 12-20522, U.S. Court of Appeals for the Fifth Circuit (October 8, 2013), which involves the use of a textualist approach to statutory interpretation from the bench.

- The addition of the Jumpstart Our Business Startups (JOBS) Act, a federal law designed to empower small businesses to raise capital more efficiently, economically, and effectively.
- New coverage of the SEC's Regulation Systems Compliance and Integrity (REG SCI) protocols, an innovative system designed to short-circuit potential cyber interruptions of the stock exchange system in the future.

Chapter 29 Personal Property and Bailments

- A new Opening Case, *Ritz v. Selma United Methodist Church*, 467 N.W.2d 266, which looks at the differences that exist among lost, abandoned, and mislaid property.
- New coverage of the concept known as natural property.
- New coverage of the concept known as a treasure trove.
- New coverage of some new trends in cultural property protection. Cultural property includes works of art, monuments, and archives that are created by and preserved for a nation, an ethnic group, a tribe, or some other cultural subdivision in order to preserve and celebrate the history, character, religion, and beliefs of that subdivision.

Chapter 30 Real Property and Landlord and Tenant Law

- A new Opening Case, *General Electric Credit Union v. Sharon K. Medow*, 2016 Ohio 3266, Court of Appeals of Ohio, First District, Hamilton County (June 3, 2016), which looks at how dower rights relate to life estates.
- New material on the concept of coverture.
- New material on dower and curtesy. Under the right of dower, a wife had an interest in her husband's property, which she would receive on his death. The husband had a similar right called the right of curtesy.
- New material on spousal rights, which replace dower and curtesy in most states.

Chapter 31 Wills, Advance Directives, and Trusts

- A new Opening Case, *Winkfield v. Children's Hospital and Research Center of Oakland*, Case Number RG 13707598 (2013), which explores the conflicts that often exist between First Amendment religious rights and the right to die with dignity.
- New, more detailed coverage of living wills.
- New, more detailed coverage of the durable power of attorney for health care.
- A new discussion of the difficulties with advance directives.
- New coverage of the physician order for life-sustaining treatment.
- New coverage of protective medical decision documents.
- New coverage of do not resuscitate orders.
- A new discussion of the right to die and the right to live.
- A new discussion of advance directives and the right to die.

Chapter 32 Professional Liability

- A new Opening Case, this one examining the unintended consequences for attorneys that result from the new version of Model Rule 8.4 (g) of the American Bar Association's Code on Ethics and Professional Responsibility.

- Coverage of the new tax code.
- New coverage of financial advisors.
- Coverage of the revised fiduciary rule.

Chapter 33 Science, Technology, and Law in the 21st Century

- A new Opening Case that examines climate change, carbon footprints, sunspots, a mysterious 1,500-year climate cycle, and the Paris Climate Agreement.
- New coverage of the California Delta Water Twin Tunnel Project and its relationship to the proposed federal science court.
- New coverage of the Solid Waste Act.
- New coverage of the Toxic Substance Abuse Act.
- New coverage of the Comprehensive Environmental Response, Compensation, and Liability Act (CERCLA).
- New coverage of the Oil Pollution Act.
- New coverage of the Paris Climate Agreement.
- New coverage of the concept of stocktake.
- Update on global population figures.
- Update on U.S. population growth figures.
- New coverage of the U.S. Supreme Court Case, *Impression Products, Inc. v. Lexmark International, Inc.*, which greatly affects patent law.
- New coverage of the patent law doctrine of the "right to tinker."

Chapter 34 International Law and the New World Order

- A new Opening Case that examines the growing global struggle between liberal democracy and authoritarianism.
- Extensive revision of the technique of predictive political history.
- New up-to-date examples of the emerging new world order.
- The addition of a current real-world example of *Realpolitik* in action.
- The addition of a current real-world example of liberal internationalism in action.
- The addition of a current real-world example of neoconservativism in action.
- The addition of a current real-world example of neoliberalism in action.
- New coverage of the relative effectiveness of liberal democracy and authoritarianism in relation to economic initial conditions.
- New coverage of the relative effectiveness of liberal democracy and authoritarianism in relation to cultural initial conditions.
- New coverage of the relative effectiveness of liberal democracy and authoritarianism in relation to the hybrid initial conditions.
- New coverage on the competing global political ideologies of liberal democracy and authoritarianism.
- New coverage of the doctrine of the Responsibility to Protect (R2P).

Acknowledgments

I am grateful to the following individuals for their review feedback. I appreciate their ideas and suggestions.

Joan Alexander
Nassau Community College

Bonnie S. Bolinger
Ivy Tech Community College

Dennis Bromley
Salt Lake Community College

Myra Bruegger
Southeastern Community College

H. Stanley Carson
Eastern Maine Community College

Machiavelli W. Chao
University of California, Irvine

Gregory L. Dalton
Genesee Community College

Nancy K. Dempsey
Cape Cod Community College

Pamela S. Evers
University of North Carolina Wilmington

John M. Golden
Slippery Rock University

Ivan Franklin Harber Jr.
Indian River State College

Warren C. Hodges
Forsyth Technical Community College

Norman Hollingsworth
Langston University

Walter E. Lippincott
Naugatuck Valley Community College

Bruce A. McKechnie
Germanna Community College

Benjamin Neil
Towson University

Michele Pickett
Cuyahoga Community College

Ricky Richardson
Tarleton State University

Beth Snodgrass
Mountain Empire Community College

Deborah Vinecour
SUNY Rockland Community College

I want to thank the following individuals who were involved with content creation.

Brad Cox
Midlands Technical College

Brian Elzweig
University of West Florida

Brian Gravely

Cheryl Harwick

Vonda Laughlin
King University

Jeff Penley
Catawba Valley Community College

Damon Scott
Atlanta Technical College

Joseph Zavaletta
Issachar Law Group–Boise, Idaho

I also extend special thanks to Jennifer A. Chiocco for her excellent photograph on the About the Author page. I also offer thanks to Gordon W. Brown, the former lead author of *Business Law with UCC Applications*, whose devotion and hard work made this book the quality product that it is today. Thanks and appreciation also go to Bob Nirkind whose patience and guidance taught me how indispensable a good editor really can be.

Acknowledgments

Finally, a book is but a raw, unsold manuscript until the skilled publishing team refines it. This manuscript benefited immeasurably from the guidance of the multiple levels of skill provided by McGraw-Hill Education: Managing Director, Tim Vertovec; our Product Developers, Jaroslaw Szymanski and Allie Kukla; Executive Brand Manager, Kathleen Klehr; and Content Project Managers, Dana Pauley and Angela Norris.

A Guided Tour

Business Law with UCC Applications, 15/e, is full of useful chapter features to make studying productive and hassle-free. The following pages show the kind of engaging, helpful pedagogical features that complement the accessible, easy-to-understand approach to teaching business law.

Business Law with UCC Applications—and Now the Applications

The fifteenth edition of *Business Law with UCC Applications* includes a new feature entitled "*Business Law with UCC Applications*—and Now the Applications." Each installment of this feature explores a political, social, or ethical aspect of the Uniform Commercial Code or the Uniform Law Commission that is not covered in the text proper but is directly related to the content of the chapter in which the feature is located. For example, the installment in Chapter 2, Sources of the Law, investigates the question of whether it is ethical for legislators to pass on their responsibility for the state's legislative agenda by turning part of that agenda over to the Uniform Law Commission, an organization that consists of legal experts appointed by the state governments but not elected by the people.

Uniform Commercial Code References

In each chapter that involves a section or sections of the Uniform Commercial Code, citations to those sections are printed under the topic heading in that chapter. This feature enables students to access the actual text of the UCC in order to double check the rule that is explained at that point in the book. Students can easily refer to the text of any individual code section by accessing the UCC through the URL printed in Appendix B of the text.

Chapter Outline

Each chapter features an outline that allows students to recognize the organization of the chapter at a glance. For reinforcement, the outline's numbering system is used throughout the body of the chapter and is repeated in the end-of-chapter Summary.

The Opening Case
A brief case opens each chapter and introduces the chapter concepts, followed by numbered questions addressing legal issues in the case. Every opening case is reexamined throughout the chapter. Those scenarios that become opening cases are chosen carefully to bring a broad spectrum of illustrations to the text. Some of these are hypotheticals, created specifically for the material in the chapters. Others are drawn from today's headlines and are not yet in the courts. Still others are classic cases that have been used in law courses for decades and thus represent the best illustrations of key points in the law.

THE OPENING CASE Round 1
The European Community v. RJR Nabisco: Euros and RICO and Nations ... Oh My!

This case starts with the sale of drugs on the streets of Europe financed by a complicated money laundering scheme allegedly masterminded by the American corporation RJR Nabisco Inc. (RJR). The European Community (EC), acting for itself and for its members, brought suit in federal court in New York against RJR under the Racketeer Influenced and Corrupt Organizations (RICO) Act, claiming that RJR had, in furtherance of its illegal scheme, committed numerous acts of money laundering, wire fraud, mail fraud, and violations of the Travel Act. For good measure, the EC added several allegations of wrongdoing under the state laws of New York. RJR filed a motion to dismiss based on two claims. The first claim stated that since RICO does not expressly authorize extraterritorial claims like this one, the presumption must be against the extraterritorial application of the statute. The second claim stated that the federal courts had no jurisdiction over the state claims because the EC was a conglomerate of nations and not a nation-state itself, which meant it did not satisfy the need for diversity that was required by the federal rules. The district court dismissed the case on both counts.

Dissatisfied with the result, the EC and its member nations filed an appeal in the U.S. Court of Appeals for the Second Circuit. In a surprise move, the appellate court reversed the District Court's ruling. In response to the first claim, the court said that the presumption that a statute like RICO does not apply to extraterritorial conduct can be overcome if a predicate offense named in RICO includes extraterritorial conduct. A **predicate offense** is generally one that provides the resources needed to commit the offenses outlined in the new statute. Racketeering, as laid out in RICO, includes money laundering as a predicate offense. Congress defines money laundering to include extraterritorial activities. Therefore, Congress intended money laundering to have an extraterritorial application in RICO. As for the charges involving mail fraud, wire fraud, and violations of the Travel Act, the appeals court held that since the complaint alleged facts that would give rise to a domestic cause of action, the fact that those facts included extraterritorial offenses did not disqualify the court from hearing the case. As for the second claim, the court decided that the federal court system had subject matter jurisdiction over the state claims because, even though the EC is not a foreign nation, it is an instrumentality that represents several foreign nations, which is enough to satisfy the requirements of the jurisdictional statute.

RJR took the case to the U.S. Supreme Court. Not surprisingly, the High Court upheld the ruling by the Court of Appeals. So far, so good for the EC. Then the High Court threw a curve. It ruled that claims brought under RICO and similar statutes by private parties (i.e., any party that is not the U.S. government; in other

Learning Objectives
Succinct, crisply written learning objectives follow the opening case at the beginning of each chapter. The numbered objectives describe what the students can expect to learn as a result of completing the chapter. Each objective is identified by a symbol in the margin where the material appears in the text.

LO Learning Objectives
1. Explain the fundamental nature of the American courts.
2. Determine when a case can be brought in federal court.
3. Recognize those cases that can be heard by the U.S. Supreme Court.
4. Identify the structure of most state court systems.
5. Define *civil litigation*.
6. List the most common discovery techniques.
7. Detail the nature of an appeal.
8. Determine the extent of cyber-jurisdiction.
9. Explain the nature of electronically stored information.
10. Describe the steps in a criminal prosecution.

New Classic Cases
A new Classic Cases feature has been included in many chapters in this edition, giving both the instructor and the students an opportunity to explore topics related to the content of the chapter in a provocative and stimulating way.

A CLASSIC CASE Healthy, Wealthy, and Wise?

Literature instructors are fond of saying that a poem, a play, a novel, or a short story is considered good, sometimes even great, if it has stood the "test of time." The same is true of many legal cases. Such is the situation with the long-standing case of *Hamer v. Sidway*, a lawsuit that most law students and paralegals encounter (or should encounter) at some time in their academic careers. *Hamer and Sidway* begins at a golden wedding anniversary celebration. At the party, Uncle William promised his nephew and namesake, William, the Younger, that if he, the nephew, would give up a long list of vices that included smoking and swearing, until his 21st birthday, he, the uncle, would pay his nephew, William, $5,000. The challenge was made in front of a room full of family members and close friends, and William, the Younger, agreed to the arrangement. Following this and in compliance with the agreement, William embarked on an extensive period of abstinence that lasted several years. Soon after his 21st birthday, William wrote to his uncle telling him of his

William brought this lawsuit. William argued that he had performed as promised and was, therefore, entitled to the money. The executor recognized that William had, indeed, refrained from smoking and swearing, but argued that, in contract law, both sides must suffer a detriment for consideration to be valid and for a contract to exist. In this case, the executor said, young William had not suffered a detriment. In fact, the opposite was true. He was much healthier than he would have been, absent the promise, and he had, therefore, benefited greatly from giving up his bad habits for such an extended period of time. In the absence of consideration, no contract ever existed and, as a result, the estate did not owe young William a single cent. The court disagreed with this analysis. The court noted that, when William gave up something that he had a legal right to do, he had suffered a detriment sufficient to provide the consideration needed to make the agreement into a *bona fide* contract. To prove its point, the court referred to a standard treatise on contract law and noted that

A Question of Ethics boxes challenge students' understanding of previously discussed chapter examples by asking questions specifically relating to ethical dilemmas.

About the Law boxes provide additional clarification of chapter concepts.

Did You Know? boxes are interesting factoids directly linked to the chapter concept being discussed.

Examples are titled and numbered throughout each chapter and use short vignettes to explain how concepts can be applied in real-life situations.

Quick Quiz boxes follow each numbered section and give students the chance to test themselves with three true/false questions. Answers are provided at the end of each chapter.

Questions for Review and Discussion provide a means for students and the instructor to reexamine and discuss the key points of law. All objectives listed at the beginning of each chapter are also reviewed.

> Questions for Review and Discussion
> 1. What are the objectives of the law?
> 2. How does the law reflect a series of complex dualities?
> 3. What are the functions of the articles and the amendments of the U.S. Constitution?
> 4. What is an executive order?
> 5. What is the role of statutory law in the legal system?
> 6. Why does this country need to set up a system of uniform state laws?
> 7. What is the role of common law in the legal system?
> 8. How does the principle of *stare decisis* provide stability to our legal system?
> 9. What is the difference between statutory interpretation and judicial review?
> 10. What is the nature of the deep state within the American legal system?

Summary Numbered to match the outline at the beginning of the chapter and the main heads within each chapter, the Summary provides an encapsulated review of the chapter's content.

Key Terms Each key term is printed in boldface and defined when introduced in the text. A list of key terms and the page number of first usage appears at the end of each chapter. A glossary of the key terms is provided at the back of the text.

Cases for Analysis have been updated extensively for the 14th edition and chosen for their relevance, ease of understanding, and interesting fact patterns. Many are abridgements of actual court decisions; some are taken from current news stories; and still others are hypothetical situations written to emphasize legal issues and concepts presented in the text.

> Cases for Analysis
> 1. David Terry was so dissatisfied with the outcome of a lawsuit that he threatened to kill Stephen J. Field, a Supreme Court Justice, whose responsibilities included acting as the Supreme Court representative in the Ninth Circuit. The Attorney General of the United States ordered a federal marshal named David Neagle to protect Justice Field. When Terry attacked Justice Field, Neagle shot and killed him. Neagle was then promptly arrested by a local sheriff and charged with murder. Neagle brought his case to the nearest federal district court under a writ of *habeas corpus*. Neagle asked the court to vacate his arrest, arguing that he had been ordered by the Attorney General of
> 2. In the wake of the disastrous events of 9/11, President George W. Bush and his advisors were concerned that the United States might be subject to further devastating attacks. Accordingly, President Bush released an executive order that authorized the establishment of a series of Military Commissions located at Guantanamo Bay designed to try individuals who were suspected of committing acts of terrorism. The order read in part, "To protect the United States and its citizens, and for the effective conduct of military operations and prevention of terrorist attacks, it is necessary for individuals subject to this order pursuant to section 2 hereof to be detained, and, when tried, to be tried

The **Case Study** at the end of each of the nine parts begins with a summary of the facts of the case, is followed by an excerpt from the court's opinion, and concludes with a series of questions.

Four appendices provide critical material for the students: The Constitution of the United States (Appendix A), Articles 1, 2, 2a, and 3 of the Uniform Commercial Code (Appendix B), the United Nations Convention for the International Sale of Goods (Appendix C), and two final documents, Patrick Henry's Tax Assessment Bill and James Madison's "Memorial and Remonstrance" (Appendix D). Marginal references throughout the text refer students to the page of the appendix where the original source of the law being discussed can be found.

> Students—study more efficiently, retain more and achieve better outcomes. Instructors—focus on what you love—teaching.

SUCCESSFUL SEMESTERS INCLUDE CONNECT

For Instructors

You're in the driver's seat.

Want to build your own course? No problem. Prefer to use our turnkey, prebuilt course? Easy. Want to make changes throughout the semester? Sure. And you'll save time with Connect's auto-grading too.

65%
Less Time Grading

They'll thank you for it.

Adaptive study resources like SmartBook® help your students be better prepared in less time. You can transform your class time from dull definitions to dynamic debates. Hear from your peers about the benefits of Connect at www.mheducation.com/highered/connect

Make it simple, make it affordable.

Connect makes it easy with seamless integration using any of the major Learning Management Systems—Blackboard®, Canvas, and D2L, among others—to let you organize your course in one convenient location. Give your students access to digital materials at a discount with our inclusive access program. Ask your McGraw-Hill representative for more information.

©Hill Street Studios/Tobin Rogers/Blend Images LLC

Solutions for your challenges.

A product isn't a solution. Real solutions are affordable, reliable, and come with training and ongoing support when you need it and how you want it. Our Customer Experience Group can also help you troubleshoot tech problems—although Connect's 99% uptime means you might not need to call them. See for yourself at **status.mheducation.com**

FOR STUDENTS

Effective, efficient studying.

Connect helps you be more productive with your study time and get better grades using tools like SmartBook, which highlights key concepts and creates a personalized study plan. Connect sets you up for success, so you walk into class with confidence and walk out with better grades.

©Shutterstock/wavebreakmedia

> " I really liked this app—it made it easy to study when you don't have your textbook in front of you. "
>
> - Jordan Cunningham,
> Eastern Washington University

Study anytime, anywhere.

Download the free ReadAnywhere app and access your online eBook when it's convenient, even if you're offline. And since the app automatically syncs with your eBook in Connect, all of your notes are available every time you open it. Find out more at **www.mheducation.com/readanywhere**

No surprises.

The Connect Calendar and Reports tools keep you on track with the work you need to get done and your assignment scores. Life gets busy; Connect tools help you keep learning through it all.

Learning for everyone.

McGraw-Hill works directly with Accessibility Services Departments and faculty to meet the learning needs of all students. Please contact your Accessibility Services office and ask them to email accessibility@mheducation.com, or visit **www.mheducation.com/about/accessibility.html** for more information.

Additional McGraw-Hill Connect Features

 McGraw-Hill Education has partnered with Roger CPA Review, a global leader in CPA Exam preparation, to provide students a smooth transition from the accounting classroom to successful completion of the CPA Exam. While many aspiring accountants wait until they have completed their academic studies to begin preparing for the CPA Exam, research shows that those who become familiar with exam content earlier in the process have a stronger chance of successfully passing the CPA Exam. Accordingly, students using these McGraw-Hill materials will have access to sample CPA Exam Multiple-Choice Questions and Task-Based Simulations from Roger CPA Review, with expert-written explanations and solutions. All questions are either directly from the AICPA or are modeled on AICPA questions that appear in the exam. Instructors may assign the auto-gradable Roger CPA Review Multiple-Choice Questions in Connect, and Task-Based Simulations are delivered via the Roger CPA Review platform, which mirrors the look, feel, and functionality of the actual exam. McGraw-Hill Education and Roger CPA Review are dedicated to supporting every accounting student along their journey, ultimately helping them achieve career success in the accounting profession. For more information about the full Roger CPA Review program, exam requirements and exam content, visit www.rogercpareview.com.

Business Law Case Repository Available in *Connect*, the Case Repository is a collection of cases from current and previous editions.

Instructor Resources

The *Connect* Instructor Resource Center is your repository for additional resources to improve student engagement in and out of class. You can select and use any asset that enhances your lecture. The *Connect* Instructor Resource Center includes:

- *eBook*
- *Test Bank*
- *Instructors Manual*
- *PowerPoint files*
- *Videos*
- *Business Law Newsletter archives*
- *Access to interactive study tools*

Tegrity Campus: Lectures 24/7

 Tegrity is a fully automated screen capture solution used in traditional, hybrid, "flipped classes" and online courses to record lessons, lectures, and skills. Automatically included within Connect for no additional charge, instructors can also use Tegrity for online proctoring. Patented search technology and real-time LMS integrations make Tegrity the market-leading solution and service.

Assurance of Learning Ready

Many educational institutions today are focused on the notion of *assurance of learning*, an important element of some accreditation standards. *Business Law with UCC Applications*, 15th edition, is designed specifically to support your assurance of learning initiatives with a simple, yet powerful solution.

Each test bank question for *Business Law with UCC Applications* maps to a specific chapter learning outcome/objective listed in the text. You can use our test bank software, EZ Test and EZ Test Online, or in *Connect* to easily query for learning outcomes/objectives that directly relate to the learning objectives for your course. You can then use the reporting features of EZ Test to aggregate student results in similar fashion, making the collection and presentation of assurance of learning data simple and easy.

AACSB Statement

The McGraw-Hill Companies is a proud corporate member of AACSB International. The AACSB leaves content coverage and assessment within the purview of individual schools, the mission of the school, and the faculty. While *Business Law*, 15th edition, and the teaching package make no claim of any specific AACSB qualification or evaluation, we have within *Business Law with UCC Applications*, 15th edition, labeled selected test bank and quiz questions according to the eight general knowledge and skills areas

Contents in Brief

Preface vii

Contents xxxii

Part One
Ethics, Law, and the Judicial System 1

Chapter 1   Ethics and the Law 2

Chapter 2   Sources of the Law 28

Chapter 3   The Judicial Process and Cyber-Procedure 62

Chapter 4   Alternative Dispute Resolution and Cyber-ADR 92

Chapter 5   Criminal Law and Cybercrimes 118

Chapter 6   Tort Law and Cybertorts 162

Case Study: Barbara Schneider, Plaintiff-Appellant v. Mark Kumpf, Defendant-Appellee 199

Part Two
Contract Law 207

Chapter 7   The Essentials of Contract Law 208

Chapter 8   Offer, Acceptance, and Mutual Assent 234

Chapter 9   Consideration and Cyber-Payments 264

Chapter 10   Capacity and Legality: The Final Elements 284

Chapter 11   Written Contracts and Cyber-Commerce 304

Chapter 12   Third Parties, Discharge, and Remedies 330

Case Study: Sylvia Burwell, Secretary of Health and Human Services, et al. v. Hobby Lobby Stores, Inc., et al. (AKA The Hobby Lobby Case) 355

Part Three
Sales and Consumer Protection 365

Chapter 13   Sales Contracts: Formation, Title, and Risk of Loss 366

Chapter 14   Sales Contracts: Rights, Duties, Breach, and Warranties 392

Chapter 15   Product Liability and Consumer Protection 414

Case Study: Norcold, Inc. v. Gateway Supply Company 441

Part Four
Negotiable Instruments and Banking 447

Chapter 16   The Nature of Negotiable Instruments 448

Chapter 17   Holders in Due Course, Defenses, and Liabilities 472

Chapter 18   Bank–Depositor Relationships and Cyber-Banking 490

Case Study: Read v. South Carolina National Bank 513

Part Five
Insurance, Secured Transactions, and Bankruptcy 519

Chapter 19   Insurance 520

Chapter 20   Mortgages, Land Contracts, and the 21st-Century Financial Crisis 548

Chapter 21   Bankruptcy Law: In Theory, in History, and in Practice 576

Case Study: Superior Savings Association v. City of Cleveland 601

Part Six
Agency and Employment 607

Chapter 22   Agency Law   608

Chapter 23   Employment Law   638

Chapter 24   Labor Law   676

Case Study: Evans v. Georgia Regional Hospital   699

Part Seven
Business Organization and Regulation 703

Chapter 25   The Business Entity: An Introduction   704

Chapter 26   The Corporate Entity   728

Chapter 27   Managing the Corporate Entity   756

Chapter 28   Government Regulation of the Corporate Entity   784

Case Study: Gries Sports Enterprises, Inc. v. Cleveland Browns Football Co., Inc.   817

Part Eight
Property Law 821

Chapter 29   Personal Property and Bailments   822

Chapter 30   Real Property and Landlord and Tenant Law   844

Chapter 31   Wills, Advance Directives, and Trusts   874

Case Study: Obergefell, et al., v. Hodges, Director, Ohio Department of Health, et al.   899

Part Nine
The Legal Environment 907

Chapter 32   Professional Liability   908

Chapter 33   Science, Technology, and Law in the 21st Century   942

Chapter 34   International Law and the New World Order   998

Case Study: Legal Consequences of the Construction of a Wall in the Occupied Palestinian Territory (Request for Advisory Opinion)   1043

Appendix A   The Constitution of the United States   1047

Appendix B   Uniform Commercial Code (Articles 1, 2, 2a, and 3)*   1056

Appendix C   United Nations Convention on Contracts for the International Sale of Goods   1057

Appendix D   Patrick Henry's Tax Assessment Bill and James Madison's "Memorial and Remonstrance"   1069

Glossary   1073

Case Index   1115

Subject Index   1120

Contents

Preface vii

©Hisham F. Ibrahim/Getty Images

Part One
Ethics, Law, and the Judicial System 1

Chapter 1 Ethics and the Law 2
- Defining the Law, Morality, and Ethics 3
- Ethical Theories 8
- Ethics and the Government 13
- Ethics and Business 17
- The Relationship between Law and Ethics 21

Chapter 2 Sources of the Law 28
- The Purpose and Operation of the Law 29
- Constitutional Law 34
- Executive Orders 41
- Statutory Law 45
- Court Decisions 48
- Administrative Regulations 50

Chapter 3 The Judicial Process and Cyber-Procedure 62
- The Court System 63
- Civil Procedure 71
- Cyber-Procedure 81
- Criminal Procedure 85

Chapter 4 Alternative Dispute Resolution and Cyber-ADR 92
- A Briefing on ADR Strategies 93
- Responsive ADR Strategies 98
- Proactive ADR Strategies 102
- Cyber Alternative Dispute Resolution 111

Chapter 5 Criminal Law and Cybercrimes 118
- Definition and Classes of Crimes 119
- Elements of a Crime 124
- Specific Crimes 133
- Cybercrimes 141
- Defenses to Criminal Liability 150

Chapter 6 Tort Law and Cybertorts 162
- Tort Law Defined 163
- Intentional Torts 167
- Negligence 176
- Strict Liability 183
- Cybertorts 184
- Remedies for Torts 187
- Developments in Tort Law 189

Case Study: *Barbara Schneider, Plaintiff-Appellant v. Mark Kumpf, Defendant-Appellee* 199

©Bacho/Shutterstock

Part Two
Contract Law 207

Chapter 7 The Essentials of Contract Law 208
- The History of Contract Law 209
- The Multidimensional Nature of Contract Law 217
- Contractual Characteristics 225

Chapter 8 Offer, Acceptance, and Mutual Assent 234
- Mutual Assent and the Offer 235
- Acceptance of an Offer 242
- Mutual Assent in Cyberspace 247
- The Destruction of Mutual Assent 253

Chapter 9 Consideration and Cyber-Payments 264

Requirements of Consideration 265
Types of Consideration 268
Problems with Consideration 272
Cyber-Payment Tactics and Concerns 277

Chapter 10 Capacity and Legality: The Final Elements 284

The Final Elements 285
Other Capacity Problems 292
Agreements to Engage in Unlawful Activity 293
Consequences of Illegality 299

Chapter 11 Written Contracts and Cyber-Commerce 304

The Statute of Frauds 305
Legal Rules for Written Contracts 312
Formalities of Construction 317
Cyber-Commerce and the Law 324

Chapter 12 Third Parties, Discharge, and Remedies 330

Contracts and Third Parties 331
The Law of Assignment 333
Assignment Rights, Duties, and Restrictions 335
Discharge by Performance 339
Discharge by Nonperformance 343
Damages and Equitable Remedies 346

Case Study: *Sylvia Burwell, Secretary of Health and Human Services, et al. v. Hobby Lobby Stores, Inc., et al. (AKA The Hobby Lobby Case)* 355

©Artifacts Images/Getty Images

Part Three
Sales and Consumer Protection 365

Chapter 13 Sales Contracts: Formation, Title, and Risk of Loss 366

The Sale and Lease of Goods 367
Rules for Sales Contracts 371
The Form of a Sales Contract 375
Title, Passage of Title, and Risk of Loss 381
Sales, Returns, and Insurable Interest 386

Chapter 14 Sales Contracts: Rights, Duties, Breach, and Warranties 392

Rights and Duties of the Parties 393
Breach of Contract 399
Warranty Protection 406

Chapter 15 Product Liability and Consumer Protection 414

Product Liability 415
Consumer Protection Laws 422
Consumer Credit Laws 430

Case Study: *Norcold, Inc. v. Gateway Supply Company* 441

©Stockbroker/Alamy

Part Four
Negotiable Instruments and Banking 447

Chapter 16 The Nature of Negotiable Instruments 448

The Essentials of Negotiable Instruments 449
Transferring Negotiable Instruments 462

Chapter 17 Holders in Due Course, Defenses, and Liabilities 472

Holder in Due Course 473
Personal Defenses 478
Real Defenses 481
Liability of the Parties 485

Chapter 18 Bank–Depositor Relationships and Cyber-Banking 490

The Bank–Depositor Relationship 491
Bank Deposits and Collections 502
Cyber-Banking 505

Case Study: *Read v. South Carolina National Bank* 513

©Plush Studios/Blend Images LLC

Part Five

Insurance, Secured Transactions, and Bankruptcy 519

Chapter 19 Insurance 520
- Risk Assessment and Peril Management 521
- Types of Insurance 526
- The Insurance Policy 540
- Cancellation of Insurance by Insurer 541

Chapter 20 Mortgages, Land Contracts, and the 21st-Century Financial Crisis 548
- A Primer on Real Property Finance and Security 549
- The 21st-Century Financial Crisis 557
- Personal Property as Security 569

Chapter 21 Bankruptcy Law: In Theory, in History, and in Practice 576
- The Checkered History of Bankruptcy in the United States 577
- Liquidation—Chapter 7, Bankruptcy Code 582
- Reorganization—Chapter 11, Bankruptcy Code 591
- Family Farmer or Fishing Business Debt Adjustment—Chapter 12, Bankruptcy Code 595
- Individual Debt Adjustment—Chapter 13, Bankruptcy Code 597

Case Study: Superior Savings Association v. City of Cleveland 601

©Keith Brofsky/Getty Images

Part Six

Agency and Employment 607

Chapter 22 Agency Law 608
- The Nature of Agency Law 609
- Principles of Agency Law 622
- Duties in Agency Law 625
- A Final View of Agency Law 628

Chapter 23 Employment Law 638
- The Employment Relationship 639
- Laws Regulating Employment Conditions 651
- Worker Benefits 654
- Equal Employment Opportunity 657
- Social Media Policies 669

Chapter 24 Labor Law 676
- Labor Law and the Economic Crisis 677
- Major Federal Labor Legislation 682
- The Collective Bargaining Process 691

Case Study: Evans v. Georgia Regional Hospital 699

©Beau Lark/Corbis/VCG/Getty Images

Part Seven

Business Organization and Regulation 703

Chapter 25 The Business Entity: An Introduction 704
- Sole Proprietorships and Other Business Entities 706
- General Partnership Characteristics 707
- Partnership Formation 712
- Partnership Property Rights and Duties 715
- Dissociation and Dissolution 721
- Other Forms of Partnership Business 723

Chapter 26 The Corporate Entity 728
- The Economic Crisis and the Corporate Entity 730
- Types of Corporate Entities 739
- Formation of the Corporate Entity 741
- Corporate Identity 745
- Financing the Corporate Entity 750

Chapter 27 Managing the Corporate Entity 756
- Management of the Corporate Entity 758
- Issues in Governing the Corporate Entity 760
- Governance Responsibilities 773
- Shareholder Rights 778
- Governance of a Limited Liability Company 779

Chapter 28 Government Regulation of the Corporate Entity 784
- The Constitution and the Corporate Entity 786
- Securities Regulation of the Corporate Entity 790
- Antitrust Regulation of the Corporate Entity 798
- Expanding the Corporate Entity 803
- The Government and the End of the Corporate Entity 810
- Dissolution of a Limited Liability Company 811

Case Study: Gries Sports Enterprises, Inc. v. Cleveland Browns Football Co., Inc. 817

©Digital Vision/Getty Images

Part Eight
Property Law 821

Chapter 29 Personal Property and Bailments 822
- Personal Property 823
- Bailments 829

Chapter 30 Real Property and Landlord and Tenant Law 844
- The Rights Related to Real Property 845
- Estates in and Co-Ownership of Real Property 848
- Subterranean Rights: Oil and Gas Developments 854
- Acquiring Title to and Managing Real Property 858
- The Landlord–Tenant Relationship 862
- Duties of the Landlord and the Tenant 866

Chapter 31 Wills, Advance Directives, and Trusts 874
- Sources and Relevance of Probate Law 875
- The Law of Wills 876
- The Law of Advance Directives 887
- The Law of Trusts 894

Case Study: Obergefell, et al., v. Hodges, Director, Ohio Department of Health, et al. 899

©Jim Arbogast/Getty Images

Part Nine
The Legal Environment 907

Chapter 32 Professional Liability 908
- The Liability of Accountants 910
- The Liability of Architects and Attorneys 924
- The Liability of Health Care Providers 932
- The Liability of Hospitals 937

Chapter 33 Science, Technology, and Law in the 21st Century 942
- Governmental Authority Regulating Science and Technology 944
- National Expenditures for Science and Technology 953
- International Authority Regulating Jurisicence 956
- Facing Global Challenges 961
- Protecting Intellectual Property 973
- Developing Global Solutions 985

Chapter 34 International Law and the New World Order 998
- The New World Order 1000
- International Law and War 1017
- The United Nations and the Global Community 1027
- International Law, Finance, and Trade 1035

Case Study: Legal Consequences of the Construction of a Wall in the Occupied Palestinian Territory (Request for Advisory Opinion) 1043

Appendix A The Constitution of the United States 1047

Appendix B Uniform Commercial Code (Articles 1, 2, 2a, and 3)* 1056

Appendix C United Nations Convention on Contracts for the International Sale of Goods 1057

Appendix D Patrick Henry's Tax Assessment Bill and James Madison's "Memorial and Remonstrance" 1069

Glossary 1073

Case Index 1115

Subject Index 1120

©Hisham F. Ibrahim/Getty Images

Part One

Ethics, Law, and the Judicial System

Chapter 1	Ethics and the Law	Chapter 5	Criminal Law and Cybercrimes
Chapter 2	Sources of the Law	Chapter 6	Tort Law and Cybertorts
Chapter 3	The Judicial Process and Cyber-Procedure	Case Study	*Barbara Schneider, Plaintiff-Appellant v. Mark Kumpf, Defendant-Appellee*
Chapter 4	Alternative Dispute Resolution and Cyber-ADR		

Chapter 1

Ethics and the Law

1-1 Defining the Law, Morality, and Ethics
The Law and Morality • Values and Ethics • Natural Law • Positive Law • Nonjudgmentalism

1-2 Ethical Theories
Social Contract Ethics • Utilitarianism • Rational Ethics

1-3 Ethics and the Government
A Governmental and Ethical Dyad • Shortcomings of the Ethical Dyad • The Threat of Failed States • The Responsibility to Protect (R2P)

1-4 Ethics and Business
The Traditional Business Culture • Reasons for Ethical Responsibility • Efforts to Promote Ethical Responsibility

1-5 The Relationship between Law and Ethics
The Need for Law in Our Society • Ethical and Legal Anarchy

THE OPENING CASE Round 1
National Security versus Human Rights

The question of whether governmental officials can detain individuals without bail in cases that involve suspected threats to national security arose again recently when the U.S. Supreme Court decided the case of *Ziglar v. Abbasi*. To understand the details of this case, we have to travel back in time to September 11, 2001. After the terror attack that brought down the Twin Towers, seriously damaged the Pentagon, and brought down United Flight 93 on 9/11, in an effort to prevent further attacks, FBI agents arrested more than 700 men of Arab and Asian descent and detained them without bail on charges of violating immigration law. Those prisoners who were later determined to be "of interest," some 84 individuals, remained in custody in Brooklyn's Metropolitan Detention Center, while the others were released. The plaintiffs in this case were six young men, five of whom are Muslim, who were held in detention for several months and were subjected to conditions that were alleged to be harsh and cruel. The defendants in the case include John Ashcroft, who was the Attorney General at the time; Robert Mueller, the former FBI Director; and the former Immigration and Naturalization Service Commissioner, James Ziglar. One of the key issues in the case involved the plaintiffs' claim that these three high-ranking government officials had conspired to detain them in harsh conditions in violation of their due process and equal protection rights on the pretext that they were illegal aliens when, in reality, the FBI used the time to investigate them for terrorist connections. The plaintiffs asked the Supreme Court for money damages against the defendants.

The right to seek money damages against high government officials like the ones in this case, for constitutional violations, was acknowledged by the High Court in a previous case, known as the *Bivens* case. However, the *Bivens* case was a very narrow ruling issued cautiously by the Court because it involved creating a cause of action that had not been expressly authorized by Congress. Therefore, the Court would not widen the grounds for such causes of action, especially when "special factors counseling hesitation" existed to convince the Court that widening the cause of action would not be in the best interests of justice. Given this interpretation of *Bivens*, the justices ruled that they would not permit a cause of action for damages in this case against the former Attorney General, the former FBI director, and the former Immigration and Naturalization Service Commissioner because there were, indeed, "special factors counseling hesitation"—namely, the extraordinary conditions surrounding the events of 9/11. Given the balancing act between an individual's constitutional rights and the rights of the rest of the people to be safe and secure in their homes, the Court opted in favor of security over freedom. So in this case, in the battle between constitutional rights and national security, national security clearly won the day. (Well, almost. The case was actually decided by a 4–2 majority. The justices who ruled in favor of national security were Roberts, Kennedy, Thomas, and Alito. Beyer and Ginsburg dissented, Sotomayor and Kagan had recused themselves, and Gorsuch had not yet joined the Court.)

[See *Ziglar v. Abbasi*, 582 U.S. ------- (2017); and *Ziglar v. Abbasi*, *Oyez*, August 26, 2017, www.oyez.org/cases/2016/15-1358#!.]

Opening Case Questions

1. Should high-ranking government officials ever be subject to having to pay money damages in a lawsuit just for doing their job? Why or why not?

2. Should the question of whether to promote national security over fundamental rights be based on how many people will be hurt if national security is sacrificed? Explain.

3. Is there ever a time when fundamental freedoms should be upheld at the expense of national security? Explain.

4. Can it ever be said that national leaders must be held to a different level of ethical responsibility than those that bind everyday citizens? If so, what is that level or responsibility; if not, why not?

5. When we enter a social contract not to harm others, have we set up an absolute and unchanging standard, or does such a contract vary from situation to situation? Explain.

Source: See: *Ziglar v. Abbasi*, 582 U.S. ------- (2017); and *Ziglar v. Abbasi*, Oyez, 26 Aug. 2017, www.oyez.org/cases/2016/15-1358#!.

 Learning Objectives

1. Define *law*, *morality*, and *ethics*.
2. Distinguish between natural law and positive law.
3. Explain the effects of nonjudgmentalism.
4. Describe social contract ethics.
5. Outline the steps in applying utilitarianism.
6. Define *rational ethics*.
7. Explain the dyadic nature of ethics in government.
8. Explore the need for ethical responsibility in business.
9. Describe the need for law in our society.
10. Clarify how the law and ethics can often benefit from anarchy.

1-1 Defining the Law, Morality, and Ethics

Often people will disagree about the most trivial of matters—whether pumpkin pie tastes best with or without whipped cream, whether London or Paris offers the best theater, and whether baseball or football is the national pastime (it's baseball, by the way). Despite this, some subjects that provoke disagreement are of great importance—whether the death penalty should be outlawed or used more frequently, whether Civil War monuments honoring Confederate soldiers and politicians should be removed from public places, whether parents or the courts should be empowered to make life-and-death decisions about children, and whether national security is more critical than constitutional rights. It would be best were we to employ a commonly understood, universally accepted ethical standard by which to measure these key issues. There is little disagreement on this basic premise. Nevertheless, once we cross that threshold, disagreement becomes the norm rather than the exception. Socrates, speaking through Plato, suggested centuries ago that we begin a study of ethics by understanding human nature. With that simple axiom in mind, we begin our study of the philosophy of ethics.

First, however, we must define a few key terms. Most legal textbooks and many treatises on ethics begin by defining these disciplines. This tradition stands in marked contrast to most other studies. Few physics textbooks pause to tell the reader what physics is. Fewer history books devote space to explaining the term *history*, and almost no math texts begin by defining *math*; however, that is as it should be. These disciplines and others like them are fixed in our minds as implacable fields of study. In history, for example, the fact that the Cleveland Cavaliers won the 2016 NBA championship (and then lost it in 2017) is not in dispute; nor is the fact that Donald Trump was elected President of the United States in 2016. Nor is our understanding that such events are historical facts. The same is true of the second law of thermodynamics in physics and the multiplication tables in mathematics. These facts are not debatable, except in the most esoteric way. [See: Jeffrie G. Murphy and Jules L. Coleman, *The Philosophy of Law* (Boulder, CO: Westview Press, 1990), p. 6; and John C. Calhoun, "A Disquisition on Government," in *Philosophy in America,* eds. Paul Russell Anderson and Max Harold Fisch (New York: Appleton-Century Crofts, 1939), pp. 356–357.]

The Law and Morality

This is not the case with morality and the law. People *will* argue about both, and when they do so, it is often in a most uncivil manner. They will dispute whether the law is a form of civil management or a way to dictate individual behavior, whether it ought to be created by a national government or a regional state system, and whether it should change regularly or stay the same indefinitely. They will even argue about whether the rules made by the government demand absolute, unquestioned obedience or simply ask for occasional recognition as optional guiding principles. As noted earlier, people will also argue about moral issues. This is why we pause at the beginning of *Business Law* to define the law and morality and to distinguish between ethics and morals, concepts that many of us usually do not think about on a daily basis.

The **law** consists of rules of conduct established by the government of a society to maintain harmony, stability, and justice. It accomplishes these objectives by defining the duties and rights of the people. The law also provides a way to protect the people by enforcing these duties and rights through the courts, the executive branch, and the legislature. The law is therefore a means of civil management. Certainly, the law usually cannot stop a person from doing wrong; however, the law can punish an individual who chooses to do that wrong, whatever it might be. The law then draws the line between conduct that is permissible and that which is not allowed, so people, at the very least, know that they can be punished if they choose to disobey the law.

EXAMPLE 1-1: The Government's Case against Jack Bauer

Once upon a time, in a mythical version of post-9/11 America, a government agent named Jack Bauer worked for a federal law enforcement agency known as the Counter Terrorist Unit (CTU). In this mythical America, as depicted on the long-running and highly successful TV show *24*, Bauer pretty much did whatever he had to do to protect American interests and save American lives, up to and including torture. Neither Bauer nor CTU escape accountability, however, and in season seven of *24*, Bauer is subpoenaed to testify before a Senate oversight committee. When asked by the chairman of the committee whether he tortured a terrorist, Bauer admits that he did (saving the lives of 45 people, 10 of whom were children). The chairman then observes that Bauer clearly believes that the ends justify the means and that he cares nothing about the law. In response, Bauer (well, okay, Kiefer Sutherland) makes an interesting observation. He says that he adapted to a situation in order to carry out his mission, which was to save the lives of those innocent civilians; however, when considering the question of whether he broke the law, Bauer does not duck, shift, or dodge responsibility. Instead, he says, "In answer to your question, am I above the law, no sir, I am more than willing to be judged by the people." As noted earlier, Bauer clearly understands that the law draws a line between conduct that is permissible and that which is not. So Bauer, as an admitted lawbreaker, knows that he can be punished for choosing to break that law and accepts that responsibility. This is what is meant when we say that the law usually cannot stop a person from doing wrong; however, the law can punish an individual who chooses to do that wrong, whatever it might be, even torture.

In contrast, **morals** are values that govern the difference between right and wrong and good and evil. As a result, we should see morality as more fundamental than law. Therefore, morality ought to serve as a guide for those bodies within our society—such as the courts, the executive branch, the legislature, and the administrative agencies—that make, interpret, and enforce the law. Most of the time, morality and legality ought to match up with each other. Indeed, many philosophers of law state that morality is a necessary element of the law. In effect, then, any law not grounded in morality cannot be considered a philosophically valid law.

Values and Ethics

So far we have defined **law** as a set of rules created by the government to establish a means of civil management that directs people to do what is right and avoid what is wrong. The purpose served by the law includes the creation of harmony, stability, and justice. The assumption is that if these purposes are met, right will be served and wrong defeated. Moreover, we have also defined **morals** as those fundamental values that determine the difference between right and wrong in the first place. What we have not explained, however, is where those values come from. This is the job of ethics. **Ethics** is the attempt to develop a means of determining what these values really are and for formulating and applying rules that enforce those values.

Natural Law

According to one system of legal thought, morality and the law are united in a common bond based on their intrinsic nature. This system of thought, which is generally known as **natural law**, sees law as originating from some objective, superior force that stands outside the everyday experience of most people. That superior force is generally God but can be referred to by a variety of other titles such as Aristotle's eternal changeless primary being, Hegel's Absolute, the Being of Eckhart Tolle, or the Kami of Shintoism. Thus, according to natural law, there exists an unbreakable link joining morality to the law in a fundamental way. This link exists because a law must, in its most basic form, be moral. Otherwise, it is not lawful. A law with an immoral purpose is not a law at all. Instead, it is an anomaly that does not fit into our concept of either law or the legal process.

It is, of course, one thing to say that laws must be firmly grounded in morality and quite another to argue that legality and morality are always the same thing. There are, in fact, some laws that have no moral content whatsoever. Thus, a city ordinance that establishes a midnight curfew for minors (those under 18 years of age) has no intrinsic moral substance, though such a law is not immoral on its face either (although most teenagers would almost certainly disagree). The natural law theorist, however, would say that such a law, if not moral in and of itself, is, at the very least, morally neutral and, therefore, has integrity as a

Did You Know?

The Koran states that the equality of all humanity serves as the basic foundation for all human rights.

law. Moreover, in a larger sense, a law that says minors must be safe at home after midnight, while not intrinsically moral, contributes to the orderly and stable functioning of society and is, therefore, moral because of its purpose and effect.

Positive Law

Natural law is sometimes confused with positive law because both depend on an outside force for their understanding of law, morality, and human rights. The difference is that positive law says that the law comes from social institutions rather than from God or some other outside force. Positive law, then, is a legal theory that says the law originates from an outside source that has emerged from within society. The process works something like this: The people of a society discover their rights as they live and work together. This discovery leads to commonly held rights that are described in a series of documents, such as the Magna Carta and the Bill of Rights. Exactly why people discover rather than invent universal rights is not clear. One argument says that rights are intuitively understood to exist within the human character. So, when people write documents such as the Bill of Rights, they include certain human rights such as the right to be treated fairly under the law. [See: Alan Dershowitz, *Rights from Wrongs: A Secular Theory of the Origin of Rights* (New York: Perseus Books Group, 2004), pp. 39-42.]

Some people say that human decency will ultimately triumph over human cruelty, giving rise to a just and moral society that will eventually abolish the worst sins of humanity. This brand of positive law is sometimes called the *Law of Peoples*. Not everyone agrees with this position, but such agreement is not necessary, so long as principles of decency and social justice can be found in certain universal documents such as the Bill of Rights in the United States Constitution or the United Nations Universal Declaration of Human Rights. Despite the differences between positive law and natural law, they hold one idea in common—namely, the belief that human values are universal, that is, they apply to all people at all times. [See: John Rawls, *The Law of Peoples* (Cambridge, MA: Harvard University Press, 1999), pp. 6-7.]

Nonjudgmentalism

Before we can discuss the process of making ethical decisions, we must make one thing absolutely clear. Making ethical decisions demands that we make judgments—period. Old default statements—such as "well, it may be right for you but it's not right for me," or "no one can ever tell any one else what is right because morals are subjective," or "who am I to judge another person's moral actions"—must be recognized for what they truly are: escape clauses that encourage people to turn a blind eye to activities that are, well, wrong. Now before you get too excited about this, you should remember that the law requires judgment too, and if you do not believe that, there is no point in reading any further because every chapter in this book will spell out actions that are wrong to make sure that you do, instead, that which is right. Moreover, if you are still uncomfortable with this, then you should reread the preceding sections that established that any law not grounded in morality cannot be considered a philosophically valid law. If you still don't believe this, then the next time a police officer pulls you over for speeding, try telling the officer that following speed limits might be right for the officer, but they are not right for you

So how did this attitude of nonjudgmentalism originate? That's fair question. Some of this results from a good-natured attempt to understand another person's behavior, especially when that behavior is difficult to talk about because it is embarrassing or controversial. While this attitude is commendable on one level, on another it can be seen as a self-focused attempt to avoid the difficulties involved in discussing such behavior with that other person. Instead of saying, "that behavior is wrong," we say, "I don't want to talk about it!" Nonjudgmentalism also originates in a culture that wants tolerance to be one of its highest virtues.

Did You Know?

The Greek word *ethos*, which forms the root of the English word *ethics*, means "character."

While tolerance is a great idea in the abstract, in reality it often degenerates into the intolerance of those who refuse to tolerate the behavior in question. Suppose, for example, an individual, in an expression of tolerance for pro-choice advocates and gay marriage supporters were to say, "If you do not tolerate pro-choice people and gay marriage supporters, then you have no place in my neighborhood." Inherent in that attempt to be tolerant of one group, is an expression of intolerance of another group.

Those who insist on being nonjudgmental make several additional errors. First, the expression of nonjudgmentalism is illogical and self-contradictory. When people say, "who am I to judge another person's morality," they are implying that anyone who decides to judge another person's morality is wrong to do so. So their expression of support for nonjudgmentalism is, in fact, a judgment against those who do judge. Second, to avoid being judgmental, nonjudgmentalists must be morally neutral on all types of behavior, including genocide, slavery, rape, and so on. On the flip side, they must also be morally neutral about honesty, justice, kindness, generosity, and so on. Imagine saying, "telling the truth might be right for you, but it is not right for me."

Finally, moral nonjudgmentalism is a slippery slope. Once you refuse to judge the telling of "little white lies," you cannot condemn covering up a burglary. Nor can you denounce committing perjury in a deposition or lying about fictitious weapons of mass destruction. Ultimately, all behavior becomes morally acceptable, and the nonjudgmentalist forfeits all right to shocked by any behavior, no matter how vile or depraved. With all this in mind, we now turn to the process of ethical decision making. (See: Regis Nicoll, "The Problem with Non-Judmentalism," *Crisis Magazine*, June 15, 2017, http://crisismagazine.com/2017/who-am-i-judge-2; and James Kalb, "The Intolerance of Liberal Toleration," *Crisis Magazine*, June 5, 2013, http://crisismagazine.com/2013/the-intolerance-of-liberal-toleration.)

Ethical Decision Making

People make ethical decisions every day; however, how they make those decisions is not always clear. Some people say that they do not think about ethics but instead act instinctively when faced with a moral problem. Others say that they just do what they "believe" is right. Still others say that they follow the rules they learned in school, in their place of worship, or in their family setting. Some professions, businesses, and organizations develop guidelines, usually called rules of conduct or canons of professional responsibility. Such rules generally describe certain levels of behavior. Some behaviors are encouraged; others are discouraged. Punishments are often included in these guidelines.

Although such rules are admirable, they are often so long and complex that they end up covering pages of text that require an in-depth study just to understand the basics. A case in point involves the Ohio Rules of Professional Conduct for attorneys. The code consists of eight different subsections, each of which includes from 4 to 18 rules. Each rule is then followed by a series of official comments that review, explain, and clarify each of the rules and any amendments that have been made to those rules. In all, the Ohio Rules cover 207 pages of text. Moreover, and more to the point, such rules are aimed at professional conduct alone and often do not even address general moral conduct. Sometimes, such codes even go so far as to excuse or ignore immoral conduct. For instance, Official Comment 2 following Rule 8.4 of the Ohio Rules covering the misconduct of an attorney, states that "matters of personal morality, such as adultery and comparable offenses ... have no specific connection to fitness for the practice of law."

Perhaps, most telling, is the fact that these rules frequently supply "loopholes" that permit people to escape culpability even when such culpability is obvious. Again, Official Comment 4 following Ohio Rule 8.4 states that "(a) lawyer may refuse to comply with an obligation imposed by law upon a good faith belief that no valid obligation exists." We can legitimately question the effectiveness of an obligation that can be avoided simply by manufacturing a "good faith belief that no valid obligation exists." The negative rights advocate would observe that the attorney is really saying, "I know what is ethically and legally correct here, but I'd rather do it my own way." Clearly, all of us need some other moral guide.

quick quiz 1-1

1. Natural law theory holds that there is no link between morality and law. true | false
2. Law has nothing to do with civil management. true | false
3. Ethical decisions are made in a variety of ways. true | false

1-2 Ethical Theories

Throughout the history of the philosophy of ethics, many scholars have offered several ethical theories for determining those values that ought to guide all ethical decisions. Theses theories include social contract ethics, utilitarianism, and rational ethics. Although these theories differ in their particulars, they all have one thing in common: Each theory is based on the assumption that people want to live ethical lives. If this were not the case, there would be no need to fashion these theories in the first place. Nevertheless, despite this common assumption, the theories differ greatly in their individual approaches to the problem of determining the nature of the values that underline ethical decision making. Our job here is to see that some of these theories work rather well, while others are less effective than we would prefer.

Social Contract Ethics

Social contract ethics holds that right and wrong are measured by the obligations imposed on each individual by an implied agreement among all the people within a particular social system. Although social contract ethics has existed in one form or another for centuries, the English philosopher Thomas Hobbes is generally credited with formulating the modern version of the theory in his book *Leviathan* (1651). At the most fundamental level, Hobbes says that human beings have two core rights that cannot be sacrificed, traded, or relinquished in any way: (1) the right to live and (2) the right to live in peace and security. In order to protect those two rights, people enter a social contract under which they agree to limit all other "rights" and to establish a central governing authority whose job it is to protect those rights by establishing an orderly, safe, and secure governmental system. Hobbes prefers a monarchy because a monarchy provides not only the type of safe and secure system that he is looking for, but also the continuity guaranteed by a clear line of succession, something oligarchies and dictatorships lack. [See: Thomas Hobbes, *Leviathan* (New York: Simon and Schuster, 1962); and George Mace, *Locke, Hobbes, and the Federalist Papers: An Essay on the Genesis of the American Political Heritage* (Carbondale: Southern Illinois University Press, 1979).]

Shortcomings of Social Contract Ethics Naturally, for the social contract to work, most people must adhere to its rules, and those who do not must be punished. If this were not the case, then the social contract would disintegrate, and the society would return to a "state of nature" in which people must fend for themselves. The existence of the social contract permits people to live together in peace and harmony, but it does not permit anyone, not even the leader, to violate the core rights of life and security. Should a leader consistently violate core rights, then the people have a duty to demand that such oppressive and dangerous behavior end. For example, should a leader begin to arrest individuals indiscriminately, the people would have the duty to seek an end to that behavior, and if such behavior continued, the people would have both a right and a duty to alter or abolish that governmental system and replace it with another, more protective system.

Another problem is that social contract ethics is descriptive rather than prescriptive. A **descriptive theory** simply describes the values at work within a social system, rather than explaining how the values originated in the first place. In contrast, a **prescriptive theory** explains how to come up with the values that permit a society to run smoothly. Of course, not everyone believes that social contract ethics is descriptive only. Some ethical theorists argue that social contract ethics is a prescriptive ethics because it places a value on the obligation to protect life and security. Thus, the people benefit by knowing that others,

A CLASSIC CASE The Declaration of Independence

Most Americans accept a paradigm that suggests that America's identity began with the Declaration of Independence as authored by Thomas Jefferson. Indeed, Jefferson himself, the third president of the United States, wanted to be remembered for only three things, one of which was the writing of the Declaration of Independence in 1776. Moreover, the common belief is that Jefferson was influenced primarily by the English philosopher John Locke (1632–1704) with assistance from the Genevan intellectual Jean-Jacques Rousseau (1712–1778). This assumption is somewhat skewed because it ignores the contribution of the social contract philosopher Thomas Hobbes who, in his landmark book *Leviathan*, outlined the core truths that Jefferson included in the Declaration. Moreover, Hobbes was influenced by Niccolo Machiavelli (1469–1527) and Francis Bacon (1469–1526), both of whom also anticipated the central core ideas of the Declaration. This unconventional view was originally promoted by George Mace, formerly of Southern Illinois University and the Brookings Institute, in his landmark book *Locke, Hobbes, and the Federalist Papers: An Essay on the Genesis of the American Political Heritage*. Mace argues, quite convincingly, that the four central truths included by Jefferson in the Declaration are pulled directly from Hobbes. To demonstrate this Mace focuses on a template of the Declaration and then proposes that we superimpose these four Hobbesian truths. What results is a fairly convincing case for the influence of Hobbes on our most sacred American scripture, the Declaration of Independence. The four truths look like this:

1. Human beings in their natural state have a common human nature.

2. Human beings need a social contract to protect themselves from one another.

3. Social contracts must protect certain essential core rights.

4. Failing social contracts can be abolished.

The pertinent section of the Declaration looks like this:

> We hold these truths to be self-evident, that all men are created equal, that they are endowed by their Creator with certain unalienable Rights, that among these are Life, Liberty and the pursuit of Happiness. That to secure these rights, Governments are instituted among Men, deriving their just powers from the consent of the governed, That whenever any Form of Government becomes destructive of these ends, it is the Right of the People to alter or to abolish it, and to institute new Government, laying its foundation on such principles and organizing its powers in such form, as to them shall seem most likely to effect their Safety and Happiness.

What do you think? Point out where in the opening section of the Declaration we find the four central truths supported by the Machiavelli–Bacon–Hobbes triad. The same triad also influenced James Madison in the writing of the Bill of Rights. See the Classic Case feature in Chapter 2 for more details on this unusual interpretation of American scripture. [See: George Mace, *Locke, Hobbes, and the Federalist Papers: An Essay on the Genesis of the American Political Heritage* (Carbondale: Southern Illinois University Press, 1979).]

Source: See: George Mace, *Locke, Hobbes, and the Federalist Papers: An Essay on the Genesis of the American Political Heritage* (Carbondale: Southern Illinois University Press, 1979).

including the sovereign himself or herself, will not violate those core rights. Social contract ethics, therefore, concentrates on each individual's obligation to everyone else and on the belief that, as long as these obligations are met, social stability will be preserved.

Utilitarianism

Utilitarianism is an ethical theory that says that the morality of an action is determined by its ultimate effects. The more good that results, the more ethical is the action. Conversely, the more bad that results, the less ethical is the action. Unlike social contract ethics, which admits the social contract is inherently unstable, utilitarianism seeks only one permanent goal: the greatest good for the greatest number. Determining the greatest good for the greatest number, however, is not as simple as it sounds. For one thing, we must resist the temptation to transform the greatest good for the greatest number principle into the "greatest good for me" principle. One way to avoid mistakes that can result from an improper application of utilitarianism is to follow its central elements by following these steps:

1. The action to be evaluated should be stated in unemotional, general terms. For example, "stealing another person's property" is emotional language; "confiscating property for one's own use" is somewhat less emotional.

THE OPENING CASE *Round 2*
National Security versus Human Rights

A brief review of the facts in the Opening Case will demonstrate the logic and the elements behind utilitarianism. Recall that after the terror attack on 9/11, FBI agents arrested more than 700 men of Arab and Asian descent and detained them without bail on charges of violating immigration law. Those prisoners who were later determined to be "of interest," some 84 individuals, remained in custody while the others were released. The plaintiffs in this case were six young men, five of whom are Muslim, who were held in detention for several months and were subjected to conditions that were alleged to be harsh and cruel. One of the key issues in the case involved the plaintiffs' claim that agents of the federal government detained them in harsh conditions in violation of their due process and equal protection rights. To evaluate the case based on utilitarianism, we must apply the five steps noted above. First, the action to be evaluated should be stated in unemotional, general terms. In this case, we would say that the action under consideration is whether, after a terrorist attack, agents of the federal government should detain, indefinitely and without bail, certain unregistered aliens of an ethnic background matching that of the terrorists until they can be cleared. Second, every person or class of people that will be affected by the action must be identified. The people who are affected are the suspects themselves, of course, plus their families and the people of the city in which the suspects we detained. Third, the good and bad consequences in relation to those people must be considered. The results of this evaluation look like this: (1) The detained individuals lost their freedom for an indefinite period of time, under harsh conditions; (2) their families lost the comfort and support of those individuals; (3) the people of the city appear to be protected from further error attacks, at least any involving theses individuals and others like them who were also detained. (4) Next, all alternatives to the action stated in step 1 must be considered. In this case, there appear to be only two options, either detain them or set them free. (5) Finally, once step 4 has been carried out, a conclusion must be reached. Whichever alternative creates the greatest good for the greatest number of people affected by the action is the one that ought to be taken. In this case, the action taken was designed to protect the inhabitants of the city. Even if we operate on the conservative side of calculating numbers and confine ourselves to Manhattan, we end up with just about 1,600,000 people. Those affected on the other side of the ledger, the suspects, did lose their freedom and did suffer many indignities, but to what end—to protect the people of New York. Therefore, the greatest good for the greatest number of people was attained. Or was it? See the Opening Case, Round 3.

2. Every person or class of people that will be affected by the action must be identified.
3. Good and bad consequences in relation to those people affected must be considered.
4. All alternatives to the action stated in step 1 must be considered.
5. Once step 4 has been carried out, a conclusion must be reached. Whichever alternative creates the greatest good for the greatest number of people affected by the action is the one that ought to be taken.

Shortcomings of Utilitarianism Despite its systematic approach to ethical questions, utilitarianism often fails to produce consistent moral judgments. The main problem with utilitarianism is developing a commonly understood definition of good. It is one thing to say that utilitarianism demands the greatest good for the greatest number of people; it is another thing entirely to define what is actually meant by the word *good*. Some people might define the greatest good as life itself, so if an action simply keeps most people affected by that action alive, that action is seen as promoting the greatest good. Others may be a bit more particular and see the greatest good in terms of the quality of life. Thus, life as a slave may be seen as less desirable than life as a free person, and any action that keeps people alive but reduces them to slavery would not be seen as promoting the greatest good. Of course, this just complicates the formula even further because people may have different ideas about the quality of life.

Some people see the quality of life in terms of creature comforts. Thus, actions that ensure that the greatest number of people will have jobs, homes, vehicles, and disposable income for clothes, travel, and entertainment would be promoting the greatest good. And actions that guarantee jobs and the good life are seen as promoting that greatest good for the greatest number. Others might see the quality of life in terms of more abstract principles, such as the need to have an environment that promotes freedom and justice. In this scenario, actions that guarantee freedom and justice would promote the greatest good, even though some people might be put at risk because promoting freedom means having strict rules about when and under what circumstances that freedom might be curtailed. The Opening Case gives us a pretty good example of this dilemma.

THE OPENING CASE Round 3
National Security versus Human Rights

Remember that, in the aftermath of 9/11, the FBI detained more than 700 men of Arab and Asian descent without bail on charges of violating immigration law. Eventually 84 prisoners, who had been determined to be "of interest" remained in custody. The plaintiffs in this case were six young men, five of whom are Muslim, who were detained for several months in conditions described as harsh and cruel. Later, the six detainees brought suit against several high-level government officials, alleging that the government had violated their due process and equal protection rights. Remember that as the last step of the utilitarian process, we must decide which alternative creates the greatest good for the greatest number of people affected by the action. In this case, the action taken deprived six individuals of their freedom without due process, in exchange for the lives of some 1,600,000 residents of Manhattan. The result seems inevitable (six lives reduced to unlawful imprisonment weighed 1,600,000 Manhattan residents). However, if the greatest good represents freedom and justice, then the result is different. Depriving six men of their freedom by unjustly denying them due process is just a start down that slippery slope we discussed earlier. It may be six people today, then 60 tomorrow, then 120,000 detained in internment camps, and then—who knows—perhaps 6 million in concentration camps. Therefore, it would seem that the greatest good for the greatest number of people was not attained. Think about it.

Rational Ethics

Rational ethics replaces the prescriptive approach of social contract theory and the result-oriented standard of utilitarianism with a system that is arguably objective, logical, and relatively consistent. Although forms of rational ethics were known in pre-Enlightenment times, the German philosopher Immanuel Kant is customarily recognized as having constructed the theory in several books including especially *Groundwork of the Metaphysics of Morals* (1785). **Rational ethics** is a philosophical theory that says ethical values can be determined by a proper application of human reason. The theory assumes, and rightfully so, that because all human beings are rational, all human beings ought to have the same ethical values. Therefore, rational ethics ought to establish universal rules of behavior that apply to all people at all times. For this reason, rational ethics is often referred to as *objective ethics*.

As rational beings, people think for themselves and, in doing so, recognize their own self-worth as individuals. Along with self-worth comes a belief in certain rights. These rights include the right to life and the right to security. Rational beings recognize that they do not want to be killed or endangered. Thus, each individual has a duty to refrain from violating the rights of all other human beings. As rational beings, people also realize that it is logical to establish rules that support the continued existence of society. A rule that destroys a society that tries to follow it would be an illogical rule. Consider the following rule: "Kill people who annoy you." A person who adheres to rational ethics would instantly recognize that such a rule is both illogical and immoral. If everyone in a society were to adopt such a rule, that society would collapse because everyone annoys someone at some time.

Shortcomings of Rational Ethics Even though rational ethics appears to be almost foolproof on the surface, it is not without its difficulties. One difficulty lies within what are referred to as penumbra rights. **Penumbra rights** are those that are found in those indeterminate or indistinct shadow areas associated with more uniformly accepted rights, such as the right to a safe and secure life. Thus, while it is clear that people have an unalienable right to a secure life, it is not quite as clear that they, therefore, have the right to arm themselves. The right to bear arms, then, is one those penumbra rights that is found within the shadow of the right to a secure life. Similarly, while it is clear that security is a core right, it is not as clear that security includes a secure reputation that is free from defamatory attacks orchestrated by other people in the media. Such penumbra rights must be interpreted by experts, most of which are found in the court system operating as judges, mediators, and magistrates. Another difficulty with rational ethics is that it does not always consider the shadowy nuances of everyday life. Rational ethics demands a clean and orderly universe wherein words, beliefs, and actions are the same for everyone. That does not always happen, as the accompanying example illustrates.

EXAMPLE 1-2: Lies and Politics: One State's Solution

The Ohio General Assembly, in an admirable if somewhat quixotic attempt to return a level of dignity to politics, made lying in political campaigns a crime. More specifically, Ohio Revised Code Section 3517.22 made it a criminal offense to "[p]ost, publish, circulate, distribute, or otherwise disseminate a false statement concerning a candidate, either knowing the same to be false or with reckless disregard for whether it was false or not, if the statement is designed to promote the election, nomination, or defeat of the candidate." The law was challenged by Susan B. Anthony List (SBAL), an advocacy group that wanted to erect a billboard that identified a state representative as having voted for federally funded abortions. The representative complained to the Ohio Elections Commission arguing that because he had never voted for federally funded abortions, the billboard would be broadcasting a lie. In reaction, the billboard company decided that it would simply not erect the troublesome sign. The SBLA believed that its right to freedom of speech had been violated, and the representative believed that his right to a safe and secure reputation had also been violated. It is at this point that rational ethics has a problem. *Rational ethics* clearly declares that it is logical to establish rules that support the continued existence of society. That much is clear; however, in this case, we have conflicting rules. On the one hand, a rule that says people must have free speech in a political debate is quite logical, while on the other hand, a rule that demands that people always tell the truth in political campaigns is also quite logical. The problem is that, in this case, as in many others, the *truth* of the matter is not clear. Under the act, insurers cannot use federal money to pay for abortions directly, and so the representative is correct. He did not vote for federally funded abortions; however, the act does support the use of federal dollars to pay for abortion-inclusive insurance coverage. So the advocacy group is also correct because, through an accounting strategy, federal money indirectly enables abortions. The difficulty with the precise and logical nature of rational ethics is that real life is not always that precise and logical. [See: *Susan B. Anthony List, et al., Petitioners v. Steven Driehaus, et al.* (No. 13-193), U.S. Court of Appeal for the Sixth Circuit (2013).]

Source: See: *Susan B. Anthony List, et al., Petitioners v. Steven Driehaus, et al.*, (No. 13-193) United States Court of Appeal for the Sixth Circuit (2013).

Notwithstanding the logical structure of rational ethics, many people are uneasy with some of its apparently incomplete parameters. As we saw in the example, one of the really difficult elements of rational ethics is that its practitioners simply assume that all concepts, terms, and ideas will have universal meaning. Thus, when Kant, for example, says that we must always tell the truth, he assumes that all things have a universally recognized meaning that is unquestionable. While such a belief works much of the time, it still falls quite short of being a consistently normative principle. If that were not the case, then we would not have the problem outlined in *Susan B. Anthony List v. Driehaus*.

quick quiz 1-2

1. Utilitarianism focuses on the consequences of an action.	true | false
2. Rational ethics is a form of nonjudgmentalism.	true | false
3. Utilitarianism and rational ethics always reach the same moral conclusion.	true | false

1-3 Ethics and the Government

If you have concluded that determining an ethical value system is difficult, then you have clearly been reading quite closely, and you have an unobstructed view of the problems associated with ethical decision making. Unfortunately, once we apply the same process to the government, matters become even more opaque. To see this, let's start with a few basics. The federal government runs the nation and, on the international scene, nations run the world. This simple reality emerges because nations possess territory, raise money through taxation, police their borders, protect their people, and if necessary, use force in a legitimate and responsible way. The government of a nation has two objectives that simultaneously justify its power and enable the proper exercise of that power. Those two objectives are (1) to protect its own existence and (2) to protect the lives, health, and well-being of its own citizens. Both of these responsibilities must be carried out in an ethical way. While this sounds like a simple and straightforward mandate, it is not. Government actions require a dyadic sense of responsibility that is often quite confusing to those officials who must act accordingly.

A Governmental and Ethical Dyad

Most people assume, and with good reason, that a single level of morality governs the behavior of both civilians and leaders. In an essay titled, "Politics as a Vocation," Max Weber suggests that this view is flawed. Weber argues, instead, that a **dyad** or a two-level system of morality exists, represented by the **ethic of ultimate ends** for individuals and an **ethic of responsibility** for national leaders. The ethic of ultimate ends must be practiced by individuals because individuals can never completely foresee "the ultimate ends" of their actions. Therefore, individuals must obey absolute moral precepts, such as "turn the other cheek" despite the fact that the ultimate consequences of those actions are unclear or uncomfortable. From this perspective, we can see why the ethic of ultimate ends is also often referred to as the ethic of benevolence.

On the other hand, the ethic of responsibility demands that the moral actor—in this case, a national leader—must consider his or her responsibilities to those people who depend on that leader for safety and security. So, for example, if a neighboring nation is belligerent, aggressive, or determined to fight ancient cultural, religious, and ethnic wars, the leaders of the first nation cannot ignore that threat, as much as they might want to. In short, they are not permitted to "turn the other cheek" because to do so would endanger the innocent people they have the duty to protect. Unfortunately, many national leaders fail to see this distinction. The leaders of the United States have been especially guilty of this shortsightedness. [See: Max Weber, "Politics as a Vocation," in *The Great Political Theories: From the French Revolution to Modern Times,* ed. Michael Curtis (New York: Harper, 2008), pp. 426–436).]

Shortcomings of the Ethical Dyad

The primary shortcoming of the ethical dyad is not the ethic itself, but the difficulty that leaders have executing one level of that ethic—the ethic of responsibility. Moreover, this is not a minor error. In a study titled *A New Pattern for a Tired World*, the essayist Louis Bromfield develops an argument that echoes the approach suggested by Weber. In doing so, Bromfield focuses on the United States, maintaining that American leaders have mishandled their basic responsibilities by focusing on what Bromfield calls "world responsibility" rather than national responsibility. What results, ironically enough, is a pattern of irresponsibility. American leaders try to help other nations as they might try to reform the poor in their local neighborhood—by giving every homeless person a handout but helping none of them get a job.

In international terms, Bromfield says this means momentarily rescuing failing nations by transferring billions into their treasuries but never dealing with the actual cause of the problem. This level of ineptitude on the part of the Americans may be understandable since the United States was ill prepared for world leadership when it assumed that role in 1918. Understandable, however, is not the same as defensible. Bromfield argues that to be truly responsible, leaders must adopt a far-reaching vision that measures what is best for the nation's citizens in terms of what is best for the economic stability of the world. Ironically, this requires disengagement from the entire world and a focus on the economic and civic health of the United States and its nearest neighbors.

Bromfield argues that the United States, Europe, Russia, China, Japan, and India must develop economic alliances with those nations closest to them, geographically and culturally. Economic alliances are crucial to global stability because, when people are fed, clothed, housed, and healthy, they do not resort to violence. Bromfield's economic alliances would look like this: The United States would join with Canada, Mexico, and other nations in the Western Hemisphere; Russia, China, and Japan would unite; the European nations would join with one another; and India would join with Pakistan (and probably with Australia and New Zealand). Once these alliances were economically healthy, they would trade with the other members in their own bloc, until they institute a network of trust. The four major economic blocs would then form trade agreements among themselves and later with smaller nations, offering help only to those nations that request assistance. This would be an effective exercise in the ethic of responsibility, first in relation to their people, and, second, in relation to the rest of the world. Bromfield goes so far as to predict a unified world economy in the far future, as long as national leaders act responsibly. He does not use the word *globalization*, but he might was well have. [See: Louis Bromfield, *A New Pattern for a Tired World* (New York: Harper, 1954).]

The Threat of Failed States

As noted above, Bromfield suggests that international decision making be based on economic motivations. His position would reduce most (all?) international decisions to market-based, value-driven decisions, aimed at preserving international peace through trade and through commerce—period. There is certainly much logic to the notion that many international problems can be solved by creating economic alliances. Of course, the success of Bromfield's plan depends upon the benevolence of the rich nations; however, the basic rule of Weber's ethical dyad is that leaders must not think benevolently but must, instead, think in terms of national responsibility. The danger is that, as the gap between the rich and poor nations grows, the rich may no longer feel it is in their national best interests to invite the poor nations into their regional alliances; therefore, the gap between the rich and poor may soon become impassable. Thus, these alliances may not lead to the global cooperation he envisions but, instead, to the global equivalent of a dual class system—the rich law abiding nations and the failed and unstable states.

Failed states are those in which the government has completely collapsed or has become so ineffective that it can no longer provide sustenance or security for its own people. **Unstable states** are those in which the government suppresses its own people thus inviting a future revolt that might destabilized a region. All of this can be avoided by taking into consideration Bromfield's other premise—that the people who live in those failed and unstable states may become so desperate they have nothing to lose by using violence. This reality is made even more unsettling because, in the modern, wireless world of global interconnectedness, asymmetrical warfare makes even the richest nation vulnerable to attack from agents of cyber-terror, chemical and biological warfare, and nuclear weapons. Thus, it may actually be in the best interests of the rich nations to make sure the people of the poor and unstable nations are cared for and protected, and thus have the chance to develop, healthy, safe and productive lives.

EXAMPLE 1-3: The Ethical Dyad in Action

In the shadow of the May 22, 2017, terror attack in Manchester, England, President Trump was involved in what was deemed to be a routine foreign policy tour. One stop on the tour led President Trump to Saudi Arabia, where he met with Saudi leaders to cement a deal that had been negotiated by Secretary of Defense Jim Mattis, Secretary of State Rex Tillerson, and National Security Adviser H. R. McMaster. Under the terms of the agreement, the United States agreed to sell Saudi Arabia weaponry, military vehicles, naval ships, and military hardware that would be used in the fight against ISIS. More importantly, in exchange for this military material and weaponry, Saudi leadership agreed to build and lead an Arab-based coalition that would be used in the battle to destroy Isis and in the crusade to keep Iran contained within its own territory. There were those on the home front who opposed this agreement because of Saudi Arabia's poor human rights record. In fact, the record has been labeled one of the worst in the region. A white paper complied by the Human Rights Watch listed numerous violations in the areas of free speech, women's rights, and criminal justice. The odd thing about this is that under Weber's doctrine, none of this would matter. Weber's ethic of responsibility would say that the president's only duty is to protect the American people. So, if the agreement manages to help the United States obtain assistance in the destruction of ISIS and the containment of Iran, thus protecting our our citizens against attack and preserving our access to oil, then the president was doing his job.

Bromfield would disagree. Bromfield would say that protecting our own people may mean protecting the rights of the citizens of other nations. Remember, an unstable state like Saudi Arabia is just as threatening to global order as a failed state. This is because the people who live in failed and unstable states have become so desperate they have nothing to lose by using violence, and violence in one nation can destabilized an entire region, thus threatening global trade. So, while Weber would approve of this military agreement with Saudi Arabia, Bromfield would not. Weber would see it as a proper exercise of the ethic of responsibility because both states would be protected from the dual threats of ISIS and Iran. In contrast, Bromfield would see it as violation of that ethic because, as long as the people of Saudi Arabia are persecuted, the state itself is unstable and open to rebellion, which could destabilize the entire region, thus threatening American interests at home and abroad. [See: Daniel Henninger, "From 9/11 to Manchester," *The Wall Street Journal,* May 16, 2017, p. A-15; "Saudi Arabia Events of 2016," *Human Rights Watch: World Report 2017,* https://www.hrw.org/world-report/2017/country-chapters/saudi-arabi; and "Saudi Arabia 2014 Human Rights Report," *Country Reports on Human Rights Practices for 2014,* U.S. Department of State, Bureau of Democracy, Human Rights and Labor, https://www.state.gov/documents/organization/236832.pdf.]

The Responsibility to Protect

So who is correct, Weber who says that the internal human rights record of a fellow nation is none of our business as long as our needs are met, or Bromfield who argues that the ethic of responsibility is only exercised properly when the safety and stability of very nation is met? Although the debate will likely go on, no matter what, it is interesting to note that the ethic of responsibility as interpreted by Bromfield recently received support from an unlikely source, the United Nations. In 2005, a new global doctrine was proposed at the United Nations World Summit. The new doctrine, which has been dubbed the **Responsibility to Protect (R2P),** declares that the leadership of every nation has a definitive duty to protect its own people from four major threats, genocide, war crimes, ethnic cleansing and crimes against humanity. Crimes against humanity include such things as slavery, torture, rape, sexual slavery, mass murder, hostage taking, terrorism, kidnapping, and apartheid, among several others. A nation-state that commits such offenses is considered to be a rogue state. Were the UN to have stopped here, R2P would clearly be a simple reiteration of Weber's position.

However, it did not stop here. Instead, it added a second layer to the doctrine. That layer declares that the international community has the duty to police all other members of the community to ensure that none of them victimize their own people. Moreover, if such offenses are discovered in a particular nation, it is the duty of all other nations to stop those offenses by resolution, by sanctions, by military intervention, or by all three. Curiously, this sounds very much like Bromfield's second premise, which reminds us that the security of the planet depends on the security of every nation. Thus, to prevent violence, terrorism, war, and so on, it is best to make sure that the people of every nation have the chance to develop healthy, stable, productive lives. Only then will the people of those nations have no reason to upset the stability of the global community. Bromfield's plan to build economic support regions would encourage this type of cooperation and might lead to the type global economic community that he once envisioned. [See: Richard Haas, *A World in Disarray: American Foreign Policy and the Crisis of the Old Order* (New York: Penguin Press, 2017), pp. 115–119. See also: Bromfield.]

> **quick quiz 1-3**
>
> 1. Weber supports the idea of a dyadic or two-level system of morality in government.   true | false
> 2. The main shortcoming of the ethical dyad is that leaders cannot execute the ethic of responsibility.   true | false
> 3. Bromfield suggests that the major powers develop military alliances.   true | false

1-4 Ethics and Business

While businesses come in every shape and size, the dominate business organization on the national and international scene is the corporation. Corporations carry a great deal of influence over the economy, the community, and the people. There are those who say that a corporation has no ethical responsibility beyond making a profit for its shareholders. This is, in fact, the traditional view of corporate responsibility. It is a view that has remained so ingrained in our system that, until recently, it was the only view built into statutory and common law. Recently, however, voices have been raised arguing that corporations have a high degree of ethical responsibility to those people affected by their decisions.

The Traditional Corporate Culture

Although all businesses affect the economy and the community, the greatest force in the American industrial state is the corporation, in general, and the multinational corporation, in particular. The reality of corporate power is revealed by the fact that philosophers on both ends of the political spectrum can point to the corporation as a guiding force in modern civilization. For instance, in his treatise, *Individualism Old and New*, the *pragmatic* American philosopher, John Dewey, notes, "The United States has steadily moved from an earlier pioneer individualism to a condition of corporate dominance." Similarly, the *theoretical* philosopher Herbert Marcuse once remarked that no one, not even the former enemies of capitalism, can escape the influence of corporate power. In fact, Marcuse goes so far as to say that in the modern global marketplace, "the socialist and communist systems are linked with capitalism." [See: John Dewey, *Individualism: Old and New* (New York: Capricorn Books, 1962); and Herbert Marcuse, *Five Lectures: Psychoanalysis, Politics, and Utopia*, trans. Jeremy J. Shapiro and Shierry M. Weber (Boston: Beacon Press, 1970).]

One reason that corporations have such power is that they are legal persons, created under the authority of federal and state statutes. This status as a "legal person" gives the corporation certain rights and abilities that other business entities do not always have. For instance, as legal persons they are accorded certain constitutional rights, such as the right not to be deprived of property without due process of law. They can also own property in their own name and have lawsuits filed to protect them or vindicate their rights. There are, of course, many types of corporations. Our focus will be on those corporations that are privately run to make a profit for their owners, who are referred to as shareholders. The traditional view says that privately owned corporations are created solely to make a profit for their shareholders. Consequently, the foremost job of any manager is to maximize those profits. In fact, under the traditional rule of shareholder dominance, the managers of a corporation could be held liable in a court of law for making decisions that do not guarantee that the shareholders would receive a maximum return on their investment.

As defined previously, the type of thinking promoted by the court in Example 1-5 is referred to as utility thinking or **cost-benefit thinking**. Using utility thinking, a corporate manager simply looks at the action he or she is about to take and asks whether the benefit to the shareholders will outweigh the cost to the corporation. If the shareholders' benefits offset corporate costs, then the action is taken. If not, the action is abandoned. Proponents of this position justify cost-benefit thinking in three ways. First, the profits to the shareholders must always come first. Second, it would be unfair to divert funds that belong to the shareholders to activities that do not directly benefit the shareholders. Third, a corporation's managers are accountable to the shareholders and to no one else. The problem with utility thinking is that it often results in actions that are clearly unethical and potentially illegal.

EXAMPLE 1-4: Corporate Culture and Utility Thinking

When Lynn Cummings discovered that the managers of a corporation in which she owned stock had made a decision that had caused shareholders to lose money in a merger plan, she sued, seeking a reversal of the merger or a suitable payment from the managers that would make up for her losses. Basically, Cummings second-guessed the way that the managers had made their decision, arguing that they had not properly researched the merger and had not placed the shareholders' profits first. The managers argued that they had made their decision based on the long-term benefits of the merger to everyone involved, including the local community and the economy of the nation and state. The court sided with Cummings, noting that the job of the managers was to look out for the shareholders' profits, not the long-term benefits to the community or the economy.

EXAMPLE 1-5: Maximum Corporate Irresponsibility

The managers of Taylor-Beechaum Pharmaceuticals Inc. received a report that the corporation's latest weight-loss drug, biomiocin, was having unpredicted side effects that caused problems for several people. The managers of Taylor-Beechaum ordered the accounting department to determine how much it would cost to recall all the biomiocin now on the market, suspend manufacturing, and conduct more tests on the drug's safety. The accountants reported that it would be more cost effective to simply leave the drug on the market and pay off anyone who might be injured and who might bring a lawsuit against Taylor-Beechaum. Keeping the drug on the shelves would allow the corporation to continue to pay dividends to the shareholders. In contrast, if the drug were taken off of the market, the payment of dividends would be suspended pending the outcome of the new testing program. Consequently, the corporate managers decided to leave biomiocin on the shelves. This decision not only violated virtually every ethical standard that we've studied thus far (except nonjudgmentalism), but also evaded the corporation's responsibility to consumers, to the government, to the shareholders, and to the public at large.

Reasons for Ethical Responsibility

The fact that corporate officers and directors have made such irresponsible decisions should not be surprising. Nor should it be surprising that until recently, the law supported such decisions. The idea that a corporation is a legal person did not spring full grown into the law when the first corporations were formed. In fact, it took jurists quite some time to see that corporations were neither partnerships nor miniature democratic states but, instead, vehicles for making a profit. Once jurists recognized the unique position that corporations hold within the hierarchy of business associations, however, they easily granted certain privileges to corporate entities. Despite this, as the jurists entered the modern age, they began to see that there were a number of reasons that corporations, like Taylor-Beechaum in Example 1-5, should accept ethical responsibility for their actions. Some of these reasons are built on the legal advantages granted to corporations. Others are based on the idea that many corporations are powerful forces in their communities. Still others focus on the self-interest of the corporation. Whatever the case, these arguments are being voiced more loudly and with more conviction with each passing fiscal year.

Legal Advantages Granted to the Corporation The first argument supporting corporate social responsibility is based on the premise that corporations are granted certain rights as a result of the incorporation process. For example, the corporate form offers limited liability to those who share in its ownership. This means that the personal assets of the corporate owners cannot be taken if the corporation defaults on a contract or commits a tort or a crime. In addition, under provisions of most incorporation statutes, a corporation is considered an artificially created person. This means that, under provisions of the U.S. Constitution and those of most state constitutions, a corporation, like a natural person, cannot be deprived of life, liberty, or property without due process of law. This also means that a corporation can own property in its own name and bring a lawsuit to vindicate its rights. Because corporations have all these rights, they owe an obligation to the public and to the community at large to act responsibly. In practical terms, this means that the decisions of corporate managers must not be narrowly focused on the profits of the shareholders.

EXAMPLE 1-6: The Andrean-Harrison Donation

As part of a downsizing campaign, the Andrean-Harrison Corporation was about to close operations in Tulsa. The company owned an office building and a small laboratory on the outskirts of Tulsa adjacent to 30 acres of undeveloped land. The corporation had a chance to sell the land at a price that would have made a profit for the shareholders of the company. Rather than take advantage of this offer, Andrean-Harrison decided to donate the land to the city. The fact that the corporation was a legal person meant that it owned the land and could donate it to the city. Corporate officials acted responsibly in this case, taking advantage of the corporation's right to own land in its own name.

The Impact of Corporate Decision Making A second reason for demanding ethical behavior from corporations is that corporate decision making clearly has an impact on more people than just the shareholders and the managers. Those who support corporate ethical responsibility often argue that many corporate decisions, such as whether to open or close a factory, will affect everyone in the local community. Those affected by such decisions include suppliers, consumers, employees, support businesses, and community members. Consequently, the argument goes, all of these groups should be taken into consideration when corporate managers make decisions. Some individuals who support this form of extreme corporate ethical responsibility would like to see representatives from the employees' union, from consumer protection groups, from environmental protection groups, and from the local chamber of commerce on every corporation's board of directors. Others, however, argue that because corporate decisions affect more individuals and groups than just the shareholders and managers, those decisions should be made by an impartial group of corporate outsiders. Often the corporate outsiders named are governmental officials.

EXAMPLE 1-7: Corporate Cooperation and Compromise

When the directors of Igar International Corporation were working on plans to diversify their operation, they considered opening a chemical plant in Santa Ana. Before making the decision, they sent a team of experts to Santa Ana to investigate the possibility of establishing an operation just within the city limits. Although the city officials promised Igar a tax abatement and agreed to donate several acres of land to the corporation, citizens' groups were against the plant because of environmental and health concerns. The corporation could have simply found a more receptive or, perhaps, a less vocal city in which to locate; however, instead of simply discarding their consideration of Santa Ana, they worked with the citizens' groups to meet their concerns. Ultimately, the two sides agreed on modifications to the project and moved forward. The willingness of the company to discuss the proposed changes in its operation reflected an understanding of the corporation's ethical responsibility based on the fact that corporate decisions have a far-ranging impact.

Enlightened Corporate Self-Interest Finally, there are those who argue, rather convincingly, that accepting ethical responsibility is actually in the long-term best interests of the corporation. This argument, which is generally referred to as enlightened self-interest, is based on the notion that ethically responsible corporations benefit by creating goodwill for themselves, thus motivating consumers to purchase their products, investors to buy their stock, and lawmakers to grant them further legal advantages. In addition, the corporation benefits because the community at large gains from such decisions. If the community at large is healthy, the argument goes, then the corporation that relies on that community will be healthy also.

EXAMPLE 1-8: Failed Negotiations Lead to Problems

The CEO of Pilder and Wesselkamper International Inc. decided to suspend negotiations with union representatives when she learned that they were about to demand a salary increase that she believed was untenable given the corporation's financial health, or lack thereof. The union threatened to file a complaint with the National Labor Relations Board, charging that the CEO and her staff were not cooperating with the collective bargaining process. The union also indicated that it was considering publishing an advertisement in *The New York Times* denouncing the CEO's decision and eventually would authorize a strike. The CEO continued to resist further negotiations and simply shut down operations. Eventually, the company filed for bankruptcy and dissolved its operation. Neither of the parties involved in this case opted to pursue a course of enlightened self-interest, which resulted in the worst possible conclusion for all those involved.

Efforts to Promote Ethical Behavior

As noted previously, the traditional view of a corporation says that its primary role is to make a profit for its shareholders. This means that corporate managers are obligated to make decisions that maximize those profits. Moreover, under the traditional role of corporate managers, those managers could be sued for making a decision that hurt the corporation's profits and thereby reduced or eliminated dividends; however, recent amendments to many corporate statutes have been designed to encourage corporate managers to make broader-based, more ethical decisions. Thus, some statutes now permit managers to consider factors beyond profit in making corporate decisions. These factors include the economic well-being of the nation, the state, and the local community; the interests of employees, consumers, and suppliers; and the betterment of the environment, the economy, and the overall social structure.

In general, it appears that the authors of these statutes have developed an ethical program based on utilitarianism. Recall that utilitarianism is not based on determining the inherent rightness or wrongness of an action. Instead, the utilitarian will measure the effects of a given action on those who will feel the impact of that action. Thus, utilitarianism seeks only one permanent goal: the greatest good for the greatest number. Also recall that before making a final choice about the ethical value of an action, the utilitarian must do his or her best to determine every person and every class of people that will be affected by the action and all (or at least most) of the good and bad consequences that will affect those individuals and those groups. When the authors of these statutes empower corporate officers to consider the economic well-being of the nation, the state, and the local community; the interests of employees, consumers, and suppliers; and the betterment of the environment, the economy, and the overall social structure, they have opened the door to a pure utilitarian evaluation. Just as long as the evaluation does not degenerate into an exercise in seeking only the greatest good for the corporation, the officers are likely to make decisions that are both ethical and legal.

EXAMPLE 1-9: Corporate Trade-Offs Mean Corporate Survival

The directors of Chindi-Mowry Enterprises Inc. were under fire because of a takeover bid against Chindi-Mowry engineered by an alien corporation known as Rixensart Industries. To stave off the assault, the directors invited a friendly bid from Sandoff Inc., a firm that promised not to dismantle Chindi-Mowry after the deal was entered. The final amount of the offer from Sandoff was less than that offered by Rixensart, and so those shareholders who sold their stock received less on the sale to Sandoff than they would have received had the directors endorsed the Rixensart plan; however, in making their decision, the directors were persuaded that the deal offered by Sandoff would save jobs, help the community, boost the national and state economy, and eventually result in a long-term gain for the corporation and for those shareholders who remained with the company.

quick quiz 1-4

1. Cost–benefit thinking will always result in ethical decisions.	true | false
2. Corporations are not allowed to own property.	true | false
3. Some statutes allow corporate managers to consider factors beyond shareholder profits in making business decisions.	true | false

1-5 The Relationship between Law and Ethics

Thus far, we have seen that ethics and morals can be distinguished from one another. We have defined values, examined the causes of unethical conduct, and determined how to develop an ethical lifestyle. Some people determine an ethical lifestyle as simply doing what is legal. Such a course of action may often result in ethical conduct; however, that is not always the case. Even when most people know that a particular type of conduct is illegal, that does not prevent some people from engaging in that conduct. For example, everyone knows that killing is illegal. Yet that knowledge does not stop the national murder rate from remaining disturbingly high. Similarly, everyone knows that child abuse, spousal abuse, and elder abuse are immoral, but that consensus has not eliminated the problem of abuse from our society.

The Need for Law in Our Society

The law is needed because, though people know better, they do not always follow ethical principles. As noted previously, the law consists of rules of conduct established by the government of a society to maintain harmony, stability, and justice in that society. It does so by defining the legal rights and duties of the people. It also provides a way to protect the people by enforcing these rights and duties through the courts and the legislature. Ethical principles can tell us what is right, but they cannot stop us from doing that which is wrong. The law also cannot stop us from doing wrong; however, the law can punish us if we choose to do wrong. The law draws the line between permissible and impermissible conduct so that people, at the very least, are punished if they hurt or cheat one another or threaten society as a whole.

Of course, the law also has other functions. For instance, the law serves as the ultimate rule maker, providing a sense of stability and harmony when order breaks down in any other area of society, from our schools and universities to the family itself. This is why each state has established a system of juvenile courts and a network of domestic relations courts to handle such disputes when they arise. The law also promotes economic growth by granting tax abatements, by rezoning certain urban areas for the establishment of stores and businesses, and by exercising the power of *eminent domain* to confiscate privately owned land for community purposes. In addition, the law guards property rights by enforcing contracts and other similar agreements and providing a forum for tort victims and their families. The law also protects the environment by regulating those industries that might overdevelop the land and those that dump waste materials and other pollutants on to the land and into the waterways. Finally, as noted, the law is responsible for advancing social justice and guaranteeing personal freedom by granting all people due process and equal protection and providing a system by which legitimate grievances can be resolved in an orderly and timely fashion.

Ethical and Legal Anarchy

Is the law perfect? Does the law always succeed in its goals and objectives? Certainly not. As is true of all institutions, the law is flawed. It is filled with loopholes, foolishness, red tape, and, at times, absolute idiocy, much of which is unintentional and most of which could be avoided if people just take the time to think coolly and rationally. For example, it makes very little sense for Congress to pass legislation to punish flag burners when it is quite clear that the Supreme Court will declare that legislation unconstitutional. Or, in a similar vein, it makes no sense for Congress to pass unfunded mandates that force the state governments to raise money to perform tasks that the federal government should have taken care of in the first place. Yet this type of thing happens all of the time. Nevertheless, having an imperfect but functioning legal system *is always preferable* to the alternative—anarchy.

Or is it? Is having an imperfect but functioning legal system always preferable to anarchy? Not everyone thinks that way. In fact, the Russian intellectual Peter Kropotkin has a different take on the entire situation. Kropotkin believes that in a utopian society, ethics and the law would always coincide. Kropotkin, along with Jean Jacques Rousseau, argues that society is dysfunctional because it ignores the fact that human nature is not competitive, as Hobbes and Madison contest, but is, instead, cooperative. They also believe that a little anarchy now and again is useful, despite the horrors that often result in such a state, but only when what emerges from that period of anarchy is a system blessed by legal and ethical harmony. To explain this further, Kropotkin introduces two human forces: (1) energy and (2) justice. Energy is found in a society that manages to redirect the collective human will toward the welfare of the entire species instead of toward individual or corporate survival measured only by monetary gain. Justice is present when all people are treated equally based on some intangible quality that has nothing to do with money. As we have seen repeatedly in our examination of the ethical theories, the difficult task is finding that intangible measuring stick. Kropotkin believes that this intangible quality is based on the self-esteem that comes from using one's talents, experience, and education to perform tasks that benefit individuals as individuals and that benefit the entire society. In short, doing one's duty in a cooperative and nonselfish way, creates harmony in the society, evokes thanks and appreciation from other members of that society, and gives each person a feeling of self-worth that goes way beyond anything that mere money can do. Kropotkin called this measure of value **appretiare**. Of course, Kropotkin's ethical and legal system based on *appretiare* is not without practical difficulties. His socioeconomic theory suffers from an inadequate, or at least unsatisfying, explanation of the mechanism by which the human race promotes cooperation over competition and establishes *appretiare*. Unlike Aldous Huxley who, in *Brave New World*, provides the reader with a genetically grounded and behavioral-based process for reprograming human nature, Kropotkin assumes that humans will, on their own, rediscover their inherent tendency to cooperate with and to respect one another finding it preferable to both anarchy and the market-based system. Given the fact that Kropotkin and others like him (Rousseau comes to mind) lack a practical venue, we will now turn to a more pragmatic, hands-on approach to the topic, the American legal system: what it is and how it came to be. For this we now turn to Chapter 2. [See: P. Eltzbacher, "Kropotkin's Teachings," *The Great Anarchists: Ideas and Teachings of Seven Major Thinkers* (Dover, New York, 1908,) pp. 144–171; Aldous Huxley, *Brave New World and Brave New World Revisited* (New York: Harper and Brothers, 1960); and James P. Hogan, *The Anguished Dawn* (Riverdale, NJ: Baen Publishing Enterprises, 1993).]

quick quiz 1-5

1. The law cannot stop us from doing wrong, but it can punish us if we choose to do wrong. — true | false
2. In a perfect society, ethics and law would always coincide. — true | false
3. The law and the legal system need not be founded on ethical considerations. — true | false

Summary

1.1 The law consists of rules of conduct established by the government of a society to maintain harmony, stability, and justice. Morals involve the values that govern a society's attitude toward right and wrong. Ethics, in contrast, attempts to develop a means for determining what those values ought to be and for formulating and applying rules in line with those values.

1.2 Social contract ethics holds that right and wrong are measured by the obligations imposed on each individual by an implied agreement among all the people within a particular social system. Utilitarianism is an ethical theory that says that the morality of an action is determined by its ultimate effects. The more good that results, the more ethical is the action. Conversely, the more bad that results, the less ethical is the action. Rational ethics is a philosophical theory that says ethical values can be determined by a proper application of human reason. The theory assumes, and rightfully so, that because all human beings are rational, all human beings ought to have the same ethical values.

1.3 The government of a nation-state has two objectives that simultaneously justify its power and enable the proper exercise of that power: (1) to protect its own existence and (2) to protect the lives, health, safety, and well-being of its own citizens. To meet those two objectives, national leaders must recognize the conflict that emerges from within a *dyad* or two-level system of morality: (1) the exercise of individual morality, represented by the ethic of ultimate ends, and (2) the exercise of national morality, represented by the ethic of responsibility.

1.4 Corporations owe society a level of responsibility because the government has granted certain legal advantages to corporations. Another reason for expecting ethically responsible decisions from corporate executives is that corporations have a great deal of power in the economic structure, and with power comes responsibility. Finally, corporations should act ethically because it is in their own best interest to do so.

1.5 In a perfect society, ethics and the law would always coincide. Our society is not perfect and is not likely to become so in the foreseeable future. Therefore, our society needs the law and the legal system to give it structure, harmony, predictability, and justice.

Key Terms

appretiare, 23
cost-benefit thinking, 18
descriptive theory, 9
dyad, 14
ethic of responsibility, 14
ethic of ultimate ends, 14
ethics, 5

failed states, 15
law, 4
morals, 5
natural law theory, 5
penumbra rights, 12
positive law, 6
prescriptive theory, 9

rational ethics, 12
Responsibility to Protect (R2P), 16
social contract ethics, 8
unstable states, 15
utilitarianism, 10

Questions for Review and Discussion

1. What is the difference between law and morality?
2. What are the differences between positive law and natural law?
3. What is nonjudgmentalism?
4. What is social contract ethics?
5. What are the steps in applying utilitarianism?
6. What is rational ethics?
7. What is the dual nature of ethics in government?
8. What are the arguments supporting corporate ethical responsibility?
9. Why is law needed in our society?
10. How can the law and ethics sometimes benefit from anarchy?

Cases for Analysis

1. In the summer of 2017, the New York Public Theater sponsored a production of Shakespeare's *Julius Caesar* at the Delacorte Theater in Central Park. By itself, there is nothing unusual about this event. In fact, the 2017 season of the Central Park Summer Shakespeare Festival marked the 55th anniversary of the program. However, this summer's program offered a bit of a twist. In the production, the character of Julius Caesar was clearly modeled after President Donald Trump. At first, this might not have been a problem, except for the fact that in this production, the character of Caesar is assassinated in a particularly bloody fashion. The production sparked instant controversy between supporters of the president, who saw it as just one more example of the left's animosity toward the president, and opponents of the president, who saw it simply as an expression of artistic creativity. What is most interesting for our purposes here is the fact that in reaction to the controversy, several

corporate sponsors, including Delta Airlines and Bank of America, withdrew all or part of their support for the Public Theater's Free Shakespeare in the Park program. Using our discussion of corporate ethical responsibility, evaluate this move by Delta and Bank of America, and determine whether the decision is in line with or opposed to corporate responsibility. One word of limitation—in the spirit of avoiding nonjudgmentalism, only two answers are acceptable: "yes" or "no." Of course, you must also explain the reasons behind your yes or no answer. [See: Michael Cooper, "In 'Julius Caesar,' an Assassination Echoes Across the Centuries," *The New York Times*, June 13, 2017, pp. A-1, A-23; and Michael Paulson and Sopan Deb, "Trump Supporters Drive Effort to Bury the Public Theater," *The New York Times*, June 13, 2017, p. A-23.]

2. It should go without saying that free speech is based on the very reasonable proposition that all beliefs, even those that many people find disagreeable, deserve to be heard in the marketplace of ideas. Historically, colleges and universities have been leaders in the preservation of this, the most fundamental of our basic human rights. Sadly, this no longer seems to be the case. It now seems that self-appointed censors have appeared on campuses around the nation demanding that individuals that they dislike or find disagreeable be prevented from speaking. Now there have always been people on campus who wanted to play the role of self-appointed censor. Generally, such people could be found somewhere high up in the administration. Today, that trend has reversed itself. Today, the censors are more likely to be found among the students themselves. A case in point is an incident that occurred at Middlebury College, where Charles Murray, a political scientist and the author of a book entitled *Coming Apart*, was invited to speak by a conservative group called the American Enterprise Institute Club. A group of Middlebury students who were opposed to some of the Murray's ideas asked the administration to cancel the speech. To their credit, the administration, in the true spirit of free speech, denied the request. This did not stop the students, however, who took matters into their own hands and succeeded in disrupting the program to such an extent that Murray never did get the chance to speak. Moreover, in a physical confrontation that followed the nonevent-event, the faculty member who was supposed to serve as moderator of a question and answer session was injured. Using rational ethics, create an argument that opposes the attempt by students at Middlebury to stop the speech by a politically unpopular speaker. Then using utilitarianism, do the same. Explain each argument, and determine which of the two positions you prefer. Explain that preference. [See: Laurie L. Patton, "The Outspoken Campus," *The Wall Street Journal*, June 10–11, 2017, p. C-1.]

3. In the wake of three devastating terror attacks in Britain in 2017, Prime Minister Theresa May laid out plans for a more proactive governmental protocol designed to make it more difficult for terrorists to plan and execute such attacks. Her plan calls for stepping up surveillance on terror suspects and increasing the investigative powers of the police. She has also proposed programs to implement additional curfews, to create stricter limits on travel, to tighten restrictions on the ability of terror suspects to associate with one another, to strengthen programs to deny terror suspects access to electronic communication devices, and to increase pretrial detention time limits for terror suspects. The most controversial aspect of her plan, however, is her pledge to change any human rights laws that might prevent or prohibit her from implementing her new protocols. Using social contract ethics, create an argument that defends the Prime Minister's anti-terror protocol. Using rational ethics, do the same. Explain each argument, and determine which of the two positions you prefer. Explain that preference. [See: Rowena Mason and Vikram Dodd, "May: I'll Rip up Human Rights Laws That Impede New Terror Legislation," *MSNNews* and *The Guardian*, June 6, 2017, http://www.msn.com/en-us/news/world/may-i%E2%80%9911-rip-up-human-rights-law-that-impede-new-terror-legislation/ar-BBCaRyG?li=BBmkt5R&ocid=spartanntp.)

4. In April 2017, U.S. military forces, operating under orders from President Trump, initiated an attack against an airbase in Syria. The attack, which involved the launching of 60 Tomahawk cruise missiles, was designed to severely disable or completely eliminate the airfield from which the Syrians had launched a chemical attack against their own people. The chemical attack, which used agents that had supposedly been removed from Syria under a

2013 international agreement, killed some 85 people, including 27 children, and severely injured 550 additional people. The American missile attack came in response to international calls for a military strike against the Syrians to cripple their ability to launch additional chemical strikes and to send a strong and definitive message that such attacks will no longer be tolerated by the international community. Using your knowledge of Max Weber's ethic of responsibility, explain whether the American attack against Syria was a proper exercise of that ethic. Now do the same using your understanding of Louis Bromfield's take on that same ethic. Finally, defend then proposition that the American missile attack is a proper exercise of R2P. [See: Gordon Lubold and Dion Nissenbaum, ."U.S. Launches Cruise Missiles at Syrian Air Base in Response to Chemical Attack" *The Wall Street Journal* Online, April 7, 2017; Haley Sweetland Edwards, "Should U.S. Colleges Be Graded by the Government?" *Time*, April 28, 2014, pp. 33-35.]

5. There seems to be little doubt today that the Democratic People's Republic of North Korea has developed a working nuclear weapon. Moreover, it also seems certain that North Korea has built and successfully launched a variety of intercontinental ballistic missiles (ICBMs). The North Korean missiles have a range of about 4,000 miles. which means that they can certainly hit South Korea, Japan, Guam, Hawaii, and Alaska, making all of these territories prime targets for a nuclear attack. As if this were not troublesome enough, at the rate at which they are developing their weapons program, the North Koreans may be able to reach the West Coast of the United States in two to three years, maybe even sooner, with a little bit of luck. The question on the table at the moment is what the United States is will do about all of this. If Max Weber had his way, the United States just might launch a preventive strike against North Korea, much like Israelis did when they attacked and destroyed the Osirak nuclear reactor in Iraq in 1981. Louis Bromfield might have a less extreme protocol in mind. It is likely that he would advise putting pressure on North Korea's Big Brother, China, which is in a position to offer economic aid to North Korea in exchange for the North Koreans stepping back from their weapons program. This much is clear. What is not clear is what the international community should do as part of the new Responsibility to Protect doctrine. Under R2P, should the international community act against North Korea based on the doctrine's mandate to prevent nations from endangering their own people? Using what you know using about R2P, defend the proposition that it would be ethical under R2P for the international community to launch a nonnuclear preventive strike against North Korea to prevent that troubled nation from starting a nuclear war on its own. [See: "Containing Mr. Kim," *The Economist*, July 8, 2017, p. 10; and "The Wrong Kind of Fireworks," *The Economist*, July 8, 2017, p. 33.]

6. The legal system in the United States has granted corporations personhood. This is significant because this status as a "legal person" gives the corporation certain powers and abilities far beyond those of mortal business entities. For instance, as legal persons, corporations are accorded certain constitutional rights, such as the right not to be deprived of property without due process of law. They can also own property in their own name and have lawsuits filed to protect them or vindicate their rights. Now in one of the most unusual, though not unexpected, twists in the law, a lawsuit has been filed on behalf of a chimpanzee that seeks a declaration from the court that such animals have human-like rights not dissimilar to the rights according corporations. The plaintiff in the case is a chimpanzee named Tommy who has been imprisoned in a small cage since his original owner's death. The suit has been brought on Tommy's behalf by the Nonhuman Rights Project (NhRP). The overall objective of the lawsuit is to alter current law, which characterizes higher cognitive animals—such as chimpanzees, gorillas, dolphins, orcas, and so on—as property. The immediate goal in the case of Tommy is to have the court, at the very least, declare that such nonhuman-cognitively superior beings (NhCSBs) have the right not to be imprisoned without good reason. The case for Tommy and others like him is based on *habeas corpus*, a legal principle that says that a person cannot be held without just cause. To seek a writ of habeas corpus is to ask the court to compel the person's keeper to bring him or her to the court so that the court can determine if the imprisonment is justified. The initial hurdle is, of course, to demonstrate that a chimpanzee is a legal person—a legal person not a human being—which may turn upon the cognitive abilities of the chimpanzee. Now explore whether such an argument can be justified using

any one of the following ethical theories: negative rights theory, rational ethics, social contract ethics, or utilitarianism. [See: Charles Siebert, "The Rights of Man and Beast," *New York Times Magazine*, April 27, 2014, pp. 28–33, 49–50, 53.]

7. In 1985, at the very beginning of the AIDS epidemic, a young family found themselves faced with a difficult decision. Their infant son was suffering from a blood disorder that would require, at least in the expert opinion of the physicians in charge of the case, the complete removal of the child's blood, followed by a transfusion with the hospital's blood products. This was a risky procedure at that point in history given the epidemic and the unpredictability of the screening process in place at the time. An alternative process suggested by the child's medically trained mother would remove half the child's blood, replacing it with a saline solution. With half of the bad blood gone and the rest diluted by the saline, the hope was that the child's body would produce healthy blood to replace the unhealthy blood. Despite the position of the experts, the parents chose the second option and the child was saved. Using rational ethics, defend the decision made by the parents as the correct one, despite the risks involved and the opinion of the experts in the case. [See: Brooks Haxton, "Playing the Cards," *New York Times Magazine*, April 27, 2014, p. 54.]

8. Peter Kropotkin is one of those philosophical economists who warned against the deepening gulf between the wealthy and the poor. Kropotkin characterized this trend as unjust and, like Marx, predicted social upheaval—anarchy—as the coming phase from which a new social system may emerge, one based on cooperation rather than competition. More than 50 years later, Louis Bromfield made a similar observation about the split between the haves and the have-nots. Bromfield's analysis was made at a global level and suggested that those nations with wealth form alliances designed to make them stable before helping the have-not nations. About 50 years after that, Thomas Piketty, a French economist, tackled the same problem in a book titled, *Capital in the Twenty-First Century*. Piketty was also troubled by the rising gap between those with capital and those who earn wages and concludes that capital will always grow faster than the economy ($r > g$). Simply put, this means that those who have wealth continue to accumulate more wealth, and those without wealth remain poor. Piketty, however, offers a different solution. He proposes gradually increasing the tax rates applied to capital, the net effect of which will ultimately be to redistribute the wealth, thus reducing the growing gulf between the two groups, reestablishing both equality and injustice on a global basis, and forestalling the revolution predicted by Kropotkin. Is Piketty's plan ethical? Before answering the question, reexamine Piketty's plan based on any one of the following ethical theories: negative rights theory, rational ethics, social contract ethics, or utilitarianism. [See: Thomas Piketty, *Capital in the Twenty-First Century* (Cambridge, MA: Harvard University Press, 2014); "Capitalism and Its Critics: A Modern Marx," *The Economist,* May 3, 2014, pp. 12–13; and "Picketty Fever: Bigger than Marx: A Wonky Book on Inequality Becomes a Blockbuster," *The Economist,* May 3, 2014, p. 67.]

Design Elements: The Opening Case: ©Sharpstock/Alamy; A Classic Case: ©Evlakhov Valeriy/Shutterstock

quick quiz Answers

1-1	1-2	1-3	1-4	1-5
1. F	1. T	1. T	1. F	1. T
2. F	2. F	2. T	2. F	2. T
3. T	3. F	3. T	3. T	3. F

Chapter 2: Sources of the Law

2-1 The Purpose and Operation of the Law
The Law as a Balancing Act • The Dualities within the Law

2-2 Constitutional Law
The Articles of Confederation • Reengineering the Articles • The Structure of the United States Constitution • State Constitutions and State Law

2-3 Executive Orders
Types of Executive Orders • Theories of Presidential Power • Challenges to Executive Orders

2-4 Statutory Law
Codes and Titles • Uniform Laws • The Uniform Commercial Code • Cyber-Law Statutes

2-5 Court Decisions
Common Law • Statutory Interpretation • Judicial Review

2-6 Administrative Regulations
Administrative Agencies • Administrative Procedures Act • The Regulatory Flexibility Act • The *Federal Register* and the *Code of Federal Regulations* • The Deep State: Dangers and Remedies

THE OPENING CASE *Round 1*
Executive Orders, Checks and Balances, and the Limits (?) of Executive Power

On June 5, 2012, President Obama issued an executive order designed to deal with the plight of many undocumented aliens who had entered the United States illegally when they were children (known in popular parlance as the "Dreamers"). The initiative, which was designated Deferred Action for Childhood Arrivals (DACA), delayed action by the Department of Homeland Security in certain cases (800,000 such cases actually) involving Dreamers who were in danger of being removed from the United States. The order also granted work authorization permits to those individuals who qualified under the guidelines set up pursuant to the order. On August 6, 2017, President Trump signed another executive order, this one ending the DACA program. Under the second order, all those already granted DACA status would retain their benefits until those benefits expired under the original order. Fifteen states and the District of Columbia filed a joint lawsuit in the Federal District Court asking that court to grant an injunction that would stop the enforcement of what they called President Trump's unconstitutional order. The attorneys general from these states argued that under terms of the rescission order, the president violated the Fifth Amendment's Due Process Clause, by using information against the immigrants that it had promised to keep secret, and the Fifth Amendment's Equal Protection Clauses, by targeting people based on national origin. The attorneys general also argued that the order violated the Administrative Procedures Act, by not following the proper rule-making process, and the Regulatory Flexibility Act, by not analyzing the impact of the changes enacted by the new order and by not posting for public comment the changes made in the original order.

Supporters of President Trump have argued that the original Obama order creating DACA was unconstitutional because it amounted to a legislative enactment that violated the underlying constitutional principle of the separation of powers. What President Obama did under the original order was to create a set of legal benefits with no legislative authority to do so. Supporters of the original Obama order countered this position by arguing that the president has the power to issue such executive orders when Congress has repeatedly "failed to act" on an issue of national importance. President

Trump's supporters have also argued that when President Obama enacted the first order, he violated the principle of prosecutorial discretion. Under prosecutorial discretion, a law enforcement official who is, in effect, "down in the trenches" may make resource distribution decisions when determining what laws to enforce and what laws to ignore. They further argue that the principle of prosecutorial discretion is meant to distribute resources at the local level, not to provide the president with a pretext to to sidestep any limitation he wants to just by invoking the magic words "prosecutorial discretion." So, which side do you think is (was?) correct—the supporters of DACA, who see the new decree as unconstitutional and a violation of federal law, or the supporters of the second order that eliminates the first order as an unconstitutional violation of the separation of powers and a misuse of prosecutorial discretion? [See: *States of New York, et al. v. Trump,* Civil Action No. 17-CV-5228 (2017); Andrew McCarthy, "To End DACA Follow the Constitution," *The National Review,* September 5, 2017, http://nationalreview.com/article/451071/donald-trump-daca-democrats-must-compromise; and Alexander Burns and Vivian Yee, "Second Chance for 'Dreamers' Seen in Courts," *The New York Times,* September 7, 2017, pp. A1, A16.]

Opening Case Questions

1. What is the difference between the Establishment Clause and the Due Process Clause of the Fifth Amendment, and how are they used in this case? Explain.
2. What is the difference between the Administrative Procedures Act and the Regulatory Flexibility Act? How do these two acts fit into this case? Explain.
3. What is the "failure to act" principle presented in this case, and how, exactly, does that principle work in this case and elsewhere? Explain.
4. What is the doctrine of the separation of powers, and how does it figure into this case? Explain.
5. What is prosecutorial discretion, and how, exactly, does that doctrine work in this case and elsewhere? Explain.

Source: See: *States of New York, et al. v. Trump,* Civil Action No. 17-CV-5228 (2017); Andrew McCarthy, "To End DACA Follow the Constitution," *The National Review,* September 5, 2017, http://nationalreview.com/article/451071/donald-trump-daca-democrats-must-compromise; Alexander Burns and Vivian Yee, "Second Chance For 'Dreamers' Seen in Courts," *The New York Times,* September 7, 2017, pp. A1 and A16.

 Learning Objectives

1. List the objectives of the law.
2. Clarify the duality of the law.
3. Outline the content of the U.S. Constitution.
4. Define and explain the use of executive orders.
5. Explain the role of statutory law in the legal system.
6. Defend the need to set up a system of uniform laws.
7. Describe how the principle of *stare decisis* provides stability within the law.
8. Differentiate between statutory interpretation and judicial review.
9. Account for the legislature's need to establish administrative agencies.
10. Clarify the nature of the deep state within the American political and legal system.

2-1 The Purpose and Operation of the Law

As explained in Chapter 1, the **law** consists of rules of conduct established by the government to maintain harmony, stability, and justice within a society. Ideally, the primary objectives of the law should be balanced equally at all times. Unfortunately, in "real life," this balance is not easy to maintain. Often, justice must be sacrificed for harmony and stability. Sometimes the opposite is true.

The Law as a Balancing Act

The law should be viewed as a delicate balancing act. One person's rights are enforced while another's are not. One group is allowed to act while another group is limited in what it is permitted to do. One person is allowed to go free while another is imprisoned, fined, and forced to forfeit his property. One corporation's contracts are upheld while another's are struck down. Trade-offs like this occur within the law on a regular basis. Generally, the objectives of harmony, stability, and justice are kept in mind when such decisions are made. Because the law is made by people, however, it is not perfect. Legislators, judges, and administrators bring their own limitations into the process. Still, many of them do their best to be as objective and fair as possible. The law is made even more complex because it involves a series of competing dualities.

The Dualities within the Law

The need to balance rights and duties within the law is not unusual. Rather, this balancing act is part of the law's fundamental nature. As Anthony Chase explains in his study, *Law and History*, the legal system is shaped by several dualities, each of which is essential to the law's success. These dualities include the balance between the spirit and the letter of the law, between legal words and their interpretation, and between abstract principles and concrete situations. This balancing act also comes into play in the application of the Uncertainty Principle to the law. [See: Anthony Chase, "Historical Jurisprudence: I. Inside/Outside," *Law and History: The Evolution of the American Legal System* (New York: The New Press, 1997), pp. 12–19.]

The Spirit and the Letter of the Law According to Chase, one of the most obvious dualities in the law is the balance between the **spirit** and the **letter of the law.** Generally, a person who follows the spirit of the law has found its actual intent, while one who is tied to the letter of the law has missed its true meaning; however, this is not always the case. Sometimes, following the letter of the law to avoid the spirit of the law can be a good thing. Thus, a shop owner who is discouraged by the complexity and intrusiveness of the law might avoid a prohibition against the sale of alcohol on Sunday by "giving away" bottles of wine to his customers who come in the next day and "give" the shop owner cash, which just happens to be equivalent to the cost of their Sunday "gift." The shop owner has met the letter of the law by not "selling" alcohol on Sunday, but he and his customers have clearly violated the spirit of the law. Is this a good thing? We'll leave that to your imagination. [See: Chase, pp. 12–14.]

Words versus Interpretation Chase explains that much of the confusion over the spirit of the law emerges when the law is written down. Because words are often ambiguous, the language of the law can become a hindrance rather than a help in the execution of the law. This is why it is sometimes necessary to manipulate the language in order to uncover the actual intent of the lawmakers and to apply that intent in a consistent and fair fashion. Certainly, this oddity opens the law to adjustments that are sometimes good and sometimes bad. However, to view this particular brand of duality, **words** versus **interpretation,** as either a strength or a weakness would be an error because it is neither. Instead, it is merely how the law works. [See: Chase, pp. 14–15.]

The Abstract and the Concrete According to Chase, duality in the law is also seen in the work of judges, legislators, and administrators. In one way or another, all three are involved in the law-making process, and as a result, all three must tackle a third type of duality, that which exists between *abstract* principles and *concrete* situations. [See: Chase, p. 15.] Thus, at times, legislators must take a principle, such as the idea that the government should be fair and equitable whenever it enacts a new tax bill, and apply that abstraction to a concrete piece of legislation. Similarly, a judge must take an abstract principle, such as the notion that all physicians must act with due care in performing their duties, and apply that principle in a case in which Dr. Jones fails to properly diagnose Mr. Smith's ailment. In all such cases, it is not possible to eliminate the tension that exists between the duality of the abstract and the concrete. The only thing that can be done is for lawmakers to deal with the concrete incident without violating the abstract principle. This is not the end to the duality issue, however. In another study of the law, Gerald Turkel points out that this duality (Turkel calls is bipolarity) exists in the very nature of a lawsuit when the plaintiff and the defendant face off against one another. This bipolarity is the essence of the adversarial system. [See: Gerald Turkel, *Law and Society: Critical Approaches* (Boston: Allyn and Bacon, 1996), p. 13.]

The Uncertainty Principle Duality also exists in the way a decision is intended and the way it is actually executed. The two—intent and result—almost never coincide, and when they do, it is generally a matter of luck, nothing more. This principle, which is generally referred

THE OPENING CASE *Round 2*
Executive Orders, Checks and Balances, and the Limits (?) of Executive Power

Recall that, in the Opening Case, President Trump signed an executive order phasing out the DACA program. Almost instantly after the order was signed, 15 states and the District of Columbia filed a joint lawsuit, asking the court to grant an injunction that would stop the enforcement of what they called President Trump's unconstitutional order. The attorneys general from these states argued that under terms of the rescission order, the president had violated the Fifth Amendment's Due Process and Equal Protection Clauses. These two abstract principles have been part of American constitutional law for more than 200 years. So far, so good. However, on the other side of the issue, supporters of the president argued that the original Obama order creating DACA was unconstitutional because it amounted to a legislative enactment that the president cannot issue without violating the separation of powers principle.

So, how is it possible for the removal of an illegal and unconstitutional order to be a violation of due process and equal protection? Good question. Here is the problem in a nutshell. These perfectly reasonable principles—due process and equal protection on one side and the separation of powers on the other—sound quite reasonable in the abstract. However, as often happens, when an abstract principle becomes concrete, everything falls apart. Guaranteeing the Dreamers due process and equal protection with an illegal order may sound good, but it simply does not work. Trying to create a legal rule illegally and then complaining when the illegal rule is challenged is a little like accepting a stolen umbrella from a kindly thief in a rainstorm and then suing the rightful owner when she demands the return of her umbrella. Sure you got wet when she claimed her umbrella, but you had no right to the umbrella in the first place. On the other hand, it seems quite unfair for you to get soaked when you quite innocently accepted the stolen umbrella from the kindly thief, who, by now, is nowhere to be found. So who is responsible for this mess: the kindly thief who gave you a stolen umbrella or the reasonable umbrella owner who demanded her umbrella and then watched you get soaked. To put it another way, who is responsible for the DACA mess: the compassionate president who created an unconstitutional program or the reasonable president who eliminates an unconstitutional program? Think about it. [See: *States of New York, et al. v. Trump,* Civil Action No. 17-CV-5228 (2017); Andrew McCarthy, "To End DACA Follow the Constitution," *The National Review*, September 5, 2017, http://nationalreview.com/article/451071/donald-trump-daca-democrats-must-compromise; and Alexander Burns and Vivian Yee, "Second Chance for 'Dreamers' Seen in Courts," *The New York Times*, September 7, 2017, pp. A1, A16.]

Source: See: *States of New York, et al. v. Trump, Civil Action No. 17-CV-5228 (2017);* Andrew McCarthy, "To End DACA Follow the Constitution," The National Review, September 5, 2017, http://nationalreview.com/article/451071/donald-trump-daca-democrats-must-compromise; Alexander Burns and Vivian Yee, "Second Chance For 'Dreamers' Seen in Courts," *The New York Times*, September 7, 2017, pp. A1 and A16.

to as the *Uncertainty Principle*, exists in physics, in politics, and in economics. John Maynard Keynes recognized the Uncertainty Principle in economics and made it one of the linchpins of his economic theory. Uncertainty between intentions and results in the law is very common. It occurs when legislators pass statutes that are vetoed by the chief executive, when a trial judge rules on a case that gets overturned by an appellate court, and when the chief executive makes an appointment that is nullified by the legislature. [See Chase, p. 19; and

THE OPENING CASE   Round 3
Executive Orders, Checks and Balances, and the Limits (?) of Executive Power

One of President Trump's campaign issues involved a promise to reform immigration law. Included in this promise was the removal of the DACA program initiated by President Obama in 2012. After the inauguration, because of problems with Congress, the bureaucracy, and the media, President Trump was slow to act on the promise to remove DACA. Part of President Trump's hesitation came from the fact that he had change of heart regarding the "incredible kids" who would be affected by the elimination of DACA. This apparent slowdown troubled many individuals who had counted on a more proactive president. Consequently, early in September 2017, President Trump found himself threatened by nine attorneys general from nine conservative states, all of whom promised to file lawsuits that would force Trump to kill DACA. To forestall the filing of these lawsuits, the president issued a new Executive Order designed to phase out DACA. As an immediate response to this move, 15 states and the District of Columbia filed a joint lawsuit in the Federal District Court Eastern District of New York, asking the court to grant an injunction that would stop the enforcement of what they called President Trump's unconstitutional order.

This experience dramatizes the Uncertainty Principle in action. The administration intended one result—to dodge the threat of nine lawsuits—only to find itself faced with one huge integrated lawsuit filed by 15 states and the District of Columbia. Additionally, the president faced a largely ineffective Congress which seemed reluctant or unable to act on his demand for immigration reform legislation. Accordingly, President Trump indicated that if Congress did not act on immigration reform, he would "revisit" the issue himself. This deliberately ambiguous statement implied that President Trump might do exactly what President Obama had done in 2012—that is, he would use executive power to fix a problem that Congress had repeatedly "failed to act" upon, despite being given multiple opportunities to do so. Ironically, such an exercise of executive power was exactly what many supporters of the president had repeatedly labeled as unconstitutional. So again we see the Uncertainty Principle in action. The president gives Congress (well, the Republican side of Congress) what it wants—the elimination of an unconstitutional program and the chance to reform immigration law. Should Congress fail to act, it may find itself faced with an unexpected and unprecedented result—a president who issues an unconstitutional order to reestablish the unconstitutional program that his constitutional order removed in the first place. Does that make any sense at all? Think about it. [See: *States of New York, et al. v. Trump,* Civil Action No. 17-CV-5228 (2017); Michael Shear and Julie Hirschfeld Davis, "U.S. Ends Program Giving 'Dreamers' Legal Protection," *The New York Times*, September 6, 2017, pp. A1, A17; Will Drabold, "We Asked Constitutional Scholars if DACA Is Legal. They're Split." *MIC,* September 6, 2017, https://mic.com/articles/184250/we-asked-constitutional-scholars-if-daca-is-legal-theyre-split#.0E5uY4kAd; and Noland D. McCaskill, "Trump Ends DACA—and Pressures Congress to Pass Immigration Reform," *POLITICO*, September 5, 2017, http://www.politico.com/story/2017/09/05/trump-dreamers-daca-work-permits-242323.)

Source: See: *States of New York, et al. v. Trump, Civil Action* No. 17-CV-5228 (2017); Michael Shear and Julie Hirschfeld Davis, "U.S. Ends Program Giving 'Dreamers' Legal Protection," *The New York Times*, September 6, 2017, pp. A1 and A17; Will Drabold, We asked constitutional scholars if DACA is legal. They're split." *MIC* September 6, 2017, https://mic.com/articles/184250/we-asked-constitutional-scholars-if-daca-is-legal-theyre-split#.0E5uY4kAd; Noland D. McCaskill, "Trump ends DACA—and pressures Congress to pass immigration reform," *POLITICO*, September 5, 2017, http://www.politico.com/story/2017/09/05/trump-dreamers-daca-work-permits-242323.

Robert Skidelsky, "Keynes's Economics: Uncertainty," *Keynes: The Return of the Master* (New York: Public Affairs, 2010), pp. 83-85.] Moreover, the legal scholar Richard Posner tells us that this inclination toward uncertainty, especially as it relates to economics, is exacerbated by the fact that some people act in unpredictable ways on a regular basis (which makes their unpredictability predictable?), while others simply sit back and react to what their neighbors have done. What is true in economics is equally true in the law. Or is it? Think about it. [See: Richard Posner, *A Failure of Capitalism* (Cambridge, MA: Harvard University Press, 2009), pp. 83-84.]

Textualism versus Pragmatism As noted earlier, the law is frequently described as a balancing act. Perhaps one of the most-often-quoted segments of this concept of balancing is seen in the attempt to balance the *spirit* of the law with the *letter* of the law. It now appears, however, that this simple and, heretofore, rarely challenged concept has several new adversaries. Supreme Court Justice Antonin Scalia and his co-author Bryan A Garner, distinguished research professor of law at Southern Methodist University, have breathed new life into a form of legal interpretation—referred to alternately as *textualism* and *originalism*—that may demonstrate the naïveté of attempting to balance the spirit with the letter of the law.

The Textualist Approach In general, the idea behind **textualism** (also called **originalism**) is for judges and attorneys to look at constitutions and statutes as literary works or as verbal icons that stand as separately created artifacts that must be judged, much like a poem or a short story, by its words and its words alone. The intent of textualism is to have legal interpreters bypass the generally biased and self-serving explanations found in legislative histories and committee reports and, instead, rely upon the meaning of the words that the legislators actually wrote and placed in the text of the constitution or the statute in question. Scalia and Garner explain the details of textualism in *Reading Law: The Interpretation of Legal Texts*. Much of the book is devoted to a detailed examination of 57 canons of interpretation and 13 false beliefs that they discredit. The very first attack on these false statements targets the idea that "the spirit of a statute should prevail over its letter." Scalia and Garner argue that the idea that the spirit of the law can somehow magically trump the letter of the law was probably born sometime in the Middle Ages when the chances of finding statutory law in England were unlikely at best. Moreover, they note that because no one has ever identified any standards by which to deduce, measure, and apply this mysterious "spirit of the law," it was most likely used as a technique to grant judges the unrestricted ability to pay no attention to the language of the law. Scalia and Garner also point out that even those judicial and philosophical giants who are alleged to have supported the spirit over letter principle really did no such thing. The leading example of those distortions is Chief Justice John Marshall, who is supposed to have depended on the spirit of the Constitution, when what he really said was that the spirit of the law should be respected just as much as the letter, and (here is the key) that the spirit itself was to be "collected chiefly from its letter." [See: Antonin Scalia and Bryan Garner, *Reading Law: The Interpretation of Legal Texts* (St. Paul, MN: West, 2012).]

The Pragmatic Approach On the other side of this issue are a number of legal experts, not the least of which is Richard Posner, chief justice of the U.S. Court of Appeals for the Seventh Circuit and the author of *Overcoming Law*. Posner's book predates Scalia and Garner's text by some 17 years. However, Posner devotes an entire chapter to textualism, largely fashioned as a critique of another champion of that theory, Robert Bork, the author of *The Tempting of America: The Political Seduction of the Law*. In *Overcoming Law*, Posner argues that textualism, whether supported by Bork or Scalia, is fine as far as it goes, but it cannot be considered as the only arrow in a judge's quiver. Textual criticism will help to get at the meaning of the words in the law; that much is true. However, to rely solely on this approach is to ignore the consequences of the law or of a singular and narrowly drawn interpretation of that law. Posner prefers, instead, a process that he labels *pragmatism*. In a nutshell, **pragmatism**

involves an approach by judges that considers the consequences of a decision to be the single most important guideline in the development of that decision. In applying a pragmatic approach, the judge must attempt to get into the mind of the framer of that law and, in doing so, see how that framer would respond to the modern circumstances in which the judge finds him- or herself. The law, Posner believes, is not static nor should it be. Moreover, in making his or her determination, the judge must not focus alone on a single interpretation, but must consider multiple interpretations in order to sort out the one that makes the most sense. This technique, Posner argues, is not "judicial lawlessness" but is, instead, an approach that looks both forward and backward and does so with a mind toward the consequences based on multiple forms of input. [See: Richard Posner, *Overcoming Law* (Cambridge, MA: Harvard University Press, 1995); and Robert Bork, *The Tempting of America: The Political Seduction of the Law* (New York: Simon and Schuster, 1990).]

quick quiz 2-1

1. The law consists of rules of conduct established by the government to maintain harmony, stability, and justice within a society.   true | false
2. Often, justice must be sacrificed for harmony and stability, but the opposite is never true.   true | false
3. Legislators and judges bring their own personal prejudices and biases into the process.   true | false

2-2 Constitutional Law

The habitual use in the media of phrases like "fake news," "alternative facts," "post-truth," and "real fake news" seems to be a phenomenon that has appeared only recently. In actuality, fake news has been a part of our heritage since the Puritans landed at Plymouth to establish religious freedom. (*Fake news alert:* The Puritans journeyed to the New World to establish a theocracy, not to establish religious freedom.) American "history" is plagued by fake news from George Washington's cherry tree to the nonexistent weapons of mass destruction hidden in Iraq. [See: Kurt Anderson, *Fantasyland: How America Went Haywire* (New York: Random House, 2017); and Hanna Rosin, "National Delusions," *New York Times Book Review*, September 10, 2017, pp. 1, 22.] The alternative facts that surround the legal process further complicate the uncertainty found in the nature, the purpose, and the operation of the law. It is true that the law can be defined as rules of conduct created by the government to maintain order, stability, and justice; however, it is also true that the law is made to regulate, control, and limit the conduct of the people. In fact, the need for a strong central government that separates the people from power and insulates the leadership from unnecessary and counterproductive contact with the people was clearly recognized by the Framers—not the least of whom was James Madison. So which is it: the post-truth that teaches us that our Founding Fathers were fine, democratically minded gentlemen or the alternative facts that reveal the Framers as fearful men determined to protect the self-interests of the ruling class? Read on.

The "historical" post-truth that we all learned about the writing of our Constitution is that the Founding Fathers (under the influence of thinkers like John Locke, David Hume, and Montesquieu) wrote the Constitution to give power to the people. The alternative facts are somewhat different from this set of post-truths. Several of the unrecognized contributors to the development of the American political system were Niccolo Machiavelli, Francis Bacon, and Thomas Hobbes. Once this reality is recognized, many of the puzzles within the

Constitution, puzzles like the Electoral College, for example, become quite clear. Separating post-truth from reality is important in the study of constitutional law, because a **constitution** is the fundamental law of a nation. The body of law that makes up the study of the constitution is called **constitutional law**. Constitutional law is rarely found in one document, one case, or one treatise, even when the Constitution itself is that one document. Make no mistake, however. A constitution need not be a single document, just so long as most everyone intuitively understands its basic concepts.

> ### EXAMPLE 2-1: Constitutional Law in the United Kingdom
>
> Unlike the U.S. Constitution, the British Constitution has never been reduced to a single document. Instead, the principles that make up the British Constitution are found in many documents, including the *Magna Carta*, an endless series of court cases, and a complex mix of statutory laws. There are problems with this fragmented approach. First, the amalgam of legal precedents that makes up the British constitution plays right into the problems associated with the Uncertainty Principle. This occurs because it is difficult to know what precedent will be called upon to support or to attack a particular legal position. Second, the absence of a written fail-safe system, like that found in the U.S. Constitution, opens the door to power abuse in the British system. On the other hand, following the dictates of the Uncertainty Principle, there are some unexpected but not unappreciated advantages to a less definite constitution. First, the British constitutional method avoids the ambiguities associated with the need to determine the difference between the words and the interpretation of those words. True, the British must still deal with this duality whenever statutes and cases are interpreted by the courts, but this is a minor issue when compared to U.S. constitutional battles. Finally, when interpreting the British Constitution, there is no need to distinguish between the letter of the law and the spirit of the law because, at least in relation to constitutional law, in the British system, there simply is no letter of the law. [See: Sarah Lyall, "As a New Government Goes to Work, the Constitution Offers Britain Few Guides," *The New York Times,* May 25, 2010, p. A6.]
>
> *Source:* See: Sarah Lyall, "As a New Government Goes to Work, the Constitution Offers Britain Few Guides," *The New York Times*, May 25, 2010, p. A6.

The Articles of Confederation

The Constitution of the United States, as it exists today, is not the nation's first constitution. The first constitution was known as the **Articles of Confederation**. The Articles of Confederation were created to hold together a fragile coalition of states, each of which was determined to maintain its own independent existence. Although the Articles of Confederation fulfilled a much-needed function during the first years in the life of the United States, they contained certain weaknesses.

One of the primary weaknesses was the fact that the United States in Congress, as the national legislature was known under the Articles, could not impose taxes or tariffs. Although a common treasury was supposed to be supplied by the states in proportion to the value of the land within each state, the states retained the power to levy and collect taxes. In essence, this rule meant that the United States in Congress had to rely on the goodwill of the states to obtain money. Such revenues were rarely forthcoming. Some states paid nothing at all; others turned over a portion of what they owed but rarely by the date the payments were due. Part of this problem was caused by the fact that the states were not about to trade one dictatorial central government for another and, therefore, simply ignored the national government.

Moreover, the desire to prevent the type of tyranny that the colonies had experienced under the rule of King George and the British Parliament led the framers of the Articles to include other limitations on the national government. For instance, all delegates to the Congress were appointed by the state legislatures and served at their pleasure. Several times, the national government found itself powerless to act, because some of the legislatures did not even bother to send delegates to Congress. In addition, whereas the United States in Congress had the authority to regulate the value of any money created under its own authority or under the authority of a state, the states retained the power to issue their own currency.

Reengineering the Articles

These problems and others like them were uppermost in the minds of the delegates to the Constitutional Convention, when they gathered in Philadelphia in 1787 to *revise* the Articles of Confederation. Also on their minds was a recent rather troubling incident in Massachusetts, an incident remembered as Shays' Rebellion. (*Fake news alert:* The rebellion was actually led by a preacher named Samuel Ely and involved more than 2,000 angry farmers.) Although the rebellion was unsuccessful, the delegates were, nevertheless, profoundly affected by the threat that it represented to the survival of the nation. In fact, some of the delegates were actually nervous about a possible new revolution. [See: Walter A. MacDougal, *Freedom Just Around the Corner* (New York: Harper Collins, 2004), p. 295.] Enter James Madison, whose broad-based educational background made him not unfamiliar with Machiavelli, Bacon, and Hobbes. In fact, Madison owned a copy of Hobbes's principal political work, *Leviathan*. We can, therefore, be relatively certain of the Hobbesian influence on Madison. [See: George Mace, *Locke, Hobbes, and the Federalist Papers* (Carbondale: Southern Illinois University Press, 1979), pp. 9, 123.] As for Bacon and Machiavelli, Hobbes worked directly with Bacon for a number of years and owed his scientific view of human nature to Bacon who, in turn, owed his views on human nature at least in part to Machiavelli. All three of these philosophers have at least one belief in common in relation to human nature: Humans will protect themselves, even if it means using violence against others, and, therefore, must be controlled by a strong central government. Madison did his best to provide that type of strong central government in the Constitution.

The Constitution itself displays a general structural orientation toward insulating the leadership of the new republic from the influence of the people. One case in point is the Electoral College (Article II, Section 1); others include the election of senators (Article I, Section 3); the Supremacy Clause (Article VI); and the religion clauses of the First Amendment. To many people, the Electoral College is a mystery both in operation and intent. In effect, the Electoral College acts as a buffer between the people and the election of the president. It is likely that many of the delegates to the convention would have actually preferred that Congress choose the president; however, such a move was viewed as a bit too extreme. The Electoral College was the compromise solution. The people would choose electors. The electors, not the people, would then "elect" the president. The Framers assumed that the electors would always be landowning, educated men of their own class, thus providing them with a dependable buffer between the chief executive and the people. [See: MacDougal, p. 302.] As an extra safeguard, the state governments would choose the method for seating the electors, thus giving the state legislators the power to guarantee the election of trustworthy electors. [See: Bernard Schwartz, *Constitutional Law* (New York: McMillan Publishing Co., 1972), pp. 135–136.]

The delegates assumed that the election of senators would require the same type of safeguard that insulated the election of the president from the vagaries of the people. Under the original Constitution (Article I, Section 3), the senators were to be elected by the state legislatures, guaranteeing that senators would always be upper-class property owners, chosen by upper-class property owners. This process remained in place until the 17th Amendment in 1913. (This was the same year, interestingly enough, that the Constitution was changed to allow an income tax under the 16th Amendment.) Senators were also given the longest term of office, six years, ensuring that the real political power at the national level would remain with the landed gentry. Even so, some of the delegates, Madison in particular, did not fully trust the state legislators to be wholly in control of the electorate in their respective states. To allay his fears, Madison campaigned to add a congressional veto to Article I of the Constitution that would empower Congress to invalidate any law passed by a state legislature that Congress deemed to be unsuitable. Some commentators argue, rather convincingly, that the only reason the congressional veto was, well, vetoed by the delegates in Philadelphia was that most of the southern representatives figured out that a congressional veto would likely sound the death knell for slavery soon after ratification. [See: Steven Waldman, *Founding Faith* (New York: Random House, 2008), p. 132.] This, of course, does not mean the federal government cannot "veto" state legislation. It just means that to do so, it must file a lawsuit and bring the case to court, arguing that the statute in question violates the Supremacy Clause of the Constitution (Article VI). The Supremacy Clause of the U.S. Constitution does in fact state that, "(t)his Constitution and the Laws of the United States . . . shall be the supreme Law of the Land."

EXAMPLE 2-2: Vetoing California's Bid to Become a Sanctuary State

Shortly after taking office in 2017, President Trump began to address the problem of illegal immigration. One of the steps that he took in this effort was to empower officers associated with Immigration and Customs Enforcement (ICE) to target not only illegal immigrants who had committed crimes, but also those who had simply been arrested. Some state officials who were familiar with the immigrant community in their own states were convinced that this move would cause unnecessary panic among many illegal immigrants, who were fearful of deportation. In an attempt to deal with this and other problems associated with the president's order, some state legislatures considered passing laws that would transform them into sanctuary states. For example, the California State Senate introduced a bill that would curtail the ability of local police officers to cooperate with federal immigration officers. The bill, designated SB 54, would limit the ability of immigration officers to access certain databanks. SB 54 would also prevent ICE officers from entering local jails and interviewing inmates who might be in the United States illegally. The fear was that, should SB 54 become law, certain dangerous inmates might be released before immigration officers could talk to them, thus increasing the possibility of further criminal activity. California state officials argued that this concern was unreasonable and was simply being used as a strategy to drum up opposition to the bill.

Many American citizens supported the California initiative. Others saw it as a blatant attempt to circumvent the president's policies. Remember that during the Constitutional Convention in Philadelphia in 1787, Madison had campaigned to add a congressional veto to Article I of the Constitution that would empower Congress to invalidate any law passed by a state legislature that Congress deemed to be unsuitable. Had Madison managed to win that contest, the Republican-dominated Congress could simply invoke its veto power and the California statute would become void, just like that. Instead, in the real world, to eliminate the law, the president threatened to cut federal funding to California and other states that followed its example. Supporters of the president argued that federal action is superior to state law because, in this case, the Constitution gave the power to control immigration to the national government. The Supremacy Clause of the U.S. Constitution does in fact state that, "(t)his Constitution and the Laws of the United States . . . shall be the supreme Law of the Land." Thus, it would seem that the federal government has a solid argument. Still the process would have been so much easier had Madison gotten his way. Right? What do you think? [See: Gustavo Solis, "California Could Become a Sanctuary State. Here Is What You Need to Know," *The Desert Sun*, February 13, 2017, http://www.desertsun.com/story/news/2017/02/10/california-could-become-sanctuary-state-heres-what-you-need-know/97751368/.]

Source: See: Gustavo Solis, "California could become a sanctuary state. Here is what you need to know," The *Desert Sun*, February 13, 2017, http://www.desertsun.com/story/news/2017/02/10/california-could-become-sanctuary-state-heres-what-you-need-know/97751368/

The last piece of textual evidence that demonstrates rather soundly that Madison and many of his fellow Framers sought protection from the masses is found in the First Amendment, in general, and, in particular, within the two religion clauses. This radical proposition, however, is best examined in relation to the structure of the Constitution. It is to that subject that we now turn.

The Structure of the United States Constitution

The Constitution of the United States is based on two fundamental principles that were supported by many of the delegates to the convention in Philadelphia. Those two principles promote, first, a separation of national powers among three distinct branches of government and, second, a checks and balances system that allows each branch to oversee the operation of the other two branches. The principle of the separation of powers set up the now familiar three branches of the national government: the executive branch, the legislative branch, and the judicial branch. The principle of checks and balances allows each branch to share in the power of the other two branches. The U.S. Constitution is divided into two parts: the articles and the amendments. The articles establish the organization of the national government. The amendments change provisions in the original articles and add ideas that the Framers did not include in those articles.

U.S. Const. Articles I–VII (see Appendix A)

The Articles The first three of the seven articles distribute the power of the government among the legislative, executive, and judicial branches. Article I establishes Congress as the legislative (statute-making) branch of the government. Article II gives executive power to the president, and Article III gives judicial power to the Supreme Court and other courts established by Congress. Article IV explains the relationships among the states and the relationship between the federal government and the states, while Article V outlines the methods for amending the Constitution. Article VI establishes the U.S. Constitution, federal laws, and treaties as the supreme law of the land. Finally, Article VII outlines how the original 13 states would go about ratifying the new Constitution. Table 2-1 outlines the content of each article in the Constitution.

Did You Know?

Roman law was first codified into The Law of the Twelve Tables in 450 BC. The Twelve Tables declared that all free citizens had certain fundamental rights.

The Bill of Rights Structurally, the Bill of Rights should have been part of the original Constitution, probably as Article V; however, from a political and a pragmatic perspective, this was not advisable. Many of the delegates to the Philadelphia convention, including Madison, believed that there was no need to add a Bill of Rights to the original Constitution. The power to regulate and protect rights, if it existed at all, was the responsibility of the states, not the national government. As the Constitution was to be written, it would be clear that the federal government, especially the legislative branch, would have only those powers that are expressly listed in the document. The Constitution would not mention rights. Therefore, Congress would have no power to enforce, eliminate, or modify rights—period. Some of the delegates also argued that, if some rights were listed, it would give the impression that those were the only rights that mattered. Therefore, it would be better to leave all mention of rights out of the Constitution.

U.S. Const. Amendments I–XXVII (see Appendix A)

These arguments were solid enough to convince New Jersey, Delaware, Connecticut, Massachusetts, Pennsylvania, and Georgia to ratify the Constitution with no Bill of Rights. However, Virginia remained unmoved, and the overwhelming fear was that, if Virginia voted down ratification, the Constitution would die a premature death. [See: Waldman, p. 136.] Still, despite the threat of defeat, Madison opposed the Bill of Rights. It was not until he saw that the Bill of Rights could be used to control political factions that he changed his mind. Madison's greatest fear was that political factions would destroy the unity of the government. To save the national government, these factions had to be brought under control, and the factions that required the greatest control were those that emerged from within the

Table 2-1 Articles of the U.S. Constitution

Articles	Content
Article I	Establishes the legislative branch of the federal government (the Congress) Defines the duties and powers of each house Outlines how Congress must conduct its business Lists legislative powers granted to Congress Lists powers denied to Congress Lists powers denied to the states
Article II	Gives executive power and responsibilities to the president Outlines the president's term of office, qualifications, and manner of election Identifies the president as commander-in-chief Gives the president power to make treaties
Article III	Establishes the Supreme Court and authorizes the establishment of other federal courts Provides for trial by jury for crimes Defines treason against the United States
Article IV	Defines interstate relations Sets up the full faith and credit clause obligating each state to recognize the public acts and proceedings of other states Provides for extradition of those accused of crimes in other states
Article V	Outlines the method of amending the Constitution
Article VI	Establishes the Constitution, federal laws, and federal treaties as the supreme law of the land
Article VII	Provides for the original ratification of the Constitution

Church. Madison (and Jefferson too, for that matter) believed that the best way to prevent religious factions from fracturing the unity of the government was to encourage them to fight among themselves, outside of the political arena. Ultimately, this conviction became one of Madison's motives for supporting the Bill of Rights.

As a dedicated Federalist and a follower of Hobbes, Madison believed that the national government needed a free hand in determining most political questions and, therefore, could not risk contradiction from any factions, but especially factions within the Church; therefore, the Church had to be "handled." From a tactical point of view, the Church could not be eliminated. However, a message had to be sent that the Church could not interfere in the political arena. The religion clause accomplished this objective by placing all religions into the same arena, giving no single religion any preference, and permitting every belief to battle on its own in the marketplace of ideas. The strategy is brilliantly conceived because it limits the power of the church without seeming to do so, in fact, while appearing to do exactly the opposite. [See: Benjamin Wiker, *Worshipping the State: How Liberalism Became Our State Religion* (Washington, DC: Regnery Publishing, 2013).]

The Post–Bill of Rights Amendments Outside of the Bill of Rights, the Constitution has been amended only 17 times. On average, this means that the Constitution is amended every 13 years; however, the amendments do not fall into neat packages that spring up every decade (plus three years). Instead, they tend to come in clusters and generally reflect some sort of flashpoint in the socioeconomic system (see Table 2-2). Thus, for example, the Civil War gave birth to Amendments 13, 14, and 15, which abolished slavery, guaranteed due process and equal protection of the law, and expanded voting rights—all within a five-year

Table 2-2 Amendments to the U.S. Constitution

The Bill of Rights	Pre–Civil War Amendments	Civil War Amendments	Progressive Amendments	Depression-Era Amendments	Modern Amendments
Amendment I Freedom of religion, speech, press, assembly	*Amendment XI* Lawsuits against the states	*Amendment XIII* Slavery is abolished	*Amendment XVI* The income tax is established	*Amendment XX* Terms of president, vice president, senators, and representatives altered	*Amendment XXII* President's terms limited to two
Amendment II The right to bear arms and set up a militia	*Amendment XII** President and vice president elected together	*Amendment XIV* Equal protection of the law, due process, citizenship	*Amendment XVII* Senators elected by direct election	*Amendment XXI* Prohibition repealed	*Amendment XXIII* Washington, DC, gets electors
Amendment III The quartering of soldiers in homes is prohibited		*Amendment XV†* Voting rights guaranteed	*Amendment XVIII‡* Prohibition established		*Amendment XXIV* Poll taxes outlawed
Amendment IV Search and seizure by probable cause			*Amendment XIX* Women given right to vote		*Amendment XXV* Disability of the president; vacancies in the vice presidency
Amendment V Grand juries, double jeopardy, self-incrimination, due process, and eminent domain					*Amendment XXVI* Vote extended to 18-year-olds
Amendment VI Procedures allowed in criminal cases					*Amendment XXVII* Congress prevented from voting itself instant pay raises
Amendment VII Jury trials in common law cases guaranteed					
Amendment VIII Bill of Rights guaranteed, cruel and unusual punishment prohibited					
Amendment IX People retain other rights					
Amendment X Powers reserved to states					

*Altered somewhat by the 20th Amendment. †Voting age changed by 26th Amendment. ‡Repealed by 21st Amendment.

span. In the second decade of the 20th century, the income tax was established, the states' election of senators was eliminated, and the vote given to women—all within seven years. Finally, the revolutionary years of the 1960s produced a widening of political inclusiveness as the District of Columbia got electors, the poll tax was eliminated, and 18-year-olds earned the right to vote. The single most important amendment outside of the Bill of Rights is the 14th Amendment, which guaranteed due process and the equal protection of the law to all people. Since its inception in 1868, the 14th Amendment has been interpreted by the courts to mean that the Bill of Rights must be enforced by the states as well as by the national government. States may expand rights but they cannot limit or eliminate them.

State Constitutions and State Law

Each state in the union adopts its own constitution. A state constitution establishes the state's government. It also sets down principles to guide the state government in making state laws and conducting state business. Most state constitutions are patterned after the U.S. Constitution; however, state constitutions tend to be longer and more detailed than the U.S. Constitution, because they must deal with local as well as statewide matters. A basic principle of constitutional law is that the U.S. Constitution is the supreme law of the land. This principle of constitutional supremacy means that all other laws must be in line with constitutional principles. If a law somehow conflicts with the Constitution, that law is said to be unconstitutional. If it does not conflict, it will be upheld by the court as constitutional.

U.S. Const. Article VI (see Appendix A)

The Constitution also says that all federal laws that are made in line with constitutional principles are to be considered the supreme law of the land. Cases that involve such conflicts, however, are not always as clear cut as those that involve state statutes that conflict with the Constitution. **Preemption** is the process by which the courts decide that a federal statute must take precedence over a state statute. The preemption of a state statute can occur in three situations. First, Congress can be very clear about its intent and explicitly state that the federal statute preempts any state statute that covers the same issues. If that is the case, then all that remains for the courts is to determine which statutes are covered by the preemption clause. Second, state statutes can be preempted by federal statutes when they conflict with the objectives of federal legislation. Third, the courts will preempt a state statute that has entered an area of the law that is traditionally an area that the federal government handles, such as foreign affairs or banking.

quick quiz 2-2

1. The present U.S. Constitution is the only constitution that the United States has ever had. — true | false
2. The principle of separation of powers was never adopted by the framers of the U.S. Constitution. — true | false
3. A basic principle of constitutional law is that state law is the supreme law of the land. — true | false

2-3 Executive Orders

An **executive order** is a device by which the president can act on his own without having to resort to the somewhat cumbersome process of going through Congress. The practice of writing and issuing an executive order is risky because the president must be careful not to violate the separation of powers principle upon which the stability of federal government depends. The process is further complicated by the fact that executive orders actually have a variety of names, such as proclamations, orders, and memoranda.

Types of Executive Orders

Technically, a **proclamation** is an executive order that addresses the public at large, while an **order** is one that is a mandatory directive aimed at a subdivision within the executive branch. In contrast, a **memorandum** is simply a suggestion issued by the president to an area of the executive branch, indicating how he would prefer that area to use its power. These designations are helpful but not determinative because some presidents are informal in their naming process. President Obama, for example, was fond of referring to his orders as memoranda.

Despite how it may seem to the public and the press, the president cannot issue an executive order on a whim. Nor should he do so without consulting proper authorities. In fact, to make sure that an executive order is legally and constitutionally sound, the president should be certain that it is founded upon a legitimate source of power. To be legally and constitutionally valid, an executive order must be based on a power that can be found in Article II of the Constitution or in a statute passed by Congress that has expressly or implicitly enabled the president to act in a certain way in a particular area within the social, political, and economic environment or, at the very least, has not forbade him to do so.

An executive order that is based on presidential authority as it appears in the Constitution is referred to as an **Article II executive order**. In contrast, an executive order issued under the authority of a congressional enactment is called a **statutory executive order**. **Hybrid executive orders** are issued using both constitutional and statutory authority. Statutory executive orders are fairly easy to spot because they will cite the statute that the president is using for the basis of his authority. Such statutes are generally rather specific about what the president can and cannot do under the authority of that statute. In contrast, Article II executive orders have fostered a bit more controversy because not all legal scholars agree on the limits of presidential power as presented in the Constitution. Admittedly, Article II contains some very expansive provisions, starting with the first line that clearly establishes the source of presidential power. Unlike Article I, which states that "All legislative power *herein granted* shall be vested in Congress," Article II begins, "The executive power shall be vested in a President." The different wording is deliberate. The Framers were determined to make certain that the legislature was limited in its power to interfere with the affairs of the individual states. Thus, they made it clear that the central government's legislative power would be restricted to that which is expressly spelled out in Article I, hence the wording *herein granted*. In contrast, the power of the president was inherent in the nature of his position as leader of the nature. The Framers could not grant power to the executive. He already held that power simply because he was the president.

Theories of Presidential Power

Despite the clear language of Article I, legal scholars, including several presidents themselves, have continued to argue about the scope of executive power. In fact, two core theories have been proposed concerning the nature of presidential power: (1) inherent executive power and (2) delegated executive power. The core theory of inherent executive power, which is sometimes referred to as the stewardship theory, was first promoted by Alexander Hamilton who, as noted earlier, simply looked at the wording of the first lines of Articles I and II and concluded that the authority of the president was not limited to the content of the article but, instead, included anything that any other national leader could do. Historically, presidents who have followed this view include Teddy Roosevelt (who first used the term "stewardship," in relation to presidential power), Woodrow Wilson, Franklin D. Roosevelt, Harry Truman, John F. Kennedy, and George W. Bush. In contrast, the core theory of delegated powers was promoted by William H. Taft, who refused to believe that the chief executive held any "undefined residuum" of authority. Instead, Taft, and others like him, such as Dwight Eisenhower, firmly believed that the president could not issue an executive order absent constitutional or congressional authority to do so. [See: Bernard Schwartz, *Constitutional Law* (New York: Macmillan, 1972, pp. 144-145; and Erwin Chemerinsky, *Constitutional Law: Principles and Policies* (New York: Aspen, 2006), pp. 339-343.]

Two intermediate theories have also been promoted to provide a sort of compromise between the two core theories: (1) interstitial executive power and (2) legislatively limited power. The interstitial theory of executive power promotes the idea that the president is free to act only so long as his actions do not violate the central principle of the separation of powers. Thus, the president cannot issue an executive order that would do something that Congress or the courts have the expressed or implied exclusive power to do. The president cannot, for example, issue an executive order that declares a law unconstitutional because that is within the purview or the courts. Nor could the president, on his own, submit a bill to Congress because only senators and representative have that power. Certainly, the president can and does pass along suggested legislative enactments, sometimes in a very lengthy and detailed way (as he does when he presents his budget to the legislature), but he still must rely on a representative or a senator to actually present the bill on the floor of Congress. In contrast, the theory of legislative limited power says that the president can do anything that has not been specifically and expressly curtailed by the Constitution or by Congress in a statute fashioned to have that effect. [See: Chemerinsky, pp. 339-343.]

THE OPENING CASE *Round 4*
Executive Orders, Checks and Balances, and the Limits (?) of Executive Power

Recall that, in the Opening Case, President Obama issued an executive order designed to deal with the plight of many undocumented aliens who had entered the United States illegally when they were children (known in popular parlance as the "Dreamers"). The initiative, which was designated Deferred Action for Childhood Arrivals (DACA), delayed action by the Department of Homeland Security in certain cases involving 800,000 Dreamers who were in danger of being removed from the United States. President Obama had been forced to issue the executive order because Congress had repeatedly "failed to act" despite being given multiple opportunities to do so. In 2017, President Trump issued his own executive order rescinding President Obama's order, arguing, in part, that it was unconstitutional because Obama's "failed to act" argument had no legitimate grounding in constitutional law. So far, so good. Trump's argument made good sense, both legally and logically. Moreover, had he stopped there, his position would have been clear. However, he did not stop there, and for good reason. It was common knowledge at the time that President Trump faced a largely paralyzed Congress, which had also "failed to act" in relation to several issues, not the least of which was immigration reform. Accordingly, the president indicated that if Congress did not act on immigration reform, he would "revisit" the issue himself. This statement implied that President Trump might do exactly what President Obama had done in 2012 if Congress, once more, "failed to act." Given the track record of Congress up to that point, this result seemed likely at that time. This move would put President Trump in the curious position of forcing DACA reform with a new executive order based on the same grounds (the Congress has "failed to act" argument) that he called unconstitutional in his first DACA order. So, if that is the case, what is the difference between what President Obama ordered in 2012 and what President Trump promised to order in 2017? Think about it. [See: Bernard Schwartz, *Constitutional Law* (New York: Macmillan, 1972, pp. 144–145; and Erwin Chemerinsky, *Constitutional Law: Principles and Policies* (New York: Aspen, 2006), pp. 339–343.]

Source: See: Bernard Schwartz, *Constitutional Law* (New York: Macmillan, 1972, pp. 144-145; Erwin Chemerinsky, *Constitutional Law: Principles and Policies* (New York: Aspen, 2006), pp. 339–343.

Challenges to Executive Orders

By now it should be obvious that executive orders can be challenged in the Courts. However, just as the president cannot issue such an order on a whim, those dissatisfied by an order cannot challenge it on a whim either. First, a challenger must demonstrate to the satisfaction of the court that he, she, they, or it have standing to sue. Second, the challenger must also demonstrate that there is sufficient grounds for bringing the suit. To prove that it has **standing to sue**, a plaintiff—that is, the party initiating the lawsuit—must demonstrate that it will suffer direct injuries should the executive order remain in effect. In the alternative, the plaintiff might also argue that although it will not suffer direct harm, it will suffer harm that somehow impacts the overall situation in which the plaintiff finds itself and that the enforcement of the order will have a continuing impact on others who are unable themselves to file for relief under the law.

Second, the challenger must also demonstrate to the satisfaction of the court that it has sufficient grounds upon which to bring the action. In the case of an executive order, this means that the plaintiff must demonstrate that the president issued the executive without proper authority to do so or that he abused his power in issuing the order. This will mean showing that the order issued by the president violates either Article II of the Constitution or the congressional law under which the order was authorized by exceeding the power granted under that law or by exercising that power in a way that violates other constitutional

THE OPENING CASE *Round 5*
Executive Orders, Checks and Balances, and the Limits (?) of Executive Power

Recall that President Trump issued an executive order to end the DACA program initiated by President Obama in 2012. Almost instantly after the order was signed, 15 states and the District of Columbia filed a joint lawsuit in the Federal District Court Eastern District of New York, asking that court to grant an injunction that would stop the enforcement of what they called President Trump's unconstitutional order. The attorneys general from these states argued that their states had standing to sue because each state had an authentic interest in protecting the health, safety, and well-being of its citizens and that the removal of the DACA program would hurt their (the states') ability to do so. In addition, each state had also expended time, money, and effort to hire and train DACA beneficiaries, and under terms of the rescission order, that time, effort, and money would be wasted. Moreover, each state also claimed to be on the verge of losing employees trained under DACA programs should the Trump order be upheld. Other conditions included in the court documents alleged how each state would be injured if President Trump's executive order remained in effect. Some states were more specific than others, but all followed this general tenor and tone. Also, to demonstrate that President Trump had issued the executive order without proper authority to do so, the attorneys general argued that even though the president had been granted congressional authority to limit immigration, he violated the Fifth Amendment's Due Process Clause, by using information against the immigrants that it had promised to keep secret, and the Fifth Amendment's Equal Protection Clause, by targeting people based on national origin. These arguments were at least partially based on the president's campaign rhetoric against certain groups of aliens that he painted in an extremely unfavorable light. Thus, the claim alleged that the president had demonstrated a deeply held discriminatory bias against that group (or at least appeared to hold such bias), which he had legitimized by using executive power. [See: See: *States of New York, et al. v. Trump,* Civil Action No. 17-CV-5228 (2017); Bernard Schwartz, *Constitutional Law* (New York: Macmillan, 1972, pp. 144–145; and Erwin Chemerinsky, *Constitutional Law: Principles and Policies* (New York: Aspen, 2006), pp. 339–343.]

Source: See: *States of New York, et al. v. Trump, Civil Action No. 17-CV-5228 (2017); Bernard Schwartz, Constitutional Law* (New York: Macmillan, 1972, pp. 144-145; Erwin Chemerinsky, *Constitutional Law: Principles and Policies* (New York: Aspen, 2006), pp. 339–343.

provisions. So, while the president may have been granted congressional authority to do something, such as issue orders as the Commander-in-Chief of the Armed Services, he cannot do so in a way that violates the Constitution. So as Commander-in-Chief of the Armed Services (Article II, Section, 2 Clause 1), the president cannot issue an executive order declaring war on North Korea, or some other rogue nation, because the power to declare war rests with Congress (Article 1 Section 8, Clause 11). [See: Peter M. Shane, et al., "State of the Union: Impact on Executive Orders," *CLE Online Seminar*, The Ohio State Bar Association, (2017), yourosba.ohiobar.org/product/26670.]

quick quiz 2-3

1. An exective order is a device by which the presidnet can act on his own without having to resort to the somewhat cumbersome process of going through Congress.   true | false

2. The core theory of inherent executive power, which is sometimes referred to as the stewardship theory, was first promoted by President Eisenhower.   true | false

3. One way to prove standing to sue is to have the injured party demonstrate that it will suffer direct harm should the executive order remain in effect.   true | false

2-4 Statutory Law

Laws passed by a legislature are known as **statutes**. At the federal level, statutes are the laws made by Congress and signed by the president. At the state level, statutes are enacted by state legislatures, such as the Ohio General Assembly or the Oregon Legislative Assembly. Many statutes prohibit certain activities. Most criminal statutes are prohibitive statutes. For instance, Ohio criminal law prohibits hazing, which is defined as coercing someone into doing an act of initiation that has a substantial risk of causing mental or physical harm. Other statutes demand the performance of some action. For instance, Ohio statutory law requires all motor vehicle drivers and passengers to wear safety belts. Some statutes, such as those that create governmental holidays or name state flowers, simply declare something.

Codes and Titles

Statutes must be arranged, cataloged, and indexed for easy reference. This is done by compiling state and federal codes. A **code** is a compilation of all the statutes of a particular state or the federal government. All federal statutes, for instance, are gathered in the United States Code (USC), while all Ohio statutory law is collected in the Ohio Revised Code (ORC). In general, codes are subdivided into **titles**, which are groupings of statutes that deal with a particular area of the law. Title 17 of the Ohio Revised Code, for example, covers corporations and partnerships. Often titles are subdivided into chapters, and chapters subdivided into sections. Thus, ORC 1701.03, *Purposes of a Corporation*, can be read from right to left as the third section of the first chapter of Title 17 of the ORC.

Uniform Laws

Because many different statutes are passed each year by the 50 state legislatures, statutory law differs from state to state. This lack of consistency can cause problems when legal matters cross state boundaries. One solution to the problem of inconsistent statutory law is for all the state legislatures to adopt the same statutes. The Uniform Law Commission (ULC) which is also called the The National Conference of Commissioners on Uniform State Laws (NCCUSL) was founded to write these uniform laws. The ULC is composed of commissioners that come from every state, the District of Columbia, Puerto Rico, and the Virgin Islands. These commissioners are usually selected by the governor. Most of the commissioners serve for a term of years set by the state. Some have no set term and can be replaced by the governor at any time. The number of commissioners from each jurisdiction is established by that jurisdiction. Some jurisdictions decide to have a lot of commissioners, while others decide to send only a few. California, for example, appoints 14, while New Hampshire limits its number to 4. The states are also responsible for sending money to the ULC to support its activities. The more populated states generally pay more than the smaller states.

BUSINESS LAW WITH UCC APPLICATIONS AND NOW—THE APPLICATIONS

The Uniform Law Commission (ULC) and a Lesson in Legal and Political Power

The people and the press often get very excited about issues like immigration reform, global warming, international trade, weapons of mass destruction, gun control, capital punishment, voter fraud, and so on. Yet very few of these same people know about the vast power that has been placed in the hands of a group of unelected legal experts who write uniform codes and then give those codes to state legislators, many of whom simply enact those uniform codes into law, sometimes without changing a single word. The Uniform Law Commission manufactures dozens of these uniform codes, covering such diverse topics as tort law, corporate law, family law, property law, domestic relations, contract law, sales law, and surrogate parenting law, just to name a few. Is it ethical for legislators to pass on their responsibility for the state's legislative agenda by turning it over to these legal experts who are appointed by the state governments but not elected by the people"? One of the purposes of *Business Law with UCC Applications* is to help students understand that powerful, but well-hidden, non-governmental institutions, such as the ULC, play a large role in the legislative process in this country. Accordingly, from time to time throughout the text, we will examine some of these organizations, including not only the ULC but also other similar institutions such as the American Bar Association and the Financial Accounting Standards Board. For now, however, we will focus on the Uniform Law Commission and its most successful, most wide ranging, and most influential code, the Uniform Commercial Code. To begin, access the ULC's website online at http://uniformlaws.org, and answer the following questions.

1. Who is the current president of the ULC?
2. What ULC codes are being considered for adoption by your state in the current year?
3. When and where will the next meeting of the ULC be held this year, and what is the topic of the meeting?
4. When will the UCC articles be reviewed in the current year?
5. What is the date and the topic of the latest press release issued by the ULC?

The Uniform Commercial Code

The most significant development in uniform state legislation has been the Uniform Commercial Code. The **Uniform Commercial Code (UCC)** is a unified set of statutes designed to govern almost all commercial transactions. The basic principles of commercial law were not changed by the UCC provisions. By defining and clarifying often misunderstood business and legal terms, the UCC helps parties involved in commercial transactions prepare their contracts.

Even the famed UCC, however, has been adjusted by various states, and not all states decide to accept the suggested amendments that come from the ULC from time to time. Some states have even eliminated some of the chapters and articles in the UCC that they have found obsolete or irrelevant or that do not fit within their established legal traditions. Louisiana, for example, which still uses the Napoleonic Code, has adopted only four of the nine articles. Nevertheless, the UCC remains one of the most successful achievements of the ULC. The Uniform Law Commission maintains a website that includes the final drafts of all uniform acts that have been approved and recommended for adoption by the state legislatures.

Cyber-Law Statutes

The advent of the information age has sparked the need for specific cyber-law statutes that address the problems associated with cyber-commerce. **Cyber-commerce** is the term applied

---

A CLASSIC CASE Memorial and Remonstrance

Statutory law is a product of the legislative process that has many stages, each of which affords a chance to push the bill forward or stop it in its tracks. Despite these safeguards and precautions, sometimes a bill succeeds or fails not on its merits, which is as it should be, but under the influence, reputation, charisma, or fortune of a famous, well-liked, or feared supporter (or opponent). Such was the case in 1785 when, in the Virginia Legislature, Patrick Henry and James Madison faced each other in a classic battle of states' rights, legislative process, and religious freedom.

Concerned about a post-war decline in the moral values of the people of Virginia, Patrick Henry introduced a bill in the Virginia legislature that was designed to help solve the problem. The bill, officially known as "A Bill for Establishing a Provision for Teachers of the Christian Religion," but generally referred to as the "Tax Assessment Bill," would assess a small property tax to support religious education. The proceeds from the tax would go to a denomination chosen by the taxpayer. The funds would be used to employ ministers and teachers who would help, "correct the morals of men, restrain their vices, and preserve the peace of society."

Madison's tract, *Memorial and Remonstrance against Religious Assessment*, has been described as a great defense of religious liberty. While the tract is certainly very well crafted and while it undoubtedly contributed to defeat of the bill, it falls far short of being a great defense of religious freedom. Yet the myth of its greatness persists. Why? A dissection of the essay, paragraph by paragraph, argument by argument, reveals its rhetorical weaknesses. This is our challenge to you. Read the Tax Assessment Bill and *Memorial and Remonstrance* (both are in Appendix D). Once you have completed reading both, make your own evaluation. Focus especially on Argument 4, which is the heart of Madison's message.

Argument 4 maintains that the most offensive consequence of the bill will be to deny religious freedom to nonbelievers. Madison finds this aspect of the bill especially reprehensible since Americans are so insistent on their own religious freedom. The problem is that the Tax Assessment Bill does none of this and here is why. (1) Taxpayers are empowered to designate where their money is to go; (2) designated denominations spend the funds as they please, just as long as it goes to the teaching of morality; (3) Quakers and Mennonists are granted an exception due to their beliefs; (4) taxpayers who belong to no sect or object to their tax money going to any religious denomination will see their money go into a general fund that will use the proceeds to support seminaries of learning.

Perhaps even more significantly, Madison's arguments never really respond to the real purpose of the bill, addressing the moral decline of the people in the aftermath of the war. That is what the bill was supposed to do. It does not persecute the church or oppress nonbelievers. The bill actually goes out of its way to be inclusive, accommodating, and compassionate to different beliefs. In fact, the bill was a model of religious tolerance for the 18th century. Think about it. [See: Steven Waldman, *Founding Faith* (New York: Random House, 2008), pp. 115–126.]

Source: See: Steven Waldman, *Founding Faith* (New York: Random House, 2008), pp. 115–26.

to all cyber-transactions. The ULC has responded to this challenge by creating several new uniform laws. For example, the Uniform Computer Information Transactions Act (UCITA) is designed to deal directly with cyber-contracts that involve the sale or licensing of digital information. Another uniform cyber-law approved by the commissioners for enactment by state legislatures is the Uniform Electronic Transactions Act (UETA). This uniform cyber-law points out those principles that should be used in every state to make certain that cyber-contracts are enforceable.

quick quiz 2-4

1. Laws passed by a legislature are known as amendments. true | false
2. Once the NCCUSL adopts a uniform law, it becomes binding in all states. true | false
3. Cyber-commerce is the term that is applied to all cyber-transactions. true | false

2-5 Court Decisions

When most people think of the law, they think of the Constitution or of statutes passed by Congress and the state legislatures. Although these two sources are important, they are not the only two sources of law in this country. The courts also make law in the following ways:

- Common law
- Interpretation of statutes
- Judicial review

Common Law

The term *common law* comes from the attempts of early English kings to establish a body of law that all the courts in the kingdom would hold in common. At that time, judges in towns and villages had instructions to settle all disputes in as consistent a manner as possible. The judges maintained this consistency by relying on previous legal decisions whenever they faced a similar set of circumstances. In this way, they established a body of common law. As the process continued, judges began to record their decisions and share them with other judges. **Common law** is the body of previously recorded legal decisions made by the courts in specific cases. The process of relying on these previously recorded legal decisions is called *stare decisis* (let the decision stand). The previously recorded legal decisions themselves are referred to as precedents.

The legal system of the United States, except Louisiana, is rooted in the common law of England. These roots derive from the early American colonists who came from England and were governed by the English monarchy. Over time, English common law has been eroded in the United States by the passing of state statutes and court decisions that better meet the needs of today's society. Nevertheless, parts of the common law as practiced in England still exist in the laws of the United States today. Courts still apply the common law when there are no modern court decisions or statutes dealing with an issue in dispute.

Today's judges make decisions in the same way as their counterparts from the Middle Ages. They rely on precedent according to the principle of *stare decisis*. A **precedent** is a model case that a court can follow when facing a similar situation.

There are two types of precedent: binding and persuasive. **Binding precedent** is precedent that a court must follow. **Persuasive precedent** is precedent that a court is free to follow or ignore. Generally, whether a precedent is binding or persuasive is determined by the court's location. For instance, decisions made by the Florida Supreme Court would be binding in all Florida state courts but persuasive in all other states' courts.

The U.S. Supreme Court has frequently emphasized the crucial role that precedent plays in the American legal system. In emphasizing the importance of precedent, the Court has outlined a series of questions that judges should ask as they contemplate whether to overturn a rule of law established in an earlier case. These questions include the following:

- Is the established rule still practical?
- Have so many people relied upon the rule that overturning it would cause difficulty and injustice?
- Is the rule still legally viable, or has it become merely a relic of an outdated and deserted legal doctrine?
- Is the rule still up to date, or has it become obsolete because of changes in society?

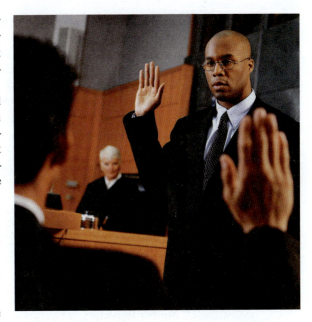

Precedents, or past decisions, form the basis of common law.
©Guy Cali/Getty Images

Only if judges can answer these questions satisfactorily should they consider overturning an established precedent.

Statutory Interpretation

A second way that court decisions make law is in the interpretation of statutes. **Statutory interpretation** is the process by which the courts analyze those aspects of a statute that are unclear or ambiguous or that were not anticipated at the time the legislature passed the statute. When legislators enact a new statute, they cannot predict how people will react to the new law. Nor can they foresee all of its future ramifications and implications. Thus, when two or more parties have a dispute that challenges the statute, they may differ as to what the legislature had in mind when it wrote the statute. Also, legislators may have purposely made the language of a statute general. The job of reacting to unforeseen circumstances and making generalities fit specific circumstances falls to the courts. As a result, a judge may be called upon to determine how a certain statute should be interpreted.

Courts are not, however, free to interpret a statute at random. A court cannot interpret a statute unless it is faced with a case involving that statute. In interpreting a statute, a court looks to a variety of sources, including the legislative history of the statute and the old statute that the new statute replaced, if any. Naturally, the court also must review any binding precedent that interprets that statute. This requirement exists because the court must still rely upon previous cases when engaged in statutory interpretation, just as it does when deciding questions of common law.

Judicial Review

A third way that courts make law is through **judicial review**, which is the process of determining the constitutionality of various legislative statutes, administrative regulations, or executive actions. In exercising the power of judicial review, a court will look at the statute, regulation, or action and compare it with the Constitution. If the two are compatible, no problem exists; however, if they are contradictory, one of the two must be declared void. Because the Constitution is the supreme law of the land, the Constitution always rules, and the statute, regulation, or action is ruled unconstitutional.

Naturally, in exercising the power of judicial review, the court also must review any binding precedent involved in the constitutional issue, because the court still must rely upon previous cases in judicial review, just as it does in common law and statutory interpretation. The lower courts in this country have the capacity to review issues of constitutionality and interpret the meaning of provisions within the U.S. Constitution; however, the ultimate authority, and therefore the final word, on such issues rests with the U.S. Supreme Court.

> **quick quiz 2-5**
>
> 1. The process of relying on previous decisions is called *stare decisis*.   true | false
> 2. Common law originated in France.   true | false
> 3. Judicial review is another name for statutory interpretation.   true | false

2-6 Administrative Regulations

Neither legislators nor judges can administer to all aspects of today's society. Moreover, legislators are generalists; they are rarely experts in all areas over which they have power. Because legislators are generalists and today's problems are so complex, statutory law, created by legislators, is very limited in what it can do. To broaden the power of statutory law, legislators delegate their power to others. They do this when they create administrative agencies.

Administrative Agencies

Federal administrative agencies administer statutes enacted by Congress in specific areas, such as communication, aviation, labor relations, working conditions, and so on. Similarly, agencies have been designated by the states to supervise intrastate activities. These agencies create rules, regulate and supervise, and render decisions that have the force of law. Their decrees and decisions are known as **administrative law**. The power to create administrative law makes the administrative agencies and their internal agents at all levels, participants in the bureaucracy, an unelected fourth branch of the government, a branch that, while subject to some limitations, such as those provided by the Administrative Procedures Act and the Regulatory Flexibility Act is, nevertheless, largely autonomous, and therefore, subject to abusive behavior. That, however, is getting ahead of the story. Let's take a detailed look, first at the types of agencies and then at the types of agency power.

Types of Agencies On paper, agencies are part of the executive branch of the government. Such agencies have a variety of names, including commission, department, agency, bureau, board, administration, directorate, office, and service, among others. Still, we can simplify this somewhat by noting that, most agencies can be placed in one of two categories: executive agencies or independent agencies. **Executive agencies** are those that are directly under the control of the president. Included in this number are departments such as the State Department, the Department of Justice, the Department of Human Services, and so on. Other lesser agencies included in the executive agencies are those such as the Internal Revenue Service, which is within the Department of the Treasury, and the Federal Bureau of Investigation, which is part of the Justice Department. Generally, the heads of these agencies are appointed by the president and serve at his pleasure. Thus, for example, despite the alternative facts presented by the media, the president appoints the head of the FBI and can remove him or her whenever he wants for any reason or for no reason.

Agencies that are labeled **independent agencies** are those that are not actually within the executive branch but, instead, act on their own authority. The theory behind the establishment of these independent agencies is the ability of Congress to distribute its power beyond its original mission. At some point during the development of the United States, senators and representatives realized that they could not be all things to all people. They recognized that they were, in fact, generalists who needed help in running an increasingly specialized and complex government. It was then that the independent agencies began to proliferate. Such agencies are often run by a team of people who are generally referred to as a commission or board. Such commissioners and board members usually serve for a set term of years. Moreover, in making such appointments, the president must follow a set of guidelines.

Types of Agency Powers The history of most agencies follows a common trajectory. First, certain members of Congress will become aware of some area or activity within the socioeconomic system that needs to be regulated in some way. Second, these bright and ambitious congressmen and -women will examine Article I of the Constitution, searching for the legislative authority needed to empower Congress to regulate that area or that activity. Third, upon finding that constitutional provision, the congressman or -woman will write a statute creating an agency that will handle the day-to-day job of policing that area or those activities. The statute is referred to as *enabling legislation* or as an *enabling statute*. Fourth, in writing the enabling statute, the author will carve out a very broad list of responsibilities and will then empower the newly created agency to carry out those responsibilities by making regulations.

Agencies have a great deal of leeway in making their own regulations, in enforcing their regulations, and in judging when people follow or break those regulations. They also often have the power to mete out punishments for those found guilty of violating a regulation or set of regulations. For this reason, many people complain that the independent agencies do exactly what the Founding Fathers wanted to prevent—that is, the concentration of legal and political power to make, enforce, and adjudicate law in one person or group of people. In addition to the rule-making power shared by all agencies, some agencies, by virtue of their enabling statute, have the authority to issue licenses. When this is the case, the license-granting agency must be sure to follow the same kind of strict protocol that is followed in making regulations. Still, the agency is empowered to decide who receives a license and who does not and when that licensee can be deprived of the license for violating some already established regulation.

Administrative Procedures Act

As noted earlier, problems often occur because many administrative agencies have the power to make the rules, enforce the rules, and interpret the rules. To help prevent any conflict of interest that could arise from these overlapping responsibilities, Congress passed the federal Administrative Procedures Act (APA). Similarly, most states have adopted a uniform law known as the Model State Administrative Procedures Act. Under these two acts, an administrative agency planning new regulations must notify the affected parties and hold hearings to allow those parties to express their views. These acts also allow the courts to review agency decisions and rulings. [See: "The Administrative Procedures Act," Electronic Privacy Information Center, 2010, https://epic.org/open_gov/Administrative-Procedures-Act.html.]

The rule-making protocol established under the authority of the federal APA applies to both executive agencies and independent agencies. Agency personnel cannot simply write a regulation in the middle of the night and then declare it a valid and binding rule the next morning. On the contrary, the APA requires the rule maker to give notice to those who will be affected by the rule. Those affected by the new rule must also have a chance to comment upon the rule before it goes operational. In fact, the agency must actually solicit comments from those who will be affected. This can be done by having a notice filed in the *Federal Register*. No limit was written into the law to control the amount of time devoted to comments, but most sessions last from 30 to 60 days. Moreover, if the first comment session turns out to be inadequate, another comment period can be opened up. Most comment periods are held in an informal way, but some require the solemnity and the detail of a court process. There are, of course, certain exceptions to the rule-making process. For instance, rules that affect the military or foreign affairs need not follow the regular rule-making protocol. [See: "The Administrative Procedures Act."]

The Regulatory Flexibility Act

The Regulatory Flexibility Act (RFA) is one of those laws passed by Congress that we hear very little about. This is unfortunate because, unlike many laws passed by Congress, this one actually does some good for people involved in small businesses and other small institutions, such as small non-profits, and small governmental subdivisions. The goal of the act is not give special treatment to small organizations, but to make sure that they get equal or nearly equal treatment in the marketplace. The RFA places an obligation on federal agencies within the bureaucracy to evaluate the effect that new regulations will have on these small institutions. The objective of this procedure is to make certain that the agencies do their best to protect small entities by keeping the negative effects produced by new regulations and orders to a minimum. [See: "The RFA in a Nutshell: A Condensed Guide to the Regulatory Flexibility Act," SBA Office of Advocacy, 2011, www.sba.gov/advo.]

The act encourages regulatory agencies to understand the financial structures of small entities and to be aware of the impact any new regulations may have on those institutions. It is also necessary for the agencies to do their best to foresee any unintended consequences that might place an undue burden on the shoulders of small institutions. The act has been amended more than once. The Small Business Regulatory Enforcement Act (SBREA) added a series of significant improvements, including empowering the courts to make sure that the agencies are following RFA rules. SBREA also added a more thorough review process to ensure that the agencies examine new rule proposals with great detail. Another amendment is the Regulatory Flexibility Improvements Act of 2011, which refines and magnifies RFA rules. [See: "The RFA in a Nutshell."]

The *Federal Register* and the *Code of Federal Regulations*

The Federal Register is a publication that produces a daily compilation of new regulations issued by federal administrative agencies. The *Federal Register* operates within the National Archives and Records Administration under the authority of the Office of the Federal Register. The Government Printing Office is responsible for actually printing the document, though today it is also available online. Most of the documents included within the *Federal Register* are directly related to the agencies. Those subdivisions devoted to the agencies include a section on rules and regulations, one on proposed rules, and one on notices of hearings, meetings, application deadlines, and administrative orders. There is also a section devoted to presidential orders and proclamations. Once a rule is finalized, it is included in the *Code of Federal Regulations (CFR)*, which is updated each year.

The Deep State: Dangers and Remedies

We have spent this chapter learning about the sources of the law and the relationships that exist among the executive branch, the legislative branch, the judicial branch, and the regulatory agencies. One problem with such a study is that it talks in terms of abstract, broadly fashioned elements. Thus, we discuss the Constitution as if it were holy scripture; judges as if they were the high priests of the temple; the executive as if he possesses a royal prerogative to do whatever he wishes; and the bureaucrats as if they hold the keys to the treasury and, thus, to the entire kingdom. In fact, this apparently monolithic structure is actually made of ordinary people who must deal with the day-to-day operation of the bureaucratic state. The bureaucratic state consists of an enormous, interlaced patchwork of agencies, departments, commissions, services, bureaus, and directorates, all of which are peopled by individuals who attempt to do their best to keep the government operating. These people generally work by themselves or with a few others in an independent fashion, but also in a strangely interdependent way that defies explanation. Lines of authority are often blurred. Job descriptions often expand and contract, while individual agents come and go and come back again.

THE OPENING CASE *Round 6*
Executive Orders, Checks and Balances, and the Limits (?) of Executive Power

President Trump ended the DACA program with an executive order issued on September 6, 2017. Immediately following the announcement of the president's newest executive order, the District of Columbia and 15 states filed a joint lawsuit asking the court to stop the enforcement of that order. The attorneys general from these states argued that the order was an unconstitutional violation of the Fifth Amendment's Due Process and Equal Protection Clauses. These arguments were expected. What was not expected were the arguments invoking the Administrative Procedures Act and the Regulatory Flexibility Act. The attorneys general argued that the order violated both these acts by not following the proper rule-making process. The arguments are similar but not identical. Let's look at both.

First, the attorneys general argue that the order should not stand because the Department of Human Services (DHS) did not follow the proper rule-making protocol mandated by the APA. This protocol requires that those affected by a new rule receive notice of the change and be given an opportunity to comment on that change. Because neither the states nor the Dreamers were given any advanced notice of the change, they had no opportunity to comment, and the order must be invalidated. Despite this logic, it is unlikely that the argument will be received favorably by the court because the APA was designed to regulate the rule-making process within the administrative agencies, of which the DHS is one. The rule, however, was not promulgated by the DHS. Rather, it came directly from the president to the DHS in its finished form. Therefore, because the APA applies only to agencies, and because the president is a person, not an agency, the APA would seem not to apply in this case.

Secondly, the attorneys general argued that the DHS failed to issue either an opening or a closing regulatory flexible analysis as required by law. This is true despite the fact that those affected by the new order include small businesses, small non-profits, and small government subdivisions—all of which are to be protected by the regulatory flexible analysis and all of which will lose employees when DACA closes down. Therefore, President Trump's order must be vacated. Again, we run into the same problem as before. The RFA was designed to regulate the rule-making process within the agencies. This rule, however, came not from the agencies, but from the president. Therefore, because the president is not an agency, the RFA does not apply.

Finally, none of this will matter if the first executive order, the one issued by President Obama, is declared illegal. It does no good for the attorneys general to argue that neither President Trump nor the agencies followed the rules in issuing an order that rescinds an illegal order. If the first order, the Obama order is—well—illegal, that ends the discussion. An illegal order cannot be enforced on its face—period, end of story. [See: *States of New York, et al. v. Trump,* Civil Action No. 17-CV-5228 (2017); Peter M. Shane, et al., "State of the Union: Impact on Executive Orders," *CLE Online Seminar*, 2017, yourosba.ohiobar.org/product/26670; and Jonathan Adler, "Assessing the Administrative Law Claims against Rescinding DACA," *Washington Post*, September 9, 2017, https://www.washingtonpost.com/news/volokh-conspiracy/wp/2017/09/09/assessing-the-administrative-law-claims-against-rescinding-daca/utm_term=.61f7f72bef0e.]

Source: See: *States of New York, et al. v. Trump, Civil Action* No. 17-CV-5228 (2017); Peter M. Shane, et al., "State of the Union: Impact on Executive Orders,"*CLE Online Seminar* (2017) yourosba. ohiobar.org/ product/26670; Jonathan Adler, "Assessing the administrative law claims against rescinding DACA," *The Washington Post,* September 9, 2017, https://www.washingtonpost.com/news/volokh-conspiracy/wp/2017/09/09/assessing-the-administrative-law-claims-against-rescinding-daca/utm_term=.61f7f72bef0e.

These agents control other agents and the public at large and are, in turn, controlled by other agents. They plan the budget; they spend their part of the budget; they move property; they build, tear down, and build again. In normal times, all of this can be explained, understood, and tolerated. In abnormal times, things change.

The Deep State Defined and Explained In abnormal times, say when a president is elected who many government agents consider a threat to, well, to any number of things (individual security, professional advancement, personally held political beliefs, religious convictions, and so on), then these government agents can find ways to use their position within the bureaucracy to undermine the president's agenda. When these disgruntled agents act individually, their tactics are merely an annoyance. However, when, they begin to work together as teams or as undetected sleeper cells, their tactics become a genuine threat to the stability of the nation. Such clandestine tactics can give rise to the emergence of a Deep State. A **Deep State** (AKA, the *Administrative State*, a *Secret State,* the *Double Government, Parapolitcs,* and *Deep Politics*) is a loosely organized group of provocateurs located within the bureaucracy who oppose the president and his administration and who work together (sometimes deliberately and sometimes just by happenstance) using guerrilla tactics to undermine and weaken the authority, the reputation, and the agenda of the president. In the short run, the goal is to neutralize the president and his agents. However, in the long run, the objective is to remove him from office in contemporary *coup d'etat* (when talk of impeachment arises, we are close to that point) and to replace the administration with one more favorable to the agenda of the Deep States' agents. (N.B. Here are two additional definitions. In an article entitled, "The Deep State, Then and Now," Cheryl Gatesworth defines the Deep State as "as sort of shadowy government staffed by unelected persons existing in parallel with the current government, occasionally intersecting with it, with the purpose of undermining the legitimate government and eventually bringing it under its complete control." John Light in "The Deep State Explained" tells us that Newt Gingrich explains the Deep State by noting that, "There is a permanent state of massive bureaucracies that do whatever they want and set up deliberate leaks to attack the president. This is what the Deep State does: They create a lie, spread it, fail to check the lie and then deny they were behind the lie"

The power of the Deep State is intensified when the bureaucrats are joined by other members of the political state who exist outside the bureaucratic framework. Such non-bureaucratic actors include members of the mainstream media; politically active organizations with an agenda; opposition party members; independent politicians, actors, and sports figures (think NFL and the National Anthem); high-ranking military officers; federal judges; independent, self-proclaimed "think tanks;" and even, at times, influential individuals outside of Washington, such as big city mayors, governors, state legislators, and corporate chief executive officers (CEOs). Some of the tactics include leaking secret information; leaking sensitive documents to the press; making private behavior public; leaking the content of private conversations; leaking information about embarrassing, idiosyncratic behavior; misplacing (losing?) important files; stonewalling investigations; delaying paperwork; filing false and misleading stories with the mainstream media; and whispering alternative facts to reporters, all with the objective of humiliating and discrediting the president and his staff and other aspects of the legitimate government.

The United States has always billed itself as "a nation of laws not of men" and this is as it should be. So when evidence surfaces that supports the existence of a Deep State, that evidence ought not to be ignored. To do so is to risk undermining the foundation of the government itself. Just as people cannot pick and choose the laws that they will obey, they cannot pick and choose the elected officials that they will follow, and that includes, especially, the president. Once an individual has been sworn in as president, that individual is due a proper expression of loyalty from people within the bureaucracy not because of his personal attributes, reputation, or past activities, but because he is the president—period. The carefully engineered system of checks and balances within our system was never intended to protect only the current president but also, and especially, the Office of the Presidency itself (along with the other branches). This reality does not mean that people cannot disagree with the chief executive. To demand so would be the height of folly. However, it does mean that, once the debate had ended, the president's mandates are to be followed. Those who continue to disagree cannot take it upon themselves to undermine those mandates. Rather, those who disagree, should have the decency to resign and seek employment elsewhere.

Despite its recent notoriety, the Deep State is not a new phenomenon. In fact, there are those historians who argue that the delegates to the Constitutional Convention of 1787 were themselves members of a Deep State, who acted illegally when they ignored the amendment process written into the Articles of Confederation, and, instead, ripped up those Articles and produced an entirely new Constitution. In essence, the men we now call the Founding Fathers, managed to get away with treason because, well, because it worked. The existence of a modern Deep State within the United States was suggested by President Dwight Eisenhower who, as early as 1961, warned the American public to "guard against the acquisition of unwarranted influence, whether sought or unsought, by the military-industrial complex. The potential for the disastrous rise of misplaced power exists and will persist." (See: Wikisource, Eisenhower's Farewell Address (press copy) https://en.wikisource.org/wiki/Eisenhower%27s_farewell_address_(press_copy). Let's look at just a few more up-to-date examples of the steps taken by individuals and by groups that might be considered Deep State activities (whether taken with a conscious and deliberate intent to disrupt or taken with good intent but illegally and with a disruptive end result).

EXAMPLE 2-3: Historical Actions by the Deep State

(1) In 1961, during the early months of his presidency, John F. Kennedy discovered that he had been misled by the Joint Chiefs of Staff and the State Department, and denied essential information by the Central Intelligence Agency (CIA), all of which might have led him to countermand the disastrous Bay of Pigs invasion of Cuba. (2) After Kennedy was killed, and Lyndon B. Johnson became president, the operation of the Deep State became more formalized. By that time, the Joint Chiefs of Staff (JSC) had allied themselves with the National Security Council (NSC), and had established a covert operation in the Executive Office Building within the JCS-NSC liaison office. The covert operation was designed to keep the Chiefs informed about Johnson's secret war decision-making process during the Vietnam War. (3) There is also ample evidence that the Nixon administration was targeted by elements of the Deep State. The FBI, under direction of J. Edgar Hoover, tasked those agents who guarded Attorney General John Mitchell with the job of informing Hoover about every conversation that took place in the Mitchell household. (4) Not to be outdone, the CIA installed E. Howard Hunt on Nixon's Plumbers Team (itself a sort of anti-Deep State, Deep State operation) and had Hunt send secret couriers to CIA Director Robert Helms with reports on the sexual activities of officials within the White House. (5) After the Nixon-Ford-Carter era, clandestine Deep State operations continued unabated. Between 1986 and 1999, both Bush and Reagan received reports from the CIA which that agency deliberately failed to label as originating from sources controlled by the Russians. (6) President Obama was counseled by advisors, allegedly with a Deep State agenda, to step back from a proposal that would have placed compensation limits on Wall Street CEOs. (7) President Obama also entangled the nation in Iraq beyond his original deadline because he listened to the biased advice of certain Think Tank consultants all of whom adopted a guise of neutrality, but who secretly supported the doctrine of military interventionism, something Obama had opposed in his 2012 presidential campaign (See: Robert Dallek, "JFK vs. the Military," *The Atlantic* (August 2013) https://www.theatlantic.com; James Rosen, "Trump, Nixon, and the Deep State," *The Washington Examiner* (March 13, 2018); Mile Lofgren, "Essay: Anatomy of the Deep State," *Moyers and Company* (February 21, 2014) http://billmoyers.com/2014/02/21/anatomy-of-the-deep-state/.)

EXAMPLE 2-4: Contemporary Actions by the Deep State

(1) In September of 2017, 201 members of Congress (all Democrats) filed a lawsuit (which would preoccupy the administration for months, even years) in federal court, arguing that President Donald Trump had violated the Emoluments Clause of the Constitution (Article I, Section 8) by continuing to do business with foreign governments, a charge that is essentially groundless. (2) Former FBI Director James Comey, in hopes that a special prosecutor would be appointed to investigate alleged Russian interference in the 2016 election (something that would tie up the administration indefinitely), turned over the contents of a government-owned memo to a university law professor with instructions to leak it to the news media. (3) A federal contractor illegally leaked a top secret National Security Agency (NSA) document concerning a Russian attempt to disrupt the 2016 election, to a news outlet called *The Intercept* (another move that would distract the president's staff). (4) The California State Senate, in deliberate defiance of federal law, introduced a bill that would limit the ability of the local police to cooperate with federal immigration officers, thus hampering the administration's attempt at immigration reform. (5) In June 2017, three CNN reporters resigned after releasing a false story on the web about a presidential aide's alleged pre-inaugural meeting with a Russian investment fund manager, a meeting that never took place. (6) Despite the fact that they have no standing to sue, several states filed lawsuits in federal court, aimed at halting the implementation of the president's executive orders on immigration, thus delaying the administration's attempts at immigration reform and simultaneously tying up the administration in another of a series of provocative, meaningless lawsuits. (7) National Security Adviser Michael Flynn was forced to resign from his post after it was revealed that he had inadvertently failed to report to Vice President Mike Pence a conversation with the Russian ambassador, something, it could be argued, that is really within the job description of incoming intelligence officers like Flynn. (8) In an attempt to discredit the Senate Majority Leader Mitch McConnell and, thus, prevent the passage of the Republican health care bill, *Occupy Democrats*, a left-wing news outlet, posted a totally false story stating that, as a child, the Majority Leader had taken advantage of a federally funded health care program, like the one he was now allegedly attempting to destroy. (9) Before leaving office, during the transition period between administrations, the National Security Adviser under the outgoing administration, allegedly for political purposes, asked for and received the names of several key associates within the new administration who were taped during routine surveillance operations, involving the Russians. (10) Finally (for now) in October 2017, in a self-confessed attempt to intimidate the president, Congressman Brad Sherman (a Democrat) filed a single impeachment article accusing the president of obstruction of justice in the firing of FBI Director James Comey, despite the fact that the FBI director serves at the pleasure of the president (See: Jon D. Michaels, "Trump and the 'Deep State:' The Government Strikes Back," *Foreign Affairs*, September/October 2017, pp. 52–56; Ed Rogers, "The 'Deep State Is Real. The 'Alt Right' Is Fake. The Inside Track on Washington Politics," *Washington Post*, February 2, 2017, https://www.washingtonpost.com/blogs/post-partisan/wp/2017/02/21/the-deep-state-is=real-thealt-right-is-fake/?utm_term=.328d812390bc; and John Tierney, "The Tyranny of the Administrative State," *The Wall Street Journal*, June 10–11, 2017, p. A13.)

The Deep State: How to Combat It The first step in counteracting a Deep State movement is to admit that the Deep State exists. Denying the existence of the Deep State or blaming reports about its operation on unstable conspiracy theorists delays the process of dealing with the debilitating effects of the Deep State and encourages its agents to do more damage. The second step is to avoid overreacting to any small victory that might be scored by agents of the Deep State. By overreacting, the president and his staff play into the hands of Deep State activists by exposing the limits of the president's ability to deal effectively with the bureaucracy. The third step is to devise a plan of action to weaken or completely nullify the work done by these Deep State activists.

One effective way to control Deep State activism is to remove, weaken, or divert the attention of the Deep State players. This can be done in a number of ways. One way is to minimize the power of the bureaucracy by turning over certain governmental operations to private corporations. This technique has been used to privatize security operations, intelligence-gathering protocols, social service programs, prison operations, and so on. Turning over these operations to profit-making contractors takes sensitive data out of the hands of Deep State activists, minimizes the likelihood that confidential data will be leaked, lessens the prevalence of filing "mistakes," and curtails the continuous revelation of sensitive information. Another related technique is to replace bureaucratic hiring, firing, evaluation, and promotion protocols with for-profit corporate protocols. For example, tying promotions and raises to on-the-job performance, rather than time served, would encourage efficient and economically healthy behavior and discourage making "mistakes" in filing, storing, accessing, retrieving, and revealing sensitive material to the press. Reclassifying employees from full-time permanent employees to at-will employees or independent contractors would make it easier to discharge activists who make the "mistakes" noted earlier. As for outside activists—such as reporters, actors, entertainers, and so on—it would be a good idea to tighten their access to members of the bureaucracy, thus hindering the ability of internal Deep State activists to leak sensitive information to those external activists.

Another way to deal with the Deep State is for the Executive Branch and Congress to cooperate in introducing legislation designed to increase the accountability of the military, the bureaucracy, and their allies in the media, private industry, and academia. This is what happened in 1972 when Congress enacted the Foreign Intelligence Surveillance Act (FISA) a measure designed to reign in a rogue intelligence community in the habit of opening surveillance activities, without probable cause, on American citizens like Attorney General John Mitchell and the White House staffers who, as noted above, were targeted during the Nixon administration.

Whatever techniques might be adopted to combat the bureaucratic Deep State, they will not be enough, by themselves, to stop the Deep State. To do that effectively, the president and his staff would also have to turn their attention to another potential source of Deep State activists—that is, the federal court system. That idea is the subject of Chapter 3, so read on. (See: Jon D. Michaels, "Trump and the 'Deep State:' The Government Strikes Back," *Foreign Affairs*, September/October 2017, pp. 52–56; Ed Rogers, "The 'Deep State Is Real. The 'Alt Right' Is Fake. The Inside Track on Washington Politics," *Washington Post*, February 2, 2017, https://www.washingtonpost.com/blogs/post-partisan/wp/2017/02/21/the-deep-state-is=real-thealt-right-is-fake/?utm_term=.328d812390bc; and John Tierney, "The Tyranny of the Administrative State," *The Wall Street Journal*, June 10–11, 2017, p. A13.)

quick quiz 2-6

1. Together, legislators and judges can administer all aspects of today's society.	true | false
2. Most legislators are specialists.	true | false
3. The decrees and decisions made by administrative agencies are known as administrative law.	true | false

Summary

2.1 The law consists of rules of conduct established by the government to maintain harmony, stability, and justice within a society. Ideally, the primary objectives of the law are to promote harmony, stability, and justice. In everyday life, the balance is not easy to maintain. The law or, more properly, the entire legal framework consists of a series of dualities that must be resolved somehow.

2.2 A constitution is the basic law of a nation or state. The U.S. Constitution provides the organization of the national government. Each state also has a constitution that determines the state's governmental structure. The body of law that forms a constitution and its interpretation is known as constitutional law.

2.3 An executive order is a device by which the president can act on his own without having to resort to the somewhat cumbersome process of going through Congress. A proclamation is an executive order that addresses the public at large. An order is aimed at a subdivision within the executive branch. A memorandum is simply a suggestion issued by the president to part of the executive branch.

2.4 The laws passed by a legislature are known as statutes. At the federal level, these are the laws made by Congress and signed by the president. At the state level, statutes are enacted by state legislatures. Statutes must be arranged, cataloged, and indexed for easy reference by compiling state and federal codes. Because many different statutes are passed each year by the 50 state legislatures, there are important differences in state statutory law throughout the nation. One solution to the problem of inconsistent statutory law is for the legislatures of all the states to adopt the same statutes. The Uniform Law Commission (ULC) was founded to write these uniform laws.

2.5 Courts make law through common law, the interpretation of statutes, and judicial review. Common law is the body of previously recorded legal decisions made by the courts in specific cases. Statutory interpretation is the process by which the courts analyze those aspects of a statute that are unclear or ambiguous or that were not anticipated at the time that the legislature passed the statute, and judicial review is the process by which the courts determine the constitutionality of various legislative statutes, administrative regulations, or executive actions.

2.6 Federal administrative agencies administer statutes enacted by Congress in specific areas, such as commerce, communication, aviation, labor relations, and working conditions. These agencies create rules, regulate and supervise, and render decisions. To help prevent any conflict of interest that could arise from these overlapping responsibilities, Congress passed the federal Administrative Procedures Act. To help small entities deal with bureaucratic red tape, Congress passed the Regulatory Flexibility Act.

Key Terms

administrative law, 50
Article II executive order, 42
Articles of Confederation, 35
binding precedent, 49
code, 45
Code of Federal Regulations (CFR), 52
common law, 48
constitution, 35
constitutional law, 35
cyber-commerce, 47
deep state, 54
executive agency, 50
executive order, 42
Federal Register, 52
hybrid executive order, 42
independent agency, 51
judicial review, 49
law, 29
memorandum, 42
persuasive precedent, 49
pragmatism, 33
precedent, 49
preemption, 41
proclamation, 42
standing to sue, 44
statutes, 45
statutory executive order, 42
statutory interpretation, 49
textualism, 33
titles, 45
Uniform Commercial Code (UCC), 47

Questions for Review and Discussion

1. What are the objectives of the law?
2. How does the law reflect a series of complex dualities?
3. What are the functions of the articles and the amendments of the U.S. Constitution?
4. What is an executive order?
5. What is the role of statutory law in the legal system?
6. Why does this country need to set up a system of uniform state laws?
7. What is the role of common law in the legal system?
8. How does the principle of *stare decisis* provide stability to our legal system?
9. What is the difference between statutory interpretation and judicial review?
10. What is the nature of the deep state within the American legal system?

Cases for Analysis

1. David Terry was so dissatisfied with the outcome of a lawsuit that he threatened to kill Stephen J. Field, a Supreme Court Justice, whose responsibilities included acting as the Supreme Court representative in the Ninth Circuit. The Attorney General of the United States ordered a federal marshal named David Neagle to protect Justice Field. When Terry attacked Justice Field, Neagle shot and killed him. Neagle was then promptly arrested by a local sheriff and charged with murder. Neagle brought his case to the nearest federal district court under a writ of *habeas corpus*. Neagle asked the court to vacate his arrest, arguing that he had been ordered by the Attorney General of the United States to protect Justice Field. He concluded that since he, Neagle, had been operating under the authority of the attorney general who had, himself, been operating under the authority of the president to "take Care that the Laws be faithfully executed" (i.e., the Faithfully Executed Clause [Article II, Section 3]), he could not be charged with murder. The attorneys for the sheriff argued that since neither the attorney general nor the president had the statutory authority to protect federal officers, the order to protect Field was illegal, and Neagle would have to respond to the murder charge. Neagle's attorney counterargued that the president's duty to protect federal officers was inherent in the duties he had by virtue of his position as the President of the United States. Which theory of presidential power will successfully defend Neagle against the murder charge? Explain. [See: *In re Neagle*, 135 U.S 1 (1890); and Bernard Schwartz, *Constitutional Law* (New York: Macmillan, 1972), pp. 144–145.]

2. In the wake of the disastrous events of 9/11, President George W. Bush and his advisors were concerned that the United States might be subject to further devastating attacks. Accordingly, President Bush released an executive order that authorized the establishment of a series of Military Commissions located at Guantanamo Bay designed to try individuals who were suspected of committing acts of terrorism. The order read in part, "To protect the United States and its citizens, and for the effective conduct of military operations and prevention of terrorist attacks, it is necessary for individuals subject to this order pursuant to section 2 hereof to be detained, and, when tried, to be tried for violations of the laws of war and other applicable laws by military tribunals." The president released the order under the authority of the Constitution making him Commander and Chief of the Armed Forces of the United States (Article II, Section 2, Clause 1); by the authority of the Uniform Code of Military Justice (UCMJ) (Title 10, U.S. Code, Sections 810 and 836); and by the authority granted to him under the Authorization of the Use of Military Force Resolution, a Joint Congressional Resolution. The Joint Resolution gave the president the power to use "all necessary and appropriate force against those nations, organizations, or persons he determines planned, authorized, committed, or aided the terrorist attacks that occurred on September 11, 2001, or harbored such organizations or persons, in order to prevent any future acts of international terrorism against the United States by such nations, organizations or persons." Salim Ahmed Hamdan, Osama bin Laden's chauffeur, was charged with conspiracy to commit

acts of terrorism. He filed for a writ of *habeas corpus*, challenging the legality of the president's executive order. The case ended in the lap of the U.S. Supreme Court. The Bush administration filed a motion, under the Detainee Treatment Act (DTA) of 2005 forbidding the inhumane treatment of prisoners at Guantanamo, but also limiting their access to both legal representation and the federal courts. The administration's motion asked the Supreme Court to have Hamdan's case dismissed. Which of the two core theories of executive power would best defend President Bush's executive order? Explain. [See: *Hamdan v. Rumsfeld*, 548 U.S 557 (2006); G. W. Bush, "Detention, Treatment, and Trial of Certain Non-Citizens in the War against Terrorism," Military Order, November 13, 2001; Authorization for the Use of Military Force, Joint Resolution of the 107th Congress, U.S. Public Law 107-40, signed into law on September 18, 2001; and Kirsten Soder, "The Supreme Court, the Bush Administration, and Guantanamo Bay," Stockholm International Peace Institute (SIPRI) Background Paper, January 2009.]

3. In San Diego in August 2009, the police stopped a car driven by David Leon Riley because the license plates on the vehicle were outdated. The police officers then discovered that Riley's driver's license had been suspended. The officers then conducted a search of Riley's car without a warrant. The officers found and seized two handguns. Further investigation connected the two handguns to a recent shooting incident. The officers also found Riley's smartphone and then, again without a warrant, searched the data that they found stored on the smartphone. The data found on the phone provided further evidence pointing to Riley's participation in gang-related activities. In addition, other data on the phone supported the belief that Riley had been involved in the shooting incident in question. Despite the warrantless nature of the searches that obtained the evidence, the court allowed the evidence to be admitted during Riley's trial. As a result, he was sentenced to 15 years to life after being convicted of attempted murder. Riley now argues that the evidence that was obtained from his smartphone was gathered by the police in violation of his Fourth Amendment right to be free from warrantless searches. The Fourth Amendment states, "The right of the people to be secure in their persons, houses, papers, and effects, against unreasonable searches and seizures, shall not be violated, and no Warrants shall issue, but upon probable cause, supported by Oath or affirmation, and particularly describing the place to be searched, and the person or thing to be seized." The appeals court upheld Riley's conviction, and the case then went to the U.S. Supreme Court. Since Riley's entire case involves the California police and was held in a California state court, how and why does the Fourth Amendment of the U.S. Constitution apply to the case? When the Fourth Amendment was enacted in the 18th century, no one even dreamed of a "smartphone." Should the Constitution be amended to include modern technological advances like smartphones? Explain. [See: *David Leon Riley v. California* (no. 13-132), U.S. Supreme Court (April 29, 2014).]

4. Barbara Rome entered Flower Memorial Hospital to undergo a series of X-rays. When she was ready for the X-rays, she was assisted by a student radiological intern. The intern placed Rome on the X-ray table and strapped her onto the table correctly; however, the intern did not properly fasten the footboard, which was located at the foot of the table. As a result of this error, Rome fell and was hurt when the table was raised. As a consequence, Rome brought a lawsuit against Flower Memorial Hospital, alleging that the ordinary negligence of the intern had caused her injury. In contrast, the hospital argued that the lawsuit involved a medical claim, as defined under the state's medical malpractice statute. Whether a case involves ordinary negligence or a medical claim would determine whether the state's two-year statute of limitations for negligence or the state's one-year statute of limitations for medical claims would apply. This case clearly involves a difference of opinion on the interpretation of a statute. What sources might the court consider when interpreting the statute in question? [See: *Rome v. Flower Memorial Hospital*, 635 N.E.2d 1239 (OH).]

5. The Heart of Atlanta Hotel brought an action against the United States seeking a judgment that would declare Title II of the Civil Rights Act of 1964 unconstitutional. Congress's power to enact the Civil Rights Act is based upon Article I, Section 8, Clause 3, which gives Congress the power to regulate commerce among the states. The Heart of Atlanta Hotel argued that the statute was an unconstitutional extension of congressional power. The hotel also

contended that the unconstitutional nature of the act especially applied to establishments like itself, which are incorporated and do business in only one state. However, because at any given time, three-fourths of the hotel's registered guests came from other states, the hotel clearly had an impact on interstate commerce. Do the lower federal courts have the authority to determine the constitutionality of Title II of the Civil Rights Act? What court has the ultimate authority to determine the constitutionality of the Civil Rights Act? Speculate on the outcome of this case. Do you think that the court should uphold the act? Explain. [See: *Heart of Atlanta Hotel v. United States*, 370 U.S. 241 (U.S. Sup. Ct.).]

Design Elements: The Opening Case: ©Sharpstock/Alamy; A Classic Case: ©Evlakhov Valeriy/Shutterstock

quick quiz Answers

2-1	2-2	2-3	2-4	2-5	2-6
1. T	1. F	1. F	1. F	1. T	1. F
2. F	2. F	2. F	2. F	2. F	2. F
3. T	3. F	3. F	3. T	3. F	3. T

Chapter 3: The Judicial Process and Cyber-Procedure

3-1 The Court System
The Federal Court System • Court Jurisdiction • State Court Systems

3-2 Civil Procedure
Commencement of the Action • Service of Process • The Pre-Answer Stage • The Answer • The Pretrial Stage • The Civil Trial • The Appeal • Execution of the Judgment

3-3 Cyber-Procedure
Cyber-Jurisdiction • Cyber-Filing • Cyber-Discovery

3-4 Criminal Procedure
The Arrest and Initial Appearance • The Preliminary Hearing • The Formal Charges • The Arraignment • The Criminal Trial

THE OPENING CASE Round 1
The European Community v. RJR Nabisco: Euros and RICO and Nations ... Oh My!

This case starts with the sale of drugs on the streets of Europe financed by a complicated money laundering scheme allegedly masterminded by the American corporation RJR Nabisco Inc. (RJR). The European Community (EC), acting for itself and for its members, brought suit in federal court in New York against RJR under the Racketeer Influenced and Corrupt Organizations (RICO) Act, claiming that RJR had, in furtherance of its illegal scheme, committed numerous acts of money laundering, wire fraud, mail fraud, and violations of the Travel Act. For good measure, the EC added several allegations of wrongdoing under the state laws of New York. RJR filed a motion to dismiss based on two claims. The first claim stated that since RICO does not expressly authorize extraterritorial claims like this one, the presumption must be against the extraterritorial application of the statute. The second claim stated that the federal courts had no jurisdiction over the state claims because the EC was a conglomerate of nations and not a nation-state itself, which meant it did not satisfy the need for diversity that was required by the federal rules. The district court dismissed the case on both counts.

Dissatisfied with the result, the EC and its member nations filed an appeal in the U.S. Court of Appeals for the Second Circuit. In a surprise move, the appellate court reversed the District Court's ruling. In response to the first claim, the court said that the presumption that a statute like RICO does not apply to extraterritorial conduct can be overcome if a predicate offense named in RICO includes extraterritorial conduct. A **predicate offense** is generally one that provides the resources needed to commit the offenses outlined in the new statute. Racketeering, as laid out in RICO, includes money laundering as a predicate offense. Congress defines money laundering to include extraterritorial activities. Therefore, Congress intended money laundering to have an extraterritorial application in RICO. As for the charges involving mail fraud, wire fraud, and violations of the Travel Act, the appeals court held that since the complaint alleged facts that would give rise to a domestic cause of action, the fact that those facts included extraterritorial offenses did not disqualify the court from hearing the case. As for the second claim, the court decided that the federal court system had subject matter jurisdiction over the state claims because, even though the EC is not a foreign nation, it is an instrumentality that represents several foreign nations, which is enough to satisfy the requirements of the jurisdictional statute.

RJR took the case to the U.S. Supreme Court. Not surprisingly, the High Court upheld the ruling by the Court of Appeals. So far, so good for the EC. Then the High Court threw a curve. It ruled that claims brought under RICO and similar statutes by private parties (i.e., any party that is not the U.S. government; in other words, a party like the EC) must allege that they, the plaintiffs, had been injured in the United States. Now, since the EC and its companion nations did not allege that they had been injured in the United States, they would not be able to proceed unless ... well, there is a bit more to this, so read on. [See: *The European Community (EC) v. RJR Nabisco, Inc. (RJR)*, 579 U.S. ----- (2016); *The European Community (EC) v. RJR Nabisco, Inc. (RJR)*, U.S. Court of Appeals, Second Circuit, Docket No. 11-2475-cv. (April 23, 2014); and Amy Howe, "Opinion Analysis: In the End RJR Prevails in European Community's RICO Lawsuit," SCOTUSblog, June 20, 2016, http://scotusblog.com/2016/06/opinion-analysis-in-the-end-rjr-prevails-in-european-communitys-rico-lawsuit/.]

Opening Case Questions

1. How is subject matter jurisdiction applied in the federal courts? Explain.
2. How does a court choose which law to apply to a case when that case touches two or more jurisdictions? Explain.
3. What is the role of the complaint in any court? Explain.
4. What is the function of a motion to dismiss in both the state and the federal courts? Explain.
5. Under what circumstances will the U.S. Supreme Court agree to review a case that it does not have to review? Explain.

Source: See: *The European Community (EC) v. RJR Nabisco, Inc. (RJR)*, 579 U.S. ----- (2016); *The European Community (EC) v. RJR Nabisco, Inc. (RJR)*, United States Court of Appeals, Second Circuit, Docket No. 11-2475-cv. (April 23, 2014); Amy Howe, "Opinion analysis: In the end RJR prevails in European Community's RICO lawsuit", *SCOTUSblog* (June 20, 2016), http://scotusblog.com/2016/06/opinion-analysis-in-the-end-rjr-prevails-in-european-communitys-rico-lawsuit/.

LO Learning Objectives

1. Explain the fundamental nature of the American courts.
2. Determine when a case can be brought in federal court.
3. Recognize those cases that can be heard by the U.S. Supreme Court.
4. Identify the structure of most state court systems.
5. Define *civil litigation*.
6. List the most common discovery techniques.
7. Detail the nature of an appeal.
8. Determine the extent of cyber-jurisdiction.
9. Explain the nature of electronically stored information.
10. Describe the steps in a criminal prosecution.

3-1 The Court System

The laws of the American government are interpreted and implemented by a system of courts authorized by either the federal or state constitutions and generally established by legislative authority. **Courts** are judicial tribunals that meet in a regular place and apply the law in an attempt to settle disputes by weighing the arguments presented by advocates for each party. Each of these official bodies is a forum for the party who presents a complaint, the party who responds to the complaint, and the jury and/or judge who settles the dispute. As noted in the previous chapter, the law involves a set of competing dualities including the spirit of the law versus the letter of the law, the words of the law versus the interpretation of those words, and the abstract principles of the law versus the concrete situations to which those principles are applied. Nowhere in the law are these dualities more obvious on a daily basis than in the court system. The same is true of the uncertainly principle that is played out every time a plaintiff and defendant place their case in the hands of a judge and jury.

The Federal Court System

U.S. Const. Article III (see Appendix A)

The federal court system is authorized by Article III of the U.S. Constitution, which states, "The Judicial Power of the United States shall be vested in one supreme court, and in such inferior courts as Congress may from time to time ordain and establish." The present federal court system includes the Supreme Court, courts of appeals, and federal district courts.

Court Jurisdiction

The authority of a court to hear and decide cases is called the court's **jurisdiction**. It is set by law and limited as to territory and type of case. A court of **original jurisdiction** has the authority to hear a case when it is first brought to court. Those courts that have the power to review a case for errors are courts of **appellate jurisdiction**. Most of the time, courts with appellate jurisdiction will be empowered to determine whether the lower courts have made errors of law. This process is referred to as **plenary review**. Sometimes an appellate court will review the factual decisions made by the judge or the jury in lower courts. Such a review, however, only occurs when the appeals court determines that the decision made in the lower court was undeniably wrong, given the facts and evidence in the case. This determination relies on the **clearly erroneous standard**. Appellate courts also have the ability to determine whether the judge in the lower court has in some way misused his or her authority. This type of review is referred to as **abuse of discretion**.

Courts with the power to hear any type of case are said to exercise **general jurisdiction**. Those with the power to hear only certain types of cases have **special jurisdiction**. Examples of courts with special jurisdiction are probate courts and courts of claims. Courts also exercise subject matter jurisdiction and personal jurisdiction. **Subject matter jurisdiction** is the court's power to hear a particular type of case. **Personal jurisdiction** is the court's authority over the parties to a lawsuit.

Federal District Courts Each state and territory in the United States has at least one federal district court. These courts are also known as *U.S. district courts*. The district courts are the courts of general jurisdiction in the federal system. Most federal cases begin in the federal district court. Not all cases belong there, however. The federal courts have subject matter jurisdiction over two types of cases: those involving federal law and those involving diversity.

Federal district courts have subject matter jurisdiction over cases that pertain to a federal question. A **federal question** could involve the U.S. Constitution, a federal statute or statutes, or a treaty. A state law issue can be included in a suit involving a federal question if the state claim is part of the same situation that created the federal question. If the federal claim is thrown out by the federal court, the state law issue usually cannot stand by itself. The people bringing the lawsuit would have to take their case to a state court.

Subject matter jurisdiction in federal court also arises in cases of diversity, even when no federal law is involved. Congress has sets up three very specific conditions under which **diversity jurisdiction** can be established in the federal court system. Those conditions include cases that are:

1. Between citizens of different states.
2. Between citizens of a state or different states and citizens of a foreign state.
3. Between citizens of a state and a foreign state as the plaintiff.

As clear cut as these classifications may seem on the surface, they often cause problems in today's complicated global community. For example, determining what Congress means by the term "foreign state" is not as simple as it seems. The first inclination is to assume that when Congress wrote the term "foreign state," it meant a nation-state. However, in the contemporary world, the term "state" can mean either a nation-state or, in many cases, a non-nation-state. Most of the time, it is easy enough to distinguish between a nation-state and a non-nation-state. Nation-states obtain sovereignty by legitimately controlling a specific territory that has visible, defensible borders. Nation-states also have a governmental structure that makes laws governing the land, the resources, and the people within its bordered territory. By virtue of its governmental responsibilities, a nation-state also has a monopoly on the legitimate use of force within its territory. Moreover, the leaders of any nation-state have one major responsibility and that is to protect the people, the resources, and the existence of the state.

In contrast, non-nation-states come in several varieties, some, but not all, of which, qualify as "foreign states" for jurisdictional purposes in the U.S. court system. Non-nation-state configurations include (1) **non-governmental organizations (NGOs)**, such as the Red Cross, that function autonomously to provide goods and services to people in need, and (2) **unified international institutions** that bring together various nation-states in a common purpose, such as the North Atlantic Treaty Organization, (NATO) and the United Nations (UN). In addition, non-nation configurations include **conglomerates**, such as the European Union (formerly the European Community [EC]), which unify several true nation-states, for a common enterprise, and which often speak with one voice that represents the members

THE OPENING CASE Round 2
Euros and RICO and Nations ... Oh My!

Recall that, in the Opening Case, the European Community (EC), acting for itself and for its members, brought suit in federal court in New York against RJR under the Racketeer Influenced and Corrupt Organizations (RICO) Act, claiming that RJR had, in furtherance of an illegal conspiracy, committed numerous acts of money laundering, wire fraud, mail fraud, and violations of the Travel Act. The EC also added several allegations of wrongdoing under the state laws of New York. RJR filed a motion to dismiss based on two claims. The first claim involved the question of whether RICO could be applied to certain extraterritorial offenses. The second claim, which is our focus here, stated that the federal courts have no jurisdiction over the state claims in the case. The district court dismissed the case, but the appellate court reversed the district court's ruling. The case ended up in the U.S. Supreme Court. In response to the second claim, the Court analyzed the statute that controls federal jurisdiction. In that analysis, the Court noted that under the statute, federal jurisdiction includes cases that involved a *foreign state* as long as the foreign state is the plaintiff (except when a foreign state promotes terrorism, in which case it can be a defendant).

Since the EC is the plaintiff in the case, the only question left is whether the EC qualifies as a foreign state. To answer this question, the Court looked at the Foreign Service Immunities Act, which defines a foreign state in the following way: "A 'foreign state' includes a political subdivision of a foreign state *or an agency or instrumentality of a foreign state* as defined in subsection (b)." So far, so good. Subsection (b) reads, "an 'agency or instrumentality of a foreign state' means an entity—(1) which is *a separate legal person*, corporate or otherwise, and (2) which is an *organ of a foreign state or a political subdivision thereof* and (3) which is neither a citizen of a State of the United States nor created under the laws of any third country." Applying this language, the court went through the following reasoning process. First, to be a foreign nation, the EC must be an agency or instrumentality of a foreign state, but to be an agency or instrumentality, it must be (1) a separate legal person and (2) an organ of a nation-state (because it cannot be a political subdivision). First, it is clear that the EC is a legal person under Article 7 of the Lisbon Treaty where it is referred to as a "legal personality." Second, it is equally clear that because the EC "serves on the collective behalf" of its members and exercises political authority over those members, it also operates as an organ of the EC. This preserves the Federal District Court's diversity jurisdiction, and the state claims remain a part of the lawsuit. [See: *The European Community (EC) v. RJR Nabisco, Inc. (RJR)*, 579 U.S. ----- (2016); *The European Community (EC) v. RJR Nabisco, Inc. (RJR)*, U.S. Court of Appeals, Second Circuit, Docket No. 11-2475-cv. (April 23, 2014); and Article 7, The Lisbon Treaty (2007), https://habitatinkling.com/project/sn406d/files/s9ml/chapter003/ch03_reader__1html.]

of that conglomerate. The difference between a conglomerate and unified-international institution is that in a unified-international institution, the nation-states retain their own separate identities, while in a conglomerate, the nation-states surrender some, but not necessarily all, control over their own affairs to the central governing body.

In diversity cases, and for other legal purposes, corporations are considered citizens of the state in which they are incorporated and the state where they have their principal place of business. In federal court, if even one defendant is a citizen of the same state as one of the plaintiffs, diversity cannot be established. In such a case, the law says that "diversity is not complete." Diversity cases must involve an amount over $75,000.

Establishing subject matter jurisdiction will not be enough to get a case into federal court if the federal court does not have personal jurisdiction over a party. To establish personal jurisdiction, the court must look at the long-arm statute in the state in which the federal court is physically located. The court must then look to see if an appropriate level of contact has been made with the home state. A long-arm statute lists circumstances in which a court can exercise personal jurisdiction over an out-of-state defendant. Typically, these circumstances include the following:

- Owning real property in the state.
- Soliciting business in the state.
- Having an office or a store in the state.
- Committing a tort within the state.
- Transacting business in the state.

Some of the circumstances listed in the long-arm statute are relatively clear. Committing a tort in a state, for instance, leaves little room for misunderstanding. Other circumstances, however, such as "transacting business in the state," are not as precise. Therefore, personal jurisdiction under a state long-arm statute also requires meeting the required minimum contacts with the state. The concept of **minimum contacts** identifies the fewest number of contacts needed to allow the court to exercise jurisdiction over the out-of-state defendant. For example, let's say that a state allows the court to establish personal jurisdiction over any person who transacts business in the state. Now suppose a person buys a newspaper at an airport during a layover in the state. Does the purchase of that single newspaper constitute "transacting business" in the state?

The question turns on whether the purchase establishes a minimum contact with the state. In this case, the answer is probably "no." In general, the courts exclude contacts that are passive or that do not rise to a level that would permit the person transacting the business to reasonably foresee that he or she would come under the court's jurisdiction as a result of that transaction. It is difficult to conclude that the casual purchase of a newspaper at an airport kiosk would lead a person to foresee that he or she has voluntarily submitted to the jurisdictional power of a state. Something more would have to be involved. For instance, if the person in question specifically targeted the airport layover time to conduct negotiations with a client, and if a contract resulted from those negotiations, then the minimum contacts requirement would have been met and jurisdiction established.

Most of the time, a court will determine subject matter jurisdiction before turning to the question of personal jurisdiction. Determining subject matter jurisdiction first, however, is not absolutely necessary. If the issue of personal jurisdiction is very obvious to the court, the court is free to dismiss the case before considering the question of subject matter jurisdiction. For example, this dismissal might happen if the defendant meets none of the categories in the long-arm statute or clearly does not meet the minimum contacts required by the case law of a state. In fact, if determining subject matter jurisdiction is especially difficult, the court is free to look at personal jurisdiction first, without even considering the question of subject matter jurisdiction.

EXAMPLE 3-1: The Stream of Commerce Theory

When attempting to establish personal jurisdiction over an out-of-state defendant, the plaintiff must convince the judge that the defendant had a set of "minimum contacts" with the state. Generally, the establishment of "minimum contacts" requires some kind of proactive strategy on the part of the defendant. This proactive strategy might involve opening a store, an office, a manufacturing plant, or a service center in the state; however, in some jurisdictions, this is not always true. In the case of *Nicastro v. McIntyre*, for example, the Supreme Court of New Jersey established a standard called the **stream of commerce theory**. In this case, the plaintiff was injured by a product made by a British manufacturer. The plaintiff sued the manufacturer for failing to warn the ultimate user of a danger involved in the operation of the product, a metal press, and for a manufacturing defect related to the absence of an appropriate safety guard. The trial court dismissed the case because the plaintiff had failed to demonstrate the needed minimum contacts. The Supreme Court of New Jersey agreed that the plaintiff had not met the minimum contact test. Oddly, this did not stop the court from establishing personal jurisdiction over the manufacturer. To establish personal jurisdiction, the New Jersey court embraced a new theory of jurisdiction: the stream of commerce test. Under the stream of commerce test, the plaintiff must demonstrate that the defendant—in this case, a foreign manufacturer—sent one of its products into "the stream of commerce" using a plan of national distribution that the manufacturer knew or at least reasonably should have known would, in some way, impact New Jersey. The New Jersey Supreme Court was satisfied that this was what had happened in the *Nicastro v. McIntyre* case. However, the New Jersey court *did limit* the stream of commerce standard to *product liability cases*—that is, cases in which the plaintiff claims to have been injured by a product manufactured or sold by the defendant. [See: *Nicastro v. McIntyre*, 2010 N.J. Lexis 19 (N.J. Feb. 2, 2010); and J. Russell Jackson, "Buy Globally, Sue Locally for Products Liability," *The National Law Journal*, March 22, 2010, p. 10.]

Source: See: *Nicastro v. McIntyre*, 2010 N.J. Lexis 19 (N.J. Feb. 2, 2010); and J. Russell Jackson "Buy Globally, Sue Locally for Products Liability," *The National Law Journal*, March 22, 2010, p. 10.

U.S. Courts of Appeals The judges at the appellate level must be guided by the standard of review that is appropriate to each case. The standard of review tells the appellate-level judges the degree to which they must remain faithful to the decision of the lower court judge. As noted previously, the three standards of review are *plenary*, *clearly erroneous*, and *abuse of discretion*. Although they do not hear as many cases each year as the district courts, there are fewer U.S. courts of appeals and, therefore, fewer judges to hear those cases. The U.S. Courts of Appeals hear appeals from the district courts, the U.S. Tax Court, and many of the administrative agencies. At present, there are 13 U.S. courts of appeals within the federal court system (see Figure 3-1). Eleven of these appellate courts cover geographical groupings of states. For example, the Sixth Circuit Court of Appeals includes Michigan, Ohio, Kentucky, and Tennessee. The Fifth Circuit includes Texas, Louisiana, and Mississippi. There is also a special appellate court for the District of Columbia called the U.S. Court of Appeals for the District of Columbia.

In addition to 12 appellate courts, organized on a geographical basis, there is a 13th appellate court that has special jurisdiction over certain types of cases. This court is known as the U.S. Court of Appeals for the Federal Circuit. The Federal Circuit was established by Congress primarily to streamline and unify patent law. However, the Federal Circuit was also given the power to hear appeals in cases that entail government contracts, trademark disputes, federal workers, veterans' benefits, and international trade, among others. Still, more than one-third of the appeals that end up in the Federal Circuit are patent cases that come either from the U.S. district courts or the U.S. Patent and Trademark Office. Some critics of the Federal Circuit have argued that the court's approach to patent law has become

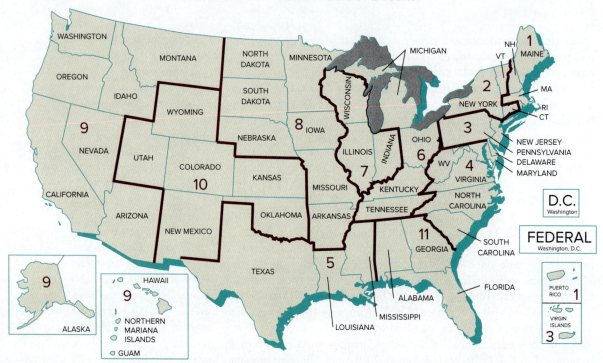

Figure 3-1 The U.S. federal court system is divided into 13 circuits, including the Washington, DC, and federal circuits. Each circuit has several district courts.

too narrow and too formalistic. [See: Marcia Cole, "Critics Target Federal Circuit," *The National Law Journal*, October 16, 2006, pp. 1, 20-21.] Others have held the opposite view. These critics contend that the standard the Federal Circuit uses to judge the patentability of abstract ideas, especially as they relate to computer software programs, has been ill advised, hopelessly vague, and virtually unusable. [See: "Difference Engine: Stalking Trolls," *The Economist Technology Quarterly*, March 8, 2014, p. 14.]

U.S. Const. Article III
(see Appendix A)

The United States Supreme Court Established by the Constitution, the U.S. Supreme Court is the court of final jurisdiction in all cases appealed from the lower federal courts and in cases coming from state supreme courts. It has original jurisdiction in cases affecting ambassadors or other public ministers and consuls and in cases in which a state is a party. The Supreme Court is composed of a chief justice and eight associate justices. They are appointed by the president with the consent of the Senate and hold office during good behavior.

In many situations, a case will reach the U.S. Supreme Court only if the court agrees to issue a writ of certiorari. A **writ of certiorari** is an order from the Supreme Court to a lower court to deliver its records to the U.S. Supreme Court for review. The Court will issue a writ of certiorari if several lower courts have dealt with an issue but cannot agree on how it should be handled. If the case involves an issue that affects a large segment of society, the Court is likely to grant a writ. Finally, the Court may also hear a case if it involves a constitutional issue.

Applicable Law When a federal court hears a case involving only federal law or the U.S. Constitution, it must follow that federal law, the Constitution, and/or any line of federal precedent that can be used to interpret the situation. Circumstances are different in diversity cases or federal law cases that also concern issues of state law. For instance, if a federal judge in Minnesota hears a diversity case between a Minnesota citizen and an Iowa citizen, would that judge use federal law, Minnesota law, or Iowa law? As a general rule, a federal court hearing a diversity case will apply the law of the state in which it is physically located and/or the state that has the most substantial connection to the case. The court is also authorized to consider whether the litigants had, at some time in the past, in a contract or agreement of some sort, specified which jurisdiction's law would apply to case of any disputes between the parties.

EXAMPLE 3-2: "Choosing" the Law

Often, the question of what law to apply in a case is crucial to the management of a lawsuit. The law of one jurisdiction may favor the plaintiff, while another may support the defendant. Frequently, whoever wins the battle of jurisdictions also wins the battle of the law and, ultimately, the war itself. Such was the situation in the case of *First W. Cap. Mgmt v. Malamed*. The case involved a provision of the new Defend Trade Secrets Act (DTSA), which forbid the federal courts from issuing injunctions that would stop an employee who knew some crucial trade secrets "from entering into a new employment agreement" after leaving his or her employer. However, Congress softened this requirement just a bit by noting that the federal court cannot impose limitations on a former employee that would somehow conflict with any state law that might forbid restrictive employment agreements. In the case of *First W. Cap. Mgmt (First) v. Malamed*, the defendant, the chief investment officer (CIO) of First, duplicated the corporation's *client book* and then left First for another job. When the officers of First learned about the CIO's surreptitious conduct, they sued, seeking an injunction that would stop him from using the client book in competition with First. The CIO argued that he was protected by the DTSA, which prohibited the court from granting injunctions that would prevent former employees "from entering into a new employment agreement." First countered by arguing that while the DTSA did, in fact, prevent injunctions that would interfere with future employment, it also included an exception that stated a court could impose an injunction protecting trade secrets, if there was "evidence of threatened misappropriation." Let's face it: duplicating the client book is pretty clear "evidence of threatened misappropriation."

Despite this roadblock, the CIO was not yet defeated. He had another argument up his sleeve. He noted that since he was a citizen of California, not Colorado, he was subject to California law. California law was much more favorable to former employees because it prohibited "restraints on the practice of a lawful profession, trade or business." The attorneys for First were not troubled by this move. If the CIO wanted to apply state law instead of the DTSA, they would apply state law. Accordingly, they pointed to a choice of law clause in the CIO's employment contract that said, quite explicitly, that in case of a dispute like this one, Colorado law would apply. Clearly, at this point, before issuing an injunction, the court had to determine which state's law would apply in the case. The general principle is that a federal court hearing a diversity case will apply the law of the state in which it is physically located and/or the state that has the most substantial connection to the case. Also, the court is empowered to consider any choice of law clause in the employment contract between the CIO and First. It should not be a shock to learn that in this case, given the principles just noted, the judge chose to apply Colorado law. The injunction was granted ordering the CIO to refrain from pursuing any former clients for two years. [See: *First W. Cap. Mgmt v. Malamed,* No. 16-cv-1961-MJW, 2016 WL 835849, at *3 (D. Colo. Sep. 30, 2016).]

Source: See: *First W. Cap. Mgmt v. Malamed,* No. 16-cv-1961-MJW, 2016 WL 835849, at *3 (D. Colo. Sep. 30, 2016).

State Court Systems

The courts of each state are organized according to the provisions of the state constitution. Despite differences from state to state, such as the names for similar types of courts, there are basic similarities. For example, each state has an arrangement of inferior, or lower-level, courts that serve as limited jurisdiction trial courts. Higher-level trial courts with broader

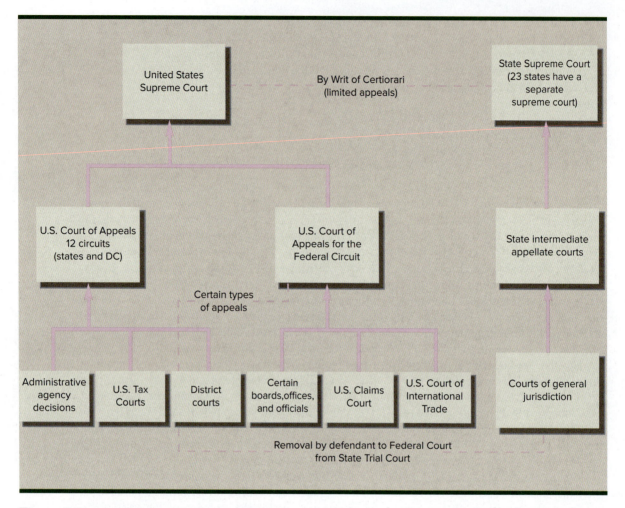

Figure 3-2 Federal and state court systems.

jurisdiction are also provided. In addition, each state has appellate courts to which questions of law (not questions of fact) may be appealed. Figure 3-2 provides a general outline of the federal and the state court systems.

State Trial Courts The state trial courts, also known as general jurisdiction courts, have the power to hear any type of case. They are often called superior courts, circuit courts, or courts of common pleas. Some states, notably New York, refer to them as supreme courts. These courts are usually organized around the counties of the state so that each county has its own trial court of general jurisdiction. Most states also have other trial courts that are lower than the general jurisdiction courts. These limited jurisdiction courts usually hear only certain types of cases. For instance, a municipal court may be empowered to hear only those cases that involve municipal ordinances, criminal cases involving crimes within the city limits, and other cases that involve monetary claims of less than $10,000. Many localities have small-claims courts that hear civil cases involving small dollar amounts, ranging from $500 to $5,000, depending on state law.

State Intermediate Appellate Courts State court systems provide for a variety of appellate court structures. Still, the purpose of the appellate courts remains the same—that is, to hear appeals on questions of law from the lower courts. Usually, appeals are heard by a three-judge panel. The panel examines the records of the lower court, reads the written arguments submitted by the attorneys, studies the law on its own, and listens to the oral arguments of the attorneys. If the panel agrees with the lower court, it will affirm the decision of that court; however, if the panel disagrees with the lower court's decision, it can set aside or modify the decision of that court.

State Supreme Courts Twenty-seven states rely on their supreme court as their only appellate court. These states have no intermediate appellate courts. The other 23 states have both intermediate appellate courts and state supreme courts. Most supreme courts consist of a panel of three to nine judges. As is true at the intermediate appellate level, the panel of judges examines the records of the lower court, reads the written arguments submitted by the attorneys, studies the law on its own, and listens to the oral arguments of the attorneys. The decisions of state supreme courts are final unless a federal issue or a constitutional right is involved.

quick quiz 3-1

1. Courts are judicial tribunals that meet in a regular place and apply the laws in an attempt to settle disputes fairly.	true | false
2. The authority of a court to hear and decide cases is called the court's jurisdiction.	true | false
3. A writ of certiorari is an order from the Supreme Court to a lower court to deliver its records to the U.S Supreme Court for review.	true | false

3-2 Civil Procedure

In a civil lawsuit, one individual, organization, or corporation brings an action against another individual, organization, or corporation. The objective of a civil suit is usually to obtain money to compensate the victim. **Civil litigation** is another name for the process of bringing a case to court to enforce a right.

Commencement of the Action

The principal parties to a lawsuit are the plaintiff and the defendant. The **plaintiff** is the person who begins the lawsuit by filing a complaint in the appropriate trial court of general jurisdiction. The **defendant** is the person against whom the lawsuit has been brought and from whom a recovery is sought.

Filing the Complaint The **complaint** sets forth the names of the parties to the lawsuit, identifying them as plaintiffs or defendants. Generally, the complaint includes the addresses of all parties. The complaint also sets forth the following:

- The facts in the case from the plaintiff's perspective.
- The alleged legal violations by the defendant.
- The injuries that the plaintiff suffered.
- The plaintiff's request for relief.

If the plaintiff wants a jury trial, this information must also be specified in the complaint. In federal court, the complaint must also include a statement of jurisdiction, which will tell the court whether the case has been brought in federal court because of a federal question or because of diversity among the plaintiffs and the defendants.

Additional Elements Needed in Some Complaints If the plaintiff wants a jury trial, this information must also be specified in the complaint. In federal court, the complaint must also include a statement of jurisdiction, which will tell the court whether the case has been brought in federal court because of a federal question or because of diversity among the plaintiffs and the defendants.

Class Action Lawsuits At times, filing a complaint is pointless because the amount of recovery for one plaintiff would be so low that it would not be worth the effort, energy, and

THE OPENING CASE Round 3
EUROS and RICO and NATIONS ... OH MY!

In the Opening Case, the European Community (EC) initiated a lawsuit in the U.S. District Court under the RICO Act. In the complaint, attorneys for the EC argued that RJR had, in an attempt to finance a global conspiracy, engaged in multiple acts of money laundering, wire fraud, mail fraud, and violations of the Travel Act. In addition, the EC alleged that RJR had committed several violations of New York state law. RJR asked the court to dismiss the case based on two arguments. First, RICO could not be applied to any crimes committed in Europe because Congress had never authorized lawsuits based on extraterritorial activities. Second, the federal courts had no jurisdiction over the state claims because the EC was not a true foreign state as required to establish diversity jurisdiction under federal law. The District Court granted RJR's request for a dismissal. The EC then filed an appeal in the U.S. appellate court. The appellate court vacated the dismissal. The appellate court noted that it could not support RJR's first claim because the presumption that a statute like RICO does not apply to extraterritorial conduct was overcome by the predicate offenses named in RICO, as well as the domestic violations alleged in the case. Nor could the appellate court support the jurisdictional claim because the statutory definition of foreign state did, in fact, apply to the EC. In effect, at this point in the case, the EC appeared to have won the day.

The Supreme Court then made a surprise move. The High Court stated that any private party bringing a lawsuit under RICO based on offenses committed in the United States would have to convince the Court that it had been injured in the United States. It appeared that the EC had made a move early in the case that now came back to haunt it. While still in the pretrial stages in the District Court, the EC had waived its right to ask for damages for injuries suffered in the United States under RICO. The District Court had accepted the waiver and permanently dismissed any damage claims for those domestic injuries. This does not mean that the EC has no remedy in the case. It is possible that it may have an equitable remedy (i.e., a non-monetary remedy) in relation to the New York state claims and, perhaps, in relation to the RICO claims. Still, even this strategy may not work because (1) up to this point, the EC had not even mentioned equitable relief for the state claims, and (2) there seems to be no precedent supporting the idea that equitable relief is possible under RICO. This is an unfortunate state of affairs for the EC. As we have just learned, stating the injuries and the outlining the relief sought for those injuries are two of the most important elements in the complaint and, therefore, in the case itself. Apparently, the EC had been so sure of its extraterritorial claims that it had been willing to waive the possibility of damages (the "relief sought" in this case) for all domestic injuries. The moral of the story is that the twin statements of injuries and relief sought in the complaint are so important to the overall case that neither the injuries nor the relief sought for those injuries should ever be waived, absent some compelling reason to do otherwise. [See: *The European Community (EC) v. RJR Nabisco, Inc. (RJR)*, 579 U.S. ----- (2016); *The European Community (EC) v. RJR Nabisco, Inc. (RJR)*, U.S. Court of Appeals, Second Circuit, Docket No. 11-2475-cv. (April 23, 2014); and Amy Howe, "Opinion Analysis: In the End RJR Prevails in European Community's RICO Lawsuit," SCOTUSblog, June 20, 2016, http://scotusblog.com/2016/06/opinion-analysis-in-the-end-rjr-prevails-in-european-communitys-rico-lawsuit/.]

Source: See: *The European Community (EC) v. RJR Nabisco, Inc. (RJR)*, 579 U.S. ----- (2016); *The European Community (EC) v. RJR Nabisco, Inc. (RJR)*, United States Court of Appeals, Second Circuit, Docket No. 11-2475-cv. (April 23, 2014); Amy Howe, "Opinion analysis: In the end RJR prevails in European Community's RICO lawsuit", *SCOTUSblog* (June 20, 2016), http://scotusblog.com/2016/06/opinion-analysis-in-the-end-rjr-prevails-in-european-communitys-rico-lawsuit/.

expense of a lawsuit. Sometimes, however, the extent of the harmful conduct is so pervasive and the number of plaintiffs so high that the cost of conducting the lawsuit is justified. This was the motivation that led to the creation of the class action lawsuit. A **class action** is a lawsuit in which one (or a small number) of the potential plaintiffs file a lawsuit on behalf of the entire class. The courts will permit a class action lawsuit provided that (1) it is not feasible for the members of the group to bring the action on their own, (2) the members of the group share common questions of law that can be tried together, and (3) the class action approach is far better than forcing the plaintiffs to file separate actions.

Forum Shopping Unfortunately, class action lawsuits are often abused. One of the most common abuses is forum shopping. **Forum shopping** occurs when a plaintiff searches for a jurisdiction with law that is favorable to its case and then files the case in that jurisdiction. The defendant can do something similar by filing a motion to remove a case filed in state court to federal court. When a case features multiple plaintiffs, as in a class action lawsuit, forum shopping becomes easier because the number of possible jurisdictions increases as the number of plaintiffs from different states increases. In order to counteract abuses, Congress enacted the Class Action Fairness Act (CAFA). The act included a number of innovations designed to limit forum shopping and to counteract some of the other abuses associated with class actions. [See: Archis Parasharami and Kevin Ranlett, "The Class Action Fairness Act, Five Years Later," *The National Law Journal*, April 12, 2010, pp. 14, 18; and Michael McNamara and Christine Henge, "'Hertz' Expands Companies Access to Federal Court," *The National Law Journal*, April 12, 2010, pp. 16–17.]

    Congress is not the only institution to show concern over the problem of forum shopping. The Supreme Court has begun to limit the options open to plaintiffs who search for courts that have a history of being biased in a way that clearly favors their position in a given case. A landmark class action lawsuit in forum shopping is the case of *Bristol-Myers Squibb v. Superior Court of California*. The case involves a class action lawsuit brought against Bristol-Myers Squibb by patients who had used and been harmed by a blood thinner known as Plavix. The plaintiffs had sought to bring dozens of plaintiffs into the class action by arguing that the California court had jurisdiction because Bristol-Meyers Squibb had performed research on the drug in California and had both advertised and marketed the drug in that state. Moreover, the plaintiffs all seemed to have the same or similar injuries as a result of using Plavix. The High Court was not convinced by these arguments. The majority opinion noted that allowing California to retain jurisdiction in this case would permit nonresidents to be brought into the case, even though the only connection they had to the state was that they had been prescribed, had purchased, had taken, and had been injured by the same drug that had injured the California residents. This "connection" to California is much too tenuous to be accepted as a valid legal connection to the state. [See: *Bristol-Myers Squibb v. Superior Court of California*, No. 16-cv-1961-MJW, 2016 WL 8358549, at *8 (D. Colo., September 30, 2016); and John Marsh, "The Defend Trade Secrets Act after One Year: Injunctions Affecting New Employment," *Trade Secret Litigator*, June 2, 2017, http://www.tradesecretlitigator.com/2017/06/the-defend-trade-secrets-act-after-one-year-injunctions-affecting-new-employment/.]

Multidistrict Litigation The federal courts also use of another procedure designed to consolidate cases in order to streamline the legal process and lighten the case load at the trial level. This procedure, known as **multidistrict litigation (MDL)**, moves a series of cases of a similar type to a single federal judge in the **MDL court** (also known as the transferee court) for preliminary case management decisions and initial discovery procedures. In this way, all critical pretrial matters can be carried out in tandem, rather than one by one in each court of origin. The cases are then returned to the court of origin (also known as the transferror court) for trial. Cases can move to the MDL court by a motion of either party or by the initiative of the original trial court. The decisions about which cases move to the MDL are made by a seven judge panel, appointed by the Chief Justice of the United States Supreme Court. The panel considers the similarities that exist in the facts among the various cases as well as any legal issues that the cases might have in common. Legislation, known as the Multidistrict Litigation Restoration Act, is pending that would transform the MDL court into a trial court so that MDL cases can be tried together in the same place by the same judge. [See: Class Action Litigation Information, http://www.classactionlitigation.com/.]

Service of Process

The complaint is presented to the appropriate court officer, usually the clerk of courts. The clerk will then see that the defendant is served with a copy of the complaint and a summons. The *summons* names the court of jurisdiction, describes the nature of the action, and demands that the defendant answer the complaint within a specified period of time, usually between 20 and 30 days, depending on the state rules of civil procedure. Giving the summons and the complaint to the defendant is called service of process.

The Pre-Answer Stage

As noted, once the defendant has been served, he or she has 20 to 30 days to file an answer. Usually, however, the defendant will ask for and receive an extension of that time period. The time between service and the answer is termed the *pre-answer stage*. During this stage, the defendant will take some time to examine the nature of the claim that has been filed by the plaintiff. The defendant may, as a result of this initial examination, decide to file one or more pre-answer motions. A *motion* is a request for the court to rule on a particular issue. One possible motion is a motion for dismissal of the case for failure to state a claim for which relief can be granted. Under the Federal Rules of Civil Procedure, this is referred to as a Rule 12(b)(6) motion. Some states call this motion a demurrer. Other motions to dismiss may be based on the grounds that the court lacks subject matter jurisdiction, that the court lacks personal jurisdiction, or that the court cannot hear the case because the statute of limitations has passed.

The Answer

The answer is the defendant's official response to the complaint. In the answer, the defendant admits or denies the allegations in the complaint. The defendant's answer can also include affirmative defenses. An affirmative defense is a set of circumstances that indicate the defendant should not be held liable, even if the plaintiff proves all of the facts in the complaint. One affirmative defense is *assumption of the risk*.

EXAMPLE 3-3: Assessing the Risk of a Risky Business

Carol Jennings took a cruise of the Mediterranean on the Underwood Cruise Line, a firm incorporated and doing business in the United States. While the cruise ship *Principia* was docked at a Greek island, Jennings joined a tour group. She was cautioned numerous times to remain with the tour group and not to wander off by herself because of the danger of being attacked and robbed. Nevertheless, Jennings ignored the warnings and left the tour group. While on her own, she wandered into a particularly dangerous part of the city where she was beaten and robbed. She later brought a lawsuit against the Underwood Cruise Line. In its answer to Jennings' complaint, the cruise line may wish to use the defense of assumption of the risk. Such a defense would argue that Jennings was aware of danger when she chose to abandon the tour group and wander off by herself. As a result, the cruise line might argue, she assumed the risk of being attacked and robbed.

THE OPENING CASE *Round 4*
EUROS and RICO and NATIONS ... OH MY!

Let's look at the case of *The European Community (EC) v. RJR Nabisco, Inc. (RJR)* one more time. Once the complaint had been filed in the federal district court, RJR decided (1) that the EC had no legitimate case under the terms laid out in the RICO Act and (2) that the federal court had no subject matter jurisdiction to hear the New York claims. Accordingly, RJR filed a Rule 12(b)(6) motion asking the court to dismiss the action because, under federal rules, the EC had failed "to state a claim for which relief can be granted." RJR's argument was based on the belief that RICO could not be applied to any crimes committed in Europe because Congress had never authorized lawsuits based on offenses committed outside of the United States. In addition, RJR also filed a Rule 12(b)(1) motion to dismiss the New York claims for lack of subject matter jurisdiction because complete diversity had not been established. As part of this motion, RJR claimed that the federal courts had no jurisdiction over the state claims because the EC was not a true foreign state as required by law, so there was no diversity as required by law to establish subject matter jurisdiction over the New York claims.

In taking the opportunity to file these motions, RJR made a smart tactical move. RJR gambled that the District Court would grant the motions, which would either cause the EC to quit right then or file an appeal. In either situation, RJR would win something. If the motion was granted, RJR might be able to walk away right then, untouched, except, of course, for attorneys' fees. However, even if the EC appealed, RJR won valuable time to prepare its case. Also recall that the need to appeal may frustrate the EC and eventually cause them to make a strategic error, like the one described earlier in the Opening Case, Round 3. RJR's gamble paid off. Both motions were granted by the district court and, while the EC did appeal, RJR got the time it wanted. Take away two lessons here. The case began in 2001, and based on RJR's two motions, the case moved upward, all the way to the U.S. Supreme Court, but it has not moved forward. It has been, in effect, stalled at the pretrial stage for 16 years. Moreover, as we saw earlier, the latest ruling by Supreme Court has cast doubt on whether the EC can recover any damages. In a case like this, the defendant's primary strategy is to delay, delay, delay. Since the Supreme Court has sent the case back to the district court where it started a decade and a half ago, RJR seems to have succeeded, at least so far. [See: *The European Community (EC) v. RJR Nabisco, Inc. (RJR)*, 579 U.S. ----- (2016); *The European Community (EC) v. RJR Nabisco, Inc. (RJR)*, U.S. Court of Appeals, Second Circuit, Docket No. 11-2475-cv. (April 23, 2014); and Amy Howe, "Opinion Analysis: In the End RJR Prevails in European Community's RICO Lawsuit," SCOTUSblog, June 20, 2016, http://scotusblog.com/2016/06/opinion-analysis-in-the-end-rjr-prevails-in-european-communitys-rico-lawsuit/.]

Source: See: *The European Community (EC) v. RJR Nabisco, Inc. (RJR)*, 579 U.S. ----- (2016); *The European Community (EC) v. RJR Nabisco, Inc. (RJR)*, United States Court of Appeals, Second Circuit, Docket No. 11-2475-cv. (April 23, 2014); Amy Howe, "Opinion analysis: In the end RJR prevails in European Community's RICO lawsuit", *SCOTUSblog* (June 20, 2016), http://scotusblog.com/2016/06/opinion-analysis-in-the-end-rjr-prevails-in-european-communitys-rico-lawsuit/.

The defendant's answer may also contain counterclaims and cross-claims. A *counterclaim* is a claim that a defendant has against a plaintiff. A *cross-claim* is a claim filed by a defendant against another defendant in the same case. At this time, a defendant may also wish to file a *third-party complaint*, which is a complaint filed by the defendant against a third party not yet named in the lawsuit.

The Pretrial Stage

After the answer has been filed, the parties must await trial. During this waiting period, cleverly dubbed the pretrial stage, several activities can be carried out, including the pretrial conference, discovery, and the filing of pretrial motions.

Pretrial Conference Some courts require cases to go to a pretrial conference after the complaint and the answer have been filed. A pretrial conference usually has two purposes.

One is to discuss the possibility of settling the case without the need for a trial. Another is to decide on the details involved in bringing the case to trial. Such a conference is generally called a *case management conference*. Issues that might be discussed at a case management conference include the way that the parties will conduct discovery or the need to place a limit on the number of expert witnesses that will be called at trial.

EXAMPLE 3-4: Frankenstein in the Federal Circuit

The Alice Corporation initiated a cause of action against the CLS Bank for patent infringement because CLS was using four Alice patents without permission or payment. When the case arrived in the District Court of the District of Columbia, the attorneys representing CLS filed a motion for a summary judgment. A summary judgment motion asks the court for a speedy judgment for the party filing the motion. This motion is filed when there is no genuine issue as to any material fact, and the party filing the motion is entitled by law to a favorable judgment. The motion must be supported by a brief that sets forth the legal arguments supporting the claim, along with applicable supporting evidence. So in this case, CLS admits it used the programs specified, it did not ask permission, and it has made no payments just as Alice has claimed. Those are the material facts (here, "material" means of "central importance"), and CLS does not deny them. In fact, when deciding the summary judgment motion, the court will examine the facts in a light that is favorable to the party that did not file the motion in question.

However—and here is the catch—despite this situation, or perhaps because of it, when the law is applied to the facts as stated, CLS contends that as a matter of law, it is entitled to a favorable judgment. The "matter of law" to which CLS refers in the motion is the patentability of the Alice programs. CLS says that those programs are abstract ideas and cannot be patented and so, once again, quite simply, no patent, no patent infringement. The district court agreed and granted the CLS summary judgment motion. Once a summary judgment motion is granted, it ends the case just as if that case had gone to trial. However, once such an order is issued, that order can appealed. That is how the case reached the Court of Appeals for the Federal Circuit, where all the fun began. So, as sometimes happens, this case will end up in the U.S. Supreme Court without ever going to trial. [See: *CLS Bank International v. Alice Corporation Pty. Ltd.*, No. 2011-130, U.S. Court of Appeals for the Federal Circuit (May 10, 2013); and "Difference Engine: Stalking Trolls," *The Economist Technology Quarterly*, March 8, 2014, p. 14.]

Source: See: *CLS Bank International v. Alice Corporation Pty. Ltd.*, No. 2011-130, United States Court of Appeals for the Federal Circuit (May 10, 2013); "Difference Engine: Stalking Trolls," *The Economist Technology Quarterly*, March 8, 2014, p. 14.

Pretrial Motions Several motions may be filed during the pretrial stage. One motion available at this time is a motion for summary judgment. A **summary judgment motion** asks the court for an immediate judgment for the party filing the motion. This motion is filed when there is no genuine issue as to any material fact, and the party filing the motion is entitled by law to a favorable judgment. The motion cannot be filed without supporting legal arguments written out in a brief and accompanied by applicable supporting evidence.

Discovery **Discovery** is the process by which the parties to a civil action search for information that is relevant to the case. The objective is to simplify the issues and avoid unnecessary arguments and surprises in the subsequent trial. Discovery techniques and tools include the following:

Depositions are oral statements made out of court under oath by witnesses or parties to the action in response to questions from the opposing attorneys. The answers are recorded by a court stenographer and can be used for later reference.

Interrogatories are written questions that must be answered in writing under oath by the opposite party. Interrogatories cannot be given to witnesses. Only plaintiffs and defendants can be required to answer interrogatories.

Requests for real evidence ask a party to produce documents, records, accounts, correspondence, photographs, or other tangible evidence. The request may also seek permission to inspect land.

Requests for physical or mental examination ask a party to undergo a physical or a mental examination. Such requests can be made only if the physical or the mental condition of the party is in controversy; it must be a central concern to the lawsuit.

Requests for admissions are made to secure a statement from a party that a particular fact is true or that a document or set of documents is genuine. An admission eliminates the need to demonstrate the truthfulness of the fact or the genuineness of the documents at trial.

Changes in the Scope of Discovery
The federal rules regarding discovery were amended recently to help control the amount of information gathering that is conducted by both sides in civil cases. Rule 26 of the Federal Rules of Civil Procedure now includes a more detailed explanation of what is allowed within the scope of discovery. The rule now reads as follows:

> Parties may obtain discovery regarding any nonprivileged matter that is relevant to any party's claim or defense and *proportional* to the *needs of the case*, considering the *importance of the issues at stake* in the action, the *amount in controversy*, the parties' relative *access* to relevant information, the parties' *resources*, the importance of the discovery in *resolving* the issues, and whether the *burden or expense of the proposed discovery outweighs its likely benefit*. Information within this scope of discovery need not be admissible in evidence to be discoverable. [See: Federal Rules of Civil Procedure, Discovery Scope and Limits, Rule 26(b)(1).]

These adjustments to Rule 26(b)(1) limit the process of discovery to a search for relevant evidence that has a genuine connection to the real issues involved in the lawsuit. Basically, the changes acknowledge the fact that the plaintiff is the party who must make most of the requests and who has very little control over the information required. Thus, the plaintiff's tendency is to ask for as much information as possible, regardless of its actual connection to the case. The defendants, on the other hand, are often tempted to either hold back as many documents as they can or to inundate the opposing parties with more information than they can handle in a lifetime or two. By requiring discovery requests to be (1) narrowed to important issues that are actually at stake in the case and (2) that are proportional to the amount of damages, the new rule forces the parties to cooperate even when they would rather not. Thus, for example, if the amount in controversy is $100,000, and the plaintiff is an employer in a wrongful discharge case, the plaintiff ought not to ask for a record of every firing that has taken place over the entire history of the company extending back 110 years, to the tune of $200,000 in expenses. Such a request is sure to be denied by the judge in the case [See: Kera Paoff and Stephen Beiting, "Discover This! Rule 26 and Employment Law Cases," Ohio State Bar Association, Online CLE, July 2017.]

The Civil Trial

Upon completion of discovery, the pretrial conference, and any hearings held on pretrial motions, the case is ready for trial. A trial by jury is an adversarial proceeding in which the judge's role is secondary to that of the jury's. Competition between attorneys permits the jury to sort out the truth and arrive at a just solution to the dispute.

Did You Know?

The single most important step in a trial is the opening statement. Studies have indicated that 80–90 percent of all jurors have made up their minds by the end of the opening statements. Although jurors may change their minds, the attorney who loses the battle of the opening statements frequently has an uphill battle to convince the jury of the validity of his or her client's position.

Prospective jurors may be selected or rejected based on their ability to render an impartial judgment.
©Fuse/Getty Images

Jury Selection
Once it is decided that the case will involve a jury, the process of *voir dire* ("to speak the truth") begins. In this process, the lawyers for both parties question prospective jurors to determine whether they will be allowed to sit on the jury. Prospective jurors may be rejected if they are unable to render an impartial judgment. One reason for rejecting a prospective juror is if he or she had a personal relationship with the litigant or with a witness. Prospective jurors may also be rejected if they have a financial interest in the outcome of the trial; however, the financial interest must be a direct, substantial interest. Remote financial interests in a trial will not disqualify a juror. Thus, the fact that the outcome of a trial may result in higher insurance rates would not disqualify a juror who has an insurance policy. Another reason might be if the prospective juror has had past experience that would prevent him or her from being impartial in the present case. Thus, a juror who has had a bad experience with a psychologist, for instance, might be unable to judge impartially the actions of a psychologist who has been sued for malpractice.

In most lawsuits, *voir dire* is conducted in the open, which means that the process is generally accessible to the press and the mass media. However, in cases that have attracted a lot of public attention, the judge may order that the media's access to the *voir dire* process be limited. Often, news reporters will be limited to reading abridged copies of the transcript of the *voir dire* process after the process has been completed. The names of the jurors may also be censored, along with personal data about those jurors. This limit on the access to *voir dire* usually occurs in notorious criminal trials, but it could also happen in high-profile civil lawsuits. Should an impartial jury be unattainable in a certain case, the defendant's attorney can file a motion to transfer the case to another district.

Opening Statements
At the beginning of the trial, both attorneys have the opportunity to make an opening statement. In the *opening statement*, an attorney presents the facts in the case and explains what he or she intends to show during the trial. Attorneys are not permitted to argue their case in the opening statement. There is widespread disagreement, however, as to what constitutes "arguing the case" during the opening statement. Consequently, the degree of argument permitted during the opening statement often depends on what the judge will allow. Attorneys must also be very careful about the facts that they include in the opening statement because such facts may later be held to be admissions before the court. Such admissions may not do any damage, but it is better to not take the risk. A "fact" carelessly dropped into the opening statement that contradicts testimony or other evidence presented later in the trial may place the attorney in the uncomfortable position of having to explain that contradiction. Conversely, each attorney should play close attention to the other attorney's opening statement just in case one of those troublesome contradictions appear, providing leverage that can be used later in the trial.

The Plaintiff's Case in Chief
The plaintiff's **case in chief** is the plaintiff's opportunity to present evidence that will prove his or her version of the case to the jury. The plaintiff's attorney calls witnesses and immediately subjects those witnesses to **direct examination**. Direct examination is designed to present the facts that will support the plaintiff's version of those facts. Opposing attorneys then have the chance to challenge the truthfulness of each piece of evidence presented. In this process of **cross-examination**, the witnesses answer questions of the defense attorney.

The Defendant's Case in Chief After the plaintiff has ended the presentation of his or her case in chief, the defendant has the opportunity to present his or her case in chief. The defendant's attorney calls witnesses for direct examination, and the plaintiff's attorney has an opportunity to cross-examine the defendant's witnesses.

The Rebuttal and the Surrebuttal Once the plaintiff and the defendant have presented their cases in chief, each attorney may present evidence to discredit the evidence presented by the opposition and reestablish the credibility of his or her own evidence. This step is called the **rebuttal**. The term **surrebuttal** is used in some states when referring to the defendant's rebuttal.

Closing Statements After the rebuttals are completed, each attorney makes a closing statement. In this statement, the attorneys emphasize aspects of the testimony and other evidence they believe will best persuade the judge or jury.

Jury Instructions Because juries comprise many people who are not familiar with particular aspects of the law, someone must explain the law to the jury. This is one of the duties of the judge. Although the attorneys may suggest to the judge what instructions ought to be used, the judge makes the decision. The judge's instructions explain the rules of law that the jurors are to apply to the facts in reaching their decision.

Verdict and Judgment After receiving the judge's instructions, the members of the jury retire to a private room, where they apply the rules stated by the judge to the evidence presented by the witnesses. If the jury cannot reach a verdict, the judge will declare a mistrial. In federal court, the jury's decision must be unanimous. Many state courts do not require a unanimous jury decision in a civil trial. Ohio, for example, requires only that three-fourths of the jurors comply. Other grounds for a mistrial include the death of a major participant in the trial such as the judge, one of the jurors, or one of the attorneys; misconduct on the part of a juror; wrongdoing during the *voir dire* process that later comes to light; and misconduct during the trial that is found to prejudice the jury. Once the judge has granted a motion for a mistrial, the plaintiff is permitted to bring the case to trial again. Most of the time, however, there is no misconduct or wrongdoing before or during the trial, and so the jury does, in fact, reach a verdict.

A **verdict** is a finding of fact. The verdict may be limited to the question of liability, or it can be extended to include the issue of damages. **Liability** means that the defendant is held legally responsible for his or her actions. The term **damages** refers to the money recovered by the plaintiff for the injury or loss caused by the defendant. The verdict is entered by the judge in the court records, and the case is said to be decided. According to the terms of the judgment, the defeated party either is required to pay the amount specified or do a specific thing, such as perform the terms of the contract. Court costs are usually paid by the losing party. If the jury is unable to reach a unanimous verdict, the judge can declare a mistrial.

In some cases, money will not be adequate to satisfy the plaintiff. In such cases, the plaintiff may seek an equitable remedy. An **equitable remedy** requires a party to do something or to refrain from doing something beyond the payment of money. One equitable remedy is **specific performance**, which would require a party to a contract to go through with the terms of the contract. Usually, specific performance is permitted only in cases involving real estate or unique, one-of-a-kind goods such as art objects or rare antiques. Another equitable remedy is an injunction. An **injunction** stops a party from doing something. For instance, an employer may seek an injunction against a former employee to prevent that employee from using a trade secret on his or her new job if that trade secret is the property of the original employer.

A QUESTION OF ETHICS

Televised Trials: Threat or Transformation

In California, Proposition 8 was placed on the ballot in order to outlaw same-sex marriages. The legality of the proposition was challenged in the federal trial court in the Northern District of California. Noting the great interest in the case and recognizing its social and political significance, the presiding judge suggested televising the trial at least within the courthouse in San Francisco where the trial was located. Later the judge, in consultation with the Chief Judge of the Ninth Circuit, suggested widening the broadcast field to include all courthouses in the Ninth Circuit. Those who supported the proposition opposed the plan to televise the trial and attempted to get a *writ of mandamus* to prevent the broadcast. The Ninth Circuit denied the *writ*, but the U.S. Supreme Court reversed the decision and stopped the broadcast indefinitely. The Supreme Court stated that it suspended the broadcast to protect witnesses who might otherwise be threatened or harassed. The ethical issue here is not the morality of Proposition 8. Rather, the question is whether a trial of this transformative significance should be broadcast or "gagged" as the Supreme Court ruled. Using both utilitarianism and rational ethics (See Chapter 1), analyze the decision made by the U.S. Supreme Court and decide whether the Supreme Court's decision can be defended using either theory. Explain your rationale using each theory. [See: David R. Fine, "Television Trials," *The National Law Journal*, January 25, 2010, p. 38.]

The Appeal

An **appeal** is the referral of a case to a higher court for review. For an appeal to be successful, it must be shown that some legal error occurred. For example, a party could argue that some of the evidence that was admitted should have been excluded or that evidence that was not allowed should have been allowed. A party could also argue that the judge's instructions were erroneous or were stated in an inappropriate manner. Generally, an appeal is filed by the party that lost the case in the trial court; however, it is also possible that the party that prevailed at trial may wish to file an appeal. This step is referred to as a **cross-appeal**. For instance, if the trial court upheld most of the claims made by the plaintiff but denied one or two key claims, the plaintiff may wish to file a cross-appeal. It may also be advisable to file a cross-appeal if the trial court did not award the appropriate amount in damages, if it refused to grant attorney's fees, or if it allowed money damages but refused to permit equitable relief. [See: Aaron S. Bayer, "Appellate Law: The Cross-Appeal," *The National Law Journal*, February 9, 2004, p. 13.]

Execution of the Judgment

In civil cases, if the judgment is not paid, the court will order the loser's property to be sold by the sheriff to satisfy the judgment. This order by the court is known as a **writ of execution**. Any excess from the sale must be returned to the loser. Execution of the judgment also may be issued against any income due to the loser, such as wages, salaries, or dividends. This process is known as execution against income, or garnishment, and the proceedings are known as garnishee proceedings. Checking accounts are also subject to garnishment.

quick quiz 3-2

1. In state court, a complaint must include a statement of jurisdiction.   true | false
2. The defendants' answer must not include either counterclaims or cross-claims.   true | false
3. *Voir dire* must always be open to the press.   true | false

3-3 Cyber-Procedure

The world of litigation has changed dramatically because of the electronic revolution. Gone are the days when litigators could wait until the last minute to conduct discovery prior to trial because they could see the limited number of paper documents sitting in a neat pile on their desks. Also gone are the days when attorney–client privilege could be protected by simply closing the office door. Electronically stored data comes in so many different formats (e-mail, texting, Facebook, LinkedIn, voicemail, spreadsheets, instant messages, databases, and so on) and is stored in so many different electronic devices (laptops, mobile phones, Kindles, GPS units, PDAs, desktop PCs, fax machines, scanners, smartphones, copiers, printers, Androids, iPads, Fitbits, iPhones, drones, and so on) that litigators have to get the jump on the process from the first moment that a lawsuit is threatened. Add to that the fact that many courts now expect—and some even require—the electronic filing of documents, and it becomes obvious that lawyers, paralegals, and businesspeople cannot ignore the electronic age even if they want to.

Cyber-Jurisdiction

Whether courts have jurisdiction over out-of-state defendants has been complicated by the electronic age. Previously, back in the age of face-to-face, U.S. mail, and over-the-phone transactions, it was fairly obvious where a corporation or an institution had its principal place of business. Of course, exactly what was meant by "principal place of business" might be at issue, but at least everyone knew the alternative sites available. Doing business on the Internet complicates all of this. Using the Internet, sellers can solicit business on their website, negotiate and enter a contract using "the point-and-click method," receive payment using PayPal, and deliver goods via FedEx or UPS without leaving the comfort of their home office and without revealing where the sellers are located, how the goods were obtained, where they were stored, and how they were transported and delivered to the seller before being loaded on a FedEx or UPS truck.

Does the type of activity described earlier reach the level of minimum contacts needed to establish personal jurisdiction? Should the minimum contacts standard be replaced by the New Jersey stream of commerce standard for electronic buying and selling? **Cyber-jurisdiction** (i.e., **electronic jurisdiction** and **e-jurisdiction**) is the power of the court to hear a case based on Internet-related transactions. While this area of the law is still in its adolescence, we can, nevertheless, extract at least one general principle: Because of its complex nature, cyber-jurisdiction is a moving target. To help attorneys, paralegals, and businesspeople hit this moving target, the courts have established a sliding scale on which several types of jurisdiction can be measured.

On one side of the scale are business transactions that are carried out from beginning to end using the Internet. These would include operations that are run like those engineered by Amazon.com and eBay. Transactions that involve solicitation, negotiation, finalization, payment, and shipping arrangements exclusively on the Internet establish the minimum contacts needed for the state of the buyer. Moreover, if a case involves product liability, the type of transaction described earlier would satisfy New Jersey's stream of commerce standard. Of course, it is possible for the seller to specify the state that will serve as the forum for settling any dispute that arises from the contract. Still, such stipulations can always be challenged if the matter actually gets to court.

On the other side of the sliding scale are those cases in which the defendant simply placed an inactive advertisement on the Internet. Such inactive

Cyber-transactions must be handled on a case-by-case basis.
©Antonio M. Rosario/Getty Images

advertisements will not usually establish jurisdiction under the minimum contacts test or the New Jersey stream of commerce test. The final type of transaction falls between the two extremes. These cases include cyber-transactions that involve more than simply placing an advertisement on the Internet. The courts have not established any single normative approach to such transactions, so the matter must be handled on a case-by-case basis.

Cyber-Filing

The federal court system officially joined the 21st century when it added a provision to the Federal Rules of Civil Procedure that permits lawyers to file court documents electronically. Moreover, under Rule 5(3), the courts can even go so far as to require that documents be filed electronically, as long as the court also accepts reasonable exceptions from those unable to comply with the new provision. Those federal courts that have adopted the new

A CLASSIC CASE "It Is Alive!" Or Is It a Moving Target?

In the case *of Diamond v. Chakrabarty*, the U.S. Supreme Court decided that it was possible to patent a life-form. As is often the case in sensitive issues like this, no one was happy with the Court's decision except, perhaps, the new patent holder. Some experts felt compelled to criticize the Supreme Court for stepping outside the bounds of its authority. Others accused the Court of a thoughtless ruling that would open the door to the abusive use of biotechnology. However, one of the most interesting points was made when a commentator noted that it was strange that the Supreme Court was willing to grant a patent for a new life-form when, in a previous case, the case of *Roe v. Wade*, the court had refused to define life. Is it ethical, or even logical, for the justices of the Supreme Court to avoid the definition of life when it comes to the rights of women and then turn around and permit a megacorporation, like General Electric, to reap potential profit from the decision? (Note: The microbiologist who developed the DNA plasmid that was the subject of *Diamond v. Chakrabarty* was employed by General Electric.) Think about it and try to come up with a rationale for each side of the issue.

Once you have done this, think about the same type of sliding scale that the Federal Circuit used in the case of *CLS Bank International v. Alice Corporation*. In that case, the Federal Circuit, sitting *en banc*, decided that a computer program, which is, in essence, an abstract idea, can be patented. Luckily, for the sake of continuity and *stare decisis*, the United States Supreme Court reversed that decision. The Supreme Court, then, in one quick decision, brought us safely back to square one, that is, back to the principle that states that abstract ideas are not patentable. Still, for a brief but not insignificant moment, uncertainty reigned in the courts over the patentability of abstract ideas.

Unfortunately, this type of uncertainty, in relation to technology, is here to stay. Moreover, legal uncertainty in relation to technology also plagues procedural law. This problem is covered at length in the section on cyber-jurisdiction. It seems that computer technology has robbed the doctrine of jurisdiction of its traditional predictability. As noted earlier, while computer law is still in its adolescence, we can, nevertheless, extract at least one general principle from its very nature: Because of the complex nature of computer law, cyber-jurisdiction is a moving target. It might be good to take a cue from this finding and generalize the rule so that it looks like this: Due to the complex nature of technology and the law, whenever the two intersect, overlap, or just pass each other at a distance, the result will be a moving target! [See: *Diamond v. Chakrabarty*, 447 U.S 303, 100 S.Ct. 204 (1980); *Roe v. Wade*, 410 U.S. 113, 93 S.Ct. 705 (1973); *CLS Bank International v. Alice Corporation Pty. Ltd*., No. 2011-130, U.S. Court of Appeals for the Federal Circuit (May 10, 2013); and "Difference Engine: Stalking Trolls," *The Economist Technology Quarterly*, March 8, 2014, p. 14.]

Source: See: *Diamond v. Chakrabarty*, 447 U.S 303, 100 S.Ct. 204 (1980); *Roe V. Wade*, 410 U.S. 113, 93 S.Ct. 705 (1973); *Alice Corp. v. CLS Bank International*, 573 U.S. ___, 134 S. Ct. 2347 (2014); *CLS Bank International v. Alice Corporation Pty. Ltd.*, No. 2011-130, United States Court of Appeals for the Federal Circuit (May 10, 2013); and "Difference Engine: Stalking Trolls," *The Economist Technology Quarterly,* March 8, 2014, p. 14.

procedure have found that *cyber-filing* (electronic filing or e-filing) is more cost effective and efficient than paper filing. Because some of the electronic systems used to keep track of court documents are accessible on the Internet, papers are no longer lost or misplaced as often as they once were. The Internet filing network also permits people to access the papers at their own convenience. This is an important feature of the electronic system because, once a party has been served properly, that party is sent a notice whenever a new document is filed electronically with the court. This eliminates the old-fashioned and time-consuming process of filing a formal notice with each party.

Still, cyber-filing does have its disadvantages. Not every law firm is properly equipped for cyber-filing, so the courts must maintain a dual filing system to accommodate "cyber-challenged" firms. Moreover, just because a firm is electronically up to date does not guarantee that its attorneys are cyber-savvy. Consequently, many courts have been forced to provide training and ongoing assistance to these attorneys at the court's expense. Also, from the attorney's perspective, since cyber-filing process is controlled by local rules, learning one set of electronic rules is rarely enough. Instead, the attorney must learn the rules for every court in which he or she does regular business. Fortunately, however, there are consistent features in these rules from one court to the next and so a diligent and conscientious attorney can survive as long as he or she is willing to be flexible.

Cyber-Discovery

The discovery process is one of the most costly and time-consuming steps in a lawsuit. As noted previously, discovery is the process by which the parties to a civil action search for information that is relevant to the case. While the goal and the philosophy behind discovery have not changed since American litigation began, the process of identifying, categorizing, evaluating, saving, and using the evidence has gone through some radical changes over the past two decades, thanks to the revolution in electronic evidence. As the use of e-evidence began to creep into the law, many attorneys were satisfied to just ignore the changes or, more frequently, to treat e-evidence as if it were just another type of paper evidence. This is no longer possible. In fact, the time is rapidly coming when attorneys who do not keep up with changes in technology may be found liable for malpractice. Once upon a time, clients hoped that their attorney would be electronically literate. Now they not only expect it, but they also demand it.

Electronically Stored Information For the sake of consistency and to prevent confusion, computerized evidence has been officially designated as **electronically stored information (ESI)**. Simply changing the name, however, does not solve the unexpected problems that have emerged because of the special nature of ESI. For example, ESI is embedded in many diverse and mysterious formats, making its retrieval difficult for most attorneys. As a result, attorneys must pay close attention to all aspects of ESI, including its preservation, storage, and communication. Attorneys who are not careful may inadvertently turn over privileged information to their opponents and not discover the error until it is too late. Fortunately, most state bar associations run continuing education seminars and annual legal conferences to help attorneys and judges keep current with these matters. The Federal Rules of Civil Procedure and most state procedural rules have also have been amended to make e-discovery more manageable.

These changes were designed to alter the behavior of attorneys so that they adjust to the peculiar characteristics of ESI. First, the rules now force attorneys to get an early start on all discovery plans or they will be unable to comply with the time limits built into the rules. Second, attorneys must now deal with the question of which electronic format will be used to request and deliver data. Third, attorneys can rest assured that the rules provide several ways to deal with those problems that arise with ESI and privilege. Fourth, attorneys can use the rules to help in the recovery of ESI that might otherwise be difficult to find. Fifth, to deal with the expenses that are involved in the identification and collection of ESI, attorneys can now refer to provisions in the rules that guarantee a fair apportionment of these expenses. Finally, attorneys can also be certain that everyone will cooperate with the new electronic discovery process because the rules have provided severe penalties for those who ignore or disobey the new ESI discovery rules.

The Discovery Protocols Pilot Project The Judicial Conference Advisory Committee on Civil Rules (Advisory Committee), which operates under the authority of the Federal Judicial Center, has introduced an innovative set of protocols aimed at simplifying and economizing the discovery process in federal employment law cases. The protocols apply only to certain employment-related lawsuits and then only to those district courts and judges that agreed to be involved in the project. The protocols themselves are grounded on three basic beliefs: (1) that the rules of discovery work best when they are adapted to certain set cases; (2) that discovery is much more efficient and economical when practitioners have no choice but to release key documents at designated times; and (3) that the litigation process works best when it starts early because an early assessment of the case, fueled by information revealed during the discovery process, can lead to earlier settlement discussions. Since the same types of records are used in most employment cases—employment manuals, employment contracts, disciplinary records, weekly work schedules, time cards, and so on—employment law seemed to be the perfect choice for this project. [See: Robert A. Steinberg, "Historical Origins of the Initial Discovery Protocols Pilot Project for Employment Cases," The Ohio State Bar Association: 2013 Annual Convention, May 10, 2013, pp. 55–56. See also: "Pilot Program Introduces Protocols for Employment Cases," *The Third Branch News*, February 2012; *Pilot Project Regarding Initial Discovery Protocols for Employment Cases Alleging Adverse Action*, The Judicial Conference Advisory Committee on Civil Rules, November 2011; and Kevin Carlson, "The Use of Initial Discovery Protocols for Employment Cases Alleging Adverse Reactions," *The Federal Lawyer*, January/February 2014.]

Update on the Pilot Project Four years into the pilot project, the Judicial Advisory Committee asked the Federal Judicial Center (FJC) to conduct a study of the program. Accordingly, the FJC examined close to 500 cases that had been involved in the protocols beginning in 2011. The study examined case processing times, case results, discovery processes used, settlement negotiations, types and numbers of motions filed, and so on. These pilot cases were then compared and contrasted to a series of similar cases, dubbed comparison cases, held outside of the pilot protocols. The results look like this: (1) Case processing times were unaffected by being part of the pilot project; (2) discovery motions were cut by 50 percent in the pilot cases; (3) pilot cases were rarely involved in motions to dismiss and summary judgment motions; (4) overall, fewer motions were filed in the pilot cases when matched to the comparison cases; and (5) settlements were reached more often in the pilot cases than in the comparison cases.

Overall Conclusions on the Pilot Project Discovery times and expenses for the pilot cases were reduced when lined up with times and expenses in the comparison cases. One of the predictions at the start of the project was that early assessment of the cases might lead to earlier settlement discussions. Because there were more settlements recorded in the pilot cases, this prediction turns out to be somewhat vindicated. However, settlements in the pilot cases did not occur any faster than those in the comparison cases. The report also noted that it was not always possible to confirm that the attorneys in these cases actually followed protocol deadlines as specified in the rules. In fact, settlement negotiations in the pilot cases may actually have delayed the exchange of evidentiary files while negotiations continued. Finally, so many random factors are involved in the process—factors such as individual judicial habits and local rule variants—that there is no way to be certain that the protocols actually led to these differences. It would seem that more research is needed to confirm the effectiveness of the protocols. [See: Emery G. Lee III and Jason A. Cantone, "Report on Pilot Project Regarding Initial Discovery Protocols for Employment Cases Alleging Adverse Action," Federal Judical Center, October 2015, http://www.fjc.gov/sites/default/files/2016/Discovery%20Protocols%20Employment.pdf.]

quick quiz 3-3

1. Cyber-jurisdiction is the power of the court to hear a case based on Internet-related transactions. true | false
2. The Federal Rules of Civil Procedure do not permit lawyers to file court documents electronically. true | false
3. The Federal Rules now refer to cyber-evidence as data compilations. true | false

3-4 Criminal Procedure

The objectives of a criminal prosecution are to protect society and to punish the wrongdoer by a fine or imprisonment. The steps in a criminal prosecution include the following:

- Arrest and initial appearance.
- Preliminary hearing.
- Formal charges.
- Arraignment.
- Trial.

The Arrest and Initial Appearance

A crime is an offense against the people. Once a law enforcement agency learns that a crime has been committed, the agency begins a criminal prosecution. The first step in a criminal prosecution is to gather evidence of the crime and identify all possible suspects. When the law enforcement agency is convinced that it has ample evidence of both the crime and the identity of the suspect, an arrest warrant is issued, and the suspect is arrested. The arrest warrant must be based on evidence that is gathered legally and, therefore, not the result of an illegal search or seizure that would violate the Fourth Amendment. If the evidence that serves as the basis for an arrest has been gathered illegally, then all evidence that flows from that illegal search and seizure will be suppressed by the court. This is called the **exclusionary rule**. The evidence gathered as a result of the illegal search is not admissible, hence it is referred to as the **fruit of the poisonous tree**.

One exception to the exclusionary rule is the attenuation doctrine. Under the **attenuation doctrine**, if a set of legally valid events intervenes between the unlawful search and the discovery of evidence, the exclusionary rule has not been violated and, because there is no poisonous tree, there can be no poisonous fruit. Two additional exceptions are the independent source doctrine and the inevitable discovery rule. Under the **independent source rule**, evidence discovered after the illegal search and separate from its operation, is admissible. Similarly, under the **inevitable discovery doctrine**, evidence that would have been discovered despite the illegal search is also admissible.

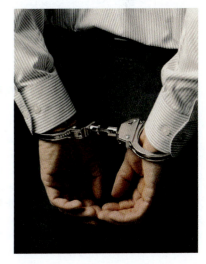

Defendants must be informed of their rights at the time of arrest. Two important rights are the right to representation by counsel and the right to remain silent.
©Photodisc/Getty Images

Another of the principal rights of the accused is the right to be represented by counsel. This right is guaranteed by the Sixth Amendment to the Constitution. Another important right is the right to remain silent, protected under the Fifth Amendment, which states that a criminal defendant cannot be compelled to be a witness against him- or herself. The U.S. Supreme Court has ruled that the 14th Amendment to the Constitution requires that both the right to remain silent and the right to representation by counsel must also be protected by state governments. The defendant is then brought before a judge or a magistrate for an initial appearance, where once again the defendant is reminded of his or her rights. At this time, a preliminary hearing is also scheduled.

The Preliminary Hearing

A **preliminary hearing** is a court procedure during which the judge decides whether probable cause exists to continue holding the defendant for the crime. The government is represented by an attorney called the **prosecutor**. In some states, this government official is called the district attorney. During the preliminary hearing, the prosecution and the defendant are permitted to make arguments and call witnesses. The case will move on to the next step if there is probable cause to hold the defendant. If not, the defendant is set free.

The Formal Charges

In the United States, formal charges against the defendant may be brought either by indictment or by information. Some states do not have a grand jury system and therefore can bring formal charges only by an information. In those states that use both, the indictment is usually used to bring formal charges for serious crimes.

A QUESTION OF ETHICS

Reading Rights: What Is Right and What Is Wrong?

Edward McDonough, assistant district attorney for the city of Middletown, has just left a session with Harold Harrison, a criminal defendant accused of armed robbery. During the session, acting under the advice of Jennifer Miller, his attorney, Harrison confessed to the crime and entered a plea bargain agreement that will place him in prison for 10 years. On his way back across the city square to his office, ADA McDonough is stopped by Sgt. Anne Wade, who confesses to him that neither she nor her partner, Sgt. Sam Newton, read Harrison his rights. McDonough knows that this admission means that the confession he just obtained is tainted and would be thrown out of court if it were challenged by Miller on behalf of Harrison. From an ethical point of view, what action should McDonough take now?

An Indictment The federal courts and many state courts bring formal charges against the defendant by issuing an indictment. An **indictment** is a set of formal charges against a defendant issued by a grand jury. A *grand jury* consists of citizens who serve as jurors for a specified period of time to review a variety of criminal cases. The objective of a grand jury review is to determine whether probable cause exists to believe that a crime has been committed and that this particular defendant may have committed the crime. Grand jury proceedings are held in secret and are directed by the prosecutor or district attorney. If the grand jury finds probable cause exists, an indictment is issued.

An Information An **information** is a set of formal charges against a defendant drawn up and issued by the prosecutor or district attorney. No grand jury is involved in this process.

Nevertheless, an information does the same thing that an indictment does. If the prosecutor has found that probable cause exists to indicate that a crime has been committed and that this particular defendant committed the crime, an information is issued.

The Arraignment

The **arraignment** is a formal court proceeding, during which the defendant, after hearing the indictment or information read, pleads either guilty or not guilty. Should the defendant enter a guilty plea, a sentence may be imposed immediately. If the defendant enters a plea of not guilty, the case moves on to the trial.

The Criminal Trial

If the defendant has requested a jury trial, a jury is selected. The jury must, of course, consist of an impartial, unbiased jurors. As is true in a civil trial, the first step in a trial is to seat a jury by going through the process of *voir dire*. As sometimes happens in a civil trial, in a criminal trial an impartial jury may be unattainable in the district in which the case was first filed. Often this happens because the press has given a certain case an enormous amount of attention. When it is not possible to seat an impartial jury in a criminal case, the defendant's attorney can file a motion to transfer the case to another district. In a federal criminal trial, in order to succeed in this motion, the defense must convince the judge that, "so great a prejudice against the defendant exists in the transferring district that the defendant cannot obtain a fair and impartial trial there." Most states use a similar standard. [See: Federal Rules of Criminal Procedure, Rule 21(a), Transfer for Trial.]

After an impartial jury, usually consisting of 12 jurors and 6 alternates, has been seated, each side makes its opening statement. Opening statements are followed by the production of evidence by both the prosecution and the defendant. One very significant difference between a criminal trial and a civil trial is the burden of proof. In a civil trial, the plaintiff must prove his or her case by a preponderance of evidence. In contrast, in a criminal case, the defendant is presumed to be innocent, and the prosecutor must prove him or her to be guilty beyond a reasonable doubt. As is the case with civil procedure, the criminal trial is completed by the attorneys' closing statements and the judge's instructions to the jury. The jury members are then allowed to retire to deliberate and decide on a verdict. In most states, a defendant can be found guilty only by the unanimous agreement of all of the jurors. A defendant who is found not guilty is released. One who has been found guilty is then sentenced by the judge. As is true in a civil case, in a criminal trial, if the jury is unable to reach a unanimous verdict, the judge can declare a mistrial. A jury that cannot reach a unanimous decision is referred to as a "hung jury." When a mistrial has been declared by the judge, the prosecution is permitted, but not required, to retry the case.

quick quiz 3-4

1. The objectives of a criminal prosecution are to protect society and to punish the wrongdoer by a fine or imprisonment.   true | false
2. The steps in a criminal prosecution include the arrest and initial appearance, the preliminary hearing, the formal charges, the arraignment, and the trial.   true | false
3. A crime is an offense against a single individual.   true | false

Summary

3.1 Courts are judicial tribunals that meet in a regular place and apply the laws in an attempt to settle disputes fairly. The federal court system is divided into three levels: the district courts, the courts of appeals, and the U.S. Supreme Court. State systems vary in structure but often consist of several levels, including lower-level limited jurisdiction trial courts, higher-level trial courts, intermediate appellate courts, and state supreme courts.

3.2 Litigation begins when the plaintiff files a complaint with the appropriate trial court. The defendant must then be given a copy of the complaint and a summons. During the pre-answer stage, the defendant may attempt to dismiss the lawsuit by filing certain pre-answer motions. In the answer stage, the defendant will file an answer, which may contain affirmative defenses, counterclaims, and/or cross-claims. The defendant at this time may also file third-party complaints. During the pretrial stage, conferences may be held, motions may be made, and discovery conducted. The trial includes the opening statement, each side's case in chief, the opportunity for rebuttal and surrebuttal, the closing arguments, and the jury instructions. The jury then renders a verdict. Either party may appeal the case if that party believes that a legal error was made during the trial that influenced the verdict unfavorably. If a judgment is not paid, the court may issue a writ of execution.

3.3 Cyber-jurisdiction (i.e., electronic jurisdiction and e-jurisdiction) is the power of the court to hear a case based on Internet-related transactions. The Federal Rules of Civil Procedure now permit federal courts to allow—and, at times, even require—lawyers to file court documents electronically. The Federal Rules now refer to cyber-evidence as electronically stored information (ESI). The rules also now deal with special situations involving ESI and discovery.

3.4 The steps in a criminal prosecution include the arrest and initial appearance, the preliminary hearing, the formal charges, the arraignment, and the trial. At the time of the arrest, the defendant must be informed of his or her rights. Immediately following the arrest, the defendant is brought before a judge or a magistrate for an initial appearance, at which time the defendant is again reminded of his or her rights. A preliminary hearing is also scheduled. A preliminary hearing is a court procedure during which the judge will decide whether probable cause exists to continue to hold the defendant pending formal charges. Formal charges against the defendant may be brought either by indictment or by information. The arraignment is a formal court proceeding, during which the defendant pleads guilty or not guilty. The trial includes the opening statement, each side's case, the closing arguments, and the jury instructions. The jury then renders a verdict.

Key Terms

abuse of discretion, 64
affirmative defense, 74
answer, 74
appeal, 80
appellate jurisdiction, 64
arraignment, 87
attenuation doctrine, 85
case in chief, 78
civil litigation, 71
class action, 73
clearly erroneous standard, 64
complaint, 71

conglomerates, 65
courts, 63
cross-appeal, 80
cross-examination, 78
cyber-jurisdiction, 81
damages, 79
defendant, 71
demurrer, 74
depositions, 76
direct examination, 78
discovery, 76
diversity jurisdiction, 64
electronic/e-jurisdiction, 81

electronically stored information (ESI), 83
equitable remedy, 79
exclusionary rule, 85
federal question, 64
forum shopping, 73
fruit of the poisonous tree, 85
general jurisdiction, 64
independent source rule, 85
indictment, 86
inevitable discovery doctrine, 85
information, 86
injunction, 79

interrogatories, 77
jurisdiction, 64
liability, 79
MDL court, 73
minimum contacts, 66
multidisciplinary litigation (MDL), 73
original jurisdiction, 64
non-governmental organization, 65
personal jurisdiction, 64
plaintiff, 71
plenary review, 64
predicate offense, 62
preliminary hearing, 86
prosecutor, 86
rebuttal, 79
request for admissions, 77
request for a physical or mental examination, 77
request for real evidence, 77
service of process, 74
special jurisdiction, 64
specific performance, 79
stream of commerce, 67
subject matter jurisdiction, 64
summary judgment motion, 76
surrebuttal, 79
unified international institutions, 65
verdict, 79
writ of certiorari, 68
writ of execution, 80

Questions for Review and Discussion

1. What is the fundamental nature of the American court system?
2. Under what circumstances might a federal court have jurisdiction to hear a case?
3. Under what circumstances might the U.S. Supreme Court hear a case?
4. What is the structure of a typical state court system?
5. What is civil litigation?
6. What are the most common discovery techniques?
7. What is involved in an appeal?
8. How is cyber-jurisdiction determined?
9. What is electronically stored information?
10. What are the steps in a criminal prosecution?

Cases for Analysis

1. After receiving an anonymous tip about drug activity, the police set up a surveillance team to watch the house named in the tip. After noting an unusual number of people entering and leaving the house, Officer Fackell stopped Edmund Strieff, the defendant in this case, as he was leaving the house. After asking for identification, as is customary, Officer Fackwell ran a check on Strieff. As it turned out, Strieff had an outstanding arrest warrant on him about a traffic violation. Fackwell arrested Strieff based on that warrant and, during a routine search, discovered drugs and drug paraphernalia. Strieff's attorneys demanded that the evidence be suppressed as "fruit of the poisonous tree." The state argued that the drugs and the drug paraphernalia were obtained legally under the authority of a valid arrest warrant and were, therefore, admissible in this case, despite the fact that the original stopping of Strieff may have violated his rights. The trial court agreed with state as did the court of appeals. The Supreme Court of Utah had different ideas and ordered the evidence suppressed. The case ended up in the U.S. Supreme Court. Should the evidence be suppressed as the fruit of the poisonous tree? Explain. [See: *Utah v. Strieff*, 2015 Utah 2; 357 P. 3d 532 (2015).]

2. Martin Shkreli was charged in the Federal District Court in Brooklyn with wire and securities fraud. Before his trial for fraud, Shkerli had made a name for himself by increasing the price of a drug known as Daraprim, which is used to help cancer and AIDS patients. After he purchased Turing Pharmaceuticals, Shkreli raised the cost of Daraprim from $13.50 per pill to $750 per pill (that's a 5,000 percent increase, by the way!). As might be expected, the press pounced on this event, and Shkreli's name became a hot topic of conversation. In most of these conversations, Shkreli was painted as the villain. In fact, the condemnation of Shkreli became so heated that even presidential candidates Donald Trump and Hillary Clinton got into the act. She called his scheme "price gouging, pure and simple," and he called Shkreli a "spoiled brat." Consequently, when the time came for choosing a jury in the fraud case (which, by the way, had nothing at all to do with the price increase), both the prosecutors and Shkreli's attorney had a very difficult time seating an impartial jury during *voir dire*.

Most potential jurors found Shkreli to be an amoral character who was simply a bad seed. What would have happened had an impartial jury never had been in found in the territory covered by the Federal District Court of Brooklyn? What federal rule would be applied here with what outcome? Explain. [See: Ryan Grenoble, "Jury Selection for 'Pharma Bro' Martin Shkrel's Trial Proving a Problem," *The HuffPost,* http://www.huffingtonpost.com/entry/martin-shkreli-pharma-bro-jury-selection-trial_us_595133f7e4b02734df2c2583; and Stephanie Clifford, "Presumed Innocent? Shkreli Is Target of Name Calling at Jury Selection," *The New York Times,* June 27, 2017.]

3. One of the most widely known criminal trials in recent memory involved that of comedian Bill Cosby, who was accused, in that case, of a single incident of sexual assault. Jury deliberations at the end of the trial lasted for 52 hours. The time devoted to jury deliberations, 12 hours per day from Monday through Saturday morning, totaled almost as much time as the entire trial. At one point on Thursday, the jurors reported that they could not reach a verdict but returned to deliberations after being asked to do so by the judge. Yet, at the end of these lengthy discussions, no verdict could be reached. Experts speculated that the many inconsistencies in the testimony of the alleged victim may have made it difficult for the jurors to reach the "guilty beyond a reasonable doubt" standard used in criminal trials. What term is used to describe a jury that cannot reach a unanimous verdict? What happens when a jury cannot reach a unanimous verdict as happened in this case? Explain. [See: Graham Bowley, Richard-Perez-Pena, and Jon Hurdle, "Jury Deadlocked, Cosby's Sex Case Ends in Mistrial," *The New York Times,* June 18, 2017, pp. 1, 20; Sydney Embrer, "Why Couldn't the Cosby Jury Reach a Verdict? Legal Experts Offer Analysis," *The New York Times,* June 18, 2017, p. 20; and J. Weston Phippen, "A Mistrial in the Cosby Case," *The Atlantic,* June 17, 2017, http://www.theatlantic.com/news/archive/2017/mistrial-bill-cosby-case/530733.]

4. The state of Alabama was required under the provisions of its own constitution to reapportion its electoral districts every 10 years; however, the state had failed to reapportion districts for more than half a century. Since then, the population of Alabama had grown to such an extent that severe inequalities existed among the electoral districts. The inequalities were so great in some cases that the votes of citizens in some parts of the state carried as much as 10 times the weight of the votes of citizens in other parts of the state. A suit was brought in federal court on the grounds that the inequalities in voting power violated certain guarantees found in the U.S. Constitution. The defendants argued that the federal court should not interfere in what is essentially a state matter and that by doing so, it would upset the delicate balance between the states and the federal government. Nevertheless, the federal district court struck down the apportionment scheme as unconstitutional. Does this case belong in the U.S. Supreme Court? Explain the reasons for your response. Should the Supreme Court uphold or overturn the federal district court's decision? Explain. [See: *Reynolds v. Sims,* 377 U.S. 533 (U.S. Sup. Ct.).]

5. Speculate on which of the following cases the U.S. Supreme Court might decide to review: a case involving a dispute over whether computer software can be copyrighted, a case involving an appeal of a zoning board's decision to limit the number of adult book stores on any single city block, a case involving the constitutionality of an abortion statute, a case involving an antitrust suit based on a violation of a federal antitrust statute between the National Football League and a former seller of NFL sports gear, a libel case against a small town newspaper involving allegations of the mayor's dishonesty, a case involving the placement of a religious scene on city property, a case brought by a steel company to enjoin employees from going on strike, a case involving the distribution of antiwar flyers at a private shopping mall, and a case involving the search of a high school student's locker without her permission. In each case, give reasons for your answer.

6. Eight limited partners filed a lawsuit in the Lucas County Court of Common Pleas, alleging that the general partners in 10 different limited partnerships had engaged in an extensive pattern of self-dealing that had involved converting partnership property for their own personal use. Also named in the lawsuit was the accounting firm of Donald J. Goldstein, CPA, a resident of Florida, and Goldstein, Lewis, and Company, a professional corporation located in Florida. The plaintiffs claimed that the accountant and the accounting firm had known of the general partners' misconduct and were therefore liable to the plaintiff for that malpractice. The accountant and the accounting firm decided to end

the suit as quickly as possible. Consequently, they filed a motion for dismissal. The motion stated that the courts of Ohio lacked personal jurisdiction over them because they were from Florida. They further stated that they did not solicit business in Ohio, maintained no place of business in Ohio, had no license to act as accountants in Ohio, owned no property in Ohio, provided all services from Florida, and filed no documents with the state of Ohio. Thus, they concluded that they fell outside the power of Ohio's long-arm statute. Conversely, the plaintiffs argued that the defendants transacted business in the state of Ohio on a continuing and ongoing basis by regularly submitting financial statements to the limited partners in Ohio and by being actively involved in the decisions of the general partnership. Did the activities of the accountant and the accounting firm place them under the jurisdiction of the Ohio court, according to the state "long-arm" statute? Explain. [See: *Goldstein v. Christiansen*, 638 N.E.2d 541 (OH).]

7. The criminal defendant in this case, a man named Gideon, broke into a pool room in Florida with the objective of committing a minor crime. Because Gideon was without any means of financial support, he could not afford an attorney. He asked for but was denied representation by a court-appointed attorney. Consequently, he represented himself at trial. Ultimately, he was found guilty and sentenced to five years in prison. Gideon later challenged his conviction on the grounds that he had been deprived of his constitutional right to representation by an attorney. In opposition, Florida argued that, though all fundamental rights guaranteed by the federal government through the Bill of Rights should also be guaranteed by state governments, the right to legal representation was not such a fundamental right. In fact, the right to a court-appointed attorney arose only when the criminal defendant had been accused of a very serious crime. The U.S. Supreme Court agreed to hear the case. How should the Supreme Court rule in this case? Is the right to an attorney a fundamental right that should be guaranteed to criminal defendants by the states, regardless of the seriousness of the crime? Explain. Examine the Constitution and find the amendment that guarantees the right to representation by an attorney. Examine the Constitution and find the amendment that extends that right to defendants in state criminal actions. [See: *Gideon v. Wainwright*, 372 U.S. 355 (U.S. Sup. Ct.).]

8. Ernesto Miranda was arrested in his own home for a serious crime and held in an interrogation room. He was not informed of his right to remain silent, nor was he informed that he could be represented by an attorney. Eventually, after a two-hour interrogation conducted by two police officers, Miranda signed a statement that indicated he had voluntarily confessed to the crime of which he was accused. On the basis of the confession, Miranda was found guilty. He appealed to the Arizona Supreme Court, which affirmed the guilty verdict. Miranda asked the U.S. Supreme Court to hear his appeal. Is this the type of case that belongs in the U.S. Supreme Court? Explain the reasons for your response. Should the Supreme Court uphold or overturn the state court's conviction of Miranda? Explain the Constitution and find the amendment that guarantees the right to remain silent when arrested for a criminal action. Examine the Constitution and find the amendment that extends that right to defendants in state criminal actions. [See: *Miranda v. Arizona*, 384 U.S. 436 (U.S. Sup. Ct.).]

Design Elements: The Opening Case: ©Sharpstock/Alamy; A Classic Case: ©Evlakhov Valeriy/Shutterstock

quick quiz Answers

3-1	3-2	3-3	3-4
1. T	1. F	1. T	1. T
2. T	2. F	2. F	2. T
3. T	3. F	3. F	3. F

Chapter 4
Alternative Dispute Resolution and Cyber-ADR

4-1 A Briefing on ADR Strategies
Problems with Litigation • The ADR Option • Shortcomings of ADR • The Federal Arbitration Act

4-2 Responsive ADR Strategies
Mediation • Arbitration Med-Arb • Early Neutral Evaluation • Summary Jury Trials • Private Civil Trials

4-3 Proactive ADR Strategies
Partnering • ADR Contract Clauses • Settlement Week • Negotiated Rule Making • Post-Appellate Procedures • International Arbitration Agreements • The Collective Science Court Proposal

4-4 Cyber Alternative Dispute Resolution
Cyber-Negotiation • Cyber-Mediation • Cyber-Arbitration • Additional Opportunities for Cyber-ADR • The European Union's Cyber-ADR Platform

THE OPENING CASE Round 1
Considine v. Brookdale Senior Living: Is Mandatory Arbitration Really Mandatory?

Alternative dispute resolution (ADR) techniques, including such things as arbitration and mediation, have become very popular recently. ADR techniques are preferred because they keep costs down, provide quick decisions, and produce unbiased results while still keeping access to the courts open—well, maybe. Case in point: Kerry Considine was hired as a physical therapist to work at Brookdale Senior Living Inc. She was later promoted to the position of ancillary service manager. As an employee of Brookdale, Considine was entitled to health and dental care coverage under Brookdale's self-financed insurance program, which is managed by United Healthcare. The plan includes an optional provision that permits health and dental care for spouses. In 2013, Considine was married to Rene Considine and, in both October and November of that year, she asked to have her spouse added to the health care plan. Both times Brookdale administrators refused to allow Considine to add Renee to the policy. Accordingly, Considine filed a discrimination claim with the Equal Employment Opportunity Commission (EEOC), alleging that she was being discriminated against based on her gender because she was married to a same-sex spouse. She alleged that Brookdale's refusal to enroll Renee violated the Civil Rights Act of 1964, the Equal Pay Act of 1963, and the Connecticut Fair Employment Practices Act. Eventually, Considine received a right to sue letter from the EEOC and took her case directly to the U.S. District Court of Connecticut.

Interestingly enough, never in these proceedings did the Brookdale administrators deny that they had withheld health care coverage from Considine's spouse based on the fact that they were dealing with a same-sex marriage. Nevertheless, Brookdale eventually granted health and dental care to Renee. That did not stop Considine from continuing to pursue the case, however. She now argued that because Brookdale had extended health care coverage voluntarily, it could just as easily withdraw that coverage at any time. This precarious state placed her at the mercy of Brookdale's administration, which constituted a case of continuing discrimination. It was at this point that Brookdale pulled a rabbit out of its hat! Brookdale pointed out that when Considine was hired, she had signed an employment contract that included a clause that said that all employment-related disputes, including any dispute involving discrimination, would be settled by mandatory binding arbitration. Moreover—and here is the beauty of Brookdale's plan—the arbitration clause also said that any dispute over whether mandatory binding arbitration had to be used would be answered by the arbitrator. Accordingly, the case went to the arbitrator, who promptly decided that (1) the case had to be presented to an arbitrator, and (2) the discrimination charge could not stand because Considine's spouse, Renee, was already enrolled in the health and dental care, so Constantine had no remedy and the case was moot. If this sounds unfair to you, read on. Much more lays ahead. [See: *Considine v. Brookdale Senior Living, Inc*, 124 F. Supp 3d 83 (2015).]

Opening Case Questions

1. What is the difference between arbitration and mediation, and which one was used in this case? Explain.

2. Why would the parties in the original employment contract agree to the mandatory binding arbitration clause in the first place? Explain.

3. Which of the alleged advantages to mandatory binding arbitration seems to have been frustrated in this case? Explain.

4. Why did the plaintiff continue to pursue the case despite the fact that her employer had already given her what she wanted in the first place? Explain.

5. What recourse does the plaintiff have now that the arbitrator has ruled that the case has ended? Explain.

Source: See: *Considine v. Brookdale Senior Living, Inc*, 124 F. Supp 3d 83 (2105).

 Learning Objectives

1. Examine the shortcomings of litigation.
2. List the advantages and the disadvantages of ADR.
3. Identify the advantages of mediation.
4. Explain the nature of an arbitration hearing.
5. Outline the med-arb process.
6. Relate the role of the early neutral evaluator.
7. Describe the process of running a summary jury trial.
8. Clarify the options available under proactive ADR.
9. Discuss the pros and cons of the collective science court proposal.
10. Identify the types of cyber-ADR platforms available today.

4-1 A Briefing on ADR Strategies

As we have seen at various points throughout the text, the law is often reflected in a series of dualities. These dualities include the symmetry sought between the spirit and the letter of the law, between legal words and their interpretation, and between abstract principles and concrete situations. This synchronization is also involved in the application of the Uncertainty Principle to legal disputes. Thus far, we have focused on the dispute-solving process known as litigation. Litigation has always been part of the American legal system. Lately, however, things have begun to change. The complexity, the expense, and the time involved in litigation have discouraged many potential litigants, who have decided to sidestep the regular court system in favor of pursuing more efficient, effective, and economical methods of settling their disputes. These unconventional methods are referred to as the alternative dispute resolution process, or simply as ADR. **Alternative dispute resolution (ADR)** occurs whenever people move outside the traditional adversarial system and try to solve their legal dispute by using creative settlement techniques, many of which have fact-finding and truth as their goals rather than simply achieving a final victory. Thus, we have a fourth duality in the law: the duality that exists between the traditional litigation system and the unorthodox ADR process.

Problems with Litigation

Many people choose a dispute resolution process that sidesteps the adversarial approach of civil litigation because they believe that it is the best way to achieve justice. Part of this belief is based on the suspicion that with an adversarial approach, victory often depends not on who is in the right, but on which advocate is the better tactician. Watching hours of television dramas such as *Suits*, *Scandal*, *NCIS*, *Better Call Saul*, *The Good Wife*, *Damages*, *The Night Of*, and *Law and Order* has probably contributed to this extreme notion of how the law operates. Unfortunately, the best tactician is often one of the most expensive advocates available, which can mean that justice often goes to those who can afford it. For this reason, many people seek an alternative that is less costly to both sides.

Litigation can also be expensive because of the initial steps that lead to the filing of a lawsuit. For instance, before an attorney can file a medical malpractice lawsuit, he or she must obtain the client's medical records, which means paying an initial copying fee that can amount to hundreds or even thousands of dollars. The attorney must then hire an expert to evaluate the records to determine whether the information in the records indicates that the client has a viable claim. Again, this expense can run into hundreds or thousands of dollars. All these expenses are encountered before the attorney even knows that a claim actually exists.

In addition to being expensive, litigation can be time consuming. The initial steps after the filing of a complaint can delay progress on a lawsuit for many months. For instance, should the defendant's motion for dismissal be granted by the court, a lengthy and time-consuming appeal process may ensue. In some cases, the appeal could even find its way to the highest court in the jurisdiction. In such a case, if the highest court reverses the lower court's dismissal of the action, the case quite literally returns to the starting line. Another time-consuming step in litigation is the process of discovery. Taking depositions, answering interrogatories, filing, and responding to requests for real evidence and handling requests for mental or physical examinations can tie up a lawsuit for months.

Moreover, some jurisdictions require litigants to submit to case management hearings and settlement hearings before they can secure a trial date. Even when a court date is secured, many court dockets, especially those in large urban areas, are backed up for months, or even years, which often means that the parties to a lawsuit must wait for long periods of time before having their day in court. Even once a trial has occurred and a decision rendered, recovery can be delayed as the parties enter a second phase of the lawsuit, the execution of the judgment phase. This process involves its own complex set of procedures, which, like the actual lawsuit, can cause expensive and time-consuming delays.

The ADR Option

ADR can, however, provide an economical and efficient alternative to litigation. Depending on the ADR technique employed, the time involved in settling a dispute can be shortened considerably and the expenses lowered significantly. Arbitration and mediation, for example, can be scheduled quickly, even before a lawsuit is filed. When scheduling either a mediation or an arbitration session, the parties need not consult the court's dockets or worry about any preliminary requirements, such as a case management conference. Moreover, even if the arbitration or mediation session does not end the dispute, it can save time by narrowing the issues or providing an evaluation of the strength of each side's case. The arbitration or mediation session may also, in some cases, provide a shortcut to discovery, thus saving time and lowering expenses.

Other ADR approaches, such as early neutral evaluation (ENE), can save money and time by providing an assessment of the issues at stake and the range of damages available, should the outcome of the case demand a remedy of some sort. Summary jury trials, private trials, and mini-trials can all be inexpensive and quick because they can be scheduled without regard to the court's docket and can be held without the expenses involved in hiring expert witnesses and providing travel and hotel accommodations for those witnesses. The cost and time involved in lengthy discovery processes can also be avoided by selecting any one of these ADR techniques.

Private proactive ADR techniques such as drafting contract clauses and entering partnering agreements can help to make litigation unnecessary from the outset. The idea behind the proactive ADR approach is to anticipate and deal with disputes before they occur. By providing a solution to problems before those problems arise, proactive ADR eliminates the uncertainty and risk inherent within the litigation process.

ADR options provide a timely, cost-efficient method for resolving legal issues.
©Fuse/Getty Images

Shortcomings of ADR

Yet ADR is not without problems. On the contrary, some critics of the process have pointed out that the private administration of justice hampers the development of the law. Because many ADR techniques sidestep the courts, critical social issues may never reach the judicial system, causing gaps in the evolution of case law and the progression of legislation. Another criticism of ADR involves its limited scope. Some legal conflicts—notably employment, contract, and tort cases—are especially well suited for ADR; however, other legal problems, primarily those involving criminal law, could never be brought before an ADR panel.

Other difficulties associated with ADR have also appeared in recent years. One problem is that ADR does not always save time and money the way it is supposed to. Typically, two of the advantages that supporters of ADR promote are the ideas that ADR is less expensive and less time consuming because such procedures do not get tangled up in the red tape of the court system. Unfortunately, this is not always the case. Sometimes, even cases that are decided by arbitration end up in the court system. Most often, this happens when one or more of the parties decide to challenge the decision of the arbitrator. When such challenges occur, there is only one place for the parties to go: to court.

EXAMPLE 4-1: Sometimes You Really Do Get What You Pay For, Even Though You'd Rather Not

Mt. Holyoke Homes LP (MHH) brought a malpractice lawsuit against Jeffer Mangels Butler and Mitchell LLP (JMBM), a law firm that had represented MHH in an earlier case. The contract between MHH and JMBM called for arbitration, and the trial court decided to enforce that requirement. Recall that one key advantage to the use of any ADR strategy is supposed to be that the process saves time and money. This case not only did not save time, but also ended up being outrageously expensive. The first problem emerged when the parties could not settle on an arbitrator. The first choice of arbitrator was rejected because she had previous dealings with the accused. The next candidate on the list was acceptable and the matter proceeded. The second problem cropped up when, after losing, MHH decided to do some post-decision web surfing and uncovered that the arbitrator had listed one of JMBM's partners as a reference on his CV. This led to a reconsideration of the case by the trial court; an appeal to the appellate court; and after that, a request that the California Supreme Court hear the case, a request that was refused. The third problem emerged from the arbitrator's original ruling, which found in favor of JMBM and ordered MHH to pay $285,000 in legal fees and $150,000 in the present action. Now, the arbitrator's decision was overturned, but that $435,000 bill is still floating out there somewhere, and someone is going to have to pay it (or JMBM will be forced to absorb the costs). Moreover, the case continued after that ruling, and more legal fees and court costs piled up and up and up. So is ADR less expensive and less time consuming? Just ask MHH and JMBM, and you'll have a fairly straightforward answer. [See: *Mt. Holyoke Homes, LP, et al. v. Jeffer Mangels Butler and Mitchell, LLP,* 219 Cal. App. 4th 1299 (Cal. Rptr. 3d. 567) (2013); and John S. Warnlof and Leslie A. Fales, "Updates on Alternative Dispute Resolution," *Contra Costa Lawyer Online,* February 1, 2014.]

Source: See: *Mt. Holyoke Homes, LP, et al. v. Jeffer Mangels Butler and Mitchell, LLP,* 219 Cal. App. 4th 1299 (Cal. Rptr. 3d. 567) (2013); John S. Warnlof and Leslie A. Fales, "Updates on Alternative Dispute Resolution," *Contra Costa Lawyer Online,* February 1, 2014.

Two additional advantages of ADR are that little discovery and very few motions are involved in the process, thus saving the litigants a lot of money. Although this argument sounds good in theory, it does not always play out in reality. Unfortunately, sometimes a case may actually take longer to resolve because there is no discovery or motion practice involved. Part of the delay is due to the fact that discovery and motion practice often help attorneys focus on the most crucial issues in a case. Also, discovery will sometimes reveal that it is necessary to settle a case rather than proceeding to trial. When there is no discovery or motion practice, the issues remain wide open. This gap means that attorneys must anticipate all the possible moves that their opponents might make. The lack of discovery also means that the small flaws in an argument may not be revealed, and a case that would have been settled during a conventional lawsuit might drag on in arbitration.

Admittedly, ADR is not intended as a replacement for the legal system. Rather, it is intended to provide potential litigants with a wider variety of choices when they are facing a legal dispute. As noted previously, because of the delays and the expense involved in litigation, many people would like to avoid that route altogether. Others would like to find a way to streamline the litigation process, so that, should the need for a trial finally present itself, the preliminary steps can be administered as painlessly as possible. With these facts in mind, we will proceed with an examination of ADR techniques.

The Federal Arbitration Act

People often get the wrong impression about ADR and its relationship to traditional litigation and the operation of the court system. Understandably enough, there may appear to be an adversarial relationship between the two systems. In fact, when ADR first began to be more popular in recent years, the courts did look at the newcomer with suspicion and hostility. However, as is often the case in such things, Congress and the Supreme Court saw the writing on the wall and decided that it was better to join the ADR effort than fight it. One crucial step in this new strategy was the passage of the Federal Arbitration Act (FAA). The FAA is designed to make certain that properly initiated arbitration agreements will be enforced by the courts. Conceptually, the process is simple enough. If a lawsuit begins that involves a contract that contains an arbitration clause, the court can stop the proceedings and require the parties to follow the requirements of that clause. Generally, the court will respond to a request by either party to obligate the other party to submit to the terms of the arbitration clause. As a first step in the process, the court must examine the arbitration

THE OPENING CASE *Round 2*
Considine v. Brookdale Senior Living: Is Mandatory Arbitration Really Mandatory?

Recall that in the Opening Case, as an employee of Brookdale Senior Living Inc., Considine was entitled to health and dental care coverage under the company's insurance program. The plan included an optional provision that permits health and dental care for spouses. Considine asked to have her spouse added to the health care plan, but Brookdale refused to do so. allow. In response, Considine filed a discrimination claim with the EEOC, alleging that she was being discriminated against based on her gender because she was married to a same-sex spouse. Eventually, Considine received a right to sue letter from the EEOC and took her case directly to the U.S. District Court. Interestingly enough, in these proceedings, Brookdale never denied that it had withheld health care coverage from Considine's spouse based on the fact that it was dealing with a same-sex marriage. Still, in due course, Brookdale did enroll Renee in the health and dental care plan. That, however, did not stop Considine from continuing to pursue the case. She altered her argument to contend that because Brookdale had acted voluntarily, it could voluntarily withdraw that coverage. She further claimed that this precarious state placed her at the mercy of Brookdale's administration, causing a case of continuing discrimination. Brookdale pointed out that, when Considine was hired, her employment contract included a clause that said that all employment-related disputes, including any dispute involving discrimination, would be settled by mandatory arbitration. Moreover, the arbitration clause also said that any dispute over whether mandatory arbitration had to be used, would be answered by the arbitrator. This is precisely the type of case that the FAA was designed to handle. Accordingly, the court ordered that the case be sent to arbitration. The rest, as they say, is history. [See: *Considine v. Brookdale Senior Living, Inc*, 124 F. Supp 3d 83 (2015).]

Source: See: *Considine v. Brookdale Senior Living, Inc,* 124 F. Supp 3d 83 (2105).

clause to make certain that arbitration really is required under the clause. If the court finds that arbitration is, indeed, required by the contract, then the court must send the case directly to arbitration, unless for some reason the court finds that the issue at hand is not one that should be decided by an arbitrator.

Under provisions of the FAA, arbitrators can call witnesses and require those witnesses to provide documentary evidence if necessary. Failure to comply would allow the arbitrator to hold the witnesses in contempt of court. The FAA does not, however, authorize arbitrators to enforce an award. That power remains under the authority of the court. Still, the FAA does empower the winner of the arbitration award to ask the court to enforce an award and the losing party to ask the court to vacate the award. Under FAA provisions, in very narrow circumstance, the court has the power to modify an arbitrator's award. The FAA also permits the federal courts to enforce international arbitration awards even though such awards are generally negotiated in foreign nation-states. Interestingly enough, the Supreme Court has also decided that the FAA controls state courts that must handle cases that involve the interpretation of arbitration clauses. Additionally, the High Court has decided that in order to make the arbitration process consistent on a national level, the FAA will take precedence over any state law that conflicts with its provisions. This does not mean, however, that the FAA is without any limits over the authority of the decisions made by arbitrators. On the contrary, the FAA does state that an arbitrator's award can be vacated if it can be shown that (1) the opposing party engaged in fraud in its attempt to win the award, (2) the arbitrators engaged in corruption or were clearly biased in favor of one of the parties in the dispute, (3) the arbitrators engaged in some other type of misconduct, or (4) the arbitrators went beyond the limits of their power in granting an award. The Supreme Court has held that these four conditions represent the only conditions under which an arbitrator's decision can be vacated by a court [See: Claudia Salomon and Samuel de Villiers, "The United States Federal Arbitration Act: A Powerful Tool for Enforcing Arbitration Agreements and Arbitral Awards," *LexisPSLArbitration* (March 17, 2014). See also *Hall St. Associates, L.L.C. v. Mattel* 552 U.S. 576 (2008).]

Did You Know?

When mediation is used to settle cases of sexual harassment in the workplace, 85 percent of those cases are resolved successfully without anyone having to go to court.

quick quiz 4-1

1. Adversarial litigation has only recently become a part of the American legal system.	true | false
2. Two of the advantages that supporters of ADR promote are the ideas that ADR is less expensive and less time consuming than litigation.	true | false
3. ADR is not intended as a replacement for the legal system.	true | false

4-2 Responsive ADR Strategies

Numerous ADR techniques can be invoked once a dispute has arisen between parties. These include but are not limited to mediation, arbitration, med-arb, early neutral evaluation, summary jury trials, and private civil trials.

Mediation

According to the American Arbitration Association, **mediation** is "a non-binding process where a neutral third party works with the parties to reach a mutually agreeable settlement." The neutral third party is referred to as a **mediator**. Some people erroneously confuse mediation with negotiation. Negotiation is the usual way that attorneys handle disputes before they end up in litigation. Such negotiation is part, or at least should be part, of every dispute that might possibly lead to litigation. In fact, negotiation is something that can take place before a lawsuit is filed, after it has been filed, before trial, and even during trial. There is no specially designated neutral third-party "negotiator" during negotiation as there is during mediation. The job of the mediator is to convince parties to adjust or settle their dispute. The mediator will try to persuade the parties to reach some sort of compromise but cannot decide what the parties will do. [See: American Arbitration Association, FAQs, retrieved June 28, 2010, from https://www.adr.org/Mediation.]

Like the timing of a negotiation conference, the timing of a mediation session can vary. Sometimes mediation follows the filing of a lawsuit, but sometimes it occurs to prevent a lawsuit from being filed. Mediation can occur before a conflict, during a conflict, after a conflict, or when a settlement following a conflict is not being followed properly. [See: The JAMS Foundation, July 28, 2010, http://www.jamsadr.com.] Mediation is often more successful than litigation because in mediation, the parties remain involved in the settlement of the dispute. Unlike litigation, which is decided by a judge or jury, a mediation session is in the hands of the parties. The mediator does not decide the disagreement. Rather, he or she serves as an intermediary who attempts to understand what brought the parties into disagreement and what issues lay at the heart of the disagreement. The mediator does not act as a therapist, a judge, or an advocate. Rather, he or she acts as an impartial outsider who can suggest solutions that will please all the parties involved in the dispute. Often, the mediator can cut to the center of a dispute in objective ways that are unavailable to the parties themselves.

EXAMPLE 4-2: Mediation: Practical Solutions to Practical Problems

Bruce Langton brought suit against David Winchester in small claims court after Winchester's daughter, Jackie, backed her car into Langton's truck, causing extensive damage to the front end of the vehicle. Langton wanted damages in the amount of $4,000. Langton's sister-in-law, Wendy Miller, suggested that the parties hire a mediator to try to reach a settlement. During the mediation session, the mediator saw that the real issue was the fact that Langton's truck was still damaged. Winchester's brother, who owned and operated an auto body shop, agreed to fix Langton's truck at no cost. This solution satisfied both parties. Langton had his truck fixed, and Winchester suffered no out-of-pocket expenses.

Arbitration

Arbitration is the process by which the parties invite a third party, called an **arbitrator**, to settle their dispute. The procedures involved in arbitration are generally more flexible than those followed in a lawsuit. The rules are either set by law or agreed to by an arbitration agreement. The hearing may be relaxed, with the arbitrator or arbitrators receiving informal testimony from the parties, or it may be rigidly controlled, with the arbitrator or arbitrators following strict rules of evidence and requiring lengthy explanations. The parties may agree in advance to be bound by the arbitrator's decision. If they do not so agree, the arbitrator's decision can be appealed in court. There is a common misconception that arbitration, and mediation for that matter, are carried out exclusively by non-lawyers. Sometimes arbitrators are lawyers and sometimes they are not. This is made clear by the American Arbitration Association, which states that arbitrators must have "senior level experience in law, business, industry or another profession." [See: American Arbitration Association, FAQs, retrieved June 28, 2010, from https://www.adr.org/Mediation.]

Some states require arbitration prior to trial in certain cases. Required arbitration is called mandatory arbitration. Some litigants have challenged government-imposed mandatory arbitration as an unconstitutional deprivation of their right to a trial by jury and equal protection under the law. Most states faced with this question have disagreed with these arguments as long as the arbitration requirement does not replace the jury trial and as long as the motives for requiring arbitration are reasonable.

An arbitration hearing can be planned and executed by the parties themselves. Generally, this step means that the parties set the ground rules for choosing the arbitrator or arbitrators, for conducting discovery, for presenting evidence, for determining the outcome, and for enforcing the reward. In addition, details such as setting the time and the place of the hearing, filling vacancies on the arbitration panel, recording the proceedings, handling objections, granting time extensions, and so on, must also be agreed upon. Because of the intricacies of such a process, many individuals who select arbitration prefer to use professional arbitration organizations such as the American Arbitration Association to handle the details of their arbitration proceeding.

Like most forms of ADR, arbitration is not without its difficulties. One shortcoming is that an arbitration hearing is run like a trial but without the safeguards that come with the rules of civil procedure, discovery, and motion practice. This characteristic may actually extend the time involved in arbitration because attorneys and negotiators must prepare a wide variety of legal arguments, some of which might have been eliminated during motion practice. Discovery also sometimes reveals facts that lead the parties into settlement negotiations that might not otherwise take place. Moreover, the wide discretion that is usually granted to arbitrators has, in some cases, led to unreasonable decisions and unjustifiable awards. Sometimes the decision made by an arbitrator comes under the review of the courts, which may result in a reversal of the arbitration order and thus frustrate the whole object of entering arbitration in the first place. Some of these difficulties can be overcome by stipulating

About the Law

The American Arbitration Association booklet, *National Rules for the Resolution of Employment Disputes*, includes rules on both mediation and arbitration.

THE OPENING CASE *Round 3*
Considine v. Brookdale Senior Living: Is Mandatory Arbitration Really Mandatory?

In the Opening Case, we learned that Brookdale Senior living refused to enroll Considine's spouse in the company's health plan. In response, Considine filed a discrimination claim with the EEOC alleging that she was being discriminated against because her spouse was a woman. Once Considine received a right to sue letter from the EEOC, she initiated a lawsuit in federal court. Meanwhile, back at the senior center, Brookdale enrolled Considine's spouse in the health care plan. Still, Considine pursued the case. In response, Brookdale noted that Considine's employment contract included a clause that said that all employment disputes had to be settled by mandatory arbitration. Accordingly, the court ordered the case to arbitration. Acting under the power of that clause and that of the Federal Arbitration Act, the arbitrator dismissed the case, saying that because Constantine had received what she had asked for in the first place, no injury existed and the arbitration was at an end. Now Constantine still believed that she had an injury that needed to be addressed. She wanted to argued that because Brookdale had extended health care coverage voluntarily, it could just as easily withdraw that coverage at any time. The precarious state she was now in placed her at the mercy of Brookdale's administration, and this state of uncertainly constituted a case of *de facto* continuing discrimination.

Now recall that some litigants continue to argue that a court-imposed order to take a case to mandatory arbitration is an unconstitutional deprivation of their right to a trial by jury and equal protection under the law. Also recall that most states faced with this question have disagreed with these arguments as long as the arbitration requirement does not replace the jury trial and as long as the motives for requiring arbitration are reasonable. In this case, under the application of the FAA, it would appear that Considine has not been granted equal protection under the law and has lost her right to a trial by jury. Defend Considine's argument. Now defend the court's ruling. Which side do you believe is correct? Explain. [See: *Considine v. Brookdale Senior Living, Inc*, 124 F. Supp 3d 83 (2015). See also: *Considine v. Brookdale Senior Living, Inc.*, GLAD, Legal Advocates and Defenders: Cases and Advocacy (2017), https://www.glad.org/cases/considine-v-brookdale-senior-living/.]

Source: See: *Considine v. Brookdale Senior Living, Inc,* 124 F. Supp 3d 83 (2105); See also: *Considine v. Brookdale Senior Living, Inc.,* GLAD, Legal Advocates and Defenders: *Cases and Advocacy* (2017), https://www.glad.org/cases/considine-v-brookdale-senior-living/.

---

that an arbitration award cannot be reversed by the courts except to correct a violation of the arbitration agreement itself.

The difficulties associated with discovery can be solved by streamlining the discovery process in arbitration, without going to the extremes represented by the way that discovery is conducted in litigation. Other problems can be solved by making sure that arbitrators follow the same rules in all hearings and insisting that they write down the reasons behind their decisions.

Med-Arb

Med-arb is an ADR process that combines mediation with arbitration. Under med-arb procedures, the parties first submit their dispute to a mediation session. If the dispute is settled via mediation, then all of the parties can leave satisfied. If, however, some matters are left undecided, the parties can move on to an arbitration hearing. During the hearing, the undecided issues would be placed before an arbitrator for final deliberation.

Early Neutral Evaluation

Early neutral evaluation (ENE) is an ADR process in which the parties permit a referee to assess their case on the basis of the facts and legal arguments alone. At the outset of an ENE process, an independent, objective referee is provided with an overview of the facts involved in the dispute and a summary of the legal arguments on which each side has built his or her case. The evaluator, after examining the facts and the law, renders an impartial assessment of the legal rights of each party and a determination of the amount of the award that should be rendered, if any. The parties can use this impartial evaluation to either settle the case or proceed to trial. Even if the ENE does not result in a final decision, it can be used to shape the issues, plan discovery, and guide any research that the attorneys must conduct as the case proceeds to trial.

Summary Jury Trials

A **summary jury trial** is a shortened version of a trial conducted in less than a day before an actual jury that then renders an advisory verdict in the case. The summary jury process offers litigants a chance to see how a jury would react to the facts of the case, as well as to the legal arguments that will be made by both sides at trial. On the day of the summary jury trial, lawyers from both sides present an abbreviated version of the case to an actual jury. The presentations are simplified, focusing on the essential facts and law. In this way, the summary jury trial eliminates much of the redundancy that occurs during a "real" trial and allows the judge and jury to focus on the essentials of the case.

As noted previously, the ultimate objective of a summary jury trial is to help both sides evaluate the effectiveness of their arguments in front of a judge and jury. This effort in turn helps the attorneys shape the issues and select the positions that are most advantageous to their case. This knowledge is enhanced by the fact that after the trial, each side has the chance to interview the jurors to see why they reacted as they did.

The success or failure of a summary jury trial depends on several factors. First, only those cases that involve a *bona fide* dispute as to the facts or authentic questions of law should be considered for a summary jury trial. Second, advanced planning is necessary to ensure a successful summary jury trial. The judge must be consulted, issues should be settled, the facts should be composed properly, the jury instructions should be determined, and a date and time established before the trial begins.

Third, during the process, strict controls and ironclad time limits must be imposed on the parties. For instance, opening statements should last no more than 20 minutes. Both sides should have no more than 1 hour for the presentation of their case in chief and 30 minutes for their rebuttal. The closing arguments should also be limited to no more than 20 minutes. Finally, a conference should be held after the trial, during which the parties have the opportunity to discuss an immediate settlement. Such a conference should be held after the jury has been polled so that their input can be factored into the settlement discussion.

EXAMPLE 4-3: Summary Jury Trials: A Posttrial, Pretrial Settlement

When Ashley Utalizar was discharged from her job with Solarpower Industries Inc., she was certain that the dismissal had been in direct violation of an implied contract that had been created by Solarpower's employee policy manual. When she brought a lawsuit against Solarpower, both parties decided to hold a summary jury trial. After the trial was held, both sides participated in a posttrial settlement conference. The results of the jury poll indicated that though the jury had decided in favor of Utalizar, they were unable to agree on the amount of damages that should be awarded to her. As a result, both Solarpower and Utalizar decided that it would be in their best interests to settle the case immediately. The attorneys for Solarpower agreed to the settlement because they saw that the jury was sympathetic to Utalizar, while Utalizar's attorneys agreed that they could not be certain that Utalizar would receive an adequate award if the jury were permitted to decide the amount of damages.

Because one reason for holding a summary jury trial is to determine how the judge and jury will react to the facts and the arguments, it is helpful to have observers gauge how the judge and the jurors react to the points made by both sides. The observers, who are often students recruited from local law schools and paralegal institutes, will record the reactions of the judge and the jurors during the trial. As an alternative, the entire process can be recorded, so that reactions can be observed later.

Private Civil Trials

A **private civil trial** is an ADR technique by which the parties hire a retired judge or magistrate to hear their dispute, following the same rules used in an official trial. Many states now permit the parties to a lawsuit to have their cases tried in a private civil trial rather than an official court. One advantage of a private trial is that the parties can hold the trial at a time and a place of their own choosing. In addition, the parties have the opportunity to choose their own judge. Decisions rendered by a judge in a private civil trial are just as binding as those made by judges on the official court docket. Moreover, private trial decisions can be appealed in the same way that public decisions are appealed.

Private civil trials are not postponed nor are they interrupted because the court has more pressing duties to perform. In addition, a private trial receives the undivided attention of the judge, who is not sidetracked by the need to attend to other matters such as the sentencing of criminal defendants. Intricate, lengthy civil cases are ideally suited for private civil trials because, in such cases, time is money. Consequently, the shorter the trial, the less expensive the final bill facing the client.

In recent years, some private firms have appeared that specialize in setting up private civil trials. Such firms will make most of the arrangements for the litigants. These arrangements include securing a judge, providing the place for the trial, and providing all necessary administrative support. These firms can also provide a jury for the trial. Jurors for private trials are generally selected from a pool of individuals who have recently served on a jury in an official trial; therefore, the jurors at the private civil trial are well acquainted with the trial procedures.

quick quiz 4-2

1. The job of a mediator is to convince the contending parties to adjust or settle their dispute. true | false
2. Some states require arbitration prior to trial in certain cases. true | false
3. The early neutral evaluation process is similar to that of a settlement hearing. true | false

4-3 Proactive ADR Strategies

All of the ADR techniques discussed thus far are invoked after a dispute has arisen. Since ADR has become so popular in recent years, some business people are taking a proactive approach to the situation by agreeing in advance to submit to one of the alternative dispute resolution tools should a disagreement between the parties arise later. These proactive ADR techniques include, but are not limited to, partnering, ADR contract clauses, settlement week, negotiated rule making, post-appellate procedures, international arbitration agreements, and the collective science court proposal.

Partnering

Partnering is a process that establishes supportive relationships among the parties to a contract to head off disputes before they occur. Generally, partnering is best used when a contract involves complex interrelationships among a wide variety of different parties. Construction agreements are ideally suited to partnering arrangements because construction contracts involve contractors and subcontractors, all of whom must perform in a cooperative manner to fulfill a contract that often takes a long period of time to complete.

Partnering attempts to deter the disorder that can arise during a dispute by drawing up certain ground rules that all the parties agree to observe. The entire process begins with a meeting held after the contract has been finalized but before the project has begun. The meeting is held at a location that is unrelated to the business of any party to the contract. In this way, the process can procede in an uninterrupted fashion.

Moreover, the meeting should be directed by an objective third party, whose job it is to help create an atmosphere of trust among the parties to the contract. The parties attempt to anticipate problems that may arise during the project as well as potential solutions to those problems. The parties agree to address all problems when they arise and to look for solutions that will mutually benefit all those involved in the project. Ultimately, the goal is to improve efficiency, ensure safety, and maximize profit by minimizing expenses, especially those that arise from cost overruns.

The parties agree to handle problems according to some ADR technique rather than by litigation. Finally, they agree to deal with one another in a fair manner within the confines of their legal relationships.

ADR Contract Clauses

An **ADR contract clause** will specify that the parties to the agreement have promised to use an alternative dispute resolution technique when a disagreement arises rather than litigating the issue. Like partnering, the drafting of ADR contract clauses is a proactive attempt to ensure that litigation will be avoided should a dispute arise. Unlike partnering, which is best suited to long-term construction contracts, ADR clauses can be included in just about any contract.

These ADR clauses can take many shapes and forms. It is possible, for instance, to insert a clause that states merely that the parties have the option of using an ADR technique. Such a clause is weak, at best, serving only to remind the parties that they do not have to sue one another to gain satisfaction. One step beyond the optional clause is a compulsory clause. This clause states that the parties are required to submit all claims that arise under the contract to an ADR technique, most often mediation or arbitration, before filing a lawsuit. The final type of clause would require the parties to submit any claim to mandatory binding arbitration. This strictest ADR clause forces the parties to abide by the decision of the arbitrator.

THE OPENING CASE *Round 4, the Final Round*
Considine v. Brookdale Senior Living: Is Mandatory Arbitration Really Mandatory?

It's time for that one final look at the Opening Case. Recall that Brookdale administrators refused to allow Kerry Considine to add her spouse to the the company's health care plan policy because her spouse was also female. Recall also that Considine filed a discrimination claim with EEOC alleging that she was being discriminated against. After Considine received a right to sue letter from the EEOC, she took her case directly to federal court. At some point during all of this, Brookdale decided to voluntarily enroll Considine's spouse in the health care plan.

Once the case was in federal court, the attorneys for Brookdale pointed out that when Considine was hired, she had signed an employment agreement that included an ADR contract clause that said that all employment-related disputes, including any dispute involving discrimination, would be settled by mandatory binding arbitration. In addition, the binding arbitration clause said that any dispute over whether mandatory arbitration had to be used would be answered by the arbitrator. Accordingly, the case went to the arbitrator, who promptly decided that (1) the case had to be presented to the arbitrator, and (2) the discrimination charge was rejected because Considine's spouse was already enrolled in the health care plan, so Constantine had no injury and, therefore required no remedy and the case was moot.

Looking at this entire situation, we must admit, whether we like it or not, that Brookdale did an excellent job covering itself in this case. First, it included an arbitration clause in its employment contract. That, in itself, is an excellent move. Second, Brookdale required employees to sign the employment contract indicating that they had read and understood all of the terms in the contract, including the mandatory binding arbitration clause. This would preclude the employees from arguing that they knew nothing about the clause. Third, probably owing to the legal climate at the time, Brookdale expressly included discrimination complaints in the list of claims that were to be brought to mandatory binding arbitration. Fourth, Brookdale precluded any claims for equitable (non-monetary) relief. Finally, and most important for what we have just learned in this chapter, Brookdale expressly stated that the agreement to submit to arbitration was *binding* and *mandatory*. Thus, Brookdale's arbitration clause is the strictest, most powerful ADR clause possible because it requires the parties to enter arbitration and compels them to bide by the decision of the arbitrator, whatever that decision might be. However we might feel about the outcome, we have to admire the job that Brookdale's legal staff did in this case. [See: *Considine v. Brookdale Senior Living, Inc*, 124 F. Supp 3d 83 (2015).]

Source: See: *Considine v. Brookdale Senior Living, Inc*, 124 F. Supp 3d 83 (2105).

Regardless of the type of clause used by the parties, the language should include certain standard provisions. For instance, the clause should specify the types of disagreements that will be submitted to ADR, the ADR technique or techniques that can be used, the scope of discovery allowed, the substantive law and the procedural rules that will be followed in the proceeding, the remedies that will be authorized, the grounds for and the procedure to follow in an appeal, and the methods of enforcing an award. The failure to follow provisions specified in an ADR clause may be grounds for the court to revoke a ruling made by an arbitrator.

Such ADR clauses have several advantages. They are especially helpful when two or more parties have embarked on an extended affiliation that may involve numerous contracts because ADR clauses clearly establish a reliable and predictable method of dealing with the disputes that will inevitably arise whenever two parties are involved in a lengthy association with each other. In addition, ADR clauses are very beneficial to those parties with the weakest position within a contractual relationship. Often, when a dispute does arise, the more powerful party will threaten litigation, secure in the knowledge that he or she can afford a lawsuit more easily than the weaker party. An ADR clause eliminates this leverage point.

Because the parties to an ADR clause agree, at least initially, to forgo the right to litigate any claims that arise among them, the courts prefer that such clauses be clear and precise. Clauses that are drafted in imprecise and ambiguous language may be invalidated by the court. If the parties intend to submit all the claims arising out of their contractual relationship to ADR, they should spell that out as precisely and completely as possible. Otherwise a party that later wishes to invoke the clause may find that the court is reluctant to support that position. When writing an ADR contract clause, it is best to use standard expressions that the court will recognize. Clauses that say the parties agree to use ADR for "any controversy or claim arising out of or relating to the agreement" will convince the court to enforce the clause for most disputes between the parties. Anything less may meet with judicial resistance.

The court will also be sensitive to any clauses, conditions, or procedures that are unconscionable. Something will be deemed unconscionable by the court if it is so outrageous that it literally "shocks the conscience of the court." Such clauses are usually engineered to produce results that are favorable to the party that has all, or at least most, of the power in the relationship and then uses that power to fashion an agreement that is almost totally in his or her favor. If the other party to the agreement must accept that agreement on a take-it-or-leave-it basis, the court is not likely to enforce it. Unconscionable clauses usually fall into one of two categories: (1) procedural unconscionability and (2) substantive unconscionability. Procedural unconscionability is generally related to the methods by which the agreement is obtained, while substantive unconscionability refers to the way that the agreement is to be carried out. The accompanying ethics case is a memorable illustration of unconscionability—perhaps even what might be called *super*-unconscionability.

A QUESTION OF ETHICS

A Blueprint for Procedural and Substantive *Super*-Unconscionability

When Zenia Chavarria applied for a job at Ralphs Grocery Company, she was required to read, fill out, and sign a fairly complex employment application that included an arbitration clause. The clause included a politely worded request for a signature ("Please sign and date the employment application . . . to acknowledge you have read, understand and agree to the following statements.") that was followed later by a statement that indicated the policy would be in effect even if the employee did not sign the document. (Nice touch!) The arbitration clause did not actually disclose the procedure that would be followed. In fact, Chavarria did not receive the policy itself for three weeks. Moreover, when she finally did have the policy in hand, what she found was a document written in complicated legalese that ran for four pages of single-spaced text. In addition, the procedure set up for choosing the arbitrator was clearly devised so that the employer would inevitably get the final binding choice. Additionally, the appointment of arbitrators from the two most reputable arbitration organizations on record, the Judicial Arbitration and Mediation Service (JAMS) and the American Arbitration Association (AAA), was forbidden by the agreement. What is more, the policy required the arbitrator to divide the fees between the arbitrating parties regardless of the merits of the case. After Chavarria left her job at Ralphs, she filed a lawsuit arguing that Ralphs violated various provisions of the California Labor Code and California Business and Professions Code.

As soon as Ralphs moved to apply the arbitration clause, Chavarria contended that the clause was unconscionable both (1) procedurally and (2) substantively. *Both* the district court *and* the court of appeals agreed with Chavarria. Why? Well, take a look: (1) Procedurally, the clause was unconscionable because it forced employees to accept the contract on a take-it-or-leave-it basis, giving them no chance to object, modify, challenge, or argue. Moreover, if employees refused to sign, the contract was still valid. Additionally, the actual policy was not revealed to the employee for three weeks and then in a document that was long, complex, and difficult to comprehend. (2) In addition, substantively, the document was unconscionable because (a) it made sure the choice of the arbitrator was up to the employer; (b) made certain that the best arbitrators in the business (those in JAMS and AAA) would not sit as arbitrator; and (c) guaranteed that the costs were shared, regardless of the outcome of the process. In short, what we have here is a memorable illustration of super-unconscionability. [See: *Chavarria v. Ralphs Grocery Company*, 733 F. 3d. 916 (9th Cir. 2013); and John S. Warnlof and Leslie A. Fales, "Updates on Alternative Dispute Resolution," *Contra Costa Lawyer Online*, February 1, 2014.]

Source: See: *Chavarria v. Ralphs Grocery Company*, 733 F. 3d. 916 (9th Cir. 2013); John S. Warnlof and Leslie A. Fales, "Updates on Alternative Dispute Resolution," *Contra Costa Lawyer Online*, February 1, 2014.

Settlement Week

Settlement week is a five-day period during which a court's docket is cleared of all business, except for settlement hearings. Prior to the opening of settlement week, all attorneys with cases pending before the court are asked to choose which of those cases might be best handled by a mediator. Judges are also permitted to nominate cases for mediation during settlement week. Also, before the opening of settlement week, a list of volunteer mediators is compiled. Cases are then matched with mediators, and a schedule is established. Attorneys are required to be present for the mediation session.

A mediation session is then held for each case. Following each session, the mediator is required to file a report with the court, stipulating the results of the session and asking for the judge's approval. Occasionally, some cases—chiefly those that do not involve determining liability—are submitted to an arbitration panel rather than to a single mediator. In such a situation, the plaintiff chooses one of the arbitrators, the defendant chooses one, and the court names the final one. Not all cases scheduled for settlement week are actually resolved during that time; however, the technique is an effective way to lighten the court's docket and is becoming more and more popular.

Negotiated Rule Making

Negotiated rule making (reg-neg) is a process by which an agency invites the people and the organizations to be affected by a new rule to have input into the writing of that rule. A working team is established that consists of representatives of the affected groups, including the agency issuing the rule. One member of the team is an objective outsider trained in the art of facilitating such discussions. The objective of negotiated rule making, of course, is to avoid disputes before they have a chance to blossom.

All representatives have the opportunity to present their point of view in relation to the proposed rule. Discussions follow, during which all of these issues are examined. Eventually, the team is expected to formulate a rule that reflects a consensus of the representatives. This consensus does not necessarily mean that all parts of the rule are enthusiastically embraced by all of the representatives. Rather, it means that all of the parties agree that they have fashioned a rule that everyone on the rule-making team can live with. The text of the proposed rule is then submitted to the rule-making agency. The success of the process depends on the willingness of the members of the team to work in a cooperative fashion and the willingness of the agency to accept the results of the team's deliberations.

Despite its advantages, negotiated rule making cannot be used in all situations. Certain subject areas are more fitting than others. A suitable subject area for reg-neg would be one

EXAMPLE 4-4: Reg-Neg: The Great Lakes Initiative

The Ohio Environmental Protection Agency (OEPA) was charged with drafting a series of rules to implement the Great Lakes Initiative. Rather than simply writing the rules and placing them before the affected parties, the OEPA decided to take a negotiated rule-making approach. Consequently, it created the Great Lakes Initiative External Advisory Group (EAG). The EAG was composed of representatives from the agency itself, from the regulated industry, and from environmental groups. The team engaged in eight months of intense negotiations. These negotiations followed a precisely planned series of steps carried out under the watchful eyes of professional facilitators. The EAG reached a firm consensus on most of the issues that arose during the negotiations. Consequently, the Joint Committee on Agency Rule Review of the Ohio General Assembly adopted a set of rules to implement the Great Lakes Initiative in a relatively harmonious atmosphere and with almost no conflict. This is an extremely successful example of reg-neg in action.

that will ultimately affect a wide range of individuals and institutions, is both complicated and controversial, and would meet with resistance if those individuals and institutions affected did not have a hand in shaping the rule. Reg-neg is also a wise course of action when the subject area affected involves nuances that fall outside the expertise of the agency representatives.

Post-Appellate Procedures

Post-appellate procedures involve taking a case that has been rejected or dismissed by a domestic court to an international organization such as the Inter-American Commission on Human Rights of the Organization of American States. In such a situation, a party that has exhausted all domestic remedies available, up to and including the United States Supreme Court, might ask such a **non-governmental organization (NGO)** to hear its case. The post-appellate case is brought against the government of the aggrieved party for allegedly failing to provide an appropriate legal remedy to redress the grievances of the victim. The claim generally involves the violation of some fundamental right, generally a due process or an equal protection right that is guaranteed by an international document such as the American Declaration of the Rights and Duties of Man or the United Nations Universal Declaration of Human Rights. The NGO then hears the case, considers the evidence, and determines whether the party's claim is justified. The NGO may demand that the government of the aggrieved party provide compensation for the injuries visited upon the victim. The NGO may also suggest actions beyond that compensation, including needed reforms in the governmental and/or judicial system to prevent such problems from occurring in the future. Whether the NGOs actually have jurisdiction over such claims is open to debate. Moreover, even if they have jurisdiction, whether their findings are actually enforceable against the government in question is problematic.

International Arbitration Agreements

An **international arbitration agreement** involves a pledge to use arbitration should the parties find themselves in disagreement as to the enforcement rights under the original contract. Generally, the agreement permits the parties to agree on a forum in which the arbitration will be held that is different from the home forum of either party. The parties also can agree to use the rules and procedures promulgated by an independent institution, such as the International Bar Association's Rules of International Commercial Arbitration.

There are several clear advantages to entering an international arbitration agreement. First, because the parties to the agreement are incorporated in different nation-states, they are free to specify whatever forum they can agree upon as the place to hold an arbitration hearing, should that become necessary. This agreement is in contrast to a litigation clause that might specify that the law of one or the other nation would apply to any legal dispute between the parties. Ultimately, such a clause can become very restrictive. The law of a particular nation-state might, for instance, specify that a dispute that arises within the borders of that nation-state would have to be tried within that nation-state. This rule can put one of the two corporations at a distinct disadvantage that may not become evident until the lawsuit has begun. Arbitration agreements can avoid this problem because the arbitration hearing can be held on neutral ground.

Second, when negotiating an arbitration agreement, the parties are also free to specify the identity of the arbitrators or leave open the option to choose the arbitrators at the time of the dispute from a large pool of potential experts. The arbitrators can thus reside in any location that satisfies all of the parties. Third, the same option is open to the parties in relation to their choice of legal representation. Rather than being limited to the forum in which the dispute is to be heard, the parties can bring in representation from any point on the globe. Fourth, using an international arbitration agreement avoids one of the most troublesome problems linked to international litigation: enforcement. Often, a party that has won a favorable decree in one nation will find it challenging to execute that decree in any other nation. International arbitration eliminates this problem because the original arbitration contract will include the terms of enforcement.

Of course, as is often the case, the best laid plans of mice and CEOs often go astray. Thus, sometimes a corporation will find that the jurisdiction that it has chosen for an arbitration hearing has different ideas about whether certain arbitrators and/or attorneys will be permitted to practice within its borders. If a country decides that certain legal representatives and certain arbitrators are not welcome in its jurisdiction, then the parties may find themselves using local attorneys and/or arbitrators, something that not only defeats the objective of the international arbitration agreement but also places the validity and acceptability of the entire arbitration process at risk. This possibility also delays the process further because when an arbitrator is dismissed, the entire action usually must begin again.

Nor are these risks trivial. The danger is especially acute in Latin America, where some nation-states still apply a 19th-century legal principle that says that foreign corporations doing business in a Latin American country or involved in an international legal dispute within the borders of such a country must apply the law of that country, regardless of any agreement made by the parties to the contrary. Sometimes this agreement means simply securing local legal assistance, but it can also mean that the foreign attorneys operating within that jurisdiction are subject to local law, which sometimes includes criminal penalties for not following the procedural rules of that jurisdiction. [Note: For a more detailed look at the problems associated with international arbitration agreements, see: Lawrence W. Newman and David Zaslowsky, "International Litigation/International Arbitration—Pitfalls for Participants," *International Litigation and Arbitration Newsletter*, November 2006, pp. 3–7, retrieved from http://www.bakernet.com. The article first appeared in *The New York Law Journal*, September 29, 2006.]

The Collective Science Court Proposal

A proposed **collective science court (CSC)** would act as a forum for disputes involving scientific and technological controversies. Individuals and institutions with concerns about certain scientific activities, such as genetic engineering, nuclear energy research, and so on, might ask the CSC to act as an impartial arbitrator in the evaluation of those concerns. The judges on the collective science court would be scientists who have had additional legal training and lawyers or judges who have received further education in scientific issues, thus allowing them to use their expertise in deciding scientific cases.

Supporters of the collective science court maintain that a panel of objective judges with scientific backgrounds would provide a neutral body capable of making unbiased, well-informed decisions. Moreover, the CSC would not necessarily provide the last word in any case held under its jurisdiction because an appellate stage would be part of the system. Finally, the decision-making process involved in science-related controversies would be centralized by the collective science court, thus providing a forum that many individuals could use to their advantage.

Critics of the CSC proposal argue that a panel made of objective judges with combined scientific and legal backgrounds would be almost impossible to convene unless some sort of specialized scientific legal academy was established to turn lawyers into scientists and scientists into lawyers. Moreover, critics also point out that the CSC would represent an additional level of bureaucratic red tape. In addition, such a forum could rapidly become buried under an avalanche of claims, many of which would be a frivolous waste of the court's time. Furthermore, some critics argue that because the issues placed before a collective science court would be highly controversial, the entire process could be plagued by political considerations that would threaten the legitimacy of the court itself.

This last group of critics also questions the basic need for a CSC. Some of these analysts point out that, in the main, scientific knowledge is a central issue in a lawsuit in only three situations: (1) when patent law is involved, especially in the evaluation of the validity of a current patent; (2) when scientific evidence must be evaluated by the judge or jury, which often happens in tort law, medical malpractice, product liability, environmental law, and cyber-law cases; and (3) when an experimental station (e.g., a supercollider) or an environmentally risky factory or power plant (read nuclear power here) is planned for a particular locality.

Patent Law Cases In relation to the first issue of *patent law*, the anti-CSC analysts argue that the Court of Appeals for the Federal Circuit is already in place to handle patent claims in an effective and efficient manner. There are merits to this outlook. The fact that the Federal Circuit is already in place and functioning would decrease the time needed to refurbish it as the new CSC. Also, the current judges have a great deal of experience managing such cases; however, as indicated in Chapter 3, the Federal Circuit has had its problems. For instance, the court's handling of a recent case has revealed its confusion over the criteria for patent approval.

A CLASSIC CASE The Case for a Collective Science Court

The classic case of *Daubert v. Merrell Dow Pharmaceuticals, Inc.*, involved a lawsuit filed by the Dauberts against Merrell Dow in which the plaintiffs argued that Bendectin, a drug produced by Merrell Dow and taken by Mrs. Daubert for nausea during her pregnancy, had caused birth defects in their children. The case depended on the issue of causation, a traditional tort law principle that says that to succeed in a negligence lawsuit, a plaintiff must prove that the defendant's action caused the plaintiff's injury; however, because of the scientific nature of the case, the court needed expert testimony to determine causation. The judges were faced with two competing lines of evidence. The defendant's evidence included peer-reviewed articles published in scientific journals and studies issued by the Federal Drug Administration (FDA). None of these reports or articles could find a link between Bendectin and birth defects. In response, the plaintiff's scientific experts offered a reanalysis of the accepted data. This reanalysis demonstrated that the original data had been badly misinterpreted by previous scientists. To determine which line of evidence should be followed, the court had to interpret Rule 702 of the Federal Rules of Evidence and *Frye v. United States*, a case that predated Rule 702, but that had, nevertheless, set up a standard that the federal courts had used for decades to evaluate expert testimony. Ultimately, the Supreme Court established the following five-stage test for determining the scientific accuracy of expert testimony:

1. Is the theory or technique subject to testing under the falsifiability principle?
2. Has the theory or technique been subjected to peer review and publication?
3. What is the known potential error rate of the theory or technique?
4. What standards of control and measurement exist for the theory or technique?
5. Is the theory or technique generally accepted by the scientific community?

The court was also quite clear that the judge in the case is charged with the responsibility of being the "gatekeeper" who determines the admissibility of scientific evidence based on these standards. The court also emphasized that it is not the results that matter, but the reliability of "the principles and the methodology" used to reach those results. What do you think? Are judges, who are educated in legal reasoning techniques and standards, capable of making scientific decisions based on these five criteria? Would scientists retrained in legal reasoning do a better job at interpreting the standards? [See: *Daubert v. Merrell Dow Pharmaceuticals, Inc.* (509 U.S. 579) (U.S.S.Ct.); and *Daubert v. Merrell Dow Pharmaceuticals, Inc.*, 43 F.3d 1311 (Ninth Circuit).]

Source: See: *Daubert v. Merrell Dow Pharmaceuticals, Inc.*, (509 U.S. 579) (U.S.S.Ct.); *Daubert v. Merrell Dow Pharmaceuticals, Inc.*, 43 F.3d 1311 (Ninth Circuit).

Scientific Evidence In relation to the second issue of *scientific evidence*, the anti-CSC lobby argues that the standard for evaluating scientific evidence, known as the *Daubert* Standard, is a clear and straightforward criteria that requires no special scientific training. While this argument seems legitimate at first glance, the *Daubert* Standard has been plagued with difficulties that are not always evident to the lay observer. The accompanying examination of the fallout from the *Daubert* case illustrates this point.

The *Daubert* standard seems to be straightforward enough and should have solved the problem of scientific evidence, but of course it did not. A survey conducted 10 years after the establishment of the standard and reported in an article that appeared in the *Ohio State Law Journal* revealed that 96 percent of the 400 judges covered by the study lacked a fundamental grasp of the first principle of falsifiability and the third principle of "error rate." These results indicate that a simple reinterpretation of the rules, even one reengineered very carefully by the Supreme Court, did not solve the problem of scientific evidence and may even have aggravated it. Additional efforts are under way short of the CSC that have helped deal with the issue of science in the courts. For example, the Advanced Science and Technology Adjudication Resources (ASTAR) in Washington, DC, was established by Congress as a scientific and technological educational resource center for judges. Also, as noted in Chapter 3, the Federal Judicial Center has inaugurated a decade-long pilot project aimed at determining what improvements might be made to the way that patent law cases are handled by the Federal Circuit. It remains to be seen whether such steps will eliminate the need for the proposed CSC. [See: Joelle Anne Moreno, "Einstein on the Bench?" *Ohio State Law Journal* 64 (2003), p. 531; "Science in the Court: NHGRI Scientists Present Latest Genomic Advances to Visiting Judges," *National Human Genome Research Institute*, June 2010; Karen Redmond, "District Courts Selected for Patent Pilot Program," *The Third Branch News*, June 7, 2011; and "The Patent Pilot Program Takes Off Around the Country," *Gibbons IP Law Alert*, October 20, 2011.] In Chapter 6, the Daubert case is revisited to examine how the Federal Rules were amended to help judges deal with scientific evidence.

Scientific Construction In relation to the third issue, the *scientific construction* of experimental stations, nuclear power plants, genetic engineering centers, supercolliders, and the like, those opposing the CSC insist that creating a science court to determine future development in a region gives too much authority to a nondemocratic institution. One vivid example of this type of struggle occurred in Minnesota. In that case, two power cooperatives, the Cooperative Power Association and the United Power Association, announced their intention to construct high-voltage power lines across Minnesota farmland. The owners of the farms involved challenged the project, arguing that the planned route of the lines would destroy their ability to use their own farmland appropriately. The governor of Minnesota called for the creation of a science court to resolve the issue. The science court would have been made of scientists, engineers, and other experts educated in the discipline and the industry involved in the dispute, thus allowing them to use their expertise in deciding the case.

The Minnesota experience seemed to confirm the fears of the anti-CSC lobby at least in two respects. First, a science court will not succeed unless it has the power to compel the parties to submit to its authority. In the Minnesota case, for instance, the co-ops saw no reason to cooperate with a voluntary court because their project had already been approved by conventional authorities. Second, a successful science court must have the power to halt work on any project that is the focus of the court's investigation. Otherwise, the court's entire process becomes an exercise in futility. On the other hand, these nondemocratic features could be overcome if the court is fashioned to ensure that all sides have the opportunity to present their views on all issues facing the court. Permitting certain parties to speak on certain issues while denying the same right to others can destroy the credibility of the court and of those involved in its creation and operation. [See: Barry Casper and Paul

Wellstone, *Powerline: The First Battle of America's Energy War* (Amherst: University of Massachusetts Press, 1981); and Barry Casper and Paul Wellstone, "Science Court on Trial in Minnesota," *Science in Context* (Cambridge, MA: MIT Press, 1982).]

quick quiz 4-3

1. The partnering process begins with a meeting held after a contract has been finalized but before the project has begun.   true | false
2. In negotiated rule making, a government agency creates a new set of regulations without the troublesome, time-consuming, expensive, and difficult step of getting input from its constituency, thus streamlining the process, saving money, and eliminating controversy.   true | false
3. The proposed science court would act as a forum for disputes involving scientific and technological controversies.   true | false

4-4 Cyber Alternative Dispute Resolution

The legal profession in the United States and in the European Union has become increasingly more comfortable with the 21st-century electronic revolution. Many courts now rely heavily on cyber-filing, cyber-messaging, and cyber-discovery. Therefore, it should come as no surprise that the next step in the cyber-evolution of the courts involves a move toward **cyber alternative dispute resolution (C-ADR)**, also known as electronic dispute resolution (e-ADR) and online dispute resolution (ODR). C-ADR has actually been in the works since the late 1990s. However, as with e-discovery and e-filing, attorneys and judges were slow to pick up on the advantage of the new process. According to the experts, C-ADR will improve the chances of getting a fair review of a case justice while, at the same time, avoiding many of the problems associated with traditional ADR methods (also sometimes called offline ADR). Proponents predict that C-ADR will be so fast, so efficient, and so economical that it will eventually replace offline ODR completely. This claim may be a bit optimistic, especially since offline ADR already claims to be faster, more efficient, and more economical than traditional litigation. The three types of C-ADR discussed here include cyber-negotiation, cyber-mediation, and cyber-arbitration. There are, however, additional C-ADR opportunities such as those involving early neutral evaluators, settlement week, summary jury trials, and private jury trials, In addition, the European Union has already launched its own online C-ADR program called the EU-ODR Platform.

Cyber-Negotiation

Cyber-negotiation (C-neg) involves an attempt to reach an agreement between two or more parties by using specialized electronic communication techniques, generally e-mail. Face-to-face negotiation can often be hampered by distance, language, and time issues. The process of engaging in cyber-negotiation can remove all three barriers, permitting parties in different countries and different time zones to come together in a timely, efficient, and cost-effective fashion unhampered by translation difficulties. However, C-neg is not without its problems. Studies in the use of e-mail, the primary means of conducting a C-neg session, have revealed that despite the prevalence of e-mail in business, its use can often cause unintentional misunderstandings, increased anger, and the appearance of dishonesty—all of which can lead to further distrust and an overall drop in cooperation. For this reason, despite the cost and time benefits associated with cyber-negotiation, it may be best to use it only when cost and distances make face-to-face negotiation impossible. [See: Julio Cesar Betancourt, "Online Dispute Resolution (ODR): What Is It, and Is It the Way Forward?" *Arbitration*, 3 (2013), Chartered Institute of Arbitrators. See also Dan DeStephen and John Helie, "OnLine Dispute Resolution: Implications for the ADR Profession," *Mediate.com: Everything Mediation*, July 2000, http://www.mediate.com/articles/helie1.cfm.]

Cyber-Mediation

Cyber-mediation (C-med) involves the addition of an impartial third party who acts as an intermediary between two opposing parties. Cyber-mediation has many of the same advantages and disadvantages as C-neg. There is no doubt distance, language, time, and money problems can be dealt with more easily with C-med than with offline mediation. However, the use of e-mail as the prime method of conducting C-med can lead to the same problems of anger, misunderstanding, and distrust as C-neg. These problems can be reduced more easily with C-med, however, because the intermediary can act as an interpreter of misconstrued content, and thus, defuse any potentially volatile situations. Still even the best mediator can be put off by accidental sarcasm, unintentional insults, and inadvertent slights. For this reason, C-med is best carried out on Skype, FaceTime, or some other equally effective electronic face-to-face technique. Electronic face-to-face meetings can eliminate or at least minimize the chance of such misunderstandings. Recall that one of the key differences between mediation and arbitration is that a mediator does not decide who wins and who loses but, instead, attempts to get each side to agree to a solution to the problem at hand. In contrast, in arbitration the arbitrator actually decides on winners and losers. This, of course, gives rise to other problems in the case of C-ADR. It is to that issue that we now turn our attention. [See: Betancourt. See also DeStephen and Helie.]

Cyber-Arbitration

Cyber-arbitration (C-arb) involves the use of an impartial third party who uses electronic communication techniques to settle disputes between two or more parties. As is true of C-neg and c-med, the primary means of online communication is the use of e-mail. Like C-med, C-arb is less susceptible to misunderstandings and misinterpretations because the arbitrator is present to iron out many of those difficulties. Of course, electronic face-to-face options are available to arbitrators just as they are available to mediators. C-arb, however, has a few problems unique to that platform. For example, both offline arbitration and C-arb make more use of evidence and witnesses than any type of negotiation or mediation. This makes both offline arbitration and C-arb more expensive and more time consuming than either type of negotiation or mediation. Specifically, the very nature of arbitration as a quasi-judicial procedure will generally require the need to call witnesses and to present evidence. Both types of arbitration also require a finished document detailing the terms of the arbitration agreement, again complicating matters further. Until recently, the absolute need for paper documents as evidence and as agreements hampered the use of C-arb. Now, however, with the advent of e-signatures, paper documents are no longer needed. This should increase the popularity of C-arb. Even so, it is unlikely that C-arb will ever truly be less time consuming and less expensive than offline arbitration except for the costs and time delays associated with travel. Still, because of the delicate and complicated nature of many arbitration hearings, C-arb may best be left for small claims matters that involve a comparatively straightforward set of facts and a relatively clear set of legal issues [See: Betancourt. See also DeStephen and Helie.]

Additional Opportunities for Cyber-ADR

So far, we have focused on negotiation, mediation, and arbitration—three traditional ADR methods that are fairly well suited for some form of cyber-ADR. However, other ADR strategies can also be easily adapted to cyber techniques, including early neutral evaluation (ENE), settlement negotiations, and both summary and private jury trials. For example, recall that in early neutral evaluation, an unbiased evaluator is brought into a case to assess the facts and the legal arguments and to offer an educated opinion about the outcome of the case. At the outset of a case, the evaluator is provided with an overview of the facts involved in the dispute and a summary of the legal arguments on which each side has built his or her case. The evaluator then offers his or her evaluation of the case, especially in terms of which party might prevail. It is easy enough to do all of this online, The evaluator can receive copies of the documents via e-mail and can send an evaluation back in the same way. The same electronic process can be used during settlement week and as part of the negotiated rule-making process. Documents and arguments can be transferred online from the parties to the mediators, who then act as online go-betweens as arguments are made by the parties for settlement consideration and for the rule-making negotiation process. The mediators in both cases can then send back their decisions online.

Both summary jury trials and private civil trials could also be handled by electronic communication techniques by assembling the participants online for face-to-face video presentations via Skype, FaceTime, or any other face-to-face online platform that might be available, now or in the future. As the use of C-ADR has increased, the need for a set for a set of ethical standards has become more and more apparent. Accordingly, the National Center for Technology and Dispute Resolution has established a set of principles designed to equip practitioners with an understanding of how to deal with a wide variety of ethical dilemmas. The principles are divided into 17 different categories that overlap and complement one another: accessibility, accountability, competence, confidentiality, empowerment, equality, fairness, honesty, impartiality, informed participation, innovation, integration, legal obligation, neutrality, protection from harm, security, and transparency. [See: DeStephen and Helie. See also: Leah Wing, "Ethical Principles for Online Dispute Resolution: A GPS Device for the Field," *International Journal of Online Dispute Resolution* 3, No. 1 (2016), pp. 12–29.]

The European Union's Cyber-ADR Platform

Recently, the European Union announced that it had has introduced a new cyber-ADR platform that will permit consumers to file complaints with sellers and to settle those complaints completely online. The multilingual platform—which is called, logically enough, the EU ODR Platform—can be accessed online by the consumer. Each company in every member state will be required to provide a link to the EU ODR Platform on its company website. Once the consumer has accessed the EU ODR Platform, he or she will fill out and submit an online form that describes the nature of the problem. The form is sent online directly to the company, which then proposes a neutral third party, referred to as an ADR entity, to hear and settle the case. The consumer and the company can then negotiate the selection of the ADR entity. Once the consumer and the company select a mutually satisfactory ADR entity, he or she will examine the complaint and render a decision. The entire process is guaranteed not to take longer than 90 days, which is considerably shorter than the time that would be spent in court for the same complaint. [See: "Commission Launches New Platform for Alternative Dispute Resolution between Customers and Online Traders," *European Commission—Daily News*, Brussels, January 8, 2016, http://europa.eu/rapid/midday-express-08-01-2016.htm; "Solving Disputes Online: New Platform for Consumers and Traders," *European Commission—Press Release*, Brussels, February 15, 2016, http://europa.eu/rapid/pres-release_IP-16-297_en.htm; and Vera Jourova, "Settling Consumer Disputes Online," *European Commission*, *Fact Sheet*, January 2016.]

quick quiz 4-4

1. Cyber-negotiation (C-neg) involves an attempt to reach an agreement between two or more parties by using specialized electronic communication techniques, generally e-mail. — true | false
2. ADR strategies such as early neutral evaluation, settlement negotiations, summary, and private jury trials are too complicated and time consuming to be use C-ADR techniques. — true | false
3. The European Union has introduced an new cyber-ADR platform that will permit consumers to file complaints with sellers and to settle those complaints completely online. — true | false

Summary

4.1 Litigation has always been a part of the American legal system. Lately, however, things have begun to change. The extensive backlog in many court systems and the perceived injustice of many verdicts have led many people to seek other methods to redress their grievances. These other methods are often grouped under the heading of alternative dispute resolution (ADR). Alternative dispute resolution occurs whenever individuals attempt to resolve a disagreement by stepping outside the usual adversarial system and applying certain creative settlement techniques, many of which have fact-finding and the discovery of truth as their goal.

4.2 There are many different ADR techniques that can be invoked once a dispute has arisen between parties. These include but are not limited to mediation, arbitration, med-arb, early neutral evaluation, summary jury trials, and private civil trials.

4.3 Since ADR has become so popular in recent years, some businesspeople are taking a proactive approach to the situation by agreeing in advance to submit to one of the alternative dispute resolution tools should a disagreement between the parties arise later. These proactive ADR techniques include, but are not limited to, partnering, ADR contract clauses, settlement week, negotiated rule making, international arbitration agreements, the post-appellate option, and the collective science court proposal.

4.4 The next step in the cyber-evolution of the courts involves a move toward cyber-alternative dispute resolution (C-ADR). Cyber-negotiation (C-neg) involves an attempt to reach an agreement between two or more parties by using electronic communication. Cyber-mediation (C-med) involves the addition of an impartial third party who acts as an intermediary between two opposing parties as they negotiate an agreement. Cyber-arbitration (C-arb) involves the use of an impartial third party who uses electronic communication techniques to settle disputes between two or more parties. The European Union has implemented a new cyber-ADR platform that will permit consumers to file complaint with sellers and to settle those complaints completely online.

Key Terms

ADR contract clause, 103
alternative dispute resolution (ADR), 93
arbitration, 99
arbitrator, 99
collective science court (CSC), 108
cyber alternative dispute resolution (C-ADR), 111
cyber-arbitration (C-arb), 112
cyber-mediation (C-med), 112
cyber-negotiation (C-neg), 111
early neutral evaluation (ENE), 100
international arbitration agreement, 107
med-arb, 100
mediation, 98
mediator, 98
negotiated rule making (reg-neg), 106

non-governmental organization (NGO), 107
partnering, 103
post-appellate procedures, 107
private civil trial, 102
settlement week, 106
summary jury trial, 101

Questions for Review and Discussion

1. What are the shortcomings of litigation?
2. What are the advantages and disadvantages of ADR?
3. What are the advantages of mediation?
4. What is the nature of an arbitration hearing?
5. What happens during the med-arb process?
6. What is the role of an early neutral evaluator?
7. What happens in the running of a summary jury trial?
8. What are the options available for proactive ADR?
9. What are the pros and cons of the collective science court proposal?
10. What cyber-ADR platforms are available today?

Cases for Analysis

1. John and Carolyn Spencer contracted with Schumacher Homes of Circleville Inc. (Schumacher) for the building of a single-family home in Mason County, West Virginia. After construction was completed and the Spencers had moved in, they discovered numerous problems with house. The Spencers contacted Schumacher, which agreed to remedy the defects. Unfortunately, Schumacher never came through and did not fulfill its promise to fix the problems. Accordingly, the Spencers sued Schumacher in state court of West Virginia, alleging negligence, fraud, breach of express and implied warranties, breach of the duty of good faith, violation of the Magnuson-Moss Warranty Act, and of more than one state law. Schumacher pointed out that the construction contract included a clause that said that all disputes between the construction company and the homeowner would be decided by an arbitrator. The Spencers argued that the arbitration clause was unconscionable and a violation of state law. Schumacher noted that the Federal Arbitration Act superseded state laws in this instance and that under the FAA, arbitration was the preferred method of settling such disputes. Schumacher also pointed to the fact that the clause itself said that questions of arbitrability were to be decided by the arbitrator, not the court. Schumacher also pointed out the FAA, which supported such arbitration clauses and the delegation of questions of arbitrability to the arbitrator, took precedence over state law. The Spencers simply reiterated their original claim that the arbitration clause was procedurally and substantively unconscionable. The trial court agreed with the Spencers. The case then went to the Supreme Court of Appeals of West Virginia. In its decision, the Supreme Court of West Virginia severely criticized past rulings by the U.S. Supreme Court upholding the validity of the FAA in relation to its provision supporting the delegation of arbitrability to the arbitrator. Accordingly, the High Court of West Virginia agreed with the trial court and declared the arbitration clause unconscionable. The case ended up in the U.S. Supreme Court. Is the Supreme Court of West Virginia correct? How will the U.S. Supreme Court rule in this case? Explain. [See: *Schumacher Homes v. Spencer*, No. 14-0441 (April 24, 2015).]

2. Eddie Lee Howard and Shane D. Schneider entered an employment agreement with Nitro-Lift Technologies LLL (Nitro) that included a confidentiality and noncompetition agreement. The employment contract also included an arbitration clause. Both Howard and Schneider, after working on projects for Nitro in Texas, Oklahoma, and Arkansas, left their jobs and began to work for a competitor. Understandably disturbed by this breach of etiquette, not to mention the breach of contract, Nitro served them both with a demand for arbitration. Howard and Schneider sued Nitro in the state court of Oklahoma arguing that under the state law of Oklahoma, the confidentiality and noncompetition agreement was void. The trial court dismissed the case filed by Howard and Schneider, finding that under the arbitration clause and the Federal Arbitration Act (FAA), the dispute had to be sent to an arbitrator. The case was accepted by the Oklahoma Supreme Court. The court sided with the employees, asking Nitro to show why the case did not fall under state law and said that, as a result, under state law, the confidentiality and noncompetition agreement was barred. Nitro pointed to the FAA and to a long

line of precedent from the U.S. Supreme Court, which supported its position that the arbitration clause was valid and that the case should be decided by an arbitrator. Howard and Schneider argued that despite the FAA and that long line of precedent, the state court could still interpret the validity of the rest of the contract, including the validity of the confidentiality and noncompetition agreement clause, which state law clearly held as invalid (or did it?). Who is correct? Does the FAA and its line of precedent supercede the state's law against confidentiality and non-competition agreement? Explain. [See: *Nitro-Lift Technologies, L.L.C. v. Howard*, 133 S. Ct. 500 (2012).]

3. Hall St. Associates LLC (Hall) entered a lease agreement with Mattel Inc. Mattel broke the lease before the appointed time and also failed to indemnify Hall for cleaning up the property in order to comply with state environmental law. The case went to trial, and the court ruled in favor of Mattel in relation to its right to terminate the lease. After this, the parties agreed to arbitrate the issue of the clean-up indemnification under the terms of the arbitration clause in the lease agreement. The arbitrator found in favor of Mattel, noting that state law did not require the indemnification. Hall asked the court to review the decision of the arbitrator, arguing that the arbitration clause in the lease agreement permitted the court to review and reverse the decision of the arbitrator, something not allowed under the FAA. The court ruled that the arbitrator had made an error of law in the decision and ordered the case sent back to the arbitrator, who changed the ruling in favor of Hall. The case then went to the court of appeals, which reversed the order in favor of Mattel, noting that the only ways that a court can overrule an arbitrator are the four ways listed in the FAA. In other words, the parties cannot, by agreement, broaden the conditions under which the arbitrator can be overruled. The case then went to the U.S. Supreme Court. Will the High Court uphold the ruling of the appeals court? Explain. [See: *Hall St. Associates, L.L.C., v. Mattel, Inc.*, 552 U.S. 576 (2008).]

4. Turner Pte. Ltd. was the main contractor in the building of *Gateway*, a long-term project to be constructed in the heart of Singapore. One of Turner's subcontractors was a company called Builders Federal Ltd. (BFL). As part of the overall contract, the two companies signed an arbitration agreement, which was designated as Clause 22 in the main contract. When the two parties found themselves in the middle of several serious disputes, they invoked Clause 22 and began arbitration. Turner asked that David Gardam be appointed as the arbitrator, and BFL asked for Douglas Smith. The court appointed Smith. From the outset, there was bad blood between Turner and Smith, which was revealed in a series of letters that went back and forth between the parties and Smith. At one point in the process, Turner realized that Clause 22 actually had no legal effect until each party activated it by giving its permission to proceed with arbitration. Smith denied that this was the case and ordered the arbitration process to continue. Turner objected, and Smith, who admitted that Turner had made a fairly convincing case, agreed to submit that argument to the High Court of Singapore. Nevertheless, Smith pushed the arbitration process forward. BFL was delighted, but Turner objected. Still the action went forward despite the precarious nature of Smith's position as arbitrator. Can the high court of Singapore dismiss Smith even though BFL is quite satisfied with his work as arbitrator? What grounds might be used to dismiss Smith? If Smith is dismissed, will the arbitration process continue or start over? [See: *Turner (East Asia) Pte. Ltd. v. Builders Federal (Hong Kong) Ltd.*, SLR 532 SGHC 47 (Singapore High Court).]

5. Jessica Gonzales obtained an official restraining order from a Colorado court that prevented her estranged husband from approaching either her or her children any closer than 100 yards. The order, however, did not stop her husband, who kidnapped their three children. Mrs. Gonzales went to the police and asked for their help. The police did very little to help her, despite the restraining order. Early the next morning, Mr. Gonzales arrived at the police station and began shooting at police officers, who shot back and eventually killed him. After the shooting was over, the police found the bodies of the three young daughters in Mr. Gonzales's truck. Mrs. Gonzales brought suit against the police department, arguing that her due process rights had been violated when the police did not enforce the restraining order. The case went from trial court to the appellate court to the U.S. Supreme Court, with no result other than a dismissal of the suit. Mrs. Gonzales, with the assistance of the American Civil Liberties Union, filed a post-appellate complaint against the United States with the Inter-American Commission on Human Rights. In her complaint, Mrs. Gonzales argued that she had been deprived of due process and equal protection under the American Declaration of the Rights and Duties of Man, an agreement that the United States was legally bound to follow. Mrs. Gonzales and her attorneys hoped that the

commission would issue a judgment in her favor and against the United States. What two initial questions must be answered first before this post-appellate case can begin? Explain. [See: *Jessica Ruth Gonzales v. The United States of America*, Petition No. P-1490-05, The Inter-American Commission on Human Rights of the Organization of American States.]

6. In a case involving an ADR clause, the parties to a contract disagreed as to whether the clause required them to submit a dispute over a trade secret problem to arbitration. The clause required the parties to submit "any controversy or claim arising out of the agreement" to arbitration. Strictly speaking, the trade secret controversy did not arise "out of" the agreement; however, it was clear that the trade secret dispute was related to the agreement. The trial court held that the language of the ADR clause was too narrow and that because the trade secret dispute did not arise out of the controversy, the parties were not required to send it to arbitration. Should the appellate court overrule the trial court's decision rejecting the requirement that the parties arbitrate the trade secret dispute? Explain your response. [See: *Tracer Research Corp. v. National Environmental Services, Co.*, 42 F.3d 1292 (9th Cir.).]

7. In the early 1990s, serious concerns about the dangers associated with genetic engineering arose after an incident pertaining to the use of certain genetically altered mice in experiments involving a highly infectious disease. In the wake of these concerns, the National Institute of Allergy and Infectious Diseases held a conference to discuss the level of safety that should be followed in laboratories involved in such research. Those involved in the conference included the researchers themselves, certain biosafety experts, representives from organizations involved in or planning to be involved in similar research, and governmental representatives from the Centers for Disease Control, the National Institutes of Health, and the Food and Drug Administration. Would this type of situation be appropriate for a reg-neg approach? Explain. Might a science court handle this type of situation even better than an agency's reg-neg procedure? Explain.

8. Adam Bontrager, the defendant, purchased a piece of land. Before the sale, the previous owner had been notified by the Department of Health that the current septic system on the property was not up to specs. Consequently, the Health Department ordered a systems upgrade. Once Bontrager bought the property, the obligation to upgrade the system passed to him. Bontrager began the process of upgrading the system and then stopped. Bontrager argued that since he was Amish and since his religion forbid him to use electricity, which the upgrade required, the Health Department order was a violation of his religious rights under the U.S. Constitution. Without the system upgrade, untreated sewage was flowing into a local stream causing a health hazard. As a result, the defendant was cited for a violation of the administrative code and fined accordingly. The case seems to be one for which ADR is well suited. Can the judge order arbitration or mediation in this case? Why or why not? [See: *State v. Bontrager*, 149 Ohio Misc.2d 33 (Newton Falls Municipal Court).]

9. Audrey Kemmelman, a freelance photographer, entered a work-for-hire agreement with *The Daily Montgomery Central Times* Corporation. During the negotiation stages, Kemmelman asked that an ADR clause be added to the contract that would compel the signatories to submit any claim to ADR. The clause stated that in the event of any dispute, the signatories to the contract would first discuss the points of conflict informally. If after 30 days, no satisfactory solution had been reached, the signatories agreed to submit the problem to the American Arbitration Association, which would assist in selecting an objective moderator who would help the signatories decide on an appropriate ADR method. Which party is likely to benefit the most from the addition of the ADR clause to the contract? Explain.

Design Elements: The Opening Case: ©Sharpstock/Alamy; A Classic Case: ©Evlakhov Valeriy/Shutterstock

quick quiz Answers

4-1	4-2	4-3	4-4
1. F	1. T	1. T	1. T
2. T	2. T	2. F	2. F
3. T	3. T	3. T	3. T

Chapter 5: Criminal Law and Cybercrimes

5-1 Definition and Classes of Crimes
Definition of a Crime • Criminal Law in the American System • Classes of Crimes

5-2 Elements of a Crime
A Criminal Act • The Required State of Mind • The Matter of Motive • The Matter of Corporate Liability • The Matter of Punishment

5-3 Specific Crimes
Crimes against People • Crimes against Property • Crimes Involving Business • Crimes against Justice

5-4 Cybercrimes
Cyber-Trespass • Crimes Committed with a Computer • Crimes That Target Computers • Federal Cybercrimes • The Global Cyber-Crisis

5-5 Defenses to Criminal Liability
The Insanity Defense • Entrapment • Justifiable Force • Mistake

THE OPENING CASE *Round 1*
United States v. Hearst: Patty, the Newspaper Heiress or Tania, the Urban Guerrilla?

This case began when 19-year-old Patty Hearst, the granddaughter of newspaper giant William Randolph Hearst, was kidnapped in California by members of an urban guerrilla outfit called the Symbionese Liberation Army (SLA). The SLA, which was dedicated to the destruction of the corporate capitalist state, demanded that the Hearst family give some $400 million in food to the poor of California, in return for the release of Hearst. The Hearst family countered with an offer of $6 million in food, which they promptly delivered. Unfortunately, the SLA was dissatisfied with quality of the food, and Hearst was never freed. A short time later, a video tape was released by the SLA on which Hearst, allegedly of her own volition, declared her membership in the SLA. A short time after that, Hearst was one of several SLA members who robbed the Hibernia Bank in San Francisco. Following the robbery, apparently to discredit reports that she had been coerced into joining the bank job, a new video was released by the SLA in which Hearst declared that she was not brainwashed but was, instead, a loyal member of the SLA. In the tape, she also declared that the bank was robbed to obtain funds to support the anti-capitalist revolution, which she joined as a dedicated soldier. A warrant was issued for her arrest and, shortly thereafter, but not before she had participated in another crime, she and several additional members of the SLA were arrested in an apartment in San Francisco.

During processing, after her arrest, when asked her profession, she replied, "urban guerrilla." Hearst was indicted for assault with intent to commit murder, assault with a deadly weapon, robbery, and kidnapping. She was tried only for the crimes of armed robbery and using a firearm to commit a felony. The Hearst family hired F. Lee Bailey, probably the most well-known, most effective criminal defense attorney in the United States at the time. Bailey knew that he could not argue that Hearst had not committed armed robbery. Aside from the eyewitnesses who were available to testify, Hearst had, herself, stated on tape that she had robbed the bank. In addition, the prosecution had tapes of conversations between Hearst and Tobin, a friend who visited her while she was incarcerated, on which she made incriminating statements. Given this damaging evidence, Bailey defended Hearst by placing her mental state at the time of the robbery in doubt. However, in an interesting move, Bailey did not use the traditional insanity plea formulas. Instead, he used a new formula known as *coercive persuasion*, which essentially means that Hearst had been "brainwashed" by members of the SLA and, therefore, had no control over her actions during the robbery at the bank. The defense painted a picture of a defeated and exhausted Hearst who had been blindfolded, isolated (locked in a closet, actually), and abused by her captors. After days of this treatment, Hearst, in a sense, lost her own identity and was subsumed into the SLA. Therefore, Bailey argued, it was not Hearst who robbed the bank, but a new personality—the urban guerrilla named "Tania," created by the coercive abuse tactics used by her captors. Despite this defense, Hearst was convicted of armed robbery and sentenced to 35 years. The sentence was eventually lowered to 7 years. She served 22 months, was released, and was ultimately pardoned by President Clinton in 2001. [See: *United States v. Hearst*, 563 F2d 1313 (9th Cir. 1978).]

Opening Case Questions

1. What is the difference between the criminal act and the required state of mind? Explain.
2. What is armed robbery? Explain.
3. What is the insanity defense, and what tests are used to demonstrate insanity within the American criminal court system? Explain.
4. What is the difference between the traditional insanity defense and coercive persuasion? Explain.
5. Who has the power under the U.S. Constitution to pardon convicted criminals? Explain.

Source: See: *United States v. Hearst,* 563 F2d 1313 (9th Cir. 1978).

Learning Objectives

1. Explain the purpose of criminal law.
2. Enumeate the various categories and classes of crimes.
3. Describe the nature of an act within the concept of criminal liabiliy.
4. Identify the four mental states to be found in the criminal code.
5. Explain the nature of corporate criminal liability.
6. Explain the various theories of punishment within criminal law.
7. Enumerate and explain the elements of several key crimes.
8. Define and explain the nature of cybercrimes.
9. Explain the standards for the insanity defense in criminal law.
10. Outline the requirements of entrapment as a defense in criminal law.

5-1 Definition and Classes of Crimes

Perhaps one of the most discussed and least understood areas of the law is criminal law. Most people think they know a lot about criminal law because they hear politicians talk about it, read about it online, or see it portrayed in the media. In fact, all three of these sources, but especially the media, spread an enormous amount of misinformation, alternative facts, post-truths, and fake news about criminal law and criminal procedure. This section of the chapter attempts to correct some of these errors by defining crime and explaining the various classes of crimes.

Definition of a Crime

A **crime** is an offense against the public at large. As such, a crime threatens the peace, safety, and well-being of the entire community. For this reason, crimes are punishable by the official governing body of a nation or state. Also for this reason, the state or federal government, representing the public at large, is the *prosecution*—that is, the one who brings the criminal action. The person accused of the crime is called the *defendant*. No act can be considered criminal unless it is prohibited by the law of the place where it is committed, and the law provides for the punishment of the offenders. These laws are created by the federal government and the governments of the 50 states.

The Objectives of Criminal Law The primary objectives of criminal law are to protect the public at large, to preserve order and stability within society, to punish those who commit criminal acts, and to discourage future criminal activity. In contrast, as we shall see, tort law is concerned with private wrongs that have caused injury to an individual's physical well-being, property, business, or reputation. Because tort law involves private wrongs rather than public ones, it focuses on the victim. Because criminal law protects the public, it seeks to eliminate crime by punishing wrongdoers and removing them from society. When a tort is committed, the victim has a cause of action against the person who has committed the tort, which may permit the victim to recover money as compensation for any injuries that he or she has suffered. In contrast, when a crime is committed, the government may prosecute the accused.

A close and unbiased analysis of the objectives of tort law and those of criminal law will reveal to even the most casual observer that criminal law is more akin to the principles supported by Thomas Hobbes and James Madison, while those of tort law sound more like those upheld by John Locke. Recall that Hobbes and Madison were both concerned with protecting two core rights: the right to life and the right to a secure life. The objectives of criminal law include protecting the public at large, preserving order and stability within society, punishing those who commit criminal acts, and discouraging future criminal activity—all of which sound very much like those two core rights. In contrast, the objectives of tort law, which include the vindication of private wrongs that have caused injury to an individual's physical well-being, property, business, or reputation, are reminiscent of Locke's focus on the rights of the individual.

Prosecutions and Lawsuits A single act can be both a crime and a tort. Thus, when a criminal battery is committed against a victim, the criminal defendant will be prosecuted for that battery in a criminal case, the results of which can include imprisonment, a fine, or both. However, the defendant can also be sued by the victim in tort law. The victim will seek damages from the defendant, which can include money for hospital bills, lost wages, pain and suffering, and so on. The standard of proof required in a criminal case differs from that required in a tort case. In a criminal case, the prosecutor or district attorney is required to prove that the criminal defendant is guilty of the crime *beyond a reasonable doubt*. In a tort case, the plaintiff's attorney must prove that the defendant is liable for the tort *by a preponderance of the evidence*. Because criminal defendants can lose their freedom; be fined; and sometimes, in capital cases, even lose their lives, the level of proof needed for a conviction is higher than what is needed to demonstrate liability in a tort case.

Double Jeopardy The U.S. Constitution protects people from being tried twice for the same crime. This principle is called the rule of **double jeopardy**. Double jeopardy, however, does not protect a defendant from being tried for a criminal offense and then being sued under tort law for that same wrongful act. This is what happened in the case of O.J. Simpson. After being found not guilty for the crime of murder, he was sued by his children for the wrongful death of their mother. This did not violate the rule of double jeopardy. Note that the Simpson case also illustrates the difference between the standard of proof in a criminal case and the standard in a tort case. Thus, although the prosecutors failed to prove Simpson guilty *beyond a reasonable doubt*, he was found liable for wrongful death *by a preponderance of the evidence*. It is also interesting to note that a single offense may trigger two prosecutions if the offense can be designated as two different crimes and can be tried in two different courts.

Thus, it is possible, for example, for a police officer to be tried in a state court for assaulting a suspect and be tried in federal court for depriving that same suspect of his civil rights.

Victim's Rights Under common law, criminal law did not focus on the victim. The theory was that if the victim needed some sort of compensation for the actions of the defendant, it was up to the victim to pursue that case in tort law. This has been altered somewhat by the legislatures that have enacted statutes that create a series of **victim's rights**. These rights often include notice to the victim that an offender has been arrested; the name of the criminal defendant; the defendant's eligibility for pretrial release; the telephone number of the law enforcement agency responsible for the defendant; and the date, time, and place of the defendant's release, if that occurs. Later in the legal process, the victim is also generally notified of the defendant's acquittal or conviction, the defendant's incarceration, the defendant's appeal, and the defendant's release date. Victims are also permitted to provide the prosecutor with a written description of his or her injuries. In addition, in many states, the victim is permitted to be present at the defendant's trial, is entitled to the return of his or her property, and is empowered to give the court a victim's impact statement before sentencing and another statement when the defendant's possible release is pending. In most cases, it is the prosecutor or the district attorney who is charged by law with enforcing the rights of victims.

Criminal Law in the American System

The American legal structure consists of the federal and the state systems. Both make and enforce criminal law; however, because there are 50 states and the District of Columbia, it is actually more accurate to say that the American system is made up of 52 systems.

A QUESTION OF ETHICS

Victim's Rights in the Texting Suicide Case

One of the most sensational trials to capture the media's attention in recent memory is the "texting suicide case" in which a teenage boy committed suicide by carbon monoxide poisoning after being told on the phone by his girlfriend to "get back in the car." The teenage defendant in the case was charged and tried for involuntary manslaughter. At a bench trial, she was found guilty. Before the sentencing, several family members, including the victim's father, mother, and sister, were permitted to make statements before the judge. After hearing those statements, the judge sentenced the defendant to 2.5 years of imprisonment. He then ordered her to serve 15 months of that sentence in the Bristol County House of Detention. The judge suspended the remainder of the sentence and ordered her to serve five years of probation after serving that 15 months. Victims are permitted to make pre-sentencing statements before the court in order to give them a chance to tell their side of the story so that the judge has an understanding of the impact that the crime in question has had on those who felt its effects most acutely. In a sense, victim statements put a face on the victims for the judge. On the other hand, part of the purpose of the law is to be as objectively fair as possible. This is why the victims of a crime do not sit on the jury. Some experts argue that victim statements make a mockery of the objective nature of the law because they unfairly prejudice the sentencing judge against the defendant right before the penalty is meted out. Using one of the ethical theories that we discussed in Chapter 1 (social contract ethics, utilitarianism, and rationale ethics), determine whether victim statements before sentencing are ethical. Explain. [See: Katharine Q. Seelye and Jess Bidgood, "Trial in Texting Suicide Lays Bare Pain of Two Teenagers," *The New York Times*, June 13, 2017, pp. A-1, A-20; and Emily Shapiro and Doug Lantz, "Michelle Carter Sentenced to 2.5 Years in Texting Suicide Case," *ABC News*, August 3, 2017, http://abcnews.go.com/US/michelle-carter-set-sentenced-texting-suicide-case/story?id=48947807.]

Nevertheless, it is helpful to limit any discussion of the law to an examination of federal and state systems. We simply must remember that each state has its own code and its own procedures, which, though similar in most respects to all other states, may have its own peculiarities.

Federal Criminal Law Another peculiarity about the American system is that the federal government has no express power in the Constitution that allows it to enact criminal law statutes or establish a national police force. Yet the federal government does enact criminal law and has set up the Federal Bureau of Investigation (FBI) as a national police force. The federal government also has a cabinet-level criminal law enforcement official called the attorney general who has the power to conduct federal criminal investigations. The existence of

A CLASSIC CASE The Outer Limits of Federal Jurisdiction

In the classic case of *Wickard v. Filburn*, the U.S. Supreme Court set the outer limits of the federal government's authority to create statutes that, under the Commerce Clause, regulate activities that cross state lines. The case was controversial at the time—and still is, among those commentators who favor limited federal power. This apprehension is understandable since the activities regulated in *Wickard v. Filburn* took place within the borders of a single state. The law in question was the Agriculture Adjustment Act of 1938 (AAA). The plaintiff was an Ohio farmer named Roscoe Filburn who grew winter wheat on his property every year. Filburn also produced and marketed eggs, chickens, and milk. Some of the wheat was sold at market. The rest Filburn kept for use on his own farm. He fed his chickens and cattle, baked bread, and kept some for the next planting. The AAA limited the amount of wheat that he could grow to 20.1 bushels per acre on 11.1 acres. Filburn didn't seem to care much for the limit, so he planted on 23 acres and produced 239 bushels on the extra 11.9 acres. He was fined by the Department of Agriculture. Believing that the best defense is a good offense, Filburn sued the government, naming then Secretary of Agriculture Claude R. Wickard a defendant in the case. The issue at hand was whether the federal government could, under the authority of the Commerce Clause, regulate an activity that occurred totally within the boundaries of a single state. The case would seem to be rather straightforward. The excess wheat that Filburn produced never left Ohio. In fact, it never left his small farm. Yet Congress not only stated the amount that he could plant and harvest, but also fined him ($117.11) for planting more than he was allowed. Filburn's case climbed the ladder all the way to the Supreme Court. Then, in one fell swoop, the Court expanded the power of Congress to almost unlimited scope. The Court held:

1. The power that Congress has under the Commerce Clause of the Constitution gives it the authority not only to regulate prices, but also to control every action that somehow impacts such prices.

2. This power exists whenever an activity has a "substantial economic effect on interstate commerce."

3. The only limit on this regulation is the requirement that congressional control over the activity be "rationally related" to the goal of Congress established in the act.

In this case the Court reasoned that, while the wheat grown and used by Filburn was minuscule, the overall effect, if left unchecked, could have a substantial effect on economic activity. After all, when Filburn and others like him grew wheat and used it for their own purposes, they were not buying wheat in the open market and, thus, we see an economic impact. Look back to the section on the Bill of Rights in Chapter 2, and answer the following question: How would James Madison evaluate the wisdom and the constitutionality of giving Congress powers not literally written down in the actual words of the Constitution, much of which he actually wrote himself? Recall Madison's arguments against the Bill of Rights, and you will have your answer here. After *Wickard v. Filburn*, does Congress have unlimited regulatory power? Explain. [See: *Wickard v. Filburn*, 317 U.S. 111, 63 S.Ct. 82 (1941).]

Source: See: *Wickard v. Filburn*, 317 U.S. 111, 63 S.Ct. 82 (1941).

the federal criminal law system and the various national law enforcement agencies is made possible by the complex adaptive processes at work within the legal system itself.

Criminal Law as Adaptation The way Congress has assumed powers never granted to it by the framers of the Constitution demonstrates how the law is a balancing act. The process works something like this: The framers of the Constitution intended that Congress have only those powers enumerated in Article I, Section 8, of the Constitution. Because the term *police power* is not mentioned anywhere in the Constitution, the Framers did not give that power to the federal government but, instead, expected the states to exercise all police power. Consequently, Congress can create criminal law statutes only in those areas over which it has jurisdiction. For instance, Congress has the power to coin money, so it can set up laws against counterfeiting. Yet, as we've seen, Congress has created criminal law statutes in areas beyond counterfeiting. If there has been no constitutional amendment explicitly handing Congress police power, how did Congress get the power to create a set of criminal law statutes and a national police force?

The answer is that Congress balanced the actual *words* of the Constitution against the need to *interpret* those words to protect the people from criminal activity. The balance occurred when Congress extended its power through a generous interpretation of the Commerce Clause. The Commerce Clause, found in Article I, Section 8, Clause 3, permits Congress to pass laws that regulate commerce "among the several States." Congress used this clause to regulate interstate criminal activities, which impact "commerce." Although the ultimate results were a long time coming, eventually the courts, through a series of cases, culminating in the case of *Wickard v. Filburn* (317 U.S. 111, 63 S.Ct. 82), gave their "stamp of approval" to the legislature's creative balancing act. In a sense then, Congress and the courts cooperated to give the federal government police power, a power it did not have under the Constitution. That power includes the authority to create federal criminal law.

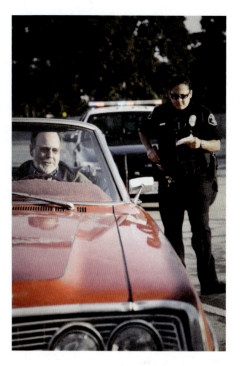

Traffic violations are usually considered petty offenses or minor misdemeanors.
©Blend Images/SuperStock

Classes of Crimes

Under common law, crimes were dealt with in the order of their seriousness: treason, felonies, and misdemeanors. Most states now divide offenses into felonies and misdemeanors. A **felony** is a crime punishable by death or imprisonment in a federal or a state prison for a term exceeding one year. Some felonies are also punishable by fines. Some states define a felony as a crime subject to "punishment by hard labor," as an "infamous crime," or as a "crime subject to infamous punishment." Manslaughter, armed robbery, and arson are examples of felonies.

Some states also have separate categories for their most serious crimes. For instance, a state might classify premeditated murder and murder as *special felonies* or *capital felonies* if these are the only two offenses that might result in a death sentence or life imprisonment. States may also have a separate category for violent offenses. Sometimes these violent offenses are termed *aggravated felonies*. Assault with a deadly weapon might be an example of an aggravated felony.

A **misdemeanor** is a less serious crime, generally punishable by a prison sentence of not more than one year. Included in this category are offenses such as disorderly conduct. Some states also have a separate category for their least serious offenses. The label for these least serious offenses varies, but two of the most common are *petty offenses* and *minor misdemeanors*. Traffic violations and building code violations are usually within this classification.

> ### quick quiz 5-1
>
> 1. A misdemeanor is a crime punishable by death or imprisonment in a federal or a state prison for a term exceeding one year.   true | false
> 2. The primary objective of criminal law is to protect victims.   true | false
> 3. It is impossible for a single act to be both a tort and a crime.   true | false

5-2 Elements of a Crime

The two elements necessary to create criminal liability are a criminal act and the required state of mind. Although it is difficult to generalize about both of these concepts, certain characteristics are common to each, regardless of jurisdiction. Nevertheless, keep in mind that criminal law is largely statutory in nature. Consequently, specific statutory definitions may vary from state to state.

A Criminal Act

Under American law, a crime cannot be committed unless some act has occurred. An individual cannot be accused of a crime for merely thinking of a criminal act; however, even a small act that appears by itself to be innocent can, in the proper context, become an illegal act. For example, even something as simple as inserting a key into the ignition of a vehicle can constitute an act under the law if the driver is intoxicated at the time. The act is such an important element to criminal liability that convictions may be avoided or overturned if defendants can show that the statute under which they were prosecuted is ambiguous in its description of the act. Often, such ambiguity will occur when the legislature passes a statute that creates a new offense; when the statute outlaws an activity that may be protected by the U.S. Constitution; or when the statute seeks to outlaw statutes or behavior that cause no imminent negative effect but may, eventually, lead to great public harm. For instance, the courts have frequently held statutes that outlaw a status, such as drug addiction or vagrancy, to be void for vagueness. The courts have also struck down statutes that are overbroad. The language of a criminal statute is overbroad if the courts cannot determine what specific activity the legislature intended to outlaw.

Omissions and Refusals to Act   At times, the failure to act, an omission, or the outright refusal to act may be considered criminal. Generally, however, an omission must be coupled with a legally imposed duty. An air traffic controller who sees two planes on a collision course, yet fails to warn the pilots, would be held criminally liable for this omission. This liability exists even though the controller did not act but instead failed to act.

Involuntary Movement or Behavior   Many states specifically exclude involuntary movement and behavior from their general definition of a criminal act. Convulsions, reflexes, movements during sleep or unconsciousness, or behavior during a seizure are all considered involuntary movement or behavior falling outside the limits of criminal liability. However, the mere fact that someone is unconscious during a seizure may not absolve that individual of criminal liability if that person knew that he or she might suffer the seizure, yet took no precautions to avoid harming people or property. A person who decides to drive an automobile knowing that she or he is subject to sudden, unpredictable epileptic seizures may be criminally liable if a seizure causes that person to lose control of the vehicle and kill or injure someone.

The Required State of Mind

In general, a crime cannot be committed unless the criminal act named in the statute is performed with the required state of mind. Many state criminal codes include the following four states of mind:

- Purpose
- Knowledge
- Recklessness
- Negligence

Purpose Individuals act with **purpose** when they intend to cause the result that in fact occurs. For example, if a person were to point a loaded gun at another person with the intention of shooting that second person, and if shots are actually fired, the person with the gun would have acted with purpose. Some states choose to call this mental state *intent*. Intent or purpose should not be confused with *premeditation*, which is often an added condition in the case of aggravated or first-degree murder. Some states specifically define premeditation as an action that results from the criminal defendant's "prior calculation and design." If, in the previous example, the person with the gun had also planned to shoot the victim, and then actually carried out this plan, the shooting would have been premeditated.

Knowledge When people act with an awareness that a particular result will probably occur, they act with **knowledge**. For instance, if the person with the gun in the preceding example took that loaded gun to a crowded shopping mall and began to fire at random, not aiming at anyone in particular, that person would be acting with the knowledge that a lot of people would be either wounded or killed. This awareness would be true even if the person with the gun were to yell, "I really don't want to shoot anyone. I hope I don't hit anybody!"

Recklessness **Recklessness** involves a perverse disregard of a known risk of negative consequences. People act recklessly when they are indifferent to a serious risk they know to exist. Two drivers who challenge each other to an illegal drag race on a public highway are acting recklessly. In other words, they have disregarded the possible serious consequences of their decision to engage in an illegal drag race.

About the Law

The definition of many legal terms varies depending on the area of the law in which they are used. For example, in tort law, negligence is defined in relation to four elements: duty, breach of duty, proximate cause, and actual harm.

EXAMPLE 5-1: Recklessness Is a Relative Factor

As noted above, recklessness involves acting with a perverse disregard of a known risk of negative consequences. Pennsylvania has a slightly different, though roughly equivalent, definition. Under Pennsylvania law, *recklessness* is defined as "consciously disregarding a substantial and unjustifiable risk." The statute goes on to add that disregarding the risk must involve, "a gross deviation from the standard of conduct that a reasonable person would observe in the actor's situation." Such an alteration in the standard definition makes little difference, until someone is accused of a crime that requires recklessness as the mental state.

A case in point involves the Philadelphia Amtrak Derailment that killed eight people. In that case, the focal point of the post-crash investigation was Brandon Bostian, the conductor. The District Attorney's Office in Philadelphia examined the evidence surrounding the incident and, in the process, considered indicting Bostian for involuntary manslaughter. To demonstrate involuntary manslaughter, the DA would have to show that the conductor was probably reckless in permitting the train to reach 106 mph on a curve limited to 50 mph. The DA's office found that Bostian was not under the influence of drugs or alcohol, nor was he on his cell phone at the time of the crash, which had been one of the first theories offered shortly after the derailment. What the DA did discover was that at the time of the crash, Bostian was concentrating on a radio distress call from a nearby train that had been hit by rock-throwing attackers. In the heat of the moment, the conductor lost "situational awareness" and, as a result, had no understanding of where the train was located at the time of the crash. Because Bostian's judgment had *not* been impaired by drugs, alcohol, or social media and because he was legitimately distracted by the emergency radio transmission, he had not been reckless but, instead, for an understandable reason (the emergency radio transmission), had been unaware of the dangerous situation that the train was in at the time. Therefore, he had not "consciously disregarded a substantial and unjustifiable risk," as the law required. Moreover, there was no "deviation from the standard of conduct that a reasonable person would observe in the actor's situation." As a result, no indictment was pursued by the Philadelphia DA.

The story does not end here, however. Shortly after the DA declared the case closed, and on the last day that charges could be filed, family members of a woman killed in the crash, using a little known and seldom invoked Pennsylvania law, filed papers with a Philadelphia Municipal Court asking that charges be brought against Bostian for involuntary manslaughter. The Court turned the papers over to the DA, who again refused to bring charges. The Court then turned the case over to the State Attorney General who agreed to file charges. Once again, the story does not end here. A Philadelphia Municipal Court Judge dismissed the Attorney General's case against Bostian, ruling that there was not enough evidence to prove recklessness on the part of the conductor. Nevertheless, the Attorney General's Office said that it would review the judge's order and just might pursue the matter further. It would appear then that recklessness, far from being definitive standard in the law, is open to a wide range of interpretations, some stricter than others. [See: Daniel Victor and Matthew Haag, "Involuntary Manslaughter Charges Filed in Amtrak Crash," *The New York Times*, May 13, 2017, p. A-17. See also: P. J. D'Annunzio, "Charges Dismissed against Amtrak Engineer in 2015 Philadelphia Derailment," *The Legal Intelligencer*, September 13, 2017, http://www.thelegalintelligencer.com.id=1202797825157/Charges-Dismissed-Against-Amtrak-Engineer-in-2015-PhilaDerailment?mcode+13952623224777&curpage+ALL.]

Source: See: Daniel Victor and Matthew Haag, "Involuntary Manslaughter Charges Filed in Amtrak Crash," *New York Times* (May 13, 2017), p. A-17; See also: P. J. D'Annunzio, "Charges Dismissed Against Amtrak Engineer in 2015 Philadelphia Derailment," *The Legal Intelligencer* (September 13, 2017) http://www.thelegalintelligencer.com.id=1202797825157/Charges-Dismissed-Against-Amtrak-Engineer-in-2015-PhilaDerailment?mcode+13952623224777&curpage+ALL.

Negligence People act with **negligence** when they fail to see the possible negative consequences of their actions. A person who cleans a hunting rifle without checking to see if it is loaded is acting with negligence because that person has not bothered to look for any possible negative consequences that could result from those actions. Criminal negligence should not be confused with negligence in tort law. Negligence in tort law is concerned with the compensation of accident victims (see Chapter 6). In contrast, negligence in criminal law is concerned with punishing the wrongdoer and protecting the public at large.

The Matter of Motive

Motive in criminal law is the wrongdoer's reason for committing the crime. One common misconception about criminal law, which is perpetuated by television programs and films, is that motive is an element of criminal liability. Such is not the case. Establishing motive may help the prosecution persuade the jury that the accused is guilty, but proving an evil motive is not necessary for a criminal conviction.

The Matter of Corporate Liability

Criminal liability requires that the prosecutor prove that the defendant possessed a particular mental state when the criminal act was committed. Such mental states are generally

THE OPENING CASE *Round 2*
United States v. Hearst: Patty, the Newspaper Heiress or Tania, the Urban Guerrilla?

Recall that in the Opening Case, Patty Hearst was kidnapped in California by members of the Symbionese Liberation Army (SLA). After a ransom payment involving food for the poor failed to satisfy the kidnappers, the SLA released a video in which Hearst allegedly declared her dedication to the SLA. Not long afterward, Hearst joined in robbery at the Hibernia Bank in San Francisco. Later, Hearst was arrested in an apartment in San Francisco. She was tried for armed robbery and using a firearm to commit a felony. Now recall that the two elements necessary to create criminal liability are a criminal act and the required state of mind. Her attorney, F. Lee Bailey, knew that he could not argue that Hearst had not committed armed robbery. Aside from the eyewitnesses who were available to testify, Hearst had, herself, stated on tape that she had robbed the bank. In addition, the prosecution had tapes of conversations with a friend on which she makes incriminating statements about the robbery. Because Bailey could not attack element 1—the act—he had to focus on element 2—the defendant's mental state at the time of the criminal act. To put it in proper legal context, he had to show that at the time of the robbery, she did not know that she was doing, or if she knew what she was doing, she did not know that what she was doing was wrong.

So far, so good. This makes perfect sense. But then Bailey did something radical. He did not use the traditional insanity plea formulas. Instead, he used a new formula known as *coercive persuasion*, which means that Hearst had been "brainwashed" by members of the SLA and, therefore, had no control over her actions during the robbery at the bank. The defense painted a picture of a defeated and exhausted Hearst who had been blindfolded, isolated (locked in a closet, actually), and abused by her captors. After days of this treatment, Hearst, in a sense, lost her own identity, and was subsumed into the SLA. Therefore, Bailey argued, it was not Hearst who robbed the bank, but a new personality, the urban guerrilla named "Tania," created by the coercive abuse tactics used by her captors. Given what you know so far about the elements of a crime, do you think that this defense will work? Explain, then read on. [See: *United States v. Hearst*, 563 F2d 1313 (9th Cir., 1978).]

Source: See: *United States v. Hearst,* 563 F2d 1313 (9th Cir. 1978).

stated quite clearly in the statute that creates the criminal offense. In fact, since criminal liability requires only two elements, the act and the mental state, legislators are very careful in drafting criminal law statutes to make certain that they explain both elements, stating both with great specificity. It is not always easy for a prosecutor to prove that a defendant possessed the required mental state. Still, when the criminal defendant is an individual, at least the prosecutor knows how to proceed. The prosecutor must produce evidence, generally consisting of actions and words, that demonstrate what was in the mind of the defendant at the time that the criminal act was committed. This is hard enough with a flesh-and-blood defendant. Corporations, on the other hand, do not have mental states, let alone mental states that can demonstrate criminal liability. Nor do they act or speak, except through their corporate officers and employees. How, then, does a prosecutor prove criminal liability when the criminal defendant is a corporation?

Corporate Personality The law provides a fairly complete picture of a corporate identity. The law has established that corporations are "legal people." As a corporate person, a corporation possesses an identity, a corporate self, that maintains an existence that is separate from those who formed it. The upside to this is that the corporation will exist long after its founders. The downside is that corporations are taxed directly for what they earn as part of the marketplace. The courts have also decided that corporations have just enough "personhood" to qualify for constitutional protections. Thus, under the 14th

Amendment, a corporation has the right to life, liberty, and property, rights that cannot be violated by the government either at the state or the federal levels. In addition, as a legal person, a corporation can institute a lawsuit or can be the target of a lawsuit.

Corporate Liability Theories Despite popular opinion, corporations are not modern inventions developed in the 19th century. In fact, we know that corporate-like organizations existed in the Middle Ages. At that time, however, common law judges could not conceive of corporate liability because corporations did not possess a mind with which to form a mental state. The modern age changed all of that. Once the courts decided that a corporation was person enough to sue or be sued, it was not a huge leap to conclude that a corporation could be held criminally liable as well. One of the earliest theories on corporate criminal liability emerged from within the doctrine of *strict liability*. Strict liability was an appropriate theory at the time because it did not require intent, something that was difficult to prove in the case of a corporation. By the beginning of the 20th century, however, the courts began to hold corporations liable for the criminal acts of their employees using the doctrine of *vicarious liability*, a theory which is also called *respondeat superior*. Under this approach, the courts decided that a corporation could be declared criminally responsible if one of its employees, who had the authority to act for the company, committed a crime while acting within the scope of his or her responsibility so long as that act was committed for the benefit of the corporation. The doctrine has been liberalized to such an extent that today, even if a worker is expressly prohibited from doing anything outside the law, the corporation might still be declared liable for a crime committed by that worker.

EXAMPLE 5-2: The Gulf Spill Vendetta and Corporate Criminal Liability

The explosion of the Deepwater Horizon drilling rig led to a massive oil spill in the Gulf of Mexico in 2010. The destruction that followed the explosion of the rig left many people demanding that three corporations—British Petroleum, Halliburton, and Transocean—be punished for what happened to the workers on the rig, to the wildlife in the gulf, and to the lives of the people living in the area because the corporations were believed to be responsible for the explosion and the oil spill. In response, the federal government set up a special panel to investigate the incident. More than six months after the accident, the panel reported that the problems aboard the drilling rig resulted from a substandard level of performance *common throughout the entire oil industry*. This finding could be a problem for prosecutors who, under the *respondeat superior* test, must demonstrate, first and foremost, that a corporate agent committed a crime. This may not sound difficult at first blush, but the more we consider the situation, the darker it becomes for the prosecutor.

The problem plays out like this: If a crime requires intent or knowledge, then the prosecutor will have to prove, *beyond a reasonable doubt*, that the corporate agent purposely or knowingly performed the wrongful act outlined in the statute. So, for example, suppose the prosecutor wants to target one of the corporations by using an aggravated arson statute to prosecute a rig operator, who was acting as a corporate agent at the time of the explosion. Aggravated arson would require the prosecutor to demonstrate that the defendant, by fire or explosion, knowingly created a risk of serious physical harm to another person or to an occupied structure. So far, this sounds like an open and shut case. But remember the explosion was not set off by the rig operator throwing a bomb. It resulted from the day-to-day operation of the rig. If the day-to-day operation of the rig was well within industry standards (OK, substandards, but standards, nonetheless), then how can the prosecutor show that the defendant "knowingly" created a "substantial risk"? How do I knowingly create a substantial risk if I am just doing what everyone in the entire industry does as a matter of day-to-day operational conduct? The answer is that I can't, and if I can't be held responsible, neither can the corporation. Of course, the prosecutor may have a case against the agent and, therefore, the corporation, for a lesser offense, perhaps one like criminal damaging, which requires only recklessness or negligence as the appropriate state of mind. However, convictions under these lesser offenses may not satisfy those victims of the oil spill who want the prosecutor to "throw the book" at the defendants, especially the defendant corporations. [See: David M. Uhlmann, "Prosecuting Crimes against the Earth," *The New York Times*, June 4, 2010, p. A-23.]

Source: See: David M. Uhlmann, "Prosecuting Crimes Against the Earth," *The New York Times,* June 4, 2010, p. A-23.

The Third Requirement Some states have added a third requirement to the three step test of corporate criminal liability. Recall, that the first two steps state that a corporation could be declared criminally responsible if one of its employees, who (1) had the authority to act for the company, committed a crime while acting within the scope of his or her responsibility so long as (2) that act was committed for the benefit of the corporation. The third requirement adds that the directors or officers of a corporation must have authorized, approved, or recklessly tolerated the criminal actions of the employees. Like the doctrine of *respondeat superior*, the directors or the officers must be acting on the job when the crimes occur. On the surface, this policy looks like an effective tool for stopping corporate criminal activity; however, in practice, the third requirement may simply encourage directors and officers to remain ignorant of the actions of their employees in order to develop a defense of "plausible deniability." The defense of plausible deniability allows corporate managers to "honestly" testify that they knew nothing about the criminal activity of which they, their employees, and the corporation are accused. [See: Eli Lederman, "Corporate Criminal Liability: The Second Generation," *Stetson Law Review* 46 (2016), pp. 71-87.]

EXAMPLE 5-3: The Gulf Spill Vendetta and the Third Requirement

Many people were outraged by the oil spill that resulted in the Gulf of Mexico from the explosion of British Petroleum's Deepwater Horizon drilling rig in 2010. Much of this anger was directed, in general, at British Petroleum and, in particular, at BP's CEO, Tony Hayward. In hearings held in Washington, DC, the CEO testified that he did not directly participate in any of the decisions made in relation to that particular rig. Those states with the third requirement require the authorization, approval, or reckless toleration of criminal activity by the board of directors or by a managing officer who is clearly responsible for establishing corporate policy, especially in relation to the incident under investigation. If, in fact, the CEO did not know what was going on at the Deepwater Horizon drilling rig then, in those states that maintain the third requirement, neither he nor the corporation can be held liable. By distancing himself from the decision-making process, the CEO had clearly adopted a defense of plausible deniability. In engineering this defense, he was undeniably acting in the corporation's best interests, as well as his own; however, he was not acting in the best interests of the shareholders, other employees, the community, and so on. Still, under the third requirement, there was nothing wrong with his conduct. In fact, his conduct was perfectly understandable and eminently reasonable. What does that tell us about the third requirement? Explain.

Variations in Foreign Law Not all law codes are created equal, and not all nations treat corporations in the same way. Such differences can motivate multinational corporations to vary their safety standards based on the final destination of a product or a series of products. Thus, for example, nations in Europe tend to be much more attentive to dangers associated with food and pharmaceuticals while the United States tends to require stricter safety measures in relation to how consumer products (vehicles, appliances, clothing, furniture, and so on) are made and what they are made of. These differences can lead to dangerous situations for consumers, for the public at large, and ultimately for the multinational, itself. Thus, multinational corporations might be inclined to sell consumer products made of cheap, but more dangerous materials in Europe because this tactic keeps the cost down and raises the multinational's profit margin. Such a strategy might seem harmless enough on the surface. After all, even (especially?) multinational corporations are designed to make money for their shareholders. However, as is often the case in the law, hidden pitfalls lurk in the midst of this seemingly harmless cost cutting tactic. That pitfall is called *corporate criminal liability*. Corporate managers must realize that, even if governmental regulations regarding materials are lax in a foreign country, the corporate criminal liability laws may not be quite so generous. Thus, for example, unlike in American law, in English law, corporations can be held criminally negligent for failing to take measures that would prevent injury even if no one in the corporation had the responsibility to perform that duty. Thus, even if no one in the corporation has the responsibility to make sure that the safest materials are used in the manufacture of a consumer item, the fact that an injury would have been prevented had the safer material been used, may mean that the corporation is criminally liable for not preventing the injury by using the safer material.

EXAMPLE 5-4: Center of London Fire and Corporate Criminal Liability in Foreign Lands

In the middle of summer in the heart of London, the worst fire in England for more than 100 years killed 79 people in a high-rise apartment known as Grenfell Tower. At first, arson was suspected, but as it turned out, this was not the case. Instead, the fire was started by an exploding refrigerator and spread rapidly because of the cheap and unsafe paneling used in the walls of the building. The villains in this tragedy turned out not to be terrorists, gang members, arsonists, or careless smokers. No, the villains turned out to be two American multinationals that may find themselves liable in a British court of law for criminal charges up to and including manslaughter. The irony is that under British building codes and according to British product manufacturing regulations, the multinationals did nothing wrong—never mind the fact that they knew that the materials with which the refrigerator and the paneling were made had been declared unsafe in the United States.

The facts look like this. The two American corporations are Whirlpool and Arconic (formerly Alcoa Aluminum). Whirlpool made the refrigerator that exploded, starting the fire, and Arconic manufactured the paneling that because it was made out of combustible materials, caused the fire to spread so rapidly that it was out of control before firefighters even arrived at the scene. The Whirlpool refrigerator was manufactured with a plastic backing. The same refrigerator, when manufactured for sale in the United States, has a fire-resistant metal backing. The Arconic paneling, which is made with a combustible polyethylene core, can only be used in American buildings that fall far below the height of Grenfell Tower. Both companies argue, correctly so it seems, that they followed British building codes and British manufacturing regulations. This will not matter to British investigators and the British prosecutors, however. Remember that under British law, despite the fact that the corporation has no duty to use the safest materials possible, the fact that injuries could have been prevented with safer material may mean that the corporations are criminally liable. To make matters worse for the two beleaguered multinational corporations, unlike in the United States, in Britain, corporations can be charged with manslaughter. That will be 79 counts of manslaughter in this case. That seems fitting enough in this case, but how is a multinational corporation to be punished if it is found guilty? It cannot be hanged, nor can it be imprisoned, so what happens? If you want to know, keep reading, the answer lies ahead. (Note: As collateral damage, Arconic's stock price plummeted into the basement after information about its role in the fire hit the newspapers on a slow news day.) [See: Danny Hakim, "Products at Center of London Fire Faced Tougher Rules in U.S.," *The New York Times*, June 27, 2017, pp. A-1, A-3.]

Source: See. Danny Hakim, "Products at Center of London Fire Faced Tougher Rules in U.S." *The New York Times* (June 27, 2017), pp. A-1 and A-3.

The Matter of Punishment

The ultimate purpose of criminal law is to protect the public. This purpose means that criminal law must outline not only the offenses that are prohibited, but also the negative consequences that result when an individual has committed one of those offenses. Many legal experts disagree about what that punishment ought to be. Still, these experts have narrowed the debate to two approaches to the sentencing of convicted criminals: (1) consequences that are designed to protect the public at large and (2) those that are tailored to fit the individual offense or the individual offender.

Protecting the Public at Large Consequences that have been created to protect the public send a message not just to the convicted felon, but also to all potential offenders. These techniques include deterrence, education, and retribution. Those experts who believe in *deterrence* advocate long and difficult prison sentences so that other people in society are dissuaded from committing similar offenses and thus suffering the same fate. Those who support the theory of *education* say that the criminal process should be presented in a public way so that the public will learn the difference between acceptable and unacceptable behavior. Finally, those who believe in *retribution* are convinced that it does society good to seek revenge against those who have disrupted the smooth running of the social system. This theory probably has the fewest supporters today. Still, some experts argue that obtaining retribution against those who seek to gratify themselves at the expense of others will prevent many potential offenders from committing similar misdeeds in the future.

Individual Offenses and Punishment Consequences that have been created to fit a particular offense or to punish a specific offender are designed to make certain that the individual offender will no longer engage in criminal activity in the future. The techniques for promoting this approach are prevention, restraint, and rehabilitation. Those experts who believe in *prevention* support long sentences in unpleasant prisons so that criminal defendants will abandon their criminal careers. Those who support *restraint* believe that criminal defendants should be incarcerated or even executed for capital offenses to prevent them from ever committing that crime—or any crime, for that matter—ever again. Finally, those who support the theory of *rehabilitation* say that convicted defendants ought to be given the opportunity to reform their conduct, restructure their lives, and start over.

Corporate Punishment As noted above, several legal theories exist under which corporations can be held criminally liable for their conduct. These theories include strict liability and at least two variations of the *respondeat superior* doctrine. Despite the great detail with which these doctrines are laid out, not one of those theories explains just how a corporation is supposed to be punished. Corporations cannot be imprisoned nor can they be given the death penalty, so it would seem that they escape the most severe levels of punishment. Nevertheless, the laws does establish a number of different ways by which corporate criminals can be punished just like their human counterparts. For example, corporations can be fined; they can be forced to hand over restitution; they can be put on probation; they can be prohibited from engaging in certain economic activities for an express period of time; they can even have property taken away from them, just so long as it is done with due process and under the equal protection of the law. [See: Charles Doyle, "Corporate Criminal Liability: An Overview of Federal Law," *Congressional Research Service*, October 30, 2013.]

The Death Penalty The use of the death penalty in criminal cases has been subject to a series of controls designed to limit the imposition of this punishment to those cases in which the criminal defendant truly deserves to be put to death. Generally, these limits are built into the criminal code and are applied by the court that is responsible for sentencing the convicted criminal defendant. The safeguards come in the form of aggravating and mitigating circumstances, which must be taken into consideration by the court at the time of sentencing.

Aggravating circumstances are those that involve offenses so appalling that the death penalty is clearly warranted. In most jurisdictions, the list of aggravating circumstances looks like this: the assassination of the president, the vice president, the governor, or the lieutenant governor of the state; a murder for hire; a murder committed to escape detection, apprehension, trial, or punishment; a murder committed while the offender was in detention; a murder by a convicted murderer; a murder of a law enforcement officer; a murder of a witness against the offender; a murder of a child under 13 years of age; or a murder during the commission of a felony. Usually, the death penalty cannot be imposed without the presence of at least one of these aggravating circumstances.

Moreover, even if aggravating circumstances are present, the death penalty might still be avoided if the mitigating circumstances outweigh the aggravating circumstances. Mitigating circumstances include the following: the victim somehow induced the offense, the offender was coerced or provoked, the offender was suffering from a mental impairment of some sort, the offender is very young, the offender has no past criminal record, the offender was not the principal actor in the offense, or the offense was subject to other factors that might be relevant to a reduced sentence. In some states, the judge also has the power, after listening to aggravating and mitigating circumstances, to set aside the jury's sentence and either order the death penalty despite the jury's recommendation or or cancel the death penalty and institute a lesser penalty. It is for this reason that those judges who administer the death penalty must be fair, impartial, and free from undue pressure, conflict of interest, and any other external influence. Some people maintain that such impartiality is difficult if not impossible in those states that elect judges because elected judges may be swayed by popular opinion, especially when facing reelection.

Death Penalty Safeguards Other safety measures are built into the judicial system that will prevent or at least minimize the dangers associated with the death penalty. Generally, the appellate court that reviews the application of the death penalty is required to evaluate the conduct of the sentencing judge for any hint of partiality, impropriety, or outside pressure. Also, normally the governor of a state has the power to commute the sentence of a defendant condemned to death, and final recourse to the U.S. Supreme Court is also possible. Nevertheless, not even these measures are air tight and so, sometimes, questionable death penalty decisions are still handed down.

EXAMPLE 5-5: Mitigating and Aggravating Circumstances: Who Decides?

Mario Dion Woodward was tried for the murder of a police officer in Montgomery, Alabama. The jury found him guilty and, after a separate sentencing hearing, voted 8-4 to give him a life sentence without the possibility of parole. Instead, the judge, after listening to aggravating and mitigating circumstances, sentenced him to death. The Supreme Court refused to grant *certiorari* in this case, although Justice Sotomayor (joined by Justice Breyer) submitted a dissent. One of the most interesting things about the Supreme Court's position on the death is that the High Court maintains that a state can still give the judge flexibility in reviewing the jury's decision. The Court's position in this matter was made clear in this case as well as in several previous cases, including *Spaziano v. Florida*, 468 U.S. 447 (1984) and *Harris v. Alabama*, 513 U.S. 504 (1995). In fact, the judge's discretion is in place in 4 of the 32 states that still use the death penalty. This is the root of Justice Sotomayor's opposition to the Court's decision not to grant *certiorari*. She argues that Alabama courts have a record of transforming life sentences into death sentences in a way that is more than a little disproportionate with the way that it is done in other states. Also, Sotomayor emphasizes that of the 27 instances of sentences moving from life to death in the past 14 years, 26 are found in the Alabama criminal courts. Her conclusion? She believes that the judicial system in Alabama is being held hostage by its need to satisfy the demands of the voting public. This is an interesting argument. Generally, the idea behind a democracy is that the power rests in the people and the people have the chance to elect officials who will represent their views or at least the views of the majority (or plurality) who elect those officials. Is Sotomayor saying, "I've had enough democracy. Let's try something else." Or is she saying, "Democracy is OK as long as the people elected agree with me?" Or is something else going on here. Recall the discussion in Chapter 2 about James Madison's fear of the people and his campaign to build a buffer between the people and public officials. Recall also that federal judges are appointed for life precisely to ensure an independent federal judiciary. Is Sotomayor agreeing with Madison? Think about it. [See: *Woodward v. Alabama*, 571 U.S.—(2013); *Gregg v. Georgia*, 428 U.S. 153 (1976); and *Furman v. Georgia*, 408 U.S. 238 (1972).]

Source: See: *Woodward v. Alabama,* 571 U.S.—(2013); *Gregg v. Georgia* 428 U.S. 153 (1976); and *Furman v. Georgia,* 408 U.S. 238 (1972).

quick quiz 5-2

1. The two elements needed to create criminal liability are a criminal act and the requisite state of mind. true | false
2. Individuals act with negligence when they act with the intention to cause the result that does in fact occur. true | false
3. Motive is an element of criminal liability. true | false

5-3 Specific Crimes

Statutory definitions and classifications of crimes vary from jurisdiction to jurisdiction. Nevertheless, several generalities can be drawn to simplify an examination of specific crimes. Crimes can be classified as crimes against people, crimes against property, crimes involving business, and crimes against justice.

Crimes against People

Crimes against people include, but are certainly not limited to, first-degree murder, second-degree murder, manslaughter, battery, and assault. A more recent addition to this list involves hate speech.

First-Degree Murder Any killing of one human being by another is labeled as a **homicide**. Criminal homicide is either murder or manslaughter. When the unlawful killing is done with premeditation and deliberate intent, it is labeled **first-degree murder**, **aggravated murder**, or **premeditated murder**, depending on the jurisdiction. The definition of first-degree murder differs from state to state; however, some of the elements are consistent. In general, most states define first-degree murder to include one of the following circumstances: killing someone with premeditation (thinking about it and planning the homicide in advance with "prior calculation and design") and/or killing someone while committing a major crime, such as

> **Did You Know?**
>
> In 1999, SabreTech Inc. was indicted by a grand jury in Miami for the 110 deaths that resulted from the crash of ValuJet Flight 592. In the case, the corporation faced 110 counts of murder.

rape, robbery, or kidnapping. Moreover, several jurisdictions have added other circumstances to the definition of first-degree murder, including causing the death of a victim under 13 years of age; causing the death of a law enforcement officer, when the offender knows or has reasonable cause to know that the victim is a police officer; causing the death of another while the offender is escaping detention for a felony; and killing someone in a cruel way such as with torture. Some states have added most or all of these to their statutory definition of first-degree murder, while others have added a combination of these new factors. It should also be obvious that these states have included some of the aggravating circumstances related to the death sentence within the definition of first-degree murder. The inclusion of these circumstance within the core definition of first-degree murder makes the application of the death penalty more likely.

Second-Degree Murder and Manslaughter If none of the conditions for first-degree murder apply, the crime is known as *second-degree murder*. In many jurisdictions, the difference between first- and second-degree murder is important because first-degree murder usually carries the death penalty, whereas second-degree murder does not. In contrast to murder, *manslaughter* is an unlawful killing of a person without the intent to kill. A killing that results when a person is in a state of extreme fright, terror, anger, or blind rage that destroys the ability to reason is known as *voluntary manslaughter*. When the killing results from negligence, it is usually called *involuntary manslaughter*.

EXAMPLE 5-6: First-Degree Murder and Voluntary Manslaughter

Brent Haywood entered a convenience store and robbed the clerk at gunpoint. As he was leaving the store, the clerk pulled a revolver from under the counter and ordered Haywood to stop. In response, Haywood fired his weapon at the clerk, who returned fire. In the exchange of gunshots, an innocent bystander, nine-year-old Teddy Newman, was shot and killed. Haywood was convicted of first-degree murder and sentenced to death by lethal injection; however, the judge, who opposed the death penalty, gave Haywood a life sentence. Teddy's father was in the courtroom when this sentence was announced. In a state of extreme rage, Teddy's father attacked and killed Haywood. Even though Teddy's father's actions were clearly intentional, they were performed in a state of extreme rage as a result of a reasonable provocation. Consequently, he was charged with voluntary manslaughter.

Battery and Assault Throughout most of English and American history, the term *battery* has been used to describe a crime in which the offender causes actual physical harm to the victim. In contrast, *assault* has generally been taken to include the threat of harm to the victim. Today, however, this simple distinction is no longer applicable because many states have created a wide variety of levels and degrees of battery and assault. Some states have even altered the actual language of the law. Ohio, for example, has eliminated the term *battery* and replaced it with the word *assault*. In Ohio, then, the term *assault* is used to describe various crimes involving the infliction of physical harm on the victim. To describe offenses that should be identified with the word *assault*, Ohio uses the terms *aggravated menacing and menacing*. Moreover, Ohio has added a few new offenses to the criminal code that are related to, but are not exactly the same as, assault and battery. These include stalking, hazing, and abuse. Given these subtle distinctions, it is always best to check the criminal code in your own jurisdiction before discussing assault and battery.

Hate Speech In recent years, many legislative bodies have attempted to criminalize the use of certain symbols, writings, and speech intended to provoke outrage or fear on the basis of race, religion, color, or gender. These statutes and ordinances are frequently referred to as laws against **hate speech**. Such statutes are constitutional only if they are not content specific. Therefore, though it may be acceptable to draft a statute that outlaws any speech designed to rouse fear or outrage, regardless of the content of that speech, it would be impermissible to outlaw speech aimed at inciting outrage or fear based solely on race, religion, color, gender, or any similar category.

Schools and New Anti-Gun Protection Laws The mass shootings at the Las Vegas Route 91 Harvest Country Music Festival that left 58 people dead and 498 injured was, at that time, the worst mass shooting event in modern American history. Unfortunately, it was only one of along line of such events, many of which have involved schools. Two of the of most tragic school related events were the Sandy Hill Elementary School shooting that took place in Connecticut in 2012 and the Marjory Stoneman Douglas High School shooting in Parkland, Florida in 2018. When events like this begin to spiral out of control, it is time to investigate what can be done and to ask who is responsible for the safety of schoolchildren.

From a legal perspective, that responsibility falls on the shoulders of school boards, school districts, state governments, and the federal government. School boards generally have the authority to supervise schools and the power to regulate the conduct of students and (everyone else, for that matter) on school property. Under the principle of *loco parentis* (in the place of the parent), school authorities must keep students safe while in school buildings, on the grounds of the school, at school activities, and on school buses. School districts also have a similar set of responsibilities. They are charged with maintaining a safe environment. Depending on state law, this can include having emergency plans; initiating fire drills; holding safety drills; practicing dangerous weather drills; preventing bullying; preventing chocking and other food-related dangers, such as dangerous allergies; maintaining a sanitary environment; policing the use of drugs on campus; and guarding against the presence of dangerous weapons on school grounds, in school buildings, at school activities, and on school buses.

State laws also impact the presence of guns in schools. Often, states make it a crime to have a deadly weapon, including guns and items that look like real guns, in school safety zones. As noted earlier, such zones generally include not just the school building itself, but also the school grounds, school buses, and school activities such as sporting events, school dances, school assemblies, field trips, and so on. Naturally, many states, as an exception to the general rule, permit school boards to hire security guards who are authorized to carry firearms and even to empower teachers and other school to employee to carry weapons in school zones. However, in most states, such people, guards, teachers, and other employees must have a concealed weapons license. Other exceptions include state or federal law enforcement officers carrying weapons onto a school zone while on duty, and parents or other authorized individuals picking up or dropping of students in school zone pick up-drop off areas, as long as such persons are duly licensed to carry such weapons.

In many ways, the responsibilities noted above are mandated not only by state law, but also by federal law. Still, the federal law that covers gun control related to schools has a long and somewhat troubled history. The statute, known officially as the Gun Free Zone Act, was first enacted in 1990. It was challenged in the courts in 1995 and was overturned by the U.S. Supreme Court in the case of *U.S. v Lopez*. In that case, the High Court decided that Congress had exceeded its power under the Commerce Clause in enacting the Gun Free Zone Act. The High Court declared that Congress had not satisfactorily demonstrated that the activities prohibited by the Gun Free Zone Act had a substantial affect on interstate commerce. Congress then refashioned the wording of the Gun Free Zone Act so that it covered only firearms that have "moved in or that otherwise affect interstate or foreign commerce." The statute says: "It shall be unlawful for any individual knowingly to possess a firearm that has moved in or that otherwise affects interstate or foreign commerce at a place that the individual knows, or has reasonable cause to know, is a school zone." The statute also defines a "school zone" as "in, or on the grounds of, a public, parochial or private school; or . . . within a distance of 1,000 feet from the grounds of a public, parochial or private school." [See: *U.S. v. Lopez,* 514 U.S. 549 (1995); and the Gun Free Zone Act (18 U.S.C. Section 922q). See also: Pamela A. Leist, "Guns and Schools: School Safety and Gun Laws," *The Ohio State Bar Association Forum,* August 2017.]

Crimes against Property

Crimes against property include but are not limited to: burglary; breaking and entering; trespass; aggravated arson; arson; aggravated robbery; robbery; theft, fraud, and related offenses.

Burglary, Breaking and Entering, and Trespass

The crime of burglary has evolved since the Middle Ages. It was once limited to the unlawful entry into a dwelling place at night. Modern legislatures have extended the definition of **burglary** to include using force, deceit, or cunning to trespass into an occupied structure with the intent to commit a crime. A more serious form of burglary is generally referred to as **aggravated burglary**. Aggravated burglary includes everything that burglary includes but adds the use of a deadly weapon, the infliction of harm, the threat of harm, or the attempt to harm another person. A third related offense is **breaking and entering**, which generally includes using force, deceit, or cunning to trespass into an unoccupied structure with the intent to commit any theft or any felony. Breaking and entering can also involve trespassing on land with the intent to commit a felony. The last offense that is related to these three offenses is **trespass**, which involves knowingly entering land without permission to do so. Some, but not all, forms of trespass include entry onto the land with the intent to commit a misdemeanor.

Aggravated Arson and Arson

Under common law rules, arson involved the burning of another person's home. Legislatures have expanded this definition so that arson now includes more than one offense. **Aggravated arson** includes using fire or explosives to create a substantial risk of physical harm to an individual or to an occupied building. Often also included in this offense is the hiring of another person to carry out the burning or the use of the explosives. A lesser offense is ordinary **arson**, which involves using fire or explosives to harm or cause a substantial risk of harm to the property of another or to do the same to another's property or to the offender's own property in order to carry out fraud. Again also included in this is hiring another to actually burn the property or use the explosives. Some states have expanded the arson statutes even further to specifically include the burning or use of explosives against government-owned buildings, government parklands, government wildlife preserves, and so on.

Aggravated Robbery and Robbery

Like many of the criminal offenses already discussed in this chapter, robbery involves more than one offense. Unlike many of the others, however, the definition of robbery has not changed much over the years. The more serious offense is generally known as aggravated robbery. **Aggravated robbery** involves attempting to commit or actually committing a theft using a deadly weapon or a dangerous ordnance or doing the same by inflicting physical harm on the victim. **Robbery** involves essentially the same elements as aggravated robbery; however, in ordinary robbery, the offender possesses a deadly weapon but neither uses nor shows the weapon. Robbery can also involve attempting to commit or actually committing a theft by inflicting or attempting to inflict physical harm on another person.

Theft, Fraud, and Related Offenses

Today, many jurisdictions will place theft, fraud, and a series of related offenses, such as receiving stolen goods or passing bad checks, together under a single heading. What each of these offenses has in common is the attempt

THE OPENING CASE *Round 3*
United States v. Hearst: Patty, the Newspaper Heiress or Tania, the Urban Guerrilla?

The Opening Case tells the tale of heiress turned urban guerrilla, Patty Hearst. After her kidnapping and a less than satisfactory ransom payment, Hearst, on a videotape, revealed that she had joined the Symbionese Libertion Army (SLA). A short time after that, Hearst was one of several SLA members who robbed the Hibernia Bank in San Francisco. Following the robbery, and to challenge reports that she had been forced into joining the robbery, the SLA released a new video in which Hearst stated, unequivocally, that she was not brainwashed but was actually a committed SLA member. In the same videotape, she said that the bank was robbed to obtain funds to support the anti-capitalism revolution, which she had joined as a dedicated soldier. A warrant was issued for her arrest and, shortly thereafter, but not before she had participated in another crime, she and several additional members of the SLA were arrested in an apartment in San Francisco. During processing, after her arrest, when asked her profession, she replied, "urban guerrilla." Hearst was indicted for assault with intent to commit murder, assault with a deadly weapon, robbery, and kidnapping. She was tried with armed robbery and using a firearm to commit a felony.

Let's focus on the armed robbery charge. The definition of armed robbery (aka first-degree robbery) in California states: "Robbery is the felonious taking of personal property in the possession of another, from his person or immediate presence, and against his will, accomplished by means of force or fear" (California Penal Code 221). Stated another way, to prove someone guilty of first-degree robbery, the prosecution must demonstrate, beyond a reasonable doubt, that the defendant took somebody's property from their immediate presence using force, fear, or threat, with the intent to keep that property permanently or long enough to make it valueless to the real owner even if returned. The Hearst family hired F. Lee Bailey, the most famous criminal defense attorney in the United States at that time. Take a look back at the definition of first-degree robbery and consider the following "portrait of a felony." The bank robbery was photographed on the bank's security cameras. Hearst and her accomplices were seen carrying automatic weapons and were heard shouting commands at customers and bank employees. On their way out of the bank, the robbers shot two people. The net amount stolen from the bank was $10,960. Given all of this, Bailey knew that he could not argue that Hearst had not committed armed robbery. Hearst and her accomplices clearly took personal property (the $10,960) in the possession of another (the bank, the bank employees, and the bank customers), from his person or immediate presence (Hearst and company were in the bank itself), and against his will, accomplished by means of force or fear (Hearst and her accomplices were armed with automatic rifles). Finally, there as no doubt that they intended to keep that $10,960 permanently to support the anti-capitalism revolution. Given all these facts, it is easy to understand why Bailey knew that he could not argue that Hearst had not committed armed robbery and would have to seek another defense. To see what that other defense might have been, read on. [See: *United States v. Hearst*, 563 F.2d 1313 (9th Cir., 1978). See also: Walter Thompson, "The Wayback Machine: When Patty Hearst Robbed a Sunset Bank," *Hoodline San Francisco*, November 21, 2015, http://www.hoodline.com/2015/11/when-patty-hearst-robbed-a-sunset-bank.]

Source: See: *United States v. Hearst*, 563 F.2d 1313 (9th Cir. 1978); See also Walter Thompson, "TheWayback Machine: When Patty Hearst Robbed a Sunset Bank," *Hoodline San Francisco* (November 21, 2015), http://www.hoodline.com/2015/11/when-patty-hearst-robbed-a-sunset-bank.

to separate the rightful owner of property from that property or to somehow profit from that separation once it has taken place. **Theft**, the simplest, and arguably the oldest of these offenses is defined in many jurisdictions as knowingly taking or obtaining control over the property of another individual without that individual's consent using deceit, threats, or coercion. **Fraud** covers a wide variety of crimes today, including such diverse activities as identity fraud, Medicaid fraud, worker's compensation fraud, telecommunications fraud, insurance fraud, defrauding a rental agency, and defrauding creditors. What each type of fraud has in common, however, is a deliberately engineered deception that the offender uses to obtain property or services that belong to another. The offenses that are related to theft and fraud cover a wide variety of situations including motion picture piracy, misuse of credit cards, trademark counterfeiting, receiving stolen property, and tampering with records.

Crimes Involving Business

Nonviolent in nature, business crimes are those carried out by a business or individual in the course of doing business to obtain a business-related advantage. Covering a wide range of illegal business practices, business crimes are directed against individuals, other businesses, the government, or the public. The business crimes discussed here include embezzlement, forgery, criminal simulation, passing bad checks, and defrauding creditors.

Embezzlement In many jurisdictions, embezzlement is defined as wrongfully taking property or funds that have been entrusted to the care of the offender. Unlike similar offenses such as theft, robbery, and burglary, a fundamental element of embezzlement is that the embezzler had control over the property or the funds that were wrongfully taken. Thus, embezzlement often occurs in a business setting and frequently involves the employees of the victim.

Forgery, Criminal Simulation, and Passing Bad Checks The crime of forgery involves the false making or changing of a writing (without proper authorization) with the intent to defraud. It is also forgery to possess or sell an altered or false writing with the intent to defraud. Some states have expressly added identity cards to their forgery statutes to emphasize the criminal nature of forged IDs. These states generally make it a crime to create, sell, use, or possess a false ID. Criminal simulation is analogous to forgery because it also involves the alteration or falsification of an object or a document with intent to defraud. However, criminal simulation involves altering or falsifying art objects, antiques, photographs, films, tapes, recordings, and/or antiquities with the intent to defraud. Passing bad checks includes issuing or transferring a check or other negotiable instrument knowing it will be dishonored and with the intent to defraud.

Defrauding Creditors Many jurisdictions have statutes that are specifically designed to protect the rights of creditors. The statute against defrauding creditors is the crime of removing, hiding, destroying, giving away, or transferring any person's property with the intent to defraud creditors. Under these statutes it is also criminal to hide, misrepresent, or refuse to disclose information about the existence, amount, or location of a person's property to a fiduciary who has been appointed to administer that person's affairs or estate. The crime of defrauding creditors can be either a felony or a misdemeanor depending on the amount of the property involved in the fraud.

Racketeer Influenced and Corrupt Organizations Act To prevent a criminal invasion of legitimate businesses, Congress enacted the Racketeer Influenced and Corrupt Organizations (RICO) Act. Under provisions of this statute, conducting a legitimate business with the funds acquired from a "pattern of racketeering activities" can give rise to criminal liability. Many of the offenses that fall within the scope of "racketeering activity"—such as arson and robbery—are serious crimes. Others, however, are less sinister. For example, both mail fraud and wire fraud fall within the definition of racketeering activities. The provisions of RICO can give rise not only to criminal charges but also to civil liability. Thus, it is not uncommon for individuals to seek damages in lawsuits filed against corporations that have violated RICO.

Crimes against Justice

Crimes against justice involve offenses committed by or with the cooperation of a public servant or a public official. Such crimes include bribery, theft in office, and dereliction of duty. Others, such as intimidation, are committed against a public official or public servant. Still others, such as obstruction of justice, resisting arrest, perjury, and tampering with evidence are committed against the justice system itself.

Bribery and Theft in Office In most states, **bribery** involves offering, promising, or actually giving something of value to a public official with the goal of influencing that official in the discharge of his or her public duties. It is also bribery when the public official solicits or accepts a thing of value in exchange for that public official's influence in whatever capacity. Many states have further expanded the crime of bribery to include witnesses who are offered or given something of value in exchange for their testimony. The bribery can be committed by the person who offers the bribe and by the witness who solicits or accepts the bribe. Another offense that involves public servants is theft in office. Most jurisdictions define **theft in office** to include any theft offense in the criminal code that is committed by a public official or a party official. The theft must involve the use of that official's governmental or party power to obtain unlawful control over governmental or party property or services.

Dereliction of Duty In most states, the crime of **dereliction of duty** can involve law enforcement officers and public servants. In relation to *law enforcement officers*, dereliction of duty is any activity that involves the officer's failure to carry out his or her lawful duties. These duties include, but are not limited to, serving lawful warrants; preventing the commission of a crime; controlling unruly prisoners; preventing the escape of prisoners; carrying out criminal proceedings; providing persons confined in a detention facility with food, shelter, and medical assistance; preserving sanitary conditions in detention facilities; and, in general, properly managing those detention facilities. *Public servants* are charged with carrying out those duties that are specifically related to the proper operation of their governmental office. In addition, many dereliction of duty statutes also expressly state that public servants have an affirmative duty to keep their department or agency within the budget set for it by the state legislature.

Intimidation The crime of **intimidation** involves threats of harm to the person or property of a public servant, party official, or witness with the intention of coercing that individual into some violation of his or her public duty. Some jurisdictions have expanded the definition of intimidation to include threats of harm to the public servant's reputation by the publication of false information. This would seem to include not only the publication of false statements in newspapers and magazines and on television, but also the posting of such false information on the Internet via the various social media outlets, such as Facebook, LinkedIn, and so on.

Obstruction of Justice and Resisting Arrest Most jurisdictions define **obstruction of justice** as any activity designed to prevent the discovery, apprehension, arrest, prosecution, conviction, or punishment of a criminal defendant. Each jurisdiction also specifies those activities that qualify as obstruction of justice. These activities include but are not necessarily limited to: hiding a criminal defendant; providing that defendant with money, transportation, weapons, disguises, and so on; warning that person of possible discovery or arrest; destroying or concealing evidence; and communicating false information to law enforcement officials about the defendant. **Resisting arrest** is defined as interfering in the lawful arrest of a criminal defendant. Most statutes defining this offense also penalize the resister for any harm that comes to a law enforcement officer involved in the arrest.

Perjury and Tampering with Evidence Under the laws of most states, **perjury** is defined as making a false statement under oath; however, many jurisdictions also add that the false statement must be material to the proceeding. A statement is material if it can have an impact on the final disposition of the case. Interestingly enough, in most cases, the fact that the perjured testimony is inadmissible as evidence makes no difference; the false statement is still perjury. However, a person cannot be convicted of perjury by a single witness. **Tampering with evidence** means altering, destroying, or removing any piece of evidence with the intent to somehow lessen the probative value of that evidence. In addition, tampering with evidence includes presenting false evidence to a public official in order to somehow destroy the effectiveness of an official investigation.

ANOTHER QUESTION OF ETHICS

The Progress of the Paramilitary Police Power

There is a difference between the police and the military. Right? The military is supposed to defend the entire nation from attacks conducted by other nations, terror groups, or perhaps even pirates on the high seas. The police, on the other hand, are supposed to serve and protect by upholding the law and protecting citizens, typically from one another. This is the traditional distinction that for decades, perhaps even centuries, worked fairly well. Today, however, it has become increasingly difficult to tell the difference between the two—not because the military has become too "police-like," but because the police have been transformed (or perhaps have transformed themselves) into military combat teams. Three decades ago, about 20 percent of our cities with populations between 20,000 and 50,000 had a SWAT (special weapons and tactics) team. Since then, that percentage has escalated to 80 percent and continues to climb. In the 1980s, the number of SWAT team raids ran around 3,000 per year, while today the number tops 50,000. Part of this is due to federal funding from the Department of Homeland Security ($35 billion between 2002 and 2011) and the Pentagon (aid has flowed to 17,000 police, sheriff, and state highway patrol departments), part is due to property seizure statutes under which crime-related resources can be confiscated by the police, and part is due to old-fashioned competition among law enforcement agencies as they battle to be the best of the best. The fact that crime-fighting agencies want to have up-to-date, state-of-the-art equipment is understandable, even admirable, and in many ways should be encouraged. However, a fundamental question remains: Are we correct that there is difference between the police and the military? Or have the two fighting forces become simple extensions of one another? If you were the mayor of a midsize city (population between 20,000 and 50,000) and, in that role, were offered a large outlay of ready cash from the Pentagon or Homeland Security to build a paramilitary SWAT team in your municipal police department, would you accept that funding? Explain the reason for your response using one of the ethical theories identified and explained in Chapter 1. [See: "Law Enforcement in the United States: Armed and Dangerous," *The Economist*, March 22, 2014, pp. 14, 16; "Paramilitary Police: Cops or Soldiers?" *The Economist*, March 22, 2014, pp. 27-28.]

Source: See: "Law Enforcement in the United States: Armed and Dangerous," *The Economist, March* 22, 2014, pp. 14, 16; "Paramilitary Police: Cops or Soldiers?" *The Economist,* March 22, 2014, pp. 27–28.

The Posse Comitatus and Insurrection Acts States' increased use of paramilitary police operatives to deal with enforcement of the law brings up an interesting legal point often overlooked in these discussions. Both the letter and the spirit of the law in this country prevent the federal government from using the U.S. military to uphold the law of an individual state. Such responsibilities rest not with the federal government, but with the state government, in general, and with the governor, in particular. The prohibition on the use of the military (first the Army, but later the Navy, Air Force, and Marines) was made official with the Posse Comitatus Act in 1878 in tandem with the Insurrection Act of 1807. The acts expressly forbid the use of the U.S. military to uphold the laws of any individual state. The laws do not cover the National Guard, which is controlled by the governor of each state, and the Coast Guard, which is now under the authority of the Department of Homeland Security. The precarious nature of this prohibition can be seen in the recent history of the law. In 2006, the act was amended to permit the use of the U.S. military to respond to natural disasters and terror attacks. In 2008, the amendment was withdrawn. Then in 2011, a narrow provision was added that permits the use of the military to deal with al-Qaeda and Taliban attacks in the United States. In 2012, the National Defense Authorization Act included a provision that permits the military to detain individuals for an undefined period of time, even though charges have not been filed against that individual. Some commentators argue, rather convincingly, that this provision effectively repeals the Posse Comitatus Act. Others contend that the Posse Comitatus Act has already been repealed in a *de facto* manner, since, as noted above, the police have morphed into a military force without any need for legislative action.

quick quiz 5-3

1. In most states, the distinction between first- and second-degree murder is important because first-degree murder usually carries the death penalty while second-degree murder does not.	true | false
2. It is acceptable to draft a statute that outlaws speech aimed at inciting outrage or fear based solely on race, religion, color, gender, or any similar category.	true | false
3. Passing bad checks includes issuing or transferring a check or other negotiable instrument knowing it will be dishonored and with the intent to defraud.	true | false

5-4 Cybercrimes

As is true of most other crimes, statutory definitions and classifications of cybercrimes (electronic crimes and e-crimes) vary from state to state. Moreover, in the case of cybercrimes, the definitions are even more varied because there is no agreement on what constitutes a cybercrime. One approach is to state that cybercrimes involve any criminal act that includes a computer. This strategy, which is often referred to as cyber-trespass, computer trespass, or e-trespass, can solve many of the problems associated with cybercrime, if only by an indirect treatment of such crimes. Another way to classify cybercrimes is to distinguish between crimes committed with a computer and crimes committed against a computer.

Cyber-Trespass

A problem arises when crimes that are already on the books are committed with a computer. As noted previously, one way to deal with this situation is to create a single generic offense called cyber-trespass, electronic trespass, or e-trespass. **Cyber-trespass** is the process of gaining access to a computer with the intent to commit a crime. In effect, in one single stroke, this strategy incorporates the rest of the criminal code into this one crime, making it an offense to use a computer to commit any other crime in the code. In a state that takes this approach, all criminal statutes—especially those pertaining to fraud, embezzlement, blackmail, and theft—become part of this one crime known as cyber-trespass.

Crimes Committed with a Computer

Another approach to dealing with cybercrime is to distinguish between using a computer to commit a crime and committing an offense against a computer. Naturally, some of these crimes will overlap. Nevertheless, enough of a distinction exists between the two to make this a viable approach to the subject. Cybercrimes that focus on the use of a computer include cyber-stalking, cyber-harassment, cyber-assault, cyber-bullying, cyber-piracy, cyber-extortion, cyber-spoofing, phishing, smishing, and vishing.

Cyber-Stalking *Cyber-stalking*, *e-stalking*, or *electronic stalking* involves targeting individuals for exploitation using computer connections. Cyber-stalkers usually target vulnerable individuals who may be searching for a genuine connection on the Internet. Minors are often targeted by cyber-stalkers. After gaining the trust of the minor or other innocent victim, the cyber-stalker arranges a meeting so that he or she can take advantage of the innocent party.

Cyber-Harassment *Cyber-harassment*, *electronic harassment*, or *e-harassment* involves using computer connections, often via e-mail or some other social media, to blanket the target with offensive sexual, racial, religious, or political comments, photographs, videos, and so on aimed at disrupting the victim's peace of mind. The psychological impact of cyber-harassment is severe, but often difficult to prove, thus making cyber-harassment an especially vicious crime.

Cyber-Assault *Cyber-assault*, *electronic assault*, or *e-assault* has several definitions depending on the jurisdiction. Cyber-assault can involve using social media to threaten to inflict immediate and severe bodily harm on the target victim. In this sense of the term, it is simply an extension of common law assault; however, cyber-assault can also mean a direct attack on a computer system with the intent to disrupt that system.

Cyber-Bullying *Cyber-bullying*, *electronic bullying*, or *e-bullying* involves intentional, aggressive, upsetting activities by a single individual or a group of individuals aimed at destroying the mental well-being of a peer. Generally, cyber-bullies use a variety of cyber-social media, including chatrooms, discussion groups, blogs, web pages, texting, instant messaging, and so on to disrupt the life of the target. The term *cyber-bullying* is generally used to describe the cyber-activities of students against one another. In most jurisdictions, it is not yet a crime.

Cyber-Piracy One of the most common, most lucrative, most covert, and most insidious of all e-crimes is cyber-piracy. Literally billions of dollars are siphoned off annually by cyber-pirates, who sometimes profit directly and sometimes indirectly from their theft. *Cyber-piracy*, *electronic piracy*, or *e-piracy* occurs when website operators take intellectual property—usually in the form of feature films, e-books, television programming, audio recordings of songs, or software—and carry them on their websites or sell them on the Internet without paying royalties to the legitimate copyright owners. The word is also sometimes used as an umbrella term for other cyber-crimes such as cyber-extortion, cyber-spoofing, phishing, smishing, and vishing.

Cyber-Extortion, Malware, and Ransomware *Cyber-extortion*, *electronic extortion*, or *e-extortion* can occur when an experienced hacker gains access to the computer records of a corporation or other institution and then disables the computer or an entire computer system. Sometimes cyber-extortion is referred to as *cyber-germ warfare*, *cyber-warfare*, or simply as *hacking*. Whatever term is used to describe the crime, once the perpetrator has disabled the computer or the computer system, he or she demands a ransom in exchange for restoring the computer or the computer system to its operational capacity. Sometimes the hacker discovers some sort of illegal, negligent, unethical, or embarrassing conduct that might damage the reputation of the target organization, but that does not have to be the case. Usually, just paralyzing the system is enough to get the attention of the owner or owners who will do anything to restore the system, including, especially, paying the ransom that the hacker has demanded. Cyber-extortion is generally carried out by a software package known as <u>malware</u> (a shortened version of *malicious software*) that infects a computer and shuts down its operation or encrypts its files making them inaccessible.

Ransomware Attacks One of the most powerful forms of malware is a program known as <u>ransomware</u>, which generally enters a computer system via an e-mail that includes a link or an attachment. Typically, the process begins when a computer operator receives a rogue e-mail (one that generally looks like an innocuous message but is sometimes sophisticated enough to closely mimic a message from a co-worker, supplier, customer, or client). The unsuspecting operator opens and reads the e-mail and then, following instructions, either clicks on the link or opens the attachment. At that point, the virus enters the system and locks down the computer or encrypts files so that they cannot be accessed, effectively shutting down the operation, not only on that one computer, but also throughout the entire system to which that computer is configured. A message follows demanding payment of a ransom in exchange for returning the computer and its network to operational status. Ransom payments are generally asked for and paid in bitcoin. [See: Russell Goldman, "Ransomware: How Hackers Hold Data Hostage," *The New York Times*, May 13, 2017, p. A-9; and "Ransomware," *Trend Micro*, https://www.trendmicro.com/vinfo/us/security/definition/Ransomware#the_Bitcoin_connection.]

The Bitcoin Factor As noted above, ransom payments in a ransomware attack are made via bitcoin. <u>Bitcoin</u> is both a digital currency (i.e., cyber-currency or e-currency) and, at the same time, a digital exchange system (i.e., cyber-currency exchange system or e-currency exchange system or cyber exchange system) that allows people to buy and sell online. Transactions are recorded on a cyber-ledger that keeps track of amounts transferred from one person or institution to another. Bitcoin value is based on supply and demand. Because there is a limited supply of bitcoins "out there" (21 million to be exact), the value climbs as bitcoins are used. The bitcoin exchange rate has gone as high as $5,000 for one bitcoin. The electronic nature of bitcoin makes it the best way for ransomware criminals to exact ransom payments from their victims. However, sometimes such payments end up being quite small. For instance, the global attack in 2017 seems to have netted the attackers only about $55,000 in bitcoin transfers. [See: Adam Shell, "What's Bitcoin Exactly, and Should I Invest in It?" *USA Today*, October 9, 2017, https://www.usatoday.com/story/money/2017/10/09/whats-bitcoin-exactly-and-should-invest-it/740598001/. See also: Paul Vigna, "Hackers Get Small Ransom in Bitcoin," *The Wall Street Journal*, May 16, 2017, p. A-6.]

Global Ransomware Attacks Early in 2017, the global community was treated to a preview of the nasty effects that can emerge from a global ransomware attack. This attack used a specialized form of ransomware known as "WannaCry" that made use of a flaw in a certain globally used software package. The malware attackers were able to encrypt critical files in thousands of computers worldwide, thus crippling systems internationally. In short order, some 200,000 computers were affected in about 150 countries including the United Kingdom, France, the Ukraine, India, Russia, China, South Korea, Taiwan, Brazil, Canada, and the United States. Some of the companies and institutions targeted included the British National Health Service, the China National Petroleum Corporation, the Russian Interior Ministry, Brazil's Social Security Agency, and the Nissan Motor Company, among others. The WannaCry hackers, it seems, have no national loyalty. In response to the crisis, the Department of Homeland Security, the Federal Bureau of Investigation, and the National Security Agency began to actively investigate the source of the ransom demands. In addition, the U.S. Computer Emergency Response Team (US-CERT) began to issue alerts aimed at informing computer uses of the WannaCry threat and advising them not to pay any ransom demands. Whether this strategy works or not is irrelevant. What is relevant is that we can expect to see more such attacks, and probably more severe ones, in the near future. [See: Nick Kostov, Jenny Gross, Stu Woo, et al., "Global Hack Pressures Officials, Victims," *The Wall Street Journal*, May 15, 2017, pp. A-1, A-6; "Cyberattack FAQs," *The Wall Street Journal*, May 15, 2017, p. A-6; and Louise Radnofsky and Shane Harris, "U.S. Agencies Work to Thwart Attack," *The Wall Street Journal*, May 15, 2017, pp. A-6.]

Cyber-Spoofing To commit *cyber-spoofing*, *electronic spoofing*, or *e-spoofing*, a cyber-criminal must falsely adopt the identity of another computer user or create a false identity on a website to commit fraud. A simple form of cyber-spoofing involves adopting the identity of an e-mailer to defraud the recipients of the original e-mail. Another type of cyber-spoofing involves creating phony websites or diverting users from legitimate websites to obtain credit card numbers, debit card numbers, PINs, passwords, or other confidential information to commit a wide variety of fraudulent activities.

Phishing and Spear Phishing Phishing and spear phishing are two forms of cyber-spoofing. *Phishing* involves sending out phony e-mails that solicit buyers and, in the process, obtain credit card information, account numbers, PINs, account balances, and so on. When the e-mail has been customized to such an extent that the recipient believes the e-mail comes from a co-worker, a friend, or a relative, the offense is called *spear phishing*. [See: "Briefing Cyberwar: War in the Fifth Domain," *The Economist*, July 3, 2010, p. 26.]

Smishing and Vishing *Smishing* links SMS (short message service) texting with phishing. *Vishing* connects phishing to voice messaging. In both situations, cyber-criminals send out messages at random, sometimes targeting a particular city, profession, or exchange number and sometimes using a particular phone list purchased or obtained illegally from an institution like a savings and loan, a credit card company, or a department store. The messages will warn the recipients that their credit card information needs to be updated or that their account is overdrawn, prompting the victims to contact a number or to access an Internet site. The victims then provide private information such as account numbers, PINs, passwords, and so on. These confidential numbers and passwords are used to infiltrate the victim's financial records, credit card accounts, debit card records, and so on. [See: "Smishing and Vishing and Other Cyber Scams to Watch Out for This Holiday," Federal Bureau of Investigation, November 2010, http://www.fbi.gov/news/stories/2010/november/cyber/112410/cyber_112410_12410.]

Crimes That Target Computers

Cybercrimes that target computers attempt to disable the computer itself, to disable the system that it operates, or to confiscate and use the information stored in the computer, sometimes after erasing the original data. Crimes that target computers include cyber-terrorism, identity theft, cyber-vandalism, and cyber-germ warfare.

Cyber-Terrorism *Cyber-terrorism*, *electronic terrorism*, or *e-terrorism* involve using a computer to disrupt or destroy one of the critical elements of the nation's cyber-infrastructure, such as the power grid, the air traffic control system, water and sanitation plants, the ground transportation system, a harbor traffic-control network, a cell tower network, the nation's stock exchange, the banking system, hospital backup generator systems, or the national defense system.

Identity Theft Another cybercrime that targets computers and computer information is identity theft. In identity theft, a perpetrator uses one of the techniques noted previously to steal credit card information, PINs, financial data, access codes, passwords, or debit card information. The perpetrator then passes himself or herself off as the victim. Using this technique, the identity thief can clean out bank accounts, run up credit card debt, divert cash transfers, buy and sell stocks, enter electronic auction networks, approve or cancel shipments, make or revoke hotel and travel reservations, and disrupt the financial and the personal life of the victim.

Cyber-Vandalism Sometimes expert vandals can attack a computer system so that a website is destroyed or paralyzed to the extent that legitimate business can no longer be conducted on that site. This type of attack is known as *cyber-vandalism*, *electronic vandalism*, or *e-vandalism*. Often, cyber-vandalism is used to cripple a business as a form of revenge for real or imagined wrongs, to exercise power over a business, or to hurt the owner of a business just for "fun."

Federal Cybercrimes

Many states have enacted legislation to combat these cybercrimes and other cyber-offenses. The federal government has also attempted to deal with the issue by passing a number of anti-cybercrime statutes. The statutes of primary importance as determined by the Computer Crime and Intellectual Property Section of the United States Department of Justice include the Computer Fraud and Abuse Act (CFAA), the Electronic Communications Privacy Act (ECPA), the Communications Assistance for Law Enforcement Act (CALEA), the Economic Espionage Act (EEA), the National Stolen Property Act (NSPA), and the Identity Theft and Assumption Deterrence Act (ITADA).

The Computer Fraud and Abuse Act (CFAA) Congress first specifically addressed the subject of cybercrime more than two decades ago when, as a part of a comprehensive crime control statute, it passed the Computer Fraud and Abuse Act (CFAA). Currently, this act outlaws accessing a protected computer in an unauthorized fashion in order to commit a wide variety of activities, including obtaining national security information, compromising the confidentiality of a computer, trespassing in a government computer, accessing a computer to defraud, damaging a computer, damaging computer information, trafficking in passwords, and threatening to damage a computer. A protected computer is any computer that is involved in interstate or foreign communication or that is involved in interstate or foreign commerce. This wide-sweeping set of qualifications also includes computers outside the territorial United States so long as foreign or interstate commerce or communication is affected in some way. For all practical purposes then, any computer—including laptops, tablets, and mobile phones—with access to the Internet would be protected computers under the provisions of the statute.

Despite the fact that the language above seems rather straightforward and unambiguous, some difficulties exist that relate to the interpretation of the CFAA. These difficulties are associated with the definition of "unauthorized access." It is very clear, for example, that a computer has been accessed in an unauthorized way whenever people work on computers that they are not permitted to access or when they have accessed a computer they are authorized to work on but have retrieved files that they are not permitted to access. However, what about a situation in which a person has been authorized to access a computer and has the authority to access a set of files but then retrieves those files in an unauthorized way (e.g., using someone else's password) or when a person has access to a computer and a set of files and retrieves those files in a legitimate way but then uses those files in an unauthorized way (e.g., accessing and then giving away trade secrets or transferring customer lists in violation of a noncompete agreement). Do these secondary scenarios also amount to unauthorized access? Widespread disagreement exists on whether these secondary scenarios amount to unauthorized access. In fact, the U.S. Courts of Appeals do not yet agree on the true meaning of "unauthorized access." A final ruling on this issue will have to come from the U.S. Supreme Court, and it will have to come soon. Stay tuned for the final decision. It is just around the corner. [See: *United States v. Nosal,* 676 F. 3d 854 (9th Cir. Ct. App. 2011). See also: "Statutory Interpretation—Computer Fraud and Abuse Act—Ninth Circuit Holds That Employees' Unauthorized Use of Accessible Information Did Not Violate the CFAA," *United States v. Nosal,* 676 F. 3d 854 (9th Cir. Ct. App. 2012) (en banc)), *Harvard Law Review* 126 (2013), p. 1454.]

The CFAA also has another interesting feature. While it is primarily a criminal law statute, it also contains provisions that authorize civil lawsuits. These provisions are designed to give a cause of action to any innocent party who has been damaged or injured in some way by a perpetrator who has accessed a protected computer in an unauthorized way. The statute empowers the innocent victim to receive money damages and/or have an injunction issued, whichever is more appropriate in the case. Of course, victims must be prepared to demonstrate that they have suffered a real loss as a result of the unauthorized entry into the computer system. Moreover, that loss actually can mean a number things, including the need to reconfigure or restore lost data, the cost involved in compiling an assessment of the damage that was done by the unauthorized entry, any income lost because of the interruption of the computer's operation, any additional losses that resulted from a discontinuation of service, any consequential damages, and so on. The minimum amount in controversy must be $5,000. [See: Shain Khoshbin and Munck Wilson Mandala, "Cybercrimes in Civil Litigation: Using the CFAA to Go 'On the Offensive,'" *Legal Tech News,* March 22, 2017, http://www.legaltechnews.com/id=1202781830294/Cybrcrimes-in-Civil-Litigation-Using-the-CFAA-To-Go-On-the-Offeb=nsive?mcode=0&curpage=All.]

The Electronic Communications Privacy Act (ECPA) Originally, the Federal Wiretap Act was designed to cover only wire and oral communications. The Electronic Communications Privacy Act (ECPA) amended the original wiretap act to cover communication by computer. The purpose of the amendment was to protect the privacy of electronic communication in the same way that wire and oral communication are protected. To do this, the act prohibits the intentional interception of electronic communication.

The Communications Assistance for Law Enforcement Act (CALEA) The ECPA was later amended to help law enforcement officials keep pace with modern advances in electronic communication. The Communications Assistance for Law Enforcement Act (CALEA) amended the earlier law by requiring communication companies to update their electronic equipment in order to make certain that such law enforcement officers could carry out their surveillance duties properly.

The Economic Espionage Act (EEA) The Economic Espionage Act (EEA) is designed to protect trade secrets. A trade secret is a plan, process, or device that is used in a business and is known only to those employees who need to know the secret to carry out their work. Examples of trade secrets include customer lists, chemical formulas, manufacturing processes, marketing techniques, pricing methods, and food or beverage recipes (think Coca-Cola). The EEA outlaws the downloading of trade secrets.

The National Stolen Property Act (NSPA) Under the National Stolen Property Act (NSPA), it is a federal crime to use interstate or foreign commerce to transport personal property, currency, or securities that an individual is aware were stolen; secured by fraud; or taken by some other illegal method, including an unauthorized electronic transfer.

The Identity Theft and Assumption Deterrence Act (ITADA) The Identity Theft and Assumption Deterrence Act (ITADA), which was amended by the Identity Theft Penalty Enhancement Act, outlaws the unauthorized transfer, possession, or use of a means of identifying another person to violate federal law. The amendment adds a new crime, called *aggravated identity theft*, to the original statute. The section on aggravated identity theft makes it clear that identity theft is much worse when it involves certain very serious felonies, including terrorism.

The CAN SPAM Act Spam is the nickname for all of those pop-up advertisements that appear on computer screens while users are tapped into the Internet. The CAN SPAM Act is designed to deal with this problem, as well as the problem of unsolicited commercial e-mail.

Stop Online Piracy Act (SOPA) As noted above, cyber-piracy occurs when website operators take some form of electronic intellectual property and carry or sell it on their websites without paying royalties. One stumbling block in dealing with cyber-piracy is that it is routinely carried out by website owners that operate far outside the jurisdiction of the United States. In an indirect attack on these offshore sites, the House of Representatives recently engineered a bill referred to as the Stop Online Piracy Act (SOPA). SOPA was designed to circuitously attack cyber-pirates by penalizing American websites that carry the pirated works and service the cyber-pirates with payment processors and advertisements. The bill would also entice Internet service providers (ISPs) to impede traffic to cyber-pirate sites using special filtering techniques. Any American entities that refuse to cooperate would be vulnerable to litigation filed by the copyright owners for infringement. The Senate version was referred to as the Protect Intellectual Property Act (PIPA). The bill caused such outrage from prominent websites such as Wikipedia and Google that the House and the Senate both postponed further consideration of their respective bills pending further investigation. [See: "Online Piracy: Stopping SOPA," *The Economist*, January 21, 2012, p. 33; and Don Reisinger, "SOPA Halted in House," *CNET Interactive*, January 20, 2012.]

The Drone Phenomenon: Federal and State Legislation A **drone** is an unpiloted remote control aircraft that can fly under its own power and move beyond the line of sight of its ground-based human operator. Drones have become a familiar feature in the skies of the United States. Like all new technological innovations, however, no one seems to know quite what to do with these drones from a legal point of view. This is one reason that, initially at least, a debate developed among city councils, state legislatures, tribal governments, and Congress as to which level of the government is best suited to have the authority to regulate the manufacture, sale, licensing, use, navigation, flight plans, pilot training, and safety of drones. Originally, Congress pointed to the U.S. Code, which seemed to establish the federal government as the political level with the power to regulate the airspace. Moreover, the Senate originally developed a federal statute to make certain that the federal government maintained control over the use of drones. The Senate bill stated, in part, that the states cannot enact legislation that relates to the "design, manufacture, testing, licensing, registration, certification, operation, or maintenance of an unmanned aircraft system, including airspace, altitude, flight paths, equipment or technology requirements, purpose, of operations, and pilot, operator, and observer qualifications, training, and certification." [See: Bart Jansen, "Senate Debates Contentious Provision against State Drone Laws," *USA Today*, April 16, 2016, http//www.usatoday.com/story/news/2016/04/19/senate-faa-bill-keeps-drone-policy-federal-hands/83241014/; and Ashton Marra, "Drone Bill Approved in W.Va. Senate," *WMKY*, March 1, 2017, http://wmky.org/post/drone-bill-approved-wva-senate.]

After much debate, however, the Senate changed direction and introduced a new bill that develops a jurisdiction-sharing plan among state, local, and tribal governments, on the one side, and the federal government, on the other. The new Senate bill is named the Drone Federalism Act (DFA) and is intended as an amendment to the Federal Aviation Administration (FAA) Modernization and Reform Act of 2012. The bill will empower state, local, and tribal governments to create regulations that cover such things as speed limits for drones, zones of drone operation, restricted areas of drone operation, drone-use curfews, and so on. The bill also specifies that such drones must not be flown beyond a 200-foot altitude limit. The bill does not eliminate the FAA's authority over the operation of drones, but it does require the FAA to justify any attempt to preempt state power in this area. The bill also proposes a pilot program under which the FAA will join with a team of representatives from 10 states to develop their own individual rules as well as procedures under which the these new regulations can be implemented and enforced. The group will also work to set up a list of "best practices" that will serve as a template for state and local governments engaged in drone rule making. The bill appears to be a reasonable compromise between state and federal factions. Accordingly, it has been endorsed by the U.S. Conference of Mayors, the National Governor's Association, the National League of Cities, the National Association of Counties, the National Association of State Aviation Officials, and the National Conference of State Legislatures. This is not the end of the story, however, so keep alert for new developments. [See: Kathryn Rattigan, "Drone Federalism Act, Seeking Regulation of Drones at the Local Level," *Robinson and Cole: Data Privacy + Security Advisor*, June 8, 2017, http://www.dataprivacyandsecurityinsider.com/2017/06/drone-federalism-act-seeking-regulation-of-drones-at-the-local-level/. See also: Jonathan Vanian, "New Senate Drone Bill Will Give Power to States and Local Governments," *Fortune*, May 25, 2017, http://fortune.com/2017/05/25/senate-drone-bill-faa-regulations/.]

The Global Cyber-Crisis

The U.S. government, U.S. corporations, and the U.S. military have become increasingly aware of both the power and the vulnerability of the Internet. National and global computer networks tie together a wide variety of systems that are used to make the global infrastructure more manageable, more efficient, and more affordable than ever before. Moreover, given the chance, very few of us would return to the days of manually controlled banking, line-of-sight air traffic control, in-person stock market trading, three-channel television, landline rotary phones, and manually operated passenger rail service. Nevertheless, with efficiency and convenience comes a trade-off. That trade-off is vulnerability. The international computer network is susceptible to collapse. A solar storm, a shift in the earth's magnetic field, a volcanic eruption, poorly written software, an incorrect file number, or inadequately maintained hardware can disrupt even the best computer system. Human operators can enter an outdated password, an inaccurate code, or the wrong person's PIN. Most of these errors are predictable and can be handled with a minimal amount of inconvenience. Other problems, those that are deliberate and knowingly target a computer system, are less easily solved.

For example, an enemy nation, a drug cartel, a crime syndicate, a gang of cyber-pirates, or a team of terrorists can, with a minimal amount of effort, send an e-mail with an attached PDF file that, when opened, will install a deadly software program in a computer system. Unlike the ransomware attacks noted above, which involve "hacking for profit," these global attacks are implemented as terrorist or military campaigns designed to undermine the safety of the infrastructure, the reliability of the electronic communications network, the continuation of power transmissions, the safety of the water supply, the security of the air traffic control network, the reliability of the international banking system, and so on. The malware used in a terror attack, for example, might command a widespread computer system to shut down; delete data; or perhaps worst of all, transfer control of the system to the attacker. Generally, when this type of terrorist or military attack occurs, no one knows what happened until the damage is done. Thus, without warning, the nation's air traffic control system might be compromised, a city's water supply contaminated, a regional power grid shut down, or the international banking system wiped clean of all transactions. Constructing a plan for dealing with a deliberate computer attack is difficult at best. Nevertheless, steps must be taken to deal with such attacks. [See: "Briefing Cyberwar: War in the Fifth Domain," *The Economist*, July 3, 2010, p. 25.]

Cyber-Strategies and Cyber-Solutions One step might be to split up data and send it along a series of different routes so that if one data stream is compromised, the others continue on their way unimpeded. This strategy is effective most of the time; however, even this tactic does not always work. One weakness in the submerged fiber-optic cable system, along which many data streams travel, is a network of bottlenecks, sites at which these streams intersect and fall under the control of a limited number of domain-name servers, making them tempting targets for cyber-criminals and cyber-terrorists. These bottlenecks appear in the Middle East, in South East Asia, and along the Eastern seaboard of the United States, any one of which is a tempting target. [See: "Briefing Cyberwar: War in the Fifth Domain," p. 25.]

Cyber-Command (Cybercom) The federal government has responded to these threats in a number of ways. First, the Pentagon has established a new cyber-command center that is charged with the job of protecting the military's computer command system. This new agency, which is officially referred to as Cyber Command or Cybercom, is under the control of the National Security Agency. It has been charged not only with protecting the American cyber-system from attack, but also with developing plans to undermine the computer systems of enemy nations. One of its goals might be to protect the "chokepoints" in the submerged fiber-optic system, but also to uncover effective ways to use the system in a way that benefits the American military [See: "Briefing Cyberwar: War in the Fifth Domain," p.25.]

Internet Crime Complaint Center (IC3) On the homefront, the federal government has taken steps to combat domestic cybercrime by establishing the Internet Crime Complaint Center (IC3). The IC3 operates as a joint venture between the National White Collar Crime Center (NW3C) and the Federal Bureau of Investigation (FBI). The IC3 handles complaints involving cybercrimes such as hacking, trade secret infringement, identity theft, cyber-extortion, and Internet fraud. Individuals and businesses can file complaints with the IC3 by accessing the agency's website. The IC3 also works closely with administrative agencies as well as with local, state, and federal law enforcement agencies. [See: Internet Crime Complaint Center, http://www.ic3.gov.]

U.S. Computer Emergency Readiness Team The U.S. Computer Emergency Readiness Team (US-CERT) was originally established as the Federal Computer Incident Response Center (FedCIRC) in 2000. The FedCIRC was renamed and moved to the Department of Homeland Security after its establishment in 2002. Since that time, the US-CERT has become one of the most reliable advisors to the federal and state governments on cyberspace security. The US-CERT also advises corporations and international non-governmental organizations (NGOs) on possible cyberthreats. In addition, the US-CERT is responsible for investigating major cyber incidents both at both the national and international levels. Recently, for example, the US-CERT was one of the leading investigating units responding to the international ransomware attack in 2017. [See: "About Us," U.S. Computer Emergency Readiness Team, Department of Homeland Security, 2016, https://www.us-cert.gov/aboutus/.]

Domestic Strategies The battle against cyber-abuse can now be fought in the home. Using a variety of computer software programs, parents can filter e-mails, text messages, and social site contacts on the Internet to prevent their children from receiving messages that are symptomatic of cyber-bullying and similar unwanted cyber-contacts. One popular weapon in this battle is the MouseMail software package developed by Safe Communications.

The MouseMail system permits parents to have e-mails, text messages, and other cyber-contacts heading to their children intercepted and filtered by a rapid comparison between the content of the message and a list of improper words. Unfamiliar senders are also tagged. The tagged messages are sent to the parents first, who handle them from that point on. Other similar software packages include Cyber/Bully/Alert.com and Social Shield.com. [See: Mike Snyder, "MouseMail Traps Kids' Cyberbullies," *USA Today*, January 5, 2011, p. 1A. See also "Welcome to Mouse Mail," http://mousemail.com.]

quick quiz 5-4

1. Statutory definitions and classifications of cybercrimes have become uniform within all jurisdictions in the United States. true | false
2. Cyber-trespass is defined as gaining access to a computer with the intent to commit a crime. true | false
3. The federal government has passed several cybercrime statutes. true | false

5-5 Defenses to Criminal Liability

Because criminal liability lies within the elements of an act and the required mental state, a logical defense would be aimed at eliminating one or both of those elements. Most defenses attempt to do just that. The most common defenses are insanity, entrapment, justifiable force, and mistake. (See Table 5-1.)

The Insanity Defense

Although the insanity defense has been around for a long time, many people do not understand the nature of the defense. One of the key points of confusion is the difference between *competency to stand trial* and the *insanity defense* itself.

Competency to Stand Trial Criminal defendants are generally presumed to be mentally competent to stand trial; however, the issue of competency to stand trial can be raised if the court, the defense attorney, or the prosecutor suspects that the defendant is not competent. If

Table 5-1 Criminal Liability and Defenses

Criminal Liability	Criminal Defenses
The act: 　Criminal behavior specifically 　　outlined by statute	Defenses to the act: 　Act as defined is "status" only 　Act as defined is ambiguous 　Act as defined is overbroad
The mental state: 　Mental state specifically 　　outlined by statute 　　Purpose 　　Knowledge 　　Recklessness 　　Negligence	Defenses to the mental state: 　Insanity 　Entrapment 　Justifiable force 　Mistake

the issue of competency is raised, the defendant will undergo psychiatric examinations to determine his or her level of competency. Generally, defendants are considered competent to stand trial if they understand the nature and the purpose of the charges against them and if they are capable of aiding their attorneys in their defense. When defendants are found to be incompetent, they are usually given treatment to improve their competency level so that they can understand what is going on and can assist in their case.

EXAMPLE 5-7: Competency and the Ability to Assist

The question of competency to stand trial was a key factor in a case in which Harold Gunther was prosecuted for the murder of one person and the attempted murder of two others. Listening at the door of an apartment, Gunther believed he heard three co-workers plotting against him. Convinced that he was about to be attacked, Gunther entered the apartment and assaulted his three co-workers, killing one and severely injuring the other two. Gunther consistently maintained that he was the intended target of a plot to destroy him. No evidence was ever presented that such a plot existed. In contrast, expert testimony indicated that Gunther was paranoid and delusional. Consequently, his defense attorney moved for a competency hearing. Despite the expert testimony, the judge in the case found Gunther competent to stand trial. The competency ruling was based on the fact that despite Gunther's mental problems, he was capable of understanding the charges against him and was able to assist in his defense. Under state law, these were the only qualifications needed for a competency finding by the court. Gunther met these qualifications and was found competent to stand trial.

Not Guilty by Reason of Insanity American law recognizes that individuals cannot be held responsible for their actions if they do not know what they are doing. In addition, it serves no practical purpose to imprison someone who needs the care of mental health professionals. For these reasons, insanity is recognized as a valid defense to criminal conduct.

The oldest test of insanity is the **M'Naughten Rule**. Under this rule, a defendant can be found not guilty by reason of insanity (NGRI) if, at the time the criminal act was committed, he or she was suffering from a mental disease that was so serious that the defendant did not know the nature of the act or did not know that act was wrong. Another test of insanity is the **irresistible impulse test**. This test holds that criminal defendants can be found NGRI if, at the time of the offense, they were stricken with a mental disease that prevented them from knowing right from wrong or that compelled them to commit the crime.

Under the **American Law Institute (ALI) test**, a person is not responsible if "as a result of mental disease or defect he lacks substantial capacity either to appreciate the criminality of his conduct or to conform his conduct to the requirements of law." The ALI test is plainly a relaxation of the usual insanity standard, as expressed in M'Naughten and the irresistible impulse test, because both of the older tests require "total" rather than "substantial" impairment. M'Naughten requires an inability to appreciate the wrongfulness of an action, and the irresistible impulse test requires a thorough loss of self-control.

It is important to understand that people found not guilty by reason of insanity do not automatically go free. Instead, they are committed to institutions and must undergo periodic psychiatric examinations. Once they are found to be sane, they may be released. Many people object to the fact that these individuals can look forward to release without serving any time in prison.

The Stockholm Syndrome and Coercive Persuasion New variations of the insanity defense are frequently offered in a creative attempt to extend the tests that will be accepted by the courts. Two such interrelated variations are the Stockholm syndrome and coercive persuasion. The Stockholm syndrome is generally related to kidnap victims but is also associated with abused children, battered spouses, hostages, prisoners of war, and cult victims, among others. The **Stockholm syndrome** is generally manifested by a victim's identification with and affection for a kidnapper or other dominant figure in the relationship (spouse, parent, cult leader, hostage takers, terrorists, enemy captors, and so on) that leads the victim to commit questionable acts at the behest of the dominant party. The victims become emotionally attached to their tormentors and display loyalty, compassion, and obedience to those tormentors, sometimes even cooperating in an attempt to rationalize and, thus, prolong the relationship. The psychological switch occurs when several factors are present. First, at the outset, the victim is convinced that the dominant party or parties will kill him or her. Second, the victim associates with no one but the dominant parties. Third, the victim is convinced that there is no way out of the situation. Finally, the victim begins to believe that the dominant party is the only one who is concerned with his or her well-being, and thus, a mutual bond of protection emerges. Given the psychological dependency that develops between the dominant party and the victim, it is possible, even likely, that the victim will lose all practical control of his or her own volition and may engage in criminal activity at the behest of the dominant party, thus leading to a defense that eliminates the mental state needed to be culpable for the crime committed.

Coercive persuasion involves a perverse relationship between a dominant party and a victim that transforms the personality of the victim so that the victim's identity undergoes a radical change. The process, which is sometimes called **brainwashing** in the popular press, involves three stages. In the first stage, the dominant party works to remove the victim's true personality. In the second stage, the victim is pushed through a long and elaborate transformation process. In the final stage, the new personality emerges and is then cemented into the victim's psychological makeup. To be successful, the victim must be motivated to enter the transformative process, must be led by the dominant party in a specific direction of change, and must receive positive reinforcement as the transformation reaches completion. Coercive persuasion is most successful when several factors are present. First, the victim must be subjected to a powerful psychological attack that weakens the victim's identity. Second, the process works best when the victim is not alone but is pushed toward change by a cooperative set of peers. Third, the victim is subjected to continuous and unrelenting pressure to comply with the new norms represented by the peer group. Finally, the victim's environment is used to reassure them of the value of the change, which then solidifies the transformation once it has been finalized. If coercive persuasion (or brainwashing) succeeds, the victim develops a new, often aberrant personality, making it possible for the victim to engage in criminal activity as a part of a new "criminal" identity, thus leading to a defense that eliminates the mental state needed to be legally liable for the crime committed. [See: *United States v. Hearst*, 563 F2d 1313 (9th Cir., 1978). See also: Lauren Bowman, Dominique Forrest, and Malissa Osei, "Social Science and Coercion as a Defense in Kidnapping Cases, Patricia Hearst: Kidnap Victim to Criminal?" Cornell University, 2010.]

Entrapment

If a law enforcement officer induces a law-abiding citizen to commit a crime, **entrapment** may be used as a defense. The person using the defense must show that the crime would not have been committed had it not been for the inducement of the officer. The defense of entrapment is not available to a defendant who would have committed the crime even without the involvement of the officer. This factor is referred to as the *propensity to commit the crime*. The entrapment defense can be used in many different types of criminal cases; however, it occurs most often when the police have engineered a sting operation designed to tempt individuals who already have the propensity to commit the crime in question. Often in a sting operation, the main players are undercover law enforcement

THE OPENING CASE *Round 4*
United States v. Hearst: Patty, the Newspaper Heiress or Tania, the Urban Guerrilla?

It is time to take one last look at the Opening Case. Recall that the case involved the kidnapping of Patty Hearst by members of an urban guerrilla outfit called the Symbionese Liberation Army (SLA). Later in the story, it was revealed that Hearst had been blindfolded, isolated, and abused by her captors. After days of this treatment, Hearst, in a sense, lost her own identity, and was subsumed into the SLA. She then lived and worked with the other members of the SLA, who, in a very real sense, became her comrades in a common cause—that is, their crusade against capitalism. A short time later, the SLA released a tape to the media on which Hearst, supposedly of her own free will, announced her alliance with the SLA. Her relationship with the SLA was now cemented. Soon after that event, Hearst and several SLA members robbed the Hibernia Bank in San Francisco. After the robbery, to discredit rumors that she had been forced to rob the bank, Hearst made a second tape and had it released to the media. On the second video tape, Hearst claimed that she was not brainwashed but was, instead, a loyal member of the SLA. In the tape, she also declared that the bank was robbed to obtain funds to support the anti-capitalism revolution, which she had joined as a dedicated soldier. A warrant was issued for her arrest and, shortly thereafter, she was arrested and put on trial for armed robbery. The Hearst family hired F. Lee Bailey. Bailey knew that he could not argue that Hearst had not committed armed robbery. Instead, he used the defense of coercive persuasion.

Recall that coercive persuasion is most successful when several factors are present. Let's look at how these factors relate to the Hearst case. First, the victim must be subjected to a powerful psychological attack that weakens the victim's identity. In this case, Hearst was isolated and abused by her captors in an effort to destroy her true personality. Second, the process works best when the victim is not alone but is pushed toward change by a cooperative set of peers. In this case, Hearst lived in the heart of a group of like-thinking, highly dedicated, self-proclaimed urban guerrillas. Third, the victim is subjected to continuous and unrelenting pressure to comply with the new norms represented by the peer group. In this case, Hearst lived with the members of the SLA as an equal, joining in their work, sharing their goals, and participating in their plans. Finally, the victim's environment is used to reassure him or her of the value of the change, which then solidifies the transformation. In this case, Hearst's relationship with the group crossed the point of no return when she participated in the robbery and then confirmed the voluntary nature of the relationship on a tape of her own making. The complete loss of her true identity is verified when she adopts a new name, Tania, and declares her profession as that of an urban guerrilla. The coercive persuasion process seemed to have succeeded. Hearst had developed a new, aberrant personality that made it possible for her to engage in an armed robbery as a part of her new "criminal" identity, thus leading to a defense that should have convinced the jury that she lacked the mental state needed to be legally liable for the robbery. Why, then, did the defense fail in her case? It is not likely that we will ever know the answer to that question, but we can speculate. It might have had something to do with the pre-trial publicity; or the fact that she was advised not to testify; or the fact that as a rich and famous heiress, she was an unsympathetic defendant. Or it may have had to do with the novelty of the defense. Think about it. [See: *United States v. Hearst*, 563 F2d 1313 (9th Cir., 1978). See also: Lauren Bowman, Dominique Forrest, and Malissa Osei, "Social Science and Coercion as a Defense in Kidnapping Cases, Patricia Hearst: Kidnap Victim to Criminal?" Cornell University, 2010.]

Source: See: *United States v. Hearst,* 563 F2d 1313 (9th Cir. 1978); See also: Lauren Bowman Dominique Forrest, and Malissa Osei, "Social Science and Coercion as a Defense in Kidnapping Cases, Patricia Hearst: Kidnap Victim to Criminal?"Cornell University (2010).

officers; however, sometimes they can be informants or reformed criminals who are used by the police to tempt individuals who are known by the police to be presently involved in a pattern of criminal activity. The fact that the police have used informants rather than undercover agents will not negate the entrapment defense, as long as all of the other elements are present.

Justifiable Force

In general, the law will not condone the use of force to solve problems. Still, special circumstances may arise that justify the use of force. Three of these situations lead to the following defenses: self-defense, defense of others, and battered spouse syndrome.

Self-Defense Normally, the law allows people to defend themselves as long as certain elements are clearly present. This action is known as **self-defense**. As indicated above, the defendant must first have a *bona fide* (good-faith) belief that his or her life was in danger or that he or she was in danger of severe bodily harm. Words by themselves, in most states, will be insufficient to prove the authentic belief that such harm is imminent. When self-defense is used in a criminal case, the defendant must show that he or she was not the one who started the altercation. Moreover, in all cases, the person claiming self-defense must not have used more force than necessary to stop the unprovoked attack. In some states, the person claiming self-defense must retreat, if possible, before resorting to force; however, a person does not have a duty to retreat before using force if the attack occurs in his or her own home. In many states, this exception has also been extended to a person's vehicle, so in those states, a person has no duty to retreat if that person is in his or her own vehicle or lawfully in a vehicle owned by a member of that person's immediate family.

Self-defense is an affirmative defense. This means that the defendant must put forth evidence that he or she has the right to that defense. This also means that the defendant must admit that he or she committed the action for which he or she has been brought to trial. Self-defense cannot be used by a defendant who has argued that he or she committed the offense by mistake ("It was an accident!") because self-defense requires the purposeful attempt to stop the assault by using force. The two defenses are, thus, incompatible with one another. Although the burden of proof to demonstrate guilt beyond a reasonable doubt still remains with the prosecution, in some states, the defendant does have the burden of proving the existence of an affirmative defense. The standard of proof in self-defense, however, is not beyond a reasonable doubt. Depending upon state law, the burden of proof is either by a preponderance of the evidence or by clear and convincing evidence. Some states do not require the defendant to prove the existence of the affirmative defense of self-defense at all. Instead, the accused is presumed to have properly defended himself or herself unless the prosecution can successfully attack the presumption.

Some states that usually declare that the defendant has the burden of proving the existence of an affirmative defense of self-defense will remove that burden when the defendant claiming self-defense was in his home or vehicle at the time of the alleged attack. In such cases, the defendant's claim of self-defense is to be treated as a rebuttable presumption. The prosecution then has the burden of rebutting the presumption by a preponderance of the evidence. Moreover, some states also provide that after a defendant has properly established that a claim of self-defense was legitimate and the prosecution drops all charges, the grand jury fails to indict, or the jury or judge finds the defendant not guilty, that defendant cannot be sued in tort case emerging from that same set of facts. [See: Philip D. Bogdanoff, "Criminal Law Boot Camp. Chapter 3: Self-Defense and the Castle Doctrine," The Ohio State Bar Association, March 18, 2014.]

Defense of Others If a person uses force to rescue another person who is the victim of an apparent attack, most states will allow the rescuer to escape criminal liability. This exception is known as **defense of others**. As in the case of self-defense, the rescuer must have a good reason to believe that the victim was in danger of severe bodily injury or even death.

Stand-Your-Ground Laws A variation on the traditional self-defense is the stand-your-ground defense, which some states have recently added to their statutory provisions in criminal procedure. Some states have stand-your-ground provisions within their common law tradition. A **stand-your-ground statute** extends self-defense by eliminating any requirement to retreat, even outside one's home or vehicle. Therefore, as long as an individual is in a place that he or she has the legal right to be, then no retreat is necessary under the law. The other elements of self-defense would still apply. Some stand-your-ground laws also include a provision that permits the defendant to seek a pretrial hearing during which the judge would decide whether to grant the defendant civil and criminal immunity. Stand-your-ground laws are also called *no-duty-to-retreat* laws in some states.

> **EXAMPLE 5-8:** Using (or Not Using) the Stand-Your-Ground Law as a Defense
>
> George Zimmerman, a volunteer neighborhood watch patrolman, was seated in his car when he spotted what he described as a suspicious individual in the neighborhood. He called in his report and was told to stay in his car. He did not do so and, instead, began to follow the individual who turned out to be an unarmed teenager. Exactly what transpired after this is open to debate, although the facts did reveal two critical points: The teenager was unarmed, and medical evidence indicated that Zimmerman sustained injuries consistent with a beating. The bottom line, however, is that Zimmerman shot and killed the teenager. Zimmerman was charged with second-degree murder. Zimmerman's primary strategy was to raise the affirmative defense of self-defense. Florida law allowed Zimmerman to use a stand-your-ground statute as his defense. He did not do so, however, because his attorneys did not want to reveal their case at a pretrial immunity hearing. Ultimately, the jury found the defendant not guilty by applying the classic principles of self-defense. Some legal experts have pointed to this as a flaw in the statute. Others believe that it is a legitimate safeguard. What do you think? [See: *State v. Zimmerman* (2012-CF001083-A).]
>
> Source: See: *State v. Zimmerman* (2012-CF001083-A).

Battered Spouse Syndrome The law also protects a married individual from being abused by his or her spouse. In most cases of spouse abuse, the wife is victimized by the violent outbursts of her husband. Many communities have established shelters where abused and battered wives can seek safety and receive counseling and legal services for themselves and their children. Wives who wish to protect themselves from the continual abuse caused by their husbands may seek legal help from the courts.

One such remedy is a *protective order*. Protective orders bar the abusing spouse from maintaining any contact with the victim. Such orders are enforced by the local police. Unfortunately, protective orders are not always effective. In some very severe cases, the victimized spouse has taken the law into her own hands and killed her tormentor. The set of circumstances that leads a woman to believe that the only way that she can escape death or severe bodily injury is to use force against her tormentor is called **battered spouse syndrome**. These circumstances are also known as *battered woman* or *battered wife syndrome*. Because the spouse had good reason to believe that she was in danger of death or severe bodily injury, battered spouse syndrome is considered a form of self-defense in some courts.

Mistake

Mistake is a defense to charges of criminal liability, as long as the mistake destroys one of the elements necessary to that crime. If the mistake does not destroy an element, it is not a valid defense. To be a successful defense, the mistake must be based on a reasonable belief. It would be no defense for a defendant to say that he shot his wife because he believed she was an invader from Mars. Note also that it is not a defense for an accused to say that she did not know that this particular conduct was prohibited by law. Nor is it a defense to a gambling charge for the defendant to argue that she did not know that the gambling law applied to her. Finally, the mistake must destroy the criminal nature of the act in the mind of the accused. It would be no defense, for example, if a defendant argued that he injured an individual by mistake when he was actually trying to injure someone else.

quick quiz 5-5

1. Most defendants who are found NGRI are released immediately. **true | false**
2. A person does not have to retreat to his or her own home before resorting to force to repel an attack. **true | false**
3. Mistake is never a defense to a charge of criminal liability. **true | false**

Summary

5.1 A crime is an offense against the public at large. As such, a crime threatens the peace, safety, and well-being of the entire community. For this reason, crimes are punishable by the official governing body of a nation or state. A felony is a crime punishable by death or imprisonment in a federal or a state prison for a term exceeding one year. Some felonies are also punishable by fines. A misdemeanor is a less serious crime that is generally punishable by a prison sentence of not more than one year.

5.2 The two elements necessary to create criminal liability are (12) an act and (2) the requisite state of mind. Generally speaking, a crime cannot be committed unless the criminal act named in the statute is performed with the requisite state of mind. Many state criminal codes include four possible states of mind: (1) purpose, (2) knowledge, (3) recklessness, and (4) negligence. Establishing motive may help investigators pinpoint the guilty party, but proving an evil motive is not necessary for a criminal conviction. Conversely, establishing the existence of a good motive will rarely absolve a defendant of criminal liability.

5.3 Crimes against people include but are not limited to first-degree murder, second-degree murder, manslaughter, battery, and assault. A more recent addition to this list involves hate speech. Crimes against property include but are not limited to burglary; breaking and entering; trespass; aggravated arson; arson; aggravated robbery; robbery; and theft, fraud, and related offenses. Crimes involving business include embezzlement, forgery, criminal simulation, passing bad checks, and defrauding creditors. RICO offenses also involve business crime. Crimes against justice include bribery, theft in office, and dereliction of duty. Others, such as intimidation, are committed against a public official or public servant. Still others, such as obstruction of justice, resisting arrest, perjury, and tampering with evidence are committed against the justice system itself.

5.4 Cybercrimes include cyber-trespass, which involves any conventional crime committed with a computer. Cybercrimes that focus on the use of a computer include cyber-extortion, cyber-stalking, cyber-harassment, cyber-assault, cyber-bullying, cyber-spoofing, phishing, smishing, and vishing. Crimes that target computers include cyber-terrorism, identity theft, cyber-vandalism, and cyber-germ warfare. Federal cybercrimes include Computer Fraud and Abuse Act (CFAA), the Electronic Communications Privacy Act (ECPA), the Communications Assistance for Law Enforcement Act (CALEA), the Economic Espionage Act (EEA), the National Stolen Property Act (NSPA), and the Identity Theft and Assumption Deterrence Act (ITADA).

5.5 Because criminal liability relies on the two essential elements of act and requisite mental state, a logical defense aims at eliminating one or both of those elements. Most defenses attempt to do just that. The most common defenses are insanity, entrapment, justifiable force, and mistake.

Key Terms

aggravated arson, 136
aggravated burglary, 136
aggravated murder, 133
aggravated robbery, 136
American Law Institute (ALI) test, 151
arson, 136
assault, 134
battered spouse syndrome, 155
battery, 134
bitcoin, 143
breaking and entering, 136
bribery, 139
burglary, 136
coercive persuasion, 152
crime, 120
criminal simulation, 138
cyber-trespass, 141
cyber-extortion, 142
defense of others, 154
defrauding creditors, 138
dereliction of duty, 139
double jeopardy, 120
drone, 147
embezzlement, 138
entrapment, 152
felony, 123
first-degree murder, 133
forgery, 138
fraud, 137
hate speech, 135
homicide, 133
intimidation, 139
involuntary manslaughter, 134
irresistible impulse test, 151
knowledge, 125
malware, 143
manslaughter, 134
misdemeanor, 123
M'Naughten Rule, 151
negligence, 126
obstruction of justice, 139
passing bad checks, 138
perjury, 140
premeditated murder, 133
purpose, 125
ransomware, 143
recklessness, 125
resisting arrest, 139
robbery, 136
second-degree murder, 134
self-defense, 154
stand your ground statute, 155
Stockholm syndrome, 152
tampering with evidence, 140
theft, 137
theft in office, 139
trespass, 136
victim's rights, 121
voluntary manslaughter, 134

Questions for Review and Discussion

1. What is the purpose of criminal law?
2. What are the various categories and classes of crimes?
3. What is the nature of an act according to the meaning of criminal liability?
4. What are the four mental states that can be found in the criminal code?
5. What is motive, and how does it differ from the elements of criminal liability?
6. What are the various crimes against people?
7. What are the various theories involved in criminal punishment?
8. What are the various ways that the federal government has dealt with cybercrime?
9. What are the standards for the insanity defense found in criminal law?
10. What are the requirements of entrapment as a defense against criminal liability?

Cases for Analysis

1. It started as a routine pledge party at Pennsylvania State University, but it turned deadly by the next morning. As part of the initiation process, each pledge at the party was plied with alcohol throughout the night—vodka, beer, wine, and so on. In fact, as they entered the frat house, each pledge received a bottle of vodka. One pledge in particular, Timothy Piazza, finished his bottle quickly. Apparently, he had many more drinks after that because he eventually became heavily intoxicated. He was so drunk that he stumbled about aimlessly and eventually injured himself when he fell down a flight of stairs. Moreover, that was not the only time he fell. In fact, he fell repeatedly. Once he hit his head on the stone

floor of the frat house. Another time, he hit his head on a railing, and still another time on some of the furniture. He vomited and passed out. All of this was caught on video, including Piazza's stumbling and falling around the frat house. By early the following morning, Piazza could not be roused by the fraternity brothers. At one point, his limp, unconscious form is seen being carried by several of the fraternity brothers. The fraternity brothers argued about what course of action to take and accessed the Internet to see what to do about someone with cold limbs. No one thought to call an ambulance until 10:48 the next morning. The call came too late. Piazza died as a result of his injuries. The investigation revealed that Piazza had a blood alcohol level that was four times the legal limit for driving. He had multiple bruises and a ruptured spleen. Apparently, his skull was also fractured. Eight of the fraternity brothers were charged with involuntary manslaughter. Does this behavior involve the mental state required to prove involuntary manslaughter? Explain. [See: Caitlin Dickerson, "Penn States Student's Dying Hours in Fraternity House Play Out in Courtroom Video," *The New York Times*, June 13, 2017, p. A-20.]

2. Edison High School in San Antonio, Texas, was the scene of an incident that later became national news, when a student brought a concealed weapon on the premises. Testimony later indicated the student did not intend to use the weapon but, instead, expected a payment for delivering the .38 caliber revolver. At first, he was charged with taking firearms onto school property in violation of a state statute. Later the state dropped its case, and the student was accused of breaking provisions of a federal statute known as the Gun-Free School Zone Act of 1990 (the GFSZ Act). Sensing that this was no ordinary case, but instead one of constitutional import, the student's attorney filed a motion to dismiss the charges based on the argument that the GFSZ Act was unconstitutional. The constitutional challenge was grounded on the argument that the GFSZ Act was an unlawful extension of congressional authority under the limits set down in the Commerce Clause. The District Court disagreed, and the case went to trial. After the student was convicted, his attorney filed an appeal with the Fifth Circuit Court of Appeals. The appeals court reversed the conviction. The Supreme Court then granted *certiorari*. Using your understanding of the Commerce Clause as interpreted by the Supreme Court in *Wickard v. Filburn*, should the Supreme Court agree with the appeals court or revert to the district court's original ruling? Explain. [See: *United States v. Lopez*, 514 U.S. 549 (1995).]

3. Fred Pomeroy was an assistant traffic manager for the New York Central and Hudson River Railroad Company. In that capacity, he handed out "rebates" to the American Sugar Refining Company in New York and New Jersey and to W. H. Edgar & Son in Detroit. The goal of the rebates was to convince the sugar refiner and the sugar dealer to use the railroad for their shipments rather than some other method. The problem with this arrangement was that the shipping rates were fixed by federal law and, thus, the rebates amounted to a bribe. Pomeroy and New York Central were prosecuted under the Elkins Act and were found guilty. On an appeal that went all the way to the U.S. Supreme Court, New York Central argued that while Pomeroy could be prosecuted under the criminal statute, the corporation could not. Can the corporation be prosecuted? What theory would you advise the court to use in this case? Explain. What will the outcome be? [See: *New York Central & Hudson River Railroad v. United States*, 212 U.S. 481 (U.S. Supreme Court).]

4. The hospitality industry in Portland, Oregon, instituted an organization that was designed to bring convention business to the city. Association members made fixed contributions to the organization, and companies in the supply business were expected to donate funds based on a percentage of their sales. Supply companies that did not contribute were boycotted by the membership. This boycott was a clear violation of the federal Sherman Antitrust Act. Both the president of Hilton Hotels Corporation and the manager of the Portland Hilton ordered the purchasing agent of the Portland Hotel to ignore the boycott and to make purchases based only on the quality of the products and service from suppliers. The purchasing agent for the Portland Hilton, however, out of personal resentment toward the sales rep of a particular supplier, enforced the boycott. After being found guilty of violating federal law, Hilton appealed, arguing that the trial court misinterpreted the law because the corporation could only be held liable if the purchasing agent committed a crime within the

scope of employment with the intention that the corporation gain some benefit from that crime. In this case, it was clear that the agent had committed a crime but the acts were not within the scope of employment because he had been expressly forbidden to continue the boycott. What was the result on appeal? Explain. [See: *United States v. Hilton Hotels Corporation*, 467 F. 2d 1000 (9th Circuit).]

5. After Charles Hood was convicted of murder, he was sentenced to death in accordance with Texas law. It was later revealed, however, that the judge who presided at Hood's trial had been involved in a lengthy affair with the prosecutor in the case. Neither the judge nor the prosecutor had revealed this relationship during the trial. Moreover, after the trial, they denied the relationship until they were compelled to tell the truth under oath. The Texas Court of Criminal Appeals later agreed to a new sentencing hearing for Hood; however, the hearing was limited to questions concerning the jury instructions and, therefore, did not involve the conflict of interest problem caused by the affair. Hood filed a petition for *certiorari* with the U.S. Supreme Court. Should the Supreme Court hear the case? Explain. [See: Mark White, "Death Penalty Must Be Fair," *The National Law Journal*, March 29, 2010, p. 43.]

6. Antonio Martinez, also known as Muhammad Hussain, discussed the killing of American soldiers with an unnamed individual who, unknown to Martinez, was actually an FBI informant. The informant passed that information to FBI agents, who arranged a sting operation during which Martinez helped build a phony car bomb. Martinez was arrested as he attempted to set off the phony car bomb in front of a recruiting center in suburban Baltimore. Martinez claimed that he was entrapped by the federal agents. Martinez's attorney argued that the defendant was not capable of developing the plan to make the bomb on his own. The federal attorney also argued that Martinez had clearly been making plans to attack U.S. soldiers before the informant contacted him. The federal attorney also argued that whether Martinez was capable of actually building a bomb on his own did not matter since he not only believed that he could do it, but also actually tried to do it—and would have done so had the bomb not been a fake. The prosecuting attorney also had a tape of Martinez arming the bomb. The video shows that Martinez enjoyed the prospect of killing the soldiers. Was Martinez entrapped? Explain by outlining the elements of entrapment. [See: "Lawyer Argues Entrapment in Bomb Plot," *The New York Times*, December 14, 2010, p. 18.]

7. Katie Roberts was wasting away from the effects of an incurable disease. She asked her husband Frank to help her commit suicide. In response to her request, Mr. Roberts mixed poison and water and placed the mixture on a chair within her reach. She took the poison and died several hours later. Mr. Roberts admitted placing the poison within her reach but denied having the required mental state for first-degree murder because he was responding to his wife's request and was motivated by love and mercy. Will he prevail? Explain. [See: *People v. Roberts*, 178 N.W.690 (MI).]

8. Several teenagers taped the broken legs of a chair together to create a cross, which they then ignited and placed on the lawn of an African American family in the neighborhood. One of the teenagers, a minor, was charged with a misdemeanor under the St. Paul Bias-Motivated Crime Ordinance. The St. Paul ordinance criminalized the placing on private property of any "symbol, object, appellation, characterization or graffiti . . . which one knows or has reasonable grounds to know arouses anger, alarm, or resentment in others on the basis of race, color, creed, religion or gender." The defendant argued that the ordinance was an unconstitutional violation of the First Amendment. The city contended that the statute was constitutional because it was necessary for the preservation of a compelling state interest—namely, the right of group members who have been discriminated against in the past "to live in peace where they wish." Is the St. Paul ordinance constitutional? Explain. [See: *R.A.V. v. St. Paul*, 505 U.S. 1992 (U.S. Sup. Ct.).]

9. Tomas Reese entered a fast-food restaurant before the restaurant had opened for business through an unlocked rear entrance. The door had been left unlocked by an accomplice who was an employee of the restaurant. After entering the restaurant, Reese pushed one employee against a soda machine and, while holding a gun to the neck of the manager, forced her to open the safe. Reese then locked the employees in a cooler and fled the scene with more than $5,000. Has Reese committed burglary, robbery, or larceny? Explain. [See: *State v. Reese*, 113 Ohio App. 3d. 642 (OH).]

10. Cuttiford and Banks lived in the same duplex; Banks lived upstairs and Cuttiford lived downstairs. The two apartments shared a common internal stairway at the back of the duplex. A confrontation began between Banks and Cuttiford in the rear stairway of the duplex. Banks became rather violent and threatened Cuttiford and Cuttiford's wife. Cuttiford went to his apartment on the bottom floor and retrieved two guns from his bedroom. When he returned to the back door near the stairway, Banks told him, "You don't have the guts to use that, because you're going to have to use it because I'm going to kill you!" Banks then came at Cuttiford, lunging from the common stairway into the kitchen of the Cuttiford's apartment. Cuttiford then shot and killed Banks. At trial, Cuttiford argued that he shot Banks in self-defense. The trial court refused to instruct the jury that Cuttiford did not have to retreat into his own home before acting to repel an attacker. The court apparently believed the prosecution, which had argued that because Banks and Cuttiford occupied the same duplex, Cuttiford had the duty to retreat before repelling Banks's attack. Was the trial court judge correct in his instruction to the jury regarding self-defense? Explain. [See: *State v. Cuttiford*, 639 N.E.2d 472 (OH).]

11. Cowen had on many occasions operated as a paid drug informant for the FBI and the Ventura Police Department. The Ventura police asked Cowen to keep in touch with them should he become involved in any deals. Subsequently, Cowen asked Busby to introduce him to any drug dealers he knew. Busby introduced Cowen to Mandell, who sold Cowen several samples of cocaine in anticipation of a $41,500 deal. Cowen then contacted the Ventura police. A police officer posed as Cowen's buyer, and both Busby and Mandell were arrested and eventually turned over to the federal authorities. Busby was convicted of possession of cocaine with the intent to distribute it. He appealed this conviction, claiming that he had been entrapped by Cowen. Will Busby's entrapment defense succeed on appeal? Explain. [See: *United States v. Busby*, 780 F.2d 804 (9th Cir.).]

Design Elements: The Opening Case: ©Sharpstock/Alamy; A Classic Case: ©Evlakhov Valeriy/Shutterstock

quick quiz Answers

5-1	5-2	5-3	5-4	5-5
1. F	1. T	1. T	1. F	1. F
2. F	2. F	2. F	2. T	2. T
3. F	3. F	3. T	3. T	3. F

Chapter 6

Tort Law and Cybertorts

6-1 Tort Law Defined
Tort Law versus Criminal Law • *Respondeat Superior* • The Element of Duty • Causation and Juriscience

6-2 Intentional Torts
Assault and Battery • False Imprisonment • Defamation and Disparagement • Fraudulent Misrepresentation • Civil Theft • Invasion of Privacy • Intentional Infliction of Emotional Distress • Misuse of Legal Procedure

6-3 Negligence
Elements of Negligence • Defenses to Negligence

6-4 Strict Liability
Grounds for Strict Liability • Product Liability

6-5 Cybertorts
The Nature of Cybertorts • Cyber-Defamation • Cyber-Disparagement • Cyber-Invasion of Privacy

6-6 Remedies for Torts
The Right to Damages • The Right to an Injunction

6-7 Developments in Tort Law
Survival Statutes and Wrongful Death • The Tort Reform Movement • Cultural Paradigms and Tort Reform • Sovereign Immunity

THE OPENING CASE Round 1
The Case of the Injured Cheerleader

Let's set the scene. Jailynn Brown, our plaintiff, belonged to a cheerleading team called the All City Airmen (ACA). The ACA was coached by Raven Evans-Harris and Kendra Fritz, two former cheerleaders. Charlotte Harris, a basketball coach and fitness trainer, also held conditioning sessions for the team. All three coaches worked on a volunteer basis. Occasionally, the team practiced on the lawn at the home of Dr. Andre T. Harris. The team had been successfully coached by Raven and Kendra for some time, and the cheerleaders had learned many of the basic routines. Two of those routines, referred to as "half stunting" and "full stunting," involve several girls who act as "bases" and another girl who acts as the "flyer." Jailynn was the flyer. The team mastered these routines very nicely and then moved on to a more complex, but still somewhat basic stunt called the "lib" or the "liberty." In half and full stunting, the bases lift the flyer by her feet. In the liberty, they lift her by one foot, and therein lies both the difference and the reason that you are reading this case today. The routine was being taught and practiced on the "uneven and sloped" front lawn of Charlotte and Dr. Harris. No mats were provided. Kendra was not at practice that day. Charlotte was at the practice but was not present as they practiced the lib. Raven taught the girls the stunt and was present during the session but was not looking at the team as they practiced. Dr. Harris had no affiliation with the team except that they sometimes practiced on his lawn. The first time that the team tried the lib, Jailynn fell but was caught by the bases. The second time she was not as lucky; she fell on her left side. Dr. Harris came out of the house to help Jailynn. However, the injury was so severe that she had to be taken to the hospital, where it was discovered that she had torn the ACL tendon in her knee. To rectify this problem, she had to have surgery.

Sometime afterward, a lawsuit was brought by Jailynn's mother, Marketa Watkins, and by Jailynn herself. Jailynn claimed that her injury was caused by the negligence of the defendants, Raven, Charlotte, and Dr. Harris. The defendants countered by arguing that when Jailynn signed up for cheerleading practice, she assumed the risk of a fall at some time during practices. Jailynn admitted that she assumed the risk but argued that the defendants had been either reckless or, worse yet, had intentionally caused her injury by conducting the practice on the uneven, slanted ground and without mats. The defendants filed a summary judgment motion arguing that even if the facts were true as stated by the plaintiffs, the defendants are not liable as a matter of law. Within this seemingly simple case, we can find several interesting aspects of tort law: the issue of duty, the nature of negligence, and the viability of the defense of assumption of the the risk. Read on for the details. [See: *Jailynn Brown, et al. v. Andre T. Harris Sr., et al.* Appellate Case No. 27069, Trial Court Case No. 2014-CV-5144 (2014).]

Opening Case Questions

1. What duty, if any, does a coach owe to his or her charges? Explain.
2. What elements will the plaintiff have to prove to win her negligence case? Explain.
3. What counterarguments can the defendant raise in this case? Explain.
4. How is assumption of the risk involved as a defense in this case? Explain.
5. What added points might be offered as part of the defense of assumption of the risk? Explain.

Source: See: *Jailynn Brown, et al. v. Andre T. Harris Sr., et al.* Appellate Case No. 27069, Trial Court Case No. 2014-CV-5144 (2014).

 Learning Objectives

1. Differentiate between the objectives of tort law and those of criminal law.
2. Outline the nature of *respondeat superior*.
3. Describe the element of duty.
4. Identify the principal intentional torts and outline the elements of each.
5. Explain the four elements of negligence.
6. Contrast contributory negligence, comparative negligence, and assumption of the risk.
7. Judge when the doctrine of strict liability applies.
8. Discuss the emerging trends in cybertort law.
9. Outline the various remedies available in tort law.
10. Point out some developments in tort reform.

6-1 Tort Law Defined

A **tort** is a private wrong that injures another person's physical well-being, emotional health, business, property, or reputation. The English word *tort* comes from the Latin word *tortus*, which can be translated as "twisted." A person who commits a tort and has thus engaged in "twisted" behavior is called a **tortfeasor**. The other party is alternately referred to as the injured party, the innocent party, the victim, or the plaintiff if a lawsuit has been filed. In the case of a lawsuit, the tortfeasor would be called a defendant.

Tort Law versus Criminal Law

One purpose of tort law is to compensate the injured party for his or her loss. Another objective is to protect potential victims by deterring future tortious behavior. In contrast, as noted in Chapter 5, criminal law involves a public wrong—that is, a wrong that affects the entire society. When a crime is committed, the government authorities begin a legal procedure that is designed to remove the offender from society and to punish that offender to the fullest extent allowed by the law. As noted in Chapter 5, however, it is possible for a single act to be both a crime and a tort. As noted in the chapter on criminal law, the U.S. Constitution protects people from being tried twice for the same crime. This rule is known as the principle of *double jeopardy*. Double jeopardy does not protect a defendant from being sued under tort law for the consequences of an action, even if that defendant has already been tried for the same wrongdoing in a criminal court using criminal law.

Respondeat Superior

About the Law

The doctrine of *respondeat superior* is also known as vicarious liability.

In criminal law the courts will hold a corporation liable when an employee commits a crime on the job to benefit the corporation. In like fashion, in tort law the courts use *respondeat superior* to hold a business or organization liable for the torts of an employee whenever an employee commits a tort while working for that business or organization. Chapter 22 will examine this concept in depth, and the proper legal terms of *master* and *servant* will be explained at length. For now, it is enough to remember that employers are at risk in tort law when their employees commit torts, and for that reason alone, both employers and employees must have some working knowledge of tort law.

The Element of Duty

One approach to the law is to think of legal liability in terms of elements. This approach emphasizes that no liability can be imposed against an individual unless all the elements are present. In tort law, the first element is duty. A **duty** is an obligation placed on individuals because of the law. The second element is a violation of that duty. A duty can be violated intentionally, through negligence, or under the theory of strict liability. To fully appreciate the concept of duty, however, we must understand its origin point. A duty is the flip side of a right. All of us have certain unalienable rights. These rights exist simply because we exist. The source of those rights is open to debate. Some of us, like Jefferson, the author of the Declaration of Independence, prefer to believe that those rights come from out Creator. Others prefer to see their origin in natural law. Still others believe that these rights emerge from the social contract, as envisioned by Niccolo Machiavelli, Sir Francis Bacon, and Thomas Hobbes (see Chapter 1).

Whatever the case, we all believe that certain rights do exist. Among these rights are the right to life, the right to be safe and secure, the right to a good reputation, the right to own and enjoy property, and so on. Because we all have these rights, every one has the duty not to violate those rights in others. So, for instance, because we have the right to life, safety, and security, we all have the duty not to kill or injure one another. Similarly, since we all have the right to a good reputation, we have the corresponding duty not lie about others. Again, since we have the right to own and enjoy property, we have the parallel duty not to steal from others, and so on. When we enter the study of tort law, we learn that these duties are the foundation upon which all other tort law principles are based. So, duty becomes the necessary first element. The problem in the law is that while certain rights and duties exist for all of us in all situations, some circumstances give rise to "special relationships" from which emerge additional specialized rights and duties. Thus, when an individual enters a hospital for treatment, for example, a special relationship arises between the patient and the health care professional. Because of that special relationship, the patient has the right to be treated properly, and the health care professional has the duty to deliver that help in a professional manner. Unfortunately, determining when these special relationships and specialized duties arise is not always easy as the following replay of the Opening Case reveals.

Causation and Juriscience

A negligence case requires the plaintiffs to prove that the defendants caused their injuries. In negligence cases, there are two kinds of causation: actual cause and proximate cause. These two types of causation will be examined at length later in the chapter; however, for now it is

THE OPENING CASE *Round 2*
The Case of the Injured Cheerleader

Let's review the facts. Jailynn Brown, our plaintiff, belonged to a cheerleading team, the All City Airmen (ACA), coached by Raven Evans-Harris and Kendra Fritz, two former cheerleaders. The team was also taught fitness by Charlotte Harris, a basketball coach and fitness trainer. All three coaches worked on a volunteer basis. The team sometimes practiced on the lawn at the home of Dr. Andre T. Harris. On the day in question, the team was practicing a new routine called the "liberty" or the "lib" for short. The stunt was being practiced on the "uneven and sloped" front lawn of Charlotte and Dr. Harris. No mats were provided. Kendra was not at practice that day. Charlotte was at the practice but was not present as they practiced the lib. Raven taught the girls the stunt and was present but not looking at the team as they practiced. Dr. Harris had no affiliation with the team except that they often practiced on his lawn. The first time that the team tried the lib, Jailynn fell but was caught by the bases. The second time she fell on her left side. Dr. Harris came out to help Jailynn. However, the injury was so severe that she had to go to the hospital, where they found out she had a torn ACL.

Sometime afterward, a lawsuit was brought by Jailynn's mother, Marketa Watkins, and by Jailynn herself. Jailynn claims that her injury was caused by the negligence of the defendants, Kendra, Charlotte, and Dr. Harris. In order to hold the defendants liable for Jailynn's injuries, the plaintiff must first show that they owed a duty to the cheerleading team. Of course, it should be clear that the defendants owe a duty not to injure the cheerleaders in the same way that they owe this duty to anyone in society. However, that is not at issue in this case because Jailynn's injury occurred within the context of a cheerleading practice session. In this case, as cheerleading coaches, Raven and Charlotte may owe an additional, specialized duty to make certain that the team practiced its routines in a safe and secure way. Let's look at the defendants one by one to determine the existence of a duty. First, Dr. Harris must be eliminated as a defendant because he never assumed any additional, specialized duties to the cheerleaders. The only connection he had to the ACA was that he allowed them to use his front lawn for practice. He did not teach, coach, advise, or schedule practices for the ACA. Second, Charlotte must also be eliminated. She does not owe any specialized duty to the cheerleaders to ensure their safety as they practice. She may owe them a duty to hold safe and secure conditioning sessions, but conditioning has nothing to do with training them for their cheerleading routines. Finally, Raven, as the cheerleading coach, does, indeed, have a specialized duty to keep the girls safe as they practice their routines. So, in regard to Raven, we must now determine if she violated that specialized duty. More on this *standard of care* will be explained as we move through the chapter . . . so keep reading. [See: *Jailynn Brown, et al. v. Andre T. Harris Sr., et al.* Appellate Case No. 27069, Trial Court Case No. 2014-CV-5144 (2014).]

Source: See: *Jailynn Brown, et al. v. Andre T. Harris Sr., et al.* Appellate Case No. 27069, Trial Court Case No. 2014-CV-5144 (2014).

enough to point out that actual cause is cause "in fact" or "real" cause. Real cause exists in the physical universe and is thus subject to experiments, tests, measurements, and other forms of proof. This means that the plaintiff will often have to use scientific evidence to demonstrate how action "A" led to effect "B." Moreover, because of the scientific nature of a case, the court generally needs to hear the testimony of an expert to determine causation. This stage in a case, where science and the law intersect, is referred to as **juriscience**. Judges at all levels, but especially those in the trial courts, must determine the validity of scientific evidence. Unfortunately, because the law is an adversarial process, judges will frequently be forced to choose between two or more competing lines of scientific proof. Judges, however, are educated in the law not science, so they need help unraveling the intricacies of scientific evidence beyond simply listening to the experts, many of whom may have hidden agendas.

After *Daubert v. Merrell Dow*, the federal rule on expert testimony was amended somewhat to help judges make this determination. The rule states that an expert may testify on a

EXAMPLE 6-1: Juriscience and Tort Law: *Daubert v. Merrell Dow Pharmaceuticals*—Revisited

The law is a balancing act that struggles to assimilate new ideas while maintaining useful and effective traditions. Sometimes this balancing act works well, and sometimes it just falls apart. A case in point is *Daubert v. Merrell Dow Pharmaceuticals, Inc.*, a U.S. Supreme Court case featured in Chapter 4, as part of our debate about the collective science court proposal. Recall that the case involves a lawsuit filed by the Dauberts against Merrell Dow in which the plaintiffs argue that Bendectin, a drug produced by Merrell Dow and taken by Mrs. Daubert for nausea during her pregnancy, had caused birth defects in their children. The case depends on the issue of causation, a traditional tort law principle that says that to succeed in a negligence lawsuit, a plaintiff must prove that the defendant's action caused the plaintiff's injury; however, because of the scientific nature of the case, the court needed expert testimony to determine causation. This point in the case, the point at which science and the law intersect, is referred to as *juriscience*.

The judges at each level, from the trial court, through the appellate court, up to the Supreme Court, and then back down to the appellate court, had to weigh the scientific evidence on causation leading from the development of the drug Bendectin to the birth defects. The judges were faced with two competing lines of evidence—one presented by the plaintiffs, the other by the defendants. The defendants' evidence included peer-reviewed articles published in scientific journals and studies issued by the U.S. Food and Drug Administration (FDA). None of these reports or articles could find a link between Bendectin and birth defects. In response, the plaintiff's scientific experts offered a reanalysis of the accepted data. This reanalysis demonstrated that the original data had been badly misinterpreted by previous scientists. To determine which line of evidence should be followed, the court had to interpret Rule 702 of the Federal Rules of Evidence and *Frye v. United States*, a case that predated Rule 702 but that had, nevertheless, set up a standard that the federal courts had used for decades to evaluate expert testimony. Ultimately, the Supreme Court decided that expert evidence did not have to be "generally accepted" as *Frye* had suggested, because some scientific discoveries may be "too particular, too new, or of too limited interest to be published." The court thus emphasized that the rules had to be interpreted liberally rather than narrowly in determining the use of expert testimony. Still, the Supreme Court concluded that such testimony did have to "rest on a reliable foundation and (be) relevant to the task at hand." Since the lower courts had used only the *Frye* standard, the case was sent back to the appeals court, which still supported Merrell Dow because the evidence produced by the plaintiffs did not demonstrate a definite causation link between Bendectin and birth defects. [See: *Daubert v. Merrell Dow Pharmaceuticals, Inc.*, (509 U.S. 579) (U.S.S.Ct.). See also *Daubert v. Merrell Dow Pharmaceuticals, Inc.*, 43 F.3d 1311 (Ninth Circuit).]

Source: See: *Daubert v. Merrell Dow Pharmaceuticals, Inc.*, (509 U.S. 579) (U.S.S.Ct.); see also *Daubert v. Merrell Dow Pharmaceuticals, Inc.*, 43 F.3d 1311 (Ninth Circuit).

scientific matter as long as "(1) testimony is based upon sufficient facts or data, (2) the testimony is the product of reliable scientific principles and methods, and (3) the witness has applied the principles and methods reliably to the facts in the case." Still, even this standard is somewhat vague and ambiguous. Many questions remain unanswered. Who is to determine when testimony has reached a level of "sufficient facts or data"? What makes a scientific principle or method "reliable"? How will the judge know when a witness has applied a principle in a reliable way? Some states have tried to be more specific in the formulation of this rule. Ohio, for example, has gone so far as to say that, if an expert witness bases an opinion on a test or an experiment, that test or experiment is reliable *only* if *all* of the following apply: "(1) the theory upon which the procedure, test, or experiment is based is objectively verifiable or validly derived from widely accepted knowledge, facts, or principles; (2) the design of the procedure, test, experiment reliably implements the theory; and (3) the particular procedure, test, or experiment was conducted in a way that will yield an accurate result."

> **quick quiz 6-1**
>
> 1. A person who commits a tort is engaged in "twisted" behavior. true | false
> 2. The purpose of tort law is to protect the public at large. true | false
> 3. Employers are never liable for the torts of their employees because such a move would violate the constitutional prohibition against double jeopardy. true | false

6-2 Intentional Torts

Intentional violations of duty include a vast variety of intentional torts, all of which have their own individual elements. Table 6-1 summarizes the primary intentional torts.

Table 6-1 Intentional Torts

Tort	Definition
Assault	An assault occurs when the victim is placed in fear or apprehension of immediate bodily harm by the tortfeasor who has the present apparent ability to inflict that harm.
Battery	A battery involves an offensive or harmful, unprivileged touching.
False imprisonment	When one party prevents another party from moving about freely, the first party has committed the intentional tort of false imprisonment.
Defamation	Any false statement communicated to others that harms a person's good name or reputation may constitute the tort of defamation.
Disparagement	Disparagement involves any false statement communicated to others that somehow questions the quality of an item of property or that raises uncertainty as to who actually has legal ownership rights to the property in question.
Food disparagement	Food disparagement laws often (1) shift the burden of proof so that the defendant, not the plaintiff, has the burden; (2) add treble damages; and (3) add criminal law elements.
Fraudulent misrepresentation	Fraudulent misrepresentation involves false statements or actions, or a combination thereof, that misrepresent facts so that an innocent party relies on those misrepresentations and suffers an injury or loss as a result.
Civil theft	Civil theft requires that the innocent victim demonstrate that the perpetrator intentionally took the victim's property in order to permanently or temporarily deprive the victim of that property.
Invasion of privacy	Invasion of privacy occurs when one person unreasonably denies another person the right to be left alone.
Intentional infliction of emotional distress	Intentional or reckless infliction of emotional distress occurs when an individual causes another to undergo emotional or mental suffering, even without an accompanying physical injury.
Misuse of legal procedures	Misuse of legal procedure occurs when one person brings a legal procedure action with malice and without probable cause.

Assault and Battery

Under U.S. tort law, assault and battery, though often closely associated with each other, are separate torts. An **assault** occurs when the victim is placed in fear or apprehension of immediate bodily harm by a tortfeasor who has the present apparent ability to inflict that harm. No actual physical contact is needed for an assault. The essence of the tort lies in the fear or apprehension that is created in the victim.

EXAMPLE 6-2: Assault with a Deadly Dart

Terry Kline and Patrick Fisher were playing a friendly game of darts at the Wood Street Tavern one evening when they invited Fred Feeney and David Ballentine to join them. Unknown to either Kline or Feeney, Ballentine was intoxicated. After losing several games, Ballentine became enraged and tried to hit Kline by throwing several darts at him. In his intoxicated state, Ballentine's aim was poor, and he did not hit Kline. Nevertheless, Ballentine has committed an assault.

A **battery** involves an offensive or harmful, unprivileged touching. Naturally, if Ballentine had actually managed to hit Kline in Example 6-2, he would have committed a battery; however, as the definition points out, a touching need not be harmful to be a battery. Moreover, a battery does not always require the touching of the actual person of the victim if the tortfeasor touches something closely associated with that victim. So, if a prankster pulls a chair out from under someone before that person sits down, and the person falls to the floor, the joker has committed a battery. Or if he or she knocks a cafeteria tray out of a diner's hands, again he or she has committed a battery, despite the fact that the actual person or the victim has not been contacted.

EXAMPLE 6-3: Battery by Antibody

Lucy Pickett works as a nurse at Garner County Hospital. Because she knows that her patient, Jim Luger, is afraid of needles, she sneaked up behind him and injected him with an antibiotic that had been ordered by his primary physician. Despite her desire to help Luger, and her wish to save him from feeling unnecessary fear, Pickett has committed a battery.

False Imprisonment

When one party prevents another party from moving about freely, the first party has committed the intentional tort of **false imprisonment**. This tort is called false arrest in some states. The victim of false imprisonment need not be locked in a prison or a jail cell. All that is required is that the person's freedom of movement be restricted. For example, a physician who refuses to return a patient's clothing until a partial payment is received for a long overdue bill has committed false imprisonment.

Store owners must be very careful about detaining suspected shoplifters because such a detention could result in a false imprisonment lawsuit if not handled properly. Still, because of the growing problem of shoplifting in society today, most states have laws that allow storekeepers to detain a suspected shoplifter if they have reasonable grounds to suspect that a shoplifting incident has occurred. This protection is ordinarily referred to as the **shopkeeper's privilege**. When the privilege is created by statute, that statute is commonly called the **merchant protection statute**. Even under such laws, the storekeeper must detain the suspect in a reasonable manner and for no longer than a reasonable length of time.

Defamation and Disparagement

Intentional torts such as battery, assault, and false imprisonment involve direct physical and psychological injury to an individual. These injuries are not the only type of harm, however, that can be imposed on individuals in tort law. Sometimes the injury results from words that damage a reputation and lead to monetary loss. Two of these word-oriented torts are defamation and disparagement.

Defamation Any false statement communicated to others that harms a person's good name or reputation may constitute the tort of **defamation**. To be defamatory, the statement must hold the victim up to ridicule, contempt, or hatred. Defamation in a temporary form, such as speech, is **slander**; in a permanent form, such as writing, it is **libel**. People can usually bring a libel suit whenever the permanent statement is damaging to their reputation, is false, and is communicated to a third party. However, under common law, individuals can bring slander lawsuits even if they have suffered no actual loss if the false statements fall into one of the following categories:

1. An accusation that the victim of the slanderous statements has committed a very serious crime, such as murder or rape.
2. An accusation that the victim has a communicable disease, such as venereal disease.
3. An accusation that the victim has engaged in improprieties in a business, trade, or profession.
4. An accusation that an unmarried female victim has been unchaste.

Individuals may speak the truth without being sued successfully for defamation as long as it is done without spite or ill will. In addition, statements made by senators and representatives on the floor of Congress and statements made in a court of law are privileged. Privileged statements are not the proper subject of a defamation lawsuit. The idea behind creating these privileges is to promote the open debate of legislative and judicial matters.

The U.S. Supreme Court has given journalists the extra protection of the actual malice test when they write about public officials. Under the **actual malice test**, a public official must prove not only that the statement made or printed was false but also that it was made with actual malice. **Actual malice** means that the statement was made or printed either with the knowledge that it was false or with a reckless disregard for its truth or falsity. Later decisions expanded the actual malice test to cover public figures. Public figures are people like television actors, sports figures, and rock stars who seek out public fame and are readily recognizable by the public at large.

EXAMPLE 6-4: In the Cross Hairs—Actual Malice

In the early morning of June 14, 2017, shortly before the Annual Congressional Baseball Game, James T. Hodgekinson fired shots at the Republican baseball team during practice, injuring Rep. Steve Scalise, among several others. Since the shooter was a Bernie Sanders follower, many people speculated that the violence had been politically motivated. Not long after that, *The New York Times* published an anti-violence editorial that accused Sara Palin's political action committee of inspiring the shooting of Democratic Congresswoman Gabby Giffords in 2011. To support the claim, the *Times* pointed to a campaign map published in 2011 that allegedly had cross hairs plastered over a likeness of Giffords. Moreover, the *Times'* editorial stated that there was a direct and clear link between the map and the shooting of Giffords. All of this proved to be false. No "clear" and "direct" link existed between the map and the shooting, as the *Times* had claimed. Moreover, the "cross hairs" were actually placed over congressional districts on the map, not on the likenesses of the congresswoman. In addition, there was substantial evidence to show that the shooter had become obsessed with Giffords as early as 2007.

Accordingly, Palin filed a lawsuit for libel against the *Times*. At first glance, Palin appears to have a perfect libel case. After all, the story hurt her reputation, was false, and was communicated to a third party. Unfortunately for Palin, she is considered a public figure. In libel law, under a case known as *The New York Times v. Sullivan*, public officials and public figures must prove more than a private citizen to succeed in a libel lawsuit. They must prove *actual malice*. Recall that actual malice means that the statement was made or printed either with the knowledge that it was false or with a reckless disregard for its truth or falsity. Palin argued that because a true version of the Giffords story had been printed in the *Times* and in a *Times* column by Charles M. Blow, *Times* staffers *knew* that the statements were false, or at the very least, they had printed the inaccurate editorial with *reckless disregard* for its truth or falsity. Ultimately, the court disagreed, noting that the fact that the *Times* had, in the past, published stories and columns with contradictory information, did not mean that *Times* staffers, operating in the present under the pressures of a deadline, actually knew about those stories and columns. Moreover, as soon as the staff knew about the errors, they quickly retracted the false information, again indicating that they had no knowledge of the false information in the editorial when it was originally printed. [See: Alberto Luperon, "Sarah Palin Is Talking to Lawyers over New York Times Article; Here's How Her Case Would Look," *MSN NEWS* and *LAW NEWZ*, June 16, 2001, http://www.msn.com/en-us/news/. See also: Callum Borchers, "The New York Times Was Negligent, but Did Not Libel Sarah Palin, a Federal Judge Says," *Washington Post*, August 29, 2017; *The New York Times v. Sullivan*, 376 U.S. 254 (1964).]

Source: See: Alberto Luperon, "Sarah Palin is Talking to Lawyers over New York Times Article; Here's How her Case Would Look," *MSN NEWS and LAW NEWZ* (June 16, 2001) http://www.msn.com/en-us/news/; See also: Callum Borchers, "The New York Times was negligent, but did not libel Sarah Palin, a federal judge says," *The Washington Post* (August 29, 2017); *The New York Times v. Sullivan,* 376 U.S. 254 (1964).

Limited-purpose public figures (also called **temporary public figures**) are people who, by their own volition, enter into a public controversy or who, by reason of their position or role, are pulled into the controversy and who, as a result, become a temporary public figure for that limited set of problems. If the plaintiff is, in fact, a limited-purpose public figure, then he or she will be judged in a defamation lawsuit by the actual malice test. In determining whether a plaintiff has become a limited-purpose public figure, the court starts with the assumption that the plaintiff is a private individual rather than a public figure. It then rests upon the shoulders of the defendant to demonstrate that the plaintiff is a limited purpose public figure. In doing this, the defendant will examine (and the court will ultimately evaluate) that status by answering these five questions: (1) Does the plaintiff have access to the mass media? (2) Has the plaintiff become part of the controversy? (3) Has the plaintiff attempted to affect the direction and/or outcome of the public controversy in question? (4) Did the controversy in question exist before the defamatory statements? (5) Has the plaintiff remained a central public figure up to the time of the defamatory printing? The key questions here are often numbers 3 and 4, so the courts will sometimes combine them before determining the applicability of the actual malice standard. In answering these two questions, the court may ask whether the plaintiff has, of his or her own free will, taken a position of importance in a particular controversy by trying to affect its resolution. If the answer is "yes," then the plaintiff is declared a limited-purpose public figure, and actual malice is used to evaluate his or her case. [See: *Ermo v. Rolling Stone*, 209 F. Supp 3d 862 (W.D. Va. 2016).]

EXAMPLE 6-5: Temporary Public Malice

Officials of the University of Virginia, including, especially, Dean Nicole Eramo, were undoubtedly shocked and dismayed by an article that appeared in *Rolling Stone Magazine* in 2014 that claimed a woman named Jackie had been raped at a party at a UVA fraternity house. Eramo was a central target of the article because her job on the campus was to handle sexual assault cases. The article accused her of being indifferent to sexual assault cases in general and to Jackie's case in particular. None of this was true. Instead, Eramo had counseled Jackie and had arranged for her to talk to the authorities, although Jackie would not cooperate with the authorities when the time came. Eramo's reputation had been hurt badly by the false accusations in the article, so she elected to sue the magazine for libel. Ordinarily, the standard for judging the case would have been the usual libel standard, which says that to succeed in a libel case, the plaintiff must prove that (1) the story is damaging to his or her reputation, (2) the story is false, and (3) the story was communicated to a third party. However, when the plaintiff is a limited-purpose public figure, the actual malice test applies. The actual malice test requires the plaintiff to prove that the defendant printed the defamatory article knowing the material in the story was false or with reckless disregard for its truth or falsity.

So, it would be much more advantageous for the plaintiff to be a private individual rather than a limited-purpose public figure. At the outset of such a determination, the court starts with the presumption that the plaintiff is a private figure and then invites the defendant to prove otherwise. Recall that the court uses five questions to determine if a private individual is a limited-purpose public figure: (1) Does the plaintiff have access to the mass media? (2) Has the plaintiff become part of the controversy? (3) Has the plaintiff attempted to affect the direction and/or outcome of the public controversy in question? (4) Did the controversy in question exist before the defamatory statements? (5) Has the plaintiff remained a central public figure up to and beyond the time of the defamatory printing? The court was satisfied that Eramo was, in fact, a limited-purpose public figure because (1) she had access to the media, even if it was primarily to the *The Cavalier Daily* and local radio stations; (2) she was featured prominently in the story that was the focal point of the controversy; (3) she was clearly part of the controversy; (4) the controversy involving sexual attacks on college campuses existed before he article was printed; and (5) the plaintiff remained a central figure up to and beyond the printing of the article. Given how these questions were answered, the plaintiff was judged to be a limited-purpose public figure and was, therefore, judged by the actual malice test.

Recall that under the actual malice test, the plaintiff must show that the defendant printed the false story with knowledge of its falsity or with reckless disregard for its truth or falsity. In this case, *Rolling Stone* had violated so many journalistic principles that *reckless disregard* was almost a foregone conclusion. The reporter who wrote the article seems, first, to have approached the story with the preconceived notion that university administrators would be unsympathetic to charges of sexual abuse. Therefore, whenever she discovered evidence that would discredit her thesis, she overlooked or ignored it. For example, she did not fully investigate the accuracy of the claims made by the alleged victim, including the identity of the alleged attacker. In addition, the reporter did not verify Jackie's report about conversations that she allegedly had with friends when she went to them for help after the alleged attack. (Later, these friends denied the versions of their conversations that Jackie had reported in the article.) Worst of all, the reporter wrote falsely that Eramo had tried to stop Jackie from reporting her charges to the authorities and that she, Eramo, had not reacted properly to Jackie's allegations about gang rape incidents at another fraternity. In the end, despite the more difficult actual malice test as used by the court, the plaintiff was victorious and was awarded $7.5 million in monetary damages. [See: *Ermo v. Rolling Stone*, 209 F. Supp 3d 862 (W.D. Va. 2016). See also: Jacob Gershman, "Rolling Stone Settles Suit on Campus Rape Story," *The Wall Street Journal*, March 13, 2017.]

Source: See: Ermo v. Rolling Stone, 209 F. Supp 3d 862 (W.D. Va. 2016); See also: Jaconb Gershman, "Rolling Stone Settles Suit on Campus Rape Story," *Wall Street Journal* (March 13, 2017).

Disparagement **Disparagement** involves any false statement communicated to others that somehow questions the quality of property or raises uncertainty as to who has legal ownership of that property. Generally, to recover for disparagement, the plaintiff must show monetary loss. Such losses may include the loss of sales, money spent to correct the public's image of a product, or expenses spent on litigation due to the disparagement. The difference between defamation and disparagement is that in defamation, the false charge is made about the victim's reputation, whereas with disparagement, the falsehood is made about a person's property or product. The falsehood usually casts doubt on the value of the product or on the property rights of the owner.

Food Disparagement Laws Some states have added a new weapon to the disparagement arsenal—food disparagement laws. **Food disparagement laws**, which are also known as "ag-gags," and "veggie libel laws," take a wide variety of forms. Some are simple extensions of conventional tort law, with a few interesting and creative twists added. For example, some states have veggie libel laws that shift the burden of proof in food disparagement cases so that the defendant, not the plaintiff, has the burden. So, instead of the plaintiff being charged with the burden of demonstrating that a story is false—or, in the case of actual malice, that it was printed (or broadcast) with knowledge of its falsity or with reckless disregard for its truth or falsity—the defendant must prove that the allegedly defamatory article was based on "reasonable and reliable" scientific research. In addition, many states permit plaintiffs to get treble (triple) damages in veggie-libel cases. Other states go much further by taking veggie libel a step higher, from tort law to criminal law. Thus, some states have made it a criminal offense to take photographs or to make videos in an agricultural operation unless the photographer or film maker first gets permission. Other states make it criminal for job applicants to lie about being associated with a journalistic operation, a labor union, or an animal rights group of any sort. Lying about such things can result in a misdemeanor or, in some states, a felony. [See: Edon Cannon, "AG-GAG and Food Disparagement Laws," Ethical Foods.com, January 3, 2017, https://ethicalfoods.com/ag-gag-and-food-disparagement-laws/; "Oprah in Trouble," *The Economist*, June 19, 1997, http://www.economist.com/node/597502.]

EXAMPLE 6-6: Is Food Defamation a Real Thing?

ABC News never saw this one coming. ABC News, a Walt Disney subsidiary, was sued by Beef Products Inc. under South Dakota's food disparagement statute for creating an erroneous impression that one of Best Products' meat products was (1) not really beef, as it was billed; (2) was absent any nutritional value; and (3) was unsafe for humans to eat. Even more dramatically, one ABC correspondent said on the air that the beef in question, something referred to as "lean finely textured beef" (LFTB), was actually nothing more than "pink slime" that was formerly used in dog food, that was sprayed with ammonia, and that was not safe for human consumption. Best Products countered by explaining that LFTB is created by a centrifuge process sanctioned by the Department of Agriculture. The process was developed specifically to take additional lean beef from cows. Moreover, Best Products added that the tiny amount of ammonia sprayed on some of the beef is designed to remove dangerous pathogens. Finally, Beef Products noted that ABC would have known this had the reporters not based their research on prejudiced "experts" and that, as a result, they broadcast the erroneous report either knowing that the information was wrong or with a reckless disregard for its truth or falsity. Despite this alleged reckless disregard for the truth, ABC ran the program, which led to a drop in sales for Best Products that led, further, to some 700 layoffs and forced the closing of three out of four of its production plants. The most dangerous aspect of this case for ABC is that Best Products has asked for $1.9 billion in damages. Now that seems bad enough but remember that South Dakota's veggie-libel law permits Best Products to seek treble damages. That elevates Best Products' $1.9 billion to almost $6 billion. Given what you know about veggie libel laws, should Best Products succeed in the suit? [See: Jacob Gershman and Lukas I. Alpert, "Food-Libel Trial Set to Begin," *The Wall Street Journal*, June 5, 2017, p. A-3; Edon Cannon, "AG-GAG and Food Disparagement Laws," *EthicalFoods.com*, January 3, 2017, https://ethicalfoods.com/ag-gag-and-food-disparagement-laws/; and "Oprah in Trouble," *The Economist*, June 19, 1997, http://www.economist.com/node/597502.]

Source: See: Jacob Gershman and Lukas I. Alpert, "Food-Libel Trial Set to Begin," *The Wall Street Journal*, (June 5, 2017, p,. A-3; Edon Cannon, "AG-GAG and Food Disparagement Laws," *EthicalFoods.com*, (January 3. 2017) https://ethicalfoods.com/ag-gag-and-food-disparagement-laws/; "Oprah in Trouble," The Economist (June 19, 1997) http://www.economist.com/node/597502.

Fraudulent Misrepresentation

Another word-oriented tort is fraudulent misrepresentation. **Fraudulent misrepresentation**, or **fraud** as it is known in some states, occurs when false statements or actions, or a combination thereof, are made by one party in a way that causes another party to rely on those misrepresentations and then to suffer an injury or loss as a result. Frequently, fraud involves a business relationship and works to destroy the mutual assent that ought to exist between the parties that are involved in a contract.

To demonstrate fraud, the complaining party (also referred to as the plaintiff) must prove the existence of five elements:

1. The complaining party will have to prove that the other party made false representations (statements) about some material fact involved in the contract. A material fact is one that is very crucial to the terms of the contract. Often, the courts say that a fact is material if it makes a difference to the outcome of the case. A fact that makes no difference, then, is immaterial.

2. The plaintiff must demonstrate convincingly that the other party made the representations knowing that they were false.

3. The plaintiff must show that the false representations were made with the intent that they be relied upon by the innocent party.

4. The complaining party must establish that there was a *reasonable* reliance on the false representations.

5. The plaintiff must verify that he or she actually suffered some loss by relying on those false representations after entering the contract.

Civil Theft

Several states have created a new intentional tort called civil theft. Civil theft emerges from state-enacted criminal law statutes that relate to theft. A lawsuit based on **civil theft** generally requires that the innocent victim demonstrate that the perpetrator intentionally took the victim's property in order to permanently or temporarily deprive the victim of that property. The burden or proof required in such a case is usually "by clear and convincing evidence," a standard that is lower than "beyond a reasonable doubt," which is used in criminal cases, and higher than "by a preponderance of the evidence," which is the usual standard in civil cases. Some civil theft statutes allow for treble damages and attorneys' fees, and others permit punitive damages. Some states require the victim to first contact the perpetrator and ask him or her to provide restitution in a dollar amount equal to what was taken. There is also a time limit added by the statute within which the perpetrator has a chance to respond and provide that restitution. Once the time limit has passed, the victim can pursue a lawsuit.

Invasion of Privacy

The courts in the United States have consistently held that people have a right to privacy. Consequently, a violation of that right would involve the tort of **invasion of privacy**. The right to privacy can be violated in several ways:

1. Revelation of confidential records.
2. Intrusion.
3. Creating a false light.
4. Exploitation.

Revelation of Confidential Records Individuals who, because of their jobs, work with confidential records containing private information must ensure that those records remain private. A failure to protect such confidential matters could result in an invasion of privacy lawsuit. Although it is not a violation of privacy for individuals to discuss confidential matters for professional reasons, it could be an invasion of privacy to discuss those same records for nonprofessional reasons. The motive of the person who releases the information does not matter. Moreover, whether there has been an invasion of privacy depends on the level of privacy expected by that person in that situation. For instance, an employee would expect privacy involving his or her employment record but not concerning the information that is printed on his or her identification badge.

Intrusion An individual's privacy can also be violated if there is an unwarranted intrusion into the person's expectation of privacy. Such an intrusion might occur if a person's photograph is taken and then published on the front page of a local newspaper. The issue at the heart of such case is the question of whether the plaintiff had a high expectation of privacy. Recall that the expectation of privacy depends on the situation. A person walking across a college campus has a very low expectation of privacy, whereas a person who is in his or her own home has a very high expectation of privacy. Thus, the publication of a photo of a person walking across campus would *not* be actionable as an invasion of privacy, but taking a similar photo while that person was in his or her home would be.

Creating a False Light Creating a false light is closely akin to defamation because it involves the publication of information about a person that paints him or her in a way that the majority of the population would see as unfavorable. A fashion model who poses for photographs for a bathing suit catalog and finds her image printed in a sexually explicit magazine would have a cause of action for being placed in a false light.

Exploitation The courts have held that an individual holds the rights to his or her own likeness to make money. An invasion of privacy can occur when one party uses an individual's photo, likeness, or name without permission for advertising, marketing, or publicity. Some courts treat the misappropriation of a person's likeness as a separate tort, calling it an invasion of the right to publicity.

Intentional Infliction of Emotional Distress

In recent years, the courts have recognized a tort called the **intentional or reckless infliction of emotional distress**. Before these more enlightened court decisions were handed down, victims who were injured emotionally by the wrongful acts of others could not recover damages without proving some sort of bodily injury. Today, in many states, someone who intentionally or recklessly causes another individual to undergo emotional or mental suffering will be responsible, even without an accompanying physical injury. The actions complained of must be extreme and outrageous and cause severe emotional suffering.

EXAMPLE 6-7: Extreme and Outrageous Silence

Marc Christian, who gained notoriety as the live-in boyfriend of Rock Hudson, sued the estate of the late actor for the intentional infliction of emotional distress. Christian argued that he had been induced to continue having "high-risk" sexual relations with the late screen star because Hudson had remained silent and failed to inform him that he had contracted AIDS. As a result of Hudson's misrepresentations, Christian contended that he suffered extreme emotional distress when he learned that Hudson was ill. This was true, Christian argued, despite the fact that he was not HIV-positive himself. Although Hudson did not attempt deliberately to transfer the virus to Christian and did not plan to cause Christian emotional distress, the inherent harmfulness of Hudson's actions could easily amount to extreme and outrageous conduct.

Misuse of Legal Procedure

The intentional tort known as the **misuse of legal procedure** occurs when one person brings a legal action with malice and without probable cause. When the misuse of the legal procedure involves the filing of a false civil lawsuit, it is called **wrongful civil proceedings**. In contrast, when the misuse involves bringing false criminal charges, it is labeled **malicious prosecution**. Some states use only the term *malicious prosecution* to refer to both forms of the tort. All of the following conditions must be present for a lawsuit based on misuse of legal procedure to succeed:

1. The defendant (the person against whom the misuse of legal procedure suit has been filed) must have brought civil or criminal charges against the plaintiff at an earlier time.
2. The earlier case must have been resolved favorably for the plaintiff.
3. The plaintiff must prove that the earlier case was brought by the defendant with malice and without probable cause.

When these conditions are present, an individual may be able to recover damages from the defendant for making the innocent party the target of a legal action without a good cause.

A related cause of action, which can easily be confused with malicious prosecution, is abuse of process. **Abuse of process** occurs when a legal procedure is used for a purpose other than that for which it is intended. It differs from malicious prosecution in that there is no requirement that the earlier case be brought without probable cause or be resolved favorably for the plaintiff. The tort can involve either a criminal or a civil case. Typically, abuse of process happens when a perfectly legal process is used as a pressure tactic to convince someone to do something he or she would not be inclined to do under ordinary circumstances.

EXAMPLE 6-8: Misuse and Abuse: Crossing the Legal Line

Janice Franklin and Karen Yalta were involved in a very difficult dissolution of their partnership. As a result of this problematic dissolution, as well as many other factors, the two young women did not like each other. Accordingly, Franklin filed a lawsuit against Yalta for defamation. The lawsuit was resolved in Yalta's favor. Yalta then sued Franklin for wrongful civil proceedings. Yalta won the case because she was able to prove that the original defamation suit against her was fabricated by Franklin, who was motivated by hatred and ill will. This suit is an example of the misuse of legal proceedings. If Franklin had filed a defamation suit to force Yalta to agree to Franklin's terms in the dissolution, she would be involved in abuse of process. This involvement would be true even if Franklin had legitimate reasons for filing the defamation suit.

quick quiz 6-2

1. Assault and battery never exist simultaneously. true | false
2. To be defamatory, a statement need not be communicated to a third party. true | false
3. The intentional infliction of emotional distress has yet to be recognized as a tort in any state jurisdiction. true | false

6-3 Negligence

People and property are sometimes injured even when no one intends that the injury occur. Such an occurrence is usually labeled an accident. Although no one acted with intent, someone was injured. The victim has experienced pain and suffering, lost wages, or incurred medical or repair bills. Justice demands that the injured party be compensated. The part of tort law that is concerned with the compensation of accident victims is called **negligence**.

Elements of Negligence

The issue before the court in a negligence action is as follows: Under what circumstances can the actions of an alleged tortfeasor be labeled negligent so that the victim can be compensated? Four elements must be present to establish negligence: legal duty, breach of duty, proximate cause, and actual harm. Table 6-2 gives an overview of these four elements.

Legal Duty A determination that a legal duty exists between the parties must be made to establish liability through negligence. This issue is solely a question of whether the tortfeasor should have reasonably foreseen a risk of harm to the injured party. Often today, the element of duty is not at issue in a lawsuit; however, there are some instances, when the existence of a duty does become a question that the court must answer. These instances generally emerge when a "special relationship" gives rise to a specialized duty. Thus, when a

Table 6-2 The Elements of Negligence

Element	Definition
Legal duty	A determination that a legal duty exists between the parties must be made to establish liability through negligence. This is solely a question of whether the tortfeasor should have reasonably foreseen a risk of harm to the injured party.
Breach of duty	The judge or the jury must determine whether the person accused of negligence has breached the duty owed to the victim. To determine if the alleged tortfeasor has met the appropriate standard of care, the court uses the reasonable person test.
Proximate cause	For the tortfeasor to be held liable, the unreasonable conduct must be the proximate cause of the victim's injuries. Proximate cause is the legal connection between the unreasonable conduct and the resulting harm.
Actual harm	The injured party in a lawsuit for negligence must show that actual harm was suffered.

teacher and several parents take a class on a field trip, for example, a special relationship arises between the teacher and the parents on one side, and the children in the other. Because of that special relationship, the children have the right to be kept safe and secure for the duration of the trip, while the teacher and the parents have the specialized duty to watch over those children to ensure their safety and security while the trip lasts. Unfortunately, determining when these specialized duties and rights arise is not always easy as the following example reveals.

EXAMPLE 6-9: *Booker v. Revco DS, Incorporated:* Duty, Duty, and More Duty

At age 74, Ramona Booker entered a drugstore by pushing her way through one door and then through a second. Both doors were extremely heavy, so Booker was compelled to use both hands, causing her cane to drag on the ground. As she entered the second door, the tip of her cane caught on the exposed coil of a security device, causing her to fall and injure herself. Booker brought a lawsuit against Revco, the retailer, to recover damages (read "money" here) for her injuries. The defendant filed a motion for summary judgment that was granted by the trial court but then reversed by the appellate court. In examining the question of whether the defendant was entitled to a judgment as a matter of law, the court held that there was no doubt that the defendant drugstore owed a duty to its customers to keep them safe from harm while on the premises. In making this judgment, the appellate court in this case quoted an earlier appellate case that held, "[It is a] well-established rule that the possessor of premises owes a duty to an invitee to exercise ordinary or reasonable care for his or her safety and protection. This duty includes maintaining the premises in a reasonably safe condition and warning an invitee of latent or concealed defects of which the possessor has or should have knowledge." [See: *Baldauf v. Kent State Univ.* (1988), 49 Ohio App.3d 46, 47-48, 550 N.E.2d 517; and *Booker v. Revco DS, Inc.*, 681 N.E.2d 499 (OH).]

Source: See: *Baldauf v. Kent State Univ.* (1988), 49 Ohio App.3d 46, 47-48, 550 N.E.2d 517; *Booker v. Revco DS, Inc.*, 681 N.E.2d 499 (OH).

Breach of Duty The judge or the jury must determine whether the person accused of negligence has breached the duty owed to the victim. A breach of duty occurs if the alleged tortfeasor has not met the appropriate standard of care. To determine if the alleged tortfeasor has met the appropriate standard of care, the court uses the reasonable person test. This test compares the actions of the tortfeasor with those of a reasonable person in a similar situation. If a reasonable person would not have done what the tortfeasor actually did, then the tortfeasor is liable. The reasonable person standard is an objective test. Circumstances may change, but the standard of care applied by a reasonable person does not. How a reasonable person would behave in one set of circumstances may not be the same in another set of circumstances.

EXAMPLE 6-10: The Case of the Unreasonable Limo Service

Luigi Tarentino hired a limousine from Highland Limo Service so that he and his wife, Maybeth, could attend their high school reunion in style. When the limousine arrived, Tarentino told the driver to take them to the Regency Hotel. Once they were on the freeway, it became clear that the driver did not know how to reach the hotel. Every time the driver took a wrong turn, Tarentino attempted to correct him. The driver continued to ignore Tarentino's instructions. Eventually, the driver, who later said he was aggravated by Tarentino's frequent interruptions, stopped the limousine and told Tarentino and his wife to walk to their reunion. He then drove off and left his passengers several miles from the hotel in the middle of an ice storm. While walking to the hotel, Tarentino slipped on a patch of ice and fell and broke his arm. Later, the Tarentinos learned that the driver had a long history of similar conduct and that the limousine company had not done a proper search into the driver's work history before hiring him. The question to the jury was, "Would a reasonable person hire an employee who will be responsible for the safety of paying passengers without checking the work history of that potential employee?" The jury said no, and Highland was held liable for the injuries that befell Tarentino from this breach of duty to protect paying passengers from harm.

If the defendant in a particular case is a professional, such as a physician or an engineer, the circumstances—not the test—change. To determine whether the defendant acted reasonably, the jury would have to know how the reasonable professional would act under similar circumstances. Determining this point may require the use of expert witnesses to testify as to a reasonable professional's conduct under the circumstances.

Actual and Proximate Cause It is not enough to simply show that the tortfeasor's actions were unreasonable. For the tortfeasor to be held liable, the unreasonable conduct must be tied to actual and proximate cause. **Actual cause**, or **cause in fact**, demonstrates that the cause (the unreasonable conduct) led to the effect (the injury to the plaintiff). The question can be viewed like a problem in physics. We look at the plaintiff's injury (the effect) and deconstruct the events that preceded it, ending with the original unreasonable behavior (the cause). Imagine a set of dominoes falling one after the other and you'll have an accurate image of this process. So, let's say that a driver is texting while driving and that inattentiveness causes him to run a red light and collide with another vehicle, injuring the other driver and totaling the other car. To find actual cause, we deconstruct events from the crash and, working backward, see that if the driver had not been texting, then the second vehicle would not have been hit. This is called the "but for" test. Using the "but for" test, the judge tells the jury to ask themselves, "Would there have been no accident, 'but for' the unreasonable conduct of the defendant?" In this case, it is clear that the accident would not have happened "but for" the unreasonable conduct (texting while driving). This gives us actual cause.

The problem with actual cause is that there is no end to the consequences that flow from the defendant's unreasonable conduct. Thus, in the car accident just mentioned, negative effects can flow from the accident for days and weeks afterward, events that would not have occurred "but for" the original unreasonable conduct (the texting while driving). Thus, our innocent victim may lose work, may have to pay medical bills, may have to buy new clothing, may have to cancel a dinner date, may lose the services of a baby sitter, may miss her favorite television show, might be unable to attend a Rotary luncheon, may be fined for an overdue library book because she has no car, may fail to defrost her refrigerator because she is distraught or has a broken arm, and so on. The law must place a limit on these effects. This policy is referred to as **proximate cause** or **legal cause**. The law says there must be a final effect for which we will hold the defendant liable. The test used to determine this "last effect" is referred to as the **foreseeability test**. In determining proximate cause, the court asks whether the harm that resulted from the original unreasonable conduct was foreseeable at the time of the original action. If the effect was foreseeable at the time of the unreasonable conduct, the defendant is liable for the damages that flow from that effect. If the effect was not foreseeable, the defendant cannot be held liable for it. In this case the driver's injuries, the damage to the car, the medical bills, and the lost wages were all foreseeable. The overdue library fines, the undefrosted refrigerator, the lost babysitter, and so on, were not.

A CLASSIC CASE The Outer Limits of Causation in Negligence

The classic case of *Overseas Tankship (UK) Ltd. v. Morts Dock and Engineering Co., Ltd.* is embedded deep within the consciousness of all law students during their first year of law school. The case, which is customarily referred to as Wagon Mound 1 (a second Wagon Mound case, *Overseas Tankship (UK) Ltd v. Miller Steamship Co Pty Ltd* (Wagon Mound 2) [1967] 1 AC 617, also involves causation but is not examined here), involves one of the most straightforward yet oddly complex elements in negligence—causation. The facts play out like this. A tanker ship named the Wagon Mound, chartered by Overseas Tankship Ltd., was docked in Sydney, Australia, and located across the harbor from Morts Dock and Engineering. Members of the crew of the Wagon Mound had carelessly let some of the bunkering oil from the ship seep into the water in the harbor. The manager of Morts had men welding on the dock at the time, so he was, understandably, just a bit apprehensive about the spilled oil. (Who wouldn't be? Right?) To allay his fears, he asked the manager of Caltex Oil, which owned the dock where the Wagon Mound was berthed, whether the oil might be a danger. He was told that since the oil was in the open and mixed with the water, it was safe. After this consultation, the welders continued to work.

At some point, molten metal from the welding process flew into the water and hit some cotton rags that were also in the harbor water. When the cotton caught fire, so did the oil and the harbor, which caused extensive damage to the wharf and a ship berthed there. Morts sued, basing the case on negligence and won at trial. Overseas appealed and the case ended up first in the New South Wales Supreme Court and, ultimately, in the Privy Council (the High Court) of Australia. The question before the Privy Council was not duty, nor breach of duty, nor even actual harm. Instead, it was causation. Now there is no question of actual cause here. Had the oil not been spilled carelessly, there would have been no fire. The real question then was one of proximate case. Was the original careless act of spilling the oil into the harbor the proximate cause of the damage to the wharf and the ship? The council rejected the old law, which was based on the distinction between direct and indirect causes, and substituted a new rule based on the foreseeability of harm and damage from the original careless actions of the defendants. The council ruled that the damage and the harm that results from the original careless actions of the defendants must be *reasonably foreseeable* at the time of those actions. So, if the injury (actual harm) is foreseeable, liability follows. If not, liability will not follow. In this case, the fact that the defendants had no way to reasonably know that the oil in the water could catch fire, there was no proximate (legal) cause and no liability. (If the damage complained of had been oil damage to the wharf and ship, a different result would have issued from the Privy Council.) [See: *Overseas Tankship (UK) Ltd. v Morts Dock and Engineering Co. Ltd.* [1961] UKPC 1, [1961] AC 388 [1961] All ER 404.]

Source: See: *Overseas Tankship (UK) Ltd. v Morts Dock and Engineering Co. Ltd.* [1961] UKPC 1, [1961] AC 388 [1961] All ER 404.

More on Proximate Cause The Wagon Mound decision regarding causation, detailed in the Classic Case, may be straightforward, but that does not mean it is simple. On the contrary, it is actually rather complex. Still, one thing is certain: The principle of foreseeability has remained as the foundation of causation after Wagon Mound, even in the United States. This realization means that the doctrine of direct and indirect causes seems to have been discredited, if not thoroughly, then nearly so. Foreseeability itself is comprised of at least four interrelated spin-offs: (1) foreseeability and types of harm, (2) foreseeability and classes of victims, (3) foreseeability and the extent of harm, and (4) foreseeability and the nature of the victim.

The first spin-off, foreseeability and types of harm, refers to the kinds of injuries that might occur from the careless actions of the initial tortfeasor. Thus, in Wagon Mound, for example, when a vessel leaks oil into a harbor, oil damage to the wharf and to ships moored in the harbor is easily foreseeable. Fire damage on the surface of the water in the harbor, however, is not. The second offshoot, foreseeability and classes of victims, refers to those individuals that a tortfeasor can foresee as being within the zone of danger. Potential victims within the zone have a cause of action against the defendant; those not in the zone, have none. In Wagon Mound, for instance, the negligent crew members (the tortfeasors) could foresee that any dock worker or crewman who might fall into the harbor that day could be harmed by the oily water. Others in the class of foreseeable victims might be dock workers and crew men who develop long-term health problems because of prolonged exposure to the oil. In contrast, firefighters as a class would not be foreseeable when the oil was first spilled and, thus, would have no cause of action against the defendants. If the fire cannot be foreseen, then firefighters on the dock cannot be foreseen either.

The third spin-off, foreseeability and the extent of harm, encompasses a range of injuries that might flow from the original negligent act. This type of foreseeability is quite extensive and, in fact, will probably not eliminate liability. Thus, the defendants in Wagon Mound will be liable for all oil damage to the cargo of all ships moored to the dock, whether that cargo is gravel or the Elgin Marbles. The final corollary, foreseeability and the nature of the victim, refers to victims with unusual and undetectable conditions. The law is straightforward on this issue, stating that "the tortfeasor takes the victim as he finds him." Thus, if a victim who falls into the oily harbor suffers extra injuries because of an allergic reaction to the oil, the defendant will be liable for those injuries, as well as for the injuries that the rest of the victims, the ones with no oil allergies, might experience. Thus the tortfeasor might not foresee the weakened condition of the victim, but the law says that has no bearing on liability. This rule is commonly referred to as the "egg-shell skull principle."

One More Note on Causation The complex nature of causation in general, and foreseeability, in particular, has led to some statutory alterations of the standard in some situations. For example, the Federal Employers Liability Act (FELA) established a negligence standard for railroads that all but eliminates the foreseeability causation doctrine. Applying its authority over interstate commerce as established by the Commerce Clause (Article I, Clause 8), Congress enacted FELA in reaction to the high number of work-related deaths and injuries in the railroad industry. More specifically, FELA is designed to help compensate railroad workers who are injured while on the job. The statute permits railroad workers to recover for work related injuries if they can demonstrate negligence, no matter how small, on the part of the railroad. The language of the statute declares that a railroad will be liable for on-the-job injuries to a worker if the railroad "caused or contributed to" a worker's injury just so long as the railroad's "negligence played a part—no matter how small—in bringing about the injury." The Supreme Court has ruled more than once that the statutory formulation of negligence and causation in FELA has replaced the common law doctrine of the foreseeability causation doctrine, as it relates to railroads.

Actual Harm The injured party in a lawsuit for negligence must show that actual harm was suffered. In most cases, the harm suffered is a physical injury and is therefore visible. Harm suffered due to fright or humiliation is difficult to demonstrate. Courts often deny damages in actions for negligence unless they can see an actual physical injury. Actual harm can also come in the form of property damage.

EXAMPLE 6-11: The Hot Coffee Myth Part 1: The Perfect Case of Negligence

Stella Liebeck, who was 79 years old at the time, purchased a cup of coffee at the drive-through window of a McDonald's restaurant in New Mexico. Her grandson, who was driving the car, parked so that she could mix cream and sugar into her coffee. While she was trying to take the top off the cup, the coffee splashed out of the cup, onto her legs and lap. As a result, she sustained third-degree burns and was in the hospital recovering for eight days. Her injuries led to skin grafts, permanent disfigurement, and 24 months of disability. The case of *Liebeck v. McDonald's* clearly involves the elements of negligence (duty, breach of duty and the standard of care, proximate cause, and actual harm). Analyze the facts in the case using the four elements of negligence. (1) Does a restaurant (even a fast-food restaurant) have a duty to protect its customers from harm? (2) Did the defendants act according to the standard of care, or did they breach their duty when they continued to hand customers foam containers containing coffee at a temperatures of 180 to 190 degrees Fahrenheit despite those 700 claims of coffee-related burns? (3) Is there a causal link (both actual and proximate) between the spilled hot coffee and third-degree burns? (4) Was Liebeck harmed by the spilled coffee? [See: *Stella Liebeck v. McDonald's Restaurants, P.T.S., Inc. and McDonald's International, Inc.*, 1995 WL 360309 (Bernalillo County, N.M. Dist. Ct. 1994); and Kevin G. Cain, "The McDonald's Coffee Lawsuit," *Journal of Consumer & Commercial Law*, August 18, 1994, pp. 14-19.]

Source: See: *Stella Liebeck v. McDonald's Restaurants, P.T.S., Inc. and McDonald's International, Inc.*, 1995 WL 360309 (Bernalillo County, N.M. Dist. Ct. 1994); Kevin G. Cain, "The McDonald's Coffee Lawsuit," *Journal of Consumer Commercial Law*, pp. 14–19.

Defenses to Negligence

Several defenses can be used by the defendant in a negligence case. These defenses include contributory negligence, comparative negligence, and assumption of the risk.

Contributory Negligence The defense of **contributory negligence** involves the failure of the injured party to be careful enough to ensure his or her personal safety. Contributory negligence prevents the injured party from recovering damages. In other words, if the injured party's negligence contributed to personal injury, the tortfeasor wins. **Last clear chance** is the injured party's defense to a charge of contributory negligence. Under this doctrine, a tortfeasor may be held liable if the injured party can show that the tortfeasor had the last clear chance to avoid injury.

Comparative Negligence To soften the harsh effects of contributory negligence, many states have adopted **comparative negligence** statutes that require courts to assign damages according to the degree of fault of each party. Rather than deny all recovery, the court weighs the relative degree of wrongdoing in awarding damages. If the tortfeasor was 80 percent negligent, the injured party may be allowed to recover 80 percent of the losses suffered. Some states have adopted the "50 percent rule." Under this rule, an injured party who was found to be more than 50 percent negligent cannot recover any damages from the tortfeasor.

Assumption of the Risk Another defense to negligence is **assumption of the risk**, which involves the voluntary exposure of the victim to a known risk. If the injured party was aware of the danger involved in a situation, and by his or her actions indicated a willingness to be exposed to the danger, then he or she has assumed that risk. An awareness of the extent of the danger is the court's primary consideration in awarding or denying damages. It is important that the victim's decision to enter the risky situation be voluntary. If he or she is forced to enter the risky situation because no other choice is available, it is not an assumption of the risk. On the other hand, if the plaintiff voluntarily enter the risky activity, then he or she has legitimately "assumed the risk" of injury. In such a case, the plaintiff can succeed in a lawsuit only if he or she can show that the defendant acted with intent or in a reckless manner.

THE OPENING CASE *Round 3*
The Case of the Injured Cheerleader

To review, Jailynn Brown, our plaintiff, belonged to the All City Airmen (ACA) cheerleading squad. The ACA was coached by Raven Evans-Harris and Kendra Fritz, two former cheerleaders. Charlotte Harris, a basketball coach and fitness trainer, also held conditioning sessions for the team. All three coaches worked on a volunteer basis. Occasionally, the team practiced on the lawn (described later as "uneven and sloped") at the home of Charlotte's father, Dr. Andre T. Harris. During one such practice, the team was trying out a new routine called the "liberty." No mats had been provided for the session. Kendra was not at practice that day, and Charlotte was at practice but not present as they practiced the liberty. Raven taught the girls the stunt and was present during the session but not looking at the team as they practiced. As team tried the liberty, Jailynn fell on her left side. Dr. Harris came out the house to help Jailynn, but the injury was bad enough to transport her to the hospital, where they learned that Jailynn had a torn ACL. Later, Jailynn's mother, Marketa Watkins, and Jailynn sued Raven, Charlotte, and Dr. Harris. The defendants countered by arguing that, when Jailynn signed up for cheerleading practice, she assumed the risk of a fall at sometime during practices. Jailynn admitted that she assumed the risk, but argued that the defendants had acted recklessly by conducting the practice without mats on uneven, slanted ground.

The defendants filed a summary judgment motion arguing that even if the facts were true as stated by the plaintiffs, the defendants are not liable as a matter of law because their conduct was not reckless. They based this conclusion on the fact that "[r]eckless conduct is characterized by the conscious disregard or indifference to a known or obvious risk of harm to another *that is unreasonable under the circumstances and is substantially greater than negligent conduct*"[1] (emphasis added by the court). In other words, the defendants were saying something like, "Yes, there was a risk of falling, but Jailynn new about that risk every time she acted as the flyer, and besides, she had performed many similar stunts in the same place under the same circumstances (read "on uneven slanted ground" and "no mats" here), so she cannot claim we were reckless. Negligent, maybe, but reckless, no." The court agreed, noting that, "Under these circumstances, we do not find that the practice location, the lack of mats, and training technique created an unreasonable risk of harm, as the fact remains that the risk amounted to falling on the grass, and falling is an inherent risk of the activity . . . Simply put, the risk of harm associated with the stunt at issue was not unreasonable under the circumstances so as to rise to the standard of recklessness."[2] End of speech. [See: *Jailynn Brown, et al. v. Andre T. Harris Sr., et al.* Appellate Case No. 27069, Trial Court Case No. 2014-CV-5144 (2014).]

Source: See: *Jailynn Brown, et al. v. Andre T. Harris Sr., et al.* Appellate Case No. 27069, Trial Court Case No. 2014-CV-5144 (2014).

The Doctrine of *Ferae Naturae* The doctrine of *ferae naturae* (wild nature) helps to determine the liability of property owners when people are injured by on their property by wild animals. As the Latin names suggests, the doctrine emerges from Roman law. Simply stated, the doctrine holds that property owners are not liable for injuries caused by wild animals on their property, just so long as the wild animals are not in the possession of the property owner. The principle is based on the quite logical idea that, in general, wild animals are not owned by anybody and are both uncontrollable and unpredictable. On the other hand, the *ferae naturae* doctrine operates as a defense when a party is injured by a wild animal *not in the possession* of the property owner. Still, property owners do have a duty to use reasonable care in maintaining their property and must warn invitees on their property of wild animals that they, the owners, know about, that the invitees do not know about and are very unlikely to discover on their own. On the other hand, property owners have no duty to warn about wild animals commonly known to exist on their property (alligators in southern Florida, for instance, or deer in central Ohio, or bears in western Pennsylvania). Be careful about this doctrine, however. When most people think about wild animals, they envision lions, and tigers, and bears (oh my!). However, property owners should be aware that wild animals can also include spiders, wasps, hornets, bees, ticks, fire ants, and so on—some of which owners might actually have *in their possession* (think honey bees here and ant farms here).

quick quiz 6-3

1. Legal duty is never at issue in any lawsuit today. true | false
2. Proximate cause is sometimes referred to as legal cause. true | false
3. Under the defense of comparative negligence, the plaintiff always loses all the damages that he or she might have been awarded, absent the defense. true | false

6-4 Strict Liability

Under certain circumstances, the courts may judge a person liable for harm even though that person was not negligent and did not commit an intentional tort. This doctrine is known as **strict liability** or absolute liability. In recent years, strict liability has also been applied to product liability cases.

Grounds for Strict Liability

Under strict liability, the court will hold a tortfeasor liable for injuries to a victim even though the tortfeasor did not intend the harm and was not in any way negligent. Strict liability is generally applied when the harm results from an ultrahazardous or very dangerous activity. Such activities include using explosives and keeping wild animals. A number of dangerous activities, such as flying an airplane, operating X-ray equipment, and laying public gas lines, are not subject to liability without fault. These activities are recognized as essential to the economic health and welfare of the public.

Product Liability

Product liability is a legal theory that imposes liability on the manufacturer and seller of a product produced and sold in a defective condition. A product in **defective condition** is unreasonably dangerous to the user, to the consumer, or to property. Anyone who produces or sells a product in defective condition is subject to liability for the physical or emotional injury to the ultimate consumer and for any physical harm to the user's property. The courts have regularly held that liability for a defective product extends to the producer of the product, the wholesaler, and the retailer. The seller or producer must be engaged in the business of selling such products. In addition, the product manufactured or sold must be expected to reach the ultimate consumer without substantial change in the conditions under which it was originally manufactured or sold.

Product liability is not without its limits. In most states, product liability also is not available as a cause of action if the only property damaged is the defective property itself. In such a situation, the product owner must seek a remedy in sales law for breach of warranty. (*Note:* People who are injured by faulty products might also be able to bring a product liability lawsuit in sales law. This issue is discussed at length in Chapter 15.)

Counterfeit Colgate toothpaste was recently imported from China and sold in dollar stores across the United States. How does this affect Colgate's reputation?

©Color China Photo/AP Images

quick quiz 6-4

1. Keeping wild animals is an ultrahazardous activity. true | false
2. Strict liability is also known as absolute liability. true | false
3. Product liability is completely unrelated to strict liability, and the two torts should never be confused with each other. true | false

6-5 Cybertorts

Computers have provided unscrupulous individuals with new ways to commit crimes and torts. In Chapter 5, we examined several cybercrimes. In this chapter, we focus on another group of legal problems, cybertorts. We look first at the nature of cybertorts and then at the problems associated with defining, describing, and preventing cybertorts.

The Nature of Cybertorts

A **cybertort** involves the invasion, distortion, theft, falsification, misuse, destruction, or exploitation of information stored in or related to electronic devices, including but not limited to desktop PCs, laptops, mobile phones, mainframe computers, phone cameras, tablets, and home computers that stand alone or are part of a computer network. Cybertorts rarely, if ever, involve any physical harm to a victim. Instead, the victim's reputation has been hurt because a false statement has been posted on Facebook; the victim's emotional state has been disturbed because his or her privacy has been invaded by a photograph passed from cell phone to cell phone; the victim has suffered extensive financial loss due to identity theft; or the victim has been terrified by repeated threats from cyber-bullies sending text messages in a relentless, ruthless fashion.

Cyber-Defamation

Cyber-defamation is the communication of false and destructive information about an individual through the use of electronic devices. Most legal moves in cyber-defamation have been designed to limit, rather than extend liability for defamatory comments disseminated electronically. For example, when the courts were first involved in cyber-defamation, they easily extended liability for defamation from the party who posted the defamation on the Internet to the Internet service provider (ISP), such as America Online (AOL), that provided the vehicle for the posting. Thus, for example, it was not difficult in one case for a court in New York to decide that the Prodigy Service Company was responsible when an investment banking firm sued for defamation after false statements were posted on a **cyber-bulletin board** that was under Prodigy's control.

After the Prodigy case, however, the Communications Decency Act was enacted by Congress to protect ISPs from future defamation lawsuits for false statements posted by other individuals on the net. Despite the passage of the law, many cases have been filed attempting to hold ISPs liable for defamatory postings. Few have succeeded, but they remain a nuisance to the providers. Still, the greater nuisance, that to the innocent victims, has not been handled adequately. In one case, AOL was found not liable for defamation even though the provider had been informed of the defamatory content of a posting and still delayed its removal. Moreover, the protection granted to ISPs has gone far beyond protection for defamatory postings. The courts have found that ISPs are not liable when hackers place a virus into a system, when piracy is involved on the Net, or when an invasion of privacy takes place via a provider's link.

Cyber-Disparagement

Disparagement involves false statements communicated to others that in some way casts doubt upon the ownership or the quality of an item of property or a product offered for sale. **Cyber-disparagement** involves the same activity on the Internet. The Facebook phenomenon has opened an avenue for the relatively new tort of cyber-disparagement. Businesses now solicit videos from their consumers for postings on their own websites. These businesses often go so far as to run games and contests in which clients and customers can submit homemade advertisements or videos that will be added to the website of the business. Unfortunately, this process is filled with legal risks, not the least of which is the possibility of a cyber-disparagement lawsuit. Such homemade videos typically target the product of a company's competitor. Thus, a company that posts such videos must make certain that the competitor's product is not subject to false statements and descriptions. This assurance requires an enormous effort aimed at monitoring the content of such submissions. Legal activity in this area has not been heavy as of yet, but that is because the tort is so new. As time goes on and competitors find themselves injured by such postings, the activity will increase, and more cyber-disparagement lawsuits will be filed.

Cyber-Invasion of Privacy

A **cyber-invasion of privacy** is the unwelcome intrusion into private matters initiated or maintained by an electronic device. Because the development of computer technology is in a constant state of flux, it is not surprising that the law is still uncertain about just what constitutes a cyber-invasion of privacy. One area that has been expanded recently involves computer-related privacy in the workplace. As the result of at least one federal case, workers employed by businesses that keep a close eye on their workers' time on the Internet have no expectation of privacy, at least in relation to their Fourth Amendment rights, provided that the employer has openly informed the workers of the surveillance.

Privacy and Employees The low expectation of privacy has long been a part of the law in relation to governmental employees. Thus, it has been clear that the Fourth Amendment right against unreasonable searches and seizures does not protect a governmental employee who knows that the government regularly monitors its employees' Internet use. The same standard now extends to employees within the private sector. How this ruling relates to the tortious invasion of privacy is problematic; however, because the standard for the invasion of privacy is based on the level of privacy expected, the fact that a worker knows that the company monitors computer use means that the expectation is low. The moral of the story is twofold: (1) Employers should routinely remind their workers that all computer use is monitored by the information technology department, and (2) workers should use computers for work-related tasks only.

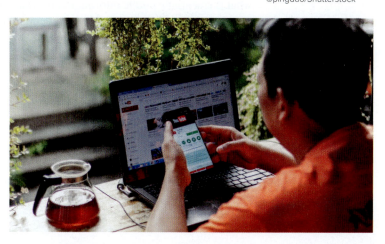

When employees know that their employer monitors their Internet use, those employees have no expectation of privacy.

©pingdao/Shutterstock

All of this assumes, however, that the computers being used in the workplace are owned and controlled by the employer. Unfortunately, this is not always the case. As small portable devices such as tablets, smartphones, laptops, and so on, proliferate, many employers are permitting their employees to use their own devices on the job. There is a certain degree of logic to this approach, which is referred to as the **bring your own device (BYOD)** tactic. Employees are usually more familiar and more comfortable with their own devices. Moreover, permitting employees to use their own devices also cuts down on costs for the employer. Regrettably, this procedure raises legal questions in relation to privacy and property ownership. Does the employer have the right, for example, to confiscate and examine the contents of a smartphone or tablet that the employee purchased and uses for both personal and business purposes? Some employers solve the problem by having the IT department configure personal devices so that certain clearly identified functions are for business use only, while others are for personal use. The smarter approach, however, may be to sidestep the issue and distribute company-owned devices (**company-owned, personally enabled devices or COPEs**) that the employee is permitted to use for personal reasons, with the caveat that the personal functions on the company-owned device may be open to inspection by the employer, who does own the device. [See: Dennis Kennedy, "Does Your Firm Have a Bring-Your-Own-Device Policy?" *ABA Journal*, January 1, 2012.]

Privacy and Clients Businesses and other organizations—such as educational institutions, health care facilities, and financial institutions—must also deal with the privacy of their customers, students, patients, and clients. Most invasions of privacy affect private records that pertain to employees who, because of their jobs, work closely with confidential files, such as educational, medical, and financial records. The failure to protect such records, whether on paper or in a computer, can result in an invasion of privacy lawsuit. Nevertheless, some courts have held that records stored in a computer require a degree of protection that is greater than the protection given to paper records because paper records can be kept hidden away or locked in a filing cabinet or a safe, whereas computer records are easy to retrieve, compile, and disseminate. Still, not every claim of a computer-related invasion of privacy automatically translates into a successful lawsuit. The law is still unsettled in several key areas, not the least of which is the question of whether ISPs are permitted to protect the privacy rights of their subscribers.

Private Privacy and Public Privacy Most of the time, **private information**, or *private private information*, as it is sometimes called, includes reports on personal matters, family relationships, sexual habits, employment records, medical data, and financial records; however, the law also recognizes a fundamental difference between *private privacy* and *public privacy*. The law is familiar with private privacy concerns about matters such as health concerns, sexual preferences, family matters, and so on. However, the computer age has given rise to another privacy issue—that is, the concern over the publication of what is essentially public information or what has been termed public-privacy matters. As noted earlier, many people believe that computer records deserve a higher degree of protection because, unlike paper documents, they are more readily vulnerable to hacking from remote sites.

Data Mining of Public Private Data The process of **data mining** takes place when a hacker links multiple strings of data together and develops a data package that the target considers a compilation of private information, despite the public sources from which the hacker composed the package. The issue here is whether the hacker's mining of public databases to construct a private data portrait violates the target's privacy. Some commentators argue that an individual's right to privacy is invaded if, in the process of gathering the data, the hacker ignores or bypasses the target's consent to produce a data portrait that embarrasses, disturbs, ridicules, bullies, exploits, or financially harms the innocent target. To the extent that the victim is harmed, he or she ought to have a cause of action against the hacker.

EXAMPLE 6-12: ATMs, Digital Cameras, and Data Mining

Frank Vilnius, a dedicated health enthusiast and avid cyclist, rode his recumbent bike into town each week to do his errands. One of the errands involved a stop at the ATM at the local branch of Superior Savings. Unknown to Vilnius, the ATM contained a digital camera that photographed the bank's customers when they used the machine. Vilnius suddenly found himself the target of spam, telemarketing calls, text messages, and snail mail ads—all selling products for cyclists. After some investigative work of his own, Vilnius discovered that one of Superior's subsidiaries, B-A-Cyclist, was a sports equipment chain with an active Internet presence. B-A regularly tapped into Superior's databank and used the photos and other customer data to target potential customers. Vilnius was not financially hurt by the intrusion, but he was annoyed enough to remove his savings from Superior Savings and move his business to the St. Georges Savings across town.

In the Vilnius case in Example 6-12, the various pieces of data that Superior Savings mined included Vilnius's address, phone number, e-mail address, mobile phone number, bank account balance, and his hobby as a cyclist. Arguably, all this data is public when looked at in isolation. Nevertheless, privacy rights emerge because the public pieces of data have been mined to produce a valuable public private data portrait that was exploited by Superior and its subsidiary without Vilnius's consent and in a manner that annoyed him enough to lead him to move his business to St. Georges. Unfortunately, there is still little case law on the issue of public private data portraits. Moreover, the law that does exist militates against the firm establishment of a public privacy right, despite the convincing case that can be made for its acceptance.

quick quiz 6-5

1. Cybertorts always involve information that has been invaded, distorted, stolen, falsified, or destroyed by an electronic device. **true | false**
2. Most legal moves in cyber-defamation have been designed to extend liability. **true | false**
3. Government employees have a high expectation of privacy in the workplace. **true | false**

6-6 Remedies for Torts

When a wrongdoer has injured another person by committing a tort, the victim can usually be compensated with monetary damages. However, at times, the equitable remedy of an injunction is more appropriate.

The Right to Damages

The compensation paid to the victims of a tort is known as **damages**. Damages can come in several forms. **Economic compensatory damages** are those that are directly quantifiable. These include damages awarded for lost wages, medical expenses, and expenses incurred in the repair or replacement of property. **Noneconomic compensatory damages** are those that result from injuries that are intangible and, therefore, not directly quantifiable. For example, damages resulting from pain and suffering, mental anguish, and loss of companionship are considered noneconomic. An award of compensatory damages may be reduced in a state that uses comparative negligence. Thus, if compensatory damages of $1 million are awarded by the jury, but the jury also finds that the plaintiff was comparatively negligent to the tune of 40 percent, as might happen, for example, if the plaintiff was injured in a car accident while not wearing a seatbelt, then instead of $1 million, the plaintiff receives $600,000. If the tortfeasor's acts are notoriously willful and malicious, a court may also impose punitive damages. These are damages above and beyond those needed to compensate the injured party. **Punitive damages** are designed to punish the tortfeasor so that similar malicious actions are avoided by others. For this reason, they are also referred to as **exemplary damages**. Some courts say that another purpose of punitive damages is to comfort the victim.

The Right to an Injunction

If a tort involves a continuing problem, such as the dumping of chemical waste into a river, the injured party may ask the court for an injunction. An **injunction** is a court order preventing someone from performing a particular act. If a tort involves some permanent fixture that harms the interests of the injured party, the court may order the wrongdoer to take positive steps to alleviate the problem. Thus, the court might order a company to clean up a landfill that has become a nuisance to neighborhood homes. If the company failed to complete the cleanup, it would be in contempt of court. Contempt of court is a deliberate violation of the order of a judge that can result in a fine or in jail time for the wrongdoer.

EXAMPLE 6-13: Fighting the Hot Coffee Myth Part 2: Damages

In Example 6-11, that the plaintiff, Stella Liebeck, purchased a cup of coffee at the drive-through window of a McDonald's restaurant in New Mexico. Her grandson, who was driving the car, parked so that she could mix cream and sugar with the coffee. While she was trying to take the top off the cup, the coffee splashed out of the cup, onto her legs and lap. As a result, she sustained third-degree burns and was in the hospital recovering for eight days. Her injuries led to skin grafts, permanent disfigurement, and 24 months of disability. Liebeck asked for $13,000 from McDonald's to cover her medical payments and an additional $5,000 for lost income. McDonald's proposed a settlement of $800. The damages awarded in this case, and the events that followed the awarding of damages, offer us a classic study on how the awarding of damages operates in the real world. The process worked like this:

1. As the first step in determining the damages, the jury decided that Liebeck should receive compensatory damages amounting to $200,000.
2. However, the jury also determined that Liebeck was 20 percent responsible for her own injuries.
3. Using comparative negligence, her award was reduced 20 percent, giving her $160,000 in compensatory damages.
4. The jury also awarded her punitive damages in the amount of $2.7 million, which amounted to two days' worth of McDonald's coffee revenue.
5. The judge lowered the punitive damages award to $480,000, which was three times the compensatory damages.

The total awarded to Liebeck turned out to be $640,000. After the award was finalized, both Liebeck and McDonald's announced that they would appeal. However, as often happens in cases like this, there was an out-of-court settlement for an undisclosed amount. [See: *Stella Liebeck v. McDonald's Restaurants, P.T.S., Inc. and McDonald's International, Inc.*, 1995 WL 360309 (Bernalillo County, N.M. Dist. Ct. 1994); and Kevin G. Cain, "The McDonald's Coffee Lawsuit," *Journal of Consumer & Commercial Law*, August 18, 1994, pp. 14–19.]

Source: See: *Stella Liebeck v. McDonald's Restaurants, P.T.S., Inc. and McDonald's International, Inc.*, 1995 WL 360309 (Bernalillo County, N.M. Dist. Ct. 1994); Kevin G. Cain, "The McDonald's Coffee Lawsuit," *Journal of Consumer Commercial Law*, pp. 14–19.

> **quick quiz 6-6**
>
> 1. Economic and noneconomic compensatory damages are essentially the same thing. true | false
> 2. Punitive damages are designed to compensate the victim of a tort. true | false
> 3. An injunction is never granted by the court in any kind of tort case. true | false

6-7 Developments in Tort Law

Tort law is in an unsettled stage of development. Much of tort law is still common law, but public dissatisfaction with the high number of tort-based lawsuits has caused some legislatures to pass statutes aimed at tort reform. Some of these moves make sense, as with the passage of wrongful death and survival statutes. The advisability of others is not quite as clear. Nevertheless, this evolutionary surge in tort law is part of the legal culture's ongoing attempt to create a balanced system. The balance this time is between the rights that victims have to be compensated for injuries caused by tortious conduct and the right that society has to be spared the heavy cost of unjustified and expensive litigation.

Survival Statutes and Wrongful Death

Under common law, if someone died from another's wrongful act, then the right to bring a lawsuit also died. This rule originated because the king would execute the wrongdoer and then take his or her property. As a result, there was no property left for the next of kin to recover in a tort suit. In the modern world, this practice makes no sense, so the state legislatures have nullified the rule with legislation. The two statutes that deal with this problem are survival statutes and statutes that deal with wrongful death.

Survival Statutes Many state legislatures have revised common law by passing survival statues. Survival statutes allow a lawsuit to be brought even if the plaintiff, or the defendant, or both are deceased. Many states also have survival statutes that preserve the right to bring a lawsuit no matter what caused the death or deaths. Most states also allow such suits if the tort involves damage to real or personal property; however, there are some limitations placed on survival statutes. For example, suits cannot be brought for libel or slander after the death of a defamed person, because such a suit is for injury to a live person's reputation. Survival suits are brought or defended by the lawful representative of the estate of the deceased.

Wrongful Death Statutes Unlike survival statutes, **wrongful death statutes** preserve the right to bring a lawsuit only if the death is caused by the negligence or the intentional conduct of the person who caused the death. Generally, only those family members who have lost the support of the deceased have the right to bring a wrongful death suit. The definition of family members generally includes husbands, wives, children, and parents. Under wrongful death statutes, creditors, business partners, and the like have no right to bring lawsuit. Wrongful death suits are also brought or defended by the lawful representative of the estate of the deceased.

The Tort Reform Movement

Other suggestions for tort reform include the introduction of statutes of repose in product liability and medical malpractice cases, the use of comparative negligence in product liability cases, and alterations in the availability of wrongful death lawsuits.

Statutes of Repose One suggested tort reform would introduce a statute of repose into product liability lawsuits. **Statutes of repose** establish a limit in years, usually but not necessarily 15 years, beyond which an injured party could not bring a lawsuit for an injury caused by a product. The limitation would be placed on end users. An *end user* is a purchaser or a user who is not involved in the production or the assembly of the product. A statute of repose differs from a statute of limitations in that the statute of limitations begins to run when the injury occurs, while the statute of repose begins to run when the product is sold. Often, such statutes carry limitations and exceptions. Thus, if the manufacturer fraudulently represented the condition of the product and that fraud led to the harm caused by the product, the statute of repose would not apply. Extremely dangerous products might also fall outside the protective zone of the statute of repose.

Statutes of repose have been suggested also as a tort reform measure in medical malpractice lawsuits. Time limits for such statutes vary from four to six years and usually begin to run when the professional services have been rendered. As is the case with statutes of repose for product liability lawsuits, the statute of repose for medical malpractice would include exceptions under which the statute would not apply. For instance, the statute would not apply if the defendant in such a lawsuit engaged in fraud in relation to the relevant facts pertaining to the professional services that form the basis of the suit.

Comparative Negligence and Product Liability Another reform that has been suggested in some states is the application of comparative negligence as an affirmative defense in some product liability cases. Under this standard, the responsibility of the manufacturer in a product liability case can be lessened by the degree to which the plaintiff's own negligence contributed to his or her injury. Some statutes even say that the manufacturer can escape liability altogether if the plaintiff's share in the responsibility exceeds 50 percent.

Wrongful Death Reform Some states have introduced a reform measure aimed at eliminating any chance of a double recovery under wrongful death statutes. Such reform provisions generally maintain that a wrongful death action cannot be instituted by family members if the deceased recovered damages from the defendant in a prior lawsuit. Thus, if during his or her lifetime, the deceased recovered damages from the defendant in a negligence action, the family cannot bring a subsequent wrongful death action based on the same facts that gave rise to the original negligence lawsuit. In essence, under such a provision, the deceased is said to have waived all rights to bring the wrongful death action when he or she recovered under the original negligence action.

Cultural Paradigms and Balance in Tort Law

There is a great deal of opposition to tort reform within the legal community, especially among attorneys who represent plaintiffs. The most fundamental complaint is that tort reform threatens the very paradigm upon which tort law is based. Fundamental to this argument is the belief that the tort law paradigm establishes a delicately balanced legal system that is threatened by the well-intentioned, but essentially clueless, supporters of tort reform.

Cultural Paradigms A **paradigm** is an unchallenged world view that establishes the rules by which everyone in a particular culture thinks, speaks, and acts. This is true whether we are dealing with a national cultural, a religious culture, a political culture, or a professional culture. The problem with tort reform is that it challenges the assumptions of the legal paradigm without offering an alternative paradigm. Instead, it offers a piecemeal, patchwork approach that borrows concepts and principles from other areas of the law and applies them in ways that are inappropriate at best. This approach to reform reveals a fundamental misunderstanding of the tort law paradigm.

Balance in Tort Law As noted earlier, the delicately balanced system of tort law is threatened by legislators and reformers who mean well, but who seem unable or unwilling to understand and appreciate the intricacies and the complexities of the tort law paradigm. In his treatise, *Law's Empire*, the legal philosopher Ronald Dworkin argues that two very strong reasons exist for preserving the current tort law paradigm. Dworkin explains it this way: "Our law as a whole recognizes two principles as pertinent to the loss people should be permitted to suffer through accidents. The first is the principle of collective sympathy. It holds that the state should try to protect people from being ruined by accidents even when the accident is their own fault. The principle is most apparent in regulative safety programs of different sorts, in workmen's compensation statutes and in state-subsidized schemes of insurance for risks to property and person not adequately covered in the private insurance market. The second is the principle of apportioning the costs of an accident among the private actors in the drama that produced it. It holds that accidental loss should be bourne by the person at fault, not the innocent victim. This principle is most evidently at work in negligence law, including legislative amendments or supplements to common law of negligence."[3] The second principle is the one that concerns us the most here. In a succinct and direct way, Dworkin has restated the fundamental rule of the tort law paradigm: People have a duty not to harm one another and when they do cause harm, whether intentionally, through carelessness, or by engaging in a dangerous activity, they pay. The principle is both logical and fair because it rehabilitates the innocent victim at the expense of the wrongdoer. It's just that simple. [See: Ronald Dworkin, *Law's Empire* (Cambridge: The Belknap Press of Harvard University, 1986) p. 269.]

Sovereign Immunity

Sovereign immunity is an ancient legal doctrine that holds that unless a nation-state grants its consent or waives its immunity, it cannot be sued. The principle extends to both the federal and the state governments. Recently, however, the doctrine has begun to fade away. The federal government, for example, passed Federal Torts Claims Act in 1946 (FCTA). Under the FCTA, tort suits are permitted, allowing individuals to recover damages for injuries caused by the actions of federal employees. Even before this, in 1887, the Tucker Act permitted lawsuits in the federal government based on contract claims. The states were also believed to have immunity simply because they existed as sovereign entities, despite being part of the federal system. Nevertheless, early on, there was some dispute over whether this immunity protected the states against suits by citizens of other states. To remove any doubt about this immunity, in 1791, the 11th Amendment was passed to establish that the states could not be sued by citizens of another state or by citizens of a foreign nation.

Moreover, the states' immunity to other lawsuits has almost completely evaporated over the years. First, state immunity was held to never have extended down to local governments and to state subdivisions such as school boards. Gradually, the courts began to remove state immunity, ruling that state government officials ought to be liable for injuries following the traditional elements of negligence—duty, breach of duty, causation, and actual harm—and that they should be liable for injuries that result from special duties created by special relationships—such as teacher to student, doctor to patient, and so on. Still, some state courts maintained the belief that public employees ought to be immune from lawsuits when the the alleged breach involves a "duty owed to the public at large." The rationale here is that public employees must be empowered to do what they have a duty to do as part of their job and should not be held back by a concern that they might make a mistake. In other words, public employees must be assured that they will not be sued if they make an error while on the job. This is know as the **public duty doctrine**. Even states that recognize this doctrine, however, will not allow a state officer to escape liability for wanton and/or reckless behavior. The bottom line is that most states have eliminated sovereign immunity by statutes, by cases, or both. The problem is that it is hard to know the situation in each individual state without doing the necessary legal research. In fact, even the courts themselves have a difficult time unraveling this complicated topic as indicated in the Case Study at the end of Part One. [See: "Sovereign Immunity," *West's Encyclopedia of American Law* (The Gale Group, 2008), http://legal-dictionary.thefreedictionay.com/Sovereign+Immunity/. See also *Schneider v. Kumpf*, 2016-Ohio-5161.]

quick quiz 6-7

1. Survival statutes allow a lawsuit to be brought even if both the plaintiff and the defendant are deceased.   true | false
2. Statutes of repose establish a limit in years beyond which an injured party could not bring a lawsuit for an injury caused by a product.   true | false
3. A paradigm is an unchallenged world view that establishes the rules by which everyone in a particular culture thinks, speaks, and acts.   true | false

Summary

6.1 A tort is a private wrong that injures another person's physical well-being, emotional health, property, or reputation. A person who commits a tort is called a tortfeasor. The other party is alternatively referred to as the injured party, the innocent party, or the victim. The primary purpose of tort law is to compensate the innocent party by making up for any loss suffered by that victim. The doctrine of *respondeat superior* may impose legal liability on employers and make them pay for the torts committed by their employees within the scope of the employer's business.

6.2 The principal intentional torts include assault, battery, false imprisonment, defamation, disparagement, food disparagement, fraudulent misrepresentation, civil theft, invasion of privacy, intentional infliction of emotional distress, and malicious prosecution.

6.3 Negligence is the failure to exercise the degree of care that a reasonable person would have exercised in the same circumstances. Negligence includes four elements: duty of care, breach of duty through a failure to exercise the appropriate standard of care, proximate cause, and actual harm. Three defenses to negligence are contributory negligence, comparative negligence, and assumption of risk.

6.4 Under the doctrine of strict liability, when people engage in ultrahazardous activities, they will be liable for any harm that occurs because of that activity, regardless of intent and regardless of care.

6.5 Cybertorts involve computer data that has been invaded, distorted, falsified, misused, destroyed, or exploited financially by an electronic device. Therefore, cybertorts rarely involve any harm to a party's physical well-being. Instead, the victim's reputation has been hurt because a false statement has been placed on the Internet, the victim's emotional state has been disturbed, because his or her privacy has been invaded by a posting on Facebook, or the victim has suffered monetary harm because of identity theft.

6.6 Tort remedies include monetary damages and injunctions.

6.7 Survival statutes allow a lawsuit to be brought even if both the plaintiff and the defendant are deceased. Wrongful death statutes preserve the rights of third parties affected by the death of the deceased to bring a lawsuit. Statutes of repose establish a limit in years beyond which an injured party could not bring a lawsuit for an injury caused by a product or by medical malpractice. Another reform that has been suggested in some states is the application of comparative negligence as an affirmative defense in some product liability cases.

Key Terms

abuse of process, 175
actual cause, 178
actual malice, 169
actual malice test, 169
assault, 168
assumption of the risk, 181
battery, 168
bring-your-own-device (BYOD), 186
cause in fact, 178
civil theft, 173
company-owned, personally enabled devices (COPE), 186
comparative negligence, 181
contributory negligence, 181
cyber-bulletin board, 184
cyber-defamation, 184
cyber-disparagement, 185
cyber-invasion of privacy, 185
cybertort, 184
damages, 187

data mining, 186
defamation, 169
defective condition, 183
disparagement, 172
duty, 164
economic compensatory damages, 187
exemplary damages, 188
false imprisonment, 168
food disparagement laws, 172
foreseeability test, 178
fraud, 173
fraudulent misrepresentation, 173
injunction, 188
intentional or reckless infliction of emotional distress, 174
invasion of privacy, 174
juriscience, 165
last clear chance, 181
libel, 169
limited-purpose public figure, 170

malicious prosecution, 175
merchant protection statute, 168
misuse of legal procedure, 175
negligence, 176
noneconomic compensatory damages, 187
paradigm, 190
private information, 186
proximate cause, 178
public duty doctrine, 191
punitive damages, 188
respondeat superior, 164
shopkeeper's privilege, 168
slander, 169
sovereign immunity, 191
statutes of repose, 190
strict liability, 183
tort, 163
tortfeasor, 163
wrongful civil proceedings, 175
wrongful death statutes, 189

Questions for Review and Discussion

1. What is the difference between a tort and a crime?
2. What is *respondeat superior*?
3. What is meant by the legal term "duty"?
4. What are the principal intentional torts?
5. What are the elements of negligence?
6. What are the differences among contributory negligence, comparative negligence, and assumption of the risk?
7. When does strict liability apply?
8. What is a cybertort?
9. What remedies are available in tort law?
10. What innovations have been suggested for contemporary state tort reform?

Cases for Analysis

1. The plaintiff in this case, Elyse Duckett, was a veteran firefighter with the San Francisco Fire Department (SFFD). During her career, she also worked as a recruitment officer assigned to hire young women and was later appointed to integrate women and minorities into the department. This case involves the death of a passenger who was thrown from an Asiana aircraft that crashed at the San Francisco Airport. Duckett was not among the first responders because she was performing other duties that had taken her away from the station house; however, after arriving at the airport driving Aircraft Rescue Firefighting 37, she learned that a passenger had been run over by one or more of

SFFD's vehicles. Later, on two occasions, Duckett was interrogated at length about the death of the passenger. Duckett informed the questioners that she and one of her colleagues had viewed a video that showed that she had not driven the vehicle that had first run over the passenger. Even so, the questioners at the first interrogation persisted in what was later described as "an aggressive, accusatory, and intimidating manner." Subsequently, a television reporter, who had tried unsuccessfully to talk to Duckett, ran a story that identified her as the driver of the vehicle that had killed the passenger. The sources for the story came from within the SFFD. The story was aired on local, national, and international news outlets. Duckett brought a lawsuit against the city and county for violations of the Firefighters Procedural Code and the California Government Code. Duckett might also pursue a defamation case against the television station that broadcast the story. Using the five-part test, determine whether Duckett is a *limited-purpose public figure*. What difference would it make if she is considered a limited-purpose public figure? Is it to her advantage or the advantage of the defendant for her to be labeled a limited-purpose public figure? Explain. [See: *Duckett v. the City and County of San Francisco, et al.* Case Number CGc-14-539201 (May 9, 2014); Dan Nakaso, "SF Firefighter . . . Alleges She Was Made a Scapegoat," *Mercury News*, May 9, 2014; and Phillip Matier and Andrew Ross, "S.F. Firefighter Claims Defamation in Asiana Crash," *SF Gate*, January 28, 2014.]

2. Warren Barrington owned and operated Toys and Tots—From Two to Twelve, a toy store that specialized in educational toys for children between 2 and 12 years of age. Barrington and his wife, who operated the store as a partnership, did their best to market only original toys made of natural materials. Electronic toys, computers, and toys made of plastic were never sold in the store. During the National Toy and Model Association of America convention, Raymond Matthews, who owned a competitive shop, started several rumors, most of which suggested that many of the toys that were being shown by the Barringtons at the convention were not made of natural materials as advertised. He also suggested that those toys that were made of natural materials involved ideas stolen from him and that the Barringtons did not have the right to market them as they were doing at the convention.

Does Matthews' behavior qualify as defamation or disparagement or both? Explain.

3. The defendant, Union Pacific RR (UPRR), was sued, under the authority of the Federal Employees Labor Act (FELA), by one of its own employees who was afflicted by West Nile virus after being bitten by a mosquito while on the job. After coming down with the virus, William Nami, the plaintiff, could not walk without a cane, could not drive, and had experienced memory loss. He argued that he was bitten by an infected mosquito while working for UPRR outside Galveston, Texas, and next to an area on UPRR's right of way, that was infested by the virus-carrying mosquitoes. He noted that the infestation had been exacerbated by UPRR's negligence in never mowing the grass and allowing the standing water to accumulate. Nami also argued that UPRR did not warn employees about the mosquitoes, did not provide insect repellent, and did not equip employees with long-sleeved shirts. UPRR replied that under the doctrine of *ferae naturae*, the company was not liable for Nami's illness because he was injured by a wild animal that was not in UPRR's possession. UPRR also claimed that because the danger was commonly understood to exist (Galveston is known by local inhabitants as the "mosquito capital of the world"), the company had neither a duty to warn nor a duty to supply employees with repellent or long-sleeved shirts. UPRR also disputed the claim that it did not mow the grass and that it let the standing water accumulate. Nami argued that UPRR was relying on common law principles, like *ferae naturae* and proximate cause, that had been deliberately superseded by FELA, which states that a railroad will be liable for on-the-job injuries to a worker if the railroad "caused or contributed to" a worker's injury just so long as the railroad's "negligence played a part—no matter how small—in bringing about the injury." The trial court held for the railroad, but the court of appeals reversed. The case then went to the Texas Supreme Court. Does FELA supersede the Roman law principle of *ferae naturae*, and if not, does the doctrine of *ferae naturae* protect UPRR from liability? Explain. [See: *Union Pacific Railroad Company v. Nami*, 498 S.W. 3d 890 (Texas 2016).]

4. In one of the worst sea tragedies in the modern era, the South Korean Ferry, Sewol, capsized during what was billed as a standard trip to a vacation island. The ship, which was loaded with high school

students, sank, claiming hundreds of lives. Although the accident happened in a foreign jurisdiction, consider the following allegations that surround the tragedy and try to determine if those allegations, one by one or in the aggregate, might be the basis for a negligence lawsuit against the marine company that owned and operated the vessel. Some of the allegations include: (a) the crew members were not properly trained in emergency techniques; (b) passengers were not instructed in emergency measures before the voyage began; (c) no more than a few of the 44 life rafts were in use during the emergency operation; (d) the captain was not on the bridge at the time of the incident; (e) the captain later deserted the ship while many of passengers were still on board; (f) before the incident, the captain assigned the third mate to steer the boat while he went back to his cabin; (g) the passengers were told to stay in their cabins below deck rather than to vacate the ship; (h) cargo on the ferry may not have been fastened down in the correct fashion, making the ship unstable during a sharp turn and causing the ship to capsize; and (i) the marine company that purchased the used ferry had added more rooms to the ship, making the vessel unsteady. Which of these allegations might make the strongest negligence case against the marine company? Which would make the weakest case? Explain. [See: Choe Sang-Hun, Su-Hyun Lee, and Jiha Ham, "Human Error Suspected as Hope Fades in Korean Ferry Sinking," *The New York Times*, April 17, 2014, pp. A1, A6; and Choe Sang-Hun, Su-Hyun Lee, "Captain and 2 Crew Members Arrested in Sinking of Korean Ferry," *The New York Times*, April 19, 2014, pp. A-4, A-8.]

5. To supply America's energy needs, more and more crude oil is being extracted from shale and shipped to refineries. Much of this crude oil is located in the northern part of the United States, especially in the Northwest. This causes a problem since the refineries are located in the South. The pipelines that would ordinarily handle these shipments cannot manage the increased load. Consequently, much of this crude oil is being transported in tank cars on the nation's railroads. Unfortunately, many of these tank cars may not be up to the task. Evidence of the dangers involved in using these tank cars for oil shipments is mounting. For example, in 2013, the following incidents occurred: (a) a derailment in Lynchburg, Virginia, causing the loss of 25,000 gallons of oil; (b) an explosion in Casselton, North Dakota, causing the loss of 475,000 gallons; and (c) a 26-car derailment in Aliceville, Alabama, leading to the loss of 630,000 gallons. In total in 2013, 1.1 million gallons of crude oil were lost in such accidents. Government and corporate authorities know about these problems and are aware of ways to make the tank cars safer for transport. Possible improvements include (a) the addition of head shields to absorb shock at both the front and the back of each tank car in case of a collision, (b) the addition of better-quality handles to stop those handles from opening in an crash, (c) the addition of housings to stop valves from breaking off should the car overturn, (d) the addition of pressure-relief valves, (e) and the addition of coverings that are impervious to heat to provide a barrier in case of a fire. Imagine that you are a newly hired in-house attorney for an oil company that uses the present unimproved cars for transporting crude oil from North Dakota to Houston, Texas. Considering this evidence, as legal counsel for the oil company, compose an e-mail that builds a *legal case* that will convince the CEO and the board of directors to make these improvements before the next accident occurs on a train hauling the company's crude oil. [See: Michael Scherer, "Spotlight-Crude Awakening: The Shale-Oil Boom Is Ferrying a New Danger to America's Freight Railways," *Time*, June 2, 2014, pp. 14–15.]

6. Violence at Rikers Island, a New York City prison on an island in the East River, has risen to epidemic proportions over the past five years. During the first four months in 2014 alone, a dozen prisoners suffered injuries that resulted from stab wounds and cuts, while prisoners and guards underwent treatment for broken bones, concussions, and punctured eardrums among many other similar injuries. Reports indicate that while the population of the prison has fallen by 15 percent since 2004, the use of force by guards has risen 240 percent over that same period. Two prisoners, one who sustained extensive injuries to his neck and back and another who has back problems and a broken nose, have filed separate lawsuits naming the City of New York as defendant. Both inmates allege that their injuries resulted from beatings conducted by corrections officers at Rikers. Using your knowledge of tort law, list and explain those torts that might form the basis of these lawsuits. [See:

Michael Schwirtz, "Mental Illness and Violence Rise at Vast Jail," *The New York Times*, March 19, 2014, pp. A18.]

7. Patrick Clawson was described by reporter Karen Branch-Brioso in a newspaper story as a "1970s era St. Louis journalist turned private eye turned FBI informant." The story was published in the *St. Louis Post-Dispatch*. The fact that he had been characterized as an informant bothered Clawson, who saw it as damaging to his reputation. Accordingly, he brought a libel case against the *Post-Dispatch*. Recall that to be libelous, a statement must be false and "hold the victim up to ridicule, contempt, or hatred." Clawson would have preferred the term *whistleblower* rather than *informant* because that term commands more respect. Why is the use of the term *informant* to describe Clawson not libelous? Explain. [See: *Clawson v. St. Louis Post-Dispatch*, No. 04-CV-486. See also "Media Law: Label of 'Informer' Is Found Not Defamatory," *The National Law Journal*, September 11, 2006.]

8. Curtis Ellison was riding as a passenger in his own vehicle when it was pulled over by the police for a parking violation. The vehicle had actually been targeted because the police had routinely checked the license plate through the department's database. This routine check had revealed that the owner of the vehicle had an outstanding warrant pending against him. When the police searched the van, they found two firearms hidden in the vehicle. As a result, Ellison was charged with felonious possession of a firearm. He argued that the search had violated his Fourth Amendment rights and that his right to privacy had been infringed. The trial court agreed and dismissed the case. The case went to the appellate court. The issue before the appellate court was whether Ellison had a high expectation of privacy about the number on his license plate. Although this is a criminal case, it is still interesting to speculate on how the court would rule on the expectation of privacy in relation to a license plate. Why should the appeals court reverse the ruling by the trial court that there is a high expectation of privacy in relation to a license plate? Explain. [See: *United States v. Ellison*, No. 04-1925. See also "Criminal Practice: No Privacy Expectation on License Plate Numbers," *The National Law Journal*, September 18, 2006, p. 16.]

9. A St. Louis police officer was speeding the wrong way down a one-way street when he collided with a vehicle being driven by Ann Martin. Martin was seriously injured in the crash and brought a lawsuit against the police officer, the City of St. Louis, and the board of police commissioners. The board of commissioners is an agency of the state of Missouri. Martin passed away, and her daughter, Kimberly Hodges, took over as the plaintiff in the case. The case was settled in relation to the board and the officer but not the city. The City of St. Louis argued that the officer could not be employed by both the board and the city at the same time. The city further argued that the officer's real employer was the board, so it, the city, could not be held liable under the doctrine of vicarious liability. Why should the city be held liable under the doctrine of vicarious liability? Explain. [See: *Hodges v. City of St. Louis*, No. SC87513. See also "Torts: Officer Is City Agent Even if Working for State Board," *The National Law Journal*, March 12, 2007, p. 15.]

10. At the height of the modern civil rights movement, *The New York Times* ran a full-page advertisement entitled "Heed Their Rising Voices." The advertisement detailed police efforts in Montgomery, Alabama, to suppress the nonviolent civil rights demonstrations being carried on there by thousands of college students. The police commissioner of Montgomery, L.B. Sullivan, filed a lawsuit against *The New York Times*, alleging that he had been libeled by information carried in the advertisement, even though he was never mentioned by name. Should the Court use the actual malice test in this case to determine whether the newspaper libeled the commissioner? Explain. [See: *New York Times Co. v. Sullivan*, 376 U.S. 254 (U.S. Sup. Ct.).]

11. Five Commerce City police officers were summoned to break up a disturbance at a local party of teenagers. At the party, Ralph Crowe, who had consumed eight cups of beer and three cups of alcoholic punch, became rowdy and had to be detained by the officers. The police released Ralph after receiving the assurances of his brother Eddie that he would drive Ralph home. After leaving the party, Eddie Crowe allowed Ralph to take the wheel. Instead of going home, Ralph drove to the site of another party, where he lost control of the car and ran down six people. The police officers were sued for negligence in releasing Ralph. Did the five officers owe a duty to the six victims of Ralph's drunk-driving accident? Explain. [See: *Leake v. Cain*, 720 P.2d 152 (CO).]

12. Myers was injured when she slipped and fell on an ice patch on the front walkway of the Canton Centre Mall. The mall is owned and operated by Forest City Enterprises. Forest City had employees who were responsible for clearing the ice off of the mall walkways every morning. On this particular morning, they had cleared the ice from the walkway a short time before Myers took her tumble. Nevertheless, an ice patch had formed, and Myers did fall, sustaining injuries. Cooper, one of the employees charged with the ice-removal task, theorized that water may have been splashed up onto the sidewalk by passing cars where it froze sometime after their initial cleaning of the day. According to Cooper, "the vehicles could have splashed this back up on there . . . we're constantly moving around the building at all times, so anything can be going on in this half of the building while you're over here doing this half coming around." Was Forest City negligent in failing to keep the sidewalk clear of ice at all times that winter? What test would be used to judge Forest City's conduct? Explain. [See: *Myers v. Forest City Enterprises, Inc.*, 635 N.E.2d 1268 (OH).]

13. Michelle Wightman was driving toward a railroad crossing at which the gates were down and the lights flashing. Wightman noted a stopped train a short distance from the gate. Believing the stopped train to be the cause of the closed gate, she drove around the gate and was struck and killed by a train that suddenly appeared from behind the stopped train. The stopped train had blocked her view of the oncoming train. Both trains were owned and operated by Consolidated Rail Corporation (CRC). Wightman's mother brought a wrongful death lawsuit and a survivorship action against CRC. In response, CRC claimed that Wightman's action of driving around the gates, in violation of both state and city law regarding the operation of a motor vehicle at a railroad crossing, constituted negligence on her part. Furthermore, CRC argued that if Wightman had not crossed the tracks, she would not have been struck by the train. Therefore, her actions were the sole cause of the accident, and the railroad corporation should not be held liable for her death. The attorney for the plaintiff argued that the placement of the first train, blocking the view of the other track, contributed to the accident and that CRC should be held liable for Wightman's death. Should Wightman's own negligence be a complete bar to the plaintiff's recovery of damages in this case? Explain. [See: *Wightman v. Consolidated Railroad Corporation*, 640 N.E.2d 1160 (OH).]

quick quiz Answers

6-1	6-2	6-3	6-4	6-5	6-6	6-7
1. T	1. F	1. F	1. T	1. T	1. F	1. T
2. F	2. F	2. T	2. T	2. F	2. F	2. T
3. F	3. F	3. F	3. F	3. F	3. F	3. T

Part 1 Case Study

Barbara Schneider, Plaintiff-Appellant v. Mark Kumpf, Defendant-Appellee
Court of Appeals of Ohio Second District, Montgomery County, No. 26855 Decided July 29, 2016 2016-Ohio-5161

©Hisham F. Ibrahim/Getty Images

Summary

The facts in this case are relatively straightforward and easy to understand, even though they might seem a bit unbelievable. The plaintiff in the case is Barbara K. Schneider, the administrator of the estate of Klonda S. Richey. The defendant is Mark Kumpf, Director of the Montgomery County Animal Resource Center (ARC) and the Montgomery County Dog Warren. The problems started for Richey when, after 24 years of quiet life at her home in Dayton, Ohio, two new neighbors moved in next door. The new neighbors owned two pit bull mastiffs, both of which play a central role in the story. The other central player in this tragedy is, of course, Kumpf, the Director of the Montgomery County ARC and the County's Dog Warden.

When Kumpf took over as ARC Director and County Dog Warden, he changed the department's philosophy from one of enforcement to one of education. Instead of focusing on citations and summonses, deputy wardens would not issue citations unless they encountered a very serious case. Kumpf made this change because he did not believe that his department was getting proper support from the courts. The courts only rarely imposed fines for the citations that were issued. Statistics indicated that during the two years leading up to the incident that ignited this lawsuit, "out of more than 20,000 calls about animals, only about 697 (about 3.4%) resulted in citations. Of 60,000 dogs in Montgomery County, only about 12 were designated as 'nuisance' or dangerous in 2013." [See: *Schneider v. Kumpf*, 2016-Ohio-5161, p. 57.]

In order to initiate his change in philosophy from enforcement to education, Kumpf instituted some far-reaching changes in the day-to-day operation of his department. For example, Kumpf indicated that, to issue a citation, an officer would have to see the dog "at large" and outside of the owner's control. Kumpf also eliminated the officer patrol times and directed dispatchers not to take calls about dog problems. In place of actually taking live calls, Kumpf had dispatchers put all such calls through to voicemail. All of Richey's calls for help concerning the two dogs that threatened her were, according to department protocol, diverted to voicemail.

Richey began to have trouble with the two mastiffs almost immediately after the new neighbors moved next door. She called the County Regional Dispatch Center repeatedly, all to no avail. In response to the trouble, she had a fence put up between the two properties and had security cameras installed to record the problems that she was having with the two dogs. Clearly, Kumpf must have known about Richey's complaints because he held regular meetings with his officers every day, during which they reported all calls that came into the center. The calls first began on August 8, 2012, when Richey notified the center that she had been chased by one of the neighbor's dogs. Receiving no response from ARC, she called the police who came out and knocked on the owner's door. When they received no answer, they left. The scene repeated itself later when an ARC officer knocked on the neighbor's door and, like the police officers before him, received no answer. He left after issuing a "dog-at-large" citation. On September 25, except for the intervention of the police, the scene was repeated. This time a written warning was issued.

Richey next attempted to get a civil protection order from the court to shield her from the neighbor's dogs. The court refused to issue the order. On March 13, Richey was again chased by one of the dogs. In addition, the dog went after Richey's cats. At this time, Richey also reported that the mailman had refused to deliver mail on the street because of neighbor's dogs. The mailman also noted that he would not deliver mail on the street until someone dealt with the dog problem. Another ARC officer knocked on the neighbor's door, again receiving no answer, and again posting a warning. On May 21, the events repeated themselves once more, only this time Richey was chased by two dogs. Once again, in response to the March 21 call, an officer showed up, knocked on the dog owner's door, received no answer, and left the property, once again after posting another in a long line of warnings.

On May 29, the events began to escalate. This time, the dog's owner had allegedly left one of the dogs outside with no food or water for a day and then ordered the dog to attack Richey. This time a complaint was issued, but the records reveal that Kumpf took no action. On July 21, the Sheriff's Department contacted the ARC about two mastiffs that were reported to be loose in Richeyvs neighborhood. The report also indicated that Richey had been chased by the dogs. Again an ARC officer failed in an attempt to meet with the owner of the dogs. However, the incident card did indicated that the dog was unlicensed. On June 22, Richey called the ARC and complained that the dogs were running about loose again. On the next day, an ARC officer finally showed up and posted yet another warning.

A new call came in on August 5. This time the dog's owner had placed one of the dog's on Richey's property in a clear effort to "scare her." The ARC officer who showed up posted another warning. On September 9, a call came in from Richey reporting a mastiff running loose in the neighborhood. An officer responded; knocked on the door; received no answer and posted a warning. Again, the incident card noted that the dog was unlicensed. On September 24, a call was received about a new dog, a bull pup, that was running loose on the street. The next day, an ARC officer repeated the ritual one more time—knock, receive no answer, post warning, leave premises. That brings us to the final chapter of the story, at least for Richey. To be accurate and authentic, this final chapter deserves to be quoted exactly as written by the court, "on February 7, 2014, the dogs killed Richey while she was on her own property." [See: *Schneider v. Kumpf*, 2016-Ohio-5161, p. 59.]

Following Richey's untimely death, Barbara Schneider, the administrator of her estate, filed a wrongful death action and personal injury lawsuit against the Board of Commissioners of Montgomery County, Montgomery County, the ARC, Kumpf, and various other unnamed persons. Subsequently, she amended the complaint, naming only Kumpf as the defendant. Schneider laid out the facts in the case and alleged that Kumpf was liable for reckless conduct in changing the basic philosophy of the ARC from enforcement to education. She also argued that he failed to follow the regulatory dog laws of Ohio. Further, she claimed that Kump was reckless in not taking action that would have labeled the dogs as dangerous, even though he had numerous reports of their dangerous nature and threatening behavior. Also Schneider alleged that Kumpf knew the dogs were nuisance but took no action to deal with the issue. Schneider also argued that Kumpf was reckless in failing to issue citations, in failing to impound the dogs, for badly misinterpreting the law, and for putting ineffective procedures into place.

For his part, Kumpf filed a motion to dismiss the entire lawsuit based on the contention that the compliant had failed to state a claim for which relief can be granted. In simple language, Kumpf was saying, "You can't sue me for that!" His position was based on two very straightforward arguments. First, using a time-worn doctrine known as sovereign immunity, Kumpf claimed that as an agent of the government, he was immune from litigation for actions that he had carried out in his role as dog warden on behalf of the state. Second, he noted that, even if sovereign immunity did not hold up as a defense, no matter, the only people who can be sued for actions carried out by a dog are owners, harborers, and keepers. Since he is clearly none of these, he cannot be sued for the actions of the dogs.

In light of the confusion that exists within the doctrine of sovereign immunity, the trial court refused to dismiss the case based on that argument alone. For a start, the trial court cited an exception that says that despite sovereign immunity, government agents can be still held liable for reckless conduct. Since, given the facts as they stand and without further argument and additional evidence, the court could not conclude that Kumpf's conduct was not reckless, the motion to dismiss the case was overruled. However, the court agreed that only owners, harborers, and keepers can be liable for a dog's action. Therefore, the motion to dismiss was granted. Since Kumpf was not an owner, harborer, or keeper of the dogs in question, the sovereign immunity question was moot, and the lawsuit was, well, over. Schneider disagreed and filed an appeal. The case went next to the Court of Appeals of Ohio, the Second

District, Montgomery County. This is the opinion that was issued by that court.

On appeal, Schneider argued, rather convincingly, that Kumpf was flat-out wrong in his contention that only owners, harborers, and keepers can be held liable for injuries caused by a dog. She then cited multiple cases that demonstrate that there are numerous situations in which liability can be assessed to others, who are not owners, harborers, or keepers. Included in that mix are landlords and other property owners who allow dangerous dogs on the common areas of their property and, thus, fail to keep those common areas reasonably safe for invitees and others legitimately on the land. Moreover, she demonstrated that this is true not only in Ohio, but also in many other jurisdictions throughout the United States.

The court of appeals saw the wisdom of this position and ran through a long list of cases, looking at the various arguments, legal rationales, and decisions by the courts. The final conclusion of the court was that such cases depend so much on the facts in a given situation that it was not possible to dismiss a case like this one based only on that flat-out rule that only owners, harborers, and keepers are liable for injuries caused by dogs.

The court then, albeit in a roundabout way, moved on to the issue of sovereign immunity. Citing cases from Tennessee and Washington, the court hinted at the possibility that sovereign immunity did not apply in this case because the actions about which the plaintiff complains may not be protected by that doctrine. The court explained that sovereign immunity is based on the principle that says that public employees are immune from lawsuits when the alleged breach involves a "duty owed to the public at large." The rationale here is that public employees must be empowered to do what they have a duty to do as part of their job and should not be held back by a concern that they might make a mistake. In other words, public employees must be assured that they will not be sued if they make an error while on the job. This is know as the public duty doctrine.

There are exceptions to this doctrine, however. One is the failure to enforce exception. This exception emerges when the governmental agents have a duty to enforce a particular law, generally one set up by a statute, and then fail to follow through on that duty. The elements look like this: "Under this exception, 'a government's obligation to the general public becomes a legal duty owed to the plaintiff when (1) government agents who are responsible for enforcing statutory requirements actually know of a statutory violation, (2) the government agents have a statutory duty to take corrective action but fail to do so, and (3) the plaintiff is within the class the statute intended to protect.'"

Kumpf argued that Ohio does not honor this failure to enforce exception. The court disagreed, noting that while Ohio generally, does not have a failure to enforce exception, that rule can be overtaken when the government agents undertake a special relationship with a member of the public. Once this affirmative act is taken and the public employee has undertaken to create a special relationship with a member of the public, then the public duty defense evaporates to be replaced by the special duty exception. The elements of the special duty exception look like this: "(1) an assumption by the municipality, through promises or actions, of an affirmative duty to act on behalf of the party who was injured; (2) knowledge on the part of the municipality's agents that inaction could lead to harm; (3) some form of direct contact between the municipality's agents and the injured party; and (4) that party's justifiable reliance on the municipality's affirmative undertaking."

Ohio has also adopted another exception to the public duty exception. That exception will not forgive wanton and reckless conduct on the part of public employees. Several questions remained open at this point int the court's opinion. One question emerges from the fact that to assert a valid cause if action against Kumpf, Schneider must demonstrate either that Kumpf has violated a statute that imposes a duty upon him or that under common law, a special duty existed that imposed upon Kumpf an obligation to make certain that Richey was not injured by the two dangerous dogs. We pick up the case with the question of statutory authority

The Court's Opinion

Delivered by Judge Wealbaun–

"Claimants who seek recovery in actions such as the present one based on purely statutory violations must still establish that the statute in question provides for a private right of action." Id. {¶ 75] The pertinent statutes here are contained in R.C. Chap. 955. We have reviewed the entire chapter, and none of the sections explicitly provides for a private cause of action. The issue remains whether a private cause of action is implied.

{¶ 76] To decide if "a private right of action should be inferred from a statute, Ohio courts have relied on a three-part test adapted from the United States Supreme Court decision in Cort v. Ash (1975), 422 U.S. 66, 95 S.Ct. 2080, 45 L.Ed.2d 26." Anderson v. -30 Smith, 196 Ohio App.3d 540, 2011-Ohio-5619, 964 N.E.2d 468, ¶ 10 (10th Dist.), citing Strack v. Westfield Cos., 33 Ohio App.3d 336, 337, 515 N.E.2d 1005 (9th Dist.1986). (Other citations omitted.) This test "examines (1) whether the statute creates a right in favor of the plaintiff, (2) whether there is any indication of legislative intent, explicit or implicit, to create or deny a remedy through private right of action, and (3) whether it is consistent with the underlying purposes of the legislative scheme to infer such a remedy." Id., citing Strack at 337. (Other citation omitted.) Recently, however, the Eighth District Court of Appeals stressed that the United States Supreme Court has gradually narrowed the Cort test by focusing "on the single factor of whether there was a legislative intent to grant a private right of action." (Citations omitted.) Grey v. Walgreen Co., 197 Ohio App.3d 418, 2011-Ohio-6167, 967 N.E.2d 1249, ¶ 8 ...

{¶ 78} Our analysis of Chapter 955 does not indicate legislative intent to create a private right of action. R.C. 955.01 requires dog owners to register their dogs with the county auditor and provide such information like the dogs' breed and ages, and the name and address of the owner. After owners register and pay a fee, the auditor will issue a metal tag for the dog. R.C. 955.08. Dogs found not wearing valid tags are prima facie evidence of lack of registration, and this lack "shall subject any dog found not wearing such a tag to impounding, sale, or destruction." R.C. 955.10.

{¶ 79} R.C. 955.12 provides for employment of county dog wardens and deputies. The statute in effect at the time of Richey's death provided, in pertinent part, that:

The warden and deputies shall make a record of all dogs owned, kept, and harbored in their respective counties. They shall patrol their respective counties and seize and impound on sight all dogs found running at large and all dogs more than three months of age found not wearing a valid registration tag, except any dog that wears a valid registration tag and is: on the premises of its owner, keeper, or harborer, under the reasonable control of its owner or some other person . . . A dog that wears a valid registration tag may be seized on the premises of its owner, keeper, or harborer and impounded only in the event of a natural disaster.

If a dog warden has reason to believe that a dog is being treated inhumanely on the premises of its owner, keeper, or harborer, the warden shall apply to the court of common pleas for the county in which the premises are located for an order to enter the premises, and if necessary, seize the dog. If the court finds probable cause to believe that the dog is being treated inhumanely, it shall issue such an order.

The warden and deputies shall also make . . . weekly reports, in writing, to the board in their respective counties of all dogs seized, impounded, redeemed, and destroyed . . .

Whenever any person files an affidavit in a court of competent jurisdiction that there is a dog running at large that is not kept constantly confined either in a dog kennel registered under this chapter or one licensed under Chapter 956. of the Revised Code or on the premises of an institution or organization of the type described in section 955.16 of the Revised Code or that a dog is kept or harbored in the warden's jurisdiction without being registered as required by law, the court shall immediately order the warden to seize and impound the dog. Thereupon the warden shall immediately seize and impound the dog complained of. The warden shall give immediate notice by certified mail to the owner, keeper, or harborer of the dog seized and impounded by the warden, if the owner, keeper, or harborer can be determined from the current year's registration list maintained by the warden and the county auditor of the county where the dog is registered, that the dog has been impounded and that, unless the dog is redeemed within fourteen days of the date of the notice, it may thereafter be sold or destroyed according to law . . .

{¶ 80} R.C. 955.222(B) further provides that: If a person who is authorized to enforce this chapter has reasonable cause to believe that a dog in the person's jurisdiction is a nuisance dog, dangerous dog, or vicious dog, the person shall notify the owner, keeper, or harborer of that dog, by certified mail or in person, of both of the following:

(1) That the person has designated the dog a nuisance dog, dangerous dog, or vicious dog, as applicable;

(2) That the owner, keeper, or harborer of the dog may request a hearing regarding the designation in accordance with this section. The notice shall include instructions for filing a request for a hearing in the county in which the dog's owner, keeper, or harborer resides.

{¶ 81} If the owner asks for a hearing, the court may allow the dog to be kept in the owner's possession, but the dog is required to be confined or restrained pending final appeal in connection with the requirements in R.C. 955.22(D) that apply to dangerous dogs. R.C. 955.222(D).3 If a dog is finally determined to be a dangerous dog, the owner will be required to follow certain provisions regarding transfer of ownership of the dog, confinement of the dog, and procurement of liability insurance. R.C. 955.222(E).

{¶ 82} A dangerous dog is defined by R.C. 955.11(A)(1)(a) as: "a dog that, without provocation, and subject to division (A)(1)(b) of this section, has done any of the following: (i) Caused injury, other than killing or serious injury, to any person; (ii) Killed another dog; (iii) Been the subject of a third or subsequent violation of division (C) of section 955.22 of the Revised Code."

{¶ 83} R.C. 955.22(C) provides that:

Except when a dog is lawfully engaged in hunting and accompanied by the owner, keeper, harborer, or handler of the dog, no owner, keeper, or harborer of any dog shall fail at any time to do either of the following:

(1) Keep the dog physically confined or restrained upon the premises of the owner, keeper, or harborer by a leash, tether, adequate fence, supervision, or secure enclosure to prevent escape;

(2) Keep the dog under the reasonable control of some person.

{¶ 84} Finally, R.C. 955.23 provides that "No county dog warden shall willfully fail to perform his duties under section 955.12 of the Revised Code or other duties required of dog wardens." On its face, this section seems to imply a private cause of action. However, the section is derived from G.C. 5652-14b, which was initially enacted in 1927. See H.B. 164, 112 Ohio Laws 347. At the time of its enactment, G.C. 5652-14g stated that: "The county dog warden of any county who willfully fails to perform his duties under section 5652-7 or other duties required of dog wardens by law shall upon conviction thereof be fined not less than twenty-five dollars nor more than fifty dollars." Id. at 352.

{¶ 85} G.C. 5652-14b was subsequently renumbered as R.C. 955.23, and it no longer contains the language about a fine and conviction. Nonetheless, R.C. 955.99(B) states that "[w]hoever violates section 955.10, 955.23, 955.24, or 955.25 of the Revised Code is guilty of a minor misdemeanor." Because the criminal penalty remains, a civil remedy is not implied by R.C. 955.23; to the contrary, the statutory scheme contemplates criminal prosecution of dog wardens for willful failure to perform their duties.

{¶ 86} Under the circumstances, we must conclude that R.C. Chap. 955 does not impliedly provide a private right of action for violation of the dog warden's statutory duties. This is consistent with a decision that Kumpf relied on in the trial court, i.e., Marshall v. Kennedy, 7th Dist. Belmont No. 86-B-3, 1988 WL 6518 (Jan. 21, 1988). In Marshall, the plaintiff filed an action against dogs owners, a dog warden, and the county commissioners, alleging that dogs came from private property onto a county highway and attacked the plaintiff. Id. at *1. The dog warden was sued for failure to carry out his duties. Id. However, the court of appeals concluded that R.C. 955.12 did not impose liability upon the dog warden or deputy dog warden for injuries allegedly caused by a dog "running at large." Id.4

{¶ 87} Furthermore, the Supreme Court of Ohio has stressed that the state is protected by conventional negligence principles from "becoming the de facto guarantor of every injury somehow attributable to the actions of a state tortfeasor." Wallace, 96 Ohio St.3d 266, 2002-Ohio-4210, 773 N.E.2d 1018, at ¶ 38. In Wallace, the court had concluded that the public duty rule was incompatible with the State's consent under R.C. 2743.02(A)(1) to have suits in the Court of Claims determined in accordance with suits between private parties. Id. at paragraph one of the syllabus. During its discussion of this issue, the court pointed out that its jurisprudence already contained safeguards that satisfy the public policy concerns of the public duty rule. First, the State already had some protection for discretionary acts. Id. at ¶ 36. In addition, "actions that do not sound in tort but seek recovery purely for a statutory violation will not necessarily lie against the state – particularly if the statute in question provides no private right of action." Id. at ¶ 37. This is the paragraph in Wallace cited by Graves, when the Supreme Court of Ohio mentioned that claimants who seek recovery "based on purely statutory violations must still establish that the statute in question provides for a private right of action." Graves, 124 Ohio St.3d 339, 2010-Ohio-168, 922 N.E.2d 201, at ¶ 24.

{¶ 88} To the extent that Schneider's action is not based on purely statutory violations like failure to classify the dogs as dangerous, Wallace also indicated that where tort liability is concerned:

A state defendant, just like any private defendant, remains protected by traditional tort concepts of duty, including foreseeability and pertinent public-policy considerations. Leake v. Cain, 720 P.2d [152] at 160 [Colo. 1986]; Chambers-Castanes v. King Cty. (1983), 100 Wash.2d 275, 292, 669 P.2d 451 (Utter, J., concurring in the result). Moreover, our tort law already requires a special relationship in order to satisfy the duty element in certain types of negligence actions, such as actions based on failure to act or failure to control the conduct of a third person. See Littleton v. Good Samaritan Hosp. & Health Ctr. (1988), 39 Ohio St.3d 86, 92, 529 N.E.2d 449; Hill v. Sonitrol of Southwestern Ohio, Inc. (1988), 36 Ohio St.3d 36, 39, 521 N.E.2d 780; see, also, 2 Restatement of the Law 2d, Torts (1965) 116-122, Sections 314-315. Thus, when a duty is neither imposed by statute nor undertaken by an instrumentality of the state, the state defendant is already insulated from liability based on a failure to act. (Footnote omitted.) Id. at ¶ 38

{¶ 89} The trial court mentioned the absence of a "special relation" between Richey and Kumpf when the court was distinguishing some cases that had found potential liability involving trailer-park owners who were not owners, keepers, or harborers of dogs. See Doc. #29, Decision, Order and Entry Granting Motion to Dismiss of Defendant Mark Kumpf, p. 15, discussing Bundy v. Sky Meadows Trailer Park, 12th Dist. Butler No. CA89 01-002, 1989 WL 125379, *1 (Oct. 23, 1989).

{¶ 90} Schneider contends that this point was not argued in the trial court and cannot be raised on appeal.

We disagree that this point was not raised. In the first place, Schneider raised the Bundy case in replying to Kumpf's motion to dismiss. See Doc. #25, Plaintiff's Memorandum in Opposition to Defendant's Motion to Dismiss, pp.14-15 and 34. In addition, Schneider also cited the Graves case in this memorandum, arguing that the decision in Marshall was distinguishable, because Graves had held that the special duty exception to sovereign immunity would not apply in cases involving reckless conduct by employees of political subdivisions. Id. at pp. 34-35, citing Graves, 124 Ohio St.3d 339, 2010-Ohio-168, 922 N.E.2d 201.

{¶ 91} Moreover, in responding to Schneider's memorandum, Kumpf noted that Schneider was arguing that he had a duty to Richey, and disputed this fact. See Doc. # 28, Defendant Mark Kumpf's Reply to Plaintiff's Memorandum in Opposition to Motion to Dismiss, p. 3. Kumpf also argued that R.C. 955.12 did not impose a duty on dog wardens for dogs running at large, and with respect to sovereign immunity, that Schneider could not show that Kumpf violated any statutory duty. Id. at pp. 6 and 7. The trial court responded to these arguments by discussing Bundy. Doc. #29 at p. 15.

{¶ 92} In Bundy, a trailer park had rules providing that animals must not run atlarge, and the park owners also knew that the dog in question had an affinity for roaming and biting small children. Bundy, 12th Dist. Butler No. CA89-01-002, 1989 WL 125379,b at 2. The court concluded that for purposes of 2 Restatement of the Law 2d, Torts, Section 315 (1965), a special relationship existed because the park knew of the dog's vicious tendencies and had rules prohibiting animals from running at large. Id. at 3. The court, therefore, concluded that the trial court erred in granting summary judgment for the trailer park owner on the plaintiff's negligence claim.

{¶ 93} In the case before us, Kumpf's alleged tortious actions consist of omissions and failure to act to prevent injury to Richey. 2 Restatement of the Law 2d, Torts, Section 302 (1965), provides that:

A negligent act or omission may be one which involves an unreasonable risk of harm to another through either

(a) the continuous operation of a force started or continued by the act or omission, or

(b) the foreseeable action of the other, a third person, an animal, or a force of nature.

{¶ 94} Comment a to Section 302 further states that: This Section is concerned only with the negligent character of the actor's conduct, and not with his duty to avoid the unreasonable risk. In general, anyone who does an affirmative act is under a duty to others to exercise the care of a reasonable man to protect them against an unreasonable risk of harm to them arising out of the act. The duties of one who merely omits to act are more restricted, and in general are confined to situations where there is a special relation between the actor and the other which gives rise to the duty. As to the distinction between act and omission, or "misfeasance" and "non-feasance," see § 314 and Comments. If the actor is under no duty to the other to act, his failure to do so may be negligent conduct within the rule stated in this Section, but it does not subject him to liability, because of the absence of duty. (Emphasis added.)

{¶ 95} 2 Restatement of the Law 2d, Torts, Section 314 (1965), also provides that "[t]he actor's realization that action on his part is necessary for another's aid or protection does not of itself impose upon him a duty to take such action."

{¶ 96} Although Chase, 971 S.W.2d 380, involved the application of the "special duty" exception to the public duty doctrine, the court's comments are somewhat instructive. In that case, the court concluded that the special duty exception applied, and the City of Memphis, therefore, was liable for the plaintiff's death by mauling, because the animal shelter and its employee "affirmatively undertook to protect the plaintiff. They issued a letter to Ms. Stidham indicating that any fencing deficiencies would be corrected. The letter further indicated that the dogs would be enrolled into obedience training. The letter indicated that failure to comply with the Animal Shelter's order would result in the animals' immediate seizure. Ms. Stidham did not appeal the order and relied upon the undertaking of Lee and the Shelter to remedy the situation." Id. at 385.

{¶ 97} In the case before us, the allegations in the complaint fall somewhat short of alleging the same type of affirmative actions as in Chase. Upon consideration, however, we conclude that this issue is more appropriately suited for resolution at the trial court level, perhaps on summary judgment, particularly since the parties did not fully discuss this issue in the specific context of whether Kumpf's actions, fairly read, could fulfill the requirements for finding the existence of a special relationship, and, therefore, a duty for purposes of tort liability.

{¶ 98} Furthermore, we agree with the trial court that a trier of fact could reasonably find that Kumpf's actions were reckless, at least based on the allegations in the complaint. Doc. #29, Decision, Order and Entry Granting Motion to Dismiss of Defendant Mark Kumpf, p. 14. As a result, we conclude that Schneider is entitled to conduct discovery on the issue of whether Kumpf owed Richey a duty, in order to give the trial court a full factual basis for ruling on the issue.

[¶ 99] Accordingly, Schneider's sole assignment of error is sustained. We disagree with the trial court that potential liability is restricted to owners, keepers, or harborers. However, the issue of whether Kumpf owed a duty to Richey requires further exploration.

III. Conclusion

[¶ 100] Schneider's sole assignment of error having been sustained, the judgment of the trial court is reversed, and this cause is remanded for further proceedings.

Questions for Analysis

1. In our study of ethics, we examined three theories of ethical conduct: utilitarianism, social contract ethics, and rationalism. Using what you know about these three theories, construct a brief argument demonstrating how the dog owner's behavior in this case violates each theory. Explain.

2. Chapter 1 also discusses the government's duty to keep citizens safe and secure. We usually think about this principle of protection in relation to the federal government and national security. This case shows that the duty of safety and security can also be violated at the local level. In what ways did the local government fail to keep its citizens safe in this case? Explain.

3. In Chapter 2, we discussed the sources of the law. This case focuses primarily on statutory law and case law. Does the defendant's liability in this case depend on whether a cause of action exists under statutory law, case law, or both? Explain.

4. In Chapter 3, we learned about civil procedure. The defendant in this case at the trial level asked the judge to dismiss the case for failure to state a claim for which relief can be granted. What is this motion called in the federal courts? The trial court granted the motion and the appellate court overturned the ruling of the trial court. What can the defendant do about this, if anything? Explain.

5. One of the reasons that the appellate court decided to allow the case to go back the trial court is so that the plaintiff can engage in discovery. What is the plaintiff looking to "discover" in this case? Also, what discovery tools might she use in this case? Explain.

6. In Chapter 4, we talked about the various forms of alternative dispute resolution (ADR). Which of the ADR techniques might have been used in settling the dispute in *Schneider v. Kumpf*? Explain.

7. In Chapter 5, the criminal law chapter, we discussed the various levels of criminal liability, the elements of a crime, and the the definitions of a few real-time crimes. This case is a civil suit, not a criminal prosecution. However, we can still speculate on what might happen in a criminal case. Can the facts here support a charge of involuntary manslaughter against the owners of the dog(s)? Explain.

8. The case against Kumpf seems to be based on negligence. What are the elements of negligence that Schneider needs to prove to hold Kumpf liable for negligence? What is the burden of proof? Explain

9. The concept of a special relationship is often at issue in a negligence case. How does the principle of special relationships fit into this case? Explain.

10. The case of *Schneider v. Kumpf* is a wrongful death lawsuit. What is a wrongful death lawsuit? Who brings a wrongful death lawsuit? Could this suit have also been brought under a survival statute? Why was the case not filed under a survival statute? Explain.

Design Elements: The Opening Case: ©Sharpstock/Alamy; A Classic Case: ©Evlakhov Valeriy/Shutterstock

©Bacho/Shutterstock

Part Two
Contract Law

Chapter 7	The Essentials of Contract Law	Chapter 11	Written Contracts and Cyber-Commerce
Chapter 8	Offer, Acceptance, and Mutual Assent	Chapter 12	Third Parties, Discharge, and Remedies

Chapter 7

The Essentials of Contract Law

7-1 The History of Contract Law
Mercantile Law, Ancient Rome, Capitalism, and the Church • The Characteristics of the Law Merchant • The Restatement of the Law of Contracts

7-2 The Multidimensional Nature of Contract Law
The Elements of a Contract • The Objectives of Contract Law • Multidimensional Principles of Contract Law

7-3 Contractual Characteristics
Valid, Void, Voidable, and Unenforceable Contracts • Unilateral and Bilateral Contracts • Express and Implied Contracts • Informal and Formal Contracts • Executory and Executed Contracts

THE OPENING CASE *Round 1*
Lynyrd Skynyrd, a Plane Crash, and a Blood Oath

At first everything was going well for the rock group known as Lynyrd Skynyrd. They had secured a contract with a record company called MCA Records Inc., and their records were selling fairly well. In fact, things looked so bright and promising that the members of the band decided to form their own corporation. They named the company Lynyrd Skynyrd Productions Inc (LSPI) and, among other things, designated it as the holder of their trade name, trademarks, and service marks. The shareholders agreement was signed by Gary Rossington, Ronnie Van Zant, Leon Wilkinson, William Powell, and Allen Collins. From that moment on, for the next two years, the band experienced nothing but success. They produced six studio albums and one album of a live performance. Moreover, their albums sold in the millions. They were literally on top of the world. Then, suddenly, and without warning, everything changed. On October 20, 1977, the plane that the band was traveling on during a tour crashed, killing Van Zant and a new guitarist named Steven Gaines. Several months after the fatal crash, Van Zant's widow, Judith, along with Rossington, Collins, and the widow of Steven Gaines, so as not to profit from the tragedy, entered an unwritten contract, agreeing to never use the name Lynyrd Skynyrd again in any way associated with the legacy of the band. They were so deadly serious about the agreement that they called it a blood oath (although the technical legal name would be a "non-use contract"). On March 4, 1978, at a shareholder's meeting of LSPI, the agreement was entered into the minutes and, at the same meeting, a written contract was drawn up and signed. The agreement was referred to as a revision of the shareholder's agreement of September 9, 1975.

One essential part of the agreement was a clause that noted that only material created for the band before Van Zant's death could be used along with the name Lynyrd Skynyrd. Everyone followed the agreement for a decade. The members of the band did perform, but only using other names, never Lynyrd Skynyrd. Van Zant's widow, Judith (later remarried and named Judith Van Zant Grondin), received many offers from book publishers and movie producers to cash in on the tragedy but, keeping her part of the 1978 blood oath, she refused every time. Now, interestingly enough, throughout all this time, recordings made by Lynryd Skynyrd, including three previous albums and one new compilation, were being put out by MCA, and the sale of that material made a large amount of money. Judith knew about the three albums but nothing about the compilation. In 1987, a Tribute Tour was planned. To accomplish the tour, LSPI formed a subsidiary called Tribute Inc. Two agreements were drawn up. The first agreement declared that Tribute Inc. would conduct the tour, produce a video, and sell merchandise (T-shirts and so on). The second agreement was a licensing agreement to perform Lynyrd Skynyrd material and to use the Lynyrd Skynyrd name. MCA was also contracted to produce a live album. Judith was pressured into going along with the tour but refused to go along with the licensing agreement. According to Judith, she repeatedly rejected any and all drafts of the licensing agreement that came her way. She was especially sensitive to any agreement that included permission to use the name Lynyrd Skynyrd. Despite this, the 1987 tour went ahead using the Lynyrd Skynyrd name. A second tour was arranged for 1988. Judith again protested. She demanded that the 1988 tour, as a violation of the non-use agreement, be canceled. She was told that it would be. This statement turned out to be somewhat misleading because the tour went forward. That was when Judith brought this lawsuit, alleging a breach of contract (the non-use agreement, also known as the original blood oath) and asking for an injunction to stop the tour.

This case highlights a number of aspects of contract law. Was mutual assent clearly expressed when the original non-use agreement was made? What served as consideration in the making of the blood oath? Was it necessary to reduce the blood oath to writing, and was that writing adequate? (*Note:* The case includes other issues, such as whether Judith was a party to the contract or a third-party beneficiary and whether there had been a violation of the Lanham Act in relation to the commercial use of the name Lynyrd Skynyrd. Since these issues are not immediately relevant here, they are not discussed in this chapter. Stay tuned, though. The issues discussed in this case never go away—ever.) [See: *Grondin v. Rossington,* 690 F. Supp. 200 (1988), United States District Court, Southern Division of New York.]

Opening Case Questions

1. What are the four elements of a contract? Does any element seem to be missing in this case? Explain.
2. Did the non-use agreement have to be in writing to be enforced? Explain.
3. What served as consideration in the non-use agreement Explain.
4. Can a plaintiff ask for and receive equitable relief in a breach of contract lawsuit like this one, or are contract lawsuits limited to money damages? Explain.
5. What are the characteristics of a contract? What contractual characteristics does the non-use agreement possess, if any? Explain.

Source: See: *Grondin v. Rossington,* 690 F. Supp. 200 (1988), United States District Court, Southern Division of New York.

 Learning Objectives

1. Define *contract*.
2. Explain the origin of the law merchant.
3. Discuss the relationship between common law and the law merchant.
4. Identify the four elements of a contract.
5. Explain the objectives of contract law.
6. Explain the place of the UCC in contract law.
7. Distinguish contracts from other agreements.
8. Explain the role of privity and agency in contract law.
9. List the contracts that must be in writing to be enforceable.
10. List the characteristics of a contract.

7-1 The History of Contract Law

A **contract** is an agreement between two or more competent parties, based on mutual promises and an exchange of things of value, to do or refrain from doing some particular thing that is neither illegal nor impossible. The agreement results in an obligation or a duty that can be enforced in a court of law. Most people understand the basic nature of a contract as a process of give and take. There are rules, however, that govern how those agreements are made, how they are carried out, how they end, and how disputes are resolved when someone yells, "no fair!" Before delving into these basic principles, however, we will pause for a moment to consider how these rules originated.

Mercantile Law, Ancient Rome, Capitalism, and the Church

The history of contract law is intertwined with the parallel development of Western mercantile law, often referred to alternately as the law merchant and *lex mercatoria*. The law merchant outlines the laws and the procedures followed by merchants in commercial transactions. As Harold J. Berman explains in his landmark study, *Law and Revolution: The Formation of the Western Legal Tradition*, mercantile law originated among the merchants themselves who needed a formalized way to deal with one another when disputes arose. According to Berman, the law merchant saw a sudden and unprecedented burst of development between the 11th and the 13th centuries in Western Europe, both on the continent and across the channel in England. This is not to say that there was no commercial law before the 11th century. Between the fall of Rome and the rise of the mercantile city-states of the late Middle Ages, which is to say during the second half of the first millennium, commercial transactions were limited to seasonal festivals, small town marketplaces, and coastal cities. The law that governed these transactions emerged from rules within the ancient traditions of the Justinian Code of the old Roman Empire. All of this began to change with a series of agricultural innovations and a sudden European population explosion. [See: Harold J. Berman, *Law and Revolution: The Formation of the Western Legal Tradition* (Cambridge, MA: Harvard University Press, 1983), pp. 333–41.]

Agriculture, Technology, and Population
Ancient Roman law was adequate at the time because commerce itself was limited during that era. The population of Europe barely topped 20 million at the end of the first millennium, and most people lived out their lives in the small villages and manors that dotted the countryside. Several irresistible complex adaptive systems (CASs) changed all of that in the 11th century. A CAS is a network of interacting conditions that reinforce one another while, at the same time, adjust to change from agents outside and inside the system. The purpose of a CAS is the survival and improvement of the system itself. Natural examples of CASs would include beehives, anthills, and the neural network of the human brain. All CASs share at least five elements. First, every CAS operates as a result of the interaction of a variety of agents (the economy, for instance, includes producers, consumers, marketers, wholesalers, retailers, shippers, investors, brokers, bankers, salespeople, and so on.) Second, in a CAS there is no central controlling agent, no single all powerful "boss" as it were. Instead, control is dispersed among various actors (think of the checks and balances system here). So no one tells anyone else what to do, even when they think that is what they are doing. Directions may be given, orders sent out, but the actors within the system will ignore, misplace, or misconstrue those orders and those directions not for personal reasons, but because those orders and directions compromise the continued existence of the entire system. Third, complex adaptive systems are just that—complex. This means that multiple levels of organization work within the system, and while those levels sometimes support one another, they just as frequently work at cross purposes, giving them the appearance of consciously opposing one another. Fourth, the longer a CAS lasts, the more change it encounters and the more adept it becomes at dealing with those changes. Finally, as part of the process, a CAS can infer the direction of future events and can adjust to those changing events. [See M. Mitchell Waldrop, *Complexity: The Emerging Science on the Edge of Chaos* (New York: Simon and Schuster, 1992, pp. 145–147. *Note:* Waldrop provides six elements; we have eliminated the last, "embedded niches."]

Recall that every complex adaptive system operates through the interaction of various agents. In the Middle Ages, these agents would include the merchants, their customers, festivals, marketplaces, royalty, the nobility, the Church, clergymen, customers, farmers, sailors, city-states, sailors, craftsmen and their apprentices, guilds, suppliers, peasants, and so on. Also remember that in a CAS, there is no controlling agent, no single all powerful "boss" as it were. In the Middle Ages, there were some very powerful rulers, including the king, his feudal lords, and the merchants. However, the one power that everyone was beholden to was the Roman Catholic Church. Within the Church, there was one controlling agent and a concentration of power, so it could be argued that in this period, the complex adaptive system was not a true complex adaptive system (a pseudo-CAS?). Still, the power of the Church was a bit unpredictable, given communication and transportation limitations. Nevertheless, as we shall see shortly, the Church still managed to maintain more control than might be expected and, oddly, that turned out to be an advantage. Recall also that complex adaptive systems always remain complex. This means that these multiple levels of organization—the church, guilds merchants, farmers, nobility, sailors, craftsmen, and so on—sometimes supported one another and sometimes did not, thus, complicating matters further. Remember also that the longer a complex adaptive remains in operation, the more change results. Last of all, do not forget that as part of the process, a CAS often anticipates future developments and alters some practices as those branch points approach.

The technological CAS at operation in the Middle Ages led to developments in agriculture (including a number of important inventions such as a new type of horse collar, a heavy plow, horseshoes, fish farming, three-field crop rotation, the overshot waterwheel, and the wind-powered post mill) that led to crop surpluses that could be sold for a profit; changes in manor law freed many peasants, who turned to selling as a livelihood; and Europe saw an unprecedented population explosion. The technological CAS overlapped and intersected with the economic CAS to empower a new group of professional sellers who developed their own system of laws (itself a new CAS) over a relatively short time. That CAS came to be called *mercantile law* or the *law merchant*. [See: Berman, pp. 333-41. See also Rodney Stark, *The Victory of Reason: How Christianity Led to Freedom, Capitalism, and Western Science* (New York: Random House, 2005), pp. 38-44.] In his book, *The Victory of Reason*, Rodney Stark notes that despite popular views to the contrary, an enormous amount of progress occurred during the Middle Ages, including the inventions listed earlier. [See: Stark, pp. 38-44.]

Development of the Law Merchant Mercantile law is also closely associated with the development of capitalism. **Capitalism** is a complex adaptive system of overlapping economic agents that operates on the basis of competition and a free market that responds to the movement of supply and demand. Contrary to the thesis proposed by Max Weber in *The Protestant Ethic: The Spirit of Capitalism*, European capitalism did not begin with the Protestant Reformation in the 16th century, but in the 11th and 12th centuries, some 400 years before Martin Luther nailed his famous 95 theses on the cathedral door in Wittenberg, Germany. Moreover, one of the driving forces behind the growth of capitalism was the Roman Catholic Church. The medieval Church had the ability to redirect capitalism as it did because, as noted earlier, the Roman Catholic Church lacked two essential elements of a pure CAS: no central leader and dispersed power bases. The medieval Church had (1) a strong central controlling agent and (2) a concentration, rather than a dispersal, of power among various actors. Much of this power was illusory, but the illusion, supported by its moral authority (inspired by the persuasive power of eternity), was more than enough within that culture. Moreover, this centralized moral authority turned out to be an advantage. Thus, the Church helped provide a rational and ethical foundation for the principles and procedures that guided the activities of merchants in their communities, in their courts, and in the making of their contracts. The Church, which is directed by a central powerful leader, refused to condemn commercial activity. Instead, it monitored how those activities were carried out. In short, the Church encouraged this new class of sellers to establish guilds that followed the law of the Church, a legal tradition that is generally referred to as **canon law**. The Church also insisted that these emerging businessmen never engage in deceit or dishonesty and always follow a good-faith approach to contract development. As long as they followed these basic precepts, the Church reassured the members of the new and expanding class of professional sellers that there was nothing inherently wrong with their chosen profession. [See: Berman, pp. 336–41; and Stark, p. xi. See also Henri Sée, *Modern Capitalism: Its Origin and Evolutions*, trans. Homer B. Vanderblue and Georges F. Doriot (New York: Adelphi Co. 1928), pp. 7–13; and Max Weber, *The Protestant Ethic: The Spirit of Capitalism* (Mineola, NY: Dover, 2003).]

A QUESTION OF ETHICS

Contract law, whether it evolved through the law merchant, the common law, or a combination of both, operates as a complex adaptive system (CAS). Each CAS emerges from a network of interacting conditions that reinforce one another while, at the same time, adjusting to change from agents outside and inside the system. Complex adaptive systems, however, do not operate within a vacuum. On the contrary, they are an integral part of a vast sea of overlapping complex systems that interact and sometimes compete with one another. The legal system; the political system; the economic system; as well as internal subsystems such the military, academia, the stock exchange, and so on, are all examples of CASs. Underlying all of these processes is the distribution of global wealth that both empowers the CASs and serves as a motive to ignite forward movement. However, the distribution of wealth is not itself a CAS; rather, it serves as the outcome of competing and cooperative CASs. At times, the competing CASs may ignite a flashpoint that causes their paths to swerve in another direction. On June 28, 1914, for example, the assassination of the Archduke Ferdinand served as a flashpoint that caused a swerve in a series of overlapping CASs (politics, the law, the economies of Europe, the military, and so on) that ultimately led to a global conflict and an economic shift that, for a while, at least, led to a lessening of this inequality.

The distribution of wealth cannot be understood absent an understanding of the interaction of two tightly interwoven CASs—the political system and the legal system. It is the interaction of these two CASs that widens or closes the inequality gap that always characterizes the flow of wealth distribution, along with the *elan vital* of Henri Bergson (*power* is a better word, but the word "power" is loaded with negative subtexts that militate against its use) that permits and, at times, forces those with wealth to hold on to it, multiply their share, or redistribute it among the economically deprived segments of the system. That is the heart of the ethical question put forward here.

Two recent books have proposed similar explanations for the unequal distribution of global wealth. In his book *Capital in the Twenty-First Century*, Thomas Piketty proposes that the unequal distribution of global wealth is empowered by the tendency of socioeconomic forces to diverge because (1) those with wealth, the 1 percent, have the power to use their capital to create more capital, and (2) the annual rate of return on capital (dividends, rents, profits, interest, and so on) climbs faster than the growth rate of the economy itself (the $r > g$ factor). Similarly, Daron Acemoglu and James Robinson, in *Why Nations Fail*, contend that those in power positions at the national and international level will always use their power to organize society in ways that increase their own wealth. In contrast, as noted earlier, during the Middle Ages, the economic activity of the 1 percent was directed by the Catholic Church. The ethical question then becomes: Should the Church, or perhaps religion in general, be given a stronger voice in the political and economic arena to help redirect and perhaps even equalize the distribution of wealth? Be careful as you consider this issue. Remember this is a question of ethics, not a question of pragmatism or practicality! [See: Daron Acemoglu and James Robinson, *Why Nations Fail* (New York: Crown, 2012); and Thomas Piketty, *Capital in the Twenty-First Century* (Cambridge: Harvard University Press, 2014).]

Source: See: Daron Acemoglu and James Robinson, *Why Nations Fail* (New York: Crown, 2012); Thomas Piketty, *Capital in the Twenty-First Century* (Cambridge: Harvard University Press, 2014).

The Characteristics of the Law Merchant

With the Roman Catholic Church supplying political and social support, with canon law providing a moral framework, and with practicality guiding their activities over a 300-year period, this new class of businessmen developed a body of effective commercial law. Berman tells us that this new system was distinguished by six characteristics: involvement, neutrality, universality, mutuality, integration, and evolution.

Involvement and Law Merchant *Involvement* requires that those affected by the law participate in its making and its execution. According to Berman, from the outset merchants were involved in the establishment and the operation of the courts that adjudicated disputes involving contracts and other commercial disagreements, such as those that might question the authenticity of negotiable instruments. Involvement meant that, as a system, the law merchant, like the Roman Catholic Church, had (1) a strong central controlling agent and (2) a concentration, rather than a dispersal, of power among various actors. This allowed the law merchant to direct, at least to a certain degree, the other characteristics of *neutrality*, *universality*, *mutuality*, *integration*, and *evolution*. Specifically, the courts held in European markets and fairs were run by businessmen who were elected to act as judges. The courts established by the guilds were run by the elected guild leaders, who often hand-picked guild members to assist in deciding certain disputes. Some territories also developed staple courts that dealt with cases involving the primary product or "staple" of a certain town or village. The courts in the Italian city-states such as Milan also elected merchants to hear disputes involving contract and other commercial transactions. Many of the coastal cities created their own local courts, sometimes referred to as admiralty courts, to handle commercial disputes involving goods carried as cargo by the ships that docked at those ports. [See: Berman, pp. 346–48.]

Neutrality of the Law Merchant The law merchant was made up of a fairly neutral system of laws and procedures. *Neutrality* characterizes any system of laws that is consistently applied in the same evenhanded way, no matter who the antagonists might be. The law was developed in the festivals, marketplaces, and coastal cities of Europe by practical men who saw the value of recording their procedures and principles in writing so that commercial activities, financial transactions, and dispute settlements could be carried out in a customary, predictable, and evenhanded way. The legal treatises and codebooks that resulted covered the making of negotiable instruments, the execution of contracts, and the procedures used in the mercantile courts. The actual process of writing these things down was authorized and supported by the ruling classes, especially those in the merchant cities of Genoa, Milan, and Pisa, and by the birth of a class of professional notaries, whose job it was to write down contracts and draft negotiable instruments, which, by virtue of this process, were lawful, valid, and enforceable. [See: Berman, pp. 341, 355.]

Universality and the Law Merchant *Universal* laws are those that apply to everyone regardless of their social status or their place of origin. The universal applicability of the law merchant was made necessary by the global nature of trade in the late Middle Ages. The city-states of Europe hosted international fairs and the coastal cities became permanent centers for international trade. Towns and coastal cities began to adhere to the law merchant rather than their local laws, which tended to be prejudiced against foreigners. In *Law and Revolution*, Berman tells us that, as the influence of the central government began to grow, some rulers agreed to incorporate the law merchant into their national documents, such as the *Magna Carta* in 1215, which contains a clause that specifically grants safe passage to foreign merchants in England. Other rulers, notably those in Italy, entered formal agreements that guaranteed that the law merchant would be used in settling any contract disagreements that might involve their people. [See: Berman, pp. 342-44.] Weber agrees with Berman that a successful capitalist system depends upon the establishment of a legal system with formal rules that emerge from a rational process. [See: Weber, p. 25.] Moreover, Henri Sée concurs that the international character of trade gave birth to modern capitalism [See: Sée, pp. 25, 29-30.]

Mutuality and the Law Merchant The concept of *mutuality* or *reciprocity* in the law merchant is the notion that commercial arrangements always involve a process of evenhanded cooperation among the parties. Mutuality in the law merchant emerged organically from within the commercial culture, which had at its foundation a belief in reciprocity. Moreover, Berman tells us that the principle of reciprocity insisted on mutuality at two levels. First, parties to any commercial transaction were expressly forbidden to cheat, lie, or trick one another. Second, all commercial transactions had to be fair to each party. This principle outlawed contracts that involved outrageous prices and those that took advantage of a party's weakened position. [See: Berman, pp. 344-46.] Of course, Weber reminds us that there is a practical foundation for the principle of reciprocity as there are for all such virtues. Honesty, he reports, has its value, if only because it will earn good credit for trustworthy merchants. [See: Weber, p. 52.] Does the utilitarian nature of reciprocity make it wrong? No. However, it does make the pursuit of reciprocity a bit less romantic.

Integration of the Law Merchant with Common Law The characteristic of *integration* permits a system to assimilate its major elements into a common core of cooperative working parts all of which contribute to the survival of the whole. The integration of mercantile law into the diverse legal traditions in Europe was especially difficult in England where a strong common law tradition had developed during the late Middle Ages. As noted in Chapter 2, common law was established in England as a way to bring all English law together into a single, consistent, comprehensive system. This program put the law merchant and the merchants who administered that law on a collision course with common law and with common law lawyers and judges. Although such collisions did occur from time to time, ultimately the law merchant was integrated into common law and the two evolved together. The first merchant courts in England were established in the 11th century as part of every royal charter that legalized a local fair. These **fair courts** (also known as **pie powder courts** because of the dusty feet, or *pie poudre*, of the merchants who took part in the proceedings) were empowered to hear cases involving commercial disputes, and since the juries were inevitably made up of merchants, the law merchant was used to adjudicate the cases. The fair courts lost their power with the creation of staple courts under the Ordinance of the Staple of 1353. **Staple courts** heard cases that involved certain set commodities. They were run by mayors who were forced to learn and apply mercantile law. This worked well for about two centuries. Then in the 16th century, the staple courts were taken over by the judges of the King's Court, and common law dominated that court. [See: E. Allan Farnsworth and John Honnold, *Commercial Law: Cases and Materials* (Mineola, NY: The Foundation Press, 1976), pp. 3-4; and Berman, pp. 348-50.]

Evolution of the Law Merchant and Common Law Finally, the *evolution* of a system permits it to adjust, change, and move forward often at the expense of competing but less pliable systems. The evolution of law merchant and common law required that the two work in tandem to deal with their chief competitor, the admiralty courts, by using both arbitration and eventually the statutory law system. **Admiralty courts** were tribunals set up in seaport towns to handle disputes involving maritime law, shipping contracts, contests over docking rights, collisions at sea, and the like. When the common law judges took over the staple courts, the merchants took their cases to the admiralty courts to ensure that the law merchant would be used to settle their disputes. This tactic became ineffective when the common law courts were given jurisdiction over most commercial cases throughout England, including those that had been handled by the admiralty courts. The merchants fought back by establishing their own arbitration groups to avoid common law altogether. The common law courts finally began to see the wisdom of incorporating common law with the law merchant; this integration practice became more accepted by the beginning of the 18th century, and the two systems finally began to evolve together. When Lord Mansfield became the chief justice, this evolutionary program kicked into high gear, and for more than three decades, the chief justice worked to combine the law merchant and common law. His work continued for the next century. Then late in the 19th century, Parliament passed the Bills of Exchange Act and the Sale of Goods Act, both of which codified common law principles, which by that time had been successfully integrated with most law merchant principles. When the National Conference of Commissioners (now known as the Uniform Law Commission) was established in 1892 in the United States, it developed two model laws, the Uniform Negotiable Instruments Act, which followed the Bills of Exchange Act and the Uniform Sales Act, which was patterned after the Sale of Goods Act. [See: Farnsworth and Honnold, pp. 4-5.] Despite the initial power struggle between common law and the law merchant, the two traditions were merged, with the principles of the law merchant dominating the law governing commercial transactions. Some of these principles are charted in Table 7-1. [See: Berman, pp. 348-350; and Sée, pp. 20-24.]

The Restatement of the Law of Contracts

This telling of the story is, at best, incomplete, and at worst, terribly flawed. Elements and players are missing. The law is, after all, a complex adaptive system that is constantly changing by design and by chance, sometimes by both, under the influence of various agents within the system. A case in point is the development of the Restatements of the Law written by the American Law Institute, an organization founded in 1923, consisting of lawyers, judges, and law professors, and funded, at that time, by the Rockefeller Foundation and the Carnegie Corporation, among other similar philanthropic institutions. The Restatements (there are many in various areas of the law such as contracts, torts, agency, property, and so on) are just what they say they are, restatements of the common law made in clear, precise, everyday prose and organized in a straightforward, easy-to-understand fashion. The Restatements, which are often updated and revised (the Restatement of the Law of Contracts, for example, is in its third edition) are not binding, but they are persuasive. They are also so adaptive that they sometimes do more than restate the law. Sometimes they create the law as the lawyers, judges, and law professors struggle to compromise on the actual meaning, intent, and objectives of the common law.

One such struggle gave support and acceptance to the concept of *promissory estoppel* in contract law. Under one of the early drafts of the original writing of the first Restatement of the Law of Contracts, the concept of consideration was grounded in bargained-for-exchange, which downplayed the benefit-detriment interpretation of consideration. This narrowly defined interpretation of consideration left no room for a situation in which, before a contract exists, a promise is made, relied on, and then broken. Under this interpretation of the law, an injured party, the one who believed in and relied on the broken promise, had no legal recourse. Later the concept of *promissory estoppel* was added to the Restatement to deal with such issues. *Promissory estoppel* restricts a party from denying that a promise was made under certain conditions, even though consideration has not been exchanged to bind an agreement. To be effective, *promissory estoppel* requires that the party making the promise know, or be presumed to know, that the other party will rely on that promise and, as a result, take action that depends on the promise being fulfilled. The party relying on the promise must actually take that action and suffer a financial loss as a result.

Table 7-1 Law Merchant Principles in Modern Law

CONTRACT LAW

The division between a law that focuses only on goods and one that centers on real property

The development of the rights of a good-faith purchaser in goods

The transfer of ownership of goods based on the transfer of documents

The development of the concept of warranties of fitness and warranties of merchantability

NEGOTIABLE INSTRUMENTS

The development of negotiable bills of exchange and promissory notes

BUSINESS ORGANIZATIONS

The invention of limited joint stock companies and the "company under a collective name"—forefathers of the modern corporation

The development of joint property ownership in partnerships

The development of survivorship rights among partners in a partnership

SECURED TRANSACTIONS

The invention of the chattel mortgage

CREDIT AND BANKING

The development of credit institutions at the great monasteries in Europe

The banking and lending operations of the Teutonic Knights and the Templars lead to modern banking procedures

INSURANCE CONTRACTS

The development of maritime insurance

The appearance of "private" insurance in the Middle Ages

The development of insurance companies in the 17th century

INTERNATIONAL LAW

The increased international trade leads to the need to develop international agreements

INTELLECTUAL PROPERTY

The creation of patents and trademarks

Sources: Harold J. Berman, *Law and Revolution: The Formation of the Western Legal Tradition,* (Cambridge: Harvard University Press, 1983), pp. 349–50 and Henri See, *Modern Capitalism: Its Origin and Evolution* (New York: Adelphi Company, 1928), pp. 20–24.

In reaching this doctrine, the lawyers, judges, law professors who wrote the first restatement accepted the principles of justice and fairness in protecting the party receiving the promise from otherwise unrecoverable losses. [See: Charles E. Clark, "The Restatement of the Law of Contracts," *Yale Law Journal* 42, no. 5 (March 1933), pp. 643-67; and Joel M. Ngugi, "Promissory Estoppel: The Life Story of an Ideal Legal Transplant," *University of Richmond Law Review* 41, no. 2 (January 2007).]

quick quiz 7-1

1. A valid contract results in an obligation that can be enforced in a court of law. true | false
2. Mercantile law, the law merchant, and *lex mercatoria* are all different names for the same area of law. true | false
3. The six characteristics of the law merchant are neutrality, universality, mutuality, involvement, integration, and evolution. true | false

7-2 The Multidimensional Nature of Contract Law

Contract law forms the basis of all other law in the corporate capitalist setting. Without contract law, there could be no buying and selling, no transfer of property rights, no properly planned and executed deliveries, no hiring of agents, no partnership agreements, no stock transfers, and so on. Like many other areas of the law, contract law is based on safeguarding people's rights. We saw this in criminal law and in tort law, and we see it now in contract law. The difference is that in criminal law and tort law, most of the time, human rights are inherent within the social setting. In other words, people have rights just because they are a part of our social structure. In contract law, people adopt new rights and duties as part of their contractual relationships, which are entered voluntarily. For this reason among a few others, contract law is a multidimensional area of the law, laying out not only what our rights and duties are, but also whether we have actually undertaken those duties and been given those rights. To explore this in more detail, we will first look at the elements of a contract and then at several additional multidimensional aspects of contract law, including the objectives of contract law, remedies in contract law, contracts and the UCC, contracts and other agreements, contracts and agency law, and contracts that must be written.

The Elements of a Contract

In order for a contract to be legally binding on all parties, four elements must be present. If even one of these elements is missing, there is no contract. This does not mean that there is no agreement. It simply means that there is no contract and no contractual relationship that can be vindicated in a court of law. The four elements are mutual assent, consideration, capacity, and legality. (*Note:* Before reading about these elements, you might want to study Table 7-2.)

Mutual Assent A valid *offer* requires that the *offeror* make a definite expression of the desire to enter a contract in terms that are clear and unambiguous and that are communicated to the *offeree*. An *acceptance* occurs when, without changing the essential terms of the offer, the offeree communicates an acceptance to the offeror. Once the offer has been properly made by the offeror and accepted properly by the offeree, then *mutual assent* exists between them. Often the courts will say that mutual assent exists when there has been a *meeting of the minds* among the parties to the agreement. If mutual assent has been destroyed, the relationship that results is said to be defective. Those situations that might destroy assent include: *fraud* (both active and passive), *misrepresentation, mistake, duress,* and *undue influence.*

Table 7-2 The Four Elements of a Contract

Element	Explanation
Mutual assent	Once the offer has been properly made by the offeror and accepted properly by the offeree, then mutual assent exists between them. Often the courts will say that mutual assent exists when there has been a meeting of the minds among the parties to the agreement. Those situations that might destroy assent include fraud (both active and passive), misrepresentation, mistake, duress, and undue influence.
Consideration	Consideration is the thing of value promised to the other party in exchange for something else of value promised by the other party. Each side in a contract must give up something, their legal detriment, and must gain something, their legal benefit. The courts are generally not concerned with the adequacy of consideration.
Capacity	The third contractual element is capacity—that is, the legal ability to make a contract. All the parties to a contract are legally permitted to assume that the other parties possess capacity. This assumption, however, is a rebuttable presumption, which means that any of the parties can attack or rebut that presumption. Many, perhaps most, capacity questions involve minors. Capacity also appears as a question in cases involving some sort of mental impairment.
Legality	The final element of a binding contract is legality. Clearly, any contract to commit a crime or a tort would be illegal and, therefore, void. Some contracts are also made illegal by statutory law. These include usurious contracts, gambling contracts, unlicensed agreements, unconscionable agreements, and some Sunday agreements. There are also some contracts that have been made illegal by the courts based on the doctrine of public policy.

Consideration *Consideration* is the thing of value promised to the other party in exchange for something else of value promised by the other party. Each side in a contract must give up something and must gain something. The legal term used to designate the gain that each party experiences is that party's legal benefit. Similarly, the legal term used to describe the sacrifice that each party must experience is that party's **legal detriment**. A legal detriment can be any of the following: (1) doing something (or promising to do something) that one has a legal right not to do, (2) giving up something (or promising to give up something) that one has a legal right to keep, and (3) refraining from doing something (or promising not to do something) that one has a legal right to do. This last type of detriment is known as **forbearance**.

The courts are generally not concerned with the adequacy of consideration. This means that the courts avoid determining "how much" consideration is enough consideration. That determination is up to the parties to the contract. However, if the consideration is *unconscionable* (ridiculously out of line with the nature of the contract), the court might intervene. The parties can settle value-related disputes on their own through a process of *accord and satisfaction*. Some things that might at first appear to be consideration are not consideration. These things include: *past consideration*, *preexisting duties*, *illusory promises*, and *future gifts*. On the other hand, those situations involving *promissory estoppel* will not eliminate a party's responsibility to compensate an innocent party, even in the absence of real consideration.

Capacity The third contractual element is *capacity*—that is, the legal ability to make a contract. All the parties to a contract are legally permitted to assume that the other parties possess capacity. This assumption, however, is a *rebuttable presumption*, which means that any one of the parties to the contract can attack or rebut that presumption. Many, perhaps most, capacity questions involve minors. The law permits a minor to rescind his or her contracts. This means that minors actually have "extra-capacity"—that is, the capacity to enter and the capacity to leave a contract. There are limits to this privilege, however. Minors must provide the reasonable value for *necessaries*—that is, materials that are needed for the minor's health, safety, and welfare that are not provided by a parent or a guardian.

Minors must also abide by certain contracts required by law, such as insurance contracts, contracts for educational loans, agency contracts, valid marriage contracts, enlistment contracts, contracts concerning child support, and pregnancy care, among others. Capacity also appears as a question in cases involving a party with a mental impairment. Some mental impairments result from physical injuries; others are genetic; some are health-related illnesses; still others are psychological in nature. Whatever the source of the difficulty, a person's mental impairment may also eliminate contractual capacity, but only if the party claiming the impairment can demonstrate that the impairment was so severe at the time the contract was made that he or she could not understand the nature, the purpose, or the effect of the agreement. If that is the case, then the contract will be voidable by the party lacking capacity. In contrast, if a person has been declared incompetent by a court, then that person's contracts are absolutely void.

Legality The final element of a binding contract is *legality*. Parties cannot be permitted to enforce a contract that involves something that the law says cannot be done. Clearly, any contract to commit a crime or a tort would be illegal and, therefore, void. Some contracts are also made illegal by statutory law. These include usurious contracts, gambling contracts, unlicensed agreements, unconscionable agreements, and some Sunday agreements. There are also some contracts that have been made illegal by the courts based on the doctrine of *public policy*. These include agreements to obstruct justice, agreements interfering with public safety, agreements to defraud creditors, agreements to escape liability (i.e., exculpatory clauses), agreements in restraint of trade, and agreements to suppress competition. In some states, several of these contracts, agreements to obstruct justice, for instance, are also made illegal by statutory law.

The Objectives of Contract Law

In general, the law is designed to promote harmony, stability, and justice. All the subdivisions within the law are charged with these same goals. Criminal law does this by defining criminal behavior with great specificity and then by providing a set of procedures that are followed fairly and consistently in order to make certain that those who threaten harmony, stability, and justice no longer walk among us. Tort law does the same thing by providing a system of compensation for the innocent victims of deliberate and accidental torts. Contract law is much more complicated and multidimensional than other areas of the law because it must not only provide the mechanism for punishment or compensation but also explain why that mechanism is used and not some other simpler and more effective method.

Rehabilitation in Contract Law The underlying objective of contract law is to determine whether the parties to the contract entered the agreement freely. If the court determines that the parties willingly entered the agreement, then the contract is valid. Then, if the court finds that one of the parties breached the contract, that party will have to **rehabilitate** the innocent party by compensating that party for any loss that results from the breach. Usually, the courts will not force a party to go through with the terms of a contract,

THE OPENING CASE *Round 2*
Lynyrd Skynyrd, a Plane Crash, and a Blood Oath

Let's review some of the facts in the Opening Case. Recall that the rock band, Lynyrd Skynyrd, formed their own corporation, naming it Lynyrd Skynyrd Productions Inc. (LSPI). The shareholder's agreement, which was entered on September 9, 1975, was signed by Gary Rossington, Ronnie Van Zant, Leon Wilkinson, William Powell, and Allen Collins. On October 20, 1977, the plane that the band was traveling on during a tour crashed, killing Van Zant and a new guitarist named Steven Gaines. Several months after the fatal crash, Van Zant's widow, Judith, along with Rossington, Collins, and the widow of Steven Gaines, entered an unwritten contract, agreeing to never use the name Lynyrd Skynyrd again in any way associated with the legacy of the band. They were so serious about the agreement that they called it a blood oath ("non-use contract"). On March 4, 1978, at a shareholder's meeting of LSPI, the agreement was entered into the minutes of the meeting, and at the same meeting, a written contract was drawn up and signed. The agreement was referred to as a revision of the shareholder's agreement of September 9, 1975.

Now remember, for a contract to be valid it must have all four elements: mutual assent, consideration, capacity, and legality. The Lynyrd Skynyrd non-use agreement would seem to have at least three of these elements. Mutual assent requires that an offer has been properly made by the offeror and accepted properly given by the offeree. Once this occurs, mutual assent is said to exist between the parties. Generally, the courts will say that mutual assent exists when there has been a *meeting of the minds* between the parties to the agreement. In this case, there was no formal offer and no formal acceptance that we are aware of. Yet, it is very clear that there was a *meeting of the minds*. The parties clearly knew what they were agreeing to and they were quite serious about the agreement, otherwise they would not referred to it as a "blood oath." Moreover, when, just a few months later, they decided to put the agreement into writing, everyone around the table had the chance to renege, deny the agreement, or demand changes. Nothing like this happened, emphasizing unanimous assent. There also seems to be no dispute as to capacity. Capacity is the legal ability to make a contract. Generally, questions of capacity involve minors and people who suffer from some sort or mental impairment. Neither situation seems to be at issue here. To be legal, the parties cannot have agreed to do something that violates the law. Again there is no evidence of legality presented in the facts of this case.

This brings us to consideration. Consideration requires that each side give up something and, at the same time, gain something. The legal term used to identify the gain that each side receives is that party's legal benefit. In like manner, the legal term that focuses on the sacrifice that each party experiences is each party's legal detriment. The law tell us that a legal detriment can be (1) doing something (or promising to do something) that a party has a legal right not to do, (2) giving up something (or promising to give up something) that a party has a legal right to keep, and (3) refraining from doing something (or promising not to do something) that a party has a legal right to do. This last type of detriment is known as forbearance. It is very clear that the "blood oath" agreement here is an example of forbearance. All the parties to the oath gave up their right to use the name Lynyrd Skynyrd in any way as part of their musical careers. This would include not using the name on tour, not placing it on album covers, not adding it to advertisements about upcoming concerts, not referring to it while on stage, and so on. All of these are examples of detriments. So, in essence, each band member gave up many things associated with the use of the name Lynyrd Skynyrd. In contrast, Judith, Van Zant's widow, was not a member of the band. So what did she give up? The answer is simple. She gave up her right to use the music and the name Lynyrd Skynyrd as well as in any other commercial enterprise, such as the creation of a movie based on Van Zant's life. This explains the detirment suffered by each party in the contract. So, what about the benefit? How do both sides benefit? The benefit lies in the nature of the non-use agreement. The agreement specifies that the name Lynyrd Skynyrd can only be used with material created and performed before the death of Van Zant. Thus, with every year that passes, the value of that music and that name, like any rare commodity, should increase. Of course, this is a gamble because, as the years go by, interest in the band may fade rather than grow. However, that is an inherent risk in many such contracts. [See: *Grondin v. Rossington,* 690 F. Supp. 200 (1988), United States District Court, Southern Division of New York.]

even when a breach has been proven. This is especially true of service contracts. However, the courts will compel the breaching party to rehabilitate the innocent party for any loss that resulted from the breach. The courts say that the objective of this rehabilitation is to place the innocent party in as good a position as he or she would have been had the contract been performed.

The Payment of Damages In contract law, the victims are compensated by the payment of money damages to make up for their losses. Generally, these damages are equal to the real financial loss suffered by the innocent victim. These damages are called *actual* or *compensatory damages*. Sometimes victims are entitled to damages for indirect losses. *Incidental damages* are those that are paid by the breaching party to make up for any expenses paid by the victim to prevent any additional loss. *Consequential damages* are indirect damages that result because of special circumstances that exist with a particular contract. **Punitive damages** are designed to punish the wrongdoer for his or her outrageous conduct. As a general rule, the courts do not award punitive damages in contract cases. Such damages are generally more appropriate in tort law cases. Nevertheless, there are exceptions to this rule. For instance, in cases of fraud, a court may approve punitive damages, because a party who commits fraud has attempted to undermine the entire contract system, something the court will not abide.

Recovery Limits and Equitable Relief There are built-in limits to the measure of the damages awarded in a contract case. For example, the innocent party cannot take advantage of the breach by deliberately raising the amount of damages that the other party must pay. This principle is called the duty to mitigate the damages or just the *duty to mitigate*. Also, there is an exception to the rule that says that the courts cannot force a party to go through with a contract. The court may force a party to perform the terms of an agreement if the contract involves land or some other unique item, such as an original work of art or a family heirloom. This is an equitable remedy called *specific performance*. *Equitable remedies* are those that are imposed by the courts when the payment of money would not compensate for the loss suffered by the innocent party. Another equitable remedy is injunction. In contract law, an *injunction* is a court order issued by a court directing a party to refrain from some activity that represents a breach of contract. Injunctions can be temporary or permanent. A temporary injunction is issued as a way to delay further activity until the court can decide whether to make the injunction permanent. A party who disobeys an injunction does so under threat of a contempt of court.

Multidimensional Principles of Contract Law

Stacked on top of the elements of a contract, the objectives of contract law, and the remedies offered in contract law are a series of additional aspects that must be examined to set the stage before entering a more detailed study of contract law. We have referred to these additional areas of the law as the multidimensional principles of contract law. These multidimensional principles include contracts and the Uniform Commercial Code, contracts and other agreements, contracts and privity, contracts and agency law, and contracts and the Statute of Frauds.

Contracts and the Uniform Commercial Code The Uniform Commercial Code (UCC) is a model set of laws designed to govern almost all commercial transactions. The UCC is organized in the following way: sale of goods contracts (Article 2); commercial paper (Article 3); bank deposits and collections (Article 4); letters of credit (Article 5); bulk transfers (Article 6); warehouse receipts, bills of lading, and other documents of title (Article 7); investment securities (Article 8); secured transactions, sales of accounts, contract rights, and chattel paper (Article 9); effective date and repealer (Article 10); and transition provisions (Article 11). All other types of contracts, such as employment contracts and real property (land) contracts, are covered by common law and by special statutes dedicated to some aspect of those contracts. Thus, employment contracts will be affected by labor law and minimum wage statutes, real property contracts will be covered by zoning laws and property tax laws, while both employment and real property contracts will be affected by civil rights legislation.

Contracts and Other Agreements All contracts are agreements, but not all agreements are contracts. An agreement may or may not be legally enforceable. To be enforceable, an agreement must conform to the law of contracts. This means at the very least that to be a legally recognized contract, an agreement must possess the four elements of a contract: mutual assent, consideration, capacity, and legality. The courts have never been inclined to enforce social agreements such as dates, dinner engagements, and so on. Many states have extended this concept to agreements to marry and agreements to live together without the benefit of a marriage contract.

BUSINESS LAW WITH UCC APPLICATIONS AND NOW— THE APPLICATIONS

Common Law, the UCC, or Something Else?

The classic case of *Tubelite Co., Inc. v. Original Sign Studio* concerns two (or is it, three?) agreements between Tubelite, the seller, and Original Sign Studio, the buyer. The first agreement was an application for credit, in which Original Sign agreed to pay for all materials shipped by Tubelite and to remit an 18 percent finance charge for overdue payments. In the second agreement, Tubelite agreed to be Original Sign's exclusive supplier. The terms of the contract were reduced to writing in a letter written by an agent of Original Sign but never signed by anyone from Tubelite. The agreement stated that Tubelite would supply Original Sign with all the material that it requested but that it would bill Original Sign only for the materials that the sign company actually used, and then, in exchange for being Original Sign's exclusive supplier, it would charge a discounted rate of somewhere between 10 and 25 percent. Tubelite also agreed to install shelving at Original Sign's warehouse for proper storing of the materials (the third contract?).

Tubelite shipped the materials that Original Sign requested and installed the shelving as per the (third?) agreement. Tubelite billed Original Sign for all the material it shipped, not just the material used. Moreover, the bill that Tubelite sent to Original Sign ignored the discounts promised under the second agreement. Original Sign ignored the bill as written by Tubelite and, instead, paid only for the materials it had used at a 25 percent discount rate. Tubelite insisted that, under the first agreement, Original Sign still owed money for the unused portion of the material. In addition, since that payment was now late, Tubelite tacked on its 18 percent penalty (remember the "finance charge"). Original Sign argued that agreement 2, the discount agreement, superseded agreement 1, the credit application. Tubelite argued that agreement 1, the credit application, was still in effect because agreement 2 was never signed by anyone from Tubelite. Therefore, the agreement failed to meet Statute of Frauds requirements (the statute that tells us what contracts must be written) and was unenforceable.

Because of the various types of contacts involved here, it is not even clear what law applies. One of these contracts is for credit. One is for the actual shipment of construction materials. One is a service agreement for the construction of the shelves. So do we have a financial contract for credit? A sale of goods contract for the materials? Or a service contract for the shelves? What law applies here? Common law, the Uniform Commercial Code (UCC), construction law, or banking law? Despite the intricate paths that seem to double back upon one another here, the appellate court saw through the maze and declared without hesitation that all three agreements, the one for credit, the one for the actual shipment of construction materials, and the one for the construction of new shelving concern goods and, therefore, fall within Article 2 of the Uniform Commercial Code. Perhaps for posterity, the appellate court felt compelled to make certain that everyone understood this because the court writes, "Goods are 'all things (including specially manufactured goods) which are movable at the time of identification to the contract for sale other than the money in which the price is to be paid, investment securities, and things in action.' R.C. 1302.01(A)(8). Here Tubelite seeks to recover payment for signage materials that it sold to Original Sign Studio. As these materials are 'movable' the Ohio Uniform Commercial Code applies to the transactions at issue." [See: *Tubelite Co., Inc. v. Original Sign Studio* 176 Ohio App.3d 241 (Tenth District).]

Source: See: *Tubelite Co., Inc. v. Original Sign Studio* 176 Ohio App.3d 241 (Tenth District).

Contracts and Privity The general rule of contract law is that the parties must stand in privity to one another. **Privity** means that all parties must have a legally recognized interest in the subject of the contract if they are to be bound by it. Parties who do not have such an interest in the subject matter of the contract may not be bound by it. Their right to bring a lawsuit in the event of a breach of contract would also be in question. Despite the privity rule, it is possible for two or more parties to provide benefits to a third party under the terms of a contract. However, the law still makes a distinction between third parties who are *intended beneficiaries* and third parties who are *incidental beneficiaries*. For example, in a life insurance contract, the parties who are named as those who will receive payment on the death of the insured would be intended beneficiaries. Given a breach of that contract, those intended beneficiaries would have a cause of action against the defaulting life insurance company. Moreover, an exception to the general rule of privity exists in cases involving warranties and product liability.

UCC 1-201(11) and (21)

Contracts and Agency Law An *agent* is a party who has been hired or appointed by a *principal* to perform some sort of work, usually of a business nature, for the principal. Agents owe several levels of duty to the principal. For example, the agent must obey the instructions of the principal, must be loyal to the principal, must exercise due care in doing work for the principal, must perform the work for the principal personally, must account for all money and property that is entrusted to his or her care by the principal, and must communicate all relevant agency information to the principal. The agent has all of these duties because, in effect, when the agent acts the principal acts. Agents can, therefore, bind the principal to a contract, even if the principal is not present. If the agent creates a contract for the principal and there is a breach of contract suit filed by the third party, the principal will be the initial target of that lawsuit. If the principal loses the lawsuit, and the fault lies with the agent, the agent will be liable to the principal for the losses he or she incurred because of that lawsuit.

Contracts and the Statute of Frauds The *Statute of Frauds* is a law that outlines those contracts that must be in writing to be enforceable in court. The original Statute of Frauds was passed by Parliament in 1677 and was officially named the Act for the Prevention of Frauds and Perjuries. The statute was part of colonial law in New England and was, thus, assimilated into American law by the states after the Revolution. It is still part of the statutory law covering contracts in every state and in the District of Columbia. Six types of contracts must be in writing to be enforceable: (1) contracts that cannot be completed within one year, (2) contracts involving land, (3) contracts in consideration of marriage, (4) contracts made by executors to pay a debt of the estate out of his or her own finances, (5) a promise to pay the debt of another, and (6) contracts for the sale of goods valued at $500 or more. If the statute of frauds demands a written contract and, for some reason, the

THE OPENING CASE Round 3
Lynyrd Skynyrd, a Plane Crash, and a Blood Oath

One last look at the Opening Case is in order here. Remember that the members of the band called Lynyrd Skynyrd were so successful that they decided to form a company known as Lynyrd Skynyrd Productions Inc. (LSPI). The company was charged with, among other things, holding their trade name, trademarks, and service marks. The shareholder agreement was signed by Gary Rossington, Ronnie Van Zant, Leon Wilkinson, William Powell, and Allen Collins. Several months after the crash that killed Van Zant and new band member Steven Gaines, Van Zant's widow, Judith, along with Rossington, Collins, and the widow of Steven Gaines, agreed never to use the name Lynyrd Skynyrd in any way associated with the legacy of the band. They called this non-use agreement a "blood oath."

Everyone followed the agreement for 10 years. In 1987, several members of the band planned a Tribute Tour. LSPI formed a subsidiary called Tribute Inc. to manage the tour. As the deal developed, two agreements were entered. The first agreement noted that Tribute Inc. would conduct the tour, produce a video, and sell merchandise. The second agreement was a licensing agreement controlling the right to use the name Lynyrd Skynyrd and to play Lynyrd Skynyrd music. MCA entered a contract to produce a live album. Judith went along with the first contract under pressure, but declined to enter the licensing agreement. Judith reportedly rejected all versions of the licensing agreement that were presented to her. She was especially against any agreement that included permission to use the Lynyrd Skynyrd name. Despite this, the 1987 tour went ahead, using the name Lynyrd Skynyrd. A second tour was arranged for 1988. Judith again protested. She demanded that the 1988 tour, as a violation of the non-use agreement, be cancelled. She was told that it would be canceled. This turned out to be a untrue. The tour went forward. Judith then brought this lawsuit, alleging a breach of contract (the non-use agreement, also known as the original blood oath), and asking for an injunction to stop the tour. The defendants pointed to the original agreement and said that, since it was an unwritten blood oath, it violated the Statute of Frauds, which required a writing to be enforceable. No writing, no enforcement—and no cancellation. Therefore, the show must go on!

Now if we look carefully at the Statute of Frauds, we begin to see some flaws in the defendants' argument. First, recall that six types of contracts must be in writing to be enforceable: (1) contracts that cannot be completed within one year, (2) contracts involving land, (3) contracts in consideration of marriage, (4) contracts made by executors to pay a debt of the estate out of his or her own finances, (5) a promise to pay the debt of another, and (6) contracts for the sale of goods valued at $500 or more. The only one of these that applies is the first one—that is, contracts that cannot be completed within one year. The court ruled that since the non-use agreement could go on indefinitely and, therefore, longer than one year, a writing was required. The court did not stop there, however. It added that, even though the one-year rule required a writing, the equitable doctrine of part performance took the contract outside of the statute of frauds. In fact, all parties involved in the contract had performed partially in a number of ways. The surviving band members had not used the name Lynyrd Skynyrd for 10 years. This non-use counted as their part performance. Moreover, Judith's continual refusal to make book deals or enter movie contracts counted as her part performance. Therefore, no writing was needed. Moreover, the court added, even if a writing were required, the agreement was still enforceable under the Statute of Frauds because it had been reduced to writing at the March 1978 shareholders meeting. That about did it, and the court went on to consider the need to issue an injunction. [See: *Grondin v. Rossington*, 690 F. Supp. 200 (1988), United States District Court, Southern Division of New York.]

Source: See: *Grondin v. Rossington*, 690 F. Supp. 200 (1988), United States District Court, Southern Division of New York.

parties never reduce that contract to writing, the contract remains valid but is unenforceable, which means that the court will dismiss the action.

Exceptions to the Statutory Rule
Several interesting exceptions apply to the rules imposed by the Statute of Frauds in relation to sale of goods contracts. The statute says that a contract for the sale of goods valued at $500 or more must be in writing unless the contract

is for specially manufactured goods. The writing also becomes unnecessary with a sale of goods contract if the goods have already been shipped and accepted or a payment has been received and accepted. Some courts say that any full performance of contract, no matter what the subject matter, will cancel the need to have a writing since the performance itself is evidence of the existence of the contract and its terms. Some courts have also held that the equitable doctrine of part performance also takes the contract out of the statute of frauds, just so long as the part performance actually resulted from the agreement, and failure to enforce the agreement would financially injure the performing party. Also, if one of the parties reduces the contract to writing and sends that writing to the other party, that unsigned paper will be sufficient as a writing under the statute unless the receiving party objects in writing within 10 days. Finally, in a court action if the party that has invoked the Statute of Frauds to escape enforcement has also admitted under oath that the contract exists, no writing is needed.

Rules of Interpretation Despite the careful precision with which the Statute of Frauds was written, whenever contracts are reduced to writing, someone is going to disagree on what was meant by the written terms. To deal with this problem, the courts have developed rules of construction to guide judges as they interpret the written word. The first rule is the *standard construction rule*, which tells judges that their primary objective in the interpretation of a written contract is to uncover the goals that the parties had when they entered the contract in the first place. As a corollary of that rule, the courts must also interpret any ambiguous clause against the party who actually wrote the contract. The goal of this rule is to encourage those parties who actually put pen to paper (or fingers to keyboard) to be as clear and straightforward as humanly possible. Otherwise, if a question of interpretation comes up later, they risk having the judge rule against them. A different problem arises when some of the terms are not just vague or ambiguous, but are actually missing from the contract. Terms such as the subject matter, the quantity, and the price to be paid are essential to a binding contractual relationship. On the other hand, at least under the UCC, it is not always necessary to have all of the terms just as long as the judge has enough information to determine a "reasonably certain basis for giving an appropriate remedy." [See: UCC 2-204 (3).]

quick quiz 7-2

1. The four elements are mutual assent, consideration, capacity, and legality. true | false
2. The courts says that the objective of rehabilitation is to place the innocent party in as good a position as he or she would have been had the contract been performed. true | false
3. All contracts must be in writing to be enforced in a court of law. true | false

7-3 Contractual Characteristics

Contractual characteristics fall into five categories: valid, void, voidable, and unenforceable; unilateral and bilateral; express and implied; informal and formal; and executory and executed. Any given contract can be classifiable in all five ways. Thus, for example, a single contract could be said to be valid, bilateral, express, formal, and executed, or any other acceptable combination of characteristics.

Valid, Void, Voidable, and Unenforceable Contracts

A **valid contract** is one that is legally binding and fully enforceable by the court. In contrast, a **void contract** is one that has no legal effect whatsoever. For example, a contract to perform an illegal act would be void. A **voidable contract** is one that may be avoided or canceled by one of the parties. Contracts made by minors or induced by fraud or misrepresentation are examples of voidable contracts. An **unenforceable contract** is one that, because of some rule of law, cannot be upheld by a court of law. An unenforceable contract may have all the elements of a complete contract and still be unenforceable.

Unilateral and Bilateral Contracts

A **unilateral contract** is an agreement in which one party makes a promise to do something in return for an act of some sort. The classic example of a unilateral contract is a reward contract. A person who promises to pay $5 to the finder of a lost driver's license does not expect a promise in return. Rather, the person expects the return of the lost license. When the license is returned, the contract arises and the promisor owes the finder $5.

In contrast, a **bilateral contract** is one in which both parties make promises. Bilateral contracts come into existence at the moment the two promises are made. A **breach of contract** occurs when one of the two parties fails to keep the promise. When there is a breach of contract, the injured party has the right to ask a court of law to somehow remedy the situation. (Breach of contract and remedies are discussed in detail in Chapter 12.)

Express and Implied Contracts

A contract can be either express or implied. An **express contract** requires some sort of written or spoken expression indicating a desire to enter the contractual relationship. An **implied contract** is created by the actions or gestures of the parties involved in the transaction.

Express Contracts When contracting parties accept mutual obligations, either through oral discussion or written communication, they have created an express contract. Oral negotiations in many cases will be reduced to writing, but this is not always necessary.

A written contract does not have to be a long, formal preprinted agreement. Although such lengthy, preprinted forms are common in some businesses, other, less formal written documents are frequently used to show that a contract exists. For example, a written contract may take the form of a letter, sales slip and receipt, notation, or memorandum. A written contract may be typed, printed, keystroked, scrawled, or written in beautiful penmanship. In some situations, state laws require certain types of contracts to be in writing. (See Chapter 11.)

A QUESTION OF ETHICS

Suppose you posted a reward notice that read, "Reward: $50 for the return of my lost college class ring." Suppose further that someone who did not know of the reward offer found your ring and returned it. Legally you would not have to pay the reward money to the person who found your ring because he or she did not know about your offer. However, would it be ethical not to pay the reward to the finder? Explain.

When a contract is placed in writing, it is essential that the content be as clear and unambiguous as possible. When faced with a dispute over an ambiguous clause, the court may be compelled to look at factual evidence to determine the actual intent of the parties. This review may mean that a case that could have been dismissed early will have to go to trial so that the court can make a factual determination of intent by looking at evidence beyond the terms in the writing.

When the law does not require a written agreement, an *oral contract* resulting from the spoken words of the parties will be enough. Parties to such an agreement, however, should anticipate the difficulty of proving the contractual relationship, should disputes arise later. Nevertheless, expressing every agreement in writing, in anticipation of a future need of proof, is impractical in the fast-paced modern world of business.

Implied Contracts One who knowingly accepts benefits from another person may be obligated for their payment, even though no express agreement has been made. An agreement of this type can be either implied-in-fact or implied-in-law. A contract implied by the direct or indirect acts of the parties is known as an **implied-in-fact contract**. Pumping gas into a car at a self-service gas station is an example of an implied-in-fact contract. Because the parties to a contract enter that contract by an exercise of free will, the court follows the **objective concept rule** in interpreting the acts and gestures of a party. Under this rule, the meaning of one's actions is determined by the impression those actions would make upon any reasonable person who might have witnessed them, not by a party's self-serving claim of what was meant or intended by the actions.

> **About the Law**
>
> The law that declares which contracts must be in writing is called the Statute of Frauds. In its original form when it was passed by Parliament in 1677, it was known as the Act for the Prevention of Fraud and Perjuries.

EXAMPLE 7-1: Implied-in-Fact Deals: Can Inaction Create a Contract?

Herbert Ward watched workers employed by the Rice Lawn and Garden Greenhouse as they chemically treated his front lawn. In fact, Ward had no contract with Rice and had not ordered any chemical treatments of his property. The treatment should have been performed on another house at 750 Maple Street, instead of at Ward's, which had an address of 570 Maple St. Ward never stopped the work crew, even though he knew that a mistake had been made. Rice would be within its rights to believe that the work was being done with Ward's consent. In assessing damages for the cost of the improvement, the court would apply the objective concept rule. A reasonable person who might have watched Rice treat the front lawn would conclude that Ward had freely consented to the work.

An **implied-in-law contract** is imposed by a court when someone is unjustly enriched. It is used when a contract cannot be enforced or there is no actual written, oral, or implied-in-fact agreement. Applying reasons of justice and fairness, a court may obligate one who has unfairly benefited at the innocent expense of another. An implied-in-law contract is also called a **quasi-contract**.

EXAMPLE 7-2: Implied-in-Law Deals: Can Injustice Be Prevented?

Karl Rapp was found unconscious in his hotel room by Jan Stevens, the third-floor maid. She immediately called 911 and then notified Ken Kramer, the hotel manager. Kramer arranged to have Rapp placed in a hospital for emergency treatment. When Rapp regained consciousness, he refused to pay for the treatment, claiming that he was not aware of what was going on and had not agreed to what had been done to him. The case illustrates a quasi-contractual situation, wherein it would be unfair to allow the injured person to benefit at the expense of the hospital. In any suit that might arise over this expense, a court would require Rapp to pay the fair value of the services rendered.

The quasi-contract concept cannot apply, however, to obtain payment for an act that a party simply feels should be done. The concept also cannot be applied when one party bestows a benefit on another unnecessarily or through misconduct or negligence. A quasi-contract is not a contract in the true sense of the word, because it is created by the court. It does not result from the mutual assent of the parties, as do express or implied-in-fact contracts.

Informal and Formal Contracts

The law sometimes requires that contracts follow formalities prescribed by statute or common law. These are called formal contracts. All others are classified as informal.

Informal Contracts Any oral or written contract that is not under seal or is not a contract of record is considered an **informal contract**. An informal contract is also known as a *simple contract*. An informal contract generally has no requirements as to language, form, or construction. It comprises obligations entered into by parties whose promises are expressed in the simplest and usually most ordinary, nonlegal language.

UCC 2-203

Formal Contracts Under common law principles, a **formal contract** differs from other types of contracts in that it has to be (1) written; (2) signed, witnessed, and placed under the seal of the parties; and (3) delivered. A *seal* is a mark or an impression placed on a written contract indicating that the instrument was executed and accepted in a formal manner. The UCC removed the requirement for a seal in sale-of-goods contracts. Some states, however, still require the use of the seal in agreements related to the sale and transfer of real property.

Today, a person's seal may be any mark or sign placed after the signature intended to be the signer's seal. In states still requiring the seal or formal contract, it is sufficient to write the word *seal* after the signature.

EXAMPLE 7-3: Formal Contracts: Is a Seal Still Needed?

Audrey Kimmel signed an agreement with Corey Baumberger to buy seven acres of farmland owned by Baumberger just outside Bellville. Later that day, Baumberger found another interested buyer who was willing to pay seven times as much as Kimmel had offered for the land. Kimmel had signed the sales agreement without including any representation of the seal. In any state that required such formality in all real property contracts, Kimmel would now be helpless in attempting to enforce the original contract that she had made with Baumberger.

Contracts of Record A special type of formal contract is known as a **contract of record**. Often, such a contract is confirmed by the court with an accompanying judgment issued in favor of one of the parties. The judgment is recorded, giving the successful litigant the right to demand satisfaction of the judgment. A contract of record is not a contract in the true sense of the word because it is court created. Although it does not have all of the elements of a valid contract, it is enforced for public policy reasons.

EXAMPLE 7-4: Contracts of Record: When Can Litigants Demand Their Money?

Mortimer Byrne installed a new roof on Alexander Harper's house in Lakeside for the agreed-upon price of $7,500. Harper paid Byrne $4,000 so that he could secure materials. After the job was completed, Byrne sent Harper a bill for $3,500. Harper sent Byrne a check for $2,500, on which was written "in full payment of all money owed." These words were in very fine print and not seen by Byrne. Byrne sued Harper in the small claims division of the Ottawa County Court of Common Pleas for the amount still owed. The court ruled in favor of Byrne and entered a judgment against Harper for the money owed. Entry of the judgment created a contract of record, which was enforceable against Harper.

Executory and Executed Contracts

A contract that has not yet been fully performed by the parties is called an **executory contract**. Such a contract may be completely executory, in which case nothing has been done, or it may be partly executory, in which case the contract is partially complete. When a contract's terms have been completely and satisfactorily carried out by both parties, it is an **executed contract**. Such contracts are no longer active agreements and are valuable only if a dispute about the agreement occurs.

quick quiz 7-3

1. A void contract is one that can be avoided by one or more of the parties. true | false
2. A formal contract is also known as a simple contract. true | false
3. A contract that has not yet been fully performed by the parties is called an executory contract. true | false

Summary

7.1 With the Roman law providing a model, the Roman Catholic Church supplying political and social support, canon law supplying a moral framework, and practicality guiding their activities over a 300-year period, the merchants of the late Middle Ages developed a body of active law that was characterized by neutrality, universality, mutuality, involvement, integration, and evolution. The law merchant was developed by the merchants themselves. The law merchant also successfully integrated itself into other legal tradition such as English common law. Many of its provisions still exist in today's court decisions and statutes.

7.2 Contract law is a multidimensional area of the law, laying out not only what our rights and duties are, but also whether we have actually undertaken those duties and been given those rights. To explore this in more detail, we looked at the elements of a contract and at several additional multidimensional aspects of contract law including the objectives of contract law, remedies in contract law, contracts and the UCC, contracts and other agreements, contracts and agency law, and contracts that must be written.

7.3 Contractual characteristics fall into five categories. These categories are valid, void, voidable, or unenforceable; unilateral or bilateral; express or implied; informal or formal; and executory or executed.

Key Terms

admiralty court, 214
bilateral contract, 226
breach of contract, 226
canon law, 212
capitalism, 211
contract, 209
contract of record, 228
executed contract, 229
executory contract, 229
express contract, 226
fair court, 214
forbearance, 218
formal contract, 228
implied contract, 226
implied-in-fact contract, 227
implied-in-law contract, 227
informal contract, 228
law merchant, 210
legal detriment, 218
mercantile law, 210
objective concept rule, 227

pie powder court, 214
privity, 223
punitive damages, 221
quasi-contract, 227
rehabilitate, 219
staple court, 214
unenforceable contract, 226
unilateral contract, 226
valid contract, 226
void contract, 226
voidable contract, 226

Questions for Review and Discussion

1. What is a contract?
2. How did the law merchant develop?
3. How did the law merchant merge with common law?
4. What are the four elements of a contract?
5. What is the objective of contract law?
6. What is the role of the UCC in contract law?
7. How do contracts differ from other agreements?
8. What are the roles of privity and agency in contract law?
9. What contracts must be in writing to be enforceable?
10. What are the characteristics of a contract?

Cases for Analysis

1. Janke Construction Company, a general contractor, was in a bidding war with several other contractors trying to obtain a contract for the construction of the marine component of a larger project that would provide a cooling system for the University of Wisconsin in Milwaukee. The bidding information packet specified that the pipe for the marine subproject had to be approved by the American Water Works Association (AWWA) as either AWWA C300 or AWWA C301 level pipe or pipe that was "equal to" those specifications. Jerry Janke, vice president of Janke Construction, talked to a representative from the Vulcan Materials Company about the piping requirements for the job. The price that was quoted by the Vulcan rep came in $40,000 less than the price quoted by Interpace, Vulcan's main competitor. No mention had been made about the exact specifications for the pipe to be used on the job. The evening before the bid was to be placed at the State Office Building in Madison, Jerry and James Janke met with Alex Barry, the general manager of Vulcan, and Peter Fox, a Vulcan sales rep. The next day, at the State Office Building, they met again with Barry who, after a quick phone call to his home office, reassured the Janke brothers that his company would supply the pipe needed for the job. With this reassurance in hand, the Jankes submitted their bid. After the Jankes won the bidding contest, they asked for and received a written quotation from Vulcan. That was when they learned that the pipe that Vulcan was going to use on the project was AWWA C302, which did not meet project specifications. The state refused to use AWWA C302 because it was not steel and, therefore, would not withstand the internal pressure of the cooling systems operation. After several meetings, it became obvious that state and university officials were not going to budge on the pipe specifications. The job was on a tight schedule and when the Jankes found that Vulcan could not supply either AWWA C300 or AWWA C301 in time to meet project deadlines, they turned to Interpace, which supplied the pipe but at a price that was $39,992.40 more than they would have paid to Vulcan. The Jankes sued Vulcan, asking for that $39,992.40 plus reimbursement for the expenses involved in the extra meetings with state officials caused by Vulcan's inability to supply the right materials. Vulcan argued that it had not breached the contract because the contract did not exist until the bid had been accepted by the state and Vulcan's written quotation was turned over to the Jankes and the Jankes signed a letter of intent. So, since there was no contract, there could be no breach of contract. Is Vulcan correct here? Does *promissory estoppel* play any role in this case? Explain. [*Janke Construction Co. v. Vulcan Materials Co.*, 386 F. Supp. 687 (1974), affirmed 527 F.2d 772 (1976) United States District Court, Western Division of Wisconsin.]
2. The Borg-Warner Protective Services Corporation and Burns International Security Services contracted to provide security for the Cleveland Institute of Art (CIA). Robert Adelman was struck

by an object thrown by a CIA student from the roof of one of the institute's buildings. Adelman sued both the CIA and the security corporations. The security corporations moved for summary judgment, arguing that they had contracted with CIA to protect the faculty and the students and that they therefore had no duty to protect pedestrians outside the buildings. Adelman argued that the contract specifically obligated the security corporations to control the activities of CIA students within the institute's buildings. The disputed clause read that the security corporations agreed "to control the movement and activities of students within the buildings at all hours." The trial court granted the summary judgment motion, and Adelman appealed. Should the appellate court reverse the decision of the lower court? Explain. If the case goes to trial, how will the court determine the meaning of the ambiguous clause? Explain. [See: *Adelman v. Timman*, 690 N.E.2d 1332 (OH).]

3. One of Stewart's clients gave him a check for $185.48. The check had been drawn up by the client's corporate employer and properly endorsed by the client. Nevertheless, the bank refused to cash the check for Stewart, even though there was enough money in the account to cover the $185.48. Could Stewart sue the bank for not cashing the check as he requested? Explain. [See: *J.E.B. Stewart v. Citizens and Southern National Bank*, 225 S.E.2d 761 (GA).]

4. Anderson, a farmer, orally agreed to buy a used tractor from the Copeland Equipment Company for $475. Copeland delivered the tractor to Anderson, who used it for 11 days. During this period, Anderson could not borrow enough funds to cover the purchase price. Anderson therefore returned the tractor to Copeland. Both parties agreed that their sales contract was canceled when the tractor was returned. However, Copeland later claimed that under the doctrine of quasi-contract, Anderson was required to pay for the 11-day use of the tractor. Do you agree with Copeland? Explain your answer. [See: *Anderson v. Copeland*, 378 P.2d 1006 (OK).]

5. B.L. Nelson & Associates Inc. entered into a contract with the city of Argyle to design and construct a sanitary sewer collection and treatment facility for the city. The city attempted to get out of the contract by citing certain provisions of the state constitution. These provisions made it illegal for the city to enter a contract for services if it did not have the money to pay for these services. Because the city did not have the funds to pay Nelson, it argued that the contract was illegal and therefore void. Was the city correct? Explain. [See: *B.L. Nelson & Associates, Inc. v. City of Argyle*, 535 S.W.2d 906 (TX).]

6. Peters entered into a contract to purchase Dowling's business. The following terms were agreed to: (a) Peters would take over all of Dowling's executory contracts, (b) Peters would purchase Dowling's tools at an agreed-to price, (c) Peters would accept full responsibility for all warranties made by Dowling on previous contracts, and (d) Dowling would remain as a consultant to the new firm for a period of five years. Analyze each part of this contract and classify each term according to whether it is executed or executory. [See: *Wagstaff v. Peters*, 453 P.2d 120 (KS).]

7. The Roman Catholic Church was not always as supportive of capitalism as it eventually became. In fact, both Henri Sée, in a study titled *Modern Capitalism*, and Harold Berman, in his book *Law and Revolution*, refer to the work of the French historian Henri Pirenne, who wrote extensively about the development of capitalism in Europe in the Middle Ages. According to Berman, Pirenne points out that the Church often took a decidedly anti-capitalist position, especially in relation to such things as moneylending and placing an unfair value on goods. On the other hand, Sée points out that, when circumstances were right in certain areas of Europe, notably the Low Countries of Holland and Zeeland, the Church was willing to support those emerging businessmen who worked diligently to create an authentic form of modern capitalism that included moneylending. Even Max Weber does not deny that certain theologians in the medieval Church managed to support the growth of capitalism. (Specifically, he refers to Anthony of Florence and Bernhard of Siena, although, to be fair, Weber does hide this reference in a lengthy footnote at the back of his book.) The question before us is this: What religious values would operate to oppose capitalism? What is it about the very nature of religious doctrine that places it in opposition to making a profit? On the other hand, what arguments can overcome this religious opposition to making a profit? Explain all your answers. [See: Harold J. Berman, *Law and Revolution: The Formation of the Western Legal Tradition* (Cambridge, MA: Harvard University Press, 1983); Henri Sée,

Modern Capitalism: Its Origin and Evolutions, trans. Homer B. Vanderblue and Georges F. Doriot (New York: Adelphi Co. 1928); and Max Weber, *The Protestant Ethic: The Spirit of Capitalism* (Mineola, NY: Dover, 2003).]

8. Mers was a sales rep for Dispatch Printing. His trainer at Dispatch assured him that as long as he was a fairly good worker, he would have continued employment. Mers did better than this, earning numerous commendations and awards for having an exemplary sales record. Unfortunately, he was arrested for a felony and shortly thereafter was suspended from Dispatch. The director of the Dispatch Employee-Labor Relations Department told Mers that he would be reinstated when he received "a clean bill of health, a clean slate." Mers was also told that he would be reinstated with back pay. Mers' felony case went to trial and the result was a hung jury. Mers had not looked for another job during this time, and so when the prosecutor announced that the case would no longer be pursued, he went back to Dispatch with his "clean slate." At that point, he was told that he could not have his job back. Mers looked for work for three years before finding another job. Mers sued Dispatch using *promissory estoppel* as one of his theories of recovery. Does Mers have a good promissory estoppel case here? Explain. [See: *Mers v. Dispatch Printing Company*, 39 Ohio App.3d 99 (1988).]

Design Elements: The Opening Case: ©Sharpstock/Alamy; A Classic Case: ©Evlakhov Valeriy/Shutterstock

quick quiz Answers

7-1	7-2	7-3
1. T	1. T	1. F
2. T	2. T	2. F
3. T	3. F	3. T

Chapter 8
Offer, Acceptance, and Mutual Assent

8-1 Mutual Assent and the Offer
The Nature of Mutual Assent • Requirements of an Offer

8-2 Acceptance of an Offer
Communication of Acceptance • Unequivocal Acceptance • Implied Acceptance • Silence as Acceptance • Rejection and Revocation • Option Contracts

8-3 Mutual Assent in Cyberspace
The E-Sign Act • The Uniform Electronic Transactions Act • The Uniform Computer Information Transactions Act • Offer and Acceptance in Cyberspace • Social Media, Offers, and Advertising • Managing "The Cloud" When Making and Accepting Offers

8-4 The Destruction of Mutual Assent
Fraud and Misrepresentation • Mistake, Duress, and Undue Influence

THE OPENING CASE *Round 1*
A Tale of E-Mails, Invoices, Letters, and a Phone Call

Using a new aerial photography technique, Oil for America (OFA) had mapped about 1 million acres of oil- and gas-rich land. The company had leased much of the land for drilling purposes but still needed title searches done on vast tracts of unleased land. The land remained unleased because it was subject to fractionalized mineral rights. Because there were time constraints and an enormous amount of land yet to be drilled, OFA entered an arrangement with two other oil companies, Petrosearch and Oxbow Energy. Kadrmas was hired to do the title searches for all three oil companies on those areas with multiple owners, referred to as "pro-splits." (It's a play on "profit splits.") Some of the pro-splits had more than 100 owners each, so this was a difficult assignment. Robert Angerer of OFA hired Kadrmas to coordinate her title searches among OFA, Petroseach, and Oxbow and to make separate but nearly identical contracts with those three firms. Accordingly, Kadrmas attempted to enter contracts with OFA, Oxbow, and Petrosearch. OFA and Petrosearch cooperated and entered into their contracts with no difficulty. Oxbow, on the other hand, turned out to be a different story. Kadrmas talked on the phone with Tony Martin of Oxbow Energy on January 10, 2004. According to Kadrmas, Martin told her to "go ahead" with the job. Kadrmas then sent Martin a letter with an agreement for the title searches, the same agreement that had gone to OFA and Petrosearch. Martin contradicted Kadrmas, saying that he did not tell Kadrmas to "go ahead" but asked, instead, for a cost estimate. He testified that, when he got the contract, he found it "unacceptable" and "too generic." So, he shredded it. He did not, however, contact Kadrmas directly by phone, e-mail, or letter, to tell her that he had done so. Moreover, while he made no counteroffer, he also did not expressly reject the terms.

In December 2003, about one month before the January phone call with Kadrmas, Martin, along with people from Petrosearch, received details, from OFA, explaining how the arrangement with Kadrmas would work. Between December and the January call (and, it seems, even after that January call), Kadrmas sent invoices to all three firms, detailing expenses, the hiring of additional people, and a record of the pro-splits that she had researched for each firm, including Oxbow. On at least two occasions during that period, Martin also updated his contact information with Kadrmas, indicating a willingness to work with her despite his initial dissatisfaction with the "generic" contract. Not realizing that she had not heard back from Martin, Kadrmas continued to handle the title searches for all three companies and to send invoices to all three, including Oxbow. On February 7, 2004, Kadrmas sent a cost estimate on future billing to Martin. Kadrmas explained that the estimate was based on previous invoices, dating back to December. At that time, she also explained that it had not been possible to estimate future billing until she had a series of past billings to show her how this unusual arrangement would work. Two days later, on February 9, 2004, Martin told Kadrmas to finish the title work she was currently involved in and to put all the rest of the work "on hold." Martin refused to pay Kadrmas for any of her work, arguing that no contract existed between Oxbow and Kadrmas. On her part, Kadrmas argued that either an express or an implied contract existed and that she was entitled to payment for the work that she had already done on behalf of Oxbow. The outcome of the case may seem very clear but, be warned, not everything in the law, especially contract law, is as it seems at first. [See: *B.J. Kadrmas, Inc. v. Oxbow Energy LLC*, 727 N.W. 2d 279 (2007).]

Opening Case Questions

1. Who is the offeror and who is the offeree in this case? Explain.
2. How was the offer made in this case, and does it include all the needed requirements? Explain.
3. Was there a binding acceptance in this case? Explain.
4. Did this contract have to be in writing, under the Statute of Frauds, to be enforceable? Explain.
5. Could the silence of the offeree, in not responding to the offeror, be construed as acceptance? Explain.

Source: See: *B.J. Kadrmas, Inc. v. Oxbow Energy LLC.* 727 N.W. 2d 279 (2007).

 Learning Objectives

1. Define *mutual assent*.
2. Identify the elements of an offer.
3. Explain the UCC's concept of offer in contract law.
4. Explain the nature of acceptance.
5. Define the mirror image rule.
6. Explain the process of revocation.
7. Identify those statutes that affect mutual assent in cyberspace.
8. Explain the elements of fraud and misrepresentation.
9. Identify the effects of mistake on mutual assent.
10. Describe duress and undue influence.

8-1 Mutual Assent and the Offer

Contractual relationships are, to a large extent, unique relationships that people enter voluntarily. Nevertheless, once a party has agreed to the terms of a contract, he or she has assumed a set of duties that are just as binding as those that are imposed automatically by law. This is why the courts and the legislatures have been very careful about spelling out the details involved in forming a contract. Many of these rules have evolved as part of the law merchant and common law. Others have been adopted by the legislature in response to social and economic changes such as the cyberspace revolution. Whatever the case, the objective of the law is to provide a proper balance between the duties of each party and their rights, both of which emerge in the contract-making process. To understand how this works, we will first examine the nature of mutual assent and the method for creating that assent through the process of offer and acceptance.

The Nature of Mutual Assent

A **contract** is an agreement between two or more competent parties based on mutual promises and an exchange of things of value, to do or refrain from doing some particular thing that is neither illegal nor impossible. The agreement results in a set of duties that can be enforced in a court of law. The power of the courts to enforce these duties comes from the fact that both parties have agreed to accept those duties. This is **mutual assent**. It is the first of the four elements of a valid contract. The courts are fond of saying that mutual assent emerges when the parties to the contract have a "meeting of the minds." In other words, both parties know what the terms of the agreement are and both willingly agree to be bound by those terms. Mutual assent can be reached quickly as in buying a Kindle on Amazon.com, or it may result from a long and involved series of negotiations as in the purchase of a house. Whatever the case, the assent that emerges comes from a communication of an open offer by an offeror that is authentically accepted by the offeree. The twin keys to mutual assent then are an "open offer" and "authentically accepted." Remember those key terms.

Requirements of an Offer

An **offer** is a proposal freely made by one party to another indicating a willingness to enter a contract. The person who makes the offer is the **offeror**, and the person to whom it is made is the **offeree**. If certain requirements are met, the court concludes that the parties intended to make and accept an offer. In the case of an open offer, the courts have established three elements that must exist: (1) serious intent, (2) clear and reasonably definite terms, and (3) communication to the offeree. We now turn to a discussion of these requirements.

Serious Intent An offeror's offer is invalid if that offeror makes the alleged offer as a joke, during an emotional outburst of rage or anger, or under circumstances that convey a lack of seriousness. The offeror's words and actions must give the offeree assurance that a binding agreement is intended. This is what makes an offer an open offer, that is, it is open to acceptance by the offeree. Serious intent will be present within the actions and the words of the offeror. (see Table 8-1)

Clear and Reasonably Definite Terms The communicated terms of an offer must be sufficiently clear to remove all doubt about the contractual intentions of the offeror. No valid offer will exist when terms are indefinite, inadequate, vague, contradictory, or confusing. To determine whether the terms in the alleged offer are clear and definite enough, ask whether the terms are so clear that if there were a breach, the court would know how to assess a remedy. If the answer is yes, the terms are probably definite enough. If the answer is no, then some critical term in the alleged offer is missing or too obscure to create a contract.

The Statute of Frauds As noted in Chapter 7, the Statute of Frauds outlines those contracts that must be in writing to be enforceable in court. This requirement makes the Statute

Table 8-1 Requirements of an Offer

Requirement	Explanation
Serious intent	The offeror's words must give the offeree assurance that a binding agreement is intended.
Clarity and reasonably definite terms	The terms of an offer must be sufficiently clear to remove any doubt about the contractual intentions of the offeror. Most courts require reasonable rather than absolute definiteness.
Communication to the offeree	The proposed offer must be communicated to the offeree by whatever means are convenient and desirable. The communication of the offer can be express or implied. Public offers are made through the media but are intended for one party whose identity or address is unknown. Invitations to trade are not offers.

THE OPENING CASE *Round 2*
A Tale of E-Mails, Invoices, Letters, and a Phone Call

Recall in the Opening Case that Oil for America (OFA) had mapped about 1 million acres of oil-rich land. It had leased much of the land for drilling but still needed title searches on vast tracts of available land. The land remained unleased because it was subject to fractionalized mineral rights. Because there were time constraints and an enormous amount of land yet to be drilled, OFA entered an arrangement with two other oil companies, Petrosearch and Oxbow Energy. Kadrmas was hired to do the title searches for all three oil companies on those areas with multiple owners, referred to as "pro-splits." Some of the pro-splits had more than 100 owners each, so this was a difficult assignment. Robert Angerer of OFA hired Kadrmas to coordinate her title searches among OFA, Petroseach, and Oxbow and to make separate but nearly identical contracts with those three firms. Oxbow Energy turned out to be the most difficult customer. Kadrmas and Tony Martin of Oxbow contacted one another by phone on January 10, 2004. Two different stories emerged from that phone call.

Kadrmas said that Martin told her to go ahead with the search. To cement the deal, Kadrmas mailed Martin a letter along with a contract for his signature to formalize the agreement for the title searches. This contract was identical to the one that went to OFA and Petrosearch. Martin had a different memory of the conversation. He said that he asked Kadrmas for a cost estimate but never told her tell to "go ahead." Martin also said that he did not like the contract that he got from Kadrmas, so he shredded it. Strangely, although he had every opportunity to do so, Martin never contacted Kadrmas directly to convey his dissatisfaction. Backing up in time, one month before the January phone call, OFA sent to Oxbow and Petrosearch a plan detailing how the arrangement with Kadrmas would work. Between that time and the January call (and even after that call), Kadrmas sent invoices to all three firms, detailing expenses, the hiring of additional people, and a record of the pro-splits that she had researched for each firm, including Oxbow. Twice during that time, Martin updated his contact information with Kadrmas, implying that he meant to carry on a continuing relationship with her. Kadrmas continued to handle the title searches for all three companies and to send invoices to all three, including Oxbow. On February 7, 2004, Kadrmas relayed a cost estimate to Martin. Kadrmas explained that the estimate was based on previous invoices, dating back to December. Moreover, she noted that a cost estimate had not been possible until she had a series of past billings to show her how this unusual arrangement would work out. On February 9, 2004, Martin told Kadrmas to finish the title work she was currently involved in and to put all the rest of the work "on hold." Martin refused to pay Kadrmas for any of her work, arguing that no contract existed between Oxbow and Kadrmas. In contrast, Kadrmas argued that, either an express or an implied contract existed and that she was entitled to payment for the work that she had already done on behalf of Oxbow.

At first blush, this may seem like a contract that must be in writing to be enforceable under the Statute of Frauds. That would be a mistake. The case involves real property leases, it is true, and real property contracts do need to be in writing. However, the case does not directly involve the leases. Rather, the case focuses on the contract for the title searches. Still, the title search contract between Kadrmas and Martin does illustrate another principle of the Statute of Frauds. That principle says that written contracts do not have to be one single continuous document. If the existence of a contract and the terms of that contract can be determined by looking at a series of written documents, then those documents can serve as a writing to satisfy the Statute of Frauds. Here we have a series of invoices to all three firms, detailing expenses, the hiring of additional people, and a record of the pro-splits that had been researched for each firm, including Oxbow. We also have a written cost estimate based on the title searches that were completed. This series of documents would have been sufficient as a written contract as required under the Statute of Frauds. [See: *B.J. Kadrmas, Inc. v. Oxbow Energy LLC*, 727 N.W. 2d 279 (2007).]

Source: See: *B.J. Kadrmas, Inc. v. Oxbow Energy LLC.* 727 N.W. 2d 279 (2007).

of Frauds a very effective legal tool for determining intent. In fact, one of the major goals of the Statute of Frauds is to provide detailed information about the terms of an agreement. Moreover, as we have seen, the first rule of contract interpretation is the *standard construction rule*, which tells judges that their primary objective in the interpretation of a written contract is to uncover the goals that the parties had when they entered the contract. To accomplish this goal, the writing must be intelligible, but it need not follow any preset format. Nor does the written contract have to be one single continuous document. The parties' goals—and, therefore, their intent—can be determined by looking at a series of written documents as long as the court can identify a continuous connection among those separate documents. Thus, intent can be found by examining letters, memos, documents, invoices, packing slips, and purchase orders that have been mailed, privately delivered, faxed, or sent electronically between the parties. It certainly helps when the parties explicitly add labels such as "Addendum C." However, the Restatement of the Law of Contracts also states that the "(e)xplicit incorporation (of the other documents) by reference is not necessary" (Section 132).

Degree of Definiteness In general, an offer should include points similar to those covered in a newspaper story—who, what, when, where, and how much—if it is to be clear, definite, and certain. This requirement means that the offer should identify (1) the parties involved in the contract, (2) the goods or services that will be the subject matter of the contract, (3) the price the offeror is willing to pay or receive, and (4) the time required for the performance of the contract. Most courts require reasonable rather than absolute definiteness. Offers will be upheld as long as the language is reasonably definite enough to enable the court to establish what the parties intended the terms to be so that, should there be a breach, a remedy can be set.

Time for Performance When the time for performance is not stated in the offer or in the final contract, then the contract must be performed within a reasonable time. A **reasonable time** is the time that may fairly, properly, and conveniently be required to do the task that is to be done, considering attending circumstances. Whether a task is performed within a reasonable time is a question of fact to be decided by the jury in a jury trial or the judge in a nonjury trial. When the time for performance is stated in the contract but there is nothing to indicate that time is of particular importance, the court will usually allow additional time to perform. When the time for performance is stated in the contract and there is something special about the contract that indicates time is essential, the time for performance will be strictly enforced. Similarly, when the phrase **time is of the essence** is included among the terms of a written contract, the time period will be enforced. The key words "time is of the essence" are the "magic words" that make it clear that time of performance is of the highest importance to the parties. Some contracts use a "best efforts" clause to avoid committing parties to a date but instead committing them to do their best to perform by a certain date.

UCC 2-204 (3)

Offers and the UCC The UCC permits offers to omit certain information. It states that "even though one or more terms are left open, a contract for sale does not fail for indefiniteness if the parties have intended to make a contract and there is a reasonably certain basis for giving an appropriate remedy." Under this section of the UCC, cost-plus contracts, output contracts, requirement contracts, and current market price contracts are enforceable even though they are not complete in certain matters. A **cost-plus contract** does not include a final price; rather, the contract price is determined by the cost of labor and materials plus an agreed-to percentage or dollar markup. A **requirements contract** is an agreement in which one party agrees to sell all of its goods to a second party, the buyer, while, in exchange, the buyer agrees to purchase those goods only from the seller specified in the contract. The terms of a requirements contract must be carefully worded. If the agreement allows the buyer to purchase only those goods that the buyer desires or wishes, the agreement is

THE OPENING CASE *Round 3*
A Tale of E-Mails, Invoices, Letters, and a Phone Call

In the Opening Case, we learned that Oil for America (OFA), using a new photo-aerial mapping technique, had located about 1 million acres of oil-rich land. OFA had managed to negotiate drilling leases for much of that land. However, OFA still had to negotiate leases on some of the remaining land. The unleased land was difficult to secure because it was subject to fractionalized mineral rights. OFA entered an agreement with Petrosearch and Oxbow Energy to help with the drilling and to share in the profits from the venture. Kadrmas was contracted to do the title searches for all three oil companies on the unleased land with multiple owners, referred to as "pro-splits." Some of the pro-splits had more than 100 owners each, so this was a difficult assignment. Robert Angerer of OFA hired Kadrmas to coordinate the title searches among OFA, Petroseach, and Oxbow and to make separate but nearly identical contracts for title search payments from each of those three firms. As noted, Oxbow Energy turned out to be the most difficult client.

Kadrmas and Tony Martin of Oxbow contacted one another by phone on January 10, 2004. In this negotiation, Kadrmas was the offeror and Martin the offeree. The terms of the offer were discussed by Kadrmas and Martin on the phone and then written into a contract that Kadrmas mailed to Martin. To be a valid offer, the agreement that Kadrmas sent to Martin would have to be characterized by four elements: (1) serious intent, (2) clear and reasonably definite terms, (3) communication to the offeree, and (4) the time required for the performance of the contract. Let's review those elements:

1. **Serious intent.** There can be little doubt that Kadrmas intended to enter an agreement with Martin to conduct the title search for the pro-splits. For one thing, she had already negotiated the same deal with OFA and Petrosearch. Moreover, by the time she and Martin got around to talking, Kadrmas had already started some of the title searches. This all indicates the existence of serious intent.

2. **Clear and reasonably definite terms.** Kadrmas and Angerer of OFA had already worked out a strategy that covered her duties and the manner of payment, and that plan had been communicated to the other two oil companies, including Oxbow. Moreover, Kadrmas and Martin discussed the terms on the phone. Finally, when Martin criticized the offer, he did not complain about the clarity of the terms. Rather, he described the offer as "unacceptable" and "too generic." Had the terms been indefinite and unclear, that would have been the time to mention it. Thus, there seems to be enough evidence to conclude that the terms were clear and indefinite.

3. **Communication to the offeree.** Kadrmas and Martin both admitted that they talked about the terms on the phone. Kadrmas admits mailing the offer and Martin admits receiving it. In fact, communication of the offer was never at issue in the case—period.

4. **Time required for the performance of the contract.** The main reason Oxbow and Petroshare were brought into the venture to begin with was that OFA knew that it would take too long to drill the land on its own before the leases would be up and the company would lose its rights altogether. So, clearly, time was of the essence, and Oxbow knew it, or the company would not have been brought into the venture in the first place. So, whatever ultimately happens to the contract, there was a definite offer in the air before the dispute arose.

[See: *B.J. Kadrmas, Inc. v. Oxbow Energy LLC*, 727 N.W. 2d 279 (2007).]

Source: See: *B.J. Kadrmas, Inc. v. Oxbow Energy LLC.* 727 N.W. 2d 279 (2007).

---

unenforceable because it is illusory in that the buyer is not really obligated to do anything. An **output contract** is an agreement in which one party consents to sell to a second party all of the goods that party makes in a given period of time. Finally, a **current market price contract** is one in which prices are determined by reference to the market price of the goods as of a specified date.

BUSINESS LAW WITH UCC APPLICATIONS AND NOW—THE APPLICATIONS

Requirements Contracts, Antitrust Law, the Consumer Welfare Doctrine, and the Uniform Law Commission (ULC)

As noted earlier, output contracts, cost plus contracts, requirements contracts, and current market price contracts are all permitted under the Uniform Commercial Code (UCC). Specifically the code states, at UCC 2-204 (1) and (3) that "A contract for sale of goods may be made in any manner sufficient to show agreement, including conduct by both parties which recognizes the existence of such a contract. . . . Even though one or more terms are left open a contract for sale does not fail for indefiniteness if the parties have intended to make a contract and there is a reasonably certain basis for giving an appropriate remedy." The provision seems simple enough. In essence, it states something eminently reasonable, that is, if two or more commercial partners are earnest about making a contract, then the mere fact that some part of the operation of the contract is uncertain should not militate against its validity. Yet, at times some of these contracts have run afoul of the law. For example, requirements contracts, in particular, have been seen as a violation of federal antitrust law. Remember that a requirements contract is an agreement in which one party promises to sell all of its goods to a second party, the buyer, while, in exchange, the buyer agrees to purchase those goods only from the seller.

In his book, *The Antitrust Paradox*, Robert Bork tells us that requirements contracts were considered illegal under the Sherman Antitrust Act and points out the absurdity of this situation. He argues, instead, that the driving principle of economics is value—that is, if a business provides a commodity that is of value to its consumers, and if the cost of operation is such that the business makes a profit, then whether the requirements contract creates vertical integration should make no difference. In an article in the *Harvard Journal of Law and Public Policy*, Professor George Priest labeled this doctrine as the *consumer welfare standard*. In defense of Bork's doctrine and the Chicago School of economics, Priest says, "Thus, there is a presumption in Chicago School analysis that individual firm practices generally benefit competition and consumers, rather than the reverse. This is the basis that led the Chicago School to be critical of, if not scathing toward, the expansion of antitrust law,"

Although he predates both Bork and Priest by a generation or two, Louis Bromfield would agree. In his landmark book, *A Few Brass Tacks*, Bromfield notes that, "No nation, however rich in real wealth, is ever richer or more secure than the wealth and economic security of its individual citizens." In other words, create an economic environment that benefits the productive wealth of your consumer-citizens, and your national security is, well, secure. Who would have thought that the Uniform Law Commission would have produced in UCC 2-204, such a forward-looking provision in such simple—and few—words? [See: Robert Bork, *The Antitrust Paradox, A Law at War with Itself* (New York: The Free Press, 1993), pp. 299–304; Louis Bromfield, *A Few Brass Tacks* (New York: Harper, 1946), p. 207; and George L. Priest, "The Abiding Influence of the Antitrust Paradox: An Essay in Honor of Robert H. Bork," Yale Law School, Yale Legal Scholar Repository, Faculty Scholarship Series Paper 643 (2003).]

Communication to the Offeree To be valid, an offer must be freely communicated to the offeree. The offeror's intent may be communicated by whatever means are convenient and desirable. For example, the offer may be communicated orally, by mail, by fax, by e-mail, by text, or by any other capable means. It may be implied. The proposing party's acts and conduct in many cases are successful in communicating the intention to make an offer to another party that witnesses them. When acts and conduct are sufficient to convey an offeror's intentions, an implied offer results.

Public Offers At times, an offer must be communicated to a party whose name, identity, or address is unknown. In such cases, the public offer is made. A **public offer** is one that is made through the public media but is intended for only one person whose identity or address is unknown to the offeror. A classic example of a public offer is an advertisement in a lost-and-found notice on an electronic bulletin board. Although it is a public offer, it is legally no different from other types of offers.

Invitations to Trade By contrast, invitations to trade are not offers. An **invitation to trade** is an announcement published to reach many persons for the purpose of creating interest and attracting responses. Newspaper and magazine advertisements, radio and television commercials, store window displays, price tags on merchandise, for rent signs, and prices in catalogs fall within this definition. In the case of an invitation to trade, no binding agreement develops until a responding party makes an offer that the advertiser accepts. Probably one of the most common invitations to trade is the listing price for real property. A **list price** for real property is the price that the seller asks initially when the property is placed on the market. The price is an invitation to the buyer to make an offer. Traditionally, there is little expectation that the buyer will actually make an offer based on that price. The expectation is that the buyer will make an offer at a price under the list price, which the seller will then respond to with a counteroffer. Counteroffers are discussed later.

In very rare circumstances, advertisements may be held to be offers. However, such advertisements would have to contain very particular promises, use phrases like "first-come, first-served," or limit the number of items to be sold. Because the number of people who can buy the product is very limited, the advertisement becomes an offer.

Auctions An **auction** is a sale that is open to the public, during which potential buyers compete for the right to purchase certain items by placing higher and higher bids until the highest bid is reached and the auctioneer accepts on behalf of the seller. Many people have the mistaken belief that in an auction the original property owner, that is, the seller, is the offeror and that the bidder is the offeree. These roles are true only if the auction has been expressly labeled as an **auction without reserve**. If the auction has not been so designated, it is considered an **auction with reserve**, which means that the bidders are the offerors and the seller is the offeree. Consequently, the seller can stop the bidding at any time that he or she wants, up to the time that the auctioneer declares a winner, generally by striking the podium with the gavel. A seller can also control the bidding somewhat if he or she establishes the lowest acceptable bid. In such a case, should the auctioneer *not* hear a bid that meets the least possible bid, he or she can reject all of those bids, and the seller retains the property.

Bait-and-Switch Confidence Games The **bait-and-switch confidence game** is a deliberately deceptive practice that entices buyers into a place of business when the seller actually has no intention of selling the item at the price stated in the advertisement. The practice has been outlawed by the Federal Trade Commission. In addition, many, and perhaps most, states have similar laws prohibiting bait-and-switch confidence games.

Did You Know?

Even though an auctioneer will say that the goods in an auction are being "offered for sale," the bidders at the auction are the parties who make the offer to buy those goods.

quick quiz 8-1

1. The person who freely makes an offer is called an offeree. true | false
2. An offer is valid only if it has (a) serious intent, (b) clear and reasonably definite terms, and (c) communication to the offeree. true | false
3. No valid offer will exist when terms are indefinite, inadequate, vague, or confusing. true | false

8-2 Acceptance of an Offer

The second major element in a binding contract is acceptance of the offer. As previously stated, **acceptance** means that the offeree agrees to be bound by the terms set up by the offeror. Only the offeree, the one to whom the offer is made, has the right to accept the offer. If another party attempts to accept, that attempt would actually be a new and independent offer.

Unilateral contracts do not usually require oral or written communication of an acceptance. When the offeror makes a promise in a unilateral contract, the offeror expects an action, not another promise in return. Performance of the action requested within the time allowed by the offeror and with the offeror's knowledge creates the contract.

In bilateral contracts, unlike unilateral ones, the offeree must communicate acceptance to the offeror. Bilateral contracts consist of a promise by one party in return for a promise by the other. Until the offeree communicates a willingness to be bound by a promise, there is no valid acceptance.

Conditions of Performance Some offers include conditions or terms that determine the rights and duties of the parties before performance, during performance, and following performance. These conditions may be classified as conditions precedent, conditions concurrent, or conditions subsequent. A **condition precedent** is a condition that requires the performance of certain acts or promises before the other party is obligated to pay money or provide any other agreed to consideration. In a *unilateral contract,* the performance of a condition precedent serves as the offeree's acceptance of the offer. In a *bilateral contract,* it is a promise that, if not performed, leads to either rescission or termination of the entire agreement. A common condition precedent is one that declares that the agreement will not be finalized and the contract will not exist until the buyer can obtain acceptable financing.

A condition that requires both parties to perform at the same time is a **condition concurrent**. A promise to deliver goods supported by the buyer's promise to pay on delivery is a very common condition concurrent. Real estate sales agreements, by custom, usually state that the owner–seller will deliver a good and complete deed to the real property on the buyer's presentation of either cash or a certified check for the amount of the purchase price. Failure of either to do as promised concurrently would be a breach of the express contract condition. A **condition subsequent** is one in which the parties agree that the contract will be terminated when a prescribed event occurs or does not occur. An agreement between a builder and a client stating that contract performance would terminate if required building permits were not obtained from the issuing public authority within 60 days after the contract is signed is a condition subsequent.

Communication of Acceptance

The communication of the acceptance of an offer may be either express or implied. In an express acceptance, the offeree chooses any method of acceptance, unless the offer states that the acceptance must be made in a particular manner. A stipulation such as "reply by fax" or "reply by e-mail" included in the offer must be carried out to achieve acceptance.

Face-to-Face and Telephone Communication No special problem as to the timing of acceptance usually arises if the parties are dealing face-to-face. The acceptance becomes complete and effective as soon as the offeror hears the words of acceptance spoken by the offeree. In a similar vein, if the parties are negotiating over the telephone, the acceptance becomes effective when the offeree speaks the words of acceptance into the telephone receiver (see Table 8-2). When the parties negotiate by mail, private courier, e-mail, or fax, problems may arise, and the law provides certain rules as to when acceptance occurs.

Table 8-2 Communication of Acceptance

Method Used	Legal Effect
Face-to-face communication	Acceptance is complete and effective when offeror hears the words of acceptance.
Telephone communication	Acceptance is complete and effective when offeror hears the words of acceptance.
Text messages	Acceptance is complete when text message is sent, if offeror has asked for a text response. If not, the acceptance is complete when sent, only if a text message is faster than the requested method.
Authorized means of communication	Acceptance is complete and effective when given by that same medium (e.g., mailed offer is accepted when acceptance is dropped in the mail).
Acceptance improperly dispatched	Acceptance is complete and effective when it actually reaches offeror.

Long-Distance Communication Under traditional common law principles, if a long-distance acceptance is made by an authorized method of communication, the acceptance is effective when it is sent. An authorized means of communication is one that has been endorsed by the offeror. The endorsement can be made either expressly or by implication. An acceptance is expressly endorsed by the offeror if he or she specifies the means of acceptance to be used by the offeror. Under traditional common law rules, an authorization of an acceptance is implied when the offeree accepts by the same means or by a means that is faster than that used to make the offer. Thus, an offer made through the mail is accepted when the acceptance is mailed or sent by a faster means such as a private courier (DHL, FedEx, or UPS), a fax, a phone call, an e-mail, or an inperson visit.

Communication Using Text Messages Text-messages have become an integral, accepted method of communicating in many people's daily routine. It is quite common for people to "text" one another about informal, personal matters. However, texting business colleagues is another matter entirely. While text messages are efficient and fast, they are also, by nature and design, without detailed content. These shortcomings probably explain why texting is still not the usual way to communicate in the business world. Nevertheless, should an offeror ask for a text message acceptance, the offeree should not hesitate to respond as requested. An acceptance will be valid when sent if the offeree uses a technique requested or endorsed by the offeror. However, it is also good practice to follow up such an acceptance with something more detailed and more permanent, such as a confirmation letter.

Communication and The Uniform Commercial Code The Uniform Commercial Code asserts that a contract comes into existence if any reasonable means is used to communicate the acceptance. The UCC is quite explicit in noting that to establish a contract for the sale of goods, unless otherwise indicated by the offeror or by the circumstances, the offeree may accept the offer in any manner and by any medium that is reasonable. A contract for the sale of goods then comes into existence when the acceptance is sent, as long as the method used to send is reasonable. The actual text of this rule is found in UCC 2-206 (1) (a).

The offer can dictate the form of acceptance required. If using an e-mail or text message to accept an offer, always follow up with a written and signed correspondence to create a permanent record.
©Lars Niki

Unequivocal Acceptance

To be effective, an acceptance must be *unequivocal*, which means that the acceptance must not change any of the terms stated in the offer. Under common law, this requirement is known as the mirror image rule.

The Mirror Image Rule Under the **mirror image rule**, the terms as stated in the acceptance must exactly "mirror" the terms in the offer. If the acceptance changes or qualifies the terms in the offer, it is not an acceptance. A qualified acceptance is actually a counteroffer. A **counteroffer** is a response to an offer in which the terms of the original offer are changed. No agreement is reached unless the counteroffer is accepted by the original offeror.

UCC 2-207

Counteroffers under the UCC The UCC has changed the mirror image rule for sale-of-goods contracts. Under the UCC, as long as there is a definite expression of acceptance, a contract will come into existence, even if an acceptance has different or additional terms. If the parties are not both merchants, the different or additional terms are treated as proposals for additions to the contract. If both parties are merchants however, the different or additional terms become part of the contract unless (1) they make an important difference

THE OPENING CASE *Round 4*
A Tale of E-Mails, Invoices, Letters, and a Phone Call

Once again, let's look back go the facts in the Opening Case. Oil for America (OFA) had leased a great deal of land for drilling purposes but still needed title searches done on vast tracts of unleased land that was subject to fractionalized mineral rights. Because of the enormous amount of land yet to be drilled, OFA entered an arrangement with two other oil companies, Petrosearch and Oxbow Energy. Robert Angerer of OFA hired Kadrmas to coordinate her title searches among OFA, Petroseach, and Oxbow and to make separate contracts with those three firms. OFA and Petrosearch cooperated and entered into their contracts with no difficulty, but Oxbow did not. On January 10, 2004, Kadrmas and Tony Martin of Oxbow Energy talked on the phone about the title search contract. Afterward, they told different stories about the phone call. Kadrmas said Martin told her to "go ahead" with the job; Martin denied that. Kadrmas did, however, send Martin a letter with an agreement for the title searches. Martin testified that he had received the contract but found it "unacceptable" and "too generic." So, he shredded it. He did not, however, contact Kadrmas directly by phone, e-mail, or letter to tell her that he had done so. Moreover, while he made no counteroffer, he also did not expressly reject the terms. Between December and the January call (and, it seems, even after that January call), Kadrmas sent invoices to all three firms, detailing expenses, the hiring of additional people, and a record of the pro-splits that she had researched for each firm, including Oxbow. On at least two occasions during that period, Martin also updated his contact information with Kadrmas, indicating a willingness to work with her despite his initial dissatisfaction with the generic contract. Kadrmas continued to handle the title searches for all three companies and to send invoices to all three, including Oxbow. On February 7, 2004, Kadrmas sent a cost estimate on future billing to Martin. Two days later, on February 9, 2004, Martin told Kadrmas to finish the title work she was currently involved in and to put all the rest of the work "on hold." Martin refused to pay Kadrmas for any of her work, arguing that no contract existed between Oxbow and Kadrmas.

In this case, Martin had continued to receive invoices, messages, a cost estimate, and periodic reports on the pro-splits that Kadrmas had completed for Oxbow. Martin also updated his contact information with Kadrmas, indicating a willingness to continue their business relationship. Given these actions, the court had no difficulty declaring that an implied contract existed between Kadrmas and Oxbow, despite Martin's objections to the contrary. [See: *B.J. Kadrmas, Inc. v. Oxbow Energy LLC*, 727 N.W. 2d 279 (2007).]

Source: See: *B.J. Kadrmas, Inc. v. Oxbow Energy LLC*. 727 N.W. 2d 279 (2007).

to the contract, (2) the offeror objects, or (3) the offer limits acceptance to its terms. This exception is discussed further in Chapter 13.

Implied Acceptance

Acceptance may result from the conduct of the offeree. Actions and gestures may indicate the offeree's willingness to enter into a binding agreement. A party's who acts as if the contract exists, by receiving bills, letters, e-mails, text messages, products, and so on, without objection may have created an implied acceptance.

Unordered Merchandise According to the Postal Reorganization Act, the recipient of unordered merchandise through the mail may treat such goods as a gift. The receiver has no obligation to pay for or return the goods or to communicate with the sender in any way. When unordered merchandise is delivered by agencies other than the Post Office, the common law rule is usually followed. Under the common law rule, the receiver is not obligated to contact the sender or to pay for the goods. There is, however, an implied obligation to retain the goods and give them reasonable care over a reasonable period of time. After that time, the receiver may consider that the sender no longer claims the goods and may use or dispose of them as desired. Some states, however, have laws similar to the postal law that allows recipients of unordered goods to consider them as gifts no matter who delivers them.

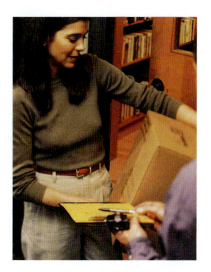

Unordered merchandise delivered by mail can be treated as a gift by the recipient. If a package is delivered by an agency other than the Post Office, the disposition of the merchandise is determined by state law.

©Keith Brofsky/Getty Images

Silence as Acceptance

As a general rule, in most situations, the offeror cannot bind the offeree just by declaring that the offeree's silence will signal an acceptance. However, should both parties agree that silence on the part of the offeree will be regarded as an acceptance, then the offeree's silence would operate as a valid acceptance. Another exception to the general rule occurs when the offeree has allowed silence to act as an acceptance. A third exception occurs when, because of the circumstances in the case, the actions of the offeree have led the offeror to the legitimate conclusion that the offeree has accepted, despite the offeree's initial silence. A fourth exception occurs when the offeree has voluntarily accepted the benefits of the transaction. On the other hand, the offeror cannot force the offeree into a contract by saying silence will mean acceptance. In contrast, the offeree can force the offeror into a contract if the offeror set up the silence condition innthe first place.

Rejection and Revocation

A **rejection** comes about when an offeree expresses or implies a refusal to accept an offer. Rejection terminates an offer and all negotiations associated with it. Further negotiations could commence with a new offer by either party or a renewal of the original offer by the offeror. Rejection is usually achieved when communicated by the offeree. A **revocation** is the calling back of the offer by the offeror. With the exception of an option contract and a firm offer, an offer may be revoked any time before it is accepted. The offeror has this right, despite what might appear to be a strong moral obligation to continue the offer. An offer may be revoked by the following methods and circumstances: communication, death or insanity of the offeror, automatic revocation, destruction of the subject matter, passage of time, and the subsequent illegality of the contract.

About the Law

Although the Ch'ing Dynasty, which ruled China from 1644 to 1911, codified the law of criminal offenses, it left civil law, for the most part, in the hands of the family and clan.

Option Contracts

An **option contract** is an agreement that binds an offeror to a promise to hold open an offer for a predetermined or a reasonable length of time. In return for this agreement, the offeror receives money or something else of value from the offeree. Parties to an option contract

THE OPENING CASE Round 5
A Tale of E-Mails, Invoices, Letters, and a Phone Call

The Opening Case can teach us one more lesson. Recall that Robert Angerer of OFA hired Kadrmas to coordinate her title searches among OFA, Petroseach, and Oxbow Energy and to make separate contracts with those three firms. On January 10, 2004, Kadrmas and Tony Martin of Oxbow Energy talked on the phone about the title search contract. Their stories about the content of that call differed quite a bit. Kadrmas said Martin gave her a "go ahead" order, but Martin denied that. On the other hand, Martin did not deny that Kadrmas sent him a letter along with a written agreement for the title searches. Moreover, he admitted that he shredded the agreement because he found it "unacceptable" and "too generic." He could have contacted Kadrmas about his dissatisfaction but, instead, chose to remain "silent." After this, Kadrmas continued to communicate with Martin, sending him invoices detailing expenses, the hiring of additional people, and a record of the pro-splits that she had researched for Oxbow. The only time that Martin communicated with Kadrmas was when he sent an update on his contact information. Kadrmas continued to handle the title searches for all three companies and continued to send invoices and reports to Oxbow. On February 7, 2004, Kadrmas sent a cost estimate on future billing to Martin. Two days later, on February 9, 2004, Martin told Kadrmas to finish the title work she was currently involved in and to put all the rest of the work "on hold."

In essence, until that moment, Martin had remained silent since the January phone call and the shredding incident. Now ordinarily under the law, an offeree's silence cannot be taken by the offeror as an acceptance. However, as we know, there are exceptions to this rule, including the following: (1) when both parties agree that silence on the part of the offeree will be regarded as an acceptance, (2) when the offeree's past behavior has allowed silence to act as an acceptance, (3) when the actions of the offeree have led the offeror to conclude that the offeree has accepted, and (4) when the offeree has voluntarily accepted the benefits of the transaction. Let's review those exceptions:

1. **An agreement between the offeror and the offeree.** Kadrmas and Martin did not agree that Martin's silence would be acceptance, so that exception does not apply here.

2. **The offeree's past behavior.** Because Kadrmas and Martin had not dealt with one another in the past, Kadrmas cannot look to Martin's past behavior to change his silence into acceptance.

3. **The actions of the offeree.** Martin's actions in accepting the invoices, title search reports, and cost estimate, as well as the fact that he updated his contact information, indicate that he had accepted the offer despite, the fact that he had remained silent up until to his February hold order. In fact, the hold order itself is evidence that he believed that Kadrmas was already acting for him under the contract. Otherwise, no hold order would have been needed.

4. **The offeree's voluntary acceptance of benefits.** Martin received and accepted the title search reports sent by Kadrmas and presumably acted on those reports. Nevertheless, even if he did not act on the reports, he had still received the only benefit that Kadrmas could bestow on him—that is, the title reports that she was hired to conduct and produce. In fact, Martin must have opened and read the reports because Oxbow Energy used the information from Kadrmas to help it produce a feasibility study for the oil exploration project.

Was Martin's silence acceptance? Yes. Given these actions, the court had no difficulty declaring that his silence acted to create an implied contract between Kadrmas and Oxbow, despite Martin's vehement and sincere objections to the contrary. [See: *B.J. Kadrmas, Inc. v. Oxbow Energy LLC*, 727 N.W. 2d 279 (2007).]

Source: See: *B.J. Kadrmas, Inc. v. Oxbow Energy LLC.* 727 N.W. 2d 279 (2007).

often agree that the consideration may be credited toward any indebtedness incurred by the offeree in the event that the offer is accepted. Should the offeree fail to take up the option, however, the offeror is under no legal obligation to return the consideration. An option contract removes the possibility of revocation through death or insanity of the offeror. The offeree who holds the option contract may demand acceptance by giving written notice of acceptance to the executor or administrator of the deceased offeror's estate or to the offeror's legally appointed guardian.

> ### EXAMPLE 8-1: Who Controls an Option Agreement?
>
> Takashi Osaka offered to sell Andras Galai a collection of rare Japanese prints for $755,000. Galai requested time to consider the offer, and Osaka agreed to hold the collection for Galai for one week in return for Galai's payment of $755. Osaka died several days later. When Galai tendered the $755,000, the executor refused to deliver the collection, claiming that death had revoked the offer. The court ruled otherwise, with judgment given to the offeree based on the option agreement between Galai and the deceased.
>
> Source: See: *B.J. Kadrmas, Inc. v. Oxbow Energy LLC.* 727 N.W. 2d 279 (2007).

Firm Offers and Sale of Goods Contracts A special rule that involves the creation of a firm offer has been developed under the Uniform Commercial Code. A **firm offer** is created when a merchant agrees in writing to hold an offer open. Under this condition, no consideration is needed to hold the offer open. A firm offer may be made for a specified period of time. If no time limit is specified, then the offer may remain open for a reasonable amount of time. However, the upper limit for a firm offer is three months. Remember that a firm offer under the UCC involves only sale-of-goods contracts.

UCC 2-205

Lease Options and Real Property A **lease option** is a contract that permits a party to lease real property while at the same time holding an option to purchase that property. Generally, to hold open the option to purchase the leased property, the person leasing the property will make an additional deposit beyond the amount that an ordinary renter would make, so that he or she retains the opportunity to purchase that property at a later time. Because a lease option involves two separate contracts, the lease contract and the option contract, it is often divided into two documents. The lease contract will detail the terms of the lease, whereas the option contract will outline the terms under which the renter can exercise the option to purchase the property.

quick quiz 8-2

1. An acceptance means that the offeree agrees to be bound by the terms set up by the offeror. — true | false
2. According to the Postal Reorganization Act, the recipient of unordered merchandise through the mail may treat such goods as a gift. — true | false
3. A rejection comes about when an offeree expresses or implies a refusal to accept an offer. — true | false

8-3 Mutual Assent in Cyberspace

The legal system, as we have seen, operates as a complex adaptive system (CAS) that emerges from a network of interacting conditions that reinforce one another while, at the same time, adjusting to change from agents outside and inside the system. These systems, however, do not act independently of one another. Rather, they overlap, interact, and sometimes compete with one another. The technological CAS has interacted with the law to produce a new subset in the legal system called cyber-law or e-law. Cyber-law helps integrate the use of computers with the orthodox operation of the legal CAS. In many situations, the courts and the legislatures have *proactively integrated* the orthodox legal system with **cyber-contracts** or **electronic contracts (e-contracts)**—that is, contracts that are made with computers or that involve computer-related products. This active approach is seen in new developments in the Uniform Commercial Code and the Restatement of the Law of Contracts. This proactive process is also seen in several laws passed by Congress and others sponsored by National Conference of Commissioners on Uniform State Laws. The new rules are found in the federal Electronic Signatures in Global and National Commerce Act (E-Sign Act), the Uniform Electronic Transactions Act, and the Uniform Computer Information Transactions Act. At other times, however, the law has simply *passively reacted* to innovative cyber breakthroughs, such as those that involve social media and cloud storage techniques.

The E-Sign Act

The E-Sign Act was passed by Congress several years ago and represents an effort to make certain that commercial cyber-documents are given the same credence as their paper counterparts. Simply stated, the act provides that cyber-contracts that are entered into over the Internet or via e-mail will be valid, provided that the parties to the e-contract have agreed that electronic signatures will be used. As long as the cyber-contract can be duplicated and stored, it will have the same validity as a paper contract. The act expressly applies to Article 2 (Sale of Goods Contracts) and Article 2A (Leases) of the UCC.

The Fair and Accurate Credit Transactions Act

The Fair and Accurate Credit Transactions Act (FACT Act) is Congress's antidote to one manifestation of the identity theft epidemic. The new law, which is actually an amendment to the Fair Credit Reporting Act (FCRA), is designed to cut down on identity theft related to the use of credit and debit cards. The act prohibits merchants from using credit and debit card receipts that show anything other than the last five credit card numbers. Receipts also cannot display credit card expiration dates. In effect, because the act outlaws such numerical displays, identity thieves will no longer be able to assume the identity of a consumer by obtaining a copy of a credit card receipt and using the credit card number and expiration date on the receipt to "verify their identity" over the phone or online. Of course, while the FACT Act helps, it does not solve every aspect of identity theft. On the other hand, if nothing else, the FACT Act does serve as an abject example of how slow lawmakers are to react to changes in society outside the beltway. The FACT Act does a fairly good job of protecting face-to-face credit and debit card transactions. So when people dine at a restaurant (including most fast-food places today), shop at mega-stores, go to the grocery, or stop at the dry cleaners or a game store, their credit card numbers and expiration dates are protected (provided a clerk or server does not memorize or write that information down on his or her sleeve).

However, most people today do at least some shopping online. One would think that the FACT Act would require online vendors to protect debit and debit card numbers and expiration dates during online transactions in the same way as face-to-face vendors. However, that is not how it works (at least as of this writing). Instead, the courts have decided that FACT Act protection extends only to paper receipts during face-to-face transactions, not to online transactions. The courts have done a good job of scouring the text of the statute and, having found no references to cyber-shopping, the Internet, electronic receipts, or e-mail, have determined that the FACT Act, as originally written, cannot be extended to cover online receipts. On the other hand, nothing prevents savvy businesspeople, with an online presence, from following the lead of the FACT Act and providing protection voluntarily.

A SOON TO BE CLASSIC CASE *Siminoff v Expedia, Inc.,* 643 F3d 793 (9th Circuit 2011)

Dimitryi Siminoff took advantage of the online airline booking service provided by Expedia Inc. At the end of the transaction, he clicked an on-screen box that indicated he would receive a receipt by e-mail. When he received the e-mailed receipt, he was astonished to see that Expedia had placed the expiration date of his credit card on the receipt. This appeared to Siminoff to be a violation of the FACT Act, so Siminoff brought this action in the federal court asking for damages. Using the late Justice Scalia's textualist approach, the court did a pretty thorough job of reading and explaining the text of the statute—all of which pointed to a dismissal of the lawsuit. This is what the the court wrote:

> Given the plain meaning of "print," the fact that the term electronically modifies the method of printing and does not alter the definition of "print," the staggered implementation schedule that applies to physical devices that print paper receipts, and the limitation of the statute to receipts produced at the point of the sale or transaction, we hold that FACTA is unambiguous in its scope. The text of FACTA simply leaves no room to doubt that "electronically printed" receipts include only receipts impressed onto a tangible medium by electronic devices at the point of the sale or transaction, not receipts that are electronically transmitted to an email account or displayed on a computer screen.

Case closed.

[See: *Siminoff v Expedia, Inc.*, 643 F3d 793 (9th Circuit 2011).]

Source: *Siminoff v Expedia, Inc.* 643 F3d 793 (9th Circuit 2011)

The Uniform Electronic Transactions Act

The Uniform Electronic Transactions Act (UETA) was written by the NCCUSL to ensure that cyber-contracts are given the same legal effect as their paper equivalents. The act does not create any new rules applying to mutual assent, consideration, capacity, and legality but, instead, makes certain that the laws that govern these elements apply to cyber-contracts just as they apply to paper contracts. There are three basic elements under the UETA. First, the participants must concur on the use of an electronic medium to create their contractual relationship. This agreement is usually not a problem because the parties to a cyber-contract are generally aware of the nature of their relationship when they sit down at a computer. Second, once the first requirement is met, the act says that the electronic record generated by the computerized transaction will have the same weight that a paper document would have in a traditional transaction. Third, once the first requirement is met, the act acknowledges that an cyber-signature is just as effective as a written signature on a paper document.

The Uniform Computer Information Transactions Act

The Uniform Computer Information Transactions Act (UCITA) arose when the Uniform Law Commission (ULC) and the ALI attempted to revise Article 2 (Sale of Goods Contracts) and Article 2A (Leases) of the UCC. Revising these articles to meet the demands of cyber-commerce and cyber-contractual relationships proved very difficult. In fact, the attempt was so difficult that the ALI dropped out of the process, leaving the ULC on its own. The ULC then elected to write an entirely new act that came to be known as UCITA. One of the problems encountered by the ULC in the writing of the new act was that many of the contracts that are entered into in cyberspace are more akin to licensing agreements than sale-of-goods contracts. The UCITA therefore covers such diverse areas as database contracts, software licensing agreements, customized software formulation, and the rights to multimedia commodities.

Many of the legal questions associated with Internet-made cyber-contracts are answered by the new act. For example, Section 102 of UCITA makes it clear that a license is to be considered "a contract that authorizes access to, or use, distribution, performance, modification, or reproduction of, information or information rights, but expressly limits the access or uses authorized or expressly grants fewer than all rights in the information, whether or not the transferee has title to a licensed copy." The UCITA has unified, streamlined, and refined the legal principles regarding such diverse areas as reverse engineering, consumer protection, shrink-wrap licenses, fair use, and consumer warranties. Despite all of this effort, the UCITA has been an extremely controversial act because many groups see it as increasing the rights and protections of software manufacturers rather than those of consumers.

Offer and Acceptance in Cyberspace

In addition to the terms included in most other offers, a cyber-offeror should insert the following terms in his or her offer: (1) payment criteria, (2) remedies that can be used by the offeree, (3) refund policies, (4) return procedures, (5) dispute settlement instructions, (6) the applicability of cyber-signatures, (7) liability disclaimers if needed, and (8) provisions relating to the offeree's manner of acceptance. There are at least two types of cyber-contracts that all online shoppers should understand: the browsewrap agreement and the clickwrap agreement (i.e., shinkwrap agreement). Browsewrap agreements are less intrusive, less obvious, and less interactive and, therefore, less likely to be binding should a dispute arise. Generally with a **browsewrap contract**, the website that contains the terms and conditions agreement is separate from the shopping website. The buyer must actively click on the website but need not do so to make purchase. In contrast, the **clickwrap agreement** requires the purchaser to read the terms of agreement page and click on that page before the transaction is complete. It is for this reason that the courts will uphold a clickwrap agreement more readily that the browsewrap agreement. With a clickwrap agreement, because purchasers must click on a statement testifying that they have read the agreement, it is more difficult for the court to accept an argument based on ignorance of the terms. Even if consumers did not read the terms, they said they did and will be required to stick by that statement.

By the way, this is no small matter. Two of the most common clauses in clickwrap agreements include arbitration clauses and forum selection clauses. An **arbitration clause** will generally have the buyers give up their right to file a lawsuit, replacing that right with mandatory binding arbitration. Usually, the clause will also specify the law that will be used in settling the dispute. As might be expected, that law is the law of the state in which the merchant is located. Similarly, a **forum selection clause**, while not requiring arbitration, will specify that all disputes will be litigated in the merchant's home state using the law of that state. The courts have ruled that as long as such clauses are easily accessible and clearly written, they will be upheld, especially because the purchaser always has the option to simply "not click" and move on to another merchant.

Social Media, Offers, and Advertising

The proliferation of social media—including Facebook, Twitter, LinkedIn, websites, blogs, and so on—has led to interesting and unintended consequences in the world of cyber-contracts. Social media, when used properly and with appropriate caution, can be just as harmless as talking to someone at a ballgame or after church. However, if handled improperly, the misuse of social media can inadvertently lead to unintended offers and perhaps, even worse, to accusations of fraud or misrepresentation. As a general rule, it is best to think of social media as a way of interacting with others unofficially. This is not to say that social media cannot be used as advertising or as a way to make or accept an offer. On the contrary, it is good business to have a visible presence online. In the 21st century, shoppers

A SOON TO BE CLASSIC CASE *Adsit Company, Inc. v. Gustin,* 18A02-1010-CV-90 Appeals Court of Indiana (2007)

Julie Gustin, who lived in Alabama, was in the market for a set of seat covers and arm rests for a classic 1967 Mercedes-Benz roadster. She was buying them for her husband, so she had her mother-in-law, Mary Gustin, who lived in Texas purchase them online from Adsit, a corporation located in Indiana using her, Julie's, credit card. In order to complete the purchase, Mary had to indicate acceptance of a clickwrap agreement that included a forum selection clause that limited all litigation to the Indiana courts and Indiana law. The seat covers and arm rest covers turned out to be the wrong color, so Julie sent them back and canceled the credit card sale with her bank So far, so good. However, the seat covers never arrived at Adsit. Accordingly, Adsit sued for breach of contract. In litigation, Julie and Mary objected to being forced to sue in Indiana using Indiana law. Here is what the court had to say about that:

> To determine whether a clickwrap agreement is enforceable, courts presented with the issue apply traditional principles of contract law and focus on whether the plaintiffs had reasonable notice of and manifested assent to the clickwrap agreement . . . the Adsit policy gave reasonable notice of its terms. To complete a transaction, a user must accept the policy, the text of which is immediately visible to the user.   The user is required to take affirmative action by clicking on the "I Accept" button; if the user refuses to agree to the terms, she cannot engage in the transaction. The entire policy is essentially three short paragraphs-one-half of a page. Moreover, the paragraph that contains the forum selection clause begins with the following heading, which is bolded and in all capital letters: "AGREEMENT ON JURISDICTION TO DAMAGES[.]" Pl.Ex. Under these circumstances, we find that Mary had reasonable notice of and manifested assent to the clickwrap agreement containing the forum selection clause.

Case closed.

[See: *Adsit Company, Inc. v. Gustin*, 18A02-1010-CV-90 Appeals Court of Indiana (2007).]

Source: Adsit Company, Inc. v. Gustin 18 A02-1010-CV-90 Appeals Court of Indiana (2007)

and clients no longer run to the Yellow Pages or to the newspaper to search for professionals. Instead, they look to the Web. However, professionals who use the Web must do so in a carefully planned way.

Businesspeople, such as accountants, architects, financial advisors, and attorneys, who are regulated by professional organizations must be especially careful about their use of social media. Attorneys, for example, must pay special attention to what the Model Rules of Professional Conduct say about advertising and soliciting business and then apply those rules on an ad hoc basis to social media. For instance, under Rule 7.2, lawyers are permitted to advertise, but under Rule 7.1 those advertisements must not be "false or misleading." Lawyers must, therefore, be especially careful not to cross these sometimes vague rules when constructing profiles on LinkedIn and Facebook, blogging, texting, and using Twitter. Exaggerating or making unsubstantiated claims in an offhanded way on a Facebook page may come very close to crossing that invisible line between an informal and harmless chat and a false advertisement.

Professionals are not the only ones who need to be careful when using social media for business purposes. Commercial speech is constitutionally protected, but to earn that protection, all commercial speech must be truthful. Blogs that guarantee the outcome of a case or that fabricate untrue stories about products and services have probably crossed the line. Creating a false identity when blogging or when offering testimonials, a practice known as sock puppetry, is also not a good idea. [See: Josh King, "Being Smart with Social Media: Ethics and Effectiveness when Engaging Online," Ohio State Bar Association 2014 Annual Convention (April 30 to May 2, 1014).]

Managing "The Cloud" when Making and Accepting Offers

Cloud storage (or cloud computing) is a cyber-technique that preserves electronic data without using local hard drives and flash drives. Instead the data is transferred to a data center that stores the data on a remote database. The data owner (or data depositor) can then access the data from anywhere by request through the Internet. Because the data is not kept on the data owner's hard drive, the owner is not tied to his or her own computer or storage device and thus gains a great deal of flexibility. Generally, the data center's storage capacity is also much greater than the storage ability of the data owner. Data centers also tend to keep current with the latest developments in web applications. Moreover, the data is accessible no matter what electronic device (smartphones, tablets, laptops, and so on) the data owner might use. All of this sounds quite good, until we recall that often the information contained in an offer—such as the asking price; the details of the negotiation process; the price mentioned in counteroffer; and the nature, timing, and technique of the acceptance—must be kept secure and confidential.

Such might be true if the transaction involves a bidding contest for a construction contract or the auctioning of a unique item, such a rare antiquity or an original work of art. This fact means that businesspeople using the cloud during the offer and acceptance steps in the creation of a contract should take the necessary steps to preserve the confidentiality of such data while it is kept within the cloud. Often, data can be kept secure by using encryption measures, a list of sanctioned users, and a verification process. Data centers should also protect stored e-data with redundancy procedures that back up the data and thus protect it from theft, hacking, and a loss of electrical service. [See: Jonathan Strickland, "How Cloud

A REAL CLASSIC CASE From Invitation, to Offer, to Acceptance

The Great Minneapolis Surplus Store published the following advertisement in a Minneapolis newspaper:

> Saturday 9 A.M. Sharp 3 Brand New Fur Coats Worth to $100.00. First Come First Served $1 Each.

On April 13, the store published another advertisement in the same newspaper:

> Saturday 9 A.M. 2 Brand New Pastel Mink 3-Skin Scarfs Selling for $89.50
> Out they go Saturday. Each . . . $1.00
> 1 Black Lapin Stole Beautiful, worth $139.50 . . . $1.00
> First Come First Served

Following the clear instructions in the advertisement, Mr. Lefkowitz traveled to the Great Minneapolis Surplus Store and arrived early enough to be the first customer to enter the store at 9 A.M. He had his dollar in hand and was ready to purchase the black lapin stole. However, he was informed that the sale was designed only for the store's women customers. Lefkowitz protested but was unable to get satisfaction from the store. Accordingly, he did what any red-blooded American would do—he filed a lawsuit. The store argued, rather convincingly, that a newspaper advertisement like the one run by the store was not an offer but was, instead, only an invitation to make an offer. The advertisement was like the "For Sale" sign in front of a house or the price posted on a motor vehicle at a used car lot. In all such cases, the buyer is the offeror and the seller is the offeree. That permits the Great Minneapolis Surplus Store to refuse to honor the customer's offer—end of story.

Lefkowitz disagreed. To prove his point, he submitted the following argument: The advertisement in the newspaper is definite enough to pinpoint every element necessary in a contract. The advertisement identifies the subject matter (one black lapin stole), the price (one American dollar), the place of the sale (the department store), the day and time of the sale (Saturday morning at 9), and the buyer as the first person to show up at the store (first come, first served). That much detail turns the invitation into an offer that he, Leftkowitz, accepted. Therefore, the store could not at that point refuse to sell, at least not without some sort of legal consequences. The court agreed. [See: *Lefkowitz v. Great Minneapolis Surplus Store, Inc.*, 86 N.W.2d 689 (Minn. 1957).]

Source: See: *Lefkowitz v. Great Minneapolis Surplus Store, Inc.*, 86 N.W.2d 689 (Minn. 1957).

Storage Works," *How Stuff Works* (2008), retrieved on January 11, 2013, from https://computer.howstuffworks.com/; and Barron Henley, "Legal Technology Tips, Tricks, Gadgets, and Websites," Ohio State Bar Association 2013 Annual Convention (May 8–10, 2013).]

quick quiz 8-3

1. The Uniform Electronic Transactions Act (UETA) was passed by Congress as a federal law. true | false
2. The Electronic Signatures in Global and National Commerce Act was written by the Uniform Law Commission. true | false
3. The process of accepting an online offer is often referred to as a "clickwrap agreement" or a "browsewrap agreement." true | false

8-4 The Destruction of Mutual Assent

As is true of most other parts of the legal system, contract law seeks to balance the rights and the duties of two or more parties. In contract law, those two parties are the offeror and the offeree, and the rights and the duties are assumed voluntarily. The balance emerges from a dialectic that pairs the offer with the acceptance and sets the stage for the development of a synthesis between the two. That synthesis is referred to as mutual assent. As the first element of a contract, mutual assent must stand on its own, without being propped up by artificial supports. Mutual assent, however, can be elusive. Unfortunately, some emergent agreements that appear to be correctly constructed at first glance are, in fact, substantively false, despite the pretty picture that they might create. Those forces that destroy assent come in five flavors: fraud, misrepresentation, mistake, duress, and undue influence.

Fraud and Misrepresentation

Both fraud and misrepresentation disrupt mutual assent. They do so by sabotaging the essential component of trust upon which all agreements, but especially contracts, are based. This is what makes both fraud and misrepresentation so insidious. They are based on deceitful practice that makes a mockery of the entire commercial process. Of the two, fraud is the more serious and the more despicable because it is deliberate. It is also the more difficult of the two to prove. This may be why many cases that should be litigated as fraud, end up in court as misrepresentation lawsuits.

Fraud To destroy mutual assent through a claim of **fraud**, the complaining or innocent party must prove the existence of five elements.

1. The complaining party will have to prove that the other party made false representations about some **material fact** (i.e., an important fact, a fact of substance) involved in the contract. A material fact is one that is very crucial to the terms of the contract.
2. The plaintiff must demonstrate convincingly that the other party made the representations knowing that they were false.
3. The plaintiff must show that the false representations were made with the intent that they be relied upon by the innocent party.
4. The complaining party must establish that there was a reasonable reliance on the false representations.
5. The plaintiff must verify that he or she actually suffered some loss by relying on the false representations after entering the contract.

A case involving either active or passive fraud must be based on these five elements.

LO8

About the Law

While the common law courts of England were quite willing to acknowledge fraud in tort law, they were not as willing to see its application in contract law.

Types of Fraud There is more than one way to commit fraud. The law distinguishes between fraud in the inception and fraud in the inducement. **Fraud in the inception** occurs when one party tricks another party into a contract by lying to the innocent party about the actual nature of the contract. In effect, because of false representations made by one party, the innocent party believes that he or she is doing "A" when he or she is actually doing "B." For example, if an insurance agent were to tell an accident victim that the paper she was signing was a privacy waiver, when it was actually an agreement releasing the insurance company from all liability, it would be fraud in the inception. **Fraud in the inducement** occurs when one party tricks another into a contract by lying about the terms of the agreement to get the innocent party to enter the contract under false pretenses. In this case, because of the false representations made by one party, the innocent party believes that he or she is doing "A," but "A" turns out to be actually "A−" or "A+" or "a" rather than simply "A." If, for instance, a loan officer at a bank were to tell a borrower that the interest rate on the loan would be 8 percent when it was actually 18 percent, that officer would have committed fraud in the inducement.

EXAMPLE 8-2: Rhodes v. Hayden

Gabriel Hayden owned a motorboat that was docked at the Butler Reservoir. Hayden, however, was about to move to the city and so was anxious to get rid of a boat for which he would have no use in the city. Kelly Rhodes, who was new in town, wanted to purchase a motorboat quickly so that she would have several weeks of summer weather left to enjoy the boat. Sensing that he could make a real killing on the deal, Hayden told Rhodes about the boat. Rhodes was impressed by Hayden's sales pitch, but she wanted to see the boat first and take it for a test run on the reservoir. Hayden agreed. Before Rhodes arrived the next day for the test run, Hayden patched up several obvious holes in the bottom of the boat with putty and poster board. Hayden knew the repairs would not make the boat seaworthy for longer than 15 minutes, but he figured that would be enough time to fool Rhodes into thinking that the boat was in good condition. Deceived by the apparently good condition of the boat, Rhodes purchased it. The next time she took it out on the reservoir, the boat quickly sank. Even though Hayden never actually told any verbal lies to Rhodes, he would still have committed fraud.

To be fraudulent, statements must involve facts. Opinions and **sales puffery** consist of the persuasive words and exaggerated claims made by salespeople to induce a customer to buy their product. As long as the comments are reserved to opinion and do not misstate facts, they cannot be considered fraud in a lawsuit, even if they turn out to be grossly wrong.

EXAMPLE 8-3: Oldacker v. Kellog Formal Wear Shoppe

Fran Holiday, a sales clerk representing the Kellog Formal Wear Shoppe, was trying to sell a tuxedo to Ken Oldacker. During the sales discussion, Holiday told Oldacker that the tux (1) came with two pairs of pants, (2) was made of 100 percent wool, (3) had a very rich texture, (4) looked very good on Oldacker, and (5) would make him look like James Bond. The first two statements are statements of material fact and could be the basis of a lawsuit for fraud if they are proven false. The others are either opinions expressed by the seller or the persuasive puffery that might induce Oldacker to buy the tux and, therefore, could not be used as the basis of a lawsuit for fraud.

Active and Passive Fraud As noted previously, **active fraud** occurs when one party actually makes a false statement intended to deceive the other party in a contract. In contrast, **passive fraud**, which is generally called **concealment** or **nondisclosure**, occurs when one party does not say something about certain facts that he or she is under an obligation to reveal. If this passive conduct is intended to deceive and does in fact deceive the other party, fraud results. In general, a party is not required to reveal every known fact related to the subject matter of a contract. Certain facts may be confidential and personal. However, if the problem or defect is hidden and the other party cannot reasonably be expected to discover the defect, provided the problem involves some material fact, the offeror may be obliged to reveal it. Some states have held that sellers are legally bound to reveal only problems so hidden that even an expert would not be able to uncover them. In these states, problems such as insect or rodent infestation would not be hidden problems because an expert could easily uncover them.

Fraud can occur in many ways. A consumer's best defense is to be knowledgeable, listen, and ask questions.

©Thinkstock/Jupiterimages

A **fiduciary relationship** is a relationship based on trust. Such relationships exist—for example, between attorneys and clients, guardians and wards, trustees and beneficiaries, and boards of directors and corporations. If one party is in a fiduciary relationship with another party, then an obligation arises to reveal what otherwise might be withheld when the two parties enter an agreement.

A QUESTION OF ETHICS

Suppose that you are showing your car to Tim Jorgenson, a potential buyer. You know that if Jorgenson takes your car for a drive, he will notice that the front end rattles at speeds in excess of 35 miles per hour and that the brakes grind badly. Jorgenson, however, does not take the car on a test drive and therefore fails to detect any defects. Would you have an ethical duty to tell Jorgenson about the car's problems? Explain.

EXAMPLE 8-4: San Rafael Motor Corporation v. Groza

Otto Groza was vice president of business and finance for the San Rafael Motor Corporation when he learned that Toth Properties Ltd. wanted to buy 12,000 acres of land owned by San Rafael. Groza was the only one at San Rafael who knew that a new extension of the interstate was going to be located on the acreage owned by the company. Moreover, Groza knew that Toth wanted the land for an outlet mall and an adjoining hotel and was willing to pay $19,000 per acre. Groza made a deal with Toth agreeing to sell the land at that price. He then went to the CEO and the board of San Rafael and offered to buy the farmland without revealing anything about the Toth deal. As a result, he purchased the acreage for $1,000 per acre and made an $18,000 profit on each acre he resold to Toth. Groza will be liable to San Rafael because he concealed a material fact that he was obligated to reveal because of his fiduciary relationship with the company.

Catfishing: A New Type of Fraud? For years, many educators were reluctant to teach online courses, despite the high demand for such courses, because there was really no way to know who was actually doing the online work. Over time, techniques have been developed to help overcome this fundamental difficulty. For example, testing centers have emerged that follow strict identification procedures to ensure that a test taker in Maine is really the student who is enrolled in a course being taught by a teacher in Nevada. As we have seen, in the law, business problems like this have been handled in variety of ways. For example, the E-Sign Act ensures that cyber-contracts that are entered into over the Internet or via e-mail will be valid, provided that the parties to the e-contract have agreed that electronic signatures will be used. Similarly, the FACT Act has cut down on identity theft by prohibiting merchants from using credit and debit card receipts that show anything other than the last five credit card numbers.

However, a new type of identify theft, called catfishing, has emerged recently, that these laws do not cover. Catfishing is not identity theft, *per se.* Instead, **catfishing** involves the creation of an entirely new online identity, a **cyber-ghost**, who then snags a gullible, but innocent, victim who becomes involved with the cyber-ghost and is then conned out of large

A SOON TO BE CLASSIC CASE *Bonhomme v. St. James,* 970 N.E.2d 1 Supreme Court of Illinois (2012)

Janna St. James entered an online relationship with Paula Bonhomme in which St. James created a fictitious online identity, a cyber-ghost, designed to gain the confidence of Bonhomme and to take advantage of that relationship. The cyber-ghost was a fictitious male named Jesse who eventually declared his love for Bonhomme. St. James also created an entire fictitious world around the cyber-ghost, including friends and relatives. Over the course of relationship, Bonhomme gave gifts to Jesse and others in the fictitious online world that amounted to more than $10,000. Later difficulties with the "relationship" caused Bonhomme to undergo therapy that led to bills that surpassed $5,000. St. James also led Bonhomme to believe that Jesse was about to move in with Bonhomme. Preparations for this "move" cost Bonhomme $700. St. James eventually led Bonhomme to believe that Jesse had committed suicide. St. James then befriended Bonhomme directly as a close friend of the "deceased" Jesse. Bonhomme then agreed to have St. James move in with her. This move cost Bonhomme more than $1,000. Eventually, the charade was uncovered by some of Bonhomme's real friends. Even after this discovery, Bonhomme continued to suffer emotional stress. This led to more therapy bills and lost wages. Eventually, Bonhomme brought this lawsuit. One of her claims was that she had been defrauded by St. James (fraudulent misrepresentation was the actual basis of the claim). As much as the court wanted to find that Bonhomme had been victimized by St. James based in fraudulent misrepresentation, it could not do so. The primary problem here was that no business relationship was involved in the case. No business relationship, no fraud. This is what the court said in dismissing the claim:

> [T]he crucial question in this case is whether the facts at issue are purely personal in nature, or whether there exists some commercial, transactional, or regulatory component that moves them beyond the purely personal. This is not a difficult question to answer. When all is said and done, what lies beneath this case is two private persons engaged in a long-distance personal relationship. To be sure, it was a personal relationship built wholly on one party's relentless deceit, but it was a purely personal relationship nonetheless. Indeed, all of the hallmarks of ordinary human relationship are present: correspondence, conversation, intimacy, trust, mutual beneficence, emotional support, affection, disappointment, and even grief. And just as importantly, there is absolutely nothing of the commercial, transactional, or regulatory at work. Plaintiff and defendant were not engaged in any kind of business dealings or bargaining, and the veracity of representations made in the context of purely private personal relationships is simply not something the state regulates or in which the state possesses any kind of valid public policy interest. Consequently, as regrettable as the alleged facts are, we hold that they are not are not the types of facts upon which a claim for fraudulent misrepresentation may be pled.

Case closed.

[See: *Bonhomme v. St. James*, 970 N.E.2d 1 Supreme Court of Illinois (2012).]

Source: Bonhomme v. St. James 970 N.E.2d 1 Supreme Court of Illinois (2012) amounts of money. While this money is allegedly used to help the cyber-ghost, it really lines the pockets of the ghost and his or her cohorts. All of this is done online so that the victim and the cyber-ghost never meet face-to-face. Laws that are designed to deal with identity theft and impersonating a person online do not apply when the identity is fabricated rather than stolen. Also, catfishing lawsuits rarely succeed when they are based on fraud because fraud requires that the injured party suffer a loss caused by relying on false representations in a business relationship. Most catfishing grievances do not involve business relationships. Rather they result from personal relationships that lead to expensive gift giving and outrageous bill paying to help the cyber-ghost financially, but do not involve business transactions between the ghost and the victim.

Misrepresentation

A false statement made innocently with no intent to deceive is **misrepresentation**. Innocent misrepresentation makes an existing agreement voidable, and the complaining party may demand rescission. **Rescission** means that both parties are returned to their original positions, before they entered into the contract. Unlike cases based on fraud, which allow rescission and damages, cases based on innocent misrepresentation allow only rescission, not monetary damages (see Table 8-3). If a party to an agreement makes an innocent misrepresentation and then later discovers that it is false, that party must reveal the truth. If the party does not reveal the truth, the innocent misrepresentation becomes fraud.

Mistake, Duress, and Undue Influence

When there has been no real meeting of the minds because of a mistake, mutual assent was never achieved, and the agreement may be rescinded. As in misrepresentation, mistake permits rescission. Both duress and undue influence rob a person of the ability to make an independent, well-reasoned decision to enter a contractual relationship freely. Both of these conditions therefore strike at the heart of contract law.

The Nature of Mistake A mistake made by only one of the contracting parties is a **unilateral mistake** and does not offer sufficient grounds for rescission or renegotiation. When both parties are mistaken, it is a **bilateral mistake**. A bilateral mistake, which is also called a **mutual mistake**, may permit a rescission by either the offeror or the offeree. Mutual mistakes are of several kinds (see Table 8-4). Some are universally accepted as grounds for rescission. Others are not grounds for rescission. Still others can give rise to

Table 8-3 Agreements Made Defective by Falsehood

Falsehood	Definition	Remedy
Active fraud	Active fraud occurs when one party to a contract makes a false statement intended to deceive the other party and thus leads that party into a deceptively based agreement.	Damages and rescission
Passive fraud	Passive fraud occurs when one party does not say something about certain facts that he or she is obligated to reveal. Obligations arise in situations involving hidden problems and fiduciary relationships.	Damages and rescission
Misrepresentation	Misrepresentation occurs when a false statement is innocently made.	Rescission

Table 8-4 Agreements Made Defective by Mutual Mistake

Mistake	Legal Effect
Mistake as to description	Rescission will be granted.
Mistake as to existence	Proof that subject matter was destroyed *before* the agreement was made gives grounds for rescission.
Mistake as to value	Rescission will not be granted since value is a matter of opinion, not fact.

lawsuits, but not in all courts or in all states. When both parties are mistaken in the identification and description of subject matter, there is a real mutual mistake, and rescission will be granted.

Proof that the subject matter had been destroyed before the agreement was made gives grounds for rescission. Thus, if one party accepted an offer to purchase a boat that both parties mistakenly believed to be berthed at a specified marina, the agreement would be voidable if it were proved that moments before acceptance, the boat had been destroyed. Had the boat been destroyed after final acceptance, there would have been no mutual mistake, and an enforceable contract would have resulted. When two parties agree on the value of the subject matter and later find they were both mistaken, it is a mutual mistake of opinion, not of fact. Mutual mistakes of opinion are not grounds for rescinding a contract.

The Nature of Duress In general, **duress** may be viewed as an action by one party that forces another party to do what need not otherwise be done. Duress forces a person into a contract through the use of physical, emotional, or economic threats (see Table 8-5). In contrast, undue influence merely involves the use of excessive pressure. Moreover, undue influence requires the existence of a special relationship, generally of a confidential or fiduciary nature. **Physical duress** involves either violence or the threat of violence against an individual or against that person's family, household, or property. If only threats are used, they must be so intense and serious that a person of ordinary prudence would be forced into the contract without any real consent. Threats of physical duress are relatively rare today. Perhaps more common are threats that create emotional duress. **Emotional duress** arises from acts or threats that would create emotional distress in the

Table 8-5 Agreements Made Defective by Force or Pressure

Type of Force or Pressure	Explanation
Physical duress	Violence or threat of violence to person, family, household, or property.
Emotional duress	Acts or threats that create emotional distress in the one on whom they are inflicted.
Economic duress	Threats of a business nature that force another party without real consent to enter a commercial agreement.
Undue influence	Dominant party in a special relationship uses excessive pressure to convince the weaker party to enter a contract.

one on whom they are inflicted. It is generally necessary that the action threatened be either illegal or illicit.

Economic duress, also known as **business compulsion**, consists of threats of a business nature that force another party without real consent to enter a commercial agreement. To establish economic duress, the complaining party must demonstrate the existence of three elements:

1. The plaintiff must prove that the other party wrongfully placed the plaintiff in a precarious economic situation.
2. The plaintiff must show that he or she had no alternative other than to submit to the contractual demands of the wrongful party.
3. The plaintiff must demonstrate that he or she acted reasonably in entering the contract.

If the plaintiff can prove the existence of these three elements, the court will rule the contract voidable on grounds of economic duress.

EXAMPLE 8-5: National Air Races Inc. v. Macon City Airport

The owners and operators of National Air Races negotiated a seven-year lease with the City of Macon for use of the Macon City Airport. Each summer, during the Fourth of July weekend celebration, the National Air Races were held at the Macon City Airport. One week before the first race of the fourth year under the contract, Macon city officials informed the owners and operators of the National Air Races that they would no longer be able to use the Macon City Airport for the Fourth of July races unless they paid a substantial rent increase. The owners and operators of the Air Races, who had already sold at least 5,000 tickets per race, had accepted entry fees from 95 pilots, and had contracts with 20 concessionaires, could not find any other suitable airport within 120 miles of Macon. As a result, they agreed to the terms. Later, the owners of the Air Races sued Macon to have the rent increase rescinded. The court ruled that the rent increase was voidable due to economic duress.

The Nature of Undue Influence The problem of **undue influence** occurs when the dominant party in a special relationship uses excessive pressure to convince the weaker party to enter a contract that greatly benefits the dominant party. A plaintiff who wants to demonstrate that he or she was enticed into a contract by undue influence must prove the existence of two elements.

1. The plaintiff must show that a special relationship existed between the parties. A special relationship can generally be characterized as one that is fiduciary in nature or one that involves domination. Examples of fiduciary relationships include the relationships of parent to child, guardian to ward, attorney to client, physician to patient, pastor to parishioner, and so forth. Relationships that involve dominance frequently occur when the stronger of the two parties is acting as a caretaker of the weaker party.
2. Second, the plaintiff must show that the other party used excessive pressure to take advantage of him or her to enter a contract that greatly benefits the party applying the pressure.

In most cases involving undue influence, one party in the special relationship has enough strength and leadership to dominate the other party, who is obviously weaker and dependent.

> **Did You Know?**
>
> It is possible for a party to ratify a contract made under duress if, after the duress has ended, the party makes a new promise to abide by the terms of the original agreement. In such a situation, the party ratifying the contract need not supply any new consideration.

quick quiz 8-4

1. Misrepresentation is a false statement made with no intent to deceive.   true | false
2. Mutual mistake is grounds for rescinding a contract.   true | false
3. Economic duress is also known as business compulsion.   true | false

Summary

8.1 If certain requirements are met, the court will conclude that the parties intended to make and accept an offer. Mutual assent is created when an offer is made by one party and accepted by the other party. An offer is valid if it is made with serious intent, displays clear and definite terms, and is communicated to the offeree.

8.2 The second major part of mutual assent is the acceptance of the offer. Communication of the acceptance may be either express or implied. Under the mirror image rule, an acceptance must not change any of the terms of the offer. The UCC has altered the mirror image rule. At any time prior to acceptance, the offeror can withdraw the offer. Still, some types of offers cannot be revoked by the offeror. These involve option contracts, firm offers, and lease option contracts.

8.3 The principal rules concerning the interpretation of the enforcement of cyber-contracts are found in the E-Sign Act, the Uniform Electronic Transactions Act (UETA), and the Uniform Computer Information Transactions Act (UCITA).

8.4 Fraud involves deliberate deception about some material fact that leads a party into an agreement that is damaging to that party. Misrepresentation is a false statement innocently made with no intent to deceive. A mutual mistake may allow for rescission by either party. Duress and undue influence rob a person of the ability to make an independent, well-reasoned decision to enter freely into a contract.

Key Terms

acceptance, 242
active fraud, 255
arbitration clauses, 250
auction, 241
auction with reserve, 241
auction without reserve, 241
bait-and-switch confidence game, 241
bilateral mistake, 257
browsewrap contract, 250
business compulsion, 259
catfishing, 256
clickwrap agreement, 250
cloud storage, 252
concealment, 255
condition concurrent, 242
condition precedent, 242
condition subsequent, 242
contract, 235
cost-plus contract, 238
counteroffer, 244
current market price contract, 239
cyber-contract, 248
cyber-ghost, 256
duress, 258
economic duress, 259
electronic contracts or e-contracts, 248
emotional duress, 258
fiduciary relationship, 255
firm offer, 247
forum selection clause, 250
fraud, 253
fraud in the inception, 254
fraud in the inducement, 254
invitation to trade, 241
lease option, 247
list price, 241
material fact, 253
mirror image rule, 244
misrepresentation, 257
mutual assent, 236
mutual mistake, 257
nondisclosure, 255

offer, 236
offeree, 236
offeror, 236
option contract, 245
output contract, 239
passive fraud, 255
physical duress, 258
public offer, 241
reasonable time, 238
rejection, 245
requirements contract, 238
rescission, 257
revocation, 245
sales puffery, 254
sock puppetry, 251
time is of the essence, 238
undue influence, 259
unilateral mistake, 257

Questions for Review and Discussion

1. What is mutual assent?
2. What are the elements of an offer?
3. What is the UCC's concept of an offer?
4. How does an acceptance come about?
5. What is the mirror image rule?
6. What is revocation?
7. What statutes affect mutual assent in cyberspace?
8. What are the elements of fraud and misrepresention?
9. What are the effects of mistake on mutual assent?
10. What are duress and undue influence?

Cases for Analysis

1. The Sharps put their house up for sale, and Andisman and Blakeley made an offer to purchase the house for $1.2 million, well sort of—that is part of the problem. The offer was dated November 2. For personal reasons, Blakeley's name was not on the offer, although he had indicated (and everyone seems to have believed) that he intended to pay cash. In contrast, Andisman's name was on the offer, but evidence indicates that she never signed it. A purchase agreement was then drawn up and signed by the Sharps on November 7. Later, despite Blakeley's promise to pay cash, an addendum was drawn up stating that the agreement was contingent on Andisman getting a loan. This document was labeled Addendum A and signed by Andisman. On November 22, Andisman's loan was preapproved. Unfortunately, after further examination of her application, the mortgage broker withdrew the preapproval. Still, this withdrawal seems to have occurred simply because the application was incomplete. The missing information was never forthcoming. Instead, a new addendum was added to the offer. This happened in May, the original closing date having long since faded into the past. This new addendum (designated Addendum C) removed the loan contingency, made Blakeley party to the agreement, and changed the closing date to June 28. Both Andisman and Blakeley signed Addendum C and faxed it to the Sharps. The new closing date came and went, again with no action from the buyers. Eventually, the sellers gave up and filed suit on September 25. In their defense, Andisman and Blakeley argued that the offer was never valid because (1) neither of them signed the offer in November, (2) acceptance was made contingent on a loan that was not approved, and (3) since "time was of the essence" in this agreement and they did not close on January 15, as noted in the offer, the agreement ended automatically by operation of law on that date. The trial court found for the Sharps and awarded them $575,000 for their losses plus more than $29,000 in special damages. Andisman and Blakeley appealed. Should the appellate court reverse the decision of the trial court? Explain. [See: *Sharp v. Andisman*, Nos. 24999, 25005 (2010-Ohio-4452).]

2. Lindbergh-Sikorsky Aircraft Corporation e-mailed an offer to Kenneth Hiebel, the owner of the Triple R-Bar Ranch in Idaho. The e-mail stated, "Please consider this our offer to purchase 20,000 acres of your 61,200-acre ranch land near Harrington, Idaho. Our offering price is between $60,000 and $65,000 per acre. Please respond soon." Look at the requirements of an offer and determine whether the e-mail quoted above constitutes a valid offer. Explain.

3. Patrick Barnes and George Layton were employed by the Sailors' Maritime Service. When they expressed dissatisfaction with their jobs, their employer offered them a new contract whereby they would receive a 10 percent bonus on company

profits if they remained with the firm. Several times they discussed the terms of the new agreement with an official of Sailors' Maritime. Eventually, they decided that the offer was a good one, and they continued on the job as usual. Sailors' Maritime later refused to pay the 10 percent bonus, claiming that its offer had never been accepted. Is Sailors' Maritime refusal to pay legally correct? Or, to pinpoint the issue more directly, was the offer accepted by Barnes and Layton? Explain. Now suppose that Sailors' Maritime had said to Barnes and Layton, "We will consider your written acceptance of this new proposal as binding us to the payment of the 10 percent bonus." Would these additional facts change your initial evaluation of this case? Why or why not?

4. Sarah Jameson read an advertisement in *The Independent* inviting her to become a member of the New Era DVD Club. Jameson chose several DVDs that were listed in the advertisement. She paid only $1 for those DVDs and became a member of the DVD club. In doing so, she also agreed to purchase four more DVDs in a year's time. Under terms clearly specified in the advertisement, Jameson knew she would receive a brochure 12 times a year listing selections. The brochure would also identify the main selections, which would be sent to her automatically unless she sent a reply form to stop the shipment. In effect, New Era has made Jameson's silence acceptance. Is this a legally effective tactic? Explain.

5. Anthony Sanderson was browsing on eBay when he located what was labeled as a 1932 edition of *Brave New World* by Aldous Huxley, produced by Chatto and Windus, the London publisher that had printed the first edition of that landmark novel. The book was advertised as coming along with a companion book by Julian Huxley, entitled *If I Were Dictator*, published in 1934 by the London-based Methuen. The seller was Juliette Straus, who set the minimum bid for the two volumes at GBP 8,700. Sanderson, who quickly bid on the two books, eventually won the auction with a successful bid of GBP 9,800. Later, after receiving the two books, Sanderson discovered that the copy of *If I Were Dictator* was actually a 1948 reprint of the original work. Is this a case of fraud or misrepresentation? Explain.

6. An advertisement appeared in the *Chicago Sun-Times* for the sale of a Volvo station wagon at Lee Calan Imports Inc., for $1,095. The advertisement had been misprinted by the *Sun-Times*. The actual price of the automobile was $1,795. O'Keefe showed up at Lee Calan and said he would buy the Volvo for $1,095. Lee Calan refused to sell the car for $1,095. O'Keefe sued, claiming that the advertisement was an offer that he accepted, creating a binding agreement. Was O'Keefe correct? Explain. [See: *O'Keefe v. Lee Calan Imports*, 262 N.E.2d 758 (IL).]

7. Morrison wanted to sell a certain parcel of land to Thoelke. He decided to make an offer by sending Thoelke a letter. When Thoelke received the letter, he decided to accept. He wrote a letter to Morrison saying that he would buy the land at the price quoted in the letter. Thoelke then mailed the letter. Before he received the letter from Thoelke, Morrison changed his mind and withdrew the offer to Thoelke. When Thoelke found out Morrison would not sell the land to him, he sued. Was Thoelke's letter a valid acceptance, binding Morrison to the sale? Explain. [See: *Morrison v. Thoelke*, 155 So.2d 889 (FL).]

8. Wholesale Coal Company ordered 25 carloads of coal from Guyan Coal and Coke Company. Guyan could not come up with 25 carloads. However, it did have seven carloads available. Before shipping the coal, Guyan wrote back to Wholesale stating, "You can be sure that if it is possible to ship the entire twenty-five carloads, we will do so. But under the circumstances, this is the best we can promise you." When Guyan heard nothing from Wholesale, it shipped the seven carloads. When Wholesale did not pay for the seven carloads, Guyan brought suit to compel payment. Wholesale countersued, claiming Guyan had not yet delivered the remaining 18 carloads. Was Wholesale correct? Explain. [See: *Guyan Coal and Coke Company v. Wholesale Coal Company*, 201 N.W. 194 (MI).]

9. Boskett offered to sell a 1916 dime to Beachcomber Coins Inc. Beachcomber examined the coin carefully and agreed to pay Boskett $500 for it. Later, Beachcomber asked a representative from the American Numismatic Society to examine the coin. The coin turned out to be counterfeit. No evidence existed to indicate fraud on Boskett's part. Beachcomber sued Boskett for rescission and a return of the $500. Beachcomber claimed this bilateral mistake of fact created grounds for a rescission. Was Beachcomber correct? Explain. [See: *Beachcomber Coins, Inc. v. Boskett*, 400 A.2d 78 (NJ).]

10. Prisoners rioted at the Iowa State Penitentiary and held prison staff members as hostages. The warden agreed in writing that no reprisals would be levied against the rioting inmates. In exchange, the prisoners released the hostages. After the hostages were released, several of the prisoners were punished for the riot. One prisoner, Wagner, was placed in solitary confinement for 30 days. He also received 180 days of administrative segregation and the loss of 1,283 days of good time earned. On what legal grounds could the warden refuse to keep his promise to the inmates? Explain. [See: *Wagner v. State*, 364 N.W.2d 246 (IA).]

11. Loral Corporation had a contract with the U.S. government to manufacture radar sets. Loral subcontracted with Austin Instrument for the production of precision parts to be used in the radar sets. In the middle of production, Austin told Loral that it would deliver no more parts unless Loral agreed to pay Austin a good deal more than originally agreed upon. Loral could not obtain the same parts in time from any other company. As a result, Loral agreed to the price increase. After delivering the radar sets, Loral sued Austin and asked the court to rescind the price increase. Did the court grant Loral's request? Explain. [See: *Austin Instrument, Inc. v. Loral Corporation*, 272 N.E.2d 533 (NY).]

Design Elements: The Opening Case: ©Sharpstock/Alamy; A Classic Case: ©Evlakhov Valeriy/Shutterstock

quick quiz Answers

8-1	8-2	8-3	8-4
1. F	1. T	1. F	1. T
2. T	2. T	2. F	2. T
3. T	3. T	3. T	3. T

Chapter 9

Consideration and Cyber-Payments

9-1 Requirements of Consideration
The Nature of Consideration • The Characteristics of Consideration

9-2 Types of Consideration
Money as Consideration • Property and Services as Consideration • Promises Not to Sue • Charitable Pledges • Bitcoin and the Cryptocurrency Revolution

9-3 Problems with Consideration
Accord and Satisfaction • Enforceable Agreements • Unenforceable Agreements

9-4 Cyber-Payment Tactics and Concerns
Cyber-Price and Competition • Cyber-Payments and Cyber-Contracts

THE OPENING CASE Round 1
To Agree or Not to Agree—That Is the Question

In December 2003, Michael Gelfand approached David Stein, an long-time family friend, and asked him to become a partner in a new investment opportunity that involved selling clusters of cellular assets in the northwestern United States. After this initial talk, Gelfand sent Stein a draft of an agreement that reflected the essence of their conversation. A short time later, Gelfand and Stein talked again and this time got serious enough to lay down some terms. Under these terms, Stein would contribute 20 percent of the investment, and Gelfand would bring in the remaining 80 percent. They also agreed to cooperate in managing the enterprise and to share profits and losses. A few months later, at another meeting, Gelfand announced that he had formed Buffalo Lake Erie Wireless Company LLC (BLEW). The purpose of BLEW was to acquire the necessary assets to go through with the deal. Gelfand also proposed that he would work with the Federal Communications Commission (FCC) to obtain the needed license. Once they had the license in hand, Stein would join the LLC. A short two months later, Gelfand had the license and had determined that $4 million would be needed to purchase the assets. Gelfand then asked Stein for a list of bullet points that would express his vision of the agreement. Stein complied promptly, and Gelfand went over the list with a fine-toothed comb. As a result of his investigation, Gelfand asked only two questions: (1) How would the two of them resolve any disagreements that might threaten to disrupt their partnership, and (2) why, under Stein's plan, would he (Gelfand) be responsible for loans from commercial lenders? In response, Stein offered a compromise provision as to the loan procedure but insisted on equal control of decision making in the business.

Several weeks later, Stein offered to pay the money that he owed under the 20 percent agreement. Gelfand did not explicitly accept the offer but, instead, in a rather cryptic response, told Stein "not to worry." Stein still worried, and as it turned out for good cause. Still, even after Gelfan's cryptic message, Stein, in good faith, helped Gelfand with the business start-up. For example, he was part of the team that negotiated buying the assets, he helped inspect the assets, he joined in finding personnel for the venture, and he worked at making additional preparations for the coming acquisition. At some point during this stage, Gelfand sent Stein another version of the operating agreement. Stein was dissatisfied with Gelfand's proposals and told him so. Still, the transaction did close on schedule. Stein and Gelfand continued to communicate but never seemed to actually close all the details of the deal. Subsequently, Stein brought this lawsuit alleging breach of fiduciary duty, breach of contract, unjust enrichment, and promissory estoppel. Stein asked for 25 percent of the present value of BLEW less the equity capital he would have invested under the original agreement. The questions relevant to us include the following: If a contract existed, what forms of consideration were part of the agreement? Since Stein did participate in the initial formation of the LLC, was that consideration adequate enough to show a contract was intended? Can Stein recover under the doctrine of promissory estoppel? Curious? Then read on. [See: *Stein v. Gelfand*, 476 F. Supp. 2d. 427 (2007).]

Opening Case Questions

1. What is consideration? Explain.
2. What does "bargained-for-exchange" mean in contract law? Explain.
3. What type of consideration is involved in the agreement between Stein and Gelfand? Explain.
4. Can the court determine the adequacy of consideration to demonstrate the existence of contract? Explain.
5. What is *promissory estoppel*, and how does it work? Explain.

Source: See: *Stein v. Gelfand*, 476 F. Supp. 2d. 427 (2007).

Learning Objectives

1. Define *consideration*.
2. Identify the different types of detriment.
3. Explain the characteristics necessary for valid consideration.
4. Define *unconscionable*.
5. Explain whether a promise not to sue can be consideration.
6. Explain whether a charitable pledge can be consideration.
7. Define *accord and satisfaction*.
8. Identify those enforceable contracts that lack consideration.
9. Explain *promissory estoppel*.
10. Describe the issues involved in cyber-payments.

9-1 Requirements of Consideration

In Chapter 8, we explored the nature of mutual assent, the first of the four elements of a contract. The second element is the mutual promise to exchange benefits and sacrifices among the parties. This exchange of things of value is called **consideration**. If an agreement has no consideration, it is not a binding contract. For example, a promise to give someone a ride to the campus in the morning is not a contract. Instead, it is simply a social arrangement because the rider has given nothing in exchange for the ride. In contrast, if the rider decides to take the bus, call a cab, use Uber, or rent a vehicle to get to campus, then a contract will exist. This is because, in the second case, the rider will have to transfer consideration in the form of a fare or a rental price in exchange for the ride to class.

The Nature of Consideration

Consideration consists of a mutual exchange of gains and losses between contracting parties. In the exchange, a gain by the offeree is at the same time a loss to the offeror. Likewise, the gain bargained for by the offeror will result in a loss or sacrifice by the offeree. The legal term used to designate the gain that each party experiences is that party's legal benefit. Similarly, the legal term used to describe the sacrifice that each party must experience is that party's **legal detriment**. A legal detriment can be any of the following: (1) doing something (or promising to do something) that one has a legal right not to do, (2) giving up something (or promising to give up something) that one has a legal right to keep, and (3) refraining from doing something (or promising not to do something) that one has a legal right to do. This last type of detriment is known as **forbearance**.

Did You Know?

When the Roman Emperor Justinian (527–565 CE) began a program of extensive legal reform, he made certain that transferring property became a relatively simple process.

Suppose Kurt promises his trainer that he will give up sugar for a year in exchange for a year of free training sessions. It is likely that Kurt improved his health by giving up sugar; however, the fact that Kurt gained a medical benefit does not eliminate his sacrifice. This "non-act" by itself is consideration. Kurt has suffered what the courts call a legal detriment, so giving up sugar has legal value, and the contract is valid.

The Characteristics of Consideration

Consideration has three characteristics: (1) The agreement must involve a bargained-for exchange, (2) the contract must involve adequate consideration, and (3) the benefits and detriments promised must themselves be legal.

Bargained-for Exchange The law will not enforce an agreement that has not been bargained for. An agreement involves a **bargained-for exchange** when (1) a promise is made in exchange for another promise, (2) a promise is made in exchange for an act, or (3) a promise is made for forbearance of an act. The concept of bargaining means that each party

A CLASSIC CASE Healthy, Wealthy, and Wise?

Literature instructors are fond of saying that a poem, a play, a novel, or a short story is considered good, sometimes even great, if it has stood the "test of time." The same is true of many legal cases. Such is the situation with the long-standing case of *Hamer v. Sidway*, a lawsuit that most law students and paralegals encounter (or should encounter) at some time in their academic careers. *Hamer and Sidway* begins at a golden wedding anniversary celebration. At the party, Uncle William promised his nephew and namesake, William, the Younger, that if he, the nephew, would give up a long list of vices that included smoking and swearing, until his 21st birthday, he, the uncle, would pay his nephew, William, $5,000. The challenge was made in front of a room full of family members and close friends, and William, the Younger, agreed to the arrangement. Following this and in compliance with the agreement, William embarked on an extensive period of abstinence that lasted several years. Soon after his 21st birthday, William wrote to his uncle telling him of his accomplishments and asking for the $5,000 due to him under the contract. Uncle William wrote a lengthy letter back in which he praised his nephew for his perseverance. He also promised to pay the money that was due. Unfortunately, Uncle William passed away before sending the money to his nephew. Undeterred, the nephew petitioned the executor of Uncle William's estate for payment. The executor refused to pay and William brought this lawsuit. William argued that he had performed as promised and was, therefore, entitled to the money. The executor recognized that William had, indeed, refrained from smoking and swearing, but argued that, in contract law, both sides must suffer a detriment for consideration to be valid and for a contract to exist. In this case, the executor said, young William had not suffered a detriment. In fact, the opposite was true. He was much healthier than he would have been, absent the promise, and he had, therefore, benefited greatly from giving up his bad habits for such an extended period of time. In the absence of consideration, no contract ever existed and, as a result, the estate did not owe young William a single cent. The court disagreed with this analysis. The court noted that, when William gave up something that he had a legal right to do, he had suffered a detriment sufficient to provide the consideration needed to make the agreement into a *bona fide* contract. To prove its point, the court referred to a standard treatise on contract law and noted that, consideration "means not so much that one party is profiting as that the other abandons some legal right in the present, or limits his legal freedom of action in the future, as an inducement for the promise of the first."[1] End of story—period. [See: *Hamer v. Sidway*, 124 N.Y. 538, 27 N.E. 256 (Court of Appeals of New York).]

Source: See: *Hamer v. Sidway*, 124 N.Y. 538, 27 N.E. 256 (Court of Appeals of New York).

will be hurt in some way if the other party fails to keep a promise. Conversely, each party gains something when the promises are kept and the exchange is made.

Adequacy of Consideration The fact that a contract has legal value is not the same as saying that it has adequate consideration. However, there are no specific requirements, other than being legal, regarding what one party may promise the other party in return for a pledge to deliver goods and services. The promise itself is adequate consideration when it represents something of value. Thus, the promise to assist another to repair an automobile would be something of value promised. The value placed on goods and services need not be street or market value. It is important only that the parties freely agreed on the value and the price. In general, the courts do not look into the adequacy of consideration; that is, they do not look to see whether the value of the consideration was fair to both parties. Ever since industrial capitalism became the primary economic system in the West, the courts no longer looked to see if the things exchanged in a contract are of equal value. Such a move would violate the profit-making principle of capitalism. Therefore, the courts let people make their own agreements, placing their own values on the goods or services exchanged. The court then enforces those agreements.

There are, however, exceptions to this general rule. In one exception, the courts give a party relief when the consideration is so outrageous that it shocks the conscience of the court. A court may refuse to enforce a contract or any clause of a contract if it considers the contract or clause **unconscionable**, that is, the consideration is so ridiculously inadequate that it shocks the court's conscience. This designation usually happens when there is a great inequality in bargaining power between the two parties. In very specific matters, usually related to taxes, some states have adopted statutes dealing with adequacy. In general though, courts remain reluctant to disturb the promises made by parties to an enforceable contract. Still some courts in some states have developed a second exception to the rule that says that courts usually do not determine how much consideration is enough consideration. That exception is generally reserved for issues involving the Statute of Frauds and the question of how much partial performance is enough partial performance to create a contract even though a writing, which is required under the law, is not available. The same principle has been used in cases that fall outside the Statute of Frauds. This is a factual question for which the courts have yet to draw a consistent standard.

The price and value of the goods exchanged need not be equal as long as the agreement is voluntary.

©Comstock Images/Jupiterimages

THE OPENING CASE Round 2
To Agree or Not to Agree—That Is the Question

In December 2003, Daniel Stein and Michael Gelfand entered into an opportunity that involved selling clusters of cellular assets in the northwestern United States. Gelfand would contribute 80 percent of the investment, and Stein would bring in the remaining 20 percent. In addition, they would share profits and losses and would operate the business together. Soon after, Gelfand formed Buffalo Lake Erie Wireless Company LLC (BLEW) to acquire the necessary assets to complete the process. Once Gelfand had the FCC license, he told Stein that that they needed $4 million to purchase the assets. Later, Stein wrote a list that would express his vision of the agreement. Gelfand read the list and asked only two questions. First, he asked how the two of them would resolve any disagreements that might threaten to disrupt their partnership. Second, he asked why, under Stein's plan, he, Gelfand, would be responsible for loans from commercial lenders. Stein offered a compromise on the loan but held fast to management rights. Stein then offered to pay his 20 percent of the agreement, but Gelfand just told him "not to worry." After this, Stein helped Gelfand start the business. For instance, Stein was on the team that negotiated the buying of the assets, he helped inspect the assets, he joined in finding personnel for the venture, and he worked at making additional preparations for the coming acquisition. At some point during this stage, Gelfand sent Stein yet another version of the operating agreement. Stein was dissatisfied with Gelfand's proposals and told him so.

Subsequently, when Stein realized that he had been passed by, he brought this lawsuit, asking for relief and alleging (1) a breach of fiduciary duty by Gelfand, (2) a breach of contract also by Gelfand, (3) that Gelfand had been unjustly enriched, and (4) that Gelfand's promises stop him from claiming that he owes nothing to Stein. What Stein wants is 25 percent of the present value of BLEW, less the equity capital he would have invested under the original agreement. Here is one of the questions faced by the court: Since Stein participated in the initial formation of the LLC, was that consideration adequate enough to show a contract was intended? The court looked at that issue in this case, and used a Statute of Frauds principle to determine whether Stein's performance was adequate enough to create a contract. The court looked at what Stein claimed to have done in his role a manager of the LLC. Remember that Stein helped negotiate the buying of the assets, he examined the assets, he helped hire new personnel, and he prepared for upcoming acquisitions. The court, in interpreting these fact in favor of the plaintiff, Stein, was forced to recognize that such activities are part of the preparation to start the business but are not part of running the business on a day-to-day basis. Consequently, the court ruled that "Stein's actions were the sorts of activities in which any party hoping or expecting to invest a million dollars in an acquisition of a business in which the party expected to have an active, post-acquisition role would have engaged. They are, in other words, almost equally consistent with a mere expectation that a contract would be concluded as with a genuine belief that a binding contract already existed."[2] The court ruled that the work that Stein did was inadequate as consideration to create a contract where none existed in the first place. The court found against Stein and for Gelfand at least on this issue. [See: *Stein v. Gelfand*, 476 F. Supp. 2d. 427 (2007).]

Source: See: *Stein v. Gelfand*, 476 F. Supp. 2d. 427 (2007).

Legality of Consideration Consideration requires that the benefits and sacrifices promised between the parties be legal. Absence of legality renders the consideration invalid. Thus, a party cannot agree to do something that he or she does not have the legal right to do. Similarly, a party cannot promise not to do something that he or she has no legal right to do. Also, a party cannot make valid consideration out of a promise to stop doing something that was illegal to do in the first place.

quick quiz 9-1

1. The fact that each party has received a benefit and suffered a detriment means that the consideration has legal value.   true | false
2. The legal term used to designate the gain that each party experiences is the party's legal benefit.   true | false
3. Consideration does not require that the benefits and sacrifices promised between the parties be legal.   true | false

9-2 Types of Consideration

Generally, consideration takes the form of money, property, or services. In certain special kinds of agreements and promises, however, the benefits and sacrifices are in some manner unique and not immediately obvious to the casual observer. Significant among these agreements are promises not to sue and charitable pledges.

Money as Consideration

Money is so closely connected with global commerce that we forget that it was not always part of the marketplace. The shift from a barter to a cash economy occurred when transporting goods to the market became difficult and hazardous. By the 9th century, the use of cash as a medium of exchange had become prevalent in medieval Europe. This shift to a cash economy was also accelerated by the need for credit. Because goods are perishable and the quality of goods can vary from transaction to transaction, contracts that required future payments were more attractive to merchants when coins rather than goods were involved. Thus, agreements based on credit backed up by coins had become commonplace throughout Europe by the 11th century, as had the practice of lending coins in exchange for interest. By the 13th century, the use of mortgage agreements based on transferring the right to receive all of the cash income from a tract of land had become routine. Today, we are once again in an era of change as we move from a cash/credit economy to one based almost totally on electronic transfers. Nevertheless, when electronic transfers are involved, people still tend to think in terms of cash, even those who have not actually handled coins or currency for some time. For this reason, it is best to always remember that hidden at the foundation of all contracts is the idea of cash equivalency. [See: Rodney Stark, *The Victory of Reason: How Christianity Led to Freedom, Capitalism, and Western Success* (New York: Random House, 2005), pp. 60-61.]

> **Did You Know?**
> Common law judges would rarely entertain arguments regarding the adequacy of consideration, even in unconscionable situations. One exception involved the promise to repay immediately a greater sum of money than that originally transferred. This is what happened in the case of *Schnell v. Nell*, an 1861 case, in which a man promised to pay $600 in return for the loan of one penny.

Property and Services as Consideration

Before money in the form of cash was accepted as a medium of exchange, consideration consisted of property and services. Sometimes, even today during recessionary or inflationary cycles, parties find it more beneficial to enter into barter agreements than to base their promises on cash payments. The courts have held that barter agreements contain valid consideration. For example, the exchange of services in return for the use of another's car or a promise to paint a house in exchange for accounting services represent benefits and sacrifices that constitute valid consideration to support a legally binding contract. Aside from this, however, services are consideration in employment contracts, independent contractor contracts, consulting contracts, acting contracts, security service contracts, cleaning service contracts, lawn maintenance contracts, agency contracts, and so on. Sometimes contracts can also involve a combination of money and services within the same agreements. Thus, when partners form a partnership, for example, all the partners may contribute both start-up capital and services based on what each partner does best. The Opening Case provides an example of this.

Promises Not to Sue

A promise not to sue, when there is the right, or at least the apparent right, to sue, is enforceable when it is supported by consideration. Promising not to sue is a forbearance. A promise not to sue in exchange for an amount of money is a customary way to settle or prevent a pending lawsuit. Settlements of this type often are preferred to expensive and time-consuming litigation. Such settlements are also better than submitting a claim to alternate dispute resolution procedures, such as arbitration or mediation.

EXAMPLE 9-1: Releases and Promises Not to Sue

Danny Hollinger was injured when a delivery van ran a red light and collided with his vehicle. Hollinger discussed his legal rights with an attorney, who suggested that he might receive compensation from the delivery company if he brought suit against the driver and the company. When faced with the suit, the delivery company's insurance company elected to offer Hollinger $250,000 if he would agree not to bring suit against the company. Hollinger agreed to these terms and signed a release in exchange for the money. The "thing of value" that Hollinger transferred to the insurance company was his right to bring a lawsuit. A court would uphold this agreement on the basis of the promise between the parties.

THE OPENING CASE Round 3
To Agree or Not to Agree—That Is the Question

Recall that in the Opening Case, Daniel Stein and Michael Gelfand had entered an agreement to sell clusters of cellular assets in the northwestern United States. Under the terms of the agreement Stein would contribute 20 percent of the investment, and Gelfand would bring in the remaining 80 percent. They also agreed to cooperate in managing the enterprise and to share profits and losses. A few months later, Gelfand formed Buffalo Lake Erie Wireless Company LLC (BLEW) to acquire assets to go through with the deal. Gelfand also obtained an FCC license. Once they had the license in hand, Stein would join the LLC. A short time later, Gelfand had the license and had determined that $4 million would be needed to purchase the assets. Several weeks later, Stein offered to pay the money that he owed under the 20 percent agreement. Gelfand did not explicitly accept the offer but, instead, in a rather cryptic response, told Stein "not to worry." Taking Gelfand at his word, Stein continued to help with the start-up the business. He was part of the team that negotiated the buying he assets, he helped inspect the assets, he joined in the finding personnel for the venture, and he worked at making additional preparations for the coming acquisition. If we look closely here at what both Stein and Gelfand have pledged, we can see there is a place for both money and services. Stein has agreed to put in 20 percent of the money need to purchase that assets in question. Gelfand would contribute 80 percent. Later in the case, we find out that they need $4 million to carry out the deal. This amounts to $3,200,000 for Gelfand and $800,000 for Stein. However, that is not the end of the story. Both parties have agreed to cooperate in managing the enterprise and to share profits and losses. We later learn that Stein helped negotiate the buying he assets, helped inspect the assets, joined in the finding personnel for the venture, and worked at making additional preparations for the coming acquisition. All of this would count as services rendered. So it is easy to see how money and services can combine in any such contract. [See: *Stein v. Gelfand*, 476 F. Supp. 2d. 427 (2007).]

Source: See: *Stein v. Gelfand,* 476 F. Supp. 2d. 427 (2007).

Acceptance of an agreement not to sue, supported by consideration, terminates one's right to continue any lawsuit, presently or in the future, on grounds described in the agreement. A promise not to sue is commonly called a **release**. Agreements of this kind are usually negotiated and agreed upon before a suit is even filed; however, occasionally they are negotiated between attorneys after a lawsuit has been filed and sometimes even after a trial has begun. In such an event, the settlement is arranged in cooperation with the court and presiding judge. Interestingly enough, some states will uphold a promise not to sue exchanged for consideration, even if circumstances later indicate that the party granting the release did not have the right to sue in the first place, as long as at the time of the agreement, the exchange was made in good faith and fraud was not involved.

Charitable Pledges

Under traditional rules, charitable pledges are not enforceable as contractual obligations because they are not supported by consideration. The dependence of charitable institutions and nonprofit organizations on the solicitation of contributions has encouraged the courts to enforce charitable pledges as though they were contractual obligations. Basically, there are three ways that the courts can seek to uphold charitable pledges. The first way involves actual consideration, which occurs when charitable contributions are made on the condition that the promisor be remembered for the gift by having his or her name inscribed in some way on a memorial associated with the project. Some courts see this promise to install a memorial to the pledgor as consideration.

A more contemporary approach is to use either promissory estoppel or public policy to support the claim. Promissory estoppel involves the detrimental reliance on a promise made by another party. If in reliance on a pledge or a series of pledges, a charity goes forward with a project, such as building an addition to the church hall or adding a wing to the synagogue, the courts will see the commencement of the project as evidence that the charity relied on the promises and will stop the promisors from denying the effects of the promise. At times, pledges are used for the general operation and maintenance of a charitable or nonprofit organization rather than for a specific project.

Courts today enforce charitable pledges by applying promissory estoppel and public policy.
©McGraw-Hill Education

When there is no promise to carry out a specific project, the courts have held that each pledge made is supported by the pledges of all others who have made similar pledges. This concept of consideration is used in support of all promises of money for undefined causes. The ultimate argument in this situation is that it would violate public policy to allow one pledgor to get away with denying his or her pledge when the other promisors relied on one another in making their individual pledges.

Bitcoin and the Cryptocurrency Revolution

Many types of currency can be used as consideration to buy and sell goods, services, and land. The most familiar means of buying and selling is through the use of money. Money is not the same as cash, however. Moreover, cash has become less and less a part of our everyday lives. In fact, many of us rely totally on credit and debit cards when we are out shopping. Others rarely leave the comfort of home and rely, instead, on their computers to shop and pay bills online. On the other hand, as noted earlier, these electronic transfers use credit and debit cards that are still dependent upon cash that is, figuratively speaking at least, held in a banking institution. Cash, in turn, is based on a precious commodity, usually gold or silver. Recently, a new form of consideration has become part of our global economy. This new form of consideration is referred to as bitcoin. Bitcoin, however, is actually a subset of **cryptocurrency**, which is a digital form of consideration that employs cryptography to make certain that contracts using bicoin as consideration are secure, controlled, and verified. Unlike traditional gold- or silver-based currencies, bitcoin is created based on a cryptographic mathematical formula. When bitcoin first appeared in 2009, it was unique because it represented the first attempt to decentralize currency. As noted earleir, most of the time, money, in its traditional form, is controlled by the banking system. Bitcoin—as a decentralized system—is controlled not by a bank, but by the people who actually use the currency, in this case, the bitcoin users themselves. As the popularity of bitcoin has increased, more and more merchants are accepting it as contractual consideration.

Using any traditional currency (dollars, euros, pounds, and so on), bitcoin users can purchase bitcoin online. Some places have established ATM-like machines that accept cash for bitcoin. In other places, buyers can use over-the-counter locations to exchange cash for bitcoin. In both situations, buyers will be connected to a bitcoin seller to effect the transfer.

Bitcoin users initiate bitcoin transactions through computers, mobile phones, and other electronic devices. Bitcoin accounts are stored on computers or in the cloud. When bitcoin users want to purchase something, they simply access the appropriate app (which can be envisioned as a safe, a money bag, a purse, or a wallet) and transfer the amount needed to finalize the contract with the seller. In one click of the mouse (or whatever), the appropriate number of bitcoin is transferred, the requirement of consideration is met, and the contract is fulfilled, at least from the buyer's perspective. One big advantage of bitcoin, as well as all other forms of cryptocurrency, is that it does not involve fees that might be attached to a transaction using conventional currency controlled by a banking institution. Another advantage is that bitcoin transactions are verified and secured by **bitcoin miners** who are paid in bitcoin to effect verification and maintain the security of bitcoin transfers. Bitcoin is also nearly inflation-proof. While bitcoin values can go up and down, the total number of bitcoin—21 million—always stays consistent. This is in contrast to traditional currencies, which can be inflated by the printing of additional paper certificates. Still, bitcoin value does change. To reflect these changes, bitcoin can be subdivided, so the number of subdivisions increases while the total number of bitcoin stays at 21 million. If the difference between bitcoin division and traditional inflation escapes you, don't be concerned. Most of us do not understand how traditional inflation works either (or how our computers, cell phones, microwave ovens, and cars work, for that matter). It may be enough that they work at all. The same is true of the bitcoin revolution (so far anyway).

quick quiz 9-2

1. Today, contractual parties never find it beneficial to enter barter agreements. — true | false
2. If a party promises not to sue another party, and it is later discovered that the first party never really had the right to sue, the original promise not to sue is invalid in every state, and the consideration must be returned. — true | false
3. Cryptocurrency is a subset of bitcoin, which is a digital form of consideration that employs cryptography to make certain that contracts using cryptocurrency as consideration are secure, controlled, and verified. — true | false

9-3 Problems with Consideration

Problems sometimes arise when the consideration involved in a contract is money and the parties disagree as to the amount of money that the debtor owes the creditor. The resolution of such problems depends on whether the transaction involves a genuine dispute as to the amount owed. One way such disputes can be settled is by an agreement known as accord and satisfaction. Additional problems arise when an agreement lacks consideration.

Accord and Satisfaction

A **disputed amount** is one on which the parties never reached mutual agreement. It may be difficult at first to see how the amount due under a contract can end up as the focal point of a dispute, until we recall that the law permits a certain degree of incompleteness in the final terms of an agreement, provided there is a way to settle on the eventual amount owed. For instance, when a contractor is hired to do work on a home or an accountant is retained to figure out a client's taxes, the final amount owed is rarely laid out in absolute terms. Instead, the custom is to settle on an amount per hour, estimate the number of hours that will be spent on the job, and then settle on the final amount once the job is finished.

If a creditor accepts as full payment an amount that is less than the amount due, the dispute has been settled by an **accord and satisfaction**. An accord and satisfaction is a new agreement resulting from a bona fide dispute between the parties as to the terms of their original agreement. The mutual agreement to the new terms is the **accord**; performance of the accord is the **satisfaction**—thus, accord and satisfaction. For accord and satisfaction to operate properly, certain elements are necessary. First, there must be a genuine dispute as to the amount due under the original agreement. Second, one of the parties, usually the one who owes the money, will suggest a way to settle the dispute, usually by tendering a lesser amount. Third, there must be acceptance of the lesser amount generally demonstrated by cashing a check for that lesser amount or some other act that signals acceptance.

In the classic accord and satisfaction scenario, the debtor tenders a check to the creditor. The check is marked "Payment in full for the amount owed on..." or words to that effect. At that point, the ball is in the creditor's court as it were. If the creditor cashes or otherwise negotiates the check, the debt has been satisfied. If the creditor does not cash the check, the debtor still owes the original amount. Great importance is placed on the written notation on the check. Generally, an oral statement that goes something like "Here is your check. That is it. I am not paying any more" is insufficient, especially if the creditor replies, "Oh, yes you are! This is not enough!" Even without the return comment by the creditor, however, the oral statement by the debtor is generally not enough, and the creditor can negotiate the check and still come back for the rest of the debt.

Enforceable Agreements

As a general rule, an agreement without consideration will not be an enforceable contract because consideration is so important as the binding element within a contractual relationship. Nevertheless, some states eliminate the requirement of consideration in specific types of agreements. Unfortunately, as is frequently the case in such matters, there is no uniformity among jurisdictions as to the types of agreements subject to such laws. Still, some typical agreements falling into this category include promises under seal, promises after discharge in bankruptcy, debts barred by the statute of limitations, promises enforced by promissory estoppel, and options governed by the UCC (see Table 9-1).

Promises under Seal A **seal** is a mark or an impression placed on a written contract indicating that the instrument was executed and accepted in a formal manner. Today, a seal is usually indicated by the addition of the word *seal* or the letters "L.S." (*locus sigilli*, meaning "place of the seal") following a party's signature. Years ago, contracts under seal required no consideration. Some states still honor a promise under seal, but most have abolished this concept, especially in relation to sale of goods contracts. In fact, the UCC has eliminated the use of the seal in all sale-of-goods contracts; however, a few states still require the use of the seal in real property and certain other types of transactions. Because there is no uniformity in this regard, it is advisable to research and consult the specific requirements in your jurisdiction.

UCC 2-205

Promises after Discharge in Bankruptcy Persons discharged from indebtedness through bankruptcy may reaffirm their obligations, prompted perhaps by moral compulsion. In the past, reaffirmation has been the subject of abuse by creditors who used pressure against those whose debts have been excused. In response, Congress passed a bankruptcy reform act that makes it more difficult for creditors to extract such promises. The bankruptcy court must now hold a hearing when a reaffirmation is intended, informing the debtor that reaffirmation is optional, not required, and of the legal consequences of reactivating a debt.

Table 9-1 Agreements without Consideration

Agreement	Legal Status
Promises under seal	Enforceable in some states for contracts not involving goods; unenforceable under the UCC for contracts involving goods
Promises after discharge in bankruptcy	Enforceable in most states
Promise to pay debts barred by statute of limitations	Enforceable
Promises enforced by promissory estoppel	Enforceable only if offeror knew that offeree would rely on the promise and offeree places himself or herself in a different and difficult position as a result of that promise
Option	Enforceable under the UCC if made by a merchant, in writing, stating the time period over which the offer will remain open
Illusory promises	Unenforceable
Promise of a gift	Unenforceable
Past considerations	Unenforceable
Preexisting duties	Unenforceable as a consideration in a new contract

It is also up to the court to approve such reaffirmations. State laws, in most cases, provide that no new consideration need be provided in support of reaffirmation. Most states require that a reaffirmation be supported by contractual intent. Some states require the new promise to be in writing; however, when there is no such provision, an oral promise or reaffirmation is usually sufficient.

Debts Barred by Statutes of Limitations State laws known as **statutes of limitations** limit the time within which a party is allowed to bring suit. The time allowed for the collection of a debt varies from state to state, usually from three to 10 years. Some states allow more time for collection when the document of indebtedness is under seal, as in the case of a promissory note containing the seal of the maker. Debtors may revive and reaffirm debts barred by the statutes of limitations without the necessity of new consideration. Affirmation will result from the part payment of the debt. When a debt is revived, the creditor again is permitted the full term, provided by the statute of limitations, to make collection. Some states require a written reaffirmation when a debt made unenforceable by the statute of limitations is reactivated. Consequently, it would be best to check the rule in your jurisdiction.

Promises Enforced by Promissory Estoppel The doctrine of **estoppel** denies rights to complaining parties that are shown to be the cause of their own injury. **Promissory estoppel** is a legal doctrine that restricts a party from denying that a promise was made under certain conditions, even though consideration has not been exchanged to bind an agreement. To be effective, promissory estoppel requires four elements: (1) The offending party must have made a clear and unambiguous promise; (2) the offending party could foresee that the innocent party would reasonably rely on that promise and might do something as a result; (3) the innocent party, relying on that promise, reasonably changes his or her position; and (4) the innocent party is hurt financially as a result. In reaching this doctrine, courts have accepted the principles of justice and fairness in protecting the party receiving the promise from otherwise unrecoverable losses.

THE OPENING CASE *Round 4*
To Agree or Not to Agree—That Is the Question

Let's look at the Opening Case just one more time. We learned that Daniel Stein and Michael Gelfand had agreed to sell clusters of cellular assets in the northwestern United States. Under the agreement Stein would contribute 20 percent of the investment and Gelfand would bring in the remaining 80 percent. They also agreed to cooperate in managing the enterprise and to share profits and losses. A few months later, Gelfand formed Buffalo Lake Erie Wireless Company LLC (BLEW) and promised to obtain an FCC license. Once they had the license in hand, Gelfand promised that Stein would join the LLC. A short time later, Gelfand had the license and had determined that $4 million would be needed to purchase the assets. During all this time, Stein and Gelfand went back and forth, proposing, examining, rejecting, and counterproposing the terms of what they hoped would eventually be a final agreement. That final agreement was never reached. Nevertheless, several weeks later, Stein offered to pay the money that he owed under the 20 percent agreement. Gelfand did not explicitly accept the offer but, instead, in a rather cryptic response, told Stein "not to worry." Stein believed that this was a promise to get back to him when it was time to pay. Consequently, relying on this promise, Stein presumably placed that money aside and did not invest it in other places that could have been more lucrative than the cell phone business. Also, relying Gelfand's promise, Stein continued to help with the start-up the business. He was part of the team that negotiated the buying he assets, he helped inspect the assets, he joined in finding personnel for the venture, and he worked at making additional preparations for the coming acquisition. Presumably, Stein could have been working for pay elsewhere at that time rater than spending all his time helping Gelfand.

When Stein sued Gelfand, one of his arguments was based on promissory estoppel. Recall that promissory estoppel requires four elements: (1) The offending party must have made a clear and unambiguous promise; (2) the offending party could foresee that the innocent party would reasonably rely on that promise and might do something as a result, (3) the innocent party, relying on that promise, in a reasonable way, actually changes his or her position; and (4) the innocent party is hurt financially as a result. In the case of *Stein v. Gelfand*, the court was not satisfied that any of the elements of *promissory estoppel* had been fulfilled. First, the promise was hardly clear and unambiguous. Stein and Gelfand had gone back and forth about the terms for months and never did reach agreement. Second, because the agreement was clearly at the negotiation stage, Gelfand could not foresee Stein would rely on it. Third, it was not reasonable for Stein to rely on such an incomplete set of promises. Finally, Stein was not injured to the tune of 25 percent of the present value of BLEW (which is what he asked for), even if we take away the equity capital that he would have invested under the original agreement. [See: *Stein v. Gelfand*, 476 F. Supp. 2d. 427 (2007).]

Source: See: *Stein v. Gelfand,* 476 F. Supp. 2d. 427 (2007).

Option An **option** is the giving of consideration to support an offeror's promise to hold open an offer for a stated or a reasonable length of time. The UCC has made an exception to the rule requiring consideration when the offer is made by a merchant. In such cases, an offer in writing by a merchant, stating the time period during which the offer will remain open, is enforceable without consideration. The offer, which is called a **firm offer** or an **irrevocable offer**, must be signed by the offeror, and the time allowed for acceptance may not exceed three months. When the time allowed is more than three months, firm offers by merchants must be supported by consideration to be enforceable.

Unenforceable Agreements

The promises just described are exceptions to the general rule that consideration must support a valid contract. The exceptions are allowed by state statute or because the courts, in the interest of fairness or justice, find it inappropriate to require consideration. There are certain promises, however, that the courts will not enforce because they lack even the rudimentary qualities of valid consideration. Included in this category are promises based on preexisting duties, promises based on past consideration, illusory promises, and promises of future gifts and legacies.

Preexisting Duties A promise to do something that one is already obligated to do by law or by some other promise or agreement cannot be made consideration in a new contract. Such obligations are called **preexisting duties**. The same rule of consideration applies to police officers, firefighters, and other public servants and officials who may pledge what appears to be some special service in exchange for a monetary reward, when all they have actually promised is to execute the duties they are already obligated to perform. Suppose, for instance, that the local fire chief, in exchange for a monetary reward, promises an apartment owner that he or she will provide protection should a fire start in the owner's building. Neither the fire chief nor the apartment owner could enforce such an agreement in court. The promise is based on the chief's empty guarantee to do what is already his or her job.

Past Consideration A promise to give another something of value in return for goods or services rendered and delivered in the past, without expectation or reward, is **past consideration**. Only when goods or services are provided as the result of bargained-for present or future promises is an agreement enforceable.

EXAMPLE 9-2: Past Consideration Is No Consideration

Gale Hansen wanted to have her hair dyed before her college graduation party but could not afford to pay the $120 fee that was expected by the local hairdresser. Without any mention of payment, her friend Marianne Everett helped Hansen dye her hair. After seeing what a good job Everett did on her hair, Hansen told Everett that she'd give her $35 for helping. Hansen's promise to Everett is not enforceable because Everett has already completed the work. Her consideration is therefore in the past.

Illusory Promises An **illusory promise** is one that seems genuine but that on close examination actually fails to obligate the promissor to do anything. A party who makes an illusory promise is the only one with any right to determine whether the other party will benefit in any way. Illusory promises fail to provide the mutuality of promises required in establishing consideration.

EXAMPLE 9-3: As Many Illusory Promises as You Might Desire

Pemberton Grocery agreed to buy such fruits and vegetables as it "might desire" for one summer season from Enchanted Farms Inc. In return for this promise, Enchanted negotiated terms whereby it would give Pemberton a special schedule of discounts for the fruits and vegetables. The promise to buy as much as it "might desire" had actually obligated Pemberton to do nothing. Its promise was illusory because Pemberton might desire absolutely no fruits and vegetables and still keep its promise. The benefits that Pemberton were to derive from the schedule of discounts were not supported by a real or enforceable promise on Pemberton's part. A suit brought by either party to enforce this agreement would fail for want of consideration.

Future Gifts and Legacies The promise of a gift to be given at some future time or in a will is not enforceable if no consideration is given for the promise. Included here are promises to provide gratuitous services or to lend one's property without expectation of any benefits in return.

quick quiz 9-3

1. If a creditor accepts as full payment an amount that is less than the amount due, the dispute has been settled by promissory estoppel. true | false
2. An option is the giving of consideration to support an offeror's promise to hold an offer open for a stated length of time. true | false
3. Although illusory promises provide the mutuality of promises required in establishing consideration, the courts will not enforce them due to the doctrine of unconscionability. true | false

9-4 Cyber-Payment Tactics and Concerns

Cyber-buying and cyber-selling has become second nature to most American consumers. Part of this process involves setting prices that are attractive to the buyer and profitable for the seller. Because the price involved in a contract is a major part of the consideration equation, and because the online marketplace has affected the pricing process, it is appropriate that we pause at this point to consider the legal ramifications of this new approach to the making of a contract. We will examine two aspects of the online pricing process: (1) cyber-price and competition and (2) cyber-payments. As these ideas develop, we will also cover several pieces of cyber-legislation.

Cyber-Price and Competition

Businesses that buy products, supplies, and services from one another have always held an advantage over the average consumer. In the commercial network of market competition, businesses could frequently negotiate with one another over the value of the consideration involved in their contracts. The same was not true of consumers who were generally paralyzed by the price set by the other party. Oddly, this was true whether the offeror was the buyer or the seller. Certainly, there have always been consumers who would comparison shop as they sought the best prices available to them. Most consumers, however, were not that ambitious. The Internet has helped improve the pricing process. Consumers can now use the Internet to seek out competitive prices, thus improving their ability to set the consideration at a level with which they are comfortable.

Cyber-Price Shopping Consumers have a wide variety of ways to comparison shop when it comes to establishing consideration in online contracts. Some online cyber-consumers now make regular use of electronic agents, referred to as a *bot* (*robot, shopping bot, cyber-bot,* or *e-bot*) to comb the vast reaches of cyberspace to find the lowest price available on an item or a service. Cyber-consumers must be aware of the legal ramifications of this process. Two model acts that cover this process are the Uniform Computer Information Transactions Act (UCITA) and the Uniform Electronic Transactions Act (UETA).

Cyber-Shopping Costs Cyber-shopping is not without its drawbacks. One such drawback involves the danger of hidden costs. One hidden cost is the Internet access fee. Most of the time, however, Internet users can track the number of minutes, or more often the number of megabytes, that they have utilized under the contract so that they can pace their time on the net, and either cut back or renegotiate a new contract with their Internet service provider (ISP). Another "hidden" cost comes in the form of shipping and handling fees. Most sellers provide shipping and handling data at the outset or at least as the contract is finalized so that the consumer enters the contract knowing the full value of the consideration paid for the goods purchased on line. Some shippers, however, will overestimate the shipping costs just to make certain that they are not caught paying more for shipping than they are prepared to spend. Buyers should be aware of this unavoidable and often untraceable hidden cost, and be ready to absorb the extra cost if they really want the merchandise.

Cyber-Shopping and the Law Cyber-shopping is not without its legal entanglements and its illegal practices. Cyber-buyers and cyber-sellers must both be attuned to the difficulties lying in wait when they enter the online cyber-commerce arena. Some traditional and recurring illegal practices, such as discriminatory price-setting and credit card fraud, are still prevalent in cyberspace. Others, such as the bait-and-switch schemes that we discussed in Chapter 8 are almost impossible to detect online until the damage is done. While both buyers and sellers can be targeted, it is the sellers who are especially vulnerable to credit card fraud and identity fraud. This is because it is much easier for buyers to use stolen credit cards and identity information online. To protect consumers, Congress passed the Identity Theft and Assumption Deterrence Act (ITADA). Later, ITADA was amended by the Identity Theft Penalty Enhancement Act (ITPEA), which outlaws the unauthorized transfer, possession, or use of a means of identifying another person to violate federal law. The amendment adds a new crime, called *aggravated identity theft*, to the original statute.

Cyber-Payments and Cyber-Contracts

Shopping online has many advantages that make it one of the fastest-growing market places on record. Most people shop online because it is quick and efficient. In addition, as noted earlier, shopping online also permits consumers to compare prices and to settle on the amount of consideration that they can afford. Additionally, some products that are not available in stores are accessible online. Hard-to-get products available online include out-of-print books, antiques, vintage clothing, rare works of art, hi-fi speaker systems, Polaroid cameras, obsolete auto parts, black-and-white TVs, rotary-dial phones, turntables and vinyl records, outdated appliances, old license plates, carbon paper, old-fashioned audio tapes, vacuum tubes, pulp magazines, out-of date VHS and Beta cassettes, Golden and Silver Age comics, and other vintage products. Despite these advantages, online shopping still has many difficulties, not the least of which is selecting a payment method.

Cyber-Payment Options Online consumers can choose from several payment methods. One of the most popular methods is by credit card or debit card. It would be very rare today for an online seller to refuse to accept credit or debit card payments. Most online sellers will accept the major credit cards such as Visa, MasterCard, Discover, and so on. Many online cyber-sellers also are moving toward the use of direct online payment systems such as PayPal. This type of system protects both the buyer and the seller. The system is so effective that at some time in the future, this may be the only way permissible to buy and sell in cyberspace. This may become the most acceptable process because most of the time when people buy and sell in cyberspace, they are dealing with strangers. The issue is especially acute in the cyber-auction industry, involving firms such as eBay. The online payment process eliminates (well, almost nearly eliminates) the identity verification problem. This is important because one of the biggest concerns about online shopping is security. Once a buyer and a seller have agreed on consideration, they both want to make certain that the contract is fulfilled as promised.

Cyber-Payment Security Update Consumers who shop online must provide the seller with a means of payment. As we have seen, the most popular method of making payment online is through the use of credit and debit cards. Unfortunately, the ease and efficiency of using such cards is frequently offset by the security concerns associated with their use. Oddly, the United States is not as up-to-date as the European Union in providing data and privacy protection to its consumers. The **EU Data Protection Directive** along with the **EU E-Privacy Directive** guarantee the rights of European citizens while, at the same time, ensuring the smooth exchange of data among those nation-states that honor the privacy and data protection standards themselves. U.S. corporations that are involved with EU corporations must demonstrate that, despite the lack of legislation in the United States, the companies themselves will promise to honor the same degree of protection to data and to privacy as guaranteed by the EU.

These guarantees have been labeled the **Safe Harbor Principles**. They are enforced by the U.S. Department of Commerce. Ironically, this means that U.S. consumers who deal with European companies or with U.S. companies that follow the EU standards will have more security protection than those who deal with purely U.S. companies. Ironically, the safe harbor dispensation is at risk of being destabilized by blowback from the discovery of the U.S. PRISM program, a project run by the National Security Agency that permitted the governments of the United States and the United Kingdom to run an extensive Internet communication collection process that compromised Google and other Internet corporations. In the wake of the PRISM revelation, the European Union has threatened to make it even more difficult for non-European companies to qualify for safe harbor exemptions.

These changes will make it more burdensome for American companies to demonstrate to the EU's satisfaction that they honor the same degree of protection to data and to privacy as guaranteed by the EU. The EU has also threatened to impose more substantial fines on American companies that violate EU privacy standards. Moreover, the EU is also preparing to raise the bar on data protection by providing a strict model for non-European companies to emulate, making it more difficult for American companies to comply with those global standards, thus fortifying the position of European companies that do comply. The EU may also establish an exclusive European cloud to make European data more secure and less accessible by American companies (although, realistically, this will not stop American intelligence gathering). [See: "Charlemagne: Reaching for the Clouds: Europe Wants Tougher Data-Privacy Rules to Deter American Snooping," *The Economist*, July 20, 2014, p. 49.]

quick quiz 9-4

1. The Internet has helped to improve the transparency of the pricing process. true | false
2. Bait and switch are almost impossible to detect online until the damage is done. true | false
3. The European Union has provided greater protection for cyber-shoppers than the United States. true | false

Summary

9.1 The fifth element necessary to any valid contract is consideration. Consideration is the mutual exchange or promise to exchange benefits and sacrifices between contracting parties. Consideration has three requirements: (1) promises made during bargaining depend on the consideration to be received, (2) the consideration must involve something of value, and (3) the benefits and detriments promised must be legal.

9.2 Generally, consideration takes the form of money, property, or services. There are certain special kinds of agreements and promises to which the benefits and sacrifices are unique. Among these are promises not to sue and charitable pledges.

9.3 Problems sometimes arise when the consideration involved in a contract is money and the parties do not agree on the amount of money owed. If there is a genuine dispute, a creditor can accept an amount as full payment even though it is less than the amount claimed. Once the creditor has accepted the lesser amount, the dispute is settled by an act of accord and satisfaction. If the dispute is not genuine, accord and satisfaction do not apply. As a general rule, contracts are not enforceable without consideration; however, some states eliminate the need for consideration in some agreements. These agreements include promises bearing a seal, promises after discharge in bankruptcy, debts barred by the statute of limitations, promises enforced by promissory estoppel, and options governed by the UCC. Other agreements that seem to involve consideration but that the courts will not enforce involve preexisting duties, past consideration, illusory promises, and gifts.

9.4 The measurement of consideration has become an issue when consumers buy and sell online. Consumers can comparison shop online using shopping search engines, patronizing user-friendly industries, and shopping with companies that provide price comparisons on their websites. Cyber-shopping hidden costs include Internet access fees and shipping and handling costs. Some illegal practices involved in online shopping include discriminatory price-setting, credit card fraud, and bait-and-switch schemes. Online consumers can choose from several payment methods including credit cards, debit cards, smart cards, and alternative cyber-payment systems such as PayPal. Privacy protection and security, however, are limited.

Key Terms

accord, 273
accord and satisfaction, 273
bargained-for exchange, 266
consideration, 265
cryptocurrency, 271
disputed amount, 272
estoppel, 274
EU Data Protection Directive, 279
EU E-Privacy Directive, 279
firm offer, 275
forbearance, 265
illusory promise, 276
irrevocable offer, 275
legal detriment, 265
locus sigilli, 273
option, 275
past consideration, 276
preexisting duties, 276
promissory estoppel, 274
release, 270
Safe Harbor Principles, 279
satisfaction, 273
seal, 273
statutes of limitations, 274
unconscionable, 267

Questions for Review and Discussion

1. What is consideration?
2. What are the different types of detriment?
3. What characteristics are necessary for consideration to be valid?
4. What is meant by the term *unconscionable*?
5. Can a promise not to sue be consideration?
6. How can a charitable pledge be consideration?
7. What is the procedure that a debtor and creditor may use to settle a claim by means of accord and satisfaction?
8. What agreements may be enforceable by a court of law even though they lack consideration?
9. What is the doctrine of promissory estoppel?
10. What issues are involved in the cyber-payment process?

Cases for Analysis

1. Rust was a partner in the firm of Woodley, Krost, & Rust. The partners hired Lightbody to take on yeoman's duties for the firm. Lightbody worked for one-half of the billings that each of his clients paid to the firm. This contract was never put in writing, but it seemed not to matter because Lightbody was paid accordingly in an honorable manner. Still, the amount of his take-home pay was a mystery from paycheck to paycheck. Moreover, the risk to Lightbody was increased by the fact that, if the client did not pay, Lightbody was not paid. One of Rust's clients ("the inventor") was caught up in a very serious patent lawsuit with the firm of Harris Company. The suit focused on an alleged infringement of the inventor's patents. The inventor was fiscally strapped at that time, and so, in lieu of cash, Rust established a contingency fee arrangement, under which Rust would not get paid unless the inventor's case was successful. The contingency fee would amount to 40 percent of the proceeds from the inventor's inventions. Rust decided that he needed help unraveling the details of the inventor's case and so he enlisted Lightbody. Lightbody agreed to add this extra work to his regular duties at the firm. However, because the inventor was paying then firm based on a contingency fee arrangement, there would be no billable hours that could be used to pay Lightbody. The solution was to pay Lightbody on a secondary contingency arrangement under which he would receive half of whatever Rust received as his contingency fee. Because Lightbody already worked for the firm, what consideration was Lightbody handing over to the the firm for this second contingency arrangement? [See: *Lightbody v. Rust*, 2003-Ohio-3937, No. 80927.]

2. Twenty-two congressional representatives proposed a bill that would permit corporate shareholders to review the consideration packages that had been granted to key corporate executives of public corporations. The bill, which was named the Shareholder Vote on Executive Compensation Act, would empower the shareholders of public corporations to evaluate and vote on the appropriateness of the compensation packages that had been granted to the corporation's top five officers. The vote, however, would not obligate the corporation to change the compensation package if the shareholders disapproved of its terms. Would such a bill, if enacted into law, conflict with established contract law principles that permit parties to negotiate their own level of consideration? Explain. [See: Donna Block, "Proposal Seeks Shareholder OK on Executive Pay," *The National Law Journal*, March 12, 2007, p. 9.]

3. Consideration can serve as a strong motivator. At least this is what a newly founded shareholder forum believes. The forum was formed to monitor the salaries of top corporate executives, especially CEOs, by matching those salaries with the executive's incentive package, which includes the corporation's latest list of objectives and the number or the percentage of those objectives that the executive must meet to receive incentive pay. The goal of incentive pay is to motivate top executives to do more than sit in the CEO's office from 9:00 to 5:00 each day. Is incentive pay a violation of the principle that says that preexisting duties cannot be used as consideration in a new contract? Explain. [See: Gretchen Morgenson, "Hear Ye, Hear Ye: Coralling Executive Pay," *The New York Times*, June 17, 2007, sec 3, pp. 1, 8.]

4. General Motors decided to move a car producing operation to Arlington, Texas, from a plant located in Ypsilanti, Michigan. As a result, the township of Ypsilanti brought a lawsuit to stop General Motors from making the move. Ypsilanti argued that GM had promised to keep the plant in Ypsilanti in exchange for certain tax privileges. The township argued further that it had relied on those promises when it granted that tax abatement to the corporation. Therefore, GM should be forced to keep its promise to maintain the Ypsilanti plant. Should the court stop this move based on the doctrine of promissory estoppel? Explain. [See: *Charter Township of Ypsilanti v. General Motors*, 508 N.W.2d 556 (Michigan Court of Appeals).]

5. Aviation Electronics entered a contract with Sky Train Institute of Montana in which Aviation agreed to supply the institute with 17,000 component parts for the development of the institute's remote control bomber. The bomber had to be operational by December 3; otherwise, the institute would lose a research grant from the Department of Defense (DoD). After delivering 5,000 parts, Aviation told Sky Train that it wanted an additional $4 million beyond the original price agreed upon to deliver the remaining parts. Sky Train attempted to obtain the parts from other firms, none of which could fill

the order in the time limit required by the DOD contract specifications. To make the deadline stipulated in the government contract, Sky Train reluctantly agreed to the new price demanded by Aviation. What "thing of value," if any, has Aviation transferred to the institute that it did not already owe the institute under the original contract? Explain.

6. Savaretti offered to pay his niece, Wilma, $2,000 if she would agree to give up eating meat and pastries and drinking caffeinated beverages for six months. Wilma agreed and gave up these activities for six months. At the end of those six months, Savaretti refused to give Wilma the $2,000, arguing that because giving up caffeine, meat, and pastries was beneficial to her health, she suffered no detriment and was owed nothing. Wilma took Savaretti to small claims court and demanded payment of the $2,000. She argued that because she had the legal right to consume the caffeine, meat, and pastries, she suffered a legal detriment and was entitled to her money. How should the referee rule in this case? Explain.

7. Daniel Davidson told Velma Evans that he would hire her to work on an architectural job. He gave her a date to show up for work and told her to leave her present job. Relying on Davidson's statements, Evans left her job. Davidson never let Evans begin work, and as a result, she was out of work for six months. Evans sued Davidson for the wages she lost during those six months. Davidson argued that because they'd never decided on the final terms of employment, no contract ever existed between the two of them. Evans argued that the principle of promissory estoppel should apply here. Is Evans correct? Explain.

8. The Mighty Fine Food Emporium agreed to buy such fruits and vegetables as it "might desire" for one summer season from Kennelsworth Farms and Vineyards. In return for this promise, Kennelsworth negotiated terms whereby it would give Mighty Fine a special schedule of discounts for the fruits and vegetables. Did the promise to buy as much as it "might desire" obligate Kennelsworth in any way? Are the benefits that Kennelsworth was to derive from the schedule of discounts supported by an enforceable promise on Kennelsworth's part? Would a suit brought by either party to enforce this agreement succeed? Explain each answer.

9. Graham O'Hanlon, without any mention of payment, helped his friend, Patricia Tippon, move from Westerville to Pepper Pike. The entire move took 48 hours to complete. At the end of the day, after she was in her new house, Tippon told O'Hanlon that she'd give him $200 for helping her move. Is Tippon's promise to O'Hanlon enforceable? Why or why not?

10. Vanoni Biological Supplies Inc. contracted with the Hayden Institute to supply the institute with 24,000 biological specimens for a series of experiments that the institute has agreed to perform for the Maritime University of Columbia. The institute must have the specimens by September 9 to meet the university's schedule. After delivering 12,000 of the specimens, Vanoni told the institute that it wanted an additional $1,600 to deliver the remaining 12,000 specimens. Can Vanoni make the delivery of the remaining 12,000 specimens consideration in a new agreement with the institute? Explain.

11. Seier agreed to pay $10,000 to Peek in exchange for all the stock in a corporation. The agreement was placed in writing. Nevertheless, when the time came for payment, Seier refused to live up to his end of the deal. His argument was that the stock was not worth the $10,000 that he had agreed to pay for it. Did the court listen to Seier's argument and attempt to determine the value of the consideration? Explain. [See: *Seier v. Peek*, 456 So.2d 1079 (AL).]

Design Elements: The Opening Case: ©Sharpstock/Alamy; A Classic Case: ©Evlakhov Valeriy/Shutterstock

quick quiz Answers

9-1	9-2	9-3	9-4
1. F	1. F	1. F	1. T
2. T	2. F	2. T	2. T
3. T	3. F	3. F	3. T

Chapter 10

Capacity and Legality: The Final Elements

10-1 The Final Elements
The Nature of Capacity and Minority • Contractual Capacity of Minors • Ratification and Disaffirmance

10-2 Other Capacity Problems
Persons Mentally Impaired • Persons Drugged or Intoxicated

10-3 Agreements to Engage in Unlawful Activity
Agreements to Commit Torts and Crimes • Agreements Illegal under Statutory Law • Agreements Contrary to Public Policy

10-4 Consequences of Illegality
In Pari Delicto Contracts • Partial Illegality in an Agreement

THE OPENING CASE Round 1
"Time Out" for a Chief Operating Officer: How Much Time Is Time Enough?

In the case of *AK Steel Corporation v. ArcelorMittal USA LLC*, two of the most competitive steel companies in the United States today battled one another to control the destiny of one corporate executive. The case began when, after 18 years of dedicated service, Keith Howell (no relation to Thurston Howell III) announced that he was leaving his position as senior vice president (VP) of operations at AK Steel (AK) to become the chief operating officer (COO) of ArcelorMittal USA (AM). During his tenure at AK, Howell had access to a large array of confidential information, trade secrets, customer lists, manufacturing techniques, company operations, strategies, logistics, capital expenditures, pricing, and so on. Howell was subject to a severance agreement that bound all AK senior executives. The agreement promised a substantial severance package when he left AK. Apparently, Howell also had a large vested retirement account from AK. Moreover, Howell had been promised a $900,000 signing bonus from AM. So, initially, at least, things looked pretty good for his chosen career path. There was just one hitch in the program. The AK severance agreement also included a noncompete agreement under which Howell had promised not to work for a competitor anywhere on the planet for one year.

The language of the noncompete agreement looked like this: "In exchange for [AK Steel's] agreement to provide you with the severance benefits opportunities set out in this Agreement . . . you agree that . . . you will not, directly or indirectly, do any of the following: serve as an employee, consultant, agent, principal, partner, owner, officer, or director of any business engaged directly or indirectly in competition with [AL Steel] . . . during the one-year period following the date when your employment with [AK Steel] terminates." Howell's inevitable departure from AK sparked a lawsuit against Howell and AM. The lawsuit included claims for breach of the noncompete agreement, misappropriation of trade secrets, and intentional interference with a contract. AK asked for a temporary restraining order and preliminary injunctive relief to stop Howell from violating the noncompete agreement. Procedurally, to succeed in obtaining such a preliminary order, AK had to show that it would probably succeed at trial, that it would be irreparably damaged if the order was not granted, that none of this would hurt any innocent third parties, and that the order would serve the public interest. Substantively, to succeed in showing that the noncompete agreement was legally permmissible, AK had to demonstrate that the noncompete (1) would prevent irreparable harm to the company, (2) would not impose undue hardship on Howell, and (3) would not harm the public at large. In this case, the third element, "public harm," was irrelevant because the noncompete agreement was purely a private matter.

Moving on, to prove the first and second points, AK offered the following arguments. First, to demonstrate irreparable harm, AK argued that since Howell knew so much about AK's price margins and negotiation plans for the upcoming year, his presence at AM would give that company an unfair advantage over AK. Second, to prove that Howell would undergo no undue hardship, AK pointed out that given his current financial health, the one-year "suspension" from work in the steel industry would be uncomfortable but tolerable. On the other side, in his own defense, Howell argued that he had been employed in the steel industry for his entire adult life and that by stopping him from working in that industry at this point in his career, even for a year, as the AK noncompete agreement contemplated, he and his family would suffer undue hardship.

Most of the time, the goal of a court in examining a contract is to determine the objectives of the parties and to enforce those objectives as much possible. The courts, in other words, either uphold or dismiss contractual claims. To be more direct, the courts do not tell the parties what they should have agreed to in the first place. From this underlying philosophy comes the general directive that the court must search for an understanding of the original terms of a contract rather than impose its will on the parties by rewriting those terms. The noncompete agreement is an exception to this rule. In fact, a court may rewrite the terms of a noncompete agreement in order to ensure that justice is done. Most noncompete agreements include a time and space factor, which a court can rewrite if it can see a fairer way to construct those limits. In this case, the AK noncompete agreement said that Howell could not work for another steel company anywhere (space) on the planet for one year (time). What do think? Are these two limits fair? If not, how should the court rewrite the term(s)? Explain. [See: *AK Steel Corp. v. ArcelorMittal USA, L.L.C*, 2016-Ohio-3285 (Court of Appeals, 12th Appellate District of Ohio, Butler County).]

Opening Case Questions

1. Can an agreement not to do something be consideration in a contract? Explain.
2. Can an individual give up his or her right to work as a part of a contract? Explain.
3. What is the general philosophy of the courts as they approach the interpretation of a contract? Explain.
4. What are the requirements of a reasonable noncompete agreement? Explain.
5. Are those limitations imposed by the employer reasonable in this case? Explain.

Source: See: *AK Steel Corp. v. ArcelorMittal USA, L.L.C*, 2016-Ohio-3285, (Court of Appeals, 12th Appellate District of Ohio, Butler County).

LO Learning Objectives

1. Identify the age of minority and the age of majority.
2. Explain the legal status of a contract made by a minor.
3. Differentiate between ratification and disaffirmance.
4. Identify the effects of mental impairment on a contract.
5. Discuss the contractual capacity of a drugged or intoxicated person.
6. Explain the legality of agreements to commit torts and crimes.
7. Identify those agreements made illegal under statutory law.
8. Enumerate those agreements contrary to public policy.
9. Explain what happens under the doctrine of *in pari delicto*.
10. Explain the effects of illegality.

10-1 The Final Elements

The final two elements of a contract are capacity and legality. A contract can have a valid offer, an effective acceptance, mutual assent, valid consideration, and still be void if it involves doing something illegal. An **illegal agreement** is one that violates criminal law or tort law, a statute, and/or public policy as established by the court. In general, the law will aid neither party involved in an illegal agreement. **Capacity** is the legal ability to enter a valid contract.

Minors are able to rescind most contracts; however, adults who contract with minors generally cannot.
©Khalid Mohammed/AP Images

Generally, a person has the ability to enter a contract if he or she possesses free will, displays a certain degree of self-knowledge and is informed about the nature, purpose, and effect of the agreement. The chapter here is designed to first explore the various factors that affect capacity and then look at what makes a contract illegal and what happens as a result of that illegality.

The Nature of Capacity and Minority

Capacity is considered a **rebuttable presumption**. This means that under the law, the parties to a contract are permitted to presume that each of them has the capacity to enter a contract. The term *rebuttable* means that presumption is not absolute. Rather, it can be challenged. Generally, in the case of capacity, the presumption is challenged by the party claiming incapacity. In other words, that party is saying something like, "I know you presumed that I had capacity to enter the contract when we negotiated this agreement and thank you for that, but, guess what, I did not have capacity and I would, therefore, like to exit the agreement." So for example, under the current state of the law, for instance, when a minor enters a contract with an adult, and the minor seeks to void the contract, he or she is challenging the presumption of capacity.

The law allows minors the privilege to **disaffirm** (negate) a contract to protect them from unscrupulous adults (or unscrupulous minors for that matter) who might take advantage of the young people who might not fully comprehend the responsibilities that they are assuming. When a minor indicates by a statement or act an intent not to live up to a contract, that minor is entitled to a return of everything given to the other party. This right exists even when the property transferred to the minor under the contract has been damaged or destroyed. A few states will deduct something from the amount due back to the minor if the goods are damaged. Most states, however, deduct nothing.

In a sense then, minors actually have extra-capacity, that is, they have the capacity to enter a contract and the capacity to exit the contract by challenging that rebuttable presumption. This is unlike someone who uses mental impairment as the grounds for disaffirming a contract. The person using mental impairment is arguing that the mental impairment took away his or her capacity to enter a contract at the time of the agreement. In contrast, the minor is using a *legal fiction* that says minors lack capacity. Another way of saying this is to note that the person with a mental impairment really did not know the nature and the purpose and the effect of the agreement and, therefore, must not be held liable. The minor may or may not have real incapacity, that is, the actual real-life inability to understand the nature, purpose, and effect of the agreement, or the minor may have legal incapacity, which is a legal fiction that says we will lump all minors together and say that they do not have capacity until they cross a magical line called the age of majority.

> **About the Law**
> A rebuttable presumption is also known as a "disputable presumption."

U.S. Const. Amendment 26 (see Appendix A).

Definition of Minority Under common law, **minority** was a term that described persons who had not yet reached the age of 21 years. Upon reaching that age, a person was said to have reached **majority**. Ratification and adoption of the 26th Amendment to the U.S. Constitution in 1971 lowered the voting age in federal elections from 21 to 18 years. To avoid the confusion that would result from having two voting ages, the states started to enact new laws that enabled 18-year-olds to vote in state and local elections. Then most states began to lower the age of majority to 18 years. (*Note:* Alabama and Nebraska use 19 and Mississippi and Puerto Rico use 21, but check the current law wherever you might live to make certain.) Some states also tie the age of majority to high school graduation. Other age requirements differ from state to state in relation to matters such as the legal ability to purchase alcoholic beverages, enter a marriage, buy tobacco products, purchase firearms, and operate motor vehicles. Recently, for instance, in response to outside influences from a variety of social organizations and governmental institutions, many states have raised the legal age for purchasing and consuming alcohol to 21 years. Also, young men must register for selective service at 18 years of age.

Emancipation and Abandonment In some jurisdictions, minors who become **emancipated**—that is, no longer under the control of their parents—are responsible for their contracts. This responsibility means that they cannot void a contract, despite their apparent minority. Emancipated minors include those who are married; those in the armed forces; and those who leave home and, in the process, give up all right to parental support. In certain states, minors are even allowed to ask the court for a legally sanctioned emancipation. In all these cases, emancipated minors are said to have **abandoned** the usual protective shield given them. Although minors in these categories are no longer protected from liability on their contracts, merchants are still reluctant to deal with them on a credit basis, fearing that they may still attempt to disaffirm, or repudiate, their contracted debts. Again, for practical, not legal, reasons, merchants often require that minors get the signature of a responsible adult who will agree to guarantee payment of money owed.

Moreover, the hesitancy felt by some merchants in relation to emancipated minors is justified because a few states still hold to the opposite rule: that emancipated minors do not give up the legal advantages associated with minority simply because they leave home or become married. To support this position, the courts in these jurisdictions note that the rule that allows minors to rescind contracts is based on the idea that minors are less experienced and less knowledgeable than adults about the consequences of their actions. It is therefore difficult to see why getting married or leaving home somehow bestows more common sense on a minor who does so. In fact, one court remarked that getting married and leaving home may actually indicate that a minor has less good sense than another minor who does neither. Because this rule differs from state to state, it would be a good idea to check the rule of law in your jurisdiction.

Misrepresentation of Age Minors sometimes lie about their age when making a contract. Despite this misrepresentation of age, most states will allow the minor to disaffirm or get out of the contract. Some jurisdictions, however, do not permit the minor to get away with the lie. Some states require the minor to place the adult party to the contract in the same situation that he or she was in before the contract. Others allow the adult to use tort law, rather than contract law, to sue the minor for fraud. Some states have also enacted statutes that allow recovery against a minor who is engaged in business and who misrepresents his or her age in a commercial contract. A number of states, for example, have statutes that deny disaffirmance if the minor has signed a written statement falsely asserting adult status. Without such a statute, the minor would be allowed to get out of the primary contract despite her or his signature on that primary contract or the contract asserting adult status.

Contractual Capacity of Minors

Executory contracts, those that have not been fully performed by both parties, may be repudiated by a minor at any time. A promise to deliver goods or render services at some future time need not be carried out by the minor who decides not to do so. This privilege is not available to an adult who contracts with a minor. If goods delivered to a repudiating minor are still in the minor's possession, it is the minor's duty to return them to the other party.

Contracts for Necessaries Goods and services that are essential to a minor's health and welfare are called **necessaries**. Thus, necessaries can include clothing, food, shelter,

A SOON TO BE CLASSIC CASE Capacity or Employment at Will? Which Dominates?

Eugene Aaron, one of the defendants in the case of *Sidco Paper Company v. Eugene Aaron and Grant Paper Company*, at the age of 17, took a position as an apprentice for the Sidco Paper Company located in Pennsylvania. At that point, he had nothing more than an oral contract with the company, and he made $60 per week. However, Aaron's apprentice period must have worked quite well because after two years, he was given a full-time position as a sales representative. This time, Sidco gave him written contract. The contract was only for a single year, but it could be renewed annually. The written contract also included an interesting term that permitted each party to terminate the agreement provided that the party gave 60 days' advanced notice. On the other hand, the contract also included a restrictive employment agreement that would be activated once Aaron's employment was terminated. The covenant would forbid Aaron from working for a Sidco competitor for two years after the end of his employment. The territory that was covered included any area starting with Richmond, Virginia, as the southern-most boundary, up to Pittsburgh as the western border, and with Boston as the northern boundary point.

When Aaron was first hired as an apprentice at 17, he was still a minor. That meant that he could void any contact at any time with no penalty. Another way to say this is that a contract made by a minor is voidable by the minor. The law allows minors to disaffirm contracts to protect them from unscrupulous adults who might take advantage of young people who might not fully comprehend the responsibilities that they are assuming. This explains why Sidco hired Aaron using only an oral agreement during his apprenticeship. Because he could leave at any time, there was no need for a written agreement. However, ironically, the written agreement that Sidco made with Aaron after he reached his majority is also one that he could disaffirm because, from all available evidence, it was an at-will agreement. Employment at-will means that an employment contract can be terminated by either party at any time for any reason or for no reason, with or without notice. This also means that the notice provision in the contract was also unnecessary and unenforceable. After all, Sidco could not make Aaron work for the company if he did not want to. That would be involuntary servitude, something we outlawed in the United States some time ago. Of course, if Aaron's employment were not at-will, there might be some monetary penalty for violating the notice provision, but that would be the extent of the negative consequences for Aaron had that occurred. [See: *Sidco Paper Company v. Aaron*, 465 Pa. 586, 315 A. 2d 250 (1976).]

Source: See: *Sidco Paper Company v. Aaron,* 465 Pa. 586, 315 A. 2d 250 (1976).

Did You Know?

Despite being designated as "necessaries," such things are not always needed to preserve or protect life. In fact, in one case the court held that funeral expenses were necessaries.

medical and dental services, tools and equipment needed for the minor to carry out his or her business, and even, in some cases, educational expenses. If a minor makes a contract for necessaries, he or she will be liable for the fair value of those necessaries. Despite the general tenor of this principle, if the necessaries have already been provided to the minor by parents or others, the rule does not apply. In addition, not everything that a party claims as a necessary will actually be a necessary. To determine whether goods and services qualify as genuine necessaries, the court will inquire into the minor's family status, financial strength, and social standing or station in life. Necessaries, then, are not the same to all persons.

Technically, a minor's contract covering necessaries is not enforceable against the minor in the truest sense of the term. Instead, the minor is required to pay the fair value of the necessaries that have been provided by the adult. The fair value is determined by the court. This approach to the law is an extension of the concept of quasi-contract. Remember that when applying the concept of quasi-contract, the court will require the parties to act as if there were a contract, even though a true contract does not exist. The point of requiring the minor to pay the fair value of the item is to play it straight with adults who carry the risk of dealing with minors in relation to necessaries. Allowing the minor to get away with completely rescinding such contracts would amount to unfair enrichment of the minor. The concept of quasi-contract is aimed at preventing this type of unjust enrichment.

Many people, including minors and the adults who deal with them, overlook an interesting corollary related to the concept of necessaries. This corollary is the standard that states that the rules related to necessaries apply only to executed contracts. An executed contract is one whose terms have been completely and satisfactorily carried out by both parties. In contrast, an executory contract is one that has not yet been fully performed by the parties. Wholly executory contracts calling for a future delivery or rendering of services may be repudiated by the minor.

Technically, parents are liable for a contract executed by a minor, even a contract for necessaries, *only* when they cosign the agreements. When a parent, or anyone else for that matter, cosigns for a loan or for a contract involving installment payments, the cosigner becomes a guarantor. A guarantor promises to pay the other party's debts if that party does not settle those debts personally. This promise is known as a guaranty of payment. In contrast, if parents do not cosign a contract, they are *not liable* for that contract, even though the contract was made by their minor child. As might be expected, there is an exception to this general rule. If a parent has neglected or deserted the minor, the parent may be held liable to a third person for the fair value of the necessaries supplied by the third party to the minor.

Other Contracts Not Voidable By statute and court decision, certain other types of contracts have been excepted from the general rule that the contracts of minors are voidable at the minor's option. For public policy reasons, minors may not, at their option, disaffirm a valid marriage or repudiate an enlistment contract in the armed forces based on a claim of incapacity to contract. Neither may a minor repudiate a contract for goods and services required by law; for example, minors may not repudiate payments for inoculations and vaccinations required for attendance at a university or college or required in securing a visa for travel in certain foreign lands. They may also be prevented from terminating contracts with banks and other financial institutions for educational loans. Some states bar minors from repudiating agency contracts and insurance contracts. Others prevent them from voiding contracts for psychological care, pregnancy care, the transfer of stocks and bonds, and contracts involving child support. These exceptions are state-by-state issues, so it is wise to check your own state statutes to determine which of these contracts are not voidable by minors in your jurisdiction.

Shield or Sword Doctrine If tempted to see the rescission rights of minors as unfair, we must keep in mind the original intent of the court in granting this power. As noted previously, the right to rescind contracts was given to minors as a protective device or "shield" against those unscrupulous adults who might try to take unfair advantage of the immaturity and inexperience of minors. This type of situation is precisely what the law envisioned when it granted minors the "shield" that allows them to rescind contracts.

The problem with this protective device is that it can be exploited by minors who use it to rescind legitimate contracts. In effect, an unprincipled minor can take this safeguard, which is meant as a protective shield, and transform it into a sword that violates the rights of the other party. Fortunately, the courts are not oblivious to this type of abuse. Because the doctrine was never meant to allow minors to take advantage of innocent people, the courts have no difficulty denying rescission rights to minors when they use it as a weapon against another contracting party.

> **About the Law**
>
> Under the Napoleonic Code, people under 30 years of age could not marry without their father's permission. In addition, a father could have his child incarcerated for as long as six months on his word alone.

EXAMPLE 10-1: The Shield and Sword Doctrine

Amber Sampson, who was 16 years of age, purchased a round-trip ticket on New England Airlines for a trip from Portland, Maine, to San Diego, California, for spring break. When spring break was over, Sampson returned to Portland and, on arrival, demanded the return of all the money that she had paid for the round-trip ticket. Her demands were based on her rescission rights as a minor. Clearly, Sampson was using her right to rescind to take advantage of New England Airlines. She was not using her rights as a minor as a protective shield, as the law intended. It is doubtful that Sampson will be permitted to recover money for her ticket.

Voidable Contracts and Innocent Third Parties Another curb on a minor's right to rescind contracts appears in the provisions of the UCC. These provisions protect the rights of an innocent third party who purchases goods from an individual who originally purchased those same goods from a minor. Although individuals who buy goods from minors have voidable ownership rights, under the UCC, those same individuals can transfer valid ownership rights to an innocent third-party purchaser of those goods. Thus, rescission by a minor will not require the innocent purchaser to return the goods.

EXAMPLE 10-2: Protecting the Innocent

David Wittmer, age 17, sold his laptop to Lustbader Electronics LLC. Lustbader refurbished the ancient laptop and then sold it to Alex Myers, an innocent third-party buyer. Before Wittmer became an adult, he decided to get back his laptop from Myers by disaffirming his contract with Lustbader. Wittmer is out of luck here. He will not be able to recover the laptop by disaffirming his contract with Lustbader. Myers is an innocent third party and is thus protected by the UCC.

The UCC rule refers to the sale of personal property. In cases in which a minor has sold real estate to one who subsequently sells it to an innocent third party, the minor, on reaching adulthood, may disaffirm the sale and recover the real property.

Ratification and Disaffirmance

People may ratify their contracts made during minority only after reaching their majority or within a reasonable time thereafter. **Ratification** or **affirmance** is the willingness to abide by contractual obligations. It may be implied by using the item purchased, making an installment payment, paying off the balance of money owed on a previously voidable contract, continuing to accept goods and services being provided under a contract, or just doing nothing about the contract after reaching majority. Affirmation may also result from the person's oral or written declaration to abide by the contract. These acts, as well as others, ratify an existing agreement and elevate it to the status of one that is enforceable against an adult.

An individual may disaffirm an agreement made during minority before or within a reasonable time after reaching adulthood. The exact period of time will vary depending on the nature of the contract and on applicable state and local laws. Failure to disaffirm within

A REAL CLASSIC CASE Minority, Majority, and the Transformative Effect of Doing Nothing

In the preceding Soon to Be Classic Case, we learned that Eugene Aaron, at the age of 17, took a position as an apprentice for the Sidco Paper Company. The hiring process involved an oral contract with the company, and he made no more than made $60 per week. Aaron's apprentice period worked quite well because after two years, he was given a full-time position as a sales representative. This time, Sidco gave him a written contract that was for a single year but that could be renewed annually. When Aaron was first hired as an apprentice at 17, he was still a minor. That meant that he could void any contact at any time with no penalty. Another way to say this is that the contract was made by a minor (Aaron) and was, therefore, voidable by the minor (Aaron). The law allows minors to disaffirm contracts to protect them from unscrupulous adults who might take advantage of young people who might not fully comprehend the responsibilities that they are assuming. This may be why Sidco hired Aaron using only an oral agreement during his apprenticeship. Because he could leave at any time, there was no need for a written agreement. Then again, the oral agreement made when Aaron was a minor might have changed into a valid, enforceable, adult-made contract. This transformation may have occurred because, after Aaron turned 18, he continued to work for Sidco, presumably under the same terms that they followed when the oral agreement was made when Aaron was 17. In this way, Aaron ratified that first contract. Ratification or affirmance is the willingness to abide by contractual obligations. In this case, ratification was implied because Aaron did nothing differently after he turned 18. He continued to work for Sidco, signaling that the new "adult" Aaron passively consented to that original contract made by the now vanished "minor" Aaron. [See: *Sidco Paper Company v. Aaron*, 465 Pa. 586, 315 A. 2d 250 (1976).]

Source: See: *Sidco Paper Company v. Aaron,* 465 Pa. 586, 315 A. 2d 250 (1976).

a reasonable period of time would imply that the contract had been ratified. The method of disaffirmance is fundamentally the same as the method of ratification. Disaffirmance may be implied by the acts of the individual after achieving majority, such as by a failure to make an installment payment. Similarly, an oral or written declaration of disaffirmance would achieve the same end. In general, there are no particular protocols attached to the act of disaffirmance by a minor. However, it is generally a good idea to make the disaffirmance in writing so that there is a record of the transaction should questions arise later. This recommendation is especially true if the contract is disaffirmed after the minor has reached the age of majority.

quick quiz 10-1

1. Executory contracts, those which have not been fully performed by both parties, may be repudiated by a minor at any time. true | false
2. Ratification is the willingness to abide by contractual obligations. true | false
3. Necessaries are the same for all persons. true | false

10-2 Other Capacity Problems

Persons deprived of the mental ability to comprehend contractual obligations have the right to disaffirm their contracts. Their rights are, in many respects, the same as the rights of minors. Agreements of mentally impaired persons are valid, voidable, or void, depending on the seriousness of their disability and whether they have been declared insane.

Persons Mentally Impaired

Under the orthodox rule of competency in contract law, a contract made by a person who is mentally infirm, has brain damage, is suffering from a physical illness such as Alzheimer's disease, or suffers from a psychological disorder may be voidable if the person's impairment is severe enough to rob that person of the ability to understand the nature, purpose, and effect of that contract. The question will be whether the mental problem existed at the time the contract was made and was so serious that the person did not understand the nature of the contract. If that is the case, the mentally impaired person may disaffirm any contract made under the influence of that mental impairment. The incompetent person must return all consideration received. This rule is true especially when the other party had no knowledge of the person's mental impairment. If, however, the other party knew about the person's mental impairment and took advantage of that knowledge, there is no requirement to return the other party to the identical place that he or she was in before the original agreement was established.

A second rule is also recognized by the Restatement of Contracts and by some states. That rule says that a person's contractual obligations may be voidable if that person suffers from a mental impairment that prevents him or her from acting in a reasonable manner. Under this version of the rule, a person may understand the nature of the contract but, because of his or her impairment, be unable to stop himself or herself from entering the contract. In such a situation, as long as the contract has yet to be executed or, if executed, can be shown to be very unjust, the impaired person may void the contract. If the contract is executed or fair, the impaired party may still void the contract but also must return the other party to the place he or she was in before the contract was entered. If returning the other party to his or her precontract condition cannot be done, the court will decide on a fair alternative.

A person declared to be insane by competent legal authority is denied the right to enter contracts. Such persons will be under the care of a guardian who acts on behalf of the impaired person, who has in effect become a ward of the court. Any contractual relationship with others results in nothing more than a void agreement. In most states, persons who knowingly take advantage of one declared insane are subject to criminal indictment and prosecution.

Persons Drugged or Intoxicated

A contract agreed to by someone under the influence of alcohol or drugs may be voidable. Incompetence related to either alcohol or drugs must be of such a degree that a contracting party would have lost the ability to comprehend or be aware of obligations being accepted under the contract. A person who enters into a contract while in this condition may either affirm or disaffirm the agreement later. Disaffirmance in such cases requires the return to the other party of all consideration that had been received. However, such a return may be refused when evidence indicates that the other party took advantage of the person's drunken or otherwise weakened condition.

EXAMPLE 10-3: Involuntary Intoxication Invalidates a Contract

Samuel K. Richardson III attended a reception at the Yakuza Gallery on Madison Avenue at 75th Street in Manhattan. Unknown to Richardson, the punch at the reception had been laced with alcohol. After drinking several glasses, Richardson became highly intoxicated. While intoxicated, he agreed to sell the original manuscript of the novel *The Bay Tree* to an antiquarian book dealer named Maynard Posner, who was also at the reception and who was quite sure that Richardson was "tipsy" at the time of the sale. When Richardson recovered, he sought to disaffirm the contract. Because his involuntary state of intoxication had robbed Richardson of his ability to comprehend the contract he was making with Posner, he would be allowed to get out of the agreement.

---

quick quiz 10-2

1. For a contract to be voidable by a person with a mental impairment, the mental problem must exist at the time the contract was made.   true | false
2. A person declared to be insane by competent legal authority cannot be denied the right to enter contracts.   true | false
3. A contract made by a person who is intoxicated is completely void.   true | false

---

10-3 Agreements to Engage in Unlawful Activity

The final element of a valid contract is legality. Ordinarily, the court will leave the parties to an illegal agreement where they placed themselves. If an illegal agreement is still executory, the court will not order it performed or award damages for breach of contract. If the illegal agreement has been executed, the court will not award damages or assist in having it annulled. The most obvious type of illegal contract is one in which parties agree to perform some sort of unlawful activity. This activity could be a crime or a tort, depending on the circumstances. However, when we use the term *unlawful activity* in this context, we are referring to activities that are clearly wrong in and of themselves. These unlawful activities include crimes and torts that most people would recognize as wrong, even if there were no statute, regulation, or court decision to tell them it was wrong.

Agreements to Commit Torts and Crimes

The law will not uphold any contract that obligates one of the parties to commit a tort. For example, a network television reporter who agrees to defame several politicians in return for a position as their opponent's press secretary would find no remedy in the law should her benefactor fail to follow through after the libelous story was printed. The agreement to commit a tort would be void in the eyes of the law. This approach only makes good sense. The law cannot lend its approval to a contract that breaks the law, no matter how complete it is in relation to the other three elements.

In like manner, the law cannot honor any agreement if the purpose of the agreement is to commit a crime. If, for example, a storekeeper would pay a known criminal to vandalize the shop of a competitor, that storekeeper would not be able to sue the criminal for breach of contract should the criminal take the money and run. As strange as it may seem, the nature of criminality is not always as clear as might be imagined. Because criminal law involves serious offenses that can result in the loss of a person's freedom or, more seriously, the loss of a person's life, all criminal statutes must be drawn as precisely and as clearly as possible. A statute that is obscure or outlines conduct that is ambiguous may be struck down by the court as void for vagueness. This ruling would mean that a contract that involves the conduct that is allegedly outlawed by a vague statute might not be void.

Agreements Illegal under Statutory Law

Most people of good faith would know, even in the absence of any statute, regulation, ordinance, rule, or court decision, that the behavior outlined in the previous examples would be wrong. It is difficult to imagine, for instance, that the shopkeeper would be surprised to discover that it is wrong to hire someone to destroy his competitor's property. Similarly, it is not easy to believe that the television reporter who agreed to lie in a television broadcast thought that her behavior was in any way admirable. In contrast, some activities that do not seem wrong on the surface may have been made wrong by specific statutory enactments. Therefore, the fact that some of these activities are illegal may catch us by surprise. For example, the shopkeeper knows vandalism is illegal but may be confused to learn that he cannot hold a garage sale without a license. Or the reporter who knows that libel is wrong may be amazed to learn that she cannot legally enforce the collection of her winnings from her Thursday night poker game (unless that game is run by a state sanctioned casino). For this reason, we will examine those activities that are wrong because a statute says they are wrong. These activities include usurious agreements, wagering agreements, unlicensed agreements, unconscionable agreements, and Sunday (Sabbath) agreements.

Usurious Agreements The illegal practice of charging more than the amount of interest allowed by law is called **usury**. To protect borrowers from excessive interest charges, each state has passed laws that specify the rate of interest that may be charged in lending money. These interest rates vary from state to state. Agreements to charge more than is allowed by law are illegal. Special statutes, however, allow small loan companies, pawn shops, and other lending agencies that accept high-risk applicants for credit to charge a higher rate of interest.

Wagering Agreements Any agreement or promise concerning a wager or some other form of gambling is invalid and may not be enforced. States make exceptions when bets are placed in accordance with laws that permit horse racing, state lotteries, church-related or charitable games of bingo, and gambling casinos regulated by state authority. However, even in states in which gambling is legal, borrowing money to gamble is frequently still illegal.

Unlicensed Agreements Certain businesses and professions must be licensed before they are allowed to operate legally. One reason for requiring a license is to provide a source of revenue, part of which is used to supervise the business or profession being licensed. A city ordinance requiring all residents to obtain a license before holding a yard or garage sale would fall into this category. Another purpose that the government has in licensing individuals is to provide supervision and regulation of businesses and professions that might inflict harm on the public if they were allowed to operate without such controls. Physicians, nurses, dentists, attorneys, engineers, architects, public school teachers, and others in public service must be supervised for the protection of the public. The law distinguishes between licenses purely for revenue and licenses for protection of the public. If a license is required simply to raise revenue, the lack of a license will not necessarily make a contract void; if a licensing requirement is designed to protect the public, unlicensed persons will not be able to enforce their contracts.

Unconscionable Agreements A court will not enforce a contract or any part of a contract that it regards as unconscionable. An agreement is considered unconscionable if its terms are so grossly unfair that they shock the court's conscience. When the court so desires, it will limit how the unconscionable clause in an agreement is carried out, provided it can do so without causing any unfair consequences.

Sunday Agreements State statutes and local ordinances that regulate the making and performing of contracts on Sunday are called blue laws because one of the first laws banning Sunday or Sabbath contracts was written on blue paper. Today, the enforcement of restrictive blue laws varies in different geographical areas. Certain states have eliminated uniform statewide laws regulating Sunday activities but permit counties and incorporated cities, towns, and villages to adopt their own ordinances under a concept known as local option. Other states have rolled back these laws almost entirely, permitting most contracts while prohibiting or limiting only a few select Sunday contracts, such as those involving the sale of alcohol. Where laws do restrict Sunday business, two rules are usually observed. First, agreements made on Sunday or any other day requiring performance on Sunday may be ruled invalid. Exceptions to this rule are those agreements necessary to the health, welfare, and safety of the community and its residents. Second, agreements made on Sunday for work to be done or goods to be delivered on a business day are valid and enforceable. However, some states still require that there be an affirmation of such agreements on a day other than Sunday if such agreements are to be enforceable. The enforcement of blue laws varies widely from state to state, county to county, and village to village.

Agreements Contrary to Public Policy

The general legal principle of public policy says no one should be allowed to do anything that injures the public at large. Agreements most commonly invalidated as contrary to public policy are those to obstruct justice, interfere with public service, defraud creditors, escape liability, and restrain trade. Some of these agreements are prohibited by statute, such as those that suppress competition and those that interfere with public service. Consequently, they could have been listed and explained in the last section. Instead, these contracts are listed here with the other public policy–related contracts, because they share one thing in common, though such contracts are made between private individuals, they would hurt the entire social structure if the law enforced them in any way.

Agreements to Obstruct Justice Agreements to obstruct justice include agreements to protect someone from arrest, to suppress evidence, to encourage lawsuits, to give false testimony, and to bribe a juror. The category also includes a promise not to prosecute someone or not to serve as a witness in a trial. Any agreement promising to perform any of these activities would be void.

Agreements Interfering with Public Service Agreements interfering with public service are illegal and void. Contracts in this group include agreements to bribe or interfere with public officials, to obtain political preference in appointments to office, to pay an officer for signing a pardon, or to illegally influence a legislature for personal gain.

Agreements to Defraud Creditors An agreement that tends to remove or weaken the rights of creditors is referred to as an agreement to defraud creditors. Such agreements are void as contrary to public policy. Thus a debtor's agreement to sell and transfer personal

ANOTHER REAL CLASSIC CASE: Public Policy, Statutory Law, and Contract Validity

New England Surrogate Parenting Advisors (NESPA) is a nonprofit organization that seeks to match potential surrogate mothers with couples who are unable to have children of their own. In this case, a surrogate mother candidate and couple entered an agreement that stipulated that the father would pay for all pregnancy expenses plus a $10,000 fee to the mother for "conceiving, carrying, and giving birth to the child." The fee was to be transferred to the surrogate mother in installments based on a structured payment plan. The final $3,500 was to be paid to the surrogate mother when the child was born. All three parties to the agreement—the surrogate mother, the father, and the father's wife—underwent psychological screening by a psychologist. The psychologist reported that the surrogate mother was a stable, considerate, and knowledgeable woman who was aware of what she was doing and would be emotionally and psychologically capable of transferring custody to the child's biological father.

For a while, everything went according to the contract. The surrogate mother conceived a child by the father. The first two payments were sent and accepted by the mother. However, at the end of the sixth month, after receiving the third payment, the mother changed her mind, returned the third payment, and told the father's attorney that the contract was ended. That was the only money returned. She kept the first two payments and the expense money she had received under the agreement. The father sued for custody, arguing that the surrogate mother had breached the contract. The judge agreed and transferred custody to the father based on the contract and because she believed such a move would ultimately be in the child's best interests. The surrogate mother appealed. The state supreme judicial court noted that, because the state had no statute covering this type of agreement, it would apply an adoption statute that was roughly analogous to the situation. Under that statute, a mother could not give up her child for adoption until four days after the child's birth. The statute also outlawed the payment of money to the mother for an adoption, although she could be paid pregnancy expenses. The state supreme court recognized that the legislature had a good reason for requiring a four-day waiting period before a mother could give up her child for adoption. The court took judicial notice of the fact that a mother comprehends the power of the connection between mother and child after the fourth day and is, therefore, in a better position to be fully aware what she is surrendering in an adoption. Using public policy, the court applied those same principles to the surrogate mother contract. In doing so, it concluded that, because the surrogate mother contract did not include a four-day waiting period, it was an illegal contract and was, therefore, void as a matter of law. [See: *R.R. v. M.H. and Another*, 426 N.E.2d 790 (Supreme Court of Massachusetts).]

Source: See: *R.R. v. M.H. and Another*, 426 N.E.2d 790 (Supreme Court of Massachusetts).

A QUESTION OF ETHICS

In February 2011, the Egyptian people displayed their dissatisfaction with the government of Hosni Mubarak by demonstrating in Tahrir Square in Cairo and in the port city of Alexandria. The demonstrations led to Mubarak's abdication and to a military takeover of the government. The military leaders pledged to develop a new constitution and to turn the government over to civilian control as soon as possible. Nevertheless, despite the movement's victory over Mubarak and his government, many protestors continued to disrupt the peaceful transition to domestic peace. Chief among these demonstrators were members of the labor movement who had created a tightly knit network of agreements under which striking textile employees, airport workers, ambulance drivers, electrical engineers, and journalists continued to cause economic disruption. All of this continued to occur despite warnings by the military government that such actions should cease. Clearly the strikers believed that their cause was moral and their actions ethical despite their dubious legality. Under American law, agreements to strike illegally would violate public policy. Should the ethical motivation of the strikers trump the illegality of their actions? Defend your response using one of the ethical theories discussed in Chapter 1.

and real property to a friend or relative for far less than actual value would be void if done for the purpose of hiding the debtor's assets from creditors with a legal claim to them.

Agreements to Escape Liability A basic policy of the law is that all parties should be liable for their own wrongdoing. Consequently, the law looks with disfavor on any agreement that allows a party to escape this responsibility. One device frequently used in the attempt to escape legal responsibility is the **exculpatory clause**. Such an agreement is usually found as a clause in a longer, more complex contract or on the back of tickets and parking stubs. The exculpatory clause will state that one of the parties, generally the one who wrote the contract, will not be liable for any economic loss of physical injury even if that party caused the loss or injury.

EXAMPLE 10-4: Newsome v. Tibbs

Pat Newsome, who worked for Van Sloane, Wentworth, and Michelson, was the chief architect on a project that involved building a new community center on the west side of Baltimore. Before the center could be built, a set of four high-rise apartment buildings, the Towers, had to come down. That job went to Tibbs TNT LLC, an expert in razing ancient buildings. When Newsome arrived at the job, he was told by Elizabeth Tibbs, the owner of Tibbs TNT, that he had to sign an additional contract with Tibbs. One of the clauses in the additional contract included an exculpatory clause that stated that Newsome would hold Tibbs blameless should Newsome be injured during the tear down of the Towers. The actual implosion of the Towers went without incident; however, afterward, Newsome was injured when the brakes on a Tibbs-owned truck failed and ran over Newsome. Newsome sued Tibbs. Tibbs pointed to the exculpatory clause and said she was not liable. The court disagreed, saying that the exculpatory clause could not protect Tibbs from liability for injuries that result from negligence on the part of Tibbs or her employees.

This exculpatory clause is an example of the type that the courts have found to be a violation of public policy. Such exculpatory clauses are not favored by the law because they permit behavior to fall below acceptable standards, which was what happened in the Newsome case. A clause simply disclaiming liability in general terms is often insufficient to release a party from his or her own negligence. Still, some courts will enforce exculpatory clauses if they do not offend public policy and there is no inequality of bargaining power between the parties. However, whenever an exculpatory provision is ambiguous, confusing, vague, incomplete, or can be interpreted in different ways, the court will construe the clause against the party it was designed to protect.

Sale of Business When a business is sold, it is common practice for the agreement to contain covenants that restrict the seller from entering the same type of business. Such **restrictive covenants** in a contract for the sale of a business will be upheld by the court if they are reasonable in time and geographical area. What is reasonable is determined by a careful examination of the business being sold. For example, an agreement by the seller of a barbershop not to open a similar shop in the same community for the next year would seem to be reasonable. In contrast, the opening of a different business, over a wider geographical area, or for a longer period of time might not be allowed by the court.

Noncompete Agreements A **noncompete agreement**, or a **restrictive employment covenant** as it is often called, limits a worker's employment options after leaving his or her present job. The idea is to protect the present employer from an employee who might take trade secrets, customer lists, or other confidential material to a competitor. In a typical noncompete agreement, an employee promises not to work for a competitor in the same field for a specified time period and within a specified geographical area after leaving the current job. Noncompete agreements must be supported by consideration and must be reasonable in the type of work they prohibit, the length of time involved in the prohibition,

THE OPENING CASE Round 2
"Time Out" for a Chief Operating Officer: How Much Time Is Time Enough?

Recall that the Opening Case began when Keith Howell decided to resign his role at AK Steel (AK) as senior VP of operations in order to accept a job as the COO of ArcelorMittal USA (AM). This gave officials at AK cause to worry because Howell had been privy to tons of confidential information, trade secrets, customer lists, manufacturing techniques, company operations, strategies, logistics, capital expenditures, pricing, and so on at AK. Howell had agreed to enter a severance contract that would kick in when he left the company. Apparently, Howell also had a large vested retirement account from AK. In addition, AM had promised Howell a $900,000 signing bonus for joining that firm. Given all of this, Howell was "sitting pretty" at this point in his career. One road block stood in the way of this nearly perfect arrangement, however. Within the pages of the AK severance agreement was a noncompete provision under which Howell had agreed not to work for a competitor anywhere on the planet for one year. Howell's decision to leave AK activated the noncompete agreement and precipitated this lawsuit. What AK wanted was a temporary restraining order and preliminary injunctive relief that would compel Howell to live up to his side of the bargain.

Substantively, to succeed in showing that the noncompete agreement was legally permissible, AK had to demonstrate that the noncompete (1) would prevent irreparable harm to the company, (2) would not impose undue hardship on Howell, and (3) would not hurt the public at large. To prove the first and second points, AK offered the following arguments. First, to demonstrate irreparable harm, AK claimed that because Howell knew so much about AK's price margins and negotiation plans for the upcoming year, his presence at AM would give that company an unfair advantage over AK. Second, to prove that Howell would undergo no undue hardship, AK pointed out that given his current financial health, the one-year "suspension" from work in the steel industry would be uncomfortable but tolerable. On the other side, Howell argued that because he had been employed in the steel industry for his entire adult life, he would most likely be unable to get a job in any other industry. Unemployment would not be so bad if he were on his own, Howell continued, but he was not on his own. In fact, he was the sole support of his entire family. As a result, his family would have no income for an entire year and that would surely qualify as an undue hardship.

Faced with these arguments, the trial court elected to reengineer the noncompete agreement and dropped the one-year limit to six months. Howell and AM were delighted. AK was not. Accordingly, AK filed an appeal. The court of appeals saw things a bit differently than the trial court. First, the appellate court was impressed by AK's argument that the timeliness of Howell's information was a key to AK's competitiveness. The fact that Howell knew so much about AK's price margins and negotiation plans for the upcoming year made him a very real threat to AK's competitiveness in relation to AM. The fact that this information had a shelf life of a single year made the one-year limit in the noncompete agreement eminently reasonable. That reasonableness would only stand, however, if the one-year limit did not cause undue hardship to Howell and his family. The appellate court took judicial notice of Howell's $900,000 signing bonus and his large vested retirement plan from AK and concluded that, while one year of unemployment would be a hardship to Howell and his family, it would not be an *undue* hardship. This was enough to convince the court of appeals that the trial court had overstepped its bounds by changing the one-year limit to six months. Accordingly, the appeals court changed the limit back to one year and sent the case back to the trial court. [See: *AK Steel Corp. v. ArcelorMittal USA, L.L.C*, 2016-Ohio-3285, (Court of Appeals, 12th Appellate District of Ohio, Butler County).]

Source: See: *AK Steel Corp. v. ArcelorMittal USA, L.L.C,* 2016-Ohio-3285, (Court of Appeals, 12th Appellate District of Ohio, Butler County).

and the geographical area (space) covered by the prohibition. To determine the reasonableness of these restrictions, the court must, in general, make sure that the limits are (1) not overly broad, but just enough to protect the employer; (2) not so strict that they impose an undue hardship on the employee; and (3) do not, in any way, cause injury to the public welfare.

More specifically, the court can use the following factors in making its decision: (1) Does the employee possess trade secrets or other confidential information that can hurt the employer? (2) Was the employee the only public face of the employer in relation to customers and clients? (3) Do the limits attempt to control unfair competition or just ordinary competition? (4) Do the limits attempt to stop the employee from exercising the ordinary skills that any employee in his or her position would possess? (5) Do the limits cut off the employee's sole way to make a living? (6) Does the agreement include geographical and temporal limits? (7) Do the limits favor the employer and hurt the employee in a disproportionate way? (8) Do the limits attempt to control peripheral duties rather than essential duties? (9) Do the limits try to control knowledge and abilities that the employee learned while on the job with the employer or knowledge and abilities that the employee had all along?

Nondisclosure Agreements A **nondisclosure agreement** requires employees to promise that, should they leave their present place of employment, they will not reveal any confidential trade secrets that they might learn while on their current job. Because the limitation is placed on the use of confidential information rather than actual employment of the worker, such agreements do not deprive people of their employment and therefore do not constitute an extensive limit on competition. Although helpful, nondisclosure agreements are often not needed to protect trade secrets. The court will generally issue an injunction to prevent the revelation or the utilization of trade secrets if the employer can convince the court that (1) the information revealed by the former employee was actually a trade secret, (2) the secret information was crucial to the running of the employer's business, (3) the employer had the right to use the trade secret, and (4) the former employee came into possession of the trade secret while in a position of trust and confidence and in such a way that it would be unfair for the former employee to disclose that trade secret in a way that would hurt his or her former employer.

---

quick quiz 10-3

1. The illegal practice of charging more than the amount of interest allowed by law is called usury.   true | false
2. If a license is required simply to raise revenue, the lack of a license will make a contract void.   true | false
3. A restrictive employment covenant limits a worker's employment options after leaving his or her present job.   true | false

---

10-4 Consequences of Illegality

Illegality of contract, as in promises to commit criminal acts, not only serves to void existing agreements, but may also lead to indictment and prosecution when sufficient evidence warrants such an action. Persons who agree to engage in criminal activity for a promised consideration are involved in what criminal law defines as a **conspiracy**. Agreements that do not violate criminal laws may still be invalid. Thus, many agreements considered contrary to public policy have been declared invalid as against the public good but not illegal in terms of criminal liability. Both types of agreements fail to have the characteristics that permit legal enforcement.

In Pari Delicto Contracts

When both parties to an illegal agreement are equally wrong in the knowledge of the operation and effect of their contract, they are said to be *in pari delicto* (in equal fault). In such cases, the court will give no aid to either party in an action against the other and will award no damages to either. When the parties are not *in pari delicto*, relief will often be allowed if sought by the more innocent of the two. Although this rule is not applicable when one may be less guilty of premeditation (plotting or planning an illegal act) and intent to achieve a gain through known illegal acts, it may be applied when one party is not aware that a law is being broken and there is no intent to do a wrong.

Partial Illegality in an Agreement

Sometimes an agreement will be partly legal and partly illegal. If the legal part of a contract can be removed from the illegal part, without changing the essential nature of the contract, then the agreement is said to be divisible. The court will enforce the legal part but not the illegal part. As long as the main purpose of the agreement can be reached without enforcing the illegal part, the courts are likely to uphold the agreement.

---

quick quiz 10-4

1. Persons who agree to commit criminal acts for a promised consideration are involved in a conspiracy. true | false

2. When both parties to an illegal agreement are equally wrong in the knowledge of the operation and effect of their contract, they are said to be *in pari delicto*. true | false

3. If the legal part of a contract can be removed from the illegal part, without changing the essential nature of the contract, the court will enforce both parts. true | false

---

Summary

10.1 The third element essential to a legally effective contract is the legal ability to enter into a contractual relationship. This legal ability is known as capacity. Under the law, there is a rebuttable presumption that anyone entering a contract has the legal capacity to do so. Because the presumption is rebuttable, a party can attack it. Minors are allowed this privilege. Minority means that an individual has not yet attained the age of majority. An exception to the rule about minors and contracts involves necessaries. By statute and court decision, certain other types of contracts have been excepted from the general rule that the contracts of minors are voidable at the minor's option.

10.2 Contracts of persons who are mentally infirm or mentally ill, but not legally declared insane, may be valid or voidable, depending on the seriousness of the mental problem. Persons declared to be insane by competent legal authority are denied the right to enter into contracts, and contracts entered into may be declared void. Incompetence related to alcohol or drugs must be of such a degree that the contracting party has lost the ability to comprehend or be aware of the obligations being accepted under the contract.

10.3 An agreement might have offer, acceptance, mutual assent, competent parties, and consideration and still be invalid if the objective of the agreement is to do something that is illegal. These contracts include those to commit crimes, to commit torts, or to violate statutory law. Public policy is a general legal principle that says no one should be allowed to do anything that tends to hurt the public at large. Agreements found void for a violation of public policy include agreements to obstruct justice, agreements interfering with public service, agreements to defraud creditors, exculpatory agreements, and agreements in restraint of trade.

10.4 Contracts that involve illegal agreements are invalid. Moreover, promises to commit illegal acts may lead to indictment and prosecution. If an entire agreement is illegal, no binding contract results. If only part of an agreement is illegal, the court may rescind only those parts found to be illegal. When both parties are equally at fault in creating an illegal agreement, the court will award no damages to either. When the parties are not in equal fault, relief will often be granted if sought by the innocent party.

Key Terms

abandoned, 287
affirmance, 290
blue laws, 295
capacity, 285
conspiracy, 299
disaffirm, 286
emancipated, 287

exculpatory clause, 297
illegal agreement, 285
in pari delicto, 300
local option, 295
majority, 286
minority, 286
necessaries, 287

nondisclosure agreement, 299
public policy, 295
ratification, 290
rebuttable presumption, 286
restrictive covenants, 297
restrictive employment covenant, 298
usury, 294

Questions for Review and Discussion

1. What is the age of minority, and what is the age of majority?
2. What is the legal status of a contract made by a minor?
3. What is the difference between ratification and disaffirmance?
4. What are the effects of mental impairment on a contract?
5. What is the contractual capacity of a drugged or intoxicated person?
6. What is the legal status of an agreement to commit a tort or a crime?
7. What agreements are illegal under statutory law?
8. What agreements are contrary to public policy?
9. What happens under the doctrine of *in pari delicto*?
10. What are the effects of illegality?

Cases for Analysis

1. After she was married, Sherri Mitchell, a young woman 17 years of age, was in an automobile accident in which she was hurt enough to require medical treatment. She was later approached by an insurance agent who offered her $2,500 as a settlement. All she had to do was sign a release that would absolve the insurance company of any complaint that she might have against it in regard to the accident. She agreed to accept the $2,500 and signed a release to that effect; however, she then changed her mind and decided to void the agreement. She argued that since she was 17 at the time she signed the release, she was a minor and could therefore void the contract. Is Mitchell correct? Explain. [See: *Mitchell v. State Farm Mutual Automobile Insurance Co.*, 963 S.W.2d (Ky. Ct. App.).]

2. Sperry Ford sold a car to Bowling when Bowling was only 16 years old. Once Bowling had paid the

full purchase price in cash, Sperry turned over the car and the certificate of title. After driving the car for only a week, Bowling discovered that the main bearing was burned out. When Bowling found out that repair costs would almost equal the price he'd paid for the car, he left the car on Sperry's lot and asked for his money back. Sperry Ford refused to give Bowling his money. Was Sperry justified in this refusal? Explain. [See: *Bowling vs. Sperry*, 184 N.E.2d 901 (IN).]

3. Quality Motors Inc. refused to sell a car to Hays because he was only 16 years old; however, Quality told Hays that it would sell the car to an adult and then show Hays how to transfer the title to his name. Hays agreed with the scheme and came back with a friend who was 23. Quality sold the car to Hays's friend. Quality then gave Hays the name of a notary public who would transfer the title to Hays. After the transfer was accomplished, Hays's father found out about the deal and tried to get Quality Motors to take the car back. Quality replied that the car had been sold to an adult, so Hays could not disaffirm the contract. Is Quality correct? Explain. [See: *Quality Motors v. Hays*, 225 S.W.2d 326 (AR).]

4. Lonchyna enlisted in the U.S. Air Force while he was still a minor. Three times he applied for and received educational delays that put off the beginning of his tour of duty. The last time, he claimed he could void the contract because he'd entered into it when he was a minor. Was Lonchyna correct? Explain. [See: *Lonchyna v. Brown, Secretary of Defense*, 491 F. Supp. 1352 (N.D. IL).]

5. Darwin Kruse was a construction worker. He was injured while working for the Coos Head Timber Company. Subsequent to the accident, Kruse signed an agreement with his employer that granted Kruse compensation in exchange for his promise not to sue. Kruse is now trying to have the agreement voided. Evidence introduced proved that Kruse had an IQ of 83 and that he dropped out of school at age 18. When he dropped out of school, he was in the eighth grade but was doing less than sixth grade-level work. Will Kruse's "slowness" necessarily invalidate the contract? Explain. [See: *Kruse v. Coos Head Timber Co.*, 432 P.2d 1009 (OR).]

6. Clear Channel Broadcasting Inc. required Diane Ignazio to sign a new contract that included an arbitration clause under which she agreed that all grievances that she might have with Clear Channel would be settled by arbitration. As part of the agreement, Ignazio gave up any right to bring a lawsuit against Clear Channel. When Ignazio was discharged, instead of moving to arbitration, she sued Clear Channel for discrimination and wrongful discharge. Clear Channel filed a motion to dismiss the case, arguing that Ignazio was bound by the arbitration agreement. Ignazio pointed to a clause in the agreement that rendered the entire agreement illegal. The clause allowed the arbitration award to be reviewed by a court based on the same broad standards used by an appeals court in reviewing a trial court's decision. This provision contradicts state law, which states that if an appeals court reviews an arbitration decision, it can only use a very limited approach to the appeal, including only such things as clerical error or misconduct. Clear Channel argued that even if the clause was illegal, it could be severed from the agreement and the rest of the agreement could be enforced. In fact, the contract even included a clause that stated that any clause found illegal ought to be removed from the contract so that the rest of the contract could be upheld. The question before the court was whether the illegal clause could be removed from the agreement without changing the essential nature of the contract. Is it legally permissible to remove the illegal part of a contract so that the court can uphold the legal part? Should the court sever the illegal clause in this case? Explain. [See: *Ignazio v. Clear Channel*, 113 Ohio St.3d 276 (Ohio Supreme Court).]

7. Cyberian Enterprises and BrandAid Marketing Corporation entered a deal under which Cyberian was supposed to purchase $21 million in BrandAid's stock. Cyberian, however, did not have the funds available to make the actual purchase, a fact that was concealed by Cyberian representatives. When BrandAid discovered the lie, it filed a lawsuit against Cyberian for fraud, breach of contract, and breaking federal securities law. Cyberian brought a countersuit against BrandAid for fraud because BrandAid had apparently failed to tell Cyberian about its own financial difficulties. BrandAid's financial problems were on file with the Securities and Exchange Commission (SEC). When the case went to District Court, the judge dismissed the case because, citing the doctrine of *in pari delicto*, he stated that both parties were at equal fault in concealing their financial difficulties. The case then went to the Second Circuit Court of Appeals, which decided that the trial court had made a mistake in dismissing the case. Why did the

appeals court overturn the decision of the trial court? Explain. [See: *BrandAid Marketing Corp. v. Biss*, 05-5243-cv (2d U.S. Cir. Ct. of App.). See also: Beth Bar, "Civil Practice: Finding of Equal Fault Is Overturned," *The National Law Journal*, September 11, 2006, p. 13.)]

8. Shannon Audley, a professional model, signed an agreement before starting work on a photo shoot at Bill Melton's studio. The agreement stated: "I, Shannon Audley, realize that working with wild and potentially dangerous animals (i.e., lion, white tiger, hawk) can create a hazardous situation resulting in loss of life or limb. I take all responsibility upon myself for any event as described above that may take place. I hold Bill Melton and T.I.G.E.R.S. or any of their agents free of any or all liability. I am signing this of my own free will." During the photo shoot, Audley was bitten on the head by the adult male lion with which she had been posing. Audley brought suit against Melton. Would the exculpatory clause be upheld by the courts? Explain. [See: *Audley v. Melton*, 640 A.2d 777 NH).]

9. Judy Myers and the Terminix International Company entered a contract in which Terminix agreed to inspect Myers's home and eliminate any termite problem found there. The service cost Myers an initial payment of $1,300 plus annual renewal fees of $85. Terminix failed to eradicate the termite infestation, causing more than $41,000 in damage to Myers's home. The contract contained a clause that required the parties to submit any disputes to arbitration under the American Arbitration Association (AAA). What the contract did not disclose was that Myers would be required to pay a filing fee to submit a claim to AAA. In this case, the filing fee amounted to $7,000. In a lawsuit filed for breach of contract, Myers asserted that the undisclosed filing fee requirement was unconscionable. Is Myers correct? Explain. [See: *Myers v. Terminix*, 697 N.E.2d 277 (OH).]

Design Elements: The Opening Case: ©Sharpstock/Alamy; A Classic Case: ©Evlakhov Valeriy/ Shutterstock

quick quiz Answers

10-1	10-2	10-3	10-4
1. T	1. T	1. T	1. T
2. T	2. F	2. F	2. T
3. F	3. F	3. T	3. F

Chapter 11

Written Contracts and Cyber-Commerce

11-1 The Statute of Frauds
Contracts That Must Be in Writing • The Contents of a Writing

11-2 Legal Rules for Written Contracts
The Standard Construction Rule • The Parol Evidence Rule • The Best Evidence Rule • The Equal Dignities Rule

11-3 Formalities of Construction
Signature Requirements • Witnesses and Acknowledgments • Special Conditions and Circumstances

11-4 Cyber-Commerce and the Law
Verification Problems • Cyber-Commerce Legislation

THE OPENING CASE Round 1
"No one can build his security on the nobleness of another person."—Willa Cather

As you read through this case, it may help to remember the old saying, "If you want something done right (or perhaps done at all), do it yourself." The owners and operators of Sole Survivor Inc., a tailor shop and shoe repair store, negotiated a 10-year lease with the Eastland Mall. The terms of the lease were spelled out in a written contract that included a clause on consideration and one on mall security, among many others. The owners of Sole Survivor agreed to pay a monthly rent that was specified in the contract along with a percentage of each month's gross receipts. Michael Johnson and Sarah Johnson agree to act as sureties for the rent. At first, things seemed to work out well, but then trouble began. The number of police reports on criminal activity at the mall rose noticeably. Many of the businesses that had been at the mall left the premises. Included in this exodus were the major anchor stores at the mall. As a result, the mall's reputation declined, and Sole Survivor lost many of its customers. Finally, as if to add insult to injury, Sole Survivor was, itself, the victim of armed robbery.

The owners of Sole Survivor notified the Eastland Mall officials about the problems repeatedly but saw no action. Sole Survivor argued that Eastland Mall had a duty to provide security and that it had failed to meet that duty. In addition, Sole Survivor claimed that the mall had failed to provide a safe and secure environment as required by the terms of the lease agreement. Further, Sole Survivor argued that the mall had breached an implied covenant of "quiet enjoyment" that would have allowed the store owners to use the premises undisturbed. Finally, taking all of this together, Sole Survivor claimed the mall's failure to provide a safe and secure working environment amounted to a constructive eviction, justifying their decision to leave the premises, which they did after eight years of occupancy. The operators of the mall disagreed with all of these allegations. Accordingly, they filed a lawsuit against Sole Survivor and the two sureties, Michael Johnson and Sarah Johnson. Eastland claims that Sole Survivor breached the lease agreement when it left the mall and, as a result, still owes rent under that agreement amounting to $96,275.48 plus late fees, interest, legal fees, and court costs. As its primary piece of evidence, Eastland produced the security clause from the original lease agreement. That clause reads: "Landlord may, from time to time and to the extent it deems appropriate in its sole discretion, determine whether to supply security services in the Common Areas and additional traffic control for the Shopping Center. Notwithstanding any other provision of this Lease, Landlord shall not be liable for any loss or damages suffered by Tenant . . . by failure to supply such services[.] . . . It is specifically understood and agreed that, by supplying such services, Landlord shall not be deemed to relieve Tenant of its duty to maintain security within the Demised Premises nor of its performance of the terms, covenants and conditions of this lease." The trial court issued a summary judgment in favor of the mall. The defendants filed an appeal.

Consider the following questions. Did this contract have to be in writing to be enforceable under the Statute of Frauds? Did the contract joining Michael Johnson and Sarah Johnson as sureties have to be in writing to be enforceable under the Statute of Frauds? Were the rental consideration terms ("a percentage of each month's gross receipts") in the contract specific enough to be enforceable? Was the security clause in the lease agreement clear or ambiguous? What principle must the court follow in its interpretation of that security clause? Who is ultimately responsible for the writing of that clause? Finally, who should prevail—the frightened, discouraged, and economically strapped tenants or the strict and determined owners of the mall? Curious? Well the answers all lay ahead. [See: *Charlotte Eastland Mall LLC v. Sole Survivor Inc.*, No. COA03-1422, Court of Appeals of North Carolina (October 19, 2004).]

Opening Case Questions

1. What law outlines those contracts that must be in writing to be enforceable? Explain.
2. Which contracts must be in writing to be enforceable? Explain.
3. Why should leases be placed in writing? Explain.
4. How definite should the terms of a written contract be? Explain.
5. What rules govern the interpretation of the terms of a written contract? Explain.

See: *Charlotte Eastland Mall LLC v. Sole Survivor Inc.*, No. COA03-1422, Court of Appeals of North Carolina (October 19, 2004).

Learning Objectives

1. Identify the goals of the Statute of Frauds.
2. Identify those contracts that must be in writing.
3. List the information that must be in the writing.
4. Explain the standard construction rule.
5. Discuss the parol evidence rule.
6. Explain the exceptions to the parol evidence rule.
7. Explain the best evidence rule.
8. Discuss the equal dignities rule.
9. Explain the problems associated with cyber-commerce.
10. Outline the latest cyber-commerce statutes.

11-1 The Statute of Frauds

Often when people hear the word *contract*, they immediately think of a piece of paper. Instead, they should think of an agreement, which may or may not be in writing. Many contracts do not have to be in writing to be enforceable. Most oral contracts are valid and upheld by the court. Although it may be desirable to put a contract in writing so that its terms are clear, only certain kinds of contracts are required to be in writing. This chapter discusses the **Statute of Frauds**, which is the law that requires certain contracts to be in writing to be enforceable.

Contracts That Must Be in Writing

According to the Statute of Frauds, applicable in most states, six types of contracts must be in writing to be enforceable:

1. Contracts that cannot be completed within one year.
2. Contracts transferring real property rights.

3. Contracts for the sale of goods of $500 or more.
4. Certain contracts entered into by executors and administrators.
5. Contracts by one party to pay a debt of another party.
6. Contracts in consideration of marriage.

The third contract on the list, contracts for the sale of goods of $500 or more, is actually included in the Uniform Commercial Code rather than the Statute of Frauds. This point is covered in depth in Chapter 13.

Contracts That Cannot Be Completed within One Year If the terms of a contract make it impossible to complete the agreement within one year, the contract must be in writing.

> **About the Law**
>
> In addition to those mentioned here, states have enacted various statutes requiring other promises to be in writing, such as promises to leave something to someone in a will, promises to pay debts that have been discharged in bankruptcy, and certain types of assignments.

Contracts Transferring Real Property Rights Under the Statute of Frauds, conveyances of real property must be in writing to be enforceable. This provision covers the sale of land; however, it also covers trusts that are created by one party, the trustor, that permit a second party, the trustee, to possess and control the land for the advantage of a third party, the beneficiary. Land contracts must be in writing because the ownership of land carries with it a bundle of rights, including the right to enter, cross, and leave the land; the right to plant, cultivate, and harvest crops on the land; the right to search for and extract minerals from the land; the right to rent or lease part or all of the land; and so on. Each of these rights can be transferred to someone other than the owner. Written contracts are needed to keep track of who owns each of these rights. Written contracts also help keep track of ownership rights for tax purposes. Moreover, real property contracts tend to be long and complicated, which also justifies the writing requirement. Whether the requirement for a writing under the Statute of Frauds includes leases is problematic because some jurisdictions permit short leases, generally those that last less than a year, to be oral. The parties to a lease are free to negotiate the time period for a lease, unless state law indicates otherwise. Most states, however, are relatively clear that leases that are designed to last longer than one year must be in writing to be enforceable. Written leases will also usually indicate what happens at the end of the time period covered in the lease. If the lease itself does not indicate what happens at the time that the lease expires, the state will generally lay down such a provision. Most states say that the lease transforms by law automatically to a month-to-month lease, although some states provide that the lease becomes valid for another year.

In addition to these provisions, the law often requires that other items be added to written leases. For example, most states require that a provision covering security deposits be added. State law also limits the amount that can be charged for security deposits. Most states limit this to one month's rent, but some can go as high as three months. States also require that security deposits be held in escrow and accrue interest that is then paid to the renters on the termination of the lease. These statutes also require that the landlord give tenants an itemization of the cost of all repairs that will be deducted from the security deposit when the lease ends. Most of these statutes also include provisions prohibiting discrimination based on race, color, creed, gender, national origin, parenthood, sexual orientation, family relationships, and even pet ownership. Another provision that should be included in any lease is the disposition of fixtures, including, especially, trade fixtures, when the lease terminates. Leases also often include provisions that indicate who will be responsible for such things as the payment of utilities, the upkeep of the premises, and security.

When a party owns land, he or she owns a bundle of rights that can be distributed among various other parties. Thus, it is possible, for example, for the owner of a parcel of land to divide the rights to that land among several different parties. One party might hold

THE OPENING CASE Round 2
"No one can build his security on the nobleness of another person."—Willa Cather

In the Opening Case, we learned that the owners and operators of Sole Survivor Inc., a tailor shop and shoe repair store entered a 10-year lease with the Eastland Mall. The owners of Sole Survivor promised to pay a monthly rent along with a percentage of each month's gross receipts. Michael Johnson and Sarah Johnson agree to act as sureties for the rent."Landlord may, from time to time and to the extent it deems appropriate in its sole discretion, determine whether to supply security services in the Common Areas and additional traffic control for the Shopping Center. Notwithstanding any other provision of this Lease, Landlord shall not be liable for any loss or damages suffered by Tenant … by failure to supply such services[.] … It is specifically understood and agreed that, by supplying such services, Landlord shall not be deemed to relieve Tenant of its duty to maintain security within the Demised Premises nor of its performance of the terms, covenants and conditions of this lease. Initially, Sole Survivor and the management of the mall worked well together. The mall provided a productive working environment, and the store paid its rent on time. Then things began to deteriorate. As the crime rate at the mall intensified, customers began to avoid shopping on the premises and sales fell off. After being victimized by an armed robbery, the owners of Sole Survivor claimed constructive eviction and abandoned the mall. The owners of Sole Survivor blamed the operators of the mall for not providing a proper level of security. The management of the mall filed a lawsuit to recover the lost rent plus attorney's fees, interest, and court costs. The management then filed a motion for a summary judgment. If granted, the summary judgment would stop the case without having to go to trial.

To succeed in convincing the court to grant the motion, the moving party, in this case, the mall, would have to show that there is no disagreement as to the essential facts in the case and that, even if the facts are interpreted in a light most favorable to the defendant, the plaintiff—in this case, the mall—would win as matter of law. It is for cases precisely like this one that the Statute of Frauds requires a writing. One of the contracts that must be in writing to be enforceable under the Statute of Frauds is a contract for the sale or lease of real property. The law requires a writing for real property contracts because the ownership of land carries with it a bundle of rights, each or all of which can be transferred to someone other than the owner. Written contracts are needed to keep track of who owns each of these rights. Written contracts also help keep track of ownership rights for tax purposes. Moreover, real property contracts tend to be long and complicated, which also justifies the writing requirement. Real property contracts, especially leases like this one, generally include provisions that indicate who will be responsible for such things as the payment of utilities, the upkeep of the premises, and security. In this case, the provision under fire was the one that covers security at the mall. When the court read this section, including the following words, "(the) Landlord may, from time to time and to the extent it deems appropriate in its sole discretion, *determine whether to supply security services in the Common Areas* and additional traffic control for the Shopping Center. Notwithstanding any other provision of this Lease, *Landlord shall not be liable for any loss or damages suffered by Tenant … by failure to supply such services."* Whatever we may think about the ethics of this provision, the written contract clearly specific who will be responsibility for security. That, however, is as it should be if the Statute of Frauds is to operate autonomously and objectively. [See: *Charlotte Eastland Mall LLC v. Sole Survivor Inc.*, No. COA03-1422, Court of Appeals of North Carolina (October 19, 2004).]

Source: See: *Charlotte Eastland Mall LLC v. Sole Survivor Inc.*, No. COA03-1422, Court of Appeals of North Carolina (October 19, 2004).

a lease to a house on the land allowing her to live there, a second could have an easement that permits him to cross the land, a third might own the right to mine the land, and so on. The Statute of Frauds requires a writing for each of these different transactions. The object of this requirement is to make certain that there is a way to follow the trail of each of these rights to determine who owns them, should a dispute arise concerning them.

An exception to the rule that contracts for the sale of land must be in writing is called **part performance** or **equitable estoppel**. The exception applies when a person relies on an owner's oral promise to sell real property and then makes improvements on the property or changes his or her position in an important way. The plaintiff in such a case must prove three elements to succeed in a lawsuit. First, the plaintiff must show that he or she made the improvement relying on the original promise and without suspecting that the other party intended to renege on the agreement. Second, the plaintiff must show that any other remedy, such as restitution for the amount spent, is not enough to satisfy his or her effort or outlay of funds. Third, the plaintiff must show that the part performance itself is evidence of the existence of the contract.

EXAMPLE 11-1: *Zuer v. Iafigliola*

Jake Iafigliola agreed in an oral contract to sell Dwight Zuer a run-down parcel of storefront property for $50,000. The storefront was located across the street from the site of a new Target that was about to be established in the neighborhood. Relying on Iafigliola's agreement, Zuer spent $20,000 improving the premises so that he could move his 24/7-365 fitness, wellness, and exercise business into the storefront. Iafigliola then backed out of the deal. Zuer sued, asking the court to order Iafigliola to go through with the contract. Iafigliola argued this was a real property contract, and it had to be in writing to be enforceable. Zuer asked the court to apply the part performance doctrine. Zuer made the following case: First, he had made the improvements relying on the original promise. Second, he pointed out that any other remedy, such as restitution for the amount spent, would not be enough because he clearly wanted the storefront in the lot across from the new Target. Third, Zuer argued that the fact that he spent $20,000 to improve the storefront could not be explained in any other way other than his reliance on the contract. The court agreed and allowed the lawsuit even without the writing.

The courts do not require a writing for a contract in which the owner of land agrees to improve the land for the use of another party who has already received a partial interest in the land. In such a situation, the courts believe that once the real interest in the land has been transferred, the contract to improve the land does not create a new interest. Instead, the new contract is solely a promise to provide labor and make changes in the land. It therefore falls outside the statute, and no writing is required.

EXAMPLE 11-2: *Dewey v. Collins*

Rene Collins owned a piece of land in rural Pennsylvania, just outside Streetsboro. Frederick Dewey received an easement across Collins's land. The easement, which was supposed to last for five years, was executed in a written document. After the first year, Dewey asked Collins to lay gravel on the small road that constituted the easement. Collins said that she would not lay the gravel herself but would permit Dewey to do so and reimburse him for the expense. Dewey laid the gravel and presented Collins with the bill. Collins refused to reimburse Dewey as agreed. Collins argued that because there was no writing, the contract, which involved land, was unenforceable. The referee disagreed, concluding that the agreement to lay gravel did not create a new interest. Instead, it simply involved a commitment to pay for improvements to land in which Dewey already owned an interest.

Contracts for the Sale of Goods of $500 or More Under the UCC, contracts for the sale of goods (movable items) for $500 or more must be in writing to be enforceable. However, there are four exceptions to this rule. Oral contracts for the sale of goods of $500 or more will be enforced in situations involving the following:

UCC 2-201

1. Oral contracts between merchants when a written confirmation has been received by one party and not objected to by the other party.
2. Specially manufactured goods that cannot be resold easily.
3. Admissions in court.
4. Executed agreements.

BUSINESS LAW WITH UCC APPLICATIONS AND NOW—THE APPLICATIONS

Of Bats, Pennies, Peppers, and Ironmen

Okay, that explanation is really quite brief. Let's try to make it a bit clearer.

First the motivation—As noted earlier, under the UCC, contracts for the sale of goods (movable items) for $500 or more must be in writing to be enforceable. However, the authors of the UCC have recognized that, even when a contract for goods valued at $500 or more is not in writing, other evidence may exist that would make the need for a writing, probably superfluous, and most likely, completely unnecessary.

Now the Application—(1) One such contract is a contract for specially manufactured goods. If a contract has begun, following the specifications of a particular buyer to construct or develop an item that is "not suitable for sale to others in the normal course of sales in the seller's business," then the writing is not needed should the buyer renege (2-201[3][a]). So, if Bruce Wayne has ordered the development and construction of a powerful, well-armed, atomic powered bat-shaped vehicle from Stark Industries, then, even without a written agreement, Tony Stark can rest assured should Mr. Wayne deny the existence of that agreement. (2) The writers of the UCC have also recognized that oral contracts between merchants that are followed by written confirmation that has been received by one party and not objected to will make that contract immune to the Statute of Frauds (2-201 [1]). So, let's say that Mr. Wayne and Mr. Stark discuss (on their respective mobile phones) a contract under which Mr. Wayne will purchase the parts needed to repair a damaged Batcopter. Mr. Wayne then mails to Mr. Stark a written confirmation, which Mr. Stark receives and does not contradict. Is that enough evidence to take us outside of the Statute of Frauds requirements? Affirmative. (3) The UCC commissioners also understand that an admission in court to the existence and terms of a contract is enough to provide the equivalent of a writing taking that situation out of the Statute of Frauds (2-201 [3][b]). Now, imagine that Mr. Wayne and Mr. Stark end up in lawsuit over an oral contract for a Kryptonite-tipped spear, which Mr. Wayne ordered from Stark Industries. The contract should have been in writing, but it is not. If either of them admits on the witness stand or in a pleading that the contract exists, no writing is needed and we are freed from the Statute of Frauds again. (*Note:* Those of you who suspected that the specially manufactures goods exception applies here too, give yourself a pat on the back. You are absolutely correct.) (4) Finally, the authors of the UCC, in their infinite wisdom, have recognized that the partial performance of a contract can serve as evidence for the existence of a contract even without a writing. So if one party accepts the goods or pays for the goods, the requirement of a writing evaporates. For instance, let's say, without any written confirmation, Mr. Wayne has ordered 1,000 Batarangs from Stark Industries, at a certain specified price ($100 per Batarang). Should Mr. Wayne's agent, Alfred Pennyworth, accept the Batarangs when delivered to stately Wayne Manor, or if Mr. Stark's agent, Pepper Potts, accepts payment from Mr. Pennyworth at Stark Tower, nobody can yell "no fair—the Statute of Frauds protects me" (2-201[3][c]).

Certain Contracts Entered by Executors and Administrators An **executor** is a person who is named in a will to oversee the distribution of the estate of a deceased according to the provisions outlined in the will. An **administrator** is a person named by the court to do the work of an executor if none is named in the will or if the executor cannot or will not perform those duties. As a general principle of law, neither an executor nor an administrator is personally liable for the debts of the decedent's estate. Executors and administrators must pay the debts of the estate, to be sure, but out of the assets of the estate, not out of their own pockets. Thus, any promise to pay the debts of the estate using the executor's or the administrator's own funds is unenforceable without a writing.

EXAMPLE 11-3: *Trautman v. Quinn*

Max Quinn was named the executor of his sister's estate. One of his sister's creditors, Nancy Trautman, demanded immediate payment of a debt of $6,600 owed by the deceased. To protect his sister's good name, Quinn promised Trautman that he would pay her the amount owed out of his own funds if the estate could not cover that amount. Trautman refused to agree unless Quinn placed the agreement in writing. Quinn agreed. After things calmed down, Trautman tried to collect the debt. Quinn refused to pay. Trautman was able to enforce the promise because she had written evidence of Quinn's agreement to pay the debt.

Contracts by One Party to Pay a Debt Incurred by Another Party A promise made by one party to pay another person's debts, if that person fails to pay the debt, falls within the statute and must be in writing to be enforceable. Several terms have been used to describe these types of transactions. They are alternately referred to as a **guaranty of payment**, a **guaranty contract**, or a **collateral contract**. The promisor is usually called a **guarantor**. Often in a commercial setting, the guarantor is referred to as a **cosigner**. The person to whom the promise is made is the **obligee**, and the person who owes the original debt is referred to as the **obligor**. It is crucial to distinguish between guaranty contracts and original contracts.

An exception to this rule is known as the primary objective test. Under the **primary objective test** (also referred to as the **leading objective test** and the **main purpose test**), if the promise to pay another party's debt is actually made to obtain a gain for the guarantor, there is no need for a writing to enforce the promise. Suppose, for instance, that Hans McKnight, the owner of Scottish Inn, depends on the Hometown Bakery for the inn's sub buns for its lunch trade. Suppose further that McKnight knows that the Hometown Bakery has had some financial trouble and may have to shut down its operations if it cannot pay Jakub's Supply for its regular flour shipment. If McKnight promises Jakub's that, if it continues to supply Hometown with flour, he will pay the bill, that promise falls under the primary objective test and need not be in writing to be enforceable.

Contracts in Consideration of Marriage Agreements made in consideration of marriage must be in writing to be enforceable. This part of the statute does not refer to the marriage contract itself or to engagement promises to marry, which are almost always oral. Rather, it refers to promises made by parties before marriage, in which they accept additional obligations not usually covered in the marriage vows. A **prenuptial agreement** (also referred to as a **premarriage agreement** and an **antenuptial agreement**) involves two people who are planning marriage and who agree to change the property rights they possess by law in a marriage. Such promises are enforceable only if they are in writing and agreed upon prior to the marriage. Many state legislatures, as well as the District of Columbia, have enacted the Uniform Premarital Ageement Act (UPAA). The UPAA supports the use of prenuptial agreements and provides for their enforcement.

Other Contracts Each state has enacted special statutes outlining other agreements that must be in writing. Other contracts that are usually required by special statutes to be in writing include the release of a party from debt (general release) and the resumption of obligations after bankruptcy. In addition, some states require real estate listing contracts and insurance binders to be in writing. Other contracts that require a writing under the UCC are contracts for the sale of securities (stocks and bonds) and agreements creating security interests.

The Contents of a Writing

The Statute of Frauds requires that the agreement be in writing—nothing more. The purpose of the writing is twofold. First, it proves that the parties entered an agreement. Second, it provides detailed information about the terms of that agreement. To accomplish these goals, the writing must be intelligible, but it need not follow any preset format. It can be found in letters, memos, documents, invoices, packing slips, and purchase orders that have been mailed, privately delivered, faxed, or sent electronically between the parties. It may be written on any surface suitable for the purpose of recording the intention of the parties, as long as all the required elements are present. A writing can even be placed in an e-mail, in a text message, or on a website, as long as it is possible to store and reproduce the electronic record of the agreement, and as long as the cyber-record includes an electronic signature as defined by the appropriate cyber-commerce statute.

Elements of a Writing To be absolutely complete, a written agreement, or **memorandum**, as it is often called, should contain the following elements:

- Terms of the agreement.
- Identification of the subject matter.
- Statement of the consideration promised.
- Names and identities of the persons to be obligated.
- Signature of the party sought to be bound to the agreement.

To determine whether the elements in the written contract are clear and definite enough, we ask whether the terms are so unambiguous that, if there were a breach, the court would know how to assess a remedy. If the answer is yes, the terms are probably definite enough. If the answer is no, then some critical term in the alleged offer is missing or too obscure to create a contract.

THE OPENING CASE Round 3
"No one can build his security on the nobleness of another person."—Willa Cather

Let's journey back to the Opening Case, where the owners and operators of Sole Survivor Inc., a tailor shop and shoe repair, store agreed to a 10-year lease with the Eastland Mall. The terms of the lease included a clause on consideration and one on mall security, among many others. The clause covering consideration noted that the owners of Sole Survivor agreed to pay a monthly rent along with a percentage of each month's gross receipts. Michael Johnson and Sarah Johnson agree to act as sureties for the rent. The security clause read as follows: "Landlord may, from time to time and to the extent it deems appropriate in its sole discretion, determine whether to supply security services in the Common Areas and additional traffic control for the Shopping Center. Although the relationship was smooth at first, that condition did not last did not last. Things started to fall apart when the crime rate at the mall climbed precipitously. Once Sole Survivor was robbed, the owners had reached their limit, broke their lease, and left the mall. To justify their actions, the owners of Sole Survivor blamed the operators of the mall for not providing a proper level of security. The management of the mall filed a lawsuit to recover the lost rent plus attorney's fees, interest, and court costs. The amount that they asked for was very precise, $96,275.48.

Now recall that the rental arrangement called for the owners of Sole Survivor to pay a set monthly rent along with a percentage of each month's gross receipts. The managers of the mall can easily determine what Sole Survivor owes in rent payments because that amount that was specified to be paid each month. All that the mall has to do is take the remaining months—say, 24 months—and multiply that by the monthly rate. So far, so good. However, what do we know about the rest of the rent? No set dollar amount per month is specified in the lease. Instead, we get a formula. The formula says that, in addition to the set rental rate, Sole Survivor will also pay a percentage of each month's gross receipts to the mall. Is this formula definite enough to satisfy a standard that require clear and definite terms? The standard asks whether the terms are definite and clear enough that, if there were a breach, the court would know how to assess a remedy. If the answer is yes, the terms are probably definite enough. If the answer is no, then some critical term in the alleged offer is missing or too obscure to create a contract. Here, the term says that rent will include a percentage of each month's gross receipts to the mall. Is this term definite and clear enough that the court will know how to assess a remedy. The answer here is yes. All the court need do is take the percentage specified in the lease, transform it into a decimal, and then multiply that decimal times the gross. Voila! The court has a set dollar amount to use as a measurement of damages! [See: *Charlotte Eastland Mall LLC v. Sole Survivor Inc.*, No. COA03-1422, Court of Appeals of North Carolina (October 19, 2004).]

Source: See: *Charlotte Eastland Mall LLC v. Sole Survivor Inc.*, No. COA03-1422, Court of Appeals of North Carolina (October 19, 2004).

quick quiz 11-1

1. A contract is said to be outside the statute if it must be in writing to show that the two objectives of the Statute of Frauds have been met.   true | false
2. An administrator is a person who is named in a will to oversee the distribution of the estate of a deceased person according to the provisions outlined in the will.   true | false
3. Agreements made in consideration of marriage must be in writing to be enforceable.   true | false

11-2 Legal Rules for Written Contracts

The legal system has developed certain basic criteria that make the construction and interpretation of written contracts as flawless as possible. These criteria act very much the way basic axioms or rules work in mathematics. Therefore, we could characterize these rules as unquestioned assumptions about the text of a writing that must be followed when an attorney, a magistrate, or a judge interprets a writing that claims to contain the terms of a contract. These four rules are (1) the standard construction rule, (2) the parol evidence rule,

(3) the best evidence rule, and (4) the equal dignities rule. The first two rules cover the interpretation of contracts, whereas the latter two govern their enforcement.

The Standard Construction Rule

LO4 Appropriately, the first of the interpretation rules is the most critical and the most fundamental of the four. The **standard construction rule** guides the entire interpretation process by directing the interpreter of a contract to determine the principal objective of the parties in the making of the contract. The *principal objective* is the primary or main goal that the parties hoped to accomplish by entering the agreement in the first place. Once this principal objective is stated, everything else must be interpreted to promote that principal objective. In line with this rule, the law also says that common words used in the contract are given their expected, everyday definition, and technical terms or professional slang will be given their technical or professional definitions. The standard construction rule also says that any standard operating procedures that are used in the parties' professions or trades should be followed whenever there is any doubt about what procedure should be used in the contract.

Because the standard construction rule is the most fundamental guideline involved in the interpretation of written contracts, it also guides the interpreter on matters of ambiguity and misinterpretation. The rule says that whenever an ambiguous term, clause, or line is found in a prewritten or preprinted contract, that ambiguity is interpreted against the party who wrote the contract. This approach should encourage those people who draft contracts to do so in clear and unambiguous terms, because if they draft a clause that is ambiguous, it will be interpreted against them. Thus, there is no profit in making things difficult to understand in any written contract.

THE OPENING CASE *Round 4*
"No one can build his security on the nobleness of another person."—Willa Cather

Let's take a look at one final application of the Opening Case. It is at this point that the old saying, "If you want something done right (or perhaps done at all), do it yourself" comes into play. In this situation, the lesson learned is that if you want a contract written correctly, then write it yourself. The story should be familiar by now. The owners and operators of Sole Survivor Inc. entered a lease agreement with the Eastland Mall. The lease was slated to last for a decade. The monthly rent was based on a set rate written that was written into the contract, plus a percentage of each month's gross receipts. As time went on, the mall's reputation suffered because it experienced a dramatic increase in criminal activity. Many of the shops that had been mainstays at the mall left for greener pastures, including the major anchor stores at the mall. Finally, after being victimized by an armed robbery, the owners of Sole Survivor decided it was time to move on. Unfortunately, they still had two years to run on the lease. Nevertheless, they packed up and left the premises. By way of explanation, they argued that Eastland Mall had a duty to provide security and that it had failed to meet that duty. In addition, Sole Survivor claimed that the mall had not provided a safe and secure environment as required by the terms of the lease agreement. The operators of the mall disagreed with these allegations. and filed a lawsuit against Sole Survivor. Eastland claimed that Sole Survivor breached the lease agreement when it left the mall and, as a result, still owed rent under that agreement amounting to $96,275.48 plus late fees, interest, legal fees, and court costs. As its main piece of evidence, Eastland produced the security clause from the original lease agreement. That clause reads: "Landlord may, from time to time and to the extent it deems appropriate in its sole discretion, determine whether to supply security services in the Common Areas and additional traffic control for the Shopping Center. Notwithstanding any other provision of this Lease, Landlord shall not be liable for any loss or damages suffered by Tenant ... by failure to supply such services[.] ... It is specifically understood and agreed that, by supplying such services, Landlord shall not be deemed to relieve Tenant of its duty to maintain security within the Demised Premises nor of its performance of the terms, covenants and conditions of this lease."

The trial court issued a summary judgment in favor of the mall. The defendants filed an appeal. The security clause turned out to be the key to the outcome of the case. Let's review the principles of contractual interpretation. The standard construction rule tells the court to uncover the principal objective of the parties in the making of the contract. Following this, the second rule states that common words used in the contract are to be given their expected, everyday definition, and technical terms or professional slang will be given their technical or professional definitions. The third rule says that whenever an ambiguous term, clause, or line is found in a prewritten or preprinted contract, that ambiguity is interpreted against the party who wrote the contract. If you apply these rules to the security clause quoted above, you should be able to guess how the appellate court ruled. In applying these rules, the court concluded (as you read, keep in mind that the Eastland Mall is the plaintiff here): "The lease clearly states, not that plaintiff is obligated to provide security, but that plaintiff may provide security in its sole discretion. Indeed, the lease expressly states that plaintiff 'shall not be liable for any loss or damages suffered by Tenant' caused by plaintiff's 'failure to supply such services.' Moreover, this paragraph explicitly provides that plaintiff's provision of security services 'shall not be deemed to relieve Tenant of its duty to maintain security within the Demised Premises nor of its performance of the terms, covenants, and conditions of this lease.' We conclude that the terms of the lease fail to support defendants' claim that plaintiff owed defendants a duty to provide 'adequate security.'"

The moral of the story is this: If you want a contract written correctly, write it yourself. The management of Eastland Mall wanted the contract written in terms that would benefit the mall, so they wrote those terms in clear and unambiguous language. By doing this, they ensured that the court, in following the standard construction rule and its corollaries, would side with them in any dispute that involved those written terms. Despite what might be seen as a set of reasonable arguments, Sole Survivor could not dodge the fact that Eastland's plain and simple language had been in the contract at the time that Sole Survivor had entered the agreement, so it was bound by those simple and direct, albeit somewhat harsh terms—period! [See: *Charlotte Eastland Mall LLC v. Sole Survivor Inc.*, No. COA03-1422, Court of Appeals of North Carolina (October 19, 2004).]

Source: See: *Charlotte Eastland Mall LLC v. Sole Survivor Inc.*, No. COA03-1422, Court of Appeals of North Carolina (October 19, 2004).

When a party owns land, he or she owns a bundle of rights that can be distributed among various other parties. Thus, it is possible, for example, for the owner of a parcel of land to divide the rights to that land among several different parties. One party might hold a lease to a house on the land allowing her to live there, a second could have an easement that permits him to cross the land, a third might own the right to mine the land, and so on. The Statute of Frauds requires a writing for each of these different transactions. The object of this requirement is to make certain that there is a way to follow the trail of each of these rights to determine who owns them, should a dispute arise concerning them.

The Parol Evidence Rule

Under the **parol evidence rule**, evidence of oral statements made before signing a written agreement is usually not admissible in court to change or contradict the terms of a written agreement. Following oral discussion and negotiation, parties may reduce their agreements to some written form. When this is done, only the terms, conditions, and promises included in the writing will be allowed as evidence in court. This provision is enforced because the court presumes that the parties will have put everything they agreed to in the writing.

EXAMPLE 11-4: *Twaine v. Krell, Inc.*

Emily Twaine purchased a $745 tablet from Krell Inc. Before all of the documents of sale were signed, the salesperson promised that she would get round-the-clock tech support from Krell technicians whenever she had a problem with her tablet or any of the software associated with the tablet. Krell subsequently refused to take care of any problems that Twaine had with the tablet. The court ruled that the salesperson's oral warranty statements were not admissible in court because they were not contained with the other conditions in the written sales agreement.

Exceptions to the Parol Evidence Rule The parol evidence rule will not apply when unfair and unjust decisions might result from its application. In cases in which a written agreement is incomplete, oral evidence may be used to supply the missing terms. Similarly, when a written contract is obscure or indistinct in certain of its terms, oral evidence may be used to clarify those terms. Also, if a written agreement contains a typographical or clerical error of some sort, the court will allow oral evidence as to the true intent of the parties.

EXAMPLE 11-5: *Bulwark v. Greene*

Edgar Bulwark was hired as an independent contractor to produce a series of magazine and journal articles that would appear under the name of a famous, and very busy, newspaper columnist named Arnold Greene. The written agreement had an error that indicated that Bulwark would receive $500 per article. The actual amount of consideration was supposed to be $5,000. The court would likely allow oral evidence to correct this obvious error.

In general, the courts allow a party to a written agreement to introduce oral testimony to show that the contract is void or voidable due to a lack of mutual assent or contractual capacity. The courts are willing to allow such testimony because it does not affect the terms of the agreement. Rather, it seeks to discredit the entire transaction. Thus, it is permissible to introduce oral evidence as to fraud, duress, misrepresentation, mistake, and undue influence. Similarly, it is appropriate to offer oral testimony as to a party's minority or mental incompetence.

EXAMPLE 11-6: *Staniland v. Morris*

James Staniland contracted with Richard Morris to purchase an original painting by Henrietta Stein, an artist who was part of the Dadaist movement in Paris during the 1920s. After signing the written contract, Staniland had the painting placed in the lobby of his business office. After one week, a customer spotted the painting and told Staniland that it was a forgery and that he had been defrauded by Morris. When Staniland took the witness stand during the trial, he was permitted to introduce evidence of the oral statements made by Morris that led him to the fraudulent conclusion that the painting was a genuine work by Stein. The court allowed the testimony because it did not affect the terms of the agreement. Rather, it sought to discredit the entire transaction.

If a written agreement depends on some event before it becomes enforceable, oral evidence may be offered regarding that condition precedent. A **condition precedent** is an act or promise that must take place or be fulfilled before the other party is obligated to perform his or her part of the agreement. The courts allow this type of oral evidence because, like the oral evidence involving assent and capacity, it does not have an impact on the terms of the agreement, but it does affect the enforceability of the entire contract.

EXAMPLE 11-7: *Lauretig v. Pierce*

Asa Pierce agreed to lease Jay Lauretig's warehouse. The terms of the lease were laid out in a lengthy, detailed written agreement. However, as a condition precedent, a credit history and background check by Lauretig on Pierce would have to come back flawless; otherwise, the deal would be canceled. When the Search and Discover Detective Agency reported that Pierce had both a bad credit rating and two criminal convictions on drug charges, Lauretig refused to go through with the contract. At court, the judge permitted oral testimony about the credit check and the criminal background search because they were precedent conditions that had to be met before the contract went into effect.

Oral evidence may be used to prove that the parties orally agreed to rescind or modify the terms of a written contract after entering into it. Subsequent negotiations to change or rescind the agreement are permitted, and evidence to that effect does not undermine the spirit of the parol evidence rule. However, if the change in the contract involves an agreement that would have to be in writing under the Statute of Frauds, then a writing would be required. Similarly, if the original written contract requires later modifications to be in writing, then that written requirement will rule.

EXAMPLE 11-8: *George Laurie Construction v. Popson*

George Laurie Construction entered into a contract with Terry and Sherrie Popson, the terms of which indicated that Laurie Construction was to place aluminum siding, downspouts, and gutters on the Popson vacation house on Kelley's Island. The agreement was written out in a long, preprinted contract with blanks for the pertinent individual information. All of the appropriate blanks were filled in, the contract was signed by all the parties, and the job began on schedule. Once Laurie was on the job for three days, Sherrie Popson decided that she wanted a window placed on the house. She discussed the cost of the additional work with George Laurie, who agreed to make the change indicated. The additional terms were not put in writing. After the job was completed, the Popsons paid the original amount but did not pay the added cost of the new window. The small claims court allowed testimony as to the terms involving the window because those terms represented negotiations subsequent to the original agreement to change the original terms.

UCC 1-205, 2-202, 2-208

As a final exception to the parol evidence rule, the UCC allows oral testimony about how the parties have done business together over a long time period. The UCC makes allowance for this type of testimony because, from a practical point of view, parties often get so used to dealing with each other in a particular way that they neglect to include certain terms in their written agreements. Similarly, some practices are so universal in a particular trade, business, or industry that the parties feel no need to include such universal practices in their written contracts. Accordingly, the UCC allows oral testimony to supplement a written agreement as to these practices.

EXAMPLE 11-9: *Commonwealth Chemical Company v. St. Clair Printing, Inc.*

St. Clair Printing Inc. and the Commonwealth Chemical Company have been doing business for 20 years. St. Clair prints all labels, business cards, letterheads, invoices, and purchase orders for Commonwealth. During their long time working together, St. Clair has always delivered orders to Commonwealth. When a new foreman took over the bindery and delivery operation for St. Clair, he decided that there would be no deliveries to any customers outside a five-mile radius of the print shop. As a result, Commonwealth did not receive an important order of labels and lost several big orders. When Commonwealth sued St. Clair for breach of contract, St. Clair pointed out that there was nothing mentioned in the written contract about delivery responsibilities falling to St. Clair. However, because of their 20-year history of consistently dealing with each other, the court allowed oral testimony about past practices to supplement the written contract.

The Best Evidence Rule

Under the **best evidence rule**, the courts generally accept into evidence only the original of a writing, not a copy. Under this rule, a written instrument is regarded as the primary or best possible evidence. Thus, the best evidence rule concurs with and supports the parol evidence rule.

The Equal Dignities Rule

The **equal dignities rule**, which is followed in some states, provides that when a party appoints an agent to negotiate an agreement that must be in writing, the appointment of the agent must also be in writing. In contrast, the appointment of an agent to negotiate an agreement that the law does not require to be in writing may be accomplished through an oral agreement.

quick quiz 11-2

1. Whenever an ambiguous term is found in a preprinted contract, that ambiguity is interpreted in favor of the party who wrote the contract. true | false
2. The principal objective is the main goal that the parties hope to accomplish by entering an agreement. true | false
3. Parol evidence is another term for written evidence. true | false

11-3 Formalities of Construction

Certain formalities are usually followed in the formation of anything other than the simplest kinds of written agreements. Although the Statute of Frauds may necessitate nothing more than the briefest written disclosure of promises, conditions, and terms, plus the signature(s) of the obligated party or parties, usually contracts in general commercial and consumer use are carefully written, researched for legal compliance, and signed. Furthermore, leases and contracts for the sale of real property may have additional requirements of content and formality that extend beyond these demands.

Signature Requirements

Written agreements should be, but need not be, signed by both parties. If signed by only one party, any obligation in the agreement would be limited to that party alone. Parties should use their usual signatures—that is, the signatures used in other matters in the regular course of business. However, any mark that the signer intends to be a signature will be the legal signature of that person. Although it is unusual, a party may adopt any name desired in creating a contractual obligation, as long as the party intends to be bound by that signature.

Facsimile Signatures With the increased use of facsimile (fax) machines, methods have been adopted to bypass the best evidence rule by giving authentication to signatures sent by way of facsimile machines. A facsimile signature will be acceptable on a contract if the contract states that facsimile signatures are valid. More commonly, however, people fax copies of signed documents to other parties, and follow it up by sending the original signed documents by overnight mail or express delivery. Some states have enacted statutes allowing certain facsimile signatures.

> **EXAMPLE 11-10:** Massachusetts General Laws Chapter 92
>
> Massachusetts has enacted the following statute relative to residence insurance agents: "A facsimile of a signature of any such resident agent imprinted on any property or casualty insurance policy issued by mail, computer modem or facsimile machine, so-called, shall have the same validity as a written signature" (Mass. Gen. Laws Chapter 92, s. 43).

In addition, some states have adopted the Uniform Facsimile Signatures of Public Officials Act. This law allows the use of facsimile signatures of public officials when certain requirements are followed.

In cases in which a party cannot sign the written agreement due to illness, physical disability, or some other physical reason, another person may sign for that person. The signature should be followed by a statement indicating that the contracting party was physically unable to sign the document and that a signature was placed on the document by another person in the contracting party's presence and at the request of the contracting party. The person who has signed for the contracting party then signs the document (see Figure 11-1). Persons who lack the ability to read or write are often obliged to sign contracts. In such

Figure 11-1 The signature for an incapacitated person bears a witness's name.

situations, the law accepts the person's mark, usually an X, properly witnessed, as a valid signature (see Figure 11-2).

Samantha X Cunningham

Her

Mark

WITNESS: I hereby attest that Samantha Cunningham made her mark as her signature and that, at her request, I added her name to her mark.

Lindsay Quartermain

Figure 11-2 The signature (*X*) of a person who does not know how to write has been witnessed.

Witnesses and Acknowledgments

Witnesses are required in the signing of a will and sometimes a deed, but in most other documents, their signatures are at the option of the contracting parties. To ensure that no misunderstanding will arise as to the acceptance and signing of a written agreement, the use of witnesses is advised. Certain official documents, such as a certificate of title to a motor vehicle and a deed to real property, require the owner's signature and an **acknowledgment** by a notary public that the signature was the person's free act and deed. The notary witnesses the signing of the document and then acknowledges this act by signing the document and adding the official seal to it. A notary is not authorized to read the document being signed and may be prevented from doing so.

Special Conditions and Circumstances

Recently, several states have begun to revise the basic requirements for some written contracts involving real property. The two revisions involve (1) contracts for the sale or lease of residential real estate and (2) real property construction projects, especially involving private homes.

Contracts for the Sale or Lease of Residential Real Estate The first type of contract that has been revised and updated by state law is a contract for the sale or lease of residential real estate. The difficulties inherent in these contracts involve their overall unpredictability. State law can outline most of the details that must be included within these agreements. However, some details depend upon local customs and traditions that are acknowledged by municipal, county, or regional real estate boards but which are foreign to brokers and attorneys who operate in other parts of the state. For example, Dayton, Ohio, was victimized by a massive flood in 1913 that led to the creation of the Miami Conservancy District, which is designed to maintain an extensive flood control system to prevent a similar disaster from happening in the future. More than a century after that flood, the conservancy district is still maintained by a yearly tax assessment on all property in the district. This tax assessment must be figured into all real property contracts in the Dayton area, something that is not involved in real property contracts in other parts of the state. Still, despite such regional differences there are some elements that must be in all real property contracts. State statutes that deal with such agreements will list the following items that must be in all real property transfer contracts:

1. A full description of the property that is the subject of the contract.
2. The price of the real property that is the subject of the contract.
3. The date of closing on the contract. Generally, there is a grace period added to this part of the agreement. The grace period can run up to 45 days.
4. An identification of the parties to the contract.
5. Any financing contingencies built into the agreement. Typically, this involves a condition precedent that the contract will not exist until the buyer has a financing plan in place.
6. An attorney approval clause that states that each party's attorney will have the power to make suggestions about any part of the contract that he or she feels might be detrimental to his or her client(s).
7. A detailed explanation of all tax assessments involved.
8. A list and description of all fixtures that stay with the property and those fixtures that can be removed. The list should also designate which fixtures are trade fixtures that can, therefore, be removed.
9. The timing of inspections. Generally, there is a statutory limit placed on this time period, something like, within 14 days of signing, or the like.
10. The home maintenance agreement. Normally, the seller warrants that a third party will fix any problems that occur within the first year of the sale.
11. A clause covering deed transfer and title insurance.
12. A clause that explains who is liable for destruction or damage to property after the inspections have occurred.
13. A statement of the earnest money put down by the buyer.
14. Any miscellaneous provisions that might be peculiar to this contract (such as a delayed possession process complete with a date of occupancy).
15. Dated and signed by all of the parties to the agreement.

The final requirement demands that all real property contracts must be written in plain English, with signed and dated duplicate originals retained by all parties. Generally, the law also requires that all alterations to the terms of the original written contract be in writing, initialed, and dated by all parties. [See: William Fergus, Deborah McDonald, and James Zitesman, "Contract and Closing Issues Relating to Residential Real Estate Transactions," Ohio State Bar Association Convention (April 30–May 2, 2014).]

Real Property Construction Projects Anyone who has built a private residence or has been involved in a residential renovation project knows that such undertakings are fraught with peril. Delays and errors are often caused by misunderstandings, mistakes, negligence, clumsiness, and impracticality. Cost overruns, time delays, work stoppages, equipment failure, property damage, and alterations in materials or construction plans can take their toll if the project is not handled properly. There is probably no way to eliminate such gaps and turnarounds whenever someone is involved in lengthy and complicated construction deals. However, some of the intensity surrounding such disputes, disagreements, and debates can be assuaged if certain terms are included in a written agreement. The trend today is for the state legislatures to develop legally binding terms that must be included in all construction contracts but especially those involving private homes. Often, state statutes that deal with such agreements will list the following items that must be in all real property construction projects contracts, but especially those involving private homes:

1. The builder and/or the construction company's name, address, phone number, e-mail address, insurance, bonding information, and tax identification number.
2. The homeowner's name, address, phone number, and e-mail address.
3. The address of the location where the home is to be constructed or the renovation, addition (shed, pool, garage, patio, deck, porch, etc.), or repairs are to be made.
4. A description of the goods and the services that will be provided by the contractor.
5. The anticipated date of completion, including cleanup.
6. The penalty for not meeting the anticipated date of completion (with some leeway built in [e.g., within two days of the anticipated date of completion]) often expressed in terms of dollars-per-day after the anticipated date of completion.
7. The estimated total cost of the project including parts, labor, subcontractors' costs, and so on.
8. Any added costs for delivering materials, installing items such as fixtures, taking paid breaks, traveling time to and from the job, and so on.
9. The contractor's certificate of insurance.
10. Signatures and dates added by all of the parties to the agreement.
11. An excess provision clause that indicates that, if there are added costs that are unexpected but necessary and the total of these added costs exceeds a set level (generally something like $5,000 in total) that such added costs must be approved in writing by the homeowner before materials are purchased or construction work involving the extra added costs begins.

A SOON TO BE CLASSIC CASE
Fixing the Identity of Fixtures

Josue Perez rented a building from Thomas Patrick without securing a written lease. Perez made comprehensive changes to the building to accommodate his plan for a bar and grill. The alterations included attaching sinks, refrigerators, freezers, coolers, furniture, and other items to the building. A wooden bar and a back bar for storing bar supplies were also added. In addition, Perez installed fire-suppression equipment, a stainless steel backsplash for the stove, and a ventilation hood. Next, Perez added a roof air conditioner for the bar. Josh's Place opened and operated successfully for 15 months. Later, Perez decided to get out of the "grill" part of the "bar and grill" business. Accordingly, he closed the restaurant and began to sell the restaurant property online. Meanwhile Patrick, the building's owner, had his own problems. He had failed to properly pay certain taxes and, to avoid foreclosure, had negotiated a payment plan with the city. Unfortunately, Patrick was unable to live up to the agreement he had made with the city and the property was sold to Schneider at a tax foreclosure auction. Perez knew about about Patrick's original tax problem and about the payment plan, but not about Patrick's inability to live up to its terms. Consequently, he was taken by surprise when Schneider, the new owner, changed the locks and argued that everything in the building belonged to him. Perez asked that his equipment, furniture, awning, stoves, coolers, sinks, refrigerators, and air-conditioning unit be returned. Schneider refused, claiming, with some conviction, to own everything inside the building.

At this point, we can see that many of Perez's problems were caused by the fact that he had no written lease. If Perez had followed the rules and insisted on a written lease, the troublesome fixtures would have been a focal point of that agreement. In fact, had Perez designated certain pieces of equipment as *trade fixtures*, he might have escaped the inconvenience of a court appearance altogether. As it was, he ended up in court. Much of what Perez would have designated as trade fixtures turned out to be just that, but not all. The trial court used a line of precedent that explained a step-by-step procedure for identifying trade fixtures. As a result, the following items were characterized as trade fixtures: the bar and the back bar, the ventilation hood (along with the fire-suppression system and the stainless steel backsplash), the sinks, and the awning (which included the name "Josh's Place"). The air-conditioning unit on the roof was designated by the trial court as a trade fixture, but according to the appellate court, this was an error by the lower court. The refrigerators, freezers, coolers, furniture, and other bar and grill type items were not mentioned by the court. It may, therefore, be assumed that the restaurant furniture, the coolers, and the refrigerators, were removable and, in fact, had already been removed from the building. The appellate court also observed that a written contract for sale had been drawn up between Perez and Patrick but had failed due to a lack of financing on the part of Perez. The fixtures were not mentioned in that agreement either. Perez and Patrick had discussed these improvements in general but never in relation to their nature as fixtures. Again, following the requirements of a written agreement would have helped Perez avoid these problems. [See: *Perez Bar & Grill v. Schneider*, 2012-Ohio-5820 (December 19, 2012).]

Source: See: *Perez Bar Grill v. Schneider,* 2012-Ohio-5820 (December 190, 2012).

As is true of the requirements for contracts for the sale or lease of residential property, the last requirement in home construction contracts is that all real property contracts be written in plain English, with signed and dated duplicate originals retained by all the parties. Generally, the law also requires that all alterations to the terms of the original written contract be in writing, initialed, and dated by all parties. These home construction contract statutes also often stipulate what cannot be in a written contract. Specifically, such statutes may define what is meant by "workmanlike conduct" or construction performed in workmanlike manner. For example, Section 47022.01(G) of the Ohio Revised Code states that **workmanlike manner** "means the home construction service supplier has engaged in construction that meets or exceeds the minimum quantifiable standards promulgated by the Ohio home builders association." Because this duty is encoded within the statutory law of the state, the written agreement between the contractor and the homeowner cannot contain a clause in which the homeowner gives up the protection provided by the statute. Home construction contract statutes will also outline other activities that contractors cannot do, such as starting construction without a written contract, failing to provide the homeowner with copies of the written contract, failing to provide the homeowner with written estimates of excess costs, and so on. Strict requirements like these for residential real estate contracts and for home construction contracts will not eliminate disagreements, disputes, and debates in these projects. Such problems are inherent within these transactions. Nevertheless, the need to provide detailed written agreements will lessen the probability that such disputes will end up in court. [See: Andrew Fredelake, J. Bradley Leach, and Jon C. Walden, "Construction Law and Public Contracting Update," Ohio State Bar Association Convention (April 30–May 2, 2014).]

A REAL CLASSIC CASE The Evolution of a Fixture in Contract Law

The evolution of real estate contracts is part of the ongoing story of the overall nature of the complex adaptive system (CAS) that is the law. Each state can tell its own story about its evolutionary journey through real estate law, and most of these journeys will somehow touch upon the evolution of the trade fixture doctrine. The court in *Perez v. Schneider* was kind enough to give us a compact and streamlined view of this history, starting with the classic case of *Teaff v. Hewitt*. In that landmark case, the court first defined a fixture. "A fixture," the court writes, "is an article [that] was a chattel, but [that] by being physically annexed or affixed to the realty, became accessory to it and part and parcel of it." [See: *Teaff v. Hewitt*, 1 Ohio St. 511, 527 (1853).] The court then outlines the basic elements of a fixture. In 1853, the justices brought in the following three elements: (1) "[a]ctual annexation to the realty, or something appurtenant thereto"; (2) "[a]ppropriation to the use or purpose of that part of the realty with which it is connected"; and (3) "[t]he intention of the party making annexation, to make the article a permanent accession to the freehold. . . ."

As straightforward and unbreakable as these elements may sound, they were not difficult to change, as the courts moved on. The first element to be revised was, appropriately enough, the first element of "attachment." As cases came and went over a century, the court decided ultimately in *Masheter v. Boehm* [37 Ohio St. 2d 68, 73 (1974)] that attachment was the least significant of the three elements. The court declared that slight attachment would not necessarily defeat the idea that the item was not a fixture and a significant degree of attachment would not make an item a fixture if the other elements held sway. [See: *Trumbull Sav. & Loan Co.*, 135 Ohio St. 48, 53 (1939).] Next the court moved to gently refine the second element—that is, the use of the item compared to the overall use of the building to which it has been attached. The court employed a somewhat convoluted explanation of this second element. However, ultimately, in the case *of Zangerle v. Republic Steel Corp.* [144 Ohio St. 529, paragraph seven of the syllabus (1945)], the principle came down to this: If an item is used for the specific purpose of the business in the building, it will likely (though not definitely; remember, the test is three-pronged) be a trade fixture. However, if the attachment can be used by whatever business enters the premises and takes up residence there, then we have a "non-trade fixture." This is what happened to the air conditioner added by Perez. An air-conditioning unit can be used by a bar or a barbershop. The court sees the second element as a deal breaker. In fact, in the *Perez* case, the court writes, "If an item fails to meet the second prong of the *Teaff* test because it is peculiar to the business being operated on the premises, it is likely to be deemed a trade fixture" (paragraph 19). That does not mean, however, that the third element carries no weight. On the contrary, it can overturn even the second element if it is strong enough because it concerns the intent of the person who placed the item on the property to begin with. Interestingly enough, the court noted that it is not the actual goal of the party that matters, but how that attachment looks to an outsider given all of the circumstances in the case. The courts have observed that as far as the third element is concerned: "[I]t is not necessarily the real intention of the owner of the chattel which governs. His apparent or legal intention to make it a fixture is sufficient" and that "ought to be apparent, from the situation and surroundings." [See: *Holland Furnace Co. v. Trumbull Sav. & Loan Co.*, 135 Ohio St. 48, 53–54 (1939), as quoted in *Perez v. Schneider.*]

Source: See: *Holland Furnace Co. v. Trumbull Sav. Loan Co.*, 135 Ohio St. 48, 53–54 (1939), as quoted in *Perez v. Schneider*.

quick quiz 11-3

1. Written agreements must always be signed by both parties to the contract. true | false
2. Real property sales contracts can be structured in an identical way in every county in a given state. true | false
3. The requirement of doing a construction job on a private residence in a workmanlike manner can be waived in the written contract. true | false

11-4 Cyber-Commerce and the Law

Cyber-commerce (computer commerce, electronic commerce, or e-commerce) involves transacting business by computer. One of the most common cyber-commerce techniques involves buying and selling directly on the Internet by accessing a company's website. Some companies, such as Amazon.com, have made a name for themselves by perfecting this e-commerce technique. Other enterprises, such as eBay, have made a business of providing a marketplace for putting buyers and sellers together in an electronic auction setting. Others, such as Orbitz and Priceline.com, have found a niche in the marketplace by providing bargain prices for airlines and hotels. There are, of course, problems associated with buying and selling on the Internet, one of which involves the difficulty of verifying the identity of the party on the other side of an Internet connection. Another problem involves how to make up for the lack of paper documents in cyber-commerce. In both cases, the law has provided a solution. We will look at the problems associated with verification first.

Verification Problems

Verification problems can be solved in a number of ways. In fact, the parties can avoid the problem by adding a term that delays the creation of the contract until the identities of the parties can be verified by some means other than computers. Or a business might elect to use its website only as an advertisement site. These solutions are unsatisfactory to most businesspeople, however, because they eliminate the advantages of doing business on the Internet. Another technique is for the parties to an Internet transaction to customize the verification process for each contract individually. However, in the interests of efficiency and cost, it would be preferable to have a process that applies to all contracts. A possible solution to this problem is the use of digital signatures. As we shall see, the Uniform Electronics Transactions Act defines a *digital signature* as "an electronic sound, symbol, or process attached to or logically associated with a record and executed or adopted by a person with the intent to sign the record." A digital signature is also referred to as a **cyber-signature**, an *electronic signature*, and an *e-signature*. Those businesses and legal practitioners who promote the use of digital signatures hope that the courts and/or the legislatures will institute a principle that states the use of a digital signature creates a rebuttable presumption that the signature is authentic and that the terms of the transaction have not been altered in transmission.

Online shopping is fast, easy, and convenient. Utilizing digital signatures is an effective method used by businesses to verify the legitimacy of the transaction.
©McGraw-Hill Education/Jill Braaten

Offer and Acceptance Online
An electronic party should always ensure that a copy of the contract is available on a hyperlink that will display the actual language of the agreement. The following terms should appear in any online agreement package: (1) payment procedures; (2) a limitation on the remedies that can be used by the parties; (3) refund policies; (4) the return process; (5) dispute settlement, forum selection, and choice-of-law provisions; (6) the applicability of cyber-signatures; (7) liability disclaimers; and (8) provisions relating to the offeree's manner of acceptance. In general, the other party accepts by clicking on a box on the computer screen that states that the party agrees to be bound by the terms of the contract. Sometimes this process is referred to as a *click-on acceptance* or *click-on agreement*. In a sense then, the *click* amounts to the party's signature. It is also critical to remember that when a cyber-agreement deals with goods, the provisions of Article 2 of the Uniform Commercial Code apply.

Cyber Contract Clauses and Hyperlinks As we have seen in this chapter, the Statute of Frauds requires that certain types of contracts must be in writing and that certain terms must be included in the writing. For example, the Statute of Frauds demands that each written contract include the terms of the agreement, the subject matter, the consideration to be paid, the names and identities of the people to be obligated, and the signature of the party sought to be bound. In addition, the law requires that written contracts contain no ambiguity, misrepresentation, or uncertainty and that if such ambiguity, misrepresentation, or uncertainty enters a written contract, it will be interpreted against the party who wrote the contract. All of this sounds good, and it works quite well when dealing with paper contracts. However, when contracts are entered online through a website such as Amazon, Barnes & Noble, Dell, Best Buy, and so on, these terms may not be as clear to the unpracticed eye as they are on paper. In fact, some terms are hidden within the ether on one of those blue hyperlinks. With virtually no assistance from the legislatures, the courts have held, rather consistently, that terms that are hidden behind one of those blue hyperlinks or their equivalent are roughly analogous to the pages of a long and drawn-out multipage paper contract. As long as the customer is notified on the screen about the clauses hidden by the hyperlink, and as long as the information in the link itself is neither ambiguous nor false nor uncertain, then the fact that the customer does not take advantage of the "click-here" invitation is no different from the customer who is told to read the unambiguous language on a multipage contract and fails to do so.

Online Advertisement "Click" Fraud One problem that arises in this area is verifying the identity of the "clicker." When companies are actually creating contracts, they police the process of verification rather closely. However, the click-on process functions not only in online contracts but also for online advertisements. Companies that advertise on the Internet often make contracts with search engines like Bing, Google, Yahoo!, or America Online. The terms of these contracts generally include a provision that states that the company that places the advertisement online will pay the search engine on the basis of the number of clicks detected on that advertisement. The clicks are supposed to be a foolproof way to gauge interest in the advertiser's service or product. However, policing the exact nature of each click has proven difficult. Thus, hundreds of thousands of phony clicks have occurred in advertisements, inflating the bills of the advertisers that pay per click. The problem arises because the search engines often farm out the actual posting of the ads to intermediary companies, called *domain parkers*, that get paid on the basis of the number of clicks on the ads for which they are responsible. The domain parkers then transfer the ads to subsidiary websites. Some of these websites display advertisements and nothing more. This scenario provides a fertile ground in which the phony click campaigns grow. Some owners of these subsidiary websites pay fraudulent clickers a small amount to click on the ads, thus driving up the cost for the advertisers and increasing the site owner's split of the proceeds. Some even use "clickbot" software, capable of mechanically clicking on certain advertisements at programmed intervals. All of the major search engines have found themselves in litigation because of this new *cyber-confidence game*. [See: Brian Grow and Ben Elgin, "Click Fraud: The Dark Side of Online Advertising," *BusinessWeek*, October 2, 2006, pp. 46–57.]

Cyber-Commerce Legislation

Cyber-commerce legislation has taken many forms over the past decade. However, the three most influential acts have been the E-Sign Act, the Uniform Electronic Transactions Act (UETA), and the Uniform Computer Information Transactions Act (UCITA). A fourth new law that deals with a slightly different but no less serious problem, that of credit cards and identity theft, is the Fair and Accurate Credit Transactions Act (FACT).

The E-Sign Act The E-Sign Act is a federal act designed to deal with problems associated with cyber-commerce, especially those related to the recognition of electronic contracts and electronic signatures. Basically, the act states that if the parties to a contract have voluntarily agreed to transact business electronically, the cyber-contract that results will be just as legally acceptable as a paper contract. The act also notes that the parties must be able to store and reproduce the cyber-record of the contract; otherwise, the cyber-record will not be legally sufficient under the act. The final word here is that under the provisions of the E-Sign Act, cyber-contracts and cyber-signatures are just as legitimate as their ink counterparts. A few documents are not covered by this statute, including court records, eviction notices, health insurance cancellations, wills, foreclosure notices, prenuptial contracts, and divorce papers. However, sale and lease of goods contracts as covered by the Uniform Commercial Code are included in the E-Sign Act.

The Uniform Electronic Transactions Act (UETA) The Uniform Electronic Transactions Act establishes the same type of legal parity between electronic records and paper records as does the E-Sign Act. It does not establish any new guidelines governing contracts just because they are entered electronically. The approach therefore is not to establish the differences between electronic contracts and paper agreements but instead to focus on the similarities. As a result, once the parties to a contract have voluntarily agreed to enter a transaction using an electronic medium, the agreement that results in electronic form, including the cyber-signatures, will be just as valid as a paper agreement. The UETA applies only to transactions that involve some sort of commercial, business, or governmental matter. The law also states that if an act, such as the Statute of Frauds, requires a writing and a signature, then a cyber-record and a cyber-signature will fulfill that requirement. Also, under provisions of the E-Sign Act, the UETA will trump the E-Sign Act provided that the state that has adopted the UETA has not altered its content. Most states, 48 at last count, have adopted the UETA. However, some states have altered provisions in the act and so it is best to check the version that has been enacted by your state. This is also why it would be smart to check the forum selection clause in any cyber-contract that you are about to enter. [See: The E-Sign Act, 15 USC Section 7002 9 (2) (A) (I).]

The Uniform Computer Information Transactions Act (UCITA) The Uniform Computer Information Transactions Act (UCITA) focuses on contracts that involve the sale or lease of computer software, computer databases, interactive products, multimedia products, and any other type of computer information. The UCITA is in line with the basic provisions of the E-Sign Act and the UETA, in that it also declares that any transaction entered into using an electronic medium is just as valid as a paper agreement. Not all states have adopted the UCITA, so it is important to check on the applicability of the statute in your jurisdiction.

The Fair and Accurate Credit Transactions Act (FACT Act) The Fair and Accurate Credit Transactions Act (FACT Act) is Congress's antidote to one manifestation of the identity theft epidemic. The new law, which is actually an amendment to the Fair Credit Reporting Act (FCRA), is designed to cut down on identity theft related to the use of credit cards. The act prohibits merchants from using credit card receipts that show anything other than the last five credit card numbers. Receipts also cannot display credit card expiration dates. In effect, because the act outlaws such numerical displays, identity thieves will no longer be able to assume the identity of a consumer by obtaining a copy of a credit card receipt and using the credit card number and expiration date on the receipt to "verify their identity" over the phone or online.

quick quiz 11-4

1. The E-Sign Act is a model act designed to deal with problems associated with cyber-commerce.   true | false
2. The Uniform Electronic Transactions Act was passed by Congress to deal with the legality of electronic transactions.   true | false
3. The UCITA is not in line with any of the provisions of the E-Sign Act or the UETA.   true | false

Summary

11.1 The Statutes of Frauds outlines six types of contracts that must be in writing to be enforceable. These include contracts that cannot be completed within one year, contracts transferring real property rights, contracts for the sale of goods of $500 or more, certain contracts entered by executors and administrators, contracts by one party to pay a debt incurred by another party, and contracts in consideration of marriage.

11.2 The legal system has developed certain basic criteria that make the construction and interpretation of written contracts consistent. These four criteria are (1) the standard construction rule, (2) the parol evidence rule, (3) the best evidence rule, and (4) the equal dignities rule.

11.3 Certain formalities are followed in the formation of contracts. Written agreements need not be signed by both parties. However, any agreement signed by only one party would obligate only that party. Facsimile signatures are allowed on a contract if the contract states that such signatures are valid. Some states have statutes allowing facsimile signatures. Persons who are illiterate usually sign written contracts with an X. Several states have begun to revise the basic requirements for the written expression of (1) contracts for the sale or lease of residential real estate and (2) real property construction projects, especially involving private homes.

11.4 There are problems associated with buying and selling on the Internet. One of these problems involves the difficulty of verifying the identity of the person on the other side of an Internet connection. Another involves the question of how to deal with the fact that electronic transactions do not produce paper documents. In both cases, the law has provided some solutions to these difficulties. Three laws that address these problems include the E-Sign Act, the Uniform Electronic Transactions Act (UETA), and the Uniform Computer Information Transactions Act (UCITA). A fourth act that deals with the problem of identity theft is the Fair and Accurate Credit Transactions Act (FACT).

Key Terms

acknowledgment, 319
administrator, 310
antenuptial agreement, 310
best evidence rule, 317
collateral contract, 310
condition precedent, 316
cosigner, 310
cyber-signature, 324
equal dignities rule, 317
equitable estoppel, 308
executor, 310
guarantor, 310
guaranty contract, 310
guaranty of payment, 310
leading objective test, 310
main purpose test, 310
memorandum, 311
obligee, 310
obligor, 310
parol evidence rule, 314
part performance, 308
premarriage agreement, 310
prenuptial agreement, 310
primary objective test, 310
standard construction rule, 313
Statute of Frauds, 305
Uniform Facsimile Signatures of Public Officials Act, 318
workmanlike manner, 322

Questions for Review and Discussion

1. What are the goals of the Statute of Frauds?
2. What contracts must be in writing under the Statute of Frauds?
3. What information must be in a writing under the Statute of Frauds?
4. What is the standard construction rule?
5. What is the parol evidence rule?
6. What are the exceptions to the parol evidence rule?
7. What is the best evidence rule?
8. What is the equal dignities rule?
9. What are the problems associated with cyber-commerce?
10. What are the latest cyber-commerce statutes?

Cases for Analysis

1. Several identity theft victims filed a series of class action lawsuits against firms that had not made the changes required by the Fair and Accurate Credit Transactions Act (FACT) by the statutory deadline. One of the issues before the court was whether the victims had to demonstrate that the offending company deliberately refused to comply or did so with reckless disregard for the new requirements. Which standard would be the appropriate one in this situation? Explain. [See: Amanda Bronstad, "Suits Multiply over Credit Card Exposure: Cash Registers Displaying Too Many Digits Spark Dozens of Class Actions," *The National Law Journal*, February 19, 2007, p. 4.]
2. Frank Strachan entered a contract with Wright Weber Construction for the building of an addition to his new home in Lakeside. The construction firm was to begin building the addition on April 2. Wright Weber agreed that the addition might be finished by March 1 of the following year, but also stipulated that May 1 of the following year was a more reasonable estimate. The details of the agreement were never reduced to writing. When Wright Weber ran into labor problems in August, it had to put the construction of the addition on hold. One month later, unable to resolve the labor dispute, Wright Weber shut the company down and abandoned the Strachan work site. As a result, Strachan had to negotiate a new contract with a new construction firm. The new contract cost $12,900 more than it would have had Weber completed the job as promised. In addition, because the Lakeside house could not be used during construction, Strachan incurred storage costs for his furniture because he had to move out of the home he was living in to accommodate the new owners. He also had to live in a hotel for four months while the Lakeside addition was completed. Strachan sued Wright Weber. Wright Weber moved for a dismissal because the contract was not in writing. Strachan argued that the contract could have been completed within one year and was therefore outside of the statute. How will the court decide the case? Explain your response.
3. Meng, a vice president at Boston University, resigned his position to protest what he regarded as the unethical and unprofessional behavior of the university's president, John Silber, in terminating a recently renewed contract with Linkage Corporation. Silber orally promised Meng, as a severance package when he resigned, 14 months of salary and benefits and free tuition for two of his children if either should attend the university. Was the oral promise enforceable? Explain. [See: *Meng v. Trustees of Boston University*, 96-9776 Appeals Court (MA).]
4. As part of an employment agreement, Bazzy orally promised to give Hall an option to buy 1,000 shares of company stock at $20 per share. Hall brought suit against the company when it refused to sell the stock to him. What legal argument may Bazzy's company use to refuse to sell the stock to Hall as agreed? [See: *Hall v. Horizon House Microwave, Inc.*, 506 N.E.2d 178 (MA).]
5. Anna Wilson was assistant manager of a Montgomery Ward store. When Montgomery Ward announced that it would be closing the store, the manager quit, leaving Wilson in charge. A district manager orally promised Wilson that if she stayed on and assisted in the closing of the store, she would receive a sum of money calculated according to a certain formula. Wilson stayed on and managed the closing of the store (which took two months) in addition to her regular duties.

Montgomery Ward refused to pay her the money, claiming that the oral promise was unenforceable. Was the store correct? Why or why not? [See: *Wilson v. Montgomery Ward*, 610 F. Supp. 1035 (DC IN).]

6. Curtis Hendrix orally agreed to compensate Beverly Spertell for services rendered in connection with their living together out of wedlock. Later, when suit was brought to collect the money, Hendrix argued that the oral contract was unenforceable under the Statute of Frauds. Do you agree with Hendrix? Explain. [See: *Spertell v. Hendrix*, 461 N.Y.S.2d 823 (NY).]

7. Walt Nicklesworth entered a lease agreement with Marblehead Properties under which Nicklesworth used the property located at 5293 Lake Shore Boulevard as a used bookstore. The terms of the lease included a right of first refusal, such that Nicklesworth could purchase the property if Marblehead ever decided to sell. Two years into the five-year lease, Marblehead sold the property to Daniel O'Donnell. Nicklesworth brought suit for breach of contract. At trial, no one could produce a written copy of the lease for the judge. The judge decided to dismiss the case. What justification did the judge use to dismiss the case? Explain.

8. Butler leased a certain piece of property from Wheeler with an option to purchase it at a later date. The agreement was handwritten and consisted of two separate documents, each listing part of the transaction. Butler later attempted to purchase the property, but Wheeler refused to sell, claiming that the agreement was unenforceable because it was contained in two documents. Was Wheeler correct? Explain. [See: *Butler v. Lovoll*, 620 P.2d 1251 (NV).]

9. Ray's Motor Sales sold a mobile home to Hathaway. Before the written contract was signed, the salesperson told Hathaway that Ray's would take care of any problems that Hathaway might have with the mobile home. This promise was not included in the written document. When Hathaway had problems with the mobile home, he asked Ray's to take care of them. Ray's refused to be of any assistance. Could Hathaway enforce Ray's promise? Explain. [See: *Hathaway v. Ray's Motor Sales*, 247 A.2d 512 (VT).]

10. In 1919, Pasha Patel owned several acres of land in the Upper Peninsula of Michigan. Half a pond was located on Patel's land. The other half of the pond was located on land owned by Brooke Brookhaven. For a small consideration, Patel transferred the right to cut ice on her side of the pond each winter to Fred Xavier. The contract was oral and supposed to last for the next five winters. Each day from early October to late March, Xavier would cut the ice and remove it. He would carefully carve the ice into large cubes that fit perfectly into the ice boxes located in the rental cabins dotting the Upper Peninsula. (This was 1919, remember.) He then sold the ice to the cabin renters. One summer Brookhaven drained her part of the pond. In October, this action meant that ice was sparse, and what was available was sunk into the mud at the bottom of the lake and thus unusable for carving and sale. Xavier brought suit against Brookhaven, arguing that her action in draining the lake made his interest in the property worthless. The court asked for a copy of the written contract transferring the right to cut the ice to Xavier. When Xavier could not produce one, the judge dismissed the case. What will be the result of the case at this point? Explain.

Design Elements: The Opening Case: ©Sharpstock/Alamy; A Classic Case: ©Evlakhov Valeriy/ Shutterstock

quick quiz Answers

11-1	11-2	11-3	11-4
1. F	1. F	1. F	1. F
2. F	2. T	2. F	2. F
3. T	3. F	3. F	3. F

Chapter 12

Third Parties, Discharge, and Remedies

12-1 **Contracts and Third Parties**
Intended Beneficiaries • Incidental Beneficiaries

12-2 **The Law of Assignment**
Assignment and Delegation • Assignment Methods

12-3 **Assignment Rights, Duties, and Restrictions**
Rights and Duties of the Assignee • Liabilities and Warranties of the Assignor • Restrictions on Assignments • Novation and Assignment

12-4 **Discharge by Performance**
Time for Performance • Satisfactory, Complete, and Substantial Performance • Conditions and Tender of Performance

12-5 **Discharge by Nonperformance**
Discharge by Agreement • Discharge by Impossibility and by Law • Operation of Law • Discharge by Breach of Contract

12-6 **Damages and Equitable Remedies**
Damages in Contract Law • Punitive or Exemplary Damages • Equitable Remedies

THE OPENING CASE Round 1
"The Repudiation Is in the Mail!"—How Not to Handle a Breach of Contract

Some lawsuits involve a series of arguments and counterarguments aimed at unraveling a complex set of facts and several perplexing legal principles. Others are fairly straightforward. This one is a little of both. The case began one day in March when Mr. Carney (oddly Mr. Carney's first name is not included in the case) enrolled his son in the fourth-grade class at Lake Ridge Academy, an independent private school located in North Ridgeville, Ohio, a suburb of Cleveland. As part of this process, Carney entered a standard school registration agreement (SRA) with Lake Ridge. Under terms of the SRA, in exchange for Lake Ridge's agreement to hold a place for his son, Carney made a down payment of $630 and promised to pay the balance at a time established by the school. Under those terms, Carney had until August 1 to repudiate the contract or be obligated to pay the remainder of the tuition, whether or not his son actually attended Lake Ridge. The SRA was written this way not only to give Lake Ridge a deadline after which it could finalize its annual budget, but also to give parents enough time to evaluate their finances before making a final commitment to the school.

As things developed, for whatever reason, Carney did not repudiate the contract by August 1. Accordingly, after that date, Lake Ridge finalized its budget based on the assumption that all parents who had not withdrawn by August 1 would pay the balance due under the terms of the SRA. So far, so good. Then Carey dropped his bombshell. In a letter postmarked August 7, he announced that he had decided to withdraw his son from the school. As far as Carney was concerned, that ended the matter. He had repudiated the contract, and he no longer owed the tuition balance under the SRA. Lake Ridge disagreed and, we are paraphrasing now, said something like, "Now, wait just a darn minute here! Read the SRA again. We gave you a five-month break—which, by the way, we did not have to do—asking in return only that you repudiate by August 1 or stick to the final tuition payment. You did not follow that simple rule, so now you are still bound under the contract. Therefore, any refusal to pay the balance is a breach of the contract—period!"

When Carney refused to come through with that final payment, Lake Ridge initiated this lawsuit, asking for the balance due ($5,610). Carney says (again paraphrasing) "No. I am not paying." He then argues: (1) He had substantially performed the terms of the SRA and, therefore, had been released from the agreement. (2) The tuition payment that Lake Ridge demanded is a penalty and thus, under law, cannot be upheld as stipulated damages. (3) Lake Ridge had not mitigated its damages, as required by law.

Lake Ridge disagreed, noting: (1) Carney had not only not substantially performed, but had also badly misunderstood what substantial performance is all about. (2) Since the payment due under the SRA accurately reflects the loss that Lake Ridge will suffer, absent the tuition payment, it is not a penalty but is, instead, a valid calculation of liquidated damages. (3) Again, Carney and his legal team have misinterpreted the doctrine of mitigation, but even under a correct statement of the doctrine, Lake Ridge was under no duty to mitigate in the first place.

The trial court ruled in favor of Carney. Lake Ridge appealed. The court of appeals reversed the trial court using an argument that emphasized the timing of Carney's attempt at repudiation. Although the Supreme Court of Ohio agreed with the appellate court's decision (Carney breached), it still decided to hear the case because, according to the High Court of Ohio, the appellate court had used the wrong reasoning to reach that conclusion. (You see, we all make errors, even appellate court judges.) [See: *Lake Ridge v. Carney*, 66 Ohio St. 3d 376, No. 2464.]

Opening Case Questions

1. What is substantial performance, and how does it work under the law? Explain.
2. What is repudiation, and how does it work? Explain.
3. What are stipulated damages? Explain.
4. What is the difference between liquidated damages (permitted as stipulated damages) and a penalty (forbidden as stipulated damages)? Explain.
5. When does mitigation become a legal requirement? Explain

Source: See: *Lake Ridge v. Carney,* 66 Ohio St. 3d 376, No. 2464.

LO Learning Objectives

1. Explain the legal rights given to all beneficiaries.
2. Identify the legal rights given to incidental beneficiaries.
3. Explain the assignment of rights and the delegation of duties.
4. Explain the nature of a novation.
5. Relate what constitutes satisfactory performance of a contract.
6. Outline the difference between complete and substantial performance.
7. List the ways that a contract can be discharged by nonperformance.
8. Clarify the concept of anticipatory repudiation.
9. Enumerate the types of damages available in the event of a breach of contract.
10. Contrast specific performance with injunctive relief.

12-1 Contracts and Third Parties

A **third party** is a person who may in some way be affected by a contract but who is not one of the contracting parties. A third party, also known as an **outside party**, is at times given benefits from a contract made between two or more other parties. A third party receiving benefits from a contract made by others is known as a **third-party beneficiary** or sometimes simply as a **beneficiary** to the contract. Although not obligated by the agreement made between those in privity, third parties may have the legal right to enforce the benefits given them by such agreements.

Intended Beneficiaries

A beneficiary in whose favor a contract is made is an **intended beneficiary**. With exceptions in some states, an intended beneficiary can enforce the contract made by those in privity of contract. Those who are most frequently recognized to be intended beneficiaries and have the right to demand and enforce the benefits promised are creditor beneficiaries, donee beneficiaries, and insurance beneficiaries.

Creditor Beneficiaries A creditor beneficiary is an outside third party to whom one or both contracting parties owe a continuing debt of obligation arising from a contract. Frequently, the obligation results from the failure of the contracting party or parties to pay for goods delivered or services rendered by the third party at some time in the past.

Donee Beneficiaries A third party who provides no consideration for the benefits received and who owes the contracting parties no legal duty is known as a donee beneficiary. However, the contracting parties owe the donee beneficiary the act promised; if it is not forthcoming, the donee beneficiary may bring suit. The consideration that supports this type of agreement is the consideration exchanged by the parties in privity of contract.

Insurance Beneficiaries An individual named as the beneficiary of an insurance policy is usually considered a donee beneficiary. The beneficiary does not have to furnish the insured with consideration to enforce payment of the policy. In some cases, an insurance beneficiary may also be a creditor beneficiary. This situation occurs in consumer or mortgage loans when the creditor requires the debtor to furnish a life-term insurance policy naming the creditor as the beneficiary. The policy will pay the debt if the debtor dies before the loan has been repaid.

Incidental Beneficiaries

An incidental beneficiary is an outside party for whose benefit a contract was not made but who would substantially benefit if the agreement were performed according to its terms and conditions. An incidental beneficiary, in contrast to an intended beneficiary, has no legal grounds for enforcing the contract made by those in privity of contract.

EXAMPLE 12-1: *Faber v. The Brotherhood of Aerospace Workers*

Mark Faber owned a hotel and restaurant in downtown Indianapolis. The Brotherhood of Aerospace Workers (BAW) had a contract with the city for the use of the municipal auditorium for the union's annual convention. One week before the convention, the union announced that it was canceling the meeting. The move was a clear violation of BAW's contract with the city. Faber brought suit against the BAW for damages due to lost business caused by the breach. The court dismissed the case on a motion for summary judgment. The court ruled that Faber was an incidental beneficiary and therefore had no grounds on which to bring the suit against the union.

quick quiz 12-1

1. A third party who provides no consideration and owes no legal duty to the contracting parties is a donee beneficiary. **true | false**
2. A creditor beneficiary is an outside third party to whom one or both contracting parties owe a continuing debt of obligation arising from the contract. **true | false**
3. Incidental and intended beneficiaries have the same rights. **true | false**

12-2 The Law of Assignment

When people enter contracts, they receive certain rights and incur particular duties. It is completely accepted today that, with some exceptions noted subsequently and unless the contract itself provides otherwise, these rights and duties can be transferred to others. An **assignment** is a transfer of a contract right, and a **delegation** is a transfer of a contract duty.

Assignment and Delegation

In general, rights are *assigned*, and duties are *delegated*. In most cases, both are governed by the same rules. If A is owed money by B, A may assign to C the right to collect the money. However, if A has agreed to pay B to harvest 200 acres of wheat for a price, B may delegate the duty of harvesting to C. Restrictions against the delegation of duties are presented later in this chapter. Three parties are associated with any assignment. Two of the parties are the ones who entered the original agreement. The party who assigns rights or delegates duties is the **assignor**. The outside third party to whom the assignment is made is the **assignee**. The remaining party to the original agreement is the **obligor**. Consideration is not required in the assignment of a contract. When there is no supporting consideration, however, the assignor may repudiate the assignment at any time before its execution. In addition, when no consideration is given for an assignment, creditors of the assignor may have the assignment rescinded on the grounds that it is a fraudulent conveyance. A **fraudulent conveyance** is a transfer of property with the intent to defraud creditors. If a fraudulent conveyance occurs, the assignor's creditors could have the assignment rescinded.

A SOON TO BE CLASSIC CASE
Two Assignments Are Better Than One . . . Perhaps

The case of *Fed. Home Loan Mtge. Corp. (FHLMC) v. Schwartzwald* began when Duane and Julie Schwartzwald negotiated a mortgage agreement with Legacy Mortgage in the amount of $251,250 to help them purchase a home. What followed was a series of assignments that greatly affected the outcome of the case for the Schwartzwalds. According to customary procedures, the Schwartzwalds executed a promissory note and gave a security interest in the home to Legacy. This is standard operating procedure in the industry. The next step was the **first assignment**. This step was also standard operating procedure, and the Schwartzwalds probably knew that this assignment was going to happen up front. The actual assignment occurred when Legacy assigned the mortgage to Wells Fargo and, as part of that second deal, endorsed the promissory note, making it payable to Wells Fargo.

Two years passed without incident during which the Schwartzwalds made their mortgage payments on a regular basis to Wells Fargo. When Duane lost his job, however, and the family moved out of state, things got rough. The Schwartzwalds made mortgage payments on the house until January when they found that they could not continue. However, they negotiated a deal with Wells Fargo under which the bank arranged to list the property for a short sale. In April, the Schwartzwalds completed a sales agreement under which the house would be sold for $259,900. The closing date was scheduled for June. Everything seemed to be proceeding smoothly when the Schwartzwalds learned in April that a foreclosure action had been started by the Federal Home Loan Mortgage Corporation (FHLMC). Unknown to the Schwartzwalds, Wells Fargo had negotiated a **second assignment** of the mortgage to FHLMC. Figure 12-1 gives a visual representation of the relationships that developed during this assignment process. [See: *Fed. Home Loan Mtge. Corp. v. Schwartzwald*, 134 Ohio St.3d 13, 2012-Ohio-5017.]

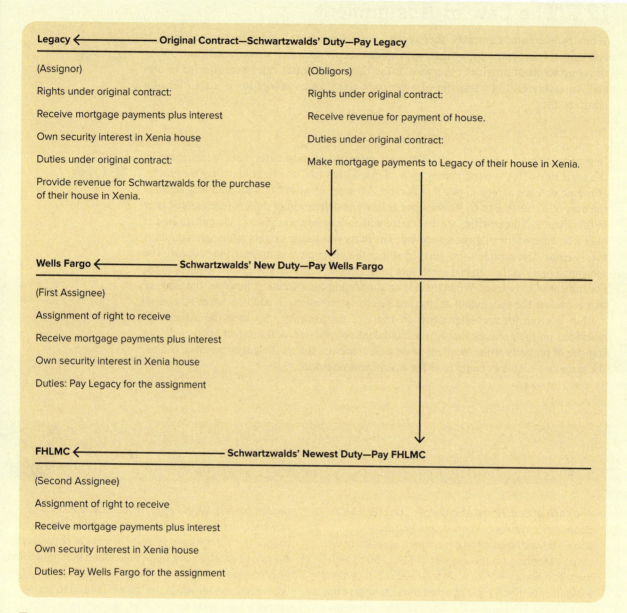

Figure 12-1 The Legacy–Schwartzwald–Wells Fargo–FHLMC Assignment Maze

Source: See: *Fed. Home Loan Mtge. Corp. v. Schwartzwald*, 134 Ohio St.3d 13, 2012-Ohio-5017.

Assignment Methods

To be valid, an assignment must follow certain accepted procedures designed to protect all of the parties. Form of assignment, notice of assignment, and the rights of parties in successive or subsequent assignments must conform to practices established by case law and state statutes. Assignment may be accomplished through written, oral, or implied agreements between the assignor and the assignee. Parties to an assignment must observe the requirement provided by the equal dignities rule discussed in Chapter 11. Under that rule, the law requires that if the agreement by the original parties must be in writing, the assignment also must be in writing.

An assignment is valid at the time it is made. As a measure of protection against subsequent assignments, the assignee should give notice of the assignment to the obligor. Although this obligation falls to the assignee, either party may give notice. Once notice is received, the obligor should deal with the assignee. If notice is not given, it would be normal practice for the obligor to render performance to the original contracting party, the assignor. If due notice has been given and the obligor makes payment to the assignor, the obligor is not excused from making payment to the assignee.

Should the assignor make a subsequent assignment of the same right, the courts must decide which of the two assignees has a superior right and claim against the obligor. A majority of the states hold that the first assignee has a superior right, even if a later assignee was the first to give notice of the assignment to the obligor. A minority of courts hold that whichever assignee was first to give notice of assignment has a superior right and claim to any assigned benefits.

quick quiz 12-2

1. A delegation is the transfer of a contractual right. — true | false
2. The equal dignities axiom has no application in the law of assignment. — true | false
3. It is the responsibility of the assignor to give notice of the assignment to the obligor. — true | false

12-3 Assignment Rights, Duties, and Restrictions

Rights can be assigned, and duties can be delegated. Although this rule seems simple enough, disagreements still arise regarding both assignment and delegation. What is generally in dispute is whether a particular right or duty can be transferred and, if so, what legal effects arise from that transfer.

Rights and Duties of the Assignee

The rights and duties of the assignee are the same as those previously held by the assignor under the original contract. It is fair to say that the assignee "steps into the shoes" of the assignor. Claims the assignor may have had against the obligor now belong to the assignee. Also, defenses the obligor may have had against the assignor's claims may now be used against the assignee.

The assignee's duty in an assignment is to give notice of the assignment to the obligor. The obligor is allowed a reasonable time to seek assurance that an assignment has been truly made. Making the assignment in writing reduces the possibility of fraudulent representation as an assignee.

About the Law

An assignment, rather than a negotiation, occurs when a check is transferred to a third party without a required endorsement.

EXAMPLE 12-2: The Quitter–Stalker Assignment, Part I

Quitter appeared at the payroll department of the Meadville Delivery Company and told the paymaster that one of Meadville's drivers, Stalker, had made an assignment of part of his paycheck to her. Under terms of the assignment, Quitter was to receive $150 of the money that Meadville owed Stalker. Meadville, the obligor, would not have to pay Quitter the $150 until the paymaster had a reasonable amount of time to verify the assignment.

A SOON TO BE CLASSIC CASE REVISITED Ignorance Is Not Bliss: At Least Not when Assignments Are Involved

The last time we saw the Soon To Be Classic Case of *Fed. Home Loan Mtge. Corp. v. Schwartzwald*, we learned Duane and Julie Schwartzwald negotiated a mortgage agreement with Legacy Mortgage in the amount of $251,250 so that they could buy a house in Xenia. The Schwartzwalds executed a promissory note and gave a security interest in the home to Legacy. Next, Legacy assigned the mortgage to Wells Fargo and endorsed the promissory note, making it payable to Wells Fargo. After Duane lost his job and the family moved out of state, the Schwartzwalds continued to make mortgage payments until January. They negotiated a deal with Wells Fargo under which the bank arranged to list the property for a short sale, and in April the Schwartzwalds completed a sales agreement under which the house would be sold for $259,900. The closing date was scheduled for June. Then suddenly in April, the Schwartzwalds learned that a foreclosure action had been started by the Federal Home Loan Mortgage Corporation (FHLMC). Unknown to the Schwartzwalds, Wells Fargo had negotiated a second assignment of the mortgage to FHLMC. However, the assignment seemed not to be complete when the foreclosure case was filed because, along with the other papers filed with the court, the FHLMC had appended a copy of the mortgage, which verified that the lender was Legacy and that the borrowers were the Schwartzwalds, *but* FHLMC failed to attach a copy of the promissory note, which it reported as being "unavailable."

This is when one of the most troublesome parts of the story begins. Julie had contacted Wells Fargo about all of this but was told it was just "standard procedure." She was also told by Wells Fargo "not to worry" because the short sale would take care of things. The Schwartzwalds relied on these representations from Wells Fargo and did not file an answer to the foreclosure filing, leaving them vulnerable to a default judgment in Common Pleas Court. In the meantime, Wells Fargo continued to work with FHLMC while also acting like the sale was going to go through. Moreover, Wells Fargo delayed so long that the buyers gave up. Now it is true that the assignor does not have the duty to inform the obligor of the assignment. However, Wells Fargo's actions here are suspect at best. There is, after all, a difference between failing to give notice and actively misleading an obligor by telling them that a foreclosure action is "standard procedure" and that they "should not worry." Moreover, continuing to work on a sale that they knew would not go through also seems to cross some sort of invisible, but no less, real ethical line. The duty to notify the Schwartzwalds (the obligors) fell on the shoulders of FHLMC (the assignee), which seems to have ignored that duty until the foreclosure notice, which would hardly constitute a valid notice in anybody's book. [See: *Fed. Home Loan Mtge. Corp. v. Schwartzwald*, 134 Ohio St.3d 13, 2012-Ohio-5017.]

Source: See: *Fed. Home Loan Mtge. Corp. v. Schwartzwald*, 134 Ohio St.3d 13, 2012-Ohio-5017.

Liabilities and Warranties of the Assignor

The assignor is obligated to any express and implied warranties that serve to protect either the assignee or the obligor. A **warranty** is a promise, statement, or other representation that a thing has certain qualities.

Warranties to the Assignee The assignor is bound by an implied warranty that the obligor will respect the assignment and make the performance, as required by the original agreement between the assignor and the obligor.

> ### EXAMPLE 12-3: The Quitter–Stalker Assignment, Part II
> Suppose, in the Quitter-Stalker assignment, that the Meadville Trucking Company had been either unwilling or unable to pay Quitter the $150. Stalker would be bound by an implied warranty to Quitter that the $150 would be paid. If the assignment were a gift to Quitter, there would be no enforceable warranty in the absence of consideration between the assignor and the assignee.

Warranties to the Obligor If the assignor delegates to an assignee duties owed the obligor, there is an implied warranty that the duties delegated will be carried out in a complete and satisfactory manner.

Restrictions on Assignments

Although most contracts may be assigned, those for personal and professional services may not. The right of assignment may also be restricted by agreement of the original parties to the contract and, in certain cases, by law.

Restrictions on Personal and Professional Service Contracts A party may not delegate duties that are of a personal or professional nature. *Personal*, in this context, means "other than routine." Musicians or artists, for example, could not delegate their services to someone else. They are chosen for their ability or artistic talent. Professional services are those rendered by physicians, lawyers, certified public accountants, ministers, and others. People in these occupations are selected because of their special abilities, and their services could not be delegated to someone else. In contrast, routine services may usually be delegated. These are services performed by electricians, mechanics, woodworkers, plumbers, waitstaff, bankers, publishers, and others whose skills and abilities are judged according to the usual customs and standards of the marketplace.

Restrictions Imposed by Original Contract Parties to a contract may include a condition that will not allow its assignment. Some courts have held that a restriction against the assignment of a debt owed by the obligor robs the assignor of a property right guaranteed by law and would be contrary to public policy. Other courts have permitted this restrictive condition.

Restrictions Imposed by Law Assignments, in special situations, may be restricted by law or declared void because they are contrary to public policy. Thus, members of the armed services may not assign any part of their pay except to a spouse or family member. Police officers, persons elected or appointed to public office, and others are likewise restricted from making assignment of their pay or of duties that they have been especially chosen to perform. Also, some states demand that if an assignee wants to

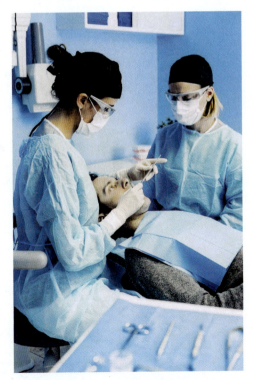

Professionals, like dentists, are chosen based on their particular skills and abilities and may not delegate their professional duties to another.

©santypan/Shutterstock

bring a lawsuit based on an assignment, as in a foreclosure action, that assignee must have already received the assignment. This is because, until the assignment has occurred, that party (assignee 2 as it were) has no personal stake in the lawsuit. Nor can the party transform itself retroactively into a party with standing after the action has begun. If the lawsuit is brought before the assignment is completed, the case will be dismissed because the party bringing lawsuit has no injury to vindicate. Once the action has been dismissed, it can be brought again, as long as the statute of limitations has not run out, the action was dismissed without prejudice, and the party obtains standing to sue. This situation must be distinguished from an action initiated by a legal representative, such as a guardian, an executor, an administrator, a trustee, and so on, brought on behalf of the real-party-in-interest. The *Schwartzwald* case illustrates the first situation, that is, a lack of standing to sue, rather than a case brought by an agent on behalf of a real-party-in-interest.

Novation and Assignment

Sometimes a party to a contract will assign all rights and delegate all duties to a third party (the assignee). Once this happens, the assignee will work directly with the obligor, performing the duties and receiving the benefits. Nevertheless, the assignor will remain in privity of contract with the obligor and be liable to the obligor if the assignee does not perform or performs improperly.

EXAMPLE 12-4: *Superfine Market v. Allgood Canning Company*

Allgood Canning Company entered into a contract to sell 1,000 cases of baked beans to Superfine Market for a specific price. Shortly thereafter, Allgood delegated its duty to ship the beans and assigned its rights to receive the money to Fastway Canning Company. The beans Fastway shipped were bad. If Superfine were to bring suit for damages, it would have to be brought against Allgood, because that was the company with which it had contracted. There was no privity between Superfine and Fastway.

In contrast, if all three parties agree, the assignor can be released from liability at the time of the assignment, and privity of contract can exist between the assignee and the obligor. Such an arrangement is called a **novation**, which is a substitution, by mutual agreement, of a new party for one of the original parties to a contract. If, in Example 12-4, Superfine and Fastway had agreed to release Allgood from responsibility under the original contract, a novation would have occurred. Privity of contract then would have been between Superfine and Fastway. Superfine's only recourse upon receiving the bad beans would have been to bring suit against Fastway because, by mutual consent, Allgood had been discharged.

quick quiz 12-3

1. The phrase "assignment of a contract" means the same thing as the phrase "assignment of rights." true | false
2. Personal and professional duties are just as transferable as all other duties. true | false
3. Novations have been outlawed under the Restatement of Contracts. true | false

12-4 Discharge by Performance

Most contracts are discharged by **performance**, which means that the parties do what they agreed to do under the terms of the contract. When performance occurs, the obligations of the parties end. Sometimes, however, the parties do not perform in a timely or satisfactory manner. At other times, they perform partially but not completely. At still other times, they do not perform at all.

Time for Performance

When the time for performance is not stated in the contract, the contract must be performed within a reasonable time. A **reasonable time** is the time that may fairly, properly, and conveniently be required to do the task that is to be done, considering attending circumstances. Whether a task is performed within a reasonable time is a question of fact to be decided by the jury in a jury trial or the judge in a nonjury trial.

EXAMPLE 12-5: *Rostow Aviation, Ltd. v. Futuregraphics, Inc.*

Rostow Aviation Ltd. entered a contract with Futuregraphics Inc. for the design and implementation of a new website for Rostow. The website was supposed to be up and operational within 60 days of the making of the contract. Futuregraphics was one week late in the completion of the site. Rostow attempted to rescind the agreement, claiming that time was of special importance. The court ruled that it had not been clearly established that time was essential for the completion of the website. Because time was not essential to the satisfactory performance of the agreement, Rostow was held to the contract.

A QUESTION OF ETHICS

The court held Rostow to the contract in Example 12-5 even though Futuregraphics was one week late in fulfilling its part of the agreement. Because time really was not essential to the agreement, and because Rostow presumably knew that, was it ethical for Rostow to raise the issue of Futuregraphics' lateness in the first place? If time had been important to the completion of the website, did Rostow have a responsibility to raise the issue of time before the contract was finalized? If Futuregraphics knew it was running behind schedule, did it have a duty to notify Rostow and offer some sort of compensation for the breach? Explain your answers.

When the time for performance is stated in the contract but there is nothing to indicate that time is of particular importance, the court will usually allow additional time to perform. When the time for performance is stated in the contract and there is something special about the contract that indicates time is essential, the time for performance will be strictly enforced.

EXAMPLE 12-6: *Carter City School System v. Arrow Images, Inc.*

Arrow Images Inc. entered a contract with the entire Carter City school system for the design, production, and distribution of the yearbooks for each of the system's three high schools. A very strict schedule was developed for each high school yearbook staff, specifying when the manuscript, art, and photos had to be e-mailed to Arrow; when the material had to be formatted and returned as pdf page proof files to the high schools; and when the pdf page proof files had to be read, corrected, and e-mailed to Arrow. The yearbooks were to be delivered to each high school 90 days after Arrow had received all pdf page proof files so that they would be ready for distribution on graduation day for each of the high schools. In such a situation, it is clear that time is an important factor in this agreement. Unfortunately, the students at two of the three schools did not return the proofs on time, and the yearbooks were late. This missed deadline caused an extra expense for the city school system, which had to send the yearbooks to students by FedEx because they were no longer on campus to pick up their books personally. When Carter City sued Arrow, the court ruled that because the students knew that time was of the essence and had not made the scheduled deadline, the city could not complain when Arrow failed to meet the delivery date.

Similarly, when the phrase "time is of the essence" is included among the terms of a written contract, the time period will be enforced. The phrase makes it clear that the time element is of the utmost importance to the parties. Some contracts use a "best efforts" clause to avoid committing parties to a date but instead committing them to do their best to perform by a certain date.

Satisfactory, Complete, and Substantial Performance

Satisfactory performance exists when either personal taste or objective standards have determined that the contracting parties have performed their contractual duties according to the agreement. Satisfactory performance is either an express or implied condition of every contract. Sales agreements for consumer goods often note this condition by including the words: "money back if not entirely satisfied." In other contracts, satisfaction may be carefully defined according to the expectations of the parties. When there is no express agreement, the law implies that work will be done in a skillful manner and the materials or goods will be free of defects. Ordinarily, the parties may be discharged from a contract only if there has been satisfactory performance. Sometimes, one person will agree to do something to another person's satisfaction. Services rendered in a beauty salon or barbershop, photographs taken at a studio, and portraits painted by an artist fall within this classification. Regardless of the skill and application of the person doing the work, dissatisfied customers may, on the basis of their personal judgment and satisfaction, refuse to make payment.

Complete performance occurs when all the parties fully accomplish every term, condition, and promise to which they agreed. **Substantial performance** occurs when a party, in good faith, executes all promised terms and conditions with the exception of minor details that do not affect the real intent of their agreement. Complete performance terminates an agreement, freeing the parties of any further obligation. Ordinarily, substantial performance also serves to discharge the agreement but with one difference: A party who correctly complains that the other party's performance has been substantial but not complete has the right to demand reimbursement from the offending party to correct those details that were not performed.

Conditions and Tender of Performance

Some contracts have conditions or terms that determine the rights and duties of the parties prior to performance, during performance, and following performance. These conditions may be classified as conditions precedent, conditions concurrent, or conditions subsequent. Also, in most situations it is necessary for a nonbreaching party to continue to offer to perform as promised. This is referred to as a tender of performance. It is discussed below at length.

THE OPENING CASE Round 2
"The Repudiation Is in the Mail"—How Not to Breach a Contract

Recall that the Opening Case began in March, when Mr. Carney enrolled his son in the fourth-grade class at Lake Ridge Academy. As part of this process, Carney agreed to enter a standard school registration agreement (SRA) with Lake Ridge. The SRA worked like this: Lake Ridge would hold a slot in the fourth grade for Carney's son and Carney would make a down payment of $630 along with a promise to pay the rest later in the year. In addition, the SRA established rather clearly that Carney had until August 1 to pull out of the contract. If he did not send notice of his plan to withdraw his son by August 1, then he agreed to pay the rest of the tuition, regardless of whether his son stayed enrolled at Lake Ridge. The SRA was written this way not only to give Lake Ridge a deadline after which it could finalize its annual budge, but also to give parents enough time to evaluate their finances before making a final commitment to the school.

As things turned out, Carney did not repudiate the contract by August 1. As part of its regular routine, after that date, Lake Ridge finalized its budget based on the assumption that all parents who had not withdrawn by August 1 would pay the balance due under the terms of the SRA. One week later, in a letter postmarked August 7, Carney notified the administration of Lake Ridge that he had withdraw his son from the school. As far as Carney was concerned, with that letter, he had ended the contract and no longer owed the tuition balance to the school. Lake Ridge officials politely explained that, under the terms of the SRA, since Carney had not notified the school of his intention to end the contract before August 1, he owed the school the rest of the tuition regardless of his son's current status.

When Carney refused to come through with that final payment, Lake Ridge initiated this lawsuit, asking for the balance due ($5,610). Carney put forth several arguments in his defense, the first of which was substantial performance. He stated, rather convincingly that he had substantially performed the terms of the SRA and, therefore, had been released from the agreement. The court disagreed. In fact, the court so strongly disagreed that it dismissed the argument immediately, noting that, "There is no reasonable argument that Carney 'substantially complied' with the provision of the contract requiring him to notify Lake Ridge of his child's withdrawal prior to August 1 . . . Carney's notice of cancellation was not received by Lake Ridge until after the August 1 deadline had passed. Thus, Carney did not comply *at all* with the requirement that cancellation take place prior to August 1."

As noted previously, an act of substantial performance occurs when a party, in good faith, executes *all promised terms* and conditions with *the exception of minor details that do not affect the real intent of their agreement*. It is difficult to see how Carney can believe that he performed *all promised terms*. Repudiating on or before August 1 was a "promised term" he did not execute. Nor could Carney in good faith call the August 1 deadline "a minor detail that did not affect the real intent of the agreement." One of the intentions of setting the August 1 date was to give parents a chance to consider all the financial factors before committing to paying rest of the tuition and to give Lake Ridge a deadline after which it could safely plan its annual budget—hardly minor details. Also recall that a party who correctly complains that the other party's performance has been substantial but not complete has the right to demand reimbursement from the offending party to correct those details that were not performed. In this case, that would amount to the $5,610 that Carney still owed. [See: *Lake Ridge v. Carney*, 66 Ohio St. 3d 376, No. 2464.]

Source: See: *Lake Ridge v. Carney*, 66 Ohio St. 3d 376, No. 2464.

Conditions of Performance A **condition precedent** is a condition that requires the performance of certain acts or promises before the other party is obligated to pay money or provide any other agreed to consideration. In a *unilateral contract*, the performance of a condition precedent serves as the offeree's acceptance of the offer. In a *bilateral contract*, it is a promise that if not performed leads to either rescission or termination of the entire agreement.

EXAMPLE 12-7: The Pressler Case

Pressler, a third-year law student, signed an agreement to accept a position with a law firm. The members of the firm agreed to hire Pressler on the condition that she receive her law degree and pass the bar examination in their state. Earning the law degree and passing the bar examination are conditions precedent to the performance of the obligation of the law firm in giving Pressler the position.

A condition that requires both parties to perform at the same time is a **condition concurrent**. A promise to deliver goods supported by the buyer's promise to pay on delivery is a very common condition concurrent. Real estate sales agreements, by custom, usually state that the owner-seller will deliver a good and complete deed to the real property on the buyer's presentation of either cash or a certified check for the amount of the purchase price. Failure of either to do as promised concurrently would be a breach of the express contract condition. A **condition subsequent** is one in which the parties agree that the contract will be terminated when a prescribed event occurs or does not occur. An agreement between a builder and a client stating that contract performance would terminate if a required building permit were not obtained from the issuing public authority within 60 days after the contract is signed is a condition subsequent. Some warranties included in contracts also illustrate these conditions.

EXAMPLE 12-8: Graham v. Metcalf

Luben Metcalf agreed to remodel Trisha Graham's back porch for $15,000. Both parties signed a written agreement. One clause in the agreement stated that Metcalf guaranteed the improvements would be free of defects for 12 months after the work was completed. Graham agreed to pay for the improvements upon completion. Metcalf's guarantee constituted a condition subsequent—that is, a condition that applies after both parties have performed their primary obligations under the contract. When, after only one month, the porch roof leaked, Graham demanded that Metcalf return and fix the problem. Metcalf repeatedly refused to do anything about the leaky roof. Graham was forced to hire another contractor to correct Metcalf's errors. Graham then successfully sued Metcalf and recovered the cost of the repairs.

Tender of Performance   In contract law, **tender of performance** means to offer to do what one has agreed to do under the terms of the contract. If someone has agreed to sell a parcel of land for $40,000, for example, tender of performance would be offering to give a signed deed to the buyer at the agreed time. Similarly, **tender of payment** would be presenting the $40,000 to the seller at the agreed time. It is important to make tender even if one knows that the other party is not going to perform the contract. This provision is necessary in some states to test the other party's willingness and ability to perform. If neither party has made tender, the court would hold that a breach of contract has not been established. Thus, neither party would be in a position to bring suit against the other. People who must perform acts (e.g., selling goods, performing services) are excused from performing if they make proper tender and it is rejected. However, people who must pay money are not excused from paying if their tender of payment is rejected. They are merely excused from paying further interest.

> **quick quiz 12-4**
>
> 1. Very few contracts are discharged by performance.   true | false
> 2. A condition precedent is a condition that requires the performance of certain actions before the other party to the contract is obligated.   true | false
> 3. Tender of performance means to offer to do what one has agreed to do under the terms of the contract.   true | false

12-5 Discharge by Nonperformance

Nonperformance may be defined as failing to fulfill or accomplish a promise, contract, or obligation according to its terms. Sometimes the failure to perform makes a party vulnerable to legal action. However, not every instance of nonperformance results in a legal action. Sometimes, nonperformance results from mutual agreement between the parties. At other times, nonperformance is excused because of conditions that make performance impossible or by operation of law. Nevertheless, under certain circumstances, nonperformance will result in a breach of contract. Discharge by nonperformance often comes about in the following ways:

- Discharge by agreement.
- Discharge by impossibility and by operation of law.
- Discharge by breach of contract.

Discharge by Agreement

Parties to a contract may stipulate the time and conditions for termination and discharge as part of their agreement. They also may subsequently agree not to do what they had originally promised. The latter is the case when there is a mutual rescission of the contract, a waiver of performance by one or more of the parties, a novation, or an accord and satisfaction to liquidate an outstanding debt or obligation.

Termination by Terms of the Contract During contract negotiations, parties may agree to certain terms that provide for automatic termination of the contract. For example, a professional athlete may contract with management that the agreement will be terminated if for any reason the player becomes either physically or mentally incapable of rendering full performance.

Mutual Rescission Contracting parties may, either before or after performance commences, rescind their contract as a result of further negotiation and by their mutual assent. **Mutual rescission**, in the majority of cases, requires both parties to return to the other any consideration already received or pay for any services or materials already rendered.

Termination by Waiver When a party with the right to complain of the other party's unsatisfactory performance or nonperformance fails to complain, **termination by waiver** occurs. It is a voluntary relinquishing (waiver) of one's rights to demand performance. A waiver differs from a discharge by mutual rescission in that a waiver entails no obligation by the parties to return any consideration that may have been exchanged up to the moment of rescission. Discharge by waiver, when made, is complete in itself.

Novation By novation, the parties to a contract mutually agree to replace one of the parties with a new party. The former, original party is released from liability under the contract. Novation is discussed in detail earlier in the chapter.

Accord and Satisfaction An accord and satisfaction is a new agreement resulting from a bona fide dispute between the parties as to the terms of their original agreement. The mutual agreement to the new terms is the accord; performance of the accord is the satisfaction—thus, accord and satisfaction. The accord, though agreed to, is not a binding agreement until the satisfaction has been made. The original agreement therefore is not discharged until the performance or satisfaction has been provided as promised.

General Release A **general release** is a document expressing the intent of a creditor to release a debtor from obligations on an existing and valid debt. A general release terminates a debt and excuses the debtor of any future payment, without the usual requirement that consideration be given in return.

Discharge by Impossibility and by Law

Occasionally, it becomes impossible to perform a contract. For example, when the subject matter of a contract, without the knowledge of the parties, had been destroyed before the contract was entered into, the contract would be discharged. Sometimes a contract that is legal when it is originally entered into by the parties becomes illegal before it is performed. This leads to a discharge by operation of law.

Types and Conditions of Impossibility Conditions that arise subsequent to the making of a contract may either void the agreement or make it voidable by one of the parties. Discharge through impossibility of performance may, in some situations, be allowed only if the specific and anticipated impossibility has been made a condition to the agreement. When the exact subject matter of an executory contract has been selected by the parties and later is destroyed, the performance obligation is discharged. In contrast, when the contract is not specific in the description or the location of the subject matter, a promisor is not discharged if the subject matter intended for delivery is destroyed. In this case, the promisor is obligated to locate and deliver subject matter of the same kind and quantity that could be secured elsewhere. Any financial losses due to the misfortune must be borne by the promisor.

When the performance of a contract requires actions declared illegal because of existing common law, statute, or public policy, the contract is void from its inception. When the performance of a contract is made illegal through the passing of laws subsequent to the formation of the contract, the contract is likewise declared void, and the parties are discharged. The death, insanity, or disability of a party obligated to perform an act that requires a special talent or skill terminates and discharges an agreement, including promises to perform by musicians, artists, writers, skilled craftspeople, and certain professionals. When promised services are to be performed for the personal benefit of a promisee, the death of the promisee will also terminate the agreement. When the contract relates to services that may be performed by others and do not demand the personal services of the contracting party, performance is not excused through death, insanity, or disability. The guardian of the party involved or the estate of the deceased may be held liable for performance.

Frustration-of-Purpose Doctrine The **frustration-of-purpose doctrine** releases a party from a contractual obligation when performing the obligations would be thoroughly impractical and senseless. The doctrine is applied only in those cases in which a party recognizes and understands possible risks and accepts them in contemplation of performance.

EXAMPLE 12-10: *Stewart v. Gaverick*

George Gaverick rented a 50th-floor apartment from Thomas Stewart for the night of December 31. The apartment had a balcony overlooking Times Square in midtown Manhattan. The rental period was for only 24 hours, and the landlord knew that the purpose of the contract was to allow Gaverick an unrestricted view of Times Square for the city's New Year's Eve celebration. Unfortunately, a terrorist alert canceled the entire Times Square celebration that year. Stewart still demanded payment from Gaverick and brought a suit in small claims court to recover the amount due. The referee refused to force Gaverick to pay for the apartment. The referee concluded that because the apartment was of no use to Gaverick, the purpose of the agreement was frustrated and Gaverick would not have to pay the rent.

Commercial Impracticability Although not identical to the frustration-of-purpose doctrine, a related concept is known as **commercial impracticability**. Under this doctrine, the courts may excuse the nonperformance of one party to a contract because an unforeseen and very severe hardship has arisen that would place an enormous hardship on that party. Commercial impracticability is not the same as impossibility because the party still can perform the contract. It is just that the performance itself would cause a great deal of adversity. Also with commercial impracticability, the purpose of the contract is not undermined by the unforeseen event, so the frustration-of-purpose doctrine does not apply. Nevertheless, under this relatively modern doctrine, some parties may escape performance if the unforeseen event was truly unforeseen and not in any way the fault of the party seeking an escape from performance.

Operation of Law

The performance of a promised act may be discharged by operation of law. Some law that causes the parties to be discharged from their obligations, such as bankruptcy or the statute of limitations, comes into play in this case. Through the provisions of the Bankruptcy Reform Act, a discharge in bankruptcy from a court will be allowed as a defense against the collection of most, but not all, debts of the bankrupt. Therefore, most contractual obligations to pay money come to an end when a party files for bankruptcy. State statutes providing time limits within which suits may be brought are known as statutes of limitations. Each state sets its own time limits. In general, actions for collection of open accounts (charge accounts) must be brought within 3 to 5 years, written agreements within 10 years, and judgments from 10 to 20 years. Those states requiring a seal on certain contracts have still other limitations and requirements that are much broader than those applied to simple contracts. The time limit for bringing suit for breach of a sales contract is four years under the Uniform Commercial Code. The statute of limitations does not technically void the debt, but it gives the debtor a defense against any demand for collection.

Discharge by Breach of Contract

When there is a breach of contract, the injured party has the right to remedy in court. There are several ways in which a breach may occur.

Deliberate Breach of Contract A breach of contract results when one of the parties fails to do what was agreed to under the terms of the contract. When time is of the essence, there is a breach if performance is not completed within the time limits agreed to by the parties. A breach also results if the performance has been negligent or unskillful. The services rendered must adhere to the standards of skill, as determined by the custom of the marketplace. Wrongful performance or nonperformance discharges the other party from further obligation and permits that party to bring suit to rescind the contract or recover money to compensate it for any loss sustained. Such compensation is known as *damages*.

Repudiation and Anticipatory Breach An anticipatory breach occurs when a party to a contract either expresses or clearly implies an intention not to perform the contract, even before being required to act. The repudiation must indicate a deliberate refusal to perform according to the terms of the contract. Breaches of this kind are also called *constructive breaches*. The injured party may either commence suit at the time of the anticipatory breach or await the date agreed to for performance, thus giving the breaching party time to reconsider and begin performance. To succeed in a case based on anticipatory repudiation, the injured party must demonstrate that he or she was ready, willing, and able to comply with the contract but could not do so because of the other party's material breach. Anticipatory breach cannot be used if the only action repudiated was the promise to pay money to another party.

Abandonment of Contractual Obligations Stopping performance once it has begun is called abandonment of contractual obligations. Leaving or deserting a party's obligations discharges the other party from any promises made and permits a suit for damages. A temporary, or short-lived, interruption of performance is not deemed abandonment. To constitute abandonment, the promisor must have inexcusably interrupted performance with the obvious intention of not returning to complete the obligations promised.

quick quiz 12-5

1. A general release is a document expressing the intent of a creditor to release a debtor from the obligations of an existing and valid debt. true | false
2. With commercial impracticability, the purpose of a contract is undermined by an unforeseen event. true | false
3. Stopping a performance once it has begun is called abandonment of contractual obligations. true | false

12-6 Damages and Equitable Remedies

A breach of contract releases the injured party from any obligations under the contract and gives that party the right to ask a court of law for a remedy. The usual remedy for breach of contract is the payment of damages in the form of money. At times, however, the payment of monetary damages is not enough to satisfy the injured party. In such situations, the injured party will ask the court for rescission, specific performance, or an injunction.

Damages in Contract Law

Damages describe money awarded to parties who have been victimized or suffered injury to their legal rights by others. Damages are of different kinds, and the nature of a claim usually determines what type of damages will apply. In some states, by statute or judicial rule, juries are charged with two decisions: They must decide which party is to be given favorable judgment and determine how much is to be awarded in damages. Appeals to a higher court are allowed when the amount of damages awarded appears to be unreasonably low or excessively high.

Actual or Compensatory Damages Actual damages are the sum of money equal to the real financial loss suffered by the injured party. Because they are intended to compensate the injured party, actual damages are also called compensatory damages. Thus, damages awarded for nondelivery of promised goods or services would be an amount equal to the difference between the price stated in the contract and what the promisee would have to pay elsewhere. Should the same goods or services be conveniently available elsewhere at the same or at a lower price, no actual loss could be claimed.

Incidental and Consequential Damages Incidental damages and consequential damages are awarded for losses indirectly but closely attributable to a breach. Incidental damages cover any expenses paid out by the innocent party to prevent further loss. Consequential damages result indirectly from the breach because of special circumstances that exist with a particular contract. To recover consequential damages, the injured party must show that such losses were foreseeable when the contract was made.

Punitive or Exemplary Damages

Damages in excess of actual losses suffered by the plaintiff awarded as a measure of punishment for the defendant's wrongful acts are punitive damages, also called *exemplary damages*. They are a court-ordered punishment rather than compensation for a known loss. Since the underlying philosophy of contract law is to compensate the innocent party for the losses that result from a breach, punitive damages are generally not permitted in the law of contracts. Sometimes public policy will permit a judge to award punitive damages, but only when a defendant is responsible for abusive and dishonest practices in consumer transactions that are unconscionable and contrary to the public good. Usually, such abusive and dishonest practices are not really associated with contract law anyway but are, instead, associated with certain business-related torts, including fraudulent misrepresentation, disparagement, the violation of an implied covenant of fairness and honesty, and intentional interference with an existing contract.

Fraudulent Misrepresentation As noted previously, fraud, or fraudulent misrepresentation, occurs when one party makes false statements or commits some sort of false action that causes another party to rely on those falsehoods then experience an injury or loss as a result. Because fraud is a deliberate attempt to subvert proper business relationships, the court views it as especially reprehensible, and those that commit fraud will find themselves paying not only compensatory damages, if applicable, but also punitive damages. The idea of punitive damages is to punish the defrauding party to such an extent that he or she will be dissuaded from any future fraudulent conduct. Punitive damages are also supposed to serve as a deterrent so that other people do not even think about committing fraud. For this reason, punitive damages are also called *exemplary damages*. Exemplary damages are used as an example for other "would-be con artists" who ought to know better than to subvert the law through fraud.

Nominal Damages Token damages awarded to parties who have experienced an injury to their legal rights but no actual loss are nominal damages. Common law usually awarded six cents to the successful plaintiff when no actual losses were shown. In today's practice, the award is usually one dollar.

Present and Future Damages Damages may be awarded for present injuries and for others that might reasonably be anticipated in the future. Thus, a party charged with fraud in the sale of a building infested with termites may be held liable for all damages revealed at the time of the suit and for damages that would reasonably be forthcoming as a result of the undisclosed and concealed infestation of the property.

A CLASSIC CASE — The Punishment Must Fit the Conduct

When one party breaks the terms of a contract, and the other party sues, the court will do its best to place the parties in as good a position as they would have been in had the contract been performed as promised. In this way, contract law differs from other areas of the law, such as criminal law, which generally seeks to punish the wrongdoer and deter the criminal conduct in the future. Contract law also differs from tort law, which is designed to compensate the victim, punish the wrongdoer, and deter tortious behavior in the future. One reason for this policy is that people voluntarily assume responsibilities when they make a contract, and those responsibilities affect only the parties and not the general public, as is the case with criminal law and, at times, tort law. All of this is fine as far as it goes, but what happens when the breaching party has deliberately undermined the basic intent of contract law by committing fraud—not just in the contract at issue, but as a pattern of conduct, perhaps even an official policy, affecting hundreds and thousands of other contracts? This is precisely what happened in *State Farm Mutual v. Campbell*. In that case, the Campbells had been involved in an automobile accident and were being sued. Their insurer, State Farm, refused to settle out of court, despite the desires of the Campbells and the advice of State Farm's own investigators. The original accident case went to trial, and the Campbells lost.

When State Farm refused to pay the full amount of the award, the Campbells sued the insurer for bad faith, fraud, and intentional infliction of emotional distress. The Campbells offered evidence that the refusal to settle was not just fraudulent in relation to their contract, but was also part of a larger pattern of conduct planned and executed by State Farm over a 20-year period against hundreds of policyholders. The conduct involved a national campaign referred to as the Performance, Planning, and Review (PP&R) Policy. Once the jury heard evidence about the systematic execution of the PP&R Policy, they awarded the Campbells $145 million in punitive damages. The judge then reduced the punitive damages to $25 million. On appeal, the Campbells stressed the fraudulent nature of the PP&R Policy, and State Farm argued that its conduct in relation to the other contracts should not be used to punish the company for its conduct in relation to the contract that it had with the Campbells. The Supreme Court of Utah agreed with the Campbells and reinstated the $145 million in punitive damages. The case made its way to the U.S. Supreme Court, which struck down that portion of the punitive damages that involved conduct unrelated to the Campbells' claim. The Court concluded that awarding punitive damage for conduct unrelated to the claim before the court in the present case violated the basic principles of due process. [See: *State Farm Mutual Automobile Ins. Co. v. Campbell*, 538 U.S. 408 (United States Supreme Court).]

Source: See: *State Farm Mutual Automobile Ins. Co. v. Campbell*, 538 U.S. 408 (United States Supreme Court).

Stipulated Damages Parties may stipulate (agree) as a condition of their contract to the amount of damages that might be assessed if there is a breach. Damages agreed to in the initial contract are called **stipulated damages**. It is the general policy of the law to permit the parties to a contract as much freedom as necessary in the construction of contractual terms. Consequently, as long as there is a legitimate way to calculate what losses might occur should there be a breach, then the parties are permitted, even encouraged in some rare cases, to add those damages to the agreement. Legitimate stipulated damages are refereed to as **liquidated damages**. It is critical to remember, of course, that the underlying philosophy of contract law is to compensate the innocent party for any losses that result from a breach, not to punish the breaching party. For this reason, the parties to a contract cannot add punitive damages to any listing of stipulated damages. Unfortunately, as is often the case in the law, it is easier to state a legal principle in the abstract than to implement it in the real world. In this case, it is very easy to say that the parties are permitted to stipulate liquidated damages but forbidden to add punitive damages to a contract. However, it is not as easy to distinguish between the two. For this reason, the courts have provided a test for implementing this ethereal principle. The test has three prongs. First,

THE OPENING CASE Round 3
"The Repudiation Is in the Mail"—How Not to Breach a Contract

The Opening Case began when Mr. Carney decided to place his son in the fourth-grade class at Lake Ridge Academy. In order to complete the entry procedure, Carney entered a standard school registration agreement (SRA) with the school, which stated that Lake Ridge would hold a seat in the fourth grade for Carney's son just as long as, in return, Carney made an initial payment of $630 and agreed to pay the rest of the tuition at a later date as specified in the agreement. To ensure that everyone was on the same page, the SRA identified August 1 as the final date that Carney had to repudiate the agreement. In the event that Carney failed to notify the school before August 1 of his plan to exit the contract, then he promised to pay the rest of the tuition, even if he took his son out of the school. The SRA was written this way to give parents enough time to evaluate their finances before making a final commitment to the school and to give Lake Ridge a deadline after which it could finalize its annual budge. August 1 came and went without any notice of repudiation from Carney. Following the terms of the contract, Lake Ridge finalized its budget based on the assumption that all parents who had not withdrawn by August 1 would pay the balance due under the terms of the SRA. A short time later, Carney sent a letter, postmarked August 7, notifying the administration of Lake Ridge that his son would not be attending the school. In Carney's mind, with that letter, he had repudiated the contract and no longer owed the school any money. Lake Ridge officials told Carney that he was mistaken. They pointed to the terms of the SRA and noted that he still owed the school the rest of his son's tuition, an amount that came to $5,610. When Carney refused to pay that amount, Lake Ridge initiated this lawsuit. Carney put forth several arguments in his defense, one of which pointed out that stipulated damages were not permitted to be punitive. Therefore, since the amount of $5,610 was punitive, he was under no obligation to send any money at all to the school, let alone an amount that topped $5,000. The court disagreed.

In Ohio, the three-prong test for distinguishing between legitimate stipulated damages (liquidated damages) and illegitimate stipulated damages (punitive damages) is named the *Samson* test after the case of *Samson Sales, Inc. v. Honeywell, Inc.* The court applied the *Samson* test to the Carney case and concluded that the $5,610 tuition payment was not a punishment but was, instead, a genuine measure of the loss that Lake Ridge had suffered due to Carney's belated response. First, given the nature of the contract, school officials would have had a difficult time determining the financial impact of a missing student or two (or three) without calculating the loss based on lost tuition. A loss based on missing tuition is easier to calculate in advance when contrasted with trying to determine the damages associated with the loss of a single student after the fact. Second, the contract must not include terms that are unconscionable, unreasonable, or disproportionate in amount. The court looked at the entire situation and first determined that the contract was not unconscionable. Looking at the entire situation, the court was convinced that the school did not force, entrap, or trick Carney into the deal. In short, there was nothing to make the contract look even a little unconscionable. Nor was there any evidence that the agreement was unreasonable. The date of August 1 was needed to give the school a chance to finalized its budget. There is nothing unreasonable involved in permitting a party the time needed to calculate the details of its own budget. Nor were the damages disproportionate to the loss suffered by the school. Because the school lost a student that it had already budgeted for, it is not disproportionate to see that loss as the equivalent of one year's tuition. Third, the contract must be clear enough for the court to see that the parties intended the amount stipulated to be awarded should a breach occur. The repudiation clause reads: "If enrollment is cancelled after August 1, parents or guardians financially responsible for student are obligated to pay the full Tuition, books and supplies charges." Looking at this clause, the court made short order of the third element of the *Samson* test. The court said, "We have no reason to believe that the plain language of the damages provision does not represent the parties' intent." Given all of this evidence, the court concluded that "The judgment of the court of appeals is affirmed. The cause is remanded to the Elyria Municipal Court to enter judgment in favor of Lake Ridge Academy for contract damages in the amount of $5,610." So there! [See: *Lake Ridge v. Carney*, 66 Ohio St. 3d 376, No. 2464.]

Source: See: *Lake Ridge v. Carney*, 66 Ohio St. 3d 376, No. 2464.

stipulated damages will be legitimate and, therefore liquidated if, given the nature of the contract, it would be difficult to judge the exact amount of the loss suffered should there be a breach. Second, the overall contract itself must not be tied up in terms that are so unconscionable, unreasonable, and disproportionate in amount that it is probable that it does not express the true intent of the parties. Third, the contract itself must be clear enough for the court to see that the parties authentically intended the amount stipulated to be awarded should a breach occur. Even this summary of the test is somewhat difficult to understand. This is not unusual, however. Sometimes it takes a real case before a difficult legal test like this one becomes clear.

Damages under *Quantum Meruit* The doctrine of *quantum meruit* (i.e., as much as one had earned) is important in assessing damages in cases founded on contracts implied in law, or quasi-contracts. Thus, when there has been no express or implied mutual agreement, a court will at times impose an obligation against a party who has been unjustly rewarded at the innocent expense of another. Damages awarded are in an amount considered reasonable in return for the benefits the one party derived through the quasi-contract relationship.

Speculative Damages Courts do not allow speculative damages. These damages are computed on losses that have not actually been suffered and that cannot be proved; they are damages based entirely on an expectation of losses that might be suffered from a breach. They differ from future damages in that speculative damages are not founded on fact but only on hope or expectation. Their basis is nothing more than a calculated guess as to the gains a party might have received had there not been a breach.

Mitigation of Damages The injured party has an obligation to do what is reasonably possible to mitigate the damages, that is, to keep damages to a minimum. A party who has been wronged by another's breach must exercise reasonable precautions to prevent the damages from becoming unfairly and unreasonably burdensome to the other party.

Equitable Remedies

When money in the form of damages is not enough to provide a fair and just award to the injured party, the court may grant an equitable remedy. Rather than simply order the breaching party to pay damages, a court issuing an equitable remedy compels the breaching party to perform an act or refrain from performing an act. The two most common equitable remedies are specific performance and injunctive relief.

Specific Performance A decree of specific performance is a court order calling for the breaching party to do what he or she promised to do under the original contract. The courts order specific performance only when the subject matter of a contract is unique or rare. The classic example of unique subject matter calling for specific performance is a contract for the sale and transfer of title to land, because each piece of land is unique. However, unique or rare subject matter could also include such items as antique, family heirlooms, original works of art, and special animals, such as a particular race horse. Obviously, an award of monetary damages would not provide the injured party satisfaction in any of these situations. Contracts for personal services are rarely enforced through specific performance. Demanding that an unwilling party perform promised personal services would be contrary to Amendment 13 of the U.S. Constitution, which prohibits human servitude. A remedy in cases of this kind, however, may be found through injunctive relief.

Injunctive Relief An *injunction* is an order issued by a court directing that a party do or refrain from doing something. An injunction may be either temporary or permanent. A temporary injunction is issued as a means of delaying further activity in any contested matter until the court determines whether a permanent injunction should be entered or the injunction should be removed entirely. One who disobeys an injunction does so under threat of penalty of contempt of court.

quick quiz 12-6

1. Actual damages are also called compensatory damages. true | false
2. Punitive damages cover any expenses paid out by the innocent party to prevent further loss. true | false
3. The courts order specific performance only when the subject matter of a contract is unique or rare. true | false

Summary

12.1 Third parties are, at times, given benefits through a contract made between two other parties. Some contracts are made specifically to benefit a third party. Such a third party is known as a third-party beneficiary. Three types of intended beneficiaries include creditor beneficiaries, donee beneficiaries, and insurance beneficiaries. Some third parties benefit from a contract even though the contract was not made for their benefit. These parties are known as incidental beneficiaries.

12.2 The transfer of contract rights to a third party outside of the original agreement is an assignment. In general, rights are assigned, and duties are delegated. However, the rules apply to both transfers in the same way. The party who assigns rights or delegates duties is the assignor. The outside third party to whom the assignment is made is the assignee. The remaining party to the original agreement is the obligor. The assignee must give notice of assignment to the obligor.

12.3 The rights and duties of the assignee are the same as those held by the assignor under the original agreement. Contracts for personal or professional services cannot be assigned. Assignments also can be limited by agreement. A novation occurs when two contracting parties agree to replace one of the parties with a new party.

12.4 Most contracts are discharged by performance, which means that the parties do what they agreed to do.

Unless the parties agree otherwise, satisfactory performance will be determined by objective standards. Substantial performance will discharge the agreement with the right to reimbursement for correcting details that were not completed. Conditions may determine the rights and duties of the parties prior to performance, during performance, and following performance. If neither party makes tender, a breach of contract is not established.

12.5 Nonperformance can discharge contractual obligations. Not every instance of nonperformance results in a breach of contract. Parties can agree to discharge a contractual obligation by terms in the contract, mutual rescission, waiver, novation, accord and satisfaction, or general release. Contractual obligations can also be discharged when it becomes impossible to perform a contract or under the frustration-of-purpose doctrine. These obligations can also be discharged by operation of law under principles of bankruptcy and the statute of limitations.

12.6 An injured party is released from any obligations under the contract following the other party's breach. In addition, the injured party has the right to ask a court of law for a remedy. The usual remedy is the payment of damages in the form of money. When the payment of monetary damages is not enough, the injured party will ask the court for rescission, specific performance, or an injunction.

Key Terms

abandonment of contractual obligations, 346
actual damages, 347
anticipatory breach, 346
assignee, 333
assignment, 333
assignor, 333
beneficiary, 331
commercial impracticability, 345
compensatory damages, 347
complete performance, 340
condition concurrent, 342
condition precedent, 341
condition subsequent, 342
consequential damages, 347
creditor beneficiary, 332
delegation, 333
donee beneficiary, 332
fraud (or fraudulent misrepresentation), 347
fraudulent conveyance, 333
frustration-of-purpose doctrine, 344
general release, 344
incidental beneficiary, 332
incidental damages, 347
injunction, 351
intended beneficiary, 331
liquidated damages, 348
mutual rescission, 343
nominal damages, 347
novation, 338
obligor, 333
outside party, 331
performance, 339
punitive damages, 347
reasonable time, 339
satisfactory performance, 340
specific performance, 350
speculative damages, 350
stipulated damages, 348
substantial performance, 340
tender of payment, 342
tender of performance, 342
termination by waiver, 343
third party, 331
third-party beneficiary, 331
warranty, 336

Questions for Review and Discussion

1. What are the legal rights given to all beneficiaries?
2. What are the legal rights given to incidental beneficiaries?
3. What is involved in an assignment of rights and a delegation of duties?
4. What is a novation?
5. What constitutes the satisfactory performance of a contract?
6. What is the difference between complete and substantial performance?
7. How can a contract be discharged by nonperformance?
8. What is anticipatory repudiation?
9. What types of damages are available in the event of a breach of contract?
10. What is the difference between specific performance and injunctive relief?

Cases for Analysis

1. Lee Wesley agreed to lay cement on the driveway leading up to Walter Lerro's house for $24,000. Plans and specifications were provided by Lerro. Wesley delegated the duties involved in laying the asphalt to Hanover Construction Inc., another contractor. Hanover then assigned the right to collect the $24,000 from Lerro to Olsen Construction Supplies Ltd. Lerro, who did not like the way his job and his money were being bounced all over the tri-county area, refused to pay Olsen. Lerro then called Wesley and ordered him to tear out the driveway because he was insulted by the fact that Wesley thought so little of his job that he had assigned it to Hanover. Identify each of the parties in this case as assignor, assignee, or obligor. Was Lerro within his rights when he refused to pay Olsen and when he ordered Wesley to remove the driveway? Explain.
2. Under a divorce decree, Blackston was ordered to pay $600 a month in child support to his former wife. The decree provided that the payments were to be paid to the clerk of the court's office. The clerk of the court assigned the right to receive the payments to the Department of Human Resources.

Who was obligated to notify Blackston of the assignment? [See: *Blackston v. State Ex Rel. Blackston*, 585 So.2d 58 (AL).]

3. Gary Jones retained the law firm of Irace and Lowry after being injured in a motorcycle accident. Later, Jones required surgery after dislocating his shoulder in an unrelated incident. Having no money to pay the surgeon, Jones signed a letter requesting that the money from the accident settlement be assigned to Dr. Herzog for treatment of a shoulder injury that occurred at a different time. The law firm was notified of the assignment. When the settlement was received by the law firm, Jones instructed the firm to pay the money to him rather than to the surgeon. It did, and the surgeon was never paid. Could Dr. Herzog recover the money owed him from the law firm? Why or why not? [See: *Herzog v. Irace*, 594 A.2d 1106 (ME).]

4. Copeland contracted with McDonald's Systems Inc. for a franchise. Copeland was granted the fast-food outlet franchise for Omaha. McDonald's also gave Copeland first refusal rights for any plans to open other franchise outlets in Omaha. Copeland exercised the right several times, opening several additional outlets. He then sold the franchise to Schupack and assigned to Schupack the right to open new McDonald's outlets in Omaha. When Schupack tried to exercise the first refusal right, McDonald's objected, claiming its relationship with Copeland developed through a special confidence in Copeland's ability to manage and promote its new franchise outlets. Was McDonald's correct? Explain. [See: *Schupack v. McDonald's Systems, Inc.*, 264 N.W.2d 827 (NE).]

5. Timbercrest built a house for the Murphys. After occupying the house for a while, the Murphys complained of several problems. Timbercrest fixed the problems, and the Murphys had no further complaints. The Litwins bought the house from the Murphys three years later. When the house was sold, neither the Litwins nor the Murphys were aware of any problems. After living in the house for two years, the Litwins became aware of several problems. The Litwins then contacted the Murphys and had the Murphys assign them their rights under the original construction agreement with Timbercrest. The Litwins then sued Timbercrest, claiming Timbercrest had breached its contract with the Murphys by not providing them with a house free of defects. Were the Litwins correct? [See: *Litwins v. Timbercrest Estates, Inc.*, 347 N.E.2d 378 (IL).]

6. Nolan wrote the song "Tumbling Tumbleweeds" and, in an agreement with Sam Fox Publishing Company, transferred all rights to the song to the company. In return, Nolan was to receive royalties according to terms laid out in the agreement. Sam Fox later assigned all rights and interests in "Tumbling Tumbleweeds" to Williamson Music Inc. Was it necessary for Sam Fox to obtain Nolan's consent before making the assignment to Williamson? Explain. [See: *Nolan v. Williamson Music, Inc.*, 300 F. Supp. 1311 (S.D. NY).]

7. When Kent contracted to have his new house constructed, he specifically noted that the plumbing must be made by Reading manufacturers. After the house had been completed, Kent did an inspection tour during which he discovered that, though much of the plumbing had come from Reading, some parts did not. After making his discovery, Kent demanded that the non-Reading plumbing fixtures be replaced with the supplies he had specified in the contract. In addition, Kent refused to pay the contractor until the proper plumbing supplies were added to the house. The contractor brought suit against Kent, arguing that though there were minor deviations from certain specified parts of the contract concerning the plumbing fixtures, he had nevertheless substantially performed his end of the deal. Kent stuck to his strict construction of the contract and labeled the contractor's performance unsatisfactory. He thus claimed to be released from the agreement unless the contractor lived up to every term in the original agreement. Who should prevail in this case? Explain. [See: *Jacob and Young v. Kent*, 129 N.E. 889.]

8. Sai Grafio agreed to paint Gerald Weaver and Katherine Brewer's house for $5,650. Weaver and Brewer paid for the paint job in installments but stopped payment on the final $1,845 check, claiming that Grafio had breached the contract by doing a poor job. The lower court judge found that the only defect in the paint job was a footprint left on the roof that would cost $50 to repair. How much money, if any, and under what legal theory, did the court allow Grafio to recover for the paint job? [See: *Weaver v. Grafio*, 595 A.2d 983 (DC).]

9. Arthur Murray Inc. and Parker entered a series of contracts under which Arthur Murray agreed to teach Parker how to dance. Under the terms of

each agreement, refunds were impossible, and the lessons could not be canceled. After the contracts were entered, Parker suffered a permanent disability that made it physically impossible for him to dance. When Arthur Murray refused to refund any part of Parker's money, he sued to rescind the contracts on grounds of impossibility. Arthur Murray claimed that the non-refund clause must be upheld by the court. Was Arthur Murray correct? Explain. [See: *Parker v. Arthur Murray, Inc.*, 295 N.E.2d 487 (IL).]

10. Bob Pagan Ford Inc. hired Smith to work as a car salesperson in Galveston County. As part of his contract, Smith agreed not to work as an auto salesperson in Galveston County for three years after leaving his employment with Bob Pagan Ford. Smith worked for Bob Pagan for only a few months. He then left and took a sales job with another dealership in Galveston County. Was injunctive relief an appropriate remedy in this case? Explain. [See: *Bob Pagan Ford, Inc., v. Smith*, 638 S.W.2d 176 (TX).]

quick quiz Answers

12-1	12-2	12-3	12-4	12-5	12-6
1. T	1. F	1. F	1. F	1. T	1. T
2. T	2. F	2. F	2. T	2. F	2. F
3. F	3. F	3. F	3. T	3. T	3. T

Part 2 Case Study

Sylvia Burwell, Secretary of Health and Human Services, et al. v. Hobby Lobby Stores, Inc., et al. (AKA *The Hobby Lobby Case*)
United States Supreme Court
Nos. 13-354 and 13-356 (June 30, 2014)
573 U.S. ____ (2014)

Summary

This case, which is usually referred to as *The Hobby Lobby Case*, began before any of the corporations involved had any knowledge that a lawsuit was in their future. The events that precipitated the lawsuit began when Congress passed the Patient Protection and Affordable Care Act (ACA) in 2012. The goal of the act was to make certain that all (well, at least most) Americans had health care insurance. The mechanism by which this was to be accomplished was a mandate that all employers who had more than 50 workers employed on a full-time basis would have to provide "a group health plan or group health insurance coverage" that would give those employees "minimum essential coverage." [26 USC Section 5000 A (f) (2); Sections 4980 H (a) and (c) (2).] To enforce the law, Congress attached stiff penalties, in the form of heavy fines, for employers who failed to obey the law. (In the case of Hobby Lobby, for example, those fines would have been more than $1.3 million daily for a total of $475 million annually.) Part of this health care package required that the insurance plan provide "preventative care and screenings" for women that would be free from "any cost sharing requirements." [42 USC Section 300gg-13(a) (4).] The statute did not identify the kind of prevention; rather, it empowered the Department of Health and Human Services (HHS) acting through the Health Resources and Services Administration (HRSA), one of the department's subdivisions, to make that determination. The HRSA took immediate steps to fulfill that assignment by calling on the Institute of Medicine. The institute endorsed the idea that employers should be compelled to provide coverage for all contraceptive procedures approved by the Food and Drug Administration. Four of these methods are designed to stop the development of an already fertilized egg. These four methods are at the heart of this case.

The HHS also issued regulations that would exempt specific not-for-profit religious institutions from participating in the coverage of these contraceptive devices. Any nonprofit religious organization that had genuine religious convictions against such methods could notify their insurer of their objection, and the insurer would then eliminate that part of the plan from the institution's coverage and cover the cost with no cost sharing penalty for the employee. Other plans that did not cover contraceptive methods were grandfathered into the new act with no penalty. This provision allowed that coverage to continue without complying with the act's contraceptive provisions. Also, based on the fundamental requirements of the ACA, employers with less than 50 workers were also exempt. Those original provisions would not compel them to participate in the offering of such contraceptive methods to their employees.

These rules and the exemptions did not anticipate religious objections from certain closely held profit-making companies that are owned and operated by a few individuals who have strong, authentic religious objections to the use of the contraceptive methods in question here. Three corporations in particular fell into this category, and each one felt so strongly about the issue that they brought suit against the secretary of the Department of Health and Human Services. These three companies are Conestoga Wood Specialties, owned and operated by Norman and Elizabeth Hahn and their three sons, who belong to the Mennonite Church; Hobby Lobby, a national chain of arts and craft stores owned and operated by David and Barbara Green and their three children, all of whom are devoted Christians; and Mardel, a chain of Christian bookstores owned and operated by one of the Greens' sons. In each of these lawsuits, the plaintiffs issued very clear and obviously sincere position statements defending their religious objection to being compelled to join in the coverage of what they considered a morally bankrupt practice. The lawsuit was brought under the authority of the Religious Freedom Restoration Act (RFRA) and the Free Exercise Clause of the Constitution.

The RFRA states that the government cannot "substantially burden a person's exercise of religion even if the burden results from a rule of general applicability" except when the government "demonstrates that the application of the burden to the person (1) is in furtherance of a compelling governmental interest; and (2) is the least restrictive means of furthering that compelling governmental interest." [42 USC Sections 2000bb-1(a)(b).] The threshold issue before the Court is whether the three corporate plaintiffs qualify as "legal persons" under the RFRA. The Court begins by noting that the goal of the RFRA is to make certain that a wide berth is given to individuals in the exercise of their religious beliefs. As the name of the act implies, congressional intent was to rebuild a layer of defense for religion that had been eroded over the years by the decisions of the judicial branch. In restoring the balance in favor of religious freedom rather than governmental power, Congress was, in essence, redirecting the courts to rebuild that lost defensive layer. Accordingly, that protection must be broadened, not narrowed. While it is true that the legal fiction of a corporation does create an entity that is separate from the founders, the purpose of that protective layer is not to protect the fiction in and of itself. Rather, that protection was built to defend real flesh and blood people. When the law defines the rights and duties of a corporation, it is actually defining the rights and duties of the people behind those corporations. They are the ones who must carry out corporate duties and who benefit from corporate rights. Thus, when the corporation is given property rights, those property rights really belong to the people. This is especially true when the right in question is a religious right. Thus, the Court in this case states with some conviction that the term *person* in the statute is not meant to protect corporate "persons" because the real protection flows to the people behind that corporate veil.

Having disposed of the "person" argument, the Court moves on to the second argument made by the defense and supported by several lower court judges as well as by the principal dissent. That argument states that Hobby Lobby, Conestoga, and Mardel do not deserve the protection afforded by the RFRA because their principal objective is to earn a profit, not to promote religious values. The Court finds this argument weak at best. The Court acknowledges that it is conceivable that a law can be enacted by the government that makes the practice of a particular religion more expensive and thus more difficult. To demonstrate this point, the Court refers to the case of *Braunfield v. Brown* [366 U.S. 599 (1961)], in which the Supreme Court acknowledged that forcing Jewish shop owners to remain closed on Sunday in addition to being closed on Saturday, which was required by their faith, might place an unfair burden on their constitutional right to the free exercise of their religion, even though the direct consequence of the prohibition was a loss of profits. Although the business owners lost the case, the right of profit-making businesses to bring free exercise cases was affirmed by the Court. The Court also notes that the several lower courts have erroneously held that the Free Exercise Clause and the RFRA do not protect profit-making businesses because their only purpose is to earn a profit, not to promote religious values. The Court points out that this is patently false in the modern view of corporate law, which has held repeatedly that corporations have civic and public duties beyond making a profit for their shareholders. Moreover, the plaintiffs in this case have repeatedly demonstrated that their corporations do have religious goals.

In a lengthy footnote, the court also makes a point that is directly related to our study of contract law. The Court notes that the dissent argues that the historical development of business in the common law does not support the notion that "lay corporations" (as opposed to ecclesiastical corporations) can have any religious function. This, as we saw in our lengthy examination of the historical development of the law merchant and its merger with common law, is simply not true. In fact, no matter which version of history we accept, the Church was closely allied with the development of the capitalist business system. Max Weber, for example, in *The Protestant Ethic: The Spirit of Capitalism*, defends the proposition that European capitalism began with the Protestant Reformation in the 16th century. Protestantism, primarily in the form of Puritanism, Separatism, and Calvinism, promoted the idea that the accumulation of wealth was a fairly good sign that the merchant who so prospered was among the elect and, therefore, bound for heaven. In a similar vein, Rodney Stark in his book, *The Victory of Reason: How Christianity Led to Freedom, Capitalism, and Western Science*, argues, rather convincingly, that one of the driving forces behind the growth of capitalism was the Roman Catholic Church. The medieval Church had the ability to redirect capitalism as it did because, as a system, the Roman Catholic Church had a strong central controlling agent and a concentration, rather than a dispersal, of power among various actors.

Thus, the Church helped provide a rational and moral foundation for the principles and procedures that guided the activities of merchants in their communities, their courts, and in the making of their contracts. The Church, which is directed by a central powerful leader, refused to condemn commercial activity. Instead, the Church monitored how those activities were carried out. In short, the Church encouraged this new class of sellers to establish guilds that followed the law of the Church, a legal tradition that is generally referred to as canon law. The Church also insisted that these emerging businessmen never engage in deceit or dishonesty and always follow a good faith approach to contract development. As long as they followed these basic precepts, the Church reassured the members of the new and expanding class of professional sellers that there was nothing inherently wrong with making a profit in their chosen profession. Finally, Berman in his study of the growth of the law merchant, *Law and Revolution: The Formation of the Western Legal Tradition*, states that from the very beginning, merchants were involved in the courts that heard and settled contract disputes and commercial differences. Involvement meant that, as a system, the law merchant, like the Roman Catholic Church, had a strong central controlling agent and a concentration, rather than a dispersal, of power. This allowed the law merchant to direct, at least to a certain degree, the other characteristics of neutrality, universality, mutuality, integration, and evolution, all of which have an ethical basis. (Reproduced below is that portion of the Court's opinion that corresponds to this analysis. Footnote numerals are included but the citations themselves and explanatory notes are omitted.)

The Court's Opinion

Delivered by Justice Alito

At issue in these cases are HHS regulations promulgated under the Patient Protection and Affordable Care Act of 2010 (ACA), 124 Stat. 119. ACA generally requires employers with 50 or more full-time employees to offer "a group health plan or group health insurance coverage" that provides "minimum essential coverage." 26 U.S.C. §5000A (f)(2); §§4980H(a), (c)(2). Any covered employer that does not provide such coverage must pay a substantial price. Specifically, if a covered employer provides group health insurance but its plan fails to comply with ACA's group-health-plan requirements, the employer may be required to pay $100 per day for each affected "individual." §§4980D (a)-(b). And if the employer decides to stop providing health insurance altogether and at least one full-time employee enrolls in a health plan and qualifies for a subsidy on one of the government-run ACA exchanges, the employer must pay $2,000 per year for each of its full-time employees. §§4980H (a), (c) (1).

Unless an exception applies, ACA requires an employer's group health plan or group-health-insurance coverage to furnish "preventive care and screenings" for women without "any cost sharing requirements." 42 U.S.C. §300gg–13(a) (4). Congress itself, however, did not specify what types of preventive care must be covered. Instead, Congress authorized the Health Resources and Services Administration (HRSA), a component of HHS, to make that important and sensitive decision. *Ibid*. The HRSA in turn consulted the Institute of Medicine, a nonprofit group of volunteer advisers, in determining which preventive services to require. See 77 Fed. Reg. 8725–8726 (2012).

In August 2011, based on the Institute's recommendations, the HRSA promulgated the Women's Preventive Services Guidelines. *See id*., at 8725–8726, and n. 1; online at http://hrsa.gov/womensguidelines (all Internet materials as visited June 26, 2014, and available in Clerk of Court's case file). The Guidelines provide that nonexempt employers are generally required to provide "coverage, without cost sharing" for "[a]ll Food and Drug Administration [(FDA)] approved contraceptive methods, sterilization procedures, and patient education and counseling." 77 Fed. Reg. 8725 (internal quotation marks omitted). Although many of the required, FDA-approved methods of contraception work by preventing the fertilization of an egg, four of those methods (those specifically at issue in these cases) may have the effect of preventing an already fertilized egg from developing any further by inhibiting its attachment to the uterus. Brief for HHS 9 Cite as: 573 U.S. ____ (2014) in No. 13-354, pp. 9-10, n. 4;[6] FDA, Birth Control: Medicines to Help You.[7]

HHS also authorized the HRSA to establish exemptions from the contraceptive mandate for "religious employers." 45 CFR §147.131(a). That category encompasses "churches, their integrated auxiliaries, and conventions or associations of churches," as well as "the exclusively religious activities of any religious order." See *ibid* (citing 26 U.S.C. §§6033(a) (3)(A)(i), (iii)). In its Guidelines, HRSA exempted these organizations from the requirement to cover contraceptive services. See http://hrsa.gov/womensguidelines.

In addition, HHS has effectively exempted certain religious nonprofit organizations, described under HHS regulations as "eligible organizations," from the contraceptive mandate. See 45 CFR §147.131(b); 78 Fed. Reg.39874 (2013). An "eligible organization" means a nonprofit organization that "holds itself out as a religious organization" and "opposes providing coverage for some or all of any contraceptive services required to be covered . . . on account of religious objections." 45 CFR §147.131(b). To qualify for this accommodation, an employer must certify that it is such an organization. §147.131(b)(4). When a group-health-insurance issuer receives notice that one of its clients has invoked this provision, the issuer must then exclude contraceptive coverage from the employer's plan and provide separate payments for contraceptive services for plan participants without imposing any cost-sharing requirements on the eligible organization, its insurance plan, or its employee beneficiaries. §147.131(c).[8] Although this procedure requires the issuer to bear the cost of these services, HHS has determined that this obligation will not impose any net expense on issuers because its cost will be less than or equal to the cost savings resulting from the services. 78 Fed. Reg. 39877.[9]

In addition to these exemptions for religious organizations, ACA exempts a great many employers from most of its coverage requirements. Employers providing "grandfathered health plans"—those that existed prior to March 23, 2010, and that have not made specified changes after that date—need not comply with many of the Act's requirements, including the contraceptive mandate. 42 U.S.C. §§18011(a), (e). And employers with fewer than 50 employees are not required to provide health insurance at all. 26 U.S.C. §4980H(c)(2).

All told, the contraceptive mandate "presently does not apply to tens of millions of people." 723 F. 3d 1114, 1143 (CA10 2013). This is attributable, in large part, to grandfathered health plans: Over one-third of the 149 million nonelderly people in America with employer-sponsored health plans were enrolled in grandfathered plans in 2013. Brief for HHS in No. 13-354, at 53; Kaiser Family Foundation & Health Research & Educational Trust, Employer Health Benefits, 2013 Annual Survey 43, 221.[10] The count for employees working for firms that do not have to provide insurance at all because they employ fewer than 50 employees is 34 million workers. See The Whitehouse, Health Reform for Small Businesses: The Affordable Care Act Increases Choice and Saving Money for Small Businesses 1.[11]

II A

Norman and Elizabeth Hahn and their three sons are devout members of the Mennonite Church, a Christian denomination. The Mennonite Church opposes abortion and believes that "[t]he fetus in its earliest stages . . . shares humanity with those who conceived it."[12]

Fifty years ago, Norman Hahn started a wood-working business in his garage, and since then, this company, Conestoga Wood Specialties, has grown and now has 950 employees. Conestoga is organized under Pennsylvania law as a for-profit corporation. The Hahns exercise sole ownership of the closely held business; they control its board of directors and hold all of its voting shares. One of the Hahn sons serves as the president and CEO.

The Hahns believe that they are required to run their business "in accordance with their religious beliefs and moral principles." 917 F. Supp. 2d 394, 402 (ED Pa. 2013). To that end, the company's mission, as they see it, is to "operate in a professional environment founded upon the highest ethical, moral, and Christian principles." *Ibid.* (internal quotation marks omitted). The company's "Vision and Values Statements" affirms that Conestoga endeavors to "ensur[e] a reasonable profit in [a] manner that reflects [the Hahns'] Christian heritage." App. in No. 13-356, p. 94 (complaint).

As explained in Conestoga's board-adopted "Statement on the Sanctity of Human Life," the Hahns believe that "human life begins at conception." 724 F. 3d 377, 382, and n. 5 (CA3 2013) (internal quotation marks omitted). It is therefore "against [their] moral conviction to be involved in the termination of human life" after conception, which they believe is a "sin against God to which they are held accountable." *Ibid.* (internal quotation marks omitted). The Hahns have accordingly excluded from the group health-insurance plan they offer to their employees certain contraceptive methods that they consider to be abortifacients. *Id.*, at 382.

The Hahns and Conestoga sued HHS and other federal officials and agencies under RFRA and the Free Exercise Clause of the First Amendment, seeking to enjoin application of ACA's contraceptive mandate insofar as it requires them to provide health-insurance coverage for four FDA approved contraceptives that may operate after the fertilization of an egg.[13] These include two forms of emergency contraception commonly called "morning after" pills and two types of intrauterine devices.[14]

In opposing the requirement to provide coverage for the contraceptives to which they object, the Hahns argued that "it is immoral and sinful for [them] to intentionally participate in, pay for, facilitate, or otherwise support these drugs." *Ibid.* The District Court denied a preliminary injunction, see 917 F. Supp. 2d, at 419, and the Third Circuit affirmed in a divided opinion, holding that "for profit, secular corporations cannot engage in religious exercise" within the meaning of RFRA or the First Amendment. 724 F. 3d, at 381. The Third Circuit also rejected the claims brought by the Hahns themselves because it concluded that the HHS "[m]andate does not impose any requirements on the Hahns" in their personal capacity. *Id.*, at 389.

B.

David and Barbara Green and their three children are Christians who own and operate two family businesses. Forty-five years ago, David Green started an arts and crafts store that has grown into a nationwide chain called Hobby Lobby. There are now 500 Hobby Lobby stores, and the company has more than 13,000 employees. 723 F. 3d, at 1122. Hobby Lobby is organized as a for-profit corporation under Oklahoma law.

One of David's sons started an affiliated business, Mardel, which operates 35 Christian bookstores and employs close to 400 people. *Ibid.* Mardel is also organized as a for-profit corporation under Oklahoma law.

Though these two businesses have expanded over the years, they remain closely held, and David, Barbara, and their children retain exclusive control of both companies. *Ibid.* David serves as the CEO of Hobby Lobby, and his three children serve as the president, vice president, and vice CEO. See Brief for Respondents in No. 13-354, p. 8.[15]

Hobby Lobby's statement of purpose commits the Greens to "[h]onoring the Lord in all [they] do by operating the company in a manner consistent with Biblical principles." App. in No. 13-354, pp. 134-135 (complaint). Each family member has signed a pledge to run the businesses in accordance with the family's religious beliefs and to use the family assets to support Christian ministries. 723 F. 3d, at 1122. In accordance with those commitments, Hobby Lobby and Mardel stores close on Sundays, even though the Greens calculate that they lose millions in sales annually by doing so. *Id.*, at 1122; App. in No. 13- 354, at 136-137. The businesses refuse to engage in profitable transactions that facilitate or promote alcohol use; they contribute profits to Christian missionaries and ministries; and they buy hundreds of full-page newspaper ads inviting people to "know Jesus as Lord and Savior." *Ibid.* (internal quotation marks omitted).

Like the Hahns, the Greens believe that life begins at conception and that it would violate their religion to facilitate access to contraceptive drugs or devices that operate after that point. 723 F. 3d, at 1122. They specifically object to the same four contraceptive methods as the Hahns and, like the Hahns, they have no objection to the other 16 FDA-approved methods of birth control. *Id.*, at 1125. Although their group-health-insurance plan predates the enactment of ACA, it is not a grandfathered plan because Hobby Lobby elected not to retain grandfathered status before the contraceptive mandate was proposed. *Id.*, at 1124.

The Greens, Hobby Lobby, and Mardel sued HHS and other federal agencies and officials to challenge the contraceptive mandate under RFRA and the Free Exercise Clause.[16] The District Court denied a preliminary injunction, see 870 F. Supp. 2d 1278 (WD Okla. 2012), and the plaintiffs appealed, moving for initial en banc consideration. The Tenth Circuit granted that motion and reversed in a divided opinion. Contrary to the conclusion of the Third Circuit, the Tenth Circuit held that the Greens' two for-profit businesses are "persons" within the meaning of RFRA and therefore may bring suit under that law.

The court then held that the corporations had established a likelihood of success on their RFRA claim. 723 F. 3d, at 1140-1147. The court concluded that the contraceptive mandate substantially burdened the exercise of religion by requiring the companies to choose between "compromis[ing] their religious beliefs" and paying a heavy fee—either "close to $475 million more in taxes every year" if they simply refused to provide coverage for the contraceptives at issue, or "roughly $26 million" annually if they "drop [ped] health-insurance benefits for all employees." *Id.*, at 1141.

The court next held that HHS had failed to demonstrate a compelling interest in enforcing the mandate against the Greens' businesses and, in the alternative, that HHS had failed to prove that enforcement of the mandate was the "least restrictive means" of furthering the Government's asserted interests. *Id.*, at 1143-1144 (emphasis deleted; internal quotation marks omitted). After concluding that the companies had "demonstrated irreparable harm," the court reversed and remanded for the District Court to consider the remaining factors of the preliminary injunction test. *Id.*, at 1147.[17]

We granted certiorari. 571 U.S. ___ (2013).

III A

RFRA prohibits the "Government [from] substantially burden[ing] a *person's* exercise of religion even if the burden results from a rule of general applicability" unless the Government "demonstrates that application of the burden to *the person*—(1) is in furtherance of a compelling governmental interest; and (2) is the least restrictive means of furthering that compelling governmental interest." 42 U.S.C. §§2000bb-1(a), (b) (emphasis added). The first question that we must address is whether this provision applies to regulations that govern the activities of for-profit corporations like Hobby Lobby, Conestoga, and Mardel.

HHS contends that neither these companies nor their owners can even be heard under RFRA. According to HHS, the companies cannot sue because they seek to make a profit for their owners, and the owners cannot be heard because the regulations, at least as a formal matter, apply only to the companies and not to the owners as individuals. HHS's argument would have dramatic consequences.

Consider this Court's decision in *Braunfeld* v. *Brown*, 366 U.S. 599 (1961) (plurality opinion). In that case, five Orthodox Jewish merchants who ran small retail businesses in Philadelphia challenged a Pennsylvania Sunday closing law as a violation of the Free Exercise Clause. Because of their faith, these merchants closed their shops on Saturday, and they argued that requiring them to remain shut on Sunday threatened them with financial ruin. The Court entertained their claim (although it ruled against them on the merits), and if a similar claim were raised today under RFRA against a jurisdiction still subject to the Act (for example, the District of Columbia, see 42 U.S.C. §2000bb-2(2)), the merchants would be entitled to be heard. According to HHS, however, if these merchants chose to incorporate their businesses—without in any way changing the size or nature of their businesses—they would forfeit all RFRA (and free-exercise) rights. HHS would put these merchants to a difficult choice: either give up the right to seek judicial protection of their religious liberty or forgo the benefits, available to their competitors, of operating as corporations.

As we have seen, RFRA was designed to provide very broad protection for religious liberty. By enacting RFRA, Congress went far beyond what this Court has held is constitutionally required.[18] Is there any reason to think that the Congress that enacted such sweeping protection put small-business owners to the choice that HHS suggests? An examination of RFRA's text, to which we turn in the next part of this opinion, reveals that Congress did no such thing.

As we will show, Congress provided protection for people like the Hahns and Greens by employing a familiar legal fiction: It included corporations within RFRA's definition of "persons." But it is important to keep in mind that the purpose of this fiction is to provide protection for human beings. A corporation is simply a form of organization used by human beings to achieve desired ends. An established body of law specifies the rights and obligations of the *people* (including shareholders, officers, and employees) who are associated with a corporation in one way or another. When rights, whether constitutional or statutory, are extended to corporations, the purpose is to protect the rights of these people. For example, extending Fourth Amendment protection to corporations protects the privacy interests of employees and others associated with the company. Protecting corporations from government seizure of their property without just compensation protects all those who have a stake in the corporations' financial well-being. And protecting the free-exercise rights of corporations like Hobby Lobby, Conestoga, and Mardel protects the religious liberty of the humans who own and control those companies.

In holding that Conestoga, as a "secular, for-profit corporation," lacks RFRA protection, the Third Circuit wrote as follows:

> "General business corporations do not, *separate and apart from the actions or belief systems of their individual owners or employees*, exercise religion. They do not pray, worship, observe sacraments or take other religiously motivated actions separate and apart from the intention and direction of their individual actors." 724 F. 3d, at 385 (emphasis added).

All of this is true—but quite beside the point. Corporations, "separate and apart from" the human beings who own, run, and are employed by them, cannot do anything at all.

B 1

As we noted above, RFRA applies to "a person's" exercise of religion, 42 U.S.C. §§2000bb-1(a), (b), and RFRA itself does not define the term "person." We therefore look to the Dictionary Act, which we must consult "[i]n determining the meaning of any Act of Congress, unless the context indicates otherwise." 1 U.S.C. §1.

Under the Dictionary Act, "the wor[d] 'person' . . . include[s] corporations, companies, associations, firms, partnerships, societies, and joint stock companies, as well as individuals." *Ibid.*; see *FCC* v. *AT&T Inc.*, 562 U.S.___, ___(2011) (slip op., at 6) ("We have no doubt that 'person,' in a legal setting, often refers to artificial entities. The Dictionary Act makes that clear"). Thus, unless there is something about the RFRA context that "indicates otherwise," the Dictionary Act provides a quick, clear, and affirmative answer to the question whether the companies involved in these cases may be heard.

We see nothing in RFRA that suggests a congressional intent to depart from the Dictionary Act definition, and HHS makes little effort to argue otherwise. We have entertained RFRA and free-exercise claims brought by nonprofit corporations, see *Gonzales* v. *O Centro Spirit Beneficiate Union do Vegetal*, 546 U.S. 418 (2006) (RFRA); *Hosanna-Tabor Evangelical Lutheran Church and School* v. *EEOC*, 565 U.S. ___ (2012) (Free Exercise); *Church of the Lucama Babel Aye, Inc.* v. *Hialeah*, 508 U.S. 520 (1993) (Free Exercise), and HHS concedes that a nonprofit corporation can be a "person" within the meaning of RFRA. See Brief for HHS in No. 13-354, at 17; 20 Reply Brief in No. 13-354, at 7-8.[19]

This concession effectively dispatches any argument that the term "person" as used in RFRA does not reach the closely held corporations involved in these cases. No known understanding of the term "person" includes some but not all corporations. The term "person" sometimes encompasses artificial persons (as the Dictionary Act instructs), and it sometimes is limited to natural persons. But no conceivable definition of the term includes natural persons and nonprofit corporations, but not for-profit corporations.[20] Cf. *Clark* v. *Martinez*, 543 U.S. 371, 378 (2005) ("To give th[e] same words a different meaning for each category would be to invent a statute rather than interpret one").

2

The principal argument advanced by HHS and the principal dissent regarding RFRA protection for Hobby Lobby, Conestoga, and Mardel focuses not on the statutory term "person," but on the phrase "exercise of religion." According to HHS and the dissent, these corporations are not protected by RFRA because they cannot exercise religion. Neither HHS nor the dissent, however, provides any persuasive explanation for this conclusion.

Is it because of the corporate form? The corporate form alone cannot provide the explanation because, as we have pointed out, HHS concedes that nonprofit corporations can be protected by RFRA. The dissent suggests that nonprofit corporations are special because furthering their religious "autonomy . . . often furthers individual religious freedom as well." *Post*, at 15 (quoting *Corporation of Presiding Bishop of Church of Jesus Christ of Latter-day Saints* v. *Amos*, 483 U.S. 327, 342 (1987) (Brennan, J., concurring in judgment)). But this principle applies equally to for-profit corporations: Furthering their religious freedom also "furthers individual religious freedom." In these cases, for example, allowing Hobby Lobby, Conestoga, and Mardel to assert RFRA claims protects the religious liberty of the Greens and the Hahns.[21]

If the corporate form is not enough, what about the profit-making objective? In *Braunfeld*, 366 U.S. 599, we entertained the free-exercise claims of individuals who were attempting to make a profit as retail merchants, and the Court never even hinted that this objective precluded their claims. As the Court explained in a later case, the "exercise of religion" involves "not only belief and profession but the performance of (or abstention from) physical acts" that are "engaged in for religious reasons." *Smith*, 494 U.S., at 877. Business practices that are compelled or limited by the tenets of a religious doctrine fall comfortably within that definition. Thus, a law that "operates so as to make the practice of . . . religious beliefs more expensive" in the context of business activities imposes a burden on the exercise of religion. *Braunfeld*, supra, at 605; see *United States* v. *Lee*, 455 U.S. 252, 257 (1982) (recognizing that "compulsory participation in the social security system interferes with [Amish employers'] free exercise rights").

If, as *Braunfeld* recognized, a sole proprietorship that seeks to make a profit may assert a free-exercise claim,[22] why can't Hobby Lobby, Conestoga, and Mardel do the same?

Some lower court judges have suggested that RFRA does not protect for-profit corporations because the purpose of such corporations is simply to make money.[23] This argument flies in the face of modern corporate law. "Each American jurisdiction today either expressly or by implication authorizes corporations to be formed under its general corporation act for any *lawful purpose* or business." 1 J. Cox & T. Hazen, Treatise of the Law of Corporations §4:1, p. 224 (3d ed. 2010) (emphasis added); see 1A W. Fletcher, Cyclopedia of the Law of Corporations §102 (rev. ed. 2010). While it is certainly true that a central objective of for-profit corporations is to make money, modern corporate law does not require for-profit corporations to pursue profit at the expense of everything else, and many do not do so. For-profit corporations, with ownership approval, support a wide variety of charitable causes, and it is not at all uncommon for such corporations to further humanitarian and other altruistic objectives. Many examples come readily to mind. So long as its owners agree, a for-profit corporation may take costly pollution-control and energy conservation measures that go beyond what the law requires. A for-profit corporation that operates facilities in other countries may exceed the requirements of local law regarding working conditions and benefits. If for-profit corporations may pursue such worthy objectives, there is no apparent reason why they may not further religious objectives as well.

HHS would draw a sharp line between nonprofit corporations (which, HHS concedes, are protected by RFRA) and for-profit corporations (which HHS would leave unprotected), but the actual picture is less clear-cut. Not all corporations that decline to organize as nonprofits do so in order to maximize profit. For example, organizations with religious and charitable aims might organize as for-profit corporations because of the potential advantages of that corporate form, such as the freedom to participate in lobbying for legislation or campaigning for political candidates who promote their religious or charitable goals.[24] In fact, recognizing the inherent compatibility between establishing a for-profit corporation and pursuing nonprofit goals, States have increasingly adopted laws formally recognizing hybrid corporate forms. Over half of the States, for instance, now recognize the "benefit corporation," a dual-purpose entity that seeks to achieve both a benefit for the public and a profit for its owners.[25]

In any event, the objectives that may properly be pursued by the companies in these cases are governed by the laws of the States in which they were incorporated—Pennsylvania and Oklahoma—and the laws of those States permit for-profit corporations to pursue "any lawful purpose" or "act," including the pursuit of profit in conformity with the owners' religious principles. 15 Pa. Cons. Stat. §1301 (2001) ("Corporations may be incorporated under this subpart for any lawful purpose or purposes"); Okla. Stat., Tit. 18, §§1002, 1005 (West 2012) ("[E]very corporation, whether profit or not for profit" may "be incorporated or organized . . . to conduct or promote any lawful business or purposes"); see also §1006(A)(3); Brief for State of Oklahoma as *Amicus Curiae* in No. 13-354.

ALITO, J., delivered the opinion of the Court, in which ROBERTS, C. J., and SCALIA, KENNEDY, and THOMAS, JJ., joined. KENNEDY, J., filed a concurring opinion. GINSBURG, J., filed a dissenting opinion, in which SOTOMAYOR, J., joined and in which BREYER and KAGAN, JJ., joined as to all but Part III-C-1. BREYER and KAGAN, JJ., filed a dissenting opinion.

Questions for Analysis

1. It should be clear that, contrary to the opinion offered by one of the dissents, that the Church played an enormous role in the development of contract law especially as it related to the growth of the law merchant. How does this realization support the majority opinion in relation to the purpose of a corporation and the relationship of that purpose to the RFRA? Explain.

2. In Chapter 7, the feature *A Question of Ethics* asks the following question: "Should the Church, or perhaps religion in general, be given a stronger voice in the political and economic arena, to help redirect and perhaps even equalize the distribution of wealth?" After reading this case, how would you answer this question? Does this answer differ from the answer you offered when you first read Chapter 7? Why or why not?

3. The history of the law merchant offered by Harold J. Berman that we looked at briefly in Chapter 7 suggests that the law merchant always involved the merchants in the law-making process. In fact, the courts established by the guilds were run by elected guild members. It is likely that these guild leaders would have understood that the law can often make merchants choose between making a profit and following their religious beliefs. Given that knowledge, speculate on just how these guild members might have decided *The Hobby Lobby Case*.

4. Also in Chapter 7, we learned that one of the essential differences between contract law and the other areas of the law is that the duties assumed by the parties to a contract are voluntary. Use that knowledge to develop an argument that supports the dissenting justices in *The Hobby Lobby Case*. Explain.

5. Max Weber, in *The Protestant Ethic: The Spirit of Capitalism*, defends the proposition that European capitalism began with the Protestant Reformation in the 16th century. In a similar vein, Rodney Stark in his book, *The Victory of Reason: How Christianity Led to Freedom, Capitalism, and Western Science*, argues that one of the driving forces behind the growth of capitalism was the Roman Catholic Church. Which view is closer to your own view on the topic? Explain.

6. In Chapter 8, we learned that sometimes the law *acts proactively* and sometimes the law simply *passively reacts*. This knowledge helped explain why the law has acted (or reacted) as it has in the area of cyber-law. Does The *Hobby Lobby Case* reflect *proactive integration* or *passive reaction*? Explain.

7. In Chapter 10, we learned that the most obvious type of illegal contract is one that is designed to obligate someone to commit a crime or a tort. Should there also be a prohibition against contracts that are designed to obligate the parties to do something unethical? Explain.

8. If corporations are legal persons, as Justice Alito suggests in the majority opinion, can they enter contracts that are binding on their shareholders, board members, and officers? Explain.

9. If corporations are legal persons, as Justice Alito suggests in the majority opinion, and if, in fact, they enter contracts that are binding on their shareholders, board members, and officers, what type of signature could they provide on any of those contracts that have to be in writing and signed by the party sought to be bound? Explain.

10. A complex adaptive system (CAS) is a network of interacting conditions that reinforce one another, while at the same time adjusting to change from agents outside and inside the system. In what ways does Justice Alito's opinion in this case reinforce the idea that the law works like a complex adaptive system? Explain.

Source: United States Supreme Court Nos. 13-354 and 13-356 (June 30, 2014) 573 U.S. ____ (2014)

Design Elements: The Opening Case: ©Sharpstock/Alamy; A Classic Case: ©Evlakhov Valeriy/Shutterstock

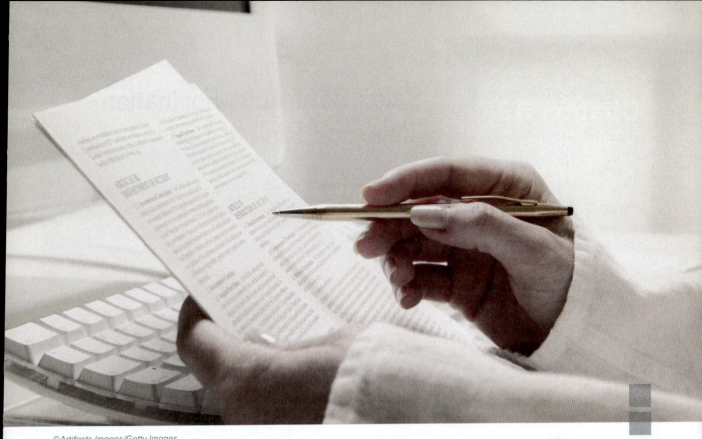

©Artifacts Images/Getty Images

Part Three

Sales and Consumer Protection

Chapter 13	Sales Contracts: Formation, Title, and Risk of Loss	Chapter 15	Product Liability and Consumer Protection
Chapter 14	Sales Contracts: Rights, Duties, Breach, and Warranties	Case Study	*Norcold, Inc. v. Gateway Supply Company*

Chapter 13

Sales Contracts: Formation, Title, and Risk of Loss

13-1 The Sale and Lease of Goods
Sales of Goods • Leases of Goods • Goods and Services

13-2 Rules for Sales Contracts
Good Faith, Course of Dealings, and Usage of Trade • Formation of a Sales Contract

13-3 The Form of a Sales Contract
The Written Sales Contract • Cyber-Sales Contracts • International Law • Auction Sales and Cyber-Auction Fraud

13-4 Title, Passage of Title, and Risk of Loss
Valid Title, Void Title, and Voidable Title • Passage of Title and Risk of Loss

13-5 Sales, Returns, and Insurable Interest
Sale on Approval • Sale or Return • Insurable Interest

THE OPENING CASE *Round 1*
"Some Legal Issues Never Get Truly Resolved. They Just Fade Away."

The story of the case known as *ePresence, Inc. v. Evolve Software, Inc.* began when ePresence entered a contract with Evolve Software, under which Evolve agreed to provide ePresence with a professional service automation system (PSA) that would help ePresence better manage its internal and customer operations. The Evolve PSA that ePresence chose (referred to officially as Evolve, Service Sphere Version 2.5, or, simply, Version 2.5) included three essential elements: (1) multi-currency, (2) international tax, and (3) intercompany capability. The system was incredibly expensive. It would cost ePresence an annual fee of $540,000. In addition, ePresence had to pay an additional $110,000 for installation and customization services and $2,000 per day for training, additional engineering work, and travel expenses. Consequently, it should not be not surprising that ePresence was upset when it learned that Version 2.5 did not feature multi-currency and international taxation support as Evolve had promised. Evolve guaranteed that if ePresence allowed them to install Version 2.5 now, they would provide Version 3.0 later. This was encouraging because Version 3.0 did, in fact, have multi-currency and international taxation support. Consequently, ePresence agreed. Unfortunately, it turned out that, although Version 3.0 had multi-currency and international taxation support, it did not have intercompany capabilities.

At this point, someone from Evolve made a clear oral promise that Evolve would get the system up and running with all the capabilities that ePresence needed, or it would refund all the money that ePresence had spent on the unsatisfactory software. Evolve even delivered a written version of that agreement to ePresence, along with a promise to provide ePresence with an initial progress report of Evolve's solution to the problem. Relying on this promise, ePresence did not terminate the relationship at that point. Unfortunately, Evolve's progress report never materialized. A short time later, the CEO of Evolve admitted that his company had done "a poor job" with the ePresence account. The CEO also reiterated the promise to return the money that ePresence had spent under the contract, if these issues were not resolved. Soon after this, Evolve reported that it would refund $150,000 to ePresence. The change in the total amount reflected what Evolve called the cost of its implementation services already performed on ePresence's behalf. With little hesitation, ePresence refused the reduced amount. Evolve countered with a refund offer of $365,000. Again ePresence refused, saying that a total refund would amount to $680,000. The two companies continued to work on a settlement agreement but failed to reach such an agreement. Through all of this, ePresence adamantly claimed that Evolve had made a clear and enforceable oral contract to pay a full refund. Eventually, once ePresence was convinced that the full refund was not forthcoming, it brought this lawsuit. [See: *ePresence, Inc. v. Evolve Software, Inc.*, 190 F. Supp. 2d 159 U.S. District Court, D. Massachusetts (February 27, 2002).]

Opening Case Questions

1. Is the agreement between ePresence and Evolve a sale-of-goods contract or a service contract? Explain.
2. What law will govern the details of the contract, if it is a sale-of-goods contract? Explain.
3. What law will govern the details of the contract if it is a service contract? Explain.
4. What difference does it make whether it is a service contract or a sale-of-goods contract? Explain.
5. In what way might following the dictates of the Statute of Frauds have solved all of these problems? Explain.

Source: See: *ePresence, Inc. v. Evolve Software, Inc.*, 190 F. Supp. 2d 159 U.S. District Court, D. Massachusetts, (February 27, 2002).

 Learning Objectives

1. Define the term *goods* and explain the nature of a sale.
2. Explain how Article 2 of the UCC applies to contractual relationships.
3. Explain the UCC rules that relate to written contracts.
4. Explain the two laws related to cyber-sales contracts.
5. Contrast an auction with reserve with an auction without reserve.
6. Explain title, void title, and voidable title.
7. Determine when title of goods passes from seller to buyer.
8. Decide when the buyer or seller must bear the risk of loss.
9. Compare a sale on approval with a sale or return.
10. Define an insurable interest.

13-1 The Sale and Lease of Goods

Previously, we discussed the general principles of contract law as they relate to common law principles regardless of what is being purchased or sold. Now we shift our focus to contracts that involve the sale or the lease of goods. Recall that goods are movable, tangible pieces of property such as vehicles, clothing, and electronic devices. As we saw in Chapter 7, much of the law regarding the sale of goods evolved from the law merchant on the European continent. With the Roman Catholic Church supplying political and social support, with canon law providing a moral framework, and with practicality guiding their activities over a 300-year period, the merchants developed a body of active law that was characterized by neutrality, universality, mutuality, involvement, integration, and evolution. The law of sales has gone through many changes over the years. However, throughout all these changes, even those that have integrated advanced cyber-technology into the sales contract, the people responsible for the Uniform Commercial Code (UCC) have attempted to preserve those six basic principles. The UCC, which has been adopted either in whole or in part by every state in the United States, will, therefore, be the focal point of our study of sales law.

UCC 2-105(1)

Sales of Goods

Some medieval version of a 21st-century Madison Avenue advertising executive knew exactly what he was doing when he branded the subject matter of every sales contracts as "goods."

UCC 2-105(2)
UCC 2-106(2)

It would hardly have attracted sales to call them "bads" or to settle on some other mundane label. Nevertheless, as we all know by the time we are old enough to read a Christmas catalog, **goods** are things (other than money, stocks, and bonds) that are tangible, movable, and valuable (to someone). They include crops, timber, and minerals if they are to be sold separately from the real property. Office furniture, mobile homes, milk, wedding pictures, electricity, vehicles, computers, waste paper, kerosene, books, clothing, jewelry, horses, toys, candy, tablets, and baseball caps are all considered goods. Goods that are not yet in existence or under the control of people are called **future goods**. They include fish in the sea, minerals in the ground, goods not yet manufactured, and commodities futures. Whenever anyone buys food in a supermarket, gasoline at a gas station, clothing at a shopping mall, a meal at a restaurant, or even a daily newspaper, a sale of goods occurs. In fact, several sales contracts usually occur for a particular item before the item reaches the consumer and sometimes even after it reaches the consumer.

EXAMPLE 13-1: Sales Contracts at Different Levels

The Steven Andrew Corporation manufactures lawn mowers. The company enters into sales contracts with its suppliers every time it purchases parts and materials to make the mowers. In addition, the company enters into sales contracts with wholesalers when it sells the mowers. Similarly, wholesalers enter into sales contracts when they sell the mowers to retailers. In the same manner, retailers enter into sales contracts when they sell the mowers to consumers. Going even further, consumers enter into sales contracts when they sell their second-hand lawn mowers to other consumers. All of these contracts are governed by the UCC.

UCC Article 2

A gift is not considered a sale because, though title passes, it is not given for a price. Similarly, a bailment (e.g., when an item is left at a store to be sold on consignment) does not meet the definition of a sale because title does not pass between the parties. Article 2 of the UCC applies whenever people buy or sell goods, whether in person, online, over the telephone, or in any other manner. This law applies to sales of goods between private parties and sales of goods by business people or merchants. To determine whether the UCC applies, ask if the contract is a contract for the sale of goods. If the answer is yes, apply the law under the UCC. If the answer is no, apply the common law of contracts. (See Table 13-1.)

BUSINESS LAW WITH UCC APPLICATIONS AND NOW—THE APPLICATIONS

"When to use the UCC and when not to use the UCC, that is the question."

The Uniform Commercial Code is difficult enough to apply to various sales contracts, without the added headache of deciding when to use it and when to call upon other legal rules such as those found in common law, consumer protection law, real property law, employment law, or even the United Nations Convention on Contracts for the International Sale of Goods. Sometimes it helps to stop thinking in terms of words alone and to visualize the relationships that exist between the law in theory and the law in practice. Table 13-1 will help as you try to unravel the differences between contract law in the abstract and contract law within the "real world" of the UCC.

Table 13-1 Different Laws as They Apply to Different Transactions

Transaction	Applicable Law
Contract for the sale of real estate	General contract law (sometimes referred to as common law) and real property law
Contract for employment	General contract law and employment law
Sale of goods between two private parties	UCC (Article 2)
Sale of goods by a merchant to a consumer	UCC (Article 2) and state consumer protection laws
Sale of goods between two merchants	UCC (Article 2)
Contract for a mixture of goods and services—consisting mostly of goods	UCC (Article 2)
Contract for a mixture of goods and services—consisting mostly of services	General contract law
Sale of goods over the Internet	UCC (Article 2)
Sale of goods at an auction	UCC (Article 2)
The leasing of goods	UCC (Article 2A)
International sales of goods	United Nations Convention on Contracts for the International Sale of Goods (CISG)
Sale of stock on the stock market	UCC (Article 8)
The writing of a check, promissory note, or draft	UCC (Article 3)

Leases of Goods

The leasing of goods is governed by Article 2A of the Uniform Commercial Code. This article includes leasing of such things as automobiles, trucks, machinery, computers, furniture, electronic equipment, and all types of tools. Many of the rules that are found in the UCC relating to the sale of goods (discussed in the following chapters) also apply to the leasing of goods under Article 2A of the UCC.

UCC 2A-101-532

Goods and Services

When a contract includes both goods and services, it is referred to as a **mixed**, **blended**, or **hybrid contract**. Such contracts have just enough of the characteristics of both types of contracts to prevent them from being pure sales or service contracts. It is important to identify whether the contract is for goods or services because the law that is applied to the contract will differ depending on the nature of the contract. Sale-of-goods contracts are governed under the UCC, while service contracts are governed by common law rules. Most contracts are clearly one or the other. However, when faced with a genuine hybrid contract, the court will still have to determine which side dominates. To choose the dominant side, the court employs one simple and straightforward rule: Determine the ultimate goal of the parties when the contract was first made. If they wanted a sales contract, they get a sales contract. If they wanted a service contract, that is what they get. Of course, the judge cannot simply ask the parties which contract they wanted because the parties will always (well usually) give conflicting answers. Instead, the court will look at three lines of evidence: (1) the *language* used in the agreement and the situation in which the contract was made; (2) the way that *compensation* was to be handled in the contract; and (3) the relationship between the goods and the services provided under the contract. If the sale of goods is dominant, as when someone purchases a furnace and has it installed, the law under the UCC applies. In contrast, if the performance of services is dominant, as when someone has a furnace repaired and a few new parts are installed, the common law of contracts applies instead.

One type of hybrid contract that has come under close scrutiny lately is any contract that involves the purchase and installation of software. Many software contracts provide both the software package itself (the goods side) and the installation of that software (the service side). These contracts are clearly hybrid contracts. However, despite the fact that software programs have been around for decades, no single test exists to determine when a software contract is a goods contract and when it is a service contract. Certainly, the courts can and do apply the standard tests noted earlier. However, there are many courts that prefer to look at software hybrid contracts as a separate breed and, thus, apply different tests to make a determination. Those courts that have settled on a test seem to favor a strategy known as the **predominant factor test**. This test directs the judge to focus on the whole contract and to take into consideration the purpose of the agreement and the degree of trust that existed between the parties in order to determine if the agreement is a goods contract, with some work involved, or a service contract, with some service involved, almost incidentally. To make this determination, some courts look at a few factors that seem to impact such agreements on a regular basis, such as (1) the language used in the agreement, (2) the value of the software package, (3) the type of business that the software seller is operating, and (4) the billing process handled by the seller.

THE OPENING CASE Round 2
"Some Legal Issues Never Get Truly Resolved. They Just Fade Away."

Evolve Software Inc. promised to provide ePresence with a professional service automation system (PSA) officially designated Evolve, Service Sphere Version 2.5 (or, simply, Version 2.5). Version 2.5 was supposed to add three essential elements to ePresence's computer system: (1) multi-currency, (2) international tax, and (3) intercompany capability. The system would cost ePresence an annual (that's right, "annual"—as in every year from now on) fee of $540,000. On top of that, ePresence had to pay $110,000 to have Evolve install and customize services and another $2,000 each day for training, additional engineering work, and travel expenses. That is probably explains why the management team at ePresence was taken aback when they found out that Version 2.5 did not feature multi-currency and international taxation support as Evolve had promised. To solve the problem, the people at Evolve guaranteed that if the ePresence management team permitted them to install Version 2.5 now, that they would provide Version 3.0 later. This made sense to the ePresence managers because Version 3.0 had the multi-currency and international taxation support they were looking for. As a result, the ePresence folks agreed. To make a long story short, although Version 3.0 had multi-currency and international taxation support, it did not have intercompany capabilities. To make things right, someone from Evolve orally promised that the Evolve techs would get the system up and running with the capabilities that ePresence needed, or Evolve would refund all the money that ePresence had spent on the unsatisfactory software. Evolve even delivered a written version of that agreement to ePresence, along with a promise to provide ePresence with an initial progress report of Evolve's solution to the problem. Because they believed the folks at Evolve, the ePresence people did not pull out of the contract. Sadly, Evolve's progress report never appeared on anyone's desk at ePresence. Remarkably, a short time later, the CEO of Evolve admitted that his company had done "a poor job" with the ePresence account. The CEO also reiterated the promise to return the money that ePresence had spent under the contract if these issues were not resolved. That all sounded good until Evolve announced that it would refund only $150,000 to ePresence. Instantly, ePresence refused the reduced amount and, almost as fast, Evolve countered with a new refund offer of $365,000. As might be expected, ePresence rejected the counteroffer, arguing that a total refund would amount to $680,000.

The case ended up in court. The lawsuit invited some very interesting questions, the first of which was the question of jurisdiction. Evolve is a California company, while ePresence calls Massachusetts its home. Determining which state would host the lawsuit was more than simply a question of who had to get on a plane and fly across the country. It was also a question of which state's law would be applied to decide the questions in the lawsuit. In this case, there were two critical questions: (1) Was the software contract a goods contract or a service contract? (2) Was the oral promise to refund all the money a binding alteration to the written agreement? The procedural issue of state law and the issues of substantive law are key elements in the case. First, the jurisdiction issue was solved by reference to the written agreement. It turned out that the written contract included a choice of forum clause. That clause read, "[t]his Agreement and all matters arising out of or relating to this Agreement shall be governed by the laws of the State of California."[1] This meant that the case would be held in California, pure and simple. The second issue, that of the nature of the contract was a bit more difficult. As we have seen, the issue of whether a software package is a goods or a service contract is not as straightforward as it appears. In fact, there are several tests for determining whether hybrid software contracts are for goods or for service.

The court here used just one element of the predominate issue test—that of price. The court concluded: "Such an analysis requires that this Court consider whether the goods or the services dominate the Agreement ... As the Agreement's price terms make plain, the software programs themselves were the essence of the Agreement."[2] If we look back at the payment schedule that Evolve laid on ePresence, the court's decision makes sense. Evolve was charging ePresence a yearly fee of $540,000. This fee was for the purchase of the "licensed software programs and maintenance service" to maintain that software package. (*Note:* The court must have had information we do not have about how little of that annual fee of $540,000 went to "service" to maintain that software package.) In contrast, ePresence paid only $110,000 to have Evolve install and customize services and another small amount, $2,000 each day, for training, additional engineering work, and travel expenses. The bill clearly focuses on the sale of the licensed software program because it charges over a half million dollars yearly for the privilege it granted to ePresence to use that licensed software. The costs associated with installing, customizing, training, engineering, and traveling ($110,000 plus that $2,000 per day)—all part of the service end of the contract—pales into insignificance when contrasted with the cost of the licensed software itself. [See: *ePresence, Inc. v. Evolve Software, Inc.*, 190 F. Supp. 2d 159 U.S. District Court, D. Massachusetts (February 27, 2002).]

Source: See: *ePresence, Inc. v. Evolve Software, Inc.*, 190 F. Supp. 2d 159 U.S. District Court, D. Massachusetts, (February 27, 2002).

quick quiz 13-1

1. A gift is considered a sale.	true | false
2. Money, stocks, and bonds are movable items that are not goods.	true | false
3. The dominant element of a contract determines whether it is a sales contract or a services contract.	true | false

13-2 Rules for Sales Contracts

The fundamental rules of contract law, discussed in Part 2, serve as a foundation for the principles found in the UCC, but the UCC is often more flexible. This flexibility is built into the UCC in order to accommodate the day-to-day reality of the world of sales. The daily operation of the commercial world requires a rapid response to the demands of customers

UCC 1-203

UCC 1-205

UCC 2-204(1)(2)

and the needs of suppliers. Unlike real property contracts, which sometimes seem to be moving in slow motion, sales contracts for goods often occur at a moment's notice with little or no preparation. Unlike collective bargaining contracts that require that all the parties agree to each word in each clause of each part of the agreement, purchase orders and invoices often have different terms hidden in the fine print, terms that might contradict one another, but which really do not matter to the actual completion of the contract. Unlike employment contracts, which will not begin until the parties know exactly what is expected of them, a shipment of goods might have to get started before all of the details of a deal are finalized. As we shall see, the UCC handles these realities in an effective and responsible way. In a very real sense, it is the almost universal adherence to the UCC that makes our commercial world work as well as it does. Some of these special rules for sales contracts are covered below.

Good Faith, Course of Dealings, and Usage of Trade

UCC 2-206(1)(a)
UCC 2-206(1)(b)
UCC 2-106(2)

Under the UCC, every contract or duty imposes an obligation of good faith. In other words, the parties to a sales contract must act and deal fairly with each other. When the parties have dealt with each other before, their prior dealings give special meaning to sales contracts. Similarly, **usage of trade**—that is, any method of dealing that is commonly used in the particular field—is given special meaning. Unless the parties express otherwise, a course of dealings or usage of trade may be used to supplement or qualify the terms of a sales contract.

Formation of a Sales Contract

A contract may be made in any manner that shows that the parties reached an agreement. It may be oral (with some exceptions) or in writing, or it may be established by the conduct of the parties. An enforceable sales contract may come about even if the exact moment of its making cannot be determined and even though some terms are not completely agreed upon.

Contracts may be formed either orally or in writing; however, a writing may be required by the Statute of Frauds for the contract to be enforceable.
©Radius Images/Getty Images

Offer and Acceptance To establish a contract for the sale of goods, unless otherwise indicated by the offeror or the circumstances, the offeree may accept the offer in any manner and by any medium that is reasonable. A contract for the sale of goods comes into existence when the acceptance is sent, as long as the method used to send it is reasonable. Unless the buyer indicates otherwise, an order or other offer to buy goods for prompt shipment may be accepted by either a prompt shipment or a prompt promise to ship. Under this rule, the goods that are shipped may be either conforming or nonconforming goods. **Conforming goods** are those that are in accordance with the obligations under the contract. **Nonconforming goods** are those that are not the same as those called for under the contract or that are in some way defective.

Firm Offer The UCC holds merchants to a higher standard than nonmerchants. A **merchant** is a person who deals in goods of the kind sold in the ordinary course of business or who otherwise claims to have knowledge or skills peculiar to those goods. Although most rules under the UCC apply to both merchants and nonmerchants alike, some rules apply only to merchants. One such rule involves a firm offer.

No consideration is necessary when a merchant promises in writing to hold an offer

A CLASSIC CASE Offer and Acceptance under the UCC

The Uniform Commercial Code (UCC) governs contracts that are made for the sale or the lease of goods. Goods, as we have seen, are movable tangible objects such as vehicles, electronic devices, and clothing. Many of the rules in the UCC are straightforward, unambiguous expressions of legal principles that have been imbedded in the law for centuries. This simple fact made the classic case of *XCEL v. DeVault* relatively easy for the court to solve. The facts in the case play out like this. DeVault Industries manufactures custom-built shotguns. XCEL had perfected a wire-cutting process that was ideally suited for the trigger assemblies in the DeVault shotguns. After an initial trial run, during which XCEL successfully produced six trigger assemblies, DeVault sent a purchase order (No. 27) to XCEL for 20 additional units (although there was enough material to produce 60 units), at a total cost of $1,080. XCEL received and accepted purchase order No. 27. Within a few days, however, Mr. Cain, the president of XCEL, phoned Mr. DeVault, the president of DeVault, and told him that XCEL could not manufacture the parts at that price. DeVault remembers the phone call differently, arguing that the two men did not talk price but, instead, discussed the quantity of the order, which was set at 20. However, DeVault did admit that Cain said he needed to produce more than 20 units to cover the setup costs for that initial 20 units. DeVault told him not to worry because they would later figure out what a fair price would be. XCEL did, in fact, manufacture the units and sent them to DeVault. Once DeVault received the units, the company sent a check to XCEL for $1,080. The check included a clear notation that read, "pymt in full PO#27 60 pcs@18.00 ea." Someone at XCEL cashed the check and deposited the proceeds in an XCEL bank account. Nevertheless, Cain continued to claim that DeVault had not paid the full amount owed under the contract. Later XCEL sent its own check for $1,080 back to DeVault. By this time, it was too late. DeVault would no longer listen to Cain, and Cain refused to hear DeVault. That was when the lawsuit erupted. The court, using the UCC, had no problem determining that a contract existed under the terms of the purchase order. As noted earlier, unless the buyer indicates otherwise, an order or other *offer to buy goods* for *prompt shipment* may be accepted by either a prompt shipment or a prompt promise to ship. The court identified DeVault's purchase order as the *offer to buy goods* and the XCEL's *prompt shipment* of the trigger assemblies as the acceptance. Moreover, because there was no indication that the goods were nonconforming, there could be no successful challenge to the existence of the contract. [See: *XCEL Mold & Machine v. DeVault Indus.*, 146 Ohio Misc. 2d 32, 2008-Ohio-269.]

See: *XCEL Mold & Machine v. DeVault Indus.* 146 Ohio Misc. 2d 32, 2008-Ohio-269.

open for the sale or lease of goods. Known as a **firm offer**, the writing must be signed by the merchant, and the time period for holding the offer open may not exceed three months. This rule differs from the general rule of contract law, which requires consideration in an option contract.

Open-Price Terms Another change that the UCC has made is that a contract for the sale of goods may be established even though the price is not settled. Such **open-price terms** may occur when the parties intend to be bound by a contract but fail to mention the price or decide to set the price later. Under non-UCC law, no contract would come about because the terms are not definite. The UCC allows such a contract to come into existence. If the parties cannot agree on the price at the later date, the UCC requires that the price will be reasonable at the time the goods are delivered.

UCC 2-104(1)
UCC 2-205
UCC 2-305(1)

Output and Requirements Terms Sometimes, a seller will agree to sell "all the goods we manufacture" or "all the crops we produce" to a particular buyer. This agreement is known as an **output contract**. At other times, a buyer will agree to buy "all the oil we need to heat our building" (or some similar requirement) from a particular seller. This agreement is called a **requirements contract**. Such contracts often were not allowed under common law

UCC 2-306

because the quantity of the goods to be bought or sold was not definite. The UCC allows output and requirements contracts for the sale of goods, as long as the parties deal in good faith and according to *reasonable expectations*.

EXAMPLE 13-2: Unreasonable Expectations

Spencer Oil Co. agreed to sell to Lopaz Manufacturing Co. all the heating oil Lopaz would need during the next year. Spencer knew that Lopaz used about 5,000 gallons of oil each year. During the summer, Lopaz enlarged its building to an extent that it would require 25,000 gallons of heating oil during the next year. Spencer would not be bound to supply that amount of oil to Lopaz because it was far beyond the amount it expected to supply.

UCC 2-207

Additional Terms in Acceptance Under the general rules of contract law, an acceptance of an offer must be an absolute, unqualified, unconditional assent to the offer. If the acceptance differs in the slightest from the offer, it is considered a rejection. The UCC changes this rule somewhat. A contract for the sale of goods occurs even though the acceptance states terms that are additional to or different from those offered or agreed upon (unless acceptance is made conditional on assent to the additional terms). The additional terms are treated as proposals for additions to the contract if the parties are not both merchants. If both parties are merchants, the additional terms become part of the contract unless they materially alter it, the other party objects within a reasonable time, or the offer limits acceptance to its terms. This rule is intended to deal with two typical situations. The first is when an agreement has been reached either orally or by informal correspondence between the parties and is followed by one or both of the parties sending formal acknowledgments or memos that contain additional terms not discussed earlier. The second situation in which this rule applies is one in which a fax or letter intended to be the closing or confirmation of an agreement adds further minor suggestions or proposals, such as "ship by Thursday" or "rush."

EXAMPLE 13-3: Additional Terms in Acceptance

Cobb and Sons Inc. reached an oral agreement with Valley Theatres Inc. for the sale of an air-conditioning system. Later, Cobb put the agreement in writing, signed it, and sent it to Valley for its signature. Valley signed the writing but added additional terms relative to the date of completion of the contract. Because both parties were merchants, the additional terms would become part of the contract unless Cobb objected to them within a reasonable time. Had one of them not been a merchant, the contract would have to come into existence without the additional terms, and the added terms would have been treated as proposals for additions to the contract.

EXAMPLE 13-4: Different Terms in Acceptance

Cal-Cut Pipe and Supply Inc. offered in writing to sell used pipe to Southern Idaho Pipe and Steel Co., specifying a delivery date. Southern Idaho accepted by sending a check but changed the delivery date. Cal-Cut mailed a confirmation containing the original delivery date with the postscript, "We will work it out." The court held that there was a binding contract between them despite the conflicting delivery terms.

Modification Under the general rules of contract law, if the parties have already entered into a binding contract, a later agreement to change that contract needs consideration to be binding. The UCC has done away with this rule in contracts for the sale of goods. An agreement modifying a contract for the sale of goods needs no consideration to be binding. Any such modification may be oral unless the original agreement is in writing and provides that it may not be modified except by a signed writing. Any such clause in a form supplied by a merchant to a nonmerchant, however, must be separately signed (such as in the margin) by the nonmerchant to be effective.

UCC 2-209(1)
UCC 2-209(2)

quick quiz 13-2

1. Under the UCC, a contract comes into existence when the acceptance is sent if the method used is reasonable.   true | false
2. No consideration is necessary to establish a firm offer when a consumer promises in writing to hold an offer open for the sale or lease of goods.   true | false
3. Under the UCC, a contract for the sale of goods may be established even though the price is not settled.   true | false

13-3 The Form of a Sales Contract

The Uniform Commercial Code also outlines the rules that must be followed in relation to written sales contracts. This is critical because many contracts in the commercial world are written. Today many sales contracts are also made online, which has required some fine-tuning of the law. As we shall see, however, there are not quite as many changes in the law as one might expect because of the cyber-revolution in sales. This is a testimony to the law of sales, which has adopted a set of rules so well adjusted to its subject matter that it can adapt to even the most radical upheavals in the economic world without missing a beat. Some of this flexibility is made possible by the members of the Uniform Law Commission (ULC) who have been willing to accommodate the needs of those involved with the new technology.

UCC 2-201(1)

The Written Sales Contract

The Statute of Frauds outlines those contracts that must be in writing to be enforceable and what the writing must contain to be complete. As long as the value of the goods involved in a sales contract does not exceed $500, the contract can be oral and still be enforceable. Once the price is $500 or more, however, the contract must be in writing to be enforceable. Also under the UCC, a lease of goods must be in writing if the total payments to be made under the lease are $1,000 or more.

UCC 2A-201(1)
UCC 2-201(2)

Exceptions to the General Rule There are four exceptions to the requirement that contracts for the sale of goods for $500 or more and the lease of goods for $1,000 or more must be in writing to be enforceable. These exceptions involve the following:

1. Oral contracts between merchants in which a confirmation has been received by one party and not objected to by the other party.
2. Specially manufactured goods.
3. Admissions in court.
4. Executed contracts.

Most of the rules that involve written contracts and the sale of goods are covered in the UCC, but some contracts involving either sale-of-goods contracts or some other type of contract fall outside the UCC. For example, contracts that cannot be completed within one year and agreements to pay the debt of another party might both involve sale-of-goods contracts. First, let's look at contracts in which one party agrees to pay another party's debt. Several terms have been used to describe these types of transactions. They are alternately referred to as a *guaranty of payment*, a *guaranty contract*, or a *collateral contract*. The promisor is usually called a *guarantor*. Often in a commercial setting, the guarantor is referred to as a *cosigner*. The person to whom the promise is made is the *obligee*, and the person who owes the original debt is referred to as the *obligor*. It is crucial to distinguish between guaranty contracts and original contracts. An exception to this rule is known as the *primary objective test*. Under the primary objective test (also referred to as the *leading objective test* and the *main purpose test*), if the promise to pay another party's debt is actually made to obtain a gain for the guarantor, there is no need for a writing to enforce the promise. The other type of contract that might involve a sale-of-goods contract in need of a writing is a contract that cannot be completed within one year. While most sale-of-goods contracts can be completed within one year, this is not always the case. In fact, this is an issue in the opening case.

THE OPENING CASE Round 3
"Some Legal Issues Never Get Truly Resolved. They Just Fade Away."

Let's look at the Opening Case one more time. Recall that Evolve Software contracted to provide ePresence with a professional service automation system (PSA) called Evolve, Service Sphere Version 2.5 (or, simply, Version 2.5), which was supposed to add three new elements to ePresence computer system: (1) multi-currency, (2) international tax, and (3) intercompany capability. The system would cost ePresence a yearly fee of $540,000. In addition, ePresence had to pay $110,000 to have Evolve install and customize services and another $2,000 each day for training, additional engineering work, and travel expenses. Unfortunately, given all this money, things went down hill very quickly and never recovered. First, Version 2.5 did not feature multi-currency and international taxation support as Evolve had promised. To solve this problem, Evolve promised that if ePresence allowed them to install Version 2.5, as it was, it would provide the more inclusive Version 3.0 later. The ePresence folks agreed, and later, Version 3.0 was installed. However, while Version 3.0 had multi-currency and international taxation support, it did not have intercompany capabilities. In an attempt to make things right, someone at Evolve orally promised that the Evolve techs would get the system up and running with the capabilities that ePresence needed, or Evolve would refund all the money that ePresence had spent on the unsatisfactory software. Evolve even delivered a written version of that agreement to ePresence, along with a promise to provide ePresence with an initial progress report of Evolve's solution to the problem. Because they believed the folks at Evolve, the ePresence people did not pull out of the contract. Sadly, Evolve's progress report never appeared on anyone's desk at ePresence. Remarkably, a short time later, the CEO of Evolve admitted that his company had done "a poor job" with the ePresence account. The CEO also repeated the promise to return the money that ePresence had spent under the contract, if these issues were not resolved. That all sounded good until Evolve announced that it would refund only $150,000 to ePresence. Instantly, ePresence refused the reduced amount. Evolve countered with a new refund offer of $365,000. The folks at ePresence rejected the counteroffer and demanded that Evolve pay a total refund of $680,000. When they could not reach an agreement, the case ended up in court.

After the court decided that California was the proper place to try the case and after the court had determined that the contract was primarily a sale of goods contract (which meant the UCC would have to be followed), the court turned to the final issue. Was the addition to the contract, promising a refund, valid, or did the parties have to abide by the original written agreement? At that point in the proceeding, the original choice of California as the forum state had a profound impact on the case. California had not only adopted the Uniform Commercial Code, but also included the entire code almost without modification. Moreover, the choice of California law meant that the court would also have to rely on California case law. This point proved to be a crucial element in the court's ultimate decision. To determine if Evolve's later modification was a valid waiver, the court looked to California Commercial Code 2-209 (2) and 2-209 (4). CCC 2-209 (2) says that "a signed agreement which excludes modification or rescission except by a signed writing cannot be otherwise modified or rescinded." This provision clearly indicates that the original written agreement must be upheld. However, the follow-up section, CCC 2-209 (4) seems to give the court the option of deferring to the modification rather than the original written agreement. That section reads, an "'attempt at modification' that does not satisfy a contractual requirement of written modifications only nonetheless 'can operate as a waiver.'" The court's final decision hinges on the interpretation of this second clause. Did this modification act as a waiver that canceled the terms of the original written contract? To answer this question, the court turned to California case law, which emphasizes that any modification must involve an "*executed* oral agreement" (italics added by the court). This focus on an "*executed*" agreement meant, to the court, at least, that words alone, even written words, were not enough to cancel out the original agreement. Since, in this case, the plaintiff, ePresence, could point only to the the words of the waiver, not to any actual conduct on the part of Evolve, sufficient to rise to the level of an executed agreement, the original contract stood. As a result, despite its reluctance to do so, given the failure of Evolve's software, the court held that the original written contract must be followed. Judgment for Evolve. [See: *ePresence, Inc. v. Evolve Software, Inc.*, 190 F. Supp. 2d 159 U.S. District Court, D. Massachusetts (February 27, 2002).]

Source: See: *ePresence, Inc. v. Evolve Software, Inc.*, 190 F. Supp. 2d 159 U.S. District Court, D. Massachusetts, (February 27, 2002).

Oral Contracts between Merchants An exception to the general rule occurs when there is an oral agreement made between two merchants. If either merchant receives a written confirmation of the oral agreement from the other merchant within a reasonable time and does not object to it in writing within 10 days, the writing is sufficient under the UCC even though it has not been signed by the other party. It is important to understand that this exception applies only to merchants, not to ordinary consumers. The UCC defines a merchant as "a person who deals in goods of the kind" that are the subject matter of the contract at hand. It is also crucial to note that any objection to the original written confirmation must be in writing. If that is not the case then the court will honor the original written confirmation, no matter how loudly and how persuasively the other party objected to the agreement.

Specially Manufactured Goods Another exception occurs when goods are to be specially manufactured for the buyer and are not suitable for sale to others in the ordinary course of the seller's business. If the seller has made either a substantial beginning in manufacturing the goods or commitments to buy them, the oral agreement will be enforceable.

UCC 2-201(3)

EXAMPLE 13-5: Specially Manufactured Goods

Lifetime Windows Inc. entered into an oral agreement to manufacture 15 oversized windows for Harold Cohen for the price of $6,000. The windows were such an odd shape that no one else would have a need for them. When the windows were manufactured, Cohen refused to take them on the ground that the oral contract was unenforceable. The court held against Cohen, however, and enforced the oral agreement. The windows were specially manufactured and were not suitable for sale to others.

UCC 2-201(3)(b)

Admissions in Court If the party against whom enforcement is sought admits in court that an oral contract for the sale of goods was made, the contract will be enforceable. The contract is not enforceable under this exception, however, beyond the quantity of goods admitted.

UCC 2-201(3)(c)

Executed Contracts When the parties carry out their agreement in a satisfactory manner, the law will not render the transaction unenforceable for want of an agreement in writing. Executed contracts (those that have been carried out) need not be in writing; the writing requirements apply only to contracts that are executory, that is, not yet performed. This provision means that contracts for goods that have been received and accepted need not be in writing. If there has been a part payment or a part delivery, the court will enforce only that portion of the agreement that has been performed.

UCC 2-201(1)

Requirements of Writing The writing that is required to satisfy the UCC must indicate that a contract for sale has been made between the parties and mention the quantity of goods being sold. It must also be signed by the party against whom enforcement is sought (the defendant). A writing is acceptable even though it omits or incorrectly states an agreed-upon term. However, a contract will not be enforceable beyond the quantity of goods shown in such writing. For that reason, it is necessary to put the quantity of goods to be bought and sold in the written agreement. Although a paper similar to the one shown in Figure 13-1 may be used, an informal note, memorandum, fax, or sales slip will satisfy the writing requirements.

UCC 1-201(39)

Signature Requirements Under the UCC, a signature includes any symbol made with the intent to authenticate a writing. Thus, in addition to a handwritten signature, the courts have held various kinds of marks, including an X and a typewritten name, qualify as a signature as long as they were written with the intent to be signatures.

Cyber-Sales Contracts

Statutes covering the problems associated with cyber-sales contracts have taken many forms over the past decade. One of the problems that required a solution was how to treat an online contract that required a written form. Two acts that have dealt with that problem are the E-Sign Act and the Uniform Electronic Transactions Act (UETA).

The E-Sign Act Congress passed the E-Sign Act to address some of the difficulties associated with cyber-commerce, especially those that involve the recognition of electronic contracts and electronic signatures. In short, the statute declares that, as long as the parties to a cyber-contract have freely decided to conduct business electronically, the cyber-contract that results will have the same legal effect as a paper contract. The statute makes it clear that the parties to the contract must have some way to store and duplicate a cyber-record of the contract; otherwise, the cyber-record will not be legally sufficient under the act. It is also important to understand that some critical documents are not covered by the act. These include court records, eviction notices, health insurance cancellations, foreclosure notices, prenuptial contracts, and divorce papers. On the other hand, UCC contracts for the sale and lease of goods are included in the E-Sign Act.

The Uniform Electronic Transactions Act (UETA) The Uniform Electronic Transactions Act (UETA), which was produced by the Uniform Law Commission, is very similar to the E-Sign Act. The UETA promises the same legal parity between electronic records and paper records that is guaranteed by the E-Sign Act. However, the UETA applies only to transactions that involve a business, governmental, or commercial situation. Still, the statute does ensure that, whenever a writing is required under the Statute of Frauds, any electronic signature that results from a cyber-transaction will fulfill that requirement. Under

CONTRACT FOR SALE OF GOODS

AGREEMENT made by and between Ozzie Caldwell (Seller) and Geordi Hasenzahl (Buyer).

It has been agreed between the two parties that:

1. Seller agrees to sell, and Buyer agrees to buy, the following described property: one regulation-size pool table now located at the residence of Ozzie Caldwell, RD #1, Box 118, Ashberry, Kentucky.

2. Buyer agrees to pay Seller the total price of $850.00;

    payable as follows:

    $600.00 deposit herewith

    $250.00 balance by cash or certified check at time of transfer

3. Seller warrants he has full legal title to said property, authority to sell said property, and that said property shall be sold free and clear of all claims by other parties.

4. Said property is sold in "as is" condition. SELLER HEREBY EXCLUDES THE WARRANTY OF MERCHANTABILITY AND FITNESS FOR A PARTICULAR PURPOSE.

5. Parties agree to transfer title on February 7, 20 - -, at RD #1, Box 118, Ashberry, Kentucky, the address of the Seller.

6. This agreement shall be binding on the parties, their successors, assigns, and personal representatives.

7. This writing is intended to represent the entire agreement between the parties.

Signed under seal this nineteenth day of January, 20 - -.

_____   _____
Buyer   Seller

Figure 13-1 With four exceptions, contracts for the sale of goods of $500 or more must be in writing to be enforceable. A formal writing such as this is not necessary to satisfy the writing requirements of the UCC, however.

the UETA an electronic signature is defined as "an electronic sound, symbol, or process attached to or logically associated with a record and executed or adopted by a person with the intent to sign the record."

International Law

Interestingly, the trend in other countries is to eliminate the requirement that a sales contract be in writing. Great Britain, for example, after having such a requirement for 277 years, did away with it in 1954. International sales law also has no writing requirements for a sales contract; instead, a sales contract may be proved by any means.

CISG Articles 1 and 2 (see Appendix C)

CISG Articles 4 and 5 (see Appendix C)

International sales law, called the United Nations **Convention on Contracts for the International Sale of Goods (CISG)**, applies only to sales between businesses whose places of business are in different countries that have adopted the law. It does not apply to sales of goods that are bought for personal, family, or household purposes. Also, the international law does not apply to auction sales; sales of stock, securities, negotiable instruments, or money; sales of ships or aircraft; or sales of electricity. The United States adopted the international sales law in 1988, and by 2007, 70 countries had made it part of their law.

UCC 2-328(2)

UCC 2-328(3)

The CISG is similar in many ways to the UCC. It also contains some differences. The CISG governs only the formation of a sales contract and the rights and duties of the parties that arise from it. The CISG is not concerned with the validity of a contract regarding, for example, the sale of illegal drugs, which would be governed by other laws. In addition, the CISG does not apply to the liability of the seller for death or personal injury caused by the goods to any person. In such a case, people would have to look to other laws for a remedy.

Auction Sales and Cyber-Auction Fraud

In an auction sale, the auctioneer presents goods for sale and invites the audience to make offers, which are known as bids. This process is similar to an invitation to trade. Bidders in the crowd respond with their offers. The highest bid (offer) is accepted by the auctioneer, usually by the drop of the gavel, together with the auctioneer's calling out the word *sold*. If, while the gavel is falling, a higher bid comes from those in the crowd, the auctioneer has two options: declare the goods sold or reopen the bidding.

UCC 2-328(4)

An auction sale is "with reserve" unless the goods are expressly put up without reserve. In an **auction with reserve**, the auctioneer may withdraw the goods at any time before announcing completion of the sale if the highest bid is not high enough. In an **auction without reserve**, after the auctioneer calls for bids on an article or lot, that article or lot cannot be withdrawn unless no bid is made within a reasonable time. In either case, a bidder may retract a bid until the auctioneer's announcement of completion of the sale. A bidder's retraction does not revive any previous bid.

Auctions are frequently used to dispose of unwanted property, satisfy judgments, and liquidate foreclosed property.
©imageBROKER/REX/Shutterstock

The practice of planting persons in the crowd for the purpose of raising bids by innocent purchasers is not allowed. Except in a forced sale, such as by a sheriff, if a seller (or the seller's agent) makes a bid at an auction without notifying other bidders, a buyer has two options. Under the UCC, a buyer may either avoid the sale or take the goods at the price of the last good faith bid prior to the completion of the sale. In a forced sale, as when a sheriff auctions property on foreclosure or to satisfy a lien creditor, the owner is allowed to bid on the property being sold.

Auctions on the Internet provide the opportunity to buy and sell goods worldwide as well as locally. An Internet auction (i.e., a cyber-auction and an e-auction) can be either person-to-person or business-to-person. In person-to-person auctions, sellers offer items directly to consumers. The highest bidder must deal directly with the seller to arrange for payment and delivery. In contrast, operators of business-to-person auctions have control of the items being offered and take charge of payment and delivery of goods bought and sold.

Cyber-auction fraud is alarming. Sometimes sellers don't deliver the goods or deliver something less valuable than they advertised. At other times, sellers don't disclose everything about a product or fail to deliver it when they say they will. The Federal Trade Commission (FTC) provides helpful information about cyber-auctions in its free brochures and on its website.

> **Did You Know?**
>
> The federal government auctions cars, trucks, real estate, airplanes, boats, jewelry, office equipment, heavy equipment, and many other items. For information about government auctions, log onto the Internet and, using the search engine Excite, type in the words "government auction." You may find something you need at a bargain price.

quick quiz 13-3

1. A lease of goods must be in writing if the total payments to be made under the lease are $500 or more.   true | false
2. The E-Sign Act was developed, written, and passed by the U.S. Congress.   true | false
3. The practice of planting persons in the crowd for the purpose of raising bids by innocent purchasers is not allowed.   true | false

13-4 Title, Passage of Title, and Risk of Loss

It is good for us to remember that the law of sales was born within the context of the law merchant and that the law merchant was closely associated with the development of capitalism. Moreover, it is also critical to recall that one of the driving forces behind the growth of capitalism was the Roman Catholic Church, which helped provide a rational and moral foundation for the principles and procedures that guided the activities of merchants in the making of their contracts. One of the things that the Church insisted upon was that merchants never engage in fraud and always follow a good faith approach to contract development. The problem of determining title to goods, especially determining just when title legitimately passes from one party to another, must be solved to ensure the basic fairness of the law of sales. After all, it is not only ownership that passes with title, but also the risk associated with that ownership. [See: Harold J. Berman, *Law and Revolution: The Formation of the Western Legal Tradition* (Cambridge, MA: Harvard University Press, 1983), pp. 336–341; and Rodney Stark, *The Victory of Reason: How Christianity Led to Freedom, Capitalism, and Western Science* (New York: Random House, 2005), p. xi. See also Henri Sée, *Modern Capitalism: Its Origin and Evolutions*, trans. Homer B. Vanderblue and Georges F. Doriot (New York: Adelphi Co. 1928), pp. 7–13.]

Valid Title, Void Title, and Voidable Title

Title, or **valid title**, is the right of ownership to goods. People who own goods have title to them. Sellers sometimes give a bill of sale to a buyer as evidence that the sale took place. A **bill of sale** is a written statement that provides evidence of the transfer of personal property from one person to another. It does not prove, however, that the seller had perfect title to the goods. The goods may have been stolen, obtained by fraud, purchased from a minor or an incompetent person, or entrusted with the seller by the true owner and sold by mistake. The question that arises in such cases is whether an innocent purchaser for value receives good title to the goods. The answer to this question depends on whether the seller's title to the goods was void or voidable and whether the goods had been entrusted to a merchant.

With the exception of voidable title, buyers of goods acquire whatever title their sellers had to the property. If a seller has **void title** (no title at all), a buyer of the goods obtains no title to them. The continued sale of the stolen property through several innocent buyers would not in any way defeat the real owner's right to the property. The rights of possession and title of successive buyers of stolen property can never be any better than the rights of the thief, who had no title. Of course, innocent purchasers may bring suit against the person from whom stolen goods were purchased for breach of warranty of title.

Anyone who obtains property as a result of another's fraud, misrepresentation, mutual mistake, undue influence, or duress holds only voidable title to the goods. **Voidable title** means title that may be voided if the injured party elects to do so. This kind of title is also received when goods are bought from a minor or a person who is mentally impaired. Some people refer to voidable title as title that is valid until voided. Anyone with voidable title to goods is able to transfer good title to others. According to the UCC, "A person with voidable title has power to transfer a good title to a good faith purchaser for value."

Entrusting Goods to a Merchant People often entrust goods that belong to them to merchants. For example, they leave their watches with jewelers and their vehicles with the body shop to be repaired. When this occurs, if the merchant sells the goods in the ordinary course of business to a third party who has no knowledge of the real owner's rights, the third party receives good title to them. The original owner who entrusted them to the merchant loses title to the goods altogether but may bring an action against the merchant for money damages caused by the loss. The reason for this rule of law is to give confidence to people who buy in the marketplace. People can be assured that they will receive good title to property (except stolen property) that they buy from a merchant who deals in goods of that kind in the ordinary course of business.

Passage of Title and Risk of Loss

It is not unusual for goods to be stolen, damaged, or destroyed while they are awaiting shipment, are being shipped, or are awaiting pickup after a sales contract has been entered. When something happens to the goods, it becomes necessary to determine who must suffer the loss: the seller or the buyer. The rules for determining the risk of loss are contained in the UCC. Except when goods are to be picked up by the buyer and in a few other cases, whoever has title to the goods bears the risk of loss. Goods must be identified in the contract before title can be transferred to the buyer. **Identified goods** are specific goods that have been selected as the subject matter of the contract. Once goods are identified, title passes to the buyer when the seller does whatever is required under the contract to deliver the goods. Contracts calling for the seller to deliver the goods are either *shipment contracts* or *destination contracts*.

Shipment Contracts A **shipment contract** is one in which the seller turns the goods over to a carrier for delivery to the buyer. The seller has no responsibility for seeing that the goods reach their destination. In a shipment contract, both title and risk of loss pass to the buyer when the goods are given to the carrier. Shipment contracts are often designated by the term *f.o.b. [the place of shipment]* (such as f.o.b. Chicago). The abbreviation **f.o.b.** means "free on board." When goods are sent **f.o.b. the place of shipment**, they will be delivered free to the place of shipment. The buyer must pay all shipping charges from there to the place of destination. The terms indicate that title to the goods and the risk of loss pass at the point of origin. Delivery to the carrier by the seller and acceptance by the carrier complete the transfer of both title and risk of loss. Thus, the buyer accepts full responsibility during the transit of the goods. (See Table 13-2.)

Table 13-2 Abbreviations

Abbreviation	Meaning
f.o.b. New York	Free on board to New York (This would be a *shipment contract* if shipped from New York.)
f.o.b. Los Angeles	Free on board to Los Angeles (This would be a *destination contract* if shipped from New York.)
c.o.d.	Collect on delivery
c.i.f.	Cost of goods shipped, insurance, and freight
c.f.	Cost of goods shipped and freight
f.a.s.	Free alongside vessel or at a dock

Destination Contracts If the contract requires the seller to deliver goods to a destination, it is called a **destination contract**. Both title and risk of loss pass to the buyer when the seller tenders the goods at the place of destination. **Tender** means to offer to turn the goods over to the buyer. Destination contracts are often designated by **f.o.b. the place of destination** (such as f.o.b. Tampa); goods shipped under such terms belong to the seller until they have been delivered to the destination shown on the contract. Similarly, the risk of loss remains with the seller until the goods are tendered at destination. Tender at destination requires that the goods arrive at the place named in the contract, the buyer is given notice of their arrival, and a reasonable time is allowed for the buyer to pick up the goods from the carrier.

When terms of shipment do not specify shipping point or destination, it is assumed to be a shipment contract. Adding the term **c.o.d.** (collect on delivery) instructs the carrier to retain possession until the carrier has collected the cost of the goods. The term **c.i.f.** (cost, insurance, and freight) instructs the carrier to collect all charges and fees in one lump sum. This sum includes the cost of goods shipped, insurance, and freight charges to the point of destination. The term **c.f.** means that insurance is not included in the sum. The term **f.a.s. vessel** (free alongside vessel) at a named port requires sellers to deliver the goods, at their own risk, alongside the vessel or at a dock designated by the buyer.

A CLASSIC CASE *(Revisited)*
Shipment and Destination Contracts

In the earlier Classic Case, we learned that DeVault, a shotgun manufacturer, sent a purchase order to XCEL for trigger-assembly units, at a total cost of $1,080. XCEL received and accepted purchase order No. 27. Within a few days, however, Mr. Cain, the president of XCEL, phoned Mr. DeVault, the president of DeVault, and told him that XCEL could not manufacture the parts at that price. DeVault told him not to worry because they would later figure out what a fair price would be. XCEL did, in fact, manufacture all 60 units and send them to DeVault. If the order had been a shipment contract, the seller, XCEL, would have turned the trigger-assembly units over to a carrier for delivery to DeVault. The seller, XCEL, would then have no responsibility for seeing that the trigger-assemblies reached DeVault. In a shipment contract, both title and risk of loss pass to the buyer when the goods are given to the carrier. In contrast, if the order had been a destination contract, then both title and risk of loss would have passed to the buyer, DeVault, when XCEL delivered the trigger-assemblies to DeVault's place of business, which was the final destination of the shipment.

Table 13-3 Passage of Title and Risk of Loss

Terms of Contract	Title Passes	Risk of Loss Passes
Shipment contract	When goods are delivered to carrier	When goods are delivered to carrier
Destination contract	When goods are tendered at destination	When goods are tendered at destination
No delivery required	When contract is made	*Merchant seller:* When buyer receives goods *Nonmerchant seller:* When seller tenders goods to buyer
Document of title	When document of title is given to buyer	When document of title is given to buyer
Agreement of the parties	At time and place agreed upon	At time and place agreed upon

No Delivery Required When the contract calls for the buyer to pick up the goods, title passes to the buyer when the contract is made. Risk of loss, however, passes at different times depending on whether the seller is a merchant. If the seller is a merchant, the risk of loss passes when the buyer receives the goods. If the seller is not a merchant, the risk of loss passes to the buyer when the seller tenders the goods to the buyer (see Table 13-3).

Fungible Goods The UCC defines **fungible goods** as "goods of which any unit is, by nature or usage of trade, the equivalent of any like unit." Wheat, flour, sugar, and liquids of various kinds are examples of fungible goods. They have no important characteristics that identify them as coming from a particular supplier, and they are usually sold by weight or measure. Title to fungible goods may pass without the necessity of separating goods sold from the bulk. Under the UCC, "an undivided share of an identified bulk of fungible goods is sufficiently identified to be sold although the quantity of the bulk is not determined."

EXAMPLE 13-6: Fungible Goods

Logan Trucking Co. owned a large fuel storage tank that was partially filled with diesel fuel. The exact quantity of fuel in the tank was not known. The company was going out of business. Interstate Trucking Co. contracted to buy half of the fuel in the tank, and Union Trucking Co. contracted to buy the other half. Both buyers agreed to send their own trucks to pick up the fuel. Title passed to the buyers when the contract was made even though the exact quantity of each sale was unknown and neither buyer had taken a share of the fuel from the entire lot.

Documents of Title Sometimes, when people buy goods, they receive a document of title to the goods rather than the goods themselves. They then give the document of title to the warehouse or carrier that is holding the goods and receive possession of them. A **document of title** is a paper giving the person who possesses it the right to receive the goods named in the document. Bills of lading and warehouse receipts are examples of documents of title. However, an automobile title certificate has not been given the legal status of a document of title, as the term is used in the UCC. When a document of title is used in a sales transaction, both title and risk of loss pass to the buyer when the document is delivered to the buyer.

Agreement of the Parties The parties may, if they wish, enter into an agreement setting forth the time that title and risk of loss pass from the seller to the buyer. With one exception, title and risk of loss will pass at the time and place agreed upon. If the agreement allows the seller to retain title after the goods are shipped, title will pass to the buyer at the time of shipment, regardless of the agreement, and the seller will have a security interest in the goods rather than title. A security interest gives the seller a right to have the property sold in the event that the buyer fails to pay money owed to the seller.

EXAMPLE 13-7: Security Interest

Raymond agreed to sell Glover her John Deere tractor for $12,000. The agreement called for Glover to pay $3,000 down and the balance in monthly installments for two years. Under the terms of the agreement, title to the tractor would not pass to Glover until the $12,000 was paid in full. Because Raymond delivered the tractor to Glover on the day that the agreement was signed, title passed to Glover at that time, regardless of the terms in the contract. The effect of those terms was to give Raymond a security interest in the tractor for the balance of the money owed to her.

Revesting of Title in Seller Buyers, after entering into sales contracts, sometimes refuse to accept the goods that are delivered or are otherwise made available to them. In all such cases, title to the goods returns to the seller. This reversion is true whether or not the buyer's rejection of the goods is justified. Similarly, title to goods returns to the seller when the buyer accepts the goods and then for a justifiable reason decides to revoke the acceptance. A justifiable reason for revoking an acceptance would be the discovery of a defect in the goods after having inspected them. When the seller sends goods to the buyer that do not meet the contract requirements and are therefore unacceptable, the risk of loss remains with the seller. For situations in which the buyer accepts the goods but later discovers some defect and rightfully revokes the acceptance, the passage of risk of loss depends on whether the buyer is insured. If the buyer has insurance, that insurance will cover the loss. If there is no insurance, the risk of loss remains with the seller from the beginning. When the buyer breaches the contract with regard to goods that have been identified to the contract, the seller may, to the extent of having no insurance coverage, treat the risk of loss as resting with the buyer.

International Sales The rules governing international sales are given in the United Nations Convention on Contracts for the International Sale of Goods (CISG). The international law does not address questions dealing with the passage of title because the laws of each country vary considerably. Instead, it leaves such questions to be decided by domestic law. This determination exists because third parties are usually involved in claiming title for themselves, and the laws of each country vary considerably. In contrast, the rules governing the passage of risk of loss are addressed in international law and are quite similar to those found in the UCC. The risk of loss passes to the buyer when the goods are handed over to the first carrier for transmission to the buyer unless the seller agrees to hand them over at a particular place. In that case, the risk of loss passes to the buyer at that time. Sometimes, goods are sold when they are in transit. When this kind of sale occurs (with some exceptions), the risk of loss passes to the buyer when the contract is made. In all other situations, the risk of loss, in general, passes when the buyer takes over the goods. The CISG has several exceptions in the contracts that it covers. It does not apply to goods bought for personal, household, or family use, or to contracts that mainly supply services. Nor does it cover the liability of the seller for death or injury caused by the goods sold.

quick quiz 13-4

1. *Void title* means title that may be voided if the injured party elects to do so. — true | false
2. *Voidable title* means no title at all. — true | false
3. Fungible goods must be separated from the bulk before title to them can pass to a buyer. — true | false

13-5 Sales, Returns, and Insurable Interest

Because of competition and a desire to give satisfaction, goods are sometimes sold with the understanding that they may be returned even though they conform to the contract. Determination of ownership and risk of loss while such goods are in the buyer's possession is sometimes necessary. Sales with the right of return are of two kinds: sale on approval and sale or return.

Sale on Approval

A sale that allows goods to be returned even though they conform to the contract is called a sale on approval when the goods are primarily for the buyer's use. When goods are sold on approval, they remain the property of the seller until the buyer's approval has been expressed. The approval may be indicated by the oral or written consent of the buyer or by the buyer's act of retaining the goods for more than a reasonable time. Using the goods in a reasonable and expected manner on a trial basis does not imply an acceptance. Grossly careless use and a failure to inform the seller of the buyer's intent to return, however, could constitute an acceptance. Goods held by the buyer on approval are not subject to the claims of the buyer's creditors until the buyer decides to accept them. In addition, the risk of loss remains with the seller until the buyer has accepted the goods.

Sale or Return

A sale that allows goods to be returned even though they conform to the contract is called a sale or return when the goods are delivered primarily for resale. When such a sale occurs, the buyer takes title to the goods with the right to revest (reinstate) title in the seller after a specified period or reasonable time. In such cases, the buyer must accept all of the obligations of ownership while retaining possession of the goods. Goods held on sale or return are subject to the claims of the buyer's creditors. While in the buyer's possession, the goods must be cared for and used in a reasonable manner, anticipating their possible return in the same condition as when received, after making allowance for ordinary wear and tear. Also, the goods must be returned at the buyer's risk and expense.

EXAMPLE 13-8: Consignment Contract

Butcher owned a gift shop in which she sold other people's goods on consignment. Hanson delivered a dozen handmade braided rugs to Butcher with the understanding that she would be paid for any that were sold. Any rugs that did not sell after three months would be returned to Hanson. This agreement was a sale or return because the rugs were delivered primarily for resale. Butcher would be required to pay Hanson for any rugs that were damaged, lost, or stolen while in Butcher's possession.

Insurable Interest

People must have an insurable interest in property to be able to place insurance on it. An **insurable interest** is the financial interest that an insured party has in the insured property. Buyers may place insurance on goods the moment a contract is made and the goods are identified to the contract. At this point, buyers receive an insurable interest in the goods they buy. They obtain an insurable interest even though they might later reject or return the goods to the seller. Notwithstanding the buyer's right to insure the goods, sellers retain an insurable interest in the goods as long as they have title to them.

EXAMPLE 13-9: Dual Insurable Interests

While shopping on vacation in an antique store in Connecticut, Maniff, who lived in Nevada, came upon a Native American totem pole she liked. She decided to buy the totem pole on the condition that the antique dealer would ship it f.o.b. Winnemucca, Nevada. The dealer agreed. Maniff received an insurable interest in the totem pole when it was identified to the contract. At the same time, the dealer retained an insurable interest in it until it was tendered at its destination in Winnemucca. Both Maniff and the antique dealer could insure the totem pole.

quick quiz 13-5

1. Goods that are sold on approval are subject to the claims of the buyer's creditors until the buyer decides to accept them. true | false
2. Goods that are sold on approval remain the property of the seller until the buyer's approval has been expressed. true | false
3. Goods that are sold on sale or return are not subject to the claims of the buyer's creditors. true | false

Summary

13.1 The Uniform Commercial Code (UCC), which contains the law of sales, has been adopted, either in whole or in part, by every state in the United States. Article 2 of the UCC applies whenever people buy or sell goods. It applies to transactions between private parties as well as transactions by businesspeople or merchants. Article 2A applies to leases of goods.

13.2 The following rules that are different from general contract law apply to sales contracts:

- A sales contract may be made in any manner that shows that the parties reached an agreement.
- Unless otherwise specified, an offeree may accept an offer in any way that is reasonable, including a prompt shipment of the goods.
- A written promise by a merchant to hold an offer open needs no consideration to be binding.
- A sales contract may be made even though the price is not settled.
- Output and requirements contracts are allowed in sales contracts as long as the parties deal in good faith and according to reasonable expectations.
- A sales contract may result even when an offeree adds different or additional terms from those offered or agreed upon.
- No consideration is necessary to modify a contract for the sale of goods.

13.3 With four exceptions, a contract for the sale of goods for $500 or more and the lease of goods for

$1,000 or more must be in writing. The exceptions are oral contracts between merchants in which a confirmation has been received by one party and not objected to by the other party, specially manufactured goods, admissions in court, and executed contracts. The United Nations Convention on Contracts for the International Sale of Goods (CISG) applies to sales between U.S. businesses and foreign businesses.

In an auction sale, offers are made by the people in the audience. The acceptance takes place when the auctioneer bangs the gavel.

13.4 Title to goods can be valid, void, or voidable. When a merchant sells goods without authority, the purchaser obtains good title. With few exceptions, such as when goods are to be picked up by the buyer, whoever has title to the goods bears the risk of loss. Once goods are identified, title passes to the buyer when the seller does whatever is required under the contract to deliver the goods. Title to fungible goods may pass without the need to separate goods sold from bulk. With a document of title, title and risk of loss pass to the buyer when the document is delivered. Title returns to the seller when the buyer refuses the goods. The risk of loss remains with the seller when the goods do not meet the requirements.

13.5 Goods sold on approval remain the property of the seller until the buyer approves. The seller retains the risk of loss. In a sale or return, the buyer takes title to the goods but is given the right to return the goods to the seller. The buyer must care for the goods in a reasonable manner and suffer the risk. Buyers have an insurable interest in goods the moment a contract is made and the goods are identified to the contract.

Key Terms

auction with reserve, 380
auction without reserve, 380
bill of sale, 381
blended contract, 369
c.f., 383
c.i.f., 383
c.o.d., 383
conforming goods, 372
Convention on Contracts for the International Sale of Goods (CISG), 380
destination contract, 383
document of title, 384

f.a.s. vessel, 383
firm offer, 373
f.o.b., 382
f.o.b. the place of destination, 383
f.o.b. the place of shipment, 382
fungible goods, 384
future goods, 368
goods, 368
hybrid contract, 369
identified goods, 382
insurable interest, 387
merchant, 372
mixed contract, 369

nonconforming goods, 372
open-price terms, 373
output contract, 373
predominant factor test, 370
requirements contract, 373
sale on approval, 386
sale or return, 386
shipment contract, 382
tender, 383
title, 381
usage of trade, 372
void title, 382
voidable title, 382

Questions for Review and Discussion

1. What are goods and what is a sale?
2. When does Article 2 of the UCC apply to contractual relationship?
3. What are the UCC rules that relate to written contracts?
4. What are the two laws that relate to cyber-sales contracts and what do they accomplish?
5. What is the difference between an auction with reserve and an auction without reserve?
6. What are valid title, void title, and voidable title?
7. When does the title to goods pass from seller to buyer?
8. When must the buyer and when must the seller bear the risk of loss?
9. What is the difference between a sale on approval and a sale or return?
10. What is an insurable interest?

Cases for Analysis

1. Brenda Brandt had a medical device implanted as part of her treatment for a serious medical condition. A charge for the device was included in the hospital bill. Later, the device was recalled by its manufacturer as substandard. Brandt had suffered serious complications, and the device was removed. She brought suit against the hospital for, among other things, breach of warranty under the Uniform Commercial Code. Was the purchase of the medical device from the hospital covered under the Uniform Commercial Code? Explain. [See: *Brandt v. Boston Scientific Corporation*, Docket No. 93982, Illinois Supreme Court (IL).]
2. Alberto Parreira, a lobsterman, contracted in writing to sell Sam Adams 1,000 pounds of fresh lobsters at a particular price during the following season. A few months later, when lobsters became plentiful and the price went down, Adams tried to get out of the contract. He argued that the contract was not enforceable because the lobsters had not yet been caught when the contract was made. Do you agree with Adams? Why or why not?
3. Harnois entered into an oral contract with Neverson to lease a compact computer and a printer for three months for $600. In an attempt to rescind the contract, Harnois claimed that the contract was unenforceable because it was not in writing. Do you agree with Harnois? Why or why not?
4. Carolina Transformer Co. Inc. brought suit against Anderson for several thousand dollars owed it for the purchase of transformers. Anderson testified in court that he had orally negotiated the contract and reached a final agreement with Carolina for the purchase of the transformers. Anderson argued, however, that he was not responsible because under the UCC, a contract for the sale of goods of $500 or more is not enforceable unless it is in writing. Do you agree with Anderson? [See: *Carolina Transformer Co. v. Anderson*, 341 So.2d 1327 (MS).]
5. Representatives of a fish marketing association (AIFMA) and a fish company (NEFCO) met at Bristol Bay, Alaska, to negotiate a marketing agreement for the forthcoming fishing season. At this meeting, NEFCO's agent, Gage, signed an agreement that contained the price that was to be paid for the fish and other details about the transaction. It omitted the quantity of fish to be purchased. Later, when suit was brought on the agreement, NEFCO argued that it was unenforceable because the written agreement failed to mention the quantity. Do you agree with NEFCO? Explain. [See: *Alaska Indus Fish Mktg. Assoc. v. New England Fish Co.*, 548 P.2d 348 (WA).]
6. Wheel Sports Center entered into a sales contract agreeing to deliver a motorcycle to Ramos for the price of $893. Ramos paid the full price for the motorcycle and immediately had it insured and registered in his name. However, before it was delivered to Ramos, the motorcycle was stolen from Wheel Sports Center. Who must suffer the loss, Wheel Sports Center or Ramos? Why? [See: *Ramos v. Wheel Sports Center*, 409 N.Y.S.2d 505 (NY).]
7. Fanning, who was 17 years old, sold her bicycle to Gerard, an adult, for $75. The next day, Gerard advertised the bicycle for sale in the classified section of a local newspaper and sold it for $150. The person who bought the bicycle was unaware that it had belonged to Fanning. When Fanning discovered what Gerard had done, she attempted to get the bicycle back from the person who bought it, claiming that Gerard had voidable title to the bicycle. Does Fanning have the legal right to the return of the bicycle? Why or why not?
8. Harold Marcus entered into a contract with Corrigan's Yacht Yard & Marine Sales Inc. to trade in his 34-foot Silverton power boat toward a later model Mainship boat. He delivered his Silverton boat to the yacht yard at the time of the contract in November. The new boat was not to be delivered until the following April. The yacht yard sold the Silverton boat to William Heiselman soon after receiving it. When the yacht yard was unable to deliver the Mainship boat to Marcus in April, Marcus took back his Silverton boat. Who had title to the boat, Marcus or Heiselman? Explain. [See: *Heiselman v. Marcus*, 488 N.Y.S.2d 571 (NY).]
9. Eberhard Manufacturing Company sold goods to Brown Industrial Sales Company without agreeing on who would bear the risk of loss. The contract contained no f.o.b. terms. Eberhard placed the goods on board a common carrier with instructions to deliver them to Brown. The goods were lost in transit. Who suffered the loss, Eberhard or Brown? Why? [See: *Eberhard Mfg. Co. v. Brown*, 232 N.W.2d 378 (MI).]

10. Henry Heide Inc. received a warehouse receipt for 3,200 100-pound bags of sugar that it bought from Olavarria. The corporation withdrew 800 bags of the sugar from the warehouse (where thousands of pounds were stored), but when it returned for the balance, it discovered that the warehouse was padlocked and empty. Some 200,000 pounds of sugar had mysteriously disappeared from it. Henry Heide carried insurance for such a loss, but its insurance company refused to pay, claiming that the corporation had no insurable interest in the sugar. Do you agree with the insurance company? Why or why not? [See: *Henry Heide, Inc., v. Atlantic Mut. Ins. Co.*, 363 N.Y.S.2d 515 (NY).]

Design Elements: The Opening Case: ©Sharpstock/Alamy; A Classic Case: ©Evlakhov Valeriy/Shutterstock

quick quiz Answers

13-1	13-2	13-3	13-4	13-5
1. F	1. T	1. F	1. F	1. F
2. T	2. F	2. T	2. F	2. T
3. T	3. T	3. T	3. F	3. F

Chapter 14

Sales Contracts: Rights, Duties, Breach, and Warranties

14-1 Rights and Duties of Parties
Tender of Performance • Buyer's Rights and Duties • Seller's Rights and Duties

14-2 Breach of Contract
Anticipatory Breach • Seller's Remedies • Buyer's Remedies • The Commercial Docket • Statute of Limitations

14-3 Warranty Protection
Express Warranties • Implied Warranties • Warranty of Title • Warranty Exclusion • Privity Not Required

THE OPENING CASE Round 1
Textualism versus Pragmatism: When Is an Acceptance Really an Acceptance (or a Rejection)?

The textualist approach to interpreting the law (the Constitution, case law, statutory law, administrative regulations, and so on) relies on a very simple principle: The only real way to know the intent of a law is to understand the words with which it is written. In contrast, the pragmatic approach to legal analysis demands that we check out a variety of ancillary resources (legislative histories, session notes, drafts of the bill, historical and contemporary sociopolitical events, social media messaging, and so on) to determine how the words of that law will bend, twist, and redefine themselves to fit into the modern world. Let's see how this plays out in the case of *Hooten v. Trimat*.

The case began when the Hooten Equipment Company (HEC), a manufacturing firm entered into a contract with a construction company named Trimat Inc. (TI) for the delivery of a range hood with an exhaust fan rated for 2,400 cubic feet. HEC complied with the order (well, sort of, anyway). Unfortunately, what HEC actually delivered to TI was a range hood with an exhaust fan rated at 3,025 cubic feet per minute. All of this was done in an even-handed, straightforward way. HEC included an invoice in the package that stated—in good, straightforward prose—that the range hood had an exhaust fan that was rated at 3,025 feet per minute rather than the 2,400 feet per minute that HEC had actually ordered. It seems that when the shipment arrived at the job site, no one from either TEC or TI bothered to check the invoice against the actual goods that were delivered. Nevertheless, all went well until TI delivered the range hood to the site where it was installed by the employees of another company. This was when things went wrong. It was at this time that TI learned that the range hood, as delivered by HEC, did not meet the guidelines established by the Ohio Industrial Department of Commerce, Division of Industrial Compliance Guidelines. The problem was that the fan was too large to permit the necessary ductwork to be installed properly.

The general manager of TI, Maurice Toler, was not pleased, so he sent a letter to HEC that informed the proper personnel that the range hood had not met the required specifications established by the state and, therefore, until HEC corrected the matter, no payment would be forthcoming. Nevertheless, HEC continued to demand payment. For its part, TI continued to refuse to pay for a range hood that it could not use. Faced with a stalemate, HEC elected to bring this lawsuit in a state court. At trial, HEC argued that TI had not only accepted the range hood as is, despite what the invoice said, but had also installed it at the construction site. Therefore, TI had not rejected the range hood but had, instead, accepted it—pure and simple. TI disagreed, noting that HEC had been informed orally and by letter that they (TI) would not pay for nonconforming goods. Given this clear and obvious rejection of the range hood, Ti continued, the company owned nothing to HEC. The trial court listened to both sides, consulted the appropriate sections of the Uniform Commercial Code (UCC), and decided that TI had, indeed, accepted the nonconforming goods and so clearly owed HEC the money due. The appropriate officials at TI thought that the only thing clear about the entire case was that they had ordered a range hood with an exhaust fan that was rated at 2,400 feet per minute and had received a range hood with an exhaust fan that was rated at 3,025 feet per minute. Therefore, they continued to refuse to pay and filed an appeal with the Fourth District Court of Appeals. The results of the appeal turned on the evidence and on the proper interpretation of the Uniform Commercial Code. Which side will win? HEC, the exhausted equipment firm, or TI, the confused construction company? Or to put it another more poetic way, which theory triumphs: textualism or pragmatism? [See: *Hooten Equipment Company v. Trimat, Inc.*, 4th District No. 03CA16 2004-Ohio-1128.]

Opening Case Questions

1. Is the agreement between HEC and TI a sales contract or a lease agreement? Explain.
2. What rights and duties generally go along with the buyer in a sales contract? Explain.
3. What rights and duties generally go along with the seller in a sales contract? Explain.
4. What is the purpose of the Magnuson–Moss Warranty Act? Explain.
5. If TI did not really accept the range hood, what happens to the contract between TI and HEC and what happens to the money that TI owes to HEC? Explain.

Source: See: *Hooten Equipment Company v. Trimat, Inc.*, 4th District No. 03CA16 2004-Ohio-1128)

 Learning Objectives

1. Describe what is meant by tender of performance.
2. Outline the rights and duties of sellers and buyers in a sales contract.
3. Explain the doctrine of anticipatory breach.
4. Discuss the seller's and the buyer's remedies in case of a breach.
5. Define the term *statute of limitations*.
6. Describe the three ways in which an express warranty may be created.
7. State the requirements of the Magnuson–Moss Warranty Act.
8. Differentiate among the implied warranties of fitness for a particular purpose, merchantability, and usage of trade.
9. Explain the meaning of a warranty of title.
10. Recognize the ways in which warranties may be excluded.

14-1 Rights and Duties of the Parties

The duties of the parties to a sales contract are simple and straightforward: The seller is obligated to turn the goods over to the buyer, and the buyer is obligated to accept and pay for the goods. In addition, all parties must act in **good faith**, which means that they must act honestly. The court need not enforce a contract or part of a contract that it finds to be unconscionable. An **unconscionable contract** is one that gives an unfair advantage to one of the parties. Unequal bargaining power, the absence of a meaningful choice by one party, and unreasonably one-sided terms, when put together, indicate unconscionability. When disputes arise between parties who have dealt together in the past, the court often looks to their past dealings to give meaning to the disputed transaction.

When interpreting the meaning of a contract, the court may also consider any usage of trade—that is, any particular methods of doing business that are commonly used in that field—and the way that the parties have dealt with one another in the past. Although terms that are expressly stated in a contract will usually control the contract's meaning, the parties' past dealings and usage of trade are often considered to supplement or qualify the express

UCC 1-205

terms. Moreover, the UCC establishes a series of rights and duties that are key elements within all sales contracts. Most of these rights and duties are based on common sense and the practicality of the commercial world. Others have been uniquely created by the Uniform Law Commission (ULC) to ensure stability in the world of sales. These rights and duties include the tender of performance, the buyer's rights and duties upon delivery of improper goods, and the seller's right to cure improper tender.

Tender of Performance

When the seller offers to turn the goods over to the buyer and when the buyer offers to pay for them, **tender of performance** occurs. It is the offering by the parties to do what they have agreed to do under the terms of the contract. Tender is necessary to test the party's ability and willingness to perform his or her part of the bargain. The seller must make tender of

THE OPENING CASE Round 2
Textualism versus Pragmatism: When Is an Acceptance Really an Acceptance (or a Rejection)?

The Opening Case began when Trimat Inc. (TI) ordered a range hood with an exhaust fan rated for 2,400 cubic feet from Hooten Equipment Company (HEC), a manufacturing firm. HEC attempted to fill the order by delivering a range hood with an exhaust fan rated at 3,025 cubic feet per minute. To its credit, HEC included an honest invoice that stated, clearly and succinctly, that the range hood had an exhaust fan that was rated at 3,025 feet per minute, which, of course, was not what TI had ordered. Curiously, no one from either HEC or TI bothered to check the invoice against the actual goods when the shipment arrived. Once the range hood was installed, however, it became clear that it did not meet the guidelines established by the Ohio Industrial Department of Commerce, Division of Industrial Compliance Guidelines. Apparently, the fan was too large to allow the proper ductwork to be installed. Maurice Toler, the general manager of TI, sent a letter to HEC that informed HEC that the range hood had not met the required specifications established by the state and, as a result, unless HEC corrected the matter, no payment would be forthcoming. Despite this, HEC continued to demand payment; at the same time, TI persisted in its refusal to pay for a range hood that was less than useless to it. To vindicate itself, HEC brought this lawsuit in a state court.

HEC argued at trial that TI had accepted the range hood as is, despite what the invoice said, and even more tellingly, had installed it at the construction site. HEC concluded that TI had not rejected the range hood but had, instead, accepted it. TI disagreed, noting that HEC had been informed orally and by letter that it (TI) would not pay for nonconforming goods. Given this clear and obvious rejection of the range hood, TI continued to say that the company owned nothing to HEC.

It is important to see that this entire lawsuit is possible because both sides have made an appropriate tender of performance. Recall that tender is required to make certain that each party is able and willing to do what is expected under the terms of the contract. HEC has fulfilled its part by making the delivery of what it thought would be an appropriate range hood. TI is willing to pay, but only when the seller delivers conforming goods. If either HEC or TI had failed to make tender, the lawsuit could not have been initiated by the party that had not made tender. Also remember that to have the right to bring suit on a sales contract, the seller of goods (HEC in this case) must make tender of delivery—that is, offer to turn the goods over to the buyer. Failure to make this offer is an excuse for the buyer not to perform its part of the bargain. Apparently, this was not a problem in this case despite the fact that nonconforming gods are at the heart of the dispute. Had it been a problem, we would not be discussing the case now. [See: *Hooten Equipment Company v. Trimat, Inc.*, 4th District No. 03CA16 2004-Ohio-1128.]

Source: See: *Hooten Equipment Company v. Trimat, Inc.*, 4th District No. 03CA16 2004-Ohio-1128)

delivery, and the buyer must make tender of payment. If one party fails to make tender and the other breaches the contract, the one not making tender cannot bring suit. To be in a position to bring suit on a sales contract, the seller of goods must make **tender of delivery**, that is, offer to turn the goods over to the buyer. Failure to make this offer is an excuse for buyers not to perform their part of the bargain.

Making Proper Tender To make proper tender, the seller must put and hold conforming goods at the buyer's disposition during a reasonable hour of the day. Sometimes goods are in the possession of a warehouse and are to be turned over to the buyer without being moved. When this situation occurs, tender requires that the seller either tender a document of title covering the goods or obtain an acknowledgment by the warehouse of the buyer's right to their possession. In a **shipment contract**, the seller must put the goods in the possession of a carrier and contract with that carrier for their transportation. Any necessary documents must be sent to the buyer, who must be promptly notified of the shipment.

UCC 2-507
UCC 2-503(1)(b)
UCC 2-504
UCC 2-503(4)

Tender of Payment by Buyer Although the seller is obligated to deliver the goods to the buyer, this obligation stands on the condition that the buyer make tender of payment, unless otherwise agreed. **Tender of payment** means offering to turn the necessary money over to the seller. Such tender may be made by any means or in any manner that is commonly used in the ordinary course of business. The seller has the right to demand payment in legal tender but must give the buyer a reasonable time to obtain it. **Legal tender** is money that may be offered legally in satisfaction of a debt and that must be accepted by a creditor when offered. Payment by check is conditional under the UCC. If the check clears, the debt is discharged. If the check is dishonored, the debt is revived. When a contract requires payment before inspection, as when goods are shipped c.o.d., the buyer must pay for them first, even if they turn out to be defective when they are inspected. Of course, if the defect is obvious, the buyer would not have to accept or pay for the goods. Payment by the buyer before inspecting the goods does not constitute an acceptance of them. Upon discovering a defect and notifying the seller, the buyer may use any of the remedies that are mentioned later in the chapter against the seller for breach of contract.

UCC 2-511(1)
UCC 2-511(3)
UCC 2-512

UCC 2-513
UCC 2-106(2)

Buyer's Rights and Duties

Except when goods are shipped c.o.d. or when the contract provides for payment against a document of title, the buyer has the right to inspect the goods before accepting or paying for them. The inspection may take place after the goods arrive at their destination. Expenses of inspection must be borne by the buyer but may be recovered from the seller if the goods do not conform to the contract and are rejected by the buyer. Goods conform to a contract when they are in accordance with the obligations under the contract. When defective goods or goods not of the kind specified in the contract are delivered, the buyer may elect to reject them all, accept them all, or accept any commercial unit or units and reject the rest. A **commercial unit** is a single whole for the purpose of sale, the division of which impairs its character or value on the market. For example, a commercial unit may be a set of articles (e.g., suite of furniture, assortment of sizes), a quantity (e.g., bale, gross, carload), or a single article (e.g., a machine) treated in the marketplace as a single whole item.

Failure of the buyer to inspect goods upon delivery results in an acceptance of the goods, even if nonconforming.

©McGraw-Hill Education/ John Flournoy

Rejection of Goods by the Buyer
A rejection occurs when a buyer refuses to accept delivery of goods tendered. A rejection must be done within a reasonable time after delivery or tender to

UCC 2-601

CISG Article 38
(see Appendix C)

UCC 2-602

the buyer. After a rejection, the buyer may not claim ownership of the goods. In addition, the buyer must notify the seller of the particular defect in the goods so as to give the seller an opportunity to correct the defect. If the goods are in the buyer's possession, the buyer must hold them with reasonable care long enough for the seller to remove them.

BUSINESS LAW WITH UCC APPLICATIONS AND NOW—THE APPLICATIONS

The Uniform Commercial Code and Learning to Live with Rejection

Now that you have a had a cursory look at rejection and the sales contract, let's get down to the real "nitty-gritty." Rejection is not as simple as it seems. The UCC does not just say, "Oh sure, if you don't like what you bought when it arrives, that's okay, just send it back." That would be too simple and, well, let's face it, just a bit unfair. Instead, the UCC gives us a fairly straightforward, if somewhat complex, set of standards for an effective rejection. The standards of rejection under the UCC look like this:

UCC 2-602 Manner and Effect of Rightful Rejection

(1) Rejection of goods must be made within a reasonable time after their delivery or tender. It is ineffective unless the buyer seasonably notifies the seller.

(2) Subject to provisions of the two following sections on rejected goods (Sections 2-603 and 2-604),

    (a) after rejection any exercise of ownership by the buyer with respect to any commercial unit is wrongful as against the seller; and

    (b) if the buyer has before rejection taken physical possession of the goods in which he does not have a security interest under the provisions of this Article (subsection (3) of section 2-711), he is under a duty after rejection to hold them with reasonable care at the seller's disposition for a time sufficient to permit the seller to remove them; but

    (c) the buyer has no further obligations with regard to goods rightfully rejected.

(3) The seller's rights with respect to goods wrongfully reject are governed by the provisions of this Article on Seller's remedies in general (Section 2-703).

Okay. That is all very nice, but what does it mean? Well, it means, first, that the buyer who finds something wrong with the goods he or she just received better speak up quickly. About what? About the fact that the are about to be rejected, that's what. Second, the buyer cannot just speak up in-house. No, no, no—that rejection must be communicated to the seller, and although UCC Section 6-602 does not say this, common sense dictates that the rejection be in writing. Third, after this communication, the buyer cannot just up and use the goods like they belong to him or her. So what does the buyer do with the rejected goods? That's number four: The buyer cannot just leave those goods out in the rain or snow. He or she better take care of them for a reasonable time, so the seller can get them back in good shape. (What's a reasonable time? That is a good question. *Reasonableness* cannot be defined, but everyone knows it when they see it. So, a reasonable time for a crate of oranges is not the same as a reasonable time for a box of auto parts. Take it from there.) Fifth, okay, that is it, the buyer has no other duties regarding those rejected goods. Oh, sorry, one more thing—all of this is subject to the seller's remedies, so you really better read ahead to UCC Section 2-703.

Alright, how does this all play out in the real world of economic transactions? That's another good question. That is why we include an Opening Case in every chapter—to give you a taste of the real world.

So before looking at the next installment of this chapter's Opening Case, *Hooten v. Trimat*, try answering the following questions:

1. Did the the representative for TI communicate the rejection of the range hood to HEC within a reasonable time? Explain.
2. Did the representatives of TI take physical possession of the goods and treat them like they belonged to TI? Explain.
3. Did the representatives of TI make a reasonable inspection of the goods on delivery? (Take a look at UCC 2-606 to answer this one.) Explain.
4. Should the fact that TI went ahead and installed (or tried to) the range hood make a difference to the outcome of the case? Why or why not?
5. How would you rule for HEC or TI? Explain.

More on the Buyer's Duties on Rejection If the seller gives no instructions within a reasonable time after being notified of the rejection, the buyer may store the goods for the seller, reship them to the seller, or resell them for the seller. In all cases, the buyer is entitled to be reimbursed for expenses. A special duty comes into existence when a buyer who is a merchant rejects goods. Merchant buyers have a duty after the rejection of goods in their possession or control to follow any reasonable instructions received from the seller with respect to the goods. If there are no such instructions, they must make reasonable efforts to sell the goods for the seller if they are perishable or threaten to decline speedily in value. Merchants who sell rejected goods are entitled to be reimbursed either by the seller or from the proceeds of the sale for reasonable expenses of caring for and selling the goods. They are also entitled to such commission as is usual in the trade or, if none, a reasonable sum not exceeding 10 percent of the proceeds of the sale. A buyer who is not a merchant has no other obligation regarding goods that are rightfully rejected.

UCC 2-604

Acceptance of Goods by the Buyer Once goods have been accepted, they cannot be rejected. Acceptance of goods takes place when the buyer, after a reasonable opportunity to inspect them, does any of the following:

UCC 2-603(1)
UCC 2-603(2)
UCC 2-606

- Signifies to the seller that the goods are conforming—that is, that they are in accordance with the obligations under the contract.
- Signifies to the seller a willingness to take them even though they are not conforming.
- Fails to reject them.
- Performs any act that is inconsistent with the seller's ownership.

When the buyer accepts goods and later discovers something wrong with them, the buyer must notify the seller within a reasonable time after the discovery. The failure to give proper notice will prevent the buyer from having recourse against the seller.

UCC 2-607(3)

Revocation of Acceptance If a buyer has accepted goods on the assumption that their nonconformity would be corrected by the seller and the seller does not do so, the buyer may revoke the acceptance. This revocation must be made within a reasonable time after the buyer discovers the nonconformity. A revocation of an acceptance is not effective until the buyer notifies the seller of it. Buyers who revoke an acceptance have the same rights and duties with regard to the goods involved as if they had rejected them.

UCC 2-608

THE OPENING CASE *Round 3*
Textualism versus Pragmatism: When Is an Acceptance Really an Acceptance (or a Rejection)

As noted earlier, this case started when the Hooten Equipment Company (HEC) agreed to deliver a range hood with an exhaust fan rated for 2,400 cubic feet to Trimat Inc. As promised, HEC delivered the range hood to the requested location. Regrettably, it was later discovered that HEC had actually delivered a range hood with an exhaust fan rated at 3,025 cubic feet per minute, not the 2,400 cubic feet requested. Unfortunately, this was discovered after the nonconforming range hood had been installed. Probably, after this problem surfaced, some bright boy or gal went back to the file, pulled out the invoice, and discovered that HEC had, indeed, noted that the range hood had a 3,025 cubic capacity. Apparently, no one had checked the invoice to see if the range hood conformed to the original order. The general manager of TI sent a letter to HEC that informed HEC that the range hood had not met the required specifications established by the state and, therefore, until HEC corrected the matter, it would not be paid. This may have been done so that TI could say that it had rejected the nonconforming goods within a reasonable time. Despite the fact that it now knew that the range hood was not what TI had requested, HEC still demanded payment. For its part, TI continued to refuse to pay for a range hood that it could not use. To move things forward, HEC sued TI, arguing that TI had accepted the range hood as is, despite what the invoice said, and had installed it at the construction site. Therefore, TI had not rejected the range hood but had, instead, accepted it—end of argument. TI disagreed, noting that HEC had been informed orally and by letter that the goods were nonconforming. TI concluded that these oral discussions and the written letter, taken together, constituted a legitimate rejection under UCC 2-602 and UCC 2-606. Given this legitimate rejection, TI owed nothing to HEC.

The trial court listened to both sides, consulted the appropriate sections of the Uniform Commercial Code (UCC), and decided that TI had accepted the nonconforming goods and so owed HEC the money due. Now, here is the most interesting part of this case. The ruling of the trial court seems almost counterintuitive, not to mention unfair. The poor folks at TI are stuck with a range hood they cannot use and, to add insult to injury, must now pay—not only for something that they cannot use, but also for something they must tear out and replace, at their expense. Despite this apparent anomaly, the court did not just pull this decision out of thin air. On the contrary, the court came to this conclusion by a careful textual reading of the statute and a mindful application of the evidence to the words of that statute. First, the court acknowledges that TI *believes* that it *did not accept* the nonconforming goods. TI tries to prove this by pointing to UCC 2-606, which reads that, (1) acceptance occurs only after the buyer has had a reasonable time to inspect the goods and then tells the seller they are conforming or that it will take the nonconforming goods despite the defects or (2) when the buyer does not make an effective rejection of the nonconforming goods. TI argues that the goods were nonconforming, and it did not accept the nonconforming goods (number 1) and it made an effective rejection (number 2). The court is willing to admit that the goods are nonconforming and that TI did not accept those nonconforming goods (number 1). So far, so good for TI. However, the statute (UCC 202-6) does not stop there.

At this point, the court delivers a masterful textualist analysis. The trial court argues, and ultimately the appellate court agrees, that the question can be reduced to whether TI made an effective rejection (number 2). Now two sections of the UCC are involved here—UCC 2-606 (1) (a) and (b), What Constitutes Acceptance, and UCC 2-602 (1), The Manner and Effect of Rightful Rejection. Now recall the exact words of these two statutes. First, UCC 2-606 (1) (a) and (b) says that "Acceptance of the goods occurs when the buyer . . . (a) after a reasonable opportunity to inspect the goods . . . (b) fails to make an effective rejection (subsection (1) of Section 2-602), but such acceptance does not occur until the buyer has had a reasonable opportunity to inspect them." So did TI (the Buyer) have a reasonable opportunity to inspect the goods, and did it fail to make an effective rejection under (subsection (1) of Section 2-203)? First, the court notes that TI had the invoice when it first received the range hood but did not take the opportunity to read it. Therefore, it had a reasonable opportunity to inspect the goods. Second, again looking at the language of the statute and the evidence, the court decides that TI failed to make an effective rejection under UCC Section 2-602 (1). Under UCC 2-602 (1), an effective rejection would be one in which the buyer makes the rejection "within a reasonable time after their delivery or tender."

The court looked at the evidence, and the best it could do was locate the delivery in December 2000 and the letter in January 2002. This seems like an inordinate amount of time between the delivery and the rejection letter. Now there may have been an oral rejection somewhere along the way, but TI could offer no evidence of such an oral rejection. Also, TI actually installed the nonconforming range hood. The court concludes that in the installation process itself, TI had many opportunities to discover the defect and yet did not do so. In this case, the plain language of the statute convinced both the trial court and the appellate court that the buyer had a reasonable amount of time and many reasonable opportunities to reject the nonconforming goods and did not do so. Thus, given the language of the statute, TI must pay for the nonconforming range hood. This result may appear unfair to many of us. However, the job of the court is to interpret the statute, not rewrite it. If the result seems unfair and the fault lies in the words of the statute, then it is the legislature's job, not the courts, to change that law. [See: *Hooten Equipment Company v. Trimat, Inc.*, 4th District No. 03CA16 2004-Ohio-1128.]

Source: See: *Hooten Equipment Company v. Trimat, Inc.*, 4th District No. 03CA16 2004-Ohio-1128)

Seller's Rights and Duties

Sellers may sometimes **cure** an improper tender or delivery of goods; that is, they may correct the defect that caused the goods to be rejected by the buyer. When the time for performance has not yet expired, the seller has the right to cure the defect and make a proper tender within the contract time. If the time for performance has expired, the seller is allowed to have an additional amount of time to substitute a conforming tender if the seller has reasonable grounds to believe that the goods that were delivered were acceptable. In all cases, sellers have a duty to notify buyers that they are going to cure the improper tender or delivery. The seller does not have the right to cure improper tender when a buyer accepts nonconforming goods, even though the buyer may later sue the seller for breach of contract. The seller has this right only when the buyer either rejects the goods tendered or revokes an acceptance of the goods.

UCC 2-508

quick quiz 14-1

1. According to the law of sales contracts, all parties must act in good faith, which means they must act honestly.	true | false
2. Tender of performance is the offering by the parties to do what they have agreed to do under the terms of the contract.	true | false
3. Buyers have no right to inspect goods before paying for them when they are shipped c.o.d.	true | false

14-2 Breach of Contract

Breach of contract occurs when one of the parties fails to do what was agreed upon in the contract. When this happens, the other party to the contract has specific remedies available under the UCC. All parties must attempt to mitigate the damages, that is, to keep them as low as possible.

Anticipatory Breach

UCC 2-610

Sometimes, one of the parties will notify the other party before the time for performance that he or she is not going to conform. This notification is known as *anticipatory breach*. It is a breach committed before there is a present duty to perform the contract. Under older contractual law, the injured party in such a case had to wait until the actual time for performance before bringing suit or taking some other action. It was necessary to wait for the actual time for performance to know for sure that the other party was indeed not going to perform. Under the UCC, when either party repudiates the contract before the time for performance, the injured party may take action immediately if waiting would be unjust or cause a material inconvenience. Any of the remedies for breach of contract are available to the aggrieved party, in addition to the right to suspend his or her own performance.

EXAMPLE 14-1: Anticipatory Breach

The Westwell Construction Company ordered 1,000 steel I-beams to be made to order from the Anaconda Steel Corporation for use in a building that Westwell was going to begin building in six months. Anaconda Steel agreed to deliver the I-beams on or before that date. Two months before the delivery date, Anaconda Steel notified Westwell that it would not be able to fill the order. Westwell could treat the contract as having been breached and use any of the buyer's remedies that are available to him under the UCC.

Seller's Remedies

UCC 2-703(a)

When a buyer breaches a sales contract, the seller may select from a number of remedies. Table 14-1 lists six remedies that sellers may employ when the buyer breaches. These remedies include withholding the delivery of goods, stopping the delivery of the goods, reselling the goods, recovering damages, suing for the price of the goods, and simply canceling the contract. Of the six remedies, the last one, canceling the contract, is the simplest and the most pain-free solution. However, from a financial perspective, it is often the most damaging. On the other hand, the most difficult and time-consuming is initiating a lawsuit. However, if it is handled properly, a lawsuit can be the fairest and the most effective remedy available in the law today.

UCC 2-705

Withhold or Stop the Delivery of Goods If the goods have not been delivered, the seller has a right to keep them upon learning of the buyer's breach. If, after shipping the goods, the seller discovers that the buyer is **insolvent** (unable to pay debts), the seller may have the delivery stopped. This right is known as **stoppage in transit** and is permitted after goods have been

Table 14-1 Seller's Remedies When the Buyer Breaches

1. Withhold delivery of any goods not yet delivered.
2. If the buyer is insolvent, stop delivery of any goods that are still in the possession of a carrier.
3. Resell any goods that have been rightfully withheld, and then sue the buyer for the difference between the agreed price and the resale price.
4. If the goods cannot be resold, sue the buyer for the difference between the agreed price and the market price.
5. Sue the buyer for the price of any goods that were accepted by the buyer.
6. Cancel the contract.

shipped but before they have reached their destination. The seller must give information to the carrier (the transportation company) to satisfy the latter that the buyer is insolvent. In addition, the seller must accept responsibility for any damage suffered by the carrier for not completing the shipment. If the insolvency information is incorrect, both the seller and the carrier could be sued for damages. The seller may also stop delivery of a carload, truckload, planeload, or larger shipments of express or freight when the buyer repudiates or fails to make a payment that is due before delivery or otherwise breaches the contract. If the seller has issued a document of title, the seller can stop delivery only by surrendering the document to the carrier. If the buyer has received the document, delivery of the goods cannot be stopped in transit.

Resell the Goods The seller may resell the goods or the undelivered balance of them. In the case of unfinished manufactured goods, a seller may either complete the manufacture and resell the finished goods or cease manufacture and resell the unfinished goods for scrap or salvage value. In such cases, the seller must use reasonable commercial judgment to avoid losses. After the sale, the injured party may sue the other for the difference between what the property brought on resale and the price the buyer had agreed to pay in the contract. Resale may be a public or private sale. If it is a private sale, the seller must give the buyer reasonable notice of its intention to resell the goods. If it is a public sale, it must be made at a place that is normally used for public sales, if such a place is available. In addition, if the goods are perishable or threaten to decline in value speedily, the seller must give the buyer reasonable notice of the time and place of resale. A purchaser who buys in good faith at a resale takes the goods free of any rights of the original buyer. Furthermore, the seller is not accountable to the buyer for any profit made on the resale. The seller who chooses to do so may buy the goods at resale.

UCC 2-706(1)
UCC 2-704(2)
UCC 2-706(4)(b)
UCC 2-706(4)(d)

Damages The seller may retain the merchandise and sue the buyer for either the difference between the contract price and the market price at the time the buyer breached the agreement or the profit (including overhead) that the seller would have made had the contract been performed. In either case, the seller is also entitled to *incidental damages*. These damages are reasonable expenses that indirectly result from the breach, such as expenses incurred in stopping delivery of goods, transporting goods, and caring for goods after the buyer's breach.

UCC 2-708
UCC 2-710

Sue for Price The seller may sue for the price of any goods that the buyer has accepted. Similarly, upon the buyer's breach, the seller may bring suit for the price of goods that cannot be resold at a reasonable price. In addition, the seller may sue the buyer for the price of any *lost* or damaged goods after the risk of their loss has passed to the buyer. In the commercial setting this remedy is sanctioned by the Uniform Commercial Code in UCC 2-709 (1) (a). The seller who sues the buyer for the price must hold for the buyer any goods that are under the seller's control. The goods may be sold, however, at any time resale is possible before the collection of a judgment in the case. The net proceeds of any resale must be credited to the buyer. Any goods that are not resold become the property of the buyer if the buyer pays for them as a result of a court judgment.

UCC 2-709

Cancel the Contract The seller can cancel the contract. This cancellation occurs when the seller ends the contract because the other party breached. When cancellation takes place in this manner, the seller may use any of the remedies mentioned for breach of contract.

UCC 2-106

Buyer's Remedies

When a seller breaches a sales contract, the buyer may select from a number of remedies. Table 14-2 lists six remedies that buyers may use whenever the seller breaches the sales contract. The first two remedies are relatively clear and straightforward. The buyer either tells the seller that the deal is off or demands a repayment of any money that has already been

Table 14-2 Buyer's Remedies When the Seller Breaches

1. Cancel the contract.
2. Sue the seller for the return of any money that has been paid.
3. Cover the sale, that is, buy similar goods from someone else and sue the seller for the difference between the agreed price and the cost of the purchase.
4. Sue the seller for the difference between the agreed price and the market price at the time the buyer learned of the breach.
5. If nonconforming goods have been accepted, notify the seller that they do not conform to the contract. Then, if no adjustment is made, sue the seller either for breach of contract or for breach of warranty.
6. When goods are unique or rare, sue for specific performance.

A CLASSIC CASE   The Case of the Disappearing Delivery or the Mystery of the Missing Merchandise

Any contract that involves clothing is covered by the Uniform Commercial Code (UCC). Keep in mind, as you read this case, that the commissioners who wrote the UCC did their best to protect all the parties involved in a contract, even those who might not deserve that protection. In this case, the plaintiff is a Los Angeles clothing manufacturer, and the defendant is a retailer doing business in Westport, Connecticut, as a clothing store named The Rage. The manufacturer received an order from The Rage for a shipment of clothing that amounted to $2,216. The clothing was packaged carefully and then turned over to a reputable and dependable shipper, the Denver-Chicago Shipping Company (Denver). Denver gave a bill of lading to the manufacturer, and the manufacturer sent along four separate invoices to The Rage. The invoices stated explicitly that the shipment was "F.O.B. Los Angeles," that the shipper was Denver-Chicago, and that the buyer bore the risk of loss. Moreover, the bill of lading stated quite clearly that all shipping charges would be paid by The Rage.

At some point between Los Angeles and Westport, exactly where is never made clear, Denver handed the shipment off to another trucking firm, the Old Colony Transportation Company of South Dartmouth, Massachusetts. When the Old Colony truck arrived at The Rage, the driver refused to deliver the goods inside the store, preferring to deliver them outside the premises. When the store manager refused to accept the eight cartons of clothing unless they ended up inside the store, the trucker drove off, still in possession of the shipment. The clothing was never seen again. The owner of The Rage sent an immediate letter of protest to the manufacturer, which filed a claim against Denver, which Denver refused to honor. Meanwhile, in Connecticut, the owner of The Rage continued to demand that the missing shipment be delivered inside the store. Whenever the manufacturer tried to contact the owner, he was unavailable. When the manufacturer finally sued, the owner of The Rage argued that he could not possibly be liable for goods he never received. Instead, he claimed that the manufacturer was responsible for the loss of the shipment because the manufacturer chose an unreliable shipper. In turn, the manufacturer argued that since the risk of loss passed to the retailer when the shipment was delivered to the trucker and since the retailer refused to accept a shipment that was quite literally on his doorstep, he must pay for the eight cartons of clothing whether he actually received them or not. The court agreed with the manufacturer. To prove its point, the court referred directly to UCC 2-709, which says quite clearly, "(1) When the buyer fails to pay the price as it becomes due, the seller may recover . . . the price (a) . . . of conforming goods lost or damaged within a commercially reasonable time after the risk of their loss has passed to the buyer." [See: *Ninth Street East, Ltd., v. Harrison*, 259 A.2d 772, 5 Conn.Cir.Ct. 597 (Connecticut Circuit Court, First Circuit).]

Source: See: *Ninth Street East, Ltd., v. Harrison*, 259 A.2d 772, 5 Conn.Cir.Ct. 597 (Connecticut Circuit Court, First Circuit).

handed over to the seller as a down payment or some other type of monetary guarantee of performance. If the seller cooperates, there is no need to go any further. However, if the seller refuses to comply, the buyer has several additional options available. These include cover the sale, sue for breach, keep the goods and seek an adjustment, or, in some rare circumstances, sue for specific performance. Of these four remedies, the last one, suing for specific performance is the most difficult and the least applicable remedy because it can only be used when the subject matter of the sales contract is something unique, such as an original work of art, or when the subject is very rare, as with an antique, a family heirloom, or a vintage automobile. On the other hand, from a financial perspective, it is often a very rewarding process for buyers because, if they are successful, they receive exactly what they bargained for in the original contract.

UCC 2-711
UCC 2-712

Cover the Sale or Sue for Breach The buyer may cover the sale, that is, buy similar goods from someone else. The buyer may then sue the seller for the difference between the agreed price and the cost of the purchase. Cover must be made without unreasonable delay. In the alternative, when a seller breaches a contract by not delivering the goods, the buyer may sue for damages if any were suffered. The measure of damages is the difference between the price that the parties agreed upon and the price of the same goods in the marketplace on the date the buyer learned of the breach. In addition, the buyer may sue for incidental and consequential damages. Damages for breach of contract may be liquidated, that is, agreed upon by the parties when they first enter into the contract. Liquidated damages will be allowed by the court if they are reasonable.

EXAMPLE 14-2: Cover of a Sales Contract

Flamme Bros. contracted to deliver a specific quantity of corn to Farmers' Union Co-op Co., a cooperative grain elevator. When Flamme Bros. failed to deliver the corn, Farmers' Union bought corn from its members over a two-week period. The court held that this purchase was cover of the contract without unreasonable delay. Farmers' Union recovered the difference between the agreed price of the corn from Flamme Bros. and the price it paid to the farmers for the corn it bought. In the alternative, Farmer's Union could have refrained from purchasing the grain from other suppliers and simply brought a lawsuit against Flamme Brothers for damages. The damages would be measured by the difference between the price that the parties agreed upon and the price of corn in the marketplace on the date Farmer's Union learned of the breach. In addition, Farmer's Union may sue for incidental and consequential damages.

Keep Goods and Seek Adjustment When improper goods are delivered, the buyer may keep them and ask the seller for an adjustment. If no adjustment is made, the buyer may sue the seller for either breach of contract or breach of warranty, whichever applies. The amount of the suit would be the difference between the value of the goods contracted for and the value of the goods received. Warranties are discussed in later in this chapter.

EXAMPLE 14-3: Swimsuit Adjustment

The Jacobs Brothers Department chain of Omaha ordered 40 dozen swimsuits from Illumination Encore Ltd., a clothing manufacturer in Fort Worth. The suits that were delivered were totally different from the samples shown by Illumination's sales rep. Because Jacobs Brothers needed swimsuits for its spring trade show, Kenneth Jacobs, the CEO of the department chain, decided to keep them. If no adjustment is made by the manufacturer, Illumination Encore, Jacobs can sue the manufacturer for damages (including loss of profits) that were suffered because of the breach of the express warranty that the goods would be the same as the sample.

UCC 2-713
UCC 2-715
UCC 2-718(1)
UCC 2-714(2)
UCC 2-716(1)

Sue for Specific Performance When the goods are unique or rare, the buyer may ask the court to order the seller to do what he or she agreed to do under the contract terms. This request is known as an action for specific performance of the contract. A decree of specific performance, if granted by the court, would require the seller to deliver to the buyer the goods described in the sales agreement. This type of action is permitted only when an award of money will not give the buyer sufficient relief. Contracts for *objets d'art*, rare gems, antiques, and goods described as one of a kind come within the scope of this type of action. Under the UCC, the decree of specific performance may include the payment of the price, damages, or other relief as the court may deem just. Buyers have a right of replevin for goods that have been identified to the contract if, after a reasonable effort, they are unable to buy the goods elsewhere. A **writ of replevin** is a court action that allows a person entitled to goods to recover them from someone who has them wrongfully.

The Commercial Docket

UCC 2-716(3)
UCC 2-725

Commercial cases have become so numerous recently that a few states have taken the extraordinary step of establishing a separate court docket dedicated exclusively to commercial cases. Those commentators who support establishing a commercial docket argue that commercial lawsuits can be handled more effectively if they are assigned to judges who have been trained to manage such cases. For example, the State of Ohio recently inaugurated a commercial docket program. The **commercial docket** provides a legal forum that is limited to commercial lawsuits handled by judges and mediators who receive special education sessions devoted exclusively to commercial law. To implement the system, the chief justice of the Ohio Supreme Court chose five trial courts to lead the way by establishing a commercial docket within their jurisdictions. The chief justice then assigned several judges to handle every case that fit within the commercial docket in their court. The program limits the commercial docket to cases that involve disputes among two or more businesses, although the court also handles a long list of similar lawsuits, including such things as the formation or dissolution of a business, the rights and duties of business partners, and so on. Each commercial docket judge chooses a cadre of mediators, referred to in Ohio as **special masters**, who are trained to handle commercial lawsuits. The special masters are the first line of defense on the commercial docket. They handle cases and make rulings that are then passed on to the commercial docket judge for evaluation and approval. The judge can uphold, reject, reverse, or resubmit the case to the special master. [See: Ohio Rules of Superintendence for the Courts of Ohio, Rules 49-49.12.]

A QUESTION OF ETHICS

The Science Court v. The Commercial Docket

As noted earlier, a planned court system that is similar to the Ohio commercial docket is the proposed science court. The science court would act as a forum for cases involving scientific and technological disputes. Like commercial docket judges, the science court judges would be trained to deal exclusively with cases of a scientific and technological nature. The science court would focus on disputes involving genetic engineering; nuclear energy research; cyber-contract law; energy law; cloning; engineering, architectural, and technological projects; medical treatments; medical research; environmental law; birth control; health care wills; health care power of attorney disputes; abortion law disputes; intellectual property problems; surrogate parenting; and so on. The plan is to use specially trained judges with scientific and technological backgrounds who will be equipped to handle the complexities of today's science-related cases. The science court and the commercial docket look good on paper, but what would happen were the science court judges to face ethical issues? Would they be able to deal with such issues effectively? What would happen when the jurisdiction of the science court clashed with the jurisdiction of the commercial docket? How would such disputes be resolved?

ETHICAL QUESTIONS

1. What happens when a commercial contract involves an ethically questionable scientific issue, such as cloning or genetic engineering? Who should handle such a case? The science court judges or the commercial docket mediators? Or should there be a third court for purely ethical questions? Explain.
2. What would happen with a case involving a surrogate parenting contract? Is that a job for the science court or the commercial docket? Should an ethical philosopher or a theologian be involved in making such decisions? Explain.
3. Would commercial docket judges begin to lean toward the best interests of merchants rather than the consumer? Would such a course of action be ethical? Again, should an ethical philosopher or a theologian be involved in making such decisions? Explain.
4. Would science court judges begin to lean toward the best interests of scientists and engineers rather than the public? Would such a course of action be ethical? Should an ethical philosopher or a theologian be involved in making such decisions? Explain.
5. There is also the ethical question of equal protection of the law. Does the commercial docket violate equal protection by giving a special forum to businesspeople? Explain. Would the science court violate equal protection by giving special forum to scientists and engineers? Why or why not? Who gets the next special forum? Politicians? Educators? Lawyers? Civil servants? Police officers and firefighters?

Statute of Limitations

Nearly all lawsuits have a time limit, set by the statute of limitations, within which a lawsuit must be brought. If the time limit is exceeded, the action is forever barred. In general, an action for breach of a sales contract must be brought within four years after the date of the breach. The parties may, if they wish provide for a shorter time period, not less than one year, in their sales agreement. They may not, however, agree to a period longer than four years.

CISG Article 49
(see Appendix C)

CISG Articles 61–64
(see Appendix C)

CISG Articles 74–77
(see Appendix C)

CISG Articles 79
(see Appendix C)

CISG Articles 81
(see Appendix C)

CISG Articles 85–88
(see Appendix C)

quick quiz 14-2

1. If the goods have not been delivered, the seller has a right to keep them upon learning of the buyer's breach. — true | false
2. The seller may sue the buyer for the price of any *lost* or damaged goods after the risk of their loss has passed to the buyer. — true | false
3. When the goods are unique or rare, the buyer may ask the court to order the seller to do what he or she agreed to do under the contract terms. — true | false

14-3 Warranty Protection

Until now in this chapter, we have focused on the actual sales agreement itself. We have looked at what constitutes performance, what constitutes nonperformance, and what happens when the seller does not deliver the goods, the buyer does not pay for the goods, or the trucking company loses the goods. Now we switch focus. Instead of looking at a contract that has not been performed, we will look at contracts that have been performed—sort of. Have you ever purchased an item that turned out to be damaged or broken when you opened the box? Have you ever paid for something that you wanted for a particular purpose, only to find that it would not do the job? Has a salesperson ever made a statement or a promise about a product that did not come true? Have you ever found an impurity or a foreign substance in food that you bought in a store or ate in a restaurant? The UCC gives you protection in all these situations under its law of warranties. A warranty is another name for a guarantee. Warranties come in all shapes and sizes. Still, in one way or another, all warranties fall into one of three categories: express warranties, implied warranties, and warranties of title.

Express Warranties

An **express warranty** is an oral or written statement, promise, or other representation about the quality of a product. Express warranties arise in three different ways: by a statement of fact or promise, by a description of the goods, or by a sample or model. In states that have adopted Article 2A of the UCC, express warranties arise when goods are leased in exactly the same way that they arise when goods are sold.

Statement of Fact or Promise Whenever a seller of goods makes a statement of fact to a buyer about the goods, that seller has created an express warranty. The seller's statement is treated legally as a guarantee that the goods will be as "they were stated to be." *This guarantee exists whether the seller is a merchant or not.* If the goods are not as they were stated to be, the seller has breached an express warranty. An express warranty also occurs when a seller makes a promise about the goods to a buyer. The promise must relate to the goods and be part of the transaction. Manufacturers often include express warranties with the products they sell. They are usually found inside the package containing the product and are sometimes referred to as *guarantees*. Formal words such as *warranty* or *guarantee* do not have to be used to create an express warranty. A seller may not intend to make a warranty, but if the language used by the seller is a statement of fact or a promise about the goods and is part of the transaction, an express warranty is created. Advertisements often contain statements and promises about goods that are express warranties.

Advertising Express Warranties The Federal Trade Commission has established specific rules for advertising express warranties on goods that are sold in interstate commerce:

- An advertisement stating that a product is warranted must tell you how to get a copy of the warranty before you buy the product.
- Advertisers who use expressions such as "Satisfaction Guaranteed," "Money-Back Guarantee," and "Free Trial Offer" must refund the full purchase price of their product at the purchaser's request. Any conditions, such as those limiting the return of the product, must be stated in the ad.
- Advertisers who warrant products for a lifetime must fully explain the terms of their promises, such as "Good for as long as you own the car."

Warranties are based on statements of fact. Therefore, the opinions of salespersons and their exaggerated and persuasive statements do not create express warranties. Courts have long indulged the temptation of salespersons to use **sales puffery** to extol their merchandise beyond the point of fact. Buyers must use common sense to recognize the difference between a salesperson's statements of fact from statements that are opinion or puffery. Such statements as "this is the best Hi Def screen on the market" or "this GPS system is a great buy" are examples of sales talk or puffery. They are not express warranties. Such statements as "this car has never been in an accident" or "this desk is made of mahogany" are factual statements that do create an express warranty.

Descriptions, Samples, and Models Any description of the goods that is made part of the basis of the bargain creates an express warranty that the goods will be as described. It is a common practice of salespeople to show samples of their products to prospective buyers. When a sample or model becomes part of the basis of the bargain, an express warranty is created. The seller warrants that the goods that will be delivered are the same as the sample or model.

Magnuson–Moss Warranty Act The federal Magnuson-Moss Warranty Act is designed to prevent deceptive warranty practices and provide consumers with more information about warranties that are made on products they buy. The act applies only when written warranties are made voluntarily for purchases of **consumer products**. These products are defined as tangible personal property normally used for personal, family, or household purposes. Because it is a federal law, the act affects only warranties on products that are sold in interstate commerce. Under the act, when a written warranty is given to a consumer on goods costing more than $10, the warranty must disclose whether it is a full or a limited warranty. When goods cost more than $15, the written warranty must be made available before the consumer decides to buy the product. The writing must express the terms and conditions of the warranty in simple and readily understood language.

A **full warranty** is one in which a defective product will be repaired without charge within a reasonable time after a complaint has been made about it. If it cannot be repaired within a reasonable time, the consumer may have either a replacement of the product or a refund of the purchase price. The consumer will not have to do anything unreasonable to get warranty service, such as ship a heavy product to the factory. A full warranty applies to anyone who owns the product during the warranty period, not only the original buyer. A full warranty must also state its duration, for example, a "full one-year warranty."

A **limited warranty** is any written warranty that does not meet all of the requirements for a full warranty. The consumer is not given the absolute, free-of-charge repair or replacement of a defective product, as in the full warranty. Something less than a complete remedy is given to the consumer. Examples of limited warranties are those that cover only parts, not labor; allow only pro rata (divided proportionately) refund or credit in the case of a defect rather than a full refund; require the buyer to return a heavy product to the store for service; or cover only the first purchaser.

Implied Warranties

Under the UCC, an **implied warranty** is a warranty that is imposed by law rather than by statements, descriptions, or samples given by the seller. It arises independently and outside the contract. The law annexes it, by implication, into the contract that the parties have made. Implied warranties are designed to promote high standards in business and to discourage harsh dealings. There are three types of implied warranties: the implied warranty of merchantability, the implied warranty of fitness for a particular purpose, and the implied warranty that is derived from a course of dealing or usage of trade.

Merchantability One of the most beneficial warranties, from the point of view of a buyer, is the implied **warranty of merchantability**. This warranty provides that, unless excluded in one of the ways discussed, whenever a merchant sells goods, the merchant warrants that the goods are **merchantable**—that is, they are reasonably fit for the purpose for which they are sold. For example, merchantability means that a lawn mower will cut grass, a sailboat will not sink, an automatic dishwasher will wash dishes, and so on. This warranty is given when the seller is a **merchant** with respect to goods of that kind. It is given by manufacturers, wholesalers, and retailers whenever they sell goods to give assurance that products sold by them are fit for the purpose for which the goods are to be used. The warranty of merchantability is not given by someone who is not a merchant. To be merchantable, goods must at least pass without objection in the trade under the contract description; if fungible goods, be of fair average quality; be fit for the ordinary purposes for which such goods are used; be of the same kind, quality, and quantity; be adequately contained, packaged, and labeled as the agreement may require; and be in conformance with any promises or statements of fact made on the container or label. A claim for breach of warranty of merchantability can be made only when a defect exists at the time the goods are purchased.

EXAMPLE 14-4: No Defect at Time of Purchase

Haven Hills Farm purchased a truck tire from Sears, Roebuck. On a trip from Mississippi to Alabama, the tire blew out, causing the truck to turn on its side, destroying 11,862 dozen eggs. At the time of the blowout, the tire was four-and-half months old and had been driven 30,000 miles. Haven Hills claimed that Sears was liable for breach of the implied warranty of merchantability. It argued that Sears sold the tire in a defective condition. In finding in favor of Sears, Roebuck, the court held that there was no evidence of a defect in the tire at the time it left the control of the manufacturer or seller.

Fitness for a Particular Purpose Sometimes buyers will have the seller select goods for them rather than select them themselves. They rely on the seller's knowledge and experience to choose the product after telling the seller of the particular use they have for the goods. This arrangement creates an implied **warranty of fitness for a particular purpose**. When the buyer relies on the seller's skill and judgment to select the goods, the seller implicitly warrants that the goods will be fit for the purpose for which they are to be used.

Usage of Trade Other implied warranties may arise from the ways in which the parties have dealt in the past or by usage of trade. For example, when a person sells a pedigreed dog, there is an implied warranty that the seller will provide pedigree papers to demonstrate the conformity of the animal to the contract. The reason this implied warranty arises is that providing such papers has become a well-established custom or practice of the trade.

Warranty of Title

Whenever goods are sold, either by a merchant or a private party, the seller warrants that the title being conveyed is good and that the transfer is rightful. This warranty is known as the **warranty of title**. It includes an implied promise that the goods will be delivered free of any liens (claims of others) about which the buyer has no knowledge. When anyone buys goods that turn out to be stolen, the rightful owner will be entitled to the return of those goods. The innocent purchaser may sue the seller for breach of warranty of title. When the buyer is aware that the person selling the goods does not personally claim title to them, the warranty of title is not made by the seller. Such is the case, for example, in sheriff's sales and sales by personal representatives of estates. To recover money damages for breach of warranty, buyers of defective goods must notify the seller of the defect within a reasonable time either after the discovery or after the defect should have been discovered. Failure to do so will prevent them from recovering damages for breach of warranty.

Warranty Exclusion

To exclude the implied warranty of merchantability in states that allow it, the word *merchantability* must be used in the disclaimer. If the exclusion is in writing, it must be in large, bold type so that it is conspicuous. To exclude the implied warranty of fitness for a particular purpose, the exclusion must be in writing and also be conspicuous. A common practice in the sale of used cars, lawn mowers, electrical appliances, and similar merchandise is for the seller to stipulate that the goods are being sold as is. The use of expressions such as *as is*, *with all faults*, and others is another way to exclude implied warranties. However, those words do not exclude express warranties or the warranty of title. Implied warranties may also be excluded under the UCC by having buyers examine the goods. When buyers have examined the goods, the sample, or the model as fully as they desire (or have refused to examine them when given the opportunity), there is no implied warranty as to defects that an examination would have revealed. Under the Magnuson–Moss Warranty Act, any clause purporting to exclude or limit consequential damages for breach of warranty must appear conspicuously on the face of the warranty. **Consequential damages** are losses that do not flow directly and immediately from an act but only from some of the consequences or results of the act.

EXAMPLE 14-5: Consequential Damages

Souci bought a freezer made by a reputable manufacturer. The freezer carried a full one-year warranty. The following sentence appeared in boldface type on the face of the warranty: "In no event shall this company be liable for consequential damages." Shortly after buying the freezer, Souci filled it with $1,500 worth of meat. Several days later, the freezer stopped working owing to a defect in its manufacture. Under the warranty, the company would have to repair or replace the freezer, but it would not be responsible for the loss of the meat. This loss would be considered consequential damage, which the company had effectively disclaimed.

Privity Not Required

Under earlier law, warranties extended only to the actual buyer of the product—that is, the one with whom the seller had dealt or was in privity of contract. People who were injured by defective products had no remedy against the seller for breach of warranty unless they themselves had purchased the goods. Thus, if children were injured by foreign objects in food that had been bought by their parents, the children could not recover for injuries because they had not purchased the goods. The UCC has abolished the requirement of privity. Instead, it provides three alternatives from which a state may choose. In all of the alternatives, warranties extend to people who would normally be expected to use the goods as well as to those who actually buy them.

Alternative A: A seller's warranty, whether express or implied, extends to any natural person who is in the family or household of his buyer or who is a guest in his home if it is reasonable to expect that such person may use, consume, or be affected by the goods and who is injured in person by breach of the warranty. A seller may not exclude or limit the operation of this section.

Alternative B: A seller's warranty, whether express or implied, extends to any natural person who may reasonably be expected to use, consume, or be affected by the goods and who is injured in person by breach of the warranty. A seller may not exclude or limit the operation of this section.

Alternative C: A seller's warranty, whether express or implied, extends to any person who may reasonably be expected to use, consume, or be affected by the goods and who is injured by breach of the warranty. A seller may not exclude or limit the operation of this section with respect to injury to the person of an individual to whom the warranty extends.

quick quiz 14-3

1. An express warranty is an oral or written statement, promise, or other representation about the quality of a product. true | false
2. An implied warranty is a warranty that is imposed by law rather than by statements, descriptions, or samples given by the seller. true | false
3. A warranty of title means that the seller warrants that the title for the goods being sold is good and that the transfer is rightful. true | false

Summary

14.1 Sellers and buyers must follow the terms of their contract and act in good faith. Tender of performance is necessary to test the other party's ability and willingness to perform. Tender of delivery requires the seller to make conforming goods available to the buyer at a reasonable hour of the day. Tender of payment may be made by any means that is commonly used in the ordinary course of business. Except when goods are shipped c.o.d. or when the contract provides for payment against a document of title, the buyer has the right to inspect goods before accepting or paying for them. When improper goods are delivered, the buyer may elect to reject all of them, accept all of them, or accept any commercial unit or units and reject the rest. Sellers may cure defects or nonconformities that caused the goods to be rejected by the buyer.

14.2 When a buyer breaches a sales contract, the seller may withhold delivery of any goods not yet delivered, stop goods that are in transit, resell the goods or the undelivered balance of them, retain the goods and bring suit for damages, bring suit for the price of any goods that the buyer has accepted, or cancel the contract. When a seller breaches a sales contract, the buyer may cancel the contract and recover any money paid out, buy similar goods from someone else and sue the seller for the difference in price, sue the seller for damages for nondelivery, keep the goods and deduct the cost of damages from any price still due, or sue for specific performance if the goods are rare or unique.

14.3 Express warranties arise by a statement of fact or promise, by a description of the goods, and by a sample or model. Other warranties may arise from the ways in which parties have dealt in the past. When goods are sold, either by a merchant or a private party, the seller warrants that the title is good and that there are no liens on the goods. Except when express warranties are made, sellers may exclude the warranties of merchantability and fitness for a particular purpose. Such an exclusion must be in writing and conspicuous. The words *as is* and *with all faults* serve to disclaim implied warranties but not the warranty of title. Warranties extend to people who would normally be expected to use the goods as well as to those who actually buy them.

Key Terms

carrier, 401
commercial docket, 404
commercial unit, 395
consequential damages, 409
consumer products, 407
cover, 403
cure, 399
express warranty, 406
full warranty, 407
good faith, 393

implied warranty, 407
insolvent, 400
legal tender, 395
limited warranty, 407
merchant, 408
merchantable goods, 408
sales puffery, 406
shipment contract, 395
special masters, 404
stoppage in transit, 400

tender of delivery, 395
tender of payment, 395
tender of performance, 394
unconscionable contract, 393
warranty of fitness for a particular purpose, 408
warranty of merchantability, 407
warranty of title, 408
writ of replevin, 404

Questions for Review and Discussion

1. What is meant by tender of performance?
2. What are the rights and duties of sellers and buyers in a sales contract?
3. What is the doctrine of anticipatory breach?
4. What are the seller's and the buyer's remedies in case of a breach?
5. What is the statute of limitations?
6. In what three ways can an express warranty be created?
7. What are the requirements of the Magnuson–Moss Warranty Act?
8. What is the nature of each of the following warranties: merchantability, fitness for a particular purpose, and usage of trade?
9. What is meant by warranty of title?
10. How can warranties be excluded?

Cases for Analysis

1. Kathleen Liarkos purchased a used Jaguar XJS automobile from Pine Grove Auto Sales. After experiencing various mechanical problems, she discovered that the vehicle's odometer had been turned back. Liarkos notified the seller that she revoked her acceptance of the vehicle. When is this remedy available to a buyer? [See: *Liarkos v. Mello*, 639 N.E.2d 716 (MA).]
2. P&F Construction Corporation ordered 338 door units for an apartment condominium project from Friend Lumber Corporation. The doors were delivered to the job site three weeks after they were ordered. Each door unit came wrapped in clear plastic. Three and one-half months after receiving the door units, P&F Construction notified Friend Lumber that the doors were one-quarter inch off size. P&F refused to pay Friend Lumber the balance due. What rule of law may Friend Lumber use to recover the money owed? [See: *P&F Const. v. Friend Lumber Corp.*, 575 N.E.2d 61 (MA).]
3. William Young had cut evergreen boughs and sold them exclusively to Frank's Nursery & Crafts Inc. for 10 years. Upon receiving a $238,000 order for 360 tons of boughs from Frank's, Young obtained cutting rights from many farmers, repaired his machinery, and made 75 new hand tiers to tie the evergreen bundles. Several months later, Frank's reduced its order to less than $60,000 for about 70 tons of boughs. Young delivered the 70 tons of boughs and sued Frank's for breach of contract. How were Young's damages computed? [See: *Young v. Frank's Nursery & Crafts, Inc.*, 569 N.E.2d 1034 (OH).]
4. Herman Googe agreed to buy an automobile from Irene Schleimer. Later, Googe changed his mind and refused to buy the car. Schleimer, without making tender of delivery, brought suit against Googe for breach of contract. Did Schleimer recover damages? Explain. [See: *Schleimer v. Googe*, 377 N.Y.S.2d 591 (NY).]

5. Mr. and Mrs. Aldridge bought a motor home from Sportsman Travel Trailer Sales, located in Texas. Two years later, after traveling more than 14,000 miles on trips to Louisiana, Colorado, and California, they attempted to reject the motor home, claiming that it was defective. Could they return the vehicle and recover damages? Explain. [See: *Explorer Motor Home Corp. v. Aldridge*, 541 S.W.2d 851 (TX).]
6. DiCintio leased for a three-year period from Adzan Auto Sales a Jeep Grand Cherokee Laredo sport utility vehicle manufactured by DaimlerChrysler. Soon after accepting delivery, the automatic transmission failed to shift gears properly, and then the vehicle started to pull to the left while being driven, after which it began to "idle rough" and stall while stopped at traffic lights. DiCintio took the vehicle to authorized dealers for repairs on six or seven occasions, but the defects persisted. When Adzan Auto Sales refused to terminate the lease or give him another car, DiContio brought suit against DaimlerChrysler for breach of the Magnuson-Moss Warranty Act. Does DiCintio have a cause of action under this law? Explain. [See: *Mark DiCintio v. DaimlerChrysler Corporation, et al*, 768 NE2d 1121 (NY).]
7. Lohr bought a mobile home from Larry's Homes. The home was damaged during delivery and never fully set up on Lohr's property. Larry's Homes attempted some repairs, but they were insufficient. An arbitrator found that the intended repairs would not have been enough even if they had been carried out. Lohr took the case to arbitration on the grounds of a breach of the warranty of merchantability under the UCC. Does the UCC apply to this case? Why or why not? [See: *Lohr v. Larry's Homes of Virginia.* Arbitrated by McCammon Group referred out of Cumberland County Circuit Court (VA).]
8. Caswell bought a gas grill to give to his friend, Kile, as a birthday present. The grill exploded the first time it was used due to a factory defect, and Kile was injured. The manufacturer of the grill argued that it was not responsible for Kile's injuries because Kile had not purchased the grill. There was no privity of contract between Kile and the manufacturer. How would you decide?
9. Shaffer ordered a glass of rosé wine at the Victoria Station Restaurant. As he took his first sip of wine, the glass broke in his hand, causing permanent injuries. Shaffer brought suit against the restaurant for breach of warranty of merchantability. The restaurant's position was that because it did not sell the wine glass to Shaffer (only its contents), it was not a merchant with respect to the glass and therefore made no warranty. Do you agree with the restaurant? Why or why not? [See: *Shaffer v. Victoria Station, Inc.*, 588 P.2d 233 (WA).]
10. McCoy bought an antique pistol from the Old Fort Trading Post for $1,000. Later, the gun was taken from McCoy by the police when they learned that it was stolen property. The police turned the gun over to the rightful owner. McCoy notified the Old Fort Trading Post of what had happened and asked for the return of his money, but the owner of the business refused to give him a refund. What remedy, if any, did McCoy have against the owner of the trading post? Explain. [See: *Trial v. McCoy*, 553 S.W.2d 199 (TX).]

Design Elements: The Opening Case: ©Sharpstock/Alamy; A Classic Case: ©Evlakhov Valeriy/Shutterstock

quick quiz Answers

14-1	14-2	14-3
1. T	1. T	1. T
2. T	2. T	2. T
3. T	3. T	3. T

Chapter 15

Product Liability and Consumer Protection

15-1 Product Liability
Social Engineering and the Law • Negligence and Product Liability • Strict Liability and Product Liability • The Consumer Product Safety Act

15-2 Consumer Protection Laws
The Federal Trade Commission • Unfair or Deceptive Practices • Trade Regulation Rules • Cyber-Law Developments and Updates • State Consumer Law Developments and Updates

15-3 Consumer Credit Laws
The Federal Truth-in-Lending Act • Equal Credit Opportunity • Unauthorized Use of Credit Cards • Fair Credit Reporting • Billing, Collecting, and Leasing

THE OPENING CASE Round 1
The Law and Social Engineering: How Far Does the Duty to Warn about Dangerous Products Extend?

The legal complex adaptive system moves in unexpected ways and, perhaps, that is as it should be. A working example of this can be found in the case of *Macrie v. SDS Biotech* (Biotech). The defendant in this lawsuit is the SDS Biotech Corporation, a manufacturing firm that develops a wide variety of chemical products used in agriculture. In general, Biotech sells its products directly to farmers who apply those chemicals directly to the crops they grow—either while the crops are in the field or after they have been harvested, depending on the instructions and warnings that accompany the chemical products. In this case, Biotech sold a product called Bravo 500 directly to a farmer named Iulianetti. Following instructions mandated by the Federal Environmental Protection Agency (EPA) and the Federal Insecticide, Fungicide, and Rodenticide Act (FIFRA), Biotech included a brochure filled with warnings and instructions about Bravo 500 in a shipment delivered to Iulianetti. Subsequently, Iulianetti either ignored, misunderstood, or misapplied the instructions because, instead of applying the Bravo 500 to the crops in the field, he applied it to the crops (in this case, squash) in storage bins. Iulianetti then sold the squash to Peter Macrie Sr., Peter Macrie Jr., and Toni Marie Macrie, all of whom worked for a family-run business that buys produce, processes it, and then resells it to another reseller down the line.

When the Macries received the squash, they unloaded it and repackaged it. Unknown to them at the time, as they unloaded the contaminated squash, they spread the dust like particles of the fungicide throughout the building. During the unloading and the repackaging of the squash, the plaintiffs breathed in the contaminated dust particles. Moreover, as they as handled the squash, they spread the contamination to to their clothing. The contamination led to illnesses, and their illnesses led to this lawsuit as a way to compensate them for their pain and suffering. The defendant, Biotech, admits that Bravo 500 is dangerous. Moreover, the company also admits that some (many?) of the farmers they deal with will misunderstand or misapply Bravo 500 despite the lengthy brochure that it, Biotech, includes with every shipment. However, Biotech argues that its duty to warn extends only to the immediate users of Bravo 500, such as farmer Iulianetti, not to those who buy and try to resell their crops (i.e., the Macries) to other resellers. Moreover, Biotech also argues that it really has no avenue available to it to send a warning to unknown intermediaries, like the Macries, who might handle the contaminated crops somewhere along the line of distribution. The Macries counterattack by saying that Biotech could give farmers warning leaflets that they could place in every shipment, or

Biotech could, in addition (or in the alternative), place advertisements in local and national newspapers that would warn potential distributors of the dangers.

To decide between the claims of Biotech and the arguments made by the Macries, the court used a classic risk-utility analysis to determine whether Biotech, and other firms in similar situations, have a duty to warn distant handlers of the dangers associated with dangerous products like fungicides. In a nutshell, the risk-utility analysis process can be boiled down to a simple, but direct question: Does the usefulness of the plan to warn remote users outweigh the risks associated with allowing those remote users to use Bravo 500 with no warning about its dangers and no information about protective steps that can be taken to minimize injury? The court decided that, in this case at least, the risks associated with the use of Bravo 500 required Biotech to issue warnings and protective measures not only to direct users, but also to remote users such as the plaintiffs. The duty to warn is inherent in the potential use of a dangerous product by all foreseeable handlers. The fact that issuing a warning and explaining protective steps are difficult tasks to accomplish logistically does not outweigh the need to warn remote handlers. If the product is dangerous, the warning must be issued properly—that is, so that it reaches all foreseeable "users." Otherwise, the product is defective—not in the way it was manufactured, but in the way the warnings were issued. [See: *Peter Macrie, Sr., Peter Macrie, Jr. and Toni Marie Macrie, Plaintiffs-Appellants v. SDS Biotech Corp., Aka Fermenta Plant Protection, Defendant-Respondent*, 267 N.J. Super. 34 (1993).]

Opening Case Questions

1. In what ways does the federal Environmental Protection Agency (EPA) protect consumers (or does it)? Explain.

2. Should corporate officers be held liable for the failure of a customer to follow its instructions about safety? Explain.

3. What is meant by the term *duty to warn*? Explain.

4. What is *risk-utility analysis* and how does it work? Explain.

5. How far down the line of distribution does the potential liability of the producer of a dangerous product extend? Explain.

Source: See: *Peter Macrie, Sr., Peter Macrie, Jr. and Toni Marie Macrie, Plaintiffs-Appellants v. SDS Biotech Corp.,* Aka Fermenta Plant Protection, Defendant-Respondent, 267 N.J. Super. 34 (1993).

 Learning Objectives

1. Describe the link between social engineering and the law.
2. Explain the difference between public interest and public policy.
3. Explain the difference between negligence and strict liability.
4. State the purpose of the Consumer Product Safety Act.
5. Explain the enforcement of the Federal Trade Commission Act.
6. Develop a list of unfair or deceptive practices.
7. Identify several FTC rules designed to protect the consumer.
8. Identify the function of the Truth-in-Lending Act.
9. Explain the latest amendments to the Truth-in-Lending Act.
10. Explain the requirements of the Consumer Leasing Act.

15-1 Product Liability

One of the fastest growing areas of consumer law is known as **product liability**. Under product liability standards, a person harmed by a product's unsafe condition may recover damages from the manufacturer, the seller, or the supplier of the product. Product liability results from the court's willingness to react to social problems and, at times, use the law to engineer social results. Because of the court's flexibility in this regard, product liability suits can now be based on one of two legal theories, negligence or strict liability, both of which are tort actions.

Social Engineering and the Law

The German philosopher Max Weber saw the law as a combination of consensus and coercion. Consensus reveals the norms by which the people of a society live, while coercion clarifies the measures taken against those who violate the consensus. Some parts of the legal community, such as the legislature are designed to proactively shape social policy. Others, like the courts, passively deal with problems on a case-by-case basis. Still others, like the administrative agencies, operate as hybrids combining both consensus and coercion, by making regulations and then enforcing those regulations through administrative hearings or in the courts. Nevertheless, all three levels—active, passive, and hybrid—must understand consensus and must use coercion. To do this properly, the courts frequently call upon the doctrine of public policy, a concept based on the assumption that no one should be permitted to do anything that harms the public interest. [See: Gerald Turkel, *Law and Society: Critical Approaches* (Boston: Allyn and Bacon, 1996), pp. 8-9.]

Public Interest and Public Policy Public policy is not the same as public interest, although the two terms are very similar and at times are used interchangeably. **Public interest** refers to the idea that certain activities affect the entire social structure and must, therefore, be regulated by the government. Public interest, then, is the equivalent of Weber's social consensus. It is in the best interests of society, for example, to have crime-free neighborhoods. **Public policy**, in contrast, seeks to implement behavior that promotes the public consensus and eliminates behavior that does not. Thus, any activity that somehow permits, encourages, or compels people to break the law and thus disrupt those crime-free neighborhoods would be against public policy and would, therefore, be outlawed. Public interest, then, is the ideal consensus, and public policy is the coercive social engineering strategy by which that consensus is implemented.

THE OPENING CASE Round 2
The Law and Social Engineering: How Far Does the Duty to Warn about Dangerous Products Extend?

Recall that in the Opening Case, we saw that the SDS Biotech Corporation sells chemical products to farmers who use those chemicals on their crops either in the field or in storage bins after the harvest. Biotech sold a fungicide named Bravo 500 directly to a farmer named Iulianetti. Following instructions mandated by the EPA and FIFRA, Biotech included a brochure filled with warnings and instructions about Bravo 500 in a shipment delivered to Iulianetti. Despite the instructions and these warnings Iulianetti did not properly apply Bravo 500 to a delivery of squash sold to Peter Macrie Sr., Peter Macrie Jr., and Toni Marie Macrie, who run a business that buys produce, processes it, and then resells it to other resellers down the line. Unknown to the Macries, the squash was contaminated with large amounts of Bravo 500. After handling the contaminated squash, the Macries became very ill, which led to this lawsuit.

The defendant, Biotech, had no problem admitting that Bravo 500 is dangerous, but it wanted to limit its duty to warn to the immediate users of Bravo 500, not to those later in the line of distribution. Eventually, the court ruled that if Biotech is going to manufacture and sell dangerous chemicals, it better make sure that it warns the people who will be affected by such products regardless of whether those people stand at near or distant points in the line of use and distribution. Without such a warning, the product will be considered defective—not in its manufacture, but in the inadequacy of the warnings that come with the product. The court made this decision by making a risk-utility analysis of the situation and concluding that the fact that issuing a warning and protective steps is difficult logistically does not outweigh the need to warn distant handlers.

Let's analyze this in terms of public interest and public policy. Recall that public interest is the equivalent of Max Weber's concept of social consensus. Public interest, then, refers to the idea that certain activities affect the entire social structure and must, therefore, be regulated by the government. In this case, public interest and social consensus both say that to protect the public at large, the government must regulate the manufacture, distribution, and use of dangerous chemicals. In contrast, public policy seeks to influence behavior in a way that promotes the public interest (or social consensus) and discourages behavior that does not promote that interest. Public policy, then, is coercive and operates on three levels. The first level is the legislative level, which makes the law that regulates the activity that is under scrutiny—in this case, the manufacture, distribution, and use of dangerous chemicals. The second level is the executive level, which involves the creation of administrative agencies, like the EPA, to implement statutory mandates. The third level involves the courts, which enforce those statutes and regulations. Public interest (or, if you prefer, Max Weber's social consensus) says, in this case at least, that people who must handle or work around dangerous chemicals, such as Bravo 500, deserve to be properly warned about the dangers associated with those chemicals and told about the ways to protect themselves from the effects of those chemicals. [See: *Peter Macrie, Sr., Peter Macrie, Jr. and Toni Marie Macrie, Plaintiffs-Appellants v. SDS Biotech Corp., Aka Fermenta Plant Protection, Defendant-Respondent,* 267 N.J. Super. 34 (1993).]

Source: See: *Peter Macrie, Sr., Peter Macrie, Jr. and Toni Marie Macrie, Plaintiffs-Appellants v. SDS Biotech Corp.,* Aka Fermenta Plant Protection, Defendant-Respondent, 267 N.J. Super. 34 (1993).

Social Engineering and Public Policy As seen briefly earlier, among the major actors in the field of social engineering and public policy are the administrative agencies. These agencies are created by the legislature and are empowered to create, enforce, and interpret regulations that carry the force of law. This legislative mandate makes these underrated and often berated agencies into hybrid operatives that use both proactive and reactive powers to engineer public policy. A case in point is the federal Environmental Protection Agency, which shapes regulations on environmental and pollution issues and then judges whether those regulations have been followed. Often this means that the EPA will exercise a policy-making role that is just as influential as the courts and the legislature. In the Opening Case about *Macrie v. SDS Biotech*, for instance, the EPA shaped the need for warnings about the manufacture, distribution, and use of hazardous chemicals like Bravo 500. Very few people hear about such cases and, therefore, maintain a negative view of all federal agencies. This is unfortunate because these agencies play a key role in defining public interest and implementing public policy. The *Macrie v. SDS Biotech* case demonstrates both functions rather well.

Public Policy and Product Liability Moreover, neither public interest nor public policy concerns are limited to dangerous chemicals. It is in the public interest to maintain a social structure that promotes health and safety and thus prevents illness and injury in all areas of the socio-economic structure. To engineer this public interest goal, public policy promotes the making of safe products. To coerce this behavior, public policy demands that manufacturers, sellers, and distributors be held responsible for any injuries that result from their products. Therefore, public policy insists that manufacturers, sellers, and distributors compensate any innocent victim who is injured by an unsafe product, regardless of whether that victim purchased, used, or simply got in the way of that unsafe product. To meet the public interest goal of a safe society, the courts have produced two legal strategies, negligence and product liability. Nevertheless, of the two standards, strict liability is more effective in reaching that goal.

Negligence and Product Liability

One legal theory available to people who are injured by faulty products is negligence. Negligence results when an individual fails to exercise the degree of care that a reasonable person would have exercised under the same circumstances. To recover for negligence in a product liability case, the victim must prove (1) that the manufacturer or seller owed a duty to the victim, (2) that the manufacturer or the seller violated that duty by not following the appropriate standard of care, (3) that the victim suffered an injury because of that careless action, and (4) that the careless action was both the actual and the proximate cause of the victim's injury.

Strict Liability and Product Liability

The doctrine of **strict liability** holds manufacturers or suppliers liable for selling goods that are unsafe, without regard to fault or negligence. The principal consideration under the doctrine of strict liability is the safety of the product, not the conduct of the manufacturer or supplier of the goods. Under this rule, manufacturers have the duty to design reasonably safe products. They must also give proper instructions for the product's use and provide warnings of possible danger. People who are injured or suffer property damage from a defective product may recover from the manufacturer or seller only if they can prove all of the following:

1. The manufacturer or seller sold the product in a defective condition.
2. The manufacturer or seller was engaged in the business of selling the product.
3. The product was unsafe to an unreasonable degree to the user or the consumer.

A CLASSIC CASE Dangerous or Unsafe? One Is OK, the Other Is Not

Whether they admit to it or not, all legal professionals will, from time to time, use the law for social engineering purposes. One example of this social engineering function is found in the doctrine of product liability, and one clear example of product liability is seen in the automotive industry. *Huff v. White Motor Co.* started a trend toward a new standard of automotive product liability. Before this case, as strange as it may seem to us today, automotive manufacturers had successfully argued that "the intended purpose of an automobile does not include its participation in collisions." (*Note:* Exactly what this means is problematic, but let's just accept it as the standard offered by the car manufacturers and see where it leads us.) The pre-*Huff* rule stated that automobile makers had no responsibility to design and manufacture cars that would protect passengers and drivers from the effects of an accident. Since *Huff* started the ball rolling three decades ago, the courts and the legislatures have altered this standard and have declared that car manufacturers must now design vehicles that have a high level of "crashworthiness." Moreover, and perhaps more to the point, the crashworthiness standard is not based on warranties or negligence. Instead, the standard is based on strict liability. This means that the consumer in an automotive product liability lawsuit does not have to demonstrate that the manufacturer violated a warranty or behaved negligently. The simple fact that the automobile was unsafe beyond what would be expected by the ordinary consumer is enough to result in liability.

Today, the strict liability standard applies to all products not just vehicles. In addition, the standard extends beyond privity and can be used to hold both the manufacturer and the seller liable. Remember, though, that the law is a balancing act. The courts have also ruled, on the opposite end of the spectrum, that the manufacturers of dangerous products are permitted to promote the sale of their products even though they know that the products are dangerous (not unsafe, but dangerous; there is a difference). As long as the product itself is legal, the corporation can advertise and sell the product despite its dangerous nature. Thus, somewhere within the intangible dimension of legal niceties there exists an invisible, largely undetectable line between manufacturing products that are unsafe and selling products that are dangerous. Manufacturing "unsafe products" is wrong; selling "dangerous products" is not. As you read the rest of the chapter, see if you can detect just where that line might be drawn. (*Hint:* Bravo 500 is not an unsafe product. It is, however, a dangerous product.) [See: *Huff v. White Motor Co.*, 565 F.2d 104 (7th Cir. App. Ct 1977); David Lauter, "Automakers Face Strict Liability," *The National Law Journal*, December 21, 1981, p. 18; Charles H. Moellenberg Jr., and Leon F. DeJulius Jr., "Remove the Tort Liability Muzzle," *The National Law Journal*, May 10, 2010, p. 34; and *Macrie v. SDS Biotech*, 267 N.J. Super. 34 (1993).]

Source: See: *Huff v. White Motor Co.*, 565 F.2d 104 (7th Cir. App. Ct 1977); David Lauter, "Automakers Face Strict Liability," *The National Law Journal,* December 21, 1981, p. 18; and Charles H. Moellenberg, Jr., and Leon F. DeJulius, Jr., "Remove the Tort Liability Muzzle," *The National Law Journal,* May 10, 2010, p. 34; Macrie v. SDS Biotech 267 N.J. Super. 34 (1993).

4. The defective condition was the proximate cause of the injury or damage.
5. The defective condition existed at the time it left the hands of the manufacturer or seller.
6. The consumer sustained physical harm or property damage by use or consumption of the product.

The Opening Case of *Macrie v. SDS Biotech* is instructive in this regard. Point 1 above requires that the plaintiff in a strict liability case demonstrate that the product was sold in a defective condition. *Macrie v. SDS Biotech* reveals that the term *defective condition* has an expanded meaning in the law. A defective condition means not only that the product itself is manufactured in a defective condition, but also that the way the product is packaged and handled can be defective. As we have seen, this is what happened in the case of *Macrie v. SDS Biotech* when Biotech failed to send out adequate warnings and precautions to the distant users of the Bravo 500. In addition to understanding the meaning of the term *defective*, however, it is also necessary to understand the difference between "unsafe" and "dangerous." The nearby Classic Case explains this difficult distinction rather well, and so, read on.

The defective condition may arise through faulty product design, faulty manufacturing, inadequate warning of danger, or improper instructions for the product's use. The manufacturer's and seller's liability extends to all persons who may be injured by the product. Injured bystanders, guests, or others who have no relationship to the product, the seller, or the manufacturer may seek damages caused by defects in the offending product.

Duty to Warn Sometimes a duty is placed on manufacturers to warn consumers that harm may result from a product. Unavoidably dangerous products may require a warning to inform the consumer of possible harm. If the warning is adequate, consumers may be required to use the product at their own risk. A warning must specify the risk presented by the product and give a reason for the warning. When the danger that is presented by a product is obvious, however, no duty to warn exists because a warning will not reduce the likelihood of injury. Despite all of this attention, the duty to warn is rarely at issue in a lawsuit. Most manufacturers will not attempt to argue that they have no duty to warn consumers about the dangers associated with their products. On the other hand, such manufacturers may be tempted to argue that their duty to warn does not extend to certain distant users. Fortunately, the courts, those perennial watchdogs of social consensus and public interest, have developed a way to determine the extent of liability for the failure to properly warn distant users. The Opening Case can provide some insight on this issue.

THE OPENING CASE Round 3
The Law and Social Engineering: How Far Does the Duty to Warn about Dangerous Products Extend?

As noted earlier, the case of *Macrie v. SDS Biotech* (Biotech) can serve as an excellent example of the extent to which the duty to warn operates. Recall that SDS Biotech Corporation sold a fungicide called Bravo 500 directly to a farmer named Iulianetti. Following instructions mandated by the EPA and the FIFRA, Biotech included a brochure filled with warnings and instructions about Bravo 500 in a shipment delivered to Iulianetti. Shortly thereafter, Iulianetti applied Bravo 500 to certain crops (in this case, squash) that was located in storage bins, something that the instructions cautioned against. Iulianetti then sold the contaminated squash to the Macries, all of whom worked for a family-run business that buys produce, processes it, and then resells it to another reseller down the line. The Macries, then, can be considered to be among the distant or remote "users" of Biotech's Bravo 500. After handling the contaminated squash, the Macries became very ill.

Their illness, clearly tied to the Bravo 500 contamination, led to this lawsuit.

Recall that Biotech, admits that Bravo 500 is dangerous (note Biotech says "dangerous," not "unsafe"). Moreover, the company also admits that some (many? most?) of the farmers that deal with the product will misunderstand or misapply Bravo 500. This means that Biotech knows that many of the distant users of Bravo 500, users like the Macries, will be exposed to its hazards. Despite this knowledge, Biotech still says, with a straight face, that its duty to warn extends only to the immediate users of Bravo 500, not to those who buy and try to resell their crops (such as the Macries) to other resellers. In addition, Biotech also maintains that even if it ahs a duty to warn the distant users, the attempt to do so would be logistically difficult, thus relieving Biotech of any duty to warn such distant users.

To decide the question of the extent of the duty to warn, the court uses a classic *risk-utility analysis* to determine whether Biotech, and other firms in similar situations, have a duty to warn distant handlers about the dangers associated with products like fungicides. In short, the risk-utility analysis process involves one question: Does the usefulness of the plan to warn remote users outweigh the risks associated with allowing those remote users to use the product with no warning about its dangers and no information about protective steps that can be taken to minimize injury? The court decided that the risks associated with the use of Bravo 500 required Biotech to issue warnings and protective measures not only to direct users, but also to remote users such as the plaintiffs in this case. The duty to warn is inherent in the potential use of a dangerous product by all foreseeable handlers. The fact that issuing a warning and protective steps is difficult logistically does not outweigh the need to warn distant handlers. If the product is dangerous the warning must be issued properly—that is, so that it reaches all foreseeable "users." Otherwise, the product is defective—not in the way it was manufactured, but in the way that the warning was issued. [See: *Peter Macrie, Sr., Peter Macrie, Jr. and Toni Marie Macrie, Plaintiffs-Appellants v. SDS Biotech Corp., Aka Fermenta Plant Protection, Defendant-Respondent,* 267 N.J. Super. 34 (1993).]

Source: See: *Peter Macrie, Sr., Peter Macrie, Jr. and Toni Marie Macrie, Plaintiffs-Appellants v. SDS Biotech Corp.,* Aka Fermenta Plant Protection, Defendant-Respondent, 267 N.J. Super. 34 (1993).

Punitive Damages In addition to recovering damages to compensate them for their losses, injured parties in strict liability cases sometimes recover punitive damages. These are monetary penalties imposed as a punishment for a wrongdoing.

A QUESTION OF ETHICS

Unsafe Products v. Dangerous Products

As we have seen many times throughout this text, the law is a balancing act. We have just examined how the courts have been willing (eager?) to use strict liability to hold manufacturers and distributors liable for injuries caused by unsafe products without any reference to negligence or warranties. Just how far will the courts go in this regard? What is the ultimate limit of strict liability as a coercive strategy of public policy? One answer to this question might be that there is no limit, that dangerous products, period, must be targeted by the law, at all cost no matter what. This is known as a *per se* rule. Literally translated from the Latin, *per se* means "in and of itself," and a rule that labels a product dangerous *per se* would assert that the product is dangerous in and of itself. In other words, such a product cannot be made "safe" because to make it "safe" would remove its basic function and render it useless. The prime target of the "dangerous *per se*" rule has been handguns. However, the rule could apply to any firearm or explosive device (read "bomb"). The argument goes something like this. Handguns, other firearms, and explosive devices are dangerous *per se* because their function is to kill. When a manufacturer designs, makes, and sells a handgun, any other firearm, or explosive device, that manufacturer knows that the product is designed to kill. Moreover, the only way to make a handgun safe is to render it unworkable, which makes it useless and, therefore, not an option. Moreover, there is no social benefit to the firearm or the explosive device that outweighs the potential harm that it can cause. Therefore, when a manufacturer places a firearm or explosive device in circulation, he or she is well aware of its potential (inevitable?) criminal use and, when such an event occurs, that manufacturer must be held strictly liable for the injuries and the harm that results—period. We will see the counterarguments to this position later in the text. For now, however, consider the "dangerous *per se*" rule and answer the following questions. [See: Donald E. Santarelli and Nicholas E. Calio, "Turning the Gun on Tort Law: Aiming at Courts to Take Products Liability to the Limit," *St. Mary's Law Journal* 14, no. 3 (1983), pp. 471–508.]

ETHICAL CONCERNS AND QUESTIONS

1. Is the function of a firearm or explosive device to kill? If you believe that the function is to kill, then what ethically justifiable reason is there for continuing to manufacture them? Explain.

2. If you believe that the function is *not* to kill, then what other ethical function does a firearm or explosive device possess? Explain.

3. Max Weber believes that the law can be used to coerce the members of a society into conforming to the general consensus. Will the "dangerous *per se*" rule eliminate killing and, thus, create crime-free neighborhoods? Explain.

4. The very first element of strict liability is that the plaintiff must prove that the manufacturer or seller sold the product in a defective condition. What is the defective condition of a firearm or explosive device that works exactly as it should? Explain.

5. What other products might be outlawed using the "dangerous *per se*" rule? Explain.

See: Donald E. Santarelli and Nicholas E. Calio, "Turning the Gun on Tort Law: Aiming at Courts to Take Products Liability to the Limit," *St. Mary's Law Journal* 14, no. 3 (1983), pp. 471–508.

Aircraft Cases and Product Liability Despite the court's willingness to impose strict liability in product liability cases involving automobiles and despite the fact that the doctrine could easily be applied to other products, there has been a curious lack of activity in this area of the law. For example, there has been a reluctance on the part of both the courts and the legislature to apply strict liability, especially as it is expressed in the crashworthiness test, to aviation accident cases. Several reasons may explain the lack of movement in this area. One reason for this apparent inactivity is that aviation crashes are rare, at least when compared to automobile accidents. Another reason may be that most aviation cases are settled out of court before litigation even begins. However, probably the most significant reason is that aviation cases tend to be more complex and difficult than automobile cases. Typically, aviation cases will require a more in-depth understanding of and appreciation for the complexity of aircraft design and operation. It may be that product liability arguments in aviation cases will have to wait for the establishment of a science court, one version of which is discussed in two earlier A Question of Ethics features, one in Chapter 4 and the other in Chapter 14. [See: Scott G. Lindvall, "Aircraft Crashworthiness: Should the Courts Set Standards?" *William and Mary Law Review* 27, no. 2 (1986), pp. 371–408.]

The Consumer Product Safety Act

Product safety has not remained solely within the purview of the courts. Congress has also gotten into the act. In an attempt to protect consumers from dangerous products, Congress passed the Consumer Product Safety Act. The act established the Consumer Product Safety Commission (CPSC) to protect consumers from unreasonable risk or injury from hazardous products. The act covers products or component parts, American-made or imported, that are manufactured or distributed for sale to a consumer for personal use, consumption, or enjoyment. The commission can order the recall of products found to be inherently unsafe and dangerous. It has the authority to impose civil fines for violations of its standards and cease-and-desist orders. Private citizens, acting on their own behalf, may bring suit to establish or enforce a safety rule if the commission fails to act.

quick quiz 15-1

1. Public interest and public policy are the same thing. — true | false
2. Negligence would usually be more effective as a legal theory in a product liability lawsuit than strict liability. — true | false
3. In addition to recovering damages to compensate them for their losses, injured parties in strict liability cases sometimes recover punitive damages. — true | false

15-2 Consumer Protection Laws

Consumer protection laws apply to transactions between business people and consumers. A *consumer* is someone who buys or leases real estate, goods, or services for personal, family, or household purposes. Thus, people who buy or rent things for personal use from a business are protected by consumer protection laws. However, if they buy the same things from another consumer or for business use, they are not, with some exceptions, protected by consumer protection law. State consumer protection offices provide information and help enforce state consumer protection laws. They sometimes assist consumers with individual problems. Consumer protection offices are located in state and county offices and, in some cities, the mayor's office.

Federal consumer protection law stems from the Federal Trade Commission Act (FTCA), which states that "unfair or deceptive acts or practices in . . . or affecting commerce are hereby declared unlawful." The act defines *commerce* as "commerce among the several states or with foreign nations or the District of Columbia." Thus, the act applies to businesses that sell real estate, goods, or services in interstate commerce or that somehow affect interstate commerce. *Interstate commerce* is business activity that touches more than one state. Purely local business activity, which has no out-of-state connections, called *intrastate commerce*, is not governed by the FTCA.

The Federal Trade Commission

The Federal Trade Commission Act transferred certain powers to the Federal Trade Commission, giving it the authority to oversee and eliminate deceptive and unfair practices in commerce. These powers include:

1. To conduct investigations into the practices of businesses.
2. To investigate possible antitrust violations.
3. To compel interstate businesses to file reports with the commission detailing their operations that fall within the FTC's jurisdiction.
4. To publish the results of the commission's investigation of interstate businesses.
5. To deal with disputes that emerge from the application of FTC regulations.
6. To deal with disputes that emerge from the application of federal antitrust law.
7. To make recommendations to Congress concerning new legislation.

In effect, the commission has become a coercive public policy instrument designed to promote the public interest. In doing so, the FTC must determine when a practice is unfair by balancing the harm that might affect consumers with the overall public good promoted by the activity under scrutiny.

If, after a thorough investigation, the FTC concludes that a violation of the law occurred, it may attempt to obtain voluntary compliance by entering into a consent order with the violating company. A **consent order** is an order under which the company agrees to stop the disputed practice without necessarily admitting that it violated the law. If an agreement cannot be reached, the FTC may issue a complaint. This action begins a formal hearing before an administrative law judge. If a violation of law is found, a cease-and-desist order or other appropriate relief may be issued. Consumers may bring individual or class action lawsuits against businesses for violating FTC rules. A **class action lawsuit** is one that is brought by one or more plaintiffs on behalf of a class of persons. Usually, a suit must be brought within one year after the violation. Alternate dispute resolutions are also available for resolving this type of problem.

Unfair or Deceptive Practices

The FTC Act prohibits unfair or deceptive practices. These practices include fraudulent misrepresentations, sending unordered merchandise, bait-and-switch schemes, and odometer tampering.

Fraudulent Misrepresentation It is unfair or deceptive for a seller to make a fraudulent misrepresentation—that is, a statement that is designed to mislead the buyer. A misrepresentation usually occurs when the seller misstates facts important to the consumer. Making false statements about the construction, durability, reliability, safety, strength, condition, or life expectancy of a product is a deceptive practice. It is also deceptive to fail to disclose to a buyer any fact that would cause the buyer to walk away from the contract. You may see ads like the following in newspapers and magazines: "Would you like to earn hundreds of dollars a week at home in your leisure time? Many people are supplementing their income in a very easy way. Let us tell you how. . . ." An offer like this may sound very attractive, particularly if you are unable to leave your home to work. Be cautious about work-at-home ads, especially ones that promise large profits in a short period of time. Although some work-at-home plans are legitimate, many are not. Home employment schemes are some of the oldest kinds of classified advertising fraud.

Unordered Merchandise Except for free samples clearly and conspicuously marked as such and merchandise mailed by charitable organizations soliciting contributions, it is a violation of the postal law and the FTCA to send merchandise through the mail to people who did not order it. Similarly, it is illegal to send a bill for such unordered merchandise or to send **dunning letters**—that is, letters requesting payments. People who receive unordered merchandise through the mail may treat it as a gift. They may keep the merchandise or dispose of it in any manner they see fit without any obligation whatsoever to the sender. In addition, senders of unordered merchandise must attach a statement to the package informing recipients of their right to keep and use the goods.

Bait-and-Switch Schemes A **bait-and-switch scheme** is an alluring but insincere offer to sell a product or service that the advertiser does not really intend to sell. Its purpose is to switch customers from buying the advertised merchandise to buying something else, usually at a higher price or on a basis more advantageous to the advertiser. There is no question that the FTCA prohibits bait-and-switch schemes. The very nature of the strategy is to trick unwary consumers into purchasing something that they neither want nor need and that is

A SOON TO BE CLASSIC CASE The CAS as Social Engineer: Multiple Definitions for a Single Concept

In the case of *Federal Trade Commission v. Kristy Ross and Innovative Marketing, Inc.*, the Federal Trade Commission brought a lawsuit against Ross, three additional officers, and a series of corporate entities. The case started when Innovative Marketing Inc (IMI, also doing business as Synergy Software) sent Internet notices that advised consumers that IMI had conducted a scan of their computer systems and had discovered that their computers had been infiltrated by a wide variety of dangerous and illegal files including viruses and spyware that put all their data at risk. IMI (or Synergy Software or some other corporate incarnation) then offered to clean up the "cyber-mess" by selling the consumer computer security software ironically dubbed "scareware." The truth was that no scans were ever performed by IMI or SS or any other affiliate of those firms. The Federal Trade Commission brought a lawsuit against Ross, IMI, SS, and all those other incarnations, as well as three other people who had acted as officers of these various corporate entities. The FTC defines *fraud* in the following way: "An act or practice is deceptive where: (1) A representation, omission, or practice misleads or is likely to mislead the consumer; (2) a consumer's interpretation of the representation, omission, or practice is considered reasonable under the circumstances; and (3) the misleading representation, omission, or practice is material." In the text, we define fraud by noting, "It is unfair or deceptive for a seller to make a fraudulent misrepresentation, that is, a statement that is designed to mislead the buyer.

A misrepresentation usually occurs when the seller misstates facts important to the consumer." In Chapter 8, we defined fraud in this way:

> To destroy mutual assent through a claim of fraud, the complaining or innocent party must prove the existence of five elements. 1. The complaining party will have to prove that the other party made a false representation about some material fact (i.e., an important fact, a fact of substance) involved in the contract. A material fact is one that is very crucial to the terms of the contract. 2. The plaintiff must demonstrate convincingly that the other party made the representation knowing that it was false. 3. The plaintiff must show that the false representations were made with the intent that they be relied upon by the innocent party. 4. The complaining party must establish that there was a reasonable reliance on the false representations. 5. The plaintiff must verify that he or she actually suffered some loss by relying on the false representation after entering the contract.

Why does the law provide three definitions for one concept (fraud)? Which definition of fraud applies in this case? Which definition is the correct definition? Which definition is the best definition? [See: *Federal Trade Commission v. Kristy Ross and Innovative Marketing, Inc., et al.*, No. 12-2340 United States Court of Appeals for the Fourth Circuit, February 25, 2014.]

Source: See: *Federal Trade Commission v. Kristy Ross and Innovative Marketing, Inc., et al.* No. 12-2340 United States Court of Appeals for the Fourth Circuit, February 25, 2014.

more expensive than the original bait that snagged their interest and pulled them into the store. The statute states quite specifically that: "No advertisement containing an offer to sell a product shall be made when the offer is not a *bona fide* effort to sell the advertised product." Any of the following activities could indicate a bait-and-switch scheme:

- A refusal to show, demonstrate, or sell the product offered in accordance with the terms of the offer.
- A "put-down" of the product by the acts or words of the seller.
- Failing to have available at all outlets listed in the advertisement a sufficient quantity of the advertised product to meet reasonably anticipated demands.
- Refusing to take orders for the advertised product to be delivered within a reasonable period of time.
- Showing a product that is defective, unusable, or impractical for the purpose represented in the advertisement.

Odometer Tampering The federal Odometer Law prohibits people from disconnecting, resetting, or altering the odometer of a motor vehicle in order to hide a vehicle's true mileage. Anyone who sells or gives away a car must provide the new owner with a written statement disclosing the odometer reading at the time of the transfer. If the seller believes that the mileage reading on the odometer is incorrect, the disclosure statement must indicate that the actual mileage is unknown. It is also a violation of the act to obtain a vehicle for resale without acquiring a finalized odometer statement from the seller. An odometer must be set at zero if it is repaired and cannot be adjusted to show the true mileage. In addition, the car owner must attach to the left doorframe a written notice showing the true mileage before the service, repair, or replacement and the date that the odometer was set at zero. It is illegal for anyone to alter or remove any such notice attached to the doorframe of a car.

Trade Regulation Rules

To correct wrongdoings in the marketplace, the FTC has also established trade regulation rules to govern the activities of interstate companies. These rules include the Used Car Rule, the Cooling-Off Rule, the negative option rule, the Mail and Telephone Order Rule, the telemarketing sales rule, and the rules connected with 900 numbers. Other rules are established by the antispam and the antislamming laws.

Used Car Rule To remedy consumer complaints involving used car sales, the FTC established the *Used Car Rule*. This rule requires used car dealers to place a *Buyer's Guide* sticker in the window of each used car they offer for sale. The Buyer's Guide provides the following information:

- A statement that the car is sold *as is* if it is sold with no warranties. (Some states do not allow used cars to be sold "as is" by car dealers.)
- A statement that the car is sold with implied warranties only if that is the case.
- A statement telling whether the warranty is "full" or "limited" and citing the length of the warranty period if the car is sold with an express warranty. In addition, the guide must list the specific systems that are covered by the warranty and state the percentage of the repair costs that will be paid by the dealer.
- A statement that tells consumers not to rely on spoken promises.
- A suggestion that consumers ask whether they may have the vehicle inspected by their own mechanic either on or off the premises.
- A list of the 14 major systems of an automobile and some of the principal defects that may occur in these systems.
- Whenever the sale of a vehicle will be carried on in Spanish, a Spanish language version of the Buyer's Guide must be placed on the window before the vehicle is marketed.

A dealer is defined as anyone who sells more than five used cars in a 12-month period. The law covers the sale of automobiles, light-duty vans, and light-duty trucks. The Buyer's Guide sticker must be printed in black ink on a white sheet of paper that is at least 11 × 7¼ inches in size. The guide becomes part of the sales contract and overrides any contrary provision that may be in the contract.

Cooling-Off Rule The FTC has established the *Cooling-Off Rule* to give consumers an opportunity to change their minds after signing contracts with people who come to their houses. Under this rule, sales of consumer goods or services over $25 made away from the seller's regular place of business, such as at a customer's home, may be canceled within three business days after the sale occurs. This rule requires the seller to give the buyer two copies of a **cancellation form**, one of which the buyer may send to the seller any time before midnight of the third business day after the contract was signed. The law also applies to consumer product parties given in private homes and to sales made in rented hotel rooms or restaurants. There are, however, several exceptions to the rule. The rule does not apply to:

- Sales that are less than $25.
- Sales that involve items used for something other than personal, household, or family reasons.
- Sales that are entered completely by phone or by mail.
- Sales that begin at the seller's regular place of business and then are simply concluded at the buyer's home.
- Sales that are made under emergency conditions.
- Sales that are involved in the repair or maintenance of personal property.

In addition, the Cooling-Off Rule does not cover insurance, securities, real estate, or craft items sold at fairs, civic centers, schools, or shopping malls. Finally, the rule does not cover vehicle sales when the seller has set up a temporary location away from his or her permanent place of business. Under the laws of some states, such as New York, the three-day right to cancel does not begin until the seller gives the buyer a written notice of the right to cancel. Until such notice is given, the buyer may use any means to notify the seller of the cancellation of the contract.

Negative Option Rule The negative option rule applies when a consumer subscribes to a magazine, or enters some other plan that sends products on a regular basis. Under such plans, the seller notifies the subscriber about the next selection before that selection is shipped. If the subscriber does nothing, the seller will ship the selection automatically. If the subscriber does not want the selection, he or she must tell the seller not to send the item before an agreed to deadline. The negative option rule does not outlaw such agreements but it does demand that sellers tell subscribers:

- The number of selections they must purchase, if any.
- The circumstances under which they can withdraw their membership.
- The notification process used to opt out of a selection.
- The timing for the return of the negative option cancellation forms.
- The circumstances under which subscribers qualify for credit in a return.
- The technique for determining postage and handling costs.
- The timing of each selection announcement.

The negative option rule does not apply to **continuity plans**. Under a continuity plan, the seller ships the goods to the subscriber on a regular basis without first sending an announcement of the upcoming delivery. While the negative option rule does not limit the use of such continuity plans, they are regulated by standard consumer protection rules. This means that the seller must notify the subscriber of all terms and conditions in a clear and unambiguous way.

The Mail and Telephone Order Rule The FTC has established a rule to protect consumers who order goods by mail, telephone, Internet, or fax machine. Under the **Mail and Telephone Order Rule**, sellers must ship orders within the time promised in their advertisements. If no time period is promised, sellers must either ship the order within 30 days or send the consumer an option notice. The option notice informs consumers of any shipping delay and gives them a chance to cancel and receive a refund. Instructions on how to cancel orders must be included in the notice. In addition, the seller must provide a free means for consumers to reply.

> **NATIONAL DO NOT CALL REGISTRY**
>
> Place your telephone number on the National Do Not Call Registry by calling toll-free 1-888-382-1222 (TTY: 1-866-290-4236) or going online to donotcall.gov. Registration is free.
>
> Placing your telephone number on the Do Not Call Registry will stop all telemarketing calls except those from political organizations, charities, and people making surveys. You can expect fewer calls within three months of the date you sign up for the registry. Your number will stay in the registry for five years, until it is disconnected, or until you delete it from the registry. You may renew your registration after five years.
>
> Telemarketers are required to search the registry every three months and avoid calling any phone numbers that are on the registry.
>
> If you receive telemarketing calls after you have registered your telephone number and it has been in the registry for three months, you can file a complaint at donotcall.gov or by calling toll-free 1-888-382-1222 (TTY: 1-866-290-4236). You will need to provide the date of the call and the name or phone number of the company that called you. Telemarketers who disregard this law can be fined up to $11,000 for each call they make.

Figure 15-1 Once your number is registered, it will remain in the National Do Not Call Registry for five years.

Telemarketing Sales Rule The FTC's Telemarketing Sales Rule is designed to protect consumers from abusive and unscrupulous telemarketers. The rule has established the *Do Not Call Registry* (see Figure 15-1) that makes it easier for consumers to reduce or eliminate unwanted sales calls. Under the Telemarketing Sales Rule:

- It is illegal for a telemarketer to call a consumer if the consumer has asked not to be called.
- Calling times are restricted to the hours between 8:00 A.M. and 9:00 P.M.
- Telemarketers must tell the consumer that it is a sales call, the name of the seller, and what they are selling before they make their pitch. If it is a prize promotion, they must tell the consumer that no purchase or payment is necessary to enter or win.
- It is illegal for telemarketers to misrepresent any information, including facts about their goods or services, earnings potential, profitability, the risk or liquidity of an investment, or the nature of a prize in a prize-promotion scheme.
- Before consumers pay, telemarketers must tell them the total cost of the products or services offered and any restrictions on getting or using them or that a sale is final or nonrefundable.

Consumers who have the slightest doubt about a telephone offer should ask for written information about the product, service, investment opportunity, or charity that is the subject of the call. They should resist high-pressure sales tactics and talk to a family member or friend before responding to the call. Consumers should never give out their bank account or credit card number to anyone who calls them. Similarly, they should never send money by courier, overnight delivery, or wire to anyone who insists on immediate payment.

900-Telephone Number Rules Telemarketers sometimes use 900 telephone numbers as part of their strategy, because the consumer, rather than the seller, pays the phone charge. To combat the abusive use of 900 telephone numbers, the Federal Trade Commission has established a series of 900-Telephone Number Rules. These rules require telemarketers who use 900 numbers to warn callers of the cost of the calls and to give those callers a chance to hang up before being charged. Under the rules, customers are also permitted to ask telephone companies to block all 900-prefix number calls. In addition, the rules require telephone companies to send customers pay-per-call disclosure statements. The FTC also prohibits the use of any prefix other than 900 as a pay-per-call service. Moreover, the FTC will not permit telephone companies to disconnect phone service to customers who refuse to pay for 900-number calls. Finally, the FTC has established a series of rules for resolving billing disputes.

AntiSpam Law The Can Spam Act is an attempt by the federal government to reduce the use of unsolicited commercial e-mail, commonly known as spam, on the Internet. Under the law, unsolicited commercial e-mail messages must be truthful and cannot use misleading subject lines or incorrect return addresses. E-mail containing pornography must be specifically labeled in the subject line. In addition, spammers cannot harvest e-mail addresses from chat rooms and other sites without permission. The rule has also been amended to include messages that are intended for mobile phones, provided that a domain name is used as part of the Internet address. This ban does not include short phone-to-phone messages

AntiSlamming Law The illegal practice of changing a consumer's telephone service without permission is referred to as slamming. New consumer protection rules created by the Federal Communications Commission (FCC) provide a remedy for consumers who have been slammed. With these rules, the FCC has taken the profit out of slamming and protected consumers from illegal charges.

Cyber-Law Developments and Updates

Cyber-commerce (computer commerce, electronic commerce, or e-commerce) involves transacting business by computer. One of the most common cyber-commerce techniques involves buying and selling directly on the Internet by accessing a company's website. One problem associated with buying and selling on the Internet involves the difficulty of verifying the identity of the party on the other side of an Internet connection. These problems have been exacerbated by the pervasive presence of handheld mobile computers such as smartphones and tablets. Two recent developments in this area involve the FTC's Children's Online Privacy Protection Rule and the Identity Theft and "Reclaim Your Name" Proposal.

Revised Children's Online Privacy Protection Rule The Children's Online Privacy Protection Rule (COPPR) has been part of the culture at the FTC since 1998 when the Children's Online Privacy Protection ACT (COPPA) was first made law. The rule mandates that website operators who have children (12 years old or younger) as their target market or who are aware that, as part of their website operation, children will provide them with personal data must inform parents and obtain consent before they are permitted to do anything with that data. The goal is to protect children and to keep the data collected from them confidential. As often happens, the rule has been updated, including a revision and an expansion of the rules for defining what is meant by personal data in relation to children. In an effort to keep pace with technology, personal data now includes information involving personal identifiers such as photos, videos, audio recordings, geolocation information, and cookies that track a child's online history. The FTC has also continued its safe harbor provisions that permit specific organizations to develop self-compliance programs. The FTC has also made available two documents designed to spread the word about the COPPA and its policies. The first document was written to help small businesses protect the privacy of the children that they deal with online. The second is designed to help parents keep up to date on COPPA protection methods for children operating online. [See: Jay Mayfield, "Revised Children's Online Privacy Protection Rule Goes Into Effect Today," Federal Trade Commission, July 1, 2013.]

Identity Theft and the "Reclaim Your Name" Program In identity theft, a perpetrator uses an electronic system or technique to steal credit card information, PINs, financial data, access codes, passwords, or debit card information. The perpetrator then passes himself or herself off as the victim. Using this technique, the identity thief can clean out bank accounts, run up credit card debt, divert cash transfers, buy and sell stocks, enter electronic auction networks, approve or cancel shipments, make or revoke hotel and travel reservations, and disrupt the financial and the personal life of the victim. To combat identity theft the FTC is exploring the initiation of a new program titled, "Reclaim Your Name," which is designed to help consumers obtain the electronic ability to monitor the use of their own personal data. The goal of the program is to empower consumers with the ability to determine when and where to share information about their personal lives, finances, employment, buying habits, bank accounts, and so on. [See: Commissioner Julie Brill, "Keynote Address: Reclaim Your Name," 23rd Computers Freedom and Privacy Conference, Washington, DC, June 26, 2013.]

State Consumer Law Developments and Updates

Most states have enacted statutes that supplement and enhance federal consumer protection laws. The Uniform Law Commission has helped in this regard by enacting a model law known as the Uniform Consumer Sales Practices Act (UCSPA), the purpose of which is to help states make adjustments to their own individual codes. State legislatures are free to adopt these statutes without change. Nevertheless, some states fashion their own statutes and others supplement the UCSPA with their own provisions that deal with some of the more troublesome aspects of consumer fraud in their own states.

Uniform Consumer Sales Practices Act

The Uniform Law Commission (ULC), which is also known as the National Conference of Commissioners of State Laws (NCCUSL), writes model laws that states are free to adopt. The ultimate goal is to develop a network of laws that are as similar as possible from state to state. As noted above, one such uniform law is the Uniform Consumer Sales Practices Act. The goal of this act is to streamline, refine, and update state statutes that regulate consumer sales contracts. The act is also designed to shield innocent buyers from unscrupulous sellers who engage in fraudulent practices. On the proactive side, the uniform law is also designed to foster the expansion of honest, impartial, and just sales techniques. Finally, the act is aimed at establishing a uniform set of laws that coordinate state laws with federal laws and state laws with one another. [See: Uniform Law Commission, Uniform Consumer Sales Practices Act, Legislative Fact Sheet and Final Act (2014).]

State Law Innovations

States are free to add, reject, ignore, or modify the Uniform Consumer Sales Practices Act. Most modifications are made to address issues that are peculiar to individual states. Some states, for example, have crossed from civil to criminal law and have authorized the state attorney general to investigate consumer fraud that is criminal in nature. Sometimes these provisions permit the use of civil and administrative subpoenas in the investigative stage of any consumer fraud case. Some states have added their own cyber-law provisions that are aimed at investigating such things as telemarketing and telecommunications fraud. On the other side of the coin, some states have tried their best to balance the scales by providing some assistance to sellers, especially after a lawsuit has been initiated. One such measure might permit a seller who has been sued to offer a "cure" that will satisfy the consumer without having to go through a long and arduous legal battle. [See: Melissa Szozda, "ID Theft, Economic Crimes, and Case Updates," *Consumer Law*, Ohio State Bar Association, July 31, 2013; and Helen M. MacMurray, "CSPA Right to Cure: Ohio's New Statutory Tool," *Consumer Law*, Ohio State Bar Association, July 31, 2013.]

State Lemon Laws

State legislatures have also attempted to protect consumers from products that are so badly flawed that they are virtually worthless. State **lemon laws** will compensate buyers for losses that result from such defective products. Some states have statutes that force sellers to give the buyer his or her money back. Other states have lemon laws that compel the manufacturer to admit to the defect and provide the consumer with a substitute product or its equivalent. At the heart of any lemon law is the manufacturer's violation of warranty. Although when most people think of lemon laws they focus on automobiles, most lemon laws involve other products too, usually appliances, machinery, and other vehicles.

> ### quick quiz 15-2
>
> 1. A consumer is someone who buys or leases real estate, goods, or services for personal, family, or household purposes.   true | false
> 2. The Federal Trade Commission Act transferred certain powers to the Federal Trade Commission, giving it the authority to oversee and eliminate deceptive and unfair practices in commerce.   true | false
> 3. To correct wrongdoings in the marketplace, the FTC has established trade regulation rules that must be followed by companies that transact business only in intrastate commerce.   true | false

15-3 Consumer Credit Laws

Consumers need just as much protection (some experts would argue more protection) in their credit transactions as in their consumer product contracts. Most Americans use credit cards as a matter of course on a daily basis, almost without thinking about it. In addition, the average American makes an installment payment on a car loan (perhaps even two) every month, almost as if it were a civic duty, like paying taxes or voting. Due to this extensive use of credit, Congress has found it necessary to pass federal laws to protect the consumer.

Consumer Financial Protection Bureau

Undoubtedly the most sweeping reform bill passed by Congress in reaction to the Economic Crisis of 2008 was the Dodd-Frank Wall Street Reform and Consumer Protection Act. Predictably, the Dodd-Frank Act is a long, involved, and complicated law that attempts to cover a whole host of financial sins. The act is comprised of 16 separate titles, many of which are often referred to as separate acts. The Consumer Finance Protection Bureau (CFPB, or simply the Bureau) was created under Title X of the Dodd-Frank Act as part of the effort to regulate the actions and the products of the consumer finance industry. The CFPB is ultimately responsible for ensuring that financial consumers are knowledgeable enough to make smart decisions regarding things like credit cards, loans from banks, and other areas of the financial world. From a pragmatic, real-world perspective, this means that the CFPB must make rules and regulations that compel financial institutions to inform consumers about such things as auto loans, bank accounts, credit cards, debt collection, payday loans, student loans, money transfers, prepaid cards, and so on. The CFPB also sponsors a website where financial consumers can get answers to financial questions online or through published guides that cover topics such as owning a home, paying for college, planning for retirement, navigating the military financial life cycle, and so on. [See: "Consumer Tools," Consumer Financial Protection Bureau, https://www.consumerfinance.gov/.]

The CFPB also has an enforcement division that is responsible for acting as an advocate for consumers to ensure that they are not mistreated, cheated, misled, or taken advantage of by the financial institutions that are under the CFPB's jurisdiction. To this end, the CFPB can introduce administrative proceedings and file lawsuits to redress grievances involving the violation of the laws and regulations that are part of its mission. The CFPB can issue warning letters to financial institutions ordering them to review and revise any policies or practices that may violate the law. The CFPB also provides a safe haven for financial industry whistleblowers who report legal violations by their present or former employer. In addition, the CFPB can secure monetary compensation for victimized consumers, either though the courts or under its own authority. Moreover, the CFPB does not operate in an unchecked or unsupervised fashion. It will respond to petitions that have been filed by financial institutions asking that orders and demands by the CFPB be set aside. The CFPB also maintains an independent ombudsman who handles problems that may have been caused by the CFPB. [See: "Policy & Compliance," Consumer Financial Protection Bureau, https://www.consumerfinance.gov/; and "CFPB Ombudsman," Consumer Financial Protection Bureau, https://www.consumerfinance.gov/cfpb-ombudsman/.]

Nevertheless, the CFPB has been the subject of many complaints from financial institutions and governmental figures, chiefly in Congress, who characterize its independent, single-leader structure as dictatorial in nature and scope. Presently, the director of the CFPB serves a set term of years and cannot be removed from office by the president, unless the president can show just cause for the removal. This is unlike most equivalent directors, such as the director of the FBI, who serves at the pleasure of the president. One proposal that has been put forth in Congress has been to replace the one-person structure with a five-person board that is similar to the board that runs the Security Exchange Commission. A more modest proposal has been to retain the single-leader structure but to remove the independent nature of that leader by making him or her subject to the president's removal power with or without cause. [See: C. Ryan Barber, "Republicans Want to Rename CFPB the 'Consumer Law Enforcement Agency,'" *The National Law Journal*, April 20, 2017, http://www.nationallawjournal.com/home/id/.]

The push to change the structure of the CFPB has come in the wake of several controversial regulations initiated by the CFPB. One such regulation forbids financial institutions such as credit card companies from adding mandatory binding arbitration clauses to their consumer credit agreements. These clauses require contractual consumers who have a grievance against a financial institution to submit to arbitration in lieu of filing a lawsuit. On the surface, the clause seems harmless enough—after all, both parties submit to the authority of the arbitrator, so the playing field is level. The real problem for the consumer appears only later when he or she wants to initiate or join a class action lawsuit against the financial institution. In effect, any financial institution with a mandatory binding arbitration clause (and there are few without such a clause) has eliminated the possibility of any class action lawsuit from being filed against it—ever. The CFPB's anti-arbitration clause regulation would reverse that trend. That is why the anti-arbitration rule, and the independent single-leader structure that made it possible, have been subjected to such vehement opposition. [See. C. Ryan Barber, "CFPB Faces 'Rock and Hard Place' in Pushing Arbitration Rule," *The National Law Journal*, April 13, 2017, http://www.nationallawjournal.com/id.]

Nor is this the only regulation under attack. Another complaint being lodged against the independent single-leader structure targets the new prepaid card rules. These regulations, which have been nicknamed the "Know Before You Owe" rules, require that a series of new disclosures, most involving fees and other features, be made known to prepaid card subscribers. The new rules cover prepaid cards, reloadable cards, mobile wallets, person-to-person payment products, payroll cards, student financial aid disbursement cards, tax refund cards, and some government benefit cards such as those that function as unemployment insurance and child support disbursement cards. The rules require that prepaid consumers have access to information about all fees, including periodic fees; per purchase fees; ATM withdrawal fees; balance inquiry fees; cash reload fees; customer service fees; and, yes, the ever present, counterintuitive, inactivity fees. The rules also include new protections for prepaid consumers who purchase such cards. One such protection compels prepaid card issuers to make certain that the consumer has the ability to pay; another rule requires prepaid card companies to give consumers monthly statements; another regulation requires that issuers set up a reasonable time period for consumers to make payments; another rule limits the amount that the card company can charge for late payments; another protection controls the amount of interest that can be charged, and so on. [See: "CFPB Finalizes Strong Federal Protections for Prepaid Account Consumers," Consumer Finance Protection Bureau, October 5, 2016, https://www.consumerfinance.gov/about-us/newsroom/cfpb-finalizes-strong-federal-protections-prepaid-account-consumers/.]

One protection that was strongly opposed by prepaid card companies was the overdraft rule. The new overdraft rule requires prepaid card companies to check a consumer's ability to pay before offering that customer overdraft protection on the card. The card companies argued that the process of checking "credit-worthiness" before making such an offer would become so onerous that most companies would simply stop making the offer. Nevertheless, those same companies argued that eliminating overdraft protection would cripple the ability of many low-income people to buy food or fill their car's gas tank before their next paycheck, thus crippling their ability to live within a budget. The opposition to these new regulations was so severe that some members of Congress even threatened to use the Congressional Review Act (CRA), a little known and seldom used statute, that gives Congress 60 "session" days to eliminate any newly enacted administrative regulation they oppose. The CRA has not been used very often over the past two decades, and there is some doubt as to its constitutionality, if only because it gives Congress the power to interfere unduly in the operation of the executive branch. Moreover, the act is inherently flawed because any override measure that Congress approves needs the president's signature. This would require the president to negate a set of rules that he might very well have initiated in the first place. Nevertheless, invoking the act would have caused serious difficulty for the CFPB. [See: C. Ryan Barber, "How a Prepaid Card Company Emerged as a 'Major Opponent' to CFPB," *The National Law Journal*, April 18, 2017, https://www.law.com/nationallawjournal/almID/1202783926090/How-a-Prepaid-Card-Company-Emerged-as-a-Major-Opponent-to-CFPB/?slreturn=20180401150748); and Maeve Carey, Alissa Dolan, and Christopher Davis, "The Congressional Review Act: Frequently Asked Questions, *Congressional Research Service*, November 17, 2016.]

ANOTHER QUESTION OF ETHICS

The Deep State Challenges the President Again

In November 2017, Richard Cordray, the director of the Consumer Financial Protection Bureau (CFPB) stepped down several months before his term of office was supposed to end. Before doing so, however, he appointed Leandra English to take his place as acting director of the CFPB. In order to accomplish this, he first appointed English, a career staffer at the CFPB, as deputy director. This move was calculated to put her in direct line to the position of acting director of the CFPB because, under the Dodd-Frank Act, the deputy director of the CFPB becomes the acting director when a vacancy occurs in the director's office. This provision in the law explains Cordray's haste in appointing English as his deputy just before he exited the CFPB. We all might be tempted to ask, "Who cares about another governmental appointment? They seem to emerge every other day in DC." True enough, but this one caused an unprecedented showdown between the president and administrative agents loyal to the previous administration.

The clash between the president and the loyalists emerged when President Trump named his own appointee to the post. That appointee was Mick Mulvaney, the head of the Office of Management and Budget. The president's authority to make this appointment comes under the Federal Vacancies Reform

Act, which empowers the president to choose acting directors of agencies that find themselves "director-less" for a time. Upping the ante, English filed a lawsuit in Federal District Court, asking the court to declare her the rightful acting director of the CFPB under the Dodd–Frank Act, which she claimed supersedes the Federal Vacancies Reform Act. English also asked the court to issue a temporary restraining order that would stop Trump's appointee from taking office.

What was at stake here was the running of a CFPB that was caught in a sea of controversy. As noted earlier, both the proposed anti-arbitration regulations and the new "Know-Before-You-Owe" rules were the source of much disagreement at the time. Unfortunately, both the moves made by the deputy director and those initiated by the president did nothing more than further destabilize an already destabilized agency. Was the strategy used by the outgoing director and his appointee another example of the tactics of the Deep State in its attempt to undermine the authority an unpopular president? Was the move by the president just a show of power that was unnecessary in view of the fact that if he had just waited, he would have been able to appoint a new director when the official term of the outgoing director expired a few months down the road? Which side seemed to hold the moral high ground in this case? Do not just rush to judgment here based solely on your opinion or only on your political preferences. Instead, take one of the ethical theories we discussed in Chapter 1—social contract ethics, utilitarianism, rational ethics, or Max Weber's ethical dyad—and construct your argument accordingly. [See: Yuka Hayashi, "Trump Sued in CFPB Battle," *The Wall Street Journal*, November 27, 2017, pp. A-1 and A-4. See also: Jim Puzzanghera, "One Job, Two Chiefs as Drama Builds at Consumer Bureau," *Tribune News Service, the Los Angeles Times, MSN NEWS*, November 28, 2017, https://www.scribd.com/article/365704700/One-Job-2-Chiefs-As-Drama-Builds-At-Consumer-Bureau.]

The Federal Truth-in-Lending Act

The Consumer Credit Protection Act (CCPA) was passed by Congress in 1968 to deal with problems associated with consumer credit. It is composed of five titles, which by today's standards is remarkably short, the first of which is the Truth-in-Lending Act. Because lending institutions and businesses charge different rates of interest to consumers, it often pays to shop around before borrowing money or buying on credit. To help consumers know the truth about the cost of borrowing money, Congress developed the Truth-in-Lending Act as a key element of the CCPA. Under the Truth-in-Lending Act, lenders must disclose two important things to borrowers: the **finance charge** (the actual cost of the loan in dollars and cents) and the **annual percentage rate (APR)** (the true rate of interest of the loan). With this information, consumers can compare the cost of loans from different lenders before deciding from which to borrow. Surprisingly, the APR sometimes turns out to be greater than it would appear at first glance.

Most consumers today rely heavily on credit card transactions. For this reason, Congress has enacted several consumer credit protection laws.
©Comstock Images/Getty Imags

EXAMPLE 15-1: True Rate of Interest

Hana borrowed $100 for one year and agreed to pay a finance charge of $10. If she kept the $100 for the year and at the end of the year paid back the full amount, together with the $10 finance charge, the APR would be 10 percent. If, however, she paid the $110 in 12 monthly installments of $9.17 each, the APR would be 18 percent. The latter rate is higher because during the course of the year, she would have the use, on the average, of only about half of the $100.

Equal Credit Opportunity

The Equal Credit Opportunity Act was passed by Congress, as amendment to the Truth-in-Lending Act, to ensure that all consumers are given an equal chance to receive credit. The law makes it illegal for banks and businesses to discriminate against credit applicants because of their sex, race, marital status, national origin, religion, or age or because they get public assistance income. The law must be followed by anyone who regularly extends credit, including banks, credit unions, finance companies, credit card issuers, and retail stores. Some of the rights to consumers under the act are as follows:

1. People who apply for credit may not be asked to reveal their sex, race, national origin, or religion; whether they are divorced or widowed; their marital status, unless they are applying for a joint account or a secured loan; information about their spouse, except in community property states, unless the spouse is also applying for credit or will use the account; their plans for having or raising children; and whether they receive alimony, child support, or separate maintenance payments if they will not be relying on that income.

2. When deciding to extend credit, creditors must not consider the applicant's sex, marital status, race, national origin, or religion; consider the applicant's age, unless the applicant is a minor or is considered favorably for being over 62; refuse to consider public assistance income in the same manner as other income; and refuse to consider income from part-time employment, pensions, or retirement programs.

3. Applicants may apply for credit under the name given to them at birth, their married name, or a combination of both. They may receive credit without a cosigner if they meet the creditor's standards. In addition, applicants have a right to know within 30 days whether their application for credit has been accepted or rejected. If rejected, they have a right to know the reasons for the rejection within 60 days.

Unauthorized Use of Credit Cards

Sometimes credit cards are lost, stolen, or used by people who have no authority to use them. Under the Truth-in-Lending Act, credit cardholders are not responsible for any unauthorized charges made after the card issuer has been notified of the loss, theft, or possible unauthorized use of the card. Such notice may be given to the card issuer by telephone, letter, or any other means. Even then, credit cardholders are responsible only for the first $50 of any unauthorized charges. Debit cards do not have this built-in protection. The credit cardholder can avoid the $50 liability if the credit card issuer has not included on the card a method to identify the user of the card, such as a signature, a photograph, or other means of identification. Card issuers must notify cardholders in advance of the potential $50 liability. As an amendment to the Truth-in-Lending Act, Congress recently launched the Consumer Financial Protection Bureau, a new federal office that is deigned to act as a watchdog in the credit industry.

Fair Credit Reporting

The Fair Credit Reporting Act was passed by Congress to ensure that consumers are treated fairly by credit bureaus and consumer reporting agencies. A consumer has the right to know all information (other than medical information) that is in his or her files. A consumer also has the right to know, in most cases, the source of the information on file. In addition, a consumer has the right to be told the name of anyone who received a credit report in the past year (or two years if the credit report relates to a job application). If errors are found, credit bureaus must investigate and then correct or delete information that is inaccurate, incomplete, or obsolete. If the credit bureau retains information that the consumer believes to be incorrect, the consumer's version of the facts must be inserted in the file. Also, creditors are required to tell consumers the specific reasons for the denial of credit.

Billing, Collecting, and Leasing

Even with all of the consumer protection laws outlined earlier, there are still a variety of ways in which consumers can be victimized. The last of these areas include billing, collecting, and leasing. In billing, retail stores, credit card companies, and other businesses that extend credit sometimes make billing errors that threaten the reputation and the credit record of innocent consumers. To make it easier for billing errors to be corrected, Congress has passed the Fair Credit Billing Act (FCBA). Improper collection procedures can also hassle innocent consumers. Under the Fair Debt Collection Practices Act, specific rules must be followed by companies that are in the business of collecting debts for others. Finally, consumers who must rent or lease products sometimes find themselves victimized by unscrupulous leasing companies. The Consumer Leasing Act is a federal law requiring leasing companies to inform consumers of all of the terms of a lease of personal property.

The Fair Credit Billing Act Under the Fair Credit Billing Act (FCBA), when consumers believe an error has been made in a bill, they must notify the creditor within 60 days after the bill was mailed. The notice must identify the consumer and give the account number, the suspected amount of error, and an explanation of why the consumer believes there is an error. The creditor must acknowledge the consumer's notice within 30 days. Then, within 90 days, the creditor must conduct an investigation and either correct the mistake or explain why the bill is believed to be correct. Another provision of the act gives consumers protection when they buy unsatisfactory goods or services with credit cards. If a consumer has a dispute with a credit card purchase, the consumer can disregard the bill for the disputed item and, instead, notify the credit card issuer of the error by telephone. The credit card issuer will put the disputed amount on hold and send the consumer a form to fill out explaining the dispute. The credit card issuer will attempt to resolve the dispute and inform the consumer of the results. Then, if the problem is not corrected and suit is brought by the credit card issuer, the consumer may use as a defense the fact that unsatisfactory goods or services were received. For this law to apply, the initial transaction must have taken place in the consumer's state or within 100 miles of the consumer's mailing address. Creditors may not give cardholders a poor credit rating for exercising their rights under this act.

Under the Fair Debt Collection Practices Act, debt collectors must follow strict guidelines when contacting consumers.

©Purestock/SuperStock

Fair Debt Collection Practices Under the Fair Debt Collection Practices Act, specific rules must be followed by companies that are in the business of collecting debts for others. Some of these rules are as follows:

1. When trying to locate someone, a debt collector may not communicate by postcard or tell others that the consumer owes money.

2. When the debt collector knows that the consumer is represented by an attorney, the debt collector may communicate only with the attorney.

3. A debt collector may not communicate with the consumer at any unusual or inconvenient time or place. Unless there are circumstances to the contrary, the convenient time for communicating with a consumer is between the hours of 8:00 A.M. and 9:00 P.M.

4. A debt collector may not communicate with the consumer at the consumer's place of employment if the debt collector knows that the employer prohibits such communication.

5. A debt collector may not communicate, in connection with the collection of a debt, with any person other than the consumer, the consumer's attorney, the creditor's attorney, or a consumer reporting agency.

6. If a consumer notifies a debt collector in writing that the consumer refuses to pay the debt or wishes the debt collector to cease further communication, the debt collector must cease communication, except to notify the consumer of a specific action.

7. Debt collectors may not harass consumers or use abusive techniques to collect debts. The use or threatened use of violence or other criminal means to harm the person, property, or reputation of consumers is not allowed. In addition, debt collectors may not use obscene or profane language or publish a list of those who allegedly refuse to pay debts. It is also illegal for a debt collector to cause a telephone to ring or to engage in repeated telephone conversations with the intent to annoy the consumer.

Debt collectors who violate this law may be sued for actual damages, punitive damages, and attorneys' fees.

The Consumer Leasing Act The Consumer Leasing Act is a federal law requiring leasing companies to inform consumers of all of the terms of a lease of personal property. Consumers can use the information to compare one lease with another or the cost of leasing with the cost of buying the same property. The law applies only to personal property leased by an individual for a period of more than four months for personal, family, or household use. It does not cover daily or weekly rentals, leases for apartments or houses, or leases to anyone for business purposes.

EXAMPLE 15-2: Businesses Not Protected

Guzman decided that her business could be managed much more efficiently if it had a computer. The cost of buying a computer, however, was more than Guzman could afford. She considered leasing one. The Consumer Leasing Act would not apply to Guzman's lease because the computer was for business rather than personal use. She would be able to make a better decision, however, if she asked the leasing company for the same information the company would be required to provide to a consumer.

The law requires that consumers be given a written statement informing them of the full cost of the lease, including the cost of any necessary licenses, taxes, or other fees. Consumers must be informed of any insurance requirements and penalties for late payment. They must also be told who is responsible for maintaining and servicing the property. In addition, they must be told whether they can buy the property and, if so, when and at what price. The law also places a limit on the amount of a **balloon payment** (a very large final payment) to no more than three times the average monthly payments. Advertisements of leases are also regulated by law. If an advertisement mentions the amount or number of payments, specifies a particular down payment, or states that no down payment is required; it must also disclose the total of regular payments, the consumer's responsibility at the end of the lease, and whether the consumer may purchase the property.

The Military Lending Act The Military Lending Act (MLA) was enacted to protect members the military, especially those on active duty, as well as their spouses and dependents, from being targeted by certain financial organizations and institutions that use questionable lending strategies to take advantage of military personnel who often find themselves in a vulnerable position because of their highly mobile, somewhat unpredictable lifestyle. The program is run under the auspices of the Department of Defense but is also enforced by the Governors of the Federal Reserve System, the Federal Deposit Insurance Corporation, the National Credit Union Administration, the Office of the Comptroller of the Currency, the Federal Trade Commission, and our old friend, the Consumer Financial Protection Bureau. Originally, the MLA provided protection from abuses related to a small set of credit practices including car loans, payday loans, and tax refund anticipation loans. Under recent amendments, protection has been extended to cover credit cards, deposit advance strategies, overdraft credit lines, and some types of installment loans. In addition, for transactions that are included under the act, the Military Annual Percentage Rate (MAPR) cannot go above 36 percent. Recent amendments have also modified some of the original provisions of the act. These amendments change the MAPR to include a number of added fees and charges. They also alter the disclosures that borrowers receive from creditors and modify some of the prohibitions on rolling over, refinancing, or renewing consumer credit contracts. Dependents under the act include children under the age of 21; children under the age of 23 who are full-time students at accredited institutions of higher learning, and who depend on a covered member for more than half of their support; children of any age who cannot support themselves because of physical incapacity and/or mental incapacity; live-in parents who depend on the covered member for more than half of their support; and former and un-remarried spouses whose marriage overlapped 20/15 years of service and who have no employer health insurance. Those who are considered covered members under the act include active duty members of the Army, Navy, Marine Corps, Air Force, and Coast Guard, as well as certain members of the Active Guard and the Reserves as specified by the certain provisions of the U.S. Code [10 USC 101 (d) (6)]. [See: Anthony Cacciatore, "The Military Lending Act: 10 U.S.C. Section 986," *The Ohio State Bar Association Forum*, August 24–25, 2017.]

quick quiz 15-3

1. Under the terms of the Truth-in-Lending Act, lenders need disclose only things to the finance charge to lenders. — true | false
2. If a credit card or a debit card is lost, the cardholder is responsible only for the first $50 of any unauthorized charges. — true | false
3. Debt collectors who violate the Fair Debt Collection Practices cannot be sued. — true | false

Summary

15.1 Public interest refers to the idea that certain activities affect the entire social structure and must, therefore, be regulated by the government. Public policy, in contrast, seeks to implement behavior that promotes the public consensus and eliminates behavior that does not. Both concepts are inherent within the legal doctrines of product liability. Under the theory of product liability, a buyer or user of a product who is injured because of the product's unsafe or defective condition may recover damages from the manufacturer, the seller, or the supplier of the goods. Product liability suits can now be based on one of two legal theories, negligence or strict liability, both of which are tort actions. Public policy has not remained solely within the purview of the courts. Congress has also entered the product safety arena by establishing the Consumer Product Safety Commission (CPSC) to protect consumers from unreasonable risk or injury from hazardous products.

15.2 The Federal Trade Commission Act gave the Federal Trade Commission (FTC) the authority to oversee and eliminate deceptive and unfair practices in commerce. The FTC and the courts have determined that certain activities are unfair or deceptive. They include fraudulent misrepresentations, sending unordered merchandise, bait-and-switch schemes, and odometer tampering. To correct wrongdoings in the marketplace, the FTC has also established trade regulation rules to govern the activities of interstate companies. These rules include the Used Car Rule, the Cooling-Off Rule, the negative option rule, the Mail and Telephone Order Rule, the telemarketing sales rule, and the rules connected with 900 numbers. Other rules are set up by the antispam law and the antislamming law.

15.3 Under Title X of the Dodd-Frank Act, Congress created the Consumer Finance Protection Bureau (CFPB) to help regulate the actions and the products of the consumer finance industry. As a part of the Truth-in-Lending Act, lenders must disclose the true nature of finance charges and the annual percentage rate. The Equal Credit Opportunity Act ensures that all consumers have an equal chance to receive credit. The Fair Credit Reporting Act guarantees fair treatment by credit bureaus and consumer reporting agencies. Under the Truth-in-Lending Act, credit card holders are not responsible for any unauthorized charges made after the card issuer has been notified of the loss, theft, or possible unauthorized use of the card. The Fair Credit Reporting Act promises that consumers will be treated fairly by credit bureaus and consumer reporting agencies. To make it easier to correct billing errors, Congress has passed the Fair Credit Billing Act (FCBA). Under the Fair Debt Collection Practices Act, specific rules must be followed by companies that are in the business of collecting debts for others. The Consumer Leasing Act requires leasing companies to inform consumers of all of the terms of a lease of personal property.

Key Terms

annual percentage rate (APR), 433
bait-and-switch scheme, 423
balloon payment, 436
Buyer's Guide, 425
cancellation form, 426
Can Spam Act, 428
class action lawsuit, 423
commerce, 422
consent order, 423
consumer, 422
continuity plan, 426
Cooling-Off Rule, 425
Dodd-Frank Wall Street Reform and Consumer Protection Act, 430
dunning letters, 423
finance charge, 433
interstate commerce, 422
intrastate commerce, 422
lemon law, 429
Mail and Telephone Order Rule, 426
product liability, 415
public interest, 416
public policy, 416
strict liability, 418
slamming, 428
spam, 428
Used Car Rule, 425

Questions for Review and Discussion

1. What is the link between social engineering and the law?
2. What is the difference between the public interest and public policy?
3. What is the difference between negligence and strict liability?
4. What is the purpose of the Consumer Product Safety Act?
5. How is the Federal Trade Commission Act enforced?
6. What are some unfair or deceptive practices?
7. What are the FTC rules designed to protect the consumer?
8. What is the function of the Truth-in-Lending Act?
9. What are some of the latest amendments to the Truth-in-Lending Act?
10. What is required by the Consumer Leasing Act?

Cases for Analysis

1. Paul and Cynthia Vance invited Carl and Jeanne Leichtamer to go for a ride in the Vances' four-wheel-drive Jeep at an "off-the-road" recreation facility called the Hall of Fame Four-Wheel Club. The club had been organized by a Jeep dealer who showed films to club members of Jeeps traveling in hilly country. This activity was coupled with a national advertising program of American Motor Sales Corporation encouraging people to buy Jeeps that could drive up and down steep hills. As the Jeep went up a 33-degree sloped, double-terraced hill, it pitched over from front to back and landed upside-down. The Vances were killed, and the Leichtamers were severely injured. The Jeep was equipped with a factory-installed roll bar attached to the sheet metal that housed the rear wheels. When the vehicle landed upside down, the flat sheet metal gave way, causing the roll bar to move forward and downward 14 inches. The Leichtamers argued that the weakness of the sheet metal housing upon which the roll bar had been attached was the cause of their injuries. The manufacturer claimed that the roll bar was provided solely for side-roll protection, not pitch over, as occurred in this case. Did the Leichtamers recover against the manufacturer on a theory of strict liability? Why or why not? [See: *Leichtamer v. American Motors Corp.*, 424 N.E.2d 568 (OH).]

2. Michael P. Babine was injured when he was thrown from an "El Toro" mechanical bull that he rode at a nightclub. The club had placed mattresses around the bull to cushion the fall of riders, but the mattresses were not adequately pushed together. Babine was thrown off during his ride and hit his head on the floor where there was a gap between the mattresses. Before riding the bull, Babine had signed a form releasing the nightclub from liability for injuries sustained from the activity. The mechanical bull had been manufactured for the purpose of being a training device for rodeo cowboys, and it was purchased second-hand by the nightclub. Babine sought to recover damages from the manufacturer under the theory of product liability. Did he succeed? Why or why not? [See: *Babine v. Gilley's Bronco Shop, Inc.*, 488 So.2d 176 (FL).]

3. Harriet Glantz lost her job. She was unable to find work for several months and fell behind in the payment of her debts. A debt collector telephoned her at 11:45 P.M., used profanity, and threatened to "take care of her" if she didn't pay the amount owed. Were Glantz's rights violated? Explain.

4. Ingram went to a used car lot in a large city and bought a used car. On his way home from the lot, the engine stopped running in the car he had just purchased. The used car lot refused to fix the car because the salesperson had written "as is" on the sales slip. Ingram had not been informed that the car was sold to him as is. Was a consumer protection law violated? Explain.

5. Prior to his marriage, Edward Garber had been in financial difficulty and had a poor credit rating. His wife, Natalie, applied for a credit card in her family name, fearing that she would be turned down if she used her married name of Garber. She was told that she must use her married name on a credit application. Could Natalie have used her family name when she applied for credit? Explain.

6. Horack bought a used Mustang from a used car lot. The odometer showed that the car had been driven only 30,000 miles. Later, while cleaning her car, Horack found a service receipt showing that the actual mileage on the car a year earlier was 45,000 miles. Was a law violated? Explain.

7. Carboni's MasterCard bill contained several charges that she had not made. Upon investigation, she discovered that her credit card was missing from her wallet. She immediately notified the bank of the lost credit card. The unauthorized charges on the bill that she received amounted to $375. Did Carboni have to pay the full amount of the bill? Explain.

8. Delores Bierlein paid a $200 deposit toward the rental of the Silver Room at Alex's Continental Inn for her wedding reception. Later, Bierlein canceled the reception because her fiancé was transferred from Ohio to New York. The inn refused to refund Bierlein's deposit. The consumer protection law of that state requires suppliers to furnish receipts when they receive deposits. Bierlein was not given a receipt for her $200 deposit. When she sued for the return of the $200, the question arose as to whether this transaction fell within the consumer protection law. Do you think it does? Explain. [See: *Bierlein v. Alex's Continental Inn, Inc.*, 475 N.E.2d 1273 (OH).]

9. In response to a radio advertisement, Mr. and Mrs. Lancet telephoned Hollywood Decorators Inc. and arranged for Mr. Wolff, a company representative, to visit their home. During Wolff's visit, the Lancets signed a contract for interior decoration and paid a $1,000 deposit. Two days later, the Lancets canceled the contract by telephone and asked for the return of their deposit. Twelve days after that, the Lancets' attorney wrote a letter to the company renewing the cancellation. Were they bound by the contract they signed? Why or why not? [See: *Hollywood Decorators, Inc., v. Lancet*, 461 N.Y.S.2d 955 (NY).]

10. After receiving an unsuccessful surgical procedure designed to facilitate weight loss, Gatten brought suit against the physician for violation of the state consumer protection law. That law read in part, "unfair methods of competition and deceptive practices in the conduct of any trade or commerce are unlawful." Gatten based her case on statements made to her about her course of treatment and the probable results of that treatment. Does the unsuccessful treatment by a physician fall within the consumer protection law? Explain. [See: *Gatten v. Merzi*, 579 A.2d 974 (PA).]

quick quiz Answers

15-1	15-2	15-3
1. F	1. T	1. F
2. F	2. T	2. F
3. T	3. F	3. F

Part 3 Case Study

Norcold, Inc. v. Gateway Supply Company
298 N.E. 2d 618
154 Ohio App. 594 (2003)

©Artifacts Images/Getty Images

Summary

The plaintiff in this case, Norcold Inc. (Norcold) makes refrigerators for recreational vehicles. The first defendant, the Gateway Supply Company, works with companies like Norcold, providing them with equipment and parts including such things as pipes, fittings, and valves. Gateway offered a revolutionary new device it had developed that would unify two separate parts into a single tap tee, which would be used to carry flammable gas for refrigerator units in a safe and efficient way. Once Norcold had agreed to use the new tap tee in its refrigeration units, Gateway contracted with Dayco, a manufacturing firm, that agreed to make the new units for Norcold. When that stage of the manufacturing process was completed, Dayco sent the tap tees to Gateway, which passed them along to Norcold, based on the purchase orders sent by Norcold. Once they had received the new tap tee, technicians at Norcold tested each tap tee twice before they had them installed in their refrigeration units. Sometime thereafter, Norcold discovered that the new tap tees were defective and, in fact, potentially hazardous. Accordingly Norcold issued a recall notice to all customers who had purchased a refrigeration unity equipped with the Gateway tap tee. The recall cost Norcold upward of $25,000. Norcold then sued Gateway for breach of contract and breach of express and implied warranties. In the meantime, Gateway filed a third-party complaint against Dayco, asking for indemnification if necessary and damages for breach of contract and for breach of both the express and implied warranties. Norcold then included Dayco in its suit. Without hesitation, Gateway then counterclaimed against Norcold for breach of contract, failure to pay, and unjust enrichment. Dayco then asked for indemnification or contribution if it were found to be liable to either Norcold or Gateway.

A series of additional summary judgment motions followed this complex array of complaints, counterclaims, cross claims and third-party complaints. The trial court granted Gateway's motion for summary judgment dismissing all claims filed by both Norcold and Dayco, but denied Dayco's summary judgment motion against Norcold. Later, after several reconsiderations of various summary judgment motions, the trial court granted both Gateway's and Dayco's summary judgment motions. Norcold appealed the dismissals, claiming that the trial court had made six separate errors in its decision. For the sake of simplicity and efficiency. we will explore the first assignment of error only.

In the first assignment of error, the court of appeals must determine whether the trial court had been correct in dismissing all consideration of the written warranties included in the tap tee contract between Norcold and Gateway. To solve this conundrum, the appellate court must determine whether the apparently express warranties included in the written agreement between Norcold and Gateway were actually relied upon by Norcold as the basis of the bargain between the two corporations. To determine this the appellate court must refer to the

Uniform Commercial Code (UCC), specifically to UCC Section 2-303 which states in part:

> **(A) Express warranties by the seller are created as follows:**
>
> (1) Any affirmation of fact or promise made by the seller to the buyer which relates to the goods and becomes part of **the basis of the bargain** creates an express warranty that the goods shall conform to the affirmation or promise. [boldface added for emphasis]

This part of the case turns on the appellate court's interpretation of the phrase "the basis of the bargain." The questions here can be summed up as follows: (1) Did the warranties in the written agreement between Norcold and Gateway become part of the contract in which Gateway promised to deliver the tap tee to Norcold? (2) If the warranties in the written agreement are, in fact, part of the contract, is it necessary that Norcold actually relied on those warranties as **the basis of the bargain** between Norcold and Gateway or, in the alternative, are the words by themselves enough to establish the warranties?

In examining the first question, the appellate court found that, in concluding that the written warranties had not been incorporated into the Norcold-Gateway tap tee contract, the trial court had followed an inappropriate precedent. The appeals court notes that the case of *Price Brothers Co. v. Philadelphia Gear Corp.* can be distinguished from the current situation because the Price Brothers case involved "pre-contract statements made by the seller, sales literature, and a journal article referring to the goods sold." These pre-contractual discussions and exhibits were, in fact, promises that had become part of the agreement. In contrast, in this case, there was no evidence of any pre-contractual statements or sales literature or journal articles. Instead, all we have are "integrated terms within the parties' written agreement."

Having decided that the written warranties had, in fact, been incorporated into the agreement, the court had to decide next whether those warranties were actually binding on Gateway. If so, Gateway would have to honor the warranties; if not, Gateway would be home free, well almost. Now, all of this may seem absurdly simple—that is, we see the word *warranty* in the written agreement and conclude that the warranty will bind the party that wrote the agreement. In truth, that may be the result. However, the court cannot jump to that conclusion without some sort of legal support. In dealing with a sales contract, legal support comes in the form of the Uniform Commercial Code, specifically, as noted earlier, form UCC 2-303. Let's repeat what it says there:

> **(A) Express warranties by the seller are created as follows:**
>
> (1) Any affirmation of fact or promise made by the seller to the buyer which relates to the goods and becomes part of **the basis of the bargain** creates an express warranty that the goods shall conform to the affirmation or promise. [boldface added for emphasis]

In its interpretation, the court of appeals rightly fixates on the phrase "the basis of the bargain." The court concludes that the plain meaning of the phrase "the basis of the bargain" appears to require that the parties discuss the warranties in the written agreement and, somehow during that discussion, talk about the warranties and expressly incorporate them into the contract. To put it simply, the folks from Norcold would have had to say something like, "Now about these warranties, unless you say right here and now that they are part of the deal, we will walk away." Then assume the folks from Gateway said something like, "Okay, sure, we don't want to lose this deal, so, sure, the express warranties are part of the agreement." If the Norcold people then say, "Great, okay, deal," then the warranties are part of the agreement. The court is not satisfied with this conclusion, so it offers a second view—that is, that the mere presence of the words in the written agreement means that the warranties are binding on the seller.

However to reach this view, the court must pull that meaning out of the statute itself. The stumbling block seems to be the phrase "the basis of the bargain." The phrase seems to suggest that the inclusion of the warranties must be "the basis of the bargain"—that is, something negotiated and accepted as part of the deal. The problem is the authors of the UCC failed to define the phrase. The judge then goes hinting for a hidden definition or clarification of the phrase. He discovers it in the comments section of the UCC. There he finds this explanation:

> Comment 3 states: [t]he present section deals with affirmations of fact by the seller, descriptions of the goods or exhibitions of samples, *exactly as any other part of a negotiation which ends in a contract is dealt with.* No specific intention to make a warranty is necessary if any of these factors is made part of the basis of the bargain. In actual practice affirmations of fact made by the seller about the goods during a bargain are regarded as part of the description of those goods; hence no particular reliance on such statements need be shown in order to weave them

into the fabric of the agreement. Rather, any fact which is to take such affirmations, once made, out of the agreement requires clear affirmative proof. The issue normally is one of fact.

The court concludes this portion of the case in this way, "Thus, comment 3 indicates that UCC section 2-313 is relevant to the question of whether an express warranty has been *created*, and the 'basis of the bargain' rule is not applicable to situations where written warranties are clear and express. A decisive majority of courts that have considered this issue have reached the similar conclusion that reliance is not an element in a claim for breach of an express written warranty normal. Express warranties 'are as much a part of the contract as any other term, and the right to damages on the breach depends on nothing more than the breach of warranty.'"

(Reproduced below is that portion of the court's opinion that reviews some of the counterarguments made to the court's decision and the rationale related to the court's analysis of "the basis of the bargain" language in UCC 2-303. Footnote numerals are included, but the citations themselves and explanatory notes are omitted.)

The Court's Opinion

Delivered by Judge Walters

OPINION.

{¶ 1} Plaintiff-Appellant, Norcold, Inc. ("Norcold"), appeals separate Shelby County Common Pleas Court decisions granting summary judgment in favor of Defendants-Appellants, Gateway Supply Company, Inc. ("Gateway") and Dayco Products, Inc. ("Dayco"). Because claims for breach of an express written warranty do not mandate reliance on the part of the buyer, we must reverse the trial court's dismissal of Norcold's express warranty claims against Gateway. With regard to Norcold's claims for breach of the implied warranties of merchantability and fitness for a particular purpose, no warranty of merchantability exists because the part in question was a newly constructed component and no average or usual standards for determining ordinary performance or quality could be determined; however, questions of material fact do remain as to whether Norcold relied on Gateway to supply parts fit for Norcoldvs particular purpose. Additionally, because a commercial purchaser of a defective product cannot maintain a claim for purely economic loss under common law tort theories of recovery and because Norcold failed to plead a contract cause of action, its claims against Dayco are barred as a matter of law.

{¶ 2} Norcold engages in the production and sale of refrigerators to manufacturers of recreational vehicles and camping trailers. For several years, Gateway has acted as a distributor of pipes, fittings, and valves to Norcold for use in refrigerator assembly. In 1992, Norcold representatives approached Gateway to discuss combining two pre-existing parts used to power Norcold's refrigerators. This combined unit would become known as a "tap tee," which is used to carry flammable gas. Thereafter, Gateway consulted with Dayco to manufacture the part.

{¶ 3} Subsequently, Dayco delivered the parts to Gateway, who then distributed them to Norcold, pursuant to Norcold's purchase orders. The purchase orders afforded Norcold the ability to test each tap tee prior to final assembly, and each part was tested twice before being integrated into the refrigerators. In summer 1999, Norcold found that the tap tees were subject to stress corrosion cracking and, thus, potentially hazardous. Accordingly, Norcold issued a recall campaign of its mobile refrigerator units and allegedly suffered damages in excess of $25,000.

{¶ 4} As a result, Norcold initiated suit against Gateway, alleging breach of contract and breach of express and implied warranties. Gateway then filed a third-party complaint against Dayco, claiming it was entitled to indemnification [Page 597] and damages for breach of contract and express and implied warranties. Thereafter, Norcold amended its complaint to include Dayco as a defendant, asserting breach of express and implied warranties. In response to the amended complaint, Gateway counter-claimed against Norcold for breach of contract, payment of an existing account, and unjust enrichment. Gateway also filed a cross-claim against Dayco, alleging breach of contract and unjust enrichment. Dayco responded to the amended complaint and cross-claim, maintaining that it was entitled to indemnification or contribution in the event it was liable to either Norcold or Gateway.

{¶ 5} After completing extensive discovery, Gateway moved for summary judgment against Norcold and Dayco, and Dayco moved for summary judgment against Norcold and Gateway. In a May 20, 2002 judgment entry, the trial court granted Gateway's motion for summary judgment in full, thus dismissing all claims of both Norcold and Dayco. In a separate judgment entry filed the same day, the trial court denied Dayco's motion for summary judgment against Norcold.

{¶ 6} Prior to the court's decisions on the summary judgment motions, Norcold moved for leave to file a second amended complaint, stating that it wanted to separate the claims against Gateway, "which are contractual in nature, from those against Dayco[,] . . . which are based in tort." The motion was initially denied; however, upon Norcold's motion to reconsider and after the claims against Gateway were dismissed, the trial court granted Norcold leave to amend its complaint for a second time. Therein, Norcold re-alleged claims against both Gateway and Dayco. Gateway and Dayco both responded with the same claims as argued in response to Norcold's first amended complaint.

{¶ 7} On September 4, 2002, pursuant to an agreed judgment entry, all claims asserted by Norcold against Gateway in the second amended complaint were dismissed in accordance with the trial court's prior grant of summary judgment. Thereafter, Dayco again moved for summary judgment against Norcold. The trial court granted the motion on December 13, 2002, finding that absent privity of contract, Ohio law does not provide a common law remedy in tort to a commercial purchaser of a defective product for purely economic loss. Following the court's entry, Norcold filed a Motion for Modification and/or Reconsideration of the court's grant of summary judgment, which was denied.

{¶ 8} From the trial court's May 20, 2002 grant of summary judgment to Gateway and December 13, 2002 grant of summary judgment to Dayco, Norcold appeals, asserting six assignments of error for our review. For purposes of brevity and clarity, we will combine our discussion of Norcold's third and fourth assignments of error. Because this appeal arises from summary judgment determinations, we will begin by setting forth our standard of review. *Page 598

Standard of Review

{¶ 9} Under Ohio law, a court may not grant a motion for summary judgment unless the record demonstrates: (1) that no genuine issue of material fact remains to be litigated; (2) that the moving party is entitled to judgment as a matter of law; and (3) that, after considering the evidence most strongly in the nonmovant's favor, reasonable minds can come but to one conclusion, and that conclusion is adverse to the party against whom the motion for summary judgment is made.[1] In ruling on a summary judgment motion, the trial court is not permitted to weigh evidence or choose among reasonable inferences; rather, the court must evaluate evidence, taking all permissible inferences and resolving questions of credibility in favor of the nonmovant.[2] Even the inferences to be drawn from the underlying facts contained in the evidentiary materials, such as affidavits and depositions, must be construed in a light most favorable to the adverse party.[3] Appellate review of summary judgment determinations is conducted on a de novo basis;[4] therefore, this court considers the motion independently and without deference to the trial court's findings.

Norcold's Claims Against Gateway

Assignment of Error I The trial court erred in granting Appellee Gateway's Motion for Summary Judgment as to Count I of Appellant Norcold's first amended complaint by finding that no genuine issue of material fact exists for resolution by a jury regarding Norcold's reliance on express warranties as a basis of its bargain with Gateway.

{¶ 10} In its first assignment of error, Norcold contends that the trial court made impermissible credibility determinations as to whether Norcold relied upon Gateway's express warranties concerning the tap tee. Neither party contests that affirmations of fact or promise were made by Gateway to Norcold within the purchase orders for the tap tees; therefore, the only issue to be [Page 599] decided by this court is whether the trial court erred in finding that the language therein was not part of the basis of the bargain between the parties.

{¶ 11} In purchasing the tap tees from Gateway, Norcold furnished purchase orders containing the following applicable language:

1. ACCEPTANCE AGREEMENT. Seller's commencement of work on the goods subject to this purchase order or shipment of such goods, whichever occurs first, shall be deemed an effective mode of acceptance of this purchase order. Any acceptance of this purchase order is limited to acceptance of the express terms contained on the front and back hereof. . .

1. WARRANTY. Seller expressly warrants that all goods or services furnished under this agreement shall conform to all specifications and appropriate standards, will be new, and will be free from defects in material or workmanship. . . . Seller warrants that all goods or services furnished here under will be merchantable, and will be safe and appropriate for the purpose for which goods or services of that kind are normally used. If seller knows or has reason to know the particular purpose for which purchaser intends to use the goods or services, seller warrants that such goods or services will fit for such particular purpose. Seller warrants that goods or services furnished will conform in all respects to samples, inspection, test, acceptance or use of the goods or services furnished here under. Such warranties shall survive inspections, tests, acceptance and use. Seller's warranty shall run to purchaser, its successors, assigns and customers, and users of products sold by purchaser. Seller agrees to replace or correct defects of any goods or services not conforming to the foregoing warranty promptly, without expense to purchaser, when notified of such nonconformity by purchaser, provided purchaser elects to provide seller with the opportunity to do so. In the event of failure of seller to correct

defects in or replace nonconforming goods or services promptly, purchaser, after reasonable notice to seller, may make such corrections or replace such goods and services and charge seller for the cost by purchaser in doing so. . . .

17. ENTIRE AGREEMENT. This purchase order, and any documents referred to on the face hereof, constitute the entire agreement between the parties.

[¶ 12] With respect to express warranties, R.C. 1302.26 (U.C.C. § 2-313) provides, in pertinent part:

(A) Express warranties by the seller are created as follows:

(1) Any affirmation of fact or promise made by the seller to the buyer which relates to the goods and becomes part of the basis of the bargain creates an express warranty that the goods shall conform to the affirmation or promise.

. . . [Page 600]

(B) It is not necessary to the creation of an express warranty that the seller use formal words such as 'warrant' or 'guarantee' or that he have a specific intention to make a warranty, but an affirmation merely of the value of the goods or a statement purporting to be merely the seller's opinion or commendation of the goods does not create a warranty.

[¶ 13] The trial court herein determined that the written warranties by Gateway did not become part of the basis of the bargain between the parties because Norcold did not actually rely on Gateway's representations. In doing so, the trial court relied upon *Price Brothers Co. v. Philadelphia Gear Corp.*, which mandated:

[i]n order to determine whether . . . pre-contract statements . . . were in fact a basis of the bargain and thus an express warranty, or whether they were merely a seller's 'puffing', the court should consider the circumstances surrounding the transaction, the reasonableness of the buyer in believing the seller, and the reliance placed on the seller's statements by the buyer.[6]

[¶ 14] The trial court's reliance thereon, however, is misplaced. Price Brothers is distinguishable from the case at bar particularly because there in the court was determining whether pre-contract statements made by the seller, sales literature, and a journal article referring to the goods sold constituted affirmations of fact or promise. In other words, the court was merely "differentiating affirmations of fact from statements of opinion."[7] In contrast, the statements in this case were not pre-contractual representations but were integrated terms within the parties' written agreement. The parties do not dispute whether the affirmations within the purchase orders constitute statements of fact or promise; their arguments entail whether the statements or affirmations were part of the basis of the bargain.

[¶ 15] Because "basis of the bargain" is not a defined term, the language has caused significant legal confusion with regard to whether a buyer's reliance upon express warranty language is a necessary part of determining the enforcement thereof.

Prior to the adoption of the Uniform Commercial Code ("UCC") in Ohio, reliance was a key inquiry as to the enforceability of an express warranty: "[a]n express warranty is an affirmation of fact by the seller as to a product or commodity to induce the purchase thereof, on which affirmation the buyer relies in making the purchase."[8] Notably, some Ohio Appellate Courts have continued to [Page 601] evaluate the enforceability of express warranties by requiring the buyer's reliance thereon, despite the absence of such language in R.C.1302.26.[9] However, these cases deal with affirmations of fact or promise during contract negotiation and not those contained in a written agreement. The parties cite no Ohio cases, nor has this court uncovered any, in which Ohio courts have grappled with the question of reliance in the context of an express written warranty.

[¶ 16] In order for this court to shed light on the meaning of "basis of the bargain," in the context of written affirmations of fact or promise in a valid contract, and any concomitant reliance requirement, we must turn to the Official Comments of the UCC for guidance. Although a review of UCC section 2-313's comments does not definitively answer whether reliance remains a necessary element for enforcement of an express warranty, the comments do seem to indicate that reliance is not required in the context of this case. Comment 3 states:

[t]he present section deals with affirmations of fact by the seller, descriptions of the goods or exhibitions of samples, exactly as any other part of a negotiation which ends in a contract is dealt with. No specific intention to make a warranty is necessary if any of these factors is made part of the basis of the bargain. In actual practice affirmations of fact made by the seller about the goods during a bargain are regarded as part of the description of those goods; hence no particular reliance on such statements need be shown in order to weave them into the fabric of the agreement. Rather, any fact which is to take such affirmations, once made, out of the agreement requires clear affirmative proof. The issue normally is one of fact.[10]

[¶ 17] Thus, comment 3 indicates that UCC section 2-313 is relevant to the question of whether an express warranty has been created, and the "basis of the bargain" rule is not applicable to situations where written warranties are clear and express. A decisive majority of courts that have considered this issue have reached the similar conclusion that reliance is not an element in a claim for breach of an express written warranty.[11] [Page 602]

[¶ 18] Express warranties "are as much a part of the contract as any other term, and the right to damages on the breach depends on nothing more than the breach of warranty."[12] In other words,

[a] warranty is an assurance by one party to a contract of the existence of a fact upon which the other party may rely. It is intended precisely to relieve the promisee of any duty to ascertain the fact for himself; it amounts to a promise to indemnify the promisee for any loss if the fact warranted proves untrue, for obviously the promisor cannot control what is already in the past.[13]

[¶ 19] Accordingly, because the warranties in this case were part of a written contract, we find that enforcement thereof is not dependent upon any reliance by Norcold. As such, we must sustain Norcold's first assignment of error.

Questions for Analysis

1. As we have seen several times, *stare decisis* is at the central core of the authority of the judicial branch. How does this case involve the use of precedent? Explain.
2. What is an express warranty? What is its purpose? Explain.
3. What authority was used by the trial court to determine whether Gateway had created a warranty in its dealings with Norcold? Explain.
4. What did the court of appeals do with the trial court's interpretation of the contract between Norcold and Gateway? Explain.
5. Has the court of appeals in this case used textualism or pragmatism in its interpretation of the phrase the "basis of the bargain"? Explain.
6. Does the warranty included in the contract between Norcold and Gateway have to be "relied upon" to be included in the agreement? Explain.
7. Why does the court return to the comments section of the UCC to determine what warranties must be relied upon? Explain.
8. Is the tap tee refrigerator unit developed by Gateway "unsafe" or "dangerous"? Explain.
9. Did Gateway fulfill its "duty to warn" in relation to Norcold? Did Gateway fulfill its "duty to warn" in relation to the customers of Norcold who were sold a defective piece of equipment? Explain.
10. A complex adaptive system is a network of interacting conditions that reinforce one another, while at the same time adjusting to change from agents outside and inside the system. In what way does the case of *Norcold, Inc., v. Gateway Supply Company* reinforce the idea that the law works like a complex adaptive system? Explain.

Design Elements: The Opening Case: ©Sharpstock/ Alamy; A Classic Case: ©Evlakhov Valeriy/ Shutterstock

©Stockbroker/Alamy

Part Four

Negotiable Instruments and Banking

Chapter 16   **The Nature of Negotiable Instruments**

Chapter 18   **Bank–Depositor Relationships and Cyber-Banking**

Chapter 16

The Nature of Negotiable Instruments

16-1 The Essentials of Negotiable Instruments
Promise and Order Instruments
• Parties to Negotiable Instruments
• Requirements of Negotiable Instruments

16-2 Transferring Negotiable Instruments
The Concept of Negotiability
• Negotiation by Indorsement
• Obligations of Indorsers • Multiple Payees, Missing and Forged Indorsements • Unauthorized or Forged Indorsements

THE OPENING CASE Round 1

Riddle Me This: "When Is a Promissory Note Not a Promissory Note?" Answer: "When It's a ..." Read on.

The riddle in this case emerged when the National Homes Corporation (National) filed a lawsuit against both N. E. Guthrie Jr. (Guthrie) and John D. Crow (Crow), alleging that they had not paid the total amount due on a promissory note. The note had been drawn by Crow in his capacity as Guthrie's agent. (*Note:* Guthrie had already paid the initial $5,000 on the note.) National argued that a balance of $780 remained outstanding. Based on the record of the trial court, Crow had little to say about the matter. Guthrie, on the other hand, had a lot to say, none of it good. To grasp the nature of Guthrie's difficulties, it will be helpful to look at the promissory note itself, which reads as follows: "$5780.00 Electra Texas 3/8 1962. Ninety (90) Days after date for Value Received I Promise To Pay to the Order of NATIONAL HOMES CORPORATION Five Thousand Eighty and 00/100 Dollars at Earl Avenue at Wallace, Lafayette, Indiana. It is hereby understood that $1000. overpayments will be made on future house deliveries until this obligation is paid. With Interest at 6.5% per annum after date. All parties to this note, including endorsers and guarantors thereof, hereby waive presentment and demand for payment, protest, and notice of dishonor. No. _____ Due _____ /s/ John D. Crow Crow Construction Co."

Guthrie had two rather fundamental complaints about the note. First, he pointed out that his name appears nowhere on the note, and so, quite understandably, he asked, "How can I be liable on a negotiable instrument on which ... (my) name nowhere appears?" He went on to explain that while Crow may have meant to execute the note on his behalf, in fact, he, Guthrie, had never authorized its making. Therefore, if anyone is liable, it is Crow. Second, Guthrie stated that even if, in some mystical-magical way, he might be considered liable for the remaining amount due, despite the absence of his name on the note, the actual amount due on the note is unclear. To demonstrate exactly what he meant by this, Guthrie pointed to the numbers on the note, that is, the $5,780.00. He then pointed to the script, which reads, "Five Thousand Eighty and 00/100 Dollars" (or $5,080.00). Guthrie then pointed out that, whenever there is a discrepancy between the numbers and the script on a negotiable instrument, the written words trump the numbers. In this case, that means that, if he owes anything, it is not $780.00 but $80.00.

The trial court addressed Guthrie's concerns in the following way. First, while it may be true that he, Guthrie, did not authorize the making of the promissory note in the first place, his subsequent behavior in paying the initial $5,000.00 indicated that he had ratified it. Therefore, it was irrelevant that he had not authorized the note when it was originally made. He was now liable due to his own voluntary ratification. As for the discrepancy in the amount, the trial court pointed out that Guthrie was correct when he noted that whenever there is a discrepancy between the numbers and the script on a negotiable instrument, the written words trump the numbers. However, the Court also added that under the same rule, a written document is to be interpreted against the parties who actually wrote the document, which, in this case, would be Crow, Guthrie's agent. This corollary to the rule permits the court to look at evidence outside the four corners of the note. The court then used oral testimony to conclude that the amount due was the amount that was recorded as a number, that is, the $5,780.00 Therefore, Guthrie owes $780.00 not $80.00.

Dissatisfied with the results of the trial, Guthrie filed for an appeal. He continued to resist the conclusions that (1) he is responsible for a note that he never authorized and (2) that the numbers recorded on a promissory note trump the written amount recorded on that instrument. The appellate court agreed to hear the case and, in its ruling, ultimately noticed some nuances in the case that neither the litigants nor the trial court itself picked up on. So, again, riddle me this: "When is a promissory note not a promissory note?" Answer: "When it is..." No, on second thought, it would really be much better if you read on. [See: *N. E. Guthrie, Petitioner v. National Homes Corporation*, 394 S. W. 2d 494 (1965); and *N. E. Guthrie, Appellant v. National Homes Corporation, Appellee*, 387 S. W. 2d 158 (1965).]

Opening Case Questions

1. What type of lawsuit did National bring against Guthrie and Crow? Was this a tort case, a contract case, or something else? Explain.

2. Is a promissory note the equivalent of a personal check, or is it more like a certified check? Explain.

3. What are the requirements of a negotiable instrument, and why does that matter in a case like this one? Explain.

4. When can the parole evidence rule be used to interpret a document, and why does it matter in a case like this one? Explain.

5. If the results that come down from the appellate court fail to satisfy Guthrie, what additional recourse might he have, if any? Explain.

Source: *N. E. Guthrie, Petitioner v. National Homes Corporation* 394 S. W. 2d 494 (1965); *N. E. Guthrie, Appellant v. National Homes Corporation, Appellee*, 387 S. W. 2d 158 (1965).

 Learning Objectives

1. State the purpose of a negotiable instrument.
2. Explain those negotiable instruments that contain a promise to pay money.
3. Explain those negotiable instruments that contain an order to pay money.
4. Differentiate among the different types of checks and money orders.
5. Identify the requirements of a negotiable instrument.
6. Explain an assignment and a negotiation of an instrument.
7. Name and describe four kinds of indorsements.
8. Identify the implied warranties related to indorsements.
9. Explain the contract that is made when people indorse negotiable instruments.
10. Describe the legal effect of a forged indorsement.

16-1 The Essentials of Negotiable Instruments

Throughout history, people have needed to transact business without carrying around large sums of money. Moreover, people have also borrowed money from one another, necessitating an orderly system of procedures and laws to govern credit transactions. The law of negotiable instruments has developed to meet these needs. Checks, drafts, and notes are used conveniently and safely as a substitute for money and to obtain credit in today's society. With the rapid development of cyber-commerce, electronic banking and online payments are now being used as a substitute for checks and other paper transactions, as well as for actual check processing through the banking system. As a result, it is estimated that the number of checks written in the United States will decline greatly during the next decade. Still, even without paper checks, the principles underlying the process of transferring funds will remain the same. It is an effective process that has stood the test of time. Sometimes, however, it is beneficial to remember just how long this financial process has been part of our culture.

A CLASSIC CASE   The Birth of Banking and the Knights Templar

The financial world owes its very existence to the work of the medieval Knights Templar. Recent popular knowledge of the Knights Templar can be attributed to Dan Brown's novel *The Da Vinci Code* and Ron Howard's film of the same name. The legends attached to the Templars are many and varied. They are pictured as the discoverers of the Holy Grail, the defenders of the Priory of Scion, a branch of the Illuminati, the forerunners of the Freemasons, and the military arm of the Cathars. Most of these legends bear no resemblance to the truth, although they do make good stories. This is unfortunate because the mystique that has been built around the Templars interferes with an understanding of their true contribution to European history, which is in the development of the European banking system.

The Templars probably began as an order of knights about 1118 or 1119. Some experts report that they were founded by Hugh de Payns (or Hugues de Payens) as an order of knights dedicated to protecting Christian pilgrims who needed armed guards to defend them as the traveled to and from the Holy Land during the Islamic occupation of that area in the Middle Ages. As their reputation grew, the Templars attracted new members to their ranks, many of whom were wealthy men with extensive land holdings and rich treasuries. Often, when these men joined the Templars, they would transfer their property and money to the control of the knights. In this way, the wealth of the Templars grew to such an extent that, at their peak, they controlled thousands of estates across Europe. Some knights and noblemen who were supportive of the Templar mission also made annual donations to the order. Eventually, the Templars would also hold the wealth of knights and other noblemen who would travel to the Holy Land and would not want to leave their valuables unattended while they were on their journeys. The Templars also established banks in their various monasteries throughout Europe and would store the riches in those banks in much the same way that safe deposit boxes do today. The Templars also devised a way by which a traveler could present a paper, called a note, to merchants and innkeepers at various points on their journey that would be redeemable for the amount of wealth that those documents represented on deposit at a Templar monastery bank. These documents are the forerunners of the modern negotiable instruments used today.

Eventually, the wealth stored in the monastery banks also became the basis for a lending system that was used by several monarchs to finance their foreign wars. Some historians argue that it was this habit of lending money to the kings of Europe that led to the downfall of the Knights Templar at the hands of Philip the Fair of France in 1313. Philip had taken out extensive loans from the Templars to fight his wars with England, and when he asked for another loan, despite having not paid back what he already owed, the Templars refused. Philip then trumped up charges against the Templars, allowing him to arrest, imprison, and execute them and then confiscate their great wealth. [See: Jefferson P. Webb, "The Knights Templar: Fathers of Modern Banking," Art of Combat European Martial Arts, *Steel Fighting*, https://steelfighting.com/2011/08/15/the-knights-templar-fathers-of-modern-banking/; and Piers Paul Read, *The Templars: The Dramatic History of the Knights Templar, the Most Powerful Military Order of the Crusades* (New York: St. Martin's Griffin, 1999).]

Source: See: Jefferson P. Webb, "The Knights Templar: Fathers of Modern Banking," *New Ulster Steel Fighting: Academy of European Martial Arts;* and Piers Paul Read, *The Templars: The Dramatic History of the Knights Templar, the Most Powerful Military Order of the Crusades* (New York: St. Martin's Griffin, 1999).

Promise and Order Instruments

The law of negotiable instruments is found in Article 3 of the Uniform Commercial Code (UCC). This article was originally drafted in 1952. Since that time, many new developments have occurred in the commercial field. To adapt to modern technology and contemporary practices, Article 3 of the UCC has been revised over the last six decades. Today under the UCC, a **negotiable instrument** is a written document signed by the maker that contains an unconditional promise *or* order to pay a fixed amount of money on demand or at a definite time to the bearer or to order. The phrase "unconditional promise or order" is one of the most central requirements of a negotiable instruments. The unconditional nature of a negotiable instrument is, however, often misunderstood and sometimes ignored. The UCC does, however, provides some help in this regard. For example UCC 3-106 outlines the characteristics that make an instrument unconditional and, therefore, a negotiable instrument. The code says that a promise will remain unconditional unless it states, "an express condition to payment that the promise or order is subject to or governed by another writing or that rights or obligations with respect to the promise or order are stated in another writing." For instance, a document would be conditional if it is payable to a single payee on one side but, on the reverse side, divides the amount due into several additional partial payments split among other payees. This would be true even though the document might look like a negotiable instrument on the front side. The conditions included on the reverse side destroy its negotiability. This principle is a time-honored requirement that predates the UCC. [See, for example: *Goldman v. Blum and Heidenheimer Bros.*, 58 Tex. 630 (1883).]

UCC Revised (1990) 3-104(e)-(j)

THE OPENING CASE *Round 2*
Riddle Me This: "When Is a Promissory Note Not a Promissory Note?" Answer: "When It's a ..." Read on.

Recall that, in the Opening Case, National Homes Corporation (National) filed a lawsuit against both N. E. Guthrie Jr. (Guthrie) and John D. Crow (Crow). The lawsuit claimed that Guthrie and Crow had been delinquent in paying the amount due on a promissory note. Crow had written the promissory note in his capacity as Guthrie's agent. By the time of the suit, Guthrie had already paid the first $5,000 on the note. National brought the suit to recover the remaining balance of $780. The note at the heart of the controversy looked like this: "$5780.00 Electra Texas 3/8 1962. Ninety (90) Days after date for Value Received I Promise To Pay to the Order of NATIONAL HOMES CORPORATION Five Thousand Eighty and 00/100 Dollars at Earl Avenue at Wallace, Lafayette, Indiana. It is hereby understood that $1000 over payments will be made on future house deliveries until this obligation is paid. With Interest at 6.5% per annum after date. All parties to this note, including endorsers and guarantors thereof, hereby waive presentment and demand for payment, protest, and notice of dishonor. No. _____ Due _____ /s/ John D. Crow Crow Construction Co." Guthrie raised two points in his defense. First, he noted that his name appeared no where on the note. Guthrie then pointed out that Crow had executed the note without his, Guthrie's, approval. Consequently, if anyone was liable it would be Crow. Second, Guthrie stated that, even if, the court saw him as liable on the note, the remaining amount due on the note was incorrect. To show what he meant, Guthrie pointed to the numbers on the note, that is, the $5,780.00. He then pointed to the script, which read, "Five Thousand Eighty and 00/100 Dollars" (or $5,080.00). According to his understanding of the law, Guthrie noted that, whenever there is a dissonance between the numbers and the words on a negotiable instrument, the written words take precedence over the numbers. Therefore, if he is found by the court to be liable on the note, he would owe $80 not the $780 claimed by National.

The trial court first addressed Guthrie's complaint about his liability for the unsigned promissory note. The trial court had no difficulty holding Guthrie liable for the note despite the missing signature. (Just how the court did this will be explained in *Round 3*.) Guthrie was upset about the court's ruling and filed an appeal. The appellate court rejected the trial court's resolution of the missing signature issue and offered its own interpretation. It is at this point that the appellate court offered a new and somewhat original interpretation of the case that neither the litigants nor the trial court had noticed. The appellate court ruled that the alleged promissory note was *not* a negotiable instrument—period. The court came to this conclusion by looking back at the definition of a negotiable instrument. Recall that a negotiable instrument is a written document signed by the maker that contains an unconditional promise or order to pay a fixed amount of money on demand or at a definite time to the bearer or to order. Recall also that one of the key requirements of a negotiable instrument is that the note must be unconditional. With this in mind, the court looked again at the instrument and noted that it was burdened with a cryptic condition. That condition stated, "It is hereby understood that $1000 over payments will be made on future house deliveries until this obligation is paid." The court saw this contingency as a condition that transformed the would-be "negotiable" instrument into an ordinary contract. Although the appellate court never explained what the condition meant in real life, it did provide a long line of precedent supporting that position. [See: *N. E. Guthrie, Petitioner v. National Homes Corporation*, 394 S. W. 2d 494 (1965); and *N. E. Guthrie, Appellant v. National Homes Corporation, Appellee*, 387 S. W. 2d 158 (1965).]

Source: *N. E. Guthrie, Petitioner v. National Homes Corporation* 394 S. W. 2d 494 (1965); *N. E. Guthrie, Appellant v. National Homes Corporation, Appellee*, 387 S. W. 2d 158 (1965).

UCC Revised (1990) 3-104(e)

Promise Instruments: Notes There are two basic kinds of negotiable instruments: promise instruments (including notes and certificates of deposit) and order instruments (including drafts and checks). A **note** (often called a **promissory note**) is a written promise by one party, called the *maker*, to pay money to the order of another party, called the *payee*. People who loan money or extend credit use notes as evidence of debt. When two or more parties sign a note, they are called *co-makers*. A **demand note**, as its name implies, is payable whenever the payee demands payment (Figure 16-1). A holder of a demand note may decide to collect the balance due at any time and for any reason. A time note, in contrast, is payable at some future time, on a date named in the instrument. Unless a note is payable in installments, the principal (face value) of the note plus interest must be paid on the date that it is due. In an **installment note**, the principal together with the interest on the unpaid balance is payable in a series of payments at specified times.

UCC Revised (1990) 3-108(a)

UCC Revised (1990) 3-104(j)

Promise Instruments: Certificates of Deposit A **certificate of deposit (CD)** is an instrument containing an acknowledgment that a bank has received a sum of money and a

No. 381 Boston, Massachusetts, October 1, 20 —
On demand, the undersigned, for value received, promise(s) to pay to the order of
CAMBRIDGE TRUST COMPANY
Two thousand four hundred and 00/100 ———— Dollars,
at its offices in Boston, Massachusetts, together with interest thereon from the
date thereof until paid at the rate of 6 percent per annum.

Address 100 Bedford Street   Victor Powell
Waltham, Massachusetts

Figure 16-1 A demand note is payable whenever the payee demands payment.

promise by the bank to repay the sum of money. A CD is a note of the bank, and CDs are written for a specific time period, such as six months, one year, two years, or five years. Banks pay higher interest for longer-term CDs and more interest than regular savings accounts because the depositor cannot withdraw the money before the due date without penalty. Some banks allow a one-time early withdrawal from a CD without penalty.

Order Instruments: Drafts In contrast to notes, which are *promises* to pay money, drafts are *orders* to pay money. They are more complicated than notes because they involve three parties rather than two. The most common type of draft in use today is the check. A less well known, but equally effective order instrument is the draft. A **draft** (also called a **bill of exchange**) is an instrument in which one party writes an instrument ordering a second party to pay money to a third party. The one who draws the draft (that is, the one who orders money to be paid) is called the *drawer*. The one who is ordered to pay the money is called the *drawee*. The one who is to receive the money is known as the *payee*. For instance, in Ernest Hemingway's novel, *A Farewell to Arms*, a story set during The Great War, one of the characters, an American Major, discusses with his friend Rinaldi the possibility of going to Milan. The tickets, however, cost a great deal of money and the Major is, as usual, somewhat short of cash. Nevertheless, being a resourceful fellow and having paid close attention to his business law instructor back home, the major has a plan which he explains to Rinaldi. "I will draw a sight draft on my grandfather, I said. A what? A sight draft. He has to pay or I go to jail. Mr. Cunningham at the bank does it. I live by sight drafts. Can a grandfather jail a patriotic grandson who is dying that Italy may live? Live the American Garibaldi, said Rinaldi. Viva the sight drafts, I said."

UCC Revised (1990) 3-104(e)

UCC Revised (1990) 3-409

EXAMPLE 16-1: Sight Draft

In Hemingway's novel, the major would be the drawer of the draft, and his grandfather would be the drawee. The story does not name the payee of the draft, but it could be the railroad ticket office or a bank in Italy—whoever is to receive the money. If this situation involved a check, the person who signed the check would be the drawer, the bank would be the drawee, and the one to whom the check were written would be the payee. You see, it really does "pay" to listen to your business law instructor.

A draft may be presented by the holder to the drawee for payment or for acceptance. When a draft is presented for payment, the drawee may decline to pay it unless it has been accepted. If the drawee refuses to pay an unaccepted draft, the draft is dishonored, and the drawee has no liability for refusing to pay it. In contrast, when a draft is presented for acceptance, the drawee is asked to become liable on the instrument. **Acceptance** is the drawee's signed agreement to pay the draft as presented. If the drawee refuses to accept the draft, it is dishonored, and again, the drawee has no liability.

Drawees are liable on drafts only when they accept them, that is, agree to become liable on them. To accept a draft, the drawee need only sign the draft across the face of the instrument. It is customary, however, when accepting a draft, for the drawee to write "accepted" across the face of the instrument, followed by the date and signature. An acceptance must be written on the draft itself; it may not be written on a separate piece of paper. By accepting a draft, the drawee agrees to pay the instrument at a later date when it became due.

Sight and Time Drafts A **sight draft** (Figure 16-2) is payable as soon as it is presented to the drawee for payment. A **time draft** (Figure 16-3) is not payable until the lapse of a particular

About the Law

A **trade acceptance** is a draft used by a seller of goods to receive payment and extend credit. Drafts are often used in combination with bills of lading, which are receipts given by freight companies to people who ship goods. A seller will ship goods to a buyer and send a bill of lading, with a trade acceptance attached, to a bank in the buyer's city. The trade acceptance orders the buyer to pay money to the seller or another party. The buyer must either pay the money or accept the draft to receive the bill of lading from the bank. The freight company will not release the goods to the buyer unless the buyer has possession of the bill of lading.

UCC Revised (1990) 3-104(f)

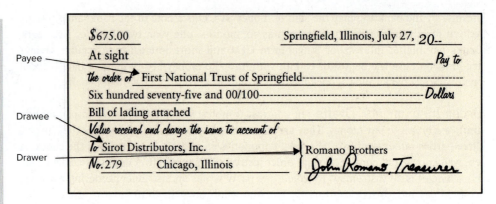

Figure 16-2 A sight draft is payable as soon as it is presented to the drawee for payment. How do you know that this draft has not been accepted by the drawee?

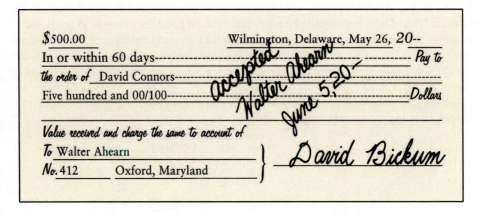

Figure 16-3 A time draft is not payable until the lapse of a particular time period stated on the draft. How do you know that this draft has been accepted by the drawee?

time period stated on the draft. Drafts that are payable "30 days after sight" and "60 days after date" are examples of time drafts.

Domestic and International Bills of Exchange A **domestic bill of exchange** is a draft that is drawn and payable in the United States. A draft that is drawn in one country but payable in another is called an **international bill of exchange** or **foreign draft**.

Order Instruments: Checks A **check** is a draft drawn on a bank and payable on demand. It is the most common form of a draft. It is drawn on a bank by a drawer who has an account with the bank and is made to the order of a specified person or business named on the check or to the bearer. A check is a safe means of transferring money, and it serves as a receipt after it has been paid and canceled by the bank. In the check shown in Figure 16-4, Margaret Evans is the drawer; she has an account with the Western National Bank. Alicia Adams Fashions Inc. is the payee. Western National Bank, on which the check is drawn, is the drawee. Ownership of a check may be transferred to another person by indorsement by the payee. In this manner, a check may circulate among several parties, taking the place of money. A bank must honor a check when it is properly drawn against a credit balance of the drawer. Failure to do so would make the bank liable to the drawer for resulting damages.

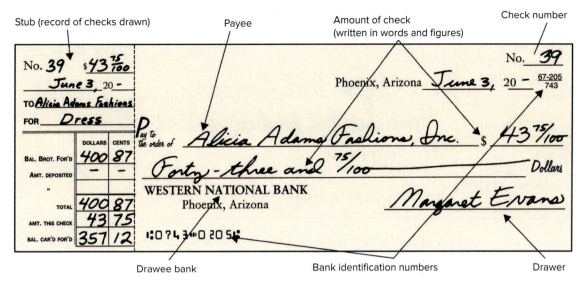

Figure 16-4 All elements of a sample check are identified.

A QUESTION OF ETHICS

Along with their bill, credit card companies often include blank checks for customers to make payable to anyone they wish, thus increasing the amount owed the credit card issuer, usually at an exceptionally high rate of interest. The practice is legal; is it ethical?

Form for Checks Banks provide regular and special printed check forms. These check forms display a series of numbers printed in magnetic ink, which make it possible to process checks speedily and accurately by computer. The first set of figures is the bank's Federal Reserve number. This number is followed by the bank's own number. The second set of numbers is the depositor's account number. The use of printed forms is not required, however. Any writing, no matter how crude, may be used as a check if it is a draft drawn on a bank and payable on demand.

UCC Revised (1990) 3-409(d)

Certified Checks A **certified check** is a check that is guaranteed by the bank. At the request of either the depositor or the holder, the bank acknowledges and guarantees that sufficient funds will be withheld from the drawer's account to pay the amount stated on the check. A prudent person will request a certified check rather than accept a personal check when involved in a business transaction with a stranger. A certified check, under the UCC, is "a check accepted by the bank on which it is drawn." The UCC places no obligation on a bank to certify a check if it does not want to do so, and the refusal to certify is not a dishonor of the check. When a check is certified, the drawer is discharged regardless of when it was done or who obtained the acceptance. Figure 16-5 illustrates a certified check.

UCC Revised (1990) 3-414(c)

UCC Revised (1990) 3-104(g)(h)

Bank Drafts and Cashier's Checks A **bank draft**, sometimes called a **teller's check** or *treasurer's check*, is a check drawn by one bank on another bank in which it has funds on deposit in favor of a third person, the payee. Many banks deposit money in banks in other areas for the convenience of depositors who depend upon the transfer of funds when

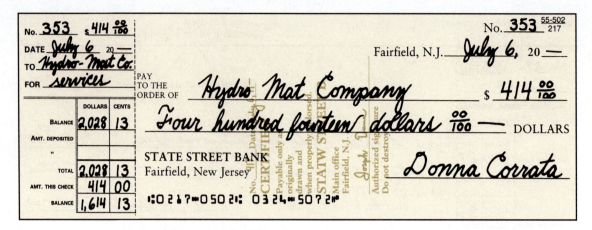

Figure 16-5 The State Street Bank became primarily liable when it certified this check.

transacting business in distant places. When the buyer is unknown to the seller, such checks are more acceptable than personal checks. A **cashier's check** is a check drawn by a bank upon itself. The bank, in effect, lends its credit to the purchaser of the check. It is the equivalent of a promissory note of the bank. Courts have held that payment cannot be stopped on a cashier's check because the bank, by issuing it, accepts the check in advance. People who will not accept personal checks will often accept cashier's checks. Such a check may be made payable either to the depositor, who purchases it from the bank, or to the person who is to cash it. If the check is made payable to the depositor, it must be indorsed to the person to whom it is transferred.

UCC Revised (1990) 3-104(i)

UCC Revised (1990) 3-104(f)

Traveler's Checks A **traveler's check** is similar to a cashier's check, in that the issuing financial institution is both the drawer and the drawee. The purchaser signs the checks in the presence of the issuer when they are purchased. To cash a check, the purchaser writes the name of the payee in the space provided and countersigns it in the payee's presence. Only the purchaser can negotiate traveler's checks, and they are easily replaced by the issuing bank if they are stolen. Traveler's checks are issued in denominations of $10 and up, and the purchaser of the checks ordinarily pays a fixed fee to the issuer.

Money Orders A **money order** is a type of draft that may be purchased from banks, post offices, telegraph companies, and express companies as a substitute for a check. Instead of being drawn on an individual's account as is a check, however, a money order is drawn on the funds of the organization that issues it. That organization promises payment from its own funds. Purchasers of money orders fill in their name and address and the name of the payee on the instrument. They are given a receipt along with the money order. If the money order is lost and the purchaser has the receipt, it will be replaced if it has not already been cashed. U.S. Postal Service money orders can be purchased for amounts up to $1,000. U.S. International Postal Service Money Orders are often used to send money to foreign countries. Telegraphic money orders may be used to send money quickly. Under the UCC, a *bank* money order is a check, even though it is described on its face as a money order, and payment can be stopped on it like an ordinary check.

Online banking and bill paying have replaced the need for paper transactions for many customers.
©Rob Daly/AGE Fotostock

A SOON TO BE CLASSIC CASE
Are Money Orders Really What They Seem to Be?

James Haas gave the Meridian Bank (Meridian) two checks—one for $22,000 and a second one for $20,000—for deposit in the Haas Mid-Way Equipment Company (HM-WEC) account at Meridian. Meridian transferred the check to the Commerce Bank. Two days later, Haas returned to Meridian and took out a money order for $35,000. The name "Meridian" was printed in prominent letters on the upper left-hand side of the money order. The money order was payable to James Haas and stamped: "Not valid for more than $35,000." Haas delivered the money order to Trump Plaza and cashed it for "use" in the casino. Meanwhile, Meridian received a return of the two original checks from Commerce Bank. The checks were apparently drawn on a closed account. Meridian then took that $42,000 out of the HM-WEC account. Haas had drawn out $35,000 for that money order, so the account was now overdrawn by $38,584. When Trump Plaza showed up with the $35,000 money order, Meridian returned it to Trump Plaza noting that the HM-WEC account at Meridian had insufficient funds to cover it.

Trump Plaza then brought a lawsuit against Haas and Meridian for the missing money. Trump Plaza argued that (1) the casino is a "holder in due course" and, therefore, must be paid by Meridian; (2) the money order was already accepted by Meridian because its name was on it and it was marked "payment stopped," indicating Meridian recognized it as its own instrument; (3) if, in fact, the cupboard was bare, it was Meridian that should suffer the loss because it was negligent in figuring out that Haas had no money in the HM-WEC account; and (4) the court relied on a case that was inappropriate, inapplicable, because a money order is not the equivalent to a check.

Meridian filed a summary judgment motion arguing that the suit should be dismissed because the money order is really the equivalent of a personal check and that it was not liable until it accepted it, and just because the bank's name was on the check or had written "payment stopped," did not mean that Meridian had accepted it. The trial court agreed and dismissed the action. Trump Plaza appealed. The appellate court upheld the dismissal. In a lengthy opinion, the court agreed with the lower court and thus disposed of Trump Plaza's arguments one by one: (1) the rights and protections of a holder in due course do not come into play unless and until the drawee bank accepts the instrument; (2) the fact that the check is imprinted with Meridian's name and has "payment stopped" written on it does not amount to an acceptance; (3) Trump Plaza had no negligence action against the bank because that cause of action is limited to the party who purchased the money order (Haas in this case). Finally, (4) Trump Plaza must have badly misread the case of *Newman v. First Nat'l State Bank of Toms River* because in that case, the court clearly said that a money order is the equivalent of a personal check. [See: *Trump Plaza v. Haas and Meridian Bank*, 692 A. 2d 86 (Superior Court of New Jersey, Appellate Division).]

Parties to Negotiable Instruments

The following are parties to negotiable instruments: maker or co-maker; drawer; issuer; drawee; payee; bearer; holder; holder in due course; indorser; indorsee; and acceptor. One by one, step by step, this is what they look like. A **maker** is a person who signs a note, that is, a person who promises to pay. **Co-makers** are two or more people who sign the same note promising to pay. A **drawer** is a person who signs a draft, that is, the one who orders payment. An **issuer** is either a maker or a drawer of an instrument. A **drawee** is a person ordered in a draft to make payment. A **payee** is a person to whom a note or draft is payable. A **bearer** is a person who is in possession of a negotiable instrument that is payable to the bearer or to cash. A person who is in possession of an instrument that has been indorsed in blank (by the payee's signature alone) is also a bearer.

A **holder** is a person who is in possession of a negotiable instrument that is issued or indorsed to that person's order or bearer. A **holder in due course** is a holder of a negotiable

UCC Revised (1990) 3-103

UCC 1-201(5)

UCC Revised (1990) 3-109(a)

Did You Know?

We are writing fewer checks! Approximately 75 percent of the working population authorizes employers to transmit their pay directly into their checking or savings accounts. The federal government now transmits Social Security payments to retirees' bank accounts each month. One-third of all households pay their mortgages by prearranged direct payments from their checking accounts. Many companies pay their vendors electronically, saving time and putting money into immediate use, thereby boosting profitability.

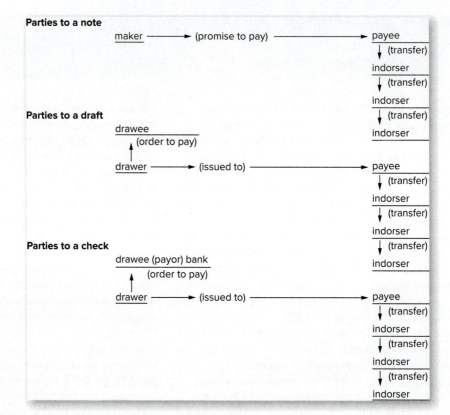

Figure 16-6 This diagram illustrates the relationship of the principal parties to negotiable instruments.

instrument who is treated as favored and given immunity from certain defenses. An **indorser** is a person who indorses a negotiable instrument, in most cases by signing one's name on the back of the paper. An **indorsee** is a person to whom a draft, note, or other negotiable instrument is transferred by indorsement. An **acceptor** is a drawee of a draft who has promised to honor the draft as presented by signing it on its face. (See Figure 16-6.)

UCC 1-201(20)

UCC Revised (1990) 3-204

Requirements of Negotiable Instruments

To be negotiable, instruments must: (1) be in writing; (2) be signed by the maker or drawer; (3) contain an unconditional promise or order to pay; (4) be made out for a fixed amount of money; (5) be payable on demand or at a definite time; and (6) except for checks, be payable to order or to bearer. As will be discussed soon, instruments that do not meet all of these requirements can be transferred to others by assignment. They cannot, however, be transferred by negotiation. Let's look at these requirements one at a time.

Written Instrument A negotiable instrument must be in writing (see Figure 16-7), which includes printing, word processing, pen or pencil writing, or any other tangible form of writing. Under the Uniform Electronic Transactions Act (UETA), an electronic record fulfills this requirement. Article 3 of the UCC has also been amended to permit electronic negotiable instruments. However, not all states have incorporated that amendment into their version of the statute and so it is best to check to see if your state has done so. Although it hardly seems worth mentioning, it is still a good idea to recognize that any negotiable instrument written in pencil is an invitation to alteration by forgery. If forgery should happen, the person who drew the instrument would be responsible for any loss caused by the negligent drawing of the instrument.

UCC Revised (1990) 3-104(a)

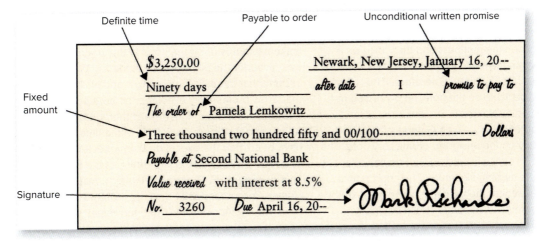

Figure 16-7 The requirements of negotiability are indicated on this 90-day note.

Signature of Maker or Drawer To be negotiable, an instrument must be signed by the maker or drawer. Any writing, mark, or symbol is accepted as a signature as long as it is the writer's intent to be a signature. It may be handwritten, typewritten, printed, or produced by a machine. A signature may be made by an agent (one who represents and acts for another) or other representative. No particular form of appointment is necessary to establish such authority. The signature may appear in the body of the instrument as well as at the end. Agents who sign their own names to an instrument are personally obligated if the instrument neither names the person represented nor shows that the agent signed in a representative capacity. However, unauthorized signatures can be ratified by the behavior of the person to whom unauthorized signature refers.

UCC 3-402
UCC 3-403
UCC 1-201 (46)
UCC Revised (1990) 3-401(a)(b)
UCC Revised (1990) 3-402
UCC Revised (1990) 3-104(a)

THE OPENING CASE Round 3

Riddle Me This: "When Is a Promissory Note Not a Promissory Note?" Answer: "When It's a ..." Read on.

In the Opening Case, both Guthrie and Crow were sued by National Homes Corporation. According to the complaint, Guthrie and Crow had not been paid the full amount due on a promissory note. Crow had signed the promissory note as Guthrie's agent. By the time of the suit, Guthrie had already paid the first $5,000, but still owed the remaining balance of $780. The note that served as the center of the suit read: "$5780.00 Electra Texas 3/8 1962. Ninety (90) Days after date for Value Received I Promise To Pay to the Order of NATIONAL HOMES CORPORATION Five Thousand Eighty and 00/100 Dollars at Earl Avenue at Wallace, Lafayette, Indiana. It is hereby understood that $1000. overpayments will be made on future house deliveries until this obligation is paid. With Interest at 6.5% per annum after date. All parties to this note, including endorsers and guarantors thereof, hereby waive presentment and demand for payment, protest, and notice of dishonor. No. _____ Due _____ /s/ John D. Crow Crow Construction Co." Guthrie defended himself by raising two arguments. First, he noted that his name appeared nowhere on the note. In addition, he argued that Crow executed the note without his approval. Therefore, if anyone is liable it is Crow. Second, Guthrie stated that, even if, the court sees him as liable on the note, the remaining amount due on the note is incorrect. To show what he means, Guthrie points to the numbers on the note, that is, the $5,780.00. He then points to the script, which reads, "Five Thousand Eighty and 00/100 Dollars"

(or $5,080.00). Guthrie notes that, should there be a difference between the numbers and the words on a negotiable instrument, the written words take precedence over the numbers. Therefore, if he is found by the court to be liable on the note, he owes $80 not the $780 claimed by National.

The trial court first addressed Guthrie's complaint about his liability on the unsigned promissory note. The trial court had no difficulty holding Guthrie liable for the note despite the missing signature. The court pointed out that subsequent to the issuance of the note, Guthrie had made payments to National. These payments constituted a valid ratification of the note. The appellate court explained its position in this way; "Under the jury findings (which are a part of the record presented to us) it was established that though the note was executed for his sole benefit Guthrie had not theretofore authorized the execution. Under further findings of the jury it was found that he did thereafter ratify its execution. Guthrie assumed the obligation to and did make payments upon the note. In the judgment credit was given for the payments so made . . . We may assume that the evidence of Crow and plaintiff showed that Crow professedly executed the note on Guthrie's account, in the belief that he was thereunto authorized. Although not binding on Guthrie at the time it could have been, had the execution been directed by him. That being true he could later ratify, as the jury found he did." [See: *N. E. Guthrie, Petitioner v. National Homes Corporation*, 394 S. W. 2d 494 (1965); and *N. E. Guthrie, Appellant v. National Homes Corporation, Appellee*, 387 S. W. 2d 158 (1965). See also: *Rakestraw v. Rodrigues*, S.F. No. 22883. Supreme Court of California (September 27, 1972); and UCC 3-402 and UCC 3-403.]

Source: *N. E. Guthrie, Petitioner v. National Homes Corporation* 394 S. W. 2d 494 (1965); *N. E. Guthrie, Appellant v. National Homes Corporation, Appellee*, 387 S. W. 2d 158 (1965).

UCC Revised (1990) 3-106(b)

UCC Revised (1990) 3-104(a)

Unconditional Promise or Order to Pay To be negotiable, an instrument must contain no conditions that might in any way affect its payment. Statements requiring that certain things be done or that specific events take place prior to payment make the instrument a simple contract rather than negotiable paper. An instrument is conditional, and thus not negotiable, if it states that it is subject to any other agreement. The same is true if an instrument states that it is to be paid only out of a particular fund. This latter rule does not apply to instruments issued by government agencies. An instrument may state that it "arises out of" another agreement without being conditional. Similarly, a negotiable instrument may indicate a particular account that is to be charged. In addition to being unconditional, a negotiable instrument must contain a promise to pay (as in a note) or an order to pay (as in a draft). A writing that says "Due Karen Osgood $600" or "IOU $600" is not negotiable because it is neither a promise nor an order to pay.

Fixed Amount of Money A negotiable instrument must be payable in a fixed amount or sum certain of money. This stipulation means an amount of money that is clearly known. *Money* is defined as a medium of exchange adopted by a domestic or foreign government as part of its currency. Thus, a fixed amount of money need not be American dollars.

Payable on Demand or at a Definite Time Negotiable instruments must be made payable on demand or at a definite time. This requirement makes it possible to determine when the debtor or promisor can be compelled to pay. Without this information, the present value of an instrument cannot be determined.

Demand Paper An instrument is payable *on demand* when it so states or when it is payable "on sight" or "on presentation." The key characteristic of demand instruments is that the holder can require payment at any time by making the demand upon the person who is obligated to pay.

Definite-Time Paper Certainty as to the time of payment of an instrument is satisfied if it is payable on or before a stated date. Instruments payable at a fixed period after a stated date or

---

Did You Know?

In a step toward enforcing one currency for Europe, 11 members of the European Union introduced the euro in 1999. The euro replaced national currencies in 2002. The initial countries participating were Belgium, Germany, Spain, France, Ireland, Italy, Luxembourg, the Netherlands, Austria, Portugal, and Finland.

at a fixed period after sight are also considered payable at a definite time. In each instance, a simple mathematical calculation makes the maturity date certain. The expressions "one year after date" and "30 days after sight" are definite as to time. An undated instrument payable 60 days after date is negotiable as a demand paper. A promise to pay only upon an act or event, the time of whose occurrence is uncertain, is not payable at a definite time. Thus, an instrument payable when a person marries, reaches a certain age, or graduates from college, or one payable within a specific period of time after a named person's death, is not negotiable.

UCC 1-201(24)

UCC Revised (1990) 3-107

UCC Revised (1990) 3-108(a)

UCC Revised (1990) 3-108(b)

Payable to Order or to Bearer Negotiable instruments, except for checks, must be payable to order or to bearer. The terms *to the order of* and *to bearer* are called words of negotiability. The most recent version of Article 3 of the UCC allows checks (but not other instruments) that are not payable to order or to bearer to be negotiable. Thus, a check, but no other instrument, payable "to Mary Harris" is negotiable in all states except those that have yet to adopt the revised Article 3.

Payable to Order An instrument is payable to order when it states that it is payable to the order of any person with reasonable certainty. The maker or drawer may state "Pay to the order of Mary Doe," "Pay to Mary Doe or order," or "Pay to Mary Doe or her assigns." An instrument may be payable to the order of the maker or drawer; the drawee; a payee who is not the maker, drawer, or drawee; two or more payees; an estate, trust, or fund; an office or officer by title; or a partnership or an unincorporated association.

Payable to Bearer An instrument is payable to bearer when it states that it is payable to bearer or the order of bearer, a specified person or bearer, cash or the order of cash, or any other indication that does not designate a specific payee. An instrument is payable to bearer when it does not state a payee. An instrument made payable to both, such as "Pay to the order of Anthony Andrews or bearer," is payable to order unless the word "bearer" is handwritten or word processed.

Dates and Controlling Words The omission of the date does not affect the negotiability of an instrument. When the date is omitted, the date on which the instrument is received is considered to be the date of issue. An instrument may be predated or postdated without affecting its negotiability. Handwritten terms control word processed and printed terms, and word processed terms control printed terms. The numbering of, or the failure to number, an instrument does not affect its negotiability. The signature may appear in the body of the instrument as well as at the end. Words control figures, except when words are ambiguous (capable of being understood in more than one way).

THE OPENING CASE Round 4
Riddle Me This: "When Is a Promissory Note Not a Promissory Note?" Answer: "When It's a ..." Read on.

Let's look at the Opening Case one more time. Recall that National Homes Corporation brought suit against both John D. Crow and N. E. Guthrie Jr. The plaintiff argued that Guthrie and Crow had failed to completely pay the amount due on a promissory note. Specifically, Guthrie had paid the first $5,000 on the note but still owed the remaining balance of $780. The note itself looked like this: "$5780.00 Electra Texas 3/8 1962. Ninety (90) Days after date for Value Received I Promise To Pay to the Order of NATIONAL HOMES CORPORATION Five Thousand Eighty and 00/100 Dollars at Earl Avenue at Wallace, Lafayette, Indiana. It is hereby understood that $1000. overpayments will be made on future house deliveries until this obligation is paid. With Interest at 6.5% per annum after date. All parties to this note, including endorsers and guarantors thereof, hereby waive presentment and demand for payment, protest, and notice of dishonor. No. _____ Due _____ /s/ John D. Crow Crow Construction Co." Guthrie made two central arguments at trial. First, he noted that his name was not on the note and that Crow had executed the note without his approval. As a result, if anyone was liable it was Crow. (*Note:* The court disposed of this argument by pointing out that Guthrie's previous payments on the note had ratified his acceptance of the note, even if he wanted to deny it now.) Second, Guthrie stated that, even if the court sees him as liable on the note, the remaining amount due on the note is incorrect. To make his point, Guthrie pointed to the numbers on the note—that is, the $5,780.00. He then pointed to the script, which read, "Five Thousand Eighty and 00/100 Dollars" (or $5,080.00). Guthrie argued that, whenever there be a discrepancy between the numbers and the words on a negotiable instrument, the written words take precedence over the numbers. Therefore, if he is found by the court to be liable on the note, he owes $80 not the $780 claimed by National.

The trial court pointed out that Guthrie was correct when he noted that, whenever there is a discrepancy between the numbers and the script on a negotiable instrument, the written words trump the numbers. However, the Court also added that, under the same rule, a written document is to be interpreted against the parties who actually wrote the document, which in this case, would be Crow, Guthrie's agent. This corollary to the rule permits the court to look at evidence outside the four corners of the note. The court then used oral testimony to conclude that the amount due was the amount that was recorded as a number—that is, the $5,780.00. Therefore, Guthrie owes $780.00 not $80.00. The appellate court disagreed, pointing out that the court is empowered to look at evidence outside the four corners of the document *only when there is ambiguity in the words* under consideration in that document. Here *there is no ambiguity* in the words—"Five Thousand Eighty and 00/100 Dollars" is $5,080.00. That's it—period—nothing could be clearer. Therefore, the court concluded that Guthrie owed National only the $80.00 he has not yet paid. [See: *N. E. Guthrie, Petitioner v. National Homes Corporation*, 394 S. W. 2d 494 (1965); and *N. E. Guthrie, Appellant v. National Homes Corporation, Appellee*, 387 S. W. 2d 158 (1965).]

Source: N. E. Guthrie, Petitioner v. National Homes Corporation 394 S. W. 2d 494 (1965); N. E. Guthrie, Appellant v. National Homes Corporation, Appellee, 387 S. W. 2d 158 (1965).

quick quiz 16-1

1. Notes are promises to pay money and drafts are orders to pay money. — true | false
2. Checks are the least common form of a draft. — true | false
3. Under the Uniform Electronic Transactions Act (UETA), an electronic record fulfills the requirement that a negotiable instrument be in writing. — true | false

16-2 Transferring Negotiable Instruments

When an instrument is first delivered by the maker or drawer for the purpose of giving rights to any person, it is said to be *issued*. When the person to whom it is issued delivers it to a third party, it is *transferred*. Instruments can be transferred by assignment or by negotiation. An **assignment** is the transfer of a contract right from one person to another. Negotiable instruments are assigned either when a person whose indorsement is required on an instrument transfers it without indorsing it or when it is transferred to another person and does not meet the requirements of negotiability. In all such transfers, the transferee has only the rights of an assignee and is subject to all defenses existing against the assignor. An assignment of negotiable instruments also occurs by operation of law when the holder of an instrument dies or becomes bankrupt. In such cases, title to the instrument vests in the personal representative of the estate or the trustee in bankruptcy.

A **negotiation** is the transfer of an instrument in such form that the transferee becomes a *holder* (a person in possession of an instrument issued or indorsed to that person, to that person's order, to bearer, or in blank). In contrast to an assignment, a negotiation gives greater rights to transferees. If an instrument is payable to order, such as "pay to the order of," it is known as **order paper**. To be negotiated, order paper must be indorsed by the payee and delivered to the party to whom it is transferred. If an instrument is payable to bearer or cash, it is called **bearer paper** and may be negotiated by delivery alone, without an indorsement. When order paper is indorsed with a blank indorsement, it is turned into bearer paper and may be further negotiated by delivery alone.

UCC Revised (1990) 3-104(c)

UCC Revised (1990) 3-109(b)

UCC Revised (1990) 3-109(a)

UCC Revised (1990) 3-113

The Concept of Negotiability

The concept of negotiability is one of the most important features of negotiable instruments. Largely because of this feature, negotiable instruments are highly trusted and used daily by millions of people. When an instrument is transferred by negotiation, the person receiving the instrument is provided with more protection than was available to the person from whom it was received. The person receiving the instrument is able, in many instances, to recover money on the instrument even when the person from whom the instrument was received could not have done so.

The payee is never guaranteed to receive payment on a check, so some small businesses choose not to accept personal checks.
©Bignai/Shutterstock

Instruments that do not meet all of the requirements of negotiability cannot be negotiated. However, they can be transferred by assignment, which is governed by the ordinary principles of contract law. People who receive instruments by assignment are not given the special protection provided those who receive instruments by negotiation, because they cannot be *holders in due course*, as explained in the next chapter.

Negotiation by Indorsement

An instrument is indorsed when the holder signs it, thereby indicating the intent to transfer ownership to another. Indorsements may be written in ink, typewritten, or stamped with a rubber stamp. They may be written or word processed on a separate paper (rider, or *allonge*), as long as the separate paper is so firmly affixed to the instrument that it becomes part of it. Although the UCC does not require indorsements to be on any particular side of the paper, for convenience, they are usually placed on the back of the instrument. Anyone who gives value for an instrument has the right to have the unqualified indorsement of the person who transferred it, unless it is payable to bearer.

Regulation CC, issued by the Federal Reserve Board under the Competitive Banking Act, has established standards for check indorsements (Figure 16-8). Under the regulation, the back of a check is divided into specific sections designed to protect the indorsement of the depositor bank (the bank of first deposit). The first one-and-a-half inches from the trailing edge of the check is reserved for the payee's indorsement. Negotiation is effective to transfer an instrument, even when it is transferred by a minor, a corporation exceeding its powers, or any other person without capacity; obtained by fraud, duress, or mistake of any kind; part of an illegal transaction; or made in breach of duty. Any such negotiations, however, may be rescinded except as against a holder in due course (defined and explained in Chapter 17), who is given special protection. There are four commonly used types of

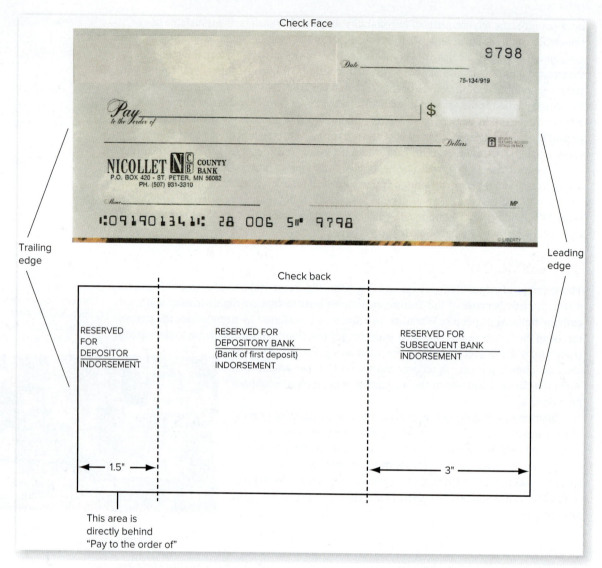

Figure 16-8 Regulation CC has issued check indorsement standards.

indorsements: blank indorsements, special indorsements, restrictive indorsements, and qualified indorsements.

Blank Indorsements A **blank indorsement** consists of the signature alone written on the instrument. No particular indorsee (person to whom an instrument is indorsed) is named. When an instrument is indorsed in blank, it becomes payable to the bearer and may be transferred by delivery alone. If the instrument is lost or stolen and gets into the hands of another holder, the new holder can recover its face value by delivery alone. For this reason, a blank indorsement should be used only in limited situations, such as at a bank teller's window. A blank indorsement turns order paper into bearer paper and may be transferred by delivery alone. When an instrument is made payable to a person under a misspelled name or a name other than that person's own, the payee may indorse in the incorrect name, in the correct name, or in both. Signatures in both names may be required by a person paying or giving value for the instrument.

EXAMPLE 16-2: Blank Indorsement

Carol Barcley received her first paycheck from the restaurant where she worked as a part-time hostess. She took the check to the bank, where she indorsed it in blank at the teller's window. This was a proper time and place to use a blank indorsement because there was no likelihood that the check would get lost or stolen.

Special Indorsements A *special indorsement* (also called an *indorsement in full*) is made by writing the words *pay to the order of* or *pay to,* followed by the name of the person to whom it is to be transferred (the indorsee) and the signature of the indorser. When indorsed in this manner, the instrument remains an order instrument and must be indorsed by the indorsee before it can be negotiated further. The holder of an instrument may convert a blank indorsement into a special indorsement by writing the words *pay to the order of a person* or *pay to a person* above the indorser's signature.

EXAMPLE 16-3: Special Indorsement

Frank Cully withdrew $3,500 from his savings account to buy a car from Glendale Motors Inc. When he made the withdrawal, Cully received a check from the bank payable to him for $3,500. He took the check to Glendale Motors, indorsed it with a special indorsement, and received title to the car. A special indorsement (indorsement in full) creates order paper, which requires the signature of the indorsee. Because the check could not be legally transferred or negotiated further until Glendale indorsed it, all parties were protected.

Restrictive Indorsements A *restrictive indorsement* limits the rights of the indorsee in some manner to protect the rights of the indorser. Indorsements for deposit or collection are restrictive indorsements designed to get an instrument into the banking system for the purpose of deposit or collection. When a check is indorsed "for deposit only," as in Figure 16-9, the amount of the instrument is credited to the indorser's account before it is negotiated further. Retail stores often stamp each check "for deposit only" when it is received. This wording provides protection in the event the check is

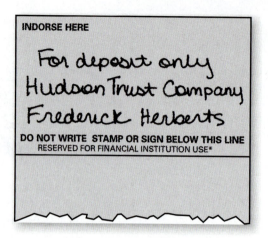

Figure 16-9 A restrictive indorsement limits the subsequent use of the instrument.

stolen. Checks mailed to the bank for deposit should always be indorsed in this way. An indorsement that purports to prohibit further transfer, such as "pay Olga Peterson only," may be further negotiated after the directions in the indorsement are carried out. Thus, after Olga Peterson is paid, any holder of the instrument may continue to negotiate it. A restrictive indorsement does not prevent further transfer or negotiation of the instrument.

A **conditional indorsement**, a type of restrictive indorsement, purports to make the rights of the indorsee subject to the happening of a certain event or condition. A person paying the instrument or taking it for value, however, may disregard the condition.

EXAMPLE 16-4: Conditional Indorsement

Gallo wished to transfer a dividend check that he received to his grandson, James Ingram, as a birthday gift (see the indorsement in the illustration). Because Gallo did not want Ingram to cash the check before his 18th birthday, he issued a conditional indorsement. However, under the UCC, a bank or anyone else who gives Ingram money or value for the check will not be affected by the condition.

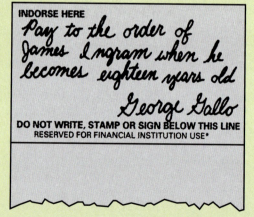

Qualified Indorsements A **qualified indorsement** is one in which words have been added to the signature that limit the liability of the indorser. By adding the words *without recourse* to the indorsement, the indorser is not liable in the event the instrument is dishonored, that is, not paid by the maker or drawer.

EXAMPLE 16-5: Qualified Indorsement

A $25,000 check was made payable to Attorney Samuel Brock in payment of a client's claim. Brock indorsed the check to the client, George Rose, "without recourse." By using this indorsement, Brock would not be responsible for payment if the check failed to clear because a qualified indorsement limits the contractual liability of the indorser.

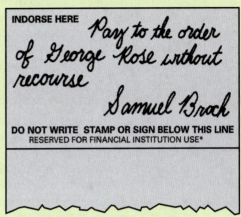

Obligations of Indorsers

Indorsements have threefold significance. In addition to being necessary to negotiate order paper, they create obligations on the part of the indorser. These obligations come in the form of implied warranties and a contractual promise to pay subsequent holders of the instrument.

Warranties of Indorsers An indorser who receives consideration for an instrument makes five warranties to subsequent transferees of the instrument. These five warranties are as follows. First, the indorser is entitled to enforce the instrument. This warranty gives assurances to subsequent holders that the person indorsing it did not steal it or come into possession of it in an unlawful manner. Second, the indorser warrants that all signatures are authentic and authorized. Third, the next warranty is that the instrument has not been altered. The indorser warrants that there has been no alteration or other irregularity. Fourth, the instrument is not subject to a defense of any party that can be asserted against the indorser. Fifth, the last warranty provides that the indorser has no knowledge of the bankruptcy of the maker, acceptor, or drawer.

Contract of Indorsers Unless an indorsement states otherwise (e.g., by words such as *without recourse*), every indorser agrees to pay any subsequent holder the face amount of the instrument if it is **dishonored** (not paid by the maker or drawee). To enforce this obligation, it is necessary for the holder to do two things. The holder of an instrument must first present it for payment to the maker or drawee when it is due. If that person refuses to pay the instrument, it is said to be dishonored. The holder then must notify the indorser or indorsers of the dishonor. If the holder is a bank, notice must be given by midnight of the next banking day. Holders other than banks must give notice within 30 days after the dishonor. Failure by the holder to make presentment and give timely notice of dishonor to an indorser has the effect of discharging that indorser from liability on the contract to pay subsequent holders of the instrument.

Multiple Payees, Missing and Forged Indorsements

If an instrument is payable to either of two payees, as in "pay to the order of Eric Foss *or* Betty Foss," the indorsement of only one of the payees is necessary to negotiate it. However, if an instrument is payable to both of two payees, as in "pay to the order of Eric Foss *and* Betty Foss," the indorsement of both payees is necessary for a proper negotiation. A bank that has taken an instrument from a customer to send through the bank collection process may supply any indorsement of the customer that is necessary to title. This rule is designed to speed up bank collections by eliminating the necessity to return to a depositor any items that were not indorsed. Such an indorsement may not be supplied by a bank, however, if the instrument contains the words *payee's indorsement required*.

Unauthorized or Forged Indorsements

An unauthorized signature or indorsement is one made without actual, implied, or apparent authority. With three exceptions and unless ratified (approved afterward), an unauthorized or forged signature does not serve as the signature of the person whose name is signed. It has no effect. In addition, when an instrument is paid on a forged indorsement, the tort of conversion takes place. For example, when a bank pays proceeds to a forger and the payee's wishes are not carried out, the bank is held liable for converting the payee's funds. **Conversion** is the wrongful exercise of dominion and control over another's personal property.

A CLASSIC CASE   Thrown by the Fictitious Payee Exception

Most of us are tempted from time to time to take the occasional shortcut or two to solve our problems. Fortunately, most of us also resist that temptation. Instead, we work for what we have; we pay our bills, and we wait patiently for our next paycheck. There are times, however, when the temptation is too great for some. An example involves Lorna Lewis, a supervisor in the credit department of Getty Petroleum. To appreciate what happened to Lewis we have to understand Getty's business. It worked something like this. Getty was in the business of distributing gasoline to its dealer-owned stations. The dealers accepted credit cards from motorists, who would pay at the pump or at the indoor cash register. The payments from the credit card companies would go directly to Getty, which would then generate checks that were made payable to the individual dealerships. The plan was foolproof—almost. There was one small glitch. The checks never went to the dealers. In a cleverly constructed accounting scheme, the checks were generated just to keep Getty's financial records straight. What actually happened was that Getty would void the checks and credit the accounts of the dealers against their future purchases.

The plan might have worked well had it not been for Lewis. Lewis was charged with voiding the checks. This gave her access to an enormous amount of money. At some point, Lewis decided to keep the checks and forge the indorsement of the payees. She then sent the checks to credit card companies to pay off her own credit card debt. The credit card companies forwarded the checks to Chemical Bank, which was where Getty kept its accounts. Eventually Lewis's game was discovered, and Getty sued the credit card companies for the lost money. Getty argued that whenever a credit card company pays money to a forger, that credit card company is liable for the lost money. Getty was correct too—well, almost. Had it not been for a very important exception to the rule, the petroleum company might have actually won the case. The fictitious payee exception says that when the maker or drawer of an instrument does not intend for the payee to have an interest in the instrument, any indorsement is effective. So, in this case, because the drawer (Getty) had no intent to transfer any interests to the payees (the service stations), anyone who signs those instruments (Lewis) has indorsed them properly and the loss falls on the shoulders of the drawer (Getty). [See: *Getty Petroleum Corp. v. American Express Travel Related Services, Co., Inc.*, 683 N.E.2d 311 (New York Court of Appeals).]

See: *Getty Petroleum Corp. v. American Express Travel Related Services, Co., Inc.* 683 N.E.2d 311 (New York Court of Appeals).

Exceptions There are three exceptions to the general rule that an unauthorized indorsement has no effect. The exceptions, shown in the following list, are designed primarily to promote negotiability of negotiable instruments.

1. *Imposters* An imposter is someone who impersonates another. When an instrument is issued to an imposter on the false belief that the imposter is the payee, the indorsement by any person in the name of the payee is treated as an effective indorsement. This rule places the loss, in such a case, on the one who is in the best position to prevent it—the maker or drawer of the instrument.
2. *Padded Payrolls* When an agent or employee of the maker or drawer pads the payroll by supplying the employer with fictitious names, an indorsement by any person in the name of each fictitious payee is effective. This rule places the burden of preventing this type of fraud on the party who is in the best position to prevent it—either the drawer (if a draft) or the maker (if a note).
3. *No Interest Intended; Fictitious Payee* When the maker or drawer of an instrument intends the payee to have no interest in the instrument or the payee is a fictitious person, an indorsement by any person in the name of the payee is effective.

quick quiz 16-2

1. An instrument is indorsed when the holder signs it, thereby indicating the intent to transfer ownership to another. true | false
2. Instruments that do not meet all of the requirements of negotiability cannot be negotiated nor transferred by assignment. true | false
3. An unauthorized signature or indorsement is one made without actual, implied, or apparent authority. true | false

Summary

16.1 The law of negotiable instruments is found in Article 3 of the UCC. Under the UCC, a negotiable instrument is a written document signed by the maker that contains an unconditional promise or order to pay a fixed amount of money on demand or at a definite time to the bearer or to order. There are two basic kinds of negotiable instruments: promise instruments (including notes and certificates of deposit) and order instruments (including drafts and checks). The following are parties to negotiable instruments: maker or co-maker; drawer; issuer; drawee; payee; bearer; holder; holder in due course; indorser; indorsee; and acceptor. To be negotiable, instruments must (1) be in writing; (2) be signed by the maker or drawer; (3) contain an unconditional promise or order to pay; (4) be made out for a fixed amount of money; (5) be payable on demand or at a definite time; and (6) except for checks, be payable to order or to bearer.

16.2 When an instrument is first delivered by the maker or drawer for the purpose of giving rights to any person, it is said to be *issued*. When the person to whom it is issued delivers it to a third party, it is *transferred*. Instruments can be transferred by assignment or by negotiation. An instrument is indorsed when the holder signs it, thereby indicating the intent to transfer ownership to another. Indorsements may be written in ink, typewritten, or stamped with a rubber stamp. There are four commonly used types of indorsements: blank indorsements, special indorsements, restrictive indorsements, and qualified indorsements. Indorsements have threefold significance. In addition to being necessary to negotiate order paper, they create obligations on the part of the indorser. These obligations come in the form of implied warranties and a contractual promise to pay subsequent holders of the instrument. An unauthorized signature or indorsement is one made without actual, implied, or apparent authority.

Key Terms

acceptance, 453
acceptor, 458
allonge, 463
assignment, 462
bank draft, 455
bearer, 457
bearer paper, 463
bill of exchange, 453
blank indorsement, 464
cashier's check, 456
certificate of deposit (CD), 452
certified check, 455
check, 454
co-makers, 457
conditional indorsement, 466
conversion, 468
demand note, 452
dishonored, 467
domestic bill of exchange, 454
draft, 453
drawee, 457
drawer, 457
foreign draft, 454
holder, 457
holder in due course, 457
indorsee, 458
indorsement in full, 465
indorser, 458
installment note, 452
international bill of exchange, 454
issuer, 457
maker, 457
money order, 456
negotiable instrument, 451
negotiation, 463
note, 452
order paper, 463
payee, 457
qualified indorsement, 466
restrictive indorsement, 465
sight draft, 453
special indorsement, 465
teller's check, 455
time draft, 453
trade acceptance, 454
traveler's check, 456

Questions for Review and Discussion

1. What is the purpose of a negotiable instrument?
2. Which negotiable instruments contain a promise to pay money?
3. Which negotiable instruments contain an order to pay money?
4. What are the different types of checks and money orders?
5. What are the requirements of a negotiable instrument?
6. What is the difference between an assignment and a negotiation of an instrument?
7. What are the four kinds of indorsements?
8. What are the implied warranties that are related to indorsements?
9. What contract is made when people indorse negotiable instruments?
10. What is the legal effect of a forged indorsement?

Cases for Analysis

1. Gail Sak wanted to give her niece, Kim Ryan, a gift of money for her 21st birthday, which was two weeks away. Because she was leaving for a trip to Europe the next day, Sak gave Ryan a check dated that day reading, "Pay to the order of Kim Ryan when she reaches the age of twenty-one (signed) Gail Sak." Was the check negotiable? Why or why not?
2. In exchange for legal services rendered to her by the law firm of Westmoreland, Hall, and Bryan,

Barbara Hall wrote the following letter: "I agree to pay to your firm as attorney's fees for representing me in obtaining property settlement agreement and tax advice, the sum of $2,760, payable at the rate of $230 per month for twelve (12) months beginning January 1, 1970. Very truly yours, Barbara Hall Hodge." Was the letter a negotiable instrument? Give the reason for your answer. [See: *Hall v. Westmoreland, Hall & Bryan*, 182 S.E.2d 539 (GA).]

3. Barton signed a promissory note promising to pay to the order of Scott Hudgens Realty & Mortgage Inc. the sum of $3,000. The note stated, "This amount is due and payable upon evidence of an acceptable permanent loan ... and upon acceptance of the loan commitment." Was the note negotiable? Why or why not? [See: *Barton v. Scott Hudgens Realty & Mortg.*, 222 S.E.2d 126 (GA).]

4. Melanie E. Regan wrote the following words on a sheet of notebook paper in her own handwriting: "Twenty years from date, I, Melanie E. Regan promise to pay to the order of Ryan M. Brown $10,000 without interest." She did not sign the paper at the end. Is the instrument negotiable? Why or why not?

5. David Shin, a silver collector, ran short of cash. He borrowed $1,500 from Vinnie Gaff, giving Gaff the following note: "Thirty days from date, I promise to pay to the order of Vinnie Gaff $1,500 worth of silver (signed) David Shin." Gaff indorsed the note and gave it to Kia Lai in exchange for services rendered by Lai. What legal term describes the transfer of the note from Gaff to Lai? Explain your answer.

6. Powell, intending to write a check to Thompson Electric Inc., instead made it payable to the order of "Tompson Electric." Thompson Electric Inc. indorsed the check with its name correctly spelled. Was the indorsement valid? Why or why not? [See: *State v. Powell*, 551 P.2d 902 (KS).]

7. Tufi forged the payee's name on the front of a U.S. Treasurer's check. When convicted of a forgery, he appealed, contending that a signature on the front of a check cannot be an indorsement. May an indorsement be written on the front of an instrument? Explain. [See: *United States v. Tufi*, 536 F.2d 855 (9th Cir.).]

8. Morse wrote a check for $2,500 payable to Reynolds for services rendered. Reynolds fraudulently raised the check to $5,500, indorsed it "without recourse," and deposited it in her bank account. Later, when the alteration was discovered, Reynolds argued that she was not responsible because her indorsement was qualified. Do you agree with Reynolds? Why or why not? [See: *Wolfram v. Halloway*, 361 N.E.2d 587 (IL).]

9. Sanders borrowed $5,000 from Waskow, giving Waskow a promissory note that read, "One year from date, I promise to pay to the order of James Waskow $5,000, without interest (signed) Mary Sanders." Six months later, Waskow died. The unindorsed note was in the possession of Waskow's landlord, who claimed that Waskow had given him the note in payment of back rent. Was the landlord a holder of the note? Why or why not? [See: *Smathers v. Smathers*, 239 S.E.2d 637 (NC).]

Design Elements: The Opening Case: ©Sharpstock/Alamy; A Classic Case: ©Evlakhov Valeriy/Shutterstock

quick quiz Answers

16-1	16-2
1. T	1. T
2. F	2. F
3. T	3. T

Chapter 17

Holders in Due Course, Defenses, and Liabilities

17-1 Holder in Due Course
The Holder in Due Course Requirements • Holder through a Holder in Due Course

17-2 Personal Defenses
Breach of Contract • Lack or Failure of Consideration • Fraud in the Inducement • Lack of Delivery • Payment of an Instrument

17-3 Real Defenses
Infancy and Mental Incompetence • Illegality and Duress • Fraud as to the Essential Nature of the Transaction • Bankruptcy • Unauthorized Signatures • Material Alteration • The FTC Legend and Consumer Notes

17-4 Liability of the Parties
Makers, Acceptors, and Certain Drawers • Other Drawers and Indorsers

THE OPENING CASE Round 1

"You may delay, but time will out."—B. Franklin

Today's story begins when Robert Stansbury made a deal with Harriet Clements to buy her laundromat. The deal was sealed when Stansbury transferred a promissory note to Clements. Shortly thereafter, Stansbury was served with a writ of garnishment by a creditor that Stansbury had failed to pay properly. The court ordered Satnsbury to make monthly payments to the court in order to pay off that debt. Fast forward about four months, and a fellow named Williams showed up and told Stansbury that he, Williams, owned the promissory note that once belonged to Clements and, from that date forward, all installments should be paid to him and not to Clements. Skeptical about the alleged transfer of his note, Stansbury demanded proof of ownership. With that demand, he also notified Williams of the garnishment order that was attached to the promissory note. Stansbury also told him that the payments that Williams expected were going to the court. Williams said something like "I care not about the garnishment, please pay me what you owe." (This is a bit of a paraphrase, of course.) He also sent the proof that Stansbury had requested. Stansbury, of course, could not pay anything to Williams. Next, Williams got tough as he turned that matter over to his lawyer with a final threat, "Pay up or face an unpleasant collection process" (Another paraphrase.)

Two years passed with no further communication from Williams. During this time, Stansbury reached an amicable settlement with his creditor. Accordingly, the court returned the sum of $8,252.85 to Stansbury who turned it over to his creditor, ending the garnishment order once and for all. Williams, of course, got nothing. Two years after this, some 44 months since his original contact with Stansbury, Williams resurfaced and sued Stansbury for the amount owed on that original promissory note. At trial, Stansbury offered two points in his defense. First, he argued that the promissory note was not a negotiable instrument because Williams took it knowing about the garnishment order. Second, Williams lost his right to recover because he waited four years to come forward and issue his notice of dishonor. The jury was sympathetic and ruled that Williams may not have known about the garnishment order when he purchased the note, but he did know about it shortly thereafter. Strangely, they did not pursue this line of inquiry further. Instead, they moved on and found that Williams had waited too long to file his notice of dishonor. Unsatisfied with this result, Williams appealed. Unfortunately for Williams, the appellate court upheld the judgment of the lower court. Williams next asked the Supreme Court of Texas to review the case, and some 13 years after the promissory note was first issued, the Supreme Court agreed to hear the second appeal. [See: *Williams v. Stansbury,* 649 S.W.2d 293, Supreme Court of Texas (1983); and, in the Texas appellate court, *Williams v. Stansbury* 634 S.W.2d 924, (Tex. App. 1982).]

Opening Case Questions

1. What are the elements that make someone (or some entity) a holder in due course? Explain.

2. Is this promissory note an authentic negotiable instrument? Explain?

3. What constitutes "good faith" in a case like this one? Explain.

4. What party in this case has the burden of proof? Explain.

5. How much time can go by before the owner of negotiable instrument must issue a notice of dishonor? Explain.

Source: See: *Williams v. Stansbury,* 649 S.W.2d 293 (1983); Inn the appellate court *Williams v. Stansbury* 634 S.W.2d 924, (Tex.App.1982).

LO Learning Objectives

1. State the characteristics of being a holder in due course.
2. Describe the special protection given to a holder in due course.
3. Define *holder*.
4. Explain the protection given to a holder through a holder in due course.
5. Name six personal defenses.
6. Discuss the protection given to people who sign consumer credit contracts.
7. Name six real defenses and explain the significance of a real defense.
8. Explain primary liability.
9. Explain secondary liability.
10. Describe the conditions that must be met to hold a secondary party liable.

17-1 Holder in Due Course

A fundamental rule of contract law states that it is not legally possible for one party to transfer rights that are greater than they actually have themselves. A key exception to that rule is found in the law of negotiable instruments. One of the basic principles of the law of negotiable instruments says that a holder in due course of negotiable instruments can receive more rights than the party or parties who held the instrument before them. For this reason, negotiable instruments are used a lot and are passed openly from one party to another. Often, the question of whether one of the parties in a lawsuit is a holder in due course will arise. Usually, the party making this claim is the holder who is trying to elevate his or her status to that of a holder in due course (a title that even sounds more important than just a plain, run of the mill, "ordinary holder"). The UCC sets the standard for determining if an ordinary **holder** is really a holder in due course. In order to demonstrate that it is a **holder in due course**, the UCC says a party must demonstrate that it took the instrument (1) for fair value, (2) in good faith, and (3) without notice that anything is wrong with it. In general, in a case involving a holder in due course, one party (party A) is holding an instrument that says that party B should fork over the ready cash to cover the face value of that instrument. Party B then raises a defense and says, because of this defense, it does not have to pay party A. The burden switches to party A, which must now prove that it is a holder in due course.

UCC Revised (1990)
3-302(a)(2)

EXAMPLE 17-1: What It Takes to Be a Holder in Due Course

Mr. Harrison of Harrison Industries receives a check from Ms. Taft of Taft Consolidated for $50,897.77. He takes the check to Garfield National Bank to cash it. Garfield tries to contact Erie City Bank on which the check is drawn with no luck because of a computer problem. Later, that "problem" turns out to have been an excuse from a not-so-industrious teller, who was outside on an extended "smoke break" when the request came across his desk. To its credit, the bank then tries to contact Ms. Taft, with no result. Because Mr. Harrison is such a good customer, Garfield still places the amount for the check in his account, which already contains $5,000. The next day, Mr. Harrison returns to Garfield National Bank and closes the account, taking out the full $55,897.77. That very afternoon, the Garfield National Bank discovers that the check has a stop payment order on it at Erie and Erie will not be sending the $50,897.77 to Garfield. After several attempts to recover the money peacefully from Harrison or Taft, Garfield National Bank sues Mr. Harrison and Ms. Taft for the $50,897.77 that it paid out beyond Mr. Harrison's original $5,000 despite the stop payment order. Ms. Taft demonstrates that she issued the stop payment order in a timely manner because Harrison had not performed the job that Mr. Harrison, as CEO of Harrison Industries, had promised. For Garfield to recover that $50,897.77 it will have to demonstrate that it is a holder in due course. In order to demonstrate that it is a holder in due course, the UCC says that Garfield must demonstrate that it took the instrument (1) for fair value, (2) in good faith, and (3) without notice that anything is wrong with it.

The Holder in Due Course Requirements

As we have seen frequently, the law operates as a complex adaptive system. Often this means that one agent within the system, a court or an agency, for example, will interact with the other agents to effect a change in the flow of information in that system, resulting in a new set of rules in that area of the law. Such was the case when the UCC was revised to take into account some of the changes in the way negotiable instruments were handled. One key target of the reform movement involved a revised explanation of the requirements needed to demonstrate the existence of holder in due course status. The requirements did not change. A holder still had to show that it took the instrument (1) for fair value, (2) in good faith, and (3) without notice that anything is wrong with it. However, measuring good faith became a bit more complicated and difficult than it had been in previous incarnations of the test.

The Value-Taking Requirement The taking for value requirement differs little from the ordinary concept of consideration in general contract law. In essence, this means that the party who took the instrument and now holds it must have given something of value (or a promise of something of value) in exchange for that instrument. The UCC explains this requirement in simple and straightforward language in Section UCC 3-303 when it says that a negotiable instrument is taken for value under the following circumstances:

1. A promise to perform has been fulfilled by the holder.
2. A security interest in or a lien on the instrument has been obtained by the holder.
3. A prior claim has been satisfied or been secured for the holder by taking the instrument.
4. A negotiable instrument is given by the holder in payment.
5. An irrevocable obligation is given by the holder in payment.

Recall that there are certain preordained situations in which consideration will never exist no matter whether the case involves negotiable instruments or regular garden-variety contracts. Gifts, for example, are not supported by consideration. That means if a party has received a negotiable instrument as a gift, that party has transferred nothing of value in exchange and, therefore, cannot be a holder in due course.

The Good-Faith Requirement Good faith is the most fluid of the holder in due course requirements. The evolution of the requirement of good faith also exemplifies the evolutionary development of the law as a complex adaptive system. Like many of the concepts in modern contract law, the concept of good faith emerged from within the practices of the medieval principles of the law merchant. As noted in Chapter 7, four of the essential characteristics of the law merchant were (1) the involvement of the merchants in the operation of the law, the need for (2) neutral and (3) universal judgments, and support for the notion of (4) mutuality (i.e., reciprocity). Nowhere in the law merchant system are the elements more clearly seen than in the concept of good faith. This is, of course, quite understandable since the merchants themselves acted as judges and carried with them a consistent and straightforward understanding of the need for their fellow merchants to be fair and just to one another and to their suppliers and buyers. The concept of good faith carried within it an appreciation for neutrality, universality, and mutuality. Of course, an understanding of good faith did not guarantee that merchants acted with good faith. If that were the case, there would be no need of the courts. Nevertheless, understanding the concept meant that, ultimately, when merchants did not act in good faith, they knew it. Ironically, it was that self-knowledge that made them effective judges in the mercantile court ("It takes a thief, to catch a thief"). [See: Harold J. Berman, *Law and Revolution: The Formation of the Western Legal Tradition* (Cambridge, MA: Harvard University Press, 1983); and Roy Goode, "The Concept of 'Good Faith' in English Law," *Pace Law School Institute of International Commercial Law*, March 1992; updated, September 11, 2009.]

When the law merchant was merged with the common law and when parts of the common law were codified, one of the concepts that flowed along with it was the concept of good faith. The assimilation process, however, was not cut from whole cloth, and its evolution into the negotiable instrument law took some time. The concept of good faith has always involved two basic elements: (1) honesty in fact and (2) conforming to accepted commercial practices of fairness. These two sides of good faith, however, were not always used in tandem in all situations. Thus, when the Uniform Commercial Code was first codified, the two-prong test of honesty and commercial fairness was restricted to a few areas:

1. It was limited to agreements covered by Article 2 of the UCC.
2. It regulated the conduct of merchants, but no one else.
3. It involved only those situations in which the actual phrase *good faith* was mentioned in Article 2 of the UCC. [See: UCC Section 1-201 General Definitions—Official Comments.]

The first prong of the test, honesty, was always part of the holder in due course requirement. It represents probably what might be considered the lowest, or perhaps the simplest, type of good faith. In its barest form, the principle says that, on a purely subjective level, the party involved in the problematic transaction was trying to be honest, or intended to be honest, but out of habit, haste, or helplessness was, objectively (in reality), a liar, a cheat, or a thief. While this principle may appear to have emerged out of *Alice in Wonderland* ("sentence first . . . verdict afterward"), the idea of subjective honesty actually makes some sense when dealing with the banking system. One court explained it this way: "The check is the major method for transfer of funds in commercial practice. The maker, payee, and endorsers of a check naturally expect it will be rapidly negotiated and collected. The wheels of commerce would grind to a halt (if an objective standard were adopted)."[1] [See: *Bowling Green Inc. v. State St. Bank & Trust*, 425 F.2d 81, 85 (1st Cir. 1970).]

This test, of course, was developed in the days before the computerized financial world had fully matured. Today, in the world of direct deposits, ATMs, debit cards, and so on, checks are no longer the "major method for the transfer of finds." Consequently, the standard was altered when the UCC was revised to include the second prong of the traditional test. Today, honesty in fact is not the only thing that is needed to create a holder in due course. Instead, a party claiming to be a holder in due course must also prove that it was acting in a way that demonstrates "conduct that meets reasonable commercial standards of fair dealing." This standard is also supported by a two-step test. Accordingly, to be operating in good faith from an objective perspective, a party who claims to be a holder in due course must act (1) according to the commercial standards of the industry, and (2) those commercial standards must themselves be reasonable. Moreover, any attempt to apply two requirements must be placed within the context of the individual transaction under scrutiny.

The Without Notice of Defect Requirement To be a holder in due course, a holder must not have notice of any claim or defense to an instrument or notice that an instrument is overdue or has been dishonored. A holder has notice of a claim or defense if the instrument bears visible evidence of forgery or alteration. The same is true if the instrument is so incomplete or irregular as to make its legal acceptance doubtful. Notice of a claim or defense is also considered given if the holder knows that the obligation of any party is voidable. A holder has notice that a demand instrument is overdue when more than a reasonable length of time has elapsed since it was issued. A check is overdue 90 days after its date. For other instruments, such as a note or draft, a reasonable time depends on the circumstances of each case. Knowledge of some facts does not in itself give the holder notice of a defense or claim. For example, the fact that an instrument is postdated or antedated does not prevent someone from being a holder in due course; neither does completing an incomplete instrument constitute having such notice, unless the holder has notice of any improper completion.

THE OPENING CASE Round 2
"You may delay, but time will out."—B. Franklin

Recall that in the Opening Case, Robert Stansbury bought Harriet Clements' laundromat and finalized the agreement with a promissory note that he transferred to Clements. Soon afterward, Stansbury received a writ of garnishment from a creditor to whom Stansbury owed a great deal of money. The court ordered Stansbury to make monthly payments to the court in order to make good on the debt. Four months later, John Williams appeared on the scene and informed Stansbury that Clements had transferred the promissory note to him and that, from that point on, all installment payments should be paid directly to him. Wisely, Stansbury asked for proof. At the same time that he made this request, Stansbury also notified Williams of the garnishment order that sent his money directly to the court. Consequently, the money that Williams had expected to receive on the promissory note went directly to the court each month. Williams continued to demand payment. Nevertheless, Stansbury could not pay anything to Williams.

Williams then turned the matter over to his lawyer, noting that if Stansbury did not pay, the matter would go into a collection process. Surprisingly, two years passed with no further contact from Williams. At about that time, Stansbury and his creditor reached a settlement. As a result, the court sent $8,252.85 to Stansbury, who transferred it to his creditor, thus ending that unpleasant chapter in his life. Two years later, Williams reappeared and sued Stansbury for the amount owed on the original promissory note.

At trial, Stansbury defended himself with two arguments. First, he pointed out that the promissory note was not a negotiable instrument because Williams took it knowing about the garnishment order. Second, he argued that Williams forfeited his recovery rights when he let so much time go by before issuing his notice of dishonor. The case went to the jury, which found that Williams did not know about the garnishment order when he purchased the note but did know about it shortly thereafter. Inexplicably, they did not pursue this line of inquiry further. Instead, they moved on and found that Williams had waited too long to file his notice of dishonor. Consequently, the jury ruled in Stansbury's favor. Williams appealed. The appellate court upheld the judgment. Williams asked the Supreme Court of Texas to review the case, and the Supreme Court agreed.

Before looking at what the Supreme Court of Texas had to say about all of this, let's consider the threshold question here: Was the promissory note that Williams had purchased from Clements a negotiable instrument? Recall that to be a negotiable instrument, a note, like the promissory note that Clements transferred to Williams, must have three characteristics. The alleged holder in due course must have taken the instrument (1) for fair value, (2) in good faith, and (3) without notice that anything was wrong with it. In this case, when he presented his case at trial and on appeal, Stansbury did not even bother to discuss the first two points. Instead, he challenged Williams' right to claim that the promissory note was a negotiable instrument because he knew about the garnishment order when he purchased it. The jury ruled that Stansbury was wrong. They ruled instead that Williams did not know about the garnishment when he purchased it but learned about it shortly thereafter. Both the trial court and the court of appeals agreed that Williams did not know about the garnishment order when he purchased the note, yet they disregarded this fact and moved instead to Williams' delay in filing his notice of dishonor.

The Supreme Court did not let this point slip by unnoticed. Instead, the Court ruled that what mattered was not what Williams learned after he received the note, but what happened at the precise moment that he purchased the note. Evidence showed that Williams did not know that the note was burdened by the garnishment at the time that he received it. Therefore, Williams took the note thinking that it was free and clear and, as a result, at that moment, the note really was a negotiable instrument and Williams was and remained a holder in due course. As a result, he was protected from all prior claims including the garnishment order. The court put it this way, "With certain exceptions not material to the present case, a holder in due course takes an instrument free from all legal and equitable claims by any person to the instrument . . . The adverse claims, against which a holder in due course is protected, are not limited to claims of ownership, but embrace rights acquired through legal process such as garnishment . . . We hold the garnishment of a debt represented by a promissory note does not affect the rights of a holder in due course, even though the garnishment is prior to the negotiation." [See: *Williams v. Stansbury,* 649 S.W.2d 293 (1983); and, in the appellate court: *Williams v. Stansbury,* 634 S.W.2d 924 (Tex. App. 1982).]

Source: See: *Williams v. Stansbury,* 649 S.W.2d 293 (1983); Inn the appellate court *Williams v. Stansbury* 634 S.W.2d 924, (Tex. App.1982).

Holder through a Holder in Due Course

A holder who receives an instrument from a holder in due course acquires the rights of the holder in due course, even though he or she does not qualify as a holder in due course. This stipulation is called a **shelter provision**. It is designed to permit holders in due course to transfer all of the rights they have in the paper to others. The shelter does not apply to a holder who has committed fraud or an illegal act.

UCC Revised (1990) 3-304

UCC Revised (1990) 3-203(b)

A QUESTION OF ETHICS

Michael Carrington, the CEO of the Ice-Fire Security Corporation, pushed his marketing division into developing a hard-hitting marketing campaign that included several new aggressive strategies. At one level, the marketing executives launched a telemarketing promotion using a customer list that Ice-Fire had purchased from several publishers who kept track of buyers interested in the types of services and products provided by Ice-Fire. Whenever a potential customer responded favorably to the telemarketer's call, he or she was placed on the company's direct mail advertising list. The direct mail department then generated a series of mailings, each of which included a document that cleverly produced a sheet of paper about the size of a dollar bill that appeared to be a valid check but lacked one of the essential requirements of negotiability, such as the words,

"Good only when applied to the purchase of. . ." Clearly, then, the entire direct mail campaign was designed to provoke the customer to open the mail, be duped by the imitation check, and make a purchase that ends up costing more than it appeared because of the implied message induced by the fictitious check. Is this publisher's sale of the customer list ethical? Is Ice-Fire's purchase and use of the lists ethical? Is a campaign that targets susceptible customers ethical? Is the use of the simulated check ethical? Give reasons for each answer. Be consistent in your responses. If you have a difficult time being consistent, then your principle itself may be flawed. Try formulating a new guiding principle. If you're stumped on the nature of a guiding principle, look back to Chapter 1. The information in that chapter should help you.

quick quiz 17-1

1. A holder is a person who is in possession of a negotiable instrument that is issued or indorsed to that person's order or to bearer. true | false
2. Able bought a book from Baker and gave Baker a $25 check. Baker indorsed the check and gave it to Charlie in payment of a debt. Charlie was not a holder in due course of the check. true | false
3. Charlie indorsed the check he received in Question 2 from Baker and gave it to David as a birthday gift. David had the rights of a holder in due course of the check. true | false

17-2 Personal Defenses

UCC Revised (1990) 3-305(b)

The favorable treatment that holders in due course receive ensures that they take instruments free from all claims to them on the part of any person and free from all personal defenses of any party *with whom they have not dealt*. **Personal defenses** (also called **limited defenses**) are defenses that can be used against a holder but not a holder in due course of a negotiable instrument. (The terms *personal defense* and *limited defense* come from common law and are not used in the UCC.) The most common personal defenses are breach of contract, failure or lack of consideration, fraud in the inducement, **lack of delivery**, and payment (see Table 17-1).

Table 17-1	Most Common Defenses
Defense	**Description**
Breach of contract	One of the parties to a contract has failed to do what he or she has previously agreed to do.
Lack of consideration	No consideration existed in the underlying contract for which the instrument was issued.
Failure of consideration	One of the parties to a contract has failed to furnish the agreed consideration.
Fraud in the inducement	The drawer or maker of an instrument is persuaded to enter a negotiable instrument into a contract because of a misrepresentation of some fact regarding the item purchased.
Non-delivery	A payee forcibly, unlawfully, or conditionally takes an instrument from a maker or drawer. The maker or drawer did not intend to deliver the instrument.
Payment of an instrument	The drawer or maker of an instrument has paid the amount of the instrument.

Breach of Contract

Negotiable instruments are often issued in exchange for property, services, or some other obligation as part of an underlying contract. Sometimes, the party to whom the instrument was issued breaches the contract by failing to perform or by performing in an unsatisfactory manner. If suit is brought on the instrument by a holder against the maker or drawer, the latter may use breach of contract as a defense. Because breach of contract is a personal defense, however, it may not be used if the holder of the instrument is a holder in due course unless the parties dealt with each other.

Lack or Failure of Consideration

Lack of consideration is a defense that may be used by a maker or drawer of an instrument when no consideration existed in the underlying contract for which the instrument was issued. The ordinary rules of contract law are followed to determine the presence or absence of consideration in such a case.

EXAMPLE 17-2: Lack of Consideration

Lowell, without any mention of payment, helped his friend Ransom move from Cambridge to Gambier. At the end of the day, after he was in his new apartment, Ransom told Lowell that he'd give him some money for helping him move. The next day, Ransom gave Lowell a $200 check. Lowell cashed the check at a local market and promptly left town. Ransom then stopped payment on the check. Ransom's promise to pay Lowell was not enforceable because Lowell had completed the work when the promise was made—it was past consideration. The local market could recover the $200 from Ransom, however, because it was a holder in due course and was not subject to the personal defense of lack of consideration.

Failure of consideration is not the same as a lack of consideration, although many people confuse the two. **Failure of consideration** is a defense that the maker or drawer may use when the other party breaches the contract by not furnishing the agreed consideration. Both lack of consideration and failure of consideration are personal defenses. They may not be used against a holder in due course.

Fraud in the Inducement

There are two kinds of fraud: fraud in the inducement and fraud as to the essential nature of the transaction. The first is a personal defense; the second is a real defense, discussed later in the chapter. The five elements of fraud are explained in depth in the contract law unit. When someone is induced by a fraudulent statement to enter into a contract, that person may have the contract rescinded. However, he or she may not use that defense against a holder in due course. A holder in due course can cut through the defense of fraud in the inducement and collect from the person who was defrauded.

Non-Delivery

Every commercial instrument may be revoked by its maker or drawer until it has been delivered to the payee. Delivery is the voluntary transfer of possession of an instrument from one person to another. If the transfer of possession is not voluntary, the instrument has not been "issued." Thus, in the event someone unlawfully takes an instrument from a drawer or some other individual or finds a lost instrument, the drawer has the defense of **non-delivery**. Non-delivery, then, is a personal defense available to the drawer which allows the drawer to refuse to pay on the instrument when the instrument has not been properly delivered. However, if the person in unlawful possession of the instrument manages to negotiate the instrument to a holder in due course, this defense is removed.

EXAMPLE 17-3: Non-Delivery

Morse wrote out a promissory note payable to the order of the "bearer," intending to give it to Marconi. On his way to see Marconi, Morse loses the note. If the check is found by Edison who then transfers it to Tesla, Tesla becomes a holder in due course, provided it was negotiated for value, in good faith, and without notice of any claim or defect. Morse would have to honor the note despite the fact that it was not delivered to Tesla by him or by Marconi. However, if Edison tried to collect from Morse, Edison could not demand payment, and Morse would not have to pay.

Payment of an Instrument

Payment of an instrument by a maker or drawee usually ends the obligations of the parties. However, if a negotiable instrument is negotiated to a holder in due course after it has been paid, it will have to be paid again. This rule exists because payment is a personal defense, which cannot be used against a holder in due course. Because of this rule, anyone who pays a demand instrument should have it marked "paid" and take possession of it. This requirement is not as important with a time instrument, unless it is paid before its due date, because no one can be a holder in due course of a past due instrument.

The protection that is given to holders in due course was not always fair to consumers who bought on credit in the past.

EXAMPLE 17-4: Former Law

In 1975, Ruby Merlin bought a car from a used car dealer. She paid a small amount down and signed a consumer sales contract agreeing to pay the balance in 24 monthly installments. The used car dealer negotiated the contract (which was actually a promissory note) to a finance company and received payment immediately. The next day, the car's transmission stopped working, and the dealer refused to fix it. Merlin would still have to pay the finance company the full amount due on the note because the finance company was a holder in due course and was not subject to personal defenses.

In 1976, the FTC adopted the **holder in due course rule**. Under this rule, holders of consumer credit contracts who are holders in due course are subject to all claims and defenses that the buyer could use against the seller, including personal defenses. Thus, if the situation described in Example 17-4 were to occur today, Merlin's defense that the car's transmission did not work could be used against the finance company, even though it was a holder in due course. When sellers of consumer products have arrangements with financial institutions to finance their customer's purchases, the financial institutions are subject to the customer's personal defenses. They lose their protection as holders in due course.

quick quiz 17-2

1. Personal defenses are defenses that can be used against a holder in due course but not a holder of a negotiable instrument.   true | false
2. The most common personal defenses are infancy and illegality.   true | false
3. If a negotiable instrument is negotiated to a holder in due course after it has been paid, it will have to be paid again.   true | false

17-3 Real Defenses

Some defenses can be used against everyone, including holders in due course. These defenses are known as **real defenses** or **universal defenses**. The terms *real* and *universal defense* come from the common law and are not used in the UCC. No one is required to pay an instrument when they have a real defense. Real defenses include infancy and mental incompetence, illegality and duress, fraud as to the essential nature of the transaction, bankruptcy, unauthorized signature, and alteration (see Table 17-2).

UCC Revised (1990) 3-305(a)(1)

Infancy and Mental Incompetence

A minor (person under the age of 18 years) or mental incompetent need not honor a negotiable instrument if it was given in payment for a contract that the minor or mental incompetent may disaffirm on the grounds of minority or incompetency. This rule is true even if the instrument comes into the hands of a holder in due course. Similarly, persons who have been found insane by a court are not liable on a negotiable instrument, because their contracts are void.

Illegality and Duress

An instrument that is associated with duress or an illegal act, such as twisting one's arm or drug trafficking, would be void and uncollectible by anyone, even a holder in due course. This provision is true even if the holder in due course is unaware of the illegal acts or conditions.

> **EXAMPLE 17-5:** Illegality—A Real Defense
>
> The Condado Aruba Caribbean Hotel loaned Tickel, who resided in Colorado, $20,000. The money was loaned for the purpose of gambling at the hotel's casino in Aruba, Netherlands Antilles, where gambling is legal. Tickel wrote two checks to repay the debt, each of which was returned for insufficient funds. When suit was brought on the checks, the Colorado court held that gambling debts are unenforceable in that state even against a holder in due course. Tickel was not liable on the checks that he had written to the hotel.

Table 17-2 Most Common Real Defenses

Defense	Description
Infancy and mental incompetence	The maker or drawer of the instrument was a minor or mentally incompetent.
Illegality and duress	Illegality—The underlying contract for which the instrument was issued was illegal. Duress—The instrument was drawn against the will of the maker or drawer because of threats of force or bodily harm.
Fraud as to the essential nature of the transaction	A false statement was made to the maker or drawer about the nature of the instrument being signed.
Bankruptcy	An order for relief was issued by the federal court that ended all the debtor's outstanding contractual obligations.
Unauthorized signature	Someone wrongfully signed another's name on an instrument without authority to do so.
Material alteration	The amount of the instrument or the payee's name was changed wrongfully after it was originally drawn by the maker or drawer.

Fraud as to the Essential Nature of the Transaction

Fraud as to the essential nature of the transaction is more serious than fraud in the inducement. When this type of fraud occurs, the defrauded party has no knowledge or opportunity to learn of the true character or terms of the matter. Because of its seriousness, it is a real defense and may be used against anyone, even a holder in due course.

EXAMPLE 17-6: Fraud as to the Essential Nature of the Transaction

Duffy, who was almost blind, was asked by Ingram to sign a receipt. Duffy signed the paper without having had it read to him. The paper was actually a note promising to pay Ingram $2,500. Duffy would not be required to pay the note, even to a holder in due course, because this kind of fraud is more critical than fraud in the inducement.

Bankruptcy

Bankruptcy may be used as a defense to all negotiable instruments, even those in the hands of a holder in due course. Holders of such instruments will receive treatment equal to that of other similar creditors when the debtor's assets are collected and divided according to the bankruptcy law.

Unauthorized Signature

UCC Revised (1990) 3-403(a)

Whenever someone signs another's name on an instrument without authority, it is a forgery. Unless ratified, it does not operate as the signature of the person whose name is signed. Instead, it operates as the signature of the person who signed it, that is, of the wrongdoer.

EXAMPLE 17-7: Forgery—A Real Defense

With no authority to do so, Parks signed Brown's name on a note, promising to pay Rivera $3,000 in 90 days. The note was negotiated by Rivera to a holder in due course. Brown would not have to pay the money to the holder in due course because the unauthorized signature is a real defense. Parks had committed a crime. The holder in due course could recover from Rivera who, in turn, could recover from the wrongdoer, Parks.

Material Alteration

Sometimes negotiable instruments are altered after they leave the hands of the maker or drawer. Usually, the alteration involves changing the payee's name or increasing the amount of an instrument. The alteration of an instrument may be used as a real defense. Unless an instrument is written negligently so that it can be easily altered, makers and drawers are not required to pay altered amounts. They must pay only the amount for which the instrument was originally written.

Writing a check in pencil is legal, but not a good idea. It leaves the check vulnerable to alteration by a dishonest person.
©Aaron Haupt/Science Source

> **EXAMPLE 17-8:** Alteration—A Real Defense
>
> Martinez wrote out a check in a proper manner for $315 and gave it to Video Sales in payment for a DVD player. Video Sales raised the check to read $815. Martinez's bank honored the altered check. Martinez could seek reimbursement from his bank for $500, the difference between the original and the altered amount.

Any person who negligently contributes to a material alteration of an instrument or an unauthorized signature may not exercise the defense of alteration or lack of authority against a holder in due course, a drawee, or other payor who pays the instrument in good faith. For example, using a pencil to write a check or not being careful to keep the figures compact and clear gives a dishonest holder an opportunity to alter the amount. The careless writer would be without defense.

UCC Revised (1990) 3-407

UCC Revised (1990) 3-406

The FTC Legend and Consumer Notes

The Federal Trade Commission requires that consumer credit contracts contain a written warning, called the **FTC legend**, which notifies the holders of those notes that they are subject to the same defenses that the original debtor had against the original seller. A **consumer credit contract** is a contract for credit to purchase an item, property, or services, for personal, family, or household use. It is not difficult to determine if a transaction is a consumer credit contract because it must exhibit certain characteristics: (1) The purchaser must be a flesh-and-blood person rather than a corporation or institution of some sort; (2) the creditor takes interest, fees, and a security interest; and (3) the creditor's business is extending credit or using credit in its business as an ordinary part of its operation. An example of a consumer credit contract would be a loan for the purchase of a vehicle. The FTC requires that the following legend be placed on such contracts:

> ANY HOLDER OF THIS CONSUMER CREDIT CONTRACT IS SUBJECT TO ALL CLAIMS AND DEFENSES WHICH THE DEBTOR COULD ASSERT AGAINST THE SELLER OF GOODS OR SERVICES OBTAINED PURSUANT HERETO OR WITH THE PROCEEDS HEREOF. RECOVERY HEREUNDER BY THE DEBTOR SHALL NOT EXCEED AMOUNTS PAID BY THE DEBTOR HEREUNDER.

The UCC has been amended to cover the consequences that flow from not placing the legend into a consumer credit contract. The amendment is found in UCC 3-305 (e) and reads as follows:

> In a consumer transaction if a law other than this article requires that an instrument include a statement to the effect that the rights of a holder or transferee are subject to a claim or defense that the issuer could assert against the original payee, and the instrument does not include such a statement: (1) the instrument has the same effect as if the instrument included such a statement; (2) the issuer may assert against the holder or transferee all claims and defenses that would have been available if the instrument included such a statement; and (3) the extent to which claims may be asserted against the holder or transferee is determined as if the instrument included such a statement. [UCC 3-305 (e)]

In summary and for emphasis, UCC 3-305 (e) says that, there is no point in not posting the FTC legend because the protections granted to the debtor by the legend remain in effect despite its absence. [See: Neil Cohen, "The Calamitous Law of Notes," *The Ohio State University Law Review* 68 (2007), pp. 161–183. See also Dan Anderson, Ice Miller, and Jeff Ferrell, "UCC Articles 3 & 4: 2017 Ohio Amendments and Recent Significant Changes," *The Ohio State Bar Association Forum*, August 24–25, 2017.]

BUSINESS LAW WITH UCC APPLICATIONS AND NOW—THE APPLICATIONS

Article 3 of the Uniform Commercial Code May be a Relic of the Past

Back in Chapter 2, we noted that the Uniform Commercial Code may be the most successful, most wide-ranging, and most influential code ever published by the Uniform National Commission. It is now time to cast some doubt on that claim. A not so recent but, nevertheless, extremely relevant law review article entitled, "The Calamitous Law of Notes," makes an interesting, well-reasoned, and virtually irrefutable argument that the addition of UCC 1-106 (d) to Article 3 makes most of the other rules laid down in that article obsolete. Here is why. UCC 1-106 (d) says this:

> If a promise or order at the time it is issued or first comes into possession of a holder contains a statement, *required by applicable statutory or administrative law*, to the effect that the rights of a holder or transferee are subject to claims or defenses that the issuer could assert against the original payee, the promise or order is not thereby made conditional for the purposes of Section 3-104 (a); but if the promise or order is an instrument, there cannot be a holder in due course of the instrument.

UCC Section 3-104 (d) asserts that if a holder has possession of an instrument that is "*required by applicable statutory or administrative law to the effect that the rights of a holder or transferee are subject to claims or defenses that the issuer could assert against the original payee,*" that holder can no longer be a holder in due course. Undoubtedly, the phrase "required by applicable statutory or administrative law" would include all consumer loan contracts that are required to display the FTC legend discussed earlier. The net effect of UCC Section 3-104 (d) then is to take all consumer credit contracts—including auto loans and loans for furniture, appliances, and so on—outside the jurisdiction of those provisions of Article 3 that apply to holders in due course and place them under the purview of ordinary contract law. The problem has become even more complicated now that the Uniform Law Commission has added UCC 3-305 (e) to Article 3. Recall that Article UCC 3-305 (e) says, in effect, that there is no point in not posting the FTC legend because the protections granted to the debtor by the legend remain in effect despite its absence from the original instrument. This would appear to mean that the holder of an instrument that lacks the FTC legend cannot answer a challenge to his or her status as a holder in due course, even if the instrument he or she owns lacks the FTC legend. This expands the number of apparent negotiable instruments that are really simple contracts, rather than contracts held by holders in due course. These contract are then subject not to Article 3, but to the ordinary laws that apply to simple contracts. That leads to a number of interesting questions. (*Note:* Before answering these questions you might want to access the original article. Neil Cohen, "The Calamitous Law of Notes," *The Ohio State University Law Review* 68 (2007), pp. 161–183. See also Dan Anderson, Ice Miller, and Jeff Ferrell, "UCC Articles 3 & 4: 2017 Ohio Amendments and Recent Significant Changes," *The Ohio State Bar Association Annual Forum*, August 24–25, 2017.]

QUESTIONS FOR RESEARCH AND DISCUSSION

1. Do the arguments presented here present a convincing argument for abandoning Article 3 in its totality? Explain.
2. What parts of Article 3 might still apply to consumer credit contracts if any? Explain.
3. What other areas of the law within and outside the UCC would apply to simple contracts? Explain.
4. What other ares of the law can you name that might become or have become obsolete? Explain.
5. Can you name any process by which an obsolete law can be removed from the books and replaced by a more relevant law? Explain.

> **quick quiz 17-3**
>
> 1. No one with a real defense is required to pay an instrument. true | false
> 2. Fraud in the inducement is more serious than fraud as to the essential nature of the transaction. true | false
> 3. If a check is written with an erasable pen and later altered by a wrongdoer, the drawer of the check would not be responsible for any loss because alteration is a real defense. true | false

UCC 3-305 (e)
UCC 3-104 (d)

17-4 Liability of the Parties

No person is liable on an instrument unless that person's signature or the signature of an authorized agent appears on the instrument. Parties to negotiable instruments have different liability depending on their function.

UCC Revised (1990) 3-401

UCC Revised (1990) 3-412, 3-413

Makers, Acceptors, and Certain Drawers

The following are obligated to pay an instrument without reservations of any kind. They are said to be primarily liable: (1) the maker of a note, (2) the issuer of a cashier's check or other draft in which the drawer and the drawee are the same person, and (3) the acceptor of a draft.

Other Drawers and Indorsers

Other drawers and indorsers have limitations on their obligation to pay an instrument. They are said to be secondarily, or conditionally, liable. The drawer of a draft that has not been accepted is obligated to pay the draft to anyone who is entitled to enforce it; however, if a bank accepts a draft, the drawer is discharged. If a drawee other than a bank accepts a draft and it is later dishonored, the obligation of the drawer is the same as an indorser stated here.

UCC Revised (1990) 3-414, 3-415 (a)(c)

Indorsers are obligated to pay an instrument only when the following conditions are met: (1) The instrument must be properly presented to the drawee or party obliged to pay the instrument, and payment must be demanded; (2) the instrument must be dishonored—that is, payment refused; and (3) notice of the dishonor must be given to the secondary party within the time and in the manner prescribed by the UCC. If all three of these conditions are not met, drawers of drafts and indorsers are discharged from their obligations.

UCC Revised (1990) 3-501

UCC Revised (1990) 3-502

Presentment **Presentment** means a demand made by a holder to pay or accept an instrument. Presentment may be made by any commercially reasonable means, including oral, written, or electronic communication. If requested by the person to whom presentment is made, the person making presentment must exhibit the instrument and provide identification.

UCC Revised (1990) 3-503 and 3-504

Dishonor **Dishonor** means to refuse to pay a negotiable instrument when it is due or to refuse to accept it when asked to do so. An instrument is dishonored when proper presentment is made and acceptance or payment is refused. Dishonor also occurs when presentment is excused and the instrument is past due and unpaid. The presenting party has recourse against indorsers or other secondary parties after notice of dishonor has been given.

EXAMPLE 17-9: Dishonor

A note was presented to Baker for payment on the date specified. Baker refused to honor it, claiming the note was a forgery. The holder would have to proceed against the indorsers to obtain payment. The note was dishonored when Baker refused to pay it.

THE OPENING CASE Round 3
"You May Delay, but Time Will Out."—B. Franklin

Let's look at the Opening Case one more time. Recall that Stansbury made a deal with Clements to buy her laundromat. To finalize the deal, Stansbury transferred a promissory note to Clements. Later, Stansbury was served with a writ of garnishment, and the court ordered Stansbury to make monthly payments in order to satisfy the debt. About four months later, John Williams arrived on the scene and told Stansbury that he, Williams, now owned the promissory note and that all installments should be paid to him and not to Clements. Concerned about the authenticity of Williams' claims, Stansbury demanded proof of ownership. At about the same time, Stansbury notified Williams of the garnishment order that was attached to the promissory note. Williams continued to press Stansbury for payment on the note. Stansbury could not and did not pay anything to Williams. Accordingly, Williams accelerated the note, demanded full payment, and turned that matter over to his lawyer. Inexplicably, Williams then vanished. In the meantime, Stansbury reached a settlement with his creditor. Two years later, Williams resurfaced and sued Stansbury for the total amount owed on the original promissory note.

At trial, Stansbury offered two points in his defense. First, he argued that the promissory note was not a negotiable instrument because Williams took it knowing about the garnishment order. Second, he argued that Williams lost his right to recover because he had waited four years to come forward and issue his notice of dishonor. The jury was sympathetic and ruled that Williams may not have known about the garnishment order when he purchased the note but did know about it shortly thereafter. Oddly, they let this point drop and moved on to Stansbury's second claim that Williams had waited too long to file his notice of dishonor. The jury found that Williams had, indeed, waited too long and that forcing Stansbury to pay Williams now would cause great hardship for him. Consequently, the jury ruled in Stansbury's favor. Williams appealed. The appellate court upheld the judgment.

Williams asked the Supreme Court of Texas to review the case, and the Supreme Court agreed. The Supreme Court had no trouble holding that Williams was a holder in due course on the promissory note that was indeed a negotiable instrument. It therefore moved on to the issue of the timing of Williams' notice of dishonor. Both the trial court and the court of appeals agreed that Williams had delayed too long to file his notice of dishonor, thus wrongfully misleading Stansbury to the conviction that Williams had abandoned the case and thus freeing him to settle the garnishment case. They also agreed that enforcing the note against Stansbury at this late date would place an unfair burden him. The Supreme Court disagreed with these conclusions quite forcefully. The Court said that the lower courts had violated Williams' rights as a holder in due course when they ruled that Williams' silence about Stansbury's failure to pay stopped him from enforcing his rights in court. A person's silence will take away his or her right to pursue a legal solution only when he or she ahs a duty to speak. Here, Williams had fulfilled that duty when he demanded payment and, getting no response, accelerated the debt and notified Stansbury that he was turning the case over to his lawyer. At that point, the duty shifted to Stansbury, who now had to bring any and all claimants into the garnishment settlement—something he had failed to do. As a result, the court ruled that Stansbury owed Williams the principal and interest accruing from the time he had purchased the note. [See: *Williams v. Stansbury*, 649 S.W.2d 293 (1983); and in the appellate court, *Williams v. Stansbury*, 634 S.W.2d 924, (Tex. App. 1982).]

Source: See: *Williams v. Stansbury*, 649 S.W.2d 293 (1983); In the appellate court *Williams v. Stansbury* 634 S.W.2d 924, (Tex. App.1982).

Notice of Dishonor Obligations of indorsers and drawers of instruments may not be enforced unless they are given notice of the dishonor or notice is excused. Notice of dishonor may be given by any reasonable means, including oral, written, or electronic communication, and is sufficient if it reasonably identifies the instrument and indicates that the instrument has been dishonored or has not been paid or accepted. The return of an instrument given to a bank for collection is sufficient notice of dishonor.

Nonbank holders must give notice of the dishonor to the drawer and indorsers within 30 days following the day of dishonor. Banks taking instruments for collection must give notice before midnight of the banking day following the day the bank was notified of the dishonor. Delay in giving notice of dishonor is excused when the holder has acted carefully and the delay is due to circumstances beyond the holder's control. Presentment and notice of dishonor are also excused when the party waived either presentment or notice of dishonor.

About the Law

Formerly, it was necessary to send a protest to drawers and indorsers when a draft payable outside the United States was dishonored. A *protest* is a certificate of dishonor that states that a draft was presented for acceptance or payment and was dishonored, together with the reasons given for refusal to accept or pay, made under the hand and seal of a United States consul or notary public. Today, under the revised (1990) UCC, a protest is no longer required but may still be used.

quick quiz 17-4

1. Indorsers never have liability to pay.   true | false
2. Presentment can be made by oral, written, or electronic communication.   true | false
3. Notice of dishonor must be given by nonbank holders to indorsers within 30 days following the day of dishonor.   true | false

Summary

17.1 A holder in due course is a holder who takes the instrument for value, in good faith, without notice that it is overdue or has been dishonored, and without notice of any defenses against it or claim to it. The concept of good faith involves two basic elements: (1) honesty in fact and (2) conforming to accepted commercial practices of fairness.

17.2 Personal defenses can be used against a holder but not a holder in due course. The most common personal defenses are breach of contract, lack or failure of consideration, fraud in the inducement, lack of delivery, and payment. Holders of consumer credit contracts who are holders in due course are subject to all claims and defenses that the buyer could use against the seller, including personal defenses.

17.3 Real defenses can be used against anyone, including a holder in due course. Real defenses are infancy and mental incompetence, illegality and duress, fraud as to the essential nature of the transaction, bankruptcy, unauthorized signature, and alteration.

17.4 Makers of notes and acceptors of drafts have an absolute liability to pay. Indorsers have a liability to pay only if an instrument is presented properly for payment, the instrument is dishonored, and proper notice of dishonor is given to the secondary party.

Key Terms

consumer credit contract, 483
dishonor, 485
failure of consideration, 479
FTC legend, 483
holder, 473
holder in due course, 473
holder in due course rule, 480
lack of consideration, 479
lack of delivery, 478
limited defenses, 478
non-delivey, 479
payment of an instrument, 480
personal defenses, 478
presentment, 485
real defenses, 481
shelter provision, 477
universal defenses, 481

Questions for Review and Discussion

1. What are the characteristics of being a holder in due course?
2. What special protection is given to a holder in due course?
3. What is a holder?
4. What protection is given to a holder through a holder in due course?
5. What are the six personal defenses?
6. What protection is given to people who sign consumer credit contracts?
7. What are the six real defenses and what is the significance of a real defense?
8. What is primary liability?
9. What is secondary liability?
10. What conditions must be met to hold a secondary party liable?

Cases for Analysis

1. Without authority to do so, Allen signed Baker's name on a note, promising to pay Cohen $5,000 in 30 days. The note was negotiated to Davidson who was a holder in due course. Will Davidson be successful in recovering the $5,000 from Baker in court? Why or why not?

2. Refrigerated Transport Co. Inc. employed a collection agency to collect some of its overdue accounts. The collection agency indorsed, without authority, checks made payable to Refrigerated Transport and deposited them in the agency's own checking account. Was the bank that accepted the checks for deposit a holder in due course? Why or why not? [See: *Nat'l Bank v. Refrigerated Transp.*, 248 S.E.2d 496 (GA).]

3. Andersen entered into a franchise agreement with Great Lake Nursery, under which Andersen was to grow and sell nursery stock and Christmas trees. Great Lake was to provide trees, chemicals, and other items. Andersen signed an installment note that read in part, "For value received, Robert Andersen promises to pay to Great Lake Nursery Corp. $6,412." Great Lake indorsed the note and transferred it to First Investment Company. Later, Andersen stopped making payments because Great Lake filed bankruptcy and failed to perform its part of the franchise agreement. May Andersen use failure of consideration as a defense when sued by First Investment Company on the note? Why or why not? [See: *First Inv. Co. v. Andersen*, 621 P.2d 683 (UT).]

4. In exchange for an asphalt paving job, Paulick gave Bucci a note promising to pay to the order of Bucci $7,593 in six months with 10 percent per annum interest. Payment was not made on the due date, and Bucci brought suit. Paulick used failure of consideration as a defense, claiming that the paving job was improperly done. The court held that Bucci was a holder in due course because he had taken the instrument for value, in good faith, and without notice of any claims or defenses of Paulick's. Could Paulick use the defense of failure of consideration against Bucci? Why or why not? [See: *Bucci v. Paulick*, 149 A.2d 1255 (PA).]

5. Carolyn Brazil wrote a check to a contractor who agreed to make certain improvements on her home. She wrote the check in reliance on the contractor's false representation that the materials for the job

had been purchased, when in fact, they had not. Brazil had the bank on which the check was drawn stop payment on it. Another bank, which cashed the check and became a holder in due course of the instrument, attempted to recover the amount of the check from Brazil. Could it do so? Explain. [See: *Citizens Nat'l Bank v. Brazil*, 233 S.E.2d 482 (GA).]

6. As part of the purchase price for a 9,040-acre ranch, Kirby gave Bergfield a $20,000 check drawn on the Bank of Bellevue. Bergfield had her banker telephone the Bank of Bellevue to inquire about Kirby's account balance to be sure that the check was good. It was learned that there was not enough money in Kirby's account to cover the check. Bergfield continued to hold the check and did not present it to the Bank of Bellevue for payment. Later, Bergfield argued that the telephone call to the bank was a presentment and demand for payment of the check. Do you agree? Why or why not? [See: *Kirby v. Bergfield*, 182 N.W.2d 205 (NE).]

7. Haik transferred his stock in Petrocomp, an oil exploration company, to Rowley in exchange for five $10,000 promissory notes. The notes were signed by Rowley and indorsed by Rowley's son, Stephen. Rowley failed to pay the notes when they became due. No presentment for payment was made by Haik on the due date, nor was a timely notice of dishonor given to Rowley's son, Stephen. Could Haik hold Stephen liable on the notes as an indorser? Explain. [See: *Haik v. Rowley*, 377 So.2d 391 (LA).]

8. David and Nettie Weiner signed seven promissory notes, totaling $89,000, in their capacity as president and secretary of NMD Realty Co. In addition, they indorsed each note on the reverse side with their individual signatures. Each note contained the following provision: "The Maker and indorser or indorsers each hereby waives presentment, demand, and notice of dishonor." The Weiners claimed that because they are secondarily liable, the bank may not proceed against them individually until after presentment, notice of dishonor, and protest have occurred. Do you agree with the Weiners? Explain. [See: *Bank of Delaware v. NMD Realty Co.*, 325 A.2d 108 (DE).]

9. Rutherford purchased real property from Ethel Stokes for $35,000. He paid $5,000 down and signed a promissory note for the balance. The note was secured by a deed of trust (a type of security interest, discussed in detail in Chapter 31). When payments on the note were overdue, Stokes considered foreclosing on the property. Prior to doing so, however, she negotiated the note to Craig, who purchased it at a discount with notice that it was in default. Was Craig a holder in due course of the note? Why or why not? [See: *Matter of Marriage of Rutherford*, 573 S.W.2d 299 (TX).]

10. Bolton wrote a check for $20,000 to his daughter, Joyce, intending to make a gift. The check was drawn on the State Bank of Wapello and mailed to Joyce in Maryland, where she was living. Joyce received the check, indorsed it, and mailed it to her bank in Baltimore with instructions to use it to establish a certificate of deposit in joint tenancy with her father. Was Joyce a holder in due course of the check? Explain. [See: *Matter of Estate of Bolton*, 444 N.W.2d 482 (IA).]

Design Elements: The Opening Case: ©Sharpstock/Alamy; A Classic Case: ©Evlakhov Valeriy/ Shutterstock

quick quiz Answers

17-1	17-2	17-3	17-4
1. T	1. F	1. T	1. F
2. F	2. F	2. F	2. T
3. T	3. T	3. F	3. T

Chapter 18

Bank–Depositor Relationships and Cyber-Banking

18-1 The Bank–Depositor Relationship
The Bank's Duties • The Depositor's Duties • Stop-Payment Rights • Insured Accounts

18-2 Bank Deposits and Collections
Bank Descriptions • A Check's Life Cycle

18-3 Cyber-Banking
The Check 21 Act • Electronic Fund Transfers • The Electronic Fund Transfer Act • The Global Financial Cyber-Crisis • The Cyber Doomsday Network

THE OPENING CASE Round 1
Forge My Signature Once, Shame on You. Forge My Signature 64 Times, Shame on Me.

Spacemakers of America Incorporated (SAI) hired Jenny Triplett (Triplett) without asking about her previous jobs and without doing a background check. This was an ill-advised move because, as it turned out, Triplett was out on probation from a forgery conviction for 13 counts of forgery in the first degree and from convictions for theft by taking and theft by deception. Had someone taken the time to conduct such a check, the officers at SAI would never had found themselves caught up in the problems that ensued.

Ironically, Triplett was hired as a bookkeeper for SAI. Her job was to handle the corporation's checkbook. Her responsibilities included working with financial reports and reconciling the corporate checkbook with the statements that SAI received from SunTrust Bank each month. Triplett reported directly to Dennis Rose, the CEO of SAI. On a regular basis, she would meet with Rose to present him with invoices and payroll records. Rose would review the invoices and tell Triplett which ones to pay. Following those instructions, she would make out the checks and hand them to Rose for his signature. No one at SAI ever double-checked her work. No one ever looked over her financial reports. No one ever examined the checkbook. In point of fact, she was virtually on her own.

A few weeks after getting the job, Triplett pulled her first con. As a test run, she forged Rose's name on a check for $3,000 (a modest amount based on her later activity) and made it payable to the Triple M Entertainment Group (TriM), a firm owned and operated by her husband. No one at SAI noticed anything amiss. Emboldened by her success, she began to churn out checks like there was no tomorrow. After only one month on the job, she managed to forge five more checks totaling some $22,320.00. Fifty-nine additional forged checks went to TriM, for a total of $475,000. Through all of this time, no one at SAI ever noticed that anything was amiss. Meanwhile, back at the bank, a loss-prevention officer became suspicious when she examined a check from SAI for $30,000 made payable to TriM. Dutifully, she faxed Rose a copy of the check and called him to make a report. Recognizing that the check was a forgery, Rose contacted the local authorities immediately, who arrested Triplett on the spot. About one month after the forged check had been discovered by SunTrust, SAI asked the bank to make good on the $523,100.03 worth of forged checks that the bank had erroneously honored. The bank officers were aghast and pointed out, with some degree of accuracy, that SAI had not notified the bank about the forgeries in a timely manner, which violated both SAI's contract with SunTrust and UCC 3-406 and 4-406.

SAI brought a lawsuit against SunTrust for negligence, conversion, and the unauthorized payment of a series of forged checks. SunTrust filed a motion for a summary judgment, which the trial court granted. On appeal, SAI argued that the granting of the summary judgment motion had been contrary to law because the court had badly misinterpreted and misapplied UCC 4-406. In the alternative, SAI argued that SunTrust had failed to use ordinary care in the processing of checks. Also in the alternative, if SAI could not recover the full $523,100.03, it should still be permitted to recover $30,670, a figure equal to what SAI had lost within the statutory grace period of 30 days as prescribed by law.

Here are some of the questions that must be answered before this case is ready for judicial determination. What are the duties that exist between a bank and its customers? Can a bank add provisions to its own contract with its customers that create new protections not provided by law? What duties are imposed on a bank's clients under UCC 4-406? Curious? Then, please read on. [See: *Spacemakers of America Inc. v. Suntrust Bank*, No: A04A2080 (Court of Appeals of Georgia) (January 21, 2005).]

Opening Case Questions

1. What is a bank? Explain.
2. Is a bank a creditor or a debtor in relation to its customers? Explain.
3. What stipulations, if any, are placed on the banks duty to honor all checks drawn by its customers? Explain.
4. Do depositors have a duty to examine the bank statements that they receive from the bank? Explain.
5. How much time does a depositor have to report an alleged forgery? Explain.

Source: See: *Spacemakers of America Inc. v. Suntrust Bank*, No: A04A2080 (Court of Appeals of Georgia) (January 21, 2005).

 Learning Objectives

1. Clarify the bank's duties in the bank–depositor relationship.
2. Clarify the depositor's duties in the bank–depositor relationship.
3. Explain a drawer's rights in relation to a stop-payment order.
4. Explain the extent of the insurance protection provided by the FDIC.
5. List the different terms used to describe banks during the bank collection process.
6. Outline a check's life cycle.
7. Describe the principal features of the Check 21 Act.
8. Describe the consumer protection features of the Check 21 Act.
9. Describe the process of an electronic fund transfer.
10. Discuss the protection given to consumers by the Electronic Fund Transfer Act.

18-1 The Bank–Depositor Relationship

We all believe that we know a bank when we see one. Banks are those respectable-looking buildings with drive-through windows and ATM machines outside and huge, heavy-duty vault doors inside. Right? Well, not always. The Uniform Commercial Code, requires us to stretch our imagination a bit and to expand our understanding of the nature of a bank. A bank, the UCC tells us is "any person engaged in the business of banking" (UCC Section 1-201 [4]). That doesn't help very much, now does it? So, let's think about it. Given this definition then, if an institution collects money from its clients, provides those clients with checking accounts, issues checkbooks to those clients for use with those accounts, identifies its clients by signature cards that the clients have voluntarily completed, sends customers statements about those accounts, and pays out money from those accounts based on the orders contained within checks that are made out by and signed by those clients, then, by

UCC 4-201*
UCC 4-212

and large, that institution is a bank—period. Whether it resides in a big fancy stone building, in a store front in a shopping center, or at the entrance to a discount mega-store seems to make no difference. In fact, this interpretation of the term *bank* is clearly in line with the objectives of the UCC, which, like almost any code, must simplify, clarify, and modernize the law, in this case, "the law of commercial transactions" (UCC Section 1-102 [2] [a]).

Banks do tend to live double lives. For instance, at times the relationship between the drawee bank and its customer is that of debtor on one side and creditor on the other. At other times, that relationship exists simultaneously as both agent and principal. Often the bank–customer relationship arises out of an express contract written in fine print legalese, but just as often, it emerges from an implied contract that occurs simply because a customer has opened a checking account with the bank. The bank becomes a debtor when money is

THE OPENING CASE Round 2
Forge My Signature Once, Shame on You. Forge My Signature 64 Times, Shame on Me.

Recall that in the Opening Case, Jenny Triplett got a job as a bookkeeper at Spacemakers of America Inc. As a bookkeeper, Triplett was responsible for handling SAI's checkbook. Her job involved working with financial reports and reconciling the corporate checkbook with the statements that SAI received from SunTrust Bank each month. Triplett reported directly to Dennis Rose, the president of SAI. Triplett met with Rose to go over the invoices from vendors each month. She would present Rose with the invoices, and Rose would then tell her which invoices to pay. After this meeting, Triplett would make out the checks and have Rose sign them. No one at SAI ever looked at her work or examined the checkbook. A little while after getting the job, Triplett forged Rose's name on a check for $3,000 and made it payable to the Triple M Entertainment Group (TriM), a corporation owned by her husband. Soon after this, Triplett managed to forge five new checks amounting to some $22,320.00 followed by 59 additional checks for a grand total of $475,000. Meanwhile, back at the bank, a SunTrust loss-prevention officer became suspicious when she examined a check from SAI for $30,000 made payable to TriM. To follow up on her suspicions she faxed Rose a copy of the check. Rose instantly saw that the check was forged. He contacted the local authorities immediately, who arrested Triplett on the spot. About one month after the forged check had been discovered by SunTrust, SAI asked the bank to make good on the $523,100.03 worth of forged checks that the bank had erroneously honored.

SAI based its request on the fundamental relationship that exists between a bank and its customer. Of course, that relationship is not simple. On the contrary, it is highly complex even when we are dealing with a single customer and a single bank. In this case, for example, the relationship is not as straightforward as it sounds. It is, in fact, a complex, multilayered relationship filled with many possible traps and pitfalls. Now recall that the relationship between the drawee bank and its customer is that of both debtor and creditor and agent and principal. The relationship arises out of the express or implied contract that occurs when the customer opens a checking account with the bank. The bank becomes a debtor when money is deposited in the bank by the customer. That means that, when the bank is called upon to pay out a certain amount of money to a third party, then it had better well do so. In this case, the bank, SunTrust, acted as a debtor that had been ordered by its creditor, SAI, to pay a third party, TRiM, a certain amount of money from its account. The problem was that the order was delivered by a party, Triplett, who had forfeited her role as a corporate agent in exchange for the ready cash that was obtained when the false check was paid to TriM by SunTrust. This much is easy enough to understand. What is problematic is the question about who should be legally responsible for the lost money: the company that allowed the forger to plunder its account or the bank that failed to find the error as the previous 63 checks passed through its hands. Curious? Well continue reading. [See: *Spacemakers of America Inc. v. Suntrust Bank*, No: A04A2080 (Court of Appeals of Georgia) (January 21, 2005).]

Source: See: *Spacemakers of America Inc. v. Suntrust Bank*, No: A04A2080 (Court of Appeals of Georgia) (January 21, 2005).

deposited in the bank by the customer. At this time, the customer is owed money by the bank and is, therefore, a creditor. When an **overdraft** occurs—that is, when the bank pays out more than the customer has on deposit—the debtor-creditor role reverses, and the bank becomes the creditor. The bank acts as the customer's agent when it collects or attempts to collect checks or other negotiable instruments made payable to the customer. If the items are deposited in the customer's account, any settlement made by the bank with the customer is provisional. A provisional settlement may be revoked by the bank if an item that the bank is attempting to collect is dishonored. The bank may charge back the amount of any credit given for the item to its customer's account or obtain a refund from its customer.

The Bank's Duties

The bank owes a duty to its depositors to honor orders and to protect funds. However, these duties carry strict limitations.

UCC 4-401*
UCC 4-402

Duty to Honor Orders The drawee bank is under a duty to honor all checks drawn by its customers when there are sufficient funds on deposit in the customer's account. If there are insufficient funds on deposit, the bank may charge the customer's account even if it creates an overdraft. If a bank fails to honor a check because of a mistake on its part, the bank is liable to the customer for any actual damages the customer suffers. The drawee bank has no liability to the holder of the check, however, unless it is certified.

EXAMPLE 18-1: Bank's Liability Extends to Actual Damages Only

Rougier, who had $178 in her checking account, wrote a check for $78.42 and mailed it to the electric company in payment of a telephone bill. Due to a mistake on its part, Rougier's bank dishonored the check and returned it to the electric company marked "insufficient funds." As soon as the error was discovered, the electric company was notified, and the check was redeposited and honored by the bank. Because Rougier suffered no loss, the bank was not liable for dishonoring the check. Had Rougier's electricity been disconnected because of the dishonored check, the bank would have been liable to her for the cost of restoring service. The bank was not liable to the electric company.

A bank is under no obligation to a customer to pay a stale check unless it is certified. A **stale check** is a check that is presented for payment more than six months after its date. A bank, however, may honor a stale check without liability to its customer if it acts in good faith.

UCC 4-404

EXAMPLE 18-2: Bank Must Act in Good Faith

The Chemical Bank paid a check that had been written by New York Flameproofing Co. 10 years earlier on a check form no longer used by that company. The account on which the check was drawn had been closed for seven years, and the company's address written on the check had changed seven years earlier. In holding against the bank for paying the check, the court said that such payment was a reckless disregard of due care, so much as to constitute bad faith. The bank was liable for the amount paid.

The drawee bank is not liable to a holder of a check for dishonoring the instrument unless it is certified. The holder's recourse is against the drawer or indorsers on their secondary liability.

UCC 4-405

Death or Incompetence of Customer The drawee bank is not liable for the payment of a check before it has notice of the death or incompetence of the drawer. In any event, a bank may pay or certify checks for 10 days after the date of death of the drawer. This rule permits holders of checks that are drawn shortly before the drawer's death to cash them without the necessity of filing a claim with the court handling the deceased's estate.

Forged and Altered Checks A *forgery* is the fraudulent making or alteration of a writing. A forgery is committed when a person fraudulently writes or alters a check or other form of negotiable instrument to the injury of another. The commission of forgery is a crime, subject to a fine and imprisonment. The offering of a forged instrument to another person when the offeror knows it to be forged is also a crime, known as *uttering*. If a bank, in good faith, pays the altered amount of a check to a holder, it may deduct from the drawer's account only the amount of the check as it was originally written. The depositor is also protected against a signature being forged. When a checking account is opened, the depositor must fill out a signature card, which is permanently filed at the bank. Thereafter, the bank is held to know the depositor's signature. The bank is liable to the depositor if it pays any check on which the depositor's signature has been forged.

Despite this list of depositor rights, the banks are not without protection against forgery. For example, banks still control the contractual relationship that exists with their customers and can, thus, add a clause or two that protects them against certain types of forgery. For instance, a bank can add a clause to a contract stipulating that it will not be liable for forgeries that result from the customer's use of a facsimile or a nonmanual signature. So, if a customer uses a rubber stamp facsimile of his or her signature, as is a common practice among corporate executives, and that stamp is used in a forgery scheme, the bank would not be liable. This is a contractual matter, however, making it something that the customer agrees to when he or she opens an account with that bank. If the customer is unhappy with that treatment, he or she is free to shop around for a bank that makes no such stipulation on their contracts.

THE OPENING CASE Round 3
Forge My Signature Once, Shame on you. Forge My Signature 64 Times, Shame on Me.

The Opening Case laid out the following set of facts. SAI hired Jenny Triplett to handle the corporation's checkbook. This meant that she was responsible for reconciling the corporate checkbook with the statements that SAI received from SunTrust Bank. As part of her job, she also paid the bills under the direction of the president of SAI, Dennis Rose. Rose would review the invoices and then tell Triplett which invoices to pay. A few weeks into her employment at SAI, Triplett forged Rose's name on a check for $3,000 and made it payable to TriM, a firm owned and operated by her husband. From that point on, her career as a forger blossomed. After one month, she had managed to forge five more checks totaling some $22,320.00. Fifty-nine additional forged checks went to TriM for a total of $475,000. A little while later, a SunTrust a loss-prevention officer did not like the looks of a check from SAI for $30,000 made payable to TriM. Following protocol, she faxed Rose a copy of the check. Recognizing that the check was a forgery, Rose contacted the local authorities immediately, who arrested Triplett. About one month after the forged check had been discovered by SunTrust, SAI asked the bank to make good on the $523,100.03 worth of forged checks that the bank had erroneously honored. The bank officers pointed out, with some degree of accuracy, that SAI had not notified the bank about the forgeries in a timely manner, which violated both SAI's contract with SunTrust and UCC 3-406 and 4-406.

SAI brought a lawsuit against SunTrust for negligence, conversion, and the unauthorized payment of a series of forged checks. SunTrust filed a motion for a summary judgment, which the trial court granted. On appeal, SAI argued that the granting of the summary judgment motion had been contrary to law because (1) the court had badly misinterpreted and misapplied UCC 4-406; (2) Suntrust had failed to use ordinary care in the processing of the checks; (3) if SAI could not recover the full $523,100.03, it should still be permitted to recover $30,670, a figure equal to what SAI had lost within the statutory grace period of 30 days as prescribed by law; and (4) under common law, SunTrust had been negligent, had wrongly converted property belonging to SAI, and had breached other statutory duties that it owed to SAI.

Let's take a look at these claims to see how SAI fared. First, the court says, rather unequivocally, that SAI is wrong about UCC 4-406, and second, the court says that SAI is incorrect about its ordinary care claim under UCC 4-406. We shall look at these two claims in the Opening Case, *Round 3*, so let's move on to the other claims. In handling the remainder of claim 2, the court takes an interesting tact. It notes that even if SAI is correct about its claim that SunTrust did not use ordinary care under provisions of the UCC (which is not, by the way, correct), the bank also engineered its own terms in a contract with SAI, regardless of what UCC 4-406 says. Moreover, that contract expressly states that because the customer is in the best position to spot a forgery, the customer is responsible for reviewing canceled checks, examining the signatures, and promptly notifying the bank of any problems. As for claim 3 that SAI should still be permitted to recover $30,670, a figure equal to what SAI had lost within the statutory grace period of 30 days as prescribed by law, the court rules that "under . . . 4-406(d), a customer's failure to timely report a wrongdoer's first forgery precludes it from recovering for any subsequent forgery by the same wrongdoer. This is true even if the subsequent forgery is discovered and timely reported to the bank pursuant to . . . 4-406(c)." Finally, in relation to the claim 4—that is, the common law claims of negligence, conversion, and breach of other statutory duties—the court concludes the case rather abruptly saying, "there is no evidence in the record of this case to support these claims." That, it would seem, would be that. (Well, not quite; we must still look at those UCC 4-406 claims. So, once again, read on and on . . . and on.) [See: *Spacemakers of America Inc. v. Suntrust Bank*, No: A04A2080 (Court of Appeals of Georgia) (January 21, 2005).]

Source: See: *Spacemakers of America Inc. v. Suntrust Bank*, No: A04A2080 (Court of Appeals of Georgia) (January 21, 2005).

On the other hand, banks sometimes put themselves at risk by permitting tellers to cash checks without verifying the depositor's signature. Many, perhaps most, banks actually have a formal policy in place that permits their tellers to cash checks under $2,500 without comparing the signature on the check with the signature on file. Most of the time this works. The checks are cashed, the funds are available, the signature is genuine, the transaction is completed and, most of all, the customer is pleased with bank's overall efficiency. When it does not work and a forged check slips through, the bank is responsible. In the long run, however, the amount of money saved by permitting the tellers to cash checks without verification far outweighs the amount of money lost on the occasional forgery.

Availability of Funds In the past, banks were not uniform in the amount of time they required before they would make funds available to their depositors. Some banks held funds longer than others, and many banks did not disclose their holding policy to their customers.

To address the issue, Congress passed the Competitive Banking Act. Under the act, the Federal Reserve Board of Governors issued Regulation CC, which requires banks to make funds available to depositors according to a prescribed schedule (Table 18-1). With exceptions, funds from checks drawn on the U.S. Treasury or any state or local government and any bank draft, cashier's check, or postal money order must be made available on the next business day following the banking day of deposit; funds from checks drawn on banks within the same Federal Reserve district must be made available within two business days following the banking day of deposit; and funds from checks drawn on banks outside the bank's Federal Reserve district must be made available within five

Table 18-1 Availability of Funds (under $5,000) You Deposit in Your Bank

Type of Check	Funds Must Be Made Available for Withdrawal
"On us" check [drawn on your bank]	1st business day* after the banking day† of deposit
Local check (except $100‡) [drawn on a bank in same check-processing region]	2nd business day* after the banking day† of deposit
Nonlocal (except $100‡) [drawn on a bank in a different check-processing region]	5th business day* after the banking day† of deposit
Electronic payment	1st business day* after the banking day† of deposit
Cashier's check	1st business day* after the banking day† of deposit
Certified check	1st business day* after the banking day of deposit
Government check	1st business day* after the banking day† of deposit
U.S. Postal Service money order	1st business day* after the banking day† of deposit

*Monday through Friday except most federal holidays.

†Any business day (up to the bank's cut-off hour) when the bank is open for substantially all of its banking activities.

‡The first $100 (or the total amount of the deposit if less than $100) must be made available on the 1st business day after the banking day of deposit.

business days following the banking day of deposit. A *business day* is defined under Regulation CC as Monday through Friday, except for most federal holidays. A *banking day* is any business day (up to the bank's cut-off hour) when the bank is open for substantially all of its banking activities.

EXAMPLE 18-3: Fund Availability

Edna Chase deposited a $500 local check that was payable to her in her bank at 3:00 P.M. on Monday. The bank's cut-off hour for the day's transactions was 2:00 P.M. Because the deposit was made after the bank's cut-off hour, it was considered received on Tuesday. The first $100 must be made available to Chase by Wednesday, and the remaining $400 must be made available by Thursday, the second business day after the banking day of deposit.

Exceptions are made for new accounts, deposits greater than $5,000, accounts that are repeatedly overdrawn, deposits of a suspicious nature, and emergency conditions. In addition, some state laws require even shorter time periods for banks to make funds available. Regulation CC also requires banks to disclose in advance their policy for making funds available to depositors. Such disclosures must be made when the account is initially opened and on conspicuously visible notices at teller stations in the bank.

Midnight Deadline Payor banks are required to either settle or return checks quickly. If they do not do so, they are responsible for paying them. If the payor bank is not the depositary bank, it must settle for an item by midnight of the banking day of receipt.

EXAMPLE 18-4: Bank's Midnight Deadline

LaPierre wrote a check to Kimberly Motors for $2,500 in payment for a secondhand car. The payor of the check (the bank on which it was drawn) was the National Bank & Trust Co. Kimberly Motors deposited the check into its account in the Southwest Mutual Bank (the depositary bank), which sent it on for collection. LaPierre's car broke down before she reached home that evening. She immediately stopped payment on the check. The National Bank & Trust Company must return the check to the Southwest Mutual Bank, with a notation that payment has been stopped, before midnight of the day that it received the check. If it keeps the check longer than that, it will be liable for payment.

If the payor bank is also the depositary bank, it must either pay or return the check or send notice of its dishonor on or before its midnight deadline. In this case, the bank's **midnight deadline** is midnight of the next banking day following the banking day on which it receives the relevant item.

UCC 4-104(h)

EXAMPLE 18-5: Longer Deadline for Depository Bank

If the National Bank & Trust Company in Example 18-4 had also been the depositary bank, it would have had an extra day to handle the check. The bank would have had until midnight of the next banking day to return the check to Kimberly Motors with the notation that payment had been stopped.

The Depositor's Duties

Depositors, in general, owe a duty to the banks in which they have checking accounts to have sufficient funds on deposit to cover checks that they write. They must also examine their bank statements and canceled checks promptly and with reasonable care and notify the bank quickly of any discrepancies.

Bad Checks Most states have statutes making it larceny or attempted larceny for a person to issue a check drawn on a bank in which the person has insufficient funds. Such statutes usually have the following provisions that must be observed in the prosecution of anyone issuing a *bad check*, sometimes called an *NSF check*: The payee has the obligation of informing the drawer of the nonpayment of the check, together with notice of the provisions of the bad-check law and of the party's legal rights and obligations. After receiving notice of nonpayment, or dishonor, the drawer is given a specified number of days, usually 5 or 10, in which to make the check good, without fear of prosecution. Failure to make full payment of the check within the number of days allowed by statute serves as presumption of guilt that the drawer issued the check with full knowledge of the facts and with intent to defraud.

Banks and their customers must both perform their responsibilities properly for the system to function effectively.
©Ryan McVay/Getty Images

> ### EXAMPLE 18-6: Bad Check Notice
> State National Bank received Yoder's check for $120 due on an installment note it held. After it was deposited, the check was returned to State National with the notification "insufficient funds." The bank's collection department sent a certified letter to Yoder, which explained his responsibility under the bad-check statute. Failure on the part of Yoder to make the check good within the period of time indicated would result in a criminal complaint being lodged against Yoder through the office of the state's prosecuting attorney.

UCC 4-406

Bad-check statutes are effectively used as a means of collection. Most bad-check writers make an effort to make full payment of the check when advised that they are subject to prosecution. Many banks offer overdraft protection service to their depositors, which covers small overdrafts that are usually caused by the mistake of the drawer in balancing the checkbook. This service is important under the Check 21 Act because checks may have a shorter float time than in the past. With this service, the bank honors small overdrafts and charges the depositor's account. This service saves the drawer the inconvenience and embarrassment of having a check returned to a holder marked "insufficient funds."

Duty to Examine Accounts The UCC imposes a duty on depositors to examine their bank statements and canceled checks promptly and with reasonable care when they are received from the bank. In the past, banks returned the canceled checks to their customers so that they could verify the authenticity of those checks and then balance their statements properly. Today, as we shall see shortly, as a standard operating procedure, banks send an electronic accounting to their customers. Banks will still send the paper checks to a customer if a customer demands that service; however, the bank will also charge the customer for that service. The electronic record that is sent to the customer will include the check number, the date the check was issued, and the amount charged to the customer's account. If, however, the customer pays bills online or has an automatic bill-paying plan in place, the bank statements will show the payees for each withdrawal.

Under common law, bank customers were responsible for examining bank statements to make certain that no forgeries passed through the bank undetected. The responsibility is based on the belief that the customer should know his or her signature better than anyone else, especially bank tellers who sometimes see dozens of signatures each day. This duty was codified when the UCC was finalized. The UCC provision reads in part, "Without regard to care or lack of care of either the customer or the bank, a customer who does not within one year after the statement or items are made available to the customer (subsection (a)) discover and report the customer's unauthorized signature on or any alteration on the item is precluded from asserting against the bank the unauthorized signature or alteration" (UCC 4-406[f]). The UCC also contains a provision that states, in the case of the same wrongdoer forging or altering more than one check, the bank must be notified of the wrongdoing within 30 days after the statement is made available to the depositor. The problem is that these duties only work if the person responsible for checking the bank statements is not the person making the forgeries, as happened in the following case.

THE OPENING CASE Round 4
Forge My Signature Once, Shame on You. Forge My Signature 64 Times, Shame on Me.

Let's look at the Opening Case one final time. Remember that Jenny Triplett was hired by SAI. No one at SAI asked about her employment record or made any effort to conduct a criminal background check. This was a mistake because Triplett was out on probation from a conviction for 13 counts of forgery in the first degree and from convictions for theft by taking and theft by deception. Interestingly enough, Triplet got a job at SAI as a bookkeeper. Her duties included reconciling the corporate checkbook with the statements that SAI received from the SunTrust Bank each month. Triplett reported to Dennis Rose, the president of the corporation. Monthly, she would present Rose with invoices, and Rose would tell Triplett which invoices to pay. Triplett then made out the checks and handed them to Rose for his signature. No one at SAI ever checked her financial reports or the checkbook. A few weeks after getting the job, Triplett forged Rose's name on a check for $3,000 and made it payable to TriM, her husband's company. No one at SAI seems to have noticed that anything was wrong. Satisfied that her scheme was working, Triplett accelerated her campaign. After one month as bookkeeper, she had successfully forged five more checks totaling some $22,320.00. Fifty-nine additional forged checks went to TriM for a total of $475,000. Then the door began to slam. A loss-prevention officer at SunTrust became suspicious when she examined a check from SAI for $30,000, made payable to TriM. She followed protocol and faxed Rose a copy of the check. Recognizing that the check was a forgery, Rose contacted the local authorities immediately, who arrested Triplett, ending her criminal career, at least temporarily.

About one month after the forged check had been discovered by SunTrust, SAI asked the bank to make good on the $523,100.03 worth of forged checks that the bank had erroneously honored. The bank officers would have none of this. They noted with confidence that SAI had not notified the bank about the forgeries in a timely manner, violating both SAI's contract with SunTrust and UCC 3-406 and 4-406. Undeterred by this clear rejection of its request, SAI brought a lawsuit against SunTrust for negligence, conversion, and the unauthorized payment of a series of forged checks. SunTrust filed a motion for a summary judgment, which the trial court granted. Still undeterred, on appeal SAI argued that the granting of the summary judgment motion had been a mistake because (1) the court had misinterpreted and misapplied UCC 4-406; (2) Suntrust had failed to use ordinary care in the processing of the checks; (3) if SAI could not recover the full $523,100.03, it should still be granted a partial recovery of $30,670; and (4) under common law, SunTrust had been negligent, had wrongly converted property belonging to SAI, and had breached other statutory duties that it owed to SAI.

In the Opening Case, *Round 3*, we covered the court's response to claims 3 and 4, so let's move back to claims 1 and 2. Here is what the court decided. The court rejected SAI's first argument that the trial court had misinterpreted UCC 4-406. On the contrary, the appellate court seems to believe that trial court did an admirable job in its interpretation of the statute. The appeals court notes that the rule expressly stated in UCC 4-406, "imposes upon a bank customer the duty to promptly examine its monthly statements and notify the bank of any unauthorized transaction. If the customer fails to report the first forged item within 30 days, it is precluded from recovering for that transaction and for any additional items forged by the same wrongdoer."[1] Because SAI had neither examined the checks nor notified the bank, it cannot recover from SunTrust. That is it, pure and simple. As for SAI's second argument, the court finds no merit in SAI's claim that SunTrust had failed to use ordinary care in the processing of SAI's checks. In fact, it seems that SunTrust went above and beyond what was practiced by other banks in the Atlanta area.

To prove its point, the court begins with the statutory definition of ordinary care as established by the UCC. Specifically, UCC 3-107 states, "'[o]rdinary care' in the case of a person engaged in business means observance of reasonable commercial standards, prevailing in the area in which the person is located, with respect to the business in which the person is engaged." The court then reviews the testimony of Jeffrey Dalrymple, a SunTrust senior vice president, who testified that "the bank's regional operations center handles between 650,000 and 1,200,000 checks per day, and its fraud detection software, ASI/16, is 'an industry standard and one of the most sophisticated rules-based fraud detection software systems available . . .' Further, commercial checks for $20,000 or greater are automatically reviewed and verified by SunTrust employees." Dalrymple concluded that "SunTrust's standards with respect to thresholds for sight inspection of checks drawn on commercial accounts not only meet but are in fact more stringent than the standards for sight inspection of such checks among other banks in the Atlanta, Georgia area and are in observance and in fact exceed reasonable commercial standards."[2] Significantly, SAI's expert could produce no evidence to refute the testimony presented by SunTrust's expert. Accordingly, the court pf appeals upheld the trial court's granting of SunTrust's summary judgment. End of case—period. [See: *Spacemakers of America Inc. v. Suntrust Bank*, No: A04A2080 (Court of Appeals of Georgia) (January 21, 2005).]

Source: See: Spacemakers of America Inc. v. Suntrust Bank, No: A04A2080 (Court of Appeals of Georgia) (January 21, 2005).

UCC 4-401(c)

Antedated and Postdated Checks

A check may be antedated or postdated. It is antedated when it is written and dated on one day and delivered later. A check is postdated when the drawer delivers it before its stated date. However, a bank may charge a postdated check against a customer's account unless the customer has notified the bank of the postdated check within a reasonable time for the bank to act on it. Any such notice by a customer to a bank is effective for the same time periods allowed for stop-payment orders, discussed subsequently. If a check is undated, its date is the date that it was first given to someone.

Stop-Payment Rights

UCC 4-403
UCC 4-403(3)

Drawers may order a bank to stop payment on any item payable on their account. The stop-payment order must be received in time and in such a manner as to afford the bank a reasonable opportunity to act on it. An oral order is binding upon the bank for 14 calendar days only, unless confirmed in writing within that period. A written order is binding for only six months, unless renewed in writing. The burden of establishing the fact and amount of loss resulting from the payment of an item contrary to a binding order to stop payment is on the customer.

A SOON TO BE CLASSIC CASE When Is a Depositor Liable?

When Arthur Woods passed away, he left an annuity payable to his wife, Dorothy. Mrs. Woods directed her attorney, Cornelius Collins, to have the insurance company, MONY Legacy Life, pay the annuity in a single payment. MONY deposited $24,900 into a MONY checking account made out to Mrs. Woods. MONY delivered the checkbook to Collins according to his instructions. Mrs. Woods was sent a statement that informed her of this transaction. Shortly after, MONY also received a change of address request that asked that all future correspondence on Mrs. Woods's MONY account be sent to Collins. MONY agreed to do so and notified Mrs. Woods of the change. During the next four months, Mrs. Woods's signature was forged on six unauthorized checks that totaled $24,448.91, effectively draining most of the funds in the account. Five months' worth of statements were sent to Collins that showed the forged drafts. Mrs. Woods, however, has stated that she did not even know about the MONY account until more than a year after it was opened in her name. At that time, she asked MONY for copies of the account and the allegedly forged checks. More than four months after receiving this information, she informed MONY that her signature had been forged. She then asked for her money back and MONY refused. Mrs. Woods brought a lawsuit against MONY. Almost immediately, MONY filed a summary judgment motion to dismiss, which the trial court granted and the court of appeals upheld. The case then went to the state supreme court.

Now, as we have just seen, under the UCC, a bank is strictly liable whenever it takes money from a customer's account based on a forged check. However, under UCC Section 4-406, the bank customer, Mrs. Woods in this case, also has a duty to examine any bank statements "sent or made available" by the bank and to report any irregularities found in that statement. Mrs. Woods makes a few creative arguments here. First she contends that, the checks that are handled by MONY are actually "payable through State Street Bank and it is State Street, not MONY that should be protected by UCC Section 4-406."[3] The court disagrees noting that, "MONY, not State Street, opened Woods's account, retained the signature card, issued the checkbook, provided monthly statements and corresponded with the customer."[4] Next, Mrs. Woods argues that she did not receive her statements in a proper and timely fashion, and so the time limit did not begin to run until she actually saw the statements. Therefore, she is well within the one-year limit. At this point, the court looks at that "made available" language in the UCC and states, without hesitation, that, "the account statements were 'made available' to Woods, and the one-year period commenced, when Collins received the monthly statements." Sadly for Mrs. Woods, that ends the case. [See: *Dorothy Woods v. MONY Legacy Life Insurance Company*, b84 N.Y2d 280, 641 N.E.2d 1070, 617 N.Y.S.2d 452 (New York).]

Source: See: *Dorothy Woods v. MONY Legacy Life Insurance Company,* b84 N.Y2d 280, 641 N.E.2d 1070, 617 N.Y.S.2d 452 (New York).

Bank's Right of Subrogation If a bank fails to stop payment on a check, it is responsible for any loss suffered by the drawer who ordered the payment stopped. The bank, however, may take the place of any holder, holder in due course, payee, or drawer who has rights against others on the underlying obligation. This right to be substituted for another is known as the bank's right of **subrogation**. It is designed to prevent loss to the bank and unjust enrichment to other parties.

UCC 4-407

Insured Accounts

The Federal Deposit Insurance Corporation (FDIC) insures deposits in banks as well as in savings and loan associations. The basic insurance coverage protects individual bank accounts for up to $250,000 and joint accounts for up to an additional $250,000. Revocable trust and payable-on-death bank accounts are protected for up to $250,000 for each beneficiary named in the account records. (See Table 18-2.)

Table 18-2 How a Husband, Wife, and One Child May Have Insured Accounts Totaling $2,500,000	
Individual Accounts:	
Husband	$ 250,000
Wife	$ 250,000
Child	$ 250,000
Joint Accounts:	
Husband and Wife	$ 250,000
Husband and Child	$ 250,000
Wife and Child	$ 250,000
Revocable Trust Accounts:	
Husband as Trustee for Wife	$ 250,000
Husband as Trustee for Child	$ 250,000
Wife as Trustee for Child	$ 250,000
Wife as Trustee for Husband	$ 250,000
	$2,500,000

A CLASSIC CASE Distressed? Fear Not! At Times the Bank Must Face Reality

The case at hand involves a forgery that resulted in the plundering of an account owned by Abdul Matin and deposited at the Chase Manhattan Bank (Chase). When Matin returned to the United States after a long period overseas, he was surprised to learn that his account at Chase had been emptied. The culprit seems to have been an unknown person who managed to file a forged change of address card with Chase and to write multiple checks that resulted in the decimation of Matin's account. When Martin, understandably enough, asked for satisfaction from Chase he was, well, disappointed by the bank's refusal to do so. He then filed a lawsuit against the bank. Unperturbed, Chase filed one of those friendly neighborhood summary judgment motions arguing that the bank had "made available" statements to Matin, who did not notify them of the forgery within the one-year statute of limitations established by UCC Section 4-406. Since Matin did not live up to his duty to report the forgery, the bank was off the hook. Unbelievably, the trial court granted Chase's motion. Stunned, Matin appealed. During that appeal, irritated and confused, and with a bit of frustration ringing in his voice, Matin could be expected to say something like (we are obviously paraphrasing here), "Now wait just a darn minute. Are you telling me that, you (the bank) made these statements available to me when you mailed them to another party?" The bank says, "Sure, how were we supposed to know it was forged?"

At this point, the court of appeals steps into the argument and gently reminds the bank that since it filed the summary judgment motion in the first place, it has the burden of demonstrating that there is no genuine issue as to any material fact. The court then says something like this to Chase, "Now, do you really think that you met that burden here, because, quite frankly, we don't." Chase, however, has another argument up its sleeve. Chase contends that it supplemented the protection given to the bank by the UCC by adding a clause to its account agreement that states that the customer, Matin in this case, must promptly and thoroughly examine any and all bank statements sent to him and to tell the bank about any and all irregularities, discrepancies, errors, and so on that are involved in those statements. Moreover, the duty emerges at the moment the statement is mailed to the customer. The court finds the argument weak at best and, thus, reverses the lower court's ruling on the summary judgment motion and sends the case back down for further deliberation. [See: *Matin v. Chase Manhattan Bank*, 10 A.S. 3d 447, 781 N.Y.S. 2d 158 (2004).]

Source: See: *Matin v. Chase Manhattan Bank*, 10 A.S. 3d 447, 781 N.Y.S. 2d 158 (2004).

quick quiz 18-1

1. The bank acts as the customer's principal when it collects checks or other negotiable instruments made payable to the customer.   true | false
2. The drawee bank has no liability to the holder of a check unless it is certified.   true | false
3. The commission of forgery is a crime, subject to a fine and imprisonment.   true | false

18-2 Bank Deposits and Collections

The tremendous number of checks handled by banks and the countrywide nature of the bank collection process require uniformity in the law of bank collections. For this reason, Article 4 of the UCC* contains rules and regulations for handling bank deposits and collections.

Bank Descriptions

During the bank collection process, banks are described by different terms, depending on their particular function in a transaction. Sometimes a bank takes a check for deposit. At other times, it pays a check as a drawee. At still other times, it takes a check for collection only. The different terms that are used to describe banks and their meanings are as follows: A **depositary bank** is the first bank to which an item is transferred for collection, even if it is also the payor bank. The term **payor bank** describes a bank by which an item is payable as drawn or accepted. It includes a drawee bank. **Intermediary bank** defines any bank to which an item is transferred in the course of collection, except the depositary or payor bank. The **collecting bank** is any bank handling the item for collection, except the payor bank, and the **presenting bank** is any bank presenting an item, except a payor bank. **Remitting bank** describes any payor or intermediary bank remitting for an item.

UCC 4-105

A QUESTION OF ETHICS

Bethany Golemen was discharged from her job as an advertising executive at Farnsworth, Yardley, and Brook. Her credit cards were maxed out, her savings account depleted, and her rent was due. On the bright side, James Farnsworth, the senior partner in the advertising firm, had given Goleman a sizable severance check as she left the office on her last day. Goleman was feeling lucky until she tried to retrieve her car from the service station where Tommy Henderson had just finished fixing the brakes on her Saturn. When Goleman tried to pay by credit card her card was rejected. Henderson refused to allow her to take her car until she gave him some type of payment. To satisfy Henderson she wrote him a check for the new brakes, even though she knew that the account was empty. She fully intended to place the severance check into the account the next morning so that the check would not bounce. Unfortunately, when she arrived at her apartment, she found that the landlord had changed the locks because her rent was six months overdue. In order to get into her apartment, she signed the severance check over to the landlord. As a result, she never deposited any money in her checking account, and her check to Henderson bounced. Was it ethical for Goleman to write Henderson the check knowing there was no money in the account? Remember that, at the time she wrote the original check out to Henderson, she fully intended to place the severance check in the account the next day. From an ethical perspective, does her intent to deposit funds in her checking account tomorrow permit her to write the bad check today? Why or why not?

A Check's Life Cycle

The life cycle of a check begins when the drawer writes a check and delivers it to the payee. The payee may take the check directly to the payor bank (the bank on which it was drawn) for payment. If that bank pays the check in cash, its payment is final, and the check is returned to the drawer with the next bank statement. However, it is more likely that the check will be deposited in the payee's own account in another bank. That bank, known as the depositary bank, acts as its customer's agent to collect the money from the payor bank. Any settlement given by the depositary bank in this case is **provisional** (not final). It may be revoked if the check is later dishonored. The check is sent (sometimes through an intermediary bank) to a collecting bank, which presents the check to the payor bank for payment. If it is honored by the payor bank, the amount will be deducted from the drawer's account, and a substitute check will be returned to the drawer with the next bank statement. If the check is dishonored for any reason, a substitute check will be returned to the payee via the same route that it was sent, and all credits given for the item will be revoked (see Figure 18-1).

UCC 4-213
UCC 4-201

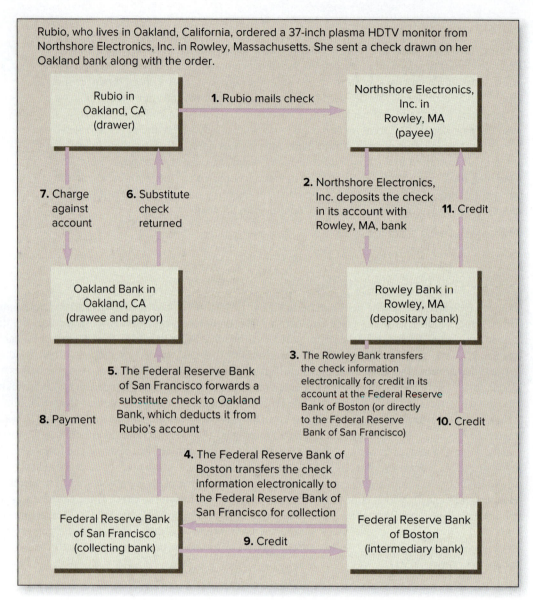

Figure 18-1 The life cycle of Rubio's check is traced through its collection and clearinghouse routes. Before the Check 21 Act became effective in October 2004, the check in this example would have had to be physically transported by plane or truck around its entire route.

18-3 Cyber-Banking

Like all of us, the world of banking has been forced to adapt to the global electronic revolution. The Internet has made the transfer of funds and the record keeping associated with those funds easier, faster, and more efficient than ever before. The new system, however, is also filled with problems. In fact, the new electronic transfer process is more precarious than the traditional process. This is because the new system is subject to hacking, viruses, identity theft, and cyber-warfare. Consequently, as is true of all parts of the social system, the banking community has been forced to interface with several new statutes designed to monitor and influence its day-to-day operation. These statutes include but are not limited to the Check 21 Act and the Electronic Fund Transfer Act.

Some banks prefer that customers use ATMs for their regular banking transactions, even featuring accounts that charge a fee for the use of live tellers.
©Andersen Ross/Getty Images

The Check 21 Act

Named for the 21st century, the **Check 21 Act** brings the check-clearing method into the modern age by the use of electronic check processing. Such processing could not be done prior to this 2004 law, because of the legal requirement that original checks be presented to the drawee bank for payment. Under this law, a new negotiable instrument called a substitute check is used. A **substitute check** (also called an *image replacement document*, or *IRD*) is a paper reproduction of both sides of an original check that can be processed just like the original check. Under the new law, banks are not required to use substitute checks, but when they do so for consideration, they make the following warranties: (1) The substitute check contains an accurate image of the front and back of the original check; (2) it is the legal equivalent of the original check; and (3) no drawer, drawee, indorser, or depositary bank will be asked to pay a check that already has paid.

UCC 4-406 (a)(b)

Original Checks No Longer Returned As noted earlier in the chapter, many banks in the past automatically returned canceled checks with their monthly bank statements to their customers, even though the UCC does not require that original checks be returned unless a customer requests them. The Check 21 Act, which takes precedence over the UCC, changes this rule. Under the Check 21 Act, the customer has a right only to a paper substitute check that is a reproduction of the front and back of the original. Bank customers no longer have an absolute right to see their original canceled checks.

Consumer Protection To protect consumers from losses related to substitute checks, the Check 21 Act includes a consumer's right to claim an *expedited credit*. This right exists if the consumer asserts in good faith the following four facts:

- The bank charged the consumer's account for a substitute check that was given to the consumer.
- Either the check was not properly charged to the consumer's account, or the consumer has a warranty claim with respect to the substitute check.
- The consumer suffered a resulting loss.
- The production of the original check or a better copy of the original check is necessary to determine the validity of any claim.

If the consumer makes a claim within 45 days after receiving the bank statement or substitute check, the bank must investigate it and make any necessary recredit to the consumer's account. If the bank needs more than 10 days to investigate and resolve the complaint, it must recredit the consumer's account for an amount up to $2,500 while it completes its investigation. The bank must recredit any remaining balance greater than $2,500 no later than 45 days after the consumer submits the claim.

Electronic Fund Transfers

Electronic banking (also called an **electronic fund transfer** or **EFT**) uses computers and electronic technology as a substitute for checks and other banking methods. People can go to automatic teller machines (ATMs) 24 hours a day to make bank deposits and withdrawals. In addition, online banking has become standard operating procedure for many people today. **Online banking** is a process by which a bank's customers can pay their bills and check their bank statements online by using their home computer, a laptop, a tablet, a smartphone, or some other other electronic device. To make this process work, the customer must access the bank's bill paying website, enter a PIN number, provide the identification number of the account, enter the amount to be paid, and identify the account number of the creditor. Some banks have arrangements for payment by **e-check** (sometimes called *electronic check conversion*), which is a system in which funds are electronically transferred from a customer's checking account, eliminating the need to process a paper check. Under one system, the customer writes out an ordinary check and gives it to a merchant when making a purchase. After obtaining the customer's written authorization, the merchant passes the check through an instrument that reads the information on the check and converts the payment from a paper check to an electronic funds transfer. The merchant then voids the check and returns it to the customer with a receipt. Payment by e-check is faster and inexpensive, thus saving time and money for everyone involved. Stored value cards have also become more and more popular over the last decade or so. A **stored value card**, which looks very much like a credit card or a hotel key card, contains a magnetic strip embedded with data. The data is read by the store's computer, generally at the check-out line, so that the merchant knows how much money the card holds before and after a purchase. The card is often issued by a merchant as a gift card or as an in-house card used as a substitute for a cash refund. A **wire transfer** (i.e., a **bank transfer** or a **credit transfer**) is a time-honored system of transferring money from one bank to another by using electronic devices. Wire transfers are controlled and operated by two networks: the Clearing House Interbank Payments System (CHIPS) and the Fedwire System. CHIPS is a private network used by commercial banks, while Fedwire is coordinated by the Federal Reserve System. Wire transfers began in the 19th century and used existing telegraph lines. This is why this type of transfer is still referred to as a "wire" transfer, although more sophisticated electronic networks are used in the 21st century.

ATM, Debit, and Combination Cards An **ATM card** is used together with a personal identification number (PIN) to gain access to an automatic teller machine either on or off the bank premises. In contrast, a **debit card** (also called a *check card* or *cash card*) is used to subtract money electronically from a bank account to pay for goods or services. Debit cards are used at stores rather than at ATM machines and usually require the use of the customer's signature rather than a PIN. Many banks now use a combination ATM–debit card that performs both functions. There are two kinds of debit cards: online and offline. *Online* debit cards make an immediate transfer of money from the customer's bank account to the merchant's bank account. *Offline* debit cards record a debit against the customer's bank account, which is processed later. A debit card offers less protection than a credit card. Unlike a credit card, a debit card payment cannot be stopped if a purchase is defective or an order is not delivered. In addition, your liability for the unauthorized use of your ATM or debit card is limited to $50 only if you notify the issuer within two business days of the loss or theft of the card. Your liability increases to $500 if notice is delayed beyond that time, and it becomes unlimited when notice is not given within 60 days. The unauthorized use of an ATM card is a criminal offense punishable by fine and/or imprisonment.

EXAMPLE 18-7: Stolen ATM Card

A thief stole Hockmeyer's purse from a grocery store shopping cart. Three days later, Hockmeyer notified the bank that her ATM card was missing. By then, however, the thief had found the card along with Hockmeyer's secret identification number and withdrawn $800 from her account. Because the bank was notified within three days of the theft, Hockmeyer lost $500. Had she notified the bank within two business days of the theft, she would have lost only $50.

The Electronic Fund Transfer Act

Regulation E, issued by the Federal Reserve Board under the Electronic Fund Transfer Act, establishes the basic rights, liabilities, and responsibilities of consumers who use electronic fund transfer services and financial institutions that offer these services. Transactions covered under the regulation include:

UCC 4A-103-505
UCC 4A-104
UCC 4A-103

- Point-of-sale purchases.
- Automated teller machine transfers.
- Telephone-initiated transfers requiring an entry password (PIN).
- Transfers resulting from debit card transactions requiring an entry password (PIN).
- Internet banking.

Under the act, consumers are entitled to receive a written receipt whenever they use an ATM. In addition, the transaction must appear on the periodic statement sent to the consumer. The consumer has 60 days to notify the bank of any error on the periodic statement or terminal receipt. After being notified, the bank has 10 business days to investigate the error. If the bank needs more time, it may take up to 45 days to complete the investigation, but only if the money in dispute is returned to the consumer's account.

Because the Electronic Fund Transfer Act is a consumer protection law, it does not apply to transactions between banks and other businesses. A different law, Article 4A of the UCC, has been adopted by many states to govern EFTs made by banks and businesses. Under the UCC, a business that orders money to be sent electronically is called the originator. The business that is to receive the money is called the beneficiary. EFTs help businesses that deal with large sums of money make quick transfers to avoid a loss of interest.

EXAMPLE 18-8: Electronic Transfers by Banks

Data Control Inc. sold a computer system to Western Sales Inc. for $2 million. When the system was installed, Western Sales ordered its bank to pay $2 million to Data Control. Because both companies had accounts in the First National Bank, the bank simply debited Western Sales' account and credited Data Control's account for $2 million. Western Sales was the originator; Data Control was the beneficiary. If Data Control had used a different bank, the First National Bank would have ordered that bank, called the beneficiary's bank, to credit Data Control's account for $2 million.

The Global Financial Cyber-Crisis

The Internet provides us with an enormous amount of flexibility and efficiency in the transfer of funds and with the record keeping associated with those funds. However, as noted earlier, the system is also often at risk. Poorly written software, an incorrect file number, a solar storm, or inadequately maintained hardware can interrupt the operation of even the most secure system. Information technicians might enter an incorrect password, an inaccurate code, or the wrong PIN, and the system might shut down or begin to act erratically. Most of these errors are handled easily enough. Other problems, those that are deliberate and knowingly target a computer system, are less easily solved.

Global Level Problems For instance, a rival firm, an enemy nation, or a crime syndicate could send an e-mail with an attached PDF file that, when opened, installs a deadly virus into a corporate computer system. The software might command the system to shut down, delete data, or, perhaps worse, transfer control of the system to the hacker. What makes this type of attack so insidious is that no one knows about it until the damage is done. Thus, without so much as a digital alarm going off, a corporation might lose all of its data or a banking system might be wiped clean of all transactions. Constructing a plan for dealing with a deliberate computer attack is difficult at best. Nevertheless, steps must be taken to deal with such attacks. [See: "Briefing Cyber-War: War in the Fifth Domain," *The Economist*, July 3, 2010, p. 25.]

Global Cyber-Targets and Cyber-Tactics One step that has been suggested is to divide the data stream so that it travels along a variety of routes so that if one line is attacked the others can continue to transmit. This solution works most of the time. Unfortunately, there are bottlenecks along the global network at which the data streams intersect and fall under the control of a limited number of domain-name servers, making them tempting targets for cyber-criminals and cyber-terrorists. These main intersection points appear in the Middle East, in South East Asia, and along the Eastern seaboard of the United States, any one of which is an inviting target. [See: "Briefing Cyber-War: War in the Fifth Domain," p. 25.]

Cyber-Command (Cyber-com) The global response to such problems has been the establishment of a new cyber-command center. The task of the new command center is to protect the military's computer command system. The National Security Agency has been given control over this new center, which has been officially named Cyber-Command or Cyber-com. Cyber-com is designed to protect the American cyber-system from attack and to formulate plans to undermine the computer systems of enemy nations. Two of its goals might be to protect the "chokepoints" in the submerged fiber-optic system and to uncover effective ways to use the system in a way that benefits the American military [See: "Briefing Cyber-War: War in the Fifth Domain," p. 25.]

Domestic Cyber-Targets and Cyber-Tactics The tactics noted previously are needed to protect the global Internet, but they do not protect individuals except in an indirect way. This is crucial because cybercriminals also frequently target individuals. Such criminals can gain access to banks account, stock portfolios, and other financial records in order to drain funds from those accounts. Or they may steal an individual's identity in order to use that person's credit cards, debit cards, checking account, and other personal financial resources. Fortunately, the federal government has taken steps to protect your bank accounts and your identity from cyber criminal attacks. These steps include the establishment of the Internet Crime Complaint Center and the passage of legislation aimed at protecting Internet transactions.

Internet Crime Complaint Center The federal government has set up the Internet Crime Complaint Center (IC3), which connects the National White Collar Crime Center

---

Did You Know?

- A *credit card* is like a loan. You agree to pay the money back later at a high interest rate unless you pay the full amount when the bill arrives. A debit card, in contrast, means "subtract"—when you use it, you subtract the money from your own bank account.

- If your *credit* card is lost or stolen, you can't lose more than $50. In contrast, if someone uses your *ATM* or *debit* card without permission, you can lose much more unless you notify your bank quickly.

- A *debit* card is often easier to obtain than a credit card and allows you to spend what is in your bank account.

- A *debit* card gives you less protection than a credit card when you purchase items that are defective or never delivered.

- Using a *debit* card instead of writing checks saves you from showing identification or giving out personal identification at the time of a transaction.

(NW3C) with the Federal Bureau of Investigation (FBI). The IC3 handles complaints involving cybercrimes such as identity theft, cyber-extortion, and Internet fraud. Individuals and businesses can file complaints with the IC3 by accessing their website online. The IC3 also works closely with administrative agencies as well as with local, state, and federal law enforcement agencies. [See: *Internet Crime Complaint Center*, http://www.ic3.gov.]

Domestic Cyber-Legislation Congress has also passed legislation aimed at solving these problems. Two such acts are the Identity Theft and Assumption Deterrence Act (ITDA) and the National Stolen Property Act (NSPA). ITDA, which was amended by the Identity Theft Penalty Enhancement Act, outlaws the unauthorized transfer, possession, or use of a means of identifying another person to violate federal law. The amendment adds a new crime, called *aggravated identity theft*, to the original statute. The section on aggravated identity theft makes it clear that identity theft is much worse when it involves certain very serious felonies, including terrorism. Under the NSPA, it is a federal crime to use interstate or foreign commerce to transport personal currency and securities that an individual is aware were stolen, were secured by fraud, or were taken by some other illegal method including an unauthorized electronic transfer.

The Cyber Doomsday Network

Recently, the banks of the United States have developed a private strategy for dealing with the threat of a cyber-attack. The project, which is referred to affectionately as Project Sheltered Harbor, is designed to stave off a potentially catastrophic run on the banks of the country, similar to the ones that ushered in the Great Depression of the 20th century. The network is the image of simplicity itself. The plan is to make certain that those banks in the Sheltered Harbor network back up their data in a systematic way. Other banks in the network would then have access to that data should a member of the Harbor network be victimized by a debilitating cyber-attack. In this way, should one bank go down, other banks in the network can serve as a surrogate to which the customers of the victimized bank can turn to access their funds. The belief is that, when the customers of the targeted bank have access to their money neither they nor the customers of the other banks, will panic and start a dreaded "run" on all the other banks in the network, thus triggering a total collapse of the nation's financial system. Ironically, the thing that makes these banks vulnerable—that is, their near total dependence on the electronic financial network—also serves as their safety net because, without the electronic system in place, the data would not be available as quickly as needed to prevent a panic (unless, of course, some clever cyber-enemy figures out how to shut down every bank in the network at precisely the same moment in time). [See: Telis Demos, "Banks Create Cyber Doomsday System," *The Wall Street Journal*, December 4, 2017, pp. B1, B10.]

quick quiz 18-3

1. Consumers have 30 days to notify the bank of any error on the periodic statement received for the use of an ATM.	true | false
2. A consumer's liability for the unauthorized use of an ATM card is limited to $500 if notice of the loss or theft of a card is given the issuer within two business days.	true | false
3. The unauthorized use of an ATM card is a criminal offense punishable by a $500 fine and/or five years in prison.	true | false

Summary

18.1 The drawee bank must honor all checks (except stale checks) drawn by its customers when there are sufficient funds on deposit. Failure to do so makes the bank liable to the customer for any actual damages the customer suffers. The drawee bank has no liability to the holder of a check unless it is certified. Banks are responsible for paying altered or forged checks. Banks must make funds available to depositors according to a specific schedule. In addition, banks must pay or return checks on or before their midnight deadline. Depositors must examine their bank statements and canceled checks promptly. It is a crime to write a check with insufficient funds in the bank. Oral stop-payment orders are binding upon the bank for 14 days; written orders to stop payment are binding for six months.

18.2 During the bank collection process, banks are described by different terms, depending on their particular function in a transaction. Sometimes a bank takes a check for deposit. At other times, it pays a check as a drawee. At still other times, it takes a check for collection only. The different terms that are used to describe banks and their meanings are as follows: depositary bank, payor bank, intermediary bank, collecting bank, presenting bank, and remitting bank. The life cycle of a check begins when the drawer writes a check and delivers it to the payee. If a payee cashes a check at a payor (drawee) bank, the payment is final. If, instead, the payee deposits a check in his or her bank, which sends it to the payor bank for collection, any payment is provisional.

18.3 The Check 21 Act establishes substitute checks, which may be returned to bank customers in place of the canceled original check and thus make check clearing much quicker through the use of electronic processing. Consumers who use EFTs have 60 days to notify the bank of an error; thereafter, the bank must investigate. A consumer's liability for the unauthorized use of an ATM card is limited to $50 if notice of the loss or theft of a card is given the issuer within two business days. Article 4A of the UCC governs EFTs made by banks and businesses. The federal government has set up the Internet Crime Complaint Center, which handles complaints involving cybercrimes such as identity theft, cyber-extortion, and Internet fraud. Congress has also passed legislation aimed at solving these problems. Two such acts are the Identity Theft and Assumption Deterrence Act and the National Stolen Property Act.

Key Terms

ATM card, 506
bank, 491
Check 21 Act, 505
collecting bank, 503
debit card, 506
depositary bank, 503
e-check, 506
electronic fund transfers (EFTs), 506
forgery, 494
intermediary bank, 503
midnight deadline, 497
online banking, 506
overdraft, 493
payor bank, 503
presenting bank, 503
provisional, 503
Regulation E, 507
remitting bank, 503
stale check, 493
stored value card, 506
subrogation, 501
substitute check, 505
uttering, 494
wire transfer, 506

Questions for Review and Discussion

1. What are the bank's duties in the bank–depositor relationship?
2. What are the depositor's duties in the bank–depositor relationship?
3. What are a drawer's rights in relation to a stop-payment order?
4. What is the extent of the insurance protection provided by the FDIC?
5. What are the different terms used to describe banks during the bank collection process?
6. What are the steps in a check's life cycle?
7. What are the principal features of the Check 21 Act?

8. What consumer protection features are found in the Check 21 Act?
9. What happens during the process of an electronic funds transfer?
10. What protection is given to consumers by the Electronic Fund Transfer Act?

Cases for Analysis

1. Kelco bought a truck from Felton, paying for it with a cashier's check she had obtained from her bank. On her way home, the truck broke down. Kelco immediately telephoned her bank and told it to stop payment on the cashier's check. Later, Kelco discovered that her bank had not stopped payment on the cashier's check and instead had paid it. Did Kelco have a claim against the bank? Explain. [See: *Taboada v. Bank of Babylon*, 408 N.Y.S.2d 734 (NY).]

2. Granite Corp. sent a check to Overseas Equipment Co. When the check was reported lost, Granite wrote to its bank telling it to stop payment on the check. Granite then sent the money to Overseas Equipment Co. by wire. Thirteen months later, the check turned up, and Granite's bank paid it. Did the bank violate its duty to stop payment on the check? Explain. [See: *Granite Equip. Leasing Corp. v. Hempstead Bank*, 326 N.Y.S.2d 881 (NY).]

3. While in the hospital during his final illness, Norris wrote a check and gave it to his sister. She deposited it in her bank account. Norris died before the check cleared, and his bank refused to pay it. May a bank honor a check when it knows of the death of the drawer? Explain. [See: *In re Estate of Norris*, 532 P.2d 981 (CO).]

4. On June 18, Templeton deposited in his bank account a $5,000 check that was payable to his order. The check reached the drawee bank through normal banking channels on June 22. That bank had received a stop-payment order on the check on May 15 and, therefore, refused to honor it. It kept the check until June 28, when it returned it to Templeton with the notification that payment had been stopped. Did the drawee bank violate a duty it owed to Templeton? Explain. [See: *Templeton v. First Nat'l Bank*, 362 N.E.2d 33 (IL).]

5. In payment for services rendered, one of Stewart's clients gave him a check for $185.48 that had been drawn by the client's corporate employer and had been made payable to the order of the client. Although properly indorsed by the client, the drawee bank flatly refused to cash the check for Stewart. The bank acknowledged that the check was good, that is, that there were sufficient funds in the account. Could Stewart sue the bank for refusing to honor the check? Why or why not? [See: *Stewart v. Citizens & Nat'l Bank*, 225 S.E.2d 761 (GA).]

6. Fitting wrote an $800 check on her account with Continental Bank. A bank employee had mistakenly placed a hold on the account, causing the bank to dishonor the check when it was presented for payment. Fitting was unable to prove that she suffered damages because of the dishonor. Could she recover damages from the bank? Explain. [See: *Continental Bank v. Fitting*, 559 P.2d 218 (AZ).]

7. Roberta Lunt deposited a $625 nonlocal check payable to her with a teller at her bank at 10:30 A.M. on Monday. The next day, Tuesday, she went to the bank to withdraw $300 and was told by the teller that she could have only $100 from the check she had deposited the day before. When must the funds be made available to Roberta? Explain why.

quick quiz Answers

18-1	18-2	18-3
1. F	1. T	1. F
2. T	2. T	2. F
3. T	3. T	3. F

Part 4 Case Study

Read v. South Carolina National Bank
286 S. C. 534, 335 S.E.2d 359, Supreme
Court of South Carolina

©Stockbroker/Alamy

Summary

This story begins when Judy Bode was hired by the Lawton Bluff Company (LBC) to work as a sales secretary. Apparently she was quite competent because she was quickly advanced to the position of executive secretary to Emerson Read, the managing partner in LBC. As part of her new duties, Bode was put in charge of a checking account that Read was responsible for in his capacity as the treasurer of an education organization, known as the South Carolina Chapter of CCIM. Shortly after assuming this position, Bode began her new career as a secret forger by making a check drawn on the CCIM account payable to herself. Forging Read's signature directly or using a facsimile rubber stamp, Bode forged 36 checks on this account. Next, Bode was given control of Read's personal checking account and proceeded to forge some 15 checks from that account. Soon after this, she was given the authority to manage several additional business accounts, including the LBC company account.

For the next four months, Bode managed to forge 14 more checks. Most of the time, she used the facsimile rubber stamp of Read's signature to forge the checks. Ironically, Read had been warned against using the stamp by the director of accounting at LBC. Following this, Bode forged Read's signature on a whole series of checking accounts that she had been given the authority to use on a regular basis. When all was said and done, the accounts she forged checks from included a Harborview Federal account, the LBC account, the CCIM account, and Read's personal account. Bode apparently had complete control over all of these accounts. No one supervised her in any way. No one checked on her work. Her job included the responsibility to reconcile the books with the statements and canceled checks mailed to LBC from the South Carolina National Bank (SCNB). No evidence was presented that countered the claim by SCNB that they sent the bank statements to LBC. However, those statements went directly to Bode, who promptly destroyed them all. Read, on his part, admitted that he never so much as opened a bank statement the entire time that Bode worked in the offices of LBC.

Once officials at LBC discovered the forgeries, they informed SCNB and asked the bank to make good on the forged checks that the bank had failed to detect and that had caused LBC to lose so much of its money. The bank refused, noting that it was not responsible for the failure of LBC personnel to supervise its own employees, especially one who had been placed in such a sensitive position. Read, as the managing general partner of LCB, then elected to bring this lawsuit against SCNB, claiming that the bank had been negligent in the handling of its accounts and was, therefore, liable for the losses that he, Read, and the company had suffered. Once the case reached the Supreme Court of Georgia, that Court correctly pointed out that the cause of action initiated by Read was not a tort action at all but was, instead, embedded within contract law, more specifically in the law as outlined by Article 4 of the Uniform Commercial Code. Accordingly, the Court based its opinion on the UCC in general and on UCC 4-406 in particular.

The court then goes through a step-by-step analysis of the behavior that led to the string of forgeries that could easily have been prevented by due diligence on the part of the people at LBC, beginning with a proper background check on Bode, which would have revealed, before she was even hired, that she "had been prosecuted, convicted and was on probation for issuing bad checks." The Supreme Court of Georgia then develops a systematic, in depth analysis that reveals that the bank had fulfilled all of its duties and that LBC had fulfilled none of its. The most intriguing thing about the opinion is that the High Court of Georgia focuses on the duties of the litigants, not on their rights. This tact is refreshing in a social system that persists in emphasizing rights and entitlements and rarely, if ever, talks about duties.

We hear a great deal about the right to choose, the right to marry, the right to a good education, the right to health care, the right to travel, the right to work, the right to free speech, the right own property, the right to control our own bodies, the right to vote, the right to be free from harassment, the right to self expression, the right to kneel during the national anthem, the right to be compensated, the rights of the victim, the rights of prisoners, the right to die, the right to . . . you name it. However, we hear very little if anything about duties and responsibilities, the duty to care for our children, the duty to be courteous, the duty to welcome the stranger, the duty to care for the sick, the duty to feed the hungry, the duty to protect the innocent, the duty to speak the truth, the duty to forgive, the duty to understand, the duty to hear both (all?) sides of the story before condemning the accused, the duty not to rush to judgment, and the duty to preserve life, all life—including the life of the condemned murderer, the life of the enemy, the life of unborn, the life of the refugee, the life of the immigrant, and even the life of the terrorist. Even Thomas Hobbes talked about the duty to adhere to the social contract. Yet, today, it is all about "me."

In his book, *The Fragile Absolute*, Slavoj Zizek, a senior researcher at the Institute for Social Studies and an avowed Marxist, as well as a respected commentator on popular culture, makes this point in a rather startling way by revealing that, when human beings construct their own value systems in such documents (although Zizek does not mention them, we can think of the United Nations Declaration of Universal Human Rights, the International Covenant of Civil and Political Rights, and the American Bill of Rights, among others), those efforts establish nothing other than temporary standards that are honored only so long as it is convenient to do so. Zizek explains this phenomenon by noting that most declarations of human rights are actually systems that tell people how to escape the prohibitions placed upon them by the absolute law of the Ten Commandments. In other words, such systems simply tell people how to justify their own selfish tendencies.

For example, Zizek argues that the right to privacy, which is frequently found in such documents, is really nothing more than the right to hide one's sins from others. Why would people demand privacy, in other words, unless they have something to hide? Similarly, the right to the free expression of ideas is actually the right to lie; the right to bear arms is clearly the right to kill; the right to the free exercise of religion is quite obviously the right to worship whatever god one might want to fashion at the moment; and the right to private property is really the right to steal, exploit, pollute, and ultimately devastate that "private property." Zizek goes on to write, "Of course, human rights do not *directly* condone the violation of the Ten Commandments—the point is simply that they keep open a marginal 'grey zone' which which should remain out of reach of (religious or secular) power: in this shady zone, I can violate these commandments, and if power probes into it, catching me . . . and trying to prevent my violations, I can cry: 'Assault on my basic human Rights.' The point is thus that it is structurally impossible, for Power, to draw a clear line of separation and prevent only the 'misuse' of a Right, while nor encroaching upon the proper use, that is, the use that does not violate the Commandments." [See: Slavoj Zizek, *The Fragile Absolute: Or Why Is the Christian Legacy Worth Fighting For?* (London: Verso, 2000), pp. 101-102.]

Now let's read how the Supreme Court of Georgia deals with duties not rights in The Case of the Runaway Forger.

After covering the facts, the Court in a *Per Curiam* (a collective, usually unanimous) opinion writes:

Although the Plaintiff couched his first cause of action in negligence, the relationship between a bank and its depositor is one of contract. This contractual relationship requires that the bank pay out funds only in accordance with the orders given by the depositor. Consequently, a bank may not charge the depositor's account for any checks containing a forged or unauthorized signature of the drawer. These rules have been incorporated into the Uniform Commercial Code. South Carolina Code of Laws § 36-4-401(1) provides that a bank may charge against its customer's account only an item which is properly payable. In § 36-3-401(1) no person is liable on an instrument unless his signature appears thereon. Section 36-3-404 provides that an unauthorized signature is wholly inoperative as that of the person whose name is signed unless he ratifies it or is *precluded* from denying it. Thus, under the Code a bank breaches its agreement with its customer when it pays a check containing a forged or unauthorized signature of the drawer. It is this breach which constitutes the customer's cause of action against the bank to recover the sums paid out on checks bearing the forged signatures. *Hardex-Steubenville Corp. v. W. Pa. National Bank*, 446 Pa. 446, 285 A.2d 874 (1971).

The defenses in this case were not that the signatures were genuine or authorized but that Read by his negligence substantially contributed to the making of the unauthorized signatures and that he failed in his duty to discover and promptly notify SCN of the forgeries and thus is precluded from denying the unauthorized signatures.

The First Defense in this case was that the Plaintiff failed in his duty to discover and promptly notify SCN of the forgeries. This duty and the effect of the customer's failure to discharge it are set forth in § 36-4-406(1) and (2).

(1) When a bank sends to its customer a statement of account accompanied by items paid in good faith in support of the debt entries or holds the statement and items pursuant to a request of instructions of its customer or otherwise in a reasonable manner makes the statement and items available to the customer, the customer must exercise reasonable care and promptness to examine the statement and items to discover his unauthorized signature or any alteration on an item and must notify the bank promptly after discovery thereof. (2) If the bank establishes that the customer failed with respect to an item to comply with the duties imposed on the customers by subsection (1) the customer is precluded from asserting against the bank: (a) his unauthorized signature or any alteration on the item if the bank also establishes that it suffered a loss by reason of such failure; and (b) an unauthorized signature or alteration by the same wrongdoer on any other item paid in good faith by the bank after the first item and statement was available to the customer for a reasonable period not exceeding fourteen calendar days and before the bank receives notification from the customer of any such unauthorized signature or alteration.

These provisions impose a duty on the depositor to check his monthly statement for unauthorized signatures on checks. If a depositor fails to do so, after the first forged check and statement relating thereto is sent him, plus a reasonable period not exceeding fourteen (14) days, he is precluded from asserting the unauthorized signature against the bank, on any subsequent item containing an unauthorized signature by the same wrongdoer.[2] The burden of proof of the depositor's negligence is on the bank. See Comment 2 to § 36-4-406.

The first forgery occurred on the Lawton Bluff account in September 1980 and would have been included in the bank statement mailed on October 1. The forgeries were not reported to SCN until January 26, 1981. Read is thus precluded from asserting forgeries which occurred after September 1980.

The preclusion under § 36-4-406(1) and (2) does not apply if the bank is negligent in paying the items.

The preclusion under subsection (2) does not apply if the customer establishes lack of ordinary care on the part of the bank in paying the item(s). § 36-4-406(3)

The burden of proving the bank's failure to exercise ordinary care under § 36-4-406(3) in paying the items rests squarely on the customer. *Nu-Way Services, Inc. v. Mercantile Trust Company*, 530 S.W.2d 743 (Mo. App. 1975). The question becomes whether there was sufficient evidence to raise a jury issue as to the lack of ordinary care on the part of SCN in paying the checks. (Check paying is the determination of whether there are sufficient funds in an account and a review of the signature on the check. This process is performed by bank's central bookkeeping department and has nothing to do with tellers in local branches who do not have signature cards).

Employees of SCN testified that when checks drawn on SCN accounts are received by SCN for payment, they are first processed through the computer where the account is automatically debited. After this, the individual checks are received in the check paying area where the check paying clerks file the checks in account number order in file trays. The accounts in those file trays are separated by plastic dividers which contain the signature card. At the same time the checks are filed in the trays, the signature on the check is compared to the signature card in the plastic guide. Check paying clerks are assigned to file checks for certain cities so they will become familiar with the accounts and the signatures.

A quality control clerk performs a random checking behind those check paying clerks to insure that the checks are filed properly and that signatures are compared. If signatures do not match, they are pulled and placed on a return sheet and transmitted back to the local office.

A representative from C & S Bank testified that their procedure is similar to that of SCN, but that the signature cards are kept in a separate place from where the checks are filed, and that signatures are only compared on checks over $10,000.00 unless the customer requests special instructions or there is an alert on the account. A representative of First National Bank testified that the procedures used by his bank were the same as those used by SCN. There was no other ntestimony of any other method of detecting forgeries employed by any other banking institution.

Although "ordinary care" is not defined in the Code, § 36-4-103(3) provides that action or nonaction consistent with general banking usage constitutes ordinary care. The only evidence as to general banking usage came from SCN and its witnesses from the area banks. Read presented no evidence to refute that SCN's procedure was consistent with general banking usage. On the contrary, Read's expert witness testified that SCN was more careful than the average bank in its examination of signatures. The only reasonable inference that could be drawn from the evidence is that SCN exercised ordinary care in paying the checks.

The Second Defense is set forth in S.C. Code of Laws § 36-3-406.

Any person who by his negligence substantially contributes to a material alteration of the instrument or to the making of an unauthorized signature is precluded from asserting the alteration or lack of authority against a holder in due course or against a drawee or other payor who pays the instrument in good faith and in accordance with the reasonable commercial standards of the drawee's or payor's business.

The evidence in this case clearly presents a situation where Read's negligence as a matter of law substantially contributed to the forgeries. He was negligent in failing to maintain proper control over the signature stamp, he allowed the same person who had possession of the checkbook to reconcile the statements with no supervision or verification and he failed to examine his bank statements. Had he examined the bank statement of the CCIM account at any time during the period January 1980 through August 1980 he would have discovered those forgeries and Bode would not have had the opportunity to forge checks on the Lawton Bluff account. SCN has clearly met its burden of proof on the issue of Read's negligence substantially contributing to the making of the unauthorized signatures.

Under § 36-3-406 the bank additionally has the burden of proving that it paid the instrument in good faith and in accordance with reasonable commercial standards of its business. Good faith is defined as "honesty in fact" § 36-1-201(19). There is no dispute as to SCN's good faith in paying the instruments. For the reasons set forth above I find as a matter of law that SCN paid the checks in accordance with reasonable commercial standards of its business.

The second cause of action was based on conversion. As stated earlier, all of the checks in the case contained forged drawer's signatures with the exception of the check drawn on the account of Rivers, Jenkins & Buist, payable to Lawton Bluff Company and deposited into the Royal Tern account at C & S Bank with no endorsement.

As to the checks which contained forged drawer's signatures there can be no cause of action for conversion. Payment by a bank of checks bearing forged signatures constitutes a breach of its agreement with its customer. Conversion of an instrument is specifically provided for in § 36-3-419(1)(c) of the Code of Laws of South Carolina. The section states that an instrument is converted when it is paid on a forged endorsement.

In *Perini v. First National Bank of Habershan, Co.*, 553 Fed. (2d) 398 (5th Cir.1977), the Fifth Circuit, in a most celebrated case, held that in cases where a defective endorsement is accompanied by a forged drawer's signature, that the loss is a forged check loss and not an endorsement loss, and no liability could be assessed on the basis of the endorsement. The court further held that no sound basis exists for extending liability for handling the endorsement beyond the unlikely event of a claim of superior right to the payment under the instrument.

In the present case all of the checks not made payable to Judy Bode were deposited into the account of the named payee and the checks made payable to Judy Bode were deposited into her son's account which was controlled by her. Therefore, the losses are a result of the forged drawer's signature, not the endorsements. Depository banks can supply the endorsement of its customer § 36-4-205.

The check payable to Lawton Bluff Company for $8,799.46 was deposited into the Royal Tern account at C & S with no endorsement. Although the check was drawn on SCN, SCN could have no way of determining into which account at C & S the check was deposited. Liability for accepting a check for deposit into an incorrect account lies with the depository bank.

In viewing all of the evidence in the light most favorable to the Plaintiff, the only inference that can be drawn from the undisputed facts is that Read's negligence substantially contributed to the making of the unauthorized signatures and that Read failed to introduce any evidence and thus to carry his burden of proof that SCN failed to exercise ordinary care in paying the terms. The SCN's motion for directed verdict is hereby granted.

Affirmed.

Footnotes by the Court

1. [She, at the time, had been prosecuted, convicted and was on probation for issuing bad checks. Read was negligent in not investigating her background before giving to her important responsibilities.]

2. Once the depositor gives notice to the bank, he would be protected on any subsequent forgeries by the same person, but notice would not revive his right to restitution on the earlier forgeries as to which notice was not given.

Questions for Analysis

1. As we have seen several times, *stare decisis* is at the central core of the authority of the judicial branch. Does this case support or contradict that description of core authority? Explain.
2. What is the Uniform Commercial Code? What goal does the Uniform Law Commission have in formulating the UCC? Explain.
3. What does UCC Section 4-406 say about the depositor's responsibilities in regard to checking bank statements and why is that relevant to this case? Explain.
4. Define the following legal terms using the text: *forgery*, *payee*, *overdraft*, and *negligence*. Which of these terms is (are) relevant in this case?
5. What is the first defense offered by the South Carolina National Bank, and how does the court respond to that defense? Explain.
6. What is the second defense offered by the South Carolina National Bank, and how does the court respond to that defense? Explain.
7. How does concept of "good faith" fit into this case? Explain.
8. How does concept of "ordinary care" fit into this case? Explain.
9. What is the court's conclusion regarding the plaintiff's behavior in this case? Explain.
10. A complex adaptive system (CAS) is a network of interacting conditions that reinforce one another, while at the same time adjusting to change from agents outside and inside the system. In what way (ways?) does the case of *Read v. S. C. National Bank* reinforce the idea that the law works like a complex adaptive system? Explain.

Source: See: Slavoj Zizek, *The Fragile Absolute: Or Why Is the Christian Legacy Worth Fighting For?* (London: Verso, 2000), pp. 101-102.

Design Elements: The Opening Case: ©Sharpstock/Alamy; A Classic Case: ©Evlakhov Valeriy/ Shutterstock

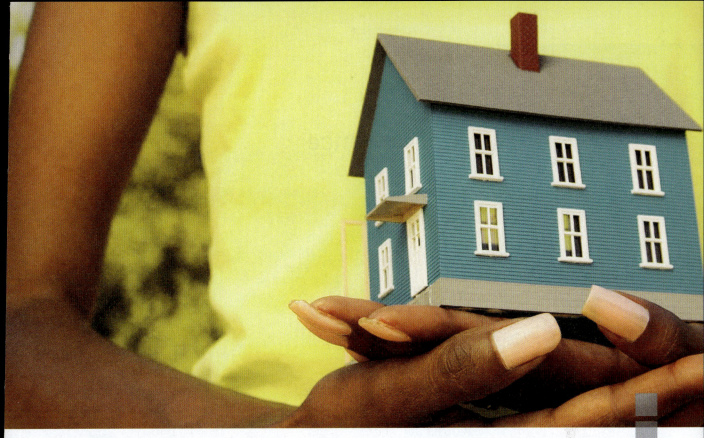
©Plush Studios/Blend Images LLC

Part Five
Insurance, Secured Transactions, and Bankruptcy

Chapter 19	Insurance	Chapter 21	Bankruptcy Law: In Theory, in History, and in Practice
Chapter 20	Mortgages, Security Interests, and the 21st-Century Financial Crisis	Case Study	*Superior Savings Association v. City of Cleveland*

Chapter 19

Insurance

19-1 Risk Assessment and Peril Management
Risks and Perils: A Double-Sided Mirror • The Insurance Contract: Parties, Elements, Interest • Insurable Interest and the Duties of the Parties

19-2 Types of Insurance
Life Insurance • Property Insurance • Automobile Insurance • Liability Insurance • Health Insurance • Umbrella Insurance • Cyber-Insurance Coverage

19-3 The Insurance Policy
Application • Binders • Premiums • Lapse

19-4 Cancellation of Insurance by Insurer
Warranties • Concealment • Misrepresentation • Estoppel

THE OPENING CASE Round 1

Owning Is Not so Satisfying a Thing, after all, as Selling. It Is Not Logical, but It Is often True.

George Ramsey (GR) and Willie Ramsey (WR), a married couple, received a warranty deed from James Sumrall as tenants-in-common to a piece of property in Bay Springs, Mississippi. The couple then executed a security deed in favor of Bay Springs Bank (SBS), granting the bank a security interest in the property. The couple then built a house on the property, in which they lived together until GR left WR and went to live with her daughter in Illinois. Shortly thereafter, the bank foreclosed on the property. It was then purchased by Don Husbands (DH) at the foreclosure sale. DH received the property through a substitute trustee deed. One year later, WR received the property back from DH through a quit claim deed. WR then tore down the old house and built a new home on the same lot and purchased a homeowner's insurance policy from State Farm Fire and Casualty (State Farm) for on the building itself for $30,000 and $15,000 on the contents of the house. Seven years later, GR took out a loan of $18,555.30 from Tower Loan of Mississippi (Tower). As security for the loan, WR conveyed a deed of trust to Tower. When WR failed to pay back the loan, Tower foreclosed on the property, the end result of which was that a trustee deed was executed conveying the property to Tower for $14,3105.20. Despite all of this, amazingly, WR continued to live in the house. (Well, why not? When there are no negative consequences, any type of behavior tends to continue unabated.) About 90 days later, a fire destroyed the house. When WR attempted to collect on the insurance policy, State Farm refused, stating that WR no longer had an insurable interest in the property. In response, WR argued that the Tower foreclosure was invalid under the deed of trust, and therefore, he remained the owner of the home and his insurable interest remained intact. GR formulated his argument using the following rationale. When Bay Springs foreclosed, WR and GR were tenants-in-common. So when WR re-purchased the property from DH, it represented a redemption of the property that both he, WR, and his wife, GR, owned as tenants-in-common. After that redemption, WR and GR held the property as tenants-in-the-entirety because they continued to be married. As a result, GR by himself could not encumber the property without WR's consent. Therefore, the transfer of the property via the deed of trust was invalid, and WR still owned the property at the time of the fire, thereby establishing his insurable interest. In the alternative, WR also argued that, even if the co-tenancy was severed when he sold the property to DH, when he (WR) bought it back, the property became the family homestead and, as a result, the home belonged to WR and GR. The bottom line then is that WR and GR held the insurable interest, not Towers.

Both GR and WR also filed claims for the contents of the house, and State Farm also denied both claims. The insurance company rejected WR's claim because she failed to properly file a detailed proof of loss form as required by the policy. Instead of filing a specific report, which would include such things as when the loss occurred, her interest in the personal property, whether another insurance policy covered the goods, and so on, she simply indicated that she did not know the cash value of the personal property, she did not know the extent of the damage to the goods, and she she did not know the cost of repair. None of this information was detailed enough for State Farm, which rejected her claim. As for WR, he knew what property had been in the house, and he did attempt to provide information as it its value. However, he also changed his mind as to the value of various pieces of property. This wavering seems to have violated one of the major prohibitions in the insurance policy. That prohibition said that that the insured was prohibited from misleading the insurance company about the value of the property. Consequently, State Farm rejected his claim also.

How do you think that things worked out for GR and WR? Do they have an insurable interest in the house? Is the house a homestead and, thus, the source of an insurable interest? Should WR be allowed to recover for the loss of her property even though she cannot identify the property? Should GR be allowed to recover for his property even though he changed his mind about the value of that property? These and other similar questions are answered, sort of, in the pages ahead. [See: *State Farm Fire and Casualty Company v. Ramsey*, 719 F.Supp. 1337 (1989) United States District Court, S.D. Mississippi, E.D.]

Opening Case Questions

1. What is an insurable interest? Explain.
2. Who can hold an insurable interest? Explain.
3. Why does the ownership of property matter in an insurance case? Explain.
4. What does an insurance company want to know about the personal property that forms the basis of a claim? Explain.
5. In this case, did the plaintiffs adhere to all of the requirements laid out in the insurance policy, and if not, will that affect their recovery under that policy? Explain.

Source: State Farm Fire and Casualty Company v. Ramsey, 719 F.Supp. 1337 (1989) United States District Court, S.D. Mississippi, E.D.

 Learning Objectives

1. Define and explain the purpose of insurance.
2. Identify the contractual elements of an insurance agreement.
3. Make clear the importance of insurable interest.
4. Differentiate among the different types of life insurance.
5. Explain how insurable interest differs with life insurance and property insurance.
6. Explain the coinsurance clause in most property insurance policies.
7. Describe coverage given by fire, marine, homeowner's, flood, and renter's insurance.
8. Differentiate among the principal kinds of automobile insurance.
9. Describe the benefits included in health insurance policies.
10. List the steps in applying for, obtaining, and maintaining an insurance policy.

19-1 Risk Assessment and Peril Management

The legal system is not a stand-alone network. Nor does it function in a void. The executive, legislative, judicial, and administrative agents often get overly connected with one another, while consistently acting at cross purposes. Yet, the emergent order within the network does exist. While this order is not always apparent on a daily basis, in the long run, the system does work, even when, logically, it should not. This paradox is especially true of the interface between insurance and the law. Strictly speaking, insurance is a business, not a branch of the law. Moreover, when insurance does interact with the law, at times it runs at counter purposes to the law. Insurance involves contracts made by agents to help people protect their lives, their health, their income, their savings, and their property against negligence, intentional torts, and criminal activity. Most insurance companies are large corporations, which themselves need protection. Some of the types of insurance available intersect with health law and property law. Others depend on an appreciation of and proper application of tort law and criminal law. Moreover, all insurance agreements are binding contracts, requiring the application of contract law. For all these reasons, and probably more, we cannot neatly package, divide, and classify insurance into well-ordered, unrelated topics. Keep this in mind and you will better understand some of the contradictory and overlapping topics that we are about to invade.

Risks and Perils: A Double-Sided Mirror

The problematic nature of insurance emerges because, at its core, it is built upon two conflicting sets of risks and perils. **Risks** are threats to those items (life, health, property, income, savings, investments, reputations, and so on) that a party wants to protect. **Perils** are the dangers that a party might pose to others and against which that party must shield itself. For example, from the risk side of the equation, when a party's life, health, property, income, savings, investments, and reputation are in danger, that party will purchase insurance to protect itself should the worst happen. So a party will purchase health insurance, home owner's insurance, automobile insurance, renter's insurance, and so on. Conversely, from the perils side of the issue, when a party's actions, business, and property endanger others, that party will buy insurance that will provide it with a legal defense team and with money to reimburse those it might injure. **Insurance**, then, is the transfer of the risk of economic loss, for a fee, from the insured to the insurer. Small contributions by a large number of people provide sufficient funds, with the help of properly managed investment opportunities, to protect the losses that are suffered by a few as they occur on an annual basis. The function of insurance then is to distribute each person's risk among all others who may not be imperiled that year or over many years. (See Table 19-1.)

The Insurance Contract: Parties, Elements, Interest

An insurance policy is actually a contract that follows the standard rules of regular contract law. This means that once you learn contract law, you already have a pretty good handle on the rules of making, writing, interpreting, enforcing, and terminating an insurance policy. That is the good news. The bad news is that you also have to learn a few things that supplement contract law and are peculiar to insurance contracts (or policies, if you will). That includes the parties to a contract as well as the concept of insurable interests, and the duties of the insured and the insurer.

Insurance policies, like other contracts, require the four elements of a contract: mutual assent, capacity, consideration, and legality. The application filled in by an applicant is an offer to the insurer, who may then accept or reject the offer. When the insurer (the offeree) accepts the offer (the application) from the applicant (the offeror), mutual assent emerges between the parties. A party to a contract must also be capable of understanding the terms of the agreement. Consideration arises from the premiums paid by the insured and the promise of the insurer to pay money to the beneficiary if a certain event happens. Finally, the subject matter must not be tainted by illegality. For example, a fire insurance policy written on a building in which the owners permitted the illegal manufacture of fireworks would be void in the event of a fire.

Table 19-1 Examples of Risk Management Strategies

Personal Event	RISKS — Financial Impact	Strategies for Reducing Financial Impact
Disability	• Loss of income • Increased expenses	• Savings and investments • Disability insurance
Death	• Loss of income	• Life insurance • Estate planning
Property loss	• Catastrophic storm damage to property • Repair or replacement • Cost of theft	• Property repair and upkeep • Auto insurance • Homeowner's insurance • Flood or earthquake insurance
Liability	• Claims and settlement costs • Lawsuits and legal expenses • Loss of personal assets and income	• Maintaining property • Homeowner's insurance • Auto insurance

Source: Gordon W. Brown, *Understanding Business and Personal Law,* 11e, p. 752.

A SOON TO BE CLASSIC CASE

Steve Granger and his partner set up a trust to cover their holdings, which included rental property in Akron, Ohio. Granger, his partner, and the trust took out a dwelling insurance policy on the rental property, and Granger added an umbrella policy all his own. The policy was held by Auto-Owners (Mutual) Insurance Company (AOMIC). Granger's problems started when he told Kozera, a potential renter, that he had no intention of renting the place in Akron to anyone with children. Kozera, the mother of a six-year-old, was insulted and humiliated by Granger's attitude and by his allegedly harsh, discriminatory words. Accordingly, she logged a complaint with the Fair Housing Contact Service (FHCS), which filed a federal lawsuit against Granger. The charges alleged that Granger's refusal to rent to Kozera was racially motivated and based on her family status. When AOMIC found out about the lawsuit, the company sent a letter to Granger indicating that the dwelling insurance policy on the Akron property did not include claims of discrimination like the one filed by Kozera, and so the company had no duty to defend Granger, his partner, or the trust. Backed into a corner, Granger settled and handed over $32,500 as compensation to Kozera. Granger then sued AOMIC.

As the case unfolded, it became clear that Granger's claim against AOMIC was based on the company's refusal to defend Granger under the umbrella policy. The trial court granted the insurance company's summary judgment motion. The appeals court, however, elected to hear counterarguments, insofar as they addressed the discrimination claim under the umbrella policy. The appellate court began by examining the language used in the umbrella policy, specifically as that language relates to the concept of personal injury. The appellate court noted at the outset that the goal of any court in the interpretation of language is to uncover the original intent of the parties. To do this, the court had to focus on the plain and ordinary meaning of the words. Moreover, the court must also interpret any ambiguous terms strictly against the insurer (AOMIC) because the insurer is the party that actually wrote the agreement and, therefore, had the opportunity and the ability to make the terms as understandable (or as garbled) as it wanted. This rule of interpretation was very important in this case because AOMIC was trying to limit its responsibilities in relation to Granger. To get at the plain language of the policy, the court used *Black's Law Dictionary* and noted that *emotional distress* is defined as "[a] highly unpleasant mental reaction (such as anguish, grief, fright, *humiliation*, or fury) that results from another person's conduct[.]" After reading this definition, the appellate court decided that Kozera *could* have suffered emotional distress when Granger humiliated her. Since any emotional distress that results from humiliation is a personal injury covered under the policy, AOMIC should have defended Granger in the lawsuit. End of case! [See: *Granger, et al. v. Auto Owners, Insurance*, 2013-Ohio-2792, Case. 26473, Court of Appeals, Ninth Judicial District (June 2013).]

Source: see: *Granger, et al. v. Auto Owners, Insurance*, 2013-Ohio-2792, Case. 26473, Court of Appeals, Ninth Judicial District (June 2013).

In addition, the courts have ruled that, in the interpretation of contractual terms, the goal of the court must be to determine the original intent of the parties when they first sat down to enter the agreement. In order to accomplish this goal, the court will focus on the plain and ordinary meaning of the words in the agreement. Moreover, the court will also interpret any ambiguous terms strictly against the insurer because the insurer is the party that actually writes the agreement and, therefore, has the opportunity and the ability to make the terms as clear (or as obscure) as it wants. This technique is especially critical when the court interprets any clause that is designed to somehow limit or narrow the coverage that the insurer is granting to the insured.

The parties to an insurance contract are the insurer (sometimes called the *underwriter*), the insured, and the beneficiary. The **insurer** accepts the risk of loss in return for a **premium** (the consideration paid for a policy) and agrees to **indemnify**, or compensate, the insured against the loss specified in the contract. The **insured** is the party (or parties) protected by the insurance contract. The contract of insurance is called the **policy**. The period of time during which the insurer assumes the risk of loss is known as the life of the policy. A third party, to whom payment of compensation is sometimes provided by the contract, is called the **beneficiary**.

Insurable Interest and the Duties of the Parties

A person or business applying for insurance must have an insurable interest in the subject matter of the policy to be insured. An **insurable interest** is the financial interest that a policyholder has in the person or property that is insured. In the case of life insurance, all people have an insurable interest in their own lives as well as the lives of their spouses and dependents. Business partners have an insurable interest in each other because they could suffer a financial loss if a partner dies. A corporation can have a financial interest in its key employees for the same reason. In the case of property insurance, anyone who would suffer a financial loss from damage to property would have an insurable interest in that property. For life insurance, the insurable interest must exist at the time the insurance is purchased. In contrast, for property insurance, the insurable interest must exist at the time of loss.

THE OPENING CASE Round 2
Owning Is Not so Satisfying a Thing, after All, as Selling. It Is Not Logical, but It Is Often True.

In the Opening Case, Willie Ramsey (WR) and his wife, Georgia Ramsey (GR), received a warranty dead from James Sumrall as tenants-in-common to a piece of property. The couple then granted a security deed to Bay Springs Bank. Subsequently, WR and GR built a house on the land and lived there until GR went to live with her daughter. Meanwhile back in Mississippi, the Bay Springs Bank foreclosed and the property was purchased by Don Husbands (DH). DH received the property through a substitute trustee deed. Later, the property went back to WR, who demolished the original dwelling and replaced it with a new one. He promptly insured his new residence with State Farm for $30,000 and the contents for $15,000. WR later defaulted on another loan with Tower Loan. Tower foreclosed. Subsequently, the house was razed by a fire and WR tried to collect on the insurance policy. State Farm, of course said no. State Farm maintained that it had no duty to pay WR because, despite the fact that he had been living in the house when it burned (why he was living there was never explained), he had no insurable interest in the property. Recall that an insurable interest requires that a person making a claim must have a financial interest in the property that was insured. In the case of property insurance, that financial interest must exist when the damage actually occurred. Thus, in the case, the fact that WR owned the property at the time he purchased the State Farm policy makes no difference. In contrast, WR may have an insurable interest in the contents of the building. Moreover, since GR and WR are still married, WR may also have a claim on the contents of the house if she had any property of value in the house when destroyed in the fire. Of course, to recover for the loss of that personal property, both of WR and GR will have to comply with any contractual requirements that State Farm may have placed in the policy. Typically, such requirements will include listing the property with specificity and stating the value of that property among several other things. Read on to see what happened to any and all of the claims made by both WR and GR on the house and its contents. [See: *State Farm Fire and Casualty Company v. Ramsey*, 719 F.Supp. 1337 (1989) United States District Court, S.D. Mississippi, E.D.]

Source: State Farm Fire and Casualty Company v. Ramsey, 719 F.Supp. 1337 (1989) United States District Court, S.D. Mississippi, E.D.

As is true of all contracts, the parties to an insurance contract (policy) voluntarily adopt the duties that emerge from that agreement. At the same time, they receive certain benefits under the contract. The insured has an initial duty to inform the insured of everything the insurer asks so that the insurer can enter the policy agreement with full knowledge of the insured's situation. In the computer age, this means that some insurers may ask for full access to a client's computer records. This approach may seem intrusive and a bit extreme. However, the contractual relationship is voluntary and the insured can always seek out another insurer if the insured is uncomfortable with the arrangement. Once the contract has been entered, the insured has the duty to (1) pay the premiums on time and in the fashion prescribed by the insurer, (2) tell the insurance company about any claims in a timely and judicious manner, and (3) work together with the insurer when the time comes for an inquiry.

The insurer has a threefold duty. Once a claim has been placed on the table, the insurer has the **duty to investigate** the claim to determine all the facts and to decide in an appropriate manner if the client is entitled to payment. If the client is covered and the claim is authentic, then the insurer has the **duty to pay** the insured directly if the insured's property must be replaced or repaired or to pay any claim by a third party based on a liability clause. Finally, if the case is disputed by a third party, then the insurer has the **duty to defend** the client. Moreover, insurance companies have the right to step into the shoes of the party they compensate and sue any party the compensated party could have sued. This substitution of one person in place of another relative to a lawful claim is known as **subrogation**.

quick quiz 19-1

1. The purpose of insurance is to spread losses among people who can most afford it.   true | false
2. An application filled in by an insurance applicant is a binding contract on the insurer.   true | false
3. Anyone can obtain insurance on another person or property, regardless of their relationship.   true | false

19-2 Types of Insurance

It is possible to obtain insurance against almost any risk if an individual or business is willing to pay the price. The premium charged will depend on the risk involved. Life insurance, property insurance, and health insurance are discussed here.

Life Insurance

Life insurance is an insurance contract that provides monetary compensation for losses suffered by another's death. Anyone has an insurable interest in the life of another if a financial loss will occur if the insured dies. For example, an insurable interest exists if the person who buys the insurance is dependent on the insured for education, support, business (partners), or debt collection. A life insurance policy will remain valid and enforceable even if the insurable interest terminates. It is necessary only that the insurable interest exists at the time the policy was issued. Premiums for life insurance are based on several factors, including the age and health of the insured, the coverage, and the type of policy. It is less expensive to buy life insurance at a young age because the death rate for young people is very low, and their health is usually at its peak. If an individual takes out insurance on him- or herself, it is not necessary for the beneficiary to have an insurable interest in the insured's life. However, if a person takes out life insurance on someone else, that person must have an insurable interest in the insured's life. The principal types of life insurance are straight life, limited-payment life, term, and endowment insurance.

Straight Life Insurance **Straight life insurance**, which is also known as **ordinary life insurance** or **whole life insurance**, requires the payment of premiums throughout the life of the insured and pays the beneficiary the face value of the policy upon the insured's death. The amount of the premium is determined by the age of the insured at the time of purchase and normally stays the same throughout the life of the policy. The younger the insured, the lower the premium, because the company expects to collect many years' worth of premiums.

Straight life insurance contains an investment feature known as the *cash surrender value*. The cash surrender value usually builds up slowly at first but in later years approaches the face amount of the policy. At some stated point (usually at the age of 95 or 100 years), it equals the face value of the policy. An insured can cancel a straight life policy at any time and receive its cash surrender value. Straight life insurance also contains a feature called a *loan value*, which is an amount of money that may be borrowed against the cash surrender value of the policy, usually at a relatively favorable rate of interest. During inflationary times, when bank interest rates are high, insurance policies are often excellent sources of loans at low interest rates.

EXAMPLE 19-1: Straight Life Insurance

At age 18 years, LaPlume purchased a straight life insurance policy with a face value of $20,000. The premiums were quite modest. At some later time, LaPlume could borrow on the policy or trade it in for its cash surrender value. Or, LaPlume could continue premium payments until death. If LaPlume died while a loan was outstanding, the insurance company would deduct the amount of the loan from the amount it paid to LaPlume's beneficiary.

A form of straight life insurance, called **universal life insurance**, allows the policy owner flexibility in choosing and changing terms of the policy. Within certain guidelines, the policy owner can modify the face value of the policy as well as the premiums in response to changing needs and circumstances in the policy owner's life. Under a typical universal life policy:

- Premiums may be increased or decreased within policy limits.
- The amount of insurance may be increased, subject to evidence of insurability, or decreased, subject to set minimums.
- The owner may borrow up to the maximum loan value at a prearranged interest rate. Policy loans reduce the cash surrender value and death benefit.
- Withdrawals may be made from the cash surrender value.

Limited-Payment Life Insurance **Limited-payment life insurance** provides that the payment of premiums will stop after a stated length of time—usually 10, 20, or 30 years. The amount of the policy will be paid to the beneficiary upon the death of the insured, whether the death occurs during the payment period or after. Because of the limited number of payments made by the insured, the premiums are proportionately higher than those for straight life; however, the cash surrender value grows faster than that of straight life insurance.

Term Insurance As the name suggests, **term insurance** is issued for a particular period, usually 10 or 20 years. The time period is known as the term. Term insurance is the least expensive kind of life insurance because term policies have no cash or loan value, as others do. Term insurance offers protection alone, in contrast to straight life, which combines protection with a savings plan. Term insurance can be renewable at the end of each period simply by paying the increased premium, without need for a new medical examination. *Convertible* term insurance policies can be converted to straight life policies without taking a new medical examination—allowing protection throughout the insured's lifetime. A modified form of term insurance is *decreasing term insurance*. The premium stays constant from year to year, but the amount of protection (death benefit) decreases over the years. This type of insurance is widely used to cover the outstanding balance of a home mortgage.

Annuity An **annuity** is guaranteed retirement income purchased by paying either a lump-sum premium or making periodic payments to an insurer. The insured may choose either (a) to receive an income for a certain fixed number of years, with a beneficiary receiving whatever is left of the annuity if the insured dies before the term expires, or (b) to receive payments as long as the insured lives and, upon death, relinquish whatever is left of the annuity, if anything.

Exemptions from Risk Many life insurance policies contain clauses that exempt the insurance company from liability in certain situations. For example, policies often do not cover the insured when riding in an airplane, violating the law, or working in certain dangerous occupations. Most policies provide that beneficiaries can recover for a death caused by suicide if the suicide occurs more than two years after the policy was taken out. They may not recover, however, when the policy contains a provision preventing such recovery or when the life insurance was purchased by someone planning suicide or who was insane. One example of a named beneficiary who could recover would be a creditor of the insured. Life insurance policies usually include an exemption from liability in times of war. The exemption states that the insurer will not be liable on the policy if the insured is killed while a member of the armed forces, generally outside the continental United States, or by service-connected causes.

Optional Provisions Life insurance policies have many optional provisions that may be purchased by the insured. Three popular options are double indemnity, waiver of premium,

> **Did You Know?**
> Young families with large financial obligations are usually better off with term life insurance rather than whole life. The substantially lower premiums may enable them to purchase needed coverage to protect against loss of income at a time when they most need it.

and guaranteed insurability. For an additional premium, the insured may purchase a benefit known as **double indemnity**, or accidental death benefit. This option provides that if the insured dies from accidental causes, the insurer will pay double the amount of the policy to the beneficiary. Death must occur within 90 days of the accident for this benefit to apply. The *waiver of premium* option excuses the insured from paying premiums if he or she becomes disabled. Some insurance policies automatically include the waiver in their provisions; others offer it as an extra-cost option. A *guaranteed insurability* option allows the insured to pay an extra premium initially in exchange for a guaranteed option to buy more insurance at certain specified times later. The additional insurance can be purchased with no questions asked; thus, no new medical examination is required even if the insured develops a serious illness before exercising the option.

Property Insurance

Property insurance can be purchased to protect both real and personal property. To establish the existence of an insurable interest in property, the insured must demonstrate a monetary interest in the property. This monetary interest means that the insured will suffer a financial loss if the property is damaged or destroyed. Unlike life insurance, this insurable interest must exist when the loss occurs. Property insurance can be made less expensive by the use of a **deductible**, which is an amount of any loss that is to be paid by the insured. It can be a specified dollar amount, a percentage of the claim amount, or a specified amount of time that must elapse before benefits are paid. The bigger the deductible, the lower is the premium charged for the same coverage.

Coinsurance Clauses **Coinsurance** is an insurance policy provision under which the insurer and the insured share costs, after the deductible is met, according to a specific formula. Most property and inland marine policies have a coinsurance clause, which limits the insurance company's liability for a loss if the property is not insured for its full replacement value. For example, if a homeowner's insurance policy has an 80 percent coinsurance clause, the building must be insured for 80 percent of its replacement value to receive full reimbursement for a loss (see Figure 19-1).

Fire Insurance A fire insurance policy is a contract in which the fire insurance company promises to pay the insured if some real or personal property is damaged or destroyed by fire. A fire insurance policy is effective on delivery to the insured, even before the

---

TYPICAL COINSURANCE CLAUSE

"The insurance company will pay that part of a loss that the insurance carried bears to 80 percent of the replacement cost of the building."

It would cost $100,000 to replace Felipe Garcia's house. If he insured it for $60,000, the insurance company would pay only three-fourths of any loss, computed as follows:

$$\frac{\text{Amount of insurance carried}}{\text{Percent of replacement cost}} = \frac{\$60,000}{80\% \text{ of } \$100,000} = \frac{\$60,000}{\$80,000} = \frac{3}{4}$$

A fire partially destroys the building, causing $40,000 worth of damage. Because of the coinsurance clause, Garcia would recover $30,000 (¾ of the loss) from the insurance company.

Figure 19-1 Here is a typical coinsurance clause found in an insurance policy. It limits the insurer's liability for a loss if the property is not insured for full, or at least 80 percent of, replacement value.

premium is paid. Even an oral agreement will make fire insurance effective. The insurer's liability under a fire policy usually covers losses other than those directly attributed to fire. Under most policies, claims may also be made for losses from water used to fight the fire; scorching; smoke damage to goods; deliberate destruction of property as a means of controlling a spreading fire; lightning, even if there is no resultant fire; riot or explosion, if a fire does result; and losses through theft or exposure of goods removed from a burning building.

Marine Insurance Marine insurance is one of the oldest types of insurance coverage, dating back to Venetian traders who sailed the Mediterranean Sea. Ocean marine insurance covers ships at sea. Inland marine insurance covers goods that are moved by land carriers such as rail, truck, and airplane. Inland marine insurance also covers such items as jewelry, fine arts, musical instruments, and wedding presents. Customers' goods in the possession of bailees, such as fur-storage houses and dry cleaners, are also covered by inland marine insurance. A *floater policy* is one that insures property that cannot be covered by specific insurance because the property is constantly changing in either value or location. A personal property floater, for example, covers personal property in general, wherever it is located.

Homeowner's Insurance Many of the leading insurance companies offer a combination policy known as the homeowner's policy. This insurance gives protection for all types of losses and liabilities related to home ownership. In general, homeowner's insurance will cover any damage that occurs to the both the outside and the inside of the house. It is also standard procedure to insure all the personal property included in the contents of the house and to insure against liability for injuries that occur on the property. Most (all?) homeowner's policies will include a deductible and a maximum amount that the insurance company agrees to pay. As noted earlier, a deductible charge is that amount that the homeowner agrees to pay up front in case of a loss. The insurance company then covers the rest of the amount of the loss up to the maximum amount agreed to in the policy. For example, if the homeowner's deductible is $5,000, the loss is $300,000, and the maximum coverage is $250,000 then the homeowners will have to pay $5,000, the insurance company will then cover the rest of loss up to the maximum of $250,000, leaving $45,000 for the homeowners to cover, unless they have supplemental homeowner's insurance to cover the remaining amount. Among the items covered are losses from fire, windstorms, burglary, vandalism, and injuries suffered by other persons while on the property. Losses from flooding generally are not covered under a homeowner's policy. However, homeowners can purchase supplemental homeowner's insurance to cover losses from flooding.

Recovering for the Property Itself To recover on a homeowner's policy, a policy holder must demonstrate that he or she had an insurable interest in the property at the time the damage wan inflicted on the property. Such proof may become somewhat problematic when more than one party claims to own the same real property in question. Real property is land and anything attached to the land. When real property is owned by more than one part each party is called a tenant. There are four types of co-tenancy: tenancy in common, joint tenancy, community property, and tenancy by the entirety. An additional type of ownership unique to American law is the homestead, at least as it relates to what is called the homestead exemption.

Tenancy in Common When two or more persons own real property as tenants in, each person owns an undivided share of the whole property. A co-tenant's share of the property transfers to that co-tenant's heirs upon his or her death rather than to the surviving co-tenants. Each co-tenant is entitled to possession of the entire premises. This rule is known as unity of possession. Tenants in common have the right to sell or deed away as a gift their share in the property without the permission of the other co-tenants. When this action occurs, any new owner becomes a tenant in common with the remaining co-tenants. One co-tenant's interest is not necessarily the same as another co-tenant's interest. In fact, under the laws of some states, when a non-co-tenant buys the tenancy-in-common at a judicial sale for the debt of all the co-tenants, and then later sells the land to one of the former co-tenants, that co-tenant has taken title to the property against the other co-tenants and, in essence, owns the property him or herself. This is due to the fact that the acquisition of title by a third person operates to terminate the original tenancy-in-common. Not all states follow this rule and so, for this reason alone, it is always best to check the laws of your home state before discussing a tenancy-in-common.

Joint Tenancy When two or more persons own real property as joint tenants, the estate created is a single estate with multiple ownership. Each tenant owns the entire estate, subject to the equal rights of the other joint tenants. Four unities must be present to create a joint tenancy: time, title, interest, and possession. (1) The unity of time means that all owners must take title at the same time. (2) The unity of title means that all owners must derive title from the same source. (3) The unity of interest means that all owners must have equal interests in the property. (4) The unity of possession means that all owners must have the equal right to possess the property.

Community Property Property (except a gift or inheritance) that is acquired by the personal efforts of either spouse during marriage is called community property. By law, community property belongs to both spouses equally. The law originated in Spain and was embraced by Mexico; it is presently followed in Puerto Rico; in some Southern states, such as Texas and Louisiana; and in many Western states, such as California and Nevada. Although state laws differ, they all operate on the theory that both spouses contribute equally to the marriage—that all property acquired during the marriage is the result of the combined efforts of both of them.

Tenancy by the Entirety A tenancy by the entirety may be held only by a husband and wife and is based upon the common law doctrine known as unity of person. Under this very old doctrine, a husband and wife were regarded, under the law, as one. In theory, each spouse owned the entire estate, and neither could destroy it by any separate act. The husband, however, had the entire control over the estate, including the exclusive right to possession and the right to all rents and profits. Many states have done away with the statute of tenancy by the entirety. Other states have enacted statutes giving equal rights to husbands and wives who own property as tenants by the entirety. Still other states require both spouses to consent to a valid mortgage on property owned as tenants by the entirety. It is, therefore, advisable to check state law first when discussing a tenancy-by-the entirety.

Homestead A homestead is the family home and the land on which the house is located, including land adjacent to the dwelling. The advantage of a homestead is that the homestead generally cannot be sold for the debts of the homeowner provided that the homeowner continues to reside on that property in that home. Of course, as is true of many (most?) protections, the protection against a forced sales of the homestead has its limits. Usually, the protection against a forced sale does not apply to mortgages or to real estate taxes. Some states do not extend the protection to mechanics liens. It is also a good idea to check state laws because some states have imposed additional limitations on the protection.

THE OPENING CASE *Round 3*
Owning Is Not so Satisfying a Thing, after All, as Selling. It Is Not Logical, but It Is often True.

We learned earlier that Georgia (GR) and Willie Ramsey (WR) purchased a parcel of land in in Mississippi. The couple received a warranty dead from James Sumrall as tenants-in-common to that property and executed a security deed in favor of Bay Springs Bank (SBS). The couple built and lived in a house on that land until GR left WR and and moved to Illinois. Later, the bank foreclosed on the property, which was purchased by Don Husbands (DH). WR received the property back from DH through a quit claim deed. WR then built a new home on the same lot and bought insurance from State Farm Fire and Casualty (State Farm) for the house at $30,000 and its contents at $15,000. WR later took out a loan of $18,555.30 on the property from Tower Loan of Mississippi (Tower). As security for the loan, WR conveyed a deed of trust to Tower. Eventually, Tower was forced to foreclose. Even after a trustee deed was executed conveying the property to Tower, WR continued to live in the house.

About 90 days later, a fire destroyed the house. When WR attempted to collect on the insurance policy, State Farm refused to pay, stating that WR no longer had an insurable interest in the property. In response, WR argued that the Tower foreclosure was invalid under the deed of trust and, therefore, he remained the owner of the home and his insurable interest remained intact. WR formulated his argument using the following rationale. When Bay Springs foreclosed, WR and GR were tenants-in-common. So when WR repurchased the property from DH, it represented a redemption of the property that both he, WR, and his wife, GR, owned as tenants-in-common. After that redemption, WR and GR held the property as tenants-in-the-entirety because they continued to be married. As a result, WR by himself could not encumber the property without GR's consent, Therefore, the transfer of the property via the deed of trust was invalid, and WR still owned the property at the time of the fire, thereby establishing his insurable interest. The Court disagreed, noting that, when DH purchased the property at the foreclosure sale for the debt owed by WR, the co-tenancy was ended and WR then acquired the property for himself alone. Therefore, when he transferred the land to Towers and Towers foreclosed, the foreclosure was valid, and Towers had the only insurable interest in the property.

In the alternative, WR also argued that even if the co-tenancy was severed when he sold the property to DH, when he (WR) bought it back, it became the family homestead and, as a result the home belonged to WR and GR, and they held the insurable interest, not Towers. Again the court disagreed. In fact, this time the court had no difficulty deciding against WR and GR because GR had not lived in the home and had only visited it sporadically. Thus, calling it a homestead would be the wildest stretch of the imagination. The court put it this way: "Mrs. Ramsey never lived in the home that is the subject of this dispute and had no interest in the home or the property on which it was situated. She was absent not only 'at the time of execution of the deed of conveyance,' but for at least five years preceding execution of that deed and at all times since the execution. Even if, as the Ramseys now claim, Mrs. Ramsey initially chose to reside apart from her husband as the result of his merciless beatings, it remains a fact that following Mr. Ramsey's repurchase and construction of a new home on the property, Mrs. Ramsey never resided there and hence it was not her homestead." [See: *State Farm Fire and Casualty Company v. Ramsey*, 719 F.Supp. 1337 (1989) United States District Court, S.D. Mississippi, E.D.]

Source: State Farm Fire and Casualty Company v. Ramsey, 719 F. Supp. 1337 (1989) United States District Court, S.D. Mississippi, E.D.

Recovering for the Contents In addition, when claim is filed, the insured will have to fill out a **proof of loss form** that details the personal property that was destroyed during the incident that gave rise to the claim. Often such a form will ask for information on the value of the property, documentation on the value of the property, the existence of other insurance policies that may cover the loss, the time of the incident, those individuals who claim the loss, their interest in the lost property, and so on. Usually, the policy will also specify a time period, often about 60 days or so, by which the proof of loss must be filed with the company. Generally, insurance policies that cover the contents of a home will disallow any claim if the insured has deliberately misled the company about the existence or the value of that lost property. Among the items covered are losses from fire, windstorms, burglary, vandalism, and injuries suffered by other persons while on the property. Losses from flooding generally are not covered under a homeowner's policy. However, as noted previously, homeowners can purchase supplemental homeowner's insurance to cover losses from flooding.

THE OPENING CASE *Round 4*
Owning Is Not so Satisfying a Thing, after All, as Selling. It Is Not Logical, but It Is often True.

Recall that in the Opening Case, a fire destroyed the second house that Willie Ramsey had constructed on a parcel of land that he and his wife, Georgia Ramsey, had purchased in Bay Springs, Mississippi. After the fire, WR tried to collect on an insurance contract that he had entered with State Farm Fire and Casualty Company for $30,000 on the house and $15,000 on its contents of the house. State Farm refused to pay, stating that WR no longer had an insurable interest in the property. We've seen how that turned out, so let's look at what happened when both GR and WR tried to recover for their lost personal property.

In a nutshell, State Farm denied both claims. The insurance company rejected WR's claim because she failed to properly file a proof of loss form as required by the policy. Instead of filing a detailed report that would include such things as when the loss occurred, her interest in the personal property, whether another insurance policy covered the goods, and so on, she simply indicated that she did not know the cash value of the personal property, she did not know the extent of the damage to the goods, and she she did not know the cost of repair. The court decided that even though WR had no direct knowledge of her own about the personal property in the house that belonged to her, she should have a chance to seek some proof that would support her claims. Therefore, the court decided that she ought to have her day in court. As for WR, he did know what was in the house that belonged to him, and he did attempt to provide information as it its value. However, he also changed his mind on the value of various pieces of property. This wavering seemed to violate one of the major prohibitions in the insurance policy—that the insured were prohibited from misleading the insurance company about the existence of the valuation of the property for which an insured had laid claim. Again, the court found against the insurance company, ruling that WR was entitled to his day in court and that the real question in his case was whether he had willfully misled the insurance company or had simply had a bad memory. [See: *State Farm Fire and Casualty Company v. Ramsey*, 719 F. Supp. 1337 (1989) United States District Court, S.D. Mississippi, E.D.]

Source: *State Farm Fire and Casualty Company v. Ramsey*, 719 F. Supp. 1337 (1989) United States District Court, S.D. Mississippi, E.D.

Flood Insurance Flooding can be caused by heavy rains, melting snow, inadequate drainage systems, failed protective devices such as levees and dams, and tropical storms and hurricanes. Nevertheless, most commercial, homeowner's, and renter's insurance policies do not cover flood damage. To obtain such coverage, special flood insurance must be obtained from an insurance agent.

Most flood insurance is backed by the National Flood Insurance Program (NFIP), established by Congress in response to the high cost of taxpayer-funded disaster relief for flood victims and the amount of damage caused by floods. Communities that agree to manage flood hazard areas by adopting minimum standards can participate in the NFIP.

However, communities that do not participate in the program cannot receive flood insurance, federal grants and loans, federal disaster assistance, or federal mortgage insurance for the acquisition or construction of structures located in flood hazard areas of their community. Most lending institutions require borrowers to obtain flood insurance when they buy, build, or improve structures in special flood hazard areas (SFHAs). Lending institutions that are federally regulated or federally insured must determine if the structure is located in an SFHA and provide written notice requiring flood insurance.

Following Hurricane Katrina, which devastated the Gulf Coast in 2005, many insurance claims were delayed, and others were not paid on the grounds that damages were caused by water rather than by wind, though most homeowners had little or no flood insurance. Hundreds of lawsuits were brought by disgruntled homeowners against insurance companies, and some million-dollar jury verdicts against the companies were settled out of court. Some of the jury awards were for punitive damages because the companies failed to pay the claims quickly enough. A federal appeals court found that many insurance policies covering property in New Orleans contained flood exclusions. The court said, "Regardless of what caused the failure of the flood-control structures that were put in place to prevent such catastrophe, their failure resulted in a widespread flood that damaged the plaintiffs' property. Their policies clearly excluded water damage caused by floods." One lower federal court case upheld the insurance company's view that homeowner policies cover damage from a hurricane's wind but not the rising water that ensues, including wind-driven surge. Several major insurers in Mississippi, which does not allow punitive damages in these cases, entered an agreement with the Mississippi attorney general to pay about $80 million to 639 policyholders whose claims were denied following Katrina. As part of the agreement, insurers were required to reopen and review claims filed by policyholders who live in that state.

Without adequate insurance, most people would be unable to even approach status quo after suffering a catastrophic event.
©ESB Essentials/Shutterstock

Renter's Insurance

Renter's insurance (or **tenant's insurance**) protects tenants against the damage or loss of personal property, stolen personal property, liability for a visitor's personal injury, and liability for negligent destruction of the rented premises. Renters can also be protected against living expenses, such as hotel charges, should the rental property become unlivable. Coverage can be obtained regardless of whether the renters are living in an apartment building, or a house, regardless of whether the house is a single family dwelling, a duplex, or a triplex. Insurance companies will sometimes customize renter's policies and may offer additional services such as identity theft coverage under the same policy. Renters also have the option of covering their personal property for the actual cash value or the replacement cost of that property. As is true of homeowner's insurance, losses from flooding generally are not covered under a renter's policy.

Dwelling Insurance

Most of the time, property insurance involves protecting property that the insured possesses and uses on a regular basis. However, some property, notably rental property, also demands protection, even though the owner may not set foot in the property for years. **Dwelling insurance** will provide this protection for the insured. A dwelling policy will protect the actual structure (a single family dwelling, an apartment building, and so on) from damage caused by fire, wind, snow, ice, lightning, and so on. However, it is also possible to add coverage for damage to the contents of the rental property. This coverage will be needed if the rental property is fully or partially furnished by the landlord or if the property contains appliances such as a range and refrigerator. Another clause can be added to a dwelling insurance policy to protect the landlord from lost rent. It is also possible, perhaps even advisable, for the insured to add liability coverage should a tenant or someone else, such as a postal worker, a contractor, or a visitor, be injured at the dwelling place. Liability insurance can also include coverage for medical payments.

Automobile Insurance

Automobile insurance provides for indemnity against losses resulting from fire, theft, or collision with another vehicle and damages arising out of injury by motor vehicles to the person or property of another. One thing to always remember about car insurance and about car accidents in general is that the law in relation to determining fault in such accidents differs a great deal from state to state. It is, therefore, always best to be very careful about choosing automobile insurance and in making certain that anyone involved in an accident contact an attorney in the state in which the accident occurs because it is the law of that state that generally applies to the accident. The following are the most common types of automobile insurance:

- Bodily injury liability insurance.
- Fault-based insurance.
- No-fault insurance.
- Add-on coverage.
- Threshold guidelines and choice-based jurisdictions.
- Uninsured-motorist insurance.
- Underinsured-motorist insurance.
- Medical payments insurance.
- Property damage liability insurance.
- Collision insurance.
- Comprehensive coverage.
- Substitute transportation insurance.
- Towing and labor insurance.

Bodily Injury Liability Insurance The risk of bodily injury or death to pedestrians and the occupants of other cars arising from the negligent operation of the insured's motor vehicle is covered by **bodily injury liability insurance**. Under liability insurance, the insurer is liable for damages up to the limit of the insurance purchased. The insurance company must also provide attorneys for the insured's defense in any civil court action.

Fault-Based Insurance Most states still base their car insurance and, therefore, the handling of car accident claims, on tort law. **Fault-based insurance** means that liability in an automobile accident will be measured by the degree of fault that can be assigned to each driver based on negligence principles. The level of fault that can be attributed to each party in the accident forms the basis for the insurance company's payment. In such a state, lawsuits may be necessary to determine damages based on pain and suffering, hospital expenses, lost wages, and so on.

No-Fault Insurance Currently no-fault insurance is required, at least to some extent, in some states. **No-fault insurance**, which is also called **personal injury protection (PIP)**, places limitations on the insured's ability to sue other drivers but allows drivers to collect damages and medical expenses from their own insurance carriers, regardless of who is at fault in an accident. This coverage helps cut down on fraudulent and excessively high claims. It also eliminates costly litigation needed to determine the negligence or lack of negligence of people involved in automobile accidents. On the other hand, even in no-fault states, a victim must sue if he or she wants to be compensated for actual property damage to the automobile itself, or to the items in the car. Some states alter the no-fault formula by adding a new element called a *threshold*. When the damages go beyond this threshold, which is defined by a set dollar amount, by injury description, or by time, the victim can file a negligence based lawsuit. Threshold injuries based on description include very serious ailments such as a permanent disability. In contrast, *time-based thresholds* are ascertained by measuring the time that the victim is incapacitated. Moreover, some jurisdictions permit both descriptive and time-based thresholds.

Add-On Coverage
In some jurisdictions, add-on coverage is legally recognized. These jurisdictions currently include Arkansas, Delaware, Maryland, and the District of Columbia. *Add-on coverage* permits a driver to buy optional coverage such as personal injury insurance that would allow him or her to receive payment without bothering to determine fault. Add-on policies, however, would not prevent the insured from bringing a lawsuit for pain and suffering and other similar injuries. Generally, threshold provisions are included in these policies.

Threshold Guidelines and Choice-Based Jurisdictions
Some no-fault jurisdictions set threshold guidelines that must be met by everyone regardless of the nature of their insurance policy. *Threshold guidelines* determine when victims can bring a lawsuit for injuries that result from an auto accident. Several states apply a strict *monetary threshold* while some no-fault jurisdictions have *descriptive thresholds*. A few states permit drivers to choose between no-fault and tort-law based insurance.

Uninsured-Motorist Insurance
Essentially, *uninsured-motorist insurance* provides protection against the risk of being injured by an uninsured motorist. The coverage applies when the person who caused the accident was at fault and had no bodily injury liability insurance to cover the loss. It protects the insured, the insured's spouse, relatives in the same household, and any other person occupying an insured automobile. It also protects people who are injured by hit-and-run drivers. No coverage is provided to an automobile used without the permission of the insured or the insured's spouse. Uninsured motorist insurance provides no reimbursement for damages to the insured's property.

Underinsured-Motorist Insurance
Basically, *underinsured-motorist insurance* provides protection against the risk of being injured by an underinsured motorist. For an insured to collect this insurance, someone without enough bodily injury coverage must have caused the accident.

Medical Payments Insurance
In essence, *medical payments insurance* pays for medical (and sometimes funeral) expenses resulting from bodily injuries to anyone occupying the policyholder's car at the time of an accident. In some states, it pays for the medical bills of all family members who are struck by a car or who are riding in someone else's car when it is involved in an accident.

Property Damage Liability Insurance
In brief, *property damage liability insurance* provides protection when other people bring claims or lawsuits against the insured for damaging property such as a car, fence, or tree. The person bringing the claim or suit must prove that the driver of the motor vehicle was at fault.

Collision Insurance
Basically, *collision insurance* provides against any loss arising from damage to the insured's automobile caused by accidental collision with another object or with any part of the roadbed. Liability under collision insurance is limited to the insured's car.

Comprehensive Coverage In short, comprehensive coverage provides protection against loss when the insured's car is damaged or destroyed by fire, lightning, flood, hail, windstorm, riot, vandalism, or theft. The insurance company's liability is limited to the actual cash value of the vehicle at the time of the loss.

Substitute Transportation Insurance Essentially, substitute transportation insurance reimburses up to specified limits for car rental or transportation costs, including taxi, bus, and train fare, while the insured's car is undergoing covered repairs.

Towing and Labor Insurance In essence, towing and labor insurance reimburses up to specified limits for towing and labor charges whenever the insured's car breaks down, whether or not an accident is involved.

Liability Insurance

As noted earlier in the chapter, perils are the dangers that a party might pose to others and against which that party must shield itself. When a party's actions, business, and property imperil others, that party should buy insurance that will provide it with a legal defense team and with the money to reimburse the victims, should the legal defense team fail to, well, to successfully defend that party. That type of coverage is generally referred to as liability insurance. Often, liability insurance is attached to another larger, more comprehensive insurance contract. Thus, an automobile contract may include a liability clause to protect the driver from medical expenses that might occur as the result of an accident. Or, as noted earlier, a landlord should demand a liability clause in his or her dwelling insurance policies. Most of the time liability coverage focuses on negligence rather than intentional torts. However, businesses sometimes carry liability policies covering intentional torts. Thus, a tavern owner should demand liability protection from the consequences of an overenthusiastic bouncer. Similarly, a security company should insist on protection from invasion of privacy lawsuits, and a newspaper should have a liability clause protecting it against defamation suits. Professionals, such as lawyers, accountants, physicians, nurses, teachers, and so on, should carry liability contracts against lawsuits based on malpractice (professional negligence).

Health Insurance

With the increasingly high costs of prescriptions, other medical products, and services, affordable health insurance is a foremost need in today's society. Many people obtain health insurance through a group insurance plan from the company for which they work. Others have individual plans that they purchase directly from an insurer. Still others have government health insurance plans through government employment, Medicare, and Medicaid. Health insurance policies often include the following benefits:

- Physician care.
- Prescription drugs.
- Inpatient and outpatient hospital care.
- Surgery.
- Dental and vision care.
- Long-term care for the elderly.

Major medical coverage pays for expenses beyond those covered by a basic plan, including long-term hospitalization and catastrophic illness.

HMOs and PPOs Health maintenance organizations (HMOs) contract with doctors and other health care professionals to provide health care services for their members. Members pay monthly premiums and must choose from a list of doctors provided by the HMO. HMOs encourage their members to have regular checkups, immunizations, and other forms of early treatment. In this way, it is hoped that people will be less likely to require more expensive kinds of treatment. Many different kinds of organizations sponsor HMOs, including doctors, community groups, insurance companies, labor unions, and corporations.

A preferred provider organization (PPO) is a group of health care providers, such as doctors or hospitals, that provide care for groups of employees at reduced rates. PPOs are usually sponsored as part of an employer's group health plan. Employees choose among the health care providers on the PPO list when they need treatment. Choosing a non-PPO provider reduces the benefits paid to the insured under the plan.

Medicare and Medicaid Most people 65 years of age and older are eligible for **Medicare**, a federally funded health insurance program. Medicare Part A helps pay for inpatient hospital care. Medicare Part B pays for 80 percent of doctors' and other medical services. Many people buy their own medigap insurance to cover the 20 percent not covered by Medicare. **Medicaid** is a health care plan for low-income people. State governments administer Medicaid, which is funded by both state and federal funds.

Disability Insurance Disability insurance pays benefits when a person cannot work because of a disability. Total, or long-term, disability pays if the insured cannot perform normal job duties for a year or longer; partial, or short-term, disability pays for shorter periods of time.

Long-Term Care Insurance Long-term care insurance helps cover care received in adult day care, assisted-living facilities, and nursing homes. Benefits are usually payable when an insured is unable to perform certain daily living activities without assistance, such as eating, bathing, dressing, or using the bathroom.

Legal Protection A variety of state and federal laws help make it easier for people with preexisting conditions to obtain and keep health insurance. A federal law known as HIPAA (Health Insurance Portability and Accountability Act) sets national standards for all health plans.

The Affordable Care Act The Affordable Care Act (ACA) was designed to make sure that all Americans have health insurance. The goal was high-minded and optimistic, but it had its problems. Still, as part of a complex adaptive system, it became, for awhile at least, a workable part of the legal network and had been somewhat successful in reaching its goals. However, complex adaptive systems rest for no one. Rather, they continually adapt to changing conditions. That is exactly what has happened in the world of health care. We will first review some of the provisions that were a part of the ACA and then take a look at some of the changes that have been introduced by the evolving health care complex adaptive system

The ACA had several features that made it a revolutionary element within the world of insurance, health care, and the law. First, it created a new document, called the Patient's Bill of Rights, which was designed to shield people from the errant practices of the health insurance trade. Another key feature related to the Patient's Bill of Right was the effort to provide as many cost-free preventive services as possible. The law also encouraged the implementation of accountable care organizations that were designed to encourage health care professionals to cooperate with one another to help patients get the best care available. The ACA also authorized the development of the health insurance marketplace, a website that was designed to assist people in enrolling in a health insurance plan by helping them see differences and similarities among available health insurance plans. People with a household income between 100 percent and 400 percent of the national poverty level as calculated by the federal government could take advantage of subsidies to purchase health insurance.

In 2013, the act introduced a pilot project labeled "bundling" under which health care providers would be paid per health care incident instead of by service rendered. The goal was to reduce costs by providing a flat rate per incident rather than an itemized step-by-step charge for each diagnostic test, each treatment, and each medication provided during that single incident. Also in 2013, the ACA instituted a funding program that would flow to state Medicaid plans to provide preventive care services. Starting in 2014, insurance providers were no longer permitted to discriminate based on preexisting conditions. Nor were they permitted to discriminate based on gender. Also in 2014, the law began to prohibit insurance companies from eliminating coverage for people who are enrolled in clinical trials for cancer treatments or treatments for other serious illnesses. In 2014, the law also provided a tax penalty for those without insurance. The maximum amount of the penalty tax was $95 for each adult not insured ($47.50 for each uninsured minor). However, the tax penalty worsened after 2014, continuing to climb until it reached a maximum in 2016. Federal tax forms were also revised in 2014 so that people could self-report a lack of insurance coverage. [See: "Key Features of the Affordable Care Act: Overview of the Health Care Law," U.S. Department of Health and Human Services, HHS.gov/HealthCare, August 31, 2014; and Alexandra B. Jeanblanc, "The Affordable Care Act and You," Ohio State Bar Association 2014 Annual Convention, Columbus, April 30–May 2, 2014.]

Changes in the Health Care Legislation Let's recall that every complex adaptive system (CAS) operates through the interaction of various agents. In the the health care system, these agents include the health care professionals and their patients, health care managers, insurance companies and their clients, pharmaceutical companies and their customers, politicians and their constituents, judges and lawyers, regulatory agencies like the Department of Health and Human Services, and so on. Also remember that in a CAS, there is no controlling agent, no single all powerful "boss" as it were. This is true even though some of these intermediary agents act as if they were the boss. (Read Congress here). Recall also that complex adaptive systems always remain complex. This means that these multiple levels of organization—health care professionals, health care managers, politicians, insurance companies, pharmaceutical companies, and so on—sometimes support one another and sometimes do not, thus complicating matters further. Remember also that the longer a CAS remains in operation, the more change results. Last of all, do not forget that as part of the process, a CAS often anticipates future developments and alters some practices as those branch points approach. That is precisely what has happened with the health care system and the Affordable Care Act. Congress has recently revised the ACA (some say repealed, others say replaced, some say revised, a few say rescued, and a few others, repaired. Take your pick.) A few of the areas that have been revamped include the individual and corporate mandates, the negative effects on older Americans, the evolving approach to preexisting conditions, and the addition of tax credits for those who do not have employer-provided health care coverage.

First, the new approach to health care will alter policies related to the individual and the corporate mandates. Recall that the ACA included a tax penalty for individuals without insurance. The new plan would eliminate this penalty. However, the new approach will not serve as a green light for people to drop their health insurance coverage completely. Under the new policy, people who do drop their insurance and then try to pick it up at a later date may find that they will be paying up to 30 percent more on the premiums for the same coverage. The goal here is to encourage those people with insurance to keep that insurance rather than dropping it wholesale and then trying to reactivate it when they get sick. Second, under the ACA, employers with a workforce topping 50 employees were compelled to provide health insurance for those employees. Under the new policy, this mandate has been eliminated. Third, under the new policies, older Americans may find themselves paying more than their younger counterparts for the same coverage. However, the same was true under the ACA. The only difference, then, is a matter of degrees. Under the ACA, insurance companies could charge older policyholders up to three times as much as their younger counterparts. Under the new policies, this percentage could go higher. Moreover, the new policies could change how insurance companies deal with preexisting conditions. Under the ACA, insurance providers could not refuse to provide insurance coverage based on a person's preexisting conditions. The new policies maintain this provision but may empower the states to apply for a waiver that would permit insurance companies to charge more on premiums that cover people with preexisting conditions who have dropped their insurance and then tried to pick it up again. Finally, under the new policies, some people who cannot get health care coverage from their employers and must pay for their own coverage will be permitted to claim tax credits for those payments. The size of the credits depends on the age of the taxpayer. These tax credits can eventually go as high as $14,000. [See: Tami Luhby, "What's Inside the Senate Republican Health Care Bill," *CNN*, June 24, 2017, http://money.cnn.com/2017/06/22/news/economy/obamacare-repeal-republican-senate-health-care-bill/index.html; and Natalie Andrews and Anna Wilde Matthews, "GOP Sets New Vote on Health Law," *The Wall Street Journal*, May 4, 2017, pp. A1, A4.]

Umbrella Insurance

Most insurance contracts have built-in ceilings to the coverage provided under the policy. Sometimes these restrictions will be expressed in terms of the risks that the insurer is willing to cover for the insured. More often, those limits will be expressed in a set limit on the funds that the insurance company is willing to pay out. An individual or a business can buy an **umbrella policy** that will grant coverage beyond the limits of the standard policy provided by the insurer in exchange for higher premium payments. Umbrella policies rarely stand alone. Most insurance companies will not even think about issuing an umbrella except as a backup for existing insurance. Umbrella policies generally lie dormant until the standard policy runs out of coverage. Thus, to mix metaphors, umbrellas function as safety nets that are available only when all other coverage has vanished. An umbrella is generally an extravagant expense that does not pay out. However, when it does kick in, the coverage is well worth the expense as.

Cyber-Insurance Coverage

It should come as no shock that computers have become ready targets for criminals who will erase data, shut down electronic systems, steal someone's identity, and extort money from businesses whose computers they have infected. Therefore, it should also come as no surprise that insurance policies are now available to protect individuals and institutions from these dangers. Such policies will cover a number of situations that might endanger or cripple a computer system or that, after a computer attack, might cause later, unanticipated difficulties. Cyber-insurance policies should, of course, provide coverage for the damage that might result from computer fraud and computer theft. Such policies should include coverage for the loss of the data (customer lists, trade secrets, and so on), for any out-of-pocket expenses involved in investigating the theft, and for the cost of restoring the lost data in terms of both time lost and the value of the data itself. Second, the policy should also cover losses that result from the disruption of computer service. Such provisions will generally be limited to losses that occur while the computer system is down. Moreover, usually the losses will be covered only if the computer system has been offline for a minimum amount of time. Finally, a good cyber-insurance policy will also provide some coverage for the payment of ransom. [See: Kerri L. Keller and P. Wesley Lambert, "Cyber and Social Engineering Fraud Insurance Coverage: Staying on the Cutting Edge of Coverage Disputes in an Evolving Insurance Landscape," *The Ohio State Bar Association*, Reference Manual Vol. No. 17-W002 (2017).]

quick quiz 19-2

1. An insured can cancel a straight life policy at any time and receive its cash surrender value. true | false
2. Term insurance is the most expensive kind of life insurance. true | false
3. With property insurance, unlike life insurance, an insurable interest must exist when a loss occurs. true | false

19-3 The Insurance Policy

In most states, the insurance policy (which is the insurance contract) comes in a standard form. These forms are carefully drafted by insurance commissioners with help from the states' legal advisors. In this way, the consumer-buyer is protected from deception or fraud. As an additional protection to consumers, some states now require that insurance contracts must be written in clear, understandable language and printed in a readable typeface. Insurance policies, nevertheless, are **adhesion contracts**—that is, contracts drawn by one party that must be accepted as is on a take-it-or-leave-it basis.

Application

The first step in obtaining an insurance policy is to fill in an application. The application is an offer made by the applicant to the insurance company. As with any offer, the offeree, in this case the insurance company, may accept or reject the offer.

Binders

The waiting period between the offer and the acceptance opens the insured to potential risk. To avoid this risk, the insured can arrange to have the insurer issue a binder. A **binder**, or binding slip, will provide temporary insurance coverage until the policy is formally accepted. The binder will include all of the usual terms that would be included in the actual policy to be issued.

Premiums

An insurance contract differs from many other contracts in that it requires the payment of premiums. The amount of the premium is determined by the nature and character of the risk and by how likely the risk is to occur. The premium increases as the chance of loss increases. Thus, a premium on a fireproof building in a city with a fire department will be much lower than the premium on a barn located where firefighting equipment is not available.

Lapse

When the insured stops paying premiums, an insurance contract is said to lapse. This feature may not mean, however, that the contract will terminate automatically on the date that the last premium is paid. It may also not lapse automatically if the insured makes a delayed payment. Although state laws differ, most states allow for a grace period in which the insured may make payments to keep life and health insurance policies in force. Beyond this period, however, the insurance contract will lapse, and the policy will terminate. Automobile and property insurance policies usually have no grace periods and will terminate when a premium is not paid when due.

quick quiz 19-3

1. An insurance binder provides permanent insurance coverage. true | false
2. Insurance premiums increase as the chance of loss increases. true | false
3. An insurance contract will terminate automatically if a premium payment is not paid on time. true | false

19-4 Cancellation of Insurance by Insurer

Under certain conditions, the insurer is given a legal right to forfeit, or cancel, an insurance policy. Proof of a forfeiture permits cancellation either before a loss or at the time the claim is made on a policy. Among the grounds permitting forfeiture are a breach of warranty and a concealment or misrepresentation of a material fact by the insured (see Table 19-2). Neither the insured nor the insurer may deny statements or acts previously made or committed that might affect the validity of the policy.

Warranties

A *warranty* is an insured's promise to abide by restrictions, especially those written into a policy that are intended to be conditions precedent to the existence of coverage. By statute in many states, an insurance company has the burden of proof in establishing that a warranty has been breached (broken) by the insured. If this breach is proved, the insurer may cancel the contract or refuse payment of loss to the insured or to a beneficiary.

EXAMPLE 19-2: Breach of Warranty

Nicole Duffy, a well-known NASCAR driver, applied for life insurance after being involved in several racing accidents. Community Life was aware of these accidents, and Duffy agreed not to race while the policy remained in force. Duffy was killed while racing in an important race. Community Life could rescind any obligation to pay Duffy's beneficiaries.

Table 19-2 Cancellation of Insurance Policies

Grounds for Cancellation	Explanation
Warranty violation	Insured fails to abide by restrictions especially written into the policy
Concealment	Insured deliberately withholds fact of material importance to insurer's decision to issue a policy
Misrepresentation	Insured gives false answers to questions in the insurance application that materially affect the insurer's risk

Concealment

Fraudulent concealment is any intentional withholding of a fact that would be of material importance to the insurer's decision to issue a policy. The applicant need only give answers to questions asked. However, the insured may not conceal facts that would be material in acceptance of a risk.

EXAMPLE 19-3: Concealment

VanDorn, an insurance agent for Canadian Life, inspected Kalintor's building before issuing a fire insurance policy. Kalintor did not show VanDorn the basement, which was filled with flammable chemicals. After the policy was issued, Kalintor's building burned to the ground. Canadian Life later learned of the secret lab and was permitted to cancel Kalintor's policy.

Misrepresentation

If an insured party gives false answers, or *misrepresentations*, to questions in an insurance application that materially affect the risk undertaken by the insurer, the contract is voidable by the insurer. A representation is material if the facts represented influence the insurer's decision to issue the policy or the rate of premium to charge.

EXAMPLE 19-4: Misrepresentation

The Clark family applied for fire insurance from the Alabama Farm Bureau Mutual Casualty Insurance Company. The Clarks answered no when asked whether they had ever been arrested. When their house was destroyed by fire and they attempted to collect under the policy, an investigation revealed that the Clarks had both been arrested on previous occasions. The court upheld the Farm Bureau's denial of benefits due to this deliberate material misrepresentation.

Although all jurisdictions agree on the effects of a deliberate deception, there is disagreement as to the effects of an innocent misrepresentation. A majority of the states hold that the intent of the insured is irrelevant. Even an innocent misrepresentation would make the policy voidable by the insurer. A minority of states would not allow the insurer to deny coverage to an insured whose misrepresentation was unintentional.

EXAMPLE 19-5: Innocent Misrepresentation

Folk took out an insurance policy with Countryside Casualty. When asked if he had any physical impairments, Folk, who suffered from epilepsy, said no. When Folk was killed in an automobile accident, his estate attempted to collect the insurance. Countryside, which had discovered Folk's epilepsy, refused to pay, claiming he had misrepresented his physical health. Evidence indicated that Folk genuinely did not consider his epilepsy, which was controlled by drugs, to be a physical impairment. In a majority of states, Folk's belief would make no difference. The policy would still be voidable by Countryside. In a minority of states, Folk's innocent misrepresentation would not allow Countryside to deny recovery under the policy.

Estoppel

An insurer may not deny acts, statements, or promises that are relevant and material to the validity of an insurance contract. This bar to denial is called an *estoppel*. When an insurer has given up the right to cancel a policy under certain circumstances by granting the insured a special dispensation, the insurer cannot deny that dispensation when the chance to cancel or deny liability arises.

EXAMPLE 19-6: Estopped from Denying Liability

Maxwell, an insurance agent for Fidelity, called on MacLaine, who wanted fire insurance to cover her new cabin. The cabin was heated by a woodburning stove that, according to Fidelity's specifications, was located too close to a wooden wall. Maxwell told MacLaine not to worry about those specifications. He then falsified the measurements on the application. Two weeks later, MacLaine's cabin burned to the ground. Due to Maxwell's behavior, Fidelity would be estopped from denying its liability to MacLaine under the policy.

When the insurance company gives up one of its rights to help the insured, the company has made a *waiver*. A waiver, which is actually a form of estoppel, can be implied from the conduct of the insurance company. For example, when an insurance company cashes the check of a lapsed policy, it has, in effect, given up or waived its right to cancel that policy. Once a right has been waived, the insurer may not later deny its waiver.

A CLASSIC CASE Sometimes the Insurance Company Wins

The classic case at hand begins with a plane crash—well—sort of. The plane in question was owned by the plaintiff, Aviation Charters Inc. At the time of the "crash," the plane had landed and was on the runway. Suddenly, the nose gear malfunctioned and the nose wheel of the plane collapsed, causing some $52,500 in damage to the plane. As a dutiful insured, Aviation Charters reported the incident to its insurance company, Avemco Insurance. The insurance company, following the duties of an insurer, investigated and discovered that the pilot of the plane (the plane that was already on the ground, mind you) did not meet the requirements spelled out in the policy. More specifically, the insurer looked at an exclusionary clause that said it would not be liable if the person piloting the craft at the time of the "crash" had less than 5,000 hours of flight time. Apparently to be "approved" under the policy, a pilot needed 5,000 hours of flight time (2,000 would not do, which was what this pilot had logged).

The investigation demonstrated that no one was really very surprised by the collapsed gear because on this particular type of aircraft, the nose gear often collapsed, usually when the plane was in taxi mode. This meant that the pilot had nothing to do with the collapsed gear, the fallen nose, or the damage to the aircraft. He could have had 500,000 hours of flight time, and the nose gear would still have collapsed. Interestingly, the insurance company makes no effort to dispute this. However, it does file a summary judgment motion stating that the case must be dismissed. The insurance company argued that it has no liability under the policy because the pilot was not "qualified." The lower court looked at the policy, interpreted the plain and ordinary language in the policy, and (probably with a resigned shrug) granted the motion for dismissal. Aviation Charters appealed.

On appeal, the plaintiff, Aviation Charters, argued that the exclusionary clause is a technicality. The plaintiff pointed to the fact that the gear could have collapsed while no one was on the plane. Moreover, Aviation Charters also brought a number of cases to the court's attention, all of which demonstrated that the pilot qualification exclusion is a technicality that should not be honored by the court if there is clear evidence that there was no causal connection between the "unqualified" pilot and the "crash." The insurance company provided no evidence to dispute the fact that the pilot did not cause the "crash." Instead, it simply pointed to the language in the exclusion clause and stated, in effect, "Sorry, but we win." The court of appeals looked at the language, looked at the facts, interpreted the language using clear and simple definitions, and concluded that, well, the insurance company is correct. Going by the strict, easy to understand, and straightforward words in the clause, the fact that an unqualified pilot was in the left seat was the key to the case, and, as a result, the insurer did not have to pay that $52,500. [See: *Aviation Charters Inc. v. Avemco Insurance Company,* Superior Court of New Jersey, Appellate Division (December 21, 2000).]

Source: See: *Aviation Charters Inc. v. Avemco Insurance Company,* Superior Court of New Jersey, Appellate Division (December 21, 2000).

A QUESTION OF ETHICS

The issues involved in the Soon to Be Classic Case on page 523 present us with a perplexing ethical issue. Just in case you missed the irony of Granger's argument, let's review what happened. Remember that Granger's first policy with AOMIC was for dwelling insurance, nothing more. As a typical dwelling contract, the agreement probably covered damage to the building and the contents from fire, wind, snow, ice, lightning, and so on. The contract would also have included coverage for unpaid rent and the like. The dwelling policy, however, did not cover discrimination. Granger, however, took out a second policy to protect him from other risks. This was the umbrella policy that is the subject of the lawsuit. Now here is where things get interesting. Remember that the present case (*Granger, et al. v. Auto Owners, Insurance*) is the second case in this scenario. The first case was the lawsuit that the FHCS and Kozera (the potential renter with the six-year-old child) brought against Granger. The second case does not give us a record of exactly what happened in that first lawsuit. However, it is likely that Granger argued that he did not discriminate against Kozera, but even if he did discriminate, the words that he spoke could not possibly have caused any type of personal injury to Kozera. In other words, Granger says something like, "I did not discriminate against Kozera and, even if I did (which I didn't) what I said did not hurt Kozera."

Despite this, at some point in the process, Granger and his attorneys saw the writing on the wall and settled. Typically, a settlement, whatever else it says, will also indicate that the defendant is not admitting any fault despite his agreement to settle. So far, so good. The next thing that Granger does is turn around and file a lawsuit against AOIMC. The lawsuit claims that AOMIC did not defend him as it should have. Then AOMIC says something like (this is a paraphrase), "Defend you for what?" To which Granger replies (paraphrasing), "For discriminating and for causing personal injury to Kozera." The insurance company says that its right to duty to defend Granger would have arisen only if he had caused personal injury to Kozera, and he did not cause personal injury because humiliation does not constitute personal injury. To which Granger replies, "I'm covered by the umbrella policy if I cause personal injury to someone, and personal injury includes mental anguish and humiliation is mental anguish. Therefore, I caused Kozera mental anguish and you should have defended me for it."

By now, the irony should be clear. In the first case, Granger claims that he did not discriminate and did not injure Kozera. Why? That is simple—because he does not want to pay Kozera any money. In this case, *Granger, et al. v. Auto Owners, Insurance,* Granger says that he did discriminate and did, in fact, injure Kozera. Why? Why does he change his position in relation to his own behavior and his own culpability? That is also simple—because he wants to get the money that he paid to Kozera back from AOMIC. Is it ethical for Granger to reinterpret his own behavior out of hope for monetary gain? Also, and perhaps more importantly, how ethical is a judicial system that not only makes this sort of alternative arguing possible, but also awards it monetarily? Think about it. Now recall that the appellate court did define humiliation as personal injury. Does that change your answer? Explain. [See: *Granger, et al. v. Auto Owners, Insurance* 2013-Ohio-2792, Case. 26473, Court of Appeals, Ninth Judicial District (June 2013).]

Source: See: *Granger, et al. v. Auto Owners, Insurance* 2013-Ohio-2792, Case. 26473, Court of Appeals, Ninth Judicial District (June 2013).

quick quiz 19-4

1. An insurance company may refuse to pay for a loss if it can prove that the insured breached a warranty to abide by certain restrictions.   true | false

2. If an insured gives false answers to questions in an insurance application, the insurance company can do nothing about it unless it discovers the fraud before any loss.   true | false

3. An insurer may not deny acts, statements, or promises that are relevant and material to the validity of an insurance contract.   true | false

Summary

19.1 Insurance is a transfer of the risk of economic loss from the insured to the insurer. Insurance policies require the elements of a contract: offer, acceptance, mutual assent, capable parties, consideration, and legality. To be insured, one must have an insurable interest in the subject matter of the policy. The parties to an insurance contract include the insurer, the insured, and the beneficiary.

19.2 It is possible to obtain insurance for a variety of risks. Life insurance provides funds to a beneficiary on the death of the insured. A beneficiary must have an insurable interest when the policy is issued but need not have that interest when the insured dies. The principal types of life insurance are straight life, limited-payment life, term, and endowment insurance. Principal types of property insurance include fire, marine, homeowner's, flood, and automobile insurance. In the case of property insurance, the insured must have an insurable interest when the loss occurs. Health insurance helps pay for such things as physician care, prescription drugs, inpatient and outpatient hospital care, surgery, dental and vision care, and long-term care for the elderly.

19.3 The first step in obtaining an insurance policy is to fill out an application. A binder provides temporary insurance coverage between the time the application is made and the time the policy becomes effective. Premiums are the consideration or payment an insured gives the insurer for its acceptance of risk. A lapse occurs when the insured stops paying premiums.

19.4 Under certain conditions, the insurer is given a legal right to cancel an insurance policy. Grounds permitting cancellation include breach of warranty, concealment of material facts, and misrepresentation on an application. Under the estoppel rule, an insurer is not allowed to deny certain statements, activities, or waivers.

Key Terms

add-on coverage, 535
adhesion contracts, 540
annuity, 527
beneficiary, 524
binder, 540
bodily injury liability insurance, 534
coinsurance, 528
collision insurance, 535
community property, 530
comprehensive coverage, 536
deductible, 528
descriptive threshold, 535
double indemnity, 528
duty to defend, 525
duty to investigate, 525
duty to pay, 525
dwelling insurance, 533
fault-based insurance, 534
homeowner's policy, 529
homestead, 530
indemnify, 524
inland marine insurance, 529
insurable interest, 524
insurance, 522
insured, 524
insurer, 524
joint tenants, 530
liability insurance, 536
life insurance, 526
limited-payment life insurance, 527
Medicaid, 537
medical payments insurance, 535
Medicare, 537

monetary threshold, 535
no-fault insurance, 534
ocean marine insurance, 529
ordinary life insurance, 526
peril, 522
personal injury protection (PIP), 534
policy, 524
premium, 524
proof of loss form, 531
property damage liability insurance, 535
real property, 529
renter's insurance, 533
risk, 522
straight life insurance, 526
subrogation, 525
substitute transportation insurance, 536
supplemental homeowner's policy, 529
tenancy by the entirety, 530
term insurance, 527
threshold, 535
threshold guideline, 535
time-based threshold, 535
towing and labor insurance, 536
umbrella policy, 539
underinsured-motorist insurance, 535
uninsured-motorist insurance, 535
universal life insurance, 526
whole life insurance, 526

Questions for Review and Discussion

1. What is insurance, and what purpose does it serve?
2. What are the contractual elements of an insurance agreement?
3. Why is insurable interest so important?
4. What are the differences among types of life insurance?
5. How does insurable interest differ with life insurance and property insurance?
6. What is a coinsurance clause?
7. What coverage is given by fire, marine, homeowner's, flood, and renter's insurance?
8. What differences exist among the principal kinds of automobile insurance?
9. What benefits are included in health insurance policies?
10. What are the steps in applying for, obtaining, and maintaining an insurance policy?

Cases for Analysis

1. Juan Ramos's wife, Maria, became concerned after a violent storm caused disastrous flooding in a community not far down the river from where their house was located. She felt comforted when her husband told her that they were fully protected against flooding by their homeowner's insurance policy. The following spring, a flood caused serious damage to their home, and Juan's insurance agent told him that his homeowner's policy did not cover flood damage. What recourse do the Ramoses have against the insurance company?
2. Al Zuni Trading Inc. purchased a $1 million life insurance policy on the life of one of its officers, Thomas McKee. Three months later, McKee resigned from the company. Two years later, McKee died. Did Al Zuni Trading have an insurable interest in the life of McKee, and thus, was it entitled to the million dollars? Explain. [See: *In re Al Zuni Trading, Inc.*, 947 F.2d 1403 (9th Cir.).]
3. U.S. Aviation Underwriters issued an aircraft insurance policy to Cash Air Inc. covering its employees. The policy stated that to be covered under the policy, the aircraft must be "flown only by a pilot or pilots described on the Coverage Summary page." Each policy coverage page stated that a pilot not named in the policy must be one who holds "an AA commercial pilot certificate with AA multi-engine and instrument ratings who has flown a minimum of 2,500 hours as pilot in command, at least 1,000 hours of which shall have been in multi-engine aircraft and at least 25 hours of which shall have been in Piper PA 31-350 aircraft." Peter Covich, an employee of Cash Air did not meet the pilot experience requirements when the Piper Seneca airplane he was piloting crashed, causing personal injuries and property damage. Must the insurance company pay for the loss? Explain. [See: *U.S. Aviation Underwriters v. Cash Air*, 568 N.E.2d 1150 (MA).]
4. Victory Container Corporation was owned by the three Radin brothers. Two of those brothers also owned the Warrensburg Paper and Board Corporation. Victory had no direct ownership of the Warrensburg plant, however. Nevertheless, Victory took out a fire insurance policy on the Warrensburg plant. When the Warrensburg property was damaged, Victory attempted to collect under the policy. Did Victory have an insurable interest in the Warrensburg property? Explain. [See: *Victory*

Container Corporation v. Calvert Fire Insurance Company, 486 N.Y.S.2d 211 (NY).]

5. Avrit and Schuring entered an agreement to purchase a certain property. Each paid $1,000 as a down payment. They were later to pay an additional $25,000. The seller of the property was to maintain insurance until the deal was finalized. Avrit and Schuring also obtained an insurance policy on the property. Before the deal was finalized, fire damaged the property. Avrit and Schuring attempted to collect on their policy, but the insurance company claimed that Avrit and Schuring had no insurable interest at the time of the fire. Did Avrit and Schuring have an insurable interest between the time of the down payment and the time the deal was finalized? Explain. [See: *Avrit v. Forest Industries Insurance Exchange*, 696 P.2d 583 (OR).]

6. Martin Searle's life insurance policy contained a standard suicide clause. Under the clause, Allstate would not be liable to the beneficiary, Alice Searle, should Martin commit suicide within the first two years of the policy even if Martin were insane at the time of his death. Martin committed suicide 10 months after the policy went into effect. Allstate refused to pay Alice any benefits under the policy. Alice sued the company, claiming that her husband had been mentally deranged at the time of the suicide and did not realize the consequences of his action. Allstate argued that the sanity clause removed the issue of mental incapacity from the case. Who would prevail in a majority of states? Explain. [See: *Searle v. Allstate Life Insurance Company*, 212 Cal. Rptr. 466 (CA).]

7. Bayer took his car to Whitaker's auto repair shop for repairs. Whitaker took the car for a test drive, with Bayer seated in the passenger seat. During the test drive, a car operated by another person drove on the wrong side of the road and collided with Bayer's vehicle, injuring Bayer. Neither Bayer's vehicle nor the vehicle owned by the wrongdoer was insured. Whitaker carried insurance on his own vehicles, including uninsured-motorist insurance. Could Bayer recover from Whitaker's insurance company under the uninsured-motorist provision of the policy? Why or why not? [See: *Bayer v. Travelers Indemnity Co.*, 267 S.E.2d 91 (VA).]

8. Riggins contacted the Hartford Insurance Company and asked for an all-risk policy for his truck. An underwriter for Hartford agreed to the policy and issued a binder on March 28. On April 2, before the full policy had been executed, Riggins left on a trip, hauling liquor. Sometime during the trip, the liquor was stolen. Hartford refused to pay, arguing that the final policy that would have been issued would not have covered the hauling of liquor. Riggins argued that the all-risk binder was in effect at the time of the theft and that he was therefore covered, even though the final policy would not have covered him. Was Riggins correct? Explain. [See: *Hilt Truck Lanes, Inc., v. Riggins*, 756 F.2d 676 (8th Cir).]

9. When Sidney Henry applied for insurance with State Farm, he was asked whether he had ever had recurrent indigestion or a hernia. Henry answered no to each question. In fact, he had experienced recurring indigestion, and it had been diagnosed as either an ulcer or a hernia. The policy was issued. Eight months later, Henry died of cancer of the esophagus. When Eula Henry applied for benefits, State Farm denied her request. Eula argued that the misrepresentations were not material because her husband died from cancer, not the illnesses he was questioned about. Was Mrs. Henry correct? Explain. [See: *Henry v. State Farm*, 465 So.2d 276 (LA).]

10. On January 13, Lax made out a check to State Farm Insurance to pay for her automobile insurance, which had lapsed 62 days earlier. Unfortunately, she forgot to mail the check. On January 22, Lax was killed when trying to pass a truck. The check was found in the wreckage and taken to a State Farm agent who mailed it to the main office. The main office, with knowledge of the accident, cashed the check. The beneficiaries argued that State Farm's conduct in cashing the check with knowledge of the accident constituted a waiver of its right to cancel the policy due to her failure to pay by the due date. Were the beneficiaries correct? Explain. [See: *VanHulle v. State Farm*, 254 N.E.2d 457 (IL).]

Design Elements: The Opening Case: ©Sharpstock/Alamy; A Classic Case: ©Evlakhov Valeriy/ Shutterstock

quick quiz Answers

19-1	19-2	19-3	19-4
1. F	1. T	1. F	1. T
2. F	2. F	2. T	2. F
3. F	3. T	3. F	3. T

Chapter 20

Mortgages, Land Contracts, and the 21st-Century Financial Crisis

20-1 A Primer on Real Property Finance and Security
Real Property as Security • Mortgage Costs • Types of Mortgages • Land Contracts • Recording the Mortgage • Rights and Duties of the Mortgagor • Rights and Duties of the Mortgagee • Purchase by Mortgage Takeover

20-2 The 21st-Century Financial Crisis
The Nature of the Crisis • The Economic-Political Dimension of the Crisis • The Causes of the Crisis • The Short-Term Solutions to the Crisis • The Long-Term Solutions to the Crisis

20-3 Personal Property as Security
Security Agreement • Attachment of a Security Interest • Perfection of a Security Interest • Priorities and Claims • Default of the Debtor

---

THE OPENING CASE Round 1
The 21st-Century Financial Crisis, Part 2: A Smart Business Strategy or Predatory Lending?

When the 21st-century financial crisis ended in June 2009, Americans everywhere let out a collective sigh of relief. Now it appears that sigh of relief came too soon. In fact, it looks as if the "end" of the original crisis actually generated a new crisis. This realization dawned on many when the City of Cincinnati sued Harbour Portfolio Advisors LLC (Harbour), a Texas investment firm engaged in buying and selling property throughout the United States. According to the complaint filed by the city, in 2011 Harbour began the process of buying up thousands of these homes, most of which had belonged to owners who could no longer make their mortgage payments and, as a result, had been evicted. At last count, Harbour had purchased 6,000 houses from Fannie Mae, 85 of which were in Cincinnati. Many of these homes were purchased for cents on the dollar—in some cases, for sales prices lower than $10,000 and in others, due to the fact that the properties were "bundled," for a completely nonexistent sales price (that's right—for $0). Harbour would then resell the home to buyers "as is" for up to five times the original purchase price.

Significantly, most of these sales were not conventional mortgages. Instead, they were land contract arrangements that charged extremely high interest rates. Land contracts also have additional terms that favor the seller and make it difficult (some say impossible) for the buyers to complete the loan payments. (*Note:* We will learn about these other terms later in the chapter.) What made these land contracts even worse was the fact that most of the houses were run down and badly in need of repair. Some had no working plumbing. Others were plagued by substandard, dangerous electrical systems. Still others had no working furnace. In one case, the amount of lead in the environment inside the home was so high that the two children living there contracted lead poisoning. (*Note:* In the lead poisoning case, Harbour had purchased the home for $7,600 and then sold it for $40,700.) Consequently, the buyers suddenly found themselves making loan payments to Harbour while trying to make expensive improvements to the property. Most of the time, the buyers would default on the loan. Harbour would then take the property back and soon sell it to another unsuspecting victim. In the suit, the city has accused Harbour of negotiating "predatory and unconscionable land sale contracts" and of not paying fines, fees, and back taxes amounting to $360,000.

The plot hatched by Harbour is bad enough, standing alone. What make the Harbour plot even more significant is that it signals that the underlying weaknesses in the system that led to the first financial crisis have not yet been solved. This would seem to indicate that the global crisis could erupt again. To truly solve the problem, financiers and lawmakers must eliminate the initial conditions that plagued the system before it imploded. Otherwise, the system remains unstable, a sure sign that "another" crisis will occur soon. As Michel Serres warns in his book *Time of Crisis*, a financial system in crisis cannot simply "recover" from that crisis; it must move away from the initial conditions that caused the crisis in the first place. Otherwise, the system remains volatile, a sure sign that another crisis will occur soon. It would seem that this second crisis is already at hand. [See: James Leggate, "Cincinnati Sues Company over 'Predatory' Land Sales Contracts, Blighted Properties," *WCPO Cincinnati*, April 14, 2017, http://www.wcpo.com/news/local-news/hamilton-county/cincinnati/cincinnati-files-lawsuit-against-predatory-land-investor?page=2; and Matthew Goldstein and Alexandra Stevenson, "Cincinnati Sues Seller of Foreclosed Homes, Claiming Predatory Acts," *The New York Times*, April 21, 2017, p. B3.]

Opening Case Questions

1. What is a mortgage? Explain.
2. What is a land contract? Explain.
3. What terms are involved in a land contract? Explain.
4. What is the 21st-century financial crisis? Explain.
5. What must happen before the financial crisis has really been resolved once and for all? Explain.

Source: See: James Leggate, "Cincinnati Sues Company over 'Predatory' Land Sales Contracts, Blighted Properties," *WCPO Cincinnati*, April 14, 2017, http://www.wcpo.com/news/local-news/hamilton-county/cincinnati/cincinnati-files-lawsuit-against-predatory-land-investor?page=2; and Matthew Goldstein and Alexandra Stevenson, "Cincinnati Sues Seller of Foreclosed Homes, Claiming Predatory Acts," *The New York Times*, April 21, 2017, p. B3.

Learning Objectives

1. Differentiate between a secured and an unsecured loan.
2. Identify the types of mortgages that are available to borrowers.
3. Explain how a land contract differs from a mortgage.
4. Describe the rights and duties of the mortgagor and those of the mortgagee.
5. Differentiate between a financial recovery and a change in the initial conditions.
6. Identify short-term solutions to the 21st-century financial crisis.
7. Explain the long-term solutions to the 21st-century financial crisis.
8. Describe how a security interest is created for personal property.
9. Decide whether security interests are perfected.
10. Determine priorities when parties claim a security interest in the same property.

20-1 A Primer on Real Property Finance and Security

When encountering a subject like finance, mortgages, land contracts, and security control, it is tempting to jump right into the crisis side of the issue, especially when that crisis has dominated the topic in the early 21st century. This temptation emerges from the dramatic nature of the subject, the seriousness of the issues at stake, and the apocalyptic aura that surrounds any crisis, but especially one that appears to have threatened the very social order upon which our culture is based. As always, however, the temptation must be resisted in favor of first gathering basic ground rules, useful concepts, and helpful definitions. This observation is not made to downplay either the seriousness or complexity of the crisis. Rather, the idea is to emphasize that the complexity and seriousness of the crisis demands

> **Did You Know?**
>
> The chances of a borrower defaulting on mortgage payments can increase dramatically with life-changing events. They jump:
> - 54 percent if the borrower has an unexpected drop in income.
> - 26 percent if the borrower gets divorced from his or her spouse.
> - 6 percent for each additional household member after the first two.

a measured and informed approach to unraveling its nature, causes, and consequences. As this study unfolds, we will learn that even the term *crisis* must be redefined and that the lessons of the recent past must not be ignored, especially as that past reveals what happens when superpowers such as the United States and Russia, for example, ignore the telltale signs of that impending crisis. This chapter will explore introductory material to lay the groundwork, and then, so armed, will enter the territory of the 21st-century financial crisis. After that, we will see how personal property plays into the larger picture of American finance. Before diving off the deep end, however, let's look at some structural details that will help build a platform of financial concepts. These details include mortgage costs, types of mortgages, land contracts, recording mortgages, and the rights and duties of the mortgagor and the mortgage.

Real Property as Security

Our economy is built upon credit, and credit is built upon trust. Trust is necessary to ensure that the money that the bank or the savings and loan company lends to the client will be repaid. Trust by itself, however, only goes so far. Bigger loans lead to a smaller level of trust, and, therefore, involve a higher need for some kind of security, or so the argument goes. **Security** is the assurance that a creditor will be paid back for any money loaned or for credit extended to a debtor. Debts are said to be secured when creditors know that somehow they will be able to recover their money. Lenders of money and people who extend credit often require a security device to protect their financial interests. A **security device** is a way for creditors to get their money back in case the borrower or debtor does not pay. A **secured loan** is one in which creditors have something of value, usually called **collateral**, from which they can be paid if the debtor does not pay. In general, if creditors are not paid the debt owed to them, they can legally gain possession of the collateral. The collateral is then sold, and the money is used to pay the debt. The right to use the collateral to recover a debt is called the creditor's **security interest**. Of course, as is true of most such things, the law must also guard against a creditor's abuse of this contractual right. If creditors lend money but do not require collateral, they have made an unsecured loan. An **unsecured loan** is one in which creditors have nothing of value that they can repossess and sell to recover the money owed to them by the debtor.

Both real property and personal property can be used to secure a debt. When real property is used as security for a loan, a device known as a mortgage is used to establish collateral for the loan. A **mortgage** is a transfer of an interest in property for the purpose of creating a security for a debt. The one who borrows the money (the **mortgagor**) conveys his or her interest in the property to the lender (the **mortgagee**) while at the same time retaining possession of the property. The borrower signs a promissory note as evidence of the loan in addition to a mortgage instrument. The mortgage creates a legal claim to the property. This legal claim, also called a **lien**, gives the lender the right to have the property sold if the debt is not paid, provided, of course, that certain legal procedures are followed to safeguard the rights of the debtor. Once the land is sold and the debt is paid, the mortgagor's obligation to the mortgagee is over. However, if the sale of the property does not satisfy the whole debt, the mortgagor will still owe the balance.

Mortgage Costs

Many costs are associated with obtaining a mortgage. Initially, a potential borrower must pay a mortgage application fee, an appraisal fee, a credit report fee, and an inspection fee. Once the loan is approved, the borrower often pays an origination fee, which is a charge for issuing the loan. Sometimes, the borrower pays interest in a lump sum upfront, called points, to get a lower rate of interest. A point is a one-time charge equal to 1 percent of the principal amount borrowed. Thus, if three points are charged on an $80,000 mortgage, the borrower will be required to pay a one-time fee of 3 percent of $80,000, which amounts to $2,400. If all IRS requirements are met, points are tax deductible. Other items charged to the borrower include charges for document preparation, attorney's fees, title insurance, surveyor fees, termite inspections, mortgage insurance, and homeowner's insurance.

Types of Mortgages

There are many different types of real property mortgages (see Table 20-1). Some of the most common mortgages are conventional fixed rate, variable-rate, interest-only, graduated payment, balloon-payment, reverse, participation, construction, deeds of trust, subprime, junior, and home equity. While strictly speaking not a mortgage, a land contact can also be used by lenders who do not qualify financially for more conventional mortgage arrangements.

Table 20-1 Some Methods of Financing a House

Types of Mortgages	Description
Conventional fixed-rate mortgage	Conventional fixed-rate mortgages have interest rates that are permanent, regardless of fluctuations in the economy.
Variable-rate mortgage	A variable- or flexible- or adjustable-rate mortgage has a rate of interest that changes according to fluctuations in the index to which it is tied.
Interest-only mortgage	With an interest-only mortgage, the borrower pays only the interest for a period of time, between one and three years or so, set by the agreement.
Graduated-payment mortgage	A graduated-payment mortgage has a fixed interest rate during the life of the mortgage; however, the monthly payments made by the mortgagor increase over the term of the loan.
Balloon-payment mortgage	A balloon-payment mortgage has comparatively low fixed payments during the life of the mortgage, followed by one large final (balloon) payment.
Reverse mortgage	A reverse mortgage is a loan that allows older homeowners to convert some of the equity in their home into cash while retaining ownership of their home.
Participation loans	In a participation loan, the borrower will transfer certain ownership (or equity) rights to the lender and in exchange, the borrower will negotiate lower interest rates or a lower down payment.
Construction loans	Construction loans authorize staggered payments at various stages of the process of building a home.
Deed of trust	Under a deed of trust, the mortgagor conveys his or her interest in the property to a trustee.
Subprime mortgages	Subprime loans are offered when a borrower does not qualify for one of the regular loans. To compensate, the lender demands that the borrower pay a much higher interest rate than more qualified lenders are required to pay.
Junior mortgages	A junior mortgage, also called a second (or subsequent) mortgage, is a mortgage subject to a prior mortgage.
Home equity loans	A home equity loan is either an outright loan or a line of credit made available to homeowners based on the value of the property over and above any existing mortgages. Home equity loans are often used to consolidate credit card balances or other debts that have higher interest rates.
Land contract	A land contract is an agreement to purchase real property in which the seller promises to finance the buyer's purchase of a tract of land and the buyer agrees to repay the seller in installment payments.

There are many different types of mortgages. Knowing which type fits your needs, both in the present and for the future, makes home ownership easier and more enjoyable.
©Ariel Skelley/Blend Images LLC

Did You Know?

The more points you pay, the lower your interest rate will be. If given a choice, you need to decide which is best for you, paying more in points and a lower rate of interest or paying less in points and a higher rate. To decide, you need to consider (1) whether you can afford to make the up-front payment now for points and (2) the length of time you expect to have the mortgage. The longer you plan to have your mortgage, the more it makes sense to pay for points now because you'll have a long time to benefit from the lower rate.

Conventional Fixed-Rate Mortgage A **conventional fixed-rate mortgage** involves no government backing by either insurance or guarantee. The loan is made by private lenders, and the risks of loss are borne exclusively by them. Conventional mortgages have interest rates that stay the same during the life of the mortgage, regardless of fluctuations in the economy. Changes in recent years, however, have resulted in the creation of variations to the fixed-interest rate mortgage, including the variable rate mortgage.

Variable-Rate Mortgage A **variable-** or **flexible-** or **adjustable-rate mortgage (ARM)** has a rate of interest that changes according to fluctuations in the index to which it is tied. The index rate may be the bank's prime rate or the Federal Reserve Board discount rate. As the index rate goes up and down, so does the rate of interest charged on the loan. This rate may be more or less than the index rate but always varies with it. The obvious advantage of the variable-rate mortgage is the drop in the amount of the mortgage payment when the rate drops. However, mortgage payments can also rise when the rate rises. In general, a change in payments, either up or down, does not occur without some advance warning. Also, variable-rate mortgages agreements must include a maximum rate that cannot be exceeded. In addition, the frequency of these changes in the rate is usually restricted by the terms of the mortgage agreement.

Interest-Only Mortgages In some situations, a borrower might negotiate an **interest-only mortgage**. In such a situation, the borrower, who very often cannot afford a down payment on a house, will agree to pay only the interest on the loan for a set period of time, anywhere between one and three years or so, set by the agreement. The idea under this approach is to wait until the borrower's financial picture brightens, allowing him or her to make the higher payments that will eventually come due.

Graduated-Payment Mortgage A **graduated-payment mortgage** has a fixed interest rate during the life of the mortgage; however, the monthly payments made by the mortgagor increase over the term of the loan. In the first years of the mortgage, the payments are low. The payments gradually increase over time, usually reaching a plateau at which the payments remain fixed. This type of mortgage is advantageous for young people, whose income may be expected to increase as their mortgage payments increase.

Balloon-Payment Mortgage A **balloon-payment mortgage** has comparatively low fixed payments during the life of the mortgage, followed by one large final (balloon) payment. The mortgage has a fixed interest rate, but it is written for a short time period, such as five years. At the end of the time period, the mortgagor usually must find new financing, either with the same or with a different lender, at the current interest rate.

Reverse Mortgage A **reverse mortgage** is a type of loan that allows older homeowners to convert some of the equity in their home into cash while retaining ownership of their home. The loan is repaid when the property is sold, or on the occurrence of some other specified event.

Participation Loans A borrower who is shopping for a loan with terms that are more favorable than usual may request a **participation loan**. In such a loan, the borrower will transfer certain ownership (or equity) rights to the lender and in exchange, the borrower will negotiate lower interest rates or a lower down payment.

Construction Loans Sometimes a borrower wants to build a new home rather than to buy an existing one. In such a case, the borrower may wish to negotiate a **construction loan** that will authorize staggered payments at various stages of the building process. Thus, the loan will issue a payment at the time the borrower buys the land, when the foundation of the house is laid, when the framing is finished, when the exterior has been constructed, and when the entire house is completed. Construction loans come in a variety of flavors including both variable and fixed rate loans.

Deeds of Trust In some states, a deed of trust is used instead of a mortgage. In a conventional mortgage, the mortgagor conveys all or part of his or her interest in the property directly to the mortgagee. Under a **deed of trust**, the mortgagor conveys his or her interest in the property to a disinterested third party, known as a trustee. The mortgagor remains on the property, but the trustee holds certain rights to that property as security for the mortgagor's creditors. If the debtor defaults, the trustee can sell the property for the benefit of those creditors. The provisions of many deeds of trust allow the trustee to sell the property without going to court. For this reason, some legal authorities do not consider a deed of trust a true mortgage, because true mortgages require a foreclosure action for the sale of the property.

Subprime Mortgages When a borrower does not qualify for one of the regular mortgages just covered, he or she might ask for and receive a **subprime loan**. Generally, these borrowers have been disqualified from conventional loan because of a bad credit history or because of a high debt-to-income ratio. These loans generally have a much higher default rate than most of the conventional loans and are thus disfavored by lenders. This is true now more than ever before because of the recent mortgage crisis that has occurred during the last few years. To compensate for the risk involved in a subprime loan, the lender demands that the borrower pay a much higher interest rate than more qualified lenders are required to pay.

Junior Mortgages Sometimes an owner of real property may execute a junior mortgage on the property. A **junior mortgage**, also called a **second** (or subsequent) **mortgage**, is a mortgage subject to a prior mortgage. For example, if a homeowner wants to improve the mortgaged property and needs another loan to do so, he or she may use the property as security for another loan. If this transaction occurs, the mortgagor is said to have executed a second mortgage on the property. Some people have three or more mortgages on one parcel of property. If all the mortgages are recorded, the holders of second and subsequent mortgages may exercise their rights against the property only after prior mortgages have been paid off. Thus, if the first mortgagee causes the property to be sold and is paid off in full, the second and subsequent mortgages are paid out of the proceeds that remain. The first mortgagee acts as a trustee of the surplus funds for the benefit of the junior mortgagees.

Home Equity Loans A **home equity loan** is an example of a junior mortgage. It is either an outright loan or a line of credit made available to homeowners based on the value of the property over and above any existing mortgages. Such a loan takes advantage of the equity that has built up in a home over a period of time. Home equity loans are often used to consolidate credit card balances or other debts that have higher interest rates. Unlike interest paid on a credit card balance, interest paid on a home equity loan is tax deductible.

Land Contracts

Strictly speaking a land contract is not a mortgage. Nevertheless, if a land contract is handled in an ethical and well-meaning way, it can be of great benefit to many buyers who otherwise do not qualify for any of the more familiar real estate buying formulas and for sellers who can negotiate to receive certain financial benefits that are unavailable in more conventional financing plans. In short, a **land contract** is an agreement to purchase real property in which the seller promises to finance the buyer's purchase of a tract of land and the buyer agrees to repay the seller in installments payment. So, unlike a mortgage in which the debtor must pay a third party, such as bank or a savings and loan, in a land contract the buyer pays the original owner who, in a sense, acts as the buyer's "bank" in providing the money for the purchase. Like borrowers who resort to subprime mortgages, those who use land contracts may have a less than stellar credit history or a low debt-to-income ratio. Also, like subprime loans, land contracts often have a somewhat higher default rate than most of the conventional loans. Because of this risk, sellers do not negotiate land contracts on a whim. Still, some sellers prefer land contracts because they have access to more buyers, can ask for and receive a higher selling price, can require a higher interest rate, and can demand a higher down payment.

THE OPENING CASE *Round 2*
The 21st-Century Financial Crisis, Part 2: Smart Business Strategy or Predatory Lending?

Recall that in the Opening Case, Harbour Portfolio Advisors, a Dallas investment firm in the business of buying and selling property throughout the United States, was sued by the City of Cincinnati. In its complaint, the city alleged that in 2011, Harbour started to buy up thousands of houses, which had been mortgaged to owners who, during the 21st-century financial crisis, had lost their homes and been evicted. In total, Habour bought 6,000 houses from Fannie Mae. Eighty-five of these houses were located in Cincinnati. Using land contracts, Harbour would resell the homes to new buyers "as is." Harbour used the land contracts approach because it knew it would attract buyers who did not qualify for any of the other forms of conventional financing. Many of these buyers had a bad credit rating and low income. Harbour also used land contracts because, by applying that technique, it could charge high interest rates and ask for large down payments. More significantly, the land contract strategy also allowed Harbour to request and receive enormously inflated purchase prices. In some cases, Harbour sold homes for up to five times the original purchase price. For example, in one instance, Harbour bought a home for $7,600 and then sold it for $40,700. Also, under the terms of a land contract, Harbour retained legal title to the property and could, thus, file a land contract forfeiture action whenever a buyer defaulted on the loan. After the forfeiture, Harbor received the house back, kept all the installments payments, and retained the down payment. The firm could then start the process over again, selling the same house to another buyer.

Standing alone, Harbour's strategy seems like nothing more than taking advantage of a lucrative investment strategy that permits it to enlarge its client base and increase its profit margin. In each transaction, Harbour invests a small amount of capital to purchase a piece of property that it can resell at a higher price, charge an increased interest rate, and a ask for a higher-than-normal down payment. The problem is that the strategy *does not* stand alone. On the contrary, it stands at the center of the 21st-century financial crisis, part 2. To see how a smart business strategy becomes predatory lending, read on. [See: *City of Cincinnati v. Harbour Portfolio Advisors, LLC*, Complaint, Court of Common Pleas Hamilton County, Ohio (April 11, 2017); James Leggate, "Cincinnati Sues Company over 'Predatory' Land Sales Contracts, Blighted Properties," *WCPO Cincinnati*, April 14, 2017, http://www.wcpo.com/news/local-news/hamilton-county/cincinnati/cincinnati-files-lawsuit-against-predatory-land-investor?page=2; and Matthew Goldstein and "Cincinnati Sues Seller of Foreclosed Homes, Claiming Predatory Acts," *The New York Times*, April 21, 2017, p. B3.]

Source: See: *City of Cincinnati v. Harbour Portfolio Advisors, LLC*, Complaint, Court of Common Pleas Hamilton County, Ohio (April 11, 2017); James Leggate, "Cincinnati Sues Company over 'Predatory' Land Sales Contracts, Blighted Properties," *WCPO Cincinnati*, April 14, 2017, http://www.wcpo.com/news/local-news/hamilton-county/cincinnati/cincinnati-files-lawsuit-against-predatory-land-investor?page=2; and Matthew Goldstein and "Cincinnati Sues Seller of Foreclosed Homes, Claiming Predatory Acts," *The New York Times*, April 21, 2017, p. B3.

Recording the Mortgage

Like a deed, a mortgage must be in writing and delivered to the recorder's office in the county where the property is located. Recording a mortgage notifies any third party who may be interested in purchasing the property or in lending money to the owner that the mortgagee has an interest in the real property covered by the mortgage. If the mortgage is not recorded and a later mortgage is given on the same property, the new mortgage is superior to the first. The second mortgagee must not know about the first mortgage and must record the mortgage properly. A failure to record the first mortgage, however, would not remove the obligation of the mortgagor to the first mortgagee. The debt would simply be unsecured.

Rights and Duties of the Mortgagor

By law and by agreement, the mortgagor has certain rights and duties in conjunction with the mortgage. First, the mortgagor has the right to possess the property. Second, the mortgagor has the right to any income produced by the property. For instance, the mortgagor would be entitled to any rent proceeds gained from leasing all or part of the property. The mortgagor could, however, assign this right to the mortgagee, which is sometimes done as a condition of executing the original mortgage agreement. Third, the mortgagor has the right to use the property for a second or third mortgage. Fourth, the mortgagor has the **equity of redemption**, that is, the right to pay off the mortgage in full, including interest, and thus discharge the debt in total.

In addition to these rights, the mortgagor has certain duties. Chief among these duties is to make payments on time. Mortgagors must preserve and maintain the mortgaged property for the benefit of the mortgagee's interest and security. Similarly, the mortgagor is often required to insure the property to the benefit of the mortgagee for the amount of the mortgaged debt. The mortgagor also must pay all taxes and assessments that may be levied against the property. Frequently, the mortgagor will ease the burden of these obligations by paying a percentage of the insurance premium and taxes each month along with the mortgage payment. The mortgagee holds the money in an escrow account. An escrow account is a special account into which money is deposited before the payment of the insurance or taxes is due. The money stays in the account until the time comes to pay the insurance or tax. The mortgagee then takes the money out of the account and makes the payments.

A SOON TO BE CLASSIC CASE Who's on First? It Looks Like Hines and Hines

Gumm and McCord agreed to buy a house from Hines and Hines for $85,000. Gumm and McCord negotiated an addendum to the contract under which Hines and Hines consented to lower the price to $73,000, by paying the buyers $12,000 and lending them $36,500. Essentially then, Hines and Hines turn into bankers for the buyers. Gumm and McCord signed a note and mortgage for the $36,500 amortized over 30 years at 8 percent interest. The closing occurred on June 6, during which Gumm and McCord signed a promissory note in favor of National City Bank. The amount of that note was $68,000. Gumm and McCord also set up a mortgage in the bank's favor for that amount. Deeds were signed and given to Gumm and McCord. On June 7, Gumm and McCord executed a mortgage in favor of the seller to secure their promissory note for $36,500. Hines and Hines recorded the mortgage on June 12. On June 19, the title company recorded both the deed and the mortgage for National City.

About two years later, Gumm and McCord defaulted on the loan. National City foreclosed. Hines and Hines entered the case at this point, claiming that their mortgage was recorded first and they were entitled to be paid first. Initially, the case went to a magistrate who ruled that the first mortgage filed is the mortgage that had a legal preference. Hines and Hines filed first and so they have preference. The common pleas court, however, disagreed and held that Gumm and McCord executed the promissory note and the mortgage with National City Bank first, so National City Bank should be given preference. Hines and Hines appealed.

The case went right to the court of appeals, which stated that the issue is who holds the preference. Who has first claim? Is it the party that executed first or the party that filed first? The appeals court said that, while National City may have executed its mortgage first, the bank failed to record the mortgage, even though it had ample time and every opportunity to do so. In fact, the record demonstrates that the bank waited seven days before bothering to make sure the mortgage was recorded. Because any recorded mortgage takes precedence, the bank's mortgage is subordinate to that of Hines and Hines. National City was not through arguing, however. The bank added that it had no notice that there was going to be a second mortgage on the property. The appeals court found this argument less than credible because the addendum was clearly attached to the original paperwork. The bank could have added a clause to the original contract that would have subordinated the Hines and Hines mortgage to the bank's mortgage, but it did not do so. Therefore, the court concluded that the magistrate was correct and that the mortgage that was recorded first—that is, the Hines and Hines mortgage—takes precedence. Period. [See: *National City Bank v. Gumm, et al.*, 2004-Ohio-1263.]

Source: See: *National City Bank v. Gumm, et al.*, 2004-Ohio-1263.

Rights and Duties of the Mortgagee

LO4

U.S. Const. Amendment 14 (see Appendix A)

Did You Know?

Since it began in 1968, Fannie Mae has helped more than 63 million families achieve the American dream of home ownership. Ginnie Mae estimates that it has helped more than 30 million American families since it began operation in 1968. Freddie Mac opened its doors two years later and has financed homes for 41 million families.

The mortgagee has the unrestricted right to sell, assign, or transfer the mortgage to a third party. Whatever rights the mortgagee had in the mortgage are then the rights of the assignee. The only way the mortgagor could stop the mortgagee from assigning the mortgage is to pay the mortgagee everything owed on the mortgage. Sometimes an assignment by the mortgagee to another mortgagee can cause unforeseen problems for the mortgagor.

Mortgagees have the right to receive each installment payment as it falls due. Frequently, mortgagees will include a term in the mortgage agreement allowing an **acceleration** of the debt if the mortgagor fails to meet an installment payment. This term means that a default on one installment payment will make the entire balance due immediately, giving the mortgagee the right to collect the full amount. In general, a clause allowing acceleration must be executed in good faith. In other words, before invoking the acceleration clause, the mortgagee must genuinely believe that the mortgagor will not be able to make good on the debt and that the mortgagee's security interest is therefore threatened. If the matter ends up in court, the mortgagor will have the burden of proving that the mortgagee did not act in good faith.

If the mortgagor has defaulted or has failed to perform some other agreement in the mortgage, the mortgagee has the right to apply to a court to have the property sold. This right is called **foreclosure**. It takes priority even when the mortgagor files for bankruptcy. Because, in a majority of jurisdictions, a mortgage is a lien on the land, a foreclosure is an equitable action. The mortgagor does not have a right to a jury trial in foreclosure action. A mortgage is foreclosed when the mortgagee proves the amount of the unpaid debt (including interest and other charges) and the property is sold by and under the direction of a court. The proceeds from the sale are then applied to the payment of the debt. Any money remaining after the claims of the mortgagee have been satisfied goes to the mortgagor or to the second and subsequent mortgagees. The mortgagee's financial interest in mortgaged property gives rise to certain constitutional rights. Under the 14th Amendment to the U.S. Constitution, mortgagees cannot lose their interest in property without due process of law.

Purchase by Mortgage Takeover

Mortgages often contain a clause providing that if the property is sold, the mortgage becomes due and payable. If the mortgage does not contain such a clause, the property may be sold with the mortgage remaining on it. In such takeovers, the transfer of title to a new buyer is subject to the buyer's payment of the seller's mortgage at the existing rate of interest. In purchasing a property already mortgaged, the buyer will either **assume the mortgage** or take the property **subject to the mortgage**. When buyers decide to assume the mortgage, they agree to pay it. When they take the property subject to a mortgage, the seller agrees to continue paying the debt.

quick quiz 20-1

1. A security device is a way for creditors to get their money back in case the borrower or debtor does not pay.	true | false
2. A home equity loan is an example of a junior mortgage.	true | false
3. The mortgagor has the right to possess the mortgaged property and to any income produced by the property unless otherwise assigned.	true | false

20-2 The 21st-Century Financial Crisis

Before we look at the financial crisis of 2008, it might be a good idea to define the term *crisis*. In his book, *Time of Crisis*, Michel Serres, a French philosopher and writer, makes several interlocking observations about the nature of any crisis that are worth examining. After reviewing the history of the word *crisis*, Serres concludes that any crisis (whether it involves medicine, law, politics, economics, religion, science, art, or the humanities) implies that the system has reached a branch point (or a flash point) of transition. In turn, the existence of a flash point within a system implies a shift in a new direction. Despite the vocabulary that we use rather habitually (and somewhat haphazardly), Serres argues, a crisis never has a real "recovery." According to Serres, the term **recovery** denotes a reversal to an earlier status. Such an about-face would actually threaten the security of the system in crisis because it indicates that no progress had been made. A lack of progress ensures that the crisis will occur again. Thus, a system must not recover from a crisis; it must move away from the initial conditions that caused the crisis. Otherwise, the system remains volatile, a sure sign that "another" crisis will occur soon. This is true of the current 21st-century financial crisis just as it is true of any healthy complex adaptive system (CAS). Before delving into this crisis, Serres asserts, somewhat forcefully, that a proper study of the current financial crisis also requires an understanding of its deep roots. In fact, like the crisis of 1929, the crisis of 2008 is not simply a financial crisis. Rather, it is a global crisis that represents a series of tectonic shifts in agriculture, transportation, health, connections, conflicts, and demographics—all of which interact with one another to signal a multi-institutional crisis that goes, in the words of Serres, "far beyond the scope of normal history." [See: Michel Serres, *Times of Crisis: What the Financial Crisis Revealed and How to Reinvent our Lives and Future* (New York: Bloomsbury, 2014), pp. ix-xiii; 1–17.]

The Nature of the Crisis

From this observation, Serres makes an interesting leap—one worth contemplating as we attempt to deal with the crisis. Serres argues, rather convincingly, that these tectonic shifts are caused by human activity, nothing more. Agricultural production, for example, is now controlled by only 2 percent of the population, which has led to a shift in living space as people move from the country to the city. Advances in transportation (and communication, for that matter, which Serres chooses not to mention—perhaps because it is so obvious, perhaps because it is too complicated to explain in the short amount of space devoted to the issue) have created what amounts to a planetary city unprecedented in human history. Advances in health and medicine have lowered infant mortality and extended the average life span, leading to a demographic leap in the size of our global population. [See: Serres, pp. 1-11.] Perhaps even more interesting, however, is Serres's observation that these tectonic shifts have given birth to a third player on the global scene, something that Serres refers to as the **biogetic system**, a socioeconomic, cultural system created by humans, which has taken on a life of its own. Serres pictures this biogetic system as a third player in a series of conflicts, each of which plays itself out with two sets of human players battling one another within that biogetic system. [See: Serres, pp. 25-44.]

Thus, in the current financial crisis, the politicians work to fix the system created by the economists, thus pitting the politicians and the economists against one another, both acting against the backdrop of the biogetic system. When politicians and lawyers pass a law (such as the Dodd-Frank Wall Street Reform and Consumer Protection Act), their opponents, the economists (and accountants, bankers, brokers, CEOs, investors, and so on), react against that law. However, emerging from within this first level of interaction (people versus people; politicians versus economists) is a second, hidden level of interaction between the people and the system itself. This system, which has taken on its own separate existence, operates in a highly reflexive (even defensive) manner, leading to unpredictable, unintended consequences. One of those consequences in the present crisis has been a defensive response from the very people that the Dodd-Frank Act is designed to protect. At the grassroots level, many people see the government's attempt to fix the system as an escalation in governmental interference. This backlash, when translated into votes, can shift the balance of the political system, leading to a new administration with new ideas on how to solve the problem. In this case, that solution may lead to less regulation rather than more. The Dodd-Frank Act has been the target of this type of backlash and, as a result, changes in that law may emerge soon. More on this issue will be discussed in Chapter 26.

The Economic-Political Dimension of the Crisis

It would be unfair and unwise to focus only on this picture of the crisis. For one thing the picture painted in *Times of Crisis* is based on philosophy and history rather than on economics and politics. When we shift to that base, the story of the crisis looks a bit more practical and, therefore, somewhat more manageable. This is the approach taken by Dmitry Orlov in his book, *Reinventing Collapse*. What Orlov suggests is that the economic crisis in the United States mirrors almost exactly the crisis that spelled the end of the Soviet Union. The Soviet Union collapsed, Orlov says, because five factors collided with one another at precisely the right place and time: (1) a rapid and unprecedented decline in the amount of energy resources (crude oil) available for production, (2) a rapid and uncontrolled widening of the international trade deficit caused by Russia's inability to produce food and goods, (3) an unrestrained level of spending on defense caused by the "star wars" initiative, (4) expanding foreign debt, and (5) a pervasive anxiety that anticipated impending disaster in the wake of the defeat in Afghanistan and the tragedy of Chernobyl. [See: Dmitry Orlov, *Reinventing Collapse: The Soviet Experience and American Prospects* (Gabriola Islands, BC, Canada: New Society Publishers, 2011), pp. 1-2.]

As a prelude to the financial crisis and as a foreshadowing of its ultimate economic collapse, Orlov declares that the United States spiraled through a series of similar events that will coincide to create the same type of disaster that the Soviet Union experienced. By 2005, the pattern of events looked like this: (1) Crude oil fabrication was down in the United States, (2) the failure to keep abreast of technological advances threatened to intensify the inequity in foreign trade, (3) the American response to the "war on terror" caused a huge increase in military spending, (4) inflation had intensified the level of foreign debt, and (5) the setbacks in Iraq and the destruction caused by Hurricane Katrina sparked new waves of insecurity and angst at home. [See: Orlov, pp. 2–3.]

Each of these elements in and of itself did not create the type of crisis that emerged in 2008. However, when these events were stacked on top of one another and interlaced with other similar problems, they helped spark the type of situation that both Serres and Orlov warn about. As these elements combined, they eroded the confidence of the American people and led to reckless speculation in real property and foolish get-rich-quick schemes that typified the 21st-century financial crisis. People agreed to schemes that appeared to create wealth with little or no effort, that promised to make a lot of money rapidly with minimal risk, and that guaranteed a huge return on a small investment that did not have to be paid up front. Moreover, in each case, the day of reckoning looked to be so far in the future that it appeared nonexistent. The problem was that the day of reckoning did arrive, and at that point scapegoats had to be found and quick-fix schemes established. People blamed Wall Street and Washington and focused on things like subprime mortgages and balloon payment schemes while ignoring the overarching underlying fundamental causes that set the stage for these abuses.

The Causes of the Crisis

As Nouriel Roubini and Stephen Mihm point out in their book, *Crisis Economics*, "Subprime mortgages were but the most obvious sign of a deep and systemic rot. This fact underscores a cardinal principle of crisis economics: The biggest and the most destructive financial disasters are not produced by something so inconsequential as subprime mortgages or a few reckless risk takers. Nor are they merely produced by the euphoria of a speculative bubble. Rather, much as with earthquakes, the pressures build for many years, and when the shock finally comes, it can be staggering." [See: Nouriel Roubini and Stephen Mihm, *Crisis Economics: A Crash Course in the Future of Finance* (New York: Penguin, 2010), p. 62.] This diagnosis is not unlike those proposed by Serres and Orlov. The pressure in the financial sector had been building for years, even decades, caused by the laundry list of elements supplied by Orlov (energy shortfalls, trade imbalance, runaway military spending, climbing foreign debt, and so on) and by Serres (changes in agriculture, transportation, communication, and demographics) and leading to a mad scramble to get rich as quickly as possible in risk-free ways.

The pressure in the current crisis resulted from these big factors, but they led to a series of small mistakes that then combined, leading to the financial disturbance the impact of which is still felt today. The upcoming causes (revealed shortly) should be seen as secondary or corollary causes that spin off from the more fundamental causes outlined by Orlov, Serres, Roubini, and Mihm, in their respective studies. However, these smaller causes must be examined and then situated in their proper place in the overall financial puzzle. These factors include the creation and later mismanagement of Fannie Mae and Freddie Mac, the development of securitization (including both mortgage-backed securities and asset-backed securities), and the increased use of faulty loans (including subprime loans, liar loans, and NINJA loans).

Fannie Mae, Ginnie Mae, and Freddie Mac
The Federal National Mortgage Association (Fannie Mae) was chartered by the Reconstruction Finance Corporation during the

Great Depression in 1938. Fannie Mae does not make mortgage loans. Rather, it purchases loans that were made based on strict guidelines set up by the Federal Housing Association (FHA) and the Veterans Administration (VA). Eventually Congress recognized a flaw in the Fannie Mae system caused by the fact that the agency had to borrow money to fund mortgages it purchased. That in and of itself was not the real problem, however. The real problem was that Congress had not properly anticipated the amount of debt that Fannie Mae would accumulate. To remedy this situation, Congress created another agency, the Government National Mortgage Association (Ginnie Mae), which then took over much of Fannie's debt, freeing Fannie to buy mortgages insured by the government. Around this same time Congress created the Federal Home Loan Mortgage Corporation (Freddie Mac), another **government-sponsored enterprise (GSE)** to help support the mortgage market. [See: Phil Angelides et al., *The Financial Crisis Inquiry Report* (New York: Public Affairs, 2011), pp. 38-39; and Roubini and Mihm, pp. 61-63.].

Securitization and Mortgage-Backed Securities

Slowly the government lifted some of the restrictions on Fannie and Freddie, first permitting them to buy loans that had not fallen within FHA or VA guidelines and then authorizing them to participate in securitization. The process of **securitization** works like this. [See: Angelides et al., pp. 38-39, 70-71; and Roubini and Mihm, pp. 62-65]. A bank or other lender lends money to a borrower who pays off the loan over time with interest. The lender makes money on the interest at a slow and steady rate over a period of years (decades actually when speaking of real property). Somewhere along the line some bright boy (or gal) decided that it would be better to bundle a bunch of these mortgages together and sell them as bonds (now called **mortgage-backed securities**) to big investors, like pension funds, which would then reap the benefit of the interest payments multiplied by the number of loans purchased in that bundle over a long period of time, while the lender received a big payment up front, allowing it to bundle more and more mortgages more and more rapidly. [See: Roubini and Mihm, p. 65]. As noted previously, Fannie, Ginnie, and Freddie were all authorized to purchase these mortgage backed securities.

Securitization and Asset-Backed Securities

Now three effects rolled off this set of circumstances. First, another bright gal (or boy) decided that, what worked for mortgages would work for car loans, furniture loans, boat loans, home improvement loans, student loans, construction loans, and so on. Thus, we witness the growing popularity of **asset-backed securities**. Second, the original lenders began to care less and less about whether the borrowers were financially qualified to pay back the loans because, well, the lenders were passing the risk on to those who purchased the securities. It was at this point that subprime loans, as well as other radical loan practices like the so-called liar loans and the NINJA ("no income, no job or assets") loans began to appear (see discussion that follows). Third, everybody got into the act, not only government-sponsored entities, like Fannie, Ginnie, and Freddie, but also commercial banks, investment banks, and dozens of private lending firms, such as Merit Financial, that appeared and vanished overnight. As a result the use of mortgage- and asset-backed securities grew by 230 percent between 2000 and 2006. This amounted to just about $2.7 trillion. [See: Charles Gasparino, *The Sellout* (New York: Harper, 2009), p. 158.] The final consequences were inevitable. The crash occurred when the high-risk borrowers could not make their payments. Land values collapsed and, in the wink of an eye, Roubini and Mihm's financial earthquake shook the very foundation of the economy.

Subprime Loans (Revisited)

Before the collapse, the use of loans experienced a huge resurgence in the middle of the first decade of the 21st century. Some of this was due to technology that allowed loans to be processed faster and for approval to be based on a mathematical probability of repayment rather than the traditional criteria of credit, capacity, capital, and collateral. [See: Angelides, pp. 67-72.] However, some of it was also caused by a push toward deregulation. This encouraged the banks and other lenders to issue subprime loans as a way to bring new homeowners into the market while simultaneously helping the lenders build handsome portfolios. [See: Roubini and Mihm, pp. 73-76.]

Liar Loans and NINJA Loans (Also Revisited) An unintended consequence of this strategy was an increase in the number of liar loans and NINJA loans that appeared on the scene with increased regularity. **Liar loans** are those that deliberately misstate the qualifications of a borrower to push a loan through the approval process. A **NINJA loan** is one that has been negotiated by a borrower with "no income, no job, and no assets." Liar loans and NINJA loans actually come in many different shapes and sizes. They include both adjustable-rate and interest-only mortgages. The idea is to somehow make it easier for someone with little or no buying power to negotiate a mortgage. [See: Gasparino, p. 151; and Roubini and Mihm, pp. 65, 89]. Securitization made such loans possible and, in a strange retroactive way, encouraged many others to jump on the securitization bandwagon, thus accelerating the securitization process. Clearly this was a recipe for disaster although only a few people realized it at the time.

Land Contracts (Another Revisit) Recall that a *land contract* is an agreement to buy real property from a seller who also finances the purchase. So in a land contract, the buyer pays the original owner who, in a sense, acts as the buyer's "bank" in providing the money for the purchase. Buyers who use land contracts avoid the long vetting process that, under normal circumstances, banks require before financing a traditional mortgage. This makes the land contract attractive to buyers with a less than perfect credit record or a low debt-to-income ratio. Buyers must remember, however, that land contracts also carry certain disadvantages. Perhaps the major disadvantage is that the buyers do not really "own" their own homes. Under a land contract, the seller retains legal title to the home, while the buyer receives only equitable title. Now there are some advantages to equitable title. For example, equitable title gives the buyer the right to inhabit and use the land and prevents the seller from selling the property to another buyer. However, the seller retains legal title until the loan is paid in full under the terms of the original agreement. The seller can also file a land contract forfeiture should the buyer default on the loan. In such cases, the buyer gets the property back, keeps all installment payments, and retains the down payment. Of course, nothing prevents the seller from conveying legal title to the buyer before the buyer has paid off the loan.

THE OPENING CASE *Round 3*
The 21st-Century Financial Crisis, Part 2: A Smart Business Strategy or Predatory Lending?

Remember that in the wake of the 21st-century financial crisis, Harbour began to buy up houses that were available as "bundled" packages after "owners" had forfeited on their mortgage loans in 2008 and 2009. Harbour, was especially successful at this practice as demonstrated by the fact that the firm managed to buy some 6,000 houses from Fannie Mae, 85 of which were located in in Cincinnati. Many of these homes were purchased for cents on the dollar—in some cases, for a sales prices lower than $10,000 and in others, due to the fact that the properties were "bundled," for $0. Harbour would then resell the homes "as is" to new buyers for up to five times the original purchase price. As noted earlier, most of these sales were made by entering land contracts with the buyers. The buyers liked land contracts because they could circumvent the detailed scrutiny that accompanied the application process for more conventional mortgages. Consequently, many—perhaps most—of these land contract buyers had less than perfect credit histories.

Now, as long as buyers kept making installment payments on time, all was well. However, when a buyer fell behind on his or her payments, trouble followed. This was because, under the terms of a land contract, the buyers do not really "own" their own homes. Under a land contract, the seller, Harbour in this case, retains legal title to the home, while the buyer receives only equitable title. There are some advantages to equitable title. For example, equitable title gives the buyer the right to inhabit and use the land and prevents the seller from selling the property to another buyer. However, the seller retains legal title until the loan is paid in full under the terms of the original agreement. Therefore, when the buyer falls behind on his or her payments, the seller can file a land contract forfeiture and take the property back. In such case, the buyer gets the property back, keeps all installments payments, and retains the down payment. Still, the land contract process could have worked for many of the buyers had Harbour not stacked the deck against them. Harbour's strategy included buying homes that were cheap not only because the initial mortgage had failed, but also because the houses were run down. Some had no working plumbing. Others were plagued by substandard, dangerous electrical systems. Still others had no working furnace. Consequently, in many cases, the buyers suddenly found themselves making loan payments to Harbour, while trying to make expensive improvements to the property. Most of the time, the buyers would default on the loan. Harbour would then take the property back, keep the installments and the down payment, and then sell the same run-down house to another unsuspecting victim.

In this way, Harbour contributed to the second wave of the 21st-century financial crisis. Those homes that had been forfeited during the first stage of the crisis now became bait to lure in unsuspecting buyers in the second wave. In this second wave, buyers promptly lost their homes too, primarily because they bought properties under land contracts that were doomed from the start because of the buyers' poor credit histories and the horrible conditions of the houses. (To be fair, Harbour sometimes sold these properties to other investors interested in fixing the house in order to "flip it" to a new buyer. Still, even in these cases, Harbour is alleged to have avoided revealing the defects to the buyer.) Of course, even after all of this was revealed, the question still remained: Did Harbour simply use a clever investment strategy, or had it crossed the line and engaged in predatory lending? You will find the answer to this question just ahead in the Opening Case, *Round 4*. [See: *City of Cincinnati v. Harbour Portfolio Advisors, LLC*, Complaint, Court of Common Pleas Hamilton County, Ohio (April 11, 2017); James Leggate, "Cincinnati Sues Company over 'Predatory' Land Sales Contracts, Blighted Properties," *WCPO Cincinnati* (April 14, 2017) http://www.wcpo.com/news/local-news/hamilton-county/cincinnati/cincinnati-files-lawsuit-against-predatory-land-investor?page=2; and Matthew Goldstein and Alexandra Stevenson, "Cincinnati Sues Seller of Foreclosed Homes, Claiming Predatory Acts," *The New York Times*, April 21, 2017, p. B3.]

Source: See: *City of Cincinnati v. Harbour Portfolio Advisors, LLC. Complaint,* Court of Common Pleas Hamilton County, Ohio, (April 11, 2017); James Leggate, "Cincinnati sues company over 'predatory' land sales contracts, blighted properties," *WCPO Cincinnati* (April 14, 2017) http://www.wcpo.com/news/local-news/hamilton-county/cincinnati/cincinnati-files-lawsuit-against-predatory-land-investor?page=2; Matthew Goldstein and Alexandra Stevenson, "Cincinnati Sues Seller of Foreclosed Homes, Claiming Predatory Acts," *The New York Times* (April 21, 2017), p. B3.

The Short-Term Solutions to the Crisis

The 21st-century financial crisis erupted when so many borrowers could not make mortgage payments that the mortgage securities market began to collapse. This collapse led to a rapid decline in the value of real property, which, like a line of dominoes falling (a snowball rolling down a hill or a house of cards collapsing), accelerated the breakdown. Those firms and individuals who had invested heavily in the mortgage-backed and asset-backed securities (and even those who had not invested all that heavily) began to experience unprecedented losses. The upcoming solutions (the short-term ones discussed herein) should be seen as quick-fix treatments that patched up the system without really targeting the underlying causes, at least as those causes are envisioned by Orlov, Serres, Rounini, and Mihm. These temporary measures include the takeover of Fannie and Freddie by the Federal Housing Finance Agency, the creation of HAMP and HARP, the establishment of the Troubled Asset Relief Program, and the passage of the Dodd-Frank Act. The first measure that we will look at is the takeover of Fannie and Freddie. This step was one of the most disheartening events that emerged from the crisis.

The Fannie and Freddie Takeover
The risky mortgages purchased by Fannie and Freddie began to take their toll on the two GSEs. The purchasing power of the two GSEs had been exaggerated by the fact that their operation was supposedly supported by the U.S. Treasury. The apparently risk-free purchases that they made were focused on mortgaged-backed and asset-backed securities, both of which were much riskier than they had appeared. Then the bottom began to fall out from under them. The two GSEs were struck by enormous losses as the housing crisis hit and mortgages began to default. The fees that had been paid to Fannie and Freddie for backing these risky mortgages did not cover their losses. Nor could they cover those losses with insurance. Moreover, and perhaps more to the point here, their portfolios were filled to capacity with mortgages purchased by subprime borrowers, ARMs, and NINJAs, and everyone knew that, as those mortgages failed, Fannie and Freddie's capital reserves would fall to zero. [See: Roubini and Mihm, p. 108; Angelides, pp. 309-323; and Gasparino, pp. 410-416.]

To prevent this disaster, and to restore confidence in the system, the government stepped in to save both institutions. The solution demanded radical steps, one of which was the formation of the **Federal Housing Finance Agency (FHFA)**. The FHFA was created in 2008 under the authority of the Housing and Economic Recovery Act of 2008. The new agency is the offspring of a merger between the Federal Housing Finance Board and the Office of Federal Housing Enterprise Oversight. In addition to its power to regulate the two wayward GSE's (Fannie and Freddie), the new group was also charged with reestablishing public faith in the mortgage market by restoring the stability, continuity, authority, and dependability of the entire lending system. The process of placing the popular and high-profile GSEs into what actually amounted to a conservatorship was deemed of critical importance to the survival of the economy. Two major programs that are operated under the auspice of the FHFA are the Home Affordable Refinance Program (HARP) and the Home Affordable Modification Program (HAMP). [See: "Who We Are and What We Do," Federal Housing Finance Agency (FHFA), http://www.fhfa.gov/.]

Modifying Fannie and Freddie One More Time
Recently, the administration and a team of senators from both sides of the aisle have been working on a plan to alter the operation of both Fannie and Freddie one more time. The ultimate goal of these two groups is to minimize the role that the federal government has in these two GSEs. (In fact, if this objective is met, they will no longer be GSEs.) The main battle in this regard is between conservative lawmakers and their neoliberal counterparts. The conservatives want to totally extract the government from both Fannie and Freddie, thus recreating a completely free real estate market. On the other side of the aisle, the standard bearers of the neoliberal movement want, at the very least, to continue to use federal power to support those 30-year, fixed-rate mortgage programs that work so well for many first-time home buyers. One plan that has been proposed would have Fannie and Freddie stop sending their earnings to the Treasury as required by a 2008 agreement. Instead of transferring those funds to the Treasury, the new proposal would make certain that Fannie and Freddie retain their own earnings, thus short-circuiting the need to use tax money to support both GSEs in case of a crisis. The downside of this newly planned program is that the process of building up a capital reserve for the two GSEs could take as much as two decades. Of course, the House has yet to speak

on this issue and may call for a complete shutdown of both GSEs. [See: Andrew Ackerman, "U.S. Focuses on Fannie and Freddie Revamp," *The Wall Street Journal*, May 2, 2017, p. B10; and Amanda Baker, "Frannie, Freddie Revamp Plan Unlikely This Year, Dividends in Focus," *US News and World Report*, March 22, 2017, https://money.usnews.com/investing/news/articles/2017-03-22/fannie-freddie-revamp-plan-unlikely-this-year-dividends-in-focus.]

Home Affordable Modification Program The Home Affordable Modification Program (HAMP) was established by the Department of the Treasury to support the efforts of homeowners who, though in default, wished to continue to make payments on their mortgages. The program provides help to the private banks and other lenders who own the mortgages and who must be convinced of the need and the value of restructuring the mortgages. Of course, not every debtor will be qualified under the HAMP guidelines. In order to take advantage of HAMP, a debtor must owe no more than $729,750 on the mortgage; the property must be the debtor's primary residence; the mortgage must have been entered no later than January 1, 2009; and the debtor must also be at least 60 days behind on payments or close to losing the home. [See: "Who We Are and What We Do," Federal Housing Finance Agency, http://www.fhfa.gov/.]

Home Affordable Refinance Program The Home Affordable Refinance Program (HARP) is a sister program to HAMP that also operates under the authority of the Federal Housing Finance Agency. Unlike HAMP, however, HARP was designed for homeowners who are not in default on their mortgage payments but who have found themselves in the unfortunate position of owing more to the bank or mortgage company than the house is actually worth. HARP is open to homeowners whose loans are owned by Fannie or Freddie. The program permits qualified individuals to receive a break on out-of-pocket mortgage expenses by introducing a lower interest rate, reducing each monthly mortgage payment, obtaining a constant fixed-rate mortgage, or stockpiling equity at a more rapid rate. [See: "Who We Are and What We Do," Federal Housing Finance Agency, http://www.fhfa.gov/.]

Another government solution is the Troubled Asset Relief Program (TARP). This program was designed to allow the government to buy many of the so-called troubled assets that had resulted from the securitization epidemic. The program was funded at a level that topped $700 billion. Under provisions in the Emergency Economic Stabilization Act (EESA), the fund is managed by the Secretary of the Treasury. The secretary has the duty to make certain that any institution that receives funds under this program agrees to permit the federal government to purchase nonvoting stock in that institution. Not all of the assets, however, went to the purchase of these troubled assets, at least not directly. Instead, they went indirectly into the bailout of several large firms such as General Motors and Chrysler. Part of the funds also went to financial institutions such as AIG and Bank of America. Many people saw this as a move that bordered on a nationalization of these financial institutions. [See: Roubini and Mihm, pp. 168–169.]

Dodd–Frank Wall Street Reform and Consumer Protection Act Undoubtedly the most sweeping reform bill enacted in this crisis is the Dodd–Frank Wall Street Reform and Consumer Protection Act. As might be expected, the Dodd–Frank Act is long, involved, and complicated. It consists of 16 separate titles, many of which are often referred to as separate acts. Thus, Title XIV of the Dodd–Frank Act is also called the Mortgage Reform and Anti-Predatory Lending Act. Title XIV is especially pertinent to our discussion of the 21st-century financial crisis because the act is designed to prevent the problems noted earlier. Some of the new provisions include the following:

1. Lenders are now required to make a good-faith attempt to insure that all borrowers have the financial ability to repay the loan taken out to finance the mortgage.

2. Lenders must also make a good-faith attempt to determine whether the borrower can also pay all taxes, insurance, and all other assessments.
3. A good-faith attempt must include an examination of specifically defined documents that provide concrete verifiable evidence of the borrower's income stream, credit history, debt-to-income situation, employment, and financial resources (not counting the equity in the real property involved in the current loan).
4. Lenders are required to use documentation supplied by the Internal Revenue Service (IRS) or some other comparable third party that is also regulated by the act.
5. Certain types of mortgage arrangements are either outlawed or limited by the act, including mortgages with balloon payments that more than double the previous payments.

The act also creates a category of mortgages called **qualified mortgages**, which have met the good-faith requirements outlined in the act. Having a qualified mortgage bestows on the lender a safe harbor privilege that creates a presumption that the lender had ample evidence demonstrating that the borrower could satisfy the loan's repayment requirements. On the other hand, the act also outlaws certain types of lender-related compensation. Thus, mortgage originators cannot be compensated based on the loan's terms, except for terms related to the principal on the loan. Also, the mortgage originator cannot be paid an origination fee, with certain exceptions, unless that fee is paid by the borrower. [See: "Dodd-Frank Act Ushers in New Regulations for Mortgage Originators," Day Pitney LLP, August 24, 2010, pp. 1–3; John ReVeal, "Mortgage Reforms Under the Dodd-Frank Act," Bryan Cave LLP, August 3, 2010, http://www.bankbryancave.com; "Summary of Mortgage Related Provisions of the Dodd-Frank Wall Street Reform and Consumer Protection Act," Mortgage Bankers Association, July 21, 2010, p. 1; and William Sweet, "Dodd-Frank Becomes Law," *Harvard Law School Forum on Corporate Governance and Financial Regulation*, July 21, 2010, p. 2, http://blogs.law.harvard.edu.]

THE OPENING CASE *Round 4*
The 21st-Century Financial Crisis, Part 2: A Smart Business Strategy or Predatory Lending?

Before moving on to the long-term solutions to the crisis, let's look at the Opening Case one more time. Recall that Harbour Portfolio Advisors is alleged to have made quite a few investment dollars by buying homes that had been foreclosed on during the worst time of the financial crisis of 2008–2009 and selling them to high-risk clients using land contracts. By using the land contract approach, Harbour could sell these houses at much more than the market value, while also charging high interest rates and demanding large down payments. Buyers with weak credit ratings often preferred to enter land contracts because they did not have to suffer through the long, and potentially futile, vetting program that accompanied the mortgage application program conducted by those banks that were engaged in the process of granting more conventional mortgages. The downside of the land contract process, however, was that the buyers did not truly own their homes. Instead, they held only equitable title, while the lender continued to own the legal title. The fact that the lender held legal title meant that when the buyer forfeited on the loan, the lender could repossess the home and keep the installment payments, as well as the down payment. Harbour then went on to sell the same run-down house to another unsuspecting victim.

To some observers, it became clear that Harbour had played a central role in the second wave of the 21st-century financial crisis. Those homes that had been forfeited during the first stage of the crisis now lured in unsuspecting buyers in the second wave. These second-wave buyers also lost their homes, too, usually because they purchased their properties with land contracts that failed not only because of the buyers' poor credit histories, but also because of the horrible conditions of the houses.

Of course, even after all of this was revealed, the question still remained: Did Harbour simply use a clever investment strategy, or had it crossed the line and engaged in predatory lending? The jury is still out (literally) on this question. However, we do know one thing for certain, the City of Cincinnati decided to battle this "predatory process" by filing a lawsuit against Harbour. In the city's strategy lies the final short-term technique for dealing with the 21st-century financial crisis—the courts. In its lawsuit, the city accused Harbour of negotiating "predatory and unconscionable land sale contracts" and of not paying fines, fees, and back taxes amounting to $360,000. The city's complaint indicates that the city had two claims against Harbour: (1) that the firm neither formally registered nor properly maintained the properties located in Cincinnati and (2) that it knew that the properties were in bad shape but never revealed any of this to the buyers and renters who ended up living there. As a consequence the city asked the court to order Harbour (1) to repair the problems that exist at their properties, (2) to pay all fines and fees that the firm owes to the city, (3) to tell clients about known property defects in the future, and (4) to repair all problems in the properties that it rents or leases. This case may turn out to be a model for other municipalities that have seen investment firms within their borders engage in similar predatory activities. Moreover, should enough cities and towns follow through on similar lawsuits, those lawsuits may serve to deter such predatory behavior before it begins. [See: *City of Cincinnati v. Harbour Portfolio Advisors, LLC*, Complaint, Court of Common Pleas Hamilton County, Ohio (April 11, 2017); James Leggate, "Cincinnati Sues Company over 'Predatory' Land Sales Contracts, Blighted Properties," *WCPO Cincinnati*, April 14, 2017, http://www.wcpo.com/news/local-news/hamilton-county/cincinnati/cincinnati-files-lawsuit-against-predatory-land-investor?page=2; and Matthew Goldstein and Alexandra Stevenson, "Cincinnati Sues Seller of Foreclosed Homes, Claiming Predatory Acts," *The New York Times*, April 21, 2017, p. B3.]

Source: See: *City of Cincinnati v. Harbour Portfolio Advisors*, LLC. Complaint, Court of Common Pleas Hamilton County, Ohio, (April 11, 2017); James Leggate, "Cincinnati sues company over 'predatory' land sales contracts, blighted properties," *WCPO Cincinnati* (April 14, 2017) http://www.wcpo.com/news/local-news/hamilton-county/cincinnati/cincinnati-files-lawsuit-against-predatory-land-investor?page=2; Matthew Goldstein and Alexandra Stevenson, "Cincinnati Sues Seller of Foreclosed Homes, Claiming Predatory Acts," *The New York Times* (April 21, 2017), p. B3.

The Long-Term Solutions to the Crisis

The previous solutions (takeover of Fannie and Freddie by the Federal Housing Finance Agency, creation of HAMP and HARP, establishment of the Troubled Asset Relief Program, and passage of the Dodd–Frank Act) should be viewed as short-term therapy rather than a long-term cure for the problems that led to the 21st-century financial breakdown. These solutions may temporarily plug certain obvious leaks, but they cannot prevent the financial dam from bursting. To head off another collapse, the entire structure must be repaired from the ground up. The long-term solutions covered in this section address the underlying cracks in the foundation of the socioeconomic system that led not just to this crisis, but to a series of overlapping disasters that have repeated themselves in a cyclical fashion over the past century.

A Philosophical Solution

A philosophical and somewhat optimistic long-term solution is offered by Serres in *Times of Crisis*. The most significant contribution that Serres makes to a long-term solution is his observation that when a crisis occurs, there can be no true recovery if *recovery* is defined as a return to the set of original initial conditions. Such an approach is self-defeating because those conditions triggered the problem. Instead of tinkering with a broken system, governmental and private authorities must alter or eliminate those initial conditions. The good news is that the initial conditions in this case were created,

Serres tells us, by human activity in agriculture, transportation, health, demographics connections, and conflicts. [See: Serres, pp. 1-15.] The bad news is that the changes that have emerged from the development of these areas have generated a new relationship between the socioeconomic-biological-ecological system (Serres calls it *Biogea*, and we have used the term the *biogetic system*) and the people who live and work within that system. [See: Serres, pp. 25-33.] Serres says we must reimmerse ourselves in the system in order to close the separation by abandoning the activities that created the initial separation. This is an interesting solution, but the law does not do well with such abstract programs. On the other hand, the notion that a new crisis will be prevented only by altering the initial conditions that led to the old crisis is a valuable observation that is related to the other two long-term solutions offered here. [See: Serres, pp. 48-72.]

An Economic-Political Solution In *Reinventing Collapse*, Orlov also implies that a new crisis will occur unless the initial conditions that produced the current crisis are abolished. It is on this point that he and Serres agree. Where they differ is in the nature of the long-term changes. Orlov believes that economic collapse is inevitable. The initial conditions that gave birth to this crisis are grounded in a political and economic social system fed by five elements: (1) a decline in energy resources, (2) a serious trade deficit, (3) unrestrained defense spending, (4) expanding foreign debt, and (5) a pervasive psychosocial anxiety leading to erratic behavior. Once these elements are in place, collapse is inevitable. Consequently, we should be more concerned with what happens in the post-collapse era than during the collapse itself. Curiously, while the post-collapse era is to be avoided, the underlying principles of that era provide a template for long-term changes in the initial conditions. [See: Orlov, pp. 2-4.]

Those principles are best seen in a concrete example. Orlov suggests a new level of governmental regulation that, while severe, can actually do some practical good. For instance, in a post-collapse (or near-post-collapse) world, energy resources in general and gasoline in particular will become so scarce that it will be rationed in a severely limited way. To address this problem, the government should prohibit the purchase of any new gas-powered vehicles—period. This prohibition would force industry to retool existing cars, making them more energy efficient. Banning new vehicles would also close all businesses related to the manufacture and sale of new vehicles, which itself results in a huge energy savings. It also leads to a drop in the use of vehicles by people; it encourages carpooling when possible and makes the development of alternative means of transportation necessary. People will ride bikes, take the bus, ride the train, develop solar-powered vehicles, fabricate steam-powered cars, and so on. [See: Orlov, pp. 132-133.]

Another measure that Orlov suggests is a post-collapse alteration in the very nature of the corporation, from one that is driven by the need for profit to one that is driven by the need to provide welfare and income for its employees. The corporation would then focus on becoming a self-perpetuating organization that does its own exploration for resources, its own manufacturing of a product, its own sales, and its own reapplication of the surplus into the development of a better corporation. Corporations become, in effect, self-perpetuating, self-sufficient communes in which people live, work, play, train, and so on, as a team. [See: Orlov, p. 129.] Both of these examples may seem highly implausible, perhaps even impossible. However, both examples focus on a solution that alters those dangerous initial conditions. Now, as we turn to Roubini and Mihm, we see how this principle can be used in the retooling of the current financial system to prevent a recurrence of an unending cycle of financial catastrophes.

A Quantifiable, Applied, Practical Solution To summarize, the Serres principle promotes altering the initial conditions of the socioeconomic system to prevent a series of repeating financial disasters. Building on this, the Orlov principle promotes a radical rethinking of financial and corporate relationships to shake up those initial conditions. Roubini and Mihm apply these two principles, without naming them, to the work-a-day world of Washington and Wall Street and construct several proposals to make those radical adjustments a reality. In one proposal, they suggest that the government make it advantageous for our largest financial institutions to subdivide and reorganize themselves into smaller, independent units. The plan would make it illegal for large financial institutions to invest in any venture from which they cannot extricate themselves with the capital reserves that they have on hand. In essence, financial institutions would be legally compelled to maintain the ability to bail themselves out of financial danger. The need to maintain self-sustaining capital reserves discourages risk-intensive ventures and discourages unchecked institutional growth. Instead, the law would encourage financial institutions to downsize so they can properly control every investment they take on. In effect, the plan would eliminate the "too-big-to-fail" syndrome that has plagued the current financial system, thus attacking a key initial condition. No institution becomes too big to fail, because there is no value any longer in being quite that "big." [See: Roubini and Mihm, p. 226; and Paul M. Barrett, "Prophet Making," *The New York Times Sunday Book Review*, June 27, 2010, p. BR13.]

In another proposal, Roubini and Mihm suggest a drastic reconfiguration of executive bonus packages. Oddly, they do not promote eliminating such bonuses. Such a move would be ill-advised. It is not "bonus as bonus" that is the problem. Rather, it is the bonus that is paid immediately with no concern for the long-term effects of the investment that earned that bonus. This technique encourages executives to support high-risk ventures that produce immediate dramatic results. Under the traditional bonus system, once an investment has produced a dramatically high return, the executive receives his or her bonus instantly. Should the investment later fail, the executive keeps that bonus. In contrast, Roubini and Mihm propose a bonus-escrow plan, referred to as the **bonus-malus** system, under which the bonus would be placed in an escrow account for several years to test the true value of the investment. The executive does not receive the bonus unless the investment demonstrates its staying power. If the investment loses money, then the bonus is reduced by an appropriate amount. Again, Roubini and Mihm have suggested a radical alteration of the initial conditions of the current system. Instead of encouraging risky "shoot-from-the-hip" investment opportunities, as the present system does, the new system encourages solid, long-term investment prospects that may even outlive the executive. [See: Roubini and Mihn, pp. 187–188; Barrett, p. BR13.]

These are only a few of the modifications that Roubini and Mihm have suggested to alter the initial conditions of the present financial situation. Others include changes in the method by which securities are approved, including a standardization of the process as well as heightened transparency that will allow investors greater access to investment ratings conducted by ratings agencies.

quick quiz 20-2

1. Subprime lending was the only cause of the 21st-century financial crisis. — true | false
2. To avoid a future crisis, the initial conditions of a financial system must be changed. — true | false
3. The federal government was forced to take over Fannie Mae but did not have to follow a similar strategy with Freddie Mac. — true | false

20-3 Personal Property as Security

Article 9 of the UCC* brings all personal property security devices, or security interests, together under one law. The property that is subject to the security interest is called *collateral*. A security interest is created by a written agreement, called a **security agreement**, which identifies the goods and is signed by the debtor. The lender or seller who holds the security interest is known as the **secured party**. A security interest is said to attach when the secured party has a legally enforceable right to take that property and sell it to satisfy the debt. It is said to be **perfected** when the secured party has done everything that the law requires to give the secured party greater rights to the goods than others have. The following definitions apply to secured transactions:

- **Consumer goods** are goods that are used or bought for use primarily for personal, family, or household purposes.
- **Equipment** is goods other than inventory, farm products, or consumer goods.
- **Farm products** are crops or livestock or supplies used or produced in farming operations.
- **Inventory** are goods other than farm products held for sale or lease or raw materials used or consumed in a business.
- **Fixtures** are goods that are so related to real estate that an interest arises in them under real estate law.
- **Purchase money security interest** is a security interest taken by a lender or a seller of an item to secure its price.
- **Buyer in the ordinary course of business** is a person who in good faith and without knowledge that the sale is in violation of ownership rights or security interest of a third party buys goods in ordinary course from a person in the business of selling goods of that kind, not including a pawnbroker.

UCC 9-102(23)
UCC 9-102(33)
UCC 9-102(34)
UCC 9-102(48)
UCC 9-102(41)
UCC 9-103
UCC 1-201(9)

Security Agreement

A security agreement is an agreement that creates a security interest. It must be in writing, be signed by the debtor, and contain a description of the collateral that is used for security.

UCC 9-105(l)

EXAMPLE 20-1: Security Agreement Must Describe Collateral

Moody Industries contracted to purchase certain robotics equipment from Universal. Moody's president signed a promissory note identifying Universal as a secured party. When Moody filed for bankruptcy, Universal claimed to have a security interest in the robotics equipment. Because the promissory note did not describe the collateral, Universal did not hold a valid security interest in the equipment.

If Universal had provided enough information about the collateral to allow the court to identify it without a detailed description, the result would have been different. Had Universal made reference to the equipment by including purchase order or invoice numbers, the court could have identified the equipment and would have upheld the validity of the security agreement.

Attachment of a Security Interest

To be effective, a security interest must be legally enforceable against the debtor. This enforceability is known as **attachment**. Attachment occurs when three conditions are met.

UCC 9-203

First, the debtor has some ownership or possessive rights in the collateral. Second, the secured party (or creditor) transfers something of value, such as money, to the debtor. Third, the secured party takes possession of the collateral or signs a security agreement that describes the collateral.

> ### EXAMPLE 20-2: Attachment of Security Interest
>
> Conroy loaned Lightfoot $5,000 for six months at 8 percent interest. Lightfoot secured the debt by giving Conroy several uncut diamonds that Lightfoot owned. Conroy agreed to return the diamonds when Lightfoot paid the debt. The security interest was legally enforceable because all three conditions were met. First, Lightfoot had ownership rights in the diamonds. Second, Conroy gave Lightfoot something of value (the $5,000). Third, Conroy took possession of the diamonds. The security interest would also have attached if Lightfoot had kept the diamonds but signed a security agreement describing them.

UCC 9-204

Creditors may obtain security interests in property acquired by the debtor after the original agreement is entered. The creditor does so by placing a provision in the security agreement that the security interest of the creditor also applies to goods the debtor acquires at a later time. It is known as a **floating lien**. This lien is important to creditors who take security interests in goods, such as food items, that are sold and replaced within short periods of time. The lien is lost when the goods are sold but regained as soon as the debtor takes possession of the new property.

Perfection of a Security Interest

When a security interest attaches, it is effective only between debtor and creditor. Such creditors, however, want to make certain that no one else can claim that collateral before they do if the debtors fail to pay them back. To preserve the right to first claim on the collateral, creditors must perfect their interest. A security interest can be perfected in one of three ways: by filing a financing statement in the appropriate government office, by attachment alone, or by possession of the collateral.

Perfection by Filing Security interests in most kinds of personal property are perfected by filing a financing statement in a public office. The office may be a central one (secretary of state's or secretary of the commonwealth's office) or a local one (county recorder or city clerk) where the debtor resides or has a place of business. The proper office for filing depends on the type of collateral and varies from state to state.

UCC 9-302

A financing statement must give the names of the debtor and the secured party. It must be signed by the debtor and give the address of a secured party from which information regarding the security interest may be obtained. It must also give a mailing address of the debtor and contain a statement indicating the types, or describing the items, of collateral. When the financing statement covers such things as fixtures, crops, timber, minerals, oil, and gas, the statement must also contain a description of the real estate concerned.

UCC 9-302(1)(d)
UCC 9-302(3)(b)

Perfection by Attachment Alone A purchase money security interest in con*sumer goods* is perfected the moment it attaches, with the exception of motor vehicles and fixtures. Security interests on motor vehicles are perfected by making a note of the lien on the certificate of title issued by the state government. Security interests on fixtures are perfected by filing a financing statement with the registry of deeds where the land is located.

EXAMPLE 20-3: Perfection of Purchase Money Security Interest

Sabatini purchased a new 60-inch Smart-4K Ultra HD TV for $1,999.99 from Steinbeck's TV Outlet. To pay for the TV, she borrowed money from the Atlantic Finance Company, which took a security interest in the TV by entering into a security agreement with Sabatini. Because this interest was a purchase money security interest and the TV set was a consumer good, the security interest would become perfected the moment it attached—that is, when Sabatini signed the agreement and received the TV set and Steinbeck received payment from the finance company.

Perfection by Possession A security interest may be perfected when the secured party (creditor) takes possession of the collateral. This possession is called a pledge. The borrower, or debtor, who gives up the property, is the pledgor. The secured party, or creditor, is the pledgee. A secured party who has possession of the collateral must take reasonable care of the property. The debtor must reimburse the secured party for any money spent to take care of the property.

UCC 9-313

EXAMPLE 20-4: Pledge of Personal Property

After Sabatini paid off the debt to the Atlantic Finance Corporation (see Example 20-3) she decided to buy a Kindle. This time, she borrowed the money from her cousin, Colter, who agreed to lend Sabatini the money only if he could have her Kindle as security until she repaid him. Colter's security interest in the Kindle became perfected when he took possession of it.

Priorities and Claims

Sometimes, two or more parties claim a security interest in the same collateral. At other times, unsecured parties claim that they have better rights than secured parties. The UCC helps resolve these conflicts. The following are some of the provisions, stating who prevails over whom in particular situations:

1. A perfected purchase money security interest in inventory has priority over a conflicting security interest in the same inventory.
2. A purchase money security interest in collateral other than inventory has priority over a conflicting security interest in the same collateral if it is perfected when the debtor receives the collateral or within 10 days thereafter.
3. Buyers of goods in the ordinary course of business (except farm products) prevail over security interests in the seller's inventory.
4. Buyers of farm products in the ordinary course of business, to the extent that they pay for and receive collateral without knowledge of the security interest, take precedence over nonperfected security interests.
5. Buyers of consumer goods are not affected by perfected security interests of which they have no knowledge.
6. In all other cases, a perfected security interest prevails over an unperfected security interest.
7. Conflicting security interests rank according to priority in time of filing or perfection.

UCC 9-312(3)
UCC 9-312(4)
UCC 9-307(1)
UCC 9-301(1)(c)

Collateral may be repossessed if the debtor defaults, but the repossession may not be conducted in a way that disturbs the peace.
©Roman.S-Photographer/Shutterstock

8. When two or more parties have unperfected security interests in the same collateral, the first to attach prevails over the other parties.

Default of the Debtor

UCC 9-307(2)
UCC 9-301
UCC 9-312(5)(a)
UCC 9-312(5)(b)
UCC 9-601

If a debtor defaults by failing to make payments when due, the secured party may satisfy the debt by taking possession of the collateral. Because of the difficulties of doing this, the perfection of a security interest by possession, as in a pledge, is better than other types of perfection. Collateral may be repossessed without going through the court if it can be done without causing a disturbance; otherwise, the creditor must use legal processes.

After repossessing the goods, the secured party (the creditor) may sell them at a public auction or private sale. The terms of the sale must be reasonable, and the debtor must be given notice of the time and place of any public auction so that he or she may bid on them personally. If the goods are consumer goods and the debtor has paid 60 percent or more of the cash price of a purchase money security interest, the secured party cannot keep the goods. They must be sold.

quick quiz 20-3

1. A security interest is perfected when the secured party has a legally enforceable right to take that property and sell it to satisfy the debt.   true | false
2. Security interests in most kinds of personal property are perfected by filing a financial statement in a public office.   true | false
3. Buyers of goods in the ordinary course of business (except farm products) prevail over security interests in the seller's inventory.   true | false

Summary

20.1 Individuals and institutions that lend money need some assurance that they will have their money returned to them. Security devices serve as this means of assurance.

20.2 A system must not recover from a crisis; it must move away from the initial conditions that caused the crisis in the first place. This is true of the current 21st-century financial crisis just as it is true of any healthy complex adaptive system (CAS). Like the crisis of 1929, the crisis of 2008 is a global crisis that must be fixed by reengineering the initial conditions that started the crisis. Some short-term solutions to the crisis include the takeover of Fannie and Freddie by the Federal Housing Finance Agency, creation of HAMP and HARP, establishment of the Troubled Asset Relief Program, and passage of the Dodd–Frank Act. Long-term solutions to the crisis must address the underlying cracks in the foundation of the socioeconomic system that led not just to this crisis, but to a series of overlapping disasters that have repeated themselves in a cyclical fashion over the past century.

20.3 When personal property is purchased on credit, the seller frequently retains a security interest in the property. Property that is subject to a security interest is called collateral. A security interest is created by a written agreement called a security agreement, which identifies the goods and is signed by the debtor. To be effective between debtor and creditor, a security interest must be made legally enforceable. This legality is known as attachment. To be effective against third parties who might also claim the secured property, the creditor must perfect the security interest. Perfection is accomplished by filing a financing statement, by attachment alone in certain cases, or by taking possession of the collateral.

Key Terms

acceleration, 556
adjustable-rate mortgage (ARM), 552
asset-backed security, 560
assume the mortgage, 557
attachment, 569
balloon-payment mortgage, 552
biogetic system, 558
bonus-malus, 568
buyer in the ordinary course of business, 569
collateral, 550
construction loan, 553
consumer goods, 569
conventional fixed-rate mortgage, 552
deed of trust, 553
Dodd–Frank Wall Street Reform and Consumer Protection Act, 564
equipment, 569
equity of redemption, 555
farm products, 569
Federal Housing Finance Agency (FHFA), 563
fixtures, 569
flexible-rate mortgage, 552
floating lien, 570
foreclosure, 556
government-sponsored enterprise (GSE), 560
graduated-payment mortgage, 552
Home Affordable Modification Program (HAMP), 564
Home Affordable Refinance Program (HARP), 564
home equity loan, 553
interest-only mortgage, 552
inventory, 569
junior mortgage, 533
land contract, 554
liar loan, 561
lien, 550
mortgage, 550
mortgage-backed security, 560
mortgagee, 550
mortgagor, 550
NINJA loan, 561
participation loan, 552
perfected, 569
purchase money security interest, 569
qualified mortgage, 565
recovery, 557
reverse mortgage, 552
second mortgage, 553
secured loan, 550
secured party, 569
securitization, 560
security, 550
security agreement, 569
security device, 550
security interest, 550
subject to the mortgage, 557
subprime loan, 553
Troubled Asset Relief Program (TARP), 564
unsecured loan, 550
variable-rate mortgage, 552

Questions for Review and Discussion

1. What is the difference between a secured and an unsecured loan?
2. What types of mortgages are available to borrowers?
3. What is the legal effect of recording a mortgage?
4. What are the rights and duties of the mortgagor and those of the mortgagee?
5. What is the difference between a financial recovery and an alteration in the initial conditions of a system?
6. What short-term solutions to the 21st-century financial crisis have been implemented?
7. What long-term solutions to the 21st-century financial crisis have been proposed to alter the initial conditions of the economy?
8. How is a security interest is created for personal property?
9. When is a security interest perfected?
10. What priorities exist when parties claim a security interest in the same property?

Cases for Analysis

1. Sanchez bought a house for $100,000, paying $10,000 down and financing the balance through a local bank. As part of the closing costs, Sanchez was required to take out private mortgage insurance to protect the bank in case she defaulted on the mortgage. She had an excellent credit rating

and always paid her mortgage payments when they were due. Two years after buying the property, she received an inheritance and used the money to pay an additional amount of $10,000 to the bank toward the principal of the loan. Hoping to cut down on her monthly payments, she asked the bank to cancel the mortgage insurance, but the bank refused. Does Sanchez have any rights in this situation? Explain.

2. Robert and Sherrell Bergeron gave a first mortgage on their property to First Colonial Bank and a second mortgage to Ford Motor Credit Company. When the Bergerons were unable to pay the mortgage, the bank foreclosed. The property was sold at a foreclosure sale for more money than the Bergerons owed the bank. The Bergerons claim that they are entitled to the surplus funds from the sale. Do you agree? Explain. [See: *First Colonial Bank for Savings v. Bergeron*, 646 N.E.2d 758 (MA).]

3. When the Prestons took out a variable mortgage with the First Bank of Marietta, their interest rate was 9 percent. The agreement allowed First Bank to raise or lower the interest rate at any time, provided that the Prestons received 30 days' notice. When the bank raised the interest rate to 11 percent, the Prestons refused to pay, arguing that the agreement was unenforceable because it set no limit on what interest rate they might be forced to pay. Were the Prestons correct? Explain. [See: *Preston v. First Bank of Marietta*, 473 N.E.2d 1210 (OH).]

4. The Woolseys ran a mink farm that was mortgaged to the State Bank of Lehi. The agreement included provisions that allowed acceleration and foreclosure if the Woolseys failed to pay their obligations under the contract. The Woolseys defaulted on several payments, and the bank foreclosed. The couple demanded a jury trial on the foreclosure action. They also argued that the bank had not acted in good faith in its acceleration and foreclosure. Were the Woolseys entitled to a jury trial? Explain. Who had the burden of proof in demonstrating the bank's good faith in accelerating payments and demanding foreclosure? [See: *State Bank of Lehi v. Woolsey*, 565 P.2d 413 (UT).]

5. Bloom executed a real estate mortgage in favor of Lakeshore Commercial Finance Corporation on September 16. On October 4, Bloom executed another mortgage on the same described real estate in favor of Northridge Bank. Northridge, without notice of the mortgage to Lakeshore, recorded its mortgage at 9:28 A.M. on October 25. On that same date, at 3:07 P.M., the prior mortgage executed in favor of Lakeshore was recorded. Bloom defaulted on the mortgages. The value of the real estate was insufficient to satisfy both mortgages fully. Which party had first rights to the property, Lakeshore or Northridge? Why? [See: *Northridge Bank v. Lakeshore Com. Fin. Corp.*, 365 N.E.2d 382 (IL).]

6. Cramer's mortgage contained a provision requiring her to pay monthly tax and insurance payments into an escrow account held by the bank in addition to principal and interest. Cramer paid the principal and interest regularly but refused to pay the tax and insurance escrow payments. The bank brought foreclosure proceedings. Did it have the right to foreclose on Cramer's mortgage? Explain. [See: *Cramer v. Metro. Sav. & Loan Ass'n.*, 258 N.W.2d 20 (MI).]

7. Matthews Motors sold a Buick Riviera to Jenkins for $11,500. Matthews then borrowed money from Averysboro National Bank, using the Buick as collateral. When Matthews defaulted on the loan, the bank attempted to repossess the Buick from Jenkins. Jenkins refused to surrender the automobile, claiming that he and not Matthews owned it. The bank brought suit, asking the court to force Jenkins to turn over the Buick. Should the court grant the bank's request? Why or why not? [See: *Averysboro National Bank v. Jenkins*, 328 S.E.2d 399 (GA).]

8. Giant Wholesale agreed to supply Hendersonville Food Center with groceries if the owner, William Page, would guarantee all debts incurred by Hendersonville. Page agreed, and a security agreement was drawn up. The security agreement gave Giant a security interest in Hendersonville's groceries and equipment. Giant failed to file a financing statement properly. When Hendersonville ran into financial difficulty, Page turned over the checking account to Giant. When this maneuver did not work, Giant repossessed all of Hendersonville's inventory. Page later went bankrupt. Gray, the bankruptcy trustee, brought a suit against Giant, claiming that the inventory was part of Page's property and thus subject to the bankruptcy proceeding. Gray argued that because the financing statement had not been filed, Giant's security interest had not been perfected. Was Gray correct? Explain. [See: *Gray v. Giant Wholesale*, 758 F.2d 1000 (4th Cir.).]

9. U.S. Electronics, a Missouri corporation with a place of business in DeKalb County, Georgia, borrowed money from a Missouri bank. The corporation gave the bank a security interest in all of its machinery and equipment. The bank filed a financing statement in Fulton County rather than in DeKalb County, as required by law. U.S. Electronics defaulted on the loan and fell behind on its rent. The corporation's landlord obtained a judgment against it for past due rent, becoming a lien creditor. The landlord claimed priority over the bank for the proceeds of a sheriff's sale of the machinery and equipment, arguing that the bank's security interest was not perfected. Do you agree? Why or why not? [See: *United States v. Waterford No. 2 Office Center*, 271 S.E.2d 790 (GA).]

10. Lallana bought a car on credit from a dealer who assigned the contract and the security agreement to Bank of America. When Lallana failed to make several payments, the bank repossessed the car. The bank notified Lallana that if she did not redeem the car or reinstate the contract within 15 days, it would sell the car. The bank then sold the car at a public auction for $5,000 and sued Lallana for $11,249, the balance due on her loan. Kelley Blue Book's estimated retail value of the car at the time of the auction was $14,820. Did the bank give Lallana proper notice of the sale? Why or why not? [See: *Bank of America v. Lallana*, 960 P.2d 1133 (CA).]

Design Elements: The Opening Case: ©Sharpstock/Alamy; A Classic Case: ©Evlakhov Valeriy/Shutterstock

quick quiz Answers

20-1	20-2	20-3
1. T	1. F	1. F
2. T	2. F	2. T
3. T	3. F	3. T

Chapter 21
Bankruptcy Law: In Theory, in History, and in Practice

21-1 The Checkered History of Bankruptcy in the United States
Re-engineering the Constitution • Federal Control of Bankruptcy • The Growth of Federal Bankruptcy Law • The Current State of Bankruptcy Law • The Authority of the States in Bankruptcy

21-2 Liquidation—Chapter 7, Bankruptcy Code
Commencing the Action • Order for Relief • Automatic Stay • Federal Exemptions • State Exemptions • Trustee's Duties • Exceptions to Discharge • Restoring Credit Following Bankruptcy

21-3 Reorganization—Chapter 11, Bankruptcy Code
Special Features of Chapter 11 • The Reorganization Plan

21-4 Family Farmer or Fishing Business Debt Adjustment—Chapter 12, Bankruptcy Code
Chapter 12 Procedures • The Chapter 12 Plan

21-5 Individual Debt Adjustment—Chapter 13, Bankruptcy Code
The Chapter 13 Plan • Plan Confirmation • Changes to Chapter 13 under BAPCPA

THE OPENING CASE Round 1
Bankruptcy or Insolvency? Federal or State Control? Traders or Traders Plus?

Once upon a time, in a galaxy far, far away, bankruptcy laws were not as clear cut, detailed, and accessible as they are today. In the past, 1902 to be exact, there was even some question, well many questions actually, about the advisability of having a federal bankruptcy law at all—period. The question of whether to establish a federal bankruptcy law was the central issue in the case of *Hanover National Bank v. Max Moyses*. In this case, Moyses was the defendant debtor, and Hanover was the plaintiff creditor. The case was brought by Hanover in the federal court in New York in 1899 in an attempt to get satisfaction on a debt that Moyses owed the bank. Moyses, however, had been declared bankrupt in a federal court in Tennessee and had already discharged all of his debts, including the one owed to Hanover. The bank admitted that Moyses had been adjudicated bankrupt under the 1898 bankruptcy statute and that the law had been followed to the letter. So far, so good, except for one major point. Hanover argued that the bankruptcy act under which Moyses had been declared insolvent was unconstitutional.

Hanover offered two reasons for the unconstitutionality of the federal bankruptcy law: (1) The law violated the Fifth Amendment prohibition against the taking of property without due process, and (2) the law violated Article I, Section 8, Clause 4 of the U.S. Constitution. Let's look at each argument one at a time. Citing the Fifth Amendment, the plaintiff claimed that the bankruptcy law was unconstitutional because, under its provisions, the process of distributing the debtor's property could be completed without notifying all those parties that had an interest in the property, Hanover being one such party. More specifically, Hanover claimed that the due process clause had been violated because (1) the statute empowered the debtor to initiate the bankruptcy proceeding (i.e., insolvency or voluntary bankruptcy) rather than the creditors, thus violating the creditors' due process rights; (2) the notice that was required under the act was so brief (10 days) that any distant creditors had no realistic chance of responding; and (3) if the creditor did manage to actually get to the bankruptcy court in a timely manner, the grounds for any objection were so limited that any retrieval of the property was almost nonexistent. As for Article I, Section 8, Clause 4, Hanover declared that the law was unconstitutional because (1) it failed to set up universal laws of bankruptcy for all states as required by the Constitution, (2) the act unconstitutionally delegated powers to the states that cannot be delegated to those states, and (3) the law unconstitutionally extended bankruptcy jurisdiction to individuals who were not traders as required by long-standing legal tradition in England and the United States.

The case reached the U.S. Supreme Court, which agreed to rule on those issues as soon as possible. Some of these questions were easy enough for the court to answer; others not so much. Working its way backward, the Court began with the question of the plaintiff's identity. Is Congress limited to passing bankruptcy legislation that protects traders alone? For the answer to this question, well, keep reading. [See:

Hanover National Bank of New York v. Max Moyses, 186 U.S. 181, 22 S.Ct. 857, 45 L.Ed. 1113 (1902).]

Opening Case Questions

1. What two provisions of the Constitution are under scrutiny here? Explain.
2. What arguments does the plaintiff use to demonstrate that the federal bankruptcy law is unconstitutional? Explain.
3. How successful do you suppose the plaintiff was in presenting these arguments? Explain.
4. What is the difference between the district courts and bankruptcy courts in the federal system? Explain.
5. What types of cases are the bankruptcy courts empowered to adjudicate on their own? Explain.

Source: See: *Hanover National Bank of New York v. Max Moyses*, 186 U.S. 181, 22 S.Ct. 857, 45 L.Ed. 1113 (1902).

LO Learning Objectives

1. Summarize the history of bankruptcy law in the United States.
2. Discuss federal and state control of bankruptcy law.
3. Identify the current state of bankruptcy law in the federal system.
4. State the criteria necessary to be eligible to file voluntarily for Chapter 7 bankruptcy.
5. State the criteria necessary for creditors to force debtors into involuntary bankruptcy.
6. Distinguish between an *order for relief* and *automatic stay* in the bankruptcy process.
7. List the federal exemptions debtors can exclude from the bankruptcy process.
8. Recognize those debts that have priority payment status under the Bankruptcy Code.
9. Explain Chapter 11 bankruptcy, emphasizing the reorganization process.
10. Discuss the requirements for Chapters 12 and 13 bankruptcy.

21-1 The Checkered History of Bankruptcy in the United States

When the framers gathered in Philadelphia in 1787 to *revise* the Articles of Confederation they were troubled by the fragile and tentative nature of those articles and by the lack of power that had paralyzed the national government. Also on their minds was the recent rebellion led by Daniel Shays, Samuel Ely, and their fellow farmers in Massachusetts. The rebellion, which involved more than 2,000 angry farmers, may have been unsuccessful, but that did not diminish the impact that it had on the delegates, many of whom were nervous about a possible new revolution. [See: Walter A. MacDougal, *Freedom Just Around the Corner* (New York: Harper Collins, 2004), p. 295.] Fearing another rebellion, the framers did not want to make the same mistakes that had been made when the Articles of Confederation had been shaped. Consequently, the Framers did their best to provide a strong central government in the Constitution.

Re-engineering the Constitution

U.S. Const., Article I, Sec. 8 (see Appendix A)

As we saw in some detail in Chapter 2, the framers of U.S. Constitution made a concerted effort to insulate the leadership of the new republic from the influence of the people. Several examples of this include the Electoral College (Article II, Section 1), the election of senators (Article I, Section 3), the supremacy clause (Article VI), and the religion clauses of the First Amendment. The bankruptcy clause in Article I, Section 8, Clause 4, is also part of this effort. Curiously, the first version of the new Constitution made no reference to bankruptcy or insolvency laws. To remedy this oversight, a bankruptcy clause was prepared and submitted to the drafting committee. This initial draft of the clause declared that Congress would have the power "to establish uniform laws upon the subject of bankruptcies and respecting the damages arising on the protest of foreign bills of exchange." The clause was added to the Constitution after nine states had voted to approve it. The final version is found in Article I, Section, 8, Clause 4, which states that Congress has the power to, "establish . . . uniform laws on the subject of Bankruptcies throughout the United States." [See: Joseph Story, *Commentaries on the Constitution of the United States* (The Constitution Society), http://www.constitution.org/js/js_005.htm.]

In his work, *Commentaries on the Constitution*, Associate Justice Joseph Story of the Supreme Court wrote in 1833 that direct mention of bankruptcy in *The Federalist Papers* occurs only once. That passage states, "The power of establishing uniform laws of bankruptcy is so intimately connected with the regulation of commerce and will prevent so many frauds, where the parties or their property may lie, or be removed into different states, that the expediency of it seems not likely to be drawn into question."[1] [See: Joseph Story, *Commentaries on the Constitution of the United States*, 4th ed., ed. Thomas Cooley (Boston: Little, Brown & Co., 1874), vol. 1.] Story also defends the addition of the bankruptcy clause. His defense is based on the idea that the bankruptcy process helps debtors to retain their ability to make a decent wage and thus to feed, clothe, and shelter their families. Story sees the bankruptcy process as a charitable system that helps the weak and powerless, and he seems convinced that the framers had this view also [See: Story, section 1100.]

Federal Control of Bankruptcy

Story then defends the use of a national law rather than a state statute to manage the distribution of a debtor's assets. First, he says that a uniform national law will foster consistency, uniformity, and justice in the distribution of a bankrupt's property. Second, he contends that a national law will avoid giving preference to one class of debtors' over another class. Third, Story argues that as a matter of constitutional law, the states have no power to control the disposition of property that lies beyond their own borders and so, passing the responsibility of controlling bankruptcy on to them will create state statutes of limited jurisdiction. In contrast, the national government does have the power to cross state lines and create rules for the distribution of property that all states must observe. Fourth, similarly the states have no power to control the disposition of property beyond the borders of the United States, and so, once again, giving the states any authority over bankruptcy will result in statutes of dubious effectiveness. On the other hand, the national government does have that authority, under its ability to negotiate treaties, and so it makes sense to reserve that responsibility to Congress [See: Story, sections 1102–1104.]

All of this makes perfect sense, of course. However, what Story forgets (or conveniently ignores) is that the framers also added the bankruptcy provision as a protective measure that would ensure that the moneyed elite (the class to which the framers belonged) would have access to a legal process that would help them get their money back (or at least part of it) from delinquent debtors without having to take matters into their own hands. The motivation for exerting this control can be seen in Madison's *Federalist Papers*, especially Federalist No. 10. Madison does not write directly about bankruptcy in this essay, but he does defend republican government at the expense of democracy, using an argument based on economics, in general, and class distinctions in particular, both of which are related to bankruptcy legislation. His rhetoric, as always, sounds highly libertarian. He wants a republic because he fears that a direct democracy in a nation as large as the United States will empower the majority to control the minority. The words *majority* and *minority* are neutral enough to mislead us into thinking that Madison had noble motives (as Story implies) and that may be the case; however, we must also understand what he means by *minority* and *majority*. [See: Charles Beard, *An Economic Interpretation of the Constitution of the United States* (New York: Macmillan, 1913).]

By *minority*, Madison meant the elite moneyed class (of which he and the other delegates were members), while by *majority*, he meant the working class (the class involved in Shays' Rebellion). To see this more vividly, we need only turn to *The Federalist Papers* where Madison writes, "But the most common and durable source of factions has been the various and unequal distribution of property. Those who hold and those who are without property have ever formed distinct interests in society. *Those who are creditors, and those who are debtors*." (emphasis added) [See: James Madison, *Federalist No. 10*, paragraph 6.] Moreover, we need not focus only on *The Federalist Papers*. The constitutional record itself can tell us something. In fact, in debate on June 26, 1787, Madison said that he feared a future in which "the property of the landed proprietors would be insecure" and that the government must be used "to support these invaluable interests, and to balance and check the other. They ought to be so constituted as to protect the minority of the opulent against the majority." [See: Robert Yates, "Notes of the Secret Debates of the Federal Convention of 1787, Taken by the Late Hon. Robert Yates, Chief Justice of the State of New York, and One of the Delegates from That State to the Said Convention," Yale Law Library, the Avalon Project, http://avalon.law.yale.edu/18th_century/yates.asp.]

The Growth of Federal Bankruptcy Law

As noted earlier, the bankruptcy clause is found in the U.S. Constitution in Article I, Section, 8, Clause 4, which states that Congress has the power to, "establish . . . uniform laws on the subject of Bankruptcies throughout the United States." In his commentaries, Justice Story reveals that the addition of this clause to the Constitution did not mean that everyone bowed to federal power. On the contrary, the issue of state-made bankruptcy laws continued to plague the legal system. Some experts in Story's era stated that the clause did, in fact, put the matter totally in the hands of the federal government. Others, however, argued that federal authority must be shared with the states. These experts claimed that, if the federal government had passed no bankruptcy laws, then the states were free to do so. Story, however, notes that any bankruptcy law passed by a state would apply only to contracts made between citizens of that state, made in that same state, after the law was passed. What happens to such laws after the federal government enacts a bankruptcy law remained uncertain. It was clear that should the federal government pass such a law, state power would be curtailed, but exactly how was not clear. As we shall see shortly the answer would not come until the 20th century. [Story, sections 1109–1110.]

Before answering that question, let's look at the checkered history of bankruptcy law at the federal level. The first federal bankruptcy law in the United States was enacted in 1800. Under that law, only creditors could begin a bankruptcy proceeding, and only merchants could qualify as debtors. That law lasted only three years before Congress repealed it. In 1840, debtor's prisons were abolished in the United States, and a year later, Congress passed a bankruptcy law that lasted only two years. Following the turmoil of the Civil War, Congress enacted a third bankruptcy law in 1867 that lasted 11 years. It wasn't until 1898 that permanent bankruptcy legislation came about in the United States with a law that gave businesses protection from creditors and lasted, with modifications during the Great Depression, for 80 years. The Bankruptcy Reform Act of 1978 again brought major changes, making it easier for businesses and individuals to obtain bankruptcy relief. It was in 1978 that Chapters 11 and 13 of the Bankruptcy Code (discussed later) were created, allowing businesses and individuals to reorganize and keep going. In addition, debtors were allowed to keep more of their assets, giving them a better chance to make a fresh start with their activities.

Despite these improvements to the process of filing for bankruptcy, the 1978 act left certain gaps in the law that had to be addressed by Congress. One job left undone was the need to clarify the authority of the bankruptcy courts themselves. Recall that Article III of the Constitution establishes the federal courts system. However, the authority to create laws of bankruptcy arises under Article I, which established the legislative branch. This means that the bankruptcy courts established by Congress under Article I do not stand on the same footing as that of the district courts, which are empowered under Article III. Before the 1978 act, the authority of the bankruptcy courts to hear cases was narrowly focused on what was termed summary jurisdiction. Summary jurisdiction gave the courts the power to apportion the debtor's estate among the creditors and little more. Other bankruptcy matters had to go through the district courts, which were deemed to have plenary rather than summary jurisdiction. The 1978 act changed this by doing away with the summary/plenary distinction and extending the power of the bankruptcy courts. Nevertheless, the bankruptcy courts suffered a set back when, in the case of *N. Pipeline Construction Company v. Marathon Pipe Line Company*, the Supreme Court declared a part of the 1978 act unconstitutional. In that case, the High Court ruled that bankruptcy courts had no jurisdiction to handle state-based contract claims that fell outside of the restructuring of debtor–creditor relations. In 1984, Congress passed the Bankruptcy Amendments and Federal Judgeship Act (BAFJ Act). that clarified the bankruptcy court's jurisdiction, noting that the authority of such courts "arises under" or "arises in" Title 11 (the Bankruptcy Code). On the other hand, cases that are "related to" Title 11 belong in the district courts which, nonetheless, can refer such cases to the bankruptcy courts. Those cases that the bankruptcy courts can hear ("arises under" or "arises in" Title 11) are referred to as **core cases**. Those that are "related to" Title 11 are called **non-core cases**. The bankruptcy courts can actually issue judgments in core cases which they cannot do in non-core cases unless the parties agree to submit the the jurisdiction of the court. When a bankruptcy court hears a non-core case, it can only pass on recommendation to the District Court which then issues an official judgment on the case. [See: *Op-Out Lenders v. Millennium Labs Holdings II, LLC, et al.*, Civ. No. 16-110-LPS (Memorandum Opinion, District Court for the District of Delaware) (March 2017); Jointly Administered Bankruptcy Case, No. 15-12284-LSS.]

The Current State of Bankruptcy Law

The 1994 Bankruptcy Reform Act continued honing the law and created the National Bankruptcy Review Commission to study the subject and make recommendations. In 2005, following a period of easy credit with many people spending far above their means, Congress decided to make filing for bankruptcy a bit more difficult by enacting far-reaching changes to the Bankruptcy Code. The result was the Bankruptcy Abuse Prevention and Consumer Protection Act of 2005 (BAPCPA). Under BAPCPA, Congress created a system that would require more debtors to file under Chapter 13 rather than Chapter 7. These changes were instituted because debtors who file under Chapter 13 must establish repayment plans that result in many more creditors being paid back in full. In addition, BAPCPA made significant alterations in the homestead exemption. Traditionally, the bankruptcy code allowed debtors to exempt all the equity in the debtor's place of residence. In fashioning BAPCPA, Congress placed new restrictions on this exemption. The current ceiling on the the homestead exemption can be found in Title 11 of the U.S. Code. As of 2016, that limit was $23,675 for individuals, and for those who are married and filing together, the ceiling is $47,350. Although Congress did its best to reengineer the code in order to tighten the exemptions provided to individuals, as often happens, the court stepped in and did some innovative reengineering of its own. Accordingly, the Court have offered a few new takes on the nature of the homestead itself. Some courts have upheld the homestead exemption as it applies to mobile homes, motor homes, and even to dry-docked boats (you know, like Travis McGee's boat, the Busted Flush, in the John McDonald series). Similarly, using a textualist approach to the interpretation of the statute, the Supreme Court has ruled that, since the homestead exemption is meant to apply to the debtor's residence and since the term *residence* refers to the place where someone resides at the present time, then it can refer to either the debtor's principal residence or to a vacation residence, but not both at the same time in the same filing [See: Sally Profeta, "Defining Residency Under The Federal Homestead Exemption," 7 *St. John's Bankr. Research Libr.* No. 19 (2015).]

BAPCPA has added a number of other restrictions beyond the adjustments to the homestead exemption. For instance, when a debtor chooses to file under Chapter 13, his or her child-support payments will no longer be discharged under the new law. Moreover, institutions that are authorized to recover delinquent child-support payments are permitted, under BAPCPA, to continue such efforts despite a bankruptcy filing. Debtors who file under either Chapter 7 or Chapter 13 are required to undergo budget, credit, and debt instruction if they intend follow through with the filing. The instruction must occur within 180 days of the actual filing. In addition, under the new law, student loans, whether public or private, cannot be discharged in a Chapter 13 filing. Still, even under BAPCPA, the debtor can receive a discharge if repaying the loan would lead to undue hardship. Moreover, a Chapter 13 debtor who owes fines or restitution following conviction for a crime cannot see those penalties discharged. BAPCPA also prohibits debtors from filing for bankruptcy under Chapters 7, 11, or 12 within six years of a Chapter 13 bankruptcy. Nor can a debtor file a new Chapter 13 filing within two years of a previous filing under Chapter 13 [See: Craig A. Gargotta, "Selected New Consumer Provisions to the Bankruptcy Abuse Prevention and Consumer Protection Act of 2005," *United States Attorney's Bulletin* (July 2006).]

The Authority of the States in Bankruptcy

By now it should be clear that the question of state control of bankruptcy in the absence of federal action was not an academic inquiry but, instead, something of practical concern long into the 20th century. The courts were openly in favor of a universally applied bankruptcy statute that would unify the operation from state to state. However, being sympathetic to the concept of a universal federal bankruptcy law is not the same as mandating that Congress pass such an act, nor justification for declaring an inconsistent, nonuniversal law as unconstitutional. Instead, the courts have held that in the absence of any federal law covering bankruptcy, the states are free to enact their own bankruptcy laws. Moreover, since the time of *Hanover National City Bank v. Moyses*, the U.S. Supreme Court has also settled on several guidelines regarding this matter. First, the Court has ruled that once Congress passes a bankruptcy law, state laws are not declared null and void but are, instead, subject to that federal law. Second, the states can plug their own provisions into state statutes that cover anything not covered by federal law, just so long as the state laws do not impair contracts (Article I, Section 10, Clause 1). Third, the states are without the power to create any bankruptcy law that affects property outside their boundary lines or that diverges from federal bankruptcy laws. Fourth, state laws regarding exemptions may differ from state to state without violating the Constitution. Finally, service of process and personal notice are not needed in a federal bankruptcy proceeding, as long as proper notice is made according to the bankruptcy statute (which in this case involved notice by mail and by publication). [See: *Hanover National Bank of New York v. Max Moyses*, 186 U.S. 181, 22 S.Ct. 857, 45 L.Ed. 1113 (1902).]

quick quiz 21-1

1. Congress passed one uniform bankruptcy statute in 1800 that has lasted until the present time.	true | false
2. The states have no power to pass any type of bankruptcy law at any time under any circumstances.	true | false
3. The bankruptcy clause in the U.S. Constitution seems to empower Congress to pass bankruptcy laws without actually requiring that Congress do so.	true | false

21-2 Liquidation—Chapter 7, Bankruptcy Code

Chapter 7 of the Bankruptcy Code, sometimes referred to as ordinary bankruptcy, provides a system in which debtors are forced to sell much of their property and use the cash to pay their creditors a portion of the amount owed each one. This process is also called **liquidation**. See Table 21-1 for a summary of different types of bankruptcy procedures.

Commencing the Action

Under Chapter 7 bankruptcy, the debtor may be an individual, partnership, corporation, or other type of business. The process may be either voluntary or involuntary. With voluntary bankruptcy, the debtor files the bankruptcy petition. With involuntary bankruptcy, creditors file the papers to force the debtor into bankruptcy and pay them off.

Voluntary Proceedings Debtors sometimes realize that their financial position can never improve without some drastic action and decide to file a bankruptcy petition on their own. Under the most recent Bankruptcy Act, however, not everyone is allowed to file for Chapter 7 bankruptcy. Under BAPCPA, to be eligible for a Chapter 7 filings, debtors must meet the following qualifications

- Satisfy the **means test**, discussed next.
- Take an approved, nonprofit budget, credit, and debt counseling course before filing for bankruptcy.
- Provide a federal income tax return for the most recent tax year.
- Take a course in financial management after filing for bankruptcy.

In addition, under BAPCPA, debtors can be disqualified from a Chapter 7 bankruptcy if they:

- Defrauded a creditor or an officer of the estate.
- Faked documents that recorded the debtor's business or financial dealings.
- Disobeyed a court order (except order to testify or produce records
- Did not explain the loss of assets that would have empowered the debtor to meet his or her liabilities.
- Received a Chapter 7 discharge within the last eight years.

Table 21-1 Types of Bankruptcy Procedures

Chapter	Who Can File?	When Used?	Special Features
Chapter 7: Ordinary Bankruptcy	Only those who (a) have income below the state's average family income for families of that size, (b) meet with an approved nonprofit credit counselor before filing, (c) provide a federal income tax return for the most recent tax year, and (d) take a course in financial management after filing.	Used when debtor wants to discharge most debts and begin with a clean slate.	Debtor's property is liquidated; some property is exempt; some debts cannot be discharged.
Chapter 11: Reorganization	Individuals, partnerships, and corporations can file; railroads can file; only commodity brokers and stockbrokers cannot; filing can be voluntary or involuntary.	Used when debtor, usually a business, wants to continue operating but needs to reorganize and liquidate debts.	Debtor-in-possession feature; plan must be fair, equitable, and feasible; creditors can also file plans; confirmation needed.
Chapter 12: Family Farmer or Fishing Business Debt Adjustment	Family farmer or fishing businesses that receive 50 percent of income from farming or fishing can file, including partnerships and corporations.	Used when debtor has a family farming or fishing business and needs a debt adjustment plan to keep running.	Debtor-in-possession feature.
Chapter 13: Individual Debt Adjustment	Individuals who meet with a credit counselor and have steady income only; no corporations or partnerships; no involuntary filings allowed.	Used when an individual debtor with a steady income voluntarily decides to adopt a debt adjustment plan.	Only the debtor can file a plan; a few debts cannot be discharged; plan lasts three years (with two-year possible extension).

If these requirements and restrictions seem somewhat harsh, remember that Congress enacted BAPCPA in 2005 to make filing for bankruptcy a bit more difficult, following a period of easy credit when many consumers took unfair advantage of the bankruptcy laws to escape that debt to the detriment of legitimate creditors. [See: Gargotta.]

The Means Test The means test consists of three steps, the passing of any one of which allows the debtor to file for Chapter 7 bankruptcy. The first step is to compare the debtor's average income during the previous six months with the median income for a family of that size in the debtor's state. If the debtor's income is less than the state's median income, the debtor is eligible to file for Chapter 7 bankruptcy. Every state's median income is provided by the U.S. Census Bureau and can be found at www.census.gov.

THE OPENING CASE Round 2
Bankruptcy or Insolvency? Federal or State Control? Traders or Traders Plus?

In the Opening Case, we learned that Moyses was the defendant debtor and Hanover was the plaintiff creditor in *Hanover National Bank v. Max Moyses*. Hanover brought the case in federal court in New York to get paid on a debt that Moyses owed the bank. Moyses, however, had been declared bankrupt in a federal court in Tennessee and had already discharged all of his debts, including the one owed to Hanover. The bank admitted that Moyses had been adjudicated bankrupt under the 1898 bankruptcy statute and that the law had been followed properly. In other words, the bank had no complaint about what had been done. Rather, at a more fundamental level, the bank argued that what had been done was illegal because the statute itself was unconstitutional.

Hanover offered two reasons for the unconstitutionality of the federal bankruptcy law: The first argument is relevant to our present study. The bank claimed that the law violated the Fifth Amendment prohibition against the taking of property without due process. Under the bankruptcy law, as it existed at that time, the debtor was empowered to initiate his (or her) own bankruptcy case. The bank feared that allowing the debtor to decide who gets notified threatened the creditors' property rights. (Exactly why the bank had this misgiving is not clear from the record, but it probably had to do with a fear that the debtor might be selective in which creditors were notified.) Today, this would not be an issue. However, in 1898 when this case was brought to court, there was still some confusion about whether individuals could initiate their own bankruptcy process. The bank based its argument on an ancient English tradition that took for granted the notion that only traders—that is, businesspeople involved in buying and selling as a profession—could declare bankruptcy. As we can see here, Chapter 7 of the current bankruptcy statute allows (even at times encourages) individuals to file for bankruptcy when necessary.

The ease by which such a provision could be added to the statute today, however, rests in part on the court's ruling in this case. The court decided that there is no need to limit bankruptcy laws to traders. In fact, such limits seem to be arbitrary and have more to do with the traditions of medieval England than with anything inherent within the process of bankruptcy in and of itself. Indeed, the court also takes judicial notice of the fact that there never really was any such restriction in the colonies, despite the model found in English law. The legislators in the colonies were not unaware of the English tradition and so it seems clear that they consciously decided that such a tradition would not be part of colonial law. The court sees no reason not to follow the colonial tradition and to reject the ancient English tradition (of traders only). [See: *Hanover National Bank of New York v. Max Moyses*, 186 U.S. 181, 22 S.Ct. 857, 45 L.Ed. 1113 (1902).]

Source: See: *Hanover National Bank of New York v. Max Moyses*, 186 U.S. 181, 22 S.Ct. 857, 45 L.Ed. 1113 (1902).

EXAMPLE 21-1: The Means Test—Median Income

Raymond and Jessica Mattik lived with their two children in a house they owned in North Carolina. They were very much in debt. Not only were they behind in their payments for their late-model car and household furnishings, but they also owed the maximum amount on five credit cards. When the interest on their adjustable-rate mortgage increased dramatically, they considered filing for bankruptcy. Together, they earned $61,113 annually. They would be eligible to file for Chapter 7 bankruptcy because their income was less than $76,382—the median income for a family of four in North Carolina. Because they qualified under this first step, they are finished with the means test.

Suppose Raymond and Jessica, in Example 21-1, had income that exceeded their state's median income for a family of four. Then, they would have to go to step two of the means test, which is more complicated. Step two requires debtors to determine whether they have enough income to pay off some of their unsecured debts. This determination requires subtracting the expenses that the debtor would be expected to spend on food, housing, utilities, clothing, out-of-pocket health care, transportation, housekeeping supplies, personal care, and some miscellaneous items from the debtor's actual income. This calculation gives the debtors their **disposable income**. Theoretically, disposable income is available to pay off the debtor's unsecured debt. The catch is that while debtors use their real income for the starting point, they must subtract the government's determination of what they should be spending on housing, utilities, and so on. The government's figures are found by accessing the forms and tables established by the federal government specifically for this purpose. If a debtor's calculations show that his or her monthly disposable income is less than what the government says it should be, he or she will be allowed to file for Chapter 7 bankruptcy. If it is more than the government's monthly figure, however, he or she cannot file for Chapter 7. The debtor may, however, be able to convert the case to another chapter of the bankruptcy code. This usually turns out to be Chapter 13.

The third step in the means test is taken only by debtors who do not qualify for Chapter 7 bankruptcy under the first two steps. Under this final step, a determination is made as to whether the debtor has the ability to pay unsecured debts over a five-year period. If a debtor's monthly disposable income is not enough to pay more than 25 percent of outstanding unsecured debts over a five-year period, the debtor will be allowed to file for Chapter 7 bankruptcy. In contrast, if the disposable income is enough to pay those debts over five years, the debtor will be required to switch over to another bankruptcy chapter, such as Chapter 13, discussed later. (*Note:* The figures tables, and forms used by the government often change, so it is best to check the most up-to-date information on the website of the federal courts [See: http://www.uscourts.gov/].)

To petition for bankruptcy, debtors file official forms with the nearest U.S. Bankruptcy Court. These courts are attached to district courts within the federal court structure (see Chapter 3). Official forms for filing bankruptcy can be obtained at legal stationery stores as well as www.uscourts.gov. The form asks debtors to name all of their creditors and indicate how much money they owe those creditors. The form also requires a listing of their property and a statement of income and expenses. Finally, the form asks debtors to list all of the property that they feel should be exempt from the sale when it comes time later in the bankruptcy proceeding to sell what they own.

Involuntary Proceedings Under Chapter 7 of the Bankruptcy Code, creditors may be able to force debtors, other than farmers, into involuntary bankruptcy if the debtor fails to pay bills generally as they become due. Creditors must prove that the outstanding debts are not subject to a bona fide dispute. Outstanding debt levels change every three years and so it is best to check the current amount of eligible debt on the federal court's website [See: http://www.uscourts.gov/.]

Order for Relief

An **order for relief** is the court's command that the liquidation begin. In a voluntary filing, the bankruptcy petition itself becomes the order for relief and is effective the moment it is filed with the court. In an involuntary case, the court does not issue the order immediately because the debtor is allowed to contest the filing, after which a hearing is held to determine whether an order for relief will be issued. When an order for relief is issued, a **case trustee** is named by the court. The trustee schedules a meeting of creditors, which the debtor is required to attend to answer questions about financial matters. Following the meeting, the trustee reports to the court as to whether the case should proceed.

THE OPENING CASE Round 3
Bankruptcy or Insolvency? Voluntary or Involuntary? Traders or Traders Plus?

Let's return to the Opening Case to explore the historic controversy over the advisability of authorizing both voluntary and involuntary bankruptcy filings. The case was brought in federal court in 1899 in New York by Hanover National Bank to retrieve some money due under a debt that Moyses owed the bank. In Tennessee, however, Moyses had filed for bankruptcy voluntarily under the federal bankruptcy act that was on the books at the time. Moyses had followed every step in the process properly. The court had also followed every step properly. The result was a declaration of Moyses's bankruptcy and a distribution of his property. The bank was clearly disappointed with that distribution. The bank, however, could not complain about what Moyses had done or how the court ruled because everything had been done by the book. So, to get around this, the bank did the only thing that it could do. It attacked the statute itself, saying that it was unconstitutional.

The argument was based on an idea that we would find somewhat bizarre today. The bank argued that the act violated due process because debtors were allowed to bring their own voluntary action for bankruptcy in federal court. According to the lawyers for the bank, this process amounted to an unconstitutional taking of their client's property under the Fifth Amendment.

Exactly why the attorneys felt that voluntary bankruptcy threatened due process is unclear, except that they seemed to doubt the debtor's objectivity and to believe that the bank had the right to start (and presumably then control) the process from the outset. This right had evaporated with the bankruptcy statute. The court disagreed. In fact, the court says that there seems no practical or legal reason to make a distinction between voluntary and involuntary bankruptcy. The court does note that some cases in English law have made a distinction from time to time between insolvency and bankruptcy. *Insolvency* was an action initiated by an imprisoned debtor to discharge his debt, while *bankruptcy* was initiated by the creditors to obtain payment. The court saw such distinctions as buried in the traditions and history of England and found no need to make the distinction between insolvency (voluntary bankruptcy) and bankruptcy (involuntary bankruptcy) in American law. Thus, Congress may call the law whatever it wants and can allow either the debtor or the creditors to initiate the process, which is what happens today. [See: *Hanover National Bank of New York v. Max Moyses*, 186 U.S. 181, 22 S.Ct. 857, 45 L.Ed. 1113 (1902).]

Source: See: *Hanover National Bank of New York v. Max Moyses*, 186 U.S. 181, 22 S.Ct. 857, 45 L.Ed. 1113 (1902).

The trustee is charged with the responsibility of liquidating the assets of the debtor for the benefit of all interested parties. Bank accounts, including debit cards, can no longer be used because they become the property of the bankruptcy trustee.

A QUESTION OF ETHICS

Carol and Michael Rothko created a limited liability company named Rosewood Acres LLC to buy, renovate, and flip homes in Sarasota, Florida. For the first four years of operation, the LLC made a neat little profit on each house flipped. At first, the Rothkos had been cautious and had flipped one house at a time. When the market was at its peak, they purchased two homes to work on simultaneously. Then the market collapsed. Up until that time, contractors who worked for the Rothkos had been willing to let overdue payments slide because they knew that the Rothkos did a very good business and the contractors did not want to jinx a good thing. Similarly, the bankers who set up the mortgages in each case were willing to accept late payments because they also knew that the Rothkos had an excellent track record in the "flipping" business. However, when the market collapsed, the contractors found themselves losing jobs left and right, so they all pressed the Rothkos for more timely payments. The bank was also less forgiving about late payments. Eventually, the Rothkos found that they could not pay the contractors, the bank, or the utility companies. Nor could they pay property taxes on the three houses. Consequently, the Rothkos decided to file a voluntary petition for bankruptcy. The court appointed Arthur M. Dent as trustee to the debtor's bankruptcy estate. Dent decided to use his own real estate firm as a consultant to assist in the sale of the debtors' property. Consider each of the following ethical issues.

1. First, was it ethical for the Rothkos to delay payments to the contractors?
2. Second, was it ethical for the contractors to suddenly demand earlier payments just because the market had shifted?
3. Third, was it ethical for the bank to demand on-time payments, after being so generous with the Rothkos?
4. Fourth, was it ethical for the court to appoint a trustee to oversee the bankruptcy process of an LLC when the court knew that the trustee was a real estate agent?
5. Finally, was it ethical for Dent to accept the position as trustee and to then use his own firm to assist in the sale of the debtors' property? Explain each point above using a consistent ethical standard.

Automatic Stay

When a voluntary or involuntary petition is filed, an **automatic stay** goes into effect. This stay is a self-operating postponement of collection proceedings against the debtor. Further efforts by creditors against the debtor to collect debts must stop immediately, except for debts caused by fraud, amounts owed for back taxes, family support, and *student loans that do not impose a hardship on the debtor*. Among other things, the stay prohibits creditors from beginning or continuing:

- Lawsuits to collect debts incurred before the filing of the petition.
- Attempts to enforce a judgment against the debtor.
- Foreclosure sales.
- Collection proceedings.
- Repossession activities.

As noted earlier, automatic stays apply to both voluntary and involuntary petitions. Creditors who knowingly ignore the stay can be held in contempt of court.

Federal Exemptions

As part of the fresh start approach under the Bankruptcy Code, debtors are permitted to exempt or exclude certain items of property from the bankruptcy process, which means that the property is kept by the debtor and cannot be sold to pay the debtor's outstanding bills. Exemptions can be doubled for married couples who file jointly.

Federal Homestead and Household Exemptions

The Bankruptcy Code allows debtors to keep a maximum amount set by law in equity in the debtor's place of residence and in property used as a burial ground. This allowance is known as the federal **homestead exemption**. Debtors can also keep a maximum amount set by law for any single item of furniture, household goods, clothes, appliances, books, crops, animals, or musical instruments. As noted earlier, BAPCPA has made significant alterations in the homestead exemption. By tradition, under provisions of the the bankruptcy code, Congress permitted debtors to exempt all the equity in the their place of residence. In fashioning BAPCPA, however, Congress placed new restrictions on this exemption. The current ceiling on the the homestead exemption can be found in Title 11 of the United States Code. Exemptions are also permitted for jewelry.

THE OPENING CASE *Round 4*
Bankruptcy or Insolvency? Voluntary or Involuntary? Traders or Traders Plus?

Recall that in theOpening Case, Hanover National Bank argued that the bankruptcy act under which the defendant-debtor Moyses had been declared insolvent was unconstitutional. The bank argued that the 1898 bankruptcy statute violated the Fifth Amendment prohibition against the taking of property without due process because the type of notice given to creditors about the initiation of the bankruptcy proceeding was so brief (10 days) that any distant creditors had no realistic chance of responding. The court had little sympathy with the bank's complaint. In fact, the court seemed a bit irritated with Hanover. Accordingly, the court ran down several points. First, the debtor must file a petition for bankruptcy with the court and along with that petition include a list of his or her property, plus a list of creditors and amounts owed to those creditors along with addresses. Second, the petition also includes a statement that asserts that the debtor is willing to have his or her property confiscated to pay those debts (except what the law exempts). Third, the property then comes under the control of the court, which then distributes it to the creditors. At that point, the 10 days' notice goes out. Fourth, the notice is actually two notices, one by mail and the other by publication. Fifth, that notice is only the first step in a series of possible notices to creditors. Sixth, the court also noted that creditors get subsequent notices at every step in the administration and distribution of the property. Seventh, and finally, at that point, the creditors get more time because the debt is not discharged for another month after the final distribution has been made, allowing more time for creditor input. The court was satisfied that this was enough time to account for due process. [See: *Hanover National Bank of New York v. Max Moyses*, 186 U.S. 181, 22 S.Ct. 857, 45 L.Ed. 1113 (1902).]

Source: See: *Hanover National Bank of New York v. Max Moyses*, 186 U.S. 181, 22 S.Ct. 857, 45 L.Ed. 1113 (1902).

Necessities Congress allows debtors to maintain a minimum standard of living by exempting certain necessary items of property. For example, debtors are allowed to exclude a maximum of amount set by law in professional tools, instruments, and books. In addition, they can exempt a set maximum amount in a motor vehicle. Finally, medical supplies that have been prescribed for the health of the debtor can be excluded.

Benefits and Support Payments Again, to allow debtors to maintain a minimum standard of living, Congress allows the exclusion of certain benefits and support payments. For instance, alimony and child support payments can be excluded. Benefits received under Social Security or a disability program are also exempt. Profits that are due under profit-sharing, pension, and annuity plans may be excluded. Furthermore, debtors are allowed to protect payments due to them under certain court orders. For example, if someone owes a debtor damages resulting from a personal injury tort case, those damages are exempt up to a maximum amount set by law. Life insurance contracts carried for the benefit of a relative or approved beneficiary that have yet to mature are also protected. Finally, tax-deferred retirement funds are exempt under the bankruptcy act.

State Exemptions

The Bankruptcy Code allows states to use exemptions created by the state legislature rather than the federal exemptions. Often, the dollar amounts included in the state statutes will be a more accurate assessment of property values within each state, because the state legislators are more flexible in such matters than members of Congress, who must consider property values across the entire country. Every state has its own set of bankruptcy exemptions. States are permitted to give debtors a choice of using the state's exemptions or requiring debtors to take the state exemptions.

Trustee's Duties

After the order for relief is granted, a trustee will be appointed to take control of the debtor's property. One of the first things the trustee does is set aside, under the trustee's avoiding powers, certain sales and property transfers made by the debtor. The property is then returned to the estate of the debtor. Included in this "pull back" are any fraudulent transfers that the debtor might have made to temporarily hide property from creditors. If the debtor is a business, the bankruptcy court may authorize the trustee to operate the business for a limited period of time. In addition, the trustee sells the debtor's property to obtain cash. The trustee then distributes the cash among the creditors according to set priorities.

Property Distribution The Bankruptcy Code provides a priority list that indicates which categories of debts are paid first (Table 21-2). Each category must be paid in full before moving on to the next category. As explained in Chapter 20, secured creditors have the right to take their collateral to satisfy the debt, and that collateral is not sold by the trustee. Although there are some narrow exceptions to this rule, most secured creditors are protected.

Table 21-2 Payment Priorities

Debt	Explanation
Secured debts	Creditors with security interests take their collateral first.
Domestic obligations	Support obligations owed to a spouse or child.
Administrative expenses	Bankruptcy trustee and others involved in bankruptcy process are paid next.
Certain unsecured debts	All unsecured debts after an involuntary petition has been filed, but before order for relief has been granted, are paid next.
Wages	Employees are paid next; a maximum is set for each employee.
Benefit plans	Contributions owed on employee benefit plans are paid next; again, a maximum is set.
Deposits and advances	Deposits made for purchase or lease of property are paid next, as are advances made for personal, family, and household services.
Taxes	Certain taxes are paid next.
Death or injury claims	Some claims for death or injury caused by debtor.
Remaining unsecured creditors	All other unsecured creditors are paid from any balance remaining.
Debtor	If anything is left, it goes back to the debtor.

EXAMPLE 21-2: Secured Creditor Protected

Perez purchased a digital camera from Digicam Corp. Perez financed the deal by signing a security agreement with the company. Under the agreement, Digicam retained a security interest in the property, allowing it to repossess the camera if Perez defaulted on the loan. Digicam was a secured creditor. The digital camera was the collateral.

Exceptions to Discharge

Once the trustee has run through all the aforementioned creditors, the debtor's debts are said to be discharged, which means that the debts are wiped away, and the debtor is allowed to begin again. If the bankruptcy debtor does not have enough money to cover the debts, they are nevertheless considered discharged. However, there are some exceptions to this general rule. Some debts cannot be discharged. In other words, even though the debtor has gone through the entire bankruptcy proceeding, money may still be owed to certain creditors.

Debts Created by Misconduct Certain debts that have fallen into the debtor's lap because of misconduct cannot be charged in bankruptcy. For example, any debts that arose because of the debtor's fraudulent behavior cannot be discharged. Similarly, the debtor cannot escape legal liability for any debt that arose from willful and malicious misconduct. Finally, if the debtor knew about a debt that was not on the original list of debts, that unlisted debt cannot be discharged.

Debts Enforced by the Government Certain debts that the debtor owes the government remain on the books even after the bankruptcy proceeding has ended. These include certain back taxes, student loans that do not impose a hardship on the debtor, and many government fines and penalties. Similarly, several types of court-enforced debts cannot be discharged, including alimony and child support or any legal liability that resulted from a court-ordered judgment for driving while intoxicated. Finally, any debts that were not discharged under a previous bankruptcy cannot be discharged under the new bankruptcy proceeding.

Debts Created by Excessive Spending Congress also refuses to allow bankruptcy debtors to discharge any excessive expenditures that occur around the time of the bankruptcy filing. This measure prevents people from running up big bills unnecessarily because they think they will not have to pay the full amount due on these bills when their assets are finally distributed. Thus, debts for luxury items that exceed $675 in value cannot be discharged if those items were purchased within 90 days before the order for relief was granted. Likewise, the debtor cannot discharge any cash advances paid to a single creditor under an open-ended credit plan that total more than $950 if those advances were made within 70 days of the relief order. (*Note:* Like other figures in the bankruptcy code, these figures changed every three years, so it is always best to check current figures on the appropriate government website.)

EXAMPLE 21-3: Nondischargeable Debt

Caswell finally realized that his financial problems were out of control. Consequently, he decided to file for bankruptcy on the following Monday. That weekend, he charged $7,000 on his credit card on a weekend trip to Atlantic City before filing for bankruptcy on Monday. Caswell would not be allowed to discharge the $7,000 debt in bankruptcy.

Restoring Credit Following Bankruptcy

A personal bankruptcy filing remains on a debtor's credit report for 10 years and has a detrimental effect on the ability to establish a line of credit. However, most debtors who file bankruptcy have already established a poor credit rating anyway, and filing bankruptcy gives them an opportunity to begin anew. A good number of their debts become discharged, which improves their debt-to-income ratio—a factor that potential creditors look at carefully. The more time that elapses after the bankruptcy filing, the easier it is to reestablish credit. Many people in this situation switch from credit cards to debit cards, which is like paying cash because instead of initiating a charge, debit cards withdraw money instantly from a bank account. Some banks offer *secured credit cards* in which customers deposit money in the bank to guarantee that their credit card charges will be paid. Until their credit is reestablished, their credit limit is the same as the amount of their bank deposit. Credit card issuers sometimes allow debtors to continue using their credit cards if they agree in writing, after the bankruptcy filing, to pay off the old debt. Often, this allowance also requires an agreement by the debtor to pay the credit card balance each month without carrying a balance. People who are able to make a down payment and have steady income may be eligible for a mortgage loan as soon as two years following a discharge in bankruptcy.

quick quiz 21-2

1. Congress no longer allows debtors to maintain a minimum standard of living by exempting certain necessary items of property. true | false
2. Under Chapter 7 bankruptcy, debtors are forced to sell most of their property and use the cash to pay their creditors a portion of the amount owed each one. true | false
3. The Bankruptcy Code allows states to use a list of exemptions created by the state legislature rather than the federal exemptions. true | false

21-3 Reorganization—Chapter 11, Bankruptcy Code

Chapter 11 of the Bankruptcy Code provides a method for businesses to reorganize their financial affairs and still remain in business. If allowed to continue in operation, companies may be able to overcome their difficulties without having to sell most of their property. In a **reorganization**, a qualified debtor creates a plan that alters the repayment schedule. A Chapter 11 filing is available to sole proprietors, partnerships, and corporations and may be either voluntary or involuntary. Individuals who file must receive credit counseling from an approved credit counseling agency before doing so. Unlike Chapter 7, Chapter 11 also allows railroads to file. The only individuals specifically excluded from filing under Chapter 11 are commodity brokers and stockbrokers, who must use Chapter 7.

Special Features of Chapter 11

One of the most attractive features of Chapter 11 for business debtors is that the business continues to operate after the filing. A debtor is referred to as a **debtor in possession** under Chapter 11

In February of 2011, Borders Group Inc. announced that it was filing for Chapter 11 bankruptcy protection.
©Ken Durden/Shutterstock

because the debtor keeps possession and control of the assets, continues to run the firm, and performs most of the functions that a trustee performs in other types of bankruptcy. However, if the problems of the business have been caused by poor judgment, mismanagement, or dishonesty, a case trustee may have to step in to examine the debtor's financial position and provide the court, creditors, and tax authorities with financial information as necessary.

As with a Chapter 7 voluntary case, the bankruptcy petition itself becomes the order for relief. The moment it is filed, the debtor assumes the position of "debtor in possession." At the same time, an automatic stay goes into effect, stopping collection proceedings against the debtor. In an involuntary case, the order for relief comes later, because the debtor is allowed time to contest the filing.

THE OPENING CASE Round 5
Bankruptcy or Insolvency? Voluntary or Involuntary? Traders or Traders Plus?

Chapter 11 bankruptcy allows a business to reorganize its debts while continuing in operation. Often, the business institutions that take advantage of this provision are large corporations that cross state lines. Such a provision would not be possible if individual states controlled the bankruptcy process. Still, it is neither advisable nor legally sound to take all such power away from the states. The case of *Hanover National Bank v. Moyses* gives us some insight into the value of permitting the states some ability to control bankruptcy procedures when necessary, just as long as the states stay within appropriate legal boundaries. To see this in more detail, let's return to the Opening Case one more time. The case was brought in federal court in New York in 1899 by Hanover National Bank to get back the money due to it on a debt that Moyses owed the bank. In Tennessee, however, Moyses had filed for bankruptcy voluntarily under the 1898 federal bankruptcy act. Moyses had followed every step in the process properly. The court had also followed every step correctly. The result was a declaration of Moyses's bankruptcy and a distribution of his property that did not please the bank. The bank, however, could not complain about what Moyses had done or how the court ruled because everything had been done by the book. So, to get around this, the bank attacked the statute itself, saying that it was unconstitutional. The bank argued that the bankruptcy statute (1) failed to set up universal laws of bankruptcy for all states as required by the Constitution under Article I, Section 8, Clause 4, and (2) unconstitutionally delegated powers to the states that cannot be delegated to those states.

The court was sympathetic to the call for a universal bankruptcy statute passed by Congress to unify principles and procedures. However, that is quite different from saying that the Constitution mandates that Congress fashion such a law and that unless it does so, the statute in effect is unconstitutional. In fact, the court indicates that in the absence of any federal law covering bankruptcy, the states are free to enact their own bankruptcy laws. Moreover, since the time of *Hanover*, the U.S. Supreme Court has also settled on several guidelines regarding this matter. First, the Court has ruled that once Congress passes a bankruptcy law, state laws do not vanish into some legal purgatory. Instead, they remain subject to federal law. Second, the states can fill in gaps that are not covered by Congress in the federal law, provided that the state laws do not impair contracts (Article I, Section 10, Clause 1). Third, states cannot enact bankruptcy legislation that affects property outside their borders or that conflicts with federal bankruptcy laws. Fourth, state laws regarding exemptions may differ from state to state without violating the Constitution. Finally, service of process and personal notice are not needed in a federal bankruptcy proceeding, as long as proper notice is made according to the bankruptcy statute (which in this case involved notice by mail and by publication). [See: *Hanover National Bank of New York v. Max Moyses*, 186 U.S. 181, 22 S.Ct. 857, 45 L.Ed. 1113 (1902).]

Source: See: Hanover National Bank of New York v. Max Moyses, 186 U.S. 181, 22 S.Ct. 857, 45 L.Ed. 1113 (1902).

The Reorganization Plan

When a Chapter 11 petition is filed, the debtor has 120 days, during which it has the exclusive right to file a reorganization plan. The 120-day period may be shortened or lengthened by the court. When the exclusive period ends, creditors (and the case trustee, if any) can file competing plans. The debtor also files a disclosure statement containing information about the debtor's assets, liabilities, and business affairs to allow creditors to make informed decisions about the reorganization plan. The disclosure statement must be approved by the court before there can be a vote by creditors on the reorganization plan.

Creditors' Committee A creditors' committee is appointed to investigate the operation of the business and assist the debtor in possession in developing and administering a reorganization plan. Membership on the committee normally consists of the creditors who hold the seven largest unsecured claims against the debtor.

Plan Qualifications The Bankruptcy Code requires fairness, equity, and feasibility in the creation of a reorganization plan. The plan will group claims against the debtor into the following classes:

- Secured creditors.
- Unsecured creditors entitled to priority (for such things as taxes and bankruptcy costs).
- General unsecured creditors.
- Equity security holders, such as shareholders and limited partners.

The law requires equal treatment for all creditors grouped in a class. In addition, the plan must be feasible; that is, there must be a good chance that the plan will actually work. The law does not require an absolute guarantee of success. A plan may be difficult to implement because of labor or supply problems and still be feasible within the meaning of the law.

A QUESTION OF ETHICS

The financial crisis that hit the United States and the international community in the early 21st century disrupted lives, ended careers, and depleted personal fortunes. It also led to a "bailout" mentality that insulated some financial institutions as untouchable while dooming others as expendable. This entire scene could have been avoided (not the crisis itself, but the bailouts) had the government "allowed" ordinary bankruptcy law to stay the course. This is the opinion offered by Michele Paige, a managing member of Paige-Capital Management, who, in a *Barron's* article entitled, "A Most Useful Tool: Bankruptcy," argues quite convincingly that the American system of bankruptcy has served us well over the decades and should be allowed to do so again. This is a rather curious statement that deserves some clarification. Bankruptcy laws, Paige argues, are designed to encourage individuals to run businesses in an aggressive way that benefits not only the entrepreneur but also suppliers, customers, employees, and the community as a whole. Sometimes these businesses fail, it's true, but when they do, bankruptcy law gives them a second chance. This does mean that there are no victims—businesses that fall and never rise again. However, these failures testify to the effectiveness of a law that weeds out firms that probably should not have been formed in the first place. Paige contends that bankruptcy law, with a few minor tweaks, would work well in the current climate because the law would permit the owners of financial firms to operate the institution while the judicial system divides the losses among the firm's creditors. Should the court run into an institution so troubled that it cannot meet its obligations even using bankruptcy, then the government could step in as a last resort. Paige offers the savings and loan crisis in the 1990s as an example of how well bankruptcy can work when it is permitted to do so. The bankruptcy alternative is better than the current situation, which burdens a financial institution with one of two fates: federal control or benign neglect, leading inevitably to failure.

ETHICAL QUESTIONS

1. Do you agree or disagree with the premise that the purpose of bankruptcy law is to stimulate business? Is this an ethical purpose?
2. Should financial institutions be forced into bankruptcy by the government or is the current strategy (federal control or benign neglect) the ethically correct one to take?
3. What changes in the bankruptcy law would have to take place to implement the plan outlined earlier?
4. If you were a creditor of a financial institution which solution would you see as ethical? A bailout, failure, or bankruptcy?
5. If you were a shareholder of a financial institution which solution would you see as ethical?—a bailout, failure, or bankruptcy? Explain each point above using a consistent ethical standard.

Source: See: Michele Paige, "Other Voices—A Most Useful Tool: Bankruptcy," *Barron's,* May 3, 2010, p. 40.

Plan Approval If the plan has not changed the legal rights of the members of a class, then no approval is required from that class. **Impaired classes**—those whose creditors receive less than full value of their claims—have the right to vote on the plan by ballot. If there are impaired classes of claims, the plan must be approved by at least one impaired class. More than one-half of the creditors who hold at least two-thirds of the amount of allowed claims in each class must accept the plan before it is approved. In addition, in the case of individual debtors, the plan cannot be confirmed over a creditor's objection without committing all of the debtor's disposable income over the next five years.

EXAMPLE 21-4: Plan Approval

The Miller Chemical Company filed for reorganization under Chapter 11 of the Bankruptcy Code. One class of creditors included unsecured creditors who were owed $2,000 or less. A second class included unsecured creditors who were owed more than $2,000. The plan called for a complete repayment of all Class 1 creditors, according to the terms of their original contracts. This provision made Class 1 an unimpaired class. The Class 2 creditors would have a choice: They could receive either a 60 percent repayment on the date of confirmation or 100 percent repayment extended over four years. The extended repayment plan called for a 30 percent repayment on the date of confirmation and seven 10 percent payments at six-month intervals. More than one-half of the Class 2 creditors would have to approve the plan. In contrast, the Class 1 creditors had no approval rights, because Class 1 was unimpaired.

Plan Confirmation The court will hold a hearing on the confirmation of the reorganization plan. A **confirmation** officially places a plan in operation. After confirmation, all property dealt with in the plan is free and clear of claims of creditors and equity security holders. The debtor is discharged from any debts that arose before the date of confirmation.

> **EXAMPLE 21-5:** Citation Corp.'s Reorganization Plan
>
> In 2007, Citation Corp. filed for Chapter 11 bankruptcy protection. In less than one month, the bankruptcy court confirmed the auto parts maker's reorganization plan. Under the plan, the company's lenders agreed to exchange $191 million in debt for a new $30 million loan and all of the company's stock. Claims by the company's unsecured creditors would be paid in full in the course of ongoing business, and stockholders were given warrants to buy new classes of stock.

quick quiz 21-3

1. Chapter 11 of the Bankruptcy Code provides a method for businesses to reorganize their financial affairs and still remain in business.	true | false
2. The automatic stay provision found in Chapter 7 of the Bankruptcy Code is not used in Chapter 11 proceedings.	true | false
3. A trustee is appointed to run the firm when a business files a Chapter 11 bankruptcy petition.	true | false

21-4 Family Farmer or Fishing Business Debt Adjustment—Chapter 12, Bankruptcy Code

The Family Farmers and Family Fishermen Protection Act is designed to help farming and fishing proprietors, with regular income, create a plan for debt repayment that will allow them to keep their family businesses running. Thus, Chapter 12 is an alternative to the ordinary bankruptcy procedure provided for by Chapter 7. To be eligible, the operation must receive 50 percent of its total income from farming or fishing. Also, 50 percent of a farmer's debt must result from farm expenses, and 80 percent of a fishing business's debt must relate to either farming or fishing. Chapter 12 is voluntary—only the debtor may file a petition for this type of bankruptcy.

LO10

Chapter 12 has some important characteristics that allow individuals to file debt adjustment plans. First, Chapter 12 sets a $4,153,150 debt ceiling for farming and $1,924,550 for fishing. Second, in addition to individuals, Chapter 12 is open to partnerships and corporations as long as one-half of the outstanding stock or equity in the business is owned by one family or by one family and its relatives. Also, the family or the family and its relatives must conduct the farming or fishing undertaking. [See: "Chapter 12 Bankruptcy Basics," U.S. Courts, http://www.uscourts.gov/service-forms/bankrupt/ bankruptcy-basics/chapter-12-bankruptcy-basics. *Note:* Like other figures in the bankruptcy code, these figures changed every three years, so it is always best to check current figures on the appropriate government website.]

The family farm gets preferential treatment in Chapter 12 bankruptcy filings.
©steverts/iStockphoto/Getty Images

Chapter 12 Procedures

Like a filing under Chapters 7 and 11, a filing under Chapter 12 creates an automatic stay of the collection of most debts. It is possible for creditors to ask the court to exempt them from the stay. However, a hearing on such a motion would have to be held, and the creditors would have to show why the court should grant exemptions.

As is the case in Chapter 7 and 11, the court will appoint a trustee to handle the farm's and fishing business's finances. The Chapter 12's trustee evaluates the case and serves as disbursing agent, collecting payments from the debtor and making disbursements to creditors.

The Chapter 12 Plan

Unlike the Chapter 11 debtor, who has a 120-day deadline to devise a reorganization plan, the Chapter 12 farming or fishing debtor is limited to 90 days. The clock starts running toward that 90-day deadline when the bankruptcy petition is filed. Debtors, however, can file for an extension.

Contents of the Plan The Chapter 12 plan must include several provisions. First, the plan must provide for payment of fixed amounts to the trustee on a regular basis over a three-year period. The trustee then distributes the funds to the creditors according to the terms of the plan, which usually offers creditors less than the amount owed. Second, the plan must make certain that all priority claims, such as taxes and bankruptcy costs, are paid in full. Secured creditors must be paid at least the value of their collateral. Unsecured creditors must receive at least as much as they would if the debtor's nonexempt assets were liquidated under Chapter 7. The plan must not take longer than three years to complete, unless the time is extended by the court. The maximum extension is for two years.

Confirmation Hearing After the plan's filing, the bankruptcy judge holds a confirmation hearing to decide whether the plan is feasible and follows the standards of the Bankruptcy Code. Creditors are notified and may appear to voice their approval or objections to the confirmation. If the judge confirms the plan, the trustee will begin disbursing funds according to the plan. If the judge does not confirm the plan, the debtor may file a modified plan, change to Chapter 7 bankruptcy, or allow the case to be dismissed and take some other course.

EXAMPLE 21-6: Court Approves Payment Plan

Bemis, who owned a dairy farm, filed for debt adjustment under Chapter 12. Bemis filed a payment plan with her bankruptcy petition. Under the plan, unsecured creditors owed more than $500 would receive 60 percent of the amount owed to them, payable monthly over a three-year period. Kimble Supply Co. objected to the plan, arguing that it would receive more if Bemis's assets were liquidated under Chapter 7 bankruptcy. Because Bemis was turning over 100 percent of her disposable income to the trustee for debt repayment, however, the court did not support Kimble's objection.

The debtor will receive a discharge after completing all payments agreed to and certifying that all domestic support obligations up to that time, if any, have been paid. The discharge releases the debtor from all debts listed in the plan.

quick quiz 21-4

1. The Family Farmers and Family Fishermen Protection Act is designed to help farming and fishing proprietors create a plan for debt repayment while maintaining the family business. true | false
2. Like a filing under Chapters 7 and 11, a filing under Chapter 12 creates an automatic stay of the collection of most debts. true | false
3. Under a Chapter 12 bankruptcy plan, secured creditors must be paid at least the value of their collateral. true | false

21-5 Individual Debt Adjustment—Chapter 13, Bankruptcy Code

Sometimes debtors overextend their credit. They have regular income, but they cannot pay all their bills. If given time, they may eventually be able to pay at least part of the amount they owe to each creditor. Rather than selling the debtor's property, Chapter 13 of the Bankruptcy Code permits an individual debtor to put in place a repayment plan. Upon completion of payments under the plan, they receive a discharge from most remaining debt. Only individual debtors, including sole proprietors and self-employed people, can take advantage of Chapter 13 provisions. Neither corporations nor partnerships can file.

To be eligible for Chapter 13, debtors must first meet with an approved nonprofit credit counselor. Their unsecured debts, such as credit cards and student loans, cannot exceed $394,725, and their secured loans, such as mortgages and car loans, cannot be more than $1,184,200. Also, the debtor must have an already established steady income. Only voluntary filings are permitted under Chapter 13. The automatic stay provision clicks into place under Chapter 13 when the relief order is issued. A trustee oversees the Chapter 13 process. [See: "Chapter 13 Bankruptcy Basics," U.S. Courts, http://www.uscourts.gov/service-forms/bankrupt/bankruptcy-basics/chapter-13-bankruptcy-basics. *Note:* Like other figures in the bankruptcy code, these figures changed every three years, so it is always best to check current figures on the appropriate government website.]

The Chapter 13 Plan

The debtor must file a repayment plan with the court, along with the Chapter 13 bankruptcy petition. Shortly thereafter, a trustee will be appointed and a meeting will be scheduled allowing the debtor to present the plan and be questioned by the trustee and creditors.

The plan must provide for payments of fixed amounts to the trustee on a regular biweekly or monthly basis. The trustee, in turn, distributes the money to creditors according to the terms of the plan. The payments must either satisfy all debts or consist of all the debtor's disposable income during the plan's period. The plan must make certain that priority debtors receive full payment.

Also, like Chapter 12, if the plan sets up groups of creditors, all group members must be treated equally. Finally, Chapter 13 debtors must abide by the rule requiring that the payment plan be completed within three to five years.

Plan Confirmation

Chapter 13 creditors have no prior input while the plan is being created. Secured creditors have approval powers, but unsecured creditors do not. Unsecured creditors may of course object to the plan at the hearing.

Excessive credit card debt is often a major contributory cause to consumer bankruptcy.
©George Doyle/Getty Images

However, similar to Chapter 12, Chapter 13 will not allow the court to go along with an objection if the debtor plans to turn over 100 percent of all disposable income to the trustee for debt repayment. The debtor must start payments within 30 days of submitting the plan to the court. If the court has yet to hold its hearing, the debtor pays the trustee. The trustee holds the money until the court upholds or rejects the plan.

Changes to Chapter 13 under BAPCPA

BAPCPA has added a number of changes to Chapter 13 bankruptcy filings. For example, under Chapter 13, a debtor's child-support payments can no longer be discharged under. In addition, agencies charged with recovering unpaid child-support payments are allowed, under BAPCPA, to continue such efforts despite a bankruptcy filing. Debtors who file under Chapter 13 must go through budget, credit, and debt counseling to follow through with the filing. The counseling must take place within 180 days of the actual filing. Also, under the BAPCPA, student loans, whether public or private, cannot be discharged in a Chapter 13 filing. On the other hand, it is possible, even under BAPCPA, for a debtor to receive a discharge if repaying the loan would lead to undue hardship. In addition, a Chapter 13 debtor who owes fines or restitution following conviction for a crime cannot see those penalties discharged. Finally, BAPCPA also forbids debtors to file for bankruptcy under Chapters 7, 11, or 12 within six years of a Chapter 13 bankruptcy. Nor can a debtor file a new Chapter 13 filing within two years of a previous filing under Chapter 13 [See: Gargotta.]

quick quiz 21-5

1. A trustee oversees the Chapter 13 process. | true | false
2. Sole proprietors can file for bankruptcy under Chapter 13 of the Bankruptcy Code, but corporations and partnerships cannot. | true | false
3. Under Chapter 13 of the Bankruptcy Code, secured creditors have approval powers of a repayment plan, but unsecured creditors do not. | true | false

Summary

21.1 The final version of the bankruptcy clause is found in the U.S. Constitution in Article I, Section 8, Clause 4, which states that Congress has the power to "establish . . . uniform laws on the subject of Bankruptcies throughout the United States." The clause empowers Congress to pass bankruptcy laws without actually requiring that Congress do so. The open-ended nature of the bankruptcy clause has led to periods in history during which no federal bankruptcy law was on the books. It wasn't until 1898 that permanent bankruptcy legislation came about in the United States, with a law that gave businesses protection from creditors and lasted, with modifications during the Great Depression, for 80 years. The Bankruptcy Reform Act of 1978 brought major changes, making it easier for businesses and individuals to obtain bankruptcy relief. In 1978, Chapters 11 and 13 of the Bankruptcy Code were created. The 1994 Bankruptcy Reform Act created the National Bankruptcy Review Commission. In 2005, following a period of easy credit with many people spending far above their means, Congress made it more difficult to declare bankruptcy by enacting far-reaching changes to the Bankruptcy Code.

21.2 Chapter 7 of the Bankruptcy Code covers ordinary bankruptcy, which is also called liquidation. To qualify, debtors must pass a means test, undergo counseling, provide a federal income tax return, and take a course in financial management. A case trustee sells the debtor's property and uses the cash to pay creditors a portion of the amount owed to each one. The process can be either voluntary or involuntary.

21.3 Reorganization under Chapter 11 of the Bankruptcy Code allows businesses to overcome financial difficulties without selling *all* their property. Instead, a reorganization plan is drawn up that changes the debtor's payment schedule. The new schedule allows the debtor to keep the business going while paying creditors.

21.4 Chapter 12 of the Bankruptcy Code applies to family farmer and fishing businesses in financial difficulty. Under Chapter 12, a family farmer or fishing business can maintain the activity while following a debt adjustment plan to satisfy creditors.

21.5 Chapter 13 of the Bankruptcy Code applies only to individual debtors with established steady incomes. Such debtors can prepare a debt-adjustment plan that will provide for repayment of outstanding debts.

Key Terms

automatic stay, 587
case trustee, 585
confirmation, 594
core cases, 580
debtor in possession, 591
disposable income, 585
homestead exemption, 587
impaired classes, 594
liquidation, 582
means test, 582
non-core cases, 580
order for relief, 585
reorganization, 591

Questions for Review and Discussion

1. What is the history of bankruptcy law in the United States?
2. What is the difference between federal and state authority to fashion bankruptcy law?
3. What is the current state of bankruptcy law in the federal system?
4. What criteria are necessary to be eligible to file voluntarily for Chapter 7 bankruptcy?
5. What criteria are necessary for creditors to force debtors into involuntary bankruptcy?
6. What is the difference between an *order for relief* and an *automatic stay*?
7. What are the federal exemptions debtors can exclude from the bankruptcy process?
8. Which debts have priority payment status under the Bankruptcy Code?
9. What is a Chapter 11 bankruptcy?
10. What are the requirements for Chapters 12 and 13 bankruptcy?

Cases for Analysis

1. Robert Marrama filed for Chapter 7 bankruptcy. In his petition, he did not disclose a vacation home that he had placed in trust. When Marrama discovered that the case trustee was going to take the vacation property as an estate asset, Marrama decided to convert his case to Chapter 13, which would allow him to keep the property and pay his debts over time. The bankruptcy court held that the failure to disclose the vacation home demonstrated bad faith by the debtor and refused to allow the conversion to Chapter 13. Do you agree with the bankruptcy court? Why or why not? [See: *Marrama v. Citizens Bank*, 05-996 U.S. Supreme Court.]

2. Soon after the birth of their second child, misfortune fell on the lives of Kurt and Leah Lyons. Kurt got laid off, the landlord raised their rent, they received notice that their car was about to be repossessed, and dunning letters arrived daily from credit card companies. Reluctantly, the couple filed for personal bankruptcy. Their disappointed parents told them that the bankruptcy would remain on their credit rating for the rest of their lives and that they would never again be able to establish a line of credit or obtain a mortgage to buy a house. Were Kurt and Leah's parents correct? Explain.

3. Lisa and William Leeper filed a Chapter 13 bankruptcy petition. One of the unsecured debts they listed on their bankruptcy petition was an amount owed to the Pennsylvania Higher Education Assistance Authority to attend college under a guaranteed student loan program. Will the loan to attend college be discharged by the bankruptcy court? Explain. [See: *Leeper v. Pennsylvania Higher Education Assistance Agency*, 94-3372 & 94-3373, U.S. Court of Appeals (3rd Cir.).]

4. When a Florida court dismissed Nellie Cortez's voluntary bankruptcy petition, it ordered her not to file another petition "under any chapter of the Bankruptcy Code for a period of 12 months." Two months later, an involuntary bankruptcy petition was filed in California by Cortez's stepfather, Thomas Bronkovic. The California court dismissed that case, finding that

Cortez had colluded with her stepfather and that the case was, in fact, her own "voluntary" petition rather than her stepfather's "involuntary" petition. While the California case was pending, the FDIC brought suit against Cortez to enforce certain promissory notes. Did FDIC violate the automatic stay provision of the Bankruptcy Code? Why or why not? [See: *Federal Deposit Insurance Corporation v. Cortez*, 96-6047, U.S. Court of Appeals (2nd. Cir.).]

5. Dyana Landrin was convicted of grand larceny after she admitted she took nearly $19,000 from the Community Mutual Savings Bank while she was employed as a teller. The county court ordered her to pay restitution to the bank—that is, return the money. Before paying restitution, Landrin filed a petition for relief under Chapter 7 of the Bankruptcy Code. Is the money owed to the bank discharged by the bankruptcy petition? Explain. [See: *In re Landrin*, 93-B-20920 (Bankr. S.D. NY).]

6. Three creditors filed an involuntary bankruptcy petition against the Manchester Lakes Association, alleging that the association was not paying its bills when they came due. Manchester fought the petition, arguing that its general partner, Dominion Federal Savings and Loan, had enough money to pay these bills as they came due, even though it was not doing so. Should the court refuse to grant the order for relief if the debtor could prove it had the ability to pay its bills? Explain. [See: *In re Manchester Lakes Association*, 47 B.R. 798 (Bankr. E.D. VA).]

7. Finding itself in great financial difficulty, Fidelity Mortgage Investors filed a voluntary bankruptcy petition in a New York bankruptcy court. When the petition was filed, the automatic suspension went into effect. Ignoring the suspension, Camelia and Farnale, two of FMI's creditors, filed suit against FMI in a Mississippi federal court. As a result, FMI was forced to pay out enormous sums of money in its own defense on the Mississippi case. FMI then returned to the bankruptcy court in New York and asked that both Camelia and Farnale be held in contempt of court for ignoring the suspension. Should the New York bankruptcy court hold Camelia and Farnale in contempt? Explain. [See: *Fidelity Mortgage Investors v. Camelia Builders, Inc.*, 550 F.2d 47 (2nd Cir.).]

8. When the Rahls filed for bankruptcy, they attempted to exclude their entire silverware set from the bankruptcy sale by listing each piece at a value far under the $200 maximum allowed for each item of individual household goods at that time. Had they listed the silverware as one item, it would have been worth more than $6,000. Thus, the entire set would not have been exempt. By listing each piece of silverware separately, the total value did not exceed $4,000, and the entire set could be saved. Should the court force the Rahls to list the silverware set as one item, thus limiting the exemption to $200? Explain. [See: *In the Matter of Rahl*, 14 B.R. 153 (Bankr. E.D. WI).]

9. Dubuque stole more than $4,000 from his employer, U-Haul. He later pled guilty to "theft by unauthorized taking or transfer." The court sentenced him to pay back the stolen money. When Dubuque filed for bankruptcy, U-Haul claimed that this debt would qualify as an exception to discharge. Was U-Haul correct? Explain. [See: *In re Dubuque*, 46 B.R. 156 (NH).]

10. U.S. Truck Company Inc. filed for a reorganization under Chapter 11 of the Bankruptcy Code. When the reorganization plan was presented for confirmation, one creditor objected to the plan. The creditor argued that the debtor was facing a possible strike and a new labor contract, both of which could place an additional strain on the debtor's finances. These potential labor problems, the creditor concluded, made the plan unfeasible. U.S. Truck admitted that the labor problems existed but noted that the company had recently rebounded from its financial problems to become very successful. Moreover, the labor union had just ratified two previous labor contracts by a 95 percent majority vote. U.S. Truck concluded that these factors made the plan workable, which was enough under the code because the code did not require a guarantee of success. Was the conclusion correct? [See: *In the Matter of U.S. Truck Co., Inc.*, 47 B.R. 932 (Bankr. E.D. MI).]

quick quiz Answers

21-1	21-2	21-3	21-4	21-5
1. F	1. F	1. T	1. T	1. T
2. F	2. T	2. F	2. T	2. T
3. T	3. T	3. F	3. T	3. T

Part 5 Case Study

Superior Savings Association v. City of Cleveland
501 F. Supp. 1244 (U.S. District Court,
Northern District of Ohio)

Summary

The Superior Savings Association, a reputable savings and loan institution with a long history of serving the Lithuanian community in Cleveland, owned a properly recorded first mortgage on a two-story brick building located at 6802 Superior Avenue in the city. The building was located just across the street from one of the branches of Superior Savings in the heart of the Lithuanian community, and one of the bank's officers passed the building every morning on his way to work. The building also held special significance in the neighborhood because it had once housed the main office of Cleveland's only Lithuanian newspaper and a neighborhood print shop owned and operated by a Lithuanian immigrant and his sons. You can, therefore, imagine the bank officer's surprise when he arrived at work one morning to find that the building had, to say it bluntly, vanished. As he gradually pieced together the story, the officer learned that the mortgagor, a fellow by the name of Hughes, had failed to keep the building in an appropriate state of repair, according to what was required by city ordinances. As a result, the city condemned the building. As a final warning, the city gave Hughes more than two months to make the needed repairs before the building would be demolished. When Hughes failed to comply, the building was torn down. At no time during the two-month grace period did anyone at Superior Savings receive any notice of the impending demolition of the building by the city. Superior Savings sued, arguing that the city had violated the association's constitutional rights by "taking away" its property without giving it proper notice. Attorneys for Superior Savings argued that the city, as an agent of the state, had deprived the banking institution of its constitutional rights under the due process clause of the 14th Amendment to the U.S. Constitution. In addition, the city had also violated its own ordinances, which also require that it give notice of the impending demolition to Superior Savings. Had the city followed its own procedures and complied with constitutional law, the bank would have been properly notified and could have taken steps to save what had become a local landmark in the Lithuanian neighborhood, despite its state of disrepair. At this point in the story, there was no way to undo the damage that had been done. The building was gone and there would be no bringing it back. Therefore, Superior Savings asked the court to grant the institution a monetary award that would provide it with money damages that would be equal to the amount that the mortgage was worth just before it was torn down and its value after being destroyed. The measurement of that value would, of course, take some fancy calculating, given the historical nature of the building, the cultural heritage of the neighborhood, and the memories that the print shop represented, but it would ultimately be worth it to Superior Savings. (Reproduced below is that portion of the Court's opinion that corresponds to this analysis. Footnote numerals are included but the citations themselves and explanatory notes are omitted.).

The Court's Opinion

Ben C. Green, Senior District Judge

Plaintiff is a savings and loan institution which holds a first mortgage on land located in the City of Cleveland, Ohio. Defendant is the City of Cleveland, which, plaintiff says, demolished a building on that land without notice to plaintiff. Plaintiff complains that the actions of the city deprived it of its property interest in the land without due process, and demands damages and attorney fees.

The city has not answered, but has filed a motion for summary judgment. That motion will be considered as a motion to dismiss for failure to state a claim upon which relief could be granted pursuant to Rule 12(b)(6), Federal Rules of Civil Procedure. Because the motion contains exhibits not part of the pleadings, the provisions of Civ.R. 56 regarding summary judgments will apply. Plaintiff has filed a brief opposing the city's motion, and has cross-moved for summary judgment.

This Court has jurisdiction to hear and decide this case pursuant to 42 U.S.C. § 1983, 28 U.S.C. § 1343.

The facts are not in dispute. In July 1977, plaintiff made a $12,000 loan to one George Hughes (who is not a party to this action), and secured the note resulting from the loan with a first mortgage on land and buildings located at 6802 Superior Avenue, Cleveland. Constructed on the land at the time was a two-story brick apartment building. The first mortgage was filed for record with the Cuyahoga County Recorder.

On October 19, 1979, the defendant, acting through its Department of Community Development, Division of Housing, inspected the subject premises and found 27 matters which were considered violations of the city's building and housing ordinances. A notice listing the violations was sent to Hughes, apparently by certified mail. The notice provided that, "This notice shall be complied with and all violations corrected by November 30, 1979." Typed in capital letters at the beginning of the itemization of the violations were the words: "THIS STRUCTURE SHALL BE DEMOLISHED AND ALL DEBRIS REMOVED FROM THE PREMISES OR THE VIOLATION SET OUT BELOW SHALL BE CORRECTED."

The notice also contains a reference that a copy thereof was to be sent to "Oper. Demo." Plaintiff did not receive a copy of the notice.

On December 14, 1979, the City's Division of Building inspected the structure, through Building Inspector John Capko and Registered Civil Engineer William L. Blankenburg. Photographs were taken at the time of the inspection and copies thereof were submitted as exhibits to the City's motion. Blankenburg's report, written that day and included as one of the exhibits, describes what is obvious from the photographs:

> The building was open, vacant, and partly vandalized. The building was only partly vandalized because the brick scavengers got there ahead of those looking for copper, and other metals. About 40 feet of brick bearing wall was removed for a height of two stories on the east side of the building. At the rear where the building juts out to the east, another 15 feet of a two-story brick bearing wall was removed from a north wall. Then at the rear, another 22 feet of a brick wall two stories high had been removed at the east wall. This last item (22 feet) was non-bearing as far as floor joists go, but it did carry parapet brick above the roof level. In every case where brick had been removed, the brick parapet was left in a dangerous condition. A heavy wind or a substantial snow load could bring down quite a bit of the building where floor or roof joists have no bearing wall to rest on.

Blankenburg concluded:

> In my opinion this building is beyond the point of economical repair. Furthermore, it is an attractive menace to the neighborhood children, and it should be torn down immediately.

In his affidavit, Inspector John Capko says that during his inspection he found a group of small children playing in and around the structure. In his handwritten report, made the day of the inspection, Capko writes:

> Comments: This structure should be razed forthwith ... (I was informed that housing has this in demo. 12-79[)].

The city asserts in its brief that on "December 18, 19[79], the City's independent contractor ... was authorized to demolish the subject property ...." The building was subsequently demolished.

From all of the above, the Court concludes that the building in question was in a manifestly deteriorated and dangerous condition from at least October 19, 1979, through the date of its demolition. The Court also concludes that the city seriously considered demolishing the building from that date onward. But at no time during that two and a half month period did the city notify the plaintiff of its intentions to raze the structure, even after the inspection of December 14 made apparent the course the city would take.

The Fourteenth Amendment to the United States Constitution reads, in pertinent part:

> "nor shall any State deprive any person of ... property without due process of law ..."

Under circumstances such as those presented here, communities have been held liable to landowners for destruction of buildings without either notice or opportunity for a hearing. *Miles v. District of Columbia*, 510 F.2d 188 (C.A.D.C., 1975). But the nature of the interests held by a mortgagor-landowner differs from those held by his mortgagee, and it has not been suggested that the interests of the mortgagor are subrogated to the mortgagee. Therefore, it will be necessary to examine the nature of the mortgagee's interests and determine to what extent constitutional protection should attach thereto.

In *Louisville Joint Stock Bank v. Radford*, 295 U.S. 555 at 594-95, 55 S.Ct. 854 at 865-866, 79 L.Ed. 1593 (1934), Justice Brandeis listed five property rights in a mortgage on real property which could not be taken from the mortgagee by Congress absent the due process required by the Fifth Amendment. Those attributes were set forth as follows:

> 1. The right to retain the lien until the indebtedness secured is paid; 2. The right to realize upon the security by a judicial public sale; 3. The right to determine when such sale shall be held, subject only to the discretion of the court; 4. The right to protect its interest in the property by bidding at such sale wherever held, and thus to assure having the mortgaged property devoted primarily to the satisfaction of the debt, either through receipt of the proceeds of a fair competitive sale or by taking the property itself; 5. The right to control meanwhile the property during the period of default, subject only to the discretion of the court, and to have the rents and profits collected by a receiver for the satisfaction of the debt.

In *W. B. Worthen Co. v. Kavanaugh*, 295 U.S. 56 at 59, 55 S.Ct. 555 at 556, 79 L.Ed. 1298 (1934), Justice Cardozo found unconstitutional a portion of a farmer's relief act, saying of Congress:

> With studied indifference to the interests of mortgagee or to his appropriate protection they have taken from the mortgage the quality of an acceptable investment for a rational investor.

And in *Wright v. Mountain Trust Bank*, 300 U.S. 440 at 457, 57 S. Ct. 556 at 559, 81 L. Ed. 736 (1937), the Court held that a federal statute violated the Fifth Amendment due process clause, since it effected a substantial impairment of the mortgagee's security. These concepts—that a mortgage confers upon the mortgagee certain specific rights of security for a debt as well as the right not to have the security impaired—remain valid today.

In *Board of Regents of State Colleges v. Roth*, 408 U.S. 564, 576-78, 92 S. Ct. 2701, 2708-2709, 33 L. Ed.2d 548 (1972), the Supreme Court held that:

> The Fourteenth Amendment's procedural protection of property is a safeguard of the security of interests that a person has already acquired in specific benefits. These interests—property interests—may take many forms.* * * * * Property interests, of course, are not created by the Constitution. Rather, they are created and their dimensions are defined by existing rules or understandings that stem from an independent source such as state law—rules or understandings that secure certain benefits and that support claims of entitlement to those benefits.

In *Paul v. Davis*, 424 U.S. 693, 710-711, 96 S.Ct. 1155, 1164-1165, 47 L.Ed.2d 405 (1976), Justice Rehnquist further defined what interests may attain the status of "property" protected by the Fourteenth Amendment:

> It is apparent from our decisions that there exists a variety of interests which are difficult of definition but are nevertheless comprehended within the meaning of either "liberty" or "property" as meant in the Due Process Clause. These interests attain the Constitutional status by virtue of the fact that they have been initially recognized and protected by state law, and we have repeatedly ruled that procedural guarantees of the Fourteenth Amendment apply wherever the State seeks to remove or *significantly alter* that protected status. (emphasis added).

The law of Ohio recognizes and protects the status of mortgages, mortgagors, and mortgagees.[1] It is further recognized that an understanding, such as a contract, may create property protected by constitutional guarantees, provided that such understandings are mutually explicit, must be such that a person claiming the interest may invoke at a hearing, and must be defined with reference to state law. *Webster v. Redmond*, 599 F.2d 793 (C.A.7, 1979). A mortgage on real property such as the one in this case fits such criteria.

This Court thus concludes that the principles set forth in *Radford, Worthen*, and *Wright* have as much force today as when they were established. No state may deprive a mortgagee of the rights set forth in *Radford* without due process. A state may not, unless via due process, substantially impair the security of a mortgage by taking from it the quality of an acceptable investment for a rational investor.

Having determined that a mortgage contains property protectable by the Fourteenth Amendment, it now must be determined whether the demolition of a building located on land deprives a mortgagee of any of those interests.

It is now well established that the value of property and the rights protected by the Fourteenth Amendment arise not from the mere possession of the property but rather from its use. *Lake Country Estates v. Tahoe Regional Planning Agency*, 440 U.S. 391, 99 S.Ct. 1171, 59 L.Ed.2d rights in a mortgage arise not just from the lien in land, but also in the maintenance of the security which makes the mortgage an acceptable investment for the rational investor.

It seems also well established that state action which "frustrates distinct investment-backed expectations" of a property owner may form the basis for a finding of a "taking" barred by the Fifth Amendment. *Penn Central Transportation Corp. v. New York City*, 438 U.S. 104, 127, 98 S.Ct. 2646, 2660, 57 L.Ed.2d 631 (1978), citing *Pennsylvania Coal Co. v. Mahon*, 260 U.S. 393, 43 S.Ct. 158, 67 L.Ed. 322 (1922).

It is apparent from the language of the mortgage deed, a copy of which was made an exhibit by plaintiff, that plaintiff took pains to take as security for its loan not just the land at 6802 Superior Avenue, but any buildings on that land as well. Plaintiff had a distinct investment-backed expectation at the time the loan was made that the apartment building on the land would remain, so as to provide security for the debt and to provide a source of funds from which the loan could be repaid.

When the defendant city caused the destruction of the building, it irrevocably foreclosed the possibility that plaintiff's protected expectations arising from the building could be realized. The city therefore deprived plaintiff of some or all of its property interest in the mortgage.

Our inquiry does not end here, as not all deprivations of property interests by a state give rise to a finding of a constitutional violation. To give rise to such a finding, the deprivation must be the result of the denial of due process. It is the task now to assess the measure of protection due to plaintiff, and determine whether the city met its burden. *Board of Regents of State Colleges v. Roth*, 408 U.S. 564, 92 S.Ct. 2701, 33 L.Ed.2d 548 (1972); *Vruno v. Schwarzwalder*, 600 F.2d 124 (C.A.8, 1979); *Colm v. Vance*, 567 F.2d 1125 (C.A.D.C., 1977).

It has been held that when emergency conditions exist, a state may take action which deprives a person of a property interest without hearing or notice provided there is a special need for very prompt action. *Fuentes v. Shevin*, 407 U.S. 67, 92 S.Ct. 1983, 32 L.Ed.2d 556 (1972). It has also been held that when faced with conditions extremely dangerous to health and safety, a municipality may, pursuant to its police power, demolish a building summarily and without notice. *Miles v. District of Columbia*, 510 F.2d 188, 192 (C.A.D.C., 1975). But where a community allows an appreciable amount of time to elapse between an inspection and demolition, the actions of the city themselves demonstrate that the exigency does not exist. *Miles v. District of Columbia, supra; cf. Pioneer Savings and Loan Co. v. City of Cleveland*, 479 F.2d 595 (C.A.6, 1973). Under such circumstances—where the city has allowed several days to elapse between identification of the problem and its resolution by demolition—it cannot claim emergency as the reason for dispensing with notice and opportunity for a hearing.

It will not be necessary to determine here, however, whether the condition of the building at 6802 Superior Avenue justified demolition without notice as an exercise of the police power.

An administrative agency is bound to observe its own regulations, and denies due process if it does not. *Service v. Dulles*, 354 U.S. 363, 77 S.Ct. 1152, 1 L. Ed.2d 1403 (1957). "Statutory authority is as much a requirement for valid [administrative action] as is constitutional reasonableness." *Wilson v. Health and Hospital Corp. of Marion County*, 620 F.2d 1201, 1217 (C.A.7, 1980).

The city was required by its own ordinances to provide notice to plaintiff of its intent to demolish the building. Section 3103.08(f) of the codified ordinances of the city reads, in pertinent part:

> The Commissioner [of Building] shall ... give written notice informing the owner or agent, *mortgagee of record*, and lien holders of record of the City's intention to demolish and remove the unsafe building or structure, at least 30 days prior to such intended action by the City. However, in cases of emergency as set forth in subsection (g) hereof, less than 30 days' notice may be given. (emphasis added).

The referenced subsection (g) authorizes the "prompt" demolition of buildings which in the opinion of the Building Commissioner present an "immediate" danger to the health and safety of others. Even though such prompt action is taken because of the emergent nature of the danger, *some* notice is required by the ordinance to be given to mortgagees of record.

When plaintiff filed the mortgage on 6804 Superior Avenue for record, it thereby gave notice to the City of Cleveland and the whole world of its interest in the land and the buildings thereon. When the city failed to observe its own ordinances and did not give plaintiff notice of its intent to demolish the building, it denied plaintiff the due process of law. Since the denial of due process deprived plaintiff of a property interest protected by the Due Process Clause of the Fourteenth Amendment, the defendant city is liable to plaintiff for the damages caused.

In *Pioneer Savings and Loan Co. v. City of Cleveland*, 479 F.2d 595, 598 (C.A.6, 1975), a case involving circumstances similar to those here, the Sixth Circuit held:

> The City was guilty of violating the [plaintiff's] constitutional right to due process of law, under the Fourteenth Amendment, and is liable to [plaintiff] in the amount due and owing on its mortgage and note, including principal and accrued interest.

Three years later, however, the Supreme Court ruled, in *Carey v. Piphus*, 435 U.S. 247, 254-255, 98 S.Ct. 1042, 1047-1048, 55 L.Ed.2d 252 (1978):

> Rights, constitutional and otherwise, do not exist in a vacuum. Their purpose is to protect persons from injuries to particular interests, and their contours are shaped by the interests they protect. Our legal system's concept of damages reflects this view of legal rights. "The cardinal principle of damages in Anglo-American law is that of *compensation* for the injury caused to plaintiff by defendant's breach of duty." 2 F. Harper and F. James, Law of Torts, § 25.1, p. 1299 (1956) (emphasis in original).

It therefore appears that any award of damages in procedural due process cases must (1) be tailored to the interests protected by the right in question, and (2) be limited to the injury actually caused to those interests by the constitutionally tortious conduct. The damages formula set forth in *Pioneer Savings and Loan Co. v. City of Cleveland, supra*, does not reflect this standard for damages; rather it presumes that the loss to the mortgagee is the value of the mortgage. The *Pioneer Savings'* formula does not take into account any (1) loss in the security of the mortgage which may have taken place pursuant to the acts or omissions of the mortgagor-landowner or others, or (2) the residual value of the parcel (and the resulting value in the mortgage) after the demolition of the building and removal of debris.

It is axiomatic that the purpose of monetary damages is, to the extent that the payment of money can do it, to place the damaged party in the same position he would have been in had the wrongful act not occurred. *See* 22 Am.Jur.2d, *Damages*, § 12, n. 11, and cases cited therein. Where compensation and not punishment is the function, the law will not put him in a better position than he would be in had the wrong not been done. *See id.*, at § 13 and cases cited therein. "[T]he law . . . remains true to the principle that substantial damages should be awarded only to compensate actual injury . . ." *Carey v. Piphus, supra*, 435 U.S. at 266, 98 S.Ct. at 1054.

It thus appears to the court that the proper measure of damages in this case would be the difference in value of plaintiff's mortgage just prior to the demolition of the building and the value of that mortgage just after the structure was razed. The precise assessment of those damages is not possible on the present record. Further actions by the parties will be required to identify the standard by which that worth may be measured, and, through application of the standard through the fact-finding process, the measure of the loss.

An order will be entered granting partial summary judgment for plaintiff and against defendant on the issue of liability, reserving for later ruling the issues of the measure and amount of damages.

Questions for Analysis

1. How does the case of *Superior Savings Association v. City of Cleveland* support or contradict the core legal principle of *stare decisis*? Explain.

2. The judge in this case relies on the Supreme Court case *Louisville Joint Stock Bank v. Radford* to outline five property rights in a mortgage on real property that cannot be taken from a mortgagee by the government absent a following of the due process rights guaranteed by the Fifth Amendment. What are those five rights? Explain.

3. The judge also relies on *Paul v. Davis*, another Supreme Court case, this time to determine what property interests emerge from the 14th Amendment. What is that (are those) interest(s)? Explain.

4. As noted previously, the judge applies the 14th Amendment to this case to reach a conclusion. Why is it necessary to use the 14th Amendment when the Fifth Amendment already guarantees that private property will not be taken by the government for public use without due process? Explain.

5. In Chapter 2 of this book, we learned that the framers added certain safeguards to the Constitution that were designed to insulate the leadership of the new republic from the influence of the people. Do the due process provisions in the Fifth and 14th Amendments support or discredit that supposition? Explain.

6. According to the judge in this case, in addition to the protections afforded by constitutional law, what other legal protections might exist for a mortgagee such as Superior Savings? Explain.

7. Would the outcome in this case have been any different had the financing for the building at 6802 Superior Avenue been negotiated as a land contract instead of a conventional mortgage? Explain.

8. What was the net effect of recording the mortgage, and how did that affect the outcome of this case? (Or did it?) Explain.

9. The judge believes that it is necessary to establish the existence of the plaintiff's (Superior Savings) rights before moving on with the case. Once that issue has been decided, what is the next step that the court must take? Explain.

10. How can the injury that emerges from a violation of due process be measured in order to supply an appropriate monetary reward to the plaintiff in a case like this one? Explain.

Design Elements: The Opening Case: ©Sharpstock/Alamy; A Classic Case: ©Evlakhov Valeriy/ Shutterstock

©Keith Brofsky/Getty Images

Part Six
Agency and Employment

Chapter 22 **Agency Law**　　Chapter 24 **Labor Law**

Chapter 22

Agency Law

22-1 The Nature of Agency Law
Agency and Other Relationships • The Question of Liability

22-2 Principles of Agency Law
Types of Principals and Agents • Liability of Principals and Agents • The Creation of an Agency • The Appointment of Subagents

22-3 Duties in Agency Law
Agent's Obligations to a Principal • The Principal's Obligations to the Agent

22-4 A Final View of Agency Law
Termination by the Acts of the Parties • Completion by Operation of Law • Agency Coupled with an Interest • Notice of Termination to Third Parties • Cyber-Agency Statutes • Agency in the Health Care Setting

THE OPENING CASE   Round 1
Vicarious Liability, Negligent Hiring, Negligent Supervision, Negligent Retention, Fiduciary Relationships, and the First Amendment

This case began more than 50 years ago when Father Francis E. Ryan (Fr. Ryan), a priest and a member of the St. Joseph's Society of the Sacred Heart (the Society), entered a romantic relationship with Anna Senna, the organist at the church where he was stationed. As a consequence of this relationship, the couple had two children, Carla Latty, born in 1952, and Adrian Senna, born sometime in the late 1940s. Adrian was raised by Anna, while Carla was put up for adoption. Anna never revealed that Fr. Ryan was the father of her children. A half a century later, when the children were in their 50s and 60s, DNA testing revealed that Carla and Adrian were siblings and that Fr. Ryan was "most probably" their father. Both Fr. Ryan and Anna Senna are deceased, and so the siblings, seeking recompense, brought suit in the state court of Maryland against the Society, the Archdiocese of Baltimore, the Archbishop of the Diocese, and the estate of the late Fr. Ryan. The claims against the the Archdiocese and the Archbishop were dismissed and the estate was never served, so the case focused on the Society as the sole defendant. The plaintiffs claimed that the Society should be held liable for fraudulent concealment, intentional infliction of emotional distress, negligent hiring, negligent supervision, negligent retention, and breach of fiduciary duty. The plaintiffs argued further that the defendant had a duty to reveal the identity of their father, and that since this was never done, they, the children, had suffered severe emotion distress. In addition, the plaintiffs argued that the defendant should have forced an end to the romantic relationship and that by not doing so, the Society had caused the children to suffer additional emotional distress. Further, the plaintiffs alleged that the Society pressured their mother into giving up Carla for adoption and then refused to provide monetary support for either child. As compensation they asked for $5 million and, as punitive damages, an additional $5 million.

The defendant filed a motion to dismiss for failure to state a claim for which relief can be granted. Before moving on, the court noted that by its very nature, the case brings up questions related to the religion clauses of the First Amendment—specifically, the question of whether the court should recognize the tort of clergy malpractice. The court refused to discuss this issue because to do so would require an in-depth dissection of religious doctrine, beliefs, and practices. Accordingly, the court decided to discuss the other issues inherent within the complaint. We will do the same, but we will focus on agency issues—specifically, vicarious liability, negligent hiring, negligent retention, and negligent supervision. [See: *Latty v. St. Joseph's Society*, 17 A.3d 155 (2011), 198 Md. App. 254 (2011).]

Opening Case Questions

1. What is agency? Explain.
2. What is vicarious liability? Explain.
3. What is negligent hiring? Explain.
4. What is negligent retention? Explain.
5. How might the First Amendment be involved in this case? Explain.

Source: See: *Latty v. St. Joseph's Society*, 17 A.3d 155 (2011), 198 Md. App. 254 (2011).

Learning Objectives

1. Describe the nature of the agency relationship.
2. Outline the doctrine of vicarious liability.
3. Distinguish among the different types of principals.
4. Distinguish among the different types of agents.
5. Distinguish among express, implied, and apparent authority.
6. Outline the duties of an agent to the principal.
7. Clarify the duties that a principal has in relation to an agent.
8. Name the ways that an agency relationship can be terminated.
9. Identify who is entitled to a notice that an agency has ended.
10. Explain electronic agency.

22-1 The Nature of Agency Law

In the essay "How Culture Changes," the anthropologist George Peter Murdock of Yale University explains, "It is a fundamental characteristic of culture that, despite its essentially conservative nature, it does change over time and from place to place." [See: George Peter Murdock. "How Culture Changes." In *Man, Culture, and Society*, ed. H. L. Shapiro (New York: Oxford University Press, 1956), pp. 247-260.] The fact that the law is a part of this process of change has been a recurring theme throughout this book. The emergence of the law of agency within our culture is another example of this tendency toward change within the legal system. Many of the changes that we have seen throughout the book emerge because the law must adapt by striking a balance between or among competing interests.

Agency and Other Relationships

The emergence of the agency law demonstrates how the legal system works as it attempts to strike a balance between doing business on your own and having other people conduct certain aspects of your business for you. To create this balance, agency law has developed its own principles, rules, doctrines, and concepts, all of which emerged independently and belong only to agency. As a result, agency law is said to be *sui generis*—that is, a law unto itself.

Principal–Agent Relationship Agency is a legal relationship in which one party, the agent, transacts business for and under the control of the second, the principal. The

Figure 22-1 The agent has the authority to represent the principal in an agency relationship.

About the Law

The definition of many legal terms varies depending on the area of the law in which they are used. *Principal* is one such term. In criminal law, a principal is defined as the chief perpetrator of a crime.

Did You Know?

In the early development of agency law, the principal was also known as the "constituent" and the "chief."

Independent contractors are not employees of the homeowner.
©Brand X Pictures/Getty Images

third party is that individual with whom the agent deals for the principal. The principal must indicate in some manner that the agent is to act for and under the control of the principal. (See Figure 22-1.) An agency relationship is always **consensual** because the agent must agree to act for the principal. The agency relationship is *fiduciary* because the agent and principal trust each other. All agency relationships are fiduciary relationships, although not all fiduciary relationships are agency relationships.

Employer–Employee Relationship The legal principles governing the relationship of principal and agent and of employer and employee are very similar. In fact, the two areas frequently intersect. Still, there are agency relationships that are not employment relationships so the two must *not* be thought of as equivalent. There are also employment relationships that are not agency relationships. The main distinction between the two relationships is that agent-employees have the authority to, and usually do, deal with third parties on behalf of the principal. Generally, we say that agent-employees conduct business for the principal, whereas non-agent-employees do not.

Master–Servant Relationship The *terms master* (employer) and *servant* (employee) continue to be used in some legal circumstances. A **master** is a person who has the right to control the activities of another person. The person whose activities are controlled is called the **servant**. A servant who has the right to conduct the business of the master is also an agent. In common usage, the terms *employer* and *employee* refer to the master–servant relationship. The terms *master* and *servant* are used instead of *employer* and *employee* in a legal setting when questions of tort liability arise.

Proprietor–Independent Contractor Relationship An **independent contractor** is a party who agrees to do a job and retains complete control over the methods employed to obtain final completion. The party for which an independent contractor works is often referred to as an employer or a **proprietor**. Independent contractors are not subject to the control of the proprietor. They maintain all required business licenses and permits and pay all job-related expenses; they are obligated only to get the job done. The proprietor has the right to specify the results of the job in question.

Moreover, he or she has the right to inspect and approve, or disapprove, the results of the independent contractor's performance. Independent contractors are not employees; however, they may be agents. The distinction depends on whether the independent contractor deals with third parties for the proprietor.

The Question of Liability

The distinctions among these relationships frequently can be crucial in determining the nature and the extent of legal liability. It is important to note, however, that the names themselves are not controlling. Instead, it is the true nature of the relationship that is critical. Calling a servant an independent contractor does not transform the nature of the relationship if the master still controls the servant's conduct.

Contract Liability An agent is appointed by a principal to negotiate and enter into contracts on behalf of the principal. Therefore, the principal is bound to the terms of those contracts. Unless an employee is also an agent, he or she has no power to negotiate and enter contracts for the employer. Moreover, an independent contractor has no power to bind the proprietor to a contract, unless expressly authorized to do so.

Tort Liability The distinction between master-servant and proprietor-independent contractor relationships is especially critical in determining the nature and the extent of tort liability. This type of liability is called **vicarious liability**. Vicarious liability is based on the principle of *respondeat superior* (let the master, or the superior, respond). To apply the doctrine of *respondeat superior* in a tort case, two questions must be answered. First, is the alleged tortfeasor a servant? Second, was the servant's action within the scope of employment. (See Figure 22-2.)

Is the Alleged Tortfeasor a Servant? To establish the existence of the master-servant relationship, the court must decide whether the alleged tortfeasor (the hired person) is a servant or an independent contractor. The most widely accepted test for determining the existence of a master-servant relationship is the control test. The **control test** requires that we look at the degree of control, or right to control, that the hiring person exercises over the hired person. The more control, or right to control, that the hiring person has over the hired person, the more likely that the court will rule that a master-servant relationship exists. The question then is a simple one: Did the alleged master (employer) have control or the right to control the alleged servant (employee)?

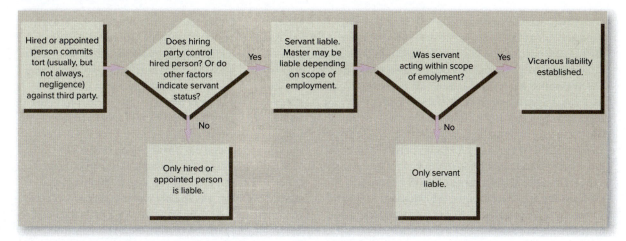

Figure 22-2 This chart shows the flow of master/servant tort liability under the *respondeat superior* doctrine.

When the degree of control is unclear or in dispute, the court has a series of factors that can be applied to bring the level of control into focus. These begin by reiterating the control test itself and then include the following additional factors:

1. Who decides the time period in which the job is performed?
2. Who owns the tools that are used on the job?
3. Who selects the overall length of the hired person's employment?
4. Who decides the method of compensating the hired person?
5. Who decides how the job is to be done?
6. What job skills are required to perform the tasks?
7. How much freedom does the hired person possess on the job?
8. Does the hired person operate a distinct business?
9. What was the understanding that existed between the parties?
10. What is the nature of the written agreement (if one exists)?

The first five questions are fairly straightforward. If the answer to a question is the hired person, then it is likely that he or she is an independent contractor (IC) at least for that question. The final five questions require a bit more analysis. For instance, in question six, the more skill involved on the job, the more likely the hired party is an IC. In question seven, the more freedom, the more likely the hired person is an IC. In question eight, a distinct business is indicative of an IC. Finally, the ninth and the tenth questions examine what transpired between the parties themselves. While the terms set up between the parties may provide evidence of an IC, those terms cannot alone prove the existence of an IC. Thus, the court will accept evidence about what the parties called themselves (IC or employee, for instance) but will not use it as final proof, absent some additional evidence.

THE OPENING CASE Round 2
Vicarious Liability, Negligent Hiring, Negligent Supervision, Negligent Retention, Fiduciary Relationships, and the First Amendment

When this case reached the court, the Society did as expected, given the issues at the heart of the case; it filed a motion to dismiss the case for failure to state a claim for which relief can be granted. Some states still call this motion a demurrer. In a motion to dismiss a case for failing to state a proper claim, the defendant asks the court (1) to assume all of the facts in the case are true and (2) to look at those facts in a light that is most favorable to the plaintiffs. The defendant's belief is that once the court has done this, it will see that there is no legal support for the plaintiff's complaint and will, therefore, dismiss the case. Despite what may look like a foregone conclusion, the court must still examine each allegation to determine its value.

To start this analysis, in the present case, the court must acknowledge that the existence of the affair is not at issue. Rather, the issue is whether the Society had a duty to the children who resulted from that affair. The plaintiffs' claims, of course, assume that the duty exists and so the court must examine each claim to determine its validity. In this case, the plaintiffs allege that the Society had a legal duty to inform the plaintiffs of their true relationship to Fr. Ryan, a duty to stop the affair, and a duty to support the children financially because the Society had control of Fr. Ryan's finances. The plaintiffs allege that these duties are based on (1) the special relationship that existed between the Society and the children, (2) the control that the Society had over Fr. Ryan's finances, (3) the fiduciary nature of the connection between the Society and the children, (4) the fact that society knew about the affair, and (5) the fact that Fr. Ryan was employed by the Society and was acting on its behalf when the affair began.

The primary claim that is relevant in this chapter is the fifth claim—that is, that the Society has a duty to the children because Fr. Ryan was its employee. Liability involving employment is generally shown by two theories: (1) the theory of vicarious liability and (2) the theory of negligence in hiring, retention, and supervision. Oddly, the plaintiffs do not use the theory of vicarious liability. Despite this oversight, we will consider that theory here before examining the theory of negligence in hiring, retention, and supervision. To hold the defendant liable under the theory of vicarious liability (which is also known as *respondeat superior*), the court must answer these questions: (1) Did a master–servant relationship exist between the Society and Fr. Ryan, and (2) was the offense (the affair) committed in pursuit of Fr. Ryan's employment with the Society? The strongest test for the existence of the master–servant relationship is the test of control. Simply stated, the test asks, Did the alleged employer have control or the right to control the alleged employee? In this case, the test can be stated in this way: Did the Society have control or the right to control the actions of Fr. Ryan while he was on the job? The answer to this question is clearly, yes. The Society would have assigned Fr. Ryan to any church at which he served, and Fr. Ryan would have had to comply. Moreover, by the very nature of his position, Fr. Ryan took a vow of obedience to the Church and its representatives, in this case, the Society. Given these facts alone, the existence of control and right to control is pretty clear. (Remember that the court must look at the facts in a way that is most favorable to the plaintiffs.) The question of scope of employment is another situation, however. For the answer to that question, please keep reading. [See: *Latty v. St. Joseph's Society*, 17 A.3d 155 (2011), 198 Md. App. 254 (2011).]

Source: See: *Latty v. St. Joseph's Society*, 17 A.3d 155 (2011), 198 Md. App. 254 (2011).

Did the Servant Act within the Scope of Employment? If the court determines that a master–servant relationship exists, it will turn to the next question, that is, "Did the servant act within the scope of employment?" The **scope of employment** involves the range of activities for which the servant is engaged. For the doctrine of *respondeat superior* to apply, a tort must be committed while the worker was performing a task for which he or she was hired, or at least one that he or she was authorized to perform by his or her employer.

To determine whether a servant was operating within the scope of employment, the court will ask the following questions:

1. Was the action committed by the employee authorized by the employer?
2. Where did the action take place?
3. Were the employer's interests and goals promoted by the action?
4. Did the employer supply the instrumentality used in the action?
5. Was this action performed by other employees on a regular basis?
6. If the action involved force, was the use of force expected by the employee as part of the job?

The Intentional Tort Factor In some situations, the court may hold the master liable for the torts of the servant even when the tort is intentional. Most of the time, vicarious liability is applied to negligence cases, because workers are not usually hired to commit intentional torts. There are, of course, exceptions to this rule. If, for example, a servant commits a tort intending to further the master's business, as when a bouncer at a casino uses force to eject an unruly patron or when a security guard at a department store commits false imprisonment, while detaining a suspected shoplifter, the master may be liable. Moreover, if the master could reasonably foresee that the servant might commit the intentional tort, as might be the case with a bouncer in a casino or a security guard in a department store, the master may be liable for that tort.

THE OPENING CASE Round 3
Vicarious Liability, Negligent Hiring, Negligent Supervision, Negligent Retention, Fiduciary Relationships, and the First Amendment

At the start of this action, the Society filed a motion to dismiss the case for failure to state a claim for which relief can be granted. Recall that in a motion to dismiss a case for failing to state a proper claim, the defendant asks the court to (1) assume all of the facts in the case are true and (2) to look at those facts in a light that is most favorable to the plaintiff. The defendant's belief is that once the court has done this, it will see that there is no legal support for the plaintiffs' complaint and will, therefore, dismiss that case. Despite what may look like a foregone conclusion, the court must still examine each allegation to determine its value.

To start this analysis in the present case, the court must acknowledge that the existence of the affair is not at issue. Rather, the issue is whether the Society had a duty to the children who resulted from that affair. We are focused here on the duty that emerges from the employment relationship between the Society and Fr. Ryan. Liability involving employment is generally shown by two theories (1) the theory of vicarious liability and (2) the theory of negligence in hiring, retention, and supervision. To hold the defendant liable under the theory of vicarious liability the court must answer these questions: (1) Did a master–servant relationship exist between the Society and Fr. Ryan, and (2) was the offense (the affair) committed in pursuit of Fr. Ryan's employment with the Society? In answer to the first question, we determined that since the Society controlled Fr. Ryan's actions on the job, a master–servant relationship did, indeed, exist between them.

Having answered that question affirmatively, we must now turn to the second question. Was the offense (the affair) committed in pursuit of the servant's employment? The traditional test for determining the scope of employment says that a servant's actions will be considered within the scope of employment if (1) the conduct at the focal point of the complaint involved actions that the servant was hired to carry out; (2) those actions were carried out where and when the work was supposed to take place; (3) those actions were carried out to further the goals of the employer; and (4) if the conduct complained of involved force, the force was expected by the employer as part of the job (as, e.g., with a security guard or a bodyguard).

Once we look at these elements, and look back at the facts, we can easily conclude that the type of romantic relationship involved in this case had absolutely nothing whatever to do with the job performed by a priest in pursuit of his duties or in furtherance of the goals of the Church. Moreover, as noted earlier, the doctrine of vicarious liability is not generally used to hold an employer liable for the intentional torts of the employee. The exception to that rule states that liability for intentional torts may be found if the employee commits a tort intending to further the master's business. Recall that we have already concluded that the romantic relationship that Fr. Ryan and Anna Senna had together had absolutely nothing to do with the job performed by a priest in pursuit of his duties. In light of this conclusion, there is no possibility of finding the Society liable for the actions of which the plaintiffs complain. (Okay, we have hedged a bit here. The romantic relationship between Fr. Ryan and Anna Senna was *not* an intentional tort. There was never any allegation that the relationship was anything other than a romantic relationship between two consenting adults. On the other hand, if we are to consider the allegations in a light most favorable to the plaintiffs we might ask whether the outcome would change were we to imagine that had Fr. Ryan actually pressured Anna Senna into the relationship. Given this scenario, Fr. Ryan would have certainly been culpable for his own actions. However, since that act of pressuring Anna Senna would also not have been within the scope of his employment, the Society would not have been be liable, and the result would have been the same.) Therefore, in relation to any claims that might have been based on vicarious liability, we must conclude that the *demurrer* must be granted, dismissing any claims based on that theory. This conclusion, however, might not completely exonerate the defendants in relation to negligent hiring, negligent retention, and negligent supervision. For that decision, please continue reading. [See: *Latty v. St. Joseph's Society*, 17 A.3d 155 (2011), 198 Md. App. 254 (2011).]

Source: See: *Latty v. St. Joseph's Society*, 17 A.3d 155 (2011), 198 Md. App. 254 (2011).

Negligent Hiring, Supervision, and/or Retention In some situations, the court may also hold the master liable for the torts of the servant even when the tort is outside the scope of employment. For instance, in some jurisdictions, if an employer (master) is negligent in checking an employee's (servant's) qualifications and consequently hires someone who is incompetent, dangerous, or even aggressive, the employer may be held liable should an innocent third party be injured by the actions of the incompetent, dangerous, or aggressive employee. Should that happen, the court may hold the employer liable for the tort of **negligent hiring** of the incompetent, dangerous, or aggressive employee. Similarly, an employer may be liable for the the tort of **negligent retention** of an incompetent, dangerous, or aggressive employee if, after hiring the employee, the employer learns that the employee is incompetent, dangerous, or aggressive and does not discharge that employee. Also, the employer may be liable if, during employee's time on the job, the employer fails to properly train, equip, and oversee the employee's activities and that lack of management injures an innocent person. This lack of proper management is referred to as the tort of **negligent supervision**.

Some courts have developed a five-element test for these employer-related torts. The five elements look like this: (1) an employment relationship existed at the time that the employee committed the tort; (2) the employee was incompetent or suffered from some other impairment that damaged his or her judgment, ability, and so on; (3) the employer had actual or constructive knowledge of that incompetence or other impairment (*Note:* Constructive knowledge means that the employer *should have known* of the impairment even if he or she did not really know about it.); (4) the employee did something related to that impairment that caused the plaintiff's injury; and (5) the employer's negligence in hiring, supervising, and or retaining the impaired employee was the proximate cause of the plaintiff's injuries. An employer may also be open to liability when the employer hires an independent contractor to perform a job that the law has not permitted the employer to delegate. This is referred to as a nondelegable duty. A **nondelegable duty** is one that the proprietor cannot delegate, or pass off, to another party. For example, an airline cannot delegate the responsibility it has for the safety of its passengers by hiring an independent contractor to do its maintenance work.

THE OPENING CASE *Round 4*
Vicarious Liability, Negligent Hiring, Negligent Supervision, Negligent Retention, Fiduciary Relationships, and the First Amendment

Recall that the real issue in this case has been whether the defendant, the St. Joseph's Society of the Sacred Heart (the Society), had a duty to the children who resulted from the affair between Fr. Ryan and Anna Senna affair. We have focused here on the duty that emerges from the employment relationship between the Society and Fr. Ryan. Recall that liability involving employment is generally shown by two theories (1) the theory of vicarious liability and (2) the theory of negligence in hiring, retention, and supervision. We have already dealt with the question of vicarious liability, so we can move on to the theory of negligence.

Now, in line with this theory, the plaintiffs have alleged that the Society was liable directly for its own behavior because it had a been negligent in hiring, supervising, and retaining Fr. Ryan. To show that the Society is liable due to its own negligence in hiring, supervising, and retaining Fr. Ryan, the plaintiffs must establish the existence of five elements: "(1) the existence of an employment relationship; (2) the employee's incompetence; (3) the employer's actual or constructive knowledge of such incompetence; (4) the employee's act or omission causing the plaintiff's injuries; and (5) the employer's negligence in hiring, [supervising] or retaining the employee as the proximate cause of plaintiff's injuries." The plaintiffs believed that the only element that needed proof was the fourth element—that is, that "the employee's act or omission (caused) . . . the plaintiff's injuries." As authority for their position, the plaintiffs pointed to a case that concludes that a religious order can be held liable for negligence in hiring, supervising, and retaining an employee who has committed sexual misconduct against a minor. The plaintiffs believed that this alone demonstrated the validity of their claim that the Society was negligent in hiring, supervising, and retaining Fr. Ryan.

The court disagreed. To make this point, the court noted that the actions complained of by the plaintiffs in the present case did not involve a minor but, instead, another consenting adult. Even so, the court was willing to imagine, just for the sake of argument, that Fr. Ryan used his position of power to entice Anna Senna into a sexual relationship. Even were that so, the court noted, the only one who would have been harmed by that liaison would have been Anna, not her children. So, even if we conclude that Anna Senna had a claim against Fr. Ryan, that does not mean that her children have the same claim. Therefore, since then plaintiffs have no claim against Fr. Ryan, by extension, they can have no claim against his employer. The court does not stop there, however. Instead, it felt compelled to take one more step, noting that were the plaintiffs to insist that they were injured by the Ryan–Senna affair, the only injury they could possibly allege would be wrongful life. The court was not prepared on go that far. Accordingly, the court wrote: "This smacks of a cause of action for wrongful life. A wrongful life cause of action includes claims 'by normal but unwanted children who seek damages either from their parents or from others negligently responsible for their conception or birth.' *Kassama v. Magat,* 368 Md. 113, 135, 792 A. 1102 (2002). Maryland does not recognize such a cause of action, nor did appellants raise it in their complaint or on appeal. *Id.* at 148, 792 A.2d 1102 (holding that 'life is not, and cannot be, an injury'). Thus, the negligence that appellants allege the society committed, as well as any possible resulting damages, presents no cognizable cause of action." [See: *Latty v. St. Joseph's Society,* 17 A.3d 155 (2011), 198 Md. App. 254 (2011).]

Source: See: *Latty v. St. Joseph's Society,* 17 A.3d 155 (2011), 198 Md. App. 254 (2011).

Fiduciary Liability *Fiduciary Duties* Some courts recognize that, when an employee breaches his or her fiduciary duty to a third party, the employer may also be liable for any injuries that result from that breach, if that employer had reason to believe that the employee might, in fact, breach that duty. In a breach of fiduciary duty lawsuit against an employer, the third party must present evidence showing that the fiduciary relationship (1) did exist, (2) was unequal in power, either (3) gave overwhelming control to the employee or (4) placed the third party in an especially vulnerable position (or both), and (5) actually injured the plaintiff. The courts generally reject such suits when the relationship is simply between a pastor and a parishioner. Instead, the relationship must have a more confidential and trusting dimension, as might exist between a counselor and a client. Moreover, the employer must have enough knowledge to reasonably believe that the third party is at risk. If all these elements fall into line, then a breach of fiduciary duty lawsuit may proceed against the employer.

THE OPENING CASE *Round 5*
Vicarious Liability, Negligent Hiring, Negligent Supervision, Negligent Retention, Fiduciary Relationships, and the First Amendment

So far our examination of the case of *Latty v. St. Joseph's Society* has focused on vicarious liability and on negligence in hiring, supervising, and retaining. However, the plaintiffs also claimed that a fiduciary relationship existed between them and the Society. Remember that a fiduciary relationship is one that is based on trust. The plaintiffs argued that because Fr. Ryan, as the father of the children, had a fiduciary relationship with them, the Society, as his employer, had that same fiduciary relationship with them. The court disagreed. In fact, the court was actually baffled as to how the plaintiffs could even raise this issue. There is also no fiduciary relationship between the parties. The court said it this way: "A fiduciary relationship is presumed to exist as a matter of law in specific situations: between a 'trustee and beneficiary, guardian and ward, agent and principal, attorney and client, partners in a partnership, [or] corporate directors and their corporation' . . . There was no agreement here between the parties from which a fiduciary duty would arise. Nor does the parties' relationship give rise to a duty presumed as a matter of law: the parties did not have an attorney-client, trustee-beneficiary, principal-agent, attorney-client, or partnership relationship, nor were they directors of a corporation. Even if a guardian-ward relationship were alleged, this would not aid appellants' claim because a guardian must be appointed by the court, and it is clear that no guardian was appointed here . . . Thus, the Josephite Fathers did not have a fiduciary duty to appellants."

Now it might be that the plaintiffs are confusing a fiduciary relationship with a confidential relationship. While similar, the two relationships are are different in several ways. However, the major difference is that with the possible exceptions of formal relationships, such as those that exist between an attorney and a client or between a trustee an a beneficiary, confidentiality is not presumed but must be proven. Thus, there is no automatic presumption of confidentiality in a parent–child relationship or in a priest–parishioner relationship. Confidentiality must be proven. It was not possible in the case of *Latty v. St. Joseph's Society* to prove a confidential relationship between the children of Anna Senna and Fr. Ryan. Nor was it possible to find such a relationship between the children and the society. The court said it this way: "There is no hint in the complaint that a confidential relationship existed between Fr. Ryan, the society and appellants. In fact, there was no allegation of any relationship between them at all. Even if we assume that appellants were automatically parishioners of Fr. Ryan's church from birth, this still does not establish a confidential relationship." [See: *Latty v. St. Joseph's Society*, 17 A.3d 155 (2011), 198 Md. App. 254 (2011).]

Source: See: *Latty v. St. Joseph's Society*, 17 A.3d 155 (2011), 198 Md. App. 254 (2011).

Criminal Liability The principal or employer ordinarily is not liable for an agent's or employee's crimes, unless the principal or employer actually aids or participates in their commission. The commission of a crime usually requires a state of mind that is specified in the criminal statute. Thus, if the principal or employer had not authorized the crime, the courts would conclude that the requisite mental state has not been shown. A principal or employer will be held criminally liable for acts done by an agent or employee to further an illegal business. In addition, most states have enacted statutes that hold a principal or employer liable for certain crimes committed by their agents or employees, even though they acted disobediently. Examples of such statutes are those that penalize the sale of impure foods or alcoholic beverages.

Independent Contractor Liability Recall that an independent contractor is someone who works for a proprietor but who maintains nearly total control over how the job is done. At the most, the proprietor can specify the outcome to be reached; the timing of that outcome; as well as the plans, materials, and colors to be used to reach that outcome. However, all other decisions are made by the contractor. Most of the time, any tort committed by an independent contractor is the responsibility of the independent contractor, not the proprietor. In fact, that is one of the advantages of hiring independent contractors rather than employees. However, this tactic does not always work. For instance, it is not legally possible for a proprietor to delegate certain duties. These duties, generally referred to as nondelegable duties, cannot be passed on to the contractor even if the contractor accepts those duties. For example, a common carrier, such as a ferry service, a bus company, or an airline, cannot delegate the responsibility it has for the safety of its passengers by hiring an independent contractor to do its maintenance work. Similarly, a hotel cannot delegate its responsibility to keep its guests secure in their rooms by hiring a private security firm. Also, proprietors can be held liable if they are not careful enough in hiring, training, supervising, and/or retaining an independent contractor. As noted earlier, like a negligent employer, a negligent proprietor can be held liable for the negligent hiring of the incompetent independent contractor. Similarly, a proprietor may be liable for the negligent supervision and the negligent retention of an incompetent independent contractor if, after hiring the independent contractor, the proprietor learns that the contractor is incompetent and does not dismiss the contractor.

Statutory Liability One of the most heavily regulated segments of the social structure is employment. Both Congress and the state legislatures create agencies, commissions, and departments that make regulations governing workplace safety, wages and hours, unemployment compensation, workers' compensation, employment discrimination, health care, layoffs and plant closings, collective bargaining and labor unions, and so on. Such statutes include Title VII of the Civil Rights Act, the Age Discrimination in Employment Act, the Worker Adjustment and Retraining Notification Act, the Family and Medical Leave Act, ERISA, the Americans with Disabilities Act, the Internal Revenue Code, the Fair Labor Standards Act, and statutes related to workers' compensation, among others. Frequently, these statutes will be written so that they apply to employees and not to independent contractors. Or, as in the case of the Internal Revenue Code, the regulations will treat employees one way and independent contractors another. This has prompted employers to simply label workers as ICs to escape or minimize the effects of the law. Consequently, the courts have created a test, called the *economic reality test*, to uncover the true nature of the employment relationship.

The Economic Realities Test The economic realities test is generally tailor made to reflect the goals of each statute and is, thus, a fairly flexible rule. Nevertheless, the rule is very similar to the control test used in *respondeat superior*; the economic realities test considers many of the same factors that are applied in the control test. These factors include determining the hired party's autonomy on the job, the length of time involved in the employment situation, and the level of skill needed to do the job. However, the economic realities test also adds some factors of its own. For example, in an attempt to determine the true nature of the financial arrangement between the parties, the economic realities test also asks about the hired party's investment in the employer's business and the degree to which the hired person's services were integrated into the employer's commercial activity.

Sovereign Immunity and the Federal Government The doctrine of sovereign immunity prevents lawsuits against a government authority without the government's consent. The doctrine is no longer as important a defense for government torts as it once was. The Federal Tort Claims Act of 1946 limits the federal government's sovereign immunity. Whenever a federal employee harms a third party or private property while driving a motor vehicle in the course of employment, the federal government is liable. However, the 1946 law explicitly preserves governmental immunity for a vaguely defined category of "discretionary" actions by officials.

A CLASSIC CASE The Free Exercise Clause of the First Amendment Does Not Shield All Behavior (or Does It?)

The defendants in this case include the pastor and the elders of a local community church. The plaintiff is a past parishioner at the same church. When an individual joins the community church, he or she agrees to abide by the disciplinary rules and procedures of the church. The constitution of the church states that the members of the governing body of the church reserve the right to discipline any member who openly engages in a pattern of behavior that violates biblical principles and who remains "unrepentant" in regard to that behavior. Such discipline can ultimately include excommunication from the church. When such an event occurs, the removal of a member is announced to the congregation at a Sunday service "in a tenderhearted and discreet manner." The announcement is followed by prayer, presumably for that former member. Because she was having difficulties in her marriage, the plaintiff sought the pastor's advice. The pastor advised her in his capacity as a professional counselor. The counseling failed to help the plaintiff, who separated from her husband and then decided to seek a divorce. When she told the pastor of her decision, she was told that she would have to give up her membership in the community church. The plaintiff says that she readily agreed to this ruling under the constitution and offered her resignation. Nevertheless, the pastor and the other elders wrote a letter that was sent to the congregation informing them of the plaintiff's situation. The letter included statements explaining that the plaintiff was leaving the congregation because she was divorcing her husband, despite the fact that she had no biblically sound reason for doing so, and, in addition, "she had engaged in a 'biblically inappropriate' relationship with another man." The letter also indicated that church members were to shun the plaintiff as a way to encourage repentance.

The plaintiff sued the pastor and the elders who had participated in the writing of the letter that was distributed to church members. The suit—which, strictly speaking, does not involve vicarious liability because the community church was unincorporated but can provide guidance on the limits of First Amendment protection—claimed that the pastor and the elders had committed the torts of intentional infliction of emotional distress, defamation, invasion of privacy, breach of fiduciary duty, and professional negligence. In response, the defendants filed motions to dismiss based on a lack of subject matter jurisdiction. In essence, by filing these motions, the defendants argued that the court had no power to hear the case because the decisions made by the elders and the actions that came from those decisions were based on internal, church-related ecclesiastical decisions that were founded on a biblical interpretation made by the elders that the court, as an arm of the government, was not permitted to examine under the First and the Fourth Amendments of the Constitution. Any attempt to interfere would, therefore, violate the Free Exercise Clause. The court agreed with the defendants and dismissed the case. The plaintiff appealed. The appellate court concurred with the trial court on those claims that were related to the disciplinary letter. Those claims cannot be examined by the court because those matters and those decisions are all related to the church's constitution and its interpretation of biblical principles. Therefore, the trial court was correct in noting that it had no subject matter jurisdiction on which to base its authority.

However, the professional negligence claim against the pastor is another matter. When it comes to that claim, the court declares that the case has removed itself from any valid First Amendment claim. The conduct that the plaintiff complains of in relation to the counseling performed by the pastor is not related to the disciplinary letter but, instead, to his secular, professional treatment of the plaintiff, even though that counseling may have been indirectly related to the decision to write the letter. Quoting another case, the appeals court says, "The free exercise clause never has immunized clergy or churches from all causes of actions alleging tortious conduct," and it does not "necessarily bar all claims which may touch on religious conduct. *Tilton v. Marshall,* 925 S.W2d 672, 677 (Tex.1996)." The court here concluded its consideration of this appeal by noting, "Having sustained (the plaintiff's) first issue, we reverse the trial court's dismissal for want of subject matter with respect only to the professional negligence claim against (the pastor) and remand that claim for trial on the merits. We affirm the trial court's dismissal in all other respects." [See: *Appellant, v. Appellee*, No. 2-02-260-CV (May 20, 2004).]

Source: See: *Appellant, v. Appellee*, No. 2-02-260-CV (May 20, 2004).

EXAMPLE 22-1: Above-Ground Radioactive Fallout

In 1982, a federal district court judge held that radioactive fallout from above-ground nuclear tests had caused at least nine people and perhaps dozens of others to die of cancer. The judge ruled that the federal government must pay damages under the Federal Tort Claims Act, explaining that while the high-level decision to conduct the tests had been discretionary, and thus was immune from liability, officials had conducted the tests in a negligent manner by failing to monitor radiation adequately or warn residents of neighboring areas in Nevada, southern Utah, and northern Arizona who lived downwind from the test site about radiation hazards and how to reduce them. A federal appeals court, however, held that all aspects of the testing program were conducted in accordance with discretionary decisions of the Atomic Energy Commission and were thus immune from liability. The U.S. Supreme Court in 1988 refused to hear an appeal from the appellate decision.

Sovereign Immunity, *Respondeat Superior*, and the States The formula for determining when a state government is liable for its own torts and for the torts of its employees, and when it retains its immunity, is often difficult to unravel. Generally, the starting point is to determine whether the state has a statute for preserving or eliminating sovereign immunity. If a statute exists that preserves immunity, the next step would be to determine whether the state has established any exceptions to the elimination of sovereign immunity. These exceptions would override sovereign immunity and permit a plaintiff to sue the state. For instance, even if immunity has been preserved in most cases, it might be forfeited if the action complained about involves a government employee's negligence while working for a state agency involved in the state's proprietary activities or its governmental functions. The final step would be to determine if any defenses are available to the state that would permit the state to escape liability, even though its sovereign immunity has been removed.

Charitable Immunity The doctrine of charitable immunity is designed to protect charitable institutions, including churches, from liability for lawsuits based on tort law. The **charitable immunity** principle, which finds its origin in English common law, is based on the belief that charities perform a useful purpose within the social network and should, therefore, not have their charitable funds diverted from charity work to tort law payments. The ultimate fear is that exposing charities to liability in tort law would impoverish many of those institutions, weaken others, and lead the rest to abandon their charitable work rather than end up on the wrong end of a lawsuit. Despite this rationale, the doctrine was eliminated in England but not before it was adopted and preserved by several jurisdictions in the United States. Since its inception in the United States in 1876, the doctrine has undergone a number of changes. Some jurisdictions, for instance, have transferred most issues surrounding the doctrine to the state legislature. Some states eliminated charitable immunity because of the widespread availability of insurance protection. In addition, many courts that kept the charitable immunity doctrine eliminated protection for charitable immunity for intentional torts. At last count, more than half of the states have eliminated charitable immunity completely. Other states, Massachusetts, for instance, have kept charitable immunity in the spirit, if not in the letter, of the law, by limiting recovery in a tort law case against a charity to nominal amounts such as $20,000. Some jurisdictions have kept charitable immunity but have made an exception for the torts of negligent supervision, thus opening church officials to liability for those torts. However, this is not true in all jurisdictions. In fact, some jurisdictions still hold that, even in cases of negligent supervision, the protection of charitable funds as a social good outweighs the good that will come from denying clerical supervisors the protection of the charitable immunity doctrine. [See: Matthew Cobb, "A Strange Distinction: Charitable Immunity and Clergy Abuse in *Pincher v. Roman Catholic Bishop of Portland*," *Maine Law Review* 62, no. 2 (2010), pp. 703–716.]

A QUESTION OF ETHICS

Clergy Malpractice, the First Amendment, and Charitable Immunity

It may seem odd to focus on the First Amendment in a chapter devoted to agency law; however, as noted earlier, the intersection of agency and constitutional law is one of the unintended consequences of the attempt to prevent the involvement of the government in the free exercise of religion. The cases noted earlier (*Latty v. St. Joseph's Society* and *Appellant, v. Appellee*) are only small clues as to the extent of the problems associated with litigation that targets the work of the clergy. These complexities are highlighted in two law review articles—"Minimizing Liability for Church Related Counseling Services: Clergy Malpractice and First Amendment Religion Clauses," by Constance Frisby Fain, and "A Strange Distinction: Charitable Immunity and Clergy Abuse in *Pincher v. Roman Catholic Bishop of Portland*," by Matthew Cobb. The first article begins by defining clergy malpractice and by recounting a history of the First Amendment in relation to that tort. The elements of the tort of clergy malpractice are defined within the bounds of ordinary tort law, as a "breach of duty of professional care by the clergy person in providing pastoral counseling or other religious services, which is factually and legally the cause of the parishioner's or the claimant's injury" [See: Fain, pp. 230-231].

The article then examines several cases involving clergy malpractice, concluding that the case for the wholesale acceptance of the tort of clergy malpractice is problematic at best, especially when the counseling in question involves a religious interpretation of church doctrines, practices, beliefs, and so on. When this entanglement occurs, the court will be unable to establish a standard of care because such a standard would involve the court in the interpretation of those religious beliefs. However, when the counseling practices under fire step outside of those bounds, then the court can, on a secular basis, determine that standard of care. At that point, the clergy member is operating as a secular counselor and can be judged in the basis of professional counseling. This would seem to indicate that the tort of clergy malpractice does not exist. The article then examines the Establishment Clause and the Free Exercise Clause of the First Amendment. Under the Establishment Clause, if a tort claim cannot be settled without interpreting church doctrine, then excessive entanglement occurs and the case is at an end. On the other hand, if the tort claim against a clergy member does not involve the theology of the church, then the lawsuit may proceed. Similarly, under the Free Exercise Clause, a lawsuit will interfere with the free exercise of religion if the court interferes with (1) an individual's freedom to follow certain religious practices or (2) the church's power to guide its own in-house concerns. [See: Constance Frisby Fain, "Minimizing Liability for Church Related Counseling Services: Clergy Malpractice and First Amendment Religion Clauses," *Akron Law Review* 44, pp. 221-260; and *Doe v. Liberatore*, 478 F.Supp.2d 742 (2007). In its discussion of fiduciary duties, the court does a good job explaining First Amendment issues related to clergy malpractice.]

The article concludes that, if a tort claim against a clergy member does not involve the theology of the church, then the lawsuit can proceed. [See: Fain, p. 251.] Does this mean that the tort of clergy malpractice does not exist? Probably. However, that does not eliminate the clergy member's or the church's liability, if the counseling "services" have crossed the line and become secular or, much worse, if the counseling becomes a tort in and of itself as when a "counseling" session turns into sexual harassment, sexual battery, or sexual abuse. In such a situation, the case no longer involves legitimate advice gone wrong but impermissible, tortious, and often even criminal behavior. The interesting thing here is that, even in such a situation, the clergy member's supervisors may have a defense. That defense is charitable immunity. As noted in the second article, the doctrine of charitable immunity is designed to protect charitable institutions, including churches, from liability for lawsuits based on tort law under the notion that charities should not have their funds diverted from their charitable mission to pay the costs of a tort action. Although most states have eliminated the defense, it still exists in several states in one form or another. Thus, in relation to agency law, the defense might still work to protect clerical supervisors from liability. On the other hand, in most cases and in most states, including Maine (which was the location of the case examined in this article), charitable immunity will not work as a defense for negligent supervision. [See: Matthew Cobb, "A Strange Distinction: Charitable Immunity and Clergy Abuse in *Pincher v. Roman Catholic Bishop of Portland*," *Maine Law Review* 62, no. 2 (2010), pp. 703-716.]

The following questions have not yet been answered. Before you consider each question, turn to Chapter 1 and review the various ethical theories noted there. Using one of those theories in a consistent way, answer the following questions on clerical malpractice, the First Amendment, charitable immunity, and the exceptions to charitable immunity. Is it ethical for clergy malpractice to be recognized as a viable tort in and of itself, despite the limits imposed by the religion clauses of the First Amendment? Is it ethical for clerical supervisors to be held liable in vicarious liability for the torts of their clergy members? Is there an ethical position that can be used to argue for the reinstatement of the defense of charitable immunity in the states to protect charitable funds from being used to pay damages in tort lawsuits? Is it ethical for the court to recognize an exception to the defense of charitable immunity when a clergy member's supervisor is being sued for negligent supervision?

quick quiz 22-1

1. An agency relationship is always consensual because the agent must agree to act for the principal.	true | false
2. All fiduciary relationships are agency relationships but not all agency relationships are fiduciary relationships.	true | false
3. Agency law is said to be *sui generis*—that is, a law unto itself.	true | false

22-2 Principles of Agency Law

Now that the different types of relationships involved in business have been discussed, the focus of the chapter can return to the principal-agent relationship. Several key guidelines help the courts distinguish among different types of principals and the different types of agents.

Types of Principals and Agents

There are three types of principals. A **disclosed principal** is one whose identity is known by third parties dealing with that principal's agent. When an agent does not reveal the existence of an agency relationship but appears to act on his or her own behalf rather than for another, an **undisclosed principal** exists. A **partially disclosed principal** exists when the agent, in dealing with third parties, reveals the existence of an agency relationship but does not identify the principal. Agents are generally classified according to the scope of their responsibility. A **general agent** is a person who is given broad authority to act on behalf of the principal in conducting the bulk of the principal's business activity on a daily basis.

A **special agent** is a person who is authorized to conduct only a particular transaction, conduct a series of related transactions, or perform only a specified act for the principal. Examples are real estate brokers, lawyers, and accountants who are retained to do a specific job and whose authority is restricted to those acts necessary to accomplish it. A **factor**, or common merchant, is a special agent who is employed to sell merchandise consigned for that purpose. The factor has possession of the goods and sells them for and on behalf of a principal. A factor who guarantees the credit of a third party to a principal and guarantees the solvency of the purchaser and performance of the contract is known as a *del credere agent*. In the event of default, the *del credere* agent is liable to the principal.

> ### EXAMPLE 22-2: The Antique Agent
>
> Edna Freeman hired Leonard Tenpenny to act as her agent in the sale of several antiques. The contract of agency included a promise by Tenpenny that Freeman would not suffer any loss because of any sales on credit that Tenpenny made with third parties. Shortly after, Tenpenny sold a rare first edition of one of Louis Bromfield's novels, valued at $50,000, to Robert Fisher on credit. Fisher later declared bankruptcy. As a *del credere* agent, Tenpenny had guaranteed the credit of Fisher and is liable to Freeman for the value of the book.

Liability of Principals and Agents

The principal is liable for all contracts that a general or special agent may enter into with third parties, as long as the agent acts within the authority conferred by the principal. An undisclosed principal can be held liable for the acts of the agent once the identity of the principal is disclosed. Once the principal's identity is revealed, a third party may sue either the principal or the agent. Following this election, however, the third party cannot later decide to sue the other, unless the principal was undisclosed at the time the choice was made. When an agent is not known to be an agent and is acting as a principal, the agent can be held liable as a principal. When a person is known to be an agent, but it is not known for whom the agent acts, the third party can also hold the agent liable. In addition, when an agent exceeds the authority conferred by the principal, the agent can be made personally liable.

The Creation of an Agency

Agents may perform only acts that have been authorized by the principal. Agents who exceed their delegated authority become personally liable. Unauthorized actions do not bind the principal unless those actions can be reasonably assumed by a third party to be within the scope of the agent's authority. Authority granted to an agent may be express, implied, or apparent. An agency is generally created by some action or conduct on the part of the principal or by operation of law. A would-be agent cannot by conduct alone or by any statement establish an agency relationship. It is therefore wise for a third party, when dealing with an agent, to determine the nature and extent of the agent's authority. An agency relationship is generally created by the following methods: by express appointment, by implication, by estoppel, by ratification, and by statute.

Agency by Express Appointment The first way that a principal can create an agency relationship is by an express appointment. This occurs when the principal either orally or in writing creates the agency relationship. The agent's *express authority* is created at the same time that the principal appoints the agent and creates the agency relationship. This happens when the principal writes down (word processes, types out, e-mails, faxes, texts, and so on) the instructions or instructs the agent by saying the words of instruction aloud. In either case, the principal uses words to transfer authority to the agent. Sometimes referred to as *actual authority*, and sometimes even as *actual express* authority, express authority may also be indicated by conduct, as when a sales representative informs the principal of travel plans, and no objection to them is expressed.

Agency by Implication Most of the time when an agency is created by an express appointment, the principal does not or cannot cover the complete extent of the agent's authority. There will always be some acts that are necessary or customary to carry out the duties that have been expressly authorized by the principal, even though those acts were not expressly authorized by the principal. For example, the express authority to sell the principal's car will include the authority to take a money order in payment for the car, even though the principal never expressly said to the agent, "You can take a money order in payment for the car." Thus, while the agency itself is not created by implication, the agent's authority to do things beyond that which has been expressed by the principal is created by implication. The agent's authority to perform acts that are necessary or customary to carry out expressly authorized duties is referred to as implied authority and sometimes as *actual implied authority*. It stems from the reasonable effort of an agent to understand the meaning of the principal's words describing what the agent is to do.

Implied authority can be described as *incidental authority* when the acts performed are reasonably necessary to carry out express authority. For example, an agent might have incidental authority to contract for the repair of the principal's van that broke down while being used to deliver perishable products that the agent had express authority to sell and deliver. Implied authority may be described as *customary authority* when the agent acts in conformity with the general trade or professional practices of the business. For example, a check-out clerk in a grocery store would have the customary authority to accept discount coupons from customers because that process conforms to the general trade practices for check-out clerks in grocery stores.

Agency by Estoppel When a principal, by words or actions, leads a third party to believe that a non-agent is an agent (or that a real agent has authority beyond that agent's actual authority), that principal has clothed that non-agent (or the over extended real agent) with apparent authority and has, thus, created an agency by estoppel. The principal may make known to the third party in a variety of ways that such authority exists. For instance, it may be generated by making a direct statement to the third party, permitting someone to have a meaningful business title, enabling someone to occupy a position of authority, or allowing someone to perform duties that give a third party reason to believe that the person has the authority to act for the principal. Sometimes apparent authority can even arise because the principal fails to act in some way. For example, apparent authority may be created if the principal terminates an agent's actual authority but fails to give proper notice of that termination to those who are entitled to receive such notice. Such apparent authority is sometimes referred to as lingering apparent authority. The party with whom the agent is dealing must reasonably believe that the agent has authority to so act, have had no notice of a lack of such authority, and act or rely on the agent's appearance of authority.

Agency by Ratification Agents sometimes perform acts on behalf of the principal that exceed their authority. Also sometimes a person who has no authority to act as an agent does so without the principal's knowledge or permission. In such cases, the principal for whom the agent claimed to act may either ignore the transaction or affirm it by *ratification*. Ratification occurs when the principal approves the unauthorized act performed by an agent or by one who has no authority to act as an agent. Although an agent generally is personally liable to third parties for actions in excess of the agent's authority, this liability is not true when the third party knows that the agent has exceeded the proper level of authority. In addition to an intent to ratify, certain other conditions must be fulfilled for ratification to be valid. The principal must have the capacity to ratify and have knowledge of all the material facts. The act to be ratified must be legal and be done on behalf of the principal. Moreover, the ratification must apply to the entire act of the agent, and ratification must occur before the third party withdraws. The principal cannot accept the benefits of an unauthorized act and then refuse to accept the obligations that are part of it. The principal becomes bound as though the agent had authority to act.

Agency by Statute In some cases, an agency is created and agency authority is bestowed upon employees by statutory law. Such authority carries with it the risk of liability for the illegal activities outlined by the statute. For example, the courts have held that some individual employees, such as corporate executives, who act as agents on behalf of the corporation, can be held personally liable for violations of the Fair Labor Standards Act. In contrast, despite the fact that the word *agent* is included in the statutory definition of *employee* the courts have held that individual employees are not liable for violations of the Americans with Disabilities Act or for violations of Title VII of the Civil Rights Act.

The Appointment of Subagents

Agents are appointed by principals because of their assumed fitness to perform some particular job. Because principals rely on the agent's personal skill and integrity, they do not ordinarily give agents the power to delegate someone else to do the job they have agreed to do. Should an agent delegate authority without authorization, the acts of the subagent do not impose any obligation or liability on the principal to third parties. In some instances, the agent is permitted to delegate authority, even if the agency agreement does not contain an express power of delegation. Such an intention may be implied from the nature of the employment or custom and usage. A real estate broker, for example, has the implied authority to delegate authority to salespersons. The nature of the business is such that it is presumed that the principal (seller) contemplates that the authority given to the agent (broker) would be exercised through the broker's agents (subagents). The purpose of agency cannot be criminal or contrary to public policy. In addition, some acts must be performed in person, not delegated to an agent. Nondelegable acts include, but are not limited to, voting, serving on juries, testifying in court, making a will, and holding public office. However, forms required by law, such as tax returns and license applications, may be executed by an agent provided that the identity of the principal, as well as the identity and capacity of the agent, are clearly shown.

quick quiz 22-2

1. A disclosed principal is one whose identity is known by third parties dealing with that principal's agent.   true | false
2. A special agent is a person who is given broad authority to act on behalf of the principal in conducting the bulk of the principal's business activity on a daily basis.   true | false
3. A factor, or common merchant, is a special agent who is employed to sell merchandise consigned for that purpose.   true | false

22-3 Duties in Agency Law

The agency relationship between agent and principal establishes rights and obligations that may be expressed in the agreement or merely implied. An individual who acts as agent for another has a fiduciary relationship with the principal. This relationship implies the placement of trust and confidence in the agent that the agent will serve the principal's interests before all others. Thus, an agent may not enter any agency transaction in which the agent has a personal interest. An agent must also not take a position in conflict with the interest of the principal.

Agent's Obligations to a Principal

In compliance with the agency contract and the fiduciary relationship, various obligations are imposed on the agent. These obligations generally involve the following duties:

1. To obey all instructions and be loyal to the principal.
2. To exercise reasonable judgment, prudence, and skill and account for all property.
3. To perform work personally and communicate fully with the principal.

Obedience and Loyalty The agent, whether being paid or acting gratuitously, must obey all reasonable and legal instructions issued by the principal that relate to the agency agreement. In obeying the instructions of the principal, the agent is duty-bound to remain within the scope of authority (i.e., the range of acts authorized by the principal). For example, if the agent were to sell equipment to a third party in violation of the principal's instructions, the agent would be liable for any injury suffered by the principal. An agent may not engage in any activity that would result in a conflict of interest with the business of the principal. This duty of loyalty implies strict and continuing faithfulness to the principal's best interests at all times. Hence, the agent must resist any temptation to use acquired confidential information to advance the agent's own interest at the expense of the principal's.

Judgment, Prudence, Skill, and the Duty to Account Agents imply that they possess the required knowledge, training, and skill to perform and carry out their agency obligations properly with reasonable care and diligence. Unless an agent claims to be an expert, the principal is entitled to expect that the agent has the degree of skill commonly displayed by others employed in similar work. An expert, such as a person in a profession requiring specific education and a special license, must use the expert judgment, prudence, and skill possessed by others who have been admitted to those professions. Whether an expert or not, the agent may be liable to the principal for losses resulting from personal neglect or incompetence.

The agent has a duty to keep a separate account of the principal's funds. Whatever money the agent receives during and as a result of the agency relationship is held in trust for the principal. An accounting must be given to the principal within a reasonable period of time after money or property is received or disbursed. Money collected by the agent must be held separate from funds belonging to the agent. If deposited in a bank, the money must be deposited in a separate account and so identified that a trust is apparent. Failure to keep such funds separate is known as *commingling*, and the agent may be held personally liable for any resulting losses.

Personal Service and Communication The agency relationship is usually one involving an agreement for personal services. In the absence of the authority to do so, an agent may not delegate duties to others unless such duties are purely mechanical in nature and require no particular knowledge, training, skill, or responsibility. The agent is duty-bound to keep the principal fully informed of all facts that materially affect the subject matter of the agency because the law assumes that if an agent receives either notice or information, it was also communicated to the principal. Therefore, the rights and liabilities of the principal to any third party are the same as if the principal had personally received the notice or information that come to the agent's attention when acting within the agent's scope of authority.

EXAMPLE 22-3: A Commitment to Communicate

Marcy Magliozzi instructed Barbara Harrison to purchase a particular furnished house on Catawba Island for her. While examining the final contract, Harrison discovered that several thousand books that were in the house would not be considered as part of the "furnishings" that went along with the sale. Despite this exception, Harrison completed the purchase for Magliozzi. A little later, Magliozzi discovered that the books did not come with the "furnished" house. Magliozzi demanded that the contract be voided. Because in the course of carrying out her duties and before buying the house, Harrison learned that the books were not part of the deal, the law assumes that Magliozzi had the same information. She cannot use the loss of the books as the basis for voiding the contract.

Remedies Available to the Principal Remedies are always available when an agent fails to observe a duty owed to a principal. For instance, the principal may do one or more of the following:

1. Terminate the agent's contract of employment.
2. Withhold compensation otherwise due the agent.
3. Recover profit the agent made in violation of agency obligations.
4. Recover money or property gained or held by the agent to which the principal is entitled.
5. Restrain the agent from continuing to breach the agency obligations.
6. Recover damages from the agent for breach of the contract of employment or assessed against the principal for the agent's wrongdoing.
7. Rescind a contract entered into by the agent based on an improper relationship between the agent and the third party.

The Principal's Obligations to the Agent

The agreement between a principal and an agent creates the duties the principal owes to the agent. Even when the agency agreement is silent, there are implied obligations owed to the agent. Among the principal's actual and implied duties are the following obligations:

1. To compensate the agent.
2. To reimburse the agent.
3. To indemnify the agent.
4. To cooperate with the performance of the agent's duties.

Compensation The principal is under a duty to pay an agent an agreed amount or the fair value for work or services that the agent performs within the scope of authority or employment. In addition, the principal must make salary deductions and payments to the government as are required by law. All states have statutes that provide for the enforcement of the payment of wages and that place penalties on delinquent employers. The agent may not recover compensation for illegal services, even though they were rendered at the request of the principal. The agent may also forfeit rights to compensation when the agent breaches his or her duties to the principal. If an agency relationship does not result from a contract, it is a **gratuitous agency**, and the agent is a **gratuitous agent**.

Reimbursement The principal is obligated to reimburse the agent for any reasonable expenses incurred while working on the principal's behalf and within the scope of the agent's authority or employment. The agent cannot recover for expenses due to the agent's own negligence. Recovery is also barred when expenses incurred by an agent are unnecessary or unreasonable in the discharge of the agency.

Indemnification Agents are also entitled to **indemnification** (i.e., payment for loss or damage suffered) if they incur a loss or are damaged as a result of a request made by the principal. The obligation to pay for the agent's personal loss or damage, which may occur in the future or is already suffered, is avoidable if the loss or damage results from an action the agent knew to be illegal or from the agent's negligence. Public policy also requires employers to indemnify employees for personal injury sustained in the course of employment, except for self-inflicted injury or intoxication. State workers' compensation laws hold that the cost of paying for such injury should be a part of the operating expense of the business.

Cooperation with the Agent The principal, having granted the agent the duty to perform certain tasks, must not interfere with the performance of those tasks. Should the principal make the agent's job difficult or impossible, the principal has breached the duty of cooperation.

Remedies Available to the Agent The remedies of an agent against a principal are based on the principal's breach of express or implied contract obligations. Where appropriate, the agent has the option of exerting one or more of the agent's rights:

1. Leave the principal's employ.
2. Recover damages for the principal's breach of contract.
3. Recover the value of services rendered.
4. Obtain reimbursement for payments made for the principal.
5. Secure indemnity for personal liability sustained while performing an authorized act for the principal.

quick quiz 22-3

1. In obeying the instructions of the principal, the agent is duty-bound to remain within the scope of authority.	true | false
2. When the agency agreement is silent, there are no implied obligations owed to the agent.	true | false
3. If an agency relationship does not result from a contract, it is a gratuitous agency and the agent is a gratuitous agent.	true | false

22-4 A Final View of Agency Law

The agency agreement may be terminated by the acts of one or both parties to the agreement or by operation of the law. When the authority of the agent is terminated, the agent loses the right to act for the principal. The only exception to the rule that either the principal or the agent may terminate an agency relationship at any time arises in the situation of an agency coupled with an interest. The principal has the duty to inform certain third parties when an agency relationship is terminated.

Termination by the Acts of the Parties

Both principal and agent may terminate an agency relationship by their acts. Most agency relationships are terminated when the parties have satisfied their contractual obligations. The relationship also may be discharged by mutual consent, as well as when either the agent or the principal breaches the agency contract.

Fulfillment of Purpose or Mutual Agreement When the purpose for which the agency was created is achieved, the agency is terminated. If an agent is appointed for a specific period of time, the arrival of that time terminates the agency. In short, when the contract is performed, the agency is at an end. The parties to an agency relationship may terminate it at any time by agreement, even before the contract is fully performed. This is referred to as mutual agreement.

Revocation or Renunciation The principal or the agent usually has the power (if not necessarily the right) at any time to terminate the agency relationship. Acting with or without cause, the principal may terminate the agreement by simply recalling the agent's authority to act (i.e., **revocation**). Even though the principal's act of revocation may be a violation of contract, the agent's authority is terminated. Agents may terminate by simply giving notice to principals that they are quitting (i.e., **renunciation**). Unless the terms of the agency agreement permit termination "at will," agents and principals who end their relationship may be liable for damages resulting from the violation of the contractual promise. Nevertheless, one cannot be forced to work against one's will.

Completion by Operation of Law

The termination of the agency agreement by operation of the law results when significant events make the continuance of the agency impossible or impractical. Termination by operation of the law occurs in instances of death, insanity, bankruptcy, or impossibility of performance.

Death or Insanity The death of the principal or agent ordinarily terminates the agency relationship automatically, even without notice. Hence, any agreement made between the agent and a third party is ineffective upon the death of the principal. Although the agent may be liable to third parties for breach of the implied warranty that the agent has authority to act, third parties cannot recover from the estate of the principal because the contract is not binding. The insanity of either the principal or the agent usually terminates the agent's authority. In some states, however, an agent has power to bind a principal who has become insane if the principal has not been legally declared insane and if the third party had no knowledge of the insanity. If the principal is only incapacitated briefly, the agent's authority may be suspended rather than terminated.

Durable Power of Attorney Generally, an agency relationship is terminated upon the incapacity of the principal. However, the trend in many states has been to enact statutes that permit the creation of a durable power of attorney. Under such statutes, a person can appoint an agent by signing a written durable power of attorney. A **durable power of attorney** preserves the authority of an agent should the principal become incapacitated. In some cases, the durable power of attorney may even activate the agent's power once the principal is incapacitated. The durable power of attorney should contain the following words: "This power of attorney shall not be affected by subsequent disability or incapacity of the principal," or "This power of attorney shall become effective upon the disability or incapacity of the principal." The Uniform Law Commission also developed the **Uniform Durable Power of Attorney Act**. Many state legislatures are in the process of adopting either a complete or a modified version of this act and so it is best to check the most up-to-date version of the law in your state.

Bankruptcy In the event of the bankruptcy of the principal, the agency is ended. All of the principal's ordinary contracts are canceled, and title to the principal's property passes to a trustee for the benefit of creditors. The bankruptcy of the agent sometimes terminates the agency for the same reasons, but the principal and the agent may continue the relationship if they choose. Usually, the bankruptcy of the agent does not prevent the agent from doing the job in the regular way, provided the agent is not using personal funds.

Impossibility of Performance An agency relationship terminates when it is impossible for the agent to accomplish the purpose of the agency for any reason. Destruction of a house by fire ends the real estate broker's agency to sell the property. A broker authorized to sell a principal's boat loses that authority if the boat is destroyed in a storm. An agent's loss of a license required to conduct the principal's business ends the authority of the agent. A change in the law that causes authorized acts to be illegal terminates the agent's authority. The authority of the agent is also terminated by notice or knowledge of a change in business conditions or values that substantially affects the agent's exercise of authority. For example, an agent hired to sell property at a specified price would have that authority terminated when the value of the property increases substantially because of zoning changes.

Agency Coupled with an Interest

The only exception to the rule that either the principal or the agent may terminate an agency relationship at any time arises in the situation of an agency coupled with an interest. An **agency coupled with an interest** is an agency agreement in which the agent is given an interest in the subject matter of the agency, in addition to compensation for services rendered to the principal. The concept protects the agent's interest in specific property belonging to the principal. The principal lacks power to revoke agencies of this kind without the consent of the agent.

EXAMPLE 22-4: An Agency Coupled with a Lot of Interest

James Heilman borrowed $9,000 from the National Security Specialty Bank of Louisville. He put up as security 200 shares of stock in the Actors Theatre Group of Louisville. Heilman then authorized the bank to sell the shares to satisfy the loan obligation should he default on that loan. In the event that it becomes necessary to sell the stock, the bank serves as Heilman's agent. Heilman may not terminate the agency except by paying off the $9,000 loan (plus interest, as per his agreement with the National Security Specialty Bank).

Notice of Termination to Third Parties

The principal has the duty to notify third parties with whom the agent has done business when the agency relationship has been terminated by the act of the parties. The exception to this rule is when the agency is terminated by operation of the law. In such instances, the principal is not required to notify anyone, and no subsequent act by the agent will bind the principal. The type of notice required depends on how the former business relations were conducted. When the third party has given credit to the principal through the agent, the third party is entitled to actual notice of termination of authority, which may be done by regular mail or by telephone. The safest way, however, is by certified mail because the Post Office provides a receipt of the notice. A notice in the classified advertisement section in a newspaper of general circulation is sufficient for third parties who have never given credit but who have had cash transactions with the agent or know that other persons have dealt with the principal through the agent. The failure to give third parties appropriate notice would make the principal liable on contracts made by a former agent with third parties.

Cyber-Agency Statutes

The Uniform Computer Information Transactions Act (UCITA) is valuable because it clearly establishes the nature of an *electronic agent*. According to UCITA, an **electronic agent** (also referred to as a *cyber-agent* or *e-agent*) can be characterized as a computer program that acts without human intervention to begin an activity, answer cyber-messages, deliver or accept *electronic mail*, or enter electronic contracts as a representative of an individual who does not intervene in the action taken by the electronic agent at the actual time of the electronic agent's activity. It is clear then that a bot (*robot, shopping bot, cyberbot,* or *e-bot*) that searches cyberspace for the lowest price in a contract, sifts through the Internet for the best accommodations, hunts cyberspace for the most economical plan, or spontaneously responds to a bidding process during an electronic auction is an electronic agent. The UCITA makes it clear that a principal, now termed an *electronic principal*, who places authority in the "hands" of an electronic agent will be liable for the electronic contracts entered by that electronic agent, even if the electronic principal remains ignorant of what the electronic agent has done because the electronic principal either ignores or forgets about the automated process.

Another model act, the Uniform Electronic Transactions Act (UETA), has legitimized the use of electronic agents by certifying that contracts made by electronic agents have the same binding effect as contracts created by human agents. The net effect of these provisions is to guarantee that a company that has used an electronic agent to receive and process an order sent by an electronic agent will not be able to deny the effectiveness of that electronic contract. The provisions also state that once an individual has received an e-mail, he or she is considered to have received notice of an e-contract, even if that person ignores or trashes the e-mail without opening or reading it. The UETA also says that e-agents must be programmed to give the other party a confirmation that the electronic contract has been entered. Otherwise, the e-contract is voidable by that party.

Agency in the Health Care Setting

In the 21st century, health care issues have increasingly crossed paths with, and sometimes even collided with, the law—and not always with favorable results. Even putting the problem of national health care legislation aside, other issues such as the mapping of the human genome, the harvesting of human organs, the cloning of human beings, the use DNA evidence in civil and criminal trials, and the prolongation of life by artificial means complicate things that used to be simple and straightforward, things such as our understanding of life and our definition of death. Sometimes these issues surface in science fiction novels, such as *The Genesis Code*, by Christopher Forrest, in which mapping the human genome leads to a new understanding of the nature of humanity; *Joshua: Son of None* by Nancy Freedman, in which a clone of John F. Kennedy relives JFK's political life with tragic consequences; or *Unisave* by Axel Madsen, in which an overpopulated world is controlled by a UN program that enforces birth and death quotas. Sometimes these issues surface in new legal devices designed to deal with the unintended consequences of changes in medical science. The latest of these devices to impact agency law are anatomical gift instruments, living wills, health care powers of attorney, and DNR notifications.

An **anatomical gift** is a donation made in advance, usually by notification on a state driver's license or a state ID, that indicates a person's desire to donate all or part of his or her body after death for the purpose of transplantation, treatment, research, or training. As noted, an anatomical gift becomes effective on death. To clarify the circumstances under which an anatomical gift becomes effective, many state legislatures have enacted statutes that define death. A typical **death statute** states that "an individual is dead if the individual has sustained either irreversible cessation of the circulatory and respiratory functions or irreversible cessation of all functions of the brain, including the brain stem, as determined in accordance with accepted medical standards" (Ohio Rev Code Section 2133.02). Some states permit individuals to challenge the state's legislative definition of death. However, such challenges must be based on religious grounds, generally under the Free Exercise Clause of the First Amendment and/or under the state's version Religion Freedom Restoration Act. [See: Kristin M. Lenhart, "Advance Medical Directives: Drafting Tips and Practical Advice," *The Ohio State Bar Association Annual Forum* (August 2017).]

A **living will** is an instrument that declares an individual's desires in relation to the withholding or the withdrawal of life-prolongation treatments. Most living will declarations include the power to end nutrition and hydration treatments. However, to terminate such treatments, the individual must be in a terminal condition or in a permanently unconscious state. To clarify the meaning of terminal condition and permanently unconscious state, most state legislatures have enacted statutes that define these terms. A typical definition of **terminal condition** states that a "(t)erminal condition means an irreversible, incurable, and untreatable condition caused by disease, illness or injury from which, to a reasonable degree of medical certainty as determined in accordance with reasonable medical standards by a declarant's attending physician and one other physician who has examined the declarant, there is no recovery, AND death is likely to occur within a relatively short time if life-sustaining treatment is not administered" (Ohio Rev Code Section 2133.01 AA). A typical definition of **permanently unconscious state** says, a "(p)ermanently unconscious state means a state of permanently unconsciousness in a declarant that to a reasonable degree of medical certainty as determined in accordance with reasonable medical standards by a declarant's attending physician and one other physician who has examined the declarant, is characterized by both an irreversible unawareness of one's being and environment, AND total loss of cerebral cortical functioning resulting in the declarant having no capacity to experience pain or suffering" (Ohio Rev Code Section 2133.01 (U)). Generally, the declarant must sign the living will before it becomes legally valid. In the alternative, a duly authorized agent can sign the instrument. Two people must witness the signing. In the alternative, the will can be notarized. It must also be dated. [See: Lenhart.]

A **durable health care power of attorney** is a document that is made by an adult, who is mentally competent, which empowers the principal's agent to decide issues of health care for the principal when that principal has lost the innate ability to decide on health care issues for himself or herself. These decisions include the ability to give informed consent to dangerous, intrusive, and/or painful procedures. The agent also has the power to withhold or to withdraw that informed consent at any time, just as if he or she were he principal. Often a durable health care power of attorney will also empower the agent to have immediate access to the principal's health care records. It is possible for the principal to terminate the health care power of attorney any time that the principal is still competent. A **DNR identification** is a document, a form, a necklace, a bracelet, or other identification technique that indicates that the declarant has previously implemented a desire not to undergo CPR or other life prolonging activities, as specified by statutory law. In the alternative, a DNR identification may also indicate that the DNR has been authorized by the declarant's attending physician. A DNR identification must be signed by a physician or by another health care professional designated by statute as authorized to issue such orders. A DNR identification may also be appended to a living will. [See: Lenhart.)

quick quiz 22-4

1. Most agency relationships are terminated when the parties have satisfied their contractual obligations.   true | false
2. The termination of the agency agreement can never happen solely by operation of law.   true | false
3. The principal has the duty to notify third parties with whom the agent has done business when the agency relationship has been terminated by the act of the parties.   true | false

Summary

22.1 Agency is the legal fiduciary relationship that exists when the principal authorizes the agent to represent the principal. The courts are often called upon to distinguish among relationships between principal and agent, employer and employee, master and servant, and proprietor and independent contractor. The terms *master* (employer) and *servant* (employee) are used when questions of tort liability arise. Even though all people are responsible for their own tortuous conduct, there are times when the law will hold not only the actual tortfeasor but also the person who engaged the tortfeasor liable for the tort. The name given to this type of liability is vicarious liability. Other liability questions include negligent hiring, negligent retention, negligent supervision, contract liability, criminal liability, statutory liability, sovereign immunity, clergy malpractice, and charitable immunity.

22.2 Any person legally capable of entering into a contract may be a principal. There are three kinds of principals—disclosed, undisclosed, or partially disclosed. Anyone may be appointed an agent. Agents are commonly classified as general agents, special agents, factor, and *del credere* agents. A principal is liable on all contracts that a general or special agent enters into, as long as the agent acts with the authority of the principal. An agent's authority may arise expressly from the written or spoken words of the principal to the agent or implied from the agent's reasonable effort to understand the meaning of the principal's words describing what the agent is to do. Apparent authority results from actions by the principal that give a third party reason to believe that an agent has the authority to act for the principal. Ratification by the principal of an unauthorized act by another person does not create agency, but it has the effect of agency.

22.3 As a result of the fiduciary relationship, the agent owes the principal the duty of obedience to instructions; loyalty; reasonable judgment, prudence, and skill; accounting for agency money and property; personal performance of agency work; and communication of all facts that affect the subject matter of the agency. In addition to the duties that the principal owes to the agent under the agency agreement, there are certain implied obligations. These obligations include the duty to compensate the agent, reimburse the agent for authorized expenses incurred, indemnify the agent for losses caused by the agency relationship through no fault of the agent, and comply with the terms of the agency contract.

22.4 An agency agreement generally terminates when its purposes are accomplished. The agency may also terminate at any time by the principal's revocation of the agent's authority or by the agent's renunciation of the agency relationship. If either party dies, becomes insane, goes bankrupt, or ceases to be qualified to act, the agency relationship is terminated by operation of the law. The principal has the duty to notify third parties with whom the agent has done business when the agency relationship has been terminated by acts of the parties. Actual notice is required when the third party has given credit to the principal through the agent. A public notice in a newspaper of general circulation is sufficient for third parties who have never given credit but who have had cash transactions with the agent.

Key Terms

agency, 609
agency coupled with an interest, 630
agent, 609
apparent authority, 624
anatomical gift, 631
charitable immunity, 620
consensual, 610
control test, 611
death statute, 632
del credere agent, 623
disclosed principal, 622
DNR identification, 632
durable health care power of attorney, 632
durable power of attorney, 629
economic realities test, 618
electronic agent, 631
express authority, 623
factor, 622
general agent, 622
gratuitous agency, 627
gratuitous agent, 627
implied authority, 624
indemnification, 628
independent contractor, 610
lingering apparent authority, 624
living will, 632
master, 610
negligent hiring, 615
negligent retention, 615
negligent supervision, 615
nondelegable duty, 615
partially disclosed principal, 622
permanently unconscious state, 632
principal, 609
proprietor, 610
ratification, 624
renunciation, 629
revocation, 629
scope of authority, 626
scope of employment, 613
servant, 610
sovereign immunity, 618
special agent, 622
sui generis, 609
terminal condition, 632
third party, 610
undisclosed principal, 622
Uniform Durable Power of Attorney Act, 629
vicarious liability, 611

Questions for Review and Discussion

1. What is an agency relationship?
2. What is vicarious liability?
3. What are the different types of principals?
4. What are the different types of agents?
5. What is express authority? Implied authority? Apparent authority?
6. What are the duties of an agent to the principal?
7. What are the duties that a principal has in relation to an agent?
8. How can an agency relationship be terminated?
9. Who is entitled to a notice that an agency has ended?
10. What are the major electronic agency laws?

Cases for Analysis

1. During batting practice in the batting cages at Howland High School, while under the supervision of baseball coach Thomas Eschman, Jeffrey Elston was injured when a ball hit a protective screen, ricocheted, and struck him in the head. Elston was life-flighted to Cleveland by helicopter, where he was treated for head injuries at Rainbow Babies and Children's Hospital. Later, Elston's parents brought suit against the high school. The school pointed to a state statute that granted state subdivisions, such as the school district, sovereign immunity. Elston's parents argued that the actions under scrutiny involved a school-related activity located on government-owned property, which clearly made it one of the exceptions to the sovereign immunity rule. The school district defended itself by arguing that the coach's actions not only represented a legitimate exercise of his professional discretion, but were also carried out in good faith and were free from wanton, reckless, or malicious conduct. Should the school district escape liability here? Explain. [See: *Elston v. Howland Local*

Schools, 113 Ohio St.3d 314 (Ohio Supreme Court).]

2. A delivery truck driver who worked for the *Evening Star* in Washington, DC, was on his route when he was commanded by a police officer to follow a traffic violator to apprehend him. The police officer then jumped onto the side of the truck and held on for the duration of the chase. During the high-speed pursuit, Balinovic was injured when the truck collided with his car. Balinovic wanted to sue both the driver and the *Evening Star* under the theory of vicarious liability. Would vicarious liability apply here? Was the driver a servant of the *Evening Star*? Was the driver operating within the scope of employment? Explain. [See: *Balinovic v. Evening Star Newspaper Co.*, 113 F.2d 505 (D.C. Cir.).]

3. Janet Young worked in an administrative capacity for the International Brotherhood of Locomotive Engineers. She was given a 10-year contract by John Sytsma, the president of the union. The president regularly engaged in hiring union employees without consulting with either the executive committee or the advisory board of the union. In addition, the president entered into other contracts on behalf of the union. Although these powers were not specified in the constitution, the union knew that he dealt with the hiring of employees and that he routinely entered nonemployment contracts on behalf of the union. Sometime after Sytsma was defeated in a reelection bid, Larry McFather, the new president, discharged Young. McFather argued that Sytsma did not have the capacity to enter a 10-year employment contract with Young because the authority to do so was not specified in the union's constitution. In addition, McFather pointed out that the contract had been entered during the union's convention, during which the power to govern the union falls to the delegates at the convention. In response, Young argued that the past practices of the union led her to the reasonable belief that the president had the power to grant her the employment contract. She also argued that even though the power to hire employees was not in the union constitution, the power to do so was implied by the powers of the president to preside over the union's administrative matters. Is Young correct on either of these points? Explain. [See: *Young v. International Brotherhood of Locomotive Engineers*, 683 N.E.2d 420 (OH).]

4. Mularchuk was employed as a part-time reserve police officer for the borough of Keansburg, New Jersey. He was never given any training, and he was not required to submit to any training with respect to the revolver he carried. A quarrel arose between McAndrew, who had car trouble, and a tow-truck driver whom McAndrew had called for assistance. Mularchuk proceeded to make arrests and, in the course of events, shot and seriously injured McAndrew. Was the borough of Keansburg liable to McAndrew under the doctrine of *respondeat superior*? Explain. [See: *McAndrew v. Mularchuk*, 162 A.2d 820 (NJ).]

5. Food Caterers Inc. had a franchise agreement with Chicken Delight Inc. Carfiro was employed by Food Caterers to deliver hot chicken bearing the trademark "Chicken Delight." While making a delivery, Carfiro was involved in an accident that killed McLaughlin. In a suit naming Chicken Delight, the franchiser, as defendant, the McLaughlin estate argued that Carfiro was an agent of Chicken Delight because Carfiro was acting for the benefit of the company. There was no evidence, however, that Carfiro was hired, paid, instructed by, or even known by Chicken Delight. The decision was for whom, and why? [See: *Estate of McLaughlin v. Chicken Delight, Inc.*, 321 A.2d 456 (CT).]

6. While Elliot was an inmate at the state-run Chillicothe Correctional Institution, he was hit in the face by Turner, a corrections officer at the institution and therefore a state employee. Elliot brought a lawsuit against the state under the doctrine of *respondeat superior*. The state argued that because Turner had acted recklessly in striking Elliot, his actions were outside the scope of his employment. Therefore, the state concluded, the court should dismiss Elliot's claim against it. Were Turner's actions outside the scope of his employment as a prison guard? Explain. [See: *Elliot v. Ohio Department of Rehabilitation and Correction*, 637 N.E.2d 106 (OH).]

7. On April 11, Fred Chapman discharged Anna Savant, the manager of his store, the Super Electronic Supply Outlet. On April 12, Chapman called *The Barnard Crossings Chronicle* and had a notice printed to the effect that Savant no longer worked for Super. On that same day, Savant ordered 12 electronic games, two computers, two laser printers, a fax machine, and a car stereo from the Global Electronic Components Corporation. As she had frequently done in the past while acting as manager for Super, she told George Pierce, the

owner of Global, to send the bill to Super. Pierce did so. Savant then kept these items for herself. Pierce did not have actual notice of Savant's discharge until April 28, when he saw the notice as he was throwing out some old newspapers. Savant could not be located, so Pierce brought suit against Chapman and Super. Chapman argued that the newspaper notice was sufficient to warn Pierce not to deal with Savant. How would the court rule? Explain.

8. Stahl was having trouble with her Volkswagen. She brought it to the service station of LePage, where it was examined and the trouble was diagnosed. LePage informed Stahl that he would not be able to do the work but that his employee, Donley, wanted to take the job on his own and could make use of the garage facilities for this purpose. A new engine was required, and Donley installed the wrong engine. The entire job had to be done over at a cost of hundreds of dollars. Stahl brought suit against LePage. She argued that she should be allowed to recover against LePage for the misdeed of Donley because Donley had apparent authority to act as LePage's agent. LePage disputed this claim, arguing that the facts did not warrant a finding of agency under any theory. How did the court find in this dispute? Why? [See: *Stahl v. LePage*, 352 A.2d 682 (VT).]

9. Castle Fabrics Inc. sold fabric to Fortune Manufacturers Inc. A dispute arose as to the acceptability of the fabric received, and Fortune returned the fabric to Castle for full credit. Castle gave Fortune only partial credit and sued Fortune for recovery of its loss. In court, Fortune showed a credit memorandum from a Castle employee indicating that Fortune would be given full credit for the fabric. Although it was within the regular responsibility of the Castle employee to send the memorandum, on this occasion, management had specifically instructed the employee not to send one. Fortune argued that the employee was an agent of Castle and thus chargeable with any mistake the agent made. Castle claimed it was not chargeable with the action of its employee because the employee had disobeyed specific instructions not to send the memorandum. The judgment was for whom and why? [See: *Castle Fabrics, Inc., v. Fortune Furniture Mfrs. Inc.*, 459 F.Supp. 409 (N.D. MS).]

10. Lloyd, an attorney, was appointed guardian of Ernest Parker. Two years later, he was appointed guardian of Virginia Hockenberry. That same year, he agreed to represent David Isaac in the purchase of a plot of real estate from Debra Taylor. On several occasions, Lloyd deposited client settlement checks into his own account. The funds received were therefore commingled with the funds in his personal account. He later used these funds to pay for his student loans, his automobile loan, his insurance, his taxes, his outstanding credit card bills, and his barber. Identify the duties that Lloyd has violated in relation to his principals, Parker, Hockenberry, and Isaac. [See: *Office of Disciplinary Counsel v. Lloyd*, 643 N.E.2d 1086 (OH).]

11. Ross needed a grinding mill and consulted Clifton, who on occasion repaired such mills but did not sell them. Ross and Clifton together selected a mill from a catalog, which Clifton happened to have on hand, that they decided would meet Ross's purposes. Ross instructed Clifton to order the mill they had selected, and Clifton did so in his own name and with his own money. When the mill arrived, Ross refused to accept it, stating that it was too small and would not do the job he intended it to do. Clifton brought suit to recover the amount he had spent. The judgment was for whom and why? [See: *Clifton v. Ross*, 28 S.W. 1085 (AR).]

Design Elements. The Opening Case: ©Sharpstock/Alamy; A Classic Case: ©Evlakhov Valeriy/ Shutterstock

quick quiz Answers

22-1	22-2	22-3	22-4
1. T	1. T	1. T	1. T
2. F	2. F	2. F	2. F
3. T	3. T	3. T	3. T

Chapter 23

Employment Law

23-1 The Employment Relationship
Employment at Will • Wrongful Discharge • After-Acquired Evidence Defense • Retaliation and Constructive Discharge • Job Qualifications and Interview Questions

23-2 Laws Regulating Employment Conditions
Health and Safety Laws • Fair Labor Standards Act • Identity and Employment Eligibility

23-3 Worker Benefits
Social Security • Unemployment Insurance • Workers' Compensation • Pension Plan Regulation • Family and Medical Leave Regulation

23-4 Equal Employment Opportunity
Civil Rights Legislation • Age Discrimination in Employment Act • Uniformed Services Employment and Reemployment Rights Act • Americans with Disabilities Act • Genetic Information Nondiscrimination Act • The Whistleblower Acts • Anti-Retaliation Safeguards

23-5 Social Media Policies
The Social Media Culture • The Nature of a Social Media Policy • The Hazards Involved in Social Media

THE OPENING CASE Round 1

"Words do not choose among their company or discriminate among the people who use them."—Dejan Stojanovic

One of the basic principles of jurisprudence is that the legislature and the court have two very different jobs to perform. The legislature makes statutory law, and the court interprets that law. On the surface, this principle appears to be simple and straightforward. It is neither, a fact made clear in the case of *Kimberly Hively v. Ivy Tech Community College* (IVY). The case involves the professional aspirations of a community college instructor named Kimberly Hively. For about five years or so, Hively taught as an adjunct faculty member at Ivy Tech Community College, the state-wide community college of Indiana. Several times during her tenure there, she applied for a full-time position at Ivy Tech. Each time, her application was rejected. Eventually she began to suspect that her rejection was based not on her academic credentials or her experience, but on her sexual orientation. Later, as if to add insult to injury, officials at Ivy Tech also notified Hively that her adjunct contract would not be renewed. That was, apparently, the last straw.

Accordingly, Hively promptly filed a complaint with Equal Employment Opportunity Commission (EEOC). The EEOC processed her claim and issued a right-to-sue letter, which empowered Hively to bring a discrimination lawsuit on her own behalf under the Civil Rights Act of 1964.

As a result, Hively filed this suit, claiming that she had been unlawfully discriminated against because of her sexual orientation. When Ivy Tech was notified of the lawsuit, it immediately filed a motion to dismiss the case for failure to state a claim for which relief can be granted, a motion that, in the federal court system, is generally referred to as a Rule 12 (b) (6) motion. Ivy Tech argued that while the Civil Rights Act of 1964 does include a prohibition against discrimination based on sex, it does not authorize a claim of discrimination based on sexual orientation. The trial court looked at the motion, read the statute, researched the appropriate line of precedent, and ruled that Ivy Tech was correct. The case was then heard by a three-judge panel in the

Seventh Circuit Court of Appeals. The panel agreed with trial court and affirmed the dismissal. Despite this, a majority of the judges in the Seventh Circuit voted to sit *en banc* and review the decision of the three-judge panel.

The main issue before the court was whether the prohibition in the Civil Right Act of 1964 against discrimination based on sex also includes a prohibition against discrimination based on sexual orientation. The court began its analysis by explaining the various options a court has in its interpretation of a statute. Although the court outlines four different interpretive techniques, these four can be reduced to two theories: textualism and pragmatism. In general, the idea behind textualism is for judges to interpret statutes by their words and their word alone. The intent of textualism is to have judges bypass the generally biased and self-serving explanations found in legislative histories and, instead, rely upon the meaning of the words that the legislators actually wrote and placed in the text of the statute in question. In contrast, pragmatism involves an approach by judges that considers the consequences of a decision to be the single most important guideline in the development of that decision. In applying a pragmatic approach, the judge must attempt to get into the mind of the framers of that law and, in doing so, see how those framers would respond to the modern circumstances in which the judge finds himself or herself. Moreover, in making this determination, the judge must not focus alone on a single interpretation but must consider multiple interpretations in order to sort out the one that makes the most sense. The court in the Ivy Tech case elected to use the pragmatic approach in its interpretation of the Civil Rights Act of 1964, at least as it refers to discrimination based on sex. In a moment, the results of that interpretation. [See: *Kimberly Hively v. Ivy Tech Community College,* No. 15-1720 (2017).]

Opening Case Questions

1. What type of employment relationship did the plaintiff have with her employer? Explain.
2. What is at-will employment, and what does it have to do with this case? Explain.
3. What exceptions exist to employment at will? Explain.
4. What are the protected classes outlined in the Civil Right of 1964? Explain.
5. What result would be expected had the court used a textualist approach in its analysis? Explain.

Source: See: *Kimberly v. Hively v. Ivy Tech Community College*, No. 15-1720 (2017).

Learning Objectives

1. Explain the doctrine of employment at will.
2. Explain the contractual situations that fall outside employment at will.
3. Itemize the statutory situations that fall outside employment at will.
4. List the wrongful discharge exceptions to employment at will.
5. Explain the after-acquired evidence rule.
6. Explain the laws regulating employee working conditions.
7. Outline the laws providing worker benefits.
8. Explain the evolution of civil rights legislation.
9. Explain the protections provided by the Age Discrimination in Employment Act.
10. Explain the nature of and the need for a social media policy.

23-1 The Employment Relationship

An employment relationship may be formed in many ways. It may result from a simple oral agreement between two individuals, or it may be created by a detailed written contract that is finalized after complex negotiations between a union and a corporation. In the United

States, the dominant legal doctrine governing most employment relationships is employment at will. Many states, however, have come to the conclusion that employment at will must be changed to ensure justice for employees. For this reason, the at-will doctrine has been modified by the addition of several wrongful discharge exceptions. Nevertheless, employment at will remains the dominant doctrine in the United States.

Employment at Will

As noted, most jurisdictions in the United States still follow the doctrine of **employment at will**, which says that an employer can dismiss an employee at any time for any reason. Under this doctrine, the employer does not even have to give a reason for the firing. The rationale for the employment-at-will doctrine is that both the employer and the employee must be free to terminate the employment relationship at any time. This principle allows both parties to end an unsatisfactory relationship or take advantage of new opportunities. Unfortunately, the principle can be abused by unscrupulous employers. Therefore, the law has created certain exceptions to the general rule. These exceptions fall into three categories: contractual exceptions, statutory exceptions, and court-created wrongful discharge exceptions. Some of these exceptions modify parts of the at-will doctrine as it applies to an employee or a group of employees. Others actually eliminate an employee's at-will status.

Contractual Exceptions Individuals with unique abilities, special talents, or a highly specialized education often have the flexibility to negotiate their own **employment contracts**. Such individuals would not be affected by employment at will. Generally, such people are in demand and can thus be selective in the choice of employers. Professional athletes, established scientists, top business executives, famous entertainers, and well-known artists and writers belong in this category. In contrast to an individual employment contract, a **collective bargaining agreement** is negotiated by the employer and the labor union. A collective bargaining agreement is a contract that covers all issues related to employment. Such agreements, which are authorized under the National Labor Relations Act (NLRA), prevent the unfair discharge of employees. The employer needs some legitimate, employment-related reason, or just cause, for the release. In general, collective bargaining contracts also provide a grievance procedure. Under a **grievance procedure**, employees have the right to appeal any employer's decision that they think violates just cause. Often, economic conditions force layoffs or plant closings. When such events occur, some or all employees may lose their jobs. Still, most collective bargaining agreements provide a negotiated procedure by which such layoffs occur. In this way, employees are at least guaranteed that the layoffs will be handled in as fair a manner as possible.

Contractual Details For an employment contract to be valid and enforceable, it must contain some key details. These details add a level of certainty, honesty, and seriousness to the employment relationship that would not exist absent their presence in the agreement. The details include the following:

1. If appropriate, a provision that outlines the length of time that the employment relationship will last or a clear statement that, even given the establishment of a contract, the employment remains at will. This provision should also include an explanation of at-will employment and a list of the legal elements of employment at will.

2. A section that identifies the names of the parties to the contract and a clear identification of which party is the employer and which party the employee. Definitions of each (employer and employee) would also be appropriate.

3. A statement that demonstrates that the employer expects the employee to know and obey all rules, regulations, procedures, guidelines, and behavioral codes established by the employer.

4. For those employment arrangements that are not at will, the agreement should contain a specifically drawn list of all reasons for discipline, plus the nature and steps in any progressive disciplinary process, and for those employment arrangements that are not at will, an explicitly written list of all causes for discharge.

5. A clause that establishes the need for confidentiality during the entire employment period.

6. A section that explains the employee's access to and limitations in regard to all electronic systems including the employer's computer system, e-mail system, and so on. In addition, clauses must be included that stress the employer's ownership of those systems. The employer must also make certain that all employees understand that they have no expectation of privacy while working on those systems and that their work on those systems will be monitored and examined from time to time.

7. A statement that makes certain that the contract is assigned only to the employer's successors.

8. A provision specifying, in the event of a dispute, which jurisdiction will hear the case. This clause is usually called the choice-of-law provision.

9. A passage that indicates whether future disputes will be heard by an arbitrator, whether the arbitration will be binding, along with any and all additional details associated with a potential arbitration hearing.

10. An article that indicates the disposition of any and all tax issues associated with the employment agreement.

11. A section that covers the details of separation pay.

12. A segment that includes the details of compensation, including all stock option details, if applicable.

13. A policy outlining the procedure to be followed in any termination process, whether initiated by the employer or the employee, including the details of a termination interview, if applicable.

14. A statement explaining any change of control provisions.

15. A restrictive employment covenant (i.e., noncompetition agreement) that includes protection for trade secrets and other confidential information, as well as provisions that include the type of work that is prohibited, the location, and the duration of the covenant.

16. A section that includes any indemnification provisions.

17. An article that permits the employee to take the agreement, examine it, and seek the advice of a lawyer about the details of the agreement before committing to the employment arrangement.

[See: Pamela S. Krivda, "Employment Contracts: Post Termination Issues," Ohio State Bar Association Convention, Columbus, Ohio (May 2, 2014).]

THE OPENING CASE Round 2
"Words Do Not Choose among Their Company or Discriminate among the People Who Use Them."–Dejan Stojanovic

In the Opening Case, we learned the plaintiff, Kimberly Hively, was an adjunct instructor at Ivy Tech Community College in South Bend, Indiana. While in her position at Ivy Tech, she applied for several full-time openings at the college and was turned down each time. After her most recent application had been turned down, she was informed that her adjunct contract would not be renewed. At this point, Hively began to suspect that her rejection had nothing to do with her teaching experience or her academic credentials. Instead, she believed that it had to do with her sexual orientation. Accordingly, she filed a complaint with the Equal Employment Opportunity Commission (EEOC). When she received her right-to-sue letter, she brought a lawsuit against Ivy Tech under the Civil Rights Act of 1964, arguing that she had been discriminated against under the act because of her sexual orientation. Ivy Tech immediately filed a motion to dismiss based on Hively's failure to state a claim for which relief can be granted. The college's argument was simple: The Civil Rights Act of 1964 forbids employment discrimination based on race, color, creed, national origin, and sex. No mention is made of sexual orientation anywhere in the law. The trial court agreed with Ivy Tech and dismissed the case.

Hively went on to appeal the case to the Seventh Circuit Court of Appeals. Had she elected to take another route, Hively might have also brought an action in state court for wrongful discharge based on the fact that her adjunct contract had been terminated without cause. Of course, in that case, Ivy Tech would have again filed another motion to dismiss for failure to state a claim for which relief can be granted based on the fact that Hively was an at-will employee. Under the doctrine of at-will employment, an employer can discharge an employee at any time, for any reason—in fact, for no reason at all. That motion would almost certainly be granted unless Hively could show that her case fell under one of several exceptions to the at-will rule. For instance, the fact that she had a contract might have canceled her at-will status, at least for the duration of the contract. In this case, however, she was not actually fired. Instead, her contract was not renewed. Technically, then, once the semester ended, so did her contract and, along with that, her protection from outright release. Of course, if the faculty members at Ivy Tech have a collective bargaining agreement, then Hively would not be an at-will employee and could not be fired without just cause. This scenario is unlikely, however, because, while it is true that many states permit instructors at public colleges and universities to form unions, those unions rarely represent adjunct faculty members. This may be one reason Hively decided to pursue a discrimination claim with the EEOC and later in the federal courts [See: *Kimberly Hively v. Ivy Tech Community College*, No. 15-1720 (2017).]

Source: See: *Kimberly v. Hively v. Ivy Tech Community College*, No. 15-1720 (2017).

Employers with 100 or more full-time employees must provide a 60-day notice to the union, or if there is no union, to the individual employees, regarding any planned layoffs or closings.
©VGstockstudio/Shutterstock

Statutory Exceptions The federal government has passed legislation that has altered the at-will doctrine in order to add a level of fairness to employment law that would not exist absent that legislation. In particular, the government has been interested in protecting employees from discrimination based on race, color, creed, national origin, and gender. Later, the legislature also developed statutory law to prevent discrimination based on age, disability, and service in the armed forces. Finally, Congress stepped in to protect workers from the hardship that results when a firm decides to close or move a business.

Civil Rights Laws The employment-at-will rule that says that an employer can discharge an employee at any time for any reason or for no reason is also limited by civil rights legislation, such as the Equal Pay Act and the various incarnations of the Civil Rights Act, as well as the Age Discrimination in Employment Act, the Uniformed Services Employment and Reemployment Rights Act, the Americans with Disabilities Act, and the Genetic Information Nondiscrimination Act. When most people consider the development of civil rights legislation, they usually think about the Civil Rights Act of 1964. This view ignores the importance of the 19th-century civil rights acts that were passed by Congress in the wake of the Civil War and under the authority of the three Civil War amendments—the 13th, 14th, and 15th Amendments. These acts include especially (but are not limited to) the Civil Rights Acts of 1866 and 1871, which are now included in the United States Code in Title 42. While most of the "action" in civil rights litigation today is associated with the 1964 act, some significant cases still emerge from time to time under these classic acts. Still, most of the focus today is on the 1964 act. As the modern prototype, the Civil Rights Act of 1964 provides a template that the other acts generally follow. The 1964 act acknowledges the existence of certain protected classes, including race, color, creed, gender, and national origin, and makes it illegal to use membership in one of those classes as a reason for employment-related decisions. Thus, it is not completely true to say that an employer can discharge an employee for "any reason or for no reason." Thanks to civil rights legislation, an employer *cannot* discharge an employee if the only reason for the discharge is membership in one or more of the protected classes. Civil rights legislation is covered at length later in this chapter.

> **Did You Know?**
> The labor movement enjoyed early success in Germany, where union membership among unskilled workers rose phenomenally in the mid-1890s.

Worker Adjustment and Retraining Notification Act Many employers who contemplate mass layoffs and/or plant closings must comply with the provisions of the Worker Adjustment and Retraining Notification Act (WARN). Under this federal statute, employers with more than 100 full-time employees must give written notice to a union official 60 days before any plant closing or mass layoff. If the employees are not represented by a union, the advance notice must go directly to all employees who will be affected by the layoff or closing. Written notice is not required if the layoff or closing is caused by a natural disaster, such as a flood or an earthquake. Notice is also not required if the closing is caused by an unpredictable business situation or if the notice might prevent the acquisition of business or capital that the employer is attempting to acquire.

Wrongful Discharge

Wrongful discharge, which is also referred to as *unjust dismissal* in some states, gives employees legal grounds for a lawsuit against employers who have dismissed them unfairly. The courts have used several theories to judge the injustice of a dismissal. These theories include promissory estoppel, fraud, implied contract, implied covenant, public policy tort, and the intentional inflection of emotional distress.

Promissory Estoppel To make a case based on promissory estoppel, the employee must demonstrate that the employer or a representative of the employer, generally a supervisor or department head, promised the employee job security despite the apparent at-will nature of the employment relationship. In promissory estoppel cases, what matters is that someone in authority made a promise to the employee that the employee believed and relied on, to his or her detriment. Promissory estoppel thus involves four elements:

1. The employer makes a promise.
2. The employer can reasonably expect the employee to rely on the promise.
3. The employee really does rely on the promise and, as a consequence, does something or refrains from doing something.
4. The employee in turn is hurt by the action or inaction in reliance on the promise.

Under these circumstances, the employer cannot deny the promise made to the employee, and the doctrine of employment at will is unavailable as a defense.

EXAMPLE 23-1: The Power of Promissory Estoppel

Bennett worked for Jameson for three years without incident. Unfortunately, on the eve of the beginning of his fourth year, Bennett was arrested for a drug-related felony, allegedly committed during his free time. Sonja Gephardt, Bennett's supervisor, told him in front of several witnesses, "We have to lay you off now, but the company bosses have promised that you can have your job back at full seniority, once the case is over. They've also promised that you'll get back pay too." When Bennett was acquitted, he attempted to be reinstated as per Gephardt's promise but was told that he was no longer needed. When Bennett brought a wrongful discharge suit against Jameson, the company filed a summary judgment motion for dismissal noting that because Bennett was an at-will employee, the company could discharge him at any time for any reason or for no reason with or without notice. The court, however, refused to grant the summary judgment motion because the judge believed that Bennett had presented a *prima facie* case for promissory estoppel. This case was established because:

1. Gephardt, representing Jameson, had made a promise to Bennett that his job with full seniority and back pay would be waiting for him after the case was resolved.
2. Gephardt, and therefore Jameson, could have reasonably expected Bennett to rely on the promise.
3. Bennett really did rely on the promise and, as a consequence, did not look for employment elsewhere.
4. Bennett was hurt by not looking for another job because he lost money while he was unemployed and while he sought a new job.

Under the circumstances of this case, the company cannot deny the promise that its agent, Gephardt, made to the employee, Bennett, and the doctrine of employment at will will be unavailable to it.

Fraud-Related Employment Cases Some states now permit an employee to bring a wrongful discharge based on fraud, a cause of action similar to promissory estoppel. A cause of action based on fraud generally applies only to false promises made by a prospective employer to a possible future employee who relies on those promises to his or her detriment. Often in such a situation, the employer induces a potential employee to take a job that the employer knows will last only a limited amount of time, without telling the employee about the short duration of that position. The employer thus exploits the employee for a limited period of time and then discharges the employee. Hiring an employee without informing him or her that the business is ending or that an office, store, or plant is about to close are circumstances that could provide the basis for employment-related lawsuits based on fraud.

Implied Contract The facts that support implied contract are similar to those that validate a promissory estoppel, so the two arguments often appear in the same case. However, there are major differences. Implied contract actually takes promissory estoppel several steps beyond a promise made by an employer and applies the principle to a general pattern of behavior by the employer that creates certain reasonable expectations on the part of the employees. Thus, **implied contract** involves an employment relationship that would have been at will had the employer or an agent of the employer not said, done, written, e-mailed, or printed something that created a workplace environment that implies the existence of a contract.

When examining a case to determine whether the employer has created an implied contract, the court can look at all of the facts involved in that employment arrangement.

The court can consider, for example, spoken and written promises made by the employer, the nature of the employment relationship, the way the parties have dealt with each other in the past, the length of the employment relationship, the customary way the employer handles such situations, and the employer's policies and procedures. To determine the employer's policies and procedures, the court can examine various company documents, including the employee handbook; letters, memos, text messages, voice mail messages, and e-mails sent to the employee; the employee's evaluation record; and any spoken promises made in face-to-face situations between the employer and the employee. The creation of the implied contract exception gives employees a fighting chance to have their day in court, a chance that previously did not exist in pure employment-at-will jurisdictions.

EXAMPLE 23-2: A Prima Facie Case for Implied Contract

When Cynthia Montalbano went to work for Holmes Enterprises, she was required to read the entire employee handbook and sign an acknowledgment indicating that she had read and understood all of the terms in that manual. One of the procedures involved a progressive disciplinary process that promised, when employees were to be disciplined for any problem, they would first receive an oral warning, followed by a written warning. Only on the third offense would employees be penalized by a suspension, and only on a fourth offense would an employee be subject to a possible discharge order. The first time Montalbano was absent without permission, she was immediately discharged. When Montalbano filed a wrongful discharge suit against Holmes Enterprises, the company filed a summary judgment motion for dismissal, noting that because Montalbano was an at-will employee, the company could discharge her at any time for any reason or for no reason with or without notice. The court would not grant the summary judgment motion because the judge believed that Montalbano had presented a *prima facie* case for the creation of an implied contract, as established by Holmes clearly indicating that the handbook was to be considered a part of the employment relationship.

Many jurisdictions that have recognized the implied contract exception still allow employers to preserve an employment-at-will arrangement by using a disclaimer. In effect, a **disclaimer** says that regardless of provisions or policies in the employee handbook and regardless of any oral promises to the contrary, an employment-at-will situation still exists between the employer and its employees. A legally effective disclaimer must include the following statements:

1. Neither the employee policy manual nor any other communication to employees is intended to create a contract between the business and its employees.
2. The employer reserves the right to dismiss an employee at any time with or without reason and with or without notice.
3. No one other than the president of the firm (or some other specified executive) can make any oral or written change in this disclaimer.

To be an effective attempt to preserve employment at will, a disclaimer also must be written in clear, unequivocal language. Moreover, it must be placed somewhere conspicuous, such as within the opening pages of the employee handbook or on a centrally located bulletin board. Finally, an effective disclaimer must be communicated to the employees or at least acknowledged by them in some way. Even then, a disclaimer might prove ineffective if the employer has made some sort of specific promise. For instance, if an employer adds a disclaimer to a handbook that also includes a very specific plan for progressive discipline, that employer might still be required to follow that disciplinary plan. Employers who fail to follow their own progressive disciplinary plan may find themselves in the midst of a wrongful discharge lawsuit, despite the disclaimer.

Implied Covenant The final wrongful discharge exception, **implied covenant**, holds that there is an implied promise in any employment relationship that the employer and the employee will be fair and honest with each other. Therefore, neither party will unfairly or dishonestly cheat the other out of anything due to the other party because of the employment relationship. The existence of an implied covenant has nothing to do with anything that the employer has said, written, or done. The implied covenant exists because the employment relationship exists. Several legal experts have argued convincingly that, once a jurisdiction embraces implied covenant, that jurisdiction is no longer an at-will jurisdiction. These experts contend that if a jurisdiction has said that a promise of fairness exists within any employment relationship, it becomes impossible to discharge an employee for "no reason" or "without notice." A discharge without cause or without notice would be inherently unfair and thus a clear violation of the ever-present, inescapable implied covenant.

A QUESTION OF ETHICS

Beth Waid was to receive a 15 percent commission on all sales she made for her employer, the Jian Computer Corporation. Waid sold a $10,000,000 computer system to the Defense Department. To avoid paying $1,500,000 to Waid, Jian fired her, despite her record as a terrific salesperson. In an employment-at-will state that did not recognize the implied covenant exception, such a discharge would be legal. However, would such a termination be ethical? Explain.

Public Policy Tort In states that still adhere to the at-will doctrine, an employee who can prove that his or her discharge somehow violated public policy may recover damages in tort. Public policy is the broad legal principle that says that the courts will not allow anyone to do anything that injures the public at large. In many jurisdictions, if an employee is fired for refusing to violate the law, such a discharge would violate public policy. For example, if an employee refuses to dump toxic waste into a river and is then fired for insubordination, that employee would have public policy grounds for a wrongful discharge lawsuit.

Similarly, if the firing itself violates the law, public policy will provide a remedy for the employee. For instance, most jurisdictions have legislation that makes it illegal for an employer to terminate an employee for missing work in order to serve on a jury. Therefore, an employer who fires an employee for absenteeism, knowing that the absent employee is actually serving as a juror, would have violated public policy and could, therefore, be targeted in a wrongful discharge lawsuit.

To succeed in a wrongful discharge lawsuit grounded on the public policy tort exception to employment at will, the employee would have to prove clarity, jeopardy, causation, and the lack of an overriding business justification for the discharge.

1. Clarity requires the existence of a definite public policy, clearly created by the U.S. Constitution, the state constitution, a statute, an administrative regulation, a common law principle, or a general governmental policy.

2. Jeopardy requires that the public will be endangered if the court does not dissuade the type of firing involved in the case.
3. Causation requires that the discharge be induced by actions that are related to the stated public policy issue.
4. The lack of an overriding business justification means that the employer had no legitimate business reason for the discharge of the employee.

In a wrongful discharge lawsuit based on public policy, the judge is charged with determining whether the first two elements, clarity and jeopardy, exist. These two elements are considered questions of law. If the case is tried before a jury, the jurors, as the triers of fact, would determine the existence of causation and the absence of an overriding business justification. In the absence of a jury, the judge would make this determination.

THE OPENING CASE Round 3
"Words do not choose among their company or discriminate among the people who use them."–Dejan Stojanovic

In the Opening Case, Kimberly Hively, an adjunct instructor at Ivy Tech Community College in South Bend Indiana, applied for a full-time position six different times between 2009 and 2014. Each time, she failed to secure a full-time job. After her sixth attempt, she began to suspect that her inability to secure a full-time post at Ivy Tech had nothing to do with her credentials or her experience. Instead, she was convinced that her inability to obtain a permanent position was directly related to her sexual orientation. Unfortunately, she never got a chance to test her theory because, in 2014, her adjunct contract was not renewed. Convinced that her firing was due to her sexual orientation, she filed a complaint with the Equal Employment Opportunity Commission. The EEOC examined her case and issued a right-to-sue letter that empowered Hively to bring her own suit in the federal courts. Shortly thereafter, she did just that.

Had she decided to take another route, Hively might have also brought an action in state court for wrongful discharge based on public policy tort. Recall that public policy is the broad legal principle that says that the courts will not allow anyone to do anything that injures the public at large. Also recall that to prove a public policy case, the employee must show the following elements: (1) that a definite public policy exists, (2) that the public will be endangered or jeopardized if the court does not dissuade the type of firing involved in the case, (3) that the discharge (or retaliation) was induced by actions that are related to public policy, and (4) that there is no justification for the firing (or retaliation).

Now let's consider the facts in *Hively v. Ivy Tech* as they relate to the elements of a public policy case. (1) Public policy would certainly support the notion that people should not lose their jobs over a characteristic that is (a) inherently part of their makeup as human beings and (b) makes no difference in their ability to do the job. It can also be argued that sexual orientation is one of these inherent characteristics. (2) It clear that if the court does not stop this type of discrimination, the rest of the working public would be in jeopardy of being fired for similar unjust reasons. (3) It is not unrealistic to argue that Hively's firing resulted from her complaints about discrimination. (4) Given her academic credentials and her experience at Ivy Tech, it is reasonable to argue that she was fired not because of poor job performance, but because of her sexual orientation. Do these arguments amount to a valid claim of wrongful discharge by a violation of public policy? It is difficult to say for certain, of course, but if Hively had no other alternative, a public policy case might have given her a fighting chance. Still, such a case is absurdly hypothetical, so it would seem that she chose the right strategy when she filed her complaint with the EEOC. Did she succeed? Well, keep reading, and you will find out! [See: *Kimberly Hively v. Ivy Tech Community College,* No. 15-1720 (2017).]

Source: See: *Kimberly v. Hively v. Ivy Tech Community College*, No. 15-1720 (2017).

Intentional Infliction of Emotional Distress Another tort claim that is being used more frequently in wrongful discharge lawsuits is the intentional infliction of emotional distress. An employee may attempt to recover damages for the intentional infliction of emotional distress if the conduct of the employer in the discharge of the employee caused serious mental and emotional suffering. To succeed in such a lawsuit, the plaintiff must prove that the employer's conduct was extreme, that the employer knew the conduct was extreme and would result in emotional distress, and that the conduct was the proximate cause of serious mental and emotional suffering.

After-Acquired Evidence Defense

A relatively new defense that employers have used successfully in wrongful discharge cases is called the *after-acquired evidence defense*. This defense is applied when an employer uncovers evidence, usually during the discovery process, that reveals that the employer could have legitimately discharged the employee, even if the employee's claims of wrongful discharge prove to be true. The defense is often raised as the grounds for the granting of a summary judgment.

> **EXAMPLE 23-3:** An After-Acquired License Problem
>
> Frank Handley was discharged from his position as a test pilot for Coastline Aviation Inc. when he was absent from work on one occasion without notifying his superior. The company's employment manual, which had no disclaimer, indicated that an employee would receive three warnings, one spoken and two in writing, for unexcused absences before being suspended. Only after a fourth unexcused absence could an employee be discharged. Handley filed a wrongful discharge suit against Coastline based on a breach of the implied contract created by the promises in the employment manual. During the discovery process, attorneys for Coastline found out that Handley's pilot's license had been suspended several years before he was hired and that Handley had lied about his license on his job application. The court ruled that even though the lack of a license had not been the reason that he was discharged, under the circumstances, because he had falsified his application and was not qualified to fly an airplane, which is clearly the function of a test pilot, he would not be entitled to receive any damages.

The after-acquired evidence defense has also been used by defendants in discrimination lawsuits. Consequently, the Equal Employment Opportunity Commission has issued a special rule that is to be applied when such a defense is raised. This rule is discussed later in the chapter.

Retaliation and Constructive Discharge

So far we have discussed only wrongful discharge in cases that involve the actual separation of the employee from the employer's workplace. This is not the only kind of discharge, however. Sometimes employers will engage in conduct that adversely affects the employee's working conditions without actually terminating the employment relationship itself. This tactic is referred to as **constructive discharge**. For example, the employee may be relocated to less than desirable jobs at the workplace, be denied raises, be deprived of continuing educational opportunities, lose seniority, be stripped of promotions, lose vacation time, be reassigned to difficult and inconvenient hours, and so on. Thus, the employee continues to come to work and to draw a paycheck, but in conditions that slowly deteriorate, making the situation at work and on the job unbearably difficult for that employee. Often, as expected (even planned), the employee will "voluntarily" leave the job because the adverse conditions become intolerable. Nevertheless, there are states in which constructive discharge, like constructive eviction, is actionable in court. Moreover, as explained later in this chapter, if the constructive discharge is conducted as **retaliation** for an employee's actions, the lawsuit may be found not only in tort law, as in public policy tort, but also in federal employment legislation, if the constructive discharge results from the filing of an employment-related claim involving federal employment legislation. Also, if the retaliation involves labor activities, recourse can be found in federal labor law (e.g., the Wagner Act) and in health and safety laws (e.g., OSHA) if the retaliation involves a complaint about health and safety issues.

A SOON TO BE CLASSIC CASE Retaliation and Constructive Discharge

Richard Ceballos was a 12-year veteran of the district attorney's office in LA. At the time that his troubles began, he was a deputy district attorney for the City of Los Angeles. The problems for both Ceballos and Gil Garcetti, the district attorney, started when Ceballos became concerned about the efficacy of a search warrant that had been issued in a case on which he was working. Ceballos was alerted to the problem when a defense attorney filed a motion to suppress the warrant because it was allegedly founded on inaccurate information. Skeptical at first, Ceballos investigated the warrant on his own and, after talking to the deputy involved in obtaining the warrant, determined that the defense attorney was correct. Accordingly, Ceballos wrote a memo that recommended dismissing the case. The case and Ceballos's recommendation were discussed at a meeting, which became less than courteous. Notwithstanding Ceballos's warnings about the inaccuracies in the warrant, the case was not dismissed by the DA. In a scene worthy of any number of *Law and Order* reruns, Ceballos testified for the defense about the problems with the warrant. Despite all this commotion about the warrant, the trial court refused to dismiss the case. The matter might have ended there had not Ceballos later been subjected to a number of apparently retaliatory moves by his supervisors. He was shipped to another court, refused a promotion, and denied access to murder cases (a requirement for promotions in the DA's office). At that point, Ceballos filed a grievance, which was denied based on a finding that no one in the DA's office had really retaliated against him for the search warrant memo, the discussion in the meeting, or his testimony for the defense. At that point, even though Ceballos had not actually been fired, he was clearly the victim of a constructive discharge. [*Note:* Ceballos later filed a claim under Section 1983 of Title 42 of the United States Code (USC).] [See: *Garcetti, et al. v. Ceballos*, 126 S. Ct. 1951 (U.S. Supreme Court).]

Source: See: *Garcetti, et al. v. Ceballos*, 126 S. Ct. 1951 (U.S. Supreme Court).

Job Qualifications and Interview Questions

At the opposite end of the problems associated with constructive discharge are the problems related to the hiring process. To avoid illegal discrimination in the hiring process, all businesses should follow three simple steps: (1) formulate nondiscriminatory job descriptions and job applications, (2) narrow the number of candidates in a nondiscriminatory fashion, and (3) ask nondiscriminatory questions during the job interview. Let's examine each of these steps one-by-one in greater detail. First, those charged with formulating the job description and the job application must make certain that none of the requirements will compel the applicants to eliminate themselves because of their race, religion, national origin, age, disabilities, military status, gender, political affiliation, children (or plans to have children), marital status, arrest record, citizenship, smoking and drinking habits, and mental health.

The most responsible strategy here is to make certain that each requirement relates to something the new employee must do on the job and is formulated using nondiscriminatory language. For example, it is not acceptable to use gender-specific terms such as *actor*, *actress*, *host*, or *hostess*, even when those terms describe what the new employee must do on the job in a single word. On the other hand, it is legally permissible to list the experience and abilities (e.g., "must have two years' experience on the stage" or "must be able to relate well to the public") that the new employee will need to perform well on the job. Second, the process of determining who will be invited for an interview should be conducted in at least two stages. In the initial stage, a committee (or an individual) examines all applications to eliminate anything that might reveal information that cannot be considered in the hiring process. In the next stage, a different group of individuals uses the redacted copies of the applications to narrow the field to those individuals who will be invited to an interview. Third, in the interview itself, the interviewers should avoid questions related to the protected classes noted earlier. This is a delicate situation that should be handled with care. Sometimes even experienced interviewers will slip during the "small talk" portion of the interview. Thus, it might seem quite natural to talk about attending a child's softball game after work, but it would be inappropriate during that informal introductory conversation to comment that the interviewee "probably knows what that's like." During the actual interview, it is best to use a list of prepared questions that have been approved by the legal department. Again, as noted above, some of these areas are problematic because the employer may need information related to the areas that are protected. A responsible procedure is to use the real qualifications rather than any incidental characteristics that have nothing to do with the job. For example, it is not appropriate to ask if an applicant has small children at home, but it is acceptable to ask if the applicant can get to work by 9 a.m. Additionally, some cities and states—notably Philadelphia, New York City, and Massachusetts—outlaw questions about former salary levels. Again, the more responsible step is to include a salary range that is available for each position on the job description so that applicants either self-select out of the job hunt or know what they are getting into salary-wise from the start of the application process. [See: Jenny Che, "10 Questions Employers Can't Ask You at a Job Interview," *Huffington Post*, March C2015, https://www.huffingtonpost.com/2015/04/ 09/off-limits-questions-job-interviews_n_7028050.html; "30 Interview Questions You Can't Ask and 30 Legal Alternatives," *Compare Business Products*, September 2013, https://www.comparebusinessproducts.com/fyi/30-interview-questions-you-cant-ask-and-30-sneaky-legal-get; and Paul Davidson, "Laws Ban 'What's Your Salary?' Question," *MSB Money and USA Today* (April 2017) https://www.usatoday.com/story/money/2017/04/27/whats-your-salary-becomes-no-no-job-interviews/100933948/.)]

quick quiz 23-1

1. Employment at will has virtually disappeared as a legal doctrine in most states thanks to the development of wrongful discharge. — true | false

2. Generally, collective bargaining agreements have eliminated grievance procedures as cumbersome and outdated because of the development of wrongful discharge. — true | false

3. Retaliation and constructive discharge are essentially the same cause of action or at least always occur in tandem with one another. — true | false

23-2 Laws Regulating Employment Conditions

Employment conditions can be divided into two distinct areas: the actual physical situation in which employees must work and the compensation received by employees. Moreover, there is a national employment verification system that affects all newly hired employees. The federal government regulates these working conditions to protect workers.

Health and Safety Laws

Various state and federal laws and administrative rules and regulations are designed to reduce preventable hazards to employees in the workplace and to provide for safe and helpful working conditions. On the state level, departments of labor and health may be charged with determining whether an employer is complying with state health and safety laws. On the federal level, the Occupational Safety and Health Act assures all workers in a business, in or affecting interstate commerce, a safe and healthful place of employment.

Occupational Safety and Health Administration
The Occupational Safety and Health Administration (OSHA), an agency responsible to the Department of Labor, establishes and enforces occupational health and safety standards with which employers must comply. To withstand a court challenge, however, it must be shown that the OSHA standards and regulations reasonably reduce the frequency or severity of employee injuries or illnesses. Employers are required to keep records of illnesses, injuries, and deaths suffered by employees and submit requested reports to the secretary of labor.

A team of OSHA inspectors enforces compliance with its many and varied health and safety regulations. Employees are permitted to request an inspection if they believe that a violation exists. The U.S. Supreme Court has ruled that an OSHA inspector must produce a search warrant if the employer refuses to admit an inspector to the job site voluntarily. When a violation of a standard is observed, the inspector issues a citation. A citation is a notice commanding the appearance of the employer in a proceeding. Employers may contest citations before the OSHA's Review Commission. If this effort fails, they may seek relief in the U.S. Court of Appeals.

Recently, OSHA instituted a new rule involving procedures that affect many businesses. The new rule, which is actually an amendment to the Code of Federal Regulations, obligates certain employers to electronically transmit data to OSHA about work-related illnesses and injuries. The amendment is designed to streamline OSHA intelligence gathering, thereby enabling the agency to find, focus on, and fix hazards that endanger employees. The amendment obligates establishments that include 250 or more employees to electronically file three forms: OSHA Form 300 (Log of Work-Related Injuries and Illnesses), OSHA Form 300A (Summary of Work-Related Injuries and Illnesses), and OSHA Form 301 (Injury and Illness Incident Report). Establishments with between 20 and 249 employees need to electronically file only OSHA Form 300 A. These reports must be sent on an annual basis. Establishments of fewer than 20 employees are not normally required to report to OSHA. The new rule, along with its preamble, also includes a number of miscellaneous provisions. For example, the preamble discourages mandatory post-incident drug testing because such policies tend to stop workers from reporting incidents. The preamble also states that OSHA is especially wary of drug testing for use rather than impairment. In addition, the preamble warns employers not to complicate the OSHA report filing process because this tactic also discourages workers from reporting. Finally, the new rule empowers OSHA to cite employers for retaliating against workers even if those workers have not actually filed a report with OSHA. [See: "Final Rule Issued to Improve Tracking of Workplace Injuries and Illnesses," The Department of Labor, Occupational Safety and Health Administration, http://www.

osha.gov/recordkeeping/finalrule/index.html; and Roman Acre, "New OSHA Final Rule: Improved Tracking of Workplace Injuries and Illnesses," Reference Manual Vol. No. 16-1295, *Ohio State Bar Association Annual Forum*, August 2017.]

Fair Labor Standards Act

The principal federal law affecting the wages and hours of employees is the Fair Labor Standards Act (FLSA), commonly referred to as the wage-hour law. Frequently amended, the act provides that workers in interstate commerce or in an industry producing goods for sale in interstate commerce must be paid no less than a specified minimum wage. Furthermore, it specifies that employees cannot work for more than 40 hours per week unless they are paid time and a half for overtime. The act prohibits the employment of children under the age of 14 years or the employment of "oppressive child labor" in any enterprise engaged in commerce or in the production of goods for commerce. Provisions of the FLSA have been duplicated by a number of states to regulate intrastate commerce and industries not covered by the federal law.

Wage and Hour Exceptions and Exemptions

The wage and hour provisions of the FLSA permit the employment of learners, apprentices, and messengers at less than the minimum wage. However, the employer must obtain express permission from the Wage and Hour Division of the Department of Labor and is subject to conditions set by it governing wages and hours. Full-time students are permitted to be employed under the same conditions in retail and service stores outside of school hours.

The wage and hour provisions of the FLSA, with certain exceptions, do not apply to people employed in an executive, administrative, or professional capacity. The exempt workers are generally identified as those who manage other employees. At least 50 percent of their primary duties must be in the performance of office or nonmanual work relating to the operations of the company or in the performance of work requiring scientific or specialized study. State, local, and federal employees; self-employed persons; and armed forces personnel are exempted from the wage and hour provisions. Also exempted are outside salespeople, employees of certain seasonal amusement or recreational businesses, and employees of small retail or service establishments.

Overtime Minimum Salary Increase

In an attempt to bring the level of overtime payments for salaried workers into the economy of the 21st century, the Obama administration increased the annual overtime pay boundary for salaried workers from $23,600 to $47,476 (or $913 weekly). In other words, salaried workers who make under $47,476 will now have to receive overtime pay. This move would mean that more than 4 million employees would likely receive a pay hike. The move, however, was stopped by a federal judge who issued a countrywide injunction against implementing the change. The judge ruled that the amount set by the Department of Labor was beyond its authority. The Department of Justice partnered with the Department of Labor to appeal this decision. The change is currently still in limbo, so you might want to check the Department of Labor website to establish the status of the overtime boundary figure. In the meantime, it is best for employers to check and double-check their internal procedures for dealing with overtime pay. Common errors include incorrectly labeling some workers as salaried workers when they should really be labeled as hourly workers. Unfortunately, it is an oversimplification to say that all salaried workers do not receive overtime. In addition, employers must be certain that they are tracking all the time that their employees are actually at work, even those moments when they are not "on the line" or "in the lab." For example, in some cases, getting dressed (as when biohazard workers must don hazmat suits) must be included as work time. [See: "Final Rule: Overtime," The Wage and Hour Division of the Department of Labor,

October 2017; Jeremy Quittner, "Obama Administration Appeals Overtime Pay Injunction," *Fortune,* December 2016, http://fortune.com/2016/6/12/01/obama-administration-appeal-overtime./; and Julie M. Young, "Employment Law under the Trump Administration," Ohio State Bar Association CLE, September 19, 2017.]

Also employers often improperly label actual employees as independent contractors. The best test for determining employee status is the economic realities test that we saw back in Chapter 22. The economic realities test is a fairly flexible rule because it considers many of the same factors that are applied in the control test used in the doctrine of *respondeat superior*. These factors include determining the hired party's autonomy on the job, the length of time involved in the employment situation, and the level of skill needed to do the job. However, the economic realities test also adds some factors of its own. For example, in an attempt to determine the true nature of the financial arrangement between the parties, the economic realities test also asks about the hired party's investment in the employer's business and the degree to which the hired person's services were integrated into the employer's commercial activity. [See: Young.]

Collective Actions under the FLSA The FSLA permits an individual employee to bring a private cause of action against an employer that has violated its provisions. The problem with this type of lawsuit is that the payments due to individual employees are rarely enough to pay for attorney fees and other litigation costs. To solve this problem, Congress passed the Portal to Portal Act, which created a new type of lawsuit under the FLSA known as a collective action. A **collective action** permits a small number of employees to bring a lawsuit representing a large collective group of employees who are "similarly situated" on the job. In bringing a collective action, the plaintiffs must get other members of the collective to voluntarily join the action. Those who do not join do not receive the benefits that might result should the plaintiffs win the case. This process is in contrast to a class action in which members of the class must "opt-out" of the class. Unlike a collective action, whoever is in the class and does not opt-out, benefits from a plaintiffs' victory. Congress created collective action litigation specifically for lawsuits brought under the authority of the FLSA in order to forestall potentially destructive lawsuits that might financially bankrupt a business. Therefore, the clear intent of Congress was to replace class action lawsuits with collective action lawsuits in FLSA cases. Despite this, in the case of *Tyson Foods, Inc. v. Bouaphakeo*, the Supreme Court permitted a collective action brought by Tyson employees under FLSA regulations to be joined with a class action brought by the same group of employees in the same suit under the state law of Iowa, thereby thwarting the will of Congress. This is another example of legislating from the bench highlighted in this chapter's Opening Case. [See: *Tyson Foods, Inc. v. Bouaphakeo*, 136 S. Ct. 1036 (2016); and "Class Actions: *Tyson Foods, Inc. v. Bouaphakeo*," 130 *Harvard Law Review* 130 (2016), p. 407.]

Working Families Flexibility Act of 2017 The Fair Labor Standards Act was recently amended by the Working Families Flexibility Act of 2017. The new act empowers employers in the private sector to offer to replace overtime pay with comp time of up to 160 hours annually for those workers who would prefer time off rather than cash. To legitimize and preserve a record of these arrangements, both the employer and the employee must sign a written agreement that testifies to the voluntary and informed nature of the new deal. This written agreement is necessary because employees cannot be compelled against their will to join a comp-time program. Moreover, the new arrangement cannot alter any existing FLSA rules related to overtime pay and the 40-hour workweek. The new act also guarantees that all unused comp time can be redeemed for cash payments at the end of each year or when the employee leaves the job. Additionally, a cash-out provision requires employers to pay workers for their accumulated comp time whenever they choose to do so. [See: Young.]

Identity and Employment Eligibility

The federal Immigration Reform and Control Act of 1986 created a national employment verification system that placed responsibility for verification of the identity and employment of all employees on the employer. The act provided that alien workers hired on or before November 6, 1986, had until May 5, 1988, to seek temporary resident status. Those who do not have documentation of their right to work in this country are not entitled to help from the National Labor Relations Board (NLRB) in labor disputes.

Employers are required to request and examine documentation of identity and employment eligibility of all new hires and rehires, including U.S. citizens, permanent residents, and nonimmigrant visa holders. Job applicants must present original documentation. After the documents are reviewed by the employer, individuals who accept an offer of employment are required to complete and sign an employment eligibility verification form in the presence of a supervisor or a human resource officer.

quick quiz 23-2

1. The Occupational Safety and Health Act is a model law created by the American Law Institute. true | false
2. The minimum wage is set by OSHA. true | false
3. The Immigration Reform and Control Act of 1986 does not affect the job application process. true | false

23-3 Worker Benefits

The law attempts to protect workers who have left a job because of retirement, injury, or disability. The law also assists workers who have been laid off or discharged. These objectives are accomplished through Social Security, unemployment insurance, and workers' compensation.

Social Security

Federal and state governments participate in programs designed to reduce the financial risk to workers caused by their unemployment, disability, hospitalization, retirement, or death. The primary federal law covering these risks is the Social Security Act of 1935. Under the Federal Insurance Contributions Act (FICA), both employers and employees are taxed equally to help pay for the worker's loss of income on retirement. The law provides that the employee's contribution is held back by the employer, who then provides a matching contribution. The amount that an employee is assessed is based on the employee's annual wage base. Each year the annual wage base is raised to accommodate changes that occur because of increases in the cost of living. The Social Security Administration will pay benefits to retired workers who are eligible under the plan. Each retired worker's benefit payments are set by law but are also raised automatically to match cost-of-living increases.

Unemployment Insurance

The unemployment insurance section of the Social Security Act provides for a joint federal and state system of unemployment insurance. Temporary financial assistance is available to individuals who are unemployed through no fault of their own and who have earned sufficient credits from prior employment. Under the Federal Unemployment Tax Act, each state operates its own unemployment insurance system, subject to conditions established by the federal government. In addition to meeting state requirements regarding length of time employed and amount of wages, former employees must be ready, willing, and able to take suitable full-time employment should it become available. Thus, claimants are ineligible to receive unemployment benefits when they refuse to work without good cause. Good cause for refusing to work must be real, not imaginary; substantial, not trivial; and reasonable, not whimsical. For example, a desire to avoid a small cut in pay does not constitute good cause to refuse an employer's offer of employment in a reasonably similar position.

Unemployment benefits help those out of work; however, the recipient must be ready, willing, and able to work should suitable employment become available.
©Chris Livingston/EPA/REX/Shutterstock

An employee who quits a job without cause or is discharged for misconduct or theft generally does not qualify for unemployment benefits. Most states disqualify workers from receiving benefits if they are on strike because of a labor dispute. Domestic workers, agricultural workers, and state and local government employees are not governed by the federal–state program. Separate federal unemployment programs exist for railroad workers and federal civilian workers.

Workers' Compensation

Workers' compensation laws are in effect in all states. These statutes compensate covered workers or their dependents for injuries, disease, or death that occur on the job or as a result of it. One form provides a fund operated only by the state government. Employers pay into a state-controlled fund. When employees suffer injuries, they apply to the state to receive their benefits.

In another form of workers' compensation, companies are required to carry insurance for their workforce, but they have the option of contributing to the state fund or purchasing insurance from a private insurer. In the third form, all employers are required to purchase workers' compensation insurance from private insurers.

To recover for work-related injuries under workers' compensation, a worker must be injured on the job. A worker traveling to work, traveling home, or traveling to some other non-work-related destination cannot recover for injuries. This restriction is also true of lunches and breaks when a worker leaves the workplace. The result is different, however, when a worker leaves the work site on a *special mission* for the employer. Then the employee would be eligible to recover if he or she is injured, especially if the trip involved a business-related lunch that the employee was required to attend away from the job site.

Generally, employees who file workers' compensation claims are immune from retaliation by their employers. Moreover, employees who are retaliated against by their employers for filing a workers' compensation claim have a cause of action against their employer and, depending on state law, can sue for lost wages if they were demoted or reassigned and for reinstatement with back pay if they were terminated. There have been some points of disagreement within various states about whether employees who are victimized by retaliation for filing workers' compensation claims must succeed in their workers' compensation claim before they can sue for retaliation. The prevailing wisdom in this matter is that employees do not need to succeed in their workers' compensation claim to bring a retaliation suit. To hold otherwise—that is, to require success in such claims—would deter workers from filing claims in the first place, something that would frustrate the

If this worker is injured on the job, his state's workers' compensation insurance will pay benefits based on the severity and duration of the injury.
©Dmitry Kalinovsky/Shutterstock

objectives of the entire workers' compensation system [See: *Onderko v. Sierra Lobo, Inc.*, 149 Ohio St.3d 157 (2017).]

Pension Plan Regulation

The Employee Retirement Income Security Act (ERISA) provides necessary supervision over employee pension plans that are established by many employers. Under the act, employers must place their pension contributions on behalf of the employees into a pension trust, independent of the employer. Under the rules of vesting, workers are guaranteed the right to receive pension benefits, regardless of whether they are working under the plan at the time of retirement. The law requires immediate vesting for all contribution made by the employee. All pension plans must also provide vested benefits for employer contributions after a worker has been on the job for five years.

Family and Medical Leave Regulation

Under the provisions of the federal Family and Medical Leave Act (FMLA), employers who have 50 or more employees at the workplace (or within 75 miles of the workplace) must give those employees up to 12 weeks of leave time in a 12-month period for child, spousal, or parental care or for the employee's own serious medical condition if that condition necessitates either in-patient treatment or medical care on a continuing basis. The 12-month period can be calculated based on a calendar year or from the time the leave actually begins. The leave time may be unpaid, but it must not jeopardize the job of the employee. To qualify for the leave time guaranteed by the FMLA, the worker must have been employed by the firm for at least one year and worked for 1,250 hours over the 12-month period before the leave is requested. Employees can draw on the 12 weeks consecutively, at intervals, or as an adjusted work plan. For example, an employee might take a half-week of leave time now and another half-week later, or an employee might reduce his or her workweek from five to four days, or a worker might adjust his or her daily work schedule from eight to six hours, and so on.

Employer Responsibilities Both the employee and the employer have responsibilities under the FMLA. For instance, the employer must keep the employee's group health insurance in effect while the employee is on leave. Furthermore, when the employee returns to work, the employer must reinstate the employee to his or her former job or a job equal to the former job. In addition, the employer must make certain that, upon returning to work, the employee receives the same pay and the same benefits that he or she received before going on leave. Employers are also forbidden to dismiss an employee or discriminate against a worker who exercises his or her leave rights under the FMLA. Similarly, the employer cannot retaliate against a worker who protests the employer's attempt to bypass the rights granted to employees under this act. Employers are also responsible for informing employees, in writing, when leave time under the FMLA has been activated.

Employee Responsibilities The FMLA also imposes certain obligations on employees. For instance, employees are required by law to give notice of their intention to take an FMLA leave whenever they can foresee the need for the leave. This notice must be given to the employer at least 30 days before the employee intends to take the leave. If the need for a leave is unpredictable, the employee must give notice as soon as doing so is practical.

Enforcement of FMLA Rules Employees who believe that their employer has violated FMLA rules can file complaints with the Employment Standards Administration. Moreover, employees who believe that their rights have been violated may file a lawsuit against their employers. Finally, a state statute or a collective bargaining agreement that gives employees more comprehensive leave coverage would supersede FMLA.

Did You Know?

One of the earliest forms of public assistance for the poor was instigated in Antwerp in the 14th century. Citizens considered deserving of the city's assistance were given identification badges. No one could receive food without the appropriate identification badge.

Military Amendments to the FMLA Congress amended the FMLA in 2009 to accommodate military caregivers. Under these new provisions, an employer must give an employee up to 26 weeks of leave time in a 12-month period to care for a family member who has sustained a serious illness or injury that occurred because of military service. This new type of leave has been labeled **military caregiver leave**. In addition, employees are permitted to use as much as 20 weeks to take care of certain nonmedical emergencies during the time that a spouse, child, or parent is on active duty in the military. This is referred to as **qualifying exigency leave**.

quick quiz 23-3

1. Most states have eliminated workers' compensation laws because they are too expensive to maintain. true | false
2. Under the Federal Unemployment Tax Act, all state unemployment compensation systems were dismantled. true | false
3. The Family and Medical Leave Act provides for 12 weeks of paid leave for all employees in any 12-month period. true | false

23-4 Equal Employment Opportunity

As noted earlier in the chapter, in recent years, the government has attempted to address the problem of discrimination in the workplace by fashioning statutes that promote equal employment opportunities. The most prominent of these statutes include Title VII of the Civil Rights Acts, the Equal Pay Act, the Age Discrimination in Employment Act, the Uniformed Services Employment and Reemployment Rights Act, the Americans with Disabilities Act, and the Genetic Information Nondiscrimination Act (GINA).

Civil Rights Legislation

Today we are so used to governmental efforts to promote equal employment opportunity that we forget that it was a long and hard struggle to reach the type of workplace equity that we enjoy today. The process began in the 19th century in the wake of the Civil War, with the adoption of three major constitutional amendments. Amendment 13 abolished slavery, Amendment 14 guarantees due process and equal protection of the law, and Amendment 15 guarantees voting rights. Each of these amendments also ends with a key section that reads, "Congress shall have the power to enforce this article by appropriate legislation." Congress exercised that authority when it passed the initial civil rights legislation in the years following the war. The first such act was the Civil Rights Act of 1866, which officially bestowed citizenship on all people born in the United States and promised them equal citizenship rights. Because of the fear that the constitutionality of the act might still be challenged, given the imprecise nature of Amendment 13, Amendment 14 was enacted to solidify the principle of equal protection and due process. A new civil rights act, the Civil Rights Act of 1871, also known as the enforcement act, was enacted by Congress to make it clear that the states must also protect these rights. More specifically the act reads:

> Every person who, *under color of any statute, ordinance, regulation, custom, or usage, of any State or Territory or the District of Columbia,* subjects, or causes to be subjected, any citizen of the United States or other person within the jurisdiction thereof *to the deprivation of*

any rights, privileges, or immunities secured by the Constitution and laws, shall be liable to the party injured in an action at law, suit in equity, or other proper proceeding for redress, except that in any action brought against a judicial officer for an act or omission taken in such officer's judicial capacity, injunctive relief shall not be granted unless a declaratory decree was violated or declaratory relief was unavailable. For the purposes of this section, any Act of Congress applicable exclusively to the District of Columbia shall be considered to be a statute of the District of Columbia. 42 United States Code, Section 1983. (Italics added)

While it took some time, it is now indisputable that all of the principles set forth in the Bill of Rights and all subsequent rights-oriented amendments must be protected by the states as well as by Congress. This is the act that Ceballos used to challenge the retaliatory action of his supervisors in his lawsuit against the District Attorney's Office in Los Angeles, California, outlined in the Soon To Be A Classic Case feature covered earlier in the chapter.

The Equal Pay Act

The stage was set for the Civil Rights Act of 1964 by the Equal Pay Act of 1963. Under provisions of the federal Equal Pay Act, employers must pay women the same amount that they pay men for the same job. The underlying motto of those who support the Equal Pay Act is "equal pay for equal work." Such a rule is easy to follow when the work in question is exactly the same. Problems occur when the work done by the women in the workplace is comparable, but not identical, to the work done by the men. To deal with this issue, the courts have ruled that as long as the work in question requires the same level of effort, ability, and accountability and is rendered in a comparable work environment, it is considered substantially equal. Substantially equal work requires equal pay. Since 1979, the Equal Pay Act has been administered by the Equal Employment Opportunity Commission (EEOC).

Title VII of the Civil Rights Act of 1964

The Civil Rights Act of 1964 covers more than employment. It also outlaws discrimination in such things as housing, travel accommodations, and education. One of its primary features is the creation of the original five protected classes. Simply stated the act prohibits discrimination on the basis of race, color, creed, gender, and national origin. Employees who believe that they have been discriminated against can file complaints with the EEOC. Moreover, some state governments have equal employment agencies that have been designated as deferral agencies under Title VII. In those states, all discrimination charges filed with the EEOC must be sent by the EEOC to the state equal employment agency. Even so, an employee who has filed such a claim can ask the EEOC, rather than the state agency, to conduct the inquiry. Discrimination claims must be registered with the EEOC no later than 180 days after the prohibited activity. In states with deferral agencies, that deadline is lengthened to 300 days.

Any discrimination claim faces a three stage analysis process. First, the claimant must present a *prima facie* case demonstrating that he or she was discriminated against by his or her employer. A *prima facie* (literally, "at first look") case means that just by viewing the facts themselves, it appears likely that the claimant has been victimized by discrimination. Second, the burden shifts to the employer who must show that while his or her action may appear to be discriminatory, he or she has a legitimate, nondiscriminatory explanation for the action. Third, the burden shifts back to the claimant to demonstrate that despite what the employer maintains, the discriminatory motive dominated his or her actions. This may be demonstrated by showing that the employer's explanation is a pretext used to cover up the discriminatory reason or that the employer had mixed motives in making the decision and that the discriminatory motive dominated the decisions made and the actions taken. Discrimination can be committed in one of two ways: disparate treatment and disparate impact.

Disparate Treatment In cases of **disparate treatment**, the employer intentionally discriminates against an individual or a group belonging to one of the protected classes. For instance, a business that advertises for "salesmen" or "saleswomen" rather than "salespersons" would be practicing this type of discrimination. The act has had a profound effect on the language of the workplace. Words and phrases that reveal a certain bias (usually a gender bias) have largely disappeared from the language. We no longer see advertisements for "waiters," "stewardesses," "actresses," "salesmen," "busboys," or "girl Fridays." Instead, we read about "servers," "flight attendants," "actors," "salespersons," "bussers," and "administrative assistants." Nevertheless, a common misconception still exists that this type of brazen discrimination has been eliminated from the workplace. Such is not the case. Even in the present day, the U.S. Supreme Court is still reviewing cases that dealt with companies that continued to discriminate in direct and obvious ways.

EXAMPLE 23-4: The Johnson Battery Discrimination Case, Part I

Johnson Controls Inc., a battery manufacturer located in Wisconsin, had an employment policy that eliminated women younger than 70 years of age from performing certain jobs in the making of batteries unless they could produce proof that they were infertile. The company argued that it was just trying to protect its workers because all the prohibited jobs involved prolonged exposure to lead. The U.S. Supreme Court disagreed and labeled the company's policy as a clear-cut example of sex discrimination.

Bona Fide Occupational Qualification Businesses have a defense against a charge of disparate treatment, called a *bona fide occupational qualification (BFOQ)*. The discrimination may be justified if the employer can prove that the job requirement is a BFOQ. Even so, a BFOQ defense can never be raised to justify racial discrimination. However, a BFOQ defense can work for some forms of sexual discrimination. For example, a requirement that all applicants for a job modeling women's bathing suits be female would be a BFOQ.

EXAMPLE 23-5: The Johnson Battery Discrimination Case, Part II

Could Johnson Controls Inc., in Example 23-4, argue that infertility in a woman is a valid BFOQ? The U.S. Supreme Court said no. A BFOQ must be related to the job performance. Both men and women can be competent battery makers, so excluding one sex or the other from that job cannot be justified.

Disparate Impact In contrast to disparate treatment, disparate impact is a more subtle form of discrimination. Discrimination through **disparate impact** or adverse impact occurs when an employer has a policy that on the surface seems neutral but that has an unequal and unfair impact on the members of one or more of the protected classes. For instance, an employer who requires all employees who work in the warehouse to be six feet tall and weigh at least 180 pounds may have discriminated against women under the doctrine of disparate impact. Although the criteria seem neutral on the surface, they would exclude women disproportionately and thus have an unfair impact on them.

Business Necessity Businesses have a defense against a charge of disparate impact known as **business necessity**. A qualification may be permitted despite its disparate impact on a protected class if the employer can show that the qualification is needed to perform the job. For example, a requirement that all job applicants have a law degree for a job as an attorney might have a disparate impact on one or more of the protected classes. However, because a law degree is needed for the job, it will be allowed. Naturally, the claimant has an opportunity to demonstrate that the challenged practice is not really needed to perform the job in question.

A CLASSIC CASE   The Establishment of "Disparate Impact"

Every legal doctrine that is not specifically written into a statute must begin somewhere and that somewhere is, more often than not, the courts. Such was the case with creation of the doctrine of disparate impact. That doctrine—the one that says some employment policies may appear neutral on their face but still violate the law because they have a disparate impact on a protected group—began in the following classic case.

The facts are straightforward enough. A group of employees were upset about the promotion policies of their employer, Dan River Steam Station, a power-generating plant owned and operated by the Duke Power Company of Draper, North Carolina. The requirements for advancement included a high school education or successful completion of a standardized general education examination. The argument made by the petitioners was that neither of these requirements was actually related to doing an effective job at the plant, that both of the requirements had the adverse effect of eliminating black employees from hiring and promotions in a proportion that was at a substantially higher rate than white employees, and the positions that required the diploma or the test were filled only by white employees and had been dominated by white employees as part of a deliberate strategy to exclude blacks. The case went to the district court, which found that the company had indeed followed a deliberately discriminatory hiring and promotion process that was consciously designed to exclude blacks from the higher-paying positions.

The plant had five departments: labor, coal handling, operations, maintenance, and the laboratory. Blacks worked exclusively in the labor department, which meant that all the high-paying jobs in the other departments were occupied by whites. Promotions in all departments were based on seniority alone. Starting in 1955, a high school diploma was needed for an initial assignment to any department except labor. After the Civil Rights Act went onto effect in 1965, the company eliminated its deliberately discriminatory hiring policies. However, at that time, a high school diploma became a requirement for moving out of labor into any of the higher-paying departments. On July 2, 1965, the date that the Civil Rights Act went into effect, the company installed a new policy. The new policy required applicants to any department but the labor department to achieve a satisfactory score on two aptitude tests and to have a high school diploma. Later, the requirement was modified somewhat to allow a transfer from the labor department or the coal department to a higher-paying department based on test scores alone.

The district court ruled that the Civil Rights Act was not designed to pass judgment on past transgressions. The appeals court believed that the case should be decided based on the intent of the employer rather than on the actual results and, finding no intent to discriminate on the part of Duke, rejected the employees' charge of discrimination. At that point, the case landed in the lap of the U.S. Supreme Court. The Supreme Court ruled that this apparently neutral policy established by the company violated the Civil Rights Act because it had a demonstrably disparate impact on blacks and was not really related to job performance. According to the Supreme Court: "What Congress has forbidden is giving these devices and mechanisms controlling force unless they are demonstrably a reasonable measure of job performance . . . Far from disparaging job qualifications as such, Congress has made such qualifications the controlling factor, so that race, religion, nationality, and sex become irrelevant. What Congress has commanded is that any tests used must measure the person for the job and not the person in the abstract." [See: *Griggs v. Duke Power Co.*, U.S. Supreme Court, 401 U.S. 424, 91 S.Ct. 849. 28 L.Ed. 158 (1971).]

Source: See: *Griggs v. Duke Power Co.*, United States Supreme Court, 401 U.S. 424, 91 S.Ct. 849. 28 L.Ed . 158 (1971).

Workplace Harassment In recent years, the courts have witnessed an increase in the number of **workplace harassment** claims. The first type of harassment claims that appeared before the EEOC were sexual harassment claims. There is no question that sexual harassment is a type of sexual discrimination and that it is forbidden by the Civil Rights Act. However, exactly what constitutes sexual harassment is misunderstood by many people. Although most people recognize *quid pro quo* harassment, they do not realize that the creation of a *hostile work environment* also constitutes sexual harassment. **Quid pro quo sexual harassment** occurs when a supervisor makes unwelcome sexual advances toward a subordinate or suggests that the subordinate trade sexual favors for preferential treatment or to avoid the threat of an adverse employment decision such as a demotion, a pay cut, or termination. The Supreme Court has also made it clear that this type of discrimination can occur between individuals of the same gender.

A **hostile work environment** occurs when misconduct, such as sexually explicit comments, photographs, pictures, text messages, e-mails, Facebook postings, cartoons, jokes, posters, or gestures, pervade the workplace to the extent that conditions become distressing, offensive, or hostile. In recent years, the law has begun to recognize that a hostile work environment need not be limited to sexual situations. In fact, a hostile workplace can be created by misconduct that creates an environment that is so offensive that it interferes with the employee's work performance. This type of harassment can result from comments, jokes, cartoons, text messages, voice mails, e-mails, Facebook postings, and so on based upon insults, attacks, sarcasm, complaints, or inappropriate jokes because of another worker's religion, color, creed, gender or national origin. The law expressly forbids employers from retaliating against employees who file harassment complaints.

THE OPENING CASE *Round 4*
"Words Do Not Choose among Their Company or Discriminate among the People Who Use Them."—Dejan Stojanovic

By now the facts in the Ivy Tech case should be fairly clear. Kimberly Hively, an adjunct instructor at Ivy Tech Community College, was dissatisfied and frustrated that she had been passed over for several full-time positions at Ivy Tech, despite her academic credentials and experience. Disappointment and frustration, however, must have turned into astonishment when she was told that after five years of dedicated service to Ivy Tech, her adjunct contract would not be renewed. Astonishment turned into action, and Hively filed a complaint with the Equal Employment Opportunity Commission, alleging sexual orientation discrimination. The EEOC issued a right-to-sue letter that empowered Hively to bring a discrimination lawsuit on her own behalf under the Civil Rights Act of 1964. Shortly thereafter, Hively filed this lawsuit, claiming that she had been unlawfully discriminated again because of her sexual orientation. When Ivy Tech was notified of the lawsuit, its attorneys did the most logical thing.

They filed a Rule 12 (b) (6) motion to dismiss the case for failure to state a claim for which relief can be granted. The motion was logical because, despite numerous cases, the federal courts, in general, had been reluctant to recognize sexual orientation as grounds for a discrimination lawsuit under the Civil Rights Act of 1964.

This reluctance is understandable because adding a new protected class to the statute would amount to "legislating from the bench," something that the courts are not permitted to do because when the courts legislate from the bench, they encroach upon the authority of the legislature. (Remember the rule: "The legislatures legislate; the courts interpret.") The district court recognized this and granted the motion to dismiss. A three-judge panel in the Seventh Circuit affirmed the dismissal. In fact, the three judges on the original panel were so reluctant to legislate, that despite their clear desire to do so, they resisted those inclinations and stuck to their proper judicial duty, that is, to interpret, not legislate. The court explained: "Perhaps the writing is on the wall. It seems unlikely that our society can continue to condone a legal structure in which employees can be fired, harassed, demeaned, singled out for undesirable tasks, paid lower wages, demoted, passed over for promotion and otherwise discriminated against solely based on who they date, love, or marry . . . But writing on the wall is not enough. Until the writing comes in the form of a Supreme Court opinion or new legislation, we must adhere to the writing of our prior precedent, and, therefore, the decision of the district court is AFFIRMED."

Despite this, a majority of the judges in the Seventh Circuit voted to sit *en banc* (all the judges sitting together to hear a case) and review the decision of the three-judge panel. The main task before these judges, however, remained the same—that is, to determine whether the prohibition in the Civil Right Act of 1964 against discrimination based on sex should be expanded to include a prohibition based on sexual orientation. There is no doubt that the judges knew what they were about to do when they agreed to review the appeal—that is, to legislate from the bench—because they went to great lengths to justify both the process and the results of that process. The judges began the opinion by explaining the various options that any court has when it interprets a statute. Although the judges outline four different interpretive techniques, these four can be reduced to two: textualism and pragmatism. The idea behind textualism is for judges to interpret a statute by focusing on the words that the legislature wrote into the statute. The intent of textualism is to have the judges bypass the generally biased and often self-serving explanations found in legislative histories and rely, instead, on the meaning of the words that the legislators used in the statute. (*Note:* The meaning of those words must, of course, be based on how those words were defined and understood at the time the statute was written.) In contrast, in applying a pragmatic approach, the judges must attempt to get into the minds of the framers of that law and, in doing so, see how those framers would respond to the modern circumstances in which the judges now finds themselves. To do this, the judges must look at the legislative history that led to the statute and to later actions taken by the legislature in relation to that statute, actions such as amending (or not amending) the statute.

The judges in the Ivy Tech case elected to use the pragmatic approach in their interpretation of the Civil Rights Act of 1964. Having made this choice, the judges offered the following rationale. Oddly, the first thing that the judges did in their rationale was to admit that legislative actions and reactions are no help in properly interpreting statutes. The judges say it this way: "In the end, we have no idea what inference to draw from congressional inaction or later enactments, because there is no way of knowing what explains each individual member's votes, much less what explains the failure of the body as a whole to change this 1964 statute." Having rejected one of the primary tools of pragmatism, the judges elect, instead, to use one Supreme Court case, the *Oncale* case, to justify its plan to legislate from the bench. The judges note that in *Oncale* (and in several cases leading to *Oncale*), the Supreme Court gave its blessing to legislating from the bench. The High Court did this by adding, over time, provisions to the Civil Rights Act that were not in that statute when it was written by Congress. In a series of cases, including *Meritor Savings Bank v. Vinson*, 477 U.S. 57 (1986), *Price Waterhouse v. Hopkins*, 490 U.S. 228 (1989), and *Oncale v. Sundowner Offshore Servs., Inc.*, 523 U.S. 75 (1998), the High Court "amended" the Civil Rights Act by transforming discrimination based on sex into (1) sexual harassment, (2) discrimination based on sexual stereotyping, and (3) male-on-male sexual harassment. Thus, the judges in *Ivy Tech* are convinced that they now have the authority to "amend" the Civil Rights Act by transforming sex discrimination into discrimination based on sexual orientation. Focusing on the language in *Oncale* in particular, the judges in Ivy Tech conclude the following: "statutory prohibitions often go beyond the principal evil to cover reasonably comparable evils, and it is ultimately the provisions of our laws rather than the principal concerns of our legislators by which we are governed. Title VII prohibits 'discriminat[ion] . . . because of . . . sex' in the 'terms' or 'conditions' of employment . . . Our holding that this includes sexual harassment must extend to sexual harassment of any kind that meets the statutory requirements. The Court could not have been clearer: the fact that the enacting Congress may not have anticipated a particular application of the law cannot stand in the way of the provisions of the law that are on the books. It is therefore neither here nor there that the Congress that enacted the Civil Rights Act in 1964 and chose to include sex as a prohibited basis for employment discrimination (no matter why it did so) may not have realized or understood the full scope of the words it chose. Indeed, in the years since 1964, Title VII has been understood to cover far more than the simple decision of an employer not to hire a woman for Job A, or a man for Job B."

Having said this, the judges wound their way through a series of arguments and counterarguments—all of which are based on their authority to "amend" the Civil Rights Act—ultimately concluding that the lower court was mistaken in granting the Rule 12 (b) (6) motion to dismiss Hively's case based on a failure to state a claim.

The case was then sent back to the district court for a determination of whether Ivy Tech did, in fact, discriminate against Hively based on sexual orientation. (*Note:* Before that happens, we may see *Hively v. Ivy Tech* again; this time in the U.S. Supreme Court. Stay tuned.) [See: *Kimberly Hively v. Ivy Tech Community College*, No. 15-1720 (2017).]

Source: See: *Kimberly v. Hively v. Ivy Tech Community College*, No. 15-1720 (2017).

Affirmative Action The term **affirmative action** refers to a practice by which an employer actively pursues a policy that will reduce the effects of past discrimination in the workplace. The term *affirmative*, in this context, means to go forth actively, and the word *action* means a definitive plan. Affirmative action is neither mandated nor prohibited by the Civil Rights Act. Generally, affirmative action plans come from a court order, but nothing prevents an employer from pursuing an affirmative action plan voluntarily. To be valid an affirmative action plan must meet several characteristics. It must, first, be required to end past discrimination that has been demonstrated to exist by empirical evidence. Second, it must not simply eliminate the hiring of members of the majority. Third, it must have a termination date. Some people are opposed to affirmative action because they see it as a form of reverse discrimination.

Reverse Discrimination Any practice (read a*ffirmative action plan* here) that is designed to eliminate discrimination against the members of a protected class but that has the opposite effect on other members of that class or on the members of another protected class is called **reverse discrimination**. To prevent this, the Supreme Court has ruled that affirmative action plans must promote a "compelling state interest" and must be finely drawn to minimize harm to those workers outside the plan. More specifically, to preserve an affirmative action plan, the government must show that the plan is necessary to fight past discrimination, has a termination date, and is the only way to reverse the discriminatory practice. In a reverse discrimination action, the claimant must take the same steps followed in a traditional discrimination case. First, the claimant must present a *prima facie* case demonstrating that he or she was victimized by reverse discrimination, usually as the result of an affirmative action plan. Second, the burden shifts to the employer who must show that, while the affirmative action plan may appear to be unlawfully discriminatory, it was designed to "eliminate manifest racial imbalances in traditionally segregated job categories." [See: *Steelworkers v. Weber*, 443 U.S., 193, 197 (1979).] Another way of saying this is to note that the affirmative action plan must meet the three requirements of all affirmative action plans, (1) be required to end past discrimination; (2) must not eliminate the hiring of members of the majority (or, to put it another way, must be finely drawn to minimize harm to those workers outside the plan) and (3) have a termination date. Third, the burden shifts back to the claimant to demonstrate that despite what the employer maintains, the affirmative action plan was improperly crafted and has resulted in unfair reverse discrimination.

Amendments to the Civil Rights Act Congress has amended the Civil Rights Act many times since its original passage in 1964. One such amendment involving pregnancy occurred in 1978. Moreover, a major overhaul of the act took place in 1991. One goal of the 1991 amendments was to revitalize the doctrine of disparate impact. The second objective involves an expansion of the remedies available under civil rights legislation. The Equal Pay Act has also been amended recently.

The Pregnancy Discrimination Act This 1978 amendment to Title VII of the Civil Rights Act of 1964 makes it clear that employers cannot discriminate against women because of pregnancy or because they recently gave birth. Stated more positively, the act provides that pregnant women must be afforded the same treatment in all employment-related decisions, including health care, as any other employee.

Strengthening Disparate Impact The first goal of the 1991 amendments was to strengthen the doctrine of disparate impact that had been weakened by the U.S. Supreme Court. The amendments make it clear that in disparate impact cases, the employer has the burden of proving that a business necessity exists for the alleged discriminatory practice that forms the basis of the complaint. The law also makes it clear that the employer must prove that the hiring or promotion qualification is directly related to the specific job in question rather than to general business needs. The party who files a complaint in a disparate impact case may also be victorious if he or she can show that the same business goal can be reached by using a nondiscriminatory employment practice.

Compensatory and Punitive Damages A second objective was to expand the availability of compensatory and punitive damages. Prior to the passage of the new act, only victims of racial discrimination could collect compensatory and punitive damages. All other victims of discrimination were limited to collecting back pay only. Under the 1991 amendments, compensatory and punitive damages were made available to people who have been discriminated against because of their sex, religion, or national origin. Other remedies that are available under Title VII are back pay, reinstatement, and attorney fees.

Other Effects of the 1991 Amendments The 1991 amendments also added a few other critical provisions designed to reinstate the actual intent of Congress in creating the original statute in 1964. For instance, the new law mandates that American businesses must give U.S. citizens working abroad the same protection against discrimination that they give workers in the United States. In addition, the new act makes it clear that an employment practice is illegal even if only a portion of the practice is discriminatory.

Amendment to the Equal Pay Act The Equal Pay Act was designed to help women undo more than 45 years of continued paycheck discrimination. This discrimination had taken place, despite the passage of the Equal Pay Act in 1963. The amendments clarify that employers cannot discriminate against women in any gender-related capacity that might be related to education, training, or background. Moreover, the amendments also specify that the 180-day time limit for filing a claim with the EEOC begins to run every time the worker is paid. Thus, the paycheck is a continuing wrong that hurts the worker each time she receives it. Finally, the statute also adds compensatory and punitive damages to the remedies available in a gender-based wage discrimination case.

After-Acquired Evidence in Relation to Discrimination Cases The EEOC has adopted an approach for discrimination cases in which after-acquired evidence reveals that the employer had a legitimate reason for discharging the employee. The rule, which applies only to cases involving the EEOC, states that the commission will not require that the employer rehire the claimant, nor will the commission attempt to recover back pay or compensatory damages that arise after the time that the after-acquired evidence was obtained. However, to avoid squelching the effectiveness of the 1991 amendments, the EEOC will still seek punitive damages in such cases.

The EEOC Strategic Enforcement Plan The Equal Employment Opportunities Commission has been proactively seeking to oversee some aspects of the equal employment arena that have been overlooked, forgotten, or ignored in the past. The Strategic Enforcement Plan of the EEOC is an essential part of this initiative. The primary goal of the initiative is to make certain that the legal system is open and accessible to all. The stated objectives of the new initiative for the years 2017–2021 include:

1. Eliminating barriers in recruitment and hiring.
2. Protecting vulnerable workers, including immigrant and migrant workers, and underserved communities from discrimination.
3. Addressing selected emerging and developing issues.
4. Ensuring equal pay protections for all workers.
5. Preserving access to the legal system.
6. Preventing systemic harassment.

Moreover, in pursuing these goals, the EEOC has promised to initiate a targeted, collaborative, effective, and efficient plan of attack that utilizes government resources in a fiscally responsible, accountable way. [See: EEOC Strategic Enforcement Plan FY (2017–2021), https://www.eeoc.gov/eeoc/plan/sepo/cfm. See also Young.]

One of these "forgotten" areas of employment law involves severance and separation agreements (Sev/Sep agreements) which have, in the past, been unfairly drawn. Given this initiative, employers must review their Sev/Sep agreements to make certain that they follow current EEOC guidelines. For example, all confidentiality and nondisclosure provisions must be narrowly drawn in clear and unambiguous language. Clauses that require employees to waive their right to file and participate in EEOC claims are forbidden. Similarly, Sev/Sep agreements can no longer require employees to give up their right to recover monetary awards in actions filed against former employers. [See: Young.]

Age Discrimination in Employment Act

The Age Discrimination in Employment Act (ADEA) prohibits discrimination on the basis of age. ADEA covers employment agencies, employers of 20 or more employees, and labor unions of more than 25 members. This act protects any person aged 40 years or older from discrimination in hiring, firing, promotion, or other aspect of employment. Like the Civil Rights Act, the ADEA is administered by the EEOC. Age discrimination claims must be registered with the EEOC no later than 300 days after the prohibited activity. Naturally, if age is a true job qualification, the law does not apply. For instance, if the job involves the modeling of junior miss fashions, it would not be discrimination to hire someone of suitable age to model the clothes. The courts, however, will carefully scrutinize all such requirements and generally be able to detect those that are merely a pretense covering age discrimination.

EXAMPLE 23-6: Taggart, Time, and the ADEA

Thomas Taggart, aged 58 years, lost his position when the subsidiary he worked for was disbanded by Time Inc., the parent corporation. All of the employees who were laid off as a result of the closing were promised preferential treatment for other jobs at Time Inc. Taggart applied for more than 30 of these positions. He was never rehired. Most of the time, the reason given for his rejection was that he was overqualified. Taggart brought an age discrimination suit under the ADEA. Time argued that Taggart was not rehired because of an overqualification barrier that had nothing to do with his age. The court disagreed. The court ruled that calling Taggart "overqualified" was just another way of saying he was too old.

In 1990, Congress amended the ADEA in response to a U.S. Supreme Court case that held that the original ADEA did not cover employee benefit plans. The amendment, which is called the Older Workers Benefit Protection Act (OWBPA), makes it clear that the ADEA forbids discrimination against older workers in the handling of their employee benefit and retirement plans. In addition, OWBPA gives older workers legal recourse if they are forced or tricked into giving up their rights under the ADEA. Usually this situation occurs when the employee is asked to sign a waiver. A waiver of rights is valid only if it is given freely and without force or coercion. The employer has the job of proving that the waiver is valid if it is introduced as evidence in court.

Uniformed Services Employment and Reemployment Rights Act

Under provisions of the Uniformed Services Employment and Reemployment Rights Act (USERA), an employee who has served in the armed forces and successfully completed his or her tour of duty is entitled, upon returning to work, to be reinstated in his or her previous position on the job. Unlike the Civil Rights Act, which is controlled by the EEOC, USERA is administered by the Veterans' Employment and Training Service (VETS). Also unlike the Civil Rights Act, under USERA, employees may file a complaint with VETS, or they can take the case directly to court. No statute of limitations is connected to USERA. However, employees are not permitted to hold back on the filing of a case for an unreasonable length of time. Employees who succeed in a case might receive damages, an injunction to prevent their termination, and sometimes, at the discretion of the judge, attorneys' fees.

Americans with Disabilities Act

The Americans with Disabilities Act (ADA) is designed to open the American workplace to this country's disabled citizens. The ADA is divided into several titles. Title I lays out the duties imposed on private-sector employers, whereas Title II covers public services and public transportation. The ADA is administered by the EEOC. The ADA carefully outlines what is considered a disability. It also explains who and what are covered by the act and what practices are specifically forbidden.

Disabilities
The ADA defines **disability** as any physical or mental impairment that substantially limits one or more of the major life activities. This definition includes paralysis, blindness, deafness, cancer, mental retardation, learning disabilities, and AIDS, among others. Excluded from protection are people with kleptomania, pyromania, or gambling disorders. Nor does the act extend to people who use illegal drugs. The definition of disability also does not include homosexuality or bisexuality. However, because the act forbids discrimination against people who are associated with a particular disability, discrimination against homosexuals, on the basis of the claim that they are more likely to contract AIDS, would be forbidden.

Activities and Individuals Covered by ADA
Discrimination is forbidden in the screening of applicants, initial hiring, and on-the-job treatment. This protection against discrimination also extends to apprenticeship programs, promotions, pay raises, and on-the-job-training opportunities. Individuals, including both employees and applicants for employment, cannot be segregated or classified because of a disability. The ADA also protects an individual from discrimination because that individual is associated with someone who has a disability. As is true of other situations, a state statute that gives individuals with disabilities more protection than the ADA would supersede the federal statute.

Forbidden Practices The ADA forbids discrimination on the basis of a disability if the disabled individual can do the essential functions of the job with "reasonable accommodations." Exactly what would qualify as a reasonable accommodation in a given set of circumstances is, at best, problematic. Nevertheless, the statute does give some guidance in determining the extent of a reasonable accommodation. An accommodation will be reasonable if it permits the disabled individual to accomplish the essential functions of the job without imposing an undue hardship on the employer. Factors used in determining whether a proposed accommodation will cause undue hardship include the type of accommodation needed, the expense involved in providing the accommodation, the financial ability of the company to provide the necessary accommodation, and the size and nature of the company involved. Because of the innovative nature of the law and the lack of precedent, the EEOC has decided to follow a case-by-case evaluation of all claims filed by disabled individuals against employers.

Genetic Information Nondiscrimination Act

Congress has become increasingly disturbed over the unauthorized use of generic information to invade the privacy of employees or to make employment decisions based on that information. To combat this threat, Congress passed the Genetic Information Nondiscrimination Act (GINA). GINA was written to protect employees by making it unlawful for employers and health insurance companies to make decisions based on any genetic information that they have acquired due to any type of genetic testing. Under the statute, the purpose of the test is immaterial. GINA targets health insurance companies, forbidding them to use genetic information to make changes in premiums or in employee contributions. On the other hand, the new statute does permit medical professionals, such as physicians, nurses, therapists, technicians, and the like, to use genetic tests and to compile genetic information for health care reasons. In fact, the law even permits health insurance providers to establish payment schedules for their clients based on genetic information. Still, GINA demands that insurers use as little of the genetic information as possible to make such decisions. In contrast, employers are forbidden to use genetic information to make hiring, firing, promotion, vacation, continuing education, professional development, transfer, budgetary, work schedule, and salary decisions. The law also forbids unions, employment agencies, and joint labor–management committees from discriminating against individuals in any employment-related decisions related to genetic information. In fact, all employment-related decisions must be made free of any influence from the genetic information. Moreover, employers, unions, employment agencies, and joint labor–management committees cannot request, require, or purchase genetic information unless required by law, used to protect individuals from toxic substances, or as part of a forensic investigation for law enforcement purposes. [See: David J. Kovach, "GINA," *Ohio State Bar Association: 2010 Annual Convention* (May 5–7, 2010), pp. 6.1-6.5. See also "The Genetic Information Nondiscrimination Act," Department of Health and Human Services, April 6, 2009, p. 1, retrieved on September 25, 2010, from http://www.genome.gov; and "H.R. 493: Genetic Information Nondiscrimination Act of 2008," *Congressional Research Service*, p. 1, retrieved on August 20, 2010, from https://www.govtrack.us/congress/bills/110/hr493.]

The Whistleblower Acts

A whistleblower can be defined as an individual who notifies official federal or state authorities about illegal activities that take place in business, government, and other similar settings. The fact that whistleblowers can often be subjected to retaliatory actions by employers, landlords, law enforcement officials, and other authority figures has prompted the passage of federal and state laws that protect individuals who have identified and reported cases of fraud, discrimination, cover-ups, and other similar illegal activities to the appropriate watchdog agencies. Many federal laws involving employment, including the Civil Rights Act of 1964, the Age Discrimination in Employment Act, the Employee Retirement Income Security Act (ERISA), the Family and Medical Leave Act, the Americans with Disabilities Act, the Equal Pay Act, the Wagner Act, the Fair Labor Standards Act, and the Occupational Safety and Health Act (OSHA), among others, contain whistleblower protection provisions. In addition, many states have enacted their own employment-related whistleblower protection acts.

Anti-Retaliation Safeguards

As noted earlier, one of the most troubling problems in employment is the danger of retaliation. Generally, employees face such retaliation after filing a complaint against an employer under the Civil Rights Act or in accordance with similar employment-related legislation. However, retaliation can also occur when employees cooperate with discrimination investigations or simply work against discrimination in the workplace. Title VII of the Civil Rights Act 1964 includes a protection against such employer retaliation. However, the EEOC has also ruled that anti-retaliation provisions can be invoked by individuals under the Americans with Disabilities Act and the Age Discrimination in Employment Act. Thus, the classes protected against retaliation include race, color, creed, national origin, gender, age, and disability. The act also protects people closely associated with people who file complaints as well as individuals who witness discrimination.

To demonstrate that retaliation has occurred, an individual must show: (1) that he or she is in a protected class, (2) that retaliation did take place, and (3) that the retaliation took place because of an action that is protected under the law. As noted earlier, the protected classes include race, color, creed, national origin, gender, age, and disability. Retaliation includes demotions, suspensions, adverse schedule changes, alterations in job descriptions, exclusion from job-related opportunities, such as continuing education, and so on. Finally, protected actions include filing discrimination claims, providing testimony and/or evidence in a discrimination case, helping in-house investigators in discrimination cases, making in-house grievances about discrimination, suggesting that official discrimination claims might be pursued with the EEOC or another official agency, and resisting employer suggestions to ignore other cases of discrimination in the workplace, among others.

quick quiz 23-4

1. The term *affirmative action* refers to a practice by which an employer actively pursues a policy that will reduce the effects of past discrimination in the workplace.   true | false

2. American businesses working in other countries need not give U.S. citizens the same protection against discrimination under the Civil Rights Act as those afforded workers in the United States itself.   true | false

3. The Uniformed Services Employment and Reemployment Rights Act (USERA) is administered by the EEOC.   true | false

23-5 Social Media Policies

There is no way to escape the social media craze that has swept through the business world in the 21st century. Employees and employers use computers as part of their jobs and they expect everyone else, customers and suppliers alike, to do the same. In fact, computers have become so commonplace in business that it is possible, perhaps even likely, that most businesspeople no longer even notice then. Nevertheless, it is crucial to remember that computers are all around us, even in places and in devices that we do not usually think of as computers. Moreover, it is also important to recall that when people become too accustomed to technology they can become careless.

The Social Media Culture

Businesspeople must remember that computers include not only mainframes, desktop PCs, tablet computers, and laptops, but also mobile phones, notebooks, personal digital assistants (PDAs), digital recorders, GPS units, smartphones, scanners, fax machines, and wireless reading devices (WRDs). It would also be helpful to remember that to the business person it is not just the devices that are important—it is the data itself. Keeping trade secrets and protecting a client's or an employee's privacy may also mean protecting data and, at times, metadata. **Metadata** is data about data and includes such things as archival metadata, administrative metadata, structural metadata, descriptive metadata, intellectual property rights, human resources metadata, planning metadata, management metadata, financial metadata, product metadata, architectural metadata, engineering metadata, research-related metadata, preservation metadata, and so on.

It is also crucial to see that employees have become so immersed in computers that they frequently act as if those computers have always been there and will always work flawlessly. They communicate with one another, customers, suppliers, wholesalers, and retailers online. They use conference calls and webinars on a daily basis. They make purchases, pay bills, and sell goods on line. They "talk" to one another on mobile phones, with text messages, by e-mail, and on Twitter. When they go home they jump on Facebook, YouTube, or LinkedIn. They make connections on dating websites; plan trips using Orbitz, Priceline, or Travelocity; purchase hard-to-get items on e-Bay or Craigslist; buy books from Amazon.com or Barnes and Noble online; they blog, read blogs, or tell others about their favorite blogs; and if that were not enough, they take college courses, attend webinars, take certification exams, and earn advanced degrees online.

The Nature of a Social Media Policy

In some ways this makes conducting business easier, more economical, and more efficient. However, the social media craze also causes problems, and a business person must be aware of the legal risks involved when employees use social media outlets and what to do about it when things go wrong. There is, therefore, no question that every business needs to write and enforce a social media policy. A **social media policy (SMP)** is a set of rules written by an employer telling employees what they can and cannot do when using electronic communication devices, formats, websites, and electronic messaging techniques, such as blogs, text messages, tweets, Skype transmissions, and e-mails. The only remaining questions are: What are the risks involved in social media? What must be included in an SMP? What is the proper way to communicate an SMP to employees? What is the most effective way to enforce an SMP?

The Hazards Involved in Social Media

As noted earlier, social media has a very important role in the business world. It can be used to communicate effectively, to contact customers and suppliers, to store data, to write proposals and reports, to conduct video conferences and webinars, to pay company bills online, to disseminate information, and so on. The purposes are limited only by the imagination of the business person at the keyboard. However, there are also risks involved. Social media can be used to disclose trade secrets, customer lists, or other company information that is best kept confidential. It can be used to harass fellow workers or customers or to defame them or perhaps to invade their privacy. There are also legal limits set down by the Federal Trade Commission that might be violated inadvertently by the improper use of social media. For these reasons, among others, it is best for every company to write, publish, distribute, and enforce a social media policy.

The Proper Way to Construct a Social Media Policy A social media policy must include certain features. First, the policy must be written in a language and a style that is precise, exact, plain, and explicit. There must be no room for misinterpretation because if the court has to interpret an ambiguous clause, its decision will likely be against the party who wrote the policy to begin with. Second, the policy must be given to the employees with the understanding that they will read and comprehend the details of the policy. Moreover, as part of this disclosure process, employees must be told up front that the employer intends to monitor their e-mail accounts and all additional online work.

The Content of a Social Media Policy First, in order to play fair with employees, the employer must let the employees know what activities are forbidden. Forbidden activities would include: sending out trade secrets, customer lists, and other private business-related data; using sexual comments and discriminatory remarks about anyone, but especially other employees, supervisors, clients, and suppliers; making remarks that are libelous, invade privacy, create emotional distress, or constitute product or ownership disparagement; and distributing any communication about company products or services that is not accompanied by a clear statement distancing the company from the author. In addition, it would be helpful to also outline what activities are appropriate using social media in the workplace.

The Procedures Associated with a Social Media Policy Once the policy has been written and explained to the employees, each of them should be given two copies of the policy, one to sign and return for their personnel file and one to keep as a reminder of what is expected of them. The employer should reserve the right to make alterations in the policy as experience reveals situations and events that were not predicted by the original policy. It is also crucial for the employer to remember that, even after the policy is distributed and the employees have been warned, there are limits to what an employer can do about violations of the policy [See: Adrienne L. Rapp, "The Responsible Employer's Social Media Policy," *Labor and Employment Update*, Ohio State Bar Association Annual Conference, May 6, 2011.]

Bring Your Own Device Clauses Social media policies must also deal with the trend that some business have adopted permitting employees to use their personal smartphones, laptops, and tablets on the job. This trend was almost inevitable given the fact that most modern electronic devices are more portable, more user-friendly, and more compact than in the past (witness the recent development of wristwatches that operate as miniature mobile computers). In light of this trend, some (many?) employers are permitting, some even encouraging, their employees to bring their own devices to the workplace. These personally owned devices are then programmed by the firm's IT experts, who create secure work areas for e-mail, employee forms, and other work-related files. This approach to such devices works well because people are accustomed to using their own devices, so the learning curve for applying those devices to work-related situations is less time-consuming and, therefore, more efficient and economical than training employees to use new, unfamiliar devices. Still, some employers prefer to provide workers with company-owned devices that are programmed by the IT department to include separate areas for the employee's personal use. Whichever technique is adopted, the employer must make certain that the SMP makes it clear that these devices are subject to surveillance and that all work-related data on such devices is company owned and must, therefore, remain confidential.

quick quiz 23-5

1. Metadata is data about data. — true | false
2. A social media policy must be given to the employees with the understanding that they will read and comprehend the details of the policy. — true | false
3. The employer should reserve the right to make alterations in the social media policy as experience reveals situations and events that were not predicted by the original policy. — true | false

Summary

23.1 The employment-at-will doctrine means that an employer can dismiss an employee at any time for any reason. Employees who belong to labor unions and individuals with the power to negotiate their own employment contracts would not be affected. Wrongful discharge gives employees legal grounds for a lawsuit against employers who have dismissed them unfairly. The courts have used several theories to judge the injustice of a dismissal. These include promissory estoppel, fraud, implied contract, implied covenant, public policy tort, and intentional inflection of emotional distress.

23.2 OSHA establishes and enforces occupational health and safety standards with which employers must comply. The principal federal law affecting the wages and hours of employees is the Fair Labor Standards Act. The act provides that workers in interstate commerce or in an industry that produces goods for sale in interstate commerce must be paid no less than a specified minimum wage. The federal Immigration Reform and Control Act of 1986 created a national employment verification system that placed responsibility on the employer for verifying the identity and employment of all employees.

23.3 Federal and state governments participate in programs designed to reduce the financial risk to workers by reason of their unemployment, disability, hospitalization, retirement, and death. The principal federal law covering these risks is the Social Security Act of 1935. Under the Federal Unemployment Tax Act, each state operates its own unemployment insurance system, subject to conditions established by the federal government. Workers' compensation laws are in effect in all states. These statutes compensate covered workers or their dependents for injuries, disease, or death that occurred on the job or as a result of it. ERISA provides needed supervision over employee pension plans established by many employers. Under provisions of the Family and Medical Leave Act (FMLA), employers who have 50 or more employees must give those employees up to 12 weeks of leave time for child, spousal, or parental care.

23.4 The Civil Rights Act of 1964 prohibits discrimination based on race, color, creed, gender, and national origin. Employees who believe they have been discriminated against can file a complaint with the EEOC. Discrimination can be committed in one of two ways: disparate treatment or disparate impact. Other steps toward equality in employment include the Age Discrimination in Employment Act, the Uniformed Services Employment and Reemployment Rights Act, and the Americans with Disabilities Act.

23.5 A social media policy must be written in a language and a style that is precise, exact, plain, and explicit. The policy must also be given to the employees with the understanding that they will read and comprehend the details of the policy. Moreover, employees must be told that the employer intends to monitor their e-mail accounts and their online work. The employer must also let the employees know what activities are forbidden. In addition, it would be helpful to outline what activities are acceptable when using social media in the workplace. Once the policy has been written and explained to the employees, they should be asked to sign a copy. The employer should reserve the right to make alterations in the policy. The employer needs to remember that even after the policy is distributed and the employees have been warned, there are limits to what an employer can do about violations of the policy.

Key Terms

affirmative action, 663
business necessity, 659
collective action, 653
collective bargaining agreement, 640
constructive discharge, 648
disability, 666
disclaimer, 645
disparate impact, 659
disparate treatment, 659
employment at will, 640
employment contracts, 640
Genetic Information Nondiscrimination Act (GINA), 667
grievance procedure, 640
hostile work environment, 661
implied contract, 644
implied covenant, 646
metadata, 669
military caregiver leave, 657
qualifying exigency leave, 657
quid pro quo sexual harassment, 661
reasonable accommodation, 667
retaliation, 649
reverse discrimination, 663
social media policy (SMP), 669
undue hardship, 667
whistleblower, 668
workers' compensation, 655
workplace harassment, 661
wrongful discharge, 643

Questions for Review and Discussion

1. What is the doctrine of employment at will?
2. What contractual situations fall outside employment at will?
3. What statutory situations fall outside employment at will?
4. What are the wrongful discharge exceptions to employment at will?
5. What is the after-acquired evidence rule?
6. What laws regulate employee working conditions?
7. What laws provide worker benefits?
8. What are the key provisions of the Civil Rights Act?
9. What protections are provided by the Age Discrimination in Employment Act?
10. What is the nature of and the need for a social media policy?

Cases for Analysis

1. The Equal Employment Opportunity Commission (EEOC) recently has been hit with many newly filed cases that allege discrimination based on caregiver status. The cases involve, for example, a police officer who was not promoted because she had young children at home, a man who was fired for taking time off to care for his sick father, a class action case against an employer that discriminated against workers who had applied for FMLA leave, and a case filed by a man who took leave time to take care of his elderly parents. Caregiver discrimination, which is officially known as family responsibility discrimination (FRD), has caused some experts to suggest that the EEOC should create guidelines that are specifically aimed at defining and outlining the elements of FRD. Others argue that there really is no such thing as FRD and that each case must be treated for what it really is—that is, gender discrimination, age discrimination, disabilities discrimination, family leave discrimination, or some other form of specifically delineated discrimination. What existing statutes could be called upon to handle FRD cases, even if those cases must go by another, more traditional name?

[See: Tresa Baldas, "EEOC Looks at Caregiver Bias: Suits Involving Family Care Rise," *The National Law Journal*, May 21, 2007, pp. 1, 18.]

2. Eugene Meade was offered a job by Cedarapids Inc. The job required moving to Eugene, Oregon, where Cedarapids had a facility called the El-Jay Plant. To entice Meade to join the Cedarapids staff, management representatives told him that business was improving, that they believed in the potential of the El-Jay plant, that El-Jay sales were growing, that production at the plant was also increasing, and that there were plans to bring in even greater numbers of new employees. On the basis of these assurances, Meade left his job and moved to Oregon. He also signed an agreement that noted that he was an at-will employee who could be fired at any time. Meade later discovered that all of the statements about the financial health of the El-Jay plant were false. Furthermore, Meade believed that the management had known all along that the statements were false. Meade learned that the El-Jay plant was actually caught in a downward economic spiral and was about to close. When Meade was discharged, he brought a lawsuit against Cedarapids, arguing that he had been defrauded into moving to Oregon. In response, the Cedarapids management team argued that they had no duty to disclose the plan to shut down the Oregon facility. The management team also pointed to the agreement that Meade had signed and concluded that, as an at-will employee, he could not complain about his firing. The trial court agreed and dismissed the case. Meade then filed an appeal. Is there enough evidence of fraud in this case to allow it to go to a jury? Explain. [See: *Meade v. Cedarapids, Inc.*, Case No. 97-35836 (The United States Court of Appeals for the Ninth Circuit).]

3. Carla McFarland was an associate professor of English literature at Highland College. She was the only single person in her department. Consequently, she was frequently assigned classes late in the evening, on weekends, and during the summer semester. She was also called upon to pick up visiting professors and serve as their escort and guide during their stays at the college. She received extra duty as adviser to *The Highland Review*, the college's literary magazine. When McFarland complained about the unequal treatment, she was told that the married professors had family responsibilities that she did not have, which took up much of their time and prevented them from having the flexibility that she had. Thus, she would continue to carry the extra load. McFarland filed a complaint with the EEOC. Can discrimination based on an employee's status as a single person be considered unlawful under the Civil Rights Act? Explain. Is this a case of disparate impact or disparate treatment? Explain. [See: Robin Wilson, "Singular Mistreatment: Unmarried Professors Are Outsiders in the Ozzie and Harriet World of Academe," *The Chronicle of Higher Education*, April 23, 2004, pp. A10–A12.]

4. Henderson worked as a chemical engineer for the Wannisky Chemical Corporation. McGuire, Henderson's supervisor, ordered him to remove the labels from several hundred steel drums that had once contained a severely corrosive acid. McGuire told Henderson that they intended to reuse the drums to ship a new chemical fertilizer. Henderson refused to remove the labels because reusing the old drums would violate both state and federal laws. When McGuire told another employee to remove the labels and reuse the drums, Henderson reported the company's activities to the state and federal authorities. Henderson was fired for his refusal to follow orders and for notifying the authorities. In a lawsuit against Wannisky, which legal exception to the employment-at-will doctrine did Henderson use? Explain.

5. Bennerson was employed by the Checker Garage Service Corporation as an auto mechanic. His duties included both assisting mechanics in the garage and making road calls to service vehicles owned and operated by his employer. During his lunch hour, Bennerson used one of his employer's taxi cabs to drive to a restaurant. En route to the restaurant, he was seriously injured when the taxi struck a pole. Bennerson filed a claim before the workers' compensation board. His claim was granted. Checker Garage appealed, arguing among other things that the taxi that Bennerson drove did not "go out of control" but that Bennerson had lost control. Was Checker correct? Explain. [See: *Bennerson v. Checker Garage Service Corporation*, 388 N.Y.S.2d 374 (NY).]

6. Nancy Barillaro and Nancy Fotia were employed in the inspection and trimming departments of Elwood Knitting Mills for approximately 16 years. Barillaro was laid off in September and Fotia in November. Both were offered the option of returning to work in March of the following year as knitting machine operators, but at an 18 percent reduction in pay. Neither accepted the offer. They

argued that the offered work would have involved a loss in seniority and a substantial reduction in pay. In addition, Fotia claimed that she was not familiar with the operation of the machine. Barillaro claimed that she was too short to operate the machine. The Pennsylvania Unemployment Compensation Board decided that neither claimant was eligible to receive benefits because they refused offers of suitable work without good cause. Was the board correct in its ruling? Explain. [See: *Barillaro v. Unemployment Compensation Bd. of Review*, 387 A.2d 1324 (PA).]

7. The Wynn Oil Company, which conducted an enormous amount of business with Latin American companies, argued that being male was a bona fide occupational qualification (BFOQ) for the position of sales executive. Wynn contended that because of certain Latin American customs, the hiring of a female sales executive would have a serious detrimental effect on the company's business. The contention was challenged in federal court. Will Wynn's argument succeed? Explain. [See: *Fernandez v. Wynn Oil Co.*, 653 F.2d 1273 (9th Cir.).]

8. The Spelling Entertainment Group hired actress Hunter Tylo to appear in the television show *Melrose Place*. Her role was to involve the seduction of another character's husband. When Tylo became pregnant, she dutifully reported her condition to Spelling. The entertainment company then discharged her, arguing that nonpregnancy was a bona fide occupational qualification (BFOQ) for the role designed for Tylo. Tylo challenged the contention that her condition disqualified her from performing her job. Can nonpregnancy be a BFOQ? Explain. [See: *Tylo v. Superior Court*, 55 Cal. App. 4th 1379 (CA).]

9. Rice, an African American woman, was denied employment as a public health representative by the City of St. Louis for lack of a college degree. Failing to obtain relief after filing a complaint with the EEOC charging racial discrimination, she filed a lawsuit in the federal district court. Rice took the position that the degree requirement had a disparate impact on African Americans and was invalid under the Civil Rights Act of 1964. She pointed out that blacks were only approximately 55 percent as likely as whites in the St. Louis area to have a college degree. Testimony showed that the satisfactory performance of public health representatives required the ability to communicate with others, frequently in emotional situations, and the ability to speak and write intelligibly. There was also a risk to the public health and safety in the employment of unqualified applicants. Did Rice prevail? Explain. [See: *Rice v. The City of St. Louis*, 607 F.2d 791 (8th Cir).]

10. The Commonwealth of Virginia required all applicants for state troopers to be between 21 and 29 years of age, at least 5 feet, 9 inches tall, and at least 156 pounds. The height and weight requirements eliminated 98 percent of the female applicants. The basic employment requirements also made it mandatory that all applicants, including applicants for civilian dispatcher positions, complete and pass written mental ability tests. The tests for dispatcher positions were not valid predictors of job performance. The tests for the trooper positions also were shown not to be predictors of job performance. The United States brought suit, charging that Virginia engaged in a pattern and practice of discrimination against African American applicants for the civilian positions and against both African American and women candidates for the trooper positions. Did the United States prevail? Explain. [See: *United States v. Commonwealth of Virginia*, 620 F.2d 1018 (4th Cir).]

11. Shirley Painter was the chief deputy clerk in the bookkeeping department of the Civil Division of the Municipal Court of the City of Cleveland. She decided to run for city council and asked for a leave of absence to pursue that goal. At first, she was granted the leave. However, two months later, she was terminated. Painter brought a wrongful discharge lawsuit against Charles Graley, the assistant personnel director in the municipal court clerk's office. Painter asked to be reinstated. She also asked for back pay and punitive damages. Her wrongful discharge suit was based on a violation of public policy. She argued that she had appropriate grounds for the suit because her termination violated the state constitution. Graley argued that a plaintiff can bring a wrongful discharge lawsuit based on public policy only if a statute exists that prohibits the firing in question. Has Painter stated sufficient legal grounds for her wrongful discharge lawsuit? Explain. [See: *Painter v. Graley*, 639 N.E.2d 51 (OH).]

Design Elements: The Opening Case: ©Sharpstock/Alamy; A Classic Case: ©Evlakhov Valeriy/ShutterstockKey Terms

quick quiz Answers

23-1	23-2	23-3	23-4	23-5
1. F	1. F	1. F	1. T	1. T
2. F	2. F	2. F	2. F	2. T
3. F	3. F	3. F	3. F	3. T

Chapter 24 Labor Law

24-1 Labor Law and the Economic Crisis
An Economic Tug-of-War • The Goals of Labor Organizations • The 21st-Century Labor Crisis

24-2 Major Federal Labor Legislation
The Wagner Act • The Taft–Hartley Act • The Landrum–Griffin Act

24-3 The Collective Bargaining Process
The National Labor Relations Board • Unfair Labor Practice Procedure • The Right to Strike in the Public Sector

THE OPENING CASE Round 1
"Of Guilds, Unions, Workers, and the Law"—Ready or Not, Here Comes UBER and the IDG

In his first novel, *The Green Bay Tree*, the American author Louis Bromfield created an intriguing character named Stepan Krylenko. Krylenko stands out in the novel as a daring, resourceful, and heroic union leader who single-handedly organizes the steel workers in a newly industrialized midwestern town at the end of the 19th century. Until recently, such tales of colorful union organizers seemed to be a thing of the past—that is, until the emergence of the Independent Drivers Guild (the IDG or the Guild), a newly formed quasi-union established to represent Uber drivers in the New York City area. The Guild appeared on the scene in 2016 as an affiliate of the International Association of Machinists and Aerospace Workers (IAMAW). The IAMAW has represented black car drivers in the New York area since the 1990s, winning for those drivers the right to form unions and to engage in collective bargaining, rights that have been taken for granted by many (most?) Americans since the 1930s. Nor was this an Pyrrhic victory because with the right to form unions and the right to engage in collective bargaining came pension plans and health care packages for drivers who had never before had the chance to obtain such benefits. The IAMAW also took a lead position in the development of the New York Black Car Operators' Injury Compensation Fund (or more directly the NYBCF), which is a state institution created to give financial assistance to drivers who cannot work because of injuries.

Enter Uber, the app-powered business enterprise that has proven to be a new convenience for those who need quick, easy, efficient, and affordable transportation for a wide variety of purposes, including such things as shopping, going to the airport, running errands, and keeping medical appointments. As is true of any innovation, Uber brought with it a series of unintended consequences, not the least of which was the fact that many independent car drivers who now worked at least part-time for Uber had no representation within the company. Many of these drivers sought help from the IAMAW, which collaborated with Uber to form the IDG, which has worked to provide the app-based drivers with a place at the bargaining table. In addition to this, the emergence of the Guild has provided sociologists, economists, and law professors with a real-life laboratory in which to study the development of the fledgling quasi-union.

In one sense, observing the birth, growth, and maturation of the Guild is like looking into the past and witnessing the development of a new union as it goes through its initial growing pains. In another sense, the birth of a union provides the opportunity to examine many of the old assumptions about labor law, assumptions that are now being retested. For example, many of us harbor certain assumptions about what a union looks like and how it operates. These assumptions, however, are built on the traditional employer–union–employee model, in which the employer wants to get as much work out of the employees as possible and the employees want to work a 40-hour workweek for a living wage, and little more. These assumptions work only if we are dealing with one-dimensional characters who bear little resemblance to real-life individuals. Nevertheless, these stereotypes stick in the minds of both employers and employees and create barriers that ought not to exist.

The Uber experience has challenged these stereotypes by creating a new class of workers who want to work for more than one employer at whatever daily (or weekly or monthly) schedule fits their life style. The app-driven world of Uber has revealed that the very nature of employment will have to be redefined. Legal pundits will have to revisit their concept of the company-run union, which, while outlawed by the Wagner Act, may yet find a valuable role in labor law today. The legal community will also be forced to rethink outlawing the type of secondary quasi-boycott that IDG has managed so successfully in recent months. Judges may be compelled to restructure the very definition of the word "union" by determining when a guild ends and a union begins. These are some of the issues that will be addressed as our study of labor law unfolds. Interested?

Then keep reading. The world of Stefan Zylenko lays just a page away. [See: "About the IDG," IDG, The Independent Drivers Guild, https://drivingguild.org/about, 2017; and Noam Scheiber, "Uber Has a Union. Sort Of," *The New York Times: Sunday Business*, May 14, 2017, pp. 1, 5. "The Black Car Fund: What We Do," The Black Care Fund, www.nybcf.org/about/.]

Opening Case Questions

1. What is the difference between a guild and a union? Explain.
2. What is a company-run union? Explain.
3. What is a secondary boycott? Explain.
4. How is a union formed? Explain.
5. What is the difference between an employee and an independent contractor? Explain.

Source: See: "About the IDG," *IDG The Independent Drivers Guild*, https://drivingguild.org/about. (2017); Noam Scheiber, "Uber Has a Union. Sort Of," *The New York Times: Sunday Business* (May 14, 2017), p. 1 and 5. "The Black Car Fund: What We Do," The Black Car Fund, www.nybcf.org/about/.]

Learning Objectives

1. Relate the historical context in which unions developed.
2. Outline the congressional–judicial tug-of-war in union history.
3. Identify the major provision of the Norris–LaGuardia Act.
4. List the basic aims of labor unions.
5. Explain the nature of the 21st-century crisis in labor law.
6. Indicate the primary tenets of the Wagner Act.
7. List the functions of the Taft–Hartley Act.
8. Explain the provisions of the Landrum–Griffin Act.
9. Describe the jurisdiction of the National Labor Relations Board.
10. Identify the possible results of a complaint filed with the NLRB.

24-1 Labor Law and the Economic Crisis

A **labor union** is an organization that acts on behalf of all employees in negotiations with the employer regarding the terms of their employment. It is a lawful assembly that is protected by the First Amendment to the U.S. Constitution and by federal and state statutes. Americans have always had a love–hate affair with unions. On the one hand, most Americans would like the marketplace to work without undue interference from the government. On the other hand, most Americans also acknowledge that businesses, when left unregulated, often take advantage of that freedom and exploit the labor market. This tension between a free market and a protective government is also seen in economics. The

John L. Lewis (left), founder of the Congress of Industrial Workers (CIO), and Samuel Gompers (right), founder of the American Federation of Labor (AFL), combined to form the AFL-CIO in 1955. Labor unions continue to shape the way companies operate. *Source: Library of Congress, Prints & Photographs Division, photograph by Harris & Ewing, [reproduction number, e.g., LC-USZ62-123456]*

two dominant schools of economic thought in academia today are the Keynesians and the Austrians. At the risk of oversimplifying things (always a danger when speaking of economics), we can say that the Keynesians, named for their founder, the British economist John Maynard Keynes, push for governmental intervention into the economy in order to protect the workers, control debt, provide support for industry, and control the money supply. The Austrian school, notably Friedrich Hayek and Joseph Schumpeter, argue that government intervention does more harm than good because it permits weak financial firms to survive, thus postponing, but not eliminating, an economic crisis, a crisis that, as strange as it may seem, is necessary for the economy to correct itself.

Labor, unfortunately, falls in the middle of this mess and is sometimes supported and sometimes victimized by both sides. The Austrians would suspend or eliminate labor unions and allow unprofitable companies to collapse to be replaced by profitable companies that rehire the unemployed workers of the collapsed firms, probably at better wages and in better workplace conditions than those that could be offered by collapsing firms. The Keynesians, in contrast, see unions as a necessary governmental control device, granting workers the power to determine their own wages and benefits, and thus permitting the government—in the form of the National Labor Relations Board, the courts, and Congress—to lawfully interfere in the operation of that business, thus preventing such economic implosions. This seesaw-like relationship is evident in the historical development of the union movement in the United States, and it provides a further example of the law as a balancing act. [See: Nouriel Roubini and Stephen Mihm, *Crisis Economics* (New York: Penguin Books, 2010), pp. 47–59.]

An Economic Tug-of-War

The history of union development in the United States provides us with a vivid example of the give-and-take between two economic theories: (1) the Keynesian strategy that approves of governmental control and (2) the Austrian school that supports a laissez-faire approach to the economy. In this case, the legislature and the courts were at odds for a long period of time and played off one another in a complicated tug-of-war as they attempted to reestablish a balance within Unions and employers are volatile enough when th the law. Although this legal tug-of-war had no definitive beginning, for convenience, we can identify the passage of the Sherman Antitrust Act in 1890 as a logical starting point. This statute was designed to break up the great anticompetitive trusts of the 19th century. As such, the passage of the Sherman Antitrust Act was an Austrian-like tactic designed to encourage competition in the capitalist economy. Ironically, in fashioning the Sherman Act to promote Austrian-like competition, Congress used its power to interfere in the economic sector, a very Keynesian-like tactic. The courts responded by issuing injunctions that permitted the corporations to use the Sherman Act to break up unions, another Keynesian tactic that, strangely, promoted Austrian principles.

The Clayton Act of 1914 Congress reacted to this example of judicial activism ("legislating from the bench" yet again) by passing the Clayton Act in 1914, another Keynesian-like tactic that forced companies to cooperate with union organizers and thus helped keep people employed. One of the goals of the Clayton Act was to hamper the federal courts' ability to issue injunctions to stop union activities. This would force businesses to recognize the role of unions as a way for employees to protect their rights. The federal judicial system, however, again reflecting an Austrian-like desire to pull the government out of the economic sector, effectively destroyed the Clayton Act when the Supreme Court (in yet another startling example of legislating from the bench) "amended" Clayton by adding two criteria that allowed the courts to issue injunctions freely to stop labor activities. The first test was *the objectives test*. Under this test, a court could issue an injunction if it determined that the goal of a strike was unlawful. Under the second test, *the means test*, the courts could stop a strike if it was conducted in an unlawful manner. The two tests were easily manipulated by big business, and the courts cooperated by routinely issuing injunctions in ways that had not been foreseen nor intended by Congress. Once again a pro-Keynesian strategy (court-issued injunctions) had been used to reestablish an Austrian-like economy (a union-free, strike-free economic system).

A QUESTION OF ETHICS

Creative Destruction or Government Regulation: The Austrians v. The Keynesians

Recall that the leading schools in economic philosophy in intellectual circles in the modern age are the Keynesians and the Austrians. Predictably, the two schools agree on almost nothing, so there is a clear dialectic split between the two groups—a split that inevitably affects labor, labor law, and the labor union concept. The two schools of thought do agree on one premise, however, and that is a belief that capitalism is unstable. Unfortunately, they disagree on what to do about that instability. The Keynesians advocate governmental involvement to protect the economy. The basic idea is that the best way to control an inherently unstable economy is to intervene in a rational way in order to reset the market's equilibrium. Conversely, the Austrians maintain that government intervention does more harm than good because it allows, even at times encourages, fragile businesses to continue, thus stalling, but not stopping, an economic collapse, a collapse that is needed for the economy to rebalance itself. To summarize, the Keynesians see instability as a harmful trend needing rational governmental correction, while the Austrians see it as the normal program of events that must remain unaffected by the government. Before you consider the following questions, turn back to Chapter 1 to review the various ethical theories noted there (social contract theory, utilitarianism, and rational ethics). Then, using one of those theories in a consistent way, answer the following questions on *creative destruction and government regulation* (or Austrianism v. Keynesianism). Is there a balancing principle hidden somewhere in this conflict, or is the Keynesian-Austrian dialectic unresolvable? Which side (the Austrians or the Keynesians) seems to have the correct approach from an ethical perspective? Would you rather see the government step in or step out of the economy? [See: Roubini and Mihm.]

Source: See: Nouriel Roubini and Stephen Mihm, Crisis Economics (New York: Penguin Books, 2010), pp. 47–59.

The Norris–LaGuardia Act of 1932 Not to be outdone, Congress reacted to this nasty subterfuge by passing another pro-Keynesian law, the Norris–LaGuardia Act, in 1932, the net effect of which was to prohibit the federal courts from issuing injunctions against union-organized strikes, thus forcing companies to do what Congress had wanted all along, to cooperate with union organizers and thus keep people working. The law also supported union activities by forbidding the courts from using injunctions to stop picketing or boycotts organized by unions, again forcing businesses to cooperate with union organizers.

The Goals of Labor Organizations

The Norris–LaGuardia Act was just one step down a long road of labor law development. Later labor laws both promoted the aims of labor unions while also preventing unions from becoming too powerful, thus perpetuating the Keynesian–Austrian balance (some might say tug-of-war). Many different types of unions have developed over the years since the advent of the Norris-LaGuardia Act. Whatever their form, however, labor unions have several objectives in common. These Keynesian-like goals include (1) creating a seniority system to protect workers' jobs from arbitrary layoffs and replacement with less demanding wage earners; (2) upgrading worker status through wage and fringe benefit increases; and (3) sponsoring laws that improve social, economic, and political conditions for worker.

The 21st-Century Labor Crisis

Over the last few years, the battle over unions has started once again. Stymied by the recent economic meltdown caused by subprime loans, falling real estate prices, and uncontrolled debt, state governments have elected to use an odd hybrid of Keynesian-Austrian tactics on themselves. In a strangely schizophrenic pattern of activity, the state governments have decided that labor unions that represent state workers must be eliminated (or in the alternative, weakened severely). In essence, the governors and the state legislatures of several midwestern states, notably Wisconsin, Ohio, Illinois, and Michigan, created and passed legislation that was deliberately and unapologetically designed to eliminate (or, in the alternative, weaken) the collective bargaining power of those unions that represent state workers (see Table 24-1). In theory, this plan would save the state governments a great deal of money, money that will not be paid in raises, health care benefits, and pension contributions. Of course, this would also mean fewer dollars in the pockets of almost 360,000 workers in Ohio alone, which, of course, decreases the buying power of state citizens, citizens who will no longer be spending quite as much money in stores, restaurants, hotels, and shops in their home states. (*Note:* Ohio voters rejected the antiunion law by a 61-39 percent margin in November 2011.)

A SOON TO BE CLASSIC CASE   Another Anti-Public Union Tactic: "One for All and All for One!—Nevermore!"

Unions and employers are volatile enough when they must confront one another one-on-one, but add the government into the mix and (with apologies to Lt. Maryk in *The Caine Mutiny*) "It's like running around dynamite with a blow torch." This is what has happened in the case of *Janus v. AFSCME*. The case began when the governor of Illinois challenged a state statute that gave public unions like the American Federation of State, County, and Municipal Employees (AFSCME) the exclusive authority to represent all state employees, even those who were opposed to the very idea of a union. The governor was especially incensed because the law robs the workers of their right to speak to their public employers as individuals or as members of a rival organization. As if adding insult to injury, the law also forces all state employees, even those who rebuff the union, to contribute part of their wages to the running of that union.

The governor's challenge arose out of the need to deal with a severe budgetary crisis in Illinois. When he found his efforts to join raises to merit and to streamline health benefits blocked by the AFSCME, he sued in federal court, arguing that the statute represented an unconstitutional block on freedom of speech for those workers opposed to the union. The governor's hope was that he would cripple the union financially by removing the statute that forced unwilling workers to contribute to the union's treasury. A few months after the governor filed his case, several public employees were added as plaintiffs to the suit. One of these plaintiffs was Mark Janus. The governor was later removed from the case because he could not show that he had been injured by the statute and, thus, had no standing to sue. Janus, however, remained as a plaintiff and the lawsuit continued. The constitutionality of state laws that authorize public unions to take operating expenses from nonmembers has been litigated before. In each case, the Supreme Court held such statutes constitutional as long as the amount paid represents the employee's fair share of the union's operating expenses and is not used to support a political agenda. The main Supreme Court Case supporting the law's constitutionality is *Abood v. Detroit Board of Education*, 431 U.S. 209 (1977).

At the time of the Janus suit, *Abood v. Detroit* had recently been challenged in the case of *Harris v. Quinn*, 134 S. Ct. 2618 (2014). When *Harris v. Quinn* reached the Supreme Court, four justices offered the following reasons for over turning *Abood*: The Court in *Abood* (1) "'fundamentally misunderstood' earlier cases concerning laws authorizing compulsory fees in the private sector; (2) failed to appreciate the difficulty of distinguishing between collective bargaining and politics in the public sector; (3) failed to appreciate the difficulty of distinguishing between collective bargaining and politics in the public sector; (4) did not foresee the difficulty in classifying union expenditures as 'chargeable or non-chargeable'; (5) 'did not foresee the practical problems that would face objecting nonmembers'; and (6) wrongly assumed forced fees are necessary to exclusive representation." The High Court would probably have overturned *Harris* had Justice Scalia not passed away. After Scalia was gone, the liberal and the conservative voices were evenly split. As a result, the ruling in *Harris* ended in a 4–4 tie. The tie meant that the *Abood* ruling was preserved.

However, since 2014, things have changed. Justice Gorsuch, the president's new appointee, is just as conservative as Justice Scalia. Consequently, in 2018, the High Court overturned Abood and in the Janus case ruled that the Illinois law is unconstitutional. Thus, we have witnessed a successful attack on public unions. The moral of the story is when the governor fails, turn the matter over the U.S. Supreme Court because those justices have no qualms about rewriting history and, in the process, destroying public unions and trampling on the will of the legislature. End of speech. [See: *Janus v. American Federation of State, County, and Municipal Employees, Council 31, et al.*; No. 16-1466 (June 27, 2018); and *Abood v. Detroit Board of Education*, 431 U.S. 209 (1977). See also: Adam Liptak, "Renewed Attack on Public Unions," *The New York Times*, June 13, 2017, p. A16.]

Source: See: *Janus v. American Federation of State, County, and Municipal Employees*, Council 31, et., al.; No. 16-1466 (June 27, 2018); *Abood v. Detroit Board of Education*, 431 U.S. 209 (1977). See also: Adam Liptak, "Renewed Attack on Public Unions," *The New York Times* (June 13, 2017), p. A16.

Table 24-1 Provisions of Ohio's Antiunion Law (2011)

Provision	Explanation
Health insurance	Employers cannot pay more than 80% into the cost of employee health insurance benefits.
Pension plans	Stops public employers from paying employee contributions to state retirement systems.
Merit pay	Mandates merit pay; takes step increases and all other automatic pay increases off the negotiating table.
Strikes and mediation	Eliminates public employees' right to strike and to submit disputes to any agreed upon dispute resolution procedure.
Collective bargaining I	Eliminates the collective bargaining rights of K–12 teachers in relation to class size, workload, and workforce size.
Collective bargaining II	Eliminates collective bargaining completely for college and university faculty members.
Fiscal emergencies	Municipalities, counties, school districts in fiscal emergency status can ignore past collective bargaining agreements. Also occurs if the state itself is in a fiscal emergency.

Sources: Nick Thomas, "Sub. S.B. 5 of the 129th G.A.," *Fiscal Note and Impact Statement: State and Local Fiscal Highlights*, Ohio Legislative Service Commission (February 2011); and Amanda Garrett, "Ohio's Senate Bill 5 Could End Collective Bargaining for Many Public College Professors," Cleveland.com (March 2011). See also *Bill Analysis*, Legislative Service Commission, Sub. S.B. 5, http://www/legislature.state.oh.us

> **quick quiz 24-1**
>
> 1. A labor union is an organization that acts on behalf of all employees in negotiations with the employer regarding the terms of their employment. — true | false
> 2. Labor union activity is not protected by the First Amendment. — true | false
> 3. The Norris–LaGuardia Act empowered the courts to issue injunctions to stop boycotts by workers. — true | false

24-2 Major Federal Labor Legislation

After the Norris-LaGuardia Act was passed by Congress in 1932, several tough labor laws were enacted. The three most important legislative enactments are the National Labor Relations Act of 1935 (generally referred to as the Wagner Act), the Labor-Management Relations Act of 1947 (popularly referred to as the Taft-Hartley Act), and the Labor Management Reporting and Disclosure Act of 1959 (often simply called the Landrum-Griffin Act). The first of these was designed to support labor's attempt to organize. The last two were designed to curb some unanticipated problems that accompanied the growth of unions in the United States. (See Table 24-2.)

Table 24-2 Federal Laws Governing Labor–Management Relations

Year	Law	Major Provisions
1914	Clayton Act	Exempted union activity from the antitrust laws
1926	Railway Labor Act	Provided for supervision of collective bargaining for railroads and airlines Established the National Mediation Board to conduct union elections and mediate employer-union disputes
1932	Norris–LaGuardia Act	Outlawed yellow-dog contracts Limited the power of federal courts to issue injunctions to halt labor disputes Guaranteed employees the right to organize into unions and to engage in collective bargaining
1935	Wagner Act	Created the National Labor Relations Board (NLRB) Authorized NLRB to conduct representative elections and to determine the bargaining unit Outlawed certain conduct by employers as unfair labor practices Authorized NLRB to hold hearings on unfair labor practic petitions
1947	Taft–Hartley Act	Outlawed certain practices by unions as unfair labor practices Allowed states to legislate right-to-work laws Provided an 80-day cooling-off period in strikes that endangered national health or safety Created a mediation and conciliation service to assist in the settlement of labor disputes
1959	Landrum–Griffin Act	Established a bill of rights for union members Required unions to adopt constitutions and bylaws Required unions to submit annual reports detailing assets, liabilities, payments, and loans Added further provisions to the list of unfair labor practices

The Wagner Act

The passage of the National Labor Relations Act in 1935 (commonly known as the Wagner Act) opened the door for the rapid growth of the union movement. It is probably the most significant U.S. labor relations statute in that it expressly sets forth the unfair labor practices prohibited for both employers and unions. The Wagner Act gives workers the right to organize by allowing them to form, join, or aid labor unions. It also establishes procedures for representative elections and collective bargaining. These basic rights are found in Title 29, Chapter 7, Subchapter II, Section 157, of the United States Code:

> Employees shall have the right to self-organization, to form, join, or assist labor organizations, to bargain collectively through representatives of their own choosing, and to engage in other concerted activities for the purpose of collective bargaining or other mutual aid or protection, and shall also have the right to refrain from any or all such activities except to the extent that such right may be affected by an agreement requiring membership in a labor organization as a condition of employment as authorized in section 158 (a) (3) of this title.

After a union has been chosen to represent the employees of a business, only that union can bargain with management. After the union has been set up at a business, individual workers cannot, on their own initiative, negotiate with management. The union has the exclusive right to bargain with the management of the business, even if the employees do not agree with how the union is handling a matter. The Wagner Act is also known for its creation of the National Labor Relations Board (NLRB), which hears and rules on charges that unfair labor practices have been committed by employers or by unions.

Employee and Labor Organization—Defined?

When first entering a subject as complex and multifaceted as labor law, and before describing the various provisions within that law, the legislature is usually very careful to define all relevant terms that will be used in that legislation. Sometimes such definitions take a great deal of space in the early sections of the law, and often people overlook these definitions. This is a mistake because the court will generally focus on such terms when litigation ensues. Unfortunately, sometimes the legislature is not much help. It may define a term in a simple and conservative way without providing much detail. In such cases, in trying to comprehend what the legislature means, the court will call on other sources such as the common law definition found in case law and those additional definitions that can be found in various restatements, legal treatises, law review articles, and so on. In the Wagner Act, for example, the legislature went to great lengths to define the term *labor organization* writing that a "'labor organization' means any organization of any kind, or any agency or employee representation committee or plan, in which employees participate and which exists for the purpose, in whole or in part, of dealing with employers concerning grievances, labor disputes, wages, rates of pay, hours of employment, or conditions of work." [See: 29 USC section 152 2(3).]

In contrast, when defining the term *employee*, the legislature was not quite as eloquent. The statutory definition of employee begins with a statement that says, quite simply, that an employee is "any employee." However, Congress then adds that the term *employee* shall

> not be limited to the employees of a particular employer, unless this subchapter explicitly states otherwise, and shall include any individual whose work has ceased as a consequence of, or in connection with, any current labor dispute or because of any unfair labor practice, and who has not obtained any other regular and substantially equivalent employment, but shall not include any individual employed as an agricultural laborer, or in the domestic service of any family or person at his home, or any individual employed by his parent or spouse, or any individual having the status of an independent contractor, or any individual

employed as a supervisor, or any individual employed by an employer subject to the Railway Labor Act [45 U.S.C. 151 et seq.], as amended from time to time, or by any other person who is not an employer as herein defined.

As can be seen here, most of the definition is devoted to covering what an employee is not. Consequently, whenever a court must define the term *employee*, that court must search through case law to find the common law definition as well as any other definitions that have been offered by various restatements, legal treatises, law review articles, and so on. Despite the need to access these sources, the process of interpretation described here does not, by itself, violate the rules of textualism. It is true that, in interpreting a statute (constitution, regulation, city ordinance, and so on), a textualist must look at the words on the page and nothing more. However, a textualist must also make certain that he or she understands those words as they were defined and used in the time period during which the statute (constitution, regulation, city ordinance, and so on) was written. This often requires some research into the etymology of the words on the page. This is especially true in labor law, which has such a deep and varied history. In the case of the word *employee*, for example, the courts have sought the contextual meaning of the the word by relying upon the common law definition as taken from the Restatement (Second) of Agency Section 2(2). That definition states, "An employee is a person who performs services for another under a contract of hire, subject to the others' control or right to control and in return for payment." [See: *Brown University*, 342 NLRB 483 49o, fn. 27 (2004) (citing *NLRB v. Town & Country Electric*, 516 U.S. at 94).]

A CONTEMPORARY CASE Students or Employees? Academic Club or Labor Organization?

The College Athletes Players Association (CAPA) filed a petition with the National Labor Relations Board, asking the NLRB to permit the football players at Northwestern University (NU) to vote on whether to unionize. NU, of course, opposed the petition. The arguments put forth by the university can be summarized as follows: (1) The football players are not employees no matter how the term is defined but are, instead, students, as determined by an earlier case known as *Brown University*, 342 NLRB 483 (2004); (2) if the NLRB decides that the students are employees, they are, at best, temporary employees who have no right to unionize; and/or (3) even if the students are full-time employees, the potential bargaining unit, the CAPA, is not a "labor organization" under the Wagner Act and, therefore, has no standing to represent the players or to present the petition. The second and third arguments are easy enough to refute. Starting from the last and moving to the first argument, the university contended that CAPA is not a proper bargaining unit because it does not fit the definition found in the Wagner Act. The NLRB rejected the argument, saying that the CAPA clearly qualified as a union because it "exists for the purpose . . . of dealing with employers on their (the employees) behalf regarding wages, hours of employment and other conditions of employment." As for the second argument, well, the NLRB easily ruled that the players are full-time workers, saying: (1) The players have a lengthy tenure at NU (four to five years), (2) they work more than 40 hours per week, (3) they work year round, and (4) they have a vested interest in their role as athletes (unlike others, such as student janitors, who focus on their studies and have no vested interest in their employment other than as a way to finance their student careers).

The first argument is the real stumbling block. Are the players employees or are they students? This question was critical because the CAPA's entire case was based on the belief that the players were employees. If they were employees, then the rest of the arguments would easily fall into place. If they were not, the rest of the arguments fell apart. The problem was that the Wagner Act defines *employees* in a simple and, to be candid, a very unproductive way. The act says that the term *employees* includes "any employee." In order to unravel the true meaning of employee, the NLRB representative had to dive into case law and examine the common law definition of employee, a definition that was probably created by a medieval judge who did not even know what a football was, let alone a football player. Calling upon the common law definition found in case law and in the Restatement (Second) of Agency, the NLRB said, "An employee is a person who performs services for another under a contract of hire, subject to the others' control or right to control and in return for payment." Looking at the evidence, the NLRB found that the coaching staff at NU uses a wide variety of techniques to control the activities of the players before, during, and after the season. Such areas of control include where they live, what vehicles they drive, whether they can leave the campus, whether they speak to the press, what they can place on the Internet, and so on. The players have a lengthy tenure at NU (four to five years) and work more than 50 to 60 hours per week before the season starts, 40 to 50 during the season, and 20 to 25 after the season. They can also receive as much as $250,000 in pay (although not as a salary, but in terms of overall financial perks) over a tenure of four to five years.

This evidence was enough for the NLRB to declare that the players were employees. However, just to add icing to the cake, the NLRB also used the *Brown University* case as further authority. In that case, the NLRB ruled that graduate students are not employees and could not unionize. However, the NLRB makes several distinctions here, all of which underline the differences between graduate students and football players: (1) The players are not primarily students (the grad students are primarily students), (2) their athletic duties are not part of their curricular requirements for graduation (the grad students' duties are part of their core requirements for their degrees), (3) the academic faculty do not supervise the players (grad students are supervised by the faculty), and (4) the compensation received by the players is not like the financial aid received by the grad students. [See: *Northwestern University, Employer v. College Athletes Players Association, Petitioner*, National Labor Relations Board, Region 13, Case Number, 13-RC-121359 (2014); and John Wolohan, "College Athletes Players Association v. Northwestern University," *Law in Sport*, April 25, 2014.]

Source: See: *Northwestern University, Employer v. College Athletes Players Association, Petitioner, National Labor Relations Board,* Region 13, Case Number, 13-RC-121359 (2014); John Wolohan, "College Athletes Players Association v. Northwestern University," *Law In Sport*, April 25, 2014.

Prohibited Activities: Unfair Labor Practices Various activities are prohibited by the Wagner Act as **unfair labor practices**, that is, improper employment practices by either an employer or the union. These activities include the following:

- Interference with employees' right to organize.
- Domination or interference with the formation or administration of any union.
- Discrimination to encourage or discourage union membership.
- Discharge for charges filed or testimony given.
- Refusal to bargain collectively.

Interference with Employees' Right to Organize An employer cannot interfere with employees when they are forming a union, selecting their representatives, voting, striking, picketing, or engaging in any other protected and legal acts. For example, an employer cannot threaten to fire or discipline a worker for union activity or reward workers who do not participate in union activities. Threats to eliminate certain benefits or privileges, to close the business, or to discharge workers for union activity also are prohibited.

EXAMPLE 24-1: Insubordination or Inconsistency: Which One Trumps the Other?

In his 10 years as a chef at the Imperial National Hotel in Houston, James Kirby might have been fired several times for violating work rules. He frequently refused to follow orders, disobeying direct instructions from his supervisor. When a union began organizing the kitchen service and housekeeping staff, Kirby strongly supported the effort. During the organizing campaign, Kirby apparently acted in an insubordinate manner and was discharged. At a subsequent NLRB hearing, his discharge was found to be tainted. On appeal, the court reasoned that though Kirby was far from the valued and trusted employee the union claimed he was, the hotel had tolerated his insubordination for 10 years. The court held that Kirby's discharge was more the result of his union activities than his work performance and reinstated him with back pay.

Domination or Interference with the Formation or Administration of Any Union An employer cannot form a company-run union for its employees. The purpose of this prohibition is to bar **company-run unions** from bowing to the wishes of management. It is also an unfair practice to aid one union over another, place employer spies at union meetings, reward some union officials, or agree with a union that a **closed shop** will be maintained. A closed shop is a work site in which the employer, by agreement, hires only union members in good standing. It is usually lawful, however, to have a provision allowing a union shop in the employment contract. A **union shop** is a place of employment in which nonunion workers may be employed for a trial period of not more than 30 days, after which the nonunion workers must join the union or be discharged.

Discrimination to Encourage or Discourage Union Membership Intentional discrimination by the employer toward an employee to encourage or discourage union membership is an unfair labor practice. Such discrimination may involve assigning an employee to less desirable work or denying an employee the opportunity to participate in overtime work. Also viewed as discriminatory is **constructive discharge**, which occurs when an employee is demoted to a job with lesser pay or authority or poorer working conditions than a previously held job or when the employee is subjected to supervisory harassment. To avoid employee complaints of intentional discrimination, employers must rely on meaningful business reasons when bestowing or denying employment opportunities.

EXAMPLE 24-2: Constructive Discharge: Nothing Trivial about It

Teresa Remington was chosen by union members to serve as their representative in collective bargaining meetings with the Harrisburg Construction Company. After her selection, Remington was harassed by the general manager of her department for trivial matters pertaining to scheduled lunch breaks and the cleanliness of her locker in the break room. Remington has the right to file a complaint with the NLRB, charging constructive discharge due to her union activities.

Discharge for Charges Filed or Testimony Given It is unlawful for employers to discharge or otherwise discriminate against employees because they file charges or give testimony under the Wagner Act. The courts interpret discrimination under this provision to include discharge, layoff, failure to rehire or recall, and transfer of covered employees.

Refusal to Bargain Collectively An employer must negotiate with employee representatives over wages, hours, the effects of business changes on employees, grievance procedures, health benefits, seniority systems, dues check-offs, and vacations. Issues must be discussed willingly, free of delaying tactics, coercion, or harassment by both sides. The employer has no duty to agree to any union demands but must meet with employee representatives at reasonable times and places to bargain in good faith. Neither party can bargain about a closed shop contract, politics, religious issues, management functions, or foreign affairs. The NLRB has no jurisdiction over religious schools, both on labor relations grounds and by virtue of the religion clauses of the First Amendment of the U.S. Constitution. The U.S. Supreme Court has ruled that the requirements of collective bargaining would represent an encroachment upon the freedom of church authorities to shape and direct teaching in accordance with the requirements of their religion. Finally, the Wagner Act does not apply to most federal employees. Nor does it apply to state or local government employees. This is why it is possible for the state governments in Wisconsin, Ohio, and Michigan to attempt to alter the collective bargaining rights of firefighters, police officers, and teachers.

THE OPENING CASE *Round 2*
"Of Guilds, Unions, Workers, and the Law"—Ready or Not, Here Comes UBER and the IDG

Recall that the Independent Drivers Guild (the IDG or the Guild) appeared on the scene in 2016 as an affiliate of the International Association of Machinists and Aerospace Workers (IAMAW). The IAMAW has represented ride-share car drivers in the New York area since the 1990s, winning for those drivers the right to form unions and to engage in collective bargaining. Enter Uber, the app-powered business enterprise that is responsible for a revolution in convenient and cost-effective personal transportation. As is true of any innovation, Uber brought with it a series of unintended consequences, not the least of which was the fact that many independent car drivers who worked at least part-time for Uber had no representation within the company. Many of these drivers asked for help from the IAMAW, which collaborated with Uber to form the IDG, which has worked to provide the app-based drivers with a place at the bargaining table. Now, however, the Independent Driver's Guild is faced with its own challenges, some of which are reflected in an institutional identity crisis. That identity crisis can be spelled out quite simply—How does the Guild fit into the traditional model of the American labor union?

In order to deal with this issue, several questions must be answered. The first, and most fundamental of all, asks whether the Guild fits into the traditional definition of labor organization as spelled out by Congress in the Wagner Act of 1935. The second inquiry asks whether Uber drivers can be considered employees within definition of employee as established by Congress in 1935 in the Wagner Act. The third question asks whether the Guild is an independent labor union, separate from the company, or simply a cleverly disguised company-run union, the type outlawed by Wagner? Finally, the last question asks whether the boycotts initiated by the Guild, with the quiet blessing of Uber, amount to the type of secondary boycott outlawed by the Taft-Hartley Act. We will address the first two questions here. The final two will be answered in the Opening Case *Round 3*.

First, is the Guild a true labor organization as defined in the Wagner Act? To answer this question, we must determine how Congress defines labor organization and how the Guild defines itself. First, the Wagner Act defines labor union in the following way: "The term labor organization means any organization of any kind, or any agency or employee representation committee or plan, in which employees participate and which exists for the purpose, in whole or in part, of dealing with employers concerning grievances, labor disputes, wages, rates of pay, hours of employment, or conditions of work." [See: 29 U.S. Code Section 152 (5).] Second, the Guild defines itself as "the first nonprofit labor organization to negotiate a seat at the table with ride share company and the first to offer crucial new protections and essential benefits while building worker power." Comparing the two definitions reveals that the Guild's self-initiated description includes some of the relevant characteristics found in the legal definition of a labor organization, including employee participation, employee benefits, and protections. Moreover, empirical evidence, such as the Guild's work in convincing Uber to raise the minimum fare from $7 to $8 and its campaign to convince the Taxi and Limousine Commission to regulate Uber's fares, indicate that the organization has acted and continues to act within the statutory definition of labor organization.

The second question ("Do Uber drivers qualify as employees under the Wagner Act?) is a different issue altogether. The statute defines employee in the following way, "The term 'employee' shall include any employee, and shall not be limited to the employees of a particular employer, unless this subchapter explicitly states otherwise, and shall include any individual whose work has ceased as a consequence of, or in connection with, any current labor dispute or because of any unfair labor practice, and who has not obtained any other regular and substantially equivalent employment, but shall not include any individual employed as an agricultural laborer, or in the domestic service of any family or person at his home, or any individual employed by his parent or spouse, or any individual having the status of an independent contractor, or any individual employed as a supervisor, or any individual employed by an employer subject to the Railway Labor Act [See: 45 U.S.C, 151 et seq.], as amended from time to time, or by any other person who is not an employer as herein defined." As noted previously, most of this definition is devoted to covering what an employee is not. However, one phrase that argues against the notion that Uber drivers are employees reads, "The term employee . . . shall not include . . . an independent contractor." The fact that Uber insists that its drivers are independent contractors suggests that Uber drivers are not employees, as does the fact that Uber drivers use their own vehicles and set their own work schedules. Whether the courts (or the NLRB) will ultimately declare Uber drivers to be independent contractors or employees remains to be seen. For now, in a moment, we will address the last two questions: Is the Guild an illegal company-run union, and is it guilty of engineering an unlawful secondary boycott? [See: "About the IDG," IDG, The Independent Drivers Guild, https://drivingguild.org/about, 2017; and Noam Scheiber, "Uber Has a Union. Sort Of," *The New York Times: Sunday Business*, May 14, 2017, pp. 1, 5.)

Source: See: "About the IDG," *IDG The Independent Drivers Guild*, https://drivingguild.org /about. (2017); Noam Scheiber, "Uber Has a Union. Sort Of," *The New York Times: Sunday Business* (May 14, 2017), p. 1 and 5.

The Taft–Hartley Act

The Labor-Management Relations Act of 1947, popularly named the Taft–Hartley Act, established a means to protect employers in collective bargaining and labor organization matters. The act also prohibits union officials from using coercive or abusive tactics against its own members. A detailed list of unfair labor activities that unions, as well as employers, were forbidden to practice was added to those of the Wagner Act.

State Right-to-Work Laws

State laws that prohibit labor–management agreements requiring union membership as a condition of getting or keeping a job are called **right-to-work laws**. These laws, in effect, outlaw both the closed shop and the union shop. Ordinarily, state labor laws have not applied to unions and businesses that are involved in interstate commerce and that are governed by federal labor laws. In fact, as noted earlier in the chapter, state labor laws generally focus only on those employees whose union activities are not regulated by federal labor law, such as state government workers. Nevertheless, the Taft–Hartley Act has created special rules with regard to state right-to-work laws. It provides that union shop contracts are legal only in states that do not forbid them. As a result, state right-to-work laws, where they exist, are applicable to most unions and businesses. All employees in the **bargaining unit** (i.e., a unit formed for the purpose of collective bargaining) are benefited by the collective bargaining agreement negotiated by the union, even if they have not paid union dues. However, nonunion employees lose all right to vote on union officers or collective bargaining agreements.

Limiting the Power of the NLRB   Some members of Congress recently proposed limiting the power of the National Labor Relations Board to pressure an employer into keeping his or her business located in a particular state. Recall that some states have passed right-to-work laws that allow employees to opt out of union membership when a union is formed or presently operates in their workplace. This feature makes such states attractive to businesses that would rather keep union membership in their business to a minimum. Some businesses have gone so far as to decide to move a plant or office from a non-right-to-work state into a state with a right-to-work law. In one case, the National Labor Relations Board issued an order that would have prevented a business from setting up a new facility in a right-to-work state. This order by the NLRB prompted some members of Congress to mount a campaign to amend the Wagner Act to limit the power of the board to frame such orders. Like the actions by the governors and the state legislatures in Wisconsin, Ohio, and Michigan, a proposal like this one in Congress further demonstrates the antiunion sentiment that has been growing within the government in the 21st century.

Free Speech Provision   The Taft–Hartley Act includes a free speech provision that allows employers to comment freely on union organizing activities. The provision states that employers do not commit an unfair labor practice by speaking to employees about unions unless they threaten reprisal or promise some benefit to employees. For instance, an employer might properly inform its employees that they should not vote for a union, but a threat to fire anyone for favoring a union shop would be an unfair labor practice.

Employee Anti-Coercion Provision   It is also an unfair labor practice for a labor union to try to coerce employees to join the union, block the employment of individuals who refuse to support a union, or encourage an employee to withdraw an unfair labor practice charge. A union can set rules for its internal operations and punish any member who refuses to follow them, but it cannot use force, violence, or intimidation against an employee. A union is also not permitted to discipline one of its members without good cause. The union has a duty to represent all of its members on an equal basis.

Secondary Boycott   It is also prohibited for a union to engage in a **secondary boycott**. This action is a conspiracy in which a union places pressure on a neutral customer or supplier with whom the union has no dispute to cause the neutral entity to cease doing business with the employer with whom the union has a dispute. Under the Taft–Hartley Act provision, it is an unfair labor practice for a union (1) to strike against an employer because another employer uses nonunion employees, (2) to strike against a general contractor to force the contractor to stop dealing with a subcontractor, (3) to ask employees of another company not to load trucks carrying the products of a company the union is striking, or (4) to refuse to work on products made by nonunion employees.

THE OPENING CASE *Round 3*
"Of Guilds, Unions, Workers, and the Law"—Ready or Not, Here Comes UBER and the IDG

Let's take one more look at the legal status of the Independent Drivers Guild. Thus far in our examination of the Guild's identity, we have established (1) that the Guild is a labor organization within the statutory definition found in 29 U.S. Code Section 152 (5) because it offers Uber drivers participation in the Guild itself, provides a voice for the drivers with Uber management, and has helped improve the lot of drivers in relation to fares and tipping. In contrast, the status of Uber drivers as employees is less clear. This is due primarily to Uber's insistence that its drivers are independent contractors and to the behavior of the drivers themselves who own their own vehicles, make their own work schedules, and sometimes work for more than one ride-service company at the same time. Now let's look at the last two identity crisis questions: (3) "Is the Guild an independent labor union that is separate from the company (Uber), or is it, in reality, a thinly disguised, illegal company-run union?" (4) "Do the boycotts initiated by the Guild, with the quiet consent of Uber, amount to the type of secondary boycott outlawed by the Taft-Hartley Act?"

The question of whether the Guild is a company-run union is difficult to answer because the quasi-union seems to have established its independence by opposing the company on issues such as tipping and minimum fares. However, on the other side of the ledger, Uber pays the Guild for its work and supplies the Guild with lists of contact information about area drivers. Moreover, the Guild avoids getting involved in issues, such as fare cuts, that Uber would just as soon not discuss. Most telling, however, is the fact that the New York Taxi Workers Alliance filed an unfair labor practice complaint with the National Labor Relations Board (NLRB) charging Uber with setting up and operating a company-run union in direct violation of the Wagner Act. [See: Section 24-3.] Interestingly enough, Uber can contest this charge because the Wagner Act applies only to unions that represent employees, not to organizations that speak for independent contractors. So, ironically, if Uber drivers really are independent contractors, then the Guild has every right to operate as a company-run union.

The final question asks whether the work interruption campaign initiated by the Guild and aimed at Uber's competitor, Lyft, will be outlawed by the NLRB as a secondary boycott under the Taft-Hartley Act. To answer this question, let's first define secondary boycott and then examine the Guild's campaign against Lyft. Recall that "a secondary boycott is a conspiracy in which a union places pressure on a neutral customer or supplier with whom the union has no dispute to cause the neutral entity to cease doing business with the employer with whom the union has a dispute." In its campaign against Lyft, the Guild encouraged its members to reserve rides with Lyft drivers in order to discuss the Guild with those drivers in defiance of Lyft's opposition to the Guild's union organizing campaign. Those Lyft drivers who refused to discuss union organizing activities would find the ride canceled. Even if the strategy failed to recruit a single driver, it would still manufacture a temporary driver shortage that would frustrate and delay regular Lyft customers. While this campaign was not a traditional, garden variety, secondary boycott, it did, nevertheless, place pressure (albeit indirectly) against a neutral customer (the delayed and frustrated Lyft client) in order to disrupt an employer (Lyft) with whom the Guild had no direct dispute (other than Lyft's reluctance to bargain with its drivers). So is the Guild's anti-Lyft campaign an illegal secondary boycott? Probably, but then only if the Guild really is a labor organization that represents employees rather than independent contractors, which it seems not to be. Satisfied? You shouldn't be. After all, the net result of our experiment has been to demonstrate that the legal status of the Guild as a union is, at best, ambiguous and, at worst, outside the boundaries of both the Wagner Act and the Taft–Hartley Act. How the court (or the NLRB) might act in the future in relation to these issues, remains to be seen. All we can say now is, "Stay tuned." [See: "About the IDG," IDG The Independent Drivers Guild, https://drivingguild.org/about, 2017; and Noam Scheiber, "Uber Has a Union. Sort Of," *The New York Times: Sunday Business*, May 14, 2017, pp. 1 5.)

Source: See: "About the IDG," *IDG The Independent Drivers Guild*, https://drivingguild.org /about. (2017); Noam Scheiber, "Uber Has a Union. Sort Of," *The New York Times: Sunday Business* (May 14, 2017), p. 1 and 5.

National Emergency Strikes

The Taft–Hartley Act gives the President of the United States special powers to deal with actual or threatened strikes that affect interstate commerce or that endanger the nation's health and safety. On the basis of a board of inquiry's findings, the president can order the attorney general to petition a federal district court to issue an injunction, stopping the strike for 60 days. The board of inquiry may then require the union members to vote on the most recent offer within an additional 15-day period and to send the results to the attorney general within five days after balloting. When the injunction ends after this 80-day period, the employees may strike. However, the president can then make legislative recommendations to Congress that would resolve the dispute.

Other Prohibited Union Practices

Under other provisions of the Taft–Hartley Act, unions cannot refuse to bargain collectively with an employer and must give notice to the employer of an intention to strike prior to the termination date of a collective bargaining contract. It is also an unfair labor practice for a labor union to require an employer to keep unneeded employees, pay employees for not working, or assign more employees to a given job than are needed (i.e., **featherbedding**). Another provision of the law prohibits a union from requiring employees who join a union to pay excessively high dues, fees, and related expenses. To determine what is excessive, the courts consider the amounts other unions charge and the employee's wages.

The Landrum–Griffin Act

The Labor Management Reporting and Disclosure Act of 1959, known as the Landrum-Griffin Act, is a tough anticorruption law. It is designed to clean up the corruption and violence that had been uncovered in the internal affairs of unions. The law requires all unions to adopt constitutions and bylaws and to register them with the secretary of labor. In addition, unions are required to submit annual reports detailing assets, liabilities, receipts, sources, payments to union members exceeding $10,000, loans to union members and businesses, and other monies paid out.

Bill of Rights Provision An important part of the Landrum-Griffin Act is the bill of rights provision for union members. This provision assures all union members of the opportunity to participate in the internal affairs of their union. They are guaranteed the right to vote in union elections, to speak at union meetings, and to receive union financial reports.

Hot-Cargo Agreement The Landrum-Griffin Act amended the Taft-Hartley Act, making it an unlawful labor practice to become involved in a **hot-cargo contract**. In this type of agreement, an employer voluntarily agrees with a union not to handle, use, or deal in nonunion-produced goods of another employer.

quick quiz 24-2

1. The Wagner Act allowed unions to organize but did not identify any unfair labor practices.	true | false
2. Right-to-work laws were outlawed by the Landrum–Griffin Act.	true | false
3. The Taft–Hartley Act outlawed secondary boycotts.	true | false

24-3 The Collective Bargaining Process

The Taft-Hartley Act established a system for helping labor and management settle their disputes without causing a major disruption in the economy or endangering the public health and safety. Central to this collective bargaining process is the NLRB and the procedures it follows in settling labor-management disputes.

The National Labor Relations Board

The NLRB is a governmental commission that has the exclusive jurisdiction to enforce the Taft-Hartley Act and related laws. It has the power to act when cases are brought before it, but only in cases in which the employer's operation or the labor dispute affects commerce. Like most government regulatory agencies, the NLRB has investigative, regulatory, administrative, enforcement, and judgmental powers. It can make its own rules of procedure, conduct investigations into unfair labor practice charges, compel individuals to appear with papers relevant to the controversy, hold hearings, and issue orders. Appeals from the five-member board go first to the appropriate U.S. Court of Appeals and then to the U.S. Supreme Court.

Unfair Labor Practice Procedure

A person, union, or employer can file notice with the NLRB of an alleged unfair labor practice within six months after it occurs. It is important to remember that unfair labor practices include not only those practices that occur between management and the labor union but also those between a union and its own members. This point is a crucial part of the union representation process, because once a collective bargaining unit is formed, the employees have only one recourse when they have a grievance, and that is through the union. Consequently, the law imposes an affirmative duty on the unions to be fair in their representation of all members. This rule does not mean that the union cannot monitor its own internal affairs, nor does it mean that unions must represent those outside of the bargaining unit. However, once a worker becomes a member of a union, he or she has the right to expect fair and equal treatment, and the union has the duty to deliver such treatment or be liable for not doing so.

If the charge has merit, a complaint is issued to notify the offending party that a hearing is to be held concerning the charges. Efforts are made through arbitration to resolve the dispute before the hearing date.

Strikes, like the 2010 nurses' strike in Minnesota, can cause major inconvenience and hardship for the general public. Unions often count on public pressure to get favorable concessions from management.
©Jim Mone/AP Images

Arbitration involves the submission of the dispute to selected persons and the substitution of their decision for the judgment of the NLRB. If arbitration efforts fail, the hearing is held. In the event that the complaint is found to be valid, a cease-and-desist order may be issued, restoring the parties to the state that existed before the unfair practice began. For example, wrongfully discharged employees may be reinstated with or without back pay. Evidence at the hearing that does not support the complaint is dismissed. Either party to the hearing may subsequently appeal the NLRB action to the appropriate U.S. Court of Appeals and then to the Supreme Court.

Mediation The Taft-Hartley Act encourages labor and management to agree freely on the settlement of disputes. To further this effort to preserve labor peace and promote prompt settlements, Congress has formed the Federal Mediation and Conciliation Service. This body can act by itself or upon the request of either side to a labor dispute. Its mediation role is to offer nonbinding suggestions for settling the dispute, require the parties to negotiate, and force a vote by employees on an employer's offers.

A CONTEMPORARY CASE Social Media Policy as a Balancing Act: Employee Rights v. Company Protection

In Chapter 23, we looked at what happens when an employer fails to implement a social media policy. Sometimes, however, the tables are turned and the mismanagement of an existing social media policy puts the employer on the spot. Such a situation occurred when an employee's use of Facebook violated her employer's social media policy. The question that emerged from the case focused on a section of the National Labor Relations Act (NLRA) that shields the speech of unionized employees who are engaged in "concerted activities for the purpose of . . . mutual aid and protection" [See: Title 29, Chapter 7, Subchapter II, Section 157 of the U.S. Code.] The exact meanings of the term "concerted activities" and the phrase "mutual aid and protection" were a bit uncertain until the case mentioned earlier brought Dawnmarie Sousa, an EMT employed by American Medical Response (AMR), to the National Labor Relations Board.

Apparently, Sousa was fired for making disparaging remarks about her supervisor on Facebook. These remarks inspired several online responses from Sousa's co-workers. Evidently, Sousa had been the target of a customer complaint. Standard operating procedure at AMR required Sousa to write a response to that complaint. Sousa asked her supervisor to allow her to get help from a Teamsters' representative in writing her response. Simply stated, her supervisor said "no." At this point, or shortly thereafter, Sousa accessed Facebook and complained about her boss. At one point, she wrote that she loved "how the company allows a 17 to become a supervisor." (It was later revealed that, at AMR, the number 17 refers to psychiatric patients.) When AMR learned about the Facebook discussion, Sousa was discharged because she had disobeyed an AMR rule that forbids workers from making unflattering remarks about AMR online.

Sousa went to the National Labor Relations Board, and the agency filed a complaint on her behalf. The NLRB ruled against AMR, stating that Sousa's remarks were protected by the NLRA precisely because she had discussed working conditions with co-workers. According to the NLRB, this activity is protected by the NLRA as "concerted activities for the purpose of . . . mutual aid and protection." The NLRB also chastised AMR for developing a social media policy that was open ended and, as a result, violated NLRA rules. It was not just the employee's termination that bothered the NLRB; it was also the entire social media policy that AMR had created. The lesson to learn from this case is that a social media policy must be tailored very carefully as a balance between protecting the company and protecting free speech rights guaranteed to workers. [See: *In re American Medical Response of Connecticut*, as discussed in Steven Greenhouse, "Company Accused of Firing Over Facebook Posting," *The New York Times*, August 11, 2010; and Adrienne L. Rapp, "The Responsible Employer's Social Media Policy," *Labor and Employment Update*, Ohio State Bar Association Annual Conference (Columbus, Ohio), May 6, 2011.]

Source: See: In re American Medical Response of Connecticut, as discussed in Steven Greenhouse, "Company Accused of Firing Over Facebook Posting," *The New York Times*, August 11, 2010; and Adrienne L. Rapp, "The Responsible Employer's Social Media Policy," *Labor and Employment Update*, Ohio State Bar Association Annual Conference (Columbus, Ohio), May 6, 2011).

The Right to Strike in the Public Sector

In the public sector, when the general welfare, safety, health, and morals of the public are involved, the right to strike is restricted. Consequently, strikes by police, firefighters, refuse collectors, air traffic controllers, postal workers, and other public employees who perform vital services are generally illegal, unless specifically authorized by statute. The U.S. Code states that "an individual may not accept or hold a position in the government of the United States or the government of the District of Columbia if he participates in a strike or asserts the right to strike against the government." The U.S. Supreme Court has affirmed lower court rulings that there is no constitutional right to strike against the federal government. Thus, strikes by federal employees are substantially more than merely unfair labor practices; they are crimes.

A QUESTION OF ETHICS

Freedom of Speech for Public and Private Employees: An Unequal Standard

In *A Contemporary Case: Retaliation and Constructive Discharge* in Chapter 23, Los Angeles County Deputy D.A. Richard Ceballos challenged a search warrant in a memo and during a meeting of law enforcement officers in the D.A.'s office. Subsequently, Ceballos was subjected to a number of retaliatory moves by his supervisors. After having a grievance rejected, Ceballos filed a claim under Section 1983 of Title 42 of the U.S. Code. In that case, Ceballos argued that he had been deprived of his constitutional right of free speech by being subjected to retaliatory moves for pointing out the conduct of some of his colleagues in obtaining a search warrant based on allegedly inaccurate information. Eventually, the U.S. Supreme Court ruled that when public employees "make statements pursuant to their official duties," they are not protected by the First Amendment.

The problem is that, whenever public employees are on the job, they are generally "commenting upon matters of public concern," and are, therefore, making statements "pursuant to their official duties." As a result, it appears that the Supreme Court has overruled the Pickering Rule and eliminated the right of public employees to speak freely on the job. The Ceballos case, then, amounts to an official gag order for public employees unless they are saying what their supervisors have told them to say. Now let's look at the recent public labor law crisis and combine what is happening there with the implications of the Ceballos case. Recall that the governors and the state legislatures of several midwestern states—notably Wisconsin, Ohio, and Michigan—attempted (often unsuccessfully) to eliminate the collective bargaining power of public employee unions. Recall also that the governor of Illinois attempted to eliminate a major source of funding for the state's public employee union by having the court declare the Illinois public union statute unconstitutional. Abolishing collective bargaining and eliminating the funding of a public employees' union are not the same as placing a gag order on public employees, but such a moves do eliminate the protection that unions give employees who want representation and who want to preserve the right to speak out about conditions on the job.

Now, taking all this into consideration, contrast these events with those noted in *Sousa v. American Medical Response of Connecticut* and the Northwestern University case. In both these cases, the NLRB protected the free speech rights of private employees: The EMT was protected in the American Medical Response case, and the football players were protected in the Northwestern University case. To summarize and simultaneously point out the contradictions among these cases, we can say the following: The private EMT has the right to text about her employer and the NU football players have the right to unionize, while the DA has no right to complain about allegedly inaccurate warrants, and police officers, firefighters, and teachers have no right to unionize in those states where the antiunion legislation is in effect. Is there an inherent unfairness within these governmental decisions? Before answering the next few questions, reconsider the different ethical theories mentioned in Chapter 1. Then, applying one, and only one, of those theories in a uniform way, respond to these questions.

1. What is the essential difference between a public worker and a private worker? Explain.
2. Should public workers have fewer rights than private sector workers? If so, why? If not, why not?
3. Does the profession of the public worker matter in determining the extent of protection for the worker's free speech rights? If so, what professionals deserve to have their freedom of speech protected and what professionals forfeit that First Amendment protection? Explain.
4. What trends in the sociopolitical economic sectors might account for this recent anti-public employee rights campaign? Explain.
5. If public workers have no right to free speech, but must remain within the "talking points" set up by their public employers, why are public officials (such as the secretary of State or the U.S. ambassador to the United Nations, for instance) subject to investigation when they simply repeat the "talking points" given to them by that employer? Ceballos is punished for speaking his mind, while other public officials are penalized for not speaking their minds but, instead, saying whatever their superiors told them to say. How can these ethical inconsistencies be solved? Or can they be? Explain.

[See: *Pickering v. Board of Ed. of Township High School Dist. 205*, Will Cty., 391 U. S. 563 (1968); *Garcetti, et al. v. Ceballos*, 126 S. Ct. 1951 (U.S. Supreme Court; *In re American Medical Response of Connecticut*, as discussed in Steven Greenhouse, "Company Accused of Firing Over Facebook Posting," *The New York Times*, August 11, 2010; Adrienne L. Rapp, "The Responsible Employer's Social Media Policy," *Labor and Employment Update*, Ohio State Bar Association Annual Conference (Columbus, Ohio), May 6, 2011; and *Northwestern University, Employer v. College Athletes Players Association, Petitioner*, National Labor Relations Board, Region 13, Case Number, 13-RC-121359 (2014).]

Source: See: *Pickering v. Board of Ed. of Township High School Dist. 205, Will Cty., 391 U. S. 563 (1968); Garcetti, et al. v. Ceballos*, 126 S. Ct. 1951 (U.S. Supreme Court; In re American Medical Response of Connecticut, as discussed in Steven Greenhouse, "Company Accused of Firing Over Facebook Posting," *The New York Times*, August 11, 2010; Adrienne L. Rapp, "The Responsible Employer's Social Media Policy," *Labor and Employment Update*, Ohio State Bar Association Annual Conference (Columbus, Ohio, May 6, 2011); *Northwestern University, Employer v. College Athletes Players Association, Petitioner*, National Labor Relations Board, Region 13, Case Number, 13-RC-121359 (2014).

quick quiz 24-3

1. There is no appeal permitted after a decision has been rendered by the National Labor Relations Board.   true | false

2. If a complaint is found valid under the NLRB procedures, a cease-and-desist order may be issued, restoring the parties to the state that existed before the unfair labor practice began.   true | false

3. The U.S. Supreme Court has repeatedly affirmed that federal employees have a constitutionally protected right to strike.   true | false

Did You Know?

Union membership in Great Britain surpassed 2 million at the beginning of the 20th century. This level made the British labor movement the most influential European union movement up to that time in history.

Summary

24.1 The first federal statute relating to labor was the Clayton Act, which attempted to prohibit federal courts from forbidding activities such as picketing and strikes. The Norris-LaGuardia Act specified acts, such as striking, picketing, and boycotting, that were not subject to federal injunctions.

24.2 The Wagner Act opened the door for the growth of labor unions. It set forth specific labor practices that were prohibited for employers and unions, established procedures for representative elections and collective bargaining, and created the NLRB. The Taft-Hartley Act outlaws specific conduct by unions as unfair labor practices and provides for an 80-day cooling off period in strikes that endanger national health or safety. The act also provides a mediation and conciliation service to assist in the settlement of labor disputes. The Landrum-Griffin Act provides a bill of rights for union members, requires unions to report to the secretary of labor, and has added to the list of unfair labor practices.

24.3 The NLRB has exclusive jurisdiction to enforce labor-management relations laws with investigative, regulatory, administrative, enforcement, and judgment powers. Any person, union, or employer can file notice with the NLRB of an alleged unfair labor practice. If the complaint has merit, a hearing is held before the NLRB. If the complaint is found to be valid, an order may be issued restoring the parties to the state existing prior to the unfair practice. Appeals of NLRB actions can be taken to the appropriate U.S. Circuit Court of Appeals and then to the U.S. Supreme Court. The Federal Mediation and Conciliation Service was formed to encourage labor and management to agree freely on the settlement of their disputes. Its mediation role is to offer nonbinding suggestions for settling the dispute, require the parties to negotiate, and force a vote by employees on employers' offers. In the public sector, the right to strike is restricted. The U.S. Code states that "an individual may not accept or hold a position in the government of the United States or the government of the District of Columbia if he participates in a strike or asserts the right to strike against the government."

Key Terms

arbitration, 692
bargaining unit, 688
closed shop, 686
company-run unions, 686
constructive discharge, 686
featherbedding, 691
hot-cargo contract, 691
labor union, 677
right-to-work laws, 688
secondary boycott, 689
unfair labor practices, 685
union shop, 686

Questions for Review and Discussion

1. What is the historical context in which unions developed?
2. What is the congressional-judicial tug-of-war in union history?
3. What are the major provisions of the Norris-LaGuardia Act?
4. What are the basic aims of labor unions?
5. What is the nature of the 21st-century crisis in labor law?
6. What are the primary tenets of the Wagner Act?
7. What are the functions of the Taft-Hartley Act?
8. What are the provisions of the Landrum-Griffin Act?
9. What is the jurisdiction of the National Labor Relations Board?
10. What are the possible results of a complaint filed with the NLRB?

Cases for Analysis

1. Nine longshoremen, all of whom were members of Local 13 of the International Longshoremen's and Warehousemen's Union, found that they were having difficulty getting jobs. The problem seemed to be that Local 13 had refused to place them on a hiring list at the union's hiring hall. Because this list was the only way that union members could get jobs as longshoremen, the nine union members were in effect being boycotted by the union and, as a result, by all potential employers. When the out-of-work union members filed grievances with Local 13, they were effectively ignored. To challenge these actions (as well as others not covered here), the out-of-work longshoremen filed a complaint with the National Labor Relations Board. The NLRB and the District Court dismissed the complaint, and the longshoremen appealed. The union argued that the question of whether to place certain members on the hiring list was a purely internal union affair that could not be challenged by the NLRB or the courts. The longshoreman contended that by refusing to place them on the list and ignoring their grievances, the union was being unfair to them. Should the appeals court overturn this ruling by the NLRB and the District Court? Explain. [See: *Richard Diaz, et al. v. International Longshoremen's and Warehousemen's Union, Local 13*, Case No. 04-56957 (U.S. Court of Appeals for the Ninth Circuit).]

2. The union representing employees of the Consolidated Manufacturing Company elected Franco and Allanson to act on their behalf at a collective bargaining session with management. At the session, Franco and Allanson demanded that the new collective bargaining agreement include terms that would require management to hire only union members in good standing. Management disagreed with this proposal. Instead, management offered a term in the agreement that would allow the company to hire nonunion workers for a trial period lasting no more than 30 days. After the 30-day trial period, the nonunion worker would have to join a union. Which of these terms in the proposed collective bargaining agreement would be allowed under federal labor law? Explain. Management also proposed that the employee union be disbanded and replaced by a company-run union. Management argued that the new company-run union would not only be more efficient but also more economical than the current union. Would this proposal be allowed under federal labor law?

3. An employee was discharged for violating the company's no-solicitation rule in its factory and offices. The employee had persisted in soliciting union membership on company property during lunch periods. The company argued that its no-solicitation rule would have been enforced against not merely union solicitation but any solicitation. How would you decide? Why? [See: *Republic Aviation Corp. v. NLRB*, 324 U.S. 793 (U.S. Sup. Ct.).]

4. Having advised Exchange Parts Co. that it was conducting an organizational campaign, the union petitioned the NLRB for an election to determine whether it would be certified as the bargaining agent of the company's employees. During the organizational campaign, while the granted certification election was pending, the company announced five additional benefits for the employees, two of which were announced only a few days before the election. In the election, the employees voted against being represented by a union. The union then filed a complaint with the NLRB, charging the company with an unfair labor practice because it granted benefits

while the campaign was taking place and the election was pending. The union argued that the company's actions interfered with the freedom of choice of the employees to determine whether they wished to be represented by the union. For whom would you decide? Why? [See: *NLRB v. Exchange Parts Co.*, 375 U.S. 405 (U.S. Sup. Ct.).]

5. Darlington Manufacturing Co. operated one textile mill that was controlled by Deering Milliken, which operated 27 other such mills. The union began an organizational campaign, which Darlington resisted. The employees filed charges of unfair labor practices with the NLRB. The board found in a subsequent hearing that the different mills controlled by Deering Milliken represented an integrated enterprise and that the closing of the Darlington mill was due to the antiunion hostility of Deering Milliken. The NLRB ordered Deering Milliken to provide back pay to the workers until they obtained similar work. The court of appeals denied enforcement of the NLRB order, holding that an independent employer has an absolute right to close a business, regardless of notice. On review by the U.S. Supreme Court, how should the Court rule on the question of whether an employer has the absolute right to close part of a business, no matter what the reason? Why? [See: *Textile Worker's Union v. Darlington Mfg. Co.*, 380 U.S. 263 (U.S. Sup. Ct.).]

6. The NLRB conducted an election among employees of Savair Manufacturing Co. to determine whether the union would represent the employees. During the election, recognition slips were distributed. The employees were told by the union that if they signed the slips before the election, they would not have to pay an initiation fee if the union won. At least 35 employees signed the slips before the election, which the union won by a vote of 22 to 20. The company refused to bargain with the union, contending that the union, by offering possible benefits to employees for signing the recognition slips, was guilty of an unfair labor practice. Did the practice of the union prevent a fair and free choice of a bargaining representative? Why or why not? [See: *NLRB v. Savair Mfg.* Co., 414 U.S. 270 (U.S. Sup. Ct.).]

7. The Department Store Employees Union was selected by the employees of the Emporium Capwell Company as their exclusive bargaining unit. Charges of discrimination in the workplace were levied against the company through the union. The union followed the grievance procedure, as established in the collective bargaining agreement. Some of the employees became dissatisfied with the union's handling of the case. Accordingly, they asked the union to begin to picket the company. Union officials advised these dissatisfied employees that according to the collective bargaining agreement, the union was bound to follow the established grievance procedure. The employees refused to cooperate with the grievance procedure and demanded that company management deal with them directly to establish an overall anti discrimination policy. Later the employees also picketed the store. Written notices were given to the picketing employees, telling them that they could be discharged if they repeated the conduct. The employees ignored the notices and, after picketing on the following weekend, were discharged. The employees filed a complaint with the National Labor Relations Board, which found that it could not support the employees. The NLRB believed that such support would challenge the exclusive bargaining power of the union and thereby subvert the statutory intent of Congress. The appeals court hearing the case reversed the board's findings, stating its belief that discrimination cases had a special position and thus fell outside the guarantee to the union of exclusive bargaining power. The case was appealed to the U.S. Supreme Court. Should the Supreme Court uphold the union's exclusive right to engage in collective bargaining with the company? Explain. [See: *Emporium Capwell, Co. v. Western Addition Community Organization*, 420 U.S. 50 (U.S. Sup. Ct.).]

quick quiz Answers

24-1	24-2	24-3
1. T	1. F	1. F
2. F	2. F	2. T
3. F	3. T	3. F

Part 6 Case Study

Evans v. Georgia Regional Hospital
830 F. 3d 1248
U.S. Court of Appeals, Eleventh Circuit (2017)

©Keith Brofsky/Getty Images

"Some stories have to be written because no one would believe the absurdity of it all."

—Shannon Adler

Summary

This case revolves around claims of discrimination and retaliation brought by Jameka Evans against Georgia Regional Hospital (the Hospital), Chief Charles Moss, Lisa Clark, and Senior Human Resources Manager Jamekia Powers—all employees of the Hospital. The facts look like this. The plaintiff, Jameka Evans, worked as a security guard at the Hospital under the supervision of Chief Charles Moss. Although she never discussed her sexuality at work, Evans alleged that it was clear from her clothing, shoes, haircut, and general demeanor that she was a lesbian. Evans further alleged that she was discriminated against and harassed at work because of her sexual orientation and because she refused to "carry herself in a 'traditional woman[ly] manner'" (gender nonconformity). Her list of complaints regarding discrimination and harassment included having her shift changed; being subjected to unnecessary, last-minute schedule alterations; being met by slamming doors; being denied equal pay and equal work; being assaulted; and being passed over for promotion by a less qualified officer, namely, Corporal Shanika Johnson, who became her immediate supervisor and who also harassed her by tampering "with her equipment, including her radio, clip, and shoulder microphone."

Evans alleged further that this pattern of discriminatory behavior was part of a deliberate retaliation campaign to punish her for filing her complaint of harassment. Evans also alleged that she had been targeted by Moss because she had filed her complaints about him with Powers in the Human Resources Division. Evans also claims that it was at that time that Powers began to question her about her sexuality. This "coincidence" led Evans to believe that her sexuality and her gender conformity (well, "nonconformity") had been the topic of conversation after she had filed the original complaint about Moss. Evans also suspected that part of the reason that she had been targeted was that she had begun a separate investigation into the possibility that the chief had broken some internal hospital policies. As evidence for these allegations, Evans produced e-mails that suggested that Moss had masterminded a plot to force her to quit by "making her employment unbearable." In addition, Evans also produced an e-mail from another employee indicating that he too had been harassed by Moss, that Moss had planned to force Evans into resigning because of the evidence she had gathered against him, and that Moss had tampered with the hiring and promotion requirements. Evans also offered a letter from yet another employee that recorded evidence of Moss's plan to force Evans to quit. Finally, despite all of this evidence, Evans produced a letter from the human resources department that reported finding no reason to believe that Evans had been the object of discrimination, harassment, or retaliation.

After hearing Evans' arguments and reviewing the evidence, the magistrate judge issued a report that made five recommendations. First, Evans' claim of discrimination based on sexual orientation had to be dismissed because sexual orientation is not a protected class under Title VII of the Civil Rights Act of 1964. Second, similarly, since Evans' claim of discrimination based on gender nonconformity is simply another way of saying discrimination based on sexual orientation, it too is not a protected class under Title VII of the Civil Rights Act of 1964; therefore, that claim must also be dismissed. Third, Evans' claim of retaliation must be dismissed because she had not demonstrated a valid discrimination claim over which she could be victimized by retaliation. Fourth, all claims against Moss, Clark, and Powers must be dismissed because, as private individuals, they cannot be defendants in a Title VII action. Fifth, and finally, none of Evans' claims can be refiled because none of the claims are actionable (appealed, yes, but amended and refiled, no). The district court reviewed the report and followed the magistrate's recommendations, dismissing Evans' entire case. Evans appealed, which is how the case arrived in the Eleventh Circuit Court of Appeals.

The Eleventh Circuit Court of Appeals reviewed the decision of the District Court with the following results. First, the court agreed that Moss, Clark, and Powers were not proper defendants in this action. Second, the court could not address the retaliation claim because Evans had failed to address it in her appeal. Third, the district court was correct in dismissing the claim based on discrimination due to sexual orientation because sexual orientation is not a protected class under the Civil Rights Act of 1964. Fourth, the district court was *incorrect* in saying that discrimination based on gender nonconformity is the same as sexual orientation. However, Evans did not present enough facts "to create a plausible inference that she suffered discrimination" based on gender nonconformity. Therefore, she must be permitted to amend her complaint to present enough evidence to create the "plausible inference" of which the court speaks. Finally, because Evans will be permitted to amend her claim of gender nonconformity, the district court's last finding must be reversed in part, and the amended claim must be given its a day in court.

[Since the facts have been covered in this summary, only the Court's analysis is reproduced here.] This analysis includes only sections III, IV, and V of the opinion. Some footnote numerals are included. Others, those located in the omitted material, are not included. In either case, the citations themselves and explanatory notes are omitted. Also, following the majority opinion, an excerpt from the concurring opinion of Judge William Pryor has been included. The concurring opinion has been added because in that concurrence, Judge Pryor eloquently and concisely sums up the role of the court and the role of the legislature. He notes, without using the term, that courts ought not to "legislate from the bench," something that many courts today have not yet learned. (*Note:* The most pertinent parts of the concurrence are **bold faced**.)

MARTINEZ, District Judge: Jameka Evans appeals the sua sponte dismissal of her employment discrimination complaint, filed pursuant to 42 U.S.C. § 2000e et seq., in which she alleged that she was discriminated against because of her sexual orientation and gender non-conformity, and retaliated against after she lodged a complaint with her employer's human resources department. We have carefully reviewed the Appellant's and amicus curiae's initial and supplemental briefs,1 and have had the benefit of oral argument. For the reasons set forth below, we affirm the district court's dismissal order in part, and vacate and remand in part . . .

III. First, Evans argues that the district court erred in dismissing her claim that she was discriminated against for failing to conform to gender stereotypes, because an LGBT person may bring a separate discrimination claim for gender non-conformity.3 She contends that her status as a lesbian supports her claim of sex discrimination, because discrimination against someone for her orientation often coincides with discrimination for gender non-conformity. Evans further asserts that discrimination based on gender stereotypes is a broad claim that encompasses more than just her appearance, but also provides for suits based on various other stereotypes, such as family structure.

Even though we hold, infra, that discrimination based on gender non-conformity is actionable, Evans's pro se complaint nevertheless failed to plead facts sufficient to create a plausible inference that she suffered discrimination. See Surtain, 789 F.3d at 1246. In other words, Evans did not provide enough factual matter to plausibly suggest that her decision to present herself in a masculine manner led to the alleged adverse employment actions. Id. Therefore, while a dismissal of Evans's gender non-conformity claim would have been appropriate on this basis, these circumstances entitle Evans an opportunity to amend her complaint one time unless doing so would be futile.

[11] [12] [13] When "a more carefully drafted complaint might state a claim, a plaintiff must be given at least one chance to amend the complaint before the district court dismisses the action with prejudice." Bryant v. Dupree, 252 F.3d 1161, 1163 (11th Cir. 2001) (citation omitted). Although a pro se litigant generally

should be permitted to amend her complaint, a district court need not allow amendment when it would be futile. Cockrell v. Sparks, 510 F.3d 1307, 1310 (11th Cir. 2007). "Leave to amend a complaint is futile when the complaint as amended would still be properly dismissed or be immediately subject to summary judgment for the defendant." Id.

Here, Evans, a pro se litigant, has not previously amended her complaint, and it cannot be said that any attempt to amend would be futile with respect to her gender non-conformity claim and possibly others . . . Accordingly, we vacate the portion of the district court's order dismissing Evans's gender non-conformity claim with prejudice and remand with instructions to grant Evans leave to amend such claim.

IV. Evans next argues that she has stated a claim under Title VII by alleging that she endured workplace discrimination because of her sexual orientation. She has not. Our binding precedent forecloses such an action. Blum v. Gulf Oil Corp., 597 F.2d 936, 938 (5th Cir. 1979)4 ("Discharge for homosexuality is not prohibited by Title VII . . ."). "Under our prior precedent rule, we are bound to follow a binding precedent in this Circuit unless and until it is overruled by this court en banc or by the Supreme Court." Offshore of the Palm Beaches, Inc. v. Lynch, 741 F.3d 1251, 1256 (11th Cir. 2014) (internal quotations omitted).

[18] The EEOC argues that the statement in Blum regarding discharge for homosexuality is dicta and not binding precedent. We disagree. Before making such statement, the panel in Blum remarked: "We comment briefly on the other issues raised on appeal." 597 F.2d at 938 (emphasis added). As a result, the statement in Blum concerning the viability of a sexual orientation claim was not dicta, but rather directly addressed a question before the Court. Even if Blum is read as disposing of the sexual orientation claim for another reason, 5 an alternative reason does not render as dicta this Court's holding that there is no sexual orientation action under Title VII.

V. Evans also argues that the district court erred in concluding that she did not meet the requirements for a retaliation claim, because a plaintiff can establish a prima facie case of unlawful retaliation if there was a good faith, reasonable belief that the employer was acting unlawfully. However, we will generally not review a magistrate judge's findings or recommendations if a party failed to object to those recommendations below. See 11th Cir. R. 3-1. Title 28 of the United States Code, Section 636(b) (1) provides that, within 14 days of being served with a copy of a magistrate judge's recommendations or findings, a party may file written objections with the court, and the court shall conduct a de novo review of the issues raised. 28 U.S.C. § 636(b)(1). Pursuant to 11th Cir. R. 3-1, a party who fails to object to a magistrate judge's findings or recommendations in an R&R "waives the right to challenge on appeal the district court's order based on unobjected-to factual and legal conclusions," provided the party was given proper notice of the objection time period and the consequences of failing to do so, as was the case here. Consequently, we will only review a waived objection, for plain error, if necessary in the interests of justice. Id. Review for plain error "rarely applies in civil cases." Ledford v. Peeples, 657 F.3d 1222, 1258 (11th Cir. 2011). Even when it does, we require a greater showing of error than in criminal appeals. United States v. Levy, 391 F.3d 1327, 1343 n.12 (11th Cir. 2004). We find nothing in the record that suggests that plain error review is appropriate in this appeal . . .

For the foregoing reasons, the district court's order dismissing Evans's action with prejudice is affirmed in part, and vacated in part and remanded for further proceedings consistent with this opinion.

AFFIRMED IN PART, VACATED IN PART AND REMANDED.

WILLIAM PRYOR, Circuit Judge, concurring: I concur in the majority opinion, but I write separately to explain the error of the argument of the Equal Employment Opportunity Commission and the dissent that a person who experiences discrimination because of sexual orientation necessarily experiences discrimination for deviating from gender stereotypes. Although a person who experiences the former will sometimes also experience the latter, the two concepts are legally distinct. And the insistence otherwise by the Commission and the dissent relies on false stereotypes of gay individuals. **I also write separately to explain that the dissent would create a new form of relief based on status that runs counter to binding precedent and would undermine the relationship between the doctrine of gender nonconformity and the enumerated classes protected by Title VII** . . .

The willingness to accept that Price Waterhouse and Glenn deal only with behaviors that deviate from gender stereotypes does not put one "at war with Glenn." Dissenting Op. at 1265. **Instead, it acknowledges that the doctrine of gender nonconformity is not and cannot be an independent vehicle for relief because the only status-based classes that provide relief are those enumerated within Title VII.** We review claims of gender nonconformity the same way in all appeals regardless of a plaintiff's sexual orientation. Any correlation that might exist between a particular sexual orientation and deviation from a particular gender stereotype does not overcome this settled rule.

Because Congress has not made sexual orientation a protected class, the appropriate venue for pressing the argument raised by the Commission and the dissent is before Congress, not this Court. And for decades, members of Congress have introduced bills for that purpose. See, e.g., Equality Act, H.R. 3185, 114th Cong. (2015); Employment Non-Discrimination Act, S. 815, 113th Cong. (2013), S. 811, 112th Cong. (2011), S. 1584, 111th Cong. (2009), H.R. 3685, 110th Cong. (2007), H.R. 3285, 108th Cong. (2003), S. 1284, 107th Cong. (2002), H.R. 2355, 106th Cong. (1999), H.R. 1858, 105th Cong. (1997), S. 2056, 104th Cong. (1996), H.R. 4636, 103d Cong. (1994); Civil Rights Act, H.R. 431, 103d Cong. (1993); Civil Rights Amendments Act, H.R. 423, 103d Cong. (1993), S. 574, 102d Cong. (1991); S. 430, 98th. Cong. (1983); S. 1708, 97th Cong. (1981); S. 2081, 96th Cong. (1979). **Contrary to the dissent's assertions, Dissenting Op. at 1272, we cite this pattern of legislation not because it does or can suggest legislative intent but because it illustrates that Congress is the appropriate branch in which to raise the arguments raised by the dissent. The dissent's disagreement boils down to incredulity that "[i]t cannot possibly be the case that"** the combination of the text of Title VII and Price Waterhouse leave some individuals unprotected from discrimination. Dissenting Op. at 1267. **But as a Court, "[o]ur province is to decide what the law is, not to declare what it should be . . . If the law is wrong, it ought to be changed; but the power for that is not with us."** Minor v. Happersett, 88 U.S. 162, 178, 21 Wall. 162, 22 L.Ed. 627 (1874).

Questions for Analysis

1. How does the case of *Evans v. Georgia Regional Hospital* support or contradict the core legal principle of *stare decisis*? Explain.
2. In what way is the case of *Evans v. Georgia Regional Hospital* similar to and different from *Hively v. Ivy Technical Community College* (the Opening Case in Chapter 23)? Explain.
3. Why does the court permit Evans to amend her claim regarding gender nonconformity? Explain.
4. Why does the court disallow Evans' request to support her claim of discrimination based on sexual orientation? Explain.
5. Why does Judge Pryor refuse to support Evans' claim of discrimination based on gender nonconformity? Explain.
6. The Supreme Court decided not to issue a *writ of certiorari* in *Evans v. Georgia Regional Hospital* but agreed to issue a writ in *Hively v. Ivy Tech Community College*. This means that the High Court will rule on the issues in *Hively* but not on those in *Evans*. Why do you suppose the High Court made this decision? Explain.
7. Should the Supreme Court uphold the appellate court's decision in *Hively* to approve the creation of sexual orientation as a new protected class in the Civil Rights Act of 1964? Explain.
8. Should the Supreme Court "amend" the Civil Rights Act of 1964 by adding sexual orientation as a protected class? Explain.
9. Why does Judge Pryor provide a list of the bills proposed by Congress to amend the Civil Rights Act of 1964? Explain.
10. What arguments can you give to support and oppose the idea that the courts ought to "legislate from the bench"? Explain.

Source: *Evans v. Georgia Regional Hospital*, 830 F. 3d 1248, U.S. Court of Appeals, Eleventh Circuit (2017).

Design Elements: The Opening Case: ©Sharpstock/Alamy; A Classic Case: ©Evlakhov Valeriy/Shutterstock

©Beau Lark/Corbis/VCG/Getty Images

Part Seven

Business Organization and Regulation

Chapter 25	The Business Entity: An Introduction	Chapter 28	Government Regulation of the Corporate Entity
Chapter 26	The Corporate Entity	Case Study	*Gries Sports Enterprises, Inc. v. Cleveland Browns Football Co., Inc.*
Chapter 27	Managing the Corporate Entity		

Chapter 25

The Business Entity: An Introduction

25-1 Sole Proprietorships and Other Business Entities
Formation of a Sole Proprietorship • Advantages and Disadvantages of a Sole Proprietorship

25-2 General Partnership Characteristics
Revised Uniform Partnership Act • Elements of a Partnership • Entity and Aggregate Theories • Alternative Business Entities

25-3 Partnership Formation
Formation of a Partnership by Contract • Formation of a Partnership by Proof of Existence

25-4 Partnership Property Rights and Duties
Partnership Liability • Partnership Property • Specific Partnership Property • Interest in the Partnership • Partnership Rights and Duties

25-5 Dissociation and Dissolution
Dissociation of a Partnership • Dissolution of a Partnership

25-6 Other Forms of Partnership Business
Registered Limited Liability Partnerships • Limited Partnerships

THE OPENING CASE Round 1
"One for All, All for One, and Two for Themselves, and Only Themselves"

This case began with the purchase of a bus line. The purchase was brokered by R. W. Keenon, Eloise Keenon (the Keenons), Harold J. Utter, and James D. Van Hooter, along with three other unnamed parties. The bus line was dubbed Western Kentucky Stages (WKS). The parties also drew up a partnership agreement, put the agreement in writing, and added a clause stipulating that "no partner should have the right to sell his or her interest in the partnership without the consent of the other partners and without first giving those partners an opportunity to buy such interest." Now, because R. W. Keenon had, for years, maintained a close relationship with Southeastern Greyhound Line, the Keenons transferred their interest in WKS to Utter, who acted as their trustee. In fact, once the partnership was formed, the Keenons had no control over their own interests in WKS despite being full partners in the venture. After about two years of operation, Utter and Van Hooser were in Chicago when officials from Greyhound Inc. (GI) made a pitch to put up $37,500 for an option to buy 60 percent of WKS, after which the WKS partners would incorporate so that Greyhound could more easily purchase 60 percent of the stock in the new WKS Corporation. The deal was engineered by Van Hooser and Utter. The other thee unnamed partners agreed. The Keenons were kept in the dark about the new arrangement with GI.

The first stage of the deal went through and, in exchange for the $37,500, GI held the option to buy that 60 percent (well, it was actually 63 percent, but who's counting?). Before this could go through, however, Utter and Van Hooser had to convince the Keenons to agree to transform the partnership into a corporation. The Keenons, quite naturally, asked something like, "Why should we agree to incorporate when we are doing a such good job as a partnership?" In response, Utter and Hooser argued that first, all the partners would be better off with the limited liability provided by the incorporation process, and second, Hooter and Utter could better deal with the Federal Revenue Department if WKS were a corporation. Nothing about the GI deal was mentioned by either Utter or Van Hooser to the Keenons. The Keenons finally agreed, but only when the others stipulated that they would never sell their shares of the new corporation without making certain the Keenons received the same deal. So far, so good. Then things began to unravel, as they often do when a "deal" is based on deception.

The GI deal fell through, and the other five partners split the $37,500 option money. When the Keenons found out about the GI deal, they, as partners, demanded their fair share of the $37,500. According to partnership law, the Keenons argued, they should receive an equal share of the $37,500 the other partners had divided among themselves. Utter and Van Hooser refused, saying that the deal was based on the amount owed to the other five partners and that the Keenons never had anything at risk when the GI deal was brokered. The Keenons argued that not withstanding how the contract with GI was brokered, the amount made on the agreement, like any amount made on any contract negotiated on behalf of the partnership, should have gone right into the WKS bank account and that each partner then owned his or her fair share of that deposit. In fact, at the next meeting of the firm, the Keenons presented a resolution saying that the $37,500 should go into the general fund. After a quick vote, the resolution failed. The Keenons then demanded their fair share of the Greyhound money.

When Van Hooser and Utter, apparently with the support of the other three partners, refused, the Keenons filed this lawsuit against Van Hooser and Utter. The commissioner of the trial court agreed with the Keenons. The trial court agreed with the commissioner. Moreover, the trial court placed responsibility solely on the shoulders of Utter and Van Hooser because they had brokered the deal and had, as trustees, dispersed the money from that deal to the other partners. Therefore, the other three unnamed partners could keep their share of the money, while Utter and Van Hooser would be compelled to divide the entire amount of $37,500 in four ways. This meant that Utter and Van Hooser had to pay the Keenons $9,375 (or $4,487.50 each). Hooser and Utter appealed the trial court's decision, and so here we are in the appellate court. Some questions you should be asking yourself are these: Is a written partnership agreement necessary when a partnership is formed? What duties exist between partners in a partnership? If two partners have a good motive for deceiving the other partners in a partnership deal, does this good motive absolve them of responsibility for deceiving the other partners? Interested? Then, all aboard for a look at partnership law . . . [See: *Van Hooser, et al. v. Keenon, et al.*, 271 S.W. 2d 270 (Court of Appeals of Kentucky).]

Opening Case Questions

1. What are the advantages and disadvantages of forming a partnership rather than a corporation? Explain.

2. Is it necessary to have a partnership agreement written out when a partnership is formed? Explain.

3. What duties do the partners in a partnership have to one another? Explain.

4. What rights do partners have in a partnership? Explain.

5. How are the profits shared in a partnership? Explain.

Source: See: *Van Hooser, et al. v. Keenoin, et al.*, 271 S.W. 2d 270 (Court of Appeals of Kentucky).

 Learning Objectives

1. List the most common forms of business associations.
2. Outline the advantages and disadvantages of a sole proprietorship.
3. Identify the two model acts that govern partnership law.
4. Describe the differences between the aggregate and entity theories of partnership.
5. Explain the nature of a partnership agreement.
6. Explain when profit sharing does not create a partnership.
7. Explain what constitutes a person in partnership law.
8. Identify the different views of specific partnership property in partnership law.
9. Distinguish between dissociation and dissolution in partnership law.
10. Distinguish between a registered limited liability partnership and a limited partnership.

25-1 Sole Proprietorships and Other Business Entities

Multiple forms of doing business are available to people who are about to enter the economic arena. Here are some of the most common forms:

1. Sole proprietorships
2. General partnerships
3. Limited partnerships
4. Limited liability partnerships
5. Private corporations
6. Public (or state-owned) corporations
7. Quasi-public corporations
8. Limited liability corporations
9. Joint ventures
10. Franchises

This chapter will focus on sole proprietorships, general partnerships, limited partnerships, and limited liability partnerships as a way of initiating our exploration of business entities and the legal rules that apply to such entities. The next three chapters will focus on the nature, organization, operation, and regulation of the corporate entity. Before that, however, this chapter will examine a series of traditional and nontraditional business persons.

Formation of a Sole Proprietorship

The easiest business organization to form is a **sole proprietorship**. In most cases, businesspeople can initiate a sole proprietorship by simply opening their doors for business. Depending on the nature, location, and extent of the business, the sole proprietor may have to check zoning restrictions, licensing laws, and filing requirements. For example, some states require a formal filing if a sole proprietor chooses to use a fictitious name.

Advantages and Disadvantages of a Sole Proprietorship

Perhaps the greatest advantage to a sole proprietorship is that the owner has complete control over the business. Another major advantage is that the owner may keep all of the profits made by the sole proprietorship. A third advantage is that a sole proprietorship is relatively simple to begin and to end.

A major disadvantage to this type of business is that the owner of a sole proprietorship is subject to unlimited liability. For example, the sole proprietor is responsible for all of the debts incurred in running the business. This liability may even extend to the owner's personal assets. Another disadvantage is that the sole proprietorship's existence depends entirely upon the sole proprietor. Finally, owners of sole proprietorships often find it difficult to raise a lot of cash quickly for expansion purposes.

quick quiz 25-1

1. Businesspeople can form a sole proprietorship only by going through the attorney general's office in the state capital. true | false
2. The greatest advantage of a sole proprietorship is that the owner has complete control over the operation of the business. true | false
3. A major disadvantage of a sole proprietorship is unlimited liability. true | false

25-2 General Partnership Characteristics

Often, a sole proprietor will decide to extend his or her business venture by joining with other people to create a partnership. The law of partnership has integrated principles associated with tort law, contract law, and agency law. However, because of its unique characteristics, it has also developed its own separate and distinct legal principles.

Revised Uniform Partnership Act

One of the most dependable sources of law affecting partnerships has been the Uniform Law Commission (ULC) which, when it was still known as the National Conference of Commissioners on Uniform State Laws, developed the **Uniform Partnership Act (UPA)** in 1914. The UPA was so successful that it was put into practice by every state in the union but one. Only Louisiana, which is devoted to the Napoleonic Code, did not adopt the UPA. Nevertheless, the UPA has been the mainstay of partnership law, in relation to general partnerships, for more than 90 years. It does, however, have its limitations and shortcomings. For instance, the act never made it clear whether a partnership should be considered an entity with an existence separate from the partners or whether it was simply an aggregate of all of the partners. These problems motivated two agents within the complex adaptive legal system, the ULC and the American Bar Association (ABA), to collaborate to develop an updated set of rules for partnerships, named the **Revised Uniform Partnership Act (RUPA)**.

The ULC offers several reasons to support states' adoption of the RUPA. Chief among those reasons is that the new act solves several problems with the UPA, not the least of which is the old act's ambiguity about the status of a partnership as an entity or an aggregate. The new act also clarifies the nature of a partner's interest in partnership property, explains the duties partners have in relation to one another, and gives partners the power to pursue a remedy when those duties are violated. It grants partnerships continuity of life, a feature that is similar but not identical to the one enjoyed by corporations. Finally, the revised act solves one of the most troubling problems of the old partnership structure, that of joint and several liability. For these reasons, among others, the RUPA has been implemented in more than half the states. The RUPA will therefore be the basis of discussion for the remainder of this chapter.

Elements of a Partnership

The RUPA says that a **partnership** is "an association of two or more persons to carry on as co-owners a business for profit." The RUPA definition emphasizes the two most essential elements of a partnership. First, partnerships must involve at least two persons. As is often the case with legal terms, *person* can have multiple meanings. In this case, the term can refer to a flesh-and-blood individual, a corporation, other partnerships, joint ventures, trusts, estates, and other commercial or legal institutions. Second, a partnership must involve a sharing of profits. This last point is so crucial that the sharing of profits is considered *prima facie* evidence of the existence of a partnership. *Prima facie* evidence in this context means that the law presumes, in the absence of evidence to the contrary, that an individual receiving profits is a partner.

Entity and Aggregate Theories

Under the Uniform Partnership Act, there was room to dispute whether a partnership should be considered an aggregate or an entity. According to the **entity theory**, a partnership exists as an individual person with its own separate identity. This unique, individual entity is separate from the identities of the partners. In contrast, under the **aggregate theory**, the partnership is seen simply as an assembly or collection of the partners who do business together. The RUPA has settled this dispute. Under the RUPA, a partnership is considered an entity in most situations. Thus, a partnership is an entity in its ability to own title to property, to sue or be sued, and to have its own separate bank accounts in its own name. Under the RUPA, partnerships also have **continuity of existence**. Continuity of existence permits a partnership to continue to operate as an entity even after the individual partners are no longer associated with it. In addition, the partners are considered agents of the partnership. However, the RUPA still considers a partnership an aggregate in relation to liability. Thus, even under the RUPA, partners still have unlimited liability for the obligations of the partnership. It is, however, possible to avoid even this problem if the partners elect to form a registered limited liability partnership. The concept of registered limited liability partnerships is discussed subsequently in this chapter.

Alternative Business Entities

As noted earlier, potential partners who are considering a business plan should think about forming a registered limited liability partnership rather than a general partnership. This simple statement, however, reveals only a very small part of the story. Starting a business, regardless of the final form of that business, is a risky endeavor. Accumulating the necessary start-up capital before opening the business and writing a comprehensive and complete operational agreement are only two of the many tasks facing new entrepreneurs. While risky, these projects are not hopeless. On the contrary, most problems can be anticipated and properly handled with well-directed, advanced research. The problems associated with the start of new business are not unlike the problems associated with establishing a stable national economy. In fact, the parallels are so close, it is worth spending a few moments considering them before moving forward.

National Economic Reform Movements According to Adam Przeworski of the University of Chicago, the goal of any national economic reform movement (NERM) is to organize the national economy so that all available funds and properties are wisely utilized in order to develop a nation-state that is economically prosperous. Przeworski notes that any properly run NERM requires (1) the development of fresh marketplaces, (2) the relaxation of prices, (3) the reduction of monopolies, and (4) the elimination of protection measures. Initiating such reforms, however, always results in unintended negative consequences (UNCs). Among these UNCs is a short-term decrease in the rate of spending that results from a transitory but seriously felt economic disruption within the nation-state, which leads to opposition from the people affected the most by the reforms. The pattern is inevitable. The relaxation of prices, for instance, leads to price increases, which leads to the decreased spending noted earlier. As competition rises, jobs are lost and people, again, spend less. The results may be so severe, Przeworski argues, that the entire reform movement may collapse under pressure for a return to the old days. However, a collapse is not inevitable as long as the managers of the NERM remember that the movement must be preceded by a fact-finding mission that uncovers the cost of the NERM, the political conditions under which the reform will be taken, and the effects of reform on the constituencies affected. [See: Adam Przeworski, *Democracy and the Market: Political and Economic Reforms in Western Europe and Latin America* (Cambridge, UK: Cambridge University Press, 1991).]

Engineering a Start-Up Plan for a New Business Like the goal of a NERM, the goal of any business plan is to organize a group of entrepreneurs and to use the capital (money, property, and expertise) provided by those entrepreneurs to fashion a product or service that is affordable and practical, the sale of which produces a profit. Like the development of a new national economy, the development of a new business requires (1) recognizing a target set of customers (fresh marketplaces), (2) developing a competitive cost structure (the relaxation of prices), and (3) outbidding of competitors (the reduction of monopolies) by selling the best product or set of services on the market. (*Note:* We removed the fourth factor here, the elimination of protective measures, because in the 21st century, this job is reserved for the government.) Again, like the reform of a national economy, the initiation of a new business always results in unintended negative consequences. Among the possible UNCs facing a new business are a short-term decrease of capital available for discretionary spending, a loss of time available for other activities, a series of profitless days (weeks, months), extended loans, increased indebtedness, discouragement among the partners (investors, employees, and so on), and the temptation to dump the entire project as a mistake. The consequences may be so hard to bear that the entire entity may collapse under the overwhelming desire to escape. Once again, the end of the business can be avoided if the managers of the new business, like the managers of a NERM, remember that the establishment of the business must be preceded by a fact-finding mission that uncovers the cost of the business, the market conditions under which the business will operate, the effects of business on the partners, and the type of business entity that is best suited for the endeavor.

Orthodox Business Entities So far we have discussed the parallels that run between creating a reformed national economy and developing a start-up plan for a new business. One of the major characteristics of any successful economic plan, whether that plan is to reform the economy or start a new business, is the ability to adapt. The development of national economic reform requires the capacity to adjust to the use of one of several orthodox business entities. An **orthodox business entity** is a conventionally run business organization that has traditionally been part of a national or state economic system. Similarly, the development of a successful start-up plan requires the ability to adapt to the possibility of forming a nontraditional, or unorthodox, business entity. Before looking at the unorthodox business entities, let's review the more conventional entities. The orthodox (or traditional) business entities include the following:

1. **Sole proprietorship** is a business operation owned and operated by one person.
2. A **general partnership** is two or more persons operating a business entity as co-owners in order to make a profit.
3. A **limited partnership** is one or more general partners joined with one or more limited partners to operate a business entity for profit.
4. A **limited liability partnership** is a general partnership in all respects except one—liability.
5. A **private corporation** is an entity formed by private persons to carry out a task best undertaken by an organization that can raise large amounts of capital quickly and that can grant the protection of limited liability.
6. A **public (or state-owned) corporation** is an entity set up by the federal, state, or local governments for governmental purposes usually involving public health, safety, or welfare.
7. A **quasi-public corporation** is a privately organized entity that makes a profit but that provides a service on which the public depends.
8. A **limited liability corporation** is a cross between a partnership and a corporation, offering the protection of limited liability like a corporation and the tax benefits of a partnership.
9. A **joint venture** (or joint undertaking) involves a contractual arrangement by which individuals unite for a limited amount of time to create a new entity in which the founders share control, expenses, and profits.

10. A franchise is a business arrangement that permits an individual, a group of investors, or another entity to lease the right to use a parent entity's business operation, trademark, goods, services, and goodwill under a fee arrangement provided to the parent.

Unorthodox Business Entities An unorthodox (or nontraditional) business entity is a non-traditional business institution that has been added to a national or state economic system to operate in an unconventional manner. Some of the unorthodox (or nontraditional) business entities, suggested by Adam Przeworski in *Democracy and the Market*, include the following:

1. A failure-proof public corporation is an entity operated by an autonomous board of directors, owned by the state, and protected from failure by the government.

2. A public-private corporation is an entity that is owned and operated by the state but that is not protected from failure by the government.

3. A cross-owned corporation is a business entity that is a public corporation owned and operated by another public corporation.

4. A public bodies corporation would not be a single corporation but would involve a project that would transform public corporations, making them into profit-making entities.

5. A social corporation is an entity run by a diverse board of directors with representatives from the employees, the state, and the general public.

6. A cooperative corporation is a business entity owned and operated by the employees or patrons of that corporation.

7. A cooperative corporation with wage-earning employees is a business owned and operated by the employees who hire nonowner employees to perform work beyond the expertise and/or availability of the owner-employees.

8. A cooperative with nonemployee owners is a business entity owned and operated by employees with some non-employee shareholders.

One of the most interesting aspects of these unorthodox business entities is that no one single entity can be labeled as the best or the worst. Often the success or the failure of a business entity depends not as much on the structure itself, as on the preliminary work done by those who plan the entity from the ground up. Again, this planning includes the ability of the members of the entity to adapt as the market, the competition, the availability of resources, and the law change. For the moment though, let's mention a few additional unorthodox entities.

Private Religiously Based Corporate Entities One innovative, unorthodox business entity that does not appear on Przeworski's list is the private religiously-based corporate entity. A private religiously based corporate entity is a dual-purpose business entity that, while not sponsored by or affiliated with a mainstream church, nevertheless seeks to promote both the goals of an established religious body and a profit for its owners. One example of this new entity is Hobby Lobby Stores Inc., which, in the case of *Burwell v. Hobby Lobby Stores, Inc.* (the *Hobby Lobby* case), characterized itself as "operating in a manner consistent with Biblical principles." In that case, the Supreme Court recognized that "organizations with religious and charitable aims might organize as for-profit corporations because of the potential advantages of that corporate form, such as the freedom to participate in lobbying for legislation or campaigning for political candidates who promote their religious or charitable goals." The High Court also noted that many states have legislatively established a unique business entity known as the benefit corporation. According to the

Supreme Court, a benefit corporation is "a dual-purpose entity that seeks to achieve both a benefit for the public and a profit for its owners." [See: *Sylvia Burwell, Secretary of Health and Human Services, et al., v. Hobby Lobby Stores, Inc., et al.*, United States Supreme Court Nos. 13-354 and 13-356 (June 30, 2014) 573 U.S. ___ (2014).]

Economic Development Special-Purpose Entities Several additional unorthodox corporate entities have appeared in some states over the last few years, the purpose of which is to facilitate public and private cooperation in community and economic development. These hybrid institutions have led the way in a variety of economic development projects such as the growth of new communities, the improvement of existing communities, the reclamation of abandoned land, the improved operation of transportation systems, and the rebuilding of failing infrastructures, among many others. Known collectively as economic development special-purpose entities (EDSPEs) these institutions promote partnerships between public and private entities in order to allow the government to assist in certain economic development projects independently from those political subdivision that establish the EDSPEs in the first place. The state of Ohio, for example, has helped engineer a number of these hybrid entities. The following list represents a small portion of the active EDSPEs in that state.

1. A special improvement district (SID) is a non-profit corporate entity instituted by the members of a community, generally including townships and municipalities, and run by a board of directors, with the purpose of working to upgrade the existing services in that community.

2. A port authority is a non-profit corporate entity established within a geographically situated area, partnering political subdivisions (municipalities, counties, and so on) to help manage the transportation industry, to promote economic growth, to help finance businesses, and to promote infrastructure redevelopment in that area (for an example, see the the Toledo Port Authority).

3. A new community authority is a corporate entity instituted by a community and run by a board of directors, the purpose of which is to coordinate with private enterprise to support the systematic growth of a diversified, strategically planned, and financially healthy community (for an example, see the New Albany Community Authority).

4. A joint economic development district (JEDD) is one of two types of joint economic development options. A JEDD, which is run by a board of directors, is designed to join resources and share costs in the economic development of two or more political subdivisions (for an example, see the Rickenbacker Global Logistics JEDD in Columbus).

5. A municipal utility district is another joint economic development option. A municipal utility district is established to develop a cost sharing program between two or more municipalities to improve the infrastructure of the participating municipalities.

6. A community improvement corporation is a non-profit corporate entity authorized by state law to either promote economic development in a community (an **economic development corporation**) or to help in reclaiming and rehabilitating empty, abandoned, and/or foreclosed real estate in the area (a **county land and reutilization corporation**).

Several additional such hybrid entities are active in Ohio. Among the greatest advantages of these hybrids is that they empower the government to mirror private institutions in areas such as wages, employment, negotiation, and so on, while at the same time giving the private entities some of the authority of the government. Time will tell just how successful these ventures will be. [See: David J. Robinson, Donell R. Grubbs, and Raymond C. Headen,

"Ohio Economic Development Special Purpose Entities," *Reference Manual,* Vol. 16-W031, The Ohio State Bar Association.]

quick quiz 25-2

1. The Revised Uniform Partnership Act has yet to be adopted by any state legislature. true | false
2. Under the RUPA, a partnership is an aggregate. true | false
3. Under the RUPA, partners are considered to be agents of the partnership. true | false

25-3 Partnership Formation

The problem with a partnership is that it can emerge simply because of the way that two or more parties are doing business with one another. That is why it is essential that businesspeople be aware of their relationships with other businesspeople with whom they work on a daily basis (see Table 25-1). Certainly the best way to form a partnership is to enter a contractual relationship by drawing up a partnership agreement. Consequently, we will examine this approach first. However, we will also look at the circumstances that can automatically create a partnership as a matter of law.

Table 25-1 Partnership Formation

Form	Definition
Partnership by contract	Express agreement drawn up by partners' articles of partnership
Partnership by proof of existence	Individuals form partnership because of their method of doing business
	Sharing of profits is *prima facie* evidence

Formation of a Partnership by Contract

One of the most common ways to form a partnership is by an express agreement between the parties. Although the agreement can be oral, it is generally best to put the terms in writing to prevent misunderstanding and disputes that might arise later in the life of the partnership. The written agreement that establishes a partnership is called a partnership agreement. The RUPA is quite specific about the nature of a partnership agreement. In fact, the RUPA defines a *partnership contract* as "the agreement, whether written, oral, or implied, among the partners concerning the partnership, including amendments to the partnership agreement." It is, of course, still possible for the partners to enter agreements subsequent to the creation of a partnership that would not be considered part of the partnership agreement. Thus, partners might enter a loan or a rental agreement that would be separate from the partnership agreement itself.

Both the RUPA and UPA are default statutes, which means that the partners are free to enter any type of agreement that they desire. However, if the partners neglect to include something in the agreement or are unsure of the interpretation of some point, the RUPA (or UPA in those states that still follow it) will "fill in the gaps." It is advisable for a partnership agreement to include the following provisions:

1. The name and duration of the partnership.
2. The names of the partners.
3. The amount of capital that each partner has contributed to the partnership.
4. The character and the extent of the business of the partnership.
5. The way that profits will be divided.
6. The way that any loss will be shared.
7. The duties of the partners.
8. Any limitations placed on the partners.
9. A section on salaries, if so desired.
10. An explanation of the dissolution process, if it is to be different from the process outlined in the RUPA.
11. A provision for determining the value of a partner's interest in the partnership.

It is also wise to recall that, though the RUPA does not require that a partnership agreement be in writing, the Statute of Frauds does dictate that certain types of contracts, such as those that will take longer than one year to complete, must be in writing. Thus, it is best to cross-reference with the Statute of Frauds just to make certain that none of those provisions apply.

THE OPENING CASE *Round 2*
"One for All, All for One, and Two for Themselves, and Only Themselves"

Recall that, in the Opening Case, R. W. Keenon, Eloise Keenon (the Keenons), Harold J. Utter, and James D. Van Hooter, along with three other unnamed parties, purchased a bus line together. Shortly thereafter, they elected to form a partnership named Western Kentucky Stages (WKS). The purpose of the partnership was to open and operate a bus line in Kentucky. The parties also entered into a partnership agreement. The agreement formalized and documented the relationship that already existed among the partners—that is, the promise to show loyalty, obedience, and due care to one another. As insurance and to make certain all points of agreement were clear and unambiguous, the partnership agreement was put in writing. Moreover, in writing the agreement, the partners included a clause stipulating that "no partner should have the right to sell his or her interest in the partnership without the consent of the other partners and without first giving those partners an opportunity to buy such interest." Now recall also that after about two years of operation, Utter and Van Hooser negotiated a deal with Greyhound Inc. (GI) under which GI put up $37,500 for an option to buy 60 percent of WKS, after which the WKS partners would incorporate so that Greyhound could more easily purchase 60 percent of the stock in the new WKS Corporation. The contract was brokered by Van Hooser and Utter, and the three unidentified partners agreed to its terms. Van Hooser and Utter, by subterfuge, also convinced the Keenons to go along with the incorporation plan. Eventually, the deal with GI fell through, and the option money was divided among Van Hooser, Utter, and the other three partners, leaving the Keenons out in the cold.

The Keenons, however, discovered the true nature of the deal and sued Utter and Van Hooser in order to receive the portion of the option money that belonged to them. In a moment, we will explore the appellate court's decision in that case. Now, however, for the moment at least, let's look at a hypothetical. Suppose the deal with GI had gone through. In that situation, Utter, Van Hooser, and the other three unknown partners would have been able to sell their shares to GI. GI would then control over 60 percent of the stock in WKS. The Keenons, however, would not have the same deal with GI. In that case, the Keenons would have been forced to sell their stock in WKS at a reduced price or would have been compelled keep their stock and hope for the best. Neither option would have been especially appealing to them, and it is likely, given their history, that they would have filed a suit against Utter and Van Hooser. The question in that case would have been: Did Utter, Van Hooser, and the other three partners violate the clause in the partnership agreement that read, "no partner should have the right to sell his or her interest in the partnership without the consent of the other partners and without first giving those partners an opportunity to buy such interest." Chances are that the answer to this question would be yes. This would be true, despite the fact that the sale of stock took place after the partnership had become a corporation because the scheme was hatched while the partnership still existed and while the clause was still valid. However, whatever the ultimate outcome would have been in this hypothetical situation, the Keenons would have had a reasonable chance of succeeding in their argument because the partnership agreement was placed in writing. Had the Keenons been forced to rely on oral testimony, Utter and Van Hooser could have made up whatever story they thought would aid their case. The moral of the story is simple, "Get a partnership agreement in writing—period!" [See: *Van Hooser, et al. v. Keenon, et al.*, 271 S.W. 2d 270 (Court of Appeals of Kentucky).]

Formation of a Partnership by Proof of Existence

The definition of a partnership offered by the RUPA establishes the parameters within which a partnership will be formed. The definition states that a business arrangement will be considered a partnership if it involves two or more persons, in association with one another, who are carrying on a business as co-owners for profit. Therefore, to show that a business is operating as a partnership by proof of existence, we must be able to point to three elements: (1) an association of two or more persons, (2) who are co-owners of (3) a business for profit.

An Association of Two or More Persons In the case of a partnership, a "person" can be a living flesh-and-blood individual, a corporation, another partnership, a joint venture, a trust, an estate, or some other commercial enterprise or legal institution. Any two of these persons working together would be sufficient to create an association.

Co-Ownership of the Business There are certain signs that indicate that the parties in a venture are co-owners. One such sign is the existence of management power. Of course, management power by itself is not enough. Employees who are not partners and even independent contractors who have control over certain projects conducted for the business may have management power without being co-owners. Still, the power to make management decisions is a persuasive piece of evidence that is helpful in establishing co-ownership. Co-ownership is also established by the sharing of profits among the partners. However, the RUPA also says that certain types of profit sharing, though real enough, will not rise to the level needed to create a partnership. These profit-sharing activities include the following:

1. The repayment of a debt.
2. Wages to an employee.
3. Payments to an independent contractor.
4. Rent payments to a landlord.
5. Annuity payments or health benefit payments to a beneficiary, representative, or designee of a retired or deceased partner.

6. Interest payments on a loan, even if the level of payments is tied to profit fluctuations.
7. Consideration for the sale of goodwill or for the sale of other property even if the payments are made in installments.

Although the sharing of profits is *prima facie* evidence of the existence of a partnership, parties can receive profits in any of the ways on this list without being saddled with the label of partner.

Carrying on a Business for Profit Finally, it is not enough for two or more persons to simply be co-owners of property, even if the property does make a profit. The association must also have the goal of running the business together. It is, of course, essential that the business in question be run for a profit. This point means that the venture cannot involve an unincorporated nonprofit venture. It is also unlikely that a solitary profit-making business transaction by itself will be enough to establish a partnership.

---

quick quiz 25-3

1. A partnership can emerge simply because of the way two or more parties are doing business with one another. | true | false
2. A "person" can be a living flesh-and-blood individual, a corporation, another partnership, a joint venture, a trust, an estate, or some other commercial enterprise or legal institution. | true | false
3. The sharing of profits is *prima facie* evidence of the existence of a partnership. | true | false

---

25-4 Partnership Property Rights and Duties

Property is an extremely critical element in partnership law because virtually every decision made by a partner deals with the disposition of partnership property. Decisions involving the use of partnership property, such as machinery, equipment, furniture, and vehicles; the purchase of raw materials; and the sale of finished products all involve the disposition of property. Even service-oriented partnerships such as shipping firms and restaurants involve the disposition of property in one way or another. Therefore, partnership duties and rights always involve partnership property. This point is also why it is critical to determine whether a given piece of property belongs to the partnership entity or to an individual partner as his or her personal property. At times it is relatively easy to distinguish between partnership property and property that belongs to individual partners. For instance, the capital contributions of all partners are considered the property of the partnership. **Capital contributions** are sums that are contributed by the partners as permanent investments and that the partners are entitled to have returned when the partnership is dissolved. In contrast, loans or later advances that partners make to the partnership and accumulated but undivided profits belong to the partners on an individual basis. Other forms of partnership property belong only to the partnership in its status as an entity.

Partnership Liability

Passage of the Revised Uniform Partnership Act has altered the type of liability that is levied against partners. **Joint liability** means that, when the partners are sued, liability will be spread among them equally. In contrast, **joint and several liability** means that the partners can be sued apart or together. Under the original Uniform Partnership Act, partners were jointly liable for contract obligations, but jointly and severally liable for any tort obligations. Under the Revised Uniform Partnership Act, liability was altered so that joint and several liability applies to suits in both contract and tort law. Basically this means that each partner could find himself or herself sued separately and could be individually liable for the entire judgment, rather than simply a proportional amount. However, because the revised act emphasizes the entity nature of the partnership, the entity itself must satisfy any judgment, contract or tort, before an individual partner can be held personally responsible. These responsibilities can, however, be altered by the partners in the partnership agreement. Also remember that some states add provisions to the revised act to restrict the application of the new law so that it applies only to partnerships formed after the date of the law's enactment.

A CLASSIC CASE   The Liability Blues

Washington Square Enteprises (WSE), a general partnership that owned and operated a shopping mall, opened a line of credit with PNC Bank for $35,000. The funds were earmarked by the partnership to help in the operation and maintenance of the mall. For almost 10 years, the account was properly maintained. Then WSE ran into financial difficulties that made it impossible for the firm to repay the $33,522.65 that it owed to PNC. In order to recoup its losses, PNC brought a lawsuit against WSE. Rather than suing the partnership, PNC sued the individual partners directly. The bank also sued only three partners, Michael Farinacci, Sam Strano, and Claire Gruttadauria, leaving the others untouched. As we shall see shortly, that was a serious error that would leave the management of the bank singing the liability blues.

The first negative consequence of this decision was the disappearance of one of the defendants, leaving only Farinacci and Gruttadauria in the case. The second negative consequence was the refusal of the trial judge to add any of the other partners, beyond Farinacci and Gruttadauria, to the lawsuit. At first, the management of PNC was confident that the failure to add the other partners would not affect the outcome of the case because, under the provisions of the Revised Uniform Partnership Act, partners are jointly and severally liable for both contract and tort debts. The defendants, however, argued that the plaintiff had made a crucial mistake. This mistake was grounded in the failure to realize that since the WSE had been formed in 1978, since the partners did not agree to be held to the new statute, and since the debt was incurred while the old statute was in effect, the RUPA did not apply in this case. Because the RUPA did not apply, the UPA had to be used to determine liability. The trial court, and later the appellate court, agreed with the defendants. That was the third negative consequence.

Under the new Revised Uniform Partnership Act, joint and several liability applies to suits in both contract and tort law. Under the original Uniform Partnership Act, the one that both courts said applied here, partners were jointly liable for contract obligations and jointly and severally liable for any tort obligations. Because this was a contract case, under the UPA, only joint liability would apply. This meant that, even though both courts decided that PNC could collect from both defendants, under the UPA, the bank could collect only each partner's proportionate share. Thus, under the UPA, the partners are jointly, not jointly and severally, liable for the debts of WSE. To emphasize this result, the trial court quoted the state supreme court in another case, wherein the court explained, "Joint liability apportions responsibility for a contractual debt equally, in the absence of a partnership agreement to the contrary, among the partners and thereby limits the creditor's execution on an individual partner's property to a pro rata share of the debt. Joint and several liability, on the other hand, allows for disproportionate satisfaction of the partnership obligation by rendering each general partner responsible for the entire amount of the partnership debt." [See: *Wayne Smith Constr. Co., Inc. v. Wolman, Duberstein & Thompson* (1992), 65 Ohio St.3d 383, 388.] The net result was that Farinacci and Gruttadauria had to pay only their proportional share of the debt. This amounted to two-eighths of the debt, or $4,190.33 each. So, while technically PNC won the case, the institution received considerably less than the full $33,522.65 that it wanted, leaving PNC management singing the liability blues. [See: *PNC Bank v. Michael Farinacci*, Eighth Appellate District, County of Cuyahoga) Case Number 96134 (2011).]

Source: See: *PNC Bank v. Michael Farinacci*, Eighth Appellate District, County of Cuyahoga) Case Number 96134 (2011).

Partnership Property

The fact that the RUPA has established the existence of a partnership as an entity has alleviated some of the difficulties once associated with identifying partnership property. The RUPA states that partnership property is any and all property that has been obtained by the partnership itself. For instance, if the property was obtained in the partnership's name, it is partnership property. If the property was obtained by a partner in his or her role as a partner, it is partnership property. If the instrument of title for the property includes the name of the partnership, it is partnership property. Finally, if the instrument of transfer indicates that the property was obtained by a partner in his or her role as a partner or if the partnership is referred to in the instrument, the property belongs to the partnership.

When it is difficult to determine whether a piece of property belongs to the partnership or to a partner, the court may ask the following questions: Has the partnership included the property in its account books? Has the partnership expended its own funds to improve or repair the property? Has the partnership paid taxes on the property? Has the partnership paid other expenses, such as maintenance costs, for the property? The more of these questions that can be answered in the affirmative, the more likely it is that the property is partnership property.

Specific Partnership Property

The RUPA has made a significant change in the rule with regard to individual pieces of partnership property. Under the UPA, each partner had a property interest in all specific items of partnership property. Each partner was therefore a co-owner of that property. This form of ownership was known as tenancy in partnership. Under the UPA, a tenancy in partnership had the following characteristics:

1. A partner had an equal right with all other partners to possess and use specific partnership property for partnership purposes but not for that partner's personal use.
2. A partner's interest in partnership property could not be assigned (i.e., transferred by sale, mortgage, pledge, or otherwise) to a nonpartner, unless the other partners agreed to the transfer.
3. Partners' rights in partnership property were not subject to attachment (i.e., taking a person's property and bringing it into the custody of the law) for personal debts or claims against the partners themselves.
4. A deceased partner's interest in real property held by the partnership passed to the surviving partners.
5. Partners' rights in specific partnership property were not subject to any allowances or rights to widows, heirs, or next of kin.

Under the RUPA, all of this has changed. The RUPA states, "A partner is not co-owner of partnership property and has no interest in partnership property which can be transferred, either voluntarily or involuntarily." Of course, partners will still be able to use partnership property. However, their right to hold and use such property is limited to partnership purposes. This significant change in relation to partnership law actually brings partnership property rights in relation to individual pieces of partnership property in line with the way property rights operate for other business associations, such as corporations.

Interest in the Partnership

The RUPA establishes that a partner has an interest in the partnership as a firm. That right consists of two parts: (1) a transferable economic interest and (2) a nontransferable interest in management rights.

Transferable Economic Interest The partner's economic interest is his or her share of the profits and losses and his or her share of the surplus. **Surplus** includes any funds that remain after the partnership has been dissolved and all other debts and prior obligations have been paid. Partners can voluntarily assign their economic interest to another party. The assignee in such an action, however, is not entitled to take part in the management of the partnership. The assignee also cannot gain access to the partnership books or the partnership financial records. Nor can an assignee demand to receive information concerning the transactions of the partnership.

> **About the Law**
> Because each partner in a partnership is an agent for all of his or her partners, any knowledge about the business of the firm that one partner has is imputed to all other partners.

Management of the Firm Participation in management decision making is not limited to the partner's proportional share of the firm. Instead, all partners have equal rights in the management of the partnership business. The day-to-day decisions of the firm are decided by a majority vote of the partners. If a vote is split evenly, then the status quo remains. If such deadlocks persist, and the very operation of the business is threatened, it may be time to dissolve the partnership. Occasionally, a unanimous vote is required in a business decision. However, such decisions must involve actions that fall outside the regular, daily operation of the business. Decisions that involve amendments to the partnership agreement also require unanimous consent.

It is, of course, possible for a partner to reduce his or her part in management voluntarily by becoming a **silent partner**. A silent partner is one who does not participate in the day-today business of the firm. This role is in contrast to a **secret partner**, whose identity and existence are not known outside the firm but who nevertheless can participate in the management of the firm. Some partnerships create their own hierarchy of partners. Thus, a firm may be divided into *junior* and *senior partners* or into *managing* and *nonmanaging partners*.

Partnership Rights and Duties

We have already pinpointed most of the individual rights that partners possess by virtue of their participation in the partnership. These rights include: (1) the right to use partnership property, as long as the property is held and used for partnership purposes; (2) the right to receive the partner's share of the profits (and losses) and his or her share of the surplus; (3) the right to manage the regular day-to-day operation of the partnership business; (4) the right to approve of serious matters outside the ordinary course of business; and (5) the right to approve of amendments to the partnership agreement. In addition, partners have certain enforcement rights, should the need arise to implement the other rights.

Enforcement Rights Under the UPA, a partner's enforcement rights are few. In fact, partners have only three enforcement rights: (1) the right to see the firm's financial records, (2) the right to compel an accounting, and (3) the right to compel a dissolution of the entire partnership. Under the RUPA, those enforcement rights are enhanced. The three rights previously noted are retained, but in addition, a partner can sue another partner directly or, under the entity theory, the partnership itself to enforce his or her partnership rights as expressed in the RUPA or granted by the partnership agreement. In such an action, the partner can ask for damages or for an equitable remedy, such as an injunction or specific performance. Of course, the reverse is also true; the partner can be sued by another partner or by the partnership itself.

Loyalty, Obedience, and Due Care The RUPA notes that partners have three critical duties: (1) loyalty, (2) obedience, and (3) due care. The first of these three, the duty of loyalty, is based on the fact that the partners are in a fiduciary relationship.

The Duty of Loyalty The duty of loyalty has become centrally important under the RUPA, unlike its position under the UPA, which devoted only a very small amount of space to the topic. According to the RUPA, the duty of loyalty includes the following items:

1. To account to the partnership for any property, profits, or benefit that comes from the partner's use of partnership property or from the winding up process after dissolution.
2. To refrain from dealing with people who may have an interest that is adverse to the best interests of the partnership.
3. To refrain from entering any competition with the partnership in the operation of partnership business.

A partner does, however, retain the right to look after himself or herself during the formation of the partnership, because the duty of loyalty does not arise until the partnership entity actually exists.

A QUESTION OF ETHICS

The End of Capitalism?

One of the premiere economists of the last century was a Harvard professor named Joseph Schumpeter, who wrote a treatise titled *Capitalism, Socialism, and Democracy* in which he foretold the ultimate end of the capitalist economic system. Oddly, Schumpeter was himself a confirmed capitalist and a dedicated member of the Austrian school of economics, so when he predicted the end of the capitalist economy, it was without joy or pleasure. In fact, it was more of a warning than a prediction, offered with the hope that something could be done to divert the path away from destruction. Schumpeter's affection for capitalism is described in the following passage, penned by Allen M. Sievers in his study, *Revolution, Evolution, and the Economic Order*:

> The capitalist, for one thing, wishes to provide for his family, and indeed capitalism is really not individual-centered but family-centered. Further, the capitalist shares in lesser degree the romantic adventuresomeness which characterized feudal society, or there would be no risky innovation or entrepreneurial exploit. Capitalism also requires a kind of symbiosis with the aristocracy and other non-bourgeois elements to run the state, and this depends on a kind of loyalty by these classes to capitalism. The masses must also be awed by the glamor or prestige of capitalist success in order to submit to the discipline necessary for business production. The business classes themselves must have an *esprit de corps* and a devotion to their way of life, as well as a code of ethics if the contract and property system is to work. We might say in sum, that Schumpeter believed that capitalist civilization is based on a rationalism qualified just a bit by other human qualities.[1]

[See: Allen M. Sievers, *Revolution, Evolution, and the Economic Order* (Upper Saddle River, NJ: Prentice-Hall, 1963), p. 41.]

We can distill from this quotation five essential qualities of the capitalist: (1) family-centeredness, (2) a willingness to take risks, (3) loyalty to the capitalist ideal, (4) awe at the success of capitalistic ventures, and (5) a code of ethics that permits the rules of contract and property law to work.

ETHICAL CONCERNS AND QUESTIONS

1. Which of the business organizations described in this chapter is best suited for realizing Sievers's capitalistic ideals? Explain. Which business entity is the most and which the least ethical? Explain.
2. According to Sievers, capitalism requires an integration of the aristocratic and the working class elements of society. Is such an integration promoted or hampered by the partnership form of

doing business? Explain. Is such an integration of the aristocratic and the working class elements of society ethical? Explain.

3. Do the alternate forms of partnership such as the limited partnership structure prove or disprove Sievers's theory? Explain.

4. Recall that Schumpeter, like F. A. Hayek, opposes governmental interference in the economy. Does this not mean that the sole proprietorship would be the perfect Schumpeter business? Why or why not?

5. Is the Austrian strategy of allowing economic collapse ethical? Explain.

The Duty of Due Care Basically, the duty of due care means that partners must do their best in the business, based on their talents, education, and abilities. It does not mean that partners must be infallible. On the contrary, the standard recognizes that a partner may make mistakes and allows for those mistakes, provided the partner acted with an ordinary level of skill and competence and in the best interests of the partnership.

THE OPENING CASE Round 3
"One for All, All for One, and Two for Themselves, and Only Themselves"

One last look at the Keenon case is in order. Recall that the Keenons, Utter, Van Hooser, and three additional unidentified parties formed a partnership called Western Kentucky Stages (WKS). The parties also drew up a partnership agreement and put that agreement in writing. After about two years of operation, Utter and Van Hooser made a deal with Greyhound Inc. (GI) under which GI put up $37,500 for an option to buy 60 percent of WKS, after which the WKS partners would incorporate so that Greyhound could more easily purchase 60 percent of the stock in the new WKS Corporation. The deal was engineered by Van Hooser and Utter. However, the other three unnamed partners went along with it. Before the deal could go through, however, Utter and Van Hooser had to convince the Keenons to agree to transform the partnership into a corporation. To make their case, Utter and Van Hooser argued that (1) the partners would be better off with the limited liability provided by the incorporation process, and (2) Van Hooser and Utter could better deal with the federal government if WKS were a corporation. While ostensibly true, these reasons were used as a cover-up to hide the real reason for incorporating—that is, to give GI easier access to WKS's stock. In addition to this series of fabrications, Utter and Van Hooser concealed the entire GI deal from the Keenons. Later, in court, Utter and Van Hooser would argue that they had to keep the Keenons in that dark because R. W. Keenon would have used his influence with GI to nix the deal, a deal that they believed was in the best interests of WKS and the other partners. Eventually, the Keenons agreed to the incorporation.

Then things fell apart. The GI deal evaporated, and the other five partners split the $37,500 option money. When the Keenons found out about the GI deal, they, as partners, demanded their fair share of the $37,500. Utter and Van Hooser refused. The Keenons argued that, not withstanding how the GI contract was brokered, the amount made in the agreement, like any amount made on any contract negotiated on behalf of the partnership should have gone into the WKS bank account and that each partner then owned his or her fair share of that deposit. When they could get no satisfaction from Van Hooser and Utter, the Keenons filed this lawsuit.

The commissioner of the trial decided the case in favor of the Keenons, and the trial court agreed. Moreover, the trial court placed full responsibility on Utter and Van Hooser because they had brokered the deal and had, as trustees, dispersed the money from that deal to the other partners. Hooser and Utter appealed the trial court's decision. In retrospect, that turned out to be a mistake. The appellate court was appalled by what Van Hooser and Utter had done. The court noted, first, that Van Hooser and Utter had unequivocally violated their duties of loyalty and due care to the other partners. Moreover, the court pointed out, rather forcefully, that the defendants' attempt to justify lying and cheating by noting that they, the defendants, had a good reason for doing so, is completely unacceptable. The court said it this way: "We should state, at the outset, that there is no relation of trust or confidence known to the law that requires of the parties a higher degree of good faith than that of a partnership. Nothing less than absolute fairness will suffice. Each partner is the confidential agent of all the others and each has a right to know all that the others know. Nor will one partner be permitted to benefit at the expense of the firm. See Hollowell v. Satterfield, 185 Ky. 397, 215 S.W. 63. In Axton v. Kentucky Bottlers' Supply Co., 159 Ky. 51, 166 S.W. 776, 778, we had this to say on the subject: 'The obligation of good faith is not even confined to persons who are actually partners. It extends to persons negotiating for a partnership, and to persons who have dissolved partnership, and have not completely wound up and settled the partnership affairs.' In Stephens v. Stephens, 298 Ky. 638, 183 S.W,2d 822, 824, we held: 'No undue advantage of one over another by misrepresentation or concealment will receive the approval of the law. A court of equity will always grant relief to the partner who has suffered from a breach of the obligation. One partner will not be permitted to obtain secretly any right that should belong to the partnership and put it to his own individual profit. Of such character is the securing of a contract. The criterion is not an actual evil motive, for the courts look to the results of any such action regardless of evil intent. If such action results in profit or advantage, the courts will require an accounting.'" [See: *Van Hooser, et al. v. Keenon, et al.*, 271 S.W. 2d 270 (Court of Appeals of Kentucky).]

Source: See: *Van Hooser, et al. v. Keenon, et al.*, 271 S.W. 2d 270 (Court of Appeals of Kentucky)

quick quiz 25-4

1. Under the RUPA, each partner has a property interest in all specific items of partnership property. true | false
2. The RUPA states that partnership property is any and all property that has been obtained by the partnership itself. true | false
3. A partner's economic interest in the partnership is nontransferrable. true | false

25-5 Dissociation and Dissolution

One of the objectives of the Uniform Law Commission and the American Bar Association in rewriting the UPA and developing the RUPA was to make certain that the new law coincided as much as possible with commercial realities. Under the UPA, whenever a partner ceased to be associated with the partnership, technically, that partnership went through the dissolution process. In present commercial realities, it no longer makes sense for partners to have to deal with the dissolution technicalities when the only thing that is really happening is the buyout of a partner who wants to leave the firm. Consequently, the RUPA now includes two methods by which a partner becomes dissociated with partnership: dissociation and dissolution.

This partnership is in the "winding up" stage and is selling its assets and inventory to satisfy creditors and hopefully distribute surplus to the former partners.
©WendellandCarolyn/Getty Images

Dissociation of a Partnership

Under the RUPA, a **dissociation** takes place whenever a partner is no longer associated with the running of the firm. It is always possible for partners to leave a partnership firm when they want. However, sometimes, a partner leaves the firm wrongfully when he or she does not have the legal right to do so. A partner's right to withdraw from a partnership may depend on whether the partnership is a term partnership or a partnership at will. A **term partnership** is one that has been set up to run for a certain set time period or to accomplish a task of some sort. A partner who leaves a term partnership before the term expires or before the task is accomplished has acted wrongfully. A **partnership at will** is one that any partner may leave without liability. The RUPA establishes the circumstances in which it is proper to leave a partnership. Some rules affect both types of partnerships; others apply only to partnerships at will. These include (1) a partner's death in either type of partnership; (2) a partner's leave-taking from a partnership at will; (3) a partner's leave-taking from either type of partnership under the rules set up by the partnership agreement; or (4) a partner's leave-taking from either type of partnership, if a court has decided that a partner cannot do what he or she is supposed to do under the partnership agreement.

Dissolution of a Partnership

The **dissolution** of a partnership occurs when a partner ceases to be associated with the partnership and the partnership ends. The dissolution of a partnership can occur in one of three ways: (1) by an action committed by the partners, (2) by operation of law, or (3) by the decree of a court of law.

An Action by the Partners
Whenever a partnership at will exists, that partnership can be dissolved whenever a partner notifies the other partners that he or she intends to leave the firm. Partnerships at will, however, are not dissolved when a partner dies or enters bankruptcy. Whenever a term partnership is involved, the RUPA says that there are several ways to dissolve the firm: (1) when the time limit has passed; (2) when the task of the partnership has been accomplished; (3) when there is express agreement among all partners to end the partnership; (4) when a partner dies; (5) when a partner becomes incapacitated; (6) when a partner goes bankrupt; and (7) when a partner produces a wrongful dissociation from the partnership and, within 90 days of that leave-taking, at least half the other partners agree to end the business.

By Operation of Law
Dissolution becomes effective by operation of law if some event occurs that makes it illegal to continue the business of the firm. If, for instance, at some time in the distant future it became illegal to manufacture and sell tobacco products, a partnership formed to produce and market cigarettes would dissolve by operation of law.

By a Court Order
When a partner has engaged in some sort of wrongdoing and, on those grounds, another partner petitions the court for a dissolution, the court may dissolve the partnership by court order. When a continuation of the business would be economically foolish, the court may dissolve the firm. Finally, when a partner does something that makes it impractical to continue the business with that partner, the court may order the dissolution of the business.

Winding Up the Partnership Business When a partnership terminates, there must be a winding up of the partnership affairs. This action includes the orderly sale of the partnership's assets, the payment of creditors, and the distribution, if any, of the remaining surplus to partners according to their profit-sharing rations.

quick quiz 25-5

1. The RUPA includes two methods by which a partner becomes dissociated with a partnership: dissociation and dissolution.	true | false
2. A partnership at will is one that any partner may leave without liability.	true | false
3. When partnership terminates, there must be a winding up of the partnership affairs.	true | false

25-6 Other Forms of Partnership Business

The changing needs of the modern marketplace and the development of new ideas in the law have combined to allow for a new form of partnership, the registered limited liability partnership. Those same forces have also cooperated to update one of the more traditional forms of the partnership business, the limited partnership.

Registered Limited Liability Partnerships

Statutory developments in several states have produced a new type of business organization known as the registered limited liability partnership. A **registered limited liability partnership (RLLP or LLP)** is a general partnership in all respects except one—liability. In a traditional general partnership, the liability for the torts committed by a partner or an employee of the partnership is joint and several. This stance means that each partner is liable and may be sued in a separate action or in a joint action. A judgment may be levied against one or more partners. The release of one partner in one action does not necessarily release the others.

The statutes usually require that the registration statement be filed by all of the partners or at least by those partners holding a majority interest in the partnership. Limited liability partnerships must update their registration statement each year or risk the loss of registration. As far as the tax laws are concerned, LLPs are considered general partnerships. When an LLP has been created, partners can no longer be held jointly or severally liable for the torts, wrongful acts, negligence, or misconduct committed by another partner or by any representative of the partnership. Naturally, partners would still be liable for their own wrongful acts and for the wrongful acts committed by other partners or employees who are under the direct control of that partner. The Revised Uniform Partnership Act includes the provisions necessary for obtaining limited liability status. Thus, states that have adopted the RUPA in its entirety do not need to pass a separate statute to allow for the creation of an LLP.

Limited Partnerships

Limited partnerships are governed by the Revised Uniform Limited Partnership Act (RULPA). The revised act defines a **limited partnership** as "a partnership formed by two or more persons . . . having one or more general partners and one or more limited partners." **General partners** take an active part in the management of the firm and have unlimited liability

> **Did You Know?**
>
> Because the dissolution of a partnership occurs whenever a partner becomes disassociated with the carrying on of partnership business, the dissolution of every partnership is inevitable. Therefore, the dissolution of a partnership is not a question of "if" but of "when."

for the firm's debts. **Limited partners** are nonparticipating investors. They contribute cash, property, or services to the partnership but do not take part in the management of the firm.

A limited partnership is advantageous for both the limited partner and the general partner. The general partner can accumulate additional capital without admitting another general partner who would be entitled to management rights. Thus, the general partner maintains control while strengthening the firm's treasury. The limited partner also benefits because a limited partnership means limited liability. **Limited liability** in turn means that the limited partner's nonpartnership property cannot be used to satisfy any debts owed by the partnership. Thus, limited partners receive a return on their investment while risking only that original investment.

Limited partnerships must follow strict filing requirements. Usually, a certificate of limited partnership must be filed with the secretary of state's office. The purpose of the certificate is to warn third parties of the limited liability of some partners. However, some state statutes indicate that neither the names of the limited partners nor the amounts of their capital contributions must be included in the certificate. This provision simplifies the formation of a limited partnership because it allows limited partners to remain anonymous.

Failure to file a certificate of limited partnership will deprive a limited partner of limited liability if third parties attempting to hold the limited partner liable did not know that they were dealing with a limited partnership. Moreover, if in the certificate of limited partnership, a limited partner is incorrectly identified as a general partner, he or she would not have limited partner status. To correct such an error, the limited partner would have to refile an amended certificate of limited partnership or leave the limited partnership altogether. Such drastic actions would be necessary unless the state statute under which the limited partnership was formed allows a limited partner who has been incorrectly named as a general partner to file with the appropriate state office a unilateral **disclaimer of general partner status**. Limited partners must also guard against becoming too involved in the business. A limited partner who exercises too much control over partnership affairs may lose the protective mantle of limited liability. Recently, however, many state legislatures have greatly expanded the types of activities that a limited partner can perform without losing the shelter provided by limited partnership status.

quick quiz 25-6

1. A registered limited liability partnership is like a general partnership in all respects except liability. — true | false
2. In most states, to become a registered limited liability partnership, the partners must file with the auditor's office in the county courthouse. — true | false
3. Limited partnerships must have at least three limited partners and no general partners. — true | false

Summary

25.1 The easiest business organization to form is a sole proprietorship. All that businesspeople have to do is open their doors for business, and a sole proprietorship is created. The greatest advantage to a sole proprietorship is that the owner has complete control over the business. The major disadvantage is that the sole proprietor is subject to unlimited liability.

25.2 The Revised Uniform Partnership Act states that a partnership is "an association of two or more persons to carry on as co-owners a business for profit." Under the RUPA, a partnership is considered an entity, or an individual unit that exists separate from the partners. A partnership is an entity in its ability to own title to property, sue or be sued, and have its own separate bank accounts in its own name. Under the RUPA, partnerships also have continuity of existence.

25.3 One of the most common ways to form a partnership is by an express agreement between the parties. It is generally best to put the terms in writing to prevent misunderstanding and disputes that might arise later in the life of the partnership. The written agreement that establishes a partnership is called a partnership agreement. To show that a business is operating as a partnership by proof of existence, three elements must exist: (1) an association of two or more persons (2) who are co-owners of (3) a business for profit.

25.4 Capital contributions are sums that are contributed by the partners as permanent investments and that the partners are entitled to have returned when the partnership is dissolved. Loans or later advances that partners make to the partnership and accumulated but undivided profits belong to the partners on an individual basis. Other forms of partnership property belong only to the partnership in its status as an entity. The RUPA states that "A partner is not co-owner of partnership property and has no interest in partnership property which can be transferred, either voluntarily or involuntarily." Partners can use a partnership only for partnership purposes. The RUPA establishes that a partner has an interest in the partnership as a firm. That interest consists of two parts: (1) a transferable economic interest and (2) a nontransferable interest in management rights.

25.5 Under the RUPA, a dissociation takes place whenever a partner is no longer associated with the running of the firm. Partners can leave a partnership firm whenever they want. A partner leaves a firm wrongfully if he or she does not have the legal right to do so. The dissolution of a partnership occurs when a partner ceases to be associated with the partnership and the partnership ends. The dissolution of a partnership can occur in one of three ways: (1) by an action committed by the partners, (2) by operation of law, or (3) by the decree of a court of law.

25.6 The changing needs of the modern marketplace and the development of new ideas in the law have combined to allow for a new form of partnership, the registered limited liability partnership. Those same forces have cooperated to update one of the more traditional forms of the partnership business, the limited partnership.

Key Terms

aggregate theory, 707
benefit corporation, 711
capital contribution, 715
community improvement corporation, 711
continuity of existence, 708
cooperative corporation, 710
cooperative corporation with wage-earning employees, 710
cooperative with nonemployee owners, 710
cross-owned corporation, 710
disclaimer of general partner status, 724

dissociation, 722
dissolution, 722
economic development special-purpose entities (EDSPEs), 711
entity theory, 707
failure-proof public corporation, 710
franchise, 710
general partner, 723
general partnership, 709
joint liability, 715
joint and several liability, 715
joint economic development district (JEDD), 711
joint venture, 709

limited liability, 724
limited liability corporation, 709
limited liability partnership, 709
limited partner, 724
limited partnership, 709, 723
municipal utility district, 711
new community authority, 711
partnership, 707
partnership at will, 722
port authority, 711
private corporation, 709
private religiously based corporate entity, 710
public corporation, 709

public bodies corporation, 710
public-private corporation, 710
quasi-public corporation, 709
registered limited liability partnership (RLLP or LLP), 723
Revised Uniform Partnership Act (RUPA), 707
secret partner, 718
silent partner, 718
social corporation, 710
sole proprietorship, 706, 709
special improvement district (SID), 711
surplus, 718
term partnership, 722
Uniform Partnership Act (UPA), 707
unorthodox (or nontraditional) business entity, 710

Questions for Review and Discussion

1. What are the most common forms of business associations?
2. What are the advantages and disadvantages of a sole proprietorship?
3. What are the two model acts that govern partnership law?
4. What are the differences between the aggregate and entity theories of partnership?
5. What is the nature of a partnership agreement?
6. When does profit sharing not create a partnership?
7. What constitutes a person in partnership law?
8. What are the different views of specific partnership property in partnership law?
9. What is the difference between dissociation and dissolution in partnership law?
10. What is the difference between a registered limited liability partnership and a limited partnership?

Cases for Analysis

1. Jennifer Yauger owned a loft in uptown Silverton. Robert Tomba and Gary Jorgen were partners in a mail-order business in Middletown called NASCAR Collectibles. To open an outlet in Silverton, Tomba and Jorgen leased the loft from Yauger. As part of the agreement, Yauger received $2,650 in rent each month. Later, Tomba and Jorgen set up a website and began an online auction house for NASCAR collectibles, similar to eBay. They were successful beyond their highest expectations, making more than $2 million in their first year of operation. When another online auction house offered Tomba and Jorgen $60 million for their site, they accepted the offer without hesitation. When Yauger heard about the deal, she claimed that she was a partner and demanded a $20 million payment, a sum equal to a one-third share of the sale price. When the case went to court, Yauger pointed to her monthly payments and labeled those payments a share of the profits. She argued that this payment demonstrated that she was a partner, based on proof of existence. Should the court grant Yauger partner status and give her a share of the proceeds from the sale of the business? Explain.

2. Kerry Taylor owned a warehouse in the industrial flats of Parke Central City. Yale Roberts and William Hull were partners in a chain of restaurants called Pirate's Seafood Carousel. Roberts and Hull leased Taylor's warehouse for their restaurant. As part of the agreement, Taylor received $7,500 in rent each month. Taylor retained office space on the top floor of the warehouse. She also agreed to allow Roberts and Hull to remodel the rest of the warehouse to meet the needs of their new restaurant. Taylor occasionally offered advice about the remodeling of the warehouse. In addition, after the restaurant opened for business, Taylor frequently signed for shipments that Roberts and Hull had ordered for the restaurant. After five years in this location, and after selling their other restaurants, Roberts and Hull decided to dissolve their partnership. During the winding up process, they were surprised to learn that Taylor claimed that she should receive a share of the surplus cash after the dissolution of the partnership because she claimed to be a partner in Pirate's Seafood Carousel. Is Taylor correct in her claim? Will Roberts and Hull have to pay her a share of their surplus cash? Explain.

3. When the father of Stephen and Chris Nuss died, the two boys, aged 15 and 12 years, began to work the family farm. While the boys were still under the age of majority, their mother, Lois, kept the books for the farm. As the boys grew older, they took more and more responsibility in running the farm.

They also rented and worked additional acres of farmland. They financed these rental agreements on their own, but their mother co-signed for the arrangements. The boys also purchased additional farmland. Again, their mother helped in this purchase by co-signing. When Chris decided to leave farming, Stephen paid him $100,000, and in exchange, Chris signed over the deed to the newly purchased land. Lois was not involved in this transaction. Stephen's farming business grew. He eventually amassed more than 1,200 acres. He and his wife, Linda, kept their own financial records and maintained their own checking account for the running of the farm. Stephen's mother was not involved in any of this detail. However, Stephen continued to pay many of the expenses involved on the original farm, where his mother still maintained her residence. Stephen also paid the insurance, maintenance, and repair expenses on all buildings and equipment on the original farm. Because Stephen continued to farm this land, in addition to the land he had subsequently purchased, these payments were always characterized as rent. No other payments went to Stephen's mother. When Stephen died, Linda, his widow and executor, claimed that a partnership existed and that the farm equipment on the original acreage and original acreage itself belonged to that partnership. Lois argued that no partnership between Stephen and her existed. Is Linda or Lois correct? Did a partnership exist? Explain. [See: *In re Estate of Nuss*, 646 N.E.2d 504 (OH).]

4. McCoy and Gugelman borrowed money from State Security Bank for their partnership, Antiques Etc. When McCoy and Gugelman failed to pay back the debt, the bank sued them as individuals. At trial, McCoy and Gugelman argued that their partnership, Antiques Etc., was an entity, not an aggregate, of the partners. Therefore, they concluded, the bank would have to show that the partnership funds were insufficient to answer the judgment before it could proceed against them individually. Are they correct? Why or why not? [See: *Security State Bank v. McCoy*, 361 N.W.2d 514 (NE).]

5. Shane ran a liquid fertilizer business. As part of the operation of the business, Shane paid Svoboda a specified amount per acre to spread the fertilizer on his clients' crops. Svoboda's per acre payments remained steady, despite Shane's profits or losses. Frisch was injured while filling a tank truck that was supposed to haul the fertilizer to Svoboda's tractor. Frisch sued both Shane and Svoboda, claiming that Svoboda was sharing in Shane's profits and was therefore a partner. Was Frisch correct? Explain. [See: *Frisch v. Svobada*, 157 N.W.2d 774 (NE).]

6. Summers and Dooley formed a partnership for the purpose of operating a trash collection business. The business was operated by the two men, and when either was unable to work, the nonworking partner provided a replacement at his own expense. Summers approached Dooley and requested that they hire a third worker. Dooley refused. Notwithstanding Dooley's refusal, Summers, on his own initiative, hired a worker. Summers paid the employee out of his own pocket. Dooley, upon discovery that a third person had been hired, objected. He stated that the additional labor was not necessary and refused to allow partnership funds to be used to pay the new employee. After paying out more than $11,000 in wages without any reimbursement from either partnership funds or his partner, Summers brought suit in the Idaho state courts. The trial court held that Summers was not entitled to reimbursement for the wages he had paid the employee. On appeal, did the Supreme Court of Idaho uphold the trial court's decision? Explain. [See: *Summers v. Dooley*, 481 P.2d 318 (ID).]

Design Elements: The Opening Case: ©Sharpstock/Alamy; A Classic Case: ©Evlakhov Valeriy/Shutterstock

quick quiz Answers

25-1	25-2	25-3	25-4	25-5	25-6
1. F	1. F	1. T	1. F	1. T	1. T
2. T	2. F	2. T	2. T	2. T	2. F
3. T	3. T	3. T	3. F	3. T	3. F

Chapter 26
The Corporate Entity

26-1 The Economic Crisis and the Corporate Entity
Crisis Management and the Corporate Entity • Capitalism and the Corporate Entity • Stabilizing Corporate Legal Principles • The Corporate Balancing Act

26-2 Types of Corporate Entities
Private, Public, and Quasi-Public Corporate Entities • Domestic, Foreign, and Alien Corporate Entities • Close and S Corporations • Limited Liability Companies, Joint Ventures, and Franchises

26-3 Formation of the Corporate Entity
Promoters and Incorporators • Articles of Incorporation • The Corporate Name • Approval of Articles • Commencement of the Business • Formation of a Limited Liability Company

26-4 Corporate Identity
De Jure and *De Facto* Corporations • Corporation by Estoppel • Piercing the Corporate Veil

26-5 Financing the Corporate Entity
Classes of Corporate Stock • Dividends

THE OPENING CASE Round 1
Piercing the Corporate Veil Is Not as Effective as You Might Think

Veil piercing, like stealing home with two outs in the bottom of the ninth, is not something to be done every afternoon. For one thing, both actions put the whole ballgame at risk. Get thrown out at home and the game is over. Pierce the veil once too often and corporate law is worthless. For another, both situations—stealing home and piercing the veil—just seem, well, unsportsmanlike. The court in *Messick v. Moring* must have had something like this in mind when it made an unpopular, but necessary, decision that finally solidified the veil-piercing doctrine in the state of Alabama. The facts in the case went something like this.

Peter Michael Gregor was out one night drinking rather heavily at restaurant-bar nicknamed "the Met." On his way home that night, he drove his vehicle through a intersection and collided with a car driven by Donna Messick Davis (Davis). The impact killed Davis. The executor of her estate, Jeffrey Messick (Messick), brought this wrongful death lawsuit on her behalf. The lawsuit was initially aimed at only three defendants: the Metropolitan Restaurant and Lounge (the Met), the Metropolitan Fixtures Corporation (MFC), and the Metropolitan Management Corporation (MMC). The three corporations had something of a symbiotic relationship. The main business was the Met, which, as noted, was a combination restaurant and bar; MFC worked to provide fixtures for the Met, and MMC supplied the Met with workers and managers. The lawsuit alleged that employees at the Met had negligently continued to serve Gregor alcoholic drinks despite the fact that he was obviously very, very drunk. This negligent behavior on the part of the employees at the Met was alleged to have led to Gregor's drunk driving, which led the the accident, which led to Davis's death. At first, the complaint named only the three corporations as defendants in the lawsuit. However, after Messick's legal team had a chance to look more closely at the organization of the three corporations, they amended the complaint to include two new defendants, Joseph Moring, MD, and William Drane, MD, who were owners, stockholders, officers, and directors of all three corporations.

Now remember, it is not supposed to work like this. As we noted in Chapter 25, the corporate form is supposed to protect the owners' investment in the corporation. This doctrine is known as *limited liability*. Unfortunately, sometimes corporate owners do not properly disengage themselves from the corporate structure and, instead, operate the business only for their own benefit, as if it were their own alter ego (you know, like Clark Kent is Superman's alter ego) or some sort of personally owned instrumentality (like the Iron Man suit is Tony Stark's personally owned instrumentality). This is exactly what Messick claimed about the relationship between Moring and Drane and their three businesses. More specifically, Messick argued that Moring and Drame were identical to the three corporations; that they operated those corporations for their own benefit alone, not for the benefit of the corporations; and that, because of this facade, the court should pierce the corporate veil and hold the two owners directly liable. When the legal team defending Moring and Drane discovered that their clients had been added to the lawsuit, they filed a summary judgment motion asking the court to dismiss the case against the two owners. The legal team argued that even if the facts as alleged by Messick were absolutely true, the law was unequivocally on the side of the defendants. Messick countered this argument by noting that the corporations had been manipulated twice for the sole benefit of the two owners: once when one of the corporations had forgiven a loan made to the two owners and once when corporate funds had been diverted from the corporations to a Merrill-Lynch account, again for the benefit of the two owners.

While it may not seem like it at first glance, there is a lot more at stake here than the fate of two defendants. The entire corporate, capitalist state is based on the faith and trust that investors have in limited liability. Corporate investors—whether they are Ma and Pa Kent in Smallville, Kansas, or Stark Industries in midtown Manhattan—rely on the protection afforded them by the corporate veil. People can invest, knowing that their losses will be limited to what they invest. If that corporate barrier is always at risk, investors may begin to find other places to put their hard-earned funds, places like foreign corporations, foreign banks, and, well, under the bedroom mattress. Before diving into the rest of this chapter, think about these questions: Should the court in *Messick v. Moring* hold Moring and Drane directly liable based on the two transactions noted earlier? What rules should apply to veil piercing, if any? Who deserves the benefit of the doubt—the plaintiff, who may have been victimized by an undercapitalized corporation or the investors, who in good faith put their hard-earned cash into the corporate capitalist structure? Oh, and finally, should Willie Mays Hayes steal home the next time he finds himself on third with two outs in the bottom of ninth? Think about it, all of it. [See: *Messick v. Moring*, 514 So. 2d 892 (The Supreme Court of Alabama).]

Opening Case Questions

1. Why did the plaintiff decide to amend his complaint in this case? Explain.
2. What is limited liability and why is it so important to the corporate-capitalist state? Explain.
3. What is veil piercing and why is it so important to the corporate-capitalist state? Explain.
4. What rules should be placed on the process of piercing the corporate veil? Explain.
5. Who stands to gain and who loses when a corporate veil is pierced? Explain.

Source: See: *Messick v. Moring* 514 So. 2d 892 (The Supreme Court of Alabama).

 Learning Objectives

1. Describe some strategies for avoiding a new 21st-century economic crisis.
2. Explain what is meant by the term *corporation*.
3. List the four methods of protecting a corporation.
4. Describe the differences among a private, a public, and a quasi-public corporation.
5. Distinguish between a close and an S corporation.
6. List the typical elements within the articles of incorporation.
7. Distinguish between the articles of organization and the operating agreement of a limited liability company.
8. Distinguish between a *de jure* and a *de facto* corporation.
9. Identify the goal of piercing the corporate veil.
10. Distinguish between common and preferred stock.

26-1 The Economic Crisis and the Corporate Entity

In Chapter 20, we analyzed the nature of the 21st-century economic crisis as it related to the financial issues of runaway mortgages and overextended lending practices, all of which led to the monetary disaster of 2008. While examining these issues, we called upon the wisdom of several modern thinkers, including Michel Serres in *Times of Crisis*, Dmitry Orlov in *Reinventing Collapse*, Nouriel Roubini and Stephen Mihm in *Crisis Economics*, and Paul M. Barrett in "Prophet-Making." To summarize their work (or our interpretation of their work), in *Times of Crisis*, Serres argues, rather persuasively, that the only way to avert any future crisis is to avoid returning to the initial conditions that created that crisis. Serres also notes that the latest economic crisis has been caused by human tampering in agriculture, transportation (communication), health, demographic connections, and conflicts. This tampering, he argues, created a biogetic (his word) system that is unstable, leading to a series of unintended consequences [See: Michel Serres, *Times of Crisis: What the Financial Crisis Revealed and How to Reinvent our Lives and Future* (New York: Bloomsbury, 2014); Dmitry Orlov, *Reinventing Collapse: The Soviet Experience and American Prospects* (Gabriola Islands, BC, Canada: New Society Publishers, 2011); Nouriel Roubini and Stephen Mihm, *Crisis Economics* (New York: Penguin, 2010); and Paul M. Barrett, "Prophet Making," *The New York Times Sunday Book Review,* (June 25, 2010) https://www.nytimes.com/2010/06/27/books/review/Barrett-t.html].

Crisis Management and the Corporate Entity

In *Reinventing Collapse*, Orlov points out that, in the Soviet Union, several factors collided that led to that nation's economic crisis. Those factors include (1) a decline in energy resources, (2) a serious trade deficit, (3) unrestrained defense spending, (4) expanding foreign debt, and (5) a pervasive psychosocial anxiety leading to erratic behavior. Without mentioning Serres, but following a strategy that seems to heed his warnings, Orlov promotes two radical strategies designed to deal with some of the most serious results of that collision. These strategies include (1) a governmental ban on the production of any new gas-powered vehicles and (2) a radical alteration in the nature of the corporation, two measures that are original and thought-provoking but ultimately too idealistic and impractical for adoption in the real world of American capitalism.

Again without referring directly to either Orlov or Serres, Roubini and Mihm appear to apply a set of integrated Serres-Orlov principles to the political and economic world of Washington and Wall Street in order to construct several proposals to make those radical adjustments a reality. In doing so, they propose two strategies, both of which focus on limiting corporate protection measures. To accomplish this objective, Roubini and Mihm suggest that (1) Congress mandate the subdivision and reorganization of the nation's largest financial institutions into smaller, independent units. This plan would make it illegal for large financial institutions to invest in any venture from which they cannot extricate themselves with the capital reserves that they have on hand. In essence, financial institutions would be legally compelled to maintain the ability to bail themselves out of financial danger. Roubini and Mihm also propose (2) a bonus-escrow plan, referred to as the "bonus-malus" system, under which the bonuses paid to top executives would be placed in escrow accounts for several years to test the true value of the programs and projects instituted by each executive. The executive does not receive the bonus unless the investment programs and projects demonstrate their staying power and profitability. If those investments lose money, then the bonus is reduced by an appropriate amount.

Capitalism and the Corporate Entity

Whether these strategies would actually be adopted by Congress is problematic. It is, after all, difficult to get politicians to do really risky things like break up corporations or freeze corporate payouts to executives (especially in election years). That is the bad news. The good news, however, is that corporate leadership does not have to wait for a congressional mandate to take the radical steps that might be needed to dodge the next financial crisis. This is because the corporation lies at the heart of the American economy and, as such, can orchestrate such changes on its own. To see why this is so, we need to examine the characteristics and the power of the corporation. A **corporation** (aka **corporate person** and **corporate entity**) is a legal entity created under the authority of a state or federal statute that gives certain individuals the capacity to operate an enterprise. As such, corporations are products of capitalism. Although capitalism originated in Europe, it flourished in the United States in the 19th century because the American economic system at that time provided the perfect engine for capitalistic progress. Much of this progress occurred because there was an enormous amount of land that needed to be developed in the United States and an influx of energetic immigrants who were willing to improve that land. Capitalism grew because those business people who worked the land as farms, factories, railroads, and stores needed an efficient and rapid way to raise capital to finance land their development projects. The corporate entity was the perfect means of raising capital quickly and using it effectively. The corporation of today, however, bears little resemblance to the corporate entity as it emerged in the 19th century. (*Note:* For detailed discussion of these radical differences, see Chapter 28.) Nevertheless, the corporate structure that exists today provides the needed power, protection, and protocols to deal with future economic problems and to profit from future economic opportunities.

Stabilizing Corporate Legal Principles

The capitalistic economic system has operated in a manner that has ensured that corporations are protected in a variety of ways. However, the basis of that protection lies within four fundamental legal principles that are designed to safeguard the corporate entity. These four principles are corporate limited liability, free transfer of ownership, central management, and the corporate person, itself.

Corporate Limited Liability Today, one of the most attractive features of the corporate way of doing business is its limited liability. **Limited liability** means that the corporate investors cannot be held personally liable for the debts of the corporation. Thus, the most that an investor can lose is the amount of money used to purchase his or her **shares** of the corporation. This liability is maintained indefinitely just so long as the corporation actually maintains its status as a self-governing, self-contained corporate person.

U.S. Const. Amendment 14 (Appendix A)

THE OPENING CASE *Round 2*
Piercing the Corporate Veil Is Not as Effective as You Might Think

In the Opening Case, we learned that Joseph Moring and William Drane had incorporated three separate businesses. These businesses were named the Metropolitan Restaurant and Lounge (the Met), the Metropolitan Fixtures Corporation (MFC), and the Metropolitan Management Corporation (MMC). Moring and Drane had clearly created these corporations to support one another. The Met, which was a combination bar and a restaurant, was the real money maker of the three. The other two businesses worked to supply and support the Met. For example, MFC worked to provide fixtures for the Met, while MMC provided the Met with employees and managers. The trouble for Moring and Drane began when someone at the Met served a customer named Peter Michael Gregor too many alcoholic drinks. By the time that Gregor left the Met, he was visibly intoxicated. While heading home that evening, Gregor drove his vehicle into the path of a car operated by Donna Messick Davis (Davis). The resulting crash led to Davis's death. Jeffrey Messick (Messick), who served as the executor of the Davis estate, brought this wrongful death lawsuit on her behalf.

When Messick first filed the suit, he named only three defendants. Those first-named defendants were the Metropolitan Restaurant and Lounge, The Metropolitan Fixtures Corporation, and the Metropolitan Management Corporation. Sometime later, once Messick had taken the opportunity to look more deeply into the relationships among these three corporations, he realized that not only were the corporations extensively entangled with one another, but they were also all owned and operated by the same two individuals, Moring and Drane. Accordingly, Messick added both Moring and Drane as defendants. This move must have taken both Moring and Drane by surprise. Both men most likely believed, and rightly so, that they were protected from liability in this case by the corporate structure that they had so carefully engineered. Remember that one of the most cited reasons to incorporate a business is to take advantage of the limited liability offered to all corporate owners and operators. Recall that limited liability means that the corporate investors cannot be held personally liable for the debts of the corporation. As a result, an investor can lose no more than the amount of money used to purchase his or her shares of the corporation. This liability lasts as long as the corporate owners and operators make certain that the corporation's separate existence is faithfully maintained. Both Drane and Moring must have realized this because they did their best to keep meticulous board records for each of the three separate corporations. Moreover, they had never done anything to use the corporate structure to defraud or cheat anyone. The fact that they were sued directly meant that the very nature of the incorporation process was at stake. As case wore on, Moring and Drane became aware that they were facing the greatest threat to the corporate way of doing business—the doctrine of piercing the corporate veil. To be continued . . . [See: *Messick v. Moring*, 514 So. 2d 892 (The Supreme Court of Alabama).]

Source: See: *Messick v. Moring* 514 So. 2d 892 (The Supreme Court of Alabama).

A NEW CLASSIC CASE
Sylvia Burwell v. Hobby Lobby Stores, Inc.: A New Spin on Corporate Personhood

The ink was hardly dry on the paper that printed the first copies of the Supreme Court's *Hobby Lobby* decision when it became clear that this case would become a classic. The case involves an insurance plan under the Affordable Care Act that would have provided "preventative care and screenings" for women employees free of "any cost sharing requirements." [42 USC Section 300gg-13(a) (4).] The statute empowered the Department of Health and Human Services (DHHS) to identify prevention techniques that would be covered under the act. To make that determination, the department enlisted the support of the Institute of Medicine, which declared that employers should provide coverage for all contraceptive procedures approved by the Food and Drug Administration. Four of these methods are designed to stop, potentially at least, the development of an already fertilized egg. These four methods violated the religious principles of the owners of Hobby Lobby, who believe that life begins at conception. Three corporations, including Hobby Lobby, brought lawsuits against the DHHS, arguing that they cannot be compelled by the government to participate in a practice that violates their religious beliefs. The lawsuit was brought under the authority of the Religious Freedom Restoration Act

(RFRA) and the Free Exercise Clause of the U.S. Constitution.

Religious Freedom Restoration Act (RFRA) The RFRA states that the government cannot "substantially burden a person's exercise of religion even if the burden results from a rule of general applicability" except when the government "demonstrates that the application of the burden to the person (1) is in furtherance of a compelling governmental interest; and (2) is the least restrictive means of furthering that compelling governmental interest." [42 USC Sections 2000bb-1(a) (b).] The first issue that the Court addresses in the opinion in *Hobby Lobby* is whether the three corporate plaintiffs qualify as "legal persons" *under this particular congressional statute*. The U.S. Supreme Court opens its opinion by making it absolutely clear that the purpose of the RFRA is to protect a person's right to exercise religious beliefs. The statute was named the Religious Freedom Restoration Act because Congress intended to reinstate a defense for religious expression that had been repeatedly weakened by the courts over the past several years (decades?). Clearly, then, the purpose of the mandate is to broaden religious protection guaranteed to all persons under the U.S. Constitution. The question then is whether a *profit-oriented* corporation qualifies as a "person" under the RFRA.

Corporate Personhood: The New Spin In this case, the Supreme Court takes the first steps toward carrying out the RFRA mandate and, in doing so, gives new life to the Free Exercise Clause of the First Amendment. However, the Court also puts a new spin on the concept of *corporate personhood*. The Court begins with the standard legal doctrine that establishes that a corporation exists as a person that is separate from its promoters, shareholders, employees, directors, and officers. So far, so good. However, as its next step, the Court applies (invents?) a novel reinterpretation of the nature of corporate personhood. The Court says that, while the corporate identity is constructed to defend the corporation, it is also created to protect the flesh-and-blood people behind that corporation. Accordingly, when the law defines the rights and duties of a corporate person, it is actually defining the rights and duties of the people behind that corporation. These people are the ones who actually carry out corporate duties and who benefit from corporate rights.

Thus, when the corporation is recognized as having rights, those rights really belong to the people behind the corporate veil. This is especially true when the "right" in question is a religious right. Thus, the Supreme Court concludes that the term *person* in the statute is meant to protect corporate "persons" *only because* the real protection flows to the people behind that corporate veil. It may be a bit hard to believe that someone on the Supreme Court actually said this, so let's take a brief look at exactly what Justice Alito states in his opinion. Alito writes:

> (I)t is important to keep in mind that the purpose of this fiction is to provide protection for human beings. A corporation is simply a form of organization used by human beings to achieve desired ends. An established body of law specifies the rights and obligations of the *people* (including shareholders, officers, and employees) who are associated with a corporation in one way or another. When rights, whether constitutional or statutory, are extended to corporations, the purpose is to protect the rights of these people. For example, extending Fourth Amendment protection to corporations protects the privacy interests of employees and others associated with the company. Protecting corporations from government seizure of their property without just compensation protects all those who have a stake in the corporations' financial well-being. And protecting the free-exercise rights of corporations like Hobby Lobby, Conestoga, and Mardel protects the religious liberty of the humans who own and control those companies.

This interpretation will undoubtedly spark controversy among corporate lawyers who are not used to such a revolutionary way of looking at the relationship between the corporate person and the people behind that person. In fact, this new way of looking at corporate identify may inspire a new wave of veil-piercing cases. [See: *Sylvia Burwell, Secretary of Health and Human Services, et al. v. Hobby Lobby Stores, Inc., et al.*, United States Supreme Court, Nos. 13-354 and 13-356 (June 30, 2014) 573 U.S. — (2014).]

Source: See: *Sylvia Burwell, Secretary of Health and Human Services, et al. v. Hobby Lobby Stores, Inc., et al.* United States Supreme Court, Nos. 13-354 and 13-356 (June 30, 2014) 573 U.S. — (2014).

Free Transfer of Ownership Corporate financing begins when the original investments are made to set up the corporation. Once the corporate person is operating, additional corporate financing may be obtained from earnings, loans, and the issuance of additional shares of stock. The issuing and selling of shares of stock to raise capital is known as *equity financing*, and equity securities give their owners a legal interest in the assets, earnings, and control of the corporation. The part of a corporation's net profits or surplus set aside for the shareholders is known as dividends. The number of shares and classes of stock that a corporation is authorized to issue are established in its certificate of incorporation. A shareholder who purchases corporate stock invests money or property in the corporation and receives a stock certificate. A **stock certificate** is written evidence of ownership of a unit of interest in the corporation.

Central Management Most state incorporation statutes provide that a corporation's business affairs are to be managed under the direction of a board of directors. The board of directors establishes broad policies, and the officers and other employees implement those policies. The shareholders are the owners of the corporation. How to keep the role of the board separate from that of executive management and that of shareholders is related to the challenge of how best to organize the board and select its members. The issues are even more complex today because a single individual often functions as a director, an officer, and a shareholder. Nevertheless, the three roles have distinct functions and should operate separately.

Corporate Personhood A corporation exists apart from its owners and is taxed directly on the income it earns. As a legal entity, a corporate person can own property and sue or be sued, just as an individual can. Moreover, the existence of a corporation is not affected by the death, incapacity, or bankruptcy of a manager or shareholder. A corporation is also considered an artificially created legal person under provisions of the U.S. Constitution. Within the context of the 14th Amendment, a corporate person—like a natural person—may not be deprived of life, liberty, or property without due process of law. Also, a corporation may not be denied equal protection of the laws within the jurisdiction of the state. A corporate person is considered a citizen of both the state in which it is incorporated and the state where it has its principal place of business. It can also be sued as a citizen of both these states. By virtue of the *due process clause* of the 14th Amendment, a state court may also exercise jurisdiction over a noncitizen corporate defendant, as long as that corporate person has had an appropriate contact with that state. Such contact can include owning property within the state, doing business in the state, or committing a tort within the state.

The Corporate Balancing Act

As we have seen at various intervals throughout the text, the law must balance several opposing factors: The letter of the law must be balanced with its spirit; the language of the law must be balanced with its interpretation; abstract legal principles must be balanced with the concrete application of those principles; and the intent of the law must be balanced with the results that emerge from the work of the lawmakers. In many ways, the corporate structure is a vivid manifestation of these balancing acts. Corporations are governed by their own bylaws, which must be balanced with federal statutes, state corporate law, and court decisions that govern the operation of those corporations. As a direct result of this, corporate officers will at times follow the letter of the law while skirting its spirit, as when they make corporate decisions that technically ought to go to the board of directors for a vote. Or they will at times interpret that language of the law to their own advantage as the big corporations did in the 19th century, when they used the Sherman Antitrust Law, specifically designed to end corporate monopolies, to break up union organizing activities and thus protect their corporate structure. None of this is to say that corporations or their officers are lawless or unethical. On the contrary, most of them are doing what they are supposed to do. They are protecting their own best interests and the best interests of their shareholders. Much of this is expressed in the balancing act among the legal watchdogs that make certain (or should make certain) that corporate officers, directors, and shareholders do not abuse the power and the privileges granted to them by the law and by the very nature of the capitalist economic system. This precarious balancing act is based upon the intervention of Congress at the federal level, the legislature at the state level, and the courts as they apply the common law.

A QUESTION OF ETHICS

The Spirit or the Letter of the Law?

As noted earlier, the law is frequently described as a balancing act. Perhaps one of the most-often-quoted segments of this concept of balancing is seen in the attempt to balance the *spirit* of the law with the *letter* of the law. It now appears, however, that this simple and, heretofore, rarely challenged concept has several new adversaries. Supreme Court Justice Antonin Scalia and his co-author Bryan A. Garner, distinguished research professor of law at Southern Methodist University, have breathed new life into a form of legal interpretation referred to alternately as *textualism* and *originalism* that may demonstrate the naïveté of attempting to balance the spirit with the letter of the law.

THE TEXTUALIST APPROACH

In general, the idea behind **textualism** (also *originalism*) is for judges and attorneys to look at constitutions and statutes as literary works or as verbal icons that stand as separately created artifacts that must be judged, much like a poem or a short story, by its words and its word alone. The intent of textualism is to have legal interpreters bypass the generally biased and self-serving explanations found in legislative histories and committee reports and instead rely upon the meaning of the words that the legislators actually wrote and placed in the text of the constitution or the statute in question. Scalia and Garner explain the details of textualism in *Reading Law: The Interpretation of Legal Texts*. Much of the book is devoted to a detailed examination of 57 canons of interpretation and 13 false beliefs that they discredit. The very first attack on these false statements targets the idea that "the spirit of a statute should prevail over its letter." Scalia and Garner argue that the idea that the spirit of the law can somehow magically trump the letter of the law was probably born sometime in the Middle Ages when the chances of finding statutory law in England were unlikely at best. Moreover, they note that, since no one has ever identified any standards by which to deduce, measure, and apply this mysterious "spirit of the law," it was most likely used as a technique to grant judges the unrestricted ability to pay no attention to the language of the law. Scalia and Garner also point out that even those judicial and philosophical giants who are alleged to have supported the spirit over letter principle really did no such thing. The leading example of those distortions is Chief Justice John Marshall who is supposed to have depended on the spirit of the Constitution, when what he really said was that the spirit of the law should be respected just as much as the letter, and (here is the key) that the spirit itself was to be "collected chiefly from its letter." [See: Antonin Scalia and Bryan Garner, *Reading Law: The Interpretation of Legal Texts* (St. Paul, MN: West, 2012).]

THE PRAGMATIC APPROACH

On the other side of this issue are a number of legal experts, not the least of which is Richard Posner, chief justice of the U.S. Court of Appeals for the Seventh Circuit and the author of *Overcoming Law*. Posner's book predates Scalia and Garner's text by some 17 years. However, Posner devotes an entire chapter to textualism, largely fashioned as a critique of another champion of that theory, Robert Bork, the author of *The Tempting of America: The Political Seduction of the Law*. In *Overcoming Law*, Posner argues that textualism, whether supported by Bork or Scalia, is fine as far as it goes, but it cannot be considered as the only arrow in a judge's quiver. Textual criticism will help to get at the meaning of the words in the law; that much is true. However, to rely solely on this approach is to ignore the consequences of the law or of a singular and narrowly drawn interpretation of that law. Posner prefers, instead, a process that he labels *pragmatism*. In a nutshell, pragmatism involves an approach by judges that considers the consequences of a decision to be the single most important guideline in the development of that decision. In applying a pragmatic approach, the judge must attempt to get into the mind of the framer of that law and, in doing so, see how that framer would respond to the modern circumstances in which the judge finds himself or herself. The law, Posner believes, is not static nor should it be. Moreover, in making his or her determination, the judge must not focus alone on a single interpretation but must consider multiple interpretations in order to sort out the one that makes the most sense. This technique, Posner argues, is not "judicial lawlessness," but is, instead, an approach that looks both forward and backward and does so with a mind toward the consequences based on multiple forms of input. [See: Richard Posner, *Overcoming Law* (Cambridge, MA: Harvard University Press, 1995); and Robert Bork, *The Tempting of America: The Political Seduction of the Law* (New York: Simon and Schuster, 1990).]

QUESTIONS YET UNANSWERED

The following questions have not yet been answered. Before you consider each question, turn to Chapter 1 to review the various ethical theories noted there (social contract theory, utilitarianism, and rational ethics). Then using one of those theories in a consistent way, answer the following questions. Is it ethical for *textualist* judges to ignore certain categories of legal research, such as legislative histories and committee reports, in their attempt to unravel the true meaning of a statute? Is it ethical for pragmatic judges to consider legislative histories and committee reports when evidence and experience have demonstrated that such reports and histories tend to be biased and prejudiced toward the position of the individual writer? Scalia and Garner argue that the spirit of the law is an invalid measuring stick because legal scholars have yet to detect any standards by which to deduce, measure, and apply this enigmatic "spirit of the law." Is this a valid argument? Why or why not? Assist Scalia and Garner by developing a standard or two that might help them identify those intangible "spiritual" standards. Posner argues that judges should always look at the possible consequences that may result from a statute once that statute goes into effect. At one level this sounds like a common-sense approach, but at another, more fundamental level, it looks like a recipe for disaster. A judge must troll through mountains of material when trying to interpret the Constitution, a statute, or a regulation. Moreover, looking backward is hard enough, but looking forward to consequences can sometimes amount to an exercise in judicial fortune-telling. That is why these results are often called "unintended consequences." Advise Posner by demonstrating the folly of trying to predict the future.

Federal Congressional Action: Congress and the Dodd–Frank Act The federal government's power to regulate business emerged directly (although some critics would say with dubious authority) and quickly from within the text of the commerce clause of the U.S. Constitution. The commerce clause is found in Article I, Section 8, Clause 3. The wording of the clause is a study in simplicity. The clause reads, "Congress shall have Power To . . . regulate Commerce with foreign Nations and among the several states." One of the first commentators to recognize the full import of these words was Supreme Court Justice William Johnson who, in his concurring opinion in *Gibbons v. Ogden*, 22 U.S. 1 (1824), wrote, "The power of a sovereign state over commerce therefore amounts to nothing more than a power to limit and restrain . . . that . . . power must be exclusive; it can reside but in one potentate, and hence the grant of this power carries with it the whole subject, leaving nothing for the State to act upon." Despite the fact that Johnson denies that he is a textualist, his study of the commerce clause in *Gibbons v. Ogden* is, nevertheless, a model of textual analysis. The words are plain and Johnson passes that plain meaning along to us.

Following Johnson's lead, the Supreme Court quickly recognized the federal government's power to regulate business. The power to regulate is so broad today that the federal government can regulate any business activity that affects interstate commerce, even if that activity takes place solely within the borders of a single state. Just about the only thing that the U.S. Supreme Court has not yet allowed the government to do is to force citizens, or anyone else for that matter, to participate in a business activity whether they want to or not. In contrast, the states do sometimes order their citizens to engage in some forms of commerce, as when they require automobile owners to buy insurance. Such legislation, however, is permitted under the state's police power. On the other hand, even that power is limited. The state can require insurance but only if a citizen actually wants to own a car. It is unlikely that a state can order a person to engage in a business activity merely because that person exists.

In Chapter 20, we learned that, in response to the 21st-century financial crisis, Congress passed several pieces of legislation, including the **Dodd-Frank Wall Street Reform and Consumer Protection Act**, aimed at fixing current economic problems and preventing such events from happening again. The problems that we discussed in Chapter 20 were related to mortgages. The mortgage industry, however, was only part of the problem. Another industry involved in the crisis was the securities industry. For that reason, Congress also included provisions in the Dodd-Frank Act to deal with the shortcomings and the errors of the securities industry, which stands at the heart of corporate ownership. As might be expected, the Dodd-Frank Act is long, involved, and complicated. It is, in fact, divided into 16 titles, many of which are named as individual acts. Two titles that affect the Securities Exchange Commission are Title VII, the Wall Street Transparency and Accountability Act, and Title IX, the Investor Protection and Securities Reform Act of 2010.

The Dodd-Frank Act was a noble experiment that attempted to reform the economic and financial community by adding more regulatory checkpoints into the system. As we have seen, however, all sectors of the sociopolitical world are subject to the complex adaptive system (CAS) in which they find themselves. The Dodd-Frank Act, with all its complexity, is no exception. Earlier, in Chapter 20, we noted that, when politicians pass a law (such as the Dodd-Frank Wall Street Reform and Consumer Protection Act), their opponents, (the economists, accountants, bankers, investors, rival politicians, and so on), react against that law. Moreover, from within that initial set of interactions, (politicians v. economists, politicians v. politicians, etc.) a second, submerged level of interaction between the people and the system itself leads to a series of unintended consequences. In the present crisis, one of these consequences has been a defensive response from the very people that the Dodd-Frank Act was designed to protect. In the last election, many people saw the government's attempt to fix the system as an escalation in governmental interference. As a result, many of these people, most of whom were potential voters, allied themselves with candidates who advocated a radical reduction in governmental regulation.

Recently, some of those reductions have begun to emerge. For example, in the case of Dodd-Frank, the House of Representatives passed an act called the Financial Creating Hope and Opportunity for Investors, Consumers, and Entrepreneurs (the Financial Choice Act), which is designed to dismantle much of what was put into place by Dodd-Frank. For instance, the Financial Choice Act called a halt to the government's ability to step in and assume control of any major financial firm that might be in danger of failing. President Trump has also joined the campaign to eliminate overregulation. To do this, the president has issued several executive orders (see Chapter 2) that, while not directly naming Dodd-Frank, may, nevertheless, have an impact on many of the new regulations that have been issued under its authority. One of these executive orders empowered the Secretary of the Treasury, "in consultation with the Administrator of the Office of

Information and Regulatory Affairs, Office of Management and Budget, to identify in an interim report to the President all such regulations that: (i) impose an undue financial burden on United States taxpayers; (ii) add undue complexity to the Federal tax laws; or (iii) exceed the statutory authority of the Internal Revenue Service." While the president's executive order and the House's version of the Choice Act may ultimately have little impact on the day-to-day operation of the economic system, they do indicate that the socioeconomic-political system is on the verge of a radical change from regulation to deregulation. [See: "Presidential Executive Order on Identifying and Reducing Tax Regulatory Burdens," issued by Donald Trump, The White House, April 27, 2017. See also: Sylvan Lane, "Trump Praises House Vote to Dismantle Dodd-Frank," *The Hill*, June 9, 2017, http://the hill.com/policy/finance/337107-trump-praises-house-vote-to-dismantle-dodd-frank.]

State Legislative Action: The Model Business Corporation Act The states have the power to regulate business under their inherent police power, a power that the federal government does not have. As noted earlier, a corporation is a legal entity created under the authority of a state or federal statute that gives certain individuals the capacity to operate an enterprise. The statutory template that most states follow in developing their corporate law statutes is the Model Business Corporation Act, often referred to as the Model Corporation Act and sometimes simply as the MBCA. The MBCA is a relatively young statute and is therefore not quite as settled as older, more traditional statutes, such as the Uniform Commercial Code and the original Uniform Partnership Act. In addition, the model act has been revised since its inception, making some of its provisions even more recent and therefore less fully developed than similar provisions in other comparable statutes.

Judicial Action: State Common Law Decisions Also, many states have a long history of common law decisions in relation to corporate law, some of which must be preempted when a state legislature adopts the MBCA. Even in the face of explicit instances of preemption, however, some state courts have been reluctant to surrender long-term common law principles and sometimes have found creative ways to interpret the MBCA within the context of that state's long-standing legal tradition. Therefore, the study of corporate law must always be tempered by a look at the state law of the jurisdiction in which a dispute is located. The process of doing business as a self-governing business association, that is, as a corporate person, is called associative corporativism, or simply corporativism. In the 19th century, each corporation was individually created by a unique legislative enactment. Each corporation had its own charter that outlined the powers and abilities of that corporation. (*Note:* For a more detailed analysis of the nature and the limits of the state's power to regulate commerce, see Chapter 28.)

quick quiz 26-1

1. A corporation is a legal entity created by either a state or federal statute authorizing individuals to operate an enterprise.   true | false

2. A corporation may not be deprived of life, liberty, or property without due process of law.   true | false

3. Limited liability means that the corporate investors rather than the corporation will be held liable for corporate debts.   true | false

26-2 Types of Corporate Entities

The previous chapter focused on sole proprietorships, general partnerships, limited partnerships, and limited liability partnerships as a way of initiating our exploration of business persons and the legal rules that apply to such persons. This chapter focuses on the nature, the formation, the identity, and the financing of the corporate entity. Before that, however, we will review the various types of traditional corporate entities. These types include:

1. Private corporations
2. Public (or state-owned) corporations
3. Quasi-public corporations
4. Domestic corporations
5. Foreign corporations
6. Alien corporations
7. Close corporations
8. S Chapter corporations
9. Limited liability corporations
10. Joint ventures
11. Franchises

Private, Public, and Quasi-Public Corporate Persons

A **private corporation** is a corporation formed by private persons to accomplish a task best undertaken by an entity that can raise large amounts of capital quickly or that can grant the protection of limited liability. Private corporations can be organized for a profit-making business purpose or for a nonprofit charitable, educational, or scientific purpose. If the corporation is organized for profit-making purposes, those profits may be distributed to the shareholders in the form of dividends. **Dividends** are the net profits, or surplus, set aside for the shareholders. **Shareholders** (or *stockholders*, as they are also known) are those individuals who own units of interest (shares of stock) in a corporation. Large private corporations generally sell their stock to the public at large and are, therefore, often referred to as public corporations. When the owners of a private corporation decide to sell stock to the public at large, financial experts report that the corporation is about to "go public." This designation can be confusing because the term **public corporation** is more properly used to describe a corporation created by the federal, state, or local government for governmental purposes. When used in the latter sense, the term includes incorporated cities, sanitation districts, school districts, transit districts, and so on. Corporations that are privately organized for profit but also provide a service on which the public depends are generally referred to as **quasi-public corporations**. In most instances, they are public utilities, which provide the public with such essentials as water, gas, and electricity. (*Note:* Unless specified otherwise, the discussion in this chapter and those that follow will focus on private corporations.)

Google Inc., headquartered in Menlo Park, California, maintains 17 corporate offices in the United States and 38 corporate offices in 23 countries throughout Asia, Europe, and North and South America.
©MariaX/Shutterstock

Domestic, Foreign, and Alien Corporate Persons

A corporation is a **domestic corporation** in the state that grants its charter. It is a **foreign corporation** in all other states. The right to do business in other states (subject to reasonable regulation) is granted by the commerce clause of the U.S. Constitution. To qualify to do business in another state, a foreign corporation must obtain a certificate of authority by providing information similar to the information provided by a domestic corporation applying for a charter. A **certificate of authority** is a document that grants a foreign corporation permission to do business in another state. A registered office and agent must be maintained within the state upon which service of process (notice of a lawsuit) may be made on behalf of the corporation. An **alien corporation** is one that, though incorporated in a nation-state other than the United States, is, nevertheless, doing business in the United States.

Close and S Corporations

A business corporation may be designated as a **close corporation** when the outstanding shares of stock and managerial control are closely held by fewer than 50 shareholders (often members of the same family) or by one person. State business corporation statutes generally accommodate closely held corporations by allowing them to have a few directors or a sole director and president, with no voting shares in the hands of the public. The Subchapter S Revision Act of 1982 gives small, closely held business corporations the option of obtaining special tax advantages by becoming an S corporation. An **S corporation** is a corporation in which shareholders have agreed to have the profits (or losses) of the corporation taxed directly to them rather than to the corporation. In this way, they avoid double taxation. There are, however, several restrictions on S corporations. These restrictions include limits on the number and types of owners that can be involved in such an entity. Consequently, many individuals now look to limited liability companies to escape double taxation.

Limited Liability Companies, Joint Ventures, and Franchises

The **limited liability company (LLC)** is best thought of as a cross between a partnership and a corporation. Like a corporation, the LLC offers the protection of limited liability to its owners. However, unlike a corporation, the LLC's tax liability flows through the LLC and to the owners. In this way, an LLC, like a partnership and an S corporation, escapes the double taxation penalty that falls on corporate entities. In addition, LLCs are statutory, which means that they may come into existence only if the owners follow the precise steps laid out in the state code by the state legislature. The owners of an LLC are called **members**. The people who run the LLC are called **managers**. Later in this chapter, we discuss the formation details of an LLC. Chapter 27 also includes a discussion of the duties and responsibilities of the members and the managers of an LLC. A **joint venture** (or **joint undertaking**) involves a contractual arrangement by which individuals unite for a limited time to create a new entity in which the founders share control, expenses, and profits. A **franchise** is a business arrangement that permits an individual, a group of investors, or another entity to lease the right to use a parent entity's business operation, trademark, goods, services, and goodwill under a fee arrangement provided to the parent.

Did You Know?

The first state statute authorizing the creation of limited liability companies in the United States was passed in Wyoming in 1977.

quick quiz 26-2

1. A private corporation is one that is formed under the authority of a state statute to perform a governmental function.	true | false
2. A certificate of authority is issued only to S corporations that have passed the test of associative liability.	true | false
3. Limited liability companies have been outlawed in most states because they limit the tax revenue that is due to the government.	true | false

26-3 Formation of the Corporate Entity

A corporation may be incorporated in any state that has a general incorporation statute. However, for many decades, Delaware has been the first place many (most?) incorporators default to as the best state in which to incorporate. Keep in mind that corporations are also subject to court decisions and the state constitution. Federal agencies such as the Securities and Exchange Commission (SEC) also regulate corporate activity. A proper understanding of effective corporate formation necessitates an examination of promoters, the articles of incorporation, the corporate name, the approval of the articles, and commencement of business. Figure 26-1 illustrates the steps of the incorporation process.

Promoters and Incorporators

The people who want to begin a new corporation or incorporate an existing business are called **promoters**. These people do the actual day-to-day work involved in the incorporation

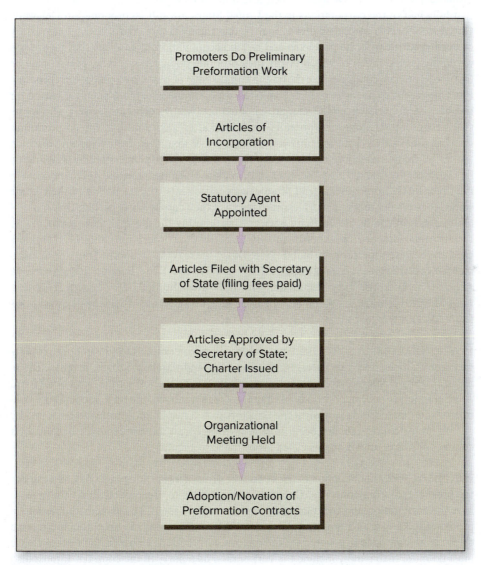

Figure 26-1 This chart shows the steps in the incorporation process.

process. **Incorporators** are the people who actually sign the articles of incorporation and submit them to the appropriate state officials. The promoters may also be the incorporators, who later become shareholders and directors of the corporation. Promoters occupy a fiduciary relationship with the nonexistent corporation and its future shareholders. Therefore, the promoter must act in the best interests of the new corporation and its shareholders. The promoter must be honest and loyal and fully reveal all information about any contracts made for the corporation.

The Delaware Factor

A business can be incorporated in any state that has a valid incorporation statute. However, for decades many (most?) promoters and incorporators headed to Delaware to incorporate (see Chapter 28). Initially, most business strategists chose Delaware as the place to incorporate because the Delaware incorporation statute was the easiest, most efficient, and most affordable statute in the nation. However, since that time, most states have liberalized their statutes so that those statutes are now just as easy, efficient, and affordable as Delaware's original statute. Yet, many incorporators and promoters still flock to Delaware when it is time to incorporate, accounting for the fact that fully half of the corporations in the United States are still incorporated in Delaware. One reason for this continued loyalty may be that the Delaware courts have a long history of dealing with corporate problems and a rich accumulation of case law that focuses on corporate issues, much of which favors the corporate managers. Another reason may be that Delaware law continues to exist on the cutting edge of new developments in corporate law. One recent study, however, has suggested a more mundane, more practical reason for this consistent preference for Delaware—momentum. Many corporate lawyers who represent first promoters and incorporators—and then, after incorporation, the corporation's managers—have always started in Delaware and, rather than task themselves with learning the law of many states, prefer, instead, to return to their traditional standby. Apparently this is especially true of those law firms that are fairly cosmopolitan and, therefore, deal in multiple states. Ironically, instead of advising their clients to incorporate in their home states, these firms recommend Delaware because they can be fairly certain that most of their cases will end up in Delaware anyway, thus limiting the law that they must know to conduct their practice. Whether this reality benefits the corporations and the shareholders, however, is, at best, problematic. [See: Daisy Maxey, "A 'Delaware Trap' for Companies," *The Wall Street Journal*, May 8, 2017, p. R11; and Kylie Larkin, "Rob Anderson Article 'The Delaware Trap' Featured in The Wall Street Journal," *Surf Report: Pepperdine Law*, May 2017, https://lawcomm.pepperdine.edu/rob-anderson-article-the-delaware trap-featured-wall-street-journal.]

Preformation Contracts

Often, promoters will enter contracts for the unborn corporation. For example, it may be necessary to lease office and warehouse space, purchase equipment, and hire employees as preliminary steps in preparing the way for the new corporation. A corporation is not bound by any of the promoter's contracts unless it adopts those contracts. Adoption occurs expressly if the directors pass a resolution agreeing to be bound by a contract. Adoption can also occur implicitly if the corporation accepts the benefits of a contract or makes any payments called for by the agreement.

Novation

Even after adoption of the contracts, promoters are still potentially liable under the pre-incorporation contracts. One way for promoters to escape potential liability is to have the corporation and the third party agree to release them. The agreement releasing a promoter is known as a **novation**. The promoter may also include an automatic release clause in all contracts negotiated for the unborn corporation. However, the release clause must do more than simply include the corporation as a party to the contract. It must also specifically release the promoters from liability.

Articles of Incorporation

The **articles of incorporation** are the written applications to the state for permission to incorporate. This written application is prepared by the corporation's incorporators. The articles, together with the state incorporation statute, represent the legal boundaries within which a corporation must conduct its business. Some state incorporation statutes are very strict, requiring detailed information in the articles of incorporation. Typically this information includes the following:

- The corporation's name.
- The duration of the corporation.
- The purpose(s) of the corporation.
- The number and classes of shares.
- The shareholders' rights in relation to shares, classes of shares, and special shares.
- The shareholders' right to buy new shares.
- The addresses of its original registered (statutory) office and its original registered (statutory) agent.
- The number of directors plus the names and addresses of the initial directors.
- Each incorporator's name and address.

The newer version of the MBCA has simplified this list somewhat, requiring only the name of the corporation, the number of shares originally authorized, the address of the original registered (statutory) office, the address of the original registered agent, and the incorporators' names and addresses.

The Corporate Name

One of the first steps in forming a corporation is to choose a corporate name. Usually, the words or an abbreviation of the words *corporation*, *company*, or *incorporated* must appear somewhere in the corporate name. Also, the corporation cannot choose a name that some other corporation already uses or a name that would confuse the new corporation with one already in existence. Even in situations in which a specific state statute does not prohibit the use of similar names, the courts will prevent such duplication if confusion or unfair competition results. Often, the secretary of state's office can tell promoters whether a name has been taken. It is also possible to reserve a name. Usually, there is a small fee for this service. Promoters also must make certain that they check the availability of a corporate name in not only the state of incorporation but also any state within which they plan to have the corporation do business.

Approval of Articles

After the articles of incorporation are submitted to the state, the appropriate state officer, often the secretary of state, will examine them to make certain that they meet all legal requirements. The secretary of state will also make certain that all filing fees have been paid and that a registered or statutory office and a registered or statutory agent have been appointed. The registered or **statutory agent** is an individual who is designated to receive service of process when a lawsuit is filed against the corporation. Once satisfied that all legal formalities have been met, the secretary of state will issue the corporation's charter, or **certificate of incorporation**. The charter, or certificate of incorporation, is the corporation's official authorization to do business in the state. After the charter is issued, the corporation becomes a fully and legally incorporated entity. The work of the promoters and incorporators ends, unless they become directors or officers of the corporation.

> **Did You Know?**
>
> A quick reference to corporate law is a book titled *Corporations: Laws of the United States*, published by Nova Publishing.

Commencement of the Business

Most state statutes provide that the first order of business upon incorporation is holding an organizational meeting. Some states require that the meeting be run by the initial directors designated in the articles. In contrast, those states that do not require naming the directors in the articles allow the organizational meeting to be run by the incorporators. Nevertheless, the first order of business at an incorporator-run meeting is to elect the directors. In addition to the appointment of the first directors, the adoption of bylaws, or regulations, also occurs at the organizational meeting. Bylaws or regulations are the rules that guide the corporation's day-to-day internal affairs. Bylaw provisions usually stipulate the time and place of shareholders' and directors' meetings, quorum requirements, qualifications and duties of directors and officers, and procedures for filling board vacancies.

Formation of a Limited Liability Company

Similar to a corporation, a limited liability company requires only one person to incorporate. However, the term *person* is liberally defined to include not only people but also corporations and other legal entities, such as partnerships, limited partnerships, trusts, estates, and so on. The term can even include another LLC. Because not all states recognize the tax advantage usually granted to limited liability companies, it is wise for persons contemplating the formation of an LLC to check the legal status of such entities in all of the states in which they intend to do business.

The Articles of Organization The articles of organization are the written application to the state for permission to form a limited liability company. These articles must include the name of the LLC, the duration of the LLC, and the address where the LLC's operating agreement and bylaws are to be kept. If neither the articles nor the operating agreement, as discussed later, include a duration statement, then some state statutes set an automatic duration period, generally of 30 years. In contrast, in the absence of a duration statement, other state statutes set an unlimited duration. The name of the LLC must include "Limited Liability Company" or those words abbreviated, or be followed by "Limited" or the abbreviation "Ltd." In addition, the name of the LLC must not be the same as the name of another LLC or corporation.

However, a problem may arise when a general partnership is transformed into an LLC. An existing general partnership may discover that it has been using a name that is reserved for a corporation or for an already existing LLC. This transformation will require changing the name of the existing partnership before it becomes an LLC. Such a change can be bothersome and complicated, not to mention expensive. The only other alternatives in such a situation would be to acquire authorization to use the common name or to abandon the effort to form an LLC. In addition, a statutory agent for the service of process must be named at the time that the articles are filed in the office of the secretary of state. Finally, proper filing fees must also be paid. Such fees are generally not exorbitant.

The Operating Agreement It is also beneficial for the members of an LLC to draw up an operating agreement. Such an agreement, though not required by law in all states, is still very helpful in establishing the bylaws of the LLC, which outline the structure and operation of an LLC. Typically the articles of organization include formation provisions, operating provisions, the nature of the business to be conducted by the LLC, distribution of profits and losses, the powers of the managers, voting rights of the members, admission and withdrawal procedures, provisions regarding the transfer of a member's interest in the LLC, and provisions involving the termination of the LLC, among others. Provisions not covered by the operating agreement are determined by the statute authorizing the creation of LLCs in that state.

Oral Modifications of the Operating Agreement Some state LLC statutes specify that operating agreements can be spoken. Under such a provision, certain procedures may inadvertently be added to the operating relationship between the members simply because of a conversation among those members. For this reason, operating agreements should be written even if state law does not require a writing. Moreover, it is wise to add a provision to the written operating agreement that asserts there can be no spoken modifications to the agreement. Fortunately, even those statutes that allow spoken additions to the operating agreement specify that certain things, such as an agreement to make a capital contribution to the LLC, must be in writing to be binding on the members.

Taxation of an LLC Under Internal Revenue Service (IRS) regulations, the status of a business under state law is not the determining factor in establishing whether a firm, such as an LLC, should be taxed as a partnership or a corporation. Rather, the tax status of such an entity depends on an election made by the owners of that entity. Under the regulations, an entity with two or more members can elect to be treated for tax purposes as an association or as a partnership. An entity owned by one person can elect either association status or a status that will, in effect, hold that the owner and the entity are identical. Election as an association in either situation means that the entity will be taxed as a corporation. The other choice will avoid the corporate tax status.

quick quiz 26-3

1. An agreement that releases a promoter is called a novation. true | false
2. Bylaws are the rules that guide the corporation's day-to-day internal affairs. true | false
3. Operating agreements for LLCs are required in all states. true | false

26-4 Corporate Identity

Corporations have a life of their own; or at least they are supposed to have such a life. That life begins when they are incorporated by their owners and continues through the choosing of a name, the appointment of an agent for service of process, the election of directors, the hiring or the appointment of managers, the selling of shares, and the paying of dividends. As we have seen, corporations have constitutional rights, citizenship (sometimes even dual citizenship), and limited liability. They are entities that can own property, buy and sell that property, sue and be sued. All of this is true, of course, provided that they are legally formed and are permitted by their owners to develop their own corporate identities. A legally formed corporation is referred to as a *de jure* corporation. A ***de jure corporation*** is one that has been formed properly by incorporators who followed all of the steps outlined by the state incorporation statute. Most corporations are *de jure* corporations. There are times, however, when the incorporation process is flawed or when the corporation loses its corporate standing. In those cases, the corporation may or may not be a ***de facto corporation***—that is, one that exists in fact, but not in law. As strange as it may seem, there are even times when a group of people never intends to incorporate but acts like a corporation to such an extent that they create a **corporation by estoppel**. Finally, there are situations when a corporation is created legally but is held back by its owners and prevented from becoming an independent entity. In that case, if the subsidiary commits a wrongful act the victim may want to pierce the corporate veil of the subsidiary to reach the parent.

De Jure and De Facto Corporations

A corporation whose existence is the result of the incorporators having fully or substantially complied with the relevant corporation statutes is a *de jure* corporation. Its status as a corporation cannot be challenged by private citizens or the state. Sometimes an error is made in the incorporation process. When this occurs, the corporation does not exist legally. Nevertheless, as long as the following conditions have been met, a *de facto* corporation (a corporation in fact) will exist:

1. A valid state incorporation statute must be in effect.
2. The parties must have made a *bona fide* (good-faith) attempt to follow the statute's requirements for incorporation.
3. The business must have acted as if it were a corporation.

Usually, if only some minor requirement has been left unsatisfied, the court will hold that there has been a good-faith attempt to incorporate. Only the state can directly challenge the existence of a *de facto* corporation. Thus, a *de facto* corporation has the same rights, privileges, and duties as a *de jure* corporation as far as anyone other than the state is concerned. The doctrine of *de facto* corporation is in a state of flux at the present time. The doctrine is itself a common law principle and, as such, can be altered by the courts and by statutory law. Moreover, it seems that the Model Business Corporation Act eliminates the doctrine altogether. Nevertheless, some states have either altered that proposition or ignored it. A state could, for example, add a section to its own version of the MBCA, which states that a corporation that forfeits its corporate status, and then recovers it, will be treated as a corporation retroactively to the day that it lost its corporate status. In effect, what this statute does is to validate the use of the *de facto* doctrine when the secretary of state retroactively reactivates a corporation's corporate status. This application is not exactly the reestablishment of the *de facto* doctrine, but it is a reasonable facsimile. Other states have found other ways around the MBCA by reinstituting a frequently ignored doctrine called corporation by *estoppel*. Given the uncertainty surrounding this issue, however, it is best to check the most recent version of a state's corporate law statute should the question ever arise.

Corporation by Estoppel

In some states, if a group of people act as if they are a corporation when in fact and in law they are not, any parties who have accepted that counterfeit corporation's existence will not be allowed to deny that acceptance. Similarly, individuals who acted as if they were a corporation will not be able to deny that the corporation exists. This doctrine has been labeled corporation by estoppel. Corporation by estoppel does not create a real corporation. Instead, it is a legal fiction used by the courts on a case-by-case basis to prevent injustice. Generally, but not always, it is applied in contract cases rather than in tort cases. Some states may have also abolished corporation by estoppel, and so, as with *de facto* corporation, it is best to check the most recent version of a state's corporate law statute.

EXAMPLE 26-1: *Valley Victory Church v. Darvin Struck and Bonnie Struck*

The Valley Victory Church lost its *de jure* corporate standing when the attorney who was responsible for filing the church's yearly reports with the secretary of state's office left the state without filing that crucial report. When the report was not filed, the secretary of state revoked Valley Victory's corporate standing and sent a letter to that effect to the truant attorney. The attorney, of course, neither received the letter nor alerted church officials, who continued to act as if the church were a corporation. In the middle of a lawsuit involving the church, Darvin Struck, one of the parties to the suit, discovered this oversight. He argued that the church had no corporate existence at the time of his gift and so the property at the heart of the dispute was still his. Church officials made two counterarguments. First, they said that at the time of the gift, they had a good-faith belief that the church was a corporation operating under the authority of a valid state incorporation statute. Therefore, under the doctrine of *de facto* corporation, they continued to operate as a corporation. Second, church officials argued that the Strucks had given the land to the congregation, not to the church. Although the court clearly wanted to accept the church's first argument, it reluctantly rejected that line of reasoning. The court, however, did decide that, under state statutory law, once the secretary of state had restored the church's corporate status, all previous corporate acts were ratified. That meant that the church's acceptance of the land was valid when it had occurred. The court also supported the church's second argument as far as it could, saying that under corporation by estoppel, the Strucks could not recognize the church as a corporation when they transferred the land and then change their minds when it suited them.

Piercing the Corporate Veil

Sometimes the courts will disregard corporate status to impose personal liability on those shareholders who have used the corporation to commit fraud or crimes or to harm the public. In such cases, the court will **pierce the corporate veil** and hold the wrongdoers (usually the controlling shareholders) personally liable for activities committed in the corporation's name. The corporate veil test has three incarnations: the alter ego test, the instrumentality test, and the three-step test for control, fraud, and injury.

The Alter Ego Test The shareholders of small close corporations are more likely to fall victim to piercing the corporate veil than are the shareholders of large corporations because the shareholders of a close corporation are often also the original incorporators, as well as the directors and officers of the corporation, and thus may neglect to follow the corporate formalities required by statute and may fail to keep corporate property and business separate from their personal property and business. Thus, the court will sometimes find that the corporation is nothing more than the **alter ego** (other self, you know, like Clark Kent is Superman's alter ego or Oliver Queen is the Arrow's alter ego) of the original incorporators. Veil piercing by the courts is less likely to occur with an LLC because corporate formalities are not required by law for LLCs as they are with a corporation. However, in many states, the shareholders of a small corporation can enter a close corporation agreement, which would allow them to escape the need to follow many corporate formalities.

The Instrumentality Test Large corporations can also fall victim to piercing the corporate veil if they set up subsidiaries, completely control those subsidiaries, and then commit fraud through those subsidiaries. In such cases, however, it is the parent corporation, rather than the individual shareholders, that the courts will hold liable. The test used to determine whether the corporate veil should be pierced to reach the parent corporation is called the **instrumentality test**. This test requires that the parent corporation so dominate the subsidiary that the subsidiary has become a "mere instrumentality of the parent." In this situation, the courts will allow the veil of the instrumentality to be pierced to reach the dominant corporation and to hold that corporation liable for any harm that has been committed through the instrumentality. The courts, however, do not engage in such veil piercing lightly. Still, while the courts respect the separate corporate identity of most subsidiaries, they cannot allow a subsidiary to be used by the parent so that the parent can escape liability, especially if the instrumentality was set up in the first place to commit fraud. When a corporation is set up as a mere instrumentality of a parent, it is sometimes referred to as a **dummy corporation** or a **corporate shell**.

The Three-Step Test

Regardless of the size or the configuration of a corporation, however, some courts have simplified matters by ignoring the distinction between large and small corporations and instead applying a three-step veil piercing test. This approach is common when the corporation has committed fraud in a fairly straightforward and obvious way. The stages in the **three-step test** for veil piercing are (1) complete control of the alleged corporate person by the owners (shareholders or members in an LLC), (2) the use of that control by the shareholders to commit fraud against the plaintiff, and (3) that fraud has caused the plaintiff to undergo some sort of injury or loss. Often, *undercapitalization* will be considered convincing evidence that the corporate owners intended to use the corporate façade to escape liability. However, by itself undercapitalization is not enough to pierce the corporate veil successfully. The court requires that the corporation's interests cannot be distinguished from those of the shareholders.

THE OPENING CASE Round 3
Piercing the Corporate Veil Is Not As Effective As You Might Think

The Opening Case started with the formation of three corporations, the Metropolitan Restaurant and Lounge (the Met), the Metropolitan Fixtures Corporation (MFC), and the Metropolitan Management Corporation (MMC). All three were incorporated by Joseph Moring, and William Drane. One evening, an employee of the Met served Peter Michael Gregor too many alcoholic drinks. In fact, Gregor had consumed so many drinks that by the time he left the restaurant, he was visibly intoxicated. On his way home, Gregor crossed through an intersection and drove his vehicle into the path of a car operated by Donna Messick Davis (Davis). Davis was killed in the resulting collision. Jeffrey Messick (Messick), the executor of the Davis estate, brought this wrongful death action on her behalf. Messick filed the suit against Metropolitan Restaurant and Lounge, the Metropolitan Fixtures Corporation, and the Metropolitan Management Corporation. After Messsick had the opportunity to do some preliminary research, he discovered two key facts: (1) The three corporations listed as defendants (the Met, MFC, and MMC) were, to a large extent, actually one large, complex corporation, and (2) this corporate complex was run by the same two men, Drane and Moring. Consequently, Messick added Drane and Moring to his amended complaint as individual defendants.

Messick asked the court to pierce the corporate veil of all three corporations in order to hold Drane and Moring personally liable for Davis's death. When Moring and Drane learned that they had been added to the lawsuit as defendants, they filed a summary judgment motion asking the court to dismiss the case. Following the formula for a summary judgment motion, Moring and Drane contended that even if the facts as alleged by Messick were absolutely true, the law was unequivocally on their side. In response, the plaintiff argued that Moring and Drane had used the corporations for their personal gain on two occasions: once when one of the three corporations had forgiven a $112,000 debt owed by the two defendants and a second time when corporate funds had been diverted from the corporations to a Merrill-Lynch account, again for the benefit of the two owners. In its consideration of the summary judgment motion, the court noted that "a corporation is a distinct entity, to be considered separate and apart from the individuals who compose it." In pointing this out, the court stressed that it is absolutely necessary for the law to first and foremost protect that corporate structure. However, the court also noted that at times, it is permissible for the court to sidestep the corporate entity to provide justice for the victims of corporate fraud. Three such times are (1) when the corporation is undercapitalized, (2) when the corporate front is designed to commit fraud, and (3) when the corporation is nothing more than the alter ego of the owners. In this case, Messick claimed that the defendants' transgression fell under the third element. In explaining this third provision, the court noted that, in order to successfully pierce the corporate veil, the plaintiff would have to prove not only that the corporation was the owners' alter ego, but also that the owners had misused the corporation and that this misuse contributed to the harm experienced by the plaintiff. Accordingly, the court developed the following three-part test to determine when it is appropriate to hold the owners liable:

1. The dominant party must have complete control and domination of the subservient corporation's finances, policy, and business practices so that at the time of the attacked transaction the subservient corporation had no separate mind, will, or existence of its own.
2. The control must have been misused by the dominant party. Although fraud or the violation of a statutory or other positive legal duty is misuse of control, when it is necessary to prevent injustice or inequitable circumstances, misuse of control will be presumed.
3. The misuse of this control must proximately cause the harm or unjust loss complained of.

Considering these three elements, the court concluded that, "While it is not necessary to prove illegality in order to establish excessive control (that is, the existence of the alter ego), it is essential that complete control and domination be proven. These two transactions (the loan and the Merrill-Lynch account) fail to establish that Moring and Drane misused their control of the corporations (parenthetical remarks added for clarity)." The bottom line is this: The three elements suggested by the court in the Messick case, with their focus on the misuse of the corporate form, have provided a poignant compromise between (1) protecting the corporate form by limiting the plaintiff's access through the corporate veil and (2) piercing the corporate veil in order to provide justice for the victims of corporate fraud. It is for these reasons that the three-prong Messick test has become the basic formula in most veil-piercing cases, at least in Alabama. [See: *Messick v. Moring*, 514 So. 2d 892 (The Supreme Court of Alabama)].

Source: See: *Messick v. Moring* 514 So. 2d 892 (The Supreme Court of Alabama).

The *Effects* of the *Hobby Lobby* Case In *William Stewart v. R. A. Eberts, Company, Inc.*, detailed in A New Classic Case, the court was charged with determining whether to pierce the corporate veil of the company and to hold its owners liable for ignoring the terms of a contract that had been made several years earlier. It is important to note that the courts do not engage in veil piercing carelessly. Veil piercing is an extraordinary action because it requires the court to disregard the essential nature of the corporate person and to hold the owners and/or the officers and directors responsible for a level of legal liability they believed had been transferred to the corporate person. Consequently, veil piercing is, or at least should be, difficult. The *Hobby Lobby* case, which we reviewed previously as the one of the newest and most significant classic cases in recent memory, seems to have changed all of this. In *Hobby Lobby*, the Supreme Court treats corporate personhood as a suggestion or an option, rather than a mandate. In the *Hobby Lobby* case itself, the Court's decision to disregard the corporate person helped the owners of Hobby Lobby because their religious rights were vindicated. However, when we transform this case into a straight veil-piercing case, the legal result is the same, but the help to the owners has vanished. Once a judge rules that the law that defines the rights and duties of a corporation *also* defines the rights and duties of the people behind that corporation, he or she has placed the owners on the same level as the corporation. The whole point of corporate personhood is to separate the owners from the corporate person so that the owners can have the protection of the corporate veil and the corporation can have a life of its own (a life that includes its own "personal" rights). Now that the corporate person and the owners are to be equated, veil piercing becomes quite easy, in fact, unnecessary, because the veil has vanished and those behind the veil are revealed as the true corporate persons (entities?).

> **quick quiz 26-4**
>
> 1. The doctrine of the *de facto* corporation requires that there be a *bona fide* attempt to incorporate under an existing incorporation statute and an exercise of corporate power.   true | false
> 2. Corporation by estoppel does not create a real corporation.   true | false
> 3. The three techniques used by the courts to determine whether the corporate veil should be pierced include the alter ego test, the instrumentality test, and the three-step test of control, fraud, and injury.   true | false

26-5 Financing the Corporate Entity

Corporate financing begins when the original investments are made to set up the corporation. Once the corporation is operating, additional corporate financing may be obtained from earnings, loans, and the issuance of additional shares of stock. The issuing and selling of shares of stock to raise capital is known as *equity financing*, and equity securities give their owners a legal interest in the assets, earnings, and control of the corporation. The part of a corporation's net profits or surplus set aside for the shareholders is known as dividends.

Classes of Corporate Stock

The number of shares and classes of stock that a corporation is authorized to issue are established in its certificate of incorporation. A shareholder who purchases corporate stock invests money or property in the corporation and receives a **stock certificate**. A stock certificate is written evidence of ownership of a unit of interest in the corporation.

Dividends

The most common type of dividend is the **cash dividend**, declared and paid out of current corporate earnings or accumulated surplus at regular intervals. A corporation's board of directors has the sole authority to determine the amount, time, place, and manner of dividend payment. Typically, the directors' declaration of a dividend sets a cutoff date—the date by which a shareholder must hold corporate stock of record to receive payment. In a few instances, a distribution of earnings is made in shares of capital stock, called a **stock dividend**.

Common Stock The most usual type of corporate stock is **common stock**. Common stock carries with it all the risks of the business, inasmuch as it does not guarantee its holder the right to profits. The shareholder is usually entitled to one vote for each share of stock held. The holders of common stock are paid dividends when the corporation elects to make such a distribution. Holders of common stock risk whatever they invest.

Preferred Stock Those classes of stock that have rights or preferences over other classes of stock are known as **preferred stock**. These preferences generally involve the payment of dividends and/or the distribution of assets on the dissolution of the corporation. Preferred stock may be either cumulative or noncumulative. Generally, dividends on cumulative preferred stock are paid every year. However, if the dividends are not paid in one year, they will be paid in later years if any dividends at all are paid by the corporation. Dividends on noncumulative preferred stock are also usually paid each year. However, with noncumulative preferred stock, dividends that are not paid in one year are lost forever.

Stock Valuation Par value is the value placed on the shares of stock at incorporation. This value, which is the same for each share of stock of the same issue, is stated on the corporation's certificate of incorporation. In the case of par value shares, the amount of the capital stock or stated capital is the total par value of all the issued stock.

The practice of placing a par value on a share of stock has been criticized as misleading. Uninformed buyers often interpret par value printed on the face of the certificate as the actual market value of the shares. To correct this condition, all states have authorized the issuance of no par value stock. *No par value stock* is corporate stock issued without any stated price. In fact, par value stock has been eliminated under provisions found in the newest version of the MBCA.

quick quiz 26-5

1. Corporate financing cannot begin until six months after the certificate of incorporation has been issued.	true | false
2. The most common type of dividend is the stock dividend.	true | false
3. The practice of placing a par value on a share of stock has been approved of and is now mandated by the American Federated Banking Commission.	true | false

Summary

26.1 The corporate entity lies at the heart of the American economy and, as such, can orchestrate change on its own. To see why this is so, we need to examine the characteristics and the power of the corporate entity. A corporation is a legal entity created under the authority of a state or federal statute that gives certain individuals the capacity to operate an enterprise. As such, corporations are products of capitalism. The capitalistic economic system has operated in a way that has ensured that corporations are protected in a variety of ways. However, the basis of that protection lies within four fundamental legal principles that are designed to protect the corporate structure. These four principles are corporate limited liability, free transfer of ownership, central management, and corporate personhood itself.

26.2 Corporations can be classified in many ways, including private, public, and quasi-public corporations; domestic and foreign corporations; and close and S corporations. The limited liability company offers the protection of limited liability but allows tax liability to flow through the LLC and to its owners.

26.3 A corporation can be incorporated in any state that has a general incorporation statute. The people who actually start the corporation are the promoters. Promoters are liable on preformation contracts until those contracts are adopted by the corporation. The articles of incorporation are drawn up by the corporation's incorporators. After reviewing the articles of incorporation, the secretary of state will issue a corporate charter, and the corporation becomes a legally incorporated entity. The members of a limited liability company must also follow precise formation procedures.

26.4 A *de jure* corporation is a legally formed corporation. Two doctrines, *de facto* corporation and corporation by estoppel, have been developed to deal with the problem of defective incorporation. A *de facto* corporation exists if there has been a good faith attempt to comply with an existing incorporation statute and an exercise of corporate power. The doctrine of corporation by estoppel prevents later denial of corporate existence by parties willing to deal with an entity as if it were a corporation. Under the doctrine of piercing the corporate veil, courts can refuse to recognize a legally formed corporation to prevent injustice and to impose liability on the wrongdoers.

26.5 Corporate financing begins when the incorporators give money to set up the business. Subsequent financing takes many forms. The issuing and selling of shares of stock to raise capital is called equity financing. The two most popular classes of stock are common stock and preferred stock. Stock can also be par value or no par value stock. Dividends can be issued as cash or as stock.

Key Terms

alien corporation, 740
alter ego, 747
articles of incorporation, 743
articles of organization, 744
associative corporativism, 738
bylaws, 744
cash dividend, 750
certificate of authority, 740
certificate of incorporation, 743
close corporation, 740
common stock, 750
corporate entity, 731
corporate person, 731
corporate shell, 748
corporation, 731
corporation by estoppel, 745
corporativism, 738
de facto corporation, 745

de jure corporation, 745
dividends, 739
Dodd–Frank Wall Street Reform and Consumer Protection Act, 737
domestic corporation, 739
dummy corporation, 748
foreign corporation, 739
franchise, 740
incorporators, 742
instrumentality test, 747
joint undertaking, 740
joint venture, 740
limited liability, 731
limited liability company (LLC), 740
managers, 740
members, 740
novation, 742

operating agreement, 744
par value, 751
pierce the corporate veil, 747
pragmatism, 736
preferred stock, 750
private corporation, 739
promoters, 741
public corporation, 739
quasi-public corporation, 739
regulations, 744
S corporation, 740
share, 731
shareholders, 739
statutory agent, 743
stock certificate, 734, 750
stock dividend, 750
textualism, 735
three-step test, 748

Questions for Review and Discussion

1. What are some of the strategies that may avoid a new 21st century economic crisis?
2. What is meant by the term *corporation*?
3. What are the constitutional rights of a corporation?
4. What are the differences among a private, a public, and a quasi-public corporation?
5. What is the difference between a close and an S corporation?
6. What are the typical elements within the articles of incorporation?
7. What is the difference between the articles of organization and the operating agreement of a limited liability company?

8. What is the difference between a *de jure* and a *de facto* corporation?
9. What is the objective of piercing the corporate veil?
10. What is the difference between common and preferred stock?

Cases for Analysis

1. Dr. Steven A. Pottschmidt was employed by Dr. Thomas J. Klosterman, who was doing business as a corporation named Thomas J. Klosterman, MD, Inc. Once Pottschmidt's original employment agreement ended, he decided to bring a breach of contract suit against Klosterman alleging that he, Pottschmidt, had not been paid the amount that was actually owed him under the agreement. Within two months of the lawsuit, Klosterman created a new corporation, called Klosterman Family Practice Inc. Klosterman Family Practice, however, did not employ anyone other than the staff of the first corporation, Thomas J. Klosterman, MD, Inc. In addition, the second corporation had not moved from the original office, had not changed its phone number, had not purchased new equipment or new furniture, and had not taken on any new patients. For a while, the two corporations held separate accounts at one bank. Eventually, however, the first company's bank account was terminated, and income for bills sent out by the first company were placed in the account of the second company. Pottschmidt wants the court to permit him to pierce the corporate veil of both Thomas J. Klosterman, MD, Inc. and Klosterman Family Practice Inc. to hold Dr. Klosterman directly liable for the money owed to him. Is there enough evidence here to permit the veil piercing requested by the plaintiff? Explain. [See: *Pottschmidt v. Thomas J. Klosterman, M.D., Inc.*, 169 Ohio App.3d 824 (Court of Appeals of Ohio, Ninth District, Medina County).]

2. The Aerenthal Financial Loan Corporation lent $578,000 to Raymond Viviani and secured the loan with a mortgage on Viviani's ski lodge, which was located south of Burlington, Vermont. Vermont decided to build a new state highway along a route that cut right through Viviani's lodge. Viviani contested the state's decision and attempted to get the highway rerouted. After several months of unsuccessful battles with the state, Viviani decided to settle for the offer from the government. The state then paid Viviani the market value for the property. Unfortunately, the state failed to notify Aerenthal Financial Loan Corporation about the transaction. When Aerenthal discovered that it had not been notified, it filed a formal protest with the state. The state sent its apologies but argued that Aerenthal had no right to be notified about what was essentially a contractual matter between Viviani and the government. Aerenthal disagreed, arguing that the government had violated its constitutional right not to be deprived of property without due process of law. The state responded by noting that under the state constitution, it had operated properly and Aerenthal was not entitled to due process. Who is correct here? Explain.

3. General Housing Assistance was incorporated as a nonprofit organization that provides low-cost housing for families who have been economically dislocated because of the downsizing of a company or the outsourcing of jobs. One year after the formation of General Housing Assistance, General Mutual Housing Assistance was incorporated in the same state. General Mutual Housing Assistance sold housing shares in condominiums to subscribers. General Mutual ran an aggressive, often obnoxious advertising campaign. After this campaign, General Housing found that people were confusing the two entities. The resulting mix-up damaged General Housing Assistance's image and threatened its charitable funding sources. Consequently, it filed suit to stop General Mutual from using the name because of the confusion between the two entities. Are the names similar enough to cause the court to order General Mutual to change its name? Explain.

4. Through Langham Engineering, Michael Langham marketed his invention, the cross-slope monitor (CSM), as an accessory to John Deere equipment. He had a plan to expand his business to include the CSM as an accessory to Caterpillar Tractor (CAT) equipment. To do this, Langham and Clark Balderson of Balderson Inc. entered a pre-incorporation agreement (PIA), in which Langham agreed to contribute his technical abilities, and Balderson agreed to contribute his leadership capabilities to

manufacture and market the CSM to CAT. No release clause was included in the PIA. The resulting corporation was named Illinois Controls Inc. Balderson was designated the president and chairman of the board, and Langham was named vice president. Over the next two years, Balderson failed to train and motivate the sales staff about the proper techniques for selling the CSM to CAT dealers. Balderson also neglected to arrange demonstrations and consignment sales, failed to employ properly trained personnel, and disregarded the need to develop, print, and distribute installation manuals for the CSM. Finally, Balderson set up another corporation named the Dymax Corporation, which dealt with CAT's competitors, thereby undermining Illinois Control's relationship with CAT. As a result, Illinois Controls was forced to shut down operations. Langham sued Balderson personally for the losses that he incurred as a result of Balderson's failure to meet his obligations as outlined in the PIA. Balderson argued that the PIA was a promoter's contract and that the corporation had adopted it. Therefore, Illinois Controls should be held liable. Was Balderson correct? Explain. [See: *Illinois Controls, Inc., v. Langham*, 639 N.E.2d 771 (OH).]

5. Harry and Kay Robinson of New York purchased a new Audi automobile from World Wide Volkswagen (WWV) in New York. After having an accident in Oklahoma, they brought a product liability action against WWV. The case was brought to court in Oklahoma. The Robinsons claimed that the injuries they suffered were caused by the defective design and placement of their automobile's gas tank and fuel system. WWV, which was incorporated in New York and did business there, contended that the Robinsons could not sue WWV in Oklahoma because it was not a citizen of Oklahoma. WWV further contended that it performed no services, owned no property, and closed no sales in Oklahoma. It solicited no business in Oklahoma either through salespersons or through advertising. It also did not indirectly through others serve or seek to serve the Oklahoma market. Did the Oklahoma state court have jurisdiction over WWV? Explain. [See: *World Wide Volkswagen Corporation v. Woodson*, 100 S.Ct. 559 (U.S. Sup. Ct.).]

6. Spence was a promoter in the incorporation of a new business. The new corporation had not yet been formed when he bought Huffman's employment agency to serve as the nucleus of that corporation. Eventually, the corporation was formed, but it never generated enough cash to pay Huffman for the employment agency. Huffman sued Spence, attempting to hold him personally liable for the amount due. Spence claimed that the corporation was liable and that his personal assets were not a proper target of the suit. Was Spence correct? Explain. [See: *Spence v. Huffman*, 486 P.2d 211 (AZ).]

7. MBI filed its original articles of incorporation under the name Montana Public Employees Benefit Services Co. Inc. After filing the articles, the corporation entered a contract with the Montana Department of Administration. Under the contract, the new corporation would have exclusive administrative control over Montana's public employee deferred-payment pension plan. The articles were not approved by the secretary of state, who requested a name change. After the corporation's name was changed to MBI, the charter was issued, and the corporation became a legal entity. The Montana Association of Underwriters, a private corporation that wanted a share in administering the state pension plan, challenged the validity of the contract, arguing that at the time the contract was signed, MBI did not legally exist. Was the Montana Association of Underwriters correct? Explain. [See: *Montana Association of Underwriters v. Department of Administration and MBI*, 563 P.2d 577 (MT).]

8. Lamas Company Inc. was incorporated in Georgia. Baldwin negotiated with Lamas, sole owner of Lamas Company Inc. to finish some electrical work on a construction site. When Baldwin was dissatisfied with the work, he decided to sue. Unfortunately, the statute of limitations ran out before he could sue Lamas Company, so he sued Lamas individually. Baldwin argued that he had dealt only with Lamas, that he did not know Lamas was an agent of the company, that Lamas did not tell him about the company, and that he understood the contract to be with Lamas individually. Lamas pointed out that Baldwin made out and sent checks directly to Lamas Company and that Lamas Company always appeared as the payee on those checks. Lamas claimed that this evidence alone would be enough to stop Baldwin from denying that he had dealt with Lamas Company Inc. The trial court rendered judgment against Lamas. On

appeal, did the appellate court reverse? Explain. [See: *Lamas v. Baldwin*, 230 S.E.2d 13 (GA).]

9. Boafo was allegedly injured while giving birth at Parkway Regional Hospital. Boafo sued both Parkway Regional and Hospital Corporation of America (HCA), asking the court to pierce the corporate veil to reach HCA, which Boafo claimed was a parent company. Boafo showed that the two corporations shared the same offices, that they purchased hospital equipment together, that HCA owned 100 percent of Parkway stock, that major financing for Parkway was performed by HCA through a national accounting system, and that Parkway was insured by another wholly owned subsidiary of HCA. In answer, HCA emphasized that Parkway handled its own daily financing, that it was free to negotiate and enter its own contracts, that it had an adequate amount of money in its treasury, and that it was not formed to promote fraud, conceal crime, or evade legal liability. The trial court granted summary judgment, dismissing the claim against HCA. Did the appellate court uphold the trial court's ruling? Explain. [See: *Boafo v. Hospital Corporation of America*, 338 S.E.2d 477 (GA).]

10. The Northeastern Corporate Institute of Technology (NCIT), a profit-oriented corporation engaged in nuclear research projects, owned and operated an experimental station in a remote region of Alaska. The Alaskan Chemical Disposal Corporation, a subsidiary of NCIT, disposed of all chemical and nuclear waste products produced by NCIT's experimental station. On a routine disposal route, an Alaskan Chemical Disposal transport convoy collided with a North Coast moving van. The lead truck in the convoy spilled chemical waste into a lake owned by Kenneth Ridgeway. Ridgeway sued both NCIT and Alaskan Chemical Disposal. NCIT argued that the disposal of NCIT's chemical was the sole responsibility of Alaskan Chemical Disposal, which it characterized as an independent contractor. Ridgeway's attorney, however, had discovered that Alaskan Chemical Disposal had no business other than providing waste disposal services to NCIT. The attorney also discovered that Alaskan Chemical Disposal was listed as a division of NCIT, was financed by NCIT, and shared the same board of directors and officers as NCIT. Moreover, the attorney found out that Alaskan Chemical Disposal was badly undercapitalized. In addition, all decisions in the running of Alaskan Chemical Disposal were made by NCIT. In light of all of this evidence, Ridgeway's attorney began to suspect that Alaskan Chemical Disposal might have been formed to allow NCIT to escape liability in just this type of situation. Will Ridgeway be allowed to maintain its suit against NCIT? Explain.

Design Elements: The Opening Case: ©Sharpstock/Alamy; A Classic Case: ©Evlakhov Valeriy/ Shutterstock

quick quiz Answers

26-1	26-2	26-3	26-4	26-5
1. T	1. F	1. T	1. T	1. F
2. T	2. F	2. T	2. T	2. F
3. F	3. F	3. F	3. T	3. F

Chapter 27: Managing the Corporate Entity

27-1 Management of the Corporate Entity
Directors of the Corporation • Officers of the Corporation • Shareholders of the Corporation • Stakeholders of the Corporation

27-2 Issues in Governing the Corporate Entity
The Corporate Balancing Act Revisited • Theories of Corporate Governance • Shareholder Voting Control • Shareholder Lawsuits

27-3 Governance Responsibilities
The Business Judgment Rule • The Fairness Rule • The Actual Authority Rule

27-4 Shareholder Rights
Right to Examine Corporate Records • Right to Share in Dividends • Right to Transfer Shares of Stock • Preemptive Rights

27-5 Governance of a Limited Liability Company
Member-Managed LLCs • Manager-Managed LLCs • Fiduciary Duties

THE OPENING CASE Round 1
Independent Directors and the Business Judgment Rule, Reconsidered, Revamped, and Reactivated (in Delaware)

Quite often, the courts operate as the passive element in the legal system. There is nothing wrong with this. In fact, one of the primary tasks of the court is to act as a brake on the tendency of the legislature to move forward without due consideration of the consequences of its legislative enactments. Still, at times, the court will independently create new doctrines that have a serious and long-lasting effect on the law. To examine this aspect of the court's role in detail, let's look at the case of *Unocal v. Mesa*. The facts in the case involve an internally generated hostile takeover bid aimed at the Unocal Corporation (Unocal) instigated by one of its own shareholders, Mesa Petroleum (Mesa). Mesa structured an offer whereby it would pay $54 a share to any and all Unocal shareholders up to the point that Mesa had purchased 37 percent of Unocal's stock (that would amount to 64 million shares). After that, any shareholders left out of the first stage would enter the second stage and would be entitled to receive only bonds and not cash. The bonds were so severely undervalued that they were called "junk bonds."

The Mesa plan was structured this way to encourage (force?) shareholders to quickly buy shares at the prices of $54 per share in order not to be left at the end of the line. At the time of the Mesa bid, the Unocal board consisted of eight independent and six internal directors. The bid was examined at a meeting of 13 board members (all eight independent members and five internal members). During that meeting, the directors were schooled in the details of the offer and informed about countermeasures that were available to defeat the bid. The countermeasure most favored would require Unocal to make a self-tender counteroffer to buy its stock for $70–$75 per share at a total cost of about $6.25 billion, with the stipulation that the offer would be available to all shareholders but Mesa. After the meeting of the 13 board members, the independent board members met separately with the corporation's lawyers and financial advisors to further consider the countermeasure. After this meeting, the five internal members rejoined the meeting. The board then voted unanimously to reject the Mesa offer. Some days later the board met again, this time to initiate the self-tender offer. The plan would be activated should Mesa actually receive tender offers amounting to its target goal of the 64 million shares. Unocal would then offer to purchase the remaining 49 percent of the outstanding shares at a price of $72 per share. As planned earlier, Mesa would be excluded from this offer (the Mesa exclusion).

Not to be outdone, Mesa filed a suit in the Chancery Court of Delaware to short-circuit Unocal's self-purchase plan. Mesa asked for a temporary restraining order designed to stop Unocal from initiating its self-tender offer on the grounds that the Mesa exclusion was discriminatory. The vice chancellor of the court granted the restraining order and Unocal appealed. Because a hearing on a preliminary injunction was pending before the Chancery Court, the Supreme Court kicked the case back to that court and recommended that the court answer the following questions as it considered the injunction: (1) Does the directors' duty of due care include protecting the corporation from being exploited by its own shareholders? (2) Is there evidence to demonstrate that the shareholders mounting the take over are out to line their own pockets at the expense of the corporation? (3) If, in fact, the hostile shareholders are a threat to the corporation, is the Unocal self-purchase strategy an appropriate exercise of business judgment rule? (4) In executing the self-purchase strategy to protect the corporation, did the directors operate in good faith?

The Chancery Court believed that the directors have a duty to protect the corporation from its own shareholders, if necessary; that there was not enough evidence to infer that the Mesa was self-dealing; and that directors directors had acted in good faith. Still, the court seemed unsure as to whether the Unocal directors could go so far as to exclude the Mesa shareholders from their offer and as to whether the Unocal directors deserved the protection of the business judgment rule. Therefore, the Chancery Court issued the preliminary injunction, and Unocal appealed. When the Supreme Court of Delaware took the appeal, it reduced the case to two basic questions: (1) Are the corporate directors rightfully and dutifully empowered to counterattack a hostile takeover bid that would substantially harm the corporation? (2) Are the directors entitled to the protection of the business judgment rule in situations like this one? The Supreme Court reexamined the facts in the case, as well as the nature of the business judgment rule, and came to a well-reasoned conclusion that extended the protection of the business judgment rule while, at the same time, imposing a few extra duties on those directors.

The case itself is an important one because it addresses a situation in which there appears to be a conflict of interest between the board's interests in perpetuating its own power and the board's duty to protect the best interests of the corporation and the corporate shareholders. The court was determined to prevent a board from simply using a corporate takeover bid as a pretense to enhance its own continued power in the corporation. To deal with this potential conflict of interest, the court will now require that decisions in cases like this be designed to protect both the corporation and the shareholders from a reasonably perceived, authentic threat to both. So, if the board wants to make sure that it is protected by the business judgment rule, it will have to convince the court that the takeover bid was a genuine danger to corporate stability and that the court's response to that danger was reasonable. To see how this all worked out in full, continue reading. [See: *Unocal Corporation v. Mesa Petroleum Company.*, 493 A. 2d 946, (1985).]

Opening Case Questions

1. Why would the board of directors of Unocal want to block the bid from Mesa Petroleum? Explain.

2. Why is it a good idea to pack the board of directors with independent directors? Explain.

3. Why is it a good idea to leave internal directors on the board of directors of a corporation? Explain.

4. What is the business judgment rule? Explain.

5. What adjustments were made to the business judgment rule by the Unocal Case? Explain.

Source: See: *Unocal Corporation v. Mesa Petroleum Company.*, 493 A. 2d 946, (1985).

LO Learning Objectives

1. Explain the central dilemma of corporate governance.
2. Describe the functions of directors, officers, and shareholders.
3. List the five theories of corporate governance.

4. Describe cumulative voting and proxy solicitation.
5. Explain shareholder proposals.
6. Distinguish between voting trusts and pooling agreements.
7. Explain shareholder direct suits, shareholder derivative suits, and the demand futility doctrine.
8. Contrast the business judgment rule with the fairness rule.
9. List the rights that belong to shareholders.
10. Explain the management of a limited liability company.

27-1 Management of the Corporate Entity

Most state incorporation statutes provide that a corporation's business affairs are to be managed under the direction of a board of directors. The board of directors establishes broad policies, and the officers and other employees implement those policies. The shareholders are the owners of the corporation. How to keep the role of the board separate from that of executive management and that of shareholders is related to the challenge of how best to organize the board and select its members. The issues are even more complex today because a single individual often functions as a director, an officer, and a shareholder. Nevertheless, the three roles have distinct functions and should be examined separately.

Directors of the Corporation

The business affairs of a corporation are managed by a board of directors elected by the shareholders. The board's responsibility is to take whatever actions are appropriate, in keeping with the corporation's rules and regulations, to further the corporation's business. Individual board members are supposed to use their own judgment in the corporate decision-making process.

Qualifications of Directors State law and corporate rules set up the qualifications that a person must have to be a corporate director. Unless prohibited by the corporation's certificate of incorporation, membership on the board of directors can be extended to anyone, including aliens, minors, and non-shareholders. Often, the certificate stipulates that at least one director must be a state resident and at least one must be a shareholder.

Time Commitment of Directors Directors are elected at the annual meeting of the shareholders. Generally, directors hold office for one or two years. The number of directors on the board varies between 8 and 12. Usually, several directors are elected as a group to maintain continuity; this procedure permits one-third of the board to be elected annually. The basic time commitment for a director is approximately 30 days per year, but depending upon need, availability, and interest, it can be 40, 60, 80, or even more days. Naturally, directors can resign from the board. However, many states require written notice of the director's resignation to the corporation.

Meetings of Directors The directors of most large corporations meet on a regular basis at a precise time and place of their choosing. The directors of many smaller corporations meet only when specific items are to be considered. Some states allow small corporations with fewer than 50 shareholders to eliminate the board of directors, as long as someone is assigned the duties that the board would have performed.

Directors are not entitled to be notified about regular board meetings unless notice is required by the corporation's bylaws. (The bylaws, or regulations of a corporation, determine how that corporation will operate.) However, directors must be notified of special meetings of the board. For example, a special meeting of the directors might be called to decide whether the corporation should institute a lawsuit. If any director is not notified of a special meeting, all actions taken at the meeting are void. A director may not specify another person to vote in her or his place. The quorum, or minimum number of directors necessary to conduct business, is usually one more than half of the total number of directors. Bylaws may require more than a quorum, perhaps 70 percent of the directors, to conduct certain types of business. This supermajority might be needed, for instance, to remove a director or sell a significant portion of the business. Generally though, the actions of a quorum constitute the official actions of the board.

EXAMPLE 27-1: Meeting the Quorum

The board of directors of Barber Enterprises Inc. consisted of seven persons. At a properly called meeting, one of the directors presented a motion calling for a stock-option purchase plan for Barber's president, vice presidents, secretary, and treasurer. Five directors attended the meeting. This constituted a quorum. Three of the five voted for the plan. This vote would constitute an official act by the board.

Officers of the Corporation

Directors are not expected to spend all of their time and energy managing the corporation. They have the authority to appoint officers and agents to run the day-to-day affairs of the corporation. By statute, the usual officers are a president, several vice presidents, a secretary, and a treasurer. Other officers, such as a comptroller, cashier, and general counsel, are often provided. The bylaws of the corporation describe the duties of each officer. Officers have the authority of general agents for the operation of the normal business of the corporation. They, in turn, delegate duties to various department heads. Although the roles of directors and officers differ, they are frequently assumed by the same people. An individual may be both chief executive officer and chair of the board of the same corporation. Directors and officers can also be shareholders in the corporation.

Shareholders of the Corporation

The shareholders are the owners of the corporation. The more shares that a shareholder owns, the more voting power that shareholder has in the running of the corporation. Therefore, the most effective way for a shareholder to obtain corporate power is to purchase more stock. Unfortunately, purchasing additional stock is not always possible—either because the shareholder does not have the financial leverage needed to purchase enough shares to gain corporate control or because there are no shares available to purchase. Another way to gain operating power is to work with the shares that the shareholder already owns but increase voting power in other ways. Before looking at those voting techniques, it is important to remember that though many shareholders are individuals, others are institutions such as union pension funds that have invested large sums of money in corporate stock to gain a return for their retirees.

Stakeholders of the Corporation

Over the past few decades, corporate law has evolved significantly to now include the stakeholders of the corporation in the decision-making process. **Stakeholders** are those individuals and coalitions who, while officially outside of the corporate decision-making structure and outside the corporate ownership establishment, are dramatically affected by the results of corporate decision making. Included in this number are representatives from employees' unions; consumer protection organizations; suppliers; customers; clients; environmental protection groups; and the local, state, national, and international communities.

> **Did You Know?**
> Although the shareholders of a corporation are the actual owners of the corporation, they are not agents of the corporation, as are the directors and officers, and therefore cannot commit the corporation to any contractual arrangements.

> **quick quiz 27-1**
>
> 1. The business affairs of a corporation are managed by a board of directors elected by the shareholders. — true | false
> 2. Membership on a board of directors can never be extended to aliens, minors, or nonshareholders. — true | false
> 3. Directors have authority to appoint officers and agents to run the day-to-day affairs of the corporation. — true | false

27-2 Issues in Governing the Corporate Entity

Under the original concept of a corporation, the shareholders are the primary reason that a corporation exists. This image has evolved over the years, so that now shareholders often take a backseat to consumers, employees, environmentalists, politicians, social science engineers, and economists. For this reason, the corporate landscape has come to resemble a battlefield in recent years. There are those who believe that the battle is a good thing because it helps make corporations more responsible. Others, however, believe that the battle has weakened, and in some cases completely dismantled, corporate power.

The Corporate Balancing Act Revisited

A more productive way of looking at the issue might be to see, not a battlefield, but an extension of the corporate balancing act that we discussed in the previous chapter. We have noted repeatedly throughout the text that the law must balance several opposing factors. For instance, we have noted that the intent of the law must be balanced against the results that emerge from the work of lawmakers; the letter of the law must be balanced with its spirit (although there is some debate about the merits of the "spirit v. letter" approach); the language of the law must be balanced with its interpretation (there is also some quarrel about the wisdom of taking a "language v. interpretation" view of the law); abstract legal principles must be balanced with the concrete application of those principles; and so on. The issue of corporate leadership is just one more aspect of this legal balancing act. Thus, as we will see in this section, the needs of the shareholders must be balanced against the needs of the stakeholders, while the needs of the stakeholders must be balanced against the needs of the economic agenda of the state and the nation. Similarly, the expertise of the managers must be balanced against the profit motive of the shareholders, the regulatory agenda of the government, and the individual needs of the stakeholders. All four groups noted above shareholders, stakeholders has offered a different solution to the problem. Which group, if any, has correctly diagnosed the problem remains to be seen. For the present, we can examine five corporate control paradigms—governmental control, independent director control, managerial control, stakeholder control, and shareholder democratic control.

Theories of Corporate Governance

Legal scholars and business experts have put forth five theories regarding how corporations should be managed: governmental control, independent director control, managerial control, stakeholder control, and shareholder democratic control.

Governmental Control Support for the governmental control theory of corporate management is based on the belief that because corporate decision making influences more individuals and groups than just the shareholders and the managers, corporate decisions should be made by an impartial group of corporate outsiders. Usually, the corporate outsiders named are government officials. These specially educated government officials would make corporate decisions in an objective manner, based on the needs of the entire society and the economy as a whole. Opponents of this theory label such an approach socialistic and point to the relatively poor record of many socialist economies as evidence of the impracticality of this approach.

Of course, those who support governmental control do not always go so far as to demand that the government have a seat in every corporate boardroom in America. A less dramatic and perhaps more effective technique is to use governmental control indirectly through regulatory legislation. One particularly effective piece of congressional legislation in this regard is the Sarbanes-Oxley Act of 2002. SarbOx, as the act is often known, was passed by Congress in the wake of a series of corporate scandals, some of which were caused by the failure of the board and the chief corporate officers to oversee activities properly within their corporations. Thus, Congress placed certain strict requirements on officers and directors and added severe penalties for the failure to meet those requirements. For example, under SarbOx, chief executive officers (CEOs), chief operating officers (COOs), and chief financial officers (CFOs) are required to present declarations that confirm the accuracy of their corporation's financial statements. They must indicate that the statements do not misrepresent the company's economic situation. The penalties for violating this particular provision include possible incarceration and monetary penalties that run into the millions.

Not everyone in the corporate community was happy about the passage of SarbOx or about the extra regulatory responsibilities that it places on corporate directors, officers, and auditors. In fact, shortly after its enactment, SarbOx was subject to a Constitutional challenge that threatened its very existence. On the surface, the challenge appeared to be a technical complaint that disputed the way that the members of the Public Company Accounting Oversight Board (PCAOB) are appointed. The PCAOB was created under provisions of SarbOx to act as an independent oversight commission designed to regulate the accounting profession. The companies that are regulated by the board make payments to support its operation. Board members are appointed by the Securities Exchange Commission (SEC)—and therein lies the heart of the problem.

The attack on the constitutionality of SarbOx was engineered by an accounting firm in partnership with the Free Enterprise Fund (FEF), a political action committee that promotes limited government interference in the free enterprise system. The heart of the attack focused on the fact that the members of the board are appointed by the Securities Exchange Commission and cannot be removed by the president except for good cause. The plaintiffs argued that this limitation on the president's authority violated the separation of powers principle and the authority of the president under the appointments clause (Article II, Section 2, Clause 2) of the Constitution. The plaintiffs further argued that the unconstitutionality of the appointment and removal process made the entire act unconstitutional. In an interesting ruling that likely satisfied no one completely, the Supreme Court decided that the limitations on the president's appointment and removal power were a violation of both the separation of powers principle and the appointments clause. However, the constitutionality of this clause did not negate the entire act. The appointment and removal authority in the act would have to be changed, but for the present, the board could continue to operate [See: *Free Enterprise Fund v. Public Company Accounting Oversight Board*, 561 U. S. 477 (2010). See also: Sarbanes-Oxley Act, Wikipedia, http://en.wikipedia.org/wiki/Sarbanes%E2%80%93Oxley_Act; Nina Totenberg, "Supreme Court Considers Sarbanes-Oxley Board," *NPR*, December 7, 2009, https://

www.npr.org/templates/story/story.php?storyID=121146830; Jayne Bryan Quinn, "Lawsuit Threatens Sarbanes-Oxley Act," *The Washington Post*, July 20, 2008, http://www.washingtonpost.com/wp-dyn/content/article/2008/07/19/AR2008071900106_2html; *Free Enterprise Fund v. Public Company Accounting Oversight Board, OYEZ: LII Supreme Court Resources*, Justia Supreme Court Center, June 28, 2010, https://www.oyez.org/cases/2009/08-861; and Free Enterprise Fund, *Source Watch: The Center for Media and Democracy*, August 11, 2008, https://www.sourcewatch.org/index.php/Free_Enterprise_Fund.)

Other serious complaints about SarbOx focused on some of the unintended consequences that emerged in the wake of its passage. Some financial experts, for instance, predicted that the United States would soon experience a loss of foreign business because of the strict rules enforced under SarbOx. These pundits feared that some alien global corporations that have the chance to place their stock for sale on an American stock exchange would move instead to a foreign exchange in search of a more lenient approach to corporate governance. Although some evidence of this trend was initially detected, other causes seem to explain why a foreign corporation might have chosen to list in London rather than New York. Some analysts argue that the epidemic of anticorporate lawsuits rather than regulatory legislation may be what actually caused some foreign firms to move away from the United States. Others suggest that the American insistence that all disputes be fashioned under American law, a trend known as legal imperialism, makes listing in the United States unpopular today. In contrast, some experts see no crisis at all, and still others suggest that the problem of attracting foreign firms to an American exchange is less troublesome than dealing with the type of widespread corruption that sparked the passage of SarbOx in the first place.

Moreover, seeking less regulation in jurisdictions outside the United States may actually end up being an effort in futility for those alien corporations that attempt to make such a change. Many foreign jurisdictions often regulate corporations more strictly than the government of the United States. For example, the European Union recently enacted the General Data Protection Regulation (GDPR), which went into effect in May 2018. Under this new regulation, many corporations, but especially insurance companies and credit card companies, that deal with European customers will have to tighten their oversight of the collection, storage, and use of any data they collect on people. More specifically, companies with European clients will have to report on their cyber-security protocol, inform customers of any breach within three days of that breach, and add a data-protection officer to their staff whose job it is to oversee how the institution compiles its electronic data. [See: Jeff Stone, "New EU Rule Will Protect Consumers in the U.S. as Well: Companies Will Have to Be More Transparent about How They Collect and Use Customer Data," *The Wall Street Journal*, April 25, 2017, p. R8.]

A QUESTION OF ETHICS

Legislating Morality: Rendering to Caesar the Things That Are Caesar's and . . .

The Sarbanes-Oxley Act (SarbOx) includes a long list of regulations that outlaw actions and procedures that most people would see as ethical problems rather than legal issues. For instance, SarbOx prevents individual loans from the corporation to board members or officers. It is difficult to see how anyone with a well-developed moral compass would even think about making or receiving such loans, let alone actually do it. Yet, here we have a federal statute that outlaws a clearly unethical practice. As if this were not surprising enough, Congress also felt the need to include a provision that expressly prohibits both altering evidence and revising, destroying, or suppressing any records needed in a government investigation of the corporation. Essentially, this is a statutory provision that tells corporate directors not to lie. It is sad to see that the Congress of the United States, of all bodies, must tell corporate managers that it is immoral to lie. Possibly even more disheartening is that the penalties for lying include incarceration. Perhaps most telling of all is that Congress believed it necessary to encourage corporate executives to develop ethical rules and regulations, as if corporate executives had never heard of the word *ethics* pre-SarbOx. Incredibly, Congress also found it necessary to remind executives that employees who provide information to federal authorities about any corporate violations are protected by the act. Finally, Congress did not trust corporate managers to follow the law on their own, and so SarbOx also set up the Public Company Accounting Oversight Board to regulate corporate auditing procedures.

QUESTIONS YET UNANSWERED

The following questions have yet to be addressed. Before you consider each question, turn to Chapter 1 to review the various ethical theories noted there (market value ethics, social contract theory, utilitarianism, and rational ethics). Then using one of those theories in a consistent way, answer the following questions.

1. In what way, if any, is SarbOx a reflection of general trends in this country concerning ethics and morality? Explain.
2. Should Congress also pass laws to regulate other institutions such as schools, churches, synagogues, and mosques, in the same way that SarbOx regulates corporations? Why or why not?
3. The text suggests that SarbOx is an example of government control over the corporate culture. In what way does SarbOx also promote independent director control and stakeholder control? Explain.
4. Is there any justifiable reason for congressional intervention into the world of ethics and morality, especially considering the Congress's poor track record in ethics? Explain.
5. In general, the trend demonstrated by SarbOx is called legislating morality. Is legislating morality ever an acceptable option? Before answering consider the rules that are promulgated by various religions. Is there a difference between Congress legislating morality and a religion teaching the Ten Commandments? Explain.

Independent Director Control A second theory of corporate control involves the establishment of independent directors. Those theorists who support the use of independent directors argue that the most effective way to ensure that corporate decisions are made in the best interests of those affected is to make certain that the decision makers themselves are not affected by those decisions. Some groups have already implemented requirements to ensure the addition of independent directors to the boards of many corporations. **Independent directors** are defined as directors who have no family members employed by the corporation, who are not themselves employed by the corporation, or, if they were at one time employed by the corporation, have not been on the staff for at least three years. The importance of the presence of independent directors on a corporate board is demonstrated by the decision of the Supreme Court of Delaware in the Opening Case.

THE OPENING CASE Round 2
Independent Directors, the Business Judgment Rule, Reconsidered, Revamped, and Reactivated (in Delaware)

In the Opening Case, Mesa Petroleum (Mesa) attempted to engineer a hostile takeover of the Unocal Corporation (Unocal). Under the terms of its takeover bid, Mesa would pay $54 a share to Unocal shareholders up to the point that Mesa had purchased 37 percent Unocal's stock (64 million shares). Any shareholders who did not get on board during this first stage would be entitled to receive only bonds and not cash for their shares. The bonds were so severely undervalued that they were called junk bonds. Under these terms, Mesa hoped to compel Unocal shareholders to rapidly sell their shares for $54 per share so as not to be left with nothing but the junk bond option. Following standard protocol, the Unocal board met to consider what to do about the Mesa bid. At the time of the Mesa takeover attempt, the Unocal board consisted of eight independent and six internal directors.

The bid was examined at a meeting of 13 board members (all eight independent members and five internal members). During that meeting, the directors were given detailed information about the the offer and about all countermeasures available to deal with the bid. The board settled on a countermeasure that would empower Unocal to make a self-tender counteroffer to buy its own stock for $70–$75 per share at a total cost of about $6.25 billion. However—and here is stipulation that troubled Mesa—the offer would be available to all shareholders *except* Mesa. After the meeting of the 13 board members, the independent board members met separately with the corporation's lawyers and financial advisors to further consider the countermeasure. After that meeting, the independent board members were rejoined by the internal members. All 13 board members voted to reject the Mesa offer. Several days after this, the board initiated its self-tender offer. The plan would go into effect when Mesa had met its target goal of the 64 million shares. Unocal would then offer to purchase the remaining outstanding shares at a price of $72 per share. As planned earlier, Mesa would be excluded from this offer (the Mesa exclusion).

Mesa filed a suit in the Chancery Court of Delaware to short circuit Unocal's self-purchase plan. Mesa asked for a temporary restraining order designed to stop Unocal from initiating its self-tender offer on the grounds that the Mesa exclusion was discriminatory. The case ended up in the Delaware Supreme Court, which reduced the case to two basic questions: (1) Are the corporate directors rightfully and dutifully empowered to counterattack a hostile takeover bid that threatens to substantially harm the corporation? (2) Are the directors entitled to the protection of the business judgment rule given the conflict of interest apparent in this situation? Ultimately, the Supreme Court believed that despite the apparent conflict of interest inherent in Unocal's countermeasure, the board had acted in good faith and had conducted a reasonable investigation. The court made it quite clear that the presence of the independent directors on the board was one of the main reasons that it decided the case in favor of Unocal. The court said it this way: "We must bear in mind the inherent danger in the purchase of shares with corporate funds to remove a threat to corporate policy when a threat to control is involved. The directors are of necessity confronted with a conflict of interest, and an objective decision is difficult . . . In the face of this inherent conflict directors must show that they had reasonable grounds for believing that a danger to corporate policy and effectiveness existed because of another person's stock ownership . . . However, they satisfy that burden 'by showing good faith and reasonable investigation.' Furthermore, such proof is materially enhanced, as here, by *the approval of a board comprised of a majority of outside independent directors* who have acted in accordance with the foregoing standards" (italics added). [See: *Unocal Corporation v. Mesa Petroleum Company*, 493 A. 2d 946, (1985).]

There is, of course, an **opt-out rule** that permits some corporations to sidestep the independent directors' rule if they are a "controlled" company. A **controlled company** is one that has more than half its voting power concentrated in one individual or a small group of people who always vote together. The opt-out provision is designed to give parent companies that are already controlled by independent boards a technique for eliminating a duplication of the independence restriction in their subsidiaries.

Legislative Support for Independent Directors Sometimes, those people who support one method of corporate governance may inadvertently lend support for another form of corporate governance, often without being aware of the contradiction. Such is the case with congressional action in the passage of SarbOx. Although the main thrust of SarbOx is to facilitate governmental control of the corporate person, some provisions have given a boost to independent control. For example, SarbOx requires all U.S corporate persons that are publicly traded and all alien corporations included on an American stock exchange to set up an **audit committee** that consists of independent members. The audit committee has the duty to oversee the operation of each accounting firm that audits the company. The committee chooses the firm, sets the amount paid to the firm, and evaluates the work of the firm. Moreover, the independent auditing committee also has the job of establishing a process for handling grievances about accounting and auditing procedures. The committee is also empowered to hire outside attorneys and/or other counselors should that need arise. Also, the law does permit the entire board to serve as an audit committee, but only if the entire board consists of independent directors. All of these measures clearly promote independent control at the expense of governmental control [See: Margaret H. McFarland, Deputy Director, Securities Exchange Commission, 17 CFR Parts, 228, 229, 249, 274, *Standards Relating to Listed Company Audit Committees*, April 9, 2004.]

Source: See: *Unocal Corporation v. Mesa Petroleum Company.,* 493 A. 2d 946, (1985).

Managerial Control The third approach to corporate governance is **managerial control**. Those who favor managerial control point out that the officers and the directors of a corporation are in the best position for judging not only the needs of the corporation but also the needs of the community and the needs of society at large. Individuals who favor managerial control would insulate the managers from shareholders by limiting the shareholders' power to vote and making it difficult for shareholders to sue managers. Opponents of managerial control argue that corporate managers may tend to be self-interested and, as a result, make relatively shortsighted decisions.

Limits on Managerial Control The idea that management should have ultimate control over corporate decision making has been with us since the first corporations opened their doors. The argument that supports this notion states that management leaders are in the best position to make such decisions based on their education, experience, and place within the corporate culture. Yet, despite this, many people object to the power given to corporate management or at least to mega-giant corporations like Amazon and Walmart. One such glaring example involves the power that has devolved to these giant corporate retailers over manufacturers. A shift in the power base began in 1975 when Congress passed the Consumer Goods Pricing Act of 1975 (CGPA). The critical feature of the CGPA, according to commentator Barry Lynn in the *CNN* story "Corporate Giants Have Too Much Power," was the ability passed on to retailers that allowed them to determine the amount charged for goods produced by manufacturers. This move, along with Reagan era policies based on "consumer welfare" in quotation marks. consumer welfare, led to a situation that empowers retail giants such as Walmart and Amazon to dictate prices at will. [See: Barry Lynn, "Corporate Giants Have Too Much Power," *CNN Opinions*, February 16, 2010, http://www.cnn.com/2010/OPINIION/02/16/lynn.amazon.power/index.html./02/.] Nevertheless, there are those who believe that the great power once wielded by corporations in general and by CEOs in particular has become a mere remnant of its former self. Much of this has to do with the fact that shareholder power has grown over the past decade or so, especially as that power is used by savvy investors who may hire expert firms to guide them through details of proxy battles. As noted earlier, the growing influence of independent board members has also played a role in this power shift. In 2012, *The Economist* reported, for example, that most corporate board members were no longer insiders but instead outsiders beyond the conventional influence of the CEO. [See: "The Shackled Boss: Corporate Bosses Are Much Less Powerful Than They Used to Be," *The Economist,* January 21, 2012, p. 76.]

Stakeholder Control Stakeholder control is based on the idea that corporate decision making affects more individuals and groups than just the shareholders and the managers of the corporation. The people who have a stake in the corporate decision-making process, beyond shareholders, directors, and officers, argue that many corporate decisions, such as a decision to open or close a factory, affect the community through consumers, suppliers, employees, and community neighbors. Consequently, all of these stakeholders and more should be represented on the boards of directors of all major corporations. Individuals who support stakeholder control would like to see representatives from employees' unions; consumer protection organizations; suppliers; customers; clients; environmental protection groups; and local, state, national, and international communities.

Environmental, Social, and Governance Issues Support for the stakeholder approach to corporate control has increased over the last few years. In fact, it has grown so much that it has acquired a new label all its own. It is now frequently referred to as ESG control—environmental, social, and governance control—and focuses on those areas that are of greatest concern to the stakeholders. Environmental concerns refer to issues related to pollution, sustainability, land reclamation, the depletion of natural resources, the preservation of energy reserves, the use of clean energy, and dealing with climate control problems. Social concerns are related to issues such as poverty, crime, drugs, disabilities, racism, sexism, immigration, disenfranchisement, and the marginalization of certain groups. Governance concerns involve internal problems that include ensuring that all stakeholders have input into corporate decision making, especially related to issues of executive pay. Interestingly enough, recent studies seem to indicate that ESG concerns have an increased effect on investment decision making. For example, a white paper entitled "ESG II: A Deeper Dive," conducted by the Bank of America's Merrill Lynch Global Research team, indicates that companies with high marks in ESG are also relatively stable and prone to long-term continuity. This makes such firms a safe bet for investors, such as pension funds, that are into the market for the long haul. [See: Andrew Ross Sorkin, "The 3 Letters More Investors Take Seriously," *The New York Times*, June 27, 2017. p. B-1; Savita Subramanian, "Why E.S.G. Is Too Critical to Ignore," Bank of America, Merrill Lynch, 2018, https://www.bofaml.com/en-us/content/esg-socially-responsible-investing-strategies.html; and "ESG Part II: A Deeper Dive," Band of America, Merrill Lynch Global Research Report, June 15, 2017.]

Shareholder Democracy Individuals who favor shareholder democracy, or corporate democracy as it is also known, believe that the shareholders have the right to run the corporation, because without their money, the corporation would not be able to survive. As the real owners of the corporation, the shareholders have a right to say how their money and their property should be used. Supporters of shareholder democracy would make management more responsive to shareholders by giving shareholders greater voting control and making it easier for them to take managers to court. Opponents of this theory point out that most shareholders are removed from the center of corporate activity and therefore cannot make the same type of informed decisions that the managers can make. Today there is a delicate balance between the theories of managerial control and shareholder democracy. Therefore, this chapter will focus on the battle between these two positions as it examines the subject of corporate control. The two most significant areas of this conflict lie in shareholder voting control and shareholder lawsuits. Shareholders can influence corporate decision making through their voting powers and through their right to initiate a lawsuit against managers (see Table 27-1).

Shareholder Voting Control

LO4

Shareholders usually receive one vote per share of common stock held. Shareholders who are dissatisfied with management can attempt to buy more shares to increase their voting

Table 27-1 Shareholder Control

Votes and Lawsuits	Explanation
Voting control: Cumulative voting	Each share of stock has as many votes as there are directors to be elected
Proxy voting	The right to vote another shareholder's stock
Voting trusts	An agreement among shareholders to transfer their voting rights to a trustee
Pooling agreements	Shareholders join in a temporary arrangement, agreeing to vote the same way on a particular issue
Shareholder proposals	A suggestion about a broad company policy or procedure submitted by a shareholder and included in management's proxy solicitation
Shareholder suits: Direct suit	A suit brought by shareholders who have been deprived of a right
Derivative suit	A suit brought by shareholders based on an injury to the corporation

power. With this increased voting power, the dissatisfied or dissident shareholders can influence the election of the board of directors. However, shareholders are not always able to buy more shares of the corporation, either because they cannot afford them or because the other shareholders are not willing to sell. In such cases, shareholders can resort to one of the other voting methods available:

- Cumulative voting
- Proxy solicitation
- Shareholder proposals
- Voting trusts
- Pooling agreements
- Shareholder nominations
- Unanimous voting restrictions

Cumulative Voting Ordinarily, each share of common stock is worth one vote. Therefore, only a majority of shareholders can elect directors of the corporation. To give minority shareholders an opportunity to elect one or more directors, some states permit **cumulative voting**. This system allows shareholders to multiply the number of their voting shares by the number of directors to be elected. All these votes may be cast for one candidate or distributed among several candidates. This procedure allows minority shareholders an opportunity to be represented on the board of directors.

EXAMPLE 27-2: Cumulative vs. Straight Voting

Beth General, James Garrett, Ken Collins, and Heather Gilliam were presented to the shareholders as candidates for the board of directors of Shopton Enterprises Inc. Three of the four were to be chosen. Because cumulative voting was authorized, the minority shareholders cast all their weighted votes for Gilliam, who had promised to represent the minority voice in corporate affairs. Had the minority voters been allowed only one vote for each share instead of three, they might have failed in their effort to elect a favored director.

Proxy Voting A **proxy** is the authority given to one shareholder to cast another shareholder's votes. **Proxy solicitation** is the process by which one shareholder asks another for his or her voting right. Proxy solicitation also refers to the actual document that is used to request the right to vote the other shareholders' votes. The minority shareholder's voting power increases as the number of proxies held rises. Because majority shareholders, including management, can also solicit proxies, a struggle between the two groups, known as a **proxy contest**, often results. Proxy contests involving large, publicly held corporations are closely regulated by the Securities and Exchange Commission (SEC). The primary federal law that controls the operation of a proxy contest is Section 14 (a) of the Securities Exchange Act of 1934. Section 14 (a) is designed to prevent fraud by requiring a complete revelation of certain facts by any individual or group that gets involved in the proxy solicitation process. Specifically, the law requires that anyone soliciting a proxy must disclose the identity of the solicitor, the reason behind the solicitation, and all other crucial facts that the shareholders will need to make an informed decision about the proxy. The document that communicates this information to the shareholders is called a **proxy statement**, which is delivered to the SEC and then sent to shareholders before the shareholders' annual meeting. Generally, the solicitation includes a card called a proxy card that can be returned to the solicitor. Rule 14 (a) of the Securities Exchange Act has recently become the focus of heated debate among shareholders and management alike. The dispute covers the question of what corporate management can and cannot exclude from proxy materials that are to be sent to shareholders.

Stockholders exercise their control through votes at annual meetings and through proxies.
©Tom Mihalek/EPA/REX/Shutterstock/Shutterstock

The Securities and Exchange Commission recently enacted several new proxy solicitation rules that have answered a few of these questions. Specifically, the SEC now requires proxies to include additional information about manager-level compensation packages. This information includes (1) risk-related elements in corporate compensation packages, (2) equity awards added to corporate compensation packages, and (3) any conflicts of interest involved in the pay packages earned by compensation consultants. The first of these reflects the fact that corporate compensation packages sometimes involve risky investment opportunities that might have a long-term effect on the value of the shareholders' shares. Such risks must now be disclosed, but only if the risks might have a "material adverse effect" on shareholders. The second disclosure reflects a change in the way that equity rewards are reported in proxy statements. Rather than the dollar figure called for under the old rules, the new rules require that the "fair value" of the award be reported. The final change requires the reporting of any money paid to consultants hired to evaluate non-executive-related salaries. The fear is that such consultants might be caught in a conflict of interest between the managers who pay their fees and the nonexecutives whose compensation packages are being evaluated. Not everyone believes that these changes will be helpful to shareholders. The fear is that the very nature of the new information (risk management, equity awards, and conflicts of interest) and the complex language needed to communicate the required facts might, at the very least, be useless to the shareholders and, at the worst, might confuse and mislead them, thus causing more harm than good. [See: Arden T. Phillips, "SEC Rules Bolster Compensation Disclosure," *The National Law Journal*, February 8, 2010, p. 7.]

Shareholder Proposals Another way for shareholders to exercise their voting power to shape corporate decision making is the shareholder proposal. Because shareholder proposals are placed in the proxy materials that are sent from corporate management to shareholders, they are closely allied with the proxy solicitation process and also governed by the Securities Exchange Act of 1934. A shareholder proposal allows shareholders to influence corporate affairs because, under SEC guidelines, shareholders of large, publicly owned corporations can compel management to include their proposals in management's proxy solicitation prior to the next shareholder meeting. A **shareholder proposal** is a suggestion about a broad company policy or procedure that is submitted by a shareholder. The proposal cannot be about the ordinary business operation of the corporation. It must concern something that affects all shareholders. A proposal to hire or fire a particular employee would not qualify, whereas a proposal to amend the corporate charter would. The rules also prohibit proposals that concern only dividend payments.

To qualify as a valid shareholder proposal under SEC rules, the proposal must be no more than 500 words long and must be received by management at least 120 days before the date of the corporation's proxy statement released to shareholders in connection with last year's annual shareholder's meeting. In addition, the shareholder must have owned at least 1 percent or $2,000 in market value of the voting stock of the corporation for one year and may submit only one proposal at a time. Even then, managers can reject the proposal if they feel that it does not qualify as a valid shareholder proposal according to a lengthy list of disqualifying characteristics cataloged by the SEC. Included on this list are proposals that are personal grievances, those beyond the corporation's power, and proposals that relate to a corporate election. However, some of these limitations recently have been challenged in a series of lawsuits filed by high-powered corporate shareholders.

Shareholder proposals, sometimes referred to as **shareholder resolutions**, have traditionally been among the weakest of shareholder voting tactics. One reason is that for many years, such proposals were not taken seriously by the directors and officers of most corporations, a situation that was exacerbated by the fact that the courts did not appear to take them seriously either. Much of this attitude was caused by the open-ended nature of the rules which permitted the corporate directors to reject most proposals made by shareholders. Moreover, many of the proposals that did make it to the ballot were filed by people with a political agenda and demanded such things as a cessation of business dealings with South African companies, a boycott of Defense Department contracts, or a campaign to redistribute shareholder dividends among needy Third World nations.

The law of balancing forces has operated over the last few years to increase the power of shareholder proposals and decrease the ability of corporate managers to short-circuit such proposals. Part of this trend has emerged because the shareholder proposal itself has become less a soapbox for political dissidents and more a tool for large institutional shareholders, thus resetting a balance that had moved heavily toward politics. Institutional shareholders, such as the American Federation of State, County, and Municipal Employees or Boston Common Asset Management, have pressed claims against corporations asking not for political action but for a share in corporate governance. Typically, such proposals demand that the corporation make some sort of amendment in voting procedures, such as a change in the bylaws to require a majority rather than a plurality vote on directors, to allow shareholders to cast advisory votes on executive salaries, or to permit shareholders to vote on anti-takeover tactics, such as the use of a white knight or a lockup agreement strategy (see Chapter 28). Sometimes, the very suggestion of a shareholder proposal will cause corporate management to change policies rather than put up with the shareholder proposal process itself.

The Wells Fargo compensation recovery case is probably the most vivid example of a change in corporate policy motivated by a shareholder proposal that was never voted upon. In that incident, two Wells Fargo executives, the CEO and the head of the community banking unit, were required, under a new corporate policy, to return some $60 million in compensation for failing to detect a fraudulent scheme under which company employees had created fake customer accounts in order to fulfill quotas. The compensation return policy had been established only three years earlier in reaction to a shareholder proposal. The proposal had suggested a new policy that would require high executives to return compensation whenever the corporation's financial situation or image is harmed by people under their command. The proposal was never voted on, but the possibility of facing a voting contest convinced the leaders of Wells Fargo to make the suggested change on their own. [See: Gretchen Morgenson, "Legislation Aims to Stifle Shareholders," *The New York Times*, June 18, 2017) p. 1, Business Section.] Corporate directors have become more amenable to such shareholder proposals in light of SarbOx and the outside support that has been provided by newly formed expert support groups, such as the Institutional Shareholder Services and Global Advisors Inc., to help shareholder activists.

The Financial Choice Act and Shareholder Proposals Not everyone favors placing power in the hands of shareholders. In fact, the Financial Choice Act of 2017 (FCA) attempts to limit the number of shareholders eligible to submit shareholder proposals. Under the current law, as noted earlier, to submit a shareholder proposal, the shareholder must own at least 1 percent or $2,000 in market value of the voting stock of the corporation for one year and may submit only one proposal at a time. These limitations make it difficult, but not impossible, for many shareholders to submit such proposals. The Financial Choice Act would change all of this. Under the new act, shareholders would have to own at least 1 percent in market value of the voting stock of the corporation for three years. Thus, the requirement of a one-year holding time has been extended to three years, and the dollar amount option has been eliminated. Also, the FCA would eliminate the ability of shareholders to use representatives to present a shareholder proposal for them. In this regard, the act reads as follows: "Shareholder Proposals by Proxies Not Permitted.—An issuer may not include in its proxy materials a shareholder proposal submitted by a person in such person's capacity as a proxy, representative, agent, 1 or person otherwise acting on behalf of a shareholder." The net effect of the FCA is to severely lower the number of shareholders who might be able to submit a shareholder proposals in the future. As of the beginning of 2018, the act has been voted on and passed only by the House of Representatives. [See: H.R. 10, Financial Choice Act of 2017, Section 844, Shareholder Proposals. See also: Morgenson.]

Voting Trusts A **voting trust** is an agreement among shareholders to transfer their voting rights to a trustee. A **trustee** is a person who is entrusted with the management and control of another's property or the rights associated with that property. Sometimes, the trustee is one of the shareholders; at other times, the trustee is an outsider. The trustee votes those shares at the annual shareholders' meeting at the direction of the shareholders. Shareholders surrender only their voting rights. All other rights, including the right to receive profits, remain with them. Generally, once a voting trust has been created, it cannot be ended until the specified time period has run its course. However, state statutes usually place a maximum time limit on the duration of a voting trust. Most state time limits run from 10 to 21 years. Voting trusts must be in writing and must be filed with the corporation.

Pooling Agreements Sometimes, shareholders join in a temporary arrangement and agree to vote the same way on a particular issue. Such agreements are known as **pooling agreements**, shareholder agreements, or voting agreements. They differ from proxies and voting trusts because the shareholders retain control of their own votes. In this sense, pooling agreements are also the weakest voting arrangement because shareholders can change their votes at the last minute. If a member of a pooling agreement changes her or his vote, however, the other members may bring a lawsuit against the shareholder who broke the agreement. In general, pooling agreements are interpreted by the court under the principles of contract law.

Shareholder Nominations Another way to increase the voting power of shareholders is to augment their ability to elect a director or directors who will represent their point of view in crucial issues facing the company. Several ways to do this include enacting state statutes, altering SEC rules, or changing stock exchange regulations so that certain events will trigger the ability of shareholders to elect board members. One such triggering event might be coupled with a shareholder proposal to permit shareholders to nominate their own directors. The rules might permit this nomination process to go forward as long as 50 percent of the votes cast (not 50 percent of the available votes, but 50 percent of those votes actually used in an election) support such a proposal. Another triggering event might be the ability of the minority shareholders to reach a 35–50 percent (depending on how the rule is worded) margin of voters who block the election of a management-nominated board candidate. Should either of these events occur, the minority shareholders would be permitted to place their own director on the next ballot at the expense of the corporation.

Unanimous Voting Restrictions An additional approach to strengthening the power of the shareholders involves a change in the corporate bylaws that makes it more difficult for the board to approve crucial issues that affect the fate of the corporation. The new voting bylaws would require unanimous agreement among all directors when the issue before the board involves a critical matter such as a merger, the sale of corporate assets, or a large increase in the salary of a top officer. Under current bylaws, one director with one vote on a board of 12 persons is of little consequence. However, under the revised regulations that require the unanimous approval of the board when major issues are decided, a single board member would have the power to block any material change contemplated by the rest of the board. The fact that a single director would have the power to stop major changes in corporate structure and policy might encourage minority shareholders to join forces in a campaign to elect their own director to the board.

Combinations Although each of these voting techniques has been discussed separately, in practice, they can be combined to increase shareholder voting power. For example, a group of minority shareholders could enter a pooling agreement in which they all agree to cast their cumulative votes for a single board candidate. It is even possible for one of the voting techniques to be used to institute another of those techniques.

Shareholder Lawsuits

The battle between management and dissident shareholders may also be waged on a front other than the annual shareholders' meeting. That front is the courtroom. Shareholders can sue management to compel a change in direction or to force management to overturn a decision. The two types of suits available to shareholders are direct suits and derivative suits.

Direct Suits A *direct suit* is brought by shareholders who have been deprived of a right that belongs to them as shareholders. These rights include the right to vote, the right to receive dividends, the right to transfer shares, the right to purchase newly issued stock, and the right to examine corporate books and records. If shareholders have been denied any of these rights, they can bring a direct suit to make up for any loss they have suffered.

Derivative Suits A *derivative suit* allows shareholders to sue corporate management on behalf of the corporation. Unlike a direct suit, a derivative suit is not based on a direct injury to a shareholder. Instead, the injury is to the corporation. The shareholders' right to sue is derived from the corporate injury. Shareholders who bring a successful derivative suit are entitled to recover attorney fees. To bring a derivative suit, shareholders must meet certain prerequisites. One prerequisite is the exhaustion of internal remedies. Before bringing suit, the shareholder must attempt to solve the problem by communicating with the board of directors and with other shareholders. In their original complaint commencing the derivative action, the shareholders must state the steps that they took to exhaust all internal remedies. If the shareholders have not exhausted internal remedies and still insist on bringing the lawsuit, the court will dismiss the case and deny any request from the shareholders for the payment of attorney fees. On the other hand, if the shareholders can show that because of a director or officer's control of the board, any attempt to bring the matter to the board would have been futile, they may convince the court to waive the requirement to exhaust internal remedies. This rule is referred to as the **demand futility doctrine**. Some legal commentators refer to an officer who has total and unquestioned control of the board of directors as a corporate **monarch**. To bring a derivative suit, a shareholder must own stock at the time of the injury and at the time of the suit. This requirement is known as the **rule of contemporary ownership**. Frequently, state corporate laws also require derivative suit plaintiffs to pay a security deposit to cover the corporation's potential expenses in defending the derivative suits. All of these requirements make it difficult for a shareholder to bring a derivative lawsuit.

A CLASSIC CASE
Derivative Suits and the Demand Futility Doctrine

The landmark case of *Aronson v. Lewis* concerned a series of arrangements between Meyers Parking Systems Inc. and Leo Fink, one of its directors. For starters, Meyers granted Fink a contract that contained a condition that permitted Fink to become a consultant at Meyers after he retired. Additional stipulations within the agreement stated that Fink would be paid $150,000 for the first three years, $125,000 for the next three, and then $100,000 each year for life. Lewis, a shareholder, took offense at this arrangement because, according to Lewis, Fink did not really perform any duties for the payments. Lewis was also upset because the board had ratified several interest-free loans to Fink. Altogether, the loans came to around $225,000. Lewis sued, asserting that the contract was "grossly excessive" and the "loans" were really just an extra added payment transferred to Fink. (*Note:* The defendant's attorney indicated later that these loans had been totally repaid.) The bottom line of Lewis's argument was that the payments to Fink represented a waste of corporate funds, for which the directors were personally liable.

The board chose to challenge Lewis's right to bring the lawsuit. Specifically, they noted that because this was a derivative lawsuit (true enough), Lewis had to exhaust internal remedies before bringing suit. This would have involved taking his complaints to the board. Lewis countered this challenge by arguing that Fink was a monarch—that is, a dictatorial officer who had complete control of the board. Therefore, the board did whatever Fink dictated. This rendered any demand on the board an exercise in futility. As evidence for this claim, the plaintiff revealed that Fink had appointed every member of the board and that each board member was, therefore, obligated to Fink. Furthermore, because all the board members had been designated as defendants in the suit, they would not approve Lewis's undertaking because, by assisting in the case, they would be suing themselves.

The court christened Lewis's strategy the *doctrine of demand futility*. However, the court said that, to succeed under the demand futility doctrine, Lewis, or any similarly situated plaintiff, would have to present much more evidence than the court had before it at the present moment. First, the court noted that the fact that an officer or director owns a lot of stock, when it is less than a majority of that stock, does not amount to complete control. Second, the court added, even majority ownership does not, by itself, amount to complete control, provided the directors exercise good judgment as they carry out their responsibilities. Third, the court noted the plaintiff had presented no evidence that the payments to Fink amounted to a waste of corporate assets. Fourth, the court declared that it is standard procedure for officers and directors to appoint new board members and that the performance of the board members is what matters, not their method of appointment. Finally, the court stated that the mere unsubstantiated claim that the directors would not sue themselves was, by itself, insufficient but, instead, must be supported by evidence that the directors violated their corporate duties. [See: *Aronson v. Lewis*, 473 A.2d 805 (March 1, 1984).]

Source: See: *Aronson v. Lewis*, 473 A.2d 805 (March 1, 1984).

quick quiz 27-2

1. Under the original concept of the corporation, the shareholders are the primay reason that a corporation exists. true | false
2. Pooling agreements have been outlawed in all states. true | false
3. A controlled company is one that has more than half its voting power concentrated in one person or a small group of persons who always vote together. true | false

27-3 Governance Responsibilities

When a court hears a case challenging a manager's decision, that court will consider the following three rules in judging that conduct: the business judgment rule, the fairness rule, and the actual authority rule (see Table 27-2).

The Business Judgment Rule

Under the **business judgment rule**, the court will not interfere with most business decisions. The rule protects managers who act legally, with due care, and in good faith, as long as their decisions are in the best interests of the corporation. The rule results from the common-sense belief that based on their education, experience, and knowledge, managers are in the best position to run the corporation. In contrast, shareholders and judges are far removed from the day-to-day operations of the business and should not be allowed to second-guess most management decisions. Protecting directors and officers in this way encourages people to become corporate managers and reassures them that they will be protected when they make difficult business decisions. The business judgment rule emerges from the duty of due diligence that a manager owes to the corporation. The **duty of due diligence** consists of four parts. It says that, when acting on behalf of the corporation, a manager must act (1) legally,

Table 27-2 Management Rule Situation Explanation

Business manager does *not* profit from decision.	**Business Judgment Rule** The decision stands if it is made (1) in good faith, (2) with due care (3) within the law, and (4) in the corporation's best interests.
Business manager profits from decision.	**Fairness Rule** The decision must be fair to the corporation decision because managers must remain loyal to the corporation.
Business manager exceeds authority.	**Actual Authority Rule** A manager may be held liable if he makes a corporate decision that exceeds corporate authority and harms the corporation.

(2) in good faith, (3) using the same level of due care that an ordinarily prudent individual would use in a comparable situation, and (4) loyally—that is, in the reasonable belief that the best interests of the company are being met.

The Fairness Rule

The Business Judgment Rule assumes that managers do not personally profit from business decisions. If managers do profit, then the decision is suspect because all managers owe a **duty of loyalty** to the corporation. To fulfill this duty, managers must place the corporation's interests above their own. When managers enter contracts with the corporation or when they are on the boards of two corporations that do business with each other, they are said to be self-dealing. Different standards are used to judge the conduct of **self-dealing managers**. For example, if a self-dealing manager seeks and obtains the approval of the board members who did not profit from the decision, or if that same manager seeks and obtains the approval of the shareholders who did not profit from the decision, then the manager's decision will be considered valid, despite the self-dealing. In the alternative, without board or shareholder approval, the manager's conduct will be judged by the fairness rule. The **fairness rule** requires managers to be fair to the corporation when they personally benefit from their business decisions. The fairness rule does not automatically declare managers disloyal if they profit from a corporate decision. Rather, it allows the court to examine the decision to determine its basic fairness to the corporation. How to measure fairness is, at best, problematic. At a minimum, it requires corporate managers to disclose all crucial information when they enter contracts with the corporation. Two rules that are offshoots of the fairness rule and the duty of loyalty are the **insider trading rule** and the corporate opportunity doctrine. Both rules give specific ways to measure a corporate manager's fairness in certain types of situations.

THE OPENING CAS   Round 3
Independent Directors and the Business Judgment Rule, Reconsidered, Revamped, and Reactivated (in Delaware)

It's time for one last look at the Opening Case. The case of *Unocal v. Mesa* began when Unocal found itself targeted for a takeover bid by Mesa Petroleum (Mesa), one of its own shareholders. Mesa set up an offer promising to pay $54 a share to Unocal shareholders until Mesa had acquired 37 percent of Unocal's stock (64 million shares.) Any shareholders left out of the first step would be eligible to receive only bonds and not cash. The method behind the Mesa plan was to make it difficult for Unocal shareholders to resist the $54 price, lest they be left with the less-attractive bond offer. Acting according to protocol, the Unocal board, which was made up of eight independent and six internal directors, met to review the Mesa bid. At this initial meeting, the directors were informed about the offer and all countermeasures that they might want to enact to short-circuit the bid. The most effective countermeasure turned out to a plan that would empower Unocal to make a self-tender counteroffer to buy its own stock for $70–$75 per share at a total cost of about $6.25 billion, with the condition that Mesa would not be permitted to buy any of those shares.

After the meeting of the 13 board members, the independent board members met separately with the corporation's lawyers and financial advisors to further consider the countermeasure. After this meeting, the entire board (minus one internal board member) reconvened and voted to turn down the Mesa offer. A few days after this, the board met again and initiated the self-tender offer. The plan would be activated should Mesa actually receive tender offers amounting to its target goal of the 64 million shares. Unocal would then offer to purchase the remaining 49 percent of the outstanding shares at a price of $72 per share. As noted earlier, Mesa would be excluded from this offer (the Mesa exclusion).

Mesa brought this lawsuit in the Chancery Court of Delaware and asked for a temporary restraining order designed to stop Unocal from initiating its self-tender offer, arguing that the Mesa exclusion was discriminatory. The vice chancellor of the court granted the restraining order, and Unocal appealed. Because a hearing on a preliminary injunction was pending before the Chancery Court, the Supreme Court sent the case back to that court. The Chancery Court decided that the directors have a duty to protect the corporation from its own shareholders, if they believe that an action by those shareholders would injure the corporation; that there was not enough evidence to infer that the Mesa was self-dealing; and that directors directors had acted in good faith. Still, the court seemed unsure as to whether the Unocal directors could go so far as to exclude the Mesa shareholder from their offer and as to whether the Unocal directors deserved the protection of the business judgement rule. Therefore, the Chancery Court issued the preliminary injunction, and Unocal appealed.

When the Supreme Court of Delaware took the appeal, it reduced the case to two basic questions: (1) Are the corporate directors rightfully and dutifully empowered to counterattack a hostile takeover bid that would substantially harm the corporation? (2) Are the directors entitled to the protection of the business judgement rule in situations like this one? To grasp how the Supreme Court dealt with these questions, let's review the requirements of the business judgment rule. Recall that the business judgment rule states that when acting on behalf of the corporation, a manager must act (1) legally, (2) in good faith, (3) using the same level of due care that an ordinarily prudent individual would use in a comparable situation, and (4) loyally in the reasonable belief that the best interests of the company are being met. However, the business judgment rule is based on the assumption that managers do not personally profit from business decisions. If managers do profit, then the decision is suspect because all managers owe a duty of loyalty to the corporation and its shareholders. To fulfill this duty, managers must place the corporation's and the shareholder's interests above their own.

In the Unocal case, Mesa argued that the Unocal board members were not entitled to the protection of the business judgment rule because, in excluding Mesa from their offer, they were not treating all shareholders fairly and, ultimately, were placing themselves in a position by which they would profit from the plan. The Court disagreed. The Court answered its first question by noting that the board members have the right and the duty to create a defense to a hostile takeover bid when that bid is not in the best interests of the corporation and the other shareholders. In this case, the board members determined that the Mesa plan was designed to force shareholders to take a price far below the actual value of the stock and that the only party gaining from the plan was Mesa itself. The Court then answered its second question, noting that Unocal was qualified to receive the protection of the business judgment rule because, while some of the directors benefited from the Unocal plan, most of them did not because they were independent board members. In addition, although some of the directors, as shareholders, profited from the plan, all the other shareholders were treated in the same way under the Unocal plan, except, of course, for Mesa. However, the exclusion of Mesa was justified because, as the Mesa plan was coercive and unfair, the board's duty of loyalty to the other shareholders and to the entire corporation superseded its duty to Mesa.

Thus, when the business judgment rule is applied to the board's action, the court found that the board's decisions were legal, made in good faith, followed the principle of due care, and were made loyally in the reasonable belief that the best interests of the corporation were being met. The Court said it this way: "The factual findings of the Vice Chancellor, fully supported by the record, establish that Unocal's board, consisting of a majority of independent directors, acted in good faith, and after reasonable investigation found that Mesa's tender offer was both inadequate and coercive. Under the circumstances the board had both the power and duty to oppose a bid it perceived to be harmful to the corporate enterprise. On this record we are satisfied that the device Unocal adopted is reasonable in relation to the threat posed, and that the board acted in the proper exercise of sound business judgment." This decision became known as the Unocal rule. In short, the rule says that board members have the right and the duty to work to block a takeover bid when that bid will damage the corporation and legitimate corporate plans. However, any countermeasure taken must be reasonably structured to meet the danger posed by the takeover bid and nothing beyond that—period. [See: *Unocal Corporation v. Mesa Petroleum Company*, 493 A. 2d 946, (1985).]

Source: See: *Unocal Corporation v. Mesa Petroleum Company.*, 493 A. 2d 946, (1985).

Insider Trading Because of their role in corporate affairs, directors and officers often possess inside information. **Inside information** is material, nonpublic, factual data that can be used to buy or sell securities at a profit. Directors, officers, and other key individuals in a corporation, such as major shareholders who are not directors or officers, qualify as insiders. **Insider trading** may or may not be illegal. Corporate insiders who buy and sell stock in their own corporation are not trading illegally provided they report these transactions to the SEC. However, insiders who use material, nonpublic, factual data that they have in their possession by virtue of their corporate office to trade securities in violation of the fiduciary duties they owe to the corporation and its shareholders have engaged in illegal insider trading. Moreover, when a corporate insider "tips" an outsider about that material, nonpublic, factual data, the "tipper" and the "tippee" who uses that data in a securities trade may both be liable for illegal insider trading. Moreover, a corporate outsider, such as a printer in a printing firm who, by virtue of his or her job, misappropriates such data and uses the data to make a securities trade is also engaged, at least potentially, in illegal insider trading. The SEC identifies the following classes of individuals who might be at risk of finding themselves on the wrong end of an insider trading case. Naturally, corporate directors, officers, and employees can easily get themselves tangled in such cases if they use material, nonpublic, factual data in their trades. However, also at risk are family members, business colleagues, and friends of such corporate insiders. Also in danger are employees who work for businesses—such as law firms, banks, brokerage houses, and printing companies—that have access to such material, nonpublic, factual data. Even government employees with ready access to such data are at risk. On the other hand, just being in these categories is not an offense. SEC Rule 10b-5-1 provides exceptions to insider trading liability when the tippees can show that, even though they had the material, nonpublic factual data, they did not use the information because the trade was already in the works before the information was obtained. [See: Electronic Code of Federal Regulations, Title 17, Chapter II, Part 240.10b-5-1 and 240.10b 5-2. See also: U.S. Securities and Exchange Commission, *Investor Information: Fast Answers*, January 15, 2013, http://www.sec.gov/answers/insider.htm.]

The Corporate Opportunity Doctrine As noted previously, along with the duty of due diligence and the duty of actual authority (see the next section), corporate managers also owe a duty of loyalty to the corporation. The duty of loyalty requires that corporate managers place the corporation's well-being ahead of their own interests. One offshoot of this duty is the idea of the corporate opportunity doctrine. The **corporate opportunity doctrine** states that corporate managers cannot take a corporate business opportunity for themselves if they know that the corporation would be interested in that opportunity as well. Before taking such an opportunity, a manager must first offer it to the corporation by informing other managers and shareholders. If the corporation rejects the opportunity, then the manager is free to take that opportunity.

The Actual Authority Rule

Corporate managers are also held to a third duty, that is, the duty to act within actual authority. The authority spoken of here includes those powers that have been granted to managers by virtue of their position within the corporation. The duties of the directors and officers of the corporation are outlined in the appropriate state statutes, in the articles of incorporation, in the regulations issued by government bodies such as the SEC, in relevant case law, and in the bylaws of the company. The **actual authority rule** states that a manager may be held liable if he or she exceeds his or her authority and the corporation is harmed as a result. Some states say that the managers will be liable for any violation of the limits of their authority on the basis of absolute or strict liability; some jurisdictions will consider the managers responsible only if the violation results in negligent or intentional conduct. This duty is also sometimes referred to as the **duty of obedience**. It is, of course, possible for a vote of the board or of the shareholders to approve a previously unauthorized act by a manager through the process of **ratification**.

Efforts to Limit Responsibility Corporate managers have come under scrutiny by regulators and the courts in recent years. As a result, many otherwise well-qualified individuals have avoided serving as corporate managers in general but, in particular, as corporate directors. To counteract this trend, some states have enacted legislation that is designed to help protect the good faith and due diligent activities of such managers. These legislative enactments take three forms: (1) voluntary protective measures, (2) automatic protective measures, and (3) protective measures that limit the amount of damages that can be recovered against directors. A voluntary protective measure is one that permits corporate shareholders to fashion their bylaws so as to limit or eliminate the liability of directors for decisions made while carrying out their duties. Such measures would allow recovery of damages only if the director deliberately broke the law, deliberately violated the duty of loyalty, deliberately violated the duty of good faith, or improperly benefited from the transaction in question. Automatic protective measures grant the same type of immunity by state law, regardless of the action or inaction of corporate shareholders. The final measure would allow lawsuits against managers even in the cases noted earlier but would place a cap on the amount of money damages that can be recovered against directors.

Efforts to Increase Responsibility At the same time that state governments are attempting to ease the liability of directors, the federal government has enacted efforts to increase director responsibilities for catching and stopping the wrongdoing of others within the corporation. One such measure is SarbOx, which places an affirmative duty on the directors of publicly traded corporations to monitor whether their corporation is conforming to all legal requirements. A second measure involves the **U.S. Sentencing Commission**, which has issued a set of rules that control the discretion of the federal courts in issuing fines against corporations found guilty of criminal activities. Under the new rules, if the directors of a corporation did not do their best to discover and stop illegal activities, the court can place very severe penalties on the corporation, once it has been found guilty of those violations. The idea behind the new rules is to force directors to pay more attention to what is going on within their own companies, especially in relation to crime-stopping activities. The new rules have led some legal commentators to suggest a series of steps that corporate directors should take when faced with suspected wrongdoing within their company. Seven steps are recommended: (1) Once a legal violation has been uncovered (or even suspected), the activity must cease instantly; (2) any and all consequences that have flowed from the violation should be uncovered and stopped immediately; (3) any attempt to engage in a cover-up, and in fact, any actions that can be remotely perceived as a cover-up, must be avoided religiously; (4) notification of the violation must be made to the proper authorities; (5) investigations must be made to uncover any similar or related activities that may be illegal; (6) the cause or causes of the legal violations must be determined; and (7) an action plan must be created and executed to punish the violators and to prevent any future violations.

quick quiz 27-3

1. The business judgment rule states that a manager's decision will stand as long as it was legal, was made with due care and in good faith, and was made in the best interests of the corporation. true | false
2. The fairness rule states that a decision made by a manager will stand if it is fair to the corporation. true | false
3. The business judgment rule is used by the courts when the manager is disinterested—that is, he or she does not personally gain from the decision. true | false

27-4 Shareholder Rights

In addition to their voting rights and their right to sue, shareholders are entitled to examine certain corporate records, share in dividends, transfer shares of stock, and buy newly issued stock.

Right to Examine Corporate Records

A shareholder's right by statute to inspect the records of the corporation is usually limited to inspections for proper purposes at an appropriate time and place. Idle curiosity and an intent that unreasonably interferes with or embarrasses corporate management would prompt officers or directors to refuse shareholders' requests to examine corporate accounts, minutes, and records. When the purpose of inspection is proper, it may be enforced by a court order.

Right to Share in Dividends

Shareholders have the right to share in dividends after they have been declared by the board of directors. Once declared, a dividend becomes a debt of the corporation and enforceable by law, as is any other debt. However, shareholders cannot force the directors to declare a dividend unless the directors are not acting in good faith in refusing to do so. Courts are not inclined to order directors to meet and declare a dividend if the court must substitute its own business judgment for that of the directors.

Right to Transfer Shares of Stock

Shareholders have the right to sell or transfer their shares of stock. The person to whom stock shares are transferred has the right to have the stock transfer entered on the corporate books. The transferee becomes a **shareholder of record** and is entitled to vote, receive dividends, and enjoy all other shareholder privileges.

Preemptive Rights

Unless the right is denied or limited by the corporate charter or by state law, shareholders have the right to purchase a proportionate share of every new offering of stock by the corporation. This right is known as the shareholder's **preemptive right**. Preemptive rights are more prevalent in small, closely held corporations than in large, publicly owned corporations. This right prevents management from depriving shareholders of their proportionate control of a corporation simply by increasing the number of shares in the corporation.

> **quick quiz 27-4**
>
> 1. Assuming a request by a shareholder to inspect the corporate books is a proper one, the courts will enforce that request.   true | false
> 2. Today, the courts will readily substitute their own judgment and declare a dividend on corporate stock, even when the directors of the corporation have voted against such a move.   true | false
> 3. Preemptive rights are more common in large, publicly held corporations than in small, closely held corporations.   true | false

27-5 Governance of a Limited Liability Company

The members of a limited liability company can choose to manage the business themselves, or they can hire outside management. An LLC that is run by the members themselves is called a member-managed LLC, whereas one operated by outside managers is referred to as a manager-managed LLC.

Member-Managed LLCs

If the managers choose to run the LLC on their own, management rights are apportioned among the members, according to the capital contributions made by each member to the LLC. Like the partners in a general partnership, the members of the LLC act as agents of the LLC. Accordingly, whenever a member performs a function within his or her apparent authority, the LLC will be bound by that action. However, as is true of a partnership, some actions fall outside the member's apparent authority. These include but are not limited to disposing of the firm's goodwill and submitting a claim of the LLC to arbitration. Naturally, the operating agreement can alter any of these statutory provisions.

Manager-Managed LLCs

If the members hire outside managers, then the LLC is run like a corporation. In the absence of an operating agreement, a single manager operates much like the CEO of a corporation, while a group of managers acts as a board of directors. Nevertheless, regardless of the number of managers involved in an LLC, both the business judgment rule and the fairness rule apply to their decisions in the same way that those rules apply to the directors of a corporation.

Fiduciary Duties

Regardless of whether the members or the managers ultimately run the LLC, both groups have a fiduciary duty to the LLC and to its members. However, as noted in the previous chapter, it would be wise to outline the specific management duties in the written operating agreement.

> **Did You Know?**
>
> Limited liability companies became more popular in the United States in 1988 when a ruling by the Internal Revenue Service declared that they could be treated as partnerships for tax purposes.

quick quiz 27-5

1. The members of an LLC have no choice in the matter of who will manage their firm. true | false
2. An operating agreement established by the LLC is not permitted to alter statutory provisions regarding governance in any way. true | false
3. Regardless of whether the members or the managers ultimately run the LLC, fiduciary duties have been suspended by provisions outlined in the latest version of the Uniform Limited Liability Company Act. true | false

Summary

27.1 The business affairs of a corporation are managed by a board of directors elected by the shareholders. The directors have the authority to appoint officers and agents to run the day-to-day affairs of the corporation.

27.2 Five theories have been put forth by legal scholars and business experts concerning how corporations should be managed. These theories are governmental control, independent director control, managerial control, stakeholder control, and shareholder democratic control. Shareholders can increase their voting power by purchasing additional stock. If they cannot purchase additional stock, they may use another device to increase their voting power, such as cumulative voting, proxies, voting trusts, pooling agreements, shareholder proposals, shareholder nominations, and unanimous voting restrictions. Shareholders can also sue the corporation. Direct suits are brought by shareholders to protect their own rights. Derivative suits are brought by shareholders when they feel that the corporation has been damaged by a management decision. Derivative suits are limited by certain rules including that shareholders must exhaust internal remedies before bringing such suits. However, the demand futility doctrine states that it is not necessary for a shareholder to exhaust internal remedies if that shareholder can demonstrate that because a manager controls the board such an approach would be futile.

27.3 Under the business judgment rule, the court will not interfere with most management decisions as long as those decisions are legal and are made with due care, in good faith, and in the best interests of the corporation. If the manager profits personally from a business decision, then the court will use the fairness rule to judge the manager's conduct.

27.4 Shareholder rights include the right to examine corporate records, the right to share dividends, the right to transfer shares of stock, and the right to buy newly issued stock.

27.5 The members of a limited liability company can choose to manage the business themselves or hire outside management. Regardless of whether the members or the managers ultimately run the LLC, both groups have a fiduciary duty to the LLC and to the members of the LLC. Nevertheless, it would be wise to outline specific management duties in the operating agreement.

Key Terms

actual authority rule, 776
audit committee, 765
business judgment rule, 773
controlled company, 764
corporate democracy, 766
corporate opportunity doctrine, 776
cumulative voting, 767
demand futility doctrine, 772
derivative suit, 771

direct suit, 771	managerial control, 765	Sarbanes–Oxley Act, 761
duty of due diligence, 773	monarch, 772	self-dealing manager, 774
duty of loyalty, 774	opt-out rule, 764	shareholder democracy, 766
duty of obedience, 777	pooling agreement, 770	shareholder of record, 778
fairness rule, 774	preemptive right, 778	shareholder proposal, 769
governmental control, 761	proxy, 768	shareholder resolutions, 769
independent director, 763	proxy contest, 768	stakeholders, 759
inside information, 776	proxy solicitation, 768	trustee, 770
insider trading, 776	proxy statement, 768	U.S. Sentencing Commission, 777
insider trading rule, 774	ratification, 777	voting trust, 770
legal imperialism, 762	rule of contemporary ownership, 772	

Questions for Review and Discussion

1. What is the central dilemma of corporate governance?
2. What are the functions of directors, officers, and shareholders?
3. What are the five theories of corporate governance?
4. What is the difference between cumulative voting and proxy solicitation?
5. What is a shareholder proposal?
6. What is the difference between a voting trust and a pooling agreement?
7. What is the difference between a shareholder direct suit and a shareholder derivative suit?
8. What is the difference between the business judgment rule and the fairness rule?
9. What are the rights that belong to shareholders?
10. How does the management of a limited liability company operate?

Cases for Analysis

1. United Missionary Baptist Church, a not-for-profit corporation, held an election for the new church pastor. Several members of the church were dissatisfied with the results of the election and with the procedures that were followed during the election. They claimed that the inclusion of absentee balloting violated the church's constitution. Without making any parliamentary moves to correct the alleged misapplication of the constitution, and despite the fact that they had used their own absentee ballots during the election, these unhappy members brought a derivative lawsuit, asking the court to compel the church to follow its own constitution. The suit was dismissed. However, the members who brought the lawsuit claimed that because the lawsuit was a derivative action, they were entitled to attorney's fees, just as the shareholders of a profit corporation were entitled to attorney's fees. The court agreed that the same rules that apply to profit corporations in derivative actions apply to derivative suits brought for nonprofit corporations. However, the court still refused to grant the request for attorney's fees. Why? [See: *Russell v. United Missionary Baptist Church*, 637 N.E.2d 82 (OH).]

2. The bylaws of Jameson Enterprises Inc. required a 70 percent supermajority to establish a quorum sufficient to hold a meeting to remove a director from the board. The bylaws also designated a meeting with such a purpose as a special meeting. The board consisted of 10 directors. Six showed up at the meeting. Of the four who failed to attend, three were in Europe. The fourth, Weinberger, was not notified of the meeting because he was the one to be removed. The six directors attending the meeting first voted to change the bylaws to require only 60 percent of the directors to establish a quorum

sufficient to hold a special meeting. The six directors then unanimously voted to remove Weinberger. When Weinberger found out about the meeting, he objected to the vote and claimed that the entire procedure was void. Was Weinberger correct? Explain.

3. Smith, a shareholder, filed suit against the board of directors of a corporation in which he had owned stock. Smith claimed that he and other shareholders had not received top dollar for their shares when their corporation had merged with another. Consequently, they sought either a reversal of the merger or payment from the directors to make up for their losses. The directors, Smith argued, had violated their duty of due care because they based their decision on a 20-minute speech by the CEO. Also, the directors had not even looked at the merger documents, let alone studied them. Furthermore, the directors had not sought any independent evaluation by outside experts. For their part, the directors argued that because their decision was made in good faith and was legal, they were protected by the business judgment rule. Were the directors correct? [See: *Smith v. Van-Gorkon*, 488 A.2d 858 (DE).]

4. Donald Lewis was a shareholder in S.L.&E. Inc., a corporation that owned land and a complex of buildings in Rochester, New York. The land and buildings were leased to LGT, a tire manufacturer. Lewis's brothers were shareholders and directors of both S.L.&E. and LGT. Lewis had no financial or managerial interest in LGT. S.L.&E. leased the land to LGT at a rate that Lewis considered damaging to S.L.&E. He pointed out that S.L.&E. collected only $14,000 per year in rent from LGT while paying out $11,000 in taxes. This rate, he argued, meant that S.L.&E. could never be a profit-making corporation. Should the directors of LGT and S.L.&E. be judged by the business judgment rule or the fairness rule? Explain. [See: *Lewis v. S.L.&E., Inc.*, 629 F.2d 764 (2nd Cir.).]

5. Jackson set up a trust for his seven children. Most of the assets in the trust consisted of stock in the two newspapers owned and run by Jackson. Over the course of 18 years, Jackson transferred all but two shares of voting stock in the newspapers. The trustee was given full power to manage the assets in the fund and sell or otherwise dispose of the newspaper stock. State law places a strict 10-year limit on voting trusts. The plaintiffs claimed that the trust, which had lasted 18 years, was no longer valid, having passed the 10-year limit. The defendants claimed that the 10-year limit did not apply to this trust. Were the defendants correct? Explain. [See: *Jackson v. Jackson*, 402 A.2d 893 (CT).]

6. Klinicki and Lundgren incorporated to form an air taxi service known as Berlinair Inc. Each of them owned one-third interest in the corporation. The final third was owned by Lelco Inc., a company owned by Lundgren. In his capacity as president of Berlinair, Lundgren learned that the Berlinair Flug Ring (BFR), a business association of Berlin's travel agents, was looking for an air charter service. Lundgren incorporated a new corporate entity called Air Berlin Charter (ABC). ABC then negotiated an air charter contract with BFR. Klinicki brought suit, demanding that Lundgren reimburse Berlinair for any profits made by ABC on the BFR contract. Was this a direct or derivative suit? Explain. Should the business judgment rule or the fairness rule be used by the court to measure Lundgren's performance? Explain. Who should have won the suit? Defend your choice. [See: *Klinicki v. Lundgren*, 695 P.2d 906 (OR).]

7. Naquin, Dubois, and Hoffpauir incorporated to form Air Engineered Systems and Services Inc. Dubois became president and Hoffpauir became secretary-treasurer. Naquin was employed by the company. Conflicts among the three caused a break down in the working relationship. Dubois and Hoffpauir offered Naquin $2,000 a month for 10 years for his share of the business if he would sign a noncompetition agreement. Naquin refused to sell until he could examine the corporate records. Dubois and Hoffpauir refused to allow Naquin to see the books until he signed the noncompetition agreement. Could Dubois and Hoffpauir attach such a condition to Naquin's request? Explain. [See: *Naquin v. Air Engineered Systems and Services, Inc.*, 463 So.2d 992 (LA).]

8. Snodgrass, a minority shareholder in the 21st Century Broadcasting Network Inc., was dissatisfied with management's decision to cancel several long-running news shows and replace them with several sitcoms and talk shows. She was also disturbed that management had decided to discharge several editorial writers and newscasters, including one who had recently won a major award for investigative journalism. Finally, she believed that a change in policy that would phase out foreign broadcast

efforts would eventually cost the company an enormous amount of money. Assuming that Snodgrass does not want to sue the corporation, what options does she have if she wants to increase her influence over the board of directors of 21st Century Broadcasting Network? Explain.

9. Keith Harris, a shareholder of Fastway Airlines Inc., discovered that Donald Fleure, chief executive officer of Fastway, had sold some of his own land to the corporation at what Harris believed to be excessive prices. Can Harris bring a direct or a derivative suit in this situation? Explain. Would the fairness rule or the business judgment rule be used to evaluate the activities of Fleure? Explain.

Design Elements: The Opening Case: ©Sharpstock/Alamy; A Classic Case: ©Evlakhov Valeriy/Shutterstock

quick quiz Answers

27-1	27-2	27-3	27-4	27-5
1. T	1. T	1. T	1. T	1. F
2. F	2. F	2. T	2. F	2. F
3. T	3. T	3. T	3. F	3. F

Chapter 28

Government Regulation of the Corporate Entity

28-1 The Constitution and the Corporate Entity
The Federal Power to Control Commerce • The Establishment of a Strong Central Government • Residual State Power over Commerce and Corporate Law

28-2 Securities Regulation of the Corporate Entity
Securities Act of 1933 • Securities Exchange Act of 1934 • Dodd–Frank Wall Street Reform and Consumer Protection Act

28-3 Antitrust Regulation of the Corporate Entity
Sherman Antitrust Act • Post–Sherman Antitrust Legislation

28-4 Expanding the Corporate Entity
Expansion Tactics and Securities Law • Expansion Tactics and Antitrust Law

28-5 The Government and the End of the Corporate Entity
Involuntary Dissolution • Voluntary Dissolution

28-6 Dissolution of a Limited Liability Company
Circumstances of Dissolution • Effects of Dissolution

THE OPENING CASE Round 1
Textualism, Purposivism, Pragmatism, Whistleblowers, and the Dodd–Frank Act

Three popular but conflicting theories of legal interpretation are textualism, purposivism, and pragmatism. *Textualism* requires judges to analyze legal documents as literary works by focusing exclusively on each document's language. In contrast, *purposivism* insists that judges consider the legislative goals of a statute, while *pragmatism* expects judges to focus on the consequences of a decision. Both pragmatism and purposivism seem to demand that judges investigate the circumstances behind the words of the text, while textualism asks judges to focus on the words as written by the legislators. To see how at least one of these techniques works, let's look at the case of *Asadi v. GE Energy*.

Khaled Asadi (Asadi) worked for GE Energy (GE) as the Iraqi Country Executive (ICE). During his tour of duty in the Middle East, Asadi lived in Amman, Jordan. In the course of his duties as ICE, Asadi attended a meeting, during which he was told by Iraqi governmental officials that GE had hired the close friend of a high Iraqi governmental figure. Asadi was told by these officials that the hiring was motivated by a desire to gain that official's support for a highly profitable partnership with the Iraqis that was being brokered at that time. Following what he considered to be the correct course of action, Asadi filed a report on this suspicious arrangement with his immediate superior and with the GE Energy ombudsman assigned to that area. Asadi was convinced that under the circumstances described by the Iraqi officials, the hiring of this individual ran afoul of the Foreign Corrupt Practices Act. Because he felt that he had followed proper protocol in filing his report, Asadi was taken aback by a negative employment evaluation he received shortly thereafter. Following this unfavorable evaluation, Asadi was pressured to leave his position as Iraqi Country Executive for GE and take a subordinate position with fewer duties and much less influence. Understandably, Asadi decided not to accept the demotion and continued in his role as the Iraqi Country Executive. One year after he had reported the suspect hiring to his supervisor, Asadi was terminated. (Well, his position as Iraqi Country Executive for GE was terminated, not Asadi himself.)

Following his firing, Asadi brought a lawsuit in the U.S. District Court for the Southern District of Texas, alleging that his termination was issued in violation of the whistleblower shield section of the Dodd–Frank Act. The GE attorneys immediately filed a Rule 12b6 motion, stating that Asadi's lawsuit failed to state claim for which relief could be granted. In arguing for a dismissal, GE claimed that Asadi was not a true whistleblower in the way the term was defined in the Dodd–Frank Act, and even if he were a whistleblower, the provisions of the act had no effect outside of the United States. The trial court ruled that GE was correct when it argued that the whistleblower provision had no effect outside the United States and dismissed the lawsuit with prejudice. Having reached this decision, the court excused itself from answering the question of whether Asadi was a true whistleblower.

Asadi filed an appeal with the Court of Appeals for the Fifth Circuit. The court of appeals began its analysis of the case by noting, without actually using the terms, that it would take a textualist rather than a purposive or a pragmatic approach to interpreting the statute. Accordingly, the court laid down the following axiom followed by two corollaries inherent in the textualist technique for statutory interpretation. The rule is "The preeminent canon of statutory interpretation requires us to 'presume that [the] legislature says in a statute what it means and means in a statute what it says.'" The two corollaries are: "In construing a statute, a court should give effect, if possible, to every word and every provision Congress used." And "Also, if possible, we interpret provisions of a statute in a manner that renders them compatible, not contradictory." Having done this, the court rendered the following analysis. The court began by looking at the exact language used by Congress to define "whistleblower." The Dodd–Frank Act defines whistleblower in retaliation cases as one who "provides" or "acting jointly" with others provides "information relating to a violation of the securities law to the Commission." (That "Commission" is, of course, the SEC.) Asadi counters by noting that while this definition may seem to limit the term "whistleblower" to those who report transgressions to the SEC, the anti-retaliation section of the same statute says that there will be no retaliation against those who make,

"disclosures that are required or protected under the Sarbanes-Oxley Act of 2002 . . . the Securities Exchange Act of 1934 . . . and any other law." No mention is made here of making a report to the SEC. Finally, Asadi points to a new SEC regulation that *expands the definition of whistleblower*. That regulation reads

> (1) For purposes of the anti-retaliation protections afforded by Section 21F(h)(1) of the Exchange Act (15 U.S.C. 78u-6(h)(1)), you are a whistleblower if:
>
> (i) You possess a reasonable belief that the information you are providing relates to a possible securities law violation (or, where applicable, to a possible violation of the provisions set forth in 18 U.S.C. 1514A(a)) that has occurred, is ongoing, or is about to occur, and;
>
> (ii) You provide that information in a manner described in Sec. 21F(h)(1)(A) of the Exchange Act (15 U.S.C. 78u-6(h)(1)(A)).

To unravel this problem, the appellate court judges, using textualism, must focus only on the words in the statute. In effect, the judges must act like poetic critics as they analyze the words themselves to determine their meaning. The question that they are trying to answer is, given the statutory language (and only that language), does the plaintiff qualify as a "whistleblower" in a retaliation case like this one? What do you think? Was Asadi a whistleblower and, therefore, entitled to protection against retaliation, or was he simple an informant entitled to no protection at all? Think about it. [See: *Asadi v. GE Energy (USA) L.L.C.*, No. 12-20522, U.S. Court of Appeals for the Fifth Circuit (October 8, 2013).]

Opening Case Questions

1. What is the objective of the Dodd–Frank Act? Explain.

2. What is a whistleblower under the terms of the Dodd–Frank Act? Explain.

3. What are textualism, purposivism, and pragmatism? Define each term.

4. In this case, did the appellate court judges use textualism, purposivism, or pragmatism? Explain.

5. Now, speculate on the judges response. What do you think they will decide? Explain.

Source: See: *Ritz v. Selma United Methodist Church*, 467 N.W.2d 266 (March 20, 1991).

Learning Objectives

1. Describe the birth of the strong central government that evolved in American politics.
2. Describe the source of state power to regulate business.
3. Explain how the Securities and Exchange Commission prevents unfair practices.
4. Explain *per se* antitrust violations of antitrust law.
5. Explain the rule-of-reason standard in antitrust law.
6. Outline the general provisions of all post–Sherman antitrust laws.
7. Define the various techniques of corporate expansion.
8. Contrast the roles of the Securities and Exchange Commission with that of the Federal Trade Commission in corporate expansion.
9. Identify the two ways that a corporation may undergo dissolution.
10. Explain the circumstances under which a limited liability company may undergo dissolution.

28-1 The Constitution and the Corporate Entity

Federal power to control commerce is found in the **commerce clause** of the U.S. Constitution. The commerce clause is located in Article I, Section 8, Clause 3, of the Constitution. Clause 3 states, "Congress shall have the Power . . . to regulate Commerce with foreign nations, and among the several States." At first glance the clause appears to be an attempt by the Framers to limit the power of the central government and, conversely, to enhance the ability of the states to regulate their own internal economic activity. However, from the very beginning the courts identified the central national government as the favored source of commercial regulatory power in the United States.

The Federal Power to Control Commerce

The federal power to control commerce in the United States appeared so early in our history that it seems to have been woven into the very fabric of the Constitution. In the case of *Gibbons v. Ogden*, 22 U.S. 1 (1824), the first major commerce case to land in the Supreme Court, the Court declared that congressional power to regulate commerce included not only the authority to control navigation, but also the power to regulate activities that occurred within a single state. Nor was the decision a close one. Five of the seven justices joined in the majority opinion. Moreover, of the two remaining justices, one was not involved in the case at any level, and the other, William Johnson, sought to extend, not limit, congressional power over all commerce. Using textual criticism, Johnson states quite clearly that

> [T]he plain and direct import of the words of the grant is consistent with this general understanding. The words of the Constitution are, "Congress shall have power to regulate commerce with foreign nations, and among the several States, and with the Indian tribes."
> It is not material, in my view of the subject, to inquire whether the article "a" or the should be prefixed to the word "power." Either or neither will produce the same result: if either, it is clear that the article "the" would be the proper one, since the next preceding grant of power is certainly exclusive, to-wit: "to borrow money on the credit of the United States."

While Johnson forswears the use of textualism, he nevertheless continues his argument by defining the word *power*, concluding that, "[t]he 'power to regulate commerce' here meant to be granted was that power to regulate commerce which previously existed in the States . . . The power of a sovereign state over commerce therefore amounts to nothing more than a power to limit and restrain . . . that . . . power must be exclusive; *it can reside but in one potentate*, and hence the grant of this power carries with it the whole subject, leaving nothing for the State to act upon." (Italics added.)

Over the next century or so, the Court generally avoided such explicit statements of full congressional power over commerce. However, in 1942 in the case of *Wickard v. Filburn*, the Court declared that the private use of wheat on a single family farm could be curtailed by the federal government. Still, the Court did manage to fashion a rationale to support this extension of power. The rationale focused on the real life problems of the American economy in the middle of the 20th century. The consumption of home-grown wheat seems to have been been the target of regulation because such consumption represented the most variable (and, therefore, the most volatile and, fortunately, most controllable) factor in the problem of the disappearing wheat crop in the U.S. at that time. In the majority opinion, the Court declared that the farmer's use of his own wheat on his own land to bake his own bread, nevertheless, affected interstate commerce. Taking all circumstances into account, the Court explained that, whenever any farmer uses his own wheat, he does not buy wheat in interstate commerce, thus weakening the entire interstate market. The justices emphasized that it was the cumulative effect of many such farmers that concerned them rather than the actions of a single farmer.

The Establishment of a Strong Central Government

The intent of the Framers to set up a strong federal government becomes clear when we place it within a proper historical context. We are generally accustomed to the childhood myth that the Framers were dedicated to individual freedom and personal liberty. As we saw in the early chapters of this book, however, the truth is almost entirely opposite to the myth. In Chapter 2, for example, we saw that James Madison, the undisputed father of the Constitution and one of the principal authors of the Bill of Rights, believed that the national government needed a free hand in determining most political questions and, therefore, could not risk contradiction from any factions, but especially factions within the states.

In addition, by 1787 on the eve of the Constitutional Convention, Madison was already campaigning for a strong central government. For example, in April 1787 Madison wrote a lengthy analysis of the Articles of Confederation in a statement titled, "Vices of the Political System of the United States." In "Vices," Madison outlines 11 such "vices," including the fact that, under the Articles of Confederation, Congress had no power to create uniform laws to regulate commerce on a national basis. Madison continued his campaign by writing private letters to Thomas Jefferson, Edmund Randolph, and George Washington. In these letters, written during March and April 1787, Madison announced his support for a unified system of federal laws to regulate trade, a federal veto by which Congress could void statutes passed by the state legislatures, and a strong central system under which the national government could force the states to do its bidding. [See: Richard K. Matthews, *If Men Were Angels: James Madison and the Heartless Empire of Reason* (Lawrence: University Press of Kansas, 1995), pp. 177–190.]

Nor was Madison alone in his convictions. Many of the delegates to the Constitutional Convention harbored similar concerns about the old system. For example, in his book, *An Economic Interpretation of the Constitution of the United States*, Charles Beard of Columbia University and Barnard College tells us that, in 1785, two years before the Constitutional Convention, several key entrepreneurs, including Thomas Fitzsimons and George Clymer, both of whom became delegates to the Constitutional Convention in Philadelphia, sent a lengthy statement to the Pennsylvania legislature in which they complained that, under the Articles of Confederation, Congress lacked "full and entire power over the commerce of the United States." In essence, they were supporting federalism, even if they did not yet use the word. Once this support for federalism is recognized as the pervading sentiment of the Framers, many of the puzzles within the Constitution, puzzles like the growth of congressional power in issues of commerce, corporate law, securities regulation, and antitrust law, for example, become quite clear. Separating myth from reality is important in the study of corporate law because, despite lip service to the opposite view, corporate law in this country is dominated (but not completely conquered) by the federal government. The states do retain some power, which is properly referred to as *residual power*, over commerce and corporate law. [See: Charles Beard, *An Economic Interpretation of the Constitution of the United States* (Mineola, NY: Dover Publications, 2004), pp. 40–41.]

Residual State Power over Commerce and Corporate Law

Despite the overwhelming power of the federal government in the regulation of corporate commercial activity, the states still retain some residual power in this arena. The power of the states to regulate commerce comes from a state's police power. **Police power** is the state's authority to restrict private rights to promote and maintain public health, safety, welfare, and morals. A state has police power simply by virtue of its existence as a legitimate governmental authority. The state government and the various subdivisions of the state government, from counties to cities to school boards to zoning districts, all play some role in the regulatory process. For example, the state grants incorporation status to corporate promoters and requires those promoters to appoint agents for the service of process. The state also collects incorporation fees, taxes corporate activities, regulates the assignment of corporate names, polices the actions of corporate managers, oversees corporate dissolutions, and creates new corporate entities, such as limited liability companies, franchises, and joint ventures. The states also police the assignment of permission for foreign and alien corporations to operate within the borders of the home state.

State Legislative Power: The Model Business Corporation Act

The states have the power to regulate business under their inherent police power, a power that, while less extensive than the constitutional power of the federal government does, nevertheless, have its place. As noted in Chapter 26, a corporation is a legal person created under the authority of a state or federal statute that gives certain individuals the capacity to operate an enterprise. Most states have contributed to a multi-state effort at establishing uniformity in corporate law by adopting the Model Business Corporation Act (MBCA), often referred to as the Model Corporation Act. The MBCA is a relatively young statute and is, therefore, not quite as settled as older, more traditional statutes, such as the Uniform Commercial Code and the original Uniform Partnership Act. In addition, the model act has been revised since its original inception, making some of its provisions even more recent and therefore less fully developed than similar provisions in other comparable statutes.

Judicial Power: Common Law Cases

Also, the common law tradition permeates the cases of many states in relation to the corporate person. While many of these cases are preempted when a state legislature adopts the MBCA, some state courts are understandably reluctant to surrender long-term common law principles and sometimes have found creative ways to interpret the MBCA within the context of that state's long-standing legal tradition. Therefore, the study of corporate law must always be tempered by a look at the state law of the jurisdiction in which a dispute is located. The process of doing business as a self-governing business association, that is, as a corporate person, is called **associative corporativism**, or simply **corporativism**.

Residual State Power

In the 19th century, each corporation was individually created by a unique legislative enactment. Moreover, the incorporation process did not follow the routine steps that are tracked today. On the contrary, each corporate entity had to be approved by the state legislature and that approval was sometimes at risk, as lengthy deliberations were conducted in the legislature to determine whether to accept this or reject that incorporation request. Each corporation had its own charter that outlined the powers and abilities of that corporation. Moreover, the officers and directors who managed the corporation could not step outside the carefully drawn bounds of that power and, if they did, the corporate charter could be revoked. Corporate managers who did exceed their authority were said to be operating *ultra vires*—that is, beyond their legal powers. Moreover, even if the corporation was never targeted for dissolution, the life of the corporation was limited to a set number of years as stated in the charter. [See: "Our Hidden History of Corporations in the United States," *Reclaim Democracy*, http://reclaimdemocracy.org/corporate-accountability-history-corporations-us/; and Robert Charles Clark, "The Meaning of Corporate Personality," *Corporate Law* (Boston: Little, Brown, and Company, 1986), pp. 675-676.]

Corporate Law in Delaware As corporate activity changed, state law changed along with it. However, the most revolutionary changes did not emerge until the waning years of the 19th century, specifically with the advent of Delaware's 1899 state corporate law statute. The Delaware statute was based on a corporate law statute in New Jersey. However, Delaware liberalized its law far beyond that of New Jersey's older law. For example, with the exception of banking, a Delaware corporation was permitted to conduct any legal business activity. Delaware incorporators were given the choice of setting a limited number of years for the existence of their corporation or accepting perpetual existence. A Delaware corporation was permitted to carry out business activities anywhere on the planet, to issue a variety of classes of stocks, to alter its charter, to unite with other corporations, to purchase other stock issued by other corporate entities, and to conduct director and shareholder meetings outside Delaware. In addition, the incorporation fee and corporate taxes were negligible, at least when compared to other states.

As a direct result of this relaxation in corporate law, out-of-state corporate promoters flocked to Delaware to incorporate (see Chapter 26). Today, most states have recognized Delaware's advantage and refashioned their corporate laws to mimic the perks that were granted by Delaware to potential incorporators. Nevertheless, Delaware still holds the advantage. Even today, the number of corporations that identify Delaware as their place of incorporation is astronomical. It is for that reason that most corporate case law that exists in the state courts today is found in Delaware. Moreover, more than anything else, Delaware corporate law focuses on the actions of the managers (officers and directors alike), and most of that activity involves the buying and selling of corporations. Also, the key focus of those decisions is on director responsibility and the primary vehicle for maintaining corporate objectivity is protecting the independent director corps. [See: Joel Seligman, "A Brief History of Delaware's General Corporation Law of 1899," *Delaware Journal of Corporate Law* 1, no. 2 (1976); and Steven Davidoff Solomon, "The Long Reach if Delaware's Corporate Influence," *The New York Times*, December 11, 2014, p. F2.]

Did You Know?

Since the Constitution was ratified, more than 10,000 amendments have been proposed by Congress. Despite all this activity, only 27 amendments have been ratified.

quick quiz 28-1

1. Federal power to control commerce is found in the commerce clause of the U.S. Constitution.   true | false
2. In Gibbons v. Ogden, the Supreme Court declared that congressional power to regulate commerce included the authority to control navigation and the power to regulate activities that occurred within a single state.   true | false
3. A state has police power only if that power is expressly granted to the state government in the state constitution.   true | false

28-2 Securities Regulation of the Corporate Entity

Two pieces of federal legislation that affect business are the Securities Act of 1933 and the Securities Exchange Act of 1934 (see Table 28-1). The primary purpose of these acts is to protect business investors by making certain that they are informed about the securities they purchase. The independent regulatory agency that carries out this function is the Securities and Exchange Commission (SEC). The SEC regulates the issuance of securities by corporations and partnerships. A **security** has been defined as a monetary investment that expects a return solely because of another person's efforts. As the following example demonstrates, a security is a security even if it is called something else.

> **EXAMPLE 28-1:** A Security by Any Other Name
>
> Osgood Minerals Inc. had to raise an enormous amount of capital quickly. One of the directors devised a scheme whereby Osgood would sell to investors parcels of land owned by the corporation and used for mining purposes. In return, the investors would be entitled to a return on their investment. The return would be calculated in relation to the amount of land owned by each investor. To avoid having to comply with SEC regulations, Osgood labeled each sale a land contract rather than a security. Because the sales were land contracts, Osgood argued, it did not have to follow SEC regulations. The SEC disagreed and brought suit to stop the sale of unregulated securities. The court held that because each investor's profits would be derived solely from the efforts of others, the investments were securities and therefore subject to SEC regulations.

Table 28-1 Securities and Antitrust Regulations

Regulation	Explanation
Securities Regulation	
Securities Act of 1933	Regulates the issuance of new securities
Securities Exchange Act of 1934	Established the Securities and Exchange Commission; act deals with subsequent trading in securities
Dodd–Frank Act Title VII	Title VII now requires that certain swaps be registered with the SEC and that they comply with certain principles enumerated in the act
Dodd–Frank Act Title IX	Title IX creates the Office of Investor Advocate and authorizes the office to appoint an ombudsman; improves the regulation of credit rating institutions; alters the use of asset-backed securities; improves shareholder democracy; and enhances whistleblowing opportunities
Antitrust Regulation	
Sherman Antitrust Act	Prohibits contracts, combinations in restraint of trade; also prohibits monopolies, attempts to monopolize, and conspiracies to monopolize
Clayton Act	Prohibits specific practices such as tying agreements and interlocking directorates
Robinson–Patman Act	Deals with product pricing, advertising, and promotional allowances
Federal Trade Commission Act	Established the Federal Trade Commission

Securities Act of 1933

The Securities Act of 1933 regulates the issuance of new securities by corporations and partnerships. Offers of securities by mail or through interstate or foreign commerce must be registered with the SEC. A registration statement and a prospectus must be filed with the SEC. A *registration statement* contains detailed information about the corporation, including data about its management, capitalization, and financial condition. A *prospectus* contains much of the same information but in a condensed and simplified form. The registration statement is designed for the experts at the SEC, whereas the prospectus is designed for potential investors.

The Securities and Exchange Commission regulates the issuance of securities by corporations and partnerships and assures that the public is protected by enforcing mandatory reporting requirements and other 1933 and 1934 Act mandates.
©Mark Wilson/Getty Images

Securities Exchange Act of 1934

The Securities Exchange Act of 1934, which actually established the SEC, deals with the subsequent trading in securities. It requires periodic reports of financial information concerning registered securities, and it prohibits manipulative and deceptive actions in the sale and purchase of securities. The act prohibits insiders, including officers and directors, from realizing profit from any purchase and sale of securities within any period of less than six months. The courts have held that insiders are not permitted to trade on information until that information has been made available to the public.

According to Section 14 (a) of the 1934 act, shareholders, including majority shareholders, who solicit proxies (see Chapter 27) must also follow strict reporting requirements. The SEC requires a written proxy solicitation to include the identity of the individual or individuals seeking the proxy, any potential conflicts of interest, and specific information about any corporate changes to be voted on. When management solicits proxies, the solicitation must also include information about management salaries. The SEC regulations also state quite specifically that all material information must be stated in readable language and be displayed prominently, rather than buried in small type somewhere in the back of the document. The regulations also explicitly forbid false or misleading information.

Dodd–Frank Wall Street Reform and Consumer Protection Act

In Chapter 20, we learned that, in response to the 21st-century financial crisis, Congress passed several pieces of legislation, including the *Dodd-Frank Wall Street and Consumer Protection Act*, aimed at fixing current economic problems and preventing such events from happening again in the future. The problems that we discussed in Chapter 20 were related to mortgages. The mortgage industry, however, was only part of the problem. Another industry involved in the crisis was the securities industry. For that reason, Congress also included provisions in the Dodd-Frank Act to deal with the shortcomings and the errors of the securities industry. As might be expected, the Dodd–Frank Act is long, involved, and complicated. It is divided into 16 different titles, many of which are named as individual acts. Two titles that affect the Securities Exchange Commission are Title VII, the Wall Street Transparency and Accountability Act, and Title IX, the Investor Protection and Securities Reform Act of 2010.

Financial institutions on Wall Street have come under increased regulation and scrutiny due to their reckless practices.
©Brand X Pictures/ PunchStock

The Wall Street Transparency and Accountability Act

The 21st-century financial crisis was caused in part by the reckless use of a financial instrument known as the derivative. A *derivative* (sometimes called a derivative contract and sometimes a derivative instrument) is a financial tool whose value emerges from a variable item, such as an interest rate, a stock index, or a commodity like fuel or crops. Derivatives can be used to manage risk as long as they are handled properly. In contrast, the misuse of derivatives can be disastrous, as was demonstrated during the 21st-century financial crisis. A **swap transaction** (or simply, a **swap**) is a derivative that is made in an over-the-counter market. The SEC has the power to regulate security-based swaps that are traded on the exchanges. According to the SEC, **security-based swaps** are "swaps based on (1) a single security, (2) a loan, (3) a narrow-based group or index of securities, or (4) events relating to a single issuer or issuers of securities in a narrow-based security index." The problem has been that, before Title VII of Dodd-Frank, referred to officially as the Wall Street Transparency and Accountability Act, the swap process was not well regulated. There was little or no transparency before, during, or after such transactions. Originally Dodd-Frank required that certain swap transactions comply with principles enumerated in the act. For example, the law required that banks place certain swaps into divisions that are not covered by federal insurance programs and that are prevented from applying to the Federal Reserve Bank for loans in a crisis. The goal of these limitations was to insulate the taxpayers from being victimized by the type of governmental bailouts that occurred in 2008. The SEC and its sister regulating body, the Commodity Futures Trading Commission, have the power to make rules in consultation with one another on the swaps over which each agency has jurisdiction. [See: "SEC Proposes Rules for Securities-Based Swap Execution Facilities," U.S. Securities and Exchange Commission, February 2, 2011, https://www.sec.gov/news/press/2011/2011-35.htm; and Marl Jickling and Kathleen Ann Ruane, "The Dodd-Frank Wall Street Reform and Consumer Protection Act: Title VII Derivatives," *Congressional Research Service,* August 30, 2010, pp. i, 1-2. See also: Victoria McGrane, "A Primer on Derivatives Provision Banks Seek," *The Wall Street Journal*, December 11, 2014, p. A4.]

Changes in the Dodd-Frank Act Some critics of the Dodd-Frank Act have long maintained that the swap limitation provisions discussed earlier actually threaten to cause more harm than good. These limitations, they argue, do not actually stop the swap process as intended. Instead, the provisions force those who configure swaps to utilize entities that are almost untouched by federal oversight provisions and, as a result, are not as well understood even by those who actually regulate them. Consequently, the provisions have merely shifted the risks to those investors who are involved in the swaps, rather than eliminating them. These same opponents also point to an increase in the cost of doing business that has resulted from implementing these provisions. Some experts also insist that these restrictions make it more difficult for American banks to compete with foreign banks that face no such limits. Those in favor of maintaining the swap limitation provisions argue that the goal is to prevent a repeat of the disastrous investments that led to the 2008 crisis and placed an undue burden on ordinary taxpayers, who bore the weight of the bailout provisions. Whatever the case, these changes were implemented as a rider to the 2015 spending bill passed by Congress in 2014. In effect, the rider to the spending bill repealed the Dodd-Frank provision requiring banks to place certain swaps in divisions that are not covered by federal insurance programs. [See: McGrane, "A Primer on Derivatives Provision Banks Seek"; and Victoria McGrane, "Swap Talk: Why Are People Fighting Over Dodd-Frank and Derivatives?" *The Wall Street Journal: Washington Wire*, December 10, 2014, http://blogs.wsj.com/washwire/2014/12/10/swap-talk-why-are-people-fighting-over-dodd-frank-and-derivatives/. See also "Dodd-Frank's 'Swaps Push-out Provision' Repealed in Omnibus Bill," *biz570.com: Northeast Pennsylvania Business Journal,* January 7, 2015, http://biz570.com/economy/dodd-frank-s-swaps-push-out-provision-repealed-inomnibus-bill-1.1810394.]

Title IX Investor Protection and Securities Reform Act The second area that Dodd-Frank now regulates more directly involves the day-to-day activities of corporations. Under Title IX, which is also known as the Investor Protection and Securities Reform Act, the rules governing the SEC have been revised so that the agency can better monitor the areas under its jurisdiction and provide more effective protection for investors. The act does several things: creates the Office of Investor Advocate and authorizes the office to appoint an ombudsman, improves the regulation of credit rating institutions, alters the use of asset-backed securities, improves shareholder democracy, and enhances whistleblowing opportunities.

The Office of Investor Advocate Subtitle A of Title IX of the Dodd-Frank Act creates a new agency, referred to as the **Office of Investor Advocate (OIA)**, the purpose of which is to help make the work of broker-dealers and investment advisors (IAs) more transparent. The law also gives the SEC the power to make new regulations that will define the fiduciary relationship between IAs and broker-dealers, on the one hand, and their clients, on the other. Section A also empowers the OIA to appoint an ombudsman and reactivates the Investor Advisory Committee, which was originally authorized in 2009.

Regulation of Credit Rating Institutions Subtitle C of Title IX authorizes the SEC to develop a new agency known as the **Office of Credit Ratings**, the purpose of which is to watch those organizations that issue credit ratings. These organizations, known in the industry as nationally recognized statistical rating organizations (NRSROs) are key elements in the financial structure of the U.S. economy because they open or close the door on the ability of investors and borrowers to enter the marketplace. Section C provides for better internal controls that will eliminate conflicts of interest and promote the reporting of irregularities, among other things.

Asset-Backed Securities Subtitle D of Title IX of Dodd-Frank mandates more effective control over the issuance of asset-backed securities. Securitization became an issue during the 21st-century financial crisis because many institutions that issued asset-backed securities sold them almost immediately. This meant that they were unconcerned about the borrower's ability to pay back the loan. To minimize the risks associated with this practice, the new law requires institutions that engage in securitization to maintain an economic stake in the assets that they securitize. More specifically, the rules now state that institutions issuing asset-backed securities must keep a minimum of 5 percent of the credit risk, although there are exceptions to this rule built into the law [See: Section 941, Regulation of Credit Risk Retention, Selected Sections of the Dodd-Frank Wall Street Reform and Consumer Act, Federal Deposit Insurance Corporation, December 8, 2011, https://www.fdic.gov/regulations/reform/dfa_selections.html#1.]

Shareholder Democracy One of the primary goals of Title IX of the Dodd-Frank Act is to enhance shareholder democracy (see Chapter 27). Recall that shareholder democracy demands that the shareholders of a corporation have more input into the decision-making process of the corporation, specifically as those decisions relate to the board of directors. To improve shareholder democracy, the following changes have been mandated by the act. The SEC is now required to make rules to ensure that shareholders have a continuing opportunity to review executive compensation. Moreover, the act specifically permits the shareholders to review and reject golden parachute contracts with executives. A **golden parachute** is a compensation package that protects executives who might lose their positions following a merger or consolidation, and so on. The SEC is also authorized to make new regulations that will empower shareholders to use management proxies to nominate board members in election contest. [See: David S. Huntington, "Summary of Dodd-Frank Financial Regulation Legislation," *The Harvard Law Forum on Corporate Governance and Financial Regulation*, July 7, 2010; and "Brief Summary of the Dodd-Frank Wall Street Reform and Consumer Protection Act," U.S. Senate Committee on Banking, Housing, and Urban Affairs, http://banking.senate.gov/public.]

Whistleblowing Enhancement Perhaps the most controversial provision included in the new act is Subtitle B of Title IX, which permits the SEC to make regulations that will improve its enforcement powers by establishing rules to implement a "whistleblowing bounty" program analogous to the one that the IRS implemented in 2006. Whistleblowers, or SEC "bounty hunters," as they are sometimes called, must meet certain minimum requirements to qualify for their "bounty." For instance, it is necessary that the evidence provided by a bounty hunter concern a security law violation and include original information. (Apparently, *original* in this situation means that the SEC did not have the new evidence until the friendly neighborhood bounty hunter showed up.) Bounty hunting can be a very lucrative enterprise. Successful hunters can pull in somewhere between 10 and 30 percent of a sanction that is over $1 million. Because such well-paid rewards can be an irresistible temptation to some, cautionary steps must be taken to prevent would-be bounty hunters from reporting unsubstantiated accusations and then racing to the SEC for their "bounty" payments. Naturally, there is some disagreement about the best way to police the whistleblowing process. Some experts argue that whistleblowing bounty hunters should be required to exhaust internal remedies before going to the SEC. These experts contend that because such reporting mechanisms are required, it makes sense to compel whistleblowers to go through those reporting systems first. On the other hand, those attorneys who have whistleblowing clients argue that such internal remedies are rarely, if ever, effective because the people who receive the complaints work for and report to the people accused in the complaint. This would be a little like requiring mugging victims to talk to a mugger's accomplice before going to the police, or so the argument goes. Also, as the following case illustrates, exhausting internal remedies is not enough to qualify as a whistleblower. Potential whistleblowers must also report transgressions to the SEC. Otherwise, under the law, as strange as it may seem, they are not really whistleblowers. [See: Whistleblower Program, U.S. Securities and Exchange Commission, 2011, https://www.sec.gov/spotlight/dodd-frank/whistleblower.shtml; David Ingram, "SEC Weighing How to Award Tipsters," *The National Law Journal*, May 16, 2011, pp. 1 and 4; *Egan v. TradingScreen, Inc.*, 10 Civ. 8202 (LBS), U.S. District Court for the Southern District of New York (2011); and *Asadi v. GE Energy (USA) L.L.C.*, No. 12-20522, U.S. Court of Appeals for the Fifth Circuit (October 8, 2013).]

THE OPENING CASE *Round 2*
Textualism, Purposivism, Pragmatism, Whistleblowers, and the Dodd-Frank Act

Recall that in the Opening Case, Khaled Asadi (Asadi) was employed by GE Energy (GE) as the Iraqi Country Executive (ICE). While attending a meeting, Asadi learned that GE had hired the friend of a high-ranking Iraqi official. Asadi's sources at the meeting reported that GE had hired in order to gain leverage with that official so that he would support a highly profitable partnership that GE was engineering with the Iraqis. Convinced that this tactic violated the Foreign Corrupt Practices Act, Asadi filed a report with his immediate superior and with the GE Energy ombudsman who was assigned to that area. Because he felt that he had followed proper protocol in filing his report, Asadi was surprised by a negative employment evaluation he received shortly thereafter. Some time after this, Asadi was pressured to resign his post as Iraqi Country Executive and accept a less attractive position with much less influence. Asadi refused to be intimidated into accepting the demotion and continued working as the Iraqi Country Executive. One year after he had reported the hiring problem to his supervisor, Asadi lost his job.

Not to be outdone, Asadi sued his former employer in the U.S. District Court for the Southern District of Texas on the grounds that his discharge violated the whistleblower protection provisions of the Dodd–Frank Act. In response, GE lawyers filed a Rule 12b6 motion stating that Asadi's lawsuit failed to state claim for which relief could be granted. In arguing for a dismissal, GE claimed that Asadi was not a whistleblower as defined in the Dodd–Frank Act. Moreover, even if Asadi were a whistleblower, these provisions of the act had no effect outside of the United States. The trial court ruled that GE was correct when it argued that the whistleblower provision was ineffective outside the United States and dismissed the lawsuit with prejudice. The court then saw no reason to address the question of whether Asadi was a true whistleblower. Asadi filed an appeal with the Court of Appeals for the Fifth Circuit.

The court of appeals began its analysis of the case by noting, without actually using the terms, that it would take a textualist rather than either a purposive or a pragmatic approach to interpreting the statute. Accordingly, the court laid down an axiom, followed by two corollaries inherent in the textualist technique for statutory interpretation. Remember, the axiom states, "The preeminent canon of statutory interpretation requires us to 'presume that [the] legislature says in a statute what it means and means in a statute what it says.'" The two corollaries are: "In construing a statute, a court should give effect, if possible, to every word and every provision Congress used." And "Also, if possible, we interpret provisions of a statute in a manner that renders them compatible, not contradictory." Having done this, the court rendered the following analysis. The court began by looking at the exact language used by Congress to define "whistleblower." The definition of whistleblower in the statute says that: "[t]he term 'whistleblower' means any individual who provides, or 2 or more individuals acting jointly who provide, information relating to a violation of the securities laws to *the Commission*, in a manner established, by rule or regulation, by the Commission" (italics added). 15 U.S.C. § 78u-6. Assuming that "[the] legislature says in a statute what it means and means in a statute what it says," a whistleblower is someone who reports illegal activity to the SEC itself. Because Asadi made his report internally and not to the SEC, he is not a whistleblower and is, therefore, not entitled to protection against retaliation.

Asadi countered by noting that the antiretaliation section of the Dodd–Frank Act forbids retaliation against those who make, "disclosures that are required or protected under the Sarbanes-Oxley Act of 2002 . . . the Securities Exchange Act of 1934 . . . including section 10A(m) of such Act . . . and any other law." This time the court applied the first corollary, which reads, "In construing a statute, a court should give effect, if possible, to *every word and every provision Congress used*" (italics added). Given this rule, the court cannot ignore the words in the opening sentence of the section that Asadi relied upon. This opening sentence reads, "No employer may discharge, demote, suspend, threaten, harass, directly or indirectly, or in any other manner discriminate against, a *whistleblower* in the terms and conditions of employment because of any lawful act done by the *whistleblower*—." Because that opening sentence makes it quite clear that the antiretaliation provision applies to whistleblowers as defined in the act, Asadi still would not qualify as a whistleblower. Finally Asadi argued that, in a new regulation, the SEC redefined whistleblower in the following way:

(1) For purposes of the anti-retaliation protections afforded by Section 21F(h)(1) of the Exchange Act (15 U.S.C. 78u-6(h)(1)), you are a whistleblower if:

(i) You possess a reasonable belief that the information you are providing relates to a possible securities law violation (or, where applicable, to a possible violation of the provisions set forth in 18 U.S.C. 1514A(a)) that has occurred, is ongoing, or is about to occur, and;

(ii) You provide that information in a manner described in Sec. 21F(h)(1)(A) of the Exchange Act (15 U.S.C. 78u-6(h)(1)(A)).

This time the court applied the second and final corollary: "Also, if possible, we interpret provisions of a statute in a manner that renders them compatible, not contradictory." The regulation defines "whistleblower" in a way that contradicts the statutory definition. Because the two definitions contradict one another, one of them must go. The court has no difficulty ruling that the definition written by Congress supersedes the definition written by the SEC. Simply stated, the court said that in fashioning this overbroad definition of whistleblower, the SEC had exceeded its authority. Only Congress can change something as fundamental as the definition of a key word in a duly authorized statute. Therefore, once again, Asadi did not qualify as a whistleblower. In conclusion, to unravel this problem, the appellate court judges, using the textualism, focused only on the words in the statute—period. In effect, the judges acted like poetic critics as they analyzed the words in the statute to determine their meaning. It is as simple as that. [See: *Asadi v. GE Energy (USA) L.L.C.*, No. 12-20522, U.S. Court of Appeals for the Fifth Circuit (October 8, 2013).]

Source: See: *Asadi v. GE Energy (USA) L.L.C.*, No. 12-20522, United States Court of Appeals for the Fifth Circuit (October 8, 2013).

A QUESTION OF ETHICS

Whistleblowing from Another Angle

Despite (or perhaps because of) the plaintiff's unsuccessful attempt to be identified as a whistleblower in the Opening Case, whistleblower vindication is still very much a part of the American legal system. A case in point is the multi-million-dollar whistleblower settlement in the lawsuits filed against the Bank of America, which ended up paying a $170 million penalty to four whistleblowers who filed suits against the bank for selling defective mortgage loans and for overvaluing mortgage properties, all of which contributed to the birth of the 21st-century financial crisis. The four record-breaking whistleblower rewards were part of a larger settlement package that was included within a variety of individual cases filed against Bank of America for financial wrongdoing.

One of the lawsuits was filed by an ex-employee of a Bank of America affiliate, Land-Safe Appraisal Services, after his work time was reduced in reaction to his reservations about the possibility that borrowers and investors would be invited to purchase inflated properties. Another complaint was issued by an employee of Countrywide Financial Corp. (another company owned by the Bank of America), who reported that Fannie Mae and Freddie Mac were actually sold defective mortgages by the bank. A third allegation from another Countrywide Financial employee indicated that the Bank of America affiliate had routinely produced mortgage loans that were hugely undervalued. The program uncovered and reported by this third employee was nicknamed the Hustle because it systematically eliminated checkpoints and evaluation processes that slowed loan approvals and rewarded brokers based on the number, rather than the quality, of the loans that they pushed through the system. The goal of the program, which was also christened the High Speed Swim Lane (HSSL), was not to produce solid mortgage loans, but to increase Countrywide's bottom line. Fannie Mae and Freddie Mac then purchased the bad loans, which collapsed because the mortgagees defaulted on their payments. Reports indicate that 57 percent of the Countrywide HSSL loans ended badly. Bank of America got into the act when it purchased a company it thought had the Midas touch, only to discover that Countrywide's success rate was a sham from day one. A fourth whistleblower case features a New Jersey mortgage company named Mortgage Now, which complained that the Federal Housing Authority had received loans from Bank of America for which the values were badly distorted.

All told, at the end of the day, Bank of America paid a $16.65 billion penalty, which included the whistleblower settlement of $1 billion, $170 million of which was parceled out to the whistleblowers themselves. [See: Christina Rexrode and Timothy Martin, "Whistleblowers Score Big," *The Wall Street Journal*, December 20–21, 2014, pp. B1–B2; and Kevin McCoy and Julie Schmit, "Jury: BofA Liable for Countrywide Mortgage Fraud," *USA Today*, October 23, 2013, http://www.usatoday.com/story/money/business/2013/10/23/bank-of-america-countrywide-mortgage-fraud/3172797/.]

QUESTIONS YET UNANSWERED

The following questions have not yet been answered. Before you consider each question, turn to Chapter 1 to review the various ethical theories noted there (market value ethics, social contract theory, utilitarianism, and rational ethics). Then, using one of those theories in a consistent way, answer the following questions.

1. Is it ethical for the courts to award such enormous amounts of money in whistleblowing cases?
2. Do you believe that justice was done in the Bank of America case? Explain.
3. Would you change the decision in this case? Explain.
4. Is whistleblowing in general an ethical practice or does it encourage betrayal and entrapment? Explain.

Source: See: Christina Rexrode and Timothy Martin, "Whistleblowers Score Big," *The Wall Street Journal*, December 20-21, 2014, pp. B1–B2; and Kevin McCoy and Julie Schmit, "Jury: BofA Liable for Countrywide Mortgage Fraud," *USA Today*, October 23, 2013, http://www.usatoday.com/story/money/business/2013/10/23/bank-of-america-countrywide-mortgage-fraud/3172797/.

Jumpstart Our Business Startups Act of 2012 The Jumpstart Our Business Startups Act of 2012 is a relatively new federal law designed to empower small businesses to raise capital more efficiently, economically, and effectively. Known affectionately as the JOBS Act, the new law is supposed to improve the job market by encouraging the expansion of small businesses that operate primarily at the local level. Aimed at streamlining some of the more detailed and problematic provisions of securities laws, the JOBS Act helps make the task of raising capital for business development more manageable and less demanding for small firms. Specifically, the JOBS act created a new class of business startups referred to in the law as emerging growth companies (EGCs). This new classification eases the initial public offering process for businesses that qualify under the act. To qualify as an EGC, a business must have recorded total gross revenues under $1 billion at the end of the most recent fiscal year. A firm that qualifies as an ESC can process an initial public offering registration statement through the Securities and Exchange Commission for a private review on a confidential basis. In keeping with the overall intent of the act and to make processing less onerous, the law requires an EGC to submit only two, rather than three, years of financials to the SEC. Before filing, an EGC can also explore financing options with qualified institutional buyers and institutional accredited investors. EGCs are also spared certain management and transparency requirements, such as revealing any ties between executive pay and financial performance, as well certain auditing requirements in place under Sarbanes–Oxley Act. The JOBS Act was amended in 2015 under terms found in the Fixing America's Surface Transportation Act (FAST Act). The amendment includes provisions that ease the timing requirements for an EGC's initial public offering registration statement, adds a grace period to cover any EGC that loses its EGC status during its IPO, and eases the burden of certain disclosure requirements. [See: Anna Pinedo, "A Quick Guide to the JOBS Act," Morrison and Foster, LLP, Practical Law Company, 2012, https://media2.mofo.com/documents/120416-pli-quick-guide-jobs-act.pdf; and "President Obama Signs FAST Act, Codifying a New Resale Exemption and Creating Additional Accommodations for EGCs," *Thomson Reuters, Practical Law*, December 14, 2015, https://content.next.westlaw.com/Document/I1b748dc9995911e598dc8b09b4f043e0/View/FullText.html?originationContext=document&transitionType=DocumentItem&contextData=(sc.Default).]

The SEC's Newest Regulation to Prevent Global Financial Collapse In response to several interruptions in various elements within the global financial trading system (read here, the National Association of Securities Dealers Automated Quotations, or Nasdaq, among others, for example), the Securities and Exchange Commission recently implemented a new collection of standards, designated Regulation Systems Compliance and Integrity rules (REG SCI) to short-circuit such potential interruptions in the future. The rules are designed to motivate stock exchanges and other designated trading systems to implement an assembly of protocols, including tighter cyber-security procedures, which will stabilize those systems and, theoretically, at least, immunize them from the types of disturbances which, of late, have threatened the entire economic trading network.

In particular, under the new regulations, all trading networks designated under the rules (there is a brief list of such entities, referred to as SCI entities, in the regulations) have been ordered to draw up written protocols, based on parameters established by the SEC, that will ensure that its systems (designated in the regulations as both its *SCI systems* and its *indirect SCI systems*) remain functioning in the face of a crisis. (*Note: SCI systems* include those operations that control trading and several other key SCI entity functions, while *indirect SCI systems* are those systems not related to trading, but that would cause problems for the SCI entity should they be compromised.) Moreover, should a crisis occur, each SCI entity must be prepared to (1) identify the cause of the crisis and fix it while, at the same time, ensuring that the trading system continues to operate and that investors are protected; (2) inform the SEC of the crisis at the time it occurs and keep the agency posted as events unfold;

(3) prepare and submit a concluding report on the incident; and (4) keep the members of the SCI entity's network notified about the incident.

Additional duties include, but are not limited to, performing a yearly review of the SCI entity's adherence to REG SCI requirements; transmitting a copy of that review to entity's upper executives, its board of directors, and the SEC; testing the operational readiness of its protocols, each year, in conjunction with the testing of other SCI entities; compiling a quarterly report on any alterations in its SCI systems; and composing a quarterly report on the safety and stability of its indirect SCI systems. Whether the requirements established under REG SCI are effective remains to be seen. Some critics applaud the effort but declare that the parameters of its control are too limited to deal with the entire problem. In fact, some pundits argue that the SEC's net of authority under REG SCI has been cast in shallow water. More specifically, while key trading networks like the New York Stock Exchange and Nasdaq are included, other large networks are not. Some critics also lament the fact that the SEC has yet to publicly issue a directory of those entities required to follow REG SCI. [See: Regulation Systems Compliance and Integrity, Securities and Exchange Commission, 17 CFR Parts 240, 242, and 240, https://www.sec.gov/rules/final/2014/34-73639.pdf; Annette Nazareth, "SEC Adopts Regulation SCI to Strengthen Securities Market Infrastructure," *Harvard Law School Forum on Corporate Governance and Financial Regulation*, 2015, https://corpgov.law.harvard.edu/2015/01/07/sec-adopts-regulation-sci-to-strengthen-securities-market-infrastructure/; and Gretchen Morgenson, "S.S.C. Cyber Rules Are Falling Short," *The New York Times*, September 24, 2017, Business, pp. 1 and 3.]

quick quiz 28-2

1. The Securities and Exchange Commission regulates the issuance of securities by corporations and partnerships. — true | false
2. The Securities Exchange Act of 1934 actually established the Securities and Exchange Commission. — true | false
3. Under the Securities Exchange Act of 1934, majority shareholders are exempt from proxy solicitation reporting requirements. — true | false

28-3 Antitrust Regulation of the Corporate Entity

Both the federal government and the states have antitrust laws to preserve the values of competition and to discourage monopolies. A **monopoly** is the exclusive control of a market by a business enterprise. At the federal level, the four principal antitrust statutes are the Sherman Antitrust Act, the Clayton Act, the Robinson–Patman Act, and the Federal Trade Commission Act.

Sherman Antitrust Act

The Sherman Antitrust Act (1890) prohibits contracts, combinations, and conspiracies in restraint of trade. It also prohibits monopolization, attempts to monopolize, and combinations or conspiracies to monopolize any part of interstate or foreign commerce. Violations of the Sherman Antitrust Act must involve at least two parties acting together. The courts use three standards to judge antitrust offenses: the per se violation standard, the rule-of-reason standard, and the quick-look standard. The three tests, however, sometimes represent moving targets that are easy to articulate but difficult to implement in a consistent and fair fashion.

The *Per Se* Standard Some restraint-of-trade practices are so serious that they are prohibited, whether or not they harm anyone. These practices are labeled *per se* **violations**, which means that the practice is so contrary to antitrust policy that harm is presumed and the practice is prohibited. For example, price fixing is inherently unreasonable and therefore considered a *per se* violation. An agreement between competitors to divide territories among themselves to minimize competition would also be unlawful, even if the agreement helps the parties compete against other parties outside the agreement. Similar unlawful activities include agreements among competitors to stop competing with one another in prices, customers, or products.

The Rule-of-Reason Standard If an alleged antitrust practice is not considered a *per se* violation, then the courts will judge the legality of that practice with the rule-of-reason approach. The **rule-of-reason standard** will stop certain practices only if they are an unreasonable restriction of competition. As a result, some practices that in fact limit competition may be legal. To determine if an anticompetitive practice is legal, the court considers such facts as the history of the restraint, the harm that results, the reason for the practice, and the purpose to be attained.

The Quick-Look Standard A third standard, the quick-look standard, has become a customary way for resolving those cases that fall into the slightly gray area between *per se* violations and the rule-of-reason standard. Under the **quick-look standard**, a court will look at the evidence in an antitrust case and determine whether an objective observer with an elementary knowledge of the financial world would see that the arrangement under scrutiny could damage competition by hurting the consumer and impairing the marketplace itself. If the court decides that this is the case, then the defendant assumes the burden of demonstrating to the court or the jury that the harm is negligible, nonexistent, or permissible.

A CLASSIC CASE Single Entity or Collection Point—*American Needle, Inc. v. The NFL*

One of the primary money-making operations that the National Football League (NFL) has engaged in over the years has been the merchandising of goods, such as ball caps, jerseys, T-shirts, and so on, all of which bear the logo and/or colors of an NFL team. Throughout the 20th century, the NFL was satisfied to deal with a variety of vendors through a legal entity that it created known as National Football League Properties (NFLP). Then, in 2000, NFLP decided to award an exclusive contract to Reebok. One former NFL merchandiser, American Needle, was unhappy with the new arrangement. Consequently, American Needle brought a lawsuit against the NFL, arguing that the Reebok contract established a monopoly that was in violation of Section 1 of the Sherman Antitrust Law. Section 1 makes it illegal to enter a contract, combination, or conspiracy in order to restrain trade. Ordinarily, under Section 1, the court would apply what is known as the rule-of-reason standard, which asks judges to balance the *pro*-competitive results of a challenged arrangement with the *anti*-competitive results. In this case, however, a different tactic was used. The Seventh Circuit Court of Appeals took a more fundamental approach and targeted the very ability of the NFL to enter a contract of any sort. The court ruled that the NFL was not a collection point around which a group of 32 teams joined forces but was, instead, a single entity. As a single entity, the NFL could not make any type of contract with itself, let alone a contract to restrain trade. This ruling means that Section 1 did not apply to the case and, as a result, the case was dismissed. The U.S. Supreme Court disagreed with the appellate court, however, and ruled that the NFL is not a single corporate person. The Court said that, although under corporate law, the NFL might be a single corporate person, under antitrust law, it is not. The NFL turns out to be, at least for purposes of antitrust law, a collection of 32 distinct constituent parts, referred to as teams and headquartered in different cities that make financial decisions on their own for their own purposes and benefit.

The case did not end here. Instead, it next went to the trial court where both sides filed motions for summary judgment. The plaintiff asked for summary judgment based on the idea that the case could be submitted to the court for a "quick look." Not to be outdone, the defendant also filed a summary judgment motion arguing that American Needle had not built a sufficient case to demonstrate that the exclusive agreement with Reebok hurt competition. To bolster its claim, the NFL presented several pieces of evidence, including a claim that NFL apparel competes with apparel from other sports and from other activities outside of sports. America Needle presented counterevidence that indicated that the sale of NFL material tends to peak during the NFL season, indicating that the market for NFL products is a common market and, therefore, is a fitting object for the antitrust complaint. The court saw this as a reasonable argument and dismissed the defendant's summary judgment motion. However, the court also dismissed the plaintiff's summary judgment motion, noting the plaintiff's evidence was insufficient to allow a quick-look solution to decide that case. Moreover, the court dismissed all the defendant's other summary judgment motions as well, thus paving the way for a trial (or a settlement).

Now, because the contract under consideration here does not appear to be a *per se* violation of the law, and because the quick-look standard cannot be applied, if the case reaches trial, the court will apply the rule-of-reason standard, which asks judges to balance the pro-competitive results of a challenged arrangement with the anti-competitive results. Take a moment to speculate on this. What might the pro-competitive results be from the single contract with Reebok? What might the anti-competitive results be? Now balance the two and predict how the court will rule. (*Note:* Of course, if you can find no appropriate balance here, you might just want to settle the case before going any further. After all, despite Jack McCoy's winning record on countless *Law and Order* reruns, sometimes surrendering is an option.) [See: *American Needle, Inc. v. New Orleans Saints, et al.*, No. 04-cv-7806, 2014 U.S. Dist. LEIXS 47527 (N.D. Ill. Apr. 4, 2014); *American Needle, Inc. v. National Football League*, 130 S.Ct. 2201 (2010). See also: Gabriel Feldman, "The NFL Is Not a Single Entity," *The National Law Journal*, February 1, 2010, p. 35; and Michael P. Waxman, "*American Needle Inc. v. National Football League*: Surprise! The Supreme Court Upholds an Existing Antitrust Doctrine," *Marquette University Law School Faculty Blog*, October 29, 2010, http://law.marquette.edu.]

Source: See: *American Needle, Inc. v. New Orleans Saints, et al.*, No. 04-cv-7806, 2014 U.S. Dist. LEIXS 47527 (N.D. Ill. Apr. 4, 2014; *American Needle, Inc. v. National Football League*, 130 S.Ct. 2201 (2010). See also Gabriel Feldman, "The NFL Is Not a Single Entity," *The National Law Journal*, February 1, 2010, p. 35; and Michael P. Waxman, "American Needle Inc. v. National Football League: Surprise! The Supreme Court Upholds an Existing Antitrust Doctrine," *Marquette University Law School Faculty Blog*, October 29, 2010, http://law.marquette.edu.

The Evolving Nature of the Triple Threat The original *per se* and rule-of-reason standards have been part of antitrust law for decades, so the line of distinction between the two is usually very clear. However, sometimes, as the law evolves, that line of distinction becomes less and less distinct. A case in point involves the court's distinction between resale price maintenance (RPM) agreements and quasi-RPM arrangements. An **RPM agreement** occurs when a retailer and a manufacturer decide that the retailer will sell certain products at a price set by the manufacturer. These RPMs have been outlawed by the court as a *per se* violation of antitrust law. In contrast, a **quasi-RPM arrangement** occurs when a manufacturer lets retailers know the price that it expects to see on an item and then declines to sell that item to any retailer that does not list the item at that price. Such arrangements are legally permissible under antitrust law because the law cannot take away the rights of manufacturers to pick those sellers with which they want to deal. While the distinction between the two seems, at best, artificial and, at worst, nonexistent, it is the law. The differences have become somewhat clearer, however, with the advent of the "quick-look" standard, the third and the newest weapon in this triple-threat arsenal of antitrust law.

Post–Sherman Antitrust Legislation

Three principal antitrust statues made the Sherman Act more specific and, as a result, more effective. The Clayton Act of 1914, the Robinson–Patman Act of 1936, the Foreign Trade Antitrust Improvements Act, and the Federal Trade Commission Act of 1914 sought to prevent practices that reduced competition or favored the creation of monopolies.

Clayton Act Congress passed the Clayton Act to police specific business practices that could be used to create a monopoly. One practice outlawed by the act is tying agreements. A **tying agreement** occurs when one party refuses to sell a product unless the buyer also purchases another product tied to the first product. The issue is the effect of the tie-in on the seller's competitors. Interlocking directorates are also outlawed by the Clayton Act. **Interlocking directorates** occur when individuals serve as directors of two corporations that are competitors. This provision is not entirely foolproof, however, because banks and common carriers are exempt. To fall under this part of the Clayton Act, at least one of the corporations must have an aggregate worth (capital, surplus, and individual profits) of more than $1 million.

Robinson–Patman Act The Robinson–Patman Act deals with product pricing, advertising, and promotional allowances. It specifically prohibits a seller from charging different prices to different customers for the same product when such differences might injure competition. However, nothing in the law is intended to prevent price differences due to cost of manufacture, sale, delivery, or bulk purchases.

Federal Trade Commission Act In addition to establishing the Federal Trade Commission (FTC), the Federal Trade Commission Act, as amended, declares that "unfair methods of competition, and unfair or deceptive practices in or affecting commerce are hereby declared unlawful." The act did not name specific unfair methods of competition. Instead, it has allowed the courts and the FTC to determine those unfair practices. The Federal Trade Commission Act was amended by the Wheeler–Lea Act and amendments in 1938 and 1975. This legislation authorized the FTC to act against unfair or deceptive acts without first proving the existence of anticompetitive behavior. The FTC was also granted the power to challenge false advertising of food, drugs, and cosmetics, regardless of the advertiser's knowledge of the advertisement's truth or falsity.

A QUESTION OF ETHICS

Textualism and Pragmatism Revisited

As we've seen in this chapter and earlier in the text, three popular but conflicting theories of legal interpretation are textualism, purposivism, and pragmatism. Textualism requires judges to analyze legal documents as literary works, by focusing exclusively on each document's language. In contrast, purposivism insists that judges consider the legislative goals of a statute, while pragmatism expects judges to focus on the consequences of a decision. Both pragmatism and purposivism seem to demand that judges investigate the circumstances behind the writing of the text. One of the most baffling aspects of the ongoing debate involving these three techniques is that often, even when a judge would rather not identify his or her analytical technique as textualism, it is textualism toward which the judge inevitably gravitates. The explanation for this paradox may rest within the incontrovertible fact that legal analysis always involves a study of language. In simple, if somewhat facetious terms, until we all engage in non-local, quantum interconnected thought transfer at the subatomic level, we will have to work our way to an understanding of any written text through the use of language. For example, in his concurring opinion in *Gibbons v. Ogden*, William Johnson determined the extent of congressional power in business by dissecting the language of the commerce clause. By doing so he came unapologetically to the conclusion that congressional commercial power would always trump state power. What is most revealing about this analysis is that Williams specifically disavows the textual approach while at the same time using it quite thoroughly. Moreover, he does so because he is forced to admit that there are no outside sources that he can use beyond that actual words of the clause. Similarly, in *Egan v. TradingScreen, Inc.*, the judge uses a carefully orchestrated textual approach because there are no committee notes and no entries in the *Congressional Record* that will allow him to do otherwise.

QUESTIONS YET UNANSWERED

The following questions have not yet been answered. Before you consider each question, turn to Chapter 1 to review the various ethical theories noted there (social contract theory, utilitarianism, and rational ethics). Using one of those theories in a consistent way, answer the following questions.

1. Is it ethical for a pragmatic judge to abandon pragmatism and use instead a textual approach? Explain.
2. Answer the preceding question for purposivism.
3. One of the defenses given in support of textualism says that the consistent use of the textual approach by the courts will encourage legislators to write clear and unambiguous laws. Is this an ethical rationale in support of textualism? Explain.
4. Some people attack textualism because it narrows the interpretation strategies available to judges. Is this an ethical rationale in support of pragmatism? Explain.
5. Do you believe that Johnson has interpreted the language of the commerce clause correctly? Why or why not?
6. Do you believe that the *Egan* court interpreted the language of the whistleblower definition correctly? Why or why not?

The Foreign Trade Antitrust Improvements Act Another antitrust measure passed by Congress is the Foreign Trade Antitrust Improvements Act (FTAIA). Unlike the other antitrust provisions supported by Congress, the FTAIA is designed to circumvent some of the restrictions placed on American companies by the Sherman Antitrust Act. The objective of the FTAIA is to permit American companies operating in foreign markets to have a fighting chance against foreign competitors that are not subject to the strict antimonopoly provisions of the act. Under terms of the bill, if an American company is operating totally in a foreign market, that company is not subject to American antitrust law.

In contrast, consumer advocates want to make it easier for plaintiffs to bring antitrust lawsuits against certain types of defendants, but especially against manufacturers. Plaintiffs frequently complain that retailers rarely bring antitrust claims against manufacturers because retailers can avoid the effects of any antitrust scheme, such as a price-fixing conspiracy, by passing the increased cost of doing business on to the consumers. The consumers, who under current rules are frequently barred from bringing lawsuits against manufacturers, have no recourse other than to pay the higher prices. For this reason, consumer advocacy groups favor making it easier for plaintiffs to file class-action lawsuits against all manufacturing firms that violate antitrust law but especially against those large cartels that are the worst offenders. Finally, state and local regulators would also like to see changes in the law. These regulators favor changes that would transfer more antitrust enforcement authority from the federal government to the states.

quick quiz 28-3

1. Price fixing is an example of a rule-of-reason practice under the Sherman Antitrust Act. true | false
2. *Per se* violations must involve actual harm to be actionable under the Sherman Antitrust Act. true | false
3. The Robinson–Patman Act has been repealed by the U.S. Antitrust Modernization Committee. true | false

28-4 Expanding the Corporate Entity

No other area of corporate activity has been scrutinized by the government more closely in recent years than the area of corporate expansion (see Table 28-2). As noted previously, several governmental agencies may be involved in any given corporate expansion venture, including the Department of Justice and the Federal Communications Commission. However, the two agencies that have the primary responsibility for regulating this activity are the Securities and Exchange Commission and the Federal Trade Commission. The two commissions have different interests in the expansion process. The SEC is concerned with regulating the expansion tactics themselves, whereas the FTC is more concerned with the competitive effects of those expansion tactics.

Expansion Tactics and Securities Law

All corporations change in size. Some grow and expand, while others shrink until they dissolve or are absorbed by a larger, more successful enterprise. Like all other corporate

Table 28-2 Types of Corporate Expansion

Technique	Explanation	Regulation
Merger and consolidation	In a merger, one company is absorbed by another; in a consolidation two companies join and a new company results	Most antifraud provisions of the SEC apply here
Asset acquisition	One corporation buys the property of another	SEC antifraud provisions apply if proxy solicitation or insider trading is involved
Stock acquisition	One corporation buys a majority of a target corporation's stock	Whenever a suitor makes an offer to acquire more than 5% of the target, the suitor must file with the SEC
Inversion	A U.S. corporation buys an alien corporation and then reincorporates in a foreign nation	New federal oversight rule in place

activities, corporate expansions are looked at very closely by government. The primary expansion techniques include mergers, consolidations, asset acquisitions, stock acquisitions, and inversions.

Merger and Consolidation Traditionally, a **merger** involves two corporations, one of which is absorbed by the other. One of the two corporations continues to carry on business under its original name, and the other simply disappears into the first. In contrast, in a **consolidation**, both companies disappear, and a new company carries on the business under a new name. Today, most legal scholars do not make any distinction between merger and consolidation. In fact, many state incorporation statutes make no reference to consolidation, preferring the term *merger* instead. A merger requires advance approval from the boards and shareholders of both corporations. In general, a two-thirds majority vote of the shareholders will be required before a merger can be approved, though some states require a supermajority of four-fifths. Shareholders who dissent are entitled to be paid for their stock if they do not wish to be a part of the merger. Written notice of a dissent is required so that the cost of purchasing the dissenter's stock can be figured as a part of the expense involved in the merger.

Most antifraud provisions of the SEC apply to the merger process. Often the merger vote will be preceded by a proxy solicitation battle. All material facts about the merger must be included in the proxy solicitation. In addition, the solicitation must not contain any false or misleading information. Similarly, the SEC prohibits insiders who know of merger plans from taking advantage of that knowledge to profit personally before the knowledge is revealed to the public.

Some state statutes apply different rules to mergers that involve a limited liability company (LLC). Under some state statutes, a merger involving an LLC requires the unanimous approval of the members rather than the two-thirds majority required of corporations. However, as is true in other circumstances, the operating agreement of an LLC could cancel this unanimous vote requirement. If the operating agreement specifies that a merger vote may be approved by less than a unanimous vote, many states give those members who are opposed to the merger the right to withdraw from the LLC and receive the cash value of their investment. However, once again, the operating agreement can alter this statutory right.

Asset Acquisition In an **asset acquisition**, one corporation purchases all the property of a second corporation. However, as in the case of mergers, SEC antifraud regulations can be applied to asset acquisitions if a proxy solicitation process is involved or if insider information is used to profit from the sale. Asset acquisition is easy and efficient, because the only formality required is approval by the directors and shareholders of the corporation that is selling its assets. A second advantage is that the buyer need not purchase all of the assets of the seller. The buyer may choose to purchase some assets while rejecting others.

Another advantage of asset acquisition is that, in general, no debts or other liabilities are transferred from seller to buyer. There are exceptions to this rule, however. In certain situations, the debts of the selling corporation will transfer to the buying corporation. For instance, if the buyer is simply a continuation of the selling corporation, the buyer will not escape the liabilities of the seller. Similarly, if the sale is structured fraudulently to escape the liabilities of the selling corporation, the debts will transfer to the buyer. It is also possible for the buyer to either expressly or implicitly assume the debts and liabilities of the seller. Finally, if, despite its label as an asset acquisition, the sale is actually a merger, the liabilities will transfer to the buyer.

Stock Acquisition In a **stock acquisition**, the buyer purchases enough stock in a corporation to gain voting control of that corporation. Stock acquisitions come in many shapes and sizes (see Table 28-3). One type of stock acquisition is the **leveraged buyout (LBO)**. In a

Table 28-3 Stock Acquisition Techniques

Technique	Explanation
Leveraged buyout	A controlling portion of stock purchased by shareholders; leveraged by loans and junk bonds.
Tender offer	Suitor makes a public offer to buy voting stock in a target corporation.
Takeover bid	Tender offer opposed by the management of the target corporation.
Corporate raid	Takeover bid opposed by management of target because corporate raider intends to dismantle target.

leveraged buyout, a controlling portion of the stock in a corporation is purchased by a group of shareholders, often several outsiders but sometimes a team of officers and directors of the company. The potential buyers can then collect the money needed to purchase the outstanding shares by enlisting the support of a bank. The bank will lend a good portion of the money to the buyers, taking an enormous payment to support that loan. If the amount produced by the bank proves inadequate, the buyers will seek the assistance of an investment firm. The investment firm produces the remainder of the needed money by issuing **junk bonds**, or bonds that are unstable but offer an elevated level of return to large, powerful investors. Because the stock purchase is made possible by these high-stakes loans, the buyout is referred to as "leveraged." The shareholders are motivated to sell because the buyout team offers them an inflated price for their shares. Sometimes after the buyers have purchased control of the corporation, they ensure their continued control by transforming the company into a private corporation. This action is referred to as "taking the company private."

A second form of stock acquisition is the **tender offer**. In a tender offer, the buyer or suitor, whether it is an individual, a consortium of like-minded individuals, or another corporation, makes a public offer to buy voting stock in a **target corporation**. A successful tender offer occurs once the buyer or buyers have purchased enough of the voting stock to satisfy the original goal, whatever that might have been. One advantage of the stock acquisition process is that it sidesteps the board of directors. The buyer deals directly with the shareholders. Again, the shareholders are motivated to sell because the buyer has made an offer that is above the current market price of the stock.

Sometimes, a tender offer is welcomed by the directors and the officers of the target because they see it as a way to strengthen the corporation and enhance their own positions within the company. At other times, however, the tender offer is seen as a corporate **takeover bid** by an **unfriendly buyer**. In a takeover bid, the unfriendly buyer, also known as an **unfriendly suitor** or a **hostile bidder**, intends to purchase enough stock to control the corporation. Often the goal of the hostile bidder is to change management and shake up the corporation after the takeover. If the suitor intends to dismantle the corporation totally or somehow integrate the target into an existing corporation to such an extent that the target ceases to exist, the suitor is referred to as a **corporate raider** and the tender offer a **corporate raid**. In both cases, hostile bidder and corporate raider, the target's management is expected to fight the takeover with every tactic available.

Inversions An **inversion** typically occurs when an American corporation buys an alien corporation and then reincorporates in that alien's national base. However, it is also possible, and sometimes easier and less obvious, for an alien corporation to buy an American corporation under a deal that is engineered at the behest of, and largely for the benefit of, the American corporation. It seems not to matter whether the purchase involves an asset acquisition, a stock acquisition, or a combination of both. Whatever the actual process involved in the sale, inversions are generally constructed as a way for the U.S. corporations to sidestep certain tax laws that do not have the same impact on the aliens as they do on America corporations. For example, a newly **inverted company** (a corporate entity that has gone through the inversion process) may immediately take advantage of the **hopscotch loan** process, which permits a tax-free loan to flow from an established alien branch into the treasury of the new alien parent. Nothing is inherently illegal about the inversion strategy itself. There is, after all, no reason anyone, even an inverted company, must voluntarily pay a high tax bill if he or she (or it) can figure out a legal way to pay those same taxes at a lower rate.

However, the tactic does bother many critics who see it as an unfair loophole that some advantageously placed corporations can use while most others cannot. It may be for that reason that the Treasury Department recently targeted inversions with a new set of tax-related rules. The new rules did not outlaw inversions as such, but they did declare that certain practices that roll off a completed inversion will no longer be tolerated. One targeted practice is the hopscotch rule noted earlier. These new rules may discourage future inversion schemes. On the other hand, the hopscotch loan is just one way for inverted companies to escape high tax rates. Thus, while future inversions may be curtailed, existing inverted companies are free to explore other loopholes in the tax laws. Moreover, since the new rules may discourage other corporate persons from using the inversion process, existing inverted companies may now have an unfair advantage over their competitors who have been discouraged from taking a similar path. [See: David Gelles, "A Brake on Reincorporating Abroad via Mergers," *The New York Times*, December 11, 2014, p. F14; and John S. Barry, "Corporate Inversions: An Introduction to the Issue and FAQ," *The Tax Foundation*, May 30, 2002, http://taxfoundation.org/article/corporate-inversions-introduction-issue-and-faq.]

Post-Offer Techniques To avoid being taken over by a hostile bidder, the management of a corporation can institute both post-offer (see Table 28-4) and pre-offer tactics (see Table 28-5). Probably the least problematic post-offer technique is the public relations initiative. Such an initiative is aimed at convincing shareholders that it is in their best interests not to sell their shares to the hostile bidder. News releases, advertisements, press conferences, and even personal letters and e-mails would attempt to convince shareholders that present management should be retained. The difficulty with this approach is that many arguments pale to insignificance when placed alongside a bid that is above the current market price of the stock.

Sometimes the most effective way for a target to shake off a bidder's hostile suit is to offer the bidder **greenmail**. A corporation that activates the greenmail defense has offered to buy the portion of the target's stock that the bidder already owns. Naturally, such an approach

Table 28-4 Post-Offer Antitakeover Tactics

Post-Offer Tactics	Explanations
Public relations campaign	Target corporation uses news releases, advertisements, and press conferences to convince shareholders to retain present management.
Greenmail	Target corporation offers to buy target's stock already owned by suitor.
White knight	Target corporation invites friendly suitor to outbid a hostile bidder.
Lockup agreement	Target corporation tags irreplaceable property for sale when hostile bidder succeeds in takeover.
Targeted shareholder agreement	Target corporation makes deal with suitor to protect management of target.

Table 28-5 Pre-Offer Antitakeover Tactics

Pre-Offer Tactic	Explanation
Supermajority provision—for takeover bids	Target corporation rewrites bylaws to require 90% vote to approve any takeover.
Supermajority provision—for amendments	Target corporation rewrites bylaws to require 90% vote to amend the bylaws.
Accelerated loans	Target corporation enters loan agreements that are due in full when the target is subject to a successful takeover.
Poison pill	Existing shareholders are empowered to buy additional shares of a potential target at bargain basement prices.

will work only if the target's offer is significantly higher than the amount that the bidder paid for the stock in the first place. Such an approach is disfavored because it robs the shareholders of the opportunity to make a profit by selling their shares and may seriously devalue the target's remaining stock, thereby victimizing the shareholders a second time.

Another post-offer technique that can be used by the target company is the white knight gambit. To implement this tactic, the target invites another suitor to outbid the hostile bidder. The second suitor is known as a **friendly suitor** or a **white knight** because the invited suitor agrees that it will retain existing management. The white knight also frequently agrees not to disrupt the smooth running of the target by selling key assets, closing plants, or laying off employees. A takeover battle usually follows. The winner is generally the suitor that can offer the highest price for the target's outstanding stock.

A fourth post-offer technique is the **lockup agreement**. A lockup agreement might be used by target management if the target owns an irreplaceable piece of property, the sale of which would seriously devalue the overall worth of the target. Such property might include rich timberland or an extremely productive coal mine. Provided that the sale of that property does not deplete virtually all the assets of the target, management could enter a contract with a white knight, giving the knight an option to buy that valuable piece of property should the hostile bidder gain control of the target corporation. The idea is to discourage the hostile bidder from buying the now-devalued target.

A fifth post-offer technique is the **targeted shareholder agreement**. Strictly speaking, a targeted shareholder agreement is not an anti-acquisition tactic as much as it is an executive protection strategy. Under the provisions of a targeted shareholder agreement, the suitor negotiates a deal with certain targeted shareholders, generally the CEO, the CFO, the CTO, and other high-ranking officers. These agreements will provide the officers/ shareholders with handsome employment-related deals that supplement the price that they will receive for the sale of their stock. Such deals might include a salary increase, a severance package, a non-compete agreement, and so on. The strategy behind negotiating a targeted shareholder agreement is not to stop the acquisition but to protect key employees who might be financially damaged or even discharged in the post-acquisition culture.

Targeted shareholder agreements were hampered in the late 1990s and early in the 21st century by two rules instituted by the SEC. These rules, known collectively as the **best-price rule**, prohibited suitors from offering different prices to different shareholders during a tender offer process. Unfortunately, the best-price rule was interpreted differently by different federal courts. Some courts, using what was called the **integral-part test**, decided that any type of price enhancement, including employment-related packages, would violate the best-price rule—period. The other rule, known as the **bright-line test**, was used by those courts that saw a violation of the best-price rule only during the actual tender offer. Thus, if an employment agreement was negotiated with a targeted shareholder before or after the actual tender offer, and the actual price that the suitor paid for the stock remained unaffected, then there was no violation of the best-price rule. The SEC eventually amended the rule to make it clear that targeted shareholder agreements that involved *only* employment-related agreements would not be subject to the best-price rule.

Pre-Offer Techniques Sometimes post-offer techniques are instituted too late to prevent takeover. For this reason, many corporations plan ahead by instituting certain pre-offer measures even before any unfriendly suitors have appeared on the horizon (see Table 28-5). For example, a corporation could institute a supermajority provision into its bylaws that would require a 90 percent affirmative vote by all shareholders for the approval of any merger. Such a move would mean that any suitor would have to acquire 90 percent of the stock of the target to assure a takeover. A backup provision requiring a supermajority to change the supermajority bylaws would also be necessary to ensure that the suitor does not simply take 51 percent of the target and then use that majority control to eliminate the supermajority merger vote provision.

An additional pre-offer technique involves the corporation in a series of accelerated loans. Under the provisions of an accelerated loan program, all major loans taken out by the corporation are due in full immediately upon the takeover of the target by an unfriendly suitor. The plan is to place the suitor in a precarious financial position because, once the target has been acquired, the suitor would be forced to pay off a series of expensive loans, thus straining the treasury of the target. The accelerated loan gambit is often unsuccessful because the financial institutions that made the loans are often willing to renegotiate the terms of the accelerated loans with the target's new owner to avoid getting a poor return on their investments.

Another pre-offer technique is the poison pill tactic. Generally, a poison pill defense is established as a pre-offer strategy that remains dormant until the right set of circumstances activates its operation. The **poison pill** defense is triggered when a potential hostile bidder manages to purchase a specified percentage (perhaps 10 to 20 percent) of the firm. At that point, the price of the remaining shares drops dramatically for all other shareholders. The hostile bidder, however, is blocked from purchasing the bargain-basement shares. The goal of this plan is to encourage existing shareholders to buy additional shares at the reduced rate in order to water down the value of the stock, thus scaring off the potential buyer. This explanation says it poorly, however, because the poison pill process can be implemented in a variety of complex modes. There are those who oppose the technique because it damages competition among potential buyers. Oddly, this is the same argument that can be used against any of the post-offer or pre-offer techniques enumerated here, so it is unclear exactly why this technique is so targeted for criticism. On the other hand, the complaint about the poison pill may lodge within the fact that the hostile bidder is frozen out of the chance to buy the bargain stock, thus placing him or her at an unfair advantage (although that is really the point, isn't it?). Moreover, some critics are uncomfortable with the fact that the strategy can be revoked by the directors whenever it suits their agenda (which is, after all, their prerogative as directors). [See: Robert Charles Clark, "Control Shifts and Insider Resistance: Tender Offers," *Corporate Law* (Boston: Little Brown, 1986), pp. 574-76; and "Shareholder Rights Plan," *Knowledge Encyclopedia*, http://www.referenceforbusiness.com/knowledge/Shareholder_rights_plan.html.]

Takeover Bids and the SEC Takeover bids are scrutinized by the SEC. Under recent amendments to federal securities law, whenever a suitor makes an offer to acquire more than 5 percent of a target, that suitor must file a statement with the SEC. The statement must indicate (1) where the money for the takeover originates, (2) why the suitor is buying the stock, and (3) how much of the target the suitor already owns. These procedures are designed to let shareholders know the identity and intention of a takeover bidder. Bidders who falsify any information on their statement may find their takeover bid stopped by a court order.

Expansion Tactics and Antitrust Law

As noted previously, antitrust law is designed to preserve competition and discourage monopolies. One way that companies can create monopolies is through a corporate expansion effort. Antitrust law does not focus on corporate expansion techniques. Instead, it looks at how an expansion attempt will affect competition in the marketplace (see Table 28-6). Section 7 of the Clayton Act forbids any corporate expansion if that expansion sets up a monopoly or otherwise hurts competition. The Clayton Act applies to horizontal, vertical, or conglomerate expansion attempts.

Expansion Attempts Because **horizontal expansion** occurs between companies that are involved in the same business, such attempts often result in monopolies. Consequently, horizontal expansion schemes are scrutinized by the FTC and are more likely to be labeled illegal. A **vertical expansion** occurs between companies that were in a customer–supplier relationship. If a manufacturer of designer jeans were to buy a chain of department stores that carried its jeans, a vertical expansion would result. A **conglomerate expansion** joins two companies that were not in competition with each other, either because they dealt in different products or services or because they operated in different geographical areas.

Hart-Scott-Rodino Antitrust Act Like the SEC, the FTC has a chance to step into expansion situations even before they become an established fact. This opportunity is provided by the Hart-Scott-Rodino Antitrust Act. Hart-Scott-Rodino is designed to police any expansion attempts that might harm competition in the marketplace. The act requires corporations that are setting up an expansion attempt to notify the FTC before the deal is completed. This advance notice allows the FTC to investigate the anticompetitive effects of the planned expansion. Should the FTC decide that the expansion will hurt competition, it can go to court and ask for an injunction to prevent the expansion.

The Tunney Antitrust Act The federal government also regulates corporate expansion through the activities of the Antitrust Division of the Department of Justice (DOJ) and through the activities of specialized agencies, such as the Federal Communications Commission (FCC). The DOJ's Antitrust Division is charged with policing mergers that affect antitrust law to ensure that in carrying out a corporate combination, the participants have not violated those laws. The primary goal of the DOJ, however, is not to stop such mergers

Table 28-6 Antitrust Law and Corporate Expansion

Technique	Explanation	Regulation
Horizontal expansion	Occurs between companies that are involved in the same business	Scrutinized by the FTC because of the likelihood of a monopoly
Vertical expansion	Occurs between companies that are in a customer-supplier relationship	Less likelihood of monopoly, therefore less FTC scrutiny
Conglomerate expansion	Occurs between two companies that are not in competition with each other	Least likelihood of monopoly, therefore least FTC scrutiny

outright but instead to help the parties negotiate a merger that can be completed without violating the law. Such agreements are referred to as **consent decrees**. The Justice Department's antitrust consent decrees are, in turn, regulated by a federal statute known as the **Antitrust Procedures and Penalties Act** or simply as the **Tunney Act**.

The Tunney Act requires that the DOJ defend its support of a consent decree by sending the decree to the federal court along with a complaint and a **competitive impact statement (CIS)**. The CIS is a document that clarifies any potential antitrust problems inherent within the expansion and the solutions to those problems suggested by the decree. The law requires that 60 days before concluding the agreement, the DOJ publish the complaint, the decree, and the CIS in the *Federal Register*. Publishing the documents gives people a chance to have input into the nature, purpose, and effects of the agreement. The *Federal Register* will then print these statements and observations. A judge must also approve the decree. In doing so, the judge takes into account two elements: (1) the effect of the decree on competition and (2) the decree's effect on the community and on any parties who might be hurt separately. The Tunney Act was amended in 2004 to make it clear that the courts have the authority to challenge consent decrees negotiated by the Justice Department.

The corporate expansion process is sometimes regulated by specialty agencies that are charged with overseeing the socioeconomic activities of the corporations involved in the expansion process. Thus, for instance, the Federal Communications Commission would be responsible for reviewing merger plans proposed by corporations involved in the communications industry. Some agency officials take this responsibility very seriously and use their power to negotiate concessions within merger agreements that permit the agency to engage in an unofficial, but effective, brand of social engineering. The FCC is one such agency. In recent years, it has exercised its review power in merger cases to protect consumers, set prices, and return jobs to the United States. Agencies that use their regulatory powers to advance social agendas that are technically outside their legislative authority are referred to as **activist agencies**.

---

quick quiz 28-4

1. Most antifraud provisions of the Securities and Exchange Commission apply to the merger process. — true | false
2. Greenmail is the least effective anti-hostile takeover technique. — true | false
3. The Hart-Scott-Rodino Act is designed to police any expansion attempts that might harm competition in the marketplace. — true | false

---

28-5 The Government and the End of the Corporate Entity

Just as the government is involved in the birth and growth (expansion) of a corporation, it is also involved in its death, or dissolution. Whether a corporation ends involuntarily or voluntarily, the government is somehow involved.

Involuntary Dissolution

If a corporation has repeatedly conducted business in an unlawful manner, the secretary of state can ask the state attorney general to bring a *quo warranto* action against that corporation. Under a *quo warranto* proceeding, the state revokes the corporation's charter. Common examples of illegal actions forming the grounds for revocation include a failure to file annual reports, a failure to pay franchise taxes, or a failure to maintain a registered or statutory agent for service of process. Corporations formed fraudulently and those exceeding their authority may also be subject to a *quo warranto* proceeding.

Courts have the power to liquidate the assets of a corporation when an action is brought by a shareholder. Grounds for involuntary dissolution at the request of a shareholder include the following:

- Evidence of illegal, oppressive, or fraudulent acts.
- A misapplication or waste of corporate assets.
- A deadlock of directors that threatens irreparable harm.
- Evidence that a dissolution is necessary to protect the rights of the complaining shareholder.

Voluntary Dissolution

Because the government grants corporate charters and regulates corporate activity, it must be informed when a corporation voluntarily dissolves. A corporation can be dissolved voluntarily by the unanimous approval of the shareholders or by a positive vote of the directors with the approval of two-thirds of the shareholders. Once the decision to dissolve has been approved, a statement of intent must be filed with the state government. The corporation will then cease business and notify creditors (by certified mail) and the public (by publication). After all claims have been received, corporate assets will be used first to pay creditors, with the surplus going to shareholders. If the existing assets cannot meet all claims, a receiver may be called in to handle matters. A *receiver* is a person appointed by law to hold property subject to diverse claims. The receiver would divide assets fairly among creditors. Following the distribution of all assets, the corporation must prepare articles of dissolution and present them to the secretary of state.

quick quiz 28-5

1. If a corporation has repeatedly conducted business in an unlawful manner, the secretary of state can require the federal Justice Department to revoke its charter.	true | false
2. Courts no longer have any power to liquidate the assets of a corporation when an action is brought by a shareholder.	true | false
3. Corporations are no longer permitted to engage in voluntary dissolution.	true | false

28-6 Dissolution of a Limited Liability Company

Because limited liability companies are created by state statutory law, the dissolution of a LLC is also regulated by state statutory law. Most state LLC statutes outline the circumstances that will trigger the dissolution of an LLC.

Circumstances of Dissolution

The dissolution of an LLC can be initiated by the unanimous agreement of all of its members. Similarly, the dissolution can be triggered by the expulsion, bankruptcy, or withdrawal of a member. However, many state statutes now declare that in both member-managed and manager-managed LLCs, a member may not leave the LLC unless such a departure is authorized by the operating agreement. Naturally, the articles of organization or the operating agreement can also specify other events that would cause a dissolution. Some state statutes also assert that the death of a member does not trigger a dissolution. Instead, the death of a member is classified as a disassociation.

Effects of Dissolution

As is true with a partnership, a limited liability company does not stop business immediately upon the dissolution event. Dissolution must be distinguished from the winding up of the LLC, which effectively puts it out of business. Winding up involves completing all of the business of the LLC and selling its property to satisfy all of the debts of the firm. As is the case with the dissolution of a partnership, the dissolution of an LLC need not be followed by a winding up of the LLC. If all of the remaining members of the LLC want to continue the LLC, they may do so. It is also possible for the operating agreement to specify that the vote to continue need not be unanimous among the remaining members. The operating agreement should also indicate that the LLC will dissolve when the number of members within the LLC falls below the number required by state law.

quick quiz 28-6

1. The dissolution of an LLC is regulated by the federal government only. true | false
2. Once an LLC has engaged in a dissolution procedure, the business does not stop immediately. true | false
3. If all the remaining members of an LLC want to continue the LLC, they may do so. true | false

Summary

28.1 The commerce clause is located in Article I, Section 8, Clause 3, of the Constitution. Clause 3 states that "Congress shall have the Power . . . to regulate Commerce with foreign nations, and among the several States." At first glance the clause appears to be an attempt by the framers to limit the power of the central government and, conversely, to enhance the ability of the states to regulate their own internal economic activity.

However, from the very beginning the courts identified the central national government as the true source of commercial regulatory power in the United States.

28.2 The primary objective of the Securities Act of 1933 and the Securities Exchange Act of 1934 is to protect investors by informing them about the securities they purchase. The Securities and Exchange Commission carries out this objective.

28.3 To preserve the value of competition and to discourage monopolies, the government has enacted several antitrust statutes. The Sherman Antitrust Act prohibits contracts, combinations, and conspiracies in restraint of trade. The Clayton Act, the Robinson-Patman Act, the Foreign Trade Improvements Act, and the Federal Trade Commission Act make the Sherman Antitrust Act more specific and more effective.

28.4 Although both securities law and antitrust law pertain to monopolies, they have different areas of focus. Securities law is concerned with regulating corporate expansion techniques, including mergers, consolidations, asset acquisitions, and stock acquisition. Antitrust law is concerned with how corporate expansion affects competition in the marketplace. Antitrust law applies to horizontal, vertical, or conglomerate expansion attempts.

28.5 Corporations can dissolve involuntarily or voluntarily. A corporation that has repeatedly conducted business in an unlawful manner may be subject to involuntary dissolution by the state. A corporation can be voluntarily dissolved by unanimous approval of the shareholders or by a positive vote of the directors with the approval of two-thirds of the shareholders. The government is involved in both involuntary and voluntary dissolution.

28.6 Because limited liability companies are created by state statutory law, the dissolution of a limited liability company is also regulated by state statutory law. Most state LLC statutes outline the circumstances that will trigger the dissolution of an LLC.

Key Terms

activist agencies, 810
associative corporatism, 788
Antitrust Procedures and Penalties Act, 810
asset acquisition, 804
best-price rule, 807
bright-line test, 807
commerce clause, 786
competitive impact statement (CIS), 810
conglomerate expansion, 809
consent decree, 810
consolidation, 804
corporate raid, 805
corporate raider, 805
corporativism, 788
derivative, 791
Dodd-Frank Wall Street and Consumer Protection Act, 791
friendly suitor, 807
golden parachute, 793

greenmail, 806
hopscotch loan, 806
horizontal expansion, 809
hostile bidder, 805
integral-part test, 807
interlocking directorates, 801
inversion, 805
inverted company, 806
junk bonds, 805
leveraged buyout (LBO), 804
lockup agreement, 807
merger, 804
monopoly, 798
Office of Credit Ratings, 793
Office of Investor Advocate (OIA), 793
per se violation, 799
police power, 788
poison pill, 808
prospectus, 791
quasi-RPM arrangement, 800

quick-look standard, 799
registration statement, 791
RPM agreement, 800
rule-of-reason standard, 799
security, 790
security-based swaps, 792
stock acquisition, 804
swap, 792
swap transaction, 792
takeover bid, 805
target corporation, 805
targeted shareholder agreement, 807
tender offer, 805
Tunney Act, 810
tying agreement, 801
ultra vires, 789
unfriendly buyer, 805
unfriendly suitor, 805
vertical expansion, 809
white knight, 807

Questions for Review and Discussion

1. How did the federal government's power to regulate business develop?
2. What is the source of state power to regulate business?
3. How does the Securities and Exchange Commission prevent unfair practices?
4. What is a *per se* antitrust violation of antitrust law?
5. What is the rule-of-reason standard in antitrust law?
6. What are the general provisions of the post–Sherman antitrust laws?
7. What are the various techniques of corporate expansion?
8. How do the interests of the Securities and Exchange Commission differ from those of the Federal Trade Commission in corporate expansion?
9. What are the two ways that a corporation may undergo dissolution?
10. Under what circumstances might a limited liability company undergo dissolution?

Cases for Analysis

1. The following lead paragraph was published in an article titled, "Why the *Times* Could Go Private," in the December 11, 2006, issue of *BusinessWeek*: "Even before restive shareholders began ramping up pressure on The New York Times Co. and insurance mogul Maurice R. 'Hank' Greenberg started buying shares, Chairman Arthur O. Sulzberger Jr. was thinking about taking the company private. In recent months, he has been quietly soliciting advice from trusted friend and financial adviser Steven Rattner, according to sources familiar with those discussions." Later, the article adds that "Rattner met with members of the Ochs-Sulzberger family, who control the voting shares of the parent company through a trust and hold 9 of the company's 13 director seats. He offered various strategic alternatives, say sources, including a leveraged buyout."[1] What does the phrase "taking the company private" mean? What is a leveraged buyout? [See: Tom Lowry and Jon Fine, "Why the *Times* Could Go Private: An LBO Would Be a Long Shot, but Sulzberger and an Adviser Are Talking It Over," *BusinessWeek*, December 11, 2006, p. 40.]

2. The W.J. Howey Co. owned a large citrus grove in Florida. The citrus grove was serviced by Howey-in-the-Hills Inc., a corporation owned and operated by the same people who ran the Howey Co. When the Howey Co. needed money, it sold tracts of land in the grove. Each buyer had to purchase both land from the Howey Co. and a service contract from Howey-in-the-Hills. The purchasers had no right to enter the land or to market the crop. All cultivating and marketing was done by the service company. Most of the buyers were from out of state. In return for their purchase, they received a share of the profits after the crops were harvested and sold. The SEC brought suit against both companies, arguing that the land and service contracts were actually securities that should have been registered with the commission. Was the SEC correct? Explain. [See: *Securities and Exchange Commission v. W.J. Howey Co.*, 66 S.Ct. 1100 (U.S. Sup. Ct.).]

3. Topco Associates Inc. is a cooperative association of small and medium-sized regional supermarket chains. Each of its member chains operates independently. All members are required to operate under exclusive territorial licenses issued by Topco. These licenses provide that members will sell Topco-controlled brands only within the marketing territory given them. The government filed suit in federal district court. It argued that this scheme of dividing markets among competing chains violated the Sherman Antitrust Act because it prohibited competition in Topco-brand products among grocery chains engaged in retail operations. Topco defended by arguing that the association actually increased competition between the smaller and the larger chains. Was Topco correct? Defend your answer. [See: *United States v. Topco Associates, Inc.*, 92 S.Ct. 1126 (U.S. Sup. Ct.).]

4. Enstrom purchased an aircraft from the Interceptor Corporation. When the aircraft crashed due to a design defect, Enstrom sued Interceptor. However, when Enstrom found out that Interceptor's assets

had been purchased by the Interceptor Company (IC), it asked the court to join IC as a new defendant. IC argued that it was a different corporation involved in a different business. IC further argued that it had simply purchased the assets of Interceptor and was now involved in selling those assets, like the aircraft, to other buyers, like Enstrom. IC concluded that it was, therefore, not liable to Enstrom. Was IC correct? Why or why not? [See: *R.J. Enstrom Corporation v. Interceptor Corporation*, 555 F.2d 277 (10th Cir.).]

5. C.E. Stumpf & Sons Inc. was formed to conduct a masonry and general contracting business. The corporation was owned in equal shares by Stumpf and his two sons, who had previously operated the same business as partners. Hostility between the two sons grew so extreme that one, Donald, ended contact with his family and was allowed no say in the operation of the business. After Donald's withdrawal from the business, he received no salary, dividends, or other revenue from the company. He brought suit seeking involuntary dissolution of the corporation. Should the court of appeals of California uphold the trial court's dissolution order? Why or why not? [See: *Stumpf v. C.E. Stumpf & Sons, Inc.*, 120 Cal. Rptr. 671 (CA).]

6. Image Technical Services Inc. (ITS), an independent service organization (ISO), provides services for companies with copying machines made by the Eastman Kodak Co. In response to such competition, Kodak tied the sale of any of its parts to an agreement not to contract for services from any ISO. Under the terms of such an agreement, a customer who wished to buy Kodak parts had to agree not to purchase service from an ISO. ITS brought a lawsuit against Kodak under the Sherman Antitrust Act. In the suit, ITS alleged that such arrangements amounted to the type of tying agreement that was specifically outlawed by the Sherman Act. Kodak filed a motion for a summary judgment, arguing that the purchase of parts and the service of the machines with those parts did not represent the purchase of two separate products. Kodak concluded that it was, therefore, entitled to a judgment as a matter of law. Should the Court grant the summary judgment motion, or is there enough evidence of a tying agreement here to allow the matter to proceed to trial? Explain. [See: *Eastman Kodak Co. v. Image Technical Services, Inc., et al.*, 504 U.S. 451 (U.S. Sup. Ct.).]

quick quiz Answers

28-1	28-2	28-3	28-4	28-5	28-6
1. T	1. T	1. F	1. T	1. F	1. F
2. T	2. T	2. F	2. F	2. F	2. T
3. F	3. F	3. F	3. T	3. F	3. T

Part 7 Case Study

Gries Sports Enterprises, Inc. v. Cleveland Browns Football Co., Inc.
Supreme Court of Ohio 496 N.E.2d 959

©John G. Mabanglo/Epa/REX/Shutterstock

Summary

Arthur Modell, president, CEO, and a director of the Cleveland Browns Football Co. Inc., owned 53 percent of that corporation. Other members of the board at that time included Pat Modell, Modell's wife; James Bailey, who was also chief counsel for and an employee of the Browns; James Berick, who was outside counsel representing the corporation and a Browns shareholder; Richard Cole; and Nate Wallack, who was also an employee of the Browns. The final member of the board of directors was Robert Gries, who owned 43 percent of the Browns and also owned Gries Sports Enterprises Inc. (GSE). Modell also owned 80 percent of the Cleveland Stadium Corporation (CSC), which leased Cleveland Stadium from the city and then subleased the stadium to the Browns and the Cleveland Indians. Other shareholders of CSC included Berick, Bailey, Cole, Wallack, Gries, and GSE. Modell was also president of CSC, and Bailey was both secretary and general counsel of that corporation.

CSC purchased 190 acres of land in Strongsville, Ohio, from Modell for $3,000,000 in cash and a promissory note for $1,000,000. Although Modell later canceled the $1,000,000 note, CSC still had debts exceeding $4,000,000. Modell decided that it would be expedient for the Browns to purchase CSC. Accordingly, he had CSC appraised by the brokerage and investment banking firm of McDonald and Company. Modell and Bailey, along with Michael Poplar, chief financial officer of CSC, determined that the Browns should pay $6,000,000 for the purchase of CSC. After this decision had been made, Modell, Bailey, Berick, and Poplar told Gries and Cole that CSC would be purchased by the Browns for $6,000,000. The purchase plan involved a payment of $120 per share of CSC to the minority shareholders, among whom were Berick, Bailey, Wallack, and Cole. Modell, the majority shareholder in CSC, was to receive a payment of $4,800,000 for his shares.

Subsequently, Gries did his own investigation into the value of CSC and concluded that Modell, Bailey, and Poplar had seriously overvalued the worth of that corporation. When the board met to consider the purchase, Modell made a presentation in support of the plan, and Gries explained his opposition. When the matter came to a vote, Bailey, Berick, Cole, and Wallack all voted for the plan. Neither Arthur nor Pat Modell participated in the vote, and Gries voted against the transaction. The following day, Gries filed a derivative lawsuit, the objective of which was to compel a reversal of the decision to purchase CSC. Gries stated that the transaction was unfair to the corporation, in that CSC was worth only $2,000,000 at the time that the Browns purchased it for $6,000,000. Gries argued that the fairness rule rather than the business judgment rule should be used to evaluate the directors' conduct because the directors who voted for the purchase were either "interested" directors due to their stock ownership or were dominated by Modell and had simply "rubber-stamped" his decision.

Moreover, Gries contended that the overvaluation of CSC was prompted by Modell's need to secure the money to pay off outstanding debts to several banks.

Modell and the other directors argued that the decision to buy CSC should be evaluated by the business judgment rule. The trial court agreed with Gries, but the appeals court reversed that decision. The case then went to the Ohio Supreme Court.

The Court's Opinion

Justice Wise

The appellees-directors herein claim that they are protected by the presumption of good faith and fair dealing that arises from the business judgment and, therefore, they do not have the burden of proving that their decision to purchase CSC was intrinsically fair to the Browns' minority shareholders.

The issue before us, then, centers on the applicability of the business judgment rule. The business judgment rule is a principle of corporate governance that has been part of the common law for at least one hundred fifty years. It has traditionally operated as a shield to protect directors from liability for their decisions. If the directors are entitled to the protection of the rule, then the courts should not interfere with or second-guess their decisions. If the directors are not entitled to the protection of the rule then the courts scrutinize the decision as to its intrinsic fairness to the corporation and the corporation's minority shareholders. . . . A party challenging a board of directors' decision bears the burden of rebutting the presumption that the decision was a proper exercise of the business judgment of the board . . . .

In a stockholders' derivative action challenging the fairness of a transaction approved by a majority of directors of a corporation a director must be (1) disinterested, (2) independent, and (3) informed in order to claim benefit of the business judgment rule. If a director fails to pass muster as to any one of these three, he is not entitled to the business judgment presumption. This does not mean that the director's decision is necessarily wrong; it only removes the protection provided by the business judgment presumption. Once this presumption is removed, the court must then inquire into the fairness of the director's decision.

(A) [A] director is interested if (1) he appears on both sides of the transaction or (2) he has or expects to derive a personal financial benefit not equally received by the stockholders; (B) a director is independent if his decision is based on the corporate merits of the subject before the board rather than extraneous considerations or influences; a director is not independent when he is dominated by or beholden to another person through personal or other relationship; and (C) a director is informed if he makes a reasonable effort to become familiar with the relevant and reasonably available facts prior to making a business judgment.

Browns' directors Modell, Gries, Bailey, Berick, Cole, and Wallack, were all stockholders in CSC. Modell was the fifty-three percent majority stockholder in the Browns and the eighty percent majority stockholder in CSC (one hundred percent after March 2, 1982). [These facts convinced the court that the directors were interested in the challenged decision and were therefore not entitled to the protection of the business judgment rule. The court then went on to apply the fairness rule to the purchase of CSC by the Browns.]

(W)hen the transaction ". . . involves insiders dealing with their corporation the test of validity of the transaction is fairness. That our courts have frequently so held is without question . . . the substance of our decisions that 'when the persons, be they stockholders or directors, who control the making of a transaction and the fixing of its terms, are on both sides, then the presumption and deference to sound business judgment are no longer present.'"

In the instant case, no arms length negotiations as to price, terms, the elements to be included (or not to be included), or any other aspect of the proposed acquisition ever took place between the Browns and CSC. The $6,000,000 price was arrived at by Messrs. AMA (Modell), Bailey and Poplar . . . prior to any disclosure to plaintiffs of the possibility of such an acquisition, and never changed despite plaintiff's objections and despite the valuations furnished the defendants by plaintiffs. The manner in which the subject transaction was initiated, structured and disclosed to plaintiffs therefore did not satisfy the reasonable concept of fair dealing. . . .

The judgment of the court of appeals is reversed, and the judgment of the trial court is reinstated.

Judgment reversed.

Questions for Analysis

1. Which party had the burden of proof in this case?
2. According to the court's opinion, what factors should be taken into consideration in determining whether a director has an interest in a transaction that is challenged by a shareholder in a derivative lawsuit?
3. According to the court's opinion, when is a director independent, and under what circumstances does the director lose that independence?

4. What circumstances does the court say will make a director informed?

5. When the business judgment rule cannot be used, as occurred in this case, what standard is applied by the court to determine whether to reverse a challenged decision made by the directors?

6. Did the court consider the purchase of the Cleveland Stadium Corporation by the Cleveland Browns to be fair to the corporation and the minority shareholders in this case? Why or why not?

Design Elements: The Opening Case: ©Sharpstock/Alamy; A Classic Case: ©Evlakhov Valeriy/ Shutterstock

©Digital Vision/Getty Images

Part Eight
Property Law

Chapter 29	Personal Property and Bailments	Chapter 31	Wills, Trusts, and Advanced Directives
Chapter 30	Real Property and Landlord and Tenant Law	Case Study	*Obergefell, et al., v. Hodges, Director, Ohio Department of Health, et al.*

Chapter 29

Personal Property and Bailments

29-1 Personal Property
Ownership of Personal Property • Lost, Misplaced, and Abandoned Property • Gifts of Personal Property • Stolen Personal Property

29-2 Bailments
Elements of a Bailment • Principles of Bailment • Bailments for Sole Benefit of Bailor • Bailments for Sole Benefit of Bailee • Mutual-Benefit Bailments Burden of Proof • Innkeepers, Carriers, Warehousers • Trends in Cultural Property Protection

THE OPENING CASE *Round 1*
The Case of the Nelson Family Treasure Trove

The case of the Nelson family treasure trove tells a story worthy of Sherwood Anderson, William Faulkner, and Louis Bromfield. Once upon a time, before pension plans, Social Security, and the SEC, Charles and Rosa Nelson, probably thinking of retirement and the Panic of 1907, began to hoard cash and coins (including silver half-dollars and gold certificates). They carefully preserved their treasure in tin cans and mason jars and secretly buried them (most likely under the dim light of an oil lantern in the dead of the night) in the ground on the site of the family home in Selma, Iowa. They continued their furtive, nocturnal deeds from the time they purchased the family home in 1922 until Charles died in 1945 and Rosa passed away in 1968. In fact, for all we know, their daughter, Opal, may have carried on the family tradition until her death in 1981. When Opal died, her estate went into probate, and her personal property was distributed according to her will. However, under the weight of unpaid property taxes and other undisclosed but substantial problems with the title to the house, the administrator of Opal's estate abandoned the property. In a tax sale, the title to the family home went to the County of Van Buren, which ultimately sold it to the Selma United Methodist Church in 1987. The church elected to have the house demolished. That was when the real crisis began.

After the house and the garage were torn down, the Nelson family treasure trove was discovered buried on the property. Among the artifacts discovered were rare silver half-dollars dating back to the 19th century and numerous gold certificates that went back to the 1920s. On its face, before conducting an appraisal of the historical significance of the coins and certificates, the value of the Nelson family treasure amounted to $24,547.74. Dutifully, and following legal protocols, the church advertised the discovery. It was at that point that more than just a few folks emerged and laid claim to the newly discovered collection. In all, at final count, 10 individuals laid claim to the Nelson family treasure. Those people included Ruth E. Ritz, H. L. Ritz, Esther A. Beck, Phillip O. Ritz, Inez E. Holland, Russell Ritz, Raymond H. Ritz, Richard T. Ritz, Randall R. Ritz, and Barry Norlin (oddly, not a single one of the plaintiffs was named Nelson). In a joint action, the plaintiffs filed a petition for a declaratory judgment, asking the trial court to decide who really owned the Nelson family treasure. The trial court had no difficulty making its determination. It said that the Nelson family treasure had originally belonged to Charles Nelson and had passed on to Opal as his heir. However, the court did not stop there. Instead, it continued and, basing its final ruling on the statute of limitations, declared that, because all actions contesting the estate had to be brought within five years of the final settlement of Opal Nelson's estate, and because more than five years had already passed, the title to the Nelson family treasure had vested in the church that had purchased the property in a legal sale.

Dissatisfied, the family members appealed the decision of the trial court. On appeal, the family members presented two relatively straightforward arguments. First, they claimed that because they were the true heirs of the Nelson estate, their claim to the Nelson family treasure superseded that of the church. Second, because the Nelson family treasure trove was newly discovered property, the court was no longer bound by the five-year statute of limitations. Not to be left out of the running, the church filed a counterappeal, arguing that the trial court was incorrect in ruling that Charles Nelson had been the true owner. Instead, the church contended that it (the church itself) was the true owner of the Nelson family treasure because some of the bills in the treasure bore dates that occurred after Charles's death. Therefore, Charles had not buried the treasure on the land; rather, someone else had done the digging and because that person or persons were unknown, the church, as the purchaser of the land in which the treasure was buried, was the true owner.

The appellate court judges were faced with several unanswered questions. Did the Nelson family treasure qualify as lost, mislaid, or abandoned property? Because the Nelson family treasure had been buried, did it became part of the natural earth? Is there really such a thing as a legal treasure trove, and if so, did the Nelson family treasure qualify as one of those treasure troves, or was it just ordinary, everyday, lost property? Curious? Then continue reading... [See: *Ritz v. Selma United Methodist Church,* 467 N.W.2d 266 (March 20, 1991).]

Opening Case Questions

1. What is the difference between lost and mislaid property? Explain.
2. What is abandoned property? Explain.
3. Under what circumstances does property become part of the natural earth? Explain.
4. What is a treasure trove? Explain.
5. Can the statute of limitations in a probate case be overridden when new property is discovered after a final probate order has been issued? Explain.

Source: See: *Ritz v. Selma United Methodist Church,* 467 N.W.2d 266 (March 20, 1991).

 Learning Objectives

1. Give examples of tangible and intangible personal property.
2. Describe the methods of owning property with others.
3. Differentiate among lost property, misplaced property, and abandoned property.
4. Identify the requirements of a completed gift.
5. Explain the law that applies to stolen property.
6. Determine when a bailment occurs.
7. Name and describe the principal types of bailments.
8. Discuss the burden of proof as it relates to bailments.
9. Make clear an innkeeper's duty to accept all guests.
10. Explain innkeepers' duties of care to their guests and their guests' property.

29-1 Personal Property

Broadly defined, **personal property** is everything that can be owned other than real estate. It is divided into two kinds, tangible and intangible. *Tangible* personal property is property that has substance and can be touched, such as a book, a pair of jeans, or a cell phone. Also called goods, or **chattels**, tangible personal property is movable and includes animals and crops. *Intangible* personal property, in contrast, is property that is not perceptible to the senses and cannot be touched. Accounts receivables and stock certificates are examples of intangible personal property. Another name for this type of property is **chose in action**, which means evidence of the right to property but not the property itself. In addition to the items mentioned, chose in action includes money due on a note or contract, damages due for breach of contract or tort, and rights under insurance policies.

Ownership of Personal Property

When personal property is owned solely by one person, it is said to be owned in **severalty**. When it is owned by more than one person, it is said to be held in **co-tenancy**. The types of co-tenancies discussed here are tenancy in common, joint tenancy, and community property. When two or more people own personal property as **tenants in common**, each co-tenant's share of the property passes to his or her heirs upon death. In contrast, when two or more people own personal property as **joint tenants** (sometimes referred to as **joint tenants with the right of survivorship**), each co-tenant's share of the property passes to the surviving joint tenants upon death. Nine states recognize **community property**, which is property (except a gift or inheritance) that is acquired by the personal efforts of either spouse during marriage and that, by law, belongs to both spouses equally. The states that recognize community property are Arizona, California, Idaho, Louisiana, Nevada, New Mexico, Texas, Washington, and Wisconsin. Spouses can leave their half of the community property by will to whomever they choose. If they die without a will, their share passes to their surviving spouse.

Lost, Misplaced, Abandoned, and Buried Property

The finder of **lost property**, that is, property which has been found in a place that the true owner did not intend and about which the owner knows nothing, has a legal responsibility, usually fixed by statute, to make an effort to learn the identity of the owner and return the property to that person. Advertising the property in a general circulation newspaper is usually evidence of the finder's honest effort to locate the owner, although today some sort of Internet posting might be even more effective. Statutes in many states provide that if the finder of lost property has made an effort to locate the owner and has not been successful within a period specified by law, the property belongs to the finder.

If lost property is found on the counter of a store, on a table in a restaurant or hotel, on a chair in a washroom, or in some similar public or semi-public place, it is considered not to be *lost* but to have been *misplaced*. **Misplaced or mislaid property** is property that has been unintentionally left behind by its owner, usually in a public place. It is reasonable to suppose that the owner will remember leaving it there and return for it. For this reason, the finder may not keep possession of the article but must leave it with the proprietor or the premises where the property is found to hold for the owner. The owner or the manager has the legal right to the possession of the misplaced property. If the property is found on the floor or in the corridor or any other place that would indicate it was not placed there intentionally, the finder may retain possession of the article while looking for the true owner. In this case, it is not likely that the owner would recall where it was lost.

EXAMPLE 29-1: Misplaced Property

While walking along a beach one morning, Carlow noticed a plastic bag near the edge of the water. She opened the bag and discovered that it contained a large sum of money. In the bag with the money was a bank deposit slip made out in the name of a nearby seafood restaurant. Carlow had a legal duty to return the money to the restaurant. Suppose the bank deposit slip had not been in the bag and Carlow was unsuccessful in an attempt to find the rightful owner. After making a sincere effort to locate the real owner, and after the period of time set by state statute, Carlow would become the owner of the money.

When lost property is found and turned over to officials of a state, without any claim registered by the finder, the property becomes the property of the state after a period of time set by statute. The same rule applies to bank deposits and other claims that have been abandoned by persons in whose names such claims were registered. In these latter instances, a period of up to 20 years may be required to establish the right of the state to take title. In some states, gift certificate money that is unclaimed after a certain number of years is supposed to be transferred to the state under the abandoned property law. When property reverts to the state, it is said to **escheat**. Some states have statutes that remove gift certificates from their abandoned property law, treating them in different ways.

Unlike lost or mislaid property, **abandoned property** is property that has been discarded by the owner without the intent to reclaim ownership of it. Courts require clear and convincing evidence of both the desertion of the property by the owner as well as the owner's intent not to return to it before determining that property was indeed abandoned. With some exceptions, anyone who finds abandoned property has the right to keep it and obtains good title to it, even against the original owner.

Old shipwrecks are often the subject of abandoned property cases. If an abandoned shipwreck is found outside the boundaries of a state, either the law of finds or the law of salvage applies under admiralty law. The **law of finds** gives ownership to the finder if all of the following apply: (a) the property is abandoned, (b) the finder intends to acquire the property, and (c) the finder has possession of the property. The **law of salvage** gives a **salvor** (one who salvages) the right to compensation for assisting a foundering vessel. **Salvage** is the reward given to persons who voluntarily assist a sinking ship or recover its cargo from peril or loss. In addition, the United Nations Convention on the Law of the Sea (UNCLOS) requires salvors to protect the historical character of shipwrecks. If an abandoned shipwreck is found in the submerged land of any state of the United States, the Abandoned Shipwreck Act of 1987 applies rather than the law of finds or the law of salvage. This act gives states the right of ownership to shipwrecks found beneath their waters.

EXAMPLE 29-2: Law of Finds

In 2004, the federal court awarded full ownership of a Civil War–era shipwreck to Odyssey Marine Exploration. The salvage company agreed to pay $1.6 million to an insurance company that had paid claims when the ship sank. The *SS Republic* was a side-wheel steamer that went down in 1865 while en route from New York to New Orleans after fighting a hurricane for two days. The salvage company discovered the shipwreck 1,700 feet below the surface of the Atlantic Ocean approximately 100 miles off the Georgia coast. Among other relics, the ship contained $400,000 (face value) of gold and silver coins, which may now be worth up to $180 million.

Sometimes, property that has been buried for such a long time that it becomes part of the natural earth itself. The finder of that property, sometimes referred to as **natural property**, is not considered the true owner. Instead, the person who owns the premises on which the property was buried becomes the legal owner. In contrast, the finder of a treasure trove becomes the rightful owner of the treasure until the real owner can be located. To be a **treasure trove**, property must consist of ancient artifacts, often, but not necessarily, money, that was deliberately hidden so long ago that the identity of the original owner has been lost in antiquity.

THE OPENING CASE *Round 2*
The Case of the Nelson Family Treasure Trove

Charles and Rosa Nelson owned a house in Selma, Iowa, where they lived together, along with their daughter Opal, from 1928 until Opal passed away in 1981. At some point during the long history of the family and the family home, Charles and Opal, probably thinking of retirement and the Panic of 1907, began to hoard cash and coins (including silver half-dollars and gold certificates). Together, they placed the silver coins and the gold certificates in mason jars and tin cans and buried their stash somewhere in the backyard. Apparently, no one, save perhaps Opal, knew anything about their unorthodox savings plan. Charles died in 1945, Rosa passed away in 1968, and Opal died in 1981. At Opal's death, her estate went into probate and her personal property was distributed according to her will. Unfortunately, because of unpaid property taxes and irregularities in the title, the family home ended in the hands of Van Buren County. In 1987, the county sold the Nelson family homestead to the Selma United Methodist Church. The church had the entire structure torn down. Unexpectedly, under the rubble of the Nelson family estate, someone unearthed the Nelson family treasure trove. Even without an appraisal, the value of the Nelson family treasure amounted to $24,547.74. Faithfully following state law, the church advertised the discovery of the hidden money. At that point, several family members surfaced and laid claim to the newly discovered treasure. In all, at final count, 10 individuals claimed a portion of the Nelson family treasure.

In a joint action, the plaintiffs filed a petition for a declaratory judgment, asking the trial court to decide who really owned the Nelson family treasure. The trial court ruled that the Nelson family treasure had belonged to Charles Nelson and had passed to Opal as his heir. The court also ruled that because all actions contesting the estate were to be brought within five years of the final settlement of Opal Nelson's estate, and because more than five years had already passed, the title to the Nelson family treasure had vested in the church that had purchased the property in a legal sale. Naturally, with more than $24,000 at stake, the plaintiffs appealed. The plaintiffs presented two arguments on appeal. First, they contended that because they were the true heirs of the Nelson estate, their claim to the Nelson family treasure superseded that of the church. Second, since the Nelson family treasure was newly discovered property, the court was no longer bound by the five year statute of limitations. The church also got into the act and filed a counterappeal, arguing that the trial court was incorrect in ruling that Charles Nelson had been the true owner. Instead, the church argued that it was the true owner of the Nelson family treasure because some of the bills and coins in the treasure bore dates that occurred after Charles's death. Therefore, the church claimed that Charles had not buried the treasure on the land. Instead, someone else had done the digging and buried the treasure. Moreover, because that person was unknown, the church, as the purchaser of the land, was the true owner.

The appellate court was faced with several unanswered questions: (1) Was the Nelson family treasure lost, mislaid, or abandoned property? (2) Because the Nelson family treasure trove had been buried in the ground, had it became part of the natural earth? (3) Finally, did the Nelson family treasure qualify as a treasure trove, or was it just ordinary, everyday, lost property? To answer these questions, the court ran through a series of definitions and principles related to lost and mislaid property. Those definitions and principles look like this: "The general rule is that the finder of *lost property* becomes the owner thereof against the whole world other than the true owner . . . Property is lost when the owner unintentionally and involuntarily parts with its possession and does not know where it is . . . *Mislaid property* is that which the owner has voluntarily placed somewhere and then forgets that it is there. . . . The right of possession of mislaid property is in the owner of the premises upon which it is found, as against all persons other than the true owner. . . . (*Natural property*) is property which has become a part of the natural earth [and] is not subject to the general rule of lost or mislaid property . . . Such property belongs to the owner of the real estate upon which it was found. Examples of this type of property are a meteorite, a prehistoric boat, valuable earthenware and gold-bearing quartz . . . *Treasure trove* is treated as lost and belongs to the finder as against all except the true owner . . . Treasure trove consists of coins or paper money which is concealed by the owner; it carries with it the thought of antiquity such that it has been hidden so long that the true owner is not discoverable . . . *Abandoned property* is that to which the owner has voluntarily relinquished all right, title, and interest with the intention of terminating his ownership. The finder who reduces abandoned property to possession acquires absolute title as against the former owner" [italics added]. The court then used these principles to come to its conclusion.

First, it is clear that the Nelson family did not lose or misplace the property. In fact, that conclusion was so clear that the court skipped right over that issue and headed directly into abandoned property. Accordingly, the court notes that because the money was placed in jars and cans, the Nelsons must have intended to retrieve it at some future date. Therefore, the treasure was not abandoned. Next, the court noted that the property cannot be considered natural property because it was still in the containers when found and had not become part of the earth. Nor is the property truly a treasure trove—despite our use of the term—because it bears none of the signs of antiquity as required under the law. Once the court had eliminated all other possibilities then, what remained had to be true. What remained was simple enough: Following the unambiguous principles of property law, whenever the original owner of a piece of property has passed away, the person's heirs are the rightful owners of that property—in this case, the plaintiffs in the lawsuit. Moreover, the plaintiffs' claim was not barred by the five-year statute of limitations because the Nelson treasure qualifies as newly discovered property. Finally, the court had no difficulty dismissing the church's claim. The church had argued that the Nelson treasure trove must have belonged to someone else because some of the coins and bills were dated after Charles had passed away. However, when pressed to produce evidence to support that allegation, the church could not do so. Moreover, the court noted that even if parts of the treasure were placed in the cans and the tins after Charles had passed away, Rose or Opal could have continued to add money to the stash after Charles was gone. Accordingly, the appellate court concluded that the trial court had been incorrect. Therefore, the Court of Appeals sent the case back to the trial court to enter a declaratory judgment in favor of the plaintiffs. [See: *Ritz v. Selma United Methodist Church*, 467 N.W.2d 266 (March 20, 1991).]

Source: See: *Ritz v. Selma United Methodist Church*, 467 N.W.2d 266 (March 20, 1991).

Gifts of Personal Property

People often make gifts of personal property. There are three requirements for a gift to be completed: the **donor** (the one giving the gift) must intend to make a gift, the gift must be delivered to the **donee** (the one receiving it), and the donee must accept the gift. Once all three requirements are met, the gift cannot be taken back by the donor. It is known as an absolute gift, or **gift *inter vivos*** (between the living). The gift of an engagement ring is a conditional gift, given in contemplation of marriage. Most courts hold that the donor of an engagement ring is entitled to its return if the engagement is broken by mutual agreement or by the donee. A few courts allow the return of the ring even when the donor breaks the engagement. These courts theorize that it is better to break the engagement without penalty than to have an unhappy marriage.

Uniform Transfers to Minors Act Problems can easily arise when gifts are given to minors. Sometimes, parents or guardians use such gifts for themselves rather than for the minor. At other times, donors make gifts to minors and then change their minds and take the gifts back. Gifts to minors are often used as tax shelters. Formerly, wealthy parents in high tax brackets often made gifts to their minor children as a way to shift unearned income to lower-bracket taxpayers. The IRS has changed this practice with the so-called kiddie tax. Unearned income (dividends and interest) of a child under the age of 19 up to $2,000 is taxed at the child's income tax rate and, above that, at the parent's income tax rate. This rule also applies to college students under the age of 24 unless they provide over half of their own support from earned income (wages and salaries). (*Note:* The amount of unearned income that can be taxed at the child's income tax rate changes periodically so it is best to check the current dollar amount allowed under the law.)

The Uniform Transfer to Minors Act (UTMA), which has been adopted by most states, also prevents some of these problems. The act establishes a procedure for gifts to be made to minors. Under the procedure, minors are assured that gifts to them will either be used for their benefit or made available to them when they become adults. The income from gifts that are given to minors is taxable according to the kiddie tax rules mentioned previously. The UTMA allows money, securities, real property, and tangible and intangible personal property to be transferred to a custodian for the minor's benefit. The age of 21 rather than 18 years is used as the age when the custodianship terminates, because the IRS uses that age to terminate certain trusts.

Gift *in Causa Mortis* A gift given during one's lifetime, in contemplation of death from a known cause, is a *gift in causa mortis*. A gift *in causa mortis* is conditional, and it is ineffective if the donor does not die as expected or if death is caused by circumstances other than those feared.

EXAMPLE 29-3: Void Gift *in Causa Mortis*

Rossano was seriously ill following an abdominal operation. Realizing that death might be near, Rossano signed over a savings account to Hall, giving Hall the savings book with necessary notations of assignment. Rossano did die three weeks later, not because of the surgery but because of a bacterial infection contracted in the hospital from contaminated surgical instruments. Rossano's executor may declare the gift *in causa mortis* void and demand the return of Rossano's savings for the benefit of the estate.

Anatomical Gifts With so many medical advancements in recent years, there is an increased need in society for gifts of human bodies, tissues, and organs for medical education, research, and transplantation. The Uniform Anatomical Gift Act was revised in 2006 to help meet present-day needs.

Stolen Personal Property

Although a presumption of title to goods usually follows possession of them, it is possible for a person to have possession of goods without having title, just as it is possible for a person to have title without having possession. Thus, a thief acquires no title to goods that are stolen and therefore cannot convey a good title. The true owner never relinquished title to the goods, and even an innocent purchaser who acquired the goods in good faith and for value would be obliged to return the goods to the owner. Title to stolen goods never left the true owner, and possession can always be regained by that owner if the goods can be found, no matter in whose possession they may be at the time.

quick quiz 29-1

1. If lost property is found on a table in a restaurant, it is considered to be misplaced rather than lost. true | false
2. A gift *in causa mortis* is conditional, and it is ineffective if the donor does not die as expected or if death is caused by circumstances other than those feared. true | false
3. An innocent purchaser who buys stolen goods from a thief acquires good title to the stolen goods. true | false

29-2 Bailments

Bailments happen all the time in everyday life. We just don't call them bailments. Ask your friend to watch your backpack in the cafeteria and you've created a bailment. Hand your keys to a valet at a parking garage and your car is in the hands of a bailee. Leave your computer at a nearby computer fix-it shop for repairs and, once again, you have set up a bailment. Most of the time this does not matter. However, when your backpack vanishes, or the valet bends a fender, or the repair shop gives you the wrong computer, then knowing about the elements, principles, and responsibilities attached to bailment comes in handy.

The Elements of a Bailment

A **bailment** is the transfer of possession and control of personal property (goods) to another with the intent that the same property will be returned later. Renting a vehicle, borrowing a friend's tablet, or leaving clothes at the cleaners are examples of bailment. The person who transfers the possession of the property to another is the **bailor**. The person to whom it is transferred is the **bailee**. The elements of bailment include the intent to transfer and accept the property, thus creating the bailment; the actual delivery of the property to the bailee; and the bailee's acceptance of that property. It is possible to create a bailment by expressly stated terms. A bailment can also be implied by circumstances. This is an **implied-in-fact bailment**, or an **implied-in-law bailment** and/or a **constructive bailment**. To figure out whether a bailment actually exists, the facts and circumstances surrounding the transaction must be analyzed. The court will look at such issues as the intent on the part of both parties to be bound to the bailment, the benefits that accrue to each party, the nature of the property involved in the transaction, and who actually retains control. One additional element that is often unstated but is, nevertheless, essential to the creation of a bailment is knowledge. Both parties, but especially the bailee, who is, after all, accepting additional responsibilities, must know what is going on. Without knowledge, there can be no proper intent and no proper acceptance on the part of either party but especially on the part of the bailee. Thus, an individual cannot simply leave an item in your home without you knowing about it and then recover for damages for the loss of that hidden item. Nor can an individual take an item of property without the owner's knowledge and then charge the owner a handsome fee for protecting the item.

A CLASSIC CASE A Late Night Halloween Caper: The Case of the Missing Intent

Richard Berglund had assumed several roles during his tenure at Roosevelt University. He was a full-time student, an editor of the campus newspaper, a paid employee, and, most critical of all, the paper's photographer. In his role as a photographer, he had to have his cameras close by and ready to go at all times. This requirement explains his preference for keeping those cameras on hand in the newspaper office. Of course, he did not come up with that idea on his own. He kept his cameras in a certain drawer in a certain filing cabinet in the darkroom because most of his predecessors had done exactly the same thing. The newspaper office was housed in a building that had security, was locked to outsiders at night, and was policed by someone at all times—to the extent that no property could be removed without written permission. Nevertheless, somehow during Halloween weekend, Berglund's expensive personal camera equipment vanished. Because the cameras were stored on university property, because the cameras were in the darkroom due to his role as photographer, and because the student activities coordinator (SAC) (for all intents and purposes, his boss) knew that he owned and used his own private cameras, Berglund demanded reimbursement from the university. When that was not forthcoming, he brought this suit against the university, alleging that a bailment had been created and that the university had failed to protect his cameras as it was required to do as bailee. The trial court agreed with Berglund.

If we look at the elements of a bailment, we might see why. The elements of bailment include the intent to transfer and accept the property, thus creating the bailment; the actual delivery of the property to the bailee; and the bailee's acceptance of that property. Berglund certainly intended to transfer the property to the filing cabinet that was owned by the university, and he certainly delivered the cameras by placing them in the filing cabinet. Moreover, because the SAC had spoken to him about his cameras and because his predecessors had stored camera equipment in exactly the same place, the university's intent to act as a bailee can be inferred. As it turned out, the trial court agreed with Berglund that a bailment had been created. Yet something seems amiss. This is why the university appealed the case. What is missing is the university's true intent to accept and protect the cameras. Because Berglund did not follow protocol and did not ask permission to store the cameras in the office, neither the university nor any of its agents, including the security guards and the SAC, had any knowledge of the cameras and could, therefore, not intentionally accept the responsibilities of a bailee. As for Berglund's arguments about the SAC and the past practices of previous photographers, the appellate court decided that neither Berglund's conversations with the coordinator nor the past practices of other photographers could rise to the level of intent. For that reason, the appellate court reversed the decision of the trial court. The ruling was simple: No intent—no bailment—period. [See: *Berglund v. Roosevelt University*, 310 NE 2d 773 Appellate Court of Illinois, First District, Third Division.]

Source: See: *Berglund v. Roosevelt University*, 310 NE 2d 773 Appellate Court of Illinois, First District, Third Division.

Principles of Bailment

In a bailment, neither the bailor nor the bailee intends any change in the title to the property involved in the bailment. The bailee has an obligation to return the same property to the bailor, or to someone the bailor designates, at a later time. A bailment does not occur when the person in possession of the property has no control over it. For example, it is not a bailment when someone parks a car in an unattended parking area. In contrast, courts have held it to be a bailment when someone parks a car in a garage or a parking lot that has an attendant present at all times to check cars going in and out. When an individual loans goods to another with the intention that the goods may be used and later replaced with an equal amount of different, but similar, goods, it is not a bailment. Instead, it is known as **mutuum**. For example, when you borrow a cup of flour from your neighbor, you will use the flour in a baking project of some sort. When you return the flour the next day, it is obviously not the same flour, but a substitute. You know this and so does your neighbor. The loan of the flour was a *mutuum* rather than a bailment because the parties did not expect that the identical particles of flour would be returned.

Bailments for Sole Benefit of Bailor

There are three principal types of bailments: bailments for the sole benefit of the bailor, bailments for the sole benefit of the bailee, and mutual-benefit bailments. In the first two types, called **gratuitous bailments**, property is transferred to another person without either party giving or asking for payment of any kind. Such bailments lack consideration; therefore, they may be rescinded at any time by either party. Parties to such agreements usually consider them only as favors. In reality, however, definite legal responsibilities are placed upon both the bailor and the bailee.

When possession of personal property is transferred to another for purposes that will benefit only the bailor, *bailments for the sole benefit of the bailor* result. In a bailment for the sole benefit of the bailor, the bailee owes a duty to use only *slight care* because the bailee is receiving no benefit from the arrangement. The bailee is required only to refrain from **gross negligence**, or very great negligence—much more serious than ordinary negligence. In a bailment for the sole benefit of the bailor, the bailor has a duty to reimburse the bailee for any expenses the bailee might have in the care of the property.

However, the bailee has no implied right to use the bailor's property in a bailment for the sole benefit of the bailor. Use without permission is technically a tort of conversion on the part of the bailee; it would make the bailee liable for any damages that might result, even if the bailee had used great care and was not guilty of negligence. (Conversion is the civil wrong that arises when one unlawfully treats another's property as one's own.)

Bailments for Sole Benefit of Bailee

Transactions in which the possession of personal property is transferred for purposes that will benefit only the bailee are gratuitous *bailments for the sole benefit of the bailee*. In a bailment for the sole benefit of the bailee, the bailee is required to use *great care* because possession of the goods is solely for the bailee's benefit. The bailee is responsible for **slight negligence**, which is the failure to use that degree of care that persons of extraordinary prudence and foresight are accustomed to use. In this type of bailment, the bailee has the right to use the property for the purposes for which the bailment was created. Use for other purposes or over a longer period of time than provided for in the agreement will make the bailee responsible for any damages that may result to the property, regardless of the amount of care exercised.

Any *ordinary* and *expected expense* incurred in the use of another's property must be borne by the bailee. For example, if you borrow your friend's car, the use of gas and oil in the operation of the car would be ordinary and expected. You as the bailee would be expected to cover those expenses. However, repairs and adjustments not caused by ordinary use or damages not attributed to the bailee's negligence become the responsibility of the bailor. The bailee is not obligated to replace parts that break down because of the gradual use and depreciation of the other's property over an extended period. If a part of the car, let's say the serpentine belt, simply reaches the point of maximum wear and tears while you are using it, through no fault of your own, then you would not be responsible for the cost of repairing that belt, even if it snaps the next time your friend drives the car right after you've returned it.

When *unusual* and *unexpected* expenses result during a bailment that are not the result of any negligence on the part of the bailee, then the bailor will be responsible for any payments that might result. If, while you are using the car, the front tire has a blowout and it is evident that the tire was badly worn in many places due to your friend's long-term neglect, then you would not be responsible. Your friend would be responsible for any unusual and unexpected expenses that might result from this problem, including your friend's obligation to reimburse you should you pay to have the tire replaced. On the other hand, if while driving your friend's car you drive it for 70 miles without releasing the emergency brake, you will be liable for ruining the brake and will have to pay for having it replaced.

Mutual-Benefit Bailments

When personal property is transferred to a bailee with the intent that both parties will benefit, a *mutual-benefit bailment* results. Ordinary bailments involving business transactions are usually mutual-benefit bailments in which the businessperson is paid for his or her services. Renting an item such as a car or a moving van, leaving a car at a garage to be repaired or a suit to be cleaned at a cleaners, placing one's property in storage, and leaving a diamond ring at a pawn shop (a *pledge*) in exchange for a loan of money are examples of mutual-benefit bailments.

A *consignment contract* is a type of mutual-benefit bailment in which the *consignor* entrusts goods to the *consignee* for the purpose of selling them. If the goods are sold, the consignee, known as the *factor*, will forward the proceeds, minus a fee, to the consignor. If they are not sold, they will be returned. In a mutual-benefit bailment, the bailee owes a duty to use *reasonable care*. Reasonable care means the degree of care that a reasonably prudent person would use under the same circumstances and conditions. The bailee is responsible for *ordinary negligence*, which is the failure to use the care that a reasonable person would use under the same circumstances.

Many courts today apply the reasonable care standard to all types of bailments, including bailments for the sole benefit of the bailor and bailments for the sole benefit of the bailee. In a mutual-benefit bailment, the bailee must use the property only for the express purposes permitted by the bailor, as provided for in the contract of bailment. The rental of a car, tools, or formal wear, for example, implies the right of reasonable use. Failing to use the property as agreed makes the bailee responsible for any damages that might result, regardless of the degree of care exercised.

Burden of Proof

Sometimes items are damaged, lost, or stolen when they are in the possession of a bailee. In the past, the bailor had to prove that the bailee was negligent to recover against the bailee for damages. This proof was very difficult to obtain because the bailor was not in a position to know what caused the loss, because the bailee had possession of the property at the time. Most courts today shift the burden of proof in bailment cases to the one who is in the best position to know what happened—that is, to the bailee. Today, when items in the possession of a bailee are damaged, lost, or stolen, the burden is on the bailee to prove that it was not negligent.

ANOTHER CLASSIC CASE   How Not to Meet the Burden of Proof: *American Ambassador Casualty Co. v. City of Chicago*

As any good citizen might do, Bruce Anderson took out an insurance policy on his automobile. The policy was taken out with American Ambassador Casualty Co. Anderson's policy insured his automobile against losses that might result if the vehicle were stolen. Moreover, the policy provided comprehensive coverage. As a result of a series of events not fully explained by the court in the case, somehow Anderson's car was impounded by officials operating under the authority of the City of Chicago. Apparently, the driver of the car had been arrested. The driver, however, was not Anderson. Therefore, Anderson was within his rights when he showed up at the impound lot and asked for his car. The city was either unwilling or unable to return Anderson's car. More than one month later, Anderson was told by the police that his car had, well, vanished. Apparently, it had been stolen and, as far as the police were concerned, that was that. Anderson applied to his insurance company for compensation, and ultimately he received a check for $10,052. The insurance company then turned around, as was its right, and sued the city. The city asked the court to dismiss the action, arguing that no bailment existed and that it could, therefore, not be held liable. (*Note:* The city also argued that it was immune under the Tort Immunity Act, but that need not concern us here.) As we have seen, and as the court explained in this case, a bailment is the transfer of possession and control of personal property (goods) to another with the intent *that the same property will be returned later* [italics added for ironic [satiric?] emphasi]. The court also notes that the elements of bailment include the intent to transfer and accept the property, thus creating the bailment; the actual delivery of the property to the bailee; and the bailee's acceptance of that property.

Now it is interesting that the city did not contest the facts. Sure, the city said, we took the car and impounded it, and, yes, Anderson asked for it back, and, no, we did not return it. The only defense that the city offered was that the plaintiff was wrong in claiming that a bailment existed because none of its agents had agreed to the bailment, period. The case sounds eerily like *Berglund v. Roosevelt University* in previous Classic Case. In both cases, we have defendants claiming that there was no agreement to create a bailment. However, there is a difference. In this case, the City of Chicago either misunderstands or just flat out twists the meaning of intent to meet its own agenda. In *Roosevelt*, neither the university nor its agents knew about the camera equipment until it came up missing. The university could not intend to keep something it did not know it had. Here, city officials not only knew they had the car, but they also took the vehicle in the first place. Moreover, the city then kept the car, despite multiple requests for its return by the rightful owner, until the car just disappeared. The court sees this as the deciding factor in the case. The city implied its agreement to the bailment by taking and keeping the car. Those actions, therefore, created an implied bailment. Call it a constructive bailment, if you want; but it is a bailment, nonetheless. [See: *American Ambassador Casualty Co. v. City of Chicago*, 563 N.E.2d 882 (1990).]

Source: See: *American Ambassador Casualty Co. v. City of Chicago*, 563 N.E.2d 882 (1990).

Innkeepers, Carriers, Warehousers

Certain types of bailees, including innkeepers, common carriers, and warehousers, have extraordinary obligations in addition to the duties imposed on all bailees.

Innkeepers An **innkeeper** is the operator of a hotel, motel, or inn that holds itself out to the public as being ready to entertain travelers, strangers, and transient guests. A **transient** is a guest whose length of stay is variable. To assist travelers in obtaining accommodations, common law imposed the duty upon innkeepers to accept all people who requested a room if one was available. In addition, innkeepers were considered insurers of their guests' property. With some exceptions, these standards are still the law today. The Civil Rights Act of 1964 prohibits discrimination in the selection of guests for reasons of race, creed, color, gender, or ethnic background. People may be turned away when all rooms are occupied or reserved. In addition, innkeepers may refuse to accommodate people whose presence might endanger the health, welfare, or safety of other guests or the safety of the establishment itself.

Innkeeper's Duty of Care Innkeepers must use reasonable care in protecting their guests from harm. They are responsible for injuries to their guests caused by the inn's negligence or the negligence of employees. Innkeepers must respect their guests' rights to privacy. Guests are guaranteed exclusive and undisturbed privacy of rooms assigned by the hotel. Interruption of the guests' privacy through unpermitted entry by hotel employees or other guests creates a liability in tort for invasion of privacy.

Innkeepers' Eliminated Liability Innkeepers are not liable as insurers in four situations:

1. Losses caused by a guest's own negligence.
2. Losses to the guest's property due to acts of God or acts of the public enemy.
3. Losses of property due to accidental fire in which no negligence may be attributed to the hotelkeeper. This exception also includes fires caused by other guests staying at the hotel at the same time. Such persons, even though on other floors, are called fellow guests.
4. Losses arising out of characteristics of the property that cause its own deterioration.

Hotels hold great responsibility and must meet obligations when it comes to their guests and travelers.
©Erik Isakson/Getty Images

A QUESTION OF LAW AND ETHICS

Footsteps in the Night, Footprints in the Morning

The Mellings arrived at their hotel in Los Alamos to attend Mr. Melling's nephew's wedding. The couple checked into the inn and unpacked their luggage. After settling in, Mr. Melling decided to shower while his wife was out shopping. After taking a shower, he opened the bathroom door and discovered a couple bringing suitcases into his room. The desk clerk had assigned the room to another couple by mistake. Following the incident, Mr. Melling was embarrassed, humiliated, and angry with the inn's employees for making such a silly mistake, but there was nowhere else in town with vacancies and so the couple decided to stay. Meanwhile, while shopping, Mrs. Melling purchased a diamond ring, which she placed in the inn's safe deposit vault. Later, Mrs. Melling withdrew the ring from the vault to wear that evening at the rehearsal dinner. When she went to return the ring to the vault later that night, she was told by the desk clerk that the vault was closed until the next morning. Before retiring for the night, the Mellings locked their outside door but did not secure the chain latch. At about 5:30 a.m., they awoke to find a masked burglar in the room at the foot of their bed. The burglar escaped with Mrs. Melling's new diamond ring and Mr. Melling's wallet. After the police had been called and a report filed, the Mellings went to the wedding. Although they were advised to lock their room before going to the church, Mr. Melling was so upset with the inn staff that he just stormed off and drove away, leaving the room unlocked. While the couple was at the wedding and the reception, their luggage disappeared from their room. Later, the couple brought suit against the Rosier Hospitality Corporation, which owned the hotel. Innkeepers have a greater duty of care toward their guests' property than is imposed in a usual mutual-benefit bailment. With exceptions (as described subsequently), innkeepers are held by law to be insurers of their guests' property. The insured property includes all personal property brought into the hotel for the convenience and purpose of the guests' stay. In the event of loss, the hotelkeeper may be held liable, regardless of the amount of care exercised in the protection of the guests' property.

A QUESTION OF LAW

Let's look again at the facts in this case and see the results of applying these principles to those facts. The inn will be held liable for the loss of the ring because it did not provide a place for its safekeeping, despite the fact that Mrs. Melling presented the ring to the staff and specifically asked for the protective measure that the staff should have been able to provide. On the other hand, the inn will not be held liable for the loss of the luggage because Mr. Melling had been specifically advised to lock the room and had failed to do so because of his inopportune temper tantrum. Moreover, in most states, innkeepers are further protected by laws limiting the amount of claim any guest may make for a single loss. The limit is usually $500 or less, depending on the state in which the hotel is located.

A QUESTION OF ETHICS

Let's look again at the facts in this case, only this time let's look at it from an ethical perspective. Before you consider each question, turn to Chapter 1 to review the various ethical theories noted there (market value ethics, social contract theory, utilitarianism, and rational ethics). Then using one of those theories in a consistent way, answer the following questions.

1. Is it ethical for an inn to set up an artificial time limit that will prevent some guests from getting the protection that they have come to expect while staying at hotels and motels? Explain.
2. Was it ethical for Mr. Melling to get angry with the hotel staff? Explain.
3. Was it ethical for Mr. Melling to storm off as he did leaving his room unlocked? Explain.
4. Was it ethical for the hotel staff to avoid checking Mr. Melling's room to see if it was locked? Explain.
5. Was it ethical for Mr. Melling to file this lawsuit given his own culpability in the situation (he did, after all, leave his own door unlocked)? Explain.

Innkeeper's Lien and Credit Card Blocking Innkeepers have a lien on their guests' property. A lien is a claim that one has against the property of another. If a guest cannot pay the bill, the innkeeper is permitted to take possession of the guest's property as security for payment at some later date. Payment of the bill releases the property and terminates the right of lien. Credit card blocking is a common method used by hotels to secure payment for a room. Under this system, guests are asked for a credit card when they register. The hotel then contacts the card issuer electronically with the estimated cost of the bill. If the card issuer approves the transaction, the guest's available line of credit is reduced by the estimated amount. This procedure is known as a block (or authorization). The final actual charge for the room will replace the block within a day or two after the guest checks out. If the guest pays the final charge with cash, check, or a different credit card, however, the block can remain on the original credit card for as long as 15 days.

Carriers The Transportation Security Administration (TSA) within the Department of Homeland Security protects the nation's transportation systems to ensure freedom of movement for people and commerce. Soon after the establishment of the TSA, Congress set up the Department of Homeland Security, which oversees the Coast Guard, Customs Service, Immigration and Naturalization Service, and TSA. Collectively, these organizations are responsible for protecting the nation's transportation system and supervising the entry of people and goods into the United States. **Carriers** are businesses that undertake to transport persons, goods, or both.

Common Carriers If a carrier holds itself out to the general public to provide transportation for compensation, it is called a common carrier. Like hotels, common carriers cannot turn away people who ask for their services, with exceptions for security reasons. Common carriers of goods are insurers of all goods accepted for shipment. They are liable as insurers regardless of whether they have been negligent. The Carmack Amendment to the Interstate Commerce Act states that a carrier is liable for damages to goods transported by it unless there is proof that the damage occurs because of one of the following exceptions:

- Acts of God (e.g., floods, tornadoes, cyclones, volcanoes, asteroid collisions, earthquakes).
- Acts of the public enemy (wartime enemies, terrorists, and the like).
- Acts of public authorities.
- Acts of the shipper.
- The inherent nature of the goods (e.g., perishable goods, evaporating and fermenting liquids, diseased animals).

EXAMPLE 29-4: Insurer of Goods

Whitehall Packing Co. engaged Amway Truck Lines to transport 40 barrels of fresh meat from its plant in Wisconsin to Howard Johnson's in New York. The federal government required plastic liners in the barrels, and Howard Johnson's would not allow dry ice in them. The refrigerator unit in Amway's truck operated properly. The truck experienced delays and took longer than its normal running time for the trip. When it arrived in New York, the meat in the barrels had a gassy odor and was not considered acceptable by the U.S. government inspector (no kidding!). An expert meat inspector testified that the barreled meat was smothered because of the use of the plastic liners and the absence of dry ice. Some hanging meat in the same truck was found to be in perfect condition. Although there was no evidence that Amway was negligent, the court held it responsible, saying that it was an insurer of the meat.

Antidiscrimination Provisions In addition to being insurers, common carriers of goods must accept *without discrimination* all goods offered to them for shipment. Under the Interstate Commerce Act, discrimination through either the selection of customers or the use of preferential rates is illegal. Exceptions to the rule against discrimination are as follows:

1. A common carrier is not required to accept goods of a type that it is not equipped to carry.
2. The carrier may refuse goods that are inherently dangerous and that would create hazard beyond the control of the carrier's usual safety facilities.
3. The common carrier may refuse goods that it does not represent itself as hauling.
4. The carrier may refuse goods that are improperly packed. Proper packaging is determined by the type of goods being shipped, the length of the haul, and the usual custom of the trade.
5. The carrier may refuse goods that are not delivered at the proper place and time.

Common carriers will not be excused from liability for losses due to strikes, mob violence, fire, and similar causes. Labor unions are required to give notice of impending strikes weeks in advance of the strike dates to allow carriers to reject shipments that might be damaged by delays caused by strikes. The carrier is required to ship goods by the proper route, protect them during shipment, and deliver them to the proper person. Carriers may limit the amount of their liability to the value stated on the bill of lading, which is the written contract between a common carrier and a shipper.

EXAMPLE 29-5: Failure to Read Contract

Bratton hired Allied Van Lines Inc. to transport her household goods from Ohio to Florida. When the goods were picked up, Bratton signed a bill of lading that contained a provision limiting the carrier's liability to $1.25 per pound (which amounted to $4,500) or the actual value of the goods as written on the bill of lading. There was a place on the bill of lading for Bratton to fill in the actual value of the goods ($10,630). She failed to do so. The shipment was destroyed in transit. Bratton argued that because she did not read the document and was unaware of any provision affecting the carrier's liability, she was not bound by the words in the bill of lading. The court held that a bill of lading containing a limitation of the carrier's liability is binding, even though the shipper had not read it.

Carrier's Lien on Goods Shipped A common carrier has the right to the payment of fees agreed upon for the shipment of the goods and a lien on all goods shipped for the amount of the shipping charges due. Should the shipper or the party receiving the goods fail to pay the charges, the carrier has the right to sell the goods at public sale.

EXAMPLE 29-6: Swift and Sure Shipping v. Harrison Printing

The Harrison Printing Company ordered paper from the Metropolis Paper Company. The paper was shipped from Metropolis, Illinois, under terms that transferred title to the paper when delivered to the carrier, Swift and Sure Shipping. Harrison Printing refused to pay shipping costs when informed of the arrival of the shipment. Notice was finally given to both firms of the carrier's intention to sell the paper to recover shipping charges. At a public sale, the paper brought a high bid of $2,237. The carrier deducted shipping costs and turned over the balance to the Harrison Printing Company.

Common Carriers of Passengers A **passenger** is defined as a person who enters the premises of a carrier with the intention of buying a ticket for a trip. One continues to be a passenger as long as one continues the trip. This relationship is terminated after the person has reached the destination printed on the ticket and left the premises of the carrier. Prior to 9/11, common carriers had an obligation to accept all passengers who sought passage over their lines. This rule has changed. By order of the U.S. Congress, the Federal Aviation Administration (FAA) has established regulations that require the screening of passengers and property before they enter an aircraft to search for dangerous weapons, explosives, and other destructive substances. Passengers who do not consent to the screening must be refused transportation.

Functioning under the Department of Homeland Security, the TSA's mission is to prevent terrorist attacks and protect the U.S. transportation network. Its work encompasses all sectors of transportation, from container ships in harbors to trucks on highways to commuter trains in subways. The approach to security on aircraft includes thorough screening of baggage and passengers by highly trained screeners, fortified cockpit doors in all airliners, thousands of federal air marshals aboard a record number of flights, and armed federal flight deck officers. A list of items that cannot be taken on board an aircraft can be found on the Internet.

More Antidiscrimination Provisions Common carriers may not discriminate in the selection of passengers on the basis of race, color, national origin, religion, sex, or ancestry. **Racial profiling**, the act of targeting a person for criminal investigation primarily because of racial or ethnic characteristics, may not be a motivating factor in a carrier's decision to refuse transportation. However, carriers may refuse passengers (1) when all available space is occupied or reserved; (2) if they are disorderly, intoxicated, insane, or infected with a contagious disease; or (3) since 9/11, when the carrier decides a passenger "is or might be inimical to safety." Moreover, a passenger who has boarded a plane that has not taken off must leave the plane if told to do so by an authorized airline representative. This is because a carrier must exercise reasonable care in the protection of passengers. Injuries that are reasonably foreseeable or preventable and that result from the carrier's negligence give the passenger a right to sue for damages. However, if injuries are not reasonably foreseeable or preventable, the carrier is not responsible.

EXAMPLE 29-7: Carrier's Duty to Protect Passengers

Three men who were intoxicated boarded a commuter train around midnight. They were talking loudly and making a lot of noise. A conductor saw them and told them not to bother passengers. At the next stop, while the conductor let passengers on and off the train, the men went to another car. There, they assaulted, hit, and kicked a passenger. As soon as the conductor reboarded the train, he sought out the three men, discovered what they had done, and had them arrested. In a suit brought by the injured passenger against the carrier, the court held in favor of the carrier. The court said that the incident occurred so quickly and unexpectedly that the conductor, acting with the highest degree of care under the circumstances, could not have averted it.

Bumped Airline Passengers When an airline flight is overbooked, the airline must first find volunteers willing to give up their seats for ones on the next available flight. If there are not enough volunteers, other passengers may be denied a seat in accordance with the airline's priority rules. Airlines are required to establish and publish priority rules for determining which passengers holding confirmed reservation space will be denied boarding on an oversold flight.

Passengers who are denied boarding involuntarily—that is, bumped—may be entitled to compensation. If the airline can arrange alternate transportation that is scheduled to arrive at the passenger's destination within one hour of the original arrival time, there is no compensation.

However, if the alternate flight gets to the destination between one and two hours late, the passenger is entitled to a cash payment. Passengers may refuse all compensation and bring private legal action. Federal regulations state: "The passenger may decline the payment and seek to recover damages in a court of law or in some other manner." The U.S. Supreme Court has confirmed that passengers who are bumped from a scheduled flight may sue the carrier for damages.

Passengers' Baggage Since 9/11, dangerous weapons, explosives, destructive items, and items that may be deemed to present a potential threat cannot be carried on board an aircraft. Many items that cannot be hand-carried may, however, be carried in the luggage compartment of planes. The law has no requirement for returning banned items that are left at airport security checkpoints. In addition, those who attempt to bring banned items through airport checkpoints are subject to civil penalties and criminal penalties. Passengers must declare any hazardous materials that they are carrying. Violators of federal hazardous materials regulations may be subject to a civil and criminal penalties. In conjunction with the carrying of passengers, a carrier is obliged to accept a reasonable amount of baggage. Excess baggage may be shipped by a passenger or through payment of additional fees. Baggage limits vary with different airlines. Personal luggage carried aboard an airline and kept at one's seat does not generally fall within the baggage weight limits permitted each passenger. When a baggage car or baggage compartment is available for checking luggage, the carrier is considered an insurer of the luggage checked by the passengers and left in these places. Property kept by passengers at their seats or in overhead compartments places upon the carrier the obligation of exercising ordinary care for its safety. Federal rules place limits on the liability of airlines for lost luggage.

Warehousers When goods are stored in a warehouse, the relationship of bailor and bailee is created between the owner of the goods and the warehouser. The UCC defines a warehouser as a person engaged in the business of storing goods for hire. A warehouse is a building or structure in which any goods, but particularly wares or merchandise, are stored. A *warehouse receipt* is a receipt issued by a person engaged in the business of storing goods for hire. Although both common carriers and warehousers are mutual-benefit bailees, they perform different functions. Common carriers are engaged in moving goods. Warehousers keep goods in storage. At times, however, one or the other will perform both functions.

Warehousers may be classified as public or private. A *public warehouser* is one that owns a warehouse in which any member of the public who is willing to pay the regular charge may store goods. Grain elevators in the Midwest, used to store farmers' grain, are sometimes established as public warehouses. A warehouser whose warehouse is not for general public use is a *private warehouser*. Most warehousers fall into this latter category. Sometimes, businesspeople will borrow money using goods that they have stored in a warehouse as security for the loan. The one who lends the money is given the warehouse receipt. If the debt is not paid, the holder of the receipt may obtain possession of the goods in storage. This practice is called *field warehousing*. A warehouser must use the amount of care that a reasonably careful person would use under similar circumstances. Failure to use such care is negligence and makes the warehouse liable for losses or damages to the goods.

EXAMPLE 29-8: Reasonable Care Required

Bekins Warehouse stored Keefe's household goods in its warehouse beneath some sprinkler system pipes. It did not inspect the area before placing the goods there. One of the pipes was unconnected, and water from the pipes leaked onto Keefe's goods, damaging them. Bekins's failure to inspect the area of storage was a negligent act that made Bekins responsible for the loss. The parties may limit the amount of liability of the warehouser by including terms to that effect in the storage agreement or warehouse receipt.

EXAMPLE 29-9: Contract Limitation

The warehouse receipt given by Bekins to Keefe in Example 29-8 limited Bekins's liability to 50 cents per pound per article. The limitation was enforceable even though it was not specifically called to Keefe's attention when the warehouse receipt was signed.

If goods are not removed from a warehouse at the end of a storage period, the warehouser may sell them. Before doing so, however, the warehouser must notify the owner that they are going to be sold and give that person the right to redeem them. If no time for storage is fixed in the agreement, the warehouser must give at least 30 days' notice to the owner before selling the goods. A warehouser has a lien on the goods that are in the warehouser's possession. A **warehouser's lien** is the right to retain possession of the goods until the satisfaction of the charges imposed on them. The lien is for the amount of money owed for storage charges, transportation charges, insurance, and expenses necessary for the preservation of the goods. The lien is a possessory one. It is lost when the warehouser voluntarily delivers the goods or unjustifiably refuses to deliver them. If the owner of the goods owes the warehouse money for the storage of other goods, the warehouser has a lien for the other debt only if it is so stated in the warehouse receipt.

If the person who stored the goods is a merchant in the course of business, the warehousers's lien may be enforced by a public or private sale at any time or place and on any terms that are commercially reasonable. Notice must be given to all persons known to claim an interest in the goods. The notice must include a statement of the amount due, the nature of the proposed sale, and the time and place of any public sale. If the person who stored the goods is not a merchant, more complicated rules must be followed to enforce the warehouser's lien. In addition to giving notice to all persons known to claim an interest in the goods, the nonmerchant must advertise the pending sale in a local newspaper. Notices and advertisements must contain specific information set forth in the UCC.

Trends in Cultural Property Protection

Cultural property includes works of art, monuments, and archives that are created by and preserved for a nation, an ethnic group, a tribe, or some other cultural subdivision in order to preserve and celebrate the history, character, religion, and beliefs of that subdivision. The Parthenon in Greece, the Pyramids in Egypt, the Forbidden City in China, and Stonehenge in the UK are larger than life examples of cultural property. However, cultural property also includes such things as Leonardo's Mona Lisa, Michelangelo's Statue of David, Jefferson's Declaration of Independence, and King John's Magna Carta. Historically, going back to ancient Rome, conquering nations had an unchallenged right to the spoils of war, which led to the wholesale transfer of works of art from the defeated lands to the home of the victors. Under Napoleon, the French took that practice to another level, declaring that, as the most advanced, most civilized, and most enlightened of all the nations on Earth, they had not only the right, but also the duty, to relocate the art and artifacts of the nations that they conquered in order to give that art and those artifacts a safe haven. It was in this way that the art of Egypt, Austria, the Papal States in Italy, and the northern Low Countries made their way to the museums and galleries of the Empire of France. By the time we reach the midpoint of the 19th century, things begin to change, albeit at a leisurely pace. The first international agreement in modern times to address the issue of cultural property was the Lieber Code, which, in 1863, recognized that, in times of war, combatants must take every effort to protect "works of art, libraries, (and) scientific collections." While this effort was a step in the right direction, it fell far short of the goal of stopping the looting of art that always followed a military campaign. In fact, the code expressly declared that the victors in a war were entitled to take whatever works of art they wanted to transport back home.

Another huge step forward came in 1933 when the International Museums Office of the League of Nations developed a document called the Roerich Pact (also known as the Treaty on the Protection of Artistic and Scientific Institutions and Historic Monuments), which declared that museums, schools, and other cultural institutions were off limits in combat zones. Eighteen nations agreed to follow the rules established by the pact. The next step came in 1945 when the United Nations established the United Nations Educational, Scientific, and Cultural Organization (UNESCO), which in 1954 sponsored the Hague Convention for the Protection of Cultural Property in the Event of Armed Conflict (the Hague Convention). In 1951, the General Conference of UNESCO formed a small committee of governmental experts who were charged with task of drafting a new convention that would cover the protection of cultural artifacts in case of war. Several drafts drawn up by the committee were reviewed by the General Conference, which sent them along to individual governments. These efforts led to an international conference attended by delegates from 52 nations. The conference produced the Hague Convention for the protection of Cultural Property in the Event of Armed Conflict. The Hague Convention sets down provisions that require each signatory to prepare protections for its own property in case of war; establishes the minimum level of respect that nations must show to all cultural property in their own nation, as well within other nation-states; creates rules for occupying forces in relation to the protection of cultural property; and institutes special protection regimes that provide a high level of protection for certain designated works of cultural significance.

In 1970, UNESCO took another step forward when it instituted the Convention on the Means of Prohibiting and Preventing the Illicit Import, Export, and Transfer of Ownership of Cultural Property. This convention went beyond the protection of cultural property in the time of war and focused, instead, on the ownership rights of nations in relation to their own cultural property. The nations that signed the convention promised to outlaw the import of stolen objects of cultural property from other nations and to take all necessary steps to send back stolen cultural property when asked to do so by another nation-state. The United States did not sign the Convention until 1972 and did not enact any legislation to activate it until 1983 when it passed the Convention on Cultural Property Implementation Act. This statute empowers the president to enter into bilateral agreements with other nations under which trade in cultural property is restricted. In 1995, the International Institute for the Unification of Private Law enacted a stricter convention entitled the Convention on Stolen or Illegally Exported Cultural Objects. This new convention allows lawsuits involving stolen cultural object to be brought in the national courts of all nations that have signed the agreement. The United States has yet to sign this convention. The United States has also enacted statutory law by its own accord without being prodded to do so by international agreements. These include the US-Mexico Treaty of Cooperation in 1971, The Regulation of Importation of Pre-Columbian Monumental or Architectural Sculpture or Murals in 1972, and the Native American Graves Protection and Repatriation of 1990. Also, the courts in the United States have been given foreign nation-states the power to bring suits into federal court to enforce ownership rights in relation to cultural property. [See: Kate Fitz Gibbon, *Who Owns the Past? Cultural Policy, Cultural Property, and the Law* (New Jersey: Rutgers University Press, 2005); "Hague Convention for the Protection of Cultural Property in the Event of Armed Conflict," *Wikipedia*, January 28, 2018, https://en.wikipedia.org./wiki/Hague_Convention_ for_the_ Protection_ of_Cultural_Property_in_the _event_of_Armed_Conflict; and "Hague Convention for the Protection of Cultural Property in the Event of Armed Conflict," The International Committee of the Red Cross, October 2010, https://www.icrc.org/en/document/protection-cultural-property-armed-conflict.)

quick quiz 29-2

1. A bailment is the transfer of possession and control of personal property to another with the intent that the same property will be returned later. **true | false**

2. An innkeeper is the operator of a hotel, motel, or inn that holds itself out to the public as being ready to entertain travelers, strangers, and transient guests. **true | false**

3. If a carrier holds itself out to the general public to provide transportation for compensation, it is called a common carrier. **true | false**

Summary

29.1 Personal property is everything that can be owned except real estate. Anyone who finds lost property must make a reasonable effort to find the owner. Misplaced property must be turned over to the manager of the place where it is found. Abandoned property is property that has been intentionally discarded by the owner and may be kept by a finder. The Abandoned Shipwreck Act gives states the right to shipwrecks beneath their waters. For a gift to be completed, the donor must intend to make a gift, it must be delivered to the donee, and the donee must accept the gift. A thief acquires no title to goods that are stolen and therefore cannot convey a good title to others.

29.2 Bailment occurs whenever someone transfers possession and control of personal property to another with the intent that the same property will be returned later. The principal types of bailments are bailments for the sole benefit of the bailor, bailments for the sole benefit of the bailee, and mutual-benefit bailments. Under modern law, bailees owe a duty to use reasonable care with the goods in their possession. When goods are lost or damaged while in the possession of a bailee, the burden is on the bailee to prove that no negligence was involved; if this proof cannot be made, the bailee will be held responsible for the loss. Innkeepers are required to accept all guests unless there are no vacancies. They must respect their guests' right of privacy. With some exceptions, innkeepers are insurers of their guests' property. The Transportation Security Administration (TSA), under the Department of Homeland Security, is responsible for protecting the United States' transportation system. Common carriers of goods are liable as insurers of the goods they ship regardless of whether they have been negligent. Public warehousers must accept goods for storage by any member of the public willing to pay for the service. Private warehouses are not for general public use.

Key Terms

abandoned property, 825
bailee, 829
bailment, 829
bailor, 829
carrier, 835
chattels, 823
chose in action, 823
community property, 824
consignee, 832
consignment contract, 832
consignor, 832
constructive bailment, 829
co-tenancy, 824
donee, 827
donor, 827
escheat, 825
gift in *causa mortis*, 828
gift *inter vivos*, 827
gratuitous bailment, 830
gross negligence, 831
implied-in-fact bailment, 829
implied-in-law bailment, 829
innkeeper, 833
joint tenants, 824
joint tenants with the right of survivorship, 824
law of finds, 825

law of salvage, 825
lost property, 824
mutuum, 830
misplaced or mislaid property, 824
natural property, 825
ordinary negligence, 832
passenger, 837
personal property, 823
racial profiling, 837
salvage, 825
salvor, 825
severalty, 824
slight negligence, 831
tenants in common, 824
transient, 833
treasure trove, 825
warehouse, 838
warehouser, 838
warehouser's lien, 839

Questions for Review and Discussion

1. What are some examples of tangible and intangible personal property?
2. What are the methods of owning property with others?
3. What are the differences among lost property, misplaced property, and abandoned property?
4. What are the requirements of a completed gift?
5. How does the law apply to stolen property?
6. When does a bailment occur?
7. What are the principal types of bailments?
8. What is the burden of proof as it relates to bailments?
9. What is an innkeeper's duty in relation to accepting guests?
10. What are innkeepers' duties of care to their guests and their guests' property?

Cases for Analysis

1. Susan Lacroix's Yerf-Dog go-kart was stolen from her driveway one evening when she went inside to have dinner. The thief placed an advertisement in the newspaper and sold it to Ronald Casey for half what it was worth. Later, Lacroix recognized the kart in Casey's yard and identified it as hers through its serial number. In a suit brought by Lacroix for the return of the go-kart, Casey argued that he now had title to the kart because he paid for it without knowledge that it had been stolen. Is Casey's argument sound? Explain.
2. David Bess rented three outdoor booth spaces at the Traders World flea market to display his inventory of Beanie Babies for sale. He stored his inventory in a locked trailer, which he left parked at the flea market overnight. When he returned the next morning, he discovered that the padlock on his trailer had been changed. Upon forcing the trailer open, he found that his entire inventory of Beanie Babies, which he estimated had a value of $60,000 to $75,000, was missing. In a suit against Traders World, Bess argued that the transaction was a bailment. Do you agree with Bess? Why or why not? [See: *Bess v. Traders World, Inc.*, CA2001-06-063 (OH).]
3. Schaeffer boarded a 30-passenger, single-aisle turboprop airplane carrying two pieces of baggage. When asked by a flight attendant to surrender one carry-on for proper storage, he refused and became verbally abusive. The captain of the plane decided not to depart with the disruptive passenger on board because he was concerned about the safety of the flight. When asked to leave the plane, Schaeffer refused, and the Port Authority police were called to remove him. Must a passenger who has boarded a plane that has not taken off leave the plane when told to do so by an authorized representative? Explain. [See: *Schaeffer v. Cavallero*, 54 F. Supp.2d 350 (S.D.N.Y.).]
4. Pollard found a valuable first edition that someone had dropped on the street. She took the book home, placing it with others in a collection of first editions. The owner's name could not be found in the lost book, and Pollard made no effort to locate the owner. Did she thus have title to the book? Explain. [See: *Doe v. Oceola*, 270 N.W.2d 254 (MI).]
5. Vincent Hartwell admired a valuable book collection on his uncle's bookshelf. To Hartwell's surprise, his uncle said that he planned to give the books to Hartwell as a gift and that he could have

them at that moment. Hartwell replied that he was living in a dormitory and had no place to keep the collection. His uncle said, "Consider the books yours. I'll keep them here, and when you're ready for them, come and get them." Hartwell thanked his uncle and left for school. His uncle died a week later. Hartwell's cousin, Kathleen Lane, inherited the uncle's entire estate. She claimed that the valuable book collection belonged to her. Who was the legal owner, Hartwell or Lane? Explain.

6. Torczyner, a diamond salesman, registered as a guest at the Hilton Hotel in Denver, Colorado. He placed his diamonds in the hotel safe when he did not need them for business purposes. On the last day of his visit, he removed the gems from the safe, left the hotel to make some business calls, and returned for the purpose of packing and checking out. Instead of placing the diamonds in the hotel safe, Torczyner carried them to his room. There, he was assaulted by two men who beat him and robbed him of the diamonds. Is the hotel responsible for the loss of the diamonds? Explain. [See: *Pacific Diamond Co. v. Superior Ct.*, 85 Cal. App. 3rd 871 (CA).]

7. In his will, Gavegnano left all his tangible personal property to his daughter, Caroline. At the time of his death, he owned 19 thoroughbred horses. In addition, a cashier's check made payable to him for $33,000 was found among his belongings. The lower court judge held that the horses and the check were tangible personal property and should be given to Caroline under the terms of the will. Caroline's brothers appealed the decision, claiming that neither the horses nor the check were tangible personal property. Were Caroline's brothers correct? Explain. [See: *Pagiarulo v. National Shawmut Bank*, 233 N.E.2d 213 (MA).]

8. Joe Scott left his automobile with Purser Truck Sales Inc. to be repaired. Purser Truck Sales turned the automobile over to Lonz Radford to make the repairs. The car was demolished while in the possession of Radford. In a suit brought by Scott against Purser, the trial court held in favor of Purser, because Scott presented no evidence indicating that Purser was negligent. Was the trial court correct? Why or why not? [See: *Scott v. Purser Truck Sales, Inc.*, 402 S.E.2d 354 (GA).]

Design Elements: The Opening Case: ©Sharpstock/ Alamy; A Classic Case: ©Evlakhov Valeriy/ Shutterstock

quick quiz Answers

29-1	29-2
1. T	1. T
2. T	2. T
3. F	3. T

Chapter 30: Real Property and Landlord and Tenant Law

30-1 The Rights Related to Real Property
Trees and Vegetation • Air and Water Rights • Fixtures and Easements

30-2 Estates in and Co-Ownership of Real Property
The Law of Estates • The Law of Co-Ownership

30-3 Subterranean Rights: Oil and Gas Developments
Subterranean Rights: The Basics • Oil and Gas Contracts: Lease, License, or Fee Simple? • Dormant Minerals Statutes

30-4 Acquiring Title to and Managing Real Property
Title to Real Property • Governmental Management of Real Property

30-5 The Landlord–Tenant Relationship
Leasing versus Other Relationships • Types of Leasehold Interests • The Lease Agreement

30-6 Duties of the Landlord and the Tenant
The Landlord's Duties • The Tenant's Duties • Tort Liability • Eviction Proceedings

THE OPENING CASE *Round 1*
The Ancient Right of Dower Still Has Power in Some of States, So Watch Out!

This case begins, as many do, with a wedding, a mortgage, and a filing. William and Sharon Medow were married in 1973. Some 34 years later, William's parents, Miriam and Martin Medow, purchased a plot of land in Cincinnati and took out a mortgage with the General Electric Credit Union (GE). On January 29, 2007, the mortgage was properly recorded by GE. Both Miriam and Martin passed away and in May 2013, the title to the property went to William. Under the statutory laws of the State of Ohio, William's wife, Sharon, received a dower interest in the property. Under the ancient concept of dower, a wife had an interest in her husband's property, which she would receive on his death. (Interestingly enough, the husband had a similar right called the right of curtesy. Curtesy was abolished by statutory law in the state of Ohio. Moreover, in Ohio, dower rights were changed to apply to both sexes. However, the term "dower" was retained. In contrast, other states that have altered the right of dower to include both sexes have adopted the gender neutral term of *spousal share*.)

The trouble in this case started when William failed to make proper payments on the mortgage. As a result, in the normal course of business, GE filed an action in the state court to foreclose on the property. Determined not to take any prisoners, GE named both William and Sharon as defendants in the action. Sharon was not pleased. In reaction, she had her attorney file a counterclaim against GE. In that counterclaim, she argued, rather convincingly, that her dower right superseded GE's claim on the property. Consequently, from the sale of the land, she demanded to be paid the value of her dower interest in the property, which would amount to some $2,000. In an unusual move, both GE and Sharon filed summary judgment motions at the same time, each one declaring that both the facts and the law were on their side. The trial court, though, had no difficulty deciding GE, not Sharon, had priority. As a result, GE's motion was granted and Sharon's was denied. Sharon, however, was not satisfied, and so she filed an appeal.

Things got a little complicated at that point. The foreclosure action was still pending, so the appellate court delayed its hearing of the appeal. This, however, did not stop GE, which decided to take matters into its own hands. It filed dual motions: (1) another summary judgment motion linked to (2) a new motion for a default judgment. In the motion for a default judgment, GE asked for a favorable ruling on its original complaint, declaring that its rights to the land superseded the defendant's dower right to the same land and asking for an official court decree that would order a proper foreclosure on the property. The trial court magistrate agreed and found in favor of GE. Sharon objected to the ruling of the magistrate. The court overruled her objections and Sharon filed an appeal. The case ended up in the Fifth District Court of Appeals in Hamilton County.

Here are some of the questions that need to be answered to properly understand what happened in this case. Why was the concept of dower created in the first place? What rights did a married woman have under the rules of dower? What limitations were placed on women because of dower? Did unmarried women have the same limitations? Is the concept of dower still prevalent in most states? What additional limitations were placed on women under common law? Did the filing by GE supersede the defendant's dower rights as GE claims, or will the defendant succeed in her claim that dower rights trump the credit union's mortgage rights? The answers to these and other similar questions are covered ahead, so don't stop now—move forward. [See *General Electric Credit Union v. Sharon K. Medow*, 2016 Ohio 3266, Court of Appeals of Ohio, First District, Hamilton County (June 3, 2016).]

Opening Case Questions

1. What is the right of dower, and how did it originate? Explain.
2. What were the advantages and the disadvantages connected to the right to dower? Explain.
3. How has the right to dower changed in the 21st century? Explain.
4. How are dower rights related to life estates? Explain.
5. What steps, if any, have been taken by the states to keep statutory dower rights gender neutral? Explain.

Source: See *General Electric Credit Union v. Sharon K. Medow*, 2016 OHIO 3266, Court of Appeals of Ohio, First District, Hamilton County (June 3, 2016).

LO Learning Objectives

1. Explain what constitutes real property.
2. Differentiate between freehold and leasehold estates.
3. Describe the different types of co-ownership of real property.
4. Explain how oil and gas rights can be transferred.
5. Discuss the goal of the dormant minerals act.
6. Identify the methods of acquiring title to real property.
7. Explain eminent domain.
8. List the five elements necessary to create a landlord–tenant relationship.
9. Identify the essential requirements of a lease.
10. Make clear the duties of landlords and tenants.

30-1 The Rights Related to Real Property

Real property and real estate are not really the same thing, although they are often treated as if they were. When real estate agents, bankers, and attorneys use the term **real estate**, they are generally referring to the actual land itself as well as everything permanently attached to it. This would include buildings, fences, and trees on the surface; earth, rocks, and minerals under the surface; and the airspace above the surface. In contrast, the term **real property** refers to the ownership rights that go along with the real estate. The problem is that very few people know about this difference, and those who do know really do not care to make the distinction. For that reason, the two terms will be used alternately in the rest of the chapter, just as if they mean the same thing. The rights that are associated with real property generally include those rights related to trees and other vegetation, air rights, subterranean rights, water rights, and the rights associated with fixtures and easements.

Trees and Vegetation

Trees, flowers, shrubs, vineyards, and field crops that grow each year without replanting (perennials) are considered real property. These plants have been planted and cultivated with the intention that they remain part of the real estate. Once planted and growing, such improvements to the land are called *fructus naturales* (fruit of nature). In contrast, crops or garden plantings that produce flowers, vegetables, or other harvest only for the year in which they are planted (annuals) are called *fructus industrials*. A tree belongs to the person on whose land the trunk is located. People who own adjoining land have the right to cut off trespassing tree branches in their airspace and trespassing roots at the boundary line of their property. Whenever property owners dig down at the very edge of their own property, however, they must provide support to their neighbor's land so that it does not cave in.

Air and Water Rights

In medieval England, landowners owned the airspace above their property to "as high as the heavens." This law changed with the increased use of the aircraft. Modern courts have held that landowners own the airspace above their land to as high as they can effectively possess or reasonably control. This height usually extends as high as the highest tree or structure on their property. It is a trespass for anyone to run wires through someone else's airspace or to use another's airspace in any way without permission. Electric and telephone companies must obtain easements for the right to run wires through the airspace of property owners.

Congress has enacted legislation that gives the public the right of freedom of transit through the navigable airspace of the United States. The **navigable airspace**, subject to FAA regulations, is the space above 1,000 feet over populated areas and above 500 feet over water and unpopulated areas. In airport cases involving planes landing and taking off, the courts try to strike a balance between the landowners' rights to the exclusive possession of their airspace, free from noise and exhaust fumes, and the public need for air travel.

Air rights are valuable and often sold to interested buyers, particularly in land-depleted metropolitan areas. For example, in New York City, developers bought air rights over the access to the George Washington Bridge and constructed multistory buildings. Two privately owned buildings have been constructed in the airspace over the Massachusetts Turnpike near Boston. Use of air rights becomes important when land is no longer available for new buildings. The private use of airspace also becomes a tax source for otherwise untaxable land owned by a city or state government.

People who own land along the bank of a river or stream are called **riparian owners**. They have certain rights and duties with respect to the water that flows over, under, and beside their land. Owners of land through which a stream flows own the soil beneath the water. If a nonnavigable stream is a boundary line between two parcels of land, the owner on each side owns to the center of the stream. If the stream is navigable, however, each owner owns only to the bank of the stream, and the bed is owned by the state. A navigable stream in some states is defined as one that ebbs and flows with the tide. In other states, it is defined as a stream that is capable of being navigated by commercial vessels. Although property owners may own the land under a stream, they do not own the water itself. Their right to the use of the water depends on the doctrine followed in their state.

Fixtures and Easements

Personal property attached to real property is known as a *fixture* and becomes part of the real property. Built-in stoves and dishwashers, kitchen cabinets, and ceiling light fixtures are examples of fixtures. If there is a question as to whether an item is a fixture, the courts ask the following questions: Has there been a temporary or permanent installation of the personal property? Can it be removed without damaging the real property? Has it been adapted to the intended use of the real property? Also, the court would ask what the intent of the party was at the time the personal property was attached to the real property. *Trade fixtures* are those items of personal property brought upon the premises by the tenant that are necessary to carry on the trade or business to which the premises will be devoted. Contrary to the general rule, trade fixtures remain the personal property of the tenant or occupier of the property and are removable at the expiration of the term of occupancy. Trade fixtures are not treated as part of the real property.

An *easement* (also called a *right of way*) is the right to use another's land for a particular purpose. Easements are used to give people the right to pass over another's land, to run wires through another's airspace, to drain water onto another's property, or to run pipes underneath someone else's ground. The one who enjoys the easement and to whom it attaches is called the *dominant tenement*. In contrast, the one on whom the easement is imposed is called the *servient tenement*.

EXAMPLE 30-1: Parties to an Easement

Hatfield owned a long, narrow strip of land that ran between a lake and a highway. She decided to sell the front half of the lot that bordered the highway to McCoy and keep the back half that bordered the lake for her own use. To give McCoy the ability to reach the lake, an easement was placed in the deed granting McCoy the right to "pass and repass" over Hatfield's property to reach the lake. In this easement, McCoy is the dominant tenement and Hatfield is the servient tenement. Also, to give Hatfield the ability to reach the highway, an easement was placed in the deed, reserving to Hatfield the right to "pass and repass" over McCoy's property to reach the highway. In this easement, Hatfield is the dominant tenement and McCoy is the servient tenement.

An easement may be created in three ways: by grant, by reservation, and by prescription. To create an *easement by grant*, the owner of the land signs a deed, giving the easement to the dominant tenement, and keeps the remainder of the land. To create an *easement by reservation*, the owner of the land grants to another person the entire parcel of land except for the easement that he or she keeps. An *easement by prescription* is an easement that is obtained by passing over another's property without permission, openly and continuously for a period of time set by state statute (20 years in many states). People claiming easements by prescription must show that they used (but did not possess) part of another's property openly, notoriously, and in a hostile manner for the prescribed period. This proof is similar to that used in adverse possession, discussed later in this chapter. A legal easement may exist even if it isn't written. For example, the law allows people access to their homes so, if the only access is by crossing through another land owner's property, the court may grant permission through an "easement by necessity." Once an easement is created, it runs with the land. This condition means that future owners will have the right to use the easement unless one of them gives it up by a deed or by not using it for a long period of time.

EXAMPLE 30-2: Easement Runs with Land

Jesse Horney conveyed the northern portion of his real estate to Wayne County Lumber Company by warranty deed in 1907. That deed included the following provision: "Said Jesse Horney hereby conveys to Wayne County Lumber Company the right of ingress and egress for teams and wagons in conducting their business through an open driveway along the South line to South Main Street." The property was conveyed to a different lumber company in 1930 and to a third lumber company in 1943. Later, in a dispute over the easement, the court held that the easement ran with the land and belonged to the third lumber company. In this case, Horney's property was the servient tenement. The lumber company's property was the dominant tenement.

A profit *à prendre* is a special type of easement with the added privilege of removing something of value from the servient property. For example, the right to enter another's property and remove sand, gravel, soil, or the like is called a profit *à prendre*. This right may be created by deed, will, or adverse use.

EXAMPLE 30-3: Profit *à Prendre*

The Bates Company and Sawyer executed an agreement that provided Bates could enter upon Sawyer's land and remove sand, gravel, and stone. Bates agreed to pay Sawyer a set rate per cubic yard or short ton for all the sand removed. The agreement stated, "Sawyer will not grant to anyone else the privilege of removing sand and stone from said parcel during the period hereof . . . but Sawyer reserves to herself, her successors and assigns, the right during said period . . . to go on and use said tract of land for any purpose they may desire, but without unreasonable interference with the rights of said Bates." The court held that Bates possessed a profit *à prendre* under the agreement.

quick quiz 30-1

1. Real property and real estate mean exactly the same thing. — true | false
2. In medieval England, landowners owned the airspace above their property to "as high as the heavens." — true | false
3. When personal property is attached to real property, it is known as a fixture and becomes part of the real property. — true | false

30-2 Estates in and Co-Ownership of Real Property

Most of the basic ownership rules regarding real property in the United States actually had their origin a millennium ago in England. After William the Conqueror won the English throne in the Battle of Hastings in 1066, he realized that he had an enormous amount of land to preserve and protect. Although he would have preferred to maintain and defend all the land on his own, he knew that he could not, and so he established a system by which he could retain the ownership of all the land in England while parceling out its maintenance and defense to the nobility. Those nobles who received large tracts of land from the king were said to hold estates, a term derived from the Latin word *status*. Although the rules that apply today emerged centuries ago on the other side of the Atlantic, they still affect us because of our English legal heritage. This heritage influences the rules that govern modern estates as well as those that relate to the co-ownership of land.

The Law of Estates

Most of the estates that were passed on to the nobility in medieval England could last infinitely because the nobles who held them were empowered to pass them on to their heirs. These estates were called **freehold estates**. Anyone with a freehold estate may transfer that interest to another by sale, gift, will, or by dying without a will. Freehold estates are either estates in fee simple or life estates.

Estates in Fee Simple Anyone owning real property outright—that is, forever—is said to have an **estate in fee simple**. The estate descends, on the death of the owner, to the owner's heirs. The owner of an estate in fee simple has absolute ownership in the real estate, with the right to use or dispose of it as desired, so long as the use of it does not interfere with others' rights.

EXAMPLE 30-4: Fee Simple Estate

When the Landers bought the land on which to build their house, they received an estate in fee simple from the former owners. They thus received full rights to the property. They may sell it, give it away, or use it as they wish. The only restrictions are those contained in the deed or required of them by law.

Life Estates A person who owns real property for life or for the life of another owns an interest in real property called a **life estate**. Such an estate may be created by deed, by will, or by law. When the terms of a deed or will state that the property is to pass at the end of a life estate to someone other than the grantor or the grantor's heirs, the future interest is a **remainder estate**. When the terms of a deed or a will state that property is to return to the grantor or the grantor's heirs at the expiration of a life estate, the future interest is a **reversion estate**.

Coverture In English common law and, by tradition, in the laws of colonial American, upon marriage a man and a woman became a single unit. (*Note:* Some legal historians believe that the custom of having the woman change her name to that of her husband emerged from the concept of marital unity. However, the practice was not codified in the United States until the mid-20th century when Hawaii became a state.) As romantic as the notion of marital unity may sound, it actually deprived married women of any power to own property. This status was referred to as **coverture**. This status also meant that she could not enter into a contract on her own nor file a lawsuit on her own behalf. Of course, she also could not be sued, but this was something of an empty privilege because her husband could be sued and she was just as much at risk as he was in any litigation affecting marital property. The powerless married woman as generally referred to as a **feme covert**, while her unmarried counterpart was called a **feme solo**. Of course, it is true that this relationship could be altered by agreement. Still, a married woman was even at risk after her husband passed away because he could also leaver her out of his will [See: Jone Johnson Lewis, "Dower and Curtesy," *ThoughtCo*, April 20, 2017, thoughtco.com/dower-and-curtesy-3529205; Daniel Doran and Mark Tosti, "Dower and Curtesy," *Oran's Dictionary of the Law* (Albany, NY: West, Thomson Learning, 2000); and "Dower and Curtesy," Cornell Law School, Legal Information Institute, https://www.law.cornell.edu/wex/ dower_and_curtesy.]

Dower and Spousal Shares The law of dower changed all that. Under the concept of dower, a wife had an interest in her husband's property, which she would receive on his death. The idea here was to make sure that widows would not be destitute. (Interestingly enough, the husband had a similar right called the right of curtesy.) During her lifetime, a wife was not permitted to sell or lease or mortgage her interest in her husband's property. On the other hand, she did have the right to her share of any income that came from the land such as rent. Also, on the plus side, she was not liable for her husband's debts. While many states have abolished dower, others have modified it to cover both sexes. Those states that still retain dower give a spouse a one-third to one-half interest in the other spouse's real property, which the first spouse will receive, should the second spouse die intestate (i.e., without a will). Many states that have retained the concept of dower have changed the name to spousal share to properly reflect its gender neutral nature. [See: Title 21 Ohio Revised Code, Sections 2101.01 to 2101. 09; Lewis, "Dower and Curtesy"; and Jone Johnson Lewis, "Coverture: Women's Nonexistence Under Law," *ThoughtCo*, April 20, 2017, thoughtco.com/coverture-in-english-american-law-3529483. See also: Doran and Tosti, "Dower and Curtesy"; "Dower and Curtesy," Cornell Law School; and Alicia Kreh, "Dower: Reigniting Equal Protection Claims in Response to the Legalization of Same-Sex Marriage and the Resulting Changes," Michigan State University College of Law (2015).]

THE OPENING CASE *Round 2*
The Ancient Right of Dower Still Has Power in Some of States, So Watch Out!

William and Sharon Medow were married in 1973. In 2007, William's parents took out a mortgage with the General Electric Credit Union (GE) and bought some property in Cincinnati. Following standard operating procedure, GE recorded the property in January 2007. Shortly thereafter, both Miriam and Martin passed away and title to the property went to William. According to Ohio law, William's wife, Sharon, received a dower interest in the property. Under common law, a wife had an interest in her husband's property, which she would receive on his death. This was referred to as dower. (Interestingly enough, the husband had a similar right called the right of curtesy. Curtesy was abolished by statutory law in the state of Ohio. However, Ohio also altered dower to include both sexes, thus preserving the husband's rights, Moreover, to simplify things, the term "dower" was retained. In contrast, other states that have changed the right of dower to include both sexes, have adopted the gender neutral term, *spousal share*.)

Unfortunately, William's payments on the mortgage fell so far behind that GE filed an action in state court to foreclose on the property. GE identified both William and Sharon as defendants in the action. In response, Sharon filed a counterclaim against GE, arguing that her dower right superseded GE's claim on the property. Consequently, from the sale of the land, she demanded to be paid the value of her dower interest in the property, which was about $2,000.

Surprisingly, both GE and Sharon filed summary judgment motions simultaneously, each one stating that both the facts and the law were on their side. The trial court, however, decided that priority rights went to GE not Sharon. As a result, GE's motion was granted and Sharon's motion was denied. Sharon, however, kept the case alive by filing an appeal. Unfortunately, since the foreclosure action was still pending, the appellate court postponed her appeal. In the meantime, GE filed a set of dual motions: (1) another summary judgment motion and

(2) a new motion for a default judgment. In the motion for a default judgment, GE demanded a ruling in its favor on its original complaint, declaring that its rights to the land superseded the defendant's dower right to the same land, and asking for an official court decree that would order a proper foreclosure on the property. The trial court magistrate ruled in favor of GE. Sharon objected to the ruling of the magistrate. The court overruled her objections, and Sharon filed this appeal. The case ended up in the Fifth District Court of Appeals in Hamilton County.

In making her claim in the court of appeals, Sharon went straight to the statute that said that, while a foreclosure proceeding can target property that includes a dower interest, that dower interest will be protected and the spouse holding the dower interest will be awarded, "a sum of money equal to the present value of the dower interest, to be paid out of the proceeds of the sale *according to the priority of the interest*" (ORC Section 2103.041). Sharon claimed that her dower right had *priority over the mortgage rights* and that she should, therefore, be paid her interest in that property, which amounted to some $2,000. The court disagreed noting, quite clearly, that the statute does not make any provision for determining "how the priority of a dower interest is to be established." Sharon countered this conclusion with a long line of cases that collectively established a rule that says that dower rights have priority over mortgage rights. The rule says that when a spouse has taken out a mortgage on property that only he (or she) has title to, that mortgage will not be effective against the non–title-holding spouse's dower interest in the property, just so long as the spouse holding the dower has not "signed the mortgage or document conveying the interest." Because she did not sign the mortgage, Sharon concluded, her dower rights take priority over that mortgage. At this point, the court noted that Sharon had misunderstood the facts in the case. William did not take out the mortgage. The mortgage was taken out by William's parents. It was at that time that the mortgage was established and GE recorded the title. When GE recorded its claim, neither Sharon nor William had any interest in the property. Her interest arose only when William received the property after his parents died. Therefore, because GE recorded the property before Sharon's dower interest existed, it holds priority—period. [See *General Electric Credit Union v. Sharon K. Medow*, 2016 Ohio 3266, Court of Appeals of Ohio, First District, Hamilton County (June 3, 2016).]

Source: See: *General Electric Credit Union v. Sharon K. Medow*, 2016 Ohio 3266, Court of Appeals of Ohio, First District, Hamilton County (June 3, 2016).

Recording the Mortgage The ruling in the Opening Case *Round 2* actually refers back to something we learned in Chapter 20 on mortgages. In that chapter, we noted that recording a mortgage notifies any third party who may be interested in purchasing the property or in lending money to the owner that the mortgagee has an interest in the real property covered by the mortgage. If the mortgage is not recorded and a later mortgage is given on the same property, the new mortgage is superior to the first. This is known as the *first in time, first in rights rule* (although some courts, for poetic purposes, have altered the rule to read, the *first in time, first in line rule*). By the way, no matter what the rule is called, to be effective, the second mortgagee must *not know* about the first mortgage and must record the mortgage properly.

The Law of Co-Ownership

Often only one person owns a tract of real estate. This type of ownership is referred to as ownership in **severalty**. It is also very common, however, for two or more people to own the same tract of land. This type of ownership is referred to as **concurrent ownership**, although the more common term is **co-ownership**. Real property may be owned individually or by two or more persons known as **co-tenants**. Co-tenant relationships include: tenancy in common, joint tenancy, community property, and tenancy by the entirety.

Tenancy in Common When two or more persons own real property as **tenants in common**, each person owns an undivided share of the whole property. A co-tenant's share of the property transfers to that co-tenant's heirs upon his or her death rather than to the surviving co-tenants. Each co-tenant is entitled to possession of the entire premises. This rule is known as *unity of possession*. Tenants in common have the right to sell or deed away as a gift their share in the property without the permission of the other co-tenants. When this action occurs, any new owner becomes a tenant in common with the remaining co-tenants. One co-tenant's interest is not necessarily the same as another co-tenant's interest.

Tenants in common may separate their interests in the property by petitioning the court for a partition of the property. If the court allows the petition, either it will divide the property into separate parcels so that each cotenant will own a particular part outright, or it will order the property sold and divide the proceeds of the sale among the cotenants. Creditors may reach the interest of a tenant in common by bringing a lawsuit against that particular cotenant and, if successful, having that cotenant's interest sold to pay the debt. By statute in most states, co-ownership of property by two or more persons is considered tenancy in common unless the relationship is expressly indicated as a joint tenancy or a tenancy by the entirety.

Tenancy by the Entirety A tenancy by the entirety may be held only by a husband and wife and is based upon the common law doctrine known as unity of person. Under this very old doctrine, a husband and wife were regarded, under the law, as one. In theory, each spouse owned the entire estate, and neither could destroy it by any separate act. However, we saw above, the husband had control over the estate, including the exclusive right to possession and the right to all rents and profits. Many states have done away with the statute of tenancy by the entirety. Other states have enacted statutes giving equal rights to husbands and wives who own property as tenants by the entirety. Still other states require both spouses to consent to a valid mortgage on property owned as tenants by the entirety. See Table 30-1.

A QUESTION OF ETHICS

Tenancy in Common or Tenancy by the Entirety: Which Is Preferred?

When the Supreme Court made its decision in the Obergefell Case (see: *Obergefell, et al. v. Hodges, Director, Ohio Department of Health, et al.* 576 U.S. ____ (2015), the Case Study at the end of Part 8), it did more than just affect marriage. It also affected property law. Here is what happened. Recall that in a tenancy in common, each person owns an undivided share of the whole property, while in a tenancy by the entirety, each spouse owns the entire estate. Before the *Obergefell* case when same-sex couples could not be married in some states, they could not own property as a tenancy by the entirety. Instead, they would own their property as a tenancy in common. The main difference is that in a tenancy in common, under *the unity possession rule*, each co-tenant is entitled to possession of the entire premises. Thus, tenants in common have the right to sell or deed away as a gift their share in the property without the permission of the other co-tenant. Also, recall that a co-tenant's share of the property transfers to that co-tenant's heirs upon his or her death rather than to the surviving co-tenant. This puts the surviving co-tenant at risk because the new co-tenant's plans for the property may be quite different from the plans of the surviving co-tenant. This could result in a conflict, which might lead to a legal battle in which the parties petition the court for a partition of the property. If the court allows the petition, either it will divide the property into separate parcels so that each co-tenant will own a particular part outright, or it will order the property sold and divide the proceeds of the sale among the co-tenants. Co-tenants are also at risk because the creditors of one of the tenants might sue that co-tenant for an outstanding debt. The suit could lead to the co-tenant's interest being sold to pay the debt.

The *Obergefell* case legalized same-sex marriage and thus opened the option of tenancy by the entirety for those couples. This removes the risks noted earlier for same-sex couples who get married now and in the future. But what about those couples who married before the *Obergefell* decision or those who registered their unions as civil contracts? Are they entitled to the protection of a tenancy by the entirety? Should those couples be forced to re-title their property to ensure that they get the protection of a tenancy by the entirety? Or should the law be changed to retroactively transform all property relationships made by same-sex couples in the past from tenancies in common to tenancies by the entirety? A retroactive change statute might wreck havoc on county recorder offices across the 50 states. Such a change would also cost a great deal—a cost that would undoubtedly be passed along to the taxpayers. On the other hand, it hardly seems fair to force same-sex couples to bear the cost and the stress of having to re-title their property just to get the same protection that traditional couples receive. Using one of the ethical theories that we discussed in Chapter 1 (social contract ethics, utilitarianism, or rational ethics), decide who should be forced to pay for these changes or, in the alternative, come up with a compromise plan that will satisfy both taxpayers and same sex couples.

Table 30-1 Co-Tenant Relationships

	Tenants in Common	Joint Tenants	Tenants by Entirety	Community Property
1. Who can be co-tenants	Any number of people	Any number of people	Only husband and wife	Only husband and wife
2. At death, deceased's share goes	To deceased's heirs*	To surviving cotenants	To surviving spouse	To deceased's heirs*
3. Title	Separate title for each cotenant	One title to the entire property	Husband has title (under the doctrine of unity)†	Title is in the community
4. Division of ownership interests	Cotenants can have equal or unequal interests	All interests must be equal	Interests equal; husband has the right to control and manage†	Both interests equal
5. Right to possession of entire premises	Equal with all cotenants	Equal with all cotenants	Husband only†	Equal with both spouses
6. Right to convey ownership interest	May convey to another without permission of cotenant	May convey to another but will end joint tenancy relationship	Husband may convey to anyone; wife's interest is protected†	May convey personal property without spouse's permission; must have written permission to convey real property
7. Right to partition the property	Yes	Yes	No	No
8. Owner's separate interest reachable by creditors	Yes	Yes	Husband's only†	No. Whole community only, depending on state law

*Either by will or the law of intestate succession if the deceased had no will.
†At common law. States have either abolished this type of tenancy or amended it to give equal rights to men and women.

Joint Tenancy When two or more persons own real property as joint tenants, the estate created is a single estate with multiple ownership. Each tenant owns the entire estate, subject to the equal rights of the other joint tenants. Four unities must be present to create a joint tenancy: time, title, interest, and possession:

1. The unity of time means that all owners must take title at the same time.
2. The unity of title means that all owners must derive title from the same source.
3. The unity of interest means that all owners must have equal interests in the property.
4. The unity of possession means that all owners must have the equal right to possess the property.

Upon the death of one joint tenant, the entire ownership remains with the other joint tenants and does not pass to the heirs or devisees of the deceased cotenant. For this reason, joint tenants are often identified as joint tenants with the right of survivorship.

A joint tenant may deed away his or her interest to a new owner without permission of the other joint tenants. The new owner, in such a case, becomes a tenant in common with the remaining joint tenants. As in the case of a tenant in common, a joint tenant may petition the court for a partition of the estate, which would end the joint tenancy. Creditors may levy upon the interests of a joint tenant on execution and take over that particular joint tenant's interest as a tenant in common with the remaining joint tenants. To levy on execution means to collect a sum of money by putting into effect the judgment of a court.

Community Property Property (except a gift or inheritance) that is acquired by the personal efforts of either spouse during marriage is called community property. By law community property belongs to both spouses equally. The law originated in Spain, was embraced by Mexico, and is presently followed in Puerto Rico, in some Southern states, such as Texas and Louisiana, and in many Western states, such as California and Nevada. Although state laws differ, they all operate on the theory that both spouses contribute equally to the marriage—that all property acquired during the marriage is the result of the combined efforts of both of them. Although one spouse may earn all the money to acquire the property, all the property acquired is considered community property.

quick quiz 30-2

1. Most of the basic ownership rules regarding real property in the United States actually had their origin a millennium ago in France. true | false
2. A person who owns real property for life or for the life of another owns an interest in real property called a life estate. true | false
3. When two or more persons own real property as tenants in common, each person owns an undivided share of the whole property. true | false

30-3 Subterranean Rights: Oil and Gas Developments

Recently, new technologies have enabled landowners (or, perhaps more correctly, land controllers) to access previously inaccessible reserve pockets of oil and gas (read "fracking" here). As is often the case, technology moves much faster than the law. Time and again technologists and investors move forward without noticing (or caring?) that certain legal difficulties have emerged. The law must, therefore, play a troublesome game of "catch-up." In this case, the very nature of the contractual relationship between landowners and gas and oil developers is unclear. Are these contracts simply leases, or are they estates? Are there existing statutes such as the dormant minerals statute that affect these agreements? Solving these problems is critical because, as is often the case when technology moves forward, unintended and unforeseen consequences emerge. Someone must be responsible for dealing with such consequences. The recent rise in earthquake activity in the fracking areas of Oklahoma and Texas is one dramatic example of this problem. However, physical damage is not the only concern. Profit distribution, ownership rights, and contract duration are also of great interest to owners, leasees, and neighbors. For these reasons, we must pause to look at this issue in some detail, even if the results uncover more questions than answers.

Subterranean Rights: The Basics

Unless excluded in the deed, the owner of land has exclusive title to material below the surface of the land. The right extends to the point determined to be the exact center of the earth. These **subterranean rights** are often sold to corporations exploring for coal, oil, or other mineral deposits. Taking out oil or minerals from below the surface would constitute trespass if such rights were not obtained from their owners. A landowner must not dig a cellar or other excavation so close to the boundary of a neighbor so as to cause the neighbor's land to cave in or the neighbor's building to be damaged. A person excavating who fails to properly shore up the adjoining land will, in all likelihood, be liable to the neighbor for damages. What happens when the damage that occurs impacts landowners, entrepreneurs, and renters who are on land not adjacent to the real property in question, but in distant areas that are affected by the search for oil and gas deposits? Or, to put it more bluntly, who pays for the earthquake damage in Fort Worth when the oil and gas exploration takes place in Dallas County?

Oil and Gas Contracts: Lease, License, or Fee Simple?

Fracking (the more scientific term is hydrocarbon fracturing) is a technological practice that involves pumping highly pressurized, chemically treated water into rock formations that are located far under the surface of the earth in order to crack open fractures in the rock so that oil and gas deposits can be pulled to the surface where the gas or oil can be drawn from the water. The seismic activity, ground water depletion, air pollution, and noise pollution caused by fracking are troublesome enough to cause some states to build strict regulations around the operation itself. But not all questions associated with oil and gas leases involve fracking or some other new drilling technology. Sometimes the issue is whether a broker can obtain a fee or how an asset is affected in a bankruptcy situation. Nevertheless, one of the main problems that must be solved is the actual nature of the contract involved in transferring (or preserving) the subterranean rights of any sort, or to put it directly, is such a contract a real property lease, a license, or a fee of some sort? [See: Ryan Fisher, "Cleveland Law Firm Provides Expert Legal Help with Fracking Problems and Opportunities," *PR Newswire*, March 12, 2012, http://www.prnewswire.com/; and "Hydraulic Fracturing," *Wikipedia, the Free Encyclopedia*, January 11, 2015, http://en.wikipedia.org/wiki/Hydraulic_fracturing.]

Fee Simple Determinable States differ on how they characterize a contract involving subterranean rights, especially as those rights relate to the extraction of gas, oil, and other minerals. Some states are quite unequivocal in declaring that a contract for oil and gas rights is neither a license nor a lease, but is instead, a fee simple determinable. As you will recall, anyone owning real property outright—that is, forever—is said to have an estate in fee simple. The estate descends, on the death of the owner, to the owner's heirs. The owner of an estate in fee simple has absolute ownership in the real estate, with the right to use or dispose of it as desired, so long as the use of it does not interfere with others' rights. Such rights can be altered by contract. In some states, for example, an oil and gas contract is considered a **fee simple determinable**. This is a fee simple that lasts as long as the ability to take the oil and gas from the earth continues. Once that ceases as an option, the fee simple reverts to the original owners. The original owners receive a royalty on the gas and oil produced by the drilling project. [See: Fisher.]

Lease Agreements In contrast, other states characterize oil and gas contracts as real property, lease agreements and others as a simple license. In a **lease** agreement, the **lessees**, those who purchase the right to enter the land from the **lessors**, those who owned the land outright, receive the ability to operate on the land as if it were their own, in exchange for an agreed to payment or a payment schedule. Thus, the lessees have the right to enter, leave, and move about the land as well as to construct the necessary drilling and extraction equipment, equipment such as derricks and pipelines, to perform their tasks. As the courts often say, in a lease agreement the lessees have been granted the ability to hold on to the land and to perform whatever tasks they reasonably need to perform in order to accomplish the objectives for which they wanted that land in the first place. Because the lease agreement is a real property contract, it must adhere to all of the legal requirements for such agreements, including the production of a written document, following all recording requirements, and so on. [See: Fisher.]

A License to Search and Extract In contrast, a **license** is a much more limited contract that bestows no property rights on the licensee. The only rights transferred are the right to enter the land, the right to search for the oil and gas, and the right to leave with a quantity of that oil and/or gas. No other property rights are transferred to the licensee. If we can use a simple analogy, the difference between a lease and a license is the difference between entering a tree farm to cut down a single evergreen to take home a Christmas tree (a license) and the right to plant, cultivate, nurture, and then cut down a tree (a lease). [See: Fisher.]

A Lease That Establishes a Fee Simple Determinable Some courts manage to mix and match a lease with a fee simple determinable. These courts would say that a lease agreement that empowers the lessees to hold on to the land and to perform whatever tasks they reasonably need to perform in order to accomplish the objectives for which they wanted that land actually creates a fee simple determinable. Ohio is one state that seems unable to make up its mind. The courts of Ohio, even the supreme court, seem to hold at one time or another to all of these positions, not simultaneously, of course, but in waves of unpredictable and somewhat exasperating change. [See: Ilya Batikov, Kevin F. Eichner, Sheila Nolan Gartland, and Matthew W. Warnock, "Title Issues and Recent Cases Relating to Oil and Gas Developments in Ohio," Ohio State Bar Association Annual Conference, April 30 to May 2, 2014; Fisher; Porter Wright, "What Is an Oil and Gas Lease? A Federal Court in Ohio Predicts Ohio Law," *Oil and Gas Law Report*, September 27, 2013, http://www.oilandgaslawreport.com/2013/09/27/; and *Rayl v. E. Ohio Gas Co.*, 348 N.E.2d 385 (9th Dist. 1973).]

A SOON TO BE CLASSIC CASE If It's Not One Technicality, It's Another

The Wellington Resource Group (WRG) brought suit against the Beck Energy Corporation (BEC) when BEC failed to pay WRG for obtaining XTO Energy (XTO) as a buyer for its oil and gas rights. Transact, a company from North Carolina, asked to enter the lawsuit because its people, not WRG, had actually found XTO. The court granted Transact's request to intervene, and the case proceeded to the next stage. At that point, BEC filed a motion to dismiss that part of the case involving Transact. BEC did not dispute the facts. Yes, it admits that Transact may have found XTO and may have secured its involvement in the contract. However, even if all that is true, BEC says, Transact cannot recover one cent because the gas and oil lease that was negotiated is a real property contract and Transact is not a licensed real estate broker in the state of Ohio, which is a requirement to receive fees in such a deal. Because Transact does not have the necessary license, it cannot collect those fees, and the case should be dismissed.

BEC's claim may appear to be a mere technicality. After all, Transact seems to have secured the buyer for BEC, and so, it only seems fair that BEC would pay Transact its fair share. However, there are some very good reasons for the state's licensing rule. Real estate negotiations are complicated and detailed procedures must be followed precisely to prevent errors in identifying real property boundaries, securing inspections, searching for deeds, uncovering liens, finding titles, and so on. That is why the state is so insistent that such contracts be negotiated by trained and experienced experts.

However, the case turns on another technicality. Is the gas and oil contract negotiated here a real property contract or something else? The question should have an easy answer, and in many states, it does. The State of Ohio, however, seems to have some difficulty in maintaining consistency in answering the question. Still, this time, the court does not hesitate. An oil and gas contract like this one, it says, is not a real property contract. Therefore, a real estate broker's license is not needed. However, before you get too enthusiastic about this definitive and fearless answer by the court, look again. The case was brought in federal court, so what we have is a federal judge interpreting state law. Is that likely to stand? Your guess, quite frankly, is as good as anyone's. [See: *Wellington Resource Group, LLC. v. Beck Energy Corporation*, Case No. 2:12-CV-104 (U.S. District Court, Southern District of Ohio, Eastern Division (September 20, 2013).]

Source: See: *Wellington Resource Group, LLC. v. Beck Energy Corporation,* Case No. 2:12-CV-104 (United States District Court, Southern District of Ohio, Eastern Division (September 20, 2013).

Dormant Minerals Statutes

A **dormant minerals statute** is designed to permit the surface owner of a plot of land to recover mineral rights that have not been utilized by a purchaser of such rights for a long time, often a period of not less than 20 years. The use of such statutes has become more popular since landowners have become more aware of the lucrative contracts that can be negotiated for oil and gas rights as discussed earlier. Some dormant mineral rights statutes, those described as "use-it-or-lose-it" statutes, include provisions that assert that mineral rights revert to the original owner once the statutory time limit has passed and the mineral rights have not been exploited. The reversion in such statutes is inevitable, so the original owner need do nothing other than sit and wait for the clock to tick on. Other more strict statutes require a series of proactive stages on the part of the original owner to jump-start the statute's application to their land. These steps may include but are not limited to the following: The surface landowner must (1) serve notice by certified mail on the holders of the dormant mineral rights indicating the surface owner's intent to assert the rights available under the act or, if the holder cannot be found, publish notice of that intent; (2) check to see if the holder of the mineral rights has recorded any new agreements in the recorder's office that might affect the surface owner's intent to assert his or her rights; and (3) file a sworn statement of abandonment in the county recorder's office. Many older versions of dormant minerals statutes did not include oil and gas as minerals. This oversight has generally been remedied in most new statutes, which specifically include or exclude oil and gas deposits in their definitions of minerals. [See: Batikov, Eichner, Gartland, and Warnock.]

quick quiz 30-3

1. A license is a limited contract that bestows no property rights on the licensee. — true | false
2. Lease agreements must adhere to all of the legal requirements for real property contracts. — true | false
3. A dormant minerals statute is designed to permit the surface owner of a plot of land to recover mineral rights that have not been used by a purchaser of such rights. — true | false

30-4 Acquiring Title to and Managing Real Property

Most of the time, property owners, unless they are causing a nuisance of a danger to others, get to decide to use, manage, and transfer the title to their own property without undue interference from the government, except, of course, for the payment of taxes and fees. Sometimes, however, the government will decide how property will be used in certain parts of a city or town, and at other more extreme times, the government may actually confiscate property for the public good. Such governmental management is exercised through zoning ordinances and eminent domain.

Title to Real Property

Title to real property refers to the ownership of that property. Saying that someone has title to a piece of property is really just a quick way of saying that a person has the evidence needed to demonstrate that he or she is entitled to possess, use, and convey that property to another. Title to real property may be acquired by sale or gift, will or descent, or by neglect.

A house deed is one example of a title to real property.
©Stockbyte/Getty Images

Title by Sale or Gift Ownership and title to real property are most frequently transferred from one owner to another by sale or by gift. This action is done by transferring a written instrument called a *deed*. The person transferring title is the **grantor**. The person to whom the title is transferred is the **grantee**. A deed becomes effective when it is delivered to the grantee. A deed to real property may be bestowed as a gift from the owner or through a sale. In the case of a gift, consideration is not given by the grantee for the deed. There are four types of deeds:

1. General warranty deed.
2. Special warranty deed.
3. Bargain-and-sale deed.
4. Quitclaim deed.

General Warranty Deed A **general warranty deed**, sometimes called a *full covenant and warranty deed*, contains express warranties under which the grantor guarantees the property to be free of encumbrances created by the grantor or by others who had title previously. It is the most desirable form of deed from the point of view of the grantee because it warrants (gives assurances) that title is good.

Special Warranty Deed A **special warranty deed** contains express warranties under which the grantor guarantees that no title defect arose during the time that the grantor owned the property, but not otherwise. No warranties are made as to defects that arose *before* the grantor owned the property.

EXAMPLE 30-5: Special Warranty Deed

Grant sold a vacant lot to Tuttle. The lot had been left to Grant through the will of a distant relative. Grant had never had the title searched, but she could guarantee Tuttle that no liens or claims against the property had been created since she inherited the property. Grant would be safe in granting title under a special warranty deed. The buyer would be protected only by making a title search that would disclose claims not covered by the seller's warranty.

Bargain-and-Sale Deed A **bargain-and-sale deed** is one that transfers title to property but contains no warranties. The form of the deed is the same as that of a warranty deed except that the warranties are omitted. Because a sale necessarily involves the idea of a valuable consideration, this type of deed is not valid without consideration. It could not be used to convey a gift of real property.

Quitclaim Deed A **quitclaim deed** (also called a *deed without covenants*) transfers to the buyer only the interest that the seller may have in a property. This type of deed merely releases a party's rights to the property. It contains no warranties. It is used when the seller gives up some right in the property, such as an easement or dower and courtesy, or to cure a defect in the chain of title.

Title by Will or Descent
When people die owning real property solely in their own name or with others as tenants in common, title passes to their heirs at the moment of death. If they die with a will, title passes to the people named in the will. If they die without a will, title passes to the heirs, as tenants in common, according to the laws of intestacy. A deed is not used when title passes to heirs in this manner. Instead, the records of the probate court establish title to the property. A deed may be used, however, by the personal representative of an estate to transfer title to real property to another. This transfer may be done in many states by authority granted in a will or by a license issued by the court.

Title by Adverse Possession
Title to real property may be obtained by taking actual possession of the property openly, notoriously, exclusively, under a claim of right, and continuously for a period of time set by state statute. This method of obtaining title to real property is called **adverse possession**. To establish such ownership rights, claimants must prove the following:

- They have had continuous use of the property for 20 years (or a period set by state statute).
- This use has been without interruption by the owner.

- It was without the owner's permission.
- It was with the owner's knowledge.

Proof of these facts in court will give a person superior rights over the one in whose name a deed is recorded. A court of equity has the power to declare the one claiming under adverse possession to be the new owner.

EXAMPLE 30-6: Adverse Possession

Wilhelm and Kupersmith were next-door neighbors. Not realizing where the true property line was, Wilhelm built a garage and driveway two feet onto Kupersmith's land. He used the garage and driveway continuously, with Kupersmith's knowledge, for the next 22 years. The error was discovered when Kupersmith sold her property to a new owner, who had it surveyed. Wilhelm, through court action, was able to obtain title to the land on which the garage and driveway were located by adverse possession.

Governmental Management of Real Property

Thomas Jefferson once said that "the care of human life and happiness, and not their destruction, is the first and only legitimate object of good government." Ideally, the governmental management of real property should promote the "care of human life and happiness." Zoning laws, on the surface at least, have as their purpose the regulation, limitation, and planning of real property for the good of the entire society. Eminent domain goes a step further declaring that there are some instances in which the "care of human life and happiness" demands the confiscation of one person's property for the preservation and the promotion of the general good.

Zoning Laws Municipal zoning laws regulate the uses that may be made of properties within specified geographical areas or districts. Residential zoning prohibits properties from being used for commercial purposes within a given area. Multifamily zoning permits construction of apartment buildings. Limited-commercial zoning allows the construction of small stores but restricts the building of large shopping malls and commercial centers. Industrial zoning allows the building of factories, and agricultural zoning allows farming in a particular area. Zoning laws help keep property values from declining and protect against the undesirable use of neighboring property.

Newly passed zoning laws do not apply to existing uses of the land. Such uses are called nonconforming uses if they are not allowed under the new zoning law. They may continue in existence but may not be enlarged or changed in kind. By appeal to the local zoning board, variances may be given to individuals or businesses when justified and reasonable. A variance is an exemption or exception that permits a use that differs from those allowed under the existing ordinance. Variances are granted in special circumstances to protect property owners who might otherwise suffer a hardship if zoning laws were applied and enforced arbitrarily. Decisions of a local zoning commission may be appealed to county commissioners, a county court, or the highest court in the state.

Eminent Domain All ownership of private property is subject to the government's superior rights if property is needed for a public purpose. Eminent domain, also called condemnation, is the right of federal, state, and local governments, or other public bodies, to take private lands, with compensation to their owners, for a public purpose. The right is exercised for such purposes as new highway construction, public parks, and state hospitals, as well as to reinvigorate depressed areas.

A CLASSIC CASE Eminent Domain and All the King's Men: *Kelo v. City of New London*

This controversy started when the leaders of New London, Connecticut, agreed to help the Pfizer Corporation, which had decided to build a research and manufacturing center in the city. To do this, the city activated the New London Development Corporation (NLDC), which began to buy the land in that area of town. Many residents in the targeted area did not want to leave their homes and simply refused to sell. Then some bright boy or gal in the city's legal department recommended invoking the city's power to confiscate land for public use under eminent domain as found in the Fifth Amendment of the Constitution. Then somebody else in the city's legal department discovered that the power to exercise eminent domain in economic development situations was granted to the city by a Connecticut statute. A homeowner named Susette Kelo, along with several other owners, sued to end the unconstitutional seizure of their property. The homeowners argued that the taking of their land for private development purposes did not fall under the heading of "public use" as visualized by the Framers when they wrote the Fifth Amendment. The property owners also argued in the alternative that, even if the annexation of their property did qualify as public use, the city had to prove with "reasonable certainty" that the appropriation of their land really would result in the public benefits predicted by the development corporation.

The suit was filed in the state court of Connecticut and eventually reached the Supreme Court of Connecticut, which supported the city. In the end, the case was heard by the U.S. Supreme Court, which granted a *writ of certiorari*. After considering the arguments, the Court, in a 5–4 ruling, held that the city's seizure of the land really was public use. The Court ruled that the government could take private property to promote private economic development. The Court said that an increased tax base, higher-paying jobs, and other benefits fulfilled a public purpose. In its decision, the Court further noted, "nothing in our opinion precludes any State from placing further restrictions on its exercise of the takings power." Within two years after the unpopular decision in the *Kelo* case, more than 80 percent of U.S. states changed their laws on the subject, making it more difficult to take private property by eminent domain. Some states, including Florida, have taken a broad approach, such as forbidding the use of eminent domain for any kind of private development. Others, including Missouri, have made guarded changes, such as not allowing farmland to be classified as "blighted." In 2007, the New Jersey high court held that before invoking eminent domain, a municipality must prove a site is truly "blighted," not simply "not fully productive." [See: *Kelo v. City of New London*, 125 S. Ct . 2655 (U.S. Supreme Court).]

Source: See: *Kelo v. City of New London*, 125 S. Ct . 2655 (U.S. Supreme Court).

Eminent domain is, at times, extended to public utilities when it can be shown that denial of a right of way for electric, telephone, gas, or other lines may interrupt construction of installations that provide needed services to an entire community. When private property is taken by eminent domain proceedings, the owner must be paid the fair value of what has been taken. The owner is not required to accept an amount offered by those assessing the value of the property. In fact, homeowners can also contest the government's decision to take their land, when they have reason to believe that the "taking" is not really for public purposes but is actual for private profit. This is precisely what happened in the classic *Kelo* case.

> **quick quiz 30-4**
>
> 1. Title to real property may be acquired by sale or gift, will or, descent, or by neglect. **true | false**
> 2. Municipal zoning laws that regulate the uses that may be made of properties within specified geographical areas or districts have been declared unconstitutional. **true | false**
> 3. Eminent domain is the right of federal, state, and local governments, or other public bodies, to take private lands, with compensation to their owners, for a public purpose. **true | false**

30-5 The Landlord–Tenant Relationship

The landlord-tenant relationship is a contractual arrangement in which the owner of real property allows another to have temporary possession and control of the premises in exchange for consideration. The agreement that gives rise to the landlord-tenant relationship is called a **lease**. The property owner who gives the lease is the **lessor** or **landlord**, and the person to whom the lease is given is the **lessee** or **tenant**. Five elements are necessary for the creation of a landlord-tenant relationship:

1. Consent of the landlord to the occupancy by the tenant.
2. Transfer of possession and control of the property to the tenant in an inferior position (in subordination) to the rights of the landlord.
3. The right by the landlord to the return of the property, called the right of reversion.
4. The creation of an ownership interest in the tenant known as a leasehold estate.
5. Either an express or implied contract between the parties that satisfies all the essentials of a valid contract (mutual assent, capacity, consideration, legality).

Although rent is usually paid by the tenant to the landlord for the arrangement, it is not essential to the creation of the landlord-tenant relationship.

Leasing versus Other Relationships

Sometimes people confuse leasing with other relationships that are similar but convey different rights and, therefore, limit certain activities that would be permissible under a leasing arrangement. The two most common relationships that may be compared with the landlord-tenant relationship are licensing and lodging.

Leasing Compared with Licensing A lease differs from a license in that a lease gives an interest in real property and transfers possession, whereas a license gives no property right or ownership interest in the property but merely allows the licensee to do certain acts that would otherwise be a trespass.

> **EXAMPLE 30-7:** License Rather than Lease
>
> The city of Topeka was given a gift of 80 acres of land for use as a public park by the heirs of Guilford G. Gage. The deed signed by the heirs contained a condition that the property would revert to them if the property were ever deeded or leased to a third party. After the park was established, the city granted the exclusive right to McCall to construct and operate, for a period of five years, a miniature train on the

premises. Under the agreement, McCall was subject in virtually all respects to the control of the city, and either party could terminate the arrangement by giving 30 days' notice. The heirs of Gage claimed that the transaction was a lease and that the property should be returned to them. In holding that McCall had a license rather than a lease, the court said that all McCall had was "the exclusive right to operate as the City may dictate."

Because a license confers a personal privilege to act and not a present possessory estate, it does not run with the land and is usually not transferable. It may be made orally or in writing and may be given without consideration. In addition, a license need not delineate the specific space to be occupied. In contrast, a lease gives the tenant exclusive possession of the premises as against all the world, including the owner. It describes the exact property leased and states the term of the tenancy and the rent to be paid. In addition, in some states, a lease must be in writing. Permission to sell Christmas trees at a gas station, to hold dance parties in a hall, and to place a sign on the outside of a building have all been held to be licenses rather than leases.

Leasing Compared with Lodging A **lodger** is one who has the use of property without actual or exclusive possession of it. A lodger is a type of licensee, with a mere right to use the property. The landlord retains control of the premises and is responsible for its care and upkeep. Unlike a tenant, a lodger has no right to bring suit for trespass or to eject an intruder from the premises. One who lives in a spare room of a house, for example, whose owner retains direct control and supervision of the entire house, is a lodger.

Types of Leasehold Interests

The interest conveyed by a lease is called a **leasehold estate** or a **tenancy**. There are four kinds of leasehold estates:

1. Tenancy at will.
2. Tenancy for years.
3. Periodic tenancy.
4. Tenancy at sufferance.

Tenancy at Will A **tenancy at will** is an ownership interest (estate) in real property for an indefinite period of time. No writing is required to create this tenancy, and it may be terminated at the will of either party by giving proper notice. The notice requirement to terminate a tenancy at will varies from state to state. It ranges from the time between rent periods to 30 days' written notice from the next day that rent is due. The rule generally followed in this country is that a tenancy at will comes to an end when the property is sold by the landlord to a third party. The notice required by state law must be given to the tenant in any event.

Tenancy for Years A **tenancy for years** is an ownership interest (estate) in real property for a definite or fixed period of time. It may be for one week, six months, one year, five years, 99 years, or any period of time, as long as it is definite. Such a tenancy automatically terminates on the expiration of the stated term. A tenancy for 100 years or more creates an estate in fee simple, transferring absolute ownership to the tenant. For this reason, leases are sometimes written for 99-year periods. In some states, a tenancy for years may be oral if the term is shorter than one year; otherwise, it must be in writing. Other states require all tenancies for years to be in writing. A tenant who remains in possession of the premises at the expiration of the term with permission of the landlord, but without a new lease, is a tenant at will in some states. In other states, such a tenant is known as a periodic tenant.

Periodic Tenancy A *periodic tenancy*, which is also known as a *tenancy from year to year* (or month to month or week to week), is a fixed-period tenancy that continues for successive periods until one of the parties terminates it by giving notice to the other party. Unless the landlord or tenant gives advance notice of an intention to terminate the lease, it will be automatically renewed at the end of each fixed period for the same term. Advance notice varies from state to state, but it generally is defined as a period of three months for periodic tenancies of one year or longer and "one period" for periodic terms of less than a year. The death of a tenant who holds a periodic tenancy does not terminate the tenancy. Rather, the interest of the tenant passes to the personal representative of the deceased's estate. A periodic tenancy may be created impliedly by a landlord accepting rent from a tenant for years whose lease has expired or who is wrongfully in possession. Some states treat the latter situation as a tenancy at will.

Tenancy at Sufferance A *tenancy at sufferance* arises when tenants wrongfully remain in possession of the premises after their tenancy has expired. It often comes about at the expiration of the term of a tenancy for years or when a tenancy at will has been properly terminated and the tenant remains in possession. Such a tenant is a wrongdoer, having no estate or other interest in the property. A tenant at sufferance is not entitled to notice to vacate and is liable to pay rent for the period of occupancy. A periodic tenancy or a tenancy at will may come about, however, instead of a tenancy at sufferance if a landlord accepts rent from a tenant whose tenancy has expired.

The Lease Agreement

The agreement between a lessor and a lessee, called a lease, creates the landlord–tenant relationship. It provides the tenant with exclusive possession and control of the real property of the landlord. Because the lease is a contract, the general rules of contract law apply to it. The essential requirements of a lease are (1) a definite agreement as to the extent and bounds of the leased property, (2) a definite and agreed term, and (3) a definite and agreed price of rental and manner of payment (see Figure 30-1).

Rent Control Some large communities have passed rent control laws to keep rents within an affordable range. These laws limit what landlords can charge for rental property and often contain procedures that must be followed before tenants may be evicted. In a number of areas, rent control laws have caused landlords to turn their apartments into condominiums, leading to shortages in rental apartments. Such laws differ from place to place. Some states, including Massachusetts, have done away with rent control laws.

Security Deposits In addition to the first month's rent, landlords often require either a security deposit or the last month's rent, or both, to be paid at the beginning of a tenancy. The deposit protects landlords against damages to their property as well as nonpayment of rent. Due to abuses of such deposits by landlords, state legislatures have passed laws regulating security deposits on residential property. Such laws spell out the rights of tenants and make it easier for tenants to prevail in court. Although these laws differ from state to state, most states limit security deposits to one, one and one-half, two, or two and one-half months' rent, and most states require that security deposits be placed in interest-bearing accounts. The interest is either paid to tenants on an annual basis or accrued in their favor. Security deposits may not be commingled with other money belonging to the landlord. Also, the landlord is given a specific period, usually 30 days after the lease ends, to account for the security deposit and return the balance due to a tenant. Many states have now "put teeth" into the law, providing for double or triple damages, court costs, and attorney's fees for tenants whose security deposits are wrongfully withheld.

LEASE

This lease made the 20th day of August, 2017, between ROBERT VICKERS, herein called Landlord, and ETHEL LOPAZ, herein called Tenant, witnesseth:

The Landlord leases to the Tenant the following described premises: Four rooms and a bath on the first floor of the premises located at 17 Rosebud Terrace, Ashmont, New Hampshire, for the term of one year commencing at noon on the first day of September 2017 and ending at noon on the 31st day of August, 2017.

The Tenant agrees to pay to the Landlord the sum of $6,000 for the said term, in eleven (11) monthly payments as follows: The first and last months' rent of $1,000, plus a security deposit of $500, payable on September 1, 2017, and $500 on the first day of each month thereafter.

The Landlord agrees that the Tenant on paying the said rent and performing the covenants herein contained shall peaceably and quietly have, hold, and enjoy the premises for said term.

The Tenant agrees that at the expiration of the time mentioned in this lease she will give peaceable possession of the said premises to the Landlord in as good a condition as they now are, the usual wear, unavoidable accidents, and loss by fire excepted, and will not make or suffer any waste thereof, nor assign this lease, nor sublet, nor permit any person to occupy the same, nor make or suffer to be made any alteration therein, without the consent of the Landlord in writing having first been obtained, and that the Landlord may enter to view and make improvements, and to show the premises to prospective tenants or purchasers.

The covenants herein shall extend to and be binding upon heirs, executors, and administrators of the parties to this lease.

IN WITNESS WHEREOF, the parties have hereunto set their hands and seals the day and year first above written.

Robert Vickers
Robert Vickers

Ethel Lopaz
Ethel Lopaz

Figure 30-1 This is an example of a lease.

EXAMPLE 30-8: Double Damages

Santos rented a $450-per-month apartment from Hollis for a term of two years. When Santos's tenancy ended, Hollis refused to return any of the $450 security deposit to Santos, claiming that the damages to the apartment fully offset the amount of the deposit. Santos hired a lawyer, who brought suit against Hollis. The landlord was able to demonstrate only $70 in damages to Santos's apartment. The court found that Hollis had wrongfully withheld $380 of Santos's security deposit. The court awarded Santos a judgment for double damages of $760 plus attorney's fees of $200. With court costs, the landlord was forced to pay over $1,000.

Option to Renew or to Purchase Many leases contain a provision allowing the lessee to have the option to renew the lease for one or more additional periods. An option to renew gives the lessee the right, at the end of the lease, to a new lease for an additional period. The new lease is on the same terms as the old one, with the possible exception of an increase in the rent. To exercise the option, the lessee must notify the lessor on or before the date set forth in the lease to do so. A lessee may, if the lease so provides, be given an option to purchase the property. This option is an agreement by the lessor to sell the property to the lessee for a stated price. To exercise the option, the lessee must notify the lessor, within the time period stated in the lease, of the decision to purchase the property.

EXAMPLE 30-9: Option to Purchase

Larson purchased a parcel of real property for $191,140 and leased it to the Panhandle Rehabilitation Center. The lease was for 10 years and contained an option to buy for $200,000. After leasing the premises for five years and spending $25,000 to improve it, Panhandle notified Larson of its intention to exercise its option. By this time, the property was worth $238,000. Larson refused to sell the property to Panhandle for $200,000. The court ordered her to do so.

Assignment and Subletting An assignment of a lease occurs when the interest in the leased premises is transferred by the lessee to another person for the balance of the term of the lease. The new party, called the *assignee*, steps into the shoes of the tenant, or assignor, and is liable for all of the original tenant's obligations and entitled to all the original tenant's rights under the lease. In contrast, it is called a **sublease** or **underlease** if the transfer is for a part of the term but not for the remainder of it. A lease may be assigned or sublet unless the lease states otherwise. Many leases are written so that they require landlord approval for an assignment or a sublease. However, in some states, the landlord cannot withhold such approval unreasonably. An assignment or sublease will be held valid if the landlord accepts rent over a period of time from either an assignee or a subtenant.

quick quiz 30-5

1. A license is just like a lease because it bestows upon the licensee the same type of property rights and ownership interests as those bestowed on a party with a lease. true | false
2. A tenancy at will is an ownership interest (estate) in real property for a definite period of time. true | false
3. An option to renew gives the lessee the right, at the end of the lease, to a new lease for an additional period. true | false

30-6 Duties of the Landlord and the Tenant

Like most of the legal relationships that we have examined in the book thus far, the landlord–tenant relationship is a balancing act that offsets the rights of one side against the duties of the other. In this case the rights are inherent within the very nature of the landlord–tenant relationship. The tenant is given the right to have temporary possession of the premises and the landlord has the right to receive consideration. The duties, in contrast, are not quite that clear.

The Landlord's Duties

A good lease agreement will carefully spell out the respective rights and duties of the landlord and the tenant. However, state and local laws may restrict or expand upon what is set forth in the lease.

Duty to Refrain from Discrimination A landlord may not discriminate in selecting tenants on the grounds of race, creed, color, national origin, or gender. In most states, a landlord may restrict rentals to persons without children but may not restrict a married couple's freedom to bear children during the leasehold. It is permissible, however, for a landlord to set up a housing complex that is open only to people 62 years of age and older and not run counter to age discrimination prohibitions. Although not directly applicable to a lease agreement, the Americans with Disabilities Act does require that owners of public accommodations such as motels and hotels have handicapped accessibility.

Landlords must ensure that the property they rent out to tenants is habitable.
©Bellurget Jean Louis/Getty Images

Duty to Maintain the Premises When real property is rented for dwelling purposes, there is an implied warranty, called the *warranty of habitability*, that the premises are fit for human habitation. This provision means that the landlord warrants there are no defects vital to the use of the premises for residential purposes. Examples of defects are unsafe electrical wiring, a malfunctioning heating or cooling system, broken windows, a leaking roof, and infestation of insects. Many municipalities have adopted ordinances to protect tenants from unsafe or unhealthy conditions created by a landlord's refusal to make necessary repairs. Building inspectors, health authorities, and other public officials are empowered to make inspections and demand improvements when they are contacted by dissatisfied tenants. In many cases, ordinances permit the tenant to cease payment of rent for the period during which the landlord fails to make the repairs or improvements needed. The majority of states hold that a landlord has a duty to clear common entryways of natural accumulations of snow and ice. Some states, nevertheless, still follow the older rule that the landlord owes no duty to tenants to clean common entryways of ice and snow unless there is an agreement on the part of the landlord to do so.

Duty to Deliver Peaceful Possession The tenant is entitled to the exclusive peaceful possession and quiet enjoyment of the rental premises. *Quiet enjoyment* is the right of a tenant to the undisturbed possession of the property. The landlord may not interfere with the tenant's rights of possession as long as the tenant abides by the conditions of the lease and those imposed by law.

EXAMPLE 30-10: Breach of Quiet Enjoyment

Smith Grocery & Variety Inc. leased one store in a two-store mall from Northern Terminals Inc. The lease entitled Smith to the use of the parking areas (between 14 and 20 spaces) abutting the leased premises. Five months after Smith opened for business, Northern Terminals added an additional store to the mall without increasing the mall's parking facilities. Smith's business declined due to the severe parking shortage caused by the opening of a Triple-S Blue Stamp Redemption Center in the new addition. The court held that Northern Terminals breached the covenant of quiet enjoyment. There was a substantial interference with the lessee's use of the premises, which was caused by the lessor's taking away of the parking spaces.

The right to exclusive possession by the tenant makes the landlord a trespasser should there be any unauthorized entry by the landlord into the rented premises.

EXAMPLE 30-11: Trespass

Benson & Childs rented a skylight suite for their architecture offices. The lease gave the owner permission to enter only when a request had been made or in the event of extreme emergency. The landlord entered the offices late one evening for what he termed was his regular safety and fire inspection. Benson & Childs may treat the landlord's trespass as a breach of their right to sole possession, giving them the right to terminate the lease and charge the landlord in either a civil or a criminal complaint.

A tenant who is wrongfully evicted is not required to return and may consider the lease as ended. An **eviction** is an act of the landlord that deprives the tenant of the enjoyment of the premises. It is called an **actual eviction** when the tenant is physically deprived of the leasehold. When the tenant is deprived of something of a substantial nature that was called for under the lease, it is termed a **constructive eviction**. The tenant is justified in abandoning the premises without paying rent when a wrongful eviction occurs. The tenant must mitigate (lessen) any damages, however, if possible.

EXAMPLE 30-12: Constructive Eviction

Sound City, U.S.A., was interested in renting space in a shopping center. An inspection of the premises disclosed portions of the ceiling tile missing or hanging loose, water marks on the ceiling, and bare fluorescent light fixtures. As a result, Sound City included in its one-year lease an addendum (addition), whereby the landlord agreed to repair and paint the ceiling tile, cover the lightbulb fixtures, panel the south wall, and erect a partition. Sound City moved into the shopping center, but after three months and many complaints, the repairs were never completed. It then moved out. The landlord brought suit for the remaining nine months' rent. The court held against the landlord, saying that there had been a constructive eviction. The physical appearance of the store was an important factor in the successful operation of Sound City's business. The failure to repair the premises properly in accordance with the lease rendered the premises unsuitable for the purpose for which they were rented.

The Tenant's Duties

The tenant has the duty to pay rent to the landlord. In addition, the landlord has the right to remove, through court procedures, a tenant for nonpayment of rent, disorderliness, or illegal or unpermitted use of the premises. A tenant has the duty to observe the valid restrictions contained in the lease. Leases may impose duties of all kinds as long as they are legal and do not deny a tenant's constitutional rights. Failure to abide by the restrictions agreed to at the time of the signing of the lease gives the landlord the right to seek the eviction of the tenant. Unless agreed otherwise, the tenant must turn over to the landlord all fixtures (except trade fixtures belonging to a business) that have been made a permanent part of the real property by the tenant during the leasehold. Tenants also have a duty to avoid damaging or destroying the property, that is, commit waste. **Waste** is defined as substantial damage to premises that significantly decreases the value of the property.

Tort Liability

When a person is injured on leased property, the one who is in control of the part of the premises where the injury occurs usually is responsible if the injury was caused by that person's negligence. The landlord, for example, is responsible for injury to others that may be caused by a defect in the common areas, such as hallways and stairways. Although landlords are not guarantors of the safety of persons in a building's common area, they are not free to ignore reasonably foreseeable risks of harm to tenants and others lawfully on the premises. Landlords must take reasonable steps to guard against foreseeable criminal acts of third parties.

Eviction Proceedings

States today do not allow landlords to use force to evict tenants. Instead, they must make use of statutory remedies that are available to them. Some states do, however, recognize the right of landlords to enter wrongfully held premises and take over possession if it can be done peacefully. **Ejectment** is the common law name given to the lawsuit brought by the landlord to have the tenant evicted from the premises. This older remedy is still available in many states; however, it is time consuming, expensive, and subject to long delays. **Unlawful detainer** is a legal proceeding that provides landlords with a quick method of evicting a tenant. The proceeding is referred to by different names in different states, including the following: summary process, summary ejectment, forcible entry and detainer, and dispossessory warrant proceedings. The remedy provides landlords with a quick method of regaining possession of their property and protects tenants from being ousted by force and violence. Strict notice requirements must be followed by the landlord, after which both parties are given their day in court. If a forcible eviction becomes necessary, it is done by the sheriff under the supervision of the court.

quick quiz 30-6

1. A landlord may not discriminate in selecting tenants on the grounds of race, creed, color, national origin, or gender.	true | false
2. Tenants also have a duty to avoid damaging or destroying the property, that is, commit waste.	true | false
3. States today do not allow landlords to use force to evict tenants.	true | false

Summary

30.1 Real property is the ground and everything permanently attached to it. It includes the airspace above the surface to as high as the owner can use and the ground under the surface. Fixtures are personal property that are so permanently attached to real property that they become part of the real property. Easements give people the right to pass over another's land, to run wires through another's airspace, to drain water onto another's property, and to run pipes underneath another's ground. Easements run with the land.

30.2 An estate in fee simple is the greatest interest that one can have in real property. It descends to one's heirs upon death and can be disposed of in any manner during one's lifetime. In contrast, a life estate lasts only for someone's life. People may own real property individually or with others. When two or more people own real property as tenants in common, the interest of a deceased owner's share passes to the heirs upon death. In contrast, when two or more people own real property as joint tenants or tenants by the entirety, the interest of the deceased owner's share passes to any other cotenants upon death.

30.3 Subterranean rights are sold to corporations exploring for coal, oil, or other mineral deposits. States differ on how they characterize a contract involving subterranean rights, especially as those rights relate to the extraction of gas, oil, and other minerals. Some states are quite unequivocal in declaring that a contact for oil and gas rights is neither a license nor a lease, but is instead a fee simple determinable. Other states characterize oil and gas contracts as real property, lease agreements, and others as a simple license. Some courts manage to mix and match a lease with a fee simple determinable. There are some states that seem unable to make up their minds. A dormant minerals statute is designed to permit the surface owner of a plot of land to recover mineral rights that have not been used by a purchaser of such rights for a long period as specified in the statute, often not less than 20 years.

30.4 A deed is used to transfer real property by sale or gift. The records of the probate court, instead of a deed, establish title to property when an owner dies. Title to real property may also be gained by adverse possession. Zoning laws regulate the uses that may be made of properties within specified geographical areas. Eminent domain is the right of federal, state, and local governments, or other public bodies, to take private lands for a public purpose. Owners must be paid the fair value of the property taken.

30.5 The landlord–tenant relationship is a contractual arrangement whereby the owner of real property allows another to have temporary possession and control of the premises in exchange for consideration. A lease is different from a license and from an agreement with a lodger. A tenancy at will is an ownership interest (estate) in real property for an indefinite period of time. A tenancy for years is an estate for a definite period of time, no matter how long or how short. A periodic tenancy is a tenancy that continues for successive periods until one of the parties terminates it by giving notice to the other party. A tenancy at sufferance arises when tenants wrongfully remain in possession of the premises after their tenancy has expired. A lease creates the landlord–tenant relationship. Because it is a contract, the general rules of contract law apply to it.

30.6 A landlord may not discriminate in selecting tenants on the grounds of race, creed, color, or gender. Landlords have the right to evict tenants for nonpayment of rent, disorderliness, and unpermitted use of the premises. Tenants must observe the valid restrictions in a lease and not commit waste. When someone is injured, the person in control of that part of the premises where the injury occurs is responsible if negligent. Peaceable entry, ejectment, and unlawful detainer are the principal methods available to landlords to regain possession of their premises.

Key Terms

actual eviction, 868
adverse possession, 859
bargain-and-sale deed, 859
community property, 854
concurrent ownership, 851
constructive eviction, 868
condemnation, 860
co-ownership, 851
co-tenants, 851
coverture, 849
curtesy, 850
dominant tenement, 847
dormant minerals statute, 857

dower, 850
easement, 847
easement by grant, 847
easement by prescription, 847
easement by reservation, 847
ejectment, 869
eminent domain, 860
estate in fee simple, 849
eviction, 868
fee simple determinable, 856
feme covert, 849
feme solo, 849
fixture, 847

fracking, 855
freehold estates, 849
general warranty deed, 859
grantee, 858
grantor, 858
joint tenants, 854
landlord, 862
lease, 856, 862
leasehold estate, 863
lessee, 856, 862
lessor, 856, 862
license, 856
life estate, 849

lodger, 863
navigable airspace, 846
nonconforming uses, 860
periodic tenancy, 864
quiet enjoyment, 867
quitclaim deed, 859
real estate, 845
real property, 845
remainder estate, 849
reversion estate, 849
right of way, 847
riparian owners, 846
servient tenement, 847
severalty, 851
special warranty deed, 859
spousal share, 850
sublease, 866
subterranean rights, 855
tenancy, 863
tenancy at sufferance, 864
tenancy by the entirety, 852
tenancy at will, 863
tenancy for years, 863
tenancy from year to year, 864
tenant, 862
tenants in common, 851
trade fixtures, 847
underlease, 866
unlawful detainer, 869
variance, 860
warranty of habitability, 867
waste, 868
zoning laws, 860

Questions for Review and Discussion

1. What constitutes real property?
2. What is the difference between freehold and leasehold estates?
3. What are the different types of co-ownership of real property?
4. What are the methods of transferring oil and gas rights?
5. What is the goal of the dormant minerals act?
6. What is eminent domain?
7. What are the methods of acquiring title to real property?
8. What are the five elements necessary to create a landlord–tenant relationship?
9. What are the essential requirements of a lease?
10. What are the duties of landlords and tenants?

Cases for Analysis

1. Aloi sold a section of her land to Bell, including in the deed an easement allowing Bell to cross Aloi's property to reach the newly acquired parcel. Three years later, Aloi sold his property to Cadd. Shortly thereafter, following an argument, Cadd put a chain across Bell's right of way, saying that he had not given permission for Bell to cross his land. How should the court rule on this case and why?
2. Alfonso DiFilippo and his brother, Pasquale, owned a parcel of real property as tenants in common. Pasquale died in 1961, leaving a life estate in the property to his widow, Annie, with the remainder estate when Annie dies to Alfonso. Annie died in 1985. Alfonso died in 1969, leaving his interest in the property to his wife, Maria. What interest did Maria own in the property when she died in 1981? [See: *DiFilippo v. DiFilippo*, 640 N.E.2d 1120 (MA).]
3. When its lease expired, Kingston Frameworks made plans to move to another building. Preparations were made to remove shelving, mat and glass cutters, display boards, benches, and other fixtures that had been built into the store when the lease first started. All the shelves and fixtures were specially designed for the picture-framing business. The landlord told the owners of Kingston Frameworks to stop removing the items from the property. Could they remove the shelves and other fixtures that were paid for and installed by them during their tenancy? Why or why not? [See: *George v. Town of Calais*, 373 A.2d 553 (VT).]
4. Smith and Dudley are next-door neighbors. The branches of a large maple tree on Smith's property hang over Dudley's driveway, dripping sap onto Dudley's car. Smith refuses to trim the branches overhanging Dudley's driveway, saying that she does not want to spoil the beauty of the tree. What are Dudley's legal rights in this situation?

5. Two years after Jean Russell was divorced from Billy Russell, Jean signed a quitclaim deed conveying her interest in their jointly owned real property to Billy. Later, she tried to have the deed set aside on the ground that Billy gave her no consideration. Was she successful? Why or why not? [See: *Russell v. Russell*, 361 So.2d 1053 (AL).]

6. Bech owned a building in which Cuevas resided as a tenant at will. Alleging that Cuevas had committed waste, Bech delivered a letter to Cuevas ordering her to vacate the premises in two days. The law of that state required 30-day notice to evict a tenant at will. Must Cuevas vacate the premises? Explain. [See: *Bech v. Cuevas*, 534 N.E.2d 1163 (MA).]

7. The following language was in a handwritten agreement signed by Harold and Saul and their respective wives: "Saul & Zelda get the option to rent the lower level of the Hope Chest store when their lease expires. If they do take it, they will pay the same rate of rent per square foot that Harold is paying for his store. Saul & Zelda will do all the fixing up at their expense. Entrance to upper level has to be maintained from Newbury Street—similar to how it is now. Saul and Zelda have to let Harold know six months ahead of time (lease expires by May 31, 1987, so that Saul and Zelda have to let Harold know by Nov. 31, 1986). Saul and Zelda cannot use the name Simon or Simon's or anything with the Simon name as a name for their store. Too confusing." Does the language contain the essential elements of a lease? Explain. [See: *Simon v. Simon*, 625 N.E.2d 564 (MA).]

8. Goldstein rented an apartment from Dunbar as a tenant at will. She paid her rent on time and took good care of the premises; she was never disorderly. Dunbar decided to evict Goldstein and rent the apartment to a college friend who was moving to the area. He sent Goldstein a proper notice to quit. Goldstein claimed that she could not be asked to leave because she had done nothing wrong. Do you agree with Goldstein? Explain. [See: *Ralo, Inc., v. Jack Graham, Inc.*, 362 So.2d 310 (FL).]

9. Sarah H. Brown and Sandy F. Soverow agreed to rent separate apartments from Osborn, the owner of an apartment complex called Nob Hill Apartments, which was being constructed. Because their single apartments were not yet completed, Brown and Soverow agreed to rent one larger apartment in the complex and live in that until their separate apartments were finished. A fire occurred in the apartment shortly after Brown put some leftover liver and gizzards for her dogs on the electric stove and left the apartment. In the lawsuit that followed, the contention was made that Brown and Soverow were lodgers rather than tenants. Do you agree with the contention? Explain. [See: *Osborn v. Brown*, 361 So.2d 82 (AL).]

10. Alabama Outdoor Advertising Co. Inc. leased part of a lot from All State Linen Service Co. to erect a commercial advertising sign. The term of the lease was for "indefinite years, beginning 1st day of January, 1973, and ending year to year thereafter." When All State sold the lot, it was argued that Alabama's lease was a tenancy at will and therefore came to an end when the lot was sold. Do you agree with this argument? Why or why not? [See: *Industrial Mach., Inc., v. Creative Displays, Inc.*, 344 So.2d 743 (AL).]

Design Elements: The Opening Case: ©Sharpstock/Alamy; A Classic Case: ©Evlakhov Valeriy/Shutterstock

quick quiz Answers

30-1	30-2	30-3	30-4	30-5	30-6
1. F	1. F	1. T	1. T	1. F	1. T
2. T	2. T	2. T	2. F	2. F	2. T
3. T	3. T	3. T	3. T	3. T	3. T

Chapter 31

Wills, Advance Directives, and Trusts

31-1 Sources and Relevance of Probate Law
Relevance of Probate to Business • Probate Terminology

31-2 The Law of Wills
Requirements for Executing a Will • Protection of Spouses and Children • Advantages and Disadvantages of the *Windsor* Ruling • The *Obergefell v. Hodges* Case • Changes in Estate Planning • Revoking, Changing, and Contesting a Will • Dying without a Will • Simultaneous Death • Settling an Estate

31-3 The Law of Advance Directives
Types of Advance Directives • The Right to Die and the Right to Life

31-4 The Law of Trusts
Types of Trusts • Obligations of the Trustee

THE OPENING CASE Round 1
Balancing the Right to Life with State Control: *Winkfield v. Children's Hospital and Research Center at Oakland*

The case of *Winkfield v. Children's Hospital and Research Center at Oakland* began innocently enough when 13-year-old Jahi McMath (Jahi) was admitted to Children's Hospital and Research Center in Oakland, California (CHRCO), for a routine tonsillectomy. At first, the procedure seemed to go according to plan. Then, unexpectedly, Jahi began to bleed profusely. The bleeding led to a large blood loss that triggered a heart attack and severe oxygen deprivation in the brain. As a result, Jahi experienced brain damage and was placed on a respirator that provided ventilation support. As long as she was on the respirator, her heart and her other organs functioned normally. However, subsequent tests revealed that she had suffered massive brain damage due to the long period that her brain had been without oxygen. At the time of the legal action noted here, Jahi was disabled and unable to do anything on her own. In fact, she was totally dependent upon the life support system.

Following standard procedures, and operating under California law (California Health, and Safety Code Section 1780) physicians at CHRCO determined that Jahi was brain dead due to an irreversible cessation of all functions within her brain, including the brain stem. Under the official protocols set up by the hospital's Task Force, CHRCO had two of their own physicians check the nature of Jahi's condition. Both physicians agreed that she had suffered brain death and that the condition was irreversible. Moreover, three additional physicians, who were not employed by the hospital, confirmed the diagnosis of brain death. Accordingly, CHRCO told Latisha Winkfield, Jahi's mother, that Jahi was brain dead and that they planned to take her off the life support system soon. Winkfield objected to this decision and brought this action, asking the court to issue a temporary restraining order. The order was designed to compel the hospital to keep Jahi on the life support system. In her complaint, Winkfield argued that, as Jahi's mother, she had the right to participate in any and all decisions that involved Jahi's health. (*Note:* Although Jahi did not have an advance directive, the First Amendment issues involved in this case would also apply to any similarly situated advance directive case.)

Winkfield argued, quite forcefully, that her case arose under the U.S. Constitution, specifically, under the Free Exercise Clause of the First Amendment. Winkfield also argued that, as Christians, she and Jahi believed that, as long as a person's heart was beating, that person was alive. It can also be assumed that they believed that taking Jahi off the life support machines would violate the Christian community's opposition to euthanasia and its belief in the sanctity of life. Despite these arguments, the trial court determined that Jahi was legally dead, and that, as a result, the hospital could take her off the life support mechanism. Winkfield appealed to the Second District California Court of Appeals and the U.S. District Court, Northern District of California. While there are convincing constitutional arguments to support Winkfield's position in this case, there are equally convincing arguments that support a constitutional right to die with dignity. This conflict is discussed in this chapter. [See: *Winkfield v. Children's Hospital and Research Center of Oakland*, Case Number RG 13707598 (2013).]

Opening Case Questions

1. What is brain death? Explain.
2. Why does the plaintiff in this case have standing to sue? Explain.
3. What type advance directive might have helped in this case? Explain.
4. What is a temporary restraining order, and how does it play into this case? Explain.
5. What is the right to life, and how does it play into this case? Explain.

Source: See: *Winkfield v. Children's Hospital and Research Center of Oakland*, Case Number RG 13707598 (2013).

 Learning Objectives

1. Give details about the sources of probate law and its relevance to business entities.
2. Identify the formal requirements for executing a will.
3. Determine whether a person who makes a will has the capacity to do so.
4. Explain how the Supreme Court's ruling involving the Defense of Marriage Act affected the law.
5. List the different methods of revoking or changing a will.
6. Outline the three grounds for contesting a will.
7. Describe who will inherit the property of someone who dies without a will.
8. Understand the steps to be taken by an executor or administrator in settling an estate.
9. Discuss the types and purposes of advance directives.
10. Differentiate among the various types of trusts and determine when they might be used.

31-1 Sources and Relevance of Probate Law

The term **probate** refers to the process of handling the will and the estate of a deceased person. Each state has its own laws passed by its legislature, different from other states, governing the writing of wills and the settling of estates. For this reason, it is necessary to check one's own state law to ascertain the rules for writing a will and to determine how property passes when someone dies. In an attempt to standardize and modernize the different state laws on this subject, the Uniform Probate Code (UPC) has been set up by the Uniform Law Commission (ULC), formerly the National Conference of Commissioners on Uniform State Laws; however, the UPC does not enjoy the popularity and universal applicability of other model laws created by the ULC, such as the Uniform Commercial Code and the Revised Uniform Partnership Act, so not all states have made it part of their law. This reluctance to act may be due to the fact that each state jealously guards its own way of handling the distribution of the estates of its own citizens and is, thus, hesitant to pitch all of that in favor of a uniform standard, which may or may not reflect the traditions of that state. Moreover, unlike commercial law, which cannot operate without crossing state lines, issues in probate law can often be handled without leaving a jurisdiction and, thus, need not fit as neatly into the network of interstate legal matters.

Relevance of Probate to Business

Because probate matters deal with the handling of people's estates, and because all businesses are owned by people in one way or another, the subject of probate law is relevant to all forms of business entities. When sole proprietors die, for example, the assets of their businesses pass to their heirs according to their states' probate laws. When owners of a corporation—that is, stockholders—die, their solely owned shares of stock pass to their heirs in a similar fashion.

Probate Terminology

It is not uncommon for people to prepare for possible future misfortune by making advance arrangements while they are still mentally and physically able to do so. One such advanced arrangement is the making of a will. A **will**, also called a **last will and testament**, is a formal document that governs the transfer of property at death. A person who dies with a will is said to die **testate**. A person who dies without a will is said to die **intestate**. The giving away of one's property by will is known as testamentary disposition. A person who makes a will is called a **testator** if a man or a **testatrix** if a woman. (The masculine forms of terms like *testator* are used for purposes of discussion here. They refer to people of either sex.) Personal property that is left by will is called a **bequest** or legacy, except in states that have adopted the Uniform Probate Code.

Real property that is left by will is known as a **devise**. Those who receive property by will are referred to as beneficiaries. They are also known as **legatees** if they receive personal property and **devisees** if they receive real property under a will. In states that have adopted the Uniform Probate Code, the term *devise* refers to both real and personal property, and the term *devisee* refers to a person who receives a gift of either real or personal property. The term **heir** is a broader term referring to a person who inherits property either under a will or from a person dying without a will. A **durable power of attorney** is a document authorizing another person to act on one's behalf with words stating that it is to either survive one's incapacity or become effective when one becomes debilitated. This authorization is not the same as an ordinary *power of attorney*, which would have questionable effect upon one's incapacity.

> **Did You Know?**
>
> It can be risky to draft one's own will or even to use a preprinted generic will found in a stationery store. The law of wills is very technical, and unique language is often used in the drafting of wills that may not be fully understood by laypeople. In addition, the law of wills varies considerably from state to state, making a generic will unreliable in many cases.

quick quiz 31-1

1. The Uniform Probate Code (UPC) has been adopted by all 50 states and Puerto Rico. true | false
2. A person who dies without a will is said to die testate. true | false
3. A person who makes a will is called a *testator* if a woman or a *testatrix* if a man. true | false

31-2 The Law of Wills

President John F. Kennedy once said, "Our problems are man-made; therefore, they can be solved by man. For in the final analysis, our most common link is that we all inhabit this small planet; we all breathe the same air; we all cherish our children's future, and we are all mortal." Kennedy was correct. As human beings we do cherish our children's future and we are all mortal. There is little we can do about the second proposition. However, the law of wills does give us some control over the first. As long as we are willing to follow the conditions set down by the law of wills, we should be able to transfer a good portion of our property to our spouse, to our children, and to others that we choose to remember.

Requirements for Executing a Will

The law governing the making and signing of wills is not uniform throughout the United States. Nevertheless, a will that is properly executed according to the laws of one state will be given full faith and credit in other states. The laws are highly technical and require strict adherence to detailed formalities. Many lawsuits have occurred over the years because people have attempted to make their own wills without consulting a lawyer. Often, in such cases, a technicality causes the will to be disallowed by the court, and the true wishes of the deceased are not carried out.

Soundness of Mind Any person who has reached the age of adulthood (18 years) and is of sound mind may make a will. The issue of soundness of mind is raised only when someone contests a will on that ground. In determining whether a testator was of sound mind when making a will, the court asks the following questions: When making the will, did the testator know, in a general way, the nature and extent of the property he or she owned? Did the testator know who would be the natural recipients of the estate? Was the testator free from delusions that might influence the disposition of the property? Did the testator know that he or she was making a will? If all of these questions are answered in the affirmative, the court will find that the testator was of sound mind when making a will.

EXAMPLE 31-1: Soundness of Mind

At the time of the execution of his will, Stein was suffering from loss of memory. His son observed his father's failing health and mental illness over a period of time. He once observed his father's failure to recognize his own wife. Stein's daughter once observed her father's failure to recognize her and another relative, both of whom he saw frequently. The court disallowed the will, saying, "The testator did not have mind and memory sound enough to know and understand the businesses upon which he was engaged at the time of execution."

Formal Requirements With the exception of a nuncupative will, discussed later, a will must be in writing, signed by the testator, and attested to in the testator's presence by the number of witnesses established by state law (see Figure 31-1). Each of the particular statutory requirements of the state where the will is made must be met for a will to be valid.

EXAMPLE 31-2: Improperly Signed and Witnessed

Dugan's will contained the following clause: "All United States Savings Bonds in safety deposit box #559 Farmers Bank 10th and Market Sts., Wilmington, Del., to be given to the people and places as marked." When Dugan died, a number of U.S. Savings Bonds were found in his safe-deposit box. There was also a handwritten list of the names of various individuals and organizations and, next to each name, serial numbers, dates, and face amounts corresponding to specific bonds. Further specific notations were written on small slips of paper and attached to each bond with a rubber band. The court held that there was no effective testamentary transfer of the bonds. Neither the list nor the envelopes nor the small slips of paper satisfied the statutory requirements for executing a will. They were not properly signed and witnessed. Dugan's wishes as stated in the will were never carried out.

LAST WILL AND TESTAMENT OF JUDITH M. DORE

I, JUDITH M. DORE, of Salem, County of Essex, Commonwealth of Massachusetts, make this my Last Will and Testament, hereby revoking all earlier wills and codicils.

ARTICLE I

I give, devise, and bequeath all my estate, real, personal, and mixed and wherever situated to my husband, PETER DORE, if he is living on the thirtieth day after my death.

ARTICLE II

If my husband, PETER DORE, is not living on the thirtieth day after my death, I give and devise all of my property of every kind and wherever located which I own at the time of my death or to which I am then in any way entitled in equal shares to my children, ALAINA DORE and DAVID DORE, but if either of them shall not be living, his or her share thereof shall pass to his or her issue then living by right of representation, and in default of such issue then his or her share shall pass to the survivor of them.

⸻

I, the undersigned testator, do hereby declare that I sign and execute this instrument as my last will, that I sign it willingly in the presence of each of said witnesses, and that I execute it as my free and voluntary act for the purposes herein expressed, this 15th day of January, 2015.

_____
Judith M. Dore

We, the undersigned witnesses, each do hereby declare in the presence of the aforesaid testator that the testator signed and executed this instrument as her last will in the presence of each of us, that she signed it willingly, that each of us hereby signs this will as witness in the presence of the testator, and that to the best of our knowledge the testator is eighteen (18) years of age or over, of sound mind, and under no constraint or undue influence.

_____   _____
(Witness)   (address)

_____   _____
(Witness)   (address)

COMMONWEALTH OF MASSACHUSETTS
COUNTY OF ESSEX

On this 15th day of January, 2017, before me, the undersigned notary public, personally appeared JUDITH M. DORE, proved to me through satisfactory evidence of identification, which was a current Massachusetts driver's license, to be the person whose name is signed on this instrument, and acknowledged to me that she signed it voluntarily for its stated purpose.

_____
Charles E. Jones, Notary Public

Figure 31-1 These are sample portions of a formal will drafted according to Massachusetts law. The laws of each state are not the same on the subject of wills.

A will may be typewritten or handwritten, or it may consist of a filled-in form. It need not be under seal. The will offered for probate must be the original and not a copy. In a case in which a testator executed both an original and a carbon copy of a will and later canceled only the carbon, the court has held that it could be presumed that the testator also intended to cancel the original. Problems of this nature can be avoided by executing only an original will.

A will must be signed by the testator. The place of the signature on the will and the requirement as to who must be present at the signing vary from state to state. In some states, a will must be signed at the end of the instrument; in other states, the signature may be placed anywhere on the paper. Similarly, some states require a will to be signed in the presence of witnesses, whereas others allow a will to be signed privately if the testator acknowledges to the witnesses when they sign that it is his or her signature. Testators who are not able to write may make a mark, such as an X, attested to by the required number of witnesses. If the testator's condition makes movement impossible, as in paralysis, another person may sign for the testator. This signing must be done at the request of the testator, in the testator's presence, and in the presence of witnesses.

With the exception of some wills that are handwritten, wills must be witnessed by the number of witnesses prescribed by state law. Almost every state today requires that a will be witnessed by two witnesses. Witnesses must sign in the presence of the testator and, in some states, each other's presence. Because the witnesses may be called upon to attest to the genuineness of the testator's signature and soundness of mind, it is advisable that witnesses be younger than the testator. In some states, no age requirements are given for witnesses. Instead, minors may witness a will as long as they are of sufficient understanding and competent to testify in court as to the facts relating to the execution of the will. In other states, witnesses must have reached a certain age, such as 14, 16, or 18 years, to qualify as a witness. In many states, persons and their spouses who witness a will may not receive gifts under the will unless there are still other witnesses. The failure to observe this provision may result in their being disinherited. Some states protect beneficiaries who witness a will by allowing them to inherit up to the amount that they would have inherited had the deceased died without a will.

Need for Accuracy Certain words often used in wills may have a legal interpretation that is different from their everyday meaning. Care must be taken to describe each bequest and devise in a manner that will satisfy the legal definition. For instance, a testator may use the word *heirs* when really meaning *children*. The differences in the meanings of the two words could result in much dispute and expensive litigation. It is also important to avoid ambiguous language.

Informal Wills A *holographic will* is one that is not witnessed but is written entirely in the handwriting of the testator. About half the states in the United States treat holographic wills as valid. The other half do not recognize them because of the lack of witnesses.

Did You Know?

The use of the "X" as a quasi-signature goes back to the beginnings of Christianity. Those people who could not sign their names would authenticate their promises by issuing an oath to Christ. They would then "sign" the oath by using the "X" which symbolized either the cross or the first letter of the Greek word for Christ (the anointed one) Xristos. By the way, often people would kiss the "X" as a sign of reverence since the "X" represented Christ. Some people speculate that this is how X's came to represent kisses.

EXAMPLE 31-3: Holographic Will

Sedmak resided in Pennsylvania. The following handwritten document was found among his papers when he died:

> My Brother Mil
> Please see that Zella Portenar receives $15,000 from my savings account it is in the Western Savings Bank.
> George A. Sedmak
> or Alexander Sedmak
> Oct 6, '02

The Pennsylvania court held the unwitnessed document to be a valid holographic will.

Oral wills made by persons in their last illness or by soldiers and sailors in actual combat are nuncupative wills. **Nuncupative wills** are valid only in some states and are restricted to the giving of personal property only. Testators must indicate their bequests and state that those hearing the statements are to be considered witnesses to the oral will.

Protection of Spouses and Children

Even though the law of wills differs from state to state, some provisions are consistent from jurisdiction to jurisdiction. Many of these identical provisions deal with the portion of an estate left to a spouse and that which is left to the children of the deceased. Most state laws contain a series of provisions that will protect the spouse. Similarly, most states have legal provisions that will protect the children. One major stipulation here is that children must have evidence that they were inadvertently left out of a parent's will. If they can do this, they are protected by state law in most jurisdictions.

Wills provide for the smooth transfer of property and assure the rights of the heirs and beneficiaries.
©Paul Edmondson/Corbis

Protection of Spouses As noted earlier, most state laws include various devices that are designed to protect all family members, but especially the spouse of the deceased. Some states provide for a **family allowance**, sometimes called a **widow's allowance**, which is an amount of money taken from the decedent's estate and given to the family to meet its immediate needs while the estate is being probated. The amount of the allowance is either a fixed, statutory amount or discretionary with the court and is not chargeable against other benefits given to the family members. Another family protection is the **homestead exemption**, which puts the family home beyond the reach of creditors up to a certain limit. Still another protective device provided by some states is known as **exempt property**, which is certain property of a decedent that passes to the surviving spouse or children and is beyond the reach of creditors. In some states, for example, $3,500 worth of personal property passes automatically to the surviving spouse or, if none, to surviving children equally. The rights of dower (for a widow) and curtesy (for a widower) are also available in some states, providing the surviving spouse with certain property rights in real property owned by the deceased spouse.

In addition to the rights mentioned, surviving spouses are assured a share of a deceased spouse's estate. A surviving spouse who does not like the provisions of a deceased spouse's will may choose to take a portion of the estate set by state statute rather than accept the amount provided in the will. In some states, this sum is referred to as a spouse's **forced share**. In other states, it is called a spouse's **elective share**. The amount the surviving spouse will receive varies from state to state. In some states, it is the amount the spouse would have received had the deceased spouse died without a will. In other states, the amount is computed by the use of a different formula.

Advantages and Disadvantages of the *Windsor* Ruling

As is often the case, when the Supreme Court rules in one area of the law other areas are affected. For example, the Supreme Court case of *Windsor v. United States,* cited in the Classic Case feature, had a tremendous impact on financial planning. Some of these changes were improvements. For example, after *Windsor*, the surviving spouse of a same-sex marriage could claim an inheritance as an exemption when paying federal taxes. This change represented progress. Another advantage was felt in health care.

A CLASSIC CASE *Windsor v. United States*: A Landmark Case in Tax Law

Edith Windsor characterized the inheritance that she had received from her spouse, Thea Spyer, as an exemption. Not surprisingly, the Internal Revenue Service disallowed the exemption and demanded an estate tax payment of $363,053, arguing that Windsor was not really Spyer's spouse under the language found in Section 3 of the Defense of Marriage Act (DOMA). Section 3 of DOMA states, "In determining the meaning of any Act of Congress, or of any ruling, regulation, or interpretation of the various administrative bureaus and agencies of the United States, the word 'marriage' means only a legal union between one man and one woman as husband and wife and the word 'spouse' refers only to a person of the opposite sex who is a husband or a wife." Since Windsor's Canadian marriage to Spyer was a union between two women, the IRS disallowed the exemption. Windsor paid the estate tax, but then filed a lawsuit against the United States, arguing that Section 3 of DOMA is an unconstitutional deprivation of equal protection and due process under the Fifth Amendment of the Constitution and asking for a return of that payment. Ultimately, the case arrived at the Supreme Court, which ruled that Section 3 of DOMA is, indeed, an unconstitutional violation of equal protection and due process. So far, so good.

However, when the Supreme Court ruled against the IRS in this case, it did more than simply return an estate tax payment to a single taxpayer. It also opened the way to altering—in a very fundamental way—the financial future of many same-sex married couples. To grasp the significance of this ruling, it is first necessary to understand what the Court did *not* do. The Court did not, as many people assume, uphold the legality of same-sex marriage. Eventually, the Court would uphold the legality of same-sex marriages, but that would not occur until the case of *Obergefell v. Hodges* [576 U.S. ____ (2015)] (see the Part 8 case study). In the *Windsor* case, the Court ruled that it is unconstitutional for the federal government to pass statutes that treat one class of citizens differently from another by creating restrictions and limitations on that class in the face of a state law designed to protect that same class of citizens. The Court put it this way, "By seeking to injure the very class New York seeks to protect, DOMA violates basic due process and equal protection principles applicable to the Federal Government. The Constitution's guarantee of equality 'must at the very least mean that a bare congressional desire to harm a politically unpopular group cannot' justify disparate treatment of that group. *Department of Agriculture v. Moreno*, 413 U.S. 528–535."

Perhaps without knowing it, and certainly without admitting it, the U.S. Supreme Court in *Windsor* initiated a wide range of legal consequences that would not be addressed until the *Obergefell v. Hodges* ruling in 2015. Moreover, the *Windsor* case is still good law. While it is true that the Court in *Windsor* talks extensively about marriage and about the statutory effects on married couples, it also talks about protecting a "state-defined class" of people. Thus, it would be logical to use the *Windsor* rationale to protect other classes of people, such as veterans, seniors, priests, illegal immigrants, and so on. Think about it. [See: *Windsor v. United States*, 570 U.S.____, 133 S.Ct. 2675, 186 L.Ed.2d 808 (2013).]

Source: See: *Windsor v. United States*, 570 U.S.____, 133 S.Ct. 2675, 186 L.Ed.2d 808 (2013).

Before *Windsor*, employer-provided health coverage for an employee's same-sex spouse was taxable. Because of the Court's ruling in *Windsor*, that coverage was no longer taxable. However, as is often the case when a ruling comes down from the Supreme Court, some unanticipated drawbacks roll off that decision. For example, after *Windsor*, same-sex married couples would no longer be able to file income tax returns as single individuals. Instead, they would have to decide whether to file jointly or separately as a married couple. Whether the married couple filed jointly or separately would depend upon a variety of tax consequences. In some cases, filing as a married couple would mean lower taxes, but in others, it may result in a tax increase, regardless of whether the couple files jointly or separately. Predictably, the new difficulties discussed here merely scratch the surface.

Protection of Children As mentioned earlier, children who can prove that they were mistakenly (rather than intentionally) left out of a parent's will are protected by the laws of most states. Forgotten children will receive the same share that they would have received had their parent died without a will. This situation does not mean that a parent may not disinherit a child. Parents are not obligated to leave children anything, but to avoid litigation, such an intention should be shown in the will. A testator who wishes to disinherit a child should name the child in the will and make the statement that the child was intentionally omitted. By doing so, the omitted child cannot claim to have been mistakenly omitted from the will. Adopted children, under modern laws, are given the same legal rights as natural children. They inherit from their adopting parents. In contrast, stepchildren, unless they have been adopted by a stepfather or stepmother, do not inherit from a stepparent. Children who have been taken into the family for one reason or another but never legally adopted have no right of inheritance.

The *Obergefell v. Hodges* Case

Windsor also had an impact on couples in those states that did not yet recognize same-sex marriages as legally legitimate. What would happen to a same-sex couple, legitimately married in a state that recognized same-sex marriages, who moved to a state that did not? That question needed an answer because many people would find themselves in that predicament very soon. The Supreme Court answered that question and many related questions when, in the case of *Obergefell v. Hodges,* five justices ruled that any state action, legislative or constitutional, that limited the definition of marriage to opposite-sex couples violated the Due Process and Equal Protection Clauses of the 14th Amendment. *Obergefell v. Hodges* was actually a consolidation of four cases filed in Ohio, Michigan, Tennessee, and Kentucky. Each of these states officially defined marriage as the union of one man and one woman. The plaintiffs in these cases included 14 couples (and two individuals whose partners were deceased) who challenged the constitutionality of the laws defining marriage in those states. Their arguments were based on the Due Process and Equal Protection Clauses of the 14th Amendment to the Constitution, which have been interpreted by the Court over the last century and a half to require the states to guarantee the same rights upheld by the federal government in the Bill of Rights.

After recognizing the historical fact that the institution of marriage has changed over the centuries, the majority in *Obergefell* reviewed the evolution of our attitudes toward homosexuality, concluding that these attitudes have gradually relaxed to the extent that, in the early part of the 21st century, many states began to legalize same-sex marriage. Next, the majority ran through a series of cases, each one ruling that under the Due Process Clause, the fundamental right to be married cannot be procedurally dismantled or limited without some compelling state reason to do so, as in the case of minors. Despite (or perhaps because of) the fact that none of these cases redefine marriage or suppose that marriage means anything other than a lawful union between a man and a woman, the majority declares that "this analysis compels the conclusion same sex couples may exercise the right to marry."

The majority pulled the Equal Protection Clause into the argument by pointing to the "synergetic" relationship between the Equal Protection Clause and the Due Process Clause, concluding, "These considerations lead to the conclusion that the right to marry is a fundamental right inherent in the liberty of the person, and under the Due Process and Equal Protection Clauses of the Fourteenth Amendment, couples of the same sex may not be deprived of that right and that liberty." [See: *Obergefell, et al., v. Hodges, Director, Ohio Department of Health, et al.* 576 U.S. ____ (2015).]

Changes in Estate Planning

Spouses in a same-sex marriage can now claim all of the protection methods available to traditional spouses in another area of the law, estate planning. This includes the family allowance, which, as noted earlier, is an amount of money taken from the decedent's estate and given to the family to meet its immediate needs while the estate is being probated. Also in estate planning, both the homestead exemption and the exempt property provision should be available to same-sex married couples. It is important to note that until the *Obergefell* case, these protections were available only in states that had made same-sex marriages legal. This changed with *Obergefell*. Now all states will be compelled to deal with these issues. In a wider sense though, the *Obergefell* ruling has simplified, perhaps even eliminated, many (most?) of these problems. Now any married couple, opposite sex or same sex, must be treated in the same way. No distinction can be made based exclusively on the gender identities of the spouses. This rule is based on the Supreme Court's belief that "the right to personal choice regarding marriage is inherent in the concept of individual autonomy." This rationale seems eminently reasonable. However, some legal experts have suggested that the Court may have overlooked or ignored some of the consequences that emerge from this principle. If "the right to personal choice regarding marriage is inherent in the concept of individual autonomy," then the government should also honor an individual's personal choice to marry several people simultaneously, or to marry someone of a close genetic relationship, or someone who is under the age of consent, and so on. Of course, it is doubtful that the Court meant to go this far. However, because the decision in *Obergefell* is based on the "right to personal choice," these issues may face the Court in the future.

Revoking, Changing, and Contesting a Will

People often make promises that are later broken, forgotten, or ignored. Broken promises come with consequences, of course, many of them unpleasant. Nevertheless, when those consequences result in fines for overdue library books, late fees for tardy car payments, or low grades for forgotten homework, the pain is bearable. However, when the broken promises relate to a will, the consequences are far more hurtful and sometimes irreparable. This is why the law has a way for handling situations that involve revoking, changing, and contesting wayward wills.

Revoking a Will With variations from state to state, a will may be revoked (canceled) in any of the following ways: (1) burning, tearing, canceling, or obliterating the will with the intent to revoke it; (2) executing a new will; and (3) in some states, the subsequent marriage of the testator. In most states, the divorce or annulment of a marriage revokes all gifts made under a will to the former spouse and revokes the appointment of the former spouse as executor of the will.

Changing a Will Sometimes testators wish to make slight changes in a will. They may do so by executing a new will or executing a **codicil**, which is a formal document used to supplement or change an existing will. A codicil must be executed with the same formalities as a will. It must be signed by the testator and properly witnessed. In addition, it must refer to the existing will to which it applies.

EXAMPLE 31-4: Properly Executed Codicil

Rueda made a will giving her entire estate to her husband. Later, Rueda enjoyed unusual financial success and felt inclined to leave $100,000 toward a new church building under construction in her parish. Rueda's attorney prepared a codicil, which Rueda formally executed in the presence of two witnesses. The bequest to the church contained in the codicil became an integral part of the will itself.

A properly executed codicil has the effect of republishing a will. It is said that a codicil breathes new life into a will, which means that the codicil will reestablish a will that had been formerly revoked or improperly executed. If, for example, a will is witnessed by only one person in a state that requires two witnesses, the will is invalid. However, if a properly signed and witnessed codicil is added at a later date, the will becomes valid.

Contesting a Will Only persons who would inherit under an earlier will or under the law of intestacy (described later in this chapter) are allowed to contest a will. A will may be contested on any of three grounds: improper execution, unsound mind, and undue influence. *Improper execution* occurs when an individual has attempted to make a will but has not followed the formal requirements. Because laypeople are not usually aware of the formal requirements for executing a will, it can be risky for them to make their own. Another grounds to contest a will is to allege that the testator was of *unsound mind*. When such an allegation is made, the burden is on the person presenting the will to the court to prove that the testator was of sound mind. This proof may occur by testimony and affidavits of witnesses and by testimony of the deceased's physician. A will may also be attacked and held invalid if a probate court finds that the testator made the will under circumstances of *undue influence*. When persons come under the influence of another to the degree that they are unable to express their real intentions in a will, the will may be declared invalid. The court must distinguish between undue influence and the kindness, attention, advice, guidance, and friendliness shown toward the testator by the one named in the will.

EXAMPLE 31-5: Undue Influence

Smolak executed a will prepared by a lawyer whom he had selected and with whom he had conferred several times before the date on which the will was signed. His niece, Sandra, was the major beneficiary under that will. A week later, he executed another will under which his nephew Michael and Michael's brother were named principal beneficiaries. This will was executed at the same time that Smolak executed a deed conveying his farm to Michael and Michael's brother (which conveyance he later sought to rescind, claiming that it was procured by fraud). The second will was executed at the office of a lawyer employed by Michael. Michael had made arrangements for a conference between his lawyer and Smolak. Michael attended that conference and also attended the execution of the resulting will. Smolak never conferred privately with Michael's lawyer concerning the second will and therefore never had an opportunity to express his true intentions out of earshot of his nephew. The court held that the second will was procured through undue influence and was therefore void.

Dying without a Will

When people die without a will, they are said to have died intestate. The property of a person who dies intestate passes to others according to the various state laws of **intestate succession**. (See an example in Figure 31-2.) These state laws, which differ from state to state, contain the rules governing the allocation of intestate property. Personal property is treated differently from real property. *Personal property* is dispersed according to the law of the state where the deceased permanently resided (his or her domicile) at the time of death and passes to the personal representative to be distributed to the heirs. In contrast, *real property* passes according to the law where the property is located and passes directly to the heirs upon the death of the owner. The personal representative receives title to real property

If the Deceased Is Survived by:	A Surviving Spouse (if any) Receives:	Any Remainder Is Distributed:
Issue (lineal descendants such as children, grandchildren, great-grandchildren)	One-half of the estate	Equally to the deceased's children. If any children are also deceased, their children divide their deceased parents' share equally.
No issue but by kindred (blood relatives)	$200,000 plus one-half of the remainder of the estate	Equally between the deceased's father and mother or to the survivor of them. *However, if both parents are deceased, then:* Equally among the deceased's brothers and sisters. If any brothers or sisters are also deceased, their children divide their deceased parents' share equally. *However, if there are no living brothers or sisters or nieces or nephews, then:* Equally among the deceased's *next of kin* (those who are most nearly related by blood, including aunts, uncles, and cousins).
No issue and no kindred	The entire estate *However, if there is no surviving spouse, issue, or kindred, then:* The entire estate *escheats* to (becomes the property of) the state.	

Figure 31-2 This is an example of the way intestate property is distributed under a typical state statute (Massachusetts).

only when it must be sold to pay debts of the estate. The following steps are taken to ascertain who will inherit from someone who dies without a will:

- Determine the rights of the surviving spouse, if any.
- Determine the rights of the other heirs.

Rights of the Surviving Spouse Under a typical state statute, if a person dies intestate, the rights of the surviving spouse are as follows: If the deceased is survived by **issue** (children, grandchildren, great-grandchildren), the surviving spouse is entitled to one-half of the estate. If the deceased is survived by no issue but by blood relatives, the surviving spouse is entitled to $200,000 plus one-half of the remainder of the estate. If the deceased is survived by no issue and no blood relatives, the surviving spouse is entitled to the entire estate. Keep in mind that this particular formula will differ from state to state.

Rights of Other Heirs Under the same typical state statute, if a person dies intestate, the property will pass, subject to the rights of the surviving spouse, as follows: If the deceased is survived by issue, the property passes in equal shares to the deceased's children, with the issue of any deceased child taking that child's share. If the deceased is survived by no issue, the property passes in equal shares to the deceased's father and mother or the survivor of them. If the deceased is survived by no issue and no father or mother, the property passes to the deceased's brothers and sisters, with the issue of any deceased brother or sister taking that brother's or sister's share. If the deceased is survived by no issue and no father, mother, brother, or sister, or issue of any deceased brother or sister, the property passes to the deceased's **next of kin** (those who are most nearly related by blood).

Simultaneous Death

When two people die in a common disaster so that it is impossible to determine who died first, the Uniform Simultaneous Death Act often comes into play. This law contains rules that are adhered to when the inheritance of property depends upon the time of death, and there is nothing to indicate that the parties died other than at the same time. The following rules are obeyed:

1. The separately owned property of each person passes as if he or she had survived unless a will or trust provides otherwise. For example, if a husband and wife die together in a plane crash, the husband's individually owned property passes to his heirs as though his wife were not living at the time of his death. Similarly, the wife's individually owned property passes to her heirs as though her husband were not living at the time of her death.

2. Property owned jointly by both of the deceased is distributed equally. In this example, half of the couple's jointly owned property passes to the husband's heirs; the other half passes to the wife's heirs.

3. When the beneficiary of an insurance policy dies at the same time as the insured, the proceeds of the insurance policy are payable as if the insured had survived the beneficiary. Suppose, in the example, the wife was the beneficiary on the husband's life insurance policy. The wife would be regarded as deceased at the time of the husband's death. The proceeds of the policy would go to the husband's estate unless an alternate beneficiary is named in the policy.

EXAMPLE 31-6: Simultaneous Death Act Not Applicable

John F. Kennedy Jr. and his wife, Carolyn Bessette Kennedy, were killed in 1999 when their plane crashed into the ocean off the coast of Martha's Vineyard. The Uniform Simultaneous Death Act did not apply because the gifts to the spouses in each will were prefaced by the phrase "if she (or he) is living on the thirtieth day after my death."

Settling an Estate

When people die owning assets, their estates must be **probated**—that is, settled under the supervision of the court. The court that supervises the procedure is called a probate court in some states and a surrogate court, or orphan's court, in others. The first step in probating an estate is to determine whether the deceased left a will. If a will exists, it usually names a personal representative called an **executor** (male) or **executrix** (female) who is the person named in the will to carry out its terms. If there is no will, or if the executor named in the will fails to perform, someone must petition the court to settle the estate. That person, if appointed, is called an **administrator (male)** or **administratrix (female)**. In states that have adopted the Uniform Probate Code, executors and administrators are called **personal representatives**.

Before an executor or administrator is appointed, notice of the petition for appointment is published in a newspaper and sent to all heirs, legatees, and devisees. Anyone with grounds to object may do so. Witnesses are sometimes asked to testify or sign affidavits about their knowledge of the execution of the will. Testimony is not necessary when all heirs and next of kin assent to the allowance of the will and no one contests it.

To ensure faithful performance, the executor or administrator is required to post a bond. A **bond** is a promise by the executor or administrator (and the sureties, if any) to pay the amount of the bond to the probate court if the duties of the position are not faithfully performed. **Sureties** are persons or insurance companies that stand behind executors or administrators and become responsible for their wrongdoing. In some states, a bond is not required if the will indicates that the executor or administrator need not post bond. In other states, a bond is always necessary, but sureties are not required if the will so dictates.

When a satisfactory bond has been filed, the court issues a certificate of appointment, called letters testamentary, to an executor or letters of administration to an administrator. The executor or administrator, called a **fiduciary** (one in a position of trust), is then authorized to proceed. The fiduciary's job consists of gathering the assets, paying the debts and taxes, and distributing the remaining assets in accordance with the will or the law of intestate succession.

quick quiz 31-2

1. A will may be typewritten or handwritten, or it may consist of a filled-in form and, whatever the case, it must be under seal and notarized. true | false
2. A will may be contested for only one reason: unsound mind. true | false
3. When people die owning assets, their estates must be probated— that is, settled, under the supervision of the court. true | false

31-3 The Law of Advance Directives

It is not uncommon for people to prepare for possible future misfortune by making advance arrangements while they are still mentally and physically able to do so. A good time to do this is when a will is executed, because all the necessary documents can be prepared, signed, and witnessed simultaneously. Part of this procedure can involve advance directives that include the making of a living will and the execution of a **health care proxy**. Advance directives are written statements in which people give instructions for their future medical care if they become unable to do so themselves.

Types of Advance Directives

In general, there are two types of **advance directives**: traditional advance directives and innovative advance directives. The traditional advance directives include the *living will* and the *durable power of attorney for health care*. The innovative and relatively new advance directives involve the *protective medical decisions document* and the *physician order for life-sustaining treatment*.

Living Wills
The most common type of traditional advance directive is the living will. A **living will** is a written expression of a person's wish to be allowed to die a natural death and not be kept alive by heroic or artificial methods. This, however, says it poorly. A living

will is actually more akin to a directive than an expression of intent, as suggested by the definition. Moreover, the living will must also be signed and either notarized or witnessed by two to three persons, depending on state law. Usually a living will concerns terminal illnesses and decisions about whether to maintain or discontinue medical treatment. Most often, the living will kicks into place when the illness is terminal and the patient can no longer make decisions on his or her own. This would include situations in which the patient is brain dead. **Brain death** is defined as the point at which all functions controlled by the brain, including the brain stem, have stopped working. Generally, a flat electroencephalogram (EEG) will provide empirical medical evidence that the brain is no longer operating properly. Other indications include the inability of the person to breathe on his or her own without the help of life support system. However, individuals may also be unable to make decisions on their own if they have slipped into a permanent vegetative state often referred to as *permanent unconsciousness*. Still, being in a state of permanent unconsciousness is not the same as being brain dead because in a state of permanent unconsciousness, some brain functions still continue. Moreover, being unable to make decisions independently may also include a situation in which a person is conscious but permanently *unaware* of his or her surroundings, as in a case of advanced dementia. Living wills can indicate the type of treatment that a person wants or does not want under any or all of these circumstances. Because of this, it is best that anyone intent on making a living will explore the nature and the effect of a such a declaration before actually activating such a document. Even so, despite what might have been said before the will has been activated and despite whatever might be written into the document, the living will, like informed consent, can be revoked by the patient at any time. Some additional items that might be included in a living will include:

- Whether to activate equipment such as ventilators or dialysis machines.
- Whether a patient desires intravenous nutrition if he or she is unable to take in food and drink.
- Whether a patient wants a "Do not resuscitate" (DNR) order added to the living will.
- Whether pain medications should be used to increase the patient's comfort (sometimes referred to as "comfort care").
- Whether the person has decided to be an organ donor.

Living wills, unlike marriage licenses, do not cross state lines. As a result, people who live and/or work in more than one state, and who are really intent on having a living will, must make sure they have a series of living wills, each one tailor made to the requirements of each state. Living wills also do not appoint agents to speak for the maker of the will. Instead, the will itself does all the talking. Those people who want to appoint an advocate must consider creating a durable power of attorney for health care. [See: "Advance Directives: Definitions," Patients Rights Council, http://www.patientsrightscouncil.org/site/advance-directives-definitions; "Types of Advance Directives," American Cancer Society, https://cancer.org/treatment/finding-and-paying-for-treatment/understanding-financial-and-legal-matters/advance-directives/types-of-advance-health-care-directives.html; and "Advance Directives," *Encyclopedia of Death and Dying*, http://www.deathreference.com/A-Bi/Advance-Directives.html.]

Durable Power of Attorney for Health Care The **durable power of attorney for health care (DPAHC)** is a written statement authorizing a person, called an agent, to make medical treatment decisions for another person, referred to as the *principal*, in the event of the principal's incapacity. Like a living will, a DPAHC must be signed and either notarized or witnessed by two to three persons. The DPAHC is not limited to situations involving terminal conditions. Once a durable power of attorney has been set up, that agent has the authority to determine what will be done for the maker of the document (i.e., the principal) in a health case situation. This authority includes the power to determine what tests, treatments, therapy, medications, and so on, will be given to the principal. Such decisions are based on what the agent and principal discussed before, during, and after the document was drawn up. If no specific instructions passed from the principal to the agent on a given set of circumstances, the agent must use his or her understanding of the principal's wishes to make such choices. On the other hand, agents are not omnipotent. They are limited to what the law allows them to do. So, for instance, in some states, agents are not permitted to stop comfort care, while in others they are not empowered to interfere with the patient's basic nutritional and hydration needs. Nevertheless, it is good planning to insist on conducting a series of long and detailed discussions between the principal and the agent so that the principal's needs and desires are well known. It is also imperative for the principal to have a "Plan B" in place that designates a second choice of agents should the number one choice be unwilling or unable to step into the role as agent. [See: "Advance Directives: Definitions," Patient Rights Council; "Types of Advance Directives," American Cancer Society; and "Advance Directives," *Encyclopedia of Death and Dying*.]

Difficulties with Advance Directives As you might have surmised by now, all is not well in the realm of advance directives. For one thing, most people (fewer than 30%) actually have an advance directive of either sort. Moreover, even when a patient has an advance directive, the health care professionals treating him or her may not know about its existence, or if they know, they might not have ready access to it. In addition, once a health care professional has access to an advance directive, he or she maybe unable to unravel the ambiguities, the missing elements, and the contradictions contained therein. For instance, an advance directive may forbid the use of "heroic measures" without explaining what is meant by that phrase. In the case of a DPAHC, the agent may be less than helpful when communicating the principal's wishes to the health care professionals either because the principal was not clear or because the agent does not remember or misunderstood what the principal wanted done in a given situation. In addition, advance directives often challenge what the physician has decided to do, which generally means that the patient's wishes are ignored despite being communicated in a clear, concise, and unambiguous way. This predicament can become especially problematic when constitutional issues such as privacy and/or religion come into play. [See: Wayne DuBois, "Advance Directives: Patient Beware," Georgia Right to Life, http://grtl.org/?q=advancs-directive-patient-beware; and "Advance Directives," *Encyclopedia of Death and Dying*.]

Additional Health Care Directives One additional protection that is available for people who are concerned about the shortcomings of living wills and DPAHCs is the physician order for life-sustaining treatment (POLST). A POLST sets up a document listing a series of medical orders, signed by a physician, and carried by a patient all the time. Such documents will state those medical procedures that paramedics, EMTs, urgent care workers, and emergency room personnel must follow. Generally, a POLST can be used to limit treatments. However, they can also be used to ensure that treatments are provided in situations that might tempt health care workers to terminate treatments too soon. A similar document is the protective medical decisions document (PMDD). The PMDD is a document that is signed by the patient and identifies an agent to make decisions for the patient in medical emergency situations when the signer is unable to make those decisions on his or her own. This document is different from standard DPAHC because it expressly forbids medical personnel from resorting to euthanasia or assisted suicide. The PMDD was developed by the International Task Force on Euthanasia and Assisted Suicide. [See: "Advance Directives: Definitions," Patients Rights Council; and "Types of Advance Directives," American Cancer Society.)

Do Not Resuscitate (DNR) Orders Any discussion of advance directives would be incomplete without touching on do not resuscitate (DNR) orders. Resuscitation involves trying to reboot a stopped heart and/or lungs. Sometimes, resuscitation involves using CPR. At other times, it can include using life support machines. **Do not resuscitate (DNR) orders** stop medical personnel from attempting to resuscitate a patient. Not all DNR orders are considered advance directives or durable powers of attorney. However, most are close enough to be considered in the same family. DNR orders come in two types: those issued in a hospital and those issued outside of the hospital. Inside a hospital, a DNR order can be added to a patient's chart if the patient asks his or her physician to issue one. However, such requests are not made in most circumstances. In fact, such a request should be made only if the patient insists on allowing a natural death. DNR orders do not "roll-over." A new order must be requested at each new admittance. Outside a hospital, a DNR order is used to notify EMTs and paramedics that a patient does not wish to be resuscitated. Such orders must be written and signed by a physician and the patient. Even so, emergency personnel are trained to use every means available to keep a patient alive during all 911 calls. Consequently, in the middle of such incidents, emergency personnel usually use all measures available to preserve life, absent clear and convincing evidence of the signed order. [See: "Types of Advance Directives," American Cancer Society.)

The Right to Die and the Right to Life

In 1990, in *Cruzon v. Director, Missouri Department of Health*, the U.S. Supreme Court ruled that the right to die was guaranteed by the due process clause of the Constitution. This was not the first time that the court system got into the business of mixing the law and science in relation to decisions regarding life and death. In 2013, in the case of *Winkfield v. Children's Hospital and Research Center at Oakland*, it did the same, that time with a different result.

The Government's Compelling Interest in Life Perhaps one of the most critical cases in the ongoing battle between the right to die and the right to life is the case of *Roe v. Wade*, in which the Supreme Court decided that the government does not have a compelling interest for interfering with a mother's own choices in relation to her pregnancy until the fetus becomes viable—that is, capable of living outside the mother's womb. At that point, the point of viability, the government has a compelling interest in preserving the life of the fetus that outweighs the mother's right to have an abortion. In 1972, the year of *Roe v. Wade*, the point of viability was after the pregnancy entered the third trimester. In a later case, the case of *Planned Parenthood v. Casey*, the Supreme Court eliminated the redline at the third trimester because medical advances allowed the fetus to become viable at an earlier time, one that could not now be drawn with any certainty. Indeed, because of scientific advances, the moment of viability had become a moving target.

Advance Directives and the Right to Die A curious disconnect exists among the use of an advance directive, the right to die, and the government's compelling interest in the preservation of life. On the one hand, the Supreme Court has said that the government has a compelling interest in preserving life and can, therefore, enact sanctions to stop the taking of a life by abortion while, on the other, it has said that the government has an interest in due process and cannot, therefore, enact sanctions that stop the taking of life by passive euthanasia. In short, the government cannot prevent passive euthanasia in accordance with a living will because it must protect due process, but it can prevent abortion because it has a compelling interest in preserving life. The next two steps in this controversy are represented by the classic case of *Gonzales, Attorney General v. Oregon* and by the Opening Case of *Winkfield v. Children's Hospital and Research Center of Oakland*.

A CLASSIC CASE   Balancing the Right to Die with Federal Control: *Gonzales, Attorney General v. Oregon*

Sometimes, the U.S. Supreme Court must dive into a controversy that has implications beyond the actual facts and issues in a particular case. In such situations, the Court may decide a case on what seems to be a narrow legal technicality but which may signal a major policy shift that will shape the future of generations to come. A case in point is the dispute in *Gonzales, Attorney General v. Oregon*. This controversy started when the citizens of Oregon authorized the establishment of a radical new measure legalizing physician-assisted suicide. The unconventional measure, which had been ironically dubbed the Oregon Death with Dignity Act (ODWDA), protected physicians from prosecution under criminal law and from litigation under civil law for prescribing drugs for terminally ill patients who wished to commit suicide. The problem arose because the drugs that would have been prescribed under the law were listed on the Controlled Substances Act (CSA) and are thus subject to federal scrutiny. The situation was, in fact, scrutinized by the U.S. Attorney General (AG), who issued an interpretive ruling that stated that any physician who prescribed such drugs under the authority of the act and with the intent to have those drugs used for suicide could lose his or her license to practice medicine. The AG reasoned that drugs controlled by the CSA were to be used only for legitimate medical purposes and, becuse suicide is not a legitimate medical purpose, a physician who prescribed controlled drugs for that purpose would be in violation of the act. Moreover, prescribing drugs for suicide was deemed by the AG to be "inconsistent with the public interest." A lawsuit was filed by several interested parties in the U.S. District Court in Oregon, which ruled in favor of the plaintiffs, and then enjoined the AG from enforcing his interpretation of the CSA. The appeals court agreed. The AG filed an appeal, which ended up in the U.S. Supreme Court. Sixteen years earlier, in a groundbreaking case known as *Cruzon v. Director, Missouri Department of Health*, 110 S.Ct. 2841 (1990), the Supreme Court had ruled that the right to die was constitutionally preserved by the due process clause.

Consequently, the Court had little problem in this case telling the AG to, in effect, "mind his own business." The CSA is supposed to stop physicians from trafficking in illegal drugs. It is not supposed to give the federal government the power to police a state's authority to regulate the practice of medicine. Consequently, the Court concluded that the AG had overstepped his authority when he tried to short-circuit the Oregon law. At least that is how the U.S. Supreme Court saw the case. Of course, in one sense, the Court in *Gonzales, Attorney General v. Oregon* avoided the real issue—that is, the question of how to balance the right to die with the government's compelling interest in preserving life. Instead, the ruling was actually based on two other issues: (1) the issue of the real purpose of the Controlled Substances Act (CSA), which is to prevent drug trafficking by physicians, and (2) the issue of the state's right to control the activities of the medical profession within its own borders. Therefore, the real problem—that is, the tug-of-war between the government's compelling interest in preserving life and an individual's right to die as guaranteed by due process—was not really addressed. However, using the facts in the case of *Winkfield v. Children's Hospital and Research Center at Oakland*, Round 2 of the Opening Case, we can speculate on one way that the courts might deal with this issue in the future. [See: *Gonzales, Attorney General v. Oregon*, 126 S.Ct. 904 (U.S. Supreme Court).]

Source: See: Gonzales, Attorney General v. Oregon, 126 S.Ct. 904 (United States Supreme Court).

THE OPENING CASE   *Round 2*
Balancing the Right to Life with State Control: *Winkfield v. Children's Hospital and Research Center at Oakland*

The case of *Winkfield v. Children's Hospital and Research Center at Oakland* gives us a potential look at how the tension between the right to life and the right to die might play themselves out. Recall that this case began when 13 year old Jahi McMath (Jahi) underwent a fairly routine tonsillectomy at Children's

Hospital and Research Center in Oakland, California. CHRCO is affiliated with the University of San Francisco, which is part of the state university system of California. The operation went forward flawlessly until Jahi began to bleed heavily. The bleeding led to a large blood loss that triggered a heart attack and severe oxygen deprivation in the brain. Consequently, Jahi experienced severe brain damage. While she was on the respirator, her heart and her other organs functioned properly. Unfortunately, later tests indicted that Jahi had suffered brain damage because she had been deprived of oxygen for too long.

Following proper protocol under California law (California Health, and Safety Code Section 1780), the physicians at CHRCO ran a series of tests and determined that Jahi's brain damage was far more serious than they thought at first. In fact, they concluded that Jahi was essentially brain dead due to an irreversible cessation of all the functions within her brain, including the brain stem. To verify these findings, CHRCO had two children's physicians check the nature of the earlier prognosis. Both physicians determined that Jahi's brain damage was irreversible. In addition, CHRCO allowed three independent physicians to run their own tests on Jahi's conditiion. They, too, concluded that Jahi was brain dead. Consequently, given all of this information, officials at CHRCO informed Jahi's mother, Latisha Winkfield, that they were going to take Jahi off the life support system. Winkfield objected to this decision and brought this lawsuit, asking the court to issue a temporary restraining order that would prevent the discontinuation of Jahi's life support system.

In her complaint, Winkfield argues that California's Uniform Determination of Death Act, under which the hospital determined that Jahi is dead and would be taken off life support, involves an unconstitutional violation of the First Amendment's free exercise of religion clause. Unfortunately, we have no further record indicating the details of the Winkfield argument. Nevertheless, by looking at the case ourselves, we can speculate on what a properly constructed First Amendment argument would look like. The statute that permits CHRCO to make a determination of brain death is California's Uniform Determination of Death Act. If this statute is to stand a constitutional challenge, it must pass the strict scrutiny test. In the case of *Sherbert v. Verner*, the U.S. Supreme Court created the gold standard for the application of the Free Exercise Clause to governmental actions. Under that standard, called the strict scrutiny standard, the government is forbidden to create statutes, regulations, and other mandates that place an undue burden on the practice of religion, unless (1) there is a compelling governmental reason for doing so and (2) the action contemplated is the least restrictive way to accomplish that compelling reason.

California's Uniform Determination of Death Act makes explicit the state's legally and medically approved definition of death. [See: Article 1. California Uniform Determination of Death Act (7180-7180).] This definition includes not only the conventional concept of death as the cessation of cardio-vascular respiratory functions, but also a relatively new definition that includes the cessation of brain function. In effect, then, the statute empowers health care facilities to withdraw life support measures from any patient who meets either prong of this definition. The problem is that the Determination of Death Act places an undue burden on the believers of any religion (including Christianity, Jahi and Winkfield's religion) that, as a doctrine, supports the right to life and that, as a result, is opposed to the type euthanasia legalized by the DDA. (*Note:* This is not a local problem, either. The Determination of Death Act has been adopted by 36 states.) Still, such a statute will stand only if it promotes a compelling governmental interest in the least restrictive way possible. The statute does promote a compelling state interest. That interest is the responsibility of the government to make certain that its citizens are guaranteed the opportunity to experience not only the right to live a full productive life, but also the right to experience a dignified death. This, however is not the end of the strict scrutiny test. To be constitutional, the statute must also meet that governmental interest in the least restrictive way possible. It is at this point that the statute fails to pass constitutional muster. This is because there are dozens of less restrictive, less religiously intrusive ways to meet the goal of guaranteeing to all the chance to experience a dignified death. It is important to note that the result would be the same whether the case involved an advance directive or, as in this case, the right of a parent to have a say in the health care decisions involving his or her child. [See: *Winkfield v. Children's Hospital and Research Center of Oakland,* Case Number RG 13707598 (2013).]

Source: See: *Winkfield v. Children's Hospital and Research Center of Oakland,* Case Number RG 13707598 (2013).

A QUESTION OF ETHICS

The future that is outlined in the novel *Unisave* by Axel Madsen is dark, depressing, and discouraging. The novel is set in the 22nd century at a time when the planet's natural resources, its energy reserves, its agriculture, and its fresh water are depleted. The earth's population has surpassed the 24 billion mark. There is very little hope for the salvation of humanity. The planet has reached a tipping point. In a desperate attempt to stall the inevitable and perhaps reverse the slide toward disaster, the United Nations has come up with several plans. One of the chief plans is established under the authority of an all-powerful global agency known as Unisave. This agency has been granted the authority to enforce a population control program that will affect everyone. There are several aspects to this program. First, the agency is equipped with the power to set quotas to control the number of children permitted to each couple. That, however, is the least strict of the new controls implemented by Unisave. Second, the agency has developed a compulsory sterilization program for some people under some circumstances. Third, it has ordered the use of drugs to suppress the sex drive among young people. Fourth, it has instituted a global program of electronic surveillance to prevent the violation of its strict anti-sex laws. Finally, it has mandated a program of compulsory **gericide**, which involves the systematic killing of the elderly. Consider each of the following ethical and legal issues.

1. When the people of Oregon supported the so-called Death with Dignity Act, did they legalize gericide in Oregon? Explain.
2. Can the Supreme Court's "compelling interest" standard be used to argue that the United States *cannot* cooperate with Unisave? Explain.
3. Could that same standard be used to compel U.S. cooperation with Unisave? Explain.
4. Can the due process standard that upheld the right to die in *Cruzan v. Director, Missouri Department of Health* be used to argue that the United States must cooperate with the gericide program? Why or why not?
5. In what way can the ruling in *Gonzales, Attorney General v. Oregon* be used to support the implementation of a gericide program? Explain.

The Science Court Revisited In Chapter 4 on alternate dispute resolution, we discussed a proposal by the governor of Minnesota for the creation of a science court to resolve legal issues related to science, medicine, engineering, and technology. The science court would be made up of scientists, engineers, and other experts educated in the discipline and the industry involved in the dispute, thus allowing them to use their expertise in deciding the case. The science court would also permit the parties to avoid the long and involved process of litigation. Since living wills, the right to die, physician-assisted suicide, and gericide involve medical issues related to life and death, cases involving them would be perfect candidates for the future science court.

A QUESTION OF ETHICS

In *Dark Age Ahead*, Jane Jacobs argues that Western civilization in general and the United States in particular stand on the verge of cultural collapse. As the cause of this collapse, she focuses on the decline of five essential mainstays of society: the family and the community, colleges and universities, the productive use of science, the government and its taxing power, and the self-regulation of the learned professions. She ends her book with a final prognosis of our culture:

> Ironically, societies (including our own) that were great cultural winners in the past are in special peril of failing to adapt successfully in the face of new realities. This is because nothing succeeds like success, and it follows that nothing hangs on past its prime like past success. Formerly vigorous cultures typically fall prey to arrogant self-deception for which the Greeks had a word, *hubris*, which we still use. Because a culture is all of

a piece, tolerance of commercial false accounting for gaining profit has military equivalents in inflated reports or enemy casualties, along with wishful intelligence about disaffection in enemy ranks. The falsities merely feed hubris; the enemy is a "public" that knows quickly whether wartime false accounting and wishful intelligence are empty bragging. The Bay of Pigs fiasco in Cuba and false body counts in the Vietnam War demonstrated an American proclivity for deception. Worse, the incentives for deception—success at sycophancy and pursuit of specious careerism—imply civilian cultural expectations that are shameful whether or not they infect military capability.[1] [See: Jane Jacobs, *Dark Age Ahead* (New York: Vintage Books, 2005), p. 175.]

Now consider each of the following ethical and legal issues.

1. When Attorney General Gonzales in the *Oregon* case argues that the government cannot be involved in supporting physicians who prescribe lethal drugs for terminally ill patients, is he "failing to successfully adapt in the face of new realities"? Explain.

2. When the Supreme Court supported the right to die in the *Cruzan* case, was it exhibiting the type of self-deceptive hubris of which Jacobs writes in *Dark Age Ahead*? Why or why not?

3. Some people have argued that the Supreme Court justices used a "technicality" to avoid the real issue in Oregon and in doing so managed to support governmentally approved suicide without actually "sticking their necks out" in the *Gonzales* case. Is this action by the justices on the Supreme Court an example of the "American proclivity for self-deception"? Explain.

4. Are the rulings in *Roe v. Wade* and *Planned Parenthood v. Casey* two examples adapting successfully to changing circumstances or another case of self-deception? Explain.

5. Both *Roe v. Wade* and *Planned Parenthood v. Casey* use a standard for personhood based on science's ability to push viability closer and closer to conception. Is this faith in science an example of hubris? Explain.

quick quiz 31-3

1. Advance directives are oral statements in which people give instructions for their future medical care if they become unable to do so themselves.	true | false
2. A living will is a written expression of a person's wishes to be kept alive using heroic and artificial methods.	true | false
3. The U.S. Supreme Court has ruled that the right to die is guaranteed by the due process clause of the U.S. Constitution.	true | false

31-4 The Law of Trusts

A **trust** is a legal device by which property is held by one person (the **trustee**) for the benefit of another (the beneficiary). The person who sets up the trust is called the *settlor*. The property that is held in trust is the *corpus*, or *trust fund*.

When a trust is established, title is split between the trustee, who holds legal title, and the beneficiary, who holds equitable or beneficial title. This separation allows the trustee to manage the trust property for the benefit of the beneficiary. Trusts are established to save taxes, provide for the needs of young children, and prevent money from being squandered, among other reasons.

Property is often placed in trust so that it will be preserved for future generations. In such cases, only the income is given out during the life of the trust, with the principal held in relatively safe investments. The rule against perpetuities prevents trusts (except charitable trusts) from lasting indefinitely. This rule in many states requires trust property to become owned by the beneficiary outright not later than 21 years after the death of some person alive at the creation of the trust.

Types of Trusts

The two principal types of trusts are testamentary trusts and living trusts. A **testamentary trust** is a trust that is created by a will. It comes into existence only upon the death of the testator. The terms of the trust, together with the names of the trustee and beneficiaries, are set out in the body of the will itself.

EXAMPLE 31-7: Spendthrift Trust

Emile Hanson died, leaving four grown sons and daughters. His children had never demonstrated any real ambition and had depended heavily on their prospects of receiving large legacies from the estate. Hanson feared that his heirs would quickly spend their inheritances and have nothing to support themselves in the years ahead. He provided for this possibility in his will by placing all assets in trust. The assets would remain intact, safely invested, and a small income would be paid from the trust income to the children. Hanson's purpose was realized in that the estate would be preserved and the surviving children would not squander their inheritance.

In a trust, such as the one illustrated in Example 31-7, provision must be made for final distribution of the trust's assets when the purpose of the trust has been served. For example, Hanson could have the trust property go to a church, college, or some other worthy nonprofit organization on the death of the last surviving child. He also could have designated a grandchild or grandchildren as the ultimate beneficiaries.

A **living trust**, also called an *inter vivos* trust, comes into existence while the settlor is alive. It is established by either a conveyance in trust or a declaration of trust. In a **conveyance in trust**, the settlor conveys away the legal title to a trustee to hold for the benefit of either the settlor or another as a beneficiary. In a **declaration of trust**, the settlor holds the legal title to the property as trustee for the benefit of some other person (the beneficiary) to whom the settlor now conveys the equitable title. A living trust may be either irrevocable or revocable. If it is *irrevocable*, the settlor loses complete control over the trust and cannot change it. The advantage of an irrevocable trust is that the income from the trust is not taxable to the settlor, and estate and inheritance taxes are avoided. The disadvantage of such a trust is that it can never be rescinded. The settlor can never get back that which has been put in an irrevocable trust, regardless of the circumstances. A *revocable* living trust may be taken back or changed at any time during the settlor's lifetime. It has neither estate tax nor income tax advantages; however, it can serve the purpose of relieving the cares of management of money or property, as well as other purposes.

A spendthrift is one who spends money profusely and improvidently. A *spendthrift trust* is designed to provide a fund for the maintenance of a beneficiary and, at the same time, secure the fund against that person's improvidence or incapacity. In some states, all trusts are considered to be of this type. In others, a clause must be placed in the trust instrument to the effect that the beneficiary cannot assign either the income or the principal of the trust and neither the income nor the principal can be reached by the beneficiary's creditors. Spendthrift trusts are not permitted in some states.

A *charitable*, or *public*, trust is one established for charitable purposes, such as the advancement of education; relief to the aged, ill, or poor; or the promotion of religion. For the trust to be valid, the identity of the person to be benefited must be uncertain. The rule against perpetuities does not apply to a charitable trust.

A *sprinkling trust*, or *spray trust*, allows the trustee to decide how much will be given to each beneficiary rather than have the settlor make the decision. The advantage of this type is that the trustee can compare the tax brackets of the beneficiaries long after the settlor is dead and cause a smaller tax liability to occur by giving more money to those beneficiaries in the lowest tax brackets. It also has built-in spendthrift provisions. The chief objection to this type of trust is that it gives the trustee too much control.

Obligations of the Trustee

The trustee is obligated by law to use a high standard of care and prudence in the investment of funds held by the trust. If real property is held in trust, it is the trustee's obligation to supervise and care for the property. When economic and other reasons indicate the need to shift trust assets to safer areas of investment, it becomes the duty of the trustee to make such changes. If investments selected by the trustee fail, the trustee is held liable unless a court rules that the action was taken with prudence and caution.

The trustee relationship is one of great and continuing responsibility. Appointment as a trustee should not be accepted by those without the knowledge and background that would afford prudent and good management. Banks, trust companies, and other kinds of fiduciary corporations offer professional services in the administration of trusts. They provide professional investment services and generally give maximum security and benefit for the fees charged.

quick quiz 31-4

1. When a trust is established, title to the trust property is held completely by the trustee. true | false
2. A *spendthrift* is one who is frugal and careful about spending money. true | false
3. Trustees are obligated by law to use an average standard of care when investing funds for the trust. true | false

Summary

31.1 Because each state's law is different on the subject of probate law, it is necessary to check one's own state law when dealing with probate matters. Furthermore, the subject of probate law is relevant to all forms of business entities.

31.2 The terms *will*, *last will and testament*, *testate*, *intestate*, *testator*, *testatrix*, *bequest*, *devise*, *legatees*, *devisees*, and *heir* are frequently used in the field of probate law. Any person who has reached adulthood and is of sound mind may make a will. Wills must be in writing, signed by the testator, and attested to in the testator's presence by two witnesses in most states. In some states, no formalities are necessary when a holographic will is made. Surviving spouses are given protection through such provisions as a family allowance, a homestead exemption, exempt property, and the rights of dower and curtesy. Spouses in states that recognize same-sex marriages can now claim all of the protection methods available to traditional spouses regarding estate planning. Also, because of the Supreme Court's rulings in the *Windsor* and *Obergefell* cases, the surviving spouse of a same-sex marriage can now claim an inheritance as an exemption when paying federal taxes. A will may be revoked by burning, tearing, canceling, or obliterating the will with the intent to revoke it; by executing a new will; and in some states, by the subsequent marriage of the testator. A will may be contested on the grounds of improper execution, unsound mind, and undue influence. When people die without a will, their property passes to others according to the law of intestate succession, which varies from state to state. Special rules apply when people die simultaneously. Separately owned property passes as if its owner had survived the other person. Property owned jointly by both decedents is distributed equally. Insurance proceeds are payable as if the insured survived the beneficiary when they both die at the same time. When people die owning assets, their estates must be probated. Heirs are notified, and an executor or administrator is appointed by the probate court.

31.3 Advance directives are written statements in which people give instructions for their future medical care if they become unable to direct their care themselves. The most common type of advance directive is the living will, which is a written expression of a person's wishes to be allowed to die a natural death and not kept alive by heroic or artificial methods. Another vehicle involving future medical cares is the durable power of attorney for health care—a written statement authorizing a person, called an agent, to make medical treatment decisions for another person, referred to as the *principal*, in the event of the principal's incapacity.

31.4 Trusts are used, among other reasons, to save taxes, provide for the needs of young children, and prevent money from being squandered easily. They may be created to take effect while a person is alive or after a person dies. When a trust is established, title is split between the trustee, who holds legal title, and the beneficiary, who holds equitable or beneficial title. The trustee manages the trust fund for the beneficiary.

Key Terms

administrator, 886
administratrix, 886
advance directives, 887
bequest, 876
bond, 887
brain death, 888
codicil, 883
conveyance in trust, 895
declaration of trust, 895
devise, 876
devisees, 876
do not resuscitate (DNR) order, 890
durable power or attorney, 876
durable power of attorney for health care (DPAHC), 888
elective share, 880
executor, 886
executrix, 886
exempt property, 880
family allowance, 880
fiduciary, 887
forced share, 880
gericide, 893
health care proxy, 887
heir, 876
homestead exemption, 880
intestate, 876
intestate succession, 884
issue, 885
last will and testament, 876
legatees, 876
living trust, 895
living will, 887
next of kin, 886
nuncupative wills, 880
personal representatives, 886
probate, 875
probated, 886
sureties, 887
testamentary trust, 895
testate, 876
testator, 876
testatrix, 876
trust, 894
trustee, 894
widow's allowance, 880
will, 876

Questions for Review and Discussion

1. What are the sources of probate law, and why is it relevant to business entities?
2. What are the formal requirements for executing a will?
3. When does a person who makes a will have the capacity to do so?
4. How did the Supreme Court ruling involving the Defense of Marriage Act affect the law?
5. What are the different methods of revoking or changing a will?
6. What are the three grounds for contesting a will?
7. Who inherits the property of someone who dies without a will?
8. What are the steps to be taken by an executor or administrator in settling an estate?
9. What are the types and purposes of advance directives?
10. What are the various types of trusts and when might they be used?

Cases for Analysis

1. Miguel Ruiz, who had a wife and two small children, did not have a will. A friend told Miguel that he should have a will because if he died without one, everything he owned would go to the state. Was the friend correct? Explain.

2. Ling Lee, who had two children, made a will leaving $1 to her husband, Seung, and the balance in equal shares to her two children. When Ling died, her husband, Seung, claimed that he was legally entitled to more than $1. Do you agree with Seung? Explain.

3. D. W. Elmer, a hospital patient, was seriously ill and unable to write his name. He executed his will, however, by making a belabored X on the paper in the presence of witnesses. Can a signature on a will made by an X be valid? Explain. [See: *In re Estate of Elmer*, 210 N.W.2d 815 (ND).]

4. James and Wanda Barns, husband and wife, were killed in a head-on automobile collision. It was impossible to determine who died first, and neither one had a will. The couple owned the following items as joint tenants: the house in which they resided and its furnishings, a savings account, and a checking account. James owned a car and some Lucent stock separately in his name. Wanda owned a car and a certificate of deposit separately in her name. James was survived by two children of another marriage; Wanda was survived by one child of another marriage. Who will inherit their property?

5. Julia Dejmal executed her will while a patient in St. Joseph's Hospital. The will was witnessed by Lucille and Catherine Pechacek. Catherine was 19 years old and employed as an assistant X-ray technician at the hospital. The age of majority at the time in that state was 21. It was contended that the will was not valid because one of the witnesses to it was a minor. Do you agree with the contention? Why or why not? [See: *Matter of Estate of Dejmal*, 289 N.W.2d 813 (WI).]

6. Lazer, a wealthy 17-year-old, learned that he was suffering from AIDS. He wrote a will leaving everything he owned to a friend he had met in school. Two years later, when Lazer died, his parents claimed that the will was not valid. Do you agree with Lazer's parents? Explain.

7. Santiago, a widower, made a will leaving $1 to his son Carlos and the balance in equal shares to his other children, Benito and Angelita. The estate, after deducting debts, taxes, and expenses, amounted to $90,000. When Santiago died, Carlos claimed that he was legally entitled to $30,000 from his father's estate. Was Carlos correct? Why or why not?

8. Evidence was introduced in court to show that, at the time she executed her will, Blanch Robinson suffered from schizophrenia. She had delusions about having had a love affair with Nelson Eddy and was suspicious, mistrustful, and perhaps deluded about her friends and acquaintances. Dixon, who had been left out of the will, contended that Robinson lacked the mental capacity to make a will. Do you agree with Dixon? Explain. [See: *Dixon v. Fillmore Cemetery*, 608 S.W.2d 84 (MO).]

9. Walsh, as settlor, executed a declaration of trust, naming himself as trustee and giving himself the income from the trust during his lifetime. After his death, the income was to be paid to his second wife for her life, and upon her death, to his two children, Edward and Margot. Upon their deaths, the income was to be paid to the children of Edward and Margot, after which it terminated. The trust expressly provided that the settlor had not made any provisions for his third child, Patricia, because "previous provisions had been made in her behalf." After executing the instrument, Walsh transferred to the trust the family residence, three farms, and a checking account. Patricia argued that the trust was testamentary and therefore invalid because it failed to comply with the statute of wills. Was this a testamentary or an *inter vivos* trust? Explain. [See: *First Nat'l Bank v. Hampson*, 410 N.E.2d 1109 (IL).]

10. Whitman Winsor's will read in part: "I give, devise, and bequeath all my property, real and personal, to my daughter Lucy T. Winsor. . . . I deem it only right and just that my said daughter Lucy T. Winsor shall have all my property . . . because she has lived with me and cared for me for many years, and it is my will that all shall be hers." Winsor had another daughter, Caroline, who was not provided for in the will. Is Caroline entitled to an intestate share of her father's estate? Why or why not? [See: *Hauptman v. Conant*, 400 N.E.2d 272 (MA).]

quick quiz Answers

31-1	31-2	31-3	31-4
1. F	1. F	1. F	1. F
2. F	2. F	2. F	2. F
3. F	3. T	3. T	3. F

Part 8 Case Study

Obergefell, et al., v. Hodges, Director, Ohio Department of Health, et al.
576 U.S. _____ (2015)

©Digital Vision/Getty Images

Summary

When the U.S. Supreme Court ruled that state statutes and constitutional provisions that limited marriage to opposite-sex couples were an unconstitutional violation of the equal protection and due process clauses of the 14th Amendment to the Constitution, very few people were surprised. Most people, however, would be surprised if they actually read the majority opinion and discovered what the case was really all about from a legal, rather than a social and cultural, perspective. The case is, in reality, a triumph for the Madisonian belief in the need for a strong central government, which can, at will, veto state legislative and state constitutional enactments in order to control the debilitating effects of factionalism. Let's take a look at what the case was all about. Although the case will probably go down in the history books as *Obergefell v. Hodges* (576 U.S._____ [2015]), it was actually a consolidation of four cases filed in Ohio, Michigan, Tennessee, and Kentucky. Each of these states officially defined marriage as the union of one man and one woman. The plaintiffs in these cases included 14 couples (and two individuals whose partners were deceased) who challenged the constitutionality of the laws defining marriage in those states. Their arguments were based on the due process and equal protection clauses of the 14th Amendment, which has been interpreted by the Court over the last 150 plus years to require the states to guarantee the same rights upheld by the federal government in the Bill of Rights.

Compared to some cases that we have examined in this text, the issues in this case are really quite simple. There are only two: (1) Does the 14th Amendment demand that state government license same sex marriage? (Michigan and Kentucky)? (2) Does the 14th Amendment demand that state governments uphold the legal validity of same-sex marriages performed legally in other states? Justice Kennedy, who wrote the majority opinion in the case, begins his explanation by reviewing the history of marriage as a cultural and social institution. Kennedy then focuses on the facts in three of the cases before the Court. The facts differ in each, but the complaint is always the same: In refusing to recognize same-sex marriage as a valid marriage, a state violates the basic rights of due process and equal protection of the law (pages 1-6 of the majority opinion). Remember what these two clauses mean. The due process clause states that the government cannot deprive individuals of life, liberty, and property without following due process of the law. This does not mean that the government cannot deprive someone of life, liberty, or property, only that it cannot do it outside proper legal procedures. The equal protection clause guarantees that the law shall protect everyone in the same way, barring some compelling state interest not to do so. These are not substantive rights, like the free exercise of religion or free speech. Rather they are procedural rights that promise that proper procedures will be used to protect substantive rights (freedom of religion, freedom of the press, and so on) in a fair and equitable way, barring a compelling reason (such as national security or crowd control) not to do so. (This distinction [procedural rights v. substantive rights] will become significant later.)

After recognizing the historical fact that the institution of marriage has changed over the centuries (although, until 2000, never straying from its fundamental and universal definition as a union between a man and a woman), Kennedy reviews the historical evolution of our cultural, social, medical, and psychological attitudes toward homosexuality, concluding that these attitudes have gradually relaxed to the extent that, in the year 2003, the State of Massachusetts legalized same-sex marriage. Shortly thereafter, in the case of the *United States v. Windsor*, the U.S. Supreme Court declared the federal Defense of Marriage Act unconstitutional to the degree that it discriminated against same-sex marriage. Next, Kennedy runs through a series of cases, each one ruling that under the due process clause, the fundamental right to be married cannot be procedurally dismantled or limited without some compelling state reason to do so, as in the case of minors (pages 6-11 of the majority opinion). Some of the cases that support Kennedy's position include *Loving v. Virginia*, 388 U.S. 1, 12 (1967), which ruled that there is no justifiable reason to outlaw interracial marriage; *Turner v. Safley*, 482 U.S. 78, 95 (1987), which concluded there is no justifiable reason to prevent a prison inmate from marrying; and *Zablocki v. Redhail*, 434 U.S. 374, 384 (1978), which ruled that there is no justifiable reason to stop a delinquent father (late on child support payments) from marrying (page 11 of the majority opinion). Despite (or perhaps because of) the fact that none of these cases redefine marriage or suppose that marriage means anything other than a lawful union between a man and a woman, Kennedy declares that "this analysis compels the conclusion same sex couples may exercise the right to marry" (page 12 of the majority opinion).

Next, Kennedy structures a rationale that explains why this is so. He notes that he will present four principles that demonstrate that the fundamental right to marry is promised by the Constitution to same-sex couples. The first premise is that the right to marry is "inherent in the concept of individual autonomy." The second principle states, "The right to marry is fundamental because it supports a two-person union unlike any other in its importance to committed individuals." The third principle is based on the belief that marriage protects children and families and "the right of child bearing, procreation, and education." The final principle declares that marriage is important because it forms the glue that holds our society together (pages 12-19).

Kennedy then pulls the equal protection clause into his argument by pointing to the "synergetic" relationship between the equal protection clause and the due process clause of the 14th Amendment, concluding, "These considerations lead to the conclusion that the right to marry is a fundamental right inherent in the liberty of the person, and under the Due Process and Equal Protection Clauses of the Fourteenth Amendment couples of the same sex may not be deprived of that right and that liberty. The Court now holds that same-sex couples may exercise the fundamental right to marry. No longer may this liberty be denied to them. *Baker v. Nelson* must be and now is overruled, and the State laws challenged by Petitioners in these cases are now held invalid to the extent they exclude same-sex couples from civil marriage on the same terms and conditions as opposite-sex couples" (pages 22-23).

Only then does Kennedy address the concerns of the appellate court, which focused on a belief that the process should wait for further debate and for legislative enactments as well as further litigation. Kennedy notes that those (see Roberts, Scalia, Thomas, and Alito) who argue for the legislative approach demanded by our democratic system ignore the fact that people who wish to exercise fundamental rights need not wait for the legislature to act, but can as a part of our republican form of government seek redress in the courts (which, by the way, is what happened here). Moreover, this principle is necessary as a way to protect the rights of a marginalized and victimized minority, which may not find support in the democratic principle of "majority rules" (pages 23-25).

The Court's Opinion

Justice Kennedy

... This analysis compels the conclusion that same-sex couples may exercise the right to marry. The four principles and traditions to be discussed demonstrate that the reasons marriage is fundamental under the Constitution apply with equal force to same-sex couples.

A **first premise** of the Court's relevant precedents is that the right to personal choice regarding marriage is inherent in the concept of individual autonomy. This abiding connection between marriage and liberty is why *Loving* invalidated interracial marriage bans under the Due Process Clause. See 388 U.S., at 12; see also *Zablocki, supra*, at 384 (observing *Loving* held "the right to marry is of fundamental importance for all individuals"). Like choices concerning contraception, family relationships, procreation, and childrearing, all of which are protected by the Constitution, decisions concerning marriage are among the most intimate that an individual can make. See *Lawrence, supra*, at 574. Indeed, the Court has noted it would respect to other matters of family life and not with respect to the decision to enter the relationship that is the foundation of the family in our society." *Zablocki, supra*, at 386.

... A **second principle** in this Court's jurisprudence is that the right to marry is fundamental because it supports a two-person union unlike any other in its importance to the committed individuals. This point was central to *Griswold v. Connecticut*, which held the Constitution protects the right of married couples to use contraception. 381 U.S., at 485. Suggesting that marriage is a right "older than the Bill of Rights," Griswold described marriage this way:

> "Marriage is a coming together for better or for worse, hopefully enduring, and intimate to the degree of being sacred. It is an association that promotes a way of life, not causes; a harmony in living, not political faiths; a bilateral loyalty, not commercial or social projects. Yet it is an association for as noble a purpose as any involved in our prior decisions." *Id.*, at 486.

And in Turner, the Court again acknowledged the intimate association protected by this right, holding prisoners could not be denied the right to marry because their committed relationships satisfied the basic reasons why marriage is a fundamental right. See 482 U.S., at 95-96. The right to marry thus dignifies couples who "wish to define themselves by their commitment to each other." *Windsor, supra*, at ___ (slip op., at 14). Marriage responds to the universal fear that a lonely person might call out only to find no one there. It offers the hope of companionship and understanding and assurance that while both still live there will be someone to care for the other.

... A **third basis** for protecting the right to marry is that it safeguards children and families and thus draws meaning from related rights of childrearing, procreation, and education. See *Pierce v. Society of Sisters*, 268 U.S. 510 (1925); *Meyer*, 262 U.S., at 399. The Court has recognized these connections by describing the varied rights as a unified whole: "[T]he right to 'marry, establish a home and bring up children' is a central part of the liberty protected by the Due Process Clause." *Zablocki*, 434 U.S., at 384 (quoting *Meyer, supra*, at 399). Under the laws of the several States, some of marriage's protections for children and families are material. But marriage also confers more profound benefits. By giving recognition and legal structure to their parents' relationship, marriage allows children "to understand the integrity and closeness of their own family and its concord with other families in their community and in their daily lives." *Windsor, supra*, at ___ (slip op., at 23). Marriage also affords the permanency and stability important to children's best interests. See Brief for Scholars of the Constitutional Rights of Children as *Amici Curiae* 22-27.

As all parties agree, many same-sex couples provide loving and nurturing homes to their children, whether biological or adopted. And hundreds of thousands of children are presently being raised by such couples. See Brief for Gary J. Gates as Amicus Curiae 4. Most States have allowed gays and lesbians to adopt, either as individuals or as couples, and many adopted and foster children have same-sex parents, see *id.*, at 5. This provides powerful confirmation from the law itself that gays and lesbians can create loving, supportive families.

Excluding same-sex couples from marriage thus conflicts with a central premise of the right to marry. Without the recognition, stability, and predictability marriage offers, their children suffer the stigma of knowing their families are somehow lesser. They also suffer the significant material costs of being raised by unmarried parents, relegated through no fault of their own to a more difficult and uncertain family life. The marriage laws at issue here thus harm and humiliate the children of same-sex couples. See *Windsor, supra*, at ___ (slip op., at 23

... **Fourth and finally**, this Court's cases and the Nation's traditions make clear that marriage is a keystone of our social order. Alexis de Tocqueville recognized this truth on his travels through the United States almost two centuries ago:

> ... There is certainly no country in the world where the tie of marriage is so much respected as in America ... [W]hen the American retires from the turmoil of public life to the bosom of his family, he finds in it the image of order and of peace. ... [H]e afterwards carries [that image] with him into public affairs." 1 Democracy in America 309 (H. Reeve transl., rev. ed. 1990).

In *Maynard v. Hill*, 125 U.S. 190, 211 (1888), the Court echoed de Tocqueville, explaining that marriage is "the foundation of the family and of society, without which there would be neither civilization nor progress." Marriage, the *Maynard* Court said, has long been "'a great public institution, giving character to our whole civil polity.'" *Id.*, at 213. This idea has been reiterated even as the institution has evolved in substantial ways over time, superseding rules related to parental consent, gender, and race once thought by many to be essential. See generally N. Cott, Public Vows. Marriage remains a building block of our national community.

For that reason, just as a couple vows to support each other, so does society pledge to support the couple, offering symbolic recognition and material benefits to protect and nourish the union. Indeed, while the States are in general free to vary the benefits they confer on all married basis for an expanding list of governmental rights, benefits, and responsibilities. These aspects of marital status include: taxation; inheritance and property rights; rules of intestate succession; spousal privilege in the law of evidence; hospital access; medical decision making authority; adoption rights; the rights and benefits of survivors; birth and death certificates; professional ethics rules; campaign finance restrictions; workers' compensation benefits; health insurance; and child custody, support, and visitation rules. See Brief for United States as *Amicus Curiae* 6-9; Brief for American Bar Association as *Amicus Curiae* 8-29. Valid marriage under state law is also a significant status for over a thousand provisions of federal law. See *Windsor*, 570 U.S., at ___ - ___ (slip op., at 15-16). The States have contributed to the fundamental character of the marriage right by placing that institution at the center of so many facets of the legal and social order.

There is no difference between same- and opposite-sex couples with respect to this principle. Yet by virtue of their exclusion from that institution, same-sex couples are denied the constellation of benefits that the States have linked to marriage. This harm results in more than just material burdens. Same-sex couples are consigned to an instability many opposite-sex couples would deem intolerable in their own lives. As the State itself makes marriage all the more precious by the significance it attaches to it, exclusion from that status has the effect of teaching that gays and lesbians are unequal in important respects. It demeans gays and lesbians for the State to lock them out of a central institution of the Nation's society. Same-sex couples, too, may aspire to the transcendent purposes of marriage and seek fulfillment in its highest meaning.

The limitation of marriage to opposite-sex couples may long have seemed natural and just, but its inconsistency with the central meaning of the fundamental right to marry is now manifest. With that knowledge must come the recognition that laws excluding same-sex couples from the marriage right impose stigma and injury of the kind prohibited by our basic charter.

Objecting that this does not reflect an appropriate framing of the issue, the respondents refer to *Washington v. Glucksberg*, 521 U.S. 702, 721 (1997), which called for a "'careful description'" of fundamental rights. They assert the petitioners do not seek to exercise the right to marry but rather a new and nonexistent "right to same-sex marriage." Brief for Respondent in No. 14-556, p. 8. *Glucksberg* did insist that liberty under the Due Process Clause must be defined in a most circumscribed manner, with central reference to specific historical practices. Yet while that approach may have been appropriate for the asserted right there involved (physician-assisted suicide), it is inconsistent with the approach this Court has used in discussing other fundamental rights, including marriage and intimacy. *Loving* did not ask about a "right to interracial marriage"; *Turner* did not ask about a "right of inmates to marry"; and *Zablocki* did not ask about a "right of fathers with unpaid child support duties to marry." Rather, each case inquired about the right to marry in its comprehensive sense, asking if there was a sufficient justification for excluding the relevant class from the right. See also *Glucksberg*, 521 U.S., at 752-773 (Souter, J., concurring in judgment); *id.*, at 789-792 (BREYER, J., concurring in judgments).

That principle applies here. If rights were defined by who exercised them in the past, then received practices could serve as their own continued justification and new groups could not invoke rights once denied. This Court has rejected that approach, both with respect to the right to marry and the rights of gays and lesbians. See *Loving* 388 U.S., at 12; *Lawrence*, 539 U.S., at 566-567.

The right to marry is fundamental as a matter of history and tradition, but rights come not from ancient sources alone. They rise, too, from a better informed understanding of how constitutional imperatives define a liberty that remains urgent in our own era. Many who deem same-sex marriage to be wrong reach that conclusion based on decent and honorable religious or philosophical premises, and neither they nor their beliefs are disparaged here. But when that sincere, personal opposition becomes enacted law and public policy, the necessary consequence is to put the imprimatur of the State itself on an exclusion that soon demeans or stigmatizes those whose own liberty is then denied. Under the Constitution, same-sex couples seek in marriage the same legal treatment as opposite-sex couples, and it would disparage their choices and diminish their personhood to deny them this right.

. . . There may be an initial inclination in these cases to proceed with caution—to await further legislation, litigation, and debate. The respondents warn there has been insufficient democratic discourse before deciding an issue as basic as the definition of marriage. In its ruling on the cases now before this Court, the majority opinion for the Court of Appeals made a cogent argument that it would be appropriate for the respondents'

States to await further public discussion and political measures before licensing same-sex marriages. See *DeBoer*, 772 F. 3d, at 409.

Yet there has been far more deliberation than this argument acknowledges. There have been referenda, legislative debates, and grassroots campaigns, as well as countless studies, papers, books, and other popular and scholarly writings. There has been extensive litigation in state and federal courts. See Appendix A, *infra*. Judicial opinions addressing the issue have been informed by the contentions of parties and counsel, which, in turn, reflect the more general, societal discussion of same-sex marriage and its meaning that has occurred over the past decades. As more than 100 *amici* make clear in their filings, many of the central institutions in American life—state and local governments, the military, large and small businesses, labor unions, religious organizations, law enforcement, civic groups, professional organizations, and universities—have devoted substantial attention to the question. This has led to an enhanced understanding of the issue—an understanding reflected in the arguments now presented for resolution as a matter of constitutional law.

Of course, the Constitution contemplates that democracy is the appropriate process for change, so long as that process does not abridge fundamental rights. Last Term, a plurality of this Court reaffirmed the importance of the democratic principle in *Schuette v. BAMN*, 572 U.S. ___ (2014), noting the "right of citizens to debate so they can learn and decide and then, through the political process, act in concert to try to shape the course of their own times." *Id.*, at ___ - ___ (slip op., at 15-16). Indeed, it is most often through democracy that liberty is preserved and protected in our lives. But as *Schuette* also said, "The freedom secured by the Constitution consists, in one of its essential dimensions, of the right of the individual not to be injured by the unlawful exercise of governmental power." *Id.*, at ___ (slip op., at 15). Thus, when the rights of persons are violated, "the Constitution requires redress by the courts," notwithstanding the more general value of democratic decision making. *Id.*, at ___ (slip op., at 17). This holds true even when protecting individual rights affects issues of the utmost importance and sensitivity.

The dynamic of our constitutional system is that individuals need not await legislative action before asserting a fundamental right. The Nation's courts are open to injured individuals who come to them to vindicate their own direct, personal stake in our basic charter. An individual can invoke a right to constitutional protection when he or she is harmed, even if the broader public disagrees and even if the legislature refuses to act. The idea of the Constitution "was to withdraw certain subjects from the vicissitudes of political controversy, to place them beyond the reach of majorities and officials and to establish them as legal principles to be applied by the courts." *West Virginia Bd. of Ed. v. Barnette*, 319 U.S. 624, 638 (1943). This is why "fundamental rights may not be submitted to a vote; they depend on the outcome of no elections." *Ibid.* [Bold face type added throughout case.]

Justice Roberts's Dissent

Roberts begins his dissent with one generalized principle, that the United States Supreme Court is not a legislative body (although, it seems to think that it is). Roberts also wants to make sure that his position is clear. In no uncertain terms he says: "Understand well what this dissent is about: It is not about whether, in my judgment, the institution of marriage should be changed to include same-sex couples. It is instead about whether, in our democratic republic, that decision should rest with the people acting through their elected representatives, or with five lawyers who happen to hold commissions authorizing them to resolve legal disputes according to law. The Constitution leaves no doubt about the answer" (page 3 of the Roberts Dissent).

What becomes evident, as Roberts continues, is that his essential objection to the majority's opinion is that five justices have taken it upon themselves to sidestep any authentic attempt to interpret the Constitution and have, instead, imposed their individual beliefs on the state governments by eliminating a "universal definition of marriage" that "has existed for millennia across civilizations" (page 4). Roberts seems especially convinced that these five members of the court have acted as self-appointed social engineers who have substituted their own view of marriage for the judgment of the duly elected legislatures of the states involved in these lawsuits and have, in effect, marginalized the people who elected those legislators. He goes on to describe Justice Kennedy's opinion in the following way: "Stripped of its shiny rhetorical gloss, the majority's argument is that the Due Process Clause gives same-sex couples a fundamental right to marry because it will be good for them and for society" (page 10).

Moreover, Roberts notes that, while Kennedy chooses cases that interpret the right to marry in a fair and even-handed way, those cases do not stand for the proposition that anyone who wishes to marry has an automatic, unquestioned right to get married. What the Court actually does in all of those cases is demand that those states that want to limit the right to marry explain and defend those limits. However, most importantly of all, the cases cited by Kennedy assume that the fundamental and traditional definition of marriage stays unchanged (pages 15–16).

Justice Scalia's Dissent

Justice Scalia objects to the fact that the majority has conjured up "liberties" that are not included in the Constitution, or the Bill of Rights or any of the other Amendments. Incredibly, the majority makes this move while extoling the virtues of "liberty," oblivious to the fact that they are neither protecting liberty nor promoting rights, but are, instead, robbing the people of the power to govern themselves. In effect, the majority has told the People of the United States that their elected officials and their democratic processes do not matter (pages 1–2 of Scalia's Dissent). Scalia notes unapologetically and with great conviction that the Court, "ends this debate, in an opinion lacking even a thin veneer of law. Buried beneath the mummeries and straining-to-be-memorable passages of the opinion is a candid and startling assertion: No matter *what* it was the People ratified, the Fourteenth Amendment protects those rights that the Judiciary, in its 'reasoned judgment,' thinks the Fourteenth Amendment ought to protect" (page 4 of Scalia's Dissent). Scalia, as an avowed and dedicated textualist, recoils in horror as the majority concludes that they alone in the history of American jurisprudence have discovered a right that everyone else seems to have missed.

Justice Thomas's Dissent

It is Justice Thomas who is most concerned about the use of procedural rights to create substantive rights out of thin air in a way never envisioned by the Framers of the Constitution. Recall in the earlier summary of this case that the due process clause states that the government cannot deprive individuals of life, liberty, or property, without properly following due process. This does not mean that the government cannot deprive someone of life, liberty, or property only that it cannot do so outside proper legal procedures. Due process and equal protection are not substantive rights, like the free exercise of religion or freedom of speech. Rather they are procedural rights that promise that proper legal measures will be used to protect substantive rights in a fair and equitable way, barring a compelling reason not to do so. Justice Thomas notes that the truly insidious nature of this legal error is that it gives judges a green light to pull "rights" out of the Constitution at will based only their personal opinion about what rights are guarded therein. Justice Thomas says it this way: "The majority's decision today will require States to issue marriage licenses to same-sex couples and to recognize same-sex marriages entered in other States largely based on a constitutional provision guaranteeing 'due process' before a person is deprived of his 'life, liberty, or property.' I have elsewhere explained the dangerous fiction of treating the Due Process Clause as a font of substantive rights. . . . It distorts the constitutional text, which guarantees only whatever 'process' is 'due' before a person is deprived of life, liberty, and property. . . . Worse, it invites judges to do exactly what the majority has done here—'roa[m] at large in the constitutional field' guided only by their personal views as to the 'fundamental rights' protected by that document" (page 2 of Thomas's Dissent).

Nor is Thomas dissuaded by the arguments put forth by the petitioners in the case, who contend that, when the voters place the time honored definition of marriage in a state constitution they have taken the issue outside the democratic system. Once the provision is in a state constitution it is out of bounds and off limits. Thomas argues, quite convincingly, that the alternative action contemplated by the petitioners does far more damage to the democratic process. Thomas, however, says it far more eloquently when he writes that, "the result petitioners seek is far less democratic. They ask nine judges on this Court to enshrine their definition of marriage in the Federal Constitution and thus put it beyond the reach of the normal democratic process for the entire Nation. That a 'bare majority' of this Court, *ante,* at 25, is able to grant this wish, wiping out with a stroke of the keyboard the results of the political process in over 30 States, based on a provision that guarantees only 'due process' is but further evidence of the danger of substantive due process" (page 3).

Justice Alito's Dissent

Alito, as a constitutional scholar, gets right to the point. He contends that the Court in the past (before this case) has held that the term *liberty* in the Due Process Clause protects rights that are "deeply rooted in this nation's history and traditions" (page 2 of Alito's Dissent). Having said this, he finds it difficult to understand how the right to engage in same sex marriage is a "deeply rooted right," especially since same sex marriage was not protected in any state prior to the year 2003 when Massachusetts passed the first law protecting that institution. Alito makes his point not to support or oppose same sex marriage but to demonstrate that the Constitution protects only "deeply rooted rights," not rights that are created by judicial belief alone (pages 2-3).

Questions for Analysis

1. How does the case of *Obergefell v. Hodges* support or contradict the core legal principle of stare decisis? Explain.

2. Throughout this textbook, but especially in Chapter 2, we examined the campaign waged by James Madison at the Constitutional Convention in Philadelphia and in the First Congress to create a strong central government under the banner of federalism (remember *The Federalist Papers*). In what way (or ways) does the *Obergefell v. Hodges* case verify the successful nature of Madison's campaign? Explain.

3. Madison wanted a federal veto added to the Constitution that would empower Congress to nullify any state legislative enactment that the federal government felt was unwise, dangerous, expensive, disruptive, or just plain inconvenient. Madison did not get his wish. Instead, he had to settle for the supremacy clause in Section VI of the Constitution. The supremacy clause was later interpreted by the Court to allow judges to invalidate statutes (executive actions, administrative regulations, and so on) that conflict with the Constitiution or with federal laws made in line with the Constitution. In what way(s) has *Obergefell v. Hodges* demonstrated that the supremacy clause is even more powerful as a tool to abrogate state action than Madison's veto power would have been? Explain.

4. Justice Roberts's concern in his dissent about the decision in the case is that the five justices in the majority have acted as self-appointed social engineers who have substituted their own view of marriage for the judgment of the duly elected legislative representatives of the people in the states involved in these lawsuits. Although this may not have been the intent of the majority, Roberts is correct in pointing out that these justices have acted as social reconstructionists rather than as judges. Is it proper for judges, at whatever level, to act as social architects or should they stick to interpreting the law as it exists on the page? Explain.

5. Justice Scalia opposes the fact that members of the majority have stepped out of their traditional roles as judges and assumed the unconstitutional role of pseudo-legislators. This transgression is labelled poetically as "legislating from the bench." Legislating from the bench occurs when judges or, in this case, justices, stop interpreting the law and start creating it, which is the exclusive role of the legislature. The offense is compounded when a pseudo-legislative act sets aside a state statute or a state constitutional provision. Without using the phrase "legislating from the bench," Scalia, nevertheless, admonishes the five justices in the majority for overstepping their constitutional roles. Unfortunately, the fact that Scalia has chastised them will have little legal effect. The reality is that, in this case at least, the court has, in one fell swoop, struck down the legislative enactments and, in some cases, the constitutional provisions, of some 30 states. What proactive steps might be taken to prevent such "legislating from the bench" in the future? Should penalties be put in place for such misconduct? Should an extra-judicial reversal process be developed by Congress to nullify unauthorized legislative mandates issued from the bench? Explain.

6. Justice Scalia is also an unapologetic, premeditated textualist who believes that the true meaning of the law lies within the words of a statute or constitutional provision. Accordingly, he reprimands the majority for concluding that they alone in the history of American jurisprudence have discovered a right that everyone else seems to have missed. Scalia is correct in his observation that the word *marriage*, from a textualist perspective, has meant the same thing for the entire collective memory of the human race, at least up until the past few decades. Should an avowed textualist like Scalia take into consideration the evolving nature of cultural standards and the corresponding attitude changes that might alter the meaning of a text or should the text remain sacrosanct as written originally? Explain.

7. Justice Thomas is authentically disturbed by the confusion that exists between procedural and substantive rights. He correctly points out that neither the due process clause nor the equal protection clause creates a substantive right. Put simply, these two rights promise that the substantive rights—things like freedom of religion, freedom of the press, freedom of assembly, freedom of speech, and so on—cannot be disrupted without due process unless some compelling governmental reason (such as national security, for example) allows it. Is Thomas correct in his assessment? If he is correct, does it really matter? Isn't this just the same "end justifies the means" argument used for centuries by governmental officials to get their way? Explain.

8. Justice Alito begins his dissent by noting that the due process clause was designed to protect rights that are "deeply rooted in the nation's history and tradition." Rights that are "deeply rooted" in the nation's history would involve things like the rights listed in question 7— freedom of religion, freedom of the press, freedom of assembly, freedom of speech, and so on. Should the majority be congratulated for creating a new right or rebuked for violating tradition? Explain.

9. The case of *Obergefell v. Hodges* altered the definition of marriage on a national scale. This change clearly affects constitutional law and the law of domestic relations. Yet, as is true of many Supreme Court decisions, the consequences of *Obergefell v. Hodges* will be felt in many other areas of the law. What other parts of the legal landscape will feel the unintended consequences of the majority ruling? In what way does the case of *Obergefell v. Hodges* highlight the problem of unintended consequences? Explain.

10. A complex adaptive system (CAS) is a network of interacting conditions that reinforce one another, while at the same time adjusting to change from agents outside and inside the system. In what ways does Kennedy's majority opinion in this case reinforce the idea that the law works like a complex adaptive system? Explain.

Source: Obergefell, et al., v. Hodges, Director, Ohio Department of Health, et al. 576 U.S. ____ (2015)

Design Elements: The Opening Case: ©Sharpstock/ Alamy; A Classic Case: ©Evlakhov Valeriy/ Shutterstock

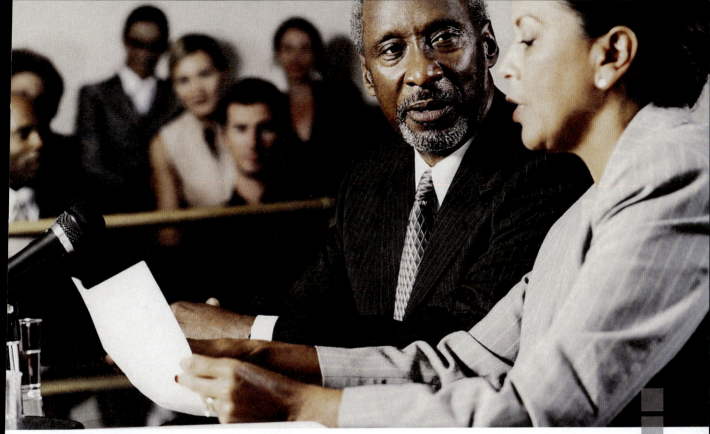
©Jim Arbogast/Getty Images

Part Nine
The Legal Environment

Chapter 32	Professional Liability	Case Study	Legal Consequences of the Construction of a Wall in the Occupied Palestinian Territory (Request for Advisory Opinion), The International Court of Justice
Chapter 33	Science, Technology, and Law in the 21st Century		
Chapter 34	International Law and the New World Order		

Chapter 32: Professional Liability

32-1 The Liability of Accountants
The Regulation of Accounting and Auditing • Accountant Registration • Accounting and Auditing • Sarbanes–Oxley Act • Conflicting Jurisdictional Problems • The Dodd–Frank Act • Duties Owed by the Accountant to the Client • Type One Accounting Arrangements • Type Two Accounting Arrangements • An Accountant's Statutory Liability • The New Tax Code • Financial Advisors and the New Fiduciary Rule

32-2 The Liability of Architects and Attorneys
The Liability of Architects • The Liability of Attorneys • Steps in a Legal Malpractice Case

32-3 The Liability of Health Care Providers
The Professional Status of Health Care Providers • The Health Care Standard of Care • Medical Records and the Patient's Rights • The Patient Protection and Affordable Care Act

32-4 The Liability of Hospitals
Ostensible Authority and Hospital Liability • Negligent Credentialing by Hospital Authorities • Tort Reform and Litigation

---

THE OPENING CASE Round 1
Cultural Engineering by Professional Organizations: Social Benefit or Constitutional Nightmare?

Lawyers have a duty to be loyal to their clients and to act with both good faith and due care as they represent those clients. Moreover, in the broader picture, they also have a duty to uphold the legal system and to ensure its smooth running. What they do not have is the duty to engineer a shift in cultural values. Or do they? The American Bar Association (ABA) would seem to have different plans for the legal profession. In a recent move, the ABA modified one of its key rules, and with that modification, has, in effect, changed the direction of the legal profession. Some experts see this move as a dangerous attempt by the ABA to suppress free speech, threaten freedom of religion, and mount a self-righteous campaign to redefine social values—all under the banner of its latest cultural reengineering project. Others hail it as a long-overdue recognition that the profession needs to accommodate 21st-century political and social sensitivities.

The new rule is referred to modestly as Model Rule 8.4 (g) and reads like this: "It is professional misconduct for a lawyer to . . . engage in conduct that the lawyer knows or reasonably should know is harassment or discrimination on the basis of race, sex, religion, national origin, ethnicity, disability, age, sexual orientation, gender identity, marital status or socioeconomic status in conduct related to the practice of law." In explaining the rationale behind this new rule, the ABA has noted, "There is a need for *a cultural shift in understanding* the inherent integrity of people regardless of their race, color, national origin, religion, age, sex, gender identity, gender expression, sexual orientation, marital status, or disability, to be captured in the rules of professional conduct." [See: ABA Standing Committee on Ethics and Professional Responsibility, Memorandum: Draft Proposal to Amend Model Rule 8.4, 2 (December 22, 2015) (italics added).] Some attorneys note that, while a such a campaign is unprecedented in its authoritative reach, it is really a harmless suggestion, made by a body with no real legislative power. Such a position ignores or overlooks the fact that state governments routinely adopt ABA rules with no changes and that those same legislatures have empowered the ABA to accredit law schools and to shape the curriculum for those schools, including its take on the ethical rules that will govern the profession for decades to come. Thus, the battle over Rule 8.4 (g) must, at the very least, be waged within the context of the ABA's real power as a quasi-governmental agency. To do otherwise is disingenuous and dangerous.

So far, this is all very abstract, so let's get a bit more concrete by looking at a few hypothetical situations. Consider the following. Would a lawyer violate Rule 8.4 (g) if, during a lunch break at a continuing education session on the *Obergefell* case, she expressed her religious belief that marriage should be limited to the traditional man–woman model? Would another lawyer at the same session violate Rule 8.4 (g) if he voiced a religious preference for recognizing same-sex marriage? Before Rule 8.4 (g), principles of free speech and freedom of religion would have tolerated both views. Now that conclusion is not as clear. Let's try two additional hypotheticals. What if a law firm refuses to take on a male client in a divorce case because the all-female staff has decided to represent only women in divorce cases? Would this violate that part of Rule 8.4 (g) that says, "It is professional misconduct for a lawyer to . . . engage in conduct that the lawyer knows or reasonably should know is . . . discrimination on the basis of . . . sex?" Similarly, what would happen if, during a meeting on the new tax law, a lawyer argues that the new tax law gives far too many benefits to the rich and that, on that basis alone, their firm should no longer represent any client who makes over $100,000 per year. Would this violate that part of Rule 8.4 (g) that says quite clearly, "It is professional misconduct for a lawyer to . . . engage in conduct that the lawyer knows or reasonably should know is . . . discrimination on the basis of . . . socioeconomic status?" Think about it. We will revisit these hypotheticals later in the chapter. First, however, we will must look at the liability of accountants and financial advisors. [See: Ronald Rotunda, "The ABA Decision to Control What Lawyers Say: Supporting 'Diversity' But Not Diversity of Thought," *The Heritage Society*, October 6, 2016, https://www.heritage.org/ report/the-aba-decision-control-what-lawyers-say-supporting-diversity-not-diversity-thought; David Hudson Jr, "States Split on New ABA Model Rule Limiting Harassing or Discriminatory Conduct," *ABA Journal*, October 2017, http://www.abajournal.com/magazine/article/ethics_model_rule_harassing_conduct; and ABA Standing Committee on Ethics and Professional Responsibility, Memorandum: Draft Proposal to Amend Model Rule 8.4 (g) (December 22, 2015) (emphasis added)].

Opening Case Questions

1. What is the function of the American Bar Association? Explain.
2. In what ways does the ABA operate like a quasi-governmental agency? Explain.
3. Why is it significant to determine whether the ABA operates as a quasi-governmental agency? Explain.
4. What is the basic substance of ABA Model Rule 8.4 (g)? Explain.
5. How might a lawyer violate Rule 8.4 (g)? Explain.

Source: See: Ronald Rotunda, "The ABA Decision to Control What Lawyers Say: Supporting 'Diversity' But Not Diversity of Thought," *The Heritage Society*, (October 6, 2016) https://www.heritage.org/ report/the-aba-decision-control-what-lawyers-say-supporting-diversity-not-diversity-thought; David Hudson, Jr, "States split on new ABA Model rule limiting harassing or discriminatory conduct," *ABA Journal* (October 2017) http://www.abajournal. com/ magazine/ article/ethics_model_rule_ harassing_c onduct; ABA Standing Comm. on Ethics and Professional Responsibility, *Memorandum: Draft Proposal to Amend Model Rule 8.4, 2* (Dec. 22, 2015) (emphasis added)

Learning Objectives

1. Distinguish between a certified public accountant and a public accountant.
2. Explain generally accepted accounting principles and generally accepted auditing standards.
3. Identify the types of auditing opinions that can be issued by auditors.
4. Distinguish between actual privity and near-privity in accounting.
5. Outline the registration requirements imposed on architects by the state.

6. Identify the duties that an architect owes to his or her clients.
7. Determine the duties that an attorney owes to his or her clients.
8. State the standard of care used to judge health care professionals.
9. Contrast the locality rule with the national standard.
10. Explain the limits of hospital liability for the torts of independent contractor.

32-1 The Liability of Accountants

As we've seen in the commercial world, the legal system and the economic culture interact with each other in such a way that they become, at times, one single system, the judicial-economic system. In Chapter 31, we also examined how the judicial-economic system acts as another aspect of the balancing process within the law. Now we turn our attention to one of the key players in the judicial-economic system, the accountant.

The Regulation of Accounting and Auditing

Accountants, like all professionals, must meet certain basic standards that are defined by the nature of their profession. A **professional** is a person who can perform a highly specialized task because of his or her special abilities, education, experience, and knowledge. Often the term professional is reserved for those individuals who perform a service for the public good. An **accountant** is a professional who can plan, direct, and evaluate a client's financial affairs. Although many accountants are charged with keeping a client's financial records, their responsibilities often go far beyond such routine tasks. Moreover, the nature of accounting means that an accountant's activities may have an impact on investors who exist outside the accountant's inner circle of clients. For these reasons, among others, accountants are regulated by the government. The federal government's power to regulate business, in general, and accounting, in particular, emerges from the commerce clause of the Constitution. The regulation of accounting by the state is part of the state's police power. The state's police power permits the state to regulate various activities to promote the general health, safety, welfare, and morals of the people.

Accountant Registration

The regulation of accounting is part of the state's police power. There are many different types of accountants. Some accountants work only for one employer. British Petroleum, for example, employs hundreds of accountants to chart the financial fortunes of the corporation. Other accountants hire themselves out to work for a wide variety of different clients. Regardless of where they work, however, accountants generally belong to one of two categories: certified public accountants or public accountants.

Certified public accountants (CPAs) have met certain age, character, education, experience, and testing requirements. These requirements are generally established by the state. For example, the state government may require CPAs to be at least 18 years of age and of good moral character. The state may also require a bachelor's degree, two or more years of experience, and a passing score on a written examination that covers accounting, auditing, and other related subject areas. **Public accountants (PAs)** are accountants who work for a variety of clients but are not certified. Frequently, states will not allow individuals to call themselves public accountants unless they have met certain requirements that are not as strict as the requirements for CPAs. State registration requirements are designed to shield citizens against people who practice accounting without the education or experience necessary to do a competent job. The state cannot, however, prevent someone from practicing accounting as a profession. The state can only stop such individuals from calling themselves CPAs, PAs, or any other title that might mislead a client into thinking the nonregistered accountant is registered.

Accounting and Auditing

Accountants perform a number of functions for their clients. They may balance accounts, reconcile bank records with account books, handle the payroll, fill out income tax returns, and handle other tax matters. Another important job that falls to the accountant is the task of auditing.

Auditing An *audit* is an examination of the financial records of an organization to determine whether those records are a fair representation of the actual financial health of the institution. To be effective, an audit is usually conducted by an outside, independent auditor. An *auditor* is an accountant who conducts an audit. The dilemma that auditors face is that they are responsible at two levels of accountability. Traditionally, auditors are hired by and work for the organization that is being audited. This is the first level of accountability. At the second level of accountability, auditors are responsible to the investors, lenders, shareholders, and others who rely on the financial statements made by those auditors. Ideally, auditors ought to be loyal to both groups of individuals. Realistically, auditors do not always overlook the fact that the organization is the one that hired them and that writes their paycheck. As a result, there is a tendency, probably unconscious in most cases, to help the organization rather than the outside investors.

> **Did You Know?**
> Because there is a tendency among accountants to settle cases out of court, many lawsuits against them never make it to trial. A lawsuit against the mega-accounting firm of Ernst & Young, for instance, was settled in the 1990s for $400 million.

Accounting Principles An independent group known as the Financial Accounting Standards Board (FASB) has established *generally accepted accounting principles (GAAP)*. The rules established by the FASB are followed by the American Institute of Certified Public Accountants (AICPA). The rules outline the procedures that accountants must use in accumulating financial data and preparing financial statements. In general, the procedures facilitate the preparation of reports that are useful, understandable, reliable, verifiable, and comparable.

Auditing Standards The Auditing Standards Board of the AICPA has set up *generally accepted auditing standards (GAAS)*. These auditing standards measure the quality of the performance of auditing procedures. In short, the auditing standards explain how an auditor can determine whether proper accounting procedures have been used. Of the 10 auditing standards, three of them relate to the auditors, three relate to their work in the field, and four relate to the opinions that they issue.

Types of Opinion An auditor's opinions may be unqualified or qualified. When auditors conclude that the financial records of the company are an accurate reflection of the company's financial status, they will issue an *unqualified opinion*. When auditors issue a *qualified opinion*, they are saying that the books represent the company's financial health as of a given date. However, auditors may qualify the opinion in one of two ways. One type of qualified opinion is the "subject to" opinion. In this case, auditors state that the books represent the company's financial health subject to some uncertainty, such as a pending lawsuit, which may affect the company in the future. The second type of qualified opinion is an "except for" opinion. Such an opinion indicates that the financial statements are an accurate reflection of the company's financial health except for some minor deviation from GAAP, not serious enough to warrant an adverse opinion. Auditors may also issue adverse opinions and disclaimers. An *adverse opinion* is rendered when the deviations from GAAP are so serious that an unqualified opinion is impossible and a qualified opinion is not justified. An adverse opinion would be rendered in the following cases:

- The financial statements do not fairly present the financial health of the organization.
- Generally accepted accounting principles are consistently ignored.

- Financial information has not been adequately disclosed.
- There are major uncertainties that could have a serious impact on the organization, and the auditor disagrees with management's presentation of those uncertainties.

A **disclaimer** declares that the auditor has decided not to give any opinion on the company's financial records. This situation generally occurs because the auditor has not had enough time to examine the books properly or was denied access to crucial records. An auditor might also issue a disclaimer if the books indicate that the organization exercised no control over the accounting process.

Accountants have a fiduciary duty with their clients and must adhere to the AICPA Code of Professional Ethics as well as GAAP and GAAS standards for the profession.
©alexraths/123RF

Ethical Rules of Accountants The AICPA has also established a **Code of Professional Ethics**, which outlines rules that govern the ethical conduct of accountants. These rules are frequently used by the courts to determine whether an accountant has breached a duty to the client in nontechnical matters not covered by GAAP and GAAS. For example, the AICPA's code has established that accountants owe their clients a duty of confidentiality even after the relationship has terminated. In this regard, an accountant cannot reveal information about a client's business to anyone outside of the accountant-client relationship unless authorized to do so by the client. Although this privilege does not extend to a court's request for information, it does cover most other situations. The ethical code also encompasses contingent fees, the independence of the auditor, promotional practices, operational practices, and quality reviews by peers.

The Sarbanes–Oxley Act

In response to some of the difficulties that can be traced to the dual identity that auditors must assume, Congress enacted the **Sarbanes-Oxley Act**. Although the Sarbanes-Oxley Act has many targets, one of the most crucial is to restore the confidence of the investment community. A key feature of the act is the creation of the **Public Company Accounting Oversight Board (PCAOB)**. This new regulatory agency is charged with the task of making certain that correct, unbiased, and comprehensive data find their way to potential investors, so that they can make informed decisions about investment opportunities. To accomplish this task, Congress gave the board responsibility for the supervision of public accounting firms. With this power came the ability to set up practical instructions for auditing procedures and philosophical canons for the ethical values that such firms must follow. To give the new federal board proper authority, the act requires the registration of all public accounting firms that are involved in auditing publicly traded corporations. The board has the authority to inspect those companies and their procedures on a regularly established schedule. The board consists of five members, only two of whom are permitted to be certified public accountants. The hope is that this approach will keep the agency objective and unbiased as it evaluates both the accounting firms and the procedures by which they operate.

The Sarbanes-Oxley Act also enacted several additional features. For example, the act specifically prohibits conflicts of interest that might arise when former auditors are hired by a company, if that company is still being audited by the same firm that once employed the former auditor. The prohibition lasts for one year and covers only the uppermost management positions of the audited company. Sarbanes-Oxley also requires that corporate audit committees receive timely and comprehensive reports from the accounting firm that is auditing the company. Alternative approaches to the way that financial data is packaged must be included in these regular reporting sessions. Under the provisions of the act,

Congress has probed the mergers that have occurred among various major accounting firms. The aim of such a probe would be to find out what led to the mergers, what fallout will result from the new configuration, and what ways exist to improve the competitive atmosphere in the accounting profession.

Conflicting Jurisdictional Problems

Although auditors and accountants are regulated by several different authorities, those authorities coexist peacefully as long as they agree with one another. Trouble results, however, when different agencies promote different agendas. This problem is further complicated whenever accountants interact with other professionals. Many of these professionals, notably attorneys, are also regulated by professional authorities, some of which promote duties that conflict with those of the accounting profession. Thus, for example, the FASB might require auditors to perform a task that calls for information that is in the hands of a client's attorney. The AICPA might support the auditor's need to obtain such information from the clients' attorneys, but the American Bar Association (ABA) might direct attorneys to withhold information from auditors to preserve attorney-client privilege or the work product privilege or both. At that point, no matter what happens, someone will violate his or her professional code and someone—the auditor, the attorney, or the client—will have to suffer the consequences.

EXAMPLE 32-1: The Hazards of Serving Too Many Masters

In the mid-1970s, in the midst of a growing litigation epidemic, the FASB released a decision that required auditors to make sure that they accrued certain losses to income while auditing any client's books, including losses that might result from possible lawsuits. To do this properly, the auditors had to get information from their clients' attorneys. To help auditors accomplish this task, the AICPA announced that auditors were now permitted to ask clients to obtain certain information from their attorneys. In reaction, the ABA declared that attorneys ought to be very careful about providing auditors with too much information, lest they violate the attorney-client or the work product privilege or both. The AICPA responded by assuring the ABA that their auditors would never go so far as to violate either the attorney-client or the work product privilege. Everything might have rested there, had the Public Company Accounting Oversight Board (PCAOB) of Sarbanes-Oxley not gotten into the act. The PCAOB muddied the waters considerably by warning auditors that they would be severely disciplined for not insisting that attorneys provide them with the necessary information, regardless of whatever arguments those attorneys might make. Does this conflict give the auditors a license to demand that attorneys violate the attorney-client privilege and the work product privilege? Certainly the ABA does not think so, but the PCAOB insists that it does. Whatever the ultimate outcome of this dispute might be, it serves to illustrate the problems that arise when too many governmental agencies regulate the same activity. [See: Peggy A. Heeg, "Auditors Are Increasingly at Odds with Attorneys," *The National Law Journal*, November 20, 2006, pp. S-1, S-6–S-7.]

Source: See: Peggy A. Heeg, "Auditors Are Increasingly at Odds with Attorneys," *The National Law Journal*, November 20, 2006, pp. S-1 and S-6–S-7.

The Dodd–Frank Act

In Chapters 20 and 29, we learned that Congress attempted to deal with the 21st-century financial crisis by passing the Dodd-Frank Act, the purpose of which is to rectify present economic problems and, thus, head off any future crisis. The problems that we discussed in Chapter 20 were related to mortgages. The problems that we looked at in Chapter 29 involved corporations. Mortgage lenders and corporate officers were not the only ones guilty of wrongdoing in the crisis. Accountants and auditors also had a hand in the mess. For that reason, Congress also included provisions in the Dodd-Frank Act for dealing with the problems peculiar to the accounting profession. As noted earlier in the book, the Dodd-Frank Act is a long, complex, and intricate statute covering over 2,000 pages. The provisions that we will concentrate on now are those that affect the potential liability of accountants.

Securities and Exchange Commission Jurisdiction
The Securities and Exchange Commission (SEC) has been charged with investigating the information that is given to investors. The goal of the study is to determine if such disclosures actually help investors. The ultimate goal of this program is to develop a new generation of literate investors who actually know what they are doing when they invest their money. (What a novel idea.) The SEC will report to Congress, specifically to the Senate Banking Committee and the House Financial Services Committee. As part of this investigation, the SEC will also look at the possibility of adding a private rights action section to the law, with an explanation of how such a proposal would affect institutional investors, among others.

Government Accountability Office/Public Company Accounting Oversight Board
The Government Accountability Office (GAO) has been charged with investigating how to regulate financial planners, especially those planners who perform income tax planning services. Similarly, the Public Company Accounting Oversight Board (PCAOB) has been empowered to develop a plan to regulate and register auditors of nonpublic broker dealers. Accordingly, the PCAOB is also now considering the development of a fresh set of audit standards.

Duties Owed by the Accountant to the Client

The concept of duty in the law is slippery at best. Still, duty commonly emerges from within the context of rights. Some rights emerge simply because people exist within a sociocultural setting. The right to remain uninjured is one such right. The right to move about freely is another. However, not all rights arise automatically. Some duties emerge from within a voluntary relationship in which, at minimum, two parties expressly (or impliedly) agree to bind themselves to one another in order to receive mutual benefits. The agreement will always involve two complementary but essential elements, the right gained (which is generally the prime motivator for joining the game in the first place) and the newly acquired duty (the obligations adopted in exchange for the rights gained). The agreement involved in purchasing a vehicle, for instance, involves such elements. One party receives the right to possess and use the vehicle, yet simultaneously accepts the obligation to make regularly scheduled payments (the duty undertaken). Such arrangements exist at the heart of contract law. However, they also exist within corporate law, agency law, employment law, insurance law, and property law, among many others, including the law of accounting.

The problem here is that in many accounting arrangements, the levels of interaction among the parties are more complicated than in an ordinary straightforward contractual arrangement. Another difference is that within the law of accounting, multiple overlapping duties exist, all of which are interlaced and may emerge even when privity does not exist or when privity is so tenuous that it remains virtually unnoticed by most (perhaps even all) of the parties. Such entanglements rarely surface until something goes wrong, and then they emerge with a vengeance. These complex entanglements emerge when accountants seek to serve more than one master, something that is rarely advisable in the law (not to mention everyday life), but unfortunately inescapable in the accounting profession. A standard industry arrangement in accounting, an arrangement that we shall call a **type one arrangement**, exists between the accountant and a client and follows ordinary contract law principles.

However, sometimes accountants must act in a dual capacity, as both accountants and as auditors. We will refer to such arrangements as **type two arrangements**. Since accountants must act in such dual positions, multiple connections emerge beyond the four walls of the original arrangement, thus complicating things. We will examine type one arrangements before advancing to the type two arrangement.

Type One Accounting Arrangements

In a standard type one accounting arrangement, the accountant enters an agreement with a client, sometimes to act as a financial manager, but more often as a tax preparer. If the accountant fails to fulfill the terms of the contract, then the client has a cause of action against the accountant. For this reason, it is very important that the terms of the contract include express duties that outline the task of the accountant and the time limits, if any, within which the tasks must be performed. Naturally, certain implied duties are included in any contract between an accountant and the client. These implied duties arise because the relationship exists. Thus, the accountant's agreement to work for the client implies an agreement to use the appropriate level of skill and due care that would be expected of any similarly situated accountant. An accountant might also be liable to clients under common law for negligence and fraud.

Negligence in Type One Arrangements The client has the right to expect the accountant to do a good job in whatever task has been assigned. From this right arises the accountant's duty of due care. The duty of due care means that the accountant must perform the job with the same skill and competence that a reasonable accounting professional would use in the same situation. **Negligence**, often called **malpractice**, occurs whenever an accountant fails to meet his or her duty of due care. Although the term *malpractice* is usually reserved for health care professionals and attorneys, it could also be applied to any form of professional negligence. How a reasonable accounting professional would handle a given situation, and thus avoid a charge of malpractice, would be determined by reference to GAAS or GAAP. Whenever accountants ignore the rules established by GAAS and GAAP, they do so at their own risk. It is fairly certain that ignoring or remaining ignorant of these principles and procedures is a one-way ticket to a malpractice suit, and there is little question that in such circumstances, the accountant would be found liable for negligence. Unfortunately, the opposite precept is not always true; that is, just because an accountant follows the GAAS or GAAP guidelines does not automatically lead to his or her vindication in a court of law. It is always possible that an accountant can follow the proper principles and procedures yet still make other errors that lead to liability. Thus, an accountant might follow GAAS, yet file a return after a required deadline, or the accountant might make a calculation error, or send the forms to the wrong agency, and so on.

A NEW CLASSIC CASE *Part One*
Monday-Morning Quarterbacking: Type One or Type Two? Duty or No Duty?

In this case, the plaintiff, Empire State Carpenters Welfare, Annuity, and Pension Fund, invested quite a bit of money in Beacon Associates LLC (BA). Subsequently, BA invested Empire's money in a firm called Bernard L. Madoff Investment Securities LLC (BLM). As things turned out, this proved to be a mistake, and Empire lost a great deal of money. The case here, however, involves the auditing firm of Friedberg, Smith & Co. P.C. (FSC).

FSC served as the auditor for BA and, as such, issued annual auditing reports on BLM. These reports affirmed that BLM's "financial statements fairly represented the financial position" of BA and of Empire Funds accounts with BLM. As it turned out, BLM was virtually valueless. Consequently, as noted earlier, Empire Funds lost a large amount of money. Distressed by the enormity of the loss, the Empire trustees sued FSC. The district court granted a motion to dismiss the claim against FSC, and Empire Funds appealed. The Second Circuit Court of Appeals shaped the case around two questions, the first of which had to be answered in the affirmative before the case could go forward: "Did FSC owe a duty of due care to Empire Funds?"

We, however, should be able to see that an even more fundamental question sits at the base of the case, and that question is: "What type of accounting arrangement existed between FSC and Empire?" Or perhaps, even more simply, "Is the arrangement between FSC and Empire a type one or a type two accounting arrangement?" If it is a type one arrangement, then duty flows automatically; however, if it is a type two arrangement, then the existence of duty is neither obvious nor direct. So which is it? Type one or type two? The answer should be obvious. Because the two firms, FSC and Empire had not entered a formal contract, we are dealing with a type two, rather than a type one, arrangement. The question of duty was then still on the table. In a moment, the answer to that question will be revealed. To reach that answer, however, you must read on. [See: *Delollis v. Friedberg*, 12-1628-cv (Second Circuit 2015).]

Source: See: *Delollis v. Friedberg*, 12-1628-cv (Second Circuit 2015).

Fraud Involving Type One Arrangements When an accountant enters a type one arrangement, he or she must perform all duties with the best interests of the client in mind. If an accountant *deliberately* misrepresents the client's financial condition or in some way *deliberately* falsifies a statement or an auditing report, that accountant will be liable to the client for fraud. Accountants may also be liable for fraud if they compile a financial report or conduct an audit recklessly. To make a proper case for fraud, it is not enough for the plaintiff to show that the accountant deliberately or recklessly attempted to falsify records and statements. In addition, the plaintiff must demonstrate that he or she actually relied on the false statements or reports. The extra effort is worth it, however, because if the plaintiff succeeds in proving that he or she was defrauded by the accountant, that plaintiff can ask for and will often be awarded punitive damages. Punitive damages, you will recall, are damages that exceed the actual financial harm to the plaintiff and are designed to punish the wayward defendant. The degree of difficulty involved in making such charges stick is directly related to whether the accountant has entered a type one or a type two arrangement.

Type Two Accounting Arrangements

As noted earlier, a type two accounting arrangement emerges when the accountant has a type one industry arrangement with one party that leads to a type two industry arrangement with at least one other party but also, frequently, with a variety of different parties. Under common law, an accountant can be held liable to some third parties who are damaged by a negligently prepared financial statement. Accountants are also liable to some third parties if they deliberately make fraudulent statements.

Negligence/Malpractice and Type Two Industry Arrangements The right to bring suit for a negligently prepared financial statement is not clear cut. In fact, the right varies from jurisdiction to jurisdiction, with some jurisdictions using more than one theory of recovery. The best that can be done is to present the various options on a track from the least to the most inclusive, or from the narrowest to the widest. The standards fall on the following spectrum: (1) actual privity (also called the Cardozo Standard), (2) near-privity (also referred to as the Actually Named Third-Party Standard), (3) near-privity plus (also dubbed the Specifically Foreseen Third-Party Standard), (4) near-privity plus-2 (frequently named the Reasonably Foreseeable Third-Party Standard), and (5) the Platonic Stabilizing Standard (also called the balancing standard). (See Table 32-1.)

Actual Privity or the Cardozo Standard The Cardozo Standard of Actual Privity emerged from within the pages of a remarkable case decided in 1932 by Judge Benjamin Cardozo of New York. The Cardozo Standard is based on a strict interpretation of the nature of duty as it is relates to privity. As we have seen, privity is a relationship that emerges when two or more parties enter a contract. The parties to the contract are said to be *in privity* and it is the actual existence of that privity that creates the obligations that the parties owe to one another. Thus, under the Cardozo

Table 32-1 Accountants' Liability to Third Parties under Common Law

Liability Theories and Explanations	
Actual privity (also the Cardozo Standard)	Privity is a relationship that emerges when two or more parties enter a contract. The parties to the contract are said to be *in privity*, and it is the actual existence of that privity that creates the obligations that the parties owe to one another. Thus, under the Cardozo Standard, unless the parties have actual privity—that is, privity that results from a type one accounting arrangement—liability does not exist.
Near-privity (also the Actually Named Third-Party Standard)	To establish a condition of near-privity, the plaintiff must show that (a) the accountant knew that the reports would be shown to a third party, (b) the accountant knew the identity of the third party and that he or she would rely on the report, and (c) the accountant's conduct revealed that he or she had knowledge of the third party's reliance. The existence of near-privity means the plaintiff did, in fact and in law, owe a duty of due care toward the third party.
Near-privity plus (also the Specifically Foreseen Third-Party Standard)	Accountants can also be liable to the limited class of third parties that is specifically foreseen (not just actually known but specifically foreseen) when the financial statement is drawn up. Thus, an accountant who prepares a financial statement, knowing that the client intends to show it to some likely investors, would be liable to any investor in that same class of specifically foreseen third parties.
Near-privity plus-2 (also the Reasonably Foreseeable Third-Party Standard)	Some courts have become very broad in holding accountants liable to third parties. These jurisdictions have adopted a test that depends on whether the plaintiff in the case was *foreseeable* (not just foreseen but foreseeable) as a possible recipient of the accountant's report.
The Platonic Stabilizing Standard (also called the Balancing Standard)	Under the moderating influence of the Platonic Stabilizing Standard, the courts should consider the following elements to determine auditor–third-party liability: (a) how extensive were the investments involved in the case, (b) how foreseeable was the injury that emerged from the conduct under scrutiny, (c) how certain was it that the auditor's behavior led to the injury, (d) how connected was the action of the auditor to the third party's financial injury, and (e) how high was the ethical responsibility of the auditor.

Standard, unless the parties have **actual privity**—that is, privity that results from a type one accounting contract, liability for negligence (aka malpractice) does not exist—period.

Near-Privity or the Actually Named Third-Party Standard If an accountant prepares a financial statement with the actual knowledge that the client is going to show the statement to a particular third party, then the accountant has entered a type two accounting arrangement. Because the accountant has actual knowledge of the existence and identity of that third party, many courts will acknowledge that, even though a state of privity does not exist in this type two arrangement, the relationship between the accountant and the third party is one in which the parties acted as if privity existed, a condition referred to as one of **near-privity**. To establish a condition of near-privity, the plaintiff must show that (1) the accountant knew that the reports would be shown to a third party, (2) the accountant knew the identity of the third party and that he or she (or it?) would rely on the report, and (3) the accountant's conduct revealed that he or she had knowledge of the third party's reliance. The existence of near-privity means the plaintiff did, in fact and in law, owe a duty of due care toward the third party. The court can move to the second issue, and that is the question of whether the defendant acted in a dutiful manner toward the third party. Another way to put this is to ask, did the actions of the defendant conform to actions that are expected of a competent, law-abiding auditor in relation to the third party? Or, to phrase it a third way, did the activity complained of (or failure to perform that activity) by the plaintiff fall within the scope of the duty owed by the defendant to the plaintiff? If this question can be answered in the affirmative, then the defendant will be held liable for any actual financial loss that occurred due to the defendant accountant's negligence (the causation and the harm spoken of earlier.) [See: *Delollis v. Friedberg*, 12-1628-cv (Second Circuit 2015). See also: *Credit Alliance Corp. v. Arthur Andersen & Co.*, Court of Appeals of New York, 65 N.Y.2d 536 (1985).]

ANOTHER CLASSIC CASE Lack of Actual Privity: The Intolerable Indeterminacy of an Indeterminate Class

Fred Stern and Company applied to the Ultramares Loan Corporation for a credit advance in support of its import business. As was its custom, Ultramares asked Stern for a detailed financial statement that included an audited balance sheet. Stern agreed and supplied Ultramares with a report from its auditors, Touche, Niven, and Company. When Stern went to Touche, Niven, and Company, the import corporation did not reveal to the accounting firm that Ultramares would see the report. The only thing that the importers told the auditors was that the report would be shown to some possible creditors. Touche, Niven, and Company filed an audit report that stated Stern had a net worth of $1 million. Satisfied with the statement, Ultramares lent the money to Stern. The report turned out to be false. Fred Stern and Company was actually worth nothing at all, zero, zilch, zip, nada, nil, naught—nothing! The auditors had filed the erroneous report because Stern had shown them a record of a series of sales that had never taken place. The importer, of course, could not hope to pay Ultramares back for the money it had borrowed, so the loan company went after someone who actually had enough money to make up the loss, and that was the accounting firm of Touche, Niven, and Company. The firm argued that the report had been prepared for Stern, and because it had no knowledge that Ultramares would see the report, it could not be liable for negligence to the loan company.

Judge Cardozo ruled that the defendant accounting firm could be liable only if it were in a state of *actual privity* with the plaintiff. Such a state of actual privity would emerge only if a real contract existed between the plaintiff and the defendant. Because no such contract existed, liability for negligence could not emerge from the relationship. Ruling otherwise, Cardozo reasoned, would create an indeterminate class of persons, corporate and otherwise, to which the accounting firm might unexpectedly find itself liable simply because its client decided to share the report with a group of outsiders. It was the *intolerable indeterminacy* of the class that bothered Cardozo, who expressed his misgivings in the following way: "The remedy is narrower where the beneficiaries of the promise are indeterminate or general. Something more must then appear than an intention that the promise shall redound to the benefit of the public or to that of a class of indefinite extension. The promise must be such as to 'bespeak the assumption of a duty to make reparation directly to the individual members of the public if the benefit is lost' (*Moch Co. v. Rensselaer Water Co.*, 247 N. Y. 160, 164; American Law Institute, Restatement of the Law of Contracts, § 145)." [See: *Ultramares Corp. v. Touche*, 255 N.Y. 70, 174 N.E. 441 (1932).]

Source: See: *Ultramares Corp. v. Touche*, 255 N.Y. 70, 174 N.E. 441 (1932).

The Near-Privity Plus or Specifically Foreseen Third-Party Standard Most states have extended this rule even further, holding that accountants are also *liable* to the limited class of third parties that is specifically foreseen (not just actually known but specifically foreseen) when the financial statement is drawn up. Thus, an accountant who prepares a financial statement, knowing that the client intends to show it to some likely investors, would *be liable* to any investor in that same class of specifically foreseen third parties. To recover from the accountant, the investors would have had to rely on the statements and suffer financial loss.

Near-Privity Plus-2 or the Reasonably Foreseeable Third-Party Standard Some courts have become very broad in holding accountants liable to third parties. These jurisdictions have adopted a test that depends on whether the plaintiff in the case was *foreseeable* (not just foreseen but foreseeable) as a possible recipient of the accountant's report. For instance, if it is reasonable for the accountant to foresee that the financial statement would be shown to bankers, suppliers, and potential investors, then the accountant is liable to any of these reasonably foreseeable classes of individuals. This ruling would be true even if the class were not specifically mentioned when the accountant was hired by the client. This version is the widest of the three tests that the courts have adopted for determining the extent of an accountant's liability to third parties in negligence cases. Cardozo would be vindicated (unhappy but vindicated nevertheless) because what these courts have done is create a test that itself creates an indeterminate class of persons, corporate and otherwise, to which the accounting firm might unexpectedly find itself liable, simply because its client decided to share the report with a group of outsiders.

A NEW CLASSIC CASE *Part Two*
Near-Privity and Actually Named Third Parties

Recall that, in Part One of our New Classic Case, the Empire State Carpenters Welfare, Annuity, and Pension Fund, the plaintiff in the suit, invested in Beacon Associates LLC (BA). Soon afterward, BA invested Empire's money in Bernard L. Madoff Investment Securities LLC (BLM). Unhappily, this move turned out to be a serious miscalculation. This lawsuit focuses not on BLM, but on the auditors Friedberg, Smith & Co. P.C. (FSC). As BLM's auditor, FSC released yearly statements on BLM's financial health. These reports confirmed that BLM's "financial statements fairly represented the financial position" of BA and of Empire Funds accounts with BLM. As it happened, this description was incorrect, and BLM was effectively worthless. Unsettled by the scale of their loss, the trustees of Empire sued FSC. The trial court granted a motion to dismiss the claim against FSC, and Empire Funds appealed.

The Second Circuit Court of Appeals focused on two questions, the first of which had to be answered in the affirmative before the case could go forward: "Did FSC owe a duty of due care to Empire Funds?" We, however, were able to see that an even more fundamental question sits at the base of the case, and that question is: "What type of accounting arrangement exists between FSC and Empire?" Or perhaps even more simply, "Is the arrangement between FSC and Empire a type one or a type two accounting arrangement?" The question is easy enough to answer. Because the two firms, FSC and Empire, entered a type two, rather a type one, arrangement, actual privity is nonexistent. In a court that follows the *Ultramares* case, the case would end at this point. In *Ultramares*, Cardozo ruled that the absence of actual privity would mean the auditor owes no duty to the third party. However, this court is just a bit more liberal and deals with the parties under a banner of near-privity. Near-privity can be established in a type two arrangement just so long as (1) the accountant knew that the reports would be shown to a third party, (2) the accountant knew the identity of the third party and that he or she (or it?) would rely on the report, and (3) the accountant's conduct revealed that he or she had knowledge of the third party's reliance. Such was the case here. The court put it this way: "We also agree that Empire has adequately pleaded near-privity between Empire and Friedberg (FSC) with regard to its Beacon investments. The proposed second-amended complaint alleges that Friedberg (FSC) addressed reports directly to Empire, that Friedberg (FSC) was aware that its reports would be used to make investments in Beacon, and that Empire would rely on its reports to do so . . . Cf. *Prudential Ins. Co. of Am. v. Dewey, Ballantine, Bushby, Palmer & Wood*, 80 N.Y.2d 377, 385 (1992)."

Now that we know that near-privity exists (and with near-privity a duty of due care). we can ask if FSC violated its duty of due care to Empire. The court says no. This is because what Empire is asking is not that FSC perform an audit on BA because Empire knows that such an audit exists. Rather Empire is demanding that, in compiling its audit of BA, FSC also request additional information directly from BLM. This is outside the scope of its duties. The court says it this way: "Empire alleges that Friedberg was obliged to obtain additional information from BLMIS [sic] to verify the existence, accuracy, and value of Beacon's BLMIS [sic] investments. Friedberg's obligation, however, was to audit Beacon, not BLMIS [sic]. Empire fails to cite any provision of the Generally Accepted Auditing Standards (GAAS) or Generally Accepted Accounting Principles that would impose such a duty. While Empire is also careful not to allege that Friedberg had a duty to actually audit BLMIS [sic], this contention is at the foundation of its claims." [See: *Delollis v. Friedberg*, 12-1628-cv (Second Circuit 2015).]

Platonic Stabilizing Standard Some state courts have had a difficult time sticking to a single standard and, as a result, have a mixed bag of results with which to examine the auditor–third-party liability issue. Perhaps the most effective way to deal with this dilemma is to use a Platonic Stabilizing Standard that balances the various liability standards and takes into account the individualized nature of each case. Like the ancient Greek philosopher Plato, who saw the middle path of balance and moderation as the way to the good life, those judges who follow the balancing standard attempt to do likewise. Platonic-minded judges who mimic his path would say that the courts should take into consideration the following elements to determine third party liability: (1) how extensive were the investments involved in the case, (b) how foreseeable was the injury that emerged from the conduct under scrutiny, (c) how certain was it that the auditor's behavior led to the injury, (d) how connected was the action of the auditor to the third party's financial injury, and (e) how high was the ethical responsibility of the auditor. Two of the hopes implied by the stabilizing standard are that, by balancing the various factors, a fair and equitable result will emerge and such conduct will be deterred in the future.

Fraud Because fraud involves a deliberate deception, the courts have no difficulty extending protection to a wide class of third parties. Thus, an accountant who prepares a fraudulent financial statement is liable to anyone who can be reasonably foreseen as relying on that statement.

An Accountant's Statutory Liability

Accountants may also be sued for violating statutory laws governing their activities. Such suits can arise under the Securities Act of 1933, the Securities Exchange Act of 1934, and various state laws.

Securities Act of 1933 Under the Securities Act of 1933, the first time a corporation issues stock for sale, it must file a registration statement (see Chapter 28). Such statements are prepared by accountants. The 1933 act allows purchasers who have lost money after buying corporate stock based on misleading or false registration statements to sue the accountants who prepared the statements. To succeed in such a lawsuit, the plaintiff must show that the registration statement included a false or misleading statement about a material matter and that he or she suffered a measurable financial setback as a result of relying on that statement. However, the accountant has a defense in such cases. Usually, if the accountant can show that he or she used due diligence in preparing the report, he or she will escape liability. Due diligence is generally demonstrated by reference to the proper application of GAAS and GAAP standards. However, the accountant will also have to show that he or she committed no additional negligent actions and made no other avoidable mistakes.

Securities Exchange Act of 1934 A second federal law, the Securities Exchange Act of 1934, also contains some provisions that affect accountants. These provisions are designed to prevent the fraudulent filing of various documents with the SEC and the fraudulent manipulation of the securities market. Both acts also contain provisions that impose criminal liability on accountants in some situations.

State Statutes In addition to these federal statutes, most states have enacted similar statutes regulating the activities of accounts as they relate to the sale of stock. State statutes that regulate the sale of stock are frequently referred to as blue sky laws because they are set up to stop the sale of securities that are as empty as several feet of blue sky.

The New Tax Code

One thing that all accountants must know inside and out is the federal tax code. Unfortunately, the tax code is a rapidly moving target that changes constantly, even under normal circumstances. In normal times, the tax code is tweaked and adjusted from time to time, as the courts hear cases, the Internal Revenue Service issues regulations, and Congress passes amendments. However, sometimes the entire code goes through a major overhaul that requires a significant adjustment in how accountants advise their clients, calculate their clients' tax liability, and adhere to the dictates of their own professional code. The new tax code, which finally became reality in 2018, has ushered in the most radical era of adjustment in more than 30 years.

The new code has introduced a novel philosophical orientation toward taxes, in general, and toward the income tax, in particular. The new philosophy of taxation (actually it would be more accurate to label it the "the newly recycled philosophy of taxation") argues that a sound economy is based on keeping more cash in the hands of consumers and more surplus capital gains in the bank accounts of businesses. This financial surplus means that individual consumers have more disposable income to spend on goods and services, which in turn motivates businesses to use their surplus gains to expand and, thus, create more jobs, which leads to more individuals with more cash to further stimulate business growth, and so on.

Moreover, the more money spent by private businesses and private citizens, the less money spent by the government on welfare, unemployment compensation, and other support programs, which leads to more spending on essential projects, such as rebuilding the infrastructure, which also leads to the creation of more private-sector jobs, and hopefully, further tax cuts. At that point, the cycle repeats itself. The ultimate goal of the cycle is to create a self-sufficient economy that depends less and less on governmental support and more on private enterprise, thus freeing the government to do what it does best—that is, to govern least.

With these factors in mind here are some of the changes that accountants must be aware of as the new code unfolds.

1. One of the key changes in the new tax code is an overhaul of the tax brackets for all levels of income. The highest bracket is now 37 percent, down from 39.6 percent, while the lowest has moved down to 10 percent. These changes apply from 2018 to 2025.
2. Personal exemptions have also been altered. In fact, all personal exemptions have been removed from the tax system. Traditionally, personal exemptions included dependent children and relatives.
3. One of the most debated changes will limit state and local tax deductions to $10,000 annually for combined state and local property taxes or state and local income taxes.
4. Home mortgage interest payments on new mortgages will now be limited to $750,000 (the limit used to be $1,000,000). In addition, the deductibility of interest payments on home equity loans has been eliminated.
5. On the other hand, for single individuals, the standard deduction has been raised from $6,000 to $12,000 and for joint filers from $12,000 to $24,000.
6. Also, cash donations to charities will now be deductible up to 60 percent of adjusted gross income (AGI).
7. Still, some miscellaneous itemized deductions will be eliminated, including the popular business expenses deduction.
8. Also eliminated are investment management fees and fees for tax return preparation.
9. On the other hand, for 2017 and 2018, the starting point for deductions for medical expenses goes back to 7.5 percent of AGI, which was the starting point before the Affordable Care Act changed things.
10. Finally, partnerships, limited liability companies, Chapter S corporations, and sole proprietorships can now claim a deduction of 20 percent on earnings. Still, there are some limitations on this last figure.

Naturally, this list is neither exhaustive nor permanent. While those alterations in the tax code that affect businesses will not change in the future, those alterations under the new code that apply only to individuals have a life expectancy of 2018 to 2025, unless Congress acts to modify them before the deadline. [See: Ken Barry, "2018 Tax Reform Law: New Tax Brackets, Credits, and Deductions," *CPA Practice Advisor*, December 22, 2017, http://www.cpapracticedvisor.com/news/12388205/2018-tax-reform-law-new-tax-brackets-credits-and-deductions; and Robert Powell, "Highlights of New Tax Law That Kick in for 2018," *The Street*, December 21, 2017, https://www.thestreet.com/story/14427666/1/highlights-of-new-tax-law-that-kick-in-for-2018.html.]

Financial Advisors and the Fiduciary Rule

Another radical change facing the financial industry is the alteration of the fiduciary rule. To understand the significance of this change, it is necessary to first understand the role of the financial advisor. **Financial advisors** are professionals who counsel clients on the handling of their financial lives. Financial advisors are highly educated individuals who go through a rigorous training process that, when completed successfully, leads to certification. A certified financial advisor is authorized to create financial plans for clients, to recommend investment strategies, and to offer advice on savings opportunities. The profession is monitored by a number of agencies including, especially, the Financial Industry Regulatory Authority (FINRA), which regulates the activities of brokerage firms. The Securities and Exchange Commission (SEC) also regulates financial advisors under the Investment

Advisors Act, which first codified the fiduciary rule in 1940. Simply stated, the **fiduciary rule** holds that registered investment advisors—that is, investment advisors who are registered with the SEC under the 1940 act—must place their clients' best interests above their own. The fiduciary rule was later reestablished under the Employee Retirement Income Security Act of 1974 (ERISA) and remains in effect today.

As we saw earlier, in the wake of the financial crisis of 2008, Congress engaged in a crusade aimed at increasing the government's control of the financial industry. One result of this crusade was the the Dodd-Frank Act which set up the Office of Investor Advocate (OIA), an agency designed to increase the transparency of the work done by broker-dealers and investment advisors. The act also empowered the SEC to expand the coverage of the fiduciary rule, a mandate the SEC failed to carry out. Subsequently, the Obama-led Department of Labor assumed that task and, under the authority of the Employee Retirement Income Security Act of 1974, greatly expanded those professionals who must abide by the fiduciary rule. Under this mandate, the "new" fiduciary rule declares that all financial professionals who work on retirement plans must put their clients' best interests above their own. While registered investment advisors were already following this rule, other financial professionals, such as insurance agents and brokers working only on a commission basis, were not. Instead, they had been operating under the less stringent suitability rule. The **suitability rule** requires only that such advisors offer investment counseling that is *suitable* to their clients' goals and nothing more. Under the expanded fiduciary rule, all financial professionals who offer investment advice to their clients must (1) avoid all conflicts of interest that might exist in the relationship; (2) guarantee that all fees are communicated to the client in understandable terms; (3) make certain that all information given to clients is correct, complete, and clear; and (4) offer investment advice that is suitable to their clients' goals.

As with any change, the application of an expanded fiduciary rule results in both an upside and a downside. The upside is that clients will be better informed on all aspects of their investments. Moreover, those advisors who were once guided only by the suitability rule will now be compelled to look out for their clients' best interests under the fiduciary rule. In many cases, this will mean that they cannot simply recommend those investment opportunities that come with the highest commissions. On the downside, the expanded rule may drive advisors who were used to the suitability rule out of business because they will be unable to deal with the compliance requirements attached to the fiduciary rule. This is, in fact, what happened when the UK initiated a similar rule. Since the enactment of the new rule, the UK has lost 22.5 percent of its financial advisors. [See: Brian Menickella, "DOL Fiduciary Rule Implementation Finally in Sight," *Forbes*, June 8, 2017), https://www.forbes.com/sites/brian menickella/2017/06/08/dol-fiduciary-rule-implementation-finally-in-sight/2/#f9d981540cf9; and Matthew Frankel, "The Fiduciary Rule: Pros and Cons, Here's What the Fiduciary Rule Means and Why Many People Are Opposed to It," *The Motley Fool*, February 3, 2017, https://www.fool.com/retirement/2017/02/03/the-fiduciary-rule-pros-and-cons.aspx.]

quick quiz 32-1

1. An accountant is a professional who can plan, direct, and evaluate a client's financial affairs.   true | false

2. An auditor's report and the accompanying financial statements will always guarantee an institution's financial health.   true | false

3. Whenever certified public accountants ignore the rules established by GAAS and GAAP, they do so with little or no risk because of their certified status.   true | false

32-2 The Liability of Architects and Attorneys

In addition to accountants, two other frequently contracted business professionals are architects and attorneys. Both are regulated by the states, and both must follow certain clearly stated duties.

The Liability of Architects

An architect is a professional who plans the construction or alteration of a variety of structures, from small, single-family dwellings to enormous skyscrapers. Generally, architects do not actually construct the building. However, they may manage the construction according to their detailed plans.

State Regulation Under its police power, the state can regulate the conduct of architects. States often establish an agency that makes the rules that architects must follow to be officially recognized as professionals in their field of expertise. The state will usually establish age, character, education, experience, and testing requirements. Often a state will maintain a list of all architects officially registered as having met all of these legal requirements.

Duties of the Architect Like any other professional, an architect owes a duty to exercise due care and skill in carrying out professional duties. This standard of care requires the architect to use the same methods, techniques, and procedures that any architect of ordinary skill would use in a similar situation. The standard does not demand that the architect's design be perfect or that the execution of the design be faultless. Architects can make mistakes, as long as those mistakes do not result from a failure to use appropriate skill and good judgment according to accepted professional standards.

Contractual Liability Sometimes the final version of a building differs from the original plan at the time the contract was made. If the deviation is actually an error caused by the architect's failure to use due care and skill, the architect may have to reimburse the client for any extra money spent to correct the error. This requirement is known as the **cost of repair rule**. A different rule is followed if the design is so defective that the structure is unusable for its originally intended purpose. In such situations, the court may declare that the architect owes the client the difference between the market value of the building as it stands and the market value of the intended structure.

Tort Liability Unlike mistakes made by accountants, errors made by architects may injure people or damage property. If the architect has failed to exercise the appropriate standard of care and if, as a result, property is damaged or people are injured, the architect may have to compensate the victims. Note, however, that the architect's mistake must cause injury or damage.

EXAMPLE 32-2: The Ironic Puzzle of Causation

Architects Lefkowitz and Rudman were hired to plan the new convention center to be located in Las Vegas. Rudman failed to check the stress specs on a balcony on the second level of the convention center's main exhibition floor. Had he made the check, his inspection would have revealed that an error had been made that could cause the balcony to collapse under its own weight. The construction firm of McMahon-Fulton Inc. ignored the Lefkowitz-Rudman specs and used their own plans. However, the McMahon-Fulton plan contained the same error that the architects' plan had contained. On the night that the convention center opened, the balcony suffered a partial collapse that injured several people. Because the contractor had ignored the Lefkowitz-Rudman plan, the architects were not held liable, despite their error.

The Liability of Attorneys

Next to the accountant, one of the most sought-after professionals by a businessperson is the attorney. An attorney is a professional because of expert knowledge, ability, and education in finding, understanding, interpreting, and applying the law. Attorneys advise their clients in a variety of different ways, all of which require good faith, loyalty, and the exercise of due care.

State Regulation of Attorneys Like accountants and architects, attorneys are regulated by the state's police power. Also like accountants and architects, attorneys are normally required to be of a certain age (usually 18) and of good moral character. They are required to possess a certain educational background and to pass a special examination, demonstrating minimum competency. Unlike architects and accountants, attorneys often do not have any experience requirements, because architects and accountants usually are required to have only a bachelor's degree, whereas attorneys obtain an advanced degree in law. This extra education often takes three to four years beyond the bachelor's degree. The experience requirement of architects and accountants frequently amounts to two years.

Ethical Rules of Attorneys The American Bar Association has established a set of ethical standards—the ABA Model Rules of Professional Conduct. The new Model Rules of Professional Conduct have simplified the old rules by dividing professional responsibility into seven areas. These areas include the client-lawyer relationship, the lawyer's duty as a counselor, the lawyer's responsibilities as an advocate, the lawyer's obligations to third parties, the responsibilities of lawyers to one another in law firms and in partnerships, the lawyer's duty to perform public service, and the lawyer's responsibilities in relation to the legal profession. Many people misunderstand the role the ABA and other similar nongovernmental institutions (NGOs). Such nongovernmental bodies are often seen as advisory organizations with the power to suggest rules and regulations, but with no binding authority over their membership. This is not the case. In the case of the ABA, for instance, once the Model Rules have been adopted by a state, those rules carry the full governmental authority of that state. Moreover, the idea that NGOs are essentially powerless, seriously underestimates the authority held by such bodies as the following case explains.

THE OPENING CASE Round 2
Cultural Engineering by Professional Organizations: Social Benefit or Constitutional Nightmare?

In the Opening Case, we learned that the American Bar Association has added a new responsibility to the list of duties placed on the shoulders of the legal profession. Prior to the addition of ABA Model Rule 8.4 (g), lawyers had several key professional responsibilities, including being dutiful and loyal to clients, acting with due care and in good faith, upholding the integrity of the legal system, and ensuring that the system, as a whole, runs well. After the addition of Rule 8.4 (g), the profession has assumed a new role, that of cultural guardian. Some lawyers hail the new rule as a long overdue recognition that the legal profession must promote new cultural norms not only in the workplace, but also in all social settings. Others, however, have characterized the move as a dangerous attempt by the ABA to suppress free speech, threaten freedom of religion, and mount a self-righteous campaign designed to redefine social values, all in the name of a fluctuating standard called political correctness.

Model Rule 8.4 (g) reads like this: "It is professional misconduct for a lawyer to . . . engage in conduct that the lawyer knows or reasonably should know is harassment or discrimination on the basis of race, sex, religion, national origin, ethnicity, disability, age, sexual orientation, gender identity, marital status or socioeconomic status in conduct related to the practice of law." With the addition of Rule 8.4 (g), the ABA has made no secret of the fact that it now expects its members to be vanguards of the political correctness fad. In defending the new rule, the ABA has argued, "There is a need for *a cultural shift in understanding* the inherent integrity of people regardless of their race, color, national origin, religion, age, sex, gender identity, gender expression, sexual orientation, marital status, or disability, to be captured in the rules of professional conduct." [See: ABA Standing Committee on Ethics and Professional Responsibility, Memorandum: Draft Proposal to Amend Model Rule 8.4, 2 (December 22, 2015) (italics added).]

Now this seems harmless enough on the surface. The ABA is, after all, simply a monitoring body that suggests, rather than legislates, professional activities within the legal community. Thus, those who acknowledge the ABA's role as the conscience of the legal profession see the new rule as nothing more than a gentle nudge toward politically correct behavior. But is it really that simple? Opponents of the rule think otherwise. They argue, with great conviction, that the ABA is not simply a benevolent coach but is, instead, a quasi-governmental body, capable of making rules that can lead to sanctions against lawyers up to and including disbarment. Consider the following: When the model rules are published by the ABA, virtually every state in the union codifies those rules so that they become binding on members of the profession. Also, every law school that wants to earn and maintain accreditation must follow the dictates of the ABA. Moreover, this power to grant accreditation is bestowed on the ABA by the state governments. In addition, as part of this government-empowered accrediting process, law schools are required to have students study the ABA rules and to pass the ABA engineered Multistate Professional Responsibility Examination (MPRE), which will soon include Rule 8.4 (g). Opponents of Rule 8.4 (g) point out that, in effect, these practices have transformed the ABA into a quasi-governmental body that must be held to the constitutional duty to guard against violations of freedom of speech and freedom of religion. Yet, Rule 8.4 (g) does precisely the opposite. In reality, it threatens both free speech and freedom of religion.

Much of this relates to the fact that the ABA has attempted to extend its control beyond the court room into the social and personal lives of attorneys. The ABA Standing Committee on Ethics and Professional Responsibility has explained the scope of Rule 8.4 (g) in the following way: "Conduct related to the practice of law includes representing clients; interacting with witnesses, coworkers, court personnel, lawyers and others while engaged in the practice of law; operating or managing a law firm or law practice; and *participating in bar association, business or social activities in connection with the practice of law.*" [See: American Bar Association, Standing Committee on Ethics and Responsibility, Report to the House of Delegates, Revised Resolution 109, August 8, 2016 (italics added).] By reaching into social settings, the ABA has attempted to regulate both speech and religious expression beyond the scope of its responsibility and its competency, and that is bad news for attorneys everywhere.

Consider the following. During a lunch break at a continuing education session on the *Obergefell* case, a lawyer expresses her religious belief that marriage should be limited to the traditional man–woman model. By making this statement, she has violated Rule 8.4 (g). Why? This is true because the ABA has expressly supported the need to follow the "*cultural shift in understanding*" toward the approval of same-sex marriage. As a result, to support traditional marriage is to discriminate on the basis of "*sexual orientation, gender identity, (and) marital status.*" Now let's consider the opposite. Let's suppose that another lawyer at the same session voices a preference for recognizing same-sex marriage. In contrast, these words do not violate the Rule 8.4 (5). Because these two statements seem to be qualitatively equal, this requires some explanation. While support for same-sex marriage follows the American Bar Association's call for a *"cultural shift in understanding,"* supporting traditional marriage runs counter to that *cultural shift* and so, by supporting traditional marriage, the first lawyer has shown herself to be opposed to the ABA's approved culture shift and is, therefore, guilty of discriminating on the basis of "*sexual orientation, gender identity, (and) marital status.*"

Nor is this a simple case of splitting interpretive hairs. In the real world, once a state legislature has adopted the ABA Rules, the courts will use those rules in malpractice lawsuits and in disciplinary actions against lawyers. Let's try two additional hypotheticals. What if a law firm refuses to take on a male client in a divorce case because the all female staff has decided to represent only women in divorce cases? Would this violate the part of Rule 8.4 (g) that says, "It is professional misconduct for a lawyer to . . . engage in conduct that the lawyer knows or reasonably should know is . . . discrimination on the basis of . . . sex?" Similarly, what would happen if, during a meeting on the new tax law, a lawyer argues that the new tax law gives far too many benefits to the rich and that, on that basis alone, their firm should no longer represent any client who makes over $100,000 per year. Would this violate that part of Rule 8.4 (g) that says quite clearly, "It is professional misconduct for a lawyer to . . . engage in conduct that the lawyer knows or reasonably should know is . . . discrimination on the basis of . . . socioeconomic status"? In both cases, the answer is "no" because discrimination against men and discrimination against the rich is not part of the cultural shift that the ABA supports. On the other hand, avoiding discrimination against women and against the poor would be part of that shift and so, if a law firm decides not to represent women clients or a law firm decides to no longer represent poor clients, those firms would both be in violation Rule 8.4 (g) because both types of discrimination are part of the ABA's supported cultural shift.

The fatal flaw in all of these examples is that cultural shifts do just that—they shift. Next time, the culture may shift against women, or Lithuanians, or Catholics, or Californians, or bald people. As a result, without a totally objective, balanced standard that defies cultural whims, injustice will follow. So what can be done about it? The good news is that, in this case at least, once codified, ABA Model Rule 8.4 (g) is subject to a constitutional challenge under the First Amendment. The challenge would work like this. If Model Rule 8.4 (g) is to stand up to a constitutional challenge, it must pass the strict scrutiny test. Under the strict scrutiny standard, the government is forbidden to create statutes, regulations, and other mandates [e.g., Model Rule 8.4 (g)] that place an undue burden on free speech and/or the practice of religion, unless (1) there is a compelling governmental purpose for doing so and

(2) the action contemplated is the least restrictive way to accomplish that compelling purpose. So assuming that the Model Rule 8.4 (g) places an undue burden on both free speech and freedom of religious expression, it will fail the strict scrutiny test and will, thus, violate the First Amendment only if (1) it does not fulfill a compelling state interest or (2) if its does promote such an interest, it fails to do so in the least restrictive way possible. Think about it. [See: Ronald Rotunda, "The ABA Decision to Control What Lawyers Say: Supporting 'Diversity' But Not Diversity of Thought," *The Heritage Society*, October 6, 2016, https://www.heritage.org/report/the-aba-decision-control-what-lawyers-say-supporting-diversity-not-diversity-thought; David Hudson Jr, "States Split on New ABA Model Rule Limiting Harassing or Discriminatory Conduct," *ABA Journal*, October 2017, http://www.abajournal.com/magazine/article/ethics_model_rule_harassing_conduct; and ABA Standing Committee on Ethics and Professional Responsibility, Memorandum: Draft Proposal to Amend Model Rule 8.4, 2 (December 22, 2015) (emphasis added)].

Source: See: Ronald Rotunda, "The ABA Decision to Control What Lawyers Say: Supporting 'Diversity' But Not Diversity of Thought," *The Heritage Society*, (October 6, 2016) https://www.heritage.org/ report/the-aba-decision-control-what-lawyers-say-supporting-diversity-not-diversity-thought; David Hudson, Jr, "States split on new ABA Model rule limiting harassing or discriminatory conduct," *ABA Journal* (October 2017) http://www.abajournal.com/ magazine/ article/ethics_model_rule_ harassing_c onduct; ABA Standing Comm. on Ethics and Professional Responsibility, *Memorandum: Draft Proposal to Amend Model Rule 8.4, 2* (Dec. 22, 2015) (emphasis added)

Ethical Problems in Dodd–Frank One the most hotly debated provisions in the Dodd–Frank Act is Subtitle B of Title IX, which permits the SEC to develop regulations that will create a "whistleblowing bounty program" analogous to the one used by the IRS.

A QUESTION OF ETHICS

Indeterminacy from Another Angle

In his essay, "The Chaotic Indeterminacy of Tort Law: Between Formalism and Nihilism," Denis J. Brion, professor of law at Washington and Lee University School of Law, explains that two very distinct interpretations of the law have existed side by side for a number of years. He calls one of these two theories *formalism* and the other *nihilism*. Brion explains the two theories in the following way:

> In "Legal Formalism: On the Immanent Rationality of Law," Ernest Weinrib offers . . . the idea that the law can be accurately described in terms of . . . its "inner coherence." He argues that the law is altogether distinct from politics and that it can only be understood from within itself. The function of judges is to "make transactions and distributions" in the social world conform to the "latent unity" of the law. The function of legal scholars is to make explicit the internal coherence and intelligibility of the law. In *The Disorder of Law: A Critique of Legal Theory*, Charles Sampford sets out to criticize the various theories of law that seek to describe it as systematic. His principal thesis is that society itself is without system—his term is the "social melee"—and that the law, as an integral part of society, is correspondingly disordered—the "legal melee." He concludes that, because of this disorder, the impact of legal doctrine on social and individual practices is strongly attenuated.

A third alternative is offered by Lawrence Friedman in his treatise *Law in America*. The law, Friedman says, is not a separate autonomous system. Rather, the law "is, essentially, a product of society; and as society changes, so does its legal system. Feudal societies have feudal legal systems; socialist societies have socialist systems; tribal societies have tribal systems; capitalist societies have capitalist legal systems. How could it be otherwise?"

Of course, the German philosopher, Max Weber, would disagree with all three of these experts. Weber offers a fourth alternative in his essay, "Politics as a Vocation." in that essay, Weber argues that the type of legal system that a nation-state develops is based on the type of authority that shapes the government of that nation-state. Bureaucratic governments produce a rational system of hierarchical rules that are developed by a legislative process. The rules are written down and those rules bind everyone, even the leader. Patriarchal government are run by personal leaders who command authority by following traditional practices. There is no need to create new law because the law has existed from the very beginning of that socio-political system and must not be changed. In fact, changes in tradition may be grounds for revolution. Finally, governments led by charismatic leaders develop legal systems that emerge from the unique qualifications (and, mystical powers) of the leader and are developed on a case-by-case basis. So charismatic law is always changing.

QUESTIONS YET UNANSWERED

The following questions have not yet been answered. Before you consider each question, turn to Chapter 1 to review the various ethical theories noted there (market value ethics, social contract theory, utilitarianism, and rational ethics). Then in a consistent way, answer the following questions.

1. Of the four theorists, which one has the more ethical view of the legal system? Explain.
2. Which view supports the idea that the judicial-economic system is a balancing act that aims at creating a flexible and responsive system? Explain.
3. Which view is supported by the evidence in this chapter concerning the regulation of the legal profession? Explain.
4. Of the four theorists, which one reflects your own personal view? Explain.
5. Of the four views, which one best explains the need for laws such as Sarbanes-Oxley and Dodd-Frank? Explain.

Whistleblowers, or SEC "bounty hunters" as they are sometimes called, must qualify for their "bounty" by providing original evidence of a securities law violation. This is not always easy. Nevertheless, bounty hunters can be a very determined group because successful hunters can earn 10 to 30 percent of a penalty over $1 million. Unfortunately, for attorneys, there are ethical problems associated with bounty hunting. If an in-house counsel discovers evidence of an in-house securities violation, and if the SEC rules demand that bounty hunters circumvent internal remedies, then the attorney has an ethical choice to make. Does the attorney remain loyal to the client and not report the violation or does the attorney help the SEC and the public by reporting the violation according to "the new whistleblower rule system"? The answer should be obvious. Client loyalty always comes before any other loyalty. However, the whistleblowing system places an enormous temptation in the path of the unsuspecting attorney. It will be interesting to see how this all plays out in the future [See: David Ingram, "SEC Weighing How to Award Tipsters," *The National Law Journal*, May 16, 2011, pp. 1, 4.]

Negligence/Malpractice An attorney has the duty to represent clients with good faith, loyalty, and due care. An attorney who does not fulfill these duties may be liable for malpractice. Usually, however, an attorney is not liable to a third party who is not a client.

Duties of the Attorney When a client hires an attorney, the client has the right to expect the attorney to act in *good faith*, which means that the attorney's duty is to act in the best interests of the client. In the absence of such good faith conduct, the attorney may face a lawsuit brought by the client and disciplinary action brought by the state. An attorney also has a duty of *loyalty* to protect the client, the client's case, and to make certain that the client receives advice and representation that is free of conflicting interests. Thus, an attorney cannot represent two clients on opposite sides of the same dispute, unless both sides have been completely informed of the dual representation and consent to it. Similarly, an attorney violates the duty of loyalty if he or she takes advantage of a client for personal profit. The duty of loyalty also gives rise to certain privileges that exist between clients and their attorneys. One of the most fundamental privileges is the **attorney–client privilege**. The attorney–client privilege guarantees that information that passes between clients and their attorneys will remain secret. The rationale that supports the attorney–client privilege is the belief that clients must feel free to tell their attorneys everything that is involved in a case so that the attorney can do his or her best as an advocate of that client. The privilege can be waived if a third party unrelated to the client is present during a discussion with the attorney, provided that third party is not a person involved in the case, such as another attorney in the firm, a paralegal, or a legal assistant.

Closely related to attorney–client privilege is the **work product privilege**. The work product privilege protects all notes, recordings, research documents, Q&As, voice mails, faxes, e-mails, computer records, memos, letters, flash drives, disks, DVDs, CDs, and so on that are prepared in anticipation of litigation. So, for instance, if an attorney interviews a client about the facts in a pending lawsuit and takes notes during that interview, those notes are protected by the work product privilege. Or if a client sends an e-mail to his or her attorney after an interview, saying something like, "Oh, by the way, when we talked yesterday, I forgot to tell you this or that about the lawsuit," that e-mail is also protected by the work product privilege. Like the attorney–client privilege, the work product privilege can be waived if the work product is revealed to a third party not related to the client or not involved in the preparation of the client's case. Moreover, the work product privilege is not an absolute privilege. This distinction means that the content of the work product may have to be disclosed if a party who needs the information wrapped up in that work product can convince a judge that he or she has a substantial need for that information and cannot obtain that information some other, more legitimate, less intrusive way.

Like all other professionals, an attorney owes a duty of *due care* to clients. This duty means that in giving legal advice, negotiating claims, litigating suits, making out wills, negotiating divorce settlements, and performing any number of other legal tasks, an attorney must exercise the same skill and care that would be expected of other attorneys in the same situation.

Steps in a Legal Malpractice Case

For a plaintiff to succeed in a malpractice case against an attorney, that plaintiff must demonstrate the existence of four specifically drawn elements. First, the plaintiff must show that the attorney owed a duty to that plaintiff. Generally, this proof is not a problem, because when the client consults the attorney, a contract is created by which the attorney assumes the duty to represent that client with the appropriate level of care. The question of duty can arise, however, when there is a factual discrepancy about whether the client actually hired the attorney to represent him or her. Thus, the duty clearly arises when the client comes to the attorney's office and asks the attorney to help him or her deal with a legal problem. In contrast, if a student were to ask a law professor a hypothetical question during a class discussion, then no duty has arisen because there is no client-attorney relationship created in such a situation.

A THIRD CLASSIC CASE
Unconstitutional or Unethical: *State of Florida, et al. v. U.S. Department of Health and Human Services*

Almost immediately after the Patient Protection and Affordable Care Act became law, the attorney general (AG) of Florida, joined by AGs from 12 other states, filed a lawsuit asking the courts to declare the act unconstitutional. In essence, the AGs claimed that the law was an unconstitutional extension of federal power that violated the commerce clause, the 10th Amendment, and Article I, Sections 2 and 9, of the Constitution. Probably the most effective argument said that penalizing someone for inactivity (not having health insurance) could not be used to support a congressional invasion of the states. This might have been the end of it had it not been for the fact some experts began to suspect the AGs had no legal justification for bringing the lawsuit. Some experts even argued that the AGs should be made to pay for the cost of the lawsuit out of their own pockets and perhaps even be disbarred because they had violated Rule 11 of the Federal Rules of Civil Procedure. Rule 11 demands that an attorney certify that, in any lawsuit filed in federal court, the "claims, defenses, and other legal contentions are warranted by existing law." The claims brought in this case were not only unwarranted but also patently false, or so the argument goes.

For one thing, the AGs had grossly misstated the law and had no evidence to support their factual contentions. The new law would not eliminate Medicare in noncomplying states, as the AGs contended; it would not require states to create an agency to help insurance consumers as the AGs said; and it would not impose a financial burden on the states, as the AGs argued, but would, instead, result in a huge savings for some states due to new federal money flowing into those states. Moreover, and perhaps more to the point, the very filing of the lawsuit was an illegal exercise of state power since, as long ago as 1923, the Supreme Court ruled in *Massachusetts v. Mellon* (262 U.S. 447), that the states have no standing to attack federal statutes on constitutional grounds.

The consequences of this lawsuit went beyond the declaratory action requested by the AGs. It could have cost a fortune in taxpayers' money to argue the case, it could have delayed the law's implementation, and it could have eliminated many needed programs that would disappear along with any truly unconstitutional parts (if there really are any). On the other hand, despite these weighty and troubling accusations, it does appear that, under the new Model Rules of Professional Conduct, the AGs actually faced an authentic ethical dilemma in this case and others like it. The Ohio version of the model rules, for instance, demands that an attorney act as an advocate for his or her clients and, at the same time, "advance the administration of justice." When lawyers become the attorneys general of their states, their duty to their constituents comes first. They appear to owe a transcendent duty to the public in the home state and to the state itself. This direct and indisputable duty comes first. This may mean that the AGs must even challenge the authority of the federal government. After all, if they do not challenge the feds, who will? [See: *State of Florida, et al. v. U.S. Department of Health and Human Services*, 3:10-CV-91 RV/EMT; Timothy Stoltzfus Jost, "Sanction the 18 State AGs," *The National Law Journal*, April 12, 2010; and "Preamble: A Lawyers Responsibilities," *Ohio Rules of Professional Conduct* (Columbus: Ohio Bar Liability Insurance Company, 2010), p. 1.]

Source: See: *State of Florida, et al. v. U.S. Department of Health and Human Services*, 3:10-CV-91 RV/EMT; Timothy Stoltzfus Jost, "Sanction the 18 State AGs," *The National Law Journal*, April 12, 2010; "Preamble: A Lawyers Responsibilities," *Ohio Rules of Professional Conduct* (Columbus: Ohio Bar Liability Insurance Company, 2010), p. 1.

Second, the attorney must have breached the duty that is owed to the client. The attorney's duty is measured by his or her compliance with a standard that holds that an attorney must represent a client in a way that demonstrates enthusiasm and dedication to the client's best interests. The attorney cannot, however, file claims or advance arguments that have no realistic chance of succeeding or that are not firmly grounded in acceptable legal principles. The attorney must act as a reasonable professional would in the same circumstances. This standard does not mean that attorneys are not permitted to make mistakes. On the contrary, mistakes are tolerated as an inevitable part of the legal profession, just as long as they do not result from carelessness, inattention, laziness, or ignorance. Third, the plaintiff must show that the attorney's questionable behavior caused the resulting harm to the plaintiff. Moreover, it is not enough that there is a factual connection between the behavior and the injury. There must also be a legal connection between the two. Such a legal connection requires foreseeability. Fourth, the plaintiff must show that he or she suffered actual harm as a result of the attorney's breach of duty.

Because attorneys are professionals and because the intricacies of the law are often mystifying to the layperson, the law requires that the elements of malpractice must be supported by expert testimony. Expert testimony can only be overlooked when the relationship between the injury suffered by the client and the behavior by the attorney is so obvious that the experience of the plaintiff is within the everyday experience of the jury. As we shall see, a very similar—in fact, an almost identical—standard is used to guide the question of whether expert testimony is needed in the case of malpractice claims that are filed against health care professionals.

Third-Party Liability In contrast to accountants and architects, attorneys are rarely held liable to third parties because the attorney's responsibilities are tied closely to the interests of the client. On the other hand, this does not mean that an attorney can be disrespectful, cruel, or vindictive to a third party. In fact, in one instance, the Ohio version of the Model Rules of Professional Conduct state quite specifically that an attorney cannot, "embarrass, harass, delay, or burden a third person." The rules also stipulate that an attorney cannot with knowledge "make a false statement of material fact or law to a third person." [See: "Rule 4.1 Truthfulness in Statements to Others" and "Rule 4.4 Respect for Rights of Third Persons," *Ohio Rules of Professional Conduct* (Columbus: Ohio Bar Liability Insurance Company, 2010), pp. 133, 139.]

Court-Driven Protection As we've seen, attorneys who are negligent can be the target of a civil suit brought by a wronged client. There are other safeguards within the legal system, however, that are designed to make certain that attorneys do not file phony lawsuits, promote unwarranted legal arguments, conduct unnecessary investigations, file unjustifiable motions, or make allegations that lack evidentiary support. The Federal Rules of Civil Procedure, for example, specifically forbid such objectionable conduct and impose severe penalties should that rule be broken. Many states have similar civil rules that are designed to deter unprofessional conduct on the part of unscrupulous attorneys. Penalties can include a payment of money to the court or to the other party. These payments may even include attorneys' fees in appropriate cases.

Criminal Liability Attorneys are not immune to criminal liability, especially when they act in collusion with their clients. Fortunately, most of the time, attorneys know what is going on within the attorney–client relationship because they are responsible for most, if not all, of the legal decisions made in that relationship. Sometimes, however, an attorney, especially an in-house attorney, might not know everything about a transaction that he or she is handling for a client. An **in-house attorney** is one who is part of the officer corps of a business and, as an employee of that business, does what he or she is told to do by his or her supervisor. Therefore, the attorney might know very little about the details behind a particular deal.

Thus, the attorney might draft a contract between a manufacturer and a retailer that appears legitimate but involves a series of unrecorded kickbacks about which the attorney knows nothing. Or an attorney might transcribe the details of a contract that involves a stock transaction based on insider trading without knowing anything about that insider's involvement in the deal. In the past, prosecuting attorneys were willing to give attorneys the benefit of the doubt. Today, however, such favoritism is fast becoming a thing of the past. In the current climate, prosecutors are less likely to be forgiving when an attorney should have known better about a suspicious contract or should have asked certain crucial questions that remained unspoken.

> **quick quiz 32-2**
>
> 1. When an architect's plan is so defective that the structure he or she has designed is unusable, the courts will invoke the cost of repair rule.   true | false
> 2. For a plaintiff to fail in a malpractice case against an attorney, that attorney must disprove the existence of all four elements of malpractice.   true | false
> 3. Because attorneys are professionals and because the intricacies of the law are often mystifying to the layperson, the law requires that the elements of malpractice be supported by expert testimony.   true | false

32-3 The Liability of Health Care Providers

Health care providers are professionals who possess the specialized knowledge, abilities, education, and experience that make it possible for them to answer some aspect of a patient's health care needs. Some businesspeople must deal with health care providers on a daily basis. Such contact is routine for hospital administrators, risk-management experts, pharmaceutical salespeople, hospital accountants, insurance adjusters, and biomedical equipment salespeople. Even individuals who do not deal regularly with health care providers in the business world may one day have to deal with them as patients. Knowledge of the liability of such professionals may be helpful in these situations.

The Professional Status of Health Care Providers

It should be obvious that physicians are professionals because they must possess the specialized knowledge, abilities, education, and experience needed to perform their jobs. Dentists, podiatrists, chiropractors, nurses, nurse practitioners, nurse technicians, radiologic technologists, respiratory therapists, and laboratory technicians are also considered health care professionals. All these professions are regulated by the state. In addition, most are regulated by independent professional organizations such as the American Society of Clinical Pathologists.

The Health Care Standard of Care

Unlike accountants, architects, and attorneys, health care professionals frequently must physically touch their patients. This physical touching can involve routine tests and examinations, as well as dangerous and painful procedures. To avoid liability for the intentional tort of battery, health care providers frequently must obtain the patient's written consent. In addition to intentional torts, health care providers might be vulnerable to charges of negligence if they do not follow the appropriate standard of care.

Consent Patients who undergo tests and treatment have the right to know about those procedures and the right to refuse to undergo them if they so desire. These rights impose a duty on the health care professional to seek the patient's consent. Consent takes two forms: general consent and informed consent. Upon entering a hospital, a patient automatically gives **general consent** for the routine tests and procedures that are needed for diagnosis and treatment. Although such consent is implied in the situation, many hospitals require patients to sign general consent forms (see Figure 32-1).

When a diagnostic test or a procedure will be dangerous or painful, the treating physician must obtain the patient's **informed consent**. For this type of consent, the physician must tell the patient in advance about the procedure and the risks involved. Informed consent must be in writing on a form that is signed by the patient and witnessed by a third party. Generally, a written consent form is considered valid by the court and precludes any suit based on battery, unless the patient can prove a lack of understanding of the information on the form or a deliberate misrepresentation as to its content.

Negligence For a patient to succeed in a negligence case against a health care professional, the patient must show that the four elements of negligence exist in the case. First, the patient must demonstrate that the health care provider owed a duty to that patient. Usually, the question of duty is not at issue in such cases. However, the question will arise whenever the relationship between the patient and the health care provider is not clear-cut or obvious. In such cases, the court may be asked to determine whether the health care provider owed a duty to the plaintiff.

CONSENT UPON ADMISSION TO HOSPITAL

Patient _____ Date _____ a.m. _____ p.m. _____

(or _____ for _____)
knowing that I, or the patient (am) (is) suffering from an illness requiring hospital care do hereby voluntarily consent to such hospital care requiring an operation, diagnostic tests or therapeutic treatment by Dr. _____ , his/her assistant or his/her designee or as necessary according to his/her judgment.

I also recognize that during the course of my operation, tests, or therapy unforeseen conditions may necessitate additional or different procedures and I am aware that inasmuch as the practice of medicine and surgery is not an exact science, there have been no guarantees made to me as the result of treatments or examinations to be performed in this hospital.

I have read the above statements and I certify that I understand them.

_____   _____
Witness   Signature of Patient

Figure 32-1 Many hospitals today require patients to sign general consent forms like this one upon admission.

Second, after establishing the existence of a duty between the health care provider and the patient, the plaintiff must show that the health care professional breached that duty. The health care professional's duty is measured by his or her compliance with a standard of care. The health care provider must act with the same level of skill, care, and knowledge that any reasonable health care provider would display in a similar situation. Determining how a reasonable health care provider would act in a given situation can be determined in several ways. One way is to refer to the hospital's policy and procedure manual. When professionals follow the standard policies and procedures as written in the manual, they are performing as any reasonable professional would, unless the procedure in the manual can be shown to be out of date, incompetently written, or incomplete in some way.

If a hospital's manual does not address a situation, if the manual is outdated, if the procedure is incompetently written, or if the steps in the procedure are incomplete, the court may judge the performance by going outside the hospital and looking at the manuals or procedures used at other hospitals. Many states today use a rule called the locality rule. The **locality rule** judges a health care provider's behavior on the basis of how other health care professionals in the same community would have acted in the same situation. Thus, rural physicians are compared to other rural physicians in the same rural community, city physicians with other city physicians in the same city, and so on. The rationale behind the locality doctrine is the commonsense notion that it is unfair to judge the professional conduct of a small-town general practitioner (GP) who is involved in a case involving a heart attack victim by comparing him or her to a big city cardiologist involved in a similar case. In such a comparison, the small-town GP will always be judged poorly because he or she will have neither the educational opportunities nor the up-to-date facilities that are available to the big city cardiologist.

Despite the widespread use of the term *locality rule*, there is no single locality doctrine. Instead, there are variations on the same theme. The most rigorous version of the doctrine is the **true locality rule**. The true locality rule requires the court to look at the standard of care used in the exact locality of the physician. This standard makes it very difficult for the plaintiff, who must use an expert witness from the same area as the defendant. Such experts are rarely forthcoming because the fraternity of local physicians is generally a closed group. A second variation on the locality rule is the **similar locality rule**. This rule permits the court to judge the actions of a local physician against those of a physician in a community of comparable size and socioeconomic character. Thus, a physician in New York would be compared to one in Chicago or Los Angeles, a physician in Cleveland with one in Pittsburgh or Buffalo, and a physician in Green Bay, Wisconsin, with one in South Bend, Indiana, or Dayton, Ohio. This rule permits the plaintiff to find an expert in one of those analogous localities an easier task because there are fewer fraternal ties among that class of physicians.

The third version of the locality rule is the **same state locality rule**. This rule, perhaps the least logical of the four variations, ignores the socioeconomic character of the physician's home base and concentrates instead on the geographical limits of a state border. Thus, a plaintiff who finds him- or herself in a state that honors the same state locality rule can call an expert from any region in that state to testify as an expert witness. The final variation of the locality rule is known as the **similar practitioner rule**. This rule actually rests on a double standard that permits GPs to be judged by one criterion and specialists by another. Thus, GPs, who are apparently expected to stay close to home, are judged by other GPs in the same community, whereas specialists, who are expected to be more cosmopolitan and therefore more educated, more up-to-date, and more competent, are judged by a standard that can be applied anywhere in the country.

Those states that no longer use the locality rule have adopted another rule called the **national rule** or the **national standard**. These states have recognized that with the advent of continuing education requirements and the presence of mass communication, online continuing education programs, and the like, there is rarely any good reason for a health care professional to be unaware of the development of medical trends on a national, or, at times, even an international basis.

Causation in a Malpractice Suit A crucial element in any malpractice case is the issue of causation. In such a case, the plaintiff must prove not only that the defendant's conduct did not conform to acceptable medical practices but also that this failure to follow acceptable procedures was the cause of the plaintiff's injury. Much of the difficulty in supplying this proof arises because the fact finder in a malpractice case must attempt to understand medical evidence that is frequently beyond his or her experience.

Expert Testimony Because many of the tasks performed by the health care provider are highly specialized, determining how the professional should act often requires expert testimony. However, expert testimony is not required if the action under examination is within the common knowledge of all people.

EXAMPLE 32-3: Experts Need Not Apply

Nurse Noel Grady was called away from Kurt Yarborough's room by another nurse. Yarborough was sedated but restless. He was thrashing about and had attempted to leave the bed several times. Despite this state, Grady left him alone, failing to raise the siderails or restrain Yarborough in any way. While Grady was absent, Yarborough tried to get out of bed. He fell and broke his leg. At Grady's negligence trial, the judge ruled that no expert testimony was needed to measure Grady's standard of care. The judge felt that the issue of whether a sedated and restless patient should be left unsupervised and unrestrained was well within the common knowledge of the jurors.

Medical Records and the Patient's Rights

In recent years, concerns about privacy matters have come to the forefront of the law. In no area of the law is this truer than in health care law. Physicians once effectively guarded the secrecy of their files by arguing that patients were apt to misinterpret or misunderstand notations made in medical jargon or hospital shorthand. These arguments are no longer acceptable. To ensure the patient's right to see his or her records, Congress passed the **Health Insurance Portability and Accountability Act (HIPAA)**. Under HIPAA, Congress has guaranteed that patients have the right to see their medical records and parents have the right to see the medical records of their children. The act also gives both groups the right to obtain duplicates of the records. There are, of course, exceptions to this rule. For instance, records that result from psychotherapy sessions receive a higher level of protection under the act. Patients are permitted to see such records only if the patient has the physician's permission. Even with permission, the patient must look through the records along with the physician. These extra limitations are placed on psychotherapy records because they are seen as somewhat emotional and open to a wide variety of false impressions.

The Health Insurance Portability and Accountability Act (HIPAA) gives patients the right to review their medical records and the records of their children.
©Ryan McVay/Getty Images

The Patient Protection and Affordable Care Act

Under provisions included in the federal Patient Protection and Affordable Care Act, the Department of Health and Human Services has developed a set of new regulations on a trial basis to help support physicians, hospitals, clinics, and other health care establishments in the creation of a system of coordinated health care institutions for Medicare patients, known as accountable care organizations (ACOs). Under the new rules, an ACO can consist of a variety of formats, including (1) ACO professionals, including physicians and hospitals in group practice arrangements; (2) networks of individual practices of ACO professionals; (3) partnerships or joint ventures between hospitals and ACO professionals; (4) hospitals employing ACO professionals; and (5) other Medicare providers and suppliers as determined by the secretary of health and human services.

The new regulations will measure the quality of an ACO under five criteria: (1) patient and caregiver experience; (2) care coordination; (3) patient safety; (4) preventive health; and (5) the handling of at-risk populations, including the frail and elderly. The ACO program is administered by the Center for Medicare and Medicaid Services (CMMS). Under the new rules, an ACO must have a board of governors with a wide-ranging membership, including representatives of all the people affected by its operation. Specifically, the rules call for a membership that involves health care providers, suppliers, and Medicare beneficiaries. To be properly certified by the CMMS, a new ACO must take responsibility for at least 5,000 beneficiaries for three years.

A THIRD CLASSIC CASE AGAIN
Unconstitutional or Unethical: *State of Florida, et al. v. U.S. Department of Health and Human Service*

Let's look at the Classic Case of *State of Florida, et al. v. U.S. Department of Health and Human Services* one more time. Recall that a lawsuit was filed by the attorney general of Florida along with 12 additional state AGs, all of whom attacked the constitutionality of the Patient Protection and Affordable Care Act. When the case reached the district court, the judge decided that the act was indeed unconstitutional, at least in part. Unfortunately, the judge also ruled that the unconstitutional portions could not be separated from the constitutional ones. Consequently, should one part of the act be lost, the entire act will be lost, including provisions like the one discussed earlier. What would then be the fate of an already established and operating accountable care organization? Explain your answer. [See: *State of Florida, et al. v. U.S. Department of Health and Human Services*, 3:10-CV-91 RV/EMT; and Timothy Stoltzfus Jost, "Sanction the 18 State AGs," *The National Law Journal*, April 12, 2010.]

See: *State of Florida, et al. v. U.S. Department of Health and Human Services*, 3:10-CV-91 RV/EMT; and Timothy Stoltzfus Jost, "Sanction the 18 State AGs," *The National Law Journal*, April 12, 2010.

quick quiz 32-3

1. For a patient to succeed in a negligence case against a health care professional, the patient must show that the four elements of negligence exist in the case.   true | false

2. Today, most courts use a rule called the national rule or the national standard to make judgments in relation to the standard of care for health care providers in negligence cases.   true | false

3. To ensure the patient's right to see his or her records, the American Law Institute and the American Bar Association collaborated to create a model act called the Health Insurance Portability and Accountability Act (HIPAA).   true | false

32-4 The Liability of Hospitals

Hospitals can be held liable for the negligence of a physician, even if that physician is not an employee of the hospital. Hospitals routinely grant physicians, who are not employed by the hospital, the privilege to treat their patients at that hospital. The granting of such **staff privileges** can be troublesome for the hospital if the staff physician becomes the defendant in a malpractice lawsuit because the patient frequently sues not only the physician, but also the hospital. Two legal theories that have been used successfully to add the hospital to the list of defendants in a malpractice lawsuit are ostensible authority and negligent credentialing.

Ostensible Authority and Hospital Liability

Ostensible authority, also known as agency by estoppel and apparent authority, has been successfully used by plaintiffs to hold the hospital, as well as the physician, liable for malpractice. **Ostensible authority** is created when a hospital presents itself to the public at large as a provider of health care services and in some way leads the patient to believe that a physician with staff privileges is an employee of the hospital. This authority can be shown if the hospital allows the physician to wear a hospital identification tag, use hospital equipment, dispense medication at the hospital, issue orders to hospital employees, and so on. Under such circumstances, the courts have been willing to hold that because it is reasonable to believe that these representations would lead the patient to the conclusion that the physician is an employee of the hospital, the patient can add the hospital to the malpractice suit as a defendant.

Negligent Credentialing by Hospital Authorities

Negligent credentialing occurs if the hospital has retained a physician that the governing body of the hospital knew or should have known was incompetent. Another form of negligent credentialing occurs if a previously competent physician with staff privileges loses that competence and the hospital governing body knows or should have known about the changed circumstances but takes no remedial action. This form of negligent credentialing is sometimes referred to as **negligent retention**. In either situation, a patient injured by the malpractice of the incompetent physician can also hold the hospital liable.

Tort Reform and Litigation

In recent years, some states have attempted to lessen the burden placed on hospitals by ostensible authority and negligent credentialing. This movement has been motivated by the belief that such lawsuits frequently pull the hospital into a lawsuit unjustly. To alleviate this injustice, tort reform provisions often place the burden of proof on the plaintiff to prove both ostensible authority and negligent credentialing. For instance, in the area of ostensible authority, some states say that the plaintiff must prove that the hospital held itself out to the public at large as a provider of health care services and that the hospital gave no notice that nonemployee staff physicians, rather than hospital employees, would render services to the patient. Moreover, these statutes also allow the hospital to escape liability by posting notices that inform patients of the independent status of staff physicians. In states that have established such a statutory protection for hospitals, a patient can hold a hospital that posts such notices liable only if the hospital directed the negligent actions that injured the patient. In negligent credentialing, some states have created a rebuttable presumption that says a hospital is presumed to have properly credentialed staff physicians if the hospital is accredited by the Joint Commission of Accreditation of Health Care Organizations. If the hospital can show that it is accredited, the burden of proof shifts to the plaintiff to show that the hospital did not follow the credentialing procedures of The Joint Commission; that the hospital knew, or should have known, of the physician's incompetence and did nothing to limit the physician's privileges; or that the credentialing process did not apply to this hospital, this physician, or the type of case that formed the basis for the lawsuit.

> **quick quiz 32-4**
>
> 1. A hospital can never be held liable for the torts of a physician unless that physician is an employee of that hospital. true | false
> 2. Ostensible authority applies only to hospitals in large urban areas. true | false
> 3. Negligent credentialing and negligent retention have been outlawed under the Restatement (Second) of Torts. true | false

Summary

32.1 Accountants are business professionals who can plan, direct, and evaluate the complex financial affairs of their clients. The most common types of accountants are certified public accountants and public accountants. Accountants must follow generally accepted accounting principles. Auditors must follow generally accepted auditing standards. They must also follow the Code of Professional Ethics of the AICPA. Accountants may be liable to both their clients and third parties. Making a determination of the extent of liability to third parties depends on understanding the nature of actual privity and near-privity.

32.2 Architects and attorneys are considered professionals and are regulated by the state. Architects may find themselves liable to clients and to third parties, whereas attorneys are generally responsible to their clients alone. Both architects and attorneys must exercise due care and skill in carrying out their professional duties.

32.3 The term *health care provider* includes physicians, dentists, chiropractors, podiatrists, nurses, nurse practitioners, nurse technicians, radiologic technologists, respiratory therapists, and laboratory technicians. Like other professionals, health care providers must act with the same skill, care, and level of knowledge that a reasonable health care professional would display in a similar situation.

32.4 Hospitals can be held liable for the negligence of a physician even if that physician is not an employee of the hospital. The granting of staff privileges can be troublesome for the hospital if the staff physician becomes the defendant in a malpractice lawsuit because the patient can sue both the physician and the hospital. Two legal theories that have been used successfully to add the hospital to the list of defendants in a malpractice lawsuit are ostensible authority and negligent credentialing.

Key Terms

accountant, 910
actual privity, 918
adverse opinion, 911
attorney-client privilege, 929
audit, 911
auditor, 911
certified public accountant (CPA), 910
Code of Professional Ethics, 912
cost of repair rule, 924
disclaimer, 912
fiduciary rule, 923
financial advisor, 922
general consent, 933
generally accepted accounting principles (GAAP), 911
generally accepted auditing standards (GAAS), 911

Health Insurance Portability and
Accountability Act (HIPAA), 935
informed consent, 933
in-house attorney, 931
locality rule, 934
malpractice, 915
national rule, 934
national standard, 934
near-privity, 918
negligence, 915
negligent credentialing, 937
negligent retention, 937
ostensible authority, 937
professional, 910
public accountant (PA), 910
Public Company Accounting
Oversight Board (PCAOB), 912
qualified opinion, 911
same state locality rule, 934
Sarbanes–Oxley Act, 912
similar locality rule, 934
similar practitioner rule, 934
staff privileges, 937
suitability rule, 923
true locality rule, 934
type one arrangement, 914
type two arrangement, 915
unqualified opinion, 911
work product privilege, 929

Questions for Review and Discussion

1. What is the difference between a certified public accountant and a public accountant?
2. What is the difference between generally accepted accounting principles and generally accepted auditing standards?
3. What are the various types of auditing opinions that can be issued by auditors?
4. What is the difference between actual privity and near-privity?
5. What are the registration requirements imposed on architects?
6. What are the duties that an architect owes to his or her clients?
7. What are the duties that an attorney owes to his or her clients?
8. What is the standard of care used to judge health care professionals?
9. What is the difference between the locality rule and the national standard in determining a health care provider's liability?
10. What are the circumstances in which hospitals can be held liable for the torts of independent contractor physicians?

Cases for Analysis

1. While she was under investigation by a grand jury, Martha Stewart penned an e-mail that explained the circumstances that led to the ImClone scandal. Stewart then dispatched the e-mail to her attorney and sent a copy to her daughter, Alexis Stewart. The e-mail was inadvertently provided to the government, along with a number of other files that had been delivered in response to a subpoena. When the e-mail was identified, government attorneys went back to the court and asked the judge to decide whether they could use the e-mail as evidence. Stewart's attorneys argued that the e-mail was under the protection of the attorney–client privilege and the work product privilege. On the other side of that argument, it is clear that the intended recipient of the e-mail was Stewart's daughter, not her attorney. Should the judge uphold the protection granted by the attorney–client privilege and the work product privilege, or should she allow the government to use the e-mail, because Stewart sent it to a third party? Explain. [See: *United States v. Stewart*, 03 Cr. 717 (U.S. District Court Southern District of New York).]

2. The Consolidata Services Company (CDS) was established to provide small businesses with payroll services. All CDS clients were required to provide CDS with an advance deposit equal to the amount of one payroll. When CDS got into a cash flow problem, it tapped into some of this deposit money to cover its own debts. Eventually, the accounting firm of Alexander Grant, which had been hired by CDS to advise it on taxes and other financial matters, discovered that the deposit account was $150,000 short. CDS assured Grant that it was

devising a plan to cover the missing $150,000. Accordingly, CDS asked Grant not to reveal the deficit. Nevertheless, Grant informed several of its own clients using the CDS payroll services and other nonclients of CDS's problem. Was Alexander Grant correct in revealing the information? What guidelines did the court use to answer this question? Explain. [See: *Wagenheim v. Alexander Grant and Co.*, 482 N.E.2d 955 (OH).]

3. Burke, an energy tycoon, hired the accounting firm of Arthur Young and Company to audit several of his operations. The SEC brought an action against Burke for fraud and for failure to meet certain SEC reporting requirements. The SEC also named Arthur Young as a defendant, claiming that the accounting firm should have discovered the fraud. Arthur Young argued that it had followed GAAS when it had audited Burke. The accounting firm concluded that this strict adherence to GAAS immunized it from liability under securities law. The SEC argued that Arthur Young should have done more to discover the fraud than what was required under GAAS. Was the SEC correct? Explain. [See: *Securities and Exchange Commission v. Arthur Young and Company*, 590 F.2d 785 (9th Cir.).]

4. Hutchins and O'Neil, as general partners in the Haddon View Investment Co., became limited partners in Car Wash Investments. The general partner in Car Wash was the Minit Man Development Company. Coopers and Lybrand accountants handled the accounting work for both Minit Man and Car Wash. They performed audits and prepared financial statements that allegedly revealed two healthy companies. Nevertheless, both Car Wash and Minit Man went out of business. As a result, Hutchins and O'Neil lost a total of $252,000. They sued Coopers and Lybrand, alleging malpractice, breach of contract, concealment, fraud, and deceit in the accountants' work for Car Wash and Minit Man. Coopers and Lybrand argued that Hutchins and O'Neil could not sue the firm because Car Wash and Minit Man were the clients, not Hutchins and O'Neil. Were the accountants correct? [See: *Haddon View Investment Co. v. Coopers and Lybrand*, 436 N.E.2d 212 (OH).]

5. Bainbridge hired the architectural firm of Seymour, Shaefer, and Lashutke to draw up plans for the alteration of Bainbridge's office building in Albuquerque, New Mexico. The plans called for the removal of the paneling in parts of the building and its replacement with Maxwell-Plus, a new, more durable material. Maxwell-Plus was specifically recommended by the architects as the best product on the market. From the beginning, the contractor had difficulty with the installation of Maxwell-Plus. In addition, two months after the work was completed, the new paneling began to deteriorate rapidly. Investigation indicated that Seymour, Shaefer, and Lashutke had failed to consider the dry, arid climate of Albuquerque, for which Maxwell-Plus was totally unsuitable. Bainbridge had to have the paneling replaced at a cost of $122,532. Subsequently, he sued the architects. Seymour, Shaefer, and Lashutke argued that they were not liable to Bainbridge because the total value of the building had not been altered by their alleged error. Were the architects correct? Explain.

6. Malcolm was a physician who ran a small private practice in Harrison, Kansas. One evening, the Sandersons brought their young daughter in for treatment of what they thought was a minor throat infection. Dr. Malcolm treated her with a standard antibiotic and sent the child home. What neither Dr. Malcolm nor the Sandersons knew was that the child had contracted a rare and often fatal blood disease. The disease, Seballian Syndrome, could only be treated with a new antibiotic called Veritrium. Had the Sanderson child been treated with Veritrium in a timely manner, her illness would have been short lived, and she would have suffered no permanent damage. As it was, the inaccurate diagnosis and the ill-advised treatment initiated by Dr. Malcolm actually made the child worse and almost caused her untimely death. Although the child eventually recovered, her hearing was permanently damaged. The Sandersons initiated a malpractice suit against Dr. Malcolm. The doctor argued that because of her location in the remote section of Kansas, she should not be expected to be as up-to-date on modern techniques as physicians who practice in large metropolitan areas. Furthermore, she argued that she could not have known about the new treatment and should, therefore, not be held liable. Is the physician correct? Explain.

Design Elements: The Opening Case: ©Sharpstock/Alamy; A Classic Case: ©Evlakhov Valeriy/Shutterstock

quick quiz Answers

32-1	32-2	32-3	32-4
1. F	1. T	1. T	1. F
2. F	2. F	2. T	2. F
3. F	3. T	3. F	3. F

Chapter 33

Science, Technology, and Law in the 21st Century

33-1 Governmental Authority Regulating Science and Technology
The Constitution and Science • The Legal Ecosystem as a Complex Adaptive System • A Federal Science Court • Residual State Regulatory Power • Judicial Power and the Common Law

33-2 National Expenditures for Science and Technology
The History of Scientific Expenditures • Office of Science and Technology Policy • Chief Technology Officer of the United States • National Institutes of Health • National Science Foundation

33-3 International Authority Regulating Juriscience
International Nongovernmental Organizations • The United Nations • International Problems • UN Educational, Scientific, and Cultural Organization • The World Health Organization and the Ebola Crisis

33-4 Facing Global Challenges
Heilbroner's Global Challenges • Regulating Energy Problems • Regulating Environmental Problems • Regulating Population Growth

33-5 Protecting Intellectual Property
The Nature of Intellectual Property • Protecting Patents • The America Invents Act • Protecting Trade Secrets • Protecting Copyright

33-6 Developing Global Solutions
Four Basic Requirements • UN Economic Security Council Proposed

THE OPENING CASE Round 1
Climate Change, Carbon Footprints, Sunspots, a Mysterious 1,500-Year Cycle, and the Paris Climate Agreement

When President Trump announced that the United States would no longer be bound by the Paris Climate Agreement, the world did not end as many people had predicted. In fact, the Paris Climate Agreement is alive and healthy despite the fact that the United States is standing on the sidelines for the moment. For example, the World Bank has declared that after 2019, it will freeze (pun intended) all requests to use its funds for oil and gas exploration projects. In addition, energy companies will find that they can no longer purchase insurance coverage from Axa, a major international insurance corporation, for any coal construction ventures they might have on the drawing board at the present time. In addition, China will continue to construct carbon-free power plants with the ultimate goal of securing up to one-fifth of its energy from such plants by 2030. So the real question is not whether the international community will continue to focus on climate change. Instead, the real question is whether the global elites have diagnosed the nature of climate change correctly because, if they have not, the rest of us may suffer from a futile scramble to escape the inevitable and a stunning failure to prepare for the predictable.

All major climate-related news stories to the contrary, there really are two sides to the issue of climate change. The first, and by far the most popular, position argues that climate change—well, global warming as the driving force behind climate change—is caused by human intervention, in general, and by the generation of greenhouse gases, especially carbon dioxide, in particular. The accumulation of greenhouse gases has led, or so the theory goes, to an increased warming of the atmosphere, the aptly named *greenhouse effect*, that then leads to the gradual melting of glaciers, Greenland, and the polar ice caps, driving fresh water into the oceans. The dumping of fresh water into the oceans causes a rise in sea levels and an interference in the northward flow of the Gulf Stream. As spin-offs from these changes, we get heavier rainfall, the flooding of many coastal areas, and, paradoxically enough, droughts in some regions. Weather patterns are also affected so that we see increased periods of violent weather, including hurricanes, typhoons, water spouts, blizzards, and tornadoes. The most serious of these changes may be, again paradoxically, the advent of a new ice age. This may occur when the addition of fresh water to the Atlantic causes the Gulf Stream to slow to a halt, thus stopping the flow of warm water to the the northern Atlantic, leading to a drastic drop in temperature in North America and Europe, thus causing an ice age in those regions (see the motion picture, *The Day After Tomorrow*).

The second, and less-well-known, theory is based on the premise that the Earth's climate goes through cycles on a regular, predictable basis. These cycles are caused by the interaction between the Earth and the Sun. Changes in the amount of radiation from the sun have a serious effect on the temperature of the Earth's atmosphere, which leads to climatic fluctuations. The waning and waxing of sunspot activity alters the amount of radiation flowing from the sun to the Earth. Sunspots are areas of intense magnetic activity on the surface of the sun that have a temperature somewhat lower than the average temperature of the Sun. Ironically, sunspots, which appear darker than the rest of the surface, actually intensify the radiation flow from the Sun because, while the sunspots themselves are cooler, those areas surrounding the sunspots are hotter than average. Thus, fewer sunspots and less radiation means a cooler Earth. The radiation flowing from the Sun, called the solar wind, blocks cosmic radiation from hitting the Earth. Thus, a less intense solar wind means more cosmic radiation, which ionizes molecules in the atmosphere, leading to cloud nuclei and creating wet clouds that act as a mirrors bouncing solar radiation back into space, thus dropping the Earth's temperature. In contrast, more sunspots means more radiation, which creates more ozone, which absorbs more ultraviolet radiation, thus increasing the atmosphere's temperature, leading to a hotter Earth. Evidence from ice core measurements, seabed sediment, fossilized pollen, cave stalagmites, and the movement of prehistoric human villages has demonstrated that these cold-to-hot climate variations happen in quasi-regular intervals roughly every 1,500 to 2,000 years. In short, based on these cycles, this theory concludes, like the first theory, that the Earth is getting warmer.

So, since both theories agree that we are headed toward a warmer climate, what difference does the difference make? The difference lies in our need to determine the correct cause of global warming. If we focus on the correct cause, we can engineer an effective response. If we focus on the incorrect cause, we will be like cavemen who decide to stop the arrival of winter by sacrificing a rabbit to the weather gods. The sacrifice may be comforting and reassuring (except for the rabbit), but winter will still arrive, and a lot of people in the tribe will die because they failed to store enough food, pile up enough animal skins, and gather enough firewood for warmth. So, if global warming is really caused by human activity, then we ought to act, and act fast, to curb that activity. However, if it is a regular, predictable pattern, then the international community would be much better off spending time and money preparing for a way to live (even to thrive) through that change. How the law and the sociopolitical system is reacting to all of this, is the subject of this chapter on juriscience—that is, the law and science. [See: S. Fred Singer and Dennis T. Avery, *Unstoppable Global Warming: Every 1,500 Years* (Lanham, MD: Rowman and Littlefield, 2008); Aurelien Breeden and Elian Peltier, "'We Are Losing the Battle,' Promises but Few Big Commitments at Macron's Climate Gathering," *The New York Times*, December 13, 2017, p. A-11; Justin Gillis, "Your Questions about Climate Change, Answered," *The New York Times National Sunday*, September 24, 2017, p. 22; and Brad Plumer, "The Paris Climate Agreement: How It Works," *The Cleveland Plain Dealer*, June 1, 2017.]

Opening Case Questions

1. What is the Paris Climate Agreement, and how does it fit into the crisis of climate change? Explain.

2. What are the two dominant theories identifying the causes of climate change? Explain each one briefly.

3. What evidence exists for each of these two theories? Explain.
4. Which of the two theories seems to be accepted by most political leaders? Why is this so?
5. What difference to global planning does it make whether we accept the carbon footprint theory or the 1,500-year cycle theory? Explain.

Source: See: S. Fred Singer and Dennis T. Avery, *Unstoppable Global Warming: Every 1,500 Years,* (Lanham, MD: Rowman and Littlefield, 2008; Aurelien Breeden and Elian Peltier, "'We Are Losing the Battle,' Promises but Few Big Commitments at Macron's Climate Gathering," *The New York Times* (December 13, 2017), p. A-11; Justin Gillis, "Your Questions About Climate Change, Answered," *The New York Times National Sunday* (September 24, 2017), p. 22; Brad Plumer, The Paris climate agreement: How it works," *The Cleveland Plain Dealer* (June 1, 2017).

Learning Objectives

1. Explain how the law permits the government to regulate science and technology.
2. Describe the function of the Office of Science and Technology Policy.
3. Define the function of the National Institutes of Health.
4. Outline the role of the National Science Foundation.
5. List Heilbroner's three challenges that face the modern world.
6. Identify the purpose of the Federal Energy Regulatory Commission.
7. Define the role of the Nuclear Regulatory Commission.
8. Describe the functions of the Clean Air Act and the Clean Water Act.
9. Explain how the law protects patents, trade secrets, and copyrights.
10. Describe the four main issues that must be considered in developing a science policy.

33-1 Governmental Authority Regulating Science and Technology

The law involves rules made by the government to promote order, stability, and justice. Science is an academic discipline that studies the natural universe, using the scientific method, with the goal of understanding the physical laws that guide the operation of the universe. Technology is the process of developing ways to enhance human control of those physical laws with the goal of extending human abilities. Science and technology, then, are involved in developing ways to create order and stability in the universe. For this reason, among others, science, technology, and the law often interact with one another. The point at which these three disciplines intersect can, for expediency, be referred to as **juriscience** or, at times, as techno-juriscience. Because the government produces and enforces the law, we must look to the sources of governmental power to determine just how much power the law has to control science and technology.

The powers to regulate, fund, and control science and technology in the United States are shared to a degree by the national government and the state governments and to a lesser extent by international convention. However, many of these functions are located in the federal government, and some of these powers and abilities reside exclusively within the federal government. For example, only the federal government is empowered to grant patents and copyrights. Some functions are shared by two levels of government, such as establishing departments, supporting education, and funding research programs. The national power emerges from the U.S. Constitution; the state power emerges from the states' residual police power. International power depends upon the type of international institution that is charged with oversight responsibilities. Depending upon which level a scientist has entered, he or she may find the road to governmental or international funding easy, difficult, or bureaucratically impossible (well, nearly impossible).

The Constitution and Science

It is often said that the Constitution revolves around two fundamental principles: (1) the separation of national powers among three distinct branches of government, and (2) a system of checks and balances to limit those powers. The principle of the separation of powers set up the three branches of the national government: the executive branch, the legislative branch, and the judicial branch. The principle of checks and balances allows each branch to share in the power of the other two branches. While all of this is true, we must also recall that the Constitution is filled with provisions designed to minimize the influence of political, social, economic, and religious factions on the national scene and to, thus, preserve the power of the central government. A **faction** is a special interest group that does its best to see that its point of view on certain issues is heard and acknowledged on Capitol Hill and in the White House. This concern over the influence of factions led the Framers (especially James Madison) to include several provisions in the Constitution to preserve and extend the power of the central government. In relation to science and technology, some of these enabling provisions are listed explicitly in Article I, such as the power "to promote the Progress of Science" by granting patents, while others have evolved over the past two centuries as the courts have interpreted the commerce clause, the taxation clause, the supremacy clause, the necessary and proper clause, and the treaty clause.

The Legal Ecosystem as a Complex Adaptive System

Recall that a complex adaptive system (CAS) is a network of interacting conditions that reinforce one another, while at the same time adjusting to change from agents outside and inside the system. Any complex adaptive system includes a variety of agents with no central controlling agent, operating at multiple complex levels as it deals with and adapts to change by inferring the direction of future events. The purpose of a CAS is the survival and improvement of the system itself. As the law adapts to science and technology, it reinforces those practices that help the system adapt and survive, while downplaying or sidestepping those that do not. Here we see how five constitutional clauses have been interpreted to either support the expansion of federal power over techno-juriscience or to reduce that expansion when necessary for the best interests of the entire system. In this complex adaptive tug-of-war, federal power over techno-juriscience has been greatly expanded under the commerce, taxation, and supremacy clauses and curbed somewhat under the necessary and proper clause and the treaty clause.

The Commerce Clause By far the most powerful clause in Article I is the commerce clause (Article I, Section 8, Clause 3). The commerce clause has been used over the past two centuries to give Congress the power to create a national police force, the FBI; to prevent employment discrimination, the Civil Rights Act of 1964; and to regulate union activity, the Wagner Act. It has also been used to empower Congress to regulate science and technology. The actual text of the **commerce clause** is deceptively simple and innocuous. It says that Congress has the power "(T)o regulate Commerce with foreign Nations, and among the several States, and with the Indian Tribes." Early in the development of constitutional law, the courts created a very narrow interpretation of this clause, arguing that Congress could only regulate commercial dealings if they passed between two or more states.

This narrow interpretation, however, did not last long. The growth of the nation and the economic shift from an agrarian to a manufacturing economy demanded that the courts grant Congress more flexibility in handling economic issues. Part of this shift involved a distribution of land under the government's land-granting program. This program demanded that Congress have the power to enforce the allocation of this land. As a result, in a case known as *Gibbons v. Ogden*, the Supreme Court ruled that any commercial operation that touched on commerce among the states could be regulated by the federal government. The implications of this ruling were not immediately clear. However, eventually, lawmakers began to realize that any commercial activity affecting commerce, even an activity that took place totally within the borders of one state could be controlled by Congress. In the case of *Wickard v. Filburn*, the U.S. Supreme Court, acting as an important agent in the complex adaptive system of the law, expanded congressional power under the commerce clause to previously unimagined lengths. In that case, the High Court ruled that a farmer's production of wheat for consumption on his own property in a single state had an impact on interstate commerce.

EXAMPLE 33-1: Strengthening the Commerce Clause

The federal power over science expanded in the case of *Gonzales v. Raich*, a case related to the federal government's science policy because it involved the regulation of marijuana use as a medical treatment. In *Raich*, the Supreme Court decided that Congress had the power to criminalize the sale and use of marijuana under the Controlled Substance Act, *even when the activity in question occurred completely within the borders of a single state.* The Court ruled, "One need not have a degree in economics to understand why a nationwide exemption for the vast quantity of marijuana (or other drugs) locally cultivated for personal use (which presumably would include use by friends, neighbors, and family members) may have a substantial impact on the interstate market for this extraordinarily popular substance. The congressional judgment that an exemption for such a significant segment of the total market would undermine the orderly enforcement of the entire regulatory scheme is entitled to a strong presumption of validity. Indeed, that judgment is not only rational, but 'visible to the naked eye,' *Lopez*, 514 U.S., at 563, under any common sense appraisal of the probable consequences of such an open-ended exemption." This case is also of critical importance because the majority opinion stresses that the Court's decisions in two high profile cases [United *States v. Lopez*, 514 U.S. 549 (1995) and *United States v. Morrison*, 529 U.S. 598 (2000)] have been repeatedly misinterpreted. In those cases, the Court struck down statutes authorized by Congress under the commerce clause. However, the majority expressly states that, it is a mistake to take either case for anything other than the Court's refusal to permit Congress to regulate activities under the authority of the commerce clause, when there is no commerce (the Court may say, "economic activities," here but it really means "commerce") involved in the prohibited conduct. [See: *Gonzales v. Raich*, 545 U.S. 1 (2005).]

Source: See: *Gonzales v. Raich*, 545 U.S. 1 (2005).

Gonzales v. Raich underscored the almost unlimited authority of the federal government to control science policy at every level of the national system. However, the complex adaptive nature of the law meant that, at some other level within the legal CAS, the system would adapt to prevent an unhealthy concentration of power in the national government that could threaten the stability of the system itself. Such an adjustment occurred in a case in which the defense used an argument based on the necessary and proper clause.

The Necessary and Proper Clause The **necessary and proper clause**, which is found in Article I, Section 8, Clause 18, of the U.S. Constitution, says that Congress has the power "(T)o make all Laws which shall be necessary and proper for carrying into Execution the foregoing Powers, and all other Powers vested by this Constitution in the Government of the United States, or any Department or Officer thereof." Generally, when

Congress invokes the necessary and proper clause, it specifically says so in the preamble to the legislative action. However, often when a case actually gets to court the interpretation of the necessary and proper clause is tied to a court's need to pull several additional clauses into the rationale in order to arrive at a decision. Occasionally, for instance, the necessary and proper clause is tied to the commerce clause, as was the case in *People for the Ethical Treatment of Property Owners v. U.S. Fish and Wildlife Service*, No. 2:13-cv-00278-DB (D. Utah, November 4, 2014). At the heart of this case is the federal government's attempt to control the treatment of the prairie dog population in the state of Utah (a case related to the federal government's science policy because it involves environmental regulation).

EXAMPLE 33-2: Challenging the Necessary and Proper Clause

In the 1970s, the Utah prairie dog was added to the endangered species list. Since that time, a coalition consisting of government workers, property owners, and conservationists developed a suitable habitat for the prairie dog population. As a result of these efforts, the prairie dog population increased steadily over the next 40 years, resulting in the prairie dog's removal from that list. However, under provisions of the federal Endangered Species Act (ESA), as interpreted by by the U.S. Fish and Wildlife Service, among several additional defendants, the prairie dog was still entitled to certain protections that interfered with the plans of Utah property owners. Specifically, ESA Section 4(d) permits *only* a "regulated take of Utah prairie dogs," something the landowners wanted to avoid. The defense argued, in part, that the necessary and proper clause empowered Congress to regulate the prairie dog population because managing the prairie dogs in Utah was part of a larger scheme by the federal government to protect those species in danger of being bought and sold into extinction. Therefore, because the wider plan was "necessary and proper," the subdivisions of that plan were too.

The court, however, saw things differently. First, the court could see no market for prairie dogs, so they could not be regulated directly. Second, the court could see no evidence that the loss of prairie dogs would affect those species, such as the bald eagle, that really were in danger of being bought and sold into extinction. Finally, the court could see no need for the government to merge the plan to regulate prairie dogs on non-federal land with other parts of its regulation scheme. Therefore, because the government's scheme was neither necessary nor proper to carry out its interstate objectives, it could not invoke the necessary and proper clause. [See: *People for the Ethical Treatment of Property Owners v. U.S. Fish and Wildlife Service*, No. 2:13-cv-00278-DB (D. Utah, November 4, 2014).]

Source: See: *People for the Ethical Treatment of Property Owners v. U.S. Fish and Wildlife Service*, No. 2:13-cv-00278-DB (D. Utah November 4, 2014).

This Utah prairie dog case, however, is not the end of the story because the complex adaptive nature of the law means that, at some other level within the legal CAS, the system will adapt to restore federal power over science. Such was the case in a lawsuit titled *State of Florida, et al. v. U.S. Department of Health and Human Services*, in which the Court was invited once again to deal with the general welfare clause.

The Taxation Clause The **taxation clause** is found in Article I, Section 8, Clause 1, of the Constitution. The clause declares, in part, that Congress is empowered to "lay and collect *taxes*, Duties, Imposts, and Excises, to pay the Debts and provide for the common defense and general welfare of the United States." Historically, the taxation clause was one of the first clauses used to justify the expansion of federal power over science and technology. Under that clause, Congress set up the Department of Agriculture in 1862 and, as part of the operation of that department, used federal money collected by taxes to hire scientists (botanists and chemists in particular) to work in that department. The power was challenged in the courts, and when the case known as *United States v. Butler* reached the Supreme Court, the Court upheld (some experts say expanded) the taxing power of Congress under the taxation clause despite the fact that it struck down the statute that was challenged in that case. Moreover, the taxing power of the federal government was strengthened once again in the case of *National Federation of Independent Business, et al., v. Sebelius*, 507 U.S.____, 132 S.Ct. 2566 (2012).

EXAMPLE 33-3: Preserving the Taxation Clause

The case of *National Federation of Independent Business, et al., v. Sebelius* is related to the federal government's science policy because it involves the maintenance of the nation's health care system. In this case, the plaintiffs challenged, as unconstitutional, that part of the Affordable Care Act that fined people who did not buy health insurance. The government defended that act, despite the fact that the law attempted to regulate nonaction (not buying insurance). The government claimed that the act was valid under the commerce clause and the necessary and proper clause. The Court refused to uphold the law under the commerce clause, arguing that the Framers did not give Congress the power to force people to engage in commercial activity. The Court also refused to sanction the act under the necessary and proper clause. However, the Court did accept the government's third argument that the "fine" was not a penalty, but a tax. Accordingly, the Court ruled by a 5–4 margin that the "penalty" for not buying insurance, as required by the act, was not a penalty at all but was, instead, a tax issued under Article I, Section 8, Clause 1. Thus, the act was a constitutional expression of the federal government's taxing power under the taxation clause. The Court's ruling was not surprising in this case because the Court has repeatedly strengthened the taxation clause of the Constitution in many cases throughout the years.

The Court has similarly strengthened the supremacy clause, which has empowered the federal government to, in effect, "veto" state law.

The Supremacy Clause The **supremacy clause**, which is found in Article VI, Clause 2, of the U.S. Constitution, says, "The Constitution, and the Laws of the United States, which shall be made in Pursuance thereof; and all Treaties made . . . shall be the supreme Law of the Land." Although it does not expressly say this, the supremacy clause has been interpreted to mean that the federal courts in general and the Supreme Court in particular have the legal authority to short-circuit state statutes, regulations, mandates, and executive orders that contradict the Constitution. The supremacy clause has also been interpreted to mean that federal law can preempt state law covering the same subject matter. State law can be preempted expressly if a preemption clause is added to a federal law or implicitly if the enforcement of the state statute makes the enforcement of the federal statute impossible. Otherwise, whenever a dispute over preemption arises the courts must determine if Congress intended to preempt. Such was the situation in the case of *Northern States Power Co. v. Minnesota*, 447 F.2d 1143 (1971), a case related to the federal government's science policy because it involves the building of a nuclear power plant.

EXAMPLE 33-4: Amplifying the Supremacy Clause

Northern States Power Company (NSPC), a Minnesota corporation, received permits from both the Atomic Energy Commission (AEC) and the Minnesota Pollution Control Agency to build a nuclear power plant in Minnesota. The Minnesota permit, however, required a more restrictive standard for waste disposal than the AEC's permit. In response, the power company sued the Minnesota agency, arguing that Minnesota had no authority to issue such a restrictive permit because once Congress set up the AEC, it had preempted the state's authority to regulate the new facility. In response, Minnesota argued that the 10th Amendment to the Constitution gave it the right to stop pollution in its territory in order to protect the health of its people. None of this seemed to matter to the trial court, which ruled in favor of NSPC. Moreover, the appellate court upheld that decision, and the Supreme Court followed suit. [See: *Northern States Power Co. v. Minnesota* 447 F.2d 1143(1971); and Allen N. Elgart, "Constitutional Law—Federal Preemption of State Regulatory Authority," *Boston College Law Review* 13, no. 4 (1972), pp. 812–26.]

Source: See: *Northern States Power Co. v. Minnesota* 447 F.2d 1143(1971); and Allen N. Elgart, "Constitutional Law—Federal Preemption of State Regulatory Authority," *Boston College Law Review* 13, no. 4 (1972), pp. 812–26.

Despite this continued expansion of federal power, at times the legal CAS readjusts and, in a remarkable turnaround, ends up limiting itself. Such was the case when, under the authority of the treaty clause, the Senate short-circuited the administration's plan to endorse the Kyoto Protocol.

The Treaty Clause The **treaty clause**, which is found in Article II, Section 2, Clause 2, of the U.S. Constitution, says the president "shall have power to make Treaties with the Advice and Consent of the Senate." Generally, treaties have little to do with science, technology, and engineering. Instead, they are concerned with such things as fishing rights, trade agreements, boundary disputes, international law, disarmament, and mutual defense agreements. Occasionally, however, treaties deal with patent and copyright law, nuclear test ban agreements, genetic engineering agreements, and climate control. Although the president is not required to consult with the Senate before a treaty is negotiated or to have a senatorial representative on his or her diplomatic team, the president is required to obtain the Senate's approval before a treaty becomes the law of the land. Today, some of the most visible and controversial treaties that the president negotiates involve juriscientific matters, especially when such matters are related to climate change and environmental clean-up projects. Such has been the case with the Kyoto Protocol and its progeny.

EXAMPLE 33-5: Questioning the Treaty Clause

One of the most troublesome science-related laws to hit the newspapers in recent years was the Kyoto Protocol, a treaty negotiated by former President Bill Clinton and signed by him in November 1998. Among other things, the protocol called for the primary industrialized nations to reduce carbon dioxide emissions below levels recorded in 1990. Although the president had signed the protocol and repeatedly indicated his support for the measure, as a treaty, it had to be approved by the Senate. Unfortunately, the Senate was strongly opposed to the measure, indicating that it could not support any proposal that would not force developing nations to reduce pollution or that would damage the American economy. The bottom line was that despite the support of the President of the United States, the Kyoto Protocol was dead in the water, so to speak, because under Article II, Section 2, Clause 2, of the U.S. Constitution, the treaty needed Senate approval. The situation deteriorated even further after the election of George W. Bush, who, like Clinton, expressed support for pollution emission reduction but, unlike Clinton, would not underwrite such measures at the expense of the United States. President Obama also did not attempt to see the protocol ratified. The legal CAS had effectively readjusted itself once again. [See: Emily C. Barbour, "International Agreements on Climate Change: Selected Legal Questions," *Congressional Research Service*, 2010, http://nationalaglawcenter.org/wp-content/uploads/assets/crs/R41175.pdf.]

Source: See: Emily C. Barbour, "International Agreements on Climate Change: Selected Legal Questions," *Congressional Research Service* (2010) http://fpc.state.gov/documents/organization/142749.pdf.

A Federal Science Court

One suggestion for handling those juriscientific issues that seem beyond the capabilities of the current political system is to establish a federal science court that would be fully dedicated to hearing all science- and technology-related cases—from patent lawsuits to cases that involve regulation and funding. The federal science court would have exclusive jurisdiction over issues involving scientific, engineering, medical, and technological cases. All judges who sit on the national science court would be expected to have a scientific background or would be required to undergo special training sessions to get up to speed on science and engineering matters. Each judge would be required to attend an internship program during which he or she would shadow a full-time science court judge to learn the ins and outs of all procedural and substantive issues peculiar to that court in regard to science and technology. The federal science court would deal with a wide variety of cases such as those involving nuclear power, cyber-terrorism, genetic engineering projects, medical malpractice suits, medical research issues, environmental protection law, intellectual property problems, and so on. As things develop, the court might even be subdivided into layers, each of which would be responsible for a different discipline. Thus, there might be a medical division, a scientific division, a technology division, and an engineering division.

A CLASSIC CASE California and the Ambitious California Delta Water Twin Tunnel Project

California has a reputation, for better or worse, as the most experimental, forward-looking state in the union. Sometimes this trend works out well, and sometimes not so much. A case in point is the California Delta Water Twin Tunnel Project (the Twin Tunnel Project), a project that just might be a prototypical case for the proposed federal science court. Currently, California must pump water from the water-rich north to the water-poor south to help irrigate more than 3 million acres of farm land and to facilitate the delivery of drinking water to the 25 million people who live in that area. The problem with the current system is that it is nearly obsolete, and therefore, highly undependable. Moreover, it causes environmental damage, including a threat to the declining fish population. The current system is also susceptible to earthquakes and subject to weather changes, including periods of severe drought.

The Twin Tunnel Project, which is designed to fix these problems and is the brain child of Governor Jerry Brown, is actually two projects: (1) the Water Fix Project and the (2) Eco Restore Project. (*Note:* Previously, it was a single project known alternately as the California Delta Water Twin Tunnel Project and the Bay Delta Conservation Plan.) The Water Fix Project will establish a new water-sharing system that is more reliable and less risky than the network in place today. The tunnel project actually involves two sets of tunnels: (1) the northern tunnels and (2) the primary tunnels. The northern tunnels consist of three different, 14-mile-long tunnels that connect the intake facilities with the Intermediate Forebay (a forebay is a type of reservoir).

The primary tunnels connect the Intermediate Forebay with the Clifton Court Forebay. These twin tunnels (for which the overall Twin Tunnel Project gets its nickname) are 30 miles in length, 40 feet in diameter, and 150 feet underground. The twin tunnels will have a $16.7 billion price tag. At this point in the project, the water is transported by two new pumping stations into the existing system and then to customers in the south. (*Note:* The twin tunnels will have a $16.7 billion price tag. However, the governor is now pushing for the construction of one tunnel for $11 billion, while waiting until later to build the second tunnel at a time when more funds are available.)

The Eco Restore Project is designed as a countermeasure to the Water Fix Project. To put it simply, if everything goes according to plan, the Eco Restore Project will fix any negative effects that flow from the Water Fix Project. More specifically, Eco Restore will rebuild the damaged habitats, the despoiled wetlands, and the ravaged floodplain affected by the Water Fix Project. Overall, the Eco Restore Project will reclaim some 30,000 acres of land.

Supporters of the new system argue that the project is needed to solve the perennial problems noted earlier—that is, the risky, undependable, and nearly obsolete system that now transports much needed water to the south and that, in its present state, damages the environment and threatens to drive some species into extinction. Opponents of the project argue that the Eco Restore part of the package has been reduced from making 21 eco-commitments to a mere 12 and has reduced the amount of land to be restored to 30,000 acres, a mere third of the amount that was originally targeted for reclamation. Opponents also point to the enormous price tag attached to the project and to the fact that the fate of both projects has been taken out of the hands of the state legislature and the voters and placed under the authority of various water regions in the state. Opponents also fear a drop in the quality of the water delivered to its customers.

For a variety of reasons, a federal science court would be an ideal forum for a battle between the supporters and the opponents of the California Two Tunnel Project. First, science court judges would be well versed in scientific matters, in general, and environmental issues, in particular. Armed with this knowledge, they would know how to deal effectively and efficiently with expert witnesses and complex scientific matters. They would know, for instance, what questions to ask, when to ask them, and whether the answers to those questions made any sense. Second, because the court would handle only scientific and technological cases, the judges would be better equipped to know whether to fast-track or slow down a case like the Twin Tunnel Project. Third, science court judges would also be able to make an intelligent evaluation of the costs involved in this project by comparing those costs to the expenditures paid out in other cases that the court has ruled on in the past. Fourth, because they are lawyers first, science court judges would also be equipped to make competent judgments regarding such things as the constitutionality of taking the approval power for projects such as the Twin Tunnel Project out of the hands of the voters and the legislature and placing that power in the hands of special interest groups such as the water regions. [See: Dale Kasler, "California Unveils Revised Blueprint for Delta Tunnel Project," *The Sacramento Bee*, July 9, 2015, http://www.sacbee.com/news/state/california/water-and-drought/article 26872906.html; Ryan Sabalow, "Southern California Water Agency Could Vote Soon on Whether to Bankroll Delta Tunnels," *The Sacramento Bee*, February 27, 2018, http://www.sacbee.com/news/state/california/water-and-drought/article 202447374.html; and "California Water Fix and Eco Restore," *Wikipedia*, https://en.wikipedia.org/wiki/California_Water_ Fix_ Eco_Restore.]

Source: See: Dale Kasler, California unveils revised blueprint for delta tunnel project," *The Sacramento Bee* (July 9, 2015) http:// www. sacbee.com/news/state/california/water-and-drought/ article 26872906.html; Ryan Sabalow, "Southern California water agency could vote soon on whether to bankroll Delta tunnels," *The Sacramento Bee* (February 27, 2018) http:// www.sacbee.com/news/state/california/water-and-drought/ article 202447374.html; "California Water Fix and Eco Restore," Wikipedia https://en.wikipedia.org/wiki/California _Water_ Fix_ Eco_Restore.

Supporters and Detractors Commentators who support the national science court argue that the complex nature of today's scientific caseload is beyond the expertise of most judges who sit on the bench at the trial level. These experts argue that it would be more effective and economical to build an entirely new league of professional *science judges* to deal with these complexities. Those who oppose the national science court contend that the training sessions to bring judges up to speed would be cost-prohibitive. Moreover, the proposed subdivision of the court into subcourts handling different disciplines would create unnecessary and expensive duplication. As you read the following issues in relation to juriscience, see if you can decide whether the science court would be a help or a hindrance. [See: Barry Casper and Paul Wellstone, *Powerline: The First Battle of America's Energy War* (Amherst, MA: University of Massachusetts Press, 1981); and Barry Casper and Paul Wellstone, "Science Court on Trial in Minnesota," *Science in Context: Readings in the Sociology of Science*, ed. Barry Barnes and David Edge (Cambridge, MA: MIT Press, 1982).]

Residual State Regulatory Power

Notwithstanding the extensive control that the national government has over science, technology, and engineering, the states still maintain a certain level of residual power in this area. The capacity of the states to regulate science and technology emerges from the states' police power. **Police power** is the states' ability to uphold and sustain the public health, safety, welfare, and morals. Every state in the union possesses police power simply because it exists as the lawful governmental authority within its own territory. The state government along with its various departments and divisions from counties or parishes; to cities, towns, and villages; to zoning districts and school boards, all have some job to play in the regulatory process. The state creates colleges and universities with research programs; regulates hospitals and clinics; standardizes laboratories and testing facilities; designs science and engineering school curricula; runs state parks and conservation programs; controls state environmental, energy, and resource programs; and so on. The state also collects incorporation fees, taxes corporate activities, polices the actions of corporate managers, and creates new corporate entities, such as limited liability companies and joint ventures, all of which may have research and development departments.

Judicial Power and the Common Law

The tradition of common law fills the law books of many state court systems with cases related to science, technology, and engineering. While many of these cases are preempted when the federal courts overturn a case or when Congress passes a statute that preempts a state law, state courts are justifiably hesitant to relinquish long-standing common law values. Consequently, state courts frequently discover imaginative ways to interpret federal guidelines within the framework of that state's established legal institutions. Consequently, the study of jurisicence must be moderated by the established principles of state law. As we have seen, that is what occurred in *People for the Ethical Treatment of Property Owners v. U.S. Fish and Wildlife Service*, No. 2:13-cv-00278-DB (D. Utah, November 4, 2014); *Northern States Power Co. v. Minnesota*, 447 F.2d 1143(1971); *Gonzales v. Raich*, 545 U.S. 1 (2005); and *National Federation of Independent Business, et al., v. Sebelius*, 507 U.S._____, 132 S. Ct. 2566 (2012); all of which are covered earlier.

quick quiz 33-1

1. A faction is a special interest group that does its best to see that its point of view on certain issues is heard and acknowledged on Capitol Hill and in the White House. | true | false

2. Congressional power to regulate science and technology is found only in the commerce clause. | true | false

3. Police power is the state's ability to uphold and sustain the public health, safety, welfare, and morals. | true | false

33-2 National Expenditures for Science and Technology

The federal government has been funding scientific and medical research for the past 150 years or more. That funding comes in many forms for a variety of purposes and with an enormously high price tag. Nevertheless, Congress and the president have agreed that the expenditure is necessary to provide for national security, to promote the health and welfare of American citizens, and to ensure the economic and social well-being of the nation. For this reason, the federal government has established a number of agencies and institutes that support, assess, coordinate, and fund scientific, medical, and technological research. The history of science funding at the national level reaches back to the 1800s and continues today at a very lucrative rate.

The History of Scientific Expenditures

Large expenditures for scientific research have a long history in the United States, extending back to the establishment of a group of land grant colleges launched in 1862 by Congress under the authority of the Morrill Act. The Morrill Act provided national monetary support for colleges and universities with the purpose of launching a set of partnerships among institutions of higher learning and the farming community. The textile industry also entered the race for progress by sending specialists into educational institutions with directions to help university researchers address issues related to technology and science in that business. Collaborations like this became so routine that they sparked the creation of huge scientific and technological educational institutions such as MIT. Paradoxically, the birth of big research universities also encouraged the establishment of research-based corporations like AT&T, Dow Chemical, Westinghouse, and GE. [See: D. Dickson, "Universities and Industry: Knowledge as Commodity," *The New Politics of Science* (Chicago: University of Chicago Press, 1988), pp. 61-62.]

Another supply of funding emerged after the Second World War when Vannevar Bush, the director of the White House Office of Scientific Research and Development, delivered a report to the president titled *Science: The Endless Frontier*, but commonly referred to as *The Bush Report*. In *The Endless Frontier*, Bush pushed for the creation of a consolidated national research institution, the National Science Foundation (NSF). The purpose of the NSF would be to provide government dollars for technological and scientific research projects, many of which would be located in the nation's colleges and universities. [See: "Introduction and Overview," *Science for the 21st Century: The Bush Report Revisited*, Ed. C. E. Barfield (Washington: AEI, 1997), pp. 3-4; D. J. Kevles, "The Changed Partnership," *Wilson Quarterly* 19 (Summer 1995), p. 42; and D. C. Mowery, "The Bush Report after Fifty Years—Blueprint or Relic," *Science for the 21st Century: The Bush Report Revisited*, Ed. C. E. Barfield (Washington: AEI, 1997), pp. 28-29.] Today, the chief national scientific agencies for scientific, medical, and technological research are the Office of Science and Technology Policy, the National Science Foundation, and the National Institutes of Health.

Office of Science and Technology Policy

The Office of Science and Technology Policy originated in 1961 as the Office of Science and Technology under President John F. Kennedy. The primary purpose of the office under Kennedy was to keep the president apprised of developments in the space program. Eventually, the purpose expanded to ensure that the president was informed about overall advances in technology and science as well as the impact that these developments might have on U.S. policy. In 1976, Congress expanded the scope and function of the office when it set up the Office of Science and Technology Policy under the National Science and Technology Policy Organization and Priorities Act. The goal of the new office is to advise the president on technological and scientific matters so that he can make informed decisions about federal programs that impact science and technology. The office is also responsible for managing science and technology policy, especially as that policy impacts the federal budget. In addition, the office integrates science policy at every level of governmental planning from the federal to the local level. This effort also includes coordinating governmental efforts with private industry to develop productive and efficient partnerships between the government and the private sector. Finally, its job is to assess the effectiveness of the overall federal science and technology program [See: "About OSTP," Office of Science and Technology Policy, The White House, http://www.whitehouse.gov/.]

Chief Technology Officer of the United States

In 2009, a new position was added to the office of the president known officially as the assistant to the president, associate director for the Office of Science and Technology Policy, but referred to generally as the chief technology officer (CTO) of the United States. The primary job of the CTO is to coordinate advances in technology and engineering as they relate to the practical jobs of improving the American economy, managing medical and health care costs, and preserving national security. The CTO works side by side with the U.S. chief information officer (CIO). The job of the CIO is to build an integrated technology policy designed to meet the needs of the national government. The position was created by Congress under the authority of the E-Government Act of 2002. All of these moves may seem new. However, even though none of these offices existed until recently, the President of the United States has had some sort of science and technology advisor on hand ever since Vannevar Bush worked for Franklin Delano Roosevelt and Harry S. Truman from 1939 to 1951. [See: "Chief Technology Officer," Office of Science and Technology Policy, The White House, http://www.whitehouse.gov/.]

National Institutes of Health

The National Institutes of Health (NIH) operate under the auspices of the Public Health Service of the Department of Health and Human Services. Their operational mission is to conduct research into all aspects of human life and health and to apply that understanding to cure illnesses, to alleviate disabilities, and to lengthen human life. The National Institutes also promote practical research that will reduce health care costs in order to improve the economic stability of the United States. The institutes also provide funding for research into the origin, prevention, and cure of diseases related to environmental problems. The institutes now invest more than $21 billion each year in medical research. Eighty percent of that figure is awarded as grants to 350,000 recipients at more than 3,000 universities, medical schools, and research organizations in the United States and around the globe. Ten percent of the original figure goes to funding the institutes' own operational laboratory in Bethesda, Maryland. The National Institutes of Health consists of 27 segments designated as institutes or as centers, each of which has an individualized research program. For example, the National Cancer Institute is charged with conducting cancer research. All but a few of these independent institutes receive their money directly from Congress. Nevertheless, the institutes handle their own administration. Funding decisions are delegated to institutes because such decisions are better handled by the experts who know how the money should be spent within their own areas of expertise. The system has the added benefit of preventing Congress from trying to use its influence to control the projects, the universities, and the individual scientists who receive the funding. The objective is to make sure the funds are spent where they should be spent. [See: "Mission," National Institutes of Health, U.S. Department of Health and Human Services, http://nih.gov.]

National Science Foundation

The National Science Foundation (NSF) is a federally funded agency that was created by Congress in 1950 to support scientific research, to stimulate the national economy, and to safeguard national security. The National Science Foundation has an annual budget that runs close to $7 billion. A substantial portion of that money is spent on scientific research in American colleges and universities. Grants from the National Science Foundation are available for practitioners in all fields of science, mathematics, and computer technology. The NSF, which is based in Arlington, Virginia, authorizes more than 120,000 grants annually. These grants are approved by a merit-based assessment process. Most of these grants fund individuals or small teams of researchers. Some grants, however, are set aside for large institutions for the purchase of equipment, facilities, and hardware. Projects that are likely to be funded are those that are clearly on the cutting edge of scientific research and development. The goal of the NSF, however, is not only to support scientific research, but also to enhance scientific education while, at the same time, building a globally competent and internationally competitive scientific labor force. Over the past 30 years, NSF researchers have been awarded more than 180 Nobel Prizes. One of the most recent Nobel Prizes went to Richard Heck of the University of Delaware, Eiichi Negishi of Purdue University, and Skira Suzuki of Hokkaido University in Japan. They won the 2010 Nobel Prize for chemistry for developing an innovative technique for joining carbon atoms together to construct effective practical complex molecules. [See: "NSF at a Glance;" and "Nobel Prizes: The NSF Connection," National Science Foundation, http://nsf.gov.]

A SECOND CLASSIC CASE Research: Driven by Science, Economics, Ethics, or Law?

The last-minute addition of an amendment to a congressional spending bill is usually seen, and rightly so, as an attempt to establish federal policy without seeming to do so. It is an effective but controversial and ethically dubious strategy. However, generally, the controversy fades as public attention is drawn elsewhere. Such has not been the case with the Dickey-Wicker (DW) Amendment, which was added to the budget in 1998 and, since then, has been the subject of renewed attention again and again. The amendment forbids the National Institutes of Health (NIH) from funding "(1) the creation of a human embryo or embryos for research purposes; or (2) research in which a human embryo or embryos are destroyed, discarded, or knowingly subjected to risk of injury or death greater than that allowed for research on fetuses in utero under 45 C.F.R. 46.204(b) and [42 U.S.C. § 289g (b)]." The NIH has interpreted that amendment to mean that any research that directly destroys a human embryo is forbidden but, and here is the rub, any research that uses cells that were already taken from an embryo through a process referred to as *derivation*, is permitted and, therefore, can be funded.

The *Sherely v. Sebelius* lawsuit under consideration here was brought by two researchers who use adult stem cells in their projects rather than stem cells taken from embryos through derivation (or some other, similar technique). The plaintiffs claim that funding research that uses derivative cells violates the DW amendment's ban on the use of "embryos . . . destroyed, discarded, or knowingly subjected to risk of injury or death." The plaintiffs argue further that their research is in danger of being underfunded (or not funded at all) because NIH generally supports research using derivative cells rather than research that, in strict compliance with the law, uses nonderivative cells. The history of the case is long, involved, and somewhat convoluted, but it amounts to this. The trial court granted an injunction to the plaintiffs, which stopped the funding of projects using derivative cells. The defendants appealed the issuance of the injunction, and the appeals court agreed, overturning the injunction. This decision reopened the door to the use of derivative cells. The appellate court's ruling turned on an interpretation of the language of the budget amendment. To interpret DW, the appeals court used a rule called the Chevron Doctrine. The Chevron Doctrine says that, when a congressional rule is truly ambiguous, a court must acquiesce to an agency's interpretation of that rule. However, if the ambiguity seems, let's say, "manufactured" by the agency to "get its way," the court must ignore the agency's self-serving interpretation and use a textualist approach to interpret the actual language of the congressional rule.

The NIH's interpretation of DW said, in effect, that derivative cells do not qualify as having been "destroyed, discarded, or knowingly subjected to risk of injury or death" and, therefore, derivative cell research can be funded. The appellate court apparently saw some sort of ambiguity in DW and, following the Chevron Doctrine, acquiesced to the NIH interpretation. This decision lifted the trial court's injunction, which, to the plaintiffs' dismay, allowed derivative cell research to be funded once again. The questions on the table now are what, if anything, is ambiguous about the words "destroyed, discarded, or knowingly subjected to risk of injury or death," and should this case be passed onto the U.S. Supreme Court? What is your opinion, and how did you formulate that opinion? [See: *Sherely v. Sebelius*, 1:09-cv-01575, U.S. District Court for the District of Columbia (2012). See also: *Sherely v. Sebelius*, No. 11-5241 (2012). *Note:* In the second appeal in the case, the Appellate Court did not revisit the issues discussed here. Therefore, this application of the Chevron Doctrine to the language of the amendment stands.]

Source: [See: *Sherely v. Sebelius*, 1:09-cv-01575, U.S. District Court for the District of Columbia (2012). See also: *Sherely v. Sebelius*, No. 11-5241 (2012) Note: In the second appeal in the case, the Appellate Court did not revisit the issues discussed here. Therefore, this application of the Chevron Doctrine to the language of the amendment stands.

quick quiz 33-2

1. The federal government did not begin funding scientific and medical research until the 20th century.	true | false
2. The National Institutes of Health operates under the auspices of the Public Health Service of the Department of Health and Human Services.	true | false
3. The National Science Foundation (NSF) is a federally funded agency that was created to support scientific research and education, to stimulate the national economy, and to safeguard national security.	true | false

33-3 International Authority Regulating Juriscience

While we will discuss international law in detail in Chapter 34, it will be helpful to look at it in this context briefly before moving on. There are four types of international nongovernmental organizations (NGOs): (1) those that are completely dependent upon the nation-states that make up their membership; (2) those that are semiautonomous organizations; (3) those that are granted or earn entity status; and (4) those that are unaffiliated transnationals that act as rogues, outlaws, criminals, or terrorists.

International Nongovernmental Organizations

NGOs that are completely dependent upon their member nations are referred to as aggregates or conglomerates of the membership. An organization such as the G-8, which is made up of the most powerful industrial nations of the world and has a floating leadership element that changes from year to year, is an excellent example. The second type is a semiautonomous organization that is initially made up of nation-states but that is actually more than the membership and is, therefore, capable of carrying out actions absent the consent of, and sometimes in defiance of, the members. Member nations might opt out of an action of which they disapprove, but the action might continue nevertheless. Member states might be able to stop some actions, depending on the structure of the organization. The United Nations is probably the best example of this type of semiautonomous international NGO.

The third type is one that achieves or is initially granted entity status. NGOs with entity status act independently because they are not at the mercy of the member states. Some are formed by an independent membership, by corporations, or by other NGOs. The International Red Cross is a good example of an entity NGO. Some commentators say NGOs evolve; they may be originally formed as conglomerates, but as they operate, they may change into semiautonomous organizations or even into entities. If, in its early history, the United States could have been conceived of as an NGO, then we can see how what was originally a loose confederation of independent states, under the Articles of Confederation, gradually evolved into a semiautonomous organization (before the Civil War the nation was referred to in the plural as in "the United States are . . .") and eventually became an entity (after the Civil War it becomes singular as in "the United States is . . ."). The European Union (EU) now appears to be going through a similar evolution. [See: Richard W. Mansbach and Kirsten L. Rafferty, *Introduction to Global Politics* (London: Routledge, 2008), pp. 403-04.]

Finally, some commentators would add a fourth category of NGO—the "transnats." **Transnats**, or transnational organizations, include terrorist groups, drug cartels, slave traders, and pirates. Transnats are unsanctioned bodies, such as al-Qaeda and ISIS, whose power comes from a willingness, some even say an eagerness, to break international law and who must, therefore, be taken into consideration when political leaders make strategic moves.

The United Nations

Despite the fact that the United Nations is a semiautonomous international NGO, it nevertheless wields a great deal of soft power on the international scene. *Soft power*, in contrast to *hard power*, which consists mostly of military force and economic influence, is waged at the emotional and psychological level. Soft power is used to persuade people, institutions, and nations that they have the same goals and objectives as the agency or person wielding the power. During the Vietnam era in the 1960s and '70s, soft power was described as the ability to earn the "hearts and minds" of the people. The United Nations has the ability to win the hearts and minds of many people in the international community. From an organizational perspective, the UN consists of three central governing agencies all located in New York City at its headquarters on the East River: the General Assembly, the Security Council, and the Secretariat.

The **General Assembly** consists of all UN member states. Each nation-state is empowered with a single vote on all matters presented to the assembly. The UN **Security Council** handles any crisis that threatens global peace. The Security Council is made up of 15 members. Five member states hold permanent seats: China, France, Russia, the United Kingdom, and the United States. The General Assembly elects the remaining 10 members for two-year terms. The secretary general is the chief administrator of the United Nations. He or she heads the **Secretariat**, which is the administrative bureaucracy of the UN. The secretary general also takes a leading role in promoting world peace. The Security Council recommends a candidate for the position of secretary general, but the General Assembly votes that person into office.

International Problems

The United Nations is a complicated and diverse organization. Many juriscientific issues related to international problems are handled by the Economic and Social Council (ECOSOC). This part of the UN is so big and so powerful that after it takes its cut of the annual budget, only 30 percent is left to be divided among the remainder of the agencies. Another key agency is the UN Educational, Scientific, and Cultural Organization (UNESCO). UNESCO promotes integrated activities in science, education, and culture and is responsible for urging nations to preserve their cultural heritage. ECOSOC has an indirect nonreporting relationship with UNESCO and with the World Health Organization (WHO).

The WHO evolved out of a similar organization that was run under the auspices of the League of Nations, the precursor of the UN. WHO's job is to promote international health care and to help prevent the spread of illness and disease. It also supports programs in medical and health research in much the same way as the National Institutes of Health in the United States. The International Atomic Energy Commission (IAEC) is an independent agency that has oversight responsibilities in relation to nuclear energy programs, while the United Nations Environment Program, another independent agency, deals with pollution issues. The World Intellectual Property Organization (WIPO) is a specialized agency that has the job of shielding intellectual property from copyright infringement, patent violations, and IP theft. All these organization have parallels in the federal systems, and all deal with the juriscientific problems of the 21st century outlined subsequently.

UN Educational, Scientific, and Cultural Organization

UNESCO is a specialized agency of the United Nations run under the auspices of the ECOSOC. UNESCO is responsible for creating outreach efforts to develop educational, cultural, and scientific ties among the member nations of the UN. Initially, the objectives of UNESCO were seen as a function of the United Nations and were thus supported by the entire membership. Evidence of its key importance is the fact that the first head of UNESCO was the world-famous British author Julian Huxley. Unfortunately, because UNESCO's mission was to allocate funds to projects run by various member states, some of these states saw themselves being marginalized while others were being rewarded. This situation fostered jealousy and resentment. As a result, UNESCO became a highly politicized organization. Eventually, it even went so far as to demand the redistribution of global resources from the developed to the underdeveloped world. In his book, *The Future of the United Nations*, Joshua Muravchik, resident scholar at the American Enterprise Institute, explains that UNESCO became more and more politicized when its leadership became tied to a bloc of underdeveloped nations within the UN.

UNESCO and The Group of 77 These underdeveloped nations referred to themselves as the Group of 77 (or just G-77). The G-77 appeared on the international stage after certain delegates attended a meeting sponsored by the United Nations Conference on Trade and Development (UNCTAD). At the time of that meeting, UNCTAD was under the leadership of the Argentine economist Raul Prebisch. Prebisch is best known as the father of dependency theory, an economic picture of the world that holds the developed world responsible for poverty in the underdeveloped world. Eventually, dependency theory became the official political position of the G-77, UNCTAD, and the United Nations. The result was a group of organizations that convinced the underdeveloped nations to adopt socialist economic structures. The G-77 also developed a manifesto called the New International Economic Order (NIEO), which was endorsed by UNESCO. [See: Linda Fasulo, *An Insider's Guide to the UN* (New Haven, CT: Yale University Press, 2004), p. 182; Robert Speaight, *Teilhard de Chardin: A Biography* (London: Collins, 1967), pp. 290–91; and Joshua Muravchik, *The Future of the United Nations: Understanding the Past to Chart a Way Forward* (Washington, DC: The American Enterprise Institute Press, 2005), pp. 69–72.]

The World Health Organization and the Ebola Crisis

In 1948, the constitution of the World Health Organization (WHO) was ratified by the member nations of the United Nations. WHO's mission is to improve the health care available to all the people of the world, but especially to those most at risk because of poverty or special health-related threats. WHO's program is based on the following basic component parts: nutrition and food; sanitation and a healthy water supply; protection against contagious diseases; containment of local illnesses; effective handling of everyday injuries and familiar diseases; adequate supplies of critical pharmaceuticals; and family planning efforts, including especially the care of mothers and children. A good portion of the work done by the WHO is aimed at building up the medical and health care facilities and professionals in poor nations so that those nations can better handle the delivery of health care and medical services to the local people.

A QUESTION OF ETHICS

Dependency Theory: A Blueprint for Injustice or a Blessing in Disguise?

The controversy surrounding UNESCO's politicization has caused an enormous amount of difficulty for the organization throughout the years. The commentators who say that UNESCO's bias in favor of the poorer nations is justified support UNESCO's critique of the developed world for exploiting the underdeveloped world, its support for dependency theory, and its adoption of the New International Economic Order (NIEO), including its demand that the rich nations compensate the poor nations. There is another side to the issue, however. The rich nations and the corporations that actually entered the underdeveloped world and drilled for oil, mined for diamonds, cut down timber, and dug for coal argue, rather convincingly, that it was their money, their equipment, and their employees that did the actual work. Their employees, with corporate money that came from investors, built roads, harbors, airports, power plants, sanitation systems, oil fields, refineries, communication systems, and so on. Moreover, the governments of the underdeveloped nations were all handsomely compensated for their fair share of the profits, or so the argument goes. Therefore, the government of each developing nation is at fault if that government failed to properly distribute a fair share of the profits to its citizens. Following this line of thought, the blessings brought by the corporations may have been disguised by the greed of the governments.

QUESTIONS YET UNANSWERED

The following questions have not yet been answered. Before you consider each question, turn to Chapter 1 to review the various ethical theories noted there (social contract theory, utilitarianism, and rational ethics). Then in a consistent way, answer the following questions.

1. Who is correct from an ethical perspective? Do the rich nations owe the underdeveloped nations because they, the rich, created the underdeveloped world's dependency on the developed world? Or does the fault lie in the hands of the governments of the underdeveloped world? Explain.

2. There is an interesting parallel situation in the operation of the National Institutes of Health and the National Science Foundation. In those institutions, the complaint is that the best and the most lucrative grants go to researchers from the big, powerful, rich mega-universities, while the small schools and the unknown researchers are largely ignored. The other side of this argument states that the unknown researchers from the small schools actually self-select themselves out of the process, either by not applying or by giving up and withdrawing their applications before the final awards are made.

    Who is correct from an ethical perspective? Do the referees from the big schools owe the representatives from small schools special attention because they, the rich, created a peer-review merit-based process that favors the big schools and the big names? Or does the fault lie in the hands of the inexperienced researchers from the small schools who "get cold feet"? Explain.

Education and Research Activities Like the National Institutes of Health at the national level, the WHO supports health and medical research programs at the international level, all of which are aimed at promoting the basic component parts of medical and health care, that serve as its foundation. More specifically, the WHO has a special research program aimed at eradicating tropical diseases that it runs in cooperation with the UN Development Program (UNDP) and the World Bank. In addition, the WHO also works with the Food and Agriculture Organization of the UN, the World Bank, and the UNDP to fight a disease known as *onchocerciasis*, or river blindness, in West Africa. The WHO is also responsible for coordinating a global effort to control infection with human immunodeficiency virus (HIV) in an attempt to eradicate the acquired immune deficiency syndrome (AIDS). [See: *Basic Facts about the United Nations* (New York: The United Nations Department of Public Relations, 1992).]

Challenges and Achievements Like UNESCO, the WHO has also had its fair share of controversy. In *The Future of the United Nations* (cited previously), Muravchik reports a case involving allegations that the director of WHO in the 1990s had granted contracts to institutions that were tied directly to members of the WHO executive board. There were also allegations at the time that threats of economic sanctions were made against certain countries if the chief of the WHO, who had been charged with these irregularities, were not reelected. Muravchik also reports, however, that the WHO has had its share of successes and has accomplished a great deal in a variety of arenas. Specifically, he praises the WHO for dealing quickly with the severe acute respiratory syndrome (SARS) crisis in 2002–2003 and thus preventing what could have been a devastating global epidemic. The WHO can also lay claim to playing a large role in the global elimination of both smallpox and polio.

The WHO and Ebola: International Health Regulations Perhaps the most visible and active involvement of the WHO in international health care problems in recent years has concerned the Ebola epidemic. The Ebola virus was first identified in 1976 during two outbreaks, one near the Ebola River in the Congo and another in the Sudan. The epidemic surfaced in March 2014 when cases were reported in Guinea. The disease quickly spread to Sierra Leone, Liberia, Nigeria, Senegal, and Mali. Six months after the first outbreak was detected, the disease had reached such proportions that the director-general of WHO was compelled to label the situation an official public health emergency of international concern. Such a state of emergency is governed by protocols found in the International Health Regulations (IHR). All nations that are official members of the WHO are required to follow IHR protocols, which include reporting requirements, treatment procedures, and containment measures.

A public health emergency of international concern must be issued when an extraordinary public health event occurs (1) that is determined to present a severe danger to the health of other nations because of the potential spread of the illness and (2) that demands an effectively managed cooperative global effort to deal with the crisis. The problem with the rules and the protocols imposed by the IHR is that the WHO has no official enforcement mechanism. Thus, despite the details of the agreement, WHO depends upon peer pressure, the principle of reciprocity, international reputation, and goodwill to ensure compliance. [See: World Health Organization, "Frequently Asked Questions about the International Health Regulations (2005)," http://www.who.int/ihr/about/faq/en/; WHO, "International Health Regulations (IHR)," http://www.who.int/ihr/publications/9789241580496/en/; and WHO, "Ebola Virus Disease," http://www.who.int/mediacentre/factsheets/fs103/en/ (updated April 2015).]

The WHO and Ebola: Ethical Considerations The global nature of the Ebola crisis raised a series of ethical concerns that officials at the World Health Organization were determined to manage quickly and effectively. For that reason, given the seriousness of the emergency, the World Health Organization convened a panel to consider the ethical ramifications of using unregistered (read "experimental" here) treatments on the most severely affected patients. After due consideration, the panel approved the use of such experimental treatments. Nevertheless, the panel also recommended that such unregistered treatments be applied only under the following conditions: Patients are to be informed about all aspects of the unregistered treatments used (including the fact that they are unregistered), patients are not to be treated until they give informed consent, patients are not to be coerced or unduly influenced into giving such consent; patients are to be promised confidentiality, patients are to be treated with dignity, and the community is to be informed about and involved in the program. The unregistered treatment programs are also to be conducted in a way that will allow for the collection and sharing of all data gathered as a result of the use of the unregistered treatments, even when that treatment occurs outside the actual clinical setting. [See: WHO, "Ethical Considerations for Use of Unregistered Interventions for Ebola Virus Disease (EVD): Summary of Panel Discussion," http://www.who.int/mediacentre/news/statements/2014/ebola-ethical-review-summary/en/.]

quick quiz 33-3

1. Five member states of the United Nations that hold permanent seats on the UN Security Council are France, Russia, Japan, the United Kingdom, and the United States. **true | false**

2. UNESCO is responsible for creating outreach efforts to develop educational, cultural, and scientific ties among the member nations of the UN. **true | false**

3. After due consideration, a task force convened by the World Health Organization approved the use of unregistered experimental treatments on the most severely affected patients in the Ebola crisis. **true | false**

33-4 Facing Global Challenges

The American bureaucratic system frequently appears complex and convoluted. The operation of the bureaucracy often seems erratic and directionless. The day-to-day activities appear to be designed to stall and block progress rather than to enhance it. The *Federal Register*, which produces a daily record of agency business, is so complex that it must include one section on rules and regulations; another on proposed rules; and one on notices of hearings, meetings, application deadlines, and administrative orders. There is also a section devoted to presidential orders and proclamations. The high level of activity within the bureaucracy could lead to the conclusion that the activity has become an end in itself, rather than the means to the end of running an efficient and effective government. While this evaluation may be discouraging, it may also be the price we pay for demanding a democratic government. Nevertheless, underneath, or perhaps above, all the activity is a series of challenges that funnel this activity in productive directions. All of the work done by the government, outside of the work needed to collect the money used to deal with the other problems themselves (think IRS here), relate in some way to four challenges: (1) the possibility of war, (2) the volatility of the marketplace, (3) the twin dangers of environmental deterioration and energy depletion, and (4) the demographic crisis. Dealing with all of these problems is part of the balancing act that is the law.

Heilbroner's Global Challenges

In 1974, the economist, author, and political scientist Robert Heilbroner wrote *An Inquiry into the Human Prospect*. In this pioneering book, Heilbroner argued that the planet Earth is faced with three challenges that must be met if humanity expects to continue into the 21st and the 22nd centuries. If these three problems are not handled, Heilbroner says with some degree of confidence, then humanity is doomed. The problems he focuses on are the possibility of war, especially nuclear war; the challenge of uncontrolled population growth (demographics); and the destruction of the environment. The list is slightly different from the one we compiled earlier. The one challenge he appears to miss is the challenge of a volatile economy. That challenge, however, is not actually missing from *An Inquiry into the Human Prospect*. In fact, the economy actually permeates the book because Heilbroner sees economic volatility as the challenge that underlies each of the other three and, ironically, is also the ultimate solution. In a sense, then, the economy is Heilbroner's mega-crisis [See: Robert Heilbroner, *An Inquiry into the Human Prospect* (New York: Norton, 1991).] We have dealt with the legal handling of the economy since we began talking about contract law in Chapter 7. Moreover, and more to the point, we focused on much of it in Chapter 30 and 31 when we discussed the government's regulation of the economy especially as it relates to the stock market, the housing market, and corporate misconduct. In Chapter 34, we will deal at length with the challenge of war. It remains, then, for us to discuss the twin challenges of energy and the environment and the inescapable problem of overpopulation, both of which fall within the realm of juriscience.

Regulating Energy Problems

The Arab oil embargo of 1973 and the subsequent energy crisis focused national attention on the power industry. In answer to these concerns, Congress created the Department of Energy and the Federal Energy Regulatory Commission. National concerns with the problems of nuclear energy, especially after the disasters involving nuclear energy in Japan, have also recently focused attention on the Nuclear Regulatory Commission. The regulation of nuclear energy for peaceful uses on a global scale is charged to the United Nations International Atomic Energy Agency (IAEA).

The Federal Energy Regulation Commission The Federal Energy Regulatory Commission (FERC) is responsible for regulating the transportation and the wholesale price of natural gas and electricity sold for use in interstate commerce. State utility commissioners regulate intrastate prices. Rates are calculated to allow companies a specific rate of return on investments (earnings divided by total assets), which they may not exceed. When utilities are confronted with increased costs due to higher fuel prices, they can apply to the commission for permission to pass these increased costs on to customers through fuel adjustment charges. The commission also licenses hydropower project proposals for the construction of interstate gas pipelines and liquefied natural gas terminals. In brief, a few of the additional duties of the FERC include regulating pipelines used in the interstate transport of oil, reviewing and approving interstate locations for natural gas lines, reviewing and approving the location of natural gas storage containers, reviewing applications for the placement of electricity transmission projects on a limited basis, licensing private and governmental (state and city) hydroelectric projects, producing mandatory standards for high-voltage interstate transmission systems, acting as a watchdog and overseeing accounting and financial reporting rules for companies regulated by the FERC, monitoring environmental risks in relation to hydroelectric and natural gas projects, and imposing civil penalties for violations of FERC regulations.

In 2005, Congress passed the Energy Policy Act, which added a series of new tasks to the FRFC's already packed agenda. One of the top initiatives in the 2005 act involves the modernization of the nation's electric power grid. Specifically, the FERC is charged with the development of a smart grid that will make optimal use of state-of-the-art technology. The goal is to apply digital technology to the nation's power network to ensure a reliable, secure, and efficient electric grid. In addition, the FERC will ensure peak operation of the grid with protection from cyber-attacks of all kinds. Moreover, the FERC is charged with the task of implementing "smart technology in grid operations, including metering, communication, and distribution automation." Other new tasks involve removing unnecessary roadblocks that are currently preventing the implementation of the smart grid and developing standards for the interoperability of equipment connected to the grid, among many others. The FERC recently unveiled its new strategic plan outlining the outcomes that will be the focus of its program for several years. Specifically, the commission has established three overall goals backed up by several objectives that explain the implementation of those goals. The goals include (1) to ensure just and reasonable rates, terms, and conditions; (2) to promote a safe, reliable, secure, and efficient infrastructure; and (3) to support the commission's mission through organizational excellence. Each goal is further supported by (1) core functions that describe the actions and the tools needed to meet each goal, (2) a specific course of action detailing practical steps to deal with the challenges and opportunities that must be handled in carrying out each goal, and (3) strategic performance measures to rate the group's movement toward accomplishing each goal. [See: "Top Initiatives," "Smart Grid," and "Strategic Plan," Federal Energy Regulatory Commission, http://ferc.gov; and Federal Energy Regulatory Commission Strategic Plan, FY 2014-2018 (March 2014).]

Nuclear Regulatory Commission Mandated by the Energy Reorganization Act, the Nuclear Regulatory Commission (NRC) is responsible for the licensing, construction, and operation of nuclear reactors. It is also responsible for regulating the possession, use, transportation, handling, and disposal of nuclear material. The NRC develops and implements rules and regulations governing licensed nuclear activities. Nuclear regulation actually began under the auspices of the Atomic Energy Commission, which was established by Congress under the Atomic Energy Act of 1946. The 1946 law was superseded by the Atomic Energy Act of 1954, which was designed to encourage the development of safe and reliable nuclear power plants. The AEC came under fire in the 1960s (What government agency didn't in the 1960s?) for developing lenient regulations regarding radiation protection, plant location, reactor safety, and protection of the environment. The AEC was eliminated in 1974 and replaced by a new agency, the current Nuclear Regulatory Commission, under the authority of the Energy Reorganization Act of 1974. The NRC was charged with overseeing various aspects of the nuclear power industry, including especially radiation shielding and reactor safety. The Three Mile Island incident in Pennsylvania in 1979 focused attention on the need for stricter regulations in relation to personnel training, energy planning, plant operation, plant operational records, and human involvement in plant operations, among several other things.

The NRC has evolved into an agency of rules and regulations for the security of nuclear materials to prevent the theft of that material, especially theft of that material by potential terrorists. The commission is also charged with developing and enforcing safety regulations in relation to radioactive waste materials. It also does its fair share of work in radiation medicine, developing standards and protecting patients from radiation overdoses. The NRC currently employs more than 4,000 employees in Maryland and four regional offices in Georgia, Illinois, Pennsylvania, and Texas. NRC inspectors also visit nuclear power plant sites and various fuel facilities across the nation. It is important to note that the NRC does not regulate nuclear weapons, military reactors, or space vehicle reactors. It does not lobby Congress, and it does not, contrary to popular opinion, operate its own reactors or its own power plants. It does, however, impose penalties for violations of its regulations. Penalties can be severe—up to $140,000 per day per violation. Licenses can also be revoked, changed, or suspended for especially egregious violations. It is even possible that a wrongdoer's violation is so severe that the violator's case is sent to the Justice Department for possible criminal proceeding. [See: "About NRC," U.S. Nuclear Regulatory Commission, http://www.nrc.gov.]

International Atomic Energy Agency

On the international scene, the United Nations has an agency with oversight responsibility for matters dealing with nuclear power. The International Atomic Energy Agency (IAEA), which was created in 1957, is responsible for making certain that, on a global basis, nuclear energy is used only for peaceful purposes. Thus, under the statute creating the agency, there is an assumption that nuclear energy is both a useful and necessary source of energy production, especially for developing nations. Nevertheless, the IAEA also exhibits a healthy respect for the dangers associated with nuclear power. IAEA's program is based on four basic component parts: setting up guidelines for the effective, economical, and environmentally safe production of nuclear energy; promoting the peaceful application of nuclear science technology; providing technical and engineering support on nuclear energy to member nations; and distributing scientific and technological knowledge about nuclear power. The agency must guard against the misplacement, loss, or theft of nuclear materials and equipment and make certain that such equipment and materials do not fall into the hands of those who would use them for military (or terrorist) operations. Much of this oversight is maintained by inspections, and by record-keeping procedures that can be verified by those inspectors. Such inspection and record-keeping strategies are involved in a variety of international agreements including: the Treaty for the Prohibition of Nuclear Weapons in Latin America and the Treaty on the Non-Proliferation of Nuclear Weapons, among others. [See: *Basic Facts about the United Nations* (New York: The United Nations Department of Public Relations, 1992).]

Unfortunately, in *The Future of the United Nations* (cited previously), Muravchik notes that such inspections and record-keeping processes are not foolproof. In fact, the IAEA inspection process has been less than 100 percent effective on a number of occasions, notably in the cases of Iraq, Iran, and North Korea. On a more positive note, other governments, in the peaceful pursuit of nuclear power, have come directly to the IAEA for equipment, for technical assistance, and for the education of its personnel. The IAEA is also responsible for setting up regulations that guide the requirements for radiation shielding and for the safe and efficient transport of nuclear materials. The agency also handles emergency operations in the case of a nuclear accident. The IAEA is also a clearinghouse of information, research, and data on all phases of nuclear energy. The clearinghouse, which is known officially as the International Nuclear Information System, is located in Vienna. The IAEA also runs the International Centre for Theoretical Physics in conjunction with UNESCO. [See: *Basic Facts about the United Nations*.]

Regulating Environmental Problems

In his book, *An Inquiry into the Human Prospect*, Heilbroner provides a succinct but poignant explanation for the nature of the environmental challenges that face the global community in the 21st century. Heilbroner writes: "Here we come to a crucial stage in our inquiry. For unlike the threats posed by population growth or war, there is an ultimate certitude about the problem of environmental deterioration that places it in a different category from the dangers we have previously examined. Nuclear attacks may be indefinitely avoided; population growth may be stabilized; but ultimately there is an absolute limit to the ability of the environment to support or tolerate the process of industrial activity, and there is a reason to believe that we are now moving to that limit very rapidly." [See: Heilbroner, p. 47.] This is a scary thought. One that should give us pause. On the national level, the responsibility for the environment has been delegated to the Environmental Protection Agency.

Important subsidiary legislation includes the Clean Air Act, the Clean Water Act, and the Oil Pollution Act. The regulation of the environment on a global scale is charged to the United Nations Environment Program (UNEP).

The Environmental Protection Agency The Environmental Protection Agency (EPA) is an independent agency in the executive branch of the federal government. It was created to carry out the provisions of the National Environmental Policy Act and other major environmental laws and executive orders dealing with air, water, solid waste, toxic substance, and noise pollution. The purpose of the 1969 National Environmental Policy Act is to establish a national policy that will combat pollution and improve the environment. The legislation encourages efforts that prevent or eliminate damage to the environment and that stimulate the health and welfare of the public. The act requires a detailed statement of environmental consequences in every recommendation or proposal for legislation and other major federal actions significantly affecting the quality of the human environment. These environmental impact statements describe in detail the expected adverse environmental consequences of a proposed action. The alternatives to the action are also described.

All major antipollution programs dealing with air, noise, solid wastes, toxic substances, and pesticides were placed under the administrative control of the Environmental Protection Agency in 1970. The EPA's primary responsibilities are to conduct research on all aspects of pollution, set and enforce pollution control standards, monitor programs to determine whether pollution abatement standards are being met, and administer grants to assist states in controlling pollution. The EPA has the power to enforce the standards and programs it initiates. It encourages voluntary compliance by industry and communities and supports state and local governments' efforts to conduct enforcement actions of their own. When such efforts fail, the EPA conducts enforcement proceedings. Moreover, state laws and local ordinances must be in line with federal regulatory policies and standards. The states and their subdivisions are not permitted to skirt federal law by creating statutes and ordinances that establish more lenient standards than those provided for in the federal statute. Congress can intentionally and expressly pass a statute or empower an agency to create regulations that are designed to preempt state law. On the other hand, it is permissible for states and their subdivisions to impose restrictions that are different from and perhaps stricter than those imposed by the federal government. Thus, it is legally permissible for a state to require special standards on resold vehicles or commercial vehicles, or to impose procedures enforcing federal standards.

Solid Waste Disposal Act Congress enacted the Solid Waste Disposal Act in 1965 (SWDA) to control the handling of solid waste. The act includes the regulation of both hazardous and non-hazardous solid waste products. Regulations set up under the act provide guidelines for storing, transporting, and disposing of hazardous waste materials using environmentally conscious protocols. The act includes the regulation of municipal, commercial, industrial, and domestic waste products. The act was amended in 1976 with the Resource Conservation and Recovery Act which extended the authority of SWDA, which Congress had deemed to be imprecise and incomplete in its original form. The new act recognized the need for the development of more effective ways to deal with the management and disposal of both hazardous and the nonhazardous solid waste. [See: "Solid Waste Disposal Act (SWDA) Law and Legal Definition," US LEGAL, https://definitions.uslegal.com/s/solid-waste-disposal-act-swda/; and "Solid Waste Disposal Act," *Wikipedia*, June 27, 2017, https://en.wikipedia.org/wiki/Solid_Waste_Disposal_Act_of_1965.)

The Clean Water Act The Clean Water Act, which was passed by Congress in 1972 as an amendment to the Federal Water Pollution Control Act of 1948, sets requirements for limiting the pollution of the nation's water sources according to a schedule and based on the most effective technology currently available. The regulations set up a system for obtaining permits for the release of pollutants into the waterways. Permits are issued provided that the pollution emissions are within legal limits. Violations of the act are punished by fines up to $25,000 daily. Often, the EPA must act against companies that pollute the environment, even if the pollution activity is unintentional. The courts have interpreted this broad prohibition to include even accidental pollution, because to hold otherwise would weaken the statute. The Clean Water Act also permits citizens suits against violators and against the administrator of the act for not properly carrying out his or her responsibilities under the act. The same definitive violation and notice provisions are applicable under this act as they are under the Clean Air Act. There is a difference between the two acts, however. Under the Clean Water Act, the party bringing the citizen's suit must be a person "having an interest which is or may be adversely affected" by the violation of the act. No such limit exists in the Clean Air Act.

The Clean Air Act In order to enforce the details of its overall environmental policy Congress has, over the years, passed subsidiary legislation regarding individual pollution problems. The three most visible acts are the Clean Air Act, the Clean Water Act, and the Oil Pollution Act. The Clean Air Act, for example, is designed to limit pollution from vehicles and from stationary sources such as factories and manufacturing centers. The act authorizes the EPA to initiate regulations to limit air pollution. Over the years, the government has added new standards that have gradually reduced the amount of pollution that can be released by vehicles. New emission control requirements were issued in 1990, regarding nitrogen oxide, hydrocarbon, and carbon monoxide. Additional emission control limits were introduced in 2009 ordering a reduction in pollution from a variety of vehicles including SUVs that must reach an 80 percent reduction level within 40 years. The penalties for violating the act are severe. Congress also added a unique feature to the Clean Air Act, which emphasizes the legislature's serious intent to see that the law is enforced. Under provisions in the act, private parties are empowered to sue violators. Private parties are also permitted to sue the act's administrator for not enforcing the act properly. There are limits to this right to bring a citizen's suit, however. The citizen bringing the suit must point to a definite violation by the perpetrator and must give advance notice to the administrator so that he or she has a chance to correct the problem before the lawsuit is initiated.

Toxic Substance Control Act In 1976, under the Toxic Substance Control Act (TSCA), Congress gave the EPA the power to regulate the use of chemical substances. The idea was to make sure that new chemical substances were adequately tested for dangers before being marketed and that hazardous chemicals already on the market were well regulated. Some chemicals such as drugs, cosmetics, food, and pesticides are not covered by the TSCA. The act has been amended several times. Those amendments include the Chemical Safety Improvement Act (CSIA) of 2013 and the Frank R. Lautenberg Chemical Safety for the 21st Century Act of 2015. The CSIA was developed to require safety tests for all chemicals already on the market. The Safety for the 21st Century Act was designed to reauthorize the TSCA and to remedy some of its shortcomings. [See: "The Toxic Substance Control Act," U.S. Environmental Protection Agency, https://www.epa.gov/enforcement/toxic-substances-control-act-tsca-and-federal-facilities#Summary; and "The Toxic Substance Control Act," *Wikipedia*, February 28, 2018 https://en.wikipedia.org/wiki/Toxic_Substances_Control_Act_of_1976.)

The Comprehensive Environmental Response, Compensation, and Liability Act The Comprehensive Environmental Response, Compensation, and Liability Act (CERCLA) empowers the EPA to compel those responsible for hazardous waste sites to decontaminate those sites or, in the alternative, to sanitize the site itself and then obtain repayment from those responsible. In an unusually creative step, Congress fashioned CERCLA to hold potentially responsible parties (PRPs) liable based on strict liability rather than intent or negligence. In other words, under CERCLA if a hazardous waste site exists, liability follows—period. Under CERCLA, a hazardous substance involves those that are included in CERCLA regulations and those designated by the Clean Water Act, the Solid Waste Disposal Act, the Clean Air Act, and the Toxic Substance Control Act. Oddly, petroleum products are not controlled by CERCLA. The act does include, however, a litany of parties who can be held strictly liable for a hazardous waste site. In particular, the act states that the present owner or operator of an establishment on which a hazardous waste site is located can be held liable; as can a past owner or a operator; as can the party who arranged for the disposal, treatment, or the transport of the hazardous waste; as can the transporter of such waste. It is especially interesting to note that a party may still be liable under CERCLA even if the method of storage, transport, or disposal of the hazardous material was legal at the time of the original act creating the hazardous waste dump. The standard is not the action (ownership, operation, arrangement, or transport) but the damage that the action caused. Unfortunately, CERCLA is a less than perfect statute. It was written very rapidly and, as result, fails to cover many problems. Those problems have been left for the courts to solve. Consequently, the act remains a moving target. [See: David E. Nash, "Environmental Law 101 for Business Lawyers," 2016 Ohio State Bar Association Business Law Conference, May 23, 2016; and "Summary of the Comprehensive Environmental Response, Compensation, and Liability Act (Superfund), Laws and Regulations," U.S. Environmental Protection Agency, https://www.epa.gov/laws-regulations/summary-comprehensive-environmental-response-compensation-and-liability-act.]

The Oil Pollution Act The Oil Pollution Act was passed by Congress in 1990 in the wake of the 1989 Exxon Valdez Alaskan oil spill. The act is designed to encourage companies that ship, drill for, and store oil to develop and use the most up-to-date equipment and the most effective safety measures possible. Sometimes, the act will require that specifically named technological and engineering steps be taken. For instance, the act mandates that, any oil tanker that wants to enter an American port must be equipped with double hulls to minimize any pollution damage should a spill occur. Under the act's provisions, any company responsible for a spill will be compelled to pay all expenses related to the clean up and will, in addition, be subject to a heavy fine. Depending on certain factors, such as the source of the spill, violators could end up paying up to $350 million.

United Nations Environment Program The United Nations Environment Program (UNEP) was created in 1972 as a consequence of work done at the United Nations Conference on the Human Environment in Stockholm that year. The UNEP, which has its central offices in Kenya, was the first UN institution located in a developing nation-state. The agency is responsible for stimulating global awareness of environmental issues and for coordinating international efforts to solve the tough problems associated with environmental deterioration. It organizes the efforts of several UN agencies as they interface with governments and private establishments, such as youth groups and women's organizations. UNEP's programs are based on 10 fundamental areas of concentration: (1) climate change, (2) the vanishing ozone layer, (3) atmospheric activity, (4) fresh water supplies, (5) desertification, (6) deforestation, (7) biological variety, (8) oceanic activity, (9) biotechnology and bioengineering, and (10) chemical safety and security. The UNEP works in a variety of ways to fulfill its environmental mission. A key activity is the Global Environmental Monitoring System (GEMS). This program controls an international system of monitoring centers run by more than 30,000 scientists located in more than 140 nation-states. The system monitors environmental activity in the oceans, in the atmosphere, in the climate, and in renewable resources. It also monitors pollution and pollution-related illnesses.

UNEP also monitors the work of INFOTERRA, a decentralized data clearinghouse that provides environmental information to institutions and individuals. Another source of environmental data monitored by UNEP is the Industry and Environment Office (IEO), which provides data to governments and industry. The IEO also promotes information and technology transfer between governments and industry dealing with environmental matters. The UNEP also develops action plans for dealing with problems in marine biology aimed at preserving marine resources. Such action plans have dealt with problems in the Mediterranean Sea, the Pacific Ocean, and the Black Sea. The UNEP also monitors a series of international agreements on the environment including the Vienna Convention and Montreal Protocol, the London Amendment to the Montreal Protocol, the Basel Convention on the Control of Transboundary Movements of Hazardous Wastes and their Disposal, and the Convention on International Trade in Endangered Species. [See: *Basic Facts about the United Nations*.]

United Nations Conference on Environment and Development The UN has also taken steps to combine environmental and energy concerns together under the auspices of the United Nations Conference on Environment and Development (UNCED). UNCED, known more popularly as the Earth Summit program, is designed to integrate economic development and environmental protection into a single well-coordinated strategy that will promote sustainable development in developing nations with the assistance and cooperation of the developed nations of the globe. The first UNCED Conference (Earth Summit I), which was held in Rio de Janeiro in 1992, resulted in an international agreement known as Agenda 21. The provisions of Agenda 21 established an in-depth set of tactics designed to activate sustainable development plans across the globe. Earth Summit I also resulted in the Rio Declaration, which defines a set of standards outlining the duties and the rights of nations in sustainable development. The summit also led to the creation of the Commission on Sustainable Development (CSD), which coordinates efforts to activate Agenda 21. The CSD also serves as a central clearing house for nations to report progress in the implementation of sustainable development plans.

A second international conference, known as the UN Framework Conference on Climate Change (UNFCCC), was held in Berlin in 1995. This conference involved 120 nations working to create a global strategy to stabilize growing levels of carbon dioxide and other greenhouse gases (GHGs) in the atmosphere. A plan was developed based on balancing (1) a timetable that will not endanger existing ecosystems, (2) a scientific strategy that will permit an adequate production of food, and (3) an economically feasible strategy that will support sustainable development. The plan, which was dubbed the Berlin Mandate, sets out a timetable for the reduction of carbon dioxide and other GHGs for various governments. The second Earth Summit held in 1997 revealed that very little progress had been made since the first conference. As a result Earth Summit II reconfirmed the goals, objectives, and plans of Agenda 21 and added a reconfirmation of the need to partner economic development with environmental protection. The new program, which was named Development Reconciling Environmental and Material Success (DREAMS), set a new set of priorities for the next five years.

A second meeting in 1997, under the auspices of UNFCCC, was held in Kyoto to discuss the lowering of greenhouse gas emissions during the first decades of the 21st century. Under terms of the agreement, known as the Kyoto Protocol, the primary industrial nations would be mandated to reduce carbon dioxide emissions below levels recorded in 1900. Unfortunately, the three major industrial nations on the planet, the United States, China, and India, refused to go along with the protocol. [See: *Basic Facts about the United Nations*; Derek Osborn and Tom Bigg, *Earth Summit II: Outcomes and Analysis* (London: Earthscan, 1998); and Christopher Flavin, "Facing Up to the Risks of Climate Change," in *State of the World 1996*, ed. Lester Brown (New York: Norton, 1996).]

The Paris Climate Agreement A new meeting under the auspices of the UN Framework Conference on Climate Change was held in Paris in 2015. The meeting produced a new pact known as the Paris Climate Agreement (also know simply as the Paris Agreement or the PCA), the purpose of which is to maintain the annual global temperature rise at a rate somewhat under 2 degrees Celsius above levels recorded before the era of industrialization. Moreover, the PCA also seeks to accomplish this task by using appropriate economic means to enhance the technological abilities of member nations to keep pace with their own voluntarily established national plans. All signatories of the PCA will issue individual national progress reports on a regular basis, and, as a unit, all the members of the PCA will produce a single global assessment, termed a stocktake, every five years starting in 2023. On Earth Day in 2016, the PCA was opened for signatures. As the early months of 2018 rolled along, 175 nations had ratified the new pact. It is important to keep in mind that individual nations are empowered to set their own nationally determined contributions and to establish their own internally monitored protocols to meet those contribution levels. However, in order to meet the temperature leveling plan noted earlier, all nations have pledged to meet a global peaking of all greenhouse gas emissions as rapidly as can be accomplished, given an understanding that many developing nations will take a bit longer to reach their own individual peaking goals than the developed nations. It is also critical to remember that the PCA is voluntary and nonbinding, which means, in effect, any nation that fails to meet its prescribed goal will not be penalized. In addition, nations can pull out of the agreement with impunity. The only glue holding the agreement together is a nation's desire to be well-thought of in the international community, something that has rarely (ever?) worked in the past. [See: "The Paris Agreement," *The United Nations Framework Convention on Climate Change*, http://unfccc.int/paris_agreement/items/9485.php; Justin Gillis, "Your Questions about Climate Change, Answered," *The New York Times National Sunday*, September 24, 2017, p. 22; and Brad Plumer, "The Paris Climate Agreement: How It Works," *The Cleveland Plain Dealer*, June 1, 2017.]

THE OPENING CASE *Round 2*
Climate Change, Carbon Footprints, Sunspots, a Mysterious 1,500-Year Cycle and the Paris Climate Agreement

Recall that, in the Opening Case, we pointed out that there are two positions on the nature of climate change. The first position argues that climate change has been caused by human activity, especially by the emission of greenhouse gases (GHGs), in general, and carbon dioxide, in particular. The second theory says that the present trend toward global warming is part of a cyclical pattern of climate change that occurs every 1,500 to 2,000 years. This pattern is not caused by human activity but by the interaction of the Sun with the Earth.

The nations that have signed the PCA, all 175 of them, have assumed that the first theory—that global warming is caused by GHGs—is the correct theory. The belief is that if the global community stops producing GHGs, global warming will be slowed to a halt. This is a fatal error. Let's look at the reasons for this conclusion.

First, as noted earlier, the PCA assumes that global warming is caused by human-activated greenhouse gas emissions. While there is some indication that the GHG emissions contribute to the warming effect, there is no conclusive proof that this is the *only* factor that ought to be considered in the overall system of global climate change. In fact, as noted in the Opening Case *Round 1*, there is ample evidence found in ice core measurements, seabed sediment, fossilized pollen, cave stalagmites, and the movement of prehistoric human villages to demonstrate that these cold-to-hot climate variations happen in quasi-regular intervals roughly every 1,500 to 2,000 years. Moreover, there is also evidence that this cycle is influenced by the appearance and the disappearance of sunspots that increase and decrease the amount of solar radiation reaching the Earth. If, in fact, this is the dominant, or perhaps even the only cause of climate change, then putting all nations to the task of lowering their GHG emissions is a little like closing all the windows in your home so that you don't hear the approaching earthquake. It may make you feel better but it won't stop your house from crashing down around you.

Even assuming that the greenhouse gases have some effect on climate change, the voluntary nature of the Paris Agreement makes it virtually unworkable. Nations are free to establish expectations that look good on paper but that do not work in real life. In effect, either way, the plan to lower GHS emissions is just not going to work. No, the better plan is to assume that climate change is going happen no matter what we do and to prepare for the changes to come. We could, for example, pour money and effort into stockpiling crops in preparation for the coming drought in some areas while, at the same time, building defenses against coastal flooding in regions like those surrounding New Orleans. We could also guide our scientific community into developing heat-resistant crops and more efficient, more widely available air-conditioned shelters. On the other hand, if the Gulf Stream scenario is correct and we are headed for an ice age then, again, we ought to be storing crops, building shelters, and developing more energy-efficient heating systems to protect us from the extreme cold that will result in an ice age. Either way, it is better to prepare for the coming change than to waste time stopping emissions that either are not the cause or that we are too late to control in a way that makes any difference. [See: "The Paris Agreement," The United Nations Framework Convention on Climate Change, http://unfccc.int/paris_agreement/items/9485.php; Justin Gillis, "Your Questions about Climate Change, Answered," *The New York Times National Sunday*, September 24, 2017, p. 22; Brad Plumer, "The Paris Climate Agreement: How It Works," *The Cleveland Plain Dealer*, June 1, 2017; and S. Fred Singer and Dennis T. Avery, *Unstoppable Global Warming: Every 1,500 Years* (Lanham, MD: Rowman and Littlefield, 2008).]

Source: See: "The Paris Agreement," The United Nations Framework Convention on Climate Change, http://unfccc.int/ paris_ agreement/items/ 9485.php; Justin Gillis, "Your Questions About Climate Change, Answered," *The New York Times National Sunday* (September 24, 2017), p. 22; Brad Plumer, The Paris climate agreement: How it works," *The Cleveland Plain Dealer* (June 1, 2017); S. Fred Singer and Dennis T. Avery, *Unstoppable Global Warming: Every 1,500 Years,* (Lanham, MD: Rowman and Littlefield, 2008.

Regulating Population Growth

The third (our fourth) challenge that Heilbroner records in his book, *An Inquiry into the Human Prospect*, is the demographic challenge of runaway population growth. Heilbroner predicts that the population will pass its tipping point within a few generations. The tipping point will be reached when the planet can no longer support its people. What follows that tipping point is a downward slide characterized by famine, fresh-water shortages, skyrocketing infant mortality rates, wars of redistribution, mega-city collapse, rolling blackouts, and a global economic depression. Heilbroner argues, rather convincingly, that this unchecked population explosion will continue unless two things happen: (1) those areas with the highest population growth rates impose strict birth control programs, and (2) strong "iron" governments rise to deal with the issues of birth control and social unrest.

Population Growth Figures If we look at population growth figures, the United States, with a population of 327 million, a growth rate of 0.8 percent, and vast amounts of unsettled land, is not a threat. Neither is much of the developed world, including the EU, which has an even smaller growth rate of only 0.4 percent. In contrast, the least developed nations of the world have a population growth rate that reaches almost 3.83 percent. Moreover, if we put the growth rates together and project into the future, we can see that by the year 2055, the population will reach 9.7 billion and 11.2 billion by 2100. [See: "Country Comparisons growth rate-United States," *Index Mundi*, January 1, 2018, https://index mundi.com/g/r.aspx?v=24; "Population Clock, United States," U.S. Census Bureau, March 6, 2018, https://www.census.gov; "Population Growth (annual %)," The World Bank, March 6, 2018, https:// data.worldbank.org/indicator/sp.pop.grow; "World Population Projected to Reach 9.7 Billion by 2010," UN Department of

Economics and Social Affairs, July 19, 2015, http://www.un.org/en/development/desa/ news/population/2016-report.html.] The significance of these figures in relation to population growth rates is difficult to imagine. So, it might be helpful to make some reverse comparisons. If we look back to the 19th century, we would find that the Earth reached its first billion in the year 1825. By 1925, 100 years later, humans had managed to add a second billion. By 1976, the population doubled again, reaching 4 billion. [See: Paul Kennedy, *Preparing for the Twenty-First Century* (New York: Random House, 1993).]

Consequences of Uncontrolled Population Growth What are the consequences of uncontrolled population growth? By the year 2050, predictions indicate that the developing world will see an increase in its labor force by some 1.8 billion workers, while the developed world will experience a loss of some 100 million workers. [See: Uri Dadush and Bennett Stancil, *The World Order in 2050* (New York: The Carnegie Endowment for World Peace, 2010).] Despite the loss of workers in the developed world, the increase in the developing world will result in more workers than job openings. This leads to poverty in the mega-cities of the developing world. Poverty leads to disease as problems develop with sanitation and waste disposal. More out of work people means a higher crime rate, an increase in violence, and a threat of social disorder. For a while, science and technology may be able to feed and provide water for these people, but at some point the numbers will outstrip the scientific ability to provide sufficient food and water. Famine follows as well as wars of redistribution. The wars of redistribution are waged when a nation (or tribe or ethnic group or revolutionary movement or terrorist organization) looks across the border to another nation and, seeing the crops and the water that they need, simply moves in and takes what it can. Depending on who is doing what to whom, the struggle my even led to a nuclear confrontation, as might happen if the Arab states attack Israel again, Pakistan attacks India, or North Korea attacks South Korea.

The American Response In light of all of this, we might believe that the United States would impose some legal incentives to participate in a birth control program that would, if nothing else, lead by example. Such a move, however, is not forthcoming. Return for a moment to Heilbroner's two solutions: (1) increased birth control and (2) the rise of iron governments to enforce both birth control and the civil peace. Neither of these is likely to emerge in the United States. First, the United States is not going to enforce birth control limitations on its citizens. The courts have a long and consistent tradition of avoiding any intrusion into the reproductive freedom of its citizens. The right to procreate without governmental interference was first recognized by the United States Supreme Court in the case of *Griswold v. Connecticut,* when the justices ruled that the government could not prevent married couples from obtaining and using contraceptives. That right was extended to unmarried couples in the case of *Eisenstadt v. Baird.* In that case, the Court wrote that "[i]f the right of privacy means anything it is the right of the individual married or single to be free from unwarranted governmental intrusion into matters so fundamentally affecting a person as the decision whether to bear or beget a child." The cap was put on the bottle, so to speak, when, in *Carey v. Population Services International,* the High Court ruled that selling and distributing contraceptives was protected by law. It is very important to note that the procreative freedom referred to by the High Court in all of these cases includes not only the right to avoid reproduction, but also to have children without any interference by the government. Thus, it is unlikely, first, that the United States will enforce birth control or, second, that it will evolve into one of Heilbroner's "iron" governments willing to violate those rights. [See: *Griswold v. Connecticut,* 381 U.S. 479, 85 S.Ct. 1678 (1965); *Eisenstadt v. Baird,* 405 U.S. 438 (1972); and *Carey v. Population Services International,* 431 U.S. 678 (1977).]

Nevertheless, there is always a difference between saying that the government *will not* do something and saying that it *cannot* do something. The flip side of the statement that the government *will not* interfere in procreative rights is that, given the right set of circumstances and the correct motivation, the government *can* interfere in procreative rights. Oddly enough that position was made clear in the case of *Roe v. Wade*. In that case, the High Court supported laws that permit abortion as long as the abortion did not occur after the fetus becomes viable. In *Roe v. Wade*, viability emerged in the third trimester, so laws that allowed abortion after that time were not permitted. According to *Planned Parenthood v. Casey*, viability comes earlier in a woman's pregnancy primarily because medical technology has pushed viability back further toward conception. Nevertheless, both cases say that the government can interfere in a woman's right to control her own body and both define that moment as the time at which the state has a **compelling interest** in the life of the child. In fact, *Planned Parenthood v. Casey* goes just a bit further, noting that the state might even have an interest in the life of the fetus *before* viability and might even be able to pass legislature limiting the rights of the woman before viability, as long as those legal limits do not cause an undue burden on the woman. The important thing to note here is that the Supreme Court has said that the government *can* interfere in the child-bearing decision of a woman if it has a compelling interest to do so. Now, up until the present time, this has been assumed to mean that the government has a compelling interest to *stop* abortion. However, this same rationale could be made to enforce the idea that the government has a compelling interest in stopping runaway birth rates, that is, by forcing an abortion or birth control or perhaps even compulsory sterilization. If, for example, there is a national or a global crisis in relation to uncontrolled population growth, the government might find that it has a compelling interest in limiting population growth by any means available including coerced abortion, forced birth control, and so on. [See: *Planned Parenthood v. Casey*, 112 S.Ct. 2791 (1992).]

The International Response The international community seems more ready, willing, and able to deal with runaway population growth than the United States. In fact, the United Nations has been involved in such work since 1947 when the **Population Commission (PC)** was created under the auspices of the Economic and Social Council. The PC investigates demographic concerns and then consults with ECOSOC on a variety of population issues. These issues include compiling accurate demographic data; developing strategies to control population growth; and gauging the relationship between a growing population, on the one hand, and economic and social issues, on the other. The authority for the commission comes from the top down, flowing as it does through the Population Division of the Department of Economic and Social Development. Moreover, and perhaps more to the point, the PC is charged with helping to implement the UN World Population Plan of Action, which was developed in 1974 at the World Population Conference in Bucharest. The plan developed strategies based on the relationships between population growth and socio economic factors. The plan has been revised since that time and now publishes an extensive list of recommendations that suggest action in relation to population-related questions. To provide funding for population-related government projects, the United Nation's Population Fund (UNPF) was set up in 1966. The UNPF provides money for family planning projects and other work in population management. [See: *Basic Facts about the United Nations*.]

quick quiz 33-4

1. The Federal Energy Regulatory Commission (FERC) is responsible for regulating the transportation and the wholesale price of natural gas alone.   true | false
2. The Nuclear Regulatory Commission owns and operates 104 civilian nuclear power plants and 63 military reactors.   true | false
3. The Clean Air Act is designed to limit pollution from vehicles but not from stationary sources such factories and manufacturing centers.   true | false

33-5 Protecting Intellectual Property

The authority of the government in the area of intellectual property has never been in doubt. However, as they say, "the devil is in the details." This is especially true of patents and copyrights because the very nature of an invention and a recorded work is originality. Originality means that every copyright and every patent application will present a new question for the patent office and, possibly, for the courts. For that reason alone the law of intellectual property is complicated and diverse. Nevertheless, the law of intellectual property plays an enormously important role in the development of scientific and technological advances that will help to combat Heilbroner's global challenges. In its most fundamental form, the entire idea behind the legal framework supporting intellectual property is that inventors, scientists, engineers, and writers must be encouraged to pursue their crafts so that the entire socioeconomic system can benefit from the advances that they produce. What the people at General Electric used to say about their own research and development applies equally well, perhaps even better, to the entire scientific community: "Progress is our most important product."

ANOTHER CLASSIC CASE Act 1
JCVI and Patent Application US2007 0264688: "To Be or Not to Be . . . Alive"

Members of the J. Craig Venter Institute (JCVI) filed patent US 2007 0264688 with the U.S. Patent Office in an attempt to patent synthetic life. What JCVI had produced was a self-replicating bacterial cell completely under the control of a synthetic genome. The development of the synthetic self-replicating cell proved that such organisms can be planned by a computer, constructed chemically in a laboratory, and then placed in a bacterium from which the original DNA had been removed. The new cell then replicated itself 1 billion times. The process will make DNA synthesis more economical and more affordable, leading to possible breakthroughs in the development of new vaccines, innovative pharmaceuticals, clean water, new food products, innovative pollution filters, and possibly even revolutionary new biofuel derivatives. This is not the first time that the legal system has faced this issue. In the case of *Diamond v. Chakrabarty*, the U.S. Supreme Court decided that it was possible to patent a lifeform. Nevertheless, the issue of patenting a self-replicating completely synthetic lifeform presents a new twist on that original theme. This is what intellectual property law is all about. [See: J. Craig Venter Institute, "First Self-Replicating Synthetic Bacterial Cell Constructed by J. Craig Venter Institute Researchers," May 20, 2010, http://www.jcvi.org; Boonsi Dickinson, "Will Patents Give Craig Venter a Monopoly Over Synthetic Life?" *Smart Planet*, May 28, 2010, www.smartplanet.com; and *Diamond v. Chakrabarty*, 447 U.S. 303, 100 S.Ct. 204 (1980).]

Source: See: J. Craig Venter Institute, "First Self-Replicating Synthetic Bacterial Cell Constructed by J. Craig Venter Institute Researchers," May 20, 2010, http://www.jcvi.org; and Boonsi Dickinson, "Will Patents Give Craig Venter a Monopoly Over Synthetic Life?" *Smart Planet*, May 28, 2010, www.smartplanet.com; *Diamond v. Chakrabarty*, 447 U.S. 303, 100 S.Ct. 204 (1980).

The Nature of Intellectual Property

Intellectual property involves an intangible ownership right in an invention, a process, a computer program, a chemical formula, an original recorded work such as a book or an article, and so on. The ownership rights bestowed on a person holding the property includes the right to give permission to use the property in exchange for some sort of consideration. This consideration is usually referred to as a **royalty**. The power of the government to grant the exclusive rights to intellectual property is expressly mentioned in Article I, Section 8, Clause 8 of the

Constitution, where the framers gave Congress the authority to grant patents and copyrights. The clause reads that Congress has the power to "promote the Progress of Science and the useful Arts, by securing for limited Times to Authors and Inventors the exclusive Right to their respective Writings and Discoveries." The granting of patents and copyrights is one of the most direct and obvious entanglements of science and the law in jurisicence.

Protecting Patents

A **patent** is a property right granted by the federal government to an inventor. A patent gives the inventor the exclusive right to make, use, and sell that invention for a period of 20 years (14 years if the patent covers a process). A patent is, in effect, a deal with the government. The inventor reveals the details of the invention in the patent application. In exchange, the inventor receives a guarantee from the government that it will protect the inventor's exclusive right to produce and profit from that invention for a specified period of time. As we shall see later, a trade secret is not revealed in any way in the open marketplace; the holder of the trade secret receives no guaranteed protection from the government. A copyright differs from a patent in that a copyright protects only the expression of an idea, whereas a patent protects the idea itself.

The Patent Application Process Each patent application requires the creation of a unique technical document. The document is then filed with the Patent and Trademark Office. To qualify for a patent, an invention must meet three requirements. First, the invention must fall within the limits defined by the statute as "patentable subject matter." Second, the invention must consist of some nonobvious, new, and useful feature not known or understood before the invention of this particular device. Third, the patent application must be so specific that individuals who are educated and experienced in the field can create the device on their own.

Patent Law and the "Right to Tinker" Like all areas of the law, the patent process is always subject to revision by the courts. In a recent landmark case, the U.S. Supreme Court has clarified the extent of control that a patent holder has over used (perhaps, "pre-owned" is a better term here) versions of an invention the patent holder has placed on the open market. The case involved a company named Lexmark International Inc. (Lexmark) that had developed a unique line of toner cartridges for use in its printers. The owners of Lexmark discovered that another firm, Impression Products Inc. (Impressions), was gathering up used (pre-owned) Lexmark cartridges, filling them with toner, and then selling them at bargain basement prices. Lexmark sued Impressions for patent infringement. The question before the court was whether a patent extended over, above, and beyond the first sale of a product. This issue, however, was actually a subdivision of a much bigger issue, that is, an issue called the "right to tinker." Proponents of the right to tinker—firms like Impressions, for example—argue that, once they have purchased a product, they have the right to do with it as they please. They can resell it, give it away, paint it, modify it, break it apart, melt it down, sell its parts individually, or even destroy it completely. The patent holders—firms such as Lexmark—argue that such "tinkering" violates their ownership rights under patent law because it interferes with their ability to sell additional copies of their invention.

Although the right to tinker is never actually named by the High Court, in its ruling, the Court has upheld the **right to tinker**. Justice Roberts noted that there was more at stake than the patent owner's property rights. Those rights must be seen in the context of the larger commercial system. Much of the commercial system is based on the repair, repainting, refurbishing, reuse, and resale of goods. The Court notes, for example, that a firm that buys, repairs, refurbishes, and then resells automobiles essentially reshapes every vehicle that rolls into its garage. What Lexmark had attempted to do was to control not only its patent rights, but also the market place beyond the sale to first purchasers. Business simply does not work that way.

Instead, after buying a product, a purchaser is free to tinker with the product and then to resell the product to other consumers, second-hand shops, vintage shops, used (pre-owned) car lots, and so on, and, coincidentally enough, to buy other products at flea markets, auctions, yard and garage sales, and so on, for further tinkering and resale. Justice Roberts says it this way, "In sum, patent exhaustion is uniform and automatic. Once a patentee decides to sell—whether on its own or through a licensee—that sale exhausts its patent rights, regardless of any post-sale restrictions the patentee purports to impose, either directly or through a license." [See: *Impression Products, Inc. v. Lexmark International, Inc.*, No. 15–1189 (argued March 21, 2017; decided May 30, 2017); Brian Fung, "Court Ruling Alters Uses of Patent Infringement Claims: Companies Cannot Wield Endless Control over Sold Items," *The Cleveland Plain Dealer*, January 1, 2017, p. A-5; and Kit Walsh, "Supreme Court Victory for the Right to Tinker in Printer Cartridge Case," The Electronic Frontier Foundation, May 20, 2017, https://www.eff.org/deeplinks/2017/05/supreme-court-victory-right-tinker-printer-cartridge-case.)

Patentable Subject Matter The law states that for the subject of a patent application to be patentable, it must be a "process, machine, manufacturer or composition of matter." In contrast, such things as laws of nature, natural phenomena, and abstract ideas cannot be patented. Neither mathematical formulas nor mathematical algorithms are patentable because they are actually laws of nature. An algorithm is a series of steps that, if followed properly, will reach a desired goal. Because many computer software programs are based on mathematical algorithms, problems arose when inventors first attempted to patent computer software. In fact, when patent applications for computer software programs began to appear in the patent office in the 1970s, most software programs were eventually found to be unpatentable. However, during the 1980s and the 1990s, the trend reversed itself. Today, more than 80 percent of all patent claims involving computers have been upheld, including those involving software alone. However, the law in this area remains somewhat unclear. Fortunately, some general guidelines can be laid down. For example, if a software program is only one part of a larger, more conventional process, the courts will allow patent protection for the whole process.

EXAMPLE 33-6: Ariya's Power packed Pup Preparation process Patent Publication Problem

Ariya Andrea, the owner, operator, and CEO of Ariya Inc., "Home of the Power Packed Pup Preparation Project," developed a new process for producing a vitamin-packed dog food. The new process allowed Ariya to produce a better-quality dog food at about half the cost of its closest competitors. Part of Ariya's success was the additional injection of several multivitamins to the dog food mix at precisely timed intervals. However, the addition of the vitamins had to be timed so precisely that each injection was controlled by a computer, following the directions of a computer program. This portion of the process was only about one-fourth of the entire operation, the rest of which was relatively conventional. The patent examiner denied Ariya's patent application because part of the process involved an unpatentable computer program. A federal court reversed the refusal because the process itself was new and could be patented. The use of the program was only one part of that process.

However, if the software stands alone, the question of whether the patent application will be granted is more difficult. The Court of Appeals for the Federal Circuit has addressed the issue in several cases and tends to affirm such patent applications. The appellate court generally upholds the patentability of software, even if it is based on a mathematical algorithm, because the software actually changes the operation of the computer. Thus, the software can be viewed as either a process or a change in the physical nature of the computer itself. To deal with the issue, the U.S. Patent and Trademark Office established a set of guidelines for computer-related inventions. The objective of the guidelines is to help eliminate ambiguity in the law regarding the patentability of software.

EXAMPLE 33-7: Forest's Finest Free Fall File Finds a Fabulous Win

Forest Gentille, the owner-operator of Forest's Finest Finance Files Inc., developed Forest's Finest Free Fall File, a software program that allowed the user to overlay on a computer screen all available trajectories for any stocks that he or she wished to purchase or sell in the near future while simultaneously displaying all changes in the data related to each pictured stock. Such a program would be invaluable to investors as they planned investment strategies. The patent examiner refused to issue a patent, arguing that Forest's program was simply the expression of a mathematical algorithm. The Board of Patent Appeals supported the examiner's position. The Court of Appeals for the Federal Circuit, however, reversed the decision and stated that, in effect, Forest's program transformed an ordinary, all-purpose computer into a specialized computer. Thus, the all-purpose computer had in effect become a new computer, capable of performing a new function by following the commands of the software program. Forest's Finest Free Fall File can be viewed as either a process creating a change or an alteration in the physical nature of the computer itself.

Until recently, a **business system** was also considered unpatentable because it was not a "process, machine, manufacturer, or composition of matter." However, in a recent court case, a computer system for analyzing information about a group of mutual funds was declared patentable by a federal court. This decision culminated in a slow erosion of the business systems category of unpatentable subjects. Even so, a computerized business system must still consist of some nonobvious, new, and useful feature not known or understood before the invention of this system. It must also be so specific that people who are educated and experienced in the field can re-create the system on their own.

Requirement 1: Usefulness The objective of patent law is to encourage inventiveness and promote progress for the benefit of all society. Thus, a device, to be patentable, must be useful, novel, and nonobvious. Many processes involving computer programs would pass the usefulness test. However, sometimes usefulness is not as clear as it seems on the surface. For an example, let's return for a moment to the requirement of "usefulness" and the classic case of the J. Craig Venter Institute and patent US 2007 0264688. Recall that the application filed with the patent office was an attempt to patent synthetic life. The development of the synthetic self-replicating cell proved that such organisms can be planned by a computer, constructed chemically in a laboratory, and then placed in a bacterium from which the original DNA had been removed. The new cell then replicated itself 1 billion times. All that is nice, but—so what? What can the synthetic life do that, well, "real" life cannot? The answer is that JCVI's new process will make DNA synthesis more economical and more affordable, leading to possible breakthroughs in the development of new vaccines, innovative pharmaceuticals, clean water, new food products, innovative pollution filters, and possibly even revolutionary new biofuel derivatives.

Requirement 2: Novelty Passing the usefulness test alone, however, is not enough to qualify for a patent. The new invention must also be novel and nonobvious. To pass the novelty test, the new device or process must be original. Copying someone else's innovation, even unintentionally, will disqualify an invention from patent eligibility.

Requirement 3: Nonobviousness Passing both the usefulness and novelty tests is still not sufficient. To be patentable a new invention must also be nonobvious. To pass the nonobviousness test, the changes or improvements must not be apparent to a person of ordinary skill in the field. If the changes are evident, then a patent will not be issued. At least that is the way it used to be. Unfortunately, the patent review process became more difficult for patent holders recently when the U.S. Supreme Court revised the traditional test of nonobviousness. The traditional test, which was referred to as the **teaching, suggestion, or motivation test**, or the **TSM standard**, compelled those who challenged a patent to demonstrate that the so-called innovation would have been discernible to anyone exposed to the same *teaching* session, the same offhand *suggestion*, or perhaps even the same *motivation* that the inventor had experienced. In essence, the test rested on the belief that any small innovation based on prior art in the field would not be patentable but that other innovations, even small ones beyond prior art, would be (see Table 33-1). **Prior art** refers to all relevant technical knowledge about the field to which the invention belongs. The test was difficult, however, because it also required the challenger to produce some sort of firm evidence to support the TSM challenge. Generally, the only factual data that the court would accept as solid evidence was information that had been printed in a professional journal or data that rose to that same high level of credibility.

In creating a new, more lenient test, the Supreme Court stressed that previous courts had been too uncompromising in their use of TSM. Accordingly, the Court suggested that challengers ought to consider using other types of evidence to contest the validity of a patent claim. Such evidence might include economic conditions, the knowledge of other inventors in the same field, or progress in the relevant technology that might show that a person of ordinary skill could easily have developed the same innovation introduced in the challenged patent. If any of these features exist, the contested innovation would not be patentable. In addition, the Supreme Court reintroduced a variation on the TSM test called the **obvious-to-try standard**, a test that had been outlawed by previous precedent. Under the newly reinstated obvious-to-try standard, if the challenger can demonstrate that anyone of ordinary skill could see that it would have been obvious to try such an innovation, the innovation would be labeled as obvious, and the invention would not be patentable.

Nonobviousness and Cyber-Inventions The new rulings make it more difficult for inventors to obtain patents and easier for challengers to demonstrate that an innovation is obvious and therefore not patentable. The decision to make the test of patent-ability harder will have a direct effect on computer-related cyber-inventions. Many innovations in computer technology that might have been patentable under the old rules will not be patentable under the new obviousness tests. For instance, under the old rules that dealt exclusively with

Table 33-1 Recent Developments in Patent Law

Standard	Explanation
Teaching, suggestion, motivation	An invention is obvious and not patentable if anyone exposed to the same teaching, suggestion, or motivation would have come up with the same invention.
Obvious-to-try standard	An invention is obvious and not patentable if the innovation was so obvious that anyone of ordinary skill could see that it was obvious to try that innovation.
Possible legislative changes	Some *possible* legislative changes slated for the future may be (1) increased ease in obtaining injunctions, (2) an 18-month publication rule, and (3) a change in the burden of proof.

TSM, a small innovation in the component parts of a laptop or a tablet might have been patentable if the new component was not made clear by teaching, suggestion, or motivation. Now, if the challenger can show that trends in engineering made the innovation a logical next step, or that it was obvious to try the change in the component parts of that tablet or laptop, the innovation, no matter how clever, will be unpatentable.

Specificity in the Application Federal law states that a patent application must describe the nature of the invention in "full, clear, concise, and exact terms." In fact, the application must be so clear that any person educated and experienced in that field can re-create the invention without having to engage in an extensive trial-and-error period. This requirement causes some difficulty in computer software patent applications, because the surest way to guarantee that someone else will be able to re-create the invention is to provide the source code in the patent application. However, many inventors are reluctant to include source code because such codes often contain trade secrets that they are unwilling to dump into the public domain. The usual compromise is to include in the patent application either a flowchart or some other visual diagram that reveals the details of the process.

ANOTHER CLASSIC CASE Act 2
JCVI and Patent Application US2007 026468: "To Be or Not to Be . . . Limited"

Members of the J. Craig Venter Institute were attempting to patent synthetic life after producing a self-replicating bacterial cell completely under the control of a synthetic genome. The development of the synthetic self-replicating cell proved that such organisms can be planned by a computer, constructed chemically in a laboratory, and then placed in a bacterium from which the original DNA had been removed. Not everyone was happy with this development, however. Some of JCVI's competitors accused the company of trying to corner the market with the patent application. The main objection to the JCVI patent application was that it was too broad. JCVI was not attempting to patent the synthetic self-replicating bacterium that the team actually created, but the process of planning, constructing, and creating any synthetic cell imaginable. Some legal experts argued that the problem may be that JCVI's patent application lacked appropriate specificity. These experts predicted that JCVI would get its patent—but not the way that it was originally written. Instead, JCVI would receive a patent for the process involving the bacterium used in the original process or, more likely, bacteria in general. JCVI would not earn a blank check to use the process on any cell imaginable.

To deal with these issues, among many others associated with the development of synthetic life technologies, a presidential commission was formed in 2010 following JCVI's announcement. In the commission's report, *New Directions: The Ethics of Synthetic Biology and Emerging Technologies*, commission members acknowledged the problems associated with the overly broad nature of the JVCI patent application but proposed no recommendations of their own beyond offering a series of alternatives that might be used to address the concerns of all affected parties. [See: Presidential Commission for the Study of Bioethical Issues, *New Directions: The Ethics of Synthetic Biology and Emerging Technologies*, December 2010, pp. 119-21; J. Craig Venter Institute, "First Self-Replicating Synthetic Bacterial Cell Constructed by J. Craig Venter Institute Researchers," May 20, 2010, http://www.jcvi.org; and Boonsi Dickinson, "Will Patents Give Craig Venter a Monopoly Over Synthetic Life?" *Smart Planet*, May 28, 2010, http://www.smartplanet.com.]

Source: See: Presidential Commission for the Study of Bioethical Issues, *New Directions: The Ethics of Synthetic Biology and Emerging Technologies*, December 2010, pp. 119-21; J. Craig Venter Institute, "First Self-Replicating Synthetic Bacterial Cell Constructed by J. Craig Venter Institute Researchers," May 20, 2010, http://www.jcvi.org; and Boonsi Dickinson, "Will Patents Give Craig Venter a Monopoly Over Synthetic Life?" *Smart Planet*, May 28, 2010, http://www.smartplanet.com.

A QUESTION OF ETHICS

The J. Craig Venter Institute classic case involved an application to patent synthetic life. JCVI had produced a self-replicating bacterial cell completely under the control of a synthetic genome. The development of the synthetic self-replicating cell proved that such organisms can be planned by a computer, constructed chemically in a laboratory and then placed in a bacterium from which the original DNA had been removed. This was not the first time that the legal system had faced this issue. In the case of *Diamond v. Chakrabarty*, the U.S. Supreme Court decided that it was possible to patent a lifeform. As is often the case in sensitive issues like this, no one was happy with the Court's decision except, perhaps, the new patent holder. Some experts felt compelled to criticize the Court for stepping outside the bounds of its authority. Others accused the Court of a thoughtless ruling that would open the door to abusive use of biotechnology. However, one of the most interesting points was made when a commentator noted that it was strange that the Supreme Court was willing to grant a patent for a new lifeform when, in the case of *Roe v. Wade*, the Court had refused to define life.

A QUESTION YET UNANSWERED

The following question has not yet been answered. Before you consider the question, turn to Chapter 1 to review the various ethical theories noted there (market value ethics, social contract theory, utilitarianism, and rational ethics). Then answer the following question:

1. Is it ethical for the justices of the Supreme Court to avoid the definition of life when it comes to the rights of women and then turn around and permit a megacorporation, like General Electric, to reap potential profit from their decision? (The microbiologist who developed the DNA plasmid that was the subject of *Diamond v. Chakrabarty* was employed by General Electric.) Try to come up with a rationale for each side of the issue. [See: *Diamond v. Chakrabarty*, 447 U.S. 303, 100 S. Ct. 204 (1980); and *Roe v. Wade*, 410 U.S. 113, 93 S.Ct. 705 (1973).]

The America Invents Act

Congress amended the patent law for the first time in over 60 years when, in 2011, it passed the America Invents Act (AIA). The new act is designed to do several things, not the least of which is to bring U.S. patent law in line with international patent law. The AIA does several important things in this regard. First, it has changed the basic principle of American patent law. The act adopts the "first-to-file" patent process, which replaces the "first-to-invent" process that had been the American standard for decades. Second, the new act has set up a series of innovative ways to dispute previous or pending patent claims.

The First-to-File Provision As noted earlier, this is a key provision that will help bring U.S. patent law in line with international patent law. Some experts predict that this change will probably increase the practice of provisional filing. Provisional filing permits an inventor or company to "hold his or her place" in line as a first filer, without having to deal with some of the formalities involved in a full-fledged filing. The net effect will be that inventors and the companies that they represent will likely file more patents earlier rather than later. The point of the early filing strategy will be to jump in line ahead of any other inventors who might be close to developing the same type of process or device that the first filer has developed, thus trumping the claims of all other inventors. The provision clearly gives the advantage to large corporate research and development departments. In contrast, those inventors who work in the family garage or in the basement of the family home and are more engrossed in the science and the technology than day-to-day business matters are likely to lose the race to the patent office. On the other hand, those inventors who are not certain about the profitability or perhaps even the marketability of their invention and, therefore, need more time to assess its cost-effectiveness can also "hold their place in line," by filing a provisional patent while they do the necessary research.

EXAMPLE 33-8: Veda's Velvet Value Shoppe

Veda Frances, the owner-operator of Veda's Velvet Value Shoppe, developed a new fabric that was stain resistant, elastic, flame retardant, durable, and shrinkproof. She had worked on it for years at home in her spare time. Once she had the process finalized, she filed her records away and went on to another equally exciting project, secure in the knowledge that as the first inventor of the fabric, her patent rights would be honored. One evening, she was having dinner with two inventor friends, Ariya Andrea and Forest Gentille. At some point in the dinner, Veda mentioned the development of her new fabric. Both Ariya and Forest urged Veda to file the invention with the Patent Office. Veda argued that she had all her records proving that she was the first inventor and that would protect her. Nevertheless, Ariya and Forest urged her to file "just to make sure." Veda agreed and did so. One week after she had he had filed, Veda found out that another inventor had tried to file a patent for an identical fabric. Fortunately, Veda had followed her friends' advice. Her invention was protected by the "first to file rule."

The New Dispute Resolution Process As indicated previously, the new law also sets up several new ways to call into question previous patent filings, including both those that have been completed and those that are still in the processing stage. There are several new ways to mount such challenges; however, the two most important are the (1) pre-issuance submission challenge and (2) the post-grant review process. The pre-submission disputes are permitted before the patent has been granted by the patent office. They can be submitted anonymously by third parties who seek to block the issuance of the patent. Naturally, proper documentation must be presented to demonstrate that the patent should not be granted. The new law also permits a post-grant review, which must be filed within nine months of the patent issuance. To be accepted for review, the post-grant challenge must show either (1) the invention did not meet the requirements of patentability, or (2) there are legal questions involved in the patent that will affect other patents and other patent applications that must be handled before proceeding further with the sale of distribution of the invention or process that is the subject of the challenged patent. [See: Ronald Abramson et al., "First Major Revision in Nearly Six Decades Changes the Patent Landscape," Hughes Hubbard and Reed LLP, September 30, 2011, retrieved on October 11, 2011, from http://www.mondaq.com; and Chris Dixon, "Summary of New Patent Act," *Business Insider*, September 16, 2011, retrieved on October 11, 2011, from http://www.businessinsider.com.]

Protecting Trade Secrets

Sometimes, an inventor or a discoverer refuses to apply for a patent. At first glance, this may seem strange. After all, the patent protects the invention or the discovery so that no one else can use it except with the patent holder's permission, and then according to the owner's terms, which will generally include royalty payments of some sort. There are disadvantages to holding a patent, however. First, a patent expires at the end of a 20-year period, and for design patents, that period is only 14 years. At the end of that period, the invention or the discovery is in the public domain, and anyone can use and profit from it. Second, to be awarded a patent, the patent applicant must fill out the patent application with great specificity. This means that anyone can access the patent and see exactly what the inventor has developed. Certainly, most people will honor the patent. However, there are people who will try to copy the process or the invention and benefit from the patent owner's work without having to pay royalties. Finally, once the patent is a public record, it is possible that someone who examines the patent might be clever enough to see the next leap in technology or science before the patent owner sees it. Thus, the work of the patent owner may inspire a competitor to take the next developmental leap before the original owner sees it, leaving the owner holding an outdated patent almost before it is approved by the patent office. For all of these reasons, and probably more, many scientists and engineers who have invented or discovered something may try to keep that discovery or that invention as secret as possible. Juriscientific principles protect these efforts as long as the holder of the secret takes certain relatively easy but very important steps.

A Primer on Trade Secrets A trade secret is a plan, process, device, procedure, formula, pattern, compilation, technique, program, design, method, or improvement used in a business and disclosed only to those employees who need to know it to do their jobs. The Uniform Trade Secrets Act sets up two conditions that must be met for a plan, process, program, and so on to gain trade secret status. First, the plan, process, or program must gain financial worth simply because it is a secret and cannot be applied by others who might use it to compete with the owner of the secret. Second, the alleged secret must be the subject of reasonable attempts to protect it from those who would use it in a way that would financially hurt the owner of the secret.

State Statutory Trade Secret Protection Various states have enacted trade secret statutes designed to protect trade secrets within the state's borders. Many of these statutes are patterned after the Uniform Trade Secrets Act, written by the Uniform Law Commission (ULC). Typically, these statutes define a trade secret, describe transgressions of the act, and provide for both damages and injunctive relief when there has been a trade secret infringement. The statutes also generally include a statute of limitations, typically about four years, and indicate that continuing use of a trade secret is a single rather than a series of transgressions. Some state statutes also allow for attorney's fees.

The Economic Espionage Act The federal government also entered the trade secrets' arena with the passage of the Economic Espionage Act in 1996. The act does not provide for any civil actions but instead outlines criminal sanctions for the theft of trade secrets and the use of fraud to obtain trade secrets. Persons convicted under the statute can face up to 10 years of imprisonment and fines that may reach as much as $500,000. The statute forbids the theft of trade secrets for distribution to a foreign government or an agent of a foreign government or for economic gain that does not benefit the actual owner of the trade secret.

Establishing Trade Secret Status In the 21st century, many of the inventors, scientists, and engineers who apply for patents know that part of the patent application will include a step involving computers. For example, the synthetic life process outlined in the JCVI case involves a computerized stage wherein the computer actually designs the synthetic genome before it is produced chemically and then placed in the bacterium. Scientists who are not overly concerned about the time limit placed on patents or with the specificity required in the patent application might file the patent application knowing full well that they have placed it at risk. Why do it then? The advantage to pursuing patent protection rather than trade secret protection is that the patent applicant can be almost certain that a patent can include a computer program. The same is not true of an engineer or a technician who wants to keep a computer program as a trade secret. The law at the moment is filled with ambiguities about the trade secret status of a computer program.

The right to characterize a computer program as a trade secret depends on the way the owners of the program treat it in relation to other people. In general, the easier it is for people to gain access to the program, the less likely it is that the program will be considered a secret should the matter be contested in court. Therefore, to protect trade secret status, the owners of a program must make certain that the program is treated as a secret from the very beginning. The goal is to grant access to the secret only to those people who need to know it to carry out their duties in the ordinary course of business. Steps that can be taken to increase the likelihood that a court will rule that a program is a trade secret include the following: (1) label the program as secret in all documents related to the program; (2) limit employee access to the program on a need-to-know basis; (3) maintain tight security in the business in general, but especially in any area where the program is required to be out in the open for business purposes; (4) keep the program and all related material under lock and key when it is not in use; (5) require employees who work with the program to sign secrecy agreements; (6) require customers who purchase the use of the program to sign licensing agreements; and (7) be especially vigilant in limiting any access to the program by competitors.

Computer Programs Denied Trade Secret Status Computer programs that have been transferred to software and then placed on the open market for wide distribution cannot claim trade secret status. Software that is widely distributed can be easily copied. Thus, it becomes difficult to demonstrate that the company has taken extensive measures to protect the information on the software. Moreover, because the purpose of placing the software on the open market is to sell it to as many people as possible, the seller must make the software readily available in bookstores and online. This availability on the open market defeats the whole trade secret concept.

Computer Programs Granted Trade Secret Status Trade secret status is available to companies that distribute their software on a limited, highly selective basis. For example, a computer company that produces and sells a program used to control the distribution of drugs by pharmaceutical firms might be able to call that program a trade secret. Such a company would not actually sell the program to the pharmaceutical firm but would instead allow the firm to use the program through a licensing agreement. A **licensing agreement** occurs when the producer of a product—in this case, a computer program—allows a purchaser to use the product only if the purchaser agrees to respect the producer's desire for secrecy. In this situation, to use the program, the pharmaceutical company would have to agree to respect the computer company's desire for secrecy. In this type of highly selective, strictly controlled transaction, trade secret status works.

Trademark Protection Before moving on to copyright law, it would be a good idea to pause momentarily just to distinguish between trade secrets and trademarks. A **trademark** is a symbol, picture, image, name, device, color, or word that a business uses to distinguish itself from its competitors. Once a business has established that it owns a trademark, that business has the exclusive right to use that mark to identify its products and services, as well as the business itself. The law provides businesspeople with several ways to establish trademark ownership: common law, state law, and federal law. To claim that trademark ownership has been established by common law, the alleged owner must show that the trademark has been used with such intensity and for such a long time that the mark has come to be identified not only with the business's products but also with the business itself. Every state legislature has also passed state trademark laws to protect the use of trademarks in intrastate commerce. Despite the use of common law and state law to protect trademarks, most of the legal action in this area takes place at the federal level. The Trademark Protection Act, also known as the Lanham Act, was passed in 1946 to provide for the registration of trademarks with the federal government. The registration authority is the U.S. Patent and Trademark

Office. Under the Lanham Act, once a trademark is properly registered with the office, it cannot be used by any other business. The act also protects trademark owners from businesses that use symbols, pictures, words, and so on that are so similar to the protected mark that consumers might be confused into thinking that the secondary mark is actually the original mark, thus leading those consumers from the owner's product to those of the competitor.

Trademark Dilution In 1995, Congress passed the Trademark Dilution Act to establish a standard for trademark infringement that would not involve direct and obvious consumer confusion. Unfortunately, the act has not always worked as well as it was supposed to, mainly because of the courts' often perplexing rules about how it ought to be interpreted. To remedy this situation, Congress amended the act in 2006. The new act, referred to as the Trademark Dilution Revision Act, established several new provisions. First, the new act allows trademark owners to obtain an injunction to stop the use of a trademark, simply by demonstrating that the effectiveness of the original mark would probably be diminished. Second, the act strengthens the eligibility of certain marks for protection, especially expressive trademarks such as Quick Lube, Fresh Way Cleaners, or Complete Comfort Heating. Third, the act provides a series of characteristics that the courts can apply to determine if the unauthorized use of a trademark really does obscure the effectiveness of the original mark.

Protecting Copyright

Copyright law is much more expansive than patent law because copyrights also protect the rights of nonscientific work. Therefore, it encompasses an area of the law that goes beyond the bounds of normal jurisience. Nevertheless, there are two areas on which jurisience and copyright law intersect dramatically. The first is in the area of scientific writing. Perhaps more than any other academic discipline—save, perhaps, law and literature—science communicates using the written word. Scientific ideas, claims, theories, antitheories, and arguments are all communicated by the written word. Scientific books, periodicals, articles, news releases, new stories, and conference poster presentations are the mainstay of the scientific community. Therefore, a clear connection exists between science and copyright law. The second, and perhaps more contemporary, way that science and copyright law intersect is in the world of computer advances. The law has had to play catch-up with scientific advances in computer technology. Scientists are responsible for these advances; they then communicate information about these advances using the advances themselves. The law must decide if the advances themselves and the way that those advances are communicated deserve copyright protection. A clear case exactly on point is the development and evolution of the computer program, something that scientists and information technologists took for granted but which the law struggled with for decades, literally.

A Primer on Copyright A *copyright* is an intangible property right granted to authors of literary, artistic, and musical compositions. A copyright gives the owner the exclusive right to reproduce, publish, and sell his or her work in a fixed, tangible medium of expression. Most people are under the mistaken impression that obtaining a copyright is a long, involved, expensive bureaucratic nightmare. Nothing could be further from the truth. In fact, a copyright, unlike a patent, emerges once an idea is fixed in a set medium—period— that's it. No filing is necessary. In fact, according to the Berne Convention, an international agreement that the United States has approved, there is no longer any need to use the traditional copyright symbol or the word *copyright* on a copyrighted work. Still, it never hurts to place this notification on a work to short-circuit any attempts to "inadvertently" violate an owner's rights. The duration of a copyright is somewhat problematic, but in general, we can say that a copyright lasts for 70 years beyond the death of the owner. Business firms owning copyrights will hold on to the rights for 95 years from the time it is was first published or 120 years from the time it is first developed, whichever deadline is passed first.

Although it was not immediately obvious to lawmakers and judges 30 year ago, a computer program is a fixed medium of expression and is, therefore, subject to copyright protection. Today, the federal Copyright Act specifically lists the following as works that are subject to copyright protection: literary works, dramatic works, musical works, pantomimes, pictorial works, sculptures, graphic works, motion pictures, audiovisual works, sound recordings, architectural works, and choreographic works. Computer programs are also specifically covered by the Copyright Act of 1980, which includes computer programs in the category of "writings" or "literary" works to which exclusive rights can be granted.

The law allows some copying to be done without permission under the **fair use doctrine**. The doctrine provides that copyrighted material may be reproduced without permission if the use of the material is reasonable and not harmful to the rights of the copyright owner. Copying items for such purposes as criticism, comment, news reporting, teaching, scholarship, and research is permissible. The fair use doctrine was codified in Title 17 USC Section 107 of the United States Code, which tells us that four factors must be weighed when figuring out whether fair use is in effect: (1) the purpose and character of the use, including whether such use is of commercial nature or is for nonprofit educational purposes; (2) the nature of the copyrighted work; (3) the amount and substantiality of the portion used in relation to the copyrighted work as a whole; and (4) the effect of the use upon the potential market for, or value of, the copyrighted work.

Juriscience has finally responded to the unprecedented changes that have occurred in computer technology. To make up for lost time, many of the recent alterations in the law were specifically designed to keep abreast of the effects of electronic communication on copyright privileges. Despite this effort, the high-speed, global, interactive nature of the Internet has caused unforeseen problems in copyright law. For example, computer technology now makes it possible for a single copy of a computer program or an individual copy of a scientific paper to be made available to millions of computer users, simply by placing that single copy on a website that is accessible to other users. This advance in computer technology may have been predictable to cyberneticists, but it went virtually unnoticed for quite some time by jurists and legislators. Nevertheless, despite the unpredictability of the problem, juriscience has provided a few solutions.

The No Electronic Theft Act

One such solution came from Congress in the form of the **No Electronic Theft Act (NET Act)**, a federal law that granted limited immunity to persons who duplicate copyrighted works on the Internet, as long as those users do not profit from the copying process. The statute does not simply grant immunity to infringers, however. Instead, it imposes criminal penalties for the violation of certain provisions. Specifically, it makes it illegal to create a duplication (including an electronic duplication) of a copyrighted work for commercial profit or private financial gain by copying or handing out one or more copies of one or more copyrighted productions within a single 180-day period.

The Digital Millennium Copyright Act

The **Digital Millennium Copyright Act (DMCA)** is designed to combat scientific and technological advances that permit users to override protection systems implanted on recorded materials to prevent that type of intellectual property theft. The law makes it illegal to use technological means to bypass, erase, or override programs specifically designed to prevent access to a copyrighted work. Another provision of the DMCA makes it illegal to use any means to circumvent a program intended to frustrate the copying of a copyrighted work.

The World Intellectual Property Organization

It would be unfair and incomplete to close any discussion of the Digital Millennium Copyright Act without mentioning its connection to the World Intellectual Property Organization (WIPO). WIPO is part of the United Nations and supported the development of two international treaties specifically designed to deal with electronic copyright problems. Two separate but closely related treaties resulted from the efforts of the WIPO. The first treaty is known as the World Intellectual Property Organization Copyright Treaty. This treaty guarantees that copyright holders will be allowed to use the Internet to post their works with full copyright protection. The second WIPO treaty, the World Intellectual Property Organization Phonograms Treaty, gives copyright holders the right to copy, publish, and distribute their works in any way, including by making video copies, audio copies, and encrypted copies. The DMCA was written to implement the provisions of these treaties into law in the United States.

quick quiz 33-5

1. A patent gives the inventor the exclusive right to make, use, and sell that invention for a period of 20 years (14 years if the patent covers a process). — true | false
2. A trade secret is a plan, process, device, procedure, formula, pattern, compilation, technique, program, design, method, or improvement used in a business and disclosed only to those employees who need to know it to do their jobs. — true | false
3. A copyright is an intangible property right granted to authors of literary, artistic, and musical compositions. — true | false

33-6 Developing Global Solutions

The goal of this chapter has been to explore the relationship between science and the law and to look at how the law helps promote discoveries in science so that those discoveries can be directed toward social and economic improvements. A central function of the law is to contribute to the civic peace by securing order, stability, and justice. There can be no more serious threat to the global social system than the challenges that Heilbroner notes earlier. Some of these challenges can be met by promoting and awarding innovation and originality in science and technology by protecting intellectual property through patents, copyrights, and trade secrets. However, there is another way to help deal with these problems and that is to actively restructure the law to direct scientific and technological activities toward solving the problems.

Four Basic Requirements

In order to solve any problem, the first thing that the government must do is to identify the parameters of the problem. At the close of the 20th century, there was an enormous amount of work done by colleges and universities, governmental institutions, corporations, and private think tanks to identify the problems that will face humanity in the 21st century. One such study was conducted by the New York Academy of Sciences (NYAS). As a result, the NYAS published a report based on 20 case studies that examined the results of government-supported science and technology polices in the United States and around the globe. The studies examined a series of successful and "less-than-successful" projects in an attempt to identify those factors that made things work and those that made them fail. The results were compiled in "Lessons from Global Experiences in Policy for Science Based Development," by Susan U. Raymond, director of the policy programs at NYAS. In the article, Raymond pinpoints six issues that became the focal point of these studies. There are, however, four main issues that we will examine here. They are (1) the necessity of focusing on long-range results; (2) the need to create partnerships among government, business, and the academic community; (3) the need to appreciate the key role played in these projects by human resources; and (4) the need to develop inventive ways to obtain capital investments in science and related projects. [See: Susan U. Raymond, "Lessons from Global Experiences in Policy for Science-Based Development," in *Science Based Economic Development: Case Studies Around the World* (New York: New York Academy of Sciences, 1996).]

Developing Long-Range Plans For decades, American science and technology programs were based on the conclusions that were contained in a blue ribbon report compiled by a committee headed by Vannevar Bush, who served as the director of the White House Office of Scientific Research and Development under Presidents Franklin D. Roosevelt and Harry S. Truman. The report, which was cleverly dubbed *Science: The Endless Frontier*, emphasized the need for pure research, the kind conducted at colleges and universities and national think tanks. Pure research, or basic research as it is generally called, is aimed at understanding the laws of nature and the principles of the physical universe without any practical goals in mind. [See: Richard Nelson, "Why the Bush Report Has Hindered an Effective Civilian Technology Policy," in *Science for the 21st Century: The Bush Report Revisited* (Washington, DC: AEI, 1997).] The Bush report promoted pure research because the committee believed that it would contribute to American economic independence, promote technological developments, while preserving the cultural and artistic aspects of human life. [See: Claude E. Barfield, "Introduction and Overview," and David C. Mowery, "The Bush Report After 50 Years—Blueprint or Relic?" both in *Science for the 21st Century: The Bush Report Revisited* (Washington, DC: AEI, 1997).]

The problem is that pure research is often underfunded because it is seen as impractical and unusable. As a result, for pure research to work it must be tied clearly to a set of long-range goals that show how such research can be applied in a practical real world setting. This is absolutely necessary in a capitalist democracy in which business people, politicians, consumers, and voters tend to look only as far as the next billing cycle or the next election. One way to do this is to create hybrid projects that include both short-term results and long-term goals. The immediate gains satisfy the politicians and the business people while the long-range goals serve to stimulate the researchers. Thus, the short-term gratification fuels support for the more long-range goals of the pure research program. Perhaps it will be of no surprise that this was the very technique used by the Benjamin Franklin Programs in Pennsylvania. Under the BF Programs, governmental long-term planning projects were designed to produce immediate results in entrepreneurship and education. The short-term accomplishments produced results that calmed critics and permitted the long-term goals to play themselves out successfully. [See: Walter H. Plosila and Susan U. Raymond, "Policies for Science Based Economic Development: The Experiences of Pennsylvania and Ohio," in *Science Based Economic Development: Case Studies Around the World* (New York: New York Academy of Sciences, 1996); and Raymond.]

Developing Partnerships The second requirement for a successful marriage between science and government is to develop partnerships among government, business, and the academic community. Such partnerships are valuable because they make use of the talents, abilities, and experience of researchers at various levels of the scientific community and in a wide variety of settings. This mixture promotes innovation, stimulates creativity, and ensures some level of success no matter what the task. Also a cross-fertilization of ideas takes place when scientists, engineers, and technicians are compelled to work together. Thus, the pure researchers in a university setting may see the practical applications of theories that they never considered before and the practical researchers in the corporations may learn about new theories that might guide them toward practical projects. Perhaps even more important is the fact that partnerships foster a sense of cooperation, camaraderie, and ownership that stimulates loyalty and motivates continued dedication to projects that, because of long-range planning, may take years to complete. [See: Plosila and Raymond; and Raymond.] This is what happened in Ohio in the last decades of the 20th century when the state government established a program known as the Ohio Technology Transfer Organization (OTTO). Under the auspices of the OTTO program, the state established representatives at colleges and universities in nearly every major industrial and business center in the state. The job of these OTTO agents was to operate as a liaison between business and industry on the one hand, and the state's academic community on the other. When an OTTO agent uncovered a problem or a project at a business or a manufacturing firm that needed assistance, he or she would contact an expert in the academic community who would work with that business to solve the problem or to join the project team. As a result of this pairing process, all of the members of a project team felt a sense of buy-in in relation to the project and developed the sense of ownership that is so critical to success.

ANOTHER CLASSIC CASE *Act 3*
JCVI and Patent Application US2007 0264688: "To Be or Not to Be . . . a Not-for-Profit Institute"

Members of the J. Craig Venter Institute sought to patent a self-replicating bacterial cell under the control of a synthetic genome. The development of the synthetic self-replicating cell proved that such organisms can be planned by a computer, constructed chemically in a laboratory, and then placed in a bacterium from which the original DNA had been removed. The new cell then replicated itself 1 billion times. (Yes, that's billion with a "b.") The process makes DNA synthesis more economical and more affordable, leading to additional breakthroughs in the development of new vaccines, innovative pharmaceuticals, cleaner water, new food products, innovative pollution filters, and possibly even revolutionary new biofuel derivatives. The J. Craig Venter Institute is a privately funded organization, not a government institution. Plus, it's a *not-for-profit* institution. This was a very intelligent and informed way for Venter to finance the institute.

Not-for-profit institutions, especially those organized as 501(c) (3) organizations, have a number of advantages. First, the surplus funds made by the institution are not distributed as dividends to shareholders or as a division of the profits to the partners. Instead, that money goes right back into the institution. Also, under federal law, any 501(c) (3) not-for-profit organization is eligible for certain tax exemptions under both federal and state tax law. Also, such institutions are eligible to receive donations that may double as tax breaks for contributors. All of these advantages would have provided Venter with a healthy source of capital for the business. All in all, the move to not-for-profit status under 501(c) (3) was an extremely creative move on Venter's part, giving him a great source of revenue and giving us an excellent example of a creative way to develop capital resources. [See: J. Craig Venter Institute, "First Self-Replicating Synthetic Bacterial Cell Constructed by J. Craig Venter Institute Researchers," May 20, 2010, http://www.jcvi.org; and Boonsi Dickinson, "Will Patents Give Craig Venter a Monopoly over Synthetic Life?" *Smart Planet*, May 28, 2010, http://www.smartplanet.com.]

Source: See: J. Craig Venter Institute, "First Self-Replicating Synthetic Bacterial Cell Constructed by J. Craig Venter Institute Researchers," May 20, 2010, http://www.jcvi.org; and Boonsi Dickinson, "Will Patents Give Craig Venter a Monopoly Over Synthetic Life?" *Smart Planet*, May 28, 2010, http://www.smartplanet.com.

Developing Education and Human Resources If long-range plans and scientific partnerships are going to be effective, they must be run by people who are well educated, who work well together, and who have a sense of loyalty to the project and to the group. This is at least partly the government's job because, like it or not, the government is entangled within education. Education at the post-secondary level is entangled with the government that "pays the bills" at the state-run institutions and monitors the operation of the private schools, as well. Moreover, the boards of trustees at the private institutions must oversee the operation of their institutions to ensure that the curriculum includes a healthy dose of science and technology.

Nor is the government's involvement in education limited to the college and university level. Programs must be developed to promote science education as part of a continuing education program for graduate students and for adults on a non-degree-seeking path. All citizens, but especially those employed in research, development, and manufacturing, must be familiar with science, medicine, engineering, and technology, especially computer technology. The first goal of the government should be to help educators produce students who can think for themselves, who are articulate and well read, who are literate in science and technology, and who can cooperate as a member of a corporate or a scientific team. The second goal should be to keep those students in the state or at least within the United States. Homegrown scientists and researchers are always a country's best employees because they are motivated and inspired by a sense of loyalty and pride. [See: Raymond.]

Developing Sources of Capital Perhaps the most important of the four requirements is that which encourages the development of creative capital sources. We have already noted how, in the United States, governmental institutions such as the National Science Foundation and the National Institutes of Health provide millions of dollars of support each year for cutting-edge scientific and medical research programs. The dollars spent by the NSF, for example, have resulted in thousands of successful projects, some of which have been recognized internationally for their accomplishments. Similar funding opportunities are available on a global level through institutions like the World Health Organization, which supports health and medical research programs at the international level, all of which are aimed at promoting advances in medical and health care. Similarly, part of UNESCO's mission is to allocate funds for educational, cultural, and scientific projects run by various member states. In the area of engineering and technology, the International Atomic Energy Agency provides funds to governments that come directly to the IAEA for equipment, for technical assistance, and for the education of its personnel in the peaceful pursuit of nuclear power.

Capital sources are also available through creative arrangements with corporate sponsors. For example, in her article, "Lessons for Global Experience," Raymond cites an example of a funding program run by a consortium of Swiss entrepreneurs, who created a foundation named FUNDES, the purpose of which was to provide financial support to Latin American businesses involved in advanced research and development programs. Private foundations are also a source of funding for research and development projects. For example, in her article, Raymond also notes how Cambridge University created two foundations, the Cambridge Capital Development Fund and Cambridge Research and Innovation. The two foundations have received funds from Cambridge itself, from nine other institutions of higher education, the government, and several financial institutions. The two foundations disperse funds for projects run by the university and by local businesses. [See: Raymond.]

UN Economic Security Council Proposed

While all of these projects are admirable and while many of them succeed, they all lack one thing. There is no centralized control point for the vast array of projects under way at any one time, at least not on the international scene. Some commentators insist that what is needed is a new way of integrating international efforts to pool global resources and to direct those resources toward solving Heilbroner's central modern challenges: environment, war, and unchecked population growth. A model of this type of organization exists if we combine the work of the Commission on Sustainable Development with the work done by the UN Security Council. The proposed institution that emerges from the marriage of these two institutions has been named the UN Economic Security Council. If we take a close look at how these two present-day institutions, the Commission on Sustainable Development (CSD) and the UN Security Council, we will see how the proposed Economic Security Council might operate. First, recall how the CSD was created. The CSD was established after the first Earth Summit in 1992 in Brazil to administer Agenda 21, which established a set of tactics designed to activate sustainable development plans across the globe. The CSD also serves as a central clearinghouse for nations to report progress in the implementation of sustainable development plans. In this way, the CSD just might be able to deal with Heilbroner's challenges were it not for two obvious drawbacks. First, the CSD deals only with the environment, while Heilbroner's challenges also deal with war, energy, and population. Second, the CSD lacks the power to enforce its recommendations under Agenda 21. In other words, the CSD has no "teeth." [See: Commission on Global Governance, *Our Global Neighborhood: The Report of the Commission on Global Governance* (Oxford: Oxford University Press, 1995).]

The second agency, the UN Security Council, provides a model for those missing teeth. The Security Council has the power to pass resolutions that have consequences for those who break those resolutions. Those consequence must be carried out by the military forces of member nations or by NATO, to be sure. However, the threat of those consequences is often enough to prevent a rogue or failed state from ignoring the decisions of the Security Council and its members. Some commentators have suggested that the UN Charter be amended to create a new Economic Security Council (ESC) that would utilize the best parts of the CSD and the Security Council to coordinate science and technology policy in order to solve the economic, environmental, and demographic problems of the globe. The ESC would first diagnose the condition of the world especially as it relates to the issues of environment, energy, and population. The council would then draw up some long-range plans that would involve specific projects for sustainable development, environmental cleanup, population control, and energy enrichment. Those plans would outline the roles that each member nation of the UN would play in the development plan, plus deadlines for those goals, plus funding resources, and, finally, consequences for noncompliance, consequences that would be carried out much like those carried out by the agents of the present Security Council.

Thus, the ESC would run much like the CSD in its planning and coordinating activities and much like the Security Council in its enforcement function, except that, instead of responding to short-range crises, as the Security Council does, the ESC would deal with long-range problems and long-range solutions. The ESC would be autonomous, much like the CSD and the Security Council. It would consist of the largest economic blocs on the planet. The blocs might be made up of a single nation—such as China, India, or the United States—or conglomerates such as the EU, or unified regions such as the Association of Southeast Asian Nations. The charter amendment creating the ESC would also include a provision to ensure that both developed and developing nations are represented proportionately based on a set formula agreed to by all member states. The ESC would not replace existing UN agencies, such as the ECOSOC. Rather, it would serve as a support mechanism that would make the projects and the plans of all agencies a reality. It might even take the UN from the level of a semi autonomous international NGO to a completely autonomous entity by giving it the teeth that it needs to be successful in its goals and objectives. [See: Commission on Global Governance.]

ANOTHER CLASSIC CASE *Act 4*
JCVI and Patent Application US2007 026468: "To Be or Not to Be . . . the G-10's Action Plan"

The J. Craig Venter Institute had produced a self-replicating bacterial cell completely under the control of a synthetic genome. The development of the synthetic self-replicating cell proved that such organisms can be planned by a computer, constructed chemically in a laboratory, and then placed in a bacterium from which the original DNA had been removed. The new cell then replicated itself a billion times. The process will make DNA synthesis more economical and more affordable, leading to the development of new vaccines, innovative pharmaceuticals, clean water, new food products, innovative pollution filters, and possibly even revolutionary new biofuel derivatives.

Now let's suppose that the United Nations Economic Security Council (ESC) has become a reality. Suppose further that the ESC has instituted an action plan that sets up a timetable for the reclamation of farmland, the recovery of clean drinking water, and the eradication of disease in a series of developing nations we will call the G-10 of the G-77. We know that the JCVI can probably use its patented process to create synthetic bacteria that can develop new vaccines and innovative pharmaceuticals to cure disease. It might also be able to develop an organism to purify the water supply and perhaps to develop crops that can grow in and revitalize the depleted soil of the G-10. In other words, all of the problems targeted by the ESC in the G-10 might be solved by the JCVI's miracle synthetic lifeforms. Should the ESC have the authority to force JCVI to hand over its work to activate the G-10 action plan? What if the ESC passed a resolution that it was ready to use military force to compel JCVI to cooperate? Does any of this seem fair to JCVI, which has put so much effort and funds into developing the synthetic lifeforms? What should the United States do in such a situation? What should JCVI do? What recourse, if any, might JCVI have in the U.S. court system? The international court system? [See: J. Craig Venter Institute, "First Self-Replicating Synthetic Bacterial Cell Constructed by J. Craig Venter Institute Researchers," May 20, 2010, http://www.jcvi.org; and Boonsi Dickinson, "Will Patents Give Craig Venter a Monopoly over Synthetic Life?" *Smart Planet*, May 28, 2010, http://www.smart planet.com.]

Source: See: J. Craig Venter Institute, "First Self-Replicating Synthetic Bacterial Cell Constructed by J. Craig Venter Institute Researchers," May 20, 2010, http://www.jcvi.org; and Boonsi Dickinson, "Will Patents Give Craig Venter a Monopoly Over Synthetic Life?" *Smart Planet*, May 28, 2010, http://www.smart planet.com.

Positive Action Plans by the ESC The JCVI Classic Case: Act 4 and the Question of Ethics exercise paint a dark, dismal, and dangerous image of the proposed ESC. However, there is a positive side to the ESC proposal. An agency that is run by unbiased, well-trained, independent, and responsible individuals would be able to draw up tough but fair action plans that must be implemented to save the planet. The task would be difficult and thankless. However, at some time in the future (the very near future if we listen to Heilbroner), such drastic measures may be needed. Remember that it was Heilbroner who stated clearly and unapologetically that drastic measures by "iron" governments might be needed to save the planet. What if another great oil spill occurs under the watchful eye and the global jurisdiction of the ESC? Suppose further that the ESC has instituted an action plan that sets up a timetable for removing the oil spill and recovering clean drinking water. We know that the JCVI can probably use its patented process to create synthetic bacteria that can filter and eliminate the pollutants in the gulf and that can purify the water supply. To put it simply, all of the problems caused by the oil spill might be solved by the JCVI's genetically engineered synthetic life-forms. In this case, the ESC might pass a resolution compelling the responsible parties to cooperate with JCVI and to compensate the institute accordingly for the use of its patented process. Because the ESC has the necessary military might to enforce the order, it is likely that the project would be carried out in record time.

The gulf would be cleaned up, JCVI would be justly compensated, and the environment would be safe again. The same technique could be used to compel a cleanup after a rogue military action such as those carried out by the terrorist groups like ISIS and al-Qaeda. Or such an action might be taken to force President Bashar al-Assad to rebuild the houses, schools, and hospitals that his military forces have destroyed in Syria. The point is that it is not the structure of the ESC that matters quite as much as the people who run it. It takes people with the proper motivation, the appropriate experience, the courage of their convictions, and just the right level of power to carry it off.

A QUESTION OF ETHICS

One of the problems that the proposed UN Economic Security Council (ESC) would face early on is population growth. Remember that one reason for modeling the ESC after the Security Council is to provide teeth for the ESC's resolutions. Suppose that the ESC decided to enforce a vigorous program of population control and to use the power of the member nation's military forces to enforce its resolutions in this regard. This is what some critics of the ESC fear. They suspect that the inauguration of the ESC might usher in the same type of world that Axel Madsen imagined in his novel *Unisave*. The novel is set in the 22nd century at a time when the planet's natural resources, its energy reserves, its agriculture, and its fresh water are depleted. The Earth's population is more than 24 billion. The planet has reached a tipping point beyond which there seems to be nowhere to go. In a desperate attempt to reverse the slide toward disaster, the United Nations establishes an agency called Unisave. If we look at Unisave closely, we will see that it resembles a runaway ESC. First, Unisave has the authority to set quotas for family size. Second, Unisave has developed a compulsory sterilization program for some people under some circumstances. Third, it has ordered the use of drugs to suppress the sex drive among young people. Fourth, it has instituted a global program of electronic surveillance to prevent the violation of its strict anti-sex laws. Finally, Unisave has mandated a program of compulsory gericide, which involves the systematic killing of the elderly.

QUESTIONS YET UNANSWERED

The following questions have not yet been answered. Before you consider each question, turn to Chapter 1 to review the various ethical theories noted there (market value ethics, social contract theory, utilitarianism, and rational ethics). Then, in a consistent way, answer the following questions.

1. What must be done (if anything) to prevent the ESC from transforming itself into Unisave? Explain
2. Is there any way to effectively stop it? Explain
3. Is it better not to start in that direction in the first place? Explain
4. Is there a justification that would approve of, or perhaps even champion, the work of the ESC and that of Unisave? Explain

quick quiz 33-6

1. A central function of the law is to contribute to the civic peace by securing order, stability, and justice.	true | false
2. Scientific partnerships are valuable because they make use of the talents, abilities, and experience of researchers at various levels of the scientific community and in a wide variety of settings.	true | false
3. The UN Economic Security Council was established in 2010.	true | false

Summary

33.1 The point at which science, technology, and the law intersect can be referred to as juriscience. The power to regulate science and technology in the United States is shared by the national government and the state governments. The national power emerges from the U.S. Constitution. The five specific clauses that relate to the national power are the commerce clause, the taxation clause, the supremacy clause, the necessary and proper clause, and the treaty clause. A proposed solution that has been suggested for dealing with the problems related to the complicated nature of scientific cases is the establishment of a national science court. Once established, the federal science court would have exclusive jurisdiction over issues involving scientific, engineering, medical, and technological cases. On the state level, the capacity of the states to regulate science and technology emerges from the state's police power. Police power is the state's ability to uphold and sustain public health, safety, welfare, and morals. In the state courts, the tradition of common law fills many law books with cases related to science, technology, and engineering.

33.2 The federal government has been funding scientific and medical research for the past 150 years. That funding comes in many forms for a variety of purposes and with a high price tag. Nevertheless, Congress and the president have agreed that the expenditure is necessary to provide for national security, to promote the health and welfare of American citizens, and to ensure the economic and social well-being of the nation. The federal government has set up a number of agencies and institutes that support, assess, coordinate, and fund scientific, medical, and technological research. The chief national agencies for scientific, medical, and technological research are the Office of Science and Technology Policy, the National Science Foundation, and the National Institutes of Health.

33.3 There are four types of international nongovernmental organizations: (1) those that are completely dependent upon the nation-states that make up their membership, (2) those that are a semiautonomous organization, (3) those that are granted or earn entity status, and (4) those that are unaffiliated transnationals that act as rogues or outlaws. International power depends upon the nature of the NGO itself. The primary international organizations under the umbrella of the UN are UNESCO and the World Health Organization. The United Nations consists of three major subdivisions, the General Assembly, the UN Security Council, and the Secretariat, which is the administrative bureaucracy of the UN. UNESCO is responsible for creating outreach efforts to develop educational, cultural, and scientific ties among the member nations of the UN. The World Health Organization's mission is to improve the health care available to all the people of the world, but especially to those most at risk because of poverty or special health-related threats.

33.4 All of the work done by the government relates in some way to four challenges: (1) the possibility of war, (2) the volatility of the marketplace, (3) the twin dangers of environmental deterioration and energy depletion, and (4) the demographic crisis. Dealing with all of these problems is part of the balancing act that is the law. The Federal Energy Regulatory Commission (FERC) is responsible for regulating the transportation and the wholesale price of natural gas and electricity sold for use in interstate commerce. State utility commissioners regulate intrastate prices. The Nuclear Regulatory Commission (NRC) is responsible for the licensing, construction, and operation of nuclear reactors. On the international scene, the International Atomic Energy Commission (IAEA) has oversight responsibility for matters dealing with nuclear power. On the national level, the responsibility for the environment has been delegated to the Environmental Protection Agency. Important subsidiary legislation includes the Solid Waste Disposal Act, the Clean Air Act, the Clean Water Act, the Toxic Substance Control Act, the Comprehensive Environmental Response, Compensation, and Liability Act. and the Oil Pollution Act. The regulation of the environment on a global scale is charged to the United Nations Environment Program (UNEP).

33.5 Intellectual property involves an intangible ownership right in an invention, a process, a computer program, a chemical formula, an original recorded work such as a book or an article, and so on. A patent is a property right granted by the federal government to an inventor. A patent gives the inventor the exclusive right to make, use, and sell that invention for a period of 20 years (14 years if the patent covers a process). These rights do not, however, override the right to tinker. A trade secret is a plan, process, device, procedure, formula, pattern, compilation, technique, program, design, method, or improvement used in a business and disclosed only to those employees who need to know it to do their jobs. A copyright is an intangible property right granted to authors of literary, artistic, and musical compositions. A copyright gives the owner the exclusive right to reproduce, publish, and sell his or her work in a fixed, tangible medium of expression.

33.6 There are four factors to consider when attempting to solve the Heilbroner challenges. They are (1) the necessity of focusing on long range results; (2) the need to create partnerships among government, business, and the academic community; (3) the need to appreciate the key role played in these projects by human resources: and (4) the need to develop inventive ways to obtain capital investments in science and related projects. The primary job of the proposed UN Economic Security Council would be to assess the condition of the world economy especially as it relates to the issues of environment, energy, and population. The council would then draw up long-range plans that would involve specific projects for sustainable development, environmental cleanup, population control, and energy enrichment.

Key Terms

business system, 976
Clean Air Act, 966
Clean Water Act, 965
commerce clause, 945
compelling interest, 972
copyright, 983
dependency theory, 958
Digital Millennium Copyright Act (DMCA), 984
Economic Espionage Act, 981
faction, 945
fair use doctrine, 984
General Assembly, 957
juriscience, 944
licensing agreement, 982

necessary and proper clause, 946
No Electronic Theft Act (NET Act), 984
obvious-to-try standard, 977
Oil Pollution Act, 967
patent, 974
police power, 952
Population Commission (PC), 972
prior art, 977
royalty, 973
right to tinker, 974
Secretariat, 957
Security Council, 957
stocktake, 969
supremacy clause, 948

taxation clause, 947
teaching, suggestions, or motivation test (TSM standard), 977
trade secret, 981
trademark, 982
transnats, 957
treaty clause, 949
Uniform Trade Secrets Act, 981
World Intellectual Property Organization (WIPO), 958, 985
World Intellectual Property Organization Copyright Treaty, 985
World Intellectual Property Organization Phonograms Treaty, 985

Questions for Review and Discussion

1. How does the law permit the government to regulate science and technology?
2. What is the function of the Office of Science and Technology Policy?
3. What is the function of the National Institutes of Health?
4. What is the role of the National Science Foundation?
5. What does Heilbroner see as the three major challenges facing the modern world?
6. What is the purpose of the Federal Energy Regulatory Commission?
7. What is the role of the Nuclear Regulatory Commission?
8. What are the functions of the Clean Air Act and the Clean Water Act?
9. How does the law protect trademarks, trade secrets, and copyrights?
10. What are the four main issues that must be considered in developing a science policy?

Cases for Analysis

1. Earth Sciences Inc. conducted gold-leaching operations in Colorado. The process involved spraying gold ore with a toxic substance. To prevent pollution, Earth Sciences had installed a reserve sump to catch any toxic runoff. An unexpected early thaw melted a snow bank, covering the ore heap. As a result, the reserve sump overflowed, dumping toxic waste into the Rito Seco Creek. The United States brought suit, alleging that Earth Sciences had violated pollution laws. Earth Sciences argued that it should not be held liable for an unintentional pollution accident. Was Earth Sciences correct? Explain. [See: *United States v. Earth Sciences, Inc.*, 559 F.2d 368 (10th Cir.).]

2. Gaskin, Ohio, is the home of Ransom College. Each August, the population of the small village triples as the students return. When this happens, the traffic in the middle of town becomes congested, and the exhaust from the cars chokes the entire downtown area. This year, the Village Council of Gaskin passed an ordinance that required the installation of emission control devices in all vehicles as a new licensing requirement. A dozen students brought suit in the U.S. District Court in Columbus, asking the court to declare the new ordinance invalid and to prevent its enforcement. The students contended that the Clean Air Act, which did not make such demands, preempted the village ordinance. Under what circumstances will a federal law like the Clean Air Act preempt state and local law? Explain. Who will prevail in this case, the village or the students? Explain.

3. The Global Environment Resistance Movement (GERM) initiated a citizen's suit under the authority of the Clean Water Act asking the court to issue an order that would shut down a plant on the Kokosing River that was dumping waste into the navigable waterways of that river. The administrator responded that GERM had acted in haste and did not meet the statutory requirement of giving him 60 days' notice. GERM responded by noting that the notice requirement had been waived by the administrator when he announced in a press conference that he did not intend to shut down the Kokosing plant . . . ever! In its argument, GERM pointed to the Clean Air Act and used that as the template for its lawsuit. Do the Clean Air Act and the Clean Water Act have identical citizen suit provisions? If they are the same, why is this so? If they are different, what are the differences? Who should win this case, GERM or the administrator? Why?

4. Officials at Semco Inc. believed that some of their most important computer files, which they characterized as trade secrets, had been appropriated by Terry Hildreth, a former vice president of Semco. Semco officials accused Hildreth of using these programs to run his new limited liability company, Hildreth Manufacturing LLC. Semco engaged in a series of harassing tactics designed to stop Hildreth's use of the alleged trade secrets. To protect himself and his new firm, Hildreth brought a lawsuit asking for a declaratory judgment that no trade secrets had been taken, despite Semco's allegations to the contrary. Semco then brought a second lawsuit alleging, among other things, that trade secrets had indeed been misappropriated by Hildreth. After the suits were decided in favor of Hildreth, the results were appealed. During both suits, the following facts came to light: Material that described the manufacturing steps that Semco now claimed were trade secrets had been routinely made available to vendors. Semco also regularly provided information about its "secret" manufacturing processes to people outside the company. Semco did not require employees to file nondisclosure or secrecy agreements. Visitors were not screened, the building was locked only after regular business hours, and the plant was open for public tours. On the basis of these facts, how should the appeals court rule on the issue of trade secrets? Explain. [See: *Hildreth Mfg., LLC. v. Semco, Inc.*, 151 Ohio App. 3d 693.]

5. Parrish and Chlarson worked for J&K Computer Systems Inc. Parrish was a computer programmer, and Chlarson was a trainee. In his capacity as programmer, Parrish wrote an accounts receivable program. Customers of J&K were granted licenses to use the program. A label on the program noted that it was J&K's property and that it could not be used without authorization under a licensing agreement. Parrish, Chlarson, and all other J&K employees were informed that the program was a secret. Nevertheless, Parrish copied it, left J&K's employ, and, along with Chlarson, opened a business similar to J&K. Parrish and Chlarson then sold the copied program to various customers. When J&K

sued, Parrish and Chlarson argued that the fact that J&K had revealed the program to customers meant it was no longer a trade secret. Were Parrish and Chlarson correct? Explain. [See: *J&K Computer Systems, Inc., v. Parrish*, 642 P.2d 732 (UT).]

6. Diehr and Latton applied for a patent to protect their development of a new process for molding raw, uncured synthetic rubber into cured products. Diehr and Latton argued that their unique contribution was to measure the temperature inside the mold and feed that temperature into a computer that was programmed to calculate the exact time needed for the curing process. The computer would then activate a mechanism to open the mold. The process, as conceived by Diehr and Latton, eliminated the guesswork usually associated with measuring the length of time for the mold to remain closed. The patent office denied the patent because it used a computer program in the process. The office said that the program was essentially a mathematical idea and was, therefore, unpatentable. Diehr and Latton argued that the mere fact that a computer program was used as part of a process did not mean that the whole process would be unpatentable. Were Diehr and Latton correct? Why or why not? [See: *Diamond v. Diehr*, 101 S.Ct. 1048 (U.S. Sup. Ct.).]

7. Hiroyuki Iwahashi, Yoshiki Nishioka, and Mitsuhiro Hakaridani applied for a patent for an autocorrelation unit for use in computers for pattern recognition—in this case, to aid in voice recognition. To achieve this type of pattern recognition, computers must perform a lengthy multiplication cycle that requires intricate circuitry and a costly multiplier unit. The computer hardware involved in this process is also large and cumbersome. The purpose of the new invention is to streamline the multiplication cycle. The elimination of the multiplier and the intricate circuitry is made possible by an algorithm that allows the computer to obtain the needed result by detouring the time-consuming multiplication cycle and using, instead, the electronic equivalent of a multiplication table. The U.S. Patent and Trademark Office rejected the patent application, and the Board of Patent Appeals and Interferences upheld that decision. Both concluded that the alleged invention was nothing more than an algorithm and could not therefore be patented. The inventors appealed the decision, arguing that the algorithm is simply part of the apparatus, which altered the operation of the computer and was therefore subject to patentability. Can a patent be rejected solely on the argument that the invention involves an algorithm? Explain. [See: *In re Iwahashi*, 888 F.2d 1370 (Fed. Cir.).]

8. Stern Electronics Inc. entered a licensing agreement with Konami Industry Co. Ltd. granting Stern exclusive rights to market the video game "Scramble" in the United States. Omni Video Games, Inc., wrote a new program that duplicated the sights and sounds of "Scramble." Stern sued Omni in federal court, asking for an injunction to prevent Omni from marketing its knockoff of "Scramble." Omni argued that Stern could not get a copyright for the "Scramble" audiovisual display because every time a player plays the game, the display is different. The display is not fixed in a tangible medium, as required by law. Because Omni had written its own program, Stern could not stop it from marketing the duplicate "Scramble" games. Was Omni correct? Explain. [See: *Stern Electronics, Inc., v. Kaufman and Omni Video Games, Inc.*, 669 F.2d 852 (2nd Cir.).]

9. In *Kelo v. City of New London*, the city fathers of New London agreed to help the Pfizer Corporation, which had decided to build a research and manufacturing center in the city. To do this, the city began to buy land in that area of town. Many residents in the targeted area refused to sell. The city invoked the government's power to confiscate land for public use under eminent domain. Kelo, along with several other owners, sued to end the unconstitutional seizure of their property. The homeowners argued that the taking of their land for private development purposes did not fall under the heading of "public use" as visualized by the founding fathers when they wrote the Fifth Amendment. The Court in a 5–4 ruling held that the city's seizure of the land really was public use. Now jump ahead in time and imagine that the ESC has been created under the UN. Could the ESC use this case as a precedent that would permit it to seize private land in the developed countries and then pass the rights and the possession of that land over to the underdeveloped countries? Explain your response. [See: *Kelo v. City of New London*, 125 S.Ct. 2655 (U.S. Supreme Court).]

10. The citizens of Oregon authorized the establishment of the Oregon Death with Dignity Act (ODWDA), which protected physicians from

prosecution under criminal law and from litigation under civil law for prescribing drugs for terminally ill patients who wished to commit suicide. The drugs would have to be prescribed under the Controlled Substances Act (CSA). The U.S. attorney general (AG) stated that any physician who prescribed such drugs with the intent to have those drugs used for suicide could lose his or her medical license. The attorney general argued that drugs controlled by the CSA could not be used for suicide because suicide is not a legitimate medical purpose. A lawsuit was filed by several interested parties in the federal district court in Oregon, which ruled in favor of the plaintiffs and which then enjoined the AG from enforcing his interpretation of the CSA. Could this case be used as precedent to promote or to fight government-enforced population control as imagined by Axel Madsen in *Unisave*? Explain. [See: *Gonzales, Attorney General v. Oregon*, 126 S.Ct. 904 (U.S. Supreme Court).]

Design Elements: The Opening Case: ©Sharpstock/Alamy; A Classic Case: ©Evlakhov Valeriy/ Shutterstock

quick quiz Answers

33-1	33-2	33-3	33-4	33-5	33-6
1. T	1. F	1. F	1. F	1. T	1. T
2. F	2. T	2. T	2. F	2. T	2. T
3. T	3. T	3. T	3. F	3. T	3. F

Chapter 34: International Law and the New World Order

34-1 The New World Order
Patterns within the New World Order • The Underlying Technique: Predictive Political History • The Theories of International Behavior • The Global Initial Conditions • Ideologies: Liberal Democracy v. Authoritarianism • Variables, Uncertainty, and Unexpected Events

34-2 International Law and War
The Just War Theory • Preventive, Preemptive, and Protective War • Substantive and Procedural Issues

34-3 The United Nations and the Global Community
The Structure of the United Nations • International Law and the United Nations • Economic Regulation and the United Nations • An Economic Security Council

34-4 International Law, Finance, and Trade
The International Monetary Fund and the World Bank • The World Trade Organization • The European Union

THE OPENING CASE Round 1
Facing the Final New World Order

In 1993, Francis Fukuyama, a relatively well-known political scientist, wrote a book entitled *The End of History and the Last Man*, in which he argued, using some fairly persuasive evidence, that with the end of the Cold War, Western liberal ideals had won the battle for the control of civilization. The future, Fukuyama declared, belonged to the ideology of liberal democracy, which would now be the dominant form of government for nations everywhere across the globe. Written in the wake of the dissolution of the Soviet Union in 1991, the book seemed more like history than the predictive political treatise that it was. Nation states like Poland, Lithuania, Estonia, Latvia, and the Ukraine adopted democratic governments (although each one calls itself a republic) as a matter of rapid political momentum, rather than as a slow and deliberative process. Not to be outdone, the Russians formed a republican government and began calling themselves the Russian Federation, which, after a tumultuous trial period under Boris Yeltsin, finally settled into a nearly stable republic (initially, at least). Even China, the most unapologetic of all communist states, experienced an impressive wave of dissent that culminated in the unforgettable march on Tiananmen Square during what is now known as the '89 Democracy Movement.

This global trend toward liberal democracy seemed to continue—even, at times, to accelerate—during the early 21st century, as witnessed by a series of flash revolutions during the Arab Spring of 2011. Then things began to change. The revolt against the strongmen in the Middle East and North Africa stalled in Syria, which is still in the midst of a seven-year civil war during which multiple factions have fought unsuccessfully to unseat the authoritarian government of President Bash al-Assad. Meanwhile, back in Russia, liberal democracy gave way to the quasi-czarist regime of President Putin, and in China, President Xi Jinping abolished term limits, setting the stage for his new role as an authoritarian president.

Curiously, this move toward the ideology of authoritarianism comes as no shock to some (many?) political scientists. For example, in his book, *An Inquiry into the Human Prospect*, economist and political philosopher Robert Heilbroner predicted in 1974 that certain unprecedented problems in the developing world, such as uncontrolled population growth, would require "the eventual rise of 'iron' governments, probably of a military-socialist cast." [See: Heilbroner, p. 38.] Similarly, other experts, including Robert Kaplan in his book

Warrior Politics, have argued that this move toward authoritarianism is inevitable given the sociopolitical trends evident in the late 20th and early 21st centuries. These sociopolitical trends include population growth, resource depletion, rapid urbanization, the growth of a new "sub-proletariat," and the use of cyberattacks and terrorism as weapons of war. These conditions have led to the growth of distorted populist movements that demand more representation within the government while failing to demonstrate the ability to contribute to the political process without taking out their xenophobic frustrations on those they see as "other."

Not unexpectedly, these issues demand more, not less, authoritarian control in the face the failure of democratic institutions to stop the tide of widespread poverty; rapid environmental deterioration; bloody civil wars; shrinking energy sources; and unstoppable instances of terrorism, piracy, drug addiction, human trafficking, and gun violence usually directed at the youngest and most innocent members of our society. The United States itself has proven to be a textbook example of dissatisfaction with traditional democratic processes. The legislative paralysis that plagued Congress for more than a decade sparked a populist backlash against the liberal elites in Washington that led to a rebellion at the ballot box in the presidential election of 2016. Those dissatisfied by the results of the constitutional election of a president they disliked staged an anti-democratic rebellion of their own, displaying signs that declared "Not My President" and establishing sanctuary cities in defiance of federal law. So, Francis Fukuyama seems to have gotten things backward. The final victor in the Cold War was not liberal democracy but, in an ending worthy of *The Twilight Zone*, the ideology of authoritarianism.

In fact, authoritarian control may provide the only truly effective solution to the global crises that we face today. Or is this a misreading of Fukuyama's work? Perhaps Fukuyama believes that, ultimately, liberal democracy will win out even if we have to endure unsettling periods like the one we live in now when authoritarianism looks like the best solution. Still, there must be more to the issue than this. Do political scientists, like Fukuyama, Heilbroner, and Kaplan have a technique that can determine the best way for the nations of the world to deal with the pressures of a growing global community? Or is this determination always bound by sheer luck and the events of the moment? Just which New World Order will actually be successful in handling global problems? Will the ideology of authoritarianism be the rule, or will liberal democracy be victorious in the long run after all? Confused? Intrigued? Good—then read on. What you discover in this chapter may surprise you. [See: Francis Fukuyama, *The End of History and the Last Man* (New York: Free Press, 1992); Robert Heilbroner, *An Inquiry into the Human Prospect* (New York: Norton, 1974); Robert Kaplan, *Warrior Politics: Why Leadership Demands a Pagan Ethos* (New York: Vintage Books, 2002); Steven Lee Myers, "China Leaps to Front of a New Authoritarian Era," *The New York Times*, February 27, 2018, p. A1, A8; and Chris Buckley, "Xi Doctrine Will Guide a Nation," *The New York Times*, February 27, 2018, p. A8.]

Opening Case Questions

1. What is the underlying thesis of Francis Fukuyama's book, *The End of History and the Last Man*? Explain.

2. What happened to the global movement toward democratic government? Explain.

3. What sociopolitical trends have set the stage for authoritarian governments? Explain.

4. What conditions in the American governmental system led to a voter revolt in 2016? Explain.

5. Which governmental system is best suited to solve the global problems of the 21st century—authoritarianism or liberal democracy? Explain.

Source: See: Francis Fukuyama, *The End of History and the Last Man* (New York: Free Press, 1992); Robert Heilbronner, *An Inquiry Into The Human Prospect* (New York: Norton, 1974); Robert Kaplan, *Warrior Politics: Why Leadership Demands a Pagan Ethos* (New York: Vintage Books, 2002); Steven Lee Myers, "China Leaps to Front of a New Authoritarian Era," *The New York Times*, (February 27, 2018), p. A1, A8; Chris Buckley, "Xi Doctrine Will Guide A Nation," *The New York Times*, (February 27, 2018), p. A8.

 Learning Objectives

1. Explain the process of predictive political history.
2. Identify and define the theories of international behavior.
3. Identify and define the various sets of global initial conditions.

4. Explain the Just War Theory.
5. Describe the mission of the International Criminal Court.
6. Identify the main goal of UNCITRAL.
7. State the differences between the UCC and the CISG.
8. Outline the structure of the World Trade Organization.
9. Relate the objectives of the Dispute Settlement Understanding.
10. Clarify the goals of the European Union.

34-1 The New World Order

The phrase *new world order* was used during the Paris peace talks in 1919 to describe the remaking of the world map following the Great War, and then again two decades later by H.G. Wells in a book that he published in 1939. George H. W. Bush used the term in the development of his defense planning document toward the close of the last century, and at the start of the 21st century, Daniel Drezner placed an original spin on the phrase when he penned an article for *Foreign Affairs* titled, "The New New World Order." The new world order, then, is a phrase frequently used to describe situations on the global stage that are unexpected, unusual, and unfamiliar. For that reason, among others, the phrase can be used to describe the situation in which we find ourselves today. The world order is a set of current initial conditions that describes how nation-states relate to one another on a global scale. The use of the word *new* to describe that world order reveals that these initial conditions have just emerged from a tectonic shift in international relations. Generally, because the conditions are so recent, no one is exactly certain what those conditions are and how they work. Thus, this changing environment must be unraveled if we are to understand the role of international law, if any, within that new environment. [See: Daniel Drezner, "The New New World Order," *Foreign Affairs*, March–April 2007; D. M. MacMillan, *Paris 1919: Six Months that Changed the World* (New York: Random House, 2001); and Zbigniew Brzezinski, *Second Chance: Three Presidents and the Crisis of American Superpower* (New York: Basic Books, 2007).]

Patterns within the New World Order

This description is not meant to imply that global conditions do not follow certain patterns, but in the new world order, those patterns have yet to be determined. These patterns are not rules exactly, but neither are they unpredictable chance events. Instead, they are indicators that are correct more often than not. The trick is to determine what the global initial conditions really are and what pattern those conditions can be expected to follow. What makes this trick so difficult is that the international players do not come into the game fresh; instead, they enter the new arena steeped in their own expectations of what the pattern should be. When the pattern shifts, sometimes the players do not, which causes diplomatic errors, international incidents, and global conflicts, some of which can be solved easily but many of which cannot. We are currently at the threshold of a changing global environment in which a volatile, unstable, yet predictable new world order is emerging.

Evidence of this emerging new world order can be seen in (1) the Russian attempt to interfere with the American presidential campaign of 2016; (2) the seemingly unending civil war in Syria, along with the plight of the refugees who have fled that war-torn nation; (3) the growing tensions between the United States and North Korea over Kim Jong Un's nuclear ambitions; (4) the United Kingdom's unprecedented exit from the European Union; (5) a potential military confrontation between the United States and China in the South China Sea; (6) and the United States's use of the most powerful non-nuclear weapon in history against an ISIS cave complex in Afghanistan. Our job during this chapter will be to determine the nature of this new world order.

It is not an easy task; not everyone agrees about what that order might be. Place 20 political commentators around a table, and you'll get 25 versions of the new world order. Still, even within this confusing collection of political theories, common themes exist. Moreover, we suggest that there may be a hidden pattern within the disorder that can be used to give direction to our study. Accordingly, we will divide this section of the chapter into four parts: (1) the underlying technique for uncovering the new world order, something that we will refer to as predictive political history; (2) the theories of international behavior that tell us how nations act; (3) the initial conditions (or possible new world orders, if you will) that offer to define the present alignment of states ranging from the most powerful nations (the United States, China, and Russia) to the most influential federation (the European Union) to failed states (Yemen, Libya, Somalia, and so on) to rogue states (North Korea and Iran) and including international nongovernmental organizations (the United Nations, the World Bank, the International Criminal Court, the Red Cross, NATO, and so on) and outlaw terror groups (such as al-Qaeda, ISIS, and Hezbollah, plus drug cartels, pirate bands, human traffickers, and so on); and (4) a final examination of the advantages and disadvantages of the two most prevalent political ideologies: liberal democracy and authoritarianism.

The Underlying Technique: Predictive Political History

Despite its name, predictive political history is not a technique for predicting the future. No such technique exists, except perhaps in the imagination of such notables as Auguste Comte, Pierre Laplace, G. W. F. Hegel, and Isaac Asimov. Instead, **predictive political history** is a technique for determining how world leaders will probably act in a given world order when facing a crisis or mapping out a future global strategy. If a political scientist wants to apply predictive political history, he or she must first determine the present state of the global system (the **international initial conditions** or the **new world order**) and then match that system to the correct set of covering laws under an accurate **theory of international behavior**. Once a set of initial conditions has been identified and a theory of international behavior chosen, our hypothetical political scientist must investigate the effectiveness of a series of political ideologies in order to determine which one is best suited for the governing of a nation-state. Simply stated, a **political ideology** is a belief system that supports a particular method of governing a nation-state. The two most prominent ideologies in the present world are liberal democracy and authoritarianism. **Liberal democracy** is a political ideology that supports placing as much political power as possible in the hands of the people. In contrast, **authoritarianism** is a political ideology that supports the notion that political power belongs in the hands of a few or even in the hands of one political figure. Under the precepts of predictive political history, a political scientist must decide which political ideology, —liberal democracy or authoritarianism—is best suited to solve the global problems represented by the initial conditions. At this point before going forward, it will be best to examine the operation of predictive political history.

As a process, predictive political history imitates science. Once a scientist knows the initial conditions of a closed system, he or she can apply the laws of an appropriate theory to make predictions about how the elements within the system, as well as the entire system itself, will act and react. For example, suppose an astronomer discovers that a mysterious cosmic cloud of interstellar dust is about to invade our solar system. That scientist might take the theory of gravity, for instance, and apply the covering laws of that theory to a set of initial conditions, including the positions of various celestial bodies, such as the Earth, the moon, the sun, the other planets, and, of course, the mysterious cloud itself, along with orbital paths, speeds, masses, directions, and so forth, of those bodies to predict when that invading interstellar dust cloud might pass between the Earth and the Sun. Then, using the laws of physics, as applied to the composition of the cloud, its density, direction, speed, and so on, the scientist could predict the effects the cloud will have on the Earth as it blocks the light from the Sun. [This scenario was imagined by the British astronomer Fred Hoyle in his book, The *Black Cloud* (New York: Signet Books, 1957).] In imitation of this process, a practitioner of predictive political history will take a theory of human political behavior on the international level, the theory of *Realpolitik*, for instance, and apply the covering laws of that theory to a set of initial conditions (the new world order) on the international scene in order to predict the future of the global community or, more often, to diagnose the seriousness and the possible direction of an international crisis.

For example, how should the United States act when one nation invades another, as happened when Russia invaded Crimea? Should the United States intervene, back off, build a coalition, protest at the United Nations, use economic sanctions, and so on? The proper application of predictive political history will help the United States formulate an appropriate strategy. The theory of international behavior will predict how the leaders of the other nations will respond to an American move, and the set of global initial conditions will tell the Americans whether, from an American perspective, the invader and the target are friends, enemies, former allies, neutrals, dangerous rogues, and so on. So, if the set of global initial conditions identifies the aggressor as an ally and the relationship between the United States and the aggressor as one based on trade and economic dependence, then the United States will act differently than if the global initial conditions identify the aggressor as a failed state, an enemy nation, or a rogue state. In addition, the theory of international behavior will predict whether the leaders of the aggressor nation will act rationally in their nation's own best interests, by negotiating, for example, or by taking the case to the UN, or if they will seek alliances with other similarly situated rogue nations and escalate the aggression. Being able to visualize such future behavior, even in terms of probabilities, far outweighs simply "shooting in the dark" with no consistent strategy and just hoping for the best. Let's look at the Russian invasion of Crimea more closely to see how predictive political history might be used to anticipate future international behavior in a real life situation.

EXAMPLE 34-1: The Russian Invasion of Crimea

Early in 2014, Russia moved more than 2,000 military personnel into Ukraine's Crimean peninsula and took command of the two major airports there. Later, armed Russian troops occupied the Crimean Parliament. The Russians, of course, claimed Crimea as their own, with some justification, since it is the home to almost 1.5 million Russians (about 60 percent of the population). The Russians also anchored their Black Sea naval fleet at a port in Crimea called Sevastopol. Yet, the president of Ukraine called the placement of troops in Crimea an unlawful invasion, which it certainly seemed to be.

The theory of predictive political history should help us visualize what the Russians will probably do next and how the American president should probably react, if at all. To envision the next Russian move and to advise the American president how best to respond, we must first identify the theory of international behavior and the global set of initial conditions that we believe dominate the international community. For the sake of the example, we will use *Realpolitik* (rationalism) as our behavioral theory and the economic theory of Thomas Barnett as our set of initial conditions. Following the covering laws of *Realpolitik*, we can say that national leaders will generally act rationally with the best interests of their own nation in mind; and following Barnett's economic set of initial conditions, Russia and the United States, as members of the stable economic core, will both want to seek a rapid and definitive solution to the problem so as not to destabilize economic activity in the region.

Now taking these two elements, the rationality of *Realpolitik* and the economic ties of Barnett's set of initial conditions, we can conclude that the Russian invasion of Crimea is a rational move in economic terms on the part of Russia because it shields the Russian fleet at Sevastopol, which is used to protect Russian shipping in the Black Sea, and that Russian troops in Crimea can better defend a Russian natural gas pipeline that runs through Ukraine. What will the Russians do next? Well, again, from a rational perspective using *Realpolitik* covering laws and Barnett's set of economic initial conditions, we can predict that the Russians will stay in Crimea, that they may even set their sights on Ukraine, and perhaps on Lithuania and Poland. Why? Because when the Russian leaders apply *Realpolitik* and Barnett's economic initial conditions to the possible actions by the United States and the EU, they can predict that the EU will do nothing, because it is in the EU's best economic interests not to provoke Russia, which supplies the European nations with natural gas.

The Russians will also predict that the Americans will likely do nothing militarily since it is currently in their best interests to avoid military action anywhere in the world beyond the Middle East, because, economically, such a move would be exorbitantly expensive; logistically the tactic would dangerously weaken their military forces; strategically, provoking the Russian Federation at this time would be counterproductive, and politically, such a move would not sit well with the electorate back home. Also, from a global perspective, the Americans do not want to destabilize their trading partners in the EU who need the natural gas supplied by Russia. In addition, the Russians know that, even if the EU and the United States do pressure them in some way, perhaps by economic sanctions, other consumer states need their natural gas and have the resources (read China here) and the motivation (read Turkey here) to pay a lot of money for it. To determine whether this scenario would actually play itself out like this, and whether it is, in fact, the correct route to take, we must study the other theories of international behavior and the other sets of global initial conditions (i.e., the other new world order options). Once this has been done, we can entertain the most difficult question of all, that is, what type of government is best suited for carrying out the protocols of predictive political history, a liberal democracy or an authoritarian system. However, for the moment, we should have some idea of how predictive political history works.

The Theories of International Behavior

Having looked at the process of predictive political history and having studied an example of that process, it is time to step back and look at the four theories of international behavior, followed by an examination of the five sets of initial conditions. The four theories of international behavior are *Realpolitik*, idealism, neoconservativism, and neoliberalism. Each international behavioral theory can be understood by examining its relationships to several covering laws. A **covering law** is a universal normative principle that follows a set pattern that can be used to understand natural processes or human behavior. Examining these patterns of covering laws will reveal how each theory shapes the actions of those leaders who adhere to its tenets. Of course, while acknowledging a leader's belief in a theory of international behavior may help predict how he or she might act in a particular strategic situation, none of this is foolproof because leaders will often act out of character or in ways that are counterproductive to their best interests and the best interests of their nation-state. Moreover, we must remember that a leader's adherence to a theory of international behavior does not necessarily have a direct correlation to his or her political party affiliation. In addition, each global situation will be plagued by wild cards, such as sudden shifts in global alliances, unexpected economic upheavals, unanticipated political changes back home, and the unpredictable actions of rogue states and terrorists. Still, as long as we acknowledge its limitations, predictive political history provides a helpful framework within which to study international politics and as such can guide both our historical analysis of past events and our attempt to forecast future global moves.

In physics, for example, a covering law, such as the law of action and reaction, identifies a physical pattern that can used to predict, in terms of probabilities, a future physical event. A series of interrelated covering laws will produce a theory, such as the theory of gravity. In predictive political history, a covering law identifies historical patterns that can be used to envision, in terms of probabilities, future international behavior. A series of interrelated covering laws will produce a theory of international behavior, such as *Realpolitik*. Some versions of these covering laws can be long and convoluted and so, in an effort to simplify each theory of international behavior, we will reduce them to four indispensable covering laws: (1) a characterization of the global scene, (2) a description of the chief actors on the global scene, (3) a claim as to how those chief actors make international decisions, and (4) a catalogue of special considerations that must be factored into any international study using the theory.

Realpolitik or realism, then, builds the four covering laws in this way: (1) characterization of the global scene—the international order can be described as a chaotic system (i.e., a system that lacks a controlling agent) [See: Tim Dunne, Milja Kurki, and Steve Smith, *International Relations Theories: Discipline and Diversity* (Oxford: Oxford University Press, 2007), p. 73]; (2) chief actors—the chief actors on the global scene are nation-states, which have a high degree of autonomy that permits them to act independently; nonetheless, that authority is not shared uniformly among those nations, since some have more power and influence than others [See: Richard W. Mansbach and Kirsten L. Rafferty, *Introduction to Global Politics* (New York: Routledge, 2008), p. 20; and John J. Mearsheimer, *The Tragedy of Great Power Politics* (New York: Norton, 2014, pp. 17]; (3) decision making—national leaders customarily look for a rational (logical) way to sustain or widen their own power and to, thus, cement or improve the power position of their nation in the global community, while simultaneously protecting their own people and property [See: Mearsheimer, *The Tragedy of Great Power Politics*, p. 17–18]; and (4) special considerations—the power that leaders have is curbed by NGOs like the United Nations, the International Criminal Court, and so on; by international corporations; and by rogue transnationals, such as terrorist groups, pirates, drug cartels, mercenaries, and so on.

Some (many?) political commentators have argued that President Trump is a textbook example of a leader who practices the theory of *Realpolitik*. The president's strategic motto "Make America Great Again" (sometimes voiced as "America First") is said to be a shorthand way of expressing the view that American interests, power, and security must guide all global policy actions. Recent decisions to pull out the Paris Climate Agreement, to enter a trade war with China, to recognize Jerusalem as the *de jure* capital of Israel, to praise the hard-line tactics of authoritarian leaders such as Rodrigo Duterte of the Philippines, to freeze legal immigration from certain Islamic nation-states, to build a border wall to act as a protection against illegal immigration, and to secure a $4 billion deal with Saudi Arabia to rebuild parts of occupied Syria are all cited as examples of *Realpolitik* at work.

Idealism or liberal internationalism constructs the four covering laws in the following way: (1) characterization—the global order is not fully chaotic but is, instead, controlled by nation-states in cooperation with the NGOs; (2) chief actors—nation-states share power with the NGOs; (3) decision making—nation-states and NGOs seek power and control but do so in the interests of international peace, by following international law and using military action within international coalitions; and (4) special considerations—the final best state of affairs that all nation-states seek (or should seek) is the formation of a democratic or a republican world government.

Political experts have long cited President Clinton as an advocate of liberal internationalism. One of Clinton's initial acts as president was to issue an order known as Presidential Decision Directive/NSC-25 (PDD-25). Under the terms of PDD-25, President Clinton wrote that "peacekeeping, peace enforcement and the establishment of a capability to conduct multilateral peace operations will become part of our National Security Strategy and National Military Strategy . . . On a case-by-case basis, I will consider placing appropriate U.S. forces and personnel under the operational control of a competent UN commander for specific UN operations authorized by the Security Council." The goal of this policy had been expressed by Clinton in a campaign speech at Georgetown University where he said that, should he take the office of the presidency, he would develop an American military force that would, "be used for purposes . . . such as standing guard at the borders of countries threatened by aggression; preventing attacks on civilians, providing humanitarian relief, and combating terrorism and drug trafficking." In other words, the U.S. military would follow the covering laws of liberal internationalism by cooperating with NGOs, in this case the UN, and by acting as an global police force in the interests of international peace. [See: William Clinton, Speech at Georgetown University, December 11, 1991, quoted in *"Command" versus "Operational Control": A Critical Review of PDD-25*, 2 by J. William Snyder, http://www.ibiblio.org/jwsnyder/wisdom/pdd25html.)

Neoconservativism sets up the following covering laws: (1) characterization—the global landscape is chaotic; (2) chief actors—nation-states are the chief actors, and all foreign policy decisions must be made to echo the "deepest values of liberal democratic societies" [See: Francis Fukuyama, *America at the Crossroads: Democracy, Power, and the Neoconservative Legacy* (New Haven, CT: Yale University Press, 2006), p. 48]; (3) decision making—the United States must be involved in global affairs and, in doing so, must promote democratic principles; and (4) special considerations—neoconservatives also voice a wariness for social reengineering missions, suspicion about the usefulness of NGOs, and a belief in the effectiveness of unilateral (as opposed to multinational) military crusades including especially preemptive and preventative strikes [See: Fukuyama, *America at the Crossroads*, p. 49].

Some political experts have noted that, in the wake of the terror attacks on 9/11, President George W. Bush promoted neoconservative values in his military and international policies, even if he never adopted the neoconservative label himself. In his National Security Strategy of 2002, Bush wrote that under his direction the United States will, among many other things, "ignite a new era of global economic growth through free markets and free trade (and) expand the circle of development by opening societies and *building the infrastructure of democracy*" (italics added). The subsequent military actions in Afghanistan and Iraq, engineered by the Bush administration, testify to the neoconservative attempt to export democracy to transitional regimes such as Iraq. [See: George W. Bush, The White House, National Security Strategy September 2002, https://georgewbush-whitehouse.archives.gov/nsc/nss/2002/.]

Neoliberalism develops the four covering laws in this way: (1) characterization—the global community scene is largely chaotic; (2) chief actors—nation-states and NGOs share the global power with international corporations; (3) decision making—international corporations cross frontiers and act to preserve their own existence, as do nation-states; however, international corporations act reasonably as they work to generate higher profits; and (4) special considerations—nation-states and international corporations act as collaborative partners and, in doing so, follow the morality of profit.

Neoliberal politicians are more difficult to identify than those who adhere to the other three theories because neoliberals must declare support for the multinational corporate culture, something that, in the current political and economic climate, is guaranteed to lose votes if not entire elections. Nevertheless, the activities of such political leaders will often reveal their neoliberal side even when campaign rhetoric claims otherwise. For example, President Ronald Reagan's unfailing faith in the capitalist system clearly marks him as a neoliberal. Reagan, and other neoliberals like him, believe that national leaders are responsible for defending the operation of the free market system; protecting the ownership of private property; maintaining an efficient and effective stock market; guaranteeing the continued operation of manufacturing, sales, and shipping; and preventing the shutdown of the economic system, or any small part of it, by unauthorized or illegal work stoppages (read strike here). Reagan's neoliberal character was showcased in 1982 when James Baker, Reagan's Treasury Secretary at the time, used the power of the International Monetary Fund (one of those NGOs we have talked about) to force Mexico to adopt a series of strict fiscal practices that prevented that nation's bankruptcy but also, in the process, protected several New York banks that had been threatened with default should the Mexican economy collapse. [See: David Harvey, *A Brief History of Neoliberalism* (Oxford: Oxford University Press, 2005), p. 73.]

When handling a crisis, the predictive political historian imitates the scientist by applying the best theory of international behavior to a set of global initial conditions that exemplify the present-day world order. In its most comprehensive version, the theory will include how a national leader will respond to and work within the initial conditions that describe the *global landscape*. The predictive history practitioner has several sets of initial conditions (new world orders) from which to choose. Still, to keep things as streamlined as possible, we will examine and explain four of these sets of initial conditions—economic, cultural, ideological, and hybrid. It is vital to determine how each set of conditions views the global order before considering international law. To study international law with no understanding of the environment in which it operates is like trying to teach the rules of baseball to someone who has never seen a baseball diamond. It can be done with great difficulty, but why try, especially if there is a real diamond on the next block.

The Global Initial Conditions

As noted previously, political scientists have offered three sets of initial conditions or new world orders for our consideration: the economic theory, the cultural theory, and the hybrid theory. Each of these new world orders has several incarnations, each different from the others. Nevertheless, within each category, the variations share more characteristics than differences, so we will focus on those common denominators.

Economic Initial Conditions
The economic new world order sees the international community as divided into two sectors: (1) those nations that are economically stable and secure and, thus, have healthy, functioning economies and (2) those nation-states that are economically dysfunctional. Thomas Barnett, senior strategic researcher at the Naval War College and author of *The Pentagon's New Map*, calls the functioning nations the "Core" and the dysfunctional nations the "Gap." Richard Haass of the Council on Foreign Relations and author of *The Opportunity* refers to the economically secure nations as the "21st-century concert." Haass does not directly name the economically unstable nations. However, given his overall theoretical bend, calling them the unintegrated nations would not be out of line. Traditionally, economically sound nations have been referred to as developed nations and economically fragile nations as developing nations. Developed nations include such nation-states as the United States, the countries in Western Europe, China, Russia, Japan, Australia, New Zealand, Canada, South Africa, Israel, India, and the ABC (Argentina, Brazil, Chile) countries of Latin America. The developing nations include nation-states in the Middle East, the Balkans, all of Africa except South Africa, South and Central America (except the ABCs), Indonesia, and Southeast Asia.

Both Barnett and Haass insist that Core nation-states must find ways to overcome or eliminate disconnectedness (Barnett's word) or to integrate (Haass's term) the Gap nations with the Core. Adopting this perspective dramatically alters the political map and, therefore, demands a change in tactics. Some nation-states, such as China and Russia, can no longer be seen by the United States as "the enemy" as they were during the Cold War. Instead, they are seen as allies within the Core, and as such, they share a common set of goals with all other Core nations. In contrast, the enemy is any individual, group, or set of circumstances that somehow separates a nation from the Core or prevents it from developing to the extent that it can become a self-sufficient member of the Core. Barnett labels these troubles spots as the "agents of disconnectedness." Under this version of the new world order, international law has certain clear and decisive objectives—namely, (1) to protect the Core nations from economic instability and political disruption; (2) to promote the integration of developing nations within the functioning Core; and (3) to fight the forces of disconnectedness that keep the Gap nations in poverty, whether those forces are terrorists in al-Qaeda, warlords in Somalia, drug runners in Colombia, or rogue governments in Iran and North Korea. [See: T. Barnett, *The Pentagon's New Map: War and Peace in the Twenty-first Century* (New York: Berkley Books, 2004); and R. N. Haass, *The Opportunity: America's Moment to Alter History's Course* (New York: Public Affairs, 2005).]

THE OPENING CASE *Round 2*
Facing the Final New World Order

One of the biggest threats to the stability of the Core is a potential contest between two or more nations within the Core itself. One potential battleground for such a contest is set between the United States and China—two members of the CORE that should see each other as allies not enemies. Yet, the continuing trade imbalance between these two superpowers threatens the stability of the CORE. Consider the following statistics:

1. The United States depends upon China to purchase its Treasury bonds and to invest in American corporations by buying stock that allows these companies to continue to exist and to place factories and retail outlets in China.
2. China owns about $1.2 trillion worth of U.S. Treasury debt.
3. Chinese defense spending has risen precipitously over the last few years reaching, as high as 10 percent of its annual budget.
4. China fields a standing army of more than 2.1 million active-duty personnel.
5. Between 1978 and 2005, 402 million Chinese were lifted out of poverty by economic reforms.

Some experts preach that the upward curve of Chinese economic development and the Chinese goal to dominate East Asia, the South China Sea, and the Western Pacific will lead inevitably to a war between the China and the United States. If we take one of the theories of international behavior, *Realpolitik*, for example, and apply that theory to the economic set of initial conditions, we get the following results. Given that *Realpolitik* believes that national leaders will act rationally to protect their own power and the lives of their people, and given that both China and the United States are, using Barnett's terminology, Core nations, these two powerful nations are not enemies at all but economic allies that must cooperate to (1) protect the stability of the Core and (2) bring Gap nations into the Core in order to ensure global stability.

The question on the table now is which political ideology, liberal democracy or authoritarianism, is best equipped to handle the dangers that are represented by a coming battle between the two most powerful nations in the Core, the United States and China. The Chinese have a relatively stable and somewhat predictable authoritarian governmental system that centers on the Chinese Communist Party (the CCP). The Communist Party of China consists of some 75 million members. However, the government itself is run by a small group of people referred to as the Communist Party elites. The actual ruling members of the government come from the highest echelons of the elites, who number about 300 to 400. The Chinese government itself is made up of the National People's Congress, the president, and the Supreme People's Court. The National People's Congress is made up of 2,900 representatives elected by people in the provinces, the regions, and the municipalities. The NPC elects the president and appoints the judges to the Court. However, these decisions are are largely guided by the CCP. Power rests primarily in the CCP, and that power is manifested in and carried out by the president, who is also the chairman of the CCP, and the Supreme Military Commander. Moreover, the president is no longer constrained by term limits and can, therefore, serve for life, if he so desires, giving him almost unlimited authoritarian power. Thus far, President Xi Jinping has demonstrated a propensity toward *Realpolitik*, making decisions that clearly place Chinese interests at the top of his agenda. Given the rise of China's economic power, it may be that the ideology of authoritarianism ought to be given a second look. [See: Noah Feldman, *Cool War: The Future of Global Competition* (New York: Random House, 2013); David C. Kang, *China Rising: Peace, Power, and Order in East Asia* (New York: Columbia University Press, 2007); and Dan Smith, *The State of the World Atlas* (New York: Penguin, 2008).]

Source: See: Noah Feldman, *Cool War: The Future of Global Competition* (New York: Random House, 2013); David C. Kang, *China Rising: Peace, Power, and Order in East Asia* (New York: Columbia University Press, 2007); S.P. Huntington, *The Clash of Civilizations and The Remaking of World Order* (New York: Simon & Schuster, 1996); Dan Smith, *The State of the World Atlas* (New York: Penguin, 2008).

Cultural Initial Conditions The cultural new world order was developed by Samuel Huntington in his book, *The Clash of Civilization*. This view sees the globe as divided into eight distinct civilizations that are more or less autonomous and more or less incapable of successfully cooperating with more than one, or at the most two, other civilizations. A **civilization** is a group of people in a series of different nation-states that share common characteristics—including history, religion, tradition, beliefs, often language, and sometimes ancestry. Huntington identifies eight such civilizations: Western civilization (the United States, Canada, Western Europe, Israel, South Africa, Australia, and New Zealand), the Sinic civilization (China, North and South Korea, and most of Southeast Asia), the Orthodox civilization (Russia and other states in Eastern Europe), the Latin American civilization (South and Central America), the Islamic civilization (Middle Eastern nation-states, the nation-states of northern Africa, and Indonesia), the African civilization (the sub-Saharan regions of Africa), the Hindu civilization (India and Sri Lanka), and the Japanese civilization (Japan alone).

Some of these civilizations contain powerful central states that serve as a sort of international "big brother" to the lesser states within a civilization. A civilization with a recognized central state is generally more stable, less warlike, and more economically prosperous than one without. The civilizations with central states include Western (the United States), Sinic (China), Hindu (India), Orthodox (Russia), and Japanese (Japan). Because most international conflicts occur between rather than within civilizations, each civilization is better off if it can limit its contact with other civilizations. To this end, Huntington has outlined a number of rules that each civilization should follow in dealing with all other civilizations. These rules include (1) the prime directive of the civilizational world order—that is, that each civilization should never interfere with the internal affairs of another civilization; (2) the rule of collective mediation, which calls for dialogue and negotiation among the central controlling states when possible whenever a dispute arises between civilizations; and (3) the commonalities rule, which encourages civilizations to emphasize those ideals that draw them together rather than those that drive them apart. Thus, it is healthier for Western civilization, for instance, to share its focus on self-determination, rather than to insist that all nations adopt Western-style democracy. Under this version of the new world order, international law has two goals: to promote civilizational autonomy and to protect civilizational rights. [See: S. P. Huntington, *The Clash of Civilizations and The Remaking of World Order* (New York: Simon & Schuster, 1996).]

THE OPENING CASE Round 3
Facing the Final New World Order

Recall that the conflict envisioned in the Opening Case involves a coming clash between two powerful political ideologies, liberal democracy and authoritarianism. One political scientist, Samuel Huntington, believes that this final clash will erupt between the two most formidable representatives of those two ideologies: China and the United States. Some commentators believe that the unprecedented growth of China and its desire to dominate, at minimum, East Asia, the South China Sea, and the Western Pacific will lead to an inevitable battle between these two nations. To prevent this spiral into cultural war, Huntington suggests that those civilizations should abandon the international community and, in a sort of self-imposed neoisolationism, withdraw totally to within their civilizational community. In this case, the United States and China would belong to two different civilizations. The United States would serve as the central controlling state of the Western civilization, while China would be the central controlling state of the Sinic civilization. Western civilization would also include Canada, Western Europe, Australia, New Zealand, South Africa, and Israel. China's civilization would include North and South Korea, and most of Southeast Asia, including the Philippines.

The establishment of the new civilizational units would require a break in trade, manufacturing, investments, and banking ties with all other civilizations, but especially those whose customs and beliefs are as different as the Americans and the Chinese. Can such disengagements actually be engineered? Huntington seems to think so. However, asking such a question is beside the point. Despite what we have just discussed here, we must realize that this take on Huntington actually misses the point. What Huntington really argues is not that the nation-states of the world should form such civilizations, but that such civilizations are already in place. The real problem is that we fail to recognize these cultural units, and as a result, we operate as if they do not exist. Moreover, Huntington adds, we do so at our own peril. When we fail to see that China exists in its own world, as do we, then we are doomed to repeat the errors of the past over and over again—errors caused, Huntington says, by operating as if no differences exist and by being surprised again and again when we find out that they do. In such a world, what matters is which ideology best suits the customs and the traditions of each civilization. In fact, if Huntington is correct, civilizational values drive the decision to be authoritarian or democratic. If the nation-states of the Western civilization are comfortable with liberal democracy, then, so be it. Similarly, if the member nations of the Sinic civilization work well in an authoritarian setting, then authoritarianism should be adopted or maintained in each of those states.

On the other hand, the contemporary trend toward authoritarianism may not be related to civilizational characteristics at all but, instead, to human nature. As Thomas Hobbes suggests in *Leviathan*, human beings may need to be constrained by a social contract that transfers all (well, most) authority to a single, all powerful leader who operates autonomously. This conjecture may explain the political movement toward authoritarianism in the West, as seen in such western nations as Austria, Italy, Poland, and, some would argue, even the United States. [See: Noah Feldman, *Cool War: The Future of Global Competition* (New York: Random House, 2013); David C. Kang, *China Rising: Peace, Power, and Order in East Asia* (New York: Columbia University Press, 2007); S. P. Huntington, *The Clash of Civilizations and the Remaking of World Order* (New York: Simon & Schuster, 1996); Dan Smith, *The State of the World Atlas* (New York: Penguin, 2008); Olaf Stapledon, *Last and First Men* (New York: Dover, 1931); Valentina Pop, "Win Slows Anti-EU Movement: Several Emboldened Nationalist Parties Have Challenged the Bloc's Existence," *The Wall Street Journal*, May 8, 2017, p. A8.]

Source: See: Noah Feldman, *Cool War: The Future of Global Competition* (New York: Random House, 2013); David C. Kang, *China Rising: Peace, Power, and Order in East Asia* (New York: Columbia University Press, 2007); S.P. Huntington, *The Clash of Civilizations and The Remaking of World Order* (New York: Simon & Schuster, 1996); Dan Smith, *The State of the World Atlas* (New York: Penguin, 2008); and Olaf Stapledon, *Last and First Men* (New York: Dover, 1931); Valentina Pop, "Win Slows Anti-EU Movement: Several emboldened nationalist parties have challenged the bloc's existence," *The Wall Street Journal* (May 8 2017, p. A8).

Hybrid Initial Conditions In *A Few Brass Tacks* and *A New Pattern for a Tired World*, essayist and political commentator Louis Bromfield develops a model for the new world order that anticipates a combined view of the work of Barnett, Haas, and Huntington and reflects the philosophical and ethical ideas of Max Weber, his contemporary. Taking a page from the ideology of *Realpolitik*, Bromfield declares unapologetically that American leaders have mismanaged their essential duties by concentrating on what Bromfield labels "world responsibility" rather than national responsibility. The United States intervenes in the affairs of other nations, intending to help but, instead, doing quite the opposite. Generally, the target nation becomes dependent on American handouts, which damages the nation's independence and erodes its self-esteem. This means that the United States momentarily rescues failing nations by transferring billions of dollars into their treasuries, but never handles the real causes of the economic crisis itself. America's lack of skill in international affairs may be understandable given its youth and inexperience, but that does not excuse the repetition of the same mistakes over and over. Bromfield maintains that, to be genuinely responsible, American leaders must accept a long view of the future, one that determines what is best for the nation's citizens in terms of what is best for the economic balance of the global community. Paradoxically, this means that the United States and other economically powerful nations must disengage from the global community and deal with the civic and economic well-being of their own people.

Bromfield proposes that the major global powers, including the United States, Europe, Russia, China, Japan, and India, establish regional economic zones among those nations closest to them. **Economic zones** are unified but isolated sectors of economic activity based on geographical areas designed to focus on the economic well-being of the nations in each zone. Bromfield's economic zones would conform to the following geographic arrangement: the Western Zone—the United States, Canada, and Mexico (possibly also South America, led by Brazil); the European Zone—essentially today's European Union; the East Asian Zone—Russia, China, and Japan (although, at times, Bromfield moves Russia into the European

Zone); and the South Central Asian Zone—India, Pakistan (at times, Bromfield adds "the rest of Asia" to this zone). Once these zones are economically and politically secure, the members of each zone will trade only with other nations within their respective zones. These exclusive trading arrangements would continue until the members of each zone developed economically secure relationships among themselves. The four major economic zones could then trade among themselves: the Western Zone with the East Asian Zone, the European Zone with the South Central Asian Zone, and so on. Eventually, each zone could enter open trade agreements with nations outside the four established zones, but only when those outside nations were ready to participate as economic equals. This strategy reflects an appropriate example of Weber's ethic of responsibility. The global giants will have demonstrated a responsible attitude toward their own people, and a mutually supportive relationship with the remainder of the globe. What's more, Bromfield foresees a future international community operating as a unified global economy. Although, he does not use the term *globalization* here, he certainly could have. So, the only question left, is to determine which ideology, liberal democracy or authoritarianism, can do the job (whether we are talking about the economic job proposed by Barnett and Haass; the civilizational job suggested by Huntington; or the hybrid job imagined by Bromfield. To find the answer to this read on. [See: Louis Bromfield, *A New Pattern for a Tired World* (New York: Harper, 1954); For an examination of the ethic of responsibility see also Max Weber, "Politics as a Vocation," in *The Great Political Theories, Volume 2*, Ed. Michael Curtis (New York: Harper, 2008), pp. 426–436.]

THE OPENING CASE *Round 4*
Facing the Final New World Order

Louis Bromfield wrote his two major political narratives, *A Few Brass Tacks* and *A New Pattern for a Tired World*, in the years immediately following World War II at a time when the United States was at the peak of its political, economic, and military power. As the only major nation untouched by the destruction of the war, the United States should have been able to manage the world's problems in a sensible, straightforward, and successful way. Unfortunately, as Bromfield has pointed out repeatedly, the United States did not live up to its potential. Instead of solving problems in Europe, Iran, Korea, Guatemala, and Viet Nam, the United States actually made things worse. Bromfield argues that America's failure to deal successfully with international problems is rooted in its inexperience and is manifested in its tendency to throw money at any problem in the hopes that money alone will make things better. As Bromfield writes in *A New Pattern*: "We pour billions of dollars into the nations of Europe, which has perhaps saved them from temporary bankruptcy, but has done nothing to solve the real and inevitable economic ills constituting the *real* causes of their decline." The United States, Bromfield says, is caught up in a repetition of past failures. As Bromfield notes: "The whole pattern of our interference and of our policies has included little but the old nineteenth-century political ideas which brought about two world wars and are perhaps bringing about a third, which could easily mean the end of civilization or even of life upon this planet."

Bromfield proposes that the United States abandon its Lone Ranger approach and, instead of trying to solve every nation's problems separately, lead a movement under which the major global powers—including the United States, Europe, Russia, China, Japan, and India—initiate economic coalitions with those nations closest to them, geographically and culturally. These economic zones would first trade among themselves until they were economically stable and would then explore relationships with other coalitions. Such a move would require a great deal of change that would be resisted both domestically and internationally. Forcing the creation of economic zones would require a unified and resource laden campaign engineered by the most powerful nation-state within each zone. It would demand cooperation on an unprecedented scale both within and between nation-states.

It would seem that such a massive undertaking would require the power of an authoritarian regime that could crush domestic resistance, defeat military opposition from neighboring nation-states, and unify a wide variety of jealous nations with competing interests. Liberal democracies with their systems of checks and balances, their reliance on political coalitions, their dependence on corporate money, their reliance on the pollsters, and their fear of the media would not be up to the task. Yet, Bromfield does not see it this way. As a fierce defender of Jeffersonian democracy, Bromfield believes that certain strong and determined liberal democracies, with their capitalist free market economy, are the best answer to global problems of economic disparity and cultural animosity. Is Bromfield correct, or is his faith in liberal democracy misplaced?

To answer this question, we must turn to the third element in predictive political history—ideology.

However, before doing so, we do have one road block to consider—economic entanglement. Recall, that China and the United States are so intertwined economically that creating the type of economic zones that Bromfield suggests might not be possible unless the United States is prepared to renege on its trade, manufacturing, and investment contracts with China. Such a move in the present economic climate would lead to an international crisis at the Dispute Settlement Board (DSB) of the

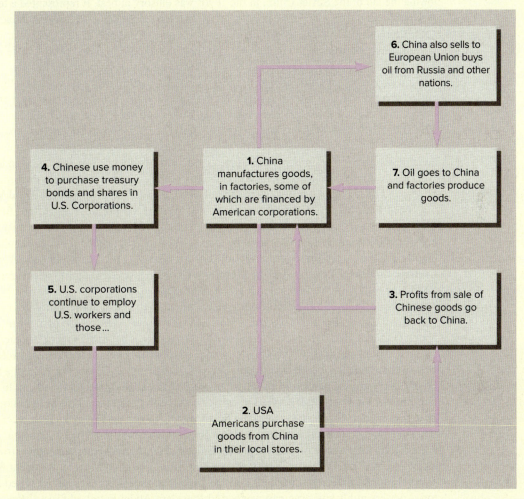

Figure 34-1 The China Economic Cycle.
Note: Bromfield proposes that the major global powers, including the United States, Europe, Russia, China, Japan, and India, establish regional economic zones among those nations closest to them. As this figure and the Opening Case Round 4 indicate, the economic entanglement of the United States and China would make Bromfield's plan difficult but not impossible.

World Trade Organization or perhaps, even to a global, armed (nuclear?) conflict. Still, Bromfield remains confident that liberal democracies are currently armed with the resources and the tools needed to see create those zones of economic trade even it it means a few

years (decades?) of hurdles, hardship, and hunger. (See Figure 34-1.) [See: Louis Bromfield, *A New Pattern for a Tired World* (New York: Harper, 1954).]

Source: See: Louis Bromfield, *A New Pattern for a Tired World* (New York: Harper, 1954).

Ideologies: Liberal Democracy v. Authoritarianism

Recall that Francis Fukuyama's book *The End of History and the Last Man* is based on the premise that, with the end of the Cold War, Western liberal ideals won the battle for the control of civilization. The future, according to Fukuyama, would be dominated by the ideology of liberal democracy, which would be the major form of government for the global community. Later events have proven that Fukuyama was overly optimistic. In fact, in the early years of the 21st century, the ideology of authoritarianism is once again challenging liberal democracy. This problem is explored by Robert Kagan in his book, *The Return of History and the End of Dreams*. Kagan believes that the period of peace and prosperity following the fall of the Soviet Union in the 1990s was illusory at best. It represented a temporary respite in the eternal political struggle between the ideologies of liberal democracy and authoritarianism. This respite would end as soon as the "losers" of the Cold War had a chance to pause, reassess their situation, regroup, and emerge as global powers once again. This, Kagan argues, is precisely what happened when the Russian people, after their failed attempt at democracy, surrendered to the *de facto* dictatorship of a new Russian oligarchy and to the promise of a return to past days of imperial glory. The Russians, Kagan argues, believe that they were victimized by the United States and the European Union during the 1990s, and they are now determined to regain their place of power in the international community. Such power they believe can only be reignited within the unified power structure of an authoritarian state. Similarly, the Chinese, who also see themselves as victimized by the West (not without good reason), have decided to use their economic strength, their military power, and their political influence to rebuild alliances with the people of the Third World who need their help to resist the temptation of Western corporate domination. Both of these great powers, Russia and China, Kagan argues, have returned to a 19th-century strategy of empire-building, and both have the ideological structure needed to see those plans of empire succeed. This return to strict authoritarianism was further cemented when the Chinese Communist Party abolished term limits for the president and thus ensured that Xi Jinping would rule with unfettered power indefinitely.

Nor is this move toward authoritarianism limited to the great autocratic states such as Russia and China. In Europe, several nation-states have seen a resurgence of anti-European Union (Euro-skeptic) parties that promote a reaffirmation of nationalism. For instance, in a recent Austrian election, a Euro-skeptic politician won 47 percent of that nation's vote in a closely contested presidential campaign. Similarly, in Poland, in October of 2015, the Euro-skeptic party won 38 percent of the legislature in a national parliamentary election. In addition, the electorate of the UK voted to extricate themselves from the European Union in a 2016 referendum, now referred to as the Brexit vote. Likewise, in Turkey in 2017, a constitutional referendum reengineered that nation's constitution, abolishing the parliamentary government, eliminating the office of prime minister, and replacing the parliamentary structure with a presidential system that bestowed extensive authoritarian powers on President Recep Tayyip Erdoğan. Similarly, President Rodrigo Duterte of the Philippines has exercised dictatorial powers in his anti-drug campaign, and President Abdel Fattah al-Sisis of Egypt has used an authoritarian approach in his dealing with dissidents, jailing thousands of them in the name of safety and security. In light of this evidence, it is easy to see why Kagan predicts a globe that will be increasingly divided into two political camps: (1) the liberal democracies, led by the United States, and (2) the authoritarian regimes, led by Russia and China. [See: Robert Kagan, *The Return of History and the End of Dreams* (New York: Public Affairs, 2005). See also: Pop, p. A-8; and "America's Foreign Policy: Goodbye to Values," *The Economist*, June 3, 2017, p. 53.]

The question in front of us right now is—why? What advantages does anyone see in an authoritarian state that would lead them to abandon a liberal democratic government, no matter how poorly run, to live under the heavy hand of an iron regime like that in China,

Russia, Turkey, Egypt, or the Philippines? Remarkably, there are several arguments offered in defense of authoritarian rule. For one thing, authoritarian regimes have one huge advantage over all liberal democracies. Authoritarian regimes are, first and foremost, efficient, effective, and fiscally competent in the handling of their resources, their territory, and their people. In simple language, authoritarian governments can do what they set out to do and do it quickly. In their book, *That Used to Be Us: How America Fell Behind in the World It Invented and How We Can Come Back*, Thomas Friedman and Michael Mandelbaum briefly relate a convincing example of authoritarian efficiency in their story about the building of the Tianjing Meijiang Convention Center in China. This huge, impressive-looking convention center includes 230,000 square meters of floor space (that is 2.5 million square feet, for you Americans). However, the most impressive thing about the building project is that it lasted just eight months. Moreover, those eight months included the winter months of November, December, January, February, and March. To make their point even more dramatically, Friedman and Mandelbaum contrast this monumental undertaking to a Washington Metro modernization project conducted on two escalators at a subway station near their homes. Friedman and Mandelbaum write, "It took China's Teda Construction Group thirty-two weeks to build a world class convention center from the ground up—including giant escalators in every corner—and it was taking the Washington Metro Crew twenty four weeks to repair two tiny escalators of twenty-two steps each." [See: Thomas Friedman and Michael Mandelbaum, *That Used to Be Us: How America Fell Behind in the World It Invented and How We Come Back* (New York: Farrar, Straus, and Giroux, 2011) p. 3.]

In addition to efficiency and economy, authoritarian regimes also offer strictly controlled security. Airports in China, for example, require airline passengers to file through no less than four security checkpoints at international airports, the last of which includes a baggage search of all carry-on luggage just before the passengers board the plane at the gate. Authoritarian governments are also capable of controlling large and diverse populations that must often be moved rapidly and efficiently to make way for industrial and electrical power projects or that must be evacuated in the face of pending natural disasters.

Despite these bright spots, authoritarian governments also have a dark side, which often outweighs the advantages gained by concentrated power. That dark side is seen in the tendency of an authoritarian government to disregard the fundamental rights of the people. Authoritarian leaders such as those listed earlier (including President Abdel Fattah al-Sisis of Egypt, President Rodrigo Duterte of the Philippines, and President Recep Tayyip Erdoğan of Turkey) must often resort to Machiavellian techniques for controlling the people, eliminating opposition voices, policing the press, and guarding their borders. Typically, authoritarian regimes are also plagued by corruption that comes in the form of bribes, kickbacks, and influence peddling. For example, in the face of widespread corruption in China, Chinese officials have mounted a campaign to clean up the system and to rid the nation of as many criminals as possible. Moreover, the widespread nature of the problem is evidenced by the fact that this anti-corruption campaign has resulted in the punishment of more than 270,000 offenders, most of whom have been placed in prison but some of whom have received the death penalty. Moreover, the campaign has been so thorough and so effective that it has netted some corrupt Politburo officials, indicating how deeply corruption is ingrained within the system. In addition, the fact that so many individuals have been caught indicates that China's reform campaign is far from over. [See: "America's Foreign Policy: Goodbye to Values," p. 53; and James Leung, "Xi's Corruption Crackdown: How Bribery and Corruption Threaten the Chinese Dream," *Foreign Affairs*, May/June 2015, p. 32.]

Of course, liberal democracies also have their problems. As we have seen, liberal democracies are often slow to act, wasteful in their spending, ineffective in their governmental programs, short-sighted in their planning, and, most of all, out of touch with their constituencies. For example, a 2016 poll run by the Rasmussen Report indicated that 73 percent of Republican voters believed that their party leaders at that time were out of touch with the majority of their party's voters. The same poll also noted that 69 percent of all voters believed that the Republicans had done a poor job representing the electorate. This might have been good news for the Democrats except that another poll, this one administered by *CBS News* in 2017, revealed that 45 percent of Democratic voters were unhappy with the Democratic party across the board at that time. The same poll reported that 75 percent of independent voters were dissatisfied with the performance of members of the Democratic Party. [See: Theodore Bunker, "Poll: 73% of Republicans Say Party Out of Touch with Voters," *Newsmax*, June 22, 2016, http://www.newsmax.com/ Politics/republicans-voters-out-of-touch-gop/2016/06/22/id/735099; and Joe Crowe, "Poll: Voters Unhappy with Both Democrats and Republicans," *Newsmax*, June 20, 2017, https://www.newsmax.com/Politics/poll-voters-unhappy-democrats/2017/06/20/id/ 797081/.]

Of course, while this evidence may show that liberal democracies are often out of touch their constituents, it does not demonstrate that liberal democracy is, in itself, a poor governmental system. On the contrary, liberal democracy, like authoritarianism, as a type of government, has its advantages. For example, liberal democracies, as an historical fact, tend to avoid war with other liberal democracies. Consequently, a rise in the number of liberal democracies within the international community ought to lead, theoretically at least, to a less violent, more secure global environment. Second, liberal democracies work best when united to a capitalistic market system. Capitalism, as a system, defends private property, encourages individual investment, creates multiple employment opportunities, guarantees labor representation in questions of wages and benefits, and promises access to the courts when things go wrong. These factors operate together to create a stable middle class that benefits from the status quo and thus, as a rule, tends to be neither dissatisfied nor rebellious, leading to a safe and stable state within a safe and stable global community. Third, liberal democracies tend to be dedicated to human rights both at home and abroad, thus reinforcing a sense of responsibility among the nations of the global community. This sense of responsibility led to the 1991 coalition of nations that reacted to the Iraqi invasion of Kuwait and freed that tiny, defenseless nation from Iraqi occupation. This informal union of liberal democracies also led to military rescue missions in Bosnia, Kosovo, Sierre Leone, Libya, Egypt, and Syria. It also led to the institutionalization of the Responsibility to Protect Doctrine at the United Nations 2005 World Summit. The Responsibility to Protect (R2P) doctrine is founded on the supposition that nation-states have a duty protect their own citizens and that those nations that endanger their own citizens will be held accountable by other law abiding nations by economic sanctions, diplomatic strategies, and when necessary, by military action. [See: "America's Foreign Policy: Goodbye to Values," pp. 53–54.]

What conclusion can we draw from all of this in relation to predictive political history? Which ideology—liberal democracy or authoritarianism—is best equipped to deal with global problems no matter which theory of international behavior and which set of initial conditions we settle on as the most accurate portrait of the new world order? Authoritarian governments can guarantee an efficient, effective, and economical strategy that is both secure and predictable, while the liberal democracies can promise the continuation of a free market, the protection of international trade, the defense of human rights, and the preservation of a relatively strife-free global community. The easy way out of this dilemma would be to default to liberal democracy because that ideology is the hallmark of Western culture, and, as Huntington would point out, we, as human beings, find it hard to think outside the box of civilizational values. Yet, there is much to admire in the strength of authoritarian efficiency and security. Perhaps the solution lies not in a dualistic "either-or" choice, but in an understanding of the existential moment in which a nation-state and its governmental system has emerged. To see what is meant by this, we will turn to the philosophy of John Dewey, who developed his theory of government after living in both the liberal democracy of his native United States and in a China that existed after the fall of the imperial system but before the emergence of the communist state.

In her book, *John Dewey in China: To Teach and to Learn*, Jessica Ching-Sze Wang tells us that Dewey views the nation-state through the lens of utilitarianism, if only because he sees the nation-state, in general, and individual existential nations in particular, as emerging from the interactions of the people who make up that nation-state. Dewey also believes, like Thomas Hobbes before him that, from a utilitarian perspective, the nation-state exists to protect the lives of the people who live in that nation-state. Therefore, nation-states are neither mystical nor magical, neither indestructible nor untouchable. Moreover, nation-states are simply one cog in the vast machinery of human society, sharing the stage with the family, the church, the school, and the economy. Nevertheless, nation-states do have a special status because, for better or worse, they remain the single most powerful unit within society. Moreover, when all other social units suffer a breakdown, it becomes the responsibility of the nation-states to fix that breakdown. No other part of society has the power, the wherewithal, or the authority to do so, not even the NGOs (like the UN) which have no separate existence without the nation-states that finance, house, and run them. [See: Jessica Ching-Sze Wang, *John Dewey in China: To Teach and to Learn* New York: State University of New York, 2007), pp. 94-96).]

Given this take on the nation-state, it should come as no surprise the Dewey rejects the idea that any one form of the nation-state and, therefore, any one ideology, either liberal democracy or authoritarianism, can take precedence over any other. There is no perfect nation-state, and there is no perfect ideology. There are only existential nation-states and individualized governmental ideologies that emerge from the interactions of the people among themselves. Therefore, to understand the nation-state, to change the nation-state, and to deal with the relationships among nation-states that exist within the global community, one must understand the people who make up each nation-state. Moreover, the fluid nature of the nation-state, and the fact that it emerges from its human participants, places a duty on the shoulders of those people to reinvent the nation-state and its global neighborhood when the need arises. Nor is this an optional activity. It is, in fact, a duty of the highest order. [See: Wang.] This may, in fact, be what is happening in China right now. Having worked with communism for 70-plus years, China has begun to experiment with Western liberalism, especially in its adoption of a quasi-capitalist economy. However, this experimentation has not prevented China's drift back to authoritarianism, as evidenced by the recent decision by the National People's Congress to eliminate presidential term limits and to, thus, further empower the president. This tenacious hold on authoritarianism can be traced to China's pragmatic need to control one of the biggest populations on the planet. So which ideology is best? The answer lies within the social context of each nation-state. This conclusion may not be as satisfactory as an answer that points to one ideology or the other, but it has the virtue if being, if nothing else, supremely realistic. Speaking of being realistic, it is time to turn to the shortcomings and the limits of the theory of predictive political history.

Variables, Uncertainty, and Unexpected Events

Despite all its virtues, predictive political history is not without its shortcomings and limitations. As John Dewey would argue, the chief shortcoming of predictive political history is that, unlike the laws of physics, the laws of predictive political history are limited by the free will of the people who operate within that system. This limitation is referred to as the volition variable. The **volition variable**, which was identified, though not named as such, by Arthur Danto in his book, *Analytical Philosophy of History*, is an unstable element within the human decision-making process imposed by the fact that humans have free will. Free will allows individuals to make arbitrary decisions that reduce the deterministic predictability of the covering laws of predictive political history. On the other hand, if we do a careful study of the volition variable, we will see decision-making patterns that make apparently unpredictable moves predictable, at least in terms of probabilities. Still, Danto would maintain that the covering laws of predictive political history must always be limited by qualifiers such as "generally," "often," "usually," and so on. Such qualifiers allow for the fact that determinism is limited by free will and that the exercise of free can still be seen as determined by events. Thus, for example, a covering law in predictive political history can never state conclusively, "When nations feel threatened, they will strike preemptively." Instead, covering "laws" should be formulated as probabilities, such as, "(Generally) when nations feel (somewhat) threatened, they will (often) strike (more or less) preemptively. [See: Arthur Danto, *Analytical Philosophy of History* (New York: Rainbow-Bridge Book Company, 1965), pp. 183-187, 212-13.] For instance, during World War II, in June 1941, Joseph Stalin, in examining the political, military, geographical, and meteorological evidence, discounted speculation that the Germans would invade Russia. Stalin should have been correct. However, he failed to factor in the volition variable including evidence that Hitler tended to make unexpected and irrational decisions, as the German dictator did when he invaded Russia that year. On the other hand, Stalin had been warned that Hitler might make such an unexpected move, and Stalin, in exercising his own free will, chose to characterize those warnings as propaganda. [See: Richard Overy, *Atlas of 20th Century History* (New York: Harper Collins, 2004), pp. 74-75.]

Predictive political history might also be disrupted by the uncertainty principle. The uncertainty principle is an unstable element within the human decision-making process that emerges because the act of making a decision in a system often alters that system. This problem results because, whenever a decision maker is also a participant in a situation, the two roles (observer and actor) interfere with one another, producing unintended consequences. In his book, *The New Paradigm for Financial Markets*, the philosopher and financial analyst George Soros calls this tendency the reflexivity principle. The uncertainty (or reflexivity) principle is rarely a problem in science (unless we are dealing with quantum physics). Thus, when a scientist determines whether a passing celestial object will cross the orbit of the Earth and be suitable for telescopic observations, her decision has no effect on the orbit of that object, its speed, composition, mass, and so on. However, when a national leader must determine whether to launch a drone on a terrorist stronghold, he (or his advisors) must determine the payload, the trajectory, the timing, and so on. In such a situation, factors that appear to be objective are actually subjective because they require evaluation and judgment. Soros says that such factors do not qualify as knowledge because they are tainted by intentions and expectations. When decisions makers do not recognize this distinction, they see things as reliable facts that may actually be unreliable value judgments. This disconnect between what is true and what the decision maker believes is true means that the decision maker has changed the situation by adding his or her value judgments into the mix of fact and fiction. Such a mix can result in unintended consequences. [See: George Soros, *The New Paradigm for Financial Markets: The Credit Crisis of 2008 and What It Means* (New York: Public Affairs, 2008).]

Finally, predictive political history can also be disrupted by unexpected, uncontrollable chaotic events. In *Warrior Politics*, Robert Kaplan calls such occurrences *sideswipes*. Chaotic events consist of unpredictable and unexpected incidents, often with a natural origin, such as earthquakes, typhoons, snowstorms, volcanic eruptions, plagues, and the like that come out of nowhere and have a debilitating effect on human decisions [See: Robert Kaplan, *Warrior Politics: Why Leadership Demands a Pagan Ethos* (New York:

Random House, 2002).] Chaotic events, however, can also result from human activity, as with the advent of cloning, genetic engineering, fusion energy, drone warfare, computer viruses, and other scientific breakthroughs; unexpected political events such as the fall of the Soviet Union, the mortgage crisis of 2008, terror attacks such as 9/11, the London tube bombing, and the Spanish train attack; or unexpected and unpredicted cultural changes such as the drug crisis, immigration reform, campaign corruption, sex scandals, and governmental spying.

quick quiz 34-1

1. A world order is a set of initial conditions that describes how nation-states relate to one another on a global scale. true | false
2. As a process, predictive political history imitates science. true | false
3. The democracies have won the ideological battle and a cooperative world has emerged. true | false

34-2 International Law and War

Karl von Clausewitz, a 19th-century Prussian soldier and political scientist, is credited with one of the most often-quoted definitions of war. "War," Clausewitz claims, "is a continuation of politics by other means." In today's world of complex multinational corporations, delicate international relationships, and instantaneous Internet transactions, Clausewitz might have added that war is also the continuation of international business by other means. As we have seen recently, international business can be affected profoundly by war, especially when it is an unpopular war that lacks international authorization and when it results in a protracted campaign of attrition that drags on for months with no clear goals and no end in sight. Such a situation can increase costs; cause shortages of raw materials; endanger shipping; and render the execution of a contract commercially impracticable, if not impossible, to perform. This scenario may be true even if the parties to a war are not citizens of the nations that are at war. Some of these problems can be solved by the internal law of a particular nation-state.

EXAMPLE 34-2: The *S.S. Christos* and the Suez Crisis

The Transatlantic Financing Corporation operated the *S.S. Christos*, a cargo ship carrying wheat from Texas to Iran, for the U.S. government. While the *S.S. Christos* was en route to Iran, Israel invaded Egypt. Two days later, France and Great Britain invaded the Suez Canal Zone. The invasion and subsequent closing of the Suez Canal made it impossible for the *S.S. Christos* to use the canal. A 3,000-mile detour around the southern coast of Africa cost Transatlantic an unexpected $44,000 above the original estimated cost of $305,842.92. When the U.S. government refused to pay the additional amount, the company brought a lawsuit. Although the United States and Transatlantic were not directly involved in the Suez hostilities, their contract had been affected by the conflict. Nevertheless, the federal court did not allow Transatlantic to recover the additional payment from the government of the United States. The court's decision was based on a traditional rule of contract law in the United States. The court declared, "While it may be an overstatement to say that increased cost and difficulty of performance never constitute impracticability, to justify relief there must be more of a variation between the expected costs and the cost of performing by an available alternative than is present in this case."

The lesson to be learned from the case in Example 34-2 is a simple one: When entering a contract that relies on the international marketplace, it is wise for all parties to be aware of the international conditions in all areas of the globe that may affect the contract. This approach is crucial because courts in the United States will take into account the foreseeability of any international crisis, including not only war but also war-related events, such as blockades, quarantines, and border closings. If the court deems that the international crisis was foreseeable, the loss suffered by the parties affected by the crisis will not be offset by the court.

A QUESTION OF ETHICS

Delusional Fantasies and Foreseeable Wars

In her influential study of the Great War, the historian Barbara W. Tuchman writes in *The Guns of August* that in 1910, two very different, yet equally popular, views on the prospect of future wars existed within Europe. One of these views was represented by Norman Angell's book, *The Great Illusion*. Angell argued that war had become an untenable option because of the economic connections among the nations of the global community. Any war would have such devastating consequences that nations could no longer afford to engage in any sort of armed conflict. In support of this view, a key British military leader, Viscount Esher, contended that a combination of factors, including "commercial disaster, financial ruin, and individual suffering," made war in the 20th century "more difficult and improbable" than ever before in the history of civilization. A contradictory position was represented by a German general, Friedrich von Bernhardi, who, in a work titled *Germany and the Next War*, argued that war was inevitable. In fact, von Bernhardi argued, war was a consequence of "natural law." Von Bernhardi insisted that war was a "biological necessity" and actually the human expression of "the struggle for existence." Von Bernhardi wrote that, among nation-states, "there can be no standing still." He concluded that any country that fails to move up the evolutionary ladder of development faces inevitable destruction. [See: Barbara Tuchman, "A Funeral," *The Guns of August* (New York: The MacMillan Company, 1962), pp. 10-11; Norman Angell, *The Great Illusion* (New York: Cosimo Classics, 1909, 2007) .]

A QUESTION YET UNANSWERED

The following question has not yet been answered. Before you consider the question, turn to Chapter 1 to review the various ethical theories noted there (social contract theory, utilitarianism, and rational ethics). Then in a consistent way, answer the following question.

> Which view, the one promoted by Norman Angell and Viscount Esher or the one promoted by General von Bernhardi, is morally correct? Explain.

Source: See: Barbara Tuchman, "A Funeral," *The Guns of August* (New York: The MacMillan Company, 1962), pp. 10–11.

The Just War Theory

One central question that cannot be answered solely by the law of a single nation-state is whether a war is just. Ethical and legal philosophers in the West have developed criteria for determining when a war can be considered legally and morally correct. This theory, termed the **just war theory**, has been invoked to defend and question the morality of many armed conflicts. In its traditional form, the theory focuses on two main areas. First, it establishes the criteria that would justify going to war. Second, it institutes criteria for the proper conduct of a war that is already in progress. A third modern feature of justifiability adds a set of criteria that establish the rules of conduct that must be followed after a war ends.

Criteria for Going to War The just war theory endorses six criteria for deciding whether a war can be morally justified: (1) just cause, (2) right intention, (3) competent authority, (4) probability of success, (5) proportionality, and (6) last resort. The first criterion, **just cause**, says that to be morally permissible, a war must be waged for honorable motives. Included among these motives are self-defense and the defense of a fellow sovereign nation-state that has been targeted by an aggressor and is unable to, defend itself properly. The second criterion, **right intention**, declares that a war must be waged only if the combatant has the correct objective. The difference between the first and the second criteria is the difference between an objective justification for war and the subjective intent of the actual combatants. A war may have an objectively justifiable cause and yet be fought for the wrong reasons. This situation could happen, for instance, if one country goes to the defense of another country but then uses that defensive campaign as a pretext to destroy the government and subjugate the civilian population of the aggressor nation-state.

The third criterion, **competent authority**, states that war can be initiated only by legitimately recognized nation-states. This standard does not mean, however, as some people have suggested, that the United Nations must declare a war for that war to have been declared by competent authority. In fact, from a legal perspective, the UN cannot declare war at all. The UN Charter is founded on the belief that all member nations maintain their sovereign authority, including the authority to declare war. This criterion also means that it is not ethically permissible for individuals, such as the late Osama bin Laden or a rogue terrorist group such as ISIS, to declare war on anyone, let alone the United States. War is a function of nation-states in their relationships with one another, not the purview of individuals, no matter how much outlaw groups like ISIS believe otherwise.

The fourth criterion, **probability of success**, declares that at the outset of a war, there must be a reasonable chance that the war will be successful; a suicidal war would fall outside this criterion. Fifth, **proportionality** holds that the good advanced by the war must exceed the negative consequences of entering the conflict. Thus, a war fought over an imaginary diplomatic insult must be considered unjust, because the objective of vindicating a spurious affront to national honor is not proportional to the death and destruction caused by war. Finally, the criterion of **last resort** means that a war can be fought only after all other means for the resolution of the dispute have been tried and failed. If both nations still have diplomatic options available for ending the crisis in a nonviolent way; if an international organization, such as the United Nations, is still willing to explore a negotiated settlement; or if time still exists to pursue a nonviolent solution, war cannot be waged as a solution to the conflict, and if one side insists on declaring war, that war will be an unjust conflict. However, the fact that all options have not been implemented is not decisive. What matters is that the nation-state that began the war gave authentic consideration to each available option, short of war.

Criteria for the Proper Conduct of War It is not enough to advocate a set of ethical and legal criteria for entering war and then ignore the criteria for conducting the war or for conduct that must be followed after the end of a war. For this reason, many, modern, legal, and moral theorists suggest several additional criteria that should guide conduct during a war and behavior after a war. The first of the criteria for conducting a war requires that the warring factions use only those military means that are proportional to the ends that they wish to achieve. Thus, because it was possible for the international coalition to subdue and eject the invading Iraqi army from Kuwait in Gulf War I by using conventional weapons, the use of nuclear weapons would have been considered a disproportionate tactic. The second criterion states that the war must be fought with discrimination. This restriction means that only combatants should be targeted in the war and that civilians must be kept out of harm's way.

A CLASSIC CASE: *Act 1*
The United States v. Bin Laden—Concerning the Just War Theory

Osama bin Laden and al-Qaeda were responsible for the 9/11 attacks on the World Trade Center in New York and the Pentagon in Washington that killed 2,996 people. Just short of a decade later, when U.S. military forces entered Pakistan for the express purpose of either capturing or killing Osama bin Laden, they were not concerned with legal niceties. They had a mission to accomplish and that was all that concerned them. Nevertheless, once the job was done, the legal questions emerged. In global operations such as the bin Laden mission, two legal spheres of influence must be addressed: the national and the international. In the international arena, there is the question of whether the uninvited use of American troops on foreign soil is legally permissible. One way to answer this question is to apply the principles of the just war theory. According to the theory, a military action is legally and morally correct as long as it passes six tests: (1) just cause, (2) right intention, (3) competent authority, (4) probability of success, (5) proportionality, and (6) last resort. The bin Laden operation passes each of these tests.

First, it was just in that it targeted the self-confessed, unrepentant mastermind of the 9/11 operation. Second, the action was fought with the right intention, bringing the man responsible for 9/11 to justice. Third, the operation was initiated by competent authority, in this case the authority of the president of the United States. Fourth, the operation had a great probability of success, given the experience, the training, and the planning used by the elite military team charged with the mission. Fifth, the action was a limited operation with one primary objective in mind: the capture or elimination of bin Laden. Sixth, the action was a last resort because all other efforts aimed at bringing bin Laden to justice had been for naught. [See: Dionne Searcey, "Killing Was Legal Under U.S. and International Law, Many Experts Say," *The Wall Street Journal*, May 6, 2011, p. A6; Jenna Greene et al., "In Bin Laden Killing, Legal Clarity," *The National Law Journal*, May 9, 2011, pp. 1, 4–5; and Michael Byers, *War Law: Understanding International Law and Armed Conflict* (New York: Grove Press, 2005), p. 7.]

Source: See: Dionne Searcey, "Killing Was Legal Under U.S. and International Law, Many Experts Say," *The Wall Street Journal*, May 6, 2011, p. A6; Jenna Greene, et al., "In Bin Laden Killing, Legal Clarity," *The National Law Journal*, May 9, 2011, pp. 1 and 4–5; Michael Byers, *War Law: Understanding International Law and Armed Conflict* (New York: Grove Press, 2005), p. 7.

Criteria for Proper Postwar Conduct Three just war principles have been established for gauging the morality of conduct following the cessation of hostilities. The first of these principles is the principle of repentance. The **principle of repentance** calls for a genuine expression of remorse by the combatants for the death and destruction caused by war. Conduct that expresses either joy or satisfaction at the death of enemy combatants, even combatants involved in a war of aggression, would violate this principle. The second criterion, the **principle of honorable surrender**, requires the victor in a war to accept the surrender of the enemy and treat the defeated combatants with dignity and respect. Refusing a genuine offer of surrender, violating that surrender after it has been implemented, or mistreating enemy combatants after surrender would all be violations of this principle. Actions that are motivated by revenge or retribution would also violate the principle of honorable surrender, as would conduct that injures or humiliates prisoners of war. Finally, the **principle of restoration** requires that the victor in a conflict act responsibly in rebuilding the defeated nation's physical environment, economy, and governmental structure.

Preventive, Preemptive, and Protective War

A nation-state starts a **preemptive war** to stop another nation-state's imminent attack on the first nation-state. A preemptive war is not the same as a preventative war, though the terms are often used as synonyms. A preemptive war is waged to stop an attack before it can begin. In contrast, a nation-state begins a **preventive war** to stop another nation-state from reaching a point that it would be capable of attacking the first nation. The doctrine adopted by the United States in 2002 was a doctrine of preemptive war, not one of preventive war. The concept of preemptive war goes back 500 years to Thomas More, who, in his work *Utopia*, noted that it would be wise to attack preemptively a force that was about to attack you. In the United States, two major military figures—General Leslie Groves, the head of the Manhattan Project, which developed the atomic bomb during World War II, and General Curtis LeMay, former commander of the Strategic Air Command (SAC)—advocated preemptive war against the Soviet Union. In the 1950s, the Joint Chiefs of Staff commissioned a study that also recommended a preemptive strike against the Soviet Union. In all of these cases, cooler heads prevailed, and preemptive war was not at that time advocated as a strategic policy of the United States.

Times changed, however, when in 2002, preemptive war became an active, strategic policy of the United States and was the primary stated motivation for the invasion of Iraq in 2003. Although it is difficult to pinpoint the exact moment of this shift in policy, the move toward preemptive war as the national policy of the United States seems to have come about less than three months after September 11, 2001, when, in the aftermath of the attacks on the World Trade Center and the Pentagon, President George W. Bush asked then-Secretary of Defense Donald Rumsfeld about war plans for an attack against Iraq. Evidence indicates that President Bush had similar strategic planning discussions with Vice President Richard Cheney and National Security Advisor Condoleezza Rice. Nevertheless, the first conscious public declaration of this change in policy occurred in a presidential address to the graduating class of West Point on June 1, 2002.

Times changed again nine years later when the concept of protective war became a weapon in the arsenal of law abiding nation-states that are wary of rogue states that have a reputation of victimizing their own people. **Protective war** is aimed at providing aid and assistance to innocent civilians who are being victimized by the military of their own nation-state. Unlike preemptive war, which is designed as a tactic to shield one nation from the unwarranted and deadly attacks of another, a protective war is waged by a nation or a coalition of nations as an intervention in the internal affairs of a sovereign state to protect the civilians of that state from their own government. This is a crucial step away from the traditions inherent within the Treaty of Westphalia, which recognized the almost sacred right of a nation-state to do what it pleased within its own borders. Even the United Nations Charter, a document aimed at unifying the nation-states of the world in a global community, still holds sovereignty as one of its central premises. Consequently, because protective war is a new and slightly controversial topic, it might be a good idea to subject it to the tests of the just war theory as well as the test of international law and, in the case of the United States, to the test of domestic legality.

Protective War and the Just War Theory The just war theory is designed to help individuals and governments make judgments about the justifiability of particular wars, rather than about the morality of war in general. Indeed, the very existence of a just war theory presumes that some wars are in fact justifiable and some are not. Therefore, it is difficult to characterize the morality of a war-making strategy, such as the strategy of protective war, without reference to the war's actual historical context. Nevertheless, all protective wars share certain characteristics that make it possible to judge such wars in theory. For example, all protective wars involve a situation in which the government of a rogue or failed nation-state has somehow victimized its own people. This victimization might involve genocide, as in Rwanda and Bosnia; anarchy, as in Somalia; or, as in the case of Syria, the use of the nation-state's military in an operation that targets its own people. Using this common context we can build a case in support of protective war using the just war theory. We will examine the criteria in reverse order: (1) last resort, (2) proportionality, (3) probability of success, (4) competent authority, (5) right intention, and (6) just cause.

First, the protector nations who initiate a protective war must demonstrate that the use of military force is a last resort. Basically, this would require the protector nations to use diplomatic channels and economic pressure to alter the behavior of the rogue nations before resorting to war. Second, a protective war should be, by definition, a war of proportional response. The object of such a war is to protect innocent civilians who have been victimized by their government. Thus, the war is not aimed at toppling the rogue government, gaining territory, aiding the rebels, or expanding the influence of the protector nations. Third, because protective wars are generally fought by coalitions with limited objectives, the probability of success is almost always ensured. Fourth, at least in the modern context, most protective wars will be channeled through the United Nations Security Council, which has a mechanism in place for dealing with such contingencies. Thus, there is little reason for a protective war to be launched outside competent authority. Fifth and sixth, as in the case of proportionality, the requirements of right intention and just cause are inherent within the reason for going to war in the first place. Protective wars, by definition "protect the innocent," a goal that involves both right intention and just cause. Thus, it is clear that a protective war like the one in Libya in 2011 or the one that could have been (or still could be) fought in Syria meet the criteria of a just war. However, this is only one-third of the battle. It is also necessary to examine the war from the perspective of international law and, in the case of the United States, from the perspective of domestic law.

Protective War and International Law Protective war has been institutionalized by the United Nations. The motivation for the institutionalization of protective war extends back to the Second World War. In the aftermath of that global conflict, there was a general outcry against the horrors of genocide and a recognition of the fact that the international community had a global responsibility to guarantee that the atrocities committed by the Nazis during that war, especially during the Holocaust, would be prevented from happening again in the future. This was, in fact, the nature of the pledge made by the United Nations when in 1948 it adopted the Convention on the Prevention and Punishment of the Crime of Genocide. In essence, that convention outlawed genocide as well as any acts that facilitated, cooperated with, or attempted to commit genocide. Unfortunately, the convention actually did very little good. Moreover, as the years went by, the convention stood as a silent reminder that the pledge against genocide had gone unfulfilled in Rwanda, Cambodia, and Bosnia. In

2001, the International Commission on Intervention and State Sovereignty (ICISS) issued a report which introduced the phrase "the responsibility to protect (R2P)." The Commission explored the nature of national sovereignty, specifically as it relates to a nation-state's responsibility to protect its own citizens from genocide, war crimes, ethnic cleansing, and crimes against humanity, as well as the responsibility of the other nations to intervene when a nation-state commits these crimes against its own citizens. The concept of the responsibility to protect was finally institutionalized in 2005 as a result of deliberations at the World Summit held in New York at the Headquarters of the United Nations. The essential terms of the **responsibility to protect (R2P)** read as follows:

1. That each individual state has the primary responsibility to protect its populations from genocide, war crimes, crimes against humanity, and ethnic cleansing. It also has a responsibility for prevention of these crimes.

2. That the international community should encourage or assist states to exercise this responsibility.

3. The international community has the responsibility to use appropriate diplomatic, humanitarian, and other peaceful means to help protect populations threatened by these crimes. When a state manifestly fails in its protection responsibilities, and peaceful means are inadequate, the international community must take stronger measures, including collective use of force authorized by the Security Council under Chapter VII.

Since its inception, the effectiveness of the R2P has been questioned by its critics. The UN Security Council activated R2P in 2011 during the Libyan Civil War. Under Resolution 1970, the UN authorized economic sanctions and an arms embargo against Libya. Under Resolution 1973, the UN established a no-fly zone over Libya and commissioned NATO troops to take "all necessary measures to protect civilians and civilian populated areas under threat or attack." The resolutions were initiated in response to threats issued by Muammar Gaddafi against the people of Libya. However, there is now some dispute as to whether Gaddafi's threats were really issued against civilians. Many reports now indicate that the threat was actually made against the armed rebels. Gaddafi had made no threat against civilians and, in fact, told rebels that if they laid down their weapons, they too would not be targeted.

The ambiguity surrounding the Libya activation highlights some of the problems with the UN's R2P policy and with protective war in general, one of which involves the difficulties in determining when civilians really are being targeted by their own government for genocide, ethnic cleansing, war crimes, or crimes against humanity. The fear is that the UN and some of the members of the Security Council might use R2P as a pretext to mobilize regime change operations against autocratic nation-states that are seen as a threat to global stability. In fact, given that, in hindsight, Gaddafi's military did not threaten civilians, the United Nations, with the blessing of the United States and other NATO member nations, seems to have engineered a *de facto* regime change in Libya. As noted earlier, should such suspicions be verified, the Libyan campaign would have crossed the line of proportionality and would, therefore, in retrospect, fail the just war test, even though it was legally authorized by the UN Security Council. Still, despite this weakness, the general consensus is that having R2P in the arsenal of the UN Security Council can act as an effective deterrent to those autocratic leaders contemplating genocide or ethnic cleansing. The final question remains. Is protective war legal under American domestic law? It is to that question that we now turn. [See: "An Introduction to the Responsibility to Protect," International Coalition for the Responsibility to Protect, http://responsibilitytoprotect.org/index.php/about-rtop/learn-about-rtop; Mohammed Nuruzzaman, "Revisiting the 'Responsibility to Protect' after Libya and Syria," *E-International Relations*, March 8, 2014, http://www.e-ir.info/2014/03/08/revisiting-responsibility-to-protect-after-libya-and-syria/; and "The 2005 World Summit

High-Level Plenary Meeting of the 60th session of the UN General Assembly," *UN Conferences, Meetings, and Events*, September 2005, http://www.un.org/en/events/pastevents/ worldsummit_2005.shtml.]

Protective War and U.S. Domestic Law When dealing with questions concerning the legality of a war, the United States generally defers to the judgment of the United Nations. In fact, the United States has a fairly good (though certainly not a perfect) record of handling armed conflict through the UN Security Council. In 1950, for instance, after North Korea invaded South Korea, the United States and its allies went to the Security Council and sought a resolution to authorize military intervention against the North Koreans. Owing to the Soviet Union's decision to boycott the Security Council's vote on the issue, the United States succeeded in obtaining the required resolution. In October 1962, when President John F. Kennedy was contemplating a blockade against Cuba to stop the influx of offensive nuclear weapons being shipped there by the Soviets, the United States again went to the UN Security Council. Deference to the UN Security Council, however, is not identical to loyalty, obedience, or surrender, to the UN, and so, at times, domestic law authorizes military action without forcing the president to go to the UN. Nevertheless, this does not mean that there is no oversight on the actions of the president in his role as commander-in-chief of the armed forces. In fact, Congress does play a role in this process—a big role.

The War Powers Resolution In the 1970s after the problems associated with the President of the United States waging war without congressional approval, Congress enacted a law that would prevent a repeat of that type of activity. The **War Powers Resolution** of 1973 is designed to limit the power of the president as commander-in-chief of the armed forces to commit American troops to the field and to maintain those troops in the field contrary to congressional approval. The resolution also requires the president to communicate to Congress on a regular basis about the military action once that action is approved by Congress. More specifically, the War Powers Resolution requires that the president inform Congress of his use of American troops within 48 hours of doing so. The notice must be in writing and must be delivered to the speaker of the House *and* the President pro Tempore of the Senate. If Congress approves of the president's use of troops, he has 60 days to accomplish the mission. At that time, 60 days after the initial written notice was given to Congress, he must withdraw the troops within 30 days unless Congress authorizes a continuation of the action. All of this assumes, of course, that Congress can actually meet and has not somehow been compromised or eliminated by enemy action on American soil. In such a case, the president is authorized to continue whatever action is needed to protect the United States.

Authorization for the Use of Military Force of 2002 The **Authorization for the Use of Military Force (AUMF)** is an act passed in 2002 by Congress in the wake of the 9/11 attacks. The proper designation of the act is Public Law 107-40 [S.J. Res. 23]. Officially, it is a joint resolution passed by both the House and the Senate. The joint resolution begins by stating that the United States is justified in using self-defense to protect its citizens and territory. The resolution also recognizes that the 9/11 attacks were an instance of the "unusual and extraordinary threat to the national security and foreign policy of the United States" and that the president has the authority "under the Constitution to take action to deter and prevent acts of international terrorism against the United States." The resolution cites the War Powers Resolution [Section 8 (A) (1)] as the statutory authority upon which the new resolution is built. Like the action authorized by UN Article 51, the authorization act relies upon self-defense as justification for the use of force, so long as that military force is used "to prevent any future acts of international terrorism" against the United States. [See: Dionne

Searcey, "Killing Was Legal Under U.S. and International Law, Many Experts Say," *The Wall Street Journal*, May 6, 2011, p. A6; Jenna Greene et al., "In Bin Laden Killing, Legal Clarity," *The National Law Journal*, May 9, 2011, pp. 1, 4–5; and Michael Byers, *War Law: Understanding International Law and Armed Conflict* (New York: Grove Press, 2005), p. 7.]

A CLASSIC CASE: *Act 2*
The United States v. Bin Laden—Concerning the Authorization for the Use of Military Force

The U.S. military entered Pakistan to capture or kill Osama bin Laden. In the Classic Case: Act 1, we asked and answered the question of whether the uninvited use of American troops on foreign soil was legally permissible. Applying the just war theory, we answered in the affirmative. Now, another unanswered question remains on the table: "Can the President of the United States use American forces *without* a congressional declaration of war in an operation aimed at capturing or assassinating a terrorist leader on foreign soil?"

To answer this question in 2011 when the attack took place, we would have applied the basic principles of the original AUMF. As part of the original AUMF, Congress declared, "The president is authorized to use all necessary and appropriate force against those nations, organizations, or persons he determines planned, authorized, committed, or aided the terrorist attack that occurred on September 11, 2001, or harbored such organizations or persons, in order to prevent any future acts of international terrorism against the United States by such nations, organizations, or persons." The resolution penned by Congress identifies Section 8 (A) (1) of the War Powers Resolution as the statutory foundation upon which the AUMF was established. Moreover, the AUMF also uses long-standing common law principles of self-defense as a valid justification for the application of military action in this case, provided the action taken is employed "to prevent any future acts of international terrorism" against the United States. So was the bin Laden operation legal under domestic statutory law? The answer is yes—at least under the AUMF of 2002. [See: Dionne Searcey, "Killing Was Legal Under U.S. and International Law, Many Experts Say," *The Wall Street Journal*, May 6, 2011, p. A6; Jenna Greene et al., "In Bin Laden Killing, Legal Clarity," *The National Law Journal*, May 9, 2011, pp. 1, 4–5; and Michael Byers, *War Law: Understanding International Law and Armed Conflict* (New York: Grove Press, 2005), p. 7.]

Source: See: Dionne Searcey, "Killing Was Legal Under U.S. and International Law, Many Experts Say," *The Wall Street Journal*, May 6, 2011, p. A6; Jenna Greene, et al., "In Bin Laden Killing, Legal Clarity," *The National Law Journal*, May 9, 2011, pp. 1 and 4–5; and Michael Byers, *War Law: Understanding International Law and Armed Conflict* (New York: Grove Press, 2005), p. 7.

Authorization for the Use of Military Force of 2015 In 2015 after two extended military campaigns in Iraq and Afghanistan and in light of the new threat imposed by the Islamic State of Iraq and Syria (also known as ISIS and ISIL, and the Islamic State in Iraq and the Levant), the president presented a reengineered version of the AUMF Act of 2002 to Congress. The new plan, officially dubbed the Authorization for the Use of Military Force of 2015, was an attempt by the president to extend the military power of the commander-in-chief without appearing to do so. Under AUMF 2015, the president would be given the authority to use military action to oppose ISIS and any "associated persons and forces." In addition, the AUMF of 2015 would eliminate the existence of "enduring offensive ground combat operations," although it would still allow other types of smaller scale operations, such as those that the United States carried out in Libya. Moreover, as a safeguard, AUMF 2015 would also include a three-year expiration date for such campaigns. AUMF 2015 would officially terminate the 2002 authorization issued by Congress for the invasion of Iraq.

Finally, the act would also expressly define **associated persons and forces** as "individuals and organizations fighting for, on behalf of, or alongside ISIL or any closely related successor entity in hostilities against the United States or its coalition partners." Despite vigorous on both sides if the political spectrum regarding the need for this resolution or one like it, as of this printing, Congress has yet to act on the AUMF of 2015. [See: 50 USC Sections 1541-48; Peter Baker, "News Analysis: A Dual View of War Power: Obama Is Proposing Limits and Leeway," *The New York Times*, February 12, 2015, pp. A1, A-12; and "Presidential Power: A Law for War," *The Economist*, February 14, 2015, p. 28. See also: Letter from the President—Authorization for the Use of United States Armed Forces in connection with the Islamic State of Iraq and the Levant, Office of the Press Secretary, The White House, February 11, 2015; and Lauren Leatherby, "Whatever Happened to the Debate over Use of Force against ISIS?" *NPR*, June 17, 2015, http://www.npr.org/2015/06/17/415203016/whatever-happened-to-the-debate-over-use-of-force-against-isis.]

A CLASSIC CASE: *Act 3*
The United States v. Bin Laden—Concerning the Authorization for the Use of Military Force 2015 Style

The president in 2011 sent a group of Navy Seals into Pakistan to capture or assassinate Osama bin Laden, the man who had masterminded the 9/11 attacks and who had repeatedly promised to launch similar attacks against the United States in the future. In the Classic Case: Acts 1 and 2, we asked and answered the question of whether the uninvited use of American troops on foreign soil was legally permissible under the just law theory and under the 2002 AUMF. In both cases the answer was yes. One final question remains: "Would the President of the United States be permitted to use military forces, absent a congressional declaration of war, in a similar operation under AUMF 2015?"

To answer this question, we must simply look at the wording of AUMF 2015. As noted earlier, AUMF 2015 recommends giving the president the power to use military action to oppose ISIS and "associated persons and forces." Taking even the most inflexible interpretation of the phrase "associated persons and forces," it is easy to see that bin Laden would fit in that category. Moreover, while AUMF 2015 would clearly abolish the use of "enduring offensive ground combat operations," it would still permit small-scale military campaigns, just like the one carried out in Pakistan against bin Laden. [See: 50 USC Sections 1541-48; Peter Baker, "News Analysis: A Dual View of War Power: Obama Is Proposing Limits and Leeway," *The New York Times*, February 12, 2015, pp. A-1, A-12; and "Presidential Power: A Law for War," *The Economist*, February 14, 2015, p. 28.]

Source: See: 50 USC Sections 1541-48; Peter Baker, "News Analysis: A Dual View of War Power: Obama Is Proposing Limits and Leeway," *The New York Times*, February 12, 2015, pp. A-1, A-12; and "Presidential Power: A Law for War," *The Economist*, February 14, 2015, p. 28.

Substantive and Procedural Issues

Most of these just war requirements were established before the advent of contemporary warfare. In the modern age, the face of war has changed. Along with these changes have come alterations in the conduct of war, including ways of dealing with prisoners of war, occupation forces, and war crimes.

Substantive Legal Changes Following World War II, in 1949, a major effort involving most of the nations of the world and sponsored by the American Red Cross was held in Geneva, Switzerland, to address the issues of prisoners of war, occupation forces, and war crimes. Out of this series of international meetings came the **Geneva Conventions**. These conventions attempt to deal with many of the problems brought on by the nature of warfare in the modern era. For instance, the first, second, and third conventions are concerned with prisoners of war, and the fourth deals with occupation forces.

Procedural and Analytical Problems Substantive changes in the law of war and international relations, such as the Geneva Conventions, are frequently complicated by procedural and analytical questions. The mere fact that a convention has been written and adopted does not mean that it will be applied properly and consistently by the nations that signed the convention. Analytical questions nearly always plague any court faced with the application of an international agreement. To facilitate this analytical process, the U.S. courts have established some guidelines for interpreting international agreements such as the Geneva Conventions.

For instance, in determining the applicability of such international pacts, the courts will first look at the literal language of the agreement, especially any definitions contained within the agreement. Second, the court will examine any supporting documentation, such as the Red Cross Commentaries in the case of the Geneva Conventions, for assistance in interpreting the settlement. Third, U.S. courts will take a liberal view in the interpretation of such agreements. This guideline means that the court will broadly and openly interpret the convention to include as many cases and situations as are justly warranted.

quick quiz 34-2

1. One central question that cannot be answered solely by the law of a single nation-state is whether a war is just. true | false
2. The just war theory was developed in the 21st century to deal with problems of modern warfare. true | false
3. The Geneva Conventions attempt to establish rules involving occupation forces and prisoners of war. true | false

34-3 The United Nations and the Global Community

As World War II drew to a close, representatives of 50 nations met in San Francisco to work out the details of the formation of the United Nations. At that meeting, called the United Nations Conference on International Organization, the 50 nations adopted a charter that on June 26, 1945, established the United Nations. The stated purposes of the United Nations are to advance human rights, to end war, to enhance human achievement, to support peaceful international coalitions, and to promote truth, justice, and the rule of law. The promotion of international law has taken many forms within the structure of the United Nations, including the International Law Commission, International Court of Justice, the UN Commission on International Trade Law, and the UN Convention on Contracts for the International Sale of Goods. Although the International Criminal Court stands outside the official system of the UN, it nevertheless has an important role to play in the administration of global justice.

The Structure of the United Nations

The United Nations is an enormous, complicated organization that consists of many agencies, organizations, courts, and commissions (see Table 34-1). The three major governing

Table 34-1 The United Nations System

THE UNITED NATIONS SYSTEM

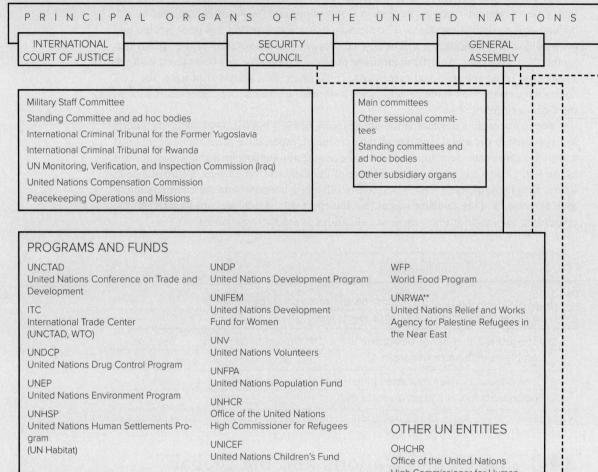

*Autonomous organizations working with the United Nations and each other through the coordinating machinery of the Economic and Social Council.

†Report only to the General Assembly.

Source: Department of Public Information, *Basic Facts about the United Nations,* New York: 2003, p. 24.

Chapter 34 International Law and the New World Order

ECONOMIC AND SOCIAL COUNCIL	TRUSTEESHIP COUNCIL	SECRETARIAT

FUNCTIONAL COMMISSIONS

Commission for Social Development
Commission on Human Rights
Commission on Narcotic Drugs
Commission on Crime Prevention and Criminal Justice
Commission on Science and Technology for Development
Commission on Sustainable Development
Commission on the Status of Women
Commission on Population and Development
Statistical Commission

REGIONAL COMMISSIONS

Economic Commission for Africa (ECA)
Economic Commission for Europe (ECE)
Economic Commission for Latin America and the Caribbean (ECLAC)
Economic Commission for Asia and the Pacific (ESCAP)
Economic Commission for Western Asia (ESCWA)
United Nations Forum on Forestry
Sessional and Standing Committees Expert, ad hoc, and related bodies

RELATED ORGANIZATIONS

IAEA
International Atomic Energy Agency

WTO (trade)
World Trade Organization

WTO (tourism)
World Tourism Organization

CTBTO
Preparatory Commission for the Comprehensive Nuclear-Test-Ban-Treaty Organization

OPCW
Organization for the Prohibition of Chemical Weapons

SPECIALIZED AGENCIES*

ILO
International Labor Organization

FAO
Food and Agriculture Organization of the United Nations

UNESCO
United Nations Educational, Scientific, and Cultural Organization

WHO
World Health Organization

WORLD BANK GROUP
 IBRD
 International Bank for Reconstruction and Development
 IDA
 International Development Association
 IFC
 International Finance Corporation
 MIG
 Multilateral Investment Guarantee Agency
 ICSID
 International Center for Settlement of Investment Disputes

IMF
International Monetary Fund

ICAO
International Civil Aviation Organization

IMO
International Maritime Organization

ITU
International Telecommunications Union

UPU
Universal Postal Union

WMO
World Meteorological Organization

WIPO
World Intellectual Property Organization

IFAD
International Fund for Agricultural Development

OSG
Office of the Secretary-General

OIOS
Office of Internal Oversight Services

OLA
Office of Legal Affairs

DPA
Department of Political Affairs

DDA
Department for Disarmament Affairs

DPKO
Department of Peacekeeping Operations

OCHA
Office for the Coordination of Humanitarian Affairs

DESA
Department of Economic and Social Affairs

DGAACS
Department of General Assembly Affairs and Conference Services

DPI
Department of Public Information

DM
Department of Management

OIP
Office of the Iraq Program

UNSECOORD
Office of the United Nations Security Coordinator

ODC
Office on Drugs and Crime

UNOG
UN Office at Geneva

UNOV
UN Office at Vienna

UNON
UN Office at Nairobi

The United Nations headquarters in New York City.
©blurAZ/Shutterstock

bodies are the Secretary General, the General Assembly, and the Security Council. The, secretary general is the chief administrator of the United Nations. He or she heads up the Secretariat, which is the administrative bureaucracy of the UN. The secretary general also takes a leading role in promoting world peace. The Security Council recommends a candidate for the position of secretary general, but the General Assembly votes that person into office. The General Assembly is made up of all the member nations of the UN. Each nation has one vote on resolutions and other matters presented to the assembly. The UN Security Council deals with crises that involve threats to international peace. The council consists of 15 members. Five of these members hold permanent seats: China, France, Russia, the United Kingdom, and the United States. The General Assembly elects the remaining 10 members for two-year terms.

International Law and the United Nations

One of the strengths of the United Nations is that it is based on a platform that continues to respect the sovereignty of each member state. Without this express guarantee built into its founding principles, it is doubtful that the United Nations Charter would have been ratified, let alone developed into the symbol for international unity that it stands for today. As is often the case with such organizations, however, the UN's main strength is also its main weakness. The sovereign nature of each member state often means that the UN's power to enforce its decrees is a matter of voluntary acquiescence. Thus, the UN must make use of its soft power more than its hard power. The UN's soft power resides in its moral authority as a platform that speaks for all nations with equal objectivity. As we saw in Chapter 33, whether this unbiased attitude exists in reality is open to debate. Nevertheless, the ideal of objective representation stands as a central core belief of the UN, one that its various organizations cannot ignore, even when they want to. The legal organizations within the UN have a special duty to be as unbiased and impartial as possible. Those legal organizations include the International Law Commission, the International Court of Justice (known more popularly as the World Court), and the International Criminal Court.

The International Law Commission The authority to codify international law is the official mission of the International Law Commission. Because all UN member nations retain their sovereign identities, the codifications drawn up by the commission must be joined voluntarily by each nation-state. The commission meets every year at a time authorized by the General Assembly. A legal topic can make its way to the commission in one of two ways. Either the General Assembly submits a legal issue to the commission or the commission itself decides to pursue a legal problem. After the commission has examined a legal topic in depth, it may draw up a draft on that aspect of international law. That draft then goes to the General Assembly for further consideration. Once the General Assembly has accepted a draft, it is codified into a convention. That convention is then submitted to the member states for their adoption. Some of the conventions that have been suggested by the commission and adopted by the General Assembly include the Convention on the Law of Treaties and the Convention on Diplomatic Relations. The General Assembly elects each of the 34 members of the International Law Commission, who each remain on the commission for five years. [See: *Basic Facts about the United Nations* (New York: United Nations, 2003), pp. 269–70.]

The International Court of Justice One of the principal vehicles for the establishment of international law and justice is the International Court of Justice (ICJ). Like many

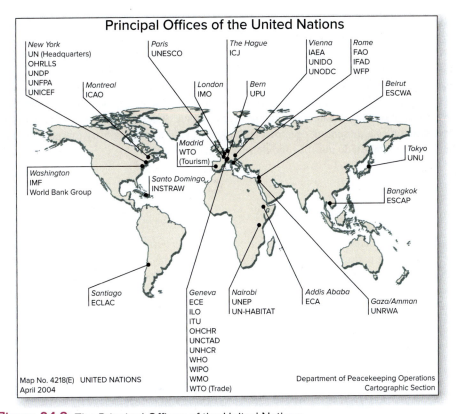

Figure 34-2 The Principal Offices of the United Nations.
Source: Department of Public Information, *Basic Facts about the United Nations* (New York: United Nations, 2003), p. 24.

of the agencies of the UN, the ICJ, which is popularly referred to as the World Court, is not located in New York City (see Figure 34-2). Situated at The Hague in the Netherlands, the ICJ was established under provisions within the UN Charter. Key features of the court include its structure and its jurisdiction.

The Structure of the ICJ The ICJ is made up of 15 judges. The Security Council and the General Assembly of the United Nations are jointly responsible for electing these judges, each of whom serves a nine-year term. All of the judges are also eligible for reelection. To ensure as much impartiality as possible, the UN Charter also specifies that no two judges can be citizens of the same country and that the judges may not have any additional employment while they sit on the court. Ideally, the judges are chosen because of their legal qualifications. Every attempt is also made to ensure that the judges exemplify the foremost legal institutions in the world. When a nation is involved in a case presented to the ICJ, that nation is permitted to appoint a single judge to the court on a temporary basis.

Standing within the ICJ Only sovereign nations have legal standing to initiate a case before the ICJ. Included within this category are nations that are member states of the United Nations. Nations that are not member states, however, may also have cases heard before the court. Questions on the legal standing of nonmember states are left up to the determination of the General Assembly and the Security Council.

Subject Matter Jurisdiction in the ICJ Subject matter jurisdiction in the ICJ is outlined within the UN Charter. This jurisdiction includes legal questions specifically referred to within the charter, as well as any legal question raised by a member nation before the court. Such legal questions may involve the interpretation of treaties and international conventions.

Unlike the courts in the federal system of the United States, which can render opinions only when faced with an actual case, the ICJ is permitted to issue advisory opinions when requested by nation-states, the General Assembly, the Security Council, or other authorized agencies within the structure of the United Nations. Those judges who disagree with the advisory opinion of the majority are empowered to issue dissenting opinions. In an advisory case, sometimes a dissenting opinion can be just as vital as the majority opinion, because the dissenter's rationale may be used in other venues.

EXAMPLE 34-3: Jurisdiction, Advisory Opinions, and the ICJ

One source of advisory opinions involves the question of how the corporate body of the United Nations relates to individual member nations. For instance, in 1949, the General Assembly solicited an advisory opinion from the ICJ concerning the assassination of a UN mediator. The mediator had been killed on a mission to Palestine. The issue before the court was whether the United Nations could hold a member state liable for any harm that befell an agent of the United Nations. The court found that the UN did indeed have that capacity.

The International Criminal Court To deal with crimes against humanity, an official **International Criminal Court (ICC)** was set up by the Rome Statute of the International Criminal Court in 1998. Unlike the ICJ, the ICC is not an official agency of the United Nations, though the UN was instrumental in its establishment. The objective of the new court, which actually began operation in 2002, is to preside over trials involving genocide, war crimes, and other human rights violations. The International Criminal Court itself and its prison are physically situated in The Hague, along with the International Court of Justice. Eighteen judges, no two of whom may be citizens of a single country, serve on the ICC for a term of nine years. The judges are elected by the states who are parties to the statute. The court also names one of the judges as president, as well as a registrar and an official prosecutor.

One of the key differences between the ICJ and the ICC is that the ICC has jurisdiction over individual defendants. On the other hand, the ICC does not have *original* jurisdiction over a defendant who has been charged with war crimes, genocide, or other offenses against humanity. Rather, the defendant's own government must prosecute the defendant before the ICC can claim original jurisdiction. Should the government fail to bring legal action against the defendant, the ICC can then step into the case. This feature has caused some concern among critics of the ICC, who argue that nation-states can protect their own citizens from prosecution in the ICC by prosecuting them in a home court that would intentionally acquit the defendant regardless of that defendant's real guilt or innocence. Supporters counter this concern by pointing out that the weight of world opinion will generally counteract this tendency of a nation-state to protect one of its own. Moreover, even though the ICC is not an official arm of the UN, the UN Security Council is empowered to intervene in a wrongful legal procedure perpetrated within or by the court. This safeguard should reassure a defendant's home nation that, once a defendant has been indicted, a strong case against that defendant has already been developed. One major drawback is that the court has very limited authority. Specifically, it can hear only cases that involve the citizens of those countries that ratified the original treaty that created the court. Several major countries, including the United States, have not ratified the treaty, which places their citizens outside the court's jurisdiction. [See: L. Fasulo, *An Insider's Guide to the UN* (New Haven, CT: Yale University Press, 2004), pp. 100–104; and *Basic Facts about the United Nations*, p. 279.]

A CLASSIC CASE: *Act 4*
The United States v. Bin Laden—Concerning the International Criminal Court

The United States has repeatedly refused to ratify the Rome Statute of the International Criminal Court. Supporters of the international new world order might see this refusal as a puzzling development. After all, if the United States must act to defend itself and others in protective wars, it ought to benefit from any additional law enforcement support it can get. However, a closer look at this situation will reveal that this interpretation is not quite the case. If the United States must engage in protective wars from time to time and must, at other times, act as the *de facto* world government, the U.S. military must act as a *de facto* world police force. A police force, by its very nature, must enter dangerous, volatile, and potentially hazardous situations. Some of these police actions call for split-second decision making. Others may involve decisions that many people in the international community, especially those who see the United States as the enemy, do not support and might even condemn.

An example is when the United States sent military personnel into Pakistan with orders to capture or kill Osama bin Laden. Many individuals, groups, and nations opposed this action. However, this is often the case when the police, even the *de facto* global police, must perform unpopular actions. If the United States were a party to the Rome treaty, the Navy Seals who risked their lives to bring a sworn enemy of the United States to justice would be in danger of a politically motivated prosecution under the authority of the ICC. Since the United States must at times act as a global police force, then the members of its military, like the Navy Seals in the bin Laden operation, need the type of legal protection from political retribution that the ICC cannot now promise to deliver.

Economic Regulation and the United Nations

The United Nations does some of its best work in the area of economics and trade. It serves as a central clearing house for international treaties, trade proposals, conventions, and trade agreements, as well as for the development of the law as it relates to the making of international contracts. Some of the chief organizations and institutions of the UN that are involved in economics and trade include the UN Commission on International Trade, the UN Convention on Contracts for the International Sale of Goods, and the Commission on Science and Technology for Development.

The UN Commission on International Trade Law In 1996, the General Assembly of the United Nations authorized the creation of the **UN Commission on International Trade Law (UNCITRAL)**. The commission consists of 36 nations, chosen to represent the primary social, economic, legal, and geographical areas of the globe. The goal of the commission is to cultivate the organization and integration of international law in relation to international trade. To this end, it coordinates the activities of institutions involved in international trade, encourages continued commitment to current treaties and conventions, and constructs new agreements for the community of international trade.

The UN Convention on CISG One of these agreements is the **UN Convention on Contracts for the International Sale of Goods (CISG)**. This agreement became effective in 1988.

It applies only to sales between businesses located in different countries. The agreement specifically excludes contracts involving goods purchased for use by individuals or families. The CISG affects the formation of an international trade contract, as well as the rights and duties that arise under such contracts. However, it deals neither with the validity of such contracts nor with the liability of the seller for harm caused by the goods. Application of the CISG is limited to businesses that are located in countries that have ratified the agreement or those that create contracts that expressly stipulate that the CISG will apply to the agreement.

The CISG governs contracts for goods within the international community in much the same way that the Uniform Commercial Code (UCC) applies to sale-of-goods contracts within the United States. There are some significant differences, however. For example, the UCC applies to contracts between merchants and to those that involve nonmerchants. The CISG, in contrast, involves only contracts between merchants. The UCC also involves not only sale-of-goods contracts but also other commercial agreements, such as leases. The CISG, in contrast, applies only to sale-of-goods contracts. Also, the UCC has modified the traditional mirror image rule to overcome problems caused by the battle of the forms. The CISG still applies the mirror image rule to the acceptance of a contractual offer. Finally, the UCC has a provision that says that any contract for the sale of goods valued at more than $500 must be in writing to be enforceable. The CISG has no such provision.

Additional UN Economic Agencies The efforts extended by the United Nations to monitor and regulate economic conditions in the global marketplace are evident in the existence of various organizations, each of which has its own mission in the financial structure of the worldwide economy. These agencies include global councils and conferences such as the Economic and Social Council (ECOSOC) and the UN Conference on Trade and Development (UNCTAD), as well as regional agencies such as the Economic Commission for Africa and the Economic Commission for Europe. Other agencies include the International Labor Organization; the World Health Organization; the United Nations Educational, Scientific, and Cultural Organization (UNESCO); the World Intellectual Property Organization (WIPO); and the Food and Agriculture Organization. Each organization makes assessments and enters judgments that influence how international business is conducted. One such organization that has special significance in this regard is the, Division for Science and Technology of UNCTAD.

The Commission on Science and Technology for Development The Commission on Science and Technology for Development was created in 1992 as part of the Economic and Social Council (ECOSOC) of the United Nations. The job of the commission is (1) to act as a clearing house for issues concerning science and technology in relation to development, (2) to support progress in determining what must be done to advance science and technology policies in developing nations, and (3) to formulate recommendations and protocols for science and technology within the UN community. Many experts see this creation as a step in the right direction but urge an even more unified response in this regard. [See: Commission on Science and Technology for Development, UNCTAD, http://unctad.org/en/Pages/CSTD.aspx (2009–2015).]

An Economic Security Council

The Commission on Global Governance, a 26-member international organization, has suggested streamlining the surveillance of international economic efforts under the auspices of an Economic Security Council (ESC). The ESC would be a single, unified international agency under the management of the United Nations that would monitor the economic activities of the member nations of the UN. The ESC would evaluate the state of the international economy and implement long-term strategic planning to promote sustainable development across the planet. However, the ESC would not take the place of existing international agencies, such as the Economic and Social Council or the UN Conference on Trade and Development, but instead would coordinate their efforts in an efficient, effective, and economic manner.

quick quiz 34-3

1. The secretary general is the chief administrator of the United Nations. true | false
2. When a nation is involved in a case presented to the ICJ, that nation must voluntarily eliminate any judge on the panel that is a citizen of that nation. true | false
3. The UCC and the CISG are identical in every way. true | false

34-4 International Law, Finance, and Trade

Not everyone who wants to enter a local business transaction has the ready cash to do so. This hurdle, however, does not necessarily prevent them from looking for ways to expand their financial base. Therefore, by their very nature, business transactions often involve buying on credit, borrowing money, and investing in risky ventures designed to make a fast profit. The same thing can be said about international business transactions. To deal with issues of finance and trade on a worldwide scale, several international organizations and agreements have emerged that are designed to make global dealings work as smoothly as local ones.

The International Monetary Fund and the World Bank

Two organizations that emerged in the aftermath of the Great Depression and World War II were the International Monetary Fund and the World Bank. Both institutions came out of a series of meetings held in Bretton Woods, New Hampshire, in the final months of World War II. The **International Monetary Fund (IMF)** is designed to serve as a way for financially strapped nations to secure loans that will help them engage in programs of sustainable economic growth and development. The IMF has 188 members, each of which has pledged to act responsibly in the pursuit of economic and developmental goals.

The **World Bank** has a mission that is quite similar to the mission of the IMF. The difference is that the IMF is dedicated to helping all nations, developed, developing, and undeveloped, with fiscal problems, whereas the World Bank works exclusively with the poorest nations in the international community. Even this mission is split between the two arms of the World Bank. The International Bank for Reconstruction and Development (IBRD) handles more conventional loans based on normal market provisions, whereas the International Development Association (IDA) handles loans to the world's most economically challenged nations.

The World Trade Organization

After the end of World War II, the primary trading nations of the international community met to work out the details of a major trade agreement. The agreement, named the **General Agreement on Tariffs and Trade (GATT)**, had as part of its original plan the creation of an

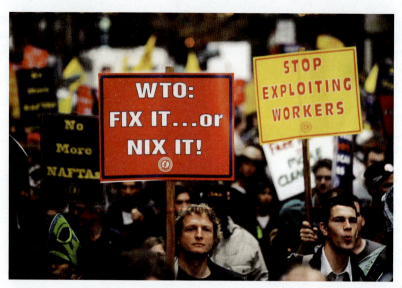

The World Trade Organization is a constant target of controversy and its summits are, frequently targeted by hostile and aggressive protesters.
©Daniel Sheehan/Getty Images

International Trade Organization (ITO). Although the ITO was never established, GATT continued to function, frequently holding international conferences on the formation and execution of international trade law. The eighth conference, which came to be known as the Uruguay Round Agreements, resulted in the creation of the **World Trade Organization (WTO)**.

The Structure of the World Trade Organization The World Trade, Organization was designed to serve as the corporate nucleus for the management of, international trade relationships. As such, the WTO replaced GATT as the focus of world trade talks. However, all agreements, treaties, and trade obligations created under GATT have been included in the WTO and thus remain in force. The structure of the WTO involves three levels: the Ministerial Conference, the General Council, and the Secretariat. The power to make key determinations under the authority of multinational trade agreements falls to the Ministerial Conference, which meets every two years. The responsibilities of the Ministerial Conference pass to the General Council whenever the Ministerial Conference is not assembled. Finally, the Secretariat, which is headed by a director general, is responsible for the administration of the WTO.

The World Trade Organization Principles The WTO has established certain overall principles that regulate how member nations must treat one another in the world of international trade. The first principle, the **national treatment principle**, states that WTO nations must apply the same standards to imports that they apply to domestic goods. The second principle, the **most-favored nation principle**, maintains that all member nations must apply the same privileges, advantages, and benefits to all other member nations in relation to similar imports. The third principle, the **tariff-based principle**, asserts that the only way that member nations can regulate the imports of other nations is through tariffs. This rule eliminates the use of more drastic techniques, such as boycotts, quotas, and quantitative limits.

The Dispute Settlement Board The **Dispute Settlement Board (DSB)** of the WTO was established to provide a forum for settling trade disputes among member, nations. The DSB follows a commonly adopted procedure known as the **Dispute Settlement Understanding (DSU)**. All member nations can be held accountable under DSU regulations. According to those regulations, only member nations have standing to initiate a case. The DSU implements a number of measures designed to improve the way that quarrels are handled. For instance, the DSU has set up a series of precise time limits for the stages in a trade conflict. The DSU ensures that a network of comprehensive guidelines is followed consistently in all such controversies. The DSU also allows effective retaliatory measures that can be implemented by one nation against another if the offending nation refuses to adhere to a decision rendered under the DSU.

> **Did You Know?**
> As of 2015, the World Trade Organization had a membership that includes 161 nations. The United States joined on January 1, 1995.

EXAMPLE 34-4: The WTO, Germany, and the Korean Retaliation

Germany and Korea were involved in a dispute concerning trade in electronic appliances and automobiles. Korea claimed that in violation of trade agreements, Germany imposed a tariff on certain electronic appliances manufactured in Korea and imported to Germany. Korea followed proper DSU procedures and received a ruling from a panel that was supported by an appellate board. The ruling indicated that Germany had indeed violated the agreement. The WTO could not directly sanction Germany. Instead, it allowed Korea to impose an enormous tariff on luxury and sports model automobiles imported from Germany to Korea. This form of sanction is known as retaliation.

The European Union

One of the most significant events to affect international law and commerce lately has been the inauguration of the **European Union (EU)**. The creation of the European Union, the attempt to formulate a common European economic policy, and the introduction of a common currency for most of Europe may transform the EU into a major competitor with the power to challenge American business interests in the global marketplace. Moreover, because many businesses within the EU have embraced cyber-commerce, American firms may face unique challenges in that arena.

The Introduction of the Euro
To adopt the **euro**, Europe's common currency, a country must first belong to the European Union. Membership in the EU alone, however, is not enough to allow a nation to adopt the euro. In addition, a nation must have a stable inflation rate, a history of interest rate convergence that falls within certain guidelines, and a pattern of fiscal responsibility. Of those nations that have qualified, 19 including Austria, Belgium, France, Germany, Ireland, Italy, Luxembourg, the Netherlands, and Spain, elected to join the effort. Several nations, including the United Kingdom, Denmark, and Sweden, opted out of the program. The use of the euro is designed to lower costs by eliminating the need to change currencies when firms in the member states deal with one another across national boundaries.

Electronic Commerce and the European Union
The EU has been active in the development of cyber-commerce directives in an attempt to head off proposed legislative initiatives in the individual member

The euro became the common currency used by European Union member states in 2002, replacing many of the, individual currencies and providing consistency for the EU.
©Getty Images

nations. Such individualized rules would complicate the rules of European cyber-commerce and defeat the purpose of a unified EU economic policy. One example of a unified directive is the Data Protection Directive. This directive assures all citizens of Europe that they will enjoy certain definitive privacy rights when they engage in cyber-commerce. Among the rights held by consumers in, Europe are the right to obtain any computer data stored about them, the right to adjust any incorrect data, the right to deny another party the use of computer data, and the right to a legal remedy for any unlawful activities in relation to computer data. Another EU directive that affects cyber-commerce is the Directive on the Protection of Consumers in Respect of Distance Contracts (ECD). This directive gives specifically enumerated privileges to consumers who deal with companies selling goods and services within the EU by electronic means. The ECD allows consumers to cancel any electronic commerce transaction without penalty within seven working days.

EXAMPLE 34-5: The Case of the Dissatisfied European Cyber-Consumer

Clay Joseph, a British citizen, was in the process of creating a new corporation that he hoped would revolutionize the comic book industry. To implement his business plan, he ordered a set of display cases from Volkmann Displays Unlimited, a German firm. On the same day, he also ordered a set of office furniture from IKEA in Sweden. When Joseph received the package from Volkmann, he discovered that the display cases could not hold the material that he wanted to store. One day later, the IKEA shipment arrived. Again he was dissatisfied, not because of any flaw in the furniture but because he had misjudged how the color of the chairs would fit into his office decor. As a European cyber-consumer, Clay Joseph's purchase of the books and the office furniture would be protected by the Directive on the Protection of Consumers in Respect of Distance Contracts (ECD), and he could rescind both deals within seven business days with no penalty whatsoever.

Did You Know?
The official symbol for the euro looks like this: €. The symbol itself is usually printed in yellow with a blue background.

National and International Law Despite the importance of focusing on international law and the laws of other countries, businesses involved in international trade must always focus on the laws of their own nation. Sometimes national law will reach into the jurisdiction of a foreign country. Although such instances are rare, they may occur when one or more of the parties to a lawsuit are citizens of the country exercise jurisdiction and when the foreign activity somehow affects the welfare of that country.

quick quiz 34-4

1. Two organizations that emerged in the aftermath of the Great Depression and World War II were the International Monetary Fund and the World Bank. true | false
2. None of the agreements, treaties, or trade obligations created under GATT have been included in the WTO. true | false
3. The EU has left the development of cyber-commerce directives up to individual nations. true | false

Summary

34.1 When a political scientist wants to use predictive political history to explain the past, to predict the future, or to handle an international crisis, he or she must first determine the present state of the global system (the international initial conditions or the new world order) and then match that system to the correct set of covering laws under an accurate theory of international behavior. The four theories of international behavior are *Realpolitik*; idealism; neoconservativism; and neoliberalism. Each international behavioral theory can be summarized by reducing it to several covering laws. A covering law is a rule of behavior that follows consistently predictable pattern such that it can be described as dictating normative decision-making processes. The four sets of initial conditions are (1) economic initial conditions, (2) cultural initial conditions, (3) ideological initial conditions, and (4) hybrid initial conditions. Once a set of initial conditions has been identified and a theory of international behavior chosen, the question becomes which political ideology—liberal democracy or authoritarianism—is best suited to solve the global problems represented by the initial conditions.

34.2 War has many significant effects on the transaction of business in the international marketplace. One of the key questions concerning the nature of war as it relates to international business is whether the war is just. Ethical and legal philosophers in the West have developed criteria for determining when a war can be considered legally and morally correct. This theory is termed the just war theory. Three types of offensive wars that are subject to scrutiny by the just war theory, international law, and domestic policy are preemptive war, preventive war, and protective war. Protective war was institutionalized by the United Nations in 2005 under the responsibility to protect (R2P) doctrine.

34.3 The stated purposes of the United Nations are to advance human rights; to end war; to enhance human achievement; to support peaceful international coalitions; and to promote international fidelity to truth, justice, and the rule of law. The promotion of international law has taken many forms within the structure of the United, Nations, including the International Court of Justice, the UN Commission on International Trade Law, and the UN Convention on Contracts for the International Sale of Goods. The International Criminal Court also plays a key role in policing international justice.

34.4 To deal with issues of finance and trade on a worldwide scale, several international organizations and agreements have emerged that are designed to make global dealings work as smoothly as local ones. These include the International Monetary Fund, the World Bank, the World Trade Organization, and the European Union.

Key Terms

associated persons and forces, 1026
authoritarianism, 1001
Authorization for the Use of Military Force (AUMF), 1024
chaotic events, 1017
civilization, 1008
Commission on Science and Technology for Development, 1034
competent authority, 1019
covering law, 1003
Dispute Settlement Board (DSB), 1036
Dispute Settlement Understanding (DSU), 1037
Economic Security Council (ESC), 1034
economic zone, 1011
euro, 1037
European Union (EU), 1037
General Agreement on Tariffs and Trade (GATT), 1035
General Assembly, 1030
Geneva Conventions, 1026
idealism, 1004
International Court of Justice (ICJ), 1030
International Criminal Court (ICC), 1032
international initial conditions, 1001
International Monetary Fund (IMF), 1035
just cause, 1019
just war theory, 1019
last resort, 1020
liberal democracy, 1001
liberal internationalism, 1004
most-favored nation principle, 1036
national treatment principle, 1036
new world order, 1001
neoconservativism, 1005
neoliberalism, 1005

political ideology, 1001
predictive political history, 1001
preemptive war, 1021
preventive war, 1021
principle of honorable surrender, 1021
principle of repentance, 1021
principle of restoration, 1021
probability of success, 1019
proportionality, 1019
protective war, 1021
realism, 1004
Realpolitik, 1004
reflexivity principle, 1016
responsibility to protect (R2P), 1023
right intention, 1019
Secretariat, 1030
secretary general, 1030
Security Council, 1030
tariff-based principle, 1036
theory of international behavior, 1001
uncertainty principle, 1016
UN Commission on International Trade Law (UNCITRAL), 1033
UN Convention on Contracts for the International Sale of Goods (CISG), 1033
volition variable, 1016
War Powers Resolution, 1024
World Bank, 1035
world order, 1000
World Trade Organization (WTO), 1036

Questions for Review and Discussion

1. What is the process of predictive political history?
2. What are the theories of international behavior?
3. What are the various sets of global initial conditions?
4. What are the principles of the Just War Theory.
5. What is the mission of International Criminal Court?
6. What is the main goal of UNCITRAL?
7. What are the differences between the UCC and the CISG?
8. What is the structure of the World Trade Organization?
9. What are the objectives of the Dispute Settlement Understanding?
10. What is the European Union?

Cases for Analysis

1. After General Manuel Noriega had come under the authority of the United States forces following the invasion of Panama, his attorneys argued that he should be treated as a prisoner of war (POW) under the Geneva Conventions. The U.S. government agreed to treat Noriega as a POW but refused to give him official POW status. Noriega's attorneys argued that this treatment as a POW could be withdrawn by the government at any time. They asked the court to declare their client a POW under the Geneva Conventions. The government argued that the events in Panama were considered hostilities rather than a war. Consequently, the government pointed out, Noriega could not be a POW. Article II of Geneva Convention III states that "the present convention shall apply to all cases of declared war and of any other armed conflict which may arise between two or more of the High Contracting Parties, even if the state of war is not recognized by one of them." Moreover, the International Red Cross Commentary on Convention III says, "Any difference between two states leading to the intervention of the armed forces is an armed conflict within the meaning of Article II." Finally, Article IV of the convention defines POWs as "persons belonging to one of the following categories, who have fallen into the power of the enemy: (1) members of the armed forces of a Party to the conflict. . . . " Taking all of this into account, as well as the U.S. courts' intent to construe the Geneva Conventions liberally, should the court declare Noriega a POW? Explain. [See: *United States of America v. Manuel Antonio Noriega*, 808 F. Supp. 791 (S.D. FL).]

2. American Rice Inc., a U.S. corporation, sold its goods in Saudi Arabia under the trade name of ABU BINT, which means "of the girl." Another American corporation, the Arkansas Rice Growers Cooperative Association, marketed similar products in Saudi Arabia using the name BINT ALARAB, which in English means "Gulf Girl." American Rice sued Arkansas in federal district

court under the Lanham Act, alleging an infringement by Arkansas of American Rice's exclusive trademark. None of the Arkansas rice products that American Rice complained of had entered any market within the United States. Arkansas argued that the federal district court had no extraterritorial power to mediate this international trade dispute. Was Arkansas correct? Explain. [See: *American Rice, Inc., v. Arkansas Rice Growers Coop. Ass'n.*, 701 F.2d 414 (5th Cir.).]

3. Gulf Oil Corporation and Eastern Air Lines entered a contract under the terms of which Gulf Oil was obligated to supply Eastern with jet fuel according to an established pricing system. In 1973, the Organization for Petroleum Exporting Countries (OPEC) established an oil embargo that precipitated the now-famous energy crisis of the 1970s. As a result of the oil embargo and the energy crisis, the price of crude oil skyrocketed. Gulf Oil asked Eastern to consent to a price increase over the price agreed to under the original contract. Eastern refused to comply with the increase. Gulf Oil then vowed to stop all jet fuel shipments to Eastern unless Eastern would reconsider its refusal to go along with the price increase. Eastern filed a lawsuit in federal district court alleging a breach of contract on Gulf Oil's part. Did the American court have jurisdiction over an exclusively American contract affected by an international incident, such as the 1973 oil embargo? Did the court agree that Gulf breached its contract with Eastern Airlines? Explain. [See: *Eastern Air Line, Inc., v. Gulf Oil Corporation*, 415 F. Supp. 429 (S.D. FL).]

4. Kenneth Armstrong, an American citizen, purchased the component parts of computers in Germany, Japan, and the United States. He took those parts to Bolivia, where he constructed the computers, stamped them with the name Starlight Computers, and sold them. Armstrong had a Bolivian registration that allowed him to use the trade name Starlight. Although none of the computers were imported into the United States by Armstrong himself, many of the counterfeit computers eventually found their way into the U.S. marketplace. Starlight Computers Inc., an American corporation, brought a lawsuit against Armstrong in U.S. District Court under the Lanham Act. Armstrong moved for a dismissal of the case, arguing that the American court did not have the authority to enforce the Lanham Act against his Bolivian operation. Is Armstrong correct? Explain.

5. France and Japan are involved in a dispute regarding trade in aircraft parts. France claims that in violation of certain trade agreements, Japan is imposing a tariff on certain types of aircraft parts that are manufactured in France and imported to Japan. France follows proper DSU procedures and receives a ruling from a panel that is supported by an appellate board. The ruling indicates that Japan has indeed violated the agreement. France asks the WTO to apply punitive sanctions directly against Japan. Will France's request be granted? Explain.

6. Helga Godel, a German citizen, placed an order for certain software items from Pascal Enterprises, a French firm. On the same day, she ordered a silverware set from Silverwings Ltd., an Austrian company. When Godel received the package from Pascal, she unwrapped the software and attempted to download the program into her computer. When she accessed the program, however, she found that though the program worked well, it was not what she had expected. Later that day, she received the silverware set. Again she was dissatisfied, this time with the quality of the product. As a European e-consumer, what rights does Godel have under the EU Directive on the Protection of Consumers in Respect of Distance Contracts? Explain.

quick quiz Answers

34-1	34-2	34-3	34-4
1. T	1. T	1. T	1. T
2. T	2. F	2. F	2. F
3. F	3. T	3. F	3. F

Part 9 Case Study

Legal Consequences of the Construction of a Wall in the Occupied Palestinian Territory (Request for Advisory Opinion)
The International Court of Justice Order of 30 January 2004

©Jim Arbogast/Getty Images

Summary

The International Court of Justice is an agency of the United Nations, established under a statute within the UN Charter. Fifteen judges sit on the ICJ. The judges are elected by the Security Council and the General Assembly of the United Nations for nine years. The judges are also eligible for reelection. To ensure as much impartiality as possible, no nation-state can have more than a single judge on the court at the same time. The statute also says that judges must work exclusively for the court during their term on the bench. Ideally, the judges on the court are chosen because of their legal qualifications. Every attempt is also made to make certain that the judges exemplify the foremost legal institutions in the world.

The statute establishing the ICJ also includes provisions to ensure the impartiality of the judges. One such provision is Article 17, paragraph 2, which states, "No Member [of the ICJ] may participate in the decision of any case in which he has previously taken part as agent, counsel, or advocate for one of the parties, or as a member of a national or international court, or of a commission of enquiry, or in any other capacity."

The present case involves the question of whether one of the judges on the ICJ ought to be permitted to participate in the case or be disqualified under this provision because of his previous involvement in the issue before the court. The case was brought to the ICJ by the government of Israel in a letter addressed to the Court Registrar, dated December 31, 2003. In that letter, the government asserted:

> Resolution A/RES/ES-10/14 requesting the advisory opinion locates the request squarely in the context of the wider Arab-Israeli/Israeli-Palestinian dispute. The essentially contentious nature of the proceedings is also recognised by the Court's invitation to Palestine to participate in the case. It is inappropriate for a Member of the Court to participate in decisions in a case in which he has previously played an active, official and public role as an advocate for a cause that is in contention in this case. Israel will be writing to the President of the Court separately on this matter pursuant to Article 34 (2) of the Rules of Court.

Israel objected to the connection that Judge Nabil Elaraby of Egypt had to the case because of his involvement in a number of initiatives that touched on several sensitive issues involved in the dispute. Specifically, Israel pointed to the judge's contributions to the 10th Emergency Session of the General Assembly of the United Nations, his employment as a legal counselor to the Egyptian Ministry of Foreign Affairs, his work as a legal consultant to the Egyptian Delegates to the Middle East Peace Initiative at Camp David in 1978, and his connection to certain actions resulting from the 1979 Israeli–Egypt Peace Treaty, especially the development of independent West Bank and Gaza Strip territories. Finally, and perhaps most significantly, the government of Israel pointed to an interview printed in a newspaper in Egypt in which the judge discussed his personal political views in relation to the nation-state of Israel.

A majority of the judges on the ICJ saw no problem with Judge Elaraby's involvement in the activities to which Israel objected. Specifically, they saw no problem with his role as legal advisor for Egypt because in that capacity, the judge had been speaking and acting as an agent of his government. In relation to the published interview, the majority pointed to the fact that Article 17, paragraph 2, detailed certain roles that a judge was prohibited from performing in a case that was before the court. Nothing on the list, the court concluded, mentioned giving interviews or publishing private political views. Therefore, the majority upheld the judge's participation in the case.

The sole dissenter was Judge Thomas Buergenthal of the United States. While Judge Buergenthal agreed with the court in relation to Judge Elaraby's official governmental roles, he disagreed about the private interview and objected to the court's strict and limited interpretation of Article 17, paragraph 2. This point is critical because, as noted previously, in an advisory case, a dissenting opinion can sometimes be just as vital as the majority opinion, because the dissenter's rationale may be used in other venues.

Dissenting Opinion of Judge Buergenthal

1. I have voted against the instant Order because I believe that the Court's decision is wrong as a matter of legal principle.

2. Israel challenges Judge Elaraby's participation in these proceedings on the ground that his previous professional involvement and personal statements on matters which go to the substance of the question before the Court in this advisory opinion request require that he not participate in these proceedings.

3. As far as Judge Elaraby's professional activities as diplomatic representative of his country and its legal adviser are concerned, the Court rejects Israel's objection by concluding that these activities, having been performed many years before the question of the construction of the wall now submitted to the Court first arose, do not fall within the activities contemplated by Article 17, paragraph 2, of the Statute to justify that he be precluded from participation in the case.

4. With regard to the newspaper interview that Judge Elaraby gave two months before his election to this Court at a time when he was no longer his country's diplomatic representative, the Court finds no basis for precluding Judge Elaraby's participation in these proceedings, because Judge Elaraby "expressed no opinion on the question put in the present case."

5. Israel seeks Judge Elaraby's disqualification on the ground, *inter alia*, that the views expressed by Judge Elaraby in the interview bear directly on issues that will have to be addressed in the advisory opinion request and that, given their nature, they create an appearance of bias incompatible with the fair administration of justice.

6. In principle, I share the Court's opinion that Judge Elaraby's prior activities, performed in the discharge of his diplomatic and governmental functions, do not fall within the scope of Article 17, paragraph 2, of the Statute of the Court so as to prevent his participation in these proceedings. . . .

7. I part company with the Court's conclusions, however, with regard to the interview Judge Elaraby gave in August of 2001, two months before his election to the Court, when he was no longer an official of his Government and hence spoke in his personal capacity. See *Al-Ahram Weekly Online*, 16–22 August 2001, issue No. 547. . . .

8. It is clear, of course, that the language of Article 17, paragraph 2, does not apply in so many words to the views Judge Elaraby expressed in the above interview. That does not mean, however, that this provision sets out the exclusive basis for the disqualification of a judge of this Court. It refers to what would generally be considered to be the most egregious violations of judicial ethics were a judge falling into one of the categories therein enumerated to participate in a case. At the same time, Article 17, paragraph 2, reflects much broader conceptions of justice and fairness that must be observed by courts of law than this Court appears to acknowledge. Judicial ethics are not matters strictly of hard and fast rules—I doubt that they can ever be exhaustively defined—they are matters of perception and of sensibility to appearances that courts must continuously keep in mind to preserve their legitimacy.

9. A court of law must be free and, in my opinion, is required to consider whether one of its judges has expressed views or taken positions that create the impression that he will not be able to consider the issues raised in a case or advisory opinion in a fair and impartial manner, that is, that he may be deemed to have prejudged one or more of the issues bearing on the subject-matter of the dispute before the court. That is what is meant by the dictum that the fair and proper administration of justice requires that justice not only be done, but that it also be seen to be done. In my view, all courts of law must be guided by this principle, whether or not their statutes or other

constitutive documents expressly require them to do so. That power and obligation is implicit in the very concept of a court of law charged with the fair and impartial administration of justice. To read them out of the reach of Article 17, paragraph 2, is neither legally justified nor is it wise judicial policy.

10. In paragraph 8 of this Order, the Court declares that, "whereas in the newspaper interview of August 2001, Judge Elaraby expressed no opinion on the question put in the present case; whereas consequently Judge Elaraby could not be regarded as having 'previously taken part' in the case in any capacity."

11. What we have here is the most formalistic and narrow construction of Article 17, paragraph 2, imaginable, and one that is unwarranted on the facts of this case. It is technically true, of course, that Judge Elaraby did not express an opinion on the specific question that has been submitted to the Court by the General Assembly of the United Nations. But it is equally true that this cannot be examined by the Court without taking account of the context of the Israeli/Palestinian conflict and the arguments that will have to be advanced by the interested parties in examining the "Legal Consequences of the Construction of a Wall in the Occupied Palestinian Territory." Many of these arguments will turn on the factual validity and credibility of assertions bearing directly on the specific question referred to the Court in this advisory opinion request. And when it comes to the validity and credibility of these arguments, what Judge Elaraby has to say in the part of the interview I quoted above creates an appearance of bias that in my opinion requires the Court to preclude Judge Elaraby's participations in the proceedings.

12. What I consider important in reaching the above conclusion is the appearance of bias. That, in my opinion, is what Article 17, paragraph 2, properly interpreted, is all about and what judicial ethics are all about. And that is why I dissent from this Order, even though I have no doubts whatsoever about the personal integrity of Judge Elaraby for whom I have the highest regard, not only as a valued colleague but also a good friend.

(*Signed*) Thomas Buergenthal

Questions for Analysis

1. Why did Israel bring this case rather than a private party? Explain.
2. What is the central issue in this case?
3. What legal statutory provision provided grounds for the complaint lodged by Israel?
4. What was the decision of the majority? Explain.
5. On what point did the dissent contest the majority opinion? Explain.

Design Elements: The Opening Case: ©Sharpstock/Alamy; A Classic Case: ©Evlakhov Valeriy/Shutterstock

Appendix A The Constitution of the United States

Preamble

We the People of the United States, in Order to form a more perfect Union, establish Justice, insure domestic Tranquility, provide for the common defence, promote the general Welfare, and secure the Blessings of Liberty to ourselves and our Posterity, do ordain and establish this Constitution for the United States of America.

Article I

Section 1. All legislative Powers herein granted shall be vested in a Congress of the United States, which shall consist of a Senate and House of Representatives.

Section 2. [1] The House of Representatives shall be composed of Members chosen every second Year by the People of the several States, and the Electors in each State shall have the Qualifications requisite for Electors of the most numerous Branch of the State Legislature.

[2] No Person shall be a Representative who shall not have attained to the Age of twenty-five Years, and been seven Years a Citizen of the United States, and who shall not, when elected, be an Inhabitant of that State in which he shall be chosen.

[3] Representatives and direct Taxes shall be apportioned among the several States which may be included within this Union, according to their respective Numbers, which shall be determined by adding to the whole Number of free Persons, including those bound to Service for a Term of Years, and excluding Indians not taxed, three fifths of all other Persons. The actual Enumeration shall be made within three Years after the first Meeting of the Congress of the United States, and within every subsequent Term of ten Years, in such Manner as they shall by Law direct. The Number of Representatives shall not exceed one for every thirty Thousand, but each State shall have at Least one Representative; and until such enumeration shall be made, the State of New Hampshire shall be entitled to chuse three, Massachusetts eight, Rhode Island and Providence Plantations one, Connecticut five, New York six, New Jersey four, Pennsylvania eight, Delaware one, Maryland six, Virginia ten, North Carolina five, South Carolina five, and Georgia three.

[4] When vacancies happen in the Representation from any State, the Executive Authority thereof shall issue Writs of Election to fill such Vacancies.

[5] The House of Representatives shall chuse their Speaker and other Officers; and shall have the sole Power of Impeachment.

Section 3. [1] The Senate of the United States shall be composed of two Senators from each State, chosen by the Legislature thereof, for six Years; and each Senator shall have one Vote.

[2] Immediately after they shall be assembled in Consequence of the first Election, they shall be divided as equally as may be into three Classes. The Seats of the Senators of the first Class shall be vacated at the Expiration of the Second Year, of the second Class at the Expiration of the fourth Year, and of the third Class at the Expiration of the sixth Year, so that one third may be chosen every second Year; and if Vacancies happen by Resignation, or otherwise, during the Recess of the Legislature of any State, the Executive thereof may make temporary Appointments until the next Meeting of the Legislature, which shall then fill such Vacancies.

[3] No Person shall be a Senator who shall not have attained to the Age of thirty Years, and been nine Years a Citizen of the United States, and who shall not, when elected, be an Inhabitant of that State for which he shall be chosen.

[4] The Vice President of the United States shall be President of the Senate, but shall have no Vote, unless they be equally divided.

[5] The Senate shall chuse their other Officers, and also a President pro tempore, in the Absence of the Vice President, or when he shall exercise the Office of President of the United States.

[6] The Senate shall have the sole Power to try all Impeachments. When sitting for that Purpose, they shall be on Oath or Affirmation. When the President of the United States is tried, the Chief Justice shall preside: And no Person shall be convicted without the Concurrence of two thirds of the Members present.

[7] Judgment in Cases of Impeachment shall not extend further than to removal from Office, and disqualification to hold and enjoy any Office of honor, Trust, or Profit under the United States: but the Party convicted shall nevertheless be liable and subject to Indictment, Trial, Judgment, and Punishment, according to Law.

Section 4. [1] The Times, Places and Manner of holding elections for Senators and Representatives, shall be prescribed in each State by the Legislature thereof; but the Congress may at any time by Law make or alter such Regulations, except as to the Places of chusing Senators.

[2] The Congress shall assemble at least once in every Year, and such Meeting shall be on the first Monday in December, unless they shall by Law appoint a different Day.

Section 5. [1] Each House shall be the Judge of the Elections, Returns, and Qualifications of its own Members, and a Majority of each shall constitute a Quorum to do Business; but a smaller Number may adjourn from day to day, and may be authorized to compel the Attendance of absent Members, in such Manner, and under such Penalties as each House may provide.

[2] Each House may determine the Rules of its Proceedings, punish its Members for disorderly Behavior, and, with the Concurrence of two thirds, expel a Member.

[3] Each House shall keep a Journal of its Proceedings, and from time to time publish the same, excepting such parts as may in their Judgment require Secrecy; and the Yeas and Nays of the Members of either House on any question shall, at the Desire of one fifth of those Present, be entered on the Journal.

[4] Neither House, during the Session of Congress, shall, without the Consent of the other, adjourn for more than three days, nor to any other Place than that in which the two Houses shall be sitting.

Section 6. [1] The Senators and Representatives shall receive a Compensation for their Services, to be ascertained by Law, and paid out of the Treasury of the United States. They shall in all Cases, except Treason, Felony and Breach of the Peace, be privileged from Arrest during their Attendance at the Session of their respective Houses, and in going to and returning from the same; and for any Speech of Debate in either House, they shall not be questioned in any other Place.

[2] No Senator or Representative shall, during the Time for which he was elected, be appointed to any civil Office under the Authority of the United States, which shall have been created, or the Emoluments whereof shall have been increased during such time; and no Person holding any Office under the United States, shall be a Member of either House during his Continuance in Office.

Section 7. [1] All Bills for raising Revenue shall originate in the House of Representatives; but the Senate may propose or concur with Amendments as on other Bills.

[2] Every Bill which shall have passed the House of Representatives and the Senate, shall, before it becomes a Law, be presented to the President of the United States; If he approve he shall sign it, but if not he shall return it, with his Objections to the House in which it shall have originated, who shall enter the Objections at large on their Journal, and proceed to reconsider it. If after such Reconsideration two thirds of that House shall agree to pass the Bill, it shall be sent together with the Objections, to the other House, by which it shall likewise be reconsidered, and if approved by two thirds of that House, it shall become a Law. But in all such Cases the Votes of both Houses shall be determined by yeas and Nays, and the Names of the Persons voting for and against the Bill shall be entered on the Journal of each House respectively. If any Bill shall not be returned by the President within ten Days (Sundays excepted) after it shall have been presented to him, the Same shall be a Law, in like Manner as if he had signed it, unless the Congress by their Adjournment prevent its Return in which Case it shall not be a Law.

[3] Every Order, Resolution, or Vote, to Which the Concurrence of the Senate and House of Representatives may be necessary (except on a question of Adjournment) shall be presented to the President of the United States; and before the Same shall take Effect, shall be approved by him, or being disapproved by him, shall be repassed by two thirds of the Senate and House of Representatives, according to the Rules and Limitations prescribed in the Case of a Bill.

Section 8. [1] The Congress shall have Power To lay and collect Taxes, Duties, Imposts and Excises, to pay the Debts and provide for the common Defence and general Welfare of the United States; but all Duties, Imposts and Excises shall be uniform throughout the United States;

[2] To borrow money on the credit of the United States;

[3] To regulate Commerce with foreign Nations, and among the several States, and with the Indian Tribes;

[4] To establish an uniform Rule of Naturalization, and uniform laws on the subject of Bankruptcies throughout the United States;

[5] To coin Money, regulate the Value thereof, and of foreign Coin, and fix the Standard of Weights and Measures;

[6] To provide for the Punishment of counterfeiting the Securities and current Coin of the United States;

[7] To Establish Post Offices and Post Roads;

[8] To promote the Progress of Science and useful Arts, by securing for limited Times to Authors and Inventors the exclusive Right to their respective Writings and Discoveries;

[9] To constitute Tribunals inferior to the supreme Court;

[10] To define and punish Piracies and Felonies committed on the high Seas, and Offenses against the Law of Nations;

[11] To declare War, grant Letters of Marque and Reprisal, and make Rules concerning Captures on Land and Water;

[12] To raise and support Armies, but no Appropriation of Money to that Use shall be for a longer Term than two Years;

[13] To provide and maintain a Navy;

[14] To make Rules for the Government and Regulation of the land and naval Forces;

[15] To provide for calling forth the Militia to execute the Laws of the Union, suppress Insurrections and repel Invasions;

[16] To provide for organizing, arming, and disciplining, the Militia, and for governing such Part of them as may be employed in the Service of the United States, reserving to the States respectively, the Appointment of the Officers, and the Authority of training the Militia according to the discipline prescribed by Congress;

[17] To exercise exclusive Legislation in all Cases whatsoever, over such District (not exceeding ten Miles square) as may, by Cession of particular States, and the Acceptance of Congress, become the Seat of the Government of the United States, and to exercise like Authority over all Places purchased by the Consent of the Legislature of the State in which the Same shall be, for the Erection of Forts, Magazines, Arsenals, dock-Yards and other needful Buildings;—And

[18] To make all Laws which shall be necessary and proper for carrying into Execution the foregoing Powers, and all other Powers vested by this Constitution in the Government of the United States, or in any Department or Officer thereof.

Section 9. [1] The Migration or Importation of Such Persons as any of the States now existing shall think proper to admit, shall not be prohibited by the Congress prior to the Year one thousand eight hundred and eight, but a Tax or duty may be imposed on such Importation, not exceeding ten dollars for each Person.

[2] The privilege of the Writ of Habeas Corpus shall not be suspended, unless when in Cases of Rebellion or Invasion the public Safety may require it.

[3] No Bill of Attainder or ex post facto Law shall be passed.

[4] No Capitation, or other direct, Tax shall be laid, unless in Proportion to the Census or Enumeration herein before directed to be taken.

[5] No Tax or Duty shall be laid on Articles exported from any State.

[6] No Preference shall be given by any Regulation of Commerce or Revenue to the Ports of one State over those of another: nor shall Vessels bound to, or from, one State be obliged to enter, clear, or pay Duties in another.

[7] No money shall be drawn from the Treasury, but in Consequence of Appropriations made by Law; and a regular Statement and Account of the Receipts and Expenditures of all public Money shall be published from time to time.

[8] No Title of Nobility shall be granted by the United States: And no Person holding any Office of Profit or Trust under them, shall, without the Consent of the Congress, accept of any present, Emolument, Office, or Title, of any kind whatever, from any King, Prince, or foreign State.

Section 10. **[1]** No State shall enter into any Treaty, Alliance, or confederation; grant Letters of Marque and Reprisal; coin Money; emit Bills of Credit; make any Thing but gold and silver Coin a Tender in Payment of Debts; pass any Bill of Attainder, ex post facto Law, or Law impairing the Obligation of Contracts, or grant any Title of Nobility.

[2] No State shall, without the Consent of the Congress, lay any Imposts or Duties on Imports or Exports, except what may be absolutely necessary for executing its inspection Laws: and the net Produce of all Duties and Imposts, laid by any State on Imports or Exports, shall be for the Use of the Treasury of the United States; and all such Laws shall be subject to the Revision and Control of the Congress.

[3] No State shall, without the Consent of Congress, lay any Duty of Tonnage, keep Troops, or Ships of War in time of Peace, enter into any Agreement or Compact with another State, or with a foreign Power, or engage in War, unless actually invaded, or in such imminent Danger as will not admit of delay.

Article II

Section 1. **[1]** The executive Power shall be vested in a President of the United States of America. He shall hold his Office during the Term of four Years, and, together with the Vice President, chosen for the same Term, be elected, as follows:

[2] Each State shall appoint, in such Manner as the Legislature thereof may direct, a Number of Electors, equal to the whole Number of Senators and Representatives to which the State may be entitled in the Congress; but no Senator or Representative, or Person holding an Office of Trust or Profit under the United States, shall be appointed an Elector.

[3] The Electors shall meet in their respective States, and vote by Ballot for two Persons, of whom one at least shall not be an Inhabitant of the same State with themselves. And they shall make a List of all the Persons voted for, and of the Number of Votes for each; which List they shall sign and certify, and transmit sealed to the Seat of the Government of the United States, directed to the President of the Senate. The President of the Senate shall, in the Presence of the Senate and House of Representatives, open all the Certificates, and the Votes shall then be counted. The Person having the greatest Number of Votes shall be the President, if such Number be a Majority of the whole Number of Electors appointed; and if there be more than one who have such Majority, and have an equal Number of Votes, then the House of Representatives shall immediately chuse by Ballot one of them for President; and if no Person have a Majority, then from the five highest on the List the said House shall in like Manner chuse the President. But in chusing the President, the Votes shall be taken by States the Representation from each State having one Vote; A quorum for this Purpose shall consist of a Member or Members from two thirds of the States, and a Majority of all the States shall be necessary to a Choice. In every Case, after the Choice of the President, the Person having the greater Number of Votes of the Electors shall be the Vice President. But if there shall remain two or more who have equal Votes, the Senate shall chuse from them by Ballot the Vice President.

[4] The Congress may determine the Time of chusing the Electors, and the Day on which they shall give their Votes; which Day shall be the same throughout the United States.

[5] No person except a natural born Citizen, or a Citizen of the United States, at the time of the Adoption of this Constitution, shall be eligible to the Office of President; neither shall any Person be eligible to that Office who shall not have attained to the Age of thirty-five Years, and been fourteen Years a Resident within the United States.

[6] In case of the removal of the President from Office, or of his Death, Resignation or Inability to discharge the Powers and Duties of the said Office, the Same shall devolve on the Vice President, and the Congress may by Law provide for the Case of Removal, Death, Resignation or Inability, both of the President and Vice President, declaring what Officer shall then act as President, and such Officer shall act accordingly, until the Disability be removed, or a President shall be elected.

[7] The President shall, at stated Times, receive for his Services, a Compensation, which shall neither be increased nor diminished during the Period for which he shall have been elected, and he shall not receive within that Period any other Emolument from the United States, or any of them.

[8] Before he enter on the Execution of his Office, he shall take the following Oath or Affirmation: "I do solemnly swear (or affirm) that I will faithfully execute the Office of President of the United States, and will to the best of my Ability, preserve, protect, and defend the Constitution of the United States."

Section 2. [1] The President shall be Commander in Chief of the Army and Navy of the United States, and of the militia of the several States, when called into the actual Service of the United States; he may require the Opinion, in writing, of the principal Officer in each of the Executive Departments, upon any subject relating to the Duties of their respective Offices, and he shall have Power to grant Reprieves and Pardons for Offenses against the United States, except in Cases of Impeachment.

[2] He shall have Power, by and with the Advice and Consent of the Senate to make Treaties, provided two thirds of the Senators present concur; and he shall nominate, and by and with the Advice and Consent of the Senate, shall appoint Ambassadors, other public Ministers and Consuls, Judges of the supreme Court, and all other Officers of the United States, whose Appointments are not herein otherwise provided for, and which shall be established by Law; but the Congress may by Law vest the Appointment of such inferior Officers, as they think proper, in the President alone, in the Courts of Law, or in the Heads of Departments.

[3] The President shall have Power to fill up all Vacancies that may happen during the Recess of the Senate, by granting commissions which shall expire at the End of their next Session.

Section 3. He shall from time to time give to the Congress Information of the State of the Union, and recommend to their Consideration such Measures as he shall judge necessary and expedient; he may, on extraordinary Occasions, convene both Houses, or either of them, and in Case of Disagreement between them, with Respect to the Time of Adjournment, he may adjourn them to such Time as he shall think proper; he shall receive Ambassadors and other public Ministers; he shall take Care that the Laws be faithfully executed, and shall commission all the Officers of the United States.

Section 4. The President, Vice President and all civil Officers of the United States, shall be removed from Office on Impeachment for, and Conviction of, Treason, Bribery, or other high Crimes and Misdemeanors.

Article III

Section 1. The judicial Power of the United States, shall be vested in one supreme Court, and in such inferior Courts as the Congress may from time to time ordain and establish. The Judges, both of the supreme and inferior Courts, shall hold their Offices during good Behaviour, and shall, at stated Times, receive for their Services a Compensation, which shall not be diminished during their Continuance in Office.

Section 2. [1] The judicial Power shall extend to all Cases, in Law and Equity, arising under this Constitution, the Laws of the United States, and Treaties made, or which shall be made, under their Authority;—to all Cases affecting Ambassadors, other public Ministers and Consuls;—to all Cases of admiralty and maritime Jurisdiction;—to Controversies to which the United States shall be a Party;—between a State and Citizens of another State; between Citizens of different States;—between Citizens of the same State claiming Lands under the Grants of different States, and between a State, or the Citizens thereof, and foreign States, Citizens or Subjects.

[2] In all Cases affecting Ambassadors, other public Ministers and Consuls, and those in which a State shall be a Party, the supreme Court shall have original Jurisdiction, In all the other Cases before mentioned, the supreme Court shall have appellate Jurisdiction, both as to Law and Fact, with such Exceptions, and under such Regulations as the Congress shall make.

[3] The trial of all Crimes, except in Cases of Impeachment, shall be by Jury; and such Trial shall be held in the State where the said Crimes shall have been committed; but when not committed within any State, the Trial shall be at such Place or Places as the Congress may by Law have directed.

Section 3. [1] Treason against the United States, shall consist only in levying War against them, or, in adhering to their Enemies, giving them Aid and Comfort. No Person shall be convicted of Treason unless on the Testimony of two Witnesses to the same overt Act, or on Confession in open Court.

[2] The Congress shall have Power to declare the Punishment of Treason, but no Attainder of Treason shall work Corruption of Blood, or Forfeiture except during the Life of the Person attainted.

Article IV

Section 1. Full Faith and Credit shall be given in each State to the public Acts, Records, and judicial Proceedings of every other State. And the Congress may by general Laws prescribe the Manner in which such Acts, Records and Proceedings shall be proved, and the Effect thereof.

Section 2. [1] The Citizens of each State shall be entitled to all Privileges and Immunities of Citizens in the several States.

[2] A Person charged in any State with Treason, Felony, or other Crime, who shall flee from Justice, and be found in another State, shall on demand of the executive Authority of the State from which he fled, be delivered up, to be removed to the State having Jurisdiction of the Crime.

[3] No Person held to Service or Labour in one State, under the Laws thereof, escaping into another, shall, in Consequence of any Law or Regulation therein, be discharged from such Service or Labour, but shall be delivered up on Claim of the Party to whom such Service or Labour may be due.

Section 3. **[1]** New States may be admitted by the Congress into this Union; but no new State shall be formed or erected within the Jurisdiction of any other State; nor any State be formed by the Junction of two or more States, or Parts of States, without the Consent of the Legislatures of the States concerned as well as of the Congress.
[2] The Congress shall have Power to dispose of and make all needful Rules and Regulations respecting the Territory or other Property belonging to the United States; and nothing in this Constitution shall be so construed as to Prejudice any Claims of the United States, or of any particular State.

Section 4. The United States shall guarantee to every State in this Union a Republican Form of Government, and shall protect each of them against Invasion; and on Application of the Legislature, or of the Executive (when the Legislature cannot be convened) against domestic Violence.

Article V

The Congress, whenever two thirds of both Houses shall deem it necessary, shall propose Amendments to this Constitution, or, on the Application of the Legislatures of two thirds of the several States, shall call a Convention for proposing Amendments, which, in either case, shall be valid to all Intents and Purposes, as part of this Constitution, when ratified by the Legislatures of three fourths of the several States, or by Conventions in three fourths thereof, as the one or the other Mode of Ratification may be proposed by the Congress; Provided that no Amendment which may be made prior to the Year One thousand eight hundred and eight shall in any Manner affect the first and fourth Clauses in the Ninth Section of the first Article; and that no State, without its Consent, shall be deprived of its equal Suffrage in the Senate.

Article VI

[1] All Debts contracted and Engagements entered into, before the Adoption of this Constitution shall be as valid against the United States under this Constitution, as under the Confederation.
[2] This Constitution, and the Laws of the United States which shall be made in Pursuance thereof; and all Treaties made, or which shall be made, under the Authority of the United States, shall be the supreme Law of the Land; and the Judges in every State shall be bound thereby, any Thing in the Constitution or Laws of any State to the Contrary notwithstanding.
[3] The Senators and Representatives before mentioned, and the Members of the several State Legislatures, and all executive and judicial Officers, both of the United States and of the several States, shall be bound by Oath or Affirmation, to support this Constitution; but no religious Test shall ever be required as a Qualification to any Office or public Trust under the United States.

Article VII

The Ratification of the Conventions of nine States shall be sufficient for the Establishment of this Constitution between the States so ratifying the Same.

Amendments

Articles in addition to, and in amendment of, the Constitution of the United States of America, proposed by Congress, and ratified by the Legislatures of the several States pursuant to the Fifth Article of the original Constitution.

Amendment 1 [1791]

Congress shall make no law respecting an establishment of religion, or prohibiting the free exercise thereof; or abridging the freedom of speech, or of the press; or the right of the people peaceably to assemble, and to petition the Government for a redress of grievances.

Amendment 2 [1791]

A well regulated Militia, being necessary to the security of a free State, the right of the people to keep and bear Arms, shall not be infringed.

Amendment 3 [1791]

No Soldier shall, in time of peace be quartered in any house, without the consent of the Owner, nor in time of war, but in a manner to be prescribed by law.

Amendment 4 [1791]

The right of the people to be secure in their persons, houses, papers, and effects, against unreasonable searches and seizures, shall not be violated, and no Warrants shall issue, but upon probable cause, supported by Oath or affirmation, and particularly describing the place to be searched, and the persons or things to be seized.

Amendment 5 [1791]

No person shall be held to answer for a capital, or other infamous crime, unless on a presentment or indictment of a Grand Jury, except in cases arising in the land or naval forces, or in the Militia, when in actual service in time of War or public danger; nor shall any person be subject for the same offence to be twice put in jeopardy of life or limb; nor shall be compelled in any criminal case to be a witness against himself, nor be deprived of life, liberty, or property, without due process of law; nor shall private property be taken for public use, without just compensation.

Amendment 6 [1791]

In all criminal prosecutions, the accused shall enjoy the right to a speedy and public trial, by an impartial jury of the State and district wherein the crime shall have been committed, which district shall have been previously ascertained by law, and to be informed of the nature and cause of the accusation; to be confronted with the witnesses against him; to have compulsory process for obtaining witnesses in his favor, and to have the Assistance of Counsel for his defence.

Amendment 7 [1791]

In Suits at common law, where the value in controversy shall exceed twenty dollars, the right of trial by jury shall be preserved, and no fact tried by jury, shall be otherwise re-examined in any Court of the United States, than according to the rules of common law.

Amendment 8 [1791]

Excessive bail shall not be required, nor excessive fines imposed, nor cruel and unusual punishments inflicted.

Amendment 9 [1791]

The enumeration in the Constitution, of certain rights, shall not be construed to deny or disparage others retained by the people.

Amendment 10 [1791]

The powers not delegated to the United States by the Constitution, nor prohibited by it to the States, are reserved to the States respectively, or to the people.

Amendment 11 [1798]

The Judicial power of the United States shall not be construed to extend to any suit in law or equity, commenced or prosecuted against one of the United States by Citizens of another State, or by Citizens or Subjects of any Foreign State.

Amendment 12 [1804]

The Electors shall meet in their respective states and vote by ballot for President and Vice President, one of whom, at least, shall not be an inhabitant of the same state with themselves; they shall name in their ballots the person voted for as President, and in distinct ballots the person voted for as Vice President, and they shall make distinct lists of all persons voted for as President, and of all persons voted for as Vice President, and of the number of votes for each, which lists they shall sign and certify, and transmit sealed to the seat of the government of the United States, directed to the President of the Senate;– The President of the Senate shall, in the presence of the Senate and House of Representatives, open all the certificates and the votes shall then be counted;–The person having the greatest number of votes for President, shall be the President, if such number be a majority of the whole number of Electors appointed; and if no person have such majority, then from the persons having the highest numbers not exceeding three on the list of those voted for as President, the House of Representatives shall choose immediately, by ballot, the President. But in choosing the President, the votes shall be taken by states, the representation from each state having one vote; a quorum for this purpose shall consist of a member or members from two thirds of the states, and a majority of all states shall be necessary to a choice. And if the House of Representatives shall not choose a President whenever the right of choice shall devolve upon them before the fourth day of March next following, then the Vice President shall act as President, as in the case of the death or other constitutional disability of the President.– The person having the greatest number of votes as Vice President, shall be the Vice President, if such number be a majority of the whole number of Electors appointed, and if no person have a majority, then from the two highest numbers on the list, the Senate shall choose the Vice President; a quorum for the purpose shall consist of two thirds of the whole number of Senators, and a majority of the whole number shall be necessary to a choice. But no person constitutionally ineligible to the office of President shall be eligible to that of Vice President of the United States.

Amendment 13 [1865]

Section 1. Neither slavery nor involuntary servitude, except as a punishment for crime whereof the party shall have been duly convicted, shall exist within the United States, or any place subject to their jurisdiction.

Section 2. Congress shall have power to enforce this article by appropriate legislation.

Amendment 14 [1868]

Section 1. All persons born or naturalized in the United States, and subject to the jurisdiction thereof, are citizens of the United States and of the State wherein they reside. No State shall make or enforce any law which shall abridge the privileges or immunities of citizens of the United States; nor shall any State deprive any person of life, liberty, or property, without due process of law; nor deny to any person within its jurisdiction the equal protection of the laws.

Section 2. Representatives shall be apportioned among the several States according to their respective numbers, counting the whole number of persons in each State, excluding Indians not taxed. But when the right to vote at any election for the choice of electors for President and Vice President of the United States, Representatives in Congress, the Executive and Judicial officers of a State, or the members of the Legislature thereof, is denied to any of the male inhabitants of such State, being twenty-one years of age, and citizens of the United States, or in any way abridged, except for participation in rebellion, or other crime, the basis of representation therein shall be reduced in the proportion which the number of such male citizens shall bear to the whole number of male citizens twenty-one years of age in such State.

Section 3. No person shall be a Senator or Representative in Congress, or elector of President and Vice President, or hold any office, civil or military, under the United States, or under any State, who having previously taken an oath, as a member of Congress, or as an officer of the United States, or as a member of any State legislature, or as an executive or judicial officer of any State, to support the Constitution of the United States, shall have engaged in insurrection or rebellion against the same, or given aid or comfort to the enemies thereof. But Congress may by a vote of two thirds of each House, remove such disability.

Section 4. The validity of the public debt of the United States, authorized by law, including debts incurred for payment of pensions and bounties for services in suppressing insurrection or rebellion, shall not be questioned. But neither the United States nor any State shall assume or pay any debt or obligation incurred in aid of insurrection or rebellion against the United States, or any claim for the loss or emancipation of any slave; but all such debts, obligations and claims shall be held illegal and void.

Section 5. The Congress shall have power to enforce, by appropriate legislation, the provisions of this article.

Amendment 15 [1870]

Section 1. The right of citizens of the United States to vote shall not be denied or abridged by the United States or by any State on account of race, color, or previous condition of servitude.

Section 2. The Congress shall have power to enforce this article by appropriate legislation.

Amendment 16 [1913]

The Congress shall have power to lay and collect taxes on incomes, from whatever source derived, without apportionment among the several States, and without regard to any census or enumeration.

Amendment 17 [1913]

[1] The Senate of the United States shall be composed of two Senators from each State, elected by the people thereof, for six years; and each Senator shall have one vote. The electors in each State shall have the qualifications requisite for electors of the most numerous branch of the State legislatures.

[2] When vacancies happen in the representation of any State in the Senate, the executive authority of such State shall issue writs of election to fill such vacancies: *Provided*, That the legislature of any State may empower the executive thereof to make temporary appointments until the people fill the vacancies by election as the legislature may direct.

[3] This amendment shall not be so construed as to affect the election or term of any Senator chosen before it becomes valid as part of the Constitution.

Amendment 18 [1919]

Section 1. After one year from the ratification of this article the manufacture, sale, or transportation of intoxicating liquors within, the importation thereof into, or the exportation thereof from the United States and all territory subject to the jurisdiction thereof for beverage purposes is hereby prohibited.

Section 2. The Congress and the several States shall have concurrent power to enforce this article by appropriate legislation.

Section 3. This article shall be inoperative unless it shall have been ratified as an amendment to the Constitution by the legislatures of the several States, as provided in the Constitution, within seven years from the date of the submission hereof to the States by the Congress.

Amendment 19 [1920]

[1] The right of citizens of the United States to vote shall not be denied or abridged by the United States or by any State on account of sex.

[2] Congress shall have power to enforce this article by appropriate legislation.

Amendment 20 [1933]

Section 1. The terms of the President and Vice President shall end at noon on the twentieth day of January, and the terms of Senators and Representatives at noon on the third day of January, of the years in which such terms would have ended if this article had not been ratified; and the terms of their successors shall then begin.

Section 2. The Congress shall assemble at least once in every year, and such meeting shall begin at noon on the third day of January, unless they shall by law appoint a different day.

Section 3. If, at the time fixed for the beginning of the term of the President, the President elect shall have died, the Vice President elect shall become President. If the President shall not have been chosen before the time fixed for the beginning of his term, or if the President elect shall have failed to qualify, then the Vice President elect shall act as President until a President shall have qualified; and the Congress may by law provide for the case wherein neither a President elect nor a Vice President elect shall have qualified, declaring who shall then act as President, or the manner in which one who is to act shall be selected, and such person shall act accordingly until a President or Vice President shall have qualified.

Section 4. The Congress may by law provide for the case of the death of any of the persons from whom the House of Representatives may choose a President whenever the right of choice shall have devolved upon them, and for the case of the death of any of the persons from whom the Senate may choose a Vice President whenever the right of choice shall have devolved upon them.

Section 5. Sections 1 and 2 shall take effect on the fifteenth day of October following the ratification of this article.

Section 6. This article shall be inoperative unless it shall have been ratified as an amendment to the Constitution by the legislatures of three fourths of the several States within seven years from the date of its submission.

Amendment 21 [1933]

Section 1. The eighteenth article of amendment to the Constitution of the United States is hereby repealed.

Section 2. The transportation or importation into any State, Territory, or possession of the United States for delivery or use therein of intoxicating liquors, in violation of the laws therefore, is hereby prohibited.

Section 3. This article shall be inoperative unless it shall have been ratified as an amendment to the Constitution by conventions in the several States, as provided in the Constitution, within seven years from the date of the submission hereof to the States by the Congress.

Amendment 22 [1951]

Section 1. No person shall be elected to the office of the President more than twice, and no person who has held the office of President, or acted as President, for more than two years of a term to which some other person was elected President shall be elected to the office of President more than once. But this Article shall not apply to any person holding the office of President when this Article was proposed by the Congress, and shall not prevent any person who may be holding the office of President, or acting as President, during the term within which this Article becomes operative from holding the office of President or acting as President during the remainder of such term.

Section 2. This article shall be inoperative unless it shall have been ratified as an amendment to the Constitution by the legislatures of three fourths of the several States within seven years from the date of its submission to the States by the Congress.

Amendment 23 [1961]

Section 1. The District constituting the seat of Government of the United States shall appoint in such manner as the Congress may direct:

A number of electors of President and Vice President equal to the whole number of Senators and Representatives in Congress to which the District would be entitled if it were a State, but in no event more than the least populous state; they shall be in addition to those appointed by the states, but they shall be considered, for the purposes of the election of President and Vice President, to be electors appointed by a state; and they shall meet in the District and perform such duties as provided by the twelfth article of amendment.

Section 2. The Congress shall have power to enforce this article by appropriate legislation.

Amendment 24 [1964]

Section 1. The right of citizens of the United States to vote in any primary or other election for President or Vice President, for electors for President or Vice President, or for Senator or Representative in Congress, shall not be denied or abridged by the United States, or any State by reason of failure to pay any poll tax or other tax.

Section 2. The Congress shall have power to enforce this article by appropriate legislation.

Amendment 25 [1967]

Section 1. In case of the removal of the President from office or of his death or resignation, the Vice President shall become President.

Section 2. Whenever there is a vacancy in the office of the Vice President, the President shall nominate a Vice President who shall take office upon confirmation by a majority vote of both Houses of Congress.

Section 3. Whenever the President transmits to the President pro tempore of the Senate and the Speaker of the House of Representatives his written declaration that he is unable to discharge the powers and duties of his office, and until he transmits to them a written declaration to the contrary, such powers and duties shall be discharged by the Vice President as Acting President.

Section 4. Whenever the Vice President and a majority of either the principal officers of the executive departments or of such other body as Congress may by law provide, transmit to the President pro tempore of the Senate and the Speaker of the House of Representatives their written declaration that the President is unable to discharge the powers and duties of his office, the Vice President shall immediately assume the powers and duties of the office as Acting President.

Thereafter, when the President transmits to the President pro tempore of the Senate and the Speaker of the House of Representatives his written declaration that no inability exists, he shall resume the powers and duties of his office unless the Vice President and a majority of either the principal officers of the executive department or of such other body as Congress may by law provide, transmit within four days to the President pro tempore of the Senate and the Speaker of the House of Representatives their written declaration and the President is unable to discharge the powers and duties of his office. Thereupon Congress shall decide the issue, assembling within, forty-eight hours for that purpose if not in session. If the Congress, within twenty-one days after receipt of the latter written declaration, or, if Congress is not in session, within twenty-one days after Congress is required to assemble, determines by two thirds vote of both Houses that the President is unable to discharge the powers and duties of his office, the Vice President shall continue to discharge the same as Acting President;

otherwise, the President shall resume the powers and duties of his office.

Amendment 26 [1971]

Section 1. The right of citizens of the United States, who are eighteen years of age or older, to vote shall not be denied or abridged by the United States or by any State on account of age.

Section 2. The Congress shall have power to enforce this article by appropriate legislation.

Amendment 27 [1992]

No law varying the compensation for the services of Senators and Representatives shall take effect, until an election of Representatives shall have intervened.

Appendix B Uniform Commercial Code (Articles 1, 2, 2a, and 3)*

The Uniform Commercial Code (UCC) was developed by the American Law Institute (ALI) and the National Conference of Commissioners on Uniform State Laws (NCCUSL) (now known as the Uniform Law Commission) as a body of rules intended to make the application of law to commercial transactions consistent across fifty states. Like all uniform laws developed by the Uniform Law Commission, the UCC and all changes to the UCC do not become law until officially adopted by the state legislatures. The UCC has been adopted in whole by all but one state legislature, Louisiana, which adopts only certain sections. Such widespread use of the UCC, even with the minor deviations some jurisdictions make from the official code, makes possible more efficient and more confident transactions across state lines. The UCC can be accessed here: https://www.law.cornell.edu/ucc. The UCC can be also be found on the official website of the Uniform Law Commission at http://uniformlaws.org/Acts.aspx. Not all states follow the same numbering sequence used in the UCC and so it is always best to check state statutory law before citing the code in any state-specific assignment.

Appendix C United Nations Convention on Contracts for the International Sale of Goods

THE STATES PARTIES TO THIS CONVENTION, BEARING IN MIND the broad objectives in the resolutions adopted by the sixth special session of the General Assembly of the United Nations on the establishment of a New International Economic Order, CONSIDERING that the development of international trade on the basis of equality and mutual benefit is an important element in promoting friendly relations among States, BEING OF THE OPINION that the adoption of uniform rules which govern contracts for the international sale of goods and take into account the different social, economic and legal systems would contribute to the removal of legal barriers in international trade and promote the development of international trade, HAVE AGREED as follows:

Part I Sphere of Application and General Provisions

Chapter I Sphere of Application

Article 1

(1) This Convention applies to contracts of sale of goods between parties whose places of business are in different States:
   (a) when the States are Contracting States; or
   (b) when the rules of private international law lead to the application of the law of a Contracting State. [Pursuant to the reservation permitted by Article 95, the United States has excluded applicability of the Convention under this subparagraph.]

(2) The fact that the parties have their places of business in different States is to be disregarded whenever this fact does not appear either from the contract or from any dealings between, or from information disclosed by, the parties at any time before or at the conclusion of the contract.

(3) Neither the nationality of the parties nor the civil or commercial character of the parties or of the contract is to be taken into consideration in determining the application of this Convention.

Article 2 This Convention does not apply to sales:

(a) of goods bought for personal, family or household use, unless the seller, at any time before or at the conclusion of the contract, neither knew nor ought to have known that the goods were bought for any such use;

(b) by auction;

(c) on execution or otherwise by authority of law;

(d) of stocks, shares, investment securities, negotiable instruments or money;

(e) of ships, vessels, hovercraft or aircraft;

(f) of electricity.

Article 3

(1) Contracts for the supply of goods to be manufactured or produced are to be considered sales unless the party who orders the goods undertakes to supply a substantial part of the materials necessary for such manufacture or production.

(2) This Convention does not apply to contracts in which the preponderant part of the obligations of the party who furnishes the goods consists in the supply of labour or other services.

Article 4 This Convention governs only the formation of the contract of sale and the rights and obligations of the seller and the buyer arising from such a contract. In particular, except as otherwise expressly provided in this Convention, it is not concerned with:

(a) the validity of the contract or of any of its provisions or of any usage;

(b) the effect which the contract may have on the property in the goods sold.

Article 5 This Convention does not apply to the liability of the seller for death or personal injury caused by the goods to any person.

Article 6 The parties may exclude the application of this Convention or, subject to Article 12, derogate from or vary the effect of any of its provisions.

Chapter II General Provisions

Article 7

(1) In the interpretation of this Convention, regard is to be had to its international character and to the need to promote uniformity in its application and the observance of good faith in international trade.

(2) Questions concerning matters governed by this Convention which are not expressly settled in it are to be settled in conformity with the general principles on which it is based or, in the absence of such principles, in conformity with the law applicable by virtue of the rules of private international law.

Article 8

(1) For the purposes of this Convention statements made by and other conduct of a party are to be interpreted according to his intent where the other party knew or could not have been unaware what that intent was.

(2) If the preceding paragraph is not applicable, statements made by and other conduct of a party are to be interpreted according to the understanding that a reasonable person of the same kind as the other party would have had in the same circumstances.

(3) In determining the intent of a party or the understanding a reasonable person would have had, due consideration is to be given to all relevant circumstances of the case including the negotiations, any practices which the parties have established between themselves, usages and any subsequent conduct of the parities.

Article 9

(1) The parties are bound by any usage to which they have agreed and by any practices which they have established between themselves.

(2) The parties are considered, unless otherwise agreed, to have impliedly made applicable to their contract or its formation a usage of which the parties know or ought to have known and which in international trade is widely known to, and regularly observed by, parties to contracts of the type involved in the particular trade concerned.

Article 10 For the purposes of this Convention:

(a) if a party has more than one place of business, the place of business is that which has the closest relationship to the contract and its performance, having regard to the circumstances known to or contemplated by the parties at any time before or at the conclusion of the contract;

(b) if a party does not have a place of business, reference is to be made to his habitual residence.

Article 11 A contract of sale need not be concluded in or evidenced by writing and is not subject to any other requirement as to form. It may be proved by any means, including witnesses.

Article 12 Any provision of Article 11, Article 29 or Part II of this Convention that allows a contract of sale or its modification or termination by agreement or any offer, acceptance or other indication of intention to be made in any form other than in writing does not apply where any party has his place of business in a Contracting State which has made a declaration under Article 96 of this Convention. The parties may not derogate from or vary the effect of this article.

Article 13 For the purposes of this Convention "writing" includes telegram and telex.

Part II Formation of the Contract

Article 14

(1) A proposal for concluding a contract addressed to one or more specific persons constitutes an offer if it is sufficiently definite and indicates the intention of the offeror to be bound in case of acceptance. A proposal is sufficiently definite if it indicates the goods and expressly or implicitly fixes or makes provision for determining the quantity and the price.

(2) A proposal other than one addressed to one or more specific persons is to be considered merely as an invitation to make offers, unless the contrary is clearly indicated by the person making the proposal.

Article 15

(1) An offer becomes effective when it reaches the offeree.

(2) An offer, even if it is irrevocable, may be withdrawn if the withdrawal reaches the offeree before or at the same time as the offer.

Article 16

(1) Until a contract is concluded an offer may be revoked if the revocation reaches the offeree before he has dispatched an acceptance.

(2) However, an offer cannot be revoked:

   (a) if it indicates, whether by stating a fixed time for acceptance or otherwise, that it is irrevocable; or

   (b) if it was reasonable for the offeree to rely on the offer as being irrevocable and the offeree has acted in reliance on the offer.

Article 17 An offer, even if it is irrevocable, is terminated when a rejection reaches the offeror.

Article 18

(1) A statement made by or other conduct of the offeree indicating assent to an offer is an acceptance. Silence or inactivity does not in itself amount to acceptance.

(2) An acceptance of an offer becomes effective at the moment the indication of assent reaches the offeror. An acceptance is not effective if the indication of assent does not reach the offeror within the time he has fixed or, if no time is fixed, within a reasonable time, due account being taken of the circumstances of the transaction, including the rapidity of the means of communication employed by the offeror. An oral offer must be accepted immediately unless the circumstances indicate otherwise.

(3) However, if, by virtue of the offer or as a result of practices which the parties have established between themselves or of usage, the offeree may indicate assent by performing an act, such as one relating to

the dispatch of the goods or payment of the price, without notice to the offeror, the acceptance is effective at the moment the act is performed, provided that the act is performed within the period of time laid down in the preceding paragraph.

Article 19

(1) A reply to an offer which purports to be an acceptance but contains additions, limitations or other modifications is a rejection of the offer and constitutes a counter-offer.

(2) However, a reply to an offer which purports to be an acceptance but contains additional or different terms which do not materially alter the terms of the offer constitutes an acceptance, unless the offeror, without undue delay, objects orally to the discrepancy or dispatches a notice to that effect. If he does not so object, the terms of the contract are the terms of the offer with the modifications contained in the acceptance.

(3) Additional or different terms relating, among other things, to the price, payment, quality and quantity of the goods, place and time of delivery, extent of one party's liability to the other or the settlement of disputes are considered to alter the terms of the offer materially.

Article 20

(1) A period of time for acceptance fixed by the offeror in a telegram or a letter begins to run from the moment the telegram is handed in for dispatch or from the date shown on the letter or, if on such date is shown, from the date shown on the envelope. A period of time for acceptance fixed by the offeror by telephone, telex or other means of instantaneous communication, begins to run from the moment that the offer reaches the offeree.

(2) Official holidays or non-business days occurring during the period for acceptance are included in calculating the period. However, if a notice of acceptance cannot be delivered at the address of the offeror on the last day of the period because that day falls on an official holiday or a non-business day at the place of business of the offeror, the period is extended until the first business day which follows.

Artcle 21

(1) A late acceptance is nevertheless effective as an acceptance if without delay the offeror orally so informs the offeree or dispatches a notice to that effect.

(2) If a letter or other writing containing a late acceptance shows that it has been sent in such circumstances that if its transmission had been normal it would have reached the offeror in due time, the late acceptance is effective as an acceptance unless, without delay, the offeror orally informs the offeree that he considers his offer as having lapsed or dispatches a notice to that effect.

Article 22 An acceptance may be withdrawn if the withdrawal reaches the offeror before or at the same time as the acceptance would have become effective.

Article 23 A contract is concluded at the moment when an acceptance of an offer becomes effective in accordance with the provisions of this Convention.

Article 24 For the purposes of this Part of the Convention, an offer, declaration of acceptance or any other indication of intention "reaches" the addressee when it is made orally to him or delivered by any other means to him personally, to his place of business or mailing address or, if he does not have a place of business or mailing address, to his habitual residence.

Part III Sale of Goods

Chapter I General Provisions

Article 25 A breach of contract committed by one of the parties is fundamental if it results in such detriment to the other party as substantially to deprive him of what he is entitled to expect under the contract, unless the party in breach did not foresee and a reasonable person of the same kind in the same circumstances would not have foreseen such a result.

Article 26 A declaration of avoidance of the contract is effective only if made by notice to the other party.

Article 27 Unless otherwise expressly provided in this Part of the Convention, if any notice, request or other communication is given or made by a party in accordance with this Part and by means appropriate in the circumstances, a delay or error in the transmission of the communication or its failure to arrive does not deprive that party of the right to rely on the communication.

Article 28 If, in accordance with the provisions of this Convention, one party is entitled to require performance of any obligation by the other party, a court is not bound to enter a judgment for specific performance unless the court would do so under its own law in respect of similar contracts of sale not governed by this Convention.

Article 29

(1) A contact may be modified or terminated by the mere agreement of the parties.

(2) A contact in writing which contains a provision requiring any modification or termination by agreement to be in writing may not be otherwise modified or terminated by agreement. However, a party may be precluded by his conduct from asserting such a provision to the extent that the other party has relied on that conduct.

Chapter II Obligations of the Seller

Article 30 The seller must deliver the goods, hand over any documents relating to them and transfer the property in the goods, as required by the contract and this Convention.

Section I. Delivery of the goods and handing over of documents

Article 31 If the seller is not bound to deliver the goods at any other particular place, his obligation to deliver consists:

(a) if the contract of sale involves carriage of the goods—in handing the goods over to the first carrier for transmission to the buyer;

(b) if, in cases not within the preceding subparagraph, the contract relates to specific goods, or unidentified goods to be drawn from a specific stock or to be manufactured or produced, and at the time of the conclusion of the contract the parties knew that the goods were at, or were to be manufactured or produced at, a particular place—in placing the goods at the buyer's disposal at the place;

(c) in other cases—in placing the goods at the buyer's disposal at the place where the seller had his place of business at the time of the conclusion of the contract.

Article 32

(1) If the seller, in accordance with the contract or this Convention, hands the goods over to a carrier and if the goods are not clearly identified to the contract by markings on the goods, by shipping documents or otherwise, the seller must give the buyer notice of the consignment specifying the goods.

(2) If the seller is bound to arrange for carriage of the goods, he must make such contracts as are necessary for carriage to the place fixed by means of transportation appropriate in the circumstances and according to the usual terms for such transportation.

(3) If the seller is not bound to effect insurance in respect of the carriage of the goods, he must, at the buyer's request, provide him with all available information necessary to enable him to effect such insurance.

Article 33 The seller must deliver the goods:

(a) if a date is fixed by or determinable from the contract, on that date;

(b) if a period of time is fixed by or determinable from the contract, at any time within that period unless circumstances indicate that the buyer is to choose a date; or

(c) in any other case, within a reasonable time after the conclusion of the contract.

Article 34 If the seller is bound to hand over documents relating to the goods, he must hand them over at the time and place and in the form required by the contract. If the seller has handed over documents before that time, he may, up to that time, cure any lack of conformity in the documents, if the exercise of this right does not cause the buyer unreasonable inconvenience or unreasonable expense. However, the buyer retains any right to claim damages as provided for in this Convention.

Section II. Conformity of the goods and third party claims

Article 35

(1) The seller must deliver goods which are of the quantity, quality and description required by the contract and which are contained or packaged in the manner required by the contract.

(2) Except where the parties have agreed otherwise, the goods do not conform with the contract unless they:

(a) are fit for the purposes for which goods of the same description would ordinarily be used;

(b) are fit for any particular purpose expressly or impliedly made known to the seller at the time of the conclusion of the contract, except where the circumstances show that the buyer did not rely, or that it was unreasonable for him to rely, on the seller's skill and judgment;

(c) possess the qualities of goods which the seller has held out to the buyer as a sample or model;

(d) are contained or packaged in the manner usual for such goods or, where there is no such manner, in a manner adequate to preserve and protect the goods.

(3) The seller is not liable under subparagraphs (a) to (d) of the preceding paragraph for any lack of conformity of the preceding paragraph for any lack of conformity of the goods if at the time of the conclusion of the contract the buyer knew or could not have been unaware of such lack of conformity.

Article 36

(1) The seller is liable in accordance with the contract and this Convention for any lack of conformity which exists at the time when the risk passes to the buyer, even though the lack of conformity becomes apparent only after that time.

(2) The seller is also liable for any lack of conformity which occurs after the time indicated in the preceding paragraph and which is due to a breach of any of his obligations, including a breach of any guarantee that for a period of time the goods will remain fit for their ordinary purpose or for some particular purpose or will retain specified qualities or characteristics.

Article 37 If the seller has delivered goods before the date for delivery, he may, up to that date, deliver any missing part or make up any deficiency in the quantity of the goods delivered, or deliver goods in replacement of any non-conforming goods delivered or remedy any lack of conformity in the goods delivered, provided that the exercise of this right does not cause the buyer unreasonable inconvenience or unreasonable expense. However, the buyer retains any right to claim damages as provided for in this Convention.

Article 38

(1) The buyer must examine the goods, or cause them to be examined, within as short a period as is practicable in the circumstances.

(2) If the contract involves carriage of the goods, examination may be deferred until after the goods have arrived at their destination.

(3) If the goods are redirected in transit or redispatched by the buyer without a reasonable opportunity for examination by him and at the time of the conclusion of the contract the seller knew or ought to have known of the possibility of such redirection or redispatch, examination may be deferred until after the goods have arrived at the new destination.

Article 39

(1) The buyer loses the right to rely on a lack of conformity of the goods if he does not give notice to the seller specifying the nature of the lack of conformity within a reasonable time after he has discovered it or ought to have discovered it.

(2) In any event, the buyer loses the right to rely on a lack of conformity of the goods if he does not give the seller notice thereof at the latest within a period of two years from the date on which the goods were actually handed over to the buyer, unless this time-limit is inconsistent with a contractual period of guarantee.

Article 40 The seller is not entitled to rely on the provisions of Articles 38 and 39 if the lack of conformity relates to facts of which he knew or could not have been unaware and which he did not disclose to the buyer.

Article 41 The seller must deliver goods which are free from any right or claim of a third party, unless the buyer agreed to take the goods subject to that right or claim. However, if such right or claim is based on industrial property or other intellectual property, the seller's obligation is governed by Article 42.

Article 42

(1) The seller must deliver goods which are free from any right or claim of a third party based on industrial property or other intellectual property, of which at the time of the conclusion of the contract the seller knew or could not have been unaware, provided that the right or claim is based on industrial property or other intellectual property:

   (a) under the law of the State where the goods will be resold or otherwise used, if it was contemplated by the parties at the time of the conclusion of the contract that the goods would be resold or otherwise used in that State; or

   (b) in any other case, under the law of the State where the buyer has his place of business.

(2) The obligation of the seller under the preceding paragraph does not extend to cases where:

   (a) at the time of the conclusion of the contract the buyer knew or could not have been unaware of the right or claim; or

   (b) the right or claim results from the seller's compliance with technical drawings, designs, formulae or other such specifications furnished by the buyer.

Article 43

(1) The buyer loses the right to rely on the provisions of Article 41 or Article 42 if he does not give notice to the seller specifying the nature of the right or claim of the third party within a reasonable time after he has become aware or ought to have become aware of the right or claim.

(2) The seller is not entitled to rely on the provisions of the preceding paragraph if he knew of the right or claim of the third party and the nature of it.

Article 44 Notwithstanding the provisions of paragraph (1) of Article 39 and paragraph (1) of Article 43, the buyer may reduce the price in accordance with Article 50 or claim damages, except for loss of profit, if he has a reasonable excuse for his failure to give the required notice.

Section III. Remedies for breach of contract by the seller

Article 45

(1) If the seller fails to perform any of his obligations under the contract or this Convention, the buyer may:

   (a) exercise the rights provided in Articles 46 to 52;

   (b) claim damages as provided in Articles 74 to 77.

(2) The buyer is not deprived of any right he may have to claim damages by exercising his right to other remedies.

(3) No period of grace may be granted to the seller by a court or arbitral tribunal when the buyer resorts to a remedy for breach of contract.

Article 46

(1) The buyer may require performance by the seller of his obligations unless the buyer has resorted to a remedy which is inconsistent with this requirement.

(2) If the goods do not conform with the contract, the buyer may require delivery of substitute goods only if the lack of conformity constitutes a fundamental breach of contract and a request for substitute goods is made either in conjunction with notice given under Article 39 or within a reasonable time thereafter.

(3) If the goods do not conform with the contract, the buyer may require the seller to remedy the lack of conformity by repair, unless this is unreasonable having

regard to all the circumstances. A request for repair must be made either in conjunction with notice given under Article 39 or within a reasonable time thereafter.

Article 47

(1) The buyer may fix an additional period of time of reasonable length for performance by the seller of his obligations.

(2) Unless the buyer has received notice from the seller that he will not perform within the period so fixed, the buyer may not, during that period, resort to any remedy for breach of contract. However, the buyer is not deprived thereby of any right he may have to claim damages for delay in performance.

Article 48

(1) Subject to Article 49, the seller may, even after the date for delivery, remedy at his own expense any failure to perform his obligations, if he can do so without unreasonable delay and without causing the buyer unreasonable inconvenience or uncertainty of reimbursement by the seller of expenses advanced by the buyer. However, the buyer retains any right to claim damages as provided for in this Convention.

(2) If the seller requests the buyer to make known whether he will accept performance and the buyer does not comply with the request within a reasonable time, the seller may perform within the time indicated in his request. The buyer may not, during that period of time, resort to any remedy which is inconsistent with performance by the seller.

(3) A notice by the seller that he will perform within a specified period of time is assumed to include a request, under the preceding paragraph, that the buyer make known his decision.

(4) A request or notice by the seller under paragraph (2) or (3) of this article is not effective unless received by the buyer.

Article 49

(1) The buyer may declare the contract avoided:

(a) if the failure by the seller to perform any of his obligations under the contract or this Convention amounts to a fundamental breach of contract; or

(b) in case of non-delivery, if the seller does not deliver the goods within the additional period of time fixed by the buyer in accordance with paragraph (1) of Article 47 or declares that he will not deliver within the period so fixed.

(2) However, in cases where the seller has delivered the goods, the buyer loses the right to declare the contract avoided unless he does so:

(a) in respect of late delivery, within a reasonable time after he has become aware that delivery has been made;

(b) in respect of any breach other than late delivery, within a reasonable time:

(i) after he knew or ought to have known of the breach;

(ii) after the expiration of any additional period of time fixed by the buyer in accordance with paragraph (1) of Article 47, or after the seller has declared that he will not perform his obligations within such an additional period; or

(iii) after the expiration of any additional period of time indicated by the seller in accordance with paragraph (2) of Article 48, or after the buyer has declared that he will not accept performance.

Article 50

If the goods do not conform with the contract and whether or not the price has already been paid, the buyer may reduce the price in the same proportion as the value that the goods actually delivered had at the time of the delivery bears to the value that conforming goods would have had at that time. However, if the seller remedies any failure to perform his obligations in accordance with Article 37 or Article 48 or if the buyer refuses to accept performance by the seller in accordance with those articles, the buyer may not reduce the price.

Article 51

(1) If the seller delivers only a part of the goods or if only a part of the goods delivered is in conformity with the contract, Articles 46 to 50 apply in respect of the part which is missing or which does not conform.

(2) The buyer may declare the contract avoided in its entirety only if the failure to make delivery completely or in conformity with the contract amounts to a fundamental breach of the contract.

Article 52

(1) If the seller delivers the goods before the date fixed, the buyer may take delivery or refuse to take delivery.

(2) If the seller delivers a quantity of goods greater than that provided for in the contract, the buyer may take delivery or refuse to take delivery of the excess quantity. If the buyer takes delivery of all or part of the excess quantity, he must pay for it at the contract rate.

Chapter III Obligations of the Buyer

Article 53 The buyer must pay the price for the goods and take delivery of them as required by the contract and this Convention.

Section I. Payment of the price

Article 54 The buyer's obligation to pay the price includes taking such steps and complying with such formalities as may be required under the contract or any laws and regulations to enable payment to be made.

Article 55 Where a contract has been validly concluded but does not expressly or implicitly fix or make provision for determining the price, the parties are considered, in the absence of any indication to the contrary, to have impliedly made reference to the price generally charged at the time of the conclusion of the contract for such goods sold under comparable circumstances in the trade concerned.

Article 56 If the price is fixed according to the weight of the goods, in case of doubt it is to be determined by the net weight.

Article 57

(1) If the buyer is not bound to pay the price at any other particular place, he must pay it to the seller:

   (a) at the seller's place of business; or
   (b) if the payment is to be made against the handing over of the goods or of documents, at the place where the handing over takes place.

(2) The seller must bear any increase in the expenses incidental to payment which is caused by a change in his place of business subsequent to the conclusion of the contract.

Article 58

(1) If the buyer is not bound to pay the price at any other specific time, he must pay it when the seller places either the goods or documents controlling their disposition at the buyer's disposal in accordance with the contract and this Convention. The seller may make such payment a condition for handling over the goods or documents.

(2) If the contract involves carriage of the goods, the seller may dispatch the goods on terms whereby the goods, or documents controlling their disposition, will not be handed over to the buyer except against payment of the price.

(3) The buyer is not bound to pay the price until he has had an opportunity to examine the goods, unless the procedures for delivery or payment agreed upon by the parties are inconsistent with his having such an opportunity.

Article 59 The buyer must pay the price on the date fixed by or determinable from the contract and this Convention without the need for any request or compliance with any formality on the part of the seller.

Section II. Taking delivery

Article 60 The buyer's obligation to take delivery consists:

(a) in doing all the acts which could reasonably be expected of him in order to enable the seller to make delivery; and
(b) in taking over the goods.

Section III. Remedies for breach of contract by the buyer

Article 61

(1) If the buyer fails to perform any of his obligations under the contract or this Convention, the seller may:

   (a) exercise the rights provided in Articles 62 to 65;
   (b) claim damages as provided in Articles 74 to 77.

(2) The seller is not deprived of any right he may have to claim damages by exercising his right to other remedies.

(3) No period of grace may be granted to the buyer by a court or arbitral tribunal when the seller resorts to a remedy for breach of contract.

Article 62 The seller may require the buyer to pay the price, take delivery or perform his other obligations, unless the seller has resorted to a remedy which is inconsistent with this requirement.

Article 63

(1) The seller may fix an additional period of time of reasonable length for performance by the buyer of his obligations.

(2) Unless the seller has received notice from the buyer that he will not perform within the period so fixed, the seller may not, during that period, resort to any remedy for breach of contract. However, the seller is not deprived thereby of any right he may have to claim damages for delay in performance.

Article 64

(1) The seller may declare the contract avoided:

   (a) if the failure by the buyer to perform any of his obligations under the contract or this Convention amounts to a fundamental breach of contract; or
   (b) if the buyer does not, within the additional period of time fixed by the seller in accordance with paragraph (1) of Article 63, perform his obligation to pay the price or take delivery of the goods, or if he declares that he will not do so within the period so fixed.

(2) However, in cases where the buyer has paid the price, the seller loses the right to declare the contract avoided unless he does so:

   (a) in respect of late performance by the buyer, before the seller has become aware that performance has been rendered; or
   (b) in respect of any breach other than late performance by the buyer, within a reasonable time:
      (i) after the seller knew or ought to have known of the breach; or
      (ii) after the expiration of any additional period of time fixed by the seller in accordance with

paragraph (1) of Article 63, or after the buyer has declared that he will not perform his obligations within such an additional period.

Article 65

(1) If under the contract the buyer is to specify the form, measurement or other features of the goods and he fails to make such specification either on the date agreed upon or within a reasonable time after receipt of a request from the seller, the seller may, without prejudice to any other rights he may have, make the specification himself in accordance with the requirements of the buyer that may be known to him.

(2) If the seller makes the specification himself, he must inform the buyer of the details thereof and must fix a reasonable time within which the buyer may make a different specification. If, after receipt of such a communication, the buyer fails to do so within the time so fixed, the specification made by the seller is binding.

Chapter IV Passing of Risk

Article 66 Loss of or damage to the goods after the risk has passed to the buyer does not discharge him from his obligation to pay the price, unless the loss or damage is due to an act or omission of the seller.

Article 67

(1) If the contract of sale involves carriage of the goods and the seller is not bound to hand them over at a particular place, the risk passes to the buyer when the goods are handed over to the first carrier for transmission to the buyer in accordance with the contract of sale. If the seller is bound to hand the goods over to a carrier at a particular place, the risk does not pass to the buyer until the goods are handed over to the carrier at that place. The fact that the seller is authorized to retain documents controlling the disposition of the goods does not affect the passage of the risk.

(2) Nevertheless, the risk does not pass to the buyer until the goods are clearly identified to the contract, whether by markings on the goods, by shipping documents, by notice given to the buyer or otherwise.

Article 68 The risk in respect of goods sold in transit passes to the buyer from the time of the conclusion of the contract. However, if the circumstances so indicate, the risk is assumed by the buyer from the time the goods were handed over to the carrier who issued the documents embodying the contract of carriage. Nevertheless, if at the time of the conclusion of the contract of sale the seller knew or ought to have known that the goods had been lost or damaged and did not disclose this to the buyer, the loss or damage is at the risk of the seller.

Article 69

(1) In cases not within Article 67 and 68, the risk passes to the buyer when he takes over the goods or, if he does not do so in due time, from the time when the goods are placed at his disposal and he commits a breach of contract by failing to take delivery.

(2) However, if the buyer is bound to take over the goods at a place other than a place of business of the seller, the risk passes when delivery is due and the buyer is aware of the fact that the goods are placed at his disposal at that place.

(3) If the contract relates to goods not then identified, the goods are considered not to be placed at the disposal of the buyer until they are clearly identified to the contract.

Article 70 If the seller has committed a fundamental breach of contract, Articles 67, 68 and 69 do not impair the remedies available to the buyer on account of the breach.

Chapter V Provisions Common to the Obligations of the Seller and of the Buyer

Section 1. Anticipatory breach and installment contracts

Article 71

(1) A party may suspend the performance of his obligations if, after the conclusion of the contract, it becomes apparent that the other party will not perform a substantial part of his obligations as a result of:

   (a) a serious deficiency in his ability to perform or in his creditworthiness; or
   (b) his conduct in preparing to perform or in performing the contract.

(2) If the seller has already dispatched the goods before the grounds described in the preceding paragraph become evident, he may prevent the handing over of the goods to the buyer even though the buyer holds a document which entitles him to obtain them. The present paragraph relates only to the rights in the goods as between the buyer and the seller.

(3) A party suspending performance, whether before or after dispatch of the goods, must immediately give notice of the suspension to the other party and must continue with performance if the other party provides adequate assurance of his performance.

Article 72

(1) If prior to the date for performance of the contract it is clear that one of the parties will commit a fundamental breach of contract, the other party may declare the contract avoided.

(2) If time allows, the party intending to declare the contract avoided must give reasonable notice to the other party in order to permit him to provide adequate assurance of his performance.

(3) The requirements of the preceding paragraph do not apply if the other party has declared that he will not perform his obligations.

Article 73

(1) In the case of a contract for delivery of goods by installments, if the failure of one party to perform any of his obligations in respect of any installment constitutes a fundamental breach of contract with respect to that installment, the other party may declare the contract avoided with respect to that installment.
(2) If one party's failure to perform any of his obligations in respect of any installment gives the other party good grounds to conclude that a fundamental breach of contract will occur with respect to future installments, he may declare the contract avoided for the future, provided that he does so within a reasonable time.
(3) A buyer who declares the contract avoided in respect of any delivery may, at the same time, declare it avoided in respect of deliveries already made or of future deliveries if, by reason of their interdependence, those deliveries could not be used for the purpose contemplated by the parties at the time of the conclusion of the contract.

Section II. Damages

Article 74 Damages for breach of contract by one party consist of a sum equal to the loss, including loss of profit, suffered by the other party as a consequence of the breach. Such damages may not exceed the loss which the party in breach foresaw or ought to have foreseen at the time of the conclusion of the contract, in the light of the facts and matters of which he then knew or ought to have known, as a possible consequence of the breach of contract.

Article 75 If the contract is avoided and if, in a reasonable manner and within a reasonable time after avoidance, the buyer has bought goods in replacement or the seller has resold the goods, the party claiming damages may recover the difference between the contract price and the price in the substitute transaction as well as any further damages recoverable under Article 74.

Article 76

(1) If the contract is avoided and there is a current price for the goods, the party claiming damages may, if he has not made a purchase or resale under Article 75, recover the difference between the price fixed by the contract and the current price at the time of avoidance as well as any further damages recoverable under Article 74. If, however, the party claiming damages has avoided the contract after taking over the goods, the current price at the time of such taking over shall be applied instead of the current price at the time of avoidance.

(2) For the purposes of the preceding paragraph, the current price is the price prevailing at the place where delivery of the goods should have been made or, if there is no current price at that place, the price at such other place as serves as a reasonable substitute, making due allowance for differences in the cost of transporting the goods.

Article 77

A party who relies on a breach of contract must take such measures as are reasonable in the circumstances to mitigate the loss, including loss of profit, resulting from the breach. If he fails to take such measures, the party in breach may claim a reduction in the damages in the amount by which the loss should have been mitigated.

Section III. Interest

Article 78 If a party fails to pay the price or any other sum that is in arrears, the other party is entitled to interest on it, without prejudice to any claim for damages recoverable under Article 74.

Section IV. Exemptions

Article 79

(1) A party is not liable for a failure to perform any of his obligations if he proves that the failure was due to an impediment beyond his control and that he could not reasonably be expected to have taken the impediment into account at the time of the conclusion of the contract or to have avoided or overcome it or its consequences.
(2) If the party's failure is due to the failure by a third person whom he has engaged to perform the whole or a part of the contract, that party is exempt from liability only if:
   (a) he is exempt under the preceding paragraph; and
   (b) the person whom he has so engaged would be so exempt if the provisions of that paragraph were applied to him.
(3) The exemption provided by this article has effect for the period during which the impediment exists.
(4) The party who fails to perform must give notice to the other party of the impediment and its effect on his ability to perform. If the notice is not received by the other party within a reasonable time after the party who fails to perform knew or ought to have known of the impediment, he is liable for damages resulting from such non-receipt.
(5) Nothing in this article prevents either party from exercising any right other than to claim damages under this Convention.

Article 80 A party may not rely on a failure of the other party to perform, to the extent that such failure was caused by the first party's act or omission.

Section V. Effects of avoidance

Article 81

(1) Avoidance of the contract releases both parties from their obligations under it, subject to any damages which may be due. Avoidance does not affect any provision of the contract for the settlement of disputes or any other provision of the contract governing the rights and obligations of the parties consequent upon the avoidance of the contract.

(2) A party who has performed the contract either wholly or in part may claim restitution from the other party of whatever the first party has supplied or paid under the contract. If both parties are bound to make restitution, they must do so concurrently.

Article 82

(1) The buyer loses the right to declare the contract avoided or to require the seller to deliver substitute goods if it is impossible for him to make restitution of the goods substantially in the condition in which he received them.

(2) The preceding paragraph does not apply:

 (a) if the impossibility of making restitution of the goods or of making restitution of the goods substantially in the condition in which the buyer received them is not due to his act or omission;

 (b) if the goods or part of the goods have perished or deteriorated as a result of the examination provided for in Article 38; or

 (c) if the goods or part of the goods have been sold in the normal course of business or have been consumed or transformed by the buyer in the course of normal use before he discovered or ought to have discovered the lack of conformity.

Article 83
A buyer who has lost the right to declare the contract avoided or to require the seller to deliver substitute goods in accordance with Article 82 retains all other remedies under the contract and this Convention.

Article 84

(1) If the seller is bound to refund the price, he must also pay interest on it, from the date on which the price was paid.

(2) The buyer must account to the seller for all benefits which he has derived from the goods or part of them:

 (a) if he must make restitution of the goods or part of them; or

 (b) if it is impossible for him to make restitution of all or part of the goods or to make restitution of all or part of the goods substantially in the condition in which he received them, but he has nevertheless declared the contract avoided or required the seller to deliver substitute goods.

Section VI. Preservation of the goods

Article 85
If the buyer is in delay in taking delivery of the goods or, where payment of the price and delivery of the goods are to be made concurrently, if he fails to pay the price, and the seller is either in possession of the goods or otherwise able to control their disposition, the seller must take such steps as are reasonable in the circumstances to preserve them. He is entitled to retain them until he has been reimbursed his reasonable expenses by the buyer.

Article 86

(1) If the buyer has received the goods and intends to exercise any right under the contract or this Convention to reject them, he must take such steps to preserve them as are reasonable in the circumstances. He is entitled to retain them until he has been reimbursed his reasonable expenses by the seller.

(2) If goods dispatched to the buyer have been placed at his disposal at their destination and he exercises the right to reject them, he must take possession of them on behalf of the seller, provided that this can be done without payment of the price and without unreasonable inconvenience or unreasonable expense. This provision does not apply if the seller or a person authorized to take charge of the goods on his behalf is present at the destination. If the buyer takes possession of the goods under this paragraph, his rights and obligations are governed by the preceding paragraph.

Article 87
A party who is bound to take steps to preserve the goods may deposit them in a warehouse of a third person at the expense of the other party provided that the expense incurred is not unreasonable.

Article 88

(1) A party who is bound to preserve the goods in accordance with Article 85 or 86 may sell them by any appropriate means if there has been an unreasonable delay by the other party in taking possession of the goods or in taking them back or in paying the price or the cost of preservation, provided that reasonable notice of the intention to sell has been given to the other party.

(2) If the goods are subject to rapid deterioration or their preservation would involve unreasonable expense, a party who is bound to preserve the goods in accordance with Article 85 or 86 must take reasonable measures to sell them. To the extent possible he must give notice to the other party of his intention to sell.

(3) A party selling the goods has the right to retain out of the proceeds of sale an amount equal to the reasonable expenses of preserving the goods and of selling them. He must account to the other party for the balance.

Part IV Final Provisions

Article 89 The Secretary-General of the United Nations is hereby designated as the depositary for this Convention.

Article 90 This Convention does not prevail over any international agreement which has already been or may be entered into and which contains provisions concerning the matters governed by this Convention, provided that the parties have their places of business in States parties to such agreement.

Article 91

(1) This Convention is open for signature at the concluding meeting of the United Nations Conference on Contracts for the International Sale of Goods and will remain open for signature by all States at the Headquarters of the United Nations, New York, until 30 September 1981.

(2) This Convention is subject to ratification, acceptance or approval by the signatory States.

(3) This Convention is open for accession by all States which are not signatory States as from the date it is open for signature.

(4) Instruments of ratification, acceptance, approval and accession are to be deposited with the Secretary-General of the United Nations.

Article 92

(1) A Contracting State may declare at the time of signature, ratification, acceptance, approval or accession that it will not be bound by Part II of this Convention or that it will not be bound by Part III of this Convention.

(2) A Contracting State which makes a declaration in accordance with the preceding paragraph in respect of Part II or Part III of this Convention is not to be considered a Contracting State within paragraph (1) of Article 1 of this Convention in respect of matters governed by the Part to which the declaration applies.

Article 93

(1) If a Contracting State has two or more territorial units in which, according to its constitution, different systems of law are applicable in relation to the matters dealt with in this Convention, it may, at the time of signature, ratification, acceptance, approval or accession, declare that this Convention is to extend to all its territorial units or only to one or more of them, and may amend its declaration by submitting another declaration at any time.

(2) These declarations are to be notified to the depositary and are to state expressly the territorial units to which the Convention extends.

(3) If, by virtue of a declaration under this article, this Convention extends to one or more but not all of the territorial units of a Contracting State, and if the place of business of a party is located in that State, this place of business, for the purposes of this Convention, is considered not to be in a Contracting State, unless it is in a territorial unit to which the Convention extends.

(4) If a Contracting State makes no declaration under paragraph (1) of this article, the Convention is to extend to all territorial units of that State.

Article 94

(1) Two or more Contracting States which have the same or closely related legal rules on matters governed by this Convention may at any time declare that the Convention is not to apply to contracts of sale or to their formation where the parties have their places of business in those States. Such declarations may be made jointly or by reciprocal unilateral declarations.

(2) A Contracting State which has the same or closely related legal rules on matters governed by this Convention as one or more non-Contracting States may at any time declare that the Convention is not to apply to contracts of sale or to their formation where the parties have their places of business in those States.

(3) If a State which is the object of a declaration under the preceding paragraph subsequently becomes a Contracting State, the declaration made will, as from the date on which the Convention enters into force in respect of the new Contracting State, have the effect of a declaration made under paragraph (1), provided that the new Contracting State joins in such declaration or makes a reciprocal unilateral declaration.

Article 95 Any State may declare at the time of the deposit of its instrument of ratification, acceptance, approval or accession that it will not be bound by subparagraph (1)(b) of Article 1 of this Convention. [The United States has made such reservation.]

Article 96 A Contracting State whose legislation requires contracts of sale to be concluded in or evidenced by writing may at any time make a declaration in accordance with Article 12 that any provision of Article 11, Article 29, or Part II of this Convention, that allows a contract of sale or its modification or termination by agreement or any offer, acceptance, or other indication of intention to be made in any form other than in writing, does not apply where any party has his place of business in that State.

Article 97

(1) Declarations made under this Convention at the time of signature are subject to confirmation upon ratification, acceptance or approval.

(2) Declarations and confirmations of declarations are to be in writing and be formally notified to the depositary.

(3) A declaration takes effect simultaneously with the entry into force of this Convention in respect of the State concerned. However, a declaration of which the depositary receives formal notification after such entry into force takes effect on the first day of the month following the expiration of six months after the date of its receipt by the depositary. Reciprocal unilateral declarations under Article 94 take effect on the first day of the month following the expiration of six months after the receipt of the latest declaration by the depositary.

(4) Any State which makes a declaration under this Convention may withdraw it at any time by a formal notification in writing addressed to the depositary. Such withdrawal is to take effect on the first day of the month following the expiration of six months after the date of the receipt of the notification by the depositary.

(5) A withdrawal of a declaration made under Article 94 renders inoperative, as from the date on which the withdrawal takes effect, any reciprocal declaration made by another State under that article.

Article 98 No reservations are permitted except those expressly authorized in this Convention.

Article 99

(1) This Convention enters into force, subject to the provisions of paragraph (6) of this article, on the first day of the month following the expiration of twelve months after the date of deposit of the tenth instrument of ratification, acceptance, approval or accession, including an instrument which contains a declaration made under Article 92.

(2) When a State ratifies, accepts, approves or accedes to this Convention after the deposit of the tenth instrument of ratification, acceptance, approval or accession, this Convention, with the exception of the Part excluded, enters into force in respect of that State, subject to the provisions of paragraph (6) of this article, on the first day of the month following the expiration of twelve months after the date of the deposit of its instrument of ratification, acceptance, approval or accession.

(3) A State which ratifies, accepts, approves or accedes to this Convention and is a party to either or both the Convention relating to a Uniform Law on the Formation of Contracts for the International Sale of Goods done at The Hague on 1 July 1964 (1964 Hague Formation Convention) and the Convention relating to a Uniform Law on the International Sale of Goods done at The Hague on 1 July 1964 (1964 Hague Sales Convention) shall at the same time denounce, as the case may be, either or both the 1964 Hague Sales Convention and the 1964 Hague Formation Convention by notifying the Government of the Netherlands to that effect.

(4) A State party to the 1964 Hague Sales Convention which ratifies, accepts, approves or accedes to the present Convention and declares or has declared under Article 92 that it will not be bound by Part II of this Convention shall at the time of ratification, acceptance, approval or accession denounce the 1964 Hague Sales Convention by notifying the Government of the Netherlands to that effect.

(5) A State party to the 1964 Hague Formation Convention which ratifies, accepts, approves or accedes to the present Convention and declares or has declared under Article 92 that it will not be bound by Part III of this Convention shall at the time of ratification, acceptance, approval or accession denounce the 1964 Hague Formation Convention by notifying the Government of the Netherlands to that effect.

(6) For the purpose of this article, ratifications, acceptances, approvals and accessions in respect of this Convention by States parties to the 1964 Hague Formation Convention or to the 1964 Hague Sales Convention shall not be effective until such denunciations as may be required on the part of those States in respect of the latter two Conventions have themselves become effective. The depositary of this Convention shall consult with the Government of the Netherlands, as the depositary of the 1964 Conventions, so as to ensure necessary co-ordination in this respect.

Article 100

(1) This Convention applies to the formation of a contract only when the proposal for concluding the contract is made on or after the date when the Convention enters into force in respect of the Contracting States referred to in subparagraph (1)(a) or the Contracting States referred to in subparagraph (1)(b) of Article 1.

(2) This Convention applies only to contracts concluded on or after the date when the Convention enters into force in respect of the Contracting States referred to in subparagraph (1)(a) or the Contracting State referred to in subparagraph (1)(b) of Article 1.

Article 101

(1) A Contracting State may denounce this Convention, or Part II or Part III of the Convention, by a formal notification in writing addressed to the depositary.

(2) The denunciation takes effect on the first day of the month following the expiration of twelve months after the notification is received by the depositary. Where a longer period for the denunciation to take effect is specified in the notification, the denunciation takes effect upon the expiration of such longer period after the notification is received by the depositary.

DONE at Vienna, this day of eleventh day of April, one thousand nine hundred and eighty, in a single original, of which the Arabic, Chinese, English, French, Russian and Spanish texts are equally authentic.

IN WITNESS WHEREOF the undersigned plenipotentiaries, being duly authorized by their respective Governments, have signed this Convention.

Appendix D: Patrick Henry's Tax Assessment Bill and James Madison's "Memorial and Remonstrance"

A Bill Establishing a Provision for Teachers of the Christian Religion (The Tax Assessment Bill)

Submitted by Patrick Henry

Whereas the general diffusion of Christian knowledge hath a natural tendency to correct the morals of men, restrain their vices, and preserve the peace of society; which cannot be effected without a competent provision for learned teachers, who may be thereby enabled to devote their time and attention to the duty of instructing such citizens, as from their circumstances and want of education, cannot otherwise attain such knowledge; and it is judged that such provision may be made by the Legislature, without counteracting the liberal principle heretofore adopted and intended to be preserved by abolishing all distinctions of pre-eminence amongst the different societies or communities of Christians;

Be it therefore enacted by the General Assembly, that for the support of Christian teachers,—per centum on the amount, or—in the pound on the sum payable for tax on the property within this Commonwealth, is hereby assessed, and shall be paid by every person chargeable with the said tax at the time the same shall become due; and the Sheriffs of the several Counties shall have power to levy and collect the same in the same manner and under the like restrictions and limitations, as are or may be prescribed by the laws for raising the Revenues of this State.

And be it enacted, That for every sum so paid, the Sheriff or Collector shall give a receipt, expressing therein to what society of Christians the person from whom he may receive the same shall direct the money to be paid, keeping a distinct account thereof in his books. The Sheriff of every County, shall, on or before the __ day of __ in every year, return to the Court, upon oath, two alphabetical lists of the payments to him made, distinguishing in columns opposite to the names of the persons who shall have paid the same, the society to which the money so paid was by them appropriated; and one column for the names where no appropriation shall be made. One of which lists, after being recorded in a book to be kept for that purpose, shall be filed by the Clerk in his office; the other shall be the Sheriff be fixed up in the Court-house, there to remain for the inspection of all concerned.

And the Sheriff, after deducting five per centum for the collection, shall forthwith pay to such person or persons as shall be appointed to receive the same by the Vestry, Elders, or Directors, however, denominated of each such society, the sum so stated to be due to that society; or in default thereof, upon the motion of such person or persons to the next or any succeeding Court, execution shall be awarded for the same against the Sheriff and his security, his and their executors or administrators; provided that ten days previous notice be given of such motion. An upon every such execution, the Officer serving the same shall proceed to immediate sale of the estate taken, and shall not accept of security for payment at the end of three months, nor to have the goods forthcoming at the day of sale; for his better direction wherein, the Clerk shall endorse upon every such execution that no security of any kind shall be taken.

And be it further enacted, That the money to be raised by virtue of this Act, shall be by the Vestres, Elders, or Directors of each religious society, appropriated to a provision for a Minister or Teacher of the Gospel of their denomination, or the providing place of divine worship, and to none other use whatsoever; except in the denominations of Quakers and Menonists, who may receive what is collected from their members, and place it in their general fund, to be disposed of in a manner which they shall think best calculated to promote their particular mode of worship.

And be it enacted, That all sums which at the time of payment to the Sheriff or Collector may not be appropriated by the person paying the same, shall be accounted for with the Court in manner as by this Act is directed; and after deducting for his collection, the Sheriff shall pay the amount thereof (upon account certified by the Court to the Auditors of Public Accounts, and by them to the Treasurer) into the public Treasury, to be disposed of under the direction of the General Assembly, for the encouragement of seminaries of learning within the Counties whence such sums shall arise, and to no other use or purpose whatsoever.

Memorial and Remonstrance against Religious Assessments– Full Text

By James Madison

To the Honorable the General Assembly of the Commonwealth of Virginia A Memorial and Remonstrance

We the subscribers, citizens of the said Commonwealth, having taken into serious consideration, a Bill printed by order of the last Session of General Assembly, entitled "A Bill establishing a provision for Teachers of the Christian Religion," and conceiving that the same if finally armed with the sanctions of a law, will be a dangerous abuse of power, are bound as faithful members of a free State to remonstrate against it, and to declare the reasons by which we are determined. We remonstrate against the said Bill,

(1) Because we hold it for a fundamental and undeniable truth, "that Religion or the duty which we owe to our Creator and the manner of discharging it, can be directed only by reason and conviction, not by force or violence." [Virginia Declaration of Rights, art. 16] The Religion then of every man must be left to the conviction and conscience of every man; and it is the right of every man to exercise it as these may dictate. This right is in its nature an unalienable right. It is unalienable, because the opinions of men, depending only on the evidence contemplated by their own minds cannot follow the dictates of other men: It is unalienable also, because what is here a right towards men, is a duty towards the Creator. It is the duty of every man to render to the Creator such homage and such only as he believes to be acceptable to him. This duty is precedent, both in order of time and in degree of obligation, to the claims of Civil Society. Before any man can be considered as a member of Civil Society, he must be considered as a subject of the Governour of the Universe: And if a member of Civil Society, who enters into any subordinate Association, must always do it with a reservation of his duty to the General Authority; much more must every man who becomes a member of any particular Civil Society, do it with a saving of his allegiance to the Universal Sovereign. We maintain therefore that in matters of Religion, no man's right is abridged by the institution of Civil Society and that Religion is wholly exempt from its cognizance. True it is, that no other rule exists, by which any question which may divide a Society, can be ultimately determined, but the will of the majority; but it is also true that the majority may trespass on the rights of the minority.

(2) Because if Religion be exempt from the authority of the Society at large, still less can it be subject to that of the Legislative Body. The latter are but the creatures and vicegerents of the former. Their jurisdiction is both derivative and limited: it is limited with regard to the co-ordinate departments, more necessarily is it limited with regard to the constituents. The preservation of a free Government requires not merely, that the metes and bounds which separate each department of power be invariably maintained; but more especially that neither of them be suffered to overleap the great Barrier which defends the rights of the people. The Rulers who are guilty of such an encroachment, exceed the commission from which they derive their authority, and are Tyrants. The People who submit to it are governed by laws made neither by themselves nor by an authority derived from them, and are slaves.

(3) Because it is proper to take alarm at the first experiment on our liberties. We hold this prudent jealousy to be the first duty of Citizens, and one of the noblest characteristics of the late Revolution. The free men of America did not wait till usurped power had strengthened itself by exercise, and entangled the question in precedents. They saw all the consequences in the principle, and they avoided the consequences by denying the principle. We revere this lesson too much soon to forget it. Who does not see that the same authority which can establish Christianity, in exclusion of all other Religions, may establish with the same ease any particular sect of Christians, in exclusion of all other Sects? That the same authority which can force a citizen to contribute three pence only of his property for the support of any one establishment, may force him to conform to any other establishment in all cases whatsoever?

(4) Because the Bill violates that equality which ought to be the basis of every law, and which is more indispensible, in proportion as the validity or expediency of any law is more liable to be impeached. If "all men are by nature equally free and independent," [Virginia Declaration of Rights, art. 1] all men are to be considered as entering into Society on equal conditions; as relinquishing no more, and therefore retaining no less, one than another, of their natural rights. Above all are they to be considered as retaining an "equal title to the free exercise of Religion according to the dictates of Conscience." [Virginia Declaration of Rights, art. 16] Whilst we assert for ourselves a freedom to embrace, to profess and to observe the Religion which we believe to be of divine origin, we cannot deny an equal freedom to those whose minds have not yet yielded to the evidence which has convinced us. If this freedom be abused, it is an offence against God, not against man: To God, therefore, not to man, must an account of it be rendered. As the Bill violates equality by subjecting some to peculiar burdens, so it violates the same principle, by granting to others peculiar exemptions. Are the Quakers and Menonists the only sects who think a compulsive support of their Religions unnecessary and unwarrantable? Can their piety alone be entrusted with the care of public worship? Ought their Religions to be endowed above all others with extraordinary privileges by which proselytes may be enticed from all others? We think too favorably of the justice and good sense of these denominations to believe that they either covet pre-eminences over their fellow citizens or that they will be seduced by them from the common opposition to the measure.

(5) Because the Bill implies either that the Civil Magistrate is a competent Judge of Religious Truth; or that he may employ Religion as an engine of Civil policy. The first is an arrogant pretension falsified by the contradictory opinions of Rulers in all ages, and throughout the world: the second an unhallowed perversion of the means of salvation.

(6) Because the establishment proposed by the Bill is not requisite for the support of the Christian Religion. To say that it is, is a contradiction to the Christian Religion itself, for every page of it disavows a dependence on the powers of this world: it is a contradiction to fact; for it is known that this Religion both existed and flourished, not only without the support of human laws, but in spite of every opposition from them, and not only during the period of miraculous aid, but long after it had been left to its own evidence and the ordinary care of Providence. Nay, it is a contradiction in terms; for a Religion not invented by human policy, must have pre-existed and been supported, before it was established by human policy. It is moreover to weaken in those who profess this Religion a pious confidence in its innate excellence and the patronage of its Author; and to foster in those who still reject it, a suspicion that its friends are too conscious of its fallacies to trust it to its own merits.

(7) Because experience witnesseth that ecclesiastical establishments, instead of maintaining the purity and efficacy of Religion, have had a contrary operation. During almost fifteen centuries has the legal establishment of Christianity been on trial. What have been its fruits? More or less in all places, pride and indolence in the Clergy, ignorance and servility in the laity, in both, superstition, bigotry and persecution. Enquire of the Teachers of Christianity for the ages in which it appeared in its greatest lustre; those of every sect, point to the ages prior to its incorporation with Civil policy. Propose a restoration of this primitive State in which its Teachers depended on the voluntary rewards of their flocks, many of them predict its downfall. On which Side ought their testimony to have greatest weight, when for or when against their interest?

(8) Because the establishment in question is not necessary for the support of Civil Government. If it be urged as necessary for the support of Civil Government only as it is a means of supporting Religion, and it be not necessary for the latter purpose, it cannot be necessary for the former. If Religion be not within the cognizance of Civil Government how can its legal establishment be necessary to Civil Government? What influence in fact have ecclesiastical establishments had on Civil Society? In some instances they have been seen to erect a spiritual tyranny on the ruins of the Civil authority; in many instances they have been seen upholding the thrones of political tyranny: in no instance have they been seen the guardians of the liberties of the people. Rulers who wished to subvert the public liberty, may have found an established Clergy convenient auxiliaries. A just Government instituted to secure & perpetuate it needs them not. Such a Government will be best supported by protecting every Citizen in the enjoyment of his Religion with the same equal hand which protects his person and his property; by neither invading the equal rights of any Sect, nor suffering any Sect to invade those of another.

(9) Because the proposed establishment is a departure from that generous policy, which, offering an Asylum to the persecuted and oppressed of every Nation and Religion, promised a lustre to our country, and an accession to the number of its citizens. What a melancholy mark is the Bill of sudden degeneracy? Instead of holding forth an Asylum to the persecuted, it is itself a signal of persecution. It degrades from the equal rank of Citizens all those whose opinions in Religion do not bend to those of the Legislative authority. Distant as it may be in its present form from the Inquisition, it differs from it only in degree. The one is the first step, the other the last in the career of intolerance. The magnanimous sufferer under this cruel scourge in foreign Regions, must view the Bill as a Beacon on our Coast, warning him to seek some other haven, where liberty and philanthrophy in their due extent, may offer a more certain repose from his Troubles.

(10) Because it will have a like tendency to banish our Citizens. The allurements presented by other situations are every day thinning their number. To superadd a fresh motive to emigration by revoking the liberty which they now enjoy, would be the same species of folly which has dishonoured and depopulated flourishing kingdoms.

(11) Because it will destroy that moderation and harmony which the forbearance of our laws to intermeddle with Religion has produced among its several sects. Torrents of blood have been spilt in the old world, by vain attempts of the secular arm, to extinguish Religious discord, by proscribing all difference in Religious opinion. Time has at length revealed the true remedy. Every relaxation of narrow and rigorous policy, wherever it has been tried, has been found to assuage the disease. The American Theatre has exhibited proofs that equal and compleat liberty, if it does not wholly eradicate it, sufficiently destroys its malignant influence on the health and prosperity of the State. If with the salutary effects of this system under our own eyes, we begin to contract the bounds of Religious freedom, we know no name that will too severely reproach

our folly. At least let warning be taken at the first fruits of the threatened innovation. The very appearance of the Bill has transformed "that Christian forbearance, love and charity," [Virginia Declaration of Rights, art. 16] which of late mutually prevailed, into animosities and jealousies, which may not soon be appeased. What mischiefs may not be dreaded, should this enemy to the public quiet be armed with the force of a law?

(12) Because the policy of the Bill is adverse to the diffusion of the light of Christianity. The first wish of those who enjoy this precious gift ought to be that it may be imparted to the whole race of mankind. Compare the number of those who have as yet received it with the number still remaining under the dominion of false Religions; and how small is the former! Does the policy of the Bill tend to lessen the disproportion? No; it at once discourages those who are strangers to the light of revelation from coming into the Region of it; and countenances by example the nations who continue in darkness, in shutting out those who might convey it to them. Instead of Levelling as far as possible, every obstacle to the victorious progress of Truth, the Bill with an ignoble and unchristian timidity would circumscribe it with a wall of defence against the encroachments of error.

(13) Because attempts to enforce by legal sanctions, acts obnoxious to so great a proportion of Citizens, tend to enervate the laws in general, and to slacken the bands of Society. If it be difficult to execute any law which is not generally deemed necessary or salutary, what must be the case, where it is deemed invalid and dangerous? And what may be the effect of so striking an example of impotency in the Government, on its general authority?

(14) Because a measure of such singular magnitude and delicacy ought not to be imposed, without the clearest evidence that it is called for by a majority of citizens, and no satisfactory method is yet proposed by which the voice of the majority in this case may be determined, or its influence secured. "The people of the respective counties are indeed requested to signify their opinion respecting the adoption of the Bill to the next Session of Assembly." But the representation must be made equal, before the voice either of the Representatives or of the Counties will be that of the people. Our hope is that neither of the former will, after due consideration, espouse the dangerous principle of the Bill. Should the event disappoint us, it will still leave us in full confidence, that a fair appeal to the latter will reverse the sentence against our liberties.

(15) Because finally, "the equal right of every citizen to the free exercise of his Religion according to the dictates of conscience" is held by the same tenure with all our other rights. If we recur to its origin, it is equally the gift of nature; if we weigh its importance, it cannot be less dear to us; if we consult the "Declaration of those rights which pertain to the good people of Virginia, as the basis and foundation of Government," it is enumerated with equal solemnity, or rather studied emphasis. Either then, we must say, that the Will of the Legislature is the only measure of their authority; and that in the plenitude of this authority, they may sweep away all our fundamental rights; or, that they are bound to leave this particular right untouched and sacred: Either we must say, that they may controul the freedom of the press, may abolish the Trial by Jury, may swallow up the Executive and Judiciary Powers of the State; nay that they may despoil us of our very right of suffrage, and erect themselves into an independent and hereditary Assembly or, we must say, that they have no authority to enact into law the Bill under consideration. We the Subscribers say, that the General Assembly of this Commonwealth have no such authority: And that no effort may be omitted on our part against so dangerous an usurpation, we oppose to it, this remonstrance; earnestly praying, as we are in duty bound, that the Supreme Lawgiver of the Universe, by illuminating those to whom it is addressed, may on the one hand, turn their Councils from every act which would affront his holy prerogative, or violate the trust committed to them: and on the other, guide them into every measure which may be worthy of his blessing, may redound to their own praise, and may establish more firmly the liberties, the prosperity and the happiness of the Commonwealth.

Glossary

abandoned In contract law, the condition that exists when a minor has left home and given up all rights to parental support.

abandoned property Property that has been discarded by the owner without the intent to reclaim ownership of it. Courts require clear and convincing evidence of both the desertion by the owner and the owner's intent never to return.

abandonment of contractual obligations The situation that exists when a party to a contract stops performance once it has begun.

abuse of discretion The determination that the judge in the lower court has misused his or her authority.

abuse of process The use of a legal procedure for a purpose other than that for which it is legitimately intended.

acceleration A provision in a mortgage agreement that allows the mortgagee to demand the entire balance due when the mortgagor misses a single installment payment.

acceptance A promise or act on the part of an offeree indicating a willingness to be bound by the terms and conditions contained in an offer. Also, the acknowledgment of the drawee that binds the drawee to the terms of a draft.

acceptor A drawee of a draft who has promised to honor the draft as presented by signing it on its face.

accord The implied or expressed acceptance of less than what the creditor billed the debtor.

accord and satisfaction An agreement (accord) whereby a creditor accepts as full payment an amount that is less than the amount due.

accountant A professional who can plan, direct, and evaluate a client's financial affairs.

acknowledgment The official recognition by a notary public that another's signature was made by that party's free will. The acknowledgment is accomplished when the notary has signed the document and added the official seal to it.

active fraud A false statement made or an action actually taken by one party with the intent to deceive a second party and thus lead that second party into a deceptively based agreement.

activist agencies Agencies that use their regulatory powers to advance social agendas that are technically outside their legislative authority.

actual authority rule A rule that states a manager may be liable for exceeding his or her authority if the corporation is harmed as a result.

actual cause In tort law, the relationship between the unreasonable conduct and the injury to the innocent party, whether the injury was or was not foreseeable. Actual cause is also referred to as cause in fact.

actual damages A sum of money equal to the real financial loss suffered by an injured party. Also called *compensatory damages.*

actual eviction An eviction in which the tenant is physically deprived of the leasehold.

actual malice The legal test used by the courts to determine defamation against a public official or a public figure. The actual malice test requires the public official or public figure to prove not only that the statement was false, negative, and communicated to a third party, but also that it was made with the knowledge that it was false or with a reckless disregard for its truth or falsity.

actual malice test A defense against libel cases that states public officials must prove not only that the statement was false, negative, and communicated to a third party, but was also made with actual malice.

actual privity Privity between a client and an accountant that results from a type one accounting arrangements.

add-on coverage In insurance law, optional coverage, such as personal injury insurance, that allows a driver to receive payments without having to determine fault.

adhesion contract A contract drawn by one party that must be accepted on a take-it-or-leave-it basis.

adjustable rate mortgage (ARM) In property law, a variable or changing rate of interest in a mortgage agreement that fluctuates based on the index (the bank's prime rate or the Federal Reserve's discount rate, and so on) to which the mortgage is tied.

administrative law That body of law, including decrees and legal decisions, generated by administrative agencies.

administrator A person appointed by a court to manage the estate of a decedent.

administrator (male); administratrix (female) A person appointed by the court to do the work of an executor if none is named in a will or if the executor either refuses to perform or is incapable of performing the duties.

admiralty court In the historical development of the law merchant, a local court established by a coastal city, usually in Italy, to handle commercial disputes regarding goods carried as cargo by ships docked at the city's port.

ADR contract clause A clause that specifies that the parties to the agreement have promised to use an alternative dispute resolution technique when a disagreement arises rather than litigating the issue.

advance directives Written statement in which people gives instructions for their future medical care.

adverse opinion An auditor's opinion that states that deviations from generally accepted accounting principles are so serious that an unqualified opinion is impossible and a qualified opinion is not justified.

adverse possession Title to real property obtained by taking actual possession of the property openly, notoriously, exclusively, under a claim of right, and continuously for a period of time set by state statute.

affirmance See *ratification*.

affirmative action A policy designed to reduce the effects of past discrimination.

affirmative defense A set of circumstances that indicates that a defendant should not be held liable, even if the plaintiff proves all of the facts in a complaint.

agency A legal agreement between two persons, whereby one is designated the agent of the other.

agency coupled with an interest An irrevocable agency agreement in which the agent is given an interest in the subject matter of the agency. Also called *irrevocable agency*.

agent A person authorized to act on behalf of another and subject to the other's control in dealing with third parties.

aggravated arson In criminal law, using fire or explosives to create a substantial risk of harm to an individual or an occupied structure, often also including the hiring of another person to carry out the offense.

aggravated burglary In criminal law, gaining unlawful entry to an occupied building by using a deadly weapon, inflicting actual harm, attempting to harm, or threatening to harm, with the intent to commit a crime.

aggravated murder In criminal law, killing someone with premeditation or with prior calculation and design, or while committing a serious felony such as rape, robbery, or kidnapping.

aggravated robbery In criminal law, attempting to commit or actually committing theft using a deadly weapon or a dangerous ordnance, or doing the same by inflicting harm on the victim.

aggregate theory A theory in partnership law that holds that a partnership is actually a conglomeration of the partners rather than a separate legal person with its own legal identity.

alien corporation A corporation that though incorporated in a foreign country does business in the United States.

allonge A strip of paper attached to a negotiable instrument for the writing of indorsements.

alter ego In corporate law, a subsidiary corporation set up by a parent corporation to do the bidding of the original parent corporation.

alternative dispute resolution (ADR) A process that occurs whenever individuals attempt to resolve a disagreement by stepping outside the usual adversarial system and applying creative settlement techniques, many of which have fact-finding and the discovery of truth as their goal.

American Law Institute (ALI) test A test under which a criminal defendant will be judged not guilty by reason of insanity "as a result of mental disease or defect he lacks substantial capacity either to appreciate the criminality of his conduct or to conform his conduct to the requirements of the law."

anatomical gift A donation made in advance, usually by notification on a state driver's license or a state ID, that indicates a person's desire to donate all or part of his or her body after death for the purpose of transplantation, treatment, research, or training.

annual percentage rate (APR) The true rate of interest on a loan.

annuity A guaranteed retirement income.

answer A defendant's official response to a complaint.

antenuptial agreement In contract law, a written agreement between two people planning marriage, who agree in writing to change the property rights they possess by law.

anticipatory breach A breach that occurs when a party to a contract either expresses or clearly implies an intention not to perform the contract even before being required to act. Also called *constructive breach*.

Antitrust Procedures and Penalties Act In federal antitrust law, a federal statute that regulates the Department of Justice's antitrust consent decrees.

apparent authority An accountability doctrine whereby a principal, by virtue of words or actions, leads a third party to believe that an agent has authority but no such authority was intended. Also called *ostensible authority* and *agency by estoppel*.

appeal The referral of a case to a higher court for review.

appellate jurisdiction The power of a court to review a case for errors.

appretiare According to Kropotkin, it is doing one's duty in a cooperative and nonselfish way, creating harmony in the society, evoking thanks and appreciation from other members of that society, and giving each person a feeling of self-worth that goes way beyond anything that mere money can do.

arbitration The process by which an outside party settles a dispute between two other parties.

arbitration clause A clause that will generally have the buyers give up their right to file a lawsuit, replacing that right with mandatory binding arbitration.

arbitrator The third party in the arbitration procedure whose job is to settle the dispute.

arraignment A formal court proceeding during which the defendant, after hearing the indictment or information read, pleads either guilty or not guilty.

arson The willful or malicious act of causing the burning of another's property.

Article II executive order An Article II executive order is one based on presidential authority as it appears in the Constitution.

Articles of Confederation The first constitution of the United States; replaced by the U.S. Constitution in 1787.

articles of incorporation A written application to a state for permission to incorporate.

articles of organization The written application to the state for permission to form a limited liability company.

assault Threatening immediate bodily harm to another person with the apparent, present ability to carry out that harm or, more simply, the attempt to commit a battery.

assault An attempt to commit a battery.

asset acquisition The purchase of all the property of a corporation by another corporation.

asset-backed securities In property law, lending money by establishing a security interest in goods such as cars, furniture, boats, and so on.

assignee A person to whom an assignment is made.

assignment The transfer of a contract right from one person to another.

assignor A person who assigns rights or delegates duties under an assignment.

associated persons and forces According to AUMF-2015, "Individuals and organizations fighting for, on behalf of, or alongside ISIL or any closely-related successor entity in hostilities against the United States or its coalition partners."

associative corporativism The process of doing business as a self-governing business association, that is, as a corporation. Also known as *corporativism*.

assume the mortgage An agreement whereby the buyer of real property already mortgaged agrees to pay the mortgage.

assumption of the risk A defense against negligence that states the victim voluntarily exposed him- or herself to a known risk.

ATM card A card used together with a personal identification number (PIN) to gain access to an automatic teller machine (ATM).

attachment The act of taking a person's property and bringing it into the custody of law.

attenuation doctrine An exception to the exclusionary rule, if a set of legally valid events intervenes between the unlawful search, and the discovery of evidence, the exclusionary rule has not been violated and, because there is no poisonous tree, there can be no poisonous fruit.

attorney–client privilege The guarantee that information that passes between clients and attorneys remains secret.

auction A sale that is open to the public, during which potential buyers compete for the right to purchase certain items by placing higher and higher bids until the highest bid is reached and the auctioneer accepts on behalf of the seller.

auction with reserve An auction at which the auctioneer has the right to withdraw goods and not sell them if acceptable bids are not made.

auction without reserve An auction at which the auctioneer cannot withdraw goods unless no bid is made within a reasonable time.

audit An examination of the financial records of an organization to determine whether those records are a fair representation of the actual financial health of the institution.

audit committee A corporate committee that consists of independent members who oversee the accounting firm that audits the corporation.

auditor The accountant who examines the financial records of an organization to determine whether those records are a fair representation of the actual financial health of the institution.

authoritarianism A political ideology that supports the notion that political power belongs in the hands of a few or even in the hands of one political figure.

Authorization for the Use of Military Force of 2015 (AUMF) An attempt by the president to extend the military power of the commander-in-chief.

automatic stay A self-operating postponement of collection proceedings against a debtor who has filed a petition for bankruptcy.

bailee The person to whom personal property is transferred under a contract of bailment.

bailment The transfer of possession and control of personal property to another with the intent that the same property will be returned later.

bailor The person who transfers personal property under a contract of bailment.

bait-and-switch confidence game An illegal promotional practice in which a seller attracts consumers by promoting a product (bait) that he or she does not intend to sell and then directs the consumers' attention to a higher-priced product (switch).

balloon payment A large final payment on a mortgage that has relatively low fixed payments during the life of the mortgage.

balloon-payment mortgage A mortgage that has relatively low fixed payments during the life of the mortgage followed by one large final (balloon) payment.

bank According to the Uniform Commercial Code a bank is "any person who engages in the business if banking" (UCC Section 1-201 (4)).

bank draft A check drawn by one bank on another bank in which it has funds on deposit in favor of a third person, the payee. Also called *teller's check*.

bargain-and-sale deed A deed that transfers title to real property but contains no warranties. This type of deed is not valid without consideration.

bargained-for exchange In reference to agreements, when a promise is made in exchange for another promise, in exchange for an act, or in exchange for a forbearance to act.

bargaining unit Employees joined together for the purpose of collective bargaining.

battered spouse syndrome A defense to criminal liability available to defendants if they can prove that they believed the only way to escape death or severe bodily injury was to use force against their tormentors.

battery The unlawful touching of another person.

bearer A person who is in possession of a negotiable instrument that is payable to the "bearer" or "cash" or that has been indorsed in blank.

bearer paper An instrument payable to bearer or cash that may be negotiated by delivery only.

beneficiary A third party receiving benefits from a contract made between two other parties. Also, the person named in an insurance policy to receive benefits paid by the insurer in event of a claim.

benefit corporation A dual-purpose entity that seeks to achieve both a benefit for the public and a profit for its owners.

bequest Personal property left in a will. Also called *legacy*.

best evidence rule The legal rule that holds that the courts generally accept into evidence only the original of a writing, not a copy.

best-price rule Rules that prohibit suitors from offering different prices to different shareholders during a tender offer process.

bilateral contract A contract in which both parties make promises.

bilateral mistake In contract law, a mistake made by both parties to a contract. Bilateral mistake allows rescission by either party. Also called *mutual mistake*.

bill of exchange See *draft*.

bill of sale A written statement evidencing the transfer of personal property from one person to another.

binder An oral or a written memorandum of an agreement for insurance intended to provide temporary insurance coverage until the policy is formally accepted.

binding precedent A previous case that a particular court must follow.

biogetic system A socioeconomic, cultural system created by humans, which has taken on a life of its own.

bitcoin Both a digital currency (i.e., cyber-currency or e-currency) and, at the same time, a digital exchange system (i.e., cyber-currency exchange system or e-currency exchange system or cyber exchange system) that allows people to buy and sell online.

blank indorsement An indorsement made by a signature alone, with no particular indorsee, written on a negotiable instrument.

blended contract In contract law, a binding agreement that has enough characteristic of a sales contract and a service contract to be considered a combination of both. See also *mixed contract* and *hybrid contract*.

blue laws State statutes and local ordinances that regulate the making and performing of contracts on Sunday.

bodily injury liability insurance A type of automobile insurance that covers the risk of bodily injury or death to pedestrians and to the occupants of other cars arising from the negligent operation of the insured's motor vehicle.

bond A certificate of indebtedness that obligates a government or corporation to pay the bondholder a fixed rate of interest on the principal at regular intervals and to pay the principal on a stated maturity date. Also, a promise by the executor or administrator (and the sureties, if any) of a will to pay the amount of the bond to the probate court if the duties of the position are not faithfully performed.

bonus-malus A plan under which an executive does not receive his/her bonus immediately but only when the investment he/she engineered proves to have appropriate profitability for the corporation.

brain death The point at which all functions controlled by the brain, including the brain stem, have stopped working.

breach of contract The failure of one of the parties to a contract to do what was previously agreed upon.

breaking and entering In criminal law, using force, deceit, or cunning to trespass into an unoccupied building with the intent to commit a felony.

bribery The act of offering, giving, receiving, or soliciting something of value to influence official action or the discharge of a public duty.

bright-line test Test used by the courts that establishes violations of the best-price rule occur only during the actual tender offer.

bring your own device (BYOD) A procedure under which employees use their own electronic units at work on the job.

browsewrap contract A website that contains the terms and conditions agreement, which is separate from the shopping website.

burglary The break-in of a dwelling or building for the purpose of carrying out a felony.

business compulsion See *economic duress*.

business judgment rule The rule that a corporate manager's decisions will not be interfered with by a court as long as the decision was made with due care, is in good faith, is lawful, and is in the best interest of the corporation.

business necessity A defense against a charge of disparate impact.

business system Until recently, business systems were considered unpatentable because they were not a "process, machine, or composition of matter." Recently, however, some computerized business systems have been patented if they consist of some nonobvious, new, and useful feature not known or understood before the invention of this system.

buyer in the ordinary course of business A person who in good faith and without knowledge that the sale is in violation of ownership rights or security interests of a third party buys goods in ordinary course from a person in the business of selling goods of that kind, not including a pawnbroker.

Buyer's Guide A window sticker that is required by the Federal Trade Commission Act to be placed in the window of each used car offered for sale by a used car dealer. The sticker discloses the warranties that are made with the sale of the car and other consumer protection information.

bylaws Rules that guide a corporation's day-to-day internal affairs. Also known as *regulations*.

c.f. Cost and freight. Terms instructing a carrier to collect the cost of goods shipped and freight charges.

c.i.f. Cost, insurance, and freight. Terms instructing a carrier to collect the cost of goods shipped, insurance, and freight charges.

c.o.d. Cash on delivery. Instructs a carrier to retain goods until it has collected the costs of the goods.

Can Spam Act A federal law designed to reduce the use of unsolicited e-mail, commonly known as spam, on the Internet.

cancellation form Under the Federal Trade Commission's Cooling-Off Rule, a document that can be filled out to terminate an order for consumer goods or services made at the buyer's home for consumer goods or services valued at $25 or more.

canon law Guilds that followed the law of the Church.

capacity In contract law, the legal ability to enter into a contractual relationship.

capital contribution The sum contributed by a business partner as a permanent investment in the business. It is then considered to be the property of the partnership.

capitalism A complex adaptive system of overlapping economic agents that operates on the basis of competition and a free market that responds to the movement of supply and demand.

carrier A business that undertakes to transport persons, goods, or both.

case in chief The collection of evidence that will prove a plaintiff's version of a case to a jury.

case trustee A person appointed by a bankruptcy court to meet with creditors and report whether the case should proceed.

cash dividend Dividend paid to shareholders in the form of cash.

cashier's check A check drawn by a bank upon its own funds.

catfishing Involves the creation of an entirely new online identity.

cause in fact In tort law, the relationship between the unreasonable conduct and the injury to the innocent party, whether the injury was or was not foreseeable. Cause in fact is also referred to as actual cause.

certificate of authority A document that grants a foreign corporation permission to do business within another state.

certificate of deposit (CD) An acknowledgment by a bank of the receipt of money and a promise to pay the money back on the due date, usually with interest.

certificate of incorporation A corporation's official authorization to do business in a state. Also called *charter* or *corporate charter*.

certified check A check that has been marked, or certified, by the bank on which it was drawn, guaranteeing payment to the holder.

certified public accountant (CPA) An accountant who has met certain age, character, education, experience, and testing requirements.

chaotic events Unpredictable and unexpected incidents, often with a natural origin, such as earthquakes, typhoons, snowstorms, volcanic eruptions, plagues and the like that come out of nowhere and have a debilitating effect on human made decisions. (See also *sideswipes*.)

charitable immunity A common law principle that grants immunity from tort law litigation to charities to protect the useful continuation of those services that such organizations make to society as a whole.

chattels Property that has substance and that can be touched.

check A draft drawn on a bank and payable on demand.

Check 21 Act A law that makes check clearing much quicker by the use of a *substitute check* in place of the original check for electronic check processing.

chose in action Evidence of the right to property but not the property itself.

civil litigation The process of bringing a case to court to enforce a right.

civil theft When the innocent victim demonstrates that a perpetrator intentionally takes a victim's property in order to permanently or temporarily deprive the victim of that property.

civilization A group of people in a series of different nation-states that share common characteristics, including history, religion, tradition, beliefs, often language, and sometimes ancestry.

class action lawsuit A lawsuit that is brought by one or more plaintiffs on behalf of a class of persons.

Clean Air Act In environmental law, a federal statute designed to limit pollution from vehicles and from stationary sources such as factories and manufacturing centers.

Clean Water Act In environmental law, a federal statute that sets requirements for limiting the pollution of the nation's water sources according to a schedule, based on the most effective technology currently available.

clearly erroneous standard The determination that the decision made in the lower court was undeniably wrong, given the facts and evidence in the case.

clickwrap agreement Requires the purchaser to read the terms of agreement page and click on that page before the transaction is complete.

close corporation A corporation whose shares of stock and managerial control are closely held by fewer than 50 shareholders (often members of the same family) or by one person.

closed shop A place of employment in which the employer, by agreement, hires only union members in good standing.

cloud storage A cyber-technique that preserves electronic data without using local hard drives or flash drives.

co-maker A person obligated, along with at least one other person, as a payor on a promissory note.

co-ownership The more common term used when two or more people own the same tract of land (i.e., concurrent ownership).

co-tenancy The quality or state of more than one owner of a single property.

co-tenants Two or more persons who own real property together.

code A compilation of all the statutes of a particular state or of the federal government.

Code of Federal Regulations (CFR) Annual listing of finalized federal rules and regulations.

Code of Professional Ethics A set of rules established by the American Institute of Certified Public Accountants that outlines rules that govern the ethical conduct of accountants.

codicil A formal document used to supplement or change an existing will.

coercive persuasion Involves a perverse relationship between a dominant party and a victim that transforms the personality of the victim so that the victim's identity undergoes a radical change.

coinsurance An insurance policy provision under which the insurer and the insured share costs, after the deductible is met, according to a specific formula.

collateral The property that is subject to a security interest.

collateral contract In contract law, a contract by which one party agrees to pay the debt of another party if that party fails to meet that obligation.

collecting bank Any bank handling an item for collection except the payor bank.

collective action Permits a small number of employees to bring a lawsuit representing a large collective group of employees who are "similarly situated" on the job.

collective bargaining agreement A contract negotiated by an employer and a labor union that covers all issues related to employment.

collective science court A proposed judicial forum that would act as a legal clearing ground for disputes involving scientific and technological issues.

collective science court (CSC) A proposed judicial forum that would act as a legal clearing ground for disputes involving scientific and technological issues.

collision insurance A type of automobile insurance that protects the insured against any loss arising from damage to the insured's automobile caused by accidental collision with another object or with any part of the roadbed.

comaker A person obligated, along with at least one other person, as a payor on a promissory note.

commerce Trade among the several states or between any foreign country and any state or territory.

commerce clause The clause in the U.S. Constitution that gives the federal government the power to regulate business among the states.

commercial impracticability A doctrine under which the courts may excuse the performance of one party to a contract because an unforeseen and very severe hardship has arisen that would place an enormous amount of hardship on that party.

commercial unit A single whole for the purpose of sale, the division of which impairs its character or value on the market, such as a set of furniture.

Commission on Science and Technology for Development A UN agency created in 1992 as part of the Economic and Social Council (ECOSOC) to act as a clearing house for issues concerning science and technology in relation to development; to support progress in determining what must be done to advance science and technology policies in developing nations, and to formulate recommendations and protocols for science and technology within the UN community.

common law The body of recorded decisions that courts refer to and rely upon when making later legal decisions.

common stock The most usual type of corporate stock. It carries with it all the risks of the business and does not guarantee its holder the right to profits.

community improvement corporation A non-profit corporate entity authorized by state law to either promote economic development in a community or to help in reclaiming and rehabilitating empty, abandoned, and/or foreclosed real estate in the area.

community property Property that is acquired by the personal effects of either spouse during marriage and which, by law, belongs to both spouses equally.

company-owned, personally enabled devices (COPE) Company-owned devices that are distributed by employers that employees are permitted to use for personal reasons with the caveat that the personal functions on the company-owned device may be open to inspection by the employer, who does own the device.

company-run unions Unions that are established by and conducted under the influence of the management of a business.

comparative negligence A form of contributory negligence that requires the court to assign damages according to the degree of fault of each party.

compelling interest The inescapable, overriding interest that the government of a nation or state has in a particular issue, such as the state or the nation's interest in the lives of its own citizens, which the government cannot ignore, and which it must pursue and protect at the risk of losing its legitimacy as the proper governing body of that state or nation.

compensatory damages See *actual damages*.

competent authority The requirement that just war may be declared and run only by legitimately recognized nation-states.

competitive impact statement (CIS) In antitrust law, a decree that clarifies any potential antitrust problems inherent within a corporate expansion and the solutions to those problems.

complaint A legal document filed by a plaintiff to begin a lawsuit. The complaint sets forth the names of the parties, the facts in the case, the alleged legal violations by the defendant, and the relief sought by the plaintiff.

complete performance In contract law, the situation that exists when both parties to a contract have fully accomplished every term, condition, and promise to which they agreed.

comprehensive coverage A type of automobile insurance that provides protection against loss when the insured's car is damaged or destroyed by fire, lightning, flood, hail, windstorm, riot, vandalism, or theft.

concealment In insurance, the intentional withholding of a fact that would be of material importance to the insurer's decision to issue a policy. In contract law, the intentional withholding of a material fact that the other party relies upon and which results in financial harm to the innocent party. See also *passive fraud*.

concurrent ownership When two or more people own the same tract of land.

condemnation See *eminent domain*.

condition concurrent A condition in a contract that requires both parties to perform at the same time.

condition precedent In contract law, an act or promise that must take place or be fulfilled before the other party is obligated to perform his or her part of the agreement.

condition subsequent A condition in a contract in which the parties agree that the contract will be terminated depending on a prescribed event occurring or not occurring.

conditional indorsement An indorsement that makes the rights of the indorsee subject to the happening of a certain event or condition.

confirmation In bankruptcy law, the official approval of a reorganization plan.

conforming goods Goods that are in accordance with the obligations under the contract.

conglomerate expansion The joining of two companies that were not in competition with each other either because they dealt in different products or services or because they operated in different geographical areas.

conglomerates Known as non-nation configurations, such as the European Union (formerly the European Community [EC]), which unify several true nation-states, for a common enterprise, and which often speak with one voice that represents the members of that conglomerate.

consensual A freely given agreement to act.

consent decree Agreements created by the Department of Justice to help parties negotiate a legal merger.

consent order Under the Federal Trade Commission Act, an order under which a company agrees to stop a disputed practice without necessarily admitting that the practice violated the law.

consequential damages Losses that do not flow directly and immediately from an act but only from some of the consequences or results of the act.

consideration In contract law, the mutual promise to exchange benefits and detriments between parties.

consignee One to whom goods are entrusted under a *consignment contract* for the purpose of selling those goods.

consignment contract A type of mutual benefit bailment in which the *consignor* entrusts goods to the *consignee* for the purpose of selling them.

consignor One who entrusts goods under *a consignment contract* to a *consignee* for the purpose of selling them.

consolidation The joining of two corporations.

conspiracy The crime that occurs when people get together with others to talk about, plan, or agree to the commission of a crime.

constitution The basic law of a nation or state.

constitutional law That body of law that involves a constitution and its interpretation.

construction loan A loan for the building of a home that permits staggered payments that fall due at various stages in the building process.

constructive bailment A bailment created by expressly stated terms that can be implied by circumstances. Also called an *implied-in-fact bailment* or an *implied-in-law bailment*.

constructive discharge Discriminatory action whereby an employee is demoted to a job with less pay, authority, or poorer working conditions than the job that person previously held or is subjected to supervisory harassment.

constructive eviction An eviction that occurs by the act of the landlord depriving the tenant of something of a substantial nature that was called for under the lease.

consumer Someone who buys or leases real estate, goods, or services for personal, family, or household purposes.

consumer credit contract A contract for credit to purchase an item, property, or services, for personal, family, or household use.

consumer goods Goods normally used for personal, family, or household purposes.

consumer products Tangible personal property normally used for personal, family, or household purposes.

continuity of existence A concept promoted by the Revised Uniform Partnership Act that permits a partnership to continue to operate as an entity even after individual partners are no longer associated with it.

continuity plan In sales law, an arrangement by which the seller of goods ships the goods to the subscriber on a regular basis without first sending an announcement of the upcoming delivery.

contract An agreement based on mutual promises between two or more competent parties to do or to refrain from doing some particular thing that is neither illegal nor impossible. The agreement results in an obligation or a duty that can be enforced in a court of law.

contract of record A special type of formal contract usually confirmed by a court with an accompanying judgment issued in favor of one of the parties.

contributory negligence A legal defense that involves the failure of an injured party to be careful enough to ensure personal safety.

control test In tort law and in agency law, the test within the doctrine of *respondeat superior* which asks that we determine the degree of control or right to control that the hiring person had over the hired person in order to determine liability.

controlled company A corporation that has more than half its voting power concentrated in one individual, or a small group of people, who always vote together.

Convention on Contracts for the International Sale of Goods (CISG) A United Nations treaty designed to govern commercial transactions between parties whose places of business are in different countries.

conventional mortgage A mortgage that involves no government backing by either insurance or guarantee.

conversion The wrongful exercise of dominion and control over another's personal property.

conveyance in trust A trust in which the settlor conveys away the legal title to a trustee to hold for the benefit of either the settlor or another as beneficiary.

Cooling-Off Rule A Federal Trade Commission rule under which sales of consumer goods or services over $25 made away from the seller's regular place of business may be canceled within three business days after the sale occurs.

cooperative corporation A business entity owned and operated by the employees of that corporation.

cooperative corporation with wage-earning employees A business owned and operated by the employees who hire non-owner employees to perform work beyond the expertise and/or availability of the owner-employees.

cooperative with non-employee owners A business entity, owned and operated by employees with some non-employee shareholders.

copyright A right granted to an author, composer, photographer, or artist to exclusively publish and sell an artistic or literary work for the life of the author plus 70 years.

core cases Title 11 bankruptcy cases that the bankrupty courts can hear ("arises under" or "arises in" Title 11).

corporate democracy See *shareholder democracy*.

corporate entity A legal entity created under the authority of a state or federal statute that gives certain individuals the capacity to operate as an enterprise.

corporate opportunity doctrine A principle that states corporate managers cannot take a business opportunity for themselves if they know their corporation would be interested in that opportunity.

corporate person A legal entity created under the authority of a state or federal statute that gives certain individuals the capacity to operate as an enterprise.

corporate raid An unfriendly takeover, designed to dismantle the target corporation.

corporate raider An unfriendly suitor that intends to dismantle the target corporation after obtaining it.

corporate shell A subsidiary corporation set up as a mere instrumentality of a parent corporation.

corporation A legal entity (or a legal person) created by either a state or federal statute authorizing individuals to operate an enterprise.

corporation by estoppel The doctrine by which parties who have benefited by dealing with a business as though it were a corporation—though in law it is not—cannot deny its existence as a corporation. Similarly, individuals who have acted as if they were a corporation would not be able to deny that the corporation existed.

corporativism The process of doing business as a self-governing association.

cosigner The guarantor in a commercial setting.

cost of repair rule The principle that states that an architect or contractor may have to reimburse a client for any extra money spent by the client to correct an error initially made by the architect or contractor.

cost-plus contract A contract in which the price is determined by the cost of labor and materials plus an agreed percentage markup.

cost–benefit thinking A system of thought that focuses on the consequences to one person or institution and then weighs the cost against the benefits of performing the action under scrutiny.

cotenancy The quality or state of more than one owner of a single property.

cotenants Two or more persons who own real property together.

counteroffer A response to an offer in which the terms and conditions of the original offer are changed.

courts Judicial tribunals that meet in a regular place and apply the law in an attempt to settle disputes by weighing the arguments presented by advocates for each party.

cover Buying similar goods from someone else when a seller breaches a contract.

covering law A universal normative principle that follows a set pattern that can be used to understand and predict, in terms of probabilities, natural processes, or human behavior.

coverture Depriving a married woman of any power to own property, enter into a contract on her own, or file a lawsuit on her own behalf.

creditor beneficiary A third party to whom one or both contracting parties owe a continuing debt of obligation arising from a contract.

crime An offense against the public at large punishable by the official governing body of a nation or state.

criminal simulation In criminal law, the altering or falsifying of art objects, antiques, photos, films, recordings, manuscripts, and/or antiquities with the intent to defraud.

cross-appeal An appeal filed by a party that has prevailed at trial.

cross-examination The questioning of witnesses by an opposing attorney.

cross-owned corporation A business entity that is a public corporation owned and operated by another public corporation.

cryptocurrency A subset of bitcoin, it is a digital form of consideration that employs cryptography to make certain that contracts using bicoin as consideration are secure, controlled, and verified.

cumulative voting A system of voting for corporate directors that is designed to benefit minority shareholders by allowing shareholders to multiply their voting shares by the number of directors to be elected.

cure The correction of a defect in goods that caused the goods to be rejected by a buyer.

current market price contract An agreement in which the prices are determined with reference to the market price of the goods on a specified date.

curtesy Under common law, the right that a widower had, if children of the marriage were born alive, to a life estate in all real property owned by the wife during the marriage.

cyber alternative dispute resolution (C-ADR) Also known as electronic dispute resolution (e-ADR) and online dispute resolution (ODR). C-ADR has actually been in the works since the late 1990s.

cyber-arbitration (C-arb) Involves the use of an impartial third party who uses electronic communication techniques to settle disputes between two or more parties.

cyber-bulletin board An electronic message board.

cyber-commerce Involves transacting business by any one of several types of electronic communication, from debit card purchases to buying and selling goods on the Internet.

cyber-contract A contract involving the sale or licensing of information in a digital format.

cyber-defamation The communication of false and destructive information about an individual through the use of a computer or other electronic device.

cyber-disparagement In tort law, disparagement committed using a computer system.

cyber-extortion Also referred to as *cyber-germ warfare*, *cyber-warfare*, or simply as *hacking*. Whatever term is used to describe the crime, once the perpetrator has disabled the computer or the computer system, he or she demands a ransom in exchange for restoring the computer or the computer system to its operational capacity.

cyber-ghost The identity that is created by catfishing, the cyber-ghost then snags a gullible, but innocent, victim who becomes involved with the cyber-ghost and is then conned out of large amounts of money.

cyber-invasion of privacy The unwelcome intrusion into private matters initiated or maintained by a computer.

cyber-jurisdiction The authority of a court to hear a case based on Internet-related transactions.

cyber-mediation (C-med) Involves the addition of an impartial third party who acts as an intermediary between two opposing parties.

cyber-negotiation (C-neg) Involves an attempt to reach an agreement between two or more parties by using specialized electronic communication techniques, generally e-mail.

cyber-signature An electronic sound or process attached to or logically associated with a record and executed or adopted by a person with the intent to sign a record.

cyber-trespass Gaining access to a computer with the intent to commit a crime.

cybertort The invasion, distortion, theft, falsification, misuse, destruction, or financial exploitation of information stored in a computer.

damages Money recovered by a party in a court action to compensate that party for injury or loss.

data mining Takes place when a hacker links multiple strings of data together and develops a data package that the target considers a compilation of private information, despite the public sources from which the hacker composed the package.

***de facto* corporation** A corporation defectively incorporated in good faith that exists in fact though not in law.

***de jure* corporation** A corporation whose existence is the result of incorporators having fully or substantially complied with the relevant corporation statutes.

death statute States that "an individual is dead if the individual has sustained either irreversible cessation of the circulatory and respiratory functions or irreversible cessation of all functions of the brain, including the brain stem, as determined in accordance with accepted medical standards."

debit card A card used to electronically subtract money from a bank account to pay for goods or services.

debtor in possession A debtor who continues to operate his or her business after filing for bankruptcy.

declaration of trust A trust in which the settlor holds the legal title to the property as trustee for the benefit of some other person (the beneficiary) to whom the settlor now conveys the equitable title.

deductible An amount of any loss that is to be paid by the insured.

deed of trust A formal written instrument that transfers legal ownership of real property to a third party while the mortgagor remains on the property. The third party holds certain rights to that property as security for the mortgagor's creditors.

deep state A loosely organized group of provocateurs located within the bureaucracy who oppose the president and his administration and who work together (sometimes deliberately and sometimes just by happenstance).

using guerrilla tactics to undermine and weaken the authority, the reputation, and the agenda of the president.

defamation The intentional tort that occurs when a false statement is communicated to others that harms a person's good name or reputation.

defective condition A condition that makes a product unreasonably dangerous to the consumer, user, or property. See *product liability*.

defendant The person against whom a lawsuit is brought and from whom recovery is sought.

defense of others A defense to criminal liability to defendants if they can show they used force to rescue another person who was the victim of an apparent attack. The rescuer must have good reason to believe the victim was in danger of severe bodily injury or death.

defrauding creditors The crime of removing, hiding, destroying, giving away, or transferring any person's property with the intent to defraud creditors.

***del credere* agent (del·KREH·de·reh)** A factor who guarantees the credit of a third party to a principal and guarantees the solvency of the purchaser and the performance of the contract.

delegation The transfer of a contractual duty.

demand futility doctrine A corporate rule that says that a shareholder need not take a complaint to the board of directors before filing a derivative lawsuit if that board is controlled by the director that is the target of the suit.

demand note A promissory note that is payable whenever the payee demands payment.

demurrer A motion for dismissal of a case on the grounds that a plaintiff has failed to state a claim for which relief can be granted.

dependency theory An economic picture of the world that holds the developed world responsible for the poverty and deprivation found in the developing world.

depositary bank The first bank to which an item is transferred for collection; the depositary bank may also be the payor bank.

deposition An oral question-and-answer session conducted under oath during which an attorney questions parties or witnesses from the opposition in a lawsuit.

dereliction of duty In criminal law, an activity that involves a law enforcement officer's failure to carry out his or her lawful duties.

derivative A financial tool the value of which emerges from a variable item, such as an interest rate, a stock index, or a commodity like fuel or crops.

derivative suit A lawsuit brought by shareholders on behalf of the corporation.

descriptive theory A system of ethical thought that describes the values at work within a social system.

descriptive threshold In insurance law, a guideline that determines when a victim can bring a lawsuit for injuries that result from an auto accident.

destination contract A contract under which the seller is required to deliver goods to a place of destination. The title and risk of loss remain with the seller until the goods reach the place of destination.

devise Real property that is left in a will. In states that have adopted the Uniform Probate Code, the term refers to both real and personal property.

devisee One who receives the real property under a will. In states that have adopted the Uniform Probate Code, the term refers to a person who receives a gift of either real or personal property under a will.

Digital Millennium Copyright Act (DMCA) A law that makes it illegal to use technological means to bypass or override programs designed to prevent access to a copyrighted work.

direct examination The questioning of witnesses by the lawyer who has called them.

direct suit A suit brought by shareholders who have been deprived of a right that belongs to them as shareholders.

disability Any physical or mental impairment that substantially limits one or more of the major life activities.

disaffirm In contract law, to indicate by a statement or act an intent not to live up to the terms of the contract.

disclaimer In employment law, a statement that regardless of provisions or policies in an employment handbook and regardless of oral promises to the contrary, an employment-at-will situation still exists between an employer and its employees. In the accounting profession, a statement declaring that an auditor has decided not to give any opinion on a firm's financial records.

disclaimer of general partner status A document filed with the appropriate state office when a limited partner has been incorrectly named as a general partner.

disclosed principal The person known by a third party to be the principal of an agent.

discovery The process by which parties to a civil suit search for information relevant to the case.

dishonor To refuse to accept or pay a negotiable instrument when it is presented.

disparagement In tort law, any false statement made to others that questions the legal ownership or raises doubts as to the quality of merchandise.

disparate impact A type of discrimination in an employer's policy that seems neutral on the surface but has an unequal or unfair impact on members of one or more of the protected classes.

disparate treatment Intentional discrimination against an individual or group belonging to a protected class. The protected classes are sex, race, color, religion, and national origin.

disposable income The amount of money left from a person's income, after subtracting certain allowable deductions.

Dispute Settlement Board (DSB) See *Dispute Settlement Understanding*.

Dispute Settlement Understanding (DSU) A series of measures administered by an international Dispute Settlement Board that are designed to improve the way trading quarrels are handled.

disputed amount Consideration on which parties to a contract never agree.

dissociation A process authorized under the Revised Uniform Partnership Act that takes place whenever a partner is no longer associated with the running of the partnership firm.

dissolution A change in the relation of partners caused by any partner ceasing to be associated in the carrying on of the business.

diversity jurisdiction Three very specific conditions under which Congress has set up specific conditions under which jurisdiction can be established in the federal court system. Those conditions include cases that are (1) between citizens of different states, (2) between citizens of a state or different states and citizens of a foreign state, and (3) between citizens of a state and a foreign state as the plaintiff.

dividends Net profits, or surplus, set aside for shareholders.

DNR indentification A document, a form, a necklace, a bracelet, or other identification technique that indicates that the declarant has previously implemented a desire not to undergo CPR or other life prolonging activities, as specified by statutory law.

do not resuscitate (DNR) order An order that stops medical personnel from attempting to resuscitate a patient.

document of title A paper that serves as evidence that the person holding the paper has title to the goods mentioned in the document.

Dodd–Frank Wall Street and Consumer Protection Act An act passed by Congress to deal with the 21st-century financial crisis.

domestic bill of exchange A draft that is drawn and payable in the United States.

domestic corporation A corporation created by or organized under the laws of the state where it is operating.

dominant tenement The property to which the right or privilege of an easement attaches.

donee One to whom a gift is given.

donee beneficiary A third party who provides no consideration for the benefits received and who owes the contracting parties no legal duty.

donor One who gives a gift.

dormant minerals statute Designed to permit the surface owner of a plot of land to recover mineral rights that have not been utilized by a purchaser of such rights for a long time, often a period of not less than 20 years.

double indemnity An optional provision in life insurance policies that provides that the insurer will pay double the amount due to a beneficiary if the insured dies from accidental causes.

double jeopardy In criminal procedure, the possibility of being tried twice for the same crime.

dower By common law, the vested rights of the wife to a one-third lifetime interest in the real property owned by her spouse. Compare *curtesy*.

draft A written order by which the party creating it orders another party to pay money to a third party. Also called *bill of exchange*.

drawee The party named in a draft who is ordered to pay the money to the payee.

drawer The party who draws a draft, that is, the party who orders that the money be paid.

drone An unpiloted, remote control aircraft that can fly under its own power and move beyond the line of sight of its ground-based human operator.

dummy corporation A corporation that is set up as a mere instrumentality of a parent corporation. Also called *corporate shell* and *empty shell*.

dunning letter A letter representing payment for goods.

durable health care power of attorney A document that is made by an adult, who is mentally competent, which empowers the principal's agent to decide issues of health care for the principal when that principal has lost the innate ability to decide on health care issues for himself or herself.

durable power of attorney A document that authorizes an agent to act on another's behalf, with the power either surviving incapacity or becoming effective upon incapacity.

durable power of attorney for health care (DPAHC) A written statement authorizing a person, called an agent, to make medical treatment decisions for another person, referred to as the principal, in the event of the principal's incapacity.

duress An action by one party that forces another party to do what need not be done otherwise.

duty An obligation placed on individuals because of the law.

duty of due diligence A duty that says that corporate managers when acting on behalf of the corporation must act (1) in good faith, (2) using the same level of care that an ordinarily prudent person would use in a comparable situation, and (3) in the reasonable belief that the best interests of the corporation are being met.

duty of loyalty A duty that states managers must place the corporation's interests above their own.

duty of obedience Managers' duty to ensure their exercise of authority is not excessive and does not harm the corporation.

duty to defend A responsibility that an insurer has in an insurance contract to defend a client when a claim is disputed by another party.

duty to investigate A responsibility that an insurer has in an insurance contract to determine if a client is entitled to payment or to any other protection guaranteed under the agreement.

duty to pay A responsibility that an insurer has in an insurance contract to replace or repair the property of an insured or to pay any claim by a third party based on a liability clause.

dwelling insurance An insurance contract under which the insurer promises to provide protection to the property owner of a single family house or an apartment building.

dyad A two-level system of morality, represented by the "ethic of ultimate ends" for individuals and the "ethic of responsibility" for national leaders.

e-check (sometimes called *electronic check conversion*) A system in which funds are electronically transferred from a customer's checking account, eliminating the need to process a paper check.

early neutral evaluation (ENE) A process similar to that of a settlement hearing, which may result in a final decision or be used to help shape the final decision.

easement The right to use the land of another for a particular purpose.

easement by grant The owner of the land signs a deed, giving the easement to the dominant tenement, and keeps the remainder of the land.

easement by prescription An easement that is obtained by passing over another's property without permission openly and continuously for a period of time set by state statute (20 years in many states).

easement by reservation The owner of the land grants to another person the entire parcel of land except for the easement that he or she keeps.

economic compensatory damages Damages that are directly quantifiable, including damages awarded for lost wages, medical expenses, and expenses incurred in the repair or replacement of property.

economic development special-purpose entities (EDSPEs) Institutions that promote partnerships between public and private entities in order to allow the government to assist in certain economic development projects independently from those political subdivision that established the EDSPEs in the first place.

economic duress Threats of a business nature that force another party without real consent to enter a commercial agreement. Also called *business compulsion*.

economic equivalent A lease agreement that has the characteristics of a sales contract, despite its name.

Economic Espionage Act Legislation that outlines criminal sanctions for the theft of trade secrets and the use of fraud to obtain trade secrets.

economic realities test In agency law, a test used by the court in vicarious liability to determine whether a worker is a servant or an independent contractor.

economic reality test In agency law, a test used by the court in vicarious liability to determine whether a worker is a servant or an independent contractor.

Economic Security Council (ESC) A single, unified international agency under the management of the United Nations that would monitor the economic activities of member nations.

economic zones Unified but isolated sectors of economic activity based on geographical areas designed to focus on the economic well-being of the nations in each zone.

ejectment The common law name given to the lawsuit brought by a landlord to have a tenant evicted from the premises.

elective share See *forced share*.

electronic agent A computer program that acts without human intervention to begin an activity, answer cyber-messages, deliver or accept electronic mail, or enter electronic contracts as a representative of an individual who does not intervene in the action taken by the electronic agent at the actual time of the electronic agent's activity. Also referred to as a cyber-agent or e-agent.

electronic contracts (e-contracts) Contracts made using computers, either via e-mail or the Internet, or that involve computer-related products, such as databases and software.

electronic fund transfer (EFT) A method of banking that uses computers and electronic technology as a substitute for checks and other banking methods.

electronic /e-jurisdiction The authority of a court to hear a case based on Internet-related transactions.

electronically stored information (ESI) Computerized evidence.

emancipated In contract law, the condition that exists when minors are no longer under the control of their parents and are responsible for their contracts.

embezzlement The act of wrongfully taking property entrusted into one's care.

eminent domain The right of federal, state, and local governments, or other public bodies, to take private lands, with compensation to their owners, for public use. Also called *condemnation*.

emotional duress Acts or threats that create emotional distress and lead a person into a contract against his or her will.

employment at will A doctrine followed by most jurisdictions in the United States that says an employer can dismiss an employee at any time for any reason.

employment contracts Individuals with unique abilities, special talents, or a highly specialized education often have the flexibility to negotiate their own contracts. These individuals would not be affected by employment at will.

entity theory A theory in partnership law that holds that a partnership is actually a separate legal person with its own legal identity.

entrapment A defense to criminal liability that claims that a previously law-abiding citizen was induced to commit a crime by a law enforcement officer.

equal dignities rule The legal rule that provides that when a party appoints an agent to negotiate an agreement that must be in writing, and the appointment of the agent must also be in writing.

equipment Goods that are used or bought for use primarily in business.

equitable estoppel See *part performance*.

equitable remedy The requirement that a party do something or refrain from doing something, beyond the payment of money.

equity of redemption A mortgagor's right to pay off the mortgage in full, including interest.

escheat When property reverts to the state.

estate in fee simple An estate in which the owner owns the land for life with the right to use it or dispose of it freely.

estoppel A legal bar to denying acts, statements, or promises.

ethic of responsibility An ethical principle developed by the 20th-century political philosopher Max Weber that holds that a leader's primary ethical guide must be the safety and security of the people of his or her nation-state.

ethic of ultimate ends An ethical principle, often referred to as the ethic of benevolence, developed by the 20th-century political philosopher Max Weber, that holds that individuals must act with compassion toward people without regard to the consequences.

ethics Rules of conduct that transcend legal rules, telling people how to act when the law does not.

EU Data Protection Directive A decree issued by the European Union (EU) that prevents European companies from sharing ESI with countries that do not provide the same level of protection for the ESI as the EU.

EU E-Privacy Directive A decree issued by the European Union (EU) that guarantees EU citizens a high level of privacy for electronically stored information.

euro The European Union's common currency.

European Union (EU) A group of countries in Europe that have joined together to formulate a common European economic policy, minimize trade barriers, and introduce a common currency with the goal of making the EU a major global competitor.

eviction An act of the landlord that deprives the tenant of the enjoyment of the premises.

exclusionary rule Any evidence that serves as the basis for an arrest that has been gathered illegally, all other evidence that flows from that illegal search and seizure will be suppressed by the court.

exculpatory clause A clause in a contract that releases a party from liability for his or her wrongful acts. These clauses are not favored by law.

executed contract A contract whose terms have been completely and satisfactorily carried out by both parties.

executive agencies Agencies that are directly under the control of the president. These include departments such as the State Department, the Department of Justice, and the Department of Human Services.

executive order An executive order is a device by which the president can act on his own without having to resort to the somewhat cumbersome process of going through Congress.

executor A person named in a will by the court to manage the estate of a testator.

executor (male); executrix (female) The party named in a will to carry out the terms of the will.

executory contract A contract that has not yet been fully performed by the parties.

exemplary damages In tort law, money payments levied by a court against a defendant designed to make an example of the defendant and, thus, deter others from the same type of unacceptable conduct.

exempt property Property of a decedent that passes to the surviving spouse or children and is beyond the reach of creditors.

express authority An agent's authority that the principal voluntarily and specifically sets forth as oral or written instructions in an agency agreement.

express contract A contract in which both parties accept mutual obligations through either oral discussion or written communication.

express warranty An oral or written statement, promise, or other representation about the quality of a product.

f.a.s vessel Free alongside vessel. Indicates that the seller must deliver goods, at the seller's own risk, alongside the vessel or at a dock designated by the buyer.

f.o.b. Free on board.

f.o.b. the place of destination Terms indicating that goods will be delivered free to the place of destination.

f.o.b. the place of shipment Terms indicating that goods will be delivered free to the place of shipment.

faction A special interest group that does its best to see that its point of view is heard, and acknowledged, supported, and funded by the government.

factor A special agent who is employed to sell merchandise consigned for that purpose.

failed states States in which the government has completely collapsed or has become so ineffective that it can no longer provide sustenance or security for its own people.

failure of consideration A personal defense that may be used by a maker or drawer of a negotiable instrument when the party with whom the maker dealt breaches the contract by not furnishing the agreed consideration.

failure-proof public corporation An entity operated by an autonomous board of directors, owned by the state and protected from failure by the government.

fair court Historically in the Middle Ages in Europe, a court set up at a festival (a fair) to handle disputes between merchants at that festival (fair).

fair use doctrine A doctrine that provides that copyright material can be used without permission if the use is reasonable and not harmful to the copyright owner.

fairness rule The rule that requires managers to be fair to the corporation when they personally benefit from their business decisions.

false imprisonment An intentional tort involving the unjustified confinement or detention of a person.

family allowance An amount of money taken from a decedent's estate and given to the family to meet its immediate needs while the estate is being probated.

farm products Crops, livestock, or supplies used or produced in farming operations.

fault-based insurance An automobile insurance policy that will measure liability in an automobile accident by the degree of fault that can be assigned to each driver using negligence principles.

featherbedding Requiring an employer, usually by a union, to keep unneeded employees, to pay employees for not working, or to assign more employees to a given job than are needed.

Federal Housing Finance Agency (FHFA) A federal agency created to oversee the operation of Fannie Mae and Freddie Mac.

federal question A matter that involves the U.S. Constitution, a federal statute or statutes, or a treaty; handled by federal district courts.

Federal Register Publication that produces a daily compilation of new regulations issued by federal administrative agencies.

fee simple determinable A fee simple that lasts as long as the ability to take the oil and gas from the earth continues. Once that ceases as an option, the fee simple reverts to the original owners.

felony A crime punishable by death or by imprisonment in a federal or state prison for a term exceeding one year.

feme covert Under common law, a married woman with no right to own property.

feme solo Under common law, an unmarried woman who has the right to own property.

fiduciary A person who acts in a position of trust or confidence.

fiduciary relationship A relationship based on trust such as exists between an attorney and a client, an agent and a principal, a guardian and a ward, a trustee and a beneficiary, or a director and a corporation.

fiduciary rule Registered investment advisors, that is, investment advisors who are registered with the SEC under the 1940 act, must place their clients' best interests above their own.

finance charge The actual cost of a loan in dollars and cents.

financial advisors Professionals who counsel clients on the handling of their financial lives.

firm offer A rule that no consideration is necessary when a merchant agrees in writing to hold an offer open for the sale of goods.

first-degree murder In criminal law, killing someone with premeditation or with prior calculation and design, or while committing a serious felony such as rape, robbery, or kidnapping.

fixture An article of personal property physically attached to real property in such a way that an interest arises in it under real estate law.

flexible-rate mortgage A mortgage that has a rate of interest that changes according to fluctuations in the index to which it is tied. Also called *variable-rate mortgage.*

floating lien A provision, placed by the creditor, in a security agreement that a security interest of the creditor also applies to goods the debtor acquires at a later time.

food disparagement laws Added by some states to the disparagement laws, these are also known as "ag-gags," and "veggie libel laws," and take a wide variety of forms. Some are simple extensions of conventional tort law. Some states have veggie libel laws that shift the burden of proof in food disparagement cases so that the defendant, not the plaintiff, has the burden.

forbearance The act of refraining from doing (or promising not to do) something that a person has a legal right to do.

forced share The portion of a decedent's estate assured to the family by state statute.

foreclosure The right of a mortgagee to apply to a court to have property sold when the mortgagor defaults or fails to perform some agreement in the mortgage.

foreign corporation A corporation created by or organized under the laws of a state other than the one in which it is operating.

foreign draft See *international bill of exchange*.

foreseeability test The final effect for which will hold the defendant liable under probably cause.

forgery The false making or alteration of a writing with the intent to defraud.

formal contract Under common law, a contract that is written; signed, witnessed, and placed under the seal of the parties; and delivered.

forum selection clause A clause, while not requiring arbitration, will specify that all disputes will be litigated in the merchant's home state using the law of that state.

forum shopping The process of locating a jurisdiction that has a friendly track record for the type of lawsuit that is about to be filed.

fracking Scientifically called hydrocarbon fracturing involves pumping highly pressurized, chemically treated water into rock formations that are located far under the surface of the earth in order to crack open fractures in the rock so that oil and gas deposits can be pulled to the surface where the gas or oil can be drawn from the water.

franchise A business arrangement that permits an individual, a group of investors, or another entity to lease the right to uses of a parent entity's business operation, trademark, goods, services, and goodwill under a fee arrangement provided to the parent.

fraud A wrongful statement, action, or concealment pertinent to the subject matter of a contract knowingly made to damage the other party.

fraud in the inception Fraud that occurs when one party tricks another into a contract by lying to the innocent party about the actual nature of the contract.

fraud in the inducement Fraud that occurs when one party tricks another into a contract by lying about the terms of the agreement to get the innocent party to enter the contract under false pretenses.

fraudulent conveyance A transfer of property with the intent to defraud creditors.

fraudulent misrepresentation A wrongful statement, action, or concealment, pertinent to the subject matter of a contract, that is knowingly made to damage the other party.

freehold estates Estates that were passed on to the nobility in medieval England could last infinitely because the nobles who held them were empowered to pass them on to their heirs.

friendly suitor See *white knight*.

fruit of the poisonous tree The evidence gathered as a result of an illegal search is not admissible in court.

frustration-of-purpose doctrine In contract law, the doctrine that releases a party from a contractual obligation when performing the obligations would be thoroughly impractical and senseless.

FTC legend Required by the Federal Trade Commission, consumer credit contracts must contain a written warning, which notifies the holders of those notes that they are subject to the same defenses that the original debtor had against the original seller.

full warranty A warranty under which a defective product will be repaired or replaced without charge within a reasonable time after a complaint has been made about it.

fungible goods Goods of which any unit is, by nature or usage of trade, the equivalent of any like unit; wheat, flour, sugar, and liquids of various kinds are examples.

future goods Goods that are not yet in existence or under the control of people; they include fish in the sea, minerals in the ground, goods not yet manufactured, and commodities futures.

general agent A person who is given broad authority to act on behalf of the principal in conducting the bulk of the principal's business activities on a daily basis.

General Agreement on Tariffs and Trade (GATT) A nonstatic agreement among the principal trading countries to reduce or eliminate tariffs and to promote free trade on a global basis.

General Assembly The member nations of the United Nations.

general consent Consent that arises automatically when a patient enters a hospital for routine tests and procedures needed for diagnosis and treatment.

general jurisdiction The power of a court to hear any type of case.

general partner A partner who takes an active part in running a partnership and has unlimited liability for the firm's debts.

general partnership Two or more persons operating a business entity as co-owners in order to make a profit.

general release A document expressing the intent of a creditor to release a debtor from obligations to an existing and valid debt.

general warranty deed A deed that contains express warranties under which a grantor guarantees property to be free of encumbrances created by the grantor or by others who had title previously. Also called *full convenant* and *warranty deed*.

generally accepted accounting principles (GAAP) Rules established by the Financial Accounting Standards Board (FASB) that outline the procedures that accountants use in accumulating financial data and in preparing financial statements.

generally accepted auditing standards (GAAS) Standards set up by the Auditing Standards Board of the American Institute of Certified Public Accountants (AICPA) that measure the quality of the performance of the auditing procedures.

Genetic Information Nondiscrimination Act (GINA) A law passed by Congress that makes it unlawful for employers or insurance companies to make decisions based on genetic information acquired by genetic testing.

Geneva Conventions International meetings that attempted to deal with many of the contemporary complications brought on by the nature of warfare in the twentieth century.

gericide Systematic killing of the elderly.

gift in *causa mortis* (in·KAWS·ah·MORE·tes) A gift given during one's lifetime in contemplation of death from a known cause.

gift *inter vivos* (IN·ter·VY·vose) A gift between the living. For an exchange to be valid, the donor must intend to make a gift, the gift must be delivered to the donee, and the donee must accept it.

golden parachute A comprehensive package that protects executives who might lose their jobs following a merger or a consolidation.

good faith Honesty in fact and observance of reasonable commercial standards of fair dealings in the trade.

goods All things (other than money, stocks, and bonds) that are movable.

government-sponsored enterprise (GSE) The Federal National Mortgage Association (Fannie Mae) was chartered by the Reconstruction Finance Corporation during the Great Depression in 1938. Another GSE, the Federal Home Loan Mortgage Corporation (Freddie Mac) was created by Congress to help support the mortgage market.

governmental control A theory of corporate control based on the belief that because corporate decision making impacts upon more individuals and groups than just shareholders and managers, those decisions should be made by a group of corporate outsiders, usually government officials. Also called *state control*.

graduated-payment mortgage A mortgage that has a fixed interest rate during the life of the mortgage; however, the monthly payments made by the mortgagor increase over the term of the loan.

grantee A person to whom title to real property is transferred in a deed.

grantor A person who transfers title to real property in a deed.

gratuitous agency An agency relationship that emerges from an agreement that is not a contract.

gratuitous agent An agent who is not under contract and, thus, performs his or her duties without payment.

gratuitous bailment A bailment for the sole benefit of either the bailor or the bailee, in which the other party receives no consideration for benefits bestowed.

greenmail A strategy used to shake off a bidder's hostile suit by offering to buy, at significantly higher cost, the portion of stock already owned by the bidder who is trying to take over the company.

grievance procedure A procedure that allows employees to appeal any decision an employer makes that employees feel violates just cause.

gross negligence Very great negligence.

guarantor The promisor.

guaranty contract In contract law, a contract by which one party agrees to pay the debt of another party if that party fails to meet that obligation.

guaranty of payment A promise to pay another's bills or to settle wrongful acts if that party does not settle them personally.

hate speech The use of certain symbols, writings, and speech intended to provoke outrage or fear on the basis of race, religion, color, or gender.

health care proxy A written statement authorizing an agent to make health care decisions for another in the event of incapacity.

Health Insurance Portability and Accountability Act (HIPAA) Legislation that guarantees patients the right to see their medical records and those of their underage children.

heir One who inherits property either under a will or through someone's dying without a will.

holder A person who is in possession of a negotiable instrument that is issued or indorsed to that person's order or to bearer.

holder in due course A holder who has taken a negotiable instrument for value, in good faith, without notice that it is overdue or has been dishonored and without notice of any defenses against it or claim to it.

holder in due course rule A rule adopted by the FTC that states that holders of consumer credit contracts who are holders in due course are subject to all claims and defenses that the buyer could use against the seller, including personal defenses.

Home Affordable Modification Program (HAMP) A program set up by the Department of the Treasury to support the efforts of homeowners who, though in default, wish to continue to make payments on their mortgages

Home Affordable Refinance Program (HARP) A federal program designed to help homeowners who owe the bank or mortgage company more than the home is worth.

home equity loan A line of credit made available to homeowners based on the value of the property over and above any existing mortgages.

homeowner's policy A type of insurance that gives protection for all types of losses and liabilities related to home ownership. Items covered include losses from fire, windstorm, burglary, vandalism, and injuries suffered by others while on the property.

homestead The family home and the land on which the house is located, including land adjacent to the dwelling.

homestead exemption A provision in the Bankruptcy Code that allows debtors to exclude a statutory amount of equity in the debtor's place of residence and in property used as a burial ground when filing for bankruptcy.

homicide The killing of one human being by another.

hopscotch loan A corporate merger process that permits a tax free loan to flow from an established alien corporation into the treasury of its new partner.

horizontal expansion The joining of companies involved in the same business.

hostile bidder See *unfriendly suitor*.

hostile work environment Occurs when misconduct, such as sexually explicit comments, photographs, pictures, text messages, e-mails, Facebook postings, cartoons, jokes, posters, or gestures, pervade the workplace to the extent that conditions become distressing, offensive, or hostile.

hot-cargo contract An agreement whereby an employer voluntarily agrees with a union not to handle, use, or deal in non–union-produced goods for another employer.

hot-cargo contract An agreement whereby an employer voluntarily agrees with a union not to handle, use, or deal in nonunion-produced goods for another employer.

hybrid contract In contract law, a binding agreement that has enough characteristic of a sales contract and a service contract to be considered a combination of both. See also *blended contract* and *mixed contract*.

hybrid executive order A hybrid executive order is one issued using both constitutional and statutory authority.

idealism A theory of international behavior that says the global order is not fully chaotic but is, instead, controlled by the NIOs; that nation-states share power with the NIOs; that nation-states and NIOs seek power and control but do so in the interests of international peace, by following international law and using military action only within international coalitions; and that the final best state of affairs that all nation-states seek (or should seek) is the formation of a democratic or a republican world government. (See also *liberal internationalism*.)

identified goods Specific goods that are selected as the subject matter of a contract.

illegal agreement In contract law, a void agreement to do something that violates the law.

illusory promise A promise that does not obligate the promisor to anything.

impaired classes Creditors who receive less than the full value of their claims in bankruptcy proceedings.

implied authority The authority of an agent to perform acts that are necessary or customary to carry out expressly authorized duties.

implied contract A contract created by the actions or gestures of the parties involved in the transaction.

implied covenant An implied promise in any employment relationship that the employer and the employee will be fair with each other.

implied warranty A warranty that is imposed by law rather than by statements, descriptions, or samples given by the seller.

implied-in-fact bailment A bailment created by circumstances rather than by intent. (See also *implied-in-law bailment*.)

implied-in-fact contract A contract implied by direct or indirect acts of the parties.

implied-in-law bailment A bailment created by circumstances rather than by intent. (See also implied-in-fact bailment.)

implied-in-law contract A remedy imposed by a court in a situation in which the parties did not create a written contract, oral, or implied-in-fact agreement but one party has unfairly benefited at the innocent expense of another. Also called *quasi-contract*.

in pari delicto (in pah·ree de·LIK·toh) In equal fault. A contract relationship when both parties to an illegal agreement are equally wrong, in the knowledge of the operation and effect of their contract.

in-house attorney A member of the officer corps of a business who is instructed in his or her duties by a supervisor.

incidental beneficiary A third party for whose benefit a contract was not made but who would substantially benefit if the agreement were performed according to its terms and conditions.

incidental damages Damages awarded for losses indirectly, but closely, attributed to a breach to cover any expenses paid out by an innocent party to prevent further loss.

incorporators The people who actually sign the articles of incorporation to start a corporation.

indemnification Payment for loss or damage suffered.

indemnify To compensate for loss or damage or insure against future loss or damage.

independent agencies Agencies that are not actually within the executive branch but, instead, act on their own authority.

independent contractor One who contracts to do a job and who retains complete control over the methods employed to obtain completion.

independent director control A theory of corporate control that states that the best way to make certain that corporate decisions are made in the best interests of the corporation is to make sure that the decision makers themselves are not affected by the decisions.

independent directors Corporate directors who have no family members employed by the corporation, who are not themselves employed by the corporation, or, if they were at one time employed by the corporation, have not been on the staff for at least three years.

independent source rule One of two additional exceptions to the attenuation doctrine, if evidence is discovered after the illegal search and is separate from its operation, it is admissible.

indictment A set of formal charges against a defendant issued by a grand jury.

indorsee A person to whom a draft, note, or other negotiable instrument is transferred by indorsement.

indorsement in full See *special indorsement*.

indorser A person who indorses a negotiable instrument.

inevitable discovery doctrine The inevitable discovery doctrine states that if evidence would have been discovered despite an illegal search that evidence is still admissible in court.

informal contract An oral or written contract that is not under a seal or is not a contract of record. Also called simple *contract*.

information A set of formal charges against a defendant drawn up and issued by the prosecutor or district attorney.

informed consent Written consent given by patients for diagnostic tests or treatments that will involve danger or pain after being told about the procedure and the risks involved.

injunction A court order preventing someone from performing a particular act.

inland marine insurance An insurance contract that covers goods that are moved by land carriers such as rail, truck, and airplane.

innkeeper An operator of a hotel, motel, or inn that holds itself out to the public as being ready to accommodate travelers, strangers, and transient guests.

inside information Material, nonpublic, factual data that can be used to buy or sell securities at a profit.

insider trading Using inside information to either cheat the corporation or take unfair advantage of corporate outsiders.

insider trading rule A rule of corporate governance that states that when managers possess important inside information, they are obligated to reveal that information before trading on it themselves.

insolvent Inability of a business entity to pay its debts as they become due in the usual course of business.

installment note A promissory note in which the principal together with interest on the unpaid balance is payable in installments at specified times.

instrumentality test The test used to determine whether the corporate veil should be pierced to reach the parent corporation.

insurable interest The financial interest that a policyholder has in the person or property that is insured.

insurance A contract whereby one party pays premiums to another party who undertakes to pay compensation for losses resulting from risks or perils specified in the contract.

insured A party that is protected by an insurer against losses caused by the risks specified in an insurance policy.

insurer A party that accepts the risk of loss in return for a premium (payment of money) and agrees to compensate the insured against a specified loss.

integral-part test A finding that any type of price enhancement violates the best-price rule.

intended beneficiary A third party in whose favor a contract is made.

intentional or reckless infliction of emotional distress A tort involving someone who intentionally or recklessly causes another to undergo emotional or mental suffering.

interest-only mortgage In property law, a mortgage in which the borrower pays only the interest for a period of time, usually one to three years, as set by the agreement.

interlocking directorates In antitrust law, a situation that occurs when individuals serve as two corporations that are competitors.

intermediary bank Any bank to which an item is transferred in the course of collection except the depositary or payor bank.

international arbitration agreement A pledge to use arbitration if parties find themselves in disagreement about enforcement rights under an original contract.

international bill of exchange A draft that is drawn in one country but is payable in another. Also called *foreign draft*.

International Court of Justice (ICJ) One of the principal vehicles for the establishment of international law and justice.

International Criminal Court (ICC) International court that presides over trials involving genocide, war crimes, and other human rights violations.

International Monetary Fund (IMF) A nongovernmental organization that is designed to help financially strapped nations to secure loans that will help them engage in programs of sustainable economic growth and development.

interrogatories Written questions to be answered in writing under oath by the opposite party in a lawsuit.

interstate commerce Business activities that touch more than one state.

intestate Having died without leaving a valid will. Compare *testate*.

intestate succession The process by which property passes to others when people die without a will.

intimidation In criminal law, threats of harm to the person or the property of a public servant, a party official, or a witness, with the intent to coerce that person into violating his or her duty under the law.

intrastate commerce Business activities that have no out-of-state connections.

invasion of privacy The intentional tort that occurs when one person unreasonably denies another person the right to be left alone.

inventory Goods held for sale or lease, or raw materials used or consumed in a business.

inversion A corporate expansion process that typically occurs when an American corporation buys an alien corporation and then reincorporates in that alien's national base or when an alien corporation buys an American corporation under a deal that is engineered at the behest of, and largely for the benefit of, the American corporation. (See also *inverted company*.)

inverted company A corporate person that has gone through the inversion process. (See also *inversion*.)

invitation to trade An announcement published for the purpose of creating interest and attracting a response by many people.

involuntary manslaughter In criminal law, the unlawful killing of another human being caused by negligence.

irresistible impulse test Under this rule, criminal defendants are judged not guilty by reason of insanity if, at the time of the action in question, they suffered from a mental disease that either prevented them from knowing right from wrong or compelled them to commit the criminal act.

irrevocable offer A rule that no consideration is necessary when a merchant agrees in writing to hold an offer open for the sale of goods. Also called *firm offer*.

issue Descendants (children, grandchildren, great-grandchildren).

issuer Either a maker or a drawer of an instrument.

joint and several liability In the law of business associations a legal principle under which the partners in a venture can be sued apart or together.

joint economic development district (JEDD) One of two types of joint economic development options. A JEDD, which is run by a board of directors, is designed to join resources and share costs in the economic development of two or more political subdivisions.

joint liability In the law of business associations a legal principle under which liability is spread among all partners when they are sued.

joint tenants Two or more persons who own property where the right of any deceased owner is automatically transferred to other surviving owners.

joint tenants with the right of survivorship See *joint tenants*.

joint venture (or joint undertaking) A business venture that involves a contractual arrangement by which individuals unite for a limited amount of time to create a new entity in which the founders share control, expenses, and profits.

judicial review The process by which a court determines the constitutionality of various legislative statutes, administrative regulations, and executive actions.

junior mortgage A mortgage subject to a prior mortgage.

junk bonds Bonds with high risk but also a high rate of return.

juriscience A discipline that explores the intersection of science and the law.

jurisdiction The authority of a court to hear and decide cases.

just cause A criterion under the just war theory, which states that to be morally permissible, a war must be waged only for honorable motives.

just war theory A theory for determining when a war can be considered legally and morally correct.

knowledge In criminal law, the awareness that a particular result will probably occur.

labor union An organization that acts on behalf of all employees in negotiations with the employer regarding terms of their employment.

lack of consideration A personal defense that may be used by a maker or drawer of a negotiable instrument when no consideration existed in the underlying contract for which the instrument was issued.

land contract An agreement to purchase real property in which the seller promises to finance the buyer's purchase of a tract of land and the buyer agrees to repay the seller in installment payments.

landlord A person who owns real property and who rents or leases it to someone else. Also called *lessor*.

last clear chance In tort law a defense used by an injured party (the plaintiff) accused of contributory negligence to show that the alleged tortfeasor (the defendant) had the final opportunity to avoid causing injury to that plaintiff.

last resort A criterion under the just war theory that states that a war must be waged only as a final course of action.

last will and testament A formal document that governs the transfer of property at death.

law A set of rules created by the governing body of a society to maintain harmony, stability, and justice in that society.

law merchant In England, the commercial law developed by merchants who needed a set of rules to govern their business transactions.

law of finds A principle that gives ownership to the finder of property as long as the property is abandoned, the finder intends to acquire the property, and the finder has possession of the property.

law of salvage A principle that gives one who engages in a salvage operation the right to compensation for assisting a foundering vessel at sea.

leading objective test In contract law, a test applied by the court to determine the real purpose of a guaranty contract.

lease A contract granting the use of certain real property to another for a specified period in return for the payment of rent.

lease option A contract that permits a party to lease real property while holding an option to purchase that property.

leasehold estate The creation of an ownership interest in the tenant. An interest in real estate that is held under a lease. Also called *tenancy*.

legal detriment In contract law, doing (or promising to do) something that one has a legal right not to do, giving up (or promising to give up) something that one has a legal right to keep, or refraining from doing (or promising not to do) something that one has a legal right to do.

legal imperialism American insistence that all disputes be resolved under American law.

legal tender Money that may be offered legally in satisfaction of a debt and that must be accepted by a creditor when offered.

legatee One who receives personal property in a will.

lemon law A statute that compensates consumers for products (especially vehicles) that are so badly flawed that they are virtually worthless.

lessee See *tenant*.

lessor See *landlord*.

leveraged buyout The purchase of a controlling portion of the stock in a corporation by a group of shareholders, usually officers and directors of the company.

leveraged buyout (LBO) The purchase of a controlling portion of the stock in a corporation by a group of shareholders, usually officers and directors of the company.

liability The legal responsibility of an individual for his or her actions.

liability insurance An insurance contract that protects an insured from injury and damage he or she has caused to a third party.

liar loans Loans that deliberately misstate the qualifications of a borrower to push a loan through the approval process.

libel Any false statement that harms another person's good name or reputation made in a permanent form, such as movies, writing, and videotape, and communicated to others.

liberal democracy A political ideology that supports placing as much political power as possible in the hands of the people.

liberal internationalism A theory of international behavior that says the global order is not fully chaotic but is, instead, controlled by the NIOs; that nation-states share power with the NIOs; that nation-states and NIOs seek power and control but do so in the interests of international peace, by following international law and using military action only within international coalitions; and that the final best state of affairs that all nation-states seek (or should seek) is the formation of a democratic or a republican world government. (See also *idealism*.)

license A grant of permission to do a particular thing, to exercise a certain privilege, to carry on a particular business, or to pursue a certain occupation; an agreement that gives no property right or interest in land but merely allows the licensee to do certain acts that would otherwise be a trespass; a privilege granted by a state or city upon payment of a fee, which is not a contract and may be revoked for cause, conferring authority to perform a designated task, such as operating a motor vehicle.

licensing agreement An agreement in which one party is given permission from another party to do a particular thing in exchange for consideration.

lien A claim that one has against the property of another.

life estate An estate in which the owner owns real property for his or her life or for the life of another.

life insurance An insurance contract that provides monetary compensation for losses suffered by another's death.

limited defense See *personal defense*.

limited liability Status that specifies that an individual's liability will not go beyond his or her original investment.

limited liability company (LLC) A business organization that borrows elements from a partnership and a corporation. LLCs may come into existence only through following the steps laid out in the state code.

limited liability corporation A cross between a partnership and a corporation, offering the protection of limited liability like a corporation and the tax benefits of a partnership.

limited liability partnership A general partnership in all respects except one—liability.

limited partner A partner who does not take part in the management of a firm and whose liability does not extend beyond his or her investment.

limited partnership One or more general partners joined with one or more limited partners to operate a business entity for profit.

limited warranty A warranty that does not meet all of the requirements of a full warranty.

limited-payment life insurance Insurance that provides that the payment will stop after a stated length of time—usually 10, 20, or 30 years.

limited-purpose public figures People who, by their own volition, enter into a public controversy or who, by reason of their position or role, are pulled into the controversy and who, as a result, become a temporary public figure for that limited set of problems.

lingering apparent authority Apparent authority that stays with an agent if the principal has terminated the agent but has failed to give proper notice to third parties entitled to such notice.

liquidated damages Stipulated damages that are legitimate.

liquidation The conversion of property into cash.

list price The price that the seller asks initially when the property is placed on the market.

living trust A trust that comes into existence while the person who establishes it is alive. Also called *inter vivos trust*.

living will A document in which individuals can indicate their desire not to be kept alive by artificial means if there is no hope for recovery.

local option The practice in a state of eliminating uniform statewide laws regulating Sunday activities and allowing the local counties, cities, towns, and villages to adopt their own special Sunday ordinances.

locality rule A means to judge a health care provider's actions on the basis of how other health care professionals in the same community would have acted in the same situation.

lockup agreement A contract between a target corporation and a white knight, giving the knight an option to buy valuable property should a hostile bidder gain control of the target corporation.

locus sigilli The place of the seal. The abbreviation L.S. is often used in place of the seal itself on formal written contracts.

lodger A person who has the use of property without actual or exclusive possession of it.

lost property The general rule is that the finder of lost property becomes the owner thereof against the whole world other than the true owner . . . Property is lost when the owner unintentionally and involuntarily parts with its possession and does not know where it is.

Mail Order and Telephone Order Rule The Federal Trade Commission rule that states that sellers must ship orders within the time promised in their advertisements.

main purpose test In contract law, a test applied by the court to determine the real purpose of a guaranty contract.

majority A term used to describe persons who have reached the legal age of adulthood.

maker A person obligated as the payor on a promissory note. See also *co-maker*.

malicious prosecution Bringing false criminal charges against an innocent victim.

malpractice Occurs when a professional accountant, health care professional, or attorney fails to meet his or her duty of care.

malware Also called malicious software, it is software that infects a computer and shuts down its operation or encrypts its files making them inaccessible.

managerial control A theory of corporate management that favors insulating managers from shareholders by limiting the shareholders' power to vote and by making it difficult for the shareholder to sue managers.

managers In the law of business associations, the people who are charged with running the day-to-day affairs of a limited liability company.

manslaughter The unlawful killing of a person without the intent to kill.

master An outdated term signifying an individual who has the right to control the physical conduct of a servant or employee.

material fact An essential or important fact; a fact of substance.

MDL court An MDL court (also known as a multidistrict litigation court or a transferee court) is one to which a series of similar cases has been moved to be handled by a single federal judge.

means test Three steps used to qualify someone for Chapter 7 bankruptcy.

med-arb A form of ADR that combines the best aspects of both mediation and arbitration. The parties first submit to a mediation session. If the matter cannot be settled, it moves to an arbitration hearing.

mediation The process by which an outside party attempts to help two other parties settle their differences.

mediator The third party in mediation whose job is to convince the contending parties to adjust or settle their dispute.

Medicaid A health care plan for low-income people that is administered by state governments but funded by both state and federal funds.

medical payments insurance A type of automobile insurance that pays for medical (and sometimes funeral) expenses resulting from bodily injuries to anyone occupying the policyholder's car at the time of an accident.

Medicare A federally funded health insurance program for people 65 years and over who are eligible for Social Security.

members In the law of business associations, the people who are the rightful owners of a limited liability company.

memorandum A memorandum is a suggestion issued by the president to an area of the executive branch, indicating how he would prefer that area to use its power.

memorandum A written agreement containing the terms of an agreement, an identification of the subject matter of the agreement, the consideration promised, the names and identities of the parties to the agreement, and the signature of the party charged to the agreement.

mercantile law An area of the law that was developed in Western Civilization almost exclusively by the merchants themselves to govern themselves and their commercial transactions.

merchant A person who deals in goods of the kind sold in the ordinary course of business or who otherwise claims to have knowledge or skills peculiar to those goods.

merchant protection statute A statute that permits a store owner to detain a person when the storeowner has reasonable cause to suspect shoplifting has occurred, also referred to as shopkeeper's privilege statute.

merchantable Whenever a merchant sells goods, the merchant warrants that the goods are reasonably fit for the purpose for which they are sold.

merger The acquisition of one corporation by another.

metadata In computer jargon, data that is used to record information about other computer data.

midnight deadline The deadline by which banks must settle or return checks or be responsible for paying them. If the payor bank is not the depository bank, it must settle for an item by midnight of the banking day of receipt. If the payor bank is also the depository bank, the deadline is midnight of the next banking day following the banking day on which it receives the relevant item.

military caregiver leave A provision under the Family and Medical Leave Act (FMLA), which states that an employer must give an employee up to 26 weeks of leave time in a 12-month period to care for a family member who has sustained a serious illness or injury that occurred because of military service.

minimum contacts The doctrine of minimum contacts identifies the fewest number of contacts that will permit a court to exercise personal jurisdiction over an out-of-state defendant.

minority A term used to describe persons who have not reached the legal age of adulthood.

mirror image rule In contract law, the rule that an acceptance must duplicate the terms in the offer.

misdemeanor A crime less serious than a felony that is generally punishable by a prison sentence of not more than one year.

misplaced or mislaid property Property that has been unintentionally left behind by its owner, usually in a public place.

misrepresentation In contract law, a false statement innocently made by one party to a contract with no intent to deceive. Also, in insurance, giving false answers to questions in an insurance application that materially affect the risk undertaken by the insurer.

misuse of legal procedure Bringing legal action without probable cause and with malice.

mixed contract In contract law a binding agreement that has enough characteristics of a sales contract and a service contract to be considered a combination of both. See also *blended contract* and *hybrid contract*.

monarch A corporate officer who has complete control of the board of directors of a corporation.

monetary threshold In insurance law, a guideline to determine when a victim can bring a lawsuit for injuries that result from an auto accident.

money order A type of draft that may be purchased from banks, post offices, telegraph companies, and express companies as a substitute for a check.

monopoly The exclusive control of a market by a business enterprise.

morals Values that govern society's attitude toward right and wrong.

mortgage A transfer of an interest in property for the purpose of creating a security for a debt.

mortgage-backed securities Bundling a bunch of FHA or VA mortgages together and selling them as bonds to big investors, like pension funds, which would then reap the benefit of the interest payments multiplied by the number of loans purchased in that bundle over a long period of time, while the lender received a big payment up front, allowing it to bundle more and more mortgages more and more rapidly.

mortgagee The party who lends money and takes back a mortgage as security for the loan.

mortgagor The party who borrows money and gives a mortgage to the lender or mortgagee as security for the loan.

most favored nation principle A principle that states that the World Trade Organization nations must apply the same privileges, advantages, and benefits to all other member nations in relation to similar imports.

multidistrict litigation (MDL) The federal courts use a procedure designed to consolidate cases in order to streamline the legal process and lighten the case load at the trial level. This procedure moves a series of cases of a similar type to a single federal judge.

municipal utility district Another joint economic development option. A municipal utility district is established to develop a cost sharing program between two or more municipalities to improve the infrastructure of the participating municipalities.

mutual assent In contract law, the state of mind that exists between an offeror and an offeree once a valid offer has been accepted and once the parties know what the terms are and have agreed to be bound by them. Also known as "a meeting of the minds."

mutual mistake See *bilaterial mistake*.

mutual recession A condition in which both parties to a contract agree to rescind the contract and return to the other any consideration already received or pay for any services or materials already rendered.

mutuum (MYOO·choo·um) A loan of goods with the intention that the goods may be used and later replaced with an equal amount of different goods.

M'Naughten Rule The oldest test for insanity whereby a criminal defendant is declared not guilty by reason of insanity if, at the time of the criminal act, he or she suffered from a mental disease that prevented him or her from understanding the nature of the act and that the act was wrong.

national rule A rule that allows a court to judge a health care provider's degree of care by determining how the same procedure is performed on a national basis.

national standard A rule that allows a court to judge a health care provider's degree of care by determining how the same procedure is performed on a national basis.

national treatment principle A principle that states that the World Trade Organization nations must apply the same standards to imports that they apply to domestic goods.

natural law theory A system of ethical thought that sees an unbreakable link joining the law and morality.

natural property Property that has been buried for such a long time that it becomes part of the natural earth itself. The finder of that property is not considered the true owner.

navigable airspace The space above 1,000 feet over populated areas and above 500 feet over water and unpopulated areas.

near-privity Privity that emerges between an accountant and a third party who is not a client. When a state of privity does not exist in a type two arrangement, the relationship between the accountant and the third party is one in which the parties acted as if privity existed.

necessaries Goods and services that are essential to a minor's health and welfare.

necessary and proper clause In constitutional law, Article I, Section 8, Clause 18, of the U.S. Constitution, which says that Congress has the power "(T)o make all Laws which shall be necessary and proper for carrying into Execution the foregoing Powers, and all other Powers vested by this Constitution in the Government of the United States, or any Department or Officer thereof."

negligence The failure to use that amount of care that a reasonably prudent person would have used under the same circumstances and conditions.

negligent credentialing Occurs if a hospital has retained a physician that the governing body of the hospital knew or should have known was incompetent.

negligent hiring The proprietor's liability for the hiring of an incompetent contractor who consequently harms an innocent third party while performing the hired-for work.

negligent retention The failure of a proprietor to dismiss an incompetent contractor after the proprietor has learned of the contractor's incompetence.

negligent supervision In employment law and tort law, the failure of the hiring party to track, regulate, and evaluate the activities of a hired party resulting in an injury to an innocent third party.

negotiable instrument A written document that is signed by the maker or drawer and that contains an unconditional promise or order to pay a certain sum of money on delivery or at a definite time to the bearer or to order.

negotiated rule making (reg-neg) Occurs when an agency that is about to create a new rule or revise existing rules enters into a cooperative process by which all parties affected by the rule have a chance to shape the final form that the rule will take.

negotiation The transfer of a negotiable instrument in such form that the transferee becomes a holder.

neoconservativism A theory of international behavior that says nation-states are the chief actors; that all foreign policy decisions must be made to echo the "deepest values of liberal democratic societies;" that the United States must be involved in global affairs and, in doing so, must promote democratic principles; that social re-engineering missions rarely work (read nation-building here); and that unilateral (as opposed to multinational) military crusades including especially preemptive and preventive strikes work and work well.

neoliberalism A theory of international behavior that the global community scene is largely chaotic; that nation-states and NIOs share the global power with international corporations; that international corporations cross frontiers and act to preserve their own existence, as do nation-states; that internationals act reasonably as they work to generate higher profits; and that nation-states and international corporations act as collaborative partners and in doing so, follow the morality of profit.

new community authority A corporate entity instituted by a community and run by a board of directors, the purpose of which is to coordinate with private enterprise to support the systematic growth of a diversified, strategically planned, and financially healthy community.

new world order A set of initial conditions that describes how nation-states relate to one another on a global scale.

next of kin Those who are most nearly related by blood.

NINJA loan A loan that has been negotiated by a borrower with "no income, no job, and no assets."

No Electronic Theft Act (NET Act) A federal law that grants limited immunity to persons who duplicate copyrighted works on the Internet, as long as those users do not profit from the copying process.

no-fault insurance A type of automobile insurance that allows drivers to collect damages and medical expenses from their own insurance carriers regardless of who is at fault in an accident.

nominal damages Token damages awarded to parties who have experienced an injury to their legal rights but no actual loss.

non-core cases Bankrupty cases that are "related to" Title 11.

non-delivery A personal defense available to the drawer of a commercial instrument that allows the drawer to refuse to pay on the instrument when the instrument has not been properly delivered, unless the delivery is to a holder in due course.

non-governmental organization (NGO) An organization that functions beyond the boundaries of any one governmental body.

nonconforming goods Goods that are not the same as those called for under a contract or that are in some way defective.

nonconforming uses Uses of land permitted to continue even though newly enacted zoning laws no longer permit similar uses.

nondelegable duty A duty that the proprietor cannot delegate, or pass off, to another party.

nondisclosure See *passive fraud*.

nondisclosure agreement An agreement that requires employees to promise that, should they leave their employment with their present employer, they will not reveal any confidential trade secrets that they may learn at their current job.

noneconomic compensatory damages Damages that result from injuries that are intangible and, therefore, not directly quantifiable. Examples include damages resulting from pain and suffering, mental anguish, and loss of companionship.

note A written promise by one party to pay money to another party. Also called *promissory note*.

novation The substitution, by mutual agreement, of another party for one of the original parties to a contract.

nuncupative wills Oral wills made by persons in their last illness or by soldiers and sailors in actual combat and are valid only in some states and are restricted to the giving of personal property only.

objective concept rule Under this rule, the meaning of one's actions is determined by the impression those actions would make upon any reasonable person who might have witnessed them, not by a party's self-serving claim of what was meant or intended by the actions.

obligee In contract law, the party to whom another party owes an obligation.

obligor In contract law, the party who is obligated to deliver on a promise or to undertake some act.

obstruction of justice In criminal law, an activity designed to prevent the discovery, apprehension, arrest, prosecution, conviction, or punishment of a criminal defendant.

obvious-to-try standard A patent challenge that asserts anyone of ordinary skill could see the invention was obvious to try, which makes the invention not be patentable.

ocean marine insurance A type of insurance that covers ships at sea.

offer In contract law, a proposal made by one party to another indicating a willingness to enter into a contract.

offeree In contract law, the person to whom an offer is made.

offeror In contract law, the person who makes the offer.

Office of Credit Ratings A new agency authorized by the SEC where the purpose is to watch those organizations that issue credit ratings. These organizations, known in the industry as nationally recognized statistical rating organizations or NRSROs, are key elements in the financial structure of the U.S. economy because they open or close the door on the ability of investors and borrowers to enter the marketplace.

Office of Investor Advocate (OIA) Subtitle A of Title XI of the Dodd–Frank Act creates a new agency, referred to as the Office of Investor Advocate (OIA), the purpose of which is to help make the work of broker-dealers and investment advisors (IAs) more transparent.

Oil Pollution Act A federal law designed to encourage companies that ship, drill for, and store oil to develop and use the most up-to-date equipment and the most effective safety measures possible.

online banking A process by which a bank's customers can pay their bills and check their bank statements online by using their home computer, a laptop, a tablet, a smartphone, or some other other electronic device.

open-price terms A contract for the sale of goods that is established even though the price is not settled.

operating agreement An agreement containing various rights, provisions, and powers that aid in establishing the bylaws of an LLC.

opt-out rule A rule that permits a corporation to sidestep the independent director's rule provided the corporation is a controlled company, that is, one that has more than half its voting power concentrated in one individual, or a small group of people, who always vote together.

option In contract law, the giving of consideration to support an offeror's promise to hold an offer open for a stated or reasonable length of time. Also called *option contract*.

order An order is an executive mandate that is a mandatory directive aimed at a subdivision within the executive branch.

order for relief In bankruptcy law, a court's command that the liquidation begin.

order paper A negotiable instrument that is payable to someone's order.

ordinary life insurance See *straight life insurance*.

ordinary negligence Failure to use that amount of care that a reasonable person would use under the same circumstance.

original jurisdiction The authority of a court to hear a case when it is first brought to court.

ostensible authority Occurs when a hospital leads a patient to believe that a physician with staff privileges is an employee of the hospital.

output contract An agreement in which a seller agrees to sell "all the goods we manufacture" or "all the crops we produce" to a particular buyer. See also *requirements contract*.

outside party See *third party*.

overdraft A payment by a bank on behalf of a customer for more than the customer has on deposit.

par value The value that is placed on the shares of stock at incorporation.

paradigm An unchallenged world view that establishes the rules by which everyone in a particular culture thinks, speaks, and acts.

parol evidence rule The rule that states that evidence of oral statements made before signing a written agreement is usually not admissible in court to change or to contradict the terms of a written agreement.

part performance An exception to the rule that contracts for the sale of land must be in writing. It applies when a person relies on an owner's oral promise to sell real estate and then makes improvements on the property or changes his or her position in an important way. Also called *equitable estoppel*.

partially disclosed principal A person, in a transaction conducted by an agent, whose existence is known to the third party but whose specific identify is unknown.

participation loan A loan in which the borrower will transfer certain ownership or equity rights to the lender in exchange for a lower interest rate or a lower down payment.

partnering A process that establishes supportive relationships among the parties to a contract to head off disputes before they occur.

partnership An association of two or more persons to carry on a business for profit.

partnership at will A partnership in which any partner may leave without liability.

passenger A person who enters the premises of a carrier with the intention of buying a ticket for a trip. One continues to be a passenger as long as the trip continues.

passing bad checks In criminal law, issuing or transferring a check or other negotiable instrument knowing it will be dishonored and with the intent to defraud.

passive fraud A failure to reveal some material fact about the subject matter of a contract that one party is obligated to reveal to the other party and that intentionally deceives that second party, leading him or her into a damaging contract. Also called *concealment* and *nondisclosure*.

past consideration A promise to give another something of value in return for goods or services rendered and delivered in the past.

patent A grant from the government that gives an inventor the exclusive right to make, use, and sell an invention for a period set by Congress.

payee The party named in a note or draft to whom payment is to be made.

payor bank A bank by which an item is payable as drawn or accepted. It includes a drawee bank.

penumbra rights A set of human rights that are found in those indeterminate or indistinct shadow areas associated with more uniformly accepted rights, such as the right to a safe and secure life.

per se **violation** In antitrust law, a restraint of trade practice so serious that it is prohibited whether or not it actually harms anyone.

perfected The state of a security interest when the secured party has done everything that the law requires to give the secured party greater rights to the goods than others have.

performance In contract law, the situation that exists when the parties to a contract have done what they had agreed to do.

peril A danger that a party might pass on to others.

periodic tenancy A leasehold estate, or tenancy, that continues for successive periods until one of the parties terminates it by giving notice to the other party.

perjury In criminal law, making false statements under oath.

permanently unconscious state Defined as a "(p)ermanently unconscious state means a state of permanently unconsciousness in a declarant that to a reasonable degree of medical certainty as determined in accordance with reasonable medical standards by a declarant's attending physician and one other physician who has examined the declarant, is characterized by both an irreversible unawareness of one's being and environment, AND total loss of cerebral cortical functioning resulting in the declarant having no capacity to experience pain or suffering."

personal defense In negotiable-instruments law, a defense that can be used against a holder but not against a holder in due course of a negotiable instrument. Also called *limited defense*.

personal injury protection (PIP) Automobile insurance that places limitations on the insured's ability to sue other drivers but allows drivers to collect damages and medical expenses from their own insurance carriers, regardless of who is at fault in an accident.

personal jurisdiction A court's authority over the parties to a lawsuit.

personal property Everything that can be owned other than real estate.

personal representative Executors and administrators of wills in states that have adopted the Uniform Probate Code.

persuasive precedent A previous case that a court is free to follow or to ignore.

physical duress Violence or the threat of violence against an individual or that person's family, household, or property that is so serious that it forces a person into a contract against his or her will.

pie powder court Historically in the Middle Ages in Europe, a court set up at a festival to handle disputes between merchants at that festival.

pierce the corporate veil The doctrine holding shareholders of a corporation personally liable when they have used the corporation as a facade to defraud or commit some other misdeed.

plaintiff The person who begins a lawsuit by filing a complaint in the appropriate trial court of general jurisdiction.

plenary review The process by which appellate courts determine if lower courts have made errors of law.

poison pill A corporate takeover defensive tactic that triggers a drop in stock prices for all but the takeover bidder.

police power A state's authority to restrict private rights to promote and maintain public health, safety, welfare, and morals.

policy The contract of insurance.

political ideology A belief system that supports a particular method of governing a nation-state.

pooling agreement An agreement made by shareholders whereby they promise to vote the same way on a particular issue. Also called *shareholder agreements* and *voting agreements*.

Population Commission (PC) A group that was created under the auspices of the UN Economic and Social Council to investigate demographic concerns and to consult with the ECOSOC on a variety of population issues.

port authority A non-profit corporate entity established within a geographically situated area, partnering political subdivisions (municipalities, counties, and so on) to help manage the transportation industry, to promote economic growth, to help finance businesses, and to promote infrastructure redevelopment in that area.

positive law In ethics, the theory that says that laws originate from an outside source that emerges within society.

post-appellate procedures The process of taking a case that has been rejected or dismissed by a domestic court to an international organization, such as the Inter-American Commission on Human Rights of the Organization of American States.

pragmatism In procedural law, a judicial interpretation technique by which a judge considers the consequences of his or her interpretation of a law.

precedent A model case that a court can follow when facing a similar situation.

predicate offense One that provides the needed resources (read money here) that are needed to commit the offense outlined in the new statute.

predictive political history A technique for determining how world leaders will probably act in a given world order when facing a crisis or mapping out a future global strategy.

predominant factor test A test that directs the judge to focus on the whole contract and to take into consideration the purpose of the agreement and the degree of trust that existed between the parties in order to determine if the agreement is a goods contract, with some work involved, or a service contract, with some service involved, almost incidentally.

preemption The process by which the courts decide that a federal statute must take precedence over a state statute.

preemptive right A shareholder's right to purchase a proportionate share of every new offering of stock by the corporation.

preemptive war A conflict waged when one nation attacks a sovereign nation to stop that nation from engaging in activities that the attacking nation has decided are against its national interests.

preexisting duty An obligation that a party is already bound to by law or by some other agreement. The party may not use this as consideration in a new contract.

preferred stock A class of stock that carries with it the right to receive payment of dividends and/or the distribution of assets on the dissolution of the corporation before other classes of stock receive their payments.

preliminary hearing A court procedure during which the judge decides whether probable cause exists to continue holding a defendant for a crime.

premarriage agreement In contract law, an agreement between two people planning marriage and who agree in writing to change the property rights they possess by law.

premeditated murder In criminal law, killing someone with prior calculation and design, or while committing a serious felony such as rape, robbery or kidnapping.

premium The consideration paid by the insured to the insurer for insurance protection.

prenuptial agreement An agreement between two people who are planning marriage and who agree to change the property rights they possess by law in a marriage.

prescriptive theory A system of ethical thought that describes how to come up with the values at work within a social system.

presenting bank Any bank presenting an item except a payor bank.

presentment A demand for acceptance or payment of a negotiable instrument made upon the maker, acceptor, or drawee by or on behalf of the holder of the instrument.

preventive war A war waged to prevent another nation-state from reaching a point that it would be capable of attacking the first nation.

primary objective test A rule that states a writing is not needed for enforcement if the promise to pay another party's debt is made to obtain a gain for the guarantor.

principal A person who authorizes an agent to act on her or his behalf and subject to her or his control.

principle of honorable surrender A criterion under a modern version of the just war theory that requires a victor to accept the surrender of the enemy and to treat the defeated combatants with dignity and respect.

principle of repentance A criterion under a modern version of the just war theory that calls for a genuine expression of remorse for the death and destruction caused by war.

principle of restoration A criterion under a modern version of the just war theory that requires a victor in a conflict to act responsibly in rebuilding the defeated nation's physical environment, economy, and governmental structure.

prior art All relevant technical knowledge about the field to which the invention belongs.

private civil trial Trials run according to the same rules of procedure and evidence as trials run under the official auspices of the court. In a private trial, the parties can hold the trial when and where they choose, and they can choose the judge. Lengthy civil cases are well-suited to this approach.

private corporation An entity formed by private persons to carry out a task best undertaken by an organization that can raise large amounts of capital quickly and that can grant the protection of limited liability.

private information Reports on personal matters, family matters, sexual habits, employment records, medical data, and financial records. Also called *private-private* information.

private religiously based corporate entity A dual-purpose business entity that, while not sponsored by or affiliated with a mainstream church, nevertheless seeks to promote both the goals of an established religious body and a profit for its owners.

privity In contract law, the relationship that exists between two parties to a contract giving each a recognized interest in the subject matter of the contract so that they are bound to that contract.

probability of success A criterion under the just war theory that states that a war must be waged only when there is a reasonable chance of success.

probate To settle the estate of a decedent under the supervision of a court.

proclamation A proclamation is an executive order that addresses the public at large.

product liability A law that imposes liability on the manufacturer and the seller of a product produced and sold in a defective condition.

professional An individual who can perform a highly specialized task because of special abilities, education, experience, and knowledge.

promissory estoppel The legal doctrine that restricts an offeror from revoking an offer under certain conditions, even though consideration has not been promised to bind the agreement. To be effective, promissory estoppel requires that the offeror know, or be presumed to know, that the offeree might otherwise make a definite and decided change of position in contemplation of promises contained in the offer.

promoters The people who do the day-to-day work involved in creating a corporation.

proof of loss form A form that details the personal property that was destroyed during the incident that gave rise to the claim.

property damage liability insurance A type of automobile insurance that provides protection when other people bring claims or lawsuits against the insured for damaging property such as a car, a fence, or a tree.

proportionality A criterion under the just war theory that states that the good advanced by the war must exceed the negative consequences of entering the conflict.

proprietor An owner, as of a business. The party for which an independent contractor works.

prosecutor An attorney that represents the government in a criminal procedure.

prospectus A document published by a corporation explaining, in simplified fashion for potential investors, the details of a stock issuance and the business making the offer.

protective war A war aimed at providing aid and assistance to innocent civilians who are being victimized by the military of their own nation-state.

provisional Not final.

proximate cause In tort law, the connection between the unreasonable conduct and the resulting harm. Proximate cause is determined by asking whether the harm that resulted from the conduct was foreseeable at the time of the original negligent act.

proxy The authority given to one shareholder to cast another shareholder's votes.

proxy contest A struggle between two factions in a corporation, usually management and a group of dissident shareholders, to obtain the votes of the other shareholders.

proxy solicitation The process by which one shareholder asks another for his or her voting right.

proxy statement A document that communicates information about the identity of a solicitor, the reason for a solicitation, and all other crucial information that shareholders need to make an informed decision about a proxy.

public (or state owned) corporation An entity set up by the federal, state, or local governments for governmental purposes usually involving public health, safety, or welfare.

public accountant (PA) An accountant who works for a variety of clients but who is not certified.

public bodies corporation A project that would transform public corporations, making them into profit making entities.

Public Company Accounting Oversight Board (PCAOB) A regulatory agency that is charged with the task of making certain that correct, unbiased, and comprehensive data finds their way to potential investors, so that they can make informed decisions about investment opportunities.

public corporation A corporation created by the federal, state, or local government for governmental purposes. Also, a large private corporation that generally sells its stock to the public at large.

public duty doctrine Public employees must be empowered to do what they have a duty to do as part of their job and should not be held back by a concern that they might make a mistake. In other words, public employees must be assured that they will not be sued if they make an error while on the job.

public interest The idea that certain activities affect the entire social structure and must, therefore, be regulated by the government.

public offer An offer made through the public media but intended for only one person whose identity or address is unknown to the offeror.

public policy The general legal principle that says no one should be allowed to do anything that tends to injure the public at large.

public-private corporation An entity that is owned and operated by the state but that is not protected from failure by the government.

public-private corporate analog An entity that is owned and operated by the state but that is not protected from failure by the government.

punitive damages Damages in excess of actual losses suffered by the plaintiff awarded as a measure of punishment for the defendant's wrongful acts. Also called *exemplary damages*.

purchase money security interest A security interest that arises when someone lends money to a consumer and then takes a security interest in the goods that the consumer buys.

purpose In criminal law, the intent to cause the result that does, in fact, occur.

qualified indorsement An indorsement in which words, such as "without recourse," have been added to the signature to limit the liability of the indorser.

qualified mortgages Mortgages that have met the good-faith requirements outlined in the Dodd–Frank Wall Street Reform and Consumer Protection Act. Having a qualified mortgage bestows on the lender a safe harbor privilege that creates a presumption that the lender had ample evidence demonstrating that the borrower could satisfy the loan's repayment requirements.

qualified opinion An opinion issued by an auditor saying that, as of a given date, the books of a firm represent its financial health; however, the auditor may qualify the opinion either because the firm is facing some uncertainty that might affect the company in the future or because the firm has deviated from generally accepted accounting principles (GAAP) in some minor way.

qualifying exigency leave Leave time that is granted to employees permitting them to use as much as 20 weeks to take care of certain nonmedical emergencies during the time that a spouse, child, or parent is on active duty in the military.

quasi-contract See *implied-in-law contract*.

quasi-public corporation A privately organized entity that makes a profit but that provides a service on which the public depends.

quasi-RPM arrangement An agreement that occurs when a manufacturer lets retailers know the price that it expects to see on an item and declines to sell that item to any retailer that does not list the item at that price.

quick-look standard A standard in antitrust law under which a judge will look at the evidence to determine whether an objective observer with elementary knowledge of the world of finance would see anticompetitive results.

quid pro quo **sexual harassment** A supervisor's unwelcome advancement or suggestion to a subordinate to trade sexual favors for preferential treatment.

quiet enjoyment The right of a tenant to the undisturbed possession of the property that he or she is renting.

quitclaim deed A deed that transfers to the buyer only the interest that the seller may have in a property and that contains no warranties.

racial profiling The act of targeting a person for criminal investigation primarily because of racial or ethnic characteristics.

ransomware One of the most powerful forms of malware, it generally enters a computer system via an e-mail that includes a link or an attachment.

ratification The principal's approval of an unauthorized act performed by an agent or by one who has no authority to act as an agent. Also, an approval of a contract made by a minor after reaching maturity.

rational ethics A system of ethical thought that uses reason as the basis for making ethical judgments.

real defense In negotiable-instruments law, any defense that can be used against everyone, including holders in due course. Also called *absolute defense* and *universal defense*.

real estate The ground and everything permanently attached to it including land, buildings, and growing trees and shrubs; the air space above the land is also included.

real property The ground and everything permanently attached to it including land, buildings, and growing trees and shrubs; the air space above the land is also included.

realism A theory of international behavior that says that the international order can be described as a chaotic system; that the chief actors on the global scene are nation-states; that national leaders customarily look for a rational way to sustain or widen their own power; and that the power leaders have is curbed by NIOs like the United Nations, the International Criminal Court, and so on, by international corporations, and by lower level transnationals, such as terrorist groups, pirates, drug cartels, mercenaries, and so on. (See also *Realpolitik*.)

Realpolitik A theory of international behavior that says that the international order can be described as a chaotic system; that the chief actors on the global scene are nation-states; that national leaders customarily look for a rational way to sustain or widen their own power; and that the power leaders have is curbed by NIOs like the United Nations, the International Criminal Court, and so on, by international corporations, and by lower level transnationals, such as terrorist groups, pirates, drug cartels, mercenaries, and so on. (See also *realism*.)

reasonable accommodation The quality of accommodation that allows a disabled worker to accomplish essential functions in the workplace without imposing undue hardship on the employer.

reasonable time In contract law, the time that may fairly, properly, and conveniently be required to do the task that is to be done, with regard to attending circumstances.

rebuttable presumption A disputable presumption that a defending party has the right to attack.

rebuttal The presentation of evidence to discredit the evidence by the opposition and to reestablish the credibility of his or her own evidence.

recklessness In criminal law, a perverse disregard for a known risk of a negative result.

recovery Denotes a reversal to an earlier status.

reflexivity principle An unstable element within the human decision-making process that emerges because the act of making a decision in a system often alters that system (See also *uncertainty principle*.)

registered limited liability partnership (RLLP or LLP) A general partnership in which partners are not jointly or severally liable for partnership liabilities caused by the act or omission of another partner or employee unless the partner had supervision over the other partner or employee.

registration statement A statement required by the Securities and Exchange Commission to indicate details about a business selling securities.

regulations Rules made by the regulatory agencies of the federal and/or state governments.

rehabilitate In contract law, the process of compensating an innocent party for losses that result from a breach of contract.

rejection The express or implied refusal by an offeree to accept an offer.

release In contract law, a promise made by one party agreeing not to sue a second party.

remainder estate A future interest in property when title is to pass to someone other than the grantor or grantor's heirs at the expiration of a life estate.

remitting bank Any payor or intermediary bank remitting for an item.

renter's insurance An insurance policy that protects tenants against loss of personal property, against liability for a visitor's personal injury, and against liability for negligent destruction of the rented premises.

renunciation A legal act by which a person abandons a right acquired, but without transferring it to another.

reorganization In bankruptcy law, a plan created by a qualified debtor that alters his or her repayment schedule and allows the debtor to stay in business.

request for admission A request made to secure a statement from a party that a particular fact is true or that a document or set of documents is genuine.

request for physical or mental examination A request for a party to undergo a physical or a mental examination.

request for real evidence A discovery device that asks the opposing party in a lawsuit to produce papers, records, accounts, correspondence, photographs, or other tangible evidence, including ESI.

requirements contract An agreement in which one party agrees to purchase all of his or her requirements of a particular product from another party. See also *output contract*.

rescission A remedy in contract law that returns both parties to a contract back to their original positions before the contract was entered into.

resisting arrest In criminal law, interfering with the lawful arrest of a criminal defendant.

respondeat superior **(re·SPOND·ee·yat se·PEER·ee·or)** The legal doctrine that imposes liability on employers and makes them pay for torts committed by their employees within the scope of the employer's business. Literally translated, it means "Let the master respond."

Responsibility to Protect (R2P) A new doctrine that declares the leadership of every nation has a definitive duty to protect its own people from four major threats: genocide, war crimes, ethnic cleansing, and crimes against humanity.

restrictive covenant A promise by an employee in an employment contract not to work for anyone else in the same field of employment for a specified time period within a particular geographical area.

restrictive employment covenant A promise by an employee in an employment contract not to work for anyone else in the same field of employment for a specified time period within a particular geographical area.

restrictive indorsement An indorsement in which words have been added to the signature of the indorser that specify the purpose of the indorsement or the use to be made of the commercial paper, such as "for deposit only."

retaliation An action or series of actions taken by a hiring party against a hired party that adversely affects the hired party, prompted by the hired party's exercise of some legal right.

reverse discrimination A practice designed to eliminate discrimination against a protected class but that has the opposite effect on members of another protected class.

reverse mortgage A type of loan that allows home owners, over the age of 62, to convert some of the equity in their home into cash while retaining ownership of their home.

reversion estate A future interest in property when title is to return to the grantor or grantor's heirs upon expiration of a life estate.

Revised Uniform Partnership Act (RUPA) The latest partnership statute written by the National Conference of Commissioners on Uniform State Laws.

revocation The calling back of an offer by the offeror.

right intention A criterion under the just war theory that states that a war must be waged only if the combatant has the correct objective.

right of way See *easement*.

right to tinker The right to do what one wants to a product once it is purchased by a company. It can be resold, given away, painted, modified, broken apart, melted, sold for parts, or even destroyed.

right-to-work laws State laws that prohibit labor-management agreements requiring union membership as a condition of getting or keeping a job.

riparian owners People who own land along the bank of a river or stream. They have certain rights and duties with respect to the water that flows over, under, and beside their land.

risk Threats to life, health, and property that an insured wants to protect against by purchasing insurance.

robbery The act of taking personal property from the possession of another against that person's will and under threat to do great bodily harm or damage.

royalty In intellectual property law, the consideration paid to an author or an inventor for permission to use the intellectual property of that author or inventor.

RPM agreement The agreement between a retailer and a manufacturer that the retailer will sell certain products at a price set by the manufacturer.

rule of contemporary ownership The rule that holds that shareholders must own stock at the time of the injury and at the time of the lawsuit if they wish to begin a derivative suit.

rule-of-reason standard In antitrust law, a doctrine that holds that a court should stop certain practices only if they are an unreasonable restriction of competition.

S corporation A corporation in which shareholders have agreed to have the profits (or losses) of the corporation taxed directly to them rather than to the corporation.

Safe Harbor Principles Principles of electronically stored information (ESI) protection established by the Department of Commerce that, if followed by American companies, will qualify them for commerce with the EU.

sale on approval A conditional sale that becomes absolute only if the buyer approves or is satisfied with the article being sold.

sale or return A sale in which the buyer takes title to goods with the right to revest title in the seller after a specified period or reasonable time.

sales puffery Persuasive words or exaggerated arguments made by salespeople to induce customers to buy their product. As long as such comments are reserved to opinion and do not misstate facts, they are not actionable as fraud, even if they turn out to be grossly in error. Also called *puffery*.

salvage A reward given to persons who voluntarily assist a sinking ship to recover its cargo from peril or loss.

salvor A person who salvages. The law of salvage gives the salvor the right to compensation for assisting a foundering vessel.

same state locality rule A means to judge a health care provider's actions on the basis of the standard of care used in the same state in which that provider practices.

Sarbanes–Oxley Act Legislation that places an affirmative duty on the directors of publicly traded corporations to monitor whether they are conforming to all legal requirements.

satisfaction The agreed-to settlement as contained in an accord.

satisfactory performance In contract law, the situation that exists when either personal taste or objective standards determine the contracting parties have performed their contractual duties according to the agreement.

scope of authority The range of acts done while performing agency duties. Also called *scope of employment*.

scope of employment See *scope of authority*.

seal A mark or impression placed on a written contract indicating that the instrument was executed and accepted in a formal manner.

second mortgage See *junior mortgage*.

second-degree murder In criminal law, the purposeful killing of another human being without premeditation.

secondary boycott Conspiracy in which a union places pressure on a neutral customer or supplier with whom the union has no dispute in order to cause the neutral entity to cease doing business with the employer with whom the union has a dispute.

secret partner A partner whose identity and existence are not known outside of the firm but who can participate in the management of the firm.

Secretariat The administrative bureaucracy of the United Nations.

secretary general The chief administrator of the United Nations.

secured loan A loan in which creditors have something of value, usually called collateral, from which they can be paid if the debtor does not pay.

secured party A lender or seller who holds a security interest.

securitization The process of bundling securities and then selling them to big investors.

security In secured transactions, the assurance that a creditor will be paid back for any money loaned or credit extended to a debtor. In corporate law, a money investment that expects a return solely because of another person's efforts.

security agreement A written agreement that creates a security interest.

Security Council The United Nations body that deals with international crises.

security device A technique for creditors to get their money back in case the borrower or debtor cannot pay.

security interest A creditor's right to use collateral to recover a debt.

security-based swaps According to the SEC, "swaps based on (1) a single security, (2) a loan, (3) a narrow-based group or index of securities, or (4) events relating to a single issuer or issuers of securities in a narrow-based security index."

self-dealing manager A corporate manager who has a stake in a decision that he or she made or is about to make.

self-defense A defense to criminal liability available to defendants if they can demonstrate (1) that they did not start the altercation, (2) that they had good reason to believe they were in danger of death or severe bodily injury, and (3) that they used only enough force to repel the attack.

servant An outdated term signifying a person employed to perform services in the affairs of another and who, with respect to the physical conduct in the performance of the service, is subject to the other's right to control.

service of process The act of giving the summons and the complaint to a defendant.

servient tenement The property through which an easement is created or through which it extends.

settlement week An ADR technique in which the court clears its docket of all business except settlement hearings.

severalty The quality or state of sole ownership of a single property.

shareholder democracy A theory of corporate management that favors making management more responsive to shareholders by giving shareholders greater voting power and by making it easier for shareholders to sue managers.

shareholder of record A person to whom stock has been transferred and whose name has been entered on the corporate books as the owner of that stock. Shareholders of record are entitled to vote, receive dividends, and enjoy all other privileges of being a shareholder.

shareholder proposal A suggestion submitted by a shareholder about a broad company policy or procedure.

shareholder resolution In corporate law, a suggestion about a broad company policy or procedure submitted by a shareholder.

shareholders Persons who own units of ownership interest called shares of stock in a corporation. Also called *stockholders*.

shares Portions of a corporation that may be owned by the various shareholders.

shelter provision A provision whereby a holder who receives an instrument from a holder in due course acquires the rights of the holder in due course even though he or she does not qualify as a holder in due course.

shipment contract A contract under which a seller turns goods over to a carrier for delivery to a buyer. Both the title and risk of loss pass to the buyer when the goods are given to the carrier.

shopkeeper's privilege A statute that permits a store owner to detain a person when the storeowner has reasonable cause to suspect shoplifting has occurred, also referred to as merchant protection statute.

sight draft A draft that is payable as soon as it is presented to the drawee for payment.

silent partner A partner who does not participate in the day-to-day business of the firm.

similar locality rule The rule that allows a court to judge a health care provider's degree of care by determining how the same procedure is performed at another hospital located in a similar locality.

similar practitioner rule A means to judge a health care provider's actions according to whether that provider is a general practitioner or a specialist.

slamming The illegal practice of changing a consumer's telephone service without permission.

slander Any false statement that harms a person's good name or reputation made in a temporary form, such as speech, and communicated to others.

slight negligence The failure to use that degree of care that persons of extraordinary prudence and foresight are accustomed to use.

social contract ethics In ethics, a theory that says that right and wrong are measured by the obligations imposed on each individual by an implied agreement among individuals within a given social system.

social corporation An entity run by a diverse board of directors with representatives from the employees, the state, and the general public.

social media policy (SMP) In employment law, a set of rules written by an employer telling employees what they can and cannot do when using electronic communication devices, formats, websites, and other electronic messaging techniques, such as blogs, text messages, tweets, skype transmissions, and e-mails.

sock puppetry The practice of creating a false identity when blogging or when offering testimonials on line.

sole proprietorship A business operation owned and operated by one person.

sovereign immunity An ancient legal doctrine that holds that unless a nation-state grants its consent or waives its immunity, it cannot be sued.

sovereign immunity The somewhat discredited doctrine preventing a lawsuit against government authority without the government's consent.

spam Unsolicited e-mail.

special agent A person who is authorized to conduct only a particular transaction or to perform only a specified act for a principal.

special improvement district (SID) A non-profit corporate entity instituted by the members of a community, generally including townships and municipalities, and run by a board of directors, with the purpose of working to upgrade the existing services in that community.

special indorsement An indorsement made by first writing on the back of a negotiable instrument an order to pay a specified person and then signing the instrument. Also called *indorsement in full*.

special jurisdiction The power of a court to hear only certain kinds of cases.

special warranty deed A deed containing express warranties under which the grantor guarantees that no defects arose in the title during the time that he or she owned the property.

specific performance A decree from a court ordering a contracting party to carry out the promises made in a contract.

speculative damages Damage computed on losses that have not actually been suffered and that cannot be proved; they are based entirely on an expectation of losses that might be suffered from a breach; the courts do not allow speculative damages.

spousal share States that have retained the concept of dower have changed the name to this to properly reflect its gender neutral nature.

staff privileges When a hospital grants physicians, who are not employed by the hospital, the privilege to treat their patients at that hospital.

stakeholders Individuals and coalitions that are officially outside a corporation but which are affected by the corporate decisions.

stale check A check that is presented for payment more than six months after its date.

stand-your-ground statute A legislative enactment in many states that extends self-defense by eliminating any requirement to retreat, even outside one's home or vehicle.

standard construction rule A theory of legal interpretation under which the court will determine the principal objective of the parties in the making of the contract.

standing to sue Standing to sue is a legal condition that a plaintiff—that is, the party initiating a lawsuit—must demonstrate to convince the court that he or she has suffered an injury that the court can redress.

staple court Historically in Europe in the Middle Ages, courts charged with the responsibility for cases involving a set type of goods or a set commodity (a staple).

statute A law passed by a legislature.

Statute of Frauds A law requiring certain contracts to be in writing to be enforceable.

statute of repose An absolute time limit for bringing a cause of action regardless of when the cause of action accrues, such as a certain number of years after a defective product has been sold to an injured customer.

statutes of limitations State laws that restrict the time within which a party is allowed to bring legal action against another.

statutes of repose Establish a limit in years, usually but not necessarily 15 years, beyond which an injured party could not bring a lawsuit for an injury caused by a product.

statutory agent An individual who is designated to receive service of process when a lawsuit is filed against a corporation or an LLC.

statutory executive order A statutory executive order is one that is issued under the authority of a congressional enactment.

statutory interpretation The process by which courts analyze aspects of a statute that are unclear or ambiguous or that were not anticipated at the time the legislature passed the statute.

stipulated damages As a condition of the contract, parties may stipulate (agree) to the amount of damages that might be assessed if there is a breach. Damages agreed to in the initial contract are called stipulated damages.

stock acquisition The purchase of enough of the voting stock of a corporation to allow the buyer to control the corporation. Also called *takeover*.

stock certificate Written evidence of ownership of a unit of interest in a corporation.

stock dividends Dividends paid to shareholders in the form of shares of capital stock.

Stockholm Syndrome A victim's identification with and affection for a kidnapper or other dominant figure in the relationship (spouse, parent, cult leader, hostage takers, terrorists, enemy captors, and so on) that leads the victim to commit questionable acts at the behest of the dominant party.

stocktake All signatories of the Paris Climate Agreement (PCA) will issue individual national progress reports on a regular basis, and, as a unit, all the members of the PCA will produce a single global assessment, known as a stocktake, every five years beginning in 2023.

stoppage in transit A right of the seller, upon learning that the buyer is insolvent, to have the delivery of goods stopped before they reach their destination.

stored value card Looks very much like a credit card or a hotel key card, contains a magnetic strip embedded with data. The data is read by the store's computer, generally at the check-out line, so that the merchant knows how much money the card holds before and after a purchase. The card is often issued by a merchant as a gift card or as an in-house card used as a substitute for a cash refund.

straight life insurance Insurance that requires the payment of premiums throughout the life of the insured and pays the beneficiary the face value of the policy upon the insured's death.

stream of commerce The principle that permits a state to exercise personal jurisdiction over a defendant if the defendant places a product in the general marketplace and the product causes injury or damage in the forum state, provided the defendant also takes other acts to establish some connection with the forum state, as by advertising there or by hiring someone to serve as a sales agent there.

strict liability The doctrine under which people may be liable for injuries to others whether or not they have been negligent or committed an international tort. Also called *absolute liability*.

subject matter jurisdiction The power of a court to hear a particular type of case.

subject to the mortgage An agreement whereby the seller of real property that is already mortgaged agrees to continue paying the mortgage payments.

sublease A lease given by a lessee to a third person conveying the same interest for a shorter term than the period for which the lessee is holding it. Also called *underlease*.

subprime loan When a borrower does not qualify for a conventional or FHA mortgage due to bad or no credit history or because of a high debt-to-income ratio. These loans generally have a much higher default rate than most of the conventional loans and are thus disfavored by lenders.

subrogation The right of one party to substitute itself for another party.

substantial performance In contract law, the situation that results when a party to a contract, in good faith, executes all the promised terms and conditions of the contract with the exception of minor details that do not affect the real intent of their agreement.

substitute check A paper reproduction of both sides of an original check that can be processed electronically.

substitute transportation insurance Insurance that reimburses the insured up to specific limits for transportation costs while a car is undergoing covered repairs.

subterranean rights The owner of land has exclusive title to material below the surface of the land. The right extends to the point determined to be the exact center of the earth.

sui generis A law unto itself. An area of the law that has developed its own independent self-contained rules.

suitability rule Advisors offer investment counseling that is *suitable* to their clients' goals and nothing more.

summary judgment motion A motion that asks a court for an immediate judgment for the party filing the motion because both parties agree on the facts in the case and because under law the party who introduced the motion is entitled to a favorable judgment.

summary jury trial A shortened version of a trial conducted in less than a day before a jury. The jury's verdict is advisory only.

supplemental homeowner's insurance Additional homeowner's insurance policy that can cover losses the full policy does not cover, such as flooding or additional amounts not covered by the maximum amount of the original policy.

supremacy clause A clause found in Article VI, Clause 2, of the U.S. Constitution that says that the Constitution and all federal laws made in line with the Constitution are the supreme law of the land.

surety One who stands behind executors or administrators and becomes responsible for their wrongdoing.

surplus Funds that remain after a partnership has been dissolved and all other debts and prior obligations have been settled.

surrebuttal A reply to the defendant's rebuttal.

swap A derivative that is made in an over-the-counter market. (See also *swap transaction*.)

swap transaction A derivative that is made in an over-the-counter market. (See also *swap*.)

takeover bid In corporate law, the offer to buy the voting stock of a corporation.

tampering with evidence In criminal law, altering, destroying, or removing any piece of evidence with the intent to somehow lessen the probative value of that evidence.

target corporation The object of a tender offer.

targeted shareholder agreement An agreement by which a suitor negotiates a deal with certain shareholders to provide them with employment-related deals that supplement the price they will receive for selling their stock.

tariff-based principle A principle that states that the only way that World Trade Organization nations can regulate the imports of other nations is through tariffs.

Taxation Clause A clause found in Article I, Section 8, Clause 1 of the United States Constitution that empowers Congress to lay and collect taxes.

teaching, suggestion, or motivation test, or TSM standard A traditional test that requires patent challengers to demonstrate that the innovation would have been obvious to anyone exposed to the same teaching session, the same off-hand suggestion, or the same motivation as the inventor had been exposed to.

teller's check See *bank draft*.

temporary public figures People who are placed against their will into the public view by some event beyond their control.

tenancy An interest in real estate that is held under a lease. Also called *leasehold estate*.

tenancy at sufferance A leasehold estate, or tenancy, that arises when a tenant wrongfully remains in possession of the premise after his or her tenancy has expired.

tenancy at will A leasehold estate, or tenancy, that continues for as long as both parties desire.

tenancy by the entirety Ownership by husband and wife, considered by the law as one, with full ownership surviving to the living spouse on the death of the other.

tenancy for years A leasehold estate, or tenancy, for a fixed period of time.

tenancy from year to year See *periodic tenancy*.

tenant A person to whom real property is rented or leased. Also called *lessee*.

tenants in common Owners of an undivided interest in property, with each owner's rights going to his or her heirs upon death rather than to the surviving cotenants.

tender To offer to turn goods over to a buyer.

tender of delivery An offer by the seller of goods to turn the goods over to the buyer.

tender of payment An offer by the buyer of goods to turn the money over to the seller.

tender of performance An offer to do what one has agreed to do under the terms of a contract.

tender offer A public offer by a suitor to buy voting stock.

term insurance Insurance that is issued for a particular period, usually 10 or 20 years.

term partnership A partnership that is set up to run for a set time period or in order to accomplish a task of some sort.

terminal condition States that a "(t)erminal condition means an irreversible, incurable, and untreatable condition caused by disease, illness or injury from which, to a reasonable degree of medical certainty as determined in accordance with reasonable medical standards by a declarant's attending physician and one other physician who has examined the declarant, there is no recovery, AND death is likely to occur within a relatively short time if life-sustaining treatment is not administered."

termination by waiver The situation that exists when a party to a contract with the right to complain of the other party's unsatisfactory performance or nonperformance fails to complain.

testamentary trust A trust that is created by a will.

testate Having made a valid will. Compare *intestate*.

testator (male); testatrix (female) A person who makes a will.

textualism In procedural law, a judicial interpretation technique by which a judge looks at a statute, constitution, regulation, or other legal document as a literary icon and, thus, considers only the words of that statute, constitution, regulation, or other legal document.

The Federal Register Publication that produces a daily compilation of new regulations issued by federal administrative agencies.

theft In criminal law, knowingly taking or obtaining control over the property of another without consent, using deceit, threats, or coercion.

theft in office In criminal law, an offense that involves the use of a governmental official's governmental or party power to obtain unlawful control over governmental or party property or services.

theory of international behavior A set of covering laws that reveal how national leaders (usually) make decisions on the global scene.

third party In contract law, a person who may, in some way, be affected by a contract but who is not one of the contracting parties. Also called *outside party*.

third-party beneficiary In contract law, a party who is not involved in an original contract but who, nevertheless, benefits from that contract.

three-step test A legal doctrine for piercing the veil of a corporation to hold the shareholders or the parent corporation liable for the actions of a corporate representative that considers (a) whether the parent has complete control of the extension; (b) whether that control was used to commit fraud; and (c) whether that fraud damaged the plaintiff in the lawsuit.

threshold Some states alter the no-fault formula by adding this element. When the damages go beyond this threshold, which is defined by a set dollar amount, by injury description, or by time, the victim can file a negligence-based lawsuit. Threshold injuries based on description include very serious ailments such as a permanent disability.

threshold guidelines In insurance law, guidelines that determine when victims can bring a lawsuit for injuries that result from an auto accident.

time draft A draft that is not payable until the lapse of a particular time period stated on the draft.

time is of the essence A contractual term indicating that the time that the contract is to be completed is critical.

time-based threshold In insurance law, a threshold ascertained by measuring the time that the victim has been incapacitated.

title The right of ownership to goods. Also, a subdivision of a code containing all the statutes that deal with a particular area of law.

tort A private wrong that injures another person's physical well-being, property, or reputation.

tortfeasor A person who commits a tort.

towing and labor insurance Insurance that reimburses up to specified limits for towing and labor charges whenever a car breaks down, whether or not an accident is involved.

trade acceptance A draft used by a seller of goods to receive payment and also to extend credit. It is often used in combination with a bill of lading.

trade fixtures Items of personal property brought upon the land by a tenant that are necessary to carry on the trade or business to which the premises will be devoted. Contrary to the general rule, trade fixtures remain the personal property of the tenant and are removable at the expiration of the terms of occupancy.

trade secret A plan, process, or device that is used in a business and is known only to employees who need to know the secret to carry out their jobs.

trademark Any word, name, symbol, or device adopted and used by a manufacturer or merchant to identify goods and distinguish them from those manufactured or sold by others.

transient A person who accepts the service of a hotel or other public accommodation without any obligation to remain a specified length of time.

transnats Transnational organizations that include terrorist cells, drug cartels, pirate groups, and slave traders.

traveler's check A draft purchased from a bank or express company and signed by the purchaser at the time of cashing as a precaution against forgery.

treasure trove Property that must consist of ancient artifacts, often, but not necessarily, money, that was deliberately hidden so long ago that the identity of the original owner has been lost in antiquity.

treaty clause A clause found in Article II, Section 2, Clause 2, of the U.S. Constitution that gives the president the power to make treaties with the advice and consent of the U.S. Senate.

trespass Involves knowingly entering land without permission to do so.

Troubled Asset Relief Program (TARP) A federal program that is designed to allow the government to buy troubled assets that resulted from the securitization epidemic.

true locality rule A means to judge a health care provider's actions on the basis of the standard of care used in the exact same locality or community.

trust A legal device by which property is held by one person for the benefit of another.

trustee A person who is entrusted with the management and control of another's property or the rights associated with that property.

Tunney or Antitrust Procedures and Penalties Act The federal statute that regulates the Justice Department's antitrust consent decrees.

tying agreement In antitrust law, an illegal practice that occurs when one party refuses to sell a given product unless the buyer also purchases another product tied to the first product.

type one arrangement An accounting arrangement by which an accountant enters an agreement with a client to act as a financial advisor and/or a tax preparer.

type two arrangement An accounting arrangement that involves a relationship with a third party that emerges because of a type one arrangement between the accountant and a client.

U.S. Sentencing Commission The commission that issues rules regarding federal courts' discretion in issuing punishments for crimes.

ultra vires An doctrine (obsolete in many jurisdictions) that describes a situation in which corporate managers have exceeded their corporate powers.

umbrella policy An insurance contract that provides protection beyond the limits of a standard policy.

UN Commission on International Trade Law (UNCITRAL) The UN organization charged with the task of organizing and integrating international law in relation to international trade.

UN Convention on Contracts for the International Sale of Goods (CISG) International agreement governing sales of goods between businesses located in different countries.

uncertainty principle An unstable element within the human decision-making process that emerges because the act of making a decision in a system often alters that system (See also *reflexivity principle*.)

unconscionable Ridiculously inadequate.

unconscionable contract A contract that is so one-sided that it is oppressive and gives unfair advantage to one of the parties.

underinsured-motorist insurance Insurance that provides protection against the risk of being injured by an underinsured motorist.

underlease See *sublease*.

undisclosed principal A person, in a transaction conducted by an agent, whose existence and identity are unknown to the third party.

undue hardship The amount of inconvenience beyond that which is required of an employer who seeks to provide reasonable accommodation for a disabled worker.

undue influence The use of excessive pressure by the dominant member of a confidential relationship to convince the weaker party to enter a contract that greatly benefits the dominant party.

unenforceable contract A contract that cannot be upheld by a court because of some rule of law.

unfair labor practices Improper employment practices by either an employer or a union.

unfriendly buyer A buyer of a corporation who intends to change management and shake up the corporation after its takeover.

unfriendly suitor A suitor of a corporation who intends to change management and shake up the corporation after its takeover.

unified international institutions Organizations that bring together various nation-states in a common purpose, such as the North Atlantic Treaty Organization, (NATO) and the United Nations (UN).

Uniform Commercial Code (UCC) A unified set of statutes designated to govern almost all commercial transactions.

Uniform Durable Power of Attorney Act (UDPA) Legislation that states a person may appoint an "attorney in fact" by signing a written durable power of attorney.

Uniform Facsimile Signatures of Public Officials Act A law that allows use of facsimile signatures of public officials when certain requirements are followed.

Uniform Partnership Act (UPA) The original partnership statute written by the National Conference of Commissioners on Uniform State Laws.

Uniform Trade Secrets Act Legislation written by the NCCUSL to define a trade secret, describe transgressions, and provide for both damages and injunctive relief when there has been a trade secret infringement.

unilateral contract An agreement in which one party makes a promise to do something in return for an act of some sort.

unilateral mistake In contract law, a mistake made by only one of the contracting parties. Unilateral mistake does not offer sufficient grounds for recession or renegotiation.

uninsured-motorist insurance A type of automobile insurance that provides protection against the risk of being injured by a motorist who does not have insurance.

union shop A place of employment where nonunion workers may be employed for a trial period of not more than 30 days, after which the nonunion workers must join the union or be discharged.

United States Sentencing Commission The commission that issues rules regarding federal courts' discretion in issuing punishments for crimes.

universal defense See *real defense*.

universal life insurance A form of straight life insurance that allows the policy owner flexibility in choosing and changing terms of the policy.

unlawful detainer A legal proceeding that provides landlords with a quick method of evicting a tenant. Also called *summary process, summary ejectment, forcible entry and detainer,* and *dispossessory warrant proceedings.*

unorthodox (or nontraditional) business entity A nontraditional business institution that has been added to a national or state economic system to operate in an unconventional manner.

unqualified opinion An opinion issued by an auditor that indicates that the financial records of a firm are an accurate reflection of the firm's financial status.

unsecured loan A loan in which creditors have nothing of value that they can repossess and sell in order to recover the money owed to them by the debtor.

unstable states States in which the government suppresses its own people thus inviting a future revolt that might destabilize a region.

usage of trade Any method of dealing that is commonly used in the particular field.

Used Car Rule A rule established by the Federal Trade Commission requiring used car dealers to place a sticker, called a *Buyer's Guide,* in the window of each used car they offer for sale. The sticker provides consumer protection information.

usury The practice of charging more than the amount of interest allowed by law.

utilitarianism A system of ethical thought that focuses on the consequences of an action.

uttering The crime of offering a forged instrument to another person, knowing it to be forged.

valid contract A contract that is legally binding and fully enforceable by the court.

variable-rate mortgage See *flexible-rate mortgage.*

variance An exemption that permits a use that differs from those allowed under the existing zoning law.

verdict A finding of fact by the jury in a court case; the jury's decision.

vertical expansion The joining of two companies that were in a customer–supplier relationship.

vicarious liability The concept of laying responsibility or blame upon one person for the actions of another.

victim's rights In criminal law, a series of rights created by the legislature for innocent people who have been victimized by crime.

void contract A contract that has no legal effect whatsoever.

void title No title at all.

voidable contract A contract that may be voided or canceled by one of the parties.

voidable title Title that may be voided if one of the parties elects to do so.

volition variable An unstable element within the human decision-making process imposed by the fact that humans will use free will to inexplicably make arbitrary decisions that throw the whole scheme out of line.

voluntary manslaughter In criminal law, a killing that results when a criminal defendant is in a state of extreme fright, terror, anger, or blind rage.

voting trust An agreement among shareholders to transfer their voting rights to a trustee.

War Powers Resolution Designed to limit the power of the president as commander-in-chief of the armed forces to commit American troops to the field and to maintain those troops in the field contrary to congressional approval.

warehouse A building or structure in which any goods, but particularly wares or merchandise, are stored.

warehouser A person engaged in the business of storing goods for hire.

warehouser's lien The right of a warehouser to retain possession of goods stored in the warehouse until the satisfaction of the charges imposed on them.

warranty A promise, statement, or other representation that an item has certain qualities; also, an insured's promise to abide by restrictions, especially those written into an insurance policy. Also, an obligation imposed by law that an item will have certain qualities. Warranties made by means of a statement or other affirmation of fact are called *express warranties;* those imposed by law are *implied warranties.*

warranty of fitness for a particular purpose An implied warranty that goods will be fit for a particular purpose. This warranty is given by the seller to the buyer of goods whenever the seller has reason to know of any particular purpose for which the goods are needed and the buyer relies on the seller's skill and judgment to select the goods.

warranty of habitability The landlord warrants that the premises are fit for human habitation.

warranty of merchantability An implied warranty that goods are fit for the ordinary purpose for which such goods are used. Unless excluded, this warranty is always given by a merchant who sells goods in the ordinary course of business.

warranty of title A warranty given by a seller to a buyer of goods that states that the title being conveyed is good and that the transfer is rightful.

waste Substantial damage to premises that significantly decreases the value of the property.

whistleblower An individual who notifies official federal or state authorities about illegal activities that take place in business, government, and other similar settings.

white knight A post-offer technique where a target company invites another suitor to outbid a hostile bidder. The second suitor agrees that it will retain the existing management.

whole life insurance See *straight life insurance*.

widow's allowance See *family allowance*.

will A legal document, not valid until the testator's death, expressing the testator's intent in distribution of all real and personal property.

wire transfer A time-honored system of transferring money from one bank to another by using electronic devices. Also known as a bank transfer or a credit transfer.

work product privilege The guarantee that all notes, recordings, research documents, Q&As, voice mails, faxes, e-mails, computer records, memos, letters, flash drives, disks, DVDs, CDs, and so on that are prepared in anticipation of litigation remain confidential.

workers' compensation Worker protection provided for by state statutes that compensates covered workers or their dependents for injury, disease, or death that occurs on the job or as a result of it.

workmanlike manner In contract law, a rule that requires that contractors use techniques on the job that meet the minimum standards of the industry.

workplace harassment Conduct at a place of employment that creates an illegally offensive environment for an employee in violation of the Civil Rights Act.

World Bank A nongovernmental organization that works exclusively with the poorest nations in the international community to help them secure loans.

World Intellectual Property Organization (WIPO) A division of the United Nations that supported the development of two international treaties designed to deal with electronic copyright problems.

World Intellectual Property Organization Copyright Treaty A treaty that guarantees copyright holders can use the Internet to post their works with full copyright protection.

World Intellectual Property Organization Phonograms Treaty A treaty that gives copyright holders the right to copy, publish, and distribute their works in any way.

world order A set of current initial conditions that describes how nation-states relate to one another on a global scale.

World Trade Organization (WTO) A corporate nucleus for the management of international trade relationships.

writ of certiorari An order from the U.S. Supreme Court to a lower court to deliver the records of a case to the Supreme Court for review.

writ of execution A court order directing the sheriff of a county to sell the property of a losing defendant to satisfy the judgment against that defendant.

writ of replevin A court order requiring a defendant to turn goods over to a plaintiff because the plaintiff has the right to immediate possession of the goods.

wrongful civil proceedings Filing a false civil lawsuit.

wrongful death statute A law that allows third parties affected by a death to bring a lawsuit only if the death is caused by the negligence or intentional conduct of the defendant.

wrongful discharge Exceptions to employment at will that give employees legal ground for lawsuits against employers who have dismissed them unfairly.

zoning law A local regulation or ordinance that restricts certain areas to specific uses; for example, areas zoned for residential, commercial, agricultural, industrial, or other uses.

Case Index

Abood v. Detroit Board of Education, 681
Adelman v. Timman, 230-231
Adsit Company, Inc. v. Gustin, 251
AK Steel Corp. v. ArcelorMittal USA, L.L.C., 284-285, 298
Alaska Indus Fish Mktg. Assoc. v. New England Fish Co., 389
American Ambassador Casualty Co. v. City of Chicago, 832-833
American Needle, Inc. v. New Orleans Saints, et al., 800
American Needle Inc. v. National Football League, 799-800
American Rice, Inc., v. Arkansas Rice Growers Coop. Ass'n., 1040-1041
Anderson v. Copeland, 231
Anderson v. Smith, 201
Appellant, v. Appellee, 618-619
Aronson v. Lewis, 772-773
Asadi v. GE Energy (USA) L.L.C., 784-785, 794-795
Audley v. Melton, 303
Austin Instrument, Inc. v. Loral Corporation, 263
Averysboro National Bank v. Jenkins, 574
Aviation Charters Inc. v. Avemco Insurance Company, 543-544
Avrit v. Forest Industries Insurance Exchange, 547
Axton v. Kentucky Bottlers' Supply Co., 721

Baker v. Nelson, 900
Baldauf v. Kent State Univ., 177
Balinovic v. Evening Star Newspaper Co., 635
Bank of America v. Lallana, 575
Bank of Delaware v. NMD Realty Co., 489
Barillaro v. Unemployment Compensation Bd. Of Review, 673-674
Barton v. Scott Hudgens Realty & Mortg., 471
Bayer v. Travelers Indemnity Co., 547
Beachcomber Coins, Inc. v. Boskett, 262
Bech v. Cuevas, 872
Bennerson v. Checker Garage Service Corporation, 673
Berglund v. Roosevelt University, 829-830, 833
Bess v. Traders World, Inc., 842
Bivens v. Six Unknown Named Agents, 2

B.J. Kadrmas, Inc. v. Oxbow Energy LLC, 234-235, 237, 239, 244, 246
B.L. Nelson & Associates, Inc. v. City of Argyle, 231
Blackston v. State Ex Rel. Blackston, 352-353
Blum v. Gulf Oil Corp., 701
Boafo v. Hospital Corporation of America, 755
Board of Regents of State Colleges v. Roth, 603, 604
Bob Pagan Ford, Inc., v. Smith, 354
Bonhomme v. St. James, 256
Booker v. Revco DS, Inc., 177
Bowling Green Inc. v. State St. Bank & Trust, 475
Bowling v. Sperry, 301-302
BrandAid Marketing Corp. v. Biss, 302-303
Brandt v. Boston Scientific Corporation, 389
Braunfeld v. Brown, 356, 360
Bristol-Myers Squibb v. Superior Court of California, 73
Bryant v. Dupree, 700
Bucci v. Paulick, 488
Bulwark v. Greene, 315
Bundy v. Sky Meadows Trailer Park, 203
Butler v. Lovoll, 329

Carey v. Piphus, 605
Carey v. Population Services International, 971
Carolina Transformer Co. v. Anderson, 389
Carter City School System v. Spectrum Images, Inc., 339-340
Castle Fabrics, Inc., v. Fortune Furniture Mfrs. Inc., 636
Chambers-Castanes v. King Cty, 203
Charlotte Eastland Mall LLC v. Sole Survivor Inc., 304-305, 307, 311-314
Charter Township of Ypsilanti v. General Motors, 281
Chavarria v. Ralphs Grocery Company, 105
Church of the Lucama Babel Aye, Inc. v. Hialeah, 361
Citizens Nat'l Bank v. Brazil, 488-489

City of Cincinnati v. Harbour Portfolio Advisors, LLC, 554, 561-562, 565-566
Clawson v. St. Louis Post-Dispatch, 196
Clifton v. Ross, 636
CLS Bank International v. Alice Corporation Pty. Ltd., 76, 82
Cockrell v. Sparks, 701
Colm v. Vance, 604
Commonwealth Chemical Company v. St. Clair Printing, Inc., 317
Considine v. Brookdale Senior Living, Inc., 92-93, 97, 100, 103-104
Continental Bank v. Fitting, 511
Corporation of Presiding Bishop of Church of Jesus Christ of Latter-day Saints v. Amos, 361
Cort v. Ash, 201
Cramer v. Metro. Sav. & Loan Ass'n., 574
Credit Alliance Corp. v. Arthur Andersen & Co., 918
Cruzon v. Director, Missouri Department of Health, 890, 891

Daubert v. Merrell Dow Pharmaceuticals, Inc., 109, 110, 165-166
David Leon Riley v. California, 60
Delollis v. Friedberg, 915-916, 918-920
Department of Agriculture v. Moreno, 881
Dewey v. Collins, 308
Diamond v. Chakrabarty, 82, 973, 979
Diamond v. Diehr, 995
DiFilippo v. DiFilippo, 871
Dixon v. Fillmore Cemetery, 898
Doe v. Liberatore, 621
Doe v. Oceola, 842
Dorothy Woods v. MONY Legacy Life Insurance Company, 500-501
Duckett v. the City and County of San Francisco, et al., 193-194

Eastern Air Line, Inc., v. Gulf Oil Corporation, 1041
Eastman Kodak Co. v. Image Technical Services, Inc., et al., 815
Eberhard Mfg. Co. v. Brown, 389
Egan v. TradingScreen, Inc., 794
Eisenstadt v. Baird, 971
Elliot v. Ohio Department of Rehabilitation and Correction, 635

Elston v. Howland Local Schools, 634-635
Emporium Capwell, Co. v. Western Addition Community Organization, 697
ePresence, Inc. v. Evolve Software, Inc., 366-367, 370-371, 376-377
Ermo v. Rolling Stone, 170-171
Estate of McLaughlin v. Chicken Delight, Inc., 635
The European Community (EC) v. RJR Nabisco, Inc. (RJR), 62-63, 65, 72, 75
Evans v. Georgia Regional Hospital, 699-702
Explorer Motor Home Corp. v. Aldridge, 412

Faber v. The Brotherhood of Aerospace Workers, 332
FCC v. AT&T Inc., 360
Fed. Home Loan Mtge. Corp. (FHLMC) v. Schwartzwald, 333-334, 336, 338
Federal Deposit Insurance Corporation v. Cortez, 600
Federal Trade Commission v. Kristy Ross and Innovative Marketing, Inc., et al., 424
Fernandez v. Wynn Oil Co., 674
Fidelity Mortgage Investors v. Camelia Builders, Inc., 600
First Colonial Bank for Savings v. Bergeron, 574
First Inv. Co. v. Andersen, 488
First Nat'l Bank v. Hampson, 898
First W. Cap. Mgmt v. Malamed, 69
Free Enterprise Fund v. Public Company Accounting Oversight Board, 761
Frisch v. Svoboda, 727
Frye v. United States, 109, 166
Fuentes v. Shevin, 604
Furman v. Georgia, 133

Garcetti, et al. v. Ceballos, 649, 694
General Electric Credit Union v. Sharon K. Medow, 844-845, 850-851
George Laurie Construction v. Popson, 316
George v. Town of Calais, 871
Gibbons v. Ogden, 736, 786, 946
Gideon v. Wainwright, 91
Goldman v. Blum and Heidenheimer Bros., 451
Goldstein v. Christiansen, 90-91
Gonzales, Attorney General v. Oregon, 890, 891, 995-996
Gonzales v. O Centro Spirit Beneficiate Union do Vegetal, 361
Gonzales v. Raich, 946, 952
Graham v. Metcalf, 342

Granger, et al. v. Auto Owners, Insurance, 523-524, 544
Granite Equip. Leasing Corp. v. Hempstead Bank, 511
Gray v. Giant Wholesale, 574
Gregg v. Georgia, 133
Grey v. Walgreen Co., 202
Gries Sports Enterprises, Inc. v. Cleveland Browns Football Co., Inc., 817-819
Griggs v. Duke Power Co., 660
Griswold v. Connecticut, 901, 971
Grondin v. Rossington, 208-209, 220, 224
Guyan Coal and Coke Company v. Wholesale Coal Company, 262

Haddon View Investment Co. v. Coopers and Lybrand, 940
Haik v. Rowley, 489
Hall St. Associates, L.L.C., v. Mattel, Inc., 116
Hall v. Horizon House Microwave, Inc., 328
Hall v. Westmoreland, Hall & Bryan, 471
Hamdan v. Rumsfeld, 59-60
Hamer v. Sidway, 266
Hanover National Bank v. Max Moyses, 576-577, 581, 584, 586, 588, 592
Hardex-Steubenville Corp. v. W. Pa. National Bank, 515
Harris v. Alabama, 132
Harris v. Quinn, 681
Hathaway v. Ray's Motor Sales, 329
Hauptman v. Conant, 898
Heart of Atlanta Hotel v. United States, 60-61
Heiselman v. Marcus, 389
Henry Heide, Inc., v. Atlantic Mut. Ins. Co., 390
Henry v. State Farm, 547
Herzog v. Irace, 353
Hildreth Mfg., LLC. v. Semco, Inc., 994
Hill v. Sonitrol of Southwestern Ohio, Inc., 203
Hilt Truck Lanes, Inc., v. Riggins, 547
Hodges v. City of St. Louis, 196
Holland Furnace Co. v. Trumbull Sav. & Loan Co., 323
Hollowell v. Satterfield, 721
Hooten Equipment Company v. Trimat, Inc., 392-394, 398-399
Hosanna-Tabor Evangelical Lutheran Church and School v. EEOC, 361
Huff v. White Motor Co., 418

Ignazio v. Clear Channel, 302
Illinois Controls, Inc., v. Langham, 753-754
Impression Products, Inc. v. Lexmark International, Inc., 974-975
Industrial Mach., Inc., v. Creative Displays, Inc., 872
In re Al Zuni Trading, Inc., 546
In re American Medical Response of Connecticut, 692-694
In re Estate of Elmer, 898
In re Estate of Norris, 511
In re Estate of Nuss, 726-727
In re Iwahashi, 995
In re Landrin, 600
In re Manchester Lakes Association, 600
In re Neagle, 59
In the Matter of Rahl, 600
In the Matter of U.S. Truck Co., Inc., 600

Jackson v. Jackson, 782
Jacob and Young v. Kent, 353
Jailynn Brown, et al. v. Andre T. Harris Sr., et al., 162-163, 165, 182
J&K Computer Systems, Inc., v. Parrish, 994-995
Janke Construction, Co. v. Vulcan Materials, Co., 230
Janus v. AFSCME, 680
Janus v. American Federation of State, County, and Municipal Employees, 681
J.E.B. Stewart v. Citizens and Southern National Bank, 231
Jessica Ruth Gonzales v. The United States of America, 116-117

Kelo v. City of New London, 861, 995
Kimberly Hively v. Ivy Tech Community College, 638-639, 641-642, 647, 661-663
Kirby v. Bergfield, 489
Klinicki v. Lundgren, 782
Kruse v. Coos Head Timber Co., 302

Lake Country Estates v. Tahoe Regional Planning Agency, 604
Lake Ridge v. Carney, 330-331, 341, 349
Lamas v. Baldwin, 754-755
Latty v. St. Joseph's Society, 608-609, 612-617, 621
Lauretig v. Pierce, 316
Leake v. Cain, 196, 203
Ledford v. Peeples, 701
Leeper v. Pennsylvania Higher Education Assistance Agency, 599-600

Lefkowitz v. Great Minneapolis Surplus Store, Inc., 252
Lewis v. S.L.&E., Inc., 782
Liarkos v. Mello, 411
Lightbody v. Rust, 281
Littleton v. Good Samaritan Hosp. & Health Ctr., 203
Litwins v. Timbercrest Estates, Inc., 353
Lohr v. Larry's Homes of Virginia, 412
Lonchyna v. Brown, Secretary of Defense, 302
Louisville Joint Stock Bank v. Radford, 603
Loving v. Virginia, 900

Macrie v. SDS Biotech Corp., 414-417, 419-420
Mark DiCintio v. DaimlerChrysler Corporation, et al., 412
Marrama v. Citizens Bank, 599
Marshall v. Kennedy, 203
Masheter v. Boehm, 323
Massachusetts v. Mellon, 930
Matin v. Chase Manhattan Bank, 502
Matter of Estate of Bolton, 489
Matter of Estate of Dejmal, 898
Matter of Marriage of Rutherford, 489
Maynard v. Hill, 901
McAndrew v. Mularchuk, 635
Meade v. Cedarapids, Inc., 673
Meng v. Trustees of Boston University, 328
Meritor Savings Bank v. Vinson, 662
Mers v. Dispatch Printing Company, 232
Messick v. Moring, 728-729, 731-732, 748-749
Miles v. District of Columbia, 603, 604
Minor v. Happersett, 702
Miranda v. Arizona, 91
Mitchell v. State Farm Mutual Automobile Insurance Co., 301
Moch Co. v. Rensselaer Water Co., 918-919
Montana Association of Underwriters v. Department of Administration and MBI, 754
Morrison v. Thoelke, 262
Mt. Holyoke Homes, LP, et al. v. Jeffer Mangels Butler and Mitchell, LLP, 95-96
Myers v. Forest City Enterprises, Inc., 197
Myers v. Terminix, 303

N. E. Guthrie, Petitioner v. National Homes Corporation, 448-449, 451-452, 459-462
N. Pipeline Construction Company v. Marathon Pipe Line Company, 580

Naquin v. Air Engineered Systems and Services, Inc., 782
National Air Races Inc. v. Macon City Airport, 259
National City Bank v. Gumm, et al., 555-556
National Federation of Independent Business, et al., v. Sebelius, 948, 952
Nat'l Bank v. Refrigerated Transp., 488
Newman v. First Nat'l State Bank of Toms River, 457
Newsome v. Tibbs, 297
New York Central & Hudson River Railroad v. United States, 158
The New York Times v. Sullivan, 170, 196
Nicastro v. McIntyre, 67
Ninth Street East, Ltd., v. Harrison, 402
Nitro-Lift Technologies, L.L.C. v. Howard, 115-116
NLRB v. Exchange Parts Co., 696-697
NLRB v. Savair Mfg. Co., 697
NLRB v. Town & Country Electric, 684
Nolan v. Williamson Music, Inc., 353
Norcold, Inc. v. Gateway Supply Company, 441-446
Northern States Power Co. v. Minnesota, 948-949, 952
Northridge Bank v. Lakeshore Com. Fin. Corp., 574
Northwestern University, Employer v. College Athletes Players Association, Petitioner, 684-685, 694
Nu-Way Services, Inc. v. Mercantile Trust Company, 515

Obergefell, et al., v. Hodges, Director, Ohio Department of Health, et al., 852-853, 881-883, 899-906
Office of Disciplinary Counsel v. Lloyd, 636
Offshore of the Palm Beaches, Inc. v. Lynch, 701
O'Keefe v. Lee Calan Imports, 262
Oldacker v. Kellog Formal Wear Shoppe, 254
Oncale v. Sundowner Offshore Servs., Inc., 662
Onderko v. Sierra Lobo, Inc., 656
Op-Out Lenders v. Millennium Labs Holdings II, LLC, et al., 580
Osborn v. Brown, 872
Overseas Tankship (UK) Ltd. v. Morts Dock and Engineering Co., Ltd., 179

Pacific Diamond Co. v. Superior Ct., 843

Pagiarulo v. National Shawmut Bank, 843
Painter v. Graley, 674
P&F Const. v. Friend Lumber Corp., 411
Parker v. Arthur Murray, Inc., 353-354
Paul v. Davis, 603
Penn Central Transportation Corp. v. New York City, 604
Pennsylvania Coal Co. v. Mahon, 604
People for the Ethical Treatment of Property Owners v. U.S. Fish and Wildlife Service, 947, 952
People v. Roberts, 159
Perez Bar & Grill v. Schneider, 321-323
Perini v. First National Bank of Habershan, Co., 516
Pickering v. Board of Ed. of Township High School Dist., 694
Pierce v. Society of Sisters, 901
Pincher v. Roman Catholic Bishop of Portland, 620-622
Pioneer Savings and Loan Co. v. City of Cleveland, 604, 605
Planned Parenthood v. Casey, 890, 972
PNC Bank v. Michael Farinacci, 716
Pottschmidt v. Thomas J. Klosterman, M.D., Inc., 753
Preston v. First Bank of Marietta, 574
Price Brothers Co. v. Philadelphia Gear Corp., 442, 445
Price Waterhouse v. Hopkins, 662
Prudential Ins. Co. of Am. v. Dewey, Ballantine, Bushby, Palmer & Wood, 920

Quality Motors v. Hays, 302

Ralo, Inc., v. Jack Graham, Inc., 872
Ramos v. Wheel Sports Center, 389
R.A.V. v. St. Paul, 159
Rayl v. E. Ohio Gas Co., 856
Read v. South Carolina National Bank, 513-517
Republic Aviation Corp. v. NLRB, 696
Reynolds v. Sims, 90
Rhodes v. Hayden, 254
Rice v. The City of St. Louis, 674
Richard Diaz, et al. v. International Longshoremen's and Warehousemen's Union, Local 13, 696
Ritz v. Selma United Methodist Church, 785, 822-823, 826-827
R.J. Enstrom Corporation v. Interceptor Corporation, 814-815
Roe v. Wade, 82, 890, 972, 979
Rome v. Flower Memorial Hospital, 60
Rostow Aviation, Ltd. v. Futuregraphics, Inc., 339
R.R. v. M.H. and Another, 296

Russell v. Russell, 872
Russell v. United Missionary Baptist Church, 781

Samson Sales, Inc. v. Honeywell, Inc., 349
San Rafael Motor Corporation v. Groza, 255
Schaeffer v. Cavallero, 842
Schleimer v. Googe, 411
Schneider v. Kumpf, 199-205
Schnell v. Nell, 269
Schuette v. BAMN, 903
Schumacher Homes v. Spencer, 115
Schupack v. McDonald's Systems, Inc., 353
Scott v. Purser Truck Sales, Inc., 843
Searle v. Allstate Life Insurance Company, 547
Securities and Exchange Commission v. Arthur Young and Company, 940
Securities and Exchange Commission v. W.J. Howey Co., 814
Security State Bank v. McCoy, 727
Seier v. Peek, 282
Service v. Dulles, 604
Shaffer v. Victoria Station, Inc., 412
Sharp v. Andisman, 261
Sherbert v. Verner, 892
Sherely v. Sebelius, 955-956
Sidco Paper Company v. Eugene Aaron and Grant Paper Company, 288, 291
Siminoff v. Expedia, Inc., 249
Simon v. Simon, 872
Smathers v. Smathers, 471
Smith v. VanGorkon, 782
Sousa v. American Medical Response of Connecticut, 694
Spacemakers of America Inc. v. Suntrust Bank, 490-492, 494-495, 499-500
Spaziano v. Florida, 132
Spence v. Huffman, 754
Spertell v. Hendrix, 329
Stahl v. LePage, 636
Staniland v. Morris, 315
State Bank of Lehi v. Woolsey, 574
State Farm Fire and Casualty Company v. Ramsey, 520-521, 524-525, 531-532
State Farm Mutual Automobile Ins. Co. v. Campbell, 348
State of Florida, et al. v. U.S. Department of Health and Human Services, 930, 936, 947
States of New York, et al. v. Trump, 28-29, 31-32, 44, 53
State v. Bontrager, 117
State v. Cuttiford, 160

State v. Powell, 471
State v. Reese, 159
State v. Zimmerman, 155
Steelworkers v. Weber, 663
Stein v. Gelfand, 264-265, 267-268, 270, 275
Stella Liebeck v. McDonald's Restaurants, 180-181, 188
Stephens v. Stephens, 721
Stern Electronics, Inc., v. Kaufman and Omni Video Games, Inc., 995
Stewart v. Citizens & Nat'l Bank, 511
Stewart v. Gaverick, 345
Strack v. Westfield Cos., 201
Stumpf v. C.E. Stumpf & Sons, Inc., 815
Summers v. Dooley, 727
Superfine Market v. Allgood Canning Company, 338
Superior Savings Association v. City of Cleveland, 601-606
Susan B. Anthony List, et al., Petitioners v. Steven Driehaus, et al., 12-13
Swift and Sure Shipping v. Harrison Printing, 836
Sylvia Burwell, Secretary of Health and Human Services, et al. v. Hobby Lobby Stores, Inc., et al., 355-363, 710, 732-733, 749-750

Taboada v. Bank of Babylon, 511
Teaff v. Hewitt, 323
Templeton v. First Nat'l Bank, 511
Textile Worker's Union v. Darlington Mfg. Co., 697
Tilton v. Marshall, 619
Tracer Research Corp. v. National Environmental Services, Co., 117
Trautman v. Quinn, 310
Trial v. McCoy, 412
Trumbull Sav. & Loan Co., 323
Trump Plaza, v. Haas and Meridian Bank, 457
Tubelite Co., Inc. v. Original Sign Studio, 222-223
Turner (East Asia) Pte. Ltd. v. Builders Federal (Hong Kong) Ltd., 116
Turner v. Safley, 900
Twaine v. Krell, Inc., 315
Tylo v. Superior Court, 674
Tyson Foods, Inc. v. Bouaphakeo, 653

Ultramares Corp. v. Touche, 918-920
Union Pacific Railroad Company v. Nami, 194
United States Aviation Underwriters v. Cash Air, 546
United States of America v. Manuel Antonio Noriega, 1040

United States v. Busby, 160
United States v. Butler, 948
United States v. Commonwealth of Virginia, 674
United States v. Earth Sciences, Inc., 994
United States v. Ellison, 196
United States v. Hearst, 118-119, 127, 137, 153
United States v. Hilton Hotels Corporation, 158-159
United States v. Lee, 361
United States v. Levy, 701
United States v. Lopez, 135, 158, 946
United States v. Morrison, 946
United States v. Nosal, 146
United States v. Stewart, 939
United States v. Topco Associates, Inc., 814
United States v. Tufi, 471
United States v. Waterford No. 2 Office Center, 575
United States v. Windsor, 900
Unocal Corporation v. Mesa Petroleum Company, 756-757, 764-765, 774-775
Utah v. Strieff, 89

Valley Victory Church v. Darvin Struck and Bonnie Struck, 746-747
Van Hooser, et al. v. Keenon, et al., 704-705, 713-714, 720-721
VanHulle v. State Farm, 547
Victory Container Corporation v. Calvert Fire Insurance Company, 547
Vruno v. Schwarzwalder, 604

W. B. Worthen Co. v. Kavanaugh, 603
Wagenheim v. Alexander Grant and Co., 939-940
Wagner v. State, 263
Wagstaff v. Peters, 231
Washington v. Glucksberg, 902
Wayne Smith Constr. Co., Inc. v. Wolman, Duberstein & Thompson, 716
Weaver v. Grafio, 353
Webster v. Redmond, 603
Wellington Resource Group, LLC. v. Beck Energy Corporation, 857
West Virginia Bd. of Ed. v. Barnette, 903
Wickard v. Filburn, 122, 123, 158, 787, 946
Wightman v. Consolidated Railroad Corporation, 197
William Stewart v. R. A. Eberts, Company, Inc., 749
Williams v. Stansbury, 472-473, 476-477, 486

Wilson v. Health and Hospital Corp. of Marion County, 604
Wilson v. Montgomery Ward, 328-329
Windsor v. United States, 880-881
Winkfield v. Children's Hospital and Research Center of Oakland, 874-875, 890-892
Wolfram v. Halloway, 471
Woodward v. Alabama, 132-133

World Wide Volkswagen Corporation v. Woodson, 754
Wright v. Mountain Trust Bank, 603

XCEL Mold & Machine v. DeVault Indus., 373, 383

Young v. Frank's Nursery & Crafts, Inc., 411

Young v. International Brotherhood of Locomotive Engineers, 635

Zablocki v. Redhail, 900
Zangerle v. Republic Steel Corp., 323
Ziglar v. Abbasi, 2-3
Zuer v. Iafigliola, 308-309

Subject Index

AAA (Agriculture Adjustment Act of 1938), 122
ABA. *See* American Bar Association
Abandoned property, 825
Abandoned Shipwreck Act of 1987, 825
Abandonment, 287
Abandonment of contractual obligations, 346
Above-ground radioactive fallout, 619-620
Abstract principles vs. concrete situations, 30-31
Abuse of discretion, 64, 67
Abuse of process, 175
ACA. *See* Patient Protection and Affordable Care Act of 2010
Acceleration of debt, 556
Acceptance of goods, 397
Acceptance of negotiable instruments, 453
Acceptance of offers, 242-247
   additional terms in, 374
   cloud storage/computing and, 252
   communication of, 242-243
   in cyberspace, 250, 324
   elements of, 217
   implied, 245
   for sale of goods, 372, 373
   silence as, 245
   UCC and, 373
   unequivocal, 244-245
Acceptors, 458, 485
Accord and satisfaction, 218, 272-273, 344
Accountable care organizations (ACOs), 936
Accountants, 910-922
   auditing and, 911-913
   defined, 910
   Dodd-Frank and, 913-914
   duties owed to clients, 914-915
   ethical rules for, 912
   jurisdictional issues for, 913
   liability to third parties under common law, 917
   registration of, 910
   Sarbanes-Oxley Act and, 912-913
   statutory liability of, 921
   tax reform and, 921-922

Accounting principles, 911
Acemoglu, Daron, 212
Acknowledgment of contract signings, 319
ACOs (accountable care organizations), 936
Acquisitions, 804-805
Act for the Prevention of Fraud and Perjuries. *See* Statute of Frauds
Active fraud, 255
Activist agencies, 810
Actual authority, 623-624
Actual authority rule, 776-777
Actual cause, 178
Actual damages, 221, 347
Actual eviction, 868
Actual express authority, 623-624
Actual harm, 180
Actual implied authority, 624
Actual malice, 169-171
Actual malice test, 169, 171
Actual privity, 918-919
ADA (Americans with Disabilities Act of 1990), 666-667
Add-on coverage, 535
ADEA (Age Discrimination in Employment Act of 1967), 665-666
Adhesion contracts, 540
Adjustable-rate mortgages (ARMs), 552
Administrative agencies, 50-51
Administrative law, 50
Administrative Procedures Act of 1946 (APA), 28, 50-53
Administrative regulations, 50-57
Administrators, 310, 886
Administratrix, 886
Admiralty courts, 214-215
Admissions in court, 378
Admissions requests, 77
Adolescents. *See* Minors
ADR. *See* Alternative dispute resolution
Adsit, 251
Advanced directives, 887-893
Advanced Science and Technology Adjudication Resources (ASTAR), 110
Adverse opinions, 911-912
Adverse possession, 859-860
Advertisements, 250-251, 325, 406-407

AEC (Atomic Energy Commission), 949, 963
Affirmance of contracts, 290-291
Affirmative action, 663
Affirmative defense, 74
Affordable Care Act. *See* Patient Protection and Affordable Care Act of 2010 (ACA)
AFSCME (American Federation of State, County, and Municipal Employees), 680
After-acquired evidence defense, 648, 664
Age Discrimination in Employment Act of 1967 (ADEA), 665-666
Agency, defined, 609
Agency coupled with an interest, 630
Agency law, 608-632. *See also* Employment law
   agent's obligations to principal in, 626-627
   case study, 608-609
   compensation in, 627
   completion by operation of law, 629-630
   contracts and, 223
   creation of an agency and, 623-625
   cyber-agency statutes, 631
   duties in, 625-628
   employer-employee relationship and, 610
   in health care setting, 631-632
   liability and, 611-618, 620, 623
   master-servant relationship and, 610
   nature of, 609-620
   notice of termination to third parties, 630-631
   principal-agent relationship and, 609-610
   principal's obligations to agent in, 627-628
   principles of, 622-625
   proprietor-independent contractor relationship and, 610-611
   reimbursement in, 627-628
   remedies in, 627, 628
   subagents in, 625
   termination by acts of parties, 629

Agenda 21, 968
Agent-principal relationship, 609-610
Agents, 223, 609, 622-623, 631
Aggravated arson, 128, 136
Aggravated burglary, 136
Aggravated felonies, 123
Aggravated identity theft, 147, 509
Aggravated menacing, 134
Aggravated murder, 133-134
Aggravated robbery, 136
Aggravating circumstances, 132
Aggregate theory, 707-708
Agreements. *See also* Contracts
  antenuptial, 310-311
  contrary to public policy, 295, 297-299
  to defraud creditors, 295, 297
  discharge by, 343-344
  enforceable, 273-275
  to engage in unlawful activity, 293-299
  to escape liability, 297
  illegal, 285, 293-299
  interfering with public service, 295
  lease, 856, 864-866
  legality of, 222
  licensing, 982
  lockup, 807
  noncompete, 284-285, 297-299
  nondisclosure, 299
  to obstruct justice, 295
  operating, 744-745
  partial illegality in, 300
  of parties, 385
  pooling, 770
  prenuptial, 310-311
  RPM, 800
  sale of business, 297
  security, 569
  Sunday, 295
  targeted shareholder, 807
  tying, 801
  unconscionable, 295
  unenforceable, 275-277
  unlicensed, 294-295
  usurious, 294
  wagering, 294
  without consideration, 274
Agriculture Adjustment Act of 1938 (AAA), 122
AIA (America Invents Act of 2011), 979-980
AICPA (American Institute of Certified Public Accountants), 911-913
AIDS/HIV, 960
Air rights, 846
AK Steel, 284-285, 298
Alabama Farm Bureau Mutual Casualty Insurance Company, 542

ALI. *See* American Law Institute
Alien corporations, 740
Allied Van Lines Inc., 836
Allonge, 463
Al-Qaeda, 141, 957, 991, 1020
Alteration of negotiable instruments, 482-483
Altered checks, 494-495
Alter ego test, 747
Alternative dispute resolution (ADR), 92-113
  advantages of, 94-96
  arbitration, 92-93, 97, 99-100, 103-104, 112, 692
  case study, 92-93
  collective science court and, 108-111
  contract clauses in, 103-105
  cyber ADR, 111-113
  defined, 93-94
  early neutral evaluation, 94-95, 100-101, 113
  Federal Arbitration Act and, 96-98, 100
  international arbitration agreements, 107-108
  med-arb, 100
  mediation, 98-99, 112, 692
  negotiated rule making, 106-107
  partnering in, 103
  post-appellate procedures, 107
  private civil trials, 95, 102, 113
  proactive strategies, 102-111
  responsive strategies, 98-102
  settlement week in, 106
  shortcomings of, 95
  summary jury trials, 95, 101-102, 113
Amazon.com, 81, 324, 669, 765
Amendments to U.S. Constitution
  Eighteenth, 1053
  Eighth, 1052
  Eleventh, 191, 1052
  Fifth (*See* Fifth Amendment)
  First (*See* First Amendment)
  Fourteenth (*See* Fourteenth Amendment)
  Fourth, 85, 185, 1051
  Nineteenth, 1053
  Ninth, 1052
  Second, 1051
  Seventeenth, 36, 1053
  Seventh, 1052
  Sixteenth, 36, 1053
  Sixth, 86, 1051-1052
  Tenth, 930, 1052
  Third, 1051
  Thirteenth, 39, 350, 643, 657, 1052
  Twelfth, 1052

  Twentieth, 1053-1054
  Twenty-fifth, 1054-1055
  Twenty-first, 1054
  Twenty-fourth, 1054
  Twenty-second, 1054
  Twenty-seventh, 1055
  Twenty-sixth, 286, 1055
  Twenty-third, 1054
America Invents Act of 2011 (AIA), 979-980
American Ambassador Casualty Co., 832-833
American Arbitration Association, 98, 99, 105
American Bar Association (ABA), 707, 908-909, 913, 925-927
American Declaration of the Rights and Duties of Man, 107
American Federation of State, County, and Municipal Employees (AFSCME), 680
American Institute of Certified Public Accountants (AICPA), 911-913
American Law Institute (ALI), 151, 215, 249, 1056
American Medical Response, 692-693
American Needle, 799-800
Americans with Disabilities Act of 1990 (ADA), 666-667
America Online (AOL), 184
Amway Truck Lines, 835
Analytical Philosophy of History (Danto), 1016
Anarchy, 22-23
Anatomical gifts, 631-632, 828
Anderson, Bruce, 832-833
Andrean-Harrison Corporation, 19
Angell, Norman, 1018
Angerer, Robert, 234, 237, 239, 244, 246
Annual percentage rate (APR), 433, 437
Annuities, 527
Answer, in civil procedure, 74-75
Antedated checks, 500
Antenuptial agreements, 310-311
Anticipatory breach of contract, 346, 400
Anti-gun protection laws, 135-136
The Antitrust Paradox (Bork), 240
Antitrust Procedures and Penalties Act of 1974, 810
Antitrust regulation, 798-803, 809-810
AOL (America Online), 184
APA (Administrative Procedures Act of 1946), 28, 50-53
Apparent authority, 624
Appeals, 80
Appellate jurisdiction, 64
Applicable law, 68-69
Applications, insurance, 540

Appretiare, 23
APR (Annual percentage rate), 433, 437
Arab Spring, 998
Arbitration, 92–93, 97, 99–100, 103–104, 112, 692
Arbitration clauses, 250
Arbitrators, 99
ArcelorMittal USA, 284–285, 298
Architects, liability of, 924
Arconic, 130
Ariya, Andrea, 975
ARMs (adjustable-rate mortgages), 552
Arraignment, 87
Arrest warrant, 85
Arson, 128, 136
Article II executive orders, 42
Articles of Confederation, 35–36, 38, 39, 577, 787
Articles of incorporation, 743
Articles of organization, 744
Asadi, Khaled, 784–785, 794–795
Ashcroft, John, 2
Assault, 134, 142, 168
Asset acquisition, 804
Asset-backed securities, 560, 793
Assignees, 333, 335, 337, 866
Assignments, 333–338
  defined, 333
  lease, 866
  liabilities and warranties of assignor, 336–337
  methods of, 334–335
  negotiable instruments and, 462
  novation and, 338
  restrictions on, 337–338
  rights and duties of assignee, 335
Assignors, 333, 336–337
Associated persons and forces, 1026
Associative corporativism, 738, 788
Assumption of mortgage, 557
Assumption of risk, 74, 181
ASTAR (Advanced Science and Technology Adjudication Resources), 110
ATM cards, 506–508
Atomic Energy Act of 1946, 963
Atomic Energy Act of 1954, 963
Atomic Energy Commission (AEC), 949, 963
Attachment of security interests, 569–570
Attenuation doctrine, 85
Attorney-client privilege, 929
Attorney general, 122
Attorneys, liability of, 925, 927–929
Auctions, 241, 380–381
Auctions without reserve, 241, 380
Auctions with reserve, 241, 380
Audit committees, 765
Auditors, 911

Audits
  defined, 911
  Dodd-Frank and, 913–914
  jurisdictional issues in, 913
  opinion types in, 911–912
  Sarbanes-Oxley Act and, 912–913
  standards for, 911
Authoritarianism, 998–999, 1001, 1009, 1012–1016
Authority, 623–624, 626
Authorization for the Use of Military Force (AUMF), 1024–1026
Automatic stay, 587
Automobile insurance, 534–536
  add-on coverage, 535
  bodily injury liability, 534
  collision, 535
  comprehensive, 536
  fault-based, 534
  medical payments, 535
  no-fault, 534–535
  property damage liability, 535
  substitute transportation, 536
  threshold guidelines, 535
  towing and labor, 536
  underinsured-motorist, 535
  uninsured-motorist, 535
Auto-Owners (Mutual) Insurance Company, 523–524, 544
Avemco Insurance, 543–544
Aviation Charters Inc., 543–544

Bacon, Francis, 9, 34, 36, 164
Bad checks, 497–498
BAFJ (Bankruptcy Amendments and Federal Judgeship) Act of 1984, 580
Bailees, 829, 831
Bailey, F. Lee, 118–119, 127, 137, 153
Bailments, 829–840
  burden of proof and, 832
  carriers and, 835–838
  constructive, 829
  defined, 829
  elements of, 829
  gratuitous, 830
  implied-in-fact, 829
  implied-in-law, 829
  innkeepers and, 833–835
  mutual-benefit, 831–832
  principles of, 830
  for sole benefit of bailee, 831
  for sole benefit of bailor, 830–831
  warehousers and, 838–839
Bailors, 829–831
Bait-and-switch confidence games, 241
Bait-and-switch schemes, 423–424
Baker, James, 1005
Balloon-payment mortgages, 552

Balloon payments, 436
Bank-depositor relationship, 491–509
  altered checks and, 494–495
  availability of funds and, 495–496
  bad checks and, 497–498
  bank's duties in, 493–497
  consumer protection and, 505–506
  cyber-banking and, 505–509
  death of customer and, 494
  depositor's duties, 497–498, 500
  deposits and collections, 502–503
  examination of accounts and, 498
  forgery and, 494–495
  incompetence of customer and, 494
  insured accounts and, 501
  midnight deadline and, 496–497
  overview, 491–493
  stop-payment rights and, 500–501
Bank drafts, 455–456
Banking days, 496
Bank money orders, 456
Bank of America, 796
Bankruptcy, 576–598. *See also specific types of bankruptcy*
  agency law and, 630
  case study, 576–577
  as defense against collection, 482
  federal control of, 578–579
  federal exemptions and, 587–588
  history and evolution of, 577–581
  homestead exemption and, 587–588
  liquidation and, 581–591
  plan approval and confirmation, 594
  promises after discharge in, 273–274
  restoration of credit following, 591
  state authority in, 581–582
  state exemptions and, 589
  types of procedures, 583
  U.S. Constitution and, 578, 579
Bankruptcy Abuse Prevention and Consumer Protection Act of 2005 (BAPCPA), 580–583, 588, 598
Bankruptcy Amendments and Federal Judgeship (BAFJ) Act of 1984, 580
Bankruptcy Code, Chapter 7 of, 581–591. *See also* Liquidation
Bankruptcy Code, Chapter 11 of, 580, 581, 591–595
Bankruptcy Code, Chapter 12 of, 580, 595–596
Bankruptcy Code, Chapter 13 of, 580, 581, 597–598
Bankruptcy Reform Act of 1978, 580
Bankruptcy Reform Act of 1994, 580
Bankruptcy Reform Act of 2005, 345
Banks. *See also* Bank-depositor relationship
  cyber-banking, 505–509
  defined, 491

Subject Index

deposits and collections, 502–503
right of subrogation, 501
types of, 497, 503
Bank transfers, 506
BAPCPA (Bankruptcy Abuse Prevention and Consumer Protection Act of 2005), 580–583, 588, 598
Barber Enterprises Inc., 759
Bargain-and-sale deeds, 859
Bargained-for exchange, 266–267
Bargaining unit, 688
Barnes and Noble, 669
Barnett, Thomas, 1002–1003, 1006
Barrett, Paul M., 730
Battered spouse syndrome, 155
Battery, 134, 168
Bay Springs Bank, 520–521, 524–525, 531–532
BCECF (Black Car Workers' Compensation Fund), 676
Beacon Associates LLC, 915–916, 919–920
Beard, Charles, 787
Bearer paper, 463
Bearers, 457
Beck Energy Corporation (BEC), 857
Beneficiaries, 223, 331–332, 524
Benefit corporations, 711
Benson & Childs, 868
Bequests, 876
Berglund, Richard, 829–830
Bergson, Henri, 212
Berman, Harold J., 210, 213–214, 357
Bernard L. Madoff Investment Securities LLC, 915–916, 919–920
Berne Convention, 983
Best evidence rule, 317
Best-price rule, 807
Beyond a reasonable doubt standard, 120, 128, 137
BFOQ (bona fide occupational qualification), 659
Bilateral contracts, 226, 242, 341
Bilateral mistake, 257
Bill of Rights, 6, 38–40, 787. *See also* Amendments to U.S. Constitution
Bill of sale, 381
Bills of exchange, 453–454
Bills of Exchange Act, 215
Binders, 540
Binding precedent, 48–49
Bin Laden, Osama, 1019, 1020, 1025–1026, 1033
Biogetic system, 558, 567
Bitcoin, 143, 271–272
Bitcoin miners, 272
Black Car Workers' Compensation Fund (BCECF), 676

Blank indorsements, 464–465
Blended contracts, 369–370
Blue laws, 295
Board of directors, 758–759
Bode, Judy, 513–514, 516
Bodily injury liability insurance, 534
Bona fide occupational qualification (BFOQ), 659
Bonds, defined, 887
Bonus-malus system, 568, 730
Booker, Ramona, 177
Bork, Robert, 33, 240, 735
Bots, 277, 631
Brain death, 888
Brainwashing, 118–119, 127, 137, 152, 153
Brave New World (Huxley), 23
Breach of contract
  anticipatory, 346, 400
  buyer's remedies in, 401–404
  cancellation of contract due to, 401
  commercial docket for, 404–405
  damages for, 401
  defined, 226
  deliberate, 345–346
  discharge by, 345–346
  as personal defense, 479
  sales contracts, 399–405
  seller's remedies in, 400–401
  statute of limitations for, 405
Breach of duty, 177–178
Breaking and entering, 136
Brexit vote, 1013
Bribery, 139
Bright-line test, 807
Bring your own device (BYOD) tactic, 186, 670–671
Brion, Denis J., 927–928
Bristol-Meyers Squibb, 73
British Petroleum, 128, 129
Bromfield, Louis, 14–17, 240, 676, 1009–1012
Brookdale Senior Living Inc., 92–93, 97, 100, 103–104
Brown, Dan, 450
Brown, Jailynn, 162–163, 165, 182
Browsewrap contracts, 250
Buffalo Lake Erie Wireless Company LLC, 264–265, 267–268, 270, 275
Bullying, 142
Bumped airline passengers, 837–838
Burden of proof, 87, 832
Burglary, 136
Bush, George H.W., 55
Bush, George W., 42, 1000, 1005, 1021
Bush, Vannevar, 953, 986
Business compulsion, 259
Business days, 496
Business entities

alternative forms of, 709–712
case study, 704–705
corporations (*See* Corporations)
national economic reform movement and, 708, 709
orthodox, 709–710
partnerships (*See* Partnerships)
sole proprietorships, 706, 709
start-up plans for, 708–709
unorthodox, 710–711
Business ethics, 17–21
Business judgment rule, 773–774
Business necessity qualification, 659–660
Buyers
  acceptance of goods by, 397
  insolvent, 400
  in ordinary course of business, 569
  rejection of goods by, 395–397
  remedies for breach of contract, 401–404
  rights and duties of, 395–397
  unfriendly, 805
Buyer's Guide, 425
By a preponderance of the evidence standard, 120
Bylaws, 744
BYOD (bring your own device) tactic, 186, 670–671

C-ADR (cyber alternative dispute resolution), 111–113
CAFA (Class Action Fairness Act of 2005), 73
CALEA (Communications Assistance for Law Enforcement Act of 1994), 146
California Delta Water Twin Tunnel Project, 950–951
Cambridge University, 988
Cancellation forms, 426
Canon law, 212
CAN SPAM Act of 2003, 147, 428
Capacity. *See* Contractual capacity
CAPA (College Athletes Players Association), 684–685
Capital contributions, 715
Capital felonies, 123
Capital in the Twenty-First Century (Piketty), 212
Capitalism, 211, 719, 731
Capitalism, Socialism, and Democracy (Schumpeter), 719
C-arb (cyber-arbitration), 112
Cardoza Standard of Actual Privity, 917–920
Car insurance. *See* Automobile insurance
Carriers, 401, 835–838
Carrington, Michael, 477
Case in chief, 78, 79

Case management conferences, 76
Case trustees, 585
Cash cards, 506
Cash dividends, 750
Cashier's checks, 456
Cash surrender value, 526
CASs. *See* Complex adaptive systems
Catfishing, 255–257
Cather, Willa, 304, 307, 311, 313
Catholic Church. *See* Roman Catholic Church
Causation, in tort law, 164–166
Cause in fact, 178
CCPA (Consumer Credit Protection Act of 1968), 433
Ceballos, Richard, 649, 658, 693
Central Intelligence Agency (CIA), 55
CERCLA (Comprehensive Environmental Response, Compensation, and Liability Act of 1980), 966–967
Certificates of authority, 740
Certificates of deposit (CDs), 452–453
Certificates of incorporation, 743
Certified checks, 455
Certified public accountants (CPAs), 910
C.f. (cost of goods and freight), 383
CFAA (Computer Fraud and Abuse Act of 1986), 145–146
CFPB (Consumer Finance Protection Bureau), 430–434
CFR (Code of Federal Regulations), 52, 651
CGPA (Consumer Goods Pricing Act of 1975), 765
Chaotic events, 1017
  "The Chaotic Indeterminacy of Tort Law: Between Formalism and Nihilism" (Brion), 927–928
Chapter 7, Bankruptcy Code, 581–591. *See also* Liquidation
Chapter 11, Bankruptcy Code, 580, 581, 591–595
Chapter 12, Bankruptcy Code, 580, 595–596
Chapter 13, Bankruptcy Code, 580, 581, 597–598
Charitable immunity, 620–622
Charitable pledges, as consideration, 270–271
Charitable trusts, 896
Chase, Anthony, 30
Chase Manhattan Bank, 502
Chattels, 823
Check 21 Act of 2003, 498, 505–506
Check cards, 506
Checks
  altered, 494–495
  antedated, 500
  bad (NSF), 497–498
  cashier's, 456
  certified, 455
  defined, 454
  e-checks, 506
  form for, 455
  life cycle of, 503–504
  postdated, 500
  stale, 493
  substitute, 505
  teller's, 455–456
  traveler's, 456
Checks and balances, 38, 55
Chemical Safety Improvement Act of 2013 (CSIA), 966
Chevron Doctrine, 956
Chicago School of economics, 240
Chief technology officers (CTOs), 954
Children. *See* Minors
Children's Hospital and Research Center, 874–875, 891–892
Children's Online Privacy Protection Act of 1998 (COPPA), 428
Children's Online Privacy Protection Rule (COPPR), 428
China
  authoritarianism in, 998, 1012–1016
  Democracy Movement in, 998
  economic alliances with, 14
  economic cycle in, 1011
  Realpolitik theory and, 1007
Chindi-Mowry Enterprises Inc., 21
CHIPS (Clearing House Interbank Payments System), 506
Chose in action property, 823
CIA (Central Intelligence Agency), 55
C.i.f. (cost, insurance, and freight), 383
CIS (competitive impact statement), 810
CISG. *See* Convention on Contracts for the International Sale of Goods
Citation Corp., 595
Civilization, defined, 1008
Civil litigation, 71
Civil procedure, 71–85
  answer in, 74–75
  appeals in, 80
  class action lawsuits, 72–74, 423
  commencement of action in, 71–74
  cyber-procedure, 81–85
  discovery in, 76–77, 83–85
  execution of judgments in, 80
  Federal Rules of Civil Procedure, 74, 77, 82, 83
  filing complaints in, 71–72
  pre-answer stage of, 74
  pretrial stage of, 75–77
  service of process in, 74
  trial phase of, 77–80
Civil Rights Act of 1866, 643, 657
Civil Rights Act of 1871, 643, 657–658
Civil Rights Act of 1964
  amendments to, 663–664
  case study, 638–639, 642, 661–663
  Commerce Clause and, 945
  EEOC strategic enforcement plan, 665
  innkeepers and, 833
  protected classes in, 643
  Title VII of, 658–661, 663
  violation of, 92
Civil theft, 173
Civil trials, 77–80, 95, 102, 113
The Clash of Civilization (Huntington), 1008
Class Action Fairness Act of 2005 (CAFA), 73
Class action lawsuits, 72–74, 423
Clayton Act of 1914, 678–679, 801
Clean Air Act of 1970, 966
Clean Water Act of 1972, 965–966
Clear and reasonably definite terms, in contract offers, 236, 239
Clearing House Interbank Payments System (CHIPS), 506
Clearly erroneous standard, 64, 67
Clergy malpractice, 621–622
Cleveland Browns Football Co., Inc., 817–819
Click-on acceptance/agreement, 250, 324
Clickwrap agreements, 250, 251
Client privacy, 186
Climate change, 942–943, 968–970
Clinton, Bill, 949–950, 1004–1005
Close corporations, 740
Closed shop, 686
Closing statements, 79, 87
Cloud storage/computing, 252
Clymer, George, 787
C-med (cyber-mediation), 112
C-neg (cyber-negotiation), 111–112
Coastline Aviation Inc., 648
C.o.d. (collect on delivery), 383
Code of Federal Regulations (CFR), 52, 651
Code of Professional Ethics (AICPA), 912
Codes, defined, 45
Codicil, 883
Coercive persuasion, 119, 127, 151–153
Coinsurance, 528
Collateral, 550, 569
Collateral contracts, 310, 376
Collecting banks, 503
Collective action, 653
Collective bargaining, 640, 687, 691–694
Collective science court (CSC), 108–111
College Athletes Players Association (CAPA), 684–685
Collision insurance, 535

Subject Index

Co-makers, 452, 457
Comey, James, 56
Commencement of business, 744
Commentaries on the Constitution (Story), 578
Commerce, defined, 422
Commerce Clause, 122, 123, 736, 786–787, 945–946
Commerce Department, U.S., 279
Commercial docket, 404–405
Commercial impracticability, 345
Commercial units, 395
Commingling, 626
Commission on Science and Technology for Development, 1034
Commission on Sustainable Development (CSD), 968, 989
Commodity Futures Trading Commission, 792
Common carriers, 835, 837
Common law, 48–49, 214–215, 788, 917, 952
Common stock, 750
Communication, 240–243, 626–627
Communications Assistance for Law Enforcement Act of 1994 (CALEA), 146
Communications Decency Act of 1996, 184
Community improvement corporations, 711
Community property, 530, 824, 854
Company-owned, personally enabled devices (COPEs), 186
Company-run unions, 686
Comparative negligence, 181, 190
Compelling interest, 972
Compensatory damages, 187–188, 221, 347, 664
Competency to stand trial, 150–151
Competent authority, in just war theory, 1019
Competitive Banking Act of 1987, 463, 495
Competitive impact statement (CIS), 810
Complaints, 71–72
Complete performance, 340
Complex adaptive systems (CASs)
  agents involved in, 210–211
  defined, 210
  evolution of, 323, 414, 538
  interaction of, 211, 247–248, 737
  legal ecosystem as, 945–949
  volatility of, 557
  wealth distribution and, 212
Comprehensive coverage, 536
Comprehensive Environmental Response, Compensation, and Liability Act of 1980 (CERCLA), 966–967

Computer commerce. *See* Cyber-commerce
Computer Fraud and Abuse Act of 1986 (CFAA), 145–146
Computer software programs, 981–982
Concealment, 255, 542
Concrete situations vs. abstract principles, 30–31
Concurrent ownership, 851
Condemnation, 860–861
Conditional indorsements, 466
Condition concurrent, 242, 342
Condition precedent, 242, 316, 341
Condition subsequent, 242, 342
Confirmation, 594, 596–598
Conforming goods, 372
Conglomerate expansion, 809
Conglomerates, 65–66
Congressional Review Act of 1996 (CRA), 432
Consensual relationships, 610
Consent decrees, 810
Consent orders, 423
Consequential damages, 221, 347, 409
Consideration, 265–277
  accord and satisfaction in, 272–273
  adequacy of, 267
  agreements without, 274
  bitcoin and cryptocurrency as, 271–272
  characteristics of, 266–268
  charitable pledges as, 270–271
  defined, 265
  elements of, 218, 220
  enforceable agreements and, 273–275
  failure of, 479
  lack of, 479
  legality of, 268
  money as, 269
  nature of, 265–266
  past, 218, 276
  problems with, 272–277
  promises not to sue as, 269–270
  promissory estoppel and, 274
  property and services as, 269
  requirements of, 265–268
  types of, 268–272
  unconscionable, 218, 267
Considine, Kerry and Renee, 92–93, 97, 100, 103–104
Consignees, 832
Consignment contracts, 386, 832
Consignors, 832
Consolidation, 804
Conspiracy, 299
Constitution, defined, 35
Constitution, U.S. *See* U.S. Constitution
Constitutional Convention (1787), 36, 37, 55, 787

Constitutional law, 34–41
Construction loans, 553
Constructive bailments, 829
Constructive breaches, 346
Constructive discharge, 648–649, 686
Constructive eviction, 868
Consumer credit contracts, 483–484
Consumer Credit Protection Act of 1968 (CCPA), 433
Consumer Finance Protection Bureau (CFPB), 430–434
Consumer goods, 569, 570
Consumer Goods Pricing Act of 1975 (CGPA), 765
Consumer Leasing Act of 1976, 436
Consumer Product Safety Act of 1972, 421–422
Consumer Product Safety Commission (CPSC), 421
Consumer product warranties, 407
Consumer protection laws, 422–437.
  See also Product liability; Warranties
  for bait-and-switch schemes, 423–424
  on billing, collecting, and leasing, 435–437
  CAN SPAM Act, 147, 428
  Consumer Leasing Act, 436
  Cooling-Off Rule, 425–426
  credit cards, unauthorized use of, 434
  credit laws, 430–437
  cyber-banking and, 505–506
  cyber-commerce and, 428–429
  Equal Credit Opportunity Act, 434
  Fair Credit Billing Act, 435
  Fair Credit Reporting Act, 248, 326, 434–435
  Fair Debt Collection Practices Act, 435–436
  Federal Trade Commission and, 422–423
  fraudulent misrepresentation and, 423
  identity theft and, 146–147, 278, 428–429, 509
  lemon laws, 429–430
  Mail and Telephone Order Rule, 426
  Military Lending Act, 436–437
  negative option rule, 426
  900-telephone number rules, 427–428
  odometer tampering and, 425
  on slamming, 428
  state laws, 429–430
  Telemarketing Sales Rule, 427
  Truth-in-Lending Act, 433
  for unfair or deceptive practices, 423–425
  unordered merchandise and, 423
  Used Car Rule, 425
Consumers, defined, 422
Consumer welfare standard, 240
Continuity of existence, 708

Continuity plans, 426
Contract clauses (ADR), 103–105
Contract law, 208–225. See also Contracts
 capacity in (See Contractual capacity)
 case study, 208–209
 consideration in (See Consideration)
 cyber-shopping and, 277–279
 damages in, 221, 346–350
 disaffirm privilege in, 286
 equitable remedies in, 221, 350–351
 history of, 209–216
 multidimensional nature and
  principles of, 217–225
 mutual assent in (See Mutual assent)
 objectives of, 219, 221
 offers in (See Offers)
 rehabilitation in, 219, 221
 restatement of, 215–216
 trade fixtures in, 322, 323
Contract liability, 611
Contracts. See also Contract law
 adhesion, 540
 agency law and, 223
 bilateral, 226, 242, 341
 breach of (See Breach of contract)
 browsewrap, 250
 cannot be completed within
  one year, 306
 collateral, 310, 376
 consignment, 386, 832
 consumer credit, 483–484
 cost-plus, 238, 240
 current market price, 239, 240
 cyber (See Cyber-contracts)
 defined, 209, 235
 destination, 383
 disaffirmance of, 290–291
 elements of, 217–219
 employment, 640–641
 entered by executors/administrators, 310
 executed, 229, 378
 executory, 229
 express, 226–227
 formal, 228
 guaranty, 310, 376
 hot-cargo, 691
 implied, 226, 227, 644–646
 of indorsers, 467
 informal, 228
 in pari delicto, 300
 insurance, 522, 524, 540–541
 land, 553–554, 561
 lease options, 247
 legality of (See Legality of contracts)
 marriage, 310–311
 negotiation of, 343
 non-use, 208–209, 220, 224
 not voidable, 289

 option, 245–247, 275
 oral, 227, 305, 306, 308, 377
 output, 239, 240, 373–374
 partnership, 712–713
 personal, 337
 preformation, 742
 privity and, 223
 professional service, 337
 quasi-contracts, 227, 288–289
 ratification of, 290–291
 real estate, 306–308, 319–320
 of record, 228
 requirements, 238–240, 373–374
 sales (See Sales contracts)
 seals on, 228, 273
 shipment, 382, 383, 395
 Statute of Frauds and (See
  Statute of Frauds)
 termination by terms of, 343
 UCC and, 221–222, 240, 309
 unconscionable, 393
 unenforceable, 226
 unilateral, 226, 242, 341
 valid, 226
 void, 226
 voidable, 226, 289, 290
 written (See Written contracts)
Contractual capacity, 285–293
 defined, 219, 220, 285
 intoxication and, 292–293
 mental impairment and, 292
 minors and, 219, 286–291
 rebuttable presumption and, 219, 286
Contractual liability, 924
Contributory negligence, 181
Controlled companies, 764
Controlled Substances Act of 1971
 (CSA), 891
Controlling words, 461
Control test, 611
Conventional fixed-rate mortgages, 552
Convention on Contracts for the
 International Sale of Goods (CISG),
 380, 385, 1033–1034, 1057–1068
Convention on Cultural Property
 Implementation Act of 1983, 840
Convention on Stolen or Illegally
 Exported Cultural Objects, 840
Convention on the Means of Prohibiting
 and Preventing the Illicit Import,
 Export, and Transfer of Ownership
 of Cultural Property, 840
Convention on the Prevention and
 Punishment of the Crime of
 Genocide, 1022–1023
Conversion, 468
Convertible term insurance, 527
Conveyance in trust, 895

Cooling-Off Rule, 425–426
Cooperative corporations, 710
Cooperative corporations with
 wage-earning employees, 710
Cooperative Power Association
 (Minnesota), 110
Cooperatives with nonemployee
 owners, 710
Co-ownership, 714–715, 848–854
COPEs (company-owned, personally
 enabled devices), 186
COPPA (Children's Online Privacy
 Protection Act of 1998), 428
COPPR (Children's Online Privacy
 Protection Rule), 428
Copyright Act of 1980, 984
Copyright law, 983–985
Cordray, Richard, 432
Core cases, 580
Corporate democracy, 766
Corporate entities. See Corporations
Corporate opportunity doctrine, 776
Corporate person. See Corporations
Corporate personhood, 17–19,
 127–128, 734
Corporate punishment, 131
Corporate raids and raiders, 805
Corporate records, right of shareholders
 to examine, 778
Corporate shell, 748
Corporate trade-offs, 21
Corporation by estoppel, 745, 746
Corporations, 728–811
 actual authority rule for, 776–777
 alien, 740
 antitrust regulation of, 798–803,
  809–810
 balancing act for, 734–738, 760
 benefit, 711
 business judgment rule for, 773–774
 capitalism and, 731
 case study, 728–729
 close, 740
 commencement of business by, 744
 community improvement, 711
 cooperative, 710
 county land and reutilization, 711
 criminal liability and, 126–130
 crisis management and, 730
 cross-owned, 710
 decision making by, 19
 de facto, 745–747
 defined, 731
 de jure, 745, 746
 directors of, 758–759
 dissolution of, 810–811
 domestic, 739–740
 dummy, 748

economic crisis and, 730-731, 733-738
economic development, 711
enlightened self-interest and, 20
expansion of, 803-810
fairness rule for, 774, 776
financing, 750-751
foreign, 739-740
foreign law variations in treatment of, 129-130
formation of, 741-745
governance of, 760-766
identity of, 745-750
independent director control of, 763
legal person status of, 17-19, 127-128, 734
legal principles related to, 19, 731, 733-738
limited liability (*See* Limited liability companies (LLCs))
management of, 758-759
managerial control of, 765
naming, 743
officers of, 759
private, 709, 739
private religiously based, 710-711
promotion of ethical behavior by, 20-21
public bodies, 710
public-private, 710
public (state-owned), 709, 710, 739
punishment of, 131
quasi-public, 709, 739
S corporations, 740
securities regulation of, 790-794, 797-798
shareholders of (*See* Shareholders)
social, 710
social responsibility of, 19-21
stakeholders of, 759, 766
traditional corporate culture, 17-18
U.S. Constitution and, 786-789
utility thinking by, 18
voting control in, 766-771
Corporativism, 738, 788
Corpus, 894
Cosigners, 310, 376
Cost-benefit thinking, 18
Cost of repair rule, 924
Cost-plus contracts, 238, 240
Co-tenancy, 529-530, 824, 851
Counterclaims, 75
Counteroffers, 244-245
County land and reutilization corporations, 711
Courts, defined, 63
Court systems, 63-71. *See also specific courts*

federal, 64
jurisdiction in, 64-69, 81-82
state, 69-71
Cover, of sales contracts, 403
Covering laws, 1003
Coverture, 849-850
CPAs (certified public accountants), 910
CPSC (Consumer Product Safety Commission), 421
CRA (Congressional Review Act of 1996), 432
Craigslist, 669
Credit cards
debit cards vs., 508
innkeepers' lien and, 835
secured, 591
unauthorized use of, 434
Credit laws, 430-437
Creditor beneficiaries, 332
Creditors, agreements to defraud, 295, 297
Creditors' committees, 593
Credit transfers, 506
Crimea, invasion by Russia, 1002-1003
Crimes. *See also* Criminal law; *specific crimes*
agreements to commit, 293-294
business-related, 138
classes of, 123
cybercrimes, 141-150
defined, 119
elements of, 124-130
against justice, 139-141
people-related, 133-136
property-related, 136-138
punishment for, 131-132
Criminal acts, 124
Criminal law, 118-156. *See also* Crimes
as adaptation, 123
case study, 118-119
corporations and, 126-130
defenses to criminal liability, 150-156
double jeopardy and, 120-121
elements necessary for criminal liability, 124-130
federal, 122-123
objectives of, 120
prosecutions and lawsuits in, 119-120
punishment in, 131-132
tort law vs., 120, 163-164
victim's rights in, 121
Criminal liability
agency law and, 617
of attorneys, 931-932
corporations and, 126-130
defenses to, 150-156
Criminal negligence, 126
Criminal procedure, 85-87
Criminal simulation, 138

Criminal trials, 87
Crisis, defined, 557. *See also* 21st century financial crisis
Crisis Economics (Roubini & Mihm), 559, 730
Cross-appeals, 80
Cross-claims, 75
Cross-examination, 78, 79
Cross-owned corporations, 710
Crow, John D., 448-449, 451, 459-462
Cryptocurrency, 143, 271-272
CSA (Controlled Substances Act of 1971), 891
CSC (collective science court), 108-111
CSD (Commission on Sustainable Development), 968, 989
CSIA (Chemical Safety Improvement Act of 2013), 966
CTOs (chief technology officers), 954
Cultural property protection, 839-840
Cumulative voting, 767
Cure, 399
Current market price contracts, 239, 240
Curtesy, 850
Customary authority, 624
Cyber-agents, 631
Cyber alternative dispute resolution (C-ADR), 111-113
Cyber-arbitration (C-arb), 112
Cyber-assault, 142
Cyber-auction fraud, 381
Cyber-banking, 505-509
Check 21 Act and, 505-506
electronic fund transfers and, 506-507
global financial cyber-crisis and, 508-509
Sheltered Harbor network and, 509
Cyber-bulletin board, 184
Cyber-bullying, 142
Cyber-buying, 277-279
Cyber Command/Cybercom, 149, 508
Cyber-commerce. *See also* Cyber-contracts
buying and selling, 277-279
"click" fraud and, 325
consumer protection laws and, 428-429
defined, 47-48
European Union and, 1037-1038
legislation related to, 325-326
sales contracts and, 378, 380
verification problems in, 324-325
Cyber-confidence game, 325
Cyber-contracts
clauses and hyperlinks, 325
defined, 247
mutual assent and, 247-250
offer and acceptance in, 250, 324
payment and, 278-279
Cybercrimes, 141-150
"click" fraud, 325

Cybercrimes—(cont.)
  computers used in, 142–144
  cyber-trespass, 141
  federal, 145–148
  global cyber-crisis, 148–150
  offenses against computers, 144–145
Cyber-defamation, 184
Cyber-discovery, 83–85
Cyber-disparagement, 185
Cyber-extortion, 142–143
Cyber-filing, 82–83
Cyber-germ warfare, 142
Cyber-ghosts, 256–257
Cyber-harassment, 142
Cyber-insurance, 539–540
Cyber-invasion of privacy, 185–187
Cyber-inventions, 977–978
Cyber-jurisdiction, 81–82
Cyber-law statutes, 47–48
Cyber-mediation (C-med), 112
Cyber-negotiation (C-neg), 111–112
Cyber-payments, 278–279
Cyber-piracy, 142, 147
Cyber-price shopping, 277
Cyber-procedure, 81–85
Cyber-sales contracts, 378, 380
Cyber-selling, 277–279
Cyber-shopping, 277–279
Cyber-signatures, 324
Cyber-solutions, 149
Cyber-spoofing, 144
Cyber-stalking, 142
Cyber-strategies, 149
Cyber-tactics, 508
Cyber-targets, 508
Cyber-terrorism, 144
Cybertorts, 184–187
Cyber-trespass, 141
Cyber-vandalism, 145

DACA. *See* Deferred Action for Childhood Arrivals
Damages
  actual, 221, 347
  for breach of contract, 401
  compensatory, 187–188, 221, 347, 664
  consequential, 221, 347, 409
  defined, 79, 187, 346
  incidental, 221, 347, 401
  liquidated, 348–350
  mitigation of, 350
  nominal, 347
  present and future, 347
  punitive, 188, 221, 347, 348, 420, 664, 916
  under *quantum meruit*, 350
  speculative, 350
  stipulated, 348–350
  in tort law, 187–188
Dangerous products vs. unsafe products, 420–421
Danto, Arthur, 1016
Dark Age Ahead (Jacobs), 893–894
Data Control Inc., 507
Data mining, 186–187
Dates on negotiable instruments, 461
Daubert standard, 110
The Da Vinci Code (Brown), 450
Dayco Products, Inc., 441, 443–444
Death
  agent-principal relationship and, 629
  bank-depositor relationship and, 494
  right to, 890–893
  simultaneous, 886
  without wills, 884–886
Death penalty, 131–132
Death statute, 632
Debit cards, 506, 508
Debtor default, 550, 572
Debtor in possession, 591–592
Debts barred by statutes of limitations, 274
Declaration of Independence, 9
Declaration of trust, 895
Decreasing term insurance, 527
Deductibles, 528
Deeds
  bargain-and-sale, 859
  defined, 858
  general warranty, 859
  quitclaim, 859
  special warranty, 859
  of trust, 553
Deep State, 52–57, 432–433
Deepwater Horizon oil spill (2010), 128–129
De facto corporations, 745–747
Defamation, 169–171, 184
Default of debtor, 550, 572
Defective condition, 183, 419
Defendants, 71, 79, 86, 87, 120
Defend Trade Secrets Act of 2016 (DTSA), 69
Defense of Marriage Act of 1996 (DOMA), 881
Defense of others, 154
Defenses
  affirmative, 74
  after-acquired evidence, 648, 664
  to criminal liability, 150–156
  entrapment, 152–153
  insanity, 150–152
  justifiable force, 154–155
  mistake, 155–156
  to negligence, 181–183
  personal (limited), 478–480
  poison pill, 808
  real (universal), 481–483
Deferred Action for Childhood Arrivals (DACA), 28–29, 31–32, 43–44, 53
Definiteness, in contract offers, 238
Definite-time paper, 460–461
Defrauding creditors, 138, 295, 297
Degree of definiteness, in contract offers, 238
De jure corporations, 745, 746
Delaware, corporations, 742, 789
Del credere agents, 623
Delegated executive power, 42–43
Delegation of duties, 333
Deliberate breach of contract, 345–346
Delivery, defined, 479
Demand futility doctrine, 772
Demand notes, 452
Demand paper, 460
Democracy and the Market (Przeworski), 710
Demurrer, 74, 614
Department of ___. *See specific name of department*
Dependency theory, 958, 959
Depositary banks, 497, 503
Depositions, 76
Depositors. *See* Bank-depositor relationship
Dereliction of duty, 139
Derivatives, 791–792
Derivative suits, 771–772
Descriptive theories, 9
Descriptive thresholds, 535
Destination contracts, 383
Deterrence, 131
Development Reconciling Environmental and Material Success (DREAMS), 968
Devise, 876
Devisees, 876
Dewey, John, 17, 1015, 1016
DFA (Drone Federalism Act), 147–148
Dickey-Wicker Amendment, 955–956
Digital Millennium Copyright Act of 1998 (DMCA), 984
Digital signatures, 324
Direct examination, 78, 79
Directors, board of, 758–759
Direct suits, 771
Disability, defined, 666
Disability insurance, 537
Disabled persons, 666–667
Disaffirmance of contracts, 290–291
Disaffirm privilege, 286
Discharge, 339–346
  by agreement, 343–344
  by breach of contract, 345–346
  for charges filed or testimony given, 686

constructive, 648-649, 686
exceptions to, 590
by impossibility, 344
by impracticability, 345
by law, 345
by nonperformance, 343-346
by performance, 339-342
Disclaimers
audits and, 912
employment-at-will and, 645
of general partner status, 724
Disclosed principals, 622
Discovery, 76-77, 83-85, 99
Discrimination, 658-665, 686, 836, 837, 867
Dishonored instruments, 467, 485, 487
The Disorder of Law: A Critique of Legal Theory (Sampford), 928
Disparagement, 172-173, 185
Disparate impact, 659, 660, 664
Disparate treatment, 659
Disposable income, 585
Disputable presumption, 286
Disputed amount, 272
Dispute resolution. *See* Alternative dispute resolution (ADR)
Dispute Settlement Board (DSB), 1036-1037
Dispute Settlement Understanding (DSU), 1037
Dissociation of partnerships, 722
Dissolution
of corporations, 810-811
of LLCs, 811-812
of partnerships, 722-723
Diversity jurisdiction, 64, 66
Dividends, 734, 739, 750-751, 778
DMCA (Digital Millennium Copyright Act of 1998), 984
DNR (do not resuscitate) orders, 890
DNR identification, 632
Document of title, 384
Dodd-Frank Wall Street Reform and Consumer Protection Act of 2010
accountants and, 913-914
backlash against, 558, 737-738
CFPB under, 430, 432-433
ethical issues in, 927-929
financial advisors and, 923
provisions of, 564-565, 737, 791, 792
Title IX of, 792-794
Title VII of, 791-792
whistleblowers and, 785, 793-795
DOMA (Defense of Marriage Act of 1996), 881
Domain parkers, 325
Domestic bills of exchange, 454
Domestic corporations, 739-740

Dominant tenement, 847
Donee beneficiaries, 332
Donees, 827
Donors, 827
Do Not Call Registry, 427
Do not resuscitate (DNR) orders, 890
Dormant minerals statutes, 857-858
Double indemnity, 528
Double jeopardy, 120-121, 163-164
Dower, 850
DPAHC (durable power of attorney for health care), 632, 888-889
Drafts, 453-454
Drane, William, 728-729, 731-732, 748-749
Drawees, 453, 457
Drawers, 453, 457, 459, 485, 487
Dreamers, 28, 31, 43
DREAMS (Development Reconciling Environmental and Material Success), 968
Drezner, Daniel, 1000
Drone Federalism Act (DFA), 147-148
Drones, 147-148
DSB (Dispute Settlement Board), 1036-1037
DSU (Dispute Settlement Understanding), 1037
DTSA (Defend Trade Secrets Act of 2016), 69
Dual insurable interests, 387
Due care, duty of, 720
Due diligence, 773-774
Due process
constitutional guarantee of, 39, 41
corporations and, 734
post-appellate procedures and, 107
violation of, 2, 10-11, 28, 31, 44, 53
Duffy, Nicole, 541
Duke Power Company, 660
Dummy corporations, 748
Dunning letters, 423
Durable power of attorney, 629-630, 632, 876
Durable power of attorney for health care (DPAHC), 632, 888-889
Duress, 258-259, 481
Duty
to account, 626
of accountants, 914-915
in agency law, 625-628
of architects, 924
of attorneys, 929
of banks, 493-497
breach of, 177-178
of buyers, 395-397
of care, 833, 834
to defend, 525

defined, 164
delegation of, 333
of depositors, 497-498, 500
of due care, 720
of due diligence, 773-774
fiduciary, 779
to honor orders, 493
of insurers, 525
to investigate, 525
of landlords, 867-868
legal, 176-177
of loyalty, 626, 718-719, 774, 908, 929
to mitigate, 221
mortgagee, 556
of mortgagor, 555
nondelegable, 615
of obedience, 626, 718, 777
of parties to sales contracts, 393-399
in partnerships, 718-720
to pay, 525
preexisting, 276
of sellers, 399
of tenants, 868
of trustees, 589
to warn, 414-417, 419-420
Dwelling insurance, 533
Dworkin, Ronald, 191
Dyads, ethical, 14-16

E-agents, 631
Early neutral evaluation (ENE), 94-95, 100-101, 113
Easement by grant, 847
Easement by prescription, 847
Easement by reservation, 847
Easements, 847-848
Eastland Mall, 304-305, 307, 311-314
eBay, 81, 278, 324, 669
Ebola epidemic, 960-961
EC. *See* European Community
E-checks, 506
E-commerce. *See* Cyber-commerce
Economic alliances, 14-15
Economic and Social Council (ECO-SOC), 957-958, 972, 1034
Economic compensatory damages, 187-188
Economic crisis. *See* 21st century financial crisis
Economic development corporations, 711
Economic development special-purpose entities (EDSPEs), 711
Economic duress, 259
Economic Espionage Act of 1996 (EEA), 146, 981
An Economic Interpretation of the Constitution of the United States (Beard), 787

Economic realities test, 618, 653
Economic Security Council (ESC), 988-991, 1034-1035
Economic zones, 1010-1012
E-contracts. *See* Cyber-contracts
ECO-SOC (Economic and Social Council), 957-958, 972, 1034
ECPA (Electronic Communications Privacy Act of 1986), 146
EDSPEs (economic development special-purpose entities), 711
Educational theory of punishment, 131
EEA (Economic Espionage Act of 1996), 146, 981
EEOC. *See* Equal Employment Opportunity Commission
EESA (Emergency Economic Stabilization Act of 2008), 564
EFTs (electronic fund transfers), 506-507
EGCs (emerging growth companies), 797
E-Government Act of 2002, 954
Eighteenth Amendment, 1053
Eighth Amendment, 1052
Eisenhower, Dwight, 43, 55
Ejectment, 869
E-jurisdiction, 81-82
Elective share, 880
Electoral College, 36, 578
Electronic agents, 631
Electronically stored information (ESI), 83-84
Electronic alternative dispute resolution (e-ADR), 111-113
Electronic check conversion, 506
Electronic commerce. *See* Cyber-commerce
Electronic Communications Privacy Act of 1986 (ECPA), 146
Electronic contracts. *See* Cyber-contracts
Electronic Fund Transfer Act of 1978, 507
Electronic fund transfers (EFTs), 506-507
Electronic jurisdiction, 81-82
Electronic mail, 631
Electronic negotiable instruments, 458
Electronic principals, 631
Electronic Signatures in Global and National Commerce (E-Sign) Act of 2000, 248, 256, 326, 378
Eleventh Amendment, 191, 1052
Ely, Samuel, 577
Emancipation, 287
Embezzlement, 138
Emergency Economic Stabilization Act of 2008 (EESA), 564

Emerging growth companies (EGCs), 797
Eminent domain, 22, 860-861
Emoluments Clause, 56
Emotional distress, 174-175, 523-524, 608, 648
Emotional duress, 258-259
Empire State Carpenters Welfare, Annuity, and Pension Fund, 915-916, 919-920
Employee, defined, 683-684
Employee Retirement Income Security Act of 1974 (ERISA), 656, 923
Employer-employee relationship, 610
Employment at will, 640-643
Employment contracts, 640-641
Employment law, 638-671. *See also* Equal employment opportunity
after-acquired evidence defense in, 648
case study, 638-639
employment at will and, 640-643
Fair Labor Standards Act and, 625, 652-653
Family and Medical Leave Act and, 656-657
health and safety in, 651-652
on identity and employment eligibility, 654
on job qualifications and interview questions, 649-650
pension plan regulation and, 656
privacy and, 185-186
retaliation and constructive discharge in, 648-649
social media policies and, 669-671
social security and, 654
unemployment insurance and, 654-655
on worker benefits, 654-657
workers' compensation and, 655-656
wrongful discharge and, 643-648
Enabling legislation, 51
Endangered Species Act of 1973 (ESA), 947
The End of History and the Last Man (Fukuyama), 998, 1012
End users, 190
ENE (early neutral evaluation), 94-95, 100-101, 113
Energy Policy Act of 2005, 962-963
Energy regulation, 962-964
Energy Reorganization Act of 1974, 963
Enforceable agreements, 273-275
English, Leandra, 432-433
Enlightened self-interest, 20
Entity theory, 707-708
Entrapment, 152-153

Environmental Protection Agency (EPA), 414, 416, 417, 419, 965
Environmental regulation, 964-970
EPA. *See* Environmental Protection Agency
ePresence, 366-367, 370-371, 376-377
Equal Credit Opportunity Act of 1974, 434
Equal dignities rule, 317
Equal employment opportunity, 657-668
Age Discrimination in Employment Act and, 665-666
Americans with Disabilities Act and, 666-667
anti-retaliation safeguards and, 668
civil rights legislation and, 657-665
Genetic Information Nondiscrimination Act and, 667
Uniformed Services Employment and Reemployment Rights Act and, 666
whistleblower acts and, 667-668
Equal Employment Opportunity Commission (EEOC)
after-acquired evidence and, 664
on anti-retaliation provisions, 668
case studies, 92, 97, 100, 103-104, 638, 642, 647, 661
Equal Pay Act administered by, 658, 664
sexual harassment claims and, 661
strategic enforcement plan, 665
Equal Pay Act of 1963, 92, 658, 664
Equal protection rights
constitutional guarantee of, 39, 41
post-appellate procedures and, 107
violations of, 2, 10-11, 28, 31, 44, 53
Equipment, defined, 569
Equitable estoppel, 308
Equitable remedies, 79, 221, 350-351
Equity financing, 734, 750
Equity of redemption, 555
ERISA (Employee Retirement Income Security Act of 1974), 656, 923
ESA (Endangered Species Act of 1973), 947
ESC (Economic Security Council), 988-991, 1034-1035
Escheat, 825
ESI (electronically stored information), 83-84
E-Sign Act. *See* Electronic Signatures in Global and National Commerce Act of 2000
Establishment Clause, 621
Estate in fee simple, 849
Estate planning, 882-883. *See also* Wills
Estate settlement, 886-887

Estoppel. *See also* Promissory estoppel
  agency by, 624
  corporation by, 745, 746
  defined, 274, 543
  equitable, 308
Ethical considerations. *See also* Ethics
  agreements to strike illegally, 296
  bankruptcy, 586-587, 593-594
  bounced checks, 503
  capitalism, 719
  checks from credit card companies, 455
  creative destruction and government regulation, 679
  Deep State, 432
  dependency theory, 959
  ebola epidemic, 960-961
  employment-at-will, 646
  fraud and, 255
  free speech, 693-694
  innkeepers' duty of care, 834
  insurance, 544
  law and, 21-23
  marketing campaigns, 477-478
  paramilitary police power, 140
  patents, 979
  population growth, 991
  reading rights, 86
  reward offers, 226
  Sarbanes-Oxley Act, 762-763
  science courts, 404-405
  spirit or letter of the law, 735-736
  televised trials, 80
  textualism and pragmatism, 801-802
  time for performance, 339
  unconscionable clauses, 105
  unsafe products vs. dangerous products, 420-421
  victim's rights in texting suicide case, 121
  war, 1018
  wealth distribution, 212
  whistleblowers, 796
Ethics, 5-23. *See also* Ethical considerations
  business and, 17-21
  in decision making, 6-8
  defined, 5
  dyads and, 14-16
  government and, 13-17
  rational (objective), 12-13
  of responsibility, 14-16, 19-21
  social contract, 8-10
  theories of, 8-13
  of ultimate ends, 14
  Uniform Law Commission and, 46
  utilitarianism, 10-11, 21
European Community (EC), 62-63, 65, 72, 75

European Union (EU)
  as conglomerate, 65
  creation of, 1037
  currency of, 460
  cyber-ADR platform of, 113
  Data Protection Directive, 279, 1038
  electronic commerce and, 1037-1038
  E-Privacy Directive of, 279
  General Data Protection Regulation, 762
Euros, 460, 1037
Evans, Jameka, 699-701
Evans-Harris, Raven, 162-163, 165, 182
Eviction, 868, 869
Evolve Software, 366-367, 370-371, 376-377
Exclusionary rule, 85
Exculpatory clause, 297
Executed contracts, 229, 378
Executive agencies, 50
Executive orders, 28-29, 31-32, 41-45, 53
Executive power, theories of, 42-43
Executors, 310, 886
Executory contracts, 229
Executrix, 886
Exemplary damages. *See* Punitive damages
Exemptions from risk, 527
Exempt property, 880
Expected expenses, 831
Expedia Inc., 249
Expedited credit, 505
Expert testimony, 109, 935
Exploitation, 174
Express authority, 623-624
Express contracts, 226-227
Express warranties, 406-407
Extortion, 142-143
Exxon Valdez Alaskan oil spill (1989), 967

FAA (Federal Aviation Administration), 148, 837
Facebook, 184, 661, 669, 692
Face-to-face communication, 242
Facsimile signatures, 318
Factions, 945
Factor, 622-623, 832
Failed states, 15, 16
Failure of consideration, 479
Failure-proof public corporations, 710
Fair and Accurate Credit Transactions (FACT) Act of 2003, 248, 249, 256, 326
Fair courts, 214
Fair Credit Billing Act of 1974 (FCBA), 435
Fair Credit Reporting Act of 1970 (FCRA), 248, 326, 434-435

Fair Debt Collection Practices Act of 1977, 435-436
Fair Housing Contact Service (FHCS), 523, 544
Fair Labor Standards Act of 1938 (FLSA), 625, 652-653
Fairness rule, 774, 776
Fair use doctrine, 984
False imprisonment, 168
False light, 174
Family allowance, 880, 882-883
Family and Medical Leave Act of 1993 (FMLA), 656-657
Family farmer debt adjustment, 595-596
Fannie Mae. *See* Federal National Mortgage Association
A Farewell to Arms (Hemingway), 453
Farm products, 569
F.a.s. vessel (free alongside vessel), 383
FASB (Financial Accounting Standards Board), 911, 913
FAST (Fixing America's Surface Transportation) Act of 2015, 797
Fault-based insurance, 534
FBI. *See* Federal Bureau of Investigation
FCA (Financial Choice Act of 2017), 737-738, 770
FCBA (Fair Credit Billing Act of 1974), 435
FCC. *See* Federal Communications Commission
FCRA (Fair Credit Reporting Act of 1970), 248, 326, 434-435
FCTA (Federal Tort Claims Act of 1946), 191, 618, 620
FDIC (Federal Deposit Insurance Corporation), 501
Featherbedding, 691
Federal Arbitration Act of 1925, 96-98, 100
Federal Aviation Administration (FAA), 148, 837
Federal Bureau of Investigation (FBI), 2, 10-11, 50, 122, 143, 149, 509
Federal Circuit, 67-68, 76, 82
Federal Communications Commission (FCC), 264, 267, 428, 809, 810
Federal Computer Incident Response Center (FedCIRC), 149
Federal court system, 64
Federal criminal law, 122-123
Federal cybercrimes, 145-148
Federal Deposit Insurance Corporation (FDIC), 501
Federal district courts, 64-66
Federal Employers Liability Act of 1908 (FELA), 180

Federal Energy Regulatory Commission (FERC), 962–963
Federal Home Loan Mortgage Corporation (Freddie Mac), 333–334, 336, 556, 559–560, 563–564
Federal Housing Association (FHA), 560
Federal Housing Finance Agency (FHFA), 563, 564
Federal Insecticide, Fungicide, and Rodenticide Act of 1910 (FIFRA), 414, 416, 419
Federal Insurance Contributions Act (FICA) taxes, 654
The Federalist Papers (Madison), 578, 579
Federal Judicial Center (FJC), 84
Federal Mediation and Conciliation Service, 692
Federal National Mortgage Association (Fannie Mae), 548, 554, 556, 559–561, 563–564
Federal question, 64
Federal Register, 51, 52, 810, 961
Federal Reserve Board, 463, 495–496, 507
Federal Rules of Civil Procedure, 74, 77, 82, 83, 931
Federal Tort Claims Act of 1946 (FCTA), 191, 618, 620
Federal Trade Commission Act of 1914 (FTCA), 422, 423, 801
Federal Trade Commission (FTC)
  bait-and-switch confidence games outlawed by, 241
  Children's Online Privacy Protection Rule from, 428
  Cooling-Off Rule from, 425–426
  corporate expansion and, 809
  cyber-auction fraud information from, 381
  establishment of, 801
  fraud as defined by, 424
  holder in due course rule from, 480
  legend requirement for consumer credit contracts, 483–484
  Mail and Telephone Order Rule from, 426
  900-telephone number rules from, 427–428
  powers of, 422–423
  Reclaim Your Name program and, 429
  Telemarketing Sales Rule from, 427
  trade regulation by, 425–428
  Used Car Rule from, 425
  on warranty protection, 406
Federal Unemployment Tax Act of 1935, 655

Federal Vacancies Reform Act of 1998, 432–433
Federal Water Pollution Control Act of 1948, 965–966
Fedwire System, 506
Fee simple determinable, 855–856
FEF (Free Enterprise Fund), 761
FELA (Federal Employers Liability Act of 1908), 180
Felonies, 123
Feme covert, 849
Feme solo, 849
Ferae naturae, 182–183
FERC (Federal Energy Regulatory Commission), 962–963
A Few Brass Tacks (Bromfield), 240, 1009–1010
FHA (Federal Housing Association), 560
FHCS (Fair Housing Contact Service), 523, 544
FHFA (Federal Housing Finance Agency), 563, 564
FICA (Federal Insurance Contributions Act) taxes, 654
Fictitious payees, 469
Fiduciary, defined, 887
Fiduciary duties, 779
Fiduciary liability, 616
Fiduciary relationships, 255, 610, 616–617
Fiduciary rule, 922–923
Field warehousing, 838
FIFRA (Federal Insecticide, Fungicide, and Rodenticide Act of 1910), 414, 416, 419
Fifteenth Amendment, 39, 643, 657, 1053
Fifth Amendment
  eminent domain and, 861
  right to remain silent and, 86
  on taking of property without due process, 576, 584, 586, 588
  text of, 1051
  violation of, 28, 31, 44, 53
Filburn, Roscoe, 122
Finance charges, 433
Financial Accounting Standards Board (FASB), 911, 913
Financial advisors, 922–923
Financial Choice Act of 2017 (FCA), 737–738, 770
Financial crisis. *See* 21st century financial crisis
Financial Industry Regulatory Authority (FINRA), 922
Fink, Leo, 772–773
Fire insurance, 528–529

Firm offers, 247, 275, 372–373
First Amendment
  free exercise clause of, 874
  labor unions and, 677
  protection from masses through, 38
  religion clauses of, 36, 608, 619, 621, 687, 733
  text of, 1051
First-degree murder, 133–134
First in time, first in rights rule, 851
First-to-file provision, 979–980
FISA (Foreign Intelligence Surveillance Act of 1972), 57
Fishing business debt adjustment, 595–596
Fitzsimons, Thomas, 787
Fixed-rate mortgages, 552
Fixing America's Surface Transportation (FAST) Act of 2015, 797
Fixtures, 322, 323, 569, 847
FJC (Federal Judicial Center), 84
Flamme Bros., 403
Flexible-rate mortgages, 552
Floater policies, 529
Floating liens, 570
Flood insurance, 532–533
FLSA (Fair Labor Standards Act of 1938), 625, 652–653
Flynn, Michael, 56
FMLA (Family and Medical Leave Act of 1993), 656–657
F.o.b. the place of destination, 383
F.o.b. the place of shipment, 382
Food and Agriculture Organization, 960, 1034
Food disparagement laws, 172–173
Forbearance, 218, 220, 265, 269
Forced share, 880
Foreclosure, 556
Foreign corporations, 739–740
Foreign drafts, 454
Foreign Intelligence Surveillance Act of 1972 (FISA), 57
Foreign Service Immunities Act of 1976, 65
Foreign Trade Antitrust Improvements Act of 1982 (FTAIA), 802–803
Foreseeability test, 178–180
Forged indorsements, 468–469
Forgery, 138, 482, 494–495
Formal charges, in criminal procedure, 86–87
Formal contracts, 228
Formalism, 928
Forrest, Christopher, 631
Forum selection clauses, 250
Forum shopping, 73
Fourteenth Amendment
  civil rights and, 643

corporate rights and, 127-128, 734
due process and equal protection in, 39, 41, 657
mortgages and, 556
state government protection of, 86
text of, 1052-1053
Fourth Amendment, 85, 185, 1051
Fracking, 855
The Fragile Absolute (Zizek), 514
Franchises, 710, 740
Fraud
 active, 255
 cyber-auction, 381
 in cyber-commerce, 325
 defined, 137-138, 424
 defrauding creditors, 295, 297
 employment cases involving fraud, 644
 as to essential nature of transaction, 482
 forgery, 138, 482, 494-495
 in inception, 254
 in inducement, 254, 479
 misrepresentation as, 173, 347, 423
 mutual assent and, 253-257
 passive, 255
 shelter provision and, 477
 in type one arrangements, 916
 types of, 254-257
 in type two arrangements, 920
Fraudulent concealment, 542
Fraudulent conveyance, 333
Fraudulent misrepresentation, 173, 347, 423
Freddie Mac. *See* Federal Home Loan Mortgage Corporation
Fred Stern and Company, 918-919
Freedman, Nancy, 631
Free Enterprise Fund (FEF), 761
Free Exercise Clause, 356, 358, 619, 621, 733, 874
Freehold estates, 849
Freeman, Edna, 623
Free speech, 13, 16, 689, 693-694, 908
Friedberg, Smith & Co. P.C., 915-916, 919-920
Friedman, Lawrence, 928
Friedman, Thomas, 1013
Friendly suitors, 807
Fritz, Kendra, 162-163, 165, 182
Fructus industriales (harvested crops), 846
Fructus naturales (fruit of nature), 846
Fruit of the poisonous tree, 85
Frustration-of-purpose doctrine, 344
Frye standard, 166
FTAIA (Foreign Trade Antitrust Improvements Act of 1982), 802-803
FTC. *See* Federal Trade Commission
FTCA (Federal Trade Commission Act of 1914), 422, 423, 801
FTC legend, 483-484

Fukuyama, Francis, 998, 999, 1012
Full warranties, 407
FUNDES, 988
Funds, availability of, 495-496
Fungible goods, 384
Future damages, 347
Future gifts and legacies, 218, 277
Future goods, 368
The Future of the United Nations (Muravchik), 958, 960, 964

GAAP. *See* Generally accepted accounting principles
GAAS. *See* Generally accepted auditing standards
Gaddafi, Muammar, 1023
GAO (Government Accountability Office), 914
Garcetti, Gil, 649
Garner, Bryan A., 33, 735
Gatesworth, Cheryl, 54
Gateway Supply Company, 441-445
GE Energy, 784-785, 794-795
Gelfand, Michael, 264-265, 267-268, 270, 275
GEMS (Global Environmental Monitoring System), 967
General agents, 622
General Agreement on Tariffs and Trade (GATT), 1035-1036
General Assembly (United Nations), 957, 1030-1032
General consent, 933
General Data Protection Regulation (GDPR), 762
General Electric Credit Union, 844-845, 850-851
General jurisdiction, 64
Generally accepted accounting principles (GAAP), 911, 912, 915, 920, 921
Generally accepted auditing standards (GAAS), 911, 912, 915, 920, 921
General partners, 723-724
General partnerships, 709
General release, 344
General warranty deeds, 859
The Genesis Code (Forrest), 631
Genetic Information Nondiscrimination Act of 2008 (GINA), 667
Geneva Conventions, 1026-1027
Genocide, 1022-1023
Gentile, Forest, 976
Gericide, 893
Germany and the Next War (von Bernhardi), 1018
Getty Petroleum, 468
GHGs (greenhouse gases), 942-943, 968-970

Giffords, Gabby, 169-170
Gifts
 anatomical, 631-632, 828
 in causa mortis, 828
 future, 218, 277
 inter vivos, 827
 of personal property, 827-828
 title by, 858-859
GINA (Genetic Information Nondiscrimination Act of 2008), 667
Gingrich, Newt, 54
Ginnie Mae (Government National Mortgage Association), 556, 560
Global challenges
 capital sources for, 988
 education and human resources for, 988
 energy regulation, 962-964
 environmental regulation, 964-970
 Heilbroner on, 962
 long-range plans for, 986
 overview, 961
 partnerships for, 986-987
 population growth, 970-972, 991
 solutions to, 985-991
Global Environmental Monitoring System (GEMS), 967
Global initial conditions, 1008-1012
Globalization, 15
Global landscape, 1006
Global warming, 942-943, 969
Golden parachutes, 793
Golemen, Bethany, 503
Gompers, Samuel, 678
Good faith
 attorneys and, 929
 defined, 393
 for holder in due course, 475-476
Goods. *See also* Sale of goods
 acceptance by buyer, 397
 conforming, 372
 consumer, 569, 570
 defined, 368
 entrusting to merchants, 382
 fungible, 384
 future goods, 368
 identified, 382
 lease of, 367, 369
 merchantable, 408
 nonconforming, 372
 rejection by buyer, 395-397
 reselling, 401
 specially manufactured, 377
 stoppage in transit, 400-401
Government Accountability Office (GAO), 914
Government action, ethics and, 13-17
Governmental control theory of corporate management, 761

Government National Mortgage Association (Ginnie Mae), 556, 560
Government-sponsored enterprises (GSEs), 560, 563
Graduated-payment mortgages, 552
Grand juries, 86
Granger, Steve, 523–524, 544
Grantees, 858
Grantors, 858
Gratuitous agency/agents, 627
Gratuitous bailments, 830
Greatest good concept, 10–11
The Great Illusion (Angell), 1018
Great Lakes Initiative External Advisory Group, 106
Great Minneapolis Surplus Store, 252
The Green Bay Tree (Bromfield), 676
Greenhouse gases (GHGs), 942–943, 968–970
Greenmail, 806–807
Grenfell Tower fire (2017), 130
Gries Sports Enterprises, Inc., 817–819
Grievance procedures, 640
Gross negligence, 831
Groundwork of the Metaphysics of Morals (Kant), 12
Group of 77 (G-77), 958
Groves, Leslie, 1021
GSEs (government-sponsored enterprises), 560, 563
Guaranteed insurability option, 528
Guarantees, 406. *See also* Warranties
Guarantors, 310, 376
Guaranty contracts, 310, 376
Guaranty of payment, 310, 376
Gulf of Mexico oil spill (2010), 128–129
Gun control legislation, 135–136
Gun Free Zone Act of 1990, 135
The Guns of August (Tuchman), 1018
Gunther, Harold, 151
Gustin, Julie and Mary, 251
Guthrie, N. E., Jr., 448–449, 451–452, 459–462

Haas Mid-Way Equipment Company, 457
Haass, Richard, 1006
Hacking, 142–143, 148
Hague Convention for the Protection of Cultural Property in the Event of Armed Conflict, 840
Halliburton, 128
Hamilton, Alexander, 42
HAMP (Home Affordable Modification Program), 563, 564
Handley, Frank, 648
Hanover National Bank, 576–577, 584, 586, 588, 592
Hanson, Emile, 895

Harassment, 142
Harassment in workplace, 661
Harbour Portfolio Advisors LLC, 548–549, 554, 561–562, 565–566
Hard power, 957
HARP (Home Affordable Refinance Program), 563, 564
Harris, Andre T., 162–163, 165, 182
Harris, Charlotte, 162–163, 165, 182
Harrisburg Construction Company, 686
Hart-Scott-Rodino Antitrust Act of 1976, 809
Hate speech, 134–135
Haven Hills Farm, 408
Hayek, Friedrich, 678
Hayward, Tony, 129
Haywood, Brent, 134
Health and Human Services Department, U.S. (HHS), 53, 355–363, 732, 935
Health and safety laws, 651–652
Health care providers, 932–936
 Affordable Care Act and, 935–936
 HIPAA and, 935
 negligence of, 933–934
 professional status of, 932
 standard of care for, 932–935
Health care proxy, 887
Health insurance, 536–539
Health Insurance Portability and Accountability Act of 1996 (HIPAA), 537, 935
Health maintenance organizations (HMOs), 537
Health Resources and Services Administration (HRSA), 355–363
Hearst, Patty, 118–119, 127, 137, 153
Heilbroner, Robert, 962, 964, 970, 971, 998
Heirs, 876, 885–886
Helms, Robert, 55
Hemingway, Ernest, 453
Henry, Patrick, 47, 1069
HHS. *See* Health and Human Services Department, U.S.
HIPAA (Health Insurance Portability and Accountability Act of 1996), 537, 935
HIV/AIDS, 960
Hively, Kimberly, 638–639, 641–642, 647, 661–663
HMOs (health maintenance organizations), 537
Hobbes, Thomas, 8–9, 22, 34, 36, 39, 120, 164, 1009
Hobby Lobby Stores Inc., 355, 356, 359–361, 710, 732–733, 749–750
Hodgkinson, James T., 169
Holder in due course, 473–487
 defined, 457–458

 good faith requirement for, 475–476
 liability of parties, 485–487
 personal defenses and, 478–480
 real defenses and, 481–483
 shelter provision and, 477
 UCC on, 473
 value-taking requirement for, 474–475
 without notice of defect requirement, 476
Holder in due course rule, 480
Holders, 457, 463
Holmes Enterprises, 645
Holographic wills, 879
Home Affordable Modification Program (HAMP), 563, 564
Home Affordable Refinance Program (HARP), 563, 564
Home equity loans, 553
Homeland Security Department, U.S., 28, 43, 140, 141, 143
Homeowner's policies, 529
Homestead exemption, 529, 530, 587–588, 880
Homicide, 133–134
Honorable surrender, principle of, 1021
Hooten Equipment Company, 392–394, 398–399
Hoover, J. Edgar, 55
Hopscotch loan process, 806
Horizontal expansion, 809
Horney, Jesse, 848
Hospitals, liability of, 937–938
Hostile bidders, 805
Hostile work environments, 661
Hot-cargo contracts, 691
Housing and Economic Recovery Act of 2008, 563
"How Culture Changes" (Murdock), 609
Howell, Keith, 284–285, 298
HRSA (Health Resources and Services Administration), 355–363
Human rights, 2–3, 6, 15–16
Hume, David, 34
Hung juries, 87
Hunt, E. Howard, 55
Huntington, Samuel, 1008–1009
Hurricane Katrina (2005), 533, 559
Husbands, Don, 520–521, 524–525, 531
Huxley, Aldous, 23
Hybrid contracts, 369–370
Hybrid executive orders, 42
Hyperlinks, 325

IAEA (International Atomic Energy Agency), 958, 964, 988
IAMAW (International Association of Machinists and Aerospace Workers), 676, 687

IBRD (International Bank for Reconstruction and Development), 1035
ICC (International Criminal Court), 1032–1033
Ice-Fire Security Corporation, 477–478
ICE (Immigration and Customs Enforcement), 37
ICISS (International Commission on Intervention and State Sovereignty), 1023
ICJ (International Court of Justice), 1030–1032, 1043–1045
IC3 (Internet Crime Complaint Center), 149, 508–509
IDA (International Development Association), 1035
Idealism, 1004–1005
Identified goods, 382
Identity theft, 144–147, 428–429, 509
Identity Theft and Assumption Deterrence Act of 1998 (ITADA), 146–147, 278, 509
Identity Theft Penalty Enhancement Act of 2004 (ITPEA), 146–147, 278
IDG (Independent Drivers Guild), 676–677, 687–690
Igar International Corporation, 20
IHR (International Health Regulations), 960
Illegal agreements, 285, 293–299
Illegality, holder in due course and, 481
Illusory promises, 218, 276
Image replacement documents (IRDs), 505
IMF (International Monetary Fund), 1005, 1035
Immigration and Customs Enforcement (ICE), 37
Immigration law, 28–29, 31–32, 37, 43–44
Immigration Reform and Control Act of 1986, 654
Impaired classes, 594
Imperial National Hotel, 686
Implied acceptance, 245
Implied authority, 624
Implied contracts, 226, 227, 644–646
Implied covenant, 304, 646
Implied-in-fact bailments, 829
Implied-in-fact contracts, 227
Implied-in-law bailments, 829
Implied-in-law contracts, 227
Implied warranties, 407–408
Impossibility, discharge by, 344
Imposters, 469
Impression Products Inc., 974–975
Improper execution of wills, 884
Incidental authority, 624
Incidental beneficiaries, 223, 332

Incidental damages, 221, 347, 401
Incompetence. *See* Mental impairment
Incorporators, 742
Indemnification, 524, 628
Independent agencies, 51
Independent contractors, 610–612, 617–618
Independent directors, 763
Independent Drivers Guild (IDG), 676–677, 687–690
Independent source rule, 85
India, economic alliances with, 14, 15
Indictments, 86
Individual debt adjustment, 597–598
Individualism Old and New (Dewey), 17
Indorsees, 458
Indorsement in full, 465
Indorsements, 463–468
  blank, 464–465
  conditional, 466
  forged, 468–469
  multiple payees and, 467–468
  qualified, 466–467
  restrictive, 465–466
  special, 465
  unauthorized, 468–469
Indorsers, 458, 467, 485–487
Inevitable discovery doctrine, 85
Informal contracts, 228
Informal wills, 879–880
Information, in criminal procedure, 86–87
Informed consent, 933
Inherent executive power, 42
In-house attorneys, 931
Injunctions, 79, 188, 221, 351
Inland marine insurance, 529
Innkeepers, 833–835
Innovative Marketing Inc., 424
In pari delicto contracts, 300
An Inquiry into the Human Prospect (Heilbroner), 962, 964, 970, 998
Insanity defense, 150–152
Inside information, 776
Insider trading, 776
Insolvency, 586
Insolvent buyers, 400
Installment notes, 452
Instrumentality test, 747–748
Insurable interest, 387, 524
Insurance, 521–543
  automobile, 534–536
  cancellation by insurer, 541–543
  cyber-insurance, 539–540
  deductibles, 528
  defined, 522
  disability, 537
  health, 536–539

  lapses in, 540–541
  liability, 536
  life, 526–528
  long-term care, 537
  parties to contract, 522, 524
  peril management and, 521–525
  policy/contract, 522, 524, 540–541
  premiums, 524, 540
  property, 528–533
  risk assessment and, 521–525
  types of, 526–540
  umbrella policies, 539
  unemployment, 654–655
Insurance beneficiaries, 332
Insured, 524, 541–542
Insurers, 524, 541–543
Insurrection Act of 1807, 141
Intangible personal property, 823
Integral-part test, 807
Intellectual property, 973–985
  copyright, 983–985
  nature of, 973–974
  patents, 82, 974–980
  trade secrets, 146, 980–983
Intended beneficiaries, 223, 331–332
Intent, 125, 236, 239
Intentional infliction of emotional distress, 174–175, 648
Intentional torts, 167–175
  assault and battery, 168
  civil theft, 173
  defamation, 169–171, 184
  disparagement, 172–173, 185
  false imprisonment, 168
  fraudulent misrepresentation, 173
  intentional infliction of emotional distress, 174–175
  invasion of privacy, 174, 185–187
  master-servant relationship and, 613
  misuse of legal procedure, 175
Interest-only mortgages, 552
Interference with employees' right to organize, 685–686
Interlocking directorates, 801
Intermediary banks, 503
Internal Revenue Service (IRS), 745, 827, 921
International arbitration agreements, 107–108
International Association of Machinists and Aerospace Workers (IAMAW), 676, 687
International Atomic Energy Agency (IAEA), 958, 964, 988
International Bank for Reconstruction and Development (IBRD), 1035
International Bar Association, 107
International bills of exchange, 454

International Commission on Intervention and State Sovereignty (ICISS), 1023
International Court of Justice (ICJ), 1030-1032, 1043-1045
International Criminal Court (ICC), 1032-1033
International Development Association (IDA), 1035
International Health Regulations (IHR), 960
International initial conditions, 1001
International law
    finance and, 1035
    protective war and, 1022-1024
    on sale of goods, 380, 385, 1033-1034, 1057-1068
    trade and, 1035-1037
    United Nations and, 1030-1033
    war and, 1017-1027
International Law Commission, 1030
International Monetary Fund (IMF), 1005, 1035
International sales, 380, 385, 1057-1068
Internet auctions, 380-381
Internet Crime Complaint Center (IC3), 149, 508-509
Internet service providers (ISPs), 147, 184, 278
Interpretation vs. words duality, 30
Interrogatories, 77
Interstate commerce, 422
Interstate Commerce Act of 1887, 836
Interstitial executive power, 43
Interview questions, 649-650
Inter vivos trusts, 895
Intestate, 876, 884
Intestate succession, 884
Intimidation, 139
Intoxication, 292-293
Intrastate commerce, 422
Intrusion, 174
Invasion of privacy, 174, 185-187
Inventory, 569
Inversions, 805-806
Inverted companies, 806
Investment Advisors Act of 1940, 922-923
Investor Protection and Securities Reform Act of 2010, 792-794
Invitations to trade, 241
Involuntary manslaughter, 134
Involuntary movement, in criminal law, 124
Involvement, law merchant and, 213
IRDs (image replacement documents), 505
Irresistible impulse test, 151

Irrevocable offers, 275
Irrevocable trusts, 895
IRS (Internal Revenue Service), 745, 827, 921
ISIS (Islamic State of Iraq and Syria), 15, 16, 957, 991, 1019, 1025-1026
ISPs (Internet service providers), 147, 184, 278
Issue, 885
Issuers, 457
ITADA (Identity Theft and Assumption Deterrence Act of 1998), 146-147, 278, 509
ITPEA (Identity Theft Penalty Enhancement Act of 2004), 146-147, 278
Ivy Tech Community College, 638-639, 641-642, 647, 661-663

J. Craig Venter Institute (JCVI), 973, 976, 978-979, 987, 990
Jacobs, Jane, 893-894
Jacobs Brothers Department Store, 403-404
Janus, Mark, 680-681
Japan, economic alliances with, 14
Jeffer Mangels Butler and Mitchell LLP (JMBM), 95-96
Jefferson, Thomas, 9, 164, 860
Jian Computer Corporation, 646
Job qualifications, 649-650
John Dewey in China: To Teach and to Learn (Wang), 1015
Johnson, Lyndon B., 55
Johnson, Michael and Sarah, 304-305, 307, 312
Johnson, William, 736, 786-787
Johnson Controls Inc., 659
Joint and several liability, 715-716
Joint Chiefs of Staff (JSC), 55
Joint Commission of Accreditation of Health Care Organizations, 937-938
Joint economic development district (JEDD), 711
Joint liability, 715-716
Joint tenants, 530, 824, 854
Joint tenants with the right of survivorship, 824
Joint ventures, 709, 740
Joseph, Clay, 1038
Joshua: Son of None (Freedman), 631
Judgments, 79, 80
Judicial Arbitration and Mediation Service (JAMS), 105
Judicial Conference Advisory Committee on Civil Rules, 84
Judicial review, 49-50
Jumpstart Our Business Startups (JOBS) Act of 2012, 797

Junior mortgages, 553
Junk bonds, 805
Juriscience, 164-166, 944
Jurisdiction, 64-69, 81-82
Jury instructions, 79
Jury selection, 78
Just cause, in just war theory, 1019
Justice Department, U.S., 809-810
Justifiable force, 154-155
Just war theory, 1019-1022
Juveniles. *See* Minors

Kadrmas, B.J., 234-235, 237, 239, 244, 246
Kagan, Robert, 1012, 1013
Kant, Immanuel, 12
Kaplan, Robert, 998-999, 1017
Katrina, Hurricane (2005), 533, 559
Keenon, Eloise and R.W., 704-705, 713-714, 720-721
Kennedy, John F., 42, 55, 876, 953, 1024
Keynes, John Maynard, 32, 678
Kimberly Motors, 497
Kirby, James, 686
Knights Templar, 450
"Know Before You Owe" rules, 431, 433
Knowledge, in criminal law, 125
Kropotkin, Peter, 22-23
Kyoto Protocol, 949-950, 968

Labor Department, U.S., 652
Labor law, 676-694
    case study, 676-677
    collective bargaining and, 640, 687, 691-694
    economic crisis and, 677-680
    federal legislation, 682-691
    Keynesians vs. Austrians, 678-680
    Landrum-Griffin Act, 691
    National Labor Relations Act, 640, 683-687
    Taft-Hartley Act, 688-691
    on unfair labor practices, 685-687, 692
Labor-Management Relations Act of 1947 (Taft-Hartley Act), 688-692
Labor Management Reporting and Disclosure Act of 1959 (Landrum-Griffin Act), 691
Labor organization, 679-680, 683-684
Labor unions
    company-run, 686
    defined, 677
    growth of, 643, 695
    prohibited practices, 685, 690-691
    strikes by, 689-690, 693
Lack of consideration, 479
Lake Ridge Academy, 330-331, 341, 349
Land contracts, 553-554, 561

Subject Index

Landlords, defined, 862
Landlord-tenant relationship, 862-869
  comparison of leasing and other relationships, 862-863
  elements necessary for creation of, 862
  eviction proceedings and, 868, 869
  landlord's duties in, 867-868
  lease agreements and, 864-866
  tenant's duties in, 868
  tort liability and, 869
  types of leasehold interests, 863-864
Landrum-Griffin Act of 1959, 691
Lanham Act of 1946, 982-983
Lapses in insurance, 540-541
Last clear chance, 181
Last resort, in just war theory, 1020
Last will and testament, 876
Las Vegas mass shooting (2017), 135
Latin America, foreign corporations in, 108
Law, 29-57
  abstract principles vs. concrete situations in, 30-31
  administrative regulations, 50-57
  agency (*See* Agency law)
  as balancing act, 30
  common, 48-49, 214-215, 788
  constitutional, 34-41
  consumer protection (*See* Consumer protection laws)
  contract (*See* Contract law)
  court decisions as, 48-50
  criminal (*See* Criminal law)
  defined, 4, 5, 29
  discharge by, 345
  dualities within, 30-34
  employment (*See* Employment law)
  of estates, 849-851
  ethics and, 21-23
  executive orders, 28-29, 31-32, 41-45
  mercantile, 210-215
  natural, 5-6
  positive, 6
  pragmatic approach to (*See* Pragmatism)
  purpose and operation of, 5, 22, 29-34
  purposivist approach to, 784-785, 795
  spirit and letter of the, 30, 33, 735
  state, 41, 429-430
  statutory, 45-48
  textualist approach to (*See* Textualism)
  tort (*See* Tort law)
  uncertainty principle and, 31-33, 35
  words vs. interpretation of, 30
Law and History (Chase), 30
Law and Revolution: The Formation of the Western Legal Tradition (Berman), 210, 213, 357

Law enforcement officers, dereliction of duty by, 139
Law in America (Friedman), 928
Law merchant
  characteristics of, 213-215
  common law integration with, 214
  defined, 210
  development of, 211-212
  evolution of, 214-215
  involvement and, 213
  mutuality and, 214
  neutrality of, 213
  principles in modern law, 216
  universality and, 213-214
Law of finds, 825
Law of Peoples, 6
Law of salvage, 825
Law of the Twelve Tables, 38
Law's Empire (Dworkin), 191
Lawsuits, 72-74, 120, 423, 771-772
Lawton Bluff Company, 513-516
LBO (leveraged buyout), 804-805
Leading objective test, 310, 376
Lease agreements, 856, 864-866
Leasehold estates, 863
Lease of goods, 367, 369
Lease options, 247
Leases
  agreements for, 856, 864-866
  assignment of, 866
  Consumer Leasing Act on, 436
  defined, 862
  interest conveyed by, 863-864
  licenses vs., 862-863
  lodging vs., 863
  option to renew or purchase, 866
  real property and, 856
Legacies, 218, 277
Legal cause, 178
Legal detriment, 218, 220, 265
Legal duty, 176-177
Legal fiction, 286
"Legal Formalism: On the Immanent Rationality of Law" (Weinrib), 928
Legal imperialism, 762
Legality of contracts
  case study, 284-285
  consequences of illegality, 299-300
  consideration and, 268
  elements of, 219
  illegal agreements, 285, 293-299
  written contracts, 312-317
Legal tender, 395
Legatees, 876
Legislatively limited power, 43
LeMay, Curtis, 1021
Lemon laws, 429-430
Lessees, 856, 862

"Lessons from Global Experiences in Policy for Science Based Development" (Raymond), 985-986, 988
Lessors, 856, 862
Letter of the law, 30, 33, 735
Leveraged buyout (LBO), 804-805
Leviathan (Hobbes), 8, 9, 36, 1009
Lewis, John L., 678
Lexmark International Inc., 974-975
Lex mercatoria, 210
Liability
  of accountants, 910-923
  agency law and, 611-618, 620, 623
  agreements to escape, 297
  of architects, 924
  of attorneys, 925, 927-929
  contract, 611
  contractual, 924
  criminal (*See* Criminal liability)
  defined, 79
  fiduciary, 616
  of health care providers, 932-936
  of hospitals, 937-938
  of independent contractors, 617-618
  joint, 715-716
  of parties to negotiable instruments, 485-487
  of partnerships, 715-716
  product (*See* Product liability)
  statutory, 618
  strict, 128, 183, 418-421
  of third parties, 931
  tort, 611-613, 615, 869, 924
  vicarious, 128, 164, 611-616
Liability insurance, 536
Liar loans, 560, 561
Libel, 169-171
Liberal democracy, 1001, 1014-1015
Liberal internationalism, 1004-1005
Licenses, 856, 862-863
Licensing agreements, 982
Liebeck, Stella, 180-181, 188
Lieber Code (1863), 839-840
Liens, 550, 570
Life estates, 849
Life insurance, 526-528
  annuity, 527
  exemptions from risk, 527
  limited-payment, 527
  optional provisions, 527-528
  straight, 526-527
  term insurance, 527
Light, John, 54
Limited defenses, 478-480
Limited liability, defined, 724, 731
Limited liability companies (LLCs)
  defined, 709, 740
  dissolution of, 811-812

Limited liability companies—(cont.)
  fiduciary duties of, 779
  formation of, 744-745
  governance of, 779
  legal principles related to, 731
  manager-managed, 779
  member-managed, 779
  taxation of, 745
Limited liability partnerships (LLPs), 709, 723
Limited partners, 724
Limited partnerships, 709, 723-724
Limited-payment life insurance, 527
Limited-purpose public figures, 170-171
Limited warranties, 407
Lingering apparent authority, 624
LinkedIn, 669
Liquidated damages, 348-350
Liquidation, 582-591
  automatic stay and, 587
  commencing action for, 582-583, 585
  defined, 582
  exceptions to discharge, 590
  federal exemptions and, 587-588
  homestead exemption and, 587-588
  involuntary proceedings, 585
  means test and, 582-585
  order for relief and, 585-586
  property distribution in, 589
  state exemptions and, 589
  trustee duties in, 589
  voluntary proceedings, 582-583
List price, 241
Litigation, 93, 94
Living trusts, 895
Living wills, 632, 887-888
LLCs. *See* Limited liability companies
LLPs (limited liability partnerships), 709, 723
Loan value, 526
Locality rule, 934
Local option, 295
Locke, Hobbes, and the Federalist Papers: An Essay on the Genesis of the American Political Heritage (Mace), 9
Locke, John, 9, 34, 120
Lockup agreements, 807
Loco parentis, 135
Locus sigilli, 273
Lodging and lodgers, 863
Long-distance communication, 243
Long-term care insurance, 537
Lost property, 824, 825
Loyalty, duty of, 626, 718-719, 774, 908, 929
Luther, Martin, 211
Lyft, 690

Lynn, Barry, 765
Lynyrd Skynyrd, 208-209, 220, 224

Mace, George, 9
Machiavelli, Niccolo, 9, 34, 36, 164
Macrie family, 414-417, 419-420
Madison, James, 9, 22, 34-39, 47, 120, 579, 787, 1069-1072
Madsen, Axel, 631, 893, 991
Magna Carta, 6, 35, 213
Magnuson-Moss Warranty Act of 1975 (MMWA), 407, 409
Mail and Telephone Order Rule, 426
Main purpose test, 310, 376
Majority, defined, 286, 579
Major medical coverage, 536
Makers, 452, 457, 459, 485
Malicious prosecution, 175
Malpractice. *See* Negligence
Malware, 143, 148
Managerial control, 765
Manager-managed limited liability companies, 779
Managers, defined, 740
Mandatory arbitration, 92-93, 97, 99, 100, 103-104
Mandelbaum, Michael, 1013
Manslaughter, 134
MAPR (Military Annual Percentage Rate), 437
Marcuse, Herbert, 17
Marine insurance, 529
Marjory Stoneman Douglas High School shooting (2018), 135
Marriage contracts, 310-311
Marshall, John, 33, 735
Martin, Tony, 234-235, 237, 239, 244, 246
Massachusetts General Laws Chapter 92, 318
Masters, 164, 610
Master-servant relationship, 610, 613, 614
Material fact, 253
Matin, Abdul, 502
Mattik, Jessica and Raymond, 584
Mattis, Jim, 15
MBCA. *See* Model Business Corporation Act
McConnell, Mitch, 56
McDonald's restaurants, 180-181, 188
McMaster, H. R., 15
MDL (multidistrict litigation), 73-74
Means test, 582-585, 679
Med-arb, 100
Mediation, 98-99, 112, 692
Mediators, 98
Medicaid, 537
Medical payments insurance, 535
Medicare, 537

Medow, Sharon, 844-845, 850-851
Meeting of the minds, 217, 220
Member-managed limited liability companies, 779
Members, defined, 740
Memorandum, 42, 311
Memorial and Remonstrance against Religious Assessment (Madison), 47, 1069-1072
Menacing, 134
Mental examination requests, 77
Mental impairment, 292, 481, 494, 629
Mercantile law, 210-215
Merchantability, warranty of, 407-409
Merchantable goods, 408
Merchant protection statute, 168
Merchants
  defined, 372, 377
  entrusting goods to, 382
  oral contracts between, 377
  rejection of goods by, 397
  warranties given to, 408
Mergers, 804-805
Meridian Bank, 457
Merlin, Ruby, 480
Mesa Petroleum, 756-757, 764-765, 774-775
Messick, Jeffrey, 728-729, 732, 748
Metadata, 669
Meyers Parking Systems Inc., 772-773
MHH (Mt. Holyoke Homes LP), 95-96
Midnight deadline, 496-497
Mihm, Stephen, 559, 563, 568, 730
Military Annual Percentage Rate (MAPR), 437
Military caregiver leave, 657
Military Lending Act of 2006 (MLA), 436-437
Miller Chemical Company, 594
Minimum contacts, 66, 67
Minitrials, 95
Minority, defined, 286, 579
Minor misdemeanors, 123
Minors
  contractual capacity and, 219, 286-291
  emancipated, 287
  as holders in due course, 481
  misrepresentation of age by, 287
  necessaries for, 287-289
  ratification and disaffirmance related to, 290-291
Mirror image rule, 244
Misdemeanors, 123
Misplaced property, 824
Misrepresentation
  of age, 287
  fraudulent, 173, 347, 423

by insured, 542
mutual assent and, 253, 257
Mistake, mutual assent and, 257-258
Mistake defense, 155-156
Mistrials, 87
Misuse of legal procedure, 175
Mitchell, John, 55, 57
Mitigating circumstances, 132
Mixed contracts, 369-370
MLA (Military Lending Act of 2006), 436-437
MMWA (Magnuson-Moss Warranty Act of 1975), 407, 409
M'Naughten Rule, 151
Model Business Corporation Act (MBCA), 738, 746, 751, 788
Model Rules of Professional Conduct (ABA), 251, 925
Model State Administrative Procedures Act, 51
Monarch, 772
Monetary thresholds, 535
Money, 269, 460
Money orders, 456-457
Monopolies, 798
Montalbano, Cynthia, 645
Montesquieu, 34
MONY Legacy Life Insurance Company, 500-501
Moody Industries, 569
Morals, defined, 5. *See also* Ethics
More, Thomas, 1021
Moring, Joseph, 728-729, 731-732, 748-749
Morrill Act of 1862, 953
Mortgage-backed securities, 560
Mortgagees, 550, 556
Mortgages, 548-568
assumption of, 557
balloon-payment, 552
case study, 548-549
conventional fixed-rate, 552
costs associated with, 550-551
defined, 550
financial crisis and, 557-568
graduated-payment, 552
interest-only, 552
junior, 553
purchase by mortgage takeover, 557
qualified, 565
recording, 555, 851
reverse, 552
second/subsequent, 553
subprime, 553, 560-561
types of, 551-553
variable-rate, 552
Mortgagors, 550, 555
Morts Dock and Engineering, 179

Most-favored nation principle, 1036
Motions, 74, 76
Motive, in criminal law, 126
Mt. Holyoke Homes LP (MHH), 95-96
MouseMail system, 149-150
Moyses, Max, 576-577, 584, 586, 588, 592
Mubarak, Hosni, 296
Mueller, Robert, 2
Multidistrict litigation (MDL), 73-74
Mulvaney, Mick, 432-433
Municipal utility district, 711
Muravchik, Joshua, 958, 960, 964
Murder, 133-134
Murdock, George Peter, 609
Mutual assent
in cyberspace, 247-253
destruction of, 253-259
duress and, 258-259
elements of, 217, 220
fraud and, 253-257
misrepresentation and, 253, 257
mistake and, 257-258
nature of, 235-236
undue influence and, 259
Mutual-benefit bailments, 831-832
Mutuality, law merchant and, 214
Mutual mistake, 257
Mutual rescission, 343
Mutuum, 830

Napoleonic Code, 47, 289, 707
NASCAR, 541
National Bankruptcy Review Commission, 580
National Center for Technology and Dispute Resolution, 113
National City Bank, 555-556
National Conference of Commissioners of State Laws (NCCUSL), 249, 429
National Conference of Commissioners on Uniform State Laws. *See* Uniform Law Commission (ULC)
National Defense Authorization Act of 2012, 141
National economic reform movement (NERM), 708, 709
National Environmental Policy Act of 1969, 965
National Flood Insurance Program (NFIP), 532-533
National Football League (NFL), 799-800
National Homes Corporation, 448-449, 451, 459, 461
National Institutes of Health (NIH), 954-956
National Labor Relations Act of 1935 (NLRA), 640, 683-687, 692-693

National Labor Relations Board (NLRB), 20, 654, 678, 683-687, 689, 691-693
Nationally recognized statistical rating organizations (NRSROs), 793
National rule, 934
National Rules for the Resolution of Employment Disputes (AAA), 99
National Science and Technology Policy Organization and Priorities Act of 1976, 953-954
National Science Foundation (NSF), 953, 955
National security, 2-3
National Security Agency, 143, 149, 279, 508
National Security Council (NSC), 55
National standard, 934
National Stolen Property Act of 1948 (NSPA), 146, 509
National treatment principle, 1036
National vs. world responsibility, 14
National White Collar Crime Center (NW3C), 149, 508-509
Native American Graves Protection and Repatriation Act of 1990, 840
NATO (North Atlantic Treaty Organization), 65
Natural law, 5-6
Natural property, 825, 826
Navigable airspace, 846
NCCUSL (National Conference of Commissioners of State Laws), 249, 429
Near-privity, 918-920
Necessaries, for minors, 287-289
Necessary and Proper Clause, 946-947
Negative option rule, 426
Negative rights, 8
Negligence, 176-183
actual harm and, 180
of attorneys, 929
causation in, 178-180, 935
comparative, 181, 190
contributory, 181
in criminal law, 126
defenses to, 181-183
defined, 125, 126
elements of, 176-180
expert testimony and, 935
gross, 831
health care providers and, 933-934
ordinary, 832
product liability and, 417
slight, 831
steps in legal case of, 930-932
in tort law, 164
in type one arrangements, 915
in type two arrangements, 916-920

Negligent credentialing, 937
Negligent hiring, 608, 613-616
Negligent retention, 608, 613-616, 937
Negligent supervision, 608, 613-616
Negotiable instruments, 449-469
　acceptance of, 453
　alteration of, 482-483
　assignment and, 462
　bearer paper, 463
　breach of contract and, 479
　certificates of deposit, 452-453
　checks (See Checks)
　defined, 451
　drafts, 453-454
　electronic, 458
　liability of parties to, 485-487
　money orders, 456-457
　notes, 452
　order paper, 463
　overview, 449-450
　parties to, 457-458
　payable on demand/definite time, 460-461
　payable to order/bearer, 461
　requirements of, 458-461
　signature requirements for, 459, 482
　transferring, 462-469
　written, 458
Negotiated rule making (reg-neg), 106-107
Negotiation
　of contracts, 343
　cyber-negotiation, 111-112
　by indorsement, 463-467
　mediation vs., 98
Nelson family treasure trove, 822-823, 826-827
Neoconservativism, 1005
Neoliberalism, 1005
NERM (national economic reform movement), 708, 709
NET (No Electronic Theft) Act of 1997, 984
Neutrality, 213
New community authority, 711
New England Surrogate Parenting Advisors (NESPA), 296
New International Economic Order (NIEO), 958, 959
The New Paradigm for Financial Markets (Soros), 1016
A New Pattern for a Tired World (Bromfield), 14, 1009-1010
New world order
　global initial conditions in, 1006, 1008-1012
　international behavior theories in, 1001, 1003-1006
　origins of term, 1000
　patterns within, 1000-1001
　predictive political history and, 1001-1003
New York Academy of Sciences (NYAS), 985-986
The New York Times, 20
Next of kin, 886
NFIP (National Flood Insurance Program), 532-533
NFL (National Football League), 799-800
NGOs (non-governmental organizations), 65, 107, 956-957
NGRI (not guilty by reason of insanity), 151
NIEO (New International Economic Order), 958, 959
Nihilism, 928
NIH (National Institutes of Health), 954-956
9/11. *See* September 11 terrorist attacks
900-telephone number rules, 427-428
Nineteenth Amendment, 1053
NINJA (no income, no job or assets) loans, 560, 561
Ninth Amendment, 1052
Nixon, Richard, 55, 57
NLRA (National Labor Relations Act of 1935), 640, 683-687, 692-693
NLRB. *See* National Labor Relations Board
No-duty-to-retreat laws, 155
No Electronic Theft (NET) Act of 1997, 984
No-fault insurance, 534-535
Nominal damages, 347
Noncompete agreements, 284-285, 297-299
Nonconforming goods, 372
Nonconforming uses, 860
Non-core cases, 580
Nondelegable duty, 615
Non-delivery defense, 479-480
Nondischargeable debt, 590
Nondisclosure, passive fraud and, 255
Nondisclosure agreements, 299
Noneconomic compensatory damages, 187-188
Non-governmental organizations (NGOs), 65, 107, 956-957
Nonjudgmentalism, 6-7
Nonperformance, discharge by, 343-346
Nontraditional business entities, 710-711
Non-use contracts, 208-209, 220, 224
No par value stock, 751
Norcold Inc., 441-446
Norris-LaGuardia Act of 1932, 679-680
North Atlantic Treaty Organization (NATO), 65
Northern States Power Company (NSPC), 949
Northern Terminals Inc., 867
Notes, 452
Not guilty by reason of insanity (NGRI), 151
Notice of dishonor, 487
Novation, 338, 344, 742
NRC (Nuclear Regulatory Commission), 963-964
NRSROs (nationally recognized statistical rating organizations), 793
NSC (National Security Council), 55
NSF checks, 497
NSF (National Science Foundation), 953, 955
NSPA (National Stolen Property Act of 1948), 146, 509
NSPC (Northern States Power Company), 949
Nuclear Regulatory Commission (NRC), 963-964
Nuncupative wills, 880
NW3C (National White Collar Crime Center), 149, 508-509
NYAS (New York Academy of Sciences), 985-986

Obama, Barack, 28-29, 31-32, 42-44, 53, 55
Obedience, duty of, 626, 718, 777
Objective concept rule, 227
Objective (rational) ethics, 12-13
Objectives test, 679
Obligees, 310, 376
Obligors, 310, 333, 337, 376
Obstruction of justice, 139, 295
Obvious-to-try standard, 977
Occupational Safety and Health Administration (OSHA), 651-652
Ocean marine insurance, 529
Odometer tampering, 425
ODR (online dispute resolution), 111-113
OEPA (Ohio Environmental Protection Agency), 106
OFA. *See* Oil for America
Offerees, 217, 236, 239-241
Offerors, 217, 236
Offers, 236-247. *See also* Acceptance of offers
　communication of, 240-241
　counteroffers, 244-245
　in cyberspace, 250, 324

Subject Index

defined, 236
firm, 247, 275, 372-373
invitations to trade, 241
irrevocable, 275
mutual assent and, 217
public, 241
rejection and revocation of, 245
requirements of, 236, 238-241
for sale of goods, 247, 372-373
social media and, 250-251
UCC and, 238-239, 243, 372-373
Office of Credit Ratings, 793
Office of Investor Advocate (OIA), 793, 923
Office of Science and Technology Policy, 953-954
Offline debit cards, 506
Ohio Antiunion Law (2011), 681
Ohio Environmental Protection Agency (OEPA), 106
Ohio Revised Code (ORC), 12, 45, 322
Ohio Rules of Professional Conduct, 7-8
Ohio Technology Transfer Organization (OTTO), 987
OIA (Office of Investor Advocate), 793, 923
Oil for America (OFA), 234, 237, 239, 244, 246
Oil Pollution Act of 1990, 966, 967
Older Workers Benefit Protection Act of 1990 (OWBPA), 666
Omissions, in criminal law, 124
Onchocerciasis, 960
Online banking, 506
Online debit cards, 506
Online dispute resolution (ODR), 111-113
Opening statements, 77, 78, 87
Open-price terms, 373
Operating agreements, 744-745
The Opportunity (Haass), 1006
Option contracts, 245-247, 275
Options to renew/purchase leases, 866
Opt-out rule, 764
Oral contracts, 227, 305, 306, 308, 377
Oral wills, 880
Orbitz, 324, 669
ORC (Ohio Revised Code), 12, 45, 322
Order for relief, 585-586
Order paper, 463
Orders, defined, 42. See also Executive orders
Ordinary bankruptcy, 582
Ordinary expenses, 831
Ordinary life insurance, 526-527
Ordinary negligence, 832
Originalism. See Textualism
Original jurisdiction, 64, 68
Orlov, Dmitry, 558, 559, 563, 567, 730

Orthodox business entities, 709-710
Osgood Minerals Inc., 790
OSHA (Occupational Safety and Health Administration), 651-652
Ostensible authority, 937
OTTO (Ohio Technology Transfer Organization), 987
Output contracts, 239, 240, 373-374
Outside parties. *See* Third parties
Overcoming Law (Posner), 33
Overdraft, 432, 493
Overseas Tankship Ltd., 179
Overtime, 652
OWBPA (Older Workers Benefit Protection Act of 1990), 666
Ownership, free transfer of, 733-734
Oxbow Energy, 234-235, 237, 239, 244, 246

Padded payrolls, 469
Paige-Capital Management, 593-594
Palin, Sara, 169, 170
Paradigm, defined, 190
Paramilitary police power, 140
Paris Climate Agreement (PCA), 942, 969-970
Parol evidence rule, 314-316
Partial illegality in agreements, 300
Partially disclosed principals, 622
Participation loans, 552
Partnering, 103
Partnership at will, 722
Partnership contracts, 712-713
Partnerships, 707-723
 characteristics of, 707-712
 defined, 707
 dissociation of, 722
 dissolution of, 722-723
 entity and aggregate theories of, 707-708
 formation of, 712-715
 general, 709
 for global challenges, 986-987
 interest in, 717-718
 liability of, 715-716
 limited, 709, 723-724
 limited liability, 709, 723
 property of, 717
 rights and duties in, 718-720
Part performance, 308
Par value, 751
PAs (public accountants), 910
Passengers, common carriers of, 837
Passing bad checks, 138
Passive fraud, 255
Past consideration, 218, 276
Patents, 974-980
 America Invents Act and, 979-980

 application process for, 974, 978
 business systems and, 976
 court system and, 67-68
 cyber-inventions and, 977-978
 defined, 974
 dispute resolution process for, 980
 first-to-file provision for, 979-980
 for life forms, 82
 nonobviousness requirement for, 977
 novelty requirement for, 976
 patentable subject matter, 975-976
 right to tinker and, 974-975
 science courts and, 109
 usefulness requirement for, 976
Patient Protection and Affordable Care Act of 2010 (ACA), 355, 357-358, 537-539, 732, 930, 935-936
Patient's Bill of Rights, 537
Patrick, Thomas, 321-322
Payees, 452, 453, 457, 469
Payns, Hugh de, 450
Payor banks, 503
PayPal, 278-279
PCAOB (Public Company Accounting Oversight Board), 761, 763, 912-914
PCA (Paris Climate Agreement), 942, 969-970
PC (Population Commission), 972
Peaceful possession, 867
Pence, Mike, 56
Pension plans, 656
The Pentagon's New Map (Barnett), 1006
Penumbra rights, 12
Perez, Josue, 321-322
Perfected security interests, 569-571
Performance
 complete, 340
 conditions of, 242, 341-342
 discharge by, 339-342
 satisfactory, 340
 specific, 350
 substantial, 340
 tender of, 342, 394-395
 time for, 238, 239, 339-340
Peril management, 521-525
Perils, defined, 522
Periodic tenancy, 864
Perjury, 140
Permanent unconsciousness, 632, 888
Per se violations, 799, 800
Personal contracts, 337
Personal defenses, 478-480
Personal injury protection (PIP), 534-535
Personal jurisdiction, 64, 66, 67
Personal property, 823-828
 abandoned, 825
 defined, 823
 dispersal upon death, 884

Personal property—(cont.)
  gifts of, 827-828
  intangible, 823
  lost, 824, 825
  misplaced, 824
  ownership of, 824
  passenger baggage, 838
  pledge of, 571, 572, 831
  as security, 569-572
  stolen, 828
  tangible, 823
Personal representatives, 886
Personal service, 626
Persuasive precedent, 48-49
Petrosearch, 234, 237, 239, 244, 246
Petty offenses, 123
Pfizer Corporation, 861
Philip the Fair (king of France), 450
Phishing, 144
Physical duress, 258
Physical examination requests, 77
Physician-assisted suicide, 891, 893
Physician order for life-sustaining treatment (POLST), 889
Pie powder courts, 214
Piercing the corporate veil, 747-750
Piketty, Thomas, 212
Pilder and Wesselkamper International Inc., 20
PIPA (Protect Intellectual Property Act), 147
PIP (personal injury protection), 534-535
Piracy, 142, 147
Plaintiffs, 71, 78, 87
Platonic Stabilizing Standard, 920
Plausible deniability, 129
Pledge of personal property, 571, 572, 831
Plenary review, 64, 67
PMDD (protective medical decisions document), 889
PNC Bank, 716
Poison pill defense, 808
Police power, 123, 140, 788, 952
Policy, insurance, 524, 540-541
Political ideologies, 1001
POLST (physician order for life-sustaining treatment), 889
Pooling agreements, 770
Population Commission (PC), 972
Population growth, 970-972, 991
Port authority, 711
Positive law, 6
Posner, Richard, 33-34, 735
Posse Comitatus Act of 1878, 141
Postal Reorganization Act of 1970, 245
Post-appellate procedures, 107
Postdated checks, 500

Power of attorney. See Durable power of attorney
PPOs (preferred provider organizations), 537
Pragmatism, 33-34, 392, 735-736, 784-785, 795, 801-802
Pre-answer stage of civil procedure, 74
Prebisch, Raul, 958
Precedent, defined, 48-49
Predicate offense, 62
Predictive political history, 1001-1003
Predominant factor test, 370
Preemption, 41
Preemptive rights, 778
Preemptive war, 1021
Preexisting duties, 218, 276
Preferred provider organizations (PPOs), 537
Preferred stock, 750-751
Preformation contracts, 742
Pregnancy Discrimination Act of 1978, 664
Preliminary hearings, 86
Premarriage agreements, 310-311
Premeditated murder, 133-134
Premeditation, 125
Premiums, 524, 540
Prenuptial agreements, 310-311
Prepaid card rules, 431-432
Prescriptive theories, 9-10
Present damages, 347
Presenting banks, 503
Presentment, 485
Presidential power, theories of, 42-43
Pretrial conferences, 75-76
Pretrial motions, 76
Pretrial stage of civil procedure, 75-77
Preventative punishment, 131
Preventive war, 1021
Priceline.com, 324, 669
Priest, George, 240
Prima facie cases, 645, 658, 663
Prima facie evidence, 707, 715
Primary objective test, 310, 376
Principal-agent relationship, 609-610
Principal objective of contracts, 313
Principals, 223, 609, 610, 622-623, 631, 888
Prior art, 977
Privacy, invasion of, 174, 185-187
Private civil trials, 95, 102, 113
Private corporations, 709, 739
Private information, 186
Private privacy, 186
Private religiously based corporate entities, 710-711
Private warehousers, 838
Privity, 223, 409-410, 917-920

Proactive ADR strategies, 102-111
  collective science court, 108-111
  contract clauses, 103-105
  international arbitration agreements, 107-108
  negotiated rule making, 106-107
  partnering, 103
  post-appellate procedures, 107
  settlement week, 106
Probability of success, in just war theory, 1019
Probate, defined, 875
Probated estates, 886
Probate law, 875-896
  advanced directives and, 887-893
  estate settlement and, 886-887
  relevance to business, 876
  simultaneous death and, 886
  terminology related to, 876
  trusts and, 894-896
  wills and (*See* Wills)
Procedural unconscionability, 105
Proclamations, 42
Prodigy Service Company, 184
Product liability, 414-421. *See also* Consumer protection laws
  aircraft cases and, 421
  case study, 414-415
  comparative negligence and, 190
  elements of, 183
  negligence and, 417
  public policy and, 417
  stream of commerce theory and, 67, 81
  strict liability and, 418-421
Professionals, defined, 910
Professional service contracts, 337
Profit *à prendre*, 848
Project Sheltered Harbor, 509
Promise instruments, 451-456
Promises after discharge in bankruptcy, 273-274
Promises not to sue, 269-270
Promissory estoppel
  charitable pledges and, 271
  consideration and, 218
  defined, 215
  promises enforced by, 274
  wrongful discharge and, 643-644
Promissory notes, 452
Promoters, 741-742
Proof of loss forms, 531-532
Propensity to commit the crime, 152
Property
  community, 530, 824, 854
  as consideration, 269
  crimes involving, 136-138
  cultural, 839-840

Subject Index 1143

distribution in liquidation, 589
exempt, 880
intellectual (*See* Intellectual property)
natural, 825, 826
in partnerships, 717
personal (*See* Personal property)
real (*See* Real property)
Property damage liability insurance, 535
Property insurance, 528-533
  coinsurance clauses in, 528
  dwelling insurance, 533
  fire insurance, 528-529
  flood insurance, 532-533
  homeowner's policies, 529
  marine insurance, 529
  recovering for contents, 531-532
  recovering for property, 529-530
  renter's insurance, 533
"Prophet-Making" (Barrett), 730
Proportionality, in just war theory, 1019
Proprietors, 610-611
Prosecutorial discretion, 29
Prosecutors/prosecution, 86, 119-120
Prospectus, 791
Pro-splits, 234, 237, 239, 244
Protect Intellectual Property Act (PIPA), 147
Protection of Artistic and Scientific Institutions and Historic Monuments Treaty (1933), 840
Protective medical decisions document (PMDD), 889
Protective orders, 155
Protective war
  defined, 1021-1022
  international law and, 1022-1024
  just war theory and, 1022
  U.S. domestic law and, 1024-1026
Protest, 487
The Protestant Ethic: The Spirit of Capitalism (Weber), 211, 356
Provisional settlements, 503
Proximate cause, 178-180
Proxy, defined, 768
Proxy contests, 768
Proxy solicitation, 768
Proxy statements, 768
Proxy voting, 768
Przeworski, Adam, 708, 710
Public accountants (PAs), 910
Public bodies corporations, 710
Public Company Accounting Oversight Board (PCAOB), 761, 763, 912-914
Public corporations, 709, 710, 739
Public duty doctrine, 191
Public interest, 416-417
Public offers, 241
Public policy
  agreements contrary to, 295, 297-299
  charitable pledges and, 271
  contract legality and, 219
  defined, 416
  product liability and, 417
  social engineering and, 417
  torts, 646-647
Public privacy, 186
Public-private corporations, 710
Public servants, dereliction of duty by, 139
Public trusts, 896
Public warehousers, 838
Punishment in criminal law, 131-132
Punitive damages, 188, 221, 347, 348, 420, 664, 916
Purchase money security interest, 569
Purpose, in criminal law, 125
Purposivism, 784-785, 795

Qualified indorsements, 466-467
Qualified mortgages, 565
Qualified opinions, 911
Qualifying exigency leave, 657
Quantum meruit, damages under, 350
Quasi-contracts, 227, 288-289
Quasi-public corporations, 709, 739
Quasi-RPM arrangements, 800
Quick-look standard, 799
Quid pro quo sexual harassment, 661
Quiet enjoyment, 867
Quitclaim deeds, 859
Quitter-Stalker assignment, 336, 337
Quo warranto proceedings, 810-811

Racial profiling, 837
Racketeer Influenced and Corrupt Organizations (RICO) Act of 1970, 62-63, 65, 72, 75, 138
Ramsey, George and Willie, 520-521, 524-525, 531-532
Ransomware, 143-144, 148
Ratification
  agency by, 624-625
  of contracts, 290-291
  in corporate governance, 777
Rational (objective) ethics, 12-13
Raymond, Susan U., 985-986, 988
Reading Law: The Interpretation of Legal Texts (Scalia & Garner), 33, 735
Reagan, Ronald, 55, 1005
Real defenses, 481-483
Real estate, defined, 845
Real estate contracts, 306-308, 319-320
Real evidence requests, 77
Realpolitik theory, 1001-1004, 1007
Real property, 845-869
  air rights, 846
  construction projects, 320-322
  co-ownership of, 848-854
  defined, 529, 845
  dispersal upon death, 884
  easements, 847-848
  estates, 849-851
  fixtures, 847
  governmental management of, 860-861
  landlord-tenant relationship and, 862-869
  lease options and, 247
  rights related to, 845-848
  as security, 550
  subterranean rights, 854-858
  title acquisition, 858-860
  transference of rights to, 306-308
  trees and vegetation, 846
  water rights, 846
Reasonable accommodations, 667
Reasonable care, 832, 833
Reasonable expectations, 374
Reasonable time standard, 238, 339
Rebuttable presumption, 219, 286
Rebuttals, 79
Receivers, defined, 811
Reckless disregard, 170, 171
Reckless infliction of emotional distress, 174-175
Recklessness, 125-126
Reclaim Your Name program, 429
Recovery, defined, 557, 566
Recovery limits, 221
Reflexivity principle, 1016-1017
Refusals to act, in criminal law, 124
Registered limited liability partnerships (RLLPs), 723
Registration statements, 791
Reg-neg (negotiated rule making), 106-107
Regulation CC (Federal Reserve Board), 463, 495-496
Regulation E (Federal Reserve Board), 507
Regulation of Importation of Pre-Columbian Monumental or Architectural Sculpture or Murals (1972), 840
Regulations, corporate, 744
Regulation Systems Compliance and Integrity (REG SCI), 797-798
Regulatory Flexibility Act of 1980 (RFA), 28, 50, 52-53
Rehabilitation, in contract law, 219, 221
Rehabilitative punishment, 131
Reinventing Collapse (Orlov), 558, 567, 730
Rejection of goods, 395-397
Rejection of offers, 245
Releases, 269-270

Religious Freedom Restoration Act of 1993 (RFRA), 356, 358-362, 732-733
Religiously based corporate entities, 710-711
Remainder estates, 849
Remington, Teresa, 686
Remitting banks, 503
Rent control, 864
Renter's insurance, 533
Renunciation of agency, 629
Reorganization (Chapter 11, Bankruptcy Code), 591-595
Repentance, principle of, 1021
Requests for admissions, 77
Requests for physical or mental examination, 77
Requests for real evidence, 77
Requirements contracts, 238-240, 373-374
Resale price maintenance (RPM) agreements, 800
Rescission, 257, 289-290, 343
Reselling of goods, 401
Residential real estate contracts, 319-320
Residual state power, 788-789, 952
Resisting arrest, 139
Resource Conservation and Recovery Act of 1976, 965
Respondeat superior, 128-129, 131, 164, 611, 613, 618, 620
Responsibility to Protect (R2P) doctrine, 16, 1014-1015, 1023
Responsive ADR strategies, 98-102
  arbitration, 92-93, 97, 99-100, 103-104, 112, 692
  early neutral evaluation, 94-95, 100-101, 113
  med-arb, 100
  mediation, 98-99, 112, 692
  private civil trials, 95, 102, 113
  summary jury trials, 95, 101-102, 113
Restatement of the Law of Contracts, 215-216, 238, 292
Restoration, principle of, 1021
Restraint theory of punishment, 131
Restrictions on assignments, 337-338
Restrictive covenants, 297
Restrictive employment covenant, 297
Restrictive indorsements, 465-466
Retaliation, 649, 668
Retribution, 131
The Return of History and the End of Dreams (Kagan), 1012
Revelation of confidential records, 174
Reverse discrimination, 663
Reverse mortgages, 552
Reversion estates, 849
Revesting of title in seller, 385

Revised Uniform Limited Partnership Act (RULPA), 723
Revised Uniform Partnership Act (RUPA), 707, 708, 712-719, 721-723
Revocable trusts, 895
Revocation of acceptance, 397
Revocation of agency, 629
Revocation of offers, 245
Revolution, Evolution, and the Economic Order (Sievers), 719
RFA (Regulatory Flexibility Act of 1980), 28, 50, 52-53
RFRA (Religious Freedom Restoration Act of 1993), 356, 358-362, 732-733
RICO Act. *See* Racketeer Influenced and Corrupt Organizations Act of 1970
Right intention, in just war theory, 1019
Right of way, 847
Right to die, 890-893
Right to life, 890-892
Right to tinker, 974-975
Right-to-work laws, 688
Riparian owners, 846
Risk assessment, 521-525
Risk of negative consequences, 125
Risks, defined, 522
Risk-utility analysis, 420
River blindness, 960
Rixensart Industries, 21
RJR Nabisco Inc., 62-63, 65, 72, 75
RLLPs (registered limited liability partnerships), 723
Robbery, 136, 137
Robinson, James, 212
Robinson-Patman Act of 1936, 801
Roerich Pact (1933), 840
Rogue states, 16
Roman Catholic Church, 211-213, 357, 367, 381
Roosevelt, Franklin D., 42, 986
Roosevelt, Theodore, 42
Roosevelt University, 829-830
Rose, Dennis, 490, 492, 494, 499
Rosewood Acres LLC, 586-587
Rothko, Carol and Michael, 586-587
Roubini, Nouriel, 559, 563, 568, 730
Rousseau, Jean-Jacques, 9, 22
Royalties, 973
RPM (resale price maintenance) agreements, 800
R2P (Responsibility to Protect) doctrine, 16, 1014-1015, 1023
Rule of contemporary ownership, 772
Rule-of-reason standard, 799, 800
Rules of International Commercial Arbitration, 107
RULPA (Revised Uniform Limited Partnership Act), 723

RUPA. *See* Revised Uniform Partnership Act
Russia
  authoritarianism in, 998
  economic alliances with, 14
  invasion of Crimea by, 1002-1003
Ryan, Francis E., 608-609, 612-617

Safe Harbor Principles, 279
Safety for the 21st Century Act of 2015, 966
Sale, title by, 858-859
Sale of business agreements, 297
Sale of goods. *See also* Sales contracts
  auctions and, 241, 380-381
  international law on, 380, 385, 1033-1034, 1057-1068
  offer and acceptance for, 247, 372-373
  open-price terms for, 373
  output contracts for, 373-374
  requirements contracts for, 373-374
  UCC and, 309, 367, 368, 375-377
Sale of Goods Act, 215
Sale on approval, 386
Sale or return, 386
Sales contracts, 369-405. *See also* Sale of goods
  breach of, 399-405
  cancellation of, 401
  cover of, 403
  cyber-sales contracts, 378, 380
  example of, 379
  for $500 or more, 309
  formation of, 372-375
  hybrid, 369-370
  insurable interest and, 387
  modification of, 375
  rights and duties of parties to, 393-399
  rules for, 371-375
  sale on approval, 386
  sale or return, 386
  tender of performance, 394-395
  title and, 381-385
  written, 375-378
Sales puffery, 254, 406-407
Salvage, 825
Salvor, 825
Same sex couples, 880-883
Same state locality rule, 934
Sampford, Charles, 928
Sanctuary states, 37
Sandoff Inc., 21
Sandy Hill Elementary School shooting (2012), 135
Sarbanes-Oxley (SarbOx) Act of 2002, 761-763, 777, 795, 912-913
SARS (severe acute respiratory syndrome), 960

Satisfaction. *See* Accord and satisfaction
Satisfactory performance, 340
Saudi Arabia, U.S. negotiations with, 15-16
SBAL (Susan B. Anthony List), 12-13
SBREA (Small Business Regulatory Enforcement Act of 1996), 52
Scalia, Antonin, 33, 249, 735
Scalise, Steve, 169
School registration agreements (SRAs), 330-331, 341, 349
Schumpeter, Joseph, 678, 719
Science: The Endless Frontier (Bush), 986
Science and technology, 944-956
  governmental authority in regulation of, 944-952
  national expenditures for, 953-956
  science courts, 404-405, 893, 950-952
  U.S. Constitution and, 945
Science courts, 404-405, 893, 950-952
Science judges, 951
Scientific construction, 110-111
Scientific evidence, 110
Scientific expenditures, 953-956
Scope of authority, 626
Scope of employment, 613
S corporations, 740
SDS Biotech Corporation, 414-417, 419-420
Seals on contracts, 228, 273
SEC. *See* Securities and Exchange Commission
Second Amendment, 1051
Secondary boycotts, 689
Second-degree murder, 134
Second/subsequent mortgages, 553
Secretariat (United Nations), 957, 1030
Secretary general (United Nations), 957, 1030
Secret partners, 718
Secured credit cards, 591
Secured loans, 550
Secured parties, 569
Securities
  asset-backed, 560, 793
  defined, 550, 790
  personal property as, 569-572
  real property as, 550
Securities Act of 1933, 791, 921
Securities and Exchange Commission (SEC)
  corporate regulation and, 741, 761, 790
  financial advisors and, 922-923
  insider trading and, 776
  jurisdiction of, 914
  proxy contests and, 768
  REG SCI from, 797-798
  shareholder proposals and, 769
  swap transactions and, 792
  takeover bids and, 808-809
  whistleblowers and, 785, 793-795, 927-929
Securities Exchange Act of 1934, 769, 785, 791, 795, 921
Securitization, 560
Security agreements, 569
Security-based swaps, 792
Security Council (United Nations), 957, 1030-1032
Security deposits, 864
Security devices, 550
Security interests, 385, 550, 569-572
Self-dealing managers, 774
Self-defense, 154
Sellers
  remedies in breach of contract, 400-401
  revesting of title in, 385
  rights and duties of, 399
Selma United Methodist Church, 822-823, 826-827
Senators, election of, 36-37
Separation of powers, 31, 38, 41-42, 945
September 11 terrorist attacks (2001), 2-3, 10-11, 1020, 1025
Serious intent, 236, 239
Serres, Michel, 549, 557-559, 563, 566-567, 730
Servants, 164, 610, 613
Service of process, 74
Services, as consideration, 269
Servient tenement, 847
Settlement week, 106
Settlors, 894
Seventeenth Amendment, 36, 1053
Seventh Amendment, 1052
Severalty, 824, 851
Severe acute respiratory syndrome (SARS), 960
Sexual harassment, 661
SFHAs (special flood hazard areas), 533
Shareholder democracy, 766, 793
Shareholders
  defined, 739, 759
  governance by, 766, 793
  lawsuits by, 771-772
  nominations by, 771
  proposals by, 768-770
  resolutions by, 769
  rights of, 778
  voting control of, 766-771
Shareholders of record, 778
Shares of corporations, 731
Shays' Rebellion, 36, 577
Shelter provision, 477
Sherman, Brad, 56
Sherman Antitrust Act of 1890, 240, 678, 734, 798-801
Shield doctrine, rescission rights as, 289-290
Shipment contracts, 382, 383, 395
Shipwrecks, 825
Shopkeeper's privilege, 168
Sideswipes, 1017
SID (special improvement district), 711
Sievers, Allen M., 719
Sight drafts, 453-454
Signature requirements
  negotiable instruments and, 459, 482
  for written contracts, 318-319, 378
Silence, as acceptance of offers, 245
Silent partners, 718
Similar locality rule, 934
Similar practitioner rule, 934
Siminoff, Dimitryi, 249
Simple contracts, 228
Simpson, O.J., 120
Simultaneous death, 886
Sixteenth Amendment, 36, 1053
Sixth Amendment, 86, 1051-1052
SLA. *See* Symbionese Liberation Army
Slamming, 428
Slander, 169
Slight negligence, 831
Small Business Regulatory Enforcement Act of 1996 (SBREA), 52
Smishing, 144
Smith Grocery & Variety Inc., 867
Social contract ethics, 8-10
Social corporations, 710
Social engineering, 414-418
Social media, offers and advertising on, 250-251
Social media policy (SMP), 669-671, 692-693
Social responsibility, corporate, 19-21
Social Security Act of 1935, 654
Sock puppetry, 251
Socrates, 3-4
Soft power, 957
Sole proprietorships, 706, 709
Sole Survivor Inc., 304-305, 307, 311-314
Solid Waste Disposal Act of 1965 (SWDA), 965
SOPA (Stop Online Piracy Act), 147
Soros, George, 1016
Sotomayor, Sonia, 132-133
Sound City, U.S.A., 868
Soundness of mind, 877
Sousa, Dawnmarie, 692-693
Sovereign immunity, 191-192, 618, 620
Spacemakers of America Incorporated, 490-492, 494-495, 499-500
Spam, 147, 428

Spear phishing, 144
Special agents, 622–623
Special felonies, 123
Special flood hazard areas (SFHAs), 533
Special improvement district (SID), 711
Special indorsements, 465
Special jurisdiction, 64
Specially manufactured goods, 377
Special masters, 404
Special warranty deeds, 859
Specific performance, 350
Specific performance remedy, 79, 221, 404
Speculative damages, 350
Spendthrift trusts, 895
Spirit of the law, 30, 33, 735
Spousal share, 844, 850
Sprinkling trusts, 896
SRAs (school registration agreements), 330–331, 341, 349
Staff privileges, 937
Stakeholders, 759, 766
Stale checks, 493
Stalin, Joseph, 1016
Stalking, 142
Standard construction rule, 225, 238, 313–314
Standing to sue, 44
Stand-your-ground statute, 154–155
Stansbury, Robert, 472–473, 476–477, 486
Staple courts, 214
Stare decisis, 48, 82
Stark, Rodney, 211, 357
Start-up plans, 708–709
State constitutions, 41
State court systems, 69–71
State Farm Insurance, 348, 520–521, 525, 531–532
State intermediate appellate courts, 70–71
State law, 41, 429–430
Statement of fact or promise, 406
State of mind, in criminal law, 125–126
State-owned corporations, 709, 710, 739
State supreme courts, 71
State trial courts, 70
Statute of Frauds
  exceptions to, 224–225
  history of, 227
  objectives of, 238
  rules of interpretation, 225
  on written contracts, 223–224, 236, 305–311
Statutes, defined, 45
Statutes of limitations, 274, 405
Statutes of repose, 190
Statutory agents, 743
Statutory executive orders, 42

Statutory interpretation, 49
Statutory law, 45-48. *See also* Uniform Commercial Code (UCC)
  agreements illegal under, 294–295
  codes and titles, 45
  cyber-law statutes, 47–48
  uniform laws, 45–46
Statutory liability, 618, 921
Stein, David, 264–265, 267–268, 270, 275
Stewardship theory, 42
Stipulated damages, 348–350
Stock acquisitions, 804–805
Stock certificates, 734, 750
Stock dividends, 750–751, 778
Stockholm syndrome, 151–152
Stocktake, 969
Stojanovic, Dejan, 638, 641, 647, 661
Stolen personal property, 828
Stop Online Piracy Act (SOPA), 147
Stoppage in transit, 400–401
Stop-payment rights, 500–501
Stored value cards, 506
Story, Joseph, 578, 579
Straight life insurance, 526–527
Stream of commerce theory, 67, 81–82
Strict liability, 128, 183, 418–421
Strikes, 689–690, 693
Subagents, 625
Subject matter jurisdiction, 64, 66
Subject to mortgage, 557
Subleases, 866
Subprime mortgages, 553, 560–561
Subrogation, 501, 525
Substantial performance, 340
Substantive unconscionability, 105
Substitute checks, 505
Substitute transportation insurance, 536
Subterranean rights, 854–858
Sui generis, 609
Suitability rule, 923
Summary judgment motions, 76
Summary jury trials, 95, 101–102, 113
Summons, 74
Sunday agreements, 295
SunTrust Bank, 490–492, 494–495, 499–500
Superior Savings Association, 601–606
Supplemental homeowner's insurance, 529
Supremacy Clause, 36, 37, 948–949
Sureties, 887
Surplus, 718
Surrebuttals, 79
Survival statutes, 189
Susan B. Anthony List (SBAL), 12–13
Swap transactions, 792

SWDA (Solid Waste Disposal Act of 1965), 965
Sword doctrine, rescission rights as, 289–290
Symbionese Liberation Army (SLA), 118–119, 127, 137, 153
Synergy Software, 424

Taft, William H., 42–43
Taft-Hartley Act of 1947, 688–692
Taggart, Thomas, 665
Tahrir Square protests (2011), 296
Takeover bids, 805, 808–809
Taliban, 141
Tampering with evidence, 140
Tangible personal property, 823
Tarentino, Luigi, 177–178
Target corporations, 805
Targeted shareholder agreements, 807
Tariff-based principle, 1036
TARP (Troubled Asset Relief Program), 564
Tax Assessment Bill (Virginia), 47, 1069
Taxation Clause, 947–948
Taylor-Beechaum Pharmaceuticals Inc., 18
Teaching, suggestion, or motivation test, 977
Technology. *See* Science and technology
Telemarketing Sales Rule, 427
Telephone communication, 242
Televised trials, 80
Teller's checks, 455–456
Temporary public figures, 170–171
The Tempting of America: The Political Seduction of the Law (Bork), 33, 735
Tenancy, defined, 863
Tenancy at sufferance, 864
Tenancy at will, 863
Tenancy by the entirety, 530, 852–853
Tenancy for years, 863–864
Tenancy from year to year, 864
Tenancy in common, 529–530, 824, 851–853
Tenants, defined, 529, 862
Tenant's insurance, 533
Tender, defined, 383
Tender of delivery, 395
Tender offer, 805
Tender of payment, 342, 395
Tender of performance, 342, 394–395
Tenpenny, Leonard, 623
Tenth Amendment, 930, 1052
Terminal conditions, 632
Termination by waiver, 343
Term insurance, 527
Term partnerships, 722
Testamentary trusts, 895
Testate, 876

Testators, 876
Testatrix, 876
Texting suicide case, victim's rights in, 121
Text messages, 243
Textualism, 33, 249, 392, 398, 735, 784-785, 795, 801-802
That Used to Be Us: How America Fell Behind in the World It Invented and How We Can Come Back (Friedman & Mandelbaum), 1013
The Fragile Absolute, Slavoj Zizek, 514
Theft, 136-137
Theft in office, 139
Theories of international behavior, 1001, 1003-1006
Third Amendment, 1051
Third parties, 331-338
  accountants' liability under common law, 917
  defined, 331, 610
  as incidental beneficiaries, 332
  as intended beneficiaries, 331-332
  law of assignment and, 333-338
  liability of, 931
  notice of termination to, 630-631
Third-party beneficiaries, 331
Third-party complaints, 75
Thirteenth Amendment, 39, 350, 643, 657, 1052
Three Mile Island accident (1979), 963
Three-step test, 748
Threshold guidelines, 535
Thresholds, 535
Tillerson, Rex, 15
Time-based thresholds, 535
Time drafts, 453-454
Time for performance, 238, 239, 339-340
Time is of the essence, 238, 340
Times of Crisis (Serres), 549, 557, 558, 566-567, 730
Title
  acquisition of, 858-860
  by adverse possession, 859-860
  defined, 45
  document of, 384
  passage and risk of loss, 382-385
  revesting in seller, 385
  by sale or gift, 858-859
  valid, 381
  void and voidable, 382
  warranty of, 408-409
  by will or descent, 859
Title IX (Dodd-Frank Act), 792-794
Title VII (Civil Rights Act of 1964), 658-661, 663
Tocqueville, Alexis de, 901
Tortfeasors, 163
Tort law, 162-192. *See also* Torts

balance in, 191
case study, 162-163
causation and jurisicence in, 164-166
criminal law vs., 120, 163-164
cultural paradigms and, 190
cybertorts, 184-187
damages in, 187-188
developments in, 189-192
duty and, 164
intentional torts, 167-175
negligence in, 176-183
objectives of, 120
reform and litigation, 937-938
reform movement in, 189-190
remedies in, 187-188
respondeat superior and, 164
sovereign immunity and, 191-192
strict liability and, 183
Tort liability, 611-613, 615, 869, 924
Torts. *See also* Tort law
  agreements to commit, 293-294
  cybertorts, 184-187
  defined, 163
  intentional, 167-175
  public policy, 646-647
  remedies for, 187-188
Towing and labor insurance, 536
Toxic Substance Control Act of 1976 (TSCA), 966
Trade acceptance, 454
Trade fixtures, 322, 323, 847
Trademark Dilution Act of 1995, 983
Trademark Protection Act of 1946 (Lanham Act), 982-983
Trademarks, 982-983
Trade regulation rules, 425-428
Trade secrets, 146, 980-983
Transatlantic Financing Corporation, 1018
Transference of real property rights, 306-308
Transients, 833
Transnats, 957
Transocean, 128
Transportation Security Administration (TSA), 835, 837
Traveler's checks, 456
Travelocity, 669
Treasurer's checks, 455-456
Treasure trove, 822-823, 825-827
Treasury Department, U.S., 564
Treaty Clause, 949-950
Trees, as real property, 846
Trespass, 136, 141, 868
Trimat Inc., 392-394, 398-399
Triplett, Jenny, 490, 492, 494, 499
Troubled Asset Relief Program (TARP), 564
True locality rule, 934

Truman, Harry S., 42, 986
Trump, Donald
  arms sales negotiated by, 15
  CFPB appointee named by, 432-433
  DACA program and, 28-29, 31-32, 43-44, 53
  on elimination of overregulation, 737
  Emoluments Clause and, 56
  on illegal immigration, 37
  on Paris Climate Agreement, 942
  Realpolitik theory and, 1004
Trump Plaza, 457
Trustees, 589, 770, 894, 896
Trust fund, 894
Trusts, 894-896
Truth-in-Lending Act of 1968, 433
TSA (Transportation Security Administration), 835, 837
TSCA (Toxic Substance Control Act of 1976), 966
TSM standard, 977
Tuchman, Barbara W., 1018
Tucker Act of 1887, 191
Tunney Act of 1974, 810
Turkel, Gerald, 31
Twelfth Amendment, 1052
Twentieth Amendment, 1053-1054
Twenty-fifth Amendment, 1054-1055
Twenty-first Amendment, 1054
21st century financial crisis, 557-568
  causes of, 559-561
  corporations and, 730-731, 733-738
  economic-political dimension of, 558-559
  homes lost during, 554, 561
  long-term solutions to, 566-568
  nature of, 558
  overview, 557
  second wave of, 548-549, 565-566
  short-term solutions to, 562-565
21st century labor crisis, 680
24 (television show), 4-5
Twenty-fourth Amendment, 1054
Twenty-second Amendment, 1054
Twenty-seventh Amendment, 1055
Twenty-sixth Amendment, 286, 1055
Twenty-third Amendment, 1054
Twitter, 669
Tying agreements, 801
Type one arrangements, 914-916
Type two arrangements, 915-920

Uber, 676-677, 687-690
UCC. *See* Uniform Commercial Code
UCITA. *See* Uniform Computer Information Transactions Act
UCSPA (Uniform Consumer Sales Practices Act), 429

UETA. *See* Uniform Electronic Transactions Act
ULC. *See* Uniform Law Commission
Ultra vires, 789
Umbrella policies, 539
UN. *See* United Nations
Unanimous voting restrictions, 771
Unauthorized indorsements, 468-469
UNCED (United Nations Conference on Environment and Development), 968
Uncertainty principle, 31-33, 35, 1016-1017
UNCITRAL (United Nations Commission on International Trade Law), 1033
UNCLOS (United Nations Convention on the Law of the Sea), 825
Unconscionable agreements, 295
Unconscionable clauses, 105, 267
Unconscionable consideration, 218, 267
Unconscionable contracts, 393
UNCs (unintended negative consequences), 708, 709
UNCTAD (United Nations Conference on Trade and Development), 958, 1034
Undercapitalization, 748
Underinsured-motorist insurance, 535
Underleases, 866
Underwriters, 524
Undisclosed principals, 622
UNDP (United Nations Development Program), 960
Undue hardships, 667
Undue influence, 259, 884
Unemployment insurance, 654-655
Unenforceable agreements, 275-277
Unenforceable contracts, 226
UNEP (United Nations Environment Program), 967-968
Unequivocal acceptance, 244-245
UNESCO. *See* United Nations Educational, Scientific, and Cultural Organization
Unexpected expenses, 831
Unfair labor practices, 685-687, 692
UNFCCC (United Nations Framework Conference on Climate Change), 968, 969
Unfriendly buyers/suitors, 805
Unified international institutions, 65-66
Uniform Commercial Code (UCC)
  acceptance of offers under, 373
  access methods, 1056
  banks as defined by, 491
  on breach of contract, 400, 401
  certified checks and, 455
  communication and, 243
  consumer credit contracts and, 483-484
  contracts and, 221-222, 240, 309, 402
  counteroffers under, 244-245
  defined, 46-47
  on duty to examine accounts, 498
  fungible goods and, 384
  holder in due course and, 473
  lease of goods and, 369
  merchants as defined by, 377
  minor's right to rescind contracts and, 290
  negotiable instruments and, 451, 458
  offers and, 238-239, 243, 372-373
  open-price terms and, 373
  organization of, 221-222
  parol evidence rule and, 316
  rejection of goods and, 396-397
  on rights and duties within sales contracts, 394
  sale of goods and, 309, 367, 368, 375-377, 1034
  seal requirement eliminated by, 273
  specific performance and, 404
  warehousers as defined by, 838
  warranty protection and, 406, 407, 409
Uniform Computer Information Transactions Act (UCITA), 48, 249-250, 277, 326, 631
Uniform Consumer Sales Practices Act (UCSPA), 429
Uniform Durable Power of Attorney Act, 629-630
Uniformed Services Employment and Reemployment Rights Act of 1994 (USERA), 666
Uniform Electronic Transactions Act (UETA)
  cyber-commerce and, 326
  cyber-contracts and, 48, 249, 378, 380
  cyber-price shopping and, 277
  electronic agents and, 631
  negotiable instruments and, 458
Uniform Facsimile Signatures of Public Officials Act, 318
Uniform Law Commission (ULC)
  cyber-commerce and, 48
  on durable power of attorney, 629
  partnerships and, 707
  predecessor to, 215
  probate law and, 875
  on rights and duties within sales contracts, 394
  structure and function of, 46, 47
  trade secrets and, 981
  UCC and, 1056
  UCITA and, 249
  UCSPA and, 429
Uniform laws, 45-46
Uniform Negotiable Instruments Act, 215
Uniform Partnership Act (UPA), 707, 713, 715-719, 721
Uniform Premarital Agreement Act (UPAA), 311
Uniform Probate Code (UPC), 875, 876
Uniform Sales Act, 215
Uniform Simultaneous Death Act, 886
Uniform Trade Secrets Act, 981
Uniform Transfer to Minors Act (UTMA), 828
Unilateral contracts, 226, 242, 341
Unilateral mistake, 257
Uninsured-motorist insurance, 535
Unintended negative consequences (UNCs), 708, 709
Unions. *See* Labor unions
Union shops, 686
Unisave (Madsen), 631, 893, 991
United Kingdom
  Brexit vote in, 1013
  common law of, 48
  constitutional law in, 35
  Grenfell Tower fire (2017) in, 130
  labor unions in, 695
United Nations Commission on International Trade Law (UNCITRAL), 1033
United Nations Conference on Environment and Development (UNCED), 968
United Nations Conference on Trade and Development (UNCTAD), 958, 1034
United Nations Convention on the Law of the Sea (UNCLOS), 825
United Nations Development Program (UNDP), 960
United Nations Educational, Scientific, and Cultural Organization (UNESCO), 840, 958, 959, 988, 1034
United Nations Environment Program (UNEP), 967-968
United Nations Framework Conference on Climate Change (UNFCCC), 968, 969
United Nations Population Fund (UNPF), 972
United Nations (UN)
  on cultural property, 840
  Economic and Social Council, 957-958, 972, 1034
  Economic Security Council, 988-991, 1034-1035

Food and Agriculture Organization, 960
General Assembly, 957, 1030-1032
on genocide, 1022-1023
international law and, 1030-1033
Responsibility to Protect doctrine, 16, 1014-1015, 1023
on sale of goods, 380, 385, 1033-1034, 1057-1068
Secretariat of, 957, 1030
secretary general of, 957, 1030
Security Council, 957, 1030-1032
structure of, 1027-1030
as unified international institution, 65
Universal Declaration of Human Rights, 6, 107
United Power Association (Minnesota), 110
Unity of possession, 852
Universal Declaration of Human Rights (United Nations), 6, 107
Universal defenses, 481-483
Universal laws, 213-214
Universal life insurance, 526-527
Unjust dismissal. *See* Wrongful discharge
Unlawful detainer, 869
Unlicensed agreements, 294-295
Unocal Corporation, 756-757, 764-765, 774-775
Unordered merchandise, 245, 423
Unorthodox business entities, 710-711
UNPF (United Nations Population Fund), 972
Unqualified opinions, 911
Unreasonable expectations, 374
Unsafe products vs. dangerous products, 420-421
Unsecured loans, 550
Unsound mind, 884
Unstable states, 15, 16
Unusual expenses, 831
UPA. *See* Uniform Partnership Act
UPAA (Uniform Premarital Agreement Act), 311
UPC (Uniform Probate Code), 875, 876
U.S. Code (USC), 45, 147, 581, 984
U.S. Computer Emergency Response Team (US-CERT), 143-144, 149
U.S. Constitution. *See also* Amendments to U.S. Constitution
Articles of Confederation, 35-36, 38, 39, 577, 787
bankruptcy and, 578, 579
Bill of Rights, 6, 38-40, 787
Commerce Clause, 122, 123, 736, 786-787, 945-946
corporations and, 786-789
on double jeopardy, 163-164
Emoluments Clause, 56
Establishment Clause, 621
Free Exercise Clause, 356, 358, 619, 621, 733, 874
on intellectual property, 973-974
motivations for creation of, 34-35
Necessary and Proper Clause, 946-947
reengineering, 36-38
science and technology regulation and, 945
structure of, 38-41
Supremacy Clause, 36, 37, 948-949
Taxation Clause, 947-948
text of, 1047-1055
Treaty Clause, 949-950
U.S. Courts of Appeals, 67-68
U.S. district courts, 64-66
U.S. Patent and Trademark Office, 67, 974, 976, 982-983
U.S. Postal Service money orders, 456
U.S. PRISM program, 279
U.S. Sentencing Commission, 777
U.S. Supreme Court
on actual malice test, 169
bankruptcy and, 578
on collective bargaining, 687
commerce regulation and, 946
jurisdiction of, 68
on precedent, 49
on right to die, 890, 891
on scope of congressional power, 122
writ of certiorari and, 68, 132-133
writ of mandamus and, 80
U.S. Tax Court, 67
Usage of trade, 372, 408
Used Car Rule, 425
USERA (Uniformed Services Employment and Reemployment Rights Act of 1994), 666
US-Mexico Treaty of Cooperation (1971), 840
Usurious agreements, 294
Usury, 294
Utilitarianism, 10-11, 21
Utility thinking, 18
UTMA (Uniform Transfer to Minors Act), 828
Utopia (More), 1021
Utter, Harold J., 704-705, 713-714, 720-721
Uttering, 494

Valid contracts, 226
Valid title, 381
Value-taking requirement, for holder in due course, 474-475
Van Hooter, James D., 704-705, 713-714, 720-721

Variable-rate mortgages, 552
Variances, 860
VA (Veterans Administration), 560
Vegetation, as real property, 846
Verdicts, 79
Vertical expansion, 809
Veterans Administration (VA), 560
Veterans' Employment and Training Service (VETS), 666
Vicarious liability, 128, 164, 611-616
Victim's rights, 121
The Victory of Reason (Stark), 211, 357
Vilnius, Frank, 187
Vishing, 144
Voidable contracts, 226, 289, 290
Voidable title, 382
Void contracts, 226
Void title, 382
Voir dire, 78, 87
Volition variable, 1016
Voluntary manslaughter, 134
Von Bernhardi, Friedrich, 1018
Von Clausewitz, Karl, 1017
Voting by shareholders, 766-771
cumulative, 767
overview, 766-767
pooling agreements, 770
proxy, 768
shareholder nominations, 771
shareholder proposals, 768-770
unanimous voting restrictions, 771
voting trusts, 770
Voting trusts, 770

Wagering agreements, 294
Wagner Act. *See* National Labor Relations Act of 1935
Wagon Mound cases, 179-180
Waid, Beth, 646
Waiver, termination by, 343
Waiver of premium option, 528
Waivers, insurance, 543
Wall Street Transparency and Accountability Act of 2010, 791-792
Walmart, 765
Wang, Jessica Ching-Sze, 1015
WannaCry ransomware attack (2017), 143-144
War, 1017-1027
just war theory, 1019-1022
overview, 1017-1018
preemptive, 1021
preventive, 1021
protective, 1021-1026
substantive and procedural issues related to, 1026-1027
Warehouse, defined, 838
Warehouse receipts, 838

Warehousers, 838-839
WARN (Worker Adjustment and Retraining Notification) Act of 1988, 643
War Powers Resolution of 1973, 1024
Warranties. *See also specific warranties*
  to assignee, 337
  of assignor, 336-337
  exclusions in, 409
  express, 406-407
  full, 407
  implied, 407-408
  of indorsers, 467
  by insured, 541
  limited, 407
  to obligor, 337
  privity not required in, 409-410
Warranty of fitness for a particular purpose, 408
Warranty of habitability, 867
Warranty of merchantability, 407-409
Warranty of title, 408-409
Warrior Politics (Kaplan), 999, 1017
Washington Square Enterprises, 716
Waste, defined, 868
Water rights, 846
Wayne County Lumber Company, 848
Weber, Max, 14-16, 211, 214, 356, 416, 928, 1012
Weinrib, Ernest, 928
Wellington Resource Group (WRG), 857
Wells, H.G., 1000
Wells Fargo, 333-334, 336, 769-770
Western Kentucky Stages, 704-705, 713-714, 720-721
Western Sales, 507
Westphalia, Treaty of (1648), 1021-1022
Westwell Construction Company, 400
Whirlpool, 130
Whistleblowers, 431, 667-668, 785, 793-796, 927-929
Whitehall Packing Co., 835
White knights, 807
Whole life insurance, 526-527
WHO (World Health Organization), 958-961, 988, 1034
Why Nations Fail (Acemoglu & Robinson), 212
Wickard, Claude R., 122
Widow's allowance, 880
Williams, John, 472-473, 476-477, 486
William the Conqueror, 848-849
Wills, 876-887
  accuracy of, 879
  administrator of, 310
  changing, 883-884
  child protection in, 882
  contesting, 884
  defined, 876
  dying without, 884-886
  executor of, 310
  formal requirements for, 877-879
  holographic, 879
  informal, 879-880
  living, 632, 887-888
  nuncupative, 880
  oral, 880
  requirements for execution of, 877-880
  revoking, 883
  same sex couples and, 880-883
  settling of estate and, 886-887
  soundness of mind and, 877
  spousal protection in, 880-881
  tenancy at, 863
  title by, 859
Wilson, Woodrow, 42
Windsor, Edith, 881
Winkfield, Latisha, 874-875, 891-892
WIPO (World Intellectual Property Organization), 958, 984-985, 1034
Wire transfers, 506
Without notice of defect requirement, for holder in due course, 476
Witnesses to contract signings, 319
Woods, Arthur and Dorothy, 500-501
Words vs. interpretation duality, 30
Worker Adjustment and Retraining Notification (WARN) Act of 1988, 643
Worker benefits, 654-657
Workers' compensation, 655-656
Working Families Flexibility Act of 2017, 653
Workmanlike manner, 322
Workplace harassment, 661
Work product privilege, 929
World Bank, 942, 960, 1035
World Health Organization (WHO), 958-961, 988, 1034
World Intellectual Property Organization (WIPO), 958, 984-985, 1034
World order, defined, 1000. *See also* New world order
World Trade Organization (WTO), 1035-1037
World vs. national responsibility, 14
WRG (Wellington Resource Group), 857
Writ of certiorari, 68, 132-133, 861
Writ of execution, 80
Writ of mandamus, 80
Writ of replevin, 404
Written contracts, 305-322
  condition precedent for, 316
  contents of, 311
  formalities of construction, 317-322
  legal rules for, 312-317
  oral evidence of, 314-316
  principal objective of, 313
  sales contracts, 375-378
  signature requirements for, 318-319, 378
  Statute of Frauds and, 223-224, 236, 305-311
Written instruments, 458
Wrongful civil proceedings, 175
Wrongful death statutes, 189, 190
Wrongful discharge, 643-648
  defined, 643
  fraud and, 644
  implied contracts and, 644-646
  implied covenant and, 646
  intentional infliction of emotional distress and, 648
  promissory estoppel and, 643-644
  public policy tort and, 646-647
WTO (World Trade Organization), 1035-1037

Xi Jinping, 998, 1007, 1012

YouTube, 669

Ziglar, James, 2
Zimmerman, George, 155
Zizek, Slavoj, 514
Zoning laws, 860-861